INFORMATION
PLEASE
ALMANAC
ATLAS & YEARBOOK
1982
36th EDITION

SIMON AND SCHUSTER
NEW YORK

Editor
Theodore B. Dolmatch
Managing Editor
Otto T. Johnson
Associate Editor
Natalie M. Aust
Senior Editors
Vera J. Dailey
George De Gregorio
Arthur Neuhauser
Arthur P. Reed, Jr.
Editors
Konrad J. A. Kundig (Science)
Blanche Ormont (Writer's Guide)
Jack Pompan (Business and the
Economy)
Don Shannon (Countries of the World)
Sanford Teller (Trivia)
Staff
Editorial Assistants: Faye
Bodner and Fred Chase
Cover Design
Martin S. Moskof and Associates
Maps
Dyno Lowenstein and Vaughn Gray

The Information Please Almanac invites comments and suggestions from readers. Because of the many letters received, however, it is not possible to respond personally to every correspondent. Nevertheless, all suggestions are most welcome, and the editors will consider them carefully. (Information Please Almanac does not rule on bets or wagers.)

Library of Congress Number: 47–845
ISBN (Hardcover): 0–671–43832–8
ISBN (Paperback): 0–671–43833–6

Previous editions of INFORMATION PLEASE were published in 1980 and 1979 by Simon & Schuster, in 1978 and 1977 by Information Please Publishing, Inc., and 1976–1947 by Dan Golenpaul Associates.

INFORMATION PLEASE ALMANAC
Editorial Office
Simon & Schuster
1230 Avenue of the Americas
New York, N.Y. 10020

CONTENTS

SPECIAL FEATURES

1981: Molecular Genetics Comes of Age by Joshua Lederberg **7**
Religion and Politics in The U.S.: The Emergence of the Christian New Right by Paul Anthony Schwartz **9**

YEAR OF THE INVESTOR   A1-A16

Special Green Centerfold Investment Section by Louis Ehrenkrantz ● Compound Annual Rates of Return for 16 Investment Categories ● The Stock Market ● Stocks as Investment Vehicles ● The Short Sale ● Options ● Fixed Income Securities ● Gemstones ● Stamps and Coins ● Art ● Art Versus Stocks ● Books ● Sports Memorabilia ● Taxes ● Bibliography

NEW HOME ENTERTAINMENT   803

The All-Seeing Eye—The Video Revolution by Theodore B. Dolmatch ● TV Today ● Video Home Recording ● Hardware ● Television Sets ● Interactive Television (QUBE) ● Software ● Video Glossary—What the New Terms Mean

CURRENT EVENTS   11

What Happened in 1980-1981: Business and the Economy ● The Courts ● Crime and Violence ● Disasters ● Education ● Energy ● Entertainment and Culture ● Environment ● Health and Medicine ● International Affairs ● National Government and Politics ● People, Places, and Things ● Religion ● Science ● Sports ● State and Local Governments ● Women ● 1981 Emmy Awards ● 1981 Nobel Prize Winners ● Deaths

ASTRONOMY   354

Astronomical Terms and Constants ● Origin of the Universe ● Brightest Stars ● Data for Sun, Moon, and Planets ● Asteroids ● Comets, Meteors, and Meteorites ● 88 Recognized Constellations ● Eclipses, 1982 ● Phenomena, 1982

AVIATION   438

Famous Firsts ● Records ● Busiest Airports ● Hijackings ● U.S. Transport and Air Force Planes ● Helicopter Records ● Hours and Earnings in Aircraft Industries

AWARDS   497

Nobel Prizes ● Grammy Awards ● Poets Laureate ● Oscars ● Other Academy Awards ● Pulitzer Prizes ● Tony Awards ● Sigma Delta Chi Awards ● Fermi Award ● New York Drama Critics' Circle Awards ● American Library Association Awards ● Peabody Awards ● Presidential Medal of Freedom ● Bollingen Prize

BUSINESS AND THE ECONOMY   34

The Economy in 1981 by Monte J. Gordon ● Employment and Unemployment ● Consumer Price Indexes ● Gross National Product ● Personal and Family Income ● Interest Rates ● Price and Production Indexes ● New Construction ● Stock Market ● Largest Corporations ● National Labor Unions ● Occupations ● Labor ● Agriculture ● Government Spending ● Social Welfare Costs ● Foreign Aid ● Freight and Passenger Traffic ● Principal Ports ● Automobile Production ● Balance of Payments ● Exports and Imports

CALENDAR AND HOLIDAYS   378

1981, 1982, 1983 Calendars ● Perpetual Calendar ● History of the Calendar ● Names of the Days and Months ● Holidays, 1982 ● World Holidays ● U.S. Legal Holidays ● Movable Holidays, 1982-1990

CANADA   282

Area and History ● Governors General and Prime Ministers ● Population ● Government ● Provinces and Territories ● House of Commons ● Trading Partners ● Holidays ● Flag and Motto ● Museums and Other Institutions ● Consumer Price Index ● Growth Statistics ● Labor Force ● Temperature and Precipitation ● Distance Between Cities ● Church Membership ● Tallest Buildings ● Awards

COUNTRIES OF THE WORLD 123

Freedom in the World: The Criteria of Freedom and *Comparative Survey of Freedom* from Freedom House • Nine–Year Record of the Survey • Treaties, Agreements, and Organization§ • Countries by Geographical and Political Groupings • Countries from Afghanistan to Zimbabwe—Rulers, Area, Population, Capitals and Largest Cities, Monetary Units, Religions, Geography, Government, History, Current Events, Economy

DISASTERS 641

Earthquakes, Volcanic Eruptions, and Floods From A.D. 79 to the Present • Storms • Fires and Explosions • Shipwrecks • Aircraft Accidents • Railroad Crashes • Miscellaneous Disasters

EDUCATION 703

Special Education in the 1980s • Federal Aid • Enrollment • Attendance Laws • High School and College Graduates • University Libraries • Endowments • Degrees Conferred • Community, Junior, and Technical Colleges • Senior Colleges and Universities • Degree Abbreviations

ENERGY 329

The Year in Energy—1981 • World Production, Trade, and Consumption • Ten Largest Electric Energy Producers • Per Capita Electric Energy Consumption • U.S. Energy Supply and Disposition • Petroleum Imported from OPEC • Production of Crude Petroleum by Countries • U.S. Nuclear Power Plants • Motor Vehicle Fuel Consumption

ENTERTAINMENT AND CULTURE 789

Notable Books • Major Symphony Orchestras • Public Libraries • Glossary of Art Movements • Top Artists and Recordings for 1980 • Radio and T.V. Statistics • Longest Running Plays • Top Money-Making Films • Museums

ENVIRONMENT 629

1981 Environmental Quality Index • Endangered Species • Sources of Information • Sources of Pollution • Pollution Abatement and Environmental Quality Expenditures • World's Water Supply • Speed of Animals • Animal Groups by Name • Animal Gestation, Incubation, and Longevity • Famous Zoological Gardens • American Zoos • National Parks • Environmental Glossary

FIRST AID 71

Treatment for Burns, Poisons, Shock • Cardiac Pulmonary Resuscitation • Heimlich Mâneuver for Food-Choking and Drowning • Severe-Bleeding Treatment

GEOGRAPHY 453

Explorations and Discoveries • Continents • Volcanoes • Mountain Peaks • Oceans and Seas • Lakes • Rivers • Waterfalls • Islands • Deserts • Caves and Caverns • Highest and Lowest Points in U.S. • U.S. Mountain Peaks • Principal U.S. Rivers • Longitude and Latitude of Cities • U.S. Coastline

GUIDE TO GROWING OLDER 688

Aging Children, Elderly Parents—And the Challenges of Growing Old Together by Barry Robinson • U.S. Population by Age • Characteristics of Persons 65 and Over • Income • Health • Employment • Marital Status • Living Arrangements • Pensions • Transportation • Crime • Sources of Help and Information • Myths and Truths about Aging • Social Security • Disability • Unemployment Insurance • State Unemployment Compensation • Medicare Program • Medicaid Services

HEADLINE HISTORY 83

Chronology of People, Places, and Events From 4500 B.C. to the Present

MAPS 472

Canada • United States • Europe • Central America and the West Indies • South America • Middle East • Africa • China • Western Pacific • Central Asia • Major Oil Producing Countries • Ancient Empires • The Moon

MEDIA 446

U.S. Daily Newspapers • U.S. and Canadian Magazines • Newspaper Circulation

MILITARY 390

Armed Forces Strength and History • Service Academies • National Guard • Pay and Allowances • Veterans' Benefits • Women and Blacks • Outlays • U.S. Military Actions • Casualties • Highest

Ranking Officers ● Military Strength of World Nations ● NATO and Warsaw Pact ● Insignia and Ranks ● Arms Exports and Imports

NUTRITION AND HEALTH 73

Capsule Profile of Health in the U.S. ● Weight Tables ● Physicians, Dentists, and Nurses ● Physicians— Median Earnings ● Daily Dietary Allowances ● Communicable Diseases ● Calories, Minerals, and Vitamins

PEOPLE 521

Famous Personalities of Past and Present

POSTAL REGULATIONS 625

Domestic and International Mail Service and Rates ● Money Order Fees ● U.N. Stamps ● 2–Letter State Abbreviations

RELIGION 407

Membership and History of Major Religions ● Leading Religious Groups in the U.S. ● U.S. Church Membership ● Other U.S. Religious Groups ● Popes ● Books of the Bible

SCIENCE 336

The Year in Science—1981 ● Table of Geologic Periods ● Chemical Elements ● Atomic Energy ● Scientific Inventions, Discoveries, and Theories

SPACE 366

The Year in Space ● Major U.S. Space Projects ● Unmanned Planetary and Lunar Programs ● Manned Space Flight Projects ● Unmanned Lunar and Interplanetary Probes ● Major Soviet Space Projects ● Manned Space Flights

SPORTS 806

Personalities ● The Olympics: 1896-1980 ● Awards ● Halls of Fame ● Organizations and Information Bureaus ● Records and Champions, from Archery to Yachting

STRUCTURES 316

Seven Wonders of the World ● Famous Structures ● Highest Dams ● Largest Hydroelectric Plants ● Tallest U.S. Buildings ● Notable Tunnels and Bridges ● Famous Canals ● Largest Dams

TAXES 428

By Touche Ross & Co. ● History of the Income Tax ● Internal Revenue Service: Auditing and Selecting Returns; Appeals ● Federal Individual Income Tax ● Legislation ● Rate Tables ● Returns Filed and Examined ● Corporation and Franchise Taxes ● Estate and Gift Taxes ● State Sales and Use Taxes ● Income and Sales Tax Rates in Selected Cities

TRAVEL 298

Air Charter Flights—Know What You're Buying ● Industry Statistics ● Passport and Customs Information ● Weather in Tourist Cities ● Expenditures ● U.S. Travel to Foreign Countries ● Passport Recipients ● Price Index for Domestic Travel ● State and City Tourism Offices ● Information Sources for Travel ● Presidential Homes and Libraries–Museums ● Road Mileages and Air Distances Between U.S. Cities ● Air Distances Between World Cities

UNITED NATIONS 324

Members ● Budget Assessments ● Headquarters ● Charter Preamble ● Secretariat ● General Assembly ● Security Council ● Court of Justice ● Agencies

U.S. HISTORY AND GOVERNMENT 546

Declaration of Independence ● Constitution ● White House ● Mayflower Compact ● Monroe Doctrine ● Order of Presidential Succession ● Star-Spangled Banner ● Emancipation Proclamation ● Confederate States ● Gettysburg Address ● Early Congresses ● Statistical History of U.S. ● Capitol ● Washington Monument ● History of the Flag ● Biographies of the Presidents ● Vice Presidents ● Burial Places of the Presidents ● Wives and Children of the Presidents ● How a President Is Nominated and Elected: Political Conventions, Electoral College ● Presidential Elections ● National Committee Chairmen ● Qualifications for Voting ● Unusual Voting Results ● Cabinet Members ● How a Bill Becomes a Law ● Federal Judiciary ● Supreme Court Justices ● Impeachments ● The Ninety-Seventh Congress ● Speakers of the House ● Floor Leaders of the Senate ● Salaries of Top Officials ● Executive Departments and Agencies ● Independent and Legislative Agencies

U.S. SOCIETIES AND ASSOCIATIONS 619

U.S. STATES AND CITIES 646
The Fifty States ● Puerto Rico ● Guam ● Non-Self-Governing Areas ● Micronesia ● State Governors ● Terms and Salaries of State Officials ● Fifty Largest Cities of U.S. ● Terms and Salaries of City Officials

U.S. STATISTICS 750
Population: 1980 Census, Metropolitan Areas, Race, States, Cities ● Immigration ● Marriage and Divorce ● Family Characteristics ● Births and Deaths ● Mortality Rates ● Expectation of Life ● Law Enforcement and Crime ● Motor Vehicle Laws

WEATHER AND CLIMATE 421
Extremes of Climate ● Tropical Storms and Hurricanes ● Climate of U.S. Cities ● Wind–Chill Factors ● Weather Glossary ● Tornadoes ● North Atlantic Hurricanes

WEIGHTS AND MEASURES 345
Metric and U.S. Equivalents ● Miscellaneous Units of Measure ● Cooking Measurements ● Conversion Factors ● Fahrenheit and Celsius Conversion Formulas ● Roman Numerals ● Mean and Median

WHERE TO FIND OUT MORE 451

WORLD STATISTICS 108
Area and Population of Countries ● Largest Cities ● Life Expectancy ● Birth and Death Rates ● Suicide Rates ● Cost of Living ● Exports and Imports ● Consumer Prices ● Production: Energy, Petroleum, Coal, Steel, Iron Ore, Grains, Meat, Sugar ● Communications

WRITER'S GUIDE 489
Punctuation, Capitalization, Abbreviation ● Forms of Address ● Foreign Words and Phrases

THE YEAR'S TOP TRIVIA 930
The light side of the news by Sanford Teller

MISCELLANEOUS FACTS
Arlington National Cemetery, p. 569 ● Assassinations, 545 ● Birthstones, 496 ● Buying Wood for Home Heating, 323 ● Chinese Calendar, 364 ● Definitions of Gold Terminology, 353 ● Energy-Saving Tips for Home Buyers, 323 ● Enforcing Your Civil Rights, 624 ● Federal Government Hotlines, 624 ● Figures and Legends in American Folklore, 545 ● Firsts in America, 544 ● The Great Seal of the U.S., 561 ● Growth of Social Security Taxes, 602 ● "In God We Trust," 611 ● How the House of Representatives Elects a President, 585 ● Labors of Hercules, 789 ● Leap Seconds, 452 ● The Liberty Bell, 584 ● Mason and Dixon's Line, 468 ● Measuring Earthquakes, 456 ● Modern Wedding Anniversary Gift List, 445 ● New Chinese Spelling, 151 ● The Pledge of Allegiance, 569 ● Plurality and Majority, 587 ● The Pony Express, 628 ● Population Center of U.S., 755 ● Portraits and Designs of U.S. Paper Currency, 353 ● Radiation Doses, 334 ● Selected CB 10-Codes, 520 ● The Statue of Liberty, 309 ● Sunbathing and Skin Cancer, 77 ● U.S. Fairs and Expositions, 795 ● World's Fair To Be Held in Knoxville, Tenn., 1982, 794 ● World Time Zones Map, 459

INDEX 931

The Comprehensive Index lists in alphabetical order all the important topics, terms, and names covered and gives the page or pages on which they appear ● To find a fact, date, or idea, begin by looking under the most specific word. For example, to find the population of Des Moines, start by looking for *Des Moines.* But that city is not listed separately. Therefore, the next step is to look under *Iowa* or *Cities, U.S.* Under *Iowa* the designated page gives the latest population of Des Moines. Under *Cities, U.S.* there is a subhead, *Population figures,* with three alternatives: *Largest* (of which Des Moines is not one), *Largest by state* (which refers back to *Iowa*), and *1970-1980 (table)* (where Des Moines is listed alphabetically). ● For President George Washington, look under *Washington,* before checking *President.* Where general headings (such as *Presidents, U.S.*) are given, they refer to a section where the subject is treated at some length.

1981: Molecular Genetics Comes of Age

Joshua Lederberg
President, Rockefeller University, New York, New York

The biology of *DNA*, the science of molecular genetics, has for the general public been a quiet sideroad on the map of "pure" scientific research for the last four decades. In 1981, it exploded into public prominence. A host of practical applications of this arcane science were announced in medicine, agriculture, energy, and the chemical industry.

Only 37 years ago, O. T. Avery, Colin MacLeod, and Maclyn McCarty at the Rockefeller University discovered that DNA was the substance that carries genetic information in bacterial cells. This finding changed the direction of all fundamental biological research. With renewed confidence scientists have striven for *chemical* explanations of structure and function in cells, tissues, and organisms.

DNA was discovered by the German pathologist Miescher in 1865. It was found to be a gummy nitrogenous substance of very high molecular weight which formed stringy threads in solution and was somehow associated with the nuclei of living cells.

But it took almost another 75 years for proof that DNA, rather than the protein and other substances in cell nuclei and chromosomes, was responsible for determining the genetic characteristics of the cell and, indeed, of all organisms. This discovery in 1944 promptly stimulated much more incisive research into the structure of DNA, culminating nine years later in the famous *double helix*, a structure proposed by Watson and Crick on the basis of the images produced when X-rays are scattered by specimens of DNA.

During the last thirty years, research into many new methods of chemical analysis and for the manipulation of segments of DNA has been carried on in laboratories throughout the world. Today we have a fairly comprehensive picture of the way this master substance is accurately reproduced at the moment of cell division in order that the information of the parent is precisely and accurately distributed to both daughter cells.

Scientists also sought to relate their findings on the DNA of simple viruses and bacteria to more complex organisms, including human cells. A further consequence of DNA research has, therefore, been the enrichment of what we know about the general biology of simpler organisms, as well as the molecular structures common to all forms of life.

At the present time, scientists believe that only about 1% of the DNA in our body is informational-ly active. The function of the remaining 99% is obscure; it may simply be "filler." The one percent, which contains about 30,000,000 nucleotides in our 23 pairs of chromosomes, is sufficient to provide the informational code for about 100,000 distinct proteins. The complexity of the research task before us can be measured by the fact that we now have detailed knowledge of less than 1,000 of these proteins.

The scientific task before us can be compared to rearranging a haystack, every straw of which is important but only one of which may correspond to the particular protein in which we are interested. One of the important recent advances in genetic engineering has been the ability to cut up or segment the huge DNA filament into a large number of manageable "straws," each of them containing a limited number of genes or units encoding a single protein. A familiar task in many laboratories today is to search for one particular straw in the huge haystack—a search that has been successful already in synthesizing such important substances as insulin and interferon. The most exciting applications of this technology are in the preparation, on a large scale, of human proteins which would otherwise be extremely costly, if not impossible, to procure.

Insulin. Insulin may be the first of these proteins on the pharmaceutical market. There is already a well-authenticated demand for it and there are a large number of diabetic patients who can benefit. Today, insulin is procured almost entirely from the pancreases of pigs, goats, or cattle and these substances, although closely related, are not identical to human insulin. While most scientists believe there will be definite advantages in using a substance identical with human insulin in place of its animal equivalents (and it is most unlikely that there will be any disadvantages!), this will not be known for sure until large-scale production and trial of biosynthetic insulin is achieved during the next few years.

Interferon. A far more precious substance than insulin, since it can be produced only in microgram quantities even from large quantities of tissue cells, is interferon. It is certainly effective in mitigating some virus infections and has had some promising results in the treatment of some forms of cancer. However, we will not know its full applicability in medicine until it also is available on a large scale for clinical trial and application. One of the more important findings about interferon is that it represents a rather large class of substances rather than one, and this encourages optimism that several variant forms of interferon will be found, each of them perhaps having an important role in medicine.

Other Applications. Besides these human proteins, genetic technology will produce an ever-increasing number of vaccines that would otherwise be most difficult to obtain. A vaccine for hoof-and-mouth disease (a serious affliction of cattle) is already in test. Improved vaccines for hepatitis and influenza will certainly be in clinical trials in the very near future. Vaccines for difficult diseases like gonorrhea and malaria are more speculative, but leads toward their development are promising and particularly important because they would be very difficult to produce by other approaches.

The engineering of microbial strains will also have important applications in the energy and chemical industries. For example, we are seeing even more efficient ways to produce fuel alcohol, not only from corn starch but also from cellulose waste. Improved processes for the production of crystalline fructose—a cheaper and slightly less caloric alternative to cane sugar—have also been announced. These are surely only the first innovations in this sphere.

DNA technology for plant cells is less advanced, but together with other innovations, it also promises a revolution in plant breeding. This will result in new crops, enhance the efficiency of fertilizer, and develop croplands that are now marginal. With the looming pressures of population on food supply in many parts of the world, and the precariousness of reserves which could be imperiled by one or a few bad crop years, these promising developments may come none too soon to protect mankind against recurrent catastrophe.

Genetics and the Law. These developments have proceeded so quickly that we are still catching our breath with respect to the legal and institutional framework which will mold this progress. Questions like the proper place of patent rights in specifically "engineered" microorganisms; the relative roles of government, the universities, and of industry; the conflicts that will arise as between the different legal systems of different countries in a large international market—these are some of the issues that will be at the center of attention during the next decade.

Although public attention naturally focuses on technological advances that have prompt practical applications, these may not be the most important result of the new genetics. The same research that has such value for industry is equally indispensible for the rapid unraveling of many scientific puzzles. Already, very important new information about the genetic basis of antibody formation, and its aberrations constituting a whole family of immunological diseases, has been found. The evolution of the aberrant genes that are connected with sickle cell and other hemoglobin diseases has been traced. Very important advances in our understanding of cancer as a lesion within the DNA of afflicted cells permitting them to escape normal bodily regulation have been made. There is no aspect of embryonic development and of aging that is not profitably being studied with these more powerful tools; and we can soon expect revolutions of insight that will be even more important than the revolutions of production in the field of biology.

The DNA technologies have already shown that it is possible to find molecular labels for individual chromosomes. This can be done to such an extent that we will soon be able to trace in a given pedigree exactly which offspring have received segments of which chromosomes. It will then be possible to trace correlations of genetic factors like heart disease or intelligence through particular chromosomal labels. Once this is done, we will be able to help people to avoid specific risks and to design individual educational strategies. Probably far more important, we all gain a better understanding of the development of these traits.

Paradoxically, the most important application of this insight is not to *do* genetics but to *transcend* genetics. At the point that we understand the operation of a specific genetic factor in the development of the individual, we can design the environmental interventions that can compensate for and enhance the working efficacy of the particular genetic code with which that individual begins his existence.

Religion and Politics in the U.S.

The Emergence of the Christian New Right

Paul Anthony Schwartz

Project Director, Center for the Study of New Religious Movements, Berkeley, California

The place of religion in American social and political life—never a settled affair—is proving to be one of the more lively issues in the United States at the beginning of a new decade. Not since the involvement of many mainline Protestant, Catholic, and Jewish ministers and rabbis in the anti-war and social movements of the 1960s and early 1970s has religious belief been so clearly linked with a specific political option or called forth such heated reaction among the public at large.

The present phenomenon can be viewed as the emergence of what is perhaps best termed the "Christian New Right," though in popular language the name of one specific group, the Moral Majority, is often taken as a generic term for the entire movement. The Moral Majority, however, is only one of several groups attempting to correct what they see as the excessive secularization of American political and cultural life. The groups constituting the Christian New Right differ from their predecessors in the 1960s in several significant ways, including the degree and sophistication of their organizational structures; their familiarity with and use of popular media, particularly television; their ability to draw upon significant financial resources to spread their message; and, in the Reagan administration, their direct access to the halls of power in Washington, D.C. For these reasons, and because public discussion concerning the role of religious and cultural pluralism appears to be up for grabs at the moment, the Christian New Right has at least temporarily stolen the thunder of the more established, traditional churches, though the latter are not without their strong response to this phenomenon.

The Moral Majority, Inc.

As noted, the Moral Majority is only one of a number of organizations that are part of the Christian New Right. It is perhaps the most well known to date, moving into media prominence during the presidential election campaign of 1980. The organization specifically refers to itself as a political group, but it is headed by the Reverend Jerry Falwell, pastor of the Thomas Road Baptist Church in Lynchburg, Virginia, where its headquarters are also located. Falwell started the group in June 1979 with the Reverend Robert Billings, using the computerized mailing lists of his "Old Time Gospel Hour," a fundamentalist radio and television program with a weekly audience estimated at between fifteen and twenty million people. Membership in the Moral Majority now stands somewhere between 300,000 and one million, including 72,000 pastors. Falwell has announced plans to have over 100,000 ministers committed to the group by the end of 1981.

The Moral Majority is, in fact, three separate legal entities: Moral Majority, Inc., The Moral Majority Foundation, and the Moral Majority Legal Defense Foundation. All three of these legal entities are tax-exempt, although only contributions to the two foundations are deductible from income taxes. Moral Majority, Inc. operates as a lobbying group with offices on Capitol Hill in Washington. This branch of the organization also runs a political action committee (PAC) which contributes funds to candidates running for state and national office who support the "pro-morality, anti-humanist" positions of the Moral Majority. The Moral Majority Foundation is the major organizing arm of the group, and was responsible for the drive to register four million Evangelical, Fundamentalist, or "born-again" Christians as voters in the 1980 elections. The Moral Majority Legal Defense Fund is conceived of as a right-wing version of the American Civil Liberties Union. Falwell has announced his intention of using the Defense Fund to legally challenge court rulings and legislation which favor such "anti-family" measures as abortion, affirmative action, women's rights, civil rights for homosexuals, etc.

The Christian Voice

The second most conspicuous organization in the Christian New Right is the Christian Voice, with headquarters in Pacific Grove, California, and Washington, D.C. It is headed by Reverend Robert Grant (Reverend Richard Zone, formerly its executive director, left the organization early in 1981 to set up his own group, In God We Trust, Inc., which has recently declared a "moral war" on San Francisco and its homosexual community).

Christian Voice was also active in the 1980 elections, publishing a "Family Voting Issues Index," and a "Report Card on Fourteen Key Moral Issues." The range of issues being linked as "pro-family" or "pro-moral" by Christian Voice demonstrates what is perhaps the Christian New Rights' most significant political achievement thus far: its ability to assemble a package of issues that appeals to both fundamentalist, "biblical" morality and to a conservative or right-wing political mentality. Thus, "family" issues like abortion, the status of women and sexual minorities, and the decline of paternal authority are joined with issues popular with the secular new right, like the Panama Canal "giveaway," increased U.S. military spending, the repudiation of the courts' "coddling" of criminal suspects, and so forth.

Colonel V. Doner is the chief strategist for the Christian Voice, and Gary Jarmin its legislative liaison on Capitol Hill. The organization has a membership/mailing list of 190,000 (representing forty-five religious denominations and the Roman Catholic Church), including an estimated 37,000 pastors. It, too, has its own political action committee: The Moral Government Fund.

9

National Christian Action Coalition

Reverend Robert Billings, co-founder with Falwell of the Moral Majority, is also Executive Director and Chairman of the third Christian New Right organization to be mentioned here, the National Christian Action Coalition. With headquarters in Washington, D.C., NCAC has a membership of 1200 churches, Christian schools, and Christian Associations. Its PAC is called the Christian Voters Victory Fund; NCAC publishes *Congressional Scoreboard* in an attempt to keep its members up to date on how members of Congress are voting on what it sees as "Christian" political issues.

Religious Roundtable

Religious Roundtable is the last of the four most significant Christian New Right organizations now operating. Its president is Edward McAteer, who also serves as National Field Director for the Conservative Caucus, a secular new right political organization. Headquarters are located in Arlington, Virginia. A council of fifty-six forms the organization's core with an estimated mailing list of from 15 to 20,000 names. Publications include *Roundtable Report*, a monthly newsletter with information on current "Christian" issues ("secular humanism," school prayer, etc.) and calls for action.

Religious Roundtable illustrates quite well the close relationship between the specifically *Christian* New Right, such as the groups mentioned above, and the more broadly *secular* New Right. Apart from McAteer's position in both camps, the Roundtable also owes a debt to individuals like Richard Viguerie (from RAVCO—a right-wing direct mailing company), Phyllis Schlafly (Eagle Forum—StopERA), Paul Weyrich (Committee for the Survival of a Free Congress), John Fisher (American Security Council), and Howard Phillips (Conservative Caucus)—all of whom were among those present at the founding session of the Religious Roundtable. This pattern of interlocking memberships on boards of directors and overlapping constituencies and mailing lists is extended by the formation of single-issue coalitions in the service of a host or right-wing political causes. At least a score—and probably many more—of these coalitions involving various combinations of Christian and secular New Right organizations now exist, including: the American Life Lobby, Concerned Women for America, Life Amendment Political Action Committee, the National Pro-Family Coalition, In God We Trust, Inc., The National Committee to Restore Internal Security, Americans Against Union Control of Government, Morality in Media, Gun Owners of America, The Coalition for The First Amendment, the American Council for Free China.

What exactly has the influence of these and other Christian New Right organizations been on American political life, and what is it likely to be in the future? Even now, the extent of the Christian New

Right's contribution to Ronald Reagan's victory is still being debated, with conservative religionists claiming credit for the size of his margin over Carter in November 1980. More likely is the impact of these groups on state and local races. A majority of senators on a "hit list" of the National Conservative Political Action Committee (NCPAC) were defeated in 1980, including McGovern in South Dakota, Javits in New York, Church in Idaho, and Nelson in Wisconsin; but even here the statistical significance of the Christian New Right's impact on these races is not totally clear.

On the other hand, the involvement of Christian New Right figures in the Reagan administration can be seen as a significant ascent to power of fundamentalists and evangelicals who have for so long been considered peripheral to mainline American religion. Reverend Robert Billings's position as religious liaison during the Reagan transition gives evidence of this. Reagan's own intention to woo this constituency was made clear by his attendance at what some have called the major religious event of 1980, a "National Affairs Briefing" for over 10,000 fundamentalist, evangelical, and "born-again" ministers held in Dallas, Texas.

On a cultural rather than a political level, the Christian New Right affiliates would also appear to be making some headway. In June 1981 the Coalition for Better Television headed by Reverend Donald Wildmon apparently exerted sufficient pressure to force Procter and Gamble, one of television's largest sponsors, to withdraw its backing from thirty shows rated "immoral" by the group's self-selected watchdog committee. Wildmon has the wholehearted support of Jerry Falwell, who has also committed Moral Majority funds to back up the campaign to "clean up TV."

But as the Christian New Right gains greater public visibility and apparent political impact, it is also galvanizing a not insignificant opposition to its attempts to define American public morality. At the end of the 1980 presidential campaign, leaders from the major Protestant, Jewish, and Catholic churches and congregations met in Washington to issue a statement roundly denouncing the efforts of Falwell and his colleagues to define the "Christian" position on what they consider complex and complicated issues of public policy. Existing liberal groups like the American Civil Liberties Union have begun organizing against the Moral Majority, with the National Organization of Women reporting its largest membership gain ever since the 1980 election. Producer Norman Lear has sponsored the formation of "People for the American Way," a group which has run television spots discussing the virtues of pluralism and religious tolerance in American life. And prominent Protestant and Catholic theologians and ethicians have joined in a coalition called "Moral Alternatives in Politics," aimed at countering Falwell's claim to exclusive truth in political analysis.

What Happened in 1980–81

The important events of the year, from November 1980 to August 1981, organized for easy reference:

11 Business and the Economy
12 The Courts
13 Crime and Violence
16 Disasters
17 Education
17 Energy
17 Entertainment and Culture
18 Environment
18 Health and Medicine

19 International Affairs
31 Late News, October 1981
25 National Government and Politics
28 People, Places, and Things
28 Religion
29 Science
20 Sports
31 State and Local Governments
31 Women

The Countries of the World section (starting on page 123) covers specific international events, country by country. Special commentaries on Business and the Economy, Energy, Medicine, Religion, Space, and Travel appear in the appropriate sections (*see* Index).

1980–81

Business and the Economy

1980

Imported Subcompacts Lowest in Auto Safety Study (Nov. 7): New report by insurance industry shows small cars continue to have worst record in accident claims.

U.S. Rejects Limit on Japanese Cars (Nov. 10): International Trade Commission finds imports are not seriously damaging domestic industry and bars higher tariffs. Ascribes Detroit's troubles to economic downturn and consumer taste for smaller cars.

1981

Scheduled U.S.-China Air Passenger Service Restored (Jan. 7): Boeing 747 with 139 Chinese passengers welcomed at San Francisco International Airport as 32-year hiatus ends. After two hours, aircraft continues to New York to start return trip next day.

Freezing Weather Damages Florida Fruit Crops (Jan. 14): Mercury at record low in at least five cities, with heavy losses to fruit and vegetable harvest.

Agreement Halts Antitrust Trial (Jan. 16): Federal judge in Washington terminates case brought by Justice Department. Bell system reported to be prepared to divest itself of up to three of 23 local telephone operating subsidiaries and certain facilities of Western Electric Co., its manufacturing subsidiary.

Consumer Prices Up 12.4% for 1980 (Jan. 23): Index rises 1.1% for December at end of second year of double-digit inflation, Bureau of Labor Statistics reports. Rise for 1979 was 13.3%.

Remaining Controls on Oil Ended (Jan. 26): President Reagan abolishes remaining price and allocation controls on domestic oil and gasoline production and distribution, carrying out Administration pledge.

G.M. Reports $763 Million Loss for 1980 (Feb. 2): Corporation suffers first full-year deficit since 1921 despite $62 million earning in fourth quarter.

Rupert Murdoch Buys Times of London (Feb. 13): Australian, 49, pays $28 million for paper and affiliates, becoming one of most powerful Fleet Street publishers of century. Agreements with unions call for new printing technology, including cold type, to eliminate about 700 jobs. Thomson Organization had lost more than $100 million in 14 years of ownership.

G.M. and Ford Give Cash Rebates (Feb. 17): Announce biggest programs in auto industry's history in response to lagging sales and pleas from dealers. Rebates range as high as $1,769.

Chrysler Reports Record Loss for 1980 (Feb. 27): Corporation puts it at $1.71 billion, eclipsing Ford record for largest deficit in U.S. corporate history. Year was its worst for automobile industry.

Standard Oil (Ohio) to Buy Kennecott Corporation (March 12): Agrees to acquire nation's largest copper producer for almost $1.8 billion in cash. This is third multi-billion-dollar takeover announced within a week. Standard Oil Company of California had offered $4 billion for 80% it does not own of Amax Inc., largest U.S. producer of molybdenum. Joseph E. Seagram & Sons, liquor company, offered $2 billion from sale of its oil properties for St. Joe Minerals Corporation.

Tokyo Agrees to Limit Auto Exports to U.S. (May 1): Three-year accord will keep them to 1.68 million in 1981–82 fiscal year, decline of 7.7%, with continued limits in next two years. U.S. car industry had sought action to increase its own sales.

OPEC Nations Freeze Petroleum Prices (May 26): Action follows Saudi Arabia's refusal to increase prices from $32-a-barrel level for light Arabian crude or cut back on huge production. Other 12 nations to cut production and keep prices for crude at current level of $36 to $41 a barrel.

Coal Miners Accept New Agreement to End Strike (May 29): U.M.W. bargaining council, 3–2, approves terms negotiated with mine operators to end walkout that has hurt regional economies and cost miners more than $50 million a week in wages. Agreement, running to October 1984, provides 38% increase in wages and benefits. **(June 8):** Most of 160,000 striking miners back at work after 72 days out. Picketing by mine construction workers, whose own contract is under negotiation, keeps thousands from returning to work in several states.

Teamsters Name Sixth President (June 4): International Brotherhood delegates elect Roy L. Williams, 66, at Las Vegas convention in union's 83rd year.

Britain Cuts Price of North Sea Oil (June 6): Agrees to $2-a-barrel reduction, lowering official price to $37.25 in move thought to enhance prospect of substantial downward move in world prices. **(June 15):** Britain agrees to cut oil price $4.25 a barrel, more than double its earlier intention.

Federal Reserve Authorizes Free Banking Zones (June 9): Will allow facilities in United States to compete for international business without federally imposed reserve requirements and interest ceilings.

Reagan Ends Import Quotas for Shoes (June 30): Refuses to extend restrictions on imports from Taiwan and South Korea, in effect four years. Action strengthens Administration's commitment to free trade.

Auto Workers Rejoin A.F.L.-C.I.O. (July 1): U.A.W. back in main labor federation 13 years after philosophical and policy differences caused it to split away.

Spraying of California Orchards Ordered (July 10): Gov. Edmund G. Brown, Jr., calls for extensive use of pesticide malathion to check infestation of crop-destroying Mediterranean fruit fly. He acts to avoid Federal quarantine of California produce. Earlier, the Governor had rejected spraying as dangerous.

Screen Writers Reach Accord in Strike (July 11): Writers Guild of America reports settlement to end 13-week walkout against Hollywood movie and TV producers. Four-year pact provides, for first time, share for writers in revenue from original programming for pay television, video cassettes, and video disks. Strike delayed start of production for 1981 TV season and threw nearly half of the 30,000 behind-scenes movie and TV workers off the job.

Bargaining Averts Postal Workers' Strike (July 21): New $4.8-billion contract agreed upon by U.S. Postal Service and two unions representing 500,000 of 667,000 postal employees. Contract calls for pay increase of 11%, or $2,100, over three years for average member of American Postal Workers Union and National Association of Letter Carriers.

Chrysler Reports First Profit Since 1978 (July 22): Corporation, near bankruptcy little more than a year previously, shows $12 million earnings in second quarter.

Washington Star Ceases Publication (July 23): Time Inc. decides to fold 128-year-old daily, long regarded as one of best afternoon newspapers in country, because of circulation and economic losses. Capital now has only one daily, the morning *Washington Post.*

U.S. Court Blocks Sale of Oil Leases Off Coast (July 27): Decision by Los Angeles judge a setback for Administration's program to accelerate exploration for oil in almost one billion acres of coastal waters. In decision involving 150,000 acres of waters off California, Judge Marian Pfaelzer rules Reagan Administration had violated 1972 law in designating development area without adequately consulting state officials. Coastal states concerned over impact on environment of projected five-year drilling.

Air Controllers Strike; Flights Disrupted (Aug. 3): The 12,-000 members of Professional Air Traffic Controllers Organization wage illegal walkout in dispute with Federal Aviation Administration over wages, workweek, and retirement plan. About half of normal 14,200 daily airline flights are grounded. Reagan warns workers to return or

lose jobs. Two days later the government dismisses the strikers. **(Aug. 11):** Air travel between U.S. and Europe snarled as Canadian controllers support strikers and refuse to handle aircraft on route. **(Aug. 12):** Two-day disruption in trans-Atlantic travel broken as Canadians end boycott in return for joint inquiry on air safety. **(Aug. 13):** 61-country international controllers' body appeals to Regan to reopen talks but delays any immediate boycotts. **(Aug. 14):** Federal labor judge recommends union be stripped of bargaining powers. **(Aug. 16):** Portuguese controllers begin 48-hour boycott of U.S. flights, but fifth of trans-Atlantic travel is rerouted. **(Aug. 17):** U.S. accepts new applications for controller jobs in two-year plan to replace striking workers. **(Aug. 29):** Many airlines, vacation business hit, report substantial financial losses as flights are curtailed. Strikers also suffer as courts bar use of union subsistence fund.

Two Financial Houses Merging (Aug. 3): Salomon Brothers, largest privately held investment banking firm, announces its acquisition, effective Oct. 1, by Phibro Corporation, huge trader in commodities.

Du Pont Wins Battle to Buy Conoco (Aug. 5): Controlling interest in America's ninth-largest oil company goes to E.I. du Pont de Nemours & Company in bidding war with Mobil Corporation and Joseph E. Seagram & Sons. Du Pont pays $7.57 billion in stock and cash to become seventh-largest industrial corporation in U.S., just behind Ford.

Six-Week Postal Strike Ends in Canada (Aug. 11): Inside mail sorters and stamp sellers return to work as Canadian Union of Postal Workers ends tie-up **(Aug. 17):** International embargo lifted as workers clear up backlog and reconnect 24 million Canadians with rest of world by post. Businessmen estimate their losses in hundreds of millions of dollars. New two-year contract improves wage and holiday benefits.

Unions Give Philadelphia Bulletin a Reprieve (Aug. 16): Threat that ailing afternoon newspaper would stop publishing lifted as they vote to grant $4.9 million in concessions demanded by publisher.

OPEC Nations Fail to Agree on Oil Prices (Aug. 21): End three-day meeting at Geneva with continuing rift on new, lower range. Saudi Arabia pledges to maintain price of $32 a barrel through 1982.

California Fights Spread of Fruit Fly (Aug. 23): Extends program of aerial spraying with malathion after 14-month futile battle by tree stripping, ground spraying, and importation of sterile Mediterranean flies. Gov. Edmund G. Brown, Jr., ordered spraying at beginning of July after Federal quarantine requiring that all produce susceptible to infestation be certified as pest-free or subjected to costly fumigation before being shipped. **(Aug. 26):** State's $14.5-billion agriculture industry hit hard as Japan requires fumigation of California produce it imports and infestation of fly reported to have spread 280 miles south to Los Angeles County.

The Courts

1980

High Court Bars Posting of Ten Commandments (Nov. 17): Justices, 5–4, upset Kentucky state law requiring display of basic Christian-Jewish tenets in every public-school classroom in state. Rules law an unconstitutional "establishment" of religion.

Justices Uphold Appeal of Lenient Sentences (Dec. 9): Supreme Court rules, 5–4, that Constitution's protection against double jeopardy does not preclude prosecutors from seeking to increase penalties regarded as too light. Decision reverses Federal Appeals Court in New York.

1981

Justices Approve Televising of Trials (Jan. 26): Supreme Court rules, 8–0, states are free to permit cameras in courts. Decision, by Chief Justice Warren E. Burger, rules coverage does not violate defendants' right to fair trial. Florida practice upheld.

Justices Uphold Democrats on Rules (Feb. 25): Supreme Court, 6–3, affirms party's right to refuse to seat delegates to national convention who were not chosen in compliance with the rules of national party.

Kansas Court Upsets Libel Ruling Against Blacks (Feb. 28): State's supreme bench voids $44,500 verdict awarded by lower court jury to Dante G. Scarpelli, a white administrator, against four medical students at University of Kansas. Dr. Scarpelli had sued for defamation of character after they had filed complaint of racial discrimination against black students.

High Court Upholds Refusal to Testify (March 9): Decides, 8–1, that defendant silent in criminal case is entitled to have judge instruct jury no inference of guilt can be drawn from decision not to take stand.

Justices Back Rape Laws That Punish Males Only (March 23): Supreme Court, 5–4, rejects challenge to California statute on intercourse with under-age partners.

Supreme Court Upholds Law on Abortion Notification (March 23): Rules a state may require doctor to inform teenaged girl's parents before performing operation, at least when she is dependent upon them and living at home. Ruling, 6–3, rejects challenge to Utah law.

Justices Curb "Bill of Rights" for Retarded (April 20): Supreme Court rules, 6–3, states are not required to provide particular level of care in institutions. Finds six-year-old U.S. law merely advisory.

Three-Year-Old School Busing Ends in Los Angeles (April 20): Mandatory program for school integration dropped after 18-year legal battle. However, only 7,000 of children affected choose to return to neighborhood schools. California Supreme Court had upheld ruling that district could not be forced to integrate schools unless there was evidence of intentional segregation.

Supreme Court Backs Alaska on Revenues (April 21): Rules, 6–3, state rather than Federal Government is entitled under law to most of income from oil and gas leases issued for Federal wildlife refuges.

Justices Widen Restriction on Search of Homes (April 21): Supreme Court rules, 7–2, that police armed with valid arrest warrant also need search warrant to enter home of person other than the one sought. Decision reverses Court of Appeals in New Orleans.

Civil Libertarian Wins Libel Action (April 22): Elmer Gertz, Chicago lawyer and lecturer, awarded $400,000 damages in retrial of 12-year-old case, constitutional landmark. Article in John Birch Society publication had linked him to alleged Communist plot to discredit Chicago police.

High Court Extends Double Jeopardy Protection (May 4): Justices rule, 5–4, that it applies beyond the question of guilt to the criminal sentence itself.

Court Expands Protection Against Self-Incrimination (May 18): Justices rule unanimously that murder suspect has right to remain silent when questioned by a psychiatrist. Also decide that a defendant cannot be deemed to have waived right to a lawyer during questioning unless he initiates new talks with police.

Justice Potter Stewart Announces Retirement (June 16): Supreme Court Associate says he will leave bench July 3 after 23 years of service. Stewart, aged 66 and in good health, gives no reason for decision.

Supreme Court Rebuffs Administration Policy (June 17): Rules, 5–3, Occupational Safety and Health Administration must protect workers from exposure to toxic substances without regard to balance between costs and benefits. Upholds limits on cotton-dust exposure.

Supreme Court Rules Against Nixon (June 22): Decides, 4–4, without formal opinion, that former President and three top aides may be required to pay monetary damages for unconstitutional wiretap of home telephone of Morton Halperin, former national security aide.

Justices Rule Draft Registration May Exclude Women (June 23): Supreme Court decides, 6–3, that Congress has power to limit registration, and presumably the draft itself. In nationwide reaction, conservatives are elated at reassertion of traditional values; feminists, civil libertarians, and opponents of Reagan defense policy are disappointed and alarmed.

Former CIA Agent Loses Appeal on Passport (June 29): Supreme Court, 7–2, backs State Department revocation of Philip Agee's passport. Ruling upholds broad legal and constitutional authority of executive branch to revoke passports on national security grounds. Agee, who spent nine years in CIA, had vowed to expose its operations, and wrote a book purporting to name hundreds of covert agents.

Justices Affirm Federal Candidates' Right to TV Time (July 1): Supreme Court, 6–3, rules stations are required to sell "reasonable" amounts of time in campaigns to candidates who request it.

Supreme Court Upholds Hostage Agreement With Iran (July 2): Unanimous ruling, on narrow basis, affirms the legal authority of Presidents Carter and Reagan to nullify court orders and suspend private lawsuits to honor the settlement. Justices act on final day of 1980–81 term, 17 days before more than $2 billion in Iranian assets are to leave the country.

Reagan Chooses Woman for Supreme Court (July 7): President to nominate Sandra Day O'Connor, 51, judge on Arizona Court of Appeals, as first of sex on high tribunal. Groups opposing abortion aroused by her record of having once sided against anti-abortion cause and favoring proposed equal rights amendment.

Judge Orders Freedom for Cuban Refugees (Aug. 17): U.S. Court in Atlanta bids government release 322 held in prison for more than year because they did not have proper entry papers upon reaching country.

Crime and Violence

1980

Radical Activist Gets Three Years in Blast (Oct. 28): Cathlyn Platt Wilkerson, 35, sentenced in Manhattan court for illegal possession of dynamite and criminally negligent homicide in Greenwich Village explosion 10 years previously that killed three persons. **(Jan. 6):** Miss Wilkerson sentenced in Chicago to nine months in jail for part in 1969 "Days of Rage" disturbance.

Six Acquitted in Five Southern Slayings (Nov. 17): All-white

North Carolina jury clears present or former members of Ku Klux Klan and Nazi Party in slaying of members of Communist Workers Party at anti-Klan rally. Jury deliberated for seven days.

U.S. Judge Dismisses Two Abscam Convictions (Nov. 26): Rules Government had "stretched" Federal statutes and "entrapped" two Philadelphia officials in racketeering and bribery case. Officials were a former Councilman, George Schwartz, 65, and Councilman Harry P. Jannotti, 56.

Two Guilty in Brooklyn Abscam Trial (Dec. 3): Federal jury convicts Rep. John M. Murphy, 54, of Staten Island of receiving unlawful gratuity, conflict of interest, and conspiracy, but acquits him on more severe charge of bribery. Jurors convict Rep. Frank Thompson, 62, of Trenton, N.J., of bribery as well as conspiracy and aiding Murphy's receipt of unlawful gratuity.

Weather Underground Leader Surrenders (Dec. 3): Bernardine Dohrn, 38, gives up to authorities 10 years after going underground to avoid Federal and local riot charges in Chicago's violent "Days of Rage" antiwar demonstration in 1969. She had been living in New York. **(Jan. 13):** In Chicago Miss Dohrn gets three years' probation and $1,500 fine.

Appeals Court Upsets "Wilmington 10" Conviction (Dec. 4): Three-judge Federal panel rules nine black men and a white woman were denied constitutional rights to fair trial in 1972 because attorneys did not have full access to testimony of major prosecution witness. Ten were arrested in firebombing of white-owned grocery store in Wilmington, N.C., during period of racial unrest that began in January 1971 when officials rejected request by black students for memorial service for Rev. Martin Luther King, Jr.

John Lennon of Beatles Shot Dead (Dec. 8): Composer and performer slain outside New York apartment house by 25-year-old former mental patient, Mark David Chapman of Honolulu. Songs Lennon wrote and played with British rock group influenced young people around the world in protest movements of the 1960s. Millions mourn him. Chapman held on murder and gun-possession charges. **(Dec. 14):** Millions across globe stand alone in silence or come together in huge crowds, heeding plea from Lennon's widow, Yoko Ono, that they take 10 minutes to remember him. **(June 22):** Chapman pleads guilty. New York judge promises sentence will not exceed 20 years to life.

Justice Dept. Clears Informer in Death (Dec. 15): Attorney General Benjamin R. Civiletti says inquiry finds "no credible evidence" that Gary Thomas Rowe, Jr., shot civil rights worker in Alabama in 1965.

1981

British Police Report Break in "Yorkshire Ripper" Case (Jan. 5): Peter Sutcliffe, 35-year-old Bradford truck driver, charged with latest murder, of 20-year-old college student. Yorkshire Ripper believed responsible for deaths of 13 women in previous five years. **(May 22):** Sutcliffe gets life sentence for each of 13 killings of women over five years. Police search cost $10 million and five million man-hours.

Pennsylvania Representative Convicted of Bribery (Jan. 9): Rep. Raymond F. Lederer, 42, Philadelphia Democrat, guilty of bribery and conspiracy in Abscam (for Arab scam) investigation, despite defense in Federal Court in Brooklyn that he had been illegally entrapped into taking $50,000 payment from Federal undercover agents posing as representatives of wealthy Arab sheiks seeking help with immigration problems.

Florida Ex-Representative Guilty of Bribery (Jan. 26): Richard Kelly, 56, Republican, sixth present or former member of Congress convicted on charges arising from Abscam investigation of political corruption. Washington Federal Court gives verdict.

Bank Charges $21.3-Million Fraud by Sports Group (Feb. 2): Wells Fargo National Bank sues in Los Angeles County Superior Court, alleging manipulation by promoters and companies called Muhammed Ali Professional Sports Inc. Former heavyweight boxing champion allowed use of name but was not involved in group and has not been accused in its activities.

Three Blacks Guilty in Miami Killing (Feb. 6): Convicted by biracial jury of second- and third-degree murder in beating of three whites in 1980 race riots. A fourth defendant is acquitted.

U.S. Jury Convicts All 10 in Terrorist Trial (Feb. 11): Upholds 13 charges of seditious conspiracy against Government, auto theft, and illegal use and possession of weapons by Chicago defendants, believed to be members of F.A.L.N., terrorist organization seeking independence for Puerto Rico. Defendants absent from courtroom.

Five Journalists Cleared in Arizona Libel Case (Feb. 19): Superior Court jury gives verdict on articles on Arizona crime that reported on 1976 car-bomb slaying of Don Bolles, *Arizona Republic* reporter. Libel charges filed by Kemper Marley, Sr., 74. Punitive damage for emotional distress awarded against one of five, Robert Greene of *Newsday*, and Investigative Reporters and Editors Inc.

Arizonian Convicted in Beating of Mexicans (Feb. 23): Federal jury in Phoenix finds Patrick W. Hanigan, 27, guilty of obstructing interstate commerce in attack on three farm workers. Brother, Thomas, acquitted.

Lowenstein Killer Found "Not Responsible" (Feb. 23): New York judge rules Dennis Sweeney, 37, former civil-rights activist, victim of "mental disease or defect." Sweeney shot Congressman Allard K. Lowenstein, his onetime mentor, in March 1980 in Lowenstein's New York law office.

Woman Convicted in Slaying of "Scarsdale Diet" Doctor (Feb. 24): Jury in White Plains, N.Y., finds Jean W. Harris, 57, former Virginia school head mistress, guilty of shooting Dr. Herman Tarnower, her companion and lover for 14 years. **(March 20):** Mrs. Harris sentenced by county judge to 15 years in prison. Angry, she protests innocence.

Bank Robbery Suspect, Age 9, Arrested (Feb. 27): Boy surrenders to FBI in New York in $100 holdup, and is placed in custody of city police. Child says he used toy gun. Allowed to return home with father.

Suspect Arrested in Theft of Wandering $1.2 Million (March 4): Joseph William Coyle, 26, unemployed longshoreman, arrested at New York's Kennedy Airport and accused of stealing money that cascaded from armored truck in Philadelphia a week previously.

Utah Jury Convicts Racist in Two Killings (March 4): Finds Joseph Paul Franklin, 30, of Alabama, guilty on Federal charges of violating rights of two young black men by shooting them as they jogged with two white girls in Salt Lake City park. **(March 23):** Franklin sentenced to two consecutive life terms in shootings. Two-hundred-pound racist subdued after attacking black U.S. prosecutor.

Berrigans and Six Others Convicted in Break-In (March 6): Antinuclear activists found guilty in Norristown,

Pa., court in damaging of missile nose cones and pouring blood on papers at General Electric Company plant. Defendants are: Rev. Daniel Berrigan and brother, Philip; Molly Rush, a housewife; Dean Hammer, Divinity student; Sister Anne Montgomery, nun; Rev. Carl Kabat, priest; John Schuchardt, lawyer, and Elmer Maas, a professor of history.

Killer of Four Executed in Indiana (March 9): Steven Timothy Judy, 24, dies at State Prison in Michigan City for murders of a mother, 21, and three children.

U.S. Juries Indict 155 on Drug Charges (March 12): Federal agents conclude two-year undercover investigation of multi-million-dollar enterprises shipping marijuana from Colombia to United States. Indictments returned in Florida, Louisiana, and Georgia.

Three Alabama White Men Held in Death of Black Youth (March 25): Charged with strangulation killing of Michael A. Donald, 19, in Mobile. Case fans racial tensions.

Italian Police Seize Hunted Terrorist (April 4): Arrest Mario Moretti, 35, an electronics expert, most senior known member of Red Brigades organization and presumed the most dangerous. Sought for nine years, he surrenders meekly at Milan rail station.

Abbie Hoffman Sentenced for Cocaine Sale (April 7): Counter culture leader of 1960s, now 44, given up to three years in prison by New York State judge. He had pleaded guilty to selling $36,000 worth of drug to undercover policemen in 1973. He calls sale "an act of stupidity." Hoffman surrendered in 1980 after spending six years in hiding after arrest of others.

Rioting Sweeps London District for Two Nights (April 11–12): Hundreds of youths, mostly black, rampage through Brixton, hurling stones, bottles, and firebombs at police. (April 13): As calm returns, Government orders judicial inquiry into rioting and looting in heavily concentrated black section. Two hundred arrested and several dozen injured, including policemen. Community leaders blame economic depression and hostility to police, rather than race, as major factors.

Barbados Orders Release of Train Robbery Fugitive (April 23): High Court rules Ronald Biggs cannot be extradited to Britain to finish 30-year prison term for "Great Train Robbery" because Barbados had never had extradition treaty with Britain.

Court Rules Agnew Took Kickbacks (April 27): Maryland judge finds that, despite denials, former Vice President Spiro T. Agnew took thousands of dollars in bribes from contractors while Governor of Maryland and Vice President. Agnew ordered to repay state $147,500 in kickbacks with interest of $101,235.

New Jersey Senator Convicted in Abscam Case (May 1): Harrison A. Williams, Jr., 60-year-old Democrat, found guilty of bribery and conspiracy charges in Brooklyn Federal Court, with Alexander Feinberg, codefendant. Senator found to have agreed illegally to use influence in immigration case and in venture in which he had concealed interest.

Teamsters' Head Indicted in Bribery Plot (May 22): Roy L. Williams, interim president of International Brotherhood of Teamsters, and four others charged by Federal grand jury with conspiring to bribe Senator Howard W. Cannon, Nevada Democrat, in futile attempt to win help in delaying trucking deregulation bill.

Two Acquitted in Retrial for Letelier Killing (May 30): Anti-Castro Cubans, Guillermo Novo Sampol and Alvin Ross Diaz, found innocent in bombing murder of former Ambassador Orlando Letelier of Chile and aide in Washington in 1976. Jury finds Novo guilty of making false statements to grand jury.

Stagehand Guilty in Metropolitan Opera Slaying (June 4): Craig S. Crimmins, 22, convicted in New York court of killing Helen Hagnes, orchestral violinist.

Former Tennessee Governor Convicted (June 9): U.S. jury in Nashville finds Ray Blanton, 51, guilty of extortion, conspiracy, and mail fraud. He is convicted of abusing official powers as Governor by accepting $23,334 bribe in plan to sell liquor licences to political friends in return for share of profits.

Earl L. Butz Sentenced on Income Tax Charge (June 19): Former Secretary of Agriculture, 71, sentenced by Federal judge to 30 days in jail and to pay $10,000 fine for filing a false Federal return. (June 29): Butz surrenders quietly at Federal Metropolitan Correctional Center in Chicago to serve term.

Suspect Arrested in Atlanta Killings (June 21): Wayne B. Williams, 23, music promoter and talent scout, charged in most recent of 28 murders of black children and young adults. Authorities doubt one person is responsible for all killings. (July 17): Williams indicted in two of the deaths. He is charged with murdering Nathaniel Cater, 27, and Jimmy Ray Payne, 21, among victims of previous two years.

Ex-Warrant Officer Seized on Espionage Charges (July 15): FBI arrests Joseph George Helmich, 44, formerly of the Army Signal Corps, who had access to top secret coding devices. He is charged with selling secret information about a sophisticated teletype coding machine to Soviet officials. He is said to have been paid $131,000 for vital secrets and to have been awarded rank of Soviet colonel.

Crime Leader Convicted in New Orleans (Aug. 3): Federal court finds Carlos Marcello, 71, reputed head of organized crime in Gulf Coast region, guilty of conspiracy in case code-named Brilab, for bribery labor. Case one of three stemming from year-long undercover inquiry into public corruption and labor racketeering in Louisiana and Southwest. Two other defendants, I. Irving Davidson, 59, Washington lobbyist, and Vincent A. Marinello, 43, a New Orleans lawyer, not guilty on all charges.

Nine Radicals Sentenced in Philadelphia (Aug. 4): Judge metes prison terms of 30 to 100 years each to members of group called Move for killing a police officer in exchange of gunfire in 1978.

3 Former Congressmen Get Three-Year Prison Terms (Aug. 13): First defendants sentenced in Federal Government's two-year Abscam investigation into political corruption. They are John M. Murphy of Staten Island, N.Y., and Michael J. Myers and Raymond F. Lederer, both of Philadelphia. U.S. Court in Brooklyn also sentences former Mayor Angelo J. Errichetti of Camden to six years and City Councilmen Louis O. Johanson of Philadelphia to three years.

Escaped Spy for Soviet Recaptured (Aug. 22): Christopher John Boyce, 28, arrested near Seattle after 19-month manhunt, through tip from informer. He had escaped from Federal prison in Lompoc, Calif., Jan. 21, 1980. Bank security photos thought to identify him as heavily disguised robber in 16 holdups.

Teen-Ager Sentenced in "Born Free" Author's Death (Aug. 28): Paul Ekai, 18, gets indefinite sentence from Kenya court in 1980 killing of Joy Adamson, naturalist. Ekai had worked at her bush camp.

Disasters

1980

Five Miners Found Dead in West Virginia Pit (Nov. 8): Men apparently victims of methane gas explosion in Westmoreland Coal Company's Ferrell mine south of Madison.

Three Mile Island Nuclear Reactor Shows Limited Damage (Nov. 14): Color videotape pictures engineers measuring radiation levels inside building, scene of nation's worst commercial nuclear accident. Tape will aid in planning six-year decontamination.

Thousands Flee Brush Fires in California (Nov. 16): Flames sweep 30,000 acres in south of state. At least 90 homes destroyed, some valued at more than $1 million. Total structural damage estimated at $25 million.

42 Killed as Korean Airlines Plane Burns in Seoul Landing (Nov. 19): Boeing 747 jetliner flying from Los Angeles and Anchorage, Alaska, bursts into flames with 215 aboard.

More Than 80 Dead in Las Vegas Fire (Nov. 21): At least 500 injured when flames sweep from kitchen through casino of MGM Grand Hotel, trapping 3,500 guests and employees. More than 1,000 guests in nightclothes rush to roof and are lifted off by helicopter. **(Dec. 18):** Investigators report significant violations of fire and building codes that they say substantially contributed to quick spread of fire.

Earthquake Kills More Than 3,000 in Italy (Nov. 24): Nation's worst temblor in 65 years devastates southern provinces of Naples, Salerno, Potenza, and Avellino. Quake destroys bridges and roads; fog and severed telephone lines also impede rescue operations. Hundreds of thousands are injured and homeless. Inefficiency of relief brings criticism of Government. **(Nov. 30):** Search for survivors abandoned as rain, hail, and wet snow impede recovery, and troops and volunteers strive to provide vaccination, water, food, clothes, and temporary shelter.

Nine Blazes Drive Thousands From California Homes (Nov. 25): Wind-driven fires blacken more than 45,000 acres in five southern counties, with four deaths, destruction or damage of 300 homes, and evacuation of tens of thousands.

26 Perish in Westchester Hotel Blaze (Dec. 4): Victims, mostly corporation executives, trapped in meeting rooms at Stouffer's conference center 10 miles north of New York City. Forty others injured. Fire worst in Westchester County's history. Blaze arouses movement for strengthening county fire codes. **(Jan. 15):** Westchester District Attorney calls fire "deliberate act of arson." **(April 29):** Luis Marin, 25, former busboy, charged with arson and murder in blaze. Pleads not guilty.

Prime Minister of Portugal Killed in Air Crash (Dec. 5): Francisco Sá Carneiro, 46, dies as light plane carrying him to political rally crashes into building after taking off from Lisbon airport. Two pilots and five others, including Defense Minister, also killed in accident three days before Presidential election.

Jetliner Crash Kills 68 in Colombia (Dec. 21): Caravelle explodes minutes after takeoff from northern coastal city of Ríohacha. Planted bomb is blamed. **(Dec. 22):** Officials of Aerovías del Cesár line report threatening call and say sabotage is apparent cause of crash.

16 Dead in Nairobi Hotel Explosion and Fire (Dec. 31): Police Commissioner hints at explosive device in New Year's Eve disaster at 76-year-old Norfolk Hotel,

packed with New Year's Eve revelers, many of them British and American tourists. **(Jan. 7):** Kenyan Government identifies bomber as Moroccan and member of Popular Front for Liberation of Palestine, Qaddura Mohammed Abd al-Hamid, 34.

1981

30 Perish in Fire at Home for Elderly (Jan. 9): At least 78 of 111 residents escape as blaze of undetermined origin burns two-story brick and stucco building at Keansburg, N.J. One victim dead of injuries in leap from window, others from smoke inhalation and carbon monoxide poisoning.

Nearly 400 Perish in Sinking of Indonesian Ship (Jan. 27): Passenger vessel *Tampomas II* catches fire in storm and sinks in Java Sea; 762 rescued.

24 Greek Fans Die in Stampede After Soccer Match (Feb. 8): Dozens injured after being trampled upon by other spectators forcing way out of crowded stadium after game in Athens attended by 45,000.

Eight Perish in Las Vegas Hilton Hotel Fire (Feb. 10): Damage estimated at $10 million in 2,700-room building; 198 injured. Busboy accused of arson.

70 Soviet Officers Killed in Plane Crash (Feb. 13): Three top commanders of Pacific Fleet among victims on Leningrad outskirts. Type of craft not disclosed.

44 Dead, 129 Injured in Dublin Dance Hall Blaze (Feb. 14): Many victims are teen-agers among 800 young people at dance competition at discothèque.

11 Workers Killed in Collapse of Condominium (March 27): Five-story building collapses at Cocoa Beach, Fla., when crane drops huge bucket of wet concrete through the freshly poured roof. Victims buried in rubble.

Freighter Pilot Blamed in Tampa Bay Crash (April 1): National Transportation Safety Board ascribes May 1980 accident in which 35 were killed to decision to cross under a bridge after ship lost bearings in storm.

Tornado Kills Six in Wisconsin (April 4): One hundred injured as storm rips through West Bend, destroying homes and other buildings. Damage estimated in millions.

U.S. Submarine and Japanese Merchantman Collide (April 9): *George Washington*, armed with nuclear missiles, and *Nissho Maru*, freighter, crash in East China Sea. Captain and first mate of freighter lost. **(April 20):** U.S. accepts liability. Claims may total $4.2 million.

15 Dead in Colorado Mine Disaster (April 17): Last body discovered in Dutch Creek No. 1 coal mine near Redstone, Colo. Victims killed by methane gas explosion as they dig high-grade coal in two spaces.

15 Killed as Two Planes Collide Over Colorado (April 17): Twin-engined Air U.S. commuter plane, a British-made Handley-Page Jetstream, and skydiving Cessna-206 crash. All 13 aboard commuter plane die, and two of six in Cessna. Four parachutists leap to safety.

Wide Snowstorm Cripples Britain (April 25): Worst April weather of century piles drifts up to six feet deep, with damage to crops and animals.

21 Killed in Explosion of Air Force Plane (May 6): Two wives of servicemen among victims in disaster at Walkersville, Md. They had been taking part in program to experience husbands' stresses while flying.

14 Killed as Aircraft Crashes on Carrier Nimitz (May 26): Marine electronic combat aircraft, EA-6B Prowler jet, blows up on flight deck off northern Florida. Three fighters destroyed, 16 other planes damaged. Navy reports 45 sailors injured in accident termed possibly worst in peacetime naval aviation. Carrier's nuclear-propulsion system is undamaged.

3,000 Reported Dead in Iran Earthquake (June 11): Large area in southeast devastated. (June 12): Many buried in mass graves. Nearly 800 rescued.

11 Dead in Glacial Break on Mount Rainier (June 21): Buried by up to 70 feet of boulder-sized chunks of ice. Victims among 29 climbers attempting to reach 14,410-foot summit of Washington State's highest peak.

Fire Destroys 25 San Francisco Buildings (July 10): Blaze called possibly city's worst since earthquake of 1906. No victims are found and no cause is discovered.

Hundreds Dead in Yangtze River Flood (July 16): Level of river highest recorded since 1905 following six days of heavy rain. Water surges from Sichuan Province through heavily populated regions toward East China Sea at Shanghai. Thousands rescued from hills and rooftops. Government seeks food and clothing for 500,000 homeless refugees. Flood crests dissipate upon reaching industrial city of Wuhan. Final toll set at 753 dead, 558 missing, 28,140 injured, and 1.5 million homeless. Flooding is worst since 1949. Damage to homes and crops set at $1.14 billion.

More Than 110 Die in Collapse of Hotel Walkways (July 18): Aerial structures suspended by steel rods in lobby of year-old Hyatt Regency Hotel in Kansas City tear loose and plummet to lobby floor as crowd dances and moves to music of Steve Miller band. Witnesses say walkways swayed until top one tore away, crashed on another beneath, and both fell to the floor, crushing dancers and observers. Injured put at 188 in major U.S. hotel disaster.

550 Reported Dead in Northwest India Floods (July 25): Waters cause heavy toll in state of Rajasthan.

Education

1981

U.S. Revokes Bilingual Teaching Regulations (Feb. 2): Secretary of Education T.H. Bell, in first official act, says proposed rules for teaching in foreign languages in public schools would have cost the taxpayers about $1 billion over next five years.

Princess Anne Named Chancellor of University of London (Feb. 18): Queen's 30-year-old daughter chosen in university's first contested election. She succeeds Queen Mother Elizabeth, in post 25 years.

Dartmouth College Names 14th President (Feb. 23): David T. McLaughlin, 49 years old, now chairman of Board of Trustees, is a 1954 Dartmouth graduate and chairman of Toro Company of Minneapolis.

Georgetown University Returns Libyan Gift (Feb. 23): Washington institution gives back more than $600,000 of endowment for professorship in Arab studies. President cites Libya's support of terrorism.

Court Upholds California Schools on Evolution Teaching (March 6): State Superior Court judge rules science textbooks do not violate fundamentalists' rights.

"Truth in Testing" Made Nationwide Policy (March 26): Trustees of College Entrance Examination Board to provide students copies of Scholastic Aptitude Test with their answer sheets and list of correct answers. Action follows discovery of errors in tests.

Swarthmore College Gets $6-Million Gift (April 2): Reports largest donation in 117-year history from Eugene M. Lang, New York City entrepreneur, a 1938 graduate of liberal college near Philadelphia.

Foundation Supports 21 in Genius Search (May 18): Names talented individuals for awards of from $24,000 to $60,000 annually for five years in hope of "significant contributions," according to donor, the John D. and Catherine MacArthur Foundation. Winners range from Robert Penn Warren, 76, poet and novelist, to Steven Wolfram, 21, a physicist.

Energy

1980

Settlement Reached in Oil Exploration Dispute (Dec. 22): U.S. and Massachusetts remove obstacle to exploration for oil and gas deposits in Georges Bank, shallow ocean bottom southeast of Cape Cod. Accord provides greater government commitment to protect fishing grounds.

1981

$35-Million Settlement for Three Mile Island Losses (Feb. 21): Owners and builders of nuclear reactor agree on payments to thousands of claimants living within 25-mile radius. Most to go for business losses. Settlement reached nearly two years after worst commercial nuclear power accident. Approved by Federal judge in Pennsylvania.

Entertainment and Culture

1980

Yale Given $4 Million in Modern Art (Nov. 7): Nearly 200 works donated to university's Art Gallery by Katharine Ordway of Weston, Conn., who died in 1979, aged 80, with additional gift of $2 million for maintenance and housing and for additional purchases. Picasso, Rouault, and Renoir among artists included.

Hawaiian Stamps Bring Record Prices (Nov. 18): Two 19th-century two-cent missionary stamps sold for $210,000 and $230,000 at New York auction. Previous record for a U.S. single stamp was $135,000.

$12 Million in Art Given New York Museum (Dec. 9): Metropolitan Museum to get collection rich in Abstract Expressionism from Chicago collector, Muriel Kallis Steinberg Newman. Paintings valued at $12–15 million.

Leonardo da Vinci Notebook Brings $5 Million (Dec. 12): Armand Hammer, American industralist and art collector, pays $5,126,000 for "Of the Nature, Weight, and Movement of Water," at London auction, highest price ever paid for a manuscript at public sale.

Museum Thieves Steal $25 Million in Paintings (Dec. 27): Break into National Museum of Fine Arts in Buenos Aires and take mostly 19th-century French Impressionist paintings and drawings and antique Chinese porcelains.

1981

Yale Gets $650,000 for Brasher Doubloon (Jan. 10): Anonymous collector in Palm Beach, Fla., pays university's asking price for one of world's most famous and valuable coins, put on sale to help finance a new library.

Composition by Mozart at Age 9 Discovered (Feb. 13): Missing symphony, written in 1765, found in Bavaria. Bought by Bavarian State Library from unidentified seller for undisclosed sum.

American Film Institute Honors Fred Astaire (April 11): Dancer, nearing 82, wins ninth Life Achievement Award in recognition of work in advancing film-making art.

Posthumous Novel Wins Pulitzer Fiction Prize (April 13): Prize board honors John Kennedy Toole, author of "A Confederacy of Dunces," about New Orleans characters. Toole committed suicide in 1969 after failing to find publisher. Mother finally got the volume published. **(April 15):** *Washington Post* says article about life of eight-year-old heroin addict for which author won a Pulitzer Prize was a fabrication. Newspaper relinquishes award, first such action in 64-year history of prizes. Janet Cooke, 26, reporter who wrote the article, resigns after admitting hoax.

Uncut "Sister Carrie" Being Published (April 16): University of Pennsylvania Press to issue version of Theodore Dreiser novel with restoration of 36,000 words deleted by wife, editors, and publisher as being too sexually explicit and rough for the early 1900s.

Chicago Unveils Joan Miró's "Chicago" (April 20): Crowd of 2,500 in Daley Square marks 88th birthday of Spanish painter and sculptor, who donated 40-foot high abstract sculpture of a woman. City and private citizens contributed $500,000 to put up figure. Artist reported too frail for trip to U.S.

Record $1 Million Paid for a Stamp (May 12): "Blue Boy" cover sold to European collector for the reportedly highest price for a philatelic item. Five-cent stamp issued in Alexandria, Va., and posted in 1846, year before first U.S. stamp was issued.

Winner of Sixth Van Cliburn International Piano Competition (May 31): André-Michel Schub, 28-year-old New Yorker, first among six finalists in contest at Fort Worth, Tex. He gains cash award of $12,000, recording contract, and two years of concerts.

Return of Paintings to East Germany Ordered (June 15): Federal judge in New York rules art collector must give back two 15th-century works by Albrecht Dürer stolen from castle occupied by U.S. troops in 1945. They are valued in millions of dollars.

Metropolitan Museum Gets $10-Million Donation (July 22): Gift to New York art institution from Harold D. Uris, building and real-estate developer, is one of largest in its history. It will endow Ruth and Harold D. Uris Center for Education at museum.

Environment

1980

Carter Signs Alaska Lands Bill (Dec. 2): Approves compromise measure passed by Congress creating more than 104 million acres of national parks, wildlife refuges, and wilderness areas from Federal holdings, ending four-year struggle between environmentalists and developers. President appeals for public support of environment, even at sacrifice of possible energy sources.

Supreme Court Approves E.P.A. Pollution Rules (Dec. 2): Decides Environmental Protection Agency can enforce water purity standards without regard to whether individual factory can afford to comply with limitations. Decision, 8–0, reverses Federal Appeals Court.

New Panel to Study Motor Vehicle Emissions (Dec. 12): Environmental Protection Agency and major automobile and truck companies, in new alliance, establish Health Effects Institute to end deep controversy over air pollution regulations.

Carter Signs Legislation Upholding Historic Landmarks (Dec. 13): Amendments to national-preservation program overcome Federal court decision regarded as threat to hundreds of existing designations.

1981

U.S. Seeks Delay in Treaty on Use of Oceans (March 3): Reagan Administration abandons agreement in United Nations Law of the Seas Conference to conclude in spring of 1981 pact on regulating use of resources. **(March 8):** Less than 48 hours before resumption of conference, Administration dismisses George H. Aldrich, acting head of U.S. delegation, and top career officials in delegation. New Head is James L. Malone, Assistant Secretary of State for Oceans and International Environmental and Scientific Affairs.

Conference Bars Trade in Products of Three Whale Species (March 6): Conservationists hail outlawing of international commerce in oil, meat, and bones of virtually only commercially hunted varieties. Japan opposes action at New Delhi conference, and Soviet Union and United States abstain in voting. The three species are sperm, sei, and fin whales.

381 Burros Slain to Clear Naval Base (March 9): Sharpshooters kill wild animals, herded by helicopters, after Navy decision that they endangered planes and ground traffic by straying onto runways and roads, at China Lake Naval Weapons Center, California.

Curb on Hunting of Sperm Whales Ordered (July 25): International Whaling Commission, meeting in Britain, orders virtual ban on hunting of species and total ban, beginning in 1983, on "cold harpoons," said to cause whales to bleed slowly to death. Conservationists hail decision, a victory for them in dramatic reversal of previous policy.

Health and Medicine

1980

Screening Test for Cystic Fibrosis Reported (Dec. 31): Reveals chemical abnormality in some skin cells, according to *New England Journal of Medicine*. Disease of respiratory tract is most common lethal inherited disease of white Americans. Report presented by scientists at Children's Hospital Medical Center and Harvard Medical School in Boston.

1981

Long-Term Study Links Cholesterol to Heart Deaths (Jan. 7): One of longest and largest analyses of its kind, lasting more than 20 years, shows consumption of large amount of cholesterol increases risk of premature coronary fatalities. Study shows higher intake of polyunsaturated fats helps protect from early coronary deaths. Analysis prepared by Dr. Richard B. Shekelle of Rush Presbyterian-St. Luke's Medical Center, Chicago.

Long-Wear Contact Lenses Approved (Jan. 14): Food and Drug Administration sanctions general use of Hydrocurbe II, first such lenses that can be worn continuously for up to two weeks.

Doctors Approve Artificial Heart for Human Use (Jan. 27): Review committee at University of Utah's College of Medicine accepts product of more than 20 years' research. Federal Food and Drug Administration must give approval for first investigational use of device in human being.

Scientists Hint New Means of Preventing Allergies (Feb. 8): Discover natural substances in body that suppress key initiator of allergic attacks in susceptible individuals. In animals, and probably humans, substances act by suppressing production of a special type of antibody called immunoglobulin that produces symptoms of allergy.

Study Finds New Drug Cuts Heart Fatalities (April 1): Report in *New England Journal of Medicine* says test of timolol in Norway suggests promise of preventing death or second heart attacks for many victims.

Artificial Skin Reported for Burn Victims (April 23): Substance made from cowhide, shark cartilage, and plastic developed by doctors at Massachusetts General Hospital in Boston. They say it performs many of the functions of real skin.

Researchers Report Powder to Make Bone (April 30): Harvard doctors implant new demineralized substance in patients with birth defects to form bone where none existed, and use it to help mend broken bones of others. Dental use held possible.

U.S. Votes No on Baby Formula Code (May 20): Dissents as World Health Organization, 93–3, adopts voluntary plan to encourage breast-feeding and restrict aggressive marketing practices. Two U.S. officials of Agency for International Development resign in protest. Bottle feeding has been associated with high levels of infant disease and death, particularly in unsanitary backward regions.

Connecticut Approves Marijuana for Patients (July 7): New law permits doctors to prescribe these cigarettes for persons suffering from glaucoma or side-effects of cancer treatments such as radiation or drugs.

Heart Transplants Prolong Man's Life (July 24): Willebrordus A. Meuffels, 36, Netherlands bus driver, in stable condition after surgeons at Houston's St. Luke's Episcopal Hospital replace organ damaged by massive heart attack during surgery to bypass clogged arteries leading to heart. They implant the second mechanical heart ever inserted in a human being. Plastic device pumps blood through a pneumatic mechanism electric-powered from a console outside body, about size of television set. Artificial heart designed and built at Texas Heart Insititute at St. Luke's. It is slightly larger than human heart. **(July 26):** Patient receives human heart from 29-year-old donor. **(Aug. 3):** Meuffels dies of kidney failure, lung problems, and infection after being kept alive 54 hours by artificial heart and for a week on transplant. Physicians say they have demonstrated that an artificial heart can maintain life and that a two-stage cardiac operation is possible.

International Affairs

1980

Labor Slate Wins in Jamaica Election (Oct. 31): Final court shows Prime Minister-elect Edward P.G. Seaga swept into office by greater margin than party predicted. Laborites win 51 of 60 Parliament seats, with record 53% of popular vote. Prime Minister Michael N. Manley retains own seat by narrow margin on People's National Party slate.

Iran Imprisons Former Foreign Minister (Nov. 7): Sadegh Ghotbzadeh under arrest for television broadcast criticizing the ruling Islamic Republican Party. He once ran state radio and television, now important tool of the theocracy. **(Nov. 10):** Ghotbzadeh freed after three days in prison, reportedly by order of Ayatollah Ruhollah Khomeini.

Polish Supreme Court Backs Trade Union Charter (Nov. 9): Rules agreement legitimizing independent labor can stand without reference to "leading role" of Communist Party in Polish society. Union leaders call off plans for nationwide strike.

Michael Foot Heads British Labor Party (Nov. 10): Its members of Parliament choose intellectual left-wing Socialist, devoted to nuclear disarmament.

Human-Rights Parley Convenes in Madrid (Nov. 11): Impasse over agenda temporarily broken, East-West conference on rights and cooperation in Europe opens. **(Nov. 14):** Conference saved from collapse as U.S. and Soviet Union accept compromise agenda.

Japanese Prime Minister Keeps Post (Nov. 27): Zenko Suzuki unanimously re-elected to two-year term as president of Liberal Democratic Party, assuring his continuation as Government leader.

Six Leftists Slain, Violence Flares in El Salvador (Nov. 29): Eleven killed as unrest spreads in capital, San Salvador, after abduction and killing of prominent opposition leaders. Crowds snarl traffic, bus service is cut, and electric power interrupted. Leftists blame National Guard troops and military-civilian junta for complicity in slayings, for which right-wing paramilitary group claims responsibility.

Blinding of Prisoners in India Charged (Dec. 1): Supreme Court and Indira Gandhi Government investigate charges of acid use by police in state of Bihar and call for punishment of those guilty of "inhuman and barbaric crime."

Poland Gets $1.3 Billion in Aid From Soviet (Dec. 1): Stanislaw Kania, Communist leader, tells party's Central Committee of help in solving economic crisis. He says close links have been maintained with Soviet Union.

Polish Communists Carry Out New Purge (Dec. 2): Central Committee dismisses four longtime members of ruling Politburo, and return to it Gen. Mieczyslaw Moczar, former Interior Minister, known for ruthlessness and conduct of anti-Zionist campaign in late 1960s. Purge, fourth since August strikes, strengthens party leader, Stanislaw Kania, as he cooperates with independent union while attempting to curb labor unrest.

Four Missing Americans Found Slain in El Salvador (Dec. 4): U.S. officials identify bodies of three nuns and lay worker of Maryknoll Order. **(Dec. 5):** U.S. suspends new economic and military aid pending clarification of role of Salvadoran security forces in killings. **(Dec. 17):** Administration restores $20 million in economic aid after reorganization of ruling junta. **(Dec. 18):** Inter-American Development Bank approves $45.4 million in loans to El Salvador for peasant cooperatives as part of plan to combat rural guerrilla violence.

President of Portugal Re-Elected (Dec. 7): Gen. António dos Santos Ramalho Eanes, 45, wins landslide victory. Onetime anti-guerrilla fighter and expert on psychological warfare had been opposed by majority conservative Democratic Alliance.

Zimbabwe Official Freed in Killing (Dec. 8): High Court rules Edgar Z. Tekere, a senior Government minister, committed murder in shooting of a white farmer, but clears him of criminal charges because he acted "in good faith" to suppress terrorism. Verdict made under law enacted by white minority regime of Ian D. Smith. Tekere is Minister of Manpower, Planning, and Development and is Secretary General of governing Zimbabwe African National Union.

Milton Obote Victor in Ugandan Election (Dec. 13): His Uganda People's Congress announced as winner of 66 of 126 parliamentary seats. Obote had been overthrown as President by Idi Amin in 1971.

El Salvador Gets First Civilian President in 49 Years (Dec. 13): Junta names José Napoleón Duarte, 55, after negotiations between armed forces and Christian Democrats, major political party.

Leading Polish Groups Appeal for Unity (Dec. 16): Roman Catholic Church, Communist Party, and new independent trade union call for reconciliation to overcome national crisis. Plea marks memorial service at Gdansk for workers slain in anti-Government riots 10 years previously.

Execution of Jewish Editor by Iran Reported (Dec. 18): Israeli television in Tel Aviv discloses death of Simon Farzami, editor of English-language *Teheran Journal*, on charges of espionage for U.S.

Seven Irish Prisoners End Hunger Strike in Belfast (Dec. 18): At least two had been nearing death of starvation after seven and a half weeks of action supporting demand that prisoners get special political status instead of treatment as common criminals. Their decision a victory for Margaret Thatcher's British Government.

Opposition Leaders Arrested in India Protest (Dec. 20): Among hundreds seized during march by thousands of farmers demanding higher prices for sugar and onion crops. Those detained include Y.B. Chavan, former Defense and Home Minister, and Sharad Pawar, former chief minister of Maharashtra state, where protest developed. Both leaders in Old Congress Party, which opposes Indira Gandhi regime. **(Dec. 28):** Many arrests and show of force by Maharashtra government foil final phase of 300-mile march by 10,000 disgruntled farmers on state legislature.

Mexico Terminates Fishing Agreements With U.S. (Dec. 28): Action reflects determination to build up fishing fleet to compete in waters traditionally dominated by U.S., Japanese, and Cuban vessels.

Marinus van der Lubbe Acquitted in Reichstag Fire (Dec. 29): West Germany quashes 1933 verdict that found Dutchman, later executed, guilty of setting blaze that enabled Nazis to carry out campaign against remaining legal opposition.

1981

Greece 10th Member of Europe's Common Market (Jan. 1): Formally joins European Economic Community. Nation will gradually integrate economy with more well-to-do members and eliminate barriers to movement of money, goods, and workers. **(Jan. 5):** Official ceremony marks accession, with left-wing opposition and confusion over price levels.

Deng Xiaoping Reportedly Takes Over High Military Post (Jan. 3): Chinese leader said to head Communist Party's Military Commission. Post had been filled by Hua Guofeng, deposed party chairman.

Two Americans Slain in San Salvador (Jan. 3): Men working in land distribution program and head of nation's agrarian program killed by gunmen in coffee shop of Sheraton Hotel in capital. Right-wing death squads blamed. Victims are: Michael P. Hammer, 42, of Potomac, Md.; Mark David Pearlman, 36, of Seattle; and José Rodolfo Viero, in mid-30s, the agrarian leader.

At Least 1,000 Killed in Nigerian Uprising (Jan. 9): Toll possibly higher over two weeks as Government forces quell attacks by members of Islamic cult. Officials report a Libyan-backed insurrection.

Prime Minister Demotes Zimbabwe Official (Jan. 10): Robert Mugabe removes Joshua Nkomo, former Patriotic Front guerrilla colleague, from Cabinet position controlling police. Mugabe also dismisses Edgar Z. Tekere as Manpower Planning Minister. Tekere recently acquitted of murder charges in killing of a white farmer.

Terrorists' Attack Destroys Military Jets in Puerto Rico (Jan. 12): Macheteros claim responsibility for setting time bombs that destroy nine fighters and damage two others at Muñiz Air National Guard base at Isla Verde. Damage estimated at $45 million.

Arab Member of Israeli Parliament Slain (Jan. 12): Gunfire from jeep kills Bedouin, Hammad Abu Rabia, in Jerusalem. Victim, in his early 50s, was chief of large tribe in Negev. He had sought compromise on Government's attempt to expropriate Bedouin land for air base.

Terrorists Release Kidnapped Magistrate in Rome (Jan. 15): Red Brigades free Giovanni D'Urso unharmed after 33 days. He is said to have given secret official information to terrorists.

Raiders Shoot Ulster Activist and Husband (Jan. 16): Bernadette Devlin McAliskey, 33, former member of Parliament and fiery opponent of British in Northern Ireland, seriously wounded by gunmen breaking into home in village near Belfast. Police blame Protestant paramilitary group.

Philippine President Ends Martial Law (Jan. 17): Ferdinand E. Marcos releases 341 prisoners hours after terminating military rule that lasted eight years and four months. At festive ceremony, Marcos signs order that all decrees and orders by which he has ruled would remain in force.

U.S.-Iran Agreement Frees 52 Hostages (Jan. 18): After three months of intense negotiations, accord is reached on procedure for releasing Americans captured in seizure of U.S. Embassy in Teheran on Nov. 4, 1979. Of $11 billion to $12 billion in frozen Iranian assets, $8 billion is put into Algerian escrow account; of this only $2.9 billion returned to Iran when hostages are freed. About $3.7 billion pays off American and other bank loans, and about $1.4 billion is left in escrow until disputed claims are settled. International claims commission to be set up. Agreement requires American companies, banks, lawyers, and government agencies to turn over to Treasury Department information about assets of late Shah, Mohammed Riza Pahlevi and family in U.S. Algeria plays major role as go-between in negotiations. **(Jan. 20):** The 52 former hostages fly to Algiers on Algerian plane under escort of Algerian diplomats and then on to U.S. military hospital in Wiesbaden, West Germany, for tests and treatment. Freedom comes only minutes after President Reagan is sworn in. **(Jan. 21):** Jimmy Carter flies to Wiesbaden as President Reagan's representative. Carter, shaken, reports hostages had been subjected to "mock firing squads" and other tortures.

52 Hostages From Iran Welcomed in U.S. (Jan. 25): Air Force VC-137 dubbed "Freedom One" flies from Wiesbaden, Germany, and lands the former captives at Stewart International Airport near U.S. Military Academy at West Point, where they are greeted by families and joyous crowds. The 139 relatives are flown to West Point from Washington, where President Reagan had told them: "America has to be very proud of you." The reunited families remain in seclusion at West Point's Thayer Hotel. **(Jan. 27):** The hostages, Richard I. Queen, a 53rd captive freed the previous summer, and 400 relatives fly to Washington, where President, in ceremony on South Lawn of White House, welcomes hostages and promises "swift and effective retribution" for attacks on U.S. employees in foreign lands. Thousands waving yellow ribbons and balloons cheer hostages' motorcade. **(Jan. 30):** Twenty-one of the hostages are cheered by New York crowds in traditional Broadway ticker tape parade.

I.R.A. Says It Killed Two Protestant Leaders (Jan. 22): Outlaw guerrillas claim responsibility for deaths of Sir Norman Stronge, 86, former Speaker of Northern Ireland Parliament, and son, James, 48, and firebombing ancestral home in North Ireland. Police believe attack is retaliation for attempted assassination of Catholic civil rights activist Bernadette Devlin McAliskey and husband, Michael.

Millions in Poland Boycott Jobs (Jan. 24): Workers heed call of Solidarity movement to take "free Saturday" to back independent union demand for five-day work week. Most major industries halted.

Former Chinese Leaders Get Long Sentences (Jan. 25): Survivors of Cultural Revolution spared execution in verdict by special court on charges of persecuting political enemies and plotting to seize power. Jiang Qing, 67, widow of Chairman Mao Zedong, and Zhang Chunqiao, 63, former Shanghai mayor, both labeled "chief culprits," get suspended two-year death sentences, which could be commuted to life in prison. Eight others sentenced to from 16 years to life in prison. The ten were found guilty of various crimes.

Spain Gets New Prime Minister (Jan. 30): Deputy Prime Minister Leopoldo Calvo Sotelo succeeds Adolfo Suárez, who resigned under attack by right-wing members of executive committee of governing Union of the Democratic Center. Committee accepts Mr. Suárez's nomination of Mr. Calvo Sotelo, a 54-year-old former industrialist in charge of economic affairs in outgoing cabinet.

Polish Workers Call Off Strike (Jan. 31): Agreement between Government and Solidarity union movement augurs labor calm. Accord after nearly 13 hours of bargaining provides for five-day, 40-hour workweek in 1982, with some non-working Saturdays in 1981.

Reagan Meets With Korean President (Feb. 2): Agrees with Chun Doo Hwan to normalize relations with South Korea. Action represents move away from Carter Administration's emphasis on human rights.

Norway Gets First Woman Prime Minister (Feb. 4): Mrs. Gro Harlem Brundtland formally installed. Pledges her Labor Government to continue policy of full employment and social welfare and to base Norway's national security on NATO alliance.

Iran Frees an American Citizen (Feb. 4): State Department reports release of Iranian-born Mohi Sobhani of Los Angeles, held since Sept. 6 on espionage charges.

Yemen Releases Two Americans Held as Spies (Feb. 8): William Thomas, Jr., 60, of Madrid, and Duwayne Terrell, 24, of Colorado Springs, say they were tortured by Yemeni authorities in effort to extract confessions. Evidence believed insufficient.

Ex-Official Breaks With British Labor Party (Feb. 9): Shirley Williams, former Education Secretary, resigns in move signaling creation of new party, "Council for Social Democracy," to work for political ideals they say Labor has abandoned in drift to left.

U.S. Human Rights Survey Finds Decline in Torture (Feb. 9): State Department also reports decrease in disappearances and inhuman treatment of prisoners during last year of Carter Administration. Report is still critical of Soviet Union's practices.

Army General Is New Polish Prime Minister (Feb. 9): Gen. Wojciech Jeruzelski, Minister of Defense, replaces Jozef Pinkowski. The general, 57, is nominated by Central Committee of Polish Communist Party. He is a Soviet-trained career officer, regarded as moderate.

Polish Farmers Lose Move to Form Trade Union (Feb. 10): Supreme Court in Warsaw rejects appeal by private growers for independent organization. Judges suggest they seek registration as a farmers' "association."

American Writer Freed by Iranians (Feb. 11): Cynthia B. Dwyer, 49, free lancer, returns to U.S. after spending more than nine months in jail as accused spy. She calls allegation "complete nonsense" and says she was probably scapegoat after abortive rescue attempt to free hostages held at U.S. Embassy.

Saudi Arabia Freeing 21 Imprisoned Americans (Feb. 18): Crown Prince Fahd calls action "gesture of goodwill" to Reagan Administration. Prisoners held on charges involving drugs, alcohol, and pornography.

Polish Students Granted an Independent Union (Feb. 18): Victory for all universities indicated as student sit-in at University of Lodz, lasting almost a month, ends with agreement by Government on independent association not under Communist control.

Rightist Military Uprising in Spain Collapses (Feb. 23): Group of Civil Guards seizes lower house of Parliament in Madrid and holds nation's leaders as hostages. Plot leaders believed to be exasperated by terrorism and granting of autonomy to Spain's regions. **(Feb. 24):** Uprising collapses 18 hours later when military leaders pledge loyalty to King Juan Carlos. In TV address, king, bemedaled and in full uniform, pledges his faith in democracy and orders the uprising crushed. **(Feb. 25):** Parliament endorses new cabinet led by Leopoldo Calvo Sotelo. A number of senior officers are implicated in abortive plot. Gen. Alfonso Armada Comyn, 61, Army's deputy chief of staff, removed from office.

Iran Bars Anglican Church (Feb. 23): Prosecutor says it will no longer be allowed to function. Most churches in country already shut down. **(Feb. 28):** Three Anglican workers freed by Iran and return to Britain. They are: John and Audrey Coleman, medical missionaries, and Jean Waddell, former church secretary. They had been held on basis of forged documents indicating cooperation with United States CIA.

Margaret Thatcher Welcomed in Washington (Feb. 26): British Prime Minister, visiting White House, praises Reagan's economic policy. **(Feb. 28):** She and President discuss possible use of British military units in international force for Persian Gulf rapid deployment. **(March 1):** She returns to London as officials report substantial agreement.

Argentina Arrests Eight Human Rights Leaders (Feb. 28): Seizes files on more than 6,000 missing persons at offices of Center for Legal and Social Studies. **(March 6):** Judge releases six, including Emilio Mignone, former high justice official, and Dr. José Westerkamp, physicist, but does not drop case. Center sought information on missing thousands.

12 M.P.'s Quit British Labor Party to Form New Group (March 2): Parliament members plan to form Social Democrats in opposition to Labor's sharp transition to the left. New grouping led by Dr. David Owen, Foreign Secretary in last Labor Government.

26th Communist Congress Ends in Moscow (March 3): Leonid I. Brezhnev, 75, unanimously re-elected as party's General Secretary. All other aging leaders of Soviet Union confirmed in office at status quo session.

U.S. Decides to Sell F-15 Equipment to Saudi Arabia (March 6): Administration will provide material to improve range and fighting power of 62 jets, over objections of Israel and many in Congress. Cites "growing threat" from Soviet Union in Middle East.

Colombia Guerrillas Kill American Missionary (March 7): Slay Chester A. Bitterman 3rd, linguist and laymissionary held hostage since abduction Jan. 19. M-19 rebels had accused him of being CIA spy and demanded that Summer Institute of Linguists, for which he worked, leave Colombia. Institute, which translated Bible into Indian dialects, had refused.

Reagan Greeted and Heckled on Visit to Canada (March 10): Hundreds outside Parliament in Ottawa denounce what they consider U.S. intervention in El Salvador and negligence on pollution, but officials report "excellent rapport" in President's discussions with Prime Minister Trudeau. **(March 11):** Reagan addresses Parliament with pledges of friendship but without concessions for resolving disputes. Private talks produce agreements on broad policy goals, but no agreements for settling Canadian grievances.

Turkey Mourns Two Diplomats Slain in Paris (March 12): Holds state funeral in Ankara for Resat Morali, 37, and Tecelli Ari, 34, murdered by gunmen who claimed to be Armenian nationalists. Nationalists have killed 17 Turkish diplomats since 1973. Turkish protests mount.

Three Pakistani Hijackers Surrender (March 14): Terrorists holding more than 100 hostages aboard Caravelle jet give up after Syria agrees to give asylum to 54 alleged political prisoners released earlier by Pakistan. Hostages, including three Americans, held 13 days. Armed captors had killed one of hostages, and threatened to kill others.

Millions in Poland Strike to Protest Violence (March 19): Riot policemen in city of Bydgoszcz break up demonstration by farmers seeking to form union, and beat some severely. **(March 20:)** Two-hour protest strikes break out in at least four cities as tension grows. Solidarity union calls nationwide strike alert but does not hold top Government officials responsible for attack. **(March 27):** Workers stage four-hour nationwide strike, largest organized protest in 36 years of Polish communism. Outbreaks draw sharp attacks from Soviet bloc nations.

Jeane Kirkpatrick Meets South African General (March 23): State Department reveals delegate to U.N. talked with senior intelligence officer despite earlier statements that no members of visiting military delegation had met policy-level U.S. officials. **(March 24):** White House says Mrs. Kirkpatrick did not know full role of high-ranking military officer.

Former British Intelligence Chief Cleared of Spying (March 26): Prime Minister Margaret Thatcher tells Commons two thorough investigations of late Sir Roger Hollis failed to reveal proof that he had been a Soviet agent and he was declared not guilty. **(March 27):** Mrs. Thatcher orders inquiry into how a British journalist had obtained information about the suspicions.

Social Democratic Party Launched in Britain (March 26): Rebel Laborites, with 14 members of Parliament and wide public support, organize formally to effect basic realignment and reject "class antagonisms."

Polish Labor Cancels Plan for General Strike (March 31): Leaders of Solidarity vote confidence in Lech Walesa, despite attacks on his agreement with Government.

Two-Day Military Coup Crushed in Thailand (April 1): Generals reported to have overthrown government of Gen. Prem Tinsulanonda, Prime Minister. **(April 3):** Thousands of loyal troops sweep into capital. Four dead and several wounded in exchanges of gunfire. Prime Minister pledges "fair judgment" for rebels.

37 Dead as Violence Erupts in Lebanon (April 2): One hundred and sixty injured as shooting erupts in Beirut and eastern Lebanon as Christian militiamen and Syrian troops exchange artillery fire in worst outbreak since cease-fire ended civil war in 1976.

Alexander Haig Visits Middle East (April 4): Secretary of State in Cairo, opening tour. Pledges Reagan Administration's desire to promote security and peace efforts in region. **(April 8):** Haig in Madrid before going to London, Paris, and Bonn on return trip. Says he has laid groundwork for stronger ties with Arab nations and Israel. In Saudi Arabia, last stop, Haig notifies Saudis of U.S. decision to sell them five Awacs electronic surveillance aircraft.

Imprisoned I.R.A. Member Elected to Parliament (April 10): Robert Sands, 27, serving 14 years for firearms violations, defeats Harold West, 63, Protestant Unionist, in Ulster ballot. Sands carrying on a hunger strike.

Polish Parliament Backs Two-Month Suspension of Strikes (April 10): Overwhelmingly approves freeze after Prime Minister Wojciech Jeruzelski threatens to resign. Approves his agreement with Solidarity union.

Four Dead in Dominican Republic Strife (April 10): Dozens injured and hundreds arrested in series of student demonstrations fueled by labor strife and charges of police brutality. Outbreaks set off by good-will visit of two United States naval vessels, which angers students.

René Lévesque's Party Victorious in Quebec (April 13): Premier and Parti Québécois win 49.2% of popular vote in legislative ballot to 46% for Liberals. Results revive hopes of Mr. Lévesque's nationalistic followers.

Britain and Belize Agree on New Constitution (April 14): Central American colony to retain existing democratic institutions upon gaining independence.

Polish Farmers Win Right to Independent Union (April 17): Government agrees with Rural Solidarity on organizational structure similar to Solidarity, union of workers. Farm union will cover country's 3.5 million private farmers. Accord removes prolonged cause of tension.

Administration Decides on Five Radar Planes for Saudis (April 21): Formally approves multibillion-dollar arms package including Awacs surveillance aircraft, despite criticism from Israel and Congress.

U.S. Offers Pakistan Five-Year Aid Package (April 21): Economic and military assistance designed to offset threat by Soviet Union from Afghanistan. It would involve $500 million for first year alone, as against Carter offer of $400 million for two years.

Reagan Lifts Curbs on Grain Exports to Soviet (April 24): Ends limitation imposed by President Carter Jan. 4, 1980, because of Russian intervention in Afghanistan. Decision announced to Cabinet in first appearance in office since attack on him.

Hunger Strikers Die in Northern Ireland Jail (May 5): Bobby Sands, 27, Irish Republican Army gunman and member of Parliament, succumbs on 66th day of fast to force British to recognize I.R.A. inmates as political prisoners. **(May 12):** Francis Hughes, 25, is second hunger striker to die in Maze Prison, Belfast, on 59th day without food. He was serving life sentence for murdering British soldier. **(May 21):** Raymond McCreesh, 24, dies after 61 days without food. He had been serving a 14-year sentence for attempting to ambush British troops. **(May 22):** Patrick O'Hara, 23, is fourth Irish Nationalist hunger striker to die, after 61 days without food. O'Hara, not an I.R.A. member, was serving eight-year term for possessing a hand grenade. **(July 8):** Fifth hunger striker, Joseph McDonnell, 30, I.R.A. member, dies in 61st day without food. **(July 13):** Martin Hurson is sixth Irish Nationalist hunger striker to die since early May, in the 45th day of his fast. **(July 14):** Street battles flare as mourners file past coffin.

François Mitterrand Elected French President (May 10): Socialist candidate wins seven-year term in biggest political shift in generation. He defeats President Valéry Giscard d'Estaing, leader of center-right coalition by about 4 percentage points. **(June 3):** Socialist Government raises minimum wage by 10% and increases Social Security benefits.

Pope John Paul II Wounded by Gunman (May 14): Shot as he stands in open car moving slowly among more than 10,000 worshipers in St. Peter's Square in Rome. Pontiff, aged 60, undergoes 5 hours 25 minutes of surgery in which parts of intestine are removed. Police seize Mehmet Ali Agca, 23, Turkish citizen, an escaped murderer who had previously threatened the Pope's life in the name of Islam. **(May 23):** Doctors report Pope out of danger and disclose details of treatment. Bullet did not injure pancreas, as had been feared at first. **(July 22):** Agca found guilty of attempting to kill Pope and two American women and is sentenced to life in prison. Rome court of two judges and six jurors rules he must spend year in solitary confinement.

Italian Voters Reject Repeal of Liberal Abortion Law (May 18): By 2–1 margin, they defeat proposal despite determined campaign by Roman Catholic Church.

Five British Soldiers Die in I.R.A. Ambush (May 19): Mine blows up their armored personnel carrier on country road. Believed detonated by remote control.

Italian Cabinet Resigns in Masonic Scandal (May 26): Government of Prime Minister Arnaldo Forlani falls as result of revelation that hundreds of high officials were members of illegal secret lodge. **(May 28):** Forlani's caretaker Government suspends five officials for belonging to secret lodge, including commanders of Italy's three intelligence services.

President of Bangladesh Shot and Killed in Coup Attempt (May 30): Ziaur Rahman, 45, slain in port city of Chittagong, with two aides and several bodyguards. Dacca radio blames little-known opposition group. **(June 1):** Army rebellion collapses with arrest of Maj. Gen. Manzur Ahmed, leader of coup. Government troops retake Chittagong, only place seized by rebels.

Israelis Destroy Iraqi Atomic Reactor (June 8): Announce planes have wrecked facility near Baghdad that would have enabled Iraq to produce atomic bombs. Prime Minister Begin defends the raid as essential to prevent attack on Israel's cities. The $275-million facility was being built by France and Italy. **(June 9):** Begin rebuts international criticism, saying, "There won't be another Holocaust in history." **(June 10):** U.S. sees possible "substantial violation" of Israel's arms agreement with U.S. and holds up delivery of four F-16 fighter-bombers. **(June 11):** In Baghdad meeting,

20 Arab nations and P.L.O. condemn raid. **(June 19):** U.N. Security Council unanimously votes resolution condemning Israel's destruction of Iraqi nuclear reactor and urges Israel to open nuclear plants to international inspection. United States backs action but stands by commitments to Israel.

Bani-Sadr Flees to Political Asylum in France (June 10): Ayatollah Ruhollah Khomeini dismisses President Abolhassan Bani-Sadr as commander in chief of Iran's armed forces, 48-year-old President's sole remaining position of authority following gradual erosion of power by clergy-dominated Government. Islamic fundamentalists suspicious because they feel he is Western-oriented, despite immense general popularity. **(June 22):** Khomeini, 81-year-old revolutionary leader, removes Bani-Sadr from office as President, leaving clergy and secular supporters in control of Government. The French-educated Bani-Sadr is reported in hiding. **(July 29):** Deposed President arrives in France after dramatic night flight from Teheran in hijacked Iranian military plane. He is granted political asylum as long as he refrains from political activity, although Iran demands extradition. Bani-Sadr is driven to apartment occupied by two teen-age daughters and his sister.

French Socialists Win Control of Parliament (June 14): Party scores landslide victory in first round of elections to National Assembly. **(June 21):** In second round voting, Socialist victory exceeds predictions and gives President François Mitterrand full Government power. Socialists go from 117 to 285 seats for majority control of 491-seat Assembly. Combined Right drops from 274 to 156, and Communists fall from 86 to 44. **(June 23):** Mitterrand, reaching agreement with Communists, appoints four Communists to 44-member Cabinet in nonsensitive posts. Communists agree to support many international and domestic policies of the Socialists.

U.S. and Pakistan Agree on $3 Billion Aid (June 15): Military and economic program designed to strengthen Pakistani defenses against threat from Soviet troops in Afghanistan. Pact calls for rapid restoration of arms assistance, suspended in 1979, including the sale of F-16 aircraft.

U.S. Agrees to Sell Arms to China (June 16): Secretary of State Alexander M. Haig, Jr., announces decision at end of successful three-day talks in Peking with Chinese leaders. Lifting of U.S. restrictions augurs major effects for U.S., China, and Soviet Union. **(June 27):** Soviet Communist Party newspaper *Pravda* attacks decision as "escalation of reckless policy" that is "highly dangerous for the cause of peace."

Minority Prime Minister Sworn in in Italy (June 28): Giovanni Spadolini, 56, secretary of small Republican Party, heads 27-member coalition as Christian Democrats lose leadership post for first time in 36 years. Formation of Government ends crisis provoked by scandal over secret Masonic lodge.

72 Dead as Blast Kills Iran Leaders (June 28): Victims include Islamic Republican Party's leader, Chief Justice Ayatollah Mohammed Beheshti, members of Parliament, and Cabinet officials as bomb destroys party's Teheran headquarters. **(June 29):** Ayatollah Ruhollah Khomeini vows that Iranian revolution will go on. He names Iran's Prosecutor General, Abdulkarim Musavi Ardebili, to succeed Beheshti.

Egypt to Get Two U.S. Atomic Reactors (June 29): Agreement signed in Washington provides also for fuel to generate electric power, with safeguards against use of material and technology for military purposes.

Chinese Reds Replace Mao's Successor (June 29): Hua Guofeng, Mao Zedong's choice, succeeded by Hu Yaobang, protégé of Deng Xiaoping, China's most powerful leader, as chairman of Communist Party. Hua declared "no longer fit" for office because of "leftist" errors in the five years of tenure.

Chinese Communists Say Mao Made Errors (June 30): Party assessment finds Mao Zedong, leader for 27 years, made both "monumental" contributions and mistakes. Present leaders, many imprisoned under Mao, attack his role in starting Cultural Revolution. Statement issued on eve of party's 60th anniversary.

Menachem Begin's Party Wins in Israel (June 30): Likud bloc wins 48 seats in parliamentary election, opposition Labor Party 47, and religious and right-wing parties 16. **(July 8):** Prime Minister Begin forms coalition government with conservative parties, National Religious Party, Agudath Israel, and Tami.

New Irish Parliament Names Prime Minister (June 30): Chooses Garret FitzGerald, former economics professor and Foreign Minister for four years, to be Ireland's seventh in office, succeeding Charles J. Haughey. FitzGerald, 55, heads coalition of his Fine Gael Party and the smaller Labor Party.

Argentine Court Releases Mrs. Isabel Martinez de Perón (July 6): Federal tribunal orders parole for former President, 50, under house arrest since military overthrew her five years previously. Thousands cheer widow of Juan Domingo Perón, Argentine strong man.

Disorders Break Out in British Cities (July 12): In wide demonstrations, youths wield bricks, gasoline bombs, spades, machetes, and other weapons in 30 major centers, including London, Liverpool, Manchester, Birmingham, Nottingham, Huddersfield, and Aldershot. High unemployment called a major cause of unrest, with racial tension one of many other causes. **(July 14):** After nearly two weeks of violence, Government reacts as thousands of arrests threaten to burden overcrowded prison system and considers Army camps as detention centers. Traditionally unarmed police will be permitted to use plastic bullets, armored vehicles, and water cannon. **(July 16):** Government plans official study of causes of unrest and ways to deal with it. Labor seeks jobs-oriented approach to reduce 2.7 million unemployed. Cabinet postpones action on $1.9-billion jobs program as Prime Minister Margaret Thatcher stands firm on austere economic program and seeks to keep emphasis on restoring and keeping law and order.

300 Dead as Israelis Bomb Beirut (July 15): As border violence escalates, Palestinian guerrillas fire dozens of rockets at northern Israeli towns in apparent retaliation for Israeli air raids into southern Lebanon. Three killed and 25 wounded. **(July 17):** Israeli jets attack densely populated section of Beirut containing Palestinian guerrilla headquarters and knock out three more bridges in southern Lebanon. Israel puts pressure on Lebanese authorities to curb Palestinian military operations and warns that she is no longer refraining from attacking guerrilla targets in civilian areas. **(July 18):** Death toll in Beirut reaches at least 300 dead and 800 wounded. Apartment houses in ruins and streets littered with household effects. **(July 20):** President Reagan indefinitely delays

delivery of F-16 fighter bombers to Israel because of "escalating level of violence" in Middle East. **(July 24):** Israeli and Palestinian forces agree separately to a cease-fire across Israeli-Lebanese frontier. U.S. negotiates agreement with Israel. U.N. deals directly with Palestine Liberation Organization. Previously the Security Council had unanimously asked end to fighting.

Polish Communists Vote by Secret Ballot (July 17): Delegates to emergency party congress support centrists and reject liberal and conservative extremists in single-ballot vote for seats on Central Committee. **(July 18):** Again by secret vote, first in Eastern Europe for such a position, delegates elect as party leader Stanislaw Kania, who led party through crisis of previous 10 months. Kania wins by 1,300 votes to 568 for Kazimierz Barcikowski, a fellow moderate, who was Kania's single opponent.

Leaders of Seven Nations Confer at Ottawa (July 19): President Reagan greeted by Prime Minister Pierre Elliott Trudeau upon arrival to work out economic and political differences with leaders of six other major industrial countries. High interest rates in U.S. and East-West relations are major topics. **(July 21):** Seventh annual conference ends with pledge to revitalize economies, but with no precise agreement on how to do so. Reagan and leaders of Britain, Canada, France, Italy, Japan, and Western Germany agree to meet again next year in France. U.S. makes no economic-policy concessions.

Britain Announces Independence for Belize (July 26): Self-governing Central American colony is Britain's last American mainland possession. After she gains full independence on Sept. 21, British forces will remain to insure country's future security.

Bani-Sadr's Successor Elected in Iran (July 26): Tally shows Prime Minister Mohammad Ali Rajai won nation's second Presidential election with more votes than predecessor had in first balloting, in 1980.

Panama's Leader Killed in Plane Crash (Aug. 1): Gen. Omar Torrijos Herrera, 52, dies with three others in bad-weather accident on inspection tour over West Panama. Torrijos known in U.S. as architect of Panama Canal Treaties and man who gave asylum to deposed ailing Shah of Iran. **(Aug. 4):** World leaders and thousands of Panamanians attend funeral.

Egypt and Israel Sign Sinai Agreement (Aug. 3): Establish 2,500-member international peacekeeping force to police their peace treaty signed in 1979.

Thousands of "Boat People" Flee Vietnam (Aug. 4): U.N. reports 12,368 were given refuge in June in camps in Malaysia, Thailand, Singapore, and Hong Kong.

U.S. and Egyptian Presidents Confer (Aug. 6): After two days of talks, Reagan assures Anwar el-Sadat of active U.S. role in future Middle East diplomacy, but avoids specific course. Sadat earlier urged U.S. to recognize Palestine Liberation Organization.

57 French Citizens Released by Iran (Aug. 10): Return to Paris after Iranian Government had held up departure in crisis following French asylum for Abolhassan Bani-Sadr, deposed president, and for a leader of the leftist People's Muhahedeen in Iran.

Jet Fighters for Israel Approved (Aug. 17): Reagan lifts 10-week suspension of shipments of 16 F-15 and F-16 jets. He makes no decision as to whether

Israel had violated agreement with U.S. in attack on Iraq.

Printers Shut Down Official Polish Press for Two Days (Aug. 18): Extraordinary job action disrupts most newspapers. Solidarity union protesting press offensive against it and demanding expanded access to state-run television, radio, and press. **(Aug. 20):** Strike ends with Solidarity threatening wider shutdown that might include television and radio.

South Africa Court Dooms Three Blacks (Aug. 19): Supreme Court in Pretoria decrees hanging for members of outlawed African National Congress opposing white rule for role in series of sabotage attempts.

U.S. Navy Jets Shoot Down Libyan Planes (Aug. 19): Two F-14s fell two Soviet-built SU-22s after being fired upon by one of the Libyan aircraft in final hours of two-day U.S. Navy exercise in southern Mediterranean and northern part of Gulf of Sidra, which the U.S. regards as international waters despite Libyan territorial claims. **(Aug. 27):** President Reagan reports Libyan pilots parachuted to safety and were picked up at sea.

I.R.A. Backer Wins Election to British Parliament (Aug. 21): Owen Carron, 28, unemployed teacher, victor in by-election in Ulster, a defeat for Protestant establishment in Northern Ireland. He succeeds late Robert Sands, elected while on hunger strike.

Two Nations Recognize El Salvador's Guerrillas (Aug. 28): Mexico and France, in joint declaration to U.N., term opposition a "representative political force," in defiance of Reagan Administration's policy.

240 Angolans Die in South African Foray (Aug. 29): South Africa also reports destroying radar installations and their antiaircraft units in five-day incursion against insurgents. Attack called largest since South Africa attempted to intervene in civil war in 1975.

Bomb Kills Top Iranian Officials (Aug. 30): President Mohammed Ali Rajai and Prime Minister Mohammed Javad Bahonar die as powerful explosion wrecks Prime Minister's offices in central Teheran. Many others in heavily guarded room killed or wounded.

U.S. Vetoes U.N. Rebuke to South Africans (Aug. 31): Breaks with Allies over Security Council resolution condemning recent raid into Angola. American officials say foray was a response to repeated attacks by guerrillas from Angola bases into Namibia.

U.S. Takes Responsibility in Sinking of Japanese Ship (Aug. 31): Says coincidental circumstances and faulty naval judgement caused loss of freighter in April after collision with U.S. submarine.

National Government and Politics

1980

Former CIA Agent Pleads Guilty to Aiding Soviet (Oct. 29): David H. Barnett, 47, admits sale of U.S. intelligence secrets and exposure of operations and agents, detailed in statement to Federal Court in Baltimore, submitted by Justice Department. **(Jan. 8):** Barnett is sentenced to 18 years by Federal District judge in Baltimore.

Ronald Reagan Elected President in Republican Sweep (Nov. 4): Wins 489 electoral votes in nationwide election to 49 for Carter. In popular tally, Reagan gets 43,201,220, or 51% to 34,913,332, or 41% for Carter, and 5,581,379 for Anderson, who with 7% thus qualifies for Federal campaign subsidy. Republicans wrest control of Senate for first

time in 26 years and gain at all other levels. Defeat of prominent Democratic liberals and other G.O.P. gains strengthen Reagan.

Two Former FBI Officials Guilty in Break-Ins (Nov. 6): W. Mark Felt, 67, and Edward S. Miller, 56, convicted in Washington Federal court of conspiring to violate constitutional rights of American citizens by illegal searches for bombing suspects in 1972 and 1973.

Reagan Makes First Appointments (Nov. 14): President-elect names as new White House chief of staff James A. Baker 3rd, Houston lawyer, 51, a former aide to President Ford and Vice President-elect George Bush. Announces appointment of Edwin Meese 3rd as counselor to President with Cabinet rank. Meese was chief of Reagan campaign staff.

Ford Settles U.S. Discrimination Case (Nov. 25): Motor Company agrees with Equal Employment Opportunity Commission to pay $23 million and provide other benefits to women and members of minorities. Settlement one of largest in recent years by a major employer.

Senate Deletes Antibusing Amendment (Dec. 10): Yields to President Carter's threat of veto and cuts from stopgap financing bill prohibition of Justice Dept. intervention in lawsuits involving busing of school children to achieve desegregation.

U.S. Drops Case Against L. Patrick Gray 3rd (Dec. 11): Justice Dept. halts prosecution of former Acting Director of FBI, accused of authorizing illegal break-ins in hunt for fugitive members of radical Weather Underground in 1972 and 1973. Prosecutor finds evidence unconvincing.

Ninety-sixth Congress Finally Adjourns (Dec. 16): Ends five-week post-election session, marking finish of 26 years of Democratic rule on Capitol Hill. Adjournment follows approval of compromise funding legislation for many key Government agencies.

President Gets Final Official 1980 Census Figures (Dec. 31): On eve of deadline, bureau certifies population count after controversy marked by bitter lawsuits. Final total is 226,504,825, which is 11.4% above 1970 count of 203,302,031. Release of figures made possible as Supreme Court overturns lower court order to block certification, pending Government appeal of New York City contention that count should be adjusted.

1981

New FBI Guidelines Bar Entrapment (Jan. 5): But Justice Department rules allow bureau's director in some cases to authorize agents to offer bribe to officials even without "reasonable indication" that individual has engaged or is engaging in crime.

Reagan Completes Cabinet; Retains Envoy to Japan (Jan. 7): President-elect, in gesture to Senate Democrats, announces that Mike Mansfield, former Senate majority leader, will continue as Ambassador.

Carter, in Farewells, Warns Nation of Dangers (Jan. 14): Fifteen-minute address televised nationally from Oval Office calls on Americans to continue struggle to avoid nuclear war, protect the environment, and enhance human rights, themes central to his Presidency. He cautions against intrusion of "single-issue groups and special-interest organizations in political process". **(Jan. 15):** President's final Budget Message proposes spending for fiscal 1982 of $739.3 billion and deficit of $27.5 billion. He asks substantial increases in military spending and cuts in nondefense programs. **(Jan. 16):** In final State of the Union Message to Congress, Carter warns that U.S. confronts "serious problems," including unemployment, unacceptably high inflation rates, and increasingly tight world oil market. (Jan. 17): Administration in final Economic Report to Congress, says only way to reduce inflation is to continue restraint in tax reduction, Government spending, and growth of money supply. Report from departing Council of Economic Advisers rejects heavy tax cuts for individuals, endorsed by incoming President Reagan.

U.S. Judge Rebuffs Louisiana Bench in Integration Case (Jan. 14): Federal official, Nauman Scott, at Alexandria, La., issues permanent court order forbidding Judge Richard Lee of State District Court or anyone else to interfere with desegregation plan for public schools of Rapides Parish. Judge Lee had defied Federal judge's temporary order by personally overseeing enrollment of three white girls in an all-white school.

Ronald Reagan Sworn In as 40th President (Jan. 20): Takes oath in first inaugural ceremony on western front of U.S. Capitol. Promising "era of national renewal," Reagan's Inaugural Address emphasizes need to limit Federal Government powers and to end unemployment and inflation. Says "Government is not the solution to our problem; government is the problem." First official act is a freeze on Government hiring. (Jan. 21): In first full day in office, Reagan swears in White House staff, seeks to dismiss hundreds of Carter Administration holdovers, and asks Cabinet help in cutting Federal budget.

Reagan Abolishes Wage-Price Board (Jan. 29): Ends unit that has monitored increases for six years, one of Carter Administration's anti-inflation weapons. Orders 60-day freeze on pending U.S. regulations. Announcement comes at first news conference.

Marine Jury Convicts Pfc. Robert R. Garwood (Feb. 5): Vietnam prisoner of war, now 34, found guilty by five officers at Camp Lejeune, N.C., court-martial of collaborating with enemy and assaulting a fellow soldier 14 years previously. His defense based on plea of insanity while confined. (Feb. 13): Garwood ordered reduced to rank of private, dishonorably discharged, and forced to forfeit some pay and allowances. Final plea for mercy blames mental illness for actions.

Reagan Approves Increase in U.S. Debt Ceiling (Feb. 7): Signs measure raising it by $50 billion to $985 billion. Retroactive law allows Government to continue borrowing to pay bills. G.O.P. traditionally against rise. It is Reagan's first legislative victory.

Reagan Administration to Observe Hostage Deal (Feb. 18): But first statement on accords with Iran says Administration would not have negotiated.

Reagan Offers Sweeping Economic Program (Feb. 18): Warning Congress of "day of reckoning," he maps drastic change in Government's direction. President proposes a $659.5-billion budget for fiscal year 1982, with $45 billion deficit. Asks budget cuts totaling $41.4 billion in 83 major programs and extensive tax reductions, including annual cut of about 10% over three years. Only military budget increased. Inflation and unemployment are targets.

Democrats Select New Chairman (Feb. 27): National Committee names Charles T. Manatt of Los Angeles, veteran party fund-raiser. He promises to develop "new American agenda" of political ideas for party.

Reagan Announces 37,000 Cut in Federal Jobs (March 6): Replaces temporary hiring freeze with "new permanent ceilings" with two-year saving of $1.3 billion.

Reagan Proposes $695-Billion Budget (March 10): Hands Congress centerpiece of plan to "stop runaway inflation" and "revitalize the economy" by decreasing Federal role. Calls election outcome "our mandate" for change, in asking Congress for support.

Five to Get $10,000 Each for FBI Violations (March 15): Justice Department agrees to pay for breach of constitutional rights by wiretaps, burglaries, or mail openings in early 1970s, in settlement of lawsuit in U.S. Court.

U.S. Drops Inquiry on Former Carter Aide (March 24): Special prosecutor finds evidence insufficient to indict Tim Kraft, once national campaign manager and White House official, on charges of cocaine use.

Congress Backs Reagan on Milk Price Supports (March 26): House takes final action on Administration plan to save $147 million by skipping April 1 increase in first test of drive to cut Federal spending.

President Reagan Wounded by Gunman (March 30): Shot as he walks to limousine after address at Washington Hilton Hotel. James S. Brady, 40, Presidential press secretary, and two law-enforcement officers also hit. In two-hour operation, surgeons remove a .22-caliber bullet that struck Reagan's seventh rib and penetrated his left lung three inches, collapsing it. A bullet pierces brain of Brady, most seriously injured. Police and Secret Service agents overpower John W. Hinckley, Jr., 25, son of a Denver oil executive. Hinckley is charged with attempted assassination of President and shooting of the three others. (March 31): President making good recovery. Vice President Bush fills in for him at White House. President signs bill eliminating increase in dairy price supports. Surgeons report Brady recovering unexpectedly well. World leaders express shock and distress at attack. (April 1): President continues "amazing recovery." Meets key aides and signs executive order amending foreign trade restrictions, but his schedule is limited. (April 11): Twelve days after shooting, President walks out of hospital, refusing to ride wheelchair to front door. He returns to White House, looking pale and walking stiffly. "Feels great."

Reagan Pardons Two Ex-FBI Officials (April 15): Grants unconditional clemency to W. Mark Felt, once second highest official in bureau, and Edward S. Miller, chief of intelligence division, who had been convicted of violating rights of citizens by authorizing break-ins into homes in search of antiwar radicals in the 1970s. President says they served nation "with great distinction."

Report Clears U.S. Officials in Billy Carter Case (April 21): Justice Department study finds none violated law in investigation of his relationship with Libya, but says brother of former President "lied to Government agents" investigating his responsibility to register as an agent for Libya.

Reagan Appeals to Congress to Pass Budget (April 28): Appears before joint session of House and Senate, calling package of spending cuts and tax reductions "the only answer we have left" to inflation and unemployment. It is first extensive public appearance since attack on life.

Convicted Representative Quits Congress (April 29): Rep. Raymond F. Lederer, 42, three-term Philadelphia Democrat, resigns day after House ethics committee recommends expulsion because of conviction in Government's Abscam investigation.

Arms Control Negotiator Appointed (April 30): Reagan names Lieut. Gen. Edward L. Rowny, an opponent of 1979 strategic arms treaty with Soviet Union, as head of talks on arms and missile limits.

Congress Approves President's Budget (May 7): House, 270–154, gives Reagan a victory as coalition of Republicans and conservative Democrats votes to curtail Federal spending and change direction of Government. Key ballot, 253–176, supports proposal for $689-billion budget for fiscal 1982, with projected deficit of $31 billion, and reduction in most spending, except for military. **(May 12):** Republican-controlled Senate, 78–20, adopts $700.8-billion Reagan budget as Democrats from West and South join Republicans in defeating moves to restore funds. Military spending increased to $188.8 billion and $1.7 billion is restored in benefits for retired Federal employees. **(May 14):** House and Senate conferees split differences and approve $695.5-billion budget, but reject full Social Security reductions proposed by Administration. Budget for fiscal 1982 has $37.6-billion deficit and $657.8-billion revenues.

Sears Settles Four U.S. Discrimination Suits (June 4): Equal Employment Opportunity Commission and Sears, Roebuck & Co., nation's largest retailer, agree on procedures to end alleged discrimination against blacks and Hispanic Americans. There will be special hiring procedures but no quotas.

Human Rights Nominee Withdraws (June 5): Ernest W. Lefever, Reagan nominee for Assistant Secretary of State for Human Rights, quits after Senate Foreign Relations Committee votes against him, 13–4. Action viewed as first defeat for Administration on a nomination. Lefever afterward rebuts accusations concerning record on human rights issues.

Two Seized on Espionage Charges (June 28): American and a Polish national arrested near Los Angeles in sale of secret weapons documents to Polish intelligence service. FBI identifies them as William Holden Bell, 61, former employee of Hughes Aircraft Company, and Marian W. Zacharski, 29, head of American operations of Polish American Machinery Company.

High CIA Official Resigns Under Fraud Charges (July 14): Max C. Hugel, chief of clandestine operations, denies allegations by two former business associates that he participated in fraudulent securities transactions when he managed an electronics business in 1970s. In letter to William J. Casey, Director of Central Intelligence, who had chosen him, he brands charges "unfounded, unproven, and untrue." Casey names John H. Stein, career CIA employee, to succeed Mr. Hugel as Deputy Director for Operations. Federal Court has found that Mr. Casey, a close adviser to President Reagan, had participated in investment offering in 1968 for a farming company that made misrepresentations to investors.

Reagan Speech Appeals for Tax-Cut Program (July 27): President, in nationwide TV address, terms it "first real tax cut for everyone in almost 20 years." He accuses Democratic Congressional leadership of "political fun and games." Democratic replies brand Administration's plan gamble with economy.

Ambassador to Saudia Arabia Resigns (July 28): Robert G. Neumann, 65-year-old foreign policy analyst, quits amidst rumors that action had been forced after a dispute with Secretary of State Alexander M. Haig, Jr. But Haig says Neumann resigned for personal reasons "for him to describe." Friends and critics of Neumann say he had been forced to resign after saying to one or more Senators he believed some statements about Middle East policy made by Mr. Haig on TV had been "unfortunate." One official says Neumann had argued that U.S. should "crack down" on Israel for some of recent actions, including bombing raids on Iraq and Beirut.

Berrigans Sentenced in Nuclear Protest (July 28): Pennsylvania judge in Norristown hands sentences of three to 10 years to Philip F. Berrigan, a former priest, and his brother, the Rev. Daniel J. Berrigan, for roles in break-in at a plant of General Electric Company at nearby King of Prussia, where missile guidance systems are made. Six others also sentenced. Before he imposes sentence, Judge Samuel W. Salus says defendants violated criminal law, and liberty has its bounds. Similar still sentences also go to Rev. Carl Kabat and John Schuchardt. Shorter sentences given Dean Hammer, Elmer Maas, Sister Anne Montgomery, and Molly Rush. Group known as the Plowshares Eight.

Senate Inquiry Finds CIA Director Fit for Post (July 29): Select Committee on Intelligence unanimously reports no basis for concluding that William J. Casey should be removed because of past financial dealings. Senator Barry Goldwater, Republican of Arizona, chairman of panel, says staff inquiry will continue into Casey's financial activities.

Reagan's Third Triumph: Victory on Tax Reductions (July 29): In key House vote, 238–195, President defeats Democratic majority with same coalition of Republicans and conservative Democrats that supported him on budget and budget reductions. Measure, similar to one voted by Senate, provides for three-year 25% cuts in individual rates and major reductions in levies paid by business and oil producers. **(Aug. 1):** In all-night session, House-Senate conferees agree on final provisions of tax legislation, designed to help spur production and stimulate the economy. **(Aug. 3):** Senate, 67–8, approves tax bill after defeating move to recommit it. **(Aug. 4):** House, 282–95, sends measure to President after visiting similar maneuver.

Congress Supports Reagan on Budget Cuts (July 31): Coalition of Republicans and conservative Democrats overturns House Democratic leadership in tumultuous debate **(June 26)** and approves, 217–211, Republican package of $38.2-billon reduction already voted by Republican Senate. House and Senate give final approval to Conference Committee's package of $35.2 billion in cuts designed to reverse Federal Government's expansion. Measure repeals or modifies long-standing programs in nation's economic and social fabric, with powerful constituencies. Steps include elimination of public service jobs under Comprehensive Employment and Training Act and reducing cash benefits in such programs as food stamps and cost-of-living adjustments. Reductions were achieved in "reconciliation" stage of legislation to meet targets of budget.

U.S. Producing Neutron Weapons (Aug. 6): President orders that Lance missile and eight-inch artillery shells be furnished with nuclear material tritium to make radiation weapons designed to kill people without severe damage to surroundings. **(Aug. 9):** Soviet Union calls Reagan's decision extremely dangerous step. Reaction in Western Europe is muted. **(Aug. 10):** Defense Secretary Caspar W. Weinberger says neutron weapons are already in production and U.S. will soon be able to deploy them overseas within a few hours of decision to do so.

People, Places, and Things

1980

Homosexual Settles Suit Against U.S. for $160,000 (Nov. 24): Leonard P. Matlovich, 37, a decorated Vietnam veteran, agrees to drop efforts for reinstatement in Air Force, which ousted him five years previously because of his homosexuality.

Romain Gary, French Novelist, Is Suicide (Dec. 3): Former diplomat, 66, dies in Paris of apparently self-inflicted gunshot wound. Gary had sent note to publisher saying death plan was not connected with suicide in 1979 of former wife, the actress Jean Seberg.

1981

Poland's Oldest Woman Dies at Age of 112 (Jan. 7): Rozalia Mielczarek, who lived in a western Poland village, had nine children and is survived by 5 grandchildren, 11 great-grandchildren, and 9 great-greatgrandchildren.

Mae West Leaves $1-Million Estate (Jan. 18): Actress, dead at 87, wills bulk, including jewelry, to sister, Mildred West. Will does not mention Paul Novak, constant companion for 25 years, formerly in stage act.

Edward M. Kennedys Divorcing After 22 Years (Jan. 21): Senator and wife, Joan, announce they will dissolve marriage "as friends." They had lived apart for much of previous two years.

British Hail Engagement of Prince Charles (Feb. 24): Buckingham Palace announces betrothal of 32-year-old heir to throne to Lady Diana Spencer, 19, an aristocrat, lifelong friend of royal family.

Lennon Leaves $5.5 Million in Britain (Feb. 28): Will of former Beatle shows assets in England and Wales in addition to $30 million in United States. Half of British estate left to Lennon's wife. Lennon's international wealth put at $250 million.

George F. Kennan Wins Einstein Peace Prize (March 16): Former diplomat and expert on Soviet affairs, 77, wins second annual award, worth $50,000, for continuing efforts to ease tensions between U.S. and U.S.S.R.

Carol Burnett Wins $1.6-Million Libel Verdict (March 26): Los Angeles jury finds *National Enquirer* libeled TV actress who contended weekly tabloid fabricated item depicting her as intoxicated in restaurant. **(May 12):** Los Angeles judge denies *Enquirer* motion for new trial but halves Miss Burnett's award.

New York's Governor Carey Weds Businesswoman (April 11): Bride is Evangeline Gouletas, 44, manager of a billion-dollar real-estate business in Illinois. Governor, on 62nd birthday, wed in Manhattan Greek Orthodox Church.

Son and Grandson of Shostakovich Defect to West (April 12): Maksim, 42, conductor of Soviet Radio Symphony Orchestra, and Dmitri, 19, its pianist, seek political asylum in West Germany after performance in Fürth, Bavaria. **(April 16):** U.S. to admit the two as refugees.

Hundreds Honor Joe Louis at Funeral (April 21): Crowds present at burial in Arlington National Cemetery of sharecropper's son who became champion prizefighter and civil rights pioneer.

Prince Charles Visits U.S. (May 3): Heir to British throne leaves after three-day private visit.

Raoul Wallenberg Voted U.S. Citizenship (June 4): Special

House subcommittee approves honorary citizenship for Swede credited with saving lives of 100,-000 Hungarian Jews threatened by Nazis in World War II.

Ex-Postal Worker Willed Millions to Blind (July 3): Clinton Teubert, who died in 1979 at the age of 91, left unexplained postscript with bequest of most of $3-million estate he amassed in lifetime of saving and investing. West Virginia court rules Huntington man's will valid despite challenges.

King and Queen of Spain Boycott Royal Wedding (July 21): Juan Carlos and Sofia decline invitation to London ceremony to protest plan of Prince Charles and bride to board honeymoon yacht at Gibraltar, British crown colony, long subject of dispute between nations.

Rose Kennedy Celebrates 91st Birthday (July 22): Mother of President and other high officials honored by many of 26 grandchildren and four great-grandchildren in celebration at family's Cape Cod home.

Millions View Wedding of Prince Charles (July 29): Heir to British throne, Prince of Wales, marries 20-year-old Lady Diana Spencer before 2,500 guests in London's baroque St. Paul's Cathedral. Hundreds of thousands watch wedding party ride in horse-drawn carriages from Buckingham Palace as an estimated 700 million around the world view pageantry on television sets. The 32-year-old Prince and Lady Diana are united by the Archbishop of Canterbury, the Most Rev. Robert Runcie, on a day that symbolizes for Britons the continuity of the monarchy and the nation itself. The Prince wears naval uniform and his bride a pearl and sequin-encrusted gown of ivory taffeta silk with a 25-foot train. Singers and musicians perform the music of Handel, Purcell, and Elgar. The processional pageantry includes the Household Cavalry with burnished breastplates and helmets with red plumes, and royal horses caparisoned in silver. Most of Europe's reigning sovereigns attend in their finery. Security is heavy, with police and troops deployed along the line of march, because of the outbreaks of violence in England and the tension in Northern Ireland. No serious incidents reported.

180-Pound Baby Elephant Born in Bronx Zoo (Aug. 20): Patty, 11-year-old Indian elephant, gives birth to pink-skinned bull calf, which is named Astor. Baby stands up in 14 minutes and walks soon afterward.

Female Whale Born at New York Aquarium (Aug. 24): Fourth beluga whale born in captivity weighs 153 pounds. Baby refuses milk from her mother, Kathy, 1,500 pounds, and is fed milky substance by hand from tube.

Religion

1980

Pope Issues Strict Rules for Remarried Catholics (Oct. 25): Says divorced persons who wed again may not receive communion unless they abstain from sexual relations, speaking at closing session of Fifth World Synod of Bishops at Vatican. Message by bishops reaffirms church's ban on contraception and divorce.

U.S. Bishops Steer Clear of Rightist Line (Nov. 13): Roman Catholic prelates, in four-day Washington meeting, move to enhance role of laity and upgrade status of women, moving some distance from hard-line thinking of Vatican and Republican Party platform. Avoid disputes over birth control and divorce.

300,000 Greet Pope on Visit to West Germany (Nov. 15): John Paul II is first Pontiff in 200 years to visit homeland of Protestant Reformation. **(Nov. 16):** In address at open-air mass outside Osnabrück, Pope exhorts Roman Catholics "to seek and intensify contacts with Protestant fellow Christians in sincere faith." **(Nov. 19):** First display of church disunity marks last day of Pope's five-day visit. Youth leaders, in statement read at mass in Munich, attack church on several issues, including sexuality, birth control, and role of women.

1981

Pope Visits Far East on 13-Day Trip (Feb. 16): John Paul II says mass in Karachi, Pakistan, stadium 20 minutes after grenade explosion near reviewing stand. Stopover called goodwill gesture toward world's 800 million Moslems. **(Feb. 17):** Pontiff arrives in Manila, most Roman Catholic of Asian nations. With President Ferdinand E. Marcos beside him, Pope extols human rights and implicitly welcomes Marcos's recent lifting of martial law. Bids for normalization of relations between church and China after 32 years' estrangement. **(Feb. 24):** Pope has 45-minute meeting in Tokyo with Japan's Emperor Hirohito and celebrates mass at baseball stadium. **(Feb. 25):** Flies to Hiroshima to deliver "peace message" and visits museum of relics from city's atomic bombing of Aug. 6, 1945. In Nagasaki, Pope is greeted by majority of 40,000 Catholics in stronghold of Catholicism. **(Feb. 26):** John Paul spends day in Nagasaki with open-air masses, speeches, and visits to survivors of 1945 atomic bombing. **(Feb. 27):** He returns to Rome, saying most moving moments of trip had been visits to the two cities devastated by atomic bombs, where he appealed to the world to make "a moral about-face" or suffer nuclear holocaust. Trip, Pope's ninth outside Italy, also included stops in Guam and Alaska and covered about 20,000 miles.

Document Casts Doubt on Mormon Leaders' Succession (March 18): Blessing by Prophet Joseph Smith, Jr., to son, Joseph Smith 3rd, said to forecast that son would become leader of church. Instead, Brigham Young became church leader in 1847 and young Joseph founded offshoot. Members of both groups see little effect.

Moon's Church Loses Libel Suit in London (March 31): Jury finds for *Daily Mail* in ruling against the Unification Church of the Rev. Sun Myung Moon. Group ordered to pay court costs estimated at nearly $2 million. Paper had charged brainwashing and kidnappings by group.

Baptist Leader Resolves Dispute With Jews (April 21): Rev. Bailey Smith, president of Southern Baptist Convention, says he would die to protect their rights. Smith had stirred controversy in 1980 when he said God did not hear the prayers of Jews.

World Anglican Bishops Convene in Washington (April 30): Twenty-seven prelates, heads of national churches, discuss concerns in week-long session. In statements condemning arms race, they say Christian doctrine of "just war" is not applicable in nuclear age, and pledge to work for "multilateral disarmament" in their countries.

New York Clergyman Heads Presbyterians (May 21): Rev. Robert M. Davidson, 52, pastor of West-Park Presbyterian Church since 1974, elected Moderator at National Assembly in Houston of 2.4-million-member United Presbyterian Church in the U.S.A. Mr. Davidson had directed ecumenical work in California.

Polish Church and State Honor Wyszynski (May 31): More than a quarter of million attend requiem mass in Warsaw's Victory Square for Stefan Cardinal Wyszynski, Roman Catholic Primate of Poland and leader of its church for nearly 33 years, dead at 79. Pope sends message of condolence.

Southern Baptists Re-Elect Conservative (June 9): Rename Rev. Bailey Smith of Oklahoma Convention's president as Fundamentalist strength gains.

Pope Names New Leader of Polish Church (July 7): Appoints Bishop Jozef Glemp of Warmia as Archbishop of Gniezno and Warsaw and Primate of Poland to succeed late Stefan Cardinal Wyszynski. Archbishop Glemp, 52, is a specialist in both canon and civil law.

Vatican Announces Deficit of $26 Million for Year (July 15): Issues rare statement at end of two-day conference of 15 non-Italian cardinals chosen by Pope to review finances of governing Curia. Cardinals call for administrative economies and appeal to wealthier dioceses to increase contributions. They also urge the streamlining of the bureaucratic structure of the Curia, including abolition or merger of several secretariats.

Pope Undergoes Successful Operation (Aug. 9): In 45 minutes of surgery, doctors restore normal functioning of intestine pierced by bullet on May 13.

Yale's President Rebukes Moral Majority (Aug. 31): A. Bartlett Giamatti attacks conservative group and others as "peddlers of coercion" in "radical assault" on pluralism, rights, and civil and religious freedom. **(Sept. 1):** Moral Majority denounces attack as "unprovoked diatribe" that had ignored truth.

Science

1980

Voyager 1 Discovers 15th Saturn Moon (Nov. 8): Third new object identified by spacecraft. It is found orbiting outer boundary of major rings; its gravitational influence is believed to be a factor in setting boundary for particles of Saturn's rings.

Voyager 1 Surveys Saturn and Its Moons (Nov. 12): Spacecraft makes first close photographic reconnaissance of the solar system's second largest planet. Cruising beneath Saturn's rings, *Voyager* reveals more ringlets within ring disk. As it sails past planet, ship discovers details of its moons, hitherto points of light in telescopes. **(Nov. 13):** Scientists analyzing data determine that moon Titan has deep, cold, and heavy atmosphere composed primarily of nitrogen.

Soviets Launch Redesigned Soyuz Spacecraft (Nov. 27): Three astronauts in bid to break 185-day endurance record set in October. *Soyuz-T3* is 39th craft in *Soyuz* series and first with three-man crew: Lieut. Col. Leonid Kizim, 39, pilot; Oleg Makarov, 47, flight engineer; and Gennady Strekalov, 40, research engineer. **(Nov. 28):** Space capsule makes computer-guided docking with *Salyut 6* orbiting laboratory. **(Dec. 10):** Three astronauts return to earth after repairing and testing *Salyut 6* on 13-day flight.

First Long-Distance Solar-Powered Flight (Dec. 3): Tiny aircraft powered only by sun's rays lands in Arizona desert six miles and 22 minutes after takeoff when motor malfunctions. Janice Brown, 32, 98-pound teacher, is pilot.

Calf Survives With Man-Made Heart (Dec. 28): Tennyson, a Jersey bull, sets world record at University of Utah, Salt Lake City, by living 222 days with artificial organ. Researchers request permission to implant similar heart in human beings.

1981

Swiss Scientists Report First Cloning of Mammal (Jan. 4): Use cells from mouse embryos to produce three mice genetically identical with original embryos. Report of transplants at University of Geneva first such to be accepted by referees of a leading scientific journal, *Cell*, published by M.I.T.

Scientists Sight Four Galaxies at Record Distance (March 1): Identify them at distances estimated about 10 billion light years away. Previous record was 8 billion light years for most distant galaxy.

Three Divers Set Pressure Chamber Record (March 6): Volunteers subjected to water pressure equal to that at 2,250 feet below sea level in 43-day test at Duke University. They are apparently unharmed. The previous record was depth of 2,165 feet.

Space Shuttle Passes Key Test, Marred by Death (March 19): *Columbia* succeeds in preflight preparations, but in countdown rehearsal in Florida one technician is killed and two others injured by lack of oxygen. **(April 2):** An injured worker, Forrest Cole, 50, dies.

Space Shuttle Columbia Succeeds in Test Flight (April 12): World's first re-usable spaceship blasts its way into earth orbit from Cape Canaveral, Fla. Astronauts, John W. Young, civilian, and Capt. Robert L. Crippen of Navy, discover several heat-shielding tiles ripped off from tail section. **(April 14):** *Columbia* rockets out of orbit and glides to safe landing on desert at Edward Air Force Base, Calif., after 36-orbit, 54-hour, and 22-minute flight. The $10-billion project expected to lead to flights with far-reaching commercial, scientific, and military applications. **(April 15):** Space agency officials report spaceship's condition is "excellent" and that it should be capable of 100 round trips into orbit. Minor damage to tiles reported.

Gene-Splicing Develops New Vaccine (June 18): Department of Agriculture announces safe, effective vaccine against foot and mouth disease, one of most serious livestock infections. This is believed to be first use of gene-splicing in developing vaccine against any disease in animals or humans.

First Sun-Powered Airplane Crosses English Channel (July 7): *Solar Challenger* flies from France to England in five and a half hours, with Stephen Ptacek, 28, of Colorado, as pilot. It maintains average speed of 30 mph and cruising altitude of 11,000 feet. The 210-pound plane has 47-foot wingspan. It is first to fly without storage battery help, powered by 16,000 photovoltaic cells on wings that convert solar energy into electricity to drive motor.

Jewish Catacomb Uncovered in Italy (July 25): Joint Italian-American archeological team excavates area near southern hill town of Venosa, apparently used as burial ground in last centuries of Roman Empire. Investigators break through to underground passages of catacomb cut in soft rock and crawl through eight galleries containing more than 1,000 grave niches over an area estimated to be size of a football field.

Soviet Has Total Solar Eclipse (July 30): It darkens 4,300-mile-long swath of southern and eastern sections. Scientists, including Americans, get extensive data on sun's influence on the weather.

Domestic Cow Mothers Wild Ox (Aug. 14): Baby gaur, native to India, born to Holstein dairy animal at Bronx Zoo. Project involved placing gaur embryo in cow's womb. It is viewed as major step in reproduction of wild and endangered animals in captivity.

Scientists Warn of Atmosphere Warming (Aug. 21): Federal team reports trend dating to 1880 as evidence of "greenhouse" effect in which carbon dioxide released by mankind's burning of fuels causes steady temperature increases. They predict global warming resulting in worldwide rise in sea level, with extensive flooding and damage to agriculture.

Voyager 2 Keeps Rendezvous With Saturn (Aug. 25): American spacecraft, after traveling 1.24 billion miles in four years, sends back data and pictures on giant planet and moons and attempts to measure strands of Saturn's rings. Plunges within 63,000 miles of planet's stormy clouds. **(Aug. 29):** Instruments on *Voyager 2* discover strange pinging radio signals and doughnut-shaped cloud of energetic particles perhaps associated with Saturn's inner moons. Some pictures missed as camera swivel platform jams, but mechanism improves with use.

Sports

1980

University of Oregon Senior Wins New York Marathon (Oct. 26): Alberto Salazar, 22, native Cuban, wins his first 26-mile, 385-yard race in 2 hours 9 minutes 41 seconds, fastest first marathon in history and eighth on world list. Grete Waltz, 27, Oslo teacher, wins women's title for third consecutive year, lowering record time to 2:25:41 and finishing 74th over-all.

Outfielder Signs $25-Million Contract With Yankees (Dec. 15): Dave Winfield's 10-year agreement carries annual cost-of-living increase with 10% maximum.

1981

$25 Million Pledged for Indianapolis Stadium (Feb. 16): Lilly Endowment Inc., set up by Eli Lilly pharmaceuticals company, pledges aid for 60,000-seat covered sports stadium. With $5 million gift from Krannert Charitable Trust, this will pay for nearly half cost of centerpiece of complex for amateur and professional sports.

First Woman to Row in Oxford's Boat (Feb. 18): Susan Brown, 22, biochemistry student, named coxswain for contest with Cambridge April 4. Her choice breaks all-male tradition dating to first race in 1929.

Tardy Reggie Jackson Fined $5,000 (March 3): Reports two days late to join Yankees for Florida spring training.

World Boxing Council Wins Antitrust Case (April 24): U.S. jury in Manhattan returns verdict for W.B.C. and president, José Sulaimán, in suit brought by Teddy Brenner, boxing promoter, against council's action in suspending him in dispute over rights to fighter Alexis Arguello.

Billie Jean King Sued for Assets (April 29): Woman alleging past lesbian relationship with professional tennis star files action in Los Angeles contending she is entitled to share in Mrs. King's property under legal doctrine in Lee Marvin case. Mrs. King describes allegations as "untrue and unfounded." **(May 1):** Mrs. King concedes former lesbian relationship with Marilyn Barnett, 32, her former secretary, but says it was "mistake" for which she accepts responsibility.

Mario Andretti Wins Indianapolis 500 (May 25): Officials void victory of Bobby Unser, penalized for illegally advancing car's position in re-entering field.

Baseball Strike Ends After Seven Weeks (July 31): Major leagues' 650 players end strike of regular-season games, second in sport's history called (June 12) after 18-month dispute with owners. Walkout has wide effect on refreshment sellers, television, airlines, players, and fans. Key issue is "free-agent" compensation. Negotiators settle differences over that issue and lengthen collective bargaining agreement to insure additional year of labor peace. Players lost estimated $28 million in salaries. Clubs' strike insurance paying benefits of $44 million, leaving $72 million in net lost revenue.

State and Local Governments
1981

Dallas Voters, 2-to-1, Reject 30% Tax Cut (Jan. 18): Defeat one of most sweeping property levy rollbacks since California's Proposition 13, in 1978.

Opponents of Busing Victors in Los Angeles (March 11): California Supreme Court lets stand as constitutional ruling upholding Proposition 1, approved by voters in 1979, which prohibits court-ordered busing unless intended to correct intentional segregation.

Women
1981

Honolulu Gets Woman Ruler Again (Jan. 2): Eileen Anderson, 51, a native of mainland U.S., takes office as mayor, first woman chief executive since Queen Liliuokalani was overthrown by American planters on Jan. 17, 1893.

Women and Labor Join in Membership Drive (March 3): Working Women association and AFL-CIO Service Employees Union form new District 925 (9-to-5) to conduct national organizing drive among office workers.

Late Events

Sadat Assassinated (Oct. 6): President Anwar el-Sadat of Egypt is shot and killed while reviewing a military parade in Cairo. A small group of men in army uniforms jump off a truck in the parade and fire rifles and hurl hand grenades at reviewing stand. At least five are killed and 40 wounded. At least one attacker was killed and several captured. They are believed to be Islamic fundamentalists, many of whom had been arrested in recent crack-down by Sadat regime. The Speaker of Parliament, Sufi Abu Taleb, was Acting President until the election of President Hosni Mubarak, 53.

Yankees Win American League Pennant (Oct. 15): The New York Yankees of the American League's Eastern Division defeated the Oakland A's of the Western Division in three straight games to win the league championship. Earlier, the Yankees beat the Milwaukee Brewers and the A's defeated the Kansas City Royals to win their division titles. The extra best three-out-of-five "mini-series" was necessitated by the unprecedented divided season as a result of the 50-day players' strike.

Dodgers Capture National League Title (Oct. 19): The Los Angeles Dodgers, National League Western Division champions, defeated the Montreal Expos, Eastern Division winner, three games to two, to win the pennant. In the division playoffs, the Dodgers beat the Houston Astros and the Expos downed the Philadelphia Phillies.

1981 Nobel Prize Winners

Peace: The Office of the United Nations High Commissioner for Refugees for aiding the growing numbers of homeless and displaced people around the world.

Medicine: Dr. Roger W. Sperry of the California Institute of Technology for research demonstrating that the right and left hemispheres of the human brain have different functions; Dr. David H. Hubel and Dr. Torsen N. Wiesel (Swedish) of Harvard University for studies of the complex manner in which the brain processes visual information.

Economics: James Tobin, Sterling Professor of Economics at Yale University, for his analyses of the financial markets and their impact on the way businesses and families spend and save.

Literature: Elias Canetti, a Bulgarian living in London who writes in German, for his "writings marked by a broad outlook, a wealth of ideas, and artistic power."

Physics: Dr. Nicolaas Bloembergen, Harvard University, and Dr. Arthur Schawlow, Stanford University, for their contribution to the development of laser spectroscopy, and Dr. Kai Siegbahn (Swedish), Uppsala University, Sweden, for his contribution to the development of high-resolution electron spectroscopy.

Chemistry: Dr. Roald Hoffmann, John A. Newman Professor of Physical Science at Cornell University, and Dr. Kenichi Fukui (Japanese), professor of physical chemistry at Kyoto University, for their work in applying the theories of quantum mechanics to predict the course of chemical reactions.

Major Emmy Awards for TV, 1981

Drama series: Hill Street Blues (NBC)
  Actress: Barbara Babcock, Hill Street Blues (NBC)
  Actor: Daniel J. Travanti, Hill Street Blues (NBC)
  Supporting actress: Nancy Marchand, Lou Grant (CBS)
  Supporting actor: Michael Conrad, Hill Street Blues (NBC)
Comedy series: Taxi (ABC)
  Actress: Isabel Sanford, The Jeffersons (CBS)
  Actor: Judd Hirsch, Taxi (ABC)
  Supporting actress: Eileen Brennan, Private Benjamin (CBS)
  Supporting actor: Danny De Vito, Taxi (ABC)
Comedy, variety, or music program: Lily: Sold Out (CBS)
Limited series: Shogun (NBC)
  Actress: Vanessa Redgrave, Playing for Time (CBS)
  Actor: Anthony Hopkins, The Bunker (CBS)
  Supporting actress: Jane Alexander, Playing for Time (CBS)
  Actor: David Warner, Masada (ABC)
Drama special: Playing for Time (CBS)
Animated program: Life is a Circus, Charlie Brown (CBS)
Information special: The Body Human: The Bionic Breakthrough (CBS)
Information series: Steve Allen's Meeting of the Minds (PBS)
Classical program in the performing arts: Live from Studio 8H, Jerome Robbins' Ballets (NBC)
Children's program: Donahue and Kids (NBC)
Network totals: NBC 20, CBS 18, ABC 12, PBS 8

Deaths in 1980–1981

Agar, Herbert, 83: won 1933 Pulitzer Prize in history for *The People's Choice,* a study of Presidents from Washington to Harding. Nov. 24, 1980.

Algren, Nelson, 72: novelist and short-story writer; author of *A Walk on the Wild Side* and *The Man With the Golden Arm.* May 9, 1981.

Astaire, Adele, 83: dancer and musical comedy star with her brother, Fred, in 1920s. Jan. 25, 1981.

Bagnold, Enid, 91: playwright and novelist wrote *National Velvet, The Chalk Garden,* and *A Matter of Gravity.* March 31, 1981.

Baldwin, Roger N., 97: founder of American Civil Liberties Union. Aug. 26, 1981.

Barber, Samuel, 70: composer won Pulitzer Prizes for his *Piano Concerto No. 1* and opera *Vanessa.* Jan. 25, 1981.

Bennett, Robert Russell, 87: orchestrated *Show Boat, Oklahoma!, My Fair Lady, Of Thee I Sing, Anything Goes.* Aug. 18, 1981.

Böhm, Karl, 87: Austrian conductor. Aug. 14, 1981.

Bondi, Beulah, 92: character actress in over 50 films. Jan. 12, 1981.

Boone, Richard, 63: actor appeared in TV series *Have Gun Will Travel.* Jan. 10, 1981.

Bradley, Omar N., 88: last five-star General of the Army was senior U.S. commander of ground troops in World War II European campaign. April 8, 1981.

Breuer, Marcel, 76: architect and designer was known for his innovative furniture. July 1, 1981.

Caetano, Marcello, 74: ex-Prime Minister of Portugal. Oct. 26, 1980.

Campora, Hector J., 71: President of Argentina in 1973. Dec. 19, 1980.

Celler, Emanuel, 92: Democratic Representative from Brooklyn from 1923 to 1973. Jan. 15, 1981.

Chayefsky, Paddy, 58: screen writer won Oscars for *Marty, The Hospital,* and *Network;* also wrote *The Americanization of Emily.* Aug. 1, 1981.

Clair, René, 82: leading French film director. March 15, 1981.

Cole, Cozy, 71: jazz drummer who played with Cab Calloway, Louis Armstrong, and Benny Goodman. Jan. 29, 1981.

Connelly, Marc, 90: playwright won Pulitzer Prize in 1930 for *The Green Pastures.* Dec. 21, 1980.

Cotter, William R., 55: Democratic Representative from Connecticut since 1971. Sept. 8, 1981.

Cronin, A(rchibald) J(oseph), 84: novelist wrote *The Citadel, The Keys of the Kingdom, The Stars Look Down, Shannon's Way.* Jan. 6, 1981.

Curran, Joseph, 75: founder of National Maritime Union in 1937. Aug. 14, 1981.

Davis Jim, 65: actor played Jock Ewing, father of the Ewing clan, on TV's *Dallas* show. April 26, 1981.

Day, Dorothy, 83: founder of Catholic Worker Movement and a crusader for social justice. Nov. 29, 1980.

Dean, Paul (Daffy), 67: star pitcher, with his brother, Dizzy Dean, on St. Louis Cardinals in 1930s. March 17, 1981.

Dodds, Harold W., 91: president of Princeton University from 1933 to 1957. Oct. 25, 1980.

Doenitz, Karl, 89: admiral commanded Germany's U-boat campaign in World War II; named by Hitler to be his successor in 1945 and then surrendered to the Allies. Dec. 24, 1980.

Dominick, Peter H., 65: Colorado Republican served two terms in Senate. March 18, 1981.

Douglas, Donald W., 88: aircraft designer brought mass air travel to the world. Feb. 1, 1981.

Douglas, Melvyn, 80: actor won two Oscars; starred in *Inherit the Wind* and *The Best Man* on stage; in *Hud* and *The Seduction of Joe Tynan* on screen. Aug. 4, 1981.

Drew, Richard, 81: inventor of Scotch tape. Dec. 14, 1980.

Farago, Ladislas, 74: wrote biography of Gen. Patton from which 1970 Oscar-winning film was adapted; also author of *The Tenth Fleet, The Broken Seal,* and *Game of the Foxes.* Oct. 15, 1980.

Fitzsimmons, Frank, 73: president of Teamsters union for 14 years. May 6, 1981.

Fox, Carol, 55: co-founder and former manager of Chicago's Lyric Opera. July 21, 1981.

Fox, Virgil, 68: concert organist played to more than six million people throughout the world. Oct. 25, 1980.

Frederika, 63: exiled Queen Mother of Greece. Feb. 6, 1981.

Gary, Romain, 66: French novelist wrote *The Roots of Heaven.* Dec. 2, 1980.

Gimbel, Bruce A., 67: retired chairman of Gimbel Brothers department store chain. Oct. 6, 1980.

Grasso, Ella T., 61: ex-Governor of Connecticut, first woman elected to a governorship in her own right. Feb. 5, 1981.

Hanson, Howard, 84: Pulitzer Prize-winning composer and ex-head of Eastman School of Music. Feb. 26, 1981.

Harding, Ann, 79: blond actress of stage and screen appeared on Broadway in long-running *The Trial of Mary Dugan.* Sept. 1, 1981.

Hirshhorn, Joseph H., 82: financier, prospector for gold, uranium, and gold; gave extensive art collection to U.S. to be displayed in Hirshhorn Museum and Sculpture Garden in Washington. Aug. 31, 1981.

Howard, Elston, 51: coach and former catcher with New York Yankees; first black to play on the team. Dec. 14, 1980.

Jessel, George, 83: comedian and actor was known as "Toastmaster General;" starred in 1925 play *The Jazz Singer.* May 25, 1981.

Kintner, Robert E., 71: former president of American Broadcasting Companies and National Broadcasting Company. Dec. 20, 1980.

Kosygin, Alexei N., 76: Premier of Soviet Union from 1964 to 1980. Dec. 18, 1980.

Kuharich, Joe, 63: former football coach at Notre Dame and of Philadelphia Eagles, Washington Redskins, and Chicago Cardinals. Jan. 25, 1981.

Leger, Jules, 67: Governor General of Canada from 1974 to 1979. Nov. 22, 1980.

Lennon, John, 40: member of the Beatles and writer of hundreds of songs. Shot, Dec. 8, 1980.

Lesage, Jean, 68: Premier of Quebec from 1960 to 1966. Dec. 11, 1980.

Levene, Sam, 75: stage and screen actor created role of Nathan Detroit in *Guys and Dolls;* also in *Three Men on a Horse, Dinner at Eight,* and *The Sunshine Boys.* Dec. 28, 1980.

Liebman, Max, 78: produced TV's *Your Show of Shows* with Sid Caesar and Imogene Coca. July 21, 1981.

Lilienthal, David E., 81: former chairman of Tennessee Valley Authority and first chairman of Atomic Energy Commission. Jan. 15, 1981.

Link, Edwin A., 77: invented Link flight simulator used in training 500,000 pilots in World War II. Sept. 7, 1981.

Loos, Anita, 93: screen writer, novelist, and playwright was author of *Gentlemen Prefer Blondes.* Aug. 18, 1981.

Louis, Joe, 66: heavyweight boxing champion from 1937 to 1948. April 12, 1981.

Maloof, George, 57: owner of Houston Rockets of National Basketball Association. Nov. 29, 1980.

McCormack, John W., 88: Speaker of the House of Representatives from 1962 to 1971; served in Congress 42 years. Nov. 22, 1980.

McLuhan, Marshall, 69: education and communications specialist believed that "the medium is the message." Dec. 31, 1980.

McQueen, Steve, 50: tough guy of films was in *The Great Escape, Bullitt, Papillon, The Sand Pebbles, The Towering Inferno.* Nov. 7, 1980.

Moses, Robert, 92: New York's "master builder" created Jones Beach, Triborough Bridge, 1964 World's Fair, and many other projects. July 29, 1981.

Mosley, Oswald, 84: former British fascist leader. Dec. 2, 1980.

Orwell, Sonia: widow of George Orwell, author of *1984,* edited her husband's collected works. Dec. 11, 1980.

Oswald, Marguerite, 73: mother of Lee Harvey Oswald, alleged assassin of President Kennedy. Jan. 17, 1981.

Piaget, Jean, 84: Swiss psychologist specialized in childhood intelligence. Sept. 17, 1980.

Ponselle, Rosa, 84: operatic soprano sang with Metropolitan for 20 years. May 25, 1981.

Raft, George, 85: film actor played typical gangster; was in *Scarface, Each Dawn I Die, They Drive by Night.* Nov. 24, 1980.

Rahman, Ziaur, 45: President of Bangladesh since 1977. Assassinated May 30, 1981.

Roberts, Rachel, 53: British actress and former wife of Rex Harrison; appeared on screen in *Murder on the Orient Express* and *Foul Play* and in many TV dramas. Nov. 26, 1980.

Roldós Aguilera, Jaime, 40: President of Ecuador. Killed in plane crash May 24, 1981.

Rose, Mauri, 74: winner of Indianapolis 500 auto race in 1941, 1947, and 1948. Jan. 1, 1981.

Roszak, Theodore, 74: sculptor in welded steel designed controversial eagle on U.S. Embassy in London. Sept. 3, 1981.

Sanders, Harlan, 90: founder of Kentucky Fried Chicken fast-food chain was honorary Kentucky colonel. Dec. 16, 1980.

Sands, Robert, 27: Irish Republican Army member succumbs after 66-day hunger strike in Belfast jail. May 5, 1981.

Saroyan, William, 72: playwright, short-story writer and novelist; wrote *The Daring Young Man on the Flying Trapeze, My Heart's in the Highlands, The Time of Your Life.* May 18, 1981.

Shawkey, Bob, 90: pitcher for New York Yankees in 1920s; pitched first game played in old Yankee Stadium. Dec. 31, 1980.

Shoumatoff, Elizabeth, 92: portrait artist was painting Franklin D. Roosevelt when he was fatally stricken in 1945. Nov. 30, 1980.

Smith, Tony, 68: sculptor of large-scale works of small objects. Dec. 26, 1980.

Smythe, Conn, 85: former owner of Toronto Maple Leafs hockey team. Nov. 18, 1980.

Soong Ching-ling, 90: widow of Sun Yat-sen, founder of modern China. May 29, 1981.

Speer, Albert, 76: Hitler's Minister of Armaments and War Production served 20 years in prison for war crimes. Sept. 1, 1981.

Stein, Jules C., 85: ophthalmologist founded MCA (Music Corporation of America) in 1924 and expanded it into billion-dollar talent agency. April 29, 1981.

Sutton, Willie, 79: bank robber known as "Willie the Actor" for his many disguises. Nov. 2, 1980.

Taurog, Norman, 82: film director won Oscar for 1930 *Skippy;* also directed *Boys Town.* April 8, 1981.

Teague, Olin E., 70: Democratic Representative from Texas for 32 years. Jan. 23, 1981.

Teale, Edwin Way, 81: writer, illustrator, photographer in field of natural history. Oct. 18, 1980.

Thomas, Billy, 49: played Buckwheat in the *Our Gang* comedy film shorts. Oct. 10, 1980.

Thomas, Lowell, 89: radio and TV commentator, author, and explorer. Aug. 29, 1981.

Torrijos Herrera, Gen. Omar, 52: chief of Panama's National Guard and formerly leader of the country for 12 years. Killed in plane crash July 31, 1981.

Trippe, Juan, 81: founder of Pan American World Airways. April 3, 1981.

Urey, Harold, 87: atomic physicist and discoverer of heavy hydrogen won 1934 Nobel Prize. Jan. 5, 1981.

Vera-Ellen, 55: dancer in stage and screen musicals appeared with Bing Crosby in *White Christmas* and with Gene Kelly and Frank Sinatra in *On the Town.* Aug. 30, 1981.

Vinson, Carl, 97: U.S. Representative from Georgia for 50 years served longer than anyone else; headed Armed Services Committee. June 1, 1981.

Waldock, Sir Humphrey, 77: president of International Court of Justice. Aug. 15, 1981.

Walker, Mickey, 79: former middleweight and welterweight boxing champion. April 28, 1981.

Wallace, DeWitt, 91: founder and editor of *Reader's Digest.* March 30, 1981.

Walsh, Raoul, 93: screen director turned out *What Price Glory?, They Died With Their Boots On, White Heat, Battle Cry.* Dec. 31, 1980.

Walsh, Stella, 69: sprinter won Olympic medals for Poland in 1932 and 1936; first woman to run 100 yards in less than 11 seconds. Dec. 4, 1980.

Ward, Barbara, 67: British economist and author. May 31, 1981.

Waugh, Alec, 83: author of over 50 books was best known for *Island In the Sun.* Sept. 3, 1981.

West, Mae, 87: Diamond Lil of stage and screen; appeared on screen in *She Done Him Wrong, I'm No Angel, Belle of the Nineties, Go West, Young Man.* Nov. 22, 1980.

Wilkins, Roy, 80: civil rights leader headed National Association for the Advancement of Colored People for 20 years. Sept. 8, 1981.

Williams, Mary Lou, 71: jazz pianist, arranger and composer. May 28, 1981.

Wyler, William, 79: directed such films as *The Best Years of Our Lives, Mrs. Miniver, Wuthering Heights, Jezebel, Roman Holiday.* July 28, 1981.

Wyszynski, Stefan, 79: Cardinal was Roman Catholic Primate of Poland. May 28, 1981.

The Economy in 1981

Monte J. Gordon
Vice President and Director of Research
The Dreyfus Corporation

The event of overpowering significance as 1981 began was the assumption of the Presidential office by Ronald Reagan in a surprising landslide victory which developed a Republican majority in the Senate although the Democrats retained a numerical advantage in the House. Buoyed by this definitive victory, President Reagan immediately embarked upon an economic and political program designed to fulfill his election promises to a surprising degree. The two major pillars of his economic program, significant budget cuts and tax cuts for individuals and business spread over three years, were passed by the Congress virtually in the form proposed although there were certain changes made reflecting the politics of gaining support from conservative Democrats in the House. The major thrust of these proposals is the objective of stimulating the economy to greater economic growth through presumed powerful incentives to individuals to save more aggressively and to business to expand capital-spending programs. According to the tenets of "Reaganomics," as this approach has come to be known, greater productivity would be gained from expansion of the supply sector of the economy, which, in turn, would create more job opportunities. The result would be growth and expansion, reduction of inflation, lower interest rates, improved revenues to the government sector, and over-all strengthening of the economy.

Along with the program of incentive to expand offered to the private sector were a number of budget cuts affecting many activities of the Federal Government with an important objective of transferring responsibilities for administering many social programs to the states and municipalities. This approach carried over into the area of regulation with the emphasis being on the reduction of the regulatory burden on business in the hope that such action would reduce costs and act to moderate and even reduce inflationary pressures.

Coupled with the major political changes was the increasing significance of monetary policy executed by the Federal Reserve Board reflecting its position as virtually the sole factor able to exert a countervailing force to the mounting pressure of inflation. In this context, the Federal Reserve developed a stance of monetary restraint which had a major effect upon the trend of interest rates. The major premise of monetary policy is emphasis upon control of the so-called monetary base which consists of required bank reserves held by the Federal Reserve and currency, while allowing interest rates to fluctuate in a rather wide band. This was in sharp contrast with past policies which pivoted around setting interest rate targets which lessened control over increases in the money supply. The effect was to keep the rate for Federal Funds, which are the most sensitive of short-term rates and reflective of overnight funds loaned between banks, to adjust reserve positions at a surprisingly high level. At a level of 20.05% at the start of the year, the federal funds rate opened 1981 consistent with the high level of the closing weeks of 1980. By mid-April the rate had declined to about 14 1/2% after which, under the pressure of increasing loan demand in the economy, the rate began to rise, reaching a level of around 20 1/2% by early July with no significant indication that monetary policy was being eased, leading to lower rates, as we neared the end of the third quarter.

Another expression of the effect of a tight monetary policy bumping against the loan demand of an economy of unanticipated strength was the rise in the prime rate charged by banks to borrowers of the highest quality. This rate reached a record high of 21 1/2% in December 1980, and declined to a level around 17% by April 2, 1981. It then began a steady ascent reaching a level of 20 1/2% by May 22, 1981, and it held this level as the year entered its closing months.

One interesting corollary of the high interest rates was growing strength of the U.S. dollar against other currencies as demand for the dollar surged to take advantage of the high yields. Record levels were set against the currencies of France, Italy, and Denmark, with five-year highs against the German mark and four-year highs against the British pound. The dollar also gained against the Japanese yen.

The rise in the federal funds' rate during the second quarter and the pattern of high money rates which has generally characterized 1981 expressed the effect of the restrictive monetary policy adopted by the Federal Reserve Board following the surprising strength of the economy in the first quarter. For that period, the gross national product rose 8.4% in real terms (adjusted for inflation), up from a preliminary figure of 6.4%. This was followed by a decline of 1.9% in real terms reported for the second quarter. The Federal Reserve Board's stringent monetary stance developed from an explosive growth in money supply during the first quarter, causing fears that a major inflation potential was building up even as the Federal Reserve noted that NOW accounts were being introduced nationwide and could cause a distortion of money market statistics. For the week ended December 31, 1980, the measure known as MI-B, which consists of currency plus demand deposits plus other checkable deposits at banks and thrift institutions, stood at $406.2 billion. The figure then surged to $418.9 billion for the week ended January 7, 1981, and in subsequent weeks rose to a level of $432.2 billion for the week ended April 22, 1981. At that point the tight monetary policy began to take hold although even as the year drew toward a close there were weeks when money supply showed a dramatic change. Indeed, the greater volatility was an expression of the persistent emphasis of monetary policy on the monetary base.

Another important effect of these developments was high rates in many short-term market instruments available to the public which included six-month money market certificates and instruments of longer maturities offered by banks which attracted people as affording means of protection against the ravages of inflation. One of the more striking developments in this regard was the growth of money market funds which offer high yields to the small and large investor by investing in short-term money market instruments with no charge for investment or withdrawal of funds. At the end of 1980, there were 96 money market funds with total assets of $74.4 billion and by early August money market fund assets had surged to $140.4 billion reflecting assets held by 129 funds. Another important effect of the high money rates and the persistent inflation was a sustained transferral of funds held in passbook deposits to six-month money market certificates offered by banks at considerably higher rates keyed to yields realized at the weekly auction of 26-week treasury bills. The figures showed about $475 billion held in such certificates. This development created significant pressures on earnings of savings and loan associations and other thrift institutions caught between higher going rates necessary to attract and hold deposits and lower income flowing from lower yielding mortgages issued in earlier years—sufficiently so that in the latter part of the year it became a matter of intense study by Congress to avert difficulties in the banking system.

Another area of the economy affected by the high money rates was the housing industry, which found demand for homes slowing as mortgage rates rose to record levels exceeding 17%. The severity of the higher mortgage rates was evident in the fact that housing starts fell from a seasonally adjusted annual rate of 1,615,000 units reported in January 1981 to a seasonally adjusted annual rate of 1,032,-000 units in June 1981. A further insight into the dimension of the decline in the housing industry is provided by the fact that in May 1980, at the trough of that period of recession, housing starts declined to a pace of 938,000 units. Reflecting a sharp decline in housing permits during June, prospects that interest rates would remain high, and a general weakening of the economy, it was not difficult to anticipate that 1981 would be a disappointing year for housing even compared with 1980 when there were a total of just under 1.3 million housing starts.

One of the most interesting developments during 1981 was the diminution of the rate of inflation to below double-digit levels despite the heady pace of economic activity in the first quarter and subsequent persistent underlying strength. In 1979 the inflation factor was 13.3% and it eased to 12.4% for 1980 with the primary causative factors in each year being energy, food, and housing. Much to the surprise of observers, the annual rate fell to 8.4% in January 1981, rose briefly to 12% in February, and then declined to 7.2% in March, with the succeeding months of April, May, and June each holding below double-digit. The effect was to reduce the rate of inflation from 9.6% in the first quarter of 1981 to 7.4% compounded annual rate in the second quarter. The major forces in this better performance were declines in energy and food costs although housing costs continued to rise.

For many observers, these factors did not reflect the level of the underlying rate of inflation, which is generally perceived to be around 9%, but rather reflected a temporary easing in certain volatile factors influencing the trend of prices. For example, another rather unexpected circumstance in 1981 was the development of an oil glut contrasting sharply with previous tight supplies and confounding those who saw no relief in either short supplies or upward price pressure. The excess supply was estimated to be about 2–3 million barrels per day and its presence brought price cuts, albeit reluctantly, from many oil-producing countries who are members of OPEC. The underlying cause of this condition was disagreement within OPEC as to a suitable pricing level, with Saudi Arabia seeking a lower price and a more definitive long-term pricing and production strategy. To achieve its point, Saudi Arabia raised its production level to 10.5 million barrels per day (including 500,000 barrels per day to offset some part of the production loss from the Iraq-Iran conflict) and maintained the level steadily. This high rate of production, coupled with conservation efforts and recessionary trends in the oil-consuming countries, resulted in excess production. As 1981 wore along, the policy appeared to be having an effect resulting in price cuts and production cuts which, in turn, brought more stable oil pricing conditions. In the U.S., the slower pace of economic activity and the efforts to conserve resulted in a pronounced decline in oil imports of about 30%.

The financial markets, both equity and debt, had an eventful year. Indeed, the financial industry itself underwent enormous structural changes, with the mergers of three leading firms making headlines—Bache Group merged into Prudential, Shearson Loeb Rhoades merged with American Express, and Salomon Bros. merged with Phibro, a major commodities trading firm. This continued the pattern of consolidation and diversification which marked the industry during the decade of the seventies. The stock market started this volatile year at around 960 on the Dow-Jones Average and rose quickly to a level of 1004.7 in terms of the Dow-Jones Average. To the disappointment of many investors, the Dow-Jones Average fell below 1000 just as quickly. It regained ground and in March crossed over the magic 1000 line to 1015.2, rising even further in April to 1024.1. By the end of April, the stock market was once again below 1000, not regaining that lofty height until June when it reached a high of 1011.9. In subsequent weeks, the stock market, beset by concerns over high interest rates, the inflationary potential of President Reagan's tax-cut program, and the restrictive monetary policy of the Federal Reserve, fell to a trading range of 920–950 in which it languished as the summer came to a close. The determination of the Federal Reserve to hold to a tight money policy in order to reduce inflation continued to hold the market in a choking grip of uncertainty. Another difficulty checking the stock market's efforts to move up were the high yields offered in the government and corporate bond market. There was considerable disarray and volatility in these markets with great reluctance to buy long-term (25–30 year) maturities. As a result, funds tended to concentrate in the short-term sector driving rates up to around 18%. An interesting corollary effect was the decline in the price of gold to around $400 an ounce as high short-term interest rates drew speculative money and discouraged buyers as a reflection of the high cost of borrowing.

Employment and Unemployment
(in millions of persons)

Category	1980	1979	1978	1975	1970	1959	1950	1945	1941	1932	1929
EMPLOYMENT STATUS[1]											
Total noninstitutional population	166.2	163.6	161.1	153.4	140.2	117.9	106.6	105.5	101.5	—	—
Total labor force	106.8	105.0	102.5	94.8	85.9	70.9	63.9	65.3	57.5	51.3	49.4
Percent of population	64.3	64.2	63.7	61.8	61.3	60.2	59.9	61.9	56.7	—	—
Civilian labor force	104.7	102.9	100.4	92.6	82.7	68.4	62.2	53.9	55.9	51.0	49.2
Employed	97.3	96.9	94.4	84.8	78.6	64.6	58.9	52.8	50.4	38.9	47.6
Agriculture	3.3	3.3	3.3	3.4	3.5	5.6	7.2	8.6	9.1	10.2	10.5
Nonagricultural industries	94.0	93.6	91.0	81.4	75.2	59.1	51.8	44.2	41.3	28.8	37.2
Unemployed	7.4	6.0	6.0	7.8	4.1	3.7	3.3	1.0	5.6	12.1	1.6
Percent of labor force	7.1	5.8	6.0	8.5	4.9	5.5	5.3	1.9	9.9	23.6	3.2
Not in labor force	59.4	58.6	58.5	58.7	54.3	47.0	42.8	40.2	44.0	—	—
INDUSTRY											
Total nonagricultural employment	90.7	89.9	86.7	76.9	70.9	53.3	45.2	40.4	36.5	23.6	31.3
Goods-producing industries	25.8	26.5	25.6	22.6	23.6	20.4	18.5	17.5	16.0	8.6	13.3
Mining	1.0	1.0	0.9	0.8	0.6	0.7	0.9	0.8	1.0	0.7	1.1
Construction	4.5	4.5	4.3	3.5	3.6	3.0	2.4	1.1	1.8	1.0	1.5
Manufacturing: Durable goods	12.2	12.8	12.3	10.7	11.2	9.4	8.1	9.1	7.0	—	—
Nondurable goods	8.1	8.3	8.2	7.6	8.2	7.3	7.1	6.5	6.2	—	—
Services-producing industries	17.7	63.4	61.1	54.3	47.3	32.9	26.7	22.9	20.6	15.0	18.0
Transportation and public utilities	5.2	5.1	5.2	4.5	4.5	4.0	4.0	3.9	3.3	2.8	3.9
Trade: Wholesale	5.3	5.2	5.0	4.4	4.0	3.1	2.6	1.9	2.0	—	—
Retail	15.3	15.1	14.6	12.6	11.0	8.0	6.8	5.4	5.3	—	—
Finance, insurance, and real estate	5.2	5.0	4.7	4.2	3.6	2.5	1.9	1.5	1.5	1.3	1.5
Services	17.7	17.1	16.3	13.9	11.5	7.1	5.4	4.2	3.9	2.9	3.4
Federal government	2.9	2.8	2.7	2.7	2.7	2.2	1.9	2.8	1.3	0.6	0.5
State and local government	13.3	13.1	12.9	11.9	9.8	5.9	4.1	3.1	3.3	2.7	2.5

1. For 1929–45, figures on employment status relate to persons 14 years and over; beginning in 1950, 16 years and over.
NOTE: Figures may not add to totals because of rounding. *Source:* Department of Labor, Bureau of Labor Statistics.

Consumer Price Index for Urban Wage Earners and Clerical Workers
(1967 = 100)

Effective January 1978, the Consumer Price Index was revised, with two indexes now being produced: A new index for All Urban Consumers covers 80% of the non-institutional population; the other index, the Consumer Price Index for Urban Wage Earners and Clerical Workers, covers about half of those included in the new index and is a major revision of the one that had been published for many years.

	1981[1]	1980	1975	1970	1965	1960	1955	1950	1945
All items	—	247.0	161.2	116.3	94.5	88.7	80.2	72.1	53.9
Food total	271.9	255.3	175.4	114.9	94.4	88.0	81.6	—	—
Apparel and upkeep	186.0	177.4	142.3	116.1	93.7	89.6	84.1	79.0	61.5
Housing total	291.3	263.2	166.8	118.9	94.9	90.2	82.3	72.8	59.1
Rent	206.4	191.3	137.3	110.1	96.9	91.7	84.3	70.4	58.8
Gas and electricity	343.2	301.2	169.6	107.3	99.4	98.6	87.5	81.2	79.6
Fuel oil, coal, bottled gas	685.1	557.2	253.3	110.1	94.6	89.2	82.3	72.7	48.0
House operation[2]	217.3	202.9	158.1	113.4	95.3	93.8	89.9	—	—
House furnishings	182.1	172.6	144.4	111.4	97.1	99.3	99.2	95.5	73.3
Transportation	278.1	250.5	150.6	112.7	95.9	89.6	77.4	68.2	47.8
Medical care	293.5	267.2	168.6	120.6	89.5	79.1	64.8	53.7	42.1
Personal care	229.7	212.7	150.7	113.2	95.2	90.1	77.9	68.3	55.1
Entertainment	217.7	203.7	144.4	113.4	95.9	87.3	76.7	74.4	62.4

1. June. 2. Combines house furnishings and operation. *Source:* Department of Labor, Bureau of Labor Statistics.

Warning on Taking Catalytic Equipped Vehicles Abroad

Catalytic equipped vehicles (1976 or later model) driven outside the United States, Canada, or Mexico will not, in most cases, meet EPA standards when brought back to the U.S. As unleaded fuel generally is not available in other countries, the catalytic converter will become inoperative and will have to be replaced. Contact Environmental Protection Agency, Public Information Center (PM-215), Washington, D.C. 20460, for details and exceptions.

Per Capita Personal Income by States

State	1980[1]	1979	1978
Alabama	$ 7,484	$ 6,962	$ 6,347
Alaska	12,406	11,219	10,485
Arizona	8,649	8,423	7,411
Arkansas	7,180	6,933	6,236
California	10,856	10,047	8,900
Colorado	9,964	9,122	8,070
Connecticut	11,445	10,129	8,973
Delaware	10,195	9,327	8,427
D.C.	11,883	10,570	9,513
Florida	8,987	8,546	7,605
Georgia	8,000	7,630	6,830
Hawaii	9,787	9,223	8,438
Idaho	8,126	7,571	6,995
Illinois	10,658	9,799	8,887
Indiana	8,978	8,570	7,701
Iowa	9,178	8,772	7,905
Kansas	9,958	9,233	7,975
Kentucky	7,718	7,390	6,618
Louisiana	8,282	7,583	6,748
Maine	7,734	7,039	6,334
Maryland	10,322	9,331	8,514
Massachusetts	9,992	8,893	7,952
Michigan	9,847	9,403	8,514
Minnesota	9,519	8,865	7,858
Mississippi	6,508	6,178	5,582
Missouri	8,846	8,251	7,341
Montana	8,445	7,684	7,067
Nebraska	8,914	8,684	7,491
Nevada	10,458	10,521	9,529
New Hampshire	8,980	8,351	7,483
New Jersey	10,755	9,747	8,792
New Mexico	7,956	7,560	6,733
New York	10,143	9,104	8,192
North Carolina	7,852	7,385	6,693
North Dakota	8,556	8,231	7,542
Ohio	9,398	8,715	7,836
Oklahoma	9,018	8,509	7,376
Oregon	9,400	8,938	8,112
Pennsylvania	9,294	8,558	7,669
Rhode Island	9,250	8,510	7,628
South Carolina	7,519	7,057	6,344
South Dakota	7,452	7,455	6,580
Tennessee	7,786	7,343	6,602
Texas	9,513	8,788	7,776
Utah	7,485	7,197	6,600
Vermont	7,839	7,329	6,609
Virginia	9,435	8,587	7,670
Washington	10,363	9,565	8,581
West Virginia	7,831	7,372	6,593
Wisconsin	9,254	8,484	7,555
Wyoming	10,692	9,922	8,668
United States	9,458	8,757	7,854

1. Preliminary. *Source:* Department of Commerce, Bureau of Economic Analysis.

Gross National Product or Expenditure
(in billions)

Item	1980	1979	1978	1977	1976	1975	1974	1970	1965	1960	1955	1950	1946	1938	1933	1929
Gross national product	$2,626	$2,414	$2,128	$1,900	$1,702	$1,529	$1,413	$982	$688	$506	$399	$286	$210	$85	$56	$103
GNP in constant (1972) dollars	1,481	1,483	1,399	1,341	1,273	1,202	1,218	1,075	926	737	655	534	477	312	222	315
Personal consumption expenditures	1,673	1,511	1,351	1,210	1,090	980	890	619	430	325	254	192	144	64	46	77
Durable goods	212	212	200	179	157	133	122	85	63	43	39	31	16	6	3	9
Nondurable goods	676	602	531	481	444	409	376	265	189	151	123	98	83	34	22	38
Services	785	696	620	550	489	438	391	269	179	131	92	63	45	24	20	30
Gross private domestic investment	395	416	352	303	243	189	215	141	112	76	68	54	31	6	1	16
Residential structures	105	119	108	92	68	52	54	36	31	24	24	20	7	2	1	4
Nonresidential structures	109	96	77	63	57	53	54	38	26	18	14	9	7	2	1	5
Producers' durable equipment	190	186	145	127	108	96	97	64	46	30	24	18	10	3	1	6
Change in business inventories	-6	18	22	22	10	-11	9	4	10	4	6	7	6	-1	-2	2
Net export of goods and services	23	13	-10	-10	8	20	6	4	8	4	2	2	8	1	(¹)	1
Government purchases	535	474	436	396	361	339	303	219	138	100	75	38	28	13	8	8
Federal	199	168	153	144	130	123	111	96	67	54	44	19	18	5	2	1
National defense	132	111	99	94	86	84	77	74	49	44	38	14	15	n.a.	n.a.	n.a.
Other	67	57	54	50	44	39	34	22	18	9	6	5	3	n.a.	n.a.	n.a.
State and local	336	306	283	252	232	216	192	123	71	47	31	20	10	8	6	7
Implicit price deflator	177	163	150	142	134	127	116	91	74	69	61	54	44	27	25	33

1. Less than $500 million. NOTE: n.a. = not available. *Source:* Department of Commerce, Bureau of Economic Analysis.

Shareholders in Public Corporations

Characteristic	1980	1975	1970	1965	1962	1959	1952
Individual shareholders (thousands)	29,840	25,270	30,850	20,120	17,010	12,490	6,490
Owners of shares listed on New York Stock Exchange (thousands)	23,520	17,950	18,290	12,430	11,020	8,510	n.a.
Adult shareowner incidence in population	1 in 5	1 in 6	1 in 4	1 in 6	1 in 6	1 in 8	1 in 16
Median household income	27,750	$19,000	$13,500	$9,500	$8,600	$7,000	$7,100
Adult shareowners with household income: under $10,000 (thousands)	1,720	3,420	8,170	10,080	10,340	9,340	n.a.
$10,000 and over (thousands)	25,410	19,970	20,130	8,410	5,920	2,740	n.a.
Adult female shareowners (thousands)	13,530	11,750	14,290	9,430	8,290	6,350	3,140
Adult male shareowners (thousands)	14,030	11,630	14,340	9,060	7,970	5,740	3,210
Median age	46	53	48	49	48	49	51

NOTE: n.a. = not available. *Source:* New York Stock Exchange.

What Americans Pay in Personal Taxes[1] and What They Save
(in billions of current dollars)

Item	1980	1975	1970	1965	1960	1955	1950
Gross personal income	$2,160.2	$1,255.5	$808.3	$538.9	$401.0	$310.9	$227.6
Social insurance contributions	87.9	50.5	28.0	13.4	9.3	5.2	2.9
Tax and non-tax payments to governments	338.5	168.8	116.6	65.7	50.9	35.5	20.7
Income available for spending and saving[2]	1,821.7	1,086.7	691.7	473.2	350.0	275.3	206.9
Income available per capita (dollars)	8,176	5,088	3,376	2,436	1,937	1,666	1,364
Personal saving	101.3	83.6	56.2	28.4	17.0	15.8	13.1
Rate of personal saving	5.6%	7.7%	8.1%	6.4%	4.9%	5.4%	6.3%

1. Personal income basis: direct taxes and payments only; corporate taxes and payments, paid by shareholders or customers, and hidden and consumption taxes not included. 2. Disposable personal income. *Source:* Department of Commerce, Bureau of Economic Analysis.

Interest Rates

Instrument	1981[1]	1980	1979	1978	1977	1976	1975	1974	1973	1972	1970
MONEY MARKET RATES											
Federal funds	18.84	13.36	11.19	7.94	5.54	5.05	5.82	10.51	8.74	4.44	7.17
Prime commercial paper											
3 months	16.35	12.66	10.97	7.94	5.54	5.24	6.26	10.05	8.20	4.66	—
6 months	15.46	12.29	10.91	7.99	5.60	5.35	6.33	9.87	8.15	4.69	7.72
Prime bankers acceptances, 3 months	16.53	12.78	11.04	8.11	5.59	5.19	6.30	9.92	8.08	4.47	7.31
Certificates of deposit, 3 months, secondary market	17.10	13.07	11.22	8.22	5.64	—	—	—	—	—	—
U.S. government securities: bills, 6-month yield	14.04	11.37	10.06	7.58	5.53	5.26	6.11	7.95	7.20	4.49	6.51
CAPITAL MARKET RATES											
U.S. Treasury											
Notes and bonds maturing in 3–5 years	—	—	9.58	8.30	6.85	6.94	7.55	7.81	6.92	5.85	7.37
5 years	14.28	11.48	9.52	8.32	6.99	7.18	7.77	7.80	—	—	—
10 years	13.88	11.46	9.44	8.41	7.42	7.61	7.99	7.56	—	—	—
State and local Moody's series:											
Aaa	9.80	7.85	5.92	5.52	5.20	5.66	6.42	5.89	—	—	—
Baa	11.25	9.01	6.73	6.27	6.12	7.49	7.62	6.53	—	—	—
Corporate bonds, seasoned issues:											
Aaa	14.04	11.94	9.63	8.73	8.02	8.43	8.83	8.57	—	—	—
Aa	14.51	12.50	9.94	8.92	8.24	8.75	9.17	8.84	—	—	—
A	15.11	12.89	10.20	9.12	8.49	9.09	9.65	9.20	—	—	—
Baa	15.97	13.67	10.69	9.45	8.97	9.75	10.61	9.50	—	—	—

1. Week ending July 3. *Source* Federal Reserve Bulletin, July 1981.

Consumer Price Indexes
(1967 = 100)

Year	Commod-ities	Ser-vices	Hous-ing	All items	Percent change[1]	Year	Commod-ities	Ser-vices	Hous-ing	All items	Percent change[1]
1940	40.6	43.6	52.4	42.0	1.0	1965	95.7	92.2	94.9	94.5	1.7
1945	56.3	48.2	59.1	53.9	2.3	1970	113.5	121.6	118.9	116.3	5.9
1950	78.8	58.7	72.8	72.1	1.0	1975	158.4	166.6	166.8	161.2	8.9
1955	85.1	70.9	82.3	80.2	−0.4	1979	208.4	234.2	227.6	217.4	11.3
1960	91.5	83.5	90.2	88.7	1.6	1980	234.1	270.9	263.2	247.0	13.5

1. Over previous year. *Source:* Department of Labor, Bureau of Labor Statistics.

Consumer Price Index for All Urban Consumers
(1967 = 100)

Group	June 1981	% increase Jan.–June	Group	June 1981	% increase Jan.–June
All items	—	8.5	Fuel oil, coal, bottled gas	682.0	35.8
Food	271.5	1.0	House operation[1]	220.7	8.7
Alcoholic beverages	199.4	7.7	House furnishings	184.6	6.8
Apparel and upkeep	185.8	3.3	Transportation	277.2	11.6
Men's and boys' apparel	176.4	4.5	Medical care	292.1	11.8
Women's and girls' apparel	155.9	−0.1	Personal care	232.1	10.4
Footwear	200.2	4.4	Tobacco products	219.1	8.0
Housing, total	291.7	10.6	Entertainment	220.4	7.4
Rent	206.8	7.3	Personal and educational		
Gas and electricity	344.7	17.0	expenses	261.8	10.3

1. Combines house furnishings and operation. *Source:* Department of Labor, Bureau of Labor Statistics.

Per Capita Personal Income

Year	Amount	Year	Amount	Year	Amount	Year	Amount	Year	Amount
1929	$705	1957	$2,050	1963	$2,460	1969	$3,667	1975	$5,851
1935	474	1958	2,074	1964	2,592	1970	3,893	1976	6,402
1940	593	1959	2,166	1965	2,773	1971	4,132	1977	7,043
1945	1,223	1960	2,219	1966	2,987	1972	4,493	1978	7,854
1950	1,501	1961	2,269	1967	3,167	1973	4,980	1979	8,757
1955	1,881	1962	2,373	1968	3,433	1974	5,428	1980	9,458

Source: Department of Commerce, Bureau of Economic Analysis.

Total Family Income
(figures in percent)

Income range	White 1980	White 1975	White 1970	White 1960	Black and other races 1980	Black and other races 1975	Black and other races 1970	Black and other races 1960
Families (thousands)[1]	52,710	49,873	46,535	41,123	7,599	6,372	5,413	4,333
Under $2,500	1.6	2.8	5.6	15.1	5.0	8.5	15.7	39.8
$2,500 to $4,999	3.3	7.4	11.4	23.8	10.2	17.7	21.5	31.2
$5,000 to $7,499	5.3	10.0	14.6	29.6	12.3	14.6	20.1	18.0
$7,500 to $9,999	6.0	10.4	16.8	16.2	9.8	12.5	14.5	6.2
$10,000 to $12,499	7.1	11.4	16.4	7.9	8.7	11.3	10.8	3.4
$12,500 to $14,999	6.8	11.2	11.5	3.3	7.4	8.8	6.5	0.9
$15,000 to $24,999	28.3	31.7	18.7	3.1	33.3	20.0	9.5	0.6
$25,000 and over	41.6	15.0	5.0	1.0	23.3	6.4	1.5	n.a.
Median income	$21,904	$14,268	$10,236	$5,835	$13,843	$9,321	$6,516	$3,230

1. As of March 1981. *Source:* Department of Commerce, Bureau of the Census.

National Income by Type
(in billions of dollars)

Type of share	1980	1980 % of total	1979	1975	1970	1965	1960	1955	1950
National income	$2,121.4	100.0	$1,963.3	$1,215.0	$800.5	$564.3	$414.5	$331.0	$241.1
Compensation of employees	1,596.5	75.3	1,460.9	931.1	603.9	393.8	294.2	224.5	154.6
Wages and salaries	1,343.6	62.5	1,235.9	805.9	542.0	358.9	270.8	211.3	146.8
Supplements to wages and salaries	252.9	11.9	225.0	125.2	61.9	35.0	23.4	13.2	7.8
Proprietors' income	130.6	6.2	131.6	87.0	66.9	57.3	46.2	41.7	37.5
Business and professional	107.2	5.1	100.7	63.5	50.0	42.4	34.2	30.3	24.0
Farm	23.4	1.1	30.8	23.5	16.9	14.8	12.0	11.4	13.5
Rental income of persons	31.8	1.5	30.5	22.4	23.9	19.0	15.8	13.9	9.4
Corporate profits[1]	182.6	8.6	196.8	95.9	69.4	76.1	49.9	46.9	37.7
Net interest	179.8	8.5	143.4	78.6	36.4	18.2	8.4	4.1	2.0

1. Includes inventory valuation adjustment. *Source:* Department of Commerce, Bureau of Economic Analysis.

Annual Budgets for 4-Person Urban Families, Autumn 1979

Item	Lower budget Amount	Lower budget Percent increase 1978–79	Intermediate budget Amount	Intermediate budget Percent increase 1978–79	Higher budget Amount	Higher budget Percent increase 1978–79
Total family consumption	$10,234	9.0	$15,353	9.7	$21,069	9.6
Food	3,911	9.4	5,044	9.4	6,360	9.5
Housing	2,409	7.9	4,594	9.9	6,971	9.9
Transportation	1,004	17.3	1,851	17.7	2,411	18.0
Clothing	866	2.2	1,235	2.2	1,804	2.0
Personal care	323	7.3	433	7.4	613	7.5
Medical Care	1,171	10.0	1,176	9.9	1,227	9.9
Other family consumption	550	6.8	1,021	6.8	1,684	6.7
Other items	539	7.4	877	8.3	1,478	8.3
Personal income taxes	1,032	10.4	3,031	10.7	6,357	10.8
Social security and disability	781	8.6	1,256	17.1	1,413	29.5
Total budget	**12,585**	**9.0**	**20,517**	**10.2**	**30,317**	**10.6**

NOTE: Above budgets illustrate three levels of living based on estimates of costs for goods and services rather than actual expenditures. Totals may not add because of rounding. *Source:* Department of Labor, Bureau of Labor Statistics. NOTE: Data are latest available.

Annual Budgets for a Retired Couple, Autumn 1979

Item	Lower Budget Amount	Lower Budget Percent increase 1978–79	Intermediate Budget Amount	Intermediate Budget Percent increase 1978–79	Higher Budget Amount	Higher Budget Percent increase 1978–79
Total family consumption	$5,763	9.2	$8,047	9.1	$11,719	9.3
Food	1,882	9.1	2,507	9.0	3,149	9.2
Housing	1,996	9.0	2,862	8.4	4,481	8.3
Transportation	420	16.7	820	17.0	1,528	17.6
Clothing	225	2.3	378	2.4	581	2.3
Personal care	169	8.3	247	7.9	362	8.1
Medical care[1]	837	9.4	842	9.5	848	9.6
Other consumption	234	6.4	390	6.6	770	6.6
Other items	259	9.3	515	9.1	950	8.6
Total budget	**6,023**	**9.2[2]**	**8,562**	**9.1[2]**	**12,669**	**9.3[2]**

1. Contains preliminary estimate for out-of-pocket costs for Medicare. 2. Largest increases since 1974. *Source:* Department of Commerce, Bureau of Labor Statistics. NOTE: Data are latest available.

Median Earnings of Full-Time Women Workers
(persons 14 years and over)

Major occupation group	1979 earnings	As percent of men's earnings
Professional and technical workers	$13,700	64.3
Nonfarm managers and administrators	11,698	53.6
Clerical workers	9,853	59.6
Sales workers	8,910	52.1
Operatives (including transport)	8,579	57.4
Service workers (except private household)	7,486	62.7
All occupations	10,168	59.6

Source: Department of Labor, Women's Bureau.

Farm Indexes
(1967 = 100)

Year	Prices paid by farmers[1]	Prices rec'd by farmers[2]	Ratio
1945	56	83	148
1950	75	103	137
1955	81	93	115
1960	88	95	108
1965	94	98	104
1970	112	110	98
1975	180	185	103
1979	250	241	96
1980	281	246	88

1. Commodities, interest, and taxes, and wage rates. 2. All crops and livestock. Source: Department of Agriculture, Economics and Statistics Service.

Median Family Income
(in current dollars)

Year	Income	Percent change	Year	Income	Percent change
1960	$ 5,620	—	1975	$13,719	6.3
1970	9,867	—	1976	14,958	9.0
1972	11,116	—	1977	16,009	7.0
1973	12,051	8.4	1978	17,640	10.2
1974	12,902	7.1	1979	19,661	11.5

Source: Department of Commerce, Bureau of the Census. NOTE: Figures are latest available.

Life Insurance in Force
(in millions of dollars)

As of Dec. 31	Ordinary	Group	Industrial	Credit	Total
1915	$16,650	$ 100	$ 4,279	—	$ 21,029
1930	78,756	9,801	17,693	73	106,413
1945	101,550	22,172	27,675	365	151,762
1950	149,071	47,793	33,415	3,844	234,168
1955	216,812	101,345	39,682	14,493	373,332
1960	341,881	175,903	39,563	29,101	586,448
1965	499,638	308,078	39,818	53,020	900,554
1970	734,730	551,357	38,644	77,392	1,402,123
1975	1,083,421	904,695	39,423	112,032	2,139,571
1978	1,425,095	1,243,994	38,080	163,081	2,870,250
1979	1,585,878	1,419,418	37,794	179,250	3,222,340
1980	1,760,474	1,579,355	35,994	165,215	3,541,038

Source: American Council of Life Insurance.

Producer Price Indexes by Major Commodity Groups
(1967 = 100)

Commodity	1980	1979	1975	1970	1965	1960	1955
All commodities	268.6	235.6	174.9	110.4	96.6	94.9	87.8
Farm products	249.3	241.4	186.7	111.0	98.7	97.2	98.2
Processed foods	241.0	222.5	182.6	112.1	95.5	89.5	85.0
Textile products and apparel	183.4	168.7	137.9	107.1	99.8	99.5	98.7
Hides, skins, and leather products	248.6	252.4	148.5	110.3	94.3	90.8	77.3
Fuels and related products and power	573.4	408.1	245.1	106.2	95.5	96.1	91.2
Chemicals and allied products	260.2	222.3	181.3	102.2	99.0	101.8	98.5
Rubber and plastic products	217.3	194.3	150.2	108.3	95.9	103.1	102.4
Lumber and wood products	288.8	300.4	176.9	113.6	95.9	95.3	97.1
Pulp, paper, and allied products	249.3	219.0	170.4	108.2	96.2	98.1	87.8
Metals and metal products	286.2	259.3	185.6	116.6	96.4	92.4	82.1
Machinery and equipment	239.6	213.9	161.4	111.4	93.9	92.0	75.7
Furniture and household durables	187.3	171.3	139.7	107.5	96.9	99.0	93.3
Nonmetallic mineral products	282.8	248.6	174.0	112.9	97.5	97.2	87.5
Transportation equipment (Dec. 1968 = 100)	206.6	188.1	141.5	104.6	98.5	98.8	—
Miscellaneous products	258.7	208.7	147.7	109.9	95.9	93.0	86.5

Source: Department of Labor, Bureau of Labor Statistics.

Foresee Auto Mechanic Shortage

The Automotive Information Council has noted a report indicating that there were 86 cars per mechanic in 1981 compared to 66 cars per mechanic in 1970. The report states that the ratio will rise to 100 cars per mechanic in 1990. In addition, the study states that the new domestic cars alone mean that distributors and repairmen must cope with 30,000 new parts.

Federal Reserve Board Indexes of Production
(1967 = 100)

Industry	1981[1]	1980	1975	1970
Total industrial production	152.7	147.1	117.8	106.7
Total manufactures	152.2	146.6	116.3	105.2
Durable manufactures	142.7	136.6	109.3	101.5
Primary metals	109.8	101.6	96.4	106.9
Fabricated metal products	140.4	135.0	109.9	109.4
Machinery	173.5	162.8	125.1	100.3
Transportation equipment	123.2	116.8	97.4	90.4
Instruments and products	169.5	171.0	132.3	110.8
Clay, glass, and stone products	151.6[2]	146.5	117.9	106.4
Lumber and products	126.2[2]	119.3	107.6	106.3
Furniture and fixtures	158.9[2]	150.0	118.2	99.4
Nondurable manufactures	165.9	161.1	126.4	110.6
Textile mill products	135.7[2]	136.8	123.3	106.3
Apparel products	124.0[3]	128.6	107.6	97.8
Leather products	70.0[2]	70.1	76.5	90.8

Industry	1981[1]	1980	1975	1970
Rubber and plastic products	276.0[2]	255.8	166.7	115.7
Paper and products	153.6	151.0	116.3	113.3
Printing and publishing	139.3	139.6	113.4	104.1
Chemicals and products	222.4[2]	206.7	147.3	120.3
Petroleum products	128.8	134.9	124.1	112.6
Foods	152.5[2]	149.2	123.4	111.7
Tobacco products	120.7[3]	119.8	111.8	100.0
Mining	141.3	132.9	112.8	109.7
Coal	124.1	146.7	113.4	105.7
Oil and gas extraction	148.3	133.8	113.3	109.7
Metal mining	121.6[2]	109.1	115.8	131.3
Stone and earth minerals	133.1[2]	131.7	107.0	98.8
Utilities	172.5	169.9	146.0	128.3

1. June estimate except where otherwise indicated. 2. May preliminary. 3. April. *Source: Federal Reserve Bulletin*, July 1981.

Value of New Construction Put in Place
(in millions of dollars)

Activity	1980	1975	1970	1960	1950	1940	1933	1929
Total new construction activity	$280,273	$135,941	$95,294	$54,738	$33,575	$8,682	$2,879	$10,973
New private construction activity	174,897	95,057	67,114	38,875	26,709	5,054	1,231	8,307
Residential	87,261	46,472	31,864	22,975	18,126	2,985	470	3,625
New dwelling units	63,139	34,408	24,272	17,279	15,551	2,560	290	3,040
Additions and alterations	21,125	10,925	6,234	4,831	2,400	335	145	340
Nonhousekeeping	2,997	1,139	1,358	865	175	90	35	245
Nonresidential building, except farm and public utility	52,434	26,407	21,412	10,149	3,904	1,025	406	2,694
Industrial	13,837	8,018	6,537	2,851	1,062	442	176	949
Commercial[1]	29,945	12,806	9,753	4,180	1,415	348	130	1,135
Other	8,652	5,582	5,122	3,118	1,427	235	100	610
Public utility	28,678	17,379	11,017	4,621	3,045	771	261	1,578
Railroads	1,153	514	304	270	309	217	115	592
Telephone and telegraph	6,733	3,683	2,968	1,088	440	122	45	354
Farm construction	5,274	3,731	1,875	849	1,522	240	49	307
New public construction activity	55,376	40,884	28,090	15,863	6,866	3,628	1,648	2,486
Residential	1,648	754	1,016	716	345	200	n.a.	n.a.
Nonresidential building	17,216	14,720	9,550	4,795	2,387	615	230	659
Industrial	1,788	918	498	407	224	164	2	n.a.
Educational	8,050	7,760	5,619	2,818	1,133	156	52	389
Hospital and institutional	1,785	1,745	838	401	499	54	49	101
Other	5,593	4,296	2,594	1,169	531	421	127	169
Military facilities	1,880	1,389	717	1,366	177	385	36	19
Highway	13,785	10,854	9,982	5,437	2,134	1,302	847	1,266
Sewer and water	10,437	6,566	2,636	1,487	659	338	95	253
Conservation and development	5,090	3,257	1,907	1,175	942	528	359	115

1. Warehouses, office and loft buildings; stores, restaurants and garages. NOTE: n.a. = not available. *Source:* Department of Commerce, Bureau of the Census.

A Profile of Your 1985 Car

Federal regulations require each car company to achieve an average of 27.5 miles per gallon for its cars made in the 1985 model year. Smaller and lighter cars will be the result. And to meet that federal average, companies will be providing some two-passenger commuter cars.

Four-passenger cars will be dominant, with only about 25% of the total capable of carrying five or six people. V-8 engines will decline to perhaps 10% of the total and will be much lower in power than the V-8's of today.

More extensive use of materials such as plastics and aluminum will be used and entire hoods and door panels might be made of plastic by 1985.

Expenditures for New Plant and Equipment[1]
(in millions of dollars)

Year	Manufacturing and mining	Transportation	All other[2]	Total
1950	$ 8,570	$ 2,380	$ 14,370	$ 25,320
1955	13,810	2,600	20,170	36,580
1960	17,650	3,190	27,800	48,630
1965	26,770	5,460	38,200	70,430
1970	39,010	6,950	59,650	105,610
1973	45,680	7,410	84,710	137,700
1974	57,830	8,230	90,920	156,980
1975	61,020	8,680	88,010	157,710
1976	67,390	8,890	95,180	171,450
1977	78,460	9,400	110,230	198,080
1978	89,930	10,670	130,640	231,240
1979	110,060	12,350	148,050	270,460
1980	129,320	12,180	154,130	295,630

1. Data exclude agriculture. 2. Includes electric and gas utilities, trade, service, communications, construction, and finance. NOTE: This series was revised in October 1980. *Source:* Department of Commerce, Bureau of Economic Analysis.

New Housing Starts[1] and Mobile Homes Shipped
(in thousands)

Year	No. of units started	Year	No. of units started	Year	Mobile homes shipped
1900	189	1965	1,510	1965	217
1910	387	1970	1,469	1970	401
1920	247	1972	2,379	1972	576
1925	937	1973	2,057	1973	567
1930	330	1974	1,352	1974	329
1935	221	1975	1,171	1975	213
1940	603	1976	1,548	1976	246
1945	326	1977	1,990	1977	277
1950	1,952	1978	2,023	1978	275
1955	1,646	1979	1,749	1979	277
1960[1]	1,296	1980	1,299	1980	222

1. Prior to 1960, starts limited to nonfarm housing; from 1960 on, figures include farm housing. *Sources:* Department of Commerce, Housing Construction Statistics, 1900–1965, and Construction Reports, Housing Starts, 1970–80; Manufactured Housing Institute, 1965–76; National Conference of States on Building Codes and Standards.

Consumer Credit
(non-installment credit; in millions of dollars)

End of year	Service credit	Charge accounts	Single-payment loans	Total credit outstanding	End of year	Service credit	Charge accounts	Single-payment loans	Total credit outstanding
1945	$ 845	$ 2,687	$ 1,491	$ 5,023	1970	9,106	9,156	19,323	37,585
1950	1,638	4,858	3,642	10,138	1975	12,027	11,739	27,378	51,144
1955	2,316	6,761	6,002	15,079	1978	16,431	12,002	35,827	64,260
1960[1]	3,734	7,235	9,084	20,053	1979	18,619	12,748	39,967	71,335
1965	5,545	8,319	15,462	29,326	1980	19,280	12,995	39,949	72,224

1. Beginning with 1960, data include Alaska and Hawaii. *Source:* Federal Reserve Board.

50 Most Active Stocks in 1980

Stock	Share volume	Stock	Share volume	Stock	Share volume
Int'l Business Machines	114,111,300	K mart Corporation	42,946,000	Chrysler Corporation	37,194,500
Texaco Inc.	108,271,200	Benguet Corporation	42,688,500	Amerada Hess	36,806,000
Mobil Corporation	92,986,200	Engelhard Minerals & Chemicals	42,490,400	Standard Oil Co. of California	36,366,600
Gulf Oil	79,211,400	Tesoro Petroleum	42,182,300	Morris (Philip) Inc.	36,247,800
Boeing Company	77,076,400	National Semiconductor	42,121,300	Norton Simon	35,747,100
American Tel. & Tel.	73,738,000	Dow Chemical	41,099,300	American Home Products	35,468,800
Sony Corporation	69,811,100	International Tel. & Tel.	40,118,900	Warner-Lambert	34,299,900
Exxon Corporation	65,894,500	Federal National Mortgage Assoc.	39,966,600	Ford Motor	33,992,100
General Motors	58,483,700	Gulf & Western Industries	38,964,200	Digital Equipment	33,961,000
Phillips Petroleum	56,310,400	General Electric	38,743,900	El Paso Company	33,858,900
Citicorp	54,116,200	Xerox Corporation	38,490,200	Middle South Utilities	33,402,900
Occidental Petroleum	51,979,700	Storage Technology	38,132,700	ASARCO Inc.	33,345,300
Sears, Roebuck	51,810,100	Ralston Purina	37,816,700	Natomas Company	32,840,800
LTV Corporation	50,016,100	City Investing	37,559,700	Williams Companies	32,652,500
Standard Oil (Indiana)	48,469,100	Colgate-Palmolive	37,395,100	McDermott Inc.	32,459,600
American Cyanamid	45,674,700			Squibb Corporation	32,260,600
Eastman Kodak	45,252,500			BankAmerica Corporation	32,258,000
Atlantic Richfield	44,912,600				

Source: New York Stock Exchange.

Business Population
(in thousands of concerns)

Item	1977[1]	1976[1]	1975[1]	1970[1]	1965[1]	1953	1949	1941	1933	1929
Total operating businesses[2]	14,740	14,559	13,979	12,001	11,417	4,188	3,984	3,276	2,782	3,029
Manufacturing	482	467	468	410	408	331	322	230	167	257
Wholesale trade	576	591	587	470	444	283	260	190	142	148
Retail trade	2,459	2,440	2,322	2,210	2,044	1,846	1,783	1,561	1,291	1,327
Service industries	4,043	3,834	3,669	2,964	2,565	750	739	615	575	591
Construction	1,279	1,221	1,144	875	876	405	339	194	185	234
All other[3]	5,901	6,007	5,788	5,072	5,080	573	541	486	422	472
New incorporations	432	376	326	264	204	352	331	290	n.a.	n.a.
Commercial and industrial failures[4]	7.9	9.6	11.4	10.7	13.5	8.9	9.2	11.8	19.9	22.9

1. Data for total operating businesses are now based on tax returns; not comparable with earlier figures. 2. 1929–33, annual average; 1941–53, as of January 1. 3. Includes agriculture, forestry, and fishing; mining; transportation, communication, electric, gas, and sanitary services; finance, insurance, and real estate; wholesale and retail trade not allocable; and nature of business not allocable. 4. Closures resulting in a known loss to creditors. NOTE: New incorporations for 1978 were 477,827; failures, 6,619. n.a. = not available. *Sources:* Departments of Commerce and the Treasury; Dun & Bradstreet. NOTE: Data are latest available.

Largest Businesses, 1980
(in thousands of dollars)
Source: Fortune magazine.

50 LARGEST INDUSTRIAL CORPORATIONS

	Sales	Assets
Exxon	$103,142,834	$56,576,558
Mobil	59,510,000	32,705,000
General Motors	57,728,500	34,581,000
Texaco	51,195,830	26,430,355
Standard Oil of California	40,479,000	22,162,000
Ford Motor	37,085,500	24,347,600
Gulf Oil	26,483,000	18,638,000
International Business Machines	26,213,000	26,703,000
Standard Oil (Ind.)	26,133,080	20,167,474
General Electric	24,959,000	18,511,000
Atlantic Richfield	23,744,302	16,604,844
Shell Oil	19,830,000	17,615,000
International Telephone & Telegraph	18,529,655	15,417,183
Conoco	18,325,400	11,036,275
E.I. du Pont de Nemours	13,652,000	9,560,000
Phillips Petroleum	13,376,563	9,844,382
Tenneco	13,226,000	13,853,000
Sun	12,945,000	10,955,000
U.S. Steel	12,492,100	11,747,600
Occidental Petroleum	12,476,125	6,629,889
United Technologies	12,323,994	7,326,270
Western Electric	12,032,100	8,047,500
Standard Oil (Ohio)	11,023,196	12,080,050
Procter & Gamble	10,772,186	6,553,359
Dow Chemical	10,626,000	11,538,000
Getty Oil	10,150,411	8,266,676
Union Carbide	9,994,000	9,659,000
Union Oil of California	9,984,100	6,772,100
Eastman Kodak	9,734,303	8,753,991
Boeing	9,426,200	5,931,300
Dart & Kraft	9,411,500	4,650,300
Chrysler	9,225,300	6,617,800
Caterpillar Tractor	8,597,800	6,098,200
Westinghouse Electric	8,514,300	6,812,600
R.J. Reynolds Industries	8,449,000	7,355,300
Goodyear Tire & Rubber	8,444,015	5,368,301
Beatrice Foods	8,290,509	3,980,279
Xerox	8,196,500	7,349,200
Marathon Oil	8,179,751	5,043,092
Ashland Oil	8,118,369	3,357,614
RCA	8,011,300	7,147,600
LTV	8,009,958	4,029,669
Amerada Hess	7,868,963	5,895,444
Cities Service	7,786,300	5,358,000
Philip Morris	7,328,300	7,366,400
Rockwell International	6,906,500	4,430,900
Bethlehem Steel	6,743,000	5,206,800
Monsanto	6,573,600	5,796,400
International Harvester	6,311,804	5,843,458
Esmark	6,108,355	1,853,895

50 LARGEST RETAILING COMPANIES

	Sales	Assets
Sears Roebuck	$25,194,900	$28,053,800
Safeway Stores	15,102,673	3,338,832
K mart	14,204,381	6,102,462
J.C. Penney	11,353,000	5,863,000
Kroger	10,316,741	1,997,545
F.W. Woolworth	7,218,176	3,171,894
Great Atlantic & Pacific Tea	6,684,179	1,230,522
Lucky Stores	6,468,682	1,400,601
American Stores Co.	6,419,884	1,292,992
Federated Department Stores	6,300,686	3,575,513
Montgomery Ward	5,496,607	3,942,230
Winn-Dixie Stores	5,388,979	903,709
Southland	4,758,656	1,495,385
City Products	4,462,378	1,283,236
Jewel Companies	4,267,922	1,288,901
Dayton Hudson	4,033,536	2,155,234
May Department Stores	3,172,976	2,259,344
Grand Union	3,137,612	707,127
Albertson's	3,039,129	627,219
Wickes Companies	2,876,973	1,705,296
ARA Services	2,806,020	1,097,065
Carter Hawley Hale Stores	2,632,921	1,651,368
Supermarkets General	2,628,851	572,884
R.H. Macy	2,373,531	1,328,254
Rapid-American	2,351,591	1,561,685
Melville	2,332,244	889,468
Allied Stores	2,298,838	1,620,270
McDonald's	2,215,463	2,643,369
Dillion Companies	2,077,265	434,943
Stop & Shop Companies	2,059,183	474,549
Associated Dry Goods	1,952,239	1,020,871
Marriott Corp.	1,718,725	1,214,264
Wal-Mart Stores	1,643,199	592,345
Zayre	1,594,235	560,737

Jack Eckerd	1,547,753	549,492
Holiday Inns	1,533,758	1,680,103
Walgreen	1,530,722	448,633
Fisher Foods	1,412,962	341,122
Tandy	1,384,637	710,298
First National Supermarkets	1,364,797	208,777
Sigmor	1,327,605	452,803
Waldbaum	1,271,624	220,008
Giant Food	1,242,620	307,447
National Tea	1,219,304	270,901
Food Fair	1,124,067	365,982
Mercantile Stores	1,108,076	653,000
Revco D.S.	1,092,797	367,144
Zale	1,041,699	718,002
Fed-Mart	1,040,415	313,446
Marshall Field	1,012,501	672,297

10 LARGEST COMMERCIAL BANKS

	Assets	Deposits
Citicorp	$114,920,000	$71,771,000
BankAmerica Corp.	111,617,291	88,426,156
Chase Manhattan Corp.	76,189,567	56,846,002
Manufacturers Hanover Corp.	55,522,249	41,744,624
J.P. Morgan & Co.	51,990,646	35,593,807
Continental Illinois Corp.	42,089,408	27,313,667
Chemical New York Corp.	41,342,220	30,067,000
Bankers Trust New York Corp.	32,325,603	23,942,285
Western Bancorp	32,110,327	24,863,703
First Chicago Corp.	28,699,441	21,361,154

10 LARGEST LIFE INSURANCE COMPANIES

	Assets	Premium and annuity income
Prudential	$59,778,470	8,668,858
Metropolitan	48,309,771	6,010,574
Equitable Life Assurance	34,599,737	4,163,345
Aetna Life	22,270,634	5,412,032
New York Life	19,725,325	2,682,329
John Hancock Mutual	18,760,598	2,436,403
Connecticut General Life	13,776,921	1,861,488
Travelers	13,351,227	3,955,025
Northwestern Mutual	11,350,786	1,193,496
Teachers Insurance & Annuity	9,748,371	1,315,944

10 LARGEST TRANSPORTATION COMPANIES

	Operating revenues	Assets
UAL	$5,041,335	$4,041,458
Trans World Corp.	5,018,281	3,184,975
CSX Corp.	4,841,350	7,523,101
United Parcel Service	4,025,169	1,346,792
Pan American World Airways	4,016,060	3,365,588
Burlington Northern	3,953,640	5,267,005
American Airlines	3,820,978	3,277,883
Eastern Air Lines	3,452,542	2,816,177
Santa Fe Industries	3,215,000	4,330,200
Delta Air Lines	2,956,960	2,042,539

10 LARGEST UTILITIES

	Assets	Operating revenues
American Telephone & Telegraph	$125,450,800	$50,791,200
General Telephone & Electronics	19,720,457	9,978,875
Southern Company	11,466,555	3,763,483
Pacific Gas & Electric	11,295,203	5,258,899
American Electric Power	10,951,984	3,756,464
Commonwealth Edison	10,177,142	3,324,043
Southern California Edison	7,733,898	3,661,117
Consolidated Edison	7,459,681	3,947,165
Middle South Utilities	7,334,879	2,342,228
Public Service Electric & Gas	6,724,860	2,994,054

10 LARGEST DIVERSIFIED FINANCIAL COMPANIES

	Assets	Revenues
Federal National Mortgage Assn.	$58,470,003	$5,202,910
Aetna Life & Casualty	35,752,700	13,318,000
Travelers Corp.	21,637,986	8,790,092
American Express	19,709,000	5,504,000
Merrill Lynch & Co.	13,245,784	3,022,473
H.F. Ahmanson	13,109,603	1,317,119
INA	10,604,000	5,255,000
Great Western Financial	10,252,838	997,222
First Charter Financial	9,676,378	955,093
Loews	9,125,112	4,535,098

Estimated Annual Retail and Wholesale Sales by Kind of Business
(in millions of dollars)

Kind of business	1980	1979
Retail trade, total	956,655	894,343
Building materials, hardware, garden supply, and mobile home dealers	48,210	50,272
Automotive dealers	167,017	177,251
Furniture, home furnishings, and equipment stores	43,918	41,868
General merchandise group stores	116,287	109,740
Food stores	217,511	195,826
Gasoline service stations	94,470	73,202
Apparel and accessory stores	44,487	42,375
Eating and drinking places	86,612	79,576
Drug stores and proprietary stores	31,557	28,107
Liquor stores	16,556	15,294
Merchant wholesale trade, total	1,043,886	915,163
Total, (excluding farm-product raw materials)	923,662	808,775
Durable goods, total	438,439	410,079
Motor vehicles and automotive parts and supplies	81,629	75,507
Furniture and home furnishings	15,580	13,940

Kind of business	1980	1979
Lumber and other construction materials	33,245	37,122
Electrical goods	46,436	41,750
Hardware, plumbing, heating and supplies	27,623	26,814
Machinery, equipment, supplies	129,048	115,952
Scrap and waste materials	16,327	16,220
Nondurable goods, total	605,447	505,084
Total (excluding farm-product raw materials)	485,223	398,696
Paper and paper products	21,643	19,271
Drugs, drug proprietaries, and druggists' sundries	13,051	11,593
Apparel, piece goods, and notions	25,790	23,009
Groceries and related products	149,889	136,529
Beer, wine, distilled alcoholic beverages	31,697	29,196
Miscellaneous nondurable goods	69,939	61,941
Tobacco and tobacco products	10,998	10,802

Source: Department of Commerce, Bureau of the Census.

50 Companies With Largest Number of Stockholders

Company	Stockholders	Company	Stockholders
American Telephone & Telegraph	3,026,000	E. I. du Pont de Nemours	213,000
General Motors	1,191,000	Niagara Mohawk Power	211,000
International Business Machines	737,000	Chrysler Corporation	209,000
Exxon Corporation	697,000	Atlantic Richfield	203,000
General Electric	524,000	Northeast Utilities	196,000
General Telephone & Electronics	486,000	Southern California Edison	193,000
Texaco, Inc.	394,000	Standard Oil (Indiana)	188,000
Sears, Roebuck	350,000	Ohio Edison	183,000
Ford Motor	346,000	Virginia Electric & Power	183,000
Southern Company	345,000	Westinghouse Electric	176,000
American Electric Power	338,000	Middle South Utilities	175,000
Gulf Oil	312,000	Consumers Power	172,000
Mobil Corporation	272,000	BankAmerica	171,000
Commonwealth Edison	269,000	Union Electric	169,000
Pacific Gas & Electric	261,000	Union Carbide Corporation	164,000
Philadelphia Electric	253,000	Occidental Petroleum	161,000
RCA	252,000	Long Island Lighting	160,000
U.S. Steel	248,000	Pennsylvania Power	157,000
Standard Oil of California	247,000	General Public Utilities	151,000
Detroit Edison	242,000	Columbia Gas System	144,000
Consolidated Edison	237,000	Pan American World Airways	140,000
Eastman Kodak	234,000	Bethlehem Steel	139,000
Tenneco Inc.	232,000	Transamerica Corporation	138,000
Public Service Electric & Gas	231,000	Duquesne Light	138,000
International Telephone & Telegraph	214,000	Greyhound Corporation	137,000

Note: As of early 1981. *Source:* New York Stock Exchange.

50 Leading Stocks in Market Value

Stock	Market value (millions)	Listed shares (millions)	Stock	Market value (millions)	Listed shares (millions)
International Business Machines	$ 39,648	584.1	Johnson & Johnson	$ 6,172	61.9
Exxon Corporation	36,540	453.2	E. I. du Pont de Nemours	6,155	146.6
American Telephone & Telegraph	35,457	740.6	Tenneco Inc.	6,142	118.4
Standard Oil Co. (Indiana)	24,308	304.3	Sun Company	6,009	123.3
Schlumberger, N.V.	23,483	200.7	Procter & Gamble	5,698	82.7
Shell Oil	17,993	308.9	Morris (Philip) Inc.	5,396	124.8
Mobil Corporation	17,167	212.6	Hewlett-Packard Company	5,367	60.0
Standard Oil of California	17,020	171.1	SmithKline Corporation	5,317	66.5
Atlantic Richfield	15,037	236.3	Superior Oil	5,257	26.6
General Electric	14,177	231.5	Xerox Corporation	5,045	84.3
General Motors	13,415	297.3	Caterpillar Tractor	5,017	86.5
Texaco Inc.	13,132	274.3	Sears, Roebuck	5,002	325.3
Eastman Kodak	11,269	161.6	Raytheon Company	4,894	44.5
Halliburton Company	9,854	118.0	Eli Lilly	4,820	75.8
Gulf Oil	9,245	211.9	Reynolds Industries	4,761	104.4
Phillips Petroleum	9,074	154.4	American Home Products	4,737	168.4
Standard Oil (Ohio)	8,697	120.8	BankAmerica Corporation	4,471	147.8
Getty Oil	8,134	88.5	Weyerhaeuser Company	4,389	128.6
Union Oil of California	7,742	173.5	Digital Equipment	4,360	45.9
Union Pacific	7,557	96.0	Marathon Oil	4,354	61.5
Conoco Inc.	7,417	113.5	Boeing Company	4,318	97.6
Teledyne Inc.	6,985	32.3	Dresser Industries	4,263	79.7
Minnesota Mining & Manufacturing	6,962	118.0	General Telephone & Electronics	4,199	154.8
Dow Chemical	6,489	202.0	Coca-Cola Company	4,138	124.0
Merck & Company	6,432	75.9	Cities Service	4,025	84.7
			Total	**$497,540**	**8,305.9**

NOTE: As of Dec. 31, 1980. Of the 1,540 common stocks listed on the New York Stock Exchange at the end of 1980, the 50 issues with the largest market value totaled $498 billion, or 41% of the total value of common stocks listed. The five largest common issues were valued at $159 billion, or 13% of the total. Four corporations joined the list in 1980: Cities Service, Dresser Industries, Digital Equipment, and Raytheon Company. *Source:* New York Stock Exchange.

Terms on Conventional First Mortgages: All Major Types of Lenders

Type of homes and year	Contract rate (percent)	Fees and charges (percent)	Effective rate (percent)	Maturity (years)	Loan amount	Purchase price	Loan-to-price ratio (percent)
New homes: 1981[1]	14.12	2.50	14.67	27.5	66,800	94,100	72.6
1980	12.25	2.09	12.65	28.2	59,200	83,400	73.2
1979	10.48	1.66	10.77	28.5	53,300	74,400	73.9
1978	9.30	1.39	9.54	28.0	45,900	62,600	75.3
1975	8.75	1.54	—	26.8	33,300	44,600	76.1
1970	8.27	1.03	—	25.1	25,200	35,500	71.7
Existing homes: 1981[1]	14.31	2.58	14.86	26.4	57,400	86,500	69.2
1980	12.58	1.90	12.95	26.8	48,000	68,000	73.3
1979	10.66	1.45	10.92	27.1	46,300	64,600	74.0
1978	9.37	1.26	9.58	26.4	39,400	54,200	75.1
1975	9.01	1.19	—	24.0	27,400	38,200	73.4
1970	8.20	0.92	—	22.8	21,000	30,000	71.1

1. June. *Source:* Federal Home Loan Bank Board.

National Labor Unions With Membership Over 100,000

Members[1]	Union
1,357,000	Automobile, Aerospace and Agricultural Implement Workers of America, International Union, United (Ind.)
160,000	Bakery and Confectionery Workers' International Union of America
145,000	Boilermakers, Iron Ship Builders, Blacksmiths, Forgers and Helpers, International Brotherhood of
135,000	Bricklayers and Allied Craftsmen, International Union of
184,000	Bridge and Structural Iron Workers, International Association of
105,000	California State Employees' Association (Ind.)
832,000	Carpenters and Joiners of America, United Brotherhood of
n.a.	Classified School Employees, American Association of (Ind.)
455,000	Clothing and Textile Workers Union of North America, Amalgamated
551,000	Communications Workers of America
1,684,000	Education Association, National (Ind.)
233,000	Electrical, Radio and Machine Workers, International Union of
162,000	Electrical, Radio and Machine Workers of America, United (Ind.)
1,041,000	Electrical Workers, International Brotherhood of
178,000	Fire Fighters, International Association of
1,300,000	Food and Commercial Workers Union, United
255,000	Government Employees, American Federation of
200,000	Government Employees, National Association of (Ind.)
400,000	Hotel and Restaurant Employees and Bartenders International Union
608,000	Laborers' International Union of North America
323,000	Ladies' Garment Workers' Union, International
230,000	Letter Carriers of the United States of America, National Association of
1,041,000	Machinists and Aerospace Workers, International Association of
101,000	Maintenance of Way Employees, Brotherhood of
185,000	Mine Workers of America, United (Ind.)
299,000	Musicians, American Federation of
180,000	Nurses' Association; American (Ind.)
107,000	Office and Professional Employees International Union
154,000	Oil, Chemical and Atomic Workers International Union
423,000	Operating Engineers, International Union of
164,000	Painters and Allied Trades of the United States and Canada, International Brotherhood of
219,000	Paperworkers International Union, United
352,000	Plumbing and Pipe Fitting Industry of the United States and Canada, United Association of Journeymen and Apprentices of the
150,000	Police, Fraternal Order of (Ind.)
251,000	Postal Workers' Union, American
122,000	Printing and Graphic Communications Union, International
180,000	Railway, Airline and Steamship Clerks, Freight Handlers, Express and Station Employees, Brotherhood of
215,000	Retail, Wholesale and Department Store Union
151,000	Rubber, Cork, Linoleum and Plastic Workers of America, United
650,000	Service Employees' International Union
154,000	Sheet Metal Workers' International Association
1,098,000	State, County and Municipal Employees of America, American Federation of
1,238,000	Steelworkers of America, United

Members[1]	Union
502,000	Teachers, American Federation of
1,891,000	Teamsters, Chauffeurs, Warehousemen and Helpers of America, International Brotherhood of (Ind.)
162,000	Transit Union, Amalgamated
130,000	Transport Workers Union of America
190,000	Transportation Union, United
112,000	Woodworkers of America, International

1. 1980. NOTE: Unless indicated by Ind. (Independent), all unions are affiliated with the AFL-CIO. n.a.=not available. *Source:* Department of Labor, Bureau of Labor Statistics.

Strikes and Lockouts

Year	Strikes and lockouts	Workers involved (thousands)	Man-days idle (thousands)	Year	Strikes and lockouts	Workers involved (thousands)	Man-days idle (thousands)
1895	1,255	407	n.a.	1950	4,843	2,410	38,800
1900	1,839	568	n.a.	1955	4,320	2,650	28,200
1905	2,186	302	n.a.	1960[1]	3,333	1,320	19,100
1915	1,593	n.a.	n.a.	1965	3,963	1,550	23,300
1920	3,411	1,463	n.a.	1970	5,716	3,305	66,414
1925	1,301	428	n.a.	1975	5,031	1,746	31,237
1930	637	183	3,320	1977	5,506	2,040	35,822
1935	2,014	1,120	15,500	1978	4,230	1,623	36,992
1940	2,508	577	6,700	1979	4,827	1,727	34,754
1945	4,750	3,470	38,000	1980[2]	3,962	1,376	30,984

1. First year for which figures include Alaska and Hawaii. 2. Preliminary. NOTE: n.a. = not available. *Source:* Department of Labor, Bureau of Labor Statistics.

Persons in the Labor Force

Year	Working population — Number (thousands)	%total population aged 10 and over[1]	Percent of working population in Farm occupation	Percent of working population in Nonfarm occupation	Year	Working population — Number (thousands)	%total population aged 10 and over[1]	Percent of working population in Farm occupation	Percent of working population in Nonfarm occupation
1830	3,932	45.5	70.5	29.5	1910	37,371	52.2	31.0	69.0
1840	5,420	46.6	68.6	31.4	1920	42,434	51.3	27.0	73.0
1850	7,697	46.8	63.7	36.3	1930	48,830	49.5	21.4	78.6
1860	10,533	47.0	58.9	41.1	1940	52,966	52.4	17.0	83.0
1870	12,925	44.4	53.0	47.0	1950	59,671	53.4	11.5	88.5
1880	17,392	47.3	49.4	50.6	1960	69,877	55.3	5.9	94.1
1890	23,318	49.2	42.6	57.4	1970	82,897	55.5	2.9	97.1
1900	29,073	50.2	37.5	62.5	1980	106,821	64.3	2.7	97.3

1. For 1830 to 1930, the data relate to the population and gainful workers at ages 10 and over. For 1940 to 1970, the data relate to the population and labor force at ages 14 and over; for 1980, the data relate to the population and labor force at age 16 and over. The farm and nonfarm percentages relate only to the experienced civilian labor force. *Source:* Department of Commerce, Bureau of the Census.

Women in the Labor Force
(16 years of age and over)

Labor force status	1980 (thousands)	1979 (thousands)	1978 (thousands)	1977 (thousands)	1976 (thousands)
In the labor force:	44,574	43,391	41,878	39,952	38,414
16 to 19 years of age	4,331	4,481	4,462	4,267	4,138
20 years and over	40,243	38,910	37,416	35,685	34,276
Employed	41,283	40,446	38,882	36,685	35,095
16 to 19 years of age	3,587	3,748	3,702	3,486	3,365
20 years and over	37,696	36,698	35,180	33,199	31,730
Unemployed	3,291	2,945	2,996	3,267	3,320
16 to 19 years of age	744	733	760	781	773
20 years and over	2,547	2,212	2,236	2,486	2,547
Not in the labor force:	41,871	41,692	41,887	42,510	42,789
Women as percent of labor force	42.6	42.2	41.7	41.0	40.5
Total civilian population	86,445	85,083	83,765	82,462	81,203

Source: Department of Labor, Women's Bureau.

Employed Persons 16 Years and Over, by Race and Occupational Groups

Race and occupational group	1980 Number	1980 Percent distribution	1979 Number	1979 Percent distribution	Percent change, 1979–80
WHITE					
White-collar workers	46,539,000	53.9	45,203,000	52.5	3.0
Professional and technical workers	14,230,000	16.5	13,714,000	15.9	3.8
Managers and administrators, except farm	10,350,000	12.0	9,945,000	11.6	4.1
Sales workers	5,859,000	6.8	5,861,000	6.8	(1)
Clerical workers	16,101,000	18.6	15,683,000	18.2	2.7
Blue-collar workers	26,896,000	31.1	28,063,000	32.6	−4.2
Craft and kindred workers	11,488,000	13.3	11,858,000	13.8	−3.1
Operatives, except transport	8,765,000	10.1	9,264,000	10.8	−5.4
Transport equipment operatives	2,938,000	3.4	3,089,000	3.6	−4.9
Nonfarm laborers	3,704,000	4.3	3,851,000	4.5	−3.8
Private household workers	694,000	0.8	728,000	0.8	−4.7
Service workers, except private household	9,748,000	11.3	9,571,000	11.1	1.8
Farm workers	2,504,000	2.9	2,460,000	2.9	1.8
Total	**86,380,000**	**100.0**	**86,025,000**	**100.0**	**0.4**
BLACK AND OTHER					
White-collar workers	4,270,000	39.2	4,140,000	37.9	3.1
Professional and technical workers	1,383,000	12.7	1,336,000	12.2	3.5
Managers and administrators, except farm	569,000	5.2	572,000	5.2	−0.5
Sales workers	313,000	2.9	302,000	2.8	3.6
Clerical workers	2,005,000	18.4	1,931,000	17.7	3.8
Blue-collar workers	3,904,000	35.8	4,003,000	36.7	−2.5
Craft and kindred workers	1,041,000	9.6	1,022,000	9.4	−1.9
Operatives, except transport	1,580,000	14.5	1,645,000	15.1	−4.0
Transport equipment operatives	530,000	4.9	523,000	4.8	1.3
Nonfarm laborers	752,000	6.9	813,000	7.4	−7.5
Private household workers	346,000	3.2	360,000	3.3	−3.9
Service workers, except private household	2,169,000	19.9	2,175,000	19.9	−0.3
Farm workers	200,000	1.8	243,000	2.2	−17.7
Total	**10,890,000**	**100.0**	**10,920,000**	**100.0**	**−0.3**

1. Less than 0.05%. *Source:* Department of Labor, Bureau of Labor Statistics.

Mothers Participating in Labor Force
(figures in percentage)

Year	Mothers with children Under 18 years	Mothers with children 6 to 17 years	Mothers with children Under 6 years[1]
1950	21.6	32.8	13.6
1955	27.0	38.4	18.2
1965	35.0	45.7	25.3
1975	47.4	54.8	38.9
1976	48.8	56.2	39.7
1977	50.7	58.3	40.9
1978	52.9	60.0	43.7
1979	54.5	61.6	45.4
1980	56.6	64.4	46.6

1. May also have older children. NOTE: For 1950 and 1955, data are for April; for 1965 and 1975–80, data are for March. *Source:* Department of Labor, Women's Bureau.

Women in the Working Population

Year[1]	Number (thousands)	Percent of female population aged 10 and over[1]	Percent of total working population aged 10 and over[1]
1880	2,647	14.7	15.2
1890	4,006	17.4	17.2
1900	5,319	18.8	18.3
1910	7,445	21.5	19.9
1920	8,637	21.4	20.4
1930	10,752	22.0	22.0
1940	12,845	25.4	24.3
1950	18,412	33.9	17.3
1960[2]	23,272	37.8	19.4
1970	31,560	43.4	22.5
1979	43,531	51.1	26.6
1980	44,733	51.7	26.9

1. For 1880–1930, data relate to population and gainful workers at ages 10 and over; for 1940, to ages 14 and over; for 1950–78, to population at ages 16 and over. 2. Beginning in 1960, figures include Alaska and Hawaii. *Sources:* Department of Commerce, Bureau of the Census, and Department of Labor, Bureau of Labor Statistics.

Where the Jobs Will Be Through the Mid-'80s
(anticipated annual job openings for selected occupations)

Occupation	Estimated employment 1978	Projected requirement 1990	Percent change 1978–90	Annual average openings 1978–90[1]
Accountants	985,000	1,275,000	29.4	61,000
Actors and actresses	13,400	18,000	34.3	850
Airplane mechanics	132,000	145,000	10.1	3,500
Airplane pilots	76,000	110,000	43.9	3,800
Anthropologists	7,000	8,600	23.1	350
Architects	54,000	77,000	42.6	4,000
Astronomers	2,000	2,100	5.0	40
Automobile mechanics	860,000	1,060,000	22.7	37,000
Bank officers	330,000	510,000	54.5	28,000
Bookkeeping workers	1,830,000	2,045,000	11.8	96,000
Building custodians	2,251,000	2,704,000	20.1	176,000
Business–machine repairers	63,000	98,000	56.0	4,200
Buyers	115,000	142,000	23.5	7,400
Carpenters	1,253,000	1,390,000	10.9	58,000
Chemists	143,000	178,000	24.0	6,100
Compositors	181,000	158,000	−12.8	3,900
Computer operating personnel	666,000	665,000	−.2	12,500
Computer programmers	247,000	320,000	29.6	9,200
Computer service technicians	63,000	121,000	92.5	5,400
Computer systems analysts	182,000	250,000	37.4	7,900
Construction laborers	860,000	970,000	12.8	49,000
Cooks and chefs	1,186,000	1,564,000	31.9	86,000
Cosmetologists	542,000	624,000	15.1	28,500
Dancers	8,000	11,000	37.5	550
Dental hygienists	35,000	65,000	85.7	6,000
Dentists	120,000	155,000	29.2	5,500
Drafters	296,000	367,000	24.0	11,000
Economists	130,000	183,000	39.2	7,800
Electricians (construction)	290,000	350,000	20.7	12,900
Engineering and science technicians	600,000	760,000	25.1	23,400
Engineers	1,136,000	1,441,000	26.8	46,500
File clerks	273,000	335,000	22.6	16,500
Firefighters	220,000	270,000	21.0	7,500
Foresters	31,200	38,000	20.6	1,400
Geographers	10,000	12,300	22.6	500
Geologists	31,000	42,000	35.5	1,700
Geophysicists	11,000	14,600	35.5	600
Health service administrators	180,000	282,000	57.1	18,000
Historians	23,000	23,000	0.0	700
Industrial machinery repairers	655,000	1,085,000	66.0	58,000
Lawyers	487,000	609,000	25.0	37,000
Librarians	142,000	160,000	12.7	8,000
Life scientists	215,000	280,000	28.4	11,200
Lithographers	28,000	45,000	61.1	2,300
Locomotive engineers	34,000	37,000	9.6	2,000
Machine tool operators	542,000	609,000	12.4	19,600
Machinists	484,000	566,000	17.0	21,000
Mathematicians	33,500	37,000	9.9	1,000
Merchant marine sailors	24,800	15,000	−36.9	−250
Meteorologists	7,300	8,800	20.0	300
Musicians	127,000	177,000	39.4	8,900
Newspaper reporters	45,000	53,000	19.6	2,400
Nurses, registered	1,060,000	1,570,000	49.9	85,000
Nurses, licensed practical	518,000	840,000	62.2	60,000
Oceanographers	3,600	4,400	21.6	150
Office machine operators	160,000	202,000	26.2	9,700
Painters	484,000	550,000	13.6	26,000
Pharmacists	135,000	185,000	37.0	7,800
Physical therapists	30,000	45,000	50.0	2,700
Physicians and osteopathic physicians	405,000	560,000	38.1	19,000
Physicists	44,000	48,000	8.9	1,000
Photographers	93,000	107,000	15.0	3,800
Plumbers and pipefitters	428,000	513,000	19.9	20,000
Police officers	450,000	550,000	22.7	16,500
Political scientists	14,000	16,100	13.8	500

Occupation	Estimated employment 1978	Projected requirements 1990	Percent change 1978–90	Annual average openings 1978–90[1]
Public relations workers	131,000	163,000	24.4	7,500
Purchasing agents	185,000	267,000	44.3	13,400
Psychologists	130,000	171,000	32.1	6,700
Private household workers	1,162,000	893,000	−23.2	45,000
Radio and TV announcers	27,000	33,500	22.2	850
Receptionists	588,000	752,000	27.9	4,000
Retail trade sales workers	2,851,000	3,785,000	32.8	226,000
Secretaries and stenographers	3,684,000	5,357,000	45.4	305,000
Singers	22,000	31,000	40.9	1,600
Social workers	385,000	475,000	24.2	22,000
Sociologists	19,000	20,700	8.1	600
Statisticians	23,000	31,100	35.2	1,500
Teachers: Kindergarten and elementary	1,322,000	1,652,000	24.9	86,000
Secondary	1,087,000	861,000	−20.8	7,200
College and university	673,000	611,000	−9.2	11,000
Truck drivers: Local	1,720,000	2,040,000	18.4	64,000
Long-distance	584,000	689,000	18.0	21,500
Typists	1,044,000	1,246,000	19.4	59,000
Urban planners	17,000	22,000	30.0	800
Veterinarians	33,500	45,000	35.6	1,700

1. Annual openings include jobs resulting from growth and deaths and retirements. Transfers to other fields of work are not reflected. *Source:* Department of Labor, Bureau of Labor Statistics.

Employed Persons by Major Occupations, 1980
(in thousands)

Occupations	Total employed	Female (Percent distribution)	Black and other (Percent distribution)
White-collar workers	50,809	53.3	8.4
Professional and technical	15,613	44.3	8.9
Accountants	1,047	36.2	8.2
Architects	90	6.7	8.9
Computer programmers	341	28.7	9.1
Computer systems analysts	201	22.4	6.0
Engineers	1,433	4.0	5.9
Aeronautical and astronautical engineers	73	2.7	5.5
Civil engineers	180	3.3	7.8
Electrical and electronic engineers	357	3.9	6.7
Industrial engineers	245	8.6	4.5
Mechanical engineers	237	2.5	5.5
Lawyers and judges	547	12.8	4.2
Librarians, archivists, and curators	199	81.4	6.5
Life and physical scientists	301	20.3	9.6
Biological scientists	64	37.5	9.4
Chemists	128	20.3	13.3
Operations and systems researchers and analysts	170	23.5	6.5
Personnel and labor relations workers	452	46.9	11.1
Dentists	140	4.3	5.0
Pharmacists	120	25.0	8.3
Physicians, medical and osteopathic	426	13.4	10.8
Registered nurses	1,302	96.5	11.4
Therapists	213	73.7	11.7
Health technologists and technicians	571	70.8	11.2
Clergy	265	4.2	6.8
Economists	138	25.4	5.1
Psychologists	106	50.9	5.7
Social workers	383	65.0	18.5
Recreation workers	116	57.8	19.0
Teachers, college and university	552	33.9	7.1
Teachers, except college and university	3,157	70.8	9.9
Adult education teachers	72	47.2	8.3
Elementary school teachers	1,383	83.7	11.9
Prekindergarten and kindergarten teachers	243	98.4	13.6
Secondary school teachers	1,243	52.1	7.9
Engineering and science technicians	1,095	17.8	8.8
Airplane pilots	76	—	—
Vocational and educational counselors	181	55.8	17.7
Writers, artists, and entertainers	1,284	39.3	5.9
Athletes and kindred workers	113	42.5	6.2
Designers	193	29.5	5.7
Editors and reporters	194	50.0	5.7
Musicians and composers	143	29.4	5.6
Painters and sculptors	195	49.7	6.2
Photographers	111	20.7	4.5
Public relations specialists and publicity writers	126	46.8	4.8
Managers and administrators, except farm	10,919	26.1	5.2
Bank officials and financial managers	643	33.6	4.7

Occupations	Total employed	Percent distribution Female	Percent distribution Black and other
Buyers and purchasing agents	452	33.6	5.1
Buyers, wholesale and retail trade	190	42.6	4.7
Health administrators	210	48.1	8.1
Office managers n.e.c.	452	66.6	2.9
Officials and administrators, public administration n.e.c.	426	28.6	10.8
Restaurant, cafeteria, and bar managers	672	39.4	9.4
Sales managers and department heads, retail trade	353	40.5	6.2
Sales managers, except retail trade	352	10.8	2.8
School administrators, elementary and secondary	298	38.6	9.1
Sales workers	6,172	45.3	5.1
Insurance agents, brokers and underwriters	532	25.2	6.2
Real estate agents and brokers	582	50.7	2.1
Stock and bond sales agents	134	16.4	2.2
Sales representatives, manufacturing industries	428	18.9	3.0
Sales representatives, wholesale trade	915	10.6	3.0
Sales clerks, retail trade	2,343	71.1	7.2
Sales workers, except clerks, retail trade	519	19.5	3.7
Clerical workers	18,105	80.1	11.1
Bank tellers	531	92.7	8.7
Billing clerks	163	90.2	8.0
Bookkeepers	1,904	90.5	5.5
Cashiers	1,554	86.6	10.8
Counter clerks, except food	350	73.4	9.4
File clerks	324	86.4	21.6
Insurance adjusters, examiners, and investigators	174	57.5	10.9
Library attendants and assistants	152	77.6	13.2
Mail carriers, post office	244	11.1	11.5
Computer and peripheral equipment operators	522	59.8	14.0
Key punch operators	266	95.9	21.8
Payroll and timekeeping clerks	232	81.0	8.6
Postal clerks	285	35.4	24.2
Receptionists	629	96.3	6.1
Secretaries	3,876	99.1	6.7
Shipping and receiving clerks	505	21.6	14.1
Statistical clerks	387	78.0	14.0
Stock clerks and storekeepers	533	32.5	12.4
Teachers aides, except school monitors	383	93.7	19.6
Telephone operators	316	91.8	15.8
Typists	1,023	96.9	15.5
Blue-collar workers	30,800	18.5	12.7
Craft and kindred workers	12,529	6.0	8.3
Carpenters	1,185	1.5	5.7
Brickmasons and stonemasons	168	.1	16.1
Electricians	648	1.2	5.7
Excavating, grading, and road machinery operators	456	.9	9.6
Painters, construction and maintenance	469	6.0	11.3
Plumbers and pipefitters	478	.6	9.2
Structural metal craft workers	74	1.4	4.1
Roofers and slaters	139	.7	10.8
Blue-collar worker supervisors n.e.c.	1,729	10.8	7.8
Machinists and job setters	658	4.0	8.7
Metal craft workers, excluding mechanics, machinists, and job setters	638	3.9	7.5
Sheetmetal workers and tinsmiths	161	3.1	6.2
Tool and die makers	176	2.8	2.3
Automobile body repairers	179	.6	5.0
Automobile mechanics	1,012	.6	9.8
Mechanics, except automobiles	2,123	2.6	7.5
Heavy equipment mechanics, including diesel	963	1.6	6.9
Household appliance and accessory installers and mechanics	141	5.0	7.8
Compositors and typesetters	174	34.5	6.9
Printing press operators	169	9.5	9.5
Bakers	133	42.9	10.5
Crane, derrick, and hoist operators	148	.7	17.6
Decorators and window dressers	114	71.1	6.1
Stationary engineers	182	1.1	9.3
Telephone installers and repairers	309	8.7	7.8
Operatives, except transport	10,346	40.1	15.3
Assemblers	1,157	53.7	15.2
Checkers, examiners and inspectors, manufacturing	736	51.6	12.4
Garage workers and gas station attendants	337	6.2	9.8
Packers and wrappers, excluding meat and produce	600	64.0	19.2
Precision machine operatives	375	11.7	8.8
Sewers and stitchers	788	95.7	19.9
Welders and flame cutters	692	5.3	11.4
Transport equipment operatives	3,468	8.0	15.3
Bus drivers	356	44.9	19.9
Delivery and route workers	584	6.7	9.9
Taxicab drivers and chauffeurs	162	9.9	25.3
Truck drivers	1,844	2.2	14.2
Nonfarm laborers	4,456	11.6	16.9
Service workers	12,958	62.0	19.4
Private households	1,041	97.5	33.2
Service workers, except private households	11,917	58.9	18.2
Cleaning workers	2,454	36.5	27.5
Food service workers	4,436	66.9	13.7
Bartenders	299	43.5	6.0
Cooks	1,331	53.3	18.4
Waiters	1,416	89.1	7.1
Health service workers	1,898	89.7	24.2
Dental assistants	138	98.6	6.5
Health aides, excluding nursing	290	84.1	22.1
Nursing aides, orderlies and attendants	1,093	87.5	28.8
Practical nurses	375	97.3	19.2
Personal service workers	1,733	76.4	15.2
Protective service workers	1,396	9.5	11.7
Fire fighters	227	1.3	7.9
Guards	548	12.4	16.8
Police and detectives	512	5.5	8.4
Farm workers	2,704	18.0	7.4
Farmers and farm managers	1,485	10.6	2.6
Farm laborers, wage workers	895	15.6	16.9
Total employed	97,270	42.4	11.2

NOTE: n.e.c. = "not elsewhere classified" and designates broad categories of occupations that cannot be more specifically identified. *Source:* Department of Labor, Bureau of Labor Statistics.

Nonmanufacturing Industries—Gross Average
Weekly Earnings and Hours Worked

Industry	1981[1] Earnings	1981[1] Hours worked	1980 Earnings	1980 Hours worked	1975 Earnings	1975 Hours worked	1970 Earnings	1970 Hours worked	1958 Earnings	1958 Hours worked
Bituminous coal and lignite mining	$460.45	39.9	$435.89	40.5	$284.53	39.2[2]	$186.41	40.8	$97.57	33.3
Metal mining	454.50	40.4	415.53	40.5	250.72	42.3	165.68	42.7	94.96	38.6
Nonmetallic minerals	350.40	43.1	327.87	43.6	213.09	43.4	155.11	44.7	88.33	43.3
Telephone communications	372.13	39.8	350.54	40.2	221.18	38.4	131.60	39.4	78.72	38.4
Radio and TV broadcasting	302.82	37.9	283.46	38.1	214.50	39.0	147.45	38.2	100.70	38.0
Electric, gas and sanitary services	409.78	41.9	371.13	41.7	246.79	41.2	172.64	41.5	98.57	40.9
Local and suburban transportation	284.59	39.2	275.01	39.4	196.89	40.1	142.30	42.1	87.29	43.0
Wholesale trade	288.75	38.5	268.35	38.5	188.75	38.6	137.60	40.0	84.02	40.2
Retail trade	156.90	30.0	146.89	30.1	108.22	32.4	82.47	33.8	54.10	38.1
Hotels, tourist courts, motels	147.67	30.7	134.81	30.5	89.64	31.9	68.16	34.6	40.89	39.7
Laundries and dry cleaning plants	161.42	33.7	151.42	33.8	106.05	35.0	77.47	35.7	45.28	38.7
General building contracting	342.49	35.9	333.04	36.2	254.88	36.0	184.40	36.3	96.92	35.5

1. May preliminary. 2. 11-month average. *Source:* Department of Labor, Bureau of Labor Statistics.

Manufacturing Industries—Gross Average
Weekly Earnings and Hours Worked

Industry	1981[1] Earnings	1981[1] Hours worked	1980 Earnings	1980 Hours worked	1975 Earnings	1975 Hours worked	1970 Earnings	1970 Hours worked	1958 Earnings	1958 Hours worked	1953 Earnings	1953 Hours worked
All manufacturing[2]	$319.20	40.1	$288.62	39.7	$189.51	39.4	$133.73	39.8	$82.71	39.2	$70.47	40.5
Durable goods	345.10	40.6	311.95	40.2	205.09	39.9	143.07	40.3	89.27	39.5	76.63	41.2
Primary metal industries	443.21	41.0	391.38	40.1	246.80	40.0	159.17	40.5	101.11	38.3	84.46	41.0
Iron and steel foundries	357.80[3]	39.8[3]	327.20	40.0	220.99	40.4	151.03	40.6	86.86	37.6	77.64	41.3
Nonferrous foundries	323.19[3]	40.5[3]	290.47	39.9	190.03	39.1	138.16	39.7	90.85	39.5	79.73	41.1
Fabricated metal products	334.96	40.7	300.58	40.4	201.60	40.0	143.67	40.7	89.78	39.9	76.49	41.8
Hardware, cutlery, hand tools	314.41[3]	39.9[3]	277.85	39.3	187.07	39.3	132.33	40.1	82.92	39.3	71.80	41.5
Other hardware	331.97[3]	39.9[3]	289.69	39.2	195.42	39.4	133.46	40.2	84.32	39.4	72.63	41.5
Structural metal products	315.97[3]	40.2	291.45	40.2	202.61	40.2	142.61	40.4	92.63	40.1	79.71	42.4
Electric and electronic equipment	303.16	40.1	277.01	39.8	180.91	39.5	130.54	39.8	83.95	39.6	70.99	40.8
Machinery, except electrical	363.85	41.3	330.44	41.1	219.22	40.9	154.95	41.1	94.33	39.8	82.68	42.4
Transportation equipment	426.63	41.3	379.20	40.6	242.61	40.3	163.22	40.3	100.40	40.0	85.28	41.6
Motor vehicles and equipment	462.09[3]	42.2[3]	394.61	39.9	262.68	40.6	170.07	40.3	101.24	39.7	89.88	42.0
Lumber and wood products	274.62	39.4	253.22	38.6	167.35	39.1	117.51	39.7	69.09	38.6	60.76	39.2
Furniture and fixtures	228.93	39.0	208.79	38.1	142.13	37.9	108.58	39.2	69.95	39.3	62.99	40.9
Nondurable goods	281.32	39.4	255.06	39.0	168.78	38.8	120.43	39.1	74.11	38.8	62.57	39.6
Textile mill products	218.97	40.4	202.80	40.0	133.28	39.2	97.76	39.9	57.51	38.6	53.18	39.1
Apparel and other textile products	181.14	36.3	161.78	35.4	111.97	35.1	84.37	35.3	54.05	35.1	48.74	36.1
Leather and leather products	185.63	37.5	167.72	36.7	120.80	37.4	92.63	37.2	57.25	36.7	50.90	37.7
Food and kindred products	293.78	39.7	272.34	39.7	184.17	40.3	127.98	40.5	79.15	40.8	63.50	41.5
Tobacco manufactures	349.60	36.8	291.85	38.1	171.38	38.0	110.00	37.8	62.17	39.1	47.63	38.1
Paper and allied products	363.80	42.6	332.06	42.3	207.58	41.6	144.14	41.9	87.99	41.9	71.81	43.0
Printing and publishing	300.88	37.1	279.73	37.1	198.32	37.0	147.78	37.7	94.62	38.0	82.29	39.0

Industry	1981[1] Earnings	1981[1] Hours worked	1980 Earnings	1980 Hours worked	1975 Earnings	1975 Hours worked	1970 Earnings	1970 Hours worked	1958 Earnings	1958 Hours worked	1953 Earnings	1953 Hours worked
Chemicals and allied products	377.39	41.7	344.04	41.5	219.63	40.9	153.50	41.6	93.20	40.7	74.21	41.0
Petroleum and coal products	494.79	43.1	421.76	41.8	267.07	41.6	182.76	42.7	111.66	40.9	90.35	40.7

1. June preliminary. 2. Average weekly earnings in 1919 = $21.84; 1929 = $24.76; 1932 = $16.89; 1939 = $23.64. Average hours worked per week in 1914 = 49.4; 1919 = 46.3; 1929 = 44.2; 1932 = 38.3; 1939 = 37.7. 3. May preliminary. *Source:* Department of Labor, Bureau of Labor Statistics.

Employment by Marital Status and Sex, March 1980
(in thousands)

Marital status and sex (persons 16 years and over)	Population	Civilian labor force Number	Civilian labor force Labor force participation rate	Civilian labor force Employed	Unemployed Number	Unemployed Percent of labor force
Men	78,217	59,376	76.8	55,466	3,911	6.6
Never married	21,519	15,134	70.7	13,224	1,910	12.6
Married, wife present	48,765	38,962	81.0	37,377	1,585	4.1
Other ever married	7,933	5,280	67.1	4,865	416	7.9
Married, wife absent	2,088	1,628	79.2	1,503	125	7.7
Widowed	1,972	565	28.7	543	22	3.9
Divorced	3,873	3,087	80.3	2,819	268	8.7
Women	86,048	43,963	51.1	41,058	2,905	6.6
Never married	17,814	10,911	61.2	9,823	1,088	10.0
Married, husband present	48,750	24,466	50.2	23,199	1,267	5.2
Other ever married	19,484	8,587	44.1	8,037	550	6.4
Married, husband absent	3,169	1,881	59.4	1,698	182	9.7
Widowed	10,479	2,359	22.5	2,265	94	4.0
Divorced	5,836	4,347	74.5	4,073	273	6.3
Total: Both sexes	164,265	103,339	63.2	96,524	6,816	6.6

NOTE: Due to rounding, sums of individual items may not equal totals. *Source:* Department of Labor, Bureau of Labor Statistics.

Characteristics of Households With Female Householder, No Husband Present, 1979

Characteristics	Number of households	Income bracket	Number of households
All households	79,108,000	Household income of female householder	
Number with female householder	22,259,000	Under $2,500	1,910,000
Percent of all households	28.1	$2,500 to $4,999	4,910,000
Persons per household	2.1	$5,000 to $7,499	3,282,000
Under 18 years	12,897,000	$7,500 to $9,999	2,542,000
Percentage under 18 years	28.3	$10,000 to $14,999	3,976,000
18 years and over	32,732,000	$15,000 to $24,999	3,697,000
Percentage 18 years and over	71.7	$25,000 to $49,000	1,716,000
Marital status of female householder		$50,000 and over	226,000
Married, husband absent	2,390,000		
Widowed	8,912,000		
Divorced	4,783,000		
Single	4,543,000	Median income	$8,511

Source: Department of Commerce, Bureau of the Census.

Occupations of Employed Women
(16 years of age and over)

Occupations	1980[1] (percent)	1979[1] (percent)	1978[1] (percent)	1977[1] (percent)	1976[1] (percent)
Professional and technical workers	16.8	16.1	15.6	15.9	16.0
Managers and administrators (except farm)	6.9	6.4	6.1	5.9	5.5
Sales workers	6.8	6.9	6.9	6.8	6.7
Clerical workers	35.1	35.0	34.6	34.7	34.9
Craft and kindred workers	1.8	1.8	1.8	1.6	1.6
Operatives, except transport	10.0	10.8	11.1	11.2	11.3
Transport equipment operatives	.7	.7	.7	.6	.6
Nonfarm laborers	1.2	1.3	1.3	1.2	1.1
Private household workers	2.5	2.6	2.9	3.1	3.1
Service workers	17.0	17.2	17.7	17.9	17.9
Farmers and farm managers	.4	.3	.3	.3	.3
Farm laborers and supervisors	.8	.9	1.0	1.0	1.0

1. Annual averages. NOTE: Details may not add up to totals because of rounding. *Source:* Department of Labor, Women's Bureau.

Earnings Distribution of Full-Time Workers, by Sex, 1979
(persons 15 years old and over)

Earnings group	Number		Distribution (percent)		Likelihood of a woman rather than a man to be in each earnings group (percent)[1]
	Women	Men	Women	Men	
Less than $3,000	673,000	877,000	3.1	2.1	1.5
$3,000 to $4,999	820,000	766,000	3.8	1.8	2.1
$5,000 to $6,999	2,820,000	1,558,000	13.0	3.7	3.5
$7,000 to $9,999	6,187,000	3,879,000	28.6	9.3	3.1
$10,000 to $14,999	7,156,000	9,558,000	33.1	22.9	1.4
$15,000 and over	3,991,000	25,141,000	18.4	60.2	0.3
Total with earnings	21,647,000	41,799,000	100.0	100.0	1.0

1. Figures obtained by dividing percentages for women by percentages for men. *Source:* Department of Commerce, Bureau of the Census.

Median Income Comparisons of Full-Time Workers by Educational Attainment 1979
(persons 25 years and over)

Years of school completed	Median income		Income gap in dollars	Women's income as a percent of men's	Percent men's income exceeded women's
	Women	Men			
Elementary school:					
Less than 8 years	$ 7,414	10,993	3,579	67.4	48.3
8 years	7,788	14,454	6,666	53.9	85.6
High School:					
1 to 3 years	8,555	15,198	6,643	56.3	77.7
4 years	10,513	18,100	7,587	58.1	72.2
College:					
1 to 3 years	11,854	19,367	7,513	61.2	63.4
4 years or more	14,885	24,007	9,122	62.0	61.3

Source: Department of Commerce, Bureau of the Census.

Comparison of Median Earnings
of Full-Time Workers by Sex
(persons 15 years and over)

Year	Median earnings		Earnings gap in dollars	Women's earnings as a percent of men's	Percent men's earnings exceeded women's	Earnings gap in constant 1979 dollars
	Women	Men				
1960	$3,257	$5,368	$2,111	60.7	64.8	$5,174
1965	3,828	6,388	2,560	60.0	66.9	5,890
1970	5,323	8,966	3,643	59.4	68.4	6,810
1971	5,593	9,399	3,806	59.5	68.0	6,821
1972	5,903	10,202	4,299	57.9	72.8	7,459
1973	6,335	11,186	4,851	56.6	76.6	7,924
1974	6,970	11,889	4,919	58.6	70.6	7,240
1975	7,504	12,758	5,254	58.8	70.0	7,086
1976	8,099	13,455	5,356	60.2	66.1	6,829
1977	8,618	14,626	6,008	58.9	69.7	7,196
1978	9,350	15,730	6,380	59.4	68.2	7,098
1979	10,169	17,045	6,876	59.7	67.6	—

Source: Department of Commerce, Bureau of the Census.

Composition of the Civilian Labor Force and Unemployment

	June 1981					June 1980				
	Civilian labor force		Unemployed			Civilian labor force		Unemployed		
Race, sex, and age	Number (thousands)	Percent distribution	Number (thousands)	Percent distribution	Rate	Number (thousands)	Percent distribution	Number (thousands)	Percent distribution	Rate
White	93,464	88.0	5,964	76.6	6.4	92,134	88.1	6,127	78.4	6.7
Men, 20 years and older	49,878	47.0	2,661	34.2	5.3	49,268	47.1	2,826	36.2	5.7
Women, 20 years and older	35,980	33.9	2,045	26.3	5.7	34,657	33.1	1,976	25.3	5.7
Teenagers, 16 to 19 years	7,605	7.2	1,258	16.2	16.5	8,209	7.8	1,325	17.0	16.1
Black and other	12,741	12.0	1,813	23.3	14.2	12,491	11.9	1,682	21.5	13.5
Men, 20 years and older	6,046	5.7	758	9.7	12.5	5,965	5.7	730	9.3	12.2
Women, 20 years and older	5,759	5.4	694	8.9	12.0	5,523	5.3	603	7.7	10.9
Teenagers, 16 to 19 years	936	0.9	361	4.6	38.6	1,003	1.0	349	4.5	34.8
All races										
Men, 20 years and older	55,876	52.6	3,425	44.0	6.1	55,182	52.8	3,658	46.8	6.4
Women, 20 years and older	41,743	39.3	2,731	35.1	6.5	40,182	38.4	2,569	32.9	6.4
Teenagers, 16 to 19 years	8,558	8.1	1,628	20.9	19.0	9,227	8.8	1,684	21.6	18.3
Total	106,176	100.0	7,784	100.0	7.3	104,591	100.0	7,811	100.0	7.5

NOTE: Totals may not add due to rounding. *Source:* Department of Labor, Bureau of Labor Statistics.

Advertising Expenditures by Medium
(in billions)

Medium	1980[1]		1975		1970		1965		1960		1950	
	Amt.	% of total	Amt.	% of total	Amt.	% of total	Amt.	% of total	Amt.	% of total	Amt.	% of total
Newspapers	$15.6	28.5	$8.4	29.9	$5.8	29.3	$4.5	29.2	$3.7	31.0	$2.1	36.4
Magazines	3.2	5.9	1.5	5.2	1.3	6.8	1.2	7.9	0.9	7.9	0.5	9.0
Business Papers	1.7	3.1	0.9	3.3	0.7	3.8	0.7	4.4	0.6	5.1	0.3	4.4
Radio	3.7	6.7	2.0	7.0	1.3	6.5	0.9	6.0	0.7	5.8	0.6	10.6
Television	11.3	20.7	5.3	18.6	3.7	18.7	2.5	16.5	1.6	13.3	0.2	3.0
Direct mail	7.7	14.0	4.2	14.8	2.7	13.9	2.3	15.2	1.8	15.3	0.8	14.1
Outdoor	0.6	1.1	0.3	1.2	0.2	1.2	0.2	1.2	0.2	1.7	0.1	2.5
Miscellaneous[2]	10.9	20.0	5.6	20.0	3.9	19.8	3.0	19.6	2.4	19.8	1.1	20.0
Total	54.7	100.0	28.2	100.0	19.6	100.0	15.3	100.0	11.9	100.0	5.7	100.0

1. Preliminary. 2. Includes regional farm papers. *Sources:* McCann-Erickson, Inc., and *Advertising Age.*

Percent Unemployed in the Civilian Labor Force

Year	Percent Unemployed	Year	Percent Unemployed
1920	5.2	1975	8.5
1922	6.7	1976	7.7
1924	5.0	1977	7.0
1926	1.8	1978	6.0
1928	4.2	1979	5.8
1930	8.7	1980	7.1
1932	23.6	Jan.	6.2
1934	21.7	Feb.	6.2
1936	16.9	March	6.3
1938	19.0	April	6.9
1940	14.6	May	7.6
1942	4.7	June	7.5
1944	1.2	July	7.6
1946	3.9	Aug.	7.6
1948	3.8	Sept.	7.4
1950	5.3	Oct.	7.6
1952	3.0	Nov.	7.5
1954	5.5	Dec.	7.4
1956	4.1	1981	
1958	6.8	Jan.	7.4
1960	5.5	Feb.	7.3
1962	5.5	March	7.3
1964	5.2	April	7.3
1966	3.8	May	7.6
1968	3.6	June	7.3
1970	4.9	July	7.0
1972	5.6	Aug.	7.2
1973	4.9		
1974	5.6		

NOTE: Estimates prior to 1940 are based on sources other than direct enumeration. *Source:* Department of Labor, Bureau of Labor Statistics.

Unemployment Rate, 1980

Race and age	Women[1]	Men[1]
All races:	7.4	6.9
16 to 19 years	17.2	18.2
20 years and over	6.3	5.9
White	6.5	6.1
16 to 19 years	14.8	16.2
20 years and over	5.6	5.2
Minority races	13.1	13.3
16 to 19 years	36.9	34.9
20 years and over	11.1	11.4

1. Annual averages. *Source:* Department of Labor, Women's Bureau.

Leading Advertising Agencies in World Billings
(in millions of dollars)

Agency	1980	1979
Young & Rubicam	$2,273.2	$1,921.1
J. Walter Thompson Co.	2,137.7	1,693.0
McCann–Erickson	1,792.1	1,670.3
Ogilvy & Mather	1,661.9	1,392.6
Ted Bates & Co.	1,404.1	1,203.0
BBDO International	1,305.0	985.5
Leo Burnett Co.	1,144.8	959.7
Foote, Cone & Belding	1,117.6	919.6
SSC&B	1,111.8	1,021.6
D'Arcy–MacManus & Masius	1,058.9	853.6

Source: Reprinted with permission from the March 18, 1981, issue of *Advertising Age.* Copyright 1981 by Crain Communications, Inc.

How Consumers Spend Their Dollar
(in billions)

	1980	1980 % of total	1979	1978	1975	1970	1960	1950	1940	1930
Food	302.9	18.1	273.2	241.4	185.2	119.6	70.5	46.0	16.6	18.0
Tobacco	20.4	1.2	19.2	18.0	14.8	10.8	6.9	4.3	1.9	1.5
Alcohol	42.8	2.6	38.9	34.9	28.4	19.2	10.6	7.9	3.6	n.a.
Clothing, accessories, and jewelry	123.5	7.4	116.2	107.8	81.6	55.8	32.2	23.7	8.9	9.7
Personal care	23.3	1.4	21.4	19.3	14.7	11.0	5.2	2.4	1.0	1.0
Housing	272.0	16.3	241.9	213.1	149.8	93.9	48.1	21.7	9.7	11.1
Household operation	228.9	13.7	206.8	183.9	132.9	84.1	46.1	29.1	10.4	9.6
Medical care	166.0	9.9	144.4	127.4	87.6	50.4	20.0	9.1	3.0	2.8
Personal business	90.8	5.4	80.3	71.3	52.2	31.6	14.2	6.6	3.2	3.7
Transportation	243.0	14.5	221.1	198.0	129.4	80.6	42.4	25.4	7.3	6.1
Recreation	106.4	6.4	99.1	89.3	65.6	41.3	17.9	11.1	3.8	4.0
Private education and research	25.1	1.5	22.8	20.6	15.8	9.9	3.7	1.7	.6	.7
Religious and welfare activities	23.3	1.4	20.8	18.9	13.9	8.9	4.9	2.3	1.0	1.2
Foreign travel and other	4.3	0.3	4.7	4.7	4.6	4.5	2.1	.7	.1	.5
Total[1]	1,672.8	100.0	1,510.9	1,348.7	976.4	621.7	324.9	192.0	71.0	69.9

1. Detail may not add to total due to rounding. *Source:* Department of Commerce, Bureau of Economic Analysis.

Highest Paid Women Executives

The top half dozen highest-paid women employed by public corporations at the beginning of the 1980s are: Jane Cahill Pfeiffer, chairman, NBC, $425,000; Rosemarie Sena, senior vice president, Shearson Hayden Stone, $300,000; Katharine Graham, president, Washington Post Co., $375,000; Olive Ann Beech, chairman, Beech Aircraft, $220,000; Joan Manley, chairman, Time-Life Books, $203,000; and Juliette M. Moran, vice president, GAF, $195,000.

Livestock on Farms
(in thousands)

Type	1981	1980	1975	1970	1965	1960	1955	1950	1945
Cattle[1]	115,013	111,192	132,028	112,369	109,000	96,236	96,592	77,963	85,573
Dairy cows[1]	10,869	10,779	11,220	13,303	16,981	19,527	23,462	23,853	27,770
Sheep[1]	11,318	11,065	14,515	20,423	25,127	33,170	31,582	29,826	39,609
Swine[1]	64,520	67,353	54,693	57,046	56,106	59,026	50,474	58,937	59,373
Chickens[2]	392,200	400,585	384,101	422,000	401,000	369,000	391,000	457,000	516,000
Turkeys[3]	3,920	3,705	3,014	6,715	6,100	5,633	4,917	5,124	7,082

1. As of Jan. 1. 2. As of Jan. 1 the previous year for 1945–60 and Dec. 1 for 1965–80. 3. Turkey breeder hens for 1975–79 and as of Dec. 1. *Source:* Department of Agriculture, Economics and Statistics Service.

Agricultural Output by States, 1980 Crops

State	Corn (1,000 bu)	Wheat (1,000 bu)	Cotton (1,000 ba[1])	Potatoes (1,000 cwt)	Tobacco (1,000 lb)	Cattle[2] (1,000 head)	Swine[3] (1,000 head)
Alabama	14,580	5,758	275	1,105	816	1,925	800
Alaska	—	—	—	—	—	8	2
Arizona	4,000	17,200	1,413	1,276	—	1,075	180
Arkansas	1,036	31,160	450	—	—	2,300	720
California	36,450	85,500	3,150	18,692	—	4,760	180
Colorado	89,680	109,900	—	12,545	—	3,125	310
Connecticut	—	—	—	405	5,475	103	12
Delaware	12,744	1,080	—	969	—	32	65
Florida	15,416	—	8	5,304	20,291	2,480	370
Georgia	54,600	19,800	86	—	110,550	1,910	2,300
Hawaii	—	—	—	—	—	220	57
Idaho	4,700	96,030	—	78,455	—	1,990	175
Illinois	1,065,780	75,360	—	414	—	2,650	6,600
Indiana	602,880	53,900	—	966	15,300	1,800	4,600
Iowa	1,463,000	3,496	—	322	—	7,450	16,100
Kansas	116,560	420,000	—	—	—	6,450	1,900
Kentucky	103,600	13,825	—	—	409,222	2,600	1,220
Louisiana	1,380	1,876	455	119	56	1,360	160
Maine	—	—	—	24,960	—	131	20
Maryland	46,080	3,686	—	306	22,575	410	220
Massachusetts	—	—	—	748	2,058	103	49
Michigan	247,000	35,200	—	9,022	—	1,380	830
Minnesota	610,130	102,556	—	11,486	—	3,800	5,100
Mississippi	2,464	7,750	1,150	—	—	1,800	410
Missouri	109,710	89,010	178	1,725	5,125	5,550	3,980
Montana	592	119,800	—	2,136	—	2,675	250
Nebraska	603,500	112,100	—	4,420	—	6,950	3,900
Nevada	—	1,800	—	—	—	640	12
New Hampshire	—	—	—	1,968	—	69	10
New Jersey	7,725	1,849	—	540	—	104	68
New Mexico	7,225	10,500	110	10,668	—	1,450	74
New York	67,890	6,000	—	2,227	—	1,831	175
North Carolina	103,800	10,500	51	15,680	763,665	1,160	2,460
North Dakota	16,820	179,650	—	2,234	—	1,850	265
Ohio	440,700	67,130	—	—	20,510	1,815	2,150
Oklahoma	5,250	195,000	216	19,745	—	5,400	350
Oregon	1,166	77,400	—	4,180	—	1,750	130
Pennsylvania	96,000	9,250	—	736	22,750	2,050	980
Rhode Island	—	—	—	—	—	8	7
South Carolina	24,720	6,912	76	—	125,125	625	700
South Dakota	121,900	162,425	—	1,072	—	4,190	1,860
Tennessee	28,800	13,300	200	196	12,544	2,400	1,140
Texas	117,000	130,000	3,305	2,306	—	13,700	930
Utah	1,500	8,942	—	1,144	—	875	58
Vermont	—	—	—	120	—	339	8
Virginia	32,725	10,582	—	1,540	108,919	1,800	750
Washington	11,280	160,220	—	43,935	—	1,450	100
West Virginia	5,162	342	—	—	2,720	570	73
Wisconsin	348,400	4,365	—	16,000	24,300	4,550	1,680
Wyoming	3,589	8,512	—	1,340	—	1,350	30
United States	6,647,534	2,369,666	11,124	301,006	1,772,001	115,013	64,520

1. 480-lb net-weight bales. 2. Number on farms as of Jan. 1, 1981. 3. Number on farms as of Dec. 1, 1980. *Source:* Department of Agriculture, Economics and Statistics Service.

Farm Income
(in millions of dollars)

Year	Cash receipts from marketings — Crops	Cash receipts from marketings — Livestock, livestock products	Government payments	Total cash income
1920	$6,644	$5,956	—	$12,600
1925	5,545	5,476	—	11,021
1930	3,868	5,187	—	9,055
1935	2,977	4,143	$ 573	7,693
1940	3,469	4,913	723	9,105
1945	9,655	12,008	742	22,405
1950	12,356	16,105	283	28,744
1955	13,523	15,967	229	29,719
1960	15,208	18,946	702	34,856
1965	17,392	21,958	2,463	41,813
1970	20,907	29,615	3,717	54,239
1973	41,132	45,936	2,607	89,675
1974	51,090	41,359	531	92,980
1975	45,150	43,059	807	89,016
1976	48,688	46,112	734	95,514
1977	48,650	47,639	1,819	98,108
1978	53,711	59,213	3,030	115,954
1979	63,394	68,522	1,375	133,291
1980	69,026	67,405	1,285	137,716

Source: Department of Agriculture, Economics and Statistics Service. NOTE: Figures are latest available.

Consumption of Principal Foods[1]
(in pounds per capita)

Foods	1980	1957–59 avg	1935–39 avg
Red meats	151.4	131.4	109.8
Poultry	62.2	33.5	15.6
Eggs[2]	35.4	45.2	36.4
Fluid milk and cream	n.a.	312.8	300.9
Cheese	17.9	7.9	5.6
Butter	4.6	8.2	17.0
Margarine	n.a.	8.9	2.9
Fats and oils[3]	n.a.	31.5	29.3
Fresh fruits	85.9	95.5	135.5
Processed fruits[4]	51.8	47.8	25.5
Fresh vegetables	n.a.	104.1	113.2
Processed vegetables	58.5	49.9	29.5
Potatoes, sweet potatoes[5]	n.a.	106.6	139.4
Sugar	85.6	96.1	97.5
Corn products[6]	69.7	27.2	37.8
Wheat flour	120.0	120.0	160.0
Coffee	n.a.	15.7	14.0
Cocoa	n.a.	3.5	4.4

1. Civilian consumption and retail equivalent basis except as noted. Data as of June 1981. 2. Pounds, not number. 3. Excludes butter and margarine. 4. Pack year. Excludes chilled fruits and juices. 5. Retail weight. 6. Corn used for cereal and baking and sweetening only. NOTE: n.a. = not available. Source: Department of Agriculture, Economics and Statistics Service.

Government Employment and Payrolls

Year and function	Employees (in thousands) Total	Federal[1]	State	Local	October 1980 payrolls (in millions) Total	Federal[1]	State	Local
1940	4,474	1,128	3,346		$566	$177	$389	
1945	6,556	3,375	3,181		1,110	642	468	
1950	6,402	2,117	1,057	3,228	1,528	613	218	96
1955	7,432	2,378	1,199	1,436	2,265	846	326	1,093
1960	8,808	2,421	1,527	4,860	3,333	1,118	524	1,691
1965	10,589	2,588	2,028	5,973	4,884	1,484	849	2,551
1970	13,028	2,881	2,755	7,392	8,334	2,428	1,612	4,294
1972	13,759	2,795	2,957	8,007	9,950	2,710	1,937	5,303
1973	14,139	2,786	3,013	8,339	11,027	3,102	2,158	5,857
1975	14,973	2,890	3,271	8,813	13,224	3,584	2,653	6,987
1976	15,012	2,843	3,343	8,826	13,924	3,565	2,894	7,465
1977	15,614	2,848	3,491	9,274	15,338	3,918	3,195	8,225
1978	15,628	2,885	3,539	9,204	16,483	4,344	3,483	8,656
1979	15,971	2,869	3,699	9,403	18,077	4,728	3,869	9,480
1980, total	16,222	2,907	3,753	9,562	$19,946	5,216	4,285	10,445
National defense and international relations	976	976	(2)	(2)	1,715	1,715	(2)	(2)
Postal service	664	664	(2)	(2)	1,265	1,265	(2)	(2)
Education	6,867	26	1,599	5,242	7,491	40	1,608	5,843
Instructional employees	3,819	(2)	467	3,352	5,261	(2)	742	4,520
Highways	563	5	258	301	671	10	346	314
Health and hospitals	1,675	266	691	718	1,919	444	761	714
Police protection	716	56	73	586	989	120	119	750
Local fire protection	308	(2)	(2)	308	355	(2)	(2)	355
Sewerage and sanitation	227	(2)	(3)	226	261	(2)	1	260
Local parks and recreation	219	(2)	(2)	219	173	(2)	(2)	173
Natural resources	519	291	192	36	732	478	220	34
Financial administration	426	110	121	195	516	172	153	191
All other	3,062	513	818	1,731	3,860	972	1,077	1,811

1. Civilians only. 2. Not applicable. 3. Fewer than 500. Source: Department of Commerce, Bureau of the Census.

Receipts and Outlays of the Federal Government
(in millions of dollars)

From 1789 to 1842, the federal fiscal year ended Dec. 31; from 1844 to 1976, on June 30; and beginning 1977, on Sept. 30.

Year	Receipts — Customs (including tonnage tax)[1]	Receipts — Internal revenue: Income and profits tax	Receipts — Internal revenue: Other	Receipts — Miscellaneous taxes and receipts	Receipts — Total receipts	Receipts — Net receipts[2]	Outlays — Department of Defense (Army, 1789–1950)	Outlays — Department of the Navy	Outlays — Interest on public debt	Outlays — All other	Outlays — Net outlays[3]	Surplus (+) or deficit (−)
1789–1791	$4	—	—	—	$4	$4	$1	—	$2	$1	$4	—
1800	9	—	1	1	11	11	3	3	3	1	11	
1810	9	—	—	1	9	9	2	2	3	1	8	+1
1820	15	—	—	3	18	18	3	4	5	6	18	
1830	22	—	—	3	25	25	5	3	2	5	15	+10
1840	14	—	—	6	20	20	7	6	—	11	24	−4
1850	40	—	—	4	44	44	9	8	4	18	40	+4
1860	53	—	—	3	56	56	16	12	3	32	63	−7
1865	85	—	209	39	334	334	1,031	123	77	66	1,298	−964
1870	195	—	185	32	411	411	58	22	129	101	310	+101
1880	187	—	124	23	334	334	38	14	96	120	268	+66
1890	230	—	143	31	403	403	45	22	36	215	318	+85
1900	233	—	295	39	567	567	135	56	40	290	521	+46
1910	334	—	290	52	675	675	190	123	21	359	694	−19
1915	210	$80	335	72	698	683	202	142	23	379	746	−63
1918	180	2,314	872	299	3,665	3,645	4,870	1,279	190	6,339	12,677	−9,032
1929	602	2,331	607	493	4,033	3,862	426	365	678	1,658	3,127	+734
1933	251	746	858	225	2,080	1,997	435	349	689	3,125	4,598	−2,602
1939	319	2,189	2,972	188	5,668	4,979	695	673	941	6,533	8,841	−3,862
1943	324	16,094	6,050	934	23,402	21,947	42,526	20,888	1,808	14,146	79,368	−57,420
1944	431	34,655	7,030	3,325	45,441	43,563	49,438	26,538	2,609	16,401	94,986	−51,423
1945	355	35,173	8,729	3,494	47,750	44,362	50,490	30,047	3,617	14,149	98,303	−53,941
1950	423	28,263	11,186	1,439	41,311	36,422	5,789	4,130	5,750	23,875	39,544	−3,122
1956[4]	705	56,639	20,564	389	78,297	74,547	35,693	—	6,787	27,981	70,460	+4,087
1960	1,123	67,151	28,266	1,190	97,730	92,492	43,969	—	9,180	39,075	92,223	+269
1965	1,478	79,792	39,996	1,598	122,863	116,833	47,179	—	11,346	59,904	118,430	−1,596
1970	2,494	138,689	65,276	3,424	209,883	193,743	78,360	—	19,304	98,924	196,588	−2,845
1975	3,782	202,146	108,371	6,711	321,010	280,997	87,471	—	32,665	205,969	326,105	−45,108
1978	6,729	278,438	148,017	7,414	440,598	401,997	105,677	—	48,695	296,386	450,758	−48,761
1979	7,640	322,995	166,848	9,154	506,721	465,955	117,900	—	59,837	315,870	493,607	−27,652
1980	7,482	359,927	192,436	12,797	572,641	520,050	136,138	—	74,860	368,013	579,011	−58,961

1. Beginning 1933, tonnage tax is included in "Other receipts." 2. Net receipts equal total receipts less (a) appropriations to federal old-age and survivors' insurance trust fund beginning fiscal year 1939 and (b) refunds of receipts beginning fiscal year 1933. 3. Includes Air Force 1950–65 (in millions): 1950—$3,521; 1956—$16,750; 1960—$19,065; 1965—$18,471. 4. Beginning 1956, computed on unified budget concepts; not strictly comparable with preceding figures. *Source:* Department of the Treasury, Bureau of Government Financial Operations.

Per Capita Social Welfare Expenditures Under Public Programs

Year	Social insur- ance	Public aid	Health and medical programs	Veterans' programs	Educa- tion	Other social welfare	All health and medical care[1]	Total[2]	Total social welfare (in millions)[3]
1950	$ 32	$ 16	$ 13	$44	$ 43	$ 3	$ 20	$ 153	$ 23,421
1955	59	18	19	28	67	4	26	195	32,512
1960	105	22	24	30	96	6	35	285	52,106
1965	142	32	32	30	143	11	48	391	76,929
1970	262	79	48	43	245	20	122	701	145,484
1975	565	188	82	78	373	35	235	1,336	289,349
1976	665	220	88	86	402	42	267	1,519	331,121
1977	730	241	93	86	430	44	307	1,642	360,645
1978	787	269	102	89	457	48	344	1,775	393,188
PERCENTAGE INCREASE FOR 1978 FROM—									
1950	2,346	1,555	661	102	951	1,536	1,623	1,064	1,579
1955	1,240	1,397	450	213	585	1,188	1,200	812	1,109
1960	647	1,098	318	202	374	666	882	522	655
1965	453	742	222	194	220	355	610	354	411
1970	200	239	114	106	86	139	183	153	170
1975	39	43	24	14	22	37	46	33	36
1976	18	22	16	3	14	15	29	17	19
1977	8	12	10	4	6	10	12	8	9

1. Combines health and medical programs with medical services provided in connection with social insurance, public aid, veterans', vocational rehabilitation, and antipoverty programs. 2. Includes housing, not shown. 3. Excludes expenditures abroad for education, veterans' benefits, civil service retirement benefits, and certain other items. Figures are latest available. *Source:* Department of Health and Human Services. *Social Security Bulletin,* May 1980.

Social Welfare Expenditures Under Public Programs
(in millions of dollars)

Year and source of funds	Social insur- ance	Public aid	Health and medical pro- grams	Veter- ans' pro- grams	Edu- cation	Hous- ing	Other social welfare	All health and medical care[1]	Total social welfare	Total social welfare as: Percent of gross national product	Percent of total gov't outlays
FEDERAL											
1950	$ 2,103	$ 1,103	$ 604	$ 6,386	$ 157	$ 15	$ 174	$ 1,362	$ 10,541	4.0	26.2
1955	6,385	1,504	1,150	4,772	485	75	252	1,948	14,623	3.9	22.3
1960	14,307	2,117	1,737	5,367	868	144	417	2,918	24,957	5.0	28.1
1965	21,807	3,594	2,781	6,011	2,470	238	812	4,625	37,712	5.7	32.6
1970	45,246	9,649	4,775	8,952	5,876	582	2,259	16,600	77,337	8.1	40.1
1975	99,715	27,205	8,547	16,570	8,629	2,541	4,264	34,126	167,470	11.5	54.0
1977	134,744	35,399	10,067	18,861	9,972	4,006	5,465	46,094	218,514	11.9	56.3
1978[2]	147,324	40,979	11,452	19,569	10,371	4,887	5,872	52,512	240,453	11.8	55.3
STATE AND LOCAL											
1950	2,844	1,393	1,460	480	6,518	(3)	274	1,704	12,967	4.9	59.2
1955	3,450	1,499	1,953	62	10,672	15	367	2,473	18,017	4.7	55.3
1960	4,999	1,984	2,727	112	16,758	33	723	3,478	27,337	5.5	60.1
1965	6,316	2,690	3,466	20	25,638	80	1,254	4,911	39,464	6.0	60.4
1970	9,446	6,839	5,132	127	44,970	120	1,886	8,791	68,519	7.1	64.0
1975	23,298	13,502	9,241	449	72,204	631	3,269	17,110	122,594	8.4	65.0
1977	26,123	17,495	10,371	155	84,448	353	4,094	21,170	143,039	7.8	65.9
1978[2]	27,778	18,641	11,552	174	90,817	337	4,711	23,686	154,010	7.5	63.6
TOTAL											
1950	4,947	2,496	2,064	6,866	6,674	15	448	3,065	23,508	8.9	37.4
1955	9,835	3,003	3,103	4,834	11,157	89	619	4,421	32,640	8.6	32.7
1960	19,307	4,101	4,464	5,479	17,626	177	1,139	6,395	52,293	10.5	38.4
1965	28,123	6,283	6,246	6,031	28,108	318	2,066	9,535	77,175	11.7	42.2
1970	54,691	16,488	9,907	9,078	50,846	701	4,145	25,391	145,856	15.2	48.2
1975	123,013	40,706	17,788	17,019	80,833	3,172	7,533	51,236	290,064	19.9	57.9

Year and source of funds	Social insurance	Public aid	Health and medical programs	Veterans' programs	Education	Housing	Other social welfare	All health and medical care[1]	Total social welfare	Total social welfare as: Percent of gross national product	Percent of total gov't outlays
1977	160,867	53,895	20,438	19,105	94,421	4,358	9,559	67,264	361,553	19.7	59.5
1978[2]	175,101	59,620	23,004	19,742	101,188	5,225	10,582	76,198	394,462	19.3	58.1

PERCENT OF TOTAL, BY TYPE

1950	21.0	10.6	8.8	29.2	28.4	0.1	1.9	13.0	100.0	(3)	(3)
1955	30.1	9.2	9.5	14.8	34.2	0.3	1.9	13.5	100.0	(3)	(3)
1960	36.9	7.8	8.5	10.5	33.7	0.3	2.2	12.2	100.0	(3)	(3)
1965	36.4	8.1	8.1	7.8	36.4	0.4	2.7	12.4	100.0	(3)	(3)
1970	37.5	11.3	6.7	6.2	34.9	0.5	3.0	17.2	100.0	(3)	(3)
1975	42.4	14.0	6.1	5.9	27.9	1.1	2.6	17.7	100.0	(3)	(3)
1977	44.5	14.9	5.7	5.3	26.1	1.2	2.6	18.6	100.0	(3)	(3)
1978[2]	44.4	15.1	5.8	5.0	25.7	1.3	2.7	19.3	100.0	(3)	(3)

FEDERAL PERCENT OF TOTAL

1950	42.5	44.2	29.2	93.0	2.3	100.0	38.9	44.4	44.8	(3)	(3)
1955	64.9	50.1	37.1	98.7	4.3	83.7	40.7	44.1	44.8	(3)	(3)
1960	74.1	51.6	38.9	98.0	4.9	81.2	36.6	45.6	47.7	(3)	(3)
1965	77.5	57.2	44.5	99.7	8.8	74.9	39.3	48.5	48.9	(3)	(3)
1970	82.7	58.5	48.2	98.6	11.6	82.9	54.5	65.4	53.0	(3)	(3)
1975	81.1	66.8	49.0	97.4	11.0	78.7	56.6	67.1	58.4	(3)	(3)
1977	83.8	66.9	49.1	99.2	10.6	91.9	57.2	68.6	60.4	(3)	(3)
1978[2]	84.1	68.7	49.0	99.1	10.2	93.5	55.5	68.9	60.9	(3)	(3)

1. Combines health and medical programs with medical services provided in connection with social insurance, public aid, veterans, and other social welfare programs. 2. Preliminary. 3. Not applicable. NOTE: Figures are latest available. *Source:* Department of Health and Human Services. *Social Security Bulletin,* May 1980.

Contributions to International Organizations
(for fiscal year 1980 in millions of dollars)

Organization	Amount[1]	Organization	Amount[1]
United Nations and Specialized Agencies	$298.48	Intergovernmental Committee for European Migration	4.12
United Nations	149.54	International Institute for Cotton	1.97
Food and Agricultural Organization	28.63	Others	4.14
International Atomic Energy Agency	21.37	Special Voluntary Programs	696.18
International Civil Aviation Organization	4.64	Consultative Group on International Agricultural Research	29.00
Joint Financing Program	2.00	Intergovernmental Committee for European Migration—Special Voluntary	138.27
International Telecommunications Union	2.76	International Atomic Energy Agency— Operational Program	12.00[2]
UNESCO	33.44	Organization of American States—Special Development Assistance Fund	6.60
World Health Organization	50.36		
World Meteorological Organization	4.51		
Others	1.23	Organization of American States—Special Multilateral Fund (education and science)	6.50
United Nations Peacekeeping Forces	59.81		
United Nations Emergency Force	50.81	United Nations Children's Fund	34.60
United Nations Force in Cyprus	9.00	United Nations Development Program	126.05
Inter-American Organizations	71.39	United Nations Environmental Program	10.00
Organization of American States	35.94	UN/FAO World Food Program	97.00
Pan American Health Organization	25.16	United Nations Fund for Population Activities	32.00
Inter-American Institute of Agricultural Sciences	7.97	United Nations High Commissioner for Refugees (6 programs)	73.14
Inter-American Tropical Tuna Commission	1.88	8 Special programs	50.31
Others	0.44	United Nations Relief and Works Agency	55.20
Regional Organizations	36.12	World Health Organization— Special Programs	8.72
NATO Civilian Headquarters	14.85		
Organization for Economic Cooperation and Development	20.22	Others	16.79
Others	1.05	**Total**	**1,177.41**
Other International Organizations	15.43		
Customs Cooperation Council	1.68		
General Agreement on Tariffs and Trade	3.52		

1. Estimated. 2. Includes cash, commodities and services and $5.1 million for Safeguard Program. *Source:* Department of State.

Foreign Assistance
(in millions of dollars)

Calendar years	Economic Assistance (net)				Military grants (net)	Net assistance[1]
	Net new grants	Net new credits	Net other assistance	Total		
July 1945–50[2]	$18,413	$ 8,086	—	$ 26,498	$ 1,981	$ 28,479
1951–55	10,459	556	$ 541	11,556	14,464	26,020
1956–60	8,291	1,503	2,226	12,021	11,327	23,348
1961–65	9,384	5,522	576	15,482	7,831	23,313
1966–70	8,808	9,430	−564	17,674	12,028	29,702
1971–75	12,939	7,524	−725	19,737	16,693	36,430
1976	2,268	3,275	−54	5,490	1,339	6,830
1977	2,283	2,861	−39	5,105	766	5,871
1978	2,676	3,691	−52	6,315	817	7,131
1979	3,036	3,308	−69	6,275	910	7,185
1980	3,898	4,656	−72	8,482	1,533	10,015
Total postwar period	82,455	50,412	1,767	134,635	69,690	204,325

1. Excludes investment in international nonmonetary financial institutions of $8,200 million. 2. Includes transactions after V-J Day (Sept. 2, 1945). NOTE: Detail may not add to total due to rounding. *Source:* Department of Commerce, Bureau of Economic Analysis.

The Public Debt

Year	Gross debt		Year	Gross debt	
	Amount (in millions)	Per capita		Amount (in millions)	Per capita
1800 (Jan. 1)	$ 83	$ 15.87	1950	$256,087[2]	$1,688.30
1860 (June 30)	65	2.06	1955	272,807[2]	1,650.63
1865	2,678	75.01	1960	284,093[2]	1,572.31
1900	1,263	16.60	1965	313,819[2]	1,612.70
1920	24,299	228.23	1970	370,094[2]	1,807.09
1925	20,516	177.12	1975	533,189	2,496.90
1930	16,185	131.51	1977(Sept. 30)	698,840	3,215.59
1935	28,701	225.55	1978	771,544	3,521.78
1940	42,968	325.23	1979	826,519	3,736.86
1945	258,682	1,848.60	1980[1]	907,701	4,063.08

1. Preliminary, Sept. 30, 1980. 2. Adjusted to exclude issues to the International Monetary Fund and other international lending institutions to conform to the budget presentation. *Source:* Department of the Treasury, Bureau of Government Financial Operations.

Domestic Freight Traffic by Major Carriers
(in millions of ton-miles)[1]

Year	Railroads		Inland waterways[2]		Motor trucks		Oil pipelines		Air carriers	
	Ton-miles	% of total	Ton-miles	% of total	Ton-miles	% of total	Ton-miles	% of total	Ton-miles	% of total
1940	379,201	61.3	118,057	19.1	62,043	10.0	59,277	9.6	14	—
1945	690,809	67.3	142,737	13.9	66,948	6.5	126,530	12.3	91	—
1950	596,940	56.2	163,344	15.4	172,860	16.3	129,175	12.1	318	—
1955	631,385	49.5	216,508	17.0	223,254	17.5	203,244	16.0	481	—
1960	579,130	44.1	220,253	16.8	285,483	21.7	228,626	17.4	778	—
1965	708,700	43.3	262,421	16.0	359,218	21.9	306,393	18.7	1,910	0.1
1970	771,168	39.8	318,560	16.4	412,000	21.3	431,000	22.3	3,274	0.2
1975	759,000	36.7	342,210	16.5	454,000	22.0	507,300	24.6	3,732	0.2
1976	799,876	36.3	372,865	16.9	510,000	23.2	515,100	23.4	3,900	0.2
1977	833,994	36.1	368,275	15.9	555,000	24.1	546,000	23.7	4,181	0.2
1978	867,982	35.1	409,316	16.6	602,000	24.4	585,800	23.7	4,630	0.2
1979[3]	927,000	35.7	431,000	16.6	628,000	24.2	605,000	23.3	5,000	0.2
1980[3]	932,000	37.3	420,000	16.9	565,000	22.6	575,000	23.0	5,000	0.2

1. Mail and express included, except railroads for 1970. 2. Rivers, canals, and domestic traffic on Great Lakes. 3. Preliminary. *Sources:* Interstate Commerce Commission; Civil Aeronautics Board; Association of American Railroads.

Intercity Passenger Traffic
(in millions of passenger-miles)

Year	Railroads Miles	Railroads % of total	Buses Miles	Buses % of total	Air carriers Miles	Air carriers % of total	Inland waterways[1] Miles	Inland waterways[1] % of total	Total commercial	Private airplanes
1940	24,766	67.1	9,800	26.5	1,052	2.8	1,317	3.6	36,935	—
1945	93,535	74.3	27,027	21.4	3,362	2.7	2,056	1.6	125,980	—
1950	32,481	46.3	26,436	37.7	10,072	14.3	1,190	1.7	70,179	—
1955	28,695	36.5	25,519	32.4	22,741	28.9	1,738	2.2	78,693	—
1960	21,574	28.6	19,327	25.7	31,730	42.1	2,688	3.6	75,319	2,228
1965	17,557	17.9	23,775	24.2	53,719	54.7	3,101	3.2	98,152	4,364
1970	10,903	7.3	25,300	16.9	109,499	73.1	4,000	2.7	149,702	9,101
1975	10,075	5.8	25,000	14.2	136,432	77.7	4,000	2.3	175,507	11,500
1976	11,000	5.8	25,000	13.2	150,000	78.9	4,000	2.1	190,000	13,000
1977	10,400	5.1	25,900	12.7	164,200	80.3	4,000	1.9	204,500	12,100
1978[2]	10,500	4.6	25,400	11.1	189,100	82.6	4,000	1.7	229,000	12,700
1979[2]	11,600	4.6	26,600	10.5	210,300	83.3	4,000	1.6	252,500	13,300
1980[2]	11,400	4.7	26,900	11.0	202,000	82.7	4,000	1.6	244,300	13,300

1. Rivers, canals, and Great Lakes. 2. Preliminary. NOTE: Beginning in 1970, data include Alaska and Hawaii. n.a. = not available. *Sources:* Interstate Commerce Commission; Civil Aeronautics Board; Association of American Railroads.

Principal U.S. Ports
(over 10 million tons annually; in thousands of tons)

Waterway title	Tonnage 1979	Tonnage 1978	Waterway title	Tonnage 1979	Tonnage 1978
New Orleans	167,135	160,612	Paulsboro, N.J., and vicinity	24,061	23,994
New York, N.Y. and N.J.	163,621	186,733	St. Louis (Metropolitan)	21,644	22,425
Houston Ship Channel, Tex.	117,551	111,936	Connsaut Harbor, Ohio	21,478	17,428
Baton Rouge, La.	76,703	74,570	Seattle Harbor, Wash.	20,039	22,482
Valdez Harbor, Alaska	65,452	55,552	Freeport Harbor, Tex.	19,984	21,712
Beaumont, Tex. (Neches R.)	58,137	52,770	Cleveland Harbor	19,470	19,659
Philadelphia Harbor	54,866	50,823	Richmond Harbor, Calif.	18,978	18,986
Baltimore Harbor and Channels	51,445	46,809	Indiana Harbor, Ind.	18,419	20,716
Norfolk Harbor, Va.	48,651	34,019	Huntington, W. Va.	16,503	16,656
Tampa Harbor, Fla.	47,885	47,077	Jacksonville Harbor, Fla.	15,278	15,713
Duluth–Superior Harbor, Minn. and Wis.	47,725	45,841	Tacoma Harbor, Wash.	15,193	13,084
Corpus Christi, Tex.	46,423	46,555	New Castle, Del., and vicinity	14,751	11,649
Pittsburgh	40,881	77,692	Ashtabula Harbor, Ohio	14,603	12,830
Chicago	38,693	39,691	Savannah Harbor, Ga.	13,528	11,426
Texas City Channel, Tex.	35,954	34,656	Escanaba, Mich.	13,453	13,207
Lake Charles Deep Water Channel, La.	35,951	38,138	Portland Harbor, Me.	13,262	22,165
Mobile Harbor, Ala.	35,265	36,261	Port Everglades Harbor, Fla.	13,031	11,964
Long Beach Harbor, Calif.	33,347	31,586	Memphis, Tenn.	12,346	13,158
Port Arthur, Tex.	32,773	33,475	Cincinnati	12,011	11,908
Marcus Hook, Pa., and vicinity	32,700	32,736	Two Harbors (Agate Bay), Minn.	11,933	10,517
Los Angeles Harbor	31,749	32,827	Taconite Harbor, Minn.	11,533	10,158
Portland, Ore.	29,146	26,573	Newport News, Va.	11,509	7,256
Toledo Harbor, Ohio	26,256	27,571	St. Paul	11,248	9,683
Boston	26,243	26,074	New Haven Harbor, Conn.	10,622	11,408
Pascagoula Harbor, Miss.	25,289	25,244	Calcite, Mich.	10,320	11,699
Detroit	24,996	25,882	Charleston Harbor, S.C.	10,056	10,841

Source: Department of the Army, Corps of Engineers.

Annual Railroad Carloadings

Year	Total	Year	Total	Year	Total	Year	Total
1920	33,754,000	1945	41,918,000	1970	27,160,000	1976	23,457,000
1925	34,783,000	1950	38,903,000	1972	26,105,000	1977	23,173,000
1930	30,173,000	1955	37,636,000	1973	27,338,000	1978	23,373,000
1935	22,015,000	1960	30,441,000	1974	26,184,000	1979	23,876,000
1940	36,358,000	1965	29,248,000	1975	23,217,000	1980	22,598,000

Source: Association of American Railroads.

Estimated Motor Vehicle Registration, 1979
(in thousands; excluding publicly owned vehicles)

State	Autos[1]	Trucks and buses	Motor-cycles	Total	State	Autos[1]	Trucks and buses	Motor-cycles	Total
Alabama	2,051	750	74	2,876	Montana	411	241	30	682
Alaska	153	88	10	251	Nebraska	856	358	55	1,269
Arizona	1,247	487	76	1,810	Nevada	404	141	23	567
Arkansas	989	501	33	1,523	New Hampshire	539	98	42	679
California	12,359	3,649	722	16,730	New Jersey	4,186	410	100	4,696
Colorado	1,721	602	117	2,440	New Mexico	657	351	47	1,055
Connecticut	2,021	158	74	2,253	New York	6,953	933	178	8,064
Delaware	315	72	11	398	North Carolina	3,331	1,010	103	4,444
D.C.	225	13	3	241	North Dakota	356	250	28	634
Florida	5,948	1,174	216	7,338	Ohio	6,167	1,441	267	7,875
Georgia	2,920	770	104	3,794	Oklahoma	1,717	832	125	2,674
Hawaii	470	82	7	558	Oregon	1,459	510	81	2,050
Idaho	466	295	51	812	Pennsylvania	5,659	1,027	217	6,903
Illinois	6,041	1,189	281	7,511	Rhode Island	508	71	23	602
Indiana	2,831	920	167	3,918	South Carolina	1,516	429	37	1,982
Iowa	1,696	616	203	2,515	South Dakota	366	219	31	616
Kansas	1,361	593	94	2,048	Tennessee	2,326	623	85	3,034
Kentucky	1,802	761	62	2,625	Texas	7,128	2,646	289	10,063
Louisiana	1,887	754	76	2,717	Utah	664	303	61	1,028
Maine	521	177	43	741	Vermont	273	70	21	364
Maryland	2,300	437	77	2,814	Virginia	2,976	480	79	3,535
Massachusetts	3,248	435	100	3,783	Washington	2,212	854	130	3,196
Michigan	5,060	1,185	251	6,496	West Virginia	869	348	37	1,254
Minnesota	2,200	772	157	3,129	Wisconsin	2,243	489	158	2,890
Mississippi	1,133	337	24	1,494	Wyoming	269	178	20	467
Missouri	2,402	813	101	3,316	**Total**	**117,410**	**31,939**	**5,404**	**154,753**

1. Includes taxicabs. NOTE: Publicly owned vehicles are as follows: autos, 812,432; trucks and buses, 1,630,976; motorcycles, 5,404,056; total vehicles, 2,472,730. Figures are latest available. *Source:* Department of Transportation, Federal Highway Administration.

Passenger Car Production by Makes

Companies and models	1980	1979	1978	1975	1970	1965
American Motors Corporation	167,802	184,636	164,351	323,704	276,127	346,367
Chrysler Corporation						
Plymouth	293,342	372,461	437,441	443,550	699,031	679,539
Dodge	263,169	380,745	408,327	354,482	405,699	547,531
Chrysler	82,462	181,427	236,504	102,940	158,614	224,061
Imperial	—	—	—	1,930	10,111	16,422
Total	**638,973**	**934,633**	**1,082,274**	**902,902**	**1,273,455**	**1,467,553**
Ford Motor Company						
Ford	929,627	1,375,775	1,698,136	1,301,414	1,647,918	2,164,902
Mercury	324,528	509,450	624,229	405,104	310,463	355,404
Lincoln	52,794	151,960	189,523	101,520	58,771	45,470
Total	**1,306,949**	**2,037,185**	**2,511,888**	**1,808,038**	**2,017,152**	**2,565,776**
General Motors Corporation						
Chevrolet	1,776,229	2,214,955	2,364,685	1,687,091	1,504,614	2,587,509
Pontiac	516,620	731,570	880,594	523,469	422,212	860,652
Oldsmobile	783,225	1,004,515	910,252	654,342	439,632	650,801
Buick	783,575	787,123	810,324	535,820	459,931	653,838
Cadillac	203,991	345,794	350,761	278,404	152,859	196,595
Total	**4,063,640**	**5,083,957**	**5,316,616**	**3,679,126**	**2,979,248**	**4,949,395**
Checker Motors Corporation	3,197	4,766	4,225	3,181	4,146	6,136
Volkswagen of America	197,106	173,192	40,194	—	—	—
Industry total	**6,377,667**	**8,418,369**	**9,119,548**	**6,716,951**	**6,550,128**	**9,335,227**

Source Automotive News, Jan. 12, 1981.

Passenger Car Data

	1979	1970	1960	1950	1940
U.S. passenger cars and taxis registered (thousands)	120,248	89,280	61,671	40,339	27,466
Total mileage of U.S. passenger cars (millions)	1,140,518	901,000	588,083	363,613	249,600
Total fuel consumption of U.S. passenger cars (millions of gallons)	79,793	65,784	41,169	24,305	16,323
World registration of cars, trucks, and buses (thousands)	396,011	248,900	126,908	70,424	n.a.
U.S. registration of cars, trucks, and buses (thousands)	154,118	108,407	73,858	49,162	32,453
U.S. share of world registration of cars, trucks, and buses	38.9%	44.0%	58.2%	69.8%	n.a.

NOTE: n.a. = not available. *Source:* Motor Vehicle Manufacturers Association of the U.S.

Domestic Passenger Car Sales

Company and model	1980	1979	1978	Company and model	1980	1979	1978
American Motors	149,438	162,057	170,739	XR-7	51,857	121,184	159,687
Spirit	49,723	54,356	24,412[1]	Capri	62,592	90,850	18,035
Concord	64,991	85,432	114,764[2]	Mercury	52,645	94,654	136,719
Pacer	2,083	8,168	20,811	Total Lincoln	69,704	131,271	188,487
Eagle	32,641	14,101	—	Versailles	4,219	13,586	15,747
Chrysler Corp.	660,017	942,207	1,146,258	Lincoln	30,114	60,797	97,009
Total Plymouth	251,312	325,523	404,371	Mark VI	35,371	56,888[5]	75,731[5]
Horizon	78,823	84,668	118,993	General Motors	4,116,482	4,911,875	5,385,282
TC3	53,971	62,072	—	Buick Division	720,368	714,508	781,364
Reliant	32,720	—	—	Skyhawk	5,388	18,768	22,221
Volare	72,116	167,091	210,125	Skylark	175,741	115,000	97,915
Voyager	—	8,265	13,895	Century	145,894	62,210	74,813
Fury	—	2,681	60,378	Regal	199,207	249,379	248,543
Plymouth	13,682	746	980	LeSabre	89,429	129,554	190,414
Total Chrysler	139,748	248,840	298,892	Electra	61,792	88,195	121,705
LeBaron	65,519	99,588	125,558	Riviera	42,917	51,402	25,753
Cordoba	44,908	61,801	105,442	Cadillac Division	213,002	314,034	350,813
Chrysler	29,321	87,451	67,892	Seville	34,709	45,317	55,721
Total Imperial	2,497	—	—	Cadillac	126,151	206,164	248,825
Total Dodge	266,460	367,844	442,995	Eldorado	52,142	62,553	46,267
Omni	61,240	69,888	89,497	Chevrolet Division	1,747,534	2,152,603	2,349,781
024	46,658	54,490	—	Chevette	373,988	375,724	247,088
Aries	25,784	—	—	Monza	150,320	141,564	158,127
Aspen	55,092	117,777	157,308	Citation/Nova	374,706	308,437	248,214
Sportsman	—	24,917	44,376	Sportvan	—	24,594	43,582
Diplomat	33,157	45,131	60,656	Camaro	116,824	204,742	260,201
Monaco	—	2,554	37,594	Malibu	267,732	344,233	374,124
Mirada/Magnum	27,595	24,784	48,326[3]	Monte Carlo	165,638	265,877	355,058
Dodge	16,934	28,303	5,238	Chevrolet	261,819	449,001	621,140
Ford Motor	1,475,232	2,132,644	2,582,702	Corvette	36,507	38,631	42,247
Ford Division	1,074,675	1,491,374	1,814,717	Oldsmobile Division	820,681	949,488	1,006,344
Pinto	142,467	187,708	167,880	Starfire	5,334	18,611	18,351
Escort	60,196	—	—	Omega	87,262	50,098	42,860
Mustang	225,290	304,053	199,760	Cutlass	210,784	114,092	113,286
Fairmont	285,272	338,819	405,780	Supreme	258,789	404,068	406,993
Club Wagon	—	31,094	45,964	Olds 88	147,997	223,699	273,384
Granada	88,371	141,737	219,026	Olds 98	73,464	92,075	123,431
LTD II	3,012	26,700	138,947	Toronado	37,051	46,845	28,039
Thunderbird	127,248	215,698	304,430	Pontiac Division	614,897	781,042	896,980
Ford	142,819	245,565	332,930	Sunbird	132,630	89,107	91,737
L-M Division	400,557	641,270	767,985	Phoenix	98,952	80,857	58,280
Total Mercury	330,853	509,999	579,498	Firebird	81,592	149,211	188,212
Bobcat	26,821	44,674	30,201	LeMans	77,911	114,993	125,020
Lynx	28,196	—	—	Grand Prix	118,414	175,573	224,195
Zephyr	87,032	99,335	120,781	Pontiac	105,398	171,301	209,536
Cougar	—	3,955	35,251	Volkswagen	177,140	166,839	23,017
Cougar/Monarch	31,710	55,347	78,824[4]	Industry total	6,578,309	8,315,622	9,307,998

1. Includes Gremlin. 2. Includes Hornet. 3. Figure is for Magnum/Charger. 4. **Monarch** only. 5. Includes Mark V. *Source:* Automotive News, Jan. 12, 1981.

Domestic and Export Factory Sales of Motor Vehicles
(in thousands)

	From plants in United States[1]								
	Passenger cars			Motor trucks and buses			Total motor vehicles		
Year	Total	Domestic	Exports	Total	Domestic	Exports	Total	Domestic	Exports
1965	9,306	9,101	205	1,752	1,616	136	11,058	10,717	341
1970	6,547	6,187	360	1,692	1,566	126	8,239	7,753	486
1975	6,713	6,073	640	2,272	2,003	269	8,985	8,076	909
1976	8,500	7,840	660	2,979	2,734	245	11,479	10,574	905
1977	9,201	8,513	688	3,442	3,179	263	12,643	11,692	951
1978	9,165	8,493	672	3,706	3,416	290	12,871	11,909	962
1979	8,419	7,678	741	3,037	2,741	296	11,456	10,419	1,037
1980	6,400	5,840	560	1,667	1,464	203	8,067	7,304	763

1. Excludes factory sales to all Federal government agencies. *Source:* Motor Vehicle Manufacturers Association of the U.S.

Balance of International Payments
(in billions of dollars)

Item	1980	1979	1978	1975	1970	1965	1960	1955	1949
Exports of goods and services (excluding transfers under military grants)	$340.9	$286.5	$221.0	$155.7	$65.7	$41.1	$28.9	$19.9	$15.8
Merchandise, adjusted, excluding military	221.8	182.1	142.1	107.1	42.5	26.5	19.7	14.4	12.2
Transfers under U.S. military agency sales contracts	7.5	7.2	8.2	3.9	1.5	0.8	0.3	0.2	n.s.s.
Receipts of income on U.S. investments abroad	76.0	66.0	43.0	25.4	11.8	7.4	4.6	2.6	1.5
Other services	35.6	31.3	27.8	19.3	9.9	6.4	4.3	2.7	2.1
Imports of goods and services	−333.8	−281.6	−230.2	−132.6	−60.0	−32.8	−23.7	−17.8	−9.6
Merchandise, adjusted, excluding military	−249.1	−211.5	−175.8	−98.0	−39.9	−21.5	−14.8	−11.5	−6.9
Direct defense expenditures	−10.8	−8.5	−7.4	−4.8	4.9	−3.0	−3.1	−2.9	−0.6
Payments of income on foreign investments in U.S.	−43.5	−33.5	−22.1	−12.6	−5.5	−2.1	−1.2	−0.5	−0.3
Other services	−30.4	−28.2	−25.0	−17.2	−9.8	−6.2	−4.6	−2.8	−1.8
Unilateral transfers, excluding military grants, net	−7.0	−5.7	−5.1	−4.6	−3.3	−2.9	−2.3	−2.5	−5.6
U.S. Government assets abroad, net	−84.5	−61.8	−61.2	−3.5	−1.6	−1.6	−1.1	−0.3	−0.7
U.S. private assets abroad, net	−71.2	−56.9	−57.3	−35.4	−10.2	−5.3	−5.1	−1.3	−0.6
U.S. assets abroad, official reserve, net	−8.2	−1.1	0.7	−0.6	2.5	1.2	2.1	0.2	−0.3
Foreign assets in U.S., net	47.6	37.6	64.1	15.6	6.4	0.7	2.3	−1.4	0.2
Statistical discrepancy	35.6	23.8	11.4	5.5	−0.2	−0.5	−1.0	0.4	0.7
Balance on goods and services	7.1	5.0	−9.25.0	23.1	5.7	8.3	5.1	2.2	6.2
Balance on goods, services, and remittances	4.6	2.8	−11.1	21.3	4.1	7.2	4.5	1.6	5.6
Balance on current account	0.1	−0.8	−14.3	18.4	2.4	5.4	2.8	−0.3	0.6

NOTE: n.s.s. = not shown separately. − denotes debits. *Source:* Department of Commerce, Bureau of Economic Analysis.

Exports and General Imports by Countries and Areas
($25 million and over; value in millions)

Area and country	Exports, including re-exports				General imports			
	1980	1970	1960	1950	1980	1970	1960	1950
NORTH AND SOUTH AMERICA								
Canada	$35,395	$9,079	$3,810	$2,039	$41,995	$11,092	$2,901	$1,960
20 Latin American Republics	36,030	5,695	3,577	2,720	31,214	4,779	3,528	2,910
Argentina	2,625	441	359	148	792	172	98	206
Bolivia	172	46	25	21	189	25	9	35
Brazil	4,344	840	464	365	4,000	670	570	715
Chile	1,354	300	203	73	559	157	193	160
Colombia	1,736	395	253	237	1,326	269	299	313
Costa Rica	498	94	45	27	405	117	35	25
Cuba	(1)	(1)	225	464	(1)	(1)	357	406
Dominican Republic	795	143	42	43	827	184	110	38

Area and country	Exports, including re-exports				General imports			
	1980	1970	1960	1950	1980	1970	1960	1950
Ecuador	864	127	57	29	938	109	65	34
El Salvador	272	64	43	33	444	48	32	51
Guatemala	553	100	64	44	466	87	59	54
Haiti	311	34	25	25	264	32	18	23
Honduras	379	89	35	24	475	102	34	20
Mexico	32,274	1,704	831	526	12,774	1,218	443	315
Nicaragua	250	77	30	19	226	61	21	19
Panama	699	208	90	112	353	76	24	10
Paraguay	109	18	9	3	85	11	8	6
Peru	1,172	214	147	76	1,443	340	183	49
Uruguay	183	41	63	41	103	19	21	106
Venezuela	4,573	759	567	406	5,547	1,082	948	324
OTHER WESTERN HEMISPHERE								
Bahamas	396	173	49	7	1,433	82	8	1
Barbados	136	22	6	1	99	9	1	(¹)
Bermuda	136	92	32	10	14	1	2	(¹)
French West Indies	67	15	4	3	7	9	(¹)	(¹)
Guyana	96	25	12	3	135	43	11	1
Jamaica	305	218	48	9	418	187	54	2
Leeward and Windward Islands	152	32	6	1	37	6	2	2
Netherlands Antilles	448	126	65	70	2,680	416	265	158
Suriname	137	35	18	7	126	56	30	13
Trinidad and Tobago	680	84	36	6	2,450	232	55	9
EUROPE								
Western Europe	67,512	14,463	7,204	3,280	48,876	11,169	4,187	1,368
Austria	448	74	80	106	407	120	49	16
Belgium and Luxembourg	6,661	1,195	467	291	2006	696	364	140
Denmark	863	227	146	65	767	284	98	12
Finland	505	99	56	21	480	114	52	35
France	7,485	1,483	699	475	5,532	942	396	132
Germany, West	10,960	2,741	1,272	(²)	12,244	3,127	897	—
Greece	922	203	103	107	320	52	33	17
Iceland	79	13	12	6	210	47	10	4
Ireland	836	112	43	47	433	135	28	2
Italy	5,511	1,353	715	369	4,676	1,316	393	109
Netherlands	8,669	1,651	817	251	2,041	528	213	85
Norway	843	196	108	95	2,734	142	66	41
Portugal	911	126	45	34	280	92	35	21
Spain	3,179	712	208	46	1,323	353	88	50
Sweden	1,767	543	301	99	1,705	399	170	71
Switzerland	3,781	700	254	130	2,851	459	198	110
Turkey	540	315	178	84	187&SFS	70	60	61
United Kingdom	12,694	2,536	1,487	548	10,184	2,194	993	335
Yugoslavia	756	168	88	43	476	96	41	19
Soviet Bloc	3,860	354	194	27	1,564	226	81	81
Bulgaria	161	15	73	857	27	2	1	2
Czechoslovakia	185	22	5	11	72	24	12	27
Germany, East	479	32	4	(²)	48	9	3	(²)
Hungary	80	28	2	3	118	6	2	2
Poland	714	70	143	9	459	98	39	11
Romania	722	66	1	2	341	13	1	(¹)
U.S.S.R.	1,513	119	39	1	485	72	23	38
ASIA AND OCEANIA								
Total Asia and Oceania	65,044	11,294	4,700	1,691	88,046	9,103	2,987	1,846
Near East	11,900	1,423	532	228	18,344	10,515	312	131
Bahrain	197	12	8	7	17	8	3	2
Iran	23	326	156	38	353	67	51	24
Iraq	724	22	37	10	369	3	27	12
Israel	2,045	592	130	(²)	971	150	27	(²)
Jordan	407	63	20	1	3	(¹)	92	8
Kuwait	886	62	41	3	498	25	124	42
Lebanon	303	64	45	28	34	13	3	4
Oman	95	—	—	—	363	—	—	—
Qatar	129	—	—	—	250	—	—	—
Saudi Arabia	5,769	141	46	34	13,323	20	65	24
Syria	239	11	38	11	28	2	7	12
United Arab Emirates	998	—	—	—	2,115	—	—	—
Yemen Arab Republic	77	—	—	—	1	—	—	—
Far East	48,269	8,682	1,979	1	65,929	8,682	2,406	1,360
Bangladesh	292	—	—	—	100	—	—	—

Area and country	Exports, including re-exports				General imports			
	1980	1970	1960	1950	1980	1970	1960	1950
Brunei	70	10[3]	—	—	293	([1] [3])	—	—
China, People's Rep. of	3,755	—	—	37	1,161	([1])	([1])	146
China (Taiwan)	4,337	527	278	40	7,362	549	20	3
Hong Kong	2,686	406	125	104	5,026	944	139	5
India	1,689	574	642	217	1,209	298	228	259
Indonesia	1,545	266	100	85	5,503	182	216	156
Japan	20,790	4,652	1,447	418	32,961	5,875	1,149	182
Korea, South	4,685	643	231	([2])	4,432	370	5	([2])
Malaysia[4]	1,337	67	18	([2])	2,688	270	156	([2])
Pakistan	642	328	170	31	140	80	36	31
Philippines	1,999	373	307	247	1,913	472	307	236
Singapore	3,033	240	42	([2])	1,984	81	19	([2])
Sri Lanka	62	12	14	7	140	26	39	66
Thailand	1,263	155	71	29	866	100	56	75
Australia	4,093	986	423	115	2,782	611	142	141
New Zealand and Samoa	599	135	78	29	795	222	119	65
Papua New Guinea	38	18	1	([1])	57	12	([1])	—
AFRICA								
Total Africa	9,060	1,425	793	376	33,605	1,067	534	494
Algeria	542	62	28	16	6,881	10	1	5
Angola	111	38	11	7	559	68	26	13
Botswana	6	—	—	—	89	63	—	—
Cameroon	93	19	—	5	638	25	6	—
Canary Islands	158	22	14	6	6	4	([1])	([1])
Congo	22	—	—	—	95	—	—	—
Egypt	1,874	77	151	34	487	23	32	55
Ethiopia	72	26	12	3	91	67	27	12
Gabon	48	7	—	—	293	9	—	—
Ghana	127	59	17	6	214	91	52	61
Guinea	34	7	—	—	96	77	—	—
Ivory Coast	185	36	—	—	303	92	—	—
Kenya	141	34	—	—	59	23	—	—
Liberia	113	46	36	25	148	51	39	21
Libya	509	108	43	([1])	7,395	39	([1])	([1])
Madagascar	7	7[5]	3	4	97	32[5]	13	8
Morocco	344	89	36	—	41	10	10	—
Mozambique	69	22	10	8	113	18	4	3
Nigeria	1,150	129	26	6	11,316	71	40	35
Senegal	41	8	—	—	10	1	—	—
Sierra Leone	21	8	—	—	80	8	—	—
South Africa[6]	2,464	563	288	129	3,428	290	108	142
Tanzania	62	12	—	—	34	24	—	—
Uganda	12	4	—	—	131	48	—	—
Zaire	155	62	27	41	370	41	58	46
Zambia	99	—	—	—	205	—	—	—
Summary:								
Developed countries	130,849	29,877	13,250	6,010	130,835	29,259	8,605	3,858
Developing countries	81,125	12,993	7,131	4,193	119,237	10,442	5,965	4,767
Total	220,705[8]	43,224[7]	20,575[7]	10,275[7]	252,804[8]	39,952[7]	14,654[7]	8,852[7]

1. Less than $500,000. 2. Not applicable. 3. Includes Bhutan, Maldives, and Portuguese Timor. 4. Excludes Sarawak and Sabah, which are included with Singapore through 1960. 5. Includes French Indian Ocean areas. 6. South-West Africa, Bechuanaland, and Swaziland included for 1950 and 1960; South-West Africa (Namibia) included for 1970 and 1979. 7. Includes Communist areas in Europe and Asia. 8. Includes exports to Communist areas in Europe and Asia, $7,616,000,000; imports, $2,728,000,000. *Source:* Department of Commerce, Bureau of the Census, Foreign Trade Division.

The Shrinking Dollar Shrinks On

The four-person household with $10,000 gross income in 1970 needed $22,477 in 1981 to keep up the same standard of living. The rise in prices over the past decade has cut the purchasing power of a dollar by more than half, taking a $9,746 bite from 1981 income. Federal income and Social Security taxes siphoned off another $4,091 last year.

State and local taxes substantially increase the tax burden on all families, but they differ widely from state to state. In the 1978–79 fiscal year, the highest ratio of state-local taxes to personal income was 15.8% in New York and the lowest was 8.6% in Oklahoma; the nationwide average was 12%. Taxes per capita tend to be lower in the South, but incomes there are also relatively low. However, the South is generally a low-tax region even in terms of taxes as a share of income.

Imports of Leading Commodities
(value in millions of dollars)

Commodity	1980	1979
Food and live animals	$15,763	$15,170
Cattle, except for breeding	228	236
Meat and preparations	2,346	2,539
Dairy products and eggs	318	304
Fish	2,612	2,639
Grains and feed for animals	331	298
Vegetables and fruit	2,047	2,062
Sugar, cane or beet	1,988	974
Coffee, green	3,872	3,820
Cocoa beans	395	555
Tea	131	126
Beverages and tobacco	2,772	2,565
Alcoholic beverages	2,220	2,013
Tobacco, unmanufactured	422	436
Crude materials, inedible, except fuels	10,496	10,653
Hides and skins, except fur skins	88	139
Fur skins, undressed	143	183
Crude rubber	816	897
Wood—simply worked	2,134	2,913
Wood pulp	1,725	1,506
Textile fibers and wastes	242	231
Industrial diamonds	119	116
Ores and metal scrap	3,696	3,249
Iron ore and concentrates	773	922
Nonferrous metal ores and concentrates	1,932	1,674
Precious metal ores and concentrates, except gold	558	271
Mineral fuels and related materials	79,058	59,998
Petroleum products	73,771	56,036
Natural gas	5,155	3,526
Animal and vegetable oils and fats	533	740
Chemicals	8,583	7,479
Organic chemicals	2,539	2,153
Inorganic chemicals	2,313	2,059
Medicinal and pharmaceutical products	508	441
Fertilizers, manufactured	1,104	976
Machinery and transport equipment	60,546	53,677
Machinery	31,904	28,044
Transport equipment	28,642	25,634
Automobiles, buses, trucks	19,163	16,870
Motor vehicle parts	4,971	5,205
Aircraft and parts	1,885	1,078
Other manufactured goods	23,711	21,006
Paper and manufactures	3,587	3,357
Glass, glassware, and pottery	1,224	1,097
Diamonds, excluding industrial	2,252	1,862
Metals and manufactures	18,718	17,457
Iron and steel-mill products	6,686	6,764
Nonferrous metals	7,623	6,320
Metal manufactures	3,731	3,671
Precious metals, except gold	2,440	1,642
Textile yarn and fabrics	2,493	2,216
Clothing	6,427	5,874
Footwear	2,808	2,861
Scientific and controlling instruments	1,418	1,158
Clocks and watches	1,097	946
Baby carriages, toys, games, and sporting goods	1,914	1,665
Artworks and antiques	2,672	1,487
Other transactions	7,183	4,905
Total	**$240,834**	**$206,256**

Exports of Leading Commodities
(value in millions of dollars)

Commodity	1980	1979
Food and live animals	$27,744	$22,251
Meat and preparations	1,293	1,127
Dairy products and eggs	255	161
Grains and preparations	18,079	14,454
Wheat, including wheat flour	6,586	5,492
Rice	1,285	850
Vegetables and fruit	2,930	2,130
Feed for animals	2,878	2,318
Beverages and tobacco	2,663	2,337
Cigarettes	1,055	909
Beverages	273	245
Crude materials, inedible, except fuels	23,791	20,756
Hides and skins, except fur skins	694	992
Soybeans, other oilseeds, peanuts	5,883	5,708
Synthetic rubber	695	579
Logs and lumber	2,675	2,797
Pulpwood and wood pulp	2,454	1,644
Raw cotton, excluding wastes	2,864	2,198
Ores and metal scrap	4,518	3,325
Mineral fuels and related materials	7,982	5,621
Coal	4,772	3,496
Petroleum and products	2,833	1,918
Animal and vegetable oils and fats	1,946	1,845
Soybean oil	705	776
Chemicals	20,740	17,308
Chemical elements and compounds	8,636	7,706
Medicines and pharmaceuticals	1,932	1,591
Fertilizers	2,265	1,404
Plastic materials and resins	3,884	3,241
Machinery and transport equipment	84,629	70,495
Machinery	55,790	44,745
Power generating machinery	8,428	6,843
Aircraft engines, parts	1,915	1,423
Automotive engines, parts	1,688	1,631
Agricultural machinery, parts	1,295	1,088
Tractors and parts	1,809	1,547
Office machines, computers	8,709	6,475
Metalworking machinery	1,756	1,391
Textile and leather machinery	693	629
Transport equipment	28,839	25,750
Road motor vehicles and parts	14,590	15,077
Aircraft, spacecraft, accessories	12,816	9,719
Other manufactured goods	16,347	12,641
Tires and tubes	511	353
Paper and manufactures	2,831	1,967
Nonmetallic mineral manufactures	2,209	1,948
Metals and manufactures	9,659	7,809
Iron and steel-mill products	2,998	2,227
Nonferrous base metals	2,964	1,609
Other manufactures of metals	4,205	3,432
Textile yarns and fabrics	3,632	3,189
Clothing	1,203	931
Scientific instruments	5,256	4,287
Photographic supplies	1,507	1,227
Printed matter	1,097	956
Other transactions	8,496	9,103
Total	**$220,705**	**$181,816**

Source: Department of Commerce, Bureau of the Census, Foreign Trade Division.

The following material was compiled from information provided by the American Red Cross, the American Heart Association, and Edumed, Inc.

First aid is the rendering of prompt and knowledgeable treatment to a person who has been injured or suddenly taken ill and for whom no immediate medical attention is available. Depending on circumstances, effective first aid can mean the difference between life and death or between temporary and permanent disability. Artificial respiration and treatment for shock that sets in after a serious accident are also important factors in the success of first aid. The best course of action to follow after taking emergency measures is to summon assistance from the local police or fire department or from the nearest available doctor.

Burns

Burns are classified according to first degree (reddened skin), second degree (blisters develop), and third degree (deep tissue damage). Face, feet, and hands are critical areas. For first-degree and small second-degree burns, submerge affected area in cold water until pain subsides. Or else apply a thick, dry sterile dressing and bandage firmly to keep air out. *Do not break blisters.* Note: Cold water may be used for any classification of burns, but not if tissue has been exposed, because of the possibility of infection. For third-degree burns, bandage as above, elevate the extremities, and obtain medical help immediately.

Eye burns: For burns of the eye, wash thoroughly with water for 15 minutes—hold the eyelid open and pour the water from the inside corner out. Put a clean pad over both closed eyelids (not only injured eye), bandage, and get medical help.

Poisoning

Speed and a clear head are vital in first aid for poison intake. If the victim loses consciousness, call for an emergency squad and give artificial respiration or cardiopulmonary resuscitation (CPR) if needed to keep the airway open. If the victim is conscious and not in convulsions, dilute the swallowed poison with a glass of water or milk, but stop at signs of nausea. The victim should also be treated for shock.

Next, call your physician or local poison-control center. Be ready to supply information on what poison, and how much of it, was taken and the weight and age of the victim, and to take down instructions for treatment and antidotes. (Antidotes suggested on a poison-container label should not be given without approval by your physician or poison-control center.)

If vomiting occurs, save a vomit specimen along with the container label for the attending physician.

Shock

Shock is caused by many types of severe injuries and severe illnesses—poisoning, damage to the respiratory system, and loss of body fluids resulting from vomiting, dysentery, or burns. It is prudent to give shock care to all seriously injured individuals.

The symptoms are: pale or bluish skin that is cold to the touch (in the case of dark-skinned persons, examine the color of the mucous membranes inside the mouth or under the eyelids, or of the nail beds); moist or clammy skin; weakness of the injured person; rapid pulse; increased rate of breathing, which may be shallow, possibly deep, and irregular; severe thirst; vomiting or retching from nausea.

With possible neck or back injury, a victim should not be moved. Otherwise, a person in shock should be kept lying down and covered only enough to keep him from losing body heat. (*Do not* add extra heat, because raising the body's surface temperature is harmful.)

A patient with severe injuries of the lower face and jaw or who is unconscious should be placed on the side, with care taken to prevent suffocation from vomit and blood. When in doubt about the proper position, keep the person lying flat, making sure the head is not lower than the rest of the body. Fluids may be given by mouth if the victim has no head or abdominal injury, if the victim would probably not need surgery, or if medical help is not immediately available. But fluids *should not* be given to persons who are unconscious, are vomiting, or are having convulsions.

Cardiac Pulmonary Resuscitation (CPR) for Cardiac Arrest[1]

The most common signal of a heart attack is uncomfortable pressure, squeezing, fullness, or pain in the center of the chest behind the breastbone; others may be sweating, nausea, shortness of breath or a feeling of weakness. These signals may subside and return. If these signals persist, activate the emergency medical services system or take the victim to the nearest hospital with 24-hour emergency cardiac care.

Airway: Determine if the collapsed person is conscious by shaking his shoulder and shouting "Are you all right?". If there is no response, you must open his airway. Be sure he is lying flat on his back. If you have to roll him over, move his entire body as a total unit.

To open the airway, lift up his neck (or chin) gently with one hand while pushing down on the forehead with the other to tilt the head back. Place your ear close to the victim's mouth. Look at his chest and stomach for movement. Listen for sounds of breathing. Feel for breath on your cheek.

If none of these signs is present, the victim is not breathing.

Breathing: Use the mouth-to-mouth technique. Turn the hand on the victim's forehead and pinch his nose shut while maintaining the head tilt with the heel of the hand. The other hand should remain under the victim's neck (or chin), lifting up.

Immediately give four quick, full breaths in rapid succession.

Check Pulse: After giving four quick breaths, locate the victim's carotid pulse to see if his heart is beating. Take the hand that is under the victim's neck and locate the voice box. Slide the tips of your index and middle fingers into the groove beside the voice box. Feel for the pulse.

If you cannot find the pulse, you must provide artificial circulation in addition to rescue breathing.

Chest Compression: To perform external chest compression, kneel at the victim's side near his chest. Locate the notch at the lowest portion of the sternum (breastbone). Place the heel of one hand about 1 to 1 ½ inches from that tip and the other on top of the first. Be sure to keep the fingers off the chest wall. You may find it easier to do by interlocking the fingers.

Bring your shoulders directly over the victim's sternum as you compress downward, keeping your arms straight. Depress the sternum about 1 ½ to 2 inches for an adult victim. Relaxation must follow compression immediately and be of equal time. Do *not* remove your hands from the sternum.

If you are the only rescuer, you must provide both rescue breathing and chest compression at the ratio of 15 chest compressions to 2 quick breaths. You must compress at the rate of 80 times per minute, since you will lose compressions when you take time to interpose these breaths.

If there is another rescuer, position yourselves on opposite sides of the victim. One should interpose a breath after every fifth compression; the other should compress the chest at a rate of 60 compressions per minute.

For Infants and Small Children: Do not exaggerate the backward position of the head tilt because it might block breathing passages.

Do not try to pinch off the nose. Cover both the mouth and nose if the victim is not breathing. Use small breaths with less volume to inflate the lungs. Give one small breath every 3 seconds.

Only one hand is used for compression. The other is slipped under the child to provide a firm support for his back.

For infants, use only the *tips* of the index and middle fingers to compress the chest at mid-sternum, depressing between ½ to ¾ inch at a rate of 100 times per minute.

For small children, use only the *heel* of one hand to compress the chest at midsternum, depressing between ¾ and 1 ½ inches, depending on the size of the child. The rate should be 80 times per minute.

For both infants and small children, breaths should be interposed after every fifth chest compression.

Neck Fracture: If the victim is injured in a diving or automobile accident, the possibility of a neck fracture should be considered. The airway should be opened by using a modified jaw thrust, keeping the victim's head in a fixed, neutral position.

The Heimlich Maneuver[2]

Food-Choking

Food-choking is caused by a piece of food lodging in the throat creating a blockage of the airway, making it impossible for the victim to breathe or speak. The victim will die of strangulation in four minutes if you do not act to save him.

Using the Heimlich Maneuver, you exert pressure that forces the diaphragm upward, compresses the air in the lungs, and expels the object blocking the breathing passage.

The victim should see a physician immediately after the rescue. Performing the Maneuver could result in injury to the victim. However, he will sur-

vive only if his airway is quickly cleared.

If no help is at hand, victims should attempt to perform the Heimlich Maneuver on themselves by pressing their own fists upward into the abdomen as described.

What to Look for: The victim of food-choking: (1) Cannot speak or breathe, (2) turns blue, (3) collapses.

Performing the Heimlich Maneuver with the rescuer standing and the victim standing or sitting: Stand behind the victim and wrap your arms around his waist.

Place your fist thumb side against the victim's abdomen, slightly above the navel and below the rib cage.

Grasp your fist with your other hand and press into the victim's abdomen with a **quick upward thrust.**

(When the victim is sitting, the rescuer stands behind the victim's chair and performs the Maneuver in the same manner.)

With the rescuer kneeling and the victim lying face up: Facing the victim, kneel astride his hips.

With one of your hands on top of the other, place the heel of your bottom hand on the abdomen slightly above the navel and below the rib cage.

Press into the victim's abdomen with a **quick upward thrust.**

Repeat several times if necessary.

Drowning

The Heimlich Maneuver is the first step used to treat drowning in order to get water out of the victim's lungs.

With the rescuer kneeling and the victim lying face up. Facing the victim, kneel astride his or her hips. Turn the victim's head to the side. This allows water to drain out of the victim's mouth when you perform the Heimlich Maneuver.

With one of your hands on top of the other, place the heel of your bottom hand on the abdomen slightly above the navel and below the rib cage.

Press into the victim's abdomen with a **quick upward thrust.**

Repeat until water no longer flows out. If the victim has not started breathing, proceed with mouth to mouth resuscitation.

Severe Bleeding

Shock and loss of consciousness may occur from the rapid loss of as little as a quart of blood. A preferred technique is to direct pressure by hand over a dressing since it prevents loss of blood from the body without interference with normal blood circulation. In an emergency, in the absence of compresses, the bare hand or fingers may be used, but only until a compress can be applied.

Apply direct pressure by placing the palm of the hand on a dressing directly over the entire area of an open wound on any surface part of the body. In most instances this technique will stop the bleeding.

A thick pad of cloth held between the hand and the wound helps to control the bleeding by absorbing the blood and allowing it to clot.

(Continued on page 79)

1. © 1977 American Heart Association. 2. © 1976 Edumed, Inc. Teaching slides, posters, wallet cards, and other instructional materials on the Heimlich Maneuver are now available. To obtain these send a self-addressed, stamped envelope to: Edumed, Inc., Box 52, Cincinnati, Ohio 45201. Heimlich Maneuver instruction for the treatment of choking and drowning can be found in the book, "Dr. Heimlich's Home Guide to Emergency Medical Situations" by Henry J. Heimlich, M.D. and Lawrence Galton (Simon and Schuster).

NUTRITION&HEALTH

A Capsule Profile of Health in the United States

Source: "Health United States 1980," U.S. Department of Health and Human Services, Public Health Service, Office of Health Research, Statistics, and Technology

Highlights

Births

- The fertility of American women remained at a low level in 1978—66.6 births per 1,000 women 15–44 years of age.
- Not only are women having fewer births, but many are also postponing them; the birth rate for women 20–24 years of age is now equal to that for women 25–29 years of age, and first births for women 30–34 years of age have increased sharply.
- In 1978, there were 32.9 births per 1,000 women 15–17 years of age, compared with 38.8 births per 1,000 in 1970.
- Although the differential has narrowed since 1970, the birth rate for black teenagers 15–17 years of age in 1978 was three times that of white teenagers in the same age group.
- Life expectancy at birth continued to increase, reaching a record 73.3 years in 1978; the difference between life expectancy for white people and all other people has narrowed, but it still remains large at 5 years.

Cesarean Deliveries

- Between 1970 and 1978, the rate of cesarean section deliveries nearly tripled to 15.2 per 100 deliveries, or more than one half million births.
- Although the United States had the highest cesarean section rate when compared to five other countries (Canada, England and Wales, Norway, Netherlands, and Sweden) for which data were available, all countries showed sharp increases in cesarean section deliveries.
- The uniformity of the increase in cesarean sections by maternal and hospital characteristics suggests that a fundamental and widespread change in obstetrical practice has taken place.
- Although a great deal of change in the age-parity composition of live births occurred, this change accounted for only 5% of the increase in cesarean section deliveries.

Mortality

- The relative difference between male and female mortality has been increasing; the ratio of the age-adjusted death rate for males to that for females increased from 1.5 in 1950 to 1.8 in 1978.
- From 1970 to 1978, heart disease mortality decreased by the same amount—18 percent—as it did the 20 years between 1950 and 1970.
- Stroke mortality decreased by a greater amount from 1970 to 1978 than it did the 20 years between 1950 and 1970—33%, compared with 25%; this recent decline has been especially large for black people who are about 60% more likely to die of stroke than are white people.
- Although it has been known for several years that control of severe hypertension leads to reduced mortality, a clinical trial completed in 1979 provided convincing evidence that control of even mild hypertension leads to reduced mortality.
- Cancer mortality has continued to decrease for people under 45 years of age and has recently begun to decline for those 45–49 years of age.
- During the 1970s, respiratory cancer death rates increased for men and women, but the rate of increase was greater for females; if current trends continue, lung cancer will replace breast cancer as the leading cause of cancer

Desirable Weights[1]

| Height[2] | | Weight[3] | | | | | |
| | | Men | | | | Women | |
in.	cm	lb		kg		lb		kg	
58	147	—	—	—	—	102	(92–119)	46	(42–54)
60	152	—	—	—	—	107	(96–125)	49	(44–57)
62	158	123	(112–141)	56	(51–64)	113	(102–131)	51	(46–59)
64	163	130	(118–148)	59	(54–67)	120	(108–138)	55	(49–63)
66	168	136	(124–156)	62	(56–71)	128	(114–146)	58	(52–66)
68	173	145	(132–166)	66	(60–75)	136	(122–154)	62	(55–70)
70	178	154	(140–174)	70	(64–79)	144	(130–163)	65	(59–74)
72	183	162	(148–184)	74	(67–84)	152	(138–173)	69	(63–79)
74	188	171	(156–194)	78	(71–88)	—	—	—	—
76	193	181	(164–204)	82	(74–93)	—	—	—	—

1. Desirable weights for men and women of different heights, based on evidence from insurance statistics of weight in relation to longevity. According to the National Center for Health Statistics, the average American male adult is 70 in. tall (178 cm) and the average female is 64 in. tall (163 cm). Accordingly, the average desirable weights are 154 lb (70 kg) and 120 lb (55 kg) throughout adult life. 2. Without shoes. 3. Without clothes. Average weight ranges in parentheses. Source: Recommended Dietary Allowances, 9th Edition (1980), with permission of the National Academy of Sciences, Washington, D.C.

mortality among women.
- Following a sustained decrease in motor vehicle accident mortality from 1968 to 1976, the age-adjusted death rate for motor vehicle accidents increased 4% between 1976 and 1977 and 7% between 1977 and 1978.
- After a steady increase since the early 1960s, the age-adjusted death rate for homicide has declined slightly since its record peak in 1974; this resulted from a sizable decrease in the rate for black people who are about six times more likely than white people to be victims of homicide.
- Following a general increase in the age-adjusted suicide rate during the 1970s, the rate declined by 5% between 1977 and 1978.
- The infant mortality rate in 1979 was 13 deaths per 1,000 live births, a 47% decline since 1965.
- Although infant mortality has been decreasing for all races, black newborns are nearly twice as likely to die during infancy as their white counterparts.
- Both white and black infant mortality rates were about 50% greater in the States with the highest rates than in the States with the lowest rates.
- One of the major factors contributing to the decline in infant mortality and especially neonatal mortality is the greatly improved survival for infants of low birth weight; about 50% of the reduction in neonatal mortality among white infants and 60% of the reduction among black infants was because of improved survival for infants weighing between 1,001 and 2,500 grams (2 lb 3 oz to 5 lb 8 oz).

Utilization of Health Resources

Between 1964 and 1978, a marked trend toward equality in the volume of physician visits between the poor and nonpoor was evident, although no convincing evidence exists that the level of use was commensurate with need.

The poor continued to use considerably fewer dental services than the nonpoor; in 1978, half the population with family incomes below $7,000 had no dental care during the 2 years preceding interview, compared with one third of those people with higher family incomes.

From 1963–65 to 1976–78, the rate of surgery for children declined, but it increased for adults, especially those 65 years of age and over.

For the period 1976–78, the North Central and South Regions generally had higher rates of surgery than the Northeast and West Regions.

In nearly every age group and geographic region, surgical utilization increased more rapidly for the poor than the nonpoor from 1963–65 to 1976–78.

In a comparison among 10 selected countries (U.S., Australia, Canada, Denmark, England and Wales, Federal Republic of Germany, Finland, France, Scotland, and Sweden), the United States, Australia, and Canada had the highest hospital discharge rates and the shortest mean lengths of stay.

The mean length of a hospital stay for people 65 years of age and over was more than 5 days shorter in the United States than in seven other countries.

The mean length of a hospital stay in the United States decreased from 8.5 days to 7.4 days in the 10-year period from 1968 to 1978; this represented an overall decrease of 13%.

Although all four geographic regions experienced decreases in lengths of stay, regional variation was more apparent in 1978 than in 1968; the Northeast had the longest stays and the West had the shortest stays.

The mean length of a hospital stay for acute myocardial infarction (heart attack) dropped from 19.2 days in 1971 to 13.8 days in 1978—a reduction of 28%.

Health Care Resources

- Between 1970 and 1979, the number of active physicians (M.D.'s) per 10,000 population increased 25% to 19.3.
- The physician supply is expected to grow rapidly in the coming years, increasing 37% between 1979 and 1990 to nearly 600,000 physicians, or 23.9 physicians per 10,000 population.
- Although the physician supply has recently been increasing in nonmetropolitan as well as in metropolitan areas, in 1978, the patient care physician-to-population ratio in nonmetropolitan areas was 7.4 per 10,000, compared with 17.1 per 10,000 in metropolitan areas.

Physicians, Dentists, and Nurses
(numbers in thousands)

Profession	1978	1977	1976	1975	1970	1965	1960	1955
Physicians, number	454	438	426	409	348	305	275	255
Rate per 100,000 resident population[1]	204	198	194	188	166	153	148	150
Active (exc. physicians in Federal serv.)	381	362	351	338	282	255	n.a.	n.a.
Rate per 100,000 resident population[1]	172	165	161	155	135	129	n.a.	n.a.
Doctors of medicine[2]	437	421	409	394	334	292	260	242
Doctors of osteopathy	17	17[3]	16[3]	15[3]	14	13	14	14
Physicians admitted to U.S. as immigrants[4]	4.4	7.1	8.1	7.1	3.2	2.0	1.6	1.0
Dentists, number[5]	121	118	n.a.	n.a.	116	109	103	95
Active (excl. dentists in Federal service)	115	113	110	108	96	86	85	76
Rate per 100,000 resident population[1]	53	52	52	50	47	45	47	47
Nurses, number (active registered)	1,059	1,011	961	906	700	613	504	430
Rate per 100,000 resident population[1]	487	465	449	427	345	319	282	259

1. Based on Bureau of the Census population estimates. 2. Excludes non-Federal physicians with temporary foreign addresses. 3. Estimated. 4. Immigration and Naturalization Service figures. 5. Beginning 1960, excludes graduates of year stated. Beginning in 1976, excludes inactive dentists. NOTE: n.a. = not available. Source: Statistical Abstract of the United States, 1980.

- Public and private initiatives have stimulated physician interest in primary care specialties; family practitioners are expected to increase from 3% of all physicians in 1975 to 10% by 1990.
- Regional variation in the supply of patient care physicians decreased between 1973 and 1978; however, the Northeast Region still had 37% more patient care physicians per 10,000 population than the South and North Central Regions.
- While the number of community hospitals was practically unchanged between 1973 and 1978, their numbers of beds, admissions, average daily census, and outpatient services substantially increased; however, occupancy rates decreased during this period.
- In 1978, 36 States had higher bed-to-population ratios and 46 States had lower occupancy rates than those recommended in the Department of Health and Human Service's National Guidelines for Health Planning.
- In 1976, the number of nursing home beds per 1,000 persons 65 years of age and over varied from 77 in the North Central Region to 51 in the South Region.

Health Care Expenditures

- Health care expenditures are continuing their rapid rise, reaching $212.2 billion, or 9.0% of the gross national product for 1979; this represents an increase of 12.5% over that for the previous year.
- Expenditures for hospital care continued to account for the largest portion of the health care dollar—40.2% in 1979; physician services accounted for 19.1%, followed by nursing home care (8.4%), drugs and drug sundries (8.0%),

and dentist services (6.4%).
- During the past three decades, hospital care and nursing home care have increased as a proportion of total health care expenditures, while physician services, drugs and drug sundries, and dentist services have decreased.
- Medical care prices more than doubled during the period 1970 to 1979; price increases alone accounted for more than two thirds of the increase in health expenditures in 1979.
- Hospital service charges generally led the increase in medical care prices, with annual increases in excess of 10% during the period 1970 to 1979.
- Third party payment for medical care services increased from 48% to 80% during the period 1966 to 1977; currently, approximately 90% of the population has some form of health insurance coverage.
- The number of employees per patient day in community hospitals increased by 19% between 1971 and 1978.
- Hospital real assets per bed increased by 28% during the period 1971 to 1977; hospital real assets per 1,000 population increased 37% during this period.
- Occupation-specific, quality-adjusted wages in the health care sector rose relative to other industries until 1972, after which these wages did not keep pace with other industries.
- Hospitals have markedly increased their reliance on debt financing of capital projects— from 35% in 1969 to 63% in 1977.

Copies of "Health United States 1980," DHHS Publication No. (PHS) 81-1232, may be ordered while they last from the Superintendent of Documents, U.S. Government Printing Office, Washington, D.C. 20402. (202) 783-3238. The cost is $7.00 per copy.

Physicians—Median Earnings
(in thousands of dollars)

Field of practice	Unincorporated				Incorporated			
	1975	1976	1977	1978	1975	1976	1977	1978
All physicians[1]	47.5	52.4	52.6	54.7	76.3	75.6	78.3	82.3
General practitioners	38.6	43.7	46.0	45.7	59.2	58.7	63.4	71.0
Internists	53.7	53.6	59.6	53.7	71.1	66.9	73.5	73.6
General surgeons	53.7	61.4	56.7	62.5	83.3	78.4	81.6	88.8
Obstetricians-gynecologists	57.5	63.4	57.3	63.7	83.4	89.2	92.9	88.4
Pediatricians	43.5	45.9	49.2	49.1	58.6	56.6	62.5	67.1
Psychiatrists	n.a.	n.a.	47.9	n.a.	n.a.	n.a.	62.3	n.a.
Family practitioners	48.2	50.7	54.8	58.1	61.9	59.4	69.4	66.9
Orthopedic surgeons	n.a.	n.a.	71.7	n.a.	87.5[2]	n.a.	98.8	n.a.

1. Includes specialties not shown separately. 2. 1974 data. Unincorporated: Represents net income from practice after payment of tax-deductible professional expenses but before payment of income taxes. Incorporated: Comprises office-based, patient care doctors of medicine (M.D.'s) of all ages who are shareholders of a medical corporation. Earnings include salary, bonuses (if any), and funds set aside by corporation for individual's retirement. *Source: Statistical Abstract of the United States, 1980.*

New Dietary Guideline Menus Available

The Department of Agriculture has issued a helpful booklet of selected menus and recipes based on the new Federal dietary guidelines. Each of the daily menus, which includes breakfast, lunch, dinner, and a snack, totals either 1,600 or 2,400 calories. The caloric levels were chosen because they represent the average adult consumption levels reported by men and women on national surveys. The menus are not intended for weight reduction.

Copies of the publication, entitled "Ideas for Better Eating," are available for $2.25 from the United States Government Printing Office, Superintendent of Documents, Washington, D.C. 20402.

Estimated Safe and Adequate Daily Dietary Intakes of Additional Selected Vitamins and Minerals[1]

Age (years)	Vitamins			Trace Elements[2]						Electrolytes		
	Vitamin K (µg)	Biotin (µg)	Pantothenic Acid (mg)	Copper (mg)	Manganese (mg)	Fluoride (mg)	Chromium (mg)	Selenium (mg)	Molybdenum (mg)	Sodium (mg)	Potassium (mg)	Chloride (mg)
Infants												
0–0.5	12	35	2	0.5–0.7	0.5–0.7	0.1–0.5	0.01–0.04	0.01–0.04	0.03–0.06	115–350	350–925	275–700
0.5–1	10–20	50	3	0.7–1.0	0.7–1.0	0.2–1.0	0.02–0.06	0.02–0.06	0.04–0.08	250–750	425–1275	400–1200
Children												
1–3	15–30	65	3	1.0–1.5	1.0–1.5	0.5–1.5	0.02–0.08	0.02–0.08	0.05–0.1	325–975	550–1650	500–1500
and 4–6	20–40	85	3–4	1.5–2.0	1.5–2.0	1.0–2.5	0.03–0.12	0.03–0.12	0.06–0.15	450–1350	775–2325	700–2100
7–10	30–60	120	4–5	2.0–2.5	2.0–3.0	1.5–2.5	0.05–0.2	0.05–0.2	0.1–0.3	600–1800	1000–3000	925–2775
Adolescents 11+	50–100	100–200	4–7	2.0–3.0	2.5–5.0	1.5–2.5	0.05–0.2	0.05–0.2	0.15–0.5	900–2700	1525–4575	1400–4200
Adults	70–140	100–200	4–7	2.0–3.0	2.5–5.0	1.5–4.0	0.05–0.2	0.05–0.2	0.15–0.5	1100–3300	1875–5625	1700–5100

1. Because there is less information on which to base allowances, these figures are not given in the main table of the RDA and are provided in the form of ranges of recommended intakes. 2. Since the toxic levels for many trace elements may be only several times usual intakes, the upper levels for the trace elements given in this table should not be habitually exceeded. NOTE: µg=microgram; mg=milligram. Source: *Recommended Dietary Allowances*, Ninth Edition (1980), with the permission of the National Academy of Sciences, Washington, D.C.

Recommended Dietary Allowances

The Recommended Dietary Allowances (RDA) given in the tables are the latest established by the National Academy of Sciences Committee on Dietary Allowances as recommendations for the average daily amounts of nutrients for healthy population groups. They should not be confused with requirements for a specific individual.

Differences in the nutrient requirements of individuals are ordinarily unknown. Therefore, RDA (except for energy) are estimated to exceed the requirements of most individuals. Intake below the recommended allowance for a nutrient is not necessarily inadequate, but the risk of its being inadequate is increased if intake falls below the level recommended as safe.

Special needs for nutrients arising from such problems as premature birth, inherited metabolic disorders, infections, chronic diseases, and the use of medications are not covered by the RDA.

These dietary allowances form the basis for the RDA set by the Food and Drug Administration and are found on food labels as "U.S.RDA." The nutritional label lists the percentage of the RDA for protein and any of 17 vitamins and minerals found in the product. This does not represent all the required nutrients.

Because individual foods are not nutritionally complete, RDA should be met by eating a wide variety of selected foods in your diet.

Allowance for Energy

The recommended allowances for energy are estimates of the average needs of population groups, not recommended intakes for individuals. These needs vary from person to person and are not easily predictable without detailed information about physical characteristics and activity of the individual. Hence, the average energy needs for each age and sex are provided only as guidelines and are not repeated in the general table of recommended allowances.

Adjustments in RDA

The RDA does not take into account special needs that may require special attention. Some of these considerations are:

Physical Activity. This increases energy expenditure. Here, the increased need for a nutrient that may be related to carbohydrate utilization is generally met by consuming a larger amount of food. Attention must be given to salt and water losses due to sweating, which if prolonged, may lead to a loss of other nutrients.

Climate. There is little evidence that nutrient requirements, other than those for energy, are altered when individuals are exposed to heat or cold. Therefore, adjustments in dietary allowances to compensate for temperature changes are not considered necessary. However, exposures to temperatures that increase sweating will also increase the need for water and salt.

Aging. It is evident from studies of adult populations that body composition changes throughout life, with fat increasing and metabolically active tissues being slowly reduced. This reduction accounts for the fall in basal energy metabolism, often with an even greater reduction in physical activity.

As a result, less food is needed to meet energy requirements, and, unless food choices are made with great care, the amounts of essential nutrients may fall below desirable levels. It is important for older people to make sure that the smaller quantities of food that they eat are selected to provide the needed amounts of essential nutrients.

It is also important that physical activity be continued in adult life and into old age.

Mean Heights and Weights and Recommended Energy Intake

Category	Age (years)	Weight (lb)	Weight (kg)	Height (in.)	Height (cm)	Energy needs (with range) (kcal)	(MJ)
Infants	0.0–0.5	13	6	24	60	kg X 115 (95–145)	kg X .48
	0.5–1.0	20	9	28	71	kg X 105 (80–135)	kg X .44
Children	1–3	29	13	35	90	1300 (900–1800)	5.5
	4–6	44	20	44	112	1700 (1300–2300)	7.1
	7–10	62	28	52	132	2400 (1650–3300)	10.1
Males	11–14	99	45	62	157	2700 (2000–3700)	11.3
	15–18	145	66	69	176	2800 (2100–3900)	11.8
	19–22	154	70	70	177	2900 (2500–3300)	12.2
	23–50	154	70	70	178	2700 (2300–3100)	11.3
	51–75	154	70	70	178	2400 (2000–2800)	10.1
	76 +	154	70	70	178	2050 (1650–2450)	8.6
Females	11–14	101	46	62	157	2200 (1500–3000)	9.2
	15–18	120	55	64	163	2100 (1200–3000)	8.8
	19–22	120	55	64	163	2100 (1700–2500)	8.8
	23–50	120	55	64	163	2000 (1600–2400)	8.4
	51–75	120	55	64	163	1800 (1400–2200)	7.6
	76 +	120	55	64	163	1600 (1200–2000)	6.7
Pregnancy						+ 300	
Lactation						+ 500	

The energy allowances for the young adults are for men and women doing light work. The allowances for the two older age groups represent mean energy needs over these age spans, allowing for a 2% decrease in basal (resting) metabolic rate per decade and a reduction in activity of 200 kcal/day for men and women between 51 and 75 years, 500 kcal for men over 75 years, and 400 kcal for women over 75. The customary range of daily energy output is shown for adults in parentheses, and is based on a variation in energy needs of ± 400 kcal at any one age, emphasizing the wide range of energy intakes appropriate for any group of people. Energy allowances for children through age 18 are based on median energy intakes of children these ages followed in longitudinal growth studies. The values in parentheses are 10th and 90th percentile of energy intake, to indicate the range of energy consumption among children of these ages. NOTE: kg—kilogram; cm—centimeter; kcal—kilocalorie; MJ—megajoule. 1 kcal is equivalent to 4.18 kilojoules. 1 megajoule is equal to 1000 kilojoules. *Source: Recommended Dietary Allowances,* Ninth Edition (1980), with the permission of the National Academy of Sciences, Washington, D.C.

National Clearinghouse for Health Information

The Department of Health and Human Services has opened a National Health Information Clearinghouse to help consumers locate specific information about health. The project has a number of referral specialists to work with questions, get in touch with resource organizations, and refer those sources to the caller or writer. The center will not give medical advice or provide referrals to individual physicians.

The project is also offering a directory of "Health Information Resources in the Department of Health and Human Services." The pamphlet includes 76 points for information on an entire range of health topics, with each entry providing a contact, address and telephone, information on the authorizing legislation and sponsor and on serial publications, automated database, and audience.

For information, write: National Health Information Clearinghouse, P.O. Box 1133, Washington, D.C. 20013, or call 800–336–4797 (in Virginia, 703–522–2590).

For the information pamphlet send a self-addressed mailing label to the address.

Sunbathing and Skin Cancer

Scientists agree that ultraviolet radiation from the sun is the leading cause of skin cancer, which is responsible for an estimated 6,500 to 7,500 deaths in the United States every year. Sunlamps also can produce ultraviolet radiation, and the Food and Drug Administration is developing performance standards for them to reduce potential hazards.

Most dermatologists consider excessive sunbathing foolhardy. To the argument that the sun stimulates the production of vitamin D on the skin, the experts reply that you can get all the vitamin D you need from proper diet.

To the contention that the use of sunscreen lotions will promote a tan without burning, the experts say that a tanned skin is a damaged skin. Besides, they add, whether you burn or tan, there always is a chance that ultraviolet radiation will damage the DNA and initiate the cancer formation process.

People can reduce the potential hazard from the sun by not exposing themselves to it unnecessarily for extended periods between 10 a.m. and 2 p.m. when most ultraviolet radiation reaches the earth's surface.

Recommended Daily Dietary Allowances[1]

Designed for the maintenance of good nutrition of practically all healthy persons in the U.S. (revised 1979)

Persons	Age (years)	Wgt. (lbs)	Wgt. (kg)	Hgt. (in.)	Hgt. (cm)	Vitamin A µg R.E.[2]	Vitamin D min µg[3]	Vitamin E mg α T.E.[4]	Ascorbic Acid (mg)	Folacin[5] (µg)	Niacin[3] (mg)	Riboflavin (mg)	Thiamin (mg)	Vitamin B6 (mg)	Vitamin B12 (µg)	Calcium (mg)	Phosphorus (mg)	Iodine (µg)	Iron (mg)	Magnesium (mg)	Zinc (mg)
Infants	0.0–0.5	13	6	24	60	420	10	3	35	30	6	0.4	0.3	0.3	0.5[6]	360	240	40	10	50	3
	0.5–1.0	20	9	28	71	400	10	4	35	45	8	0.6	0.5	0.6	1.5	540	360	50	15	70	5
Children	1–3	29	13	35	90	400	10	5	45	100	9	0.8	0.7	0.9	2.0	800	800	70	15	150	10
	4–6	44	20	44	112	500	10	6	45	200	11	1.1	0.9	1.3	2.5	800	800	90	10	200	10
	7–10	62	28	52	132	700	10	7	45	300	16	1.4	1.2	1.6	3.0	800	800	120	10	250	10
Males	11–14	99	45	62	157	1,000	10	8	50	400	18	1.6	1.4	1.8	3.0	1,200	1,200	150	18	350	15
	15–18	145	66	69	176	1,000	10	10	60	400	18	1.7	1.4	2.0	3.0	1,200	1,200	150	18	400	15
	19–22	154	70	70	177	1,000	7.5	10	60	400	19	1.7	1.5	2.2	3.0	800	800	150	10	350	15
	23–50	154	70	70	178	1,000	5	10	60	400	18	1.6	1.4	2.2	3.0	800	800	150	10	350	15
	51+	154	70	70	178	1,000	5	10	60	400	16	1.4	1.2	2.2	3.0	800	800	150	10	350	15
Females	11–14	101	46	62	157	800	10	8	50	400	15	1.3	1.1	1.8	3.0	1,200	1,200	150	18	300	15
	15–18	120	55	64	163	800	10	8	60	400	14	1.3	1.1	2.0	3.0	1,200	1,200	150	18	300	15
	19–22	120	55	64	163	800	7.5	8	60	400	14	1.3	1.1	2.0	3.0	800	800	150	18	300	15
	23–50	120	55	64	163	800	5	8	60	400	13	1.2	1.0	2.0	3.0	800	800	150	18	300	15
	51+	120	55	64	163	800	5	8	60	400	13	1.2	1.0	2.0	3.0	800	800	150	10	300	15
Pregnant	—	—	—	—	—	+200	+5	+2	+20	+400	+2	+0.3	+0.4	+0.6	+1.0	+400	+400	+25	[7]	+150	+5
Lactating	—	—	—	—	—	+400	+5	+3	+40	+100	+5	+0.5	+0.5	+0.5	+1.0	+400	+400	+50	[7]	+150	+10

1. Allowances provide for individual variances among most normal persons living in the United States under usual environmental stresses. 1 Retinol equivalent = 1 µg retinol.
2. Retinol equivalents. 1 Retinol equivalent = 1 µg retinol, the average 1 mg of niacin is derived from each 60 mg of dietary tryptophan.
3. As cholecalciferol. 10 µg cholecalciferol = 400 I.U. vitamin D. 4. α tocopherol equivalents. 1 mg d-α-tocopherol = 1 α T.E. 5. Although expressed as niacin, the average 1 mg of niacin is derived from each 60 mg of dietary tryptophan. 6. The RDA for vitamin B12 in infants is based on average concentration of the vitamin in human milk. 7. Cannot be met by ordinary diets: use of supplemental iron is recommended. NOTE: mg—milligram; µg—microgram; IU—International Units; lbs—pounds; Wgt.—Weight; Hgt.—Height. *Source: Recommended Dietary Allowances*, Ninth Edition (1980), with the permission of the National Academy of Sciences, Washington, D.C.

SEVERE BLEEDING

(Continued from page 72)

Do not disturb blood clots after they have formed within the cloth. If blood soaks through the entire pad without clotting, do not remove the pad, but add additional thick layers of cloth and continue to direct pressure even more firmly.

Tourniquet Warning. The use of a tourniquet is dangerous, and the tourniquet should be used only for a severe life-threatening hemorrhage that cannot be controlled by other means.

The decision to apply a tourniquet is in reality a decision to risk sacrifice of a limb in order to save life. Once a tourniquet is applied, care by a physician is imperative. (NOTE: A tourniquet should be at least two inches wide.)

Communicable Diseases

Disease	Incubation period[1]	Period of communicability
Chickenpox (varicella)	2 to 3 weeks	From 5 days before appearance of vesicles to 6 days after
Common Cold	12 to 72 hours; usually 24 hrs	From 1 day before onset to 5 days after
Conjunctivitis	1 to 3 days	During course of active infection
Diphtheria	2 to 5 days	Usually 2 weeks or less; seldom more than 4 weeks
Dysentery, amebic	2 to 4 weeks (varies widely)	During intestinal infection; possibly for years if untreated
Enterobiasis (pinworm)	3 to 6 weeks	Not directly transmitted
Food poisoning: Botulism	12 to 36 hours	Not applicable
Salmonella infection	6 to 72 hours; usually 36	3 days to 3 weeks (extremely variable)
Staphylococcus intoxication	2 to 4 hours	Not applicable
German measles (rubella)	8 to 10 days; usually 14	1 week before and at least 4 days after onset of rash
Gonorrhea	2 to 5 days; sometimes longer	Indefinite unless treated
Hepatitis (serum)	45 to 160 days; usually 80 to 100	Many weeks before onset of symptoms
Herpes Simplex	Up to 2 weeks	As long as 7 weeks after recovery
Impetigo contagiosa	4 to 10 days; sometimes longer	Until lesions are healed
Infectious mononucleosis	Varies 2 to 6 weeks	Unknown
Influenza	Usually 1 to 3 days	Probably limited to 3 days from clinical onset
Measles (rubeola)	10 days (to onset): 14 days (to rash)	From beginning of prodromal period to 4 days after onset of rash
Meningitis, meningococcal	2 to 10 days	Usually 1 day after appropriate medication
Mumps	12 to 26 days; commonly 18	From 6 days before distinctive symptoms up to 9 days after
Pediculosis	Apprx. 2 weeks	While lice remain alive
Pneumonia: Bacterial	Usually 1 to 3 days	Unknown
Viral	Believed to be 1 to 3 days	Unknown
Poliomyelitis	3 to 21 days; commonly 7 to 12	7 to 10 days before and after onset of symptoms
Rabies	2 to 8 weeks or longer	From animals, 3 to 5 days before onset and during course of the disease
Respiratory (acute viral)	Few days to 1 week or more	Duration of active disease
Ringworm (of body)	4 to 10 days	As long as lesions are present
(Athlete's foot)	Unknown	As long as lesions are present
Scarlet fever and streptococcal sore throat	1 to 3 days	Uncomplicated cases apprx. 10 to 21 days; in untreated cases, weeks or months
Smallpox	7 to 17 days; commonly 10 to 12	During first week
Syphilis	10 days to 10 weeks; usually 3 weeks	Variable and indefinite
Tetanus	4 days to 3 weeks	Not applicable
Trichinosis	2 to 28 days after ingestion of infected meat; usually 9 days	Not directly transmitted
Tuberculosis	4 to 12 weeks (to primary phase)	As long as tubercle bacilli are discharged by patient
Typhoid fever	1 to 3 weeks, average 2 weeks	As long as typhoid bacilli appear in excreta; 2 to 5% of patients become permanent carriers
Whooping cough (pertussis)	Commonly 7 days, almost uniformly within 10 days, and not exceeding 21 days	From 7 days after exposure to 3 weeks after onset of typical paroxysms

1. Usual limits. NOTE: This list is incomplete, but includes those diseases that are most common and widespread.

Death Rate Is Rising for Youths

While the over-all death rate for Americans has dropped by 20% from 1960 to 1978, the rate for young people 15 to 24 has increased by 11% according to a Public Health Service report, "Health: United States, 1980." The chief causes for the deaths among the 15-to-24-year-old group were motor vehicle accidents, other kinds of accidents, suicide, drug abuse, and murder. Many of these deaths are related to alcohol and drug abuse.

Calories, Minerals, and Vitamins of Selected Foods

Food and amount	Energy (calories)	Protein (gm)	Fat (gm)	Calcium (mg)	Iron (mg)	Vitamin A (IU)	Vitamin B₁ (thiamin) (mg)	Vitamin B₂ (riboflavin) (mg)	Niacin (mg)	Vitamin C (ascorbic acid) (mg)
Apple, 1 medium, raw	80	—	1	10	.4	120	.04	.03	.1	6
Applesauce, 1 cup, canned, unsweetened	100	—	—	10	1.2	100	.05	.02	.1	2
Bacon, 2 slices, crisp	85	4	8	2	.5	—	.08	.05	.8	—
Banana, 1 medium	100	1	—	10	.8	230	.06	.07	.8	12
Beans, snap green, 1 cup cooked	30	2	1	63	.8	680	.09	.11	.6	15
Beans, red kidney, 1 cup canned	230	15	1	74	4.6	10	.13	.10	1.5	—
Beans, baked, pork and molasses, 1 cup	385	16	12	161	5.9	—	.15	.10	1.3	—
Beef cuts, cooked: Chuck, boned, 3 ounces	245	23	16	10	2.9	30	.04	.18	3.6	—
Hamburger, 3 ounces	235	20	17	9	2.6	30	.07	.17	4.4	—
Rib roast, 3 ounces boned	375	17	33	8	2.2	70	.05	.13	3.1	—
Round, 3 ounces boned	220	24	13	10	3.0	20	.07	.19	4.8	—
Sirloin, 3 ounces boned	330	20	27	9	2.5	50	.05	.15	4.0	—
Beef stew with vegetables, 1 cup	220	16	11	29	2.9	2,400	.15	.17	4.7	17
Beets, 1 cup cooked	55	2	—	24	.5	30	.05	.07	.5	10
Breads: Cracked wheat, average slice	65	2	1	22	.7	—	.08	.06	.8	—
Italian, average slice, enriched	85	3	1	5	.6	—	.12	.07	1.0	—
Raisin, average slice enriched	65	2	1	18	.5	—	.09	.06	.6	—
Rye (American), average slice	60	2	1	19	.6	—	.07	.05	.7	—
White, average slice enriched	70	2	1	21	.6	—	.10	.06	.8	—
Whole wheat, average slice	65	3	1	24	.8	—	.09	.03	.8	—
Butter, 1 tbsp	100	—	12	3	—	430	—	—	—	—
Cabbage, 1 cup, raw, coarsely shredded	15	1	—	34	.3	90	.04	.04	.2	33
Cake: Sponge, average slice	195	5	4	20	1.1	300	.09	.14	.6	—
Pound, average slice	160	2	10	6	.5	80	.05	.06	.4	—
Candies: Caramels, 1 ounce	115	1	3	42	.4	—	.01	.05	.1	—
Chocolate, milk, 1 ounce	145	2	9	65	.3	80	.02	.10	.1	—
Cantaloup, ½ melon	80	2	—	38	1.1	9,240	.11	.08	1.6	90
Carrot, raw, 1 average size	30	1	—	27	.5	7,930	.04	.04	.4	6
Catsup, 1 tbsp	15	—	—	3	.1	210	.01	.01	.2	2
Cheese: Cheddar, 1 ounce	115	7	9	204	.2	300	.01	.11	—	—
Cottage, creamed, 1 cup	235	28	10	135	.3	370	.05	.37	.3	—
Cottage, uncreamed, 1 cup	125	25	1	46	.3	40	.04	.21	.2	—
Cream cheese, 1 ounce	100	2	10	23	.3	400	—	.06	—	—
Swiss, natural, 1 ounce	105	8	8	272	—	240	—	.10	—	—
Swiss, process, 1 ounce	95	7	7	219	.2	230	.01	.08	—	—
Chicken, broiled, 3 ounces	115	20	3	8	1.4	80	.05	.16	7.4	—

Food	Calories	Protein (g)	Fat (g)	Calcium (mg)	Iron (mg)	Vitamin A (I.U.)	Thiamine (mg)	Riboflavin (mg)	Niacin (mg)	Vitamin C (mg)
Chicken, fried, ½ breast, 3.3 ounces	160	26	5	9	1.3	70	.04	.17	11.6	3
Chicken, canned, boned, 3 ounces	170	18	10	18	1.3	200	.03	.11	3.7	8
Clams, raw, 3 ounces	65	11	1	59	5.2	90	.08	.15	1.1	2
Cocoa, 1 cup, homemade	220	9	9	298	.8	320	.10	.44	.4	—
Coffee; black, 1 cup	—	—	—	—	—	—	—	—	—	—
Cola, carbonated, 12 ounces	145	—	—	—	—	—	—	—	—	—
Corn, average ear	70	2	1	2	.5	310	.09	.08	1.1	7
Corn flakes, 1 cup	95	2	—	3	.6	1,180	.29	.35	2.9	9
Crabmeat, canned, 3 ounces	85	15	2	38	.7	—	.07	.07	1.6	—
Crackers, Graham, 4	110	2	3	11	1.0	—	.04	.16	1.0	—
Saltines, 4	50	1	1	2	.5	—	.05	.05	—	2
Cream: Light, table, 1 cup	470	6	46	231	.1	1,730	.08	.36	.1	1
Heavy, whipping, 1 cup	820	5	88	154	.1	3,500	.05	.26	—	2
Sour, 1 cup	495	7	48	268	.1	1,820	.08	.34	.1	—
Whipped topping (pressurized), 1 cup	155	—	13	61	—	550	.02	.04	.2	—
Doughnut, 1 plain	100	6	5	10	.4	20	.04	.05	—	5
Egg: Raw or cooked in shell, 1	80	6	6	28	1.0	260	.04	.14	.4	—
Omelet, scrambled, 1	95	7	7	47	.9	310	.08	.16	—	—
Frankfurter, 1	170	1	15	3	.8	—	.05	.11	1.4	—
Fruit cocktail, 1 cup canned	195	—	—	23	1.0	360	.08	.03	1.0	5
Grapefruit: Raw, ½	45	2	—	19	.5	10	.10	.02	.2	44
Canned, syrup, 1 cup	180	1	—	33	.8	30	.03	.05	.5	76
Juice, fresh, 1 cup	95	—	—	22	.5	20	—	.05	.5	93
Haddock, breaded, fried, 3 ounces	140	17	5	34	1.0	—	.05	.01	2.7	2
Honey, strained, 1 tbsp.	65	—	—	1	.1	—	—	—	.1	—
Ice cream, 1 cup	270	5	14	176	—	540	.05	.33	—	1
Jellies, 1 tbsp	50	—	—	4	.1	—	—	.01	.1	1
Lamb: Rib chop, boned, 4 ounces	400	25	33	10	1.5	—	.14	.25	5.6	—
Leg roast, 3 ounces, boned	235	22	16	9	1.4	—	.13	.23	4.7	—
Lemon, 1 medium	20	—	—	19	.4	10	.03	.01	.1	39
Liver: Beef, fried, 2 ounces	130	15	6	6	5.0	30,280	.15	2.37	9.4	15
Luncheon meat: Boiled ham, 2 ounces	135	11	10	6	1.6	—	.25	.09	1.5	—
Canned, spiced or unspiced, 2 ounces	165	8	14	5	1.2	—	.18	.12	1.6	—
Macaroni, enriched, 1 cup	—	5	1	11	1.3	—	.20	.11	1.5	—
Macaroni and cheese, 1 cup	430	17	22	362	1.8	860	.20	.40	1.8	—
Margarine, 1 tbsp	100	—	12	3	—	470	—	—	—	—
Mayonnaise, 1 tbsp	100	—	11	3	.1	40	—	.01	—	—
Milk: Whole, 1 cup	150	8	8	291	.1	310	.09	.40	.2	2
Skim (non-fat), 1 cup	85	8	—	302	.1	500	.09	.34	.2	2
Buttermilk, 1 cup	100	8	—	285	.1	80	.08	.38	.1	2
Mushrooms, canned, 1 cup	40	5	—	15	1.2	—	—	.60	4.8	4
Nuts: Almonds, 1 cup shelled	850	26	77	332	6.7	—	.34	1.31	5.0	—
Peanuts, roasted, 1 cup	840	37	72	107	3.0	—	.46	.19	24.8	—
Oatmeal, 1 cup cooked	130	5	2	22	1.4	—	.19	.05	.2	—
Oils, salad, cooking, 1 tbsp	120	—	14	—	—	—	—	—	—	—
Orange, 1 medium	65	1	—	54	.5	260	.13	.05	.5	66

| | Nutrients | | | Minerals | | Vitamins | | | | |
Food and amount	Energy (calories)	Protein (gm)	Fat (gm)	Calcium (mg)	Iron (mg)	Vitamin A (IU)	Vitamin B₁ (thiamin) (mg)	Vitamin B₂ (riboflavin) (mg)	Niacin (mg)	Vitamin C (ascorbic acid) (mg)
Orange juice, fresh, 1 cup	110	2	—	27	.5	500	.22	.07	1.0	124
Frozen, diluted with 3 parts water, 1 cup	120	2	—	25	.2	540	.23	.03	.9	120
Oysters, raw, 1 cup	160	20	4	226	13.2	740	.34	.43	6.0	—
Pancake, wheat, 1 average	60	2	2	27	.4	30	.06	.07	.5	—
Peach, raw, 1 medium	40	1	—	9	.5	1,330	.02	.05	1.0	7
Peanut butter, 1 tbsp	95	4	8	9	.3	—	.02	.02	2.4	—
Peas, green, 1 cup	110	8	—	30	3.0	960	.43	.14	2.7	21
Pie: Apple, 4-inch wedge	345	3	15	11	.9	40	.15	.11	1.3	2
Cherry, 4-inch wedge	350	4	15	19	.9	590	.16	.12	1.4	—
Lemon meringue, 4-inch wedge	305	4	12	17	1.0	200	.09	.12	.7	4
Pineapple, raw, 1 cup diced	80	1	—	26	.8	110	.14	.05	.3	26
Pineapple juice, canned, 1 cup	140	1	—	38	.8	130	.13	.05	.5	23
Pizza (cheese), 4¾-inch wedge	145	6	4	86	1.1	230	.16	.18	1.6	4
Pork: Roast, 3 ounces	310	21	24	9	2.7	—	.78	.22	4.8	—
Chop, with bone, 2.7 ounces	305	19	25	9	1.1	—	.75	.22	4.5	—
Potatoes: Baked, 1 medium	145	4	—	14	.7	—	.15	.07	2.7	31
French fried, deep fat, 10 pieces	135	2	7	8	.7	40	.07	.04	1.6	11
Mashed with milk, 1 cup	135	4	2	50	.8	—	.17	.11	2.1	21
Potato chips, 10	115	1	8	8	.4	—	.04	.01	1.0	3
Prune juice, 1 cup canned	195	1	—	36	1.8	30	.03	.03	1.0	5
Rice: White, enriched, 1 cup cooked	225	4	—	21	1.8	—	.23	.02	2.1	—
Puffed, 1 cup	60	1	—	3	.3	—	.07	.01	.7	—
Salad dressings: Mayonnaise type, 1 tbsp	65	—	6	2	—	30	—	—	—	—
French, 1 tbsp	65	—	6	2	.1	—	—	—	—	—
French, low calorie, 1 tbsp	15	—	1	2	.1	—	—	—	—	—
Salmon: Canned, 3 ounces	120	17	5	167	.7	60	.03	.16	6.8	—
Sardines, canned, 3 ounces	175	20	9	372	2.5	190	.02	.17	4.6	—
Spaghetti, 1 cup cooked	155	5	1	11	1.3	—	.20	.11	1.5	—
Spinach, 1 cup cooked	40	5	1	167	4.0	14,580	.13	.25	.9	50
Sugar, 1 teaspoon	15	—	—	—	—	—	—	—	—	—
Tomato juice, canned, 1 cup	45	2	—	17	2.2	1,940	.12	.07	1.9	39
Tuna fish, 3 ounces	170	24	7	7	1.6	70	.04	.10	10.1	—
Veal, 3-ounce cutlet	185	23	9	9	2.7	—	.06	.21	4.6	—
Yogurt, from lowfat milk, 8-oz. container, plain	145	12	4	415	.2	150	.10	.49	.3	2

NOTE: Gm—gram; Mg—milligram; IU—International Unit. A dash in a column indicates little or no basis for assigning value. *Source:* Department of Agriculture, Science and Education Administration.

HEADLINE HISTORY

In any broad overview of history, arbitrary compartmentalization of facts is self-defeating (and makes locating interrelated people, places, and things that much harder). Therefore, Headline History is designed as a "timeline"—a chronology that highlights both the march of time and interesting, sometimes surprising, juxtapositions.

Also see related sections of *Information Please,* particularly the Statistical History of the United States, Inventions and Discoveries, Countries of the World, etc.

B.C.

Before Christ or Before Common Era (B.C.E.)

4500–3000 B.C. Sumerians in the Tigris and Euphrates valleys develop a city-state civilization; first phonetic writing (**c.3500 B.C.**). Egyptian agriculture develops. Western Europe is neolithic, without metals or written records. Earliest recorded date in Egyptian calendar (**4241 B.C.**). First year of Jewish calendar (**3760 B.C.**). Copper used by Egyptians and Sumerians.

3000–2000 B.C. Pharaonic rule begins in Egypt. Cheops, 4th dynasty (**2700–2675 B.C.**). The Great Sphinx of Giza. Earliest Egyptian mummies. Papyrus. Phoenician settlements on coast of what is now Syria and Lebanon. Semitic tribes settle in Assyria. Sargon, first Akkadian king, builds Mesopotamian empire. The Gilgamesh epic (**c.3000 B.C.**). Abraham leaves Ur (**c.2000 B.C.**). Systematic astronomy in Egypt, Babylon, India, China.

2000–1500 B.C. Hyksos invaders drive Egyptians from Lower Egypt (**17th century B.C.**). Amosis I frees Egypt from Hyksos (**c.1600 B.C.**). Assyrians rise to power —cities of Ashur and Nineveh. Twenty-four-character alphabet in Egypt. Israelites enslaved in Egypt. Cuneiform inscriptions used by Hittites. Peak of Minoan culture on Isle of Crete—earliest form of written Greek. Hammurabi, king of Babylon, develops oldest existing code of laws (**18th century B.C.**). In Britain, Stonehenge erected on some unknown astronomical rationale.

1500–1000 B.C. Ikhnaton develops monotheistic religion in Egypt (**c.1375 B.C.**). His successor, Tutankhamen, returns to earlier gods. Moses leads Israelites out of Egypt into Canaan—Ten Commandments. Greeks destroy Troy (**c.1193 B.C.**). End of Greek civilization in Mycenae with invasion of Dorians. Chinese civilization develops under Shang dynasty. Olmec civilization in Mexico—stone monuments; picture writing.

1000–900 B.C. Solomon succeeds King David, builds Jerusalem temple. After Solomon's death, kingdom divided into Israel and Judah. Hebrew elders begin to write Old Testament books of Bible. Phoenicians colonize Spain with settlement at Cadiz.

900–800 B.C. Phoenicians establish Carthage (**c.810 B.C.**). The *Iliad* and the *Odyssey,* perhaps composed by Greek poet Homer.

800–700 B.C. Prophets Amos, Hosea, Isaiah. First recorded Olympic games (**776 B.C.**). Legendary founding of Rome by Romulus (**753 B.C.**). Assyrian king Sargon II conquers Hittites, Chaldeans, Samaria (end of Kingdom of Israel). Earliest written music. Chariots introduced into Italy by Etruscans.

700–600 B.C. End of Assyrian Empire (**616 B.C.**)—Nineveh destroyed by Chaldeans (Neo-Babylonians) and Medes (**612 B.C.**). Founding of Byzantium by Greeks (**c.660 B.C.**). Building of the Acropolis in Athens. Solon, Greek lawgiver (**640–560 B.C.**). Sappho of Lesbos, Greek poetess. Lao-Tse, Chinese philosopher and founder of Taoism (born **c.604 B.C.**).

600–500 B.C. Babylonian king Nebuchadnezzar builds empire, destroys Jerusalem (**586 B.C.**). Babylonian Captivity of the Jews (starting **587 B.C.**). Hanging Gardens of Babylon. Cyrus the Great of Persia creates great empire, conquers Babylon (**539 B.C.**), frees the Jews. Athenian democracy develops. Aeschylus, Greek dramatist (**525–465 B.C.**). Confucius (**551–479 B.C.**) develops philosophy-religion in China. Buddha (**563–483 B.C.**) founds Buddhism in India.

500–400 B.C. Greeks defeat Persians: battles of Marathon (**490 B.C.**), Thermopylae (**480 B.C.**), Salamis (**480 B.C.**). Peloponnesian Wars between Athens and Sparta (**431–404 B.C.**)—Sparta victorious. Pericles comes to power in Athens (**462**

Some Ancient Civilizations

Name	Approximate dates	Location	Major cities
Akkadian	2350–2230 B.C.	Mesopotamia, parts of Syria, Asia Minor, Iran	Akkad, Ur, Erich
Assyrian	1800–889 B.C.	Mesopotamia, Syria	Assur, Nineveh, Calah
Babylonian	1728–1686 B.C. (old) 625–539 B.C. (new)	Mesopotamia, Syria, Palestine	Babylon
Cimmerian	750–500 B.C.	Caucasus, northern Asia Minor	—
Egyptian	2850–715 B.C.	Nile valley	Thebes, Memphis, Tanis
Etruscan	900–396 B.C.	Northern Italy	
Greek	900–200 B.C.	Greece	Athens, Sparta, Thebes, Mycenae, Corinth
Hittite	1640–1200 B.C.	Asia Minor, Syria	Hattusas, Nesa
Lydian	700–547 B.C.	Western Asia Minor	Sardis, Miletus
Mede	835–550 B.C.	Iran	Media
Minoan	3000–1100 B.C.	Crete	Knossos
Persian	559–330 B.C.	Iran, Asia Minor, Syria	Persepolis, Pasargadae
Phoenician	1100–332 B.C.	Palestine (colonies: Gibralter, Carthage Sardinia)	Tyre, Sidon, Byblos
Phrygian	1000–547 B.C.	Central Asia Minor	Gordion
Roman	500 B.C.– A.D. 300	Italy, Mediterranean region, Asia Minor, western Europe	Rome, Byzantium
Scythian	800–300 B.C.	Caucasus	—
Sumerian	3200–2360 B.C.	Mesopotamia	Ur, Nippur

B.C.). Flowering of Greek culture during the Age of Pericles (450–400 B.C.). Sophocles, Greek dramatist (496–c.406 B.C.). Hippocrates, Greek "Father of Medicine" (born 460 B.C.). Xerxes I, king of Persia (rules 485–465 B.C.).

400–300 B.C. Pentateuch—first five books of the Old Testament evolve in final form. Philip of Macedon assassinated (336 B.C.) after conquering Greece; succeeded by son, Alexander the Great (356–323 B.C.), who destroys Thebes (335 B.C.), conquers Tyre and Jerusalem (332 B.C.), occupies Babylon (330 B.C.), invades India, and dies in Babylon. His empire is divided among his generals; one of them, Seleucis I, establishes Middle East empire with capitals at Antioch (Syria) and Seleucia (in Iraq). Trial and execution of Greek philosopher Socrates (399 B.C.). Dialogues recorded by his student, Plato. Euclid's work on geometry (323 B.C.). Aristotle, Greek philosopher (354–322 B.C.). Demosthenes, Greek orator (384–322 B.C.). Praxiteles, Greek sculptor (400–330 B.C.).

300–251 B.C. First Punic War (264–241 B.C.): Rome defeats the Carthaginians and begins its domination of the Mediterranean. Temple of the Sun at Teotihuacan, Mexico (c.300 B.C.). Invention of Mayan calendar in Yucatán —more exact than older calendars. First Roman gladiatorial games (264 B.C.). Archimedes, Greek mathematician (287–212 B.C.).

250–201 B.C. Second Punic War (219–201 B.C.): Hannibal, Carthaginian general (246–142 B.C.), crosses the Alps (218 B.C.), reaches gates of Rome (211 B.C.), retreats, and is defeated by Scipio Africanus at Zama (202 B.C.). Great Wall of China built (c.215 B.C.).

200–151 B.C. Romans defeat Seleucid King Antiochus III at Thermopylae (191 B.C.)—beginning of Roman world domination. Maccabean revolt against Seleucids (167 B.C.).

150–101 B.C. Third Punic War (149–146 B.C.): Rome destroys Carthage, killing 450,000 and enslaving the remaining 50,000 inhabitants. Roman armies conquer Macedonia, Greece, Turkey, Balearic Islands, and southern France. Venus de Milo (c.140 B.C.). Cicero, Roman orator (106–43 B.C.).

100–51 B.C. Julius Caesar (100–44 B.C.) invades Britain (55 B.C.) and conquers Gaul (France) (c.50 B.C.). Spartacus leads slave revolt against Rome (71 B.C.). Romans conquer Seleucid empire. Roman general Pompey conquers Jerusalem (63 B.C.). Cleopatra on Egyptian throne (51–31 B.C.). Chinese develop use of paper (c.100 B.C.). Virgil, Roman poet (70–19 B.C.). Horace, Roman poet (65–8 B.C.).

50–1 B.C.   Caesar crosses Rubicon to fight Pompey (**50** B.C.). Herod made Roman governor of Judea (**47** B.C.). Caesar murdered (**44** B.C.). Caesar's nephew, Octavian, defeats Mark Antony and Cleopatra at Battle of Actium (**31** B.C.), and establishes Roman empire as Emperor Augustus—rules **27** B.C.-A.D. **14**. Birth of Jesus Christ (variously given from **4** B.C. to A.D. **7**). Ovid, Roman poet (**43** B.C.-A.D. **18**).

A.D.
The Christian or Common Era (C.E.)

1–49   After Augustus, Tiberius becomes emperor (dies, **37**), succeeded by Caligula (assassinated, **42**), who is followed by Claudius. Crucifixion of Jesus (probably **30**). Han dynasty in China founded by Emperor Kuang Wu Ti. Buddhism introduced to China.

50–99   Claudius poisoned (**54**), succeeded by Nero (commits suicide, **68**). Missionary journeys of Paul the Apostle (**34–60**). Jews revolt against Rome; Jerusalem destroyed (**70**). Roman persecutions of Christians begin (**64**). Colosseum built in Rome (**71–80**); Trajan (rules **98–116**); Roman empire extends to Mesopotamia, Arabia, Balkans. First Gospels of St. Mark, St. John, St. Matthew.

100–149   Hadrian rules Rome (**117–138**); codifies Roman law, establishes postal system, builds wall between England and Scotland. Jews revolt under Bar Kokhba (**122–135**); final *Diaspora* (dispersion) of Jews begins.

150–199   Marcus Aurelius (rules Rome **161–180**). Oldest Mayan temples in Central America (c.**200**). Mayan civilization develops writing, astronomy, mathematics.

200–249   Goths invade Asia Minor (c.**220**). Roman persecutions of Christians increase. Persian (Sassanid) empire re-established. End of Chinese Han dynasty.

250–299   Increasing invasions of the Roman empire by Franks and Goths. Buddhism spreads in China.

300–349   Constantine the Great (rules **312–337**) reunites eastern and western Roman empires, with new capital (Constantinople) on site of Byzantium (**330**); issues Edict of Milan legalizing Christianity (**313**); becomes a Christian on his deathbed (**337**). Council of Nicaea (**325**) defines orthodox Christian doctrine. First Gupta dynasty in India (c.**320**).

350–399   Huns (Mongols) invade Europe (c.**360**). Theodosius the Great (rules **392–395**)—last emperor of a united Roman empire. Roman empire permanently divided in **395**: western empire ruled from Rome; eastern empire ruled from Constantinople.

400–449   Western Roman empire disintegrates under weak emperors. Alaric, king of the Visigoths, sacks Rome (**410**). Attila, Hun chieftain, attacks Roman provinces (**433**). St. Patrick returns to Ireland (**432**). St. Augustine's *City of God* (**411**).

450–499   Vandals destroy Rome (**455**). Western Roman empire ends as Odoacer, German chieftain, overthrows last Roman emperor, Romulus Augustulus, and becomes king of Italy (**476**). Ostrogothic kingdom of Italy established by Theodoric the Great (**493**). Clovis, ruler of the Franks, is converted to Christianity (**496**). First schism between western and eastern churches (**484**). Peak of Mayan culture in Mexico (c.**460**).

500–549   Eastern and western churches reconciled (**519**). Justinian I, the Great (**483–565**), becomes Byzantine emperor (**527**), issues his first code of civil laws (**529**), conquers North Africa, Italy, and part of Spain. Plague spreads through Europe (from **542**). Arthur, semi-legendary king of the Britons (killed, c.**537**). Boëthius, Roman scholar (executed, **524**).

550–599   Beginnings of European silk industry after Justinian's missionaries smuggle silkworms out of China (**553**). Mohammed, founder of Islam (**570–632**). Buddhism in Japan (c.**560**). St. Augustine of Canterbury brings Christianity to Britain (**597**). After killing about half the population, plague in Europe subsides (**594**).

600–649   Mohammed flees from Mecca to Medina (the *Hegira*); first year of the Muslim calendar (**622**). Muslim empire grows (**634**). Arabs conquer Jerusalem (**637**), destroy Alexandrian library (**641**), conquer Persians (**641**). Fatima, Mohammed's daughter (**606–632**).

650–699   Arabs attack North Africa (**670**), destroy Carthage (**697**). Venerable Bede, English monk (**672–735**).

700–749   Arab empire extends from Lisbon to China (by **716**). Charles Martel, Frankish leader, defeats Arabs at Tours/Poitiers, halting Arab advance in Europe (**732**). Charlemagne (**742–814**).

750–799   Caliph Harun al-Rashid rules Arab empire (**786–809**): the "golden age" of Arab culture. Vikings begin attacks on Britain (**790**), land in

Ireland (**795**). Charlemagne becomes king of the Franks (**771**). City of Machu Picchu flourishes in Peru.

800–849 Charlemagne (Charles the Great) crowned first Holy Roman Emperor in Rome (**800**). Arabs conquer Crete, Sicily, and Sardinia (**826–827**). Charlemagne dies (**814**), succeeded by his son, Louis the Pious, who divides France among his sons (**817**).

850–899 Norsemen attack as far south as the Mediterranean but are repulsed (**859**), discover Iceland (**861**). Alfred the Great becomes king of Britain (**871**), defeats Danish invaders (**878**). Russian nation founded by Vikings under Prince Rurik, establishing capital at Novgorod (**855–879**).

900–949 Vikings discover Greenland (**c.900**). Arab Spain under Abd ar-Rahman III becomes center of learning (**912–961**).

950–999 Eric the Red establishes first Viking colony in Greenland (**982**). Mieczyslaw I becomes first ruler of Poland (**960**). Hugh Capet elected King of France in **987**; Capetian dynasty to rule until **1328**. Musical notation systematized (**c.990**). Vikings and Danes attack Britain (**988–999**). Holy Roman Empire founded by Otto I, King of Germany since **936**, crowned by Pope John XII in **962**.

c.1000 Hungary and Scandinavia converted to Christianity. Viking raider Leif Ericson discovers North America, calls it *Vinland*. Chinese invent gunpowder. *Beowulf*, Old English epic.

1009 Moslems destroy Holy Sepulchre in Jerusalem.

1013 Danes control England. Canute takes throne (**1016**), conquers Norway (**1028**), dies (**1035**); kingdom divided among his sons: Harold Harefoot (England), Sweyn (Norway), Hardecanute (Denmark).

1040 Macbeth murders Duncan, king of Scotland.

1053 Robert Guiscard, Norman invader, establishes kingdom in Italy, conquers Sicily (**1072**).

1054 Final separation between Eastern (Orthodox) and Western (Roman) churches.

1055 Seljuk Turks, Asian nomads, move west, capture Baghdad, Armenia (**1064**), Syria, and Palestine (**1075**).

1066 William of Normandy invades England, defeats last Saxon king, Harold II, at Battle of Hastings, crowned William I of England ("the Conqueror").

1073 Emergence of strong papacy when Gregory VII is elected. Conflict with English and French kings and German emperors will continue throughout medieval period.

1095 *(See* special material on "The Crusades.")

1150–67 Universities of Paris and Oxford founded in France and England.

1162 Thomas à Becket named Archbishop of Canterbury, murdered by Henry II's men (**1170**). Troubadours (wandering minstrels) glorify romantic concepts of feudalism.

1189 Richard I ("the Lionhearted") succeeds Henry II in England, killed in France (**1199**), succeeded by King John.

1211 Genghis Khan invades China, captures Peking (**1214**), conquers Persia (**1218**), invades Russia (**1223**), dies (**1227**).

1215 King John forced by barons to sign Magna Carta at Runneymede, limiting royal power.

1233 The Inquisition begins as Pope Gregory IX assigns Dominicans responsibility for combatting heresy. Torture used (**1252**). Ferdinand and Isabella establish Spanish Inquisition (**1478**). Tourquemada, Grand Inquisitor, forces conversion or expulsion of Spanish Jews (**1492**). Forced conversion of Moors (**1499**). Inquisition in Portugal (**1531**). First Protestants burned at the stake in Spain (**1543**). Spanish Inquisition abolished (**1834**).

1241 Mongols defeat Germans in Silesia, invade Poland and Hungary, with-

Omar Khayyám, *Persian poet* (1027?–1123)

El Cid, *Spanish national hero* (1040–1099)

Peter Abelard, *French theologian* (1079–1142)

Judah Halevi, *Jewish poet* (1085–1140)

Thomas à Becket, *English prelate and martyr* (1118–1170)

Moses Maimonides, *Jewish philosopher* (1135–1204)

Genghis Khan, *Mongol emperor* (1162–1227)

St. Francis of Assisi, *founder of Franciscans* (1182–1226)

Roger Bacon, *English scientist* (1214–1294)

Kublai Khan, *Mongol ruler* (1216–1294)

St. Thomas Aquinas, *Catholic theologian* (1225–1274)

Marco Polo, *Venetian explorer* (1254–1323)

Dante Alighieri, *Italian poet* (1265–1321)

THE CRUSADES (1096–1291)

In 1095 Pope Urban II calls for war to rescue Holy Land from Moslem infidels at Council of Clermont. *First Crusade* (**1096**)—about 500,000 peasants led by Peter the Hermit prove so troublesome that Byzantine Emperor Alexius ships them to Asia Minor; only 25,000 survive return after massacre by Seljuk Turks. Followed by organized army, led by nobility, which reaches Constantinople (**1097**), conquers Jerusalem (**1099**), Acre (**1104**), establishes Latin Kingdom protected by Knights of St. John the Hospitaller (**1100**), and Knights Templar (**1123**). Seljuk Turks start series of counterattacks (**1144**). *Second Crusade* (**1146**) led by King Louis VIII of France and Emperor Conrad III. Crusaders perish in Asia Minor (**1147**).

Saladin controls Egypt (**1171**), unites Islam in Holy War (*Jihad*) against Christians, recaptures Jerusalem (**1187**). *Third Crusade* (**1189**) under kings of France, England, and Germany fails to reduce Saladin's power. *Fourth Crusade* (**1200–1204**)—French knights sack Greek Christian Constantinople, establish Latin empire in Byzantium. Greeks re-establish Orthodox faith (**1262**).

Children's Crusade (**1212**)—Only 1 of 30,000 French children and about 200 of 20,000 German children survive to return home. Other Crusades—against Egypt (**1217**), *Sixth* (**1228**), *Seventh* (**1248**), *Eighth* (**1270**). Mamelukes conquer Acre; end of the Crusades (**1291**).

draw from Europe after Ughetai, Mongol leader, dies.

1251 Kublai Khan governs China, becomes ruler of Mongols **(1259)**, establishes Yuan dynasty in China **(1280)**, invades Burma **(1287)**, dies **(1294)**.

1271 Marco Polo of Venice travels to China, in court of Kublai Khan **(1275–1292)**, returns to Genoa **(1295)** and writes *Travels*.

1272 English King Edward I conquers Wales and Scotland; Great Britain unified. Summons the Model Parliament in **1295**.

1312–37 Mali Empire reaches its height in Africa under King Mansa Musa.

1337–1453 Hundred Years' War—English and French kings fight for control of France.

c.1325 The beginning of the Renaissance in Italy: writers Dante, Petrarch, Boccaccio; painter Giotto. Development of *No* drama in Japan. Aztecs establish capital on site of modern Mexico City. Peak of Moslem culture in Spain. Small cannon in use.

1347–1351 At least 25 million people die in Europe's "Black Death" (bubonic plague).

1368 Ming dynasty begins in China.

1376–82 John Wycliffe, pre-Reformation religious reformer and followers translate Latin bible into English.

1378 The Great Schism **(to 1417)**—rival popes in Rome and Avignon, France, fight for control of Roman Catholic Church.

c.1387 Chaucer's *Canterbury Tales*.

1415 Henry V defeats French at Agincourt, Jan Hus, Bohemian preacher and follower of Wycliffe, burned at stake in Constance as heretic.

1418–60 Portugal's Prince Henry the Navigator sponsors exploration of Africa's coast.

1428 Joan of Arc leads French against English, captured by Burgundians **(1430)** and turned over to the English, burned at the stake as a witch after ecclesiastical trial **(1431)**.

1438 Inca rule in Peru.

1450 Florence becomes center of Renaissance arts and learning under the Medicis.

1453 Turks conquer Constantinople, end of the Byzantine empire. Hundred Years' War between France and England ends.

1455 The Wars of the Roses, civil wars between rival noble factions, begin in England **(to 1485)**. Having invented printing with movable type at Mainz, Germany, Johann Gutenberg completes first bible.

1462 Ivan the Great rules Russia until **1505** as first czar; ends payment of tribute to Mongols.

1492 Moors conquered in Spain by troops of Ferdinand and Isabella. Columbus discovers Caribbean islands, returns to Spain **(1493)**. Second voyage to Dominica, Jamaica, Puerto Rico **(1493–1496)**. Third voyage to Orinoco **(1498)**. Fourth voyage to Honduras and Panama **(1502–1504)**.

1497 Vasco da Gama sails around Africa and discovers sea route to India **(1498)**. Establishes Portuguese colony in India **(1502)**. John Cabot, employed by England, reaches and explores Canadian coast. Michelangelo's *Bacchus* sculpture.

Leonardo da Vinci, *Renaissance artistic and scientific genius* (1452–1519)

Vasco da Gama, *Portuguese explorer* (1460–1524)

Juan Ponce de León, *Spanish explorer* (1460–1521)

Hans Holbein (the Elder), *German painter* (1465?–1524)

Niccolo Machiavelli, *Italian author* (1468–1527)

Albrecht Dürer, *German painter* (1471–1528)

Nicolaus Copernicus, *Polish scientist* (1473–1543)

Michelangelo Buonarroti, *Italian painter, sculptor, architect* (1475–1564)

Cesare Borgia, *Renaissance prince* (1476–1507)

Titian, *Italian painter* (1477–1576)

Sir Thomas More, *English statesman* (1478–1535)

Lucrezia Borgia, *Italian patron of the arts* (1480–1519)

Ferdinand Magellan, *Portuguese explorer* (1480–1521)

Martin Luther, *German Reformation leader* (1483–1546)

Raphael, *Italian painter* (1483–1520)

Ulrich Zwingli, *Swiss humanist* (1484–1531)

Hernando Cortes, *Spanish Conquistador* (1485–1547)

Andrea del Sarto, *Florentine painter* (1486–1531)

Thomas Cranmer, *English churchman* (1489–1556)

François Rabelais, *French writer* (1490–1553)

Jacques Cartier, *French explorer* (1491–1557)

St. Ignatius de Loyola, *founder of Jesuits* (1491–1556)

Paracelsus, *Swiss physician* (1493–1541)

Correggio, *Italian painter* (1494–1534)

Hans Holbein (the Younger) *German painter* (1497–1543)

Hernando De Soto, *Spanish explorer* (1499–1542)

Duns Scotus, *Scottish theologian* (1265–1308)

Giotto, *Italian painter* (1276–1337)

Guillaume de Machaut, *French composer* (1300–1377)

Petrarch (Francesco Petrarca), *Italian poet* (1304–1374)

Giovanni Boccaccio, *Florentine novelist* (1313–1375)

John Wycliffe, *English church reformer* (1320–1384)

Geoffrey Chaucer, *English writer* (c.1340–1400)

Jan Hus, *Bohemian religious reformer* (c.1369–1415)

Thomas à Kempis, *German mystic* (1380–1471)

Donatello, *Italian sculptor* (1386–1466)

Fra Angelico, *Italian painter* (1387–1455)

Johann Gutenberg, *inventor of movable type* (1398–1468)

Luca della Robbia, *Italian sculptor* (1400–1482)

Guillaume Dufay, *French composer* (c.1400–1474)

Fra Filippo Lippi, *Italian painter* (1406–1469)

Joan of Arc, *French saint and national heroine* (1412–1431)

Tomas de Torquemada, *Spanish Inquisitor* (1420–1498)

Giovanni Bellini, *Italian painter* (1430–1516)

François Villon, *French poet* (1431–1465?)

Sandro Botticelli, *Italian painter* (1444–1510)

Lorenzo de'Medici, *Renaissance ruler* (1449–1492)

Hieronymus Bosch, *Dutch painter* (1450–1516)

Josquin des Prés, *Dutch composer* (1450–1521)

Isabella I, *Queen of Spain* (1451–1504)

Christopher Columbus, *Italian explorer* (1451–1506)

Amerigo Vespucci, *Italian navigator* (1451–1512)

Savonarola, *Italian churchman* (1452–1498)

1501 First black slaves in America brought to Spanish colony of Santo Domingo.
c.1503 Leonardo da Vinci paints the *Mona Lisa.*
1506 St. Peter's Church started in Rome; designed and decorated by such artists and architects as Bramante, Michelangelo, da Vinci, Raphael, and Bernini before its completion in 1626.
1509 Henry VIII ascends English throne. Michelangelo paints the ceiling of the Sistine Chapel.
1517 Turks conquer Egypt, control Arabia. Martin Luther posts his 95 theses denouncing church abuses on church door in Wittenberg—start of the Reformation in Germany.
1519 Ulrich Zwingli begins Reformation in Switzerland. Hernando Cortes conquers Mexico for Spain. Charles I of Spain is chosen Holy Roman Emperor Charles V. Portuguese explorer Fernando Magellan sets out to circumnavigate the globe.
1520 Luther excommunicated by Pope Leo X. Suleiman I ("the Magnificent") becomes Sultan of Turkey, invades Hungary (1521), Rhodes (1522), attacks Austria (1529), annexes Hungary (1541), Tripoli (1551), makes peace with Persia (1553), destroys Spanish fleet (1560), dies (1566). Magellan reaches the Pacific, is killed by Philippine natives (1521). One of his ships under Juan Sebastián del Cano continues around the world, reaches Spain (1522).
1524 Verrazano, sailing under the French flag, explores the New England coast and New York Bay.
1527 Troops of the Holy Roman Empire attack Rome, imprison Pope Clement VII—the end of the Italian Renaissance. Castiglione writes *The Courtier.* The Medici expelled from Florence.
1532 Pizarro marches from Panama to Peru, kills the Inca chieftain, Atahualpa, of Peru (1533). Machiavelli's *Prince* published posthumously.
1535 Reformation begins as Henry VIII makes himself head of English Church after being excommunicated by Pope. Sir Thomas More executed as traitor for refusal to acknowledge king's religious authority. Jacques Cartier sails up the St. Lawrence River, basis of French claims to Canada.
1536 Henry VIII executes second wife, Anne Boleyn. John Calvin establishes Presbyterian form of Protestantism in Switzerland, writes *Institutes of the Christian Religion.* Danish and Norwegian Reformations. Michelangelo's *Last Judgment.*
1541 John Knox leads Reformation in Scotland, establishes Presbyterian church (1560).
1543 Publication of *On the Revolution of Heavenly Bodies* by Polish scholar Nicolaus Copernicus—giving his theory that the earth revolves around the sun.
1545 Council of Trent to meet intermittently until 1563 to define Catholic dogma and doctrine, reiterate papal authority.
1547 Ivan IV ("the Terrible") crowned as Czar of Russia, begins conquest of Astrakhan and Kazan (1552), battles nobles (boyars) for power (1564), kills his son (1580), dies, and is succeeded by a son who gives power to Boris Godunov (1584).
1553 Roman Catholicism restored in England by Queen Mary I, who rules until 1558. Religious radical Michael Servetus burned as heretic in Geneva by order of John Calvin.
1554 Benvenuto Cellini completes the bronze *Perseus.*
1556 Akbar the Great becomes Mogul emperor of India, conquers Afghanistan (1581), continues wars of conquest (until 1605).
1558 Queen Elizabeth I ascends the throne (rules to 1603). Restores Protestantism, establishes state Church of England (Anglicanism). Renaissance will reach height in England—Shakespeare, Marlowe, Spenser.
1561 Persecution of Huguenots in France stopped by Edict of Orleans. French religious wars begin again with massacre of Huguenots at Vassy. St. Bartholomew's Day Massacre—thousands of Huguenots murdered (1572). Amnesty granted (1573). Persecution continues periodically until Edict of Nantes (1598) gives Huguenots religious freedom (until 1685).
1568 Protestant Netherlands revolts against Catholic Spain; independence will be acknowledged by Spain in 1648. High point of Dutch Renaissance —painters Rubens, Van Dyck, Hals, and Rembrandt.
1570 Japan permits visits of foreign ships. Queen Elizabeth I excommunicated by Pope. Turks attack Cyprus and war on Venice. Turkish fleet defeated at Battle of Lepanto by Spanish and Italian fleets (1571). Peace of Constantinople (1572) ends Turkish attacks on Europe.
1580 Francis Drake returns to England after circumnavigating the globe. Knighted by Queen Elizabeth I (1581). Montaigne's *Essays* published.
1583 William of Orange rules The Netherlands; assassinated on orders of Philip II of Spain (1584).

Benvenuto Cellini, *Florentine sculptor* (1500–1571)
Nostradamus, *French astrologer* (1503–1566)
John Knox, *Scottish church reformer* (1505–1572)
St. Francis Xavier, *Jesuit missionary* (1506–1552)
John Calvin, *Swiss theologian* (1509–1564)
Giorgio Vasari, *Italian art historian* (1511–1574)
Andreas Vesalius, *Dutch anatomist* (1515–1564)
Andrea Palladio, *Italian architect* (1518–1580)
Tintoretto (Jacopo Robusti), *Italian painter* (1518–1594)
Pieter Brueghel (the Elder), *Dutch painter* (1520–1569)
Pierre de Ronsard, *French poet* (1524–1585)
Giovanni Palestrina, *Italian composer* (1526–1594)
Paolo Veronese, *Italian painter* (1528–1588)
Queen Elizabeth, *English ruler* (1533?–1603)
Michel de Montaigne, *French author* (1533–1592)
El Greco, *Spanish-Greek painter* (1542–1614)
Tycho Brahe, *Danish astronomer* (1546–1601)
Miguel de Cervantes, *Spanish writer* (1547–1616)
Giordano Bruno, *Italian philosopher* (1548–1600)
Sir Walter Raleigh, *English courtier* (1552–1618)
Edmund Spenser, *English poet* (1552–1599)
Giovanni Gabrieli, *Italian composer* (c.1557–1612)
Francis Bacon, *English philosopher* (1561–1626)
Christopher Marlowe, *English dramatist* (1564–1593)
Galileo Galilei, *Italian scientist* (1564–1642)
William Shakespeare, *English dramatist and poet* (1564–1616)
Michelangelo da Caravaggio, *Italian painter* (c.1565–1609)
Claudio Monteverdi, *Italian composer* (1567–1643)
Johannes Kepler, *German astronomer* (1571–1630)
John Donne, *English poet* (1573–1631)
Inigo Jones, *English architect* (1573–1652)
Ben Jonson, *English dramatist* (1573–1637)
Peter Paul Rubens, *Flemish painter* (1577–1652)
William Harvey, *English physician and anatomist* (1578–1657)

1587 Mary, Queen of Scots, executed for treason by order of Queen Elizabeth I. Monteverdi's *First Book of Madrigals.*

1588 Defeat of the Spanish Armada by English. Henry, King of Navarre and Protestant leader, recognized as Henry IV, first Bourbon king of France. Converts to Roman Catholicism in **1593** in attempt to end religious wars.

1590 Henry IV enters Paris, wars on Spain **(1595)**, marries Maria de Medici **(1600)**, assassinated **(1610)**. Spenser's *The Faerie Queen,* El Greco's *St. Jerome.* Galileo's experiments with falling objects.

1598 Boris Godunov becomes Russian Czar. Tycho Brahe describes his astronomical experiments.

1600 Giordano Bruno burned as a heretic. Ieyasu rules Japan, moves capital to Edo (Tokyo). Shakespeare's *Hamlet* begins his most productive decade. English East India Company established to develop overseas trade.

1607 Jamestown, Virginia, established—first permanent English colony on American mainland.

1609 Samuel de Champlain establishes French colony of Quebec.

1611 Gustavus Adolphus elected King of Sweden. King James Version of the Bible published in England. Rubens paints his *Descent from the Cross.*

1614 John Napier discovers logarithms.

1618 Start of the Thirty Years' War (to **1648**)—Protestant revolt against Catholic oppression; Denmark, Sweden, and France will invade Germany in later phases of war. Kepler proposes his Third Law of planetary motion.

1620 Pilgrims, after three-month voyage in *Mayflower,* land at Plymouth Rock. Francis Bacon's *Novum Organum.*

1633 Inquisition forces Galileo to recant his belief in Copernican theory.

1642 English Civil War. Cavaliers, supporters of Charles I, against Roundheads, parliamentary forces. Oliver Cromwell defeats Royalists **(1646)**. Parliament demands reforms. Charles I offers concessions, brought to trial **(1648)**, beheaded **(1649)**. Cromwell becomes Lord Protector **(1653)**. Rembrandt paints his *Night Watch.*

1644 End of Ming Dynasty in China—Manchus come to power. Descartes' *Principles of Philosophy.* John Milton's *Areopagitica* on the freedom of the press.

1648 End of the Thirty Years' War. German population about half of what it was in **1618** because of war and pestilence.

1658 Cromwell dies; his son, Richard, resigns and Puritan government collapses.

1660 English Parliament calls for the restoration of the monarchy; invites Charles II to return from France.

1661 Charles II is crowned King of England. Louis XIV begins personal rule as absolute monarch; starts to build Versailles.

1664 British take New Amsterdam from the Dutch. English limit "Nonconformity" with re-established Anglican Church. Isaac Newton's experiments with gravity.

1665 Great Plague in London kills 75,000.

1666 Great Fire of London. Molière's *Misanthrope.*

1683 War of European powers against the Turks (to **1699**). Vienna withstands three-month Turkish siege; high point of Turkish advance in Europe.

Frans Hals, *Dutch painter* (1581–1666)

Phineas Fletcher, *English dramatist* (1582–1650)

Francis Beaumont, *English dramatist* (1584–1616)

Cardinal Richelieu, *French prelate* (1585–1642)

Thomas Hobbes, *English philosopher* (1588–1679)

John Winthrop, *first governor of Massachusetts* (1588–1649)

Robert Herrick, *English poet* (1591–1674)

Johann Amos Comenius, *Moravian educational reformer* (1592–1670)

Peter Stuyvesant, *Dutch administrator in America* (1592–1672)

George Herbert, *English poet* (1593–1633)

Izaak Walton, *English biographer* (1593–1683)

Nicola Amati, *Italian violin maker* (1594–1684)

Nicolas Poussin, *French painter* (1594–1665)

Pocahontas, *Indian princess* (1595–1617)

René Descartes, *French philosopher* (1596–1650)

Oliver Cromwell, *English general and statesman* (1599–1658)

Anthony Van Dyck, *Flemish painter* (1599–1641)

Diego Velázquez, *Spanish painter* (1599–1660)

Pedro Calderón de la Barca, *Spanish dramatist* (1600–1681)

Roger Williams, *American religious leader* (1604–1683)

Pierre Corneille, *French dramatist* (1606–1684)

Rembrandt van Rijn, *Dutch painter* (1606–1669)

THE FOUNDING OF THE AMERICAN NATION

Colonization of America begins: Jamestown, Va. **(1607)**; Pilgrims in Plymouth **(1620)**; Massachusetts Bay Colony **(1630)**; New Netherland founded by Dutch West India Company **(1623)**, captured by English **(1664)**. Delaware established by Swedish trading company **(1638)**, absorbed later by Penn family. Proprietorships by royal grants to Lord Baltimore (Maryland, **1632**); Captain John Mason (New Hampshire, **1635**); Sir William Berkeley and Sir George Carteret (New Jersey, **1663**); friends of Charles II (the Carolinas, **1663**); William Penn (Pennsylvania, **1682**); James Oglethorpe and others (Georgia, **1732**).

Increasing conflict between colonists and Britain on western frontier because of royal edict limiting western expansion **(1763)**, and regulation of colonial trade and increased taxation of colonies (Writs of Assistance allow search for illegal shipments, **1761**; Sugar Act, **1764**; Currency Act, **1764**; Stamp Act, **1765**; Quartering Act, **1765**; Duty Act, **1767**.) Boston Massacre **(1770)**. Lord North attempts conciliation **(1770)**. Boston Tea Party **(1773)**, followed by punitive measures passed by Parliament—the "Intolerable Acts."

First Continental Congress **(1774)** sends "Declaration of Rights and Grievances" to King, urges colonies to form Continental Association. Paul Revere's Ride and Lexington and

Concord battle between Massachusetts minutemen and British **(1775)**.

Second Continental Congress **(1775)**, while sending "olive branch" to the king, begins to raise army, appoints Washington commander-in-chief, and seeks alliance with France. Some colonial legislatures urge their delegates to vote for independence. Declaration of Independence **(July 4, 1776)**.

Major Battles of the Revolutionary War: *Long Island:* Howe defeats Putnam's division of Washington's Army in Brooklyn Heights, but Americans escape across East River **(1776)**. *Trenton and Princeton:* Washington defeats Hessians at Trenton, British at Princeton, winters at Morristown **(1776–77)**. Howe winters in Philadelphia; Washington at Valley Forge **(1777–78)**. Burgoyne surrenders British army to General Gates at *Saratoga* **(1777)**.

France recognizes American independence **(1778)**. The War moves south: Savannah captured by British **(1778)**; Charleston occupied **(1780)**; Americans fight successful guerrilla actions under Marion, Pickens, and Sumter. In the West, George Rogers Clark attacks Forts Kaskaskia and Vincennes **(1778–1779)**, defeating British in the region. Cornwallis surrenders at *Yorktown,* Virginia **(Oct. 19, 1781)**. By **1782**, Britain is eager for peace because of conflicts with European nations. *Peace of Paris* **(1783)**: Britain recognizes American independence.

1685 James II succeeds Charles II in England, calls for freedom of conscience **(1687)**. Protestants fear restoration of Catholicism and demand "Glorious Revolution." William of Orange invited to England and James II escapes to France **(1688)**. William III and his wife, Mary, crowned. In France, Edict of Nantes of 1598, granting freedom of worship to Huguenots (French Protestants), is revoked by Louis XIV; thousands of Protestants flee.

1689 Peter the Great becomes Czar of Russia—attempts to westernize nation and build Russia as military power. Defeats Charles XII of Sweden at Poltava **(1709)**. Beginning of the French and Indian Wars (to 1763), campaigns in America linked to a series of wars between France and England for domination of Europe.

1690 William III of England defeats former King James II and Irish rebels at Battle of the Boyne in Ireland. John Locke's *Human Understanding.*

Jan Vermeer, *Dutch painter* (1632–1675)

Baruch Spinoza, *Dutch philosopher* (1632–1677)

Christopher Wren, *English architect* (1632–1723)

Samuel Pepys, *English diarist* (1633–1703)

Jean Baptiste Lully, *French composer* (1639–1687)

Jean Racine, *French dramatist* (1639–1699)

Sir Isaac Newton, *English philosopher and mathematician* (1642–1727)

William Penn, *founder of Pennsylvania* (1644–1718)

Antonio Stradivari, *Italian violin maker* (1644–1737)

Gottfried W. von Leibniz, *German scientist* (1646–1716)

Arcangelo Corelli, *Italian composer* (1653–1713)

Jacques Bernoulli, *Swiss scientist* (1654–1705)

Edmund Halley, *English astronomer* (1656–1742)

Henry Purcell, *English composer* (1658–1695)

Daniel Defoe, *English author* (1659–1731)

Alessandro Scarlatti, *Italian composer* (1659–1725)

Cotton Mather, *Massachusetts churchman* (1663–1728)

François Couperin, *French composer* (1668–1733)

Giovanni Battista Vico, *Italian philosopher* (1668–1744)

William Congreve, *English dramatist* (1670–1730)

Peter the Great, *Russian czar* (1672–1725)

Antonio Vivaldi, *Italian composer* (1678–1741)

George Phillip Telemann, *German composer* (1681–1767)

Jean Philippe Rameau, *French composer* (1683–1764)

Jean Antoine Watteau, *French painter* (1684–1721)

J.S. Bach, *German composer* (1685–1750)

George Frederick Handel, *German-English composer* (1685–1759)

Domenico Scarlatti, *Italian composer* (1685–1757)

Gabriel Fahrenheit, *German physicist* (1686–1736)

Alexander Pope, *English poet* (1688–1744)

Emanuel Swedenborg, *Swedish mystic* (1688–1772)

Baron de Montesquieu, *French philosopher* (1689–1755)

François de Voltaire, *French philosopher* (1694–1778)

Canaletto (Antonio Canale), *Italian painter* (1697–1768)

William Hogarth, *English painter* (1697–1764)

John Milton, *English poet* (1608–1674)

François de La Rouchefoucauld, *French author* (1613–1680)

Henry More, *English philosopher* (1614–1687)

Cyrano de Bergerac, *French poet* (1619–1655)

Andrew Marvell, *English poet* (1621–1678)

Molière (Jean-Baptiste Poquelin), *French dramatist* (1622–1673)

Blaise Pascal, *French philosopher* (1623–1662)

Robert Boyle, *English scientist* (1627–1691)

John Bunyan, *English author* (1628–1688)

John Dryden, *English dramatist* (1631–1700)

John Locke, *English philosopher* (1631–1704)

Luca Giordano, *Italian painter* (1632–1705)

Anton van Leeuwenhoek, *Dutch zoologist* (1632–1723)

1701 War of the Spanish Succession begins—the last of Louis XIV's wars for domination of the continent. The Peace of Utrecht **(1714)** will end the conflict and mark the rise of the British Empire. Called Queen Anne's War in America, it ends with the British taking New Foundland, Acadia, and Hudson's Bay Territory from France, and Gibraltar and Minorca from Spain.

1704 Deerfield (Conn.) Massacre of English colonists by French and Indians. Bach's first cantata. Jonathan Swift's *Tale of a Tub. Boston News Letter* —first newspaper in America.

1707 United Kingdom of Great Britain formed—England, Wales, and Scotland joined by parliamentary Act of Union.

1729 J. S. Bach's *St. Matthew's Passion.* Isaac Newton's *Principia* translated from Latin into English.

1735 John Peter Zenger, New York editor, acquitted of libel in New York, establishing press freedom.

1740 Capt. Vitus Bering, Dane employed by Russia, discovers Alaska.

1746 British defeat Scots under Stuart Pretender Prince Charles at Culloden Moor. Last battle fought on British soil.

1751 Publication of the *Encyclopédie* begins in France, the "bible" of the Enlightenment.

1755 Samuel Johnson's *Dictionary* first published. Great earthquake in Lisbon, Portugal—over 60,000 die.

1756 Seven Years' War (called French and Indian War in America) (to 1763), in which Britain and Prussia defeat France, Spain, Austria, and Russia.

François Boucher, *French painter* (1703–1770)

Jonathan Edwards, *American theologian* (1703–1758)

John Wesley, *founder of Methodism* (1703–1791)

Benjamin Franklin, *American statesman* (1706–1790)

Henry Fielding, *English novelist* (1707–1754)

Leonhard Euler, *Swiss mathematician* (1707–1783)

Linnaeus (Carl von Linné), *Swedish botanist* (1707–1778)

Samuel Johnson, *English author* (1709–1784)

William Boyce, *English composer* (1710–1779)

Giovanni Pergolesi, *Italian composer* (1710–1736)

David Hume, *Scottish philosopher* (1711–1776)

France loses North American colonies; Spain cedes Florida to Britain in exchange for Cuba. In India, over 100 British prisoners die in "Black Hole of Calcutta."

1757 Beginning of British Empire in India as Robert Clive, British commander, defeats Nawab of Bengal at Plassey.

1759 British capture Quebec from French. Voltaire's *Candide*. Haydn's *Symphony No. 1*.

1762 Catherine II ("the Great") becomes Czarina of Russia. J. J. Rousseau's *Social Contract*. Mozart tours Europe as six-year-old prodigy.

1769 Sir William Arkwright patents a spinning machine—an early step in the Industrial Revolution.

1772 Joseph Priestley and Daniel Rutherford independently discover nitrogen. Partition of Poland—in **1772, 1793,** and **1795,** Austria, Prussia, and Russia divide land and people of Poland, end its independence.

1775 The American Revolution *(see* "The Founding of the American Nation"). James Watt invents the steam engine. Priestley discovers hydrochloric and sulfuric acids.

1776 Adam Smith's *Wealth of Nations.* Edward Gibbon's *Decline and Fall of the Roman Empire.* Thomas Paine's *Common Sense.* Fragonard's *Washerwoman.* Mozart's *Haffner Serenade.*

1778 Capt. James Cook discovers Hawaii. Franz Mesmer uses hypnotism.

1781 Immanuel Kant's *Critique of Pure Reason.* Herschel discovers Uranus.

1783 End of Revolutionary War *(see* special material on "The Founding of the American Nation"). William Blake's poems. Beethoven's first printed works.

1784 Crimea annexed by Russia. John Wesley's *Deed of Declaration,* the basic work of Methodism.

1785 Russians settle Aleutian Islands.

1787 The Constitution of the United States signed. Lavoisier's work on chemical nomenclature. Mozart's *Don Giovanni.*

1788 French *Parlement* presents grievances to Louis XVI who agrees to convening of Estates-General in **1789**—not called since **1613.** Goethe's *Egmont.* Laplace's *Laws of the Planetary System.*

1789 French Revolution *(see* special material on the "French Revolution"). In U.S., George Washington elected President with all 69 votes of the Electoral College, takes oath of office in New York City. Vice President: John Adams. Secretary of State: Thomas Jefferson. Secretary of Treasury: Alexander Hamilton.

Jean-Jacques Rousseau, *French philosopher* (1712–1778)

Denis Diderot, *French encyclopedist* (1713–1784)

Laurance Sterne, *English novelist* (1713–1768)

K.P.E. Bach, *German composer* (1714–1788)

David Garrick, *English actor* (1717–1779)

Horace Walpole, *English statesman and novelist* (1717–1797)

Thomas Chippendale, *English artisan* (1718?–1779)

Bernardo Canaletto, *Italian painter* (1720–1780)

Giambattista Piranesi, *Italian artist* (1720–1778)

Baron von Münchhausen, *German anecdotist* (1720–1797)

Mme. de Pompadour, *French courtesan* (1721–1764)

Tobias Smollet, *English novelist* (1721–1771)

Samuel Adams, *American patriot* (1722–1803)

Joshua Reynolds, *English painter* (1723–1792)

Adam Smith, *English economist* (1723–1790)

Immanuel Kant, *German philosopher* (1724–1804)

Giovanni Casanova, *Italian adventurer* (1725–1798)

Thomas Gainsborough, *English painter* (1727–1788)

Oliver Goldsmith, *English writer* (1728–1774)

Catherine II (Catherine the Great), *Russian empress* (1729–1796)

Edmund Burke, *English statesman* (1729–1797)

William Cowper, *English poet* (1731–1800)

George Washington, *first American President* (1732–1799)

J.H. Fragonard, *French painter* (1732–1800)

Josef Haydn, *Austrian composer* (1732–1809)

Franz Anton Mesmer, *Austrian hypnotist* (1733–1815)

Joseph Priestley, *English scientist* (1733–1804)

John Adams, *American President* (1735–1826)

Daniel Boone, *American frontiersman* (1735–1820)

Patrick Henry, *American patriot* (1736–1799)

James Watt, *Scottish inventor* (1736–1819)

John S. Copley, *American painter* (1737–1815)

Edward Gibbon, *English historian* (1737–1794)

Thomas Paine, *American author and patriot* (1737–1809)

William Herschel, *English astronomer* (1738–1822)

Prince Potemkin, *Russian statesman* (1739–1791)

James Boswell, *Scottish writer* (1740–1795)

Marquis de Sade, *French libertine and writer* (1741–1814)

Benedict Arnold, *American general and traitor* (1741–1801)

Luigi Boccherini, *Italian composer* (1743–1805)

Antoine Lavoisier, *French chemist* (1743–1794)

Jean-Paul Marat, *French revolutionist* (1743–1793)

Thomas Jefferson, *American President* (1743–1826)

Jean-Baptiste de Lamark, *French scientist* (1744–1829)

Alessandro Volta, *Italian scientist* (1745–1827)

Francisco de Goya, *Spanish painter* (1746–1828)

Johann Pestalozzi, *Swiss educator* (1746–1827)

John Paul Jones, *American naval officer* (1747–1792)

Jeremy Bentham *English economist* (1748–1832)

Jacques David, *French painter* (1748–1825)

Count Casimir Pulaski, *Polish-American patriot* (1748–1779)

Johann Wolfgang von Goethe, *German writer* (1749–1832)

FRENCH REVOLUTION (1789–1799)

Revolution begins when Third Estate (Commons) delegates swear not to disband until France has a constitution. Paris mob storms Bastille, symbol of royal power (July 14, 1789). National Assembly votes for Constitution, Declaration of the Rights of Man, a limited monarchy, and other reforms (1789–90). Legislative Assembly elected, Revolutionary Commune formed, and French Republic proclaimed (1792). War of the First Coalition—Austria, Prussia, Britain, Netherlands, and Spain fight to restore French nobility (1792–97). Start of series of wars between France and European powers that will last, almost without interruption, for 23 years. Louis XVI and Marie Antoinette executed. Committee of Public Safety begins Reign of Terror as political control measure. Interfactional rivalry leads to mass killings. Danton and Robespierre executed. Third French Constitution sets up Directory government (1795).

1790 H.M.S. *Bounty* mutineers settle on Pitcairn Island. Aloisio Galvani experiments on electrical stimulation of the muscles. Philadelphia temporary capital of U.S. as Congress votes to establish new capital on Potomac. U.S. population about 3,929,000, including 698,000 slaves. Lavoisier formulates *Table of 31 chemical elements.*

1791 U.S. Bill of Rights ratified. Boswell's *Life of Johnson.*

1794 Kosciusko's uprising in Poland quelled by the Russians. In U.S., Whiskey Rebellion in Pennsylvania as farmers object to liquor taxes. U.S. Navy and Post Office Department established.

1796 Napoleon Bonaparte, French general, defeats Austrians. In the U.S., Washington's Farewell Address (**Sept. 17**); John Adams elected President; Thomas Jefferson, Vice President. Edward Jenner introduces smallpox vaccination.

1798 Napoleon extends French conquests to Rome and Egypt.

1799 Napoleon leads coup that overthrows Directory, becomes First Consul —one of three who rule France.

James Monroe, *American President* (1758–1831)

Horatio Nelson, *English admiral* (1758–1805)

Maximilien de Robespierre, *French revolutionist* (1758–1794)

Noah Webster, *American lexicographer* (1758–1843)

Robert Burns, *Scottish poet* (1759–1796)

Katsuhika Hokusai, *Japanese artist* (1760–1849)

Luigi Cherubini, *Italian composer* (1760–1842)

Robert Fulton, *American inventor* (1765–1815)

Eli Whitney, *American inventor* (1765–1825)

John Dalton, *English chemist* (1766–1844)

T. R. Malthus, *English economist* (1766–1834)

John Quincy Adams, *American President* (1767–1848)

Andrew Jackson, *American President* (1767–1845)

Jacques Lafitte, *French pirate* (1767–1844)

Tecumseh, *American Indian chief* (1768?–1813)

Napoleon Bonaparte, *French emperor* (1769–1821)

Duke of Wellington, *English general* (1769–1852)

Ludwig van Beethoven, *German composer* (1770–1827)

G. W. F. Hegel, *German philosopher* (1770–1831)

William Wordsworth, *English writer* (1770–1850)

Robert Owen, *English social reformer* (1771–1858)

Walter Scott, *Scottish novelist* (1771–1832)

Friedrich von Schlegel, *German philosopher* (1772–1829)

Prince K. von Metternich, *Austrian statesman* (1773–1859)

Jane Austen, *English novelist* (1775–1817)

J. W. Turner, *English painter* (1775–1851)

John Constable, *English painter* (1776–1837)

Henry Clay, *American statesman* (1777–1852)

Heinrich von Kleist, *German poet* (1777–1811)

Karl von Clausewitz, *German military strategist* (1780–1831)

J.A. Ingres, *French painter* (1780–1867)

Nicolo Paganini, *Italian composer* (1782–1840)

Daniel Webster, *American statesman* (1782–1852)

Simón Bolívar, *Latin American patriot* (1783–1830)

Washington Irving, *American writer* (1783–1859)

Stendhal (Marie Henri Beyle), *French novelist* (1783–1842)

J. J. Audubon, *American naturalist* (1785–1851)

James Madison, *American President* (1751–1836)

Richard Brinsley Sheridan, *Irish dramatist* (1751–1816)

Fanny Burney, *English writer* (1752–1840)

Betsy Ross, *American flagmaker* (1752–1836)

C. de Talleyrand-Périgord, *French statesman* (1754–1838)

Marie Antoinette, *French queen* (1755–1793)

Alexander Hamilton, *American statesman* (1755–1804)

Gilbert Stuart, *American painter* (1755–1828)

Aaron Burr, *American statesman* (1756–1836)

Wolfgang Amadeus Mozart, *Austrian composer* (1756–1791)

William Blake, *English poet* (1757–1827)

Marquis de Lafayette, *French general in America* (1757–1834)

1800 Napoleon conquers Italy, firmly establishes himself as First Consul in France. In the U.S., Federal Government moves to Washington. Robert Owen's social reforms in England. William Herschel discovers infrared rays. Alessandro Volta produces electricity.

1801 Austria makes temporary peace with France. United Kingdom of Great Britain and Ireland established with one monarch and one parliament; Catholics excluded from voting.

1803 U.S. negotiates Louisiana Purchase from France: For $15 million, U.S. doubles its domain, increasing its territory by 827,000 sq mi. (2,144,500 sq km), from Mississippi River to Rockies and from Gulf of Mexico to British North America.

1804 Haiti declares independence from France; first black nation to gain freedom from European colonial rule. Napoleon proclaims himself emperor of France, systematizes French law under *Code Napoleon.* In the U.S., Alexander Hamilton is mortally wounded in duel with Aaron Burr. Lewis and Clark expedition begins exploration of what is now northwestern U.S.

1805 Lord Nelson defeats the French-Spanish fleets in the Battle of Trafalgar. Napoleon victorious over Austrian and Russian forces at the Battle of Austerlitz.

1807 Robert Fulton makes first successful steamboat trip on *Clermont* between New York City and Albany.

Davy Crockett, *American frontiersman* (1786–1836)

Carl Maria von Weber, *German composer* (1786–1826)

Louis Daguerre, *French photographic pioneer* (1787–1851)

Lord Byron, *English poet* (1788–1824)

Arthur Schopenhauer, *German philosopher* (1788–1860)

James Fenimore Cooper, *American writer* (1789–1851)

Michael Faraday, *English physicist* (1791–1867)

Samuel F. B. Morse, *American inventor* (1791–1872)

1808	French armies occupy Rome and Spain, extending Napoleon's empire. Britain begins aiding Spanish guerrillas against Napoleon in Peninsular War. In the U.S., Congress bars importation of slaves. Beethoven's *Fifth* and *Sixth Symphonies* performed.	Percy Bysshe Shelley, *English poet* (1792–1822)
1812	Napoleon's Grand Army invades Russia in June. Forced to retreat in winter, most of Napoleon's 600,000 men are lost. In the U.S., war with Britain declared over freedom of the seas for U.S. vessels. U.S.S. *Constitution* sinks British frigate. *(See* special material on the "War of 1812.")	Gioacchino Rossini, *Italian composer* (1792–1868)
1814	French defeated by allies (Britain, Austria, Russia, Prussia, Sweden, and Portugal) in War of Liberation. Napoleon exiled to Elba, off Italian coast. Bourbon King Louis XVIII takes French throne. George Stephenson builds first practical steam locomotive.	Sam Houston, *Texas political leader* (1793–1863)
1815	Napoleon returns: "Hundred Days" begin. Napoleon defeated by Wellington at Waterloo, banished again to St. Helena in South Atlantic. Congress of Vienna: victorious allies change the map of Europe.	John Keats, *English poet* (1795–1821)
1817	Simón Bolívar establishes independent Venezuela, as Spain loses hold on South American countries. Bolívar named President of Colombia **(1819)**. Peru, Guatemala, Panama, and Santo Domingo proclaim independence from Spain **(1821)**.	Thomas Carlyle, *British historian* (1795–1881)
1820	Missouri Compromise—Missouri admitted as slave state but slavery barred in rest of Louisiana Purchase north of 36°30' N.	Heinrich Heine, *German poet* (1797–1856)
1822	Greeks proclaim a republic and independence from Turkey. Turks invade Greece. Russia declares war on Turkey **(1828)**. Greece also aided by France and Britain. War ends and Turks recognize Greek independence **(1829)**. Brazil becomes independent of Portugal. Schubert's *Eighth Symphony* ("The Unfinished").	Ando Hiroshige, *Japanese painter* (1797–1858)
1823	U.S. Monroe Doctrine warns European nations not to interfere in Western Hemisphere.	Franz Schubert, *Austrian composer* (1797–1828)
1824	Mexico becomes a republic, three years after declaring independence from Spain. Beethoven's *Ninth Symphony*.	Adam Mickiewicz, *Polish poet* (1798–1855)
1825	First passenger-carrying railroad in England.	Auguste Comte, *French philosopher* (1798–1857)
1830	French invade Algeria. Louis Philippe becomes "Citizen King" as revolution forces Charles X to abdicate. Mormon church formed in U.S. by Joseph Smith.	Ferdinand Delacroix, *French painter* (1798–1863)
1831	Polish revolt against Russia fails. Belgium separates from the Netherlands. In U.S., Nat Turner leads unsuccessful slave rebellion.	Honoré de Balzac, *French novelist* (1799–1850)
1833	Slavery abolished in British Empire.	Aleksander Pushkin, *Russian poet* (1799–1837)
1834	Charles Babbage invents "analytical engine," precursor of computer. McCormick patents reaper.	John Henry Newman, *English prelate* (1801–1890)
1836	Boer farmers start "Great Trek"—Natal, Transvaal, and Orange Free State founded in South Africa. Mexican army besieges Texans in Alamo. Entire garrison, including Davy Crockett and Jim Bowie, wiped out. Texans gain independence from Mexico after winning Battle of San Jacinto. Dickens's *Pickwick Papers*.	Brigham Young, *Mormon leader* (1801–1877)
1837	Victoria becomes Queen of Great Britain. Mob kills Elijah P. Lovejoy, Illinois abolitionist publisher.	Lajos Kossuth, *Hungarian patriot* (1802–1894)
1839	First Opium War (to **1842**) between Britain and China, over importation of drug into China.	Alexander Dumas, père, *French novelist* (1802–1870)
1840	Lower and Upper Canada united.	Victor Hugo, *French novelist* (1802–1885)
1841	U.S. President Harrison dies **(April 4)** one month after inauguration; John Tyler becomes first Vice President to succeed to Presidency.	Ralph Waldo Emerson, *American philosopher* (1803–1882)
1844	Democratic convention calls for annexation of Texas and acquisition of Oregon ("Fifty-four-forty-or-fight"). Five Chinese ports opened to U.S. ships. Samuel F. B. Morse patents telegraph.	Hector Berlioz, *French composer* (1803–1869)
1845	Congress adopts joint resolution for annexation of Texas.	Benjamin Disraeli, *British statesman* (1804–1881)
1846	Failure of potato crop causes famine in Ireland. U.S. declares war on Mexico. California and New Mexico annexed by U.S. Brigham Young leads Mormons to Great Salt Lake. W. T. Morton uses ether as anesthetic. Sewing machine patented by Elias Howe.	Nathaniel Hawthorne, *American novelist* (1804–1864)
1848	Revolt in Paris: Louis Philippe abdicates; Louis Napoleon elected President of French Republic. Revolutions in Vienna, Venice, Berlin, Milan, Rome, and Warsaw. Put down by royal troops in **1848–49**. U.S.-Mexico War ends; Mexico cedes claims to Texas, California, Arizona, New Mexico, Utah, Nevada. U.S. treaty with Britain sets Oregon Territory boundary at 49th parallel. Karl Marx and Friedrich Engels' *Communist Manifesto*.	George Sand, *French writer* (1804–1876)
1849	California gold rush begins.	Giuseppe Mazzini, *Italian patriot* (1805–1872)
		Hans Christian Andersen, *Danish writer* (1805–1875)
		Alexis de Tocqueville, *French writer* (1805–1859)
		Elizabeth Barrett Browning, *English poet* (1806–1861)
		John Stuart Mill, *English philosopher* (1806–1873)
		Giuseppe Garibaldi, *Italian patriot* (1807–1882)
		Henry Wadsworth Longfellow, *American poet* (1807–1882)
		Honoré Daumier, *French artist* (1808–1879)

WAR OF 1812

British interference with American trade, impressment of American seamen, and "War Hawks" drive for western expansion lead to war. American attacks on Canada foiled; U.S. Commodore Perry wins battle of Lake Erie **(1813)**. British capture and burn Washington **(1814)** but fail to take Fort McHenry at Baltimore. Andrew Jackson repulses assault on New Orleans after treaty of Ghent ends war **(1815)**. War settles little but strengthens U.S. as independent nation.

Year	Event	Person
1850	Henry Clay opens great debate on slavery, warns South against secession.	Abraham Lincoln, *American president* (1809–1865)
1851	Herman Melville's *Moby Dick*. Harriet Beecher Stowe's *Uncle Tom's Cabin*.	Nicolai Gogol, *Russian writer* (1809–1852)
1852	South African Republic established. Louis Napoleon proclaims himself Napoleon III ("Second Empire").	Edgar Allan Poe, *American writer* (1809–1849)
1853	Crimean War begins as Turkey declares war on Russia. Commodore Perry reaches Tokyo.	Alfred, Lord Tennyson, *English poet* (1809–1892)

1850 Henry Clay opens great debate on slavery, warns South against secession.

1851 Herman Melville's *Moby Dick*. Harriet Beecher Stowe's *Uncle Tom's Cabin*.

1852 South African Republic established. Louis Napoleon proclaims himself Napoleon III ("Second Empire").

1853 Crimean War begins as Turkey declares war on Russia. Commodore Perry reaches Tokyo.

1854 Britain and France join Turkey in war on Russia. In U.S., Kansas-Nebraska Act permits local option on slavery; rioting and bloodshed. Japanese allow American trade. Antislavery men in Michigan form Republican Party. Tennyson's *Charge of the Light Brigade*. Thoreau's *Walden*.

1855 Armed clashes in Kansas between pro- and anti- slavery forces. Florence Nightingale nurses wounded in Crimea. Walt Whitman's *Leaves of Grass*.

1856 Flaubert's *Madame Bovary*.

1857 Supreme Court, in Dred Scott decision, rules that a slave is not a citizen. Financial crisis in Europe and U.S. Great Mutiny (Sepoy Rebellion) begins in India. India placed under crown rule as a result.

1858 Pro-slavery constitution rejected in Kansas. Abraham Lincoln makes strong antislavery speech in Springfield, Ill.: " . . . this Government cannot endure permanently half slave and half free." Lincoln-Douglas debates. First trans-Atlantic telegraph cable completed by Cyrus W. Field.

1859 John Brown raids Harpers Ferry; is captured and hanged. Work begins on Suez Canal. Unification of Italy starts under leadership of Count Cavour, Sardinian premier. Joined by France in war against Austria. Edward Fitzgerald's *Rubaiyat of Omar Khayyam*. Charles Darwin's *Origin of Species*. J. S. Mill's *On Liberty*

1861 U.S. Civil War begins as attempts at compromise fail *(see* special material on "The Civil War"). Congress creates Colorado, Dakota, and Nevada territories; adopts income tax; Lincoln inaugurated. Serfs emancipated in Russia. Pasteur's theory of germs. Independent Kingdom of Italy proclaimed under Sardinian King Victor Emmanuel II.

1863 French capture Mexico City; proclaim Archduke Maximilian of Austria emperor.

1865 Lincoln fatally shot at Ford's Theater by John Wilkes Booth. Vice President Johnson sworn as successor. Booth caught and dies of gunshot wounds; four conspirators are hanged. Joseph Lister begins antiseptic surgery. Gregor Mendel's Law of Heredity. Lewis Carroll's *Alice's Adventures in Wonderland*.

1866 Alfred Nobel invents dynamite. Seven Weeks' War: Austria defeated by Prussia and Italy.

1867 Austria-Hungary Dual Monarchy established. French leave Mexico; Maximilian executed. Dominion of Canada established. U.S. buys Alaska from Russia for $7,200,000. South African diamond field discovered. Volume I of Marx's *Das Kapital*. Strauss's *Blue Danube*.

1868 Revolution in Spain; Queen Isabella deposed, flees to France. In U.S., Fourteenth Amendment giving civil rights to blacks is ratified. Georgia under military government after legislature expels blacks.

Abraham Lincoln, *American president* (1809–1865)

Nicolai Gogol, *Russian writer* (1809–1852)

Edgar Allan Poe, *American writer* (1809–1849)

Alfred, Lord Tennyson, *English poet* (1809–1892)

William Ewart Gladstone, *British statesman* (1809–1898)

Charles Darwin, *English scientist* (1809–1882)

Felix Mendelssohn, *German composer* (1809–1847)

Louis Braille, *French inventor of touch alphabet for blind* (1809–1852)

Frédéric Chopin, *Polish composer* (1810–1849)

Robert Schumann, *German composer* (1810–1856)

Phineas T. Barnum, *American showman* (1810–1891)

Harriet Beecher Stowe, *American writer* (1811–1896)

William M. Thackeray, *English novelist* (1811–1863)

Franz Liszt, *Hungarian composer* (1811–1896)

Robert Browning, *English poet* (1812–1889)

Charles Dickens, *English novelist* (1812–1870)

Alfred Krupp, *German munitions magnate* (1812–1887)

Sören Kierkegaard, *Danish philosopher* (1813–1855)

Giuseppe Verdi, *Italian composer* (1813–1901)

Richard Wagner, *German composer* (1813–1883)

Otto von Bismarck, *Prussian statesman* (1815–1898)

Charlotte Brontë, *English writer* (1816–1855)

THE CIVIL WAR (1861–1865)
(The War Between the States or the War of the Rebellion)

Apart from the matter of slavery, the Civil War arose out of both the economic and political rivalry between an agrarian South and an industrial North and the issue of the right of states to secede from the Union.

1861 After South Carolina secedes (**Dec. 20, 1860**), Mississippi, Florida, Alabama, Georgia, Louisiana, and Texas follow, forming the Confederate States of America, with Jefferson Davis as president (**Jan.-March**). War begins as Confederates fire on Fort Sumter (**April 12**). Lincoln calls for 75,000 volunteers. Southern ports blockaded by superior Union naval forces. Virginia, Arkansas, Tennessee, and North Carolina secede to complete 11-state Confederacy. Union army advancing on Richmond repulsed at first Battle of Bull Run (**July**).

1862 Edwin M. Stanton named Secretary of War (**Jan.**). Grant wins first important Union victory in West, at Fort Donelson; Nashville falls (**Feb.**). Ironclads, Union's *Monitor* and Confederate's *Virginia* (*Merrimac*) duel at Hampton Roads (**March**). New Orleans falls to Union fleet under Farragut; city occupied (**April**). Grant's army escapes defeat at Shiloh. Memphis falls as Union gunboats control upper Mississippi (**June**). Confederate general Robert E. Lee victorious at second Battle of Bull Run (**Aug.**). Union army under McClellan halts Lee's attack on

Washington in the Battle of Antietam (**Sept.**). Lincoln removes McClellan for lack of aggressiveness. Burnside's drive on Richmond fails at Fredericksburg (**Dec.**). Union forces under Rosecrans chase Bragg through Tennessee; battle of Murfreesboro (**Oct.-Jan. 1863**).

1863 Lee defeats Hooker at Chancellorsville; "Stonewall" Jackson, Confederate general, dies (**May**). Confederate invasion of Pennsylvania stopped at Gettysburg by George Meade—Lee loses 20,000 men—the greatest battle of the War (**July**). It and the Union victory at Vicksburg mark the war's turning point. Union general George H. Thomas, the "Rock of Chickamauga," holds Bragg's forces on Georgia-Tennessee border (**Sept.**). Sherman, Hooker, and Thomas drive Bragg back to Georgia. Tennessee restored to the Union (**Nov.**).

1864 Ulysses S. Grant named commander-in-chief of Union forces (**March**). In the Wilderness campaign, Grant forces Lee's Army of Northern Virginia back toward Richmond (**May-June**). Sherman's Atlanta campaign and "march to the sea" (**May-Sept.**). Farragut's victory at Mobile Bay (**Aug.**). Hood's Confederate army defeated at Nashville. Sherman takes Savannah (**Dec.**).

1865 Sheridan defeats Confederates at Five Forks; Confederates evacuate Richmond (**April**). On **April 9**, Lee surrenders to Grant at Appomattox.

1869 First U.S. transcontinental rail route completed. James Fisk and Jay Gould attempt to control gold market causes Black Friday panic. Suez Canal opened. Mendeleev's periodic table of elements.

1870 Franco-Prussian War (to **1871**): Napoleon III capitulates at Sedan. Revolt in Paris; Third Republic proclaimed.

1871 France surrenders Alsace-Lorraine to Germany; war ends. German Empire proclaimed with Prussian King as Kaiser Wilhelm I. Fighting with Apaches begins in American West. Boss Tweed corruption exposed in New York. The Chicago Fire, with 250 deaths and $196-million damage. Stanley meets Livingston in Africa.

1872 Congress gives amnesty to most Confederates. Jules Verne's *Around the World in 80 Days*.

1873 Economic crisis in Europe. U.S. establishes gold standard.

1875 First Kentucky Derby.

1876 Sioux kill Gen. George A. Custer and 264 troopers at Little Big Horn River. Alexander Graham Bell patents the telephone.

1877 After Presidential election of **1876**, Electoral Commission gives disputed Electoral College votes to Rutherford B. Hayes despite Tilden's popular majority. Russo-Turkish war (ends in **1878** with power of Turkey in Europe broken). Reconstruction ends in the American South. Thomas Edison patents phonograph.

1878 Congress of Berlin revises Treaty of San Stefano ending Russo-Turkish War; makes extensive redivision of southeastern Europe. First commercial telephone exchange opened in New Haven, Conn.

1880 U.S.-China treaty allows U.S. to restrict immigration of Chinese labor.

1881 President Garfield fatally shot by assassin; Vice President Arthur succeeds him. Charles J. Guiteau convicted and executed (in **1882**).

1882 Terrorism in Ireland after land evictions. Britain invades and conquers Egypt. Germany, Austria, and Italy form Triple Alliance. In U.S., Congress adopts Chinese Exclusion Act. Rockefeller's Standard Oil Trust is first industrial monopoly. In Berlin, Robert Koch announces discovery of tuberculosis germ.

1883 Congress creates Civil Service Commission. Brooklyn Bridge and Metropolitan Opera House completed.

1885 British Gen. Charles G. "Chinese" Gordon killed at Khartoum in Egyptian Sudan.

1886 Bombing at Haymarket Square, Chicago, kills seven policemen and injures many others. Eight alleged anarchists accused—three imprisoned, one commits suicide, four hanged. (In **1893**, Illinois Governor Altgeld, critical of trial, pardons three survivors.) Statue of Liberty dedicated. Geronimo, Apache Indian chief, surrenders.

1887 Queen Victoria's Golden Jubilee. Sir Arthur Conan Doyle's first Sherlock Holmes story, "A Study in Scarlet."

1888 Historic March blizzard in Northeast U.S.—many perish, property damage exceeds $25 million. George Eastman's box camera (the Kodak). J.B. Dunlop invents pneumatic tire. Jack the Ripper murders in London.

1889 Second (Socialist) International founded in Paris. Indian Territory in Oklahoma opened to settlement. Thousands die in Johnstown, Pa., flood. Mark Twain's *A Connecticut Yankee in King Arthur's Court*.

1890 Congress votes Sherman Antitrust Act. Sitting Bull killed in Sioux uprising.

1892 Battle between steel strikers and Pinkerton guards at Homestead, Pa.; union defeated after militia intervenes. Silver mine strikers in Idaho fight non-union workers; U.S. troops dispatched. Diesel engine patented.

1894 Sino-Japanese War begins (ends in **1895** with China's defeat). In France, Capt. Alfred Dreyfus convicted on false treason charge (pardoned in **1906**). In U.S., Jacob S. Coxey of Ohio leads "Coxey's Army" of unemployed on Washington. Eugene V. Debs calls general strike of rail workers to support Pullman Company strikers; strike broken, Debs jailed for six months. Thomas A. Edison's kinetoscope given first public showing in New York City.

1895 X-rays discovered by German physicist, Wilhelm Roentgen.

1896 Supreme Court's *Plessy* v. *Ferguson* decision—"separate but equal"

Henry David Thoreau, *American writer* (1817–1862)

Ivan Turgenev, *Russian writer* (1818–1883)

Karl Marx, *German political philosopher* (1818–1883)

Queen Victoria, *British monarch* (1819–1901)

George Eliot, *English novelist* (1819–1880)

Walt Whitman, *American poet* (1819–1892)

Friedrich Engels, *German political philosopher* (1820–1895)

Florence Nightingale, *English nurse* (1820–1910)

Charles Baudelaire, *French poet* (1821–1867)

Feodor Dostoevsky, *Russian writer* (1821–1881)

Gustave Flaubert, *French novelist* (1821–1880)

Mary Baker Eddy, *founder of Christian Science* (1821–1910)

Ulysses S. Grant, *American President* (1822–1885)

Gregor Mendel, *Austrian scientist* (1822–1884)

Louis Pasteur, *French scientist* (1822–1895)

Alexandre Dumas, fils, *French writer* (1824–1895)

Johann Strauss, *Austrian "waltz king"* (1825–1899)

Stephen Foster, *American composer* (1826–1864)

Joseph Lister, *English surgeon* (1827–1912)

Henrik Ibsen, *Norwegian dramatist* (1828–1906)

Leo Tolstoi, *Russian novelist* (1828–1910)

Jules Verne, *French author* (1828–1905)

William Booth, *Salvation Army founder* (1829–1912)

Emily Dickinson, *American poet* (1830–1886)

James Clerk Maxwell, *Scottish astronomer and physicist* (1831–1879)

Louisa May Alcott, *American author* (1832–1888)

Horatio Alger, *American author* (1834–1899)

Lewis Carroll (Charles Lutwidge Dodgson), *English author* (1832–1898)

SPANISH-AMERICAN WAR (1898–1899)

War fires stoked by "jingo journalism" as American people support Cuban rebels against Spain. American business sees economic gain in Cuban trade and resources and American power zones in Latin America. Outstanding events: Submarine mine explodes U.S. battleship *Maine* in Havana Harbor (**Feb. 15**); 260 killed; responsibility never fixed. Congress declares independence of Cuba (**April 19**). Spain declares war on U.S. (**Apr. 24**); Congress (**Apr. 25**) formally declares nation has been at war with Spain since Apr. 21. Commodore George Dewey wins seven-hour battle of Manila Bay (**May 1**). Spanish fleet destroyed off Santiago, Cuba (**July 3**); city surrenders (**July 17**). Treaty of Paris (ratified by Senate in **1899**) ends war. U.S. given Guam and Puerto Rico and agrees to pay Spain $20 million for Philippines. Cuba independent of Spain; under U.S. military control for three years until **May 20, 1902**. Yellow fever is eradicated and political reforms achieved.

doctrine. Alfred Nobel's will establishes prizes for peace, science, and literature. Marconi receives first wireless patent in Britain. William Jennings Bryan delivers "Cross of Gold" speech at Democratic Convention in Chicago. First modern Olympic games held in Athens, Greece.

1898 Chinese "Boxers," anti-foreign organization, established. They stage uprisings against Europeans in **1900**; U.S. and other Western troops relieve Peking legations. Spanish-American War *(see* special material on the "Spanish-American War"). Pierre and Marie Curie discover radium and polonium.

1899 Boer War (or South African War). Conflict between British and Boers (descendants of Dutch settlers of South Africa). Causes rooted in longstanding territorial disputes and in friction over political rights for English and other "uitlanders" following 1886 discovery of vast gold deposits in Transvaal. (British victorious as war ends in **1902**.) Casualties: 5,774 British dead, about 4,000 Boers. Union of South Africa established in **1908** as confederation of colonies; becomes British dominion in **1910**.

1900 Hurricane ravages Galveston, Tex.; 6,000 drown. Sigmund Freud's *The Interpretation of Dreams.*

1901 Queen Victoria dies; succeeded by son, Edward VII. As President McKinley begins second term, he is shot fatally by anarchist Leon Czolgosz. Theodore Roosevelt sworn in as successor.

1902 Enrico Caruso's first gramophone recording.

1903 Wright brothers, Orville and Wilbur, fly first powered, controlled, heavier-than-air plane at Kitty Hawk, N.C. Henry Ford organizes Ford Motor Company.

1904 Russo-Japanese War—competition for Korea and Manchuria: In **1905**, Port Arthur surrenders to Japanese and Russia suffers other defeats; President Roosevelt mediates Treaty of Portsmouth, N.H., ending war with concessions for Japan. *Entente Cordiale:* Britain and France settle their international differences. General theory of radioactivity by Rutherford and Soddy. New York City subway opened.

1905 General strike in Russia; first workers' soviet set up in St. Petersburg. Sailors on battleship *Potemkin* mutiny; reforms including first Duma (parliament) established by Czar's "October Manifesto." Albert Einstein's special theory of relativity and other key theories in physics. Franz Lehar's *Merry Widow.*

1906 San Francisco earthquake and three-day fire; 500 dead. Roald Amundsen, Norwegian explorer, fixes magnetic North Pole.

1907 Second Hague Peace Conference, of 46 nations, adopts 10 conventions on rules of war. Financial panic of **1907** in U.S.

1908 Earthquake kills 150,000 in southern Italy and Sicily. U.S. Supreme Court, in Danbury Hatters' case, outlaws secondary union boycotts.

1909 North Pole reached by American explorers Robert E. Peary and Matthew Henson.

1910 Boy Scouts of America incorporated.

1911 First use of aircraft as offensive weapon in Turkish-Italian War. Italy defeats Turks and annexes Tripoli and Libya. Chinese Republic proclaimed after revolution overthrows Manchu dynasty. Sun Yat-sen named president. Mexican Revolution: Porfirio Diaz, president since 1877, replaced by Francisco Madero. Triangle Shirtwaist Company fire in New York; 145 killed. Richard Strauss's *Der Rosenkavalier.* Irving Berlin's *Alexander's Ragtime Band.* Amundsen reaches South Pole.

1912 Balkan Wars (**1912–13**) resulting from territorial disputes: Turkey defeated by alliance of Bulgaria, Serbia, Greece, and Montenegro; London peace treaty (**1913**) partitions most of European Turkey among the victors. In second war (**1913**), Bulgaria attacks Serbia and Greece and is defeated after Romania intervenes and Turks recapture Adrianople. *Titanic* sinks on maiden voyage; over 1,500 drown.

1913 Suffragettes demonstrate in London. Garment workers strike in New York and Boston; win pay raise and shorter hours. Sixteenth Amendment (income tax) and 17th (popular election of U.S. senators) adopted. Bill creating U.S. Federal Reserve System becomes law. Stravinsky's *The Rite of Spring.*

1914 World War I begins *(see* special material on "World War I"). Panama Canal officially opened. Congress sets up Federal Trade Commission, passes Clayton Antitrust Act. U.S. Marines occupy Veracruz, Mexico, intervening in civil war to protect American interests.

1915 U.S. protests German submarine actions and British blockade of Germany. U.S. banks lend $500 million to France and Britain. D. W. Griffith's film *Birth of a Nation.* Albert Einstein's *General Theory of Relativity.*

1916 Congress expands armed forces. Tom Mooney arrested for San Francisco bombing (pardoned in **1939**). Pershing fails in raid into Mexico in

Edouard Manet, *French painter* (1832–1883)

Johannes Brahms, *German composer* (1833–1897)

Alfred Nobel, *Swedish industrialist* (1833–1896)

Edgar Dégas, *French painter* (1834–1917)

James McNeill Whistler, *American painter* (1834–1903)

Dmitri Mendeleev, *Russian chemist* (1834–1907)

Mark Twain (Samuel L. Clemens), *American author* (1835–1910)

Camille Saint-Saëns, *French composer* (1835–1910)

Andrew Carnegie, *American industrialist* (1835–1919)

W. S. Gilbert, *English librettist* (1836–1911)

Bret Harte, *American novelist* (1836–1902)

Winslow Homer, *American painter* (1836–1910)

Sitting Bull, *American Indian chief* (1837–1890)

J. P. Morgan, *American financier* (1837–1913)

Georges Bizet, *French composer* (1838–1875)

Paul Cézanne, *French painter* (1839–1906)

John D. Rockefeller, *American industrialist* (1839–1937)

Thomas Hardy, *English novelist* (1840–1928)

Emile Zola, *French novelist* (1840–1902)

Claude Monet, *French painter* (1840–1926)

Pierre Renoir, *French painter* (1840–1919)

Auguste Rodin, *French sculptor* (1840–1917)

Peter Ilich Tchaikovsky, *Russian composer* (1840–1893)

Ambrose Bierce, *American author* (1842–1914)

William James, *American philosopher* (1842–1910)

Arthur Sullivan, *English composer* (1842–1900)

Henry James, *American novelist* (1843–1916)

Edvard Grieg, *Norwegian composer* (1843–1907)

Sarah Bernhardt, *French actress* (1844–1923)

Anatole France (Jacques Anatole Thibault), *French author* (1844–1924)

Gerard Manley Hopkins, *English poet* (1844–1899)

Friedrich Nietzsche, *German philosopher* (1844–1900)

Nikolai Rimski-Korsakov, *Russian composer* (1844–1908)

quest of rebel Pancho Villa. U.S. buys Virgin Islands from Denmark for $25 million. President Wilson re-elected with "he kept us out of war" slogan. "Black Tom" explosion at munitions dock in Jersey City, N.Y., $40,000,000 damages; traced to German saboteurs. Margaret Sanger opens first birth control clinic. Easter Rebellion in Ireland put down by British troops.

1917 First U.S. combat troops in France as U.S. declares war **(April 6)**. Russian Revolution—climax of long unrest under czars. February Revolution—Czar forced to abdicate, liberal government created. Kerensky becomes prime minister and forms provisional government **(July)**. In October Revolution, Bolsheviks seize power in armed coup d'état led by Lenin and Trotsky. Kerensky flees. Revolutionaries execute the czar and his family **(1918)**. Reds set up Third International in Moscow **(1919)**. Balfour Declaration promises Jewish homeland in Palestine. Sigmund Freud's *Introduction to Psychoanalysis.*

1918 Russian Civil War between Reds (Bolsheviks) and Whites (anti-Bolsheviks); Reds win in **1920**. Allied troops (U.S., British, French) intervene **(March)**; leave in **1919**. Japanese hold Vladivostok until 1922. World-wide influenza epidemic strikes; by **1920**, nearly 20 million are dead. In U.S. alone, 500,000 perish.

1919 Third International (Comintern) establishes Soviet control over international Communist movements. Paris peace conference. Versailles Treaty, incorporating Wilson's draft Covenant of League of Nations, signed by Allies and Germany; rejected by U.S. Senate. Congress formally ends war in **1921**. Eighteenth (Prohibition) Amendment adopted. Alcock and Brown make first trans-Atlantic non-stop flight.

1920 League of Nations holds first meeting at Geneva, Switzerland. U.S. Dept. of Justice "red hunt" nets thousands of radicals; aliens deported. Woman suffrage (19th) amendment ratified. First Agatha Christie mystery. Sinclair Lewis's *Main Street.*

1921 Reparations Commission fixes German liability at 132 billion gold marks. German inflation begins. Major treaties signed at Washington Disarmament Conference limit naval tonnage and pledge to respect territorial integrity of China. Irish Free State formed in southern Ireland as self-governing dominion of British Empire. In U.S., Nicola Sacco and Bartolomeo Vanzetti, Italian-born anarchists, convicted of armed robbery murder; case stirs world-wide protests; they are executed in **1927**.

1922 Mussolini marches on Rome; forms Fascist government. Irish Free State officially proclaimed.

1923 Adolf Hitler's "Beer Hall Putsch" in Munich fails; in **1924** he is sentenced to five years in prison where he writes *Mein Kampf;* released after eight months. Occupation of Ruhr by French and Belgian troops to enforce reparations payments. Widespread Ku Klux Klan violence in U.S. George Gershwin's *Rhapsody in Blue.*

1924 Death of Lenin; Stalin wins power struggle, rules as Soviet dictator until death in **1953**. Italian Fascists murder Socialist leader Giacomo Matteotti. Interior Secretary Albert B. Fall and oilmen Harry Sinclair and Edward L. Doheny are charged with conspiracy and bribery in the Teapot Dome scandal, involving fraudulent leases of naval oil reserves. In **1931**,

Wilhelm Conrad Roentgen, *German discoverer of X-rays* (1845–1923)

Gabriel Fauré, *French composer* (1845–1924)

Thomas Alva Edison, *American inventor* (1847–1931)

Alexander Graham Bell, *American inventor* (1847–1922)

Paul Gauguin, *French painter* (1848–1903)

August Strindberg, *Swedish dramatist* (1849–1912)

Luther Burbank, *American horticulturist* (1849–1926)

Guy de Maupassant, *French author* (1850–1893)

Robert Louis Stevenson, *English author* (1850–1894)

Vincent Van Gogh, *Dutch painter* (1853–1890)

George Eastman, *American photographic pioneer* (1854–1932)

George Bernard Shaw, *Irish dramatist* (1856–1950)

Oscar Wilde, *Anglo-Irish author* (1856–1900)

Sigmund Freud, *Austrian founder of psychoanalysis* (1856–1939)

Robert E. Peary, *American explorer* (1856–1920)

Booker T. Washington, *American educator* (1856–1915)

Joseph Conrad, *Anglo-Polish novelist* (1857–1924)

Giacomo Puccini, *Italian composer* (1858–1924)

Theodore Roosevelt, *American President* (1858–1919)

Max Planck, *German physicist* (1858–1947)

WORLD WAR I (1914–1918)

Imperial, territorial, and economic rivalries lead to the "Great War" between the Central Powers (Austria-Hungary, Germany, Bulgaria, and Turkey) and the Allies (U.S., Britain, France, Russia, Belgium, Serbia, Greece, Romania, Montenegro, Portugal, Italy, Japan). About 10 million combatants killed, 20 million wounded.

1914 Austrian Archduke Francis Ferdinand and wife assassinated in Sarajevo by Serbian nationalist, Gavrilo Princip **(June 28)**. Austria declares war on Serbia **(July 28)**. Germany declares war on Russia **(Aug. 1)**, on France **(Aug. 3)**, invades Belgium **(Aug. 4)**. Britain declares war on Germany **(Aug. 4)**. Germans defeat Russians in Battle of Tannenberg on Eastern Front **(Aug.)**. First Battle of the Marne **(Sept.)**. German drive stopped 25 miles from Paris. By end of year, war on the Western Front is "positional" in the trenches.

1915 German submarine blockade of Great Britain begins **(Feb.)**. Dardanelles Campaign—British land in Turkey **(April)**, withdraw from Gallipoli **(Dec. to Jan. 1916)**. Germans use gas at second Battle of Ypres **(April-May)**. *Lusitania* sunk by German submarine—1,198 lost, including 128 Americans **(May 7)**. On Eastern Front, German and Austrian "great offensive" conquers all of Poland and Lithuania; Russians lose 1 million men **(by Sept. 6)**. "Great Fall Offensive" by Allies results in little change from 1914 **(Sept.-Oct.)**. Britain and France declare war on Bulgaria **(Oct. 14)**.

1916 Battle of Verdun—Germans and French each lose about 350,000 men **(Feb.)**. Extended submarine warfare begins **(March)**. British-German sea battle of Jutland **(May)**; British lose more ships, but German fleet never ventures forth again. On Eastern front, the Brusilov offensive demoralizes Russians, costs them 1 million men **(June-Sept.)**. Battle of the Somme—British lose over 400,000; French, 200,000; Germans, about 450,000; all with no strategic results **(July-Nov.)**. Romania declares war on Austria-Hungary **(Aug. 27)**. Bucharest captured **(Dec.)**.

1917 U.S. declares war on Germany **(April 6)**. Submarine warfare at peak **(April)**. On Italian Front, Battle of Caporetto—Italians retreat, losing 600,000 prisoners and deserters **(Oct.-Dec.)**. On Western Front, Battles of Arras, Champagne, Ypres (third battle), etc. First large British tank attack **(Nov.)**. U.S. declares war on Austria-Hungary **(Dec. 7)**. Armistice between new Russian Bolshevik government and Germans **(Dec. 15)**.

1918 Great offensive by Germans **(March-June)**. Americans' first important battle role at Château-Thierry—as they and French stop German advance **(June)**. Second Battle of the Marne **(July-Aug.)**—start of Allied offensive at Amiens, St. Mihiel, etc. Battles of the Argonne and Ypres panic German leadership **(Sept.-Oct.)**. British offensive in Palestine **(Sept.)**. Germans ask for armistice **(Oct. 4)**. British armistice with Turkey **(Oct.)**. German Kaiser abdicates **(Nov.)**. Hostilities cease on Western Front **(Nov. 11)**.

Fall is sentenced to year in prison; Doheny and Sinclair acquitted of bribery. Nellie Tayloe Ross elected governor of Wyoming; first woman governor elected in U.S. Nathan Leopold and Richard Loeb convicted in "thrill killing" of Bobby Franks in Chicago; defended by Clarence Darrow; sentenced to life imprisonment. (Loeb killed by fellow convict in **1936**; Leopold paroled in **1958**, dies in **1971**.)

1925 Locarno conferences work to secure European peace by mutual guarantees. John T. Scopes convicted and fined for teaching evolution in a public school in Tennessee "Monkey Trial"; sentence set aside. John Logie Baird, Scottish inventor, transmits human features by television. Adolf Hitler publishes Volume I of *Mein Kampf*.

1926 General strike in Britain brings nation's activities to standstill. U.S. marines dispatched to Nicaragua during revolt; they remain until **1933**. Gertrude Ederle of U.S. is first woman to swim English Channel.

1927 German economy collapses. Socialists riot in Vienna; general strike follows acquittal of Nazis for political murder. Trotsky expelled from Russian Communist Party. Charles A. Lindbergh flies first successful solo non-stop flight from New York to Paris. Ruth Snyder and Judd Gray convicted of murder of Albert Snyder; they are executed at Sing Sing prison in **1928**. *The Jazz Singer*, with Al Jolson, first part-talking motion picture.

1928 Kellogg-Briand Pact, outlawing war, signed in Paris by 65 nations. Alexander Fleming discovers penicillin. Richard E. Byrd starts expedition to Antarctic; returns in **1930**.

1929 Trotsky expelled from U.S.S.R. Lateran Treaty establishes independent Vatican City. In U.S., stock market prices collapse, with U.S. securities losing $26 billion—first phase of Depression and world economic crisis. St. Valentine's Day gangland massacre in Chicago.

1930 Britain, U.S., Japan, France, and Italy sign naval disarmament treaty. Nazis gain in German elections. Cyclotron developed by Ernest O. Lawrence, U.S. physicist.

1931 Spain becomes a republic with overthrow of King Alfonso XIII. German industrialists finance 800,000-strong Nazi party. British parliament enacts statute of Westminster, legalizing dominion equality with Britain. Mukden Incident begins Japanese occupation of Manchuria. In U.S., Hoover proposes one-year moratorium of war debts. Harold C. Urey discovers heavy hydrogen. Gangster Al Capone sentenced to 11 years in prison for tax evasion (freed in **1939**; dies in **1947**).

1932 Nazis lead in German election with 230 Reichstag seats. Famine in U.S.S.R. In U.S., Congress sets up Reconstruction Finance Corporation to stimulate economy. Veterans march on Washington—most leave after Senate rejects payment of cash bonuses; others removed by troops under Douglas MacArthur. U.S. protests Japanese aggression in Manchuria. Amelia Earhart is first woman to fly Atlantic solo. Charles A. Lindbergh's baby son kidnapped, killed. (Bruno Richard Hauptmann arrested in **1934**, convicted in **1935**, executed in **1936**.)

1933 Hitler appointed German chancellor, gets dictatorial powers. Reichstag fire in Berlin; Nazi terror begins. (*See* special material on "The Holocaust.") Germany and Japan withdraw from League of Nations. Giuseppe Zangara executed for attempted assassination of President-elect Roosevelt in which Chicago Mayor Cermak is fatally shot. Roosevelt inaugurated ("the only thing we have to fear is fear itself"); launches New Deal. Prohibition repealed. U.S.S.R. recognized by U.S.

Arthur Conan Doyle, *English writer* (1859–1930)
Knut Hamsun, *Norwegian novelist* (1859–1952)
Henri Bergson, *French philosopher* (1859–1941)
John Dewey, *American philosopher* (1859–1952)
Georges Seurat, *French painter* (1859–1891)
Pierre Curie, *French physicist* (1859–1906)
Anton Chekhov, *Russian dramatist* (1860–1904)
Gustav Mahler, *German composer* (1860–1911)
Rabindranath Tagore, *Indian poet* (1861–1941)
Alfred North Whitehead, *British philosopher-mathematician* (1861–1947)
Edith Wharton, *American author* (1862–1937)
Claude Debussy, *French composer* (1862–1918)
David Lloyd George, *British statesman* (1863–1945)
Henry Ford, *American automobile pioneer* (1863–1947)
William Randolph Hearst, *American newspaper magnate* (1863–1951)
Henri Toulouse-Lautrec, *French painter* (1864–1901)
George Washington Carver, *American botanist* (1864–1943)
Richard Strauss, *German composer* (1864–1949)
Rudyard Kipling, *English writer* (1865–1936)
William Butler Yeats, *Irish poet* (1865–1939)
Jean Sibelius, *Finnish composer* (1865–1957)
Sun Yat-sen, *Chinese statesman* (1866–1927)
Benedetto Croce, *Italian philosopher* (1866–1952)

THE HOLOCAUST (1933–1945)

"Holocaust" is the term describing the Nazi annihilation of about 6 million Jews (two thirds of the pre-World War II European Jewish population), including 4,500,000 from Russia, Poland, and the Baltic; 750,000 from Hungary and Romania; 290,000 from Germany and Austria; 105,000 from The Netherlands; 90,000 from France; 54,000 from Greece; etc.

The Holocaust was unique in its being *genocide*—the systematic destruction of a people solely because of religion, race, ethnicity, or nationality—on an unmatched scale. Along with the Jews, another 9 to 10 million people—Gypsies, Slavs (Poles, Ukrainians, and Belorussians)—were exterminated.

The only comparable act of genocide in modern times was launched in April 1915, when an estimated 600,000 Armenians were massacred by the Turks.

1933 Hitler named German Chancellor (**Jan.**). Dachau, first concentration camp, established (**March**). Boycotts against Jews begin (**April**).

1935 Anti-Semitic Nuremberg Laws passed by Reichstag (**Sept.**).

1937 Buchenwald concentration camp opens (**July**).

1938 Extension of anti-Semitic laws to Austria after annexation (**March**). *Kristallnacht* (Night of Broken Glass)—anti-Semitic riots in Germany and Austria (**Nov. 9**). 26,000 Jews sent to concentration camps; Jewish children expelled from schools (**Nov.**). Expropriation of Jewish property and businesses (**Dec.**).

1940 As war continues, Nazi acts against Jews extended to German-conquered areas.

1941 Deportation of German Jews begins; massacres of Jews in Odessa and Kiev—68,000 killed (**Nov.**); in Riga and Vilna—almost 60,000 killed (**Dec.**).

1942 Unified Jewish resistance in ghettos begins (**Jan.**). 300,000 Jews from Warsaw Ghetto deported to Treblinka death camp (**July**).

1943 Warsaw Ghetto uprisings (**Jan. and April**); Ghetto exterminated (**May**).

1944 476,000 Hungarian Jews sent to Auschwitz (**May–June**). D-day (**June 6**). Soviet Army liberates Maidanek death camp (**July**). Nazis try to hide evidence of death camps (**Nov.**).

1945 Americans liberate Buchenwald, Bergen-Belsen camps (**April**). Nuremberg War Crimes Trial (**Nov. 1945 to Oct. 1946**).

1934 Chancellor Dollfuss of Austria assassinated by Nazis. Hitler becomes Führer. U.S.S.R. admitted to League of Nations. Dionne sisters, first quintuplets to survive beyond infancy, born in Canada.

1935 Saar incorporated into Germany after plebiscite. Nazis repudiate Versailles Treaty, introduce compulsory military service. Mussolini invades Ethiopia; League of Nations invokes sanctions. Roosevelt opens second phase of New Deal in U.S., calling for social security, better housing, equitable taxation, and farm assistance. Huey Long assassinated in Louisiana.

1936 Germans occupy Rhineland. Italy annexes Ethiopia. Rome-Berlin Axis proclaimed (Japan to join in **1940**). Trotsky exiled to Mexico. King George V dies; succeeded by son, Edward VIII, who soon abdicates to marry American-born divorcée, and is succeeded by brother, George VI. Spanish civil war begins. (Franco's fascist forces defeat Loyalist forces by **1939**, when Madrid falls.) War between China and Japan begins, to continue through World War II. Japan and Germany sign anti-Commintern pact; joined by Italy in **1937**.

1937 Hitler repudiates war guilt clause of Versailles Treaty; continues to build German power. Italy withdraws from League of Nations. U.S. gunboat *Panay* sunk by Japanese in Yangtze River. Japan invades China, conquers most of coastal area. Amelia Earhart lost somewhere in Pacific on round-the-world flight.

1938 Hitler marches into Austria; political and geographical union of Germany and Austria proclaimed. Munich Pact—Britain, France, and Italy agree to let Germany partition Czechoslovakia. Germany occupies Sudetenland, about one third of Czechoslovakia. Douglas "Wrong-Way" Corrigan flies from New York to Dublin.

1939 Germany occupies Bohemia and Moravia; renounces pacts with Poland and England and concludes 10-year non-aggression pact with U.S.S.R. Russo-Finnish War begins; Finns to lose one tenth of territory in **1940** peace treaty. World War II begins *(see* special material on "World War II"). In U.S., Roosevelt submits $1,319-million defense budget, proclaims U.S. neutrality, and declares limited emergency. Einstein writes FDR about feasibility of atomic bomb. New York World's Fair opens.

1940 Trotsky assassinated in Mexico. Estonia, Latvia, and Lithuania annexed by U.S.S.R. U.S. trades 50 destroyers for leases on British bases in Western Hemisphere. Selective Service Act signed.

1941 Japanese surprise attack on U.S. fleet at Pearl Harbor brings U.S. into World War II. Manhattan Project (atomic bomb research) begins. Roosevelt enunciates "four freedoms," signs lend-lease act, declares national emergency, promises aid to U.S.S.R.

Wilbur Wright, *American aviation pioneer* (1867–1912)

Arturo Toscanini, *Italian conductor* (1867–1957)

Marie (Sklodowska) Curie, *Polish-French scientist* (1867–1937)

Maxim Gorki, *Russian writer* (1868–1936)

Robert A. Millikan, *American physicist* (1869–1953)

Mohandas Gandhi, *Indian leader* (1869–1948)

André Gide, *French author* (1869–1951)

Henri Matisse, *French painter* (1869–1954)

Frank Lloyd Wright, *American architect* (1869–1959)

Nikolai Lenin, *Russian revolutionist* (1870–1924)

Orville Wright, *American aviation pioneer* (1871–1948)

Rasputin, *Russian monk* (1871–1916)

Stephen Crane, *American author* (1871–1900)

Theodore Dreiser, *American novelist* (1871–1945)

Marcel Proust, *French author* (1871–1922)

Bertrand Russell, *English philosopher* (1872–1970)

Enrico Caruso, *Italian tenor* (1873–1921)

Chaim Weizmann, *first president of Israel* (1874–1952)

WORLD WAR II (1939–1945)

Axis powers (Germany, Italy, Japan, Hungary, Romania, Bulgaria) *vs.* Allies (U.S., Britain, France, U.S.S.R., Australia, Belgium, Brazil, Canada, China, Denmark, Greece, Netherlands, New Zealand, Norway, Poland, South Africa, Yugoslavia).

1939 Germany invades Poland and annexes Danzig; Britain and France give Hitler ultimatum (Sept. 1), declare war (Sept. 3). Disabled German pocket battleship Admiral Graf Spee blown up off Montevideo, Uruguay, on Hitler's orders (Dec. 17). Limited activity ("Sitzkrieg") on Western Front.

1940 Nazis invade Netherlands, Belgium, and Luxembourg (May 10). Chamberlain resigns as Prime Minister; Churchill takes over (May 10). Germans cross French frontier (May 12) using air/tank/infantry "Blitzkrieg" tactics. Dunkerque evacuation—about 335,000 out of 400,000 Allied soldiers rescued from Belgium by British civilian and naval craft (May 26-June 3). Italy declares war on France and Britain; invades France (June 10). Germans enter Paris; city undefended (June 14). France and Germany sign armistice at Compiègne (June 22). Nazis bomb Coventry, England (Nov. 14).

1941 Germans launch attacks in Balkans. Yugoslavia surrenders—General Mihajlovic continues guerrilla warfare; Tito leads left-wing guerrillas (April 17). Nazi tanks enter Athens; remnants of British Army quit Greece (April 27). Hitler attacks Russia (June 22). Atlantic Charter—FDR and Churchill agree on war aims (Aug. 14). Japanese attacks on Pearl Harbor, Philippines, Guam force U.S. into war; U.S. Pacific fleet crippled (Dec. 7). U.S. and Britain declare war on Japan. Germany and Italy declare war on U.S.; Congress declares war on those countries (Dec. 11).

1942 British surrender Singapore to Japanese (Feb. 15). U.S. forces on Bataan peninsula in Philippines surrender (April 9). U.S. and Filipino troops on Corregidor island in Manila Bay surrender to Japanese (May 6). Village of Lidice in Czecho-

slovakia razed by Nazis (June 10). U.S. and Britain land in French North Africa (Nov. 8).

1943 Casablanca Conference—Churchill and FDR agree on unconditional surrender goal (Jan. 14–24). German 6th Army surrenders at Stalingrad—turning point of war in Russia (Feb. 1–2). Remnants of Nazis trapped on Cape Bon, ending war in Africa (May 12). Mussolini deposed; Badoglio named premier (July 25). Allied troops land on Italian mainland after conquest of Sicily (Sept. 3). Italy surrenders (Sept. 8). Nazis seize Rome (Sept. 10). Cairo Conference: FDR, Churchill, Chiang Kai-shek pledge defeat of Japan, free Korea (Nov. 22–26). Teheran Conference: FDR, Churchill, Stalin agree on invasion plans (Nov. 28-Dec. 1).

1944 U.S. and British troops land at Anzio on west Italian coast and hold beachhead (Jan. 22). U.S. and British troops enter Rome (June 4). D-Day—Allies launch Normandy invasion (June 6). Hitler wounded in bomb plot (July 20). Paris liberated (Aug. 25). Athens freed by Allies (Oct. 13). Americans invade Philippines (Oct. 20). Germans launch counteroffensive in Belgium—Battle of Bulge (Dec. 16).

1945 Yalta Agreement signed by FDR, Churchill, Stalin—establishes basis for occupation of Germany, returns to Soviet Union lands taken by Germany and Japan; U.S.S.R. agrees to friendship pact with China (Feb. 11). Mussolini killed at Lake Como (April 28). Admiral Doenitz takes command in Germany; suicide of Hitler announced (May 1). Berlin falls (May 2). V-E Day—Germany signs unconditional surrender terms at Rheims (May 7). Potsdam Conference—Truman, Churchill, Atlee (after July 28), Stalin establish council of foreign ministers to prepare peace treaties; plan German postwar government and reparations (July 17-Aug. 2). A-bomb blasts Hiroshima (Aug. 6). U.S.S.R. declares war on Japan (Aug. 8). Nagasaki hit by A-bomb (Aug. 9). Japan surrenders (Aug. 14). V-J Day—Japanese sign surrender terms aboard battleship *Missouri* (Sept. 2).

1942 Declaration of United Nations signed in Washington. Women's military services established. Enrico Fermi achieves nuclear chain reaction. Japanese and persons of Japanese ancestry moved inland from Pacific Coast. Coconut Grove nightclub fire in Boston kills 491.

1943 President freezes prices, salaries, and wages to prevent inflation. Income tax withholding introduced.

1944 G.I. Bill of Rights enacted. Bretton Woods Conference creates International Monetary Fund and World Bank. Dumbarton Oaks Conference—U.S., British Commonwealth, and U.S.S.R. propose establishment of United Nations.

1945 Yalta Conference (Roosevelt, Churchill, Stalin) plans final defeat of Germany **(Feb.)**. San Francisco Conference establishes U.N. **(April-June)**. FDR dies **(April 12)**. Potsdam Conference (Truman, Churchill, Stalin) establishes basis of German reconstruction **(July-Aug)**.

1946 First meeting of U.N. General Assembly opens in London **(Jan. 10)**. League of Nations dissolved **(April)**. Italy abolishes monarchy **(June)**. Verdict in Nuremberg war trial: 12 Nazi leaders (including 1 tried in absentia) sentenced to hang; 7 imprisoned; 3 acquitted **(Oct. 1)**. Goering commits suicide a few hours before 10 other Nazis are executed **(Oct. 15)**. Winston Churchill's "Iron Curtain" speech warns against Soviet expansion. Xerography invented by Chester Carlson.

1947 Britain nationalizes coal mines **(Jan. 1)**. Peace treaties for Italy, Romania, Bulgaria, Hungary, Finland signed in Paris **(Feb. 10)**. Soviet Union rejects U.S. plan for U.N. atomic-energy control **(March 4)**. Truman Doctrine proposed—the first significant U.S. attempt to "contain" communist expansion **(March 12)**. Marshall Plan for European recovery proposed—a coordinated program to help European nations recover from ravages of war **(June)**. (By **1951**, this "European Recovery Program" had cost $11 billion.) India and Pakistan gain independence from Britain **(Aug. 15)**. Cominform (Communist Information Bureau) founded under Soviet auspices to rebuild contacts among European Communist parties, missing since dissolution of Comintern in **1943 (Sept.)**. (Yugoslav party expelled in **1948** and Cominform disbanded in **1956.**)

1948 Gandhi assassinated in New Delhi by Hindu fanatic **(Jan. 30)**. Communists seize power in Czechoslovakia **(Feb. 23-25)**. Burma and Ceylon granted independence by Britain. Organization of American States (OAS) Charter signed at Bogotá, Colombia **(April 30)**. Nation of Israel proclaimed; British end Mandate at midnight; Arab armies attack **(May 14)**. Berlin airlift begins **(June 21)**; ends May 12, 1949. Stalin and Tito break **(June 28)**. Independent Republic of Korea is proclaimed, following election supervised by U.N. **(Aug. 15)**. Verdict in Japanese war trial: Tojo and six others sentenced to hang (hanged **Dec. 23**); 18 imprisoned **(Nov. 12)**. United States of Indonesia established as Dutch and Indonesians settle conflict **(Dec. 27)**. Alger Hiss, former U.S. State Department official, indicted on perjury charges after denying passing secret documents to communist spy ring. Convicted in second trial **(1950)** and sentenced to five-year prison term.

1949 Cease-fire in Palestine **(Jan. 7)**. Truman proposes Point Four Program to help world's backward areas **(Jan. 20)**. Israel signs armistice with Egypt **(Feb. 24)**. Start of North Atlantic Treaty Organization (NATO)—treaty signed by 12 nations **(April 4)**. German Federal Republic (West Germany) established **(Sept. 21)**. Truman discloses Soviet Union has set off atomic explosion **(Sept. 23)**. Communist People's Republic of China formally proclaimed **(Oct. 1)**.

1950 Truman orders development of hydrogen bomb **(Jan. 31)**. Korean War *(see special material on the "Korean War")*. Assassination attempt on President Truman by Puerto Rican nationalists **(Nov. 1)**. Brink's robbery in Boston; almost $3 million stolen **(Jan. 17)**.

1951 Six nations agree to Schuman Plan to pool European coal and steel **(March 19)**—in effect **Feb. 10, 1953**. Julius and Ethel Rosenberg sentenced to death for passing atomic secrets to Russians **(March)**. Japanese peace treaty signed in San Francisco by 49 nations **(Sept. 8)**. Color television introduced in U.S.

1952 George VI dies; his daughter becomes Elizabeth II **(Feb. 6)**. NATO

Winston Churchill, *British statesman* (1874–1965)

Gertrude Stein, *American writer* (1874–1946)

Arnold Schönberg, *Austrian composer* (1874–1951)

Guglielmo Marconi, *Italian physicist* (1874–1935)

Thomas Mann, *German novelist* (1875–1955)

C. G. Jung, *Swiss psychiatrist* (1875–1961)

Carl Sandburg, *American poet* (1878–1967)

Martin Buber, *Jewish philosopher* (1878–1965)

Joseph Stalin, *Russian dictator* (1879–1953)

Leon Trotsky, *Russian revolutionist* (1879–1940)

Paul Klee, *Swiss painter* (1879–1940)

Albert Einstein, *German-American physicist* (1879–1955)

Douglas MacArthur, *American general* (1880–1964)

Pablo Picasso, *Spanish-born French painter* (1881–1973)

Béla Bartók, *Hungarian composer* (1881–1945)

Alexander Fleming, *English scientist* (1881–1955)

Franklin D. Roosevelt, *American President* (1882–1945)

Eamon de Valera, *Irish statesman* (1882–1975)

James Joyce, *Irish author* (1882–1941)

Georges Braque, *French painter* (1882–1963)

Igor Stravinsky, *Russian composer* (1882–1971)

Benito Mussolini, *Italian dictator* (1883–1945)

Franz Kafka, *Czechoslovakian-born Austrian author* (1883–1924)

John Maynard Keynes, *English economist* (1883–1946)

Walter Gropius, *German architect* (1883–1969)

Harry S. Truman, *American President* (1884–1972)

Eduard Benes, *Czechoslovakian statesman* (1884–1948)

D. H. Lawrence, *English writer* (1885–1930)

KOREAN WAR (1950–1953)

1950 North Korean Communist forces invade South Korea **(June 25)**. U.N. calls for cease-fire and asks U.N. members to assist South Korea **(June 27)**. Truman orders U.S. forces into Korea **(June 27)**. North Koreans capture Seoul **(June 28)**. Gen. Douglas MacArthur appointed commander of unified U.N. forces **(July 8)**. Pusan Beachhead—U.N. forces counterattack and capture Seoul **(Aug.-Sept.)**, capture Pyongyang, North Korean capital **(Oct.)**. Chinese Communists enter war **(Oct. 26)**, force U.N. retreat toward 39th parallel **(Dec.)**.

1951 Gen. Matthew B. Ridgeway replaces MacArthur after he threatens Chinese with massive retaliation **(April 11)**. Armistice negotiations **(July)** continue with interruptions until June **1953**.

1953 Armistice signed **(June 26)**. Chinese troops withdraw from North Korea **(Oct. 26, 1958)**, but over 200 violations of armistice noted to **1959**.

conference approves European army **(Feb.)**. AEC announces "satisfactory" experiments in hydrogen-weapons research; eyewitnesses tell of blasts near Enewetak **(Nov.)**.

1953 Gen. Dwight D. Eisenhower inaugurated President of United States **(Jan. 20)**. Stalin dies **(March 5)**. Malenkov becomes Soviet Premier; Beria, Minister of Interior; Molotov, Foreign Minister **(March 6)**. Dag Hammarskjold begins term as U.N. Secretary-General **(April 10)**. Edmund Hillary, of New Zealand, and Tenzing Norkay, of Nepal, reach top of Mt. Everest **(May 29)**. East Berliners rise against Communist rule; quelled by tanks **(June 17)**. Egypt becomes republic ruled by military junta **(June 18)**. Julius and Ethel Rosenberg executed in Sing Sing prison **(June 19)**. Korean armistice signed **(July 27)**. Moscow announces explosion of hydrogen bomb **(Aug. 20)**.

1954 First atomic submarine *Nautilus*, launched **(Jan. 21)**. Five U.S. Congressmen shot on floor of House as Puerto Rican nationalists fire from spectators' gallery; all five recover **(March 1)**. Army *vs.* McCarthy inquiry—Senate subcommittee report blames both sides **(Apr. 22-June 17)**. Dien Bien Phu, French military outpost in Vietnam, falls to Vietminh army **(May 7)**. *(See* special material on the "Vietnam War.") U.S. Supreme Court (in *Brown* v. *Board of Education of Topeka*) unanimously bans racial segregation in public schools **(May 17)**. Eisenhower launches world atomic pool without Soviet Union **(Sept. 6)**. Eight-nation Southeast Asia defense treaty (SEATO) signed at Manila **(Sept. 8)**. West Germany is granted sovereignty, admitted to NATO and Western European Union **(Oct. 23)**. Dr. Jonas Salk starts innoculating children against polio. Algerian War of Independence against France begins **(Nov.)**; France struggles to maintain colonial rule until 1962 when it agrees to Algeria's independence.

1955 Nikolai A. Bulganin becomes Soviet Premier, replacing Malenkov **(Feb. 8)**. Churchill resigns; Anthony Eden succeeds him **(April 6)**. Federal Republic of West Germany becomes a sovereign state **(May 5)**. Warsaw Pact, east European mutual defense agreement, signed **(May 14)**. Argentina ousts Perón **(Sept. 19)**. President Eisenhower suffers coronary thrombosis in Denver **(Sept. 24)**. Martin Luther King, Jr., leads black boycott of Montgomery, Ala., bus system **(Dec. 1)**; desegregated service begun **(Dec. 21)**. AFL and CIO become one organization—AFL-CIO **(Dec. 5)**.

1956 Nikita Khrushchev, First Secretary of U.S.S.R. Communist Party, denounces Stalin's excesses **(Feb. 24)**. First aerial H-bomb tested over Namu islet, Bikini Atoll—10 million tons TNT equivalent **(May 21)**. Worker's uprising against Communist rule in Poznan, Poland, is crushed **(June 28–30)**. Egypt takes control of Suez Canal **(July 26)**. Israel launches attack

Ezra Pound, *American poet* (1885–1972)

Sinclair Lewis, *American novelist* (1885–1951)

Alban Berg, *Austrian composer* (1885–1935)

Niels Bohr, *Danish physicist* (1885–1962)

David Ben-Gurion, *Israeli statesman* (1886–1973)

Chiang Kai-shek, *Chinese statesman* (1887–1975)

Le Corbusier (C.E. Jeanneret), *Swiss-born French architect* (1887–1965)

T. S. Eliot, *Anglo-American poet* (1888–1965)

Eugene O'Neill, *American dramatist* (1888–1953)

Ludwig Wittgenstein, *Austrian philosopher* (1889–1951)

Adolf Hitler, *German dictator* (1889–1945)

Charles Chaplin, *English screen actor-director* (1889–1977)

Dwight D. Eisenhower, *American President* (1890–1969)

Charles de Gaulle, *French soldier and statesman* (1890–1970)

Sergei Prokofiev, *Russian composer* (1891–1953)

Frederick Banting, *Canadian discoverer of insulin* (1891–1941)

VIETNAM WAR (1950–1975)
U.S., South Vietnam, and Allies versus North Vietnam and National Liberation Front (Viet Cong). Outstanding events:

1950 President Truman sends 35-man military advisory group to aid French fighting to maintain colonial power in Vietnam.

1954 After defeat of French at Dienbienphu, Geneva Agreements (July) provide for withdrawal of French and Vietminh to either side of demarcation zone (DMZ) pending reunification elections, which are never held. Presidents Eisenhower and Kennedy (from 1954 onward) send civilian advisors and, later, military personnel to train South Vietnamese.

1960 Communists form National Liberation Front in South.

1963 Ngo Dinh Diem, South Vietnam's premier, slain in coup (Nov. 1).

1961–1963 U.S. military advisors rise from 2,000 to 15,000.

1964 North Vietnamese torpedo boats reportedly attack U.S. destroyers in Gulf of Tonkin (Aug. 2). President Johnson orders retaliatory air strikes. Congress approves Gulf of Tonkin resolution (Aug. 7) authorizing President to take necessary steps to "maintain peace."

1965 U.S. planes begin combat missions over South Vietnam. In June, 23,000 American advisors committed to combat. By end of year over 184,000 U.S. troops in area.

1966 B-52s bomb DMZ, reportedly used by North Vietnam for entry into South (July 31).

1967 South Vietnam National Assembly approves election of Nguyen Van Thieu as President (Oct. 21).

1968 U.S. has almost 525,000 men in Vietnam. In Tet offensive (Jan.-Feb.), Viet Cong guerrillas attack Saigon, Hue, and some provincial capitals. President Johnson orders halt to U.S. bombardment of North Vietnam (Oct. 31). Saigon and N.L.F. join U.S. and North Vietnam in Paris peace talks.

1969 President Nixon announces Vietnam peace offer (May 14)

—begins troop withdrawals (June). Viet Cong forms Provisional Revolutionary Government. U.S. Senate calls for curb on commitments (June 25). Ho Chi Minh, 79, North Vietnam president, dies (Sept. 3); collective leadership chosen. Some 6,000 U.S. troops pulled back from Thailand and 1,000 marines from Vietnam (announced Sept. 30). Massive demonstrations in U.S. protest or support war policies (Oct. 15).

1970 Nixon announces sending of troops to Cambodia (April 30). Last U.S. troops removed from Cambodia (June 29).

1971 Congress bars use of combat troops, but not air power, in Laos and Cambodia (Jan. 1). South Vietnamese troops, with U.S. air cover, fail in Laos thrust. Many American ground forces withdrawn from Vietnam combat. *New York Times* publishes Pentagon papers, classified material on expansion of war (June).

1972 Nixon responds to North Vietnamese drive across DMZ by ordering mining of North Vietnam ports and heavy bombing of Hanoi-Haiphong area (April 1). Nixon orders "Christmas bombing" of north to get North Vietnamese back to conference table (Dec.).

1973 President orders halt to offensive operations in North Vietnam (Jan. 15). Representatives of North and South Vietnam, U.S., and N.L.F. sign peace pacts in Paris, ending longest war in U.S. history (Jan. 27).

1974 Both sides accuse each other of frequent violations of cease-fire agreement.

1975 Full-scale warfare resumes. Communists victorious (April 30). South Vietnam Premier Nguyen Van Thieu resigns (April 21). American troops evacuated (April 30). More than 140,000 Vietnamese refugees leave by air and sea, many to settle in U.S. Provisional Revolutionary Government takes control (June 6).

1976 Election of National Assembly paves way for reunification of North and South.

on Egypt's Sinai peninsula and drives toward Suez Canal (**Oct. 29**). British and French invade Egypt at Port Said (**Nov. 5**). Cease-fire forced by U.S. pressure stops British, French, and Israeli advance (**Nov. 6**). Revolt starts in Hungary—Soviet troops and tanks crush anti-Communist rebellion (**Nov.**).

1957 Eisenhower Doctrine calls for aid to Mideast countries which resist armed aggression from Communist-controlled nations (**Jan. 5**). Eisenhower sends troops to Little Rock, Ark., to quell mob and protect school integration (**Sept. 24**). Russians launch *Sputnik I*, first earth-orbiting satellite—the Space Age begins (**Oct. 4**).

1958 Army's Jupiter-C rocket fires first U.S. earth satellite, *Explorer I*, into orbit (**Jan. 31**). Egypt and Syria merge into United Arab Republic (**Feb. 1**). European Economic Community (Common Market) established by Rome Treaty becomes effective **Jan. 1, 1958**. Khrushchev becomes Premier of Soviet Union as Bulganin resigns (**Mar. 27**). Gen. Charles de Gaulle becomes French premier (**June 1**), remaining in power until **1969**. New French constitution adopted (**Sept. 28**), de Gaulle elected president of 5th Republic (**Dec. 21**). Eisenhower orders U.S. Marines into Lebanon at request of President Chamoun, who fears overthrow (**July 15**).

1959 Cuban President Batista resigns and flees—Castro takes over (**Jan. 1**). Tibet's Dalai Lama escapes to India (**Mar. 31**). St. Lawrence Seaway opens, allowing ocean ships to reach Midwest (**April 25**).

1960 American U-2 spy plane, piloted by Francis Gary Powers, shot down over Russia (**May 5**). Khrushchev kills Paris summit conference because of U-2 (**May 16**). Powers sentenced to prison for 10 years (**Aug. 19**)—freed in **February 1962** in exchange for Soviet spy. Top Nazi murderer of Jews, Adolf Eichmann, captured by Israelis in Argentina (**May 23**)—executed in Israel in **1962**. Communist China and Soviet Union split in conflict over Communist ideology. Belgium starts to break up its African colonial empire, gives independence to Belgian Congo (Zaire) on **June 30**. Cuba begins confiscation of $770 million of U.S. property (**Aug. 7**).

1961 U.S. breaks diplomatic relations with Cuba (**Jan. 3**). John F. Kennedy inaugurated President of U.S. (**Jan. 20**). Kennedy proposes Alliance for Progress—10-year plan to raise Latin American living standards (**Mar. 13**). Moscow announces putting first man in orbit around earth, Maj. Yuri A. Gagarin (**April 12**). Cuba invaded at Bay of Pigs by an estimated 1,200 anti-Castro exiles aided by U.S.; invasion crushed (**April 17**). First U.S. spaceman, Navy Cmdr. Alan B. Shepard, Jr., rockets 116.5 miles up in 302-mile trip (**May 5**). Virgil Grissom becomes second American astronaut, making 118-mile-high, 303-mile-long rocket flight over Atlantic (**July 21**). Gherman Stepanovich Titov is launched in Soviet spaceship *Vostok II;* makes 17½ orbits in 25 hours, covering 434,960 miles before landing safely (**Aug. 6**). East Germans erect Berlin Wall between East and West Berlin to halt flood of refugees (**Aug. 13**). U.S.S.R. fires 50-megaton hydrogen bomb, biggest explosion in history (**Oct. 29**).

1962 Lt. Col. John H. Glenn, Jr., is first American to orbit earth—three times in 4 hr 55 min (**Feb. 20**). Adolf Eichmann hanged in Israel for his part in Nazi extermination of six million Jews (**May 31**). France transfers sovereignty to new republic of Algeria (**July 3**). Cuban missile crisis—U.S.S.R. to build missile bases in Cuba; Kennedy orders Cuban blockade, lifts blockade after Russians back down (**Aug.-Nov.**). James H. Meredith, escorted by Federal marshals, registers in University of Mississippi (**Oct. 1**). Pope John XXIII opens Second Vatican Council (**Oct. 11**)—Council holds four sessions, finally closing Dec. 8, 1965. Cuba releases 1,113 prisoners of 1961 invasion attempt (**Dec. 24**).

1963 France and West Germany sign treaty of cooperation ending four centuries of conflict (**Jan. 22**). Pope John XXIII dies (**June 3**)—succeeded June 21 by Cardinal Montini, who becomes Paul VI. U.S. Supreme Court rules no locality may require recitation of Lord's Prayer or Bible verses in public schools (**June 17**). Civil rights rally held by 200,000 blacks and whites in Washington, D.C. (**Aug. 28**). Washington-to-Moscow "hot line" communications link opens, designed to reduce risk of accidental war (**Aug. 30**). President Kennedy shot and killed by sniper in Dallas, Tex. Lyndon B. Johnson becomes President same day (**Nov. 22**). Lee Harvey Oswald, accused assassin of President Kennedy, is shot and killed by Jack Ruby, Dallas nightclub owner (**Nov. 24**).

1964 U.S. Supreme Court rules that Congressional districts should be roughly equal in population (**Feb. 17**). Jack Ruby convicted of murder in slaying of Lee Harvey Oswald; sentenced to death by Dallas jury (**March 14**)—conviction reversed Oct. 5, 1966; Ruby dies Jan. 3, 1967, before second trial can be held. Three civil rights workers—Schwerner, Goodman, and Cheney—murdered in Mississippi (**June**). Twenty-one arrests result in trial and conviction of seven by Federal jury. President's Commission on the Assassination of President Kennedy issues Warren Report con-

Tito (Josip Broz), *Yugoslavian President* (1892–1980)

Haile Selassie, *Ethiopian emperor* (1892–1975)

Hermann Goering, *Nazi leader* (1893–1946)

Mao Zedong, *Chinese Communist leader* (1893–1976)

Nikita Khrushchev, *Russian leader* (1894–1971)

Martha Graham, *American dancer* (1894–   )

Paul Hindemith, *German-American composer* (1895–1963)

Bertolt Brecht, *German dramatist* (1898–1956)

Ernest Hemingway, *American author* (1898–1961)

Federico García Lorca, *Spanish author* (1899–1936)

Francis Poulenc, *French composer* (1899–1963)

Kurt Weill, *German-American composer* (1900–1950)

Aaron Copland, *American composer* (1900–   )

Werner Heisenberg, *German physicist* (1901–   )

Walt Disney, *American cartoonist* (1901–1966)

Enrico Fermi, *Italian-American physicist* (1901–1954)

John Steinbeck, *American novelist* (1902–1968)

Dmitri Shostakovich, *Russian composer* (1906–1975)

W. H. Auden, *English poet* (1907–1973)

Albert Camus, *French author* (1913–1960)

John F. Kennedy, *American President* (1917–1963)

cluding that Lee Harvey Oswald acted alone.

1965 Rev. Dr. Martin Luther King, Jr., and more than 2,600 other blacks arrested in Selma, Ala., during three-day demonstrations against voter-registration rules (**Feb. 1**). Malcolm X, black-nationalist leader, shot to death at Harlem rally in New York City (**Feb. 21**). U.S. Marines land in Dominican Republic as fighting persists between rebels and Dominican army (**April 28**). Medicare, senior citizens' government medical assistance program, begins (**July 1**). Blacks riot for six days in Watts section of Los Angeles: 34 dead, over 1,000 injured, nearly 4,000 arrested, fire damage put at $175 million (**Aug. 11–16**). Power failure in Ontario plant blacks out parts of eight northeastern states of U.S. and two provinces of southeastern Canada (**Nov. 9**).

1966 Black teen-agers riot in Watts, Los Angeles; two men killed and at least 25 injured (**March 15**). Michael E. De Bakey implants artificial heart in human for first time at Houston hospital; plastic device functions and patient lives (**April 21**).

1967 Three Apollo astronauts—Col. Virgil I. Grissom, Col. Edward White II, and Lt. Cmdr. Roger B. Chaffee—killed in spacecraft fire during simulated launch (**Jan. 27**). Israeli and Arab forces battle; six-day war ends with Israel occupying Sinai Peninsula, Golan Heights, Gaza Strip, and east bank of Suez Canal (**June 5**). Red China announces explosion of its first hydrogen bomb (**June 17**). Racial violence in Detroit; 7,000 National Guardsmen aid police after night of rioting. Similar outbreaks occur in New York City's Spanish Harlem, Rochester, N.Y., Birmingham, Ala., and New Britain, Conn. (**July 23**). Thurgood Marshall sworn in as first black U.S. Supreme Court justice (**Oct. 2**). Dr. Christiaan N. Barnard and team of South African surgeons perform world's first successful human heart transplant (**Dec. 3**)—patient dies 18 days later.

1968 North Korea seizes U.S. Navy ship *Pueblo;* holds 83 on board as spies (**Jan. 23**). President Johnson announces he will not seek or accept presidential renomination (**March 31**). Martin Luther King, Jr., civil rights leader, is slain in Memphis (**April 4**)—James Earl Ray, indicted in murder, captured in London on **June 8**. In **1969** Ray pleads guilty and is sentenced to 99 years. Sen. Robert F. Kennedy is shot and critically wounded in Los Angeles hotel after winning California primary (**June 5**)—dies **June 6**. Sirhan B. Sirhan convicted **1969**. Czechoslovakia is invaded by Russians and Warsaw Pact forces to crush liberal regime (**Aug. 20**).

1969 Richard M. Nixon is inaugurated 37th President of the U.S. (**Jan. 20**). Apollo 11 astronauts—Neil A. Armstrong, Edwin E. Aldrin, Jr., and Michael Collins—take man's first walk on moon (**July 20**). Sen. Edward M. Kennedy pleads guilty to leaving scene of fatal accident at Chappaquiddick, Mass. (**July 18**) in which Mary Jo Kopechne was drowned—gets two-month suspended sentence (**July 25**).

1970 Biafra surrenders after 32-month fight for independence from Nigeria (**Jan. 12**). Rhodesia severs last tie with British Crown and declares itself a racially segregated republic (**March 1**). Four students at Kent State University in Ohio slain by National Guardsmen at demonstration protesting April 30 incursion into Cambodia (**May 4**). Senate repeals Gulf of Tonkin resolution (**June 24**).

1971 Supreme Court rules unanimously that busing of students may be ordered to achieve racial desegregation (**April 20**). Anti-war militants attempt to disrupt government business in Washington (**May 3**)—police and military units arrest as many as 12,000; most are later released. Twenty-sixth Amendment to U.S. Constitution lowers voting age to 18. U.N. seats Communist China and expels Nationalist China (**Oct. 25**).

1972 President Nixon makes unprecedented eight-day visit to Communist China (**Feb.**). Britain takes over direct rule of Northern Ireland in bid for peace (**March 24**). Okinawa reverts to Japan after 27 years of U.S. rule (**May 14**). Gov. George C. Wallace of Alabama is shot by Arthur H. Bremer at Laurel, Md., political rally (**May 15**)—Wallace paralyzed for life from the waist down. Bremer is sentenced to 63 years in prison on **Aug. 4**. Five men are apprehended by police in attempt to bug Democratic National Committee headquarters in Washington D.C.'s Watergate complex—start of the Watergate scandal (**June 17**). Supreme Court rules that death penalty is unconstitutional (**June 29**). Bobby Fischer becomes first American world chess champion, defeating Boris Spassky of U.S.S.R. (**Sept. 1**). Eleven Israeli athletes at Olympic Games in Munich are killed after eight members of an Arab terrorist group invade Olympic Village; five guerrillas and one policeman are also killed (**Sept. 5**).

1973 Great Britain, Ireland, and Denmark enter European Common Market (**Jan. 1**). Indians hold 10 hostages after seizing settlement of Wounded Knee, S.D., demand Government discuss their grievances (**Feb. 28**)—surrender on **May 9**. Nixon, on national TV, accepts responsibility, but

not blame, for Watergate; accepts resignations of advisers H. R. Haldeman and John D. Ehrlichman, fires John W. Dean III as counsel. **(April
30)**. Greek military junta abolishes monarchy and proclaims republic
(June 1). U.S. bombing of Cambodia ends, marking official halt to 12 years
of combat activity in Southeast Asia **(Aug. 15)**. Violent military coup in
Chile deposes President Salvador Allende Gossens, who reportedly
commits suicide **(Sept. 11)**. Fourth and biggest Arab-Israeli War begins as
Egyptian and Syrian forces attack Israel as Jews mark Yom Kippur,
holiest day in their calendar. **(Oct. 6)**. Spiro T. Agnew resigns as Vice
President and then, in Federal Court in Baltimore, pleads no contest to
charges of evasion of income taxes on $29,500 he received in 1967
while Governor of Maryland. He is fined $10,000 and put on three years'
probation **(Oct. 10)**. In the "Saturday Night Massacre," Nixon fires special
Watergate prosecutor Archibald Cox and Deputy Attorney General
William D. Ruckelshaus; Attorney General Elliot L. Richardson resigns
(Oct. 20). Egypt and Israel sign U.S.-sponsored cease-fire accord **(Nov. 11)**.

1974 Patricia Hearst, 19-year-old daughter of publisher Randolph Hearst,
kidnapped by Symbionese Liberation Army. **(Feb. 5)**—Bloodless coup
restores Portuguese democracy **(April 25)**. House Judiciary Committee
adopts three articles of impeachment charging President Nixon with
obstruction of justice, failure to uphold laws, and refusal to produce
material subpoenaed by the committee **(July 30)**. Richard M. Nixon announces he will resign the next day, the first President to do so **(Aug. 8)**.
Vice President Gerald R. Ford of Michigan is sworn in as 38th President
of the U.S. **(Aug. 9)**. Ford grants "full, free, and absolute pardon" to
ex-President Nixon **(Sept. 8)**.

1975 John N. Mitchell, H. R. Haldeman, John D. Ehrlichman, and Robert C.
Mardian found guilty of Watergate cover-up. Mitchell, Haldeman, and
Ehrlichman are sentenced on Feb. 21 to 30 months-8 years in jail and
Mardian to 10 months-3 years **(Jan. 1)**. American merchant ship
Mayaguez, seized by Cambodian forces, is rescued in operation by U.S.
Navy and Marines, 38 of whom are killed **(May 15)**. Suez Canal reopens
after eight years **(June 5)**. *Apollo* and *Soyuz* spacecraft take off for
U.S.-Soviet link-up in space **(July 15)**. Federal jury clears Gov. James A.
Rhodes of Ohio; Robert J. White, former Kent State University Presi-
dent, and 27 Ohio National Guardsmen in $46-million damage suit
brought by 9 wounded students and parents of 4 slain on campus in 1970
(Aug. 27). President Ford escapes assassination attempt in Sacramento,
Calif., **(Sept. 5)**. Patricia Hearst apprehended by FBI. **(Sept. 18)**. President
Ford escapes second assassination attempt in 17 days. **(Sept. 22)**.

1976 Palestine Liberation Organization seated at U.N. **(Jan 13)**. U.S. and Spain
sign five-year treaty of friendship and cooperation **(Jan. 25)**. Supreme
Court rules that blacks and other minorities are entitled to retroactive
job seniority **(March 24)**. Senate Select Intelligence Committee reports
that FBI, CIA, Army intelligence, and other agencies illegally investigated citizen groups, makes sweeping recommendations to control intelligence community **(April 28)**. Ford signs Federal Election Campaign
Act **(May 11)**. Many killed and wounded when South African police fire
on students in Soweto, near Johannesburg, largest black urban center in
country **(June 16)**. Francis E. Meloy, Jr., U.S. Ambassador to Lebanon,
assassinated in Beirut; all Americans advised to leave country as civil
war continues; deaths exceed 30,000 **(June 17)**. Supreme Court rules that
death penalty is not inherently cruel or unusual and is a constitutionally
acceptable form of punishment **(July 3)**. Nation celebrates Bicentennial
(July 4). Israeli airborne commandos attack Uganda's Entebbe Airport
and free 103 hostages held by pro-Palestinian hijackers of Air France
plane; one Israeli and several Ugandan soldiers killed in raid **(July 4)**. New
York disbars ex-President Nixon **(July 8)**. Britain's Ambassador to Ireland
and aide are killed when land mine explodes under their car in Dublin
(July 22). Mysterious disease that eventually claims 29 lives strikes American Legion convention in Philadelphia **(Aug. 4)**. Prince Bernhard of The
Netherlands, caught up in Lockheed Aircraft bribery scandal, resigns all
military and business posts **(Aug. 26)**. Supreme Court lifts stay on death
penalties **(Oct. 4)**. Jimmy Carter elected U.S. President **(Nov. 2)**. Chinese
explode atmospheric nuclear device; fallout over U.S. **(Nov. 17)**.

1977 First woman Episcopal priest ordained **(Jan. 1)**. Scientists identify previously unknown bacterium as cause of mysterious "legionnaire's disease"
(Jan. 18). Astronomers discover water outside of Earth's galaxy, indicating possibility of life in outer space **(Jan. 19)**. New Chinese Government
allows films, plays, and artists previously banned by Cultural Revolution
(Jan. 21). Carter pardons Vietnam draft evaders **(Jan. 21)**. TV adaptation
of *Roots* has total of 130 million viewers, breaking all records **(Jan. 30)**.
Supreme Court upholds use of racial quotas in state reapportionment
plans **(March 1)**. U.S. extends its control of the seas to 200-mile limit **(March

1). NASA reports planet Uranus has five rings (**March 30**). Spain legalizes Communist Party after 38-year ban (**April 9**). Israeli Labor Government defeated in general election by "hawkish" Likud Party (**May 17**). Scientists report using bacteria in lab to make insulin (**May 23**). Lockheed under-the-table payments to foreign nationals to win aircraft contracts revealed to reach $38 million (**May 26**). Tongsun Park identified as Korean agent who allegedly spent millions to influence U.S. officials (**June 4**). Soviets charge Anatoly Shcharansky, Jewish human-rights activist, with treason (**June 4**). Laetrile found useless as cancer cure (**June 15**). Supreme Court rules that states are not required to spend Medicaid funds on elective abortions (**June 20**). Deng Xiaoping, purged Chinese leader, restored to power as "Gang of Four" is expelled from Communist Party (**July 22**). First oil from Alaska's Prudhoe Bay fields pours from 799-mile pipeline at ice-free port of Valdez (**July 28**). U.S. and Cuban Missions open as significant step to restore official relations (**Sept. 1**). Tongsun Park charged by U.S. Justice Department with influence-buying (**Sept. 8**). Nuclear-proliferation pact, curbing spread of nuclear weapons, signed by 15 countries, including U.S. and U.S.S.R. (**Sept. 21**). Thirty-eight persons killed as earthen dam at Toccoa, Ga., collapses during heavy rains (**Nov. 6**). Vatican and Italy agree on accord replacing 1929 concordat; Roman Catholicism no longer state religion (**Nov. 7**). Inquiry into prison death of Steven Biko, black leader, absolves South African security police; U.S. State Department expresses shock (**Dec. 2**). Carter names G. William Miller to replace Arthur F. Burns as Federal Reserve Board Chairman (**Dec. 28**).

1978 Crown of St. Stephen, symbol of sovereignty, returned to Hungary from U.S. (**Jan. 6**). President chooses Federal Appeals Court Judge William H. Webster as FBI director (**Jan. 19**). Soviet spy satellite with atomic reactor breaks up over northwest Canada (**Jan. 24**); signs of radiation found (**Jan. 28**). Rhodesia's Prime Minister Ian D. Smith and three black leaders agree on transfer to black majority rule (**Feb. 15**). Soviet revokes citizenship of expatriate cellist-conductor Mstislav Rostropovich and wife, singer Galina Vishnevskaya (**March 15**). Former Italian Premier Aldo Moro kidnapped by left-wing terrorists, who kill five bodyguards (**March 16**); he is found slain (**May 9**). U.S. Senate approves Panama Canal neutrality treaty (**March 16**); votes treaty to turn canal over to Panama by year 2000 (**April 18**). *Holocaust*, four-night TV dramatization of Nazi extermination of Jews, viewed by 120 million in nation (**April 20**). Supreme Court upholds corporate spending in elections under constitutional right of free speech (**April 26**). All 51 construction workers killed in collapse of power plant cooling tower under construction at St. Mary's, W. Va. (**April 27**). David Berkowitz pleads guilty and gets 25 years to life in each of New York's six "Son of Sam" killings (**May 8**). New 15-cent first-class postage rate takes effect (**May 28**). Californians in referendum approve Proposition 13 for nearly 60% slash in property tax revenues (**June 6**). Mormon Church ends ban on blacks (**June 9**). Supreme Court, in Bakke case, bars quota system in college admissions, but affirms constitutionality of programs giving advantage to minorities (**June 28**); Justices support affirmative action to remedy past discrimination in employment (**July 3**). Baby girl born in England from egg fertilized outside womb in what is believed world's first such case (**July 26**). *New York Times* reporter, M.A. Farber, jailed after losing fight against turning over files in New Jersey murder case; paper fined $5,000 a day (**Aug. 4**); Farber released after 27 days in jail as Jersey Supreme Court suspends contempt citation against him and the *Times* (**Aug. 30**). Pope Paul VI, dead at 80, mourned (**Aug. 6**); new Pope, John Paul I, 65, dies unexpectedly after 34 days in office (**Sept. 28**); succeeded by Karol Cardinal Wojtyla of Poland as John Paul II (**Oct. 16**). William and Emily Harris plead guilty in Symbionese Liberation Army kidnapping of Patricia Hearst (**Aug. 31**). "Framework for Peace" in Middle East signed by Egypt's President Anwar el-Sadat and Israeli Premier Menachem Begin after 13-day conference at Camp David led by President Carter (**Sept. 17**). Senate extends deadline for equal rights amendment ratification until June 30, 1982 (**Oct. 8**). Exodus of Vietnam refugees in small boats hits record; thousands perish at sea (**Nov. 7**). Republicans score gains in Congressional and state elections; Democrats retain political domination (**Nov. 8**). Carter signs energy act including provision to spur conversion from oil and gas to coal (**Nov. 9**). 911 in cult die in mass murder-suicide in Guyanan jungle after California Congressman and four others perish in ambush (**Nov. 20**). Coastal States Gas Corp. reports pact for first oil imports from Communist China (**Nov. 21**). San Francisco Mayor and a city supervisor slain (**Nov. 27**). Former supervisor convicted (**May 21, 1979**). U.S. and China agree to begin diplomatic relations; Carter reassures Taiwan (**Dec. 15**). Oregon man acquitted of raping wife in nation's first such trial (**Dec. 27**).

1979 Oil spills pollute ocean waters in Atlantic and Gulf of Mexico (**Jan. 1, June 8, July 21**). Ohio agrees to pay $675,000 to families of dead and injured in Kent State University shootings (**Jan. 4**). Vietnam and Cambodian insurgents it backs announce fall of Phnom Penh, Cambodian capital, and collapse of Pol Pot regime (**Jan. 7**). Shah leaves Iran after year of turmoil (**Jan. 16**); revolutionary forces under Moslem leader, Ayatollah Ruhollah Khomeini, take over (**Feb. 1**, et seq.). Pope John Paul II acclaimed on visit to Latin America (**Jan 25–31**). Senior Deputy Prime Minister of China, Deng Xiaoping, acclaimed on visit to U.S.; confers with President Carter (**Jan. 28-Feb. 5**). Chinese invade Vietnam (**Feb. 18**); withdraw troops (**March 5**); report 20,000 casualties, with probably 5,000 deaths (**May 2**). Conservatives win British election; Margaret Thatcher new Prime Minister (**March 28**). Nuclear power plant accident at Three Mile Island, Pa., releases radioactivity (**March 28**). Former Prime Minister Zulfikar Ali Bhutto hanged in Pakistan (**April 4**). Government bans interstate shipment of aerosol propellants (**April 15**). Supreme Court backs Federal bugging powers (**April 18**). Los Angeles court orders Lee Marvin to pay $104,000 to singer with whom actor lived out of wedlock for six years (**April 18**). Bishop Abel T. Muzorewa wins interracial Rhodesia election (**April 24**). Gasoline shortage spreads across nation; many states adopt odd-even rationing (**May 10**, et seq.). Florida executes John Arthur Spenkelink, 30, for murder after pleas fail, first involuntary execution in nation since 1967 (**May 25**). Millions cheer Pope on triumphal visit to native Poland (**June 2–10**). Carter offers $18.2-billion health plan for poor and elderly (**June 12**). Carter and Brezhnev sign SALT II agreement (**June 14**). Supreme Court upholds Federal ban on controversial cancer drug laetrile (**June 18**). Nationwide truckers' protest halts 40% of major carriers' hauling capacity (**June 21**). Jeremy Thorpe, former British Liberal Party leader, acquitted in London of plotting to murder alleged former homosexual lover (**June 22**). Supreme Court upholds preference for blacks in jobs (**June 27**). China signs three-year trade treaty with U.S. (**July 7**). President's energy address calls for conservation and increases in oil and gas production (**July 15**). Carter shakes up Cabinet and White House staff (**July 17**). House committee finds conspiracy in John Kennedy assassination (**July 17**). Nicaraguan President Gen. Anastasio Somoza Debayle resigns and flees to Miami (**July 17**); Sandinists form government (**July 19**). Congress votes international trade liberalization (**July 23**). Andrew Young resigns as U.N. delegate from U.S. after reprimand for unauthorized talks with P.L.O. (**Aug 15**). Carter lifts controls on price of domestic crude oil (**Aug. 17**). Diana Nyad, 30, swims from Bahamas to Florida (**Aug. 20**). Earl Mountbatten of Burma, 79, British World War II hero, and three others killed by blast on fishing boat off Irish coast (**Aug. 27**); two I.R.A. members accused (**Aug. 30**). Hurricane David takes heavy death toll in Caribbean; thousands injured and homeless (**Aug. 30**). Spacecraft *Pioneer II* gets first close photos of Saturn (**Sept. 1**). Carter decides on mobile missile system, MX (**Sept. 7**). Worst smog in 24 years hits Southern California (**Sept. 14**). British and French wind up Concorde production (**Sept. 21**). Carter approves controversial Tellico hydroelectric dam on Little Tennessee River (**Sept. 25**). Vietnamese start offensive against Pol Pot regime in Cambodia (**Sept. 25**). Thousands cheer Pope on visit to Ireland and U.S. (**Sept. 29-Oct. 7**). Congress approves Carter proposal for new Department of Education (**Sept. 27**). Carter announces response to Soviet troops in Cuba; reports Russian assurance force has no combat function (**Oct. 1**). Chilean Supreme Court bars extradition of three indicted in U.S. for planning murder of Chilean exile leader (**Oct. 1**). W. A. Boyle, 78, former UMW president, again sentenced to life after new trial in Yablonski killings (**Oct. 11**). Senate votes to denounce Senator Herman E. Talmadge of Georgia on expense account and campaign fund charges (**Oct. 11**). Special investigator clears Carter family business on fund diversion charges in 1976 campaign (**Oct. 16**). Nevada executes Jesse Walter Bishop, 46, Las Vegas casino murderer, in state's first execution in 18 years (**Oct. 22**). Congress votes stand-by gasoline rationing (**Oct. 23**). U.S. surgeons operate on deposed Shah of Iran (**Oct. 24**); Shah dies at 60 (**July 27, 1980**). Park Chung Hee, 62, South Korean President for 18 years, assassinated by intelligence chief (**Oct. 26**). Long-lost da Vinci mural reported discovered in Florence (**Nov. 1**). Iranian militants seize U.S. embassy in Teheran and hold hostages (**Nov. 4**). Times of London resumes publication after shutdown of nearly a year in technology dispute (**Nov. 13**). Lane Kirkland succeeds George Meany as AFL-CIO president (**Nov. 19**). Eleven rock fans killed in crush at Cincinnati's Riverfront Coliseum (**Dec. 3**). Soviet invasion of Afghanistan stirs world protests (**Dec. 27**).

1980 Indira Gandhi wins landslide victory in India (**Jan. 6**). Scientists announce gene splitting produces natural virus-fighting substance (**Jan. 16**). Soviet arrests dissident nuclear physicist Andrei D. Sakharov and wife

(**Jan. 22**). Shigato Nakano, Japanese Army chief, resigns in spy inquiry (**Jan. 28**). Six U.S. Embassy aides escape from Iran with Canadian help (**Jan. 29**). FBI's two-year undercover operation "Abscam" (for Arab scam) implicates public officials (**Feb. 2**). Thirty-three dead in rioting at New Mexico prison (**Feb. 4**). U.S. creates 40 million-acre wildlife refuge in Alaska (**Feb. 12**). Supreme Court upholds CIA's right to censor employees' writings (**Feb. 19**). Arizona court reverses two convictions in killing of reporter (**Feb. 26**). Terrorists hold diplomats hostage for 61 days in Bogota embassy (**Feb. 27-April 27**). Thirty-six dead as snow and cold sweep Southeastern U.S. (**March 3**). Three studies find little saccharin link to cancer (**March 5**). Dr. Herman Tarnower, 69, "Scarsdale diet" doctor, slain (**March 10**). John Wayne Gacy, 37, convicted in Chicago in murders of 33 young men and boys (**March 12**). Indiana jury clears Ford Motor Co. in three Pinto deaths (**March 13**). Robert Muncie enthroned as 102nd Archbishop of Canterbury (**March 25**). Silver price collapse shakes Hunts' $2-billion silver empire (**March 27**). Congress approves "windfall" tax on oil profits (**March 27**). Thousands of Cubans find refuge in U.S. (**April 6** et seq.). U.S. breaks diplomatic ties with Iran (**April 7**). Two Soviet astronauts rendezvous with space station (**April 9**). John B. Anderson, Republican, declares independent candidacy in Presidential campaign (**April 24**). Eight U.S. servicemen are killed and five are injured as helicopter and cargo plane collide in abortive desert raid to rescue American hostages in Teheran (**April 25**); President Carter attacks Iranians for exhibiting bodies (**April 28**). Cyrus R. Vance resigns as U.S. Secretary of State (**April 28**); Senator Edward S. Muskie of Maine succeeds him (**April 29**). Three gunmen seize Iran's embassy in London (**April 30**); British forces storm embassy and free hostages (**May 5**). Georgia Federal court jury acquits Bert Lance, former U.S. Budget Director, on nine bank fraud charges (**April 30**). Death toll 17 in Miami race rioting after acquittal of four white former policemen in fatal beating of black (**May 17**). First women graduate from service academies (**May 21, 28**). Three U.S. computer errors signal Soviet attack (**June 3**). Congress overrides Carter veto of oil-import fee repeal (**June 5, 6**). Congress votes $3.3 million for draft registration (**June 12, 25**). High court upholds patents for new forms of life (**June 16**). Crack in Milan church wall endangers da Vinci's *Last Supper* (**June 16**). Many dead as police and demonstrators clash in South Africa (**June 17**). Carter approves shipment of nuclear fuel to India (**June 19**). Congress votes $20-billion synthetic fuels program (**June 26**). Supreme Court upholds limits on Federal aid for abortions (**June 30**). Justices approve affirmative action for minority contractors in Federal works program (**July 2**). Court affirms public and press right of access to criminal trials (**July 2**). Billy Carter registers as agent of Libya (**July 14**). Women's second world conference opens in Copenhagen (**July 14**). Synanon founder and two aides guilty in rattlesnake death plot (**July 15**). Republican National Convention nominates Reagan-Bush slate (**July 16, 17**). Federal Court rules draft registration unconstitutional because of exclusion of women (**July 18**). Olympic games open in Moscow, boycotted by U.S. and other nations (**July 19**). Woman violinist slain at Metropolitan Opera House in New York (**July 24**). U.S. strengthens guidelines for bilingual education (**Aug. 5**). Giant panda born in Mexico City zoo; lives for eight days (**Aug. 12**). Democratic Convention renominates Carter and Mondale (**Aug. 13, 14**). Vatican rules married Anglican priests can join Catholic clergy (**Aug. 20**). Polish workers end 18-day walkout with Government pledges of political and economic concessions (**Sept. 1**). Drought ravages crops across much of Eastern U.S. (**Sept. 11**). EPA postpones auto pollution limits (**Sept. 17**). Anastasio Somoza Debayle, ousted Nicaragua ruler, and two aides assassinated in Asunción, Paraguay capital (**Sept. 17**). Screen actors and producers agree to formula for settling nine-week strike over pay-TV recompense (**Sept. 17**). Iraqi troops hold 90 square miles of Iran after invasion (**Sept. 19**); as scale of warfare grows, U.N. Security Council appeals to both sides to cease fighting (**Sept. 23**); Iraqis pushing deep into Iran (**Sept. 24**). New Turkish Prime Minister forms civilian cabinet (**Sept. 21**). Procter & Gamble recalls Rely Tampon after U.S. studies find toxic shock risk (**Sept. 22**). New law gives Gandhi Government in India power to imprison without trial (**Sept. 23**). U.S. decides to send radar aircraft to Saudi Arabia (**Sept. 30**). Aleksei N. Kosygin, 76, ailing Soviet Prime Minister, resigns (**Oct. 23**). Four-party coalition government is formed in Italy (**Oct. 25**). Carter and Reagan meet in nationally televised debate (**Oct. 28**). *Voyager I* photographs two more Saturnian moons (**Oct. 28**).

(For later events, *See* Current Events, 1980–81, in Table of Contents.)

WORLD STATISTICS

Area and Population by Country
Mid-1981 Estimates

Country	Area[1]	Population	Country	Area[1]	Population
Afghanistan	251,000	16,250,000	Hungary	35,919	10,725,000
Albania	11,100	2,800,000	Iceland	39,702	235,000
Algeria	919,951	20,250,000	India[7]	1,229,737	683,810,000
Andorra	175	30,000	Indonesia[8]	735,268	155,300,000
Angola	481,350	7,250,000	Iran	636,363	37,400,000
Argentina	1,972,067	27,400,000	Iraq	172,000	13,400,000
Australia	2,967,909	14,900,00	Ireland	26,600	3,460,000
Austria	32,375	7,515,000	Israel	7,992[9]	4,000,000
Bahamas	4,404	225,000	Italy	116,304	57,150,000
Bahrain	240	400,000	Ivory Coast	124,502	8,500,000
Bangladesh	55,126	90,700,000	Jamaica	4,411	2,225,000
Barbados	166	250,000	Japan	143,574	117,650,000
Belgium	11,781	9,870,000	Jordan	37,297	3,300,000
Belize	8,867	160,000	Kenya	224,960	16,300,000
Benin	43,483	3,675,000	Kiribati	264	60,000
Bhutan	19,305	1,325,000	Korea, North	46,768	18,350,000
Bolivia	424,162	5,750,000	Korea, South	38,031	38,800,000
Botswana	222,000	750,000	Kuwait	7,780	1,440,000
Brazil	3,286,470	127,000,000	Laos	91,429	3,800,000
Bulgaria	42,823	8,875,000	Lebanon	4,015	3,230,000
Burma	261,789	34,350,000	Lesotho	11,720	1,375,000
Burundi	10,747	4,650,000	Liberia	43,000	1,920,000
Cambodia	70,000	9,000,000	Libya	679,536	3,100,000
Cameroon	183,569	8,650,000	Liechtenstein	61	30,000
Canada	3,851,809	24,000,000	Luxembourg	999	80,000
Cape Verde	1,557	330,000	Madagascar	230,035	9,000,000
Central African Republic	241,313	2,500,000	Malawi	45,747	6,125,000
Chad	495,752	4,650,000	Malaysia	128,328	14,000,000
Chile	286,396	11,275,000	Maldives	115	150,000
China, People's Republic of[2]	3,691,521	970,000,000	Mali	464,873	7,100,000
China, Republic of[3]	13,592	18,000,000	Malta	122	350,000
Colombia	455,355	28,500,000	Mauritania	419,229	1,675,000
Comoros	692	330,000	Mauritius	787	975,000
Congo	132,046	1,580,000	Mexico	761,600	74,500,000
Costa Rica	19,652	2,300,000	Monaco	(10)	30,000
Cuba	44,218	9,990,000	Mongolia	604,250	1,725,000
Cyprus	3,572	635,000	Morocco	171,953	20,500,000
Czechoslovakia	49,374	15,400,000	Mozambique	303,073	10,750,000
Denmark[4]	16,615	5,130,000	Nauru	8.2	8,000
Djibouti	8,996	330,000	Nepal	54,362	14,325,000
Dominica	300	85,000	Netherlands	13,967	14,250,000
Dominican Republic	18,704	5,580,000	New Zealand[11]	103,736	3,150,000
Ecuador	105,685	8,625,000	Nicaragua	57,143	2,750,000
Egypt	386,872	43,000,000	Niger	489,206	5,550,000
El Salvador	8,260	4,750,000	Nigeria	356,700	79,575,000
Equatorial Guinea	10,830	370,000	Norway	125,182	4,150,000
Ethiopia	457,142	32,000,000	Oman[12]	82,000	920,000
Fiji	7,055	625,000	Pakistan[13]	342,750	85,000,000
Finland	130,119	4,800,000	Panama	29,306	2,000,000
France	212,973	53,950,000	Papua New Guinea	183,540	3,250,000
Gabon	102,317	550,000	Paraguay	157,047	3,165,000
Gambia	4,016	625,000	Peru	496,222	18,300,000
Germany, East[5]	40,646	16,730,000	Philippines	115,707	49,000,000
Germany, West[6]	95,815	61,400,000	Poland	120,359	35,900,000
Ghana	92,100	11,750,000	Portugal	35,340	10,000,000
Greece	50,547	9,700,000	Qatar	4,000	230,000
Grenada	133	110,000	Romania	91,700	22,500,000
Guatemala	42,042	7,470,000	Rwanda	10,169	5,200,000
Guinea	94,925	5,115,000	St. Lucia	238	125,000
Guinea-Bissau	13,948	580,000	St. Vincent and the Grenadines	250	120,000
Guyana	83,000	890,000	San Marino	23.6	20,500
Haiti	10,714	5,100,000	São Tomé and Príncipe	372	90,000
Honduras	43,277	3,825,000	Saudi Arabia	873,000	8,650,000

Country	Area[1]	Population	Country	Area[1]	Population
Senegal	76,124	5,800,000	Turkey	301,380	45,500,000
Seychelles	171	60,000	Tuvalu	10	7,000
Sierra Leone	27,925	3,560,000	Uganda	91,134	14,000,000
Singapore	238	2,420,000	U.S.S.R.	8,649,489	267,600,000
Solomon Islands	11,500	225,000	United Arab Emirates	32,000	850,000
Somalia	246,155	3,750,000	United Kingdom	94,249	55,900,000
South Africa[14]	322,061	24,000,000	United States	3,540,939	230,000,000
Spain[15]	194,885	37,750,000	Upper Volta	105,870	7,100,000
Sri Lanka	25,332	15,000,000	Uruguay	68,548	2,925,000
Sudan	967,491	18,750,000	Vanuatu (New Hebrides)	5,700	110,000
Suriname	63,251	400,000	Vatican City State	[17]	1,000
Swaziland	6,704	550,000	Venezuela	352,143	14,300,000
Sweden	173,665	8,330,000	Vietnam	126,436	53,550,000
Switzerland	15,941	6,375,000	Western Samoa	1,133	160,000
Syria	71,498	9,325,000	Yemen, People's Democratic		
Tanzania[16]	362,820	19,000,000	Republic of[18]	111,000	1,950,000
Thailand	198,455	48,175,000	Yemen Arab Republic	75,290	6,100,000
Togo	21,853	2,600,000	Yugoslavia	98,766	22,550,000
Tonga	290	100,000	Zaire	905,063	29,450,000
Trinidad and Tobago	1,980	1,145,000	Zambia	290,724	6,000,000
Tunisia	63,379	6,500,000	Zimbabwe	150,333	7,580,000

1. Square miles. 2. Including Manchuria and Tibet. 3. Excluding Quemoy and Matsu. 4. Excluding Faeroe Islands and Greenland. 5. Including East Berlin. 6. Excluding West Berlin. 7. Including Jammu and Kashmir and Sikkim. 8. Including Portuguese East Timor, annexed in 1976, and Irian Jaya (former Netherlands New Guinea and later West Irian). 9. Excluding territory occupied in 1967 war. 10. 0.65 square mile. 11. Excluding dependencies. 12. Excluding Kuria Muria Islands. 13. Excluding Jammu and Kashmir. 14. Excluding South-West Africa (Namibia), Bophuthatswana, Transkei, and Venda. 15. Including Balearic and Canary Islands. 16. Including Zanzibar. 17. 0.17 square mile. 18. Excluding Perim and Kamaran Islands.

Largest Cities of the World

Census figures and population estimates in the following table are based on data reflecting different years. Some cities include metropolitan areas or contiguous suburbs, while others report only those residing within precise geographical or physical boundaries. Therefore, the ratings in this listing must be considered approximate.

City	Population	Year	City	Population	Year
São Paulo, Brazil	12,578,045	1980C	Manila	7,500,000	1977E
Shanghai	11,000,000	1979E	New York	7,071,030	1980C
Mexico City	9,200,000	1979E	London	6,877,000	1979E
Calcutta	9,165,650	1980C	Jakarta, Indonesia	6,400,000	1980E
Rio de Janeiro	9,011,981	1980C	Cairo	5,423,000	1977E
Peking	9,000,000	1979E	Bangkok, Thailand	5,000,000	1980E
Tokyo	8,500,000	1980E	Karachi, Pakistan	5,000,000	1980E
Seoul, South Korea	8,400,000	1980E	Lima, Peru	4,900,000	1979E
Bombay	8,202,759	1980C	Leningrad	4,588,000	1979C
Moscow	8,011,000	1979C	Teheran, Iran	4,496,000	1976C

Source: United Nations *Demographic Yearbook, 1978,* and official estimates. NOTE: E = estimate: C = census.

Some Other Large Foreign Cities

City	Population	Year[1]	City	Population	Year[1]
Addis Ababa, Ethiopia	1,250,000	1980E	Barranquilla, Colombia	868,000	1979E
Ahmedabad, India	2,515,195	1980C	Belfast, Northern Ireland	354,000	1978E
Alexandria, Egypt	2,318,655	1976C	Belgrade, Yugoslavia	1,000,000	1980E
Algiers	2,500,000	1979E	Belo Horizonte, Brazil	2,534,576	1980C
Alma Ata, U.S.S.R.	910,000	1979C	Berlin[3]	3,034,000	1979E
Amsterdam	957,700	1979E	Bern, Switzerland	142,800	1979E
Ankara, Turkey	2,561,765	1980C	Birmingham, England	1,034,000	1979E
Antwerp, Belgium	927,200[2]	1978E	Bogotá, Colombia	4,300,000	1980E
Athens	3,000,000[2]	1981E	Bonn, West Germany	285,000	1977E
Auckland, New Zealand	753,100[2]	1980E	Brasilia, Brazil	1,000,000	1980E
Baghdad, Iraq	3,205,600	1977E	Brisbane, Australia	1,004,500[2]	1978E
Baku, U.S.S.R.	1,550,000	1979C	Brussels	1,029,000[2]	1978E
Badung, Indonesia	1,201,730	1971C	Bucharest	1,807,000	1977E
Bangalore, India	2,913,537	1980C	Budapest	2,100,000	1980E
Barcelona	1,725,000	1981E	Buenos Aires	3,000,000	1980E

City	Population	Year[1]	City	Population	Year[1]
Calgary, Canada	469,917	1976C	Melbourne	2,717,600[2]	1978E
Cali, Colombia	1,189,000	1979E	Milan, Italy	1,696,250	1978E
Canton, China	2,300,000	1970E	Minsk, U.S.S.R.	1,276,000	1979C
Cape Town, South Africa	892,000	1980E	Monterrey, Mexico	1,054,000	1978E
Caracas, Venezuela	2,950,000	1980E	Montevideo, Uruguay	1,229,700	1975E
Casablanca, Morocco	2,220,000	1979E	Montreal	1,080,546	1976C
Chongqing (Chungking), China	3,500,000	1970E	Munich, West Germany	1,299,800	1979E
Cologne, West Germany	794,200	1979E	Nagoya, Japan	2,080,000	1976E
Copenhagen	660,000	1980E	Nanjing (Nanking), China	2,000,000	1970E
Córdoba, Argentina	781,600	1975E	Nantes, France	263,689	1975C
Dacca, Bangladesh	2,500,000	1980E	Naples, Italy	1,226,100	1978E
Damascus, Syria	1,150,000	1979E	Nice, France	346,620	1975C
Delhi, India	6,196,414	1980C	Novosibirsk, U.S.S.R.	1,312,000	1979C
Dnepropetrovsk, U.S.S.R.	1,066,000	1979C	Odessa, U.S.S.R.	1,046,000	1979C
Donetsk, U.S.S.R.	1,021,000	1979C	Osaka, Japan	2,750,500	1976E
Dublin	543,600	1979E	Oslo	460,400	1978E
Düsseldorf, West Germany	596,600	1979E	Ottawa	394,462	1976C
Edinburgh, Scotland	455,000	1979E	Paris	2,150,000	1980E
Florence, Italy	463,300	1978E	Port-au-Prince, Haiti	745,000	1978E
Frankfurt, West Germany	629,000	1979E	Porto Alegre, Brazil	2,332,370[2]	1980C
Fukuoka, Japan	1,039,300[2]	1977E	Prague	1,188,600	1979E
Geneva	152,700	1980E	Pusan, South Korea	3,160,000	1980E
Genoa, Italy	789,500	1978E	Pyongyang, North Korea	1,500,000	1976E
Glasgow, Scotland	794,000	1979E	Quebec	177,082	1976C
Gorki, U.S.S.R.	1,344,000	1979C	Quezon City, Philippines	994,700	1975E
Guadalajara, Mexico	1,813,000	1978E	Quito, Ecuador	775,000	1980E
Guatemala City	1,000,000	1980E	Rangoon, Burma	2,200,000	1979E
Guayaquil, Ecuador	1,100,000	1980E	Recife, Brazil	2,346,196[2]	1980C
The Hague	671,500	1979E	Riyadh, Saudi Arabia	1,250,000	1980E
Haifa, Israel	227,200	1976E	Rome	2,900,000	1980E
Hamburg, West Germany	1,658,100	1979E	Rosario, Argentina	750,500	1975E
Harbin, China	2,750,000	1970E	Rostov-on-Don, U.S.S.R.	934,000	1979C
Havana	2,000,000	1979E	Rotterdam	1,014,800	1979E
Helsinki, Finland	484,000	1981E	Salvador, Brazil	1,766,075[2]	1980C
Ho Chi Minh City (Saigon), Vietnam	3,460,500	1976E	Santiago, Chile	3,850,000	1980E
Hyderabad, India	1,607,396	1971C	Santo Domingo, Dominican Republic	1,103,400	1979E
Hyderabad, Pakistan	628,310	1972C	Sapporo, Japan	1,307,700[2]	1977E
Ibadan, Nigeria	847,000	1975E	Seville, Spain	630,000	1981E
Istanbul	2,990,680	1980C	Shenyang, China	3,750,000[2]	1970E
Jerusalem	412,000	1981E	Singapore, Singapore	2,308,200	1977E
Johannesburg, South Africa	1,500,000	1980E	Sofia, Bulgaria	1,000,000	1979E
Kanpur, India	1,685,308	1980C	Stockholm	1,400,000	1980E
Kharkov, U.S.S.R.	1,444,000	1979C	Stuttgart, West Germany	582,100	1979E
Kiev, U.S.S.R.	2,144,000	1979C	Surabaja, Indonesia	1,556,255	1971C
Kinshasa, Zaire	2,500,000	1979E	Sverdlovsk, U.S.S.R.	1,211,000	1979C
Kobe, Japan	1,366,500[2]	1977E	Sydney, Australia	3,200,000[2]	1980E
Kuala Lumpur, Malaysia	1,000,000	1980E	Taipai, Taiwan	2,225,000	1980E
Kuibyshev, U.S.S.R.	1,216,000	1979C	Tashkent, U.S.S.R.	1,779,000	1979C
Kunming, China	1,700,000	1970E	Tbilisi, U.S.S.R.	1,066,000	1979C
Lagos, Nigeria	4,000,000[2]	1980E	Tel Aviv-Jaffa, Israel	336,000	1979E
Lahore, Pakistan	2,165,372	1972C	Tianjin (Tientsin), China	4,280,000	1970E
La Paz, Bolivia	700,000	1979E	Toronto	633,318	1976C
Lausanne, Switzerland	131,000	1980E	Tunis, Tunisia	960,000[2]	1976E
Liège, Belgium	617,000[2]	1978E	Turin, Italy	1,172,900	1978E
Lisbon	861,500	1979E	Valparaiso, Chile	248,500	1978E
Liverpool, England	520,000	1979E	Valencia, Spain	770,000	1981E
Lódz, Poland	830,800	1980E	Vancouver, Canada	410,188	1976C
Luda, China	4,000,000	1970E	Venice	358,400	1978E
Lyallpur, Pakistan	822,263	1972C	Vienna	1,580,600	1978E
Lyons, France	462,841	1975C	Volgograd, U.S.S.R.	929,000	1979C
Madras, India	2,469,449	1971C	Warsaw	1,576,600	1980E
Madrid	3,275,000	1981E	Wellington, New Zealand	326,000	1980E
Marseilles, France	914,356	1975C	Winnipeg, Canada	560,874	1976C
Mecca, Saudi Arabia	500,000	1980E	Yokohama, Japan	2,694,500[2]	1977E
Medellín, Colombia	1,748,000	1979E	Zurich	377,300	1980E

1. E = estimated; C = census. 2. Figure is for metropolitan area and may include suburbs or some rural population. 3. West Berlin, 1,905,000; East Berlin, 1,129,000. NOTE: The population of many other cities will be found throughout the World History section under individual countries. *See* Table of Contents.

Expectation of Life by Age and Sex for Selected Countries

Country	Period	Males 0	1	10	20	40	60	Females 0	1	10	20	40	60
NORTH AMERICA													
United States	1975	68.7	68.9	60.3	50.8	32.6	16.8	76.5	76.6	67.9	58.1	39.0	21.8
Canada	1970–72	69.3	69.8	61.2	51.7	33.2	17.0	76.4	76.6	67.9	58.2	39.0	21.4
Mexico	1975	62.8	68.0	59.2	49.9	32.7	17.9	66.6	69.3	62.6	53.1	35.3	19.1
Puerto Rico	1976	70.2	70.8	62.1	52.3	34.8	19.0	77.1	77.5	68.7	58.9	39.7	22.0
Trinidad and Tobago	1970	64.1	65.6	57.3	47.8	29.5	13.6	68.1	69.3	60.9	51.3	32.7	16.3
CENTRAL AND SOUTH AMERICA													
Brazil	1960–70	57.6	—	56.2	47.0	30.0	15.0	61.1	—	58.9	49.7	32.5	16.6
Chile	1969–70	60.5	64.9	56.7	47.3	29.9	15.5	66.0	70.0	62.2	52.7	34.5	18.0
Colombia	1950–52	44.2	50.4	48.2	39.6	24.8	11.8	45.9	51.1	49.4	40.9	26.6	12.8
Costa Rica	1972–74	66.3	69.1	61.3	51.8	33.8	17.4	70.5	72.7	64.9	55.2	36.5	19.2
Ecuador	1962–74	54.9	60.5	55.5	47.1	31.3	16.2	58.1	62.8	58.0	49.3	33.0	17.3
Guatemala	1963–65	48.3	52.5	51.3	43.2	28.1	14.8	49.7	53.4	52.8	44.6	29.2	14.7
Panama	1970	64.3	66.4	59.9	50.8	33.4	17.0	67.5	69.4	62.7	53.6	36.1	19.9
Uruguay	1963–64	65.5	68.0	59.5	50.0	31.7	15.9	71.6	73.7	65.2	55.5	36.7	19.5
Venezuela[1]	1961	66.4	68.8	61.8	52.4	34.6	18.9	—	—	—	—	—	—
EUROPE													
Austria	1976	68.1	—	59.9	50.4	32.0	15.7	75.1	—	66.6	56.8	37.6	19.7
Belgium	1968–72	67.8	68.4	59.9	50.3	31.6	15.2	74.2	74.5	65.9	56.1	36.9	19.2
Cyprus	1973	70.0	70.7	62.1	52.3	33.5	16.5	72.9	74.2	65.7	55.8	36.4	18.5
Czechoslovakia	1970	66.2	67.0	58.4	49.9	30.6	14.6	72.9	72.6	64.9	55.2	35.9	18.3
Denmark[2]	1975–76	71.1	70.9	62.3	52.6	33.7	17.1	76.8	76.5	67.7	57.9	38.5	21.1
Finland	1975	67.4	67.1	58.5	48.9	30.6	15.0	75.9	75.6	66.8	57.0	37.7	19.7
France	1976	69.2	69.2	60.5	51.0	32.5	16.7	77.2	77.0	68.3	58.6	39.3	21.5
Germany, East[3]	1976	68.8	69.0	60.4	50.8	32.2	15.9	74.4	74.3	65.6	55.9	36.6	18.8
Germany, West[3]	1975–77	68.6	69.0	60.4	50.9	32.3	15.8	75.2	75.4	66.7	56.9	37.7	19.9
Greece	1970	70.1	72.2	63.8	54.1	35.1	17.5	73.6	75.3	66.9	57.1	37.8	19.3
Hungary	1974	66.5	68.2	59.5	49.9	31.5	15.5	72.4	73.7	65.1	55.3	36.1	18.7
Ireland	1970–72	68.8	69.2	60.6	51.0	32.1	15.6	73.5	73.8	65.1	55.3	40.8	18.7
Italy	1970–72	69.0	70.1	61.6	52.0	33.2	16.7	74.9	75.8	67.1	57.3	38.1	20.2
Netherlands	1977	72.0	71.8	63.2	53.5	34.4	17.4	78.4	78.1	69.4	59.6	40.2	22.1
Norway	1976–77	72.1	71.9	63.2	53.6	34.7	17.7	78.4	78.1	69.4	59.5	40.0	21.8
Poland	1970–72	66.8	68.0	59.4	49.8	31.6	15.5	73.8	74.6	66.0	56.2	37.0	19.3
Portugal	1974	65.3	67.2	59.0	49.6	31.5	15.4	72.0	73.5	65.3	55.6	36.5	18.7
Spain	1970	69.7	—	62.0	52.4	33.7	17.0	75.0	—	66.9	57.1	38.0	20.1
Sweden	1972–76	72.1	71.9	63.1	53.5	34.7	17.6	77.8	77.4	68.6	58.8	39.5	21.4
Switzerland	1968–73	70.3	70.5	62.0	52.4	33.6	16.7	76.2	76.2	67.6	57.8	38.4	20.4
U.S.S.R.	1971–72	64.0	—	—	—	—	—	74.0	—	—	—	—	—
United Kingdom													
England and Wales	1974–76	69.6	—	—	—	—	—	75.8	—	—	—	—	—
Northern Ireland	1975–77	67.5	67.9	59.3	49.7	31.2	14.9	73.8	74.2	65.5	55.7	36.4	19.0
Scotland	1971–73	67.2	67.8	59.2	49.8	31.3	15.0	73.6	74.1	65.4	55.6	36.3	18.9
Yugoslavia	1970–72	65.4	68.0	59.7	50.1	31.8	15.7	70.2	72.8	64.6	54.9	35.8	18.2
ASIA													
Bangladesh	1974	45.8	53.5	50.5	42.5	28.1	14.4	46.6	53.5	50.3	42.2	27.7	14.1
India	1951–60	41.9	48.4	45.2	36.9	22.1	11.8	40.6	46.0	43.8	35.6	22.4	12.9
Iran	1973–76	57.6	63.5	59.1	49.7	31.4	16.1	57.4	64.0	60.9	51.6	33.7	17.9
Israel	1977	71.3	71.7	63.0	53.5	34.6	17.6	74.7	74.9	66.3	56.5	37.1	19.2
Japan[4]	1974	71.2	71.0	62.5	52.8	33.0	17.0	76.3	76.0	67.4	57.5	38.3	20.3
Korea, South	1970	63.0	66.0	58.0	49.0	31.0	16.0	67.0	69.0	61.0	52.0	34.0	17.0
Pakistan	1962	53.7	60.6	57.0	47.8	30.8	15.6	48.8	53.9	51.7	42.9	27.7	15.5
Sri Lanka	1967	64.8	67.4	60.5	51.2	33.2	17.0	66.9	68.9	62.4	53.0	35.0	17.8
Syria	1970	54.5	60.7	56.4	47.4	30.5	15.2	58.7	64.1	59.5	50.5	33.3	17.3
AFRICA													
Egypt	1960	51.6	56.2	56.6	47.7	30.5	15.1	53.8	59.9	62.0	52.9	35.0	18.0
Kenya	1969	46.9	52.6	51.0	43.0	28.3	14.5	51.2	56.6	54.1	45.7	30.3	15.7
South Africa (white population)	1959–61	64.7	65.9	57.5	48.0	30.2	15.0	71.7	72.5	64.1	54.4	35.5	18.6
OCEANIA													
Australia[5]	1965–67	67.6	68.1	59.5	50.0	31.4	15.8	74.2	74.4	65.8	56.0	36.9	19.5
New Zealand	1970–72	68.5	—	—	—	—	—	74.6	—	—	—	—	—

1. Figures for male and female together. 2. Excluding data for Faeroe Islands and Greenland. 3. Includes relevant data relating to Berlin. No separate data have been supplied. 4. Japanese nationals in Japan only. 5. Excludes full-blooded aborigines. NOTE: Figures are latest available. *Source:* United Nations *Demographic Yearbook, 1978.*

Estimates of World Population by Regions

				Estimated population in millions				
Year	North America[1]	Latin America[2]	Europe[3]	U.S.S.R.	Asia[4]	Africa	Oceania	World total
1650	1	7	103	[5]	257	100	2	470
1750	1	10	144	[5]	437	100	2	694
1850	26	33	274	[5]	656	100	2	1,091
1900	81	63	423	[5]	857	141	6	1,571
1930	134	108	355[6]	179	1,120[7]	164	10	2,070
1950	166	164	392[6]	180	1,368[7]	219	13	2,501
1960	199	216	425[6]	214	1,644[7]	273	16	2,986
1970	226	283	459[6]	243	2,027[7]	352	19	3,610
1975	264	297	4,736	255	2,256[7]	401	21	3,967
1977	240	340	478[6]	259	2,413[7]	430	22	4,182
1978	242	349	480[6]	262	2,461[7]	442	22	4,258

1. U.S. (including Alaska and Hawaii), Bermuda, Canada, Greenland, and St. Pierre and Miquelon. 2. Mexico, Central and South America, and Caribbean Islands. 3. Includes Russia 1650–1900. 4. Excludes Russia (U.S.S.R.). 5. Included in Europe. 6. Excludes European Turkey, which is included in Asia. 7. Includes both Asian and European Turkey. NOTE: Figures are latest available. *Sources:* W.F. Willcox, 1650–1900; United Nations, 1930–78.

Crude Birth and Death Rates for Selected Countries
(per 1,000 population)

	Birth rates					Death rates				
Country	1980	1979	1975	1970	1965	1980	1979	1975	1970	1965
Australia	15.4	15.5	16.9	20.6	19.6	7.4	7.4	7.9	9.0	8.8
Austria	12.0	11.4	12.5	15.2	17.9	12.2	12.2	12.8	13.4	13.0
Belgium	12.7	12.6	12.2	14.7	16.4	11.6	11.4	12.2	12.3	12.5
Canada	n.a.	15.5	15.8	17.4	21.4	n.a.	7.1	7.4	7.3	7.5
Czechoslovakia	16.4	17.8	19.6	15.9	16.4	12.1	11.5	11.5	11.6	10.0
Denmark	11.2	11.6	14.2	14.4	18.2	10.9	10.7	10.1	9.8	10.1
El Salvador	34.7	39.1	38.9	40.0	46.5	7.9	7.4	7.9	9.9	10.6
Finland	13.1	13.3	13.9	14.0	17.0	9.4	9.2	9.3	9.6	7.9
France	14.8	14.1	14.1	16.8	17.7	10.1	10.2	10.6	10.7	11.1
Germany, East	14.6	14.0	10.8	13.9	16.5	14.2	13.9	14.3	14.1	13.3
Germany, West	10.0	9.5	9.7	11.4	17.9	11.5	11.6	12.1	12.1	11.2
Greece	n.a.	15.9	15.7	16.5	17.7	n.a.	8.7	8.9	8.4	7.9
Hungary	13.9	15.0	18.4	14.7	13.1	13.6	12.8	12.4	11.6	10.7
Ireland	n.a.	21.5	21.5	21.8	22.2	n.a.	9.7	10.6	11.4	11.5
Israel	24.1	24.7	28.2	26.9	25.4	6.7	6.9	7.1	7.1	6.2
Italy	11.2	11.8	14.8	16.8	19.2	9.7	9.4	9.9	9.7	10.0
Japan	13.7	14.3	17.2	18.9	18.6	6.2	6.0	6.4	6.9	7.1
Luxembourg	11.5	11.2	11.2	13.2	15.6	11.3	11.0	12.2	12.3	11.8
Malta	15.4	16.6	18.3	16.3	17.6	9.1	8.9	8.8	9.4	9.4
Mauritius	27.0	27.5	25.1	26.0	35.4	7.2	7.3	8.1	7.8	8.6
Mexico	n.a.	n.a.	37.5	42.1	45.3	n.a.	n.a.	7.2	9.6	9.5
Netherlands	n.a.	12.5	13.0	18.3	19.9	n.a.	8.0	8.3	8.4	8.0
New Zealand	n.a.	16.7	18.4	22.1	22.8	n.a.	8.2	8.1	8.8	8.7
Norway	12.5	12.8	14.1	16.6	17.5	10.0	10.1	9.9	10.0	9.1
Panama	26.8	29.4	32.3	37.2	39.1	n.a.	n.a.	n.a.	8.8[1]	7.3
Poland	19.4	19.5	18.9	16.8	17.3	9.7	9.2	8.7	8.2	7.4
Portugal	n.a.	n.a.	19.1	20.0	22.9	n.a.	n.a.	10.4	10.8	10.1
Singapore	17.3	17.3	17.8	23.0	31.1	5.2	5.3	5.1	5.2	5.6
Spain	n.a.	16.1	19.1	19.5	21.3	n.a.	7.8	8.2	8.3	8.7
Sweden	11.7	11.6	12.6	13.7	15.9	11.0	11.0	10.8	9.9	10.1
Switzerland	11.9	11.3	12.3	15.8	18.7	9.2	9.0	8.7	9.1	9.3
Tunisia	n.a.	n.a.	36.6	36.4	44.3	n.a.	n.a.	n.a.	17.6[1]	11.8
United Kingdom	13.5	13.1	12.5	16.3	18.4	12.0	12.1	11.9	11.8	11.5
United States	16.2	15.8	14.8	18.3	19.4	8.9	8.7	8.9	9.4	9.4
Yugoslavia	17.0	17.1	18.2	17.8	20.9	9.0	8.5	8.7	8.9	8.7

1. 1969–70 figure. NOTE: n.a. = not available. *Source:* United Nations, *Monthly Bulletin of Statistics*, June 1981.

Suicide Rates for Selected Countries
(per 100,000 population)

Country	Year	Rate	Country	Year	Rate	Country	Year	Rate
Angola	1972	1.0	Guatemala	1972	3.4	Singapore	1977	9.7
Australia	1977	11.1	Hong Kong	1977	12.3	South Africa		
Argentina	1977	7.8	Hungary	1977	40.3	Black	1971	5.6
Austria	1976	22.7	Iceland	1977	10.4	White	1971	14.5
Barbados	1975	1.2	Ireland	1975	4.7	Spain	1975	3.9
Belgium	1976	16.6	Israel	1977	6.5	Sweden	1975	19.4
Bulgaria	1976	14.1	Italy	1972	5.8	Switzerland	1977	23.8
Canada	1976	12.8	Jamaica	1971	1.0	Trinidad and		
Chile	1976	5.7	Japan	1977	17.8	Tobago	1976	8.9
Costa Rica	1977	4.4	Mexico	1975	1.7	Turkey	1971	1.9
Cuba	1971	15.0	Netherlands	1977	9.2	United Kingdom		
Czechoslovakia	1976	20.8	New Zealand	1976	9.2	England and		
Denmark	1976	23.9	Norway	1977	11.4	Wales	1976	7.8
Ecuador	1975	2.7	Panama	1975	2.6	Northern		
El Salvador	1971	8.7	Paraguay	1977	1.8	Ireland	1977	4.6
Finland	1974	25.1	Peru	1972	1.8	Scotland	1977	8.1
France	1970	15.4	Philippines	1974	1.1	United States	1976	12.5
Germany, East	1970	30.5	Poland	1977	12.4	Uruguay	1976	10.8
Germany, West	1976	21.7	Portugal	1975	8.5	Venezuela	1977	4.6
Greece	1976	2.8	Puerto Rico	1977	9.5	Yugoslavia	1975	13.4

NOTE: Figures are latest available. *Source:* United Nations *Demographic Yearbook, 1978.*

Cost of Living of United Nations Personnel in Selected Cities as Reflected by Index of Retail Prices, 1980
(New York City = 100)

City	Index	City	Index	City	Index
Addis Ababa, Ethiopia	95	Dar es Salaam, Tanzania	93	New Delhi, India	86
Algiers, Algeria	127	Geneva	142	Nicosia, Cyprus	84
Amman, Jordan	120	Guatemala City, Guatemala	99	Paris	139
Ankara, Turkey	79	The Hague, the Netherlands	134	Quito, Ecuador	86
Athens	108	Havana	81	Rabat, Morocco	126
Baghdad, Iraq	93	Jakarta, Indonesia	109	Rangoon, Burma	79
Bangkok, Thailand	89	Kabul, Afghanistan	89	Rio de Janeiro	88
Beirut, Lebanon	97	Islamabad, Pakistan	89	Rome	100
Belgrade, Yugoslavia	92	Katmandu, Nepal	86	San José, Costa Rica	105
Bogotá, Colombia	93	Kingston, Jamaica	70	San Salvador, El Salvador	100
Bonn, West Germany	134	Kinshasha, Zaire	147	Santiago, Chile	116
Brazzaville, Congo	137	La Paz, Bolivia	103	Seoul, South Korea	113
Brussels, Belgium	137	Lagos, Nigeria	119	Sofia, Bulgaria	97
Budapest	83	Lima, Peru	100	Sydney, Australia	104
Buenos Aires	216	London	140	Teheran, Iran	99
Cairo	86	Madrid	114	Tokyo	160
Caracas, Venezuela	138	Manila	100	Tripoli, Libya	145
Colombo, Sri Lanka	74	Mexico City	95	Tunis, Tunisia	128
Copenhagen	134	Montevideo, Uruguay	115	Vienna	130
Dacca, Bangladesh	95	Montreal	79	Vientiane, Laos	71
Dakar, Senegal	124	Nairobi, Kenya	103	Warsaw	69
Damascus, Syria	134	Nassau, Bahamas	115	Washington, D.C.	95

Source: United Nations, *Monthly Bulletin of Statistics, March 1981.*

Smaller Families Preferred Worldwide

The World Fertility Survey, begun in 1972, reports that fertility in both developed and less developed countries has declined. In the less developed countries a growing preference for smaller families (especially in Asia and Latin America), increased family planning, and modernizing influences—along with education and urbanization—were cited as factors.

In some developed countries deaths exceeded births. In Austria, Belgium, Denmark, England, Finland, France, East Germany, West Germany, Italy, The Netherlands, Norway, Sweden, and Switzerland fertility rates were below replacement level.

Value of Exports and Imports
(in millions of U.S. dollars)

Country	Exports[1]	Imports[1]	Country	Exports[1]	Imports[1]
Afghanistan	$ 494[2]	$ 686[2]	Libya	9,907[4]	5,311[2]
Algeria	9,545[2]	8,537[2]	Madagascar	394[2]	641[2]
Angola	1,227[3]	625[3]	Malawi	295	439
Argentina	7,810[2]	6,713[2]	Malaysia	8,711[2]	7,027[2]
Australia	22,053	20,332	Mali	177[2]	180[2]
Austria	17,508	24,495	Malta	497	938
Bahamas	3,495[2]	3,949[2]	Mauritania	147[2]	259[2]
Bahrain	2,492[2]	2,481[2]	Mauritius	377[2]	609
Bangladesh	662[2]	1,537[2]	Mexico	8,768[2]	11,829[2]
Barbados	219	521	Morocco	2,403	4,185
Belgium–Luxembourg	64,066	71,185	Mozambique	129[6]	278[6]
Benin	26[4]	267[4]	Netherlands	73,871	76,881
Bolivia	942	814	New Zealand	5,414	5,464
Brazil	15,244[2]	19,804[2]	Nicaragua	646[4]	594[4]
Bulgaria	10,372	9,586	Niger	134[5]	127[5]
Burma	363[2]	319[2]	Nigeria	18,073[2]	12,399[2]
Burundi	105[2]	167	Norway	18,476	16,957
Cameroon	1,129[2]	1,271[2]	Oman	2,284[2]	1,387[2]
Canada	64,252	58,545	Pakistan	2,588	5,350
Central African Republic	79[2]	55[4]	Panama	292[2]	1,187[2]
Chad	59[5]	118[5]	Papua New Guinea	964[2]	788[2]
Chile	4,820	5,805	Paraguay	310	494
Colombia	3,410[2]	3,365[2]	Peru	3,474[2]	2,090[2]
Congo	119[4]	242[4]	Philippines	4,601[2]	6,613[2]
Costa Rica	1,002	1,457	Poland	16,998	18,871
Cuba	4,456[4]	4,687[4]	Portugal	3,468[2]	6,086[2]
Cyprus	525	1,202	Qatar	3,896[2]	1,425[2]
Czechoslovakia	14,891	15,148	Romania	9,724[2]	10,916[2]
Denmark	16,485	19,363	Rwanda	115	190
Dominican Republic	995	1,433	Saudi Arabia	63,427[2]	24,254[2]
Ecuador	2,013[2]	2,248	Senegal	421[4]	756[4]
Egypt	3,046	4,860	Sierra Leone	205[2]	297[2]
El Salvador	1,029[2]	979[2]	Singapore	14,233[2]	17,635[2]
Ethiopia	418[2]	567[2]	Solomon Islands	67[2]	57[2]
Fiji	350	561	Somalia	111[2]	249[2]
Finland	14,155	15,580	Spain	20,721	34,080
France	111,251	134,912	Sri Lanka	924	2,029
Gabon	1,106[4]	616[4]	Sudan	581[2]	869[2]
Gambia	53	280	Suriname	444[2]	411[2]
Germany, East	17,312	19,082	Sweden	30,914	33,441
Germany, West	192,930	188,001	Switzerland	29,634	36,356
Ghana	1,096[4]	993[4]	Syria	1,644	3,329
Greece	3,855[2]	9,640[2]	Tanzania	523[2]	1,084[2]
Guatemala	1,270[2]	1,504[2]	Thailand	5,288[2]	9,212
Guyana	291[2]	317[2]	Togo	241[4]	450[4]
Haiti	185[2]	212[4]	Tonga	8[2]	29[2]
Honduras	733[2]	830[2]	Trinidad and Tobago	4,077	3,178
Hungary	8,677	9,235	Tunisia	1,766[2]	2,830[2]
Iceland	931	1,000	Turkey	2,261[2]	4,946[2]
India	7,608[2]	9,546[2]	Uganda	427[2]	187[6]
Indonesia	21,909	10,834	U.S.S.R.	76,481	68,523
Iran	19,872[2]	9,738[2]	United Arab Emirates	13,652[2]	6,960[2]
Iraq	26,429	4,213[4]	United Kingdom	115,350	120,095
Ireland	8,489	11,192	United States	216,668	255,643
Israel	5,265	7,910	Upper Volta	85[2]	593[2]
Italy	77,667	99,452	Uruguay	788[2]	1,231[2]
Ivory Coast	2,515[2]	2,493[2]	Vanuatu	33[4]	45[4]
Jamaica	769[2]	1,010[2]	Venezuela	14,159[2]	9,618[2]
Japan	129,807	140,528	Western Samoa	18[2]	73[2]
Jordan	402[2]	1,949[2]	Yemen, People's Dem.		
Kenya	1,104[2]	1,658[2]	Republic of	248[2]	379[2]
Korea, South	17,548	22,292	Yemen Arab Republic	7[4]	1,283[4]
Kuwait	18,252[2]	5,204[2]	Yugoslavia	8,367	14,029
Laos	11[3]	65[3]	Zaire	1,324[2]	597[2]
Lebanon	436[6]	1,701[6]	Zambia	1,377[2]	755[2]
Liberia	537[2]	487[2]	Zimbabwe	1,194[2]	940[2]

1. 1980 unless otherwise indicated. 2. 1979. 3. 1974. 4. 1978. 5. 1976. 6. 1977. *Source:* United Nations, *Monthly Bulletin of Statistics,* June 1981.

Consumer Price Indexes for Selected Countries
(1967—100)

Country	Total Indexes				Average annual percent change. 1975–1979	Indexes for Selected Items, 1979			
	1979	1978	1975	1970		Food[1]	Clothing	Housing[2]	Transportation
Australia	268.3	245.8	178.7	109.8	10.7	258.4	282.3	295.8	n.a.
Austria	191.2	184.4	157.2	110.6	5.0	178.4	166.7	215.7	202.4
Canada	221.0	202.5	160.1	112.4	8.4	261.8	174.9	224.6	206.7
France	259.1	233.9	178.9	117.1	9.7	268.7	240.0	263.7	291.5
Germany, West	169.9	160.6	144.1	107.0	4.2	153.9	168.6	181.4	174.3
Italy	332.7[3]	289.8	186.9	109.2	15.5	330.8[3]	359.6[3]	298.7[3]	384.5[3]
Japan	261.5	252.1	204.5	119.3	6.3	271.9	269.1	212.9	287.3
Netherlands	222.3[3]	212.5	175.3	115.5	6.1	187.8[3]	245.5[3]	225.3[3]	204.9[3]
Sweden	238.0	222.0	164.3	112.0	9.7	253.0	183.8	261.1	n.a.
United Kingdom	359.0	316.6	216.5	117.4	13.5	417.5	279.2	341.5	379.2
United States	217.4	195.4	161.2	116.3	7.8	234.5	166.6	227.6	212.0

1. Restaurant meals, alcohol, and tobacco are included for some countries, excluded for others. 2. Includes shelter, utilities, and household furnishings and operations. However, actual coverage and measurement methods vary significantly from country to country. 3. Preliminary. NOTE: n.a. = not available. *Source:* United States Department of Labor, Bureau of Labor Statistics.

Energy, Petroleum, and Coal, by Country

Country	Energy consumed[1] (coal equiv.)				Electric energy production[2] (bil. kwh)		Crude petroleum production[3] (mil. metric tons)		Coal production[4] (mil. metric tons)	
	Total (mil. metric tons)		Per capita (kilograms)							
	1978	1970	1978	1970	1978	1970	1978	1970	1978	1970
Algeria	12.7	6.6	687	460	4.7	2.0	54.0	49.0	z	—
Argentina	49.4	39.2	1,873	1,691	34.2	21.7	22.7	20.0	.4	.6
Australia	94.4	67.2	6,622	5,375	86.0[6]	53.9[6]	20.9	8.5[7]	73.0	45.2
Austria	30.4	25.3	4,048	3,424	38.2	30.0	1.8	2.8	n.a.	n.a.
Bahrain	3.6	1.0	10,302	4,720	1.2	.2[8]	2.7	3.8	n.a.	n.a.
Belgium	59.8	59.3	6,078	5,923	49.0	30.5	n.a.	n.a.	6.6	11.4
Brazil	91.7	44.6	794	478	110.6[5]	45.5[5]	8.1	8.0	4.3[9]	2.4
Bulgaria	44.2	33.4	5,020	3,937	29.7	19.5	.1	.3	.3	.4
Canada	233.3	201.1	9,930	9,393	327.1[5]	204.7[5]	63.6	60.4	25.0	11.6
Chile	10.8	12.5	997	1,287	10.2	7.6	.8	1.5	1.1	1.4
China, People's Republic of	766.3	391.2	837	515	225.0	n.a.	104.1	23.9	618.0	360.0[11] [12]
China, Republic of[12]	37.7	15.3	2,202	1,055	35.7	14.0	.2[13]	.1[13]	2.9	4.5
Colombia	18.1	12.7	700	601	15.5	8.8	6.8	11.3	4.0	2.3
Cuba	11.8	9.4	1,168	1,109	7.8	4.9	.1	.2	n.a.	n.a.
Czechoslovakia	114.0	93.3	7,531	6,510	68.9	45.2	.1	.2	28.5	28.2
Denmark	27.7	28.8	5,423	5,838	22.2	20.0	.4	—	n.a.	n.a.
Ecuador	3.9	1.8	505	293	2.4	.9	9.8	.2	n.a.	n.a.
Egypt	18.3	8.8	463	265	13.5	7.6	21.0	16.4	n.a.	—
Finland	24.7[14]	19.2	5,205[14]	4,159	33.4[5]	21.2[5]	n.a.	n.a.	n.a.	n.a.
France	232.7	192.8	4,368	3,794	218.2	147.0	1.9	2.3	21.5[9]	37.8[9]
Germany, East	119.3	102.1	7,121	5,984	96.0	67.7	.1	.1	.3	1.0
Germany, West	368.8	317.8	6,015	5,239	352.1	242.6	5.1	7.5	90.1	116.3[15]
Greece	18.1	11.2	1,925	1,274	19.1	9.8	n.a.	—	n.a.	n.a.
Hong Kong	7.6	4.0	1,657	1,010	9.1[8]	5.1[8]	n.a.	n.a.	n.a.	n.a.
Hungary	36.9	32.9	3,451	3,185	25.4	14.5	2.3	1.9	3.0[9]	4.2[9]
India	113.6	96.8	178	179	107.1[16]	61.2[16]	11.2	6.8	100.8	73.7
Indonesia	40.8	13.3	278	112	4.7	2.1[8]	90.0	42.6	.3	.2
Iran	63.7	27.1	1,808	945	18.5	7.0	261.0	191.3	.9[17]	.5[10] [17]
Iraq	7.8	5.8	633	617	7.0	1.9[8]	129.0	76.5	n.a.	n.a.
Ireland	10.6[14]	9.0[14]	3,292[14]	3,064[14]	10.0[16]	6.1[16]	n.a.	n.a.	.1	.2
Israel	8.7	7.4	2,362	2,524	11.2	6.9	z	5.0[18]	n.a.	n.a.
Italy	183.1	144.1	3,230	2,689	173.4	117.4	1.4	1.4	n.a.	.3
Jamaica	3.9	2.6	1,823	1,377	2.1	1.5	n.a.	n.a.	n.a.	n.a.
Japan	439.5	332.4	3,825	3,215	565.1[16]	359.5[16]	.5	.8	19.0	39.7[19]
Korea, Dem. Peo. Rep.	46.1	28.2	2,702	2,027	n.a.	n.a.	n.a.	n.a.	35.0	21.8[10]
Korea, Republic of	50.3	25.4	1,359	819	31.2	9.6	n.a.	n.a.	17.8	12.4

Country	Energy consumed[1] (coal equiv.)				Electric energy production[2] (bil. kwh)		Crude petroleum production[3] (mil. metric tons)		Coal production[4] (mil. metric tons)	
	Total (mil. metric tons)		Per capita (kilograms)							
	1978	1970	1978	1970	1978	1970	1978	1970	1978	1970
Kuwait	8.1	10.0	6,771	13,352	7.0	2.2[8]	105.2[20]	150.6[20]	n.a.	n.a.
Libya	4.7	1.1	1,889	577	1.6[8]	.4[8]	95.3	159.8	n.a.	n.a.
Malaysia	9.5	4.3[21]	716	468[21]	7.9	3.3[21]	9.7	.9	n.a.	n.a.
Mexico	92.6	60.7	1,384	1,241	53.6[5]	28.7[5]	56.5	21.5	7.1	3.0
Netherlands	74.2	66.0	5,327	5,066	61.5	40.9	1.4	1.9	n.a.	4.3
New Zealand	11.8	8.0	3,790	2,835	21.6[8 16]	13.7[8 16]	.7	.1[7]	1.9	2.2
Nigeria	7.3	2.5	106	45	3.5	1.6	89.0	54.2	.3	.1
Norway	22.6	18.7	5,571	4,822	78.6	57.6	17.3	—	.5	.5
Pakistan	13.2	12.2[22]	172	93[22]	11.1[6]	8.7[6 22]	.5	.5	1.1[6]	1.3[6 11]
Peru	10.9	8.6	649	633	8.9	5.5	7.0	3.6	n.a.	.2
Philippines	15.7	10.8	339	292	17.0	8.7	n.a.	n.a.	.2	z
Poland	195.8	138.9	5,596	4,270	114.8	64.5	.3	.4	192.6	140.1
Portugal	10.1	6.1	1,030	702	13.2	7.5	n.a.	n.a.	.2	.3
Romania	87.7	58.4	4,042	2,883	61.6	35.1	14.6	13.4	7.2	6.4[9]
Saudi Arabia	12.8	6.3	1,306	808	3.5	.7[8]	410.3[20]	188.4[20]	n.a.	n.a.
Singapore	5.7	1.7	2,461	808	5.8	2.2[8]	n.a.	n.a.	n.a.	n.a.
South Africa	96.4[23]	63.2[23]	3,178[23]	2,618[23]	84.9	50.8	n.a.	n.a.	88.9	54.6
Spain	88.3	50.2[24]	2,405	1,485[24]	100.3	56.5	.9	.2	12.2[9]	10.8[9]
Sweden	49.3	49.7	5,954	6,183	89.0	60.6	z	n.a.	z	z
Switzerland	23.4	21.6	3,690	3,475	43.5[5 25]	33.2[5 25]	n.a.	n.a.	n.a.	n.a.
Syria	7.8	2.9	968	457	2.1	.9	10.0	4.2	n.a.	n.a.
Thailand	14.7	8.8	327	256	12.5	4.5	z	z[10]	n.a.	n.a.
Trinidad and Tobago	5.6	4.7	4,965	4,542	1.6	1.2	12.0	7.2	n.a.	n.a.
Tunisia	3.3	1.3	543	257	1.7	.8	4.3	4.2	n.a.	n.a.
Turkey	34.3	16.9	793	480	21.2	8.6	2.5	3.5	4.3	4.6
U.S.S.R.	1,445.4[14]	1,054.7[14]	5,500[14]	4,345[14]	1,190.6	740.9	572.5[7]	353.0[7]	504.3	432.7
United Arab Emirates	4.5	1.4	18,548	7,446	.8	.1[26]	90.0	37.7	n.a.	n.a.
United Kingdom	290.9	300.2	5,212	5,377	288.9	249.0	51.0	.1	123.2[9]	147.1[9]
United States	2,502.1	2,269.5	11,374	11,077	2,328[5]	1,640[5]	425.0	475.3	530.0	550.4
Uruguay	3.0	2.6	1,054	913	3.3	2.2	n.a.	n.a.	n.a.	n.a.
Venezuela	39.2	25.6	2,989	2,457	24.3	12.7	109.4	194.3	.1	z
Vietnam	6.1	5.5[27]	125	302[27]	3.5	1.2[27]	n.a.	n.a.	6.0	3.0[9 28]
Yugoslavia	44.6	29.3	2,035	1,438	50.5	26.0	4.1	2.9	.5	.6
Zaire	1.9	1.8	69	81	4.1	3.2	1.1	—	.1	.1
Zambia	2.6	2.1	474	494	8.7[5]	.9[5]	n.a.	n.a.	.7	.6
World total	8,755.2	6,820.1	2,074	1,892	7,617	4,923	2,986	2,277	2,538	2,143

1. Based on apparent consumption of coal, lignite, petroleum products, natural gas, and hydro and nuclear electricity. 2. Comprises utilities generating primarily for public use. Relates to production at generating centers, including station use and transmission losses. 3. Includes shale oil, but excludes natural gasoline. 4. Excludes lignite and brown coal, except as noted. 5. Net production, i.e., excluding station use. 6. Year ending June 30. 7. Includes gas condensates. 8. Excludes production by industrial establishments for own use. 9. Includes slurries. 10. Data from United States Department of the Interior, Bureau of Mines. 11. Includes lignite and brown coal. 12. *Source:* United States Department of Commerce, Bureau of the Census. Data from Republic of China publications. 13. In million kiloliters. 14. Includes peat. 15. Includes low-grade coal at its hard-coal equivalent. 16. Year beginning April. 17. Year beginning March 21. 18. Includes estimated production in the occupied Sinai Peninsula (1970: 4.9 million metric tons). 19. Includes brown coal. 20. Includes share of production and consumption in the Neutral Zone. 21. West Malaysia only. 22. Includes Bangladesh. 23. Includes data for Botswana, Lesotho, Namibia, and Swaziland. 24. Includes Canary Islands and Ceuta. 25. Year ending Sept. 30. 26. Abu Dhabi only. 27. Data for former Republic of South Vietnam only. 28. Data for former Democratic Republic of Vietnam only. NOTES: metric ton = 1.1023 short tons. n.a. = not available. z = less than 50,000 metric tons. A dash represents zero. *Source:* Except as noted, Statistical Office of the United Nations, New York, N.Y., *Statistical Yearbook* (Copyright).

World Population to Level at 10.5 Billion in 2110

The world's population will most likely stabilize at 10.5 billion in the year 2110, according to a 1981 United Nations Fund for Population Activities report. This forecast revises earlier predictions by others that the population would increase to 14 or 16 billion before stabilizing. The lower assessment is a result of improved world population control.

The over-all growth rate of 1.73% between 1975 and 1980 will decline to 1.5% annually by the year 2000. However, there is a sharp difference in the growth for industrialized and nonindustrialized nations. People in industrialized countries, who ac-

counted for 24% of the world's population in 1980, will account for only 13% in the year 2110.

The U.S. population will level off in the year 2060 at 320 million, while the U.S.S.R. will stabilize in 2100 at 380 million. The forecast predicts that by 2110 there will be 6.3 billion people in South Asia and Africa.

Today's global population is 4.4 billion, and although current grain output can feed 6 billion, 450 million go hungry, mostly due to inadequate grain distribution.

Labor Force, Manufacturing, Steel, Iron Ore, Cement, Cotton Yarn, and Fish, 1977

Country	Economically active population[1] (thousands)	Persons engaged in Manufacturing[2] (thousands)	Steel Production[3] (mil. metric tons)	Steel Consumption[4] Total (mil. metric tons)	Steel Consumption[4] Per capita (kilograms)	Iron ore[5] (iron content) (mil. metric tons)	Cement[6] (mil. metric tons)	Cotton yarn[7] (thousands metric tons)	Fish catches[8] (thousands metric tons)
Algeria	2,565	n.a.	.2	2.0	110	1.7	1.8	9[12]	44
Argentina	9,011	n.a.	2.7	3.6	140	.3	6.0	95[13]	393
Australia	5,330	1,175[14 15]	7.5[14]	5.1	365	60.2[14]	5.0	20[13 14]	128[14]
Austria	3,098	677[12 16 17]	4.1	2.5	335	1.1	6.0	20	3
Belgium	3,638	n.a.	11.3	4.0[18]	388[18]	z	7.8	41	45
Brazil	29,557	3,638[16 19 20]	11.2	12.0	107	56.6[21]	20.5	70[22 23]	790[24]
Bulgaria	4,268	1,180[25]	2.6	2.4	276	.7	4.7	86	138
Canada	8,162[26]	1,748[22]	13.6	12.8	550	31.8[27]	9.9	63[22]	1,280
Chile	2,607	236[12 28]	.5[29]	.6	60	4.9	1.1	23[13 30]	1,285
China, People's Republic of	n.a.	n.a.	27.0[21]	32.5	38	32.5[21]	40.0[21]	1,450[13]	6,880[24]
China, Republic of[31]	5,748	1,735	.6	3.2	192	n.a.	10.3	277[32]	855
Colombia	5,134	457[12 16 33]	.2	.8	31	.5	3.3	28[19]	75[24]
Cuba	2,633	n.a.	.3	.5	53	n.a.	2.7	24[13]	185
Czechoslovakia	6,996	2,489[25]	15.1	10.5	700	6	9.8	126	18
Denmark	2,313	380[22 34]	.7	1.8	356	z	2.3	2	1,807
Dominican Rep.	856	n.a.	n.a.	.1	28	n.a.	.6[21]	z[22 35]	5
Ecuador	1,443	75[12 16 36]	n.a.	.4	46	n.a.	.6[20]	1[22]	476
Egypt	7,782	693[30 37]	.3[21]	1.0	26	.7	3.2	210[13]	105
El Salvador	1,315	51[12 16 38]	n.a.	.1	21	n.a.	.3	6[13]	8
Finland	2,129	498[20]	2.2	1.5	326	.8	1.7	18[22]	117
France	20,439	5,760[39]	22.1	19.5	368	11.1	29.0	238	760
Germany, East	8,214	3,112[40]	6.9	9.9	591	z	12.1	135[41]	209
Germany, West	26,494	6,915[42]	39.0	33.0	538	.9	32.2	178[41]	432
Ghana	3,332	61[43 44 45]	n.a.	.1	11	n.a.	.7[22]	n.a.	383
Greece	3,388[46]	573[12]	.5[21]	1.6	176	.9	10.6	87[13 22]	106[24]
Guatemala	1,364	69[12 20]	n.a.	.2	26	n.a.	.5	n.a.	3
Hong Kong	1,655	755	n.a.	1.2	262	—	1.0	200	158
Hungary	4,989	1,331[40]	3.7	3.7	343	.1	4.6	60[47]	35
India	180,373	5,662[22 48 49]	9.8[29]	10.2	16	26.5	19.2	1,034[50]	2,540
Indonesia	40,100	759[12 51]	n.a.	1.2	8	n.a.	2.9	54[30]	1,545
Iran	7,584	396[12 33 52]	n.a.	4.7	137	.7[21 53]	6.0[22]	65[22 35]	2[24]
Iraq	n.a.	134[12 54]	n.a.	.7	60	n.a.	2.5[21]	1[12 13]	26
Ireland	1,120	203[30 55]	z[21]	.5	150	n.a.	1.6	4[56]	96
Israel	956	255[20 43]	.1[21]	.7	195	n.a.	2.0	26	24
Italy	18,750	3,624[12 57]	23.3	20.8	368	.2	38.2	212	427
Japan	53,321	11,212[16 22 58]	102.4	58.2	512	.5[59]	73.1	441	10,733
Korea, North	n.a.	n.a.	3.1[21]	3.2	190	3.8[21]	7.0[21]	n.a.	1,600[24]
Korea, South	10,378	1,717[20 22 44]	2.7[29]	6.8	186	.4	14.2	189	2,419
Lebanon	n.a.	n.a.	n.a.	.2	79	n.a.	1.4[21]	5[13 30]	3[24]
Liberia	412	n.a.	n.a.	z	19	12.0	.1[21]	n.a.	16[24]
Luxembourg	131	45[12 57]	4.3	[18]	[18]	.5	.3	n.a.	n.a.
Malaysia	3,430	261[16 19 60]	n.a.	.6	50	.2	1.8[61]	18[13 61]	619
Mexico	12,910	n.a.	5.5	6.5	100	3.6	13.3	158[12 13]	670
Morocco	3,981	n.a.	z[12 62]	.8	44	.2	2.6	14[19]	261
Netherlands	4,169	1,022[63 64]	4.9	4.5	322	n.a.	3.9	28	313
New Zealand	1,026[9]	299[22 48 65]	n.a.	.9	280	—	.9	n.a.	111
Nigeria	18,036	186[19 44 54]	n.a.	1.8	27	n.a.	1.3	5[12 13]	506
Norway	1,469	367[20 22]	.7	1.6	405	2.4	2.3	1	3,562
Pakistan	39,591	258[20 30]	.7	.7	9	n.a.	3.1[14]	283[13 14 50]	249
Peru	3,872	258[20 30]	.4[21]	.6	37	4.0	2.0[21]	n.a.	2,530
Philippines	11,355	532[19 20]	n.a.	1.4	31	—	4.1	31[13 47]	1,511
Poland	16,944	4,284[66]	17.3	18.7	.5	.2[67]	21.3	219[41]	665
Portugal	3,424	629[16 22 60]	.4	1.5	156	z	4.3	85[13]	310
Rhodesia[79]	110	n.a.	.3[21]	.5	74	.3[21]	5	n.a.	2[24]
Romania	10,362	1,635[68]	11.5	9.8[12]	464[12]	.6	13.1	171[41 47]	151
South Africa	7,986	1,315[58 69]	7.2[29 70]	4.9[71]	161[71]	16.6	6.6	67	603
Spain	11,865	2,279[16 22 72]	10.9	9.1	249	4.2	28.0	66	1,455
Sri Lanka	3,459	n.a.	z		2	n.a.	.4	5[13]	139
Sweden	3,413	925	4.0	3.8	463	16.1	2.5	7[22]	192
Switzerland	3,005	675[16 73]	.7[74]	2.3	356	n.a.	3.6	45	4

Country	Economically active population[1] (thousands)	Persons engaged in Manufacturing[2] (thousands)	Steel Production[3] (mil. metric tons)	Steel Consumption[4] Total (mil. metric tons)	Per capita (kilograms)	Iron ore[5] (iron content) Production (mil. metric tons)	Cement[6] (mil. metric tons)	Cotton yarn[7] (thousands metric tons)	Fish catches[8] (thousands metric tons)
Syria	1,525	176	n.a.	.6	76	n.a.	1.4	28[13]	2
Thailand	16,850	n.a.	.3[21]	1.4	31	z	5.1	73[13 22 47]	1,778
Tunisia	1,094	84[16 22 75]	.2[62]	.4	63	z	.6	7[13 22]	38
Turkey	15,829	738[22 33]	1.5	4.7	112	1.4	13.4	167[22 50]	155[24]
U.S.S.R.	115,204	30,562	146.7	145.6[22]	567[22]	131.4	127.1	1,597	9,352
United Kingdom	22,754[76]	7,472[12]	20.4	19.5	349	.9	15.5	126	1,004
United States	82,897[9]	n.a.	113.7[10]	133.9	618	35.0[11]	72.6	1,145	3,102
Uruguay	1,012	239	z	2	16	—	.7[21]	n.a.	48
Venezuela	3,015	324[12]	.8[21]	3.6	285	8.5	3.3	16[43]	152
Vietnam	5,742[77]	n.a.	n.a.	.3	7	n.a.	.7[21]	10[13 30 77]	1,014[24 77]
Yugoslavia	8,890	1,811[22 78]	2.4	5.2	239	1.5	8.2	121	61
World, total	n.a.	n.a.	667.0	n.a.	n.a.	482.8	759.0	n.a.	73,500

1. Comprises all persons engaged in or actively seeking productive work in some branch of the economy during a specified period of time. Generally, data are for a specific date in the 1960's and 1970's. 2. Comprises average number of employees, working proprietors, and unpaid family workers engaged in production of manufactured goods, including assembly of component parts and, except in the case of consumer goods, repair services. Except as noted, excludes gas manufacture and electricity. 3. Total production of crude steel, both ingots and steel for castings. Excludes wrought (puddled) iron. 4. Data represent apparent consumption (i.e., production plus imports minus exports) and do not take into account changes in stocks. 5. Refers generally to iron content of marketable ores mined, including manganiferous iron ores but excluding pyrites. Some data are rough estimates obtained by applying a fixed percentage to figures for crude ore production. 6. Covers, as far as possible, all hydraulic cements used for construction (portland, metallurgic, aluminous, natural, etc.). 7. Covers pure and mixed yarn and excludes tire cord yarn, except as noted. 8. Covers both sea and inland fisheries, in terms of live weight. Includes shellfish; excludes whales, dolphins, etc. 9. Excludes Armed Forces abroad. 10. Excludes steel for castings made in foundries operated by companies not producing ingots. 11. Includes iron content of byproduct ore. 12. For 1975. 13. Pure cotton yarn only. 14. Year ending June 30. 15. All establishments except single-establishment enterprises with fewer than 4 employees. 16. For one period of the year indicated. 17. Establishments with 20 or more employees. 18. Luxembourg included with Belgium. 19. For 1974. 20. Establishments with 5 or more engaged. 21. Data from U.S. Bureau of Mines. 22. For 1976. 23. Production in the State of São Paulo only. 24. FAO estimate. 25. All enterprises in socialist sector except publishing. 26. Excludes armed services. 27. Shipments from mines. 28. Establishments with 50 or more engaged. 29. Ingots only. 30. For 1973. 31. *Source:* United States Department of Commerce, Bureau of the Census. Data from Republic of China publications. 32. For 1969. 33. Establishments with 10 or more engaged. 34. Establishments with 6 or more employees. 35. Mixed yarn only. 36. Establishments with 7 or more engaged. 37. Private establishments with 10 or more engaged and all public establishments. 38. Establishments with 5 or more engaged. 39. Total mining and manufacturing. 40. All enterprises. 41. Includes tire cord yarn. 42. Establishments with 20 or more engaged. 43. For 1972. 44. Includes homeworkers. 45. Establishments with 30 or more engaged. 46. Includes Armed Forces abroad. 47. Excludes yarn made from waste. 48. Year ending March 31. 49. Establishments with 10 or more engaged using power, or with 20 or more engaged not using power. 50. Mill production only. 51. Establishments with 20 or more workers. 52. Year ending March 20. 53. Year beginning March 21. 54. Establishments with 10 or more employees. 55. Establishments with 3 or more engaged. 56. Data from International Cotton Advisory Committee. 57. Enterprises with 20 or more engaged. 58. All private establishments. 59. Includes iron content of iron sand and pyrites. 60. Establishments in selected industries. 61. West Malaysia only. 62. Crude steel for casting only. 63. Work-years. 64. All kind-of-activity units in mining and manufacturing. 65. Establishments with 2 or more engaged. 66. All establishments in the socialist sector, except publishing. 67. Includes iron content of iron pyrites. 68. State enterprises under direction of central government. 69. For one period of year ending June 30, 1976. 70. Includes concast steel billets. 71. Includes data for Botswana, Lesotho, Namibia, and Swaziland. 72. All establishments, but certain industries not covered. 73. Establishments subject to labor laws. 74. Data from United Nations Economic Commission for Europe. 75. All units with 5 or more employees. 76. For England and Wales only. 77. Data for former Republic of South Vietnam only. 78. All enterprises in the socialist sector, except licensed handicrafts. 79. Now Zimbabwe. NOTES: n.a. = not available. z = less than 50,000 metric tons (metric ton = 1.1023 short tons. *Source:* Except as noted, Statistical Office of the United Nations, New York, N.Y., *Statistical Yearbook* and *Demographic Yearbook.* (Copyright.) NOTE: Figures are the latest available.

Wheat and Rice—Production by Country
(in thousands of metric tons)[1]

COUNTRY	Wheat 1979	1978	1977	1976	1971-75 average	Rice[1] 1979	1978	1977	1976	1971-75 average
Afghanistan	2,200	2,813	2,652	2,936	2,533	450	428	400	448	405
Argentina	7,800	8,100	5,300	11,000	6,936	326	310	320	309	302
Australia	16,100	18,250	9,370	11,825	10,104	692	490	530	417	331
Austria	850	1,195	1,072	1,234	965	—	—	—	—	—
Bangladesh	494	348	259	218	109	19,355	19,273	19,441	17,628	16,793
Belgium	1,010[2]	1,022[2]	795[2]	939[2]	958[2]	—	—	—	—	—
Brazil	2,924	2,677	2,066	3,216	1,934	7,589	7,242	8,994	9,757	7,012
Bulgaria	3,000[3]	3,466	3,028	3,152	3,123	65[3]	61	68	41	63

COUNTRY	Wheat 1979	1978	1977	1976	1971-75 average	Rice[1] 1979	1978	1977	1976	1971-75 average
Burma	41	92	75	56	39	10,000	10,500	9,462	9,319	8,386
Cambodia	—	—	—	—	—	1,569	1,800[3]	1,800[3]	1,500[3]	1,000[3]
Canada	17,746	21,146	19,862	23,587	15,092	—	—	—	—	—
Chile	995	893	1,219	866	1,050	181	105	120	98	64
China, People's Republic of[3]	60,003	52,002	45,001	50,001	36,601	143,400	138,202	129,470	129,054	121,532
China, Republic of[4]	n.a.	2	1	1	2	n.a.	2,444[5]	2,649[5]	2,713[5]	2,397[5]
Colombia	38	38	29	45	58	1,932	1,715	1,307	1,560	1,231
Cuba	—	—	—	—	—	500	458	459	451	375
Czechoslovakia	4,400[3]	5,601	5,214	4,807	4,360	—	—	—	—	—
Denmark	573	642	606	593	566	—	—	—	—	—
Ecuador	19	29	40	65	57	303	233	328	368	241
Egypt	1,856	1,942	1,699	1,962	1,821	2,507	2,351	2,275	2,300	2,396
Ethiopia	449	429	605	532	648	—	—	—	—	—
Finland	208	241	295	654	516	—	—	—	—	—
France	19,393	20,970	17,350	16,126	17,022	45[3]	45	23	32	56
Germany, East	3,226	3,147	2,914	2,715	2,797	—	—	—	—	—
Germany, West	7,971	8,118	7,235	6,702	7,132	—	—	—	—	—
Greece	2,411	2,734	1,766	2,376	1,934	94[3]	93	94	69	87
Hungary	3,706	5,677	5,319	5,148	4,299	48[3]	27	35	32	64
India	34,982	31,749	29,010	28,846	24,172	69,000	80,743	79,006	63,052	64,510
Indonesia	—	—	—	—	—	26,350	25,781	23,356	23,301	21,151
Iran	5,000	5,700	5,517	6,044	4,644	1,212	1,280	1,400	1,566	1,265
Iraq	1,492	910	696	1,302	1,318	284	172	199	163	172
Ireland	260	247	250	200	264	—	—	—	—	—
Israel	128	167	220	206	252	—	—	—	—	—
Italy	9,140	9,332	6,347	9,516	9,528	1,014	979	693	907	950
Japan	440	367	236	222	280	15,600	16,354	17,000	15,292	15,689
Korea, North	370[3]	350[3]	310[3]	340[3]	292[3]	4,800[3]	4,500[3]	4,610[3]	4,150[3]	3,195[3]
Korea, South	42	36	45	82	123	8,051	8,342	8,291	7,202	5,915
Laos	—	—	—	—	—	900[3]	796	847	858	865
Madagascar	—	—	—	—	—	2,327	1,914	2,154	2,043	1,855
Malaysia	—	—	—	—	—	2,161	1,527	1,922	1,995	1,942
Mexico	2,272	2,654	2,456	3,363	2,264	489	397	567	463	476
Nepal	415	411	362	387	275	2,500[3]	2,339	2,282	2,386	2,365
Netherlands	836	792	661	710	676	—	—	—	—	—
New Zealand	327	329	354	388	297	—	—	—	—	—
Pakistan	9,944	8,367	9,144	8,691	7,222	4,953	4,908	4,424	4,106	3,593
Panama	—	—	—	—	—	200	162	186	144	157
Peru	95	113	120	127	124	545	468	587	570	516
Philippines	—	—	—	—	—	7,000[3]	7,318	6,895	6,461	5,386
Poland	4,220	6,029	5,308	5,745	5,605	—	—	—	—	—
Portugal	233	255	229	694	624	135	135	112	97	151
Romania	4,684	6,243	6,463	6,724	5,399	55	58	47	37	57
South Africa	2,220	1,690	1,860	2,239	1,735	3[3]	3[3]	3[3]	3	3
Spain	4,118	4,806	4,064	4,436	4,564	427	401	379	406	368
Sri Lanka	—	—	—	—	—	1,806	1,890	1,677	1,253	1,355
Sweden	1,113	1,290	1,522	1,765	1,352	—	—	—	—	—
Switzerland	417	406	323	400	386	—	—	—	—	—
Syria	1,319	1,651	1,217	1,790	1,249	—	—	—	1	1
Thailand	—	—	—	—	—	15,640	17,530	13,921	15,068	13,948
Turkey	17,631	16,769	16,720	16,578	12,372	224	305	270	251	248
U.S.S.R.	90,100	120,824	92,165	96,882	88,935	2,400	2,096	2,217	2,001	1,753
United Kingdom	7,140	6,613	5,274	4,740	5,045	—	—	—	—	—
United States	58,289	48,922	55,420	58,307	47,792	6,199	6,040	4,501	5,246	4,579
Uruguay	380	174	173	505	354	248	226	228	217	148
Venezuela	1	1	1	1	1	653	544	496	206	256
Vietnam	—	—	—	—	—	10,500[3]	10,040	10,885	12,076	10,732
Yugoslavia	4,512	5,355	5,595	5,979	5,177	34	34	36	23	33
World total	425,478	450,079	390,697	424,744	358,794	379,814	386,303	369,729	350,456	329,180

1. Rice data cover rough and paddy, except as noted. Data for each country pertain to the calendar year in which all or most of the crop was harvested. 2. Includes Luxembourg. 3. FAO estimate. 4. Source: United States Department of Commerce, Bureau of the Census. Data from Republic of China publications. 5. Paddy only. NOTES: metric ton = 1.1023 short tons, n.a. = not available. *Source:* Except as noted, Statistical Office of the United Nations, New York, N.Y. *Statistical Yearbook.* (Copyright.)

Corn, Meat, and Sugar—Production by Country
(in thousands of metric tons)

Country	Corn 1979	Corn 1978	Corn 1972–1977, average	Meat[1] 1978	Meat[1] 1977	Meat[1] 1971–1976, average	Sugar[2] 1977	Sugar[2] 1976	Sugar[2] 1971–1975, average
Argentina	8,700	9,700	7,885	3,540	3,269	2,683	1,666	1,559	1,364
Australia	168	130	145	2,843[3]	2,722	2,268[3]	3,452	3,395	2,810
Austria	1,347	1,166	938	504[4]	492	460	506	426	396
Belgium[5]	37	37	28	921	872	855	757	721	723
Brazil	16,309	13,533	16,449	3,148	3,343	2,909	8,759	7,236	6,323
Bulgaria	3,300[4]	2,236	2,589	466[4]	453	387	240	230	225
Canada	4,963	4,032	3,251	1,635	1,687	1,578	155	156	122
Chile	489	257	313	248	253	247	120	240	152
China, People's Republic of	40,620[4]	31,607[4]	29,018[4]	17,017[4]	16,536[4]	13,899[4]	3,800	4,000	3,480
China, Republic of[6]	n.a.	107	114[7]	n.a.	n.a.	n.a.	n.a.	n.a.	n.a.
Colombia	870	862	783	547[4]	531[4]	518[4]	853	935	849
Cuba	95[4]	95[4]	92[4]	208[4]	202[4]	200[4]	6,953	6,151	5,675
Czechoslovakia	600[4]	619	664	1,214[4]	1,136	1,053	924	620	752
Denmark	n.a.	n.a.	n.a.	1,031	987	962	472	432	372
Dominican Republic	15	40	47	62	59	55	1,258	1,287	1,177
Egypt	2,938	3,117	2,687	292[4]	284[4]	273	657	576	549
El Salvador	521	507	360	48	47	41[8]	364	261	216
Ethiopia	1,067	982	977	343[4]	338[4]	337	137	136	131
France	10,293	9,531	8,332	3,507[4]	3,414	3,382	3,908	2,721	2,859
Germany, East	2[4]	2	8	1,616[4]	1,608	1,395	700	609	561
Germany, West	655	617	541	3,999[4]	3,856	3,651	n.a.	2,844	2,435
Ghana	380	340	359	29[4]	27[4]	32[4]	25	12	8
Greece	627	513	520	341	343	306	294	386	187
Guatemala	850	760	725	93	83	77	487	517	299
Hungary	7,400	6,655	6,014	1,031[4]	1,002	894	476	395	307
India	5,000[4]	6,219	6,224	646[4]	642[4]	620[4]	5,019	5,033	4,238
Indonesia	3,200	4,029	2,929	328[4]	326[4]	301	1,100	1,380	907
Iran	57	60	44	366[4]	358[4]	331[4]	752	650	603
Ireland	n.a.	n.a.	n.a.	556	551	469	n.a.	n.a.	176[9]
Italy	6,260	6,221	5,337	2,075[4]	2,000	1,812	n.a.	1,758	1,196
Japan	5	7	14	1,590[4]	1,526	1,288	566	506	600
Kenya	1,800	2,169	2,404[4]	181[4]	164[4]	161[4]	185	182	149
Malaysia	30[4]	30[4]	21[4]	62[9]	63[9]	62[10]	60	50	19
Mexico	9,255	10,909	8,672	1,033	1,028	899	2,790	2,710	2,672
Morocco	312	390	337	135	133	159	260	250	246
Netherlands	5	5	8	1,444	1,369	1,221	n.a.	947	822
Nigeria	1,500[4]	1,480[4]	1,123[4]	339[4]	330[4]	314[4]	40	30	34
Pakistan	846	798	768	570[4]	559	424	764	677	506[11]
Peru	600	623	657	186	182	190	900	930	918[8]
Philippines	3,300	2,860	2,418	535	518	484	2,624	2,984	2,338
Poland	187	119	97	2,601	2,279	2,261	1,810	1,774	1,774
Portugal	456	500	506	252	249	224	10	12	13[12]
Romania	12,380	10,208	9,265	1,108[4]	1,165	978	590	561	577
South Africa	8,240	9,930	8,505	744[4]	708	683	2,369	2,113	1,944
Spain	2,237	1,969	1,864	1,358	1,310	1,106	1,262	1,162	847
Sweden	n.a.	n.a.	n.a.	459	455	417	339	301	280
Switzerland	101	105	117	417[4]	413	374	85	83	71
Thailand	3,300	2,791	2,237	363[4]	352[4]	365[4]	2,361	1,757	1,101[13]
Turkey	1,358	1,300	1,184	624[4]	616	563	1,158	1,090	810
Uganda	500[4]	660[4]	516	94[4]	93[4]	84	20	20	86
U.S.S.R.	8,400	8,951	10,599	13,085[4]	12,732	12,258	8,885	8,500	8,880
United Kingdom	1	2	4	2,005	2,133	2,186	978	657	930
United States	197,208	180,008	145,940	17,605	18,013	16,936	5,523	6,163	5,409
Uruguay	71	172	181	405	404	393	120	120	82
Venezuela	848	804	560	384	372	313	445	510	523
Vietnam	520[4]	485	325[4]	550[4]	511[4]	470[4]	80	—	—
Yugoslavia	10,082	7,585	8,763	1,057[4]	1,048	850	647	580	448
Zaire	350[4]	500	483	60[4]	59[4]	55[8]	65	65	55
Zimbabwe	1,000[4]	1,400	1,327	171[4]	189[4]	163[4]	200	220	227
World total	394,231	363,927	318,245	104,360	102,494	93,407	91,826	86,573	77,610

1. Beef and veal (incl. buffalo meat), pork (incl. bacon and ham), and mutton and lamb (incl. goat meat). Refers to meat from animals slaughtered within the national boundaries irrespective of origin of animals, and relates to commercial and farm slaughter. In terms of carcass weight. Excludes lard, tallow, and edible offals, except as noted. 2. Beet and cane. Data generally

in terms of raw sugar. 3. Year ending June 30. 4. FAO estimate. 5. Includes Luxembourg for corn and meat. 6. *Source:* United States Department of Commerce, Bureau of the Census. Data from Republic of China publications. 7. Data for 1974–77. 8. Excludes data for 1971. 9. Excludes data for 1975. 10. West Malaysia only. 11. 1971 data for Bangladesh included with Pakistan. 12. Data for 1975 only. 13. Data for 1974 and 1975. NOTES: Data for each country pertain to the calendar year in which all or most of the crop was harvested. Metric ton = 1.1023 short tons, n.a. = not available. *Source:* Except as noted, Statistical Office of the United Nations, New York, N.Y., *Statistical Yearbook.* (Copyright.)

Communications
(telephones, mail, newspapers, radio, and television)

Country	Telephones, in use,[1] 1977 (thousands)	Telephones per 100 population, 1977	Pieces of mail sent, domestic,[2] 1977 (millions)	Daily newspapers,[3] 1975 Number	Circulation Total (thousands)	Copies per 1,000 population	Receiving sets, 1976 Radio[4] (thousands)	Television[5] (thousands)
Algeria	298	1.6	218	4	285	17	173	30
Argentina	2,342	9.0	620[9]	164	2,773[10]	n.a.	838[7]	180[7]
Australia	5,685[11]	40.4[11]	2,069[12]	70	5,320	394	770[13]	351[13]
Austria	2,443	32.5	1,618	30	2,405	320	291[13]	236[13]
Bangladesh	98	.1	251	30	356[14]	n.a.	n.a.	n.a.
Belgium	3,100	31.5	2,581	30	2,340	239	409[13]	268[13]
Bolivia	49[15]	.9[15]	3	14	199	35	74	n.a.
Brazil	4,836	4.1	2,178	280[15]	4,050[15]	39[15]	158[7]	96
Bulgaria	946	10.7	n.a.	13	2,023	232	314[13]	176[13]
Burma	32	.1	75[7]	7	319	10	22[13]	—
Cambodia	71[7]	11.2[7]	1[15]	16	n.a.	n.a.	14[7]	4
Canada	14,488	61.8	5,638[16][17]	121	4,872[18]	n.a.	1,011	428
Chile	467	4.8	68[8]	47	n.a.	n.a.	172	68
China, People's Republic of	n.a.	n.a.	n.a.	n.a.	n.a.	n.a.	16[19]	1[15]
China, Republic of[20]	1,690	10.1	690	31[9]	n.a.	n.a.	90	55
Colombia	1,396	5.6	119[21]	40	1,248[22]	n.a.	117	70
Costa Rica	151	7.2	9	6	174	88	74	77
Cuba	321	3.3	42[7]	15	53[23]	n.a.	222	69
Cyprus	83	13.5	14	12	78[24]	n.a.	313[13]	89[13]
Czechoslovakia	2,863	19.0	2,216[15][25]	29	4,436	300	263[13]	254[13]
Denmark	2,718[26]	53.4[26]	1,268[16]	49	1,723	341	365[13]	323[13]
Dominican Republic	127[9]	2.6[9]	6[7]	10	197	42	41	33
Ecuador	221	2.9	7	29	331	49	279[19]	41
Egypt	503[21]	1.4[21]	206	14[21]	773[21]	21[21]	138	17[7]
El Salvador	72	1.9	21[27]	12	234[28]	n.a.	340	33
Ethiopia	79	.3	21[15]	8	70	3	7	1
Finland	2,032	42.9	676[8]	60	n.a.	n.a.	461[13]	363[13]
France	17,519	32.9	11,382[9]	98	11,341	214	330[13]	274[13]
Germany, East	2,860	17.1	968	40	7,946	472	367[13]	309[13]
Germany, West	22,932	37.4	12,368	334	19,298	312	329[13]	311[7][13]
Ghana	67	.7	58[16]	4	500	51	105	3
Greece	2,320	25.0	283	106	n.a.	n.a.	300	127
Guatemala	53[15]	1.0[15]	27[9]	11	165[29]	n.a.	42	19
Honduras	19[9]	.7[9]	21	8	99[30]	n.a.	57	17
Hong Kong	1,132[9]	25.5[9]	157[16]	82	n.a.	n.a.	527	191[13]
Hungary	1,104	10.3	1,611[8]	27	2,454	233	241[7][13]	236[13]
Iceland	95	42.9	188	5	94	431	291[13]	241
India	2,096	.3	7,421[16]	835	9,383	16	24[13]	1[13]
Indonesia	347	.3	189	172	2,171[31]	n.a.	37[13]	2
Iran	782[9]	2.3[9]	858[32]	20	484	15	63	51
Iraq	320[9]	2.8[9]	33[9]	7	192[33]	n.a.	113[7]	37
Ireland	519	16.1	320[8][16]	7	693	222	300[13]	207[13]
Israel	993[34]	27.1[34]	316[16]	23	1,337[35]	n.a.	189	137
Italy	16,125	28.5	3,031[9]	78	6,296	113	232[13]	220[13]
Jamaica	109[9]	5.4[9]	77[9]	3	131[23]	n.a.	270	54
Japan	48,646[34]	42.4[34]	12,186[9][16]	108[21]	57,820[21]	526[21]	530	239[7]
Kenya	144	1.0	106	3	134	10	37	4
Korea, South	1,976	5.4	720	36	6,010	173	139	64[13]
Kuwait	155	13.8	5[16]	6[21]	80[21]	86[21]	487	183[7]
Lebanon	192[19]	6.8[19]	26[36]	33	283[37]	n.a.	540	144
Luxembourg	186	52.3	46	7	161[38]	n.a.	575	293
Madagascar	32[9]	.4[9]	22[7]	9[21]	59[21]	9[21]	74	1

Country	Telephones, in use,[1] 1977 (thousands)	Telephones per 100 population, 1977	Pieces of mail sent, domestic,[2] 1977 (millions)	Daily newspapers[3] 1975 Number	Circulation Total (thousands)	Copies per 1,000 population	Radio[4] (thousands)	Television[5] (thousands)
Malaysia	375	3.0	330[8 39]	31	1,038	87	118	45
Mexico	3,712	5.9	1,068[9]	256	n.a.	n.a.	301[7]	84[7]
Morocco	210	1.2	101	9	360	21	84	29[13]
Netherlands	5,846	41.8	3,737	95[19]	4,100[19]	315[19]	290[13]	274[13]
New Zealand	1,674[40]	53.3[40]	578[8 16 17]	39	n.a.	n.a.	865	259[13]
Nigeria	121[9]	.2[9]	959	12	613[24]	n.a.	79	2
Norway	1,563	38.6	1,008[12]	80	1,657	412	320[13]	270[13]
Pakistan	259[9]	.3[9]	502[9]	102	358[41]	n.a.	17[13]	5
Panama	155[9]	9.0[9]	7[15]	6	131	79	157	108
Paraguay	40[9]	1.4[9]	n.a.	8	73[30]	n.a.	66	20
Peru	403	2.6	n.a.	35	n.a.	n.a.	129	37
Philippines	567	1.3	630[36]	15	686[42]	n.a.	43	18
Poland	2,925	8.4	1,730[8 9]	44	8,429	248	239[13]	198[13]
Portugal	1,175	12.0	462	30	612	70	161[13]	76[13]
Puerto Rico	515[9]	16.0[9]	n.a.	5[21]	405[21]	132[21]	549	196
Rhodesia[47]	190[9]	2.9[9]	112	3	116	18	39	11
Romania	1,196[7]	5.6[7]	686[7]	20[21]	2,716[21]	129[21]	145[13]	138[13]
Saudi Arabia	160[9]	2.1[9]	52	11[21]	96[21]	11[21]	28	14
Singapore	395[34]	17.1[34]	116	10[21]	n.a.	n.a.	156[13]	129[13]
South Africa	2,191	8.3	1,383	24	1,776	70	96	n.a.
Spain	9,528	26.1	3,578	115	3,491	98	259	185
Sri Lanka	72[7]	.5[7]	580[16]	18	n.a.	n.a.	58	—
Sudan	62	.3	32[8]	4	n.a.	n.a.	77[7 13]	6[7]
Sweden	5,930	71.7	2,551[8]	135	4,678	572	390[13]	363[13]
Switzerland	4,145	65.7	2,929	95	2,573	402	332[13]	285[13]
Syria	193	2.5	23[15]	6	n.a.	n.a.	224[19]	30
Thailand	367	.8	184	56	n.a.	n.a.	131[7]	18
Trinidad and Tobago	70[9]	6.5[9]	21[43]	3	100[23]	n.a.	253	103
Tunisia	144	2.5	70	4	190	33	141	36
Turkey	1,131[9]	2.8[9]	608	437[19]	n.a.	n.a.	105[13]	44
U.S.S.R.	19,600[44]	7.5[44]	5,069	691	100,928	397	481[7]	217[7]
United Kingdom	23,182	41.5	8,840[8 16 17 27]	111	21,700	388	706[13]	317[13]
United States	162,072	74.4	88,970[6 7 8]	1,812	61,222	287	1,882[7]	571[7]
Uruguay	268	9.5	17	30	637[36]	n.a.	516	114
Venezuela	742[9]	6.0[9]	202[21]	49	1,067[45]	n.a.	407	116
Vietnam[46]	47[15]	.3[15]	59[15 27]	n.a.	n.a.	n.a.	24[19]	—
Yugoslavia	1,556	7.1	644	26	1,896	89	210[13]	161[13]
World total	423,082	10.4	n.a.	n.a.	n.a.	n.a.	n.a.	n.a.

1. Comprises public and private telephones installed which can be connected to a central exchange. 2. Items mailed for distribution within national territories. Comprises letters, postcards, printed matter, merchandise samples, small packets and phonopost packets. Includes mail carried without charge, but excludes ordinary packages, and insured letters and boxes. 3. Publications containing general news and appearing at least 4 times a week; may range in size from a single sheet to 50 or more pages. Circulation data include copies sold outside the country. 4. Data cover estimated number of receivers in use, except as noted, and apply to all types of receivers for radio broadcasts to the public, including receivers connected to a radio "redistribution system" but excluding television sets. 5. Estimated number of sets in use, except as noted. 6. Includes ordinary packages as well as insured letters and boxes. 7. For 1975. 8. Excludes small packets. 9. For 1976. 10. 147 dailies. 11. Year ending June 30. 12. Year beginning July 1. 13. Number of licenses issued. 14. 27 dailies. 15. For 1973. 16. Year beginning April 1. 17. Excludes printed matter. 18. 117 dailies. 19. For 1970. 20. *Source:* United States Department of Commerce Bureau of the Census. Data from Republic of China publications. 21. For 1974. 22. 34 dailies. 23. 2 dailies. 24. 10 or more dailies. 25. Domestic and foreign. 26. Includes Faeroe Islands and Greenland. 27. Excludes postcards. 28. 8 dailies. 29. 7 dailies. 30. 4 dailies. 31. 55 dailies. 32. For 1971. 33. 5 dailies. 34. As of March 31 of the following year. 35. 19 dailies. 36. For 1969. 37. 17 dailies. 38. 6 dailies. 39. Data refer to West Malaysia only. 40. Year ending March 31. 41. 18 dailies. 42. 12 dailies. 43. For 1972. 44. Excludes telephone systems of the military forces. 45. 30 dailies. 46. Data are for former Republic of South Vietnam. 47. Now Zimbabwe. NOTE: n.a. = not available. *Source:* Except as noted, Statistical Office of the United Nations, New York, N.Y., *Statistical Yearbook.* (Copyright.)

Foreign Currency Exchange

Visitors to foreign countries can usually change their U.S. dollars into the appropriate currency at their point of departure. Most airports have currency exchange facilities, generally open from 9:00 A.M. to 10:00 P.M. The Deak-Perera Group, the largest private organization specializing in foreign money exchange, has offices in some airports. It is generally advisable for an American traveling to a foreign destination to have a small amount of the foreign currency on hand on arrival. Currency can usually be exchanged at foreign entry points.

Visitors to the United States can usually exchange their currency into U.S. dollars at their port of entry. A large number of banks also exchange foreign currency during normal banking hours.

COUNTRIES OF THE WORLD

Freedom in the World

One of the most important aspects of any country is the state of human freedom within its borders. Freedom is not a concept that lends itself to simple tabulation. As basic as freedom is, its measures are subtle and complex. For this reason, the editors of *Information Please* have once again turned to Freedom House for its annual Comparative Survey of Freedom.

Freedom House is a national organization dedicated to strengthening democratic institutions.

"For 35 years," said former President Carter, "the vigilance of Freedom House in the pursuit of democratic ideals has nourished those ideals throughout the world."

Readers may obtain Freedom House's bimonthly, *Freedom at Issue,* or its complete annual survey, *Freedom in the World: Political Rights and Civil Liberties,* from Freedom House, 20 W. 40th St., New York, N.Y. 10018.

The Criteria of Freedom

The Freedom House Survey defines freedom in terms of both civil and political freedoms, as traditionally understood in constitutional democratic countries.

Political Rights

In the area of *political rights* the Survey asks whether leaders are chosen, or decisions made, on the basis of an open voting process. If they are, then the question arises whether recent votes suggest that a significant opposition is allowed to compete. This would be demonstrated by the size of the opposition and, particularly, whether a recent change of government had resulted from an election or vote. Are there multiple political parties, or at least candidates not selected by the government? Does the polling and counting of votes appear to be generally without coercion and fraud? What share of the political power is exercised by elected representatives?

Also, how is political power allocated among central, regional, and local authorities? A wide dispersion of power is particularly critical in large states, or in states in which most people are isolated from participation in national life by lack of educational and economic development. Even if elections are not important in a country, one needs to ask if power is divided among a wide variety of persons and groups. In some cases a *de facto* balance of power may offer as much political freedom as an ineffective electoral system. Finally, the Survey asks how free the political system is from foreign or military control or influence.

Civil Liberties

Civil liberties generally imply independent news media, free from censorship. The Survey is interested primarily in censorship that is applied in defense of a ruling party or its policies; it has only marginal interest in censorship applied for social or religious reasons. Perhaps the most important civil liberties for the average person are the right to openly express oneself, the right to discuss public affairs with one's fellows without fear, and the right

to belong to an independent private organization free of government supervision. Civil liberties include the right to a fair trial, and thus imply that the judiciary is to a degree independent. There is little detailed information readily available on the behavior of many judicial systems, but there often are indications as to whether an individual in a particular country can win a case against the government in court.

Closely allied to this question is the degree to which the security forces of a state respect individual rights. The number of political prisoners (arrested for opinions rather than violent action) and the existence of torture or brutality are important indicators. Finally, civil liberties are usually more operative when a nation is at peace, for increasing numbers of persons feel cowed into silence as levels of political violence rise. The Freedom House Survey also takes some account of the partial denial of rights implied by illiteracy, except on the local level.

The reader should be aware that judgments of civil and political rights are always on a comparative basis, and that Freedom House bases its conclusions on behavior rather than laws or formal systems. One might realize the imperfections of all systems and that the *pattern* of rights, not a simple list of pluses and minuses, is critical.

Political and Economic Systems

Freedom House further classifies countries according to their political and economic systems.

These classifications appear under each country in the Countries, Territories, and Dependencies section.

Theoretically, the most democratic countries should be those with *decentralized multi-party systems.* More common are *centralized multi-party systems* (such as in France or Japan) in which the central government organizes lower levels of government primarily for reasons of efficiency.

Dominant party systems allow the forms of democracy, but structure the political process so that opposition groups do not have a realistic chance of achieving power.

The now classical form of one-party rule is that of the *communist one-party states* (such as the U.S.S.R. or Vietnam). The slightly larger number of *socialist one-party states* are ruled by groups that use Marxist-Leninist rhetoric and organize ruling parties much along communist lines, but either do not have the disciplined organization of communist states or have explicitly rejected one or another aspect of communism. A final group of *nationalist one-party states* adopt the political form popularized by the communists (and the fascists in the last generation), but the leaders either reject entirely the revolutionary ideologies of socialist or communist states or show little inclination to develop the totalitarian controls that characterize these states. There are several borderline states that might be switched between socialist and nationalist categories (*e.g.*, Libya or Syria). It should also be noted that "socialist" is used here to designate a political rather than economic system. A socialist "vanguard party" will almost surely develop a socialist economy, but a state with a socialist economy need not be ruled by a quasi-communist vanguard party.

Non-party systems can be relatively democratic, as in the small island of Nauru, but generally they are not. Such systems may be *traditional non-party systems*, ranging from Tonga to Saudi Arabia. Much more important are the many *military non-party systems*, such as that in Argentina.

States with *inclusive capitalist* forms are generally developed states in which the ruling assumption remains reliance on the operation of the market and on private provision for industrial welfare. A larger number of states are classified as *noninclusive capitalist* such as Liberia or Thailand, and they do not have over 50% of the population involved in a capitalist modern economy and the bulk of the population still living in traditional terms. In such states the traditional economy may be individual, communal, or feudal, but the direction of change as development proceeds is capitalistic.

Capitalist-statist nations (such as Brazil, Turkey, or Saudi Arabia) have very large government productive enterprises, either because of an elitist development philosophy or major dependence on a key resource such as oil. Government interferes in the economy in a major way in such states, but not primarily because of egalitarian motives.

Capitalist-socialist systems (such as those in Israel, the Netherlands, or Sweden) provide social services on a large scale through governmental or other nonprofit institutions. These nations still see capitalism as legitimate, but its legitimacy is accepted grudgingly by many in government. Governments of other states grouped here (such as Egypt or Poland) proclaim themselves to be socialist, but in fact allow rather large portions of the economy to remain in the private domain. Both variants also have *noninclusive versions* (such as India or Madagascar).

Socialist economies, on the other hand, strive to place an entire national economy under direct or indirect government control. States such as the U.S.S.R. or Cuba may allow some modest private productive property, but this is only by exception, and right to such property can be revoked at any time. The leaders of *noninclusive socialist states* have the same goals as the leaders of industrial socialist states, but their relatively primitive economies and untrained peoples cannot yet be completely socialized. Such states generally have a small socialized modern economy and a large preindustrial economy in which the organization of production and trade is still largely traditional. It should be understood that the classifications given are impressionistic; along the continuum between capitalist and socialist systems the division into categories must, of course, be judgmental.

Freedom in the World—1981

The percentage of people now living in freedom compared to last year dropped by 1.1 points to 35.9% of the world's population. There are 1.613 million persons residing in 51 free nations and 29 related territories. The percentage of partly free and not free increased. There are 970.9 million (21.6%) living in 76 partly free places, and 1,911.9 million (42.5%) residing in 62 countries and territories regarded as not free.

The human population has increased to 4,495.8 million, so that the number living in free countries rose while the percentage diminished.

In 17 countries with 1,455 million people, reductions in political rights and/or civil liberties were noted by our Comparative Survey of Freedom. In 7 of these, with populations of 68.7 million, deteriorations in human freedom moved the country to a lower category. Turkey and Upper Volta went from free to partly free; Surinam from free to not free; and Bolivia, Liberia, Seychelles, and Syria from partly free to not free.

The loss of freedom in 10 other nations with 1,380 million population was not sufficient to move the country to a lower category. Losses, however, were noted in partly free China (Taiwan), El Salva-dor, Grenada, Guatemala, Korea (South), and Western Samoa; and in not free China (Mainland), Haiti, the Soviet Union, and Zambia.

For 45.9 million persons in 4 countries there were major improvements in status. Ghana and Peru went from partly free to free, and Uganda and Uruguay from not free to partly free.

Improvements within categories were recorded for 8 countries with 123.3 million: Honduras, Nepal, Panama, Poland, Thailand, Vanuatu, and Zimbabwe among the partly free, and Iraq among the not free.

At the outset of 1981, the following levels of political rights and civil liberties are shown in our Comparative Survey:

Not free: 1,911.9 million (42.5% of the world's population), of whom 1,910.1 million live in 58 countries (35.8% of the nations), and 1.8 million reside in 4 (11.2%) of the related territories.

Partly free: 970.9 million (21.6%), of whom 962 million live in 53 nations (32.7%), and 8.9 million reside in 23 (41.1%) of the territories.

Free: 1,613 million (35.9%), of whom 1,607.6 million inhabit 51 countries (31.4%), and 5.4 million live in 29 (51.8%) of the related territories.

Nine-Year Record of the Survey
(population in millions)

Survey date	World population	Free Number	Free Percent	Partly free Number	Partly free Percent	Not free Number	Not free Percent
Jan. 1973	3,334	1,029	32	720	21	1,583	47
Jan. 1974	3,784	1,351	36	812	22	1,618	42
Jan. 1975	3,867	1,366	35	899	23	1,602	42
Jan. 1976	4,063	804	20	1,436	35	1,823	45
Jan. 1977	4,020	790	20	1,464	36	1,766	44
Jan. 1978	4,083	1,455	36	874	21	1,754	43
Jan. 1979	4,227	1,483	35	1,043	25	1,701	40
Jan. 1980	4,326	1,601	37	921	21	1,804	42
Jan. 1981	4,495	1,613	35.9	970.9	21.6	1,911	42.5

The Comparative Survey of Freedom
Table of Nations

	Political Rights[1]	Civil Liberties[1]	Status of Freedom[2]	Outlook[3]		Political Rights[1]	Civil Liberties[1]	Status of Freedom[2]	Outlook[3]
Afghanistan	7	7	NF	0	Fiji	2	2	F	0
Albania	7	7	NF	0	Finland	2	2	F	0
Algeria	6	6	NF	0	France	1	2	F	0
Angola	7	7	NF	0	Gabon	6	6	NF	0
Argentina	6	5	NF	0	Gambia	2	2	F	0
Australia	1	1	F	0	Germany, East	7	6	NF	0
Austria	1	1	F	0	Germany, West	1	2	F	0
Bahamas	1	2	F	0	Ghana	2+	3+	F+	0
Bahrain	5	4	PF	0	Greece	2	2	F	0
Bangladesh	3	3	PF	0	Grenada	5—	5	PF	—
Barbados	1	1	F	0	Guatemala	5—	6—	PF	0
Belgium	1	1	F	0	Guinea	7	7	NF	0
Benin	7	6	NF	0	Guinea-Bissau	6	6	NF	0
Bhutan	5	5	PF	0	Guyana	4	4—	PF	0
Bolivia	7—	5—	NF—	0	Haiti	6	6—	NF	0
Botswana	2	3	F	0	Honduras	4+	3	PF	+
Brazil	4	3	PF	0	Hungary	6	5	NF	0
Bulgaria	7	7	NF	0	Iceland	1	1	F	0
Burma	7	6	NF	0	India	2	3—	F	0
Burundi	7	6+	NF	0	Indonesia	5	5	PF	0
Cambodia	7	7	NF	0	Iran	5	5	PF	0
Cameroon	6	6	NF	0	Iraq	6+	7	NF	0
Canada	1	1	F	0	Ireland	1	1	F	0
Cape Verde	6	6	NF	0	Israel	2	2	F	0
Central African Republic	7	6	NF	0	Italy	1+	2	F	0
Chad	6	6	NF	0	Ivory Coast	6	5	PF	0
Chile	6	5	PF	0	Jamaica	2	3	F	0
China, People's Republic of	6	6—	NF	+	Japan	1+	1	F	0
China, Republic of	5	6—	PF	+	Jordan	6	6	NF	0
Colombia	2	3	F	0	Kenya	5	4	PF	0
Comoros	4	5	PF	0	Kiribati	2	2	F	0
Congo	7	7	NF	0	Korea, North	7	7	NF	0
Costa Rica	1	1	F	0	Korea, South	5—	6—	PF	0
Cuba	6	6	NF	0	Kuwait	6	4	PF	+
Cyprus	3	3+	PF	0	Laos	7	7	NF	0
Czechoslovakia	7	6	NF	0	Lebanon	4	4	PF	0
Denmark	1	1	F	0	Lesotho	5	5	PF	0
Djibouti	3	4	PF	0	Liberia	6	6—	NF—	+
Dominica	2	2	F	+	Libya	6	6	NF	0
Dominican Republic	2	3	F	0	Luxembourg	1	1	F	0
Ecuador	2	2	F	0	Madagascar	6	6	NF	0
Egypt	5	5	PF	0	Malawi	6	7	NF	0
El Salvador	6—	4—	PF	0	Malaysia	3	4	PF	0
Equatorial Guinea	7	6	NF	0	Maldives	5	5	PF	0
Ethiopia	7	7	NF	0	Mali	7	6	NF	0
					Malta	2	3—	F	—

	Political Rights[1]	Civil Liber- ties[1]	Status of Free- dom[2]	Outlook[3]
Mauritania	7	6	NF	0
Mauritius	2	4	PF	+
Mexico	3	4	PF	0
Mongolia	7	7	NF	0
Morocco	4	4	PF	0
Mozambique	7	7	NF	0
Nauru	2	2	F	0
Nepal	3+	4	PF	0
Netherlands	1	1	F	0
New Zealand	1	1	F	0
Nicaragua	5	5	PF	—
Niger	7	6	NF	0
Nigeria	2	3	F	0
Norway	1	1	F	0
Oman	6	6	NF	0
Pakistan	7—	5	NF	0
Panama	4+	4+	PF	0
Papua New Guinea	2	2	F	0
Paraguay	5	5	PF	0
Peru	2+	3+	F+	0
Philippines	5	5	PF	0
Poland	6	4+	PF	0
Portugal	2	2	F	0
Qatar	5	5	PF	0
Romania	7	6	NF	0
Rwanda	6	6	NF	0
St. Lucia	2	3	F	0
St. Vincent	2	2	F	0
São Tomé and Príncipe	6	6	NF	0
Saudi Arabia	6	6	NF	0
Senegal	4	4	PF	+
Seychelles	6	6—	NF—	0
Sierra Leone	5	5	PF	0
Singapore	5	5	PF	0
Solomon Islands	2	2	F	0
Somalia	7	7	NF	0

	Political Rights[1]	Civil Liber- ties[1]	Status of Free- dom[2]	Outlook[3]
South Africa	5	6	PF	+
Spain	2	3	F	0
Sri Lanka	2	3	F	0
Sudan	5	5	PF	+
Suriname	7—	5—	NF—	0
Swaziland	5	5	PF	0
Sweden	1	1	F	0
Switzerland	1	1	F	0
Syria	5	6	NF—	0
Tanzania	6	6	NF	0
Thailand	3+	4	PF	0
Togo	7	6	NF	0
Tonga	5	3	PF	0
Transkei	5	6	PF	0
Trinidad and Tobago	2	2	F	0
Tunisia	6	5	PF	0
Turkey	5—	5—	PF—	+
Tuvalu	2	2	F	0
Uganda	5+	5+	PF+	0
U.S.S.R.	6	7—	NF	0
United Arab Emirates	5	5	PF	0
United Kingdom	1	1	F	0
United States	1	1	F	0
Upper Volta	6—	5—	PF—	0
Uruguay	5+	5+	PF+	0
Venezuela	1	2	F	0
Vietnam	7	7	NF	0
Western Samoa	4	3—	PF	0
Yemen Arab Republic	6	5	NF	0
Yemen, People's Dem. Republic of	6	7	NF	0
Yugoslavia	6	5	NF	0
Zaire	6	6	NF	0
Zambia	5	6—	PF	0
Zimbabwe	3+	4+	PF	—

1. The scales use the numbers 1–7, with 1 comparatively offering the highest level of political or civil rights, and 7 the lowest. A plus or minus following a rating indicates an improvement or decline in the rating since January 1979. For further information on the scale and survey see Freedom in the World: Political Rights and Civil Liberties, 1980. available from Freedom House. 2. A free state is designated by F, a partly free state by PF, and a not free state by NF. 3. A positive outlook for freedom is indicated by a plus sign, a negative outlook, by a minus sign, and relative stability of ratings by a zero. The outlook for freedom is based on the problems the country is facing, the way the government and people are reacting to these problems, and the longer run political traditions of the society. A judgment of outlook may also reflect an imminent change, such as the expected adoption of a meaningful new constitution.

International Treaties, Agreements, and Organizations

Association of Southeast Asian Nations

A non-military alliance of Thailand, Malaysia, Singapore, Indonesia, and the Philippines, formed in Bangkok in 1967. Its goal of regional economic integration along the lines of the European Economic Community has not been achieved. However, cooperation on international, political, and economic issues has been evolving. ASEAN took its first major political stand in January 1979 when it condemned Vietnam's invasion of Cambodia.

Papua New Guinea now has observer status in the ASEAN.

Arab League

Formed at Cairo on March 22, 1945, as a loose confederation of Arab states seeking Arab unity. Founding members were Egypt, Iraq, Jordan, Lebanon, Saudi Arabia, Syria, and the Yemen Arab Republic, joined later by Algeria, Bahrain, Djibouti, Kuwait, Libya, Mauritania, Morocco, Oman, Qatar, Somalia, the Sudan, Tunisia, the United Arab Emirates, the Yemen People's Democratic Republic, and the Palestine Liberation Organization. Military cooperation has been hampered by differences among the members, except in the Suez Canal crisis of 1956. The league has proved more effective in economic and cultural affairs. A permanent secretariat was set up at Cairo.

Alliance for Progress Agreement

Embodied in the Declaration of Punta del Este, adopted Aug. 17, 1961, by the U.S. and 19 other American republics, Cuba abstaining. The U.S. agreed to provide most of $20 billion needed over the next 10 years for Latin-American economic development. The other nations pledged themselves to increase their own contributions to economic and social development and to make the reforms necessary for all to share fully in the benefits gained under the Alliance for Progress.

Central Treaty Organization (CENTO)

Created in 1955 to provide a defense shield on the northern tier of the Middle East against Soviet penetration. Its original members were Turkey, Iran, U.K., Pakistan, and Iraq (which withdrew in 1959). In 1958, the U.S. signed a declaration of collective security to cooperate with the member states. CENTO was known as the Baghdad Pact until 1958, when its headquarters were moved to Ankara, Turkey. Iran and Pakistan withdrew in 1979.

Commonwealth of Nations

An association of equal and independent nations and subordinate areas formerly part of the old British Empire and united by their symbolic allegiance to the Crown. Member nations gained equal status with the U.K. under the Statute of Westminster of 1931, which formally initiated the Commonwealth. Its members consult and cooperate and share trade and other economic benefits. For a list of members, *see* Countries of the World by Groupings.

The European Community

In 1950, the then French Foreign Minister, Robert Schuman, proposed a "Community" of the French and German coal and steel industries, with membership open to other European countries. The *European Coal and Steel Community (ECSC)* was established in 1952; it eliminated customs duties and reduced currency and trade restrictions on coal, iron ore, and scrap. Original members were France, Germany, Italy, Belgium, the Netherlands, and Luxembourg.

By 1955, discussions began on other ways of increasing European economic integration. The *European Economic Community* (the *Common Market* or *EEC*) was established by a treaty, signed in Rome in 1957, by the original members of the ECSC. In 1970, the U.K., Ireland, Denmark, and Norway were invited to join. All except Norway did so in 1972; the enlarged "Community of the Nine" formally came into existence on January 1, 1973. Greece became the tenth EEC member in 1979 and joined formally Jan. 1, 1981.

The purposes of the EEC include the removal of trade barriers, coordination of economic policies, and increased mobility of labor and capital among its members—much of which had been achieved by 1978. Its aim is eventual economic union of the member nations and ultimate political confederation.

A second treaty was signed in Rome in 1957 establishing the *European Atomic Energy Community (Euratom)* to integrate activities of member nations concerned with nuclear power and technology.

The three Communities (ECSC, EEC, and Euratom) make up the *European Community*, with a Council of Ministers and a European Parliament. A European Court of Justice and the European Investment Bank also function within the European Community. (*See* R.C. Mowat, *Creating the European Community*, 1973.)

European Free Trade Association (EFTA)

Formed in 1959 (formally begun 1960) to promote economic growth and fair competition, equalize the supply of raw materials among the member states, and to expand world trade. Members now include Austria, Iceland, Norway, Portugal, Sweden, Switzerland, and Finland (associate). Denmark and the U.K., originally members, withdrew before becoming members of the EEC in 1973: at that time a new trade agreement was made between the EFTA and the Common Market. By 1966, custom duties between members had virtually been eliminated. The EFTA is based in Geneva.

The Helsinki Agreement

Popular name for declaration adopted Aug. 1, 1975, by 35 nations—including the United States and the Soviet Union—participating in the Conference on Security and Cooperation in Europe held at Helsinki, Finland. The declaration particularly stressed "fundamental rights, economic and social progress and well-being for all peoples," as well as the need for joint action to promote world peace and security. The participating states reaffirmed their full support for the United Nations and pledged to respect each other's "sovereign equality and individuality. . . . " They pledged to broaden and deepen détente, and renounced the "threat or use of force" and subversion in settling international disputes.

Outstanding in the declaration was the section on cooperation in humanitarian and cultural fields. The signers pledged themselves to respect "fundamental freedoms, including the freedom of thought, conscience, religion or belief."

Among the stated objectives were: Freer movement among persons, institutions, and organizations; wider exchange of information; increased cultural exchanges and broader dissemination of books, films, other media, and artistic works. The agreement was reviewed in an eight-month conference at Belgrade, Yugoslavia, ending in March 1978, which was attended by representatives of the U.S. and Canada, 32 European countries, and the Vatican. After bitter debate, the conference adopted a summary document that did not mention human rights or other issues dividing East and West.

Another review conference began in Madrid in

the autumn of 1980 and adjourned the following July 24 until Oct. 27 without reaching agreement on the major issues of human rights or military security. The protracted negotiations ranged from terrorism to measures to ease emigration, and a proposal to hold a later conference on military security in Europe.

Marshall Plan (European Recovery Program)

Proposed in June 1947 by Gen. George C. Marshall, U.S. Secretary of State, to meet the need for integrated recovery efforts against "hunger, poverty, desperation, and chaos" in Europe. A July conference of 16 nations (the U.S.S.R. and its satellites refusing to participate) estimated four-year-aid requirements at $22.4 billion. In April 1948, Congress appropriated $5.4 billion. The U.S. established the Economic Cooperation Administration; European nations set up the Organization for European Economic Cooperation (OEEC). Each participating country set aside, in its own currency, sums matching the aid it received. The ERP ended in December 1951, a year ahead of schedule, with a total cost of $11 billion. Emphasis by then had been shifted to rearmament. (*See* S.E. Harris, ed., *Foreign Economic Policy for the U.S.*, 1948, 1968.)

North Atlantic Treaty Organization (NATO)

Set up April 4, 1949, under a regional defense treaty for the North Atlantic area stating that "an armed attack against one . . . shall be considered an attack against . . . all" and that participating nations will take necessary joint counteraction under the United Nations Charter, including the use of armed force. The founding members were the U.S., Canada, Iceland, Norway, Great Britain, the Netherlands, Denmark, Belgium, Luxembourg, Portugal, France, and Italy. Greece, Turkey, and West Germany were added later. NATO marked the first time that the United States pledged to go to war to support allies before the outbreak of hostilities. The member nations are represented on the governing NATO Council. Its organization comprises their top foreign, economic, defense, and financial ministers. Its major military commands are SACEUR for Europe and SACLANT for the Atlantic Ocean area. (*See* James Huntley, *The NATO Story*, 1969.)

Organization for Economic Cooperation and Development (OECD)

Founded in 1961 to encourage world trade and economic progress and aid underdeveloped nations. The OECD superseded the Organization for European Economic Cooperation, which had been established under the Marshall Plan in 1948. Members are Australia, Austria, Belgium, Canada, Denmark, Finland, France, West Germany, Greece, Iceland, Ireland, Italy, Japan, Luxembourg, the Netherlands, New Zealand, Norway, Portugal, Spain, Sweden, Switzerland, Turkey, the U.K. and the U.S. (Yugoslavia has a special association). Its structure is consultative; its decisions, not binding.

Organization of African Unity (OAU)

Founded in May 1963 by 32 African countries, the OAU has grown to include most independent African countries; South Africa is specifically excluded; as was Rhodesia; Zimbabwe, formerly Rhodesia, was admitted as 50th member upon gaining independence in 1980. Its charter reflects historical Pan-African concern for the political sovereignty, economic advancement, and cultural cooperation of all African peoples. The charter affirms allegiance to United Nations principles; its key section emphasizes the eradication of colonialism and promotion of international cooperation. The OAU has assisted in the relaxation or settlement of border disputes and helped resolve internal crises. In economic cooperation, it has stressed transportation and telecommunications. It maintains a close relationship with the U.N. OAU headquarters are at Addis Ababa, Ethiopia.

Organization of American States (OAS)

Created in April 1948 as a regional agency working with the UN to promote peace, justice, hemispheric solidarity, and economic development; and to defend the sovereignty of member nations. Original members were Argentina, Bolivia, Brazil, Chile, Colombia, Costa Rica, Cuba, Dominica, the Dominican Republic, Ecuador, El Salvador, Guatemala, Haiti, Honduras, Mexico, Nicaragua, Panama, Paraguay, Peru, the U.S., Uruguay, and Venezuela. Barbados, Grenada, Jamaica, Santa Lucia, Surinam, and Trinidad and Tobago were admitted later. In 1962 Cuba was suspended. The permanent body of the OAS is the General Secretariat, formerly the Pan-American Union Headquarters, Washington, D.C.

Organization of Petroleum Exporting Countries (OPEC)

Founded in 1960 at Baghdad, Iraq, to advance its members' interests in trade and development and in relations with other oil-producing nations. Venezuela took the initiative; other founders were Iran, Iraq, Kuwait, and Saudi Arabia. They were joined by Algeria, Ecuador, Gabon, Indonesia, Libya, Nigeria, Qatar, and the United Arab Emirates. Through such practices as the 1973–74 embargo, OPEC has maintained high oil prices and has generally fixed the price of oil in international trade.

Panama Canal Treaties

Approved by the U.S. Senate in March and April of 1978. The basic treaty provides for turning the canal over to Panama by the year 2000. Until noon Dec. 31, 1999, the canal will be operated by a new U.S. agency, the Panama Canal Commission, with five Americans and four Panamanians on the board. Until 2000 the U.S. will have primary responsibility for defending the canal; Panama will assume jurisdiction over the 533-square-mile Canal Zone.

The Neutrality Treaty, also effective Dec. 31, 1999, provides that the U.S. and Panama will each have the right to defend the canal against threats to its neutrality or the peaceful passage of ships. A Senate reservation gave the U.S. the unilateral right to use force if necessary to reopen the canal or restore its operations. The Senate specified that any intervention would be only to keep the canal open, not to interfere in Panama's internal affairs. (See *Panama.*)

Treaty for a Partial Nuclear Test Ban

Agreement, effective Oct. 10, 1963, signed in Moscow Aug. 8, 1963, by the U.S., U.K., and the U.S.S.R. Although over 100 nations have since signed, France and China have not. The treaty banned nuclear testing in the atmosphere, in outer space, or under water. The signatories can withdraw under certain conditions.

The Potsdam Declaration

Issued at Potsdam, Germany, July 26, 1945, after a conference of President Truman, Prime Minister Churchill (later, Clement Attlee), and Prime Minister Stalin. Pending entry of the U.S.S.R. into the war against Japan, it was issued in the names of Truman, Churchill, and Chiang Kai-shek (reached by radio). The declaration, designed to clarify and implement the Yalta Agreement, demanded unconditional surrender of Japan and outlined surrender terms. It called for elimination of "irresponsible militarism" and for Allied occupation until Japan's war-making power was destroyed. Other major points included "stern justice" for war criminals, democratic reforms, and respect for fundamental human rights. Successful U.S. testing of the atom bomb was revealed to Stalin at Potsdam.

Strategic Arms Limitation Talks (SALT I)

Two agreements limiting American and Soviet nuclear weapons were signed in Moscow in 1972 after three years of negotiations. One was a five-year interim pact limiting some offensive strategic weapons and the number of launchers for intercontinental ballistic missiles carrying nuclear warheads. The other, a treaty of indefinite duration, restricted antiballistic or defensive missiles to 200 on each side. (That number was reduced to 100 in a 1974 amendment.) The agreements were signed by President Richard M. Nixon and Leonid I. Brezhnev, the Soviet Communist Party leader. The talks originated with discussions at Glassboro, N.J., in 1967 between President Lyndon B. Johnson and the Soviet Prime Minister, Aleksei N. Kosygin. On Nov. 24, 1974, President Gerald R. Ford reached agreement in principle with Mr. Brezhnev at Vladivostok on limiting the numbers of all offensive strategic weapons and delivery systems until Dec. 31, 1985.

(SALT II)

A treaty resulting from the second round of strategic arms limitation talks was signed in Vienna on June 18, 1979, by President Carter and Soviet leader Brezhnev and went to the U.S. Senate for ratification. The treaty runs to 1985 and limits each side to 2,400 intercontinental ballistic missile launchers and long-range bombers within six months. The U.S. is already under this ceiling, but the Russians will have to destroy 100 of their launchers or bombers. By the end of 1981, a new ceiling of 2,250 is to come into effect. The treaty allows each country to develop one new missile and to modernize its existing weapons within certain restrictions. Each side would verify the other's compliance by its own technical means. The agreement ran into sharp opposition in the Senate. A substantial increase in spending on armaments appeared to be the price many senators would set for their affirmative votes. President Carter delayed ratification efforts indefinitely following the Soviet invasion of Afghanistan in December 1979. Controversy over the treaty continued well into the Reagan Administration.

Warsaw Pact

Signed May 14, 1955, by Albania, Bulgaria, Czechoslovakia, East Germany, Hungary, Poland, Romania, and the U.S.S.R. Albania, barred from meetings in 1962, withdrew in 1968 after ideological differences. The pact is the Communist equivalent of NATO, providing that an attack on one shall be regarded as an attack on all.

The Yalta Agreement

Signed Feb. 11, 1945, at conference of President Roosevelt and Prime Ministers Churchill and Stalin. The U.S., U.K., and the U.S.S.R. agreed to require Germany's unconditional surrender and on dividing Germany into separate zones for occupation, with France invited to join as the fourth occupying power. The agreement pledged disarmament of Germany, breakup of the arms industry, punishment of war criminals, reparations for destruction by the Germans, and the wiping out of nazism and militarism. The conference also agreed on terms for Russia to enter the war against Japan. (See R.F. Fenno, ed., *The Yalta Conference,* 2nd ed., 1972.)

Countries of the World by Groupings

KEY

1—Member of the Organization of American States (OAS)
2—Member of the Organization of African Unity (OAU)
3—Member of the Organization of Petroleum Exporting Countries (OPEC)
4—Member of the North Atlantic Treaty Organization (NATO)
5—Member of the Association of Southeast Asian Nations
6—Member of the Central Treaty Organization (CENTO)
7—Member of the Arab League

8—Member of the Warsaw Pact
9—Member of the European Economic Community (EEC)
10—Member of the European Free Trade Association (EFTA)
11—Member of the Commonwealth
12—Member of the Economic Community of West African States (ECOWAS)
13—Member of the Organization for Economic Cooperation and Development (OECD)

NORTH AMERICA

Canada: 4, 11, 13
Mexico: 1
United States: 1, 4, 13

SOUTH AMERICA

Argentina: 1
Bolivia: 1
Brazil: 1
Chile: 1
Colombia: 1
Ecuador:1, 3
Guyana: 11
Paraguay: 1
Peru: 1
Suriname: 1
Uruguay: 1
Venezuela: 1,3

CENTRAL AMERICA

Belize: 11
Costa Rica: 1
El Salvador: 1
Guatemala: 1
Honduras: 1
Nicaragua: 1
Panama: 1

CARIBBEAN REGION

Bahamas: 11
Barbados: 1, 11
Cuba
Dominica: 1, 11
Dominican Republic: 1
Grenada: 1, 11
Haiti: 1
Jamaica: 1, 11
St. Lucia: 1, 11
St. Vincent and the Grena-
  dines: 11
Trinidad and Tobago: 1, 11

EUROPE

Albania
Andorra
Austria: 10, 13
Belgium: 4, 9, 13
Bulgaria: 8
Cyprus: 11

Czechoslovakia: 8
Denmark: 4, 9, 13
Finland: 10 (assoc. mem.), 13
France: 4, 9, 13
Germany, East: 8
Germany, West: 4, 9, 13
Greece: 4, 9, 13
Hungary: 8
Iceland: 4, 10, 13
Ireland: 9, 13
Italy: 4, 9, 13
Liechtenstein
Luxembourg: 4, 9, 13
Malta: 11
Monaco
Netherlands: 4, 9, 13
Norway: 4, 10, 13
Poland: 8
Portugal: 4, 10, 13
Romania: 8
San Marino
Spain: 13
Sweden: 10, 13
Switzerland: 10, 13
U.S.S.R.: 8
United Kingdom: 4, 6, 9, 11, 13
Vatican City State
Yugoslavia

MIDDLE EAST

Bahrain: 7
Iran: 3
Iraq: 3, 7
Israel
Jordan: 7
Kuwait: 3, 7
Lebanon: 7
Oman: 7
Qatar: 3, 7
Saudi Arabia: 3, 7
Syria: 7
Turkey: 4, 6, 13
United Arab Emirates: 3, 7
Yemen, People's Democratic
  Republic of: 7
Yemen Arab Republic: 7

FAR EAST

China, People's Republic of

China, Republic of
Japan: 13
Korea, North
Korea, South
Mongolia
Philippines: 5

SOUTHEAST ASIA

Cambodia
Indonesia: 3, 5
Laos
Malaysia: 5, 11
Singapore: 5, 11
Thailand: 5
Vietnam

SOUTH ASIA

Afghanistan
Bangladesh: 11
Bhutan
Burma
India: 11
Maldives
Nepal
Pakistan
Sri Lanka: 11

OCEANIA

Australia: 11
Fiji: 11
Kiribati: 11
Nauru: 11
New Zealand: 11,13
Papua New Guinea: 11
Solomon Islands: 11
Tonga: 11
Tuvalu: 11
Vanuatu (New Hebrides)
Western Samoa: 11

AFRICA

Algeria: 2, 3, 7
Angola: 2
Benin: 2, 12
Bophuthatswana
Botswana: 2, 11
Burundi: 2
Cameroon: 2, 12
Cape Verde: 2

Central African Republic: 2
Chad: 2, 12
Comoro Islands: 2
Congo: 2
Djibouti: 7
Egypt: 2, 7
Equatorial Guinea: 2
Ethiopia: 2
Gabon: 2, 3
Gambia: 2, 11, 12
Ghana: 2, 11, 12
Guinea: 12
Guinea-Bissau: 2, 12
Ivory Coast: 2, 12
Kenya: 2, 11
Lesotho: 2, 11
Liberia: 2, 12
Libya: 2, 3, 7
Madagascar: 2
Malawi: 2, 11
Mali: 2, 12
Mauritania: 2, 7, 12
Mauritius: 2, 11
Morocco: 2, 7
Mozambique: 2
Niger: 2, 12
Nigeria: 2, 3, 11, 12
Rwanda: 2
Sao Tomé and Príncipe: 2
Senegal: 2, 12
Seychelles: 11
Sierra Leone: 2, 11, 12
Somalia: 2, 7
South Africa, Rep. of
Sudan: 2, 7
Swaziland: 2, 11
Tanzania: 2, 11
Togo: 2, 12
Transkei
Tunisia: 2, 7
Uganda: 2, 11
Upper Volta: 2, 12
Venda
Zaire: 2
Zambia: 2, 11
Zimbabwe: 2, 11

Countries, Territories, and Dependencies

For later developments, *see* Current Events

Economic data for each country have been drawn from reports of the United States State Department, the World Bank and the National Foreign Assessment Center. Population figures are mid-1981 estimates.

AFGHANISTAN

Democratic Republic of Afghanistan
President: Babrak Karmal (1979)
Premier: Sultan Ali Kishtmand (1981)
Area: 251,000 sq mi. (650,090 sq km)
Population (est. 1981): 16,250,000 (growth rate: 2.2%)
Density per square mile: 64.7
Capital: Kabul
Largest cities (est. 1979): Kabul, 891,700; (est. 1975 by U.N.): Kandahar, 209,000; Herat, 157,000; (est. 1973 by U.N.): Baghlan, 110,900
Monetary unit: Afghani
Languages: Pushtu and Dari Persian (both official)
Religion: Islam (Sunni, 90%; Shiah, 10%)
National name: Jamhouriati Democratici Afghanistan
Freedom House classification: Socialist pre-industrial, one-party communist
Economic summary: Gross national product (1979): $3.4 billion. Average annual growth rate (1976–79): 4.5%. Per capita income: $130. Labor force in agriculture: 68%; principal products: wheat, grains, cotton, fruits, nuts. Labor force in industry: 10%; major products: soap, furniture, shoes, carpets, textiles, cement, coal. Natural resources: natural gas, oil, coal, copper, sulfur, lead, zinc, iron, salt, precious and semi-precious stones. Exports: fresh and dried fruits, natural gas, karakul skins, carpets, hides, wool, cotton. Imports: petroleum products, yarns and textiles, transportation equipment, wheat. Major trading partners: U.S.S.R., India, U.K., Pakistan, West Germany, Japan, U.S.

Geography. Afghanistan, approximately the size of Texas, lies wedged between the U.S.S.R., China, Pakistan, and Iran. The country is split east to west by the Hindu Kush mountain range, rising in the east to heights of 24,000 feet (7,315 m). With the exception of the southwest, most of the country is covered by high snow-capped mountains and is traversed by deep valleys.

Government. A limited monarchy ended July 17, 1973, in a coup that ousted King Mohammad Zahir Shah. Mohammed Daud, a former Prime Minister and brother-in-law of the King, proclaimed a republic, suspended the 1964 Constitution, and abolished the Shura (parliament). On April 27, 1978, Daud himself was overthrown and Noor Mohammad Taraki installed as president of a 35-member Revolutionary Council.

History. Afghanistan occupies the land route to India trod by many conquerors, among them Darius I and Alexander the Great. The Moslems conquered the country from the west, beginning in the 7th century A.D. Genghis Khan in the 13th century and Tamerlane in the 14th century were later conquerors. Tamerlane's descendant, Baber, used the Afghanistan town of Kabul from 1504 to achieve the Mogul conquest of India. The country was torn by tribal and family warfare until Nadir Shah of Persia conquered the area in the 18th century. His commander, Ahmad Shah, established an emirate in 1747 and unified the country.

A later ruler, Dost Mohammed, reigned as the British and Czarist Russia began their struggle for central Asia. The Afghan Wars (1838–42 and 1878–81) that he, his son, and his grandson waged against the British are remembered for the massacre of the British at Kabul in 1842 and for the subsequent assaults on the Khyber Pass.

Afghanistan regained independence, though still under British influence, by the Anglo-Russian agreement of 1907, and full sovereignty by the Treaty of Rawalpindi in 1919. Emir Amanullah founded the kingdom in 1926.

The 1973 coup that ended the monarchy also cut off a 10-year experiment in democracy when Mohammed Daud seized all powers. The April 27, 1978, coup that brought Noor Mohammed Taraki to power resulted not only in the death of Daud but also, according to press reports, in the deaths of thousands of officials and supporters of his government.

Taraki's attempts to create a Marxist state with Soviet aid brought armed resistance from conservative Muslim opposition. Rebels kidnapped U.S. Ambassador Adolph Dubs in an attempt to ransom comrades held by the Taraki government. Dubs was killed on Feb. 14, 1979, when Afghan police attacked his captors and Soviet advisers ignored U.S. appeals for restraint.

Taraki resigned on Sept. 16, 1979, reportedly because of poor health, and was succeeded by Prime Minister Hafizullah Amin. As disorder spread, it was announced on Dec. 28 that Amin had been killed and replaced by Babrak Karmal, who had called for Soviet troops under a mutual defense treaty. Pakistan and other Moslem nations called for a U.N. Security Council session and charged that Amin had been executed on Dec. 27 by Soviet troops already present in Kabul. The Council's call for immediate withdrawal of an estimated 40,000 Soviet troops was vetoed by the U.S.S.R. on Jan. 8, 1980.

With 85,000 reported in the invasion force by June, the U.S.S.R. and government forces were still unable to quell the rebels. Despite cuts in U.S. exports of high-technology goods and restrictions on food exports, together with a boycott of the Moscow Olympics by Western and Moslem nations, the Soviet Union refused to withdraw its troops.

Resistance by six Afghan guerrilla organizations continued to be strong late in 1980, with U.S. official sources estimating 10,000 to 12,000 Soviet casualties since the beginning of the Soviet occupation. Soviet-U.S. contacts were reported to have met with failure as Moscow insisted that only Western recognition of the Karmal regime would bring about a Soviet withdrawal.

ALBANIA

People's Socialist Republic of Albania
President of Presidium: Haxhi Leshi (1953)
Premier: Mehmet Shehu (1954)
Area: 11,100 sq mi. (28,748 sq km)
Population (est. 1981): 2,800,000 (growth rate: 2.1%)
Density per square mile: 252.3
Capital and largest city (est. 1976): Tirana, 192,300
Monetary unit: Lek
Language: Albanian
Religions: Historically Islam 70%; Greek Orthodox, 20%; Roman Catholic, 10%
National name: Republika Popullore Socialiste e Shqipërisë
Freedom House classifications: Socialist industrial, one-party communist
Economic summary: Gross national product (1979): $2.2 billion. Average annual growth rate (1970–78): 4.2%. Per capita income (1972): $520. Land used for agriculture: 43%; labor force: 61%; principal products: wheat, corn, potatoes, sugar beets, cotton, tobacco. Labor force in industry: 18%; major products: textiles, timber, construction materials, fuels, semi-processed minerals. Exports: metal ores, crude petroleum, bitumen, tobacco. Imports: machinery, construction materials, foodstuffs, wheat. Major trading partners: East European countries.

Geography. Albania is situated on the eastern shore of the Adriatic Sea, with Yugoslavia to the north and east and Greece to the south. Slightly larger than Maryland, it is a mountainous country, mostly over 3,000 feet (914 m) above sea level, with a narrow, marshy coastal plain crossed by several rivers. The centers of population are contained in the interior mountain plateaus and basins.

Government. Under the Constitution that Albania adopted in 1946, supreme power is vested in the popularly elected National Assembly, to which the Cabinet, headed by the Premier, is responsible. The 240 members of the National Assembly all belong to the Labor Party and Democratic Front. The only political party is Labor (Communist), led by First Secretary Enver Hoxha.

History. Albania proclaimed its independence on Nov. 28, 1912, after a history of Roman, Byzantine, and Turkish domination.

A battlefield in World War I, Albania reasserted its independence in 1920. A chief, Ahmet Zogu, proclaimed himself president in 1925 and monarch (King Zog) in 1928. Italy, under Benito Mussolini, drove him into exile in 1939 and annexed the country. The Communists under Enver Hoxha established a government in 1944, issuing a Constitution in 1946 (amended in 1950) declaring the country a people's republic. Close relations with the U.S.S.R. ended in 1961 with the Soviet-Chinese rupture. Thereafter, Albania functioned as a Peking satellite, receiving massive Chinese aid to offset the Soviet boycott.

In 1967, the regime closed all of the nation's 2,169 churches and mosques in a move to make the country "the first atheist state in the world."

Albania's long alliance with China ended with the announcement in 1978, that China was cutting off all aid to its one-time partner. Albanian criticism of Peking following the death of Mao Zedong was cited as the reason, but Tirana called the action "arbitrary." There was no indication from Tirana that Albania was ready to return to the Soviet sphere.

ALGERIA

Democratic and Popular Republic of Algeria
President: Chadli Bendjedid (1979)
Prime Minister: Mohammed Benahmed Abdelghani (1979)
Area: 919,951 sq mi. (2,382,673 sq km)
Population (est. 1981): 20,250,000 (growth rate: 3.2%)
Density per square mile: 22.0
Capital: Algiers
Largest cities (est. 1979): Algiers, 2,500,000; Oran, 600,000; Constantine, 500,000; Annaba, 300,000
Monetary unit: Dinar
Languages: Arabic (official), French
Religion: Islam
National name: République Algérienne Democratiqe et Populaire—El Djemhouria El Djazaïria Demokratia Echaabia
Freedom House classifications: Socialist industrial, one-party socialist
Economic summary: Gross national product (1979): $28.9 billion. Average annual growth rate (1970–78): 2.6%. Per capita income: $1,720. Average rate of inflation (1976): 15%. Land used for agriculture: 19%; labor force: 50%; principal products: wheat, barley, oats, wine, fruits, olives, vegetables, livestock. Labor force in industry: 20%; major products: petroleum, gas, petrochemicals, fertilizers, iron and steel, textiles, transport equipment. Natural resources: petroleum, natural gas, iron ore, phosphates, lead, zinc, mercury. Exports: petroleum products, wine. Imports: food, capital and consumer goods. Major trading partners: U.S., West Germany, France, Italy.

Geography. Nearly four times the size of Texas, Algeria is bordered on the west by Morocco and on the east by Tunisia and Libya. To the south are Mauritania, Mali, and Niger. Low plains cover small areas near the Mediterranean coast, with 68% of the country a plateau between 2,625 and 5,250 feet (800 and 1,600 m) above sea level. The highest point is Mount Tahat in the Sahara, which rises 9,850 feet (3,000 m).

Government. Algeria is governed by the President, whose term runs for 5 years. A new Constitution was approved on Nov. 19, 1976.

A National Popular Assembly of 261 members was elected Feb. 25, 1977, the first since the dismissal of a predecessor body early in 1965. The National Liberation Front, which led the struggle for independence from France, is the only legal party.

History. As ancient Numidia, Algeria became a Roman colony at the close of the Punic Wars (145 B.C.). Conquered by the Vandals about A.D. 440, it fell from a high state of civilization to virtual barbarism, from which it partly recovered after invasion by the Moslems about 650.

In 1492 the Moors and Jews, who had been expelled from Spain, settled in Algeria. Falling under Turkish control in 1518, Algiers served for three centuries as the headquarters of the Barbary pirates. The French took Algeria in 1830 and made it a part of France in 1848.

The fight by Algerian nationalists for independence had widespread political, diplomatic, military, and financial repercussions in France. Politically, it brought Gen. Charles de Gaulle to power when the army and extremist French colonist virtually seceded, set up a "Committee of Public Safety," and demanded that de Gaulle be given power. Ironically, it was de Gaulle who resolved to end the fighting by granting Algeria self-determination and independence, while his former army and French colonial supporters in Algeria joined to create the Secret Army Organization (OAS), a terrorist group that tried to block independence. But metropolitan France, weary of continued warfare, voted by some 15 million to 5 million in January 1961 to approve de Gaulle's proposals.

On July 5, 1962, Algeria was proclaimed independent. In October 1963, Ahmed Ben Bella was elected President. He began to nationalize foreign holdings and aroused opposition. He was overthrown in a military coup on June 19, 1965, by Col. Houari Boumediène, who suspended the Constitution and sought to restore financial stability. While retaining close economic and financial relations with France and the U.S., Algeria entered the Arab bloc and joined the war against Israel in 1967. Thereafter, the U.S.S.R. stepped up development aid.

Friction with Morocco intensified in 1976 as Algeria opposed the annexation of the Spanish Sahara by Morocco and Mauritania following a mass invasion of the former Spanish colony by Moroccan civilians. Algeria formally recognized a Saharan Arab Democratic Republic—composed of Polisario front leaders who fought unsuccessfully for an independent Sahara—on Feb. 27, 1976. The move was accompanied by a break in diplomatic relations with Morocco.

From an agricultural economy closely linked to France even after independence, Algeria became an exporter of energy in the form of petroleum products and then liquefied natural gas. The U.S. replaced France as Algeria's chief trading partner in 1976, buying 40% of Algerian crude oil production. In common with other oil-exporting countries in 1977 and 1978, however, Algeria slowed its general industrial expansion and shifted investment toward increasing oil and gas output and strengthening agriculture. Non-energy industry had proved too costly in relation to income produced and agricultural imports had become a drain on a weakened economy.

Boumediène died in December 1978 after a long illness. Chadli Bendjedid, Secretary-General of the National Liberation Front, took the presidency in a smooth transition of power. On July 4, 1979, he released from house arrest former President Ahmed Ben Bella, who had been confined for 14 years since his overthrow.

Algeria played a key role in the ultimate release of U.S. hostages from Iran, when Iran named the Algerian government as its intermediary for negotiations with Washington in November 1980. On Jan. 17, Behzad Nabavi, Algerian Minister of Executive Affairs, was credited with achieving the breakthrough when he persuaded the Iranians to allow U.S. banks to retain $3.7 billion in Iranian assets against which the banks had legal claims. Three days later, the 52 hostages were released to Algerian custody in Teheran and flown to Algiers, where they were greeted by U.S. officials.

ANDORRA

Valleys of Andorra

Episcopal Co-Prince: Msgr. Joan Martí Alanis, Bishop of Urgel (1974)

French Co-Prince: François Mitterrand, President of France (1981)

First Syndic: Julià Reiq-Ribó (1981)
Area: 175 sq mi. (453 sq km)
Population (est. 1981): 30,000
Density per square mile: 171.4
Capital (est. 1975): Andorra la Vella, 10,900
Monetary units: French franc and Spanish peseta
Languages: Catalán (official); French, Spanish
Religion: Roman Catholic
National names: Les Vallées d'Andorre-Valls d'Andorra
Economic summary: Land used for agriculture: 4%; labor force: 20%; principal products: oats, barley, tobacco, cattle, sheep. Labor force in industry: 80%; major products: tobacco products and electric power; tourism. Natural resources: water power, mineral water. Major trading partners: France, Spain, West Germany, Japan.

Geography. Andorra lies high in the Pyrenees Mountains on the French-Spanish border. The country is drained by the Valira River.

Government. A General Council of 24 members, elected for four years, chooses the First Syndic and Second Syndic. In 1976 the Andorran Democratic Association, the principality's first political party, was formed.

History. An autonomous and semi-independent co-principality, Andorra has been under the joint suzerainty of the French state and the Spanish bishops of Urgel since 1278.

ANGOLA

People's Republic of Angola

President: José Eduardo dos Santos (1979)
Area: 481,350 sq mi. (1,246,700 sq km)
Population (est. 1981): 7,250,000 (growth rate: 2.4%)
Density per square mile: 15.1
Capital and largest city (est. 1970): Luanda, 475,300
Monetary unit: Kwanza
Languages: Bantu, Portuguese (official)
Religions: Animist, 45%; Roman Catholic, 43%; Protestant, 12%
Freedom House classifications: Socialist pre-industrial, one-party socialist
Economic summary: Gross national product (1979): $3.1 billion. Average annual growth rate (1970–78): −10.5%. Per capita income: $440. Principal agricultural products: coffee, sisal, corn, cotton, sugar, tobacco, bananas. Major industrial products: oil, diamonds, processed fish, tobacco, textiles, cement, processed food and sugar. Natural resources: diamonds, gold, iron, oil. Exports: oil, coffee, diamonds, fish and fish products, iron ore, timber, corn. Imports: machinery and electrical equipment, bulk iron, steel and metals, textiles, clothing. Major trading partners: Cuba, U.S.S.R., Portugal, U.S.

Geography. Angola, more than three times the size of California, extends for more than 1,000 miles (1,609 km) along the South Atlantic in southwestern Africa. Zaire is to the north and east; Zambia to the east, and South-West Africa (Namibia) to the south. A plateau averaging 6,000 feet (1,829 m) above sea level rises abruptly from the coastal lowlands. Nearly all the land is desert or savanna, with hardwood forests in the northeast.

Government. Last of Portugal's African colonies to gain independence, Angola was born amid civil war Nov. 11, 1975. Four months later, the Popular

Movement for the Liberation of Angola (MPLA) claimed victory over two rival factions with the aid of Soviet weapons and advisers and Cuban troops. Cuban Premier Fidel Castro's pledge to withdraw all his troops by the end of 1976 was still unredeemed two years later, and the situation in Angola remained one of the root causes of U.S.-U.S.S.R. conflict in Africa.

Because of the troop presence, the U.S. vetoed Angolan membership in the U.N. on June 23, 1976. It abstained in a second vote on Nov. 22, 1976, and Angola on December 1 became the 147th member of the world organization.

History. Discovered by the Portuguese navigator Diego Cao in 1482, Angola became a link in trade with India and the Far East. Later it was a major source of slaves for Portugal's New World colony of Brazil. Development of the interior began after the Treaty of Berlin in 1885 fixed the colony's borders, and British and Portuguese investment pushed mining, railways, and agriculture.

Following World War II, independence movements began but were sternly suppressed by military force. The April revolution of 1974 brought about a reversal of Portugal's policy, and the next year President Francisco da Costa Gomes signed an agreement to grant independence to Angola. The plan called for election of a constituent assembly and a settlement of differences by the MPLA and the National Front for the Liberation of Angola (FNLA) and the National Union for the Total Independence of Angola (UNITA).

Despite covert aid to FNLA by the U.S. and open support by neighboring Zaire for the Front's leader, Holden Roberto, the MPLA had the initial advantage of strength in the capital region. Cuban troops were introduced in October and soon routed the poorly trained and equipped FNLA and UNITA forces.

The Organization of African Unity, split over the issue earlier, recognized the MPLA government led by Agostinho Neto on Feb. 11, 1976, and the People's Republic of Angola became the 47th member of the organization.

The new government nationalized 19 major industries on May 19, mostly Portuguese-owned. This, together with Lisbon's objection to the refueling of Cuban troop transports in the Azores, led to a break between the former mother country and Angola.

Although militarily victorious, Neto's regime had yet to consolidate its power in opposition strongholds in the east and south. Less militantly Marxist than their colleagues in the former East African colony of Mozambique, the new leaders sought help from both the Western and Eastern worlds.

In March 1977, Zairean refugees in Angola invaded Zaire's Shaba Province, bringing charges by Zairean President Mobutu Sese Seko that the unsuccessful invasion was Soviet-backed with the collaboration of Angola. The Neto regime, the U.S.S.R., and Cuba all denied complicity. In May 1978, another invasion took place, and this time the U.S. and France joined Mobutu in accusing Angola, the U.S.S.R., and Cuba, all of which again denied guilt.

Neto died in Moscow of cancer on Sept. 10, 1979. The Planning Minister, José Eduardo dos Santos, was named President.

In March 1981, President Reagan asked Congress to repeal a 1976 ban on military aid to UNITA rebels led by Joseph Savimbi but strong opposition caused the administration to abandon its efforts. U.S. firms doing business with Angola, led by Gulf Oil, which has exploited the Cabinda oil field since its discovery, has supported the central government and urged establishment of diplomatic relations between Washington and Luanda.

ARGENTINA

Argentine Republic
President: Gen. Roberto Eduardo Viola (1981)
Area: 1,072,067 sq mi. (2,776,654 sq km)
Population (est. 1981): 27,400,000 (growth rate: 1.6%)
Density per square mile: 25.6
Capital: Buenos Aires
Largest cities (est. 1980): Buenos Aires, 3,000,000; (est. 1975 by U.N.): Córdoba, 781,600; Rosario, 750,500; La Plata, 391,200; San Miguel de Tucumán, 321,600
Monetary unit: Peso
Language: Spanish
Religion: Predominantly Roman Catholic
National name: República Argentina
Freedom House classifications: Capitalist-statist industrial, non-party military
Economic summary: Gross national product (1979): $61.0 billion. Average annual growth rate (1970–78): 1.5%. Per capita income: $1,840. Rate of inflation (1980): 112%. Land used for agriculture: 57%; labor force: 19%; principal products: grains, oilseeds, livestock products. Labor force in industry: 40%; major products: processed foods, motor vehicles, consumer durables, textiles, chemicals. Natural resources: minerals, lead, zinc, tin, copper, iron, manganese, oil, uranium. Exports: meats, grains, wool. Imports: machinery and electric equipment, wood and lumber, newsprint, crude oil, automotive equipment and parts, iron and steel products, chemicals. Major trading partners: Western European and South American countries, U.S., Japan, U.S.S.R.

Geography. With an area slightly less than one third of the United States and second in South America only to its eastern neighbor, Brazil, in size and population, Argentina is a plain, rising from the Atlantic to the Chilean border and the towering Andes peaks. Aconcagua (23,034 ft.; 7,021 m) is the highest peak in the world outside Asia. It is bordered also by Chile on the west, Bolivia and Paraguay on the north, and by Uruguay on the east.

The northern area is the swampy and partly wooded Gran Chaco, bordering on Bolivia and Paraguay. South of that are the rolling, fertile pampas, rich for agriculture and grazing and supporting most of the population. Next southward is Patagonia, a region of cool, arid steppes with some wooded and fertile sections. The eastern part of Tierra del Fuego, the island southern tip of South America, belongs to Argentina.

Government. Argentina is a federal union of 22 provinces, one national territory, and the Federal District. Under the Constitution of 1853 (restored by a Constituent National Convention in 1957 and amended in 1972), the President and Vice President were elected every four years by direct vote. The President appointed his Cabinet. The Vice President presided over the Senate but had no other powers. The Congress consisted of two houses: a 69-member Senate and a 243-member Chamber of Deputies. All legislators were elected by direct vote for four-year terms.

All political parties have been suspended, along with Congress, since the military coup of March 24, 1976. Meetings or statements by political parties are forbidden.

History. Discovered in 1516 by Juan Díaz de Solis, Argentina developed slowly under Spanish colonial rule. Buenos Aires was settled in 1580; the cattle industry was thriving as early as 1600.

Invading British forces were expelled in 1806–07, and when Napoleon conquered Spain, the Argentinians set up their own government in the name of the Spanish King in 1810. On July 9, 1816, independence was formally declared.

As in World War I, Argentina proclaimed neutrality at the outbreak of World War II, but in the closing phase declared war on the Axis on March 27, 1945, and became a founding member of the United Nations. Juan D. Perón, an army colonel, emerged as the strongman of the postwar era, winning the Presidential elections of 1946 and 1951.

Opposition to Perón's increasing authoritarianism, fanned by worsening relations with the Roman Catholic Church, led to a coup by the armed forces that sent Perón into exile in 1955. The Peronist Party and Congress dissolved, and Argentina entered a long period of military dictatorships with brief intervals of constitutional government.

In the first free election since 1951, a Perón-endorsed candidate, Hector Campóra, narrowly won the Presidency in 1973. He resigned July 13, seven weeks after his inauguration, in an effort to hand power back to Perón. The former dictator returned from exile and, with his third wife, Maria Estela (Isabel) Martinez de Perón, as Vice-Presidential candidate, swept the election on Sept. 23, 1973, winning 61% of the vote.

Perón launched a three-year plan to double the economic growth rate and boost family incomes by a third; it involved price freezes, wage boosts, and increased government spending. He persuaded subsidiaries of two U.S. auto manufacturers to sell vehicles to Cuba under a $1.2-billion export grant. It was an early break in the hemispheric boycott of Cuba.

Perón died of a heart attack at the age of 78 on July 1, 1974. His widow became the hemisphere's first woman chief of state, but she took over a nation racked by acute economic and political polarization reflected in mounting civil disorders.

Mrs. Perón was re-elected head of the Peronist movement Aug. 24, 1975, at a tumultuous party Congress at which 118 of 238 delegates walked out before the vote. In mid-September she announced she would take a month-long leave of absence to recover from nervous strain and turned the presidential duties over to Italo A. Luder, president of the Senate.

Returning to take up her duties again October 16, Mrs. Perón was greeted with demands for her resignation as both the economic recession and terrorism increased. The inflation rate for 1975 was 334.8%, compared with 40% for 1974, and labor protest mounted despite massive wage boosts.

The long-anticipated military revolt came March 24, 1976, with a junta composed of Army Lt. Gen. Jorge Rafaél Videla, Adm. Eduardo Massera, and Air Force Brig. Gen. Orlando Agosti taking power. Mrs. Perón and her closest advisers were arrested and subsequently charged with misuse of government funds, while thousands of Peronist government officials and labor leaders were placed under detention.

Videla took office as President on March 29 and formed a government of six military officers and two civilians, one of them the industrialist José Martinéz de Hoz, as Minister of the Economy. The new regime suspended the Justicialista (Peronist) Party as well as all others and decreed new security laws and censorship.

Political murders and terrorism under the Videla regime mounted, together with allegations of police torture. Testimony at the United Nations Human Rights Commission in 1977 said 2,300 had died, 10,000 had been jailed for political reasons, and more than 20,000 had disappeared since the new government took power.

The twin plagues of inflation and terrorism continued in 1980, the former somewhat diminished by stringent economic measures. From a 1978 record 169.5% increase in the cost of living, the 1979 increase was held to below 90%, with unemployment at less than 4%.

Gen. Roberto Eduardo Viola, former Army Chief of Staff, was sworn in as President on March 29, 1981. Earlier, he had visited Washington and assured members of Congress that he would try to improve Argentina's human-rights record. State Department officials said the Carter Administration's ban on military aid to Argentina because of human-rights violations would be reviewed, and no more public reports would be issued. On July 6, Viola released Mrs. Perón from house arrest and she left for Spain.

New fears for the economy arose when the government announced a 30% devaluation of the peso in June, making a total of 64% for the year and triggering new inflation.

AUSTRALIA

Commonwealth of Australia
Sovereign: Queen Elizabeth II
Governor-General: Sir Zelman Cowen (1977)
Prime Minister: Malcolm Fraser (1975)
Area: 2,967,909 sq mi. (7,686,843 sq km)
Population (est. 1981): 14,900,000 (average annual growth rate, 1975–79, 1.2%)
Density per square mile: 5.0
Capital (est. 1980): Canberra, 241,300
Largest cities (1980 for metropolitan area): Sydney, 3,200,000; Hobart (on Tasmania), 166,500; **(est. 1978 for metropolitan area):** Melbourne, 2,717,600; Brisbane, 1,004,500; Adelaide, 930,500; Perth, 864,900
Monetary unit: Australian dollar
Language: English
Religions (1971 census): Anglican, 31%; Roman Catholic, 27%; Uniting Church, 17%
Member of Commonwealth of Nations
Freedom House classifications: Capitalist industrial, multi-party decentralized
Economic summary: Gross national product (1979): $130.7 billion. Average annual growth rate (1970–78): 1.5%. Per capita income (1977): $6,830. Land used for agriculture: 63%; labor force: 14%; principal products: wool, meat, cereals, sugar, wine grapes, sheep, cattle, dairy products. Labor force in industry: 32%; major products: machinery, motor vehicles, iron and steel, textiles, chemicals. Natural resources: gold, iron ore, bauxite, zinc, lead, tin, coal, oil, uranium, timber. Exports: coal, wool, iron ore, wheat,

sugar, beef, veal. Imports: transport equipment, petroleum and petroleum products, machinery, appliances, textiles. Major trading partners: U.S., U.K., Japan, New Zealand.

Geography. The continent of Australia, with the island state of Tasmania, is approximately equal in area to the United States (excluding Alaska and Hawaii), and is nearly 50% larger than Europe (excluding the U.S.S.R.).

Mountain ranges run from north to south along the east coast, reaching their highest point in Mount Kosciusko (7,308 ft; 2,228 m). The western half of the continent is occupied by a desert plateau that rises into barren, rolling hills near the west coast. It includes the Great Victoria Desert to the south and the Great Sandy Desert to the north. The Great Barrier Reef, extending about 1,245 miles (2,000 km), lies along the northeast coast.

The island of Tasmania (26,178 sq mi.; 67,800 sq km) is off the southeastern coast.

Government. The Federal Parliament consists of a bicameral legislature. The House of Representatives has 124 members elected for three years by popular vote. The Senate has 64 members elected by popular vote for six years. One half of the Senate is elected every three years. Voting is compulsory at 18. Federal judicial power is vested in the High Court of Australia, which consists of seven justices, appointed by the Governor-General in Council. Each of the states has its own judicial system.

The major political parties are the Liberal Party (54 seats in the House of Representatives), led by Prime Minister Malcolm Fraser; Australian Labor Party (51 seats), led by William G. Hayden; National Country Party (20 seats), led by J. Douglas Anthony.

History. Dutch, Portuguese, and Spanish ships sighted Australia in the 17th century; the Dutch landed at the Gulf of Carpentaria in 1606. In 1642, Abel Tasman (for whom Tasmania was named) proved that Australia was not part of the Antarctic Continent. Australia was called New Holland, Botany Bay, and New South Wales until about 1820.

Captain James Cook, in 1770, claimed possession for Great Britain. A British penal colony was set up at what is now Sydney, then Port Jackson, in 1788, and about 161,000 transported English convicts were settled there until the system was suspended in 1839.

Free settlers established six colonies: New South Wales (1786), Tasmania (then Van Diemen's Land) (1825), Western Australia (1829), South Australia (1834), Victoria (1851), and Queensland (1859).

Sheep raising and wheat growing built the economy, and the white population, which had dwindled to 34,000 in 1820, grew to 400,000 by 1850. Discovery of gold in Victoria in 1851 led immigrants to pour in. The six colonies became states and in 1901 federated into the Commonwealth of Australia with a Constitution that incorporated British parliamentary tradition and U.S. federal experience. Australia became known for liberal legislation: free compulsory education, protected trade unionism with industrial conciliation and arbitration, the "Australian" ballot facilitating selection, the secret ballot, women's suffrage, maternity allowances, and sickness and old age pensions.

The Labor Government of Prime Minister Gough Whitlam, elected in 1972, was itself a victim of the twin economic troubles that hit Australia along with most of the rest of the world—inflation and recession. Opposition parties blocked passage of government budget requests to force Whitlam to resign and, in what was called an unconstitutional action, Governor-General Sir John Kerr dissolved both houses of Parliament in November, 1975. Kerr asked Malcolm Fraser, the Liberal Party chief, to form a caretaker government until a new general election in December. Kerr resigned in 1977.

Following a narrow re-election victory in October 1980, Fraser embarked on a program of spending cuts and incentive to private industry. He announced a 10% cut in federal employment and plans to return government bookshops, home loans, and other activities to private industry. On a visit to the U.S. in July 1981, Fraser encouraged President Reagan, saying private-sector growth had resulted from budget cuts and tax incentives.

Australian External Territories

Norfolk Island (14 sq mi.; 36.3 sq km) was placed under Australian administration in 1914. Population in 1979 was about 2,200.

The Ashmore and Cartier Islands (.8 sq mi.), situated in the Indian Ocean off the northwest coast of Australia, came under Australian administration in 1934. In 1938 the islands, which are uninhabited, were annexed to the Northern Territory.

The Australian Antarctic Territory (2,360,000 sq mi.; 6,112,400 sq km), comprises all the islands and territories, other than Adélie Land, situated south of lat. 60° S and lying between long. 160° to 45° E. It came under Australian administration in 1936.

Heard Island and the McDonald Islands (158 sq mi.; 409.2 sq km), lying in the sub-Antarctic, were placed under Australian administration in 1947. The islands are uninhabited.

The Cocos (Keeling) Islands (5.5 sq mi.; 14.2 sq. km) consist of 27 small coral islands lying in the Indian Ocean. They came under Australian administration in 1955. Population in 1979 was 392.

Christmas Island (52 sq mi.; 134.7 sq km) is situated in the Indian Ocean. It came under Australian administration in 1958. Population in 1979 was 3,264.

Coral Sea Islands (400,000 sq mi.; 1,036,000 sq km, but only a few sq mi. of land) became a territory of Australia in 1969. There is no permanent population on the islands.

AUSTRIA

Republic of Austria
President: Rudolf Kirchschläger (1974)
Chancellor: Bruno Kreisky (1970)
Area: 32,375 sq mi. (83,851 sq km)
Population (est. 1981): 7,515,000 (growth rate: 0.0%)
Density per square mile: 232.1
Capital: Vienna
Largest cities (est. 1978): Vienna, 1,580,600; (est. 1976 by

U.N.): Graz, 250,900; Linz, 208,000; Salzburg, 139,000; Innsbruck, 120,400
Monetary unit: Schilling
Language: German
Religion: Roman Catholic, 90%
National name: Republik Österreich
Freedom House classifications: Capitalist-socialist industrial, multi-party centralized
Economic summary: Gross national product (1979): $64.6 billion. Average annual growth rate (1970–78): 3.6%. Per capita income (1977): $6,360. Average rate of inflation (1976–77): 5.5%. Labor force in agriculture: 18%; principal products: livestock, forest products, grains, sugar beets, potatoes. Labor force in industry: 49%; principal products: iron and steel, chemicals, machinery, paper and pulp. Natural resources: iron ore, petroleum, timber, magnesite, aluminum, coal, lignite, cement, copper. Exports: iron and steel products, timber, paper, textiles, electrotechnical machines, chemical products. Imports: machinery, vehicles, chemicals, iron and steel, metal goods, raw materials, fuels, food stuffs. Major trading partners: U.S., West Germany, Italy, Switzerland, U.K.

Geography. Slightly smaller than Maine, Austria includes much of the mountainous territory of the eastern Alps (about 75% of the area). The country contains many snowfields, glaciers, and snow-capped peaks, the highest being the Grossglockner (12,530 ft; 3,819 m). The Danube is the principal river. Forests and woodlands cover about 40% of the land area.

Almost at the heart of Europe, Austria has as its neighbors Italy, Switzerland, West Germany, Czechoslovakia, Hungary, Yugoslavia, and Liechtenstein.

Government. Austria is a federal republic composed of nine provinces (Bundesländer), including Vienna. The President is elected by the people for a term of six years. The bicameral legislature consists of the Bundesrat, with 58 members chosen by the provincial assemblies, and the Nationalrat, with 183 members popularly elected for four years. Presidency of the Bundesrat revolves every six months, going to the provinces in alphabetical order.

The major political parties are the Social Democratic Party (95 of 183 seats in Nationalrat), led by Chancellor Bruno Kreisky; People's Party (77 seats); Freiheitliche Partei (11 seats).

History. Settled in prehistoric times, the Central European land that is now Austria was overrun in pre-Roman times by various tribes, including the Celts. Charlemagne conquered the area in 788 and encouraged colonization and Christianity. In 1252, Ottokar, King of Bohemia, gained possession, only to lose the territories to Rudolf of Hapsburg in 1278. Thereafter, until World War I, Austria's history was largely that of its ruling house, the Hapsburgs.

Austria emerged from the Congress of Vienna in 1815 as the Continent's dominant power. The *Ausgleich* of 1867 provided for a dual sovereignty, the empire of Austria and the kingdom of Hungary, under Francis Joseph I, who ruled until his death on Nov. 21, 1916. He was succeeded by his grandnephew, Charles I.

During World War I, Austria-Hungary was one of the Central Powers with Germany, Bulgaria, and Turkey, and the conflict left the country in political chaos and economic ruin. Austria, shorn of Hun-

gary, was proclaimed a republic in 1918, and the monarchy was dissolved in 1919.

A parliamentary democracy was set up by the Constitution of Nov. 10, 1920. To check the power of Nazis advocating union with Germany, Chancellor Engelbert Dollfuss in 1933 established a dictatorship, but was assassinated by the Nazis on July 25, 1934. Kurt von Schuschnigg, his successor, struggled to keep Austria independent, but on March 12, 1938, German troops occupied the country, and Hitler proclaimed its *Anschluss* (union) with Germany, annexing it to the Third Reich.

After World War II, the U.S. and Britain declared the Austrians a "liberated" people. But the Russians prolonged the occupation. Finally Austria concluded a state treaty with the U.S.S.R. and the other occupying powers and regained its independence on May 15, 1955. The second Austrian republic, established Dec. 19, 1945, on the basis of the 1920 Constitution (amended in 1929), was declared by the federal parliament to be permanently neutral. Austria became a member of the Council of Europe in 1956.

Vienna has become a headquarters for international organizations, such as the International Atomic Energy Agency and the Organization of Petroleum Exporting Countries (OPEC). In June 1979, Presidents Jimmy Carter and Leonid Brezhnev met in Vienna to sign the second U.S.-Soviet Strategic Arms Limitation Treaty—SALT II.

BAHAMAS

Commonwealth of the Bahamas
Sovereign: Queen Elizabeth II
Governor-General: Sir Gerald Cash (1979)
Prime Minister: Lynden O. Pindling (1967)
Area: 4,404 sq mi. (11,406 sq km)
Population (est. 1981): 225,000 (growth rate, 3.4%)
Density per square mile: 56.8
Capital and largest city (est. 1980 for metropolitan area): Nassau, 143,000
Monetary unit: Bahamian dollar
Language: English
Religions: Baptist, 29%; Anglican, 23%; Roman Catholic, 23%; Methodist, 7%
Member of Commonwealth of Nations
Freedom House classifications: Capitalist industrial, multi-party centralized
Economic summary: Gross national product (1979): $640 million. Average annual growth rate (1970–78): —6.4%. Per capita income: $4,178. Principal agricultural products: fruits, vegetables. Major industrial products: fish, petroleum, pharmaceutical products; tourism. Natural resources: salt, aragonite, timber. Exports: petroleum products, pharmaceuticals, cement, rum. Imports: crude oil, foodstuffs, manufactured goods. Major trading partners: U.S., U.K., Canada.

Geography. The Bahamas are an archipelago of about 700 islands and 2,400 uninhabited islets and cays lying 50 miles off the east coast of Florida. They extend from northwest to southeast for about 760 miles (1,223 km). Only 22 of the islands are inhabited; the most important is New Providence (80 sq mi.; 207 sq km), on which Nassau is situated. Other islands include Grand Bahama, Abaco, Eleuthera, Andros, Cat Island, San Salvador (or Watling's Island), Exuma, Long Island, Crooked Island, Acklins Island, Mayaguana, and Inagua.

The islands are mainly flat, few rising above 200 feet (61 m). There are a few streams and one large lake (on Inagua).

Government. The Bahamas moved toward greater autonomy in 1968 after the overwhelming victory in general elections of the Progressive Liberal Party, led by Prime Minister Lynden O. Pindling. The black leader's party won 29 seats in the House of Assembly to only 7 for the predominantly white United Bahamians, who had controlled the islands for decades before Pindling became Prime Minister in 1967.

With its new mandate from the 85%-black population, Pindling's government negotiated a new Constitution with Britain under which the colony became the Commonwealth of the Bahama Islands in 1969. On July 10, 1973, The Bahamas became an independent nation as the Commonwealth of the Bahamas.

In the 1977 election, Pindling's Progressive Liberal Party won 30 of 38 seats in Parliament; the Bahamian Democratic Party, 6; the Free National Movement, 2.

History. The islands were reached by Columbus in October 1492, and were a favorite pirate area in the early 18th century. The Bahamas were a crown colony from 1717 until they were granted internal self-government in 1964.

BAHRAIN

State of Bahrain
Amir: Sheik Isa bin-Sulman al-Khalifa (1961)
Prime Minister: Khalifa bin Sulman al-Khalifa (1970)
Area: 240 sq mi. (622 sq km)
Population (est. 1981): 400,000 (growth rate: 4.0%)
Density per square mile: 1,666.7
Capital (est. 1980): Manama, 150,000
Monetary unit: Bahrain dinar
Languages: Arabic (official); English
Religion: Islam
Freedom House classifications: Capitalist-statist industrial, non-party non-military
Economic summary: Gross national product (1979): $2.1 billion. Average annual growth rate (1970–78): −1.4%. Per capita income (1977): $2,500. Average rate of inflation (1975–77): 15%. Land used for agriculture: 10%; labor force: 5%; principal products: eggs, vegetables, fruits. Labor force in industry: 90%; major products: oil, aluminum, fish. Natural resources: oil, fish. Exports: oil, aluminum, fish. Imports: machinery, oil-industry equipment, motor vehicles, foodstuffs. Major trading partners: U.K., U.S., Japan, Saudi Arabia.

Geography. Bahrain is an archipelago in the Persian Gulf off the coast of Saudi Arabia. The islands for the most part are level expanses of sand and rock.

Government. A new Constitution was approved in 1973. It created the first elected parliament in the country's history. Called the National Council, it consisted of 30 members elected by male citizens for four-year terms, plus up to 14 Cabinet ministers as ex-officio members. In August 1975, the Amir dissolved the National Council.

History. A sheikdom that passed from the Persians to the al-Khalifa family from Arabia in 1782, Bah-

rain became, by treaty, a British protectorate in 1820. It has become a major Middle Eastern oil center and, through use of oil revenues, is one of the most developed of the Persian Gulf sheikdoms. The Amir, Sheik Isa bin-Sulman al-Khalifa, who succeeded to the post in 1961, is a member of the original ruling family. Bahrain announced its independence on Aug. 14, 1971.

BANGLADESH

People's Republic of Bangladesh
Acting President: Abdus Sattar (1981)
Prime Minister: Shah Azizur Rahman (1979)
Area: 55,126 sq mi. (142,776 sq km)
Population (est. 1980): 90,700,000 (growth rate: 2.7%)
Density per square mile: 1,645.3
Capital and largest city (est. 1980): Dacca, 2,500,000
Monetary unit: Taka
Principal languages: Bengali (official), English
Religions: Islam, 85%; Hindu, 13%
Member of Commonwealth of Nations
Freedom House classifications: Capitalist-statist pre-industrial, multi-party centralized
Economic summary: Gross national product (1979): $8.3 billion. Average annual growth rate (1970–78): 0.2%. Per capita income: $85. Land used for agriculture: 66%; labor force, 75%; principal products: rice, jute, tea, sugar, wheat. Labor force in industry, 11%; major products: jute goods, textiles, leather, sugar, fertilizer, paper, pharmaceuticals. Natural resources: natural gas. Exports: jute goods, jute, tea, leather, seafood. Imports: food grains, fuels, raw cotton, yarn, manufactured goods. Major trading partners: U.S., U.S.S.R., Japan.

Geography. Bangladesh, on the northern coast of the Bay of Bengal, is surrounded by India, with a small common border with Burma in the southeast. It is approximately the size of Wisconsin. The country is low-lying riverine land traversed by the many branches and tributaries of the Ganges and Brahmaputra rivers. Elevation averages less than 600 feet (183 m) above sea level. Tropical monsoons and frequent floods and cyclones inflict heavy damage in the delta region.

Government. Executive power is vested in the President, elected by universal suffrage for a term of five years. Legislative power is held by a National Assembly of 330 members, 30 of whom are women elected by the majority party. The major parties are the Bangladesh Nationalist Party (207 of 330 seats), the Bangladesh Awami League (39 seats), Muslim League (20 seats), and the Nationalist Socialist Party (8 seats). The remaining seats are held by splinter parties and 16 independents.

History. Like West Pakistan and India, the former East Pakistan was part of imperial British India until Britain withdrew in 1947. The two Pakistans were united by religion (Islam), but their peoples were separated by culture, physical features, and 1,000 miles of Indian territory. Bangladesh consists primarily of East Bengal (West Bengal is part of India and its people are primarily Hindu) plus the Sylhet district of the Indian state of Assam. For almost 25 years after independence from Britain, its history was as part of Pakistan (*see* Pakistan).

The East Pakistanis unsuccessfully sought greater autonomy from West Pakistan. The first general elections in Pakistani history, in December 1970, saw virtually all 171 seats of the region (out of 300 for both East and West Pakistan) go to Sheik Mujibur Rahman's Awami League, with the rest to other similarly independence-minded minor parties.

Attempts to write an all-Pakistan Constitution to replace the military regime of Gen. Yahya Khan failed. General strikes in East Pakistan followed at Mujibur's direction; he also told his followers to stop paying taxes. Yahya bloodily put down his revolt in March 1971. An estimated one million Bengalis were killed in the fighting or later slaughtered. Ten million more took refuge in India.

In December 1971, India invaded East Pakistan, routed the West Pakistani occupation forces, and created Bangladesh. The U.S. opposed its violent creation, but recognized Bangladesh in April 1972 and provided several hundred million dollars in relief aid.

In February 1974, Pakistan agreed to recognize the independence of Bangladesh. India, Pakistan, and Bangladesh signed an agreement two months later that provided for release of all Pakistani prisoners, improved conditions for the Bihari minority seeking to emigrate from Bangladesh to Pakistan, and negotiations to restore normal communication among the three states.

The charismatic Mujibur had a following of millions and near-dictatorial powers, but he failed to cope with poverty, starvation, sporadic political violence, and widespread government corruption.

Before dawn on Aug. 15, 1975, Mujibur, his wife, and several relatives were assassinated in a coup led by young Army officers. As president, they installed Khondakar Mushtaque Ahmed, a founder of the Awami League who was then Minister of Foreign Trade and Commerce.

A military coup forced Ahmed from power Nov. 6, 1975, and installed former Supreme Court Chief Justice Abu Sadat Mohammed Sayem as president and "chief martial law administrator." On Nov. 30, 1976, Gen Ziaur Rahman, Army Chief of Staff, took over Sayem's powers and blocked the national elections scheduled for early 1977. On April 21, 1977, Ziaur became president following Sayem's resignation. Two years later, Ziaur ended the martial law originally imposed in 1975 and in 1979 permitted parliamentary elections, in which his Bangladesh Nationalist Party won an absolute majority.

On May 30, 1981, Ziaur, two aides, and six bodyguards were killed by a group of army officers in an attempted coup. The rebels, led by Gen. Manzar Ahmed, were arrested by loyal troops after a day of fighting, and Ahmed and two other officers were slain by "enraged guards." Vice President Abdus Sattar assumed power as Acting President, and an election to choose a new leader was scheduled for Oct. 15.

BARBADOS

Sovereign: Queen Elizabeth II
Governor-General: Sir Deighton L. Ward (1976)
Prime Minister: J. M. G. Adams (1976)
Area: 166 sq mi. (431 sq km)
Population (est. 1981): 250,000 (average annual growth rate, 1977–80, 0.4%)
Density per square mile: 1,506.0
Capital and largest city (est. 1980): Bridgetown, 8,000
Monetary unit: Barbados dollar
Language: English

Religions: Anglican, 53%; Methodist, 9%; Roman Catholic, 4%
Member of Commonwealth of Nations
Freedom House classifications: Capitalist industrialist, multi-party centralized
Economic summary: Gross national product (1979): $610 million. Average annual growth rate (1970–78): 2.1%. Per capita income (1977): $1,840. Principal agricultural products: sugar cane, subsistence foods. Major industrial products: light manufactures, sugar milling; tourism. Exports: sugar and sugar cane byproducts, clothing. Imports: foodstuffs, machinery, manufactured goods. Major trading partners: U.S., Caribbean nations, U.K., Canada.

Geography. An island in the Atlantic about 300 miles (483 km) north of Venezuela, Barbados is only 21 miles long (34 km) and 14 miles across (23 km) at its widest point. It is circled by fine beaches and narrow coastal plains. The highest point is Mount Hillaby (1,105 ft; 337 m) in the north central area.

Government. The Barbados legislature dates from 1627. It is bicameral, with a Senate of 21 appointed members and an Assembly of 24 elected members.

The major political parties are the Barbados Labor Party (17 seats in Assembly), led by Prime Minister J. M. G. Adams; Democratic Labor Party (7 seats), led by Errol Barrow.

History. Barbados, with a population 90% black, was settled by the British in 1627. It became a crown colony in 1885. It was a member of the Federation of the West Indies from 1958 to 1962. Britain granted the colony independence on Nov. 30, 1966, and it became a parliamentary democracy.

While retaining membership in the Commonwealth of Nations and economic ties with Britain, Barbados seeks broader economic and political relations with Western Hemisphere countries. Diplomatic ties with Cuba were established in 1972.

BELGIUM

Kingdom of Belgium
Sovereign: King Baudouin I (1951)
Premier: Mark Eyskens (1981)
Area: 11,781 sq mi. (30,513 sq km)
Population (est. 1981): 9,870,000 (growth rate, 1978–79, 0.1%)
Density per square mile: 837.8
Capital: Brussels
Largest cities (est. 1978 for metropolitan area): Brussels, 1,029,000; Antwerp, 927,200; Liège, 617,600; Ghent, 486,000
Monetary unit: Belgian franc
Languages: Dutch, 56%; French, 32%; bilingual (Brussels), 11%
Religion: Roman Catholic, 97%
National name: Royaume de Belgique—Koninkrijk België
Freedom House classifications: Capitalist industrial, multi-party decentralized
Economic summary: Gross national product (1979): $107.3 billion. Average annual growth rate (1970–78): 3.0%. Per capita income: $8,040. Land used for agriculture: 47%; labor force: 3.2%; principal products: livestock, poultry, grain, sugar beets, flax, tobacco, potatoes, vegetables, fruits. Labor force in industry: 35%; major products: fabricated metal, iron and steel, coal, textiles, chemicals. Exports: metal products, transport equipment, textiles,

glassware, ceramics. Imports: mineral ores, chemicals, machinery and equipment, petroleum products, grains, fruits, natural fibers, processed foods. Major trading partners: West Germany, France, Netherlands, U.K., U.S., Italy.

Geography. A neighbor of France, West Germany, the Netherlands, and Luxembourg, Belgium has about 40 miles of seacoast on the North Sea at the Strait of Dover. In area, it is approximately the size of Maryland. The northern third of the country is a plain extending eastward from the seacoast. North of the Sambre and Meuse Rivers is a low plateau; to the south lies the heavily wooded Ardennes plateau, attaining an elevation of about 2,300 feet (700 m).

The Schelde River, which rises in France and flows through Belgium, emptying into the Schelde estuaries, enables Antwerp to be an ocean port.

Government. Belgium, a parliamentary democracy under a constitutional monarch, consists of nine provinces. Its bicameral legislature has a Senate, with its 181 members elected for four years—106 by general election, 50 by provincial councillors and 25 by the Senate itself. The 212-member Chamber of Representatives is directly elected for four years by proportional representation. There is universal suffrage, and those who do not vote are fined.

Belgium joined the North Atlantic Alliance in 1949 and is a member of the European Community. NATO and the European Community have their headquarters in Brussels. The present Cabinet is a coalition of the Social Christians, Socialists, Flemish nationalists, and Brussels Francophones.

The sovereign, Baudouin I, was born Sept. 7, 1930, the son of King Leopold III and Queen Astrid. He became King on July 17, 1951, after the abdication of his father. He married Doña Fabiola de Mora y Aragón on Dec. 15, 1960. Since he has no children, his brother, Prince Albert, is heir to the throne.

The major political parties are the Flemish-Speaking Social Christian Party (51 Senators, 57 Representatives); French-Speaking Social Christian Party (22 Senators, 25 Representatives); Flemish-Speaking Socialist Party (21 Senators, 26 Representatives); French-Speaking Socialist Party (32 Senators, 32 Representatives); Flemish-Speaking Liberal Party (18 Senators, 22 Representatives); Party for Liberty and Progress of Wallonia (9 Senators, 15 Representatives); Flemish People's Party (11 Senators, 14 Representatives); French-Speaking Brussels Party (9 Senators, 11 Representatives.)

History. Belgium occupies part of the Roman province of Belgica, named after the Belgae, a people of ancient Gaul. The area was conquered by Julius Caesar in 57–50 B.C., then was overrun by the Franks in the 5th century. It was part of Charlemagne's empire in the 8th century, then in the next century was absorbed into Lotharingia and later into the Duchy of Lower Lorraine. In the 12th century it was partitioned into the Duchies of Brabant and Luxembourg, the Bishopric of Liège, and the domain of the Count of Hainaut, which included Flanders.

The rise of the wool industry brought prosperity and power to the country, particularly to the semi-independent cities—Ghent, Bruges, and Ypres. In the 16th century, Belgium, with most of the area of the Low Countries, passed to the Duchy of Burgundy and was the marriage portion of Archduke Maximilian of Hapsburg and the inheritance of his grandson, Charles V, who incorporated it into his empire. Then, in 1555, they were united with Spain.

By the treaty of Utrecht in 1713, the country's sovereignty passed to Austria. During the wars that followed the French Revolution, Belgium was occupied and later annexed to France. But with the downfall of Napoleon, the Congress of Vienna in 1815 gave the country to the Netherlands. The Belgians revolted in 1830 and declared their independence.

Germany's invasion of Belgium in 1914 set off World War I. The Treaty of Versailles (1919) gave the areas of Eupen, Malmédy, and Moresnet to Belgium. Leopold III succeeded Albert, King during World War I, in 1934. In World War II, Belgium was overwhelmed by Nazi Germany, and Leopold III was made prisoner. When he attempted to return in 1950, Socialists and Liberals revolted. He abdicated July 16, 1951, and his son, Baudouin, became King the next day.

The country has long been torn by language disputes between the Dutch-speaking Flemish people and the French-speaking Walloons. In 1972, a major clash occurred over transferring six small hamlets from Flemish to Walloon administrative jurisdiction. When a balancing change was not implemented, the government fell. A new one under Edmond Leburton was formed; this, in turn, was replaced in 1974 by one under Léo Tindemans of the Flemish Social Christian party.

Early in 1978, Tindemans' coalition reached agreement on a plan to begin in January 1979 the transformation of the nation into a federated state by the mid-80's. The plan would divide Belgium into Dutch- and French-speaking areas.

A financial crisis, building for more than a year, brought down the government on March 31, 1981, when Socialists in the majority coalition opposed the suspension of the automatic linkage of wage increases to rising prices. Premier Wilfried Martens proposed that after the suspension, wage increases should be given in fixed amounts, eliminating the indexing system which Belgium pioneered. Mark Eyskens, taking office on April 6, retained Socialist support by instituting a temporary price freeze, thus blocking wage hikes without dismantling the wage-price linkage.

BELIZE

Area: 8,867 sq mi. (22,965 sq km)
Population (est. 1981): 160,000 (growth rate, 1970–80: 1.9%)
Density per sq mi.: 18.1
Capital (est. 1980): Belmopan, 4,500
Monetary unit: Belize dollar
Languages: English (official) and Spanish
Religions: 50% Roman Catholic; Anglican, and other Protestant sects
Economic summary: Gross national product (1979): $130 million. Average annual growth rate (1970–78): 5.0%. Per capita income: $700. Land used for agriculture: 38%; labor force: 39%; principal products: sugar cane, citrus fruits, corn, molasses, rice, bananas, livestock. Labor force in industry: 20%; major products: timber, processed foods, furniture, rum, soap. Natural resource: timber.

Exports: sugar, molasses, clothing, lumber, citrus fruits, fish. Imports: vehicles, building materials, petroleum, foodstuffs, textiles, machinery. Major trading partners: U.S., U.K., Mexico, Canada, Jamaica.

Geography: Belize (formerly British Honduras) is situated on the Caribbean Sea south of Mexico and east and north of Guatemala. Most of the country is heavily forested with mahogany, cedar, and logwood. Mangrove swamps and cays along the coast give way to hills and mountains in the interior. The highest point is Victoria Peak, 3,681 feet (11,220 m).

BENIN

People's Republic of Benin
President: Lt. Col. Mathieu Kerekou (1972)
Area: 43,483 sq mi. (112,622 sq km)
Population (est. 1981): 3,675,000 (growth rate, 2.8%)
Density per square mile: 84.5
Capital: Porto-Novo
Largest cities (est. 1979): Cotonou, 327,000; Porto-Novo, 132,000
Monetary unit: Franc CFA
Ethnic groups: Fons and Adjas, Baribas, Yorubas, Mahis
Languages: French, African languages
Religions: Animist, Christian, Islam
National name: République Populaire du Benin
Freedom House classifications: Socialist pre-industrial, one-party socialist
Economic summary: Gross national product (1979): $860 million. Average annual growth rate (1970–78): 1.4%. Per capita income (1977): $200. Labor force in agriculture: 85%; principal products: oil palms, peanuts, cotton, coffee, tobacco, corn, rice, livestock, fish. Major industrial products: processed palm oil, palm kernel oil. Natural resources: low-grade iron ore, limestone, some offshore oil. Exports: palm and agricultural products. Imports: clothing, consumer goods, lumber, fuels, foodstuffs, machinery, transportation equipment. Major trading partners: France and other Western European countries.

Geography. This West African nation on the Gulf of Guinea, between Togo on the west and Nigeria on the east, is about the size of Tennessee. It is bounded also by Upper Volta and Niger on the north. The land consists of a narrow coastal strip that rises to a swampy, forested plateau and then to highlands in the north. A hot and humid climate blankets the entire country.

Government. The change in name from Dahomey to Benin was announced by President Mathieu Kerekou in November 1975. Benin commemorates an African kingdom that flourished in the 17th century. At the same time, Kerekou announced the formation of a political organization, the Party of the People's Revolution of Benin, to mark the first anniversary of his declaration of a "new society" guided by Marxist-Leninist principles.

History. One of the smallest and most densely populated states in Africa, Benin was annexed by the French in 1893. The area was incorporated into French West Africa in 1904. It became an autonomous republic within the French Community in 1958, and on Aug. 1, 1960, was granted its independence within the Community.

Gen. Christophe Soglo deposed the first president, Hubert Maga, in an army coup in 1963. He dismissed the civilian government in 1965, proclaiming himself chief of state. A group of young army officers seized power in December 1967, deposing Soglo. They promulgated a new Constitution in 1968.

In December 1969, Benin had its fifth coup of the decade, with the army again taking power. In May 1970, a three-man presidential commission was created to take over the government. The commission had a six-year term; each member serves as president for two years. Maga turned over power as scheduled to Justin Ahomadegbe in May 1972, but six months later yet another army coup ousted the triumvirate and installed Lt. Col. Mathieu Kerekou as President.

BHUTAN

Kingdom of Bhutan
Ruler: King Jigme Singye Wangchuk (1972)
Area: 19,305 sq mi. (49,421 sq km)
Population (est. 1981): 1,325,000 (growth rate, 2.3%)
Density per square mile: 68.6
Capital (est. 1980): Thimphu, 10,000
Monetary unit: Ngultrum
Language: Dzongkha
Religions: Buddhist, 75%; Hindu, 25%
National name: Druk-yul
Freedom House classifications: Capitalist pre-industrial, non-party non-military
Economic summary: Gross national product (1979): $110 million. Average annual growth rate (1970–78): −0.2%. Per capita income (1976): $70. Labor force in agriculture: 99%; principal products: rice, barley, wheat, potatoes, fruit. Major industrial product: handicrafts. Natural resources: timber, hydroelectric power. Exports: rice, dolomite, handicrafts. Major trading partner: India.

Geography. Mountainous Bhutan, half the size of Indiana, is situated on the southeast slope of the Himalayas, bordered on the north and east by Tibet and on the south and west by India. The landscape consists of a succession of lofty and rugged mountains running generally from north to south and separated by deep valleys. In the north, towering peaks reach a height of 24,000 feet (7,315 m).

Government. Bhutan is a constitutional monarchy. The King rules with a Council of Ministers and a nine-member Advisory Council, of whom five are elected by the people; two represent the monastic order and two are named by the King. There is a National Assembly (Parliament), which meets semiannually, but no political parties.

History. After almost a century of conflict, British troops invaded the country in 1865 and negotiated an agreement under which Britain undertook to pay an annual allowance to Bhutan on condition of good behavior. A treaty with India in 1949 increased this subsidy and placed Bhutan's foreign affairs under Indian control.

In the 1960s, Bhutan undertook modernization, abolishing slavery and the caste system, emancipating women, breaking up estates, and limiting farms to 30 acres.

BOLIVIA

Republic of Bolivia
President: Gen. Luis García Meza Tejada (1980)
Area: 424,162 sq mi. (1,098,581 sq km)
Population (est. 1981): 5,750,000 (growth rate, 2.6%)
(Indian, 53%; mestizo, 32%; white, 15%)
Density per square mile: 13.6
Judicial capital (est. 1979): Sucre, 90,000
Administrative capital: La Paz
Largest cities (est. 1979): La Paz, 700,000; (est. 1976 by
U.N.): Santa Cruz, 237,100; Cochabamba, 194,150; Oruro,
124,100
Monetary unit: Peso boliviano
Languages: Spanish, Quechua, Aymara
Religion: Roman Catholic, 94%
National name: República de Bolivia
Freedom House classifications: Capitalist pre-industrial,
non-party military
Economic summary: Gross national product (1979): $3.0
billion. Average annual growth rate (1970–78): 3.1%. Per
capita income (1979): $636. Labor force in agriculture:
70%; principal products: potatoes, corn, rice, sugar cane,
bananas. Labor force in industry: 10%; major products:
refined petroleum, processed foods, tin, textiles, clothing.
Natural resources: petroleum, natural gas, tin, lead, zinc,
copper, tungsten, bismuth, antimony, gold, sulfur, silver,
iron ore. Exports: tin, petroleum, lead, zinc, silver,
antimony, gold, coffee, sugar, cotton, natural gas.
Imports: foodstuffs, chemicals, capital goods,
pharmaceuticals, transport equipment. Major trading
partners: Western European and Latin American
countries, U.S., Japan.

Geography. Landlocked Bolivia, equal in size to
California and Texas combined, lies to the west of
Brazil. Its other neighbors are Peru and Chile on
the west and Argentina and Paraguay on the south.
The country is a low alluvial plain throughout
60% of its area toward the east, drained by the
Amazon and Plata river systems. The western part,
enclosed by two chains of the Andes, is a great
plateau—the Altiplano, with an average altitude of
12,000 feet (3,658 m). More than 80% of the population lives on the plateau, which also contains La
Paz. At an altitude of 11,910 feet (3,630 m), it is the
highest capital city in the world.
Lake Titicaca, half the size of Lake Ontario, is
one of the highest large lakes in the world, at an
altitude of 12,507 feet (3,812 m). Islands in the lake
hold ruins of the ancient Incas.

Government. Faltering steps toward the restoration
of civilian government were abruptly halted on
July 17, 1980, when Gen. Luis García Meza Tejada
seized power in the 189th coup in Bolivia's 155
years of independence. He chose a 15-member
cabinet—only two civilians among them—to replace the interim administration of Bolivia's first
woman President, Lydia Gueiler Tejada.

History. Famous since Spanish colonial days for its
mineral wealth, modern Bolivia was once a part of
the ancient Incan Empire. After the Spaniards defeated the Incas in the 16th century, Bolivia's
predominantly Indian population was reduced to
slavery. The country won its independence in 1825
and was named after Simón Bolívar, the famed liberator.
Since 1825 Bolivia has had more than 60 revolutions, 70 Presidents, and 11 Constitutions.
Harassed by internal strife, Bolivia lost great
slices of territory to three neighbor nations. Several

thousand square miles and its outlet to the Pacific
were taken by Chile after the War of the Pacific
(1879–84). In 1903 a piece of Bolivia's Acre province, rich in rubber, was ceded to Brazil. And in
1938, after a war with Paraguay, Bolivia gave up
claim to nearly 100,000 square miles of the Gran
Chaco.
Great prosperity came with World War II and its
demand for two important Bolivian products, tin
and wolframite. But rising prices provoked strikes
that were ruthlessly broken and promoted growth
of the leftist National Revolutionary Movement.
The movement seized power in 1943 but was ousted by a moderate government in 1947.
In 1965 a guerrilla movement mounted from
Cuba and headed by Maj. Ernesto (Ché) Guevara
began a revolutionary war. With the aid of U.S.
military advisers, the Bolivian army, helped by the
peasants, smashed the guerrilla movement, wound-
ing and capturing Guevara on Oct. 8, 1967, and
shooting him to death the next day.
Bolivia's first elections in 11 years were authorized in July 1977 by Col. Hugo Banzer Suarez, who
had seized the presidency seven years before. Gen.
Juan Pereda Asbun, his claimed victory disputed as
fraudulent, declared himself the winner with the
backing of the armed forces. In August 1978, the
U.S. suspended military aid to Bolivia (the combined economic and military-aid program of $56.1
million for fiscal 1979 was the largest in Latin
America) as a protest against Pereda's coup. Although he had ruled out elections before 1980,
Pereda yielded to external and internal pressure
and permitted presidential and congressional elections on July 1, 1979.
Former President Hernan Siles Suazo led in the
voting but failed to win a majority, and the Congress chose Walter Guevara Arze as provisional
President pending new elections. But in November 1979, Col. Alberto Natusch staged a coup that
lasted only 16 days. An interim civilian regime, led
by Lydia Gueiler Tejada, was installed and elections rescheduled for June 1980. Again Siles led but
fell short of a majority in a three-way race that
included two other former Presidents, Gen. Banzer
and Victor Paz Estenssoro.
Gen. Luis Garcia Meza, who had become army
commander only nine months earlier, seized power
on July 17, 1980, in a carefully prepared action that
had the support of almost the entire military establishment and the reported aid of Argentina's military regime. U.S. Senator Dennis DeConcina,
Arizona Democrat, charged that Garcia Meza and
his colleagues were heavily involved in the lucra-
tive cocaine trade.
Garcia Meza in February 1981 dismissed two
ministers, both of them reported to be deeply involved in the drug trade. On June 27, an attempted
coup by Gen. Lucio Anez Rivera, army chief of
staff, was defeated by loyal troops but there was
widespread public discontent because of the failure of Garcia Meza to stabilize the economy.

BOPHUTHATSWANA
See South Africa

BOTSWANA

Republic of Botswana
President: Quett Masire (1980)
Area: 222,000 sq mi. (576,000 sq km)

Population (est. 1981): 750,000 (growth rate, 2.6%)
Density per square mile: 3.8
Capital and largest city (est. 1979): Gaborone, 50,000
Monetary unit: Pula
Languages: English, Setswana
Religions: Christian, 60%; Animist
Member of Commonwealth of Nations
Freedom House classifications: Capitalist pre-industrial, multi-party decentralized
Economic summary: Gross national product (1979): $560 million. Average annual growth rate (1970–78): 13.2%. Per capita income: $480. Land used for agriculture: 5%; labor force: 75%; principal products: livestock, sorghum, corn, millet, cowpeas, beans. Labor force in industry: 56%. Major products: diamonds, copper, nickel, salt, soda ash, potash, coal, frozen beef; tourism. Natural resources: diamonds, copper, nickel, salt, soda ash, potash, coal. Exports: meat products, diamonds, hides, copper, nickel. Imports: machinery, transport equipment, manufactured goods, food, chemicals, mineral fuels. Major trading partners: U.K., South Africa.

Geography. Twice the size of Arizona, Botswana is in south central Africa, bounded by South-West Africa, Zambia, Zimbabwe, and South Africa. Most of the country is near-desert, with the Kalahari occupying the western part of the country. The eastern part is hilly, with salt lakes in the north.

Government. The Botswana Constitution provides, in addition to the unicameral National Assembly, for a House of Chiefs, which has a voice on bills affecting tribal affairs. There is universal suffrage.

The major political parties are the Democratic Party (29 of 32 elective seats in 36-man Legislative Assembly), led by President Quett Masire; National Front (2 seats), led by Kenneth Koma; People's Party (1 seat), led by Kenneth Nkhwa.

History. Botswana is the land of the Batawana tribes, which, when threatened by the Boers in Transvaal, asked Britain in 1885 to establish a protectorate over the country, then known as Bechuanaland. In 1961, Britain granted a Constitution to the country. Self-government began in 1965, and on Sept. 30, 1966, the country became independent. Since 1975, it has been an associate member of the European Common Market.

BRAZIL

Federative Republic of Brazil
President: Gen. João Baptista de Oliveira Figueiredo (1979)
Area: 3,286,470 sq mi. (8,511,957 sq km)
Population (est. 1981): 127,000,000 (growth rate, 2.3%) (approx.: white, 60%; mestizo, 26%; black, 11%)
Density per square mile: 38.6
Capital (est. 1980): Brasília, 1,000,000
Largest cities (1980 census): São Paulo, 12,578,045; Rio de Janeiro, 9,011,981; Belo Horizonte, 2,534,576; Recife, 2,346,196; Porto Alegre, 2,332,370; Salvador, 1,766,075
Monetary unit: Cruzeiro
Language: Portuguese
Religion: Roman Catholic, 91%
National name: Brasil
Freedom House classifications: Capitalist-statist industrial, multi-party decentralized
Economic summary: Gross national product (1979): $207.3 billion. Average annual growth rate (1970–78): 6%. Per capita income (1976): $1,191. Land used for agriculture: 17%; labor force: 31%; principal products: coffee, rice, beef, corn, milk, sugar cane, soybeans, cocoa. Labor force in industry: 33%; major products: steel, chemicals, petrochemicals, machinery, motor vehicles, cement, lumber. Natural resources: iron ore, manganese, bauxite, nickel, other industrial metals. Exports: coffee, iron ore, soy meal, soybeans, transport equipment, machinery, cocoa beans, footwear. Imports: capital and consumer goods, petroleum, machinery, chemicals, pharmaceuticals. Major trading partners: U.S., West Germany, Netherlands, Argentina, Spain, U.K., France, Japan.

Geography. Brazil covers nearly half of South America, extends 2,965 miles (4,772 km) north-south, 2,691 miles (4,331 km), east-west, and borders every nation on the continent except Chile and Ecuador. It is the fifth largest country in the world, ranking after the U.S.S.R., Canada, China, and the U.S.

More than a third of Brazil is drained by the Amazon and its more than 200 tributaries. The Amazon is navigable for ocean steamers to Iquitos, Peru, 2,300 miles (3,700 km) upstream. Southern Brazil is drained by the Plata system—the Paraguay, Uruguay, and Paraná Rivers. The most important stream entirely within Brazil is the Sao Francisco, navigable for 1,000 miles (1,903 km), but broken near its mouth by the 275-foot (84 m) Paulo Afonso Falls.

Government. Under the Constitution, Brazil is a union of 22 states, 4 territories, and 1 federal district. The President is elected for a six-year term by an electoral college made up of members of the National Congress. The National Congress is composed of two houses—the Senate, whose members serve eight-year terms, and the Chamber of Deputies, elected for four-year terms. Members of Congress are elected by equal, direct, compulsory, and secret suffrage under proportional representation.

The military took control in 1964, ousting the last elected civilian President and installing a series of military men (with the Congress ratifying the junta's choice).

The major political parties are the Partido Democrático Social, led by Senator José Sarney (the pro-government party formerly called ARENA, for Aliança Renovadora Nacional); Partido do Movimento Democrático Brasileiro, led by Representative Ulysses Guimarães; Partido Popular, led by Senator Tancredo Neves; and the Partido Trabalhista Brasileiro, led by Yvette Vargas.

History. Brazil is the only Latin American nation deriving its language and culture from Portugal. Adm. Pedro Alvares Cabral claimed the territory for the Portuguese in 1500. He brought to Portugal a cargo of wood, pau-brasil, from which the land received its name. Portugal began colonization in 1532 and made the area a royal colony in 1549.

During the Napoleonic wars, King João VI, then Prince Regent, fled the country in 1807 in advance of the French armies and in 1808 set up his court in Rio de Janeiro. João was drawn home in 1820 by a revolution, leaving his son as Regent. When Portugal sought to reduce Brazil again to colonial status, the prince declared Brazil's independence on Sept. 7, 1822, and became Pedro I, Emperor of Brazil.

Harassed by his parliament, Pedro I abdicated in 1831 in favor of his five-year-old son, who became Emperor in 1840 as Pedro II. The son was a popular monarch, but discontent built up and, in 1889, following a military revolt, he had to abdicate. Although a republic was proclaimed, Brazil was under two military dictatorships during the next four years. A revolt permitted a gradual return to stability under civilian Presidents. Slavery was abolished in 1888.

The President during World War I, Wenceslau Braz, cooperated with the Allies and declared war on Germany. The President from 1926 to 1930, Washington Luiz Pereira da Souza, was overthrown by a revolutionary group under Getulio Vargas, who took over as provisional President.

Vargas' 1934 Constitution curtailed states' rights and established a nationalistic policy. In 1937, Vargas seized absolute power and adopted another Constitution, extending his term indefinitely. In World War II, Brazil cooperated with the Western Allies, welcoming Allied air bases, patrolling the South Atlantic, and joining the invasion of Italy after declaring war on the Axis.

Vargas was overthrown on Oct. 29, 1945. Succeeding presidents were Gen. Eurico Gaspar Dutra (1945–50); Getulio Vargas (1950–54); João Cafe Filho (1954–55); Juscelino Kubitschek de Oliveira (1955–60); Janio Quadros (1960); João Goulart (1960–63); Gen. Humberto de Alencar Castelo Branco (1963–66); Gen. Arthur Costa e Silva (1966–69); Gen. Emilio Garrastazu Médici (1970–74).

In 1974, Gen. Ernesto Geisel was elected President. The election was the freest in a decade and the least violent in many years. Press censorship was relaxed under a policy of "decompression."

Geisel tightened political controls in 1977, suspending Congress on April 1 when opposition legislators balked at approving election procedures guaranteeing ARENA control over state governments.

Relations with the U.S. remained cool following Geisel's 1977 repudiation of a mutual defense pact after a U.S. State Department report cited the military regime's repression of human rights, and Brazil emphasized that President Carter was coming on his own request when he visited Brazil in March. The U.S. also opposed Brazil's purchase of German nuclear equipment capable of reprocessing spent nuclear fuel into weapons-grade plutonium.

National elections on Nov. 15, 1978, saw the ruling ARENA party lose its majority by a slight margin in popular voting but it retained control of both houses of Congress by a narrow edge. In the 1979 presidential election, Geisel's hand-picked candidate, Gen. João Baptista de Oliveira Figueiredo, was elected.

Figueiredo had pledged a return to democracy when he took office in 1979 and granted amnesty to 5,000 political exiles. He aroused international protest, however, when the leader of a metalworkers' strike, Luis da Silva, was sentenced in March 1981 to three and a half years in prison. The strike halted Brazilian automobile production and cost the industry $500 million in lost sales.

BULGARIA

People's Republic of Bulgaria
Chairman of the State Council: Todor Zhivkov (1971)
Prime Minister (Chairman of Council of Ministers): Grisha Filipov (1981)

Area: 42,823 sq mi. (110,912 sq km)
Population (est. 1981): 8,875,000 (growth rate: 0.4%)
Density per square mile: 207.4
Capital: Sofia
Largest cities (est. 1979): Sofia, 1,000,000; (est. 1976 by U.N.): Plovdiv, 307,400; Varna, 257,700; Ruse, 161,600; Burgas, 146,700; Stara Zagora, 123,900
Monetary unit: Lev
Language: Bulgarian
Religions: Orthodox, 83%; Islam, 13%
National name: Narodna Republika Bulgariya
Freedom House classifications: Socialist industrial, one-party communist
Economic summary: Gross national product (1979): $32.7 billion. Average annual growth rate (1970–78): 5.7%. Labor force in agriculture: 27%; principal products: grains, tobacco, fruits, vegetables. Labor force in industry: 26%; major products: processed agricultural products, machinery, textiles, clothing. Natural resources: metals, minerals, lumber. Exports: machinery and transport equipment, fuels, minerals, raw materials, agricultural products. Imports: machinery and transportation equipment, fuels, raw materials, metals, agricultural raw materials. Major trading partners: U.S.S.R., Soviet bloc countries.

Geography. Two mountain ranges and two great valleys mark the topography of Bulgaria, a country the size of Tennessee. Situated on the Black Sea in the eastern part of the Balkan peninsula, it shares borders with Yugoslavia, Romania, Greece, and Turkey. The Balkan belt crosses the center of the country, almost due east-west, rising to a height of 7,800 feet (2,377 m). The Rhodope range breaks off from the Balkans in the west, curves, and then straightens out to run nearly parallel along the southern border. Between the two ranges, is the valley of the Maritsa, Bulgaria's principal river. Between the Balkan range and the Danube, which forms most of the northern boundary with Romania, is the Danubian tableland.

Southern Dobruja, a fertile region of 2,900 square miles (7,511 sq km), below the Danube delta, is an area of low hills, fens, and sandy steppes.

Government. The present Constitution has been in effect since May 18, 1971. The National Assembly, consisting of 400 members elected for five-year terms, is the governing body. It elects the State Council and the Council of Ministers.

The Communist Party is led by the chairman of the State Council, Todor Zhivkov.

History. The first Bulgarians, a tribe of wild horsemen akin to the Huns, crossed the Danube from the north in A.D. 679 and subjugated the Slavic population of Moesia. They adopted a Slav dialect and Slavic customs and twice conquered most of the Balkan peninsula between 893 and 1280. After the Serbs subjected their kingdom in 1330, the Bulgars gradually fell prey to the Turks, and from 1396 to 1878 Bulgaria was a Turkish province. In 1878, Russia forced Turkey to give the country its independence; but the European powers, fearing that Bulgaria might become a Russian dependency, intervened. By the Treaty of Berlin in 1878, Bulgaria became autonomous under Turkish sovereignty.

In 1887, Prince Ferdinand of Saxe-Coburg-Gotha was elected ruler of Bulgaria; on Oct. 5, 1908, he declared the country independent and took the title of Tsar.

Bulgaria joined Germany in World War I and lost. On Oct. 3, 1918, Tsar Ferdinand abdicated in favor of his son, Tsar Boris III. Boris assumed dictatorial powers in 1934–35. When Hitler awarded Bulgaria southern Dobruja, taken from Romania in 1940, the weak but land-hungry Boris joined the Nazis in war the next year and occupied parts of Yugoslavia and Greece. Later the Germans tried to force Boris to send his troops against the Russians. Boris resisted and died under mysterious circumstances on Aug. 28, 1943.

Simeon II, infant son of Boris, became nominal ruler under a regency. Russia declared war on Bulgaria on Sept. 5, 1944. An armistice was agreed to three days later, after Bulgaria had declared war on Germany. Russian troops streamed in the next day, and under an informal armistice a coalition "Fatherland Front" Cabinet was set up under Kimon Georgiev.

A peace treaty negotiated in 1947 permitted Bulgaria to keep southern Dobruja. A Constitution was adopted in 1947 establishing a Soviet-type people's republic.

BURMA

Socialist Republic of the Union of Burma
President: U Ne Win (1974)
Prime Minister: U Maung Maung Kha (1977)
Area: 261,789 sq mi. (678,036 sq km)
Population (est. 1981): 34,350,000 (growth rate, 2.4%)
Density per square mile: 131.2
Capital: Rangoon
Largest cities (est. 1979): Rangoon, 2,200,000 (est. 1977 for metropolitan area by U.N.): Mandalay, 458,000; Moulmein, 188,000; Bassein, 138,000; Pegu, 135,000
Monetary unit: Kyat
Language: Burmese
Religions: Buddhist, 80%; Christian, Islam, Hindu
National name: Pyidaungsu Socialist Thammada Myanma Naingngandau
Freedom House classifications: Capitalist-socialist pre-industrial, one-party socialist.
Economic summary: Gross national product (1979): $5.1 billion. Average annual growth rate (1970–78): 1.7%. Per capita income (1977): $120. Labor force in agriculture: 67%; principal products: sugar cane, corn, rice, peanuts. Labor force in industry: 9%; major products: textiles, footwear, processed agricultural products, wood and wood products, refined petroleum. Natural resources: timber, nickel, cobalt, copper, gold, rubies, sapphires, jade. Exports: rice, teak. Imports: machinery and transportation equipment, textiles, manufactured goods. Major trading partners: Singapore, Western European countries, China, U.K., Japan.

Geography. Burma occupies the northwest portion of the Indochinese peninsula. India lies to the northwest and China to the northeast. Bangladesh, Laos, and Thailand are also neighbors. The Bay of Bengal touches the southwestern coast.

Slightly smaller than Texas, the country is divided into three natural regions: the Arakan Yoma, a long, narrow mountain range forming the barrier between Burma and India; the Shan Plateau in the east, extending southward into Tenasserim; and the Central Basin, running down to the flat fertile delta of the Irrawaddy in the south. This delta contains a network of intercommunicating canals and nine principal river mouths.

Government. On March 2, 1962, the government of U Nu was overthrown and replaced by a Revolu-

tionary Council, which assumed all power in the state. Gen. U Ne Win, as chairman of the Revolutionary Council, became the chief executive.

A new Constitution was approved in 1973 and took effect Jan. 4, 1974. Under it, Burma is a Socialist Democratic Republic with a 451-seat unicameral legislature called the People's Congress. In 1972, Ne Win and his colleagues resigned their military titles and thereafter ruled as "civilians." In 1974, Ne Win dissolved the Revolutionary Council and became President under the new Constitution; he is also chairman of the Council of State. The Burmese Socialist Program Party, the only legal party, is led by Ne Win.

History. In 1612, the British East India Company sent agents to Burma, but the Burmese long resisted efforts of British traders, and Dutch and Portuguese as well, to establish posts on the Bay of Bengal. By the Anglo-Burmese War in 1824–26 and two following wars, the British East India Company expanded to the whole of Burma by 1886. Burma was annexed to India. It became a separate colony in 1937.

During World War II, Burma was a key battleground; the 800-mile Burma Road was the Allies' vital supply line to China. The Japanese invaded the country in December 1941, and by May 1942 had occupied most of it, cutting the Burma Road. After one of the most difficult campaigns of the war, Allied forces liberated most of Burma prior to the Japanese surrender in August 1945.

Burma became independent on Jan. 4, 1948. The new government was soon faced by armed uprisings of Communists and of Karen tribesmen. In 1949 the Karen rebels won a large degree of autonomy. In 1951 and 1952 the Socialists achieved power, and Burma became the first Asian country to introduce social legislation.

In 1968, after the government had made headway against the Communist rebels, the military regime adopted a policy of strict nonalignment and followed "the Burmese Way" to socialism. But the insurgents, reportedly numbering several thousand and armed by China, continued active.

In August 1981, Ne Win announced that he would resign from the Presidency in November after 19 years in power.

BURUNDI

Republic of Burundi
Head of Government: Lt. Col. Jean-Baptiste Bagaza (1978)
Area: 10,747 sq mi. (27,834 sq km)
Population (est. 1981): 4,650,000 (growth rate, 2.5%)
Density per square mile: 432.7
Capital and largest city (1979 census): Bujumbura, 151,000
Monetary unit: Burundi franc
Languages: Kirundi (official), French
Religions: Roman Catholic, 53%; Animist, 38%; Protestant, 7%
National name: Republika Y'Uburundi
Freedom House classifications: Capitalist-socialist pre-industrial, one-party socialist
Economic summary: Gross national product (1979): $720 million. Average annual growth rate (1970–78): 1.3%. Per capita income (1977): $128. Average rate of inflation (1974–78): 15%. Principal agricultural products: coffee, tea, cotton, food crops. Major industrial products: light consumer goods. Natural resources: nickel, uranium, cobalt, unexploited copper and platinum deposits.

Exports: coffee, tea, hides. Imports: textiles, food, transport equipment, petroleum products. Major trading partners: Belgium, West Germany, France, U.S.

Geography. Wedged among Tanzania, Zaire, and Rwanda in east central Africa, Burundi occupies a high plateau divided by several deep valleys. It is equal in size to Maryland.

Government. Legislative and executive power is vested in the president.

Burundi's first Constitution, approved July 11, 1974, placed UPRONA (Unity and National Progress), the only political party, in control of national policy and automatically made Lt. Gen. Michel Micombero president.

History. Burundi was once part of German East Africa. An integrated society developed among the Watusi, a tall, warlike people and nomad cattle raisers, and the Bahutu, a Bantu people, who were subject farmers. Belgium won a League of Nations mandate in 1923, and subsequently Burundi, with Rwanda, was transferred to the status of a United Nations trust territory.

In 1962, Burundi gained independence and became a kingdom under Mwami Mwambutsa IV, with his son, Louis Rwangasore, as premier. Shortly after, the son was assassinated. The second man to succeed him, Pierre Ngendandumwe, who took office in 1963, was assassinated in 1965 when an unsuccessful coup against the Watusi led to the massacre of many Bahutus.

Crown Prince Charles, returning from Europe, rallied Watusi extremists, ousted the premier, suspended the Constitution, and renewed relations with Communist China. He deposed his father in 1966, reigned as Ntare V, with Micombero as premier. Three months later, Micombero, in a military coup, overthrew the Mwami and established a republic, installing himself as president.

One of Africa's worst tribal wars, which became genocide, occurred in Burundi in April 1972, following the return of Ntare. He was given a safe-conduct promise in writing by Micombero but was "judged and immediately executed" by the Burundi leader. His return was apparently attended by an invasion of exiles of Burundi's Hutu tribe. Although Hutus make up 85% of the population, they have been dominated for centuries by the minority Tutsi tribe of Micombero. Whether Hutus living in Burundi joined the invasion is unclear, but after it failed, the victorious Tutsis proceeded to massacre some 100,000 persons in six weeks, with possibly 100,000 more slain by summer.

On Nov. 1, 1976, a military coup led by Lt. Col. Jean-Baptiste Bagaza ousted Micombero, who was serving his second term. Bagaza assumed the presidency Nov. 3, suspended the Constitution, and announced that a 30-member Supreme Revolutionary Council would be the governing body.

Early in 1977, the Council gave Bagaza a mandate for a renewable five-year term and proposed its own dissolution, once UPRONA is reorganized.

CAMBODIA

Democratic Kampuchea
President: Heng Samrin (1979)
Area: 70,000 sq mi. (181,300 sq km)

Population (est. 1981): 9,000,000
Density per square mile: 128.6
Capital and largest city (est. 1979 for metropolitan area): Phnom Penh, 270,000
Monetary unit: Riel
Ethnic groups: Khmer, 93%; Vietnamese, 4%; Chinese, 3%
Languages: Khmer (official), French, Vietnamese, Chinese
Religion: Theravada Buddhist
Freedom House classifications: Socialist industrial, one-party communist
Economic summary: Gross national product (1971): $500 million. Principal agricultural products: rice, rubber, corn. Major industrial products: fish, wood and wood products, milled rice. Natural resources: timber, gemstones, iron ore, manganese, phosphate. Exports: natural rubber, rice, pepper, wood. Imports: foodstuffs, fuel, machinery. Major trading partners: China, North Korea.

Geography. Situated on the Indochinese peninsula, Cambodia is bordered by Thailand and Laos on the north and Vietnam on the east and south. The Gulf of Siam is off the western coast. The country, the size of Missouri, consists chiefly of a large alluvial plain ringed in by mountains and on the east by the Mekong River. The plain is centered on Lake Tonle Sap, which is a natural storage basin of the Mekong.

Government. A bloodless coup toppled Prince Sihanouk in 1970. It was led by Lon Nol and Prince Sisowath Sirik Matak, Sihanouk's cousin. Sihanouk moved to Peking to head a government-in-exile. On Oct. 9, 1970, Cambodia became the Khmer Republic, and Lon Nol proclaimed himself President.

The Lon Nol regime was overthrown in April 1975 by Pol Pot, a leader of the Communist Khmers Rouges forces, who instituted a xenophobic reign of terror. Pol Pot was in turn ousted on Jan. 8, 1979, by Heng Samrin, a dissident backed by strong Vietnamese forces.

History. Cambodia came under Khmer rule about A.D. 600. Under the Khmers, magnificent temples were built at Angkor. The Khmer kingdom once ruled over most of Southeast Asia, but attacks by the Thai and the Vietnamese almost annihilated the empire until the French joined Cambodia, Laos, and Vietnam into French Indochina.

Under Norodom Sihanouk, enthroned in 1941, and particularly under Japanese occupation during World War II, nationalism revived. After the ouster of the Japanese, the Cambodians sought independence, but the French returned in 1946, granting the country a Constitution in 1947 and independence within the French Union in 1949. Sihanouk won full military control during the French-Indochinese War in 1953. He abdicated in 1955 in favor of his parents, remaining head of the government, and when his father died in 1960, became chief of state without returning to the throne. In 1963, he sought a guarantee of Cambodia's neutrality from all parties to the Vietnam War.

Sihanouk first favored the Communist-backed Vietcong in Vietnam, but in 1967 he accused the Communists of planning a revolt and veered away from them. In 1968 he announced that under certain conditions he would not oppose "hot pursuit" by American troops of Communist forces across the Cambodian border.

On March 18, 1970, while Sihanouk was abroad trying to get North Vietnamese and the Vietcong out of border sanctuaries near Vietnam, anti-Vietnamese riots occurred, and Sihanouk was overthrown, a move legalized by the legislature. The historically anti-Vietnamese (North and South) Cambodians largely stayed with the government.

North Vietnamese and Vietcong units in border sanctuaries began moving deeper into Cambodia, threatening rapid overthrow of Lon Nol. President Nixon sent South Vietnamese and U.S. troops across the border on April 30. U.S. ground forces, limited to 30-kilometer penetration, withdrew by June 30.

The Vietnam peace agreement of 1973 stipulated withdrawal of foreign forces from Cambodia, but fighting continued between Hanoi-backed insurgents and U.S.-supplied government troops. U.S. air support for the government forces was ended by Congress on Aug. 15, 1973. Lon Nol made overtures for a negotiated settlement, but neither Sihanouk nor leaders of the Khmer Rouge rebels would deal with him.

Fighting continued through 1974, then reached a quick climax early in 1975. In January, the rebels cut off the Mekong River as a supply route to Phnom Penh and fought their way to the outskirts of the capital and began shelling it. In February, the U.S. Congress ignored a request from President Ford for $222 million to supplement Phnom Penh's dwindling arms stores, but a U.S. food airlift to the besieged capital went forward.

As government troops fell back in bitter fighting, there were student protests in Phnom Penh, and foreigners began leaving the country. Lon Nol fled by air April 1, leaving the government under the interim control of Premier Long Boret. On April 16, the government's capitulation ended the five-year war, but not the travails of war-ravaged Cambodia.

The new regime embarked immediately on a sweeping, inward-looking agrarian revolution. Cambodian borders were closed, but 6,000 refugees escaped to Thailand. They reported that all cities had been evacuated, with inhabitants relocated to found new farm settlements in the jungle. They said policy was enforced by Communist troops and teen-aged revolutionaries who summarily shot dissidents and former government soldiers.

Khieu Samphan, an early Khmer Rouge leader, appeared to be the strong man of the new regime. Sihanouk, the nominal chief of state, returned from exile in Peking in 1975 for the first time since the 1970 coup. A new Constitution was proclaimed in December 1975, establishing a 250-member People's Assembly, a State Presidium headed by Pol Pot, and a Supreme Judicial Tribunal. Samphan replaced Sihanouk as head of state in April 1976, and the former monarch became a virtual prisoner.

In the next two years, from 2 to 4 million Cambodians are estimated to have died under the brutality of the regime, which President Carter called "the worst violator of human rights in the world." Border clashes with Vietnam developed into a Vietnamese invasion and by the end of 1978 the Pol Pot government appeared to be collapsing.

Sihanouk, held under house arrest since 1976, was freed by Pol Pot early in 1979 and sent as a spokesman for the regime to protest the Vietnamese invasion before the U.N. Security Council. Sihanouk eloquently attacked Vietnam while conceding that the Pol Pot regime was inhumane. His call for Vietnam's withdrawal was barred only by a Soviet veto.

Despite the capture of Phnom Penh on Jan. 8 by Heng Samrin, a dissident Khmer Rouge backed by

Vietnamese troops, fighting continued in isolated areas. Retreating Pol Pot forces and refugees totaling 40,000 were driven into Thailand by May. Thai authorities forced 15,000 to return, admitting that "several hundred" may have been killed by waiting Vietnamese troops.

Due largely to the support of China and the Association of Southeast Asian Nations (ASEAN), the defeated regime retained the Cambodian seat at the United Nations. A conference on Cambodia met at the United Nations, July 13–17, 1981, and approved unanimously a resolution calling for Vietnamese withdrawal.

The 92-nation conference also asked for U.N.-supervised elections and guarantee of Cambodian independence. Vietnam and the Soviet Union, together with all Soviet bloc supporters, boycotted the conference. Earlier, Deputy Premier and Foreign Minister Ieng Sary of the Nationalist regime said Pol Pot has been dropped and the regime, admitting error, now wished to join with all Nationalist forces in a common front to defeat the Vietnamese invaders.

CAMEROON

United Republic of Cameroon
President: Ahmadou Ahidjo (1960)
Prime Minister: Paul Biya (1975)
Area: 183,569 sq mi. (475,442 sq km)
Population (est. 1981): 8,650,000 (growth rate: 2.6%)
Density per square mile: 46.6
Capital: Yaoundé
Largest cities (est. 1980): Douala, 500,000; Yaoundé, 350,000
Monetary unit: Franc CFA
Languages: French and English (both official); Foulbé, Bamiléke, Ewondo, Donala, Mungaka, Bassa
Religions: Animist, Christian, Islam
National name: République Unie du Cameroun
Freedom House classifications: Capitalist pre-industrial, one-party nationalist
Economic summary: Gross national product (1979): $4.6 billion. Average annual growth rate (1970–78): 2.8%. Per capita income: $460. Land used for agriculture: 35%; labor force: 80%; principal products: coffee, cocoa, tropical agricultural products. Labor force in industry: 10–15%. Major products: small manufacturing, consumer goods, aluminum. Natural resources: timber, some oil, bauxite. Exports: cocoa, coffee, timber, aluminum, cotton. Imports: manufactured consumer goods, capital goods, food, beverages, tobacco, fuel. Major trading partners: France, U.S., neighboring African states, Western European nations.

Geography. Cameroon is a West African nation on the Gulf of Guinea, bordered by Nigeria, Chad, the Central African Republic, the Congo, Equatorial Guinea, and Gabon. It is nearly twice the size of Oregon.

The interior consists of a high plateau, rising to 4,500 feet (1,372 m), with the land descending to a lower, densely wooded plateau and then to swamps and plains along the coast. Mount Cameroon (13,350 ft.; 4,069 m), near the coast, is the highest elevation in the country. The main rivers are the Benue, Nyong, and Sanaga.

Government. After a 1972 plebiscite, a unitary nation was formed out of East and West Cameroon to replace the former Federal Republic. A Constitution was adopted, providing for election of a president every five years and of a 120-seat National Assembly, whose nominal five-year term can be extended or shortened by the president. The Cameroon National Union is the only political party.

History. The United Republic of Cameroon is inhabited by Hamitic and Semitic peoples in the north, where Islam is the principal religion, and by Bantu peoples in the central and southern regions, where native animism prevails. The tribes were conquered by many invaders.

The land escaped colonial rule until 1884, when treaties with tribal chiefs brought the area under German domination. After World War I, the League of Nations gave the French a mandate over 80% of the area, and the British 20% adjacent to Nigeria. After World War II, when the country came under a U.N. trusteeship in 1946, self-government was granted, and the Cameroun People's Union emerged as the dominant party by campaigning for reunification of French and British Cameroon and for independence. Accused of being under Communist control, it waged a campaign of revolutionary terror from 1955 to 1958, when it was crushed. In British Cameroon, unification was pressed also by the leading party, the Kamerun National Democratic Party, led by John Foncha.

France set up Cameroun as an autonomous state in 1957, and the next year its legislative assembly voted for independence by 1960. In 1959 a fully autonomous government of Cameroun was formed under Ahmadou Ahidjo. Cameroun became an independent republic on Jan. 1, 1960, adopted a Constitution in a referendum in February, and chose a National Assembly in April. The Assembly elected Ahidjo president. A federal Constitution was approved in 1961, and the Federal Republic of Cameroon came into being in October, headed by Ahidjo and Foncha.

Ahidjo was re-elected in 1975 for a fourth five-year term. Paul Biya was named prime minister.

one-party socialist

Economic summary: Gross national product (1979): $80 million. Average annual growth rate (1970–77): −2.1%. Per capita income (1978): $180. Principal agricultural products: bananas, corn, sugar cane, sweet potatoes. Major industry: fishing, salt mining. Natural resources: salt, siliceous rock, minerals. Exports: fish and shellfish, bananas, salt. Imports: machinery, textiles, petroleum products. Major trading partners: Portugal, U.K., Japan, neighboring African states.

Geography: Cape Verde, only slightly larger than Rhode Island, is an archipelago in the Atlantic 385 miles (620 km) west of Dakar, Senegal.

The islands are divided into two groups: Barlavento in the north, comprising Santo Antão (291 sq mi.; 754 sq km), Boa Vista (240 sq mi.; 622 sq km), São Nicolau (132 sq mi.; 342 sq km), São Vicente (88 sq mi.; 246 sq km), Sal (83 sq mi.; 298 sq km), and Santa Luzia (13 sq mi.; 34 sq km); and Sotavento in the south, consisting of São Tiago (383 sq mi.; 992 sq km), Fogo (184 sq mi.; 477 sq km), Maio (103 sq mi.; 267 sq km), and Brava (25 sq mi.; 65 sq km). The islands are mostly mountainous, with the land deeply scarred by erosion. There is an active volcano on Fogo.

Government. The islands became independent on July 5, 1975, under an agreement negotiated with Portugal in 1974. The 56-member National Assembly chose Aristides Pereira as President and Maj. Pedro Pires as Premier. All members of the Assembly belong to the African Party for the Independence of Portuguese Guinea and Cape Verde, then the only party that entered candidates in the election. It is committed to union with Guinea-Bissau, another former Portuguese colony.

History. Uninhabited upon their discovery in 1456, the Cape Verde islands became part of the Portuguese empire in 1495. A majority of their modern inhabitants are of mixed Portuguese and African ancestry. A coaling station developed during the 19th century on the island of São Vicente has grown in recent years to an oil and gasoline storage depot for ships and aircraft.

CANADA

See separate Canada section

CAPE VERDE

Republic of Cape Verde
President: Aristides Pereira (1975)
Premier: Maj. Pedro Pires (1975)
Area: 1,557 sq mi. (4,033 sq km)
Population: (est. 1981): 330,000 (growth rate, 2.1%)
Density per square mile: 211.9
Capital (est. 1980): Praia, 35,000
Largest city (est. 1980): Mindelo, 50,000
Monetary unit: Cape Verde escudo
Language: Portuguese
Religions: Mainly Roman Catholic, Protestant, and Christian Racionalist
National name: República de Cabo Verde.
Freedom House classifications: Socialist pre-industrial,

CENTRAL AFRICAN REPUBLIC

Head of Government: Gen. André Kolingba (1981)
Area: 241,313 sq mi. (625,000 sq km)
Population (est. 1981): 2,500,000 (growth rate, 2.6%)
Density per square mile: 10.4
Capital and largest city (est. 1979): Bangui, 350,000
Monetary unit: Franc CFA
Ethnic groups: Mandja-Baya, Banda, Mbaka, Azande
Languages: French (official) and Sango
Religions: Animist, 60%; Christian, 35%; Islam, 5%
National name: République Centrafricain
Member of French Community
Freedom House classifications: Capitalist pre-industrial, one-party non-military
Economic summary: Gross national product (1979): $560 million. Average annual growth rate (1970–78): 1.0%. Per capita income: $177. Land used for agriculture: 10%; labor force: 80%; principal products: cotton, coffee,

peanuts, food crops, livestock. Major industrial products: timber, textiles, soap, cigarettes, processed food. Natural resources: diamonds, uranium, timber. Exports: diamonds, cotton, timber, coffee. Imports: machinery and electrical equipment, petroleum products, textiles. Major trading partners: France, Yugoslavia, Japan, U.S.

Geography. Situated about 500 miles north (805 km) of the equator, the Central African Republic is a landlocked nation bordered by Cameroon, Chad, the Sudan, Zaire, and the Congo. Twice the size of New Mexico, it is covered by tropical forests in the south and semidesert land in the east. The Ubangi and Shari are the largest of many rivers.

Government. On Dec. 4, 1976, the Central African Republic became the Central African Empire. Marshal Jean-Bédel Bokassa, who had ruled the republic since he took power in a military coup Dec. 31, 1965, was declared Emperor Bokassa I. He was overthrown in a coup on Sept. 20, 1979. Former President David Dacko, returned to power and changed the country's name back to the Central African Republic. An army coup on Sept. 1, 1981, deposed Dacko and suspended the Constitution and all political parties. A Military Committee of National Redress was set up to run the country.

History. As the colony of Ubangi-Shari, what is now the Central African Republic was united with Chad in 1905 and joined with Gabon and the Middle Congo in French Equatorial Africa in 1910. After World War II a rebellion in 1946 forced the French to grant self-government. In 1958 the territory voted to become an autonomous republic within the French Community, but on Aug. 13, 1960, President David Dacko proclaimed the republic's independence from France.

Dacko undertook to move the country into Peking's orbit, but was overthrown in a coup on Dec. 31, 1965, by the then Col. Jean-Bédel Bokassa, Army Chief of Staff. In August 1977, the U.S. State Department protested the Emperor's jailing of American and British newsmen.

Bokassa staged an elaborate coronation ceremony on the first anniversary of the Empire, inviting 3,500 guests to see him place a diamond-studded crown on his head and sit on a 2.5-ton gilded bronze throne in the shape of an eagle. The cost of the ceremony was one fourth of the annual foreign-exchange earnings of the country, one of the 25 poorest in the world.

CHAD

Republic of Chad
President: Goukouni Oueddei (1979)
Area: 495,752 sq mi. (1,284,000 sq km)
Population (est. 1981): 4,650,000 (growth rate, 2.3%)
Density per square mile: 9.4
Capital and largest city (est. 1979): N'djamena, 300,000
Monetary unit: Franc CFA
Ethnic groups: Baguirmiens, Kanembous, Saras, Massas, Arabs, Toubous, Goranes
Languages: French (official), Sara, Kanembou, Ouddai, Massa, Arabic, Gorane
Religions: Islam, 45%; Animist, 45%; Christian, 10%
National name: République de Tchad
Freedom House classifications: Capitalist pre-industrial, non-party military

Economic summary: Gross national product (1979): $490 million. Average annual growth rate (1970–78): −0.6%. Per capita income: $70. Land used for agriculture: 50%; labor force: 90%; principal products: cotton, cattle, fish, sugar, subsistence crops. Labor force in industry: 4%; major products: livestock and livestock products, beer, bicycle and radio assembly, textiles, cigarettes. Natural resources: petroleum, unexploited uranium, kaolin. Exports: cotton, livestock and livestock products. Imports: food, motor vehicles and parts, petroleum products, machinery, construction materials. Major trading partners: Western European countries.

Geography. A landlocked country in north central Africa, Chad is about 85% the size of Alaska. Its neighbors are Niger, Libya, the Sudan, the Central African Empire, Cameroon, and Nigeria.

Lake Chad, from which the country gets its name, lies on the western border with Niger and Nigeria. In the north is a desert that runs into the Sahara.

Government. After a coup on April 13, 1975, a nine-member military council took over all governmental functions, including those of the 75-member Legislative Assembly. Political parties were banned.

History. Chad was absorbed into the colony of French Equatorial Africa, as part of Ubangi-Shari, in 1910. France began the country's development after 1920, when it became a separate colony. In 1946, French Equatorial Africa was admitted to the French Union. By referendum in 1958 the Chad territory became an autonomous republic within the French Union.

An independence movement led by the first Premier and President, François (later Ngarta) Tombalbaye, achieved complete independence on Aug. 11, 1960. After a coup failed in 1963, Tombalbaye as President and chief of state promulgated a new Constitution and organized a new government.

A six-year sub-Sahara drought caused mass migrations, thousands of deaths, and famine conditions for some 2 million Chadians in 1974. International relief efforts were disrupted October 25, when President Tombalbaye ordered rejection of U.S. grain shipments (45% of the total). He charged that U.S. officials had barred Chadians from policy roles.

Tombalbaye was killed in the 1975 coup and was succeeded by Gen. Félix Malloum, who faced a Libyan-financed rebel movement, the Chadian National Liberation Front (Frolinat), throughout his tenure in office. A ceasefire backed by Libya, Niger, and the Sudan early in 1978 failed to end the fighting, and French military aid, both troops and supplies, was increased.

Nine rival groups meeting in Lagos, Nigeria, in March 1979, agreed to form a provisional government headed by Goukouni Oueddi, a former Frolinat leader. Fighting broke out again in Chad in March 1980, when Defense Minister Hissene Habre challenged Oueddi. French troops evacuated most of the whites from N'djamena, including the staff of the U.S. embassy, as Habre's followers secured the capital. By the year's end, Libyan troops supporting Oueddi had retaken the city and Libyan President Muammar Qaddafi proposed a merger with Chad. But the Organization of African Unity summit meeting in June called for an international peacekeeping force to replace Libyan troops and permit the holding of elections, a proposal endorsed by France.

CHILE

Republic of Chile

President: Gen. Augusto Pinochet Ugarte (1973)
Area: 286,396 sq mi. (741,766 sq km)
Population (est. 1981): 11,275,000 (growth rate, 1.5%)
Density per square mile: 39.4
Capital: Santiago
Largest cities (est. 1980): Santiago, 3,850,000; Viña del Mar, 262,100; Valparaiso, 248,200; Talcahuano, 204,100; Concepción, 172,800; Antofagasta, 157,000
Monetary unit: Peso
Language: Spanish
Religion: Roman Catholic
National name: República de Chile
Freedom House classifications: Capitalist industrial, non-party military
Economic summary: Gross national product (1979): $18.4 billion. Average annual growth rate (1970–78): 2.1%. Per capita income: $970. Land used for agriculture: 21%; labor force 20%; principal products: grains, fruits, potatoes, vegetables, wine, livestock. Labor force in industry: 22%; major products: processed fish, transportation equipment, iron and steel, pulp, paper. Natural resources: copper, timber, iron ore, nitrates. Exports: copper, cellulose, iron ore. Imports: food, petroleum, capital goods. Major trading partners: U.S., Japan, Western European and Latin American countries.

Geography. Situated south of Peru and west of Bolivia and Argentina, Chile fills a narrow 1,800-mile (2,897 km) strip between the Andes and the Pacific. Its area is nearly twice that of Montana.

One third of Chile is covered by the towering ranges of the Andes. In the north is the mineral-rich Atacama Desert, between the coastal mountains and the Andes. In the center is a 700-mile-long (1,127 km) valley, thickly populated, between the Andes and the coastal plateau. In the south, the Andes border on the ocean.

At the southern tip of Chile's mainland is Punta Arenas, the southernmost city in the world, and beyond that lies the Strait of Magellan and Tierra del Fuego, an island divided between Chile and Argentina. The southernmost point of South America is Cape Horn, a 1,390-foot (424-m) rock on Horn Island in the Wollaston group, which belongs to Chile.

The Juan Fernández Islands, in the South Pacific about 400 miles (644 km) west of the mainland, and Easter Island, about 2,000 miles (3,219 km) west, are Chilean possessions.

Government. Under the pre-coup Constitution, the nation elected a President every six years, a Senate of 50 members every eight years (one-half renewable every four years), and a Chamber of Deputies of 150 members every four years.

Leftist parties were abolished immediately after the 1973 military coup that ousted President Salvador Allende Gossens. Other parties were placed "in recess," and on March 12, 1977, the government officially dissolved them.

History. Chile was originally under the control of the Incas in the north and the fierce Araucanian people in the south. In 1541, a Spaniard, Pedro de Valdivia, founded Santiago. Chile won its independence from Spain in 1818 under Bernardo O'Higgins and an Argentinian, José de San Martin. O'Higgins, dictator until 1823, laid the foundations of the modern state with a two-party system and a centralized government.

The dictator from 1830 to 1837, Diego Portales, fought a war with Peru in 1836–39 that expanded Chilean territory. The Conservatives were in power from 1831 to 1861. Then the Liberals, winning a share of power for the next 30 years, disestablished the church and limited presidential power. Chile fought the War of the Pacific with Peru and Bolivia from 1879 to 1883, winning Antofagasta, Bolivia's only outlet to the sea, and extensive areas from Peru. A revolt in 1890 led by Jorge Montt overthrew, in 1891, José Balmaceda and established a parliamentary dictatorship that existed until a new Constitution was adopted in 1925. Industralization began before World War I and led to the formation of Marxist groups.

Juan Antonio Ríos, President during World War II, was originally pro-Nazi but in 1944 led his country into the war on the side of the U.S. After the war, Gabriel González Videla, elected by a coalition including the Communists, turned on them. The Communist Party was outlawed until 1958.

A small abortive army uprising in 1969 raised fear of military intervention to prevent a Marxist, Salvador Allende Gossens, from taking office after his election to the presidency on Sept. 4, 1970, with 36.3% of the vote in a three-way battle. Dr. Allende was the first President in a non-Communist country freely elected on a Marxist-Leninist program.

Allende quickly established relations with Cuba and the People's Republic of China and nationalized several American companies. He promised compensation but imposed retroactive taxes to cancel out most claims, leading to cool but proper relations with the U.S. By 1972, inflation was running over 100% annually.

A middle-class general strike led to a military coup Sept. 11, 1973, then to Allende's overthrow and mysterious death in an army assault on the presidential palace. More than 2,700 deaths were reported in the coup, and many thousands were arrested. The coup ended a 46-year era of constitutional government in Chile, which had boasted the longest such record in Latin America.

The takeover was led by a four-man junta headed by Army Chief of Staff Augusto Pinochet Ugarte, who assumed the office of President and governed under a state of siege that was kept in force by extensions every six months. In March 1978, Pinochet lifted the state of siege because of "support for government" by the public, reported by a Gallup poll to be 75%.

Committed to "exterminate Marxism," the junta embarked on a right-wing dictatorship. It suspended parliament, banned political activity, and broke relations with Cuba.

The Human Rights Commission of the Organization of American States charged the junta with "most grave violations" of basic liberties, but the O.A.S. voted in May 1975 not to hear the report until further evidence was supplied. In July, Chile denied entry to a U.N. investigatory panel. On June 9, 1978, the government reversed that policy to permit the U.N. Human Rights Commission to send an investigative mission to Cuba.

In 1974, it was disclosed that the U.S. Central Intelligence Agency had secretly aided Allende's opponents before his election and had later worked covertly to "destabilize" his government.

In 1977, Pinochet, in a speech marking his fourth

year in power, promised elections by 1985 if conditions warranted. Earlier, he had abolished DINA, the secret police, and decreed an amnesty for political prisoners, an action Amnesty International said might affect only 200–400 of some 1,500 political prisoners. In 1978, Pinochet permitted the deportation of Michael V. Townley to the U.S., where he and three Cuban exiles were charged with the murder of Orlando Letellier, a former Chilean foreign minister who had taken refuge in Washington.

Townley, given a reduced sentence in May 1979 because he gave evidence to convict the Cubans, testified that all four had been ordered to act by the secret police. A Chilean court refused to extradite three Chilean officers the U.S. accused of complicity in the assassination.

Pinochet was inaugurated on March 11, 1981, for an eight-year term as President, at the end of which, according to the Constitution adopted six months earlier, the junta would nominate a civilian as successor.

CHINA

People's Republic of China
Head of State: Ye Jianying (1978)
Premier: Zhao Ziyang (1980)
Area: 3,691,521 sq mi. (9,561,000 sq km)[1]
Population (est. 1981): 970,000,000 (growth rate, 1.4%)
Density per square mile: 262.7
Capital: Peking
Largest cities (est. 1979): Shanghai, 11,000,000; Peking, 9,000,000; **(est. 1970):** Tianjin (Tientsin), 4,280,000; Wuhan, 4,250,000; Luda (Port Arthur and Dairen), 4,000,000; Shenyang (Mukden), 3,750,000; Chongqing (Chungking), 3,500,000; Harbin, 2,750,000; Taiyuan, 2,725,000; Canton, 2,300,000; Nanjing (Nanking), 2,000,000
Monetary unit: Yuan
Language: Chinese, (Mandarin, Cantonese, and local dialects)
Religions: Principally Confucianist, Buddhist, and Taoist
National name: Zhonghua Renmin Gongheguo
Freedom House classifications: Socialist industrial, one-party communist
Economic summary: Gross national product (1979): $517 billion. Average annual growth rate (1970–77): 4.5%. Per capita income: $390. Labor force in agriculture: 75%; principal products: rice, wheat, grains, cotton. Major industrial products: iron and steel, textiles, armaments, petroleum. Natural resources: coal, natural gas, limestone, marble. Exports: agricultural products, oil, minerals, metals, manufactured goods. Imports: grains, chemical fertilizer, steel, industrial raw materials, machinery and equipment. Major trading partners: Japan, Hong Kong, West Germany, Australia, Romania, Canada, U.S.S.R., U.K., France.

Geography. China, which occupies the eastern part of Asia, is slightly larger in area than the U.S. Its coastline is roughly a semicircle, about 2,150 miles (3,460 km) long. The greater part of the country is mountainous, and only in the lower reaches of the Yellow and Yangtze Rivers are there extensive low plains.

The principal mountain ranges are the Tien Shan, to the northwest; the Kunlun chain, running south of the Taklimakan and Gobi Deserts; and the Trans-Himalaya, connecting the Kunlun with the borders of China and Tibet. Manchuria is largely an undulating plain connected with the north China plain by a narrow lowland corridor. Inner Mongolia contains the relatively fertile southern and eastern portions of the Gobi. The large island of Hainan (13,500 sq mi.; 34,965 sq km) lies off the southern coast.

Hydrographically, China proper consists of three great river systems. The northern part of the country is drained by the Yellow River (Huang Ho), 2,900 miles long (4,667 km) and mostly unnavigable. The central part is drained by the Chang Jiang (Yangtze Kiang), the fourth longest river in the world 3,602 miles (5,797 km). The Xi Jiang (Si Kiang) in the south is 1,236 miles long (1,989 km) and navigable for a considerable distance. In addition, the Amur (2,704 mi.; 4,352 km) forms part of the northeastern boundary.

Government. With 3,040 deputies, elected for four-year terms by universal suffrage, the National People's Congress is the chief legislative organ. A State Council has the executive authority. The Congress elects the Premier and Deputy Premiers. All ministries are under the State Council, headed by the Premier.

The Communist Party controls the government.

History. By 2000 B.C., the Chinese were living in the Hwang Ho basin, and they had achieved an advanced stage of civilization by 1200 B.C. The great philosophers Lao-tse, Confucius, Mo Ti, and Mencius lived during the Chou dynasty (1122–249 B.C.). The warring feudal states were first united under Emperor Ch'in Shih Huang Ti, during whose reign (246–210 B.C.) work was begun on the Great Wall. Under the Han dynasty (206 B.C.-A.D. 220) China prospered and traded with the West.

In the T'ang dynasty (618–907), often called the golden age of Chinese history, painting, sculpture, and poetry flourished, and printing made its earliest known appearance.

The Mings, last of the native rulers (1368–1644), overthrew the Mongol, or Yuan, dynasty (1280–1368) established by Kublai Khan. The Mings in turn were overthrown in 1644 by invaders from the north, the Manchus.

China closely restricted foreign activities, and by the end of the 18th century only Canton and the Portuguese port of Macao were open to European merchants. Following the Anglo-Chinese War of 1839–42, however, several treaty ports were opened, and Hong Kong was ceded to Britain.

New Chinese Spelling

Starting in 1978, China has adopted a new system for spelling most Chinese names in the Roman alphabet. The Pinyin ("transcription") system will be used by *Information Please* for current names of people and places, with certain exceptions (e.g., *Tibet* rather than *Xizang* and *Peking* rather than *Beijing*). The new spelling is an attempt to use the Roman alphabet to render more precisely the sounds of Mandarin Chinese. A few letters in Pinyin have unique sounds: x, as in *she*; q, as in *cheek*; zh, as in *jump*.

Provinces and Regions of China

Name	Area (sq mi.)	Capital
Provinces		
Anhui (Anhwei)	54,015	Hefei (Hofei)
Fujian (Fukien)	47,529	Fuzhou (Fukien)
Gansu (Kansu)	137,104	Lanzhou (Lanchow)
Guangdong (Kwangtung)	89,344	Canton
Guizhou (Kweichow)	67,181	Guiyang (Kweiyang)
Hebei (Hopei)	81,479	Shijiazhuang (Shitikiachwang)
Heilongjiang (Heilungkiang)[1]	178,996	Harbin
Henan (Honan)	64,479	Zhengzhou (Chengchow)
Hubei (Hupeh)	72,394	Wuhan
Hunan	81,274	Changsha
Jiangsu (Kiangsu)	40,927	Nanjing (Nanking)
Jiangxi (Kiangsi)	63,629	Nanchang
Jilin (Kirin)[1]	72,201	Changchun
Liaoning[1]	53,301	Shenyang
Quinghai (Chinghai)	278,378	Xining (Sining)
Shaanxi (Shensi)	75,598	Xian (Sian)
Shandong (Shantung)	59,189	Jinan (Tsinan)
Shanxi (Shansi)	60,656	Taiyuan
Sichuan (Szechwan)	219,691	Chengdu (Chengtu)
Yunnan	168,417	Kunming
Zhejiang (Chekiang)	39,305	Hangzhou (Hangchow)
Autonomous Region		
Guangxi Zhuang (Kwangsi Chuang)	85,096	Nanning
Nei Monggol (Inner Mongolia)[1]	454,633	Hohhot (Huhehot)
Ningxia Hui	30,039	Yinchuan (Yinchwan)
Xinjiang Uygur (Sinkiang Uighur)[1]	635,829	Urumqi (Urumchi)
Xizang (Tibet)	471,660	Lhasa

1. Together constitute (with Taiwan) what has been traditionally known as Outer China, the remaining territory forming the historical China Proper. NOTE: Names are in Pinyin, with conventional spelling in parentheses.

Treaties signed after further hostilities (1856–60) weakened Chinese sovereignty and removed foreigners from Chinese jurisdiction. The disastrous Chinese-Japanese War of 1894–95 was followed by a scramble for Chinese concessions by European powers, leading to the Boxer Rebellion (1900), suppressed by an international force.

The death of the Empress Dowager Tzu Hsi in 1908 and the accession of the infant Emperor Hsüan T'ung (Pu-Yi) were followed by a nationwide rebellion led by Dr. Sun Yat-sen, who became first President of the Provisional Chinese Republic in 1911. The Manchus abdicated on Feb. 12, 1912. Dr. Sun resigned in favor of Yuan Shih-k'ai, who suppressed the republicans but was forced by a serious rising in 1915–16 to abandon his intention of declaring himself Emperor. Yuan's death in June 1916 was followed by years of civil war between rival militarists and Dr. Sun's republicans.

Nationalist forces, led by Gen. Chiang Kai-shek and with the advice of Communist experts, soon occupied most of China, setting up a Kuomintang regime in 1928. Internal strife continued, however, and Chiang broke with the Communists.

An alleged explosion on the South Manchurian Railway on Sept. 18, 1931, brought invasion of Manchuria by Japanese forces, who installed the last Manchu Emperor, Henry Pu-Yi, as nominal ruler of the puppet state of "Manchukuo." Japanese efforts to take China's northern provinces in July 1937 were resisted by Chiang, who meanwhile had succeeded in uniting most of China behind him.

Within two years, however, Japan seized most of the ports and railways. The Kuomintang government retreated first to Hankow and then to Chungking, while the Japanese set up a puppet government at Nanking headed by Wang Jingwei.

Japan's surrender in 1945 touched off civil war between Nationalist forces under Chiang and Communist forces led by Mao Zedong, the party chairman. Despite U. S. aid, the Chiang forces were overcome by the Maoists, backed by the Soviet bloc, and were expelled from the mainland. The Mao regime, established in Peking as the new capital, proclaimed the People's Republic of China on Oct. 1, 1949, with Zhou Enlai Premier.

The soviet-type government, after prolonged negotiations, signed a 30-year treaty of friendship and mutual aid with the U.S.S.R. on Feb. 14, 1950. Its published terms provided for return of the Changchun railroad to China and the eventual return of Port Arthur and Dairen, occupied by Soviet troops. Later in the year, Chinese troops invaded Tibet and began its subjugation, a campaign that brought China into conflict with India. After the Korean War began in June 1950, China led the Communist bloc in supporting North Korea, and on Nov. 26, 1950, the Mao regime intervened openly.

A deterioration of relations between Peking and Moscow was indicated in 1958 when Peking emerged as an independent center of Communist power, challenging the leadership role of the U.S.S.R. in the Soviet bloc.

In 1958, Mao undertook the "Great Leap Forward" campaign, which combined the establishment of rural communes with a crash program of village industrialization. These efforts also failed, causing Mao to lose influence to Liu Shaoqi, who became President in 1959, to Premier Zhou, and to Party Secretary Deng Xiaoping. Meanwhile China's backing of subversive movements in Asia soured relations with India and Burma, although it very nearly achieved the conquest of Indonesia, and culminated in war on the borders of India late in 1962. By the next year, the break with the U.S.S.R. was complete.

Zhou proposed the movement that became known as the Cultural Revolution at the party congress in 1964, the same year China exploded its first atomic (fission) bomb (it produced a fusion bomb in 1967).

Mao moved to Shanghai, and from that base he and his supporters waged their own Cultural Revolution. President Liu and the party secretary, Deng, took over, and their followers denounced hundreds of party and government officials at rallies and in wall posters. Then, in 1966, Chen became director of the Cultural Revolution; the Army Chief of Staff, Lo Ruiqing, was purged; and Lin replaced Liu as second in the hierarchy. In the spring of 1966 the Mao group formed Red Guard units dominated by youths and students, closing the schools to free the students for agitation.

The Red Guards campaigned against "old ideas, old culture, old habits, and old customs." Often they were no more than uncontrolled mobs, and brutality was frequent. Early in 1967 efforts were made to restore control. The Red Guards were urged to return home. Schools started opening. But the height of violence was only reached in September 1967 when in Canton the opposing factions used tanks and artillery against each other.

Persistent overtures by the Nixon Administration (relaxed trade and travel restrictions) abruptly climaxed in an invitation to a U.S. table tennis team to visit Peking in April 1971. This was followed by the dramatic announcement in July that Henry Kissinger, Mr. Nixon's national security adviser, had secretly visited Peking and reached agreement on a visit by the President to China.

The movement toward reconciliation, which signaled the end of the U.S. containment policy toward China, provided irresistible momentum for Chinese admission to the U.N. Despite U.S. opposition to expelling Taiwan (Nationalist China), the world body overwhelmingly ousted Chiang in seating Peking.

Mr. Nixon went to Peking for a week early in 1972, meeting Mao as well as Chou. The summit ended with a historic communiqué on February 28, in which both nations promised to work toward improved relations. They differed over Vietnam as well as Taiwan, although the U.S. noted it was withdrawing from Vietnam and said its ultimate goal was withdrawal from Taiwan as well, with interim reductions of those forces as tension in the area diminished.

In 1973, the U.S. and China agreed to set up "liaison offices" in each other's capitals, which constituted de facto diplomatic relations. Full diplomatic relations were barred by China as long as the U.S. continued to recognize Nationalist China.

The National People's Congress held its first meeting in a decade in Peking, Jan. 13–17, 1975. With Mao absent, it re-elected Zhou as Premier. It approved a government realignment that placed Marshal Ye Jianying in the post of Defense Minister, vacant since Lin's death. It revised the 1954 Constitution to reassert the primacy of the Communist Party and to specify limited rights of citizens to strike and demonstrate, to hold private farm plots, and to work for themselves.

Zhou predicted in a keynote address that "fierce contention" between the U.S. and the U.S.S.R. "is bound to lead to world war some day." He said there is "no détente, let alone lasting peace in the world today."

The same warnings against détente were made during President Ford's visit to China, Dec. 8–12, 1975, by Vice Premier Deng Xiaoping. Deng served as chief host because Zhou was now seriously ill with cancer and Mao, visibly failing, saw the visitor only briefly.

On Jan. 8, 1976, amid a national outpouring of grief, Zhou died. Demonstrations in the capital turned into near riots when mourners suspected the government of trying to suppress the display of emotion. Deng, who had been rehabilitated by Zhou and designated as his successor, was supplanted within a month by Hua Guofeng, former Minister of Public Security. Hua, believed to be a compromise between radicals and the moderates represented by the ousted Deng, became permanent Premier in April. In October he was named successor to Mao as Chairman of the Communist Party.

Mao died September 10, apparently of Parkinson's disease, and China for the second time in a year went into a period of national mourning. Almost immediately afterward, a campaign against his widow, Jiang Qing, and three of her "radical" colleagues began. The "Gang of Four" was denounced for having undermined the party, the government, and the economy.

Jiang was brought to trial in 1980 and sentenced on Jan. 25, 1981, to die within two years unless she showed repentance, in which case she would be imprisoned for life. She showed no remorse at the trial, shouting defiance as she was taken away.

While the despised four were reviled throughout China, there was evidence by late 1976 that Deng was to be rehabilitated. At the Central Committee meeting of 1977, Deng was reinstated as Deputy Premier, Chief of Staff of the Army, and member of the Central Committee of the Politburo. He was ranked behind Ye Jianying, the Defense Minister, in the third-ranking place in the government.

At the same time, Jiang Qing, Wang Hongwen, Zhang Chunqiao, and Yao Wenyuan—the notorious "Gang of Four"—were removed from all official posts and banished from the party. The final resolution of the committee meeting declared national unity restored and "a new leap forward taking shape in the national economy."

In August 1977, the 11th national Communist Party Congress and the election of a new Politburo took place as U.S. Secretary of State Cyrus Vance visited China to call for efforts by both China and the U.S. to normalize relations.

The Fifth National People's Congress adopted a new Constitution on March 5, 1978, strengthening civil rights such as free speech and the right to file complaints against the government. The Congress also approved a 10-year plan to increase farm production and add 120 industrial complexes to the nation's industrial base. Hua Guofeng was affirmed as Premier despite rumors that Deputy Premier Deng might take the post.

In May 1978, expulsion of ethnic Chinese by Vietnam produced an open rupture. China withdrew aid technicians and announced a complete cutoff, disclosing for the first time that it had given

$10 billion to Vietnam in the past 20 years. Peking sided with Cambodia in the border fighting that flared between Vietnam and Cambodia, charging Hanoi with aggression.

On Aug. 12, 1978, China and Japan signed a treaty of peace and friendship, a treaty attacked by Moscow as hostile to the Soviet Union. Peking and Washington then announced that they would open full diplomatic relations on Jan. 1, 1979. Over Congressional objections, the Carter administration abrogated the Taiwan defense treaty, the last obstacle to full relations. Deputy Premier Deng sealed the agreement with a visit to the United States that coincided with the opening of embassies in both capitals on March 1.

Peking protested Congressional guarantees of Taiwan's defense that were inserted in legislation governing future U.S. relations with the island. The Chinese nevertheless went ahead with the drafting of a trade pact that gave them most-favored-nation status. China agreed to pay $80 million compensation for American property seized after the 1949 Communist take-over of the mainland.

A near proxy war with the Soviet Union erupted on Deng's return from the U.S. as 200,000 to 300,000 Chinese troops invaded Vietnam to avenge alleged violations of Chinese territory. The action was seen as more a reaction to Vietnam's invasion of Cambodia, where China had been the dominant outside influence since 1975. While the Soviet Union stepped up supply airlifts, the Chinese inflicted damage on the northern border, then withdrew.

At home, a political trend that had seen a "freedom wall" in Peking where individuals could publish their opinions without censorship was dampened. But if individual expression was curbed, the leadership encouraged a radical shift from traditional Marxism toward private enterprise in every phase of the national economy.

The first People's Congress in five years marked the culmination of Deng's post-Mao modernization efforts. On Sept. 10, the Congress confirmed Zhao Ziyang, an economic planner, as Premier replacing Hua Guofeng, who had held the post since 1976. Hua retained his chairmanship of the Communist Party.

At the Central Committee meeting of June 27–29, 1981, another Deng protégé, Hu Yaobang, was elevated to the party chairmanship and Hua retired. The 66-year-old Hu had served as party Secretary-General, a post he retained. Deng became chairman of the military commission of the central committee, giving him control over the army. The committee's 215 members concluded the session with a statement holding Mao Zedong responsible for the "grave blunder" of the Cultural Revolution.

Teng's triumph was somewhat dulled by the recognition that his modernization program had outpaced Chinese resources. The 1981 budget had to be reduced by $9.8 billion to $64.6 billion, cutting capital spending for oil and coal production and even for defense. Inflation was blamed for casualties such as the Baoshan steel plant in Shanghai, which was to have been a showpiece of industrial modernization.

Despite economic problems, U.S.-China trade was expected to total $6 billion in 1981, up from $4.3 billion in 1980 and $2.3 billion the year before. Diplomatic relations continued to develop as Secretary of State Alexander M. Haig, Jr., announced during a visit to Peking, June 14–16, that

the Reagan administration would remove restrictions to permit China to buy U.S. weapons and high-technology equipment. At the end of his visit, it was announced that Premier Zhao Ziyang would visit Washington in 1982.

CHINA (TAIWAN)

Republic of China
President: Chiang Ching-kuo (1978)
Premier: Sun Yun-hsuan (1978)
Area: 13,592 sq mi. (35,203 sq km)[1]
Population (est. 1981): 18,000,000 (growth rate, 2.0%)
Density per square mile: 1,324.3
Capital: Taipei
Largest cities (est. 1980): Taipei, 2,225,000; Kaohsiung, 1,063,000; Taichung, 579,000; Tainan, 557,000; Chilung (Keelung), 342,300.
Monetary unit: New Taiwan dollar
Language: Chinese (Mandarin) and various dialects
Religions: Confucianist, Buddhist, Christian, Taoist
Freedom House classifications: Capitalist-statist industrial, dominant party
Economic summary: Gross national product (1979): $32 billion. Average annual growth rate (1970–77): 5.5%. Per capita income: $1,170. Labor force in agriculture: 22%; principal products: rice, sweet potatoes, sugar cane, bananas, pineapples, citrus fruits. Labor force in industry: 42%; major products: textiles, clothing, chemicals, processed foods, electronic equipment, cement, ships, plywood. Natural resources: timber, camphor. Exports: textiles, electrical machinery, plywood. Imports: machinery, basic metals, crude oil, chemicals. Major trading partners: U.S., Japan.

1. Excluding Quemoy and Matsu.

Geography. The Republic of China today consists of the former Taiwan Province, including Taiwan, an island 100 miles (161 km) off the Asian mainland in the Pacific; two offshore islands, Quemoy and Matsu; and the nearby islets of the Pescadores chain. It is slightly larger than the combined areas of Massachusetts and Connecticut.

The country is divided by a central mountain range that runs from north to south, rising sharply on the east coast and descending gradually to a broad western plain, where cultivation is concentrated.

Government. The President and the Vice President are elected by the National Assembly for a term of six years. There are five major governing bodies called Yuans: Executive, Legislative, Judicial, Control, and Examination. Taiwan's internal affairs are administered by the Taiwan Provincial Government under the supervision of the Provincial Assembly, which is popularly elected.

The majority and ruling party is the Kuomintang (Nationalist Party) led by President Chiang Ching-kuo. There are also two minority parties: the China Democratic Socialist Party and the Young China Party.

History. Taiwan was inhabited by aborigines of Malayan descent when Chinese from the areas now designated as Fukien and Kwangtung began settling it beginning in the 7th century, becoming the majority.

The Portuguese explored the area in 1590, naming it The Beautiful (Formosa). In 1624 the Dutch set up forts in the south, the Spanish in the North. The Dutch threw out the Spanish in 1641 and controlled the island until 1661, when the Chinese General Koxinga took it over, established an independent kingdom, and expelled the Dutch. The Manchus seized the island in 1683 and held it until 1895, when it passed to Japan after the first Sino-Japanese War. Japan developed and exploited it, and it was heavily bombed by American planes during World War II, after which it was restored to China.

After the defeat of its armies on the mainland, the Nationalist Government of Generalissimo Chiang Kai-shek retreated to Taiwan in December 1949. With only 15% of the population consisting of the 1949 immigrants, Chiang dominated the island, maintaining a 600,000-man army in the hope of eventually recovering the mainland. Japan renounced its claim to the island by the San Francisco Peace Treaty of 1951.

By stationing a fleet in the Strait of Formosa the U.S. prevented a mainland invasion in 1953, and in 1955 the U.S. signed a mutual defense treaty by which it is committed to defend Taiwan and the neighboring islands.

The "China seat" in the U.N., which the Nationalists held with U.S. help for over two decades, was lost in October 1971, when the People's Republic of China was admitted and Taiwan ousted by the world body.

President Nixon's summit meeting with Chinese leaders and the 1972 Sino-American communiqué further eroded Taiwan's position. In it, the U.S. said its eventual goal was complete withdrawal of its forces from Taiwan and progressive cutbacks as tensions in the area eased. With the end of U.S. participation in the war in Vietnam, withdrawal of U.S. air-support forces on the island began in 1973.

Chiang died at 87 of a heart attack on April 5, 1975. His son, Chiang Ching-kuo, continued as Premier and dominant power in the Taipei regime. He assumed the presidency in 1978, and Sun Yun-suan became Premier.

President Carter's announcement that the U.S. would recognize only the People's Republic of China after Jan. 1, 1979, and that the U.S. defense treaty would end aroused protests in Taiwan and in the U.S. Congress. Against Carter's wishes, Congress, in a bill governing future relations with Taiwan, guaranteed U.S. action in the event of an attack on the island. The legislation also provided for the continuation of trade and other relations through an American Institute in Taipei, housed in the former American Embassy.

COLOMBIA

Republic of Colombia
President: Julio César Turbay Ayala (1978)
Area: 455,355 sq mi. (1,179,369 sq km)
Population (est. 1981): 28,500,000 (growth rate, 2.1%) (mestizo, 68%; white, 20%; Indian, 7%; black, 5%)
Density per square mile: 62.5
Capital: Bogotá
Largest cities (est. 1980): Bogotá, 4,300,000; Medellín,

1,748,000; Cali, 1,189,000; Baranquilla, 868,000; Bucaramanga, 443,000; Cartagena, 355,000
Monetary unit: Peso
Language: Spanish
Religion: Roman Catholic
National name: República de Colombia
Freedom House classifications: Capitalist industrial, multi-party centralized
Economic summary: Gross national product (1979): $26.4 billion. Average annual growth rate (1970–78): 3.6%. Per capita income: $830. Land used for agriculture: 30%; labor force: 30%; principal products: coffee, bananas, rice, corn, sugar cane, cotton, tobacco, flowers. Labor force in industry: 15%; major products: textiles, processed food, clothing and footwear, beverages, chemicals, metal products, cement. Natural resources: petroleum, natural gas, coal, iron ore, nickel, gold, copper, emeralds. Exports: coffee, agricultural products, apparel, chemicals, metals. Imports: machinery, electrical equipment, chemical products, metals and metal products, transport equipment. Major trading partners: U.S., West Germany, Japan, Venezuela, Netherlands.

Geography. Colombia, in the northwestern part of South America, is the only country on that continent that borders on both the Atlantic and Pacific Oceans. It is nearly equal to the combined areas of California and Texas.

Through the western half of the country, three Andean ranges run north and south, merging into one at the Ecuadorean border. The eastern half is a low, jungle-covered plain, drained by spurs of the Amazon and Orinoco, inhabited mostly by isolated, tropical-forest Indian tribes. The fertile plateau and valley of the eastern range are the most densely populated parts of the country.

Government. Colombia's President, who appoints his own Cabinet, serves for a four-year term. The Senate, the upper house of Congress, has 112 members elected for four years by direct vote. The Chamber of Deputies of 199 members is directly elected for four years.

The major political parties are the Liberal Party (62 of 112 seats in Senate, 112 of 199 seats in House), Conservative Party (49 seats in Senate, 83 seats in House), and National Opposition Union, a leftist coalition (1 seat in Senate, 4 seats in House).

History. Spaniards in 1510 founded Darien, the first permanent European settlement on the American mainland. In 1538 the Spaniards established the colony of New Granada, the area's name until 1861. After a 14-year struggle, in which Simón Bolívar's Venezuelan troops won the battle of Boyacá in Colombia on Aug. 7, 1819, independence was attained in 1824. Bolívar united Colombia, Venezuela, Panama, and Ecuador in the Republic of Greater Colombia (1819–30), but lost Venezuela and Ecuador to separatists. Bolívar's Vice President, Francisco de Paula Santander, founded the Liberal Party as the Federalists while Bolívar established the Conservatives as the Centralists.

Santander's presidency (1832–36) re-established order, but later periods of Liberal dominance (1849–57 and 1861–80), when the Liberals sought to disestablish the Roman Catholic Church, were marked by insurrection and even civil war. Rafael Nuñez, in a 15-year-presidency, restored the power of the central government and the church, which led in 1899 to a bloody civil war and the loss in 1903 of Panama over ratification of a lease to the

U.S. of the Canal Zone. For 21 years, until 1930, the Conservatives held power as revolutionary pressures built up.

The Liberal administrations of Enrique Olaya Herrera and Alfonso López (1930–38) were marked by social reforms that failed to solve the country's problems, and in 1946, insurrection and banditry broke out, claiming hundreds of thousands of lives by 1958. Laureano Gómez (1950–53); the Army Chief of Staff, Gen. Gustavo Rojas Pinilla (1953–56), and a military junta (1956–57) sought to curb disorder by repression.

Subsequent Presidents were Alberto Lleras Camargo (1957–62); Guillermo León Valencia (1962–66); Carlos Lleras Restrepo (1966–70); Misael Pastrana Borrero (1970–74); and Alfonso López Michelson (1974–78).

Julio César Turbay Ayala, Liberal Party candidate in 1978, won a narrow victory—approximately 140,000 of a total of nearly 2.5 million votes—over the Conservative Party candidate. The Liberals also retained control of both the Senate and House.

Government hopes to suppress the Movement of April 19 (M-19), an urban guerrilla organization which had threatened public order, rose with the capture of 74 members of the group in a battle with army troops on the Ecuador border on March 18, 1981. Included in the captives and 19 killed were believed to be the top leadership, some of whom confessed that they had been trained in Cuba. Turbay suspended diplomatic relations with Cuba in protest and prepared an amnesty program offering freedom for M-19 and other rebels who turned in their weapons. As the amnesty deadline approached, M-19 bands combined with the older, pro-Soviet Colombian Armed Revolutionary Forces (FARC) to seize control of much of Caqueta province 230 miles south of Bogotá. As Turbay prepared to report to Congress on the failure of the amnesty offer, three M-19 mortar rounds struck the Presidential palace.

COMOROS

Federal and Islamic Republic of the Comoros
President: Ahmed Abdallah (1978)
Premier: Salim Ben Ali (1978)
Area: 692 sq mi. (1,792 sq km)
Population (est. 1981): 330,000 (growth rate, 2.8%)
Density per square mile: 476.9
Capital and largest city (est. 1979): Moroni (on Grande Comoro), 16,000
Monetary unit: Franc CFA
Language: French
Religions: Islam and Christian
National name: État Comorien
Freedom House classifications: Capitalist pre-industrial, non-party non-military
Economic summary: Gross national product (1979): $90 million. Average annual growth rate (1970–78): −5.3%. Per capita income: $153. Principal agricultural products: perfume essences, copra, coconuts, cloves, vanilla, cinnamon, yams; major industrial products: perfume distillations. Exports: perfume essences, vanilla, copra, cloves. Imports: foodstuffs, fuels, chemicals, cotton textiles, cement. Major trading partners: France, Madagascar, U.S., West Germany, Kenya, Italy.

Geography. The Comoros Islands—Grande Comoro, Anjouan, Mohéli, and Mayotte (which retains ties to France)—are an archipelago of volcanic origin in the Indian Ocean between Mozambique and Madagascar.

Government. A coup by foreign mercenaries on May 13, 1978, deposed President Ali Soilih, who had held power since 1975. A "political and military directorate" headed by Ahmed Abdallah and Mohammed Ahmed governed until the adoption of a constitution on Oct. 1 ushered in a republic. With the resignation of Ahmed two days later, Abdallah became president.

History. Under French rule since 1886, the Comoros declared themselves independent July 6, 1975. However, Mayotte, with a Christian majority, voted against joining the other, mainly Islamic, islands, in the move to independence and remains French.

A month after independence, Justice Minister Ali Soilih staged a coup with the help of mercenaries, overthrowing the new nation's first president, Ahmed Abdallah. Soilih lowered the voting age to 14, destroyed all records and killed many Comorans. He was overthrown on May 13, 1978, when a small boatload of French mercenaries, some of whom had aided him three years earlier, seized government headquarters.

CONGO

People's Republic of the Congo
President: Col. Denis Sassou-Nguessou (1979)
Prime Minister: Col. Louis-Sylvain Ngoma (1975)
Area: 132,046 sq mi. (342,000 sq km)
Population (est. 1981): 1,580,000 (growth rate, 2.8%)
Density per sq mi.: 12.0
Capital and largest city (est. 1977): Brazzaville, 310,000
Monetary unit: Franc CFA
Ethnic groups: Vilis, Bakongo, Batekes, Mbochis
Languages: French, Lingala, Kokongo
Religions: Animist, 60%; Roman Catholic, 38%
National name: République Populaire du Congo
Member of French Community
Freedom House classifications: Capitalist-socialist pre-industrial, one-party socialist.
Economic summary: Gross national product (1979): $950 million. Average annual growth rate (1970–78): 0.2%. Per capita income: $490. Principal agricultural products: sugar cane, wood, coffee, cocoa, peanuts, tobacco. Labor force in industry: 20%; major products: crude oil, cigarettes, soap, beverages, milled sugar. Natural resources: wood, potash, petroleum, natural gas. Exports: oil, lumber, tobacco, veneer and plywood. Imports: machinery, transportation equipment, manufactured consumer goods, iron and steel, foodstuffs. Major trading partners: France and other Western European countries.

Geography. The Congo is situated in west central Africa astride the Equator. It borders on Gabon, Cameroon, the Central African Republic, Zaire, and the Angola exclave of Cabinda, with a short stretch of coast on the South Atlantic. Its area is nearly three times that of Pennsylvania.

Most of the inland is tropical rain forest, drained

by tributaries of the Zaire (Congo) River, which flows south along the eastern border with Zaire to Stanley Pool. The narrow coastal plain rises to highlands separated from the inland plateaus by the 200-mile-wide Niari River Valley, which gives passage to the coast.

Government. Since the coup of September 1968 the country has been governed by a National Council of the Revolution. The Congolese Labor Party is the only party.

History. The inhabitants of the former French Congo, mainly Bantu peoples with Pygmies in the north, were subjects of several kingdoms in earlier times.

The Frenchman Pierre Savorgnan de Brazza signed a treaty with Makoko, ruler of the Bateke people, in 1880, which established French control. The area, with Gabon and Ubangi-Shari, was constituted the colony of French Equatorial Africa in 1910. It joined Chad in supporting the Free French cause in World War II. The Congo proclaimed its independence without leaving the French Community in 1960.

Maj. Marien Ngouabi, head of the National Council of the Revolution, took power as president on Jan. 1, 1969. He was sworn in for a second five-year term in 1975. A visit to Moscow by Ngouabi in March ended with the signing of a Soviet-Congolese economic and technical aid pact.

A four-man commando squad assassinated Ngouabi in Brazzaville on March 18, 1977. Five days later the assassination of Émile Cardinal Biayenda, Archbishop of Brazzaville, was announced. Former President Alphonse Massamba-Débat, accused of plotting both deaths, was executed.

Col. Joachim Yhombi-Opango, Army Chief of Staff, assumed the presidency on April 4. In June, the new government agreed to resume diplomatic relations with the U.S., ending a 12-year rift. Yombhi-Opango resigned on Feb. 4, 1979, and was replaced by Col. Denis Sassou-Nguessou.

COSTA RICA

Republic of Costa Rica
President: Rodrigo Carazo Odio (1978)
Area: 19,652 sq mi. (50,898 sq km)
Population (est. 1981): 2,300,000 (growth rate, 2.6%)
Density per square mile: 117.0
Capital and largest city (est. 1980 for metropolitan area): San José, 635,000
Monetary unit: Colón
Language: Spanish
Religion: Roman Catholic
National name: República de Costa Rica
Freedom House classifications: Capitalist industrial, multi-party centralized
Economic summary: Gross national product (1979): $3.9 billion. Average annual growth rate (1970–78): 3.3%. Per capita income: $1,370. Labor force in agriculture: 33%; principal products: bananas, coffee, sugar cane, rice, corn, cocoa, livestock. Labor force in industry: 20%; major products: processed foods, textiles and clothing, construction materials, fertilizer. Natural resource: timber. Exports: coffee, bananas, beef, sugar, cacao.

Imports: manufactured products, machinery, transportation equipment, chemicals, foodstuffs, fuels, fertilizer. Major trading partners: U.S., Central American countries, West Germany, Japan.

Geography. This Central American country lies between Nicaragua to the north and Panama to the south. Its area slightly exceeds that of Vermont and New Hampshire combined.

Most of Costa Rica is tableland, from 3,000 to 6,000 feet (914 to 1,829 m) above sea level. Cocos Island (10 sq mi.) (26 sq km), about 300 miles (483 km) off the Pacific Coast, is under Costa Rican sovereignty; although it is mostly tropical jungle, it is of potential strategic importance in defense of the Panama Canal.

Government. Under the 1949 Constitution, the president and the one-house Legislative Assembly of 57 members are elected for terms of four years.

The army was abolished in 1949. There is a civil guard of 3,000 and a rural guard of 2,500.

The major political parties are Unity Party (27 of 57 seats in Legislative Assembly), led by Rafael A. Grillo; National Liberation Party (25 seats), led by Armando Arauz; Pueblo Unido Party (3 seats), led by Humberto Vargas Carbonel; Agricola Cartagines Party (1 seat), led by Martin Brenes; Frente Popular Party (1 seat), led by Dr. Rodolfo Cerdas Cruz.

History. Costa Rica was inhabited by 25,000 Indians when Columbus discovered it and probably named it in 1502. Few of the Indians survived the Spanish conquest, which began in 1563. The region was administered as a Spanish province. Costa Rica achieved independence in 1821 but was absorbed for two years by Agustín de Iturbide in his Mexican Empire. It was established as a republic in 1848.

Except for the military dictatorship of Tomás Guardia from 1870 to 1882, Costa Rica has enjoyed one of the most democratic governments in Latin America.

On Feb. 5, 1978, Rodrigo Carazo Odio, leader of a four-party opposition coalition called the Unity Party, defeated the candidate of the ruling National Liberation Party. His victory was attributed partly to the fact that the government had granted protection to Robert L. Vesco, a fugitive U.S. financier. On his inauguration in May, Carazo ordered that Vesco be barred from Costa Rica.

CUBA

Republic of Cuba
President (1976) and Premier (1959): Fidel Castro
Area: 44,218 sq mi. (114,524 sq km)
Population (est. 1981): 9,900,000 (growth rate, 1.1%)
Density per square mile: 223.9
Capital: Havana
Largest cities (est. 1979): Havana, 2,000,000; (est. 1975 by U.N.): Santiago de Cuba, 315,800; Camagüey, 221,800; Holguín, 151,900; Guantánamo, 148,800; Santa Clara, 146,650
Monetary unit: Peso
Language: Spanish
Religion: Roman Catholic
National name: República de Cuba

Freedom House classifications: Socialist industrial, one-party communist

Economic summary: Gross national product (1979): $13.9 billion. Average annual growth rate (1970–78): 4.7%. Per capita income (constant 1957 prices): $840. Land used for agriculture: 65%; labor force: 33%; principal products: sugar, tobacco, coffee, rice, meat, vegetables, fruits. Labor force in industry: 17%; major products: refined oil products, textiles, chemicals, processed food, metals, light consumer products. Natural resources: metals, primarily nickel. Exports: sugar, textiles, chemicals, tobacco, fish, rum, fruits. Imports: capital equipment, raw materials, petroleum, consumer products. Major trading partners: U.S.S.R., other Communist bloc countries.

Geography. The largest island of the West Indies group (equal in area to Pennsylvania), Cuba is also the westernmost—just west of Hispaniola (Haiti and the Dominican Republic), and 90 miles (145 km) south of Key West, Fla., at the entrance to the Gulf of Mexico.

The island has mountainous areas in the southeast, central area, and the west (Sierra Maestra). The rest of the country is flat or rolling.

Government. There have been no national elections since 1958. Fidel Castro heads the Council of Ministers, the chief governing body.

The only political party is the Cuban Communist Party, with a 100–member Central Committee; the power rests with a Politbureau of 8 and a Secretariat of 6.

History. Cuba was occupied by the Arawak Indians when Columbus discovered the island in 1492; they died off from diseases brought by sailors and settlers. By 1511, Spaniards under Diego Velásquez were founding settlements that served as bases for Spanish exploration. Cuba soon after served as an assembly point for treasure looted by the conquistadores, attracting French and English pirates.

Black slaves and free laborers were imported to work sugar and tobacco plantations, and waves of chiefly Spanish immigrants maintained a European character in the island's culture. Early slave rebellions and conflicts between colonials and Spanish rulers laid the foundation for an independence movement that turned into open warfare from 1867 to 1878. The poet, José Marti, in 1895 led the struggle that finally ended Spanish rule, thanks largely to U.S. intervention in 1898 after the sinking of the battleship *Maine* in Havana harbor.

An 1899 treaty made Cuba an independent republic under U.S. protection. The U.S. occupation, which ended in 1902, suppressed yellow fever and brought large American investment. From 1906 to 1909, Washington invoked the Platt Amendment to the treaty, which gave it the right to intervene in order to suppress any revolt. U.S. troops came back in 1912 and again in 1917 to restore order.

Gerardo Machado, President during the Depression, planned vast social reforms but abandoned them. The U.S., under President Franklin D. Roosevelt, scrapped the Platt Amendment in 1934. Fulgencio Batista, an army sergeant, led a revolt in 1934 that overthrew the Machado regime and developed into a Batista dictatorship. A succession of constitutionally elected Presidents—Ramón Grau San Martín, Carlos Mendieta, Miguel Mariano Gómez, Carlos Prío Socarrás—pushed through social reforms, hampered by overwhelming corruption manipulated by Batista, who seized power in 1952.

Fidel Castro staged a hopeless revolt in 1953. Captured and paroled, he went to Oriente Province and, aided by an Argentinian adventurer, Ernesto (Ché) Guevara, rebuilt his forces and waged a guerrilla war. The U.S. withdrew support from Batista in 1958. With funds from Soviet sources, Castro bought off the leaders of Batista's army. This and popular support from the intellectual and laboring classes demoralized the army, and Castro's forces grew as he marched on Havana. Batista fled to the Dominican Republic on Jan. 1, 1959.

Executions and torture by the new Castro regime caused a world outcry. Castro antagonized the U.S. in 1959 by confiscating U.S. investments in banks and industries and by seizing large U.S. landholdings, turning them at first into collective farms, then into Soviet-type state farms.

The U.S. broke off relations on Jan. 3, 1961, and Castro disclosed his alliance with the U.S.S.R. and the Soviet bloc. Thousands of Cubans fled to the U.S. From their ranks an invasion force was recruited by an all-party coalition financed and guided by the U.S. Central Intelligence Agency and trained in Florida and Guatemala. It landed in the Bay of Pigs, Cuba, on April 17, 1961, but when President Kennedy refused it air support under Soviet and Latin American pressure, the effort collapsed.

In 1962 the U.S.S.R. built missile sites in Cuba and provided Castro's army with troops, planes, and submarines. Alarmed, Kennedy on Oct. 22, 1962, served notice that the U.S. was willing to risk war to enforce a demand that the Soviet Union remove weapons and troops considered to threaten U.S. security. The U.S. confronted Soviet vessels with U.S. warships. Soviet Premier Nikita Khrushchev agreed to remove the missiles, and the blockade was lifted on November 20. Shortly before Christmas, Castro released 1,113 Bay of Pigs prisoners.

Russia, spending over $1 million a day (about $400 million a year) to keep Cuba afloat, had to increase its contribution by over $100 million in 1971, but gained greater control over Cuba's economy by setting up a joint Soviet-Cuban economic commission on management and efficiency.

Neither nation formally admitted it, but U.S.-Cuban relations began to thaw with negotiation of a 1973 agreement to end air hijacking. Except for political refugees, criminal hijackers will be extradited to their home country or tried for the crime where they land; also, both nations pledged to forbid attacks on the other to be mounted from their territory.

In 1975, both sides signaled readiness to improve relations. U.S. curbs on travel by Cuba'a United Nations delegation were eased and the U.S. joined 15 Latin American republics in voting to scrap economic and diplomatic sanctions the O.A.S. had imposed against Cuba in 1964.

The improving U.S.-Cuban climate cooled in late 1975 with the disclosure that Cuban troops were aiding the Popular Movement for the Liberation of Angola as the Marxist organization fought to gain control of the former Portuguese African colony. Despite Cuba's intervention in Africa, the Carter administration signed fishing agreements with Havana in 1977, removed restrictions on travel to the island, and eased the 1960 embargo to permit Cuba to buy essential goods.

In September 1977, Cuban diplomats opened an interests section in the old Cuban embassy in

Washington and 10 Americans—later 20—opened a similar office in the former U.S. embassy in Havana. Hopes that full diplomatic relations would be restored were shattered early in 1978 when Washington charged that 10,000 to 11,000 Cubans were fighting for the Marxist government of Ethiopia. Castro himself denied taking any part in the 1978 invasion of Zaire staged from Angola, but U.S. intelligence sources said a total of 40,000 Cuban troops were serving in Africa and had suffered 1,500 casualties.

Late in 1978, Castro offered to free 3,600 remaining political prisoners if the U.S. would accept them, to which he later added 7,000 former prisoners and up to 50,000 persons having relatives living abroad. Small numbers began to leave, but both Castro and Cuban exiles complained that U.S. immigration processing was too slow.

Emigration increased dramatically after April 1, 1980, when Castro, irritated at the granting of asylum to would-be refugees by the Peruvian embassy, removed the guards and allowed 10,000 Cubans to swarm into the embassy grounds. As an airlift began taking them to Costa Rica for distribution to other countries, Castro insisted that they must go directly to their final destination. When he ordered the port of Mariel opened and a "freedom flotilla" of small boats from the U.S. arrived to find that the government had consigned criminals, homosexuals, and others considered undesirable to be taken along with relatives of Cuban-Americans. The total of departures soared past 125,000 despite efforts by the Carter administration to halt the traffic and it was not until Castro, embarrassed by the reported application of 1 million Cubans to join the exodus, closed the port Sept. 26.

At the second party Congress, Dec. 17–20, Castro threatened to reopen Mariel if the U.S. did not cooperate in solving future immigration problems. He pronounced Cuba willing to improve relations with the new Reagan administration but received no encouragement. Secretary of State Alexander M. Haig, Jr., early declared Cuba a proxy for Soviet subversion of the nations of the Caribbean. The State Department later named Cuba as the principal source of arms and training for the leftist guerrillas in El Salvador, apparently foreclosing a rapprochement. Castro, however, after confessing to economic difficulties at the party Congress, announced in June that limited foreign investment would be accepted in order to attract hard currency needed to pay a current foreign debt of $2.9 billion.

CYPRUS

Republic of Cyprus
President: Spyros Kyprianou (1977)
Area: 3,572 sq mi (9,251 sq km)
Population (est. 1981): 635,000 (growth rate, 0.8%) (Greek, 82%, Turkish, 18%)
Density per square mile: 177.8
Capital and largest city (est. 1978): Nicosia, 160,000
Monetary unit: Cyprus pound
Languages: Greek, Turkish, English
Religions: Greek Orthodox, 77%; Islam, 18%
National name: Kypriaki Dimokratia—Kibris Cumhuriyeti
Member of Commonwealth of Nations

Freedom House classifications: Capitalist industrial, multi-party decentralized
Economic summary: Gross national product (1979): $1.9 billion. Average annual growth rate (1970–78): 1.4%. Per capita income: $1,580. Land used for agriculture: 47%; labor force: 36%; principal products: vine products, citrus, potatoes, other vegetables. Labor force in industry: 47%; major products: beverages, footwear, clothing, cement, asbestos mining. Natural resources: copper, asbestos, gypsum, building stone, marble, clay, salt. Exports: asbestos, copper, pyrites, citrus, raisins. Imports: manufactured goods, machinery and transportation equipment, petroleum products, foodstuffs. Major trading partners: U.K., Saudi Arabia, Italy, Greece, U.S., Syria, Lebanon, Libya.

Geography. The third largest island in the Mediterranean (one and one half times the size of Delaware), Cyprus lies off the southern coast of Turkey and the western shore of Syria. Most of the country consists of a wide plain lying between two mountain ranges that cross the island. The highest peak is Mount Olympus at 6,406 feet (1,953 m).

Government. Under the republic's Constitution, for the protection of the Turkish minority the vice president as well as three of the 10 Cabinet ministers must be from the Turkish community, while the House of Representatives is elected by each community separately, 70% Greek Cypriote and 30% Turkish Cypriote representatives.

The Greek and Turkish communities are self-governing in questions of religion, education, and culture. Other governmental matters are under the jurisdiction of the central government. Each community is entitled to a Communal Chamber.

The Greek Communal Chamber, which had 23 members, was abolished in 1965 and its function was absorbed by the Ministry of Education. The Turkish Communal Chamber, however, has continued to function.

The following is a breakdown of the 35 seats held by Greeks: Democratic Front of Spyros Kyprianou (18); AKEL Progressive Party of the Working People (12); Democratic Rally (12); Socialist Party of Dr. Vassos Lyssarides (3). The 15 Turkish members have not attended sessions of the House since 1964.

History. Cyprus was the site of early Phoenician and Greek colonies. For centuries its rule passed through many hands. It fell to the Turks in 1571, and a large Turkish colony settled on the island.

In World War I, on the outbreak of hostilities with Turkey, Britain annexed the island. It was declared a crown colony in 1925.

For centuries the Greek population, regarding Greece as its mother country, has sought self-determination and reunion with it (*enosis*). The resulting quarrel with Turkey threatened NATO. Cyprus became an independent nation on Aug. 16, 1960, with Britain, Greece, and Turkey as guarantor powers.

After troubled years, a crisis was averted in 1968 when an American mediator, Cyrus R. Vance, induced Turkey, Greece, and Cyprus to accept a solution proposed by U.N. Secretary General U Thant for withdrawal of the Greek troops and the dismantling of Turkish invasion forces. The ethnic blocs began long direct negotiations for a new Constitution.

Archbishop Makarios, president since 1959, was overthrown July 15, 1974, by a military coup led by the Cypriot National Guard. The new regime named Nikos Giorgiades Sampson as president and Bishop Gennadios as head of the Cypriot Church to replace Makarios. The rebels were led by rightist Greek officers who supported *enosis.*

Diplomacy failed to resolve the crisis. Turkey invaded Cyprus by sea and air July 20, 1974, asserting its right to protect the Turkish Cypriote minority. Greece rejected a Turkish demand for withdrawal of the 650 Greek officers who had engineered the coup. The crisis forced resignation of the military junta that had ruled Greece for seven years.

Geneva talks involving Greece, Turkey, Britain, and the two Cypriote factions failed in mid-August, and the Turks subsequently gained control of 40% of the island. Greece made no armed response to the superior Turkish force, but bitterly suspended military participation in the NATO alliance.

On Cyprus, U.S. Ambassador Rodger P. Davies was shot to death in August during Greek Cypriote riots. The tension continued after Makarios returned to become President on Dec. 7, 1974. He offered self-government to the Turkish minority, but rejected any solution "involving transfer of populations and amounting to partition of Cyprus."

Turkish Cypriots proclaimed a separate state in the northern part of the island and proposed a "biregional federation." Some 200,000 Greek Cypriots demanded return to their homes in the Turkish zone and an estimated three fourths of the 45,000 ethnic Turks in the Greek zone crossed into the Turkish area.

Makarios died on Aug. 3, 1977, and Spyros Kiprianou was elected to serve the remaining five months of his term. Kiprianou, running unopposed, won a full five-year term in 1978.

Despite intense pressure from the U.S. and other NATO allies anxious to end the dispute that kept both Greece and Turkey from functioning as defenders of the strategic eastern Mediterranean, intercommunal negotiations have remained deadlocked.

CZECHOSLOVAKIA

Czechoslovak Socialist Republic
President: Gustav Husak (1975)
Premier: Lubomir Strougal (1970)
Area: 49,374 sq mi. (127,877 sq km)
Population (est. 1981): 15,400,000 (growth rate, 0.6%) (Czech, 64%; Slovak, 30%)
Density per square mile: 311.9
Capital: Prague
Largest cities (est. 1979): Prague, 1,188,600; **(est. 1976):** Brno, 359,500; Bratislava, 340,900; Ostrava, 300,900; Kosice, 174,400; Plzeň, 156,500
Monetary unit: Koruna
Languages: Czech, Slovak, Hungarian
Religions: Roman Catholic, 70%; Czechoslovak Church, 8%; Protestant, 7%; Greek Orthodox, 5%.
National name: Československá Socialistická Republika
Freedom House classifications: Socialist industrial, one-party communist
Economic summary: Gross national product (1979): $80.5 billion. Average annual growth rate (1970–78): 4.3%. Per capita income (1976): $3,985. Labor force in agriculture: 14%; principal products: wheat, rye, oats, corn, barley, potatoes, sugar beets, hogs, cattle, horses. Labor force

in industry: 39%; major products: iron and steel, machinery and equipment, cement, sheet glass, motor vehicles, armaments, chemicals, ceramics. Natural resources: coal/coke, timber, lignite, uranium, magnesite. Exports: machinery, motor vehicles, iron and steel, chemicals. Imports: machinery, equipment, fuels, raw materials, food, consumer goods. Major trading partners: U.S.S.R. and Soviet bloc, Austria, U.K.

Geography. Czechoslovakia lies in central Europe, a neighbor of East and West Germany, Poland, the U.S.S.R., Hungary, and Austria. It is equal in size to New York State. The principal rivers—the Elbe, Danube, Oder, and Moldau—are vital commercially to this landlocked country, for both waterborne commerce and agriculture, which flourishes in fertile valleys irrigated by these rivers and their tributaries.

Government. Since 1969 the supreme organ of the state has been the Federal Assembly, which has two equal chambers: the Chamber of People, with 200 deputies, and the Chamber of Nations, with 150 deputies (75 from the Czech Socialist Republic and 75 from the Slovak Socialist Republic). The chief executive is the President, who is elected by the Federal Assembly for a five-year term. The Premier and his Cabinet are appointed by the President but are responsible to the Federal Assembly.

The major political parties are the Communist Party, led by First Secretary Gustav Husak in both republics; Socialist Party; People's Party in the Czech Socialist Republic; Slovak Freedom Party and Slovak Reconstruction Party in the Slovak Socialist Republic. Together with trade unions, youth organizations, and other organizations, they form the National Front.

History. Probably about the 5th century A.D., Slavic tribes from the Vistula basin settled in the region of modern Czechoslovakia. Slovakia came under Magyar domination. The Czechs founded the kingdom of Bohemia, the Premyslide dynasty, which ruled Bohemia and Moravia from the 10th to the 16th century. One of the Bohemian kings, Charles IV, Holy Roman Emperor, made Prague an imperial capital and a center of Latin scholarship. The Hussite movement founded by Jan Hus (1369?–1415) linked the Slavs to the Reformation and revived Czech nationalism, previously under German domination. A Hapsburg, Ferdinand I, ascended the throne in 1526. The Czechs rebelled in 1618. Defeated in 1620, they were ruled for the next 300 years as part of the Austrian Empire.

In World War I, Czech and Slovak patriots, notably Thomas G. Masaryk and Milan Stefanik, promoted Czech-Slovak independence from abroad while their followers fought against the Central Powers. On Oct. 28, 1918, Czechoslovakia proclaimed itself a republic. Shortly thereafter Masaryk was unanimously elected first President.

Hitler provoked the country's German minority in the Sudetenland, led by Konrad Henlein, to agitate for autonomy. At the Munich Conference on Sept. 30, 1938, France and the U.K., seeking to avoid World War II, agreed that the Nazis could take the Sudetenland. Dr. Eduard Beneš, who had succeeded Masaryk, resigned on Oct. 5, 1938, and fled to London. Czechoslovakia became a state within the German orbit and was known as Czecho-Slovakia. In March 1939, the Nazis occupied the country. Beneš organized a government-in-exile in London in 1940.

Soon after Czechoslovakia was liberated in World War II and the government returned in April 1945, it was obliged to cede Ruthenia to the U.S.S.R. In 1946, a Communist, Klement Gottwald, formed a six-party coalition Cabinet. Pressure from Moscow increased until Feb. 23–25, 1948, when the Communists seized complete control in a coup. Following constituent assembly elections in which the Communists and their allies were unopposed, a new Constitution was adopted.

Beneš refused to sign it and resigned; he died mysteriously on Sept. 3, 1948. The Constitution was promulgated June 9. Thereafter, agriculture was collectivized, industry almost completely socialized, and foreign trade conducted chiefly with the Soviet bloc. Industrialization was intensified and concentrated upon heavy industry. The "people's democracy" was converted into a "socialist" state by a new Constitution adopted June 11, 1960.

After the death of Stalin and the relaxing of Soviet controls, Czechoslovakia witnessed a nationalist awakening. In 1968 conservative Stalinists were driven from power and replaced by more liberal, reform-minded Communists.

In more orthodox circles of the U.S.S.R. and its European satellites, fears arose that the trend was undermining Communist rule. Soviet military maneuvers on Czechoslovak soil in May 1968 were followed in July by a meeting of the U.S.S.R. with Poland, Bulgaria, East Germany, and Hungary in Warsaw that demanded an accounting, which Prague refused. Czechoslovak-Soviet talks on Czechoslovak territory, at Cierna, in late July led to an accord. But the Russians charged that the Czechoslovaks had reneged on pledges to modify their policies, and on Aug. 20–21, troops of the five powers, estimated at 600,000, executed a lightning invasion and occupation.

Soviet secret police seized the top Czechoslovak leadership and detained it for several days in Moscow. But Soviet efforts to establish a puppet regime failed. President Ludvik Svoboda negotiated an accord providing for a gradual troop withdrawal in return for "normalization" of political policy.

The purge of liberals was virtually completed in 1970. Only Svoboda remained from 1968. Husak, who became Secretary General of the Communist Party in 1969, promised no show trials, but most liberals were punished. Czechoslovakia signed a new friendship treaty with the U.S.S.R. that codified the "Brezhnev doctrine," under which Russia can invade any Eastern European socialist nation that threatens to leave the satellite camp.

Continuing ferment surfaced early in 1975 with publication in the West of a long letter of protest against repression written by Alexander Dubcek, First Secretary of the Czechoslovak Communist Party during the 1968 "Prague Spring." The letter, addressed to the Presidium of Czechoslovakia's Federal Assembly, charged that the regime had purged thousands of creative workers. Dubcek was later reported transferred to a menial forester's job.

One of the most vigorous of the Eastern European groups formed to support human rights in the wake of the 1975 Helsinki Conference on Security and Cooperation in Europe was the Czech "Charter 77," an association of 240 intellectuals who signed a New Year manifesto protesting the suppression of freedom. Detentions of the signers began immediately, and a second manifesto appeared on January 8 with 300 signatures condemning the official reaction to the first. On Jan. 28, the government offered to let five of the dissidents leave the country, but they refused.

Charter 77 adherents marked their first anniversary with a manifesto Jan. 1, 1978, calling for open debate on the observance of human rights in Czechoslovakia. Enough of the group remained in May 1981 for the government to jail 36 persons in the biggest roundup of dissidents since 1971, as part of the precautions against any show of sympathy for Polish workers. The Czech Communist Party was among the most severe of the Eastern European states in condemning what Husak called an attempted "counterrevolutionary coup" in Poland.

DENMARK

Kingdom of Denmark
Sovereign: Queen Margrethe II (1972)
Prime Minister: Anker Jørgensen (1975)
Area: 16,615 sq mi. (43,033 sq km)[1]
Population (est. 1981): 5,130,000[1] (growth rate: 0.2%)
Density per square mile: 308.8
Capital: Copenhagen
Largest cities (est. 1980): Copenhagen, 660,000; (est. 1976 by U.N.): Arhus, 246,100; Odense, 167,900; Alborg, 154,600
Monetary unit: Krone
Language: Danish
Religion: Lutheran (established)
National name: Kongeriget Danmark
Freedom House classifications: Capitalist-socialist industrial, multi-party centralized
Economic summary: Gross national product (1979): $60.8 billion. Average annual growth rate (1970–78): 2.1%. Per capita income: $9,663; average rate of inflation (1977–78): 10%. Labor force in agriculture: 9%; principal products: meat, dairy products, fish, fur. Labor force in industry: 33%; major products: industrial and construction equipment, electronics, furniture, textiles. Natural resources: oil and gas, zinc, lead, iron ore, coal, molybdenum, cryolite, uranium. Exports: farm products, manufactured goods, fish, furs, furniture. Imports: industrial raw materials, fuel, machinery and equipment, transport equipment, chemicals, textile fibers. Major trading partners: West Germany, Sweden, U.K., U.S., Norway.

---

1. Excluding Faeroe Islands and Greenland.

Geography. Smallest of the Scandinavian countries (half the size of Maine), Denmark occupies the Jutland peninsula, which extends north from Germany between the tips of Norway and Sweden. To the west is the North Sea and to the east the Baltic.

The country also consists of several Baltic islands; the two largest are Sjaelland, the site of Copenhagen, and Fyn. The narrow waters off the north coast are called the Skagerrak and those off the east, the Kattegat.

Government. Denmark has been a constitutional monarchy since 1849. Legislative power is held jointly by the Sovereign and parliament. The Constitution of 1953 provides for a unicameral parliament called the Folketing, consisting of 179 popularly elected members who serve for four years. The Cabinet is presided over by the Sovereign, who appoints the Prime Minister.

The Sovereign, Queen Margrethe II, was born

April 16, 1940, and became Queen—the first in Denmark's history—Jan. 15, 1972, the day after her father, King Frederik IX, died at 72 in the 25th year of his reign. Margrethe was the eldest of his three daughters (by Princess Ingrid of Sweden). The nation's Constitution was amended in 1953 to permit her to succeed her father in the absence of a male heir to the throne. (Denmark was ruled six centuries ago by Margrethe I, but she was never crowned Queen since there was no female right of succession.) Margrethe's sisters are Benedikte (born 1944) and Anne Marie (born 1946), now the former Queen of Greece.

The major political parties are the Social Democratic Party (68 seats in the Folketing), led by Prime Minister Anker Jørgensen; Liberal Democratic Party (22 seats), led by Henning Christophersen; Conservative Party (22 seats), led by Poul Schlüter; Progress Party (20 seats), led by Mogens Glistrup; Socialist People's Party (11 seats), led by Gert Petersen; Radical Liberal Party (10 seats); Center Democratic Party (6 seats); Left Socialist Party (6 seats); Single Tax Party (5 seats); Christian People's Party (5 seats).

History. Denmark emerged with establishment of the Norwegian dynasty of the Ynglinger in Jutland at the end of the 8th century. Danish mariners played a major role in the raids of the Vikings, or Norsemen, on Western Europe and particularly England. The country was Christianized by St. Ansgar and Harald Blaatand (Bluetooth)—the first Christian king—in the 10th century. Harald's son, Sweyn, conquered England in 1013. His son, Canute the Great, who reigned from 1014 to 1035, united Denmark, England, and Norway under his rule; the southern part of Sweden was part of Denmark until the 17th century. On Canute's death, civil war tore the country until Waldemar I (1157–82) re-established Danish hegemony over the north.

In 1282, the nobles won the Great Charter, and Eric V was forced to share power with parliament and a Council of Nobles. Waldemar IV (1340–75) restored Danish power, checked only by the Hanseatic League of north German cities allied with ports from Holland to Poland. His daughter, Margrethe, in 1397 united under her rule Denmark, Norway, and Sweden. But Sweden later achieved autonomy and in 1523, under Gustavus I, independence.

Denmark supported Napoleon, for which it was punished at the Congress of Vienna in 1815 by the loss of Norway to Sweden. In 1864, Bismarck, together with the Austrians, made war on the little country as an initial step in the unification of Germany. Denmark was neutral in World War I.

In 1939, Denmark signed a 10-year pact with Hitler, but less than a year later it was invaded by the Nazis. King Christian X reluctantly cautioned his countrymen to accept the occupation, but there was widespread resistance against the Nazis. In 1944, Iceland declared its independence from Denmark, ending a union that had existed since 1380.

Liberated by British troops in May 1945, the country staged a fast recovery in both agriculture and manufacturing and was a leader in liberalizing trade. It joined the United Nations in 1945 and NATO in 1949.

The Social Democrats largely ran Denmark after the war but were ousted in 1973 when, in an election dominated by protests against high taxes, all established parties lost heavily. The big winner was

the new Progress Party. A minority government was formed by the Liberal Democrats, with their leader, Poul Hartling, as Premier. After losing a vote of confidence in January 1975, Hartling resigned and was succeeded by Anker Jørgensen, a Social Democrat who was Premier in 1972–73.

Outlying Territories of Denmark
FAEROE ISLANDS

Status: Autonomous part of Denmark
Commissioner: L. Groth (1972)
Area: 540 sq mi. (1,399 sq km)
Population (est. 1981): 43,000 (growth rate: 1.0%)
Density per square mile: 79.9
Capital (1977 census): Thorshavn, 11,600
Monetary unit: Faeroese krone
Economic summary: Gross national product (1979): $430 million. Average annual growth rate (1970–78): 6.1%. Per capita income: $4,340. Principal agricultural products: sheep and cattle. Major industrial product: fish. Exports: fish and fish products. Imports: machinery and transport equipment, foodstuffs, petroleum and petroleum products. Major trading partners: Denmark, U.S., Norway, U.K.

This group of 21 islands, lying in the North Atlantic about 200 miles (322 km) northwest of the Shetland Islands, joined Denmark in 1386 and has since been part of the Danish kingdom. The islands were occupied by British troops during World War II, after the German occupation of Denmark.

The Faeroes have home rule under a bill enacted in 1948; they also have two representatives in the Danish Folketing.

GREENLAND

Status: Autonomous part of Denmark
Area: 840,000 sq mi. (incl. 708,069 sq mi. covered by icecap) (2,175,600 sq km).
Population (est. 1981): 50,000 (growth rate, 1978–79: 0.4%)
Capital (est. 1979): Godthaab, 8,800
Monetary unit: Krone
Economic summary: Gross national product (1979): $390 million. Average annual growth rate (1970–78): 5.5%. Principal agricultural products: hay, sheep, garden produce. Major industries: mining, slaughtering, fishing, sealing. Natural resource: cryolite. Exports: fish and fish products, metalic ores and concentrates. Imports: petroleum and petroleum products, machinery and transport equipment, foodstuffs. Major trading partners: Denmark, U.S., Finland, West Germany, U.K.

Greenland, the world's largest island, was colonized in 985–86 by Eric the Red. Danish sovereignty, which covered only the west coast, was extended over the whole island in 1917. In 1941 the U.S. signed an agreement with the Danish minister in Washington, placing it under U.S. protection during World War II but maintaining Danish sovereignty. A definitive agreement for the joint defense of Greenland within the framework of NATO was signed in 1951. A large U.S. air base at Thule in the far north was completed in 1953.

Under 1953 amendments to the Danish Constitution, Greenland became part of Denmark, with two representatives in the Danish Folketing. On May 1, 1979, Greenland gained home rule, with its own local parliament (Landsting), replacing the Greenland Provincial Council.

Greenland is the world's only source of natural cryolite, important in making aluminum.

DJIBOUTI

Republic of Djibouti
President: Gouled Aptidon Hassan (1977)
Prime Minister: Gourad Hamadou Barkat (1978)
Area: 8,996 sq mi. (23,300 sq km)
Population (est. 1981): 330,000 (growth rate: 5.1%)
Density per sq mi.: 36.7
Capital (est. 1978): Djibouti, 160,000
Monetary unit: Djibouti franc
Languages: Arabic, French, Afar, Somali
Religion: Islam
Freedom House classifications: Capitalist industrial, one-party nationalist
Economic summary: Gross national product (1979): $140 million. Average annual growth rate (1970–78): —1.2%. Per capita income: $360. Principal agricultural products: goats, sheep, camels. Industries: port and maritime support, construction. Exports: hides, cattle, coffee (in transit from Ethiopia). Imports: machinery, transport equipment, foodstuffs. Major trading partners: France, Ethiopia, Japan.

Geography. Djibouti lies in northeastern Africa on the Gulf of Aden at the southern entrance to the Red Sea. It borders on Ethiopia and Somalia. The country, the size of Massachusetts, is mainly a stony desert, with scattered plateaus and highlands.

Government. On May 8, 1977, the population of the French Territory of the Afars and Issas voted by more than 98% for independence. Voters also approved a 65-member interim Constituent Assembly. France transferred sovereignty to the new nation of Djibouti on June 27. Later in the year it became a member of the Organization of African Unity and the Arab League. The People's Progress Assembly is the only political party.

History. The territory that is now Djibouti was acquired by France between 1843 and 1886 by treaties with the Somali sultans. Small, arid, and sparsely populated, Djibouti is important chiefly because of the capital city's port, the terminal of the Djibouti-Addis Ababa railway that carries 60% of Ethiopia's foreign trade.

Originally known as French Somaliland, the colony voted in 1958 and 1967 to remain under French rule. It was renamed the Territory of the Afars and Issas in 1967 and took the name of its capital city on attaining independence.

Somali rebels in Ethiopia's Ogaden Province cut the railway to Djibouti in June 1977 and there was fear that the new nation might be absorbed by Somalia. In July 1980, Djibouti granted base rights to United States ships and planes in exchange for undisclosed amounts of aid.

DOMINICA

Commonwealth of Dominica
President: Aurelius Marie (1980)
Prime Minister: Mary Eugenia Charles (1980)
Area: 300 sq mi. (777 sq km)
Population: (est. 1981): 85,000 (growth rate: 0.6%)
Density per square mile: 283.3
Capital and largest city (est. 1978): Roseau, 16,800
Monetary unit: East Caribbean dollar
Languages: English and French patois
Religions: Roman Catholic, Anglican, Methodist
Member of Commonwealth of Nations
Freedom House classifications: Capitalist industrial, multi-party centralized
Economy: Gross national product (1979): $30 million. Average annual growth rate (1970–78): —3.4%. Labor force in agriculture: 50%; principal products: bananas, citrus fruits, coconuts, cocoa. Major industries: agricultural processing; tourism. Exports: bananas, lime juice, oil, cocoa. Imports: machinery and equipment, foodstuffs, manufactured goods, cement. Major trading partners: U.K., Commonwealth and Caribbean countries, U.S., Canada.

Geography. Dominica is an island of the Lesser Antilles in the Caribbean south of Guadeloupe and north of Martinique.

Government. Dominica is a republic, with a president elected by the House of Assembly as head of state and a prime minister appointed by the president on the advice of the Assembly. The Freedom Party (17 of 21 seats in the Assembly) is led by Prime Minister Mary Eugenia Charles. The Opposition Democratic Labor Party holds two seats and independents the remaining two.

History. Discovered by Columbus in 1493, Dominica was claimed by Britain and France until 1815, when Britain asserted sovereignty. Dominica, along with other Windward Isles, became a self-governing member of the West Indies Associated States in free association with Britain in 1967.

Full independence was granted on Nov. 3, 1978, in ceremonies at which the first Prime Minister, Patrick R. John, declared a socialist course for the new republic. John aroused strong opposition when he proposed laws curbing the right to strike and freedom of the press. During a demonstration in Roseau in May 1979, police fired at the crowd, killing three. After a general strike, John dissolved the Assembly and set new elections for Dec. 1, but continued disorder forced his resignation and replacement by Oliver Seraphin.

Dissatisfaction over the slow pace of reconstruction after Hurricane David struck the island in September 1979 brought a landslide victory for the opposition Freedom Party in July 1980. The vote gave the prime ministership to Mary Eugenia Charles, a strong advocate of free enterprise.

DOMINICAN REPUBLIC

President: Antonio Guzmán (1978)
Area: 18,704 sq mi. (48,442 sq km)
Population (est. 1981): 5,580,000 (growth rate: 2.5%) (approx.): mestizo, 75%; white, 15%; Negro, 10%
Density per square mile: 298.3
Capital: Santo Domingo[1]
Largest cities (est. 1979): Santo Domingo, 1,103,400; **(1970 census):** Santiago de los Caballeros, 155,151
Monetary unit: Peso
Language: Spanish
Religion: Roman Catholic
National name: República Dominicana
Freedom House classifications: Capitalist industrial, multi-party centralized
Economic summary: Gross national product (1979): $5.2 billion. Average annual growth rate (1970–78): 4.2%. Per capita income: $880. Labor force in agriculture: 73%; principal products: sugar cane, coffee, cocoa, tobacco, rice, corn. Labor force in industry: 8%; major products: processed sugar, textiles, cement, nickel, bauxite, and

gold mining. Natural resources: nickel, bauxite, gold, silver. Exports: sugar, nickel, coffee, tobacco, cocoa, bauxite. Imports: foodstuffs, petroleum, industrial raw materials, capital equipment. Major trading partner: U.S.

---

1. Called Cuidad Trujillo from 1936 to 1961.

Geography. The Dominican Republic in the West Indies, occupies the eastern two thirds of the island of Hispaniola, which it shares with Haiti. Its area equals that of Vermont and New Hampshire combined.

Crossed from northwest to southeast by a mountain range with elevations exceeding 10,000 feet (3,048 m), the country has fertile, well-watered land in the north and east, where nearly two thirds of the population lives. The southwest part is arid and has poor soil, except around Santo Domingo.

Government. The president is elected by direct vote every four years. Legislative powers rest with a Senate and a Chamber of Deputies, both elected by direct vote, also for four years. All citizens must vote when they reach 18 years of age, or even earlier if they are married.

The major political parties are the Dominican Revolutionary Party, the party of the Administration, led by Dr. José Francisco Peña Gomez; the Reformist Party, led by former President Joaquín Balaguer; Dominican Liberation Party, led by Juan Bosch; Partido Quisquellano Demócrata, led by Elías Wessin y Wessin; Movimiento de Integración Democrática Anti-Releccionista, led by Augusto Lora.

History. The Dominican Republic was discovered by Columbus in 1492. He named it La Española, and his son, Diego, was its first viceroy. The capital, Santo Domingo, founded in 1496, is the oldest European settlement in the Western Hemisphere. Spain ceded the colony to France in 1795, and Haitian blacks under Toussaint L'Ouverture conquered it in 1801.

In 1808 the people revolted and the next year captured Santo Domingo, setting up the first republic. Spain regained title to the colony in 1814. In 1821 the people overthrew Spanish rule, but in 1822 they were reconquered by the Haitians. They revolted again in 1844, threw out the Haitians, and established the Dominican Republic, headed by Pedro Santana. Uprisings and Haitian attacks led Santana to make the country a province of Spain from 1861 to 1865. The U.S. Senate refused to ratify a treaty of annexation. Disorder continued until the dictatorship of Ulíses Heureaux; in 1916, when disorder broke out again, the U.S. sent in a contingent of marines, who remained until 1934.

A sergeant in the Dominican army trained by the marines, Rafaél Leonides Trujillo Molina, overthrew Horacio Vásquez in 1930 and established a dictatorship that lasted until his assassination 31 years later. To end border clashes, Trujillo mounted an invasion of Haiti in 1937, killing more than 10,000 Haitians. Trujillo developed the country but ran it for his own benefit and that of his followers; he wound up owning much of the economy.

After Trujillo's assassination on May 30, 1961, disorders forced out the President, Joaquín Balaguer, but a governing council, in spite of an abortive military coup, steered the country to a return to constitutional government.

A new Constitution was adopted in 1962, and the first free elections since 1924 put Juan Bosch, a leftist leader, in office. A planned program of reforms with U.S. support was cut off by a rightwing military coup that replaced Bosch with a civilian triumvirate.

Leftists rebelled April 24, 1965, and President Lyndon Johnson sent in 400 marines to help evacuate U.S. citizens. After an OAS ceasefire request May 6, a compromise installed Hector Garcia-Godoy as provisional president. Balaguer won in free elections in 1966 against Bosch, and an OAS force of 9,000 U.S. troops and 2,000 from other countries withdrew. Balaguer restored political and economic stability and launched a 15-year development program.

Balaguer's longtime support for free elections faltered in May 1978, when the army suspended the counting of ballots as he trailed in a fourth-term bid. After a warning from President Jimmy Carter, however, Balaguer accepted the victory of Antonio Guzmán of the opposition Dominican Revolutionary Party.

Guzmán began a rural development and land reform program despite the destruction caused by Hurricane David in September 1979. In June 1981, Guzmán announced that he would not seek re-election at the end of his term in August 1982, the first time in Dominican history that a President voluntarily relinquished power.

ECUADOR

Republic of Ecuador
President: Osvaldo Hurtado Larrea (1981)
Area: 105,685 sq mi. (273,724 sq km)
Population (est. 1981): 8,625,000 (growth rate: 3.0%)
Density per square mile: 81.6
Capital: Quito
Largest cities (est. 1980): Guayaquil, 1,100,000; Quito, 775,000; Cuenca, 135,000
Monetary unit: Sucre
Languages: Spanish, Quéchua, Jibaro
Religion: Roman Catholic
National name: República del Ecuador
Freedom House classifications: Capitalist pre-industrial, multi-party centralized
Economic summary: Gross national product (1979): $8.5 billion. Average annual growth rate (1970–78): 5.6%. Per capita income: $1,099. Land used for agriculture: 15%; labor force: 56%; principal products: bananas, coffee, cocoa, sugar cane, fruits, corn, potatoes, rice. Labor force in industry: 18%; major products: processed foods, textiles, chemicals, fish, petroleum. Natural resources: petroleum, fish, timber, minerals. Exports: petroleum, bananas, coffee, cocoa, sugar, fish products. Imports: agricultural and industrial machinery, industrial raw materials, building supplies, chemical products, transportation and communication equipment. Major trading partners: U.S., Latin American and Western European countries, Japan.

Geography. Ecuador, equal in area to Nevada, is in the northwest part of South America fronting on the Pacific. To the north is Colombia and to the east and south is Peru. Two high and parallel ranges of the Andes, traversing the country from north to south, are topped by tall volcanic peaks. The highest is Chimborazo at 20,577 feet (6,272 m).

The Galápagos Islands (or Colón Archipelago) (3,029 sq mi.; 7,845 sq km) in the Pacific Ocean about 600 miles (966 km) west of the South American mainland, became part of Ecuador in 1832.

Government. A 1978 Constitution returned Ecuador to civilian government after eight years of military rule. Under its terms, the President is elected by universal suffrage to a term of five years and a House of Representatives of 69 members popularly elected for the same period. A faction of the Concentration of Popular Forces Party controls a majority of the legislature. An opposing faction of the party, led by Assad Bucaram, holds approximately 20 seats.

History. The tribes in the northern highlands of Ecuador formed the Kingdom of Quito around A.D. 1000 It was absorbed, by conquest and marriage, into the Inca Empire. Pizarro conquered the land in 1532, and through the 17th century a thriving colony was built by exploitation of the Indians. The first revolt against Spain occurred in 1809. Ecuador then joined Venezuela, Colombia, and Panama in a confederacy founded by Simón Bolívar and known as Greater Colombia.

On the collapse of this union in 1830, Ecuador became independent. Subsequent history was one of revolts and dictatorships; it had 48 presidents during the first 131 years of the republic. Conservatives ruled until the Revolution of 1895 ushered in nearly a half century of Radical Liberal rule, during which the church was disestablished and freedom of worship, speech, and press was introduced.

In 1970, following six months of strife between university students and police, President José María Velasco Ibarra, who was elected in 1968 for the fifth time, took supreme powers to "avoid social and economic chaos." He closed universities, jailed some professors and businessmen, and demanded "reform" of the Supreme Court. Opposition political leaders were arrested and a military shake-up ensued.

Velasco was ousted nine months later by a junta, which sharply increased fees charged to foreign oil companies.

A three-man military junta headed by Vice Adm. Alfredo Poveda, which had taken power in a 1976 coup, agreed to a free presidential election on July 16, 1978. Jaime Roldós Aguilera won the runoff on April 29, 1979, backed by a "center leftist" coalition, the Concentration of Popular Forces.

The 40-year-old President, his wife and Ecuador's minister of defense died in the crash of a small plane May 24, 1981. Vice President Osvaldo Hurtado Larrea became President. In March, Roldos had reached a truce with Peru in a border clash which had broken out January 28 in the Cordilleras del Condor mountains. In February, Ecuador released without charge a U.S. tuna boat seized a month earlier and fined $1.2 million for unauthorized entry into the 200-mile "economic zone" claimed by Ecuador.

EGYPT

Arab Republic of Egypt
President (1970) and Premier (1980): Anwar el-Sadat
Area: 386,872 sq mi. (1,001,998 sq km)
Population (est. 1981): 43,000,000 (growth rate: 2.6%)
Density per square mile: 111.1
Capital: Cairo
Largest cities (est. 1979): Cairo, 5,423,000; (1976 census): Alexandria, 2,318,655; Giza, 1,246,713; Shubra el Khema, 393,700; El Mahalla el Kubra, 292,853; Tanta, 284,636; Port Said, 262,620; Mansura, 257,866

Monetary unit: Egyptian pound
Language: Arabic
Religions: Islam, 93%; Christian (mostly Copt), 7%
Freedom House classifications: Capitalist-socialist industrial, dominant party
Economic summary: Gross national product (1979): $18.6 billion. Average annual growth rate (1970–78): 6.3%. Per capita income: $280. Land used for agriculture: 3%; labor force: 50%; principal products: cotton, wheat, rice, corn. Labor force in industry: 13%; major products: textiles, processed foods, tobacco manufactures, chemicals, fertilizer, petroleum and petroleum products. Natural resources: manganese ore, phosphates, petroleum, gold, nickel, tungsten. Exports: cotton, rice, petroleum, manufactured goods. Imports: foodstuffs, machinery, fertilizers, woods. Major trading partners: West Germany, Italy, France, U.K., U.S.

Geography. Egypt, at the northeast corner of Africa on the Mediterranean Sea, is bordered on the west by Libya, on the south by the Sudan, and on the east by the Red Sea and Israel. It is nearly one and one half times the size of Texas.

The historic Nile flows through the eastern third of the country. On either side of the Nile valley are desert plateaus, spotted with oases. In the north, toward the Mediterranean, plateaus are low, while south of Cairo they rise to a maximum of 1,015 feet (309 m) above sea level. At the head of the Red Sea is the Sinai Peninsula, between the Suez Canal and Israel.

Navigable throughout its course in Egypt, the Nile is used largely as a means of cheap transport for heavy goods. The principal port is Alexandria. The Nile delta starts 100 miles (161 km) south of the Mediterranean and fans out to a sea front of 155 miles between the cities of Alexandria and Port Said. From Cairo north, the Nile branches into many streams, the principal ones being the Damietta and the Rosetta.

Except for a narrow belt along the Mediterranean, Egypt lies in an almost rainless area, in which high daytime temperatures fall quickly at night.

Government. Executive power is held by the President, who is also serving as Premier, and can appoint one or more Vice Presidents.

The major political parties are the National Democratic Party, Free Socialist Party, Nationalist Progressive Party, and Independent Front.

History. Egyptian history dates back to about 4000 B.C., when the kingdoms of upper and lower Egypt, already highly civilized, were united. Egypt's "Golden Age" coincided with the 18th and 19th dynasties (16th to 13th centuries B.C.), during which the empire was established. Persia conquered Egypt in 525 B.C.; Alexander the Great subdued it in 332 B.C.; and then the dynasty of the Ptolemies ruled the land until 30 B.C., when Cleopatra, last of the line, committed suicide and Egypt became a Roman province. From 641 to 1517 the Arab caliphs ruled Egypt, and then the Turks took it for their Ottoman Empire.

Napoleon's armies occupied the country from 1798 to 1801. In 1805, Mohammed Ali, leader of a band of Albanian soldiers, became Pasha of Egypt. After completion of the Suez Canal in 1869, the French and British took increasing interest in Egypt.

British troops occupied Egypt in 1882, and British resident agents became its actual administrators, though it remained under nominal Turkish sovereignty. In 1914, this fiction was ended, and Egypt became a protectorate of Britain.

Pressure by Egyptian nationalists forced Britain to declare Egypt an independent, sovereign state on Feb. 28, 1922, although the British reserved rights for the protection of the Suez Canal and the defense of Egypt. In 1936, by an Anglo-Egyptian treaty of alliance, all British troops and officials were to be withdrawn, except from the Suez Canal Zone. When World War II started, Egypt remained neutral. British imperial troops finally ended the Nazi threat to Suez in 1942 in the battle of El Alamein, which took place west of Alexandria.

In 1951, Egypt abrogated the 1936 treaty and the 1899 Anglo-Egyptian condominium of the Sudan (*See* Sudan.) Rioting and attacks on British troops in the Suez Canal Zone followed, reaching a climax in January 1952. The army, led by Gen. Mohammed Naguib, seized power on July 23, 1952. Three days later, King Farouk abdicated in favor of his infant son. Naguib took over the premiership in September and promised far-reaching reforms. The monarchy was abolished and a republic proclaimed on June 18, 1953, with Naguib holding the posts of Provisional President and Premier. He relinquished the latter in 1954 to Gamal Abdel Nasser, leader of the ruling military junta. Naguib was deposed seven months later. Nasser was confirmed as President in a popular referendum on June 23, 1956.

Nasser's policies embroiled his country in continual conflict. In 1956, the U.S. and Britain withdrew their pledges of financial aid for the building of the Aswan High Dam. In reply, Nasser nationalized the Suez Canal and expelled British oil and embassy officials. Israel, barred from the Canal and exasperated by terrorist raids, invaded the Gaza Strip and the Sinai Peninsula. Britain and France, after demanding Egyptian evacuation of the Canal Zone, attacked Egypt on Oct. 31, 1956. Worldwide pressure forced Britain, France, and Israel to halt the hostilities. A U.N. emergency force occupied the Canal Zone, and all troops were evacuated in the spring of 1957.

On Feb. 1, 1958, Egypt and Syria formed the United Arab Republic, which was joined by Yemen in an association known as the United Arab States. However, Syria withdrew from the United Arab Republic in 1961 and Egypt dissolved its ties with Yemen in the United Arab States. On Sept. 2, 1971, Egypt finally shed the name United Arab Republic.

On June 5, 1967, Israel invaded the Sinai Peninsula, the East Bank of the Jordan River, and the zone around the Gulf of Aqaba. Only a U.N. ceasefire on June 10 saved the Arabs from complete rout. The war left the U.A.R. army, its prestige, and its economy in ruins. The Suez Canal was blocked by wrecks and closed to all traffic. Nasser at first resigned as President, then withdrew the resignation, getting increased power to rebuild the stricken nation. He obtained economic and financial help from the U.S.S.R., China, Kuwait, and former King Saud of Saudi Arabia.

Nasser declared the 1967 cease-fire void along the Canal in April 1969 and began a war of attrition. Egyptian artillery fire across the canal sparked Israeli "deep penetration" raids that attempted to topple Nasser. He went to Moscow in January 1970, and by March, Russians were flying planes with Egyptian markings to defend the Nile delta and were manning some antiaircraft missiles. An estimated 10,000 to 12,000 Russians were in Egypt in 1970. Missiles were moved into the Canal Zone,

challenging Israeli air superiority. The U.S. peace plan of June 19, 1970, resulted in Egypt's agreement to reinstate the cease-fire for at least three months, (from August) and to accept Israel's existence within "recognized and secure" frontiers that might emerge from U.N.-mediated talks. In return, Israel accepted the principle of withdrawing from occupied territories.

Then, on Sept. 28, 1970, Nasser died, at 52, of a heart attack in the midst of Jordanian-Palestinian guerrilla hostilities and the hijacking by these guerrillas of four Western jet planes. The new President was Anwar el-Sadat, an associate of Nasser and a former newspaper editor.

The Aswan High Dam, whose financing by the U.S.S.R. was its first step into Egypt, was completed and dedicated in January 1971.

In July 1972, Sadat ordered the expulsion of Soviet "advisors and experts" from Egypt because the Russians had not provided the sophisticated weapons he felt were needed to retake territory lost to Israel in 1967. Moscow pulled out virtually all of its 18,000 men.

The fourth major Arab-Israeli war broke out Oct. 6, 1973, while Israelis were commemorating Yom Kippur, the Jewish high holy day. Egypt swept deep into the Sinai, while Syria strove to throw Israel off the Golan Heights. Arab oil-producing countries cut off shipments to the U.S. and other Western nations, helping to precipitate a worldwide energy crisis.

A U.N.-sponsored truce was accepted on October 22 after an Israeli thrust across the Suez into Egypt itself cut off Egyptian forces in the Sinai. In January 1974, both sides agreed to a settlement negotiated by U.S. Secretary of State Henry A. Kissinger that gave Egypt a narrow strip along the entire Sinai bank of the Suez Canal. In June, President Nixon made the first visit by a U.S. President to Egypt and full diplomatic relations were established. An Egyptian-American economic commission was established to channel aid to Egypt, including nuclear power reactors. The Suez Canal was cleared and it reopened on June 5, 1975.

Kissinger pursued "shuttle diplomacy" between Cairo and Jerusalem to extend areas of agreement. Israel yielded on three points—the possession of the Mitla and Giddi passes in the Sinai and the Abu Rudeis oil field in the peninsula—and both sides committed themselves to annual renewal of the U.N. peacekeeping force in the Sinai. Although not a peace treaty, the agreement established the U.S. mediating position.

Sadat, defying Arab charges of betrayal in dealing with Israel, gained U.S. aid and the security to turn his attention to an economy beset by 30% inflation and serious unemployment. A 1976 referendum gave Sadat, running unopposed for a second six-year term, a 99.9% vote of approval.

Sadat won promises of major economic help in 1977, when Saudi Arabia and other Arabian Gulf states agreed to lend Egypt $1.5 billion. A consortium of the International Monetary Fund, the European Economic Community, and others recommended loans and credits of $13.1 billion for 1977–80. And the Ford Motor Co. said it would resume manufacture of trucks and diesel engines in an Alexandria plant shut down by the Arab boycott in the 1960s. Goodyear, Union Carbide, and Coca-Cola also began operations in Egypt.

In the most audacious act of his career, Sadat flew to Jerusalem at the invitation of Prime Minister Menachem Begin and pleaded before Israel's Knesset on Nov. 20, 1977, for a permanent peace settlement. The Arab world reacted with fury—only Morocco, Tunisia, Sudan, and Oman voiced approval—and Egyptian Foreign Minister Ismail Fahmy resigned. Hope for progress cooled when political talks in Jerusalem snagged, and Sadat ordered his negotiators home Jan. 17, 1978. The Egyptian was angered by Begin's defense of new settlements on the West Bank and his refusal to discuss the ultimate status of the West Bank and Gaza Strip, which Sadat proposed be placed under Jordanian and Egyptian administration respectively.

Sadat maintained an image of cooperation while Begin reflected intransigence, a perception shared by the U.S. Congress as it voted for Carter's requested package sale of jet fighters to Egypt, Saudi Arabia, and Israel over Israeli protests.

Egyptian and Israeli officials met in the Sinai desert on April 26, 1979, to implement the peace treaty calling for the phased withdrawal of occupation forces from the peninsula. On May 27 ahead of schedule, Israel turned over the gateway town of El Arish to Egyptian administration. By mid-1980, two thirds of the Sinai was transferred, but progress here was not matched in the other area covered by the treaty—the negotiation of Arab autonomy in the Gaza Strip and the West Bank.

Sadat, who angrily called a halt to further autonomy talks in August 1980 because of continued Israeli settlement of the West Bank, traveled to Washington a year later to urge President Reagan to recognize the Palestine Liberation Organization as a means of resuming the talks. Sadat warned of Saudi impatience, and Secretary of State Alexander M. Haig, Jr., for the first time indicated that Reagan might accept some form of compromise, such as negotiating with West Bank mayors who are also members of the PLO, despite the U.S. commitment not to deal with the guerrilla organization as such.

Suez Canal. The Suez Canal, in Egyptian territory between the Arabian Desert and the Sinai Peninsula, is an artificial waterway about 100 miles (161 km) long between Port Said on the Mediterranean and Suez on the Red Sea. Construction work, directed by the French engineer Ferdinand de Lesseps, was begun April 25, 1859, and the Canal was opened Nov. 17, 1869. The cost was 432,807,882 francs. The concession was held by an Egyptian joint stock company, *Compagnie Universelle du Canal Maritime de Suez,* in which the British government held 353,504 out of a total of 800,000 shares. The concession was to expire Nov. 17, 1968, but the company was nationalized July 26, 1956, by unilateral action of the Egyptian government.

The Canal was closed in June 1967 after the Arab-Israeli conflict. With the help of the U.S. Navy, work was begun on clearing the Canal in 1974, after the cease-fire ending the Arab-Israeli war. It was reopened to traffic June 5, 1975.

EL SALVADOR

Republic of El Salvador
President: José Napoleón Duarte (1980)
Area: 8,260 sq mi. (21,393 sq km)
Population (est. 1981): 4,750,000 (growth rate: 3.0%)
Density per square mile: 575.1
Capital: San Salvador

Largest cities (est. 1980): San Salvador, 430,000; (est. 1969): Santa Ana, 168,000
Monetary unit: Colón
Language: Spanish
Religion: Roman Catholic
National name: República de El Salvador
Freedom House classifications: Capitalist industrial, non-party military
Economic summary: Gross national product (1979): $3.0 billion. Average annual growth rate (1970–78): 2.2%. Per capita income: $610. Land used for agriculture: 58%; labor force: 57%; principal products: coffee, cotton, corn, sugar, rice, beans. Labor force in industry: 14%; major products: processed foods, clothing and textiles, petroleum products. Natural resources: timber, balsam, gold, silver, coal, copper, iron, zinc, mercury, sulfur. Exports: coffee, cotton, sugar. Imports: machinery, automotive vehicles, petroleum, foodstuffs, fertilizer. Major trading partners: U.S., Caribbean countries, Japan.

Geography. Situated on the Pacific coast of Central America, El Salvador has Guatemala to the west and Honduras to the north and east. It is the smallest of the Central American countries, its area equal to that of Massachusetts, and the only one without an Atlantic coastline.

Most of the country is a fertile volcanic plateau about 2,000 feet (607 m) high. There are some active volcanoes and many scenic crater lakes.

Government. The Constitution provides for a President, popularly elected for five years and ineligible to succeed himself, and a unicameral legislature, the National Assembly, consisting of 52 members elected by popular suffrage for two years.

A junta that took power on Oct. 15, 1979, remained in power even after choosing a civilian member, José Napoleón Duarte, as President on Dec. 13, 1980.

History. Pedro de Alvarado, a lieutenant of Cortés, conquered El Salvador in 1525. El Salvador, with the other countries of Central America, declared its independence from Spain on Sept. 15, 1821, and was part of a federation of Central American states until that union was dissolved in 1838. Its independent career for several decades thereafter was marked by numerous revolutions and wars against other Central American republics.

In 1931, the first free election in 20 years was held, but Gen. Maximiliano Hernández Martínez took power in December of that year and maintained a dictatorship until he was ousted in 1944. For nearly two decades, politics remained turbulent and unstable, until the 1962 elections.

The new President, Julio Adalberto Rivera, restored free elections. In 1968, a drop in exports of coffee and cotton produced a slump. Widespread unemployment in El Salvador and land hunger in Honduras resulted in a conflict between the two nations in 1969. Deportation from Honduras of several thousand Salvadorans led to an invasion by El Salvador. Under threats of economic sanctions and military intervention, El Salvador withdrew its troops.

Presidential elections in 1972 gave none of four candidates a clear majority; therefore, the National Assembly, in which the National Conciliation Party had an overwhelming majority, proclaimed its candidate, Col. Arturo Armando Molina, as President.

The 1977 presidential elections were marked by at least eight deaths and massive protest demonstrations by the National Opposition Union, which charged extensive voter fraud. Gen. Carlos Humberto Romero, candidate of the governing National Conciliation Party, claimed victory over Lt. Col. Ernesto Claramount, the National Opposition Union candidate, who chose exile rather than prison after the election.

On Oct. 15, 1979, a junta composed of two army officers and three civilians deposed the President, Gen. Carlos Humberto Romero, seeking to halt increasingly violent clashes between leftist and rightist forces. The military officers were Col. Jaime Abdul Gutierrez Avendaño and Col. Adolfo Arnoldo Majano. The civilian members resigned in January and were replaced by two Christian Democrats, José Napoleón Duarte and José Antonio Morales Ehrlich, and a non-party member, José Ramón Avalos Navarrete. The junta strove to halt civil strife but found itself attacked from the left as too conservative and from the right as too liberal, with bloody conflicts continuing.

On Dec. 4, 1980, three American nuns and an American lay worker were killed in an ambush near San Salvador, causing the Carter administration to suspend all aid pending an investigation. The naming of José Napoleón Duarte, a Christian Democrat who had joined the military junta earlier, as President brought a resumption of U.S. aid.

Leftist guerrillas announced a "final offensive" aimed at victory before the Reagan administration took office Jan. 20, but Salvadoran forces beat down rebel attacks. The new U.S. administration sent 56 military advisers and increased military and economic aid to the beleaguered government and launched a campaign to dissuade other countries from supporting the rebels, asserting that the guerrillas were receiving Soviet arms via Cuba and Nicaragua. Violence from both the right and left continued, with the death toll averaging 1,000 a month.

EQUATORIAL GUINEA

Republic of Equatorial Guinea
Head of state: Lieut. Col. Teodoro Nguema Menzogo (1979)
Area: 10,830 sq mi. (28,051 sq km)
Population (est. 1981): 370,000 (growth rate: 2.1%)
Density per square mile: 34.6
Capital and largest city (est. 1970): Malabo (formerly Santa Isabel), 19,300
Monetary unit: Ekuele
Languages: Spanish, Fang, Bubi
Religions: Roman Catholic, Protestant, Animist
National name: República de Guinea Ecuatorial
Freedom House classifications: Capitalist-statist pre-industrial, non-party military
Economic summary: Gross national product (1972): $70 million. Per capita income: $240. Land used for agriculture: 85–90%; labor force: 95%; principal products: cocoa, wood, coffee. Natural resource: wood. Exports: cocoa, wood, coffee, bananas, palm oil. Imports: foodstuffs, beverages, tobacco, textiles, machinery. Major trading partner: Spain.

Geography. Equatorial Guinea, formerly Spanish Guinea, consists of Rio Muni (10,045 sq mi.; 26,117 sq km), on the western coast of Africa, and several islands in the Gulf of Guinea, the largest of which is Macias Nguema Biyogo (formerly Fernando Po) (785 sq mi.; 2,033 sq km). The other islands

are Pagalu (formerly Annobón), Corisco, Elobey Grande, and Elobey Chico. The total area is twice that of Connecticut.

Government. Executive power is vested in a Council of Ministers appointed by and responsible to the president. Legislative power is vested in a 60-member People's National Assembly.

A new Constitution was approved in 1973 and the capital's name was changed from Santa Isabel to Malabo.

The Partido Unico Nacional de Trabajadores, headed by the president, is the only political party.

History. Fernando Po and Annobón came under Spanish control in 1778. From 1827 to 1844, with Spanish consent, Britain administered Fernando Po, but in the latter year Spain reclaimed the island. Río Muni was given to Spain in 1885 by the Treaty of Berlin.

Negotiations with Spain led to independence on Oct. 12, 1968.

In 1969, anti-Spanish incidents in Río Muni, including the tearing down of a Spanish flag by national troops, caused 5,000 Spanish residents to flee for their safety, and diplomatic relations between the two nations became strained. A month later, President Masie Nguema Biyogo Negue Ndong charged that a coup had been attempted against him. He seized dictatorial powers and arrested 80 opposition politicians and even several of his Cabinet ministers and the secretary of the National Assembly.

A coup on Aug. 3, 1979, deposed Masie, and a junta led by Lieut. Col. Teodoro Nguema Menzogo took over the government. Menzogo expelled Soviet technicians and reinstated cooperation with Spain.

ETHIOPIA

Head of State: Lt. Col. Mengistu Haile Mariam (1977)
Area: 457,142 sq mi. (1,183,998 sq km)
Population (est. 1981): 32,000,000 (growth rate: 0.7%)
Density per square mile: 70.0
Capital: Addis Ababa
Largest cities (est. 1980): Addis Ababa, 1,250,000; (est. 1978 by U.N.): Asmara, 393,800
Monetary unit: Birr
Languages: Amharic (official), Galligna, Tigrigna
Religions: Copt (Christian), Islam
Freedom House classifications: Socialist pre-industrial, non-party military
Economic summary: Gross national product (1979): $4.0 billion. Average annual growth rate (1970–78): −0.1%. Per capita income: $100. Land used for agriculture: 65%; labor force: 90%; principal products: coffee, barley, wheat, corn, sugar cane, cotton, oilseeds, livestock. Labor force in industry: 10%; Major industrial products: cement, cotton textiles, refined sugar, processed foods, refined oil. Natural resources: potash, salt, gold, copper, platinum. Exports: coffee, hides and skins, oilseeds. Imports: petroleum. Major trading partners: Saudi Arabia, Japan, Italy, West Germany, Iran, U.K., France, U.S.

Geography. Ethiopia is in east central Africa, bordered on the west by the Sudan, the east by Somalia and Djibouti, the south by Kenya, and the north by the Red Sea. It is nearly three times the size of California.

Over its main plateau land, Ethiopia has several high mountains, the highest of which is Ras Dashan at 15,158 feet (4,620 m). The Blue Nile, or Abbai, rises in the northwest and flows in a great semicircle east, south, and northwest before entering the Sudan. Its chief reservoir, Lake Tana, lies in the northwestern part of the plateau.

Government. A provisional military government headed by a 120-member officers' committee (the Dirgue) deposed Ethiopia's traditional monarchy in 1974, suspended parliament, and ruled by decree. It proclaimed Ethiopia a socialist state.

History. Black Africa's oldest state, Ethiopia can trace 2,000 years of recorded history. Its now-deposed royal line claimed descent from King Menelik I, traditionally believed to have been the son of the Queen of Sheba and King Solomon. The present nation is a consolidation of smaller kingdoms that owed feudal allegiance to the Ethiopian Emperor.

Hamitic peoples migrated to Ethiopia from Asia Minor in prehistoric times. Semitic traders from Arabia penetrated the region in the 7th century B.C. Its Red Sea ports were important to the Roman and Byzantine Empires. Coptic Christianity came to the country in A.D. 341, and a variant of that communion became Ethiopia's state religion.

Ancient Ethiopia reached its peak in the 5th century, then was isolated by the rise of Islam and weakened by feudal wars. Modern Ethiopia emerged under Emperor Menelik II, who established its independence by routing an Italian invasion in 1896. He expanded Ethiopia by conquest.

Disorders that followed Menelik's death brought his daughter to the throne in 1917, with his cousin, Tafari Makonnen, as Regent, heir presumptive, and strongman. When the Empress died in 1930, Tafari was crowned Emperor Haile Selassie I.

As Regent, Haile Selassie outlawed slavery. As Emperor, he worked for centralization of his diffuse realm, in which 70 languages are spoken, and for moderate reform. In 1931, he granted a Constitution, revised in 1955, that created a parliament with an appointed Senate and an elected Chamber of Deputies, and a system of courts. But basic power remained with the Emperor.

Bent on colonial empire, fascist Italy invaded Ethiopia on Oct. 3, 1935, forcing Haile Selassie into exile in May 1936. Ethiopia was annexed to Eritrea, then an Italian colony, and Italian Somaliland to form Italian East Africa, losing its independence for the first time in recorded history. In 1941, British troops routed the Italians, and Haile Selassie returned to Addis Ababa.

The Emperor's gradual reforms failed to make headway against key problems. Although 85% of Ethiopians were subsistence farmers, feudal laws vested ownership of 55% of its land in the crown, the church, and the nobility; there was strong pressure for land reform. There was also mounting insurgency in Eritrea, a culturally distinct province where Christians and Moslems have long vied for control, which the United Nations placed under Ethiopian rule in 1952. Violent agitation for Eritrean independence was begun in 1969 by the Moslem-led Eritrean Liberation Front, which used Arab-supplied arms to field a 4,000-man guerrilla force.

Deep discontent erupted in the fall of 1973. A long drought had caused famine that killed 100,-000 peasants and drove thousands of others to cities, where food was scarce and inflation was rampant. Charges of mismanagement of drought relief sparked riots in Addis Ababa in 1974, and unpaid troops in Asmara, capital of Eritrea, mutinied to protest conditions. The Cabinet headed by Prime Minister Aklilou Habte-wold resigned.

The Emperor named Endalkachew Makonnen, a moderate, as Prime Minister and agreed to call a constitutional convention. But there was a general strike, students rioted, and mutiny spread to the air force. In mid-April, with disorders growing, army and police units arrested over 200 prominent persons. Late in June the army took virtual control of Addis Ababa and made more arrests.

Endalkachew was ousted on July 24, arrested, and later executed. Under his successor, Michael Imru, a draft Constitution proposing a constitutional monarchy was put forward, but power shifted relentlessly to a new Armed Forces Committee.

In August, the Armed Forces Committee nationalized Haile Selassie's palace and estates and directed him not to leave Addis Ababa. On Sept. 12, 1974, He was peacefully deposed after nearly 58 years as Regent and Emperor. The 82-year-old "Lion of Judah" was placed under guard. Parliament was dissolved and the Constitution suspended.

On December 20, the Armed Forces Committee announced that Ethiopia would become a socialist state directed by one political organization called the Supreme Progressive Council. All financial concerns were nationalized in 1975 and the regime proclaimed nationalization of all rural land, ending 2,000 years of feudal tenure.

On Aug. 27, 1975, Haile Selassie died in a small apartment in his former Addis Ababa palace where he had been treated as a state prisoner. He was 83.

After the coup, revolt in Eritrea escalated from guerrilla conflict to open war. The Eritrean Liberation Front, armed by Libya and other Arab states, demanded full independence. The regime tried and failed to negotiate with the Front and then began vigorous military action. Some 22,000 government troops were in combat in Eritrea by February 1975, and 6,000 deaths, mostly of civilians, were said to have resulted in March.

U.S. military aid, which had been going to Ethiopia since World War II, was suspended after the 1974 coup and only briefly resumed in 1976 as the military government turned increasingly toward the U.S.S.R. In retaliation for the Carter Administration's ruling out further aid to Ethiopia because of human rights violations, the regime in April and May of 1977 shut down the Kagnew communications center in Asmara and other U.S. military and diplomatic offices, ordering some 300 Americans to leave.

Lt. Col. Mengistu Haile Mariam was named head of state Feb. 2, 1977, to replace Brig. Gen. Teferi Benti, who was killed in a factional fight of the Dirgue after having ruled since 1974. The government was losing its fight to hold Eritrea and in the southeastern region of Ogaden, Somali guerrillas backed by Somali regular forces threatened the ancient city of Harar. In October, the U.S.S.R. announced it would end military aid to Somalia and henceforth back its new ally, Ethiopia. This, together with the intervention of Cuban troops in Ogaden, turned the tide for Mengistu. By March 1978, the badly beaten Somalis had retreated to their homeland.

In late July 1978, the Ethiopian government reported that it had gained its first victory over Eritrean rebels in three years in a campaign aimed at cutting them off from their supply lines to the Sudan. In both Eritrea and Ogaden, however, guerrilla resistance was still strong in 1980 and large areas were reported under only sporadic government control.

FIJI

Dominion of Fiji
Sovereign: Queen Elizabeth II
Governor General: Sir George Cakobau (1973)
Prime Minister: Sir Kamisese Mara (1970)
Area: 7,055 sq mi. (18,272 sq km)
Population (est. 1981): 625,000 (average annual growth rate, 1975–79: 1.8%)
Density per square mile: 88.6
Capital (1976 census): Suva (on Viti Levu), 63,600
Monetary unit: Fijian dollar
Languages: Fijian, Hindustani, English
Religions: Christian, Hindu, Islam
Member of Commonwealth of Nations
Freedom House classifications: Capitalist pre-industrial, multi-party centralized
Economic summary: Gross national product (1979): $1.0 million. Average annual growth rate (1970–78): 3.1%. Per capita income (1977): $1,100. Average rate of inflation (1975–77): 9.3%. Labor force in agriculture: 44%; principal products: sugar, copra, bananas, ginger. Labor force in industry: 16%; major industrial products: refined sugar, gold, lumber. Natural resources: timber, fish, gold, copper. Exports: sugar, copra. Imports: foodstuffs, machinery, manufactured goods, fuels, chemicals. Major trading partners: Australia, Japan, U.K., New Zealand, U.S.

Geography. Fiji consists of more than 500 islands in the southwestern Pacific Ocean about 1,960 miles (3,152 km) from Sydney, Australia. The two largest islands are Viti Levu (4,109 sq mi.; 10,642 sq km) and Vanua Levu (2,242 sq mi.; 5,807 sq km). The island of Rotuma (18 sq mi.; 47 sq km), about 400 miles (644 km) to the north, is a dependency of Fiji. Overall, Fiji is nearly as large as New Jersey.

The largest islands in the group are mountainous and volcanic, with the tallest peak being Mount Victoria (4,341 ft; 1,323 m) on Viti Levu. The islands in the south have dense forests on the windward side and grasslands on the leeward.

Government. Executive authority is vested in the Cabinet and legislative authority in a bicameral 74-member Parliament. The major political parties are the Alliance Party, led by Prime Minister Sir Kamisese Mara; National Federation Party, led by Jai Ram Reddy, and Fijian Nationalist Party, led by Sakeasi Butadroka.

History. In 1874, an offer of cession by the Fijian chiefs was accepted, and Fiji was proclaimed a possession and dependency of the British Crown.

During World War II, the archipelago was an important air and naval station on the route from the U.S. and Hawaii to Australia and New Zealand.

Fiji became independent on Oct. 10, 1970. The next year it joined the five-island South Pacific Forum, which intends to become a permanent regional group to promote collective diplomacy of the newly independent members. The Forum also includes Western Samoa, Tonga, Nauru, and the self-governing segments of the Cook Islands.

FINLAND

Republic of Finland
President: Urho K. Kekkonen (1956)
Premier: Mauno Koivisto (1979)
Area: 130,119 sq mi. (337,009 sq km)
Population (est. 1981): 4,800,000 (growth rate: 0.3%) (Finnish, 93%; Swedish, 6%)
Density per square mile: 36.9
Capital: Helsinki
Largest cities (est. 1981): Helsinki, 484,000; Tampere, 166,250; Turku, 163,500
Monetary unit: Markka
Languages: Finnish, Swedish
Religions: Lutheran, 98%; Orthodox, 1.6%
National name: Suomen Tasavalta—Republiken Finland
Freedom House classifications: Capitalist-socialist industrial, multi-party centralized
Economic summary: Gross national product (1979): $39.4 billion. Average annual growth rate (1970–78): 2.2%. Per capita income (1979): $9,900. Per capita income: $6,110. Land used for agriculture: 8%; labor force: 17%; principal products: dairy products, cereals, sugar beets, potatoes. Labor force in industry: 39%; major products: metal manufactures, forestry and wood products, refined copper, ships. Natural resource: timber. Exports: timber, paper and pulp, ships, machinery, iron and steel, clothing, footwear. Imports: foodstuffs, petroleum and petroleum products, chemicals, transportation equipment, iron and steel, machinery textile yarns. Major trading partners: Western European countries, U.S.S.R., Sweden.

Geography. Finland stretches 700 miles (1,127 km) from the Gulf of Finland on the south to Soviet Petsamo, north of the Arctic Circle. The U.S.S.R. extends along the entire eastern frontier. In area, Finland is three times the size of Ohio.

Off the southwest coast are the Åland Islands, controlling the entrance to the Gulf of Bothnia. Finland has more than 60,000 lakes. Of the few rivers, only the Oulu (Ulea) is navigable to any important extent.

The Swedish-populated Åland Islands (581 sq mi.; 1,505 sq km) have an autonomous status under a law passed in 1951.

Government. The president, chosen for six years by the popularly elected Electoral College of 300 members, appoints the Cabinet. The one-chamber Diet, the Eduskunta, consists of 200 members elected for four-year terms by proportional representation.

The major political parties are the Social Democratic Party (52 seats in the Eduskanta), led by former Premier Kalevi Sorsa; Conservative Party (46 seats); Center Party (37 seats); People's Democratic League (Communist) (35 seats); Swedish People's Party (10 seats); Christian League (9 seats); Rural Party (7 seats); Liberal Party (4 seats). Premier Mauno Koivisto leads a coalition of Social Democratic, Communist, Center, and Swedish People's Party members totaling 134 seats.

History. At the end of the 7th century, the Finns came to Finland from their Volga settlements, taking the country from the Lapps, who retreated northward. The Finns' repeated raids on the Scandinavian coast impelled Eric IX, the Swedish King, to conquer the country in 1157 and bring it into contact with Western Christendom. By 1809 the whole of Finland was conquered by Alexander I of Russia, who set up Finland as a Grand Duchy.

The first period of Russification (1899–1905) resulted in a lessening of the powers of the Finnish

Diet. The Russian language was made official, and the Finnish military system was superseded by the Russian. The pace of Russification was intensified from 1908 to 1914. When Russian control was weakened as a consequence of the March Revolution of 1917, the Diet on July 20, 1917, proclaimed Finland's independence, which became complete on Dec. 6, 1917.

Finland rejected Soviet territorial demands, and the U.S.S.R. attacked on Nov. 30, 1939. The Finns made an amazing stand of three months and finally capitulated, ceding 16,000 square miles (41,440 sq km) to the U.S.S.R. Under German pressure, the Finns joined the Nazis against Russia in 1941, but were defeated again and ceded the Petsamo area to the U.S.S.R. In 1948, a 20-year treaty of friendship and mutual assistance was signed by the two nations and renewed for another 20 years in 1970.

In 1970 Finland entered into a trade agreement with the enlarged European Economic Community (Common Market), which includes Norway and Denmark, and also with Comecom, the Communist East European Economic Group.

The world oil crisis added a practical new reason for maintenance of an unimpaired relationship with Moscow, for Finland imports two thirds of its oil from the U.S.S.R. In 1974, the two nations signed a 10-year energy cooperation pact providing for delivery to Finland of two 440-megawatt nuclear power stations scheduled to go into operation in 1981–82.

Helsinki was the site in 1975 of a summit conference of 35 heads of government convened for the signing of a European security agreement.

The agreement, signed by every European government except Albania and by the United States and Canada, established procedures for the promotion of international peace and periodic meetings to assess results.

FRANCE

French Republic
President: François Mitterrand (1981)
Premier: Pierre Mauroy (1981)
Area: 212,973 sq mi. (551,600 sq km)
Population (est. 1981): 53,950,000 (average annual growth rate, 1975–80, 0.4%)
Density per square mile: 253.3
Capital: Paris
Largest cities (est. 1980): Paris, 2,150,000; **(1975 census):** Marseilles, 914,356; Lyons, 462,841; Toulouse, 383,176; Nice, 346,620; Nantes, 263,689; Strasbourg, 257,300; Bordeaux, 226,281
Monetary unit: Franc
Religion (est.): Roman Catholic, 90%; Protestant, Jewish, Islam, and others, 10%
National name: République Française
Freedom House classifications: Capitalist industrial, multi-party centralized
Economic summary: Gross national product (1979): $531.5 billion. Average annual growth rate (1970–78): 3.1%. Per capita income (1978): $8,759. Rate of inflation (1979): 12.9%. Land used for agriculture: 60%; labor force: 10%; principal products: cereals, feed grains, livestock and dairy products, wine, fruits, vegetables. Labor force in industry: 37%; major products: chemicals, automobiles, processed foods, iron and steel, aircraft, textiles, clothing. Natural resources: coal, iron ore, bauxite, fish, forests. Exports: textiles and clothing, iron and steel

products, machinery and transport equipment, agricultural products, wine. Imports: machinery, crude petroleum, iron and steel products, textile fibers, coal and coke, foodstuffs. Major trading partners: West Germany, Italy, U.S., Belgium-Luxembourg, U.K., Netherlands.

Geography. France (80% the size of Texas) is second in size to the U.S.S.R. among Europe's nations. In the Alps near the Italian and Swiss borders is Europe's highest point—Mont Blanc (15,781 ft; 4,810 m). The forest-covered Vosges Mountains are in the northeast, and the Pyrenees are along the Spanish border.

Except for extreme northern France, which is part of the Flanders plain, the country may be described as four river basins and a plateau. Three of the streams flow west—the Seine into the English Channel, the Loire into the Atlantic, and the Garonne into the Bay of Biscay. The Rhône flows south into the Mediterranean. For about 100 miles (161 km), the Rhine is France's eastern border.

West of the Rhône and northeast of the Garonne lies the central plateau, covering about 15% of France's area and rising to a maximum elevation of 6,188 feet (1,886 m). In the Mediterranean, about 115 miles (185 km) east-southeast of Nice, is Corsica (3,367 sq mi.; 8,721 sq km).

Government. The president is elected for seven years by universal suffrage. He appoints the premier, and the Cabinet is responsible to Parliament. The president has the right to dissolve the National Assembly or to ask Parliament for reconsideration of a law. The Parliament consists of two houses: the National Assembly and the Senate.

The major political parties are the Socialists (285 of 491 seats in the National Assembly), led by Pierre Joxe; Rally for the Republic (88 seats), led by Claude Labbe; Union for French Democracy (62 seats), led by Jean-Claude Gaudin; and Communists (44 seats), led by André Lajoinie.

History. The history of France, as distinct from ancient Gaul, begins with the Treaty of Verdun (843), dividing the territories corresponding roughly to France, Germany, and Italy among the three grandsons of Charlemagne. Julius Caesar had conquered part of Gaul in 57–52 B.C., and it remained Roman until Franks invaded it in the 5th century.

Charles the Bald, inheritor of *Francia Occidentalis,* founded the Carolingian dynasty, which ruled over a kingdom increasingly feudalized. By 987, the crown passed to Hugh Capet, a princeling who controlled only the Île-de-France, the region surrounding Paris. For 350 years, an unbroken Capetian line added to its domain and consolidated royal authority until the accession in 1328 of Philip VI, first of the Valois line. France was then the most powerful nation in Europe, with a population of 15 million.

The missing pieces in Philip's domain were the French provinces still held by the Plantagenet kings of England, who also claimed the French crown. Beginning in 1338, the Hundred Years' War eventually settled the contest. English longbows defeated French armored knights at Crécy (1346) and the English also won the second landmark battle at Agincourt (1415), but the final victory went to the French peasant girl, Joan of Arc, at Orléans (1429).

Absolute monarchy reached its apogee in the reign of Louis XIV (1643–1715), the Sun King,

Rulers of France

Name	Born	Ruled[1]
CAROLINGIAN DYNASTY		
Pepin the Short	c. 714	751–768
Charlemagne[2]	742	768–814
Louis I the Debonair[3]	778	814–840
Charles I the Bald[4]	823	840–877
Louis II the Stammerer	846	877–879
Louis III[5]	c. 863	879–882
Carloman[5]	?	879–884
Charles II the Fat[6]	839	884–887[7]
Eudes (Odo), Count of Paris	?	888–898
Charles III the Simple[8]	879	893–923[9]
Robert I[10]	c. 865	922–923
Rudolf (Raoul), Duke of Burgundy	?	923–936
Louis IV d'Outremer	c. 921	936–954
Lothair	941	954–986
Louis V the Sluggard	c. 967	986–987
CAPETIAN DYNASTY		
Hugh Capet	c. 940	987–996
Robert II the Pious[11]	c. 970	996–1031
Henry I	1008	1031–1060
Philip I	1052	1060–1108
Louis VI the Fat	1081	1108–1137
Louis VII the Young	c.1121	1137–1180
Philip II (Philip Augustus)	1165	1180–1223
Louis VIII the Lion	1187	1223–1226
Louis IX (St. Louis)	1214	1226–1270
Philip III the Bold	1245	1270–1285
Philip IV the Fair	1268	1285–1314
Louis X the Quarreler	1289	1314–1316
John I[12]	1316	1316
Philip V the Tall	1294	1316–1322
Charles IV the Fair	1294	1322–1328
HOUSE OF VALOIS		
Philip VI	1293	1328–1350
John II the Good	1319	1350–1364
Charles V the Wise	1337	1364–1380
Charles VI the Well-Beloved	1368	1380–1422
Charles VII	1403	1422–1461
Louis XI	1423	1461–1483
Charles VIII	1470	1483–1498
Louis XII the Father of the People	1462	1498–1515
Francis I	1494	1515–1547
Henry II	1519	1547–1559
Francis II	1544	1559–1560
Charles IX	1550	1560–1574
Henry III	1551	1574–1589
HOUSE OF BOURBON		
Henry IV of Navarre	1553	1589–1610
Louis XIII	1601	1610–1643
Louis XIV the Great	1638	1643–1715
Louis XV the Well-Beloved	1710	1715–1774
Louis XVI	1754	1774–1792[13]
Louis XVII (Louis Charles de France)[14]	1785	1793–1795

Name	Born	Ruled[1]
FIRST REPUBLIC		
National Convention	—	1792–1795
Directory (Directoire)	—	1795–1799
CONSULATE		
Napoleon Bonaparte[15]	1769	1799–1804
FIRST EMPIRE		
Napoleon I	1769	1804–1815[16]
RESTORATION OF HOUSE OF BOURBON		
Louis XVIII le Désiré	1755	1814–1824
Charles X	1757	1824–1830[17]
BOURBON-ORLEANS LINE		
Louis Philippe ("Citizen King")	1773	1830–1848[18]
SECOND REPUBLIC		
Louis Napoleon[19]	1808	1848–1852
SECOND EMPIRE		
Napoleon III (Louis Napoleon)	1808	1852–1870[20]
THIRD REPUBLIC (PRESIDENTS)		
Louis Adolphe Thiers	1797	1871–1873
Marie E. P. M. de MacMahon	1808	1873–1879
François P. J. Grévy	1807	1879–1887
Sadi Carnot	1837	1887–1894
Jean Casimir-Périer	1847	1894–1895
François Félix Faure	1841	1895–1899
Émile Loubet	1838	1899–1906
Clement Armand Fallières	1841	1906–1913
Raymond Poincaré	1860	1913–1920
Paul E. L. Deschanel	1856	1920–1920
Alexandre Millerand	1859	1920–1924
Gaston Doumergue	1863	1924–1931
Paul Doumer	1857	1931–1932
Albert Lebrun	1871	1932–1940
VICHY GOVERNMENT (CHIEF OF STATE)		
Henri Philippe Pétain	1856	1940–1944
PROVISIONAL GOVERNMENT (PRESIDENTS)		
Charles de Gaulle	1890	1944–1946
Félix Gouin	1884	1946–1946
Georges Bidault	1899	1946–1947
FOURTH REPUBLIC (PRESIDENTS)		
Vincent Auriol	1884	1947–1954
René Coty	1882	1954–1959
FIFTH REPUBLIC (PRESIDENTS)		
Charles de Gaulle	1890	1959–1969
Georges Pompidou	1911	1969–1974
Valéry Giscard d'Estaing	1926	1974–1981
François Mitterrand	1916	1981–

1. For Kings and Emperors through the Second Empire, year of end of rule is also that of death, unless otherwise indicated. 2. Crowned Emperor of the West in 800. His brother, Carloman, ruled as King of the Eastern Franks from 768 until his death in 771. 3. Holy Roman Emperor 814–840. 4. Holy Roman Emperor 875–877 as Charles II. 5. Ruled jointly 879–882. 6. Holy Roman Emperor 881–887 as Charles III. 7. Died 888. 8. King 893–898 in opposition to Eudes. 9. Died 929. 10. Not counted in regular line of Kings of France by some authorities. Elected by nobles but killed in Battle of Soissons. 11. Sometimes called Robert I. 12. Posthumous son of Louis X; lived for only five days. 13. Executed 1793. 14. Titular King only. He died in prison according to official reports, but many pretenders appeared during the Bourbon restoration. 15. As First Consul, Napoleon held the power of government. In 1804, he became Emperor. 16. Abdicated first time June 1814. Re-entered Paris March 1815,

after escape from Elba; Louis XVIII fled to Ghent. Abdicated second time June 1815. He named as his successor his son, Napoleon II, who was not acceptable to the Allies. He died 1821. 17. Died 1836. 18. Died 1850. 19. President; became Emperor in 1852. 20. Died 1873.

whose brilliant court was the center of the Western world. Neither Louis XV, nor his grandson, Louis XVI, could sustain the role, however, and the Ancien Régime tottered under the weight of an outmoded society, crushing taxes, and the infiltration of egalitarian philosophy. The monarchy lost French Canada in the Battle of Quebec Sept. 13, 1759, and in its last gasp under Louis XVI aided the American British colonists to gain their freedom.

Revolution plunged France into a blood bath beginning in 1789 and ending with a new authoritarianism under Napoleon Bonaparte, who had successfully defended the infant republic from foreign attack and then made himself First Consul in 1799 and Emperor in 1804. Napoleon set patterns in government, education, and law visible today, and his conquests spread them throughout Europe.

The Congress of Vienna (1815) sought to restore the pre-Napoleonic order in the person of Louis XVIII, but industrialization and the middle class, both fostered under Napoleon, built pressure for change, and a revolution in 1848 drove Louis Phillipe, last of the Bourbons, into exile.

A second republic elected as its president Prince Louis Napoleon, a nephew of Napoleon I, who declared the Second Empire in 1852 and took the throne as Napoleon III. His opposition to the rising power of Prussia ignited the Franco-Prussian War (1870–71), ending in his defeat and abdication.

A new France emerged from World War I as the continent's dominant power. But four years of hostile occupation had reduced northeast France to ruins. The postwar Third Republic was plagued by political instability and economic chaos.

From 1919, French foreign policy aimed at keeping Germany weak through a system of alliances, but it failed to halt the rise of Adolf Hitler and the Nazi war machine. On May 10, 1940, mechanized Nazi troops attacked, and, as they approached Paris, Italy joined with Germany. The Germans marched into an undefended Paris and Marshal Henri Philippe Pétain signed an armistice June 22. France was split into an occupied north and an unoccupied south, the latter becoming a totalitarian state with Pétain as its chief.

Allied armies liberated France in August 1944. The French Committee of National Liberation, formed in Algiers in 1943, established a provisional government in Paris headed by Gen. Charles de Gaulle. The Fourth Republic was born Dec. 24, 1946.

The Empire became the French Union; the National Assembly was strengthened and the presidency weakened; and France joined the North Atlantic Treaty Organization. A war against communist insurgents in Indochina was abandoned after the defeat at Dien Bien Phu. A new rebellion in Algeria (*see* Algeria) threatened a military coup, and on June 1, 1958, the Assembly invited de Gaulle to return as premier with extraordinary powers. He drafted a new Constitution for a Fifth Republic, adopted Sept. 28, which strengthened the presidency and reduced legislative power. He was elected president Dec. 21.

The new president negotiated the independence of Algeria on July 5, 1962. De Gaulle cultivated the former colonies along with other new nations of what he called the Third World—nations aligned with neither the West nor the Soviet bloc—

as a base for French leadership. In 1960, de Gaulle exploded an atomic bomb; in 1963 he negotiated a Franco-German friendship treaty; and the following year he recognized Peking, at the same time improving relations with the U.S.S.R.

De Gaulle took France out of NATO in 1967 and expelled all foreign-controlled troops from the country. Although he had been re-elected to a seven-year term in 1965, the end of his reign was foreshadowed in 1968 by a rebellion of students. The disorders spread to the workers, resulting in a general strike supported by half the labor force. De Gaulle offered and then canceled a referendum and held elections on the promise of reforms, which gave his supporters an overwhelming victory.

De Gaulle went on to attempt to achieve a long-cherished plan of regional reform. This, however, aroused wide opposition. He decided to stake his fate on a referendum. At the voting in April 1969, the electorate defeated the plan. His successor, Georges Pompidou, de Gaulle's premier for six years, reversed the de Gaulle policy of opposing the unification of Europe.

Pompidou continued the de Gaulle policies of seeking to expand France's influence in the Mideast and Africa, selling arms to South Africa (despite the U.N. embargo), to Libya, and to Greece, and in 1971 he endorsed British entry into the Common Market.

Pompidou died of cancer in April 1974 and the special election to choose a successor was won by Valéry Giscard d'Estaing, who had served as de Gaulle's Finance Minister but was not a Gaullist party member. Giscard defeated François Mitterrand, the Socialist and Communist candidate, by less than 1% of the 26 million votes cast.

To retain a parliamentary majority, Giscard required Gaullist support. He upheld the General's foreign policy—an independent nuclear deterrent, staying away from NATO military ties—but espoused domestic liberalism in lowering the voting age and easing restrictions on divorce and abortion. Giscard pushed nuclear-power development to lessen French dependence on imported fuel.

Jacques Chirac, the Gaullist Premier, resigned in 1976 because he said he lacked power to deal with growing economic problems and Giscard refused to delegate presidential authority. Chirac's successor was Raymond Barre, a technician without political background.

Although the launching of the Republic of Djibouti June 27, 1977, meant the end of the last French colony on Africa's mainland, Giscard continued to play a strong hand in African affairs.

A surprise victory in parliamentary elections in 1978, resulting from a split between Socialists and Communists, gave Giscard a solid majority, but the following year a cut in subsidies to industry generated a wave of strikes and the worst rioting in Paris since the student rebellion of 1968. Giscard concentrated on foreign policy, attacking the U.S. at the Tokyo economic summit of 1979 for failing to conserve oil and continuing his criticism at the Venice summit the following year. To the further annoyance of the Carter Administration, he met with Soviet President Leonid I. Brezhnev in Warsaw earlier without prior consultation with Washington.

174 Countries of the World—France

Giscard's African strongman image began to fade with the collapse of his one-time protégé, Jean-Bedel Bokassa, whose Central African Empire dissolved in a cloud of scandal in 1979. Alleged gifts of diamonds to the French President by the short-lived Emperor Bokassa became the basis of a whispering campaign against Giscard, worsened by Government efforts to suppress it legally. The defeat of President Goukouni Oueddi of Chad by Libyan-aided dissidents in January 1981, despite the presence of French troops, added no luster to Giscard's African record.

Mitterrand's stunning defeat on May 10 of the Gaullist alliance that had held power since 1958 was attributed to the challenger's skill in maintaining the Communists' support while holding them at arm's length and to the failure of Giscard to hold Gaullist support. Chirac only reluctantly supported the President in the final round of voting after having run against him in the first.

Mitterrand's ultimate triumph came in the final round of parliamentary voting when his Socialist Party, which in 1971 had polled only 5% of the votes in a similar election, swept to absolute power in the Assembly with 285 of the 491 seats. The Gaullist Rassemblement pour la République (Rally for the Republic) was cut in half, together with its allied Union pour la Democratie Française (Union for French Democracy), and the Communists fell to their lowest strength since World War II.

Although Communist support was not needed, Mitterrand named four Communist ministers to his 44-member Cabinet, the first since the postwar period and the cause for some alarm among NATO allies. Mitterrand reassured Vice President George Bush in June, pointing to the statement signed by the Communist Party as the price of joining the government, endorsing Western European defense against the Soviet Union and calling for Soviet withdrawal from Afghanistan. Mitterrand also met with German Chancellor Helmut Schmidt to support the stationing of U.S. nuclear weapons in Western Europe.

The victors immediately moved to carry out campaign pledges to nationalize major industries, halt nuclear testing, suspend nuclear power plant construction, and impose new taxes on the rich. Premier Pierre Mauroy called for the nationalization of military production of the Dassault-Breguet aircraft corporation, the Sacinor and Usinor steel companies, some remaining privately owned commercial banks, and the major manufacturing companies in generators, chemicals, glass appliances, and nonferrous metals.

Mauroy said the government would negotiate for subsequent takeover of important foreign-owned businesses such as Honeywell-Bull computers and ITT-France (U.S.) and Roussel-Uclaf (a West German-controlled drug and chemical business).

The Socialist program also called for a job-creation program to ease unemployment, which reached 1.8 million in June. The program was to be partly financed by income surtaxes and taxes on expense-account spending and luxury hotels and restaurants.

A foreign-policy crisis soon arose when the ousted Iranian President, Abolhassam Bani-Sadr, took refuge in Paris. The Iranian government on Aug. 6 announced that it would hold 110 French citizens, including diplomats, unless Bani-Sadr were extradited. Mitterrand initially refused to permit extradition although he ordered the former President to refrain from political activity. A few days later, the French nationals were flown out of Iran.

Overseas Departments and Territories of France

FRENCH GUIANA (including ININI)

Status: Overseas Department
Prefect: Désiré Carli (1980)
Area: 35,135 sq mi. (91,000 sq km)
Population (est. 1981): 65,000 (growth rate: 2.9%)
Capital (est. 1980): Cayenne, 35,000
Monetary unit: Franc
Language: French
Religion: Roman Catholic
Economic summary: Gross national product (1975): $100 million. Per capita income: $800. Labor force in agriculture: 21%; principal agricultural products: rice, corn, manioc, cocoa, bananas, sugar cane. Labor force in industry: 8%; major industrial products: timber, rum, rosewood essence, gold mining. Natural resources: bauxite, timber, cinnabar, low-grade iron ore. Exports: shrimp, timber, rum, rosewood essence. Imports: food, consumer and producer goods, petroleum. Major trading partners: U.S., France, Martinique.

French Guiana, lying north of Brazil and east of Suriname on the northeast coast of South America, was first settled in 1626. Penal settlements, embracing the area around the mouth of the Maroni River and the Iles du Salut (including Devil's Island), were founded in 1852; they have since been abolished.

During World War II, French Guiana at first adhered to the Vichy government, but the Free French took over in 1943. French Guiana accepted in 1958 the new Constitution of the French Fifth Republic and remained an Overseas Department of the French Republic.

FRENCH POLYNESIA

Status: Overseas Territory
High Commissioner: Paul Cousseran (1977)
Area: 1,544 sq mi. (4,000 sq km)
Population (est. 1981): 160,000 (growth rate: 2.1%)
Monetary unit: Colonial franc Pacifique
Religions: Protestant, 55%; Roman Catholic, 32%.
Capital (1977 census): Papeete (on Tahiti), 62,700
Economic summary: Gross national product (1979): $970 million. Average annual growth rate (1970–78): 2.8%. Principal agricultural product: coconuts. Major industries: tourism, maintenance of French nuclear test base. Exports: coconut products, mother of pearl. Major trading partners: France, U.S.

The term French Polynesia is applied to the scattered French possessions in the eastern Pacific—Mangareva (Gambier), Makatea, the Marquesas Islands, Rapa, Rurutu, Rimatara, the Society Islands, the Tuamotu Archipelago, Tubuai, Raivavae, and the island of Clipperton—which were organized into a single colony in 1903. There are 120 islands, of which 25 are uninhabited.

The High Commissioner is assisted by a Privy Council and a popularly elected Representative Assembly. The principal and most populous island —Tahiti, in the Society group—was claimed as French in 1768. In 1958, French Polynesia voted in favor of the new Constitution of the French Fifth Republic and remained an Overseas Territory of the French Republic. The natives are mostly Polynesians.

The Pacific Nuclear Test Center on the atoll of Mururoa, 744 miles (1,200 km) from Tahiti, was completed in 1966.

GUADELOUPE

Status: Overseas Department
Prefect: Guy Maillard (1978)
Area: 687 sq mi. (1,779 sq km)
Population (est. 1981): 330,000 (average annual growth rate, 1975–79: −0.5%)
Capital (est. 1977): Basse-Terre, 15,800
Largest city (est. 1978): Pointe-à-Pitre, 25,000
Monetary unit: Franc
Languages: French, Creole patois
Religions: Roman Catholic
Economic summary: Gross national product (1979): $1.1 billion. Average annual growth rate (1970–78): 3.1%. Per capita income: $828. Land used for agriculture: 33%; labor force: 25%; principal agricultural products: sugar cane, bananas, rum, pineapples. Major industries: construction, public works. Exports: sugar, bananas, rum. Imports: foodstuffs, clothing, consumer goods, petroleum. Major trading partner: France.

Guadeloupe, in the West Indies about 300 miles (483 km) southeast of Puerto Rico, was discovered by Columbus in 1493. It consists of the twin islands of Basse-Terre and Grande-Terre and five dependencies—Marie-Galante, Les Saintes, La Désirade, St. Barthélemy, and the northern half of St. Martin. The volcano Soufrière (4,813 ft; 1,467 m), also called La Grande Soufrière, is the highest point on Guadeloupe. Violent activity in 1976 and 1977 caused thousands to flee their homes.

French colonization began in 1635. In 1958, Guadeloupe voted in favor of the new Constitution of the French Fifth Republic and remained an Overseas Department of the French Republic.

MARTINIQUE

Status: Overseas Department
Prefect: Marcel Julia (1979)
Area: 431 sq mi. (1,116 sq km)
Population (est. 1981): 330,000 (average annual growth rate, 1975–79: −0.7%)
Capital (1974 census): Fort-de-France 98,800
Monetary unit: Franc
Languages: French, Creole patois
Religion: Roman Catholic
Economic summary: Gross national product (1979): $1.5 billion. Average annual growth rate (1970–78): 6.2%. Per capita income (1975): $1,366. Land used for agriculture: 47%; labor force: 23%; principal agricultural products: sugar cane, bananas, rum, pineapples. Labor force in industry: 9%; major industries: sugar, rum, oil, cement, tourism. Natural resource: fish. Exports: iron ore, fish, copper. Imports: foodstuffs, capital goods. Major trading partners: France, U.S

Martinique, lying in the Lesser Antilles about 300 miles (483 km) northeast of Venezuela, was probably discovered by Columbus in 1502 and was taken for France in 1635. Following the Franco-German armistice of 1940, it had a semiautonomous status until 1943, when authority was relinquished to the Free French. The area, administered by a Prefect assisted by an elected council, is represented in the French Parliament. In 1958, Martinique voted in favor of the new Constitution of the French Fifth Republic and remained an Overseas Department of the French Republic.

MAYOTTE

Status: Territorial collectivity
Representative of French Government: Philippe Kessler (1980)

Area: 146 sq mi. (378 sq km)
Population (est. 1980): 48,600
Capital: Dzaoudzi (about 3,200)
Principal products: vanilla, essential oils, copra

The most populous of the Comoro Islands in the Indian Ocean, with a Christian majority, Mayotte voted in 1974 and 1976 against joining the other, predominantly Moslem islands, in declaring themselves independent. It continues to retain its ties to France.

NEW CALEDONIA AND DEPENDENCIES

Status: Overseas Territory
High Commissioner: Claude Charbonniaud
Area: 8,548 sq mi. (22,139 sq km)[1]
Population (est. 1981): 150,000 (growth rate: 0.5%)
Capital (1976 census): Nouméa, 56,100
Monetary unit: Colonial franc Pacifique
Language: Melanesian and Polynesian dialects
Religion: Christian
Economic summary: Gross national product (1979): $870 million. Average annual growth rate (1970–78): −4.9%. Per capita income (1971): $1,800. Principal agricultural products: coffee, vegetables, beef. Major industrial product: nickel. Natural resources: nickel, chromite, iron ore. Export: nickel. Imports: machinery, transport equipment, foodstuffs. Major trading partners: France, Japan, U.S., Australia.

1. Including dependencies.

New Caledonia (6,466 sq mi.; 16,747 sq km), about 1,070 miles (1,722 km) northeast of Sydney, Austrialia, was discovered by Capt. James Cook in 1774 and annexed by France in 1853. The government also administers the Isle of Pines, the Loyalty Islands (Uvéa, Lifu, and Maré), the Belep Islands, the Huon Island group, and the Chesterfield Islands.

New Caledonia chose in 1958 to remain an Overseas Territory of the French Republic. The natives are Melanesians; about one third of the population is white and one fifth Indochinese and Javanese.

REUNION (BOURBON)

Status: Overseas Department
Prefect: Bernard Landouzy
Area: 970 sq mi. (2,510 sq km)
Population (est. 1981): 500,000 (average annual growth rate, 1975–79: 0.7%)
Capital (est. 1980): Saint-Denis, 105,000
Monetary unit: Franc
Languages: French, Creole
Religion: Roman Catholic
Economic summary: Gross national product (1979): $2.2 billion. Average annual growth rate (1970–78): −1.0%. Principal agricultural products: sugar cane, vanilla, bananas, perfume plants. Major industrial products: rum, cigarettes, processed sugar. Exports: sugar, perfume essences, rum, molasses. Imports: manufactured goods, foodstuffs, beverages, machinery and transportation equipment, petroleum products. Major trading partners: France, Mauritius.

Discovered by Portuguese navigators in the 16th century, the island of Réunion, then uninhabited, was taken as a French possession in 1643. It is located about 450 miles (724 km) east of Madagascar, in the Indian Ocean. In 1958, Réunion approved the Constitution of the Fifth French Republic and remained an Overseas Department of the French Republic.

ST. PIERRE AND MIQUELON

Status: Overseas Department
Prefect: Clément Bouhin (1979)
Area: 93 sq mi. (242 sq km)
Population (est. 1980): 6,300
Capital (est. 1980): Saint Pierre, 5,800
Economic summary: Major industries: fishing, canneries.
Exports: petroleum products, cattle, fish. Major trading
partners: Canada, France, U.S.

The sole remnant of the French colonial empire
in North America, these islands were first occupied
by the French in 1604. Their only importance
arises from proximity to the Grand Banks, located
10 miles south of Newfoundland, making them the
center of the French Atlantic cod fisheries. On July
19, 1976, the islands became an Overseas Depart-
ment-of the French Republic.

SOUTHERN AND ANTARCTIC LANDS

Status: Overseas Territory
Administrator: Francis Jacquemont
Area: 169,614 sq mi. (439,300 sq km)
Capital: Port-au-Français

This territory is uninhabited except for the personnel of scientific bases. It consists of Adélie Land
(166,752 sq mi.; 431,888 sq km) on the Antarctic
mainland and the following islands in the southern
Indian Ocean: the Kerguelen and Crozet archipelagos and the islands of Saint-Paul and New
Amsterdam.

WALLIS AND FUTUNA ISLANDS

Status: Overseas Territory
Administrator Superior: Pierre Isaac (1979)
Area: 77 sq mi. (200 sq km)
Population (est. 1980): 9,200
Capital (1980): Mata-Utu (on Uvea), 600

The two islands groups in the South Pacific between Fiji and Samoa were settled by French missionaries at the beginning of the 19th century. A
protectorate was established in the 1880s. Following a referendum by the Polynesian inhabitants,
the status was changed to that of an Overseas Territory in 1961.

GABON

Gabonese Republic
President: Omar Bongo (1967)
Premier: Léon Mébiame (1975)
Area: 102,317 sq mi. (265,001 sq km)
Population (est. 1981): 550,000 (growth rate: 1.3%)
Density per square mile: 5.4
Capital and largest city (est. 1978): Libreville, 225,200
Monetary unit: Franc CFA
Ethnic groups: Bateke, Obamba, Bakota, Shake, Pongwés,
Adumas, Chiras, Punu, and Lumbu
Languages: French (official) and Bantu dialects
Religions: Animist, Christian, Islam
National name: République Gabonaise
Member of French Community
Freedom House classifications: Capitalist pre-industrial,
one-party nationalist
Economic summary: Gross national product (1979): $2.1
billion. Average annual growth rate (1970–78): 8.6%. Per
capita income: $250. Labor force in agriculture: 70%;
principal products: cocoa, coffee, wood, palm, rice,
bananas, peanuts. Labor force in industry: 30%; major
products: petroleum, natural gas, processed wood,

manganese, uranium. Natural resources: wood, petroleum,
iron ore, manganese, uranium. Exports: crude petroleum,
wood and wood products, minerals, coffee. Imports:
mining and road-building machinery, electrical equipment,
foodstuffs, textiles, transport vehicles. Major trading
partners: France, U.S., West Germany.

Geography. This West African land with the Atlantic as its western border is also bounded by
Equatorial Guinea, Cameroon, and the Congo. Its
area is slightly less than Kentucky's.

From mangrove swamps on the coast, the land
becomes divided plateaus in the north and east and
mountains in the north. Most of the country is covered by a dense tropical forest.

Government. The president is elected for a seven-
year term. Legislative powers are exercised by a
National Assembly, which is elected for a seven-
year term. After his conversion to Islam in 1973,
President Bongo changed his given name, Albert
Bernard, to Omar. The Parti Démocratique Gabo-
nais (all National Assembly seats) is led by President Bongo. He was re-elected without opposition
in 1973 and in 1980.

History. Little is known of Gabon's history, even in
oral tradition, but Pygmies are believed to be the
original inhabitants. Now there are many tribal
groups in the country, the largest being the Fang
people who constitute a third of the population.

Gabon was first visited by the Portuguese navigator Diego Cam in the 15th century. In 1839, the
French founded their first settlement on the left
bank of the Gabon Estuary and gradually occupied
the hinterland during the second half of the 19th
century. It was organized as a French territory in
1888 and became an autonomous republic within
the French Union after World War II and an independent republic on Aug. 17, 1960.

Immense resources in oil, uranium, manganese,
and iron help give Gabon's inhabitants a per capita
annual income of $225 to $250, the highest in black
Africa. To speed exploitation of a billion-ton iron
ore reserve in the Belinga-Mekambo region, the
government began work in 1969 on a 350-mile railroad leading from the coast into the area. The
project was initiated by President León Mba, who
died in 1967, and has been continued by his hand-
picked successor, Omar Bongo.

In 1974, Bongo negotiated 60% control of an
iron-ore venture half-owned by the Bethlehem
Steel Corp. In October of that year, he visited Peking and concluded an economic and technical
agreement with China.

GAMBIA

Republic of the Gambia
President: Sir Dawda K. Jawara (1970)
Area: 4,016 sq mi. (10,403 sq km)
Population (est. 1981): 625,000 (growth rate: 2.8%)
Density per square mile: 155.6
Capital and largest city (est. 1980) Banjul, 48,000
Monetary unit: Dalasi
Languages: Native tongues, English (official)
Religions: Islam, Christian, Animist
Member of Commonwealth of Nations
Freedom House classifications: Capitalist pre-industrial,
multi-party centralized
Economic summary: Gross national product (1979): $150
million. Average annual growth rate (1970–78): 2.9%. Per

capita income: $210. Land used for agriculture: 55%; labor force: 85%; principal products: peanuts, rice, palm kernels. Major industrial products: processed peanuts. Natural resources: fish. Exports: peanuts and peanut products. Imports: textiles, foodstuffs, tobacco, machinery, petroleum products. Major trading partners: U.K., France, Japan.

Geography. Situated on the Atlantic coast in westernmost Africa and surrounded on three sides by Senegal, Gambia is twice the size of Delaware. The Gambia River flows for 200 miles (322 km) through Gambia on its way to the Atlantic. The country, the smallest on the continent, averages only 20 miles (32 km) in width.

Government. The president's five-year term is linked to the 35-member unicameral House of Representatives, from which he appoints his Cabinet members and the vice president.

The major political party is the People's Progressive Party (29 seats in House of Representatives), led by President Jawara.

History. During the 17th century, Gambia was settled by various companies of English merchants. Slavery was the chief source of revenue until it was abolished in 1807. Gambia became a crown colony in 1843 and an independent nation within the Commonwealth of Nations on Feb. 18, 1965.

A proposal to convert from a monarchy to a republic was approved in a 1970 referendum, and on April 24 of that year Gambia proclaimed itself a republic.

Tourism increased after 1977 because of Alex Haley's book *Roots*. In it, he traced his family's origins back to the Mandinka tribe in Juffure, a Gambian village.

GERMANY, EAST

German Democratic Republic
Chairman of Council of State: Erich Honecker (1976)
Chairman of Council of Ministers: Willi Stoph (1976)
Area: 40,646 sq mi. (195,273 sq km)[1]
Population (est. 1981): 16,730,000 (growth rate: −0.1%)
Density per square mile: 41.2
Capital: Berlin (eastern sector)
Largest cities (est. 1979): East Berlin, 1,129,000; (est. 1978 by U.N.): Leipzig, 565,200; Dresden, 511,200; Karl-Marx Stadt, 309,450; Magdeburg, 280,550; Halle, 233,000; Rostock, 219,000; Erfurt, 206,300
Monetary unit: Mark of the Deutsche Demokratische Republik
Language: German
Religions: Protestant, 53%; Roman Catholic, 8%
National name: Deutsche Demokratische Republik
Freedom House classifications: Socialist industrial, one-party communist
Economic summary: Gross national product (1979): $107.6 billion. Average annual growth rate (1970–78): 4.8%. Per capita income: $4,120. Land used for agriculture: 43%; labor force: 9%; principal products: grains, potatoes, sugar beets, meat and dairy products. Labor force in industry: 39%; major products: steel, chemicals, machinery, electrical and precision engineering products, fishing vessels. Natural resources: brown coal, potash, uranium. Exports: machinery and equipment, chemical products, textiles, clothing. Imports: raw materials, fuels, agricultural products, machinery and equipment. Major

trading partners: U.S.S.R., Soviet bloc, West Germany.

1. Including East Berlin (156 square miles), which has been incorporated into the German Democratic Republic.

Geography. East Germany lies on the Baltic Sea with Poland to the east and Czechoslovakia to the south. The border with West Germany is roughly a line running south from Lübeck for about 250 miles. The main river is the Elbe, which flows from Dresden in the southeast to the North Sea in the northwest. The Oder and Neisse Rivers form the border with Poland. Most of the country, which is the size of Tennessee, is situated in the north German plain.

Government. The People's Chamber, composed of 500 deputies elected for five-year terms, chooses the chairman and Council of State and the chairman and Council of Ministers, which carries on executive functions.

The major political party is the Socialist Unity (Communist) Party, led by Secretary General Erich Honecker. Others are Christian Democratic Union, Liberal Democratic Party, Democratic Farmers' Party, National Democratic Party.

History. (For history before 1945, *see* Germany, West.) The area now occupied by East Germany, as well as adjacent areas in Eastern Europe, consists of Mecklenburg, Brandenburg, Lusatia, Saxony, and Thuringia. Soviet armies conquered the five territories by 1945. In the division of 1945 they were allotted to the U.S.S.R. Soviet forces created a State controlled by the secret police with a single party, the Socialist Unity (Communist) Party. The Russians appropriated East German plants to restore their war-ravaged industry.

When the Federal Republic of Germany was established in West Germany, the East German states adopted a more centralized constitution for the Democratic Republic of Germany, and it was put into effect on Oct. 7, 1949. The U.S.S.R. thereupon dissolved its occupation zone, but Soviet troops remained. The Western Allies declared that the East German Republic was a Soviet creation undertaken without self-determination and refused to recognize it. It was recognized only within the Soviet bloc.

In 1953, the U.S.S.R. transferred control of East Germany from the military commander to a civilian commissioner and announced a more liberal policy. Continued austerity and political repression led to workers' riots in East Berlin and other cities, allegedly instigated by the Soviet secret police as part of a power struggle within the Kremlin. Soviet troops ruthlessly reestablished order.

In 1955, Walter Ulbricht, hard-line dictator, won Soviet recognition of the East German republic and joined the Warsaw Treaty Organization, organizing troops under the guise of police forces. In the middle and late 1960s, East Germany also came to enjoy economic prosperity.

East German troops took part in the Soviet-bloc occupation of Czechoslovakia in August 1968, but reportedly were withdrawn after the U.S.S.R. questioned whether the 1945 Potsdam agreements permitted German troops on foreign soil.

A constitution adopted in April 1968 reaffirmed one-party rule and narrowed civil rights. Ulbricht continued pressure on West Berlin, opposed liberalization in Czechoslovakia and other parts of the Soviet bloc, impeded Bonn's establishment of ties with East Europe, and pressured Bonn to acknowledge the existence of the two German states.

Talks between the two German states on normalization began in 1970, with the East seeking recognition of its existence and the West wanting easing of pressure on Berlin. West Germany's nonaggression treaty with the U.S.S.R. was cooly received by Ulbricht. In 1971 he resigned and rapprochement between the two Germanys accelerated with agreement on a variety of issues (for details, *see* Germany, West). By 1973, normal relations were established, and the two states entered the United Nations.

A new Constitution unanimously approved by the East German parliament on Sept. 27, 1974, pointedly deleted any reference to eventual reunification of the two Germanys, a principle maintained in the West German constitution.

The 25-year diplomatic hiatus between East Germany and the U.S. ended Sept. 4, 1974, with the establishment of formal relations.

The East German government has repeatedly challenged the Western powers' right of access to Berlin, most recently at the time of President Carter's July 15, 1978, visit to West Berlin. Autobahn traffic between the city and West Germany was deliberately slowed and, as in a similar 1977 case, the U.S., U.K., and France protested to the U.S.S.R. and the East Germans that such action was illegal under the 1971 Four Power Agreement.

Increased Soviet action in Africa in 1978 revealed that East Germany as well as Cuba was actively engaged as a Soviet agent. Defense Minister Heinz Hoffmann visited Angola just before the invasion of Zaire's Shaba Province was launched in May. In Angola, 1,000 East German troops were reported serving with the army, and a small number of pilots were flying combat strikes.

Chairman of the Council of State Erich Honecker gave strong backing to the Soviet Union's stern policy toward Poland as the workers' demand for democratic rights advanced in 1980 and 1981. On Oct. 28, 1980, he closed the border, which had been open between the two states for 10 years, permitting only certified relatives or invited friends to visit. Five million Poles had visited East Germany in the previous year, largely to find cheaper and more abundant consumer goods.

In February 1981, Honecker, in a surprise gesture, declared at his party's 16th Congress that German reunification might eventually be possible, something the Communist regime had ruled out 10 years earlier. He also eased border restrictions on exchanges with West Germany imposed a few months before.

GERMANY, WEST

Federal Republic of Germany
President: Karl Carstens (1979)
Chancellor: Helmut Schmidt (1974)
Area: 95,815 sq mi. (248,161 sq km)[1]
Population (est. 1981): 61,400,000 (average annual growth rate, 1976–80, −0.1%)
Density per square mile: 640.8
Capital (est. 1977): Bonn, 285,000
Largest cities (est. 1979): Hamburg, 1,658,100; Munich, 1,299,800; Cologne, 974,200; Essen, 654,900; Frankfurt, 629,000; Dortmund, 611,100; Düsseldorf, 596,600; Stuttgart, 582,100; Bremen, 557,600; Hannover, 536,000
Monetary unit: Deutsche Mark
Language: German
Religions: Protestant, 49%; Roman Catholic, 45%
National name: Bundesrepublik Deutschland

Freedom House classifications: Capitalist industrial, multi-party decentralized
Economic summary: Gross national product (1979): $717.7 billion. Average annual growth rate (1970–78): 2.4%. Per capita income (1978): $10,300. Labor force in agriculture: 5%; principal products: grains, potatoes, sugar beets. Labor force in industry: 43%; major products: iron, steel, coal, cement, chemicals, machinery, ships, vehicles. Natural resources: timber, coal, potash. Exports: machines and machine tools, chemicals, motor vehicles, iron and steel products. Imports: manufactured and agricultural products, raw materials, fuels. Major trading partners: France, Netherlands, Belgium-Luxembourg, Italy, U.S., U.K.

1. Excluding West Berlin (184 square miles with 1979 population of 1,905,000).

Geography. The Federal Republic of Germany occupies the western half of the central European area historically regarded as German. This was the part of Germany occupied by the United States, Britain, and France after the German defeat in World War II, when the eastern half of prewar Germany was split roughly between a Soviet-occupied zone, which became the present German Democratic Republic, and an area annexed by Poland.

West Germany's neighbors are France, Belgium, Luxembourg, and the Netherlands on the west, Switzerland and Austria on the south, Czechoslovakia and East Germany on the east, and Denmark on the north.

The northern plain, the central hill country, and the southern mountain district constitute the main physical divisions of West Germany, which is slightly smaller than Oregon. The Bavarian plateau in the southwest averages 1,600 feet (488 m) above sea level, but it reaches 9,721 feet (2,963 m) in the Zugspitze Mountains, the highest point in the country.

Important navigable rivers are the Danube, rising in the Black Forest and flowing east across Bavaria into Austria, and the Rhine, which rises in Switzerland and flows across the Netherlands in two channels to the North Sea and is navigable by smaller vessels as far as Cologne. The Rhine and the Elbe, which also empties into the North Sea, are navigable within Germany for ships of 400 tons. The Weser, flowing into the North Sea, and the Main and Mosel (Moselle), both tributaries of the Rhine, are also important.

Government. Under the Constitution of May 23, 1949, the Federal Republic was established as a parliamentary democracy. The Parliament consists of the Bundesrat, an upper chamber representing and appointed by the 10 Länder, or states (plus West Berlin), and the Bundestag, a lower house elected for four years by universal suffrage. Each house has non-voting representatives from West Berlin. The entire legislature elects the President of the Republic for a five-year term; the Bundestag alone chooses the Chancellor, or Prime Minister. Each of the Länder and West Berlin have an assembly popularly elected for a four-year or five-year term.

The major political parties are the Christian Democratic Union-Christian Social Union (226 of 497 seats in the Bundestag), led by Helmut Kohl; Social Democratic Party (218 seats) led by former Chancellor Willy Brandt; and the Free Democratic Party (53 seats), led by Hans-Dietrich Genscher. Chancellor Helmut Schmidt's government is a coalition with the Free Democrats.

History. Immediately before the Christian era, when the Roman Empire had pushed its frontier to the Rhine, what is now Germany was inhabited by several tribes believed to have migrated from Central Asia between the 6th and 4th centuries B.C. One of these tribes, the Franks, attained supremacy in western Europe under Charlemagne, who was crowned Holy Roman Emperor A.D. 800. By the Treaty of Verdun (843), Charlemagne's lands east of the Rhine were ceded to the German Prince Louis. Additional territory acquired by the Treaty of Mersen (870) gave Germany approximately the area it maintained throughout the Middle Ages. For several centuries after Otto the Great was crowned King in 936, the German rulers were also usually heads of the Holy Roman Empire.

Relations between state and church were changed by the Reformation, which began with Martin Luther's 95 theses, and came to a head in 1547, when Charles V scattered the forces of the Protestant League at Mühlberg. Freedom of worship was guaranteed by the Peace of Augsburg (1555), but a Counter Reformation took place later, and a dispute over the succession to the Bohemian throne brought on the Thirty Years' War (1618–48), which devastated Germany and left the empire divided into hundreds of small principalities virtually independent of the Emperor.

Meanwhile, Prussia was developing into a state of considerable strength. Frederick the Great (1740–86) reorganized the Prussian army and defeated Maria Theresa of Austria in a struggle over Silesia. The conflict with revolutionary France hastened the disintegration of the empire. After the defeat of Napoleon at Waterloo (1815), the struggle between Austria and Prussia for supremacy in Germany continued, reaching its climax in the defeat of Austria in the Seven Weeks' War (1866) and the formation of the Prussian-dominated North German Confederation (1867).

The architect of German unity was Otto von Bismarck, a conservative, monarchist, and militaristic Prussian Junker who had no use for "empty phrasemaking and constitutions." From 1862 until his retirement in 1890 he dominated not only the German but also the entire European scene. He unified all Germany in a series of three wars against Denmark (1864), Austria (1866), and France (1870–71), which many historians believe were instigated and promoted by Bismarck in his zeal to build a nation through "blood and iron."

On Jan. 18, 1871, King Wilhelm I of Prussia was proclaimed German Emperor in the Hall of Mirrors at Versailles. The North German Confederation, created in 1867, was abolished, and the Second German Reich, consisting of the North and South German states, was born. With a powerful army, an efficient bureaucracy, and a loyal bourgeoisie, Chancellor Bismarck consolidated a powerful centralized state.

Wilhelm II dismissed Bismarck in 1890 and embarked upon a "New Course," stressing an intensified colonialism and a powerful navy. His chaotic foreign policy culminated in the diplomatic isolation of Germany and the disastrous defeat in World War I (1914–18).

The Second German Empire collapsed following the defeat of the German armies in 1918, the naval mutiny at Kiel, and the flight of the Kaiser to the Netherlands on November 10. The Social Democrats, led by Friedrich Ebert and Philipp Scheidemann, crushed the Communists and established a moderate republic with Ebert as President.

The Weimar Constitution of 1919 provided for a President to be elected for seven years by universal suffrage and a bicameral legislature, consisting of the Reichsrat, representing the states, and the Reichstag, representing the people. It contained a model Bill of Rights. It was weakened, however, by a provision that enabled the President to rule by decree.

President Ebert died Feb. 28, 1925, and on April 26, Field Marshal Paul von Hindenburg was elected president.

The mass of Germans regarded the Weimar Republic as a child of defeat, imposed upon a Germany whose legitimate aspirations to world leadership had been thwarted by a world conspiracy. Added to this were a crippling currency debacle, a tremendous burden of reparations, and acute economic distress.

Adolf Hitler, an Austrian war veteran and a fanatical nationalist, fanned discontent by promising a Greater Germany, abrogation of the Treaty of Versailles, restoration of Germany's lost colonies, and destruction of the Jews. When the Social Democrats and the Communists refused to combine against the Nazi threat, President Hindenburg made Hitler chancellor on Jan. 30, 1933.

With the death of Hindenburg on Aug. 2, 1934, Hitler repudiated the Treaty of Versailles and began full-scale rearmament. In 1935 he withdrew Germany from the League of Nations, and the next year he reoccupied the Rhineland and signed the anti-Comintern pact with Japan, at the same time strengthening relations with Italy. Austria was annexed in March 1938. By the Munich agreement in September 1938 he gained the Czech Sudetenland, and in violation of this agreement he completed the dismemberment of Czechoslovakia in March 1939. But his invasion of Poland on Sept. 1, 1939, precipitated World War II.

On May 8, 1945, Germany surrendered unconditionally to Allied and Soviet military commanders, and on June 5 the four-nation Allied Control Council became the *de facto* government of Germany.

(For details of World War II, *see* Headline History.)

At the Berlin (or Potsdam) Conference (July 17–Aug. 2, 1945) President Truman, Premier Stalin, and Prime Minister Clement Attlee of Britain set forth the principles by which the Allied Control Council was to be guided. They were Germany's complete disarmament and demilitarization, destruction of its war potential, rigid control of industry, and decentralization of the political and economic structure. Pending final determination of territorial questions at a peace conference, the three victors agreed in principle to the ultimate transfer of the city of Königsberg (now Kaliningrad) and its adjacent area to the U.S.S.R. and to the administration by Poland of former German territories lying generally east of the Oder-Neisse Line.

For purposes of control Germany was divided in 1945 into four national occupation zones, each headed by a Military Governor, assisted by appropriate supervisory and operating staffs.

Efforts to unify Germany were unsuccessful, and the Western powers were unable to agree with the U.S.S.R. on any fundamental issue. Work of the Allied Control Council was hamstrung by repeated Soviet vetoes; and finally, on March 20, 1948, Russia walked out of the Council. Meanwhile, the U.S. and Britain had taken steps to merge their zones economically (Bizone); and on May 31, 1948,

Rulers of Germany and Prussia

Name	Born	Ruled[1]	Name	Born	Ruled[1]
KINGS OF PRUSSIA			Adolf Hitler[6] [7]	1889	1934–1945
Frederick I[2]	1657	1701–1713	Karl Doenitz[6]	1891	1945–1945
Frederick William I	1688	1713–1740			
Frederick II the Great	1712	1740–1786	**GERMAN FEDERAL REPUBLIC**		
Frederick William II	1744	1786–1797	**(WEST) (PRESIDENTS)**		
Frederick William III	1770	1797–1840	Theodor Heuss	1884	1949–1959[9]
Frederick William IV	1795	1840–1861	Heinrich Luebke	1895	1959–1969[8]
William I	1797	1861–1871[3]	Gustav Heinemann[10]	1899	1969–1974
			Walter Scheel	1919	1974–1979
EMPERORS OF GERMANY			Karl Carstens	1914	1979–
William I	1797	1871–1888			
Frederick III	1831	1888–1888	**GERMAN DEMOCRATIC REPUBLIC**		
William II	1859	1888–1918[4]	**(EAST)**		
			Wilhelm Pieck[5]	1876	1949–1960
HEADS OF THE REICH			Walter Ulbricht[11]	1893	1960–1973
Friedrich Ebert[5]	1871	1919–1925	Willi Stoph[12]	1914	1973–1976
Paul von Hindenburg[5]	1847	1925–1934	Erich Honecker[12]	1912	1976–

1. Year of end of rule is also that of death, unless otherwise indicated. 2. Was Elector of Brandenburg (1688–1701) as Frederick III. 3. Became Emperor of Germany in 1871. 4. Died 1941. 5. President. 6. Führer. 7. Named Chancellor by President Hindenburg in 1933. 8. Died 1972. 9. Died 1963. 10. Died 1976. 11. Chairman of Council of State. Died 1973. 12. Chairman of Council of State.

the U.S., Britain, France, and the Benelux countries agreed to set up a German state comprising the three Western Zones.

The U.S.S.R. reacted by clamping a blockade on all ground communications between the Western Zones and Berlin, an enclave in the Soviet Zone. The Western Allies countered by organizing a gigantic airlift to fly supplies into the beleaguered city, assigning 60,000 men to it. The U.S.S.R. was finally forced to lift the blockade on May 12, 1949.

The Federal Republic of Germany was proclaimed on May 23, 1949, with its capital at Bonn. In free elections, West Germany voters gave a majority in the Constituent Assembly to the Christian Democrats, with the Social Democrats largely making up the opposition. Konrad Adenauer became chancellor, and Theodor Heuss of the Free Democrats was elected first president.

With admission into the European Coal and Steel Community and later into the Common Market, West Germany prospered. In 1950 a West Berlin Constitution provided for autonomous municipal government and representation in the Bundestag. A peace contract was given West Germany on May 26, 1952, that created within the North Atlantic Treaty Organization, a European Defense Community, but it was later vetoed by France.

Agreements in Paris in 1954 giving the Federal Republic full independence and complete sovereignty came into force on May 5, 1955. Under it, West Germany and Italy became members of the Brussels treaty organization created in 1948 and renamed the Western European Union. West Germany also became a member of NATO. In 1955 the U.S.S.R. recognized the Federal Republic. The Saar territory, under an agreement between France and West Germany, held a plebiscite and despite economic links to France voted to rejoin West Germany. It became a state of West Germany on Jan. 1, 1957.

In 1963, Chancellor Adenauer concluded a treaty of mutual cooperation and friendship with France and then retired. He was succeeded by his chief inner-party critic, Ludwig Erhard, who was followed in 1966 by Kurt Georg Kiesinger. He, in turn, was succeeded in 1969 by Willy Brandt, former mayor of West Berlin.

The division between West Germany and East Germany was intensified when the Communists erected the Berlin Wall in 1961. In 1968, the East German Communist leader, Walter Ulbricht, imposed restrictions on West German movements into West Berlin. The Soviet-bloc invasion of Czechoslovakia in August 1968 added to the tension.

Willy Brandt's Socialist government pushed through an "Ostpolitik" policy that led to the first official meetings of leaders of East and West Germany, in 1970. A treaty with the U.S.S.R. was signed in Moscow in August 1970 in which force was renounced and respect for the "territorial integrity" of present European states declared.

Three months later, West Germany signed a similar treaty with Poland, renouncing force and setting Poland's western border as the Oder-Neisse Line, thus acknowledging Poland's post-war annexation of 40,000 square miles (103,600 sq km) of former German territory. It subsequently resumed formal relations with Czechoslovakia in a pact that "voided" the Munich treaty that gave Nazi Germany the Sudetenland.

Both German states were admitted to the United Nations in 1973.

Brandt, winner of a Nobel Peace Prize for his foreign policies, was forced to resign in 1974 when an East German spy was discovered to be one of his top staff members. Succeeding him was a moderate Social Democrat, Helmut Schmidt.

West Germany was host to the fourth annual summit meeting of the seven leading industrial nations July 16–17, 1978. Schmidt, whose economy was Europe's strongest with a trade surplus of $5 billion in 1977, was critical of U.S. failure to curb its oil consumption and inflation. Schmidt had differed with Carter previously, questioning his emphasis on human rights as a threat to détente and refusing to accept U.S. restrictions on the export of nuclear reactors unless all nations accepted such controls.

The Christian Social Union of Bavaria broke its 30-year alliance with the Christian Democratic

Party in 1979 to run its leader, Franz Josef Strauss, in a three-way race against the Christian Democrats' Ernst Albrecht and Chancellor Schmidt in the 1980 elections. Schmidt, campaigning on a tough policy of stationing U.S. nuclear weapons in West Germany despite Soviet threats, won the Oct. 5 contest easily with a new coalition majority of 271.

Schmidt had made an unsuccessful trip to Moscow four months before the vote to urge President Leonid I. Brezhnev to withdraw from Afghanistan. He canceled a scheduled visit to East Germany in August because of the Soviet and East bloc pressure on the Polish labor movement. Smarting from Reagan Administration criticism of German defense weakness, Schmidt threatened to resign in May 1981 in order to win Bundestag approval of the stationing of U.S. nuclear weapons in West Germany.

At the "big seven" economic summit in Ottawa in July, Schmidt forcefully presented European demands for lowering U.S. interest rates but was unable to persuade Reagan to take action.

BERLIN

Status: West Berlin: State of West Germany; East Berlin: capital of East Germany
Governing Mayor, West Berlin: Richard von Weizsäcker (1981)
Mayor, East Berlin: Erhard Krack
Area: 340 square miles (West Berlin, 184; East Berlin, 156
Population (est. 1979): 3,034,000 (West Berlin, 1,905,000; East Berlin, 1,129,000)

Berlin, the capital of prewar Germany, lies entirely within the borders of East Germany. After the war, the city was occupied by the forces of the U.S., Britain, France, and the U.S.S.R. The three western sectors, now known as West Berlin, contain 55% of the area and two thirds of the population.

West Berlin is a state of the Federal Republic of Germany, but supreme authority remains in the hands of the three Western powers in accordance with postwar agreements. The government is composed of the governing mayor, the 11-member Senate (his Cabinet), and the House of Representatives, a popularly elected legislative body that elects the governing mayor and the Senate.

East Berlin is governed by a City Assembly elected by Communist Party members, and a Magistrat (City Council) chosen by the Assembly and headed by the mayor. In violation of the Four Power Agreements, the Soviet Sector has been incorporated into the German Democratic Republic and is now the capital of that country.

Major anti-Communist riots broke out in East Berlin in June 1953 and, since Aug. 13, 1961, the Soviet Sector has been virtually sealed off by a Communist-built wall, 26½ miles (43 km) long, running through the city. It was built to stem the flood of refugees seeking freedom in the West, 200,000 having fled in 1961 before the wall was erected.

GHANA

Republic of Ghana
President: Hilla Limann (1979)
Area: 92,100 sq mi. (238,537 sq km)
Population (est. 1981): 11,750,000 (growth rate: 3.3%)

Density per square mile: 127.6
Capital: Accra
Largest cities (est. 1975): Accra, 716,600; (est. 1972): Kumasi, 342,982; Sekondi-Takoradi, 161,071
Monetary unit: Cedi
Languages: Native tongues (Twi, Fanti, Ga, Ewe, Dagbani); English
Religions: Christian 43%, Islam, 12%, Animist 38%
Member of Commonwealth of Nations
Freedom House classifications: Capitalist-statist industrial, multi-party centralized
Economic summary: Gross national product (1979): $4.5 billion. Average annual growth rate (1970–78): −3.0%. Per capita income: $790. Land used for agriculture: 19%; labor force: 60%; principal products: cocoa, timber, coconuts, coffee, subsistence crops, rubber. Labor force in industry: 17%; major products: mining products, lumber, light manufactured goods, fish, aluminum. Natural resources: gold, diamonds, bauxite, manganese, fish. Exports: cocoa beans and products, gold, timber, manganese ore. Imports: petroleum, food, industrial raw materials, machinery, transport equipment. Major trading partners: U.K., U.S., Western European countries, Japan.

Geography. A West African country bordering on the Gulf of Guinea, Ghana has the Ivory Coast to the west, Upper Volta to the north, and Togo to the east. It compares in size to Oregon.

The coastal belt, extending about 270 miles (435 km), is sandy, marshy, and generally exposed. Behind it is a gradually widening grass strip. The forested plateau region to the north is broken by ridges and hills. The largest river is the Volta.

Government. Ghana, under military rule since 1972, returned to civilian government in 1979. In elections held June 18, 1979, the People's National Party won 71 seats in a reconstituted 140-seat Parliament. Hilla Limann, candidate of the People's National Party, won the presidency in a run-off on July 9 against Victor Owusa, leader of the Popular Front Party, which won 42 seats. Splinter parties shared the balance.

History. Created an independent country on March 6, 1957, Ghana is the former British colony of the Gold Coast. The area was first seen by Portuguese traders in 1470. They were followed by the English (1553), the Dutch (1595), and the Swedes (1640). British rule over the Gold Coast began in 1820, but it was not until after quelling the severe resistance of the Ashanti in 1901 that it was firmly established. British Togoland, formerly a colony of Germany, was incorporated into Ghana by referendum in 1956. As the result of a plebiscite, Ghana became a republic on July 1, 1960.

Premier Kwame Nkrumah attempted to take leadership of the Pan-African Movement, holding the All-African People's Congress in his capital, Accra, in 1958 and organizing the Union of African States with Guinea and Mali in 1961. But he oriented his country toward the Soviet Union and China and built an autocratic rule over all aspects of Ghanaian life.

In February 1966, while Nkrumah was visiting Peking and Hanoi, he was deposed by a military coup led by Gen. Emmanuel K. Kotoka. The U.S. recognized the new regime and gave it financial aid. In April 1967, a military junta was crushed, but Kotoka was killed. The military leaders took steps to restore civilian rule and a new Constitution was approved in May 1969.

Another military group took over in January

1972. Its leader, Col. Ignatius Acheampong, proclaimed himself Head of State and chairman of the National Redemption Council, which replaced Parliament. The new regime proposed a union government of military, police, and civilian elements in a referendum approved by the voters in March 1978. Before the plan could be implemented, however, Lt. Gen. Frederick W. K. Akuffo of the military governing council ousted Acheampong on July 5. The shift was apparently related to food shortages and Ghana's raging inflation, running at an annual rate of more than 100%.

A military coup led by Flight Lieutenant Jerry Rawlings, imprisoned after an earlier attempt, overthrew Akuffo on June 4, 1979. Rawlings promised that the election of a civilian president would go ahead as scheduled, and Hilla Limann, candidate of the People's National Party, became President-elect in July.

GREECE

Hellenic Republic
President: Constantine Karamanlis (1980)
Premier: George Rallis (1980)
Area: 50,547 sq mi. (130,917 sq km)
Population (est. 1981): 9,700,000 (average annual growth rate, 1969–79, 0.7%)
Density per square mile: 191.9
Capital: Athens
Largest cities (est. 1981 for metropolitan area): Athens, 3,000,000; **(1971 census):** Salonika, 345,799; Piraeus, 187,362; Péristéri, 118,413; Patrai, 111,607
Monetary unit: Drachma
Language: Greek
Religion: Greek Orthodox
National name: Elliniki Dimokratia
Freedom House classifications: Capitalist industrial, multi-party centralized
Economic summary: Gross national product (1979): $36.7 billion. Average annual growth rate (1970–78): 3.8%. Per capita income (1979): $3,665. Labor force in agriculture: 38%; principal products: grains, fruits, vegetables, olives, olive oil, tobacco, cotton, livestock, dairy products. Labor force in industry: 27%; major products: textiles, metals, chemicals, electrical equipment, cement, glass. Natural resources: bauxite, lignite, forests. Exports: fruits, vegetables, textiles, tobacco. Imports: machinery and automotive equipment, petroleum, consumer goods, chemicals, meat, live animals. Major trading partners: West Germany, Japan, Italy, France, Saudi Arabia, U.S., U.K.

Geography. Greece, on the Mediterranean Sea, is the southernmost country on the Balkan Peninsula in Eastern Europe. It is bordered on the north by Albania, Yugoslavia, and Bulgaria; on the west by the Ionian Sea; and on the east by the Aegean Sea and Turkey. It is slightly smaller than Alabama.

North central Greece, Epirus, and western Macedonia all are mountainous. The main chain of the Pindus Mountains rises to 9,000 feet (2,743 m) in places, separating Epirus from the plains of Thessaly. Mt. Olympus, rising to 9,570 feet (2,909 m) in the north near the Aegean Sea, is the highest point in the country. Greek Thrace is mostly a lowland region separated from European Turkey by the lower Evros River.

Among the many islands are the Ionian group off the west coast; the Cyclades group to the southeast; other islands in the eastern Aegean, including Lesbos, Samos, and Chios; and Crete, the fourth largest Mediterranean island.

The Dodecanese, a group of islands in the Aegean Sea near the coast of Asia Minor, were ceded to Greece by the 1947 Italian peace treaty and were formally transferred on March 7, 1948.

Government. Greece returned to democratic government when the military dictatorship imposed in April 1967, collapsed July 23, 1974. A referendum in December 1974, resulted in 69% support for a republic to replace the monarchy.

The major political parties are the New Democracy Party (177 of 300 seats in the unicameral parliament), led by Premier George Rallis; Panhellenic Socialist Movement (94 seats), led by Andreas Papandreou; Communist Party (11 seats); Party of Democratic Socialism (3 seats); Union of Democratic Center (3 seats); National Alignment (2 seats).

History. Greece, with a recorded history going back to 766 B.C., reached the peak of its glory in the 5th century B.C., and by the middle of the 2nd century B.C., it had declined to the status of a Roman province. It remained within the Eastern Roman Empire until Constantinople fell to the Crusaders in 1204.

In 1453, the Turks took Constantinople, and by 1460 Greece was a Turkish province. The insurrection made famous by the poet Lord Byron broke out in 1821, and in 1827 Greece was set up as an independent nation, with sovereignty guaranteed by the U.K., France, and Russia.

The protecting powers chose Prince Otto of Bavaria as the first king of modern Greece in 1832 to reign over an area only slightly larger than the Peloponnese Peninsula. Chiefly under the next king, George I, chosen by the protecting powers in 1863, Greece acquired much of its present territory. During his 57-year reign, a period in which he encouraged parliamentary democracy, Thessaly, Epirus, Macedonia, Crete, and most of the Aegean islands were added from the disintegrating Turkish empire. An unsuccessful war against Turkey after World War I brought down the monarchy, to be replaced by a republic in 1923.

Two military dictatorships and a financial crisis brought George II back from exile, but only until 1941, when Italian and German invaders defeated tough Greek resistance. After British and Greek troops liberated the country in October 1944, Communist guerrillas staged a long campaign in which the government received U.S. aid under the Truman Doctrine, the predecessor of the Marshall Plan.

A military junta seized power in April 1967, sending young King Constantine II into exile December 14. Col. George Papadopoulos, as premier, converted the government to republican form in 1973 and as President ended martial law. He was moving to restore democracy when he was ousted in November of that year by his military colleagues. The regime of the "colonels," which had tortured its opponents and scoffed at human rights, resigned July 23, 1974, after having bungled an attempt to seize Cyprus.

Former Premier Karamanlis returned from exile to become premier of Greece's first civilian government since 1967. The election in November gave him 54% backing, and a new republican Constitution was adopted June 7, 1975.

Greece cut its military ties with the North Atlantic Treaty Organization in 1974 because of U.S. failure to restrain Turkey from invading Cyprus. It was not until Oct. 20, 1980, that Greece returned as a military partner in NATO, even then with some public protest. A lengthy dispute with Turkey over air and sea rights in the Aegean advanced toward settlement with the return to the alliance. An air-rights agreement was announced in March 1981, and the demarcation of the continental shelf in order to resolve oil-exploration problems was expected to follow.

On Jan. 1, 1981, Greece became the 10th member of the European Community. In the organization's Council of Ministers, Greece will have five votes, ranking with the Netherlands and Belgium but behind the "big four"—Britain, West Germany, France, and Italy—which have 10 votes each.

GRENADA

State of Grenada
Sovereign: Queen Elizabeth II
Prime Minister: Maurice Bishop (1979)
Governor General: Paul Scoon (1978)
Area: 133 sq mi. (344 sq km)
Population (est. 1981): 110,000 (black, 53%; mixed, 42%) (growth rate, 1.0%)
Density per square mile: 827.1
Capital and largest city (est. 1978): St. George's, 30,000
Monetary unit: East Caribbean dollar
Ethnic groups: Caribs and Indians
Language: English
Religions: Roman Catholic, Anglican, Methodist
Member of Commonwealth of Nations
Freedom House classifications: Capitalist-socialist industrial, dominant party
Economic summary: Gross national product (1979): $70 million. Average annual growth rate (1970–78): −1.8%. Per capita income: $500. Land used for agriculture: 44%; labor force: 40%; principal products: spices, cocoa, bananas. Exports: nutmeg, cocoa beans, bananas, mace. Imports: foodstuffs, machinery, building materials. Major trading partners: U.K., West Indies countries, West Germany, Netherlands, U.S.

Geography. Grenada (the first "a" is pronounced as in "gray") is the most southerly of the Windward Islands, about 100 miles (161 km) from the South American coast. It is a volcanic island traversed by a mountain range, the highest peak of which is Mount St. Catherine (2,756 ft.; 840 m).

History. Grenada was discovered by Columbus in 1498. After more than 200 years of British rule, most recently as part of the West Indies Associated States, it became independent Feb. 7, 1974.

The country began its independence in chaos, as opponents of Prime Minister Eric M. Gairy's curbs on civil liberties—notably the professionals and educated class, as well as some union leaders and businessmen—paralyzed Grenada with a general strike that ended after two weeks when Gairy promised to disband his secret police force.

In 1975, Grenada became a member of the Organization of American States. In June 1977, it was host to the OAS General Assembly.

The government of Prime Minister Gairy was ousted March 13, 1979, by the New Jewel Movement of Maurice Bishop. Bishop, a protégé of Cuban President Fidel Castro, invited Cuban military advisers to Grenada and on June 20, 1980,

called on Grenadians to join a "people's militia" to fight a "people's war" against imperialism.

GUATEMALA

Republic of Guatemala
President: Gen. Romeo Lucas García (1978)
Area: 42,042 sq mi. (108,889 sq km)
Population (est. 1981): 7,470,000 (annual growth rate: 3.0%)
Density per square mile: 177.7
Capital and largest city (est. 1980): Guatemala City, 1,000,000
Monetary unit: Quetzal
Languages: Spanish, Indian dialects
Religion: Roman Catholic
National name: República de Guatemala
Freedom House classifications: Capitalist pre-industrial, multi-party centralized
Economic summary: Gross national product (1979): $6.9 billion. Average annual growth rate (1970–78): 3.3%. Per capita income: $1,020. Labor force in agriculture: 53%; principal products: corn, beans, coffee, cotton, cattle, sugar, bananas, essential oils, timber. Labor force in industry: 14%; principal products: prepared foods, textiles, construction materials, tires, pharmaceuticals. Natural resources: nickel, timber, shrimp. Exports: coffee, cotton, sugar, meat, bananas. Imports: fuels and lubricants, industrial machinery, motor vehicles, iron and steel. Major trading partners: U.S., Central American nations, West Germany, Japan, Venezuela.

Geography. The northernmost of the Central American nations, Guatemala is the size of Tennessee. Its neighbors are Mexico on the north, west, and east and Belize, Honduras, and El Salvador on the east. The country consists of two main regions —the cool highlands with the heaviest population and the tropical area along the Pacific and Caribbean coasts. The principal mountain range rises to the highest elevation in Central America and contains many volcanic peaks. Volcanic eruptions are frequent.

The Petén region in the north contains important resources and archaeological sites of the Mayan civilization.

Government. Executive power is vested in the president, who is elected for a term of four years, and his Cabinet of 12 members. Legislative power lies with the 61-member National Congress.

The major political parties are National Liberation Movement (20 seats in the National Congress); Democratic Institutional Party (17 seats); Revolutionary Party (14 seats); Christian Democratic Party (7 seats); and the Central Aranista National Party (3 seats).

History. Once the site of the ancient Mayan civilization, Guatemala, conquered by Spain in 1524, set itself up as a republic in 1839. From 1898 to 1920, the dictator Manuel Estrada Cabrera ran the country, and from 1931 to 1944, Gen. Jorge Ubico Castaneda was the strongman. In 1944 the National Assembly elected Gen. Federico Ponce president, but he was overthrown in October. In December, Dr. Juan José Arévalo was elected as the head of a leftist regime that continued to press its reform program. Jacobo Arbenz Guzmán, administration candidate with pro-Communist leanings, won the 1950 elections.

Arbenz expropriated the large estates, including

plantations of the United Fruit Company, and exterminated his political enemies. With covert U.S. backing, a revolt was led by Col. Carlos Castillo Armas, and Arbenz took refuge in Havana. Castillo Armas became president but was assassinated in 1957. Constitutional government was restored in 1958, and Gen. Miguel Ydigoras Fuentes was elected president. He was host to the Cuban force that trained for the disastrous landing at the Bay of Pigs in April 1961.

In 1963 the Ydigoras government was overthrown by Enrique Peralta Azurdia, who ruled until 1966, when elections, under a new Constitution, led to Congress's choice of Dr. Julio César Méndez Montenegro.

A wave of terrorism, by left and right, began in 1967, and in August 1968 U.S. Ambassador John Gordon Mein was killed when he resisted kidnappers. Fear of anarchy led to the election in 1970 of Army Chief of Staff Carlos Araña Osorio, who had put down a rural guerrilla movement at the cost of nearly 3,000 lives. Araña, surprisingly, pledged social reforms when he took office. Another military candidate, Gen. Kjell Laugerud, won the presidency in 1974 amid renewed political violence.

A devastating earthquake on Feb. 4, 1976, killed 22,000 and injured 74,000, doing little damage to the country's growing industrial base, however.

In 1977, Britain's announcement of its intention to grant independence to Belize, formerly British Honduras, brought a threat by Guatemala to fight for the territory. Guatemala eventually signed a treaty in March 1981, pledging to negotiate territorial claims and recognize the new state on its attaining independence in September 1981.

Civil strife increased again under the presidency of Gen. Romeo Lucas García, who was elected in 1978. Amnesty International charged in February 1981 that Lucas had been directly responsible for 5,000 deaths, including those of 76 leaders of the opposition Christian Democratic Party. Although the Carter Administration had cut off military aid in 1978 because of human-rights violations, the Reagan Administration was reported ready to restore aid.

GUINEA

Revolutionary People's Republic of Guinea
President: Ahmed Sékou Touré (1958)
Premier: Louis Lansana Béavogui (1972)
Area: 94,925 sq mi. (245,857 sq km)
Population (est. 1981): 5,115,000 (growth rate: 2.8%)
Density per square mile: 53.9
Capital and largest city (est. 1980): Conakry, 765,000
Monetary unit: Syli
Languages: French (official), native tongues (Malinké, Susu, Fulani)
Religions: Islam and Animist
National name: République Populaire Revolutionnaire de Guinée
Freedom House classifications: Socialist pre-industrial, one-party socialist
Economic summary: Gross national product (1979): $1.5 billion. Average annual growth rate (1970–78): 0.8%. Per capita income: $140. Principal agricultural products: rice, cassava, millet, corn, coffee, bananas, palm products, pineapples. Major industrial products: bauxite, alumina, light manufactured and processed goods. Natural resources: bauxite, iron ore, diamonds, gold, water power. Exports: bauxite, alumina, pineapples, bananas, coffee. Imports: petroleum, machinery, transport equipment, foodstuffs, textiles. Major trading partners: Communist bloc, Western Europe, U.S.

Geography. Guinea, in West Africa on the Atlantic, is also bordered by Guinea-Bissau, Senegal, Mali, the Ivory Coast, Liberia, and Sierra Leone. Slightly smaller than Oregon, the country consists of a coastal plain, a mountainous region, a savanna interior, and a forest area in the Guinea Highlands. The highest peak is Mount Nimba at about 6,000 feet (1,829 m).

Government. The National Assembly has 150 members elected by universal suffrage from a list prepared and presented by the Parti Démocratique de Guinée, the only political party, led by President Ahmed Sékou Touré, Secretary General of the party.

History. Previously part of French West Africa, Guinea achieved independence by rejecting the new French Constitution, and on Oct. 2, 1958, became an independent state with Sékou Touré as president. Touré led the country into being the first avowedly Marxist state in Africa. Diplomatic relations with France were suspended in 1965, with the Soviet Union replacing France as the country's chief source of economic and technical assistance.

In 1966, when a Ghanaian military coup deposed Kwame Nkrumah as President, Touré welcomed him to Guinea and declared him joint president and party leader. The titles proved to be only honorary. Touré accused Ghana of being an American imperialist puppet, and the U.S. Embassy in his capital, Conakry, was sacked. In retaliation the United States ended financial aid. An exchange of letters between the Guinean and U.S. presidents restored relations.

Prosperity came in 1969 after the start of exploitation of bauxite deposits. Touré was re-elected to a seven-year term in 1974 and again in 1981.

GUINEA-BISSAU

Republic of Guinea-Bissau
President of Revolutionary Council: João Bernardo Vieira (1980)
Area: 13,948 sq mi. (36,125 sq km)
Population (est. 1981): 580,000 (growth rate: 1.9%)
Density per square mile: 41.6
Capital and largest city (est. 1979 for metropolitan area): Bissau, 109,500
Monetary unit: Guinea-Bissau peso
Language: Portuguese
Religions: Animist, 66%; Islam, 30%; Roman Catholic, 4%
National name: Guiné Bissau
Freedom House classifications: Socialist pre-industrial, one-party socialist
Economic summary: Gross national product (1979): $140 million. Average annual growth rate (1970–78): 2.9%. Per capita income: $230. Labor force in agriculture: 90%; principal products: palm oil, root crops, rice, coconuts, peanuts. Natural resources: potential bauxite deposits. Exports: peanuts, coconuts, shrimp, fish, wood. Imports: foodstuffs, manufactured goods, fuels, transportation equipment. Major trading partner: Portugal.

Geography. A neighbor of Senegal and Guinea in West Africa, on the Atlantic coast, Guinea-Bissau is about half the size of South Carolina.

The country is a low-lying coastal region of swamps, rain forests, and mangrove-covered wetlands, with about 25 islands off the coast. The Bijagos archipelago extends 30 miles (48 km) out to sea. Internal communications depend mainly on deep estuaries and meandering rivers, since there are no railroads. Bissau, the capital, is the main port.

Government. The 15-member Council of State was elected in 1977 by a National Assembly of 150 members chosen from regional councils elected from lists provided by the sole political party, the African Party for the Independence of Guinea-Bissau and Cape Verde.

History. Guinea-Bissau was discovered in 1446 by the Portuguese Nuno Tristao, and colonists in the Cape Verde Islands obtained trading rights in the territory. In 1879 the connection with the Cape Verde Islands was broken. Early in the 1900s the Portuguese managed to pacify some tribesmen, although resistance to colonial rule remained.

The African Party for the Independence of Guinea-Bissau and Cape Verde was founded in 1956 and several years later began guerrilla warfare that grew increasingly effective. By 1974 the rebels controlled most of the countryside, where they formed a government that was soon recognized by scores of countries. The military coup in Portugal in April 1974 brightened the prospects for freedom, and in August the Lisbon government signed an agreement granting independence to the province as of Sept. 10. The new republic took the name Guinea-Bissau. Its government was immediately recognized by the United States.

In November 1980, Premier João Bernardo Vieira headed a coup that deposed Luis Cabral, President since 1974. A Revolutionary Council assumed the powers of government, with Vieira as its head.

GUYANA

Cooperative Republic of Guyana
President: Forbes Burnham (1980)
Prime Minister: Ptolemy A. Reid (1980)
Area: 83,000 sq mi. (214,969 sq km)
Population (est. 1981): 890,000 (growth rate: 1.4%) (East Indian, 52%; African, 31%; mixed 10%; Amerindian, 5%)
Density per square mile: 10.7
Capital and largest city (est. 1976 by U.N.): Georgetown, 72,000
Monetary unit: Guyana dollar
Languages: English (official), Hindi, Urdu
Religions: Hindu, 37%; Protestant, 32%; Roman Catholic, 13%
Member of Commonwealth of Nations
Freedom house classifications: Capitalist-socialist industrial, multi-party centralized
Economic summary: Gross national product (1979): $480 million. Average annual growth rate (1970–78): —0.2%. Per capita income: $510. Labor force in agriculture: 29%; principal products: sugar, rice. Labor force in industry: 31%; major products: bauxite, alumina. Natural resources: bauxite, gold, diamonds, hardwood timber, shrimp. Exports: sugar, bauxite, alumina, rice, shrimp. Imports: consumer and manufactured goods. Major trading partners: Canada, Caribbean nations, U.K., U.S.

Geography. Guyana is situated on the northern coast of South America east of Venezuela, west of Suriname, and north of Brazil. The country consists of a low coastal area and the Guiana Highlands in the south. There is an extensive north-south network of rivers. Guyana is the size of Idaho.

Government. Guyana, formerly British Guiana, proclaimed itself a republic on Feb. 23, 1970, ending its tie with Britain while remaining in the Commonwealth.

Guyana has a unicameral legislature, the National Assembly, with 53 members directly elected for four-year terms and 12 elected by local councils. A 24-member Cabinet is headed by the President.

The major political parties are the People's National Congress (41 of 53 seats in National Assembly), led by President Forbes Burnham; People's Progressive Party (10 seats), led by Dr. Cheddi B. Jagan.

History. British Guiana won internal self-government in 1952. The next year the People's Progressive Party, headed by Cheddi B. Jagan, an East Indian dentist, won the elections and Jagan became Prime Minister. British authorities deposed him for alleged Communist connections. A coalition ousted Jagan in 1964, installing a moderate Socialist, Forbes Burnham, a black, as Prime Minister. On May 26, 1966, the country became an independent member of the Commonwealth and resumed its traditional name, Guyana.

The government nationalized mining operations of the U.S.-owned Reynolds Metals Co. in 1975.

In 1978, the International Monetary Fund approved an $18.7-million loan for Guyana, which is trying to overcome a $60-million deficit in balance of payments.

One of the most bizarre incidents in modern history occurred when 911 persons died in a mass murder-suicide on Nov. 19, 1978, at a remote settlement in Guyana founded by a U.S. sect known as the People's Temple. The victims were either shot or forced to drink poisoned Kool-Aid by the Rev. Jim Jones, for whom the site, Jonestown, was named.

Jones ordered his followers to die after his aides had killed U.S. Representative Leo J. Ryan of California and three newsmen who accompanied Ryan on an investigative trip to the colony.

HAITI

Republic of Haiti
Life President: Jean-Claude Duvalier (1971)
Area: 10,714 sq mi. (27,750 sq km)
Population (est. 1981): 5,100,000 (growth rate: 2.4%)
Density per square mile: 476.0
Capital and largest city (est. 1978): Port-au-Prince, 745,000
Monetary unit: Gourde
Languages: French, Creole
Religion: Roman Catholic
National name: République d'Haïti
Freedom house classifications: Capitalist pre-industrial, dominant party
Economic summary: Gross national product (1979): $1.3 billion. Average annual growth rate (1970–78): 2.2%. Per capita income: $230. Land used for agriculture: 31%; labor force: 79%; principal products: coffee, sugar cane, rice, corn, sorghum. Labor force in industry: 7%; major products: refined sugar, textiles, flour, cement, bauxite, light assembly products. Natural resource: bauxite. Exports: coffee, light industrial products, bauxite, sugar, essential oils, sisal. Imports: consumer goods, foodstuffs, industrial equipment, petroleum products, construction

materials. Major trading partner: U.S.

Geography. Haiti, in the West Indies, occupies the western third of the island of Hispaniola, which it shares with the Dominican Republic. About the size of Maryland, Haiti is two thirds mountainous, with the rest of the country marked by great valleys, extensive plateaus, and small plains. The most densely populated region is the Cul-de-Sac plain near Port-au-Prince.

Government. In 1964, the late President, François Duvalier, known as "Papa Doc," made himself president for life. His son, Jean-Claude, then 19, known as "Baby Doc," inherited the title on his father's death on April 21, 1971. Under a Constitution revised in 1964, the president in periods of crisis may dismiss the National Assembly and Cabinet and govern by decree. The Parti d'Unité Nationale (57 of the 58 seats in the National Assembly), led by President Duvalier, is the only legal party in the country.

History. Discovered by Columbus, who landed at Môle Saint Nicolas on Dec. 6, 1492, Haiti in 1697 became a French possession known as Saint Domingue. An insurrection among a slave population of 500,000 in 1791 ended with a declaration of independence by Pierre-Dominique Toussaint l'Ouverture in 1801. Napoleon Bonaparte suppressed the independence movement, but it eventually triumphed in 1804 under Jean-Jacques Dessalines, who gave the new nation the aboriginal name Haiti.

Its prosperity dissipated in internal strife as well as disputes with neighboring Santo Domingo during a succession of 19th-century dictatorships, a bankrupt Haiti accepted a U.S. customs receivership from 1905 to 1941. Direct U.S. rule from 1915 to 1930 brought a measure of stability and a population growth that made Haiti the most densely populated nation in the hemisphere.

In 1949, after four years of democratic rule by President Dumarsais Estimé, dictatorship returned under Gen. Paul Magloire, who was succeeded by François Duvalier in 1957.

Duvalier established a dictatorship based on secret police, known as the "Ton-ton Macoutes," who gunned down opponents of the regime. Duvalier's son, Jean-Claude, or "Baby Doc," succeeded his father in 1971 as ruler of the poorest nation in the Western Hemisphere.

Limited economic improvement followed an increase in foreign investment under the new regime as 150 foreign companies established Haitian branches to take advantage of low wages. A steady exodus of refugees continued toward the United States, reaching a high of 15,000 in 1980. Previously denied refugee status, Haitian "boat people" were accorded the same temporary entrance rights as Cubans who arrived by boat.

On May 27, 1980, Duvalier married Michelle Bennett in a wedding attended by 5,000 guests and estimated to cost from $3 million to $5 million.

HONDURAS

Republic of Honduras
Provisional President: Gen. Policarpo Paz García (1980)
Area: 43,277 sq mi. (112,088 sq km)
Population (est. 1981): 3,825,000 (growth rate: 3.4%) (60% mestizo)

Density per square mile: 88.4
Capital and largest city (est. 1980): Tegucigalpa, 375,000
Monetary unit: Lempira
Languages: Spanish, some Indian dialects, English in Bay Islands Department
Religion: Roman Catholic
National name: República de Honduras
Freedom House classifications: Capitalist pre-industrial, multi-party centralized
Economic summary: Gross national product (1979): $1.9 billion. Average annual growth rate (1970–78): 0.4%. Per capita income: $490. Labor force in agriculture: 66%; principal products: bananas, coffee, corn, beans, cotton, sugar cane, tobacco. Labor force in industry: 8%; major products: processed agricultural products, textiles and clothing, wood products. Natural resources: timber, gold, silver, lead, zinc, antimony. Exports: bananas, coffee, lumber, meat, petroleum products. Imports: manufactured goods, machinery, transportation equipment, chemicals, petroleum. Major trading partners: U.S., Caribbean countries, West Germany, Venezuela, Japan.

Geography. Honduras, in the north central part of Central America, has a 400-mile (644-km) Caribbean coastline and a 40-mile (64-km) Pacific frontage. Its neighbors are Guatemala to the west, El Salvador to the south, and Nicaragua to the east. Honduras is slightly larger than Tennessee.

Generally mountainous, the country is marked by fertile plateaus, river valleys, and narrow coastal plains.

Government. The military regime in power since 1972 authorized the election of a Constitutional Assembly on April 20, 1980. The Partido Liberal, led by Roberto Suazo Córdova, won 35 of the Assembly seats; the Partido Nacional, led by Ricardo Zuñiga, won 33; the balance were won by a minor party. President Policarpo Paz García formally transferred power to the Assembly on July 20, but remained Provisional President until the election of a new leader, scheduled for November 29, 1981.

History. Columbus discovered Honduras on his last voyage in 1502. Honduras, with four other countries of Central America, declared its independence from Spain in 1821 and was part of a federation of Central American states until 1838. In that year it seceded from the federation and became a completely independent country.

It has been troubled by revolution and war ever since. U.S. Marines intervened in 1903 and 1923. In 1931, 1932, and 1937, major revolutions were crushed by force.

In July 1969, El Salvador invaded Honduras after Honduran landowners had deported several thousand Salvadorans. The fighting left 1,000 dead and tens of thousands homeless. By threatening economic sanctions and military intervention, the OAS induced El Salvador to withdraw.

In June 1970, Honduras and El Salvador agreed to a demilitarized zone of 1.8 miles on each side of their ill-defined border and accepted an OAS police force. A year later they agreed, despite two more border flare-ups, to negotiate a peace settlement.

In 1971, Ramon Ernesto Cruz, a lawyer, diplomat, and teacher, became Honduras's first freely elected president since 1949. But strongman Oswaldo López Arellano, citing "chaos and weakness" under the coalition, again seized control (for the third time in two decades). He served until his ouster in 1975.

On Aug. 7, 1978, the military ousted Juan Alberto Melgar Castro as president, naming Gen. Policarpo Paz Garcia as chief of state. This was the second military-originated change of government in three years resulting from charges of corruption.

HUNGARY

Hungarian People's Republic
President: Pál Losonczi (1967)
Premier: Gyorgy Lazar (1975)
Area: 35,919 sq mi. (93,030 sq km)
Population (est. 1981): 10,725,000 (growth rate: 0.2%)
Density per square mile: 298.6
Capital: Budapest
Largest cities (est. 1980): Budapest, 2,100,000; (est. 1977 by U.N.): Miskolc, 205,600; Debrecen, 194,000; Szeged, 174,600; Pécs, 167,700; Györ, 123,200
Monetary unit: Forint
Language: Magyar
Religions: Roman Catholic, 60%; Protestant, atheist
National name: Magyar Népköztársaság
Freedom House classifications: Socialist industrial, one-party communist
Economic summary: Gross national product (1979): $41.3. Average annual growth rate (1970–78): 5.1%. Per capita income: $2,750. Land used for agriculture: 75%; labor force: 20%; principal products: corn, wheat, potatoes, sugar beets, vegetables, wine grapes, fruits. Labor force in industry: 33%; major products: precision and measuring equipment, pharmaceuticals, textiles, transport equipment. Natural resources: some bauxite and brown coal. Exports: machinery and tools, industrial and consumer goods, raw materials. Imports: machinery, raw materials. Major trading partners: U.S.S.R., Warsaw Pact countries.

Geography. This central European country the size of Indiana is bordered by Austria to the west, Czechoslovakia to the north, the U.S.S.R. and Romania to the east, and Yugoslavia to the south.

Most of Hungary is a fertile, rolling plain lying east of the Danube River and drained by the Danube and Tisza rivers. In the extreme northwest is the Little Hungarian Plain. South of that area is Lake Balaton (250 sq mi.; 648 sq km).

Government. Hungary is a People's Republic with legislative power vested in the unicameral National Assembly, whose 352 members are elected directly for four-year terms. The supreme body of state power is the 21-member Presidential Council elected by the National Assembly. The supreme administrative body is the Council of Ministers, headed by the Premier.

The Hungarian Socialist Workers (Communist) Party, led by János Kádár, is the only political party.

History. About 2,000 years ago, Hungary was part of the Roman provinces of Pannonia and Dacia. In A.D. 896 it was invaded by the Magyars, who founded a kingdom. Christianity was accepted during the reign of Stephen I (St. Stephen) (997–1038).

The peak of Hungary's great period of medieval power came during the reign of Louis I the Great (1342–82), whose dominions touched the Baltic, Black, and Mediterranean seas.

War with the Turks broke out in 1389, and for more than 100 years the Turks advanced through the Balkans. When the Turks smashed a Hungarian army in 1526, western and northern Hungary accepted Hapsburg rule to escape Turkish occupa-

tion. Transylvania became independent under Hungarian princes. Intermittent war with the Turks was waged until a peace treaty was signed in 1699.

After the suppression of the 1848 revolt against Hapsburg rule, led by Louis Kossuth, the dual monarchy of Austria-Hungary was set up in 1867.

The dual monarchy was defeated with the other Central Powers in World War I. After a short-lived republic in 1918, the chaotic Communist rule of 1919 under Béla Kun ended with the Romanians occupying Budapest on Aug. 4, 1919. When the Romanians left, Adm. Nicholas Horthy entered the capital with a national army. The Treaty of Trianon of June 4, 1920, cost Hungary 68% of its land and 58% of its population. Meanwhile, the National Assembly had restored the legal continuity of the old monarchy; and, on March 1, 1920, Horthy was elected Regent.

Following the German invasion of Russia on June 22, 1941, Hungary joined the attack against the Soviet Union, but the war was not popular and Hungarian troops were almost entirely withdrawn from the eastern front by May 1943. German occupation troops set up a puppet government after Horthy's appeal for an armistice with advancing Soviet troops on Oct. 15, 1944, had resulted in his overthrow. The German regime soon fled the capital, however, and on December 23 a provisional government was formed in Soviet-occupied eastern Hungary. On Jan. 20, 1945, it signed an armistice in Moscow. Early the next year, the National Assembly approved a constitutional law abolishing the thousand-year-old monarchy and establishing a republic.

By the Treaty of Paris (1947), Hungary had to give up all territory it had acquired since 1937 and to pay $300 million reparations to the U.S.S.R., Czechoslovakia, and Yugoslavia. In 1948 the Communist Party, with the support of Soviet troops seized control. Hungary was proclaimed a People's Republic and one-party state in 1949. Industry was nationalized, the land collectivized into state farms, and the opposition terrorized by the secret police.

The terror, modeled after that of the U.S.S.R., reached its height with the trial of Jozsef Cardinal Mindszenty, Roman Catholic primate. He confessed to fantastic charges under duress of drugs or brainwashing and was sentenced to life imprisonment in 1949. Protests were voiced in all parts of the world.

On Oct. 23, 1956, anti-Communist revolution broke out in Budapest. To cope with it, the Communists set up a coalition government and called former Premier Imre Nagy back to head it. But he and most of his ministers were swept by the logic of events into the anti-Communist opposition, and he declared Hungary a neutral power, withdrawing from the Warsaw Treaty and appealing to the United Nations for help.

One of his ministers, János Kádár, established a counter-regime and asked the U.S.S.R. to send in military power. Soviet troops and tanks suppressed the revolution in bloody fighting after 190,000 people had fled the country and Mindszenty, freed from jail, had taken refuge in the U.S. Embassy. By treachery, Nagy and some of his ministers were abducted by the Soviet occupation troops and executed.

Kádár was succeeded as Premier, but not party secretary, by Gyula Kallai in 1965. Continuing his program of national reconciliation, Kádár emptied prisons, reformed the secret police, and eased travel restrictions.

Hungary developed the reputation of being the freest East European state, with Kádár's new motto —"If you're not against us, you're with us"—replacing previous police state suspicions. Significant Western capitalist investment was welcomed and some capitalistic methods embraced.

After 15 years' asylum in the U.S. Embassy, Mindszenty, under an agreement between the Vatican and the Hungarian regime, was allowed to travel into exile to Rome in 1971. In a move applauded by Kádár, Pope Paul VI removed Mindszenty from his honorary post as Primate of Hungary in 1974. The Cardinal died in Vienna in 1975.

Relations with the U.S. improved in 1972 when World War II debt claims between the two nations were settled. On Jan. 6, 1978, the U.S. returned to Hungary, over anti-Communist protests, the 977-year-old crown of St. Stephen, held at Fort Knox since World War II.

ICELAND

Republic of Iceland
President: Vigdis Finnbogadottir (1980)
Prime Minister: Gunnar Thoroddsen (1980)
Area: 39,702 sq mi. (102,828 sq km)
Population (est. 1981): 235,000 (growth rate: 1.1%)
Density per square mile: 5.9[1]
Capital and largest city (est. 1980): Reykjavik, 83,500
Monetary unit: Króna
Language: Icelandic
Religion: Evangelical Lutheran
National name: Lýdveldid Island
Freedom House classifications: Capitalist industrial, multi-party centralized
Economic summary: Gross national product (1979): $2.4 billion. Average annual growth rate (1970–78): 3.3%. Per capita income (1977): $5,450. Labor force in agriculture: 9%; fishing and fish processing: 13%; principal agricultural products: livestock, hay, fodder, cheese. Labor force in industry: 17%; major products: processed aluminum, fish. Natural resources: fish, diatomite, hydroelectric and geothermal power. Exports: fish, aluminum. Imports: petroleum products, machinery, transport equipment, food, textiles. Major trading partners: U.S., U.S.S.R., Western European countries.

1. Including some offshore islands.

Geography. Iceland, a bleak island about the size of Kentucky, lies in the north Atlantic Ocean east of Greenland and just touches the Arctic Circle. It is one of the most volcanic regions in the world.

Small fresh-water lakes are to be found throughout the island, and there are many natural phenomena, including hot springs, geysers, sulfur beds, canyons, waterfalls, and swift rivers. More than 13% of the area is covered by snowfields and glaciers, and most of the people live in the 7% of the island comprising fertile coastlands.

Government. The president is elected for four years by popular vote. Executive power resides in the prime minister and his Cabinet. The Althing (Parliament) is composed of 60 members in two houses. They elect 20 of themselves to constitute the Upper House, the remaining 40 representing the Lower House.

The major political parties are the Independence Party (22 of 60 seats in the Althing), led by Geir Hallgrimsson; Progressive Party (17 seats), led by Steingrimur Hermannsson; People's Alliance (11 seats), a Marxist group, led by Svavar Gestsson; So-cial Democratic Party (10 seats), led by Kjartan Johannsson. Prime Minister Gunnar Thoroddsen of the Independent Party leads a coalition of the Progressives and the People's Alliance supported by a few of his own party.

History. Iceland was first settled shortly before 900, mainly by Norse. A Constitution drawn up about 930 created a form of democracy and provided for an Althing, or General Assembly.

In 1262–64, Iceland came under Norwegian rule and passed to ultimate Danish control through the formation of the Union of Kalmar in 1483. In 1874, Icelanders obtained their own Constitution. In 1918, Denmark recognized Iceland as a separate state with unlimited sovereignty but still nominally under the Danish king.

On June 17, 1944, after a popular referendum, the Althing proclaimed Iceland an independent republic.

The British occupied Iceland in 1940, immediately after the German invasion of Denmark. In 1942, the U.S. took over the burden of protection. Iceland refused to abandon its neutrality in World War II and thus forfeited charter membership in the United Nations, but it cooperated with the Allies throughout the conflict. Iceland joined the North Atlantic Treaty Organization in 1949.

Iceland unilaterally extended its territorial waters from 12 to 50 nautical miles in 1972, precipitating a running dispute with Britain known as the "cod war." Icelandic warships harassed British trawlers, which then received aid from British gunboats; some trawlers were shelled, and Icelandic and British warships collided in 1973. The World Court ruled in 1974 that the 50-mile limit could not be applied unilaterally, but Iceland rejected the ruling.

An agreement calling for registration of all British trawlers fishing within 200 miles of Iceland and a 24-hour time limit on incursions was finally reached in 1976.

INDIA

Republic of India
President: Neelam Sanjiva Reddy (1977)
Prime Minister: Indira Gandhi (1980)
Area: 1,229,737 sq mi. (3,185,019 sq km)
Population (1981 census): 683,810,000 (growth rate: 1.8%)
Density per square mile: 556.0
Capital (1980 census): New Delhi, 619,417
Largest cities (1980 census): Calcutta, 9,165,650; Greater Bombay, 8,202,759; Delhi, 6,196,414; Madras, 4,276,635; Bangalore, 2,913,537; Ahmedabad, 2,515,195; Kanpur, 1,685,308
Monetary unit: Rupee
Principal languages: Hindi (official), Bengali, Sindhi, Gujarati, Kannarese, Kashmiri, Malayalam, Marathi, Oriya, Punjabi, Tamil, Telugu, Urdu, Kannada, Assamese (all recognized by the Constitution)
Religions: Hindu, 83%; Islam, 11%; Christian, 3%; Sikh, 2%
National name: Bharat
Member of Commonwealth of Nations
Freedom House classifications: Capitalist-statist, pre-industrial, multi-party decentralized
Economic summary: Gross national product (1979): $126.0 billion. Average annual growth rate (1970–78): 1.6%. Per capita income (1979): 140. Land used for agriculture: 54%; labor force: 70%; principal products: rice, wheat, oilseeds, cotton, tea. Major industrial products: jute, processed food, steel, machinery, transport machinery, cement. Natural resources: Iron ore, coal, manganese, mica,

Political Subdivisions of Republic of India

Subdivisions	Area sq mi.	Population 1971 census	Subdivisions	Area sq mi.	Population 1971 census
STATES			Sikkim[4]	2,744	215,000
Andhra Pradesh	106,052	43,502,708	Tamil Nadu[5]	50,132	41,199,168
Assam	30,400[1]	14,625,152[1]	Tripura	4,022	1,556,342
Bihar	67,198	56,353,369	Uttar Pradesh	113,452	88,341,144
Gujarat	72,154	26,697,475	West Bengal	33,928	44,312,011
Haryana	16,670	10,036,808			
Himachal Pradesh	10,880	3,460,434	**UNION TERRITORIES**		
Jammu and Kashmir[2]	85,861	4,616,632	Andaman and Nicobar Islands	3,215	115,133
Karnataka[3]	74,122	29,299,014	Arunachal Pradesh	31,400	467,511
Kerala	15,003	21,347,375	Chandigarh	44	257,251
Madhya Pradesh	171,210	41,654,119	Dadra and Nagar-Haveli	189	74,170
Maharashtra	118,530	50,412,235	Delhi	573	4,065,698
Manipur	8,628	1,072,753	Goa, Daman, and Diu	1,619	857,771
Meghalaya	8,700[1]	1,011,699[1]	Lakshadweep[6]	11	31,810
Nagaland	6,236	516,449	Mizoram	8,100	332,390
Orissa	60,182	21,944,615	Pondicherry	196	471,707
Punjab	21,630	13,551,060			
Rajasthan	132,151	25,765,806			

1. After reorganization of North East Frontier Agency in December 1971. 2. Status in dispute with Pakistan. 3. Formerly Mysore. 4. Sikkim became an Indian state in May 1975. Population figure is 1974 estimate. 5. Formerly Madras. 6. Formerly Laccadive, Minicoy, and Amindivi Islands.

bauxite, limestone. Exports: engineering goods, cotton apparel and fabrics, handicrafts, tea, iron and steel. Imports: petroleum, food grains, nonelectrical machinery, fertilizer. Major trading partners: U.S., Japan, U.K., U.S.S.R.

Geography. One third the area of the United States, the Republic of India occupies most of the subcontinent of India in south Asia. It borders on China in the northeast. Other neighbors are Pakistan on the west, Nepal and Bhutan on the north, and Burma and Bangladesh on the east.

The country contains a large part of the great Indo-Gangetic plain, which extends from the Bay of Bengal on the east to the Afghan frontier on the Arabian Sea on the west. This plain is the richest and most densely settled part of the subcontinent. Another distinct natural region is the Deccan, a plateau of 2,000 to 3,000 feet (610 to 914 m) in elevation, occupying the southern portion of the subcontinent.

Forming a part of the republic are several groups of islands—the Laccadives (14 islands) in the Arabian Sea and the Andamans (204 islands) and the Nicobars (19 islands) in the Bay of Bengal.

India's three great river systems, all rising in the Himalayas, have extensive deltas. The Ganges flows south and then east for 1,540 miles (2,478 km) across the northern plain to the Bay of Bengal; part of its delta, which begins 220 miles (354 km) from the sea, is within the republic. The Indus, starting in Tibet, flows northwest for several hundred miles in the Kashmir before turning southwest toward the Arabian Sea; it is important for irrigation in Pakistan. The Brahmaputra, also rising in Tibet, flows eastward, first through India and then south into Bangladesh and the Bay of Bengal.

Government. India is a federal republic. It is also a member of the Commonwealth of Nations, a status defined at the 1949 London Conference of Prime Ministers, by which India recognizes the Queen as

head of the Commonwealth. Under the Constitution effective Jan. 26, 1950, India has a parliamentary type of government.

The constitutional head of the state is the President, who is elected every five years. He is advised by the Prime Minister and a Cabinet based on a majority of the bicameral Parliament, which consists of a Council of States (Rajya Sabha), representing the constituent units of the republic and a House of the People (Lok Sabha), elected every five years by universal suffrage.

The major political parties are Congress Party I (351 of 542 seats in the Lok Sabha), led by Prime Minister Indira Gandhi; Lok Dal (secular Janata) Party (41 seats), led by former Prime Minister Charan Singh; Congress II (anti-Gandhi) Party (13 seats); Communist (Marxist independent) Party (35 seats); Communist (pro-Soviet) Party of India (10 seats).

History. The Aryans, or Hindus, who invaded India between 2400 and 1500 B.C. from the northwest found a land already well civilized. Buddhism was founded in the 6th century B.C. and spread through northern India. The earliest exact date in Indian history is 327 B.C., when Alexander the Great invaded India.

In 1526, Mohammedan invaders founded the great Mogul empire, centered on Delhi, which lasted, at least in name, until 1857. Akbar the Great (1542–1605) strengthened this empire and became the ruler of a greater portion of India than had ever before acknowledged the suzerainty of one man. The long reign of his great-grandson, Aurangzeb (1658–1707), represents both the culmination of Mogul power and the beginning of its decay.

Vasco da Gama, the Portuguese explorer, visited India first in 1498, and for the next 100 years the Portuguese had a virtual monopoly on trade with the subcontinent. Meanwhile, the English founded the East India Company, which set up its first factory at Surat in 1612 and began expanding its influence, fighting the Indian rulers and the French,

Dutch, and Portuguese traders simultaneously.

Bombay, taken from the Portuguese, became the seat of English rule in 1687. The defeat of French and Islamic armies by Lord Clive in the decade ending in 1760 laid the foundation of the British Empire in India. From then until 1858, when the administration of India was formally transferred to the British Crown following the Sepoy Mutiny of native troops in 1857, the East India Company suppressed native uprisings and extended British rule.

After World War I, in which the Indian states sent more than 6 million troops to fight beside the Allies, Indian nationalist unrest rose to new heights under the leadership of a little Hindu lawyer, Mohandas K. Gandhi, called Mahatma Gandhi. His tactics called for nonviolent revolts against British authority. He soon became the leading spirit of the All-India Congress Party, which was the spearhead of revolt. In 1919 the British gave added responsibility to Indian officials, and in 1935 India was given a federal form of government and a measure of self-rule.

In 1942, with the Japanese pressing hard on the eastern borders of India, the British War Cabinet tried and failed to reach a political settlement with nationalist leaders. The Congress Party took the position that the British must quit India. In 1942, fearing mass civil disobedience, the government of India carried out widespread arrests of Congress leaders, including Gandhi.

Gandhi was released in 1944 and other leaders later. Negotiations for a settlement were resumed, but they proved fruitless. Finally, in February 1947, the Labor government announced its determination to transfer power to "responsible Indian hands" by June 1948 even if a Constitution had not been worked out.

Lord Mountbatten as Governor-General, by June 1947, achieved agreement on the partitioning of India along religious lines (a plan previously opposed by the predominant Hindus and by Britain) and on the splitting of the provinces of Bengal and the Punjab, which the Moslems had claimed.

The Indian Independence Act, passed quickly by the British Parliament, received royal assent on July 18, 1947, and on August 15 the Indian Empire passed into history.

Jawaharlal Nehru, leader of the Congress Party, was made Prime Minister. Before an exchange of populations could be arranged, bloody riots occurred among the communal groups, and armed conflict broke out over rival claims to the princely state of Jammu and Kashmir. Peace was restored only with the greatest difficulty. In 1949 a Constitution, along the lines of the U.S. Constitution, was approved making India a sovereign republic. Under a federal structure the states were organized on linguistic lines.

The dominance of the Congress Party contributed to stability. In 1956 the republic absorbed the former French settlements. Five years later, it forcibly annexed the Portuguese enclaves of Goa, Damao, and Diu.

Communist China provoked a border dispute in 1957 that proceeded by local skirmishes until Oct. 20, 1962, when the Chinese mounted a massive offensive against Ladakh in the Kashmir and against the North East Frontier Agency. After gaining much territory claimed by India, the Chinese announced a cease-fire on Nov. 20, 1962.

Nehru died in 1964. His successor, Lal Bahadur Shastri, died on Jan. 10, 1966, a few hours after having concluded talks with President Ayub Khan of Pakistan arranging for an interim settlement of their differences. Nehru's daughter, Indira Gandhi, became Prime Minister, and she continued the policy of nonalignment.

In 1971 the Pakistani Army moved in to quash the independence movement in East Pakistan that was supported by clandestine aid from India, and some 10 million Bengali refugees poured across the border into India, creating social, economic, and health problems. In August, India signed a friendship treaty with the U.S.S.R. and quantities of Soviet arms began to enter India. After numerous border incidents, India invaded East Pakistan and in two weeks forced the surrender of the Pakistani army and took 93,000 prisoners. East Pakistan was established as an independent state and renamed Bangladesh.

India moved further toward the U.S.S.R. in 1973 with a 15-year economic, technological, and trade cooperation agreement.

India startled the world in 1974 by exploding an atomic device made of plutonium it had surreptitiously removed from a peaceful reactor given by Canada.

In the summer of 1975, the world's largest democracy veered suddenly toward authoritarianism when a judge in Allahabad, Mrs. Gandhi's home constituency, found her landslide victory in the 1971 elections invalid because civil servants had illegally aided her campaign. An appeal to the Supreme Court produced an interim order permitting her to continue as Prime Minister but without a vote in Parliament.

Amid demands for her resignation, Mrs. Gandhi decreed a state of emergency on June 26 and ordered mass arrests of her critics, including all opposition party leaders except the Communists. Rigid censorship was clamped on both the national press and foreign correspondents.

Legislation extending the emergency indefinitely passed Parliament July 23. Opposition members walked out after the vote. Their boycott was still in force during the next two weeks, when unhampered Congress Party majorities successively enacted: a bill forbidding courts to invalidate the government's emergency decrees; a constitutional amendment retroactively barring lawsuits challenging the elections of high government officers, including the Prime Minister, and a bill retroactively wiping out Mrs. Gandhi's conviction in the 1971 election case.

In 1976, India and Pakistan formally renewed diplomatic relations. Air and land transportation between the two nations was also restored.

Despite strong opposition to her repressive measures and particularly the resentment against compulsory birth control programs, Mrs. Gandhi in 1977 announced parliamentary elections for March. At the same time, she freed most political prisoners, including her former Deputy Prime Minister, Morarji R. Desai, and L. K. Advani, a rightwing Hindu nationalist. Press censorship was relaxed and serious defections from the ruling Congress Party began.

The landslide victory of Desai and his allies unseated Mrs. Gandhi and also defeated a bid for office by her son, Sanjay, himself a focus of much criticism as the recipient of official favors. Taking office, the 81-year-old Desai promised to "drive fear from the society" and restore morality to government.

In state elections in April, Desai's Janata Party toppled the Congress Party in eight of 10 states where the Congress Party had held power, as in the national government, since independence.

In July, Neelam Sanjiva Reddy was elected President, replacing Fakhruddin Ali Ahmed, who died February 11.

Desai moved away from Mrs. Gandhi's pro-Soviet policy, receiving a visit from President Carter Jan. 1–3, 1978, and himself visiting Carter in June. A dispute over the supply of enriched uranium to India, in which the U.S. Nuclear Regulatory Agency sought greater safeguards over its use, was resolved by Carter in India's favor in the hope that India would eventually sign the Non-Proliferation Treaty. Desai's success abroad was not matched at home, however, as economic problems and party squabbles lowered enthusiasm for the new regime.

One of the unifying factors of the Janata Party was the threat of a comeback attempt by former Prime Minister Gandhi, who regrouped a faction of the Congress Party under her leadership. Her announcement in May 1979 that she would not run for a seat in Parliament released the Janata Party's shaky bonds. The party had already been split over the inclusion of a right-wing Hindu element. Deputy Prime Minister Charan Singh's formation of a new "secular" Janata Party brought down the Desai government in mid-July and he became Prime Minister. However, he resigned the next month, but agreed to stay on and head a caretaker government.

Mrs. Gandhi staged a spectacular comeback in elections in January 1980. She followed her triumph with victories in eight of nine state legislative elections. Returned to power, Mrs. Gandhi showed a less hostile attitude toward the United States, condemning the Soviet invasion of Afghanistan and obtaining from the Carter administration approval for continued uranium shipments for India's nuclear program. She suffered a personal blow in the death of her son, Sanjay, a close personal aide, in a plane crash on June 23.

The visit of Soviet President Leonid I. Brezhnev to India in December 1980 altered Mrs. Gandhi's stand on Afghanistan to an acceptance of the Soviet assertion that its troops were there only because of U.S. and Chinese "interference" in that country. A joint statement called for dismantling all foreign bases in the Indian Ocean but named only one, the U.S. naval base on Diego Garcia Island.

In February 1981 after Washington announced a review of the 1963 agreement under which the Tarapur nuclear reactor was being supplied with U.S. fuel, Indian officials indicated that they were preparing to explode a new nuclear device, the first since 1976. U.S. Senator Alan Cranston of California said that intelligence reports had confirmed that India and Pakistan were making "final preparations" for nuclear weapons testing before the end of 1982.

Native States. Most of the 560-odd native states and subdivisions of pre-1947 India acceded to the new nation, and the central government pursued a vigorous policy of integration. This took three forms: merger into adjacent provinces, conversion into centrally administered areas, and grouping into unions of states. Finally, under a controversial reorganization plan effective Nov. 1, 1956, the unions of states were abolished and merged into adjacent states, and India became a union of 15 states and 8 centrally administered areas. A 16th state was added in 1962, and in 1966, the Punjab was partitioned into two states.

The status of the large princely state of Jammu and Kashmir on the northwest frontier is in dispute with Pakistan. It is 85% Islamic, but its Hindu ruling prince acceded to India, which took over administration following invasion by Moslem troops in late 1947. The part occupied by India was incorporated into India in 1957.

The controversy over Jammu and Kashmir was waged in the halls of the U.N. until 1965, when India announced that its civil servants would assume administration of the state. Pakistan sent guerrillas into the territory, and India, in response, invaded in August 1965. In September the U.N. sponsored a cease-fire and stationed observers to make sure it was honored, but there were violations.

The U.S.S.R. intervened and arranged a meeting in Tashkent between Prime Minister Shastri of India and President Ayub Khan of Pakistan. With the U.S.S.R. as mediator, they reached an interim settlement, the Declaration of Tashkent, in January 1966. It provided for the withdrawal of troops, observance of the U.N. cease-fire, and continued attempts to resolve their disputes by diplomatic means.

Resolution of the territorial dispute over Kashmir grew out of peace negotiations following the two-week India-Pakistan war of 1971. After sporadic skirmishing, an accord reached July 3, 1972, committed both powers to withdraw troops from a temporary cease-fire line after the border was fixed. Agreement on the border was reached Dec. 7, 1972.

In April 1975, the Indian Parliament voted to make the 300-year-old kingdom of Sikkim a full-fledged Indian state, and the annexation took effect May 16.

Situated in the Himalayas, Sikkim was a virtual dependency of Tibet until the early 19th century. Under an 1890 treaty between China and Great Britain, it became a British protectorate, and was made an Indian protectorate after Britain quit the subcontinent.

INDONESIA

Republic of Indonesia
President and Prime Minister: General Suharto (1969)[1]
Area: 735,268 sq mi. (1,904,344 sq km)[2]
Population (est. 1981): 155,300,000 (growth rate: 2.1%)
Density per square mile: 211.2
Capital: Jakarta
Largest cities (est. 1980): Jakarta, 6,400,000; (1971 census): Surabaja, 1,556,255; Bandung, 1,201,730; Semarang, 646,590; Medan, 635,562; Palembang, 582,961
Monetary unit: Rupiah
Languages: Bahasa Indonesia (official), Dutch, and more than 60 regional languages
Religions: Islam, 89%; Christian, 7%; Hindu, Buddhist
National name: Republik Indonesia
Freedom House classifications: Capitalist-statist pre-industrial, dominant party
Economic summary: Gross national product (1979): $52.2 billion. Average annual growth rate (1970–78): 5.3%. Per capita income: $310. Land used for agriculture: 11%; labor force: 64%; principal products: rice, cassava, soybeans, copra, rubber, coffee, palm oil, tea. Labor force in industry: 7%; major products: textiles, food and beverages, light manufactures, cement, fertilizer. Natural resources: oil, timber, nickel, natural gas, tin, bauxite, copper. Exports: oil, timber, rubber, tin. Imports: food, chemicals, textiles. Major trading partners: Japan, U.S., West Germany, Singapore.

1. General Suharto served as Acting President of Indoesia from 1967 to 1969. 2. Includes West Irian (former Nether-

lands New Guinea), renamed Irian Jaya in March 1973 (159,355 sq mi.; 412,731 sq km), and former Portuguese Timor (5,763 sq mi.; 14,925 sq km), annexed in 1976.

Geography. Indonesia is part of the Malay archipelago in Southeast Asia with an area nearly three times that of Texas. It consists of the islands of Sumatra, Java, Madura, Borneo (except Sarawak in the north), the Celebes, the Moluccas, and about 30 smaller archipelagos, totaling 13,677 islands, of which about 6,000 are inhabited. Its neighbor to the north is Malaysia and to the east Papua New Guinea.

A backbone of mountain ranges extends throughout the main islands of the archipelago. Earthquakes are frequent, and there are many active volcanoes.

Government. The President is elected by the People's Consultative Assembly, whose 920 members include the functioning legislative arm, the 460-member House of Representatives. Meeting at least once every five years, the Assembly has broad policy functions. The House, 100 of whose members are appointed by the President, meets at least once annually. General Suharto was elected unopposed to a third five-year term in 1978.

The major political parties are Sekber Golkar, 232 of 360 contested seats in the House; Islamic United Development Party, 99 seats; Democratic Party, 29 seats.

History. Indonesia is inhabited by Malayan and Papuan peoples ranging from the more advanced Javanese and Balinese to the more primitive Dyaks of Borneo. Invasions from China and India contributed Chinese and Indian admixtures.

During the first few centuries of the Christian era, most of the islands came under the influence of Hindu priests and traders, who spread their culture and religion. Moslem invasions began in the 13th century, and most of the area was Moslem by the 15th. Portuguese traders arrived early in the 16th century but were ousted by the Dutch about 1595. After Napoleon subjugated the Netherlands homeland in 1811, the British seized the islands but returned them to the Dutch in 1816. In 1922 the islands were made an integral part of the Netherlands kingdom.

In World War II, the Japanese military occupation with nominal native self-government continued until August 1945. About the time of the Japanese surrender, a self-styled Indonesian Republic headed by Achmed Sukarno took over effective control of parts of Sumatra and Java. Allied forces, mostly British Indian troops, moved in, and fought the nationalists until November 1946, when Dutch-Indonesian parleys resulted in a draft agreement that contemplated the formation by Jan. 1, 1949, of a Netherlands-Indonesian Union. This would consist on the one hand of the Netherlands, the Netherlands Antilles, and Surinam and on the other of the United States of Indonesia, which was to be a sovereign nation composed of three equal states—the Republic of Indonesia, East Indonesia, and Borneo. Differences of interpretation ensued, and the Dutch resorted to force in July 1947. Both sides issued cease-fire orders the next month in response to a call from the U.N. Security Council.

On Nov. 2, 1949, Dutch and Indonesian leaders agreed upon the terms of union. Sukarno was elected president of the federation and the first all-Indonesian Cabinet was formed with Mohammed Hatta as premier. The transfer of sovereignty took place at Amsterdam on December 27, 1949.

In 1963, Netherlands New Guinea was transferred to Indonesia, and renamed West Irian. In 1973 it became Irian Jaya.

Sukarno, who had himself declared "President for Life," launched a series of guerrilla raids in 1963 to scuttle formation of the new Federation of Malaysia. A treaty between Indonesia and Malaysia in 1966 ended the open conflict. Meanwhile, with Sukarno's encouragement, Communist influence increased.

Early in 1966, Moslem students led an anti-Communist campaign that is believed to have assassinated more than 300,000 Indonesians suspected of Communist ties. Sukarno was forced in March 1966 to yield power to General Suharto, army Chief of Staff. He began a series of trials of Sukarno's associates. The Communist Party was outlawed. Sukarno was forced to give up all power on Feb. 22, 1967, and Suharto became acting president the next month.

He ended hostilities with Malaysia and established close ties with the West. Suharto introduced a "New Order" emphasizing austerity and fiscal responsibility and with Western aid of $200 million —one third provided by the U.S.—began rebuilding the country. In 1968, the Consultative Assembly elected Suharto president for a five-year term.

Suharto also permitted national elections, which moved the nation back toward representative government. The Consultative Assembly elected him unanimously for a second five-year term in 1973.

The economic and political stability achieved by the Suharto regime was tested by external events in 1975. Tightening of world money markets put serious pressures on ambitious industrial development plans underwritten by Pertamina, the state-owned oil company. Communist triumphs in Vietnam and Cambodia encouraged Jakarta toward a policy of non-alignment with any great power and toward closer relationships with other members of the Association of Southeast Asian Nations, a regional grouping of five non-Communist states.

Indonesia annexed the former Portuguese half of the island of Timor in 1976 after the provisional government of the area requested annexation.

Bankruptcy of Pertamina in 1976, and the arrest of Gen. Ibnu Sutowo as an investigation of $10 billion in debts began, dramatically reduced foreign investment. A total of $2 billion in 1975 was cut to $423 million in 1976. The government estimated that debt service for 1977–78 would offset an expected 18% gain in oil revenues.

Indonesia, as one of the countries receiving an influx of "boat people" from Vietnam, was host to a 24-nation conference in May 1979 to consider the problem. Indonesia offered Galang Island, 25 miles south of Singapore, as a refugee processing center, but took none on a permanent basis.

IRAN

Islamic Republic of Iran
President: Vacant
Prime Minister: Vacant
Area: 636,363 sq mi. (1,648,180 sq km)
Population (est. 1981): 37,400,000 (growth rate: 2.9%)
  (Iranian, Kurdish, Azerbaijani)
Density per square mile: 58.7
Capital: Teheran
Largest cities (1976 census): Teheran, 4,496,159; Isfahan, 671,825; Mashed, 670,180; Tabriz, 598,576

Monetary unit: Rial
Languages: Farsi (Persian), Kurdish, Azerbaijani
Religions: Shi'ite Moslem, 93%; Sunni Moslem, 5%
Freedom House classifications: Capitalist-statist pre-industrial, dominant party
Economic summary: Gross national product (1979): $81.7 billion. Per capita income: $2,170. Land used for agriculture: 14%; labor force: 33%; principal products: wheat, barley, rice, sugar beets, cotton, dates, raisins, sheep, goats. Labor force in industry: 21%; major products: crude and refined oil, textiles, cement, processed foods, steel and copper fabrication. Natural resources: oil, gas, iron, copper. Exports: petroleum, carpets, raw cotton, fruits and nuts, hides and leather. Imports: machinery, iron and steel products, chemicals, pharmaceuticals, electrical equipment, agricultural products. Major trading partners: Japan, West Germany, U.K., Italy, Netherlands, Spain, France.

Geography. Iran, a Middle Eastern country south of the Caspian Sea and north of the Persian Gulf, is three times the size of Arizona. It shares borders with Iraq, Turkey, the U.S.S.R., Afghanistan, and Pakistan.

In general, the country is a plateau averaging 4,000 feet (1,219 m) in elevation. There are also maritime lowlands along the Persian Gulf and the Caspian Sea. The Elburz Mountains in the north rise to 18,603 feet (5,670 m) at Mt. Damavend. From northwest to southeast, the country is crossed by a desert 800 miles (1,287 km) long.

Government. The Pahlavi dynasty was overthrown on Feb. 11, 1979, by followers of the Ayatollah Ruhollah Khomeini. After a referendum endorsed the establishment of a republic, Khomeini drafted a Constitution calling for a President to be popularly elected every four years, an appointed Prime Minister, and a unicameral National Consultative Assembly, popularly elected every four years.

Khomeini also instituted a Revolutionary Council to insure the adherence to Islamic principles in all phases of Iranian life. The Council formally handed over its powers to the Assembly after the organization of the legislature in July 1980, but continued to exercise power as a sort of shadow government.

History. Oil-rich Iran was called Persia before 1935. Its key location blocks the lower land gate to Asia and also stands in the way of traditional Russian ambitions for access to the Indian Ocean. After periods of Assyrian, Median, and Achaemenidian rule, Persia became a powerful empire under Cyrus the Great, reaching from the Indus to the Nile at its zenith in 525 B.C. It fell to Alexander in 331–30 B.C. and to the Seleucids in 312–02 B.C., and a native Persian regime arose about 130 B.C. Another Persian regime arose about A.D. 224, but it fell to the Arabs in 637. In the 12th century, the Mongols took their turn ruling Persia, and in the early part of the 18th century, the Turks occupied the country.

An Anglo-Russian convention of 1907 divided Persia into two spheres of influence. British attempts to impose a protectorate over the entire country were defeated in 1919. Two years later, Gen. Reza Pahlavi seized the government and was elected hereditary Shah in 1925. Subsequently he did much to modernize the country and abolished all foreign extraterritorial rights.

Increased pro-Axis activity led to Anglo-Russian occupation of Iran in 1941 and deposition of the Shah in favor of his son, Mohammed Reza Pahlavi. Ali Razmara became premier in 1950 and

pledged to restore efficient and honest government, but he was assassinated after less than nine months in office and Mohammed Mossadegh took over. Mossadegh was ousted in August 1953, by Fazollah Zahedi, whom the Shah had named premier.

Iran established closer relations with the U.S. and the West, and the U.S. began a vast program of economic and military aid. In 1955 the country joined the Central Treaty Organization (then called the Baghdad Pact). At the Shah's insistence, the government undertook a broad program of reform, especially agrarian land reform, distributing crown lands and estates to the landless peasants.

Despite Iran's role as a founding member of the Organization of Petroleum Exporting Countries, Iran did not participate in OPEC's 1973 embargo on oil shipments to the West. Iran's oil profits financed an extraordinary modernization program of education, industrialization, and construction, expected to cost over $400 billion over a 13-year period.

Iran led nine other members of OPEC in raising oil prices at the end of 1976, and the refusal of Saudi Arabia and the United Arab Emirates to go along resulted in a 38% drop in Iranian oil exports. The loss of revenues forced the government to curtail its aid program. In 1977, a $2.2-billion final contract for the purchase of 160 F-16 fighter planes was signed with the U.S.

Opposition to the Shah spread, despite the imposition of martial law in September 1978, and massive demonstrations demanded the return of the exiled Ayatollah Ruhollah Khomeini. Riots and strikes continued despite the appointment of an opposition leader, Shahpur Bakhtiar, as premier on Dec. 29. The Shah and his family left Iran on Jan. 16, 1979, for a "vacation," leaving power in the hands of a regency council.

Khomeini returned on Feb. 1 to a nation in turmoil as military units loyal to the Shah continued to support Bakhtiar and clashed with revolutionaries. Khomeini appointed Mehdi Bazargan as premier of a provisional government and in two days of fighting, revolutionaries forced the military to capitulate on Feb. 11.

The new government canceled contracts for U.S. military equipment and training and began a program of nationalization of insurance companies, banks and industries both locally and foreign-owned. Oil production fell amid the political confusion, precipitating a fuel crisis in the U.S.

Khomeini, ignoring opposition, proceeded with his plans for revitalizing Islamic traditions. He urged women to return to the veil, or chador; banned alcohol and mixed bathing, and prohibited music from radio and television broadcasting, declaring it to be "no different from opium."

Revolutionary militants invaded the U.S. Embassy in Teheran on Nov. 4, 1979, seized staff members as hostages, and precipitated an international crisis. The regime denied responsibility but eventually took the militants' view that the diplomats could legitimately be imprisoned until the Shah and his assets were returned to Iran.

Khomeini refused all appeals, even a unanimous vote by the U.N. Security Council demanding immediate release of the hostages. On a New Year's trip to Teheran, U.N. Secretary-General Kurt Waldheim never saw Khomeini, and a subsequent U.N. commission of inquiry met a similar rebuff.

Election of Abolhassan Bani-Sadr as President on Jan. 25, 1980, raised hopes that his moderate stance might bring a change.

Iranian hostility toward Washington was reinforced by the Carter administration's ineffective economic boycott and deportation order against Iranian students in the U.S., the break in diplomatic relations and ultimately an aborted U.S. raid in April aimed at rescuing the hostages.

Even the death of the deposed Shah Mohammed Reza Pahlavi on July 17 had no effect. As the first anniversary of the embassy seizure neared, Khomeini and his followers insisted on their original conditions: guarantee by the U.S. not to interfere in Iran's affairs, cancellation of U.S. damage claims against Iran, release of $8 billion in frozen Iranian assets, an apology, and the return of the assets held by the former imperial family.

These conditions were largely met in an agreement signed by Deputy Secretary of State Warren Christopher in Teheran on Jan. 19 and the 52 American hostages were released the following day, ending 444 days in captivity. The $8 billion was subject to claims of U.S. creditors, however, and the delivery of the late Shah's assets under U.S. control was made subject to court decisions.

From the release of the hostages onward, Bani-Sadr and the conservative clerics of the dominant Islamic Republican Party clashed with growing frequency. He was stripped of his command of the armed forces by Khomeini on June 6 and ousted as President on June 22. Bani-Sadr went into hiding and emerged in Paris, vowing to fight Khomeini. On June 28, four Cabinet members and 68 other prominent Khomeini backers were killed by a bomb planted in the Islamic Republican Party headquarters. On July 24, Prime Minister Mohammed Ali Rajai was elected overwhelmingly to the Presidency.

Rajai and Prime Minister Mohammed Javad Bahonar were killed on Aug. 30 by a bomb in Bahonar's office.

IRAQ

Republic of Iraq
President: Saddam Hussein (1979)
Area: 172,000 sq mi. (445,480 sq km)
Population (est. 1981): 13,400,000 (growth rate: 3.5%)
(Arab, 75%; Kurdish, 15%; Iranian, 3.8%)
Density per square mile: 77.9
Capital: Baghdad
Largest cities (est. 1977): Baghdad, 3,205,600; (1965 census): Basra, 310,950, Mosul, 264,146; Kirkuk, 175,303; An Najaf, 134,027
Monetary unit: Iraqi dinar
Languages: Arabic and Kurdish
Religions: Islam, 96%; Christian, 3%
National name: Al Jumhouriya Al Iraqia
Freedom House classifications: Socialist pre-industrial, one-party socialist
Economic summary: Gross national product (1979): $30.4 billion. Average annual growth rate (1970–78): 7.7%. Per capita income (1977): $1,550. Average rate of inflation (1976–78): 10%. Land used for agriculture, 18%; labor force, 30%; principal products: livestock, wheat, barley, cotton, fruits, vegetables. Labor force in industry: 27%; major products: petroleum, cement, textiles. Natural resources: oil, natural gas, phosphates, sulfur. Exports: petroleum, dates. Imports: manufactured goods, food grains, machinery, construction materials, livestock. Major trading partners: France, Italy, U.S.S.R., Japan, West Germany, Turkey, Brazil, U.K.

Geography. Iraq, a triangle of mountains, desert, and fertile river valley, is bounded on the east by Iran, on the north by Turkey, the west by Syria and Jordan, and the south by Saudi Arabia and Kuwait. It is twice the size of Idaho.

The country has arid desertland west of the Euphrates, a broad central valley between the Euphrates and Tigris, and mountains in the northeast. The fertile lower valley is formed by the delta of the two rivers, which join about 120 miles (193 km) from the head of the Persian Gulf. The gulf coastline is 26 miles (42 km) long. The only port for seagoing vessels is Basra, which is on the Shatt-al-Arab River near the head of the Persian Gulf.

Government. Since the coup d'etat of July 1968, Iraq has been governed by the Arab Ba'ath Socialist Party through a Council of Command of the Revolution headed by the President. There is also a Council of Ministers headed by the President.

History. From earliest times Iraq was known as Mesopotamia—the land between the rivers—for it embraces a large part of the alluvial plains of the Tigris and Euphrates.

An advanced civilization existed by 4000 B.C. Sometime after 2000 B.C. the land became the center of the ancient Babylonian and Assyrian empires. It was conquered by Cyrus the Great of Persia in 538 B.C., and by Alexander in 331 B.C. After an Arab conquest in A.D. 637–40, Baghdad became capital of the ruling caliphate. The country was cruelly pillaged by the Mongols in 1258, and during the 16th, 17th, and 18th centuries was the object of repeated Turkish-Persian competition.

Nominal Turkish suzerainty imposed in 1638 was replaced by direct Turkish rule in 1831. In World War I, an Anglo-Indian force occupied most of the country, and Britain was given a mandate over the area in 1920. The British recognized Iraq as a kingdom in 1922 and terminated the mandate in 1932 when Iraq was admitted to the League of Nations. In World War II, Iraq generally adhered to its 1930 treaty of alliance with Britain, but in 1941, British troops were compelled to put down a pro-Axis revolt led by Premier Rashid Ali.

Iraq became a charter member of the Arab League in 1945, and Iraqi troops took part in the Arab invasion of Palestine in 1948. The 1930 treaty of alliance with Britain was terminated in 1955, and replaced by a defense cooperation agreement.

Faisal II, born on May 2, 1935, succeeded his father, Ghazi I, who was killed in an automobile accident on April 4, 1939. Faisal and his uncle, Crown Prince Abdul-Ilah, were assassinated in August 1958 in a swift revolutionary coup that brought to power a military junta headed by Abdul Karem Kassim. The short-lived "Arab Union," formed by the federation of Iraq and Jordan in February 1958, came abruptly to an end with recognition by the United Arab Republic (Egypt) of the rebel government of Iraq. Kassim, in turn, was overthrown and killed in a coup staged March 8, 1963, by the Ba'ath Socialist Party.

President Abdel Salam Arif, a leader in the March coup, staged another coup in November, driving the Ba'ath members of the revolutionary council from power. He adopted a new constitution in 1964. In 1966, he, two Cabinet members, and other supporters died in a helicopter crash. His brother, Gen. Abdel Rahman Arif, assumed the presidency, crushed the opposition, and won an indefinite extension of his term in 1967. His regime was ousted in July 1968 by a junta led by Maj. Gen. Ahmed Hassan al-Bakr.

In 1970, the Baghdad government announced a settlement of the 8½-year sporadic war with the Kurds of northeastern Iraq (who spread over the border into Turkey and Iran), accepting two nationalities in Iraq (Arabs and Kurds) and promising a Kurdish vice president of Iraq and proportional Kurdish representation in a new parliament. The Kurds ultimately refused the government's terms.

The Kurdish rebellion flared anew in 1974, following collapse of an Iraqi plan for Kurdish self-rule. The rebels, armed and reinforced from Iran, withstood Soviet-supplied Iraqi forces for 11 months until Iran ended its aid under an agreement with Iraq. Some 200,000 Kurds fled to Iran and the revolt was liquidated within a month.

A long-standing dispute over control of the Shatt el-Arab waterway between Iraq and Iran broke into full-scale war on Sept. 20, 1980. Iraqi planes attacked Iranian airfields and the Abadan refinery, and Iraqi ground forces moved into Iranian territory. Within a week, the waterway was blocked and Iraqi bombing of Kharg Island in the Persian Gulf halted Iranian oil exports.

Jordan offered the port of Aqaba and overland transport to enable Iraq to obtain supplies, but Iran, already suffering from trade embargos resulting from its holding U.S. diplomats as hostages, was hit harder. Despite the smaller size of its armed forces, Iraq took and held the initiative by seizing Abadan and Khurramshahr together with substantial Iranian territory by December and beating back Iranian counterattacks in January. Peace efforts by the Islamic nations, the nonaligned, and the United Nations failed as 1981 wore on and the war stagnated.

The Israeli surprise bombing attack on Iraq's Oshirak nuclear reactor outside Baghdad on July 7 rallied the Arab world almost unanimously behind Iraq and the U.N. Security Council's condemnation of the raid on June 19 won a unanimous vote and a rebuke to Israel by U.S. Ambassador Jeane Kirkpatrick.

IRELAND

President: Patrick J. Hillery (1976)
Taoiseach (Prime Minister): Garret M. D. FitzGerald (1981)
Area: 26,600 sq mi. (68,894 sq km)
Population (est. 1981): 3,460,000 (average annual growth rate, 1966–79, 1.2%)
Density per square mile: 130.1
Capital: Dublin
Largest cities (est. 1979): Dublin, 543,600; (1971 census): Cork, 128,235
Monetary unit: Irish pound (punt)
Languages: Irish, English
Religions: Roman Catholic, 95%; Protestant, 5%
National name: Eire
Freedom House classifications: Capitalist industrial, multi-party centralized
Economic summary: Gross national product (1979): $13.8 billion. Average annual growth rate (1970–78): 2.3%. Per capita income: $3,000. Average rate of inflation (1978): 8%. Land used for agriculture, 67%; labor force in agriculture and fishing: 26%; principal products: cattle and dairy products, potatoes, barley, sugar beets, hay, silage, wheat. Labor force in industry: 26%; major products: processed foods, beverages, textiles, chemicals and pharmaceuticals, machinery and construction equipment. Natural resources: zinc, lead, natural gas, barite, copper, gypsum, limestone, dolomite, peat, silver. Exports: livestock, meat, dairy products, machinery,

chemicals, textiles, and clothing. Imports: grains, petroleum products, machinery, transport equipment, chemicals, textile yarn. Major trading partners: U.K., Western European countries, U.S., Canada.

Geography. Ireland is situated in the Atlantic Ocean and separated from Britain by the Irish Sea. Half the size of Arkansas, it occupies the entire island except for the six northern counties of Ulster.

Ireland resembles a basin—a central plain rimmed with mountains, except in the Dublin region. The mountains are low, with the highest peak, Carrantuohill in County Kerry, rising to 3,415 feet (1,041 m).

The principal river is the Shannon, which begins in the north central area, flows south and southwest for about 240 miles (386 km), and empties into the Atlantic.

Government. Ireland is a parliamentary democracy. The National Parliament (Oireachtas) consists of the president and two Houses, the House of Representatives (Dáil Eireann) and the Senate (Seanad Eireann), whose members serve for a maximum term of five years. The House of Representatives has 166 members elected by proportional representation; the Senate has 60 members of whom 11 are nominated by the prime minister, 6 by the universities and the remaining 43 from five vocational panels. The prime minister (Taoiseach), who is the head of government, is appointed by the president on the nomination of the House of Representatives, to which he is responsible.

The major political parties are Fianna Fáil (78 of 166 seats in the Dáil), led by former Prime Minister Charles J. Haughey; Fianna Gael (65 seats), led by Prime Minister Garret FitzGerald; Labor Party (15 seats), led by Michael O'Leary; Independents (8 seats).

History. In the Stone and Bronze Ages, Ireland was inhabited by Picts in the north and a people called the Erainn in the south, the same stock, apparently, as in all the isles before the Anglo-Saxon invasion of Britain. About the fourth century B.C., tall, red-haired Celts arrived from Gaul or Galicia. They subdued and assimilated the inhabitants and established a Gaelic civilization.

By the beginning of the Christian Era, Ireland was divided into five kingdoms—Ulster, Connacht, Leinster, Meath, and Munster. St. Patrick introduced Christianity in 432 and the country developed into a center of Gaelic and Latin learning. Irish monasteries, the equivalent of universities, attracted intellectuals as well as the pious and sent out missionaries to many parts of Europe and, some believe, to North America.

Norse depredations along the coasts, starting in 795, ended in 1014 with Norse defeat at the Battle of Clontarf by forces under Brian Borv. In the 12th century, the Pope gave all Ireland to the English Crown as a papal fief. In 1171, Henry II of England was acknowledged "Lord of Ireland," but local sectional rule continued for centuries, and English control over the whole island was not reasonably absolute until the 17th century. By the Act of Union (1800), England and Ireland became the "United Kingdom of Great Britain and Ireland."

A steady decline in the Irish economy followed in the next decades. The population had reached 8.25 million when the great potato famine of 1846–48 took many lives and drove millions to emigrate to America. By 1921 it was down to 4.3 million.

In the meantime, anti-British agitation continued along with demands for Irish home rule. The advent of World War I delayed the institution of home rule and resulted in the Easter Rebellion in Dublin (April 24–29, 1916), in which Irish nationalists unsuccessfully attempted to throw off British rule. Guerrilla warfare against British forces followed proclamation of a republic by the rebels in 1919.

The Irish Free State was established as a dominion on Dec. 6, 1921, with the six northern counties as part of the United Kingdom. Ireland was neutral in World War II.

In 1948, Éamon de Valera, American-born leader of the Sinn Fein, who had won establishment of the Free State in 1921 in negotiations with Britain's David Lloyd George, was defeated by John A. Costello, who demanded final independence from Britain. The Republic of Ireland was proclaimed on April 18, 1949. It withdrew from the Commonwealth but in 1955 entered the United Nations. Since 1949 the prime concern of successive governments has been economic development.

De Valera, who retired in 1973 after two terms in the largely ceremonial presidency, died Aug. 29, 1975, at the age of 92.

Through the 1960s, two antagonistic currents dominated Irish politics. One sought to bind the wounds of the rebellion and civil war, symbolized in 1967 by the merger of Protestant Trinity College and Catholic University College into the University of Dublin. The other was the effort of the outlawed extremist Irish Republican Army to bring Northern Ireland into the republic. Despite public sympathy for unification of Ireland, the Dublin government dealt rigorously with IRA guerrillas caught inside the republic's borders.

The 1973 election brought to power Liam Cosgrave, at the head of a coalition of the Fianna Gael and the Labor Party, unseating the Fianna Fáil, which had governed for 35 of 41 years of the republic. Cosgrave cooperated with the British government in attempts to control IRA terrorism and, after the assassination of the British Ambassador to Ireland in 1976, pushed through an Emergency Powers Act to strengthen police and court powers in combating terrorists.

The 1977 election gave the Fianna Fáil a record 84 seats in the Dáil and put John Lynch into the prime minister's post.

Although Lynch drew protests from Britain and Ulster for publicly advocating unification in 1978, he resigned on Dec. 5, 1979, amid intra-party complaints that he was too conciliatory on the issue. Health Minister Charles J. Haughey, the party's choice to suceed Lynch, was under no such handicap. An ardent nationalist, he had been forced to resign as Finance Minister in 1970 because he was accused of smuggling weapons to IRA rebels in the North.

Elections on June 11, 1981, failed to provide Haughey with a majority and Garret M. D. Fitz-Gerald, leader of the Fianna Gael, was elected Prime Minister by 81 to 78 with the support of 15 Labor Party members and one independent Socialist added to his own party's 65 members. Other independents abstained, among them Kieran Doherty, a prisoner in Northern Ireland's Maze Prison, who with another prisoner had won election to the Southern Parliament (the Republic's Constitution extends citizenship to anyone born in Northern Ireland).

Doherty's death from a hunger strike on Aug. 3, the eighth such death (the ninth occurred within the week) since prisoners in the Maze began fasting in March, could mean a realignment following a by-election.

ISRAEL

State of Israel
President: Yitzhak Navon (1978)
Prime Minister: Menachem Begin (1977)
Area: 7,992 sq mi. (20,699 sq km)[1]
Population (est. 1981): 4,000,000 (average annual growth rate, 1975–80, 2.3%)
Density per square mile: 500.5
Capital: Jerusalem
Largest cities (est. 1981): Jerusalem, 412,000[2]; (est. 1979): Tel Aviv, 336,000; Haifa, 229,000; Ramat Gan, 120,000
Monetary unit: Shekel
Languages: Hebrew, Arabic, English
Religions: Jewish, 85%; Islam, Christian
National name: Medinat Israel
Freedom House classifications: Capitalist-socialist industrial, multi-party centralized
Economic summary: Gross national product (1979): $15.7. Average annual growth rate (1970–78): 1.6%. Per capita income (est. 1979): $3,200. Rate of inflation (1980): 131.5%. Land used for agriculture: 20%; labor force: 6%; principal products: citrus and other fruits, vegetables, beef, dairy and poultry products. Labor force in industry: 25%; major products: processed foods, cut diamonds, clothing and textiles, chemicals, metal products, transport and electrical equipment, plastics. Natural resources: sulfur, limestone, rock salt, phosphates, potash, bromine. Exports: polished diamonds, citrus and other fruits, clothing and textiles, processed foods, fertilizer and chemical products. Imports: military equipment, rough diamonds, chemicals, machinery, iron and steel, cereals, textiles, vehicles, ships, aircraft. Major trading partners: Western European countries, U.S., U.K., Japan.

1. Excluding 26,473 sq mi. (68,565 sq km) occupied in 1967 war. As of mid-1980, two thirds of the Sinai had been returned to Egypt. 2. Includes East Jerusalem.

Geography. Israel, slightly smaller than Massachusetts, lies at the eastern end of the Mediterranean Sea. It is bordered by Egypt on the west, Syria and Jordan on the east, and Lebanon on the north.

Northern Israel is largely a plateau traversed from north to south by mountains and broken by great depressions, also running from north to south.

The maritime plain of Israel is remarkably fertile. The southern Negev region, which comprises almost half the total area, is largely a wide desert steppe area. The National Water Project irrigation scheme is now transforming it into fertile land. The Jordan, the only important river, flows from the north through Lake Hule (Waters of Merom) and Lake Kinneret (Sea of Galilee or Sea of Tiberias), finally entering the Dead Sea, 1,290 feet (393 m) below sea level. This "sea," which is actually a salt lake (394 sq mi.; 1,020 sq km), has no outlet, its water balance being maintained by evaporation.

Government. Israel, which does not have a written constitution, has a republican form of government headed by a president elected for a five-year term by the Knesset. He may serve no more than two terms. The Knesset has 120 members elected by universal suffrage under proportional representation for four years. The government is administered by the Cabinet, which is headed by the prime minister.

The Knesset decided in June 1950 that Israel would acquire a constitution gradually through the years by the enactment of fundamental laws. Israel grants automatic citizenship to every Jew who desires to settle within its borders, subject to control of the Knesset.

The major political parties are Likud (48 of 120 seats in the Knesset), led by Prime Minister Menachem Begin; Labor Alignment (47 seats), led by Shimon Peres; National Religious Party (6 seats), led by Yossef Burg; Agudath Israel (4 seats); Communist Party (4 seats).

History. Palestine, cradle of two great religions and homeland of the modern state of Israel, was known to the ancient Hebrews as the "Land of Canaan." Palestine's name derives from the Philistines, a people who occupied the southern coastal part of the country in the 12th century B.C.

A Hebrew kingdom established in 1000 B.C. was later split into the kingdoms of Judah and Israel; they were subsequently invaded by Assyrians, Babylonians, Egyptians, Persians, Macedonians, Romans, and Byzantines. The Arabs took Palestine from the Byzantine Empire A.D. 634–40. With the exception of a Frankish Crusader kingdom from 1099 to 1187, Palestine remained under Moslem rule until the 20th century (Turkish rule from 1516), when British forces under Gen. Sir Edmund Allenby defeated the Turks and captured Jerusalem Dec. 9, 1917. The League of Nations granted Britain a mandate to govern Palestine, effective in 1923.

Jewish colonies—Jews from Russia established one as early as 1882—multiplied after Theodor Herzl's 1897 call for a Jewish state. The Zionist movement received official approval with the publication of a letter Nov. 2, 1917, from Arthur Balfour, British Foreign Secretary, to Lord Rothschild, a British Jewish leader. Balfour promised support for the establishment of a Jewish homeland in Palestine on the understanding that the civil and religious rights of non-Jewish Palestinians would be safeguarded.

A 1937 British proposal called for an Arab and a Jewish state separated by a mandated area incorporating Jerusalem and Nazareth. Arabs opposed this, demanding a single state with minority rights for Jews, and a 1939 British White Paper retreated, offering instead a single state with further Jewish immigration to be limited to 75,000. Although the White Paper satisfied neither side, further discussion ended on the outbreak of World War II, when the Jewish population stood at nearly 500,000, or 30% of the total. Illegal and legal immigration during the war brought the Jewish population to 678,000 in 1946, compared with 1,269,000 Arabs. Unable to reach a compromise, Britain turned the problem over to the United Nations in 1947, which on November 29 voted for partition—despite strong Arab opposition.

Britain did not help implement the U.N. decision and withdrew on expiration of its mandate May 14, 1948. Zionists had already seized control of areas designated as Jewish, and, on the day of British departure, the Jewish National Council proclaimed the State of Israel.

U.S. recognition came within hours. The next day, Jordanian and Egyptian forces invaded the new nation. At the cease-fire Jan. 7, 1949, Israel increased its original territory by 50%, taking west-

ern Galilee, a broad corridor through central Palestine to Jerusalem, and part of modern Jerusalem. (In April 1950, Jordan annexed areas of eastern and central Palestine that had been designated for an Arab state, together with the old city of Jerusalem.)

The provisional leaders of the Jewish state, Chaim Weizmann and David Ben-Gurion, became Israel's first president and prime minister. The new government was admitted to the U.N. May 11, 1949.

The next clash with Arab neighbors came when Egypt nationalized the Suez Canal in 1956 and barred Israeli shipping. Coordinating with an Anglo-French force, Israeli troops seized the Gaza Strip and drove through the Sinai to the east bank of the Suez Canal, but withdrew under U.S. and U.N. pressure. In 1967, Israel threatened retaliation against Syrian border raids, and Syria asked Egyptian aid. Egypt demanded the removal of U.N. peace-keeping forces from Suez, staged a national mobilization, closed the Gulf of Aqaba, and moved troops into the Sinai. On June 5, with a simultaneous air attack against Syrian, Jordanian, and Egyptian bases and in a six-day war totally defeated its Arab enemies. Expanding its territory by 200%, Israel at the cease-fire held the Golan Heights, the West Bank of the Jordan River, the Old City, and all of the Sinai and the east bank of the Suez Canal.

Israel demanded as its new terms for peace with its Arab neighbors a guarantee that any occupied territory returned could never be used as a base for aggression. It also insisted that Jerusalem remain a unified city and that peace negotiations be conducted directly, something the Arab states had refused to do because it would constitute a recognition of their Jewish neighbor.

Egypt's President Gamal Abdel Nasser renounced the 1967 cease-fire in 1969 and began a "war of attrition" against Israel, firing Soviet artillery at Israeli forces on the east bank of the canal. Nasser died of a heart attack on Sept. 28, 1970, and was succeeded by Anwar el-Sadat.

In the face of Israeli reluctance even to discuss the return of occupied territories, the fourth Mideast war erupted Oct. 6, 1973, with a surprise Egyptian and Syrian assault on the Jewish high holy day of Yom Kippur. Initial Arab gains were reversed when a cease-fire took effect two weeks later, but Israel suffered heavy losses in manpower.

U.S. Secretary of State Henry A. Kissinger arranged a disengagement of forces on both the Egyptian and Syrian fronts, which permitted the two Arab nations to recover small amounts of territory they lost in 1967. The disengagement was supervised by U.N. peace-keeping forces, with the U.S.S.R. for the first time sharing the cost. Geneva talks, aimed at a lasting peace, foundered, however, when Israel balked at inclusion of the Palestine Liberation Organization, a guerrilla front increasingly active in terrorism directed against Israel.

At home, criticism of the ruling Labor Party's lack of preparedness cost it five seats in 1973 election, and Prime Minister Golda Meir was forced to head a minority government until her retirement on April 10, 1974. Yitzhak Rabin, a former general formed a successor government, which won narrow approval in the Knesset and, in October assembled a majority coalition.

In the same month, the PLO won recognition as the "representative of the Palestine people" in a resolution passed by the U.N. General Assembly and at an Arab summit meeting in Rabat, Morocco, where the Arab states pledged $2.3 billion in military aid to Israel's neighbors.

When Kissinger sought a second-stage agreement between Israel and Egypt for disengagement in the Sinai in January 1975, Israel insisted on a formal Egyptian pledge of non-belligerency but eventually signed a three-year agreement in Geneva in September.

The agreement required Israel to give up the strategic Mitla and Gidi passes and to return the captured Abu Rudeis oil fields. Egypt guaranteed passage of Israeli cargoes through the reopened Suez Canal, and both sides renounced force in the settlement of disputes. Two hundred U.S. civilian technicians were stationed in a widened U.N. buffer zone to monitor and warn either side of truce violations.

A U.S. commitment to give Israel $400 million in economic aid and $1 billion in weapons was then disclosed, along with the assurance of a coordinated U.S.-Israeli position in any renewed Geneva negotiations. Nevertheless, an estrangement between Washington and Jerusalem, which began with the 1974 Arab oil boycott, persisted and the solidity of the alliance became increasingly an issue in domestic politics.

For the Israelis, the July 4, 1976, rescue of 103 hostages in a hijacked Air France airliner at Entebbe, Uganda, was a stunning victory against Arab terrorism. The hijacking was the first in a year and a half to be carried out by Palestinians, in this case the Popular Front for the Liberation of Palestine. Rabin contravened government policy in opening negotiations with the terrorists but secretly prepared a commando raid on the airport. When he learned that the hostages faced death in any event, Rabin launched the airborne raid, which killed the terrorists and a score of soldiers, losing only two hostages and one rescuer.

With no progress toward permanent peace and rampant inflation causing severe economic strain, the malaise in the Labor Party deepened in early 1977 when Rabin confessed to maintaining an illegal bank account in the United States. He resigned April 8 and Defense Minister Shimon Peres was named the party's leader for general elections May 17, in which the Labor Party was defeated for the first time since Israel's founding.

Menachem Begin, 63, took office June 21 as the leader of the Likud, a coalition of conservative parties. Begin founded the Irgun Zvai Leumi (National Military Organization) to fight British rule during the Palestine Mandate. His election victory provoked a wave of negative reaction throughout the Arab world and misgivings on the part of Western proponents of a Mideast peace. Attempting to modify his image, the Likud platform on the inauguration of the new government omitted an election claim of permanent sovereignty over the West Bank and agreed to suspend the application of Israeli law to the occupied territories in general while peace negotiations were under way.

A dramatic breakthrough in the tortuous history of Mideast peace efforts occurred Nov. 9, 1977, when Egypt's President Sadat declared his willingness to go anywhere to talk peace Begin on November 15 extended an invitation to the Egyptian leader to address the Knesset. Sadat's arrival in Israel four days later raised worldwide hopes. But optimism ebbed even before Begin was invited to Ismailia by Sadat, December 25–26.

An Israeli peace plan unveiled by Begin on his return, and approved by the Knesset, offered to end military administration in the West Bank and the Gaza Strip, with a degree of Arab self-rule but no relinquishment of sovereignty by Israel. Sadat severed talks on January 18 and, despite U.S. condemnation, Begin approved new West Bank settlements by Israelis. Dissidents within the cabinet, notably Defense Minister Ezer Weizman, kept the door open for negotiations, however, and a foreign ministerial meeting of the two antagonists with U.S. Secretary of State Cyrus Vance took place in England on July 18.

Amid the continuing tension over peace negotiations, a PLO raid on Israel's coast on March 11 killed 30 civilians and provoked a full-scale invasion of southern Lebanon by Israel three days later to attack PLO bases. Israel withdrew three months later, turning over strongpoints to Lebanese Christian militia wherever possible rather than to a U.N. peacekeeping force installed in the area.

Peace talks resumed their painful progress in October as Israeli Foreign Minister Moshe Dayan and Egyptian Defense Minister Kamel Hassan Ali, with the participation of President Carter, agreed on a U.S. draft treaty.

On March 14, 1979, after a visit by Carter, the Knesset approved a final treaty, and 12 days later Begin and Sadat signed the document, together with Carter, in a White House ceremony. Israel began its withdrawal from the Sinai on May 25 by handing over the coastal town of El Arish and the two countries opened their border on May 29, the same day Israeli navy landing craft transited the Suez Canal for the first time.

On Palestinian automony, there was little progress. On Feb. 10, 1980, Israel inflamed Arab opinion with the Cabinet's approval of Jewish settlements in Hebron, until then an exclusively Arab West Bank city. A right-wing Israeli terrorist campaign that maimed three Arab West Bank mayors and finally, the Knesset's passage of a law annexing East Jerusalem further antagonized the Arabs and stalled the autonomy talks. The Jerusalem action drew a unanimous condemnation—in which the U.S. joined—from the U.N. Security Council and caused the last eight countries still maintaining embassies in Jerusalem to remove them in response to a Council appeal.

One of the most difficult periods in Israel's history began with a confrontation with Syria over the placing by Syria of Soviet surface-to-air missiles in the Bekaa Valley of Lebanon in April 1981. President Reagan dispatched Philip C. Habib to prevent a clash. While Habib was seeking a settlement, Begin ordered a bombing raid against an Iraqi nuclear reactor on June 7, invoking the theory of pre-emptive self-defense because he said Iraq was planning to make nuclear weapons to attack Israel. Only through strenuous diplomatic efforts was the U.S. able to stave off Arab demands for sanctions against Israel in the Security Council in a vote on June 19 that condemned the action.

Begin's belligerence was credited with his narrow victory over Shimon Peres' Labor Party on June 30. He followed it with a bombing raid against PLO headquarters in Beirut on July 17 that killed 300 persons and injured 700. Begin's assertion that the attack was again in self-defense against PLO raids and bombardment across the border caused questions even among his supporters and drew the strongest criticism of Israel yet from Washington. Although Habib eventually got Begin to agree to a cease-fire on July 23, the Reagan Administration was forced to suspend indefinitely the delivery of

F-16 jets promised to Israel. By the two actions, Israel appeared to have blocked any resumption of work toward a permanent Mideast settlement, an effort that was faltering anyway.

ITALY

Italian Republic
President: Sandro Pertini (1978)
Premier: Giovanni Spadolini (1981)
Area: 116,304 sq mi. (301,225 sq km)
Population (est. 1981): 57,150,000 (growth rate: 0.3%)
Density per square mile: 491.4
Capital: Rome
Largest cities (est. 1980): Rome, 2,900,000; (est. 1978): Milan, 1,696,250; Naples, 1,226,100; Turin, 1,172,900; Genoa, 789,500; Palermo, 687,250; Bologna, 476,800; Florence, 463,300; Catania, 399,100; Venice, 358,400.
Monetary unit: Lira
Language: Italian
Religion: Roman Catholic
National name: Repubblica Italiana
Freedom House classifications: Capitalist industrial, multi-party centralized
Economic summary: Gross national product (1980): $394 billion. Average annual growth rate (1970–80): 3.0%. Per capita income: $3,470. Land used for agriculture: 50%; labor force: 12%; principal products: wheat, rice, grapes, olives, citrus fruits. Labor force in industry: 43%; major products: automobiles, machinery, chemicals, textiles, shoes. Natural resources: fish, dwindling natural gas reserves. Exports: machinery and transport equipment, textiles, foodstuffs, chemicals, footwear. Imports: crude oil, machinery and transport equipment, foodstuffs, ferrous and nonferrous metals, wool, cotton. Major trading partners: West Germany, France, Netherlands, U.S., U.K.

Geography. Italy is a long peninsula shaped like a boot bounded on the west by the Tyrrhenian Sea and on the east by the Adriatic. Slightly larger than Arizona, it has for neighbors France, Switzerland, Austria, and Yugoslavia.

Approximately 600 of Italy's 708 miles (1,139 km) of length are in the long peninsula that projects into the Mediterranean from the fertile basin of the Po River. The Apennine Mountains, branching off from the Alps between Nice and Genoa, form the peninsula's backbone, and rise to a maximum height of 9,560 feet (2,912 m) at the Gran Sasso d'Italia (Corno). The Alps form Italy's northern boundary.

Several islands form part of Italy. Sicily (9,926 sq mi.; 25,708 sq km) lies off the toe of the boot, across the Strait of Messina, with a steep and rockbound northern coast and gentler slopes to the sea in the west and south. Mount Etna, an active volcano, rises to 10,741 feet (3,274 m), and most of Sicily is more than 500 feet (3,274 m) in elevation. Sixty-two miles (100 km) southwest of Sicily lies Pantelleria (45 sq mi.; 117 sq km), and south of that are Lampedusa and Linosa. Sardinia (9,301 sq mi.; 24,090 sq km), which is just south of Corsica and about 125 miles (200 km) west of the mainland, is mountainous, stony, and unproductive.

Italy has many northern lakes, lying below the snow-covered peaks of the Alps. The largest are Garda (143 sq mi.; 370 sq km), Maggiore (83 sq mi.; 215 sq km), and Como (55 sq mi.; 142 sq km).

The Po, the principal river, flows from the Alps on Italy's western border and crosses the Lombard plain to the Adriatic.

Government. The president is elected for a term of seven years by Parliament in joint session with regional representatives. The president nominates the premier and, upon the premier's recommendations, the members of the Cabinet. Parliament is composed of two houses: a Senate with 315 elective members and a Chamber of Deputies of 630 members elected by the people for a five-year term.

The major political parties are: Christian Democratic Party (262 seats of 630 in Chamber of Deputies), led by Flaminio Piccoli; Communist Party (201 seats), led by Enrico Berlinguer; Socialist Party (62 seats), led by Bettino Craxi; Social Movement Party (30 seats), led by Giorgio Almirante; Social Democratic Party (20 seats), led by Pietro Longo; Radical Party (18 seats), led by Francesco Rutelli; Republican Party (16 seats), led by Premier Giovanni Spadolini; Liberal Party (9 seats), led by Valerio Zanone; and Proletarian Unity Party (6 seats), led by Lucio Magri.

History. Until A.D. 476, when the German Odoacer became head of the Roman Empire in the west, the history of Italy was largely the history of Rome. From A.D. 800 on, the Holy Roman Emperors, Popes, Normans, and Saracens all vied for control over various segments of the Italian peninsula. Numerous city states, such as Venice and Genoa, and many small principalities flourished in the late Middle Ages.

In 1713, after the War of the Spanish Succession, Milan, Naples, and Sardinia were handed over to Austria, which lost some of its Italian territories in 1735. After 1800, Italy was unified by Napoleon, who crowned himself King of Italy in 1805; but with the Congress of Vienna in 1815, Austria once again became the dominant power in Italy.

Austrian armies crushed Italian uprisings in 1820, 1821, and 1831. In the 1830s Giuseppe Mazzini, brilliant liberal nationalist, organized the Risorgimento (Resurrection), which laid the foundation for Italian unity.

Disappointed Italian patriots looked to the House of Savoy for leadership. Count Camille di Cavour (1810–61), Premier of Sardinia in 1852 and the architect of a united Italy, joined England and France in the Crimean War (1853–56), and in 1859 helped France in a war against Austria, thereby obtaining Lombardy. By plebiscite in 1860, Modena, Parma, Tuscany, and the Romagna voted to join Sardinia. In 1860, Giuseppe Garibaldi conquered Sicily and Naples and turned them over to Sardinia. Victor Emmanuel II, King of Sardinia, was proclaimed King of Italy in 1861.

Allied with Germany and Austria-Hungary in the Triple Alliance of 1882, Italy declared its neutrality upon the outbreak of World War I on the ground that Germany had embarked upon an offensive war. In 1915, Italy entered the war on the side of the Allies.

Benito (Il Duce) Mussolini, a former Socialist, organized discontented Italians in 1919 into the Fascist Party to "rescue Italy from Bolshevism." He led his Black Shirts in a march on Rome and, on Oct. 28, 1922, became premier. He transformed Italy into a dictatorship, embarking on an expansionist foreign policy with the invasion and annexation of Ethiopia in 1935 and allying himself with Adolf Hitler in the Rome-Berlin Axis in 1936. He was executed by Partisans on April 28, 1945 at Dongo on Lake Como.

Following the overthrow of Mussolini's dictatorship and the armistice with the Allies (Sept. 3,

1943), Italy joined the war against Germany as a co-belligerent. King Victor Emmanuel III abdicated May 9, 1946, and left the country after having installed his son as King Humbert II. However, a provisional government held a popular plebiscite three weeks later and the Italians voted to establish a republic. On June 13, King Humbert followed his father into exile.

The peace treaty that took effect Sept. 15, 1947, required Italian renunciation of all claims in Ethiopia and Greece and the cession of the Dodecanese to Greece and of five small Alpine areas to France. In addition, the major part of the Istrian Peninsula, including Fiume and Pola, went to Yugoslavia.

The Trieste area west of the new Yugoslav territory was made a free territory (until 1954, when the city and a 90-square-mile zone were transferred to Italy and the rest to Yugoslavia).

The government of Mario Rumor fell in 1974. After a 51-day crisis, a government was formed under Aldo Moro, a left-centrist Christian Democrat who had been Premier three times before.

Withdrawal of the Socialists from Moro's coalition—the 32nd government since World War II—brought his resignation Jan. 7, 1976. In the June elections, the Communists gained but the Christian Democrats still led and, warned by the U.S. and West Germany against a Communist coalition, they chose to govern as a minority under Giulio Andreotti. Petro Ingrao, a Communist, became President of the Chamber of Deputies, however, and Communists won 7 of 26 parliamentary chairmanships.

Andreotti had Communist cooperation in imposing wage limits and taxes to meet International Monetary Fund conditions for a $530-million loan. He also got Communist backing to combat a wave of kidnappings and political terrorism that culminated in the seizure of former Premier Moro in Rome on March 16, 1978, by the ultra-left Red Brigades. The discovery on May 9 of Moro's bullet-ridden body near the site of his kidnapping caused worldwide shock.

A second political shock was the resignation of President Giovanni Leone on June 15, six months before the end of his term, because of his involvement in Lockheed bribery scandals. Moro had been the leading candidate to replace him, but in the wide-open contest that ensued, 81-year-old Sandro Pertini became Italy's first Socialist president.

Tacit Communist support that had enabled Andreotti to govern ended on March 31, 1979, as the Communists insisted on seats in Andreotti's fifth cabinet and joined with the Socialists to defeat the government. Elections in June produced only one surprise—a drop in Communist strength in national voting for the first time since the beginning of the republic. The 4% loss went to splinter parties rather than to the Christian Democrats, however, leaving the political situation stalemated unless Andreotti were to accept Communist ministers.

The long crisis ended on Aug. 5, when Francesco Cossiga, a Christian Democrat, was able to form a minority coalition with the Social Democrats and Liberals. A Christian Democratic decision to bar Communists from Cabinet posts forced his resignation on March 19, 1980, but Cossiga persuaded the Socialists to join a majority coalition despite the ban on Communists. The majority held firm in his support when Communists and neo-Fascists

pressed for his impeachment in July on charges that he had warned the son of a colleague to flee Italy to avoid arrest as a terrorist.

Disaster and scandal brought the long reign of the Christian Democrats to an end when Italy's 40th premier since World War II, Arnaldo Forlani, was forced to resign in the wake of disclosure that many high-ranking Christian Democrats and civil servants belonged to a secret Masonic lodge known as "P-2." The scandal followed the disastrous earthquake that struck southern Italy on Nov. 23, 1980, killing 3,105, injuring 7,671, and leaving 1,575 missing and presumed dead. Delay in providing relief for survivors, amid reports of theft of supplies, cast a pall over the nation.

When the Socialists deserted the coalition, Forlani was forced to resign on May 26, 1981, leaving to Giovanni Spadolini of the small Republican Party the task of forming a new government. Spadolini declared his intention to outlaw the secret lodge, combat Italy's 20% inflation by cutting social services and government borrowing, fight the terrorism plaguing society, and support NATO's plans for the stationing of nuclear weapons in Western Europe.

Religion. Although Italy is predominantly Roman Catholic, religious freedom is permitted. Catholic religious teaching is given in all elementary and intermediate schools. Relations with the Church were regulated until 1977, by the treaty with the Holy See of Feb. 11, 1929, which established the temporal power of the Pope over Vatican City. In November 1977, a new accord replaced the 1929 Corcordat; Catholicism is no longer to be considered as the state religion and Vatican influence on education and marriage has been reduced.

IVORY COAST

Republic of Ivory Coast
President: Félix Houphouët-Boigny (1960)
Area: 124,502 sq mi. (322,462 sq km)
Population (est. 1981): 8,500,000 (growth rate: 3.3%)
Density per square mile: 68.3
Capital and largest city (est. 1980): Abidjan, 1,000,000
Monetary unit: Franc CFA
Ethnic groups: Agnis, Baoulés, Senoufos, Kroumen, Mandes, Dan-Gouros
Languages: French and African languages
Religions: Animist, 65%; Islam, 23%; Christian, 12%
National name: République de la Côte d'Ivoire
Freedom House classifications: Capitalist pre-industrial, one-party nationalist
Economic summary: Gross national product (1979): $8.6 billion. Average annual growth rate (1970–78): 0.9%. Per capita income (1978): $1,200. Labor force in agriculture: 85%; principal products: coffee, cocoa, timber, palm oil, sugar, bananas. Major industrial products: food, textiles, shoes, metals. Natural resources: petroleum, iron ore. Exports: coffee, cocoa. Imports: raw materials, consumer goods, fuels. Major trading partners: France, U.S., Western European countries.

Geography. The Ivory Coast, in western Africa on the Gulf of Guinea, is a little larger than New Mexico. Its neighbors are Liberia, Guinea, Mali, Upper Volta, and Ghana.

The country consists of a coastal strip in the south, dense forests in the interior, and savannas in the north. Rainfall is heavy, especially along the coast.

Government. The government is headed by a President who is elected every five years by popular vote, together with a National Assembly of 147 members.

The Parti Démocratique de la Côte d'Ivoire, a member of the Rassemblement Démocratique Africain, is the only political party.

History. The Ivory Coast attracted both French and Portuguese merchants in the 15th century. French traders set up establishments early in the 19th century, and in 1842, the French obtained territorial concessions from local tribes, gradually extending their influence along the coast and inland. The area was organized as a territory in 1893, became an autonomous republic in the French Union after World War II, and achieved independence on Aug. 7, 1960.

The Ivory Coast formed a customs union in 1959 with Dahomey (Benin), Niger, and Upper Volta. The country is one of the most prosperous and stable in West Africa. It succeeded in getting a $10-million loan from European and U.S. private capital in 1960 for low-cost housing and other development work. It also obtained a $30-million U.S. loan to assist in construction of a $96.5-million hydro-electric project.

JAMAICA

Sovereign: Queen Elizabeth II
Governor-General: Florizel Glasspole (1973)
Prime Minister: Edward P. G. Seaga (1980)
Area: 4,411 sq mi. (11,424 sq km)
Population (est. 1981): 2,225,000 (growth rate: 1.2%)
Density per square mile: 504.4
Capital and largest city (est. 1974): Kingston, 169,800
Monetary unit: Jamaican dollar
Language: English
Religions: Anglican, Baptist, Roman Catholic
Member of Commonwealth of Nations
Freedom House classifications: Capitalist-statist industrial, multi-party centralized
Economic summary: Gross national product (1979): $2.7 billion. Average annual growth rate (1970–78): −1.4%. Per capita income: $1,610. Land used for agriculture: 42%; labor force: 28% (includes fishing and mining); principal products: sugar cane, citrus fruits, bananas, pimentos, coconuts, coffee, cocoa. Labor force in industry: 12%; major products: bauxite, textiles, processed foods, light manufactures. Natural resources: bauxite, gypsum, limestone. Exports: alumina, bauxite, sugar, bananas, citrus fruits, rum, cocoa. Imports: fuels, machinery, transport and electrical equipment, food, fertilizer. Major trading partners: U.S., U.K., Canada.

Geography. Jamaica is an island in the West Indies, 90 miles (145 km) south of Cuba and 100 miles (161 km) west of Haiti. It is a little smaller than Connecticut.

The island is made up of a plateau and the Blue Mountains, a group of volcanic hills, in the east. Blue Mountain (7,402 ft.; 2,256 m) is the tallest peak.

Government. The legislature is a 60-member House of Representatives elected by universal suffrage and an appointed Senate of 21 members. The Prime Minister is appointed by the Governor-General and must, in the Governor-General's opinion, be the person best able to command the confidence of a majority of the members of the House of Representatives.

The major political parties are the Jamaica Labor Party (52 seats in the House of Representatives), led by Prime Minister Edward P. G. Seaga; and the People's National Party (8 seats), led by former Prime Minister Michael Manley.

History. Jamaica was inhabited by Arawak Indians when Columbus discovered it in 1494 and named it St. Iago. It remained under Spanish rule until 1655, then became a British possession. The island prospered from wealth brought by buccaneers to their base, Port Royal, the capital, until the city disappeared in the sea in 1692 after an earthquake. The Arawaks died off from disease and exploitation, and slaves, mostly black, were imported to work sugar plantations. Abolition of the slave trade (1807), emancipation of the slaves (1833), and a gradual drop in sugar prices led to depressed economic conditions that resulted in an uprising in 1865.

The following year Jamaica's status was changed to that of a colony, and conditions improved considerably. Introduction of banana cultivation made the island less dependent on the sugar crop for its well-being. Overpopulation and problems inherited from the colonial era, such as illiteracy, produced chronic substantial unemployment, leading to much emigration to the Caribbean countries and to the U.S.

On May 5, 1953, Jamaica attained internal autonomy, and in 1958 it led in organizing the West Indies Federation. This effort at Caribbean unification failed. A nationalist labor leader, Sir Alexander Bustamante, led a campaign for withdrawal from the Federation. As the result of a popular referendum in 1961, Jamaica became independent on Aug. 6, 1962.

Michael Manley became Prime Minister in 1972 and initiated a socialist program, with higher taxes on land and luxuries and on the production of bauxite. In 1977, the government agreed to buy 51% of the Kaiser and Reynolds bauxite operations in Jamaica, ending a dispute with the U.S. companies over heavy taxes imposed earlier.

Elections on Oct. 30, 1980, offered a sharp contrast between Manley's socialism trending toward the Cuban model of his friend, Fidel Castro, and the aggressive capitalism of Labor Party leader Edward P. G. Seaga. A campaign marked by violence ended with 57% of the popular vote and 51 of 60 House seats for Seaga, who immediately banished the Cuban ambassador. Seaga was the first foreign head of government to visit the newly installed President Reagan, on Jan. 28, 1981, to appeal for aid. The International Monetary Fund granted a loan of $650 million in April and a group of industrialized nations, together with the Interamerican Development Bank, offered credits of $350,000.

JAPAN

Emperor: Hirohito (1926)
Prime Minister: Zenko Suzuki (1980)
Area: 143,574 sq mi. (371,857 sq km)
Population (est. 1981): 117,650,000 (growth rate: 0.8%)
Density per square mile: 819.4
Capital: Tokyo
Largest cities (est. 1980)[1]: Tokyo, 8,500,000; (est. 1977 by

U.N.): Osaka, 2,723,700; Yokohama, 2,694,500; Nagoya, 2,083,500; Kyoto, 1,465,000; Kobe, 1,366,500; Sapporo, 1,307,700; Kitakyshu, 1,068,000

Monetary unit: Yen

Language: Japanese

Religions: Shintoist, Buddhist, Christian

National name: Nippon

Freedom House classifications: Capitalist industrial, multi-party centralized

Economic summary: Gross national product (1979): $1,019.5 billion. Average annual growth rate (1970–78): 7.8%. Per capita income: $6,010. Land used for agriculture, 16%; labor force, including fishing, 11%; principal products: rice, vegetables, fruits, meat, natural silk. Labor force in industry: 34%; major products: machinery and equipment, metals and metal products, textiles, autos, chemicals, electrical and electronic equipment. Natural resource: fish. Exports: machinery and equipment, metals and metal products, textiles. Imports: fossil fuels, metal ore, raw materials, foodstuffs, machinery and equipment. Major trading partners: U.S., U.K., Canada.

1. Except for Tokyo, figures refer to *shi*, a minor division that may include some scattered or rural population as well as an urban center.

Geography. An archipelago extending more than 2,360 miles (3,776 km) from north to south in the Pacific, Japan is separated from the east coast of Asia by the Sea of Japan. It is approximately the size of Montana.

Japan's four main islands are Honshu, Hokkaido, Kyushu, and Shikoku. The Ryukyu chain to the southwest was U.S.-occupied and the Kuriles to the northeast are Russian-occupied. The surface of the main islands consists largely of mountains separated by narrow valleys. There are about 50 more or less active volcanoes, of which the best-known is Mount Fuji.

Government. Japan's Constitution, promulgated on Nov. 3, 1946, replaced the Meiji Constitution of 1889. The 1946 Constitution, sponsored by the U.S. during its occupation of Japan, brought fundamental changes to the Japanese political system, including the abandonment of the Emperor's divine rights. The Diet (Parliament) consists of a House of Representatives of 511 members, elected for four years, and a House of Councilors of 252 members, half of whom are elected every three years for six-year terms. Executive power is vested in the Cabinet, which is headed by a Prime Minister, nominated by the Diet from its members.

Emperor Hirohito, who was born April 29, 1901, succeeded his father, Yoshihito, on Dec. 25, 1926. He was married on Jan. 26, 1924, to Princess Nagako, born in 1903. They have two sons—Crown Prince Akihito (born Dec. 23, 1933) and Prince Hitachi (born Nov. 28, 1935)—and four daughters. Succession to the Japanese throne is in the male line only.

The major political parties are the Liberal Democratic Party (286 of 511 seats in the House of Representatives), led by Prime Minister Zenko Suzuki; Socialist Party (107 seats), led by Kazuo Asukada; Clean Government (Komeito) Party (33 seats), led by Yoshikatsu Takeiri; Communist Party (29 seats), led by Sanzo Nosaka; Democratic Socialist Party (28 seats), led by Ikko Kasuga; New Liberal Club (12 seats).

History. A series of legends attributes creation of Japan to the sun goddess, from whom the later emperors were allegedly descended. The first of them

was Jimmu Tenno, supposed to have ascended the throne in 660 B.C.

Recorded Japanese history begins with the first contact with China in the 5th century A.D. Japan was then divided into strong feudal states, all nominally under the Emperor, but with real power often held by a court minister or clan. In 1185, Yoritomo, chief of the Minamoto clan, was designated Shogun (Generalissimo) with the administration of the islands under his control. A dual government system —Shogun and Emperor—continued until 1867.

First contact with the West came about 1542, when a Portuguese ship off course arrived in Japanese waters. Portuguese traders, Jesuit missionaries, and Spanish, Dutch, and English traders followed. Suspicious of Christianity and of Portuguese support of a local Japanese revolt, the shoguns prohibited all trade with foreign countries; only a Dutch trading post at Nagasaki was permitted. Western attempts to renew trading relations failed until 1853, when Commodore Matthew Perry sailed an American fleet into Tokyo Bay.

Japan now quickly made the transition from a medieval to a modern power. Feudalism was abolished and industrialization was speeded. An imperial army was established with conscription. The shogun system was abolished in 1868 by Emperor Meiji, and parliamentary government was established in 1889. After a brief war with China in 1894–95, Japan acquired Formosa (Taiwan), the Pescadores Islands, and part of southern Manchuria. China also recognized the independence of Korea (Chosen), which Japan later annexed (1910).

In 1904–05, Japan defeated Russia in the Russo-Japanese War, gaining the territory of southern Sakhalin (Karafuto) and Russia's port and rail rights in Manchuria. In World War I, Japan, which took a negligible part in military operations, seized Germany's Pacific islands and leased areas in China. The Treaty of Versailles then awarded it a mandate over the islands.

At the Washington Conference of 1921–22, Japan agreed to respect Chinese national integrity. The series of Japanese aggressions that was to lead to the nation's downfall began in 1931 with the invasion of Manchuria. The following year, Japan set up this area as a puppet state, "Manchukuo," under Emperor Henry Pu-Yi, last of China's Manchu dynasty. On Nov. 25, 1936, Japan joined the Axis by signing the anti-Comintern pact. The invasion of China came the next year and the Pearl Harbor attack on the U.S. on Dec. 7, 1941.

(For details of World War II (1939–45), *see* Headline History.)

Japan surrendered formally on Sept. 2, 1945, aboard the battleship *Missouri* in Tokyo Bay after atomic bombs had hit Hiroshima and Nagasaki. Southern Sakhalin and the Kurile Islands reverted to the U.S.S.R., and Formosa (Taiwan) and Manchuria to China. The Pacific islands remained under U.S. occupation. General of the Army Douglas MacArthur was appointed Supreme Commander for the Allied Powers on Aug. 14, 1945.

A new Japanese Constitution went into effect in 1947. In 1949, many of the responsibilities of government were returned to the Japanese. Full sovereignty was granted to Japan by the Japanese Peace Treaty in 1951.

The treaty took effect on April 28, 1952, when Japan returned to full status as a nation. It was admitted into the United Nations in 1958.

Following the visit of Prime Minister Eisaku Sato to Washington in 1969, the U.S. agreed to return Okinawa and other Ryukyu Islands to Japan in

1972, and both nations renewed the security treaty in 1970.

Events of the 1970s tested Japan's special relationship with the U.S. Trade ties were strained in 1972 by Washington's inconclusive effort to curb textile imports from Japan. The focus of Japanese diplomacy was altered when President Nixon opened a dialogue with Peking in 1972. Prime Minister Kakuei Tanaka, who succeeded Sato in 1972, quickly established diplomatic relations with the mainland Chinese and severed ties with Formosa.

The jump in world oil prices that followed the 1973 Arab boycott squeezed Japan, which imports 85% of its oil from the Middle East. Japan greatly expanded its exports to the oil states and accepted some Arab investments.

Following Communist triumphs in Southeast Asia in the spring of 1975, Japan began moving into the diplomatic and commercial vacuum that followed U.S. withdrawal from the area.

Spending on defense in 1975 was less than 1% of the gross national product, and Japan's all-volunteer Self-Defense Forces numbered only 232,000 —12% below authorized strength.

President Ford visited Japan Nov. 18–24, 1974, the first U.S. President to do so. Substantive results were minimized by Tanaka's domestic political troubles. Tanaka resigned two days after Ford's departure, and was succeeded by Takeo Miki, a compromise choice from the progressive wing of the Liberal Democrats.

While economic recovery continued in 1976, the Lockheed scandal pursued the ruling Liberal Democrats. With the disclosure by the U.S. Senate that $6.3 million in "promotion" money had been paid by the aircraft company to Yoshio Kodama, a rightwing political "fixer," Miki was placed under strong pressure to investigate the ultimate recipients.

Former Prime Minister Tanaka himself was jailed in August, charged with having received $1.7 million of the Lockheed money in violation of exchange controls. The scandal cost the party its control of the House of Representatives in the December election, but nine independents affiliated with the Liberal Democrats to provide a narrow majority. Miki resigned, accepting responsibility for the first defeat since the party took control of the government in 1955, turning over leadership to Takeo Fukuda.

Fukuda, concentrating on economic recovery, achieved a record year in 1977, with exports exceeding imports by $9 billion, nearly twice the previous record of $5.1 billion in 1972. With the U.S. alone, Japan's favorable balance was $7.3 billion, despite a steadily falling dollar in yen terms.

Visiting Washington in May 1978, Fukuda promised "massive efforts" to reduce Japan's surplus, currently running at an annual rate of $14 billion, by cutting automobile, color television, and steel exports and by buying U.S. aircraft. In return, like other U.S. trade partners, he urged Washington to curb inflation at home and support the dollar in foreign markets.

On Aug. 12, 1978, Japan and China signed a treaty of peace and friendship that was viewed by both countries as a foreign-policy landmark. This pact followed an 8-year, $20-billion economic pact in which Japanese business leaders agreed to provide China with modern technology in return for Chinese natural resources.

Despite pledges to its economic partners at the Bonn summit of industrial powers in July 1978 that it would reduce its trade surplus, Japan reported an all-time high figure of $18.3 billion for the year.

But, Japan's oil bill of $39.5 billion for the year ended March 31, 1980, produced a record trade deficit of $14.4 billion in contrast to a $13.4 billion surplus the previous year.

A $6-billion favorable balance in trade with the U.S. brought strong pressure from the U.S. auto industry and unions for a reduction in exports of Japanese cars although an earlier voluntary restraint on television exports was dropped.

Masayoshi Ohira, Prime Minister since November 1978, died on June 12, 1980, and in national elections held June 22, the ruling Liberal Democrats reversed an eight-year decline in public support, winning a firm parliamentary majority. The party chose Zenko Suzuki, a little-known 66-year-old follower of Ohira, as the new Prime Minister.

Suzuki's first contact with the Reagan Administration, in May 1981, went badly as reports of a U.S.-Japan "alliance" and weapons build-up emerged from the White House, causing the resignation of Masayoshi Ito as Foreign Minister for "misinterpreting" events. The sinking of a Japanese freighter by a U.S. nuclear submarine in the China Sea on April 9 and the statement by Former U.S. Ambassador Edwin O. Reischauer that U.S. ships carrying nuclear weapons regularly entered Japanese ports in the 1960s despite the Constitutional ban so aroused public opinion that Secretary of State Alexander M. Haig, Jr., canceled plans to visit Tokyo on his Far East tour in June.

Announcement on June 19 that Japan's gross national product grew at a rate of nearly 5% for the fiscal year ending March 31 brought new demands for increased imports of manufactured goods by Japan, which international trade experts charged was still creating barriers against trade despite repeated promises by Tokyo to relax such restrictions. To placate the ailing U.S. automobile industry, Japan announced that it would limit exports of cars to the United States to 1,680,000 units for the year ending March 31, 1982.

JORDAN

The Hashemite Kingdom of Jordan
Ruler: King Hussein I (1952)
Prime Minister: Mudar Badran (1980)
Area: 37,297 sq mi. (96,599 sq km)[1]
Population (est. 1981): 3,300,000 (growth rate: 3.0%)
Density per square mile: 88.5
Capital: Amman
Largest cities (est. 1979): Amman, 700,000; (est. 1977 by U.N.): Zarka, 263,500; Irbid, 136,800
Monetary unit: Jordanian dinar
Language: Arabic
Religions: Islam, 94%; Christian, 6%
National name: Al Mamlaka al Urduniya al Hashemiyah
Freedom House classifications: Capitalist industrial, non-party non-military
Economic summary: Gross national product (1979): $2.6 billion (East Bank only). Average annual growth rate (1972–78): 7.0%. Per capita income: $870. Land used for agriculture: 11%; labor force: 23%; principal products: wheat, fruits, vegetables, olive oil. Labor force in industry: 67%; major products: phosphate, refined petroleum products, cement. Natural resources: phosphate, potash. Exports: fruits, vegetables, phosphate. Imports: machinery, transport equipment, cereals, petroleum products. Major trading partners: U.S., U.K., West Germany, Japan, Lebanon, Saudi Arabia.

1. Includes territory occupied by Israel in 1967 war.

Geography. The Middle East kingdom of Jordan is bordered on the west by Israel and the Dead Sea, on the north by Syria, on the east by Iraq, and on the south Saudi Arabia. It is comparable in size to Indiana.

Arid hills and mountains make up most of the country. The southern section of the Jordan River flows through the country.

Government. Jordan is a constitutional monarchy with a bicameral parliament. Its Chamber of Deputies of 60 members is elected for four years by the people, and the 30 members of the Senate are appointed by the King.

All political parties were banned in 1957.

History. In biblical times, the country that is now Jordan contained the lands of Edom, Moab, Ammon, and Bashan. In A.D. 106 it became part of the Roman province of Arabia and in 633–36 was conquered by the Arabs.

Taken from the Turks by the British in World War I, Jordan (formerly known as Transjordan) was separated from the Palestine mandate in 1920, and in 1921, placed under the rule of Abdullah ibn Hussein.

In 1923, Britain recognized Jordan's independence, subject to the mandate. In 1946, grateful for Jordan's loyalty in World War II, Britain abolished the mandate. That part of Palestine occupied by Jordanian troops was formally incorporated by action of the Jordanian Parliament in 1950.

King Abdullah was assassinated in 1951. His son Talal was deposed as mentally ill the next year. Talal's son Hussein, born Nov. 14, 1935, succeeded him.

From the beginning of his reign, Hussein had to steer a careful course between his powerful neighbor to the west, Israel, and rising Arab nationalism, frequently a direct threat to his throne. Riots erupted when he joined the Central Treaty Organization (the Baghdad Pact) in 1955, and he incurred further unpopularity when Britain, France, and Israel attacked the Suez Canal in 1956, forcing him to place his army under nominal command of the United Arab Republic of Egypt and Syria.

The 1961 breakup of the UAR eased Arab national pressure on Hussein, who was the first to recognize Syria after it reclaimed its independence. Jordan was swept into the 1967 Arab-Israeli war, however, and lost the old city of Jerusalem and all of its territory west of the Jordan river, the West Bank. Embittered Palestinian guerrilla forces virtually took over sections of Jordan in the aftermath of defeat, and open warfare broke out between the Palestinians and government forces in 1970.

Despite intervention of Syrian tanks, Hussein's Bedouin army defeated the Palestinians, suffering heavy casualties. A U.S. military alert and Israeli armor massed on the Golan Heights contributed psychological weight, but the Jordanians alone drove out the Syrians and invited the departure of 12,000 Iraqui troops who had been in the country since the 1967 war. Ignoring protests from other Arab states, Hussein by mid-1971 crushed Palestinian strength in Jordan and shifted the problem to Lebanon, where many of the guerrillas had fled.

In the Arab-Israeli war of 1973, Jordan remained aloof, whether in deference to $30 million in annual arms aid from the U.S. or in fear of losing more territory. But in October 1974, Hussein concurred in an Arab summit resolution calling for an independent Palestinian state and endorsing the Pales-

tine Liberation Organization as the "sole legitimate representative of the Palestinian people." This apparent reversal of policy changed with the growing disillusion of Arab states with the P.L.O., however, and by 1977 Hussein referred again to the unity of people on both banks of the Jordan.

As Egypt and Israel neared final agreement on a peace treaty early in 1979, Hussein met with Yassir Arafat, the PLO leader, on March 17 and issued a joint statement of opposition. Although the U.S. pressed Jordan to break Arab ranks on the issue, Hussein elected to side with the great majority, cutting ties with Cairo and joining the boycott against Egypt.

On June 15, 1978, Hussein, who had celebrated his 25th anniversary on the throne, married Elizabeth Halaby, 26, daughter of Najeeb Halaby, former president of Pan American World Airways. In an unexpected gesture, the monarch's fourth wife —his previous wife was killed and the first two divorced—was proclaimed Queen and given the name Noor al-Hussein.

Hussein visited Washington in July, and despite his refusal to soften his opposition to the Camp David agreements, he won the Carter administration's promise to sell Jordan U.S. tanks.

In September 1980, Jordan declared itself with Iraq in its conflict with Iran and, despite threats from Syria, opened ports to war shipments for Iraq unable to go directly to Baghdad because of the blocking of the Shatt al-Arab waterway.

KAMPUCHEA

See Cambodia

KENYA

Republic of Kenya
President: Daniel Arap Moi (1978)
Area: 224,960 sq mi. (582,646 sq km)
Population (est. 1981): 16,300,000 (growth rate: 4.0%)
Density per square mile: 72.5
Capital: Nairobi
Largest cities (est. 1980): Nairobi, 835,000; Mombasa, 400,000
Monetary unit: Kenyan shilling
Languages: Swahili (official), Bantu, Kikuyu, English
Religions: Protestant, 33%; Roman Catholic, 17%; Islam, 24%; Animist
Member of Commonwealth of Nations
Freedom House classifications: Capitalist pre-industrial, one-party nationalist
Economic summary: Gross national product (1979): $5.8 billion. Average annual growth rate (1970–78): 2.5%. Per capita income: $270. Land used for agriculture: 10–15%; labor force in agriculture: 23%; principal products: coffee, sisal, tea, pyrethrum, cotton, livestock. Labor force in industry: 14%; major products: plastic goods, furniture, batteries, textiles, soap, cigarettes, refined oil. Natural resources: wildlife. Exports: coffee, tea, livestock products, pyrethrum, tanning extract. Imports: machinery, transport equipment, crude oil, paper and paper products, iron and steel products, textiles. Major trading partners: Western European countries, Japan, Iran, U.S., Zambia, Uganda.

Geography. Kenya lies on the equator in east central Africa on the coast of the Indian Ocean. It is twice the size of Nevada. Kenya's neighbors are Tanzania, Uganda, the Sudan, Ethiopia, and Somalia.

In the north, the land is arid; the southwestern

corner is in the fertile Lake Victoria Basin; and a length of the eastern depression of Great Rift Valley separates western highlands from those that rise from the lowland coastal strip. Large game reserves have been developed.

Government. Under its Constitution of 1963, amended in 1964, Kenya has a one-house National Assembly of 171 members, elected for five years by universal suffrage. Since 1969, the president has been chosen by a general election.

The Kenya African National Union, led by the president, is the only political party.

President Jomo Kenyatta died in his sleep on Aug. 22, 1978. Vice President Daniel Arap Moi was elected to succeed him on Oct. 10.

History. Kenya, formerly a British colony and protectorate, was made a crown colony in 1920. The whites' domination of the rich plateau area, the White Highlands, long regarded by the Kikiyu people as their territory, was a factor leading to native terrorism, called the Mau Mau movement, in 1952. In 1954 the British began preparing the territory for African rule and independence. In 1961 Jomo Kenyatta was freed from banishment to become leader of the Kenya African National Union.

Internal self-government was granted in 1963; Kenya became independent on Dec. 12, 1963, with Kenyatta the first president. Kenya obtained economic and technical assistance from Communist China beginning in 1964 and later a World Bank loan.

In 1967, Kenya, Uganda, and Tanzania agreed to establish an East African trading community and a development bank. Kenya also sought to end dominance of retail trade by the Indian community of 188,000. In 1968 it began a drive against the Asians, and 20,000 left the country. In 1972, Kenyatta ordered all Asians with Kenyan passports to leave, allegedly because of foreign-currency manipulations.

KIRIBATI

Republic of Kiribati
Sovereign: Queen Elizabeth II
Governor General: Reginald J. Wallace (1980)
President: Ieremia Tabai (1979)
Area: 264 sq mi. (683 sq km)
Population (est. 1981): 60,000 (growth rate: 1.6%)
Density per square mile: 227.3
Capital (est. 1974): Bairiki (on Tarawa Atoll), 17,100
Monetary unit: Australian dollar
Language: English
Religions: Roman Catholic, 48%; Protestant, 45%
Freedom House classifications: Capitalist-statist pre-industrial, non-party non-military
Economic summary: Gross national product (1979): $40 million. Principal agricultural products: copra, vegetables. Exports: phosphates, copra. Imports: foodstuffs, fuel, transportation equipment. Major trading partners: New Zealand, Australia.

Geography. Kiribati, formerly the Gilbert Islands, consists of three widely separated main groups of Southwest Pacific islands, the Gilberts on the equator, the Phoenix Islands to the east, and the Line Islands further east. Ocean Island, producer of phosphates, which constitute 99% of the new nation's annual income of $18 million, is also included in the two million square miles of ocean, which will give Kiribati an important fishery resource.

Government. The president holds executive power. The legislature consists of a House Assembly with 37 members.

History. A British protectorate since 1892, the Gilbert and Ellice Islands became a colony in 1915–16. The two island groups were separated in 1975 and given internal self-government.

Tarawa and others of the Gilbert group were occupied by Japan during World War II. Tarawa was the site of one of the bloodiest battles in U.S. Marine Corps history when Marines landed in November 1943 to dislodge the Japanese defenders.

Princess Anne, representing Queen Elizabeth II, presented the independence documents to the new government on July 12, 1979.

KOREA, NORTH

Democratic People's Republic of Korea
President: Marshal Kim Il Sung (1972)
Premier: Li Jong-ok (1977)
Area: 46,768 sq mi. (121,129 sq km)
Population (est. 1981): 18,350,000 (growth rate: 3.2%)
Density per square mile: 392.4
Capital and largest city (est. 1976): Pyongyang, 1,500,000
Monetary unit: Won
Language: Korean
Religions: None
National name: Chosun Minchu-chui Inmin Konghwa-guk
Freedom House classifications: Socialist industrial, one-party communist
Economic summary: Gross national product (1979): $19.7 billion. Average annual growth rate (1970–78): 3.8%. Per capita income: $590. Land used for agriculture: 17%; labor force, 48%; principal products: corn, rice, vegetables. Major industrial products: machines, electric power, chemicals, textiles, processed foods, metallurgical products. Natural resources: coal, iron ore. Exports: minerals, chemical and metallurgical products. Imports: machinery and equipment, petroleum, foodstuffs, coking coal. Major trading partners: U.S.S.R., China, Japan.

Geography. Korea is a 600-mile (966 km) peninsula jutting from Manchuria and China (and a small portion of the U.S.S.R.) into the Sea of Japan and the Yellow Sea off eastern Asia. North Korea occupies an area slightly smaller than Pennsylvania north of the 38th parallel.

The country is almost completely covered by a series of north-south mountain ranges separated by narrow valleys. The Yalu River forms part of the northern border with Manchuria.

Government. The elected Supreme People's Assembly, as the chief organ of government, chooses a Presidium and a Cabinet. The Cabinet, which exercises executive authority, is subject to approval by the Assembly and the Presidium.

The Korean Workers (Communist) Party, led by President Kim Il Sung, is the only political party.

History. According to myth, Korea was founded in 2333 B.C. by Tangun. In the 17th century, it became a vassal of China and was isolated from all but Chinese influence and contact until 1876, when Japan forced Korea to negotiate a commercial treaty, opening the land to the U. S. and Europe. Japan achieved control as the result of its war with China (1894–95) and with Russia (1904–05) and annexed Korea in 1910. Japan developed the country but never won over the Korean nationalists.

After the Japanese surrender in 1945, the country was divided into two occupation zones, the U.S.S.R. north of and the U.S. south of the 38th parallel. When the cold war developed between the U.S. and U.S.S.R., trade between the zones was cut off. In 1948, the division between the zones was made permanent with the establishment of separate regimes in the north and south. By mid-1949, the U.S. and U.S.S.R. withdrew all troops. The Democratic People's Republic of Korea (North Korea) was established on May 1, 1948. The Communist Party, headed by Kim Il Sung, was established in power.

On June 25, 1950, the North Korean army launched a surprise attack on South Korea. On June 26, the U.N. Security Council condemned the invasion as aggression and ordered withdrawal of the invading forces. On June 27, President Harry S. Truman ordered air and naval units into action to enforce the U.N. order. The British government did the same, and soon a multinational U.N. command was set up to aid the South Koreans. The North Korean invaders took Seoul and pushed the South Koreans into the southeast corner of their country.

Gen. Douglas MacArthur, U.N. commander, made an amphibious landing at Inchon on September 15 behind the North Korean lines, which resulted in the complete rout of the North Korean army. The U.N. forces drove north across the 38th parallel, approaching the Yalu River. Then Communist China entered the war, forcing the U.N. forces into headlong retreat. Seoul was lost again, then regained; ultimately the war stabilized near the 38th parallel but dragged on for two years while the belligerents negotiated. An armistice was agreed to on July 27, 1953.

North Korea became embroiled with the U.S. again on Jan. 23, 1968, when it seized the American intelligence ship *Pueblo* and its crew of 83. After more than a year, the crew was released.

When a U.S. helicopter strayed across the 38th parallel July 13, 1977, and was shot down by North Koreans, with the loss of three crewmen, the reaction was much more restrained. President Carter acknowledged U.S. error and, after seven hours of talks at Panmunjom, the North Koreans sent back the three bodies and the lone survivor.

Although Kim appears to be revered, economic troubles have beset his rigidly collectivist country. World bankers say a record of unpaid accounts due the U.S.S.R., as well as non-Communist states, has demolished North Korea's international credit standing. Its armed forces, numbering 467,000, are about three fourths of the South's military establishment, but the North's 600-plane air force holds a 3-to-1 edge over its potential foe, who has relied on U.S. air support in the event of war.

President Carter, visiting Seoul from June 29 to July 1, 1979, proposed that the U.S., North Korea, and South Korea meet "to promote dialogue and reduce tensions in the area," possibly leading to reunification of the two Koreas. Pyongyang's official party newspaper rejected the proposal, saying the North favors reunification talks but without the "alien interference" of the U.S.

Kim again rejected as a 'foolish burlesque' an invitation on Jan. 12, 1981, by South Korea's military chief, Chun Doo Hwan, to hold reunification talks in Seoul. Kim refused again when Chun re-

peated the invitation on March 3 during his inauguration as President of the Southern republic.

KOREA, SOUTH

Republic of Korea
President: Chun Doo Hwan (1980)
Preimer Nam Duk Woo (1980)
Area: 38,031 sq mi. (98,500 sq km)
Population (est. 1981): 38,800,000 (growth rate: 1.6%)
Density per square mile: 1,020.2
Capital: Seoul
Largest cities (est. 1980): Seoul, 8,400,000; Pusan, 3,160,000; Taegu, 1,600,000; Inchon, 1,100,000; Kwangju, 725,000; Taejon, 650,000; Chonju, 370,000; (1975 census): Pusan, 2,453,200; Taegu, 1,310,800; Inchon, 800,000; Kwangju, 607,700; Taejon, 506,700; Chonju, 311,400
Monetary unit: Won
Language: Korean
Religions: Buddhist, 47%; Christian, 18%; Confucian, 13%
National name: Dae Han Min Kook
Freedom House classifications: Capitalist industrial, non-party military
Economic summary: Gross national product (1979): $55.9 billion. Average annual growth rate (1970–78): 8.1%. Per capita income: $880. Land used for agriculture: 23%; labor force, including fishing, 36%; principal products: rice, barley. Labor force in industry: 24%; major products: clothing and textiles, processed foods, chemical fertilizers, chemicals, plywood, steel, electronics equipment. Natural resources: iron and copper ore, tungsten, graphite, limestone, coal, gold, silver. Exports: clothing and textiles, electric machinery, plywood, footwear, steel, ships. Imports: oil, ships, steel, wood, wheat, organic chemicals, machinery. Major trading partners: U.S., Japan.

Geography. Slightly larger than Indiana, South Korea lies below the 38th parallel on the Korean peninsula. It is mountainous in the east; in the west and south are many harbors on the mainland and offshore islands.

Government. A national referendum in October 1980 approved a new Constitution that provides for election of the President by an electoral college chosen by popular vote. The term of office is for seven years, limited to one term. A unicameral National Assembly has 276 members, 184 elected directly by popular vote, the remainder appointed in proportion to party strength in the election.

Major parties are the Democratic Justice Party (151 of 276 National Assembly seats), led by Prime Minister Nam Duk Woo; the opposition Democratic Korea Party (81 seats), led by Yoo Chi Song, and the Korea National Party (25 seats); Independents hold 11 seats and the remaining eight are held by splinter parties.

History. South Korea came into being in the aftermath of World War II as the result of a 1945 agreement making the 38th parallel the boundary between a northern zone occupied by the U.S.S.R. and a southern zone occupied by U.S. forces. (For details, *see* North Korea.)

Elections were held in the U.S. zone in 1948 for a national assembly, which adopted a republican Constitution and elected Syngman Rhee president. The new republic was proclaimed on August 15 and was recognized as the legal government of Korea by the U.N. on Dec. 12, 1948.

On June 25, 1950, South Korea was attacked by

North Korean Communist forces. U.S. armed intervention was ordered on June 27 by President Harry S. Truman, and on the same day the U.N. invoked military sanctions against North Korea. Gen. Douglas MacArthur was named commander of the U.N. forces. U.S. and South Korean troops fought a heroic holding action but, by the first week of August, they had been forced back to a 4,000-square-mile beachhead in southeast Korea.

There they stood off superior North Korean forces until September 15, when a major U.N. amphibious attack was launched far behind the Communist lines at Inchon, port of Seoul. By September 30, U.N. forces were in complete control of South Korea. They then invaded North Korea and were nearing the Manchurian and Siberian borders when several hundred thousand Chinese Communist troops entered the conflict in late October. U.N. forces were then forced to retreat below the 38th parallel.

On May 24, 1951, U.N. forces recrossed the parallel and had made important new inroads into North Korea when truce negotiations began on July 10. An armistice was finally signed at Panmunjom on July 27, 1953, leaving a devastated Korea in need of large-scale rehabilitation. The armistice contemplated an international political conference on the status of Korea, but negotiations for arranging it broke down.

The U.S. and South Korea signed a mutual-defense treaty on Oct. 1, 1953.

Rhee, president since 1948, resigned in 1960 in the face of rising disorders. Posun Yun was elected to succeed him, but political instability continued. In 1961, Gen. Park Chung Hee took power in a coup. He built up the country, maintaining an average growth rate in the economy of 8.5%. The U.S. stepped up military aid, building up South Korea's armed forces to 600,000 men. The South Koreans sent 50,000 troops to Vietnam, most of their cost paid by the U.S.

In mid-1972, following President Nixon's summit meetings in Moscow and Peking, the two Koreas issued a mutual declaration setting a goal of peaceful reunification. (For details, *see* Korea, North).

An announcement by President Carter in March 1977 that he would withdraw U.S. ground troops from South Korea within four to five years brought protests from both the Park government and opposition leaders. A U.S. pledge of $2 billion in arms aid—close to the estimated amount of savings in the troop reduction—together with a commitment that U.S. air and naval forces would stay indefinitely appeared to have reassured Koreans.

Tension between Seoul and Washington also arose over human rights as South Korean dissidents appealed for U.S. support in their demands that Park rescind both the 1972 Constitution and his 1975 emergency powers. Park responded to pressure by releasing 14 political detainees, including several Christian leaders, but not Kim Dae Jung, a former opposition presidential candidate kidnapped from Tokyo in 1973 by the Korean Central Intelligence Agency.

A growing scandal over Korean bribery of U.S. Congressmen accelerated in 1977 with testimony by a defecting ex-Director of the KCIA who named a Washington influence man, Tongsun Park, as a KCIA agent. Two former Democratic Representatives, Richard T. Hanna of California and Otto E. Passman of Louisiana, were indicted in 1978 for accepting bribes, with Hanna sentenced to six months in prison.

A Congressional investigation in 1978 charged four sitting Democratic Representatives, Charles H. Wilson, Edward R. Roybal, and John J. McFall of California, and Edward J. Patten of New Jersey, with having accepted money improperly from Park. The House voted to cut $56 million in food aid for Korea because President Park had refused to permit his former Ambassador to the U.S., Kim Dong Jo, to testify before Congressional committees.

Park's assassination on Oct. 26, 1979, by Kim Jae Kyu, head of the Korean Central Intelligence Agency, brought a liberalizing trend as Choi Kyu Hah, the new President, freed imprisoned dissidents. The release of opposition leader Kim Dae Jung in February 1980 generated anti-government demonstrations that turned into riots by May. Choi resigned on Aug. 16. Chun Doo Wha, head of a military Special Committee for National Security Measures, was the sole candidate as the electoral college confirmed him as President on Aug. 27. On Sept. 17, Kim Dae Jung was sentenced to death by a military court on charges of high treason. Chun commuted the sentence on Jan. 23, 1981, and lifted martial law the next day.

Elected to a full seven-year term on Feb. 11, Chon had visited Washington on Feb. 2 to receive President Reagan's assurance that U.S. troops would remain in South Korea and that the sale of U.S. F-16 jet aircraft would be authorized to modernize the Republic's air force. General elections on March 25 gave the ruling Democratic Justice Party a solid majority of the National Assembly.

KUWAIT

State of Kuwait
Emir: Sheik Jaber al-Ahmad al-Sabah (1977)
Prime Minister: Sheik Sa'ad Abdullah al-Sabah (1978)
Area: 7,780 sq mi. (20,150 sq km)
Population (est. 1981): 1,440,000 (growth rate: 6.3%)
Density per square mile: 185.1
Capital (est. 1980): Kuwait, 60,000
Largest city (est. 1980): Hawalli, 152,000
Monetary unit: Kuwaiti dinar
Languages: Arabic and English
Religions: Islam, 95%; Christian, 5%
National name: Dowlat al Kuwait
Freedom House classifications: Capitalist-statist industrial, non-party non-military
Economic summary: Gross national product (1979): $21.9 billion. Average annual growth rate (1970–78): 0.6%. Land used for agriculture: 1%. Labor force in industry: 22%; major products: crude and refined oil, fertilizer, chemicals, building materials, shrimp. Natural resources: petroleum, fish, shrimp. Exports: crude and refined petroleum, shrimp. Imports: foodstuffs, automobiles, building materials, machinery, textiles. Major trading partners: Japan, U.S., U.K., West Germany.

Geography. Kuwait is situated northeast of Saudi Arabia at the northern end of the Persian Gulf, south of Iraq. It is slightly larger than Hawaii. The low-lying land is mainly sandy and barren.

Government. Sheik Jaber al-Ahmad al-Sabah rules as Emir of Kuwait and appoints the Prime Minister, who appoints his Cabinet (Council of Ministers). The National Assembly, consisting of 50 members elected by adult males, has been suspended. There are no political parties in Kuwait.

History. Kuwait obtained British protection in 1897 when the Sheik feared that the Turks would take over the area. In 1961, Britain ended the protectorate, giving Kuwait independence, but agreed to give military aid on request. Iraq immediately threatened to occupy the area and Sheik Sabah al-Salem al-Sabah called in British troops in 1961. Soon afterward the Arab League sent in troops, replacing the British. The prize was oil.

Oil was discovered in the 1930s. Kuwait proved to have 20% of the world's known oil resources. It has been a major producer since 1946, the world's second largest oil exporter, with the main concession held by a British-American concern. The Sheik, who gets half the profits, devotes most of them to the education, welfare, and modernization of his kingdom. In 1966, Sheik Sabah designated a relative, Jaber al-Ahmad al-Sabah, as his successor. By 1968, the sheikdom had established a model welfare state, and it sought to establish dominance among the sheikdoms and emirates of the Persian Gulf.

Kuwait contributed generously to Egypt and Jordan after the 1967 war with Israel and supported the 1973 war against Israel with funds and by joining the Arab oil boycott of Western nations.

In 1975, the government nationalized Kuwaiti operations of Gulf Oil and British Petroleum. The acquisition, which cost about $180 million, gave Kuwait full control of an estimated 60 billion barrels of petroleum reserves.

In 1981, the World Bank classed Kuwait as the world's richest country, with a per capita gross national product of $15,970.

LAOS

Lao People's Democratic Republic
President: Souphanouvong (1975)
Premier: Kaysone Phomvihane (1975)
Area: 91,429 sq mi. (236,800 sq km)
Population (est. 1981): 3,800,000 (growth rate: 1.1%)
Density per square mile: 41.6
Capital and largest city (est. 1978): Vientiane, 200,000
Monetary unit: New kip
Languages: Lao (official); French, English
Religion: Buddhist
Freedom House classifications: Socialist pre-industrial, one-party communist
Economic summary: Gross national product: (1978): $300 million. Per capita income (1976): $70. Land used for agriculture, 8%; labor force, 85%; principal products: rice, corn, vegetables. Major industrial products: tin, timber, tobacco, textiles, electric power. Natural resources: tin, timber, hydroelectric power. Exports: electric power, forest products, tin concentrates, coffee. Imports: rice, foodstuffs, petroleum products, machinery, transport equipment. Major trading partners: Thailand, U.S.S.R., Malaysia, France, China, Vietnam.

Geography. A landlocked nation in Southeast Asia occupying the northwestern portion of the Indochinese peninsula, Laos is surrounded by China, Vietnam, Cambodia, Thailand, and Burma. It is twice the size of Pennsylvania.

Laos is a mountainous country, especially in the north, where peaks rise above 8,000 feet (2,438 m). Dense forests cover the northern and eastern areas. The Mekong River flows through the country for 300 miles (483 km) of its course.

Government. Laos is a people's democratic republic with executive power in the hands of the premier. The monarchy was abolished Dec. 2, 1975, when the Pathet Lao ousted a coalition government and King Sisavang Vatthana abdicated. The King was appointed "Supreme Adviser" to the President, the former Prince Souphanouvong. Former Prince Souvanna Phouma, Premier since 1962, was made an "adviser" to the government. The Lao People's Revolutionary Party (Pathet Lao), led by President Souphanouvong and Premier Kaysone Phomvihane, is the only political party.

History. Laos became a French protectorate in 1893, and the territory was incorporated into the union of Indochina. A strong nationalist movement developed during World War II, but France reestablished control in 1946 and made the King of Luang Prabang constitutional monarch of all Laos. France granted semiautonomy in 1949 and then, spurred by the Viet Minh rebellion in Vietnam, full independence within the French Union in 1950. In 1951, Prince Souphanouvong organized the Pathet Lao, a Communist independence movement, in North Vietnam. The Viet Minh in 1953 established the Pathet Lao in power at Samneua. Viet Minh and Pathet Lao forces invaded central Laos, and civil war resulted.

By the Geneva agreements of 1954 and an armistice of 1955, two northern provinces were given the Pathet Lao, the royal regime the rest. Full sovereignty was given the kingdom by the Paris agreements of Dec. 29, 1954. In 1957, Prince Souvanna Phouma, the royal Premier, and the Pathet Lao leader, Prince Souphanouvong, the Premier's half-brother, agreed to re-establishment of a unified government, with Pathet Lao participation and integration of Pathet Lao forces into the royal army. The agreement broke down in 1959, and armed conflict broke out again.

In 1960, the struggle became three-way as Gen. Phoumi Nosavan, controlling the bulk of the royal army, set up in the south a pro-Western revolutionary government headed by Prince Boun Gum. General Phoumi took Vientiane in December, driving Souvanna Phouma into exile in Cambodia. The Soviet bloc supported Souvanna Phouma. In 1961, a cease-fire was arranged and the three princes agreed to a coalition government headed by Souvanna Phouma.

But North Vietnam, the U.S. (in the form of Central Intelligence Agency personnel), and China remained active in Laos after the settlement. North Vietnam used a supply line (Ho Chi Minh trail) running down the mountain valleys of eastern Laos into Cambodia and South Vietnam, particularly after the U.S.-South Vietnamese incursion into Cambodia in 1970 stopped supplies via Cambodian seaports.

An agreement, reached in 1973 revived coalition government. Royal Laotian rule continued in populous areas, the Pathet Lao controlled the mountainous east, and the two groups exercised joint rule over Vientiane Province. With Souvanna Phouma as premier and Souphanouvong as president of a 42-member National Political Council representing both factions, joint operation of the government began.

Laotian officials confirmed in March 1979 the presence of 30,000 Vietnamese troops in Laos and their use of the country as a staging area for the Vietnamese invasion of Cambodia. They also confirmed that 1,000 Laotian troops were in Cambodia in support of the Heng Samrin regime, which overthrew the Pol Pot government in January.

LEBANON

Republic of Lebanon
President: Elias Sarkis (1976)
Premier: Shafiq al-Wazan (1980)
Area: 4,015 sq mi. (10,400 sq km)
Population (est. 1981): 3,230,000 (growth rate: 2.6%)
Density per square mile: 804.5
Capital: Beirut
Largest cities (est. 1975): Beirut, 1,172,000; (est. 1964): Tripoli, 127,600
Monetary unit: Lebanese pound
Languages: Arabic (official); French, English
Religions: Christian and Islam
National name: Al-Joumhouriya al-Lubnaniya
Freedom House classifications: Capitalist industrial, multi-party decentralized
Economic summary: Gross national product (1973): $3 billion. Annual growth rate: 7–10%. Per capita income: $730. Land used for agriculture: 27%; labor force: 49%; principal products: fruits, wheat, corn, barley, potatoes, tobacco, olives, onions. Labor force in industry: 11%; major products: processed foods, textiles, cement, chemicals, refined oil; tourism. Exports: fruits, vegetables, textiles. Imports: metals, machinery, foodstuffs. Major trading partners: U.S., Western European and Arab countries.

Geography. Lebanon lies at the eastern end of the Mediterranean Sea north of Israel and west of Syria. It is four fifths the size of Connecticut.

The Lebanon Mountains, which parallel the coast on the west, cover most of the country, while on the eastern border lies the Anti-Lebanon range. Between the two lies the El Bika Valley, the principal agricultural area.

Government. Lebanon is governed by a President, elected by Parliament for a six-year term, and a Cabinet of Ministers appointed by the President but responsible to Parliament.

Parliament has 99 members elected for a four-year term by universal suffrage and chosen by proportional division of religious groups.

Party breakdown of the Chamber of Deputies is difficult because of the religious groupings required by law and because many deputies join in major parliamentary blocs—Democratic Front, Tri-Partite Coalition, and National Struggle Front. The parties represented in Parliament are: Al-Kataib, led by Pierre Al-Jumayeh; Al-Wataniyin Al-Ahrar, led by Camille Chamoun; Al-Takadumi Al-Ishteraki; Al-Kutla Al-Wataniya, led by Raymond Edde; Al-Dimocrati Al-Eshteraki, led by Kamel El-Assad.

History. In ancient times Lebanon was the mountainous hinterland of the Phoenician coast towns. From the 7th to the 11th century there infiltrated into southern Lebanon the heretics of Islam, who finally coalesced into the Druse community.

In the 19th century the Turkish Sultanate encouraged the Druses to wage civil war against the Christian Maronites. After a massacre of 2,500 Christians in 1860, Lebanon was occupied by the French for a year. From 1864 to 1914, a Christian military government ruled the area under nominal Turkish sovereignty. After World War I, France received a League of Nations mandate over Syria and Lebanon. The French drew a Lebanese border

in 1920 to offset predominantly Moslem Syria and proclaimed the area a republic under French control on May 23, 1926. Complete independence came on Nov. 26, 1941. Lebanon joined the Arab League and took part in the invasion of Palestine on May 15, 1948.

In 1958, a civil war broke out, with the Moslems Kamal Jumblatt and Saeb Salam leading the opposition to the Maronite Christian government. Threatened with defeat, President Camille Chamoun obtained the intervention of U.S. military forces. In September, a Maronite Christian military man, Gen. Fouad Chehab, took over the presidency. After a U.N. resolution demanded it, the U.S. forces withdrew.

Palestinian guerrillas using Lebanese territory drew Lebanon into conflict with Israel. Terrorist attacks on Israeli airliners led to an Israeli raid on Arab airlines at Beirut, and terrorist assaults on Israel's northern settlements drew punitive raids against guerrillas in Lebanon by Israeli army and air units. Lebanon appeared powerless.

Intensifying civil war through 1976 led to the ousting of President Suleiman Franjieh by Parliament in May after the virtual destruction of Beirut. Franjieh refused to step down until the end of his six-year term in October when his successor, Elias Sarkis, took office.

At the time of Sarkis' inauguration, Lebanon was divided into a northern sector, controlled by Syrian troops who had entered the country to restore order, and a coastal region under Christian control, with enclaves where leftist Moslems and the Palestine Liberation Organization dominated. With the economy shattered and an estimated 40,000 dead in 18 months of war, many felt that the country might be dismembered.

Notwithstanding flare-ups of civil strife, an Arab League committee of Syria, Egypt, Saudi Arabia, and Kuwait appeared by mid-1977 to have stabilized a reunited Lebanon. Banks had reopened and reconstruction of Beirut began.

A new crisis began for Lebanon on March 14, 1978, with the invasion of Israeli forces across the entire 60-mile northern border to a depth of from 4 to 10 miles. The invasion was in retaliation for a PLO terrorist raid on Israel and the chief targets were PLO bases in southern Lebanon. On March 19, the U.N. Security Council called for immediate withdrawal and authorized a 4,000-man peace-keeping force to occupy the area, a force later enlarged to 6,000.

Israeli troops withdrew by June but turned over more strongpoints to Lebanese Christian militia than to UNIFIL, the U.N. force. Israel asserted that UNIFIL was allowing PLO guerrillas to infiltrate the border region, threatening Israel as well as the Lebanese Christians in the area. Efforts to establish a Lebanese army "presence" in southern Lebanon failed, and UNIFIL was still supervising a shaky peace in 1981, with little prospect of a return to normal.

Tension escalated in April 1981 when Israeli jets intervened for the first time in fighting between Syrian troops and Christian militia east of Beirut, shooting down two Syrian helicopters. Syria then moved Soviet surface-to-air (SAM-6) missiles into the Bekaa Valley and Israel announced that it would use force if necessary to remove them. While a special U.S. Mideast peace envoy, Philip C. Habib, sought to mediate, Israel on July 17 bombed a densely populated section of Beirut, claiming that it was done in retaliation for PLO rockets and artillery fired from Lebanon into northern Israel.

The bombing left 300 dead and 800 wounded and brought an appeal by the Security Council for a cease-fire. Not until July 24 was Habib able to win Begin's consent to a cease-fire, difficult to arrange because the Israeli Prime Minister refused to negotiate with the PLO. The PLO agreement was secured by Lebanese allies of the PLO working through Gen. William Callaghan, Irish commander of UNIFIL.

LESOTHO

Kingdom of Lesotho
Sovereign: King Moshoeshoe II (1966)
Prime Minister: Chief Leabua Jonathan (1966)
Area: 11,720 sq mi. (30,355 sq km)
Population (est. 1981): 1,375,000 (growth rate: 2.2%)
Density per square mile: 117.3
Capital and largest city (est. 1976): Maseru, 14,700
Monetary unit: Maloti
Languages: English and Sesotho (official)
Religions: Roman Catholic, 39%; Lesotho Evangelical Church, 24%; Anglican, 10%; non-Christian, 18%
Member of Commonwealth of Nations
Freedom House classifications: Capitalist pre-industrial, dominant party
Economic summary: Gross national product (1979): $440 million. Average annual growth rate (1970–78) 9.3%. Per capita income: $270. Land used for agriculture: 15%; labor force: 87%; principal products: corn, wheat, sorghum, barley, livestock. Labor force in industry: 2%. Natural resources: diamonds. Exports: wool, mohair, wheat, cattle, diamonds, hides and skins. Imports: corn, building materials, clothing, vehicles, machinery. Major trading partner: South Africa.

Geography. Mountainous Lesotho, the size of Maryland, is surrounded by the Republic of South Africa in the east central part of that country except for short borders on the east and south with two discontinuous units of the Republic of Transkei. The Drakensberg Mountains in the east are Lesotho's principal chain. Elsewhere the region consists of rocky tableland.

Government. There is a 93-member interim National Assembly made up of 60 representatives of various political parties, 22 leading chiefs, and 11 appointees.

The major political parties are the Basotho National Party, led by Prime Minister Leabua Jonathan and the Basutoland Congress Party led by G. P. Ramoreboli.

History. Lesotho (formerly Basutoland) was constituted a native state under British protection by a treaty signed with the native chief Moshesh in 1843. It was annexed to Cape Colony in 1871, but in 1884 it was restored to direct control by the Crown.

The colony of Basutoland became the independent nation of Lesotho on Oct. 4, 1966.

In the 1970 elections, Ntsu Mokhehle, head of the Basutoland Congress Party, claimed a victory, but Jonathan declared a state of emergency, suspended the Constitution, and arrested Mokhehle. The major issue in the election was relations with South Africa, with Jonathan for close ties to the surrounding white nation, while Mokhehle was for a more independent policy. Jonathan jailed 45 opposition politicians, declared the King had "techni-

cally abdicated" by siding with the opposition party, exiled him to the Netherlands, and named his Queen and her seven-year-old son as Regent.

The King returned after a compromise with Jonathan in which the new Constitution would name him head of state but forbid his participation in politics.

LIBERIA

Republic of Liberia
President: Master Sgt. Samuel K. Doe (1980)
Area: 43,000 sq mi. (111,370 sq km)
Population (est. 1981): 1,920,000 (growth rate: 3.1%)
Density per square mile: 44.7
Capital and largest city (est. 1978): Monrovia, 229,300
Monetary unit: Liberian dollar
Languages: English (official) and tribal dialects
Religions: Protestant Christian, Islam, Catholic, Animist
Freedom House classifications: Capitalist pre-industrial, non-party military
Economic summary: Gross national product (1979): $890 million. Average annual growth rate (1970–78): 0.2%. Per capita income: $600. Land used for agriculture: 20%; labor force: 75%; principal products: rubber, rice, palm oil, cassava, coffee, cocoa. Labor force in industry: 25%; major products: iron ore, diamonds, processed rubber, processed food, construction materials. Natural resources: iron ore, rubber, timber, diamonds. Exports: iron ore, rubber, timber, diamonds. Imports: machinery, petroleum products, transport equipment, foodstuffs. Major trading partners: U.S., West Germany, Netherlands, Italy, Belgium.

Geography. Lying on the Atlantic in the southern part of West Africa, Liberia is bordered by Sierra Leone, Guinea, and the Ivory Coast. It is comparable in size to Tennessee.

Most of the country is a plateau covered by dense tropical forests, which thrive under an annual rainfall of about 160 inches a year.

Government. Since April 25, 1980, Liberia has been under military rule by the 17-member People's Redemptive Council, which suspended the Constitution after overthrowing the civilian government.

History. Liberia was founded in 1822 as a result of the efforts of the American Colonization Society to settle freed American slaves in West Africa. In 1847, it became the Free and Independent Republic of Liberia.

The government of Africa's first republic was modeled after that of the United States, and Joseph J. Roberts of Virginia was elected the first president. He laid the foundations of a modern state and initiated efforts, never too successful but pursued for more than a century, to bring the aboriginal inhabitants of the territory to the level of the emigrants. The English-speaking descendants of U.S. blacks, known as Americo-Liberians, were the intellectual and ruling class. The indigenous inhabitants, divided, constitute 99% of the population.

The country's only big enterprises are the million-acre concession granted in 1925 to the Firestone Plantations Co. for rubber cultivation, and a large iron ore concession developed by the Republic Steel Corp., beginning in 1951. After 1920, considerable progress was made toward opening up the interior, a process that was spurred in 1951 by the establishment of a 43-mile (69-km) railroad to the Bomi Hills from Monrovia.

In July 1971, while serving his sixth term as president, William V. S. Tubman died following surgery and was succeeded by his long-time associate, Vice President William R. Tolbert, Jr.

Tolbert was ousted in a military coup carried out April 12, 1980, by army enlisted men led by Master Sgt. Samuel K. Doe. Tolbert and 27 other high officials were executed and a civilian Cabinet was briefly installed. But on April 25, the 17-member People's Redemptive Council, an exclusively military body, suspended the Constitution and assumed all executive power. Doe and his colleagues based their action on the grievances of "native" Liberians against corruption and misrule by the Americo-Liberians who had ruled the country since its founding.

LIBYA

People's Socialist Libyan Arab Public
Head of State: Col. Muammar el-Qaddafi (1969)
Secretary-General of the General People's Congress: 'Abd al-Ati Ubaydi (1979)
Premier: Jadallah Azzuz et Talhi (1979)
Area: 679,536 sq mi. (1,759,998 sq km)
Population (est. 1981): 3,100,000 (growth rate: 3.4%)
Density per square mile: 4.4
Capital: Tripoli
Largest cities (est. 1980): Tripoli, 1,000,000; **(1973 census):** Benghazi, 282,192
Monetary unit: Libyan dinar
Language: Arabic
Religion: Islam
National name: Al-Jumhuria al-Arabia al-Libya
Freedom House classifications: Capitalist-statist industrial, one-party socialist
Economic summary: Gross national product (1979): $23.4 billion. Average annual growth rate (1970–78): —2.6%. Per capita income: $6,260. Land used for agriculture: 7%; labor force: 20%; principal products: wheat, barley, olives, dates, citrus fruits, peanuts. Labor force in industry: 10%; major products: petroleum, processed foods, textiles, handicrafts. Natural resources: petroleum, natural gas. Export: petroleum. Imports: machinery, foodstuffs, manufactured goods. Major trading partners: Italy, West Germany, U.S., U.K., France.

Geography. Libya stretches along the northeastern coast of Africa between Tunisia and Algeria on the west and Egypt on the east; to the south are the Sudan, Chad, and Niger. It is one sixth larger than Alaska.

A greater part of the country lies within the Sahara. There are many oases along the Mediterranean coast; farther inland is arable plateau land.

Government. In a bloodless coup d'etat on Sept. 1, 1969, the military seized power in Libya. King Idris I, who had ruled since 1951, was deposed and the Libyan Arab Republic proclaimed. The official name was changed in 1977 to People's Socialist Libyan Arab Public. The Revolutionary Council that had governed since the coup was renamed the General Secretariat of the General People's Congress. The Arab Socialist Union Organization is the only political party.

History. Libya was a part of the Turkish dominions from the 16th century until 1911. Following the outbreak of hostilities between Italy and Turkey in that year, Italian troops occupied Tripoli; Italian sovereignty was recognized in 1912.

Libya was the scene of much desert fighting during World War II. After the fall of Tripoli on Jan. 23, 1943, it came under Allied administration. In 1949, the U.N. voted that Libya should become independent by 1952.

Discovery of oil in the Libyan Desert promised financial stability and funds for economic development. The flow of oil was halted in June, when Libya joined the Arab oil boycott of Britain and the U.S. as a result of the Middle East war but was soon resumed thereafter.

In 1974, President Muammar el-Qaddafi gave up his domestic political powers to Premier Abdul Salam Jallud, but remained the leader in foreign affairs.

In 1975, following a visit by Soviet Premier Alexei N. Kosygin, a major deal for Soviet arms sales to Libya, reported to involve $1 billion to $4 billion in modern military equipment, was concluded. It was followed by a Soviet agreement to supply Libya with a nuclear research reactor in the 2–10 megawatt range.

On July 21, 1977, a four-day war broke out between Libya and Egypt, with Egypt charging that Libyans had attacked a frontier post. Superior Egyptian air power and armor inflicted losses on their opponents and the clash ended after Algerian President Houari Boumediène intervened as peacemaker.

Another military adventure by Qaddafi ended ignominiously in April 1979 with the defeat of a Libyan force of 2,000 sent to the aid of Uganda's President Idi Amin against Ugandan rebels and Tanzanian forces. Qaddafi offered asylum to the ousted Amin and his family.

The United States closed its embassy in Tripoli on Feb. 7 amid growing U.S.-Libyan tension. Four members of the Libyan embassy in Washington were expelled on May 11 for threatening Libyan students in the United States and on July 14 a scandal erupted as Billy Carter, brother of the President, was disclosed to have registered as a Libyan agent. Subsequent information that Billy had received $220,000 from Libyan officials launched a Senate investigation, and the case became an important issue in the presidential election.

Libyan troops supporting Chad's President Goukoumi Oueddi entered the capital city of Djamena on Dec. 16, 1980. After a visit to Benghazi in January by Oueddi, Libya announced a merger of the two nations despite protests from France and African nations. (Plans for a similar merger with Syria announced in September were indefinitely postponed by Qaddafi and Syrian President Ḥafez al-Assad in a meeting Dec. 18.)

The Reagan Administration, accusing Libya of supporting international terrorism, closed the Libyan embassy in Washington on May 6, 1981. After talks with Libyan officials in July, the U.S. concluded that no improvement in relations was possible, although U.S. oil companies remained active in Libya and 2,000 U.S. citizens continued to work there.

LIECHTENSTEIN

Principality of Liechtenstein
Ruler: Prince Franz Josef II (1938)

Prime Minister: Hans Brunhart (1978)
Area: 61 sq mi. (157 sq km)
Population (est. 1981): 30,000 (average annual growth rate, 1975–78: 1.9%)
Density per square mile: 491.8
Capital and largest city (est. 1979): Vaduz, 4,900
Monetary unit: Swiss franc
Language: German (Alemannish dialect)
Religion: Roman Catholic
Economic summary: Per capita income: $16,864. Labor force in agriculture: 4%; principal products: livestock, vegetables, corn, wheat, potatoes, grapes. Labor force in industry: 50%; major products: high-technology products, building equipment, food products, machinery, industrial goods. Natural resources: timber, hydroelectric power, salt. Exports: manufactured metal products, machines and instruments, textiles, chemical products. Imports: raw materials, machinery, processed foods and goods. Major trading partners: Finland, Switzerland and other Western European countries.

Geography. Tiny Liechtenstein, not quite as large as Washington, D.C., lies on the east bank of the Rhine River south of Lake Constance between Austria and Switzerland. It consists of low valley land and Alpine peaks. Falknis (8,401 ft; 2,561 m) and Naatkopf (8,432 ft; 2,570 m) are the tallest.

Government. The Constitution of 1921, amended in 1972, provides for a legislature, the Landtag, of 15 members elected by direct suffrage.

The ruler, Prince Franz Josef II, was born in 1906 and succeeded his great-uncle, Franz I, in 1938. In 1943 he married Countess Gina Wilczek of Austria.

The major political parties are the Homeland Union (8 of 15 seats in the Landtag) and the Progressive Citizens Party (7 seats).

History. Founded in 1719, Liechtenstein was a member of the German Confederation from 1815 to 1866, when it became an independent principality. It abolished its army in 1868 and has managed to stay neutral and undamaged in all European wars since then. It also remained free of ties until after World War I. Since then, it has been oriented toward Switzerland.

LUXEMBOURG

Grand Duchy of Luxembourg
Ruler: Grand Duke Jean (1964)
Premier: Pierre Werner (1979)
Area: 999 sq mi. (2,586 sq km)
Population (est. 1981): 365,000. (Luxembourgian, French, German)
Density per square mile: 365.4
Capital and largest city (est. 1980): Luxembourg, 80,000 (average annual growth rate, 1976–80: 0.2%)
Monetary unit: Luxembourg franc
Languages: Letzeburgesch, French, German
Religion: Mainly Roman Catholic
National name: Grand-Duché de Luxembourg
Freedom House classifications: Capitalist industrial, multi-party centralized
Economic summary: Gross national product (1979): $4.5 billion. Average annual growth rate (1970–78): 4.1%. Per capita income: $6,900. Land used for agriculture: 42%; labor force: 6%; principal products: livestock, dairy products, wine. Labor force in industry: 46%; major products: steel, rubber, synthetic fibers. Natural

resource: Iron ore. Export: steel. Imports: machinery, textiles, transport equipment, plastics. Major trading partners: European Common Market countries.

Geography. Luxembourg is a neighbor of Belgium on the west, West Germany on the east, and France on the south. The Ardennes Mountains extend from Belgium into the northern section of Luxembourg.

Government. Luxembourg's unicameral legislature, the Chamber of Deputies, consists of 59 members elected for five years.

The major political parties are the Christian Social Party (24 of 59 seats in Chamber of Deputies), led by Jacques Senter; Socialist-Labor (14 seats), led by Lydie Schmit; Democratic Party (15 seats), led by Premier Pierre Werner; Social Democratic Party (5 seats), led by Henry Cravatte; Communist Party (5 seats), led by René Urbany.

History. Sigefroi, Count of Ardennes, an offspring of Charlemagne, was Luxembourg's first sovereign ruler. In 1060, the country came under the rule of the House of Luxembourg. From the 15th to the 18th century, Spain, France, and Austria held it in turn. The Congress of Vienna in 1815 made it a Grand Duchy and gave it to William I, King of the Netherlands. In 1839 the Treaty of London ceded the western part of Luxembourg to Belgium.

The eastern part, continuing in personal union with the Netherlands and a member of the German Confederation, became autonomous in 1848 and a neutral territory by decision of the London Conference of 1867, governed by its Grand Duke. Germany occupied the duchy in World Wars I and II. Allied troops liberated the enclave in 1944.

In 1961, Prince Jean, son and heir of Grand Duchess Charlotte, was made head of state, acting for his mother. She abdicated in 1964, and Prince Jean became Grand Duke.

By a customs union between Belgium and Luxembourg, which came into force on May 1, 1922, to last for 50 years, customs frontiers between the two countries were abolished. On Jan. 1, 1948, a customs union with Belgium and the Netherlands (Benelux) came into existence. On Feb. 3, 1958, it became an economic union.

MADAGASCAR

Democratic Republic of Madagascar
President and Head of State: Comdr. Didier Ratsiraka (1975)
Prime Minister: Lt. Col. Desiré Rakotoarijaona (1977)
Area: 230,035 sq mi. (595,791 sq km)
Population (est. 1981): 9,000,000 (growth rate: 2.5%)
Density per square mile: 39.1
Capital and largest city (est. 1976): Antananarivo, 468,000
Monetary unit: Malagasy franc
Languages: Malagasy, French
Ethnic groups: Merina (or Hova), Betsimisaraka, Betsileo, Tsimihety, Antaisaka, Sakalava, Antandroy
Religions: Animist, 55%; Catholic, 21%; Protestant, 18%; Islam, 7%
National name: Repoblika Demokratika Malagasy
Freedom House classifications: Capitalist-socialist pre-industrial, one-party nationalist
Economic summary: Gross national product (1979): $2.5 billion. Average annual growth rate (1970–78): −2.7%.

Per capita income: $250. Average rate of inflation: 9%. Land used for agriculture: 63%; labor force: 26%; principal products: rice, livestock, coffee, vanilla, sugar, cloves, cotton, sisal, peanuts, tobacco. Labor force in industry: 15%; major products: processed food, textiles, refined petroleum products, assembled automobiles, soap, mining products. Natural resources: graphite, chromium, coal, bauxite, ilmenite, tar sands, semiprecious stones. Exports: coffee, cloves, vanilla. Imports: machinery and equipment, chemicals, crude petroleum, rice. Major trading partners: France, U.S.

Geography. Madagascar lies in the Indian Ocean off the southeast coast of Africa opposite Mozambique. The world's fourth-largest island, it is twice the size of Arizona. The country's low-lying coastal area gives way to a central plateau. The once densely wooded interior has largely been cut down.

Government. The Constitution of Dec. 30, 1975, approved by referendum following a military coup, provides for direct election by universal suffrage of a president for a seven-year term, a Supreme Council of the Revolution as a policy-making body, a unicameral People's National Assembly of 137 members (elected for five-year terms), and a military Committee for Development. The new constitution followed a period of martial rule that began with the suspension of the republic's original bicameral legislature in 1972.

History. The present population is of black and Malay stock, with perhaps some Polynesian, called Malagasy. The French took over a protectorate in 1885, and then in 1894–95 ended the monarchy, exiling Queen Rànavàlona III to Algiers. A colonial administration was set up, to which the Comoro Islands were attached in 1908, and other territories later. In World War II, the British occupied Madagascar, which retained ties to Vichy France.

An autonomous republic within the French Community since 1958, Madagascar became an independent member of the Community in 1960. In May 1973, an army coup led by Maj. Gen. Gabriel Ramanantsoa ousted Philibert Tsiranana, president since 1959.

With unemployment and inflation both high, Ramanantsoa resigned Feb. 5, 1975. His leftist-leaning successor, Interior Minister Richard Ratsimandrava, an Army lieutenant colonel, was killed six days later by a machine-gun ambush in Antananarivo, the capital.

On June 15, 1975, Comdr. Didier Ratsiraka was named President. He announced that he would follow a socialist course and, after nationalizing banks and insurance companies, declared all mineral resources nationalized.

MALAWI

Republic of Malawi
Life President: Hastings Kamuzu Banda (1966)
Area: 45,747 sq mi. (118,484 sq km)
Population (est. 1981): 6,125,000 (growth rate: 3.0%)
Density per square mile: 133.9
Capital (1977 census): Lilongwe, 102,900
Largest city (1977 census): Blantyre, 222,200
Monetary unit: Kwacha
Languages: English (official), Chichewa
Religion: Animist, 65%; Christian, 33%

Member of Commonwealth of Nations
Freedom House classifications: Capitalist pre-industrial, one-party nationalist
Economic summary: Gross national product (1979): $1.2 billion. Average annual growth rate (1970–78): 3.1%. Per capita income: $154. Average rate of inflation (1974–78): 10%. Land used for agriculture: 30%; labor force: 90%; principal products: tobacco, tea, sugar, corn, peanuts. Labor force in industry: 24%; major products: food, beverages, tobacco, textiles, footwear. Natural resource: limestone. Exports: tobacco, tea, sugar, peanuts. Imports: machinery, transport equipment, manufactured goods, oil. Major trading partners: U.K., U.S., South Africa, Netherlands, Japan, West Germany.

Geography. Malawi is a landlocked country the size of Pennsylvania in southeastern Africa, surrounded by Mozambique, Zambia, and Tanzania. Lake Malawi, formerly Lake Nyasa, occupies most of the country's eastern border. The north-south Rift Valley is flanked by mountain ranges and high plateau areas.

Government. Under a Constitution that came into effect on July 6, 1966, the president is the sole head of state; there is neither a prime minister nor a vice president. The National Assembly has 87 members.

There is only one national party—the Malawi Congress Party (all 87 seats in the National Assembly), led by President Hastings K. Banda.

History. The first European to make extensive explorations in the area was David Livingstone in the 1850s and 1860s. In 1884, Cecil Rhodes's British South African Company received a charter to develop the country. The company came into conflict with the Arab slavers in 1887–89. After Britain annexed the Nyasaland territory in 1891, making it a protectorate in 1892, Sir Harry Johnstone, the first high commissioner, using Royal Navy gunboats, wiped out the slavers.

Nyasaland became the independent nation of Malawi on July 6, 1964. Two years later, it became a republic within the Commonwealth of Nations.

Dr. Hastings K. Banda, Malawi's first Prime Minister, became its first President. He pledged to follow a policy of "discretionary nonalignment." Banda alienated much of Black Africa by maintaining good relations with such white-ruled nations as South Africa and Rhodesia. He argued that his landlocked country had to rely on white-ruled countries for access to the sea and trade.

MALAYSIA

Paramount Ruler: Sultan Haji Ahmad Shah, Sultan of Pahang (1979)
Prime Minister: Mahathir Bin Mohamed (1981)
Area: 128,328 sq mi. (332,370 sq km)
Population (est. 1981): 14,000,000 (growth rate: 2.4%)
Density per square mile: 109.1
Capital: Kuala Lumpur
Largest cities (est. 1980 by U.N.): Kuala Lumpur, 1,000,000; George Town (Pinang), 300,000; Ipoh, 275,000
Monetary unit: Ringgit
Languages: Malay (official), Chinese, Tamil, English
Religions: Islam, (official), Buddhist, Hindu, Christian, Confucian, Taoist
Member of Commonwealth of Nations
Freedom House classifications: Capitalist-industrial, dominant party

Economic summary: Gross national product (1979): $18 billion. Average annual growth rate (1970–78): 4.8%. Per capita income: $990. Labor force: 12%; principal products: natural rubber, palm oil, tin, petroleum, rice, timber. Major industrial products: processed rubber, timber, and palm oil, tin, petroleum, light manufactures, electronics equipment. Natural resources: tin, oil, copper, timber. Exports: natural rubber, palm oil, tin, timber, petroleum. Imports: machinery, transport equipment, chemicals. Major trading partners: Japan, Singapore, U.S., U.K.

Geography. Malaysia is at the southern end of the Malay Peninsula in southeast Asia. The nation also includes Sabah and Sarawak on the island of Borneo to the southeast. Its area slightly exceeds that of New Mexico.

Most of Malaysia is covered by dense jungle and swamps, with a mountain range running the length of the peninsula. Extensive forests provide ebony, sandalwood, teak, and other woods.

Government. Malaysia is a sovereign constitutional monarchy within the Commonwealth of Nations. The Paramount Ruler is elected for a five-year term by the hereditary rulers of the states from among themselves. He is advised by the prime minister and his cabinet. There is a bicameral legislature. The Senate, whose role is comparable more to that of the British House of Lords than to the U.S. Senate, has 68 members, partly appointed by the Paramount Ruler to represent minority and special interests, and partly elected by the legislative assemblies of the various states.

The House of Representatives, or lower house, is made up of 154 members, who are elected for five-year terms.

The major political parties are the National Front, a coalition of 10 parties (131 of 154 seats in the House of Representatives); Democratic Action Party (16 seats); Islamic Party (5 seats).

History. Malaysia came into existence on Sept. 16, 1963, as a federation of Malaya, Singapore, Sabah (North Borneo), and Sarawak. In 1965, Singapore withdrew from the federation. Since 1966, the 11 states of former Malaya have been known as West Malaysia, and Sabah and Sarawak have been known as East Malaysia.

The Union of Malaya was established April 1, 1946, being formed from the Federated Malay States of Negri Sembilan, Pahang, Perak, and Selangor; the Unfederated Malay States of Johore, Kedah, Kelantan, Perlis, and Trengganu; and two of the Straits Settlements—Malacca and Penang. The Malay states had been brought under British administration during the late 19th and early 20th centuries.

It became the Federation of Malaya on Feb. 1, 1948, and the Federation attained full independence within the Commonwealth of Nations in 1957.

Sabah, constituting the extreme northern portion of the island of Borneo, was a British protectorate administered under charter by the British North Borneo Company from 1881 to 1946, when it assumed the status of a colony. It was occupied by Japanese troops from 1942 to 1945.

Sarawak extends along the northwestern coast of Borneo for about 500 miles (805 km). In 1841, part of the present territory was granted by the Sultan of Brunei to Sir James Brooke. Sarawak continued to be ruled by members of the Brooke family until the Japanese occupation.

From 1963, when Malaysia became independent, it was the target of guerrilla infiltration from Indonesia, but beat off invasion attempts. In 1966, when Sukarno fell and the Communist Party was liquidated in Indonesia, hostilities ended.

In the late 1960s, the country was torn by communal rioting directed against Chinese and Indians, who controlled a disproportionate share of the country's wealth. Beginning in 1968, the government moved to achieve greater economic balance through a rural development program.

Malaysia felt the impact of the "boat people" fleeing Vietnam early in 1978. Because the refugees were mostly ethnic Chinese, the government was apprehensive about any increase of a minority that previously had been the source of internal conflict in the country. In November, authorities banned landings and reversed the order only after several hundred refugees drowned when their fragile boats were towed offshore by Malaysian police. By August 1980, the number of refugees was reported down to 20,000 from a high of 76,500 in July 1979, but at year end a new influx of Vietnamese rather than Chinese was reported—persons fleeing economic conditions or young men escaping conscription.

MALDIVES

Republic of Maldives
President: Maumoon Abdul Gayoom (1978)
Area: 115 sq mi. (298 sq km)
Population (est. 1981): 150,000 (growth rate: 3.0%)
Density per square mile: 1,304.3
Capital and largest city (est. 1978): Malé, 29,600
Monetary unit: Maldivian rupee
Language: Divehi
Religion: Islam
Freedom House classifications: Capitalist pre-industrial, non-party non-military
Economic summary: Gross national product (1979): $30 million. Average annual growth rate (1970–78): −2.1%. Per capita income: $150. Principal agricultural products: coconuts, millet. Labor force in industry: 50%; major products: fish, processed coconuts. Natural resource: fish. Export: fish. Imports: rice, wheat flour, sugar, drugs, textiles. Major trading partners: Sri Lanka, Japan, India, Singapore.

Geography. The Republic of Maldives is a group of atolls in the Indian Ocean about 500 miles (805 km) southwest of Sri Lanka. Its 1,087 coral islets stretch over an area of 45,000 square miles (116,550 sq km).

Government. The 9-member Cabinet is headed by the president. The Majlis (Parliament) is a unicameral legislature consisting of 48 members. Eight of these are appointed by the president. The others are elected for three-year terms, 2 from the capital island of Malé and 2 from each of the 19 administrative atolls.

There are no political parties in the Maldives.

History. The Maldives (formerly called the Maldive Islands) are inhabited by an Islamic seafaring people. Originally the islands were under the suzerainty of Ceylon. They came under British protection in 1887 and were a dependency of the then colony of Ceylon until 1948. The independence agreement with Britain was signed July 26, 1965.

For centuries a sultanate, the islands adopted a republican form of government in 1952, but the sultanate was restored in 1954. In 1968, however, as the result of a referendum, a republic was again established in the islands.

Ibrahim Nasir, president since 1968, was removed from office by the Majlis in November 1978 and replaced by Maumoon Abdul Gayoom. A national referendum confirmed the new leader.

MALI

Republic of Mali
Chief of State (1968) and Head of Government (1969):
  Gen. Moussa Traoré
Area: 464,873 sq mi. (1,204,021 sq km)
Population (est. 1981): 7,100,000 (growth rate, 2.7%)
Density per square mile: 15.3
Capital and largest city (est. 1980): Bamako, 450,000
Monetary unit: Mali franc
Ethnic groups: Bambara, Peul, Soninke, Malinke, Songhai, Dogon, Senoufo, Minianka, Berbers, and Moors
Languages: French (official), African languages
Religions: Islam, 65%; Animist, 30%; Christian
National name: République de Mali
Freedom House classifications: Capitalist-socialist pre-industrial, one-party nationalist
Economic summary: Gross national product (1979): $930 million. Average annual growth rate (1970–78): 1.8%. Per capita income (1977): $96. Principal agricultural products: millet, sorghum, corn, rice, sugar, cotton, peanuts, livestock. Major industrial products: processed foods, textiles, cigarettes, fish. Natural resources: bauxite, iron ore, maganese, lithium, phosphate, kaolin, salt, limestone, gold. Exports: meat, livestock, cotton, fish, peanuts, tannery products. Imports: food, machinery, vehicles, petroleum products, chemicals and pharmaceuticals, textiles. Major trading partners: France, Ivory Coast, Senegal, U.K., West Germany, U.S.S.R., China.

Geography. Most of Mali, in West Africa, lies in the Sahara. A landlocked country four fifths the size of Alaska, it is bordered by Guinea, Senegal, Mauritania, Algeria, Niger, Upper Volta, and the Ivory Coast.

The only fertile area is in the south, where the Niger and Senegal Rivers provide irrigation.

Government. The army overthrew the government on Nov. 19, 1968, and formed a provisional government. The Military Committee of National Liberation consists of 14 members and forms the decision-making body.

In late 1969 an attempted coup was foiled, and Lt. Moussa Traoré, president of the Military Committee took over as chief of state and later as head of government, ousting Capt. Yoro Diakité as Premier.

The Malian People's Democratic Union, established in 1976, is the only political party.

History. Subjugated by France by the end of the 19th century, this area became a colony in 1904 (named French Sudan in 1920) and in 1946 became part of the French Union. On June 20, 1960, it became independent and, under the name of Sudanese Republic, was federated with the Republic of Senegal in the Mali Federation. However, Senegal seceded from the Federation on Aug.

20, 1960, and the Sudanese Republic then changed its name to the Republic of Mali on September 22.

In the 1960s, Mali concentrated on economic development, continuing to accept aid from both Soviet bloc and Western nations, as well as international agencies. In the late 1960s, it began retreating from close ties with China. But a purge of conservative opponents brought greater power to President Modibo Keita, and in 1968 the influence of the Chinese and their Malian sympathizers increased. By a treaty signed in Peking in 1968, China agreed to help build a railroad from Mali to Guinea, providing Mali with vital access to the sea.

Mali, with Mauritania, the Ivory Coast, Senegal, Dahomey (Benin), Niger, and Upper Volta signed a treaty establishing the Economic Community for West Africa to promote economic development among the seven nations. It came into force on Jan. 1, 1973.

A six-year sub-Sahara drought devastated Mali before disastrously heavy rains began in 1974. Emergency shipments from a dozen nations and international organizations helped alleviate a famine that affected 1.8 million Malians and killed thousands.

MALTA

Republic of Malta
President: Anton Buttigieg (1976)
Prime Minister: Dom Mintoff (1971)
Area: 122 sq mi. (316 sq km)
Population (est. 1981): 350,000 (average annual growth rate, 1972–79: 1.2%)
Density per square mile: 2,868.9
Capital (est. 1979): Valetta, 14,000
Largest city (est. 1979): Sliema, 20,100
Monetary unit: Maltese pound
Languages: Maltese and English
Religion: Roman Catholic
National name: Repubblika Ta Malta
Member of Commonwealth of Nations
Freedom House classifications: Capitalist-statist industrial, multi-party centralized
Economic summary: Gross national product (1979): $890 million. Average annual growth rate (1970–78): 11.2%. Per capita income (1980): $2,380. Land used for agriculture, 45%; labor force: 6%; principal products: fodder crops, potatoes, onions, fruits and vegetables. Labor force in industry: 27%; major products: textiles, yarn, knitted goods, processed foods, plastics, electronic equipment. Natural resources: limestone, salt. Exports: textiles, yarns, manufactured goods, ships. Imports: manufactured goods, machinery, transport equipment. Major trading partners: West Germany, U.K., Italy.

Geography. The five Maltese islands—with a combined land area smaller than Philadelphia—are in the Mediterranean about 60 miles (97 km) south of the southeastern tip of Sicily.

Government. The government is headed by a Prime Minister, responsible to a 65-member House of Representatives elected by universal suffrage.

The major political parties are Malta Labor Party (34 of 65 seats in House of Representatives), led by Prime Minister Dom Mintoff; Nationalist Party (31 seats), led by Edward Fenech Adami.

History. The strategic importance of Malta was recognized by the Phoenicians, who occupied it, as did in their turn the Greeks, Carthaginians, and Romans. The apostle Paul was shipwrecked there in A.D. 58.

The Knights of St. John (Malta), who obtained the three habitable Maltese islands of Malta, Gozo, and Comino from Charles V in 1530, reached their highest fame when they withstood an attack by superior Turkish forces in 1565.

Napoleon seized Malta in 1798, but the French forces were ousted by British troops the next year, and British rule was confirmed by the Treaty of Paris in 1814.

Malta was heavily attacked by German and Italian aircraft during World War II, but was never invaded by the Axis.

Malta became an independent nation on Sept. 21, 1964, and a republic Dec. 13, 1974, but remained in the British Commonwealth. The Governor-General, Sir Anthony Mamo, was sworn in as first president and Dom Mintoff remained prime minister.

The new government proposed a seven-year plan to end economic dependence on foreign military bases by 1980. It called for a $568-million investment program to create 20,000 new jobs. Britain withdrew its last troops from Malta in 1979, thus ending its annual subsidy of $33 million for use of the island's port facilities.

For a time, Libya appeared to be substituting for Britain as a source of outside income, as President Muammar el-Qaddafi extended generous credits and concessionary prices for oil on condition that Malta's Labor government keep the North Atlantic Treaty Organization from using the island's port facilities. But a conflict over oil rights, in which Libyan ships threatened a Maltese-licensed drilling rig in the waters between Malta and Libya in August 1980 forced Mintoff to break with Qaddafi, expel most of the Libyan military advisers, and negotiate a treaty of friendship and aid with Italy.

MAURITANIA

Islamic Republic of Mauritania
Chief of State and Head of Government: Lt. Col. Mohamed Khouna Ould Haydalla (1980)
Premier: Lieut. Col. Maaouya Ould Sidi Ahmed Taya (1981)
Area: 419,229 sq mi. (1,085,803 sq km)
Population (est. 1981): 1,675,000 (growth rate: 1.9%)
Density per square mile: 4.0
Capital and largest city (est. 1977): Nouakchott, 135,000
Monetary unit: Ouguyia
Ethnic groups: Moors; a black minority (Poulars, Soninkes, and Wolofs)
Languages: Arabic and French
Religion: Islam
National name: République Islamique de Mauritanie
Freedom House classifications: Capitalist-statist pre-industrial, non-party military
Economic summary: Gross national product (1979): $510 million. Average annual growth rate (1970–78): —0.6%. Per capita income: $376. Principal agricultural products: livestock, millet, maize, wheat, dates, rice. Major industrial products: iron ore, processed fish. Natural resources: copper, iron ore, gypsum, fish. Exports: iron ore, fish, copper. Imports: foodstuffs, capital goods. Major trading partners: France, Spain, U.S., U.K., Italy.

Geography. Mauritania, three times the size of Arizona, is situated in northwest Africa with about 350 miles (592 km) of coastline on the Atlantic Ocean. It is bordered by Morocco on the north,

Algeria and Mali on the east, and Senegal on the south.

The country is mostly desert, with the exception of the fertile Senegal River valley in the south and grazing land in the north.

Government. An Army coup on July 10, 1978, deposed Moktar Ould Daddah, who had been President since Mauritania's independence in 1960. Since then, a 13-man Committee for National Recovery has exercised executive and legislative power, having replaced the National Assembly and the single political party that existed before the coup.

History. Mauritania was first explored by the Portuguese. The French organized the area as a territory in 1904.

Mauritania became an independent nation on Nov. 28, 1960, and was admitted to the United Nations in 1961 over the strenuous opposition of Morocco, which claimed the territory. With Moors, Arabs, Berbers, and blacks frequently in conflict, the government in the late 1960s sought to make Arab culture dominant to unify the land.

Mauritania and Morocco planned to divide the territory of the former Spanish Sahara after the departure of the colonial administration. Mauritanian troops moved into the territory but encountered resistance from the Polisario Front, a Saharan independence movement backed by Algeria. Mauritania broke diplomatic relations with Algeria in 1976, after Algerian recognition of the area as an independent state.

The task of pacifying one-third of the former Spanish Sahara (the exact amount of territory acquired by Mauritania in the division with Morocco is unknown) proved a heavy burden. Increased military spending and rising casualties contributed to the discontent that brought down the civilian government of Ould Daddah in 1978. His military replacement, Lt. Col. Moustapha Saleck, was forced to resign after Premier Ahmed Bouceif and other military leaders were killed in a plane crash on May 27, 1979. Lt. Col. Mohamed Mahmoud Ould Louly held power for only six months and was removed by the junta on Jan. 4, 1980, for unsatisfactory performance. Lt. Col. Mohamed Khouna Ould Haydalla was named new chief of state and government.

MAURITIUS

Governor-General: Sir Dayendranath Burrenchobay (1978)
Prime Minister: Sir Seewoosagur Ramgoolam (1961)
Area: 787 sq mi. (2,040 sq km)
Population (est. 1981): 975,000 (average annual growth rate, 1971–79: 1.4%) (Indian, 51%; Creole, 33%)
Density per square mile: 1,238.9
Capital and largest city (est. 1980): Port Louis, 155,000
Monetary unit: Mauritian rupee
Languages: English (official), French, Creole, Hindi, Urdu, Chinese
Religions: Hindu, 51%, Christian (mainly Roman Catholic), 30%; Islam, 16%; Buddhist, 3%
Member of Commonwealth of Nations
Freedom House classifications: Capitalist industrial, multi-party centralized
Economic summary: Gross national product (1979): $970 million. Average annual growth rate (1970–78): 6.9%. Per capita income: $640. Land used for agriculture: 50%; labor force: 50%; principal products: sugar cane, rice.

Labor force in industry: 6%; major products: processed sugar and tea, tobacco, cut diamonds, textiles, electronic equipment. Natural resources: iron ore, gypsum, fish. Exports: sugar, tea, molasses. Imports: foodstuffs, manufactured goods. Major trading partners: Western European countries, U.S., U.K.

Geography. Mauritius is a mountainous island in the Indian Ocean east of Madagascar.

Government. Mauritius is a member of the British Commonwealth, with Queen Elizabeth II as head of state. She is represented by a governor-general, who chooses the prime minister from the unicameral Legislative Assembly. The Legislative Assembly has 70 members, 62 of whom are elected by direct suffrage. The remaining 8 are chosen from among the unsuccessful candidates.

The major parties are a governing coalition of the Labor Party and the Parti Mauricien Social Democrate (34 of 70 seats in the Legislative Assembly), led by Prime Minister Sir Seewoosagur Ramgoolam, and the opposition Mouvement Militant Mauricien (33 seats). Independents comprise the balance of the Assembly.

History. Mauritius was seized from France by British troops in 1810 and ceded to Britain by the Treaty of Paris in 1814. Until 1903, Mauritius and the Seychelles were administered as a single colony. The colony of Mauritius became an independent nation on March 12, 1968.

The nation has an Indian majority, descendants of laborers imported from India to work the sugar plantations after the abolition of slavery in 1834. The native blacks speak French and are Roman Catholics.

Overpopulation and unemployment continue to be major problems.

MEXICO

United Mexican States
President: José López Portillo (1976)
Area: 761,600 sq mi. (1,972,547 sq km)
Population (est. 1981): 74,500,000 (growth rate: 2.4%) (55% mestizo; 29% Indian)
Density per square mile: 97.8
Capital: Mexico City
Largest cities (est 1979): Mexico City, 9,200,000; (est. 1978 by U.N.): Guadalajara, 1,813,000; Monterrey, 1,054,000; Puebla de Zaragoza, 678,000
Monetary unit: Peso
Languages: Spanish, Indian languages
Religion: Mainly Roman Catholic
National name: Estados Unidos Mexicanos
Freedom House classifications: Capitalist-statist industrial, dominant party
Economic summary: Gross national product (1979): $107.6 billion. Average annual growth rate (1970–78): 1.3%. Land used for agriculture, 12%; labor force: 33%; principal products: corn, cotton, coffee, sugar cane, vegetables. Labor force in industry: 33%; major products: processed foods, chemicals, basic metals and metal products, petroleum. Natural resources: petroleum, silver, copper, gold, lead, zinc, natural gas, timber. Exports: coffee, cotton, fruits and vegetables, petroleum, sulfur. Imports: machinery, equipment, industrial vehicles, intermediate goods. Major trading partners: U.S., Japan, Western European countries.

Geography. The United States' neighbor to the south, Mexico is about one fifth its size. Baja California in the west, an 800-mile (1,287-km) peninsula, forms the Gulf of California. In the east are the Gulf of Mexico and the Bay of Campeche, which is formed by Mexico's other peninsula, the Yucatán.

Mexico is a great, high plateau, open to the north, with mountain chains on east and west and with ocean-front lowlands lying outside of them.

Government. The President, who is popularly elected for six years and is ineligible to succeed himself, governs with a Cabinet of ministers. Congress has two houses—a 400-member Chamber of Deputies, elected for three years, and a 64-member Senate, elected for six years.

Each of the 31 states has considerable autonomy, with a popularly elected governor, a legislature, and a local judiciary. The President of Mexico appoints the governor of the Federal District.

The major political parties are the Partido Revolucionario Institucional, Authentic Party of the Mexican Revolution; National Action Party; Communist Party; Worker's Party; Democratic Party; and Popular Socialist Party.

History. Mexico's early history is shrouded in mystery. At least two civilized races—the Mayas and later the Toltecs—preceded the wealthy Aztec empire, conquered in 1519–21 by the Spanish under Hernando Cortés. Spain ruled for the next 300 years until 1810 (the date was Sept. 16 and is now celebrated as Independence Day), when the Mexicans first revolted. They continued the struggle and finally won independence in 1821.

Turbulent years followed. From 1821 to 1877, there were two emperors, several dictators, and enough presidents and provisional executives to make a new government on the average of every nine months. Mexico lost Texas (1836), and after defeat in the war with the U.S. (1846–48) it lost the area comprising the present states of California, Nevada, and Utah, most of Arizona and New Mexico, and parts of Wyoming and Colorado.

In 1855, the Indian patriot Benito Juárez began a series of liberal reforms, including the disestablishment of the Catholic Church, which had acquired vast property. A subsequent civil war was interrupted by the French invasion of Mexico (1861), the crowning of Maximilian of Austria as Emperor (1864), and then his overthrow and execution by forces under Juárez, who again became President in 1867.

The years after the fall of the dictator Porfirio Diaz (1877–80 and 1884–1911) were marked by bloody political-military strife and trouble with the U.S., culminating in the punitive expedition into northern Mexico (1916–17) in unsuccessful pursuit of the revolutionary Pancho Villa. There was a continuous succession of various presidents and of internal strife until 1917, when a new Congress was elected and a liberal Constitution adopted. Since a brief period of civil war in 1920, Mexico has enjoyed a period of gradual agricultural, political, and social reforms. Relations with the U.S. were again disturbed in 1938 when all foreign oil wells were expropriated. Agreement on compensation was finally reached in 1941.

Lázaro Cardenas (1934–40), president during the oil seizures, also began a program of distributing land to the peasants and of broad labor reforms. Manuel Avila Camacho, president during World War II, followed Cardenas' policy at home but cooperated closely with the United Nations, and established cordial relations with the U.S. His policy was followed by his immediate successors, Miguel Alemán, Adolfo Ruíz Cortines, and Adolfo López Mateos. López Mateos redefined Mexican foreign policy as "independent" rather than neutral or partial, a course followed by Gustavo Díaz Ordaz, who became president in 1964.

Mexico maintained ties with Cuba after the Organization of American States approved a U.S.-sponsored boycott of Fidel Castro's regime in 1962. Mexico opposed the boycott until the OAS repealed it in 1975.

Luis Echeverría Alvarez, who was elected president in 1970, worked vigorously in Latin America and elsewhere in the underdeveloped world to promote more benefits for developing nations from the raw materials they export.

Mexico and Venezuela proposed formation of a Latin American economic system (SELA) to promote regional economic development, and the organization held its first meeting in Caracas in 1976.

Drastically devaluing the peso in 1976, the government still cut the rate of inflation by mid-1977 to 20%, compared to the 45% rate of the previous year. Continued improvement of the economy—the trade deficit fell to $887 million for the first half of 1980, less than three quarters of that for the same period of 1979—was largely a result of Mexico's rise from 15th place in 1976 to fourth in world oil production at the beginning of 1981.

Oil production averaged 2 million barrels a day in February 1981, when the growing world surplus prompted the government to announce that it would cut output to 1.5 million barrels a day. On June 1, not a member of the Organization of Petroleum Exporting Countries, became the first major producer to reduce oil prices, a move expected to cut export income by $1.3 billion for the second half of 1981.

The country's oil reserves were estimated to be the world's fifth largest in 1981, following the discovery of a huge offshore field in the Gulf of Mexico. It was here that the world's biggest oil spill was capped in March 1980 after 3.1 million barrels were lost in nine months. The disaster caused a dispute with the United States when Mexico refused to pay the cost of cleaning up Texas beaches. Another conflict arose over the Mexican navy's seizure of U.S. fishing boats off the West Coast in the summer of 1980, causing the Carter Administration to ban importation of Mexican tuna.

With the election of Ronald Reagan as U.S. President, a new era of "personal relationship" was proclaimed by him and López Portillo at a border meeting on Jan. 5, 1981. López Portillo came to Washington in June, and after a long meeting with Reagan at Camp David, a new U.S. immigration policy designed to ease Mexican concerns was disclosed. As elaborated later, the program called for 100,000 "guest workers" to be admitted from Mexico over a two-year test period. Also proposed was an increase to 40,000 a year in visas for legal immigration from Mexico, with the possibility of borrowing additional visas from the Canadian allotment, historically never filled.

López Portillo also pressed for economic, rather than military, aid to combat Communist penetration of the Caribbean area. With Venezuela, he led the way in pledging oil to help poor nations in the region. He urged Reagan to follow his policy and invited him to a 22-nation conference on aid for developing nations sponsored by Mexico at Cancun in October 1981. Reagan accepted after assurances that Cuba, with which López Portillo maintained friendly relations, would not be invited.

MONACO

Principality of Monaco
Ruler: Prince Rainier III (1949)
Minister of State: Jean Herly (1981)
Area: 0.73 square mile (465 acres)
Population (est. 1981): 30,000, of whom 5,500 are Monégasque citizens
Density per square mile: 41,095.9
Capital: Monaco-Ville
Monetary unit: French franc
Languages: French and Monégasque
Religion: Roman Catholic
National name: Principauté de Monaco

Geography. Monaco is a tiny, hilly wedge driven into the French Mediterranean coast nine miles east of Nice.

Government. Prince Albert of Monaco gave the principality a Constitution in 1911, creating a National Council of 18 members popularly elected for five years. The head of government is the Minister of State.

Prince Rainier III, born May 31, 1923, succeeded his grandfather, Louis II, on the latter's death, May 9, 1949. Rainier was married April 18, 1956, to Grace Kelly, U.S. actress. A daughter, Princess Caroline Louise Marguerite, was born on Jan. 23, 1957 (married to Philippe Junot June 28, 1978 and divorced in 1980); a son, Prince Albert Louis Pierre, on March 14, 1958; and another daughter, Princess Stéphanie Marie Elisabeth, on Feb. 1, 1965.

The special significance attached to the birth of descendants to Prince Rainier stems from a clause in the Treaty of July 17, 1919, between France and Monaco stipulating that in the event of vacancy of the Crown, the Monégasque territory would become an autonomous state under a French protectorate.

The National and Democratic Union (all 18 seats in National Council), led by Auguste Medecin, is the only political party.

History. The Phoenicians, and after them the Greeks, had a temple on the Monacan headland honoring Hercules. From *Monoikos*, the Greek surname for this mythological strong man, the principality took its name. After being independent for 800 years, Monaco was annexed to France in 1793 and was placed under Sardinia's protection in 1815. In 1861, it went under French guardianship but continued to be independent.

By a treaty in 1918, France stipulated that the French government be given a veto over the succession to the throne.

Monaco is a little land of pleasure with a tourist business that runs as high as 1.5 million visitors a year. It had popular gaming tables as early as 1856. Five years later, a 50-year concession to operate the games was granted to François Blanc, of Bad Homburg. This concession passed into the hand of a private company in 1898.

Monaco's practice of providing a tax shelter for French businessmen resulted in a dispute between the countries. When Rainier refused to end the practice, France retaliated with a customs tax. In 1967, Rainier took control of the Société des Bains de Mer, operator of the famous Monte Carlo gambling casino, in a program to increase hotel and convention space. He paid $8 million to Greek shipping magnate Aristotle Onassis for his shares.

MONGOLIA

Mongolian People's Republic
Chairman of Presidium of the Great People's Khural (President): Yumjaagiin Tsedenbal (1974)
Chairman of Council of Ministers (Premier): Jambyn Batmunkh (1974)
Area: 604,250 sq mi. (1,565,000 sq km)
Population (est. 1981): 1,725,000 (growth rate, 1978–79: 2.6%)
Density per square mile: 2.9
Capital and largest city (est. 1979): Ulan Bator, 400,000
Monetary unit: Tugrik
Language: Khalkha Mongolian
Religion: Lamaistic Buddhism
National name: Bugd Nairamdakh Mongol Ard Uls
Freedom House classifications: Socialist industrial, one-party communist
Economic summary: Gross national product (1979): $1.3 billion. Average annual growth rate (1970–78): 3.1%. Principal agricultural products: livestock, wheat, oats, barley. Major industrial products: animal products, building materials, minerals. Natural resources: coal, copper, molybdenum. Exports: livestock, animal products, nonferrous metals. Imports: machinery and equipment, clothing, petroleum, sugar, tea. Major trading partners: U.S.S.R. and Soviet bloc countries.

Geography. Mongolia lies in eastern Asia between Soviet Siberia on the north and China on the south. It is slightly larger than Alaska.

The productive regions of Mongolia—a tableland ranging from 3,000 to 5,000 feet (914 to 1,524 m) in elevation—are in the north, which is well drained by numerous rivers, including the Hovd, Onon, Selenga, and Tula.

Much of the Gobi Desert falls within Mongolia. There several mountain ranges, one of which, the Altai Mountains, contains the highest peak in the country—Tabun Bogdo at 15,266 feet (4,653 m).

Government. The Mongolian People's Republic is a socialist state in the form of a people's democracy. The highest organ of state power is the Great People's Khural (Parliament), which is elected for a term of four years and is convened once a year. The Great People's Khural elects the Presidium, which consists of a chairman, two vice chairmen, a secretary, and six members. The Council of Ministers is set up by the Great People's Khural and consists of a chairman, vice chairmen, and ministers.

The Mongolian People's Revolutionary Party, led by President Yumjaagiin Tsedenbal, is the only political party.

History. The Mongolian People's Republic, formerly known as Outer Mongolia, is a Russian satellite. It contains the original homeland of the historic Mongols, whose power reached its zenith during the 13th century under Kublai Khan. The area ac-

cepted Manchu rule in 1689, but after the Chinese Revolution of 1911 and the fall of the Manchus in 1912, the northern Mongol princes expelled the Chinese officials and declared independence under the Khutukhtu, or "Living Buddha."

In 1921, Soviet troops entered the country and facilitated the establishment of a republic by Mongolian revolutionaries in 1924 after the death of the last Living Buddha. China, meanwhile, continued to claim Outer Mongolia but was unable to back the claim with any strength. Under the 1945 Chinese-Russian Treaty, China agreed to give up Outer Mongolia, which, after a plebiscite, became a nominally independent country.

The country allied itself with the U.S.S.R. in its dispute with China. It has mobilized troops along its borders since 1968 when the two powers became involved in border clashes on the Kazakh-Sinkiang frontier to the west and on the Amur and Ussuri Rivers. Under a 20-year treaty of friendship and cooperation signed in 1966, it was entitled to call upon the U.S.S.R. for military aid in the event of invasion.

MOROCCO

Kingdom of Morocco
Ruler: King Hassan II (1961)
Premier: Mohamed Boucetta (1981)
Area: 171,953 sq mi. (445,358 sq km)
Population (est. 1981): 20,500,000 (growth rate, 2.9%)
Density per square mile: 119.2
Capital: Rabat
Largest cities (est. 1979): Casablanca, 2,220,000; Rabat, 770,000; (est. 1975 by U.N.): Marrakech, 330,400; Fez, 321,450; Meknès, 244,500
Monetary unit: Dirham
Languages: Arabic, French, Spanish
Religions: Chiefly Islam
National name: al-Mamlaka al-Maghrebia
Freedom House classifications: Capitalist pre-industrial, multi-party centralized
Economic summary: Gross national product (1979): $14.5 billion. Average annual growth rate (1970–78): 3.9%. Per capita income (1977): $520. Land used for agriculture: 32%; labor force: 50%; products: barley, wheat, citrus fruits, vegetables, sugar beets, wool. Labor force in industry, 15%; major products: textiles, fish, chemicals. Natural resources: phosphates, iron, manganese, lead, fisheries. Exports: phosphates, citrus fruits, vegetables, canned fruits and vegetables, canned fish, carpets. Imports: industrial capital goods, fuels, foodstuffs, consumer goods. Major trading partners: France, Italy, West Germany.

Geography. Morocco, about one tenth larger than California, is just south of Spain across the Strait of Gibraltar and looks out on the Atlantic from the northwest shoulder of Africa. Algeria is to the east and Mauritania to the south.

On the Atlantic coast there is a fertile plain. The Mediterranean coast is mountainous. The Atlas Mountains, running northeastward from the south to the Algerian frontier, average 11,000 feet (3,353 m) in elevation.

Government. The King, after suspending the 1962 Constitution and dissolving Parliament in 1965, promulgated a new Constitution in 1972. He continued to rule by decree until June 3, 1977, when the first free elections since 1962 took place. The

264-member Chamber of Deputies has 176 elected seats, with the balance chosen by local councils and groups.

A coalition of independents loyal to the King and small right-wing parties has 114 of the 176 elected seats in the Chamber of Deputies; Istiqlal, principal opposition group, 45 seats; Socialist Union of Popular Forces, 16 seats; and the Communist Party of Progress and Socialism, one seat.

History. Morocco was once the home of the Berbers, who helped the Arabs invade Spain in A.D. 711 and then revolted against them and gradually won control of large areas of Spain for a time after 739.

The country was ruled successively by various native dynasties and maintained regular commercial relations with Europe, even during the 17th and 18th centuries when it was the headquarters of the famous Salé pirates. In the 19th century, there were frequent clashes with the French and Spanish. Finally, in 1904, France and Spain divided Morocco into zones of French and Spanish influence, and these were established as protectorates in 1912.

Meanwhile, Morocco had become the object of big-power rivalry, which almost led to a European war in 1905 when Germany attempted to gain a foothold in the rich mineral country. By terms of the Algeciras Conference (1906), Morocco was internationalized economically, and France's privileges were limited.

The Tangier Statute, concluded by Britain, France, and Spain in 1923, created an international zone at the port of Tangier, permanently neutralized and demilitarized. In World War II, Spain occupied the zone, ostensibly to ensure order, but was forced to withdraw in 1945.

Sultan Mohammed V was deposed by the French in 1953 and replaced by his uncle, but nationalist agitation forced his return in 1955. On his death on Feb. 26, 1961, his son, Hassan, became King.

France and Spain recognized the independence and sovereignty of Morocco in 1956. Later the same year, the Tangier international zone was abolished.

In the Middle East war of 1967, Morocco joined the Arab states in their attack on Israel.

In 1975, tens of thousands of Moroccans crossed the border into Spanish Sahara to back their government's contention that the northern part of the territory was historically part of Morocco. At the same time, Mauritania occupied the southern half of the territory in defiance of Spanish threats to resist such a takeover. Abandoning its commitment to self-determination for the territory, Spain withdrew, and only Algeria protested. Algerian recognition of a Saharan republic in 1976 led to a break in relations among the three North African states, and Algerian-backed Polisario Front guerrillas continued to fight Moroccan and Mauritanian forces, preventing exploitation of the region's rich phosphate deposits.

Although Polisario guerrillas were still active in 1977, Hassan dispatched 1,500 troops to Zaire in April to help President Mobutu Sese Seko defeat an invasion from Angola. Radical African states criticized Morocco, but most hailed the successful operation, in which France supplied the airlift.

In the May 1978 invasion of Zaire's Shaba Province, Morocco once again supplied troops, this time only a small number, who were transported to Zaire by the U.S. Air Force.

With the Sahara problem still unresolved in 1981, Hassan, under pressure from other African leaders at the Organization of African Unity summit in Nairobi, Kenya, on June 26 agreed to a cease-fire with a referendum under international supervision to decide the future of the territory. No details were fixed, although the O.A.U. was expected to ask for a U.N. peace-keeping force to insure a fair vote.

MOZAMBIQUE

People's Republic of Mozambique
President: Samora Moises Machel (1975)
Area: 303,073 sq mi. (784,959 sq km)
Population (est. 1981): 10,750,000 (growth rate: 2.8%)
Density per square mile: 35.5
Capital and largest city (est. 1980): Maputo, 750,000
Monetary unit: Metical
Languages: Portuguese (official); Bantu languages
Religions: Animist, 66%; Christian, 22%; Islam, 11%
National name: República Popular de Moçambique
Freedom House classifications: Socialist pre-industrial, one-party socialist.
Economic summary: Gross national product (1979): $2.6 billion. Average annual growth rate (1970–78): −5.5%. Per capita income: $220. Principal agricultural products: cotton, cashew nuts, sugar, tea, copra, wheat, peanuts. Labor force in industry: 5%; major products: processed foods, petroleum products, beverages, textiles, tobacco. Natural resources: coal, iron ore, fluorite, tantalite, timber. Exports: cashew nuts, cotton, sugar, mineral and timber products, tea, copra. Imports: machinery and electrical equipment, cotton textiles, vehicles, petroleum products, iron and steel. Major trading partners: Portugal, South Africa, U.S., U.K., West Germany.

Geography. Mozambique stretches for 1,535 miles (2,470 km) along Africa's southeast coast. It is nearly twice the size of California. Tanzania is to the north; Malawi, Zambia, and Zimbabwe to the west; and South Africa and Swaziland to the south.

The country is generally a low-lying plateau broken up by 25 sizable rivers that flow into the Indian Ocean. The largest is the Zambezi, which provides access to central Africa. The principal ports are Maputo and Beira, which is the port for Zimbabwe.

Government. After having been under Portuguese colonial rule for 470 years, Mozambique became independent on June 25, 1975. It is a Marxist state. The first President, Samora Moises Machel, is a militant Maoist and a former nurse who headed the National Front for the Liberation of Mozambique (FRELIMO) in its 10-year guerrilla war for independence.

History. Mozambique was discovered by Vasco da Gama in 1498, although the Arabs had penetrated into the area as early as the 10th century. It was first colonized in 1505, and by 1510, the Portuguese had control of all the former Arab sultanates on the east African coast.

FRELIMO was organized in 1963. Guerrilla activity had become so extensive by 1973 that Portugal was forced to dispatch 40,000 troops to fight the rebels. A cease-fire was signed in September 1974, when Portugal agreed to grant Mozambique independence.

After a brief period of cooperation with neighboring white-ruled Rhodesia, Mozambique closed its border in 1976, cutting off Rhodesia's most direct link to the sea. A series of border clashes between Rhodesian forces and guerrillas based in

Mozambique continued until Zimbabwe achieved independence in April 1980, when rail and highway communications between the two countries were reopened.

NAMIBIA
See South Africa

NAURU

Republic of Nauru
President and Premier: Hammer DeRoburt (1978)
Area: 8.2 sq mi. (21 sq km)
Population (est. 1981): 8,000
Density per square mile: 1,000.0
Capital: Yaren
Monetary unit: Australian dollar
Languages: Nauruan, English
Religions: Protestant, 60%; Catholic, 33%
Special relationship within the Commonwealth of Nations
Freedom House classifications: Capitalist-statist industrial, non-party non-military
Economic summary: Gross national product (1977): $155 million. Major industrial products: phosphates. Natural resources: phosphates. Exports: phosphates. Imports: foodstuffs, fuel. Major trading partners: Australia, New Zealand, U.K., Japan.

Geography. Nauru is an island in the Pacific just south of the equator, about 2,500 miles (4,023 km) southwest of Honolulu.

Government. Legislative power is invested in a popularly elected 18-member Parliament, which elects the President from among its members. Executive power rests with the President, who is assisted by a five-member Cabinet.

History. Nauru was annexed by Germany in 1888. It was placed under joint Australian, New Zealand, and British mandate after World War I, and in 1947 it became a U.N. trusteeship administered by the same three powers. On Jan. 31, 1968, Nauru became an independent republic.

NEPAL

Kingdom of Nepal
Ruler: King Birendra Bír Bikram Shah Dev. (1972)
Prime Minister: Surya Bahadur Thapa (1979)
Area: 54,362 sq mi. (140,797 sq km)
Population (est. 1981): 14,325,000 (growth rate: 2.4%)
Density per square mile: 263.5
Capital and largest city (est. 1976): Katmandu, 171,400
Monetary unit: Nepalese rupee
Languages: Nepali (official), Newari, Bhutia
Religions: Hindu, 89%; Buddhist, 8%
Freedom House classifications: Capitalist pre-industrial, non-party non-military
Economic summary: Gross national product (1979): $1.8 billion. Average annual growth rate (1970–78): 0.3%. Per capita income: $108. Labor force in agriculture: 95%; principal products: rice, maize, wheat, millet, jute, sugar cane, oilseed, potatoes. Labor force in industry: 5%; major products: cigarettes, bricks, sugar, lumber, jute, hydroelectric power, cement. Natural resources: water, timber, hydroelectric potential. Exports: agricultural products and timber. Imports: textiles, manufactured goods. Major trading partner: India.

Geography. A landlocked country the size of Arkansas, lying between India and the Tibetan Autonomous Region of China, Nepal contains Mount Everest (29,028 ft.; 8,848 m), the tallest mountain in the world. Along its southern border, Nepal has a strip of level land that is partly forested, partly cultivated. North of that is the slope of the main section of the Himalayan range, including Everest and many other peaks higher than 20,000 feet (6,096 m).

Government. A new Constitution promulgated by King Mahendra in 1962 provided for a unicameral legislature called the National Panchayat. All political parties were banned in 1960.

History. The Kingdom of Nepal was unified in 1768 by King Prithwi Narayan Shah. A commercial treaty was signed with Britain in 1792, and in 1816, after more than a year's hostilities, the Nepalese agreed to allow British residents to live in Katmandu, the capital. In 1923, Britain recognized the absolute independence of Nepal. Between 1846 and 1951, the country was ruled by the Rana family, which always held the office of prime minister. In 1951, however, the King took over all power and proclaimed a constitutional monarchy.

Mahendra Bir Bikram Shah became King in 1955. Nepal and China settled their differences in 1956, and thereafter Nepal accepted economic aid from the Chinese. The U.S. and the U.S.S.R. also provide aid.

After Mahendra, who had ruled since 1955, died of a heart attack in 1972, Prince Birendra, at 26, succeeded to the throne.

In the first election in 22 years, on May 2, 1980, voters approved the continued autocratic rule by the King with the advice of a partyless Parliament. The King promised, however, that he would eventually permit the election of a new legislature to which the Prime Minister and Cabinet would be responsible.

THE NETHERLANDS

Kingdom of the Netherlands
Sovereign: Queen Beatrix (1980)
Premier: Andries van Agt (1977)
Area: 13,967 sq mi. (36,175 sq km)
Population (est. 1981): 14,250,000 (growth rate: 0.8%)
Density per square mile: 1,040.4
Capital: Amsterdam; seat of government: The Hague
Largest cities (est. 1979): Rotterdam, 1,014,800; Amsterdam, 957,700; The Hague, 671,500; Utrecht, 476,400
Monetary unit: Guilder
Language: Dutch
Religions: Roman Catholic, 40%; Dutch Reformed, 24%; unaffiliated, 24%
National name: Koninkrijk der Nederlanden
Freedom House classifications: Capitalist-socialist industrial, multi-party centralized
Economic summary: Gross national product (1979): $143.2 billion. Average annual growth rate (1970–78): 2.3%. Per capita income: $7,597. Land used for agriculture: 70%; labor force, 10%; principal products: wheat, barley, sugar beets, potatoes, flax, bulbs, meat and dairy products. Labor force in industry: 30%; major products: metal fabrication, textiles, chemicals, electronic equipment. Exports: foodstuffs, machinery, natural gas, chemicals, petroleum products, textiles. Imports: machinery, crude petroleum, chemicals, textiles, mineral ores. Major

trading partners: West Germany, Belgium, France, U.K.

Geography. The Netherlands, on the coast of the North Sea, has West Germany to the east and Belgium to the south. It is twice the size of New Jersey.

Part of the great plain of north and west Europe, the Netherlands has maximum dimensions of 190 by 160 miles (360 by 257 km) and is low and flat except in Limburg in the southeast, where some hills rise to 300 feet (92 m). About half the country's area is below sea level, making the famous Dutch dikes a requisite to the use of much land. Reclamation of land from the sea through dikes has continued through recent times.

All drainage reaches the North Sea, and the principal rivers—Rhine, Maas (Meuse), and Schelde—have their sources outside the country. The Rhine is the most heavily used waterway in Europe.

Government. The Netherlands and its former colony of the Netherlands Antilles form the Kingdom of the Netherlands.

The Netherlands is a constitutional monarchy with a bicameral Parliament. The Upper Chamber has 75 members elected for six years by representative bodies of the provinces, half of the members retiring every three years. The Lower Chamber has 150 members elected by universal suffrage for four years. The two Chambers have the right of investigation and interpellation; the Lower Chamber can initiate legislation and amend bills.

The Sovereign, Queen Beatrix Wilhelmina Armgard, born Jan. 31, 1938, was married on March 11, 1966, to Claus von Amsberg, a former West German diplomat. The marriage drew public criticism because of the bridegroom's service in the German army during World War II. In 1967, Beatrix gave birth to a son, Willem-Alexander Claus George Ferdinand, the first male heir to the throne since 1884. She also has two other sons, Johan Friso Bernhard Christian David, born in 1968, and Constantijn Christof Frederik Aschwin, born the next year.

Premier Andries van Agt leads a minority government. The Christian Appeal (48 of 150 seats in the Lower Chamber), led by van Agt, is the largest of 10 parties. Other major parties are the opposition Labor Party (44 seats), led by former Prime Minister Joop den Uyl; the Liberal Party for Freedom and Democracy (26 seats), and Democrats '66 (17 seats).

History. Julius Caesar found the low-lying Netherlands inhabited by Germanic tribes—the Nervii, Frisii, and Batavi. The Batavi on the Roman frontier did not submit to Rome's rule until 13 B.C., and then only as allies.

A part of Charlemagne's empire in the 8th and 9th centuries A.D., the area later passed into the hands of Burgundy and the Austrian Hapsburgs, and finally in the 16th century came under Spanish rule.

When Philip II of Spain suppressed political liberties and the growing Protestant movement in the Netherlands, a revolt led by William of Orange broke out in 1568. Under the Union of Utrecht (1579), the seven northern provinces became the Republic of the United Netherlands.

The Dutch East India Company was established in 1602, and by the end of the 17th century Holland was one of the great sea and colonial powers of Europe.

The nation's independence was not completely established until after the Thirty Years' War (1618–48), after which the country's rise as a commercial and maritime power began. In 1814, all the provinces of Holland and Belgium were merged into one kingdom, but in 1830 the southern provinces broke away to form the Kingdom of Belgium. A liberal Constitution was adopted by the Netherlands in 1848.

In spite of its neutrality in World War II, the Netherlands was invaded by the Nazis in May 1940, and the East Indies were later taken by the Japanese. The nation was liberated in May 1945. In 1948, after a reign of 50 years, Queen Wilhelmina resigned and was succeeded by her daughter Juliana.

In 1949, after a four-year war, the Netherlands granted independence to the East Indies, which became the Republic of Indonesia. In 1963, it turned over the western half of New Guinea to the new nation, ending 300 years of Dutch presence in Asia. Attainment of independence by Suriname on Nov. 25, 1975, left the Dutch Antilles as the Netherlands' only overseas territory.

Prime Minister Andries van Agt ended a seven-month constitutional crisis in December 1977 when he was able to form a center-right majority coalition. Early in 1980, Queen Juliana announced her intention to abdicate on her 71st birthday, April 30, in favor of the 42-year-old Crown Princess Beatrix. She had delayed her retirement to repair the damage to the monarchy caused by charges in 1976 that her husband, Prince Bernhard, had accepted payments from the Lockheed Aircraft Corp. to influence purchases of military planes. Beatrix was invested as Queen on April 30 in a ceremony marred by protests of Amsterdam squatters against eviction.

Van Agt lost his narrow majority in elections on May 26, 1981, in which the major issue was the deployment of U.S. cruise missiles on Dutch soil. The Prime Minister personally endorsed the proposal as a NATO defense measure but could not win his party's endorsement.

Netherlands Autonomous Country

NETHERLANDS ANTILLES

Status: Part of the Kingdom of the Netherlands
Governor: Bernardito M. Leito (1970)
Premier: Domenico F. Martina
Area: 817 sq mi. (821 sq km)
Population (est. 1981): 275,000 (growth rate: 1.0%)
Capital (est. 1978): Willemstad, 152,000
Economic summary: Gross national product (1979): $920 million. Average annual growth rate (1970–78): 0.3%. Per capita income: $1,700. Principal agricultural products: pigs, goats. Major industries: oil refining, tourism. Natural resource: phosphate. Export: petroleum. Import: petroleum. Major trading partners: Venezuela, U.S., Netherlands.

Geography. The Netherlands Antilles comprise two groups of Caribbean islands 500 miles (805 km) apart: one, about 40 miles (64 km) off the Venezuelan coast, consists of Curaçao (173 sq mi.; 448 sq km), Bonaire (95 sq mi.; 246 sq km), and Aruba (69 sq mi.; 179 sq km); the other, lying to the northeast, consists of three small islands with a total area of 34 square miles (88 sq km). The Dutch acquired Curaçao from Spain in 1643.

Government. There is a constitutional government formed by the Governor and Cabinet and an elected Legislative Council. The area has complete autonomy in domestic affairs.

NEW ZEALAND

Dominion of New Zealand
Sovereign: Queen Elizabeth II
Governor-General: Sir David S. Beattie (1980)
Prime Minister: Robert D. Muldoon (1975)
Area: 103,736 sq mi. (268,676 sq km) (excluding dependencies)
Population (est. 1981): 3,150,000 (average annual growth rate, 1977–80: 0.0%) (European, 90%; Maori and other Polynesian, 10%)
Density per square mile: 30.4
Capital: Wellington
Largest cities (est. 1980 for metropolitan area): Auckland, 753,100; Wellington, 326,000; Christchurch, 295,100; Dunedin, 118,700
Monetary unit: New Zealand dollar
Languages: English, Maori
Religions: Church of England, 29%; Presbyterian, 18%; Roman Catholic, 15%
Member of Commonwealth of Nations
Freedom House classifications: Capitalist industrial, multi-party centralized
Economic summary: Gross national product (1979): $19.2 billion. Average annual growth rate (1970–78): 0.9%. Per capita income (1976): $4,106. Labor force in agriculture: 13%; principal products: wool, meat, dairy products, livestock. Labor force in industry: 33%; major products: processed foods, textiles, machinery, transport equipment, wood and paper products. Natural resources: forests, coal, gold, tungsten, iron ore, asbestos. Exports: meat, dairy products, wool. Imports: machinery, minerals, chemicals, consumer goods. Major trading partners: Australia, U.K., Japan, U.S.

Geography. New Zealand, about 1,250 miles (2,012 km) east of Australia, consists of two main islands and a number of smaller, outlying islands so scattered that they range from the tropical to the antarctic. The country is the size of Colorado.

New Zealand's two main components are North Island and South Island, separated by Cook Strait, which varies from 16 to 190 miles (26 to 396 km) in width. North Island (44,281 sq mi.; 114,688 sq km) is 515 miles (829 km) long and volcanic in its south-central part. It contains many hot springs and beautiful geysers. South Island (58,093 sq mi.; 150,461 sq km) has the Southern Alps along its west coast, with Mount Cook (12,349 ft; 3,764 m) the highest point.

The largest of the outlying islands are the Auckland Islands (234 sq mi.; 606 sq km), Campbell Island (44 sq mi.; 114 sq km), the Antipodes Islands (24 sq mi.; 62 sq km), and the Kermadec Islands (13 sq mi.; 34 sq km).

Government. New Zealand was granted self-government in 1852, a full parliamentary system and ministries in 1856, and dominion status in 1907. The Queen is represented by a Governor-General, and the Cabinet is responsible to a unicameral Parliament of 92 members, who are elected by popular vote for three years.

The major political parties are the National Party (51 of 92 seats in the House of Representatives), led by Prime Minister Robert D. Muldoon; Labor Party (49 seats) led by Wallace E. Rowling; and Social Credit Party (2 seats).

History. New Zealand was discovered and named in 1642 by Abel Tasman, a Dutch navigator. Captain James Cook explored the islands in 1769. In 1840, Britain formally annexed them.

From the first, the country has been in the fore-front in instituting social welfare legislation. It adopted old age pensions (1898); a national child welfare program (1907); social security for the aged, widows, and orphans, along with family benefit payments; minimum wages; a 40-hour week and unemployment and health insurance (1938); and socialized medicine (1941).

New Zealand supported U.S. policy in Vietnam and supplied military aid to South Vietnam in the orientation of its policy toward the U.S. and Asian neighbors after Britain's entry into the European Common Market. To replace the lost British market —the once prosperous islands had fallen into a local recession since 1972—New Zealand sought to sell more agricultural products to Japan. In 1978, Prime Minister Muldoon announced a pact with Japan enlarging quotas for New Zealand beef, reducing the tariffs on New Zealand fish, and providing for Japanese purchase of butter, skim milk, and other food products.

Cook Islands and Overseas Territories

The Cook Islands (93 sq mi.; 241 sq km) were placed under New Zealand administration in 1901. They achieved self-governing status in association with New Zealand in 1965. Population in 1978 was about 19,600. The seat of government is on Rarotonga Island.

Chief exports in 1978 were citrus juice (37%), clothing (22%), canned fruit (10%), pineapple juice (8%). Leading customer in 1978 was New Zealand (98%). Leading suppliers were New Zealand (83%), Japan (5%).

Niue (100 sq mi.; 259 sq km) was formerly administered as part of the Cook Islands. It was placed under separate New Zealand administration in 1901 and achieved self-governing status in association with New Zealand in 1974. The capital is Alofi. Population in 1980 was about 3,300.

Chief exports in 1975 were passion fruit (42%), copra (37%), plaited ware (11%), honey (6%), limes (3%). Leading customer in 1975 was New Zealand (73%). Leading supplier was New Zealand (80%).

The Ross Dependency (160,000 sq mi.; 414,400 sq km), an Antarctic region, was placed under New Zealand administration in 1923.

Tokelau (4 sq mi.; 10 sq km) was formerly administered as part of the Gilbert and Ellice Islands colony. It was placed under New Zealand administration in 1925. Its population in 1980 was about 1,600.

NICARAGUA

Republic of Nicaragua
Executive power is held by the nine-member Directorate of the Sandinista Front (1979)
Area: 57,143 sq mi. (148,000 sq km)
Population (est. 1981): 2,750,000 (growth rate: 2.8%) (mestizo, 70%; white, 17%; black, 9%; Indian, 4%)
Density per square mile: 48.1
Capital and largest city (est. 1978): Managua, 517,500
Monetary unit: Cordoba
Language: Spanish
Religion: Roman Catholic
National name: República de Nicaragua
Freedom House classifications: Capitalist-socialist industrial,

non-party non-military

Economic summary: Gross national product (1979): $1.7 billion. Average annual growth rate (1970–78): 1.7%. Per capita income: $980. Land used for agriculture: 7%; labor force: 43%; principal products: cotton, coffee, sugar cane, rice, corn, beans, cattle. Labor force in industry: 15%; major products: processed foods, chemicals, metal products, clothing and textiles. Natural resources: timber, fisheries. Exports: cotton, coffee, chemical products, meat, sugar. Imports: food and non-food agricultural products, chemicals and pharmaceuticals, transport equipment, clothing, petroleum. Major trading partners: U.S., Caribbean and Western European countries.

Geography. Largest but most sparsely populated of the Central American nations, Nicaragua borders on Honduras to the north and Costa Rica to the south. It is slightly larger than New York State.

Nicaragua is mountainous in the west, with fertile valleys. A plateau slopes eastward toward the Caribbean.

Two big lakes—Nicaragua, about 100 miles long (161 km), and Managua, about 38 miles long (61 km)—are connected by the Tipitapa River. The Pacific coast is bald and rocky. The Caribbean coast, swampy and indented, is aptly called the "Mosquito Coast."

Government. A nine-member Directorate for the Sandinista National Liberation Front has replaced the five-member junta that took power July 19, 1979, with the overthrow of President Anastasio Somoza Debayle. Although members of the Directorate share authority in principle, Humberto Ortega Saavedra, commander of the armed forces, and his brother, Daniel Ortega Saavedra, a member of the original junta, are believed to dominate the group.

History. Nicaragua, which established independence in 1838, was first visited by the Spaniards in 1522. The chief of the country's leading Indian tribe at that time was called Nicaragua, from whom the nation derived its name. A U.S. naval force intervened in 1909 after two American citizens had been executed, and a few U.S. Marines were kept in the country from 1912 to 1925. The Bryan-Chamorro Treaty of 1916 (terminated in 1970) gave the U.S. an option on a canal route through Nicaragua, and naval bases. Disorder after the 1924 elections brought in the marines again.

A guerrilla leader, Gen. César Augusto Sandino, began fighting the occupation force in 1927. He fought the U.S. troops successfully until their withdrawal in 1933. They trained Gen. Anastasio (Tacho) Somoza García to head a National Guard. In 1934, Somoza assassinated Sandino and overthrew the Liberal President Juan Batista Sacassa, establishing a military dictatorship with himself as president. He spurred the economic development of the country, meanwhile enriching his family through estates in the countryside and investments in air and shipping lines. On his assassination in 1956, he was succeeded by his son Luis, who alternated with trusted family friends in the presidency until his death in 1967. Another son, Maj. Gen. Anastasio Somoza Debayle, became President in 1967.

One of the worst earthquakes in Nicaragua's history struck Managua on Dec. 23, 1972, destroying an estimated 90% of its commercial establishments and 70% of its housing. Over 6,000 were killed, 20,000 injured, and 300,000 made homeless, and 60,000 were jobless as a result. Rebuilding costs were put at $772 million. Somoza obtained loans

from the U.S. and international banks totaling $127 million for the reconstruction of Managua. Shortly afterward, he declared martial law after leftist guerrillas had kidnapped 14 prominent officials.

Although the Somoza regime was cited in 1977 by a U.S. State Department report for human-rights violations and Nicaragua's Catholic hierarchy testified to the government's repression and terror, it was not until 1978 that the Carter Administration moved to cut military aid to Somoza.

The situation was aggravated by the murder on January 10 of Pedro Joaquin Chamorro, editor of an opposition newspaper, causing student strikes and wide public protest. In an uncharacteristic response, Somoza made concessions to protesters and announced an inquiry into Chamorro's death. On May 16, the U.S. Congress acted to restore $12 million in military aid to Nicaragua.

Sandinista guerrillas, leftists who took their name from Gen. Sandino, launched a civil war in May 1979, occupying parts of Managua and holding several provincial towns. Somoza ordered bombings to drive the rebels out, an action that embittered Nicaraguans of all classes. He defied appeals by the U.S. and the Organization of American States to step down and permit a peaceful transition to an all-party government. The U.S. sought to win Sandinista agreement to the incorporation of Somoza's National Guard into the armed forces of the new government, but the President flew to exile in the U.S. on July 17 without reaching a settlement.

Although the original five-member junta included two non-Sandinista members who resigned in April 1980, and were replaced by two other non-Sandinistas, exclusive power was moving to the Sandinista Directorate. The prominence of Cuban President Fidel Castro at the celebration of the first anniversary of the revolution and the indefinite delay of elections strengthened debate over the true political color of the Sandinistas. U.S. Congressional doubts delayed release of $75 million in aid until September 1980, when President Jimmy Carter certified that Nicaragua was not "exporting violence."

On Jan. 23, 1981, the Reagan Administration suspended aid after the U.S. Ambassador to El Salvador claimed that Nicaragua was supplying Salvadoran rebels. In June, State Department reports that Soviet T-55 tanks were being shipped to Nicaragua were denied by Daniel Ortega.

NIGER

Republic of Niger

Chief of State: Col. Seyni Kountché (1974)

Area: 489,206 sq mi. (1,267,044 sq km)

Population (est. 1981): 5,550,000 (growth rate: 2.9%)

Density per square mile: 11.2

Capital and largest city (est. 1977): Niamey, 225,000

Monetary unit: Franc CFA

Ethnic groups: Hausa, 54%; Djerma and Songhai, 24%; Peul, 11%

Languages: French (official); Hausa, Songhai; Arabic

Religions: Islam, 85%; Animist, 15%

National name: République du Niger

Freedom House classifications: Capitalist pre-industrial, non-party military

Economic summary: Gross national product (1979): $1.4 billion. Average annual growth rate (1970–78): −0.6%. Per capita income: $100. Land used for agriculture: 3%; labor force: 90%; principal products: peanuts, cotton, livestock, millet, sorghum, vegetables. Major industrial products: uranium, cement, bricks, light industrial products. Natural resources: uranium, coal, iron. Exports: uranium, peanuts, livestock, hides, skins. Imports: fuels, machinery, transport equipment, foodstuffs, consumer goods. Major trading partners: France, other Western European countries, Nigeria.

Geography. Niger, in West Africa's Sahara region, is four fifths the size of Alaska. It is surrounded by Mali, Algeria, Libya, Chad, Nigeria, Benin, and Upper Volta.

The Niger River in the southwest flows through the country's only fertile area. Elsewhere the land is semiarid.

Government. After a military coup on April 15, 1974, Lt. Col. Seyni Kountché suspended the Constitution and instituted rule by decree. Previously, the President was elected by direct universal suffrage for a five-year term and a National House of Assembly of 50 members was elected for the same term.

The Parti Progressiste Nigérien-Rassemblement Démocratique Africain, the only political party, was dissolved in 1974.

History. Niger was incorporated into French West Africa in 1896. There were frequent rebellions, but when order was restored in 1922, the French made the area a colony. In 1958, the voters approved the French Constitution and voted to make the territory an autonomous republic within the French Community. The republic adopted a Constitution in 1959 and the next year withdrew from the Community, proclaiming its independence.

The 1974 army coup ousted President Hamani Diori, who had held office since 1960. He was charged with having mishandled relief for the terrible drought that had devastated Niger and five neighboring sub-Saharan nations for several years. An estimated 2 million people were starving in Niger, but 200,000 tons of imported food, half U.S.-supplied, substantially ended famine conditions by the year's end. The new President, Lt. Col. Seyni Kountché, Chief of Staff of the army, installed a 12-man military government. A predominantly civilian government was formed by Kountché in 1976.

NIGERIA

Federal Republic of Nigeria
President: Alhaji Shehu Shagari (1979)
Area: 356,700 sq mi. (923,853 sq km)
Population (est. 1981): 79,575,000[1] (growth rate: 3.3%)
Density per square mile: 223.1
Capital: Lagos
Largest cities (est. 1980): Lagos (metropolitan area): 4,000,000; (est. 1975 by U.N.): Ibadan, 847,000; Ogbomosho, 432,000; Kano, 399,000
Monetary unit: Naira
Languages: English (official) and native tongues
Religions: Islam, 47%; Christian, 34%; Animist
Member of Commonwealth of Nations
Freedom House classifications: Capitalist-statist pre-industrial, multi-party decentralized
Economic summary: Gross national product (1979): $55.3 billion. Average annual growth rate (1970–78): 4.4%. Per capita income: $500. Land used for agriculture: 13%; labor force: 70%; principal products: peanuts, cotton, cocoa, rubber, yams, cassava, livestock. Labor force in

industry: 10%; major products: crude oil, natural gas, coal, tin, processed rubber, cotton, petroleum, wood, hides, textiles, cement, footwear, chemicals. Natural resources: petroleum, tin, columbite, iron ore, coal, limestone, lead, zinc, timber. Exports: oil, cocoa, palm products, rubber, timber, tin. Imports: machinery and transport equipment, manufactured goods, chemicals. Major trading partners: U.K., Western European countries, U.S.

1. While U.N. and similar sources continue to report figures in this area, interpretations of election data by demographers suggest that, in reality, the population of Nigeria is close to 100 million.

Geography. Nigeria, one third larger than Texas and black Africa's most populous nation, is situated on the Gulf of Guinea in West Africa. Its neighbors are Benin, Niger, Cameroon, and Chad.

The lower course of the Niger River flows south through the western part of the country into the Gulf of Guinea. Swamps and mangrove forests border the southern coast; inland are hardwood forests.

Government. Beginning in 1966, a Supreme Military Council governed the country. In 1977, new local-government councils elected a 203-member national Constituent Assembly, which completed a new draft constitution in 1978. With the election of Alhaji Shehu Shagari, a former finance minister, as President in August 1979, the country returned to civilian rule on Oct. 1 with a United States type of presidential administration.

History. Between 1879 and 1914, private colonial developments by the British, with reorganizations of the Crown's interest in the region, resulted in the formation of Nigeria as it exists today. During World War I, native troops of the West African frontier force joined with French forces to defeat the German garrison in the Cameroons.

Nigeria became independent on Oct. 1, 1960.

Organized as a loose federation of self-governing states, the independent nation faced an overwhelming task of unifying a country with 250 ethnic and linguistic groups. The largest were the Hausa and Fulani in the north and the Ibo and Yoruba in the south, each of which had kingdoms in the late Middle Ages.

Rioting broke out again in 1966, the military commander was seized, and Col. Yakubu Gowon took power. Also in that year, the Moslem Hausas in the north massacred the predominantly Christian Ibos in the east, many of whom had been driven from the north. Thousands of Ibos took refuge in the Eastern Region. The military government there asked Ibos to return to the region and, in May 1967, the assembly voted to secede from the federation and set up the Republic of Biafra. Civil war broke out.

In January 1970, after 31 months of civil war, Biafra surrendered to the federal government. An estimated one million persons, mostly Ibos of the defeated state, were homeless and hungry, but a massive international relief operation kept the death toll down. The overall cost of the civil war was estimated at $840 million.

Gowon's nine-year rule was ended in 1975 by a bloodless coup that made Army Brigadier Muritala Rufai Mohammed the new chief of state. Mohammed was assassinated the next year 1976 by a group of seven young officers, who failed to seize control of the government. The 20-member Supreme Military Council chose Lt. Gen. Olusegun Obasanjo, Chief of Staff of the armed forces, as the new head of the Council and President. The assassins were publicly executed by firing squads.

Although Nigeria ranked seventh in world oil production in 1977 with revenues of $10 billion, a deficit in its balance of payments of $960 million for the year forced the government to impose severe restrictions on imported consumer goods. Nevertheless, Nigeria's prestige as the richest black African nation was emphasized by the visit of President Carter to Lagos on March 31, 1978, the first visit by an American President to black Africa since a brief stopover in Liberia by President Franklin D. Roosevelt during World War II.

NORWAY

Kingdom of Norway
Sovereign: King Olav V (1957)
Prime Minister: Kare Willoch (1981)
Area: 125,182 sq mi. (324,219 sq km)
Population (est. 1981): 4,150,000 (growth rate: 0.3%)
Density per square mile: 33.2
Capital: Oslo
Largest cities (est. 1979): Oslo, 457,300; Bergen, 212,750; Trondheim, 135,550; Stavanger, 88,100
Monetary unit: Krone
Language: Norwegian
Religions: Evangelical Lutheran (state), 94%
National name: Kongeriket Norge
Freedom House classifications: Capitalist-socialist industrial, multi-party centralized
Economic summary: Gross national product (1979): $43.5 billion. Average annual growth rate (1970–78): 3.9%. Per capita income: $8,316. Land used for agriculture: 3%; labor force, including fishing: 11%; principal products: dairy products, livestock, grain, vegetables, fruits, furs, wool. Labor force in industry: 16%; major products: oil and gas, fish, pulp and paper, ships, aluminum, iron, steel, nickel, fertilizers, transportation equipment, hydroelectric power, petrochemicals, electronic equipment. Natural resources: fish, timber, hydroelectric power, ores, oil, gas. Exports: oil, natural gas, ships, fish products, chemicals, pulp and paper. Imports: machinery, motor vehicles, foodstuffs, iron and steel, textiles and clothing. Major trading partners: Sweden, West Germany, U.K., U.S., Denmark.

Geography. Norway is situated in the western part of the Scandinavian peninsula. It extends about 1,100 miles (1,770 km) from the North Sea along the Norwegian Sea to more than 300 miles (483 km) above the Arctic Circle, the farthest north of any European country. It is slightly larger than New Mexico. Sweden borders on most of the eastern frontier, with Finland and the U.S.S.R. in the northeast.

Nearly 70% of Norway is uninhabitable and covered by mountains, glaciers, moors, and rivers. The hundreds of deep fiords that cut into the coastline give Norway an overall oceanfront of more than 12,000 miles (19,312 km). Nearly 150,000 islands off the coast form a breakwater and make a safe coastal shipping channel.

Government. Norway is a constitutional hereditary monarchy. Executive power is vested in the King together with a Cabinet, or Council of State, consisting of a Prime Minister and at least seven other members. The Storting, or Parliament, is composed of 155 members elected by the people under pro-

portional representation. The Storting discusses and votes on political and financial questions, but divides itself into two sections (Lagting and Odelsting) to discuss and pass on legislative matters. The King cannot dissolve the Storting before the expiration of its term.

The sovereign is Olav V, born July 2, 1903, only son of Haakon VII and Princess Maud (1869–1938), third daughter of Edward VII of England. He succeeded to the throne on the death of his father Sept. 20, 1957. He married Princess Märtha of Sweden (1901–1954) on March 21, 1929. Their children are Princess Ragnhild Alexandra (born 1930), Princess Astrid (born 1932), and Crown Prince Harald (born 1937). In 1968, the Crown Prince married Sonja Haraldsen, a commoner.

The major political parties are the Labor Party (76 of 155 seats in the Storting), led by Prime Minister Gro Harlem Brundtland; Conservative Party (41 seats), led by Käre Willoch, Christian Democrats (22 seats), led by Lars Korvald; Center Party (12 seats), led by Johan J. Jakobsen; Socialist Left Party (2 seats), led by Hanna Kranmo.

History. Norwegians, like the Danes and Swedes, are of Teutonic origin. The Norsemen, also known as Vikings, ravaged the coasts of northwestern Europe from the 8th to the 11th century.

In 1815, Norway fell under the control of Sweden. The union of Norway, inhabited by fishermen, sailors, merchants, and peasants, and Sweden, an aristocratic country of large estates and tenant farmers, was not a happy one, but it lasted for nearly a century. In 1905, the Norwegian Parliament arranged a peaceful separation and invited a Danish prince to the Norwegian throne—King Haakon VII. A treaty with Sweden provided that all disputes be settled by arbitration and that no fortifications be erected on the common frontier.

When World War I broke out, Norway joined with Sweden and Denmark in a decision to remain neutral and to cooperate in the joint interest of the three countries. In World War II, Norway was invaded by the Germans on April 9, 1940. It resisted for two months before the Nazis took over complete control. King Haakon and his government fled to London, where they established a government-in-exile. Maj. Vidkun Quisling, whose name is now synonymous with traitor or fifth columnist, was the most notorious Norwegian collaborator with the Nazis. He was executed by the Norwegians on Oct. 24, 1945.

Despite severe losses in the war, Norway recovered quickly. The country led the world in social experimentation. A neighbor of the U.S.S.R., Norway sought to retain good relations with the Soviet Union without losing its identity with the West. It entered the North Atlantic Treaty Organization in 1949.

Verification of U.S. and Soviet oil strikes in separated areas of Norway's sector of the North Sea bottom led the Storting in 1975 to impose stiff tax and royalty rates on concession holders. Following discovery of a North Sea field expected to produce 900,000 barrels a day by 1984, Parliament in 1976 approved establishment of a national refining and distributing company to market petroleum products at home and abroad.

Dependencies of Norway

Svalbard (23,957 sq mi.; 62,049 sq km), in the Arctic Ocean about 360 miles north of Norway, consists of the Spitsbergen group and several smaller islands, including Bear Island, Hope Island, King

Charles Land, and White Island (or Gillis Land). It came under Norwegian administration in 1925. The population in 1979 was 3,640.

Bouvet Island (23 sq mi.; 60 sq km), in the South Atlantic about 1,600 miles south-southwest of the Cape of Good Hope, came under Norwegian administration in 1928.

Jan Mayen Island (144 sq mi.; 273 sq km), in the Arctic Ocean between Norway and Greenland, came under Norwegian administration in 1929. Its population in 1973 was 37.

Peter I Island (96 sq mi.; 249 sq km), lying off Antarctica in the Bellinghausen Sea, came under Norwegian administration in 1931.

Queen Maud Land, a section of Antarctica, came under Norwegian administration in 1939.

OMAN

Sultanate of Oman
Sultan: Qabus Bin Said (1970)
Area: 82,000 sq mi. (212,380 sq km)
Population (est. 1981): 920,000[1] (growth rate: 3.0%)
Density per square mile: 11.2
Capital (est. 1973): Muscat, 15,000
Largest city (est. 1973): Matrah, 18,000
Monetary unit: Omani rial
Language: Arabic
Religion: Islam
National name: Saltanat Oman
Freedom House classifications: Capitalist-statist
pre-industrial, non-party non-military
Economic summary: Gross national product (1979): $2.6 billion. Average annual growth rate (1970–78): 3.7%. Per capita income: $4,880. Principal agricultural products: dates, alfalfa, onions, wheat, tobacco, bananas. Major industries: petroleum drilling, fishing, construction. Natural resources: oil, asbestos, marble, copper, limestone, chromium, manganese, iron. Exports: oil. Imports: machinery and transport equipment, food, mineral fuels, tobacco. Major trading partners: U.K., U.S., India, Australia, China, Japan.

1. Excluding the Kuria Muria Islands.

Geography. Oman is a 1,000-mile-long (1,609-km) coastal plain at the southeastern tip of the Arabian peninsula lying on the Arabian Sea and the Gulf of Oman. The interior is a plateau. The country is the size of Kansas.

Government. The Sultan of Oman (formerly called Muscat and Oman), an absolute monarch, is assisted by several Personal Advisers, 17 Ministers, and other government officials.
There are no political parties.

History. Although Oman is an independent state under the rule of the Sultan, it has been under British protection since the early 19th century.
Muscat, the capital of the geographical area known as Oman, was occupied by the Portuguese from 1508 to 1648. Then it fell to Persian princes and later was regained by the Sultan.
The Kuria Muria Islands, formerly part of Aden, were given to Oman by the British in 1967.
In a palace coup on July 23, 1970, the Sultan, Sa'id bin Taimur, who had ruled since 1932, was overthrown by his son, who promised to establish a modern government and use new-found wealth to aid the people of this very isolated state.

PAKISTAN

Islamic Republic of Pakistan
President: Gen. Mohammad Zia ul-Haq (1978)
Area: 342,750 sq mi. (877,723 sq km)[1]
Population (est. 1981): 85,000,000 (growth rate: 2.8%)
Density per square mile: 248.0
Capital (1972 census): Islamabad, 77,000
Largest cities (est. 1980 for metropolitan area): Karachi, 5,000,000; (1972 census): Lahore, 2,165,372; Lyallpur, 822,263; Hyderabad, 628,310; Rawalpindi, 615,392
Monetary unit: Pakistan rupee
Principal languages: Urdu (national), English (official), Punjabi, Sindhi, Pashtu, and Baluchi
Religions: Islam, 97%; Hindu, Christian
Freedom House classifications: Capitalist-statist
pre-industrial, non-party military
Economic summary: Gross national product (1979): $21.0 billion. Average annual growth rate (1970–78): 1.5%. Per capita income: $200. Land used for agriculture: 24%; labor force: 54%; principal products: wheat, rice, cotton. Labor force in industry: 18%; major products: cotton textiles, processed foods, tobacco, chemicals, natural gas. Natural resources: natural gas, limited petroleum, iron ore. Exports: raw and manufactured cotton, rice, carpets, leather. Imports: food grains, edible oil, crude oil, machinery, chemicals, transport equipment. Major trading partners: U.S., U.K., Japan, West Germany, Saudi Arabia, China, U.S.S.R.

1. Excluding Kashmir and Jammu.

Geography. Pakistan is situated in the western part of the Indian subcontinent, with Afghanistan and Iran on the west, India on the east, and the Arabian Sea on the south.
Nearly twice the size of California, Pakistan consists of towering mountains, including the Hindu Kush in the west, a desert area in the east, the Punjab plains in the north, and an expanse of alluvial plains. The 1,000-mile-long (1,609 km) Indus River flows through the country from the Kashmir to the Arabian Sea.

Government. On July 5, 1977, martial law returned to Pakistan when Gen. Mohammad Zia ul-Haq, Army Chief of Staff, ousted the civilian government of Prime Minister Zulfikar Ali Bhutto. Zia declared himself Chief Administrator of Martial Law as head of a four-man council. The national and state assemblies were dissolved and all political parties banned, while the Chief Justices of the four states replaced the governors.

History. Pakistan was one of the two original successor states to British India. For almost 25 years following independence in 1947, it consisted of two separate regions. East and West Pakistan, but now comprises only the western sector. It consists of Sind, Baluchistan, the former North-West Frontier Province, western Punjab, the princely state of Bahawalpur, and several other smaller native states.
The British became the dominant power in the region in 1797 following Lord Clive's military victory, but rebellious tribes kept the northwest in turmoil. In the northeast, the formation of the Moslem League in 1906 estranged the Moslems from the Hindus. In 1930, the league, led by Mohammed Ali Jinnah, demanded creation of a Moslem state wherever Moslems were in the majority. He sup-

ported Britain during the war. Afterward, the league received almost a unanimous Moslem vote in 1946 and Britain agreed to the formation of Pakistan as a separate dominion.

Pakistan was proclaimed a republic March 23, 1956. Iskander Mirza, then Governor General, was elected Provisional President and H. S. Suhrawardy became the first non-Moslem League Prime Minister.

In 1958, Mirza surrendered his power to Gen. Ayub Khan, who purged corrupt and inefficient officeholders, broke up the feudal land system, eliminated much of the black market, tax evasion, and hoarding, and revolutionized education. A vote of confidence in 1960 extended Ayub's dictatorial rule for five years and gave him power to write a new Constitution, which went into effect in 1962. In 1969, Gen. Yahya Khan ousted Ayub and took over as President.

The election of 1970—the first direct general balloting in Pakistani history—set the stage for bloody civil war. The Awami League, led by Sheik Mujibur Rahman, swept all National Assembly seats allotted the more populous East Pakistan, while the major West Pakistani party, the People's Party, led by Zulfikar Ali Bhutto, won only 82 seats.

Yahya directed the newly elected Assembly to meet March 1, 1971, and in 120 days write a Constitution. The Assembly never convened. Mujibur called general strikes, which turned bloody, and told East Pakistanis to stop paying taxes to the central government. West Pakistan troops moved in and fighting began. The independent state of Bangladesh, or Bengali nation, was proclaimed March 26, 1971.

The intervention of Indian troops permitted the new state to emerge and brought Yahya down. Bhutto took over and accepted Bangladesh as an independent entity. India appeared to have also gained a permanent partition of the Kashmir along cease-fire lines of 1971. The overall effect was to leave Pakistan a much smaller and weaker nation, no longer able to challenge India seriously.

Diplomatically, 1976 saw the resumption of formal relations between India and Pakistan. At the same time, civilian air traffic between the two nations was restored after an 11-year interruption.

Pakistan's first elections under civilian rule took place in March 1977 and provoked bitter opposition protest when Bhutto's party was declared to have won 155 of the 200 elected seats in the 216-member National Assembly. A rising tide of violent protest and political deadlock led to a military takeover on July 5. Gen. Mohammed Zia ul-Haq became Chief Martial Law Administrator.

Bhutto was tried and convicted for the 1974 murder of a political opponent, and despite worldwide protests was executed on April 4, 1979, touching off riots by his supporters. The execution was another step in the consolidation of power by Zia, who had declared himself President on Sept. 16, 1978, a month after Fazel Elahi Chaudhry left office upon the completion of his 5-year term. Under the Constitution, he was to remain in office until his successor took over, but he refused because of disagreement over certain policies of Zia.

In April 1981, a five-year U.S. military and economic aid program, with $500 million to be delivered in the first year, was pronounced acceptable by Pakistan, which had rejected a two-year, $400-million package offered by the Carter administration as inadequate to meet the Soviet threat. While Zia continued to repress political opposition at home, he became increasingly active in world

affairs. Pakistan took the leadership in Islamic efforts to settle the war between Iran and Iraq and in opposing the Soviet presence in Afghanistan and the Soviet-backed Vietnamese invasion of Cambodia.

PANAMA

Republic of Panama
President: Aristides Royo (1978)
Area: 29,306 sq mi. (75,903 sq km)
Population (est. 1981): 2,000,000 (growth rate: 2.2%) (mestizo, 65%; black, 13%; white, 11%; Indian, 10%)
Density per square mile: 68.2
Capital and largest city (est. 1980): Panama City, 400,000
Monetary unit: Balboa
Language: Spanish (official)
Religion: Roman Catholic, 86%, Protestant
National name: República de Panamá
Freedom House classifications: Capitalist-statist industrial, dominant party
Economic summary: Gross national product (1979): $2.5 billion. Average annual growth rate (1970–78): 0.5%. Per capita income (1977): $1,252. Land used for agriculture: 24%; labor force: 40%; principal products: bananas, corn, sugar, rice, cattle. Labor force in industry: 18%; major industrial products: refined petroleum, sugar. Natural resources: copper (unexploited). Exports: bananas, refined petroleum, sugar, shrimp. Imports: crude oil, capital goods, food. Major trading partners: U.S., West Germany, Venezuela, Saudi Arabia, Ecuador.

Geography. The southernmost of the Central American nations, Panama is south of Costa Rica and north of Colombia. The Panama Canal bisects the isthmus at its narrowest and lowest point, allowing passage from the Caribbean Sea to the Pacific Ocean.

Panama is slightly smaller than South Carolina. It is marked by a chain of volcanic mountains in the west, moderate hills in the interior, and a low range on the east coast. There are extensive forests in the fertile Caribbean area.

Government. Following a military coup in 1968, a two-man junta ruled briefly but was in turn overthrown by Gen. Omar Torrijos, head of the National Guard (army).

In 1972, a new Constitution was approved by a new 505-seat National Assembly of Community Representatives (corregidores), which was created in the first election in five years. The Charter provides for indirect election of the President by the Assembly. The Assembly elected Demetrio Lakas Bahas President but named Torrijos as Head of Government with all civil and military powers for six years. Otherwise the Assembly is more a consultative than legislative body. Torrijos named a legislative committee to assist him in drafting laws.

In the 1978 election, Dr. Aristides Royo was elected president, succeeding Lakas Bahas.

History. Visited by Columbus in 1502 on his fourth voyage and explored by Balboa in 1513, Panama was the principal transshipment point for Spanish treasure and supplies to and from South and Central America in colonial days. In 1821, when Central America revolted against Spain, Panama joined Colombia, which already had declared its independence. For the next 82 years, Panama attempted unsuccessfully to break away from Colombia. After U. S. proposals for canal rights over the narrow isthmus had been rejected by Colombia, Panama proclaimed its independence with U.S. backing in 1903.

For canal rights in perpetuity, the U.S. paid Panama $10 million and agreed to pay $250,000 each year, increased to $430,000 after devaluation of the U.S. dollar in 1933 and was further increased under a revised treaty signed in 1955. In exchange, the U.S. got the Canal Zone—a 10-mile-wide strip across the isthmus—and a considerable degree of influence in Panama's affairs.

In 1968, Dr. Arnulfo Arias was elected President for the third time in three decades. And for the third time, he was thrown out of office by the military. A two-man junta, Col. José M. Pinilla and Col. Bolívar Urrutia, took control. They were ousted by Gen. Omar Torrijos Herrera, who named a new junta, with Demetrio Lakas Bahas as President.

Panama and the U.S. agreed in 1974 to negotiate the eventual reversion of the canal to Panama, despite strongly expressed opposition in the U.S. Congress. The texts of two treaties—one governing the transfer of the canal and the other guaranteeing its neutrality after transfer—were negotiated by August 1977 and were signed by Torrijos and President Carter in Washington on September 7. A Panamanian referendum approved the treaties by more than two thirds on October 23, but further changes were insisted upon by the U.S. Senate.

The principal change was a reservation sponsored by Senator Dennis De Concini, an Arizona Democrat, specifying that despite the neutrality treaty's specification that only Panama shall maintain forces in its territory after transfer of the canal Dec. 31, 1999, the U.S. should have the right to use military force to keep the canal operating if it should become obstructed. After lengthy debate, the Senate approved the neutrality treaty on March 16, 1978, by 68–32 and by the same vote approved the basic treaty governing the transfer on April 18. On June 16, Carter and Torrijos exchanged instruments of ratification in Panama City.

The basic treaty provides an increase from the present $2.3 million a year in royalties to $10 million a year during the transition period, with an additional annual payment of $10 million if it can be obtained from tolls. It also requires the use of more Panamanians as canal employees in the interim and pledges the U.S. not to pursue the development of another canal without the agreement of Panama.

Panama Canal. First conceived by the Spaniards in 1534, when King Charles V of Spain ordered a survey of a waterway across the Isthmus, a construction concession was granted by the Colombian government in 1878 to St. Lucien N. B. Wyse, representing a French company. Two years later, the French Canal Company, inspired by Ferdinand de Lesseps, began construction of what was to have been a sea-level canal. The effort ended in bankruptcy nine years later and the United States ultimately paid the French $40 million for their rights and assets.

The U.S. project, built on territory controlled by the United States, and calling for the creation of an interior lake connected to both oceans by locks, got under way in 1904. Completed in 1914, the Canal is 40.27 miles long and lifts ships 85 feet above sea level through a series of three locks on the Pacific and Atlantic sides. Enlarged in later years, each lock now measures 1,000 feet in length, 110 feet in width, and 40 feet in depth of water.

PAPUA NEW GUINEA

Sovereign: Queen Elizabeth II
Prime Minister: Sir Julius Chan (1980)
Governor General: Sir Tore Lokoloko (1977)
Area: 183,540 sq mi. (475,369 sq km)
Population (est. 1981): 3,250,000 (average annual growth rate, 1971–79: 2.7%)
Density per square mile: 17.7
Capital and largest city (est. 1979): Port Moresby, 120,000
Monetary unit: Kina
Languages: English, Melanesian pidgin, and 717 distinct native languages
Religions: Roman Catholic, 31%; Lutheran, 27%; Anglican, United Church
Member of Commonwealth of Nations
Freedom House classifications: Capitalist pre-industrial, multi-party decentralized
Economic summary: Gross national product (1979): $1.9 billion. Average annual growth rate (1970–78): 0.2%. Labor force in agriculture, including fishing: 85%; principal products: sweet potatoes, coffee, copra, palm oil, cocoa, tea, rubber, cattle. Major industrial products: soap, concrete products, clothing, light fabricated metal products, paint, furniture. Natural resources: copper, gold, silver, timber, tuna. Exports: copper, coffee and cocoa beans, copra, timber. Imports: food, machinery, transport equipment, fuels, chemicals. Major trading partners: Australia, U.K., Japan.

Geography. Papua New Guinea occupies the eastern half of the island of New Guinea, just north of Australia, and many outlying islands. The Indonesian province of Irian Jaya is to the west. To the north and east are the islands of Manus, New Britain, New Ireland, and Bougainville, all part of Papua New Guinea.

Papua New Guinea is about one tenth larger than California. Its mountainous interior has only recently been explored. The high-plateau climate is temperate, in contrast to the tropical climate of the coastal plains. Two major rivers, the Sepik and the Fly, are navigable for shallow-draft vessels.

Government. Papua New Guinea attained independence Sept. 16, 1975, ending a United Nations trusteeship under the administration of Australia. Parliamentary democracy was established by a Constitution that invests power in a single-chamber national legislature.

The Pangu Party, People's Progress Party, and United Party are the largest of half a dozen political parties.

History. The eastern half of New Guinea was first visited by Spanish and Portuguese explorers in the 16th century, but a permanent European presence was not established until 1884, when Germany declared a protectorate over the northern coast and Britain took similar action in the south. Both nations formally annexed their protectorates and, in 1901, Britain transferred its rights to a newly independent Australia. Australian troops invaded German New Guinea in World War I and retained control under a League of Nations mandate that eventually became a United Nations trusteeship, incorporating a territorial government in the southern region, known as Papua.

Australia granted limited home rule in 1951 and, in 1964, organized elections for the first House of Assembly. Autonomy in internal affairs came nine years later.

Just before independence, dissidents on the island of Bougainville, whose copper resources provide the chief foreign earnings for the central government, declared their intention to secede. The central government responded by taking direct control in October 1975, amid warnings from Australia that it would oppose secession. Prime Minister Michael Somare met with pro-secessionists early in 1976 and, after conceding extra powers for a restored provincial government, resolved the dispute.

Somare lost a vote of confidence on March 11, 1980, and was succeeded by Sir Julius Chan, head of the People's Progress Party and former Finance Minister.

PARAGUAY

Republic of Paraguay
President: Gen. Alfredo Stroessner (1954)
Area: 157,047 sq mi. (406,752 sq km)
Population (est. 1981): 3,165,000 (growth rate: 2.4%)
(mestizo, 95%; white, 3%; Indian, 2%)
Density per square mile: 20.2
Capital and largest city (est. 1980): Asunción, 530,000
Monetary unit: Guaraní
Languages: Spanish (official), Guaraní
Religion: Roman Catholic (official)
National name: República del Paraguay
Freedom House classifications: Capitalist-statist
pre-industrial, dominant party
Economic summary: Gross national product (1979): $3.2
billion. Average annual growth rate (1970–78): 4.5%. Per
capita income: $1,035. Labor force in agriculture: 53%;
principal products: oilseeds, cotton, wheat, sweet
potatoes, tobacco, corn, rice, sugar cane. Labor force in
industry: 19%; major products: packed meats, crushed
oilseeds, beverages, textiles, light consumer goods,
cement. Natural resource: timber. Exports: cotton,
oilseeds, meat products, tobacco, timber, coffee,
essential oils. Imports: fuels and lubricants, machinery
and motors, motor vehicles, beverages, tobacco,
foodstuffs. Major trading partners: Brazil, Argentina,
West Germany, U.S., Netherlands, U.K., Japan.

Geography. California-size Paraguay is surrounded by Brazil, Bolivia, and Argentina in south central South America. Eastern Paraguay, between the Paraná and Paraguay Rivers, is upland country with the thickest population settled on the grassy slope that inclines toward the Paraguay River. The greater part of the Chaco region to the west is covered with marshes, lagoons, dense forests, and jungles.

Government. The President is elected by popular vote for five years. The legislature is bicameral, consisting of a Senate of 30 members and a Chamber of Representatives of 60 members. There is also a Council of State, whose members are nominated by the government.

The governing Partido Colorado was further strengthened in 1977 when the Partido Liberal Unido, a merger of the Partido Liberal Radical and Partido Liberal, was declared illegal.

History. In 1526 and again in 1529, Sebastian Cabot explored Paraguay when he sailed up the Paraná and Paraguay Rivers. From 1608 until their expulsion from the Spanish dominions in 1767, the Jesuits maintained an extensive establishment in the south and east of Paraguay. In 1811, Paraguay revolted against Spanish rule and became a nominal republic under two Consuls.

Actually, Paraguay was governed by three dictators during the first 60 years of independence. The third, Francisco López, waged war against Brazil and Argentina in 1864–65, a conflict in which the male population was almost wiped out. A new Constitution in 1870, designed to prevent dictatorships and internal strife, failed to do so, and not until 1912 did a period of comparative economic and political stability begin. The dispute between Paraguay and Bolivia over the Chaco region led to war in 1932 and was finally settled by the 1935 Buenos Aires Peace Conference, which gave most of the Chaco to Paraguay.

After World War II, politics became particularly unstable. Juan Natalicio González was elected President in 1948. Successive revolts on Jan. 30 and Feb. 26, 1949, ousted him and his successor. The leader of the second revolt, Felipe Molas López, was elected President in April but gave way to Federico Chaves. Re-elected in 1953, Chaves was ousted by the army, and Gen. Alfredo Stroessner was elected to complete his term.

Stroessner ruled under a state of siege until 1965, when the dictatorship was relaxed and exiles returned. The Constitution was revised in 1967 to permit Stroessner to be re-elected, and press freedom was briefly restored before the regime again moved to repress opposition.

U.S. companies began exploration for oil in 1974 in the desolate Chaco Boreal section of northwest Paraguay under 40-year contracts that the regime's critics denounced as overgenerous. No oil has been found.

Paraguay was criticized by the U.S. State Department for violation of human rights, but was not one of the countries for which the Carter Administration recommended aid cuts. Amnesty International estimated that about 350 political prisoners were held in Paraguayan jails.

PERU

Republic of Peru
President: Fernando Belaúnde Terry (1980)
Premier: Manuel Ulloa (1980)
Area: 496,222 sq mi. (1,285,216 sq km)
Population (1981): 18,300,000 (growth rate: 2.6%) (white
and mestizo, 52%; Indian, 46%)
Density per square mile: 36.9
Capital: Lima
Largest cities (est. 1979 for metropolitan area): Lima,
4,900,000; (est. 1978): Arequipa, 410,000; Trujillo,
350,000; Chiclayo, 260,000; Piura, 165,000; Cuzco, 150,000
Monetary unit: Sol
Languages: Spanish, Quéchua
Religion: Roman Catholic
National name: República del Perú
Freedom House classifications: Capitalist-statist
pre-industrial, multi-party centralized
Economic summary: Gross national product (1979): $12.6
billion. Average annual growth rate (1970–78): 0.3%. Per
capita income (1980): $796. Land used for agriculture:
2%; labor force: 42%; principal products: corn, sugar,
cotton, coffee, wool. Labor force in industry: 13%; major
products: processed minerals, fish meal, refined
petroleum, textiles. Natural resources: minerals and
metals, fish, petroleum, timber. Exports: copper, fish
products, cotton, sugar, coffee, lead, silver, zinc, wool,
iron ore. Imports: machinery, cereals, chemicals,
pharmaceuticals. Major trading partners: U.S., Japan,
Western European, and Latin American countries.

Geography. Peru, in western South America, extends for nearly 1,500 miles (2,414 km) along the Pacific Ocean. Colombia and Ecuador are to the north, Brazil and Bolivia to the east, and Chile to the south.

Five sixths the size of Alaska, Peru is divided by the Andes Mountains into three sharply differentiated zones. To the west is the coastline, much of it arid, extending 50 to 100 miles (80 to 160 km) inland. The mountain area, with peaks over 20,000 feet (6,096 m), lofty plateaus, and deep valleys, lies centrally. Beyond the mountains to the east is the heavily forested slope leading to the Amazonian plains.

Government. The President, elected by universal suffrage for a five-year term, holds executive power. A Senate of 60 members and a Chamber of Deputies of 180 members, both elected for five-year terms, share legislative power.

The major political parties are: Acción Popular (98 of 180 seats in the Chamber and 26 of 60 seats in the Senate), led by President Fernando Belaúnde Terry; Partido Popular Cristiano (10 Chamber seats and 6 Senate seats), led by Luis Bedoya Reyes; and the opposition Partido Aprista Peruano (58 Chamber seats and 18 Senate seats), led by Luis Alberto Sanchez. The Partido Popular Cristiano is allied with Belaúnde.

History. Peru was once part of the great Incan empire and later the major vice-royalty of Spanish South America. It was conquered in 1531–33 by Francisco Pizarro. On July 28, 1821, Peru proclaimed its independence, but the Spanish were not finally defeated until 1824. For a hundred years thereafter, revolutions were frequent, and a new war was fought with Spain in 1864–66.

Peru emerged from 20 years of dictatorship in 1945 with the inauguration of President José Luis Bustamante y Rivero after the first free election in many decades. But he served for only three years and was succeeded in turn by Gen. Manuel A. Odria, Manuel Prado y Ugarteche, and Fernando Belaunde Terry. On Oct. 3, 1968, Belaunde was overthrown by Gen. Juan Velasco Alvarado.

Velasco nationalized the nation's second biggest bank and turned two large newspapers over to Marxists in 1970, but he also allowed a new agreement with a copper-mining consortium of four American firms.

On May 31, 1970, the country suffered the hemisphere's worst natural disaster, an earthquake which, together with a mud slide it caused, took an estimated 50,000 lives.

The World Bank granted Peru $470 million in credits in 1973, which appeared to end a boycott by international financial institutions in which the U.S. has a strong influence. American copper and fishing firms were seized in 1974, but compensation was paid. Peru also became in 1974 the first nation in the Western Hemisphere to receive Soviet military advisers.

On Aug. 29, 1975, Velasco was replaced in a bloodless coup by his Premier, Gen. Francisco Morales Bermúdez. To meet International Monetary Fund requirements for the extension of credit, Morales decreed a severe economic austerity program in 1977, touching off student and leftist demonstrations. Even stiffer measures, ranging from 50% to 100% increases in the prices of essentials, were ordered in 1978.

Fulfilling a pledge to restore civilian government, Morales scheduled elections for May 18, 1980, in which Belaúnde Terry, the last civilian President, won 43% of the vote in a field of 15 candidates. Allied with the small Partido Popular Cristiano, Belaúnde Terry's Acción Popular party was assured of a parliamentary majority. In one of his first moves, the new President returned to private ownership newspapers that had been seized under the Morales regime.

THE PHILIPPINES

Republic of the Philippines
President (1965): Ferdinand E. Marcos
Prime Minister: César Virata (1981)
Area: 115,707 sq mi. (299,681 sq km)
Population (est. 1981): 49,000,000 (growth rate: 2.5%)
Density per square mile: 423.5
Capital: Quezon City
Largest cities (est. 1977 for metropolitan area): Manila, 7,500,000 (est. 1975 by U.N.): Quezon City, 994,700; Davao, 515,500; Cebu, 418,500
Monetary unit: Peso
Languages: Pilipino, English, Spanish; dialects: Tagalog, Visayan
Religions: Roman Catholic, 85%; Islam, 4%; Aglipayan (Independent Philippine Christian), 4%; Protestant, 3%
National name: Republika ng Pilipinas
Freedom House classifications: Capitalist pre-industrial, one-party dominant-party
Economic summary: Gross national product (1979): $28.1 billion. Average annual growth rate (1970–78): 3.7%. Per capita income (1980): $765. Land used for agriculture: 26%; labor force: 47%; principal products: rice, corn, coconuts, sugar cane, bananas, tobacco. Labor force in industry: 12%; major products: processed agricultural products, textiles, chemicals and chemical products. Natural resources: forests, metallic and non-metallic minerals. Exports: coconut products, sugar, logs and lumber, copper concentrates, bananas, garments, nickel. Imports: petroleum, industrial equipment, wheat. Major trading partners: U.S., Japan.

Geography. The Philippine Islands are an archipelago of over 7,000 islands lying about 500 miles (805 km) off the southeast coast of Asia. The overall land area is comparable to that of Arizona. The northernmost island, Y'Ami, is 65 miles (105 km) from Taiwan, while the southernmost, Saluag, is 40 miles (64 km) east of Borneo.

Only about 7% of the islands are larger than one square mile, and only one third have names. The largest are Luzon in the north (40,420 sq mi.; 04,687 sq km), Mindanao in the south (36,537 sq mi.; 94,631 sq km), Samar (5,124 sq mi.; 13,271 sq km), Negros (4,903 sq mi.; 12,699 sq km), and Palawan (4,550 sq km).

The islands are of volcanic origin, with the larger ones crossed by mountain ranges. The highest peak is Mount Apo (9,690 ft; 2,954 m) on Mindanao.

Government. President Ferdinand E. Marcos proclaimed a new Constitution in 1973, replacing the previous presidential style of government with a parliamentary system. The president became the symbolic head of state and the prime minister the head of government, with Marcos holding both posts. Marcos has ruled by decree since Sept. 21, 1972, and the new Constitution dissolved the previous legislature. A new National Assembly of 186 elected and 31 appointed members was chosen April 7, 1978. Its powers are limited, within the framework of what Marcos has called "constitutional authoritarianism."

History. Fernando Magellan, the Portuguese navigator in the service of Spain, discovered the Philippines in 1521. Twenty-one years later, a Spanish exploration party named the group of islands in honor of Price Philip, later Philip II of Spain. Spain retained possession of the islands for the next 350 years.

The Philippines were ceded to the U.S. in 1899 by the Treaty of Paris after the Spanish-American War. Meanwhile, the Filipinos, led by Emilio Aguinaldo, had declared their independence. They continued guerrilla warfare against U.S. troops until the capture of Aguinaldo in 1901. By 1902, peace was established except among the Moros.

The first U.S. civilian Governor-General was William Howard Taft (1901–04). The Jones Law (1916) provided for the establishment of a Philippine Legislature composed of an elective Senate and House of Representatives. The Tydings-McDuffie Act (1934) provided for a transitional period until 1946, at which time the Philippines would become completely independent.

Under a Constitution approved by the people of the Philippines in 1935, the Commonwealth of the Philippines came into being, with Manuel Quezon y Molina as president.

On Dec. 8, 1941, the Philippines were invaded by Japanese troops. Following the fall of Bataan and Corregidor, Quezon established a government-in-exile, which he headed until his death in 1944. He was succeeded by Vice President Sergio Osmeña.

U.S. forces led by Gen. Douglas MacArthur reinvaded the Philippines in October 1944 and, after the liberation of Manila in February 1945, Osmeña re-established the government.

The Philippines achieved full independence on July 4, 1946. Manuel A. Roxas y Acuña was elected first president. Subsequent presidents have been Elpidio Quirino (1948–53), Ramón Magsaysay (1953–57). Carlos P. García (1957–61), Diosdado Macapagal (1961–65), and Ferdinand E. Marcos (since Dec. 30, 1965).

Marcos became the first president in Philippine history to win re-election in 1969, when he overwhelmingly defeated Sergio Osmeña, Jr., with campaign promises to become less dependent on the U.S. and to establish ties with Communist countries. The campaign violence led to 59 deaths. After his inauguration, the worst peacetime riots in Philippine history occurred when a student-led demonstration tried to storm the presidential palace, with 5 dead and 157 injured, to protest government corruption.

Political, civil, and religious unrest was responsible for the deaths of almost 500 persons in 1971, and disastrous month-long rains that caused enormous flooding added to the toll in 1972. In September 1972, Marcos declared martial law and arrested hundreds of political opponents, journalists, and leftists.

Nearly 8,000 persons died Aug. 17, 1976, when an earthquake measuring 8 on the Richter scale hit Mindanao and other southern islands. The disaster temporarily quelled a rebellion by the Moslem majority in Mindanao, but fighting resumed until a truce was reached in December. Rebel representatives and Manila officials signed an agreement in Tripoli in 1977, providing a degree of autonomy for the Moslem region.

The Philippines was one of six nations criticized by the U.S. State Department for human-rights violations in a report made public in 1977, although the department recommended continuing aid because of the importance of U.S. bases in the Philippines. Marcos at first declared he would reject any aid and threatened to close the bases but later softened, saying they could remain if the U.S. pledged that the bases would be used to defend the Philippines in the event of an attack. He also announced that he would phase out the military tribunals he established in 1972 and in two months freed about 1,000 of 4,774 prisoners being held for military trial.

Political restraints were eased for the legislative elections of 1978. The suppressed Liberal Party and other opposition groups formed the People's Force Party and contested the 21 seats assigned to Manila. Amid charges of fraud, Marcos' New Society Movement won all 21. Marcos freed many political prisoners before his inauguration as prime minister on June 12 and pledged to move toward "making democracy real", although he retained his powers under martial law.

Marcos, who had freed the last of the national leaders still in detention, former Senator Benigno S. Aquino, Jr., in 1980 and permitted him to go to the United States, ended eight years of martial law on January 17, 1981. On April 7, a plebiscite approved changes to the 1973 Constitution establishing a ministerial government and authorizing re-election of the President. On June 16, Marcos won a second six-year term with 86% of the vote as most opposition parties boycotted the election.

POLAND

Polish People's Republic
President of the Council of State: Henryk Jablonski (1972)
Premier: Gen Wojciech Jaruzelski (1981)
Area: 120,359 sq mi. (311,730 sq km)
Population (est. 1981): 35,900,000 (growth rate: 1.0%)
Density per square mile: 298.3
Capital: Warsaw
Largest cities (est. 1980): Warsaw, 1,576,600; Lodz, 830,800; Krakow, 706,100; Wroclaw, 609,100; Poznan, 545,600; Gdansk, 443,200; Szczecin, 388,000; Katowice, 351,300
Monetary unit: Zloty
Language: Polish (more than 90%)
Religions: Roman Catholic, Greek Orthodox, Protestant, Jewish
National name: Polska Rzeczpospolita Ludowa
Freedom House classifications: Capitalist-socialist industrial, one-party communist
Economic summary: Gross national product (1979): $135.5 billion. Average annual growth rate (1970–78): 5.9%. Per capita income: $2,740. Labor force in agriculture: 32%; principal products: grains, sugar beets, potatoes, hogs and other livestock. Labor force in industry: 26%; major products: iron and steel, chemicals, textiles, processed foods, transport equipment. Natural resources: coal, sulfur, copper, natural gas. Exports: fuels, machinery and equipment, agricultural products. Imports: oil, iron ore, raw materials, grain. Major trading partners: Communist bloc countries, U.K., Italy, U.S., West Germany, France.

Geography. Poland, a country the size of New Mexico in north central Europe, borders on East Germany to the west, Czechoslovakia to the south, and the U.S.S.R. to the east. In the north is the Baltic Sea.

Most of the country is a plain with no natural boundaries except the Carpathian Mountains in the south and the Oder and Neisse Rivers in the east. Other major rivers, which are important to commerce, are the Vistula, Warta, and Bug.

Government. The 1952 Constitution describes Poland as a people's republic. The supreme organ of state authority is the Sejm (Parliament), which is composed of 460 members elected for four years.

The major political parties are the Polish United Workers' (Communist) Party (255 of 460 seats in the Sejm), led by First Secretary Stanislaw Kania; United Peasant Party (117 seats), led by Stefan Ignar; Democratic Party (39 seats), led by Edward Kowalczyk; non-party members and Catholic organizations (49 seats).

History. Little of certainty is known about Polish history before the 11th century, when King Boleslaus I (the Brave) ruled over Bohemia, Saxony, and Moravia. Mongol invasions in 1241 and 1259 were repelled. Meanwhile, the Teutonic knights were erecting in Prussia a state that included part of Poland and barred the latter's access to the Baltic. The knights were defeated by Wladislaus II at Tannenberg in 1410 and became Polish vassals, and Poland regained a Baltic shoreline. Poland reached the peak of power between the 14th and 16th centuries, scoring military successes against the Russians and Turks. In 1683, John III (John Sobieski) turned back the Turkish tide at Vienna.

These successes did not halt the process of decline that resulted from the lack of strong central authority, and Prussia, Russia, and Austria were able to carry out a first partition of the country in 1772, a second in 1792, and a third in 1795–96. For more than a century thereafter, there was no Polish state, but the Poles never ceased their efforts to regain their independence.

The independence of Poland was formally proclaimed in November 1918, and Marshal Josef Pilsudski was made Chief of State. In 1919, Ignace Paderewski, the famous pianist and patriot, became the first premier. In 1926, Pilsudski seized complete power in a coup and ruled the country dictatorially until his death on May 12, 1935, when he was succeeded by Marshal Edward Smigly-Rydz.

Despite a 10-year nonaggression pact signed with Germany in 1934, Hitler attacked Poland on Sept. 1, 1939. Russian troops invaded from the east on September 17, and on September 28 a German-Russian agreement was signed dividing Poland between Russia and Germany. Wladyslaw Raczkiewicz formed a government-in-exile in France with Gen. Wladyslaw Sikorski as premier. This government moved to London after France's defeat in 1940.

All of Poland was occupied by Germany after the Nazi attack on the U.S.S.R. in June 1941. On July 30, 1941, the government-in-exile signed an agreement with the U.S.S.R. in which the latter voided all German-Soviet agreements effected after Sept. 1, 1939.

The legal Polish government soon fell out with the Russians, however, and, in 1944, a Communist-dominated Polish Committee of National Liberation received Soviet recognition. Moving to Lublin after that city's liberation, it proclaimed itself the Provisional Government of Poland. Some former members of the Polish government in London joined with the Lublin government to form the Polish Government of National Unity, which Britain and the U.S. recognized.

On Aug. 2, 1945, in Berlin, President Harry S. Truman, Joseph Stalin and Prime Minister Clement Attlee of Britain established a new *de facto* western frontier for Poland along the Oder and Neisse Rivers. (The border was finally agreed to by West Germany in a nonaggression pact signed Dec. 7, 1970.) On Aug. 16, 1945, the U.S.S.R. and Poland signed a treaty delimiting the Soviet-Polish frontier. Under these agreements, Poland was shifted westward. In the east it lost 69,860 square miles (180,934 sq km) with 10,772,000 inhabitants; in the west it gained (subject to final peace-conference approval) 38,986 square miles (100,973 sq km) with a prewar population of 8,621,000.

In 1946, a unicameral Parliament was established by referendum. A limited legal opposition was countenanced at first. Then, in 1947, the government bloc won a huge majority in government-controlled elections and after much fighting the underground opposition was suppressed and the Sovietization of Poland begun, with Soviet Marshal Konstantin Rokossovsky as Defense Minister and army commander.

In 1952, a Constitution was promulgated making Poland a "people's democracy" of the Soviet type. In 1955, Poland, which had joined the Council for Economic Mutual Assistance in 1949, became a member of the Warsaw Treaty Organization, and its foreign policy became identical with that of the U.S.S.R. The government undertook persecution of the Roman Catholic Church as one of the remaining source of opposition and in 1953 arrested the primate, Stefan Cardinal Wyszynski. But in June 28–30, 1956, worker and student riots in Poznan forced reconsideration of the repression.

Wladyslaw Gomulka was elected leader of the United Workers (Communist) Party in 1956. He denounced the Stalinist terror, ousted many Stalinists, relieved Rokossovsky, freed Wyszynski, and improved relations with the church. Most collective farms were dissolved, and the press became freer.

Much as the Poznan bread riots of 1956 brought Gomulka to power, so pre-Christmas rioting in 1970 in Gdansk and other Baltic coastal towns caused Gomulka to fall and elevated Edward Gierek to the key post of party boss. Cause of the worker riots, in which at least 45 and probably over 200 died when police and army troops crushed the protest, was steep price rises on meat and other foods. Significantly, no students or intellectuals were involved.

Serious resistance to increased food prices again brought rioting in Polish cities in the summer of 1976 after the government announced a new schedule of prices.

As a result of the riots, the government in 1977 revised its economic goals to put more emphasis on production of consumer goods and reduced foreign borrowing for capital investment, slowing industrial development. Indicative of a growing force to ease government policies, a group of professionals formed the Movement for the Defense of Human and Civil Rights to cooperate with the Workers Defense Committee and to seek freedom of expression for all political groups.

An event of profound importance to Poland's 90% Catholic population was the election in October 1978 of Karol Cardinal Wojtila of Krakow as Pope John Paul II. His visit to his homeland from June 2 to June 11, 1979, the first papal journey to a Marxist state, met with nervous apprehension from the government and an outpouring of emotion from not only Polish Catholics but also those from neighboring Communist countries who were able to attend events.

A strike that began in shipyards and spread to other industries in August 1980 produced a stunning victory for workers on Aug. 31 when the economically hard-pressed government accepted for the first time in a Marxist state the right of workers to organize in independent unions. In addition, the strikers won curbs on media censorship and the privileges of Communist Party members over ordinary workers in state enterprises. The strike was supported financially by Western unions and vocally by Pope John Paul II.

The strike also led to major changes in Polish leadership. Edward Babuich, who became Premier early in 1980, was replaced by Jozef Pinkowski, and Edward Gierek, longtime Communist Party head, was ousted in favor of Stanislaw Kania.

Led by Solidarity, a free union founded by Lech Walesa, workers launched a drive for liberty and improved conditions. A national strike for a five-day week in January 1981 led to the dismissal of Premier Pinkowski and the naming of the fourth Premier in less than a year, Gen. Wojciech Jaruzelski. He and Kania defended workers' gains against Soviet and Polish hardline criticism, but warned of the deteriorating economy, which required Western creditors in April to defer repayment of $2.6 billion of $27 billion in foreign debt. In July, for the first time within the Soviet bloc, an emergency party congress voted by secret ballot and confirmed Kania and moderate leaders, rejecting right-wing, pro-Soviet members of the Politburo.

PORTUGAL

Portuguese Republic
President: Gen. António Ramalho Eanes (1976)
Premier: Francisco Pinto Balsemão (1980)
Area: 35,340 sq mi. (91,531 sq km)
Population (est. 1981): 10,000,000 (growth rate: 0.5%)
Density per square mile: 283.0
Capital: Lisbon
Largest cities (est. 1979): Lisbon, 861,500; (est. 1975 by U.N.): Opporto, 335,700
Monetary unit: Escudo
Language: Portuguese
Religion: Roman Catholic
National name: República Portuguesa
Freedom House classifications: Capitalist-socialist industrial, multi-party centralized
Economic summary: Gross national product (1979): $21.3 billion. Average annual growth rate (1970–78): 2.0%. Land used for agriculture: 48%; labor force: 31%; principal products: grains, potatoes, olives, wine grapes. Labor force in industry: 35%; major products: textiles, footwear, wood pulp, paper, cork, metal products, refined oil, chemicals, canned fish, wine. Natural resources: fish, cork, tungsten ore. Exports: cotton, textiles, cork and cork products, canned fish, wine, timber and timber products, resin. Imports: petroleum, cotton, industrial machinery, iron and steel, chemicals. Major trading partners: U.K., West Germany, U.S., France, Italy.

Geography. Portugal occupies the western part of the Iberian Peninsula, bordering on the Atlantic Ocean to the west and Spain to the north and east. It is slightly smaller than Indiana.

The country is crossed by many small rivers, and also by three large ones that rise in Spain, flow into the Atlantic, and divide the country into three geographic areas. The Minho (Miño in Spain) River, part of the northern boundary, cuts through a mountainous area that extends south to the vicinity of the Douro (Duero) River. South of the Douro, the mountains slope to the plains about the Tagus

(Tejo) River. The remaining division is the southern one of Alentejo.

The Azores, stretching over 340 miles (547 km) in the Atlantic, consist of nine islands divided into three groups, with a total area of 924 square miles (2,393 sq km). The nearest continental land is Cape da Roca, Portugal, about 900 miles (1,448 km) to the east. The Azores are an important station on Atlantic air routes, and Britain and the U.S. established air bases there during World War II.

Madeira, consisting of two inhabited islands, Madeira and Porto Santo, and two groups of uninhabited islands, lies in the Atlantic about 535 miles (861 km) southwest of Lisbon.

Government. A new Constitution, adopted in April 1976, provides for popular election of a President for a five-year term and for a legislature, the Assembly of the Republic, for four years.

The major political parties are the Democratic Alliance (136 of 250 seats in the Assembly), led by Premier Francisco Pinto Balsemão; Socialist Party (73 seats), led by former Premier Mário Soares, and Communist Party (40 seats), led by Alvaro Cunhal.

History. Portugal was a part of Spain until it won its independence in the middle of the 12th century. King John I (1385–1433) unified his country at the expense of the Castilians and the Moors of Morocco. The expansion of Portugal was brilliantly coordinated by John's son, Prince Henry the Navigator. In 1488, Bartolomew Diaz reached the Cape of Good Hope, proving that the Far East was accessible by sea. In 1498, Vasco da Gama reached the west coast of India. By the middle of the 16th century, the Portuguese Empire included West and East Africa, Brazil, Persia, Indochina, and Malaya.

In 1581, Philip II of Spain invaded Portugal and held it captive for 60 years. There followed a catastrophic decline of Portuguese commerce. Courageous and shrewd explorers, the Portuguese proved to be inefficient and corrupt colonizers. By the time the Portuguese dynasty was restored in 1640, Dutch, English, and French competitors began to seize the lion's share of the world's colonies and commerce. Portugal retained Angola and Mozambique in Africa, and Brazil (until 1822).

In the first half of the 19th century, Portugal's political history was distinguished by dynasty quarrels and factional strife. The corrupt King Carlos, who ascended the throne in 1889, made João Franco the Premier with dictatorial power in 1906. In 1908, Carlos and his heir were shot dead on the streets of Lisbon. The new King, Manoel II, was driven from the throne in the Revolution of 1910. Portugal was proclaimed a republic with a system modeled upon that of France.

Traditionally friendly to Britain, Portugal fought in World War I on the Allied side in Africa as well as on the Western Front. Weak postwar governments and a revolution in 1926 brought Antonio Oliveira Salazar to power. He kept Portugal neutral in World War II but gave the Allies naval and air bases after 1943.

Portugal lost the tiny remnants of its Indian empire—Goa, Daman, and Diu—to Indian military occupation in 1961, the year an insurrection broke out in Angola. For the next 13 years, Salazar, who died in 1970 after two years in a coma, and his successor, Marcello Caetano, fought independence movements amid growing world criticism. Leftists in the armed forces, weary of a losing battle, launched the "Happy Revolution" of April 25, 1974. They installed Gen. António de Spínola as Provisional President with promises of peace in

Africa and reforms at home.

Spínola's moderate left Cabinet failed to satisfy the military leadership, who named Col. Vasco dos Santos Gonçalves as Premier on July 14. After Spínola's resignation on Sept. 30, Gen. Francisco da Costa Gomez, Chief of Staff of the armed forces, became President of an increasingly leftist regime. But conservatism in the country outside Lisbon manifested itself in the 1975 election of delegates to draft a new Constitution, as Socialists led with 38% of the delegates, Popular Democrats captured 28%, and the Communists trailed with only 12.5%.

Anti-Communist violence in rural areas and pressure from non-Communists in the government and military forced Gonçalves out on Aug. 29, 1975, and he was replaced by the more moderate Vice Adm. José Pinheiro. Elections under a new Constitution in 1976 gave Gen. António Ramalho Eanes, Army Chief of Staff, a landslide victory even though he campaigned for a program of economic austerity. With Mário Soares as Premier, tough economic policies slowed inflation but proved unpopular with legislators, who forced Soares out on July 27, 1978.

Pursuit of economic austerity measures brought down Soares' centrist successor, Carlos Alberto Mota Pinto, less than a year later, giving Portugal its first woman Premier, Maria Lurdes Pintassilgo, who acted as caretaker until the victory of Francisco Manoel Lumbrales de Sá Carneiro's Democratic Alliance on Dec. 2, 1979. Sá Carneiro's coalition of his own Social Democratic Party, the Christian Democrats and the small Popular Monarchist Party won a majority of three seats, the first absolute majority for a governing party since the 1974 revolution.

On Dec. 4, 1980, Sá Carneiro, who had increased his coalition's majority in parliamentary elections in October, died in an air crash while campaigning against the re-election of President Eanes. Three days later, Eanes won a second four-year term with 57% of the popular vote, a victory for the left-leaning general that countered the rightward trend led by Sá Carneiro.

Portuguese Overseas Territory

After the April 1974 revolution, the military junta moved to grant independence to the territories, beginning with Portuguese Guinea in September 1974, which became the Republic of Guinea-Bissau.

Mozambique and Angola followed, leaving only Portuguese Timor and Macao of the former Empire. Despite Lisbon's objections, Indonesia annexed Timor.

MACAO

Status: Territory
Governor: Gen. Nuno Viriato Tavares de Melo Egídio (1978)
Area: 6 sq mi. (15.5 sq km)
Population (est. 1981): 280,000 (growth rate: 2.1%)
Capital (1970 census): Macao, 241,413
Monetary unit: Patacá
Economic summary: Gross national product (1979): $540 million. Annual average growth rate (1970–78): 16%. Labor force in agriculture: 5%; principal products: rice and vegetables; Labor force in industry: 30%; major products: textiles, fireworks, fish products. Exports: textiles and clothing, manufactured goods, foodstuffs. Imports: consumer goods, foodstuffs. Major trading partners: Hong Kong, China, U.S., West Germany, France.

Macao comprises the peninsula of Macao and the two small islands of Taipa and Colôane on the South China coast, about 35 miles (53 km) from Hong Kong. Established by the Portuguese in 1557, it is the oldest European outpost in the China trade, but Portugal's sovereign rights to the port were not recognized by China until 1887, and its boundaries are still not delimited. The port has been eclipsed in importance by Hong Kong, but it is still a busy distribution center and also has an important fishing industry. It is notorious for its opium trade and gambling houses. Most of the population is Chinese.

QATAR

State of Qatar
Ruler: Sheik Khalifa bin Hamad al-Thani (1972)
Area: 4,000 sq mi. (19,360 sq km)
Population (est. 1981): 230,000 (growth rate: 4.4%)
Density per square mile: 57.5
Capital (est. 1979): Doha, 180,000
Monetary unit: Qatari riyal
Language: Arabic
Religion: Islam
Freedom House classifications: Capitalist-statist industrial, non-party non-military
Economic summary: Gross national product (1979): $3.8 billion. Average annual growth rate (1970–78): −2.5%. Major industrial product: oil. Natural resource: oil. Export: oil. Major trading partners: U.K., U.S., France, Japan, West Germany.

Geography. Qatar occupies a small peninsula that extends into the Persian Gulf from the east side of the Arabian Peninsula. Saudi Arabia is to the west and the United Arab Emirates to the south. The country is mainly barren.

Government. Qatar, one of the Persian Gulf sheikdoms, lies between Bahrain and United Arab Emirates. For a long time, it was under Turkish protection, but in 1916, the sultan accepted British protection. After the discovery of oil in the 1940s and its exploitation in the 1950s and 1960s, political unrest spread to the sheikdoms. Qatar declared its independence in 1971. The next year the current Sheik, Khalifa bin Hamad al-Thani, ousted his cousin in a bloodless coup.

ROMANIA

Socialist Republic of Romania
President: Nicolae Ceausescu (1967)
Premier: Ilie Verdet (1979)
Area: 91,700 sq mi. (237,500 sq km)
Population (est. 1981): 22,500,000 (Romanian, 88%; Hungarian, 8%) (growth rate: 0.7%)
Density per square mile: 245.4
Capital: Bucharest
Largest cities (est. 1977 by U.N.): Bucharest, 1,807,000; Timisoara, 268,800; Iasi, 265,000; Cluj-Napoca, 262,400; Brasov, 257,100; Constanta, 256,900; Galati, 239,300; Craiova, 222,400
Monetary unit: Leu
Languages: Romanian, Hungarian, Serbian, German, Turkish
Religions: Romanian Orthodox, 70%; Greek Orthodox, 10%
National name: Republica Socialista România
Freedom House classifications: Socialist industrial,

one-party communist
Economic summary: Gross national product (1979): $41.8 billion. Average annual growth rate (1970–78): 9.6%. Per capita income: $2,360. Land used for agriculture: 63%; labor force: 36%; principal products: corn, wheat, oil seeds, potatoes. Labor force in industry: 26%; major products: power, mining, forestry, metal production and processing, chemicals, food processing, textiles. Natural resources: oil, timber, natural gas, coal. Exports: foodstuffs, lumber, fuel, manufactures. Imports: machinery, rolled steel, iron ore, coke and coking coal, minerals. Major trading partners: U.S.S.R., East Germany, West Germany.

Geography. A country in southeastern Europe slightly smaller than Oregon, Romania is bordered on the west by Hungary and Yugoslavia, on the north and east by the U.S.S.R., on the east by the Black Sea, and on the south by Bulgaria.

The Carpathian Mountains divide Romania's upper half from north to south and connect near the center of the country with the Transylvanian Alps, running east and west.

North and west of these ranges lies the Transylvanian plateau, and to the south and east are the plains of Moldavia and Walachia. In its last 190 miles (306 km), the Danube River flows through Romania only. It enters the Black Sea in northern Dobruja, just south of the border with the Soviet Union.

Government. The supreme body of state power and the sole legislative body is the Grand National Assembly, with 465 members elected for five-year terms. It elects a State Council, which provides for the continuity of state power and settles problems between sessions of the Assembly. The supreme executive and administrative body is the Council of Ministers elected by the Assembly.

The Communist Party, led by Secretary General Nicolae Ceausescu, is the only political party.

History. Most of Romania was the Roman province of Dacia from about A.D. 100 to 275. From the 6th to the 12th century, wave after wave of barbarian conquerors—Vlachs, Bulgars, and others—passed over the area. By the 15th century, the main Romanian principalities of Moldavia and Walachia had become satellites within the Ottoman Empire, although they retained much independence. After the Russo-Turkish War of 1828–29, they became Russian protectorates. In 1848, the Romanians rebelled but were suppressed by the Russians. The nation became a kingdom in 1881 after the Congress of Berlin.

King Ferdinand ascended the throne in 1914. At the start of World War I, Romania proclaimed its neutrality, but later joined the Allied side and in 1916 declared war on the Central Powers. The armistice of Nov. 11, 1918, gave Romania vast territories from Russia and the Austro-Hungarian Empire.

The gains of World War I, making Romania the largest Balkan state, included Bessarabia, Transylvania, and Bukovina. The Banat, a Hungarian area, was divided with Yugoslavia.

In 1925, Crown Prince Carol renounced his rights to the throne, and when King Ferdinand died in 1927, Carol's son, Michael (Mihai) became King under a regency. However, Carol returned from exile in 1930, was crowned King Carol II, and gradually became a powerful political force in the country. In 1938, he abolished the democratic Constitution of 1923.

In 1940, the country was reorganized along Fascist lines, and the Fascist Iron Guard became the nucleus of the new totalitarian party. On June 27, the Soviet Union occupied Bessarabia and northern Bukovina. By the Axis-dictated Vienna Award of 1940, two fifths of Transylvania went to Hungary, after which Carol dissolved Parliament and granted the new premier, Ion Antonescu, full power. He abdicated and again went into exile.

Romania subsequently signed the Axis Pact on Nov. 23, 1940, and the following June joined in Germany's attack on the Soviet Union, reoccupying Bessarabia. Following the invasion of Romania by the Red Army in August 1944, King Michael led a coup that ousted the Antonescu government. An armistice with the Soviet Union was signed in Moscow on Sept. 12, 1944.

A Communist-dominated government bloc won elections in 1946, Michael abdicated on Dec. 30, 1947, and Romania became a "people's republic." In 1955, Romania joined the Warsaw Treaty Organization and the United Nations. A decade later, with the adoption of a new Constitution emphasizing national autonomy, and especially after Nicolae Ceausescu came to power in 1967, Bucharest became an increasingly dissident voice in the Soviet bloc.

Alone of the Warsaw Pact members, Romania maintained ties with China and Albania after the two broke with Moscow. Almost as annoying to the Soviet leadership was Ceausescu's continuing of ties with Israel, a relationship that made possible the secret preparations for the visit to Israel by Egypt's President Anwar el-Sadat in November 1977. Ceausescu also exchanged cultural and scientific accords with Washington in 1974 and visited the United States in 1978. In a New Year's Day speech, 1980, the Romanian leader became the first and only Eastern European voice to protest the Soviet invasion of Afghanistan.

Despite his liberal international record, at home Ceausescu has harshly suppressed dissidents calling for freedom of expression in the wake of the Helsinki agreements.

RWANDA

Republic of Rwanda
President: Maj. Gen. Juvénal Habyarimana (1973)
Area: 10,169 sq mi. (26,338 sq km)
Population (est. 1981): 5,200,000 (growth rate: 3.2%)
Density per square mile: 511.4
Capital and largest city (1978 census): Kigali, 118,000
Monetary unit: Rwanda franc
Languages: Kinyarwanda and French
Religions: Roman Catholic, 45%; Protestant, 9%; Animist
Freedom House classifications: Capitalist-socialist pre-industrial, one-party nationalist
Economic summary: Gross national product (1979): $970 million. Average annual growth rate (1970–78): 1.4%. Per capita income: $106. Land used for agriculture: 33%; labor force: 95%; principal products: coffee, tea, pyrethrum, beans, potatoes. Labor force in industry: less than 5%; major products: processed foods, light consumer goods, minerals. Natural resources: cassiterite, wolfram. Exports: cassiterite, tea, pyrethrum, wolfram. Imports: textiles, foodstuffs, machinery, and equipment. Major trading partners: Belgium, West Germany, U.S., Kenya.

Geography. Rwanda, in east central Africa, is surrounded by Zaire, Uganda, Tanzania, and Burundi.

It is slightly smaller than Maryland.

Steep mountains and deep valleys cover most of the country. Lake Kivu in the northwest, at an altitude of 4,829 feet (1,472 m) is the highest lake in Africa. Extending south of it are the Virunga Mountains, which include Volcan Karisimbi (14,187 ft.; 4,324 m), Rwanda's highest point.

Government. Grégoire Kayibanda was President from 1962 until he was overthrown in a bloodless coup on July 5, 1973, by the military led by Gen. Juvénal Habyarimana.

In a plebiscite in December 1978, Habyarimana was elected to a five-year term as president and a new constitution adopted that provides for an elected Assembly and a single official party, the National Revolutionary Development Movement.

History. Rwanda, which was part of German East Africa, was first visited by European explorers in 1854. During World War I, it was occupied in 1916 by Belgian troops. After the war, it became a Belgian League of Nations mandate, along with Burundi, under the name of Ruanda-Urundi. The mandate was made a U.N. trust territory in 1946. Until the Belgian Congo achieved independence in 1960, Ruanda-Urundi was administered as part of that colony.

Ruanda became the independent nation of Rwanda on July 1, 1962.

ST. LUCIA

Commonwealth of St. Lucia
Governor-General: Boswell Williams (acting) (1980)
Prime Minister: Winston Cenac (1981)
Area: 238 sq mi. (616 sq km)
Population (est 1981): 125,000 (growth rate: 1.7%)
Density per square mile: 525.2
Capital (est. 1979): Castries, 45,000
Monetary unit: East Caribbean dollar
Languages: English, patois
Religion: Roman Catholic 91%; Anglican, 3%; Seventh-day Adventist, 2%
Member of Commonwealth of Nations
Freedom House classifications: Capitalist-socialist industrial, multi-party centralized
Economic summary: Gross national product (1979): $90 million. Average annual growth rate (1970–78): 2.3%. Labor force in agriculture: 50%; principal products: bananas, coconuts, sugar, cocoa, spices. Major industrial products: processed limes. Exports: bananas, cocoa. Imports: foodstuffs, machinery and equipment, fertilizers, petroleum products. Major trading partners: U.K., U.S., Canada.

Geography. One of the Windward Isles of the Eastern Caribbean, St. Lucia lies just south of Martinique. It is of volcanic origin. A chain of wooded mountains runs from north to south, and from them flow many streams into fertile valleys.

Government. A governor-general represents the sovereign, Queen Elizabeth II. A prime minister is head of government, chosen by a 17-member House of Assembly elected by universal suffrage for a maximum term of five years.

History. Discovered by Spain in 1503 and ruled by Spain and then France, St. Lucia became a British territory in 1803. With other Windward Isles, St. Lucia was granted home rule in 1967 as one of the West Indies Associated States. On Feb. 22, 1979,

St. Lucia achieved full independence in ceremonies boycotted by the opposition St. Lucia Labor Party, which had advocated a referendum before cutting ties with Britain.

Unrest and a strike by civil servants forced Prime Minister John Compton to hold elections in July, in which his United Workers Party lost its majority for the first time in 15 years. The Labor Party, with 12 of 17 seats in the Assembly, elected Allan Louisy as prime minister, and Deputy Prime Minister George Odlum told a victory rally the party will take from the rich to give to the poor—"That's not communism, that's Christianity."

Formerly dependent on a single crop, bananas, St. Lucia has sought to expand tourism and industry to lower its 17% unemployment and a payments deficit of $28 million in 1978. The government provided tax incentives to a U.S. corporation, Amerada Hess, to facilitate location of a $150-million oil refinery and transhipment terminal on the island.

ST. VINCENT

Commonwealth of St. Vincent and the Grenadines
Sovereign: Queen Elizabeth II
Governor-General: Sir Sydney Gunn-Munro (1979)
Prime Minister: Milton Cato (1979)
Area: 150 sq mi. (389 sq km)
Population (est. 1981): 120,000 (growth rate: 2.9%)
Density per square mile: 800.0
Capital and largest city (est. 1979): Kingstown, 23,650
Monetary unit: East Caribbean dollar
Language: English
Religions: Anglican, 47%; Methodist, 28%; Roman Catholic, 13%
Member of Commonwealth of Nations
Freedom House classifications: Capitalist-socialist industrial, multi-party centralized
Economic summary: Gross national product (1979): $50 million. Average annual growth rate (1970–78): −1.8%. Principal agricultural products: bananas, arrowroot, coconuts. Major industry: food processing. Exports: bananas, arrowroot, copra. Imports: fertilizers, transportation equipment, chemicals, fuels, clothing. Major trading partners: U.K., U.S., Canada, Caribbean nations.

Geography. St. Vincent, chief island of the Commonwealth, is 18 miles (29 km) long and 11 miles (18 km) wide. One of the Windward Islands in the Lesser Antilles, it is 100 miles (161 km) west of Barbados. The island is mountainous and well forested. The Grenadines, a chain of nearly 600 islets with a total area of only 17 square miles (27 sq km), extend for 60 miles (96 km) from northeast to southwest between St. Vincent and Grenada, southernmost of the Windwards.

St. Vincent is dominated by the volcano La Soufrière, part of a volcanic range running north and south, which rises to 4,048 feet (1,234 m). The volcano erupted over a 10-day period in April 1979, causing the evacuation of the northern two thirds of the island. (There is also a volcano of the same name on Basse-Terre, Guadeloupe, which became violently active in 1976 and 1977.)

Government. A Governor-General represents the sovereign, Queen Elizabeth II. A Prime Minister, elected by a 13-member unicameral legislature, holds executive power. The Labor Party, led by Prime Minister Milton Cato, holds 11 of the 13 seats.

History. Discovered by Columbus in 1498, and alternately claimed by Britain and France, St. Vincent became a British colony by the Treaty of Paris in 1783. The islands won home rule in 1969 as part of the West Indies Associated States and achieved full independence Oct. 26, 1979. Prime Minister Milton Cato's government quelled a brief rebellion Dec. 8, 1979, three days after elections had given the ruling Labor Party 11 of 13 seats in the Assembly. The rebellion was attributed to economic problems following the eruption of La Soufrière in April, 1979. Unlike a 1902 eruption which killed 2,000, there was no loss of life but widespread losses to agriculture.

SAN MARINO

Most Serene Republic of San Marino
Co-Regents: Two selected every six months by Grand and General Council
Area: 23.6 sq mi. (62 sq km)
Population (est. 1981): 20,500 (mostly Italian)
Density per square mile: 868.6
Capital and largest city (est. 1980 for metropolitan area): San Marino, 8,500
Monetary unit: Italian lira
Language: Italian
Religion: Roman Catholic
National name: Repubblica di San Marino
Economic summary: Principal agricultural products: wheat and other grains, grapes, fruits, vegetables. Major industrial products: textiles, paper, leather, cement and other building materials. Exports: building stone, lime, chestnuts, wheat, hides, baked goods. Imports: manufactured consumer goods. Major trading partner: Italy.

Geography: One tenth the size of New York City, San Marino is surrounded by Italy. It is situated in the Apennines, a little inland from the Adriatic Sea near Rimini.

Government. The country is governed by two coregents. Executive power is exercised by two secretaries of state—one for foreign and political affairs and one for internal affairs. In 1959, the Grand Council granted women the vote.

The major political parties are the Christian Democratic Party (26 of 60 seats in the Grand and General Council); Communist Party (16 seats), Democratic Socialist Party (11 seats), Socialist Party (7 seats).

History. According to tradition, San Marino was founded about A.D. 350 and had good luck for centuries in staying out of the many wars and feuds on the Italian peninsula. It is the oldest republic in the world.

A person born in San Marino remains a citizen and can vote no matter where he lives.

SÃO TOMÉ AND PRÍNCIPE

Democratic Republic of Sao Tomé and Príncipe
President: Manuel Pinto da Costa (1975)
Area: 372 sq mi. (964 sq km)
Population (est. 1981): 90,000 (growth rate: 1.1%)
Density per square mile: 241.9
Capital and largest city (est. 1977): Sao Tomé, 20,000
Monetary unit: Dobra
Language: Portuguese

Religions: Roman Catholic, Evangelical Protestant, Seventh-Day Adventist
Freedom House classifications: Socialist industrial, one-party socialist
Economic summary: Gross national product (1979): $52 million. Average annual growth rate (1970–77): 8.0%. Per capita income (1974): $160. Average rate of inflation (1972–74): 25%. Principal agricultural products: cocoa, copra, coconuts, palm oil, coffee, bananas. Major industrial products: beer, palm oil, copra. Exports: cocoa, coffee, copra, palm oil. Imports: foodstuffs, textiles, machinery, beverages, fuels, lubricants. Major trading partners: Portugal, Netherlands, West Germany.

Geography. The tiny volcanic islands of São Tomé and Príncipe lie in the Gulf of Guinea about 150 miles (241 km) off West Africa. São Tomé (about 330 sq mi.; 855 sq mi.) is covered by a dense mountainous jungle, out of which have been carved large plantations. Príncipe (about 40 sq mi.; 104 sq km) consists of jagged mountains. Other islands in the republic are Pedras Tinhosas and Rolas.

History. São Tomé and Príncipe became independent of Portugal on July 12, 1975. The islands were discovered by the Portuguese in 1471. The majority of the early inhabitants were convicts, Jews from Portugal, and slaves from Brazil and the mainland.

SAUDI ARABIA

Kingdom of Saudi Arabia
Ruler and Prime Minister: King Khalid Bin Abdul-Aziz (1975)
Area: 873,000 sq mi. (2,261,070 sq km)
Population (est. 1981): 8,650,000 (growth rate: 5.6%)
Density per square mile: 9.9
Capital: Riyadh
Largest cities (est. 1980): Riyadh, 1,250,000; Jeddah, 750,000; Mecca, 500,000
Monetary unit: Riyal
Language: Arabic
Religion: Islam
National name: Al-Mamlaka al-'Arabiya as-Sa'udiya
Freedom House classifications: Capitalist-statist industrial, non-party non-military
Economic summary: Gross national product (1979): $62.6 billion. Average annual growth rate (1970–78): 4.9%. Labor force in agriculture: 24%; principal products: dates, grains, livestock. Labor force in industry: 39%; major products: petroleum, cement, plastic products, furniture. Natural resource: oil. Exports: petroleum and petroleum products. Imports: manufactured goods, transport equipment, construction materials, processed food. Major trading partners: U.S., Western European countries, Japan, West Germany.

Geography. The Middle East oil-producing country of Saudi Arabia occupies most of the Arabian Peninsula, with the Red Sea and the Gulf of Aqaba on the west and the Persian Gulf on the east. Neighbors are Jordan, Iraq, and Kuwait in the north, and, along the perimeter from southwest to east, the two Yemens, Oman, and the United Arab Emirates. The country is more than three times the size of Texas.

Saudi Arabia's oil region lies along the Persian Gulf. The country is mostly desert. The Asir Mountains inland rise to a height of 9,000 feet (2,743 m).

Government. Saudi Arabia is a monarchy whose legitimacy rests on *Shariah* (the Law of Islam) and custom. A Council of Ministers was formed in 1953. It acts as a Cabinet under the leadership of the King and is composed of 21 ministries.

Royal and ministerial decrees account for most of the promulgated legislation, treaties, and conventions.

There are no political parties in Saudi Arabia.

History. Mohammed united the Arabs in the 7th century, and his followers, led by the caliphs, founded a great empire, with its capital at Medina. Later, the caliphate capital was transferred to Damascus and then Baghdad, but Arabia retained its importance because of the holy cities of Mecca and Medina. In the 16th and 17th centuries, the Turks established at least nominal rule over much of Arabia, and in the middle of the 18th century, it was divided into separate principalities.

The Kingdom of Saudi Arabia is almost entirely the creation of King Ibn Saud (1882–1953). A descendant of earlier Wahabi rulers, he seized Riyadh, the capital of Nejd, in 1901 and set himself up as leader of the Arab nationalist movement. By 1906 he had established Wahabi dominance in Nejd. He conquered Hejaz in 1924–25, consolidating it and Nejd into a dual kingdom in 1926. In 1932, Hejaz and Nejd became a single kingdom, which was officially named Saudi Arabia. A year later the region of Asir was incorporated into the kingdom.

Oil was discovered in 1936, and commercial production began during World War II. Saudi Arabia was neutral until nearly the end of the war, but it was permitted to be a charter member of the United Nations. The country joined the Arab League in 1945 and took part in the 1948–49 war against Israel, but followed a less extremist policy as opposed to the line of the 1958–61 United Arab Republic. In 1951, the U.S. was allowed to build an air base at Dhahran.

On Ibn Saud's death in 1953, his eldest son, Saud, began an 11-year reign marked by an increasing hostility toward the radical Arabism of Egypt's Gamal Abdel Nasser. In 1964, the ailing Saud was deposed and replaced by the Premier, Crown Prince Faisal, who gave vocal support but no military help to Egypt in the 1967 Mideast war.

Faisal's assassination by a deranged kinsman in 1975 shook the Middle East, but failed to alter his kingdom's course. His successor was his brother, Prince Khalid. Khalid gave influential support to Egypt during negotiations on Israeli withdrawal from the Sinai desert. His government made it clear to the industrial West that Saudi Arabia's relatively moderate oil-pricing policies could change if consumer nations flouted Saudi views.

Saudi Arabia exercised a moderating influence in the Organization for Petroleum Exporting Countries (OPEC) to restrain prices. In July 1979 President Carter disclosed Crown Prince Fahd's promise to increase Saudi oil production by one million barrels a day for three months to ease the world oil shortage.

Although Carter had hoped that Saudi Arabia would support the Egyptian-Israeli peace treaty—the U.S. sold 60 F-15 fighters to the Saudis in 1978 and sent a fleet to the Arabian Sea when border clashes between the two Yemens alarmed Riyadh—Arab solidarity doomed this hope in 1979. Saudi Arabia joined the majority in condemning Egypt, broke diplomatic relations with Cairo and canceled its commitment to pay for $525 million worth of F-15's for Egypt.

A takeover by an unknown group of the Grand Mosque in Mecca on Nov. 20, 1979, spread fears that the Saudi monarchy might be under internal threat. There were conflicting stories about the uprising's origin, including an Iranian charge of U.S. involvement, which led to anti-American demonstrations in Pakistan and elsewhere in the Moslem world. After the recapture of the mosque by the Army on Dec. 4 at the cost of 130 lives, Saudi officials denied reports of uprisings elsewhere. On Jan. 9, 1980, 63 persons—41 Saudis and the remainder aliens—were beheaded for their participation in the takeover. A tightening of Islamic law and a shakeup in the Army's top command were linked to the incident.

Saudi concern over possible Iranian attack after the outbreak of the war between Iran and Iraq, added to the tension created by the Soviet invasion of Afghanistan, prompted a Saudi request for U.S. arms. Despite Israeli protests, Washington announced on April 21, 1981, that it would sell five Advance Warning and Command Systems (AWAC) planes to the Saudis, together with seven KC-135 tanker planes, which would increase the range of 62 F-15 fighter-interceptors already delivered.

Sheikh Ahmed Zaki Yamani, the Oil Minister, earlier announced that his government would maintain the 10.3-million-barrels-a-day oil production rate it set when Iran and Iraq cut their production. The Saudi action was a key element in the reduction of world oil prices, which was part of the arms deal, but Congressional objection to the plane sales forced a postponement of delivery.

SENEGAL

Republic of Senegal
President: Abdou Diouf (1981)
Premier: Habib Thiam (1981)
Area: 76,124 sq mi. (197,161 sq km)
Population (est. 1981): 5,800,000 (growth rate: 2.7%)
Density per square mile: 76.2
Capital and largest city (est. 1978): Dakar, 915,000
Monetary unit: Franc CFA
Ethnic groups: Wolofs, Sereres, Peuls, Tukulers, and others
Languages: French (official); Wolof, Serer, other tribal dialects
Religion: Islam, 86%; Animist, 9%; Christian, 5%
National name: République du Sénégal
Freedom House classifications: Capitalist-socialist industrial, dominant party.
Economic summary: Gross national product (1979): $2.4 billion. Average annual growth rate (1970–78): −0.3%. Per capita income: $353. Land used for agriculture: 12%; labor force: 80%; principal products: peanuts, millet, cotton, rice, sorghum. Labor force in industry: 8%; major products: peanut oil, fertilizer, cement, processed food and fish, refined petroleum. Natural resources: fish, phosphate. Exports: peanuts, phosphate rock, canned fish. Imports: foodstuffs, consumer goods, machinery, transport equipment. Major trading partners: France, African neighbors.

Geography. The capital of Senegal, Dakar, is the westernmost point in Africa. The country, slightly smaller than South Dakota, surrounds Gambia on three sides and is bordered on the north by Mauritania, on the east by Mali, and on the south by Guinea and Guinea-Bissau.

Senegal is mainly a low-lying country, with a semidesert area in the north and northeast and forests in the southwest. The largest rivers include the Senegal in the north and the Gambia in the central region.

Government. There is a National Assembly of 100 members, elected every five years. There is universal suffrage and a constitutional guarantee of equality before the law.

The major political party is the Socialist Party, led by President Abdou Diouf. Legal opposition was reconstituted in 1974 with formation of the Senegalese Democratic Party, headed by Abdoulaye Wade, which urged reduction in French and Western influences. The African Independence Party was reorganized in 1976.

History. The Portuguese had some stations on the banks of the Senegal River in the 15th century, and the first French settlement was made at Saint-Louis about 1650. The British took parts of Senegal at various times, but the French gained possession in 1840 and organized the Sudan as a territory in 1904. In 1946, together with other parts of French West Africa, Senegal became part of the French Union. On June 20, 1960, it became an independent republic federated with the Sudanese Republic in the Mali Federation, from which it withdrew two months later.

On Jan. 1, 1973, Senegal joined with six other states to create the West African Economic Community to promote economic development within the region.

SEYCHELLES

Republic of Seychelles
President: Albert René (1977)
Area: 171 sq mi. (443 sq km)
Population (est. 1981): 60,000 (average annual growth rate, 1975–79: 1.5%)
Density per square mile: 350.9
Capital (est. 1977): Victoria, 23,000
Monetary unit: Seychelles rupee
Languages: English, French (both official), Creole patois
Religions: Roman Catholic, 90%; Anglican, 8%
Member of Commonwealth of Nations
Freedom House classifications: Capitalist-socialist industrial, one-party socialist
Economic summary: Gross national product (1979): $90 million. Average annual growth rate (1970–78): 3.9%. Per capita income: $710. Land used for agriculture: 54%; labor force: 27%; principal products: vanilla, copra, cinnamon. Labor force in industry: 55%; major products: processed copra and vanilla, coconut oil. Exports: cinnamon, coconut products, fish. Imports: food, tobacco, manufactured goods, machinery, petroleum products, textiles, transport equipment. Major trading partners: U.K., Kenya, India, South Africa, Australia.

Geography. Seychelles consists of an archipelago of 92 islands in the Indian Ocean northeast of Madagascar. The principal islands are Mahé (55 sq mi.; 142 sq km), Praslin (15 sq mi.; 38 sq km), and La Digue (4 sq mi.; 10 sq km). The Aldabra, Farquhar, and Desroches groups are included in the territory of the republic.

Government. Seized from France by Britain in 1810, the Seychelles Islands remained a colony until June 29, 1976. The state is an independent republic within the Commonwealth.

On June 5, 1977, Prime Minister Albert René ousted the islands' first President, James Mancham, suspending the Constitution and the 25-member National Assembly. Mancham, whose "lavish spending" and flamboyance were cited by René in

seizing power, charged that Soviet influence was at work. The new president denied this and, while more left than his predecessor, pledged to keep the Seychelles in the Commonwealth.

A new Cabinet was formed with members only from Seychelles People's United Party, none from Mancham's Seychelles Democratic Party.

SIERRA LEONE

Republic of Sierra Leone
President: Dr. Siaka P. Stevens (1971)
First Vice President: Sorie I. Koroma (1978)
Second Vice President: Christian A. Kamara-Taylor (1978)
Area: 27,925 sq mi. (72,326 sq km)
Population (est. 1981): 3,560,000 (growth rate: 2.2%)
Density per square mile: 127.5
Capital and largest city (est. 1974): Freetown, 314,340
Monetary unit: Leone
Languages: English (official), Mende, Temne, Creole
Religions: Animist, 54%; Islam, 40%; Christian, 6%
Member of Commonwealth of Nations
Freedom House classifications: Capitalist pre-industrial, one-party socialist
Economic summary: Gross national product (1979): $840 million. Average annual growth rate (1970–78): −1.3%. Per capita income: $176. Average rate of inflation (1972–77): 15%. Land used for agriculture: 2.3%; labor force: 75%; principal products: coffee, cocoa, ginger, rice. Labor force in industry: 15%; major products: diamonds, bauxite, beverages, cigarettes, construction goods. Natural resources: diamonds, bauxite, chromite, iron ore, rutile. Exports: diamonds, iron ore, palm kernels, cocoa, coffee. Imports: food, petroleum products, chemicals, machinery. Major trading partners: U.K., U.S., Western European and Communist countries.

Geography. Sierra Leone, on the Atlantic Ocean in West Africa, is half the size of Illinois. Guinea, in the north and east, and Liberia, in the south, are its neighbors.

Mangrove swamps lie along the coast, with wooded hills and a plateau in the interior. The eastern region is mountainous.

Government. Sierra Leone became an independent nation on April 27, 1961, and declared itself a republic, with former Prime Minister Siaka P. Stevens as president for a five-year term, on April 19, 1971.

Sierra Leone became a one party state under the aegis of the All Peoples Congress Party in April 1978.

History. The coastal area of Sierra Leone was ceded to English settlers in 1788 as a home for blacks discharged from the British armed forces and also for runaway slaves who had found asylum in London. The British protectorate over the hinterland was proclaimed in 1896.

After elections in 1967, the British Governor-General replaced Sir Albert Margai, head of SLPP, which had held power since independence, with Dr. Stevens, head of APC, as prime minister. The Army took over the government; then another coup in April 1968 restored civilian rule and put the military leaders in jail.

A coup attempt early in 1971 by the army commander was apparently foiled by loyal army officers, but the then Prime Minister Stevens called in troops of neighboring Guinea's army, under a 1970 mutual defense pact, to guard his residence. After perfunctorily blaming the U.S. for the coup attempt, Stevens switched Governors-General, changed the Constitution, and ended up with a republic, of which he was first president. He was accused of taking "sweeping dictatorial powers," but was re-elected in 1976.

SINGAPORE

Republic of Singapore
President: Benjamin Sheares (1971)
Prime Minister: Lee Kuan Yew (1959)
Area: 238 sq mi. (616 sq km)
Population (est. 1981): 2,420,000 (growth rate, 1978–79: 1.2%) (Chinese, 76%; Malay, 15%; Indian, 7%)
Density per square mile: 10,168.1
Capital (est. 1978): Singapore, 2,335,000
Monetary unit: Singapore dollar
Languages: Malay, Chinese (Mandarin), Tamil, English
Religions: Islam, Christian, Buddhist, Hindu, Confucianist, Taoist
Member of Commonwealth of Nations
Freedom House classifications: Capitalist-statist industrial, dominant party
Economic summary: Gross national product (1979): $9.1 billion. Average annual growth rate (1970–78): 6.6%. Per capita income: (1980): $4,224. Land used for agriculture: 22%; labor force: 2%; principal products: poultry, hogs, orchids, vegetables, fruits. Labor force in industry: 27%; major industries: petroleum refining, oil exploration, ship repair, rubber processing, electronics and other light industry. Exports: electrical machinery, electronics, textiles. Imports: rice, machinery, petroleum. Major trading partners: U.S., Japan, U.K., Western European and Communist countries.

Geography. The Republic of Singapore consists of the main island of Singapore, off the southern tip of the Malay Peninsula between the South China Sea and the Indian Ocean, and 54 nearby islands.

There are extensive mangrove swamps extending inland from the coast, which is broken by many inlets.

Government. The head of state is the President. There is a Cabinet, headed by the Prime Minister, and a Parliament of 69 members elected by universal suffrage.

The People's Action Party, led by Prime Minister Lee Kuan Yew, is the only political party represented in Parliament.

History. Singapore, founded in 1819 by Sir Stamford Raffles, became a separate crown colony of Britain in 1946, when the former colony of the Straits Settlements was dissolved. The other two settlements—Penang and Malacca—were transferred to the Union of Malaya, and the small island of Labuan was transferred to North Borneo. The Cocos (or Keeling) Islands were transferred to Australia in 1955 and Christmas Island in 1958.

Singapore attained full internal self-government in 1959. On Sept. 16, 1963, it joined Malaya, Sabah (North Borneo), and Sarawak in the Federation of Malaysia. It withdrew from the Federation on Aug. 9, 1965, and proclaimed itself a republic the next month.

SOLOMON ISLANDS

Sovereign: Queen Elizabeth II
Governor-General: Baddeley Devesi (1978)
Prime Minister: Peter Kenilorea (1978)
Area: 11,500 sq mi. (29,785 sq km)
Population (est. 1981): 225,000 (average annual growth rate, 1970–79: 3.4%)
Density per square mile: 19.6
Capital and largest city (est. 1980): Honiara (on Guadalcanal), 18,500
Monetary unit: Solomon Islands dollar
Languages: Pidgin English, English, Melanesian dialects
Religions: Anglican, 34%; Roman Catholic, 19%; South Seas Evangelical, 17%; other Protestant, 25%
Member of British Commonwealth.
Freedom House classifications: Capitalist pre-industrial, non-party non-military
Economic summary: Gross national product (1978): $90 million. Average annual growth rate (1970–77): 1.7%. Principal agricultural products: copra, palm oil, rice, cocoa, cattle, spices. Major industrial products: processed fish, timber, jute, soap, canned meat, handicrafts. Natural resources: fish, timber. Exports: fish, timber, copra, palm oil. Imports: machinery and transport equipment, foodstuffs, fuel, manufactured goods. Major trading partners: Australia, Japan, U.K., U.S.

Geography. Lying east of New Guinea, this island nation consists of the southern islands of the Solomon group: Guadalcanal, Malaita, Santa Isabel, San Cristóbal, Choiseul, New Georgia, and numerous smaller islands.

Government. After 85 years of British rule, the Solomons achieved independence July 7, 1978. The Crown is represented by a Governor-General and legislative power is vested in a unicameral legislature of 38 members, led by the Prime Minister.

History. Discovered in 1567 by Alvaro de Mendana, the Solomons were not visited again for about 200 years. In 1886, Great Britain and Germany divided the islands between them. In 1914, Australian forces took over the German islands and the Solomons became an Australian mandate in 1920. In World War II, most of the islands were occupied by the Japanese. American forces landed on Guadalcanal on Aug. 7, 1942. The islands were the scene of several important U.S. naval and military victories. They are still largely undeveloped, with only 60 miles of paved road and fewer than 1,000 motor vehicles.

SOMALIA

Somali Democratic Republic
President: Maj. Gen. Mohamed Siad Barre (1969)
Area: 246,155 sq mi. (637,541 sq km)
Population (est. 1981): 3,750,000 (growth rate: 9.5%)
Density per square mile: 15.2
Capital and largest city (est. 1980 by U.N.): Mogadishu, 377,000
Monetary unit: Somali shilling
Language: Somali
Religion: Islam
National name: Al Jumhouriya As-Somalya Dimocradia
Freedom House classifications: Capitalist-socialist pre-industrial, one-party socialist
Economic summary: Gross national product (1978): $470 million. Average annual growth rate (1970–77): −1.1%. Per capita income: $110. Labor force in agriculture: 30%; principal products: livestock, bananas, sorghum, peanuts, sugar cane, cotton, maize. Labor force in industry: 3%; major products: textiles, meat, fish, canned fruit juices.

Natural resources: timber, uranium. Exports: livestock, skins and hides, bananas. Imports: machinery, manufactured goods, transport equipment. Major trading partners: Arab countries, Italy.

Geography. Somalia, situated in the Horn of Africa, lies along the Gulf of Aden and the Indian Ocean. It is bounded by Djibouti in the northwest, Ethiopia in the east, and Kenya in the southwest. In area it is slightly smaller than Texas.

Generally arid and barren, Somalia has two chief rivers, the Shebeli and the Juba.

Government. Maj. Gen. Mohamed Siad Barre took power on Oct. 21, 1969, in a bloodless coup that established a Supreme Revolutionary Council as the governing body, replacing a parliamentary government. On July 1, 1976, Barre dissolved the Council, naming its members to the Somali Socialist Party, organized that day as the nation's only legal political party. In December 1979, a 171-member People's Assembly was elected under a new Constitution adopted in August. The Assembly confirmed Barre as President for a six-year term.

History. From the 7th to the 10th century, Arab and Persian trading posts were established along the coast of present-day Somalia. Nomadic tribes occupied the interior, occasionally pushing into Ethiopian territory. In the 16th century, Turkish rule extended to the northern coast and the Sultans of Zanzibar gained control in the south.

After British occupation of Aden in 1839, the Somali coast became its source of food. The French established a coaling station in 1862 at the site of Djibouti and the Italians planted a settlement in Eritrea. Egypt, which for a time claimed Turkish rights in the area, was succeeded by Britain. By 1920, a British protectorate and an Italian protectorate occupied what is now Somalia. The British ruled the entire area after 1941, with Italy returning in 1950 to serve as United Nations trustee for its former territory.

In mid-1960, Britain and Italy granted independence to their respective sectors, enabling the two to join as the Republic of Somalia on July 1. Somalia broke diplomatic relations with Britain in 1963 when the British granted the Somali-populated Northern Frontier District of Kenya to the Republic of Kenya.

On Oct. 15, 1969, President Abdi Rashid Ali Shermarke was assassinated and the army seized power, dissolving the legislature and arresting all government leaders. Maj. Gen. Mohamed Siad Barre, as President of a renamed Somali Democratic Republic, leaned heavily toward the U.S.S.R., which had largely trained and equipped the nation's 9,000-man army. A Soviet naval base was established at Berbera.

In 1977, Somalia openly backed rebels in the westernmost area of Ethiopia, the Ogaden desert, which had been seized by Ethiopia at the turn of the century. The action was an embarrassment to the U.S.S.R., which was heavily involved in Ethiopia's new Marxist government after the ouster of Emperor Haile Selassie in 1974.

After denying Barre's pleas for aid, the U.S.S.R. announced in 1977 the cutoff of military aid to Somalia and the providing of "defensive weapons" to Ethiopia. Somalia then expelled an estimated 1,500 Soviet military and civilian aides and broke diplomatic relations with Cuba, which had furnished military advisers to the Ethiopian troops fighting in the Ogaden.

Somalia acknowledged defeat in an eight-month war against the Ethiopians, having lost many of what had become a 32,000-man army and most of its tanks and planes. In March 1978, the U.S. agreed to supply $7 million in food over six months, in addition to $6 million in emergency food relief provided in December. The U.S. refused to consider weapons sales, however, unless Somalia gave up all claims to northern Kenya, the Ogaden, and the Republic of Djibouti, all once claimed as "Greater Somalia." Barre refused to do this.

A U.S. announcement on Jan. 9, 1980, that bases for U.S. ships and planes in the Indian Ocean would be sought in Somalia, Oman, and Kenya, brought a request from Somalia for $1 billion worth of modern arms and an equal amount of economic aid. In August, an agreement was signed giving the U.S. use of military bases in Somalia in return for $25 million in military aid in 1981 and more in subsequent years.

SOUTH AFRICA

Republic of South Africa
State President: Marais Viljoen (1979)
Prime Minister: Pieter W. Botha (1978)
Area: 322,061 sq mi. (834,135 sq km)[1]
Population (est. 1981): 24,000,000[1] (growth rate: 2.1%) (black, 67%; white, 19%; colored [mixed], 11%; Asian, 3%)
Density per square mile: 74.5[1]
Administrative capital: Pretoria
Legislative capital: Cape Town
Judicial capital: Bloemfontein
Largest cities (est. 1980): Johannesburg, 1,500,000; Cape Town, 892,000; Pretoria, 600,000; Bloemfontein, 180,000; **(est. 1975):** Durban, 837,000; Port Elizabeth, 468,800
Monetary unit: Rand
Languages: English, Afrikaans, Bantu languages
Religions (1970): Dutch Reformed, 16%; Methodist, 10%; Roman Catholic, 9%; Anglican, 8%; other Christian, 55%
National name: Republiek van Suid-Afrika
Freedom House classifications: Capitalist-statist industrial, multi-party centralized
Economic summary: Gross national product (1979): $49.0 billion. Average annual growth rate (1970–78): 0.7%. Per capita income: $1,450. Labor force in agriculture: 53%; principal products: corn, wool, wheat, sugar cane, tobacco, citrus fruits. Labor force in industry: 15%; major products: assembled automobiles, machinery, textiles, iron and steel, chemicals, fertilizer, fish. Natural resources: gold, diamonds, platinum, uranium, coal, iron ore, asbestos, manganese. Exports: wool, diamonds, corn, uranium, sugar, fruits, hides and skins, asbestos, fish products. Imports: motor vehicles, machinery, metals, petroleum products, chemicals, textiles. Major trading partners: U.S., West Germany, Japan, U.K.

1. Excluding South-West Africa (Namibia), Transkei, Bophuthatswana, and Venda.

Geography. South Africa, on the continent's southern tip, is washed by the Atlantic Ocean on the west and by the Indian Ocean on the south and east. Its neighbors are South-West Africa (Namibia) in the northwest, Zimbabwe and Botswana in the north, and Mozambique and Swaziland in the northeast. Bophuthatswana, Transkei, and Venda are independent enclaves within South Africa, which occupies an area nearly three times that of California.

The country has a high interior plateau, or veld, nearly half of which averages 4,000 feet (1,219 m) in elevation.

There are no important mountain ranges, although the Great Escarpment, separating the veld from the coastal plain, rises to over 11,000 feet (3,350 m) in the Drakensberg Mountains in the east. The principal river is the Orange, rising in Lesotho and flowing westward for 1,300 miles (2,092 km) to the Atlantic.

The southernmost point of Africa is Cape Agulhas, located in Cape Province about 100 miles (161 km) southeast of the Cape of Good Hope.

Government. The Republic is divided into four provinces (Cape, Transvaal, Orange Free State, and Natal), each with a Provincial Council. A 50-member Senate and 165-member House of Assembly make up the Parliament. Members have five-year terms unless Parliament is dissolved earlier. The President is chosen by Parliament for a seven-year term.

Six "Bantustans," or black homelands, exist within the country. They have unicameral legislatures elected by black voters. (Only whites vote in parliamentary elections.) There are also a Colored (mixed race) Representative Council of 60 members (40 elected) and an Indian Council of 30 members (all elected), which give some representation for these minorities.

The major political parties are the National Party (131 of 165 seats in the House of Assembly), led by Prime Minister Pieter W. Botha; Progressive Federal Party (26 seats), led by Frederick van Zyl Slabbert. New Republic Party (18 seats), led by Vause Raw.

History. Dutch settlers arrived in South Africa in 1652 and by the beginning of the 18th century numbered nearly 2,000.

Britain seized the Cape Colony in 1814 and within seven years settled 5,000 Britons there, freeing the slaves on whom the Boer (Dutch) farmers relied for labor. The Boers pushed north of the Orange and Vaal rivers to escape the British, but in 1877 the British annexed the Transvaal territory. Although the Dutch relinquished the territory in 1881, resentment continued to smolder, and the Jameson Raid of 1899 touched off the Boer War, ending in Dutch defeat in 1902.

The four provinces were united in the Union of South Africa in 1910. Louis Botha, the first Prime Minister and a Boer, allied the dominion with Britain in World War I. The Unionist Party, led by Jan Christiaan Smuts, advocated a pro-British line and a more liberal racial policy in the period between wars, while the Nationalist Party urged withdrawal from the Commonwealth and racial separation.

Smuts brought the nation into World War II on the Allied side against Nationalist opposition, and South Africa became a charter member of the United Nations in 1945, but refused to sign the Universal Declaration of Human Rights. Apartheid—racial separation—dominated domestic politics as the Nationalists gained power and imposed greater restrictions on Bantus, Coloreds, and Asians.

Boer hostility to Britain triumphed in 1961 with the declaration on May 31 of the Republic of South Africa and the severing of ties with the Commonwealth. Nationalist Prime Minister H. F. Verwoerd's government in 1963 asserted the power to restrict freedom of those who opposed rigid racial laws. Three years later, amid increasing racial tension and criticism from the outside world, Verwoerd was assassinated. His Nationalist successor, Balthazar J. Vorster, launched a campaign of conciliation toward conservative black African states,

offering development loans and trade concessions. He accelerated the program for developing Bantustans, giving independence to the Transkei in 1976 and to Bophuthatswana in 1977.

The late 1960s and early 1970s were economic boom years for South Africa, giving blacks there the highest incomes in Africa, even though two thirds of the national income was going to the white fifth of the population.

A critical issue was South-West Africa, the former German territory ruled by South Africa since World War I, a rule challenged by the United Nations when it asserted responsibility for the territory in 1974 under the name Namibia. African demands for immediate freedom for Namibia led to an attempt to expel South Africa from the U.N. in 1974, a move blocked by a U.S., British, and French veto. The General Assembly barred South Africa from its seat anyway, and the seat has remained empty.

In the 1975–76 Angolan civil war, Vorster engaged 4,000 troops on the side of the National Union for the Total Independence of Angola, which lost to the Soviet-backed Popular Movement for the Liberation of Angola. Defeat in Angola was followed by a wave of riots in black townships in South Africa, originating in protests against the use of the Afrikaans language in schools.

At the same time, outside pressure forced Vorster to withdraw military aid to Rhodesia in mid-1976. He met with U.S. Secretary of State Henry A. Kissinger in Zurich in September. As a result, Premier Ian Smith of Rhodesia's white government agreed to negotiate with nationalists in Rhodesia for a majority rule.

Unrest in Soweto, the principal black township near Johannesburg, continued through 1978 despite the elimination of compulsory schooling in Afrikaans and relaxation of "petty apartheid." Under white as well as black pressure, the government desegregated theaters and opera houses, although movie theaters in white areas remained segregated. The death of Steven Biko on Sept. 12, 1977, caused widespread protest when the anti-apartheid activist was discovered to have died from a brain injury while jailed.

Economic restrictions tightened on South Africa following a vote by the Security Council imposing a mandatory embargo on arms in retaliation for South Africa's crackdown on opponents of apartheid. Although the U.S., Britain, and France vetoed mandatory economic sanctions against South Africa, U.S. and European businesses, unions, and church groups acted to cut trade with it.

Scandal rocked the Nationalist government in 1979 with the disclosure of the diversion of secret propaganda funds by former Information Minister Connie Mulder. He was alleged to have advanced $11 million to John McGoff, an American Publisher, to buy *The Washington Star*, which was used instead to buy *The Sacramento Union*. Mulder's linking of Vorster with the scandal forced Vorster's resignation on June 4, 1979, from the State Presidency to which he had been elected after leaving the prime ministership in September.

The new Prime Minister, Peter W. Botha, moved toward a more liberal racial policy by easing job restrictions on blacks and extending black union rights. He appointed a multiracial advisory council, to assist in a proposed Constitutional revision and to replace the largely ceremonial Senate. The new group, composed of 39 whites, 15 Asians and mixed bloods, but including no blacks, met for the first time on Feb. 3, 1981.

Botha's policy brought right-wing defection from the ruling party in parliamentary elections on April 29, as the Nationalist popular vote dropped from nearly 65% in 1977 to 55% and the number of seats from 137 to 131. Although winning no seats, the splinter right Herstigte (Reconstituted) Nationalist Party gained nearly 10% in the popular vote. At the same time, the opposition Progressive Federal Party, capitalizing on urban whites' support for faster change, gained nine seats for a total of 26 in the new Parliament.

Negotiations for the independence of Namibia, stalled since 1978, made no progress in the Botha government's first encounter with the Reagan Administration. Foreign Minister Roelof F. Botha conferred with President Reagan and high U.S. officials in May. According to leaked State Department documents, he was offered "strategic cooperation" in return for a commitment to genuine independence in Namibia and movement away from apartheid at home.

BOPHUTHATSWANA

Republic of Bophuthatswana
President: Chief Lucas Mangope (1977)
Area: 15,610 sq mi. (40,430 sq km)
Population (est. 1981): 1,255,000 (growth rate: 2.4%)
Density per square mile: 80.4
Capital: Mmabatho
Largest city (est. 1980): Ga-Rankuwa, 80,000
Monetary unit: South African rand
Languages: Central Tswana, English, Afrikaans
Religions: Methodist, Lutheran, Anglican, and Bantu Christian

Geography. Bophuthatswana consists of half a dozen discontinuous areas within the boundaries of South Africa, most of them in the northern sector near Botswana.

Government. The republic has a 99-member Legislative Assembly, approximately half of whom are elected and the others appointed. President Mangope's Democratic Party is the majority party.

History. Bophuthatswana was given independence by South Africa on Dec. 6, 1977, following Transkei as the second "homeland" to be established by Pretoria. The new state and Transkei are recognized only by South Africa and each other.

Mangope, as chief minister in the pre-independence period, sought linkage of the six units into a consolidated area, but was unable to achieve his objective. A second issue, the citizenship of Tswanas in South Africa who wished to remain South African nationals, was settled by enabling them to have citizenship in South African homelands not yet independent.

About two thirds of the population of Bophuthatswana live permanently or as migrants in white areas of South Africa.

Economy. Bophuthatswana is richer than many other South African homelands, as it has more than half of the republic's platinum deposits. All foreign trade is included with South Africa's, and it is economically dependent at present on that country.

SOUTH-WEST AFRICA (NAMIBIA)

Status: Mandate
Area: 318,261 sq mi. (824,296 sq km)
Population (est. 1981): 1,000,000 (growth rate: 3.0%)
Density per square mile: 3.1
Administrator-General: Danie Hough (1980)
Capital (est. 1980): Windhoek, 85,000
Summer capital (est. 1980): Swakopmund 17,500
Monetary unit: South African rand
National name: Suidwes-Afrika/Namibië; South-West Africa/Namibia
Economic summary: Gross national product (1979): $1.2 billion. Growth rate (1970–78): 0.6%. Land used for agriculture: 30%; labor force: 68%; principal products: corn, millet, sorghum, livestock. Labor force in industry: 4%; major products: canned meat, dairy products, tanned leather, textiles, clothing. Natural resources: diamonds, copper, lead, zinc, uranium, fish. Exports: diamonds, copper, lead, zinc, beef cattle, karakul pelts. Imports: construction materials, fertilizer, grain, foodstuffs. Major trading partner: South Africa.

Geography. The mandate, bounded on the north by Angola and Zambia and on the east by Botswana and South Africa, was discovered by the Portuguese explorer Diaz in the late 15th century. It is for the most part a portion of the high plateau of southern Africa with a general elevation of from 3,000 to 4,000 feet.

History. The territory became a German colony in 1884 but was taken by South African forces in 1915, becoming a South African mandate by the terms of the Treaty of Versailles.

South Africa's application for incorporation of the territory was rejected by the U.N. General Assembly in 1946 and South Africa was invited to prepare a trusteeship agreement instead. By a law passed in 1949, however, the territory was brought into much closer association with South Africa—including representation in its Parliament.

In 1969, South Africa extended its laws to the mandate over the objection of the U.N.; particularly its black African members. When South Africa refused to withdraw them, the Security Council condemned it.

Under a 1974 Security Council resolution, South Africa was required to begin the transfer of power to the Namibians by May 30, 1975, or face U.N. action, but 10 days before the deadline Prime Minister Balthazar J. Vorster rejected U.N. supervision. He said, however, that his government was prepared to negotiate Namibian independence, but not with the South-West African People's Organization, the principal black separatist group. Meanwhile, the all-white legislature of South-West Africa eased several laws on apartheid in public places.

Despite international opposition, the Turnhalle Conference in Windhoek drafted a constitution to organize an interim government based on racial divisions, a proposal overwhelmingly endorsed by white voters in the territory in 1977. At the urging of ambassadors of the five Western members of the Security Council—the U.S., Britain, France, West Germany, and Canada—South Africa on June 11 announced rejection of the Turnhalle constitution and acceptance of the Western proposal to include the South-West Africa People's Organization (SWAPO) in negotiations.

With the approval of SWAPO, a militant nationalist group, Justice Marthinus T. Steyn was appointed by South Africa to serve as administrator of the territory during the transition to independence. At the same time, Pretoria announced that it would retain control of Walvis Bay, the territory's only deepwater port.

Apartheid laws were repealed by Steyn, and South-West representation in the South African parliament ended.

TRANSKEI

Republic of Transkei

President: Paramount Chief Daliwonga Matanzima (1980)
Prime Minister: Paramount Chief George Matanzima (1979)
Area: 15,831 sq mi. (41,002 sq km)
Population (est. 1981): 2,500,000 (growth rate: 2.2%)
Density per square mile: 157.9
Capital (est. 1980): Umtala, 32,500
Monetary unit: South African rand
Languages: English, Xhosa, Southern Sotho
Religions: Christian, 66%; tribal, 24%
Freedom House classifications: Capitalist pre-industrial, dominant party
Economic summary: Gross domestic product: $150 million. Per capita income: $86. Principal agricultural products: tea, corn, sorghum, dry beans. Major industrial products: timber, textiles. Natural resource: timber. Exports: timber, tea, sacks. Imports: foodstuffs, machines, equipment. Major trading partner: South Africa.

Geography. Transkei occupies three discontinuous enclaves within southeast South Africa that add up to twice the size of Massachusetts. It has a 270-mile (435 km) coastline on the Indian Ocean. A port is being developed at Port St. Johns. The capital, Umtata, is connected by rail to the South African port of East London, 100 miles (161 km) to the southwest.

Government. Transkei was granted independence by South Africa as of Oct. 26, 1976. A constitution called for organization of a parliament composed of 75 representative chiefs and 75 elected members, with a ceremonial president and executive power in the hands of a prime minister.

The Organization of African States and the chairman of the United Nations Special Committee Against Apartheid denounced the new state as a sham and urged governments not to recognize it.

History. British rule was established over the Transkei region between 1866 and 1894, and the Transkeian Territories were formed in 1903. Under the Native Land Act of 1913, the Territories were reserved for black occupation. In 1963, Transkei was given internal self-government and a legislature that elected Paramount Chief Kaiser Matanzima as Chief Minister, a post he retained in elections in 1968 and 1973.

Economy. Some 60% of Transkei is cultivated, producing corn, wheat, beans, and sorghum. Grazing is important. Some light industry has been established.

VENDA

Republic of Venda

President: Chief Patrick R. Mphephu (1979).
Area: 2,448 sq mi. (6,340 sq km)
Population (est. 1981): 525,000
Density per square mile: 214.5
Capital: Thohoyandou
Largest town (est. 1980): Makearela, 2,500
Monetary unit: South African rand
Languages: Venda, English, Afrikaans
Religions: Christian, tribal
Economic Summary: Gross domestic product: $156 million. Per capita income: $312. Principal agricultural products:

meat, tea, fruit, sisal, corn. Major industrial products: timber, graphite, magnetite.

Geography. Venda is composed of two noncontiguous territories in northeast South Africa with a total area of about half that of Connecticut. It is mountainous but fertile, well-watered land, with a climate ranging from tropical to subtropical.

Government. The third of South Africa's homelands to be granted independence, Venda became a separate republic on Sept. 13, 1979, unrecognized by any government other than South Africa and its sister homelands, Transkei and Bophuthatswana. The President is popularly elected. An 84-seat legislature is half elected, half appointed.

History. The first European reached Venda in 1816, but the isolation of the area prevented its involvement in the wars of the 19th century between blacks and whites and with other tribes. Venda came under South African administration after the Boer War in 1902. Limited home rule was granted in 1962. Chief Patrick R. Mphephu, leader of one of the 27 tribes that historically made up the Venda nation, became Chief Minister of the interim government in 1973 and President upon independence in 1979.

SOVIET UNION

Union of Soviet Socialist Republics

Chairman of Presidium (President): Leonid I. Brezhnev (1977)
Chairman of Council of Ministers (Premier): Nikolai A. Tikhonov (1980)
Area: 8,649,489 sq mi. (22,402,200 sq km)
Population (est. 1981): 267,600,000 (growth rate: 0.8%) (Russian, 52%; Ukrainian, 17%; Uzbek, 5%; Byelorussian, 4%; Kazak, 3%; Tatar, 2%)
Density per square mile: 30.9
Capital: Moscow
Largest cities (1979 census): Moscow, 8,011,000; Leningrad, 4,588,000; Kiev, 2,144,000; Tashkent, 1,779,000; Baku, 1,550,000; Kharkov, 1,444,000; Gorki, 1,344,000; Novosibirsk, 1,312,000; Minsk, 1,276,000; Kuibyshev, 1,216,000; Sverdlovsk, 1,211,000; Dnepropetrovsk, 1,066,000; Tbilisi, 1,066,000; Odessa, 1,046,000; Chelyabinsk, 1,031,000; Donetsk, 1,021,000; Yerevan, 1,019,000; Omsk, 1,014,000
Monetary unit: Ruble
Languages: *See* Population, above
Religions: Russian Orthodox (predominant), Islam, Roman Catholic, Jewish, Lutheran
National name: Soyuz Sovyetskikh Sotsialisticheskikh Respublik
Freedom House classifications: Socialist industrial, one-party communist
Economic summary: Gross national product (1979): $1,082 billion. Average annual growth rate (1970–78): 4.3%. Per capita income: $3,990. Land used for agriculture: 10%; labor force: 23%; principal products: wheat, rye, corn, oats, potatoes, sugar beets, cotton and flax, cattle, pigs, sheep. Labor force in industry: 76%; major products: ferrous and nonferrous metals, fuels and power, building materials, chemicals, machinery. Natural resources: fossil fuels, water power, timber, manganese, lead, zinc, nickel, mercury, potash, phosphate. Exports: fossil fuels, raw materials, machinery and equipment, semifinished products. Imports: machinery and equipment, foodstuffs, raw materials. Major trading partners: Soviet bloc, Western industrialized countries.

Republics of the U.S.S.R.

Republic and capital	Area sq mi.	Population est. 1977 (thousands)
Russian S.F.S.R. (Moscow)	6,593,391	135,600
Ukraine (Kiev)	233,089	49,300
Kazakhstan (Alma-Ata)	1,064,092	14,498
Byelorussia (Minsk)	80,154	9,414
Uzbekistan (Tashkent)	158,069	14,474
Georgia (Tbilisi)	26,872	4,999
Azerbaijan (Baku)	33,475	5,776
Lithuania[1] (Vilnius)	25,174	3,342
Moldavia (Kishinev)	13,012	3,885
Latvia[1] (Riga)	24,595	2,512
Kirghizia (Frunze)	76,641	3,443
Tadzhikistan (Duschambe)	55,019	3,591
Armenia (Erevan)	11,506	2,893
Turkmenistan (Ashkhabad)	188,417	2,650
Estonia[1] (Tallinn)	17,413	1,447

1. Soviet jurisdiction not recognized by the United States.

Geography. The U.S.S.R. is the largest unbroken political unit in the world, occupying more than one seventh of the land surface of the globe. The greater part of its territory is a vast plain stretching from eastern Europe to the Pacific Ocean. This plain, relieved only occasionally by low mountain ranges (notably the Urals), consists of three zones running east and west: the frozen marshy tundra of the Arctic; the more temperate forest belt; and the steppes or prairies to the south, which in southern Soviet Asia become sandy deserts.

The topography is more varied in the south, particularly in the Caucasus between the Caspian and Black Seas, and in the Tien-Pamir mountain system bordering Afghanistan, Sinkiang, and Mongolia. Mountains (Stanovoi and Kolyma) and great rivers (Amur, Yenisei, Lena) also break up the sweep of the plain in Siberia.

In the west, the major rivers are the Volga, Dnieper, Don, Kama, and Southern Bug.

Government. Legislative authority is vested in the Supreme Soviet of the U.S.S.R., which consists of two chambers—the Soviet of the Union, with 767 members, and the Soviet of Nationalities, with 750 members. All members of the Supreme Soviet are elected for five years by the people.

A Presidium is elected by the Supreme Soviet to deal with state matters when the latter is not in session. It consists of a chairman, first vice chairman, 15 vice chairmen (one for each union republic), 21 members, and a secretary. The chairman of the Presidium is sometimes referred to as the President.

Executive authority rests with the Council of Ministers. It is appointed by the Supreme Soviet and includes a chairman, a first vice chairman, and various vice chairmen, chairmen of state committees, ministers, etc. The chairman of the Council of Ministers is often referred to as the Premier.

Judicial authority is vested in the Supreme Court of the U.S.S.R. It consists of a chairmen, vice chairman, members, and people's assessors, who are elected by the Supreme Soviet for five years.

Each of the 15 union republics and the 20 autonomous republics has a Supreme Soviet (with a Presidium), a Council of Ministers, and a Supreme Court. Each of the eight autonomous regions has a Soviet of People's Deputies.

The Communist Party of the Soviet Union is the only party. It is the basic power in the country and today has a membership of 17,480,000.

The supreme organ of the party is the Party Congress, which meets at least once in five years. It elects a Central Committee, consisting of 320 members and 151 candidate members, to carry on party work between sessions of the Congress.

Within the Central Committee is a Political Bureau (Politburo), which was called the Presidium from 1952 to 1966. It functions between sessions of

Rulers of Russia Since 1533

Name	Born	Ruled[1]	Name	Born	Ruled[1]
Ivan IV the Terrible	1530	1533–1584	Nicholas I	1796	1825–1855
Theodore I	1557	1584–1598	Alexander II	1818	1855–1881
Boris Godunov	c.1551	1598–1605	Alexander III	1845	1881–1894
Theodore II	1589	1605–1605	Nicholas II	1868	1894–1917[7]
Demetrius I[2]	?	1605–1606			
Basil IV Shuiski	?	1606–1610[3]	**PROVISIONAL GOVERNMENT (PREMIERS)**		
"Time of Troubles"	—	1610–1613			
Michael Romanov	1596	1613–1645	Prince Georgi Lvov	1861	1917–1917
Alexis I	1629	1645–1676	Alexander Kerensky	1881	1917–1917
Theodore III	1656	1676–1682			
Ivan V[4]	1666	1682–1689[5]	**U.S.S.R. (PREMIERS)**		
Peter I the Great[4]	1672	1682–1725	N. Lenin	1870	1917–1924
Catherine I	c.1684	1725–1727	Aleksei Rykov	1881	1924–1930
Peter II	1715	1727–1730	Vyacheslav Molotov	1890	1930–1941
Anna	1693	1730–1740	Joseph Stalin[8]	1879	1941–1953
Ivan VI	1740	1740–1741[6]	Georgi M. Malenkov	1902	1953–1955
Elizabeth	1709	1741–1762	Nikolai A. Bulganin	1895	1955–1958
Peter III	1728	1762–1762	Nikita S. Khrushchev	1894	1958–1964
Catherine II the Great	1729	1762–1796	Aleksei N. Kosygin	1904	1964–1980
Paul I	1754	1796–1801	Nikolai A. Tikhonov	1905	1980–
Alexander I	1777	1801–1825			

1. For Tsars through Nicholas II, year of end of rule is also that of death, unless otherwise indicated. 2. Also known as Pseudo-Demetrius. 3. Died 1612. 4. Ruled jointly until 1689, when Ivan was deposed. 5. Died 1696. 6. Died 1764. 7. Killed 1918. 8. General Secretary of Communist Party, 1924–53.

the Central Committee. Also within the Central Committee is the Secretariat. The present General Secretary of the Central Committee, Leonid I. Brezhnev, has served since Oct. 15, 1964. Named President in June 1977 to succeed Nikolai V. Podgorny, he is the first man in Soviet history to hold both posts simultaneously.

History. Tradition says the Viking Rurik came to Russia in A.D. 862 and founded the first Russian dynasty in Novgorod. The various tribes were united by the spread of Christianity in the 10th and 11th centuries; Vladimir "the Saint" was converted in 988. During the 11th century, the grand dukes of Kiev held such centralizing power as existed. In 1240, Kiev was destroyed by the Mongols, and the Russian territory was split into numerous smaller dukedoms, out of which three large centers emerged—Galicia, Moscow, and Novgorod. The early dukes of Moscow extended their dominions through their office of tribute collector for the Mongols.

In the late 15th century, Duke Ivan III acquired Novgorod and Tver and threw off the Mongol yoke. Ivan IV, the Terrible (1533–84), first Muscovite Tsar, is considered to have founded the Russian state. He crushed the power of rival princes and boyars (great landowners), but Russia remained largely medieval until the reign of Peter the Great (1682–1725), grandson of the first Romanov Tsar, Michael (1613–45). Peter made extensive reforms aimed at westernization and, through his defeat of Charles XII of Sweden at the Battle of Poltava in 1709, he extended Russia's boundaries to the west.

Catherine the Great (1762–96) continued Peter's westernization program and also expanded Russian territory, acquiring the Crimea and part of Poland. During the reign of Alexander I (1801–25), Napoleon's attempt to subdue Russia was defeated (1812–13), and new territory was gained, including Finland (1809) and Bessarabia (1812). Alexander originated the Holy Alliance, which for a time crushed Europe's rising liberal movement.

Alexander II (1855–81) pushed Russia's borders to the Pacific and into central Asia. Serfdom was abolished in 1861, but heavy restrictions were imposed on the emancipated class. Revolutionary strikes following Russia's defeat in the war with Japan forced Nicholas II (1894–1917) to grant a representative national body (Duma), elected by narrowly limited suffrage. It met for the first time in 1906. Nicholas continued in his reactionary course, however, and the overwhelmingly liberal Duma had little or no influence.

World War I demonstrated tsarist corruption and the inefficiency of the tsarist regime, although the call of patriotism held the poorly equipped army together for a time. Disorders broke out in Petrograd (now Leningrad) in March 1917, and defection of the Petrograd garrison launched the revolution. Nicholas II was forced to abdicate on March 15, 1917, and he and his family were killed by revolutionists on July 16, 1918.

A provisional government composed of conservative and radical elements under the successive premierships of Prince Lvov and a moderate, Alexander Kerensky, lost ground to the radical, or Bolshevik, wing of the Socialist Democratic Labor Party. On Nov. 7, 1917, the Bolshevik revolution, engineered by N. Lenin[1] and Leon Trotsky, took place. The Kerensky government was overthrown,

and authority was vested in a Council of People's Commissars, with Lenin as Premier.

The humiliating Treaty of Brest-Litovsk (March 3, 1918) concluded the war with Germany, but civil war and foreign intervention delayed Communist control of all Russia until 1920. A brief war with Poland in 1920 resulted in Russian defeat.

The Union of Soviet Socialist Republics was established as a federation on Dec. 30, 1922.

The death of Lenin on Jan. 21, 1924, precipitated an intraparty struggle between Joseph Stalin, General Secretary of the party, and Trotsky, who favored swifter socialization at home and fomentation of revolution abroad. Stalin won. Trotsky was dismissed as Commissar of War in 1925 and banished from the Soviet Union in 1929. He was murdered in Mexico City on Aug. 21, 1940, by a political agent.

Stalin further consolidated his power by a series of purges in the late 1930s, liquidating prominent party leaders and military officers. Stalin assumed the premiership May 6, 1941.

Soviet foreign policy, at first friendly toward Germany and antagonistic toward Britain and France and then, after Hitler's rise to power in 1933, becoming anti-Fascist and pro-League of Nations, took an abrupt turn on Aug. 24, 1939, with the signing of a nonaggression pact with Nazi Germany. The next month, Moscow joined in the German attack on Poland, seizing territory later incorporated into the Ukrainian and Byelorussian S.S.R.'s. The war with Finland, 1939-40, added territory to the Karelian S.S.R. set up March 31, 1940; the annexation of Bessarabia and Bukovina from Romania became part of the new Moldavian S.S.R. on Aug. 2, 1940; and the annexation of the Baltic republics of Estonia, Latvia, and Lithuania in June 1940 (still unrecognized by the U.S.) created the 14th, 15th, and 16th Soviet Republics. (The number of so-called "Union" republics was reduced to 15 in 1956 when the Karelian S.S.R. became one of the 20 Autonomous Soviet Socialist Republics based on ethnic groups.)

The Soviet-German collaboration ended abruptly with a lightning attack by Hitler on June 22, 1941, which seized 500,000 square miles of Russian territory before Soviet defenses, aided by U.S. and British arms, could halt it. The Soviet resurgence at Stalingrad from November 1942 to February 1943 marked the turning point in a long battle, ending in the final offensive of January 1945.

Then, after denouncing a 1941 nonaggression pact with Japan in April 1945, when Allied forces were nearing victory in the Pacific, the Soviet Union declared war on Japan on Aug. 8, 1945, and quickly occupied Manchuria, Karafuto, and the Kurile islands.

Postwar territorial acquisitions include the Carpatho-Ukraine (12,617 sq mi.; 32,678 sq km) obtained from Czechoslovakia June 29, 1945, incorporated into the Ukrainian S.S.R.; the Republic of Tannu Tuva in central Asia (64,000 sq mi.; 165,760 sq km), incorporated early in 1945 into the Russian Soviet Federal Socialist Republic (R.S.F.S.R.); Karafuto or southern Sakhalin (13,935 sq mi.; 36,092 sq km) and the Kurile Islands (3,944 sq mi.; 10,215 sq km), occupied by Soviet troops in August 1945 and incorporated into the R.S.F.S.R.; the northern part of eastern Prussia (about 7,000 sq mi.; 18,130 sq km), placed under *de facto* Soviet administration at the Potsdam Conference and incorporated into the R.S.F.S.R.; the Petsamo district of Finland, obtained *de jure* under the 1947 treaty and incorporated into the R.S.F.S.R.; and Poland

1. N. Lenin was the pseudonym taken by Vladimir Ilich Ulyanov. It is sometimes given as Nikolai Lenin or V. I. Lenin.

east of the Curzon Line (69,860 sq mi.; 180,937 sq km), under terms of the Soviet-Polish treaty of Aug. 16, 1945, incorporated into the Ukrainian and Byelorussian S.S.R.'s.

The U.S.S.R. built a cordon of Communist states running from Poland in the north to Albania and Bulgaria in the south, including East Germany, Czechoslovakia, Hungary, and Romania, composed of the territories Soviet troops occupied at the war's end. With its Eastern front solidified, the Soviet Union launched a political offensive against the non-Communist West, moving first to block the Western access to Berlin. The Western powers countered with an airlift, completed unification of West Germany, and organized the defense of Western Europe in the North Atlantic Treaty Organization.

Stalin died on March 6, 1953, and was succeeded the next day by G. M. Malenkov as Premier. His chief rivals for power—Lavrenti P. Beria (chief of the secret police), Nikolai A. Bulganin, and Lazar M. Kaganovich—were named first deputies. Beria was purged in July and executed on Dec. 23, 1953.

The new power in the Kremlin was Nikita S. Khrushchev, First Secretary of the party. He replaced Malenkov with Bulganin in the premiership and then removed Malenkov, Kaganovich, and Vyacheslav M. Molotov from the Politburo. At the 20th Party Congress in 1956, Khrushchev denounced the "personality cult" of Stalin and in 1958 unseated Bulganin to become head of the government as well as of the party.

Khrushchev formalized the Eastern European system into a Council for Mutual Economic Assistance (Comecon) and a Warsaw Pact Treaty Organization as a counterweight to NATO. Tiny Albania was allowed to break away to join China in contesting Soviet domination of the Communist world, as Yugoslavia had done earlier. However, no mercy was shown to the Hungarians who rebelled in 1956, nor to the Czechs in their political struggle for liberation 12 years later.

In its technological race with the U.S., the Soviet Union exploded a hydrogen bomb in 1953, developed an intercontinental ballistic missile by 1957, sent the first satellite into space (Sputnik I) in 1957, and put Yuri Gagarin in the first orbital flight around the earth in 1961. On July 24, 1975, the 44-hour linkup of a Soviet Soyuz space vehicle (with two crewmen) with a U.S. Apollo spacecraft and its crew of three) demonstrated—for the first time openly—the level of Soviet space capability.

Although he had denounced personality cults, Khrushchev wielded enormous power. His downfall stemmed from his decision to place Soviet nuclear missiles in Cuba and then, when challenged by the U.S., backing down and removing the weapons. He was also blamed for the ideological break with China after 1963.

Khrushchev was forced into retirement on Oct. 15, 1964, and was replaced by Leonid I. Brezhnev as First Secretary of the Party and Aleksei N. Kosygin as Premier.

President Nixon visited the U.S.S.R. for summit talks in May 1972, concluding agreements on strategic-arms limitation and a declaration of principles on future U.S.-Soviet relations. The welcome given Nixon at a time when the U.S. was bombing North Vietnam, a Soviet ally, was regarded as proof that 25 years of cold war had ended.

The 1972 Strategic Arms Limitation Treaty (SALT I) set a ceiling of 200 anti-ballistic missiles (ABM's) for each side and the U.S.S.R. was frozen at 1,618 land-based intercontinental missiles (ICBM's), with the U.S. held to 1,054. Submarine-based missiles were restricted by a complicated formula giving the U.S.S.R. a numerical advantage, balanced by permitting the U.S. more warheads for its more reliable and accurate missiles.

Brezhnev visited the U.S. in 1973 to discuss further arms limitations, but a return visit to Moscow by Nixon the following year failed to produce an expected permanent treaty. The two sides agreed to reduce ABM's to 100 each and to restrict underground nuclear testing (air, sea, and space tests were already prohibited), but there was no agreement to stop the proliferation of multi-warhead missiles (MIRV's).

Presidents Gerald R. Ford and Brezhnev met in Vladivostok in November 1974 and reached tentative agreements to be incorporated into a treaty at the Geneva SALT talks in 1975. They proposed a ceiling of 2,400 ICBM's for each side, of which no more than 1,320 could have MIRV's. There was hard bargaining but no decision on verification methods nor on whether the new U.S. subsonic Cruise missile and the Soviet Backfire bomber should be covered.

Ford and Brezhnev renewed the discussions without progress at the 35-nation Conference on Security and Cooperation in Europe at Helsinki in 1975.

President Carter, actively pursuing both human rights and disarmament, joined with the Soviet Union in September 1977 to declare that the SALT I accord, which would have expired Oct. 1 without further action, be maintained in effect while the two sides sought a new agreement (SALT II).

Despite recurrent friction, desire for détente appeared to moderate the Kremlin's policies toward the U.S. after the 1972 summit. There was a near-confrontation during the Arab-Israeli war of October 1973, when a Soviet threat to intervene to aid trapped Egyptian forces led Washington to call a world-wide nuclear alert, but the crisis was eased when the United Nations approved a truce plan developed by the U.S. and the U.S.S.R. The Kremlin made no overt move to capitalize on the fall of U.S.-backed governments in Indochina in the spring of 1975, but hailed the war's end as an incentive to improvement in relations with the U.S.

Brezhnev's 1977 election to the presidency followed publication of a new Constitution supplanting the one adopted in 1936. It specified the dominance of the Communist Party, previously unstated, and in what was taken to be a weapon against dissidents, declared that "rights and freedoms shall be inseparable from the performance by citizens of their duties." This was thought to restrict dissidents when they cited constitutional guarantees of individual freedom.

Although Brezhnev promised an end to the "illegal repressions" of the Stalin era, the issue of human rights remained a major one in both domestic and foreign policy. Dissidents continued to cite the Helsinki Agreement, and Carter's public support for Anatoly Shcharansky drew the angry charge from Brezhnev that Carter was conducting "ideological warfare" against the U.S.S.R. Amid the verbal fireworks, there was serious concern about the extent to which human rights might become an obstacle to SALT negotiations and to Soviet-U.S. relations in general.

Charges of Soviet interference by Carter and particularly by Security Adviser Zbigniew Brezezinski in Africa brought heated comments from Moscow in 1978. The State Department warned, after Brezhnev had complained of SALT delays, that Soviet military aid to Ethiopia threatened all U.S.-Soviet relations. The Soviet news agency,

Tass, said on February 26 that Soviet aid to Ethiopia was to counter Somali aggression and would end with a ceasefire. Similar friction occurred following the May invasion by rebels from Soviet-allied Angola, culminating in a speech by Carter to graduates of the U.S. Naval Academy telling the Russians they must "choose either confrontation or cooperation."

A crisis arose July 10 when, despite warnings from the Carter Administration, the government brought two prominent Jewish dissidents to trial, only two days before the opening of a new round of SALT negotiations in Geneva. Amid worldwide protest, a Moscow judge sentenced Anatoly Scharansky to three years in prison and 10 years in a forced labor camp on charges of treason. Scharansky, a leading spokesman for Jews seeking to emigrate to Israel, was accused of passing classified information to U.S. agents.

Aleksandr Ginzburg, manager of a fund established by exiled writer Aleksandr Solzhenytsin to aid political prisoners, was sentenced to eight years in a labor camp. Ginzburg was found guilty of "anti-Soviet agitation."

Carter condemned the action and temporarily halted the export of high technology goods to the Soviet Union. In April 1979, the issue was partly resolved with the exchange of Ginzburg and four other dissidents for two Soviet spies held by the United States. For 1979, the final count of Soviet Jews allowed to emigrate was 51,320, the highest number since emigration was permitted.

Carter and the ailing Brezhnev signed the SALT II treaty in Vienna on June 18, 1979, setting ceilings on each nation's arsenal of intercontinental ballistic missiles. Doubts about Senate ratification grew, and became a certainty on Dec. 27, when Soviet troops invaded Afghanistan. Despite protests from the Moslem and Western worlds, Moscow insisted that Afghan President Hafizullah Amin had asked for aid in quelling a rebellion.

In the face of evidence that Amin had been liquidated by Soviet advisers before the troops arrived, the Soviet Union vetoed a Security Council resolution on Jan. 7, 1980, that called for a withdrawal. Carter ordered a freeze on grain exports and high-technology equipment and stated that his "opinion of the Russians has changed more drastically in the last week than even in the previous two-and-a-half years."

On Jan. 20, Carter called for a world boycott of the Summer Olympic Games scheduled for Moscow. The boycott, less than complete, nevertheless marred the first Olympics to be held in Moscow as the United States, Canada, Japan, and to a partial extent all the western allies except France and Italy shunned the event.

Through 1981, an estimated 100,000 Soviet troops remained in Afghanistan, with guerrilla resistance continuing, and Moscow's motives still unclear. The invasion was regarded by some U.S. theoreticians as having been prompted by the weak response of the Carter administration to the seizure of the U.S. Embassy in Teheran. Others suggested that Soviet leaders were only routinely backing a Marxist regime threatened with overthrow. With Iran racked by internal struggles, there was also the opportunity for Soviet military power to intervene from a flanking position, possibly gaining for Moscow both Iranian oil and the access to the Indian Ocean, coveted since tsarist days.

While the Soviet Union maintained a stony defense in the face of criticism from Western Europe

and the U.S., and a summit meeting of 37 Islamic nations that unanimously condemned the "imperialist invasion" of Afghanistan, the growing crisis in Poland increasingly drew world attention. The Kremlin adopted an equally unyielding policy, sternly warning Warsaw against concessions to Polish workers and threatening military intervention.

The Reagan Administration took an initial hard line, with Secretary of State Alexander M. Haig, Jr., talking of a total trade embargo in the event of a Soviet military move into Poland. But at the Party's 26th Congress on Feb. 23, 1981, Brezhnev appeared to soften his approach with a call for an East-West summit and new arms-control talks.

Making no direct response, Reagan on April 24 lifted the Carter-imposed embargo on grain sales to the U.S.S.R. Soviet commentators asserted that the action benefited U.S. farmers more than Moscow. The delivery of only a third of the grain anticipated in the previous 15 months was known to have reduced Soviet beef and milk production, and the need to buy from other sources at higher prices further strained the Soviet economy.

SPAIN

Spanish State
Ruler: King Juan Carlos I (1975)
Premier: Leopoldo Calvo Sotelo (1981)
Area: 194,885 sq mi. (504,750 sq km)[1]
Population (est. 1981): 37,750,000 (growth rate, 1978–79: 0.9%) (Spanish, Basque, Catalan, Galician)
Density per square mile: 193.7
Capital: Madrid
Largest cities (est. 1981): Madrid, 3,275,000; Barcelona, 1,725,000; Valencia, 770,000; Seville, 630,000; Zaragoza, 600,000; Vizcaya (Bilbao), 450,000
Monetary unit: Peseta
Languages: Spanish, Basque, Catalan, Galician
Religion: Roman Catholic
National name: Estado Español
Freedom House classifications: Capitalist industrial, multi-party centralized.
Economic summary: Gross national product (1979): $162.3 billion. Average annual growth rate (1970–78): 3.1%. Per capita income: $3,190. Land used for agriculture: 41%; labor force: 19%; principal products: cereals, vegetables, citrus fruits, wine, olives and olive oil, livestock. Labor force in industry: 37%; major products: processed foods, textiles, footwear, petro-chemicals, steel, automobiles, ships. Natural resources: coal, lignite, water power, uranium, mercury, pyrites, fluorospar, gypsum, iron ore, zinc, lead, tungsten, copper. Exports: fresh fruits, iron and steel products, textiles, footwear, mercury, ships, canned fruits and vegetables. Imports: machinery and transportation equipment, chemicals, automobiles, machinery, iron, steel. Major trading partners: Western European nations.

1. Including the Balearic and Canary Islands.

Geography. Spain occupies 85% of the Iberian Peninsula in southwestern Europe, which it shares with Portugal; France is to the northeast. It is touched by the Bay of Biscay in the north, the Atlantic Ocean in the west, and the Mediterranean Sea in the south and east.

Spain, less than 10 miles (16 km) from Africa at the Strait of Gibraltar, is separated from France by the Pyrenees. The country is generally a broad plateau sloping to south and east and crossed by a series of mountain ranges and river valleys.

Principal rivers are the Ebro in the northeast, the

Tagus in the central region, and the Guadalquivir in the south.

Off Spain's east coast in the Mediterranean are the Balearic Islands (1,936 sq mi.; 5,014 sq km), the largest of which is Majorca. Sixty miles (97 km) west of Africa are the Canary Islands (2,808 sq mi.; 7,273 sq km).

Government. King Juan Carlos I (born Jan. 5, 1938) succeeded Generalissimo Francisco Franco Bahamonde as Chief of State Nov. 22, 1975.

The Cortes, or Parliament, consists of a Chamber of Deputies of 350 members and a Senate of 208, all elected by universal suffrage. The new Cortes, replacing one that was largely appointed or elected by special constituencies, was organized under a constitution adopted by referendum Dec. 6, 1978.

The major political parties are the 12-party coalition of the Union of the Democratic Center (168 of 350 seats in the Chamber of Deputies, 120 of 208 elected Senate seats), led by Leopoldo Calvo Sotelo; Spanish Socialist Workers Party (121 seats in Chamber, 68 in Senate); Communist Party (23 seats in Chamber, none in Senate), led by Santiago Carrillo; Democratic Coalition (9 seats in Chamber, 3 in Senate); Convergencia i Unión (Catalonian Party) (8 seats in Chamber, 1 in Senate); Basque Party (7 seats in Chamber, 8 in Senate).

History. Spain, originally inhabited by Celts, Iberians, and Basques, became a part of the Roman Empire in 201 B.C., when it was conquered by Scipio Africanus. In A.D. 412, the barbarian Visigothic leader Ataulf crossed the Pyrenees and ruled Spain, first in the name of the Roman emperor and then independently. In 711, the Moslems under Tariq entered Spain from Africa and within a few years completed the subjugation of the country. In 732, the Franks, led by Charles Martel, defeated the Moslems near Poitiers, thus preventing the further expansion of Islam in southern Europe. Internal dissension of Spanish Islam invited a steady Christian conquest from the north.

Aragon and Castile were the most important Spanish states from the 13th to the 15th century, in time absorbing all the other peoples of Spain. Aragon and Castile were consolidated by the marriage of Ferdinand II and Isabella I. The last Moslem stronghold, Granada, was captured in 1492. With Moslem control ended, Roman Catholicism was established as the official state religion. The Jews (1492) and the Moslems (1502) were expelled at the cost of incalculable suffering and loss of life.

In the era of exploration, discovery, and colonization, Spain amassed tremendous wealth and a vast colonial empire. The conquest of Peru by Pizarro (1532–33) and of Mexico by Cortés (1519–21) brought great prosperity to the motherland. The Spanish Hapsburg monarchy, through wars, diplomatic negotiations, and marriages, became for a time one of the most powerful in the world.

In 1588, Philip II sent his Invincible Armada to invade England, but its destruction cost Spain its supremacy on the seas and paved the way for England's colonization of America. Spain then sank rapidly to the status of a second-rate power and never again played a major role in European politics. Its colonial empire in the Americas and the Philippines vanished in wars and revolutions during the 18th and 19th centuries.

In World War I, Spain maintained a position of neutrality. In 1923, Gen. Miguel Primo de Rivera became dictator. In 1930, King Alfonso XIII revoked the dictatorship, but a strong antimonarchist and republican movement led to his leaving Spain in 1931.[2] The new Constitution declared Spain a workers' republic, broke up the large estates, separated church and state, and secularized the schools. The elections held in 1936 returned a strong Popular Front majority, with Manuel Azaña as President.

But political chaos persisted. On July 18, 1936, a conservative army officer in Morocco, Francisco Franco Bahamonde, led a mutiny against the government. The civil war that followed lasted three years and cost the lives of nearly a million people. Franco was aided by Fascist Italy and Nazi Germany, while Soviet Russia helped the Loyalist side. Several hundred leftist Americans served in the Abraham Lincoln Brigade on the side of the republic. The war ended when Franco took Madrid on March 28, 1939.

Franco became head of the state, national chief of the Falange Party (the governing party), and Premier and Caudillo (leader). The country was ruled by Franco's Cabinet, the National Council of the Falange Party, and the Cortes, which formulated laws subject to Franco's veto.

In a referendum in 1947, the Spanish people approved a Franco-drafted succession law declaring Spain a monarchy again. Franco, however, continued as Chief of State.

In 1969, Franco and the Cortes designated Prince Juan Carlos Alfonso Victor María de Borbón (who married Princess Sophia of Greece on May 14, 1962) to become King of Spain when the provisional government headed by Franco came to an end. He is the grandson of Alfonso XIII and the son of Don Juan, pretender to the throne.

In 1967 Spain concluded its first economic-social development plan, which had raised levels of living dramatically within a decade and, combined with Spanish migration to higher-wage countries in Western Europe, had virtually eradicated unemployment. A new Constitution, adopted in 1966, allowed for the direct election of one fourth of the Cortes.

Franco died of a heart attack on Nov. 20, 1975, after more than a year of ill health, and Juan Carlos was proclaimed King two days later.

Over strong rightist opposition, the government legalized the Communist Party in advance of the 1977 elections and permitted the return of Dolores Ibarruri, "La Pasionaria" of the 1930s, from long exile in Moscow. Premier Adolfo Suaraz Gonzalez's Union of the Democratic Center, a coalition of a dozen centrist and rightist parties, claimed 34.3% of the popular vote in the election.

The Spanish Socialist Workers Party (PSOE) ran the strongest opposition campaign to win 28.5% of the vote, with the Communists following at 9% and the right-wing Popular Alliance trailing with 8.2%.

The strong stand for the "Eurocommunist" philosophy of separation from Moscow's leadership taken by Santiago Carrillo, the Communist Party leader, was a feature of the election and drew a sharp attack from the Soviet Union.

Under pressure from Catalonian and Basque nationalists, Suárez granted home rule to these regions in 1979, but centrists backed by him did poorly in the 1980 elections for local assemblies in the two areas. Economic problems persisted, along with new incidents of terrorism, and Suárez resigned on Jan. 29, 1981, recommending Leopoldo Calvo Sotelo as his successor.

---

2. However, he did not abdicate. In 1941, shortly before his death, he renounced his claim to the throne in favor of his third son, Don Juan.

While the Cortes was debating Calvo's confirmation, 200 right-wing Civil Guardsmen invaded the chamber on Feb. 23 and held the Cabinet and 350 legislators hostage. King Juan Carlos made a televised appeal for support of the government, the attempt failed and the Prime Minister was subsequently confirmed by a vote of 186–158.

SRI LANKA

Democratic Socialist Republic of Sri Lanka
President: J. R. Jayawardene (1978)
Prime Minister: Ranasinghe Premadasa (1978)
Area: 25,332 sq mi. (65,610 sq km)
Population (est. 1981): 15,000,000 (growth rate: 1.7%)
Density per square mile: 592.1
Capital: Colombo
Largest cities (est. 1980): Colombo, 640,000; (est. 1976): Dehiwela, 166,000; Jaffna, 117,000
Monetary unit: Sri Lanka rupee
Languages: Sinhala, Tamil, English
Religions: Buddhist, 67%; Hindu, 18%; Christian, 8%; Islam, 7%
Member of Commonwealth of Nations
Freedom House classifications: Capitalist-statist industrial, multi-party centralized.
Economic summary: Gross national product (1979): $3.4 billion. Average annual growth rate (1970–78): 1.9%. Per capita income: $220. Land used for agriculture: 25%; labor force: 53%; principal products: tea, coconuts, rubber, rice, spices. Labor force in industry: 15%; major products: consumer goods, textiles, chemicals, paper and paper products. Natural resources: limestone, graphite, gems. Exports: tea, rubber. Imports: rice, flour, petroleum, fertilizer. Major trading partners: Pakistan, U.K., Saudi Arabia, Iran.

Geography. An island in the Indian Ocean off the southeast tip of India, Sri Lanka is about half the size of Alabama. Most of the land is flat and rolling; mountains in the south central region rise to over 8,000 feet (2,438 m).

Government. After 24 years as a British dominion, Ceylon became an independent republic and reverted to the traditional name Sri Lanka (resplendent island) on May 22, 1972. A new Constitution was adopted, replacing that of 1948. William Gopallawa, the former Governor-General, was named President and Mrs. Sirimavo R. D. Bandaranaike remained Prime Minister.

The new Constitution set up the National State Assembly, which consists of as many elected representatives of the people as a Delimitation Commission may determine. The 168-member Assembly is a unicameral legislature and serves for six years unless dissolved earlier.

The major political parties are the United National Party (141 of 168 seats in the National Assembly), led by President J.R. Jayawardene; Tamil United Liberation Front (17 seats); Sri Lanka Freedom Party (9 seats), led by former Prime Minister Bandaranaike.

History. Following Portuguese and Dutch rule, Ceylon became an English crown colony in 1798. The British developed coffee, tea, and rubber plantations and granted six Constitutions between 1798 and 1924. The Constitution of 1931 gave a large measure of self-government.

Ceylon became a self-governing dominion of the Commonwealth of Nations in 1948. Rioting by the Tamils seeking a separate state within a federal system occurred in 1958 and 1961, resulting in the outlawing of their party. In 1962, the Prime Minister, Mrs. Bandaranaike, a radical, nationalized Western oil and other business facilities and became embroiled with the U.S. and Britain over compensation. She was ousted in the 1965 elections by a multiparty coalition.

Following considerable pre-election violence, Mrs. Bandaranaike was returned to power in a landslide victory in 1970, with her three-party leftist coalition capturing over two thirds of parliament. An important factor was the 800,000 youths 18-to-21 years old given the vote for the first time; they proved largely left-leaning.

Worsening economic conditions and charges of corruption combined to produce a crushing defeat for Mrs. Bandaranaike in general elections of 1977. Junius Richard Jayawardene, 73-year-old leader of the small United National Party, became Prime Minister.

Amid opposition criticism, Jayawardene was sworn in as president on Feb. 3, 1978, in a constitutional change to the presidential system of government. He named his deputy party leader, Ranasinghe Premadasa, as prime minister.

SUDAN

Democratic Republic of the Sudan
President: (1971): Maj. Gen. Gaafar Mohamed Nimeiri
Area: 967,491 sq mi. (2,505,802 sq km)
Population (est. 1981): 18,750,000 (growth rate: 3.0%)
Density per square mile: 19.4
Capital: Khartoum
Largest cities (est. 1980): Khartoum, 1,600,000; (est. 1973): Omdurman, 250,000; Port Sudan, 130,000
Monetary unit: Sudanese pound
Languages: Arabic, English, tribal dialects
Religions: Islam, 66%; Animist, 29%; Christian, 5%
National name: Jamhuryat es-Sudan Al Demogratia
Freedom House classifications: Capitalist-socialist pre-industrial, one-party nationalist
Economic summary: Gross national product (1979): $6.6 billion. Average annual growth rate (1970–78): 2.6%. Per capita income: $165. Land used for agriculture: 3%; labor force: 86%; principal products: cotton, peanuts, sesame seeds, gum arabic, sorghum, wheat sugar cane. Labor force in industry: 6%; major products: cement, textiles, pharmaceuticals, shoes, processed foods. Natural resources: some iron ore, copper, chrome, industrial metals. Exports: cotton, peanuts, gum arabic, livestock. Imports: manufactured goods, machinery and transport equipment, food, livestock. Major trading partners: U.K., West Germany, Italy, India, China, France, Japan.

Geography. The Sudan, in northeast Africa, is the largest country on the continent, measuring about one fourth the size of the United States. Its neighbors are Chad and the Central African Republic on the west, Egypt and Libya on the north, Ethiopia on the east, and Kenya, Uganda, and Zaire on the south. The Red Sea washes about 500 miles of the eastern coast.

The country extends from north to south about 1,200 miles (1,931 km) and west to east about 1,000 miles (1,609 km). The northern region is a continuation of the Libyan Desert. The southern region is fertile, abundantly watered and, in places, heavily forested. It is traversed from north to south by the Nile, all of whose great tributaries are partly or entirely within its borders.

Government. Under the 1975 Constitution, executive power is vested in a president elected by universal suffrage for a term of six years. Legislative authority is exercised by a 350-member People's Assembly. The Sudanese Union is the only authorized political party.

History. The early history of the Sudan (known as the Anglo-Egyptian Sudan between 1898 and 1955) is linked with that of Nubia, where a powerful local kingdom was formed in Roman times with its capital at Dongola. After conversion to Christianity in the 6th century, it joined with Ethiopia and resisted Mohammedanization until the 14th century. Thereafter the area was broken up into many small states until 1820–22, when it was conquered by Mohammed Ali, Pasha of Egypt. Egyptian forces were evacuated during the Mahdist revolt (1881–93), but the Sudan was reconquered by the Anglo-Egyptian expeditions of 1896–98, and in 1899 became an Anglo-Egyptian condominium, which was reaffirmed by the Anglo-Egyptian treaty of 1936.

Egypt and Britain agreed in 1953 to grant self-government to the Sudan under an appointed Governor-General. An all-Sudanese Parliament was elected in November-December 1953, and an all-Sudanese government was formed. In December 1955, the Parliament declared the independence of the Sudan, which, with the approval of Britain and Egypt, was proclaimed on Jan. 1, 1956.

In October 1969, Maj. Gen. Gaafar Mohamed Nimeiri, the president of the Council for the Revolution, took over as prime minister. He was elected the nation's first president in 1971 by a reported 98.6% of the vote in a national referendum. His term was for six years.

On March 2, 1973, eight Palestinian terrorists invaded the Saudi Arabian embassy in Khartoum and killed one Belgian and two American diplomats after their demands for the release of Arab terrorist prisoners in different countries were refused. The terrorists surrendered after three days and were captured, but Nimeiri postponed bringing them to trial in the face of Arab calls for their release.

The terrorists were convicted of murder June 24, 1974, but Nimeiri freed them the next day and turned them over to the Palestine Liberation Army, which flew them to Cairo. The U.S. withdrew its Ambassador in protest, but he returned in October 1974 after the men were imprisoned in Egypt.

In 1976, a third attempted coup against Nimeiri left 1,000 rebels and loyal troops dead after a fierce battle in Khartoum. Nimeiri accused President Muammar el Qaddifi of Libya of having instigated the attempt and broke relations with Libya. Firing squads executed 81 convicted rebels.

Nimeiri also charged Soviet involvement in the attempt and in 1977 expelled 90 Soviet advisers. He moved closer to Egypt—he was one of the few Arab leaders who supported Sadat's dramatic visit to Israel in November 1977—and the U.S. Nimeiri publicly backed the Eritrean rebel movement in 1977 in its fight against the pro-Soviet Ethiopian central government, which accused him of giving material aid as well as moral support to the rebels.

SURINAME

Republic of Suriname
President: Dr. Henk R. Chin A Sen (1980)

Area: 63,251 sq mi. (163,820 sq km)
Population (est. 1981): 400,000 (growth rate: —0.6%)
  (Hindi, 37%; Creole, 31%; Indonesian, 15%; Bush Negro, 10%)
Density per square mile: 6.3
Capital and largest city (est. 1973): Paramaribo, 150,000
Monetary unit: Suriname guilder
Language: Dutch, Surinamese (lingua franca)
Religions: Protestant, Roman Catholic, Hindu, Islam
Freedom House classifications: Capitalist industrial, non-party military.
Economic summary: Gross national product (1979): $950 million. Average annual growth rate (1970–78): 4.7%. Per capita income: $1,240. Land used for agriculture: 0.3%; labor force: 29%; principal products: rice, citrus fruits, sugar, coffee. Labor force in industry: 15%; major products: aluminum, alumina, processed foods, lumber, bricks, cigarettes. Natural resources: bauxite, iron ore, timber, fish, shrimp. Exports: bauxite, alumina, aluminum, lumber and wood products. Imports: food and beverages, machinery, petroleum, textiles, vehicles. Major trading partners: U.S., Western European countries.

Geography. Suriname lies on the northeast coast of South America, with Guyana to the west, French Guiana to the east, and Brazil to the south. It is about one tenth larger than Michigan. The principal rivers are the Corantijn on the Guyana border, the Marowijne in the east, and the Suriname, on which the capital city of Paramaribo is situated. The Tumuc-Humac Mountains are on the border with Brazil.

Government. Suriname, formerly known as Dutch Guiana, became an independent republic on Nov. 25, 1975. The first prime minister, Henck A. E. Arron, was ousted by a seven-man military junta on Feb. 25, 1980, and replaced by Dr. Henk R. Chin A Sen.

Chin A Sen was elevated to the office of President by the junta on Aug. 14, 1980, and the 39-member National Assembly was abolished. A military cabinet was designated to conduct the government.

History. England established the first European settlement on the Suriname River in 1650 but transferred sovereignty to the Dutch in 1667 in the Treaty of Breda, by which the British acquired New York. Colonization was confined to a narrow coastal strip, and until the abolition of slavery in 1863, African slaves furnished the labor for the plantation economy. After 1870, laborers were imported from British India and the Dutch East Indies.

In 1948, the colony was integrated into the Kingdom of the Netherlands and two years later was granted full home rule in other than foreign affairs and defense. After race rioting over unemployment and inflation, the Netherlands offered complete independence in 1973. Henck A. E. Arron, leader of a coalition of Creole (Surinamese of African descent) parties, advocated independence, while Jaggernath Lachmon, leader of the Surinamese of East Indian descent, urged delay.

Arron retained power in the first post-independence elections in 1977 but held only a one-seat margin over Lachmon's group early in 1980. He had promised early elections when seven Army sergeants and a lieutenant staged a coup on Feb. 25 and installed a civilian, Dr. Henk R. Chin A Sen, as Prime Minister. A subsequent military intervention made Chin A Sen President, abolishing the legislature and instituting a military government.

SWAZILAND

Kingdom of Swaziland
Ruler: King Sobhuza II (1921)
Prime Minister: Prince Mabandla Dlamini (1979)
Area: 6,704 sq mi. (17,363 sq km)
Population (est. 1981): 550,000 (growth rate: 2.8%)
Density per square mile: 82.0
Capital and largest city (est. 1976): Mbabane, 23,000
Monetary unit: Lilangeni
Languages: English and Siswati (official)
Religions: Christian, 60%; Animist, 40%
Member of Commonwealth of Nations
Freedom House classifications: Capitalist pre-industrial, non-party non-military
Economic summary: Gross national product (1979): $350 million. Average annual growth rate (1970–78): 4.8%. Per capita income: (1975): $440. Land used for agriculture: 8%; labor force: 31%; principal products: corn, livestock, sugar cane, citrus fruits, cotton, rice, pineapples. Labor force in industry: 25%; major products: milled sugar, ginned cotton, processed meat and wood, iron ore. Natural resources: iron ore, asbestos, coal. Exports: sugar, wood products, iron ore, asbestos, citrus fruits, canned fruits. Imports: motor vehicles, fuels and lubricants, foodstuffs, clothing. Major trading partners: South Africa, U.K., U.S.

Geography. Swaziland, 85% the size of New Jersey, is surrounded by South Africa and Mozambique. The country consists of a high veld in the west and a series of plateaus descending from a maximum of 6,000 feet (1,829 m) to a low veld of 1,500 feet (457 m).

Government. In 1967, a new Constitution established King Sobhuza II as head of state and provided for an Assembly of 24 members elected by universal suffrage, together with a Senate of 12 members—half appointed by the Assembly and half by the King. In 1973, the King renounced the Constitution, suspended political parties, and took total power for himself. In 1977, he replaced the Parliament with an assembly of tribal leaders. The Parliament reconvened in 1979.

History. Bantu peoples migrated southwest to the area of Mozambique in the 16th century. A number of clans broke away from the main body in the 18th century and settled in Swaziland. In the 19th century they organized as a tribe, partly because they were in constant conflict with the Zulu. Their ruler, Mswazi, applied to the British in the 1840s for help against the Zulu. The British and the Transvaal governments guaranteed the independence of Swaziland in 1881. In 1890 a provisional government, representing the Swazi, the British, and the Transvaal, was established.

South Africa held Swaziland as a protectorate from 1894 to 1899, but after the Boer War, in 1902, Swaziland was transferred to British administration. The Paramount Chief was recognized as the native authority in 1941.

In 1963, the territory was constituted a protectorate, and on Sept. 6, 1968, it became the independent nation of Swaziland.

SWEDEN

Kingdom of Sweden
Sovereign: King Carl XVI Gustaf (1973)
Prime Minister: Thorbjörn Fälldin (1980)
Area: 173,665 sq mi. (449,792 sq km)
Population (est. 1981): 8,330,000 (growth rate: 0.2%)
Density per square mile: 48.0
Capital: Stockholm
Largest cities (est. 1980): Stockholm, 1,400,000; Göteborg, 700,000; Malmö, 450,000
Monetary unit: Krona
Language: Swedish
Religion: Swedish Lutheran, 95%
National name: Konungariket Sverige
Freedom House classifications: Capitalist-socialist industrial, multi-party centralized
Economic summary: Gross national product (1979): $98.6 billion. Average annual growth rate (1970–78): 1.1%. Per capita income: (1980): $14,340. Principal agricultural products: dairy products, grains, sugar beets, potatoes, wood. Labor force in industry: 33%; major products: machinery, instruments, metal products, automobiles. Natural resources: forests, iron ore, hydroelectric power, unmined uranium. Exports: wood products, iron ore, machinery, iron and steel bearings, ships, instruments, automobiles. Imports: machinery, instruments, petroleum, yarns, foodstuffs. Major trading partners: Norway, West Germany, U.K., Denmark, Finland, U.S.

Geography. Sweden occupies the eastern part of the Scandinavian peninsula, with Norway to the west, Finland and the Gulf of Bothnia to the east, and Denmark and the Baltic Sea in the south. It is one tenth larger than California.

The country slopes eastward and southward from the Kjölen Mountains along the Norwegian border, where the peak elevation is Kebnekaise at 6,965 feet (2,123 m) in Lapland. In the north are mountains and many lakes. To the south and east are central lowlands and south of them are fertile areas of forest, valley, and plain.

Along Sweden's rocky coast, chopped up by bays and inlets, are many islands, the largest of which are Gotland and Öland.

Government. Sweden is a constitutional monarchy. Under the 1975 Constitution, the Riksdag is the sole governing body. The prime minister is the political chief executive.

In 1967, agreement was reached on part of a new Constitution after 13 years of work. It provided for a single-house Riksdag of 350 members (later amended to 349 seats) to replace the 104-year old bicameral Riksdag. The members are popularly elected for three years. Ninety-two present members of the Riksdag are women.

The King, Carl XVI Gustaf, was born April 30, 1946, and succeeded to the throne Sept. 19, 1973, on the death at 90 of his grandfather, Gustaf VI Adolf. Carl Gustaf was married on June 19, 1976, to Silvia Sommerlath, a West German commoner. Their first child, Princess Victoria, was born on July 14, 1977. Their second, Prince Carl Philip, was born on May 13, 1979. Under the new Act of Succession, effective Jan. 1, 1980, the first child of the reigning monarch, regardless of sex, is heir to the throne.

The major political parties are the Social Democratic Party (154 seats in the Riksdag), led by former Prime Minister Olof Palme; Conservative Party (73 seats), led by Gösta Bohman; Center Party (64 seats), led by Prime Minister Thorbjörn Fälldin; Liberal Party (38 seats), led by former Prime Minister Olla Ullsten; Communist Party (20 seats), led by Lars Werner. The Center and Liberal parties form the coalition government.

History. The earliest historical mention of Sweden is found in Tacitus' *Germania*, where reference is made to the powerful king and strong fleet of the Suiones. Toward the end of the 10th century, Olaf Sköttkonung established a Christian stronghold in Sweden. Around 1400, an attempt was made to unite the northern nations into one kingdom, but this led to bitter strife between the Danes and the Swedes.

In 1520, the Danish King, Christian II, conquered Sweden and in the "Stockholm Bloodbath" put leading Swedish personalities to death. Gustavus Vasa (1523–60) broke away from Denmark and fashioned the modern Swedish state.

Sweden played a leading role in the second phase (1630–35) of the Thirty Years' War (1618–48). By the Treaty of Westphalia (1648), Sweden obtained western Pomerania and some neighboring territory on the Baltic. In 1700, a coalition of Russia, Poland, and Denmark united against Sweden and by the Peace of Nystad (1721) forced it to relinquish Livonia, Ingria, Estonia, and parts of Finland.

Sweden emerged from the Napoleonic Wars with the acquisition of Norway from Denmark and with a new royal dynasty stemming from Marshal Jean Bernadotte of France, who became King Charles XIV·(1818–44). The artificial union between Sweden and Norway led to an uneasy relationship, and the union was finally dissolved in 1905.

Sweden maintained a position of neutrality in both World Wars.

An elaborate structure of welfare legislation, imitated by many larger nations, began with the establishment of old-age pensions in 1911. Economic prosperity based on its neutralist policy enabled Sweden, together with Norway, to pioneer in public health, housing, and job security programs.

Forty-four years of Socialist government were ended in 1976 with the election of a conservative coalition headed by Thorbjörn Fälldin, a 50-year-old sheep farmer. The surprise conservative victory was credited to public opposition to a nuclear power program backed by the Socialists and to a program that would have given control of all businesses to labor unions within 20 years.

Nuclear-power policy dominated Swedish policy in the ensuing years. Fälldin resigned on Oct. 5, 1978, when his conservative parties partners demanded less restrictions on nuclear power, and his successor, Ola Ullsten, resigned a year later after failing to achieve a consensus on the issue. Returned to office by his coalition partners, Fälldin said he would follow the course directed by a national referendum. On March 23, 1980, voters backed the development of 12 nuclear plants and use of them for at least 25 years to supply 40% of national energy needs while the search for alternative sources continued.

SWITZERLAND

Swiss Confederation
President: Fritz Honegger (1981)
Vice President: Kurt Furgler (1981)
Area: 15,941 sq mi. (41,288 sq km)
Population (est. 1981): 6,375,000 (growth rate: −0.2%)
  (Swiss, 85%; Italian, 8%; German, 2%; Spanish, 2%;
  French, 1%—figures by place of birth)
Density per square mile: 399.9
Capital: Bern
Largest cities (est. 1980): Zurich, 377,300; Basel, 183,200; Geneva, 152,700; Lausanne, 131,000; Winterthur, 86,400
Monetary unit: Swiss franc
Languages: German, 65%; French, 18%; Italian, 12%; Romansch, 1%
Religions: Roman Catholic, 49%; Protestant, 48%
National name: Schweiz/Suisse/Svizzera
Freedom House classifications: Capitalist industrial, multi-party decentralized
Economic summary: Gross national product (1979): $89.9 billion. Average annual growth rate (1970–78): 0.0%. Per capita income: $11,606. Land used for agriculture: 49%; labor force: 8%; principal products: cheese and other dairy products, livestock, fruits, grains, wine. Labor force in industry: 43%; major products: watches and clocks, precision instruments, machinery, chemicals, pharmaceuticals, textiles, generators, turbines. Natural resources: water power, timber, salt. Exports: electrical machinery and appliances, textile yarns, dyestuffs, chemicals. Imports: nonelectrical machinery, transport equipment, iron and steel. Major trading partners: West Germany, France, U.S., Netherlands, Italy, U.K.

Geography. Switzerland, in central Europe, is the land of the Alps. Its tallest peak is the Dufourspitze at 15,203 feet (4,634 m) on the Swiss side of the Italian border, one of 10 summits of the Monte Rose massif in the Pennine Alps. The tallest peak in all of the Alps, Mont Blanc (15,771 ft; 4,807 m), is actually in France.

Most of Switzerland comprises a mountainous plateau bordered by the great bulk of the Alps on the south and by the Jura Mountains on the northwest. About one fourth of the total area is covered by mountains and glaciers.

The country's largest lakes—Geneva, Constance (Bodensee), and Maggiore—straddle the French, German-Austrian, and Italian borders, respectively.

The Rhine, navigable from Basel to the North Sea, is the principal inland waterway. Other rivers are the Aare and the Rhône.

Switzerland, twice the size of New Jersey, is surrounded by France, West Germany, Austria, Liechtenstein, and Italy.

Government. The Swiss Confederation consists of 26 sovereign cantons, of which three are divided into half-cantons. Federal authority is vested in a bicameral legislature. The Ständerat, or State Council, consists of 46 members, two from each canton. The lower house, the Nationalrat, or National Council, has 200 deputies, elected for four-year terms.

Executive authority rests with the Bundesrat, or Federal Council, consisting of seven members chosen by parliament. The parliament elects the President, who serves for one year and is succeeded by the Vice President. The federal government regulates foreign policy, railroads, postal service, and the national mint. Each canton reserves for itself important local powers.

A constitutional amendment adopted in 1971 by referendum gave women the vote in federal elections and the right to hold federal office. An equal rights amendment passed in a national referendum June 14, 1981, barring discrimination against women under canton as well as federal law, ending the legal basis for barring women's votes in the last canton which maintained the restriction.

The major political parties are the Social Democratic Party (51 of 200 seats in National Council), led by Helmut Hubacher; Radical Democratic Party (51 seats), led by Yann Richter; Conservative Christian-Social Party (44 seats), led by Hans Wyer;

People's Party (23 seats), led by Fritz Hofmann. These four parties constitute the ruling coalition.

History. Called Helvetia in ancient times, Switzerland in the Middle Ages was a league of cantons of the Holy Roman Empire. Fashioned around the nucleus of three German forest districts of Schwyz, Uri, and Unterwalden, the Swiss Confederation slowly added new cantons. In 1648 the Treaty of Westphalia gave Switzerland its independence from the Holy Roman Empire.

French revolutionary troops occupied the country in 1798 and named it the Helvetic Republic, but Napoleon in 1803 restored its federal government. By 1815, the French- and Italian-speaking peoples of Switzerland had been granted political equality.

In 1815, the Congress of Vienna guaranteed the neutrality and recognized the independence of Switzerland. In the revolutionary period of 1847, the Catholic cantons seceded and organized a separate union called the *Sonderbund*. In 1848 the new Swiss Constitution established a union modeled upon that of the U.S. The Federal Constitution of 1874 established a strong central government while maintaining large powers of control in each canton.

National unity and political conservatism grew as the country prospered from its neutrality. Its banking system became the world's leading repository for international accounts. Strict neutrality was its policy in World Wars I and II. Geneva was the seat of the League of Nations, and Geneva, along with The Hague in the Netherlands, became the headquarters of a number of international organizations.

In 1971, the Swiss Supreme Court ruled that Swiss banks must show U.S. tax officials records of U.S. citizens suspected of tax fraud, thus significantly modifying a 1934 law that had seemed to forbid any bank disclosures.

SYRIA

Syrian Arab Republic
President: Hafez al-Assad (1971)
Premier: Abdel Raouf al-Kasm (1980)
Area: 71,498 sq mi. (185,180 sq km)
Population (est. 1981): 9,325,000 (growth rate: 3.4%)
Density per square mile: 130.4
Capital: Damascus
Largest cities (est. 1979): Damascus, 1,150,000; (est. 1978 by U.N.): Aleppo, 878,000; Homs, 306,000; Hama, 180,000
Monetary unit: Syrian pound
Language: Arabic
Religions: Islam, 85%; Christian, 14%
National name: Al-Jamhouriya al Arabiya As-Souriya
Freedom House classifications: Capitalist-socialist industrial, dominant party
Economic summary: Gross national product (1979): $8.9 billion. Average annual growth rate (1970–78): 6.0%. Per capita income: $780. Land used for agriculture: 47%; labor force: 32%; principal products: cotton, wheat, sugar beets, sheep, goats. Labor force in industry: 26%; major products: textiles, cement, glass, petroleum, processed food, soap. Natural resources: chrome, manganese, asphalt, iron ore, rock salt, phosphate, oil, natural gas. Exports: petroleum, textiles, tobacco, fruits and vegetables, cotton. Imports: machinery and metal products, textiles, fuels, foodstuffs. Major trading partners: Italy, West Germany, U.S.S.R., Yugoslavia, Switzerland, Saudi Arabia.

Geography. Slightly larger than North Dakota, Syria lies at the eastern end of the Mediterranean Sea. It is bordered by Lebanon and Israel on the west, Turkey on the north, Iraq on the east, and Jordan on the south.

Coastal Syria is a narrow plain, in back of which is a range of coastal mountains, and still farther inland a steppe area. In the east is the Syrian Desert, and in the south is the Jebel Druze Range. The highest point in Syria is Mount Hermon (9,232 ft; 2,814 m) on the Lebanese border.

Government. Syria's first permanent Constitution was approved in 1973, replacing a provisional charter that had been in force for 10 years. It provided for an elected People's Council as the legislature. No national religion is specified, although Islamic law is the basis of the state law.

In the first election in 10 years, in 1973, the Ba'ath Arab Socialist Party of President Hafez al-Assad, running on a unified National Progressive ticket with the Communist and Socialist parties, won 70% of the vote and a commensurate proportion of the seats for a four-year term in the People's Council. In the 1977 Council elections, the ruling Ba'athists won 125 of the now 195 seats; the National Progressive Front coalition, 34 seats; various rightist candidates, 36 seats.

History. Ancient Syria was conquered by Egypt about 1500 B.C., and after that by Hebrews, Phoenicians, Assyrians, Chaldeans, Persians, and Greeks. From 64 B.C. until the Arab conquest in A.D. 636, it was part of the Roman Empire except during brief periods. The Arabs made it a trade center for their extensive empire, but it suffered severely from the Mongol invasion in 1260 and fell to the Ottoman Turks in 1516. Syria remained a Turkish province until World War I.

A secret Anglo-French pact of 1916 put Syria in the French zone of influence. The League of Nations gave France a mandate over Syria after World War I, but the French were forced to put down several nationalist uprisings. In 1930, France recognized Syria as an independent republic, but still subject to the mandate. After nationalist demonstrations in 1939, the French High Commissioner suspended the Syrian Constitution. In 1941, British and Free French forces invaded Syria to eliminate Vichy control. During the rest of World War II, Syria was an Allied base.

Again in 1945, nationalist demonstrations broke into actual fighting, and British troops had to restore order. Syrian forces met a series of reverses while participating in the Arab invasion of Palestine in 1948. In 1958, Egypt and Syria formed the United Arab Republic, with Gamal Abdel Nasser of Egypt as President. However, Syria became independent again on Sept. 29, 1961, following a revolution.

In the war of 1967, Israel quickly vanquished the Syrian army. Before acceding to the U.N. cease-fire, the Israeli forces took over control of the fortified Golan Heights commanding the Sea of Galilee.

Syria joined Egypt in attacking Israel in October 1973 in the fourth Arab-Israeli war, but was pushed back from initial successes on the Golan Heights to end up losing more land. However, in the settlement worked out by U.S. Secretary of State Henry A. Kissinger in 1974, the Syrians recovered all the territory lost in 1973 and a token amount of territory, including the deserted town of Quneitra, lost in 1967.

Resumption of relations with the U.S. in 1974 moderated Syria's tone, but not the goals of its policy toward Israel. Syria initiated a resolution declaring the Palestine Liberation Organization to be the sole representative of the Palestinian people, a measure that was adopted by the U.N. General Assembly in October 1974 and became the vehicle for legitimizing the insurgent organization. As Israeli-Egyptian peace negotiations continued, Syria's hostility toward Egypt increased.

At the Arab League conference in Baghdad in March 1979, Syria demanded even harsher measures against Egypt than the break in diplomatic relations and economic boycott proposed by the conference. Syria asked that the boycott, including oil supplies, be applied to the U.S. as well.

Syrian troops, in Lebanon since 1976 as part of an Arab peace-keeping force whose other members subsequently departed, intervened increasingly during 1980 and 1981 on the side of Moslem Lebanese in their clashes with Christian militants supported by Israel. When Israeli jets shot down Syrian helicopters operating in Lebanon in April 1981, Syria moved Soviet-built surface-to-air (SAM 6) missiles into Lebanon's Bekaa Valley. Israel demanded that the missiles be removed because they violated a 1976 understanding between the governments. The demand, backed up by bombing raids, prompted the Reagan Administration to send veteran diplomat Philip C. Habib as a special envoy to avert a new conflict between the nations.

TANZANIA

United Republic of Tanzania
President: Julius K. Nyerere (1964)
Prime Minister: Edward Sokoine (1977)
Area: 362,820 sq mi. (939,704 sq km)[1]
Population (est. 1981): 19,000,000 (growth rate, 1978–79: 3.1%)
Density per square mile: 52.4
Capital and largest city (est. 1980): Dar es Salaam, 900,000
Monetary unit: Tanzanian shilling
Languages: Swahili, Bantu, Arabic, English
Religions: Animist, 35%; Christian, 31%; Islam, 31%
Member of Commonwealth of Nations
Freedom House classifications: Socialist pre-industrial, one-party socialist
Economic summary: Gross national product (1979): $4.7 billion. Average annual growth rate (1970–78): 1.7%. Per capita income: $200. Land used for agriculture: 60%; labor force: 90%; Principal products: sugar, maize, rice, wheat, cotton, coffee, sisal, cashew nuts, tea, tobacco, pyrethrum, cloves. Major industrial products: textiles, light manufactures, refined oil, processed agricultural products, diamonds, cement, fertilizer. Natural resources: hydroelectric potential, unexploited iron and coal, natural gas. Exports: coffee, cotton, sisal, diamonds, cloves, cashew nuts. Imports: manufactured goods, textiles, machinery and transport equipment, crude oil, foodstuffs. Major trading partners: U.K., China, India, Hong Kong, West Germany, U.S., Japan.

1. Including Zanzibar.

Geography. Tanzania is in East Africa on the Indian Ocean. To the north are Uganda and Kenya; to the west, Burundi, Rwanda, and Zaire; and to the south, Mozambique, Zambia, and Malawi. Its area is three times that of New Mexico.

Tanzania contains three of Africa's best-known lakes—Victoria in the north, Tanganyika in the west, and Nyasa in the south. Mount Kilimanjaro in the north, 19,340 feet (5,895 m), is the highest point on the continent.

Government. Under the republican form of government, Tanzania has a President elected by universal suffrage who appoints the Cabinet ministers. The 218-member National Assembly is composed of 96 elected members from the mainland, 10 members appointed by the President (from both Tanganyika and Zanzibar), 35 national members (elected by the National Assembly after nomination by various national institutions), 32 members of the Zanzibar Revolutionary Council, 20 other Zanzibar members appointed by the President in agreement with the President of Zanzibar, and up to 20 other Zanzibar members appointed by the President in agreement with the first Vice President, who represents Zanzibar.

The Tanganyika African National Union, the only authorized party on the mainland, and the Afro-Shirazi Party, the only party in Zanzibar and Pemba, merged in 1977 as the Revolutionary Party (Chama Cha Mapinduzi) and elected Julius K. Nyerere as its head.

History. Arab traders first began to colonize the area in A.D. 700. Portuguese explorers reached the coastal regions in 1500 and held some control until the 17th century, when the Sultan of Oman took power. With what are now Burundi and Rwanda, Tanganyika became the colony of German East Africa in 1885. After World War I, it was administered by Britain under a League of Nations mandate and later as a U.N. trust territory.

Although not mentioned in old histories until the 12th century, Zanzibar was believed always to have had connections with southern Arabia. The Portuguese made it one of their tributaries in 1503 and later established a trading post, but they were driven out by Arabs from Oman in 1698. Zanzibar was declared independent of Oman in 1861 and, in 1890, it became a British protectorate.

Tanganyika became independent on Dec. 9, 1961; Zanzibar, on Dec. 10, 1963. On April 26, 1964, the two nations merged into the United Republic of Tanganyika and Zanzibar. The name was changed to Tanzania six months later.

In 1975, the 1,163-mile (1,872 km) Tanzam railway linking the Tanzanian port of Dar es Salaam with Zambia was officially opened. Built and financed by China, the railway provided a direct route for Zambian copper exports to the sea, replacing a longer route through white-ruled Rhodesia to Mozambique.

In 1977, Tanzania closed its border with Kenya because of a dispute over the operation of East African Airways, an entity of the East African Community. The breakup of the airline left the East African Posts and Telecommunications Corporation as the only community agency still functioning.

An invasion by Ugandan troops in November 1978 was followed by a counterattack in January 1979, in which 5,000 Tanzanian troops were joined by 3,000 Ugandan exiles opposed to President Idi Amin. Within a month, full-scale war developed and the Tanzania/exile force pushed north and captured Kampala on April 11.

Nyerere kept troops in Uganda in open support of former Ugandan President Milton Obote, despite protests from opposition groups, until the national elections in December 1980. Although

Obote asked that the Tanzanians remain after his victory in order to control guerrilla resistance, Nyerere ordered their withdrawal in May 1981, citing the $1-million-a-month drain on his precarious finances.

THAILAND

Kingdom of Thailand

Ruler: King Bhumibol Adulyadej (1946)
Premier: Gen. Prem Tinsulanonda (1980)
Area: 198,455 sq mi. (514,000 sq km)
Population (est. 1981): 48,175,000 (growth rate: 2.3%) (incl. 2.5 million of Chinese descent born in Thailand)
Density per square mile: 242.8
Capital and largest city (est. 1980): Bangkok, 5,000,000
Monetary unit: Baht
Languages: Thai (Siamese), Chinese, English
Religions: Buddhist, 95%; Islam, 4%
National name: Muang Thai
Freedom House classifications: Capitalist pre-industrial, multi-party centralized
Economic summary: Gross national product (1979): $26.9 billion. Average annual growth rate (1970–78): 4.5%. Per capita income (1979): $575. Land used for agriculture: 71%; labor force: 78%; principal products: rice, rubber, corn, tapioca, sugar, pineapples. Labor force in industry: 7%; major products: processed food, textiles, wood, cement, tin, tungsten. Natural resources: fish, natural gas, forests, fluorite, tin, tungsten. Exports: rice, tapioca, sugar, rubber, maize, tin, pineapples, textiles. Imports: machinery and transport equipment, nonelectrical machinery, crude oil, fuels and lubricants, base metals, chemicals. Major trading partners: Japan, U.S., Singapore, West Germany, Netherlands, U.K., Hong Kong.

Geography. Thailand occupies the western half of the Indochinese peninsula and the northern two thirds of the Malay peninsula in southeast Asia. Its neighbors are Burma on the north and west, Laos on the east, and Cambodia and Malaysia on the south. Thailand is about three fourths the size of Texas.

Most of the population is supported in the fertile central alluvial plain, which is drained by the Chao Phnaya River and its tributaries.

Government. King Bhumibol Adulyadej, who was born Dec. 5, 1927, second son of Prince Mahidol of Songkhla, succeeded to the throne on June 9, 1946, when his brother, King Ananda Mahidol, died of a gunshot wound. He was married on April 28, 1950, to Queen Sirikit; their son, Vajiralongkorn, born July 28, 1952, is the Crown Prince.

After three years of civilian government ended with a military coup on Oct. 6, 1976, Thailand reverted to military rule. The junta permitted national elections in 1979, however, which confirmed the junta's designated premier, Gen. Kriangsak Chamanan. When Chamanan resigned on March 12, 1980, the National Assembly was allowed to elect his successor. Political parties, banned after the coup, gained limited freedom in 1980.

History. The Thais first began moving down into their present homeland from the Asiatic continent in the 6th century A.D. and by the end of the 13th century ruled most of the western portion. During the next 400 years, the Thais fought sporadically with the Cambodians and the Burmese. The British obtained recognition of paramount interest in

Thailand in 1824, and in 1896 an Anglo-French accord guaranteed the independence of Thailand.

A coup in 1932 changed the absolute monarchy into a representative government with universal suffrage. After five hours of token resistance on Dec. 8, 1941, Thailand yielded to Japanese occupation and became one of the springboards in World War II for the Japanese campaign against Malaya.

After the fall of its pro-Japanese puppet government in July 1944, Thailand pursued a policy of passive resistance against the Japanese, and after the Japanese surrender, Thailand repudiated the declaration of war it had been forced to make against Britain and the U.S. in 1942. By a treaty signed with Britain and India in 1946, Thailand renounced all wartime acquisitions of Malayan territory.

Thailand's major problem in the late 1960s was suppressing guerrilla action by Communist invaders in the north.

Although Thailand had received $2 billion in U.S. economic and military aid since 1950 and had sent troops (paid by the U.S.) to Vietnam while permitting U.S. bomber bases on its territory, the collapse of South Vietnam and Cambodia in the spring of 1975 brought rapid changes in the country's diplomatic posture.

At the Thai government's insistence, the U.S. agreed to withdraw all 23,000 U.S. military personnel remaining in Thailand by March 1976. Diplomatic relations with China were established in 1975. Meanwhile, overtures toward an accommodation with the new regime in South Vietnam were initiated.

Thailand protested vigorously when 1,100 U.S. Marines were airlifted to Thai bases May 14, 1975, for use in the rescue of the crew of the cargo ship Mayaguez after its seizure by a Cambodian gunboat. The marines were withdrawn the next day, and Thailand later accepted a U.S. apology for unauthorized use of its territory.

In 1973, when Field Marshal Thanom Kittikachorn resigned under the pressure of massive student demonstrations, Thailand returned to a civilian government and in 1975 had its first general elections. Premier Seni Pramoj was ousted in 1976 by Admiral Sa-Ngad Chaloryu and the National Administrative Reform Council after rioting by leftist students. The junta appointed Thanin Kraivichien, a supreme court justice, as premier and appointed a 340-member National Assembly, 110 of them military officers.

As insurgent activity increased and skirmishes along the Cambodian border continued despite Thai efforts to make peace with the Communist regime in Phnom Penh, the military, in 1977, ousted Thanin as "weak," replacing him with Gen. Kriangsak Chamanan.

Refugees from Laos, Cambodia, and Vietnam flooded into Thailand in 1978 and 1979, and despite efforts by the United States and other Western countries to resettle them, a total of 130,000 Laotian and Vietnamese refugees were living in camps along the Cambodian border in mid-1980. A drive by Vietnamese occupation forces on western Cambodian areas loyal to the Pol Pot government, culminating in invasions of Thai territory in late June, drove an estimated 100,000 Cambodians across the line as refugees, adding to the 200,000 of their countrymen already in Thailand. The total of 430,000 were being fed by United Nations and church relief organizations but the Thai government complained of the burden of their presence.

The Vietnamese incursions, notwithstanding Hanoi's claim that the troops were only seeking guerrillas hidden in the refugee camps, prompted a Thai appeal to Washington for military aid. In July, 35 reconditioned tanks and other weapons were flown to Thailand, and the Carter administration pledged its help in the event of a larger attack.

By November 1980, U.N. officials said that 150,-000 Cambodians had gone back to their homeland, and on Dec. 16 the Red Cross announced that it would end food distribution across the border and henceforth feed only the 90,000 refugees remaining in camps on the Thai side.

On April 3, 1981, a military coup against the Prem government failed. King Bhumibol Adulyadej took refuge outside Bangkok with Prem and his cabinet and the rebels found neither public nor sufficient military support.

TOGO

Republic of Togo
President: Gen. Gnassingbé Eyadema (1967)
Area: 21,853 sq mi. (56,599 sq km)
Population (est. 1981): 2,600,000 (growth rate: 3.0%)
Density per square mile: 119.0
Capital and largest city (est. 1980): Lomé, 285,000
Monetary unit: Franc CFA
Languages: Ewé, Mina (south), Kabyé, Cotocoli (north), French (official), and many dialects
Religions: Animist, 60%; Christian, 25%; Islam, 8%
National name: République Togolaise
Freedom House classifications: Capitalist-socialist pre-industrial, one-party nationalist
Economic summary: Gross national product (1979): $860 million. Average annual growth rate (1970–78): 1.7%. Per capita income: $300. Land used for agriculture: 15%; labor force: 90%; principal products: yams, manioc, millet, sorghum, cocoa, coffee, rice, cotton. Labor force in industry: 22%; major products: phosphate, textiles. Natural resources: marble, iron, manganese, phosphate, limestone. Exports: phosphate, cocoa, coffee. Imports: consumer goods, fuels, machinery, foodstuffs. Major trading partners: France, U.K., West Germany, Netherlands.

Geography. Togo, twice the size of Maryland, is on the south coast of West Africa bordering on Ghana to the west, Upper Volta to the north and Benin to the east.

The Gulf of Guinea coastline, only 32 miles long (51 km), is low and sandy. The only port is at Lomé. The Togo hills traverse the central section.

Government. The government of Nicolas Grunitzky was overthrown in a bloodless coup on Jan. 13, 1967, led by Lt. Col. Etienne Eyadema (now Gen. Gnassingbé Eyadema). A National Reconciliation Committee was set up to rule the country. In April, however, Eyadema dissolved the Committee and took over as President. In December 1979, a 67-member National Assembly was voted in by national referendum. The Assembly of the Togolese People is the only political party.

History. Brazilians were the first traders to settle in Togo. Established as a German colony (Togoland) in 1884, the area was split between the British and the French as League of Nations mandates after World War I and subsequently administered as U. N. trusteeships. The British portion voted for incorporation with Ghana.

Togo became independent on April 27, 1960. Sylvanus Olympio, its first President, was assassinated in 1963 and succeeded by Nicolas Grunitzky.

TONGA

Kingdom of Tonga
Sovereign: King Taufa'ahau Tupou IV (1965)
Prime Minister: Prince Fatafehi Tu'ipelehake (1965)
Area: 290 sq mi. (751 sq km)
Population (est. 1981): 100,000
Density per square mile: 370.4
Capital (est. 1976): Nuku'alofa, 18,300
Monetary unit: Pa'anga
Languages: Tongan, English
Religions: Free Wesleyan, 47%; Roman Catholic, 16%; Free Church of Tonga, 14%; Mormon, 9%; Church of Tonga, 9%
Member of Commonwealth of Nations
Freedom House classifications: Capitalist pre-industrial, non-party non-military
Economic summary: Gross national product (1979): $40 million. Average annual growth rate (1970–78): 1.2%. Land used for agriculture: 80%; labor force: 75%; principal products: yams, taro, papaya, pineapples, coconuts, tobacco, peanuts, bananas, copra. Major industrial products: copra, desiccated coconut. Natural resources: fish, timber. Exports: copra, coconut products, bananas. Imports: manufactures, foodstuffs, transport equipment, petroleum. Major trading partners: New Zealand, Australia, Netherlands, Norway.

Geography. Situated east of the Fiji Islands in the South Pacific, Tonga (also called the Friendly Islands) consists of some 150 islands, of which 36 are inhabited.

Most of the islands contain active volcanic craters; others are coral atolls.

Government. Tonga is a constitutional monarchy. Executive authority is vested in the Sovereign, a Privy Council, and a Cabinet headed by the Prime Minister. Legislative authority is vested in the Legislative Assembly.

History. The present dynasty of Tonga was founded in 1831 by Taufa'ahau Tupou, who took the name George I. He consolidated the kingdom by conquest and in 1875 granted a Constitution.

In 1900, his great-grandson, George II, signed a treaty of friendship with Britain, and the country became a British protected state. The treaty was revised in 1959.

Queen Salote Tupou reigned from 1918 to 1964 and was succeeded by her son, who became King Taufa'ahau Tupou IV.

Tonga became independent on June 4, 1970.

TRANSKEI
See South Africa

TRINIDAD AND TOBAGO

Republic of Trinidad and Tobago
President: Ellis Clarke (1976)
Prime Minister: George M. Chambers (1981)
Area: 1,980 sq mi. (5,128 sq km)
Population (est. 1981): 1,145,000 (growth rate: 1.5%) (black, 43%; East Indian, 40%; mixed, 14%)

Density per square mile: 578.3
Capital and largest city (est. 1976): Port-of-Spain, 47,300
Monetary unit: Trinidad and Tobago dollar
Languages: English (official); Hindi, French, Spanish
Religions: Roman Catholic, 31%; Protestant, 27%; Islam, 13%; Hindu, 6%
Member of Commonwealth of Nations
Freedom House classifications: Capitalist industrial, multi-party centralized
Economic summary: Gross national product (1979): $3.9 billion. Average annual growth rate (1970–78): 2.4%. Per capita income: $3,040. Land used for agriculture: 26%; labor force: 13%; principal products: sugar cane, cocoa, coffee, rice, bananas. Labor force in industry: 33%; major products: petroleum, processed food, cement; tourism. Natural resources: petroleum. Exports: petroleum, sugar. Imports: crude oil, foodstuffs, machinery and equipment. Major trading partners: U.S., U.K., Saudi Arabia, Indonesia, Iran, Japan, Netherlands.

Geography. Trinidad and Tobago lies in the Caribbean Sea off the northeast coast of Venezuela. The area of the two islands is slightly less than that of Delaware.

Trinidad, the larger, is mainly flat and rolling, with mountains in the north that reach a height of 3,085 feet (940 m) at Mount Aripo. Tobago is heavily forested with hardwood trees.

Government. The legislature consists of a 24-member Senate and a 36-member House of Representatives.

The major political parties are the People's National Movement, led by Prime Minister George M. Chambers (24 seats in the House of Representatives); United Labor Front (10 seats), led by Raffique Shah and Basdeo Panday; Democratic Action Congress (2 seats).

History. Trinidad was discovered by Columbus in 1498 and remained in Spanish possession, despite raids by other European nations, until it capitulated to the British in 1797 during a war between Britain and Spain.

Trinidad was ceded to Britain in 1802, and in 1899 it was united with Tobago as a colony. From 1958 to 1962, Trinidad and Tobago was a part of the West Indies Federation, and on Aug. 31, 1962, it became independent.

On Aug. 1, 1976, Trinidad and Tobago cut its ties with Britain and became a republic, remaining within the Commonwealth and recognizing Queen Elizabeth II only as head of that organization.

TUNISIA

Republic of Tunisia
President: Habib Bourguiba (1957)
Premier: Mohammed Mzali (1980)
Area: 63,379 sq mi. (164,152 sq km)
Population (est. 1981): 6,500,000 (growth rate: 2.5%)
Density per square mile: 102.6
Capital and largest city (est. 1976 for metropolitan area): Tunis, 960,000
Monetary unit: Tunisian dinar
Languages: Arabic, French
Religions: Predominantly Islam; Roman Catholic, Jewish, Greek Orthodox
National name: Al-Djoumhouria Attunusia
Freedom House classifications: Capitalist-socialist industrial, one-party socialist
Economic summary: Gross national product (1979): $7.0 billion. Average annual growth rate (1970–79): 5.7%. Per capita income: $930. Labor force in agriculture: 40%; principal products: wheat, olives, citrus fruits, grapes, dates. Labor force in industry: 21%; major products: crude oil, olive oil, textiles, and leather, chemical fertilizers, petroleum. Natural resources: oil, phosphates, iron ore, lead, zinc. Exports: petroleum, phosphates, olive oil. Imports: machinery and equipment, consumer goods, foodstuffs. Major trading partners: France, West Germany, Italy.

Geography. Tunisia, at the northernmost bulge of Africa, thrusts out toward Sicily to mark the division between the eastern and western Mediterranean Sea. Twice the size of South Carolina, it is bordered on the west by Algeria and by Libya on the south.

The country is covered by plains in the east and projects southward to the Sahara. In the north, the Atlas Mountains continue from Algeria but do not reach great height.

Government. Executive power is vested by the Constitution in the president, elected for five years and eligible for re-election to two additional terms. Legislative power is vested in a National Assembly elected by universal suffrage.

In 1975, the National Assembly amended the Constitution to make Habib Bourguiba President for life. At 71, Bourguiba was re-elected to a fourth five-year term when he ran unopposed in 1974. The only party, the Socialist Destourian, is led by Bourguiba.

History. Tunisia was settled by the Phoenicians and Carthaginians in ancient times. Except for an interval of Vandal conquest in A.D. 439–533, it was part of the Roman Empire until the Arab conquest of 648–69. It was ruled by various Arab and Berber dynasties until the Turks took it in 1570–74. French troops occupied the country in 1881, and the Bey signed a treaty acknowledging a French protectorate.

Nationalist agitation forced France to grant internal autonomy to Tunisia in 1955 and to recognize Tunisian independence and sovereignty in 1956. The Constituent Assembly deposed the Bey on July 25, 1957, declared Tunisia a republic, and elected Habib Bourguiba as President.

Bourguiba maintained a pro-Western foreign policy that earned him enemies. Tunisia refused to break relations with the U.S. during the Israeli-Arab war in June 1967, and it cracked down on anti-U.S. demonstrators.

Tunisia ended its traditionally neutral role in the Arab world when it joined with the majority of Arab League members to condemn Egypt for concluding a peace treaty with Israel. The Tunisian capital was offered as the temporary headquarters of the League, following the expulsion of Egypt and the shutting of the Cairo offices. At the League's first session in Tunis on June 28, 1979, Tunisian Minister of Information Chedli Klibi was elected Secretary-General to replace Mahmoud Riad of Egypt, who resigned.

TURKEY

Republic of Turkey
President and Head of National Security Council: Gen. Kenan Evren (1980)

Area: 301,380 sq mi. (incl. 9,121 in Europe) (780,576 sq km)
Population (est. 1981): 45,500,000 (growth rate: 2.3%)
Density per square mile: 151.0
Capital: Ankara
Largest cities (1980 census): Istanbul, 2,990,680; Ankara, 2,561,765; Izmir, 1,049,000; Adana, 834,050; Bursa, 657,500; Gaziantep, 510,650
Monetary unit: Turkish lira
Language: Turkish
Religion: Islam
National name: Türkiye Cumhuriyeti
Freedom House classifications: Capitalist-statist industrial, non-party military
Economic summary: Gross national product (1979): $58.8 billion. Average annual growth rate (1970–78): 4.1%. Per capita income (1979): $1,330. Rate of inflation (1980): 118%. Land used for agriculture: 35%; labor force: 60%; principal products: cotton, tobacco, cereals, sugar beets, fruits, nuts. Labor force in industry: 16%; major products: textiles, processed foods, steel, petroleum. Natural resources: coal, chromite, copper, boron, oil. Exports: cotton, tobacco, fruits, nuts, livestock products, textiles. Imports: machinery, transport equipment, metals, mineral fuels, fertilizer, chemicals, crude oil. Major trading partners: West Germany, U.S., Italy, France, Iraq, U.S., U.S.S.R.

Geography. Turkey is at the northeastern end of the Mediterranean Sea in southeast Europe and southwest Asia. To the north is the Black Sea and to the west the Aegean Sea. Its neighbors are Greece and Bulgaria to the west, the U.S.S.R. to the north, Iran to the east, and Syria and Iraq to the south. Overall, it is more than twice the size of Montana.

The country is divided into two natural areas by the historic waterway formed by the Dardanelles, the Sea of Marmara, and the Bosporus.

Turkey in Europe comprises an area about equal to the state of Massachusetts. It is hilly country drained by the Maritsa River and its tributaries.

Turkey in Asia, or Anatolia, about the size of Texas, is roughly a rectangle in shape with its short sides on the east and west. Its center is a treeless plateau rimmed by mountains.

Government. The President is elected by the Grand National Assembly for a seven-year term and is not eligible for re-election.

In a military coup on Sept. 11, 1980, led by Gen. Kenan Evren, the Army Chief of Staff, Premier Süleyman Demirel was ousted, the Grand National Assembly dissolved and the Constitution suspended. Demirel, former Premier Bülent Ecevit, and some 100 legislators and political figures were detained. Martial law was declared and all political parties were dissolved.

A six-man National Security Council was set up to run the country.

History. The Ottoman Turks first appeared in the early 13th century in Anatolia, subjugating Turkish and Mongol bands pressing against the eastern borders of Byzantium. They gradually spread through the Near East and Balkans, capturing Constantinople in 1453 and storming the gates of Vienna two centuries later. At its height, the Ottoman Empire stretched from the Persian Gulf to western Algeria.

Defeat of the Turkish navy at Lepanto by the Holy League in 1571 and failure of the siege of Vienna heralded the decline of Turkish power. By the 18th century, Russia was seeking to establish itself as the protector of Christians in Turkey's Balkan territories. Russian ambitions were checked by Britain and France in the Crimean War (1854–56), but the Russo-Turkish War (1877–78) gave Bulgaria virtual independence and Romania and Serbia liberation from their nominal allegiance to the Sultan.

Turkish weakness stimulated a revolt of young liberals known as the Young Turks in 1909. They forced Sultan Abdul Hamid to grant a constitution and install a liberal government. Reforms were no barrier to further defeats, however, in a war with Italy (1911–12) and the Balkan Wars (1912–13). Under the influence of German military advisors, Turkey signed a secret alliance with Germany on Aug. 2, 1914, that led to a declaration of war by the Allied powers and the ultimate humiliation of the occupation of Turkish territory by Greek and other Allied troops.

In 1919, the new Nationalist movement, headed by Mustafa Kemal, was organized to resist the Allied occupation and, in 1920, a National Assembly elected him President of both the Assembly and the government. Under his leadership, the Nationalist government was recognized by foreign powers, the Greeks were driven out of Smyrna, and other Allied forces were withdrawn.

The present Turkish boundaries (with the exception of Alexandretta, ceded to Turkey by France in 1939) were fixed by the Treaty of Lausanne (1923) and later negotiations. The caliphate and sultanate were separated, and the sultanate was abolished in 1922. On Oct. 29, 1923, Turkey formally became a republic, with Mustafa Kemal, who took the name Kemal Atatürk, as its first President. The caliphate was abolished in 1924, and Atatürk proceeded to carry out an extensive program of reform, modernization, and industrialization.

Gen. Ismet Inönü was elected to succeed Atatürk in 1938 and was re-elected in 1939, 1943, and 1946. Defeated in 1950, he was succeeded by Celâl Bayar. In 1939, a mutual assistance pact was concluded with Britain and France. Turkey followed a neutral course during most of World War II. However, on Feb. 23, 1945, it declared war on Germany and Japan, but took no active part in the conflict.

Turkey became a full member of NATO in 1952. In 1971, the Turkish military demanded the ouster of Ismet Inönü, Premier since 1961, who was replaced by Nihat Erim. He pushed through a law that forbade growing of opium poppies after 1972.

The poppy-growing ban was shelved after Bülent Ecevit, a liberal, became Premier in 1974. Instead, the government required bulk-harvesting of all poppies and consignment of dried "poppy hay" to legal refineries abroad, maintaining that the method would prevent farmers from diverting raw opium to illicit channels. The system was continued after conservative Premier Süleyman Demirel took over the government in 1975.

Turkey invaded Cyprus by sea and air July 20, 1974, following the failure of diplomatic efforts to resolve the crisis caused by the ouster of Archbishop Makarios. Turkey, asserting its right to protect the minority Turkish Cypriot community, demanded the withdrawal of the 650 Greek officers who had led the coup. Greece refused the demand.

Talks in Geneva involving Greece, Turkey, Britain, and Greek Cypriot and Turkish Cypriot leaders broke down in mid-August. Turkey unilaterally announced a cease-fire August 16, after having gained control of 40% of the island.

More than a year of diplomatic negotiations failed to produce a settlement on Cyprus, where tensions were compounded after Turkish Cypriots established their own state in the north on Feb. 13, 1975.

U.S.-Turkish relations, excellent for a generation, were seriously damaged when Congress voted to end arms sales to Turkey in 1975 because arms the U.S. had supplied for mutual defense had been used in the invasion of Cyprus. Congress maintained the ban despite warnings from President Ford that it would imperil the future of 20 U.S. air and intelligence bases in Turkey and could affect Turkey's role as NATO's anchor in the Eastern Mediterranean.

In July 1975, after a 30-day warning, Turkey took over control of all the installations except the big joint defense base at Incirlik, which it reserved for "NATO tasks alone." Some 7,000 U.S. military men remained on duty under Turkish orders, but relations between Ankara and Washington hit a 30-year low.

In August 1978, the Carter administration won a reluctant Congressional reversal of the arms embargo, but a year later there was renewed Congressional opposition to granting military aid because Turkey had balked at allowing U.S. U-2 reconnaissance planes to use its air space. The planes were to check on Soviet compliance with SALT II, the strategic arms limitation treaty. Ecevit said the U-2's would be acceptable only if the Soviet Union agreed to their presence.

Economic problems and civil disturbances plagued the government in 1979, and a $1.45-billion aid package organized by the U.S. and Western European nations—conditioned on economic reforms—was advanced to help Turkey finance imports. Meanwhile, the Soviet Union agreed to build an atomic power plant for Turkey and supply fuel for it, the first such agreement with a NATO member. Moscow also increased its oil shipments to Turkey.

After conservative gains in the elections of Oct. 14, 1979, Ecevit resigned and Demirel returned to power at the head of a minority government. Strikes and terrorism, stimulated by continuing inflation and rising unemployment, brought Turkey to the brink of anarchy in 1980. In March, a mission of the Organization for Economic Cooperation and Development abandoned efforts to negotiate Ankara's request for a $3-billion loan to stabilize the economy.

The establishment of a military government in September 1980 brought a measure of internal stability. Gen. Evren, head of the National Security Council, promised to form a Constituent Assembly in 1981 that would revise the Constitution and function as a legislature until elections were held and civilian government restored.

TUVALU

Sovereign: Queen Elizabeth II
Governor-General: Sir Fiatau Penitala Teo (1978)
Prime Minister: Toalipi Lauti (1978)
Area: 10 sq mi. (26 sq km)
Population (est. 1981): 7,000
Density per square mile: 700.0
Capital and largest city (est. 1979): Funafuti, 2,200
Monetary unit: Australian dollar
Languages: Samoan and Gilbertese
Member of the Commonwealth of Nations

Freedom House classifications: Capitalist pre-industrial, non-party non-military
Economic summary: Gross national product (1975): $1 million. Principal agricultural products: copra and coconuts. Export: copra. Imports: food and mineral fuels. Major trading partners: Australia, U.K.

Geography. Formerly the Ellice Islands, Tuvalu consists of nine small islands scattered over 500,000 square miles of the western Pacific, just south of the equator.

Government. Official executive power is vested in a Governor-General, representing the Queen, who is appointed by her on the recommendation of the Tuvalu government. Actual executive power lies with a Prime Minister, who is responsible to a House of Assembly composed of eight elected members.

History. The Ellice Islands became a British protectorate in 1892 and were annexed by Britain in 1915–16 as part of the Gilbert and Ellice Islands Colony. The Ellice Islands were separated in 1975, given home rule, and renamed Tuvalu. Full independence was granted on Sept. 30, 1978.

UGANDA

Republic of Uganda
President: Milton Obote (1980)
Prime Minister: Otema Alimadi (1980)
Area: 91,134 sq mi. (236,036 sq km)
Population (est. 1981): 14,000,000 (growth rate: 3.1%)
Density per square mile: 153.6
Capital and largest city (est. 1980): Kampala, 500,000
Monetary unit: Ugandan shilling
Languages: English (official), Swahili, Luganda, Ateso, Luo
Religions: Christian, Islam
Member of Commonwealth of Nations
Freedom House classifications: Capitalist-statist, pre-industrial, multi-party centralized
Economic summary: Gross national product (1979): $3.7 billion. Average annual growth rate (1970–78): −2.8%. Per capita income: $240. Land used for agriculture: 21%; labor force: 90%; principal products: coffee, tea, cotton, tobacco, sugar, fish. Labor force in industry: 3%; major products: processed agricultural products, copper, cement, shoes, fertilizer, sheet iron, beverages. Natural resources: copper, miscellaneous minerals. Exports: coffee, cotton, tea, copper. Imports: petroleum products, machinery, transport equipment. Major trading partners: U.S., U.K., Kenya.

Geography. Uganda, twice the size of Pennsylvania, is in east central Africa. It is bordered on the west by Zaire, on the north by the Sudan, on the east by Kenya, and on the south by Tanzania and Rwanda.

The country, which lies across the Equator, is divided into three main areas—swampy lowlands, a fertile plateau with wooded hills, and a desert region. Lake Victoria forms part of the southern border.

Government. Executive power is held by the President, chosen for a five-year term by the party winning a majority in parliamentary elections. Legislative power is held by the National Assembly. Major parties are the Uganda People's Congress (72 of 126 seats), led by Prime Minister

Alimedi; the Democratic Party (53 seats); and the Uganda Patriotic Movement (1 seat).

History. Uganda was first visited by European explorers as well as Arab traders in 1844. An Anglo-German agreement of 1890 declared it to be in the British sphere of influence in Africa, and the Imperial British East Africa Company was chartered to develop the area. The company did not prosper financially, and in 1894 a British protectorate was proclaimed.

Uganda became independent on Oct. 9, 1962. As its first president, the country chose Mutesa II, King of the ancient kingdom of Buganda. Dr. Milton Obote had been Prime Minister. In 1965, he suspended the Constitution and assumed the powers of the government, later abolishing the offices of President and Vice President.

Obote in 1970 passed laws declaring that 40,000 British Asians—Asian-born persons, mostly Indian, who lived in Uganda but chose British citizenship in 1962 rather than Ugandan—needed a variety of passes and permits to remain in the country. In 1971, Idi Amin, an unpredictable army sergeant, ousted Obote and made himself President. The next year, he began expelling the Asians. He also expelled Israeli advisors rather than pay Israel's military aid bill and applauded Hitler's treatment of Jews.

With his country's potentially rich agricultural economy in turmoil, partly because of large purchases of weapons for its 20,000-man army, Amin nationalized all land in 1975, without compensation to former owners.

In 1976, Amin had himself proclaimed President for Life by the Defense Council, which replaced the Council of Ministers as Uganda's ruling body.

An Israeli commando raid against Entebbe airport on July 4, 1976, freed 103 hostages in a hijacked French airliner that had been held at the airport for a week by Palestinian guerrillas. Hostages, and the government of Israel, charged that Amin had collaborated with the hijackers.

The world condemned Amin's atrocities—Amnesty International reported in 1977 that 300,-000 may have died under his rule, including Cabinet ministers and church leaders. Few African leaders denounced him, however, until President Julius K. Nyerere of Tanzania launched an invasion in November 1978, with the tacit acquiescence of most of Africa. Libya's chief, Muammar el-Qaddafi, came to Amin's defense with troops and arms, but the Libyans only temporarily halted the invaders. Kampala was taken on April 11, 1979, and Amin fled to Libya.

A brief interim government in which Yusufe Lule and Godfrey Binaisa served as President in rapid succession ended when a Military Commission, headed by Paulo Muwanga, took power on May 12, 1980. Elections on Dec. 10–11, the first in 18 years, restored constitutional government.

UNION OF SOVIET SOCIALIST REPUBLICS
See Soviet Union

UNITED ARAB EMIRATES

Head of State: Sheik Zayed Bin Sultan Al-Nahayan (1971)
Prime Minister: Sheik Rashid bin Said al-Maktoum (1979)
Area: 32,000 sq mi. (82,880 sq km)
Population (est. 1981): 850,000 (Arab, 42%; South Asian, 50%) (growth rate: 4.0%)
Density per square mile: 26.6
Capital and largest city (est. 1975): Abu Dhabi, 95,000
Monetary unit: Dirham
Language: Arabic
Religion: Islam
Freedom House classifications: Capitalist-statist industrial, non-party non-military
Economic summary: Gross national product (1979): $13.0 billion. Average annual growth rate (1970–78): −5.6%. Per capita income: $18,500. Land used for agriculture: 8%; labor force: 10%; principal products: vegetables, meats, dates, tobacco, fruit. Labor force in industry: 65%; major products: fish, light manufactures, petroleum, construction materials. Natural resources: oil. Exports: petroleum, pearls, fish. Imports: machinery, consumer goods, food. Major trading partners: Western European nations, U.K., Japan, U.S., India.

Geography. The United Arab Emirates, in the eastern part of the Arabian Peninsula, extends along part of the Gulf of Oman and the southern coast of the Persian Gulf. The nation is the size of Maine. Its neighbors are Saudi Arabia in the west and south, Qatar in the north, and Oman in the east. Most of the land is barren and sandy.

Government. The United Arab Emirates was formed in 1971 by seven emirates known as the Trucial States—Abu Dhabi (the largest), Dubai, Sharjah, Ajman, Fujairah, Ras al Khaimah and Umm al-Qaiwain.

The loose federation allows joint policies in foreign relations, defense, and development, with each member state keeping its internal local system of government headed by its own ruler. A 40-member legislature consists of eight seats each for Abu Dhabi and Dubai, six seats each for Ras al Khaimah and Sharjah, and four each for the others. It is a member of the Arab League.

History. Originally the area was inhabited by a seafaring people who were converted to Islam in the seventh century. Later, a dissident sect, the Carmathians, established a powerful sheikdom, and its army conquered Mecca. After the sheikdom disintegrated, its people became pirates.

Threatening the sultanate of Muscat and Oman early in the 19th century, the pirates provoked the intervention of the British, who in 1820 enforced a partial truce and in 1853 a permanent truce. Thus what had been called the Pirate Coast was renamed the Trucial Coast.

UNITED KINGDOM

United Kingdom of Great Britain and Northern Ireland
Sovereign: Queen Elizabeth II (1952)
Prime Minister: Margaret Thatcher (1979)
Area: 94,250 sq mi. (244,108 sq km)
Population (est. 1981): 55,900,000 (growth rate, 1977–79: 0.0%) (English, Scottish, Welsh, Northern Irish)
Density per square mile: 593.1
Capital: London, England
Largest cities (est. 1979): Greater London, 6,877,000; Birmingham, England, 1,034,000; Glasgow, Scotland, 794,000; Leeds, England, 724,000; Sheffield, England, 544,000; Liverpool, England, 520,000; Manchester, England, 479,000; Bradford, England, 462,000; Edinburgh, Scotland, 455,000; Bristol, England, 408,000
Monetary unit: Pound sterling (£)

Area and Population of United Kingdom

Subdivision	Area sq mi.	Area sq km	Population (est. 1979)
England and Wales	58,381	151,207	49,250,000
Scotland	30,416	78,777	5,153,000
Northern Ireland	5,452	14,121	1,550,000
Total	94,249	244,105	55,953,000

Languages: English, Welsh, Gaelic
Religions: Church of England (established church); Church of Wales (disestablished); Church of Scotland (established church—Presbyterian); Church of Ireland (disestablished); Roman Catholic; Methodist; Congregational; Baptist; Jewish
Freedom House classifications: Capitalist-socialist industrial, multi-party centralized
Economic summary: Gross national product (1979): $353.6 billion. Average annual growth rate (1970–78): 1.9%. Per capita income: $4,360. Principal agricultural products: cereals, livestock and livestock products. Major industrial products: steel, heavy engineering and metal manufactures, textiles, motor vehicles and aircraft, electronics, chemicals. Natural resources: coal, oil, gas. Exports: machinery, transport equipment, chemicals, beverages. Imports: foodstuffs, petroleum, machinery, crude materials. Major trading partners: Western European nations, U.S., Canada, France.

Geography. The United Kingdom, consisting of England, Wales, Scotland, and Northern Ireland, is twice the size of New York State. England, in the southeast part of the British Isles, is separated from Scotland on the north by the granite Cheviot Hills; from them the Pennine chain of uplands extends south through the center of England, reaching its highest point in the Lake District in the northwest. To the west along the border of Wales—a land of steep hills and valleys—are the Cambrian Mountains, while the Cotswolds, a range of hills in Gloucestershire, extend into the surrounding shires.

The remainder of England is plain land, though not necessarily flat, with the rocky sand-topped moors in the southwest, the rolling downs in the south and southeast, and the reclaimed marshes of the low-lying fens in the east central districts.

Scotland is divided into three physical regions—the Highlands, the Central Lowlands, containing two-thirds of the population, and the Southern Uplands. The western Highland coast is intersected throughout by long, narrow sea-lochs, or fiords. Scotland also includes the Outer and Inner Hebrides and other islands off the west coast and the Orkney and Shetland Islands off the north coast.

Wales is generally hilly; the Snowdon range in the northern part culminates in Mount Snowdon (3,560 ft, 1,085 m), highest in both England and Wales.

Important rivers flowing into the North Sea are the Thames, Humber, Tees, and Tyne. In the west are the Severn and Wye, which empty into the Bristol Channel and are navigable, as are the Mersey and Ribble.

Government. The United Kingdom is a constitutional monarchy, with a Queen and a Parliament that has two houses: the House of Lords with about 830 hereditary peers, 26 spiritual peers, about 270 life peers and peeresses, and 9 law-lords, who are hereditary, or life, peers, and the House of Commons, which since 1974 has had 635 popularly elected members. Supreme legislative power is vested in Parliament, which sits for five years unless sooner dissolved.

The executive power of the Crown is exercised by the Cabinet, headed by the Prime Minister. The latter, normally the head of the party commanding a majority in the House of Commons, is appointed by the Sovereign, with whose consent he or she in turn appoints the rest of the Cabinet. All ministers must be members of one or the other house of Parliament; they are individually and collectively responsible to the Crown and Parliament. The Cabinet proposes bills and arranges the business of Parliament, but it depends entirely on the votes in the House of Commons. The Lords cannot hold up "money" bills, but they can delay other bills for a maximum of one year.

By the Act of Union (1707), the Scottish Parliament was assimilated with that of England, and Scotland is now represented in Commons by 71 members. The Secretary of State for Scotland, a member of the Cabinet, is responsible for the administration of Scottish affairs.

The major political parties are the Conservative Party (336 of the 635 seats in the House of Commons), led by Prime Minister Margaret Thatcher; Labor Party (256 seats), led by Michael Foote; Social Democrats (15 seats), led by David Owens; Liberal Party (11 seats), led by David Steel; Ulster Unionists and other Northern Irish parties (12 seats); Scottish Nationalist Party (2 seats); Welsh Nationalist Party (2 seats).

Ruler: Queen Elizabeth II, born April 21, 1926, elder daughter of King George VI and Queen Elizabeth, succeeded to the throne on the death of her father on Feb. 6, 1952; married Nov. 20, 1947, to Prince Philip, Duke of Edinburgh, born June 10, 1921; their children are Prince Charles[1] (heir presumptive), born Nov. 14, 1948; Princess Anne, born Aug. 15, 1950; Prince Andrew, born Feb. 19, 1960; and Prince Edward, born March 10, 1964. The Queen's sister is Princess Margaret, born Aug. 21, 1930.

History. Roman invasions of the 1st century B.C. brought Britain into contact with the Continent. When the Roman legions withdrew in the 5th century A.D., Britain fell easy prey to the invading hordes of Angles, Saxons, and Jutes from Scandinavia and the Low Countries. Seven large kingdoms were established, and the original Britons were forced into Wales and Scotland. It was not until the 11th century that the country finally became united under the Danish King Canute. Following the death of Edward the Confessor (1066), a dispute about the succession arose, and William, Duke of Normandy, invaded England, defeating the Saxon King, Harold II, at the Battle of Hastings (1066). The Norman conquest introduced Norman law and feudalism.

The reign of Henry II (1154–89), first of the Plantagenets, saw an increasing centralization of royal power at the expense of the nobles, but in 1215 John (1199–1216) was forced to sign the Magna Carta, which awarded the people, especially the nobles, certain basic rights. Edward I (1272–1307)

---

1. The title Prince of Wales, which is not inherited, was conferred on Prince Charles by his mother on July 26, 1958. The investiture ceremony took place on July 1, 1969. The previous Prince of Wales was Prince Edward Albert, who held the title from 1911 to 1936 before he became Edward VIII.

Rulers of England and Great Britain

Name	Born	Ruled[1]	Name	Born	Ruled[1]
SAXONS[2]			**HOUSE OF YORK**		
Egbert[3]	c. 775	828–839	Edward IV	1442	1461–1483[5]
Ethelwulf	?	839–858	Edward V	1470	1483–1483
Ethelbald	?	858–860	Richard III	1452	1483–1485
Ethelbert	?	860–866			
Ethelred I	?	866–871	**HOUSE OF TUDOR**		
Alfred the Great	849	871–899	Henry VII	1457	1485–1509
Edward the Elder	c. 870	899–924	Henry VIII	1491	1509–1547
Athelstan	895	924–939	Edward VI	1537	1547–1553
Edmund I the Deed-doer	921	939–946	Jane (Lady Jane Grey)[6]	1537	1553–1553
Edred	c. 925	946–955	Mary I ("Bloody Mary")	1516	1553–1558
Edwy the Fair	c. 943	955–959	Elizabeth I	1533	1558–1603
Edgar the Peaceful	943	959–975			
Edward the Martyr	c. 962	975–979	**HOUSE OF STUART**		
Ethelred II the Unready	968	979–1016	James I[7]	1566	1603–1625
Edmund II Ironside	c. 993	1016–1016	Charles I	1600	1625–1649
DANES			**COMMONWEALTH**		
Canute	995	1016–1035	Council of State	—	1649–1653
Harold I Harefoot	c.1016	1035–1040	Oliver Cromwell[8]	1599	1653–1658
Hardecanute	c.1018	1040–1042	Richard Cromwell[8]	1626	1658–1659[9]
SAXONS			**RESTORATION OF HOUSE OF**		
Edward the Confessor	c.1004	1042–1066	**STUART**		
Harold II	c.1020	1066–1066	Charles II	1630	1660–1685
			James II	1633	1685–1688[10]
HOUSE OF NORMANDY			William III[11]	1650	1689–1702
William I the Conqueror	1027	1066–1087	Mary II[11]	1662	1689–1694
William II Rufus	c.1056	1087–1100	Anne	1665	1702–1714
Henry I Beauclerc	1068	1100–1135			
Stephen of Blois	c.1100	1135–1154	**HOUSE OF HANOVER**		
			George I	1660	1714–1727
HOUSE OF PLANTAGENET			George II	1683	1727–1760
Henry II	1133	1154–1189	George III	1738	1760–1820
Richard I Coeur de Lion	1157	1189–1199	George IV	1762	1820–1830
John Lackland	1167	1199–1216	William IV	1765	1830–1837
Henry III	1207	1216–1272	Victoria	1819	1837–1901
Edward I Longshanks	1239	1272–1307			
Edward II	1284	1307–1327	**HOUSE OF SAXE-COBURG**[12]		
Edward III	1312	1327–1377	Edward VII	1841	1901–1910
Richard II	1367	1377–1399[4]			
			HOUSE OF WINDSOR[12]		
HOUSE OF LANCASTER			George V	1865	1910–1936
Henry IV Bolingbroke	1367	1399–1413	Edward VIII	1894	1936–1936[13]
Henry V	1387	1413–1422	George VI	1895	1936–1952
Henry VI	1421	1422–1461[5]	Elizabeth II	1926	1952–

1. Year of end of rule is also that of death, unless otherwise indicated. 2. Dates for Saxon kings are still subject of controversy. 3. Became King of West Saxons in 802; considered (from 828) first King of all England. 4. Died 1400. 5. Henry VI reigned again briefly 1470–71. 6. Nominal Queen for 9 days; not counted as Queen by some authorities. She was beheaded in 1554. 7. Ruled in Scotland as James VI (1567–1625). 8. Lord Protector. 9. Died 1712. 10. Died 1701. 11. Joint rulers (1689–1694). 12. Name changed from Saxe-Coburg to Windsor in 1917. 13. Was known after his abdication as the Duke of Windsor; died 1972.

continued the conquest of Ireland, reduced Wales to subjection and made some gains in Scotland. In 1314, however, English forces led by Edward II were ousted from Scotland after the Battle of Bannockburn. The late 13th and early 14th centuries saw the development of a separate House of Commons with tax-raising powers.

Edward III's claim to the throne of France led to the Hundred Years' War (1338–1453) and the loss of almost all the large English territory in France. In England, the great poverty and discontent caused by the war were intensified by the Black Death, a plague that reduced the population by about one third. The Wars of the Roses (1455–85), a struggle for the throne between the House of

York and the House of Lancaster, ended in the victory of Henry Tudor (Henry VII) at Bosworth Field (1485).

During the reign of Henry VIII (1509–47), the Church in England asserted its independence from the Roman Catholic Church. Under Edward VI and Mary, the two extremes of religious fanaticism were reached, and it remained for Henry's daughter, Elizabeth I (1558–1603), to set up the Church of England on a moderate basis. In 1588, the Spanish Armada, a fleet sent out by Catholic King Philip II of Spain, was defeated by the English and destroyed during a storm. During Elizabeth's reign, England became a world power.

Elizabeth's heir was a Stuart—James VI of Scot-

British Prime Ministers Since 1770

Name	Term	Name	Term
Lord North (Tory)	1770–1782	Marquis of Salisbury (Conservative)	1886–1892
Marquis of Rockingham (Whig)	1782–1782	William E. Gladstone (Liberal)	1892–1894
Earl of Shelburne (Whig)	1782–1783	Earl of Rosebery (Liberal)	1894–1895
Duke of Portland (Coalition)	1783–1783	Marquis of Salisbury	
William Pitt, the Younger (Tory)	1783–1801	(Conservative)	1895–1902
Henry Addington (Tory)	1801–1804	Earl Balfour (Conservative)	1902–1905
William Pitt, the Younger (Tory)	1804–1806	Sir H. Campbell-Bannerman	
Baron Grenville (Whig)	1806–1807	(Liberal)	1905–1908
Duke of Portland (Tory)	1807–1809	Herbert H. Asquith (Liberal)	1908–1915
Spencer Perceval (Tory)	1809–1812	Herbert H. Asquith (Coalition)	1915–1916
Earl of Liverpool (Tory)	1812–1827	David Lloyd George (Coalition)	1916–1922
George Canning (Tory)	1827–1827	Andrew Bonar Law (Conservative)	1922–1923
Viscount Goderich (Tory)	1827–1828	Stanley Baldwin (Conservative)	1923–1924
Duke of Wellington (Tory)	1828–1830	James Ramsay MacDonald	
Earl Grey (Whig)	1830–1834	(Labor)	1924–1924
Viscount Melbourne (Whig)	1834–1834	Stanley Baldwin (Conservative)	1924–1929
Sir Robert Peel (Tory)	1834–1835	James Ramsay MacDonald	
Viscount Melbourne (Whig)	1835–1841	(Labor)	1929–1931
Sir Robert Peel (Tory)	1841–1846	James Ramsay MacDonald	
Earl Russell (Whig)	1846–1852	(Coalition)	1931–1935
Earl of Derby (Tory)	1852–1852	Stanley Baldwin (Coalition)	1935–1937
Earl of Aberdeen (Coalition)	1852–1855	Neville Chamberlain (Coalition)	1937–1940
Viscount Palmerston (Liberal)	1855–1858	Winston Churchill (Coalition)	1940–1945
Earl of Derby (Conservative)	1858–1859	Clement R. Attlee (Labor)	1945–1951
Viscount Palmerston (Liberal)	1859–1865	Sir Winston Churchill (Conservative)	1951–1955
Earl Russell (Liberal)	1865–1866	Sir Anthony Eden (Conservative)	1955–1957
Earl of Derby (Conservative)	1866–1868	Harold Macmillan (Conservative)	1957–1963
Benjamin Disraeli (Conservative)	1868–1868	Sir Alec Frederick Douglas-Home	
William E. Gladstone (Liberal)	1868–1874	(Conservative)	1963–1964
Benjamin Disraeli (Conservative)	1874–1880	Harold Wilson (Labor)	1964–1970
William E. Gladstone (Liberal)	1880–1885	Edward Heath (Conservative)	1970–1974
Marquis of Salisbury		Harold Wilson (Labor)	1974–1976
(Conservative)	1885–1886	James Callaghan (Labor)	1976–1979
William E. Gladstone (Liberal)	1886–1886	Margaret Thatcher (Conservative)	1979–

land—who joined the two crowns as James I (1603–25). The Stuart kings incurred large debts and were forced either to depend on Parliament for taxes or to raise money by illegal means. In 1642, war broke out between Charles I and a large segment of the Parliament; Charles was defeated and executed in 1649, and the monarchy was then abolished. After the death in 1658 of Oliver Cromwell, the Lord Protector, the Puritan Commonwealth fell to pieces and Charles II was placed on the throne in 1660. The struggle between the King and Parliament continued, but Charles II knew when to compromise. His brother, James II (1685–88), possessed none of his ability and was ousted by the Revolution of 1688, which confirmed the primacy of Parliament. James's daughter, Mary, and her husband, William of Orange, were now the rulers.

Queen Anne's reign (1702–14) was marked by the Duke of Marlborough's victories over France at Blenheim, Oudenarde, and Malplaquet in the War of the Spanish Succession. England and Scotland meanwhile were joined by the Act of Union (1707). Upon the death of Anne, the distant claims of the elector of Hanover were recognized, and he became King of Great Britain and Ireland as George I.

The unwillingness of the Hanoverian kings to rule resulted in the formation by the royal ministers of a Cabinet, headed by a Prime Minister, which directed all public business. Abroad, the constant wars with France expanded the British Empire all over the globe, particularly in North America and India. This imperial growth was checked by the revolt of the American colonies (1775–81).

Struggles with France broke out again in 1793 and, during the Napoleonic Wars, which ended at Waterloo (1815), Britain was pitted at one time against almost all of Europe.

The Victorian era, named after Queen Victoria (1837–1901), saw the growth of a democratic system of government that had begun with the Reform Bill of 1832. The two important wars in Victoria's reign were the Crimean War against Russia (1853–56) and the Boer War (1899–1902), the latter enormously extending Britain's influence in Africa.

Increasing uneasiness at home and abroad marked the reign of Edward VII (1901–10). Within four years after the accession of George V in 1910, Britain entered World War I when Germany invaded Belgium. The nation was led by coalition Cabinets, headed first by Herbert Asquith and then, starting in 1916, by the Welsh statesman David Lloyd George. Postwar labor unrest culminated in the general strike of 1926.

King Edward VIII succeeded to the throne on Jan. 20, 1936, at his father's death, but abdicated on Dec. 11, 1936 (in order to marry an American divorcee, Wallis Warfield Simpson) in favor of his brother, who became George VI.

The efforts of Prime Minister Neville Chamberlain to stem the rising threat of Nazism in Germany failed with the German invasion of Poland on Sept. 1, 1939, which was followed by Britain's entry into World War II on September 3. Allied reverses in the spring of 1940 led to Chamberlain's resignation and the formation of another coalition war Cabinet by the Conservative leader, Winston Churchill, who led Britain through most of World War II. Churchill resigned shortly after V-E Day, May 7, 1945, but then formed a "caretaker" government that remained in office until after the parliamentary elections in July, which the Labor Party won overwhelmingly. The government formed by Clement R. Attlee began a moderate socialist program.

For details of World War II (1939–45), *see* Headline History.

In 1951, Churchill again became Prime Minister at the head of a Conservative government. George VI died Feb. 6, 1952, and was succeeded by his daughter Elizabeth II.

Churchill stepped down in 1955 in favor of Sir Anthony Eden, who resigned on grounds of ill health in 1957, and was succeeded by Harold Macmillan and Sir Alec Douglas-Home. In 1964, Harold Wilson led the Labor Party to victory.

Wilson, the first Labor Prime Minister in 13 years, was a skilled strategist from the party's center who instituted no great changes domestically. His ambition for success abroad was thwarted by the French veto of Britain's bid for entry into the European Economic Community and by his own inept handling of the unilateral declaration of independence by Southern Rhodesia, the last sizable British colony.

A lagging economy brought the Conservatives back to power in 1970. Prime Minister Edward Heath won Britain's admission to the European Community, a move affirmed by 67.2% in the nation's first referendum. Heath narrowly lost a February 1974 election overshadowed by a coal strike, returning Wilson to the leadership and the first minority government since 1929.

Party elections after Wilson's announcement of his intention to retire elevated James Callaghan from the Foreign Ministry to the Prime Minister's office in 1976.

Despite economic troubles, unemployment, and continuing conflict in Northern Ireland and Rhodesia, Britons in June 1977 celebrated the Silver Jubilee of Queen Elizabeth II with genuine affection. The Queen's first grandchild, Peter Mark Andrew Phillips, son of Princess Anne, was born November 14. On May 24, 1978, the first divorce in the immediate royal family in more than 150 years took place when Princess Margaret's 18-year marriage to the Earl of Snowdon was legally ended.

Margaret Thatcher became Britain's first woman Prime Minister as the Conservatives won 339 seats for a 43-seat majority in elections on May 3, 1979. The 53-year-old, Oxford-educated daughter of a grocer campaigned for lower taxes, curbs on labor unions, and less government at home coupled with a more decisive foreign policy.

Mrs. Thatcher moved quickly to implement her domestic program but was blocked by African and U.S. resistance from granting early recognition to the Muzorewa government in Zimbabwe (Rhodesia). In September 1979, a bold initiative by her foreign minister, Lord Carrington, brought all parties in the conflict to a conference in London at which she threatened and cajoled the white minority and black factions until all agreed on a new Constitution. The successful conduct of elections in February and the transfer of sovereignty on April 18, 1980, was a political triumph for the Conservatives.

A similar gamble, with Mrs. Thatcher threatening to pull Britain out of the European Economic Community, brought a major reduction in the British contribution to the E.E.C. Although the victory avoided sharp increases in food prices, the dispute strengthened the growing sentiment in Britain for withdrawal from the E.E.C.

Despite rising income from North Sea oil production, the economy sagged in 1980 and continued to slide in 1981 as the government pursued a harsh deflationary policy. With unemployment nearing 6 million, rioting broke out in London, Liverpool, Manchester, and other cities. Lack of jobs and discontent among black and Asian minorities were blamed for the upheavals, which resulted in thousands of arrests, but Mrs. Thatcher only called for stronger police measures and public discipline.

The rioting cast a shadow on the wedding of Prince Charles and Lady Diana Spencer, held on July 20 at St. Paul's Cathedral rather than historic Westminster Abbey, the usual site for royal ceremonies.

NORTHERN IRELAND

Status: Part of United Kingdom
Secretary of State: Humphrey Atkins (1979)
Area: 5,452 sq mi. (14,121 sq km)
Population (est. 1979): 1,525,000
Density per square mile: 279.7
Capital and largest city (est. 1978): Belfast, 354,000
Monetary Unit: British pound sterling
Languages: English, Gaelic
Religions: Roman Catholic, 35%; Presbyterian, 29%; Church of Ireland, 24%; Methodist, 5%

Geography. Northern Ireland comprises the counties of Antrim, Armagh, Down, Fermanagh, Londonderry, and Tyrone, which make up predominantly Protestant Ulster and form the northern part of the island of Ireland, westernmost of the British Isles. It is slightly larger than Connecticut.

Government. Northern Ireland is an integral part of the United Kingdom (it has 12 representatives in the British House of Commons), but under the terms of the Government of Ireland Act in 1920, it had a semiautonomous government. But in 1972, after three years of internal strife which resulted in over 400 dead and thousands injured, Britain suspended the Ulster parliament. The Ulster counties became governed directly from London after an attempt to return certain powers to an elected Assembly in Belfast.

The Northern Ireland Assembly was dissolved in 1975 and a Constitutional Convention was elected to write a Constitution acceptable to Protestants and Catholics. The convention failed to reach agreement and closed down the next year.

The major political parties are the United Ulster Unionist Coalition (Protestant) (46 of 78 delegates to the Constitutional Convention); Social Democratic Labor Party (Catholic) (17 delegates); Alliance Party (8 delegates); New Unionist Party of Northern Ireland (Protestant) (5 delegates).

History. Ulster was part of Catholic Ireland until the reign of Elizabeth I (1558–1603) when, after crushing three Irish rebellions, the crown confiscated lands in Ireland and settled in Ulster the Scot Presbyterians who became rooted there. Another rebellion in 1641–51, crushed as brutally by Oliver Cromwell, resulted in the settlement of Anglican Englishmen in Ulster. Subsequent political policy favoring Protestants and disadvantaging

Catholics encouraged further settlement in Northern Ireland.

But the North did not separate from the South until William Gladstone presented in 1886 his proposal for home rule in Ireland as a means of settling the Irish Question. The Protestants in the North, although they had grievances like the Catholics in the South, feared domination by the Catholic majority. Industry, moreover, was concentrated in the north and dependent on the British market.

When World War I began, civil war threatened between the regions. Northern Ireland, however, did not become a political entity until the six counties accepted the Home Rule Bill of 1920. This set up a semiautonomous Parliament in Belfast and a Crown-appointed Governor advised by a Cabinet of the Prime Minister and eight ministers, as well as a 12-member representation in the House of Commons in London.

As the Republic of Ireland gained its sovereignty, relations improved between North and South, although the Irish Republican Army, outlawed in recent years, continued the struggle to end the partition of Ireland. In 1966–69, communal rioting and street fighting between Protestants and Catholics occurred in Londonderry, fomented by extremist nationalist Protestants, who feared the Catholics might attain a local majority, and by Catholics demonstrating for civil rights.

Rioting, terrorism, and sniping killed more than 2,000 people from 1969 through 1981, and the religious communities, Catholic and Protestant, became hostile armed camps. British troops were brought in to separate them but themselves became a target of Catholics.

In 1973, a new British charter created a 78-member Assembly elected by proportional representation that gave more weight to Catholic strength. It created a Province Executive with committee chairmen of the Assembly heading all government departments except law enforcement, which remained under London's control. Assembly elections in 1973 produced a majority for the new Constitution that included Catholic assemblymen.

Ulster's leaders agreed in 1973 to create an 11-member Executive Body with six seats assigned to Unionists (Protestants) and four to members of Catholic parties. Unionist leader Brian Faulkner headed the Executive. Also agreed to was a Council of Ireland, with 14 seats evenly divided between Dublin and Belfast, which could act only by unanimous vote.

Although the Council lacked real authority, its creation sparked a general strike by Protestant extremists in 1974. The two-week strike caused Faulkner's resignation from the Executive and resumption of direct rule from London.

In April 1974, London instituted a new program that responded to some Catholic grievances, but assigned more British troops to cut off movement of arms and munitions to Ulster's violence-racked cities.

Violence continued unabated, with new heights reached early in 1976 when the British government announced the end of special privileges for political prisoners in Northern Ireland. British Prime Minister James Callaghan visited Belfast in July and pledged that Ulster would remain part of the United Kingdom unless a clear majority wished to separate.

In October 1977, the 1976 Nobel Prize for Peace was awarded to Mairead Corrigan and Betty Williams for their campaign for peace in Northern Ireland. Intermittent violence continued, however, and on Aug. 27, 1979, an I.R.A. bomb killed Earl Mountbatten as he was sailing off southern Ireland. The death of the 79-year-old cousin of the Queen, a World War II hero and the last Viceroy of India, shocked the world. Mrs. Thatcher visited Ulster two days later and denounced terrorism. After Mountbatten's state funeral in Westminster Abbey on Sept. 5, Mrs. Thatcher met with Irish Premier John Lynch to discuss security measures against the I.R.A. Lynch urged an attack on the "root cause," the division of Ireland.

New talks aimed at a restoration of home rule in Northern Ireland began and quickly ended in January 1980. In May, Mrs. Thatcher met with the new Prime Minister of the Irish Republic, Charles Haughey, but she insisted that the future of Ulster must be decided only by its people and the British Parliament. Haughey declared that an internal solution "cannot and will not succeed."

Civil disturbances reached new heights in the summer of 1981 as Irish nationalist prisoners went on hunger strikes in Maze Prison to attain their demands for "political" status. By August, ten had died, each death followed by violent demonstrations. The British government, despite appeals from outside agencies, refused to yield, insisting that privileges could be granted only within prison rules.

Dependencies of the United Kingdom
ANGUILLA, ANTIGUA
See West Indies Associated States

BERMUDA

Status: Self-governing dependency
Governor: Sir Peter Ramsbotham (1977)
Prime Minister: J. David Gibbons (1977)
Area: 20 sq mi. (52 sq km)
Population (est. 1981): 65,000 (growth rate: 1.3%)
Capital (est. 1978): Hamilton, 2,500
Monetary unit: Bermuda dollar
Economic summary: Gross national product (1979): $560 million. Average annual growth rate (1970–78): 1.4%. Per capita income: $7,540. Land used for agriculture: 12%; labor force: 1.3%; principal products: bananas, vegetables, citrus fruits, dairy products. Labor force in industry: 6.2%; major products: structural concrete, paints, perfumes, furniture. Natural resource: limestone. Exports: semi-tropical produce, light manufactures. Imports: foodstuffs, manufactured goods. Major trading partners: U.S., U.K., Canada.

Bermuda is an archipelago of about 360 small islands, 580 miles (934 km) east of North Carolina. The largest is (Great) Bermuda, or Long Island. Discovered by Juan de Bermúdez, a shipwrecked Spaniard, early in the 16th century, the islands were settled in 1612 by an offshoot of the Virginia Company and became a crown colony in 1684.

In 1940, sites on the islands were leased for 99 years to the U.S. for air and navy bases. Bermuda is also the headquarters of the West Indies and Atlantic squadron of the Royal Navy.

In 1968, Bermuda was granted a new Constitution, its first Prime Minister, and autonomy, except for foreign relations, defense, and internal security. The predominantly white United Bermuda Party has retained power in three elections against the opposition—the black-led Progressive Laborites—although Bermuda's population is 60% black. Serious rioting occurred in December 1977 after two blacks were hanged for a series of murders, including the 1973 assassination of the Governor, Sir Richard Sharples, and British troops were summoned to restore order.

BRITISH ANTARCTIC TERRITORY

Status: Dependency
High Commissioner: Rex Masterson Hunt (1980)
Area: 500,000 sq mi. (1,395,000 sq km)
Population (1976): 55

The British Antarctic Territory consists of the South Shetland Islands, South Orkney Islands, and Nearby Graham Land on the Antarctic continent, largely uninhabited. They were dependencies of the British crown colony of the Falkland Islands but received a separate administration in 1962, being governed by a British-appointed High Commissioner who is Governor of the Falklands.

BRITISH INDIAN OCEAN TERRITORY

Status: Dependency
Commissioner: John Adam Robson (1979)
Administrator: P. A. Raftery (1981)
Administrative headquarters: Victoria, Seychelles
Area: 85 sq mi, (220 sq km)

This dependency, consisting of the Chagos Archipelago and other small island groups, was formed in 1965 by agreement with Mauritius and the Seychelles. There is no permanent civilian population in the territory.

BRITISH VIRGIN ISLANDS

Status: Dependency
Governor: James A. Davidson (1978)
Area: 59 sq mi. (153 sq km)
Population (est. 1979): 12,000
Capital (est. 1975): Road Town (on Tortola): 3,500
Monetary unit: U.S. dollar

Some 36 islands in the Caribbean Sea northeast of Puerto Rico and west of the Leeward Islands, the British Virgin Islands are economically interdependent with the U.S. Virgin Islands to the south. They were formerly part of the administration of the Leeward Islands. They received a separate administration in 1956 as a crown colony. In 1967 a new Constitution was promulgated that provided for a ministerial system of government headed by the Governor. The principal islands are Tortola, Virgin Gorda, Anegada and Jost Van Dyke.

BRUNEI

Status: Independent state
Sultan: Hassanel Bolkiah (1968)
High Commissioner: A. C. Watson
Area: 2,226 sq mi. (5,765 sq km)
Population (est. 1981): 225,000 (growth rate, 1978–79: 5.8%)
Capital (est. 1978): Bandar Seri Begawan, 70,000
Monetary unit: Brunei dollar
Economic summary: Gross national product (1979): $2.2 billion. Average annual growth rate (1970–78): 4.9%. Per capita income: $2,970. Land used for agriculture: 3%; labor force: 31%; principal agricultural products: rubber, rice, pepper. Labor force in industry: 33%; major industrial products: crude petroleum, liquefied natural gas. Natural resources: petroleum, natural gas. Exports: crude petroleum, liquefied natural gas. Imports: machinery, transport equipment, manufactured goods, foodstuffs. Major trading partners: Japan, U.S., U.K., Singapore.

A sultanate on the northwest coast of the island of Borneo on the South China Sea, Brunei consists of two prongs into the territory of Sarawak, East Malaysia. It was a powerful state from the 16th to the 19th century, ruling over the northern part of Borneo and adjacent island chains. But it fell into decay and lost Sarawak in 1841, becoming a British protectorate in 1888 and a British dependency in 1905.

The Sultan regained control over internal affairs by a Constitution he instituted in 1959, along with an agreement with the Crown delegating responsibility for defense and foreign affairs. Britain, which is responsible for foreign affairs, is represented by a High Commissioner; government is by a Privy Council and Council of Ministers, both presided over by the Sultan, and a Legislative Council.

Sultan Bolkiah was crowned in 1968 at the age of 22. He succeeded his father, Sir Omar Ali Saifuddin, who had abdicated.

Most of the inhabitants are Malays, Borneans, and Chinese. The majority of the population lives in and around the capital, situated on the Brunei River nine miles from its mouth.

CAYMAN ISLANDS

Status: Dependency
Governor: Thomas Russell (1974)
Area: 118 sq mi. (306 sq km)
Population (est. 1978): 14,000
Capital (est. 1980): Georgetown (on Grand Cayman), 7,600
Monetary unit: Cayman Islands dollar

This dependency consists of three islands—Grand Cayman (76 sq mi; 197 sq km), Cayman Brac (22 sq mi; 57 sq km), and Little Cayman (20 sq mi; 52 sq km)—situated about 180 miles (290 km) northwest of Jamaica. They were dependencies of Jamaica until 1959, when they became a unit territory within the Federation of the West Indies. In 1962, upon the dissolution of the Federation, the Cayman Islands became a British dependency. The islands' chief export is turtle products.

CHANNEL ISLANDS

Status: Crown dependencies
Lieutenant Governor of Jersey: Gen. Sir Peter Whiteley (1980)
Lieutenant Governor of Guernsey: Air Chief Marshal Sir Peter Le Cheminant
Area: 75 sq mi. (194 sq km)
Population (est. 1978): 125,000
Capital of Jersey: St. Helier
Capital of Guernsey: St. Peter Port
Monetary units: Guernsey pound; Jersey pound

This group of islands, lying in the English Channel off the northwest coast of France, is the only portion of the Duchy of Normandy belonging to the English Crown, to which it has been attached since the conquest of 1066. It was the only British possession occupied by Germany during World War II.

For purposes of government, the islands are divided into the Bailiwick of Jersey (45 sq mi.; 117 sq km) and the Bailiwick of Guernsey (30 sq mi.; 78 sq km), including Alderney (3 sq mi.; 7.8 sq km); Sark (2 sq mi.; 5.2 sq km), Herm, Jethou, etc. The islands are administered according to their own laws and customs by local governments. Acts of Parliament in London are not binding on the islands unless they are specifically mentioned. The Queen is represented in each Bailiwick by a Lieutenant Governor.

English is now the language in daily use, although the French patois is still spoken by some people. New legislation is drafted in English, but French has been retained for ceremonial purposes in the legislative bodies.

FALKLAND ISLANDS AND DEPENDENCIES

Status: Dependency
Governor: Rex Masterson Hunt (1980)
Area: 4,700 sq mi. (12,173 sq km)
Population: est. (1978): 2,000
Capital (est. 1978): Stanley (on East Falkland), 1,100
Monetary unit: Falkland Island pound

This sparsely inhabited dependency consists of a group of islands in the South Atlantic, about 250 miles (402 km) east of the South American mainland. The largest islands are East Falkland and West Falkland. Dependencies are South Georgia Island (1,450 sq mi.; 3,756 sq km), the South Sandwich Islands, and other islets. Three former dependencies—Graham Land, the South Shetland Islands, and the South Orkney Islands—were established as a new British dependency, the British Antarctic Territory, in 1962.

The chief industry is sheep raising and, apart from the production of wool, hides and skins, and tallow, there are no known resources. The whaling industry is carried on from South Georgia Island. The chief export is wool.

GIBRALTAR

Status: Self-governing dependency
Governor: Sir William Jackson (1978)
Chief Minister: Sir Joshua Hassan
Area: 2.25 sq mi. (5.8 sq km)
Population (est. 1980): 30,000
Monetary unit: Gibraltar pound
Economic summary: Gross national product (1979): $130 million. Average annual growth rate (1970–78): 5.0%. Exports: re-exports of tobacco, petroleum, wine. Imports: manufactured goods, fuels, foodstuffs. Major trading partners: U.K., Morocco, Portugal, Netherlands.

Gibraltar, at the south end of the Iberian Peninsula, is a rocky promonotory commanding the western entrance to the Mediterranean. Aside from its strategic importance, it is also a free port, naval base, and coaling station. It was captured by the Arabs crossing from Africa into Spain in A.D. 711. In the 15th century, it passed to the Moorish ruler of Granada and later became Spanish. It was captured by an Anglo-Dutch force in 1704 during the War of the Spanish Succession and passed to Great Britain by the Treaty of Utrecht in 1713. Most of the inhabitants of Gibraltar are of Spanish, Italian, and Maltese descent.

Spanish efforts to recover Gibraltar culminated in a referendum in 1967 in which the residents voted overwhelmingly to retain their link with Britain. Spain sealed Gibraltar's land border in 1969 and did not open communications until April 1980, after the two governments had agreed to solve their dispute in keeping with a United Nations resolution calling for restoration of the "Rock" to Spain.

HONG KONG

Status: Dependency
Governor: Sir Murray MacLehose (1971)
Area: 398 sq mi. (1,031 sq km)
Population (est. 1981): 5,156,000 (growth rate, 1975–80: 2.7%)
Capital (1976 census): Victoria (Hong Kong Island), 501,700
Monetary unit: Hong Kong dollar
Economic summary: Gross national product (1979): $18.7 billion. Average annual growth rate (1970–78): 6.9%. Per capita income (1976): $2,176. Labor force in agriculture: 2%; principal products: vegetables, rice, dairy products. Labor force in industry: 51%; major industrial products: textiles, clothing, toys, transistor radios, watches, electronic components. Exports: clothing, textiles, toys, watches, transistor radios, electronic components. Imports: raw materials, consumer goods, food. Major trading partners: U.S., U.K., Japan, West Germany, China.

The crown colony of Hong Kong comprises the island of Hong Kong (32 sq mi.; 83 sq km), Stonecutters' Island, Kowloon Peninsula, and the New Territories on the adjoining mainland. The island of Hong Kong, located at the mouth of the Pearl River about 90 miles (145 km) southeast of Canton, was ceded to the Britain in 1841.

Stonecutters' Island and Kowloon were annexed in 1860, and the New Territories, which are mainly agricultural lands, were leased from China in 1898 for 99 years. Hong Kong was attacked by Japanese troops Dec. 7, 1941, and surrendered the following Christmas. It remained under Japanese occupation until August 1945.

Possessing an excellent natural harbor, the only safe deep-sea anchorage between Shanghai and Southeast Asia, Hong Kong is the transshipment center for trade throughout southern China and the western Pacific.

The cities of Victoria and Kowloon contain the greater part of the population, which is overwhelmingly Chinese. Besides those Chinese engaged in agriculture or industry, many live in sampans or junks either in Victoria harbor or neighboring bays, supporting themselves by fishing or by performing labor on the wharves.

In 1974, Hong Kong rescinded a policy of accepting illegal immigrants from China that had, since 1968, made the crowded city a sanctuary for thousands of Chinese refugees.

ISLE OF MAN

Status: Dependency
Lieutenant Governor: Rear Adm. Sir Nigel Amherst Cecil
Area: 227 sq mi. (588 sq km)
Population (est. 1978): 60,500
Capital (est. 1976): Douglas, 20,300
Monetary unit: Isle of Man pound

Situated in the Irish Sea, equidistant from Scotland, Ireland, and England, the Isle of Man is administered according to its own laws by a government composed of the Lieutenant Governor, a Legislative Council, and a House of Keys, one of the most ancient legislative assemblies in the world.

The chief exports are beef and lamb, fish, and livestock.

LEEWARD ISLANDS

See British Virgin Islands; Montserrat; West Indies Associated States

MONTSERRAT

Status: Dependency
Governor: D. K. H. Dale
Area: 40 sq mi. (104 sq km)
Population (est. 1978): 13,500
Capital (est. 1975): Plymouth, 1,260
Monetary unit: East Caribbean dollar

The island of Montserrat is in the Lesser Antilles of the West Indies. Until 1956, it was a division of the Leeward Islands. It did not join the West Indies Associated States established in 1967.

The chief exports are cattle, potatoes, cotton, lint, recapped tires, mangoes, tomatoes.

PITCAIRN ISLAND

Status: Dependency
Governor: R. J. Stratton (1980)
Island Magistrate: Ivan Christian
Area: 1.75 sq mi. (4.5 sq km)
Population (est. 1980): 63
Capital: Adamstown

Pitcairn Island, in the South Pacific about midway between Australia and South America, consists of the island of Pitcairn and the three uninhabited islands of Henderson, Duicie, and Oeno. The island of Pitcairn was settled in 1790 by British mutineers from the ship *Bounty*, commanded by Capt. William Bligh. It was annexed as a British colony in 1838. Overpopulation forced removal of the settlement to Norfolk Island in 1856, but about 40 persons soon returned.

The colony is governed by a 10-member Council presided over by the Island Magistrate, who is elected for a three-year term.

ST. HELENA

Status: Dependency
Governor: G. C. Guy (1976)
Area: 47 sq mi. (122 sq km)
Population (est 1979): 7,300
Capital (est. 1978): Jamestown, 1,500
Monetary unit: Pound sterling

St. Helena is a volcanic island in the South Atlantic about 1,100 miles (1,770 km) from the west coast of Africa. It is famous as the place of exile of Napoleon (1815–21).

It was taken for England in 1659 by the East India Company and was brought under the direct government of the Crown in 1834.

St. Helena has two dependencies: Ascension (34 sq mi.; 88 sq km), an island about 700 miles (1,127 km) northwest of St. Helena; and Tristan da Cunha (40 sq mi.; 104 sq km), a group of six islands about 1,500 miles (2,414 km) south-southwest of St. Helena.

Leading suppliers in 1968 were U.K. (61%), South Africa (28%).

ST. KITTS-NEVIS

See West Indies Associated States

TURKS AND CAICOS ISLANDS

Status: Dependency
Governor: J. C. Strong
Area: 193 sq mi. (500 sq km)
Population (est. 1978): 6,200
Capital (est. 1977): Grand Turk, 2,900
Monetary unit: U.S. dollar

These two groups of islands are situated at the southeast end of the Bahamas. The principal islands in the Turks group are Grand Turk and Salt Cay; the principal ones in the Caicos group are South Caicos, East Caicos, Middle (or Grand) Caicos, North Caicos, Providenciales, and West Caicos.

The Turks and Caicos Islands were dependencies of Jamaica until 1959, when they became a unit territory within the Federation of the West Indies. In 1962, when Jamaica became independent, the Turks and Caicos became a British crown colony. The present Constitution has been in force since 1969.

Chief exports in 1974 were crayfish (73%) and conch (25%).

VIRGIN ISLANDS

See British Virgin Islands

WEST INDIES ASSOCIATED STATES

Status: Self-governing territories in free association with the United Kingdom, which is responsible for defense and external affairs. The British Government conducts its affairs with the West Indies Associated States through an official representative, whose office is in Bridgetown, Barbados.
British Representative: J. S. Arthur (1978)
Area: Antigua, 171 sq mi. (443 sq km); St. Christopher (Kitts)-Nevis-Anguilla, 153 sq mi. (397 sq km)
Population (est. 1980): Antigua, 80,000; St. Christopher (Kitts)-Nevis-Anguilla, 70,000
Capitals: Antigua: St. Johns, 23,500; St. Christopher (Kitts)-Nevis-Anguilla: Basseterre (on St. Kitts), 15,900
Monetary unit: East Caribbean dollar
Economic summary: Antigua: Gross national product (1978): $70 million. Average annual growth rate (1970–77): −3.7%. Per capita income: $720. Principal agricultural product: cotton. Major industries: oil refining, tourism. Exports: petroleum products, cotton. Imports: crude oil, foodstuffs, clothing. Major trading partners: U.K., U.S., Commonwealth Caribbean countries. St. Christopher–Nevis–Anguilla: Gross domestic product (1977): $32 million. Per capita income: $580. Principal agricultural products: sugar, cotton. Major industries: sugar processing, salt extraction. Exports: sugar, molasses, cotton, salt, copra. Imports: foodstuffs, fuel, manufactured goods. Major trading partners: U.S., U.K., Japan.

The West Indies Associated States were established in 1967 and consisted of Antigua and St. Kitts-Nevis-Anguilla of the Leeward Islands, and Dominica, Grenada, St. Lucia, and St. Vincent of the Windward Islands. Statehood for St. Vincent was held up until 1969 because of local political uncertainties. (Grenada became independent in 1974, Dominica in 1978, and St. Lucia and St. Vincent in 1979.)

Two members of the Leeward group—the British Virgin Islands and Montserrat—did not become Associated States.

Each of the Associated States is fully self-governing in its internal affairs.

The association between Britain and each state is to be free and voluntary. As a guarantee of its voluntary nature, association will be terminable by either party. On termination of association, the state would become independent of Britain.

In 1967, Anguilla declared its independence from the St. Kitts-Nevis-Anguilla federation. Britain however, did not recognize this action. In February 1969, Anguilla voted to cut all ties with Britain and become an independent republic. In March, Britain landed troops on the island and, on March 30, a truce was signed. In July 1971, Anguilla became a dependency of Britain and two months later Britain ordered the withdrawal of all its troops.

A new Constitution for Anguilla, effective in February 1976, provides for separate administration and a government of elected representatives. The Associated State of St. Kitts-Nevis-Anguilla remains in being, but Anguilla has a separate relationship with Britain.

WINDWARD ISLANDS
See West Indies Associated States

UPPER VOLTA

Republic of Upper Volta
President of Military Committee of Reform for National Progress: Col. Sayé Zerbo
Area: 105,870 sq mi. (274,200 sq km)
Population (est 1981): 7,100,000 (growth rate, 2.3%)
Density per square mile: 67.1
Capital and largest city (est. 1980): Ouagadougou, 235,000
Monetary unit: Franc CFA
Ethnic groups: Mossis, Bobos
Languages: French, African languages
Religion: Animist, 50%; Islam, 17%; Roman Catholic, 8%
National name: République de Haute-Volta
Freedom House classifications: Capitalist-socialist pre-industrial, non-party military
Economic summary: Gross national product (1979): $1 billion. Average annual growth rate (1970–78): −1.0%. Per capita income (1977): $113. Average rate of inflation: 12%. Labor force in agriculture: 95%; principal products: millet, sorghum, corn, rice, livestock, peanuts, sugar cane, cotton. Major industrial products: processed agricultural products, light industrial items, brick, brewed products. Natural resources: manganese, limestone, marble, gold, uranium, bauxite, copper. Exports: livestock, peanuts, cotton. Imports: textiles, food and consumer goods, transport equipment, machinery, fuels. Major trading partners: Ivory Coast, France, Ghana, Western European nations.

Geography. Slightly larger than Colorado, Upper Volta is a landlocked country in West Africa. Its neighbors are the Ivory Coast, Mali, Niger, Benin, Togo, and Ghana. The country consists of extensive plains, low hills, high savannas, and a desert area in the north.

Government. Under a Constitution adopted by referendum in 1977, executive power is vested in a President elected by popular vote for a four-year term. Legislative power rests with a 57-member National Assembly elected for four years.

History. Upper Volta consists chiefly of the lands of the Mossi Empire, where France established a protectorate over the Kingdom of Ouagadougou in 1897. Upper Volta became a separate colony in 1919, was partitioned among Niger, the Sudan, and the Ivory Coast in 1933 and was reconstituted in 1947. An autonomous republic within the French Community, it became independent on Aug. 5, 1960.

President Maurice Yameogo was deposed on Jan. 3, 1966, by a military coup led by Col. Sangoulé Lamizana, who dissolved the National Assembly and suspended the Constitution. A new Constitution was adopted later that year and a new Assembly was elected. However, dissension within the Volta Democratic Union, the major party, led to renewed military rule. Constitutional rule returned in 1978 with the election of an Assembly and a presidential vote in June in which Gen. Lamizana won by a narrow margin over three other candidates.

In 1973, Upper Volta formed, with six other nations, the Economic Community for West Africa to promote economic development in the region.

On Nov. 25, 1980, there was a bloodless coup which placed Gen. Lamizana under house arrest. Col. Sayé Zerbo took charge as the President of the Military Committee of Reform for National Progress.

URUGUAY

Oriental Republic of Uruguay
President: Gen. Gregorio Alvarez (1981)
Area: 68,548 sq mi. (177,539 sq km)
Population (est. 1981): 2,925,000 (growth rate: 0.6%)
Density per square mile: 42.7
Capital and largest city (est. 1980): Montevideo, 1,250,000
Monetary unit: New peso
Language: Spanish
Religion: Roman Catholic
National name: República Oriental del Uruguay
Freedom House classifications: Capitalist-socialist industrial, non-party military
Economic summary: Gross national product (1979): $6.1 billion. Average annual growth rate (1970–78): 1.8%. Per capita income (1976): $1,090. Land used for agriculture: 85%; labor force: 8%; principal products: livestock, grains. Labor force in industry: 34%; major products: processed meats, wool and hides, textiles, shoes, handbags and leather wearing apparel, cement, refined petroleum. Natural resources: hydroelectric power potential. Exports: meat, hides, shoes, leather products, furs, wool, fish. Imports: fuels, chemicals, machinery, metals. Major trading partners: U.S., Brazil, Argentina.

Geography. Uruguay, on the east coast of South America south of Brazil and east of Argentina, is comparable in size to the State of Washington.

The country consists of a low, rolling plain in the south and a low plateau in the north. It has a 120-mile (193 km) Atlantic shore line, a 235-mile (378 km) frontage on the Rio de la Plata, and 270 miles (435 km) on the Uruguay River, its western boundary.

Government. The President serves for a term of five years. He appoints a Council of 11 ministers to assist him. Before it was dissolved, Congress consisted of the Senate and the House of Deputies. Members remained in office for five years.

In June 1973, President Juan María Bordaberry yielded to military pressure and dissolved Congress, thus ending 40 years of constitutional rule. His decree announced creation of a Council of State to perform Congressional functions, oversee presidential activities, and formulate constitutional reforms for a national plebiscite.

Political activity has been banned since 1973.

History. Juan Díaz de Solis, a Spaniard, discovered Uruguay in 1516, but the Portuguese were first to settle it when they founded Colonia in 1680. After a long struggle, Spain wrested the country from Portugal in 1778. Uruguay revolted against Spain in 1811, only to be conquered in 1816–20 by the Portuguese from Brazil. Independence was reasserted with Argentine help in 1825, and the republic was set up in 1830.

Independence, however, did not restore order, and a revolt in 1836 touched off nearly 50 years of factional strife, with occasional armed intervention from Argentina and Brazil.

Alberto Heber, who became President in 1966, vigorously championed reform, and a referendum authorized revision of the Constitution to vest executive powers in a President and a Cabinet of Ministers. Oscar Diego Gestido, elected President later that year, devoted much effort to improving the ailing economy. But he died the next year and was succeeded by Jorge Pacheco Areco.

Siege-state regulations were instituted after the Tupámaros first urban guerrilla organization launched a series of spectacular kidnappings, bank and casino robberies (one gold haul netted over $250,000), and arms raids on military arsenals to embarrass what was then the most democratic government in South America. In 1970, the Tupámaros kidnapped a U.S. aid adviser, Dan Mitrione, and killed him when their ransom demands were not met.

The continuing economic, political, and guerrilla problems precipitated impeachment proceedings against Pacheco in 1971. A bitterly fought election followed, with Juan María Bordaberry, Pacheco's hand-picked choice, the winner.

Disputes between the government and the military, coupled with worsening economic problems (the peso was devalued 32 times during Bordaberry's first three years in office), led to a military revolt in February 1973 that ended in an agreement with Bordaberry in which the military promised to maintain the constitutional system but virtually took over control of the government.

Despite the military takeover, inflation soared at a 100% yearly rate and the Tupámaros continued to be active. Their assassinations and bombings were matched by government repression; an estimated 3,500 persons were arrested on political charges in the year after Congress was dissolved, and the press was kept tightly in line.

Military leaders, citing Bordaberry's opposition to the return of constitutional government, removed him from office in 1976. The National Council of 25 military officers and 21 civilians designated Aparicio Méndez to take over the Presidency for a five-year term.

Although the government in 1977 reported that sentences for political prisoners would be reduced, Amnesty International estimated that 5,000 such prisoners were being held in Uruguay, more than in any other Latin nation. The Carter Administration cut economic aid from $220,000 to $25,000 and eliminated military sales credits of $3 million for Uruguay because of the human-rights situation. The Uruguayan government then declared that it would refuse any U.S. aid.

In November 1980, voters rejected by 58% a Constitution that would have given the military permanent power. The government later announced that following the selection of a new President by the National Council in 1981, the restoration of civilian government would be discussed with the former political parties. In August, the Council designated General Gregorio Alvarez, retired commander in chief of the army, as the next head of state. He assumed the Presidency Sept. 1.

VANUATU

Republic of Vanuatu
President: George Sokomanu (1980)
Prime Minster: Rev. Walter Lini (1980)
Area: 5,700 sq mi. (14,763,sq km)
Population (est. 1981): 110,000 (growth rate: 2.7%)
Density per square mile: 19.3
Capital (est. 1976): Vila (metropolitan area): 17,400
Monetary unit: Australian dollar and Vanuatu franc

Religions: Presbyterian, 40%; Roman Catholic, 16%; Anglican, 14%; other Christian, 15%; Animist, 15%
Freedom House classifications: Capitalist-statist pre-industrial, multi-party centralized.
Economic Summary: Gross national product (1979): $60 million. Average annual growth rate (1970–78): 1.9%. Principal agricultural products: copra, cocoa, coffee, livestock. Exports: copra, cocoa, coffee, frozen fish. Major trading partners: France, U.S., Japan.

Geography. Formerly known as the New Hebrides, Vanuatu is an archipelago of some 80 islands lying between New Caledonia and Fiji in the South Pacific. Largest of the islands is Espiritu Santo (875 sq mi.; 2,266 sq km); others are Efate, Malekula, Malo, Pentecost, and Tanna. The population is largely Melanesian of mixed blood.

Government. The constitution by which Vanuatu achieved independence on July 30, 1980, vests executive authority in a President, elected by an electoral college for a five-year term. A unicameral legislature of 39 members exercises legislative power. The Vanuaaku party, led by Prime Minister Walter Lini, holds 26 seats.

History. The islands were discovered by Pedro Fernandes de Queiros of Portugal in 1606 and were charted and named by the British navigator James Cook in 1774. Conflicting British and French interests were resolved by a joint naval commission that administered the islands from 1887. A condominium government was established in 1906.

The islands' plantation economy, based on imported Vietnamese labor, was prosperous until the 1920s, when markets for its products declined. The New Hebrides escaped Japanese occupation in World War II and the French population was among the first to support the Gaullist Free French movement.

A brief rebellion by French settlers and plantation workers on Espiritu Santo led by Jimmy Stevens in May 1980 threatened the scheduled independence of the islands. Britain sent a company of Royal Marines and France a contingent of 50 policemen to quell the revolt, which the new government said was financed by the Phoenix Foundation, a right-wing U.S. group. With the British and French forces replaced by soldiers from Papua New Guinea, independence ceremonies took place on July 30. The next month it was reported that Stevens had been arrested and the revolt quelled.

VATICAN CITY STATE

Ruler: Pope John Paul II (1978)
Area: 0.17 sq mi. (0.44 sq km)
Population (est. 1981): 1,000 (Italian, 85%; Swiss and others, 15%)
Density per square mile: 5,882.4
Monetary unit: Lira
Languages: Latin, Italian
Religion: Roman Catholic
National name: Stato della Città del Vaticano

Geography. The Vatican City State is situated on the Vatican hill, on the right bank of the Tiber River, within the commune of Rome.

Government. The Pope has full legal, executive, and judicial powers. Executive power over the area is in the hands of a Commission of Cardinals appointed by the Pope. The College of Cardinals is the Pope's chief advisory body, and upon his death the cardinals elect his successor for life. The cardinals themselves are created for life by the Pope.

In the Vatican the central administration of the Roman Catholic Church throughout the world is carried on by 11 congregations, three tribunals, three main secretariats, and numerous councils, committees, and commissions. In its diplomatic relations, the Holy See is represented by the Papal Secretary of State.

History. The Vatican City State, sovereign and independent, together with the Lateran palaces, have been intimately associated with the history of the Roman Catholic Church since the martyrdom of St. Peter. From these areas the Pope exercised temporal sway for many centuries over a large part of central Italy; in 1859, the Papal States comprised an area of some 17,000 square miles (44,030 sq km). During the struggle for Italian unification, from 1860 to 1870, most of this area became part of Italy.

By an Italian law of May 13, 1871, the temporal power of the Pope was abrogated, and the territory of the Papacy was confined to the Vatican and Lateran palaces and the villa of Castel Gandolfo. The Popes consistently refused to recognize this arrangement and, by the Lateran Treaty of Feb. 11, 1929, between the Vatican and the Kingdom of Italy, the exclusive dominion and sovereign jurisdiction of the Holy See over the city of the Vatican was again recognized, thus restoring the Pope's temporal authority over the area.

The first session of Ecumenical Council Vatican II was opened by John XXIII on Oct. 11, 1962, to plan and set policies for the modernization of the Roman Catholic Church. Pope Paul VI continued the Council, opening the second session on Sept. 29, 1963.

On Aug. 26, 1978, Cardinal Albino Luciani was chosen by the College of Cardinals to succeed Paul VI, who had died of a heart attack on Aug. 6. The new Pope, who took the name John Paul I, was born on Oct. 17, 1912, at Forno di Canale in Italy.

Pope John Paul I succeeded a pontiff who stood implacably against relaxing the church's traditional stand against birth control, on the Latin rite's insistence upon clerical celibacy, and on conservatism in theological speculation. During his reign, however, he paid much attention to improving ecumenical relations with other denominations.

(For a listing of all the Popes, *see* the Index.)

Only 34 days after his election, John Paul I died of a heart attack, ending the shortest reign in 373 years. On Oct. 16, Cardinal Karol Wojtyla, 58, was chosen Pope and took the name John Paul II. The first Polish Pope was also the first to have been named from a communist nation.

John Paul II visited his homeland in June 1979, exhorting millions to "never lose your spiritual freedom" and telling workers that Christ would not accept that man be considered "merely as a means of production." The trip was a triumph for the warm, outgoing Pontiff despite the Polish government's undisguised efforts to dampen the public impact of his visit.

A visit to the Irish Republic and to the United States in September and October 1979, followed by a 12-nation African tour in May 1980 and a visit in July to Brazil, the most populous Catholic nation, further established John Paul's image as a "people's" Pope. But he also used his travels to preach a more conservative doctrine, cautioning U.S. nuns against seeking priestly functions and sternly opposing abortion and contraception. During his African journey, he reaffirmed long-ignored canon laws against political roles for the clergy. On May 13, 1981, a Turkish terrorist shot the Pope in St. Peter's Square, the first assassination attempt against the pontiff in modern times. Mehmet Ali Agca was sentenced on July 22 to life imprisonment by an Italian Court.

VENEZUELA

Republic of Venezuela
President: Luis Herrera Campíns (1979)
Area: 352,143 sq mi. (912,050 sq km)
Population (est. 1981): 14,300,000 (growth rate: 3.3%) (mestizo, 69%; white, 20%; black, 9%; Indian, 2%)
Density per square mile: 40.6
Capital: Caracas
Largest cities (est. 1980 for metropolitan area): Caracas, 2,950,000; (est. 1976 by U.N.): Maracaibo, 792,000; Valencia, 439,000; Maracay, 301,000
Monetary unit: Bolívar
Language: Spanish
Religion: Roman Catholic
National name: República de Venezuela
Freedom House classifications: Capitalist-statist industrial, multi-party centralized
Economic summary: Gross national product (1979): $45.2 billion. Average annual growth rate (1970–78): 3.1%. Per capita income: $2,590. Land used for agriculture: 2%; labor force, 24%; principal products: rice, coffee, corn, sugar, bananas, dairy, meat, and poultry products. Labor force in industry, 23%; principal products: refined petroleum products, iron and steel, paper products, aluminum, textiles, transport equipment. Natural resources: petroleum, natural gas, iron ore, gold, hydroelectric power. Exports: petroleum, iron ore, cocoa, coffee. Imports: machinery and transport equipment, manufactures, chemicals, foodstuffs. Major trading partners: U.S., West Germany, Japan.

Geography. Venezuela, a third larger than Texas, occupies most of the northern coast of South America on the Caribbean Sea. It is bordered by Colombia to the west, Guyana to the east, and Brazil to the south.

Mountain systems break Venezuela into four distinct areas: (1) the Maracaibo lowlands; (2) the mountainous region in the north and northwest; (3) the Orinoco basin, with the llanos (vast grass-covered plains) on its northern border and great forest areas in the south and southeast; (4) the Guiana Highlands, south of the Orinoco, accounting for nearly half the national territory. About 80% of Venezuela is drained by the Orinoco and its tributaries.

Government. Venezuela is a federal republic consisting of 20 states, the Federal District, two territories and 72 islands in the Caribbean. There is a bicameral Congress, the 52 members of the Senate and the 213 members of the Chamber of Deputies being elected by popular vote to five-year terms. The President is also elected for five years. He must be a Venezuelan by birth and over 30 years old. He is not eligible for re-election until 10 years after the end of his term.

The major political parties are the Democratic Action Party, with 23 of 52 Senate seats and 83 of 213 seats in the Chamber of Deputies; Social Christian Party, with 22 Senate seats and 83 Chamber seats, People's Electoral Movement, Democratic

Republican Union.

History. Columbus discovered Venezuela on his third voyage in 1498. A subsequent Spanish explorer gave the country its name, meaning "Little Venice." There were no important settlements until Caracas was founded in 1567. Simón Bolívar, who led the liberation of much of the continent from Spain, was born in Caracas in 1783. With Bolívar taking part, Venezuela was one of the first South American colonies to revolt against Spain, in 1810, but it was not until 1821 that independence was won. Federated at first with Colombia and Ecuador, the country set up a republic in 1830 and then sank for many decades into a condition of revolt, dictatorship, and corruption.

From 1908 to 1935, Gen. Juan Vicente Gómez ruled tyrannically, picking satellites to alternate with him in the presidential palace. Thereafter, there was a struggle between democratic forces and those backing a return to strong-man rule. Dr. Rómulo Betancourt and the liberal Acción Democrática Party won a majority of seats in a constituent assembly to draft a new Constitution in 1946. A well-known writer, Rómulo Gallegos, candidate of Betancourt's party, easily won the presidential election of 1947. But, the army ousted Gallegos the next year and instituted a military junta.

Following elections in 1952, the junta presented its resignations to the army, which named Col. Marcos Pérez Jiménez as Provisional President. He re-established strongman rule. But the country overthrew the dictatorship in 1958 and thereafter enjoyed democratic government. Rafael Caldera Rodríguez, President from 1969 to 1974, legalized the Communist Party and established diplomatic relations with Moscow.

Venezuela and neighboring Guyana in 1970 called a 12-year moratorium on their border dispute (Venezuela claims 50,000 square miles of Guyana's 83,000).

As a charter member of the Organization of Petroleum Exporting Countries (OPEC), Venezuela shared the benefits of the tripled oil prices engineered by OPEC, but did not join the 1973 Arab oil boycott. President Carlos Andrés Pérez took office in 1974, committed to give all Venezuelans a stake in the oil bonanza that made his country the richest in South America.

In 1976, Venezuela nationalized 21 oil companies, mostly subsidiaries of U.S. firms, offering compensation of $1.28 billion. Oil income in that year was $9.9 billion, and although production decreased 2.2%, revenue remained at the same level in 1977 because of higher prices, largely financing an ambitious social welfare program.

A continuing decline in oil production as world markets slackened forced the government to impose austerity measures early in 1978.

Despite his difficulties at home, Pérez continued to play an active foreign role in extending economic aid to Latin neighbors, in backing the human—rights policy of President Carter, and in supporting Carter's return of the Panama Canal to Panama.

Opposition Christian Democrats capitalized on Pérez's domestic problems to elect Luis Herrera Campíns President in Venezuela's fifth consecutive free election, on Dec. 3, 1978. At his inauguration in March 1979, Herrera called for "fiscal discipline" to reduce a record foreign debt of $7.4 billion despite soaring oil revenues.

Venezuela was host to the OPEC meeting on Dec. 20, 1979, that abandoned uniform pricing and permitted Venezuela to raise its own price to an average of $26 a barrel in January 1980. Despite its position as the largest Latin producer (2.35 million barrels a day in 1979, of which 1.9 million were exported), Venezuela's continuing balance of payments deficit forced the government to seek foreign loans to pay a debt estimated in January at $13.3 billion.

VIETNAM

Socialist Republic of Vietnam
President: Truong Chinh (1981)
Premier: Pham Van Dong (1976)
Area: 126,436 sq mi. (327,469 sq km)
Population (est. 1981): 53,550,000 (growth rate: 2.5%)
Density per square mile: 423.5
Capital Hanoi
Largest cities (est. 1976): Ho Chi Minh City (Saigon),[1] 3,460,500; Hanoi, 1,443,500; (est. 1973): Da Nang, 492,200; Na Trang, 216,200; Qui Non, 213,750; Hue, 209,000; **(1960 census):** Haiphong, 182,490
Monetary unit: Dong
Languages: Vietnamese, French, Chinese
Religions: Buddhist, Roman Catholic, Cao-Dai, Hoa-Hao, Confucian, Animist
National name: Công Hòa Xa Hôi.Chú Nghia Viêt Nam
Freedom House classifications: Socialist industrial, one-party communist
Economic summary: Gross national product (1978): $8.9 billion. Per capita income: $140. Labor force in agriculture: 70%; principal products: rice, rubber, fruits and vegetables, corn, sugar cane, fish. Labor force in industry, 8%; major products: processed foods, textiles, cement, chemical fertilizers, glass, tires. Natural resources: forests, coal. Exports: agricultural products, coal, mineral ores. Imports: petroleum, steel products, railroad equipment, chemicals, medicines, raw cotton, fertilizer, grain. Major trading partners: U.S.S.R., Soviet bloc nations, Japan.

1. Includes suburb of Cholon.

Geography. Vietnam occupies the eastern and southern part of the Indochinese peninsula in Southeast Asia, with the South China Sea along its entire coast. China is to the north and Laos and Cambodia to the west. Long and narrow on a north-south axis, Vietnam is about twice the size of Arizona.

The Mekong River delta lies in the south and the Red River delta in the north. Heavily forested mountain and plateau regions make up most of the country.

Government. Less than a year after the capitulation of the former Republic of Vietnam (South Vietnam) on April 30, 1975, a joint National Assembly convened with 249 deputies representing the North and 243 representing the South. The Assembly set July 2, 1976, as the official reunification date. Hanoi became the capital and Ton Duc Thang, President of the Northern regime since 1969, became President of the new republic.

(By 1981, the National Assembly had increased to 496 members.)

Pham Van Dong, Premier in Hanoi since 1955, took over the new administration, and the Northern flag, anthem, and crest became the symbols of the new Vietnam. The only concession to the former Provisional Revolutionary Government of South Vietnam, which nominally administered the South in the interim period of less than a year after South Vietnam surrendered, was the installation of its President, Nguyen Huu Tho, as one of two Vice Presidents.

Dang Cong san Vietnam (Communist Party), led by First Secretary Le Duan, is the only political party.

History. The Vietnamese are descendants of Mongoloid nomads from China and migrants from Indonesia. They recognized Chinese suzerainty until the 15th century, an era of nationalistic expansion, when Cambodians were pushed out of the southern area of what is now Vietnam.

A century later, the Portuguese were the first Europeans to enter the area. France established its influence early in the 19th century and within 80 years conquered the three regions into which the country was then divided—Cochin-China in the south, Annam in the center, and Tonkin in the north.

France first unified Vietnam in 1887, when a single governor-generalship was created, followed by the first physical links between north and south—a rail and road system. Even at the beginning of World War II, however, there were internal differences among the three regions.

Japan took over military bases in Vietnam in 1940 and a pro-Vichy French administration remained until 1945. A veteran Communist leader, Ho Chi Minh, organized an independence movement known as the Vietminh to exploit a confused situation. At the end of the war, Ho's followers seized Hanoi and declared a short-lived republic, which ended with the arrival of French forces in 1946.

Paris proposed a unified government within the French Union under the former Annamite emperor, Bao Dai. Cochin-China and Annam accepted the proposal, and Bao Dai was proclaimed emperor of all Vietnam in 1949. Ho and the Vietminh withheld support, and the revolution in China gave them the outside help needed for a war of resistance against French and Vietnamese troops armed largely by the U.S.

A bitter defeat at Dien Bien Phu in northwest Vietnam on May 5, 1954, broke the French military campaign and brought the division of Vietnam at the conference of Geneva that year.

In the new South, Ngo Dinh Diem, Premier under Bao Dai, deposed the monarch in 1955 and established a republic with himself as President. Diem used strong U.S. backing to create an authoritarian regime that suppressed all opposition but could not eradicate the Northern-supplied Communist Viet Cong.

Skirmishing grew into a full-scale war, with escalating U.S. involvement. A military coup, U.S.-inspired in the view of many, ousted Diem Nov. 1, 1963, and a kaleidoscope of military governments followed. The most savage fighting of the war occurred in early 1968, during the Tet holidays.

Although the Viet Cong failed to overthrow the Saigon government, U.S. public reaction to the apparently endless war forced a limitation of U.S. troops to 550,000 and a new emphasis on shifting the burden of further combat to the South Vietnamese. Ho Chi Minh's death on Sept. 3, 1969, brought a quadrumvirate to replace him but no flagging in Northern will to fight.

U.S. bombing and invasion of Cambodia in the summer of 1970—an effort to destroy Viet Cong bases in the neighboring state—marked the end of major U.S. participation in the fighting. Most American ground troops were withdrawn from combat by mid-1971 as heavy bombing of the Ho Chi Minh trail from North Vietnam appeared to cut the supply of men and matériel to the South.

Secret negotiations for peace by Secretary of State Henry A. Kissinger with North Vietnamese officials during 1972 after heavy bombing of Hanoi and Haiphong brought the two sides near agreement in October. When the Northerners demanded the removal of the South's President Nguyen Van Thieu as their price, President Nixon ordered the "Christmas bombing" of the North. The conference resumed and a peace settlement was signed in Paris on Jan. 27, 1973. It called for release of all U.S. prisoners, withdrawal of U.S. forces, limitation of both sides' forces inside South Vietnam, and a commitment to peaceful reunification.

Despite Chinese and Soviet endorsement, the agreement foundered in a welter of charges and countercharges—the North asserting that the U.S. was violating the limitation on arms supplies, Washington and Saigon accusing Hanoi of infiltrating troops to the south. U.S. bombing of Communist-held areas in Cambodia was halted by Congress in August 1973, and in the following year Communist action in South Vietnam increased.

An armored attack across the 17th parallel in January 1975 panicked the South Vietnamese army and brought the invasion within 40 miles of Saigon by April 9. Thieu resigned on April 21 and fled, to be replaced by Vice President Tran Van Huong, who quit a week later, turning over the office to Gen. Duong Van Minh. "Big Minh" surrendered Saigon on April 30, ending a war that took 1.3 million Vietnamese and 56,000 American lives, at the cost of $141 billion in U.S. aid.

Although the new regime in the South at first appeared to be taking a moderate line, "re-education" of former South Vietnamese government and army personnel began immediately. By mid-1976, virtually all foreigners were expelled, even those married to Vietnamese.

On May 3, 1977, the U.S. and Vietnam opened negotiations in Paris to normalize relations. One of the first results was the withdrawal of U.S. opposition to Vietnamese membership in the United Nations, formalized in the Security Council on July 20 when the Council accepted the application without a vote. Two major issues remained to be settled, however: the return of the bodies of some 2,500 U.S. servicemen missing in the war and the claim by Hanoi that former President Nixon had promised reconstruction aid under the 1973 agreement.

Negotiations failed to resolve these issues, and the question of recognition appeared to have been shelved indefinitely when the U.S. expelled the Vietnamese Ambassador to the United Nations, Dinh Ba Thi, early in 1978. Thi was accused of complicity in an espionage case in which a U.S. citizen and a Vietnamese refugee were later convicted of delivering U.S. intelligence to Hanoi.

The new year also brought an intensification of border clashes between Vietnam and Cambodia and accusations by China that Chinese residents of Vietnam were being subjected to persecution. Peking cut off all aid and withdrew 800 technicians.

By June, 133,000 ethnic Chinese were reported to have fled Vietnam, and a year later as many as 500,000 of the 1.8 million Vietnamese of Chinese ancestry were believed to have escaped. Half of these had gone by land or sea to China, where the government made it clear that no more refugees were welcome and tens of thousands more had survived boat passage to Thailand, Malaysia, Indonesia, or Hong Kong. U.S. officials said 100,000 may have died. Survivors said they had paid up to $5,000 in bribes to leave Vietnam, and U.S. and British officials charged Hanoi with a deliberate extortion policy.

Replying to worldwide criticism, Premier Pham Van Dong said only that he would try to limit the outflow. Other Vietnamese officials dismissed the "boat people" as misfits the government was unwilling and unable to keep in the country.

Hanoi was undoubtedly preoccupied with a continuing war in Cambodia, where 60,000 Vietnamese troops were aiding the Heng Samrin regime in suppressing the last forces of the pro-Chinese Pol Pot regime. In early 1979, Vietnam was conducting a two-front war, defending its northern border against a Chinese invasion and at the same time supporting its army in Cambodia.

Only a Soviet veto prevented Vietnam from being labeled an aggressor by the U.N. Security Council as Prince Shihanouk of Cambodia, released from house arrest by the Pol Pot regime, presented the case against Hanoi after the fall of Phnom Penh. Vietnam's ambassador, backed by the Soviet Union and the Soviet bloc, sought condemnation of Peking's invasion but could find no sympathizers.

Despite Hanoi's claims of total victory, resistance in Cambodia continued through 1981, prompting Vietnamese troops to raid guerrilla and refugee camps across the Thai border. Vietnam's second conflict, on its border with China, also flared sporadically.

(For a Vietnam War chronology, see Headline History.)

WESTERN SAMOA

Independent State of Western Samoa
Head of State: Malietoa Tanumafili II (1962)
Prime Minister: Taisi Tupuola Efi (1976)
Area: 1,133 sq mi. (2,934 sq km)
Population (est. 1981): 160,000 (growth rate: 1.0%)
Density per square mile: 141.2
Capital and largest city (1980): Apia, 33,400
Monetary unit: Tala
Languages: Samoan and English
Religions: Congregational, 50%; Roman Catholic, 22%; Methodist, 16%
National name: Samoa i Sísifo
Member of Commonwealth of Nations
Freedom House classifications: Capitalist pre-industrial, non-party non-military
Economic summary: Gross national product (1978): $70 million. Per capita income: $290. Land used for agriculture: 50%; labor force: 50%; principal products: copra, cocoa, bananas, timber. Labor force in industry: 10%; major products: timber, light industrial products. Natural resource: timber. Exports: copra, cocoa, bananas, foodstuffs. Major trading partners: Australia, New Zealand, Netherlands, Japan.

Geography. Western Samoa, the size of Rhode Island, is in the South Pacific Ocean about 2,200 miles (3,540 km) south of Hawaii midway to Sydney, Australia, and about 800 miles (1,287 km) northeast of Fiji. The larger islands in the Samoan chain are mountainous and of volcanic origin. There is little level land except in the coastal areas, where most cultivation takes place.

Government. Western Samoa has a 47-member Legislature, consisting mainly of the titleholders (chiefs) of family or tribal groups, with two members elected by universal suffrage to represent those not belonging to such groups. When the present Chiefs of State die, successors will be elected by the Legislature.

History. The Samoan islands were discovered in the 18th century and visited by Dutch and French traders. Toward the end of the 19th century, conflicting interests of the U.S., Britain, and Germany resulted in a treaty signed in 1899. It recognized the paramount interests of the U.S. in those islands east of 171° west longitude (American Samoa) and Germany's interests in the other islands (Western Samoa); the British withdrew in return for recognition of their rights in Tonga and the Solomons.

New Zealand occupied Western Samoa in 1914, and was granted a League of Nations mandate. In 1947, the islands became a U.N. trust territory administered by New Zealand.

Western Samoa became independent on Jan. 1, 1962.

YEMEN

People's Democratic Republic of Yemen
President: Ali Nasser (1980)
Area: 111,000 sq mi. (287,490 sq km)[1]
Population (est. 1981): 1,950,000[1] (growth rate: 2.4%)
Density per square mile: 17.6[1]
National capital and largest city (est. 1980): Aden, 343,000
Administrative capital: Madinat ash Sha'b
Monetary unit: Yemen dinar
Language: Arabic
Religion: Islam
National name: Jumhurijah al-Yemen al Dimuqratiyah al Sha'abijah
Freedom House classifications: Socialist pre-industrial, one-party socialist
Economic summary: Gross national product (1979): $890 million. Average annual growth rate (1973–78): 12.7%. Per capita income: $290. Land used for agriculture: 0.3%; labor force: 70–80%; principal products: sorghum, millet, wheat, cotton, coffee. Labor force in industry: 2–3%; major products: refined oil products, salt, fish meal, cloth. Natural resource: fish. Exports: petroleum products, textiles, cotton. Imports: crude oil, foodstuffs, manufactured goods. Major trading partners: U.K., Japan, Iran, Kuwait, Yemen Arab Republic.

1. Excluding Perim and Kamaran islands.

Geography. Formerly known as Southern Yemen, the People's Democratic Republic of Yemen extends along the southern part of the Arabian Peninsula on the Gulf of Aden and the Indian Ocean. It is comparable in size to Nevada. The Yemen Arab Republic is to the northwest, Saudi Arabia to the north, and Oman to the east.

A 700-mile (1,130-km) narrow coastal plain gives way to a mountainous region and then a plateau area.

Government. On June 23, 1969, President Qahtan Mohammed al Shaabi resigned and was replaced by a five-man Presidential Council.

A Constitution published in 1970 changed the state's name from Southern Yemen and established a 111-seat legislature, the People's Supreme Council of which Ali Nasser is chairman, and thus head of state. The only legal political party is the Yemeni Socialist Party.

History. The People's Republic of Southern Yemen was established Nov. 30, 1967, when Britain granted independence to the Federation of South

Arabia. This Federation consisted of the state (once the colony) of Aden and 16 of the 20 states of the Protectorate of South Arabia (once the Aden Protectorate). The four states of the Protectorate that did not join the Federation later became part of Southern Yemen.

Salim Robea Ali, Chairman of the Presidential Council since its establishment in 1969, was ousted and executed June 26, 1978, two days after the assassination of President Ahmed Hussein al-Ghashmi of the Yemen Arab Republic. Premier Ali Nasser Mohammed assumed the added duty of Council head.

Abdul Fattah Ismail, Secretary General of the ruling party who was elected President by the Supreme Council on Dec. 27, 1978, reversed Robea's movement toward reconciliation with the Yemen Arab Republic and an accommodation with Saudi Arabia. Despite Fattah Ismail's acquiescence to the continuing build-up of Soviet military strength in the country in conjunction with the Soviet invasion of Afghanistan, he proved to be an embarrassment to Moscow. His sudden resignation on April 21, 1980, was reported to have stemmed from the new Soviet desire to win friends in the Yemen Arab Republic and Saudi Arabia.

YEMEN ARAB REPUBLIC

Chief of State: Lieut. Col. Ali Abdulla Saleh (1978)
Premier: Abdel Karim al-Iriani (1980)
Area: 75,290 sq mi. (195,000 sq km)
Population (est. 1981): 6,100,000 (growth rate: 2.3%)
Density per square mile: 81.0
Capital and largest city (est. 1975): San'a', 134,600
Monetary unit: Rial
Language: Arabic
Religion: Islam
National name: Al Jamhuriya al Arabiya Yamaniya
Freedom House classifications: Capitalist pre-industrial, non-party military
Economic summary: Gross national product (1979): $2.4 billion. Per capita income: $180. Land used for agriculture: 42%; labor force: 73%; principal products: wheat, sorghum, cattle, sheep, cotton, fruits. Major industrial products: consumer goods, construction materials. Natural resources: traces of copper, sulfur, coal, quartz. Exports: cotton, coffee, hides and skins. Imports: foodstuffs, manufactures, machinery and transport equipment, chemicals, fuel, lubricants, tobacco. Major trading partners: Japan, Australia, Arab nations, U.S.S.R., U.K.

Geography. The Yemen Arab Republic occupies the southwestern tip of the Arabian Peninsula, with its western coast on the Red Sea opposite Ethiopia. Its neighbors are Saudi Arabia to the north and east and the People's Democratic Republic of Yemen to the south. Its area is slightly less than that of South Dakota.

A north-south coastal plain 20–50 miles wide (32 –80 km) lies in the west; eastward, there are the interior highlands, which attain a height of 12,000 feet (3,660 m), and the expanse of the Rub 'al-Khali Desert.

Government. The country's first permanent Constitution was submitted to the National Assembly in 1971. It provided for a 179-member legislature, the Consultative Council, 20 of whose members would be chosen by the President and the rest elected every four years. A five-man executive Presidential

Council was to be chosen by the Consultative Council.

A merger agreement between Yemen and the People's Democratic Republic of Yemen (Southern Yemen) was signed by the two states in 1972 after bitter border clashes between them over a five-year period. A new Constitution was to be drafted, but meanwhile the joint government was to be "republican, nationalist, and democratic," ruled by a single, merged Presidential Council and unified legislative, executive, and judicial branches.

In 1974, the army ousted the government in a bloodless coup and suspended the Constitution and its various legislative bodies. No political organizations are permitted.

History. The history of Yemen dates back to the Minaean kingdom (1200–650 B.C.). It accepted Islam in A.D. 628, and in the 10th century came under the control of the Rassite dynasty of the Zaidi sect. The Turks occupied the area from 1538 to 1630 and from 1849 to 1918. The sovereign status of Yemen was confirmed by treaties signed with Saudi Arabia and Britain in 1934.

Yemen joined the Arab League in 1945 and established diplomatic relations with the U.S. in 1946.

In 1962, a military revolt of elements favoring President Gamal Abdel Nasser of Egypt broke out. A ruling junta proclaimed a republic, and Yemen became an international battleground, with Egypt and the U.S.S.R. supporting the revolutionaries, and King Saud of Saudi Arabia and King Hussein of Jordan the royalists. The civil war continued until the war between the Arab states and Israel broke out in June 1967. Nasser had to pull out many of his troops and agree to a cease-fire and withdrawal of foreign forces. The war finally ended with the defeat of the royalists in mid-1969.

In 1977, Col. Ibrahim al-Hamidi was assassinated after three years as head of government and was succeeded by Lt. Col. Ahmed Hussein al-Ghashmi as head of the Presidential Council. On June 24, 1978, al-Ghashmi was killed by a bomb as he received the credentials of a new ambassador from the People's Democratic Republic of Yemen. The People's Council elected Col. Ali Abdulla Saleh as President on July 17.

YUGOSLAVIA

Socialist Federal Republic of Yugoslavia
President: Sergej Krajger (1981)
President of Federal Executive Council (Premier): Veselin Djuranovic (1977)
Area: 98,766 sq mi. (255,804 sq km)
Population (est. 1981): 22,550,000 (growth rate: 0.8%)
(Serbian, 42%; Croatian, 24%; Slovene, 9%; Macedonian, 5%; Albanian, 4%)
Density per square mile: 228.3
Capital: Belgrade
Largest cities (est. 1980): Belgrade, 1,000,000; (1971 census): Zagreb, 566,224; Skopje, 312,980; Sarajevo, 243,980; Ljubljana, 173,853; Split, 152,905
Monetary unit: Dinar
Languages: Serbo-Croatian, Slovene, Macedonian (all official)
Religions: Greek Orthodox, 41%; Roman Catholic, 32%; Islam, 12%
National name: Socijalisticka Federativna Republika Jugoslavija
Freedom House classifications: Capitalist-socialist industrial, one-party communist

Economic summary: Gross national product (1979): $53.8 billion. Average annual growth rate (1970–78): 5.0%. Per capita income: $2,210. Land used for agriculture: 33%; labor force: 48%; principal products: corn, wheat, tobacco, sugar beets. Labor force in industry: 52%; major products: wood, processed food, nonferrous metals, machinery, textiles. Natural resources: bauxite, timber, antimony, chromium, lead, zinc, asbestos, mercury, cadmium. Exports: timber, nonferrous metals, machinery and metal products, textiles, iron and steel. Imports: machinery and metal products, chemicals, textiles, iron, petroleum, steel. Major trading partners: U.S.S.R., West Germany, Italy, U.S.

Geography. Yugoslavia fronts on the eastern coast of the Adriatic Sea opposite Italy. Its neighbors are Austria, Italy, and Hungary to the north, Romania and Bulgaria to the east, and Greece and Albania to the south. It is slightly larger than Wyoming.

About half of Yugoslavia is mountainous. In the north, the Dinaric Alps rise abruptly from the sea and progress eastward as a barren limestone plateau called the Karst. Montenegro is a jumbled mass of mountains, containing also some grassy slopes and fertile river valleys. Southern Serbia, too, is mountainous. A rich plain in the north and northeast, drained by the Danube, is the most fertile area of the country.

Government. Yugoslavia is a federal republic composed of six socialist republics—Serbia (which includes the provinces of Vojvodina and Kosovo), Croatia, Slovenia, Bosnia-Herzegovina, Macedonia, and Montenegro. Actual administration is carried on by the Federal Executive Council and its secretaries.

The League of Communists and the Socialist Alliance of the Working People are the major political parties.

History. Yugoslavia was formed Dec. 1, 1918, from the patchwork of Balkan states and territories where World War I began with the assassination of Archduke Ferdinand of Austria at Sarajevo on June 28, 1914. The new Kingdom of Serbs, Croats, and Slovenes included the former kingdoms of Serbia and Montenegro; Bosnia-Herzegovina, previously administered jointly by Austria and Hungary; Croatia-Slavonia, a semi-autonomous region of Hungary, and Dalmatia, formerly administered by Austria. King Peter I of Serbia became the first monarch, his son acting as Regent until his accession as Alexander I on Aug. 16, 1921.

Croatian demands for a federal state forced Alexander to assume dictatorial powers in 1929 and to change the country's name to Yugoslavia. Serbian dominance continued despite his efforts, amid the resentment of other regions. A Macedonian associated with Croatian dissidents assassinated Alexander in Marseilles, France, on Oct. 9, 1934, and his cousin, Prince Paul, became Regent for the King's son, Prince Peter.

Paul's pro-Axis policy brought Yugoslavia to sign the Axis Pact on March 25, 1941, and opponents overthrew the government two days later. On April 6 the Nazis occupied the country, and the young King and his government fled. Two guerrilla armies —the Chetniks under Draza Mihajlovic supporting the monarchy and the Partisans under Tito (Josip Broz) leaning toward the U.S.S.R.—fought the Nazis for the duration of the war. In 1943, Tito established an Executive National Committee of Liberation to function as a provisional government.

Tito won the election held in the fall of 1945, as monarchists boycotted the vote. A new Assembly abolished the monarchy and proclaimed the Federal People's Republic of Yugoslavia, with Tito as Prime Minister.

Ruthlessly eliminating opposition, the Tito government executed Mihajlovic in 1946. With Soviet aid, Tito annexed the greater part of Italian Istria under the 1947 peace treaty with Italy but failed in his claim to the key port of Trieste. Zone B of the former free territory of Trieste went to Yugoslavia in 1954.

Tito broke with the Soviet bloc in 1948 and Yugoslavia has since followed a middle road, combining orthodox Communist control of politics and general overall economic policy with a varying degree of freedom in the arts, travel, and individual enterprise. Tito, who became President in 1953 and President for life under a revised Constitution adopted in 1963, has played a major part in the creation of a "non-aligned" group of states, the so-called "third world."

The Marshal supported his one-time Soviet mentors in their quarrel with Communist China, but even though he imprisoned the writer Mihajlo Mihajlov and other dissenters at home, he criticized Soviet repression of Czecholovakia in 1968.

Tito welcomed President Nixon to Yugoslavia in 1970 for the first U.S. Presidential visit, and he went to the U.S. the following year, but the relationship has been touchy.

Tito's death on May 4, 1980, three days before his 88th birthday, removed from the scene the last World War II leader. A rotating presidency designed to avoid internal dissension was put into effect immediately, and the feared clash of Yugoslavia's multiple nationalities and regions appeared to have been averted. On May 15, Cvijetin Mijatovic of the Serbian republic began a one-year term. A collective presidency, rotated annually among the six republics and two autonomous provinces of the federal republic, was to continue to govern according to a constitutional change made in 1974.

In March 1981, the Albanian minority, which forms 80 per cent of the population of the autonomous province of Kosovo, backed Albanian students demonstrating against conditions at the university. By April, the demonstrations had swelled to riots in which 11 were killed as 100,000 people demanded the status of a separate republic, which would enable Kosovo to secede from the Yugoslav federation. Albania's government and press applauded the nationalist movement.

ZAIRE

Republic of Zaire
President: Mobutu Sese Seko (1965)
Prime Minister: Joseph Nsigna (1981)
Area: 905,063 sq mi. (2,344,113 sq km)
Population (est. 1981): 29,450,000 (growth rate: 2.9%)
Density per square mile: 32.5
Capital: Kinshasa
Largest cities (est. 1979): Kinshasa, 2,500,000; (est. 1974 by U.N.): Kananga, 601,250; Luluabourg, 506,000; Lubumbashi, 403,600
Monetary unit: Zaire
Languages: French; Bantu dialects, mainly Swahili, Lingala, Ishiluba, and Kikongo
Religions: Animist, 50%; Roman Catholic, Protestant, Islam
Ethnic groups: Bantu, Sudanese, Nilotics, Pygmies, Hamites
National name: République du Zaïre
Freedom House classifications: Capitalist-statist pre-industrial, one-party nationalist

Economic summary: Gross national product (1979): $7.0 billion. Average annual growth rate (1970–78): −2.2%. Per capita income (1976): $132. Land used for agriculture: 2%; labor force: 70–80%; principal products: coffee, palm oil, rubber, tea, cotton, cocoa, manioc, bananas, plantains, vegetables, fruits. Major industrial products: processed and unprocessed minerals, consumer products, metal and chemical products, construction materials, steel. Natural resources: copper, cobalt, zinc, industrial diamonds, manganese, tin, gold, rare metals, bauxite, iron, coal, 13% of world hydroelectric potential. Exports: copper, cobalt, diamonds, gold, manganese, coffee, palm oil, wood. Imports: crude petroleum, petroleum products, chemicals, transport equipment, textiles, food. Major trading partners: Belgium, France, West Germany, U.S., U.K.

Geography. Zaire is situated in west central Africa and is bordered by the Congo, the Central African Empire, the Sudan, Uganda, Rwanda, Burundi, Tanzania, Zambia, Angola, and the Atlantic Ocean. It is one quarter the size of the U.S.

The principal rivers are the Ubangi and Bomu in the north and the Zaire (Congo) in the west, which flows into the Atlantic. The entire length of Lake Tanganyika lies along the eastern border with Tanzania and Burundi.

Government. Under the Constitution approved by referendum in 1967 and amended in 1974, the third Constitution since 1960, the president and a unicameral Legislature are elected by universal suffrage for five-year terms.

In 1971, the government proclaimed that the Democratic Republic of the Congo would be known as the Republic of Zaire, since the Congo River's name had been changed to the Zaire. In addition, President Joseph D. Mobutu took the name Mobutu Sese Seko and Katanga Province became Shaba.

There is only one political party: the Popular Movement of the Revolution, led by President Mobutu.

History. Formerly the Belgian Congo, this territory was inhabited by ancient Negrito peoples (Pygmies), who were pushed into the mountains by Bantu and Nilotic invaders. The American correspondent Henry M. Stanley navigated the Congo River in 1877 and opened the interior to exploration. Commissioned by King Leopold II of the Belgians, Stanley made treaties with native chiefs that enabled the King to obtain personal title to the territory at the Berlin Conference of 1885.

Criticism of forced labor under royal exploitation prompted Belgium to take over administration of the Congo, which remained a colony until agitation for independence forced Brussels to grant freedom on June 30, 1960. Moise Tshombe, Premier of the then Katanga Province seceded from the new republic on July 11, and another mining province, South Kasai, followed. Belgium sent paratroopers to quell the civil war, and with President Joseph Kasavubu and Premier Patrice Lumumba of the national government in conflict, the United Nations flew in a peacekeeping force.

Kasavubu staged an army coup in 1960 and handed Lumumba over to the Katangan forces. A U.N. investigating commission found that Lumumba had been killed by a Belgian mercenary in the presence of Tshombe. Dag Hammarskjold, U.N. Secretary-General, died in a plane crash en route to a peace conference with Tshombe on Sept. 17, 1961.

U.N. Secretary-General U Thant submitted a national reconciliation plan in 1962 that Tshombe rejected. Tshombe's troops fired on the U.N. force in December, and in the ensuing conflict Tshombe capitulated on Jan. 14, 1963. The peacekeeping force withdrew, and, in a complete about-face, Kasavubu named Tshombe Premier to fight a spreading rebellion. Tshombe used foreign mercenaries and, with the help of Belgian paratroops airlifted by U.S. planes, defeated the most serious opposition, a Communist-backed regime in the northeast.

Kasavubu abruptly dismissed Tshombe in 1965 and was himself ousted by Gen. Joseph-Desiré Mobutu, Army Chief of Staff. The new President nationalized the Union Minière, the Belgian copper mining enterprise that had been a dominant force in the Congo since colonial days. The plane carrying the exiled Tshombe was hijacked in 1967 and he was held prisoner in Algeria until his death from a heart attack was announced June 29, 1969.

Mobutu eliminated opposition to win election in 1970 to a term of seven years, which was renewed in a 1977 election. He invited U.S., South African, and Japanese investment to replace Belgian interests. In 1975, he nationalized much of the economy, barred religious instruction in schools, and decreed the adoption of African names.

In the Angolan civil war of 1975–76, Mobutu backed the National Front for the Liberation of Angola, whose leader, Holden Roberto, is related to him by marriage. The Zairean government opposed the recognition of the Soviet-backed Popular Movement for the Liberation of Angola and reluctantly accepted its victory.

On March 8, 1977, invaders from Angola calling themselves the Congolese National Liberation Front pushed into Shaba and threatened the important mining center of Kolwezi. France and Belgium responded to Mobutu's pleas for help with weapons, but the U.S. gave only nonmilitary supplies.

In April, France flew 1,500 Moroccan troops to Shaba to defeat the invaders, who were, Mobutu charged, Soviet-inspired, and Cuban-led. U.S. intelligence sources, however, confirmed Soviet and Cuban denials of any participation and identified the rebels as former Katanga gendarmes who had fled to Angola after their 1963 defeat.

On May 15, 1978, a new assult from Angola resulted in the capture of Kolwezi and the death of 100 whites and 300 blacks. In this second invasion, France and Belgium intervened directly as 1,000 Foreign Legion paratroopers repelled the Katangese and 1,750 Belgian soldiers helped evacuate 2,000 Europeans. The U.S. supplied 18 air transports for both the troop movement and the evacuation. This time President Carter himself backed Mobutu's renewed assertions of Soviet-Cuban participation.

France led in organizing Western aid for the restoration of the shattered mining operations at Kolwezi, an important part of the Shaba industry that is the mainstay of Zaire's economy.

ZAMBIA

Republic of Zambia
President: Kenneth D. Kaunda (1964)
Prime Minister: Nalumino Mundia (1981)
Area: 290,724 sq mi. (752,975 sq km)
Population (est. 1981): 6,000,000 (growth rate: 3.2%)
Density per square mile: 20.1
Capital: Lusaka

Largest cities (est. 1980 for metropolitan area): Lusaka, 684,000; **(est. 1978 by U.N.):** Kitwe, 310,000; Ndola, 291,000; Chingola, 173,000; Mufulira, 170,000
Monetary unit: Kwacha
Languages: English and local dialects
Religions: Animist, Roman Catholic, Protestant, Hindu, Islam
Member of Commonwealth of Nations
Freedom House classifications: Capitalist-socialist pre-industrial, one-party socialist
Economic summary: Gross national product (1979): $2.8 billion. Average annual growth rate (1970–78): −0.9%. Per capita income: $480. Land used for agriculture: 70%; labor force: 85%; principal products: maize, tobacco, cotton, sugar cane. Labor force in industry: 15%; major products: foodstuffs, beverages, chemicals, textiles, fertilizers. Natural resources: copper, zinc, lead, cobalt, coal. Exports: copper, zinc, lead, cobalt, tobacco. Imports: manufactured goods, machinery and transport equipment, foodstuffs. Major trading partners: U.K., Japan, South Africa, U.S., West Germany, China.

Geography. Zambia, a landlocked country in south central Africa, is about one tenth larger than Texas. It is surrounded by Angola, Zaire, Tanzania, Malawi, Mozambique, Zimbabwe, Botswana, and South-West Africa (Namibia). The country is mostly a plateau that rises to 8,000 feet (2,434 m) in the east.

Government. Zambia (formerly Northern Rhodesia) is governed by a president, elected by universal suffrage, and a Legislative Assembly, consisting of 105 members elected by universal suffrage and up to 10 additional members nominated by the president.

In 1972, the Assembly passed a law making the ruling United National Independence Party, led by President Kenneth D. Kaunda, the only legal political party.

History. Empire builder Cecil Rhodes obtained mining concessions in 1889 from King Lewanika of the Barotse and sent settlers to the area soon thereafter. It was ruled by the British South Africa Company, which he established, until 1924, when the British government took over the administration.

From 1953 to 1964, Northern Rhodesia was federated with Southern Rhodesia and Nyasaland in the Federation of Rhodesia and Nyasaland. On Oct. 24, 1964, Northern Rhodesia became the independent nation of Zambia.

Kenneth Kaunda, the first president, kept Zambia within the Commonwealth of Nations. The country's economy, dependent on copper exports, was threatened when Rhodesia declared its independence from British rule in 1965 and defied U.N. sanctions, which Zambia supported, an action that deprived Zambia of its trade route through Rhodesia. The U.S., Britain, and Canada organized an airlift in 1966 to ship gasoline into Zambia. In 1967, Britain agreed to finance new trade routes for Zambia.

Kaunda visited China in 1967, and China later agreed to finance a 1,000-mile railroad from the copper fields to Dar es Salaam in Tanzania. A pipeline was opened in 1968 from Ndola in Zambia's copper belt to the Indian Ocean at Dar es Salaam, ending the three-year oil drought.

In 1969, Kaunda announced the nationalization of the foreign copper-mining industry, with Zambia to take 51% (over $1 billion, estimated), and an agreement was reached with the companies on payment. He then announced a similar take-over of foreign oil producers.

Zambia suffered heavy damage from bombing raids by the former Rhodesian air force on Zimbabwean guerrilla bases and on its transportation links. These actions, combined with falling prices for copper and cobalt, forced Kaunda to declare a state of economic austerity in January 1981.

A strike by copper-belt workers, directed partly against cuts in consumer subsidies and partly at UNIP, the regime's single party, brought a quick victory for the workers after they shut down production. In February, Kaunda installed a new Prime Minister and a new party chief, both more acceptable to the powerful copper-belt unions, and in April, UNIP readmitted union leaders who had been expelled at the time of the strike.

ZIMBABWE

President: Rev. Canaan Banana (1980)
Prime Minister: Robert Mugabe (1980)
Area: 150,333 sq mi. (389,362 sq km)
Population (est. 1981): 7,580,000 (growth rate: 2.5%) (black, 96%; white, 4%)
Density per square mile: 50.4
Capital: Salisbury
Largest cities (est. 1980 for metropolitan area): Salisbury,[1] 655,000; Bulawayo, 375,000
Monetary unit: Zimbabwean dollar
Languages: English (official), Sindebele, Shona
Religions: Christian, 20%; Animist
Freedom House classifications: Capitalist-statist pre-industrial, multi-party centralized
Economic summary: Gross national product (1979): $3.4 billion. Average annual growth rate (1970–78): −1.0%. Per capita income (1979): $530. Principal agricultural products: tobacco, corn, sugar, cotton, livestock. Major industrial products: steel, textiles, chemicals, vehicles, gold, copper. Natural resources: gold, copper, cobalt, nickel, tin, asbestos. Exports: gold, tobacco, asbestos, copper, meat, chrome, nickel, clothing, sugar. Imports: machinery, petroleum products, wheat, transport equipment. Major trading partner: South Africa.

1. To be changed to Harare in late 1981.

Geography. Zimbabwe, a landlocked country in south central Africa, is slightly smaller than California. It is bordered by Botswana on the west, Zambia on the north, Mozambique on the east, and South Africa on the south.

A high veld up to 6,000 feet (1,829 m) crosses the country from northeast to southwest. This is flanked by a somewhat lower veld that contains ranching country. Tropical forests that yield hardwoods lie in the southeast.

In the north, on the border with Zambia, is the 175-mile-long (128-m) Kariba Lake, formed by the Kariba Dam across the Zambezi River. It is the site of one of the world's largest hydroelectric projects.

Government. Executive power rests with the 26-member Cabinet, headed by the Prime Minister. The President, elected by a majority of the House of Assembly, exercises formal executive powers. The legislature is composed of a 100-member House of Assembly, 80 of whom are elected by black voters and 20 by whites, and a 40-member Senate. Black House members elect 14 Senators and whites elect 10. Ten tribal chiefs—five from Mashonaland and five from Matabeleland—are elected by their peers and six appointed by the President complete the Senate membership.

Major political parties are the Zimbabwe African National Union (57 seats in the House of Assembly), led by Prime Minister Robert Mugabe; Zimbabwe African People's Union (20 seats), led by Joshua Nkomo; and the United African National Council (3 seats), led by former Prime Minister Abel Muzorewa. The Republican Front, led by former Prime Minister Ian Smith, holds all 20 seats reserved for whites.

History. Zimbabwe, formerly called Rhodesia, was colonized by Cecil Rhodes's British South Africa Company at the end of the 19th century. In 1923, European settlers voted in a referendum to become the self-governing British colony of Southern Rhodesia rather than merge with what was then the Union of South Africa. After a brief federation with Northern Rhodesia and Nyasaland in the post-World War II period, Southern Rhodesia chose to remain a colony when its two partners voted for independence in 1963.

On Nov. 11, 1965, the white-minority government of Rhodesia unilaterally declared its independence from Britain.

In 1967, Rhodesia became the first country against which the United Nations ever imposed mandatory sanctions. The U.S. stopped virtually all trade with Rhodesia. The country refused to cave in, but began a slow movement toward meeting the demands of the black Africans. The white-minority regime of Prime Minister Ian Smith withstood British pressure, economic sanctions, guerrilla attacks, and a right-wing assault.

On March 1, 1970, Rhodesia formally proclaimed itself a republic, and within the month nine nations, including the U.S., closed their consulates there.

In 1972 the international economic boycott of Rhodesia began to break down. The U.S. was one country that resumed trade by buying Rhodesian chrome ore, but restored the ban a year later.

Black terrorism, which began late in 1972, resulted in the death of several hundred black rebels and several dozen white citizens and soldiers. The army draft size was doubled and other steps were taken to counter the security threat, including uprooting 8,000 black Africans from the area bordering Mozambique in an attempt to create a 200-mile-long (322 km) buffer zone.

Heightened guerrilla war and a withdrawal of South African military aid—particularly helicopters—marked the beginning of the collapse of Smith's 11 years of resistance in the spring of 1976. Under pressure from South Africa's Prime Minister, Johannes Vorster, Smith agreed with U.S. Secretary of State Henry A. Kissinger that majority rule should come within two years.

In the fall, Smith met with black nationalist leaders in Geneva. The meeting broke up six weeks later when the Rhodesian Premier insisted that whites must retain control of the police and armed forces during the transition to majority rule. A British proposal called for Britons to take over these powers.

Divisions between Rhodesian blacks—Bishop Abel Muzorewa of the African National Congress and Ndabaningi Sithole as moderates versus Robert Mugabe and Joshua Nkomo of the Patriotic Front as advocates of guerrilla force—sharpened in 1977 and no agreement was reached. In July, with white residents leaving in increasing numbers and the economy showing the strain of war, Smith rejected outside mediation and called for general

elections in order to work out an "internal solution" of the transfer of power.

On March 3, 1978, Smith, Muzorewa, Sithole, and Chief Jeremiah Chirau signed an agreement to transfer power to the black majority by Dec. 31, 1978. They constituted themselves an Executive Council, with chairmanship rotating but Smith retaining the title of Prime Minister. Blacks were named to each cabinet ministry, serving as co-ministers with the whites already holding these posts. African nations and the Patriotic Front leaders immediately denounced the action, but Western governments were more reserved, although none granted recognition to the new regime.

Despite continuing fighting, white voters ratified a new constitution on Jan. 30, 1979, enfranchising all blacks, establishing a black majority Senate and Assembly, and changing the country's name to Zimbabwe Rhodesia. A general election on April 24 gave Muzorewa's party 67.3% of the vote, and although the Patriotic Front urged a boycott, more than 60% of the eligible blacks went to the polls.

As black African states refused recognition and the United Nations sanctions remained in force, Muzorewa agreed to negotiate with Mugabe and Nkomo in British-sponsored talks beginning Sept. 9. By December, all parties accepted a new draft constitution, a cease-fire, and a period of British administration pending a general election. Lord Christopher Soames arrived on Dec. 12 to head the government, followed by British and Commonwealth troops who were to serve as peace-keeping forces as Patriotic Front guerrillas were grouped at 40 assembly points throughout the country.

The United Nations Security Council ended sanctions on Dec. 21, the day the formal agreement was signed by all parties.

In voting completed on Feb. 29, 1980, Mugabe's ZANU-Patriotic Front party won 57 of the 80 Assembly seats reserved for blacks. Nkomo's ZAPU-Patriotic Front party won 20 seats and Muzorewa's United African National Council only three. In an earlier vote on Feb. 14, the Rhodesian Front won all 20 seats reserved for whites in the Assembly.

At a ceremony on April 18, Prince Charles of Britain handed to President-elect Rev. Canaan Banana the symbols of independence. Mugabe, a Marxist, had already pledged his support for continuation of the existing free-market economy. Britain announced a two-year $165-million aid program for the new government, and the United States, opening the first embassy in Salisbury, offered $15 million for rural rehabilitation and $2 million to rebuild rural clinics.

In January 1981, Mugabe dismissed Nkomo as Home Minister and his onetime rival left the government in protest. At the same time, the Prime Minister discharged Edgar Z. Tekere, Manpower and Planning Minister, who had been tried and acquitted of the murder of a white farmer.

Mugabe survived both tests and scored an unprecedented triumph when, in response to his appeal for economic aid, Western nations pledged $1.8 billion for the next three years. The United States promised to give $225 million in grants in addition to $50 million in low-interest loans to replace war-damaged housing. Despite the successes of the new government, whites continued to leave the country in 1981, threatening Zimbabwe's farm and industrial production.

(For late reports, see Current Events of 1980–81)

CANADA

Sovereign: Queen Elizabeth II
Governor General: Edward R. Schreyer (1979)
Prime Minister: Pierre Elliott Trudeau (1980)
Area: 3,851,809 sq mi. (9,976,139 sq km)
Population (est. 1981): 24,000,000 (British, 44.6%; French, 28.7%; other European, 23%) (growth rate, 1979–80, 0.9%)
Density per square mile: 6.2
Capital: Ottawa, Ont.
Largest cities (1979) Winnipeg, Man. 578,000; Calgary, Alta. 530,846; Edmonton, Alta., 491,359; Regina, Sask., 153,848; **(1976 census)** Montreal, Que., 1,080,546; Toronto, Ont., 633,318; Vancouver, B.C., 410,188; Hamilton, Ont., 312,003; Ottawa, Ont., 304,462; London, Ont., 240,392; Windsor, Ont., 196,526; Quebec, Que., 177,082
Monetary Unit: Canadian dollar
Languages: English, French
Religions: Roman Catholic, 46.2%; United Church, 17.5%; Anglican, 11.8%; Presbyterian, 4%; Lutheran, 3.3%; Baptist, 3.1%; others, 14.1%
Gross national product (1979): $228.4 billion
Average annual growth rate (1970–78): 3.0%
Freedom House classifications: Capitalist industrial, multi-party decentralized

Geography. Covering most of the northern part of the North American continent and with an area larger than that of the United States, Canada has an extremely varied topography. The northeastern region, including most of Quebec, northern Ontario and Manitoba, and the Northwest Territories, with Hudson Bay in the center, is an important source of minerals, wood pulp, and water power. In the east the mountainous maritime provinces have an irregular coast line on the Gulf of St. Lawrence and the Atlantic. The St. Lawrence plain, covering most of southern Quebec and Ontario, and the interior continental plain, covering southern Manitoba and Saskatchewan and most of Alberta, are the principal cultivable areas. They are separated by a forested plateau rising from lakes Superior and Huron.

Westward toward the Pacific, most of British Columbia, Yukon, and part of western Alberta are covered by parallel mountain ranges including the Rockies. The Pacific border of the coast range is ragged with fiords and channels. The highest point in Canada is Mount Logan (19,850 ft; 6,050 m), which is in the Yukon.

Canada has an abundance of large and small lakes. In addition to the Great Lakes on the U.S. border, there are 9 others that are more than 100 miles long (161 km) and 35 that are more than 50 miles long (80 km).

The two principal river systems are the Mackenzie and the St. Lawrence. The St. Lawrence, with its tributaries, is navigable for over 1,900 miles (3,058 km).

Government. Canada, a self-governing member of the Commonwealth of Nations, is a federal union of 10 provinces whose powers are laid down in the British North America Act of 1867. The executive powers nominally rest in the hands of the Governor General, who represents the Queen and is appointed by her upon the recommendation of the Canadian government.

Actually the Governor General acts only with the advice of the Canadian Prime Minister and the members of the Cabinet, who also sit in the federal Parliament. The Parliament has two houses: a Senate of 104 members appointed for life, and a House of Commons of 264 members apportioned according to provincial population. Elections are held at least every five years or whenever the party in power is voted down in the House of Commons or considers it expedient to appeal to the people. The Prime Minister is the leader of the majority party in the House of Commons—or, if no single party holds a majority, the leader of the party able to command the support of a majority of members of the House. Laws must be passed by both houses of Parliament and signed by the Governor General in the Queen's name.

The 10 provincial governments are nominally headed by Lieutenant Governors appointed by the federal government, but the executive power in each actually is vested in a Cabinet headed by a Premier, who is leader of the majority party. The provincial legislatures are composed of one-house assemblies whose members are elected for four-year terms. They are known as Legislative Assemblies, except in Newfoundland, where it is the House of Assembly, and in Quebec, where it is the National Assembly.

The judicial system consists of a Supreme Court in Ottawa (established in 1875), with appellate jurisdiction, and a Supreme Court in each province, as well as county courts with limited jurisdiction in most of the provinces. The Governor General in Council appoints these judges.

The major political parties are the Liberal (147 of 282 seats in House of Commons), led by Prime Minister Pierre Elliott Trudeau; Progressive Conservative Party (102 seats), led by former Prime Minister Charles Joseph Clark; New Democratic Party (33), led by John Edward Broadbent; Social Credit Party (no seats) led by Fabien Roy. No Independents hold a seat and there are no vacancies.

History. The Norse explorer Leif Ericson probably reached the shores of Canada (Labrador or Nova Scotia) in A.D. 1000, but the history of the white man in the country actually began in 1497, when John Cabot, an Italian in the service of Henry VII of England, reached Newfoundland or Nova Scotia. Canada was taken for France in 1534 by Jacques Cartier. The actual settlement of New France, as it was then called, began in 1604 at Port Royal in what is now Nova Scotia; in 1608, Quebec was founded. France's colonization efforts were not very successful, but French explorers by the end of the 17th century had penetrated beyond the Great Lakes to the western prairies and south along the Mississippi to the Gulf of Mexico. Meanwhile, the English Hudson's Bay Company had been established in 1670. Because of the valuable fisheries and fur trade, a conflict developed between the French and English; in 1713, Newfoundland, Hudson Bay, and Nova Scotia (Acadia) were lost to England.

During the Seven Years' War (1756–63), England extended its conquest, and the British Maj. Gen. James Wolfe won his famous victory over Gen. Louis Montcalm outside Quebec on Sept. 13,

Canadian Governors General and Prime Ministers Since 1867

Term of office	Governor General	Term	Prime Minister	Party
1867–1868	Viscount Monck[1]	1867–1873	Sir John A. Macdonald	Conservative
1869–1872	Baron Lisgar	1873–1878	Alexander Mackenzie	Liberal
1872–1878	Earl of Dufferin	1878–1891	Sir John A. Macdonald	Conservative
1878–1883	Marquess of Lorne	1891–1892	Sir John J. C. Abbott	Conservative
1883–1888	Marquess of Lansdowne	1892–1894	Sir John S. D. Thompson	Conservative
1888–1893	Baron Stanley of Preston	1894–1896	Sir Mackenzie Bowell	Conservative
1893–1898	Earl of Aberdeen	1896	Sir Charles Tupper	Conservative
1898–1904	Earl of Minto	1896–1911	Sir Wilfrid Laurier	Liberal
1904–1911	Earl Grey	1911–1917	Sir Robert L. Borden	Conservative
1911–1916	Duke of Connaught	1917–1920	Sir Robert L. Borden	Unionist
1916–1921	Duke of Devonshire	1920–1921	Arthur Meighen	Unionist
1921–1926	Baron Byng of Vimy	1921–1926	W. L. Mackenzie King	Liberal
1926–1931	Viscount Willingdon	1926	Arthur Meighen	Conservative
1931–1935	Earl of Bessborough	1926–1930	W. L. Mackenzie King	Liberal
1935–1940	Baron Tweedsmuir	1930–1935	Richard B. Bennett	Conservative
1940–1946	Earl of Athlone	1935–1948	W. L. Mackenzie King	Liberal
1946–1952	Viscount Alexander	1948–1957	Louis S. St. Laurent	Liberal
1952–1959	Vincent Massey	1957–1963	John G. Diefenbaker	Progressive-Conservative
1959–1967	George P. Vanier			
1967–1973	Roland Michener	1963–1968	Lester B. Pearson	Liberal
1974–1979	Jules Léger	1968–1979	Pierre Elliott Trudeau	Liberal
1979–	Edward R. Schreyer	1979–1980	Charles Joseph Clark	Conservative
		1980–	Pierre Elliott Trudeau	Liberal

1. Became Governor General of British North America in 1861.

1759. The Treaty of Paris in 1763 gave England control.

At that time the population of Canada was almost entirely French, but in the next few decades, thousands of British colonists emigrated to Canada from the British Isles and from the American colonies. In 1849, the right of Canada to self-government was recognized. By the British North America Act of 1867, the Dominion of Canada was created through the confederation of Upper and Lower Canada, Nova Scotia, and New Brunswick. Prince Edward Island joined the Dominion in 1873.

In 1869 Canada purchased from the Hudson's Bay Company the vast middle west (Rupert's Land) from which the provinces of Manitoba (1870), Alberta, and Saskatchewan (1905) were later formed. In 1871, British Columbia joined the Dominion. The country was linked from coast to coast in 1885 by the Canadian Pacific Railway.

During the formative years between 1866 and 1896, the Conservative Party, led by Sir John A. Macdonald, governed the country, except during the years 1873–78. In 1896, the Liberal Party took over and, under Sir Wilfrid Laurier, an eminent French Canadian, ruled until 1911.

In World War I, more than 500,000 Canadian soldiers fought for the Allied cause. After the Treaty of Versailles, Canada, a full-fledged nation, was admitted to the League of Nations and appointed its own representatives in foreign countries. By the Statute of Westminster in 1931 the British Dominions, including Canada, were formally declared to be partner nations with Britian, "equal in status, in no way subordinate to each other," and bound together only by allegiance to a common Crown.

Newfoundland became Canada's 10th province on March 31, 1949, following a plebiscite. Besides the provinces, Canada includes two territories—the Yukon Territory, the area north of British Columbia and east of Alaska, and the Northwest Territories, including all of Canada north of 60° north latitude except Yukon and the northernmost sections of Quebec and Newfoundland. This area includes all of the Arctic north of the mainland, Norway having recognized Canadian sovereignty over the Svendrup Islands in the Arctic in 1931.

The Liberal Party, led by William Lyon Mackenzie King, dominated Canadian politics from 1921 until 1957, when it was succeeded by the Progressive Conservatives. The Liberals, under the leadership of Lester B. Pearson, returned to power in 1963. Pearson remained Prime Minister until 1968, when he retired and was replaced by a former law professor, Pierre Elliott Trudeau. Trudeau maintained Canada's defensive alliance with the United States, but began moving toward a more independent policy in world affairs.

Trudeau set about creating what he termed a "just society," stressing domestic reforms. His election was considered in part a response to the most serious problem confronting the country, the division between French- and English-speaking Canadians, which had led to a separatist movement in the predominantly French province of Quebec. Trudeau, himself a French Canadian, supported programs for bilingualism and an increased measure of provincial autonomy, although he would not tolerate the idea of separatism. In 1974, the provincial government voted to make French the official language of Quebec.

Capturing the Quebec provincial government from the long-entrenched local Liberal Party, René Lévesque and his separatist Parti Québécois pledged that they would seek independence for the province. He shocked English-speaking Canadians with a New York speech two months after his election in which he said the question was not when but *how* Quebec would attain independence.

Conflicts over the law establishing French as the dominant language in Quebec, particularly in schooling, kept separatism as a national issue, but by-elections in 1977 produced easy victories for

Trudeau's ruling Liberals in four Quebec seats in the national legislature, and polls showed a decline in separatist support both in the province and elsewhere in Canada. Early in 1978, Trudeau declared that he would use force to prevent any illegal declaration of independence by Lévesque.

Economic problems appeared to take precedence over politics in 1978, as the Sun Life Assurance Company of Canada, the nation's largest insurance firm, announced that it would move its headquarters from Montreal to Toronto. Many businesses had left the province earlier, but Sun Life was the first to cite the language law as the reason for its departure.

Despite Trudeau's removal of price and wage controls in 1978, continuing inflation and a high rate of unemployment caused him to delay elections until May 22, 1979, the first time since 1935 that a Canadian government had retained office for the allowable five-year term. The delay gave Trudeau no advantage—the Progressive Conservatives under Charles Joseph Clark defeated the Liberals everywhere except in Quebec, New Brunswick, and Newfoundland. The Liberals actually won the larger share of the popular vote with 40%, but because their strength was concentrated in Quebec they won only 114 seats to the Conservatives' 136 and 36% of the popular vote.

Clark took office as the head of Canada's fifth minority government in the last 20 years, needing the support of 26 New Democratic Party members and six Social Credit members to obtain an absolute majority in the 282-seat House.

Trudeau's defeat after 11 years in power was attributed to 9.8% inflation, to western opposition to his energy policies, and, in the opinion of some, public distaste over a sensational autobiography written by the Prime Minister's estranged wife. Trudeau's proposed changes in the Canadian constitution aroused the opposition of provincial premiers, even including Quebec's separatist leader, Lévesque, who opposed constitutional changes until federal-provincial relationships were clarified.

Clark's government collapsed after only six months when a motion to defeat the Tory budget carried by 139–133 on Dec. 13, 1979. On the same day, the Quebec law making French the exclusive official language of the province—an issue which had been expected to provide Clark's first major internal test—was voided by the Canadian Supreme Court.

In national elections Feb. 18, 1980, the resurgent Liberals under Trudeau scored an unexpectedly big victory, winning 146 seats (147 when a vacancy was filled a month later), while the Conservatives fell from 136 to 103 and the New Democrats won 32 seats. The House became a three-party legislature for the first time in half a century when the Social Credit party failed to win a single seat.

Trudeau promised to hold down energy costs—an 18-cents-a-gallon gasoline tax proposal was blamed for the Tory defeat—and to renew his efforts to reform ferderal-provincial relations. The Quebec challenge suffered a setback shortly after Trudeau took power when a referendum for the negotiation of a separate status for the province went down to a crushing defeat.

Renewed attempts to "patriate" the Canadian Constitution, which under the British North America Act required Britain's assent to changes, failed to win provincial agreement. When Trudeau sought to remove British parliamentary authority without consent of the provinces, they sued and the dispute was not expected to be resolved by Canada's Supreme Court until late in 1981.

Nor was Trudeau more successful in reviving a lagging economy, which registered zero growth in 1980. In July 1981, the Canadian dollar fell to a new low of less than 83 U.S. cents. One phase of Trudeau's new economic program created friction with the United States—tighter controls on U.S. oil and gas producers working in Canada. Talks between Trudeau and President Reagan in an exchange of visits before the Ottawa summit of industrialized nations brought no early compromise.

Economy. Agriculture, including horticulture, fruit growing, and the raising of stock and poultry, is the largest single industry. Canada is one of the world's greatest wheat-exporting countries; production is concentrated in Manitoba, Saskatchewan, and Alberta.

Stock raising and dairy farming have grown greatly since 1920. Ontario and Quebec are the

Population of Canada by Provinces and Territories

Province	1981 (Jan. Estimate)	1980 (Jan. Estimate)	1979 (Jan. Estimate)	1971 (Census)	1961 (Census)
Alberta	2,135,900	2,053,100	1,985,200	1,627,874	1,331,944
British Columbia	2,687,000	2,611,700	2,555,800	2,184,621	1,629,082
Manitoba	1,027,000	1,026,200	1,029,900	988,247	921,686
New Brunswick	709,100	704,800	699,200	634,557	597,936
Newfoundland	583,600	577,400	572,900	522,104	457,853
Nova Scotia	858,100	851,000	845,400	788,960	737,007
Ontario	8,600,500	8,543,300	8,479,900	7,703,106	6,236,092
Prince Edward Island	124,100	123,900	122,300	111,641	104,629
Quebec	6,325,200	6,288,300	6,289,600	6,027,764	5,259,211
Saskatchewan	975,700	965,300	952,500	926,242	925,181
Northwest Territories	42,800	43,100	43,100	34,807	22,998
Yukon Territory	21,500	21,800	21,800	18,388	14,628
Total	24,088,700	23,809,800	23,597,600	21,568,311	18,238,247
Rural	—	—	—	5,157,525	5,537,857
Urban	—	—	—	16,410,785	12,700,390

Source: Statistics Canada.

most important dairying provinces.

Canadian manufactures rely mainly on domestic raw materials; growing industries that depend largely on material imported in a raw or semi-finished state include the manufacture of automobiles, sugar, and rubber goods, as well as the iron and steel industry in Nova Scotia, Quebec, and Ontario. The latter two provinces account for more than 80% of all manufactures. The abundance of cheap water power is one of the chief factors in the growth of Canadian industry.

The most important industries in terms of output are pulp and paper, nonferrous-metals smelting and refining, petroleum products, meatpacking, motor vehicles, and sawmill products.

Canada's mineral resources are both rich and varied. Metals come mainly from two widely separated regions, the mountain ranges of the Pacific coast and the province of Ontario. Copper ore also exists in Quebec, Manitoba, and Newfoundland. Production of petroleum centers in Alberta. There are deposits of uranium in the Northwest Territories.

The total area of land covered by forests is estimated at 1,300,000 square miles (3,367,000 sq km), of which only 435,000 square miles (1,126,650 sq km) are commercially productive and accessible. The manufacture of pulp and paper is one of the leading industries.

Fishing, Canada's oldest industry, is carried on along the Atlantic and Pacific coasts and on the inland lakes.

Chief exports in 1979 were motor vehicles (17%); machinery (10%); timber (6%); metal ores (6%); crude oil and products (6%); natural gas (5%); chemicals (5%); newsprint (5%); wood-pulp (5%); cereals (5%); nonferrous metals (5%). Leading customers were U.S. (68%); Japan (6%). Leading suppliers were U.S. (73%); Japan (3%).

In 1979 Canada's exports totaled about $68.1 billion, while imports were $66.5 billion. Tourism in 1978 accounted for gross receipts of $1.7 billion from 12.7 million visitors.

In 1980, Canada's inflation rate was 10.7% and unemployment remained at 7.4%.

Government of Canada

Governor General and Commander-in-Chief: His Excellency The Right Honorable Edward R. Schreyer

GOVERNOR GENERAL'S HOUSEHOLD
Secretary to the Governor General and Secretary General of the Order of Canada, and Secretary General of the Order of Military Merit: Esmond U. Butler, Esq., C.V.O.
Comptroller of the Household: D. C. McKinnon, C.V.O.
Director of Honors: Roger de C. Nantel, Esq. C.D.
Administrative Secretary: Alain C. E. Joly de Lotbiniere
Cultural Advisor to the Governor General: Robert H. Hubbard
Press Secretary: René Chertier

THE CANADIAN MINISTRY
Prime Minister: The Right Hon. Pierre Trudeau
Deputy Prime Minister and Minister of Finance: The Hon. Allan MacEachen
Minister of Transport: The Hon. Jean-Luc Pepin
Minister of Justice and State for Social Development: The Hon. Jean Chrétien
Minister of Indian Affairs and Northern Development: The Hon. John Munro
Minister of State for Economic Development and Senate House Leader: The Hon. H. A. (Bud) Olson
Minister of Industry, Trade and Commerce: The Hon. Herb Gray
Minister of Agriculture: The Hon. Eugene Whelan
Minister of Consumer and Corporate Affairs and Postmaster General: The Hon. André Ouellet
Minister of Energy, Mines and Resources: The Hon. Marc Lalonde
Leader of the Government in the Senate: The Hon. Ray Perrault
Minister of Fisheries and Oceans: The Hon. Roméo Le Blanc

Minister of State for Science and Technology and Minister of the Environment: The Hon. John Roberts
Minister of National Health and Welfare: The Hon. Monique Bégin
Minister of Supply and Services: The Hon. Jean-Jacques Blais
Secretary of State and Minister of Communications: The Hon. Francis Fox
Minister of National Defense and Veterans Affairs: The Hon. Gilles Lamontagne
Minister of Regional Economic Expansion: The Hon. Pierre De Bané
Minister of State for the Wheat Board: The Hon. Hazen Argue
Minister of Labor and Minister of State for Sports: The Hon. Gerald Regan
Secretary of State for External Affairs: The Hon. Mark MacGuigan
Solicitor General: The Hon. Robert Kaplan
Minister of State for Multiculturalism: The Hon. James Fleming
Minister of National Revenue: The Hon. William Rompkey
Minister of State in the Department of Finance: The Hon. Pierre Bussières
Minister of State for Small Business: The Hon. Charles Lapointe
Minister of State for Trade: The Hon. Ed Lumley
President of the Privy Council and Government House Leader: The Hon. Yvon Pinard
President of the Treasury Board: The Hon. Donald Johnston
Minister of Employment and Immigration and Minister of State for the Status of Women: The Hon. Lloyd Axworthy
Minister of Public Works with Responsibility for C.M.H.C.: The Hon. Paul Cosgrove
Minister of State for Mines: The Hon. Judy Erola

Federal Courts

Federal courts in Canada include the Supreme Court of Canada, the Federal Court of Canada, and various Specialized tribunals such as the Tax Review Board, the Court Martial Appeal Court, and the Immigration Appeal Board. These courts and tribunals are created by Parliament.

Provinces and Territories

ALBERTA

Capital: Edmonton
Lieut. Governor: The Hon. Frank Lynch-Staunton
Premier: The Hon. Peter Lougheed
Provincial Treasurer: Hon. Louis D. Hyndman
Atty. General: Hon. Neil Crawford
Entered Confederation: September 1, 1905
Provincial flower: Wild rose (1930)
Population (1980 est.): 2,063,800
Area: 255,200 sq mi.
Largest cities: (1979) Edmonton (491,359) Calgary (530,816) Lethbridge (51,668) Medicine Hat (36,356) Red Deer (39,370)
Provincial parks: 54 (4,184 sq mi.)
Province revenue (1980 est.): $6.367 billion
Province expenditure (1980 est.): $6.703 billion

Alberta was inhabited by various Indian groups for at least 10,000 years. European explorers first appeared in the 1750s to extend the fur trade. By the last quarter of the 18th century The Hudson's Bay Company and the North West Company had established trading posts. From 1821, when the companies merged, until 1870 the Hudson's Bay Company governed the area. In 1870 it was transferred to the Dominion of Canada, and officially became a province in 1905.

Alberta today has become the most dynamic and fastest growing of Canada's ten provinces. Economic progress, spurred on in recent years by developments in the energy resources sector is rapidly transforming the province into a leading North American economic region. Out of a Gross Domestic Product of $28.4 billion in 1978, the net value of production of commodity producing industries was $16.9 billion. The relative shares of this production were: mining (particularly oil and natural gas), 53%; construction, 20%; manufacturing, 16%; agriculture, 9%; logging, fisheries, and trapping, 2%.

Among Alberta's attractions are Elk Island National Park, Banff and Jasper National Parks in the Rocky Mountains, Wood Buffalo National Park which straddles the Alberta-Northwest Territories border, Dinosaur Provincial Park, fur trading post of Rocky Mountain House, Provincial Museum and Archives of Alberta in Edmonton, and Heritage Park in Calgary.

BRITISH COLUMBIA

Capital: Victoria
Lieut. Governor: The Hon. Henry P. Bell-Irving
Premier: The Hon. William R. Bennett
Deputy Premier: The Hon. Grace McCarthy
Minister of Finance: The Hon. Hugh A. Curtis
Atty. General: The Hon. L. Allan Williams
Entered Confederation: July 20, 1871
Provincial flower: Dogwood (1956)
Population (Oct. 1980 est.): 2,662,000
Area: 366,255 sq mi.
Largest cities (1976 census): Vancouver (410,188); Burnaby (131,599); Surrey (116,497); Richmond (80,034); Victoria (62,551)
Provincial parks: 352 (17,524.8 sq mi.)
Province revenue (1980–81): $5.8 billion
Province expenditure (1980–81): $5.5 billion

British Columbia was one of the last regions of the North American continent to be explored and settled, with the impetus coming from the fur trade and the gold that lay in its mountains. Spanish ships visited the coast in 1774, followed by Capt. James Cook, whose account of the fur wealth led to the influx of fur traders. The first trading post was established in 1805 at McLeod Lake. The gold strike of 1858 made Fort Victoria into a city, opened up the mainland to settlement, and resulted in its proclamation as the Colony of British Columbia in 1858. With the arrival of the Canadian Pacific Railway at Port Moody in 1885, a new era opened with permanent railroad and lumbering settlements established along the route.

The chief elements of the province's economy are: forest industries, mining, tourism, shipping, and agriculture, with forest industries the leader. The mining sector is also a large contributor to the economy with copper, crude oil, molybdenum, zinc lead, and natural gas the most valuable products.

Among British Columbia's attractions are the re-created gold rush town of Barkerville, Pacific Rim National Park, the fur trading post of Fort St. James, and Fort Langley where the province's salmon export industry began.

MANITOBA

Capital: Winnipeg
Lieut. Governor: Hon. Francis L. Jobin
Premier: Hon. Sterling R. Lyon
Minister of Finance: Hon. Brian Ransom
Atty. General: Hon. Gerald W.J. Mercier
Entered Confederation: July 15, 1870
Provincial flower: Prairie crocus (1906)
Population (1980 est.): 1,028,300
Area: 251,000 sq mi.
Largest cities: Winnipeg (578,000); Brandon (34,901); Thompson (17,291); Portage la Prairie (12,555); Selkirk (9,862)
Provincial parks: 56 (3,960 sq mi.)
Province revenue (1981–82): $2,161,200,533
Province expenditure (1981–82): $2,381,015,800

Sir Thomas Button, an English explorer, came through Hudson Bay in 1612. After its foundation in 1670, the Hudson's Bay Company began to build forts in the area. Britain's claim to the Hudson Bay region was recognized by the Treaty of Utrecht in 1713, but meanwhile the French entered Manitoba from the east. La Verendrye explored and built several forts in Manitoba between 1733 and 1738. Later, British and French traders from Montreal reopened trade routes in southern and central Manitoba. In 1783, the North West Company based in Montreal began to compete for furs with the Hudson's Bay Company. A fur war ensued which ended in 1821 when the companies merged. The first European settlement of Manitoba came in 1812 when Thomas Douglas, 5th earl of Selkirk, received a grant of land on the Red River from the Hudson's Bay Company. The Dominion of Canada acquired all of the Hudson's Bay Company territory in 1869–70 and part of it became the province of Manitoba under the Manitoba Act of 1870.

Its southern farmlands are the backbone of the province's economy. Wheat is the main crop. Mineral production and forest products are other leading contributors to the economy. The major minerals are nickel, copper, oil, cement, zinc, and sand/gravel. Pulpwood for paper manufacture accounts for 60% of the timber cut. Manufacturing accounts for more than one third of the value of goods and services produced in the province every year.

Among Manitoba's attractions are Lower Fort Garry near Selkirk, restored to recreate a 19th century Hudson's Bay Company post, and Riding Mountain National Park.

NEW BRUNSWICK

Capital: Fredericton
Lieut. Governor: The Hon. Hedard Robichaud
Premier: The Hon. Richard B. Hatfield
Minister of Finance: The Hon. Fernand G. Dube
Minister of Justice: The Hon. Rodman E. Logan
Entered Confederation: July 1, 1867
Provincial flower: Purple violet (1936)
Coat of Arms: Assigned by Queen Victoria in 1868
Motto: Spem Reduxit (Hope Restored)
Provincial flag: Adopted 1965
Provincial tartan: Adopted 1959
Geographic center: Boiestown
Number of counties: 15
Language: French is the first language of 36% of the population. New Brunswick is the only officially bilingual province in Canada.
Population (1980 est.): 707,100
Area: 27,633 sq mi.
Largest cities (1980): St. John (metro 116,300); Moncton (82,900); Fredericton (47,500); Bathurst (15,900); Edmundston (12,000); Campbellton (8,400)
Provincial parks: 59 (83.26 sq mi.)
Province revenue (1979–80): $1,449.5 million
Province expenditure (1979–80): $1,321.7 million

New Brunswick is one of the four original provinces making up the national Confederation in 1867. It was first known to Europeans as a portion of a region called Acadia, settled by the French. By the mid-18th century, British expansion on the neighboring Nova Scotian peninsula led to confrontation with the French. The Acadians were expelled after the British victory of 1755. A British proclamation of 1763 incorporated the area into Nova Scotia but in 1784 it was separated from it and was established as the province of New Brunswick. The first English settlement was established at Maugerville in 1792. During the American Revolution, 14,000 Loyalists settled on the banks of the St. John and St. Croix rivers. Responsible home government was granted by Britain in 1848 and New Brunswick entered the Confederation in 1867.

Since approximately 80% of the province is forested, it is no surprise that New Brunswick's major industries are forest-related, including the manufacture of pulp and paper. Fishing is another economic mainstay on the Bay of Fundy and northeast coasts with herring, lobster, and cod the top catches. New Brunswick is also an important mining center, ranking first in the nation in the production of antimony and bismuth, with zinc following second, silver third, lead fourth, and copper fifth. New Brunswick agriculture and potatoes are synonymous. The dairy industry ranks first. Food process-

ing is a major employer. Tourism is a growing sector.

Among the province's attractions are King's Landing, a recreated Loyalist village where approximately 70 buildings and a costumed staff portray the 1780–1890 era; Village Historique Acadien which depicts the Acadian way of life between 1780–1880; Fundy and Kouchibouguac National Parks; F.D. Roosevelt's summer home on Campobello Island; the N.B. Museum, one of the oldest in the country; more than 90 covered bridges; beaches; golf courses; numerous crafts festivals.

NEWFOUNDLAND

Capital: St. John's
Lieut. Governor: Hon. Gordon A. Winter
Premier: The Hon. A. Brian Pickford
Minister of Finance: The Hon. Dr. John Collins
Minister of Justice: Hon. G. Ottenheimer
Entered Confederation: March 31, 1949
Provincial flower: Pitcher plant (1954)
Population (1977 est.): 562,500
Area: 156,185 sq mi.
Largest cities: St. John's (86,576); Corner Brook (35,198); Stephenville (10,284); Mount Pearl (10,193); Conception Bay South (9,743)
Provincial parks: 72 (3,099.0 sq mi.)
Province revenue (1981–82): $1,515,361,000
Province expenditure (1981–82): $1,499,862,200

John Cabot, sailing under the English flag, reached the island of Newfoundland in 1497 and is its official discoverer. His enthusiastic reports led to international rivalries over the region, with English, French, Basque, and Portuguese fishermen contesting for catches. By 1600 England and France were the chief rivals. Attempts at colonization during the 17th century were met with hostility by the English fishermen and after 1634 by the English crown. In 1699 Parliament prohibited settlement except for maintaining fisheries. French-English rivalries were settled by treaties in 1713 and 1783 recognizing British sovereignty. The island's population increased despite repressive legislation, and in 1729 Britain appointed a naval governor and in 1792 established a judicial system. With the appointment of a resident governor and council in 1824, it was acknowledged as a settled colony. A popularly elected assembly was established in 1832 and in 1855 the island was granted full responsible government. Between 1864 and 1869 and again in 1895, the subject of Newfoundland joining the Canadian Confederation was broached but was rejected at the polls. Not until 1948, in the second of two referenda, was there a clear majority for confederation. The administration of Labrador remained unsettled until 1927 when it was awarded to Newfoundland.

Newfoundland's economy is dependent upon mineral production, pulp and paper products, and fish products, with mining playing the major role as a consequence of western Labrador's vast iron reserves. Oil has been discovered at the Hybernia Well, some 200 miles offshore from St. John's on Eastern Grand Banks.

Among Newfoundland's attractions are an ancient Indian burial ground at Port aux Choix and a Norse settlement at L'Anse aux Meadows.

NORTHWEST TERRITORIES

Capital: Yellowknife
Commissioner: John H. Parker
Deputy Commissioner: Robert S. Pilot
Created: July 15, 1870
Reconstituted: Sept. 1, 1905
Flower: Mountain avens (1959)
Population (1979 est.): 46,257
Area: 1,304,903 sq mi.
Largest cities: Yellowknife (10,112), Hay River (3,345), Inuvik (2,892), Frobisher Bay (2,454), Fort Smith (2,234)
Territories revenue (Fiscal 1980): $307,530,000
Territories expenditure (Fiscal 1980): $236,472,000

The Athabascan Indian people have lived in the forested and barrenland regions of what is now the Northwest Territories during the last 2,500 years. The Inuit (Eskimo) have lived in the Arctic regions for about 1,000 years.

Many believe the first Europeans to visit the Northwest Territories were the Norse. According to their history, they sailed by an icy and mountainous land they called Helluland, which was probably what we now call Baffin Island.

In the late 16th century, British trading companies began searching for a shorter more secure shipping route to the Pacific Ocean and the Orient, and Arctic exploration began. In 1576 Martin Frobisher took possession of Baffin Island. In 1668 the ship *Nonsuch* entered Hudson Bay to establish a trade in furs. This led to the establishment of the Hudson's Bay Company in 1670, a company which continues to this day.

In 1818 the British Admiralty began a serious effort to find the Northwest Passage. Ten expeditions were mounted over the next 30 years. But it wasn't until 1903, when *The Gjoa*, commanded by Norwegian Roald Amundsen, sailed from Europe, that the Passage was finally navigated, after three winters in the Arctic.

Meanwhile land expeditions by Sir John Franklin, Thomas Simpson, and others had resulted in exploration and mapping of the Mackenzie District and northern coastline during the 1820s and 1830s.

Commercial ventures followed in the footsteps of the explorers. Many fur trading posts were established in the Mackenzie Valley. Whaling fleets began in Baffin Bay, Hudson Bay and later the western Arctic.

Not far behind were the missionaries, followed by the Royal Canadian Mounted Police, who were made responsible for maintaining law and order.

In 1920 oil was struck north of Fort Norman. There was a dramatic increase in traffic on the Mackenzie River. The introduction of the airplane increased the demand for fuel and the refinery expanded at Norman Wells in 1939.

The first gold brick was poured in 1938 at Yellowknife and two gold mines are still producing. Mining became the principal industry. Today lead and zinc are the main products. They are mined in Pine Point. Exploration for oil and gas is proceeding at a high pitch with good potential for the future.

There has been an evolution toward more responsible government in the Northwest Territories. In 1967 Yellowknife was named capital of the N.W.T. and the Territorial Government was located there. By 1970 most provincial-type responsibilities had been transferred from the federal government to the Territorial Government. The exception was and still is nonrenewable resources which remain with the federal administration. The Territorial Council has developed from a combination of elected representatives and federal appointees to a fully elected legislative assembly with up to seven of its members responsible for government departments and forming an Executive Committee or cabinet along with the Commissioner and Deputy Commissioner who are public servants.

Among the Northwest Territories' attractions are Wood Buffalo National Park, which straddles the Alberta-Northwest Territories border, home of the largest herd of bison on the continent; Nahanni National Park with its spectacular Virginia Falls; and Auyuittuq, on Baffin Island, Canada's first national park above the Arctic Circle.

NOVA SCOTIA

Capital: Halifax
Lieut. Governor: The Hon. John Elvin Shaffner
Premier: The Hon. John M. Buchanan
Mayor: His Worship Ron Wallace
Minister of Finance: The Hon. Joel Matheson
Atty. General: The Hon. Henry W. How
Entered Confederation: July 1, 1867
Provincial flower: Trailing Arbutus (1901) "Mayflower"
Population (1981): 856,100
Area: Land 20,743 sq mi. Water 325 sq mi.
Highest Point: 1,747 ft
Origin of Name: Latin for New Scotland. Derived from the Latin charter by which New Scotland was granted to Sir Wm. Alexander (afterwards Earl of Stirling) in 1621
Slogan: Canada's Ocean Playground
Flag: Consists of the ancient Arms granted in 1625 by King Charles I, with the cross of Saint Andrew extended in a rectangle three-quarters as wide as its length. Colors: Red, yellow, royal blue, and white
Tartan: The Nova Scotia tartan was the first provincial tartan in Canada. Originally designed in 1953, the popular tartan was registered in 1956 in Her Majesty's Register Office in Edinburgh, Scotland. Colors: red, gold, blue, white, and green
No. of counties: 18
Largest cities: Halifax (117,882); Dartmouth (65,341); Sydney (30,645); Glace Bay (21,836); Truro (12,840)
Provincial parks: 103 (25.1 sq mi.)
Province revenue: $1,410,577,486. Recoveries: $125,106,848
Province expenditure: $1,518,354,250

Nova Scotia is one of the four British colonies federated into the Dominion of Canada in 1867. It was the site of the first permanent North American settlement north of Florida, established by the French in 1605. The 17th and 18th centuries were characterized by struggles for power between the British and French. In 1713 the French began construction of Louisbourg fortress and Halifax was founded in 1749 as a counterbalance. In 1848 Nova Scotia became the first British colony to have a government responsible to the people through elected representatives. There was economic and political opposition to the proposed confederation with Ontario, Quebec, and New Brunswick, but the union was carried out in 1867.

The chief components of the province's economy are fisheries, agriculture (livestock, poultry, dairying), the pulp industry, and mining (coal and industrial minerals).

Among Nova Scotia's attractions are Fort Ann, the first national historic park; the restored fortress of Louisbourg; Champlain's habitation at Port Royal; the Halifax Citadel; Alexander Graham Bell National Historic Park; and Cape Breton Highlands National Park.

ONTARIO

Capital: Toronto
Lieut. Governor: The Hon. John Black Aird
Premier: The Hon. William G. Davis
Provincial Treasurer: The Hon. Frank S. Miller
Atty. General: The Hon. Roy McMurtry
Entered Confederation: July 1, 1867
Provincial flower: White trillium (1937)
Population (1980 est.): 8.6 million
Area: 412,582 sq mi.
Largest cities: Toronto (633,318); North York (558,398); Scarborough (387,149); Hamilton (312,003); Ottawa (304,462)
Provincial parks: 127 (20,503.8 sq mi.)
Province revenue (1980–81): $15.3 billion
Province expenditure (1980–81): $16.7 billion

The first known white man in the province was the French explorer Étienne Brûlé on an expedition to the Ottawa River in 1610-11. He was followed by Samuel de Champlain, other French explorers, fur traders, and missionaries. France established Fort Frontenac (present-day Kingston) in 1673 to provide military protection to its fur empire. However, no French colonization had taken place, except for a small farming settlement near Detroit, by the time Canada was ceded to Great Britain in 1763. The Quebec Act of 1774 established Ontario as part of an extended colony ruled from Quebec. The Constitution Act of 1791 divided Quebec colony into Lower Canada (French–Quebec) and Upper Canada (Loyalist–Ontario). John Graves Simcoe, the first lieutenant governor of Upper Canada fixed the capital at York (now Toronto). In 1841 the provinces were united. Responsible cabinet government was achieved in 1848. Canadian federation—in 1867—was brought about in large part by John A. Macdonald and George Brown, Ontario politicians.

Leading elements of the province's economy are agriculture, mining (the province mines 51% of the world's nickel), forest products, and manufacturing (steel, automobiles, industrial machinery).

Among Ontario's attractions are Upper Canada Village near Morrisburg, a recreation of a 19th century Ontario community; Fort Henry at Kingston, and Fort George at Niagara Falls; and "Canada's Wonderland," the nation's first theme park located in Maple.

PRINCE EDWARD ISLAND

Capital: Charlottetown
Lieut. Governor: The Hon. J.A. Doiron
Premier: The Hon. J. Angus MacLean
Minister of Finance: The Hon. Lloyd G. MacPhail
Atty. General: The Hon. Horace B. Carver
Entered Confederation: July 1, 1873
Provincial flower: Lady's slipper (1947)
Population (1981 est.): 124,000
Area: 2,184 sq mi.
Largest cities: Charlottetown (17,063); Summerside (8,592); Sherwood (5,602); St. Elanors (2,495); Parkdale (2,172)

Provincial parks: 40 (12.2 sq mi.)
Province revenue: $352,556,900
Province expenditure: $351,486,200

John Cabot may have seen the island in 1497 but Jacques Cartier, the French navigator, is credited with its discovery in June 1534. Samuel de Champlain claimed it for France in 1603 but it was not colonized until 1720. The British occupied the island in 1758 and it was formally ceded to Great Britain in 1763. Representative government reached the island in 1851. A conference in 1864 to discuss the possible union of the three Maritime Provinces was the forerunner of the Quebec Conference of 1864 which resulted in the founding of the Dominion of Canada. Thus Prince Edward Island has been known as the "Cradle of Confederation" although it did not join the union until 1873.

Agriculture is the basic element in the island's economy, followed by the tourist industry and fisheries. Manufacturing and processing are becoming more important, especially electronic equipment and frozen french fries.

Among the province's attractions are Province House in Charlottetown, which is a national historic site; 1,100 miles of pink, sandy beaches; and Fort Amherst National Historic Park, with a full-sized reproduction of a Micmac Indian village nearby.

QUEBEC

Capital: Quebec City
Lieut. Governor: The Hon. Jean-Pierre Côté
Premier: Rene Levesque
Vice Premier: Jacques-Yvan Morin
Minister of Finance: Jacques Parizeau
Minister of Justice: Marc-André Bédard
Entered Confederation: July 1, 1867
Provincial flower: White garden (Madonna) lily (1963)
Population (1979): 6,301,200
Area: 636,400 sq mi.
Largest cities: Montreal (1,080,546); Laval (246,243); Quebec (177,082); Longueuil (122,429); St. Léonard 78,452)
Provincial parks: 100
Province revenue (1980–81): $14,655,000,000
Province expenditure (1980–81): $17,640,000,000

Jacques Cartier landed at present-day Gaspé in 1534 and took possession of the land in the name of the King of France. New France began with the founding of Quebec City by Samuel de Champlain in 1608, Trois-Rivière in 1616, and Montreal in 1642. Following capitulation of the French army to the British in 1760, the land was ceded to Britain in 1763. The Quebec Act of 1774 created what is now Quebec and tried to fuse British and French institutions in the new political entity. In 1791 Canada was divided into Lower Canada (French) and Upper Canada (English). An attempt to unite them in 1822 failed but in 1841 an Act of Union joined the provinces and in 1867 the British North American Act created the Confederation of Canada.

The economy of the province breaks down as follows: 61% service industries, 30% manufacturing-processing industries, 8% agricultural-extractive. Iron ore, electric power, and forest products (pulp and paper plants) are the chief resources.

Among the province's attractions are Cartier-

Brebeuf Park in Quebec City, which marks Jacques Cartier's first wintering spot in the New World; La Mauricie National Park in the Laurentian Mountains; Forillon National Park, on the Gaspé peninsula; and Laurentide Park, established for the conservation of caribou.

SASKATCHEWAN

Capital: Regina
Lieut. Governor: The Hon. Irwin McIntosh
Premier: The Hon. Allan E. Blakeney
Minister of Finance: The Hon. E.L. (Ed) Tchorzewski
Atty. General: The Hon. Roy J. Romanow
Entered Confederation: September 1, 1905
Provincial flower: Western red lily (1941)
Provincial bird emblem: Prairie sharp-tailed grouse
Population (1979 est.): 960,000
Area: 251,700 sq mi.
Largest cities: Regina (153,848); Saskatoon (144,269); Moose Jaw (33,441); Prince Albert (30,121); Yorkton (15,077)
Provincial and Regional parks: 116 (2,191 sq mi.)
National Park: 1 (1,500 sq mi.)
Province revenue (Preliminary 1981): $2,416,328,000
Province expenditure (Preliminary 1981): $2,183,718,000

The first white man known to see the Saskatchewan River was Henry Kelsey in 1691. The area which became the Province of Saskatchewan was first granted to the Hudson's Bay Company. In 1868 it was surrendered back to the British crown by the Rupert's Land Act to be turned over to the newly formed Dominion of Canada, which was done in 1870. In 1873 Canada created the North West Mounted Police to maintain law and order. The territories were granted an executive council in 1875 and by 1897 had won responsible parliamentary government. Saskatchewan entered the Confederation in 1905 under the Saskatchewan Act.

The chief elements of the province's economy are agriculture, oil, gas, potash, coal and uranium.

Among its attractions are Prince Albert National Park, Cypress Hills Provincial Park, and Fort Walsh, the first headquarters of the North West Mounted police, R.C.M.P. Training Depot, Provincial and Western Development Museums.

YUKON TERRITORY

Capital: Whitehorse
Commissioner: Douglas Bell
Created a separate territory: June 1898
Flower: Fireweed (1957)
Population (March 1981): 26,011
Area: 207,000 sq mi.
Largest cities: Whitehorse (17,610); Faro (1,960); Watson (1,449)
Government revenue[1]: $102,829,978
Government expenditures[1]: $115,582,792

The Yukon was among the last areas of the North American continent to be explored by white men. Two explorers for the Hudson's Bay Company, John Bell and Robert Campbell, first entered the region around 1840. Fort Yukon was established in 1847 on the Yukon River in what was Russian territory. It was relocated in 1867 after the United States purchased Alaska from Russia, and it was relocated again in 1890. It was a center for a small fur trade. Gold discoveries in the 1870s brought some prospectors into the area, but it was the discovery of rich deposits in Bonanza Creek in 1896 that led to the gold rush of 1898. In the same year the Canadian Parliament separated the rapidly growing area from the Northwest Territories and gave it separate territorial status.

The territory's economy is dependent upon mining, with tourism, a rapidly expanding industry, second. Logging is carried out in some southern areas.

Among the Yukon's attractions are Klune National Park, which contains Canada's highest peak, Mount Logan; and Dawson City, the old gold rush boom town, which has been restored.

1. Includes Crown corporations.

Party Standings—House of Commons
Thirty-second Parliament—Speaker, Jeanne Sauvé; The Clerk of the House of Commons, C.B. Koester

Province	Lib.[1]	P.C.[2]	N.D.P.[3]	S.Cr.[4]	Ind.	Vacancies	Seats by provinces
Alberta	0	21	—	—	—	—	21
British Columbia	—	16	12	—	—	—	28
Manitoba	2	5	7	—	—	—	14
New Brunswick	7	3	—	—	—	—	10
Newfoundland	5	2	—	—	—	—	7
Nova Scotia	5	6	—	—	—	—	11
Ontario	52	37	6	—	—	—	95
Prince Edward Island	2	2	—	—	—	—	4
Quebec	74	1	—	—	—	—	75
Saskatchewan	—	7	7	—	—	—	14
Yukon/NWT	—	2	1	—	—	—	3
National totals	**147**	**102**	**33**			**0**	**282**

1. Liberal Party—Leader, Rt. Hon. Pierre Elliott Trudeau. 2. Progressive Conservative Party—Leader, Joseph Clark. 3. New Democratic Party—Leader, John Edward Broadbent. 4. Social Credit Party—Leader, Fabien Roy. NOTE: Last three General Elections were held on July 8, 1974, May 22, 1979 and Feb. 18, 1980. The legal duration is five years.

Principal Trading Partners in 1980
(in millions of Canadian dollars)

Selected countries	Imports	Exports
United States	$48,414.2	$48,058.4
United Kingdom	1,977.3	3,239.0
Belgium/Luxembourg	250.6	1,000.5
France	770.0	1,018.9
West Germany	1,448.5	1,664.1
Italy	609.5	997.4
Netherlands	263.0	1,435.7
Norway	—	335.8
U.S.S.R.	—	1,540.5
Saudi Arabia	2,445.8	—
Republic of South Africa	—	205.0
India	94.0	350.2
Japan	2,792.2	4,387.4
People's Republic of China	—	869.0
Australia	506.6	677.2
Brazil	347.7	
Venezuela	2,164.4	678.1
Mexico		494.1
Total selected countries	$62,083.8	$66,951.3
Total all countries	$68,979.4	$75,902.9

National Holidays

	1980	1981	1982
New Year's Day	Jan. 1	Jan. 1	Jan. 1
Good Friday	April 4	April 17	April 9
Easter Monday	April 7	April 20	April 12
Victoria Day	May 19	May 18	May 24
Dominion Day	July 1	July 1	July 1
Labor Day	Sept. 1	Sept. 7	Sept. 6
Thanksgiving	Oct. 13	Oct. 12	Oct. 11
Remembrance Day	Nov. 11	Nov. 11	Nov. 11
Christmas Day	Dec. 25	Dec. 25	Dec. 25

National Flag and Motto

The National Flag of Canada, otherwise known as the Canadian Flag, was approved by Parliament and proclaimed by Her Majesty the Queen on February 15, 1965, and is described as a red flag of the proportions two by length and one by width, containing in its center a white square the width of the flag, bearing a single red maple leaf.

The Flag is flown on land daily from sunrise to sunset at all federal government buildings, airports, and military bases and establishments within and outside Canada, and may appropriately be flown or displayed by individuals and organizations.

The Canada Shipping Act provides that the National Flag is the proper national colors for all Canadian ships and boats; and it is the flag flown on Canadian Naval vessels.

The motto—*A mari usque ad mare* ("From sea to sea")—is from the Latin version of Psalm LXXII: 8: "He shall have dominion also from sea to sea, and from the river unto the ends of the earth."

Canadian Museums and Related Institutions

Region	Art galleries	History museums	Restorations	Science and technology museums	Living science museums[1]	General museums	Community museums	Archives	Other institutions[2]	Total
Atlantic	10	9	65	8	2	3	44	14	5	160
Quebec	11	19	16	4	11	1	27	11	6	106
Ontario	35	22	73	14	12	3	106	19	9	293
Central	19	39	45	10	8	7	113	12	8	261
British Columbia	11	12	14	9	8	2	49	7	6	118
Yukon and Northwest Territories	—	—	2	—	—	1	3	1	—	7
Total	86	101	215	45	41	17	342	64	34	945

1. Aquaria, zoos, botanical gardens, arboretums, and conservatories. 2. Including nature park museums or nature centers. *Source:* Statistics Canada, July 1979, based on a 1976 survey.

Percentage Distribution of Canadian Population by Provinces and Territories

Province or territory	1979 (est.)	1978 (est.)	1971	1961	1951	1941	1931
Alberta	8.49	8.31	7.55	7.30	6.71	6.92	7.05
British Columbia	10.84	10.77	10.13	8.93	8.32	7.11	6.69
Manitoba	4.35	4.40	4.58	5.05	5.54	6.34	6.75
New Brunswick	2.96	2.96	2.94	3.28	3.68	3.97	3.94
Newfoundland	2.43	2.42	2.42	2.51	2.58	—	—
Nova Scotia	3.58	3.58	3.66	4.04	4.59	5.02	4.94
Ontario	35.91	35.96	35.71	34.19	32.82	32.92	33.07
Prince Edward Island	0.52	0.52	0.52	0.58	0.70	0.83	0.85
Quebec	26.61	26.77	27.95	28.84	28.95	28.96	27.70
Saskatchewan	4.04	4.03	4.29	5.07	5.94	7.79	8.88
Northwest Territories	0.18	0.19	0.16	0.13	0.11	0.10	0.09
Yukon Territory	0.09	0.09	0.09	0.08	0.06	0.04	0.04
Totals	**100.00**	**100.00**	**100.00**	**100.00**	**100.00**	**100.00**	**100.00**

Canadian Motor Vehicle Registrations, 1979

Province or territory	Passenger cars[1]	Motor trucks	Motor buses	Motor-cycles	Other motor vehicles[2]	Total motor vehicles
Alberta	1,040,277	438,302	6,827	44,712	[3]	1,530,118
British Columbia	1,098,821	434,185[4]	[5]	36,860[6]	[3]	1,569,866
Manitoba	452,984	175,830	342[7]	15,653[6]	748[8]	645,552
New Brunswick	250,388	84,964	326	10,869	9,720	356,267
Newfoundland	140,394	53,305	n.a.	3,971[6]	n.a.	197,670
Nova Scotia	316,257	123,325	1,309	15,943	682	457,516
Ontario	3,390,837	834,284	21,602	90,933	[3]	4,637,656
Prince Edward Island	47,632	18,498	422	1,734	[3]	68,361
Quebec	2,568,665	373,768	17,193	98,387	45,251	3,103,264
Saskatchewan	366,164	298,652	4,792	12,170	809	682,587
N.W.T.	6,067	8,719	114	1,081[6]	148	16,129
Yukon T.	6,660	10,385	[5]	620[6]	[3]	17,665
Total	**9,985,146**	**2,854,217**	**52,927**	**332,933**	**57,353**	**13,282,576**

1. Includes taxis and for-hire cars. 2. Ambulances, fire trucks, etc. 3. Included with passenger cars or trucks. 4. Includes taxicabs. 5. Included in trucks. 6. Includes mopeds. 7. Excludes school buses which are licensed as passenger cars. 8. Includes only antique vehicles and vehicles for road testing. n.a. = not available. *Source:* Statistics Canada.

Canadian Consumer Price Index
(1971 = 100)

Year	Food	Housing	Clothing	Trans-portation	Health and personal care	Recreation and reading	Tobacco and alcohol	All-item index
1962	77.5	74.0	78.4	76.9	71.6	74.3	78.8	75.9
1963	80.0	74.8	80.3	76.9	73.5	75.4	78.9	77.2
1964	81.3	76.0	82.4	77.8	75.8	76.6	80.4	78.6
1965	83.4	77.3	83.8	80.7	79.4	77.9	81.7	80.5
1966	88.7	79.5	87.0	82.6	81.8	80.1	83.7	83.5
1967	89.9	82.9	91.4	86.1	86.0	84.1	85.8	86.5
1968	92.8	86.7	94.1	88.3	89.5	88.3	93.6	90.0
1969	96.7	91.2	96.7	92.4	93.8	93.5	97.2	94.1
1970	98.9	95.7	98.5	96.1	98.0	96.8	98.4	97.2
1971	100.0	100.0	100.0	100.0	100.0	100.0	100.0	100.0
1972	107.6	104.7	102.6	102.6	104.8	102.8	102.7	104.8
1973	123.3	111.4	107.7	105.3	109.8	107.1	106.0	112.7
1974	143.4	121.1	118.0	115.8	119.4	116.4	111.8	125.0
1975	161.9	133.2	125.1	129.4	133.0	128.5	125.3	138.5
1976	166.2	145.7	132.0	143.3	144.3	136.2	134.3	148.9
1977	180.1	161.9	141.0	153.3	155.1	142.7	143.8	160.8
1978	208.0	170.8	146.4	162.2	166.2	148.2	155.5	175.2
1979	235.4	186.2	159.9	178.0	181.2	158.4	166.7	191.2
1980	260.6	201.4	178.7	200.7	199.3	173.5	185.3	210.6

Source: Statistics Canada

Growth Statistics
(in Canadian dollars)

Year	Exports (including re-exports (millions of dollars)	Imports (millions of dollars)	Industry selling price indexes for manufacturing (1971=100)	Railway gross revenues[1] (millions of dollars)	Railway operating expenses[1] (millions of dollars)	Tons of revenue freight carried one mile[1] (millions)	Freight carried on welland canal (thousands of tons)	Vessels other than coastal entered & cleared (thousands of reg net tons)
1891	n.a.	n.a.	n.a.	$ 48	$ 35	n.a.	975	18,803
1901	n.a.	n.a.	n.a.	73	50	n.a.	620	26,030
1911	n.a.	n.a.	n.a.	189	131	16,048	2,538	47,430
1921	$ 814	$ 799	n.a.	458	423	26,622	3,076	54,649
1941	1,640	1,449	n.a.	538	404	49,982	13,230	64,766
1951	3,963	4,085	n.a.	1,089	978	64,300	16,198	100,259
1961	5,896	5,771	82.4	1,156	1,053	65,828	31,404	156,987
1965	8,767	8,633		1,369	1,288	87,052	53,437	199,454
1966	10,326	9,866	n.a.	1,476	1,367	94,944	59,137	202,170
1967	11,411	11,075	n.a.	1,514	1,438	92,239	52,850	197,422
1968	13,624	12,358	92.3	1,528	1,433	93,147	58,105	204,777
1969	14,890	14,130	95.8	1,579	1,496	94,688	53,532	197,391
1970	16,819	13,952	98.1	1,672	1,570	108,210	62,963	217,621
1971	17,820	15,618	100.0	1,797	1,693	119,412	63,058	228,561
1972	20,140	18,669	104.4	1,843	1,750	119,135	64,194	243,376
1973	25,301	23,303	116.1	2,029	1,935	125,471	67,195	244,466
1974	32,177	31,639	138.1	2,476	2,394	133,554	52,360	227,175
1975	32,755	34,668	153.7	2,618	2,668	130,997	59,849	231,345
1976	38,028	37,391	161.6	3,058	2,927	132,589	64,340	124,071
1977	44,375	42,156	174.3	3,388	3,186	137,745	71,736	264,425
1978	52,605	49,606	190.4	3,709	3,500	141,747	72,389	277,433
1979	65,514	62,724	217.9	4,601	4,259	152,085	66,165	n.a.

1. Six major railways, representing about 95% of the industry in terms of operating revenues and other performance indicators. NOTE: n.a. = not available. *Source:* Statistics Canada.

Growth Statistics
(in Canadian dollars)

Year	Motor vehicle registrations (thousands)	Telephones in use (thousands)	Post office and money order revenue (thousands)	Index numbers of weekly earnings[1] 1961 = 100	Strikes and lockouts Employees affected (thousands)	Strikes and lockouts Time lost working days (thousands)	Federal finance Total revenue (millions of dollars)	Federal finance Total expenditure (millions of dollars)	Federal finance Net debt (millions of dollars)
1881	n.a.	n.a.	1,345	n.a.	n.a.	n.a.	$ 30	$ 34	$ 155
1891	n.a.	n.a.	2,516	n.a.	n.a.	n.a.	39	41	238
1901	n.a.	n.a.	3,421	n.a.	24	738	53	58	268
1911	22	303	9,147	n.a.	29	1,821	118	123	340
1921	465	902	26,331	n.a.	28	1,049	436	528	2,341
1931	1,201	1,364	30,416	n.a.	11	204	356	442	2,262
1941	1,573	1,562	40,383	34.1	87	434	872	1,250	3,649
1951	2,872	3,114	90,455	64.0	103	902	3,113	2,901	11,645
1961	5,517	6,014	202,004	100.0	98	1,335	5,618	5,958	12,437
1965	6,669	7,445	263,704	116.2	172	2,350	7,180	7,218	15,504
1966	7,035	7,883	275,994	127.8	411	5,178	7,696	7,735	15,543
1967	7,482	8,358	295,529	130.6	252	3,975	8,358	8,780	15,965
1968	7,877	8,818	337,023	140.3	224	5,083	9,029	9,824	16,760
1969	8,254	9,296	374,902	150.8	307	7,752	10,163	11,938	17,336
1970	8,497	9,750	444,069	162.8	262	6,540	12,321	11,928	16,943
1971	9,022	10,269	432,911	176.7	240	2,867	12,803	13,182	17,322
1972	9,481	10,987	504,211	191.4	706	7,754	14,227	14,841	17,937
1973	10,158	11,677	563,159	205.4	348	5,776	16,602	16,121	17,456
1974	11,002	12,454	591,133	227.6	592	9,255	19,383	20,056	18,128
1975	11,443	13,165	617,743	261.7	479	10,859	24,909	26,055	19,275
1976	11,786	13,885	568,190	295.8	1,571[2]	11,685	29,956	33,978	23,296
1977	12,547	14,488	774,860	326.2	218	3,742	32,721	39,011	29,586
1978	12,975	15,172	945,763	350.3	402	7,393	32,846	42,879	39,619
1979	n.a.	n.a.	1,108,543	381.6	463	7,786	35,216	46,923	55,807

1. In manufacturing. 2. This figure includes 830,000 affected by "day of protest." NOTE: n.a. = not available. *Source:* Statistics Canada

Estimates of the Civilian Labor Force and Its Main Components, Annual Averages
(in thousands)

Year	Civilian population[1]	Civilian labor force[1]			Persons not in the labor force[1]	Un-employ-ment rate percent	Partici-pation rate percent
		Employed	Unem-ployed	Total labor force			
1966	13,475	7,152	267	7,420	6,055	3.6	55.1
1967	13,874	7,379	315	7,694	6,179	4.1	55.5
1968	14,264	7,537	382	7,919	6,344	4.8	55.5
1969	14,638	7,780	382	8,162	6,475	4.7	55.8
1970	15,016	7,879	495	8,374	6,642	5.9	55.8
1971	15,388	8,079	552	8,631	6,757	6.4	56.1
1972	15,747	8,329	562	8,891	6,856	6.3	56.5
1973	16,125	8,759	520	9,279	6,846	5.6	57.5
1974	16,562	9,137	525	9,662	6,900	5.4	58.3
1975	16,470	9,363	697	10,060	6,410	6.9	61.1
1976	16,873	9,572	736	10,308	6,565	7.1	61.1
1977	17,250	9,754	862	10,616	6,634	8.1	61.5
1978[2]	17,381	9,972	911	10,882	6,499	8.4	62.6
1979[2]	17,691	10,369	838	11,207	6,484	7.5	63.3
1980[2]	18,004	10,655	867	11,522	6,483	7.5	64.0

1. 14 years of age, or over. 2. 15 years of age, or over. *Source:* Statistics Canada.

Average Temperature and Precipitation Data

Station	Temperature °C				Average frost date		Average total annual precip. (mm)	Aver. ann. snow-fall (cm)
	Mean Jan.	Mean July	Extreme Max.	Extreme Min.	Last in spring	First in fall		
St. John's A, Nfld.	−3.8	15.3	30.6	−23.3	June 3	Oct. 12	1511.5	363.7
Charlottetown A, P.E.I.	−6.7	18.4	34.4	−27.8	May 17	Oct. 15	1127.8	305.1
Halifax, N.S.	−3.2	18.3	34.4	−25.0	May 1	Nov. 1	1318.8	210.8
Sydney A, N.S.	−4.4	17.9	35.0	−25.6	May 23	Oct. 16	1340.9	288.0
Yarmouth A, N.S.	−2.7	16.4	30.0	−21.0	May 2	Oct. 24	1283.2	204.5
Chatham A, N.B.	−9.3	19.2	37.8	−35.0	May 22	Sept. 21	1051.2	309.4
Moncton A, N.B.	−7.9	18.6	37.2	−32.2	May 23	Sept. 23	1099.3	313.7
Saint John A, N.B.	−7.1	17.1	34.4	−36.7	May 18	Oct. 2	1400.3	204.7
Fort Chimo A, Que.	−23.4	11.4	32.2	−46.7	June 27	Aug. 30	483.8	236.7
Montreal McGill, Que.	−8.9	21.6	36.1	−33.9	April 22	Oct. 23	999.0	243.1
Quebec A, Que.	−11.6	19.2	35.6	−36.1	May 18	Sept. 28	1088.6	326.6
Schefferville (Knob Lake) A, Que.	−22.7	12.6	31.7	−50.6	June 18	Aug. 31	722.5	335.5
Sherbrooke, Que.	−9.6	20.1	36.7	−41.1	May 12	Sept. 27	972.6	244.6
London A, Ont.	−6.0	20.5	36.7	−31.7	May 9	Oct. 6	924.5	201.2
Ottawa A, Ont.	−10.9	20.7	37.8	−36.1	May 11	Oct. 1	850.9	215.6
Thunder Bay A, Ont.	−14.8	17.5	37.2	−41.1	May 31	Sept. 10	738.5	222.0
Toronto, Ont.	−4.4	21.8	40.6	−32.8	April 20	Oct. 30	789.9	141.0
Churchill A. Man.	−27.6	12.0	33.9	−45.0	June 22	Sept. 12	396.6	183.9
The Pas A, Man.	−22.4	17.9	36.7	−49.4	May 28	Sept. 20	449.7	157.2
Winnipeg A, Man.	−18.3	19.7	40.6	−45.0	May 25	Sept. 21	535.2	131.3
Regina A, Sask.	−17.3	18.9	43.3	−50.0	May 27	Sept. 12	397.9	114.8
Saskatoon A, Sask.	−18.7	18.8	40.0	−47.8	May 27	Sept. 15	352.6	112.5
Beaverlodge CDA, Alta.	−14.9	15.6	36.7	−47.8	May 22	Sept. 7	454.7	183.6
Calgary A, Alta.	−10.9	16.5	36.1	−45.0	May 28	Sept. 12	437.1	153.9
Edmonton Ind. A, Alta.	−14.7	17.5	34.4	−48.3	May 14	Sept. 19	446.5	132.1

Station	Temperature °C Mean Jan.	Mean July	Extreme Max.	Min.	Average frost date Last in spring	First in fall	Average total annual precip. (mm)	Aver. ann. snow-fall (cm)
Kamloops A, B.C.	−6.0	20.9	40.6	−37.2	May 5	Sept. 28	260.6	77.0
Prince George A, B.C.	−11.8	14.9	34.4	−50.0	June 10	Aug. 28	620.7	233.4
Prince Rupert, B.C.	1.8	13.6	32.2	−21.1	April 19	Nov. 5	2414.5	113.0
Vancouver A, B.C.	2.4	17.4	33.3	−17.8	March 31	Oct. 30	1068.1	52.3
Dawson, Y.T.	−28.6	15.5	35.0	−58.3	May 26	Aug. 27	325.5	136.4
Whitehorse A, Y.T.	−18.9	14.1	34.4	−52.2	June 5	Sept. 1	260.3	127.8
Coppermine, N.W.T.	−29.4	9.3	32.2	−50.0	June 27	Aug. 21	216.3	101.9
Fort Simpson A, N.W.T.	−27.6	16.1	35.0	−53.3	May 31	Aug. 29	343.2	137.9
Frobisher Bay A, N.W.T.	−26.2	7.9	24.4	−45.6	June 30	Aug. 29	415.2	246.9
Resolute A, N.W.T.	−32.6	4.3	18.3	−52.2	July 10	July 20	136.4	78.7

A = Airport, Ind. A = Industrial Airport CDA = Canada Department of Agriculture. Source: Canada Year Book 1978-79, Statistics Canada.

Highest Elevations

Province or territory	Height in feet	Height in meters
Alberta—Mount Columbia	12,294	3,747
British Columbia—Mt. Fairweather	15,300	4,663
Manitoba—Baldy Mountain	2,729	832
New Brunswick—Mount Carleton	2,690	820
Newfoundland—Cirque Mt., Labrador Penin.	5,160	1,573
Nova Scotia—North Barren Mt., Cape Breton Island	1,747	532
Ontario—Ogidaki Mt.	2,183	665
Prince Edward Island—highest point Queens County	465	142
Quebec—Mt. Jacques Cartier, Gaspé Penin.	4,160	1,268
Saskatchewan—Cypress Hills	4,546	1,386
Northwest Territories—Mt. Sir James MacBrien	9,062	2,762
Yukon Territory—Mount Logan	19,850	6,050

Mileage Between Principal Points in Canada
(via rail or water)

Approximate distances by rail or water	Nfld. St. John's	N.S. Halifax	P.E.I. Charlottetown	N.B. Saint John	N.B. Fredericton	Que. Quebec	Que. Montreal	Ont. Ottawa	Ont. Toronto	Ont. Thunder Bay	Man. Winnipeg	Sask. Regina	Sask. Saskatoon	Alta. Calgary	Alta. Edmonton	B.C. Vancouver	B.C. Victoria	B.C. Pr. Rupert
St. John's	0	930	1,041	1,081	1,094	1,466	1,563	1,675	1,897	2,521	2,797	3,153	3,268	3,531	3,646	4,262	4,362	4,543
Halifax	930	0	239	279	292	664	761	873	1,095	1,719	1,995	2,351	2,466	2,729	2,844	3,460	3,560	3,741
Charlottetown	1,041	239	0	215	230	600	684	795	1,018	1,653	1,950	2,305	2,421	2,772	2,751	3,413	3,498	3,707
Saint John	1,081	279	215	0	67	425	482	594	816	1,470	1,894	2,250	2,374	2,726	2,699	3,368	3,324	3,655
Fredericton	1,094	292	230	67	0	403	454	565	788	1,423	1,753	2,108	2,224	2,575	2,554	3,216	3,301	3,510
Quebec City	1,466	664	600	425	403	0	164	276	498	1,152	1,521	1,877	1,992	2,353	2,323	2,995	2,898	3,279
Montreal	1,563	761	684	482	454	164	0	112	334	988	1,357	1,713	1,828	2,244	2,151	2,886	2,900	3,115
Ottawa	1,675	873	795	594	565	276	112	0	247	887	1,301	1,658	1,772	2,133	2,098	2,775	2,789	3,054
Toronto	1,897	1,095	1,018	816	788	498	334	247	0	809	1,233	1,590	1,704	2,065	2,030	2,707	2,755	2,986
Thunder Bay	2,521	1,719	1,653	1,470	1,423	1,152	988	877	809	0	424	781	895	1,256	1,221	1,898	1,967	2,177
Winnipeg	2,797	1,995	1,950	1,894	1,753	1,521	1,357	1,301	1,233	424	0	356	471	832	797	1,474	1,548	1,753
Regina	3,153	2,351	2,305	2,250	2,108	1,877	1,713	1,658	1,590	781	356	0	161	476	487	1,118	1,193	1,443
Saskatoon	3,268	2,466	2,421	2,374	2,224	1,992	1,828	1,772	1,704	895	471	161	0	399	326	1,097	1,131	1,282
Calgary	3,531	2,729	2,772	2,726	2,575	2,353	2,244	2,133	2,065	1,256	832	476	399	0	195	642	727	1,151
Edmonton	3,646	2,844	2,751	2,699	2,554	2,323	2,151	2,098	2,030	1,221	797	487	326	195	0	771	846	956
Vancouver	4,262	3,460	3,413	3,368	3,216	2,995	2,886	2,775	2,707	1,898	1,474	1,118	1,097	642	771	0	85	546
Victoria	4,362	3,560	3,498	3,324	3,301	2,898	2,900	2,789	2,755	1,967	1,548	1,193	1,131	727	846	85	0	631
Prince Rupert	4,543	3,741	3,707	3,655	3,510	3,279	3,115	3,054	2,986	2,177	1,753	1,443	1,282	1,151	956	546	641	0

Air Distances Between Cities
(via Air Canada)

From	To	Miles[1]	From	To	Miles[1]
Gander	Montreal	1,109	Montreal	Vancouver	2,444
Gander	Toronto	1,494	Montreal	Windsor	521
Halifax	Moncton	120	Ottawa	Winnipeg	1,174
Halifax	Montreal	571	St. John's, Nfld.	Montreal	1,147
Halifax	North Bay	1,034	Sydney	Halifax	200
Halifax	Ottawa	665	Toronto	Chicago	435
Halifax	Toronto	897	Toronto	Cleveland	195
Halifax	Vancouver	3,015	Toronto	Edmonton	1,693
Halifax	Winnipeg	1,893	Toronto	New York	375
Lethbridge	Calgary	124	Toronto	Tampa	1,119
Lethbridge	Edmonton	301	Toronto	Vancouver	2,118
Montreal	Boston	778	Toronto	Winnipeg	942
Montreal	Edmonton	2,019	Vancouver	Victoria	47
Montreal	Goose Bay	824	Winnipeg	Calgary	750
Montreal	Moncton	451	Winnipeg	Edmonton	753
Montreal	New York	350			
Montreal	Ottawa	94			
Montreal	Toronto	326			

1. Statute miles. *Source:* Air Canada.

Land and Fresh Water Areas of Canada

Province, territory, or district	Land sq miles	Fresh water sq miles	Total sq miles	Percent of total area
Alberta	248,800	6,485	255,285	6.6
British Columbia	359,279	6,976	366,255	9.5
Manitoba	211,775	39,225	251,000	6.5
New Brunswick	27,835	519	28,354	0.7
Newfoundland	143,045	13,140	156,185	4.1
Nova Scotia	20,402	1,023	21,425	0.6
Ontario	344,092	68,490	412,582	10.7
Prince Edward Island	2,184	—	2,184	0.1
Quebec	523,860	71,000	594,860	15.4
Saskatchewan	220,182	31,518	251,700	6.5
Northwest Territories	1,253,438	51,465	1,304,903	33.9
Franklin	541,753	7,500	549,253	14.3
Keewatin	218,460	9,700	228,160	5.9
Mackenzie	493,225	34,265	527,490	13.7
Yukon Territory	205,346	1,730	207,076	5.4
Totals	3,560,238	291,571	3,851,809	100.0

Canadian Church Membership

Religious group	Churches	Members	Clergy
Protestant and others[1]	17,068	4,520,032	18,130
Roman Catholics	5,836	9,991,243	13,050
Jewish congregations	112	305,000	n.a.
Eastern churches[2]	232	425,736	170
Polish National Catholic, Armenian churches	18	31,000	15
Buddhist	15	2,543	10
Miscellaneous	19	4,603	13
Total	23,300	15,280,157	31,388

1. Includes such groups as Latter-Day Saints and Jehovah's Witnesses. 2. Includes Coptic church. NOTE: n.a. = not available. *Source: Yearbook of American and Canadian Churches 1981.*

Canada's 25 Tallest Buildings

City	Building	Stories	Height ft	Height m	City	Building	Stories	Height ft	Height m
Toronto	CN Tower	—	1,821	555	Calgary	Norcen Tower	33	508	155
Toronto	First Bank Tower	72	952	290	Calgary	Scotia Centre	38	504	154
Toronto	Commerce Court West	57	784	239	Montreal	Le Complexe Desjardins			
Toronto	Toronto–Dominion Tower	56	758	231		La Tour du Sud	40	498	152
Calgary	Calgary Tower	—	626	191	Toronto	Two Bloor West	34	486	148
Montreal	Place Victoria	47	624	190	Toronto	Commerce Court North	34	476	145
Montreal	Place Ville Marie	42	616	188	Toronto	Simpson Tower	33	473	144
Montreal	Canadian Imperial Bank				Toronto	Sun Life Centre	35	470	143
	of Commerce	43	604	184	Vancouver	Royal Bank Tower	37	468	142
Toronto	Royal Trust Tower	46	600	183	Toronto	Continental Place	34	466	142
Toronto	Royal Bank Plaza—South				Calgary	Oxford Square North	34	463	141
	Tower	41	589	180	Calgary	Shell Tower	34	460	140
Vancouver	Harbour Center (incl.				Toronto	Palace Pier (2 bldgs.)	46	452	138
	100-ft pylon)	32	581	177	Vancouver	Scotiabank Tower	36	451	137
Toronto	Manulife Centre	53	545	166					

Major Canadian Awards, 1980

Governor General's Literary Awards

Fiction: English: George Bowering, *Burning Waters;* French: Pierre Turgeon, *La Premiere Personne*
Poetry: English: Stephen Scobie, *McAlmon's Chinese Opera;* French: Michel Van Schendel, *De L'Oeil et De L'Ecoute*
Nonfiction: English: Jeffrey Simpson, *Discipline of Power: The Conservative Interlude and the Liberal Restoration;* French: Maurice Champagne-Gilbert, *La Famille et L'Homme a Delivrer du Pouvoir*

Juno Award Winners

Female Vocalist: Anne Murray
Male Vocalist: Bruce Cockburn
Group: Prism
Country Female Vocalist: Anne Murray
Country Male Vocalist: Eddie Eastman
Country Group: The Good Brothers
Best New Female Vocalist: Carole Pope
Best New Male Vocalist: Graham Shaw
Best New Group: Powder Blues
Folksinger: Bruce Cockburn
Instrumental Artist: Frank Mills
Composer: Eddie Schwartz
Best Jazz Recording: Rob McConnell and the Boss Brass for *Present Perfect*
Best Classical Recording: Arthur Ozolins for *Stravinsky-Chopin Ballad*

Actra Awards

The Earle Grey Award for the Best Acting Performance in Television in a Leading Role: Al Waxman, *Winnings of Frankie Walls*
The Andrew Allan Award for the Best Acting Performance in Radio: Zoe Caldwell, *Fifth Business*
Best Variety Performance in Television: Dinah Christie
Best Supporting Actor in Television: Mary Pirie, *Lyon's Den*
Du Maurier Award for Best New Television Performer: Lally Cadeau, *Harvest*
Best Television Host–Interviewer: Patrick Watson
Best Radio Host–Interviewer: Bronwyn Drainie and Patrick Martin

The Foster Hewitt Award for Excellence in Sportcasting: Jim Robson
Gordon Sinclair Award for Outspoken Opinions and Integrity in Broadcasting: Eric Malling
The John Drainie Award for Distinguished Contribution to Broadcasting: Francis Hyland
Best Television Program of the Year: *Store Wars* and *10 Toronto Street*
Best Radio Program: *Sunday Morning*
Best Dramatic Writer—Television: Grahame Woods, *War Brides*
Best Dramatic Writer—Radio: Sharon Pollock, *Sweet Land of Liberty*

The Royal Bank Award

In 1967, as a Canadian centennial project, The Royal Bank of Canada established the Royal Bank Award to honor "a Canadian citizen or person domiciled in Canada whose outstanding achievement is of such importance that it is contributing to human welfare and the common good." The award consists of a gold medal and a cash grant of $50,000.

1967	Dr. Wilder Penfield, neurosurgeon
1968	Dr. C. J. Mackenzie, engineer
1969	His Eminence Paul-Émile Cardinal Léger
1970	Morley Callaghan, novelist
1971	Arthur Erickson, architect
1972	Dr. Gustave Gingras, rehabilitation expert
1973	Dr. J. A. Corry, educationalist
1974	Jean Gascon, actor/director
1975	Dr. R. Keith Downey and Dr. Baldur R. Stefansson, agricultural scientists
1976	Mary Pack, organizer of the Canadian Arthritis and Rheumantism Society
1977	Dr. W. A. Paddon and Dr. Gordon W. Thomas, frontier medical pioneers
1978	Dr. H. Northrop Frye, literary scholar
1979	Dr. Lotta Hitschmanova, founder and executive director, Unitarian Service Committee of Canada
1980	Dr. Jacques Genest, founder and director, Clinical Research Institute of Montreal
1981	Harry E. Foster, founder and president, Canadian Special Olympics Inc.

TRAVEL

Air Charter Flights—Know What You're Buying

(Source: Civil Aeronautics Board, Bureau of Consumer Protection)

All Charters Are Not Alike

Over the past several years the United States has relaxed its charter rules to make lower cost air transportation available to more and more people. Public charters can now be purchased from a tour operator, a travel agent, or directly from the airline. If you deal directly with the airline, you must purchase the transportation at least seven days before flight time.

If your flight has been arranged by a club or other organization for its members, it may be what is called an "affinity" charter flight. These charters do not carry the consumer protection provisions of public charters. Be sure you know what kind of charter flight you are purchasing.

Read Your Contract Carefully

A public charter may include only the flights, or it may be sold as a complete package, including hotels, guided tours, and ground transportation. Either way, your rights are spelled out in a contract you have with the tour operator. The operator or your travel agent should give you a contract to read and sign when you pay for your trip. If you find legalese you don't understand, ask for a written explanation in plain English of conditions you find unclear.

The CAB requires tour operators to disclose certain information in your contract about the restrictions and regulations that apply to your charter.
1. You usually pay penalties if you cancel. The closer to departure you cancel, the less of your money you get back. On some charters, if a substitute can go in your place, you don't lose your money.
2. You can buy trip cancellation insurance. The policy protects your fare in case you must cancel due to illness or death in the family. Your travel agent or tour operator can tell you how to buy the insurance and what health conditions it does or doesn't cover. Usually charter cancellation insurance won't pay you if you must cancel because of a pre-existing sickness.
3. The tour operator or airline can cancel a public charter for any reason up until ten days before departure. The chance that your flight might be canceled if it doesn't sell well, or for some other reason, is a risk you take in return for a low fare.
4. All charter flights and ground arrangements are subject to changes. Signing a contract does not guarantee that prices won't go up or that itineraries won't change. But if there is a major change in your flight or tour, you don't have to accept it. Major changes include those in:
   - departure or return city
   - departure or return date, unless the date change results from a flight delay
   - hotels
   - price, if the increase is more than 10% of what you paid

If your tour operator knows of a major change in time to let you know before departure, you can cancel with a full refund if you don't like it. However, if the operator changes the departure or return city, and you accept that change, the operator doesn't have to provide transportation to the new city. You must get there on your own. If you don't find out about a change until your trip has begun, you can reject the changed flight or hotel, make and pay for your own alternative plans instead, and get a partial refund for the changed component when you get home.

5. Your contract must clearly state if your charter is an "Operator's Option Plan." The Operator's Option Plan is a special kind of public charter that may appeal to the gambler in you. Your contract will say that the charter could leave and return from any city on a list drawn up by the operator, and on any of several flight dates offered. You agree to depart and return from the cities the charterer selects on the dates he chooses. In making its choices, the tour operator will consider, among other things, which cities and dates are preferred by most passengers. The tour operator will let you know the final decisions at least 10 days before departure. Even if the choices from among the cities and dates offered are not your favorites, you can't get a refund once you've paid and signed the contract, which must clearly state that yours is an "Operator's Option Plan." The extra flexibility the charterer has in arranging this plan can result in a low cost that may well be worth the compromise you might make.
6. Getting a refund takes time. If you are due a refund after either you or the tour operator cancels, he has two weeks to return your money.
7. The tour operator has to take specific steps to protect your money. The tour operator must be fully bonded or have special bank arrangements called escrow accounts that hold your money until your flight returns. If your money is going into a charter escrow account, the bank will be named in your contract. You should make your check out either to the charter escrow account or to your travel agent, who will send it to the escrow for you. If a tour operator goes out of business you should contact the bonding company or bank identified in your contract for a refund.

Some Advice

There are a few other things you should know about public charters before you sign up for one.
1. No "Open Returns" are allowed on round trip public charters. Be sure you have a specific return date, city, and flight, so you won't be stranded.
2. You and you alone are responsible for knowing if you need a visa and passport for your trip. You can be certain of the visa and passport rules of the countries you plan to visit by calling or writing their embassies in Washington, D.C., or their Consul Offices in some major cities.
3. If your luggage gets lost during your trip, the

tour operator may refuse to accept responsibility. To cover yourself, make sure your renters' or homeowners' insurance policy covers losses that happen when you're away from home. You might also ask your travel agent if there's a one-shot baggage insurance policy available for your trip to cover losses when your bags are not in the airlines' hands. The charter airlines, of course, only pay claims for bags when there's evidence the luggage was lost or damaged while in their possession.

4. Your charter may be delayed. Like any other flight, a charter is subject to delays. An international flight may be delayed up to 48 hours before the charterer or airline must come up with substitute transportation or offer you a refund. On domestic flights, substitute transportation or refunds must be offered if the delay exceeds six hours.

If the return portion of an international charter flight is delayed more than six hours, the airline must pay incidental expenses for the passengers. Payment is calculated at the rate of $16 for each 24-hour period of delay. The airline may choose to offer food and lodging instead of issuing compensation.

5. Charters and scheduled flights operate independently of each other. If there's a delay on the scheduled flight connecting you to the city where your charter departs, causing you to miss your charter, you lose your flight and money. Charter reservations are only good for one flight. If you miss it for any reason, you're probably out of luck. Check with the tour operator to see if he has another charter flying to your destination (sometimes on back-to-back packages, there's a little hope).

If your charter is late returning and causes you to miss a scheduled connecting flight back to your home, you have to pay your own expenses while you wait for the next connection. If you have a discount fare on a scheduled connecting flight you could lose it if your returning charter is delayed. Then you, not the airlines or tour operator, have to pay more for a regular fare on your connection.

Baggage and Other Problems

Your baggage can't be automatically checked from a scheduled flight to a charter, and vice versa. You have to check it yourself. When planning a charter, allow plenty of time to check in at the airport from which your charter leaves, or from which you have a connecting flight. On international trips, remember that you may encounter delays in customs.

You might find seating space for your charter plane to be more crowded than you're used to. A charter's financial success depends on all of the seats being filled, with cost spread over a greater number of people.

If a charter flight hasn't sold out shortly before departure, the operator can sell seats at bargain basement prices to the latecomers. Some who've paid the regular price well in advance may object, but should realize that the operator's alternative may be to cancel the flight altogether for economic reasons.

Charter fares are relatively low but might not be the cheapest to your destination. Ask your travel agent to compare fares on scheduled and charter flights for you.

Charters can be a wise travel investment when you find one within your price range, and if you can be flexible in your travel plans. Just be sure you know the conditions for the trip you're buying before you pay for it.

U.S. Travel Industry Statistics

Volume, receipts, employment	1980	1979	1977	1975
Domestic travel volume[1] (in millions of passenger-miles)				
Automobile	975.9	996.0	1,104.4	n.a.
Air	189.8	200.6	154.8	131.8
Bus	17.5	17.1	16.6	n.a.
Rail	4.7	4.8	4.2	3.8
Total (billions)	1,187.9	1,218.5	1,280.1	n.a.
Industry receipts[2] (in billions of dollars)				
Transportation	$114.5	$ 90.1	$ 67.7	$ 57.7
Lodging	25.1	23.5	17.1	13.7
Food service	82.2	75.1	63.8	51.4
Amusements	28.3	25.8	22.8	18.0
Total (billions)	$250.1	$214.5	$171.4	$140.8
Employment[3] (in millions of jobs)				
Transportation	1.06	1.05	1.04	1.02
Lodging	1.01	1.02	.86	.82
Food service	4.82	4.58	3.85	3.33
Total (billions)	6.89	6.65	5.76	5.17

1. Includes: Auto: Main rural road passenger-miles; Air: Domestic certified air carrier revenue passenger-miles; Bus: All intercity bus passenger-miles; Rail: Amtrak passenger-miles. 2. Includes: Transportation: Air and rail transportation companies, gasoline service stations; Lodging: Commercial lodging places; Food Service: Eating and drinking places; Amusements: Amusement and recreation services. 3. Includes: Transportation: Air transportation, intercity highway transportation and gasoline service stations; Lodging: Commercial lodging places; Food Service: Eating and drinking places. NOTE: n.a. = not available. *Source:* U.S. Travel Data Center, Washington, D.C.

Winter Sports Gain in National Forests

Department of Agriculture Forest Service officials predict a 23% increase in winter sports in the 154 national forests over the next ten years. This gain is twice the expected increase in sports for other times of the year. Part of the reason is attributed to the growing popularity of the back country in the winter time.

U.S. Passport and Customs Information

Source: Department of State, Passport Services and Department of the Treasury, Customs Service

Passports

With a few exceptions, a passport is required for all United States citizens to depart from and enter the United States and to enter most foreign countries. A United States citizen is not required by United States laws or regulations to have a valid passport for travel to or in North, South, or Central America, except Cuba. It is, however, recommended that a passport be obtained for travel to Central and South America since many of the countries require that United States citizens be in possession of a valid passport. United States travelers should carry documentary evidence of their United States citizenship and identity to facilitate re-entry into the United States. Travelers should check passport and visa requirements with consular officials of the countries to be visited well in advance of their departure date.

Applications for passport may be made to any Passport Agent; to a clerk of any Federal court or State court of record, or a judge or clerk or any probate court, accepting applications; or at a Post Office selected to accept passport applications. Passport agencies are located in Boston; Chicago; Detroit; Honolulu; Houston; Los Angeles; Miami; New Orleans; New York; Philadelphia; San Francisco; Seattle; Stamford, Conn.; and Washington, D.C.

A first passport must be applied for in person. Applicants must present evidence of citizenship (e.g., a birth certificate), personal identification (e.g., driver's license), two identical photographs taken within six months (2 x 2 inches, with the image size measured from the bottom of the chin to the top of the head [including hair] not less than 1 inch nor more than 1⅜ inches, signed in the center on the reverse; vending machine photographs not acceptable), plus the application. A fee of $10 plus a $5 execution fee is charged.

You may apply by mail if you have been the bearer of a passport issued within eight years prior to the date of a new application; are able to submit your most recent United States passport with your new application; your previous passport was not issued before your 18th birthday. This procedure may be used only in the United States. If you are eligible to apply by mail, include your previous passport, completed and signed Application for Passport by Mail, new signed photographs, and the $10 passport fee. The $5 execution fee is not required when applying by mail.

If you claim citizenship by naturalization, a Certificate of Naturalization is required.

Passports may be amended to show a married name or legal change of name, to correct descriptive data, or to exclude a person previously included.

Any alterations by the bearer other than change of address and notification data appearing in the passport are forbidden.

Your passport is valid for five years from date of issue unless specifically limited by the Secretary of State to a shorter period of validity.

The passport is a traveler's principal means of identification abroad, and its loss is very serious. It should be reported immediately to the nearest United States embassy or consular office. Loss of a passport in the United States should be reported in writing to Passport Services, Department of State, Washington, D.C. 20524, or the nearest Passport Agency.

NOTE: The period of validity of passports, passport fees, and criteria for use of the passport-by-mail and amendment procedures may change. This information should be checked with your nearest Passport official.

Customs

United States residents must declare all articles acquired abroad and in their possession at the time of their return. In addition, articles acquired in the U.S. Virgin Islands, American Samoa, or Guam and not accompanying you must be declared at the time of your return. The wearing or use of an article acquired abroad does *not* exempt it from duty. Customs declaration forms are distributed on vessels and planes, and should be prepared in advance of arrival for presentation to the immigration and customs inspectors.

If you have not exceeded the duty-free exemption allowed, you may make an oral declaration to the customs inspector. A written declaration is necessary when (1) total fair retail value of articles exceeds $300 (keep your sales slips); (2) over 1 liter of liquor, 200 cigarettes, or 100 cigars are included; (3) items are not intended for your personal or household use, or articles brought home for another person; and (4) when a customs duty or internal revenue tax is collectible on any article in your possession.

An exception to the above are regulations applicable to articles purchased in the Virgin Islands, American Samoa, or Guam where you may receive a customs exemption of $600. Not more than $300 of this exemption may be applied to merchandise obtained elsewhere than in these islands. Four liters of alcoholic beverages and 2000 cigarettes may be included provided not more than one liter and 200 cigarettes were acquired elsewhere than in these islands. Articles acquired in and sent from these islands to the United States may be claimed under your duty-free personal exemption if properly declared at the time of your return.

Articles accompanying you, in excess of your personal exemption, up to $600 will be assessed at a flat rate of duty of 10% based on fair retail value in country of acquisition. (If articles were acquired in the insular possessions, the flat rate of duty is 5% and these goods may accompany you or be shipped home.) These articles must be for your personal use or for use as gifts and not for sale. This provision may be used every 30 days, excluding the day of your last arrival. Any items which have a "free" duty rate will be excluded before duty is calculated.

Other exemptions include in part: automobiles, boats, planes, or other vehicles taken abroad for noncommercial use. Foreign-made personal articles (e.g., watches, cameras, etc.) taken abroad should be registered with Customs before departure. Gifts of not more than $25 can be shipped back to the United States tax and duty free ($40 if mailed from the Virgin Islands, American Samoa, or Guam). Household effects and tools of trade which you take out of the United States are duty free at time of return.

Prohibited and restricted articles include in part: absinthe, narcotics and dangerous drugs, obscene articles and publications, seditious and treasonable materials, hazardous articles (e.g., fireworks, dangerous toys, toxic and poisonous substances) and switchblade knives, biological materials of public health or veterinary importance, fruit, vegetables and plants, meats, poultry and products thereof, birds, monkeys, and turtles.

If you understate the value of an article you declare, or if you otherwise misrepresent an article in your declaration, you may have to pay a penalty in addition to payment of duty. Under certain circumstances, the article could be seized and forfeited if the penalty is not paid.

If you fail to declare an article acquired abroad, not only is the article subject to seizure and forfeiture, but you will be liable for a personal penalty in an amount equal to the value of the article in the United States. In addition, you may also be liable to criminal prosecution.

If you carry more than $5,000 into or out of the United States in currency (either United States or foreign money), negotiable instruments in bearer form, or travelers checks, a report must be filed with United States Customs at the time you arrive or depart with such amounts.

As U.S. restrictions on travel to Cuba, North Korea, Vietnam, and Cambodia have been eased, the Office of Foreign Assets Control (FAC) issued a general license, effective March 21, 1977, which allows visitors to those countries to purchase a maximum of $100 worth of goods. This amount is based on foreign market or retail value in the country where acquired. These articles must be for personal use—not for resale—and must accompany the traveler on his entry into the U.S. This allowance may be used only once every 6 months.

International Tourist Arrivals and Receipts, 1979–1980

Area	Arrivals (millions)		Receipts (billions)	
	1979[1]	1980[2]	1979[1]	1980[2]
Africa	5.3	5.8	1.8	2.0
Americas	50.0	52.5	16.0	18.5
East Asia and the Pacific	13.8	15.0	5.0	6.0
Europe	196.0	208.0	54.0	64.0
Middle East	3.6	3.0	1.4	1.5
South Asia	2.0	1.5	0.8	0.5
Total	270.7	285.8	79.0	92.5

1. Revised estimates. 2. Preliminary estimates. *Source:* World Tourism Organization

Volume of Domestic Travel by U.S. Residents
(in millions of person-trips)

Domestic Travel	1980
Mode of Transportation:	
Auto, truck, recreational vehicle	748.2
Airplane	142.5
Bus	19.7
Train	9.9
Other	14.8
Purpose of trip:	
Visiting friends and relatives	331.8
Other pleasures	351.3
Business and convention	135.0
Other	117.0
Type of trip:	
Vacation	578.2
Weekend	451.5
Total person–trips	935.1

Source: U.S. Travel Data Center, Washington, D.C.

Average Daily Temperatures (°F) in Tourist Cities

Location	January High	January Low	April High	April Low	July High	July Low	October High	October Low
U.S. CITIES (See Weather and Climate Section)								
CANADA (See Canadian Section)								
MEXICO								
Acapulco	85	70	87	71	89	75	88	74
Mexico City	66	42	78	52	74	54	70	50
OVERSEAS								
Australia (Sydney)	78	65	71	58	60	46	71	56
Austria (Vienna)	34	26	57	41	75	59	55	44
Bahamas (Nassau)	77	65	81	69	88	75	85	73
Bermuda (Hamilton)	68	58	71	59	85	73	79	69
Brazil (Rio de Janeiro)	84	73	80	69	75	63	77	66
Denmark (Copenhagen)	36	29	50	37	72	55	53	42
Egypt (Cairo)	65	47	83	57	96	70	86	65
France (Paris)	42	32	60	41	76	55	59	44
Germany (Berlin)	35	26	55	38	74	55	55	41
Greece (Athens)	54	42	67	52	90	72	74	60

Location	January High	January Low	April High	April Low	July High	July Low	October High	October Low
Hong Kong	64	56	75	67	87	78	81	73
India (Calcutta)	80	55	97	76	90	79	89	74
Italy (Rome)	54	39	68	46	88	64	73	53
Israel (Jerusalem)	55	41	73	50	87	63	81	59
Japan (Tokyo)	47	29	63	46	83	70	69	55
Nigeria (Lagos)	88	74	89	77	83	74	85	74
Netherlands (Amsterdam)	40	34	52	43	69	59	56	48
Puerto Rico (San Juan)	81	67	84	69	87	74	87	73
South Africa (Cape Town)	78	60	72	53	63	45	70	52
Spain (Madrid)	47	33	64	44	87	62	66	48
United Kingdom (London)	44	35	56	40	73	55	58	44
United Kingdom (Edinburgh)	43	35	50	39	65	52	53	44
U.S.S.R. (Moscow)	21	9	47	31	76	55	46	34
Venezuela (Caracas)	75	56	81	60	78	61	79	61
Yugoslavia (Belgrade)	37	27	64	45	84	61	65	47

Expenditures of U.S. Travelers to Foreign Countries
(in millions of dollars)

Type of expense	1980	1979	1978	1977	1975
Transportation fare payments	$6,111	$5,162	$4,680	$4,473	$3,726
Foreign flag carriers	3,607	3,184	2,896	2,748	2,263
U.S. flag carriers	2,504	1,978	1,784	1,725	1,463
Travel payments in foreign countries	10,397	9,413	8,475	7,451	6,417
Canada	1,817	1,599	1,407	1,433	1,306
Mexico	2,564	2,460	2,121	1,918	1,637
Mexican border zone	1,416	1,291	1,128	1,165	1,047
Total overseas areas	6,016	5,354	4,947	4,100	3,474
Europe and Mediterranean[1]	3,412	3,185	2,942	2,398	1,918
Western Europe	3,021	2,842	2,600	2,103	1,709
United Kingdom	903	826	771	585	404
France	383	355	287	233	226
Italy	360	300	260	240	194
Switzerland	150	158	153	145	121
West Germany	322	283	220	203	174
Austria	104	84	75	73	65
Denmark	49	54	70	51	43
Sweden	42	38	52	40	29
Norway	51	47	49	37	44
Netherlands	95	71	65	49	60
Belgium and Luxembourg	44	50	37	34	39
Spain	173	200	213	151	135
Portugal	69	58	53	37	19
Ireland	103	115	110	97	55
Greece	139	163	140	102	73
Other Western Europe	34	40	45	26	28
Other Europe and Mediterranean	391	343	342	295	209
Israel	179	157	144	146	57
Other[2]	212	186	198	149	152
Caribbean Area and Central America	1,134	1,019	888	790	787
Bermuda	191	164	136	123	118
Bahama	262	224	198	158	161
Jamaica	118	122	118	100	118
Other British West Indies	189	190	153	144	103
Netherlands West Indies	157	138	114	106	97
Other West Indies and Central America	217	181	169	159	190
South America	392	288	306	254	242
Other overseas areas	1,078	862	811	658	527
Japan	185	142	155	149	131
Hong Kong	145	137	113	87	75
Australia and New Zealand	234	153	123	92	54
Other	514	430	420	330	267
Total expenses[3]	16,508	14,575	13,155	11,924	10,143

1. Includes Algeria, Cyprus, Egypt, Israel, Lebanon, Libya, Malta, Morocco, Syria, Tunisia, and Turkey. 2. Includes U.S.S.R. 3. Cruise passenger fare payments included in transportation payments (predominantly foreign flag carriers). Shore expenditures included in regional and country totals. *Source:* Department of Commerce, Bureau of Economic Analysis.

Expenditures of Visitors in U.S.
(in millions of dollars)

Country or region of permanent residence	1980	1979	1978	1977	1975
Transportation—U.S. Flag Carriers	$2,053	$1,677	$1,238	$1,025	$ 767
Expenditures in U.S.	10,090	8,383	7,186	6,150	4,697
Canada	2,428	2,092	2,248	2,150	1,561
Mexico	2,554	1,869	1,459	1,316	1,311
U.S. border area	1,646	1,160	954	967	972
Overseas Visitors	5,108	4,422	3,479	2,684	1,825
Western Europe	1,942	1,715	1,323	1,003	611
United Kingdom	469	375	308	205	144
Germany	500	440	333	263	145
France	216	180	140	121	68
Italy	96	84	70	61	41
Netherlands	108	97	84	57	36
Belgium	n.a.	48	34	29	14
Sweden	n.a.	n.a.	54	40	23
Switzerland	n.a.	n.a.	72	51	32
Other	n.a.	n.a.	228	176	108
Caribbean and Central America	417	375	322	276	206
South America	977	793	660	455	303
Other Areas	1,772	1,539	1,174	950	705
Japan	774	699	539	450	410
Total expenditures	**12,143**	**10,060**	**8,424**	**7,175**	**5,464**

NOTE: n.a. = not available. *Source:* Department of Commerce, Bureau of Economic Analysis.

Travelers from the U.S. to Foreign Countries[1]
by Country and Region Visited
(in thousands)

Country or region visited	1980	1979	1978	1977	1975
Canada[2]	10,963[3]	10,909	11,277	11,451	12,499
Mexico[4]	4,144	4,000[4]	3,073	2,735	2,786
Total Overseas	8,163	7,835	7,790	7,390,	6,354
Europe and Mediterranean	3,934	4,068	4,105	3,920	3,185
Western Europe	3,746	3,866	3,914	3,663	2,990
Austria	420	419	426	359	377
Belgium-Luxembourg	243	257	234	240	289
Denmark	181	206	271	238	230
France	888	943	882	786	809
Greece	284	309	284	257	178
Ireland	239	278	296	303	191
Italy	749	718	718	715	650
Netherlands	395	379	363	317	416
Norway	118	137	165	147	135
Portugal	185	195	195	134	95
Spain	368	443	524	334	370
Sweden	135	136	213	180	150
Switzerland	529	535	572	620	567
United Kingdom	1,580	1,617	1,725	1,559	1,199
West Germany	787	864	765	768	733
Other Western Europe	159	167	219	122	142
Israel	289	258	277	316	138
Other Europe and Mediterranean[5]	497	509	606	489	515
Caribbean Area and Central America	2,624	2,533	2,365	2,203	2,065
South America	594	434	515	483	447
Other Overseas Areas	1,011	800	805	784	657
Total	23,270	22,744	22,140	21,576	21,639

1. Excludes travel by military personnel and other government employees stationed abroad; also excludes cruise travelers. 2. Visitors staying one or more nights. 3. Preliminary figure. 4. Mexican National Tourist Council. Visitors staying one or more nights. 5. Includes the U.S.S.R. *Sources:* Department of Commerce, Bureau of Economic Analysis, and *Statistics Canada.*

Object of Travel by Passport Recipients[1]

Object	1980	1979	1978	1977
Personal reasons	41.2%	48.6	48.5%	32.4%
Pleasure	27.5	17.4	25.4	35.5
Business	5.3	6.4	5.1	6.1
Education	2.6	2.9	2.3	2.5
Religious	.4	.4	.3	.3
Scientific	.09	.04	.05	.03
Health	.03	.02	.03	.04
Government	4.5	4.6	4.4	5.0
Not Stated	18.3	19.5	13.9	18.2

1. Percentages rounded off. *Source: Summary of Passport Statistics,* Department of State, Bureau of Consular Affairs.

Passport Recipients by Sex and Age Groups, 1980

Age group	Male	Female	Total
Under 5	50,360	48,030	98,390
5–14	95,700	101,810	197,510
15–24	204,350	281,190	485,540
25–44	546,440	483,500	1,029,940
45–59	360,090	330,340	690,430
60–69	165,530	181,970	347,500
70–Over	74,730	96,428	171,158
Total	1,497,200	1,523,268	3,020,468

Source: Summary of Passport Statistics: Department of State, Bureau of Consular Affairs.

Price Index Figures for Domestic Travel and Selected Components, 1976–1980
(1967 = 100)

	1976	1977	1978	1979	1980
Travel price index	169.9	187.8	203.3	234.3	283.2
Gasoline	177.9	188.2	196.3	265.6	369.1
Common carrier transportation fares					
Taxicab	176.9	189.9	203.5	221.7	259.5
Intercity train	165.3	180.6	194.6	212.4	250.1
Air	172.2	182.0	190.6	205.8	284.8
Bus	196.9	223.5	240.2	260.0	297.1
Lodging	172.9	187.0	212.7	245.8	280.7
Food service	186.1	200.3	218.4	242.9	267.0
Entertainment services	127.4	166.2	175.4	187.6	201.0
Incidentals	—	161.5	168.7	178.0	193.3

Source: U.S. Travel Data Center.

State and City Tourism Offices

The following is a selected list of state, territorial, and city tourism offices. Where a toll-free 800 number is available, it is given. However, the numbers are subject to change.

ALABAMA
Bureau of Publicity and Information
State Highway Building
Montgomery, Ala. 36130
205–832–5510 or
800–633–5761

ALASKA
Alaska Division of Tourism
Pouch E
Juneau, Alaska 99811
907–465–2010

AMERICAN SAMOA
Director of the Office of Tourism
Pago Pago, American Samoa 96799

ARIZONA
Arizona Office of Tourism
1700 W. Washington
Phoenix, Ariz. 85007
602–252–5962

Phoenix
Phoenix & Valley of the Sun Convention and Visitor's Bureau
2701 E. Camelback Road
Phoenix, Ariz. 85016

Tucson
Visitor's Bureau
P.O. Box 991
Tucson, Ariz. 85702

ARKANSAS
Arkansas Department of Parks and Tourism
149 State Capitol Building
Little Rock, Ark. 72201
501–371–7777 or
800–643–8383

Hot Springs
Hot Springs Chamber of Commerce Convention and Visitors Division
P.O. Box 1500
Hot Springs, Ark. 71901

CALIFORNIA
Office of Visitor Services
Department of Economics and Business Development
1120 N. St.
Sacramento, Calif. 95814
916–322–1396

San Francisco
San Francisco Convention and Visitor's Bureau
1390 Market Street, Suite 260
San Francisco, Calif. 94102

COLORADO
Office of Tourism
Colorado Division of Commerce and Development
313 Sherman St., Room 500
Denver, Colo. 80203
303–839–3045 or
800–525–3083

CONNECTICUT
Tourism Promotion Service

Connecticut Department of
Commerce
210 Washington St.
Hartford, Conn. 06106
203-566-3385 or
800-243-1685

DELAWARE
State Visitors Service
Division of Economic
Development
630 State College Rd.
Dover, Del. 19901
302-678-4254

DISTRICT OF COLUMBIA
Washington Convention and
Visitors Association
Suite 250
1575 Eye Street, NW
Washington, D.C. 20005
202-789-7000

FLORIDA
Department of Commerce
Visitors Inquiry
126 Van Buren Street
Tallahassee, Fla. 32301
904-487-1462

Miami
Miami Metro Department of
Publicity & Tourism
499 Biscayne Blvd.
Miami, Fla. 33132

GEORGIA
Tourist Division
P.O. Box 1776
Atlanta, Ga. 30301
404-656-3590 or
800-241-8444

GUAM
Guam Visitors Bureau
P.O. Box 3520
Agana, Guam 96910

HAWAII
Hawaii Visitors Bureau
2270 Kalakana Ave. Suite 801
Honolulu, Hawaii 96815
808-823-1811

IDAHO
Division of Tourism and
Industrial Development
State Capitol Building, Room
108
Boise, Idaho 83720
208-384-2470

ILLINOIS
Office of Tourism
222 South College
Springfield, Ill. 62706
217-782-7139

Chicago
Convention and Tourism
Bureau
332 S. Michigan Avenue, Room
2050
Chicago, Ill. 60604

INDIANA
Tourism Development Division
State House, Room 336
Indianapolis, Ind. 46204
317-232-8860

IOWA
Travel Development Division
250 Jewett Building
Des Moines, Iowa 50309
515-281-3100 or 3679

KANSAS
Tourist Division
Department of Economic
Development
503 Kansas Ave.
6th Floor
Topeka, Kan. 66603
913-296-3481

KENTUCKY
Kentucky Department of
Tourism
Capital Plaza Tower
Frankfort, Ky. 40601
502-564-4930

LOUISIANA
Louisiana Tourist Development
Commission
P.O. Box 44291, Capitol
Station
Baton Rouge, La. 70804
504-342-4900

New Orleans
Greater New Orleans Tourist &
Convention Commission
334 Royal Street
New Orleans, La. 70130

MAINE
Maine Publicity Bureau
97 Winthrop Street
Hallowell, Maine 04347
207-289-2423

MARYLAND
Division of Tourist Development
1748 Forest Drive
Annapolis, Md. 21401
301-269-3517 or
800-638-5252 (out of
state)

MASSACHUSETTS
Division of Tourism
100 Cambridge Street
Boston, Mass. 02202
617-727-3201

Boston
Convention and Tourist Bureau,
Inc.
900 Boylston Street
Boston, Mass. 02215

MICHIGAN
Travel Bureau
Department of Commerce
P.O. Box 30226
Law Building
Lansing, Mich. 48909
517-373-1195 or

800-248-5703 (out of
state)

MINNESOTA
Tourism Division
480 Cedar St., Hanover Bldg.
St. Paul, Minn. 55101
612-296-5029

MISSISSIPPI
Department of Tourism and
Development
Mississippi Agricultural and
Industrial Board
P.O. Box 849
Jackson, Miss. 39205
601-354-6715 or
800-647-2290

MISSOURI
Missouri Division of Tourism
308 E. High St.
P.O. Box 1055
Jefferson City, Mo. 65101
314-751-4133

MONTANA
Travel Promotion Unit
Department of Highways
Helena, Mont. 59601
406-449-2654

NEBRASKA
Division of Travel and Tourism
P.O. Box 94666, State Capitol
Lincoln, Neb. 68509
420-471-3111

NEVADA
Nevada Division of Tourism
Capitol Complex
1100 E. William Street
Suite 106
Carson City, Nev. 89710
702-885-4322

Las Vegas
Las Vegas Chamber of
Commerce
2301 E. Sahara Avenue
Las Vegas, Nev. 89104

NEW HAMPSHIRE
Office of Vacation Travel
P.O. Box 856
Concord, N.H. 03301
603-271-2665

NEW JERSEY
Division of Travel and Tourism
P.O. Box 400
Trenton, N.J. 08625
609-292-2470

Atlantic City
Greater Atlantic City Chamber
of Commerce
10 Central Pier
Atlantic City, N.J. 08401

NEW MEXICO
Commerce and Industry
Department
Travel Division

Bataan Memorial Building
Santa Fe, N.M. 87503
505–827–5571 or
800–545–2040

NEW YORK
Travel Bureau
New York State
99 Washington Avenue
Albany, N.Y. 12245
518–474–4166

New York City
New York Convention and
Visitor's Bureau
2 Columbus Circle
New York, N.Y. 10019

NORTH CAROLINA
Travel and Tourism Division
Department of Commerce
Box 25249
Raleigh, N.C. 27611
919–733–4171

NORTH DAKOTA
North Dakota Travel Division
State Highway Department
Capitol Grounds
Bismarck, N.D. 58505
701–224–2525 or
800–437–2077 (out of
state)

OHIO
Ohio Office of Travel
P.O. Box 1001
Columbus, Ohio 43216
614–466–8844 or
800–848–1300 (out of
state)

OKLAHOMA
Tourism Promotion Division
505 Will Rogers Building
Oklahoma City, Okla. 73105
405–521–2464

OREGON
Travel Information Section
101 Transportation Building
Salem, Oreg. 97310
503–378–6309 or
800–547–4901

PENNSYLVANIA
Bureau of Travel Development
206 South Office Building

Harrisburg, Pa. 17120
717–787–5453 or
800–323–1717

Philadelphia
Convention and Visitor's
Bureau
1525 John F. Kennedy Blvd.
Philadelphia, Pa. 19102

PUERTO RICO
Puerto Rico Tourism
Development Company
P.O. Box 3072
Old San Juan Station
San Juan, Puerto Rico 00913

RHODE ISLAND
Department of Economic
Development
Tourist Division
1 Weybosset Hill
Providence, R.I. 02903
401–277–2601

SOUTH CAROLINA
South Carolina Division of
Tourism
Box 71
Columbia, S.C. 29202
803–758–8735

SOUTH DAKOTA
South Dakota Division of
Tourism
221 South Central
Pierre, S.D. 57501
605–773–3301 or
1–800–843–1390 (out of
state)

TENNESSEE
Tennessee Tourist Development
P.O. Box 23170
Nashville, Tenn. 37203
615–741–2158

TEXAS
Texas
P.O. Box 5064
Austin, Texas 78763
512–475–7123

UTAH
Utah Travel Council
Council Hall, Capitol Hill

Salt Lake City, Utah 84114
801–533–5681

VERMONT
Agency of Development and
Community Affairs
Travel Division
61 Elm Street
Montpelier, Vt. 05602
802–828–3236

VIRGIN ISLANDS
Division of Tourism
P.O. Box 1692
St. Thomas, Virgin Islands
00801

VIRGINIA
Virginia State Travel Service
6 North Sixth Street
Richmond, Va. 23219
804–786–4484

WASHINGTON
Washington State Dept. of
Commerce and Economic
Development
General Administration Bldg.
G-3
Olympia, Wash. 98504
206–753–5630 or
800–443–2784

WASHINGTON, D.C.
See District of Columbia

WEST VIRGINIA
Travel Development Division
1900 Washington Street, East
Charleston, W.Va. 25305
304–348–2286

WISCONSIN
Division of Tourism
Box 7606
Madison, Wis. 53707
608–266–2161

WYOMING
Wyoming Travel Commission
Frank Norris, Jr. Travel
Center
Cheyenne, Wyo. 82002
307–777–7777 or
800–843–1930 (out of
state)

Information Sources for Travel

Many government and private organizations provide tourist information as a public service. Almost all of the 50 states and the various territories of the U.S. have government-financed tourism offices to provide information about their areas. Many states have welcome centers located on major highways near their borders. Nearly every city has a visitor's bureau, convention center, or chamber of commerce—people very willing to inform visitors about their city or region. Travel agencies—which are business organizations financed by commissions from airlines, cruise lines, hotels, and other elements of the travel industry—make available a variety of travel brochures and general information,

almost always without charge. International travel organizations, like American Express, also offer travel information.

Libraries and bookstores have many tour guides to the United States on their shelves. Among the best known are:

Fodor's USA (1 volume and 11 regional guides) (David McKay)

Exxon Travel Club Guides (Exxon Travel Club) 7 guides on U.S., Canada, Mexico, Caribbean and Bahamas/Bermuda.

Mobil Travel Guides (7 volumes) (Mobil Oil Corp. and Rand McNally)

National Park Guide (Rand McNally)

Vacationland, USA (National Geographic Society)
Some publications covering accommodations are:
AYH Hostel Guide and Handbook (American Youth Hostels)
Country Inns and Back Roads (Berkshire Traveller Press)
Directory (Budget Motels & Hotels of America)
National Directory of Budget Motels (Pilot Industries)
Hotel and Motel Red Book (American Hotel Association)
Where to Stay USA (Frommer/Pasmantier) For camping—including recreational vehicles and trailers. Accommodations in all 50 states from $3 to $20 per night.
Campground and Trailer Park Guide (Rand McNally)
KOA Kampground Directory and RV Buyers Guide (Kampgrounds of America)
Trailering Parks & Campgrounds (Woodall)
Many foreign governments maintain tourist offices in major American cities. International airlines generally have available detailed information about cities and countries along their routes. Travel agencies and international travel organizations like American Express and Thomas Cook also offer travel information, almost always without charge.
Libraries and bookstores have many guides to specific countries. Among the best known are:
$-A-Day Guides (Frommer/Pasmantier) 15 in-depth U.S. and World guides to low-cost tourist accommodations and facilities.
Dollarwise Guides (Frommer/Pasmantier) 12 U.S. and World guides to the best tourist values in every price range, from budget to deluxe, with emphasis on the medium-priced.
The Arthur Frommer Guides (Frommer/Pasmantier) 17 pocket-size guides to U.S. and foreign cities covering tourist accommodations and facilities in all price ranges.
Special Editions (Frommer/Pasmantier): **How to Beat the High Cost of Travel; and Frommer's Guide to China** (Spring 1982) The latest opportunities for China travel. Includes complete phrase section.
Fodor's Europe (David McKay) (plus 19 guides to individual countries)
Fielding's Travel Guide to Europe (Fielding)
Let's Go: Europe (Harvard Student Agencies)
Let's Go: Britain & Ireland (Harvard Student Agencies)
Let's Go: France (Harvard Student Agencies)
Michelin Guides (Michelin Tyre Co.)
Eurail Guide (Saltzman)
Nagel's Guides (Nagel) (76 guides in English)

Homes of the Presidents and Presidential Libraries–Museums

Source: American Automobile Association *Tour Books* and *Information Please* questionnaires.

GEORGE WASHINGTON
George Washington Birthplace National Monument: Washingtons Birthplace, Va. 22575. Open: daily 9–5 (closed Jan. 1, Dec. 25). Free admission.
Mount Vernon: on George Washington Memorial Parkway, Mount Vernon, Va. 22121 (16 mi. south of Washington, D.C.). Open: March 1–Oct. 31 daily 9–5; Nov. 1–Feb. 28–daily 9–4. Adm. $3 (senior citizens, $2.50; children 6–11, $1.50 under 6, free).
Washington's home.

JOHN ADAMS and JOHN QUINCY ADAMS
John Adams and John Quincy Adams Birthplaces: 133 and 141 Franklin St., Quincy, Mass. 02169. Open: April 19–Oct. 15, daily 9–5. Adm. Free. Tour of grounds while houses undergo restoration.
Family home of the Adamses.

Adams National Historic Site: 135 Adams St., Quincy, Mass. 02169. Open: April 19–Nov. 10—daily 9–5. Adm. 50¢ (children under 16 free).
Home of Adams family from 1788 to 1927; built in 1731. Contains furnishings used by four Adams generations.

THOMAS JEFFERSON
Monticello: on Route 53, 3 mi. southeast of Charlottesville, Va. 22902. Open: March 1–Oct. 31—daily 8–5; Nov. 1–Feb. 28—daily. 9–4:30 (closed Dec. 25). Adm. $3 (children 6–11, $1).
Home of Jefferson; begun in 1769; finished in 1809. National shrine contains Jefferson mementos.

JAMES MADISON
Montpelier: Montpelier Station, Va., 22957; on Route 20, 5 mi. west of Orange, Va. Estate not open to public, but graveyard may be visited.
Madison's home.

JAMES MONROE
Ash Lawn: off Route 53, 2½ mi. beyond Monticello, near Charlottesville, Va. 22901. Open: daily, March–Oct. 9–6, Nov.-Feb. 10–5. (closed Jan. 1, Thanksgiving, Dec. 25). Adm. $2.50 (children 6–11, 75¢; under 6, free).
Monroe's home from 1799 to 1823; a working farm planned in 1798 by Jefferson; craft demonstrations; owned by College of William and Mary.

ANDREW JACKSON
The Hermitage: off I–40 east on U.S. 70N, 12 mi. east of Nashville, Tenn. 37076. Open: daily 9–5 (closed Dec. 25). Adm. $3 (children 6–13, $1; under 6, free).
Jackson's home.

MARTIN VAN BUREN
Martin Van Buren National Historic Site (Lindenwald): on Route 9H, 2 mi. south of Kinderhook, N.Y. 12106. Open: Wed.-Sun., May-Sept.
Van Buren's home from 1839 to 1862. Designated a National Historic Site in 1974, the house is now undergoing restoration by the National Park Service; not open to visitors. Guided tours of grounds, Memorial Day weekend to Sept. 30.

WILLIAM HENRY HARRISON
Berkeley Plantation (Harrison's Landing): halfway between Richmond and Williamsburg, Va., on Virginia Route 5. Open daily 8–5 (closed Dec. 25). Adm. $3.50 (children 6–12, $1.75; over 60, $2.50).
Birthplace of William Henry Harrison and ancestral home of Benjamin Harrison. Site of first official Thanksgiving in America, in 1619.

JOHN TYLER
Sherwood Forest: on Virginia Route 5, 20 mi. west of Colonial Williamsburg, Charles City, Va. 23030. Open: daily 9–5 (closed Dec. 25). Adm. $3 (students

and senior citizens, $2.50, children 6–12, $1.50).
Tyler's home; built circa 1730, it is the longest frame residence in America—300 feet in length. Original furnishings. Still occupied by Tyler family.

FRANKLIN PIERCE

Franklin Pierce Homestead: near junction of Routes 9 and 31, northwest of Hillsboro, N.H. 03244. Open: mid-June-Labor Day, Tues.-Sun. 9–5. Adm. 50¢ (visitors under 18 free).
Pierce's home.

JAMES BUCHANAN FOUNDATION

Wheatland: 1120 Marietta Ave., Route 23, Lancaster, Pa. 17603. Open: April 1–Nov. 30, daily, 10–4:30. Adm. $2.50 (students, $1.20; children under 12, 60¢). Group rate $1.
Restored 1828 mansion of nation's only bachelor President. Contains American Empire and Victorian decorative-arts collections.

ABRAHAM LINCOLN

Lincoln Home National Historic Site: 430 South 8th St., Springfield, Ill. 62703. Open: daily, 8–5 (closed Jan. 1, Dec. 25). Adm. Free.
House is only home owned by Lincoln.

ANDREW JOHNSON

Andrew Johnson National Historic Site: Greeneville, Tenn. 37743. Open: daily 9–5 (closed Dec. 25). Adm. to Homestead (June 1–Sept. 15): 50¢ (children under 16 free).
Contains two houses where Johnson lived, tailor shop where he worked, and Andrew Johnson National Cemetery.

ULYSSES S. GRANT

U. S. Grant Home State Historic Site: 510 Bouthillier, Galena, Ill. 61036. Open: daily 9–5 (closed Jan. 1, Thanksgiving, Dec. 25). Free admission.

RUTHERFORD B. HAYES PRESIDENTIAL CENTER

Rutherford B. Hayes Library and Museum State Memorial: 1337 Hayes Ave., Fremont, Ohio 43420. Museum open: Mon.-Sat 9–5, Sun and hldys. 1:30–5. Adm.: $1.25 (children 6–12, 50¢). Library open: Mon.-Sat. 9–5 (closed Sun.); free. Home open (tours only): Wed.-Sat. 9–5, Sun.-Tues. and hldys. 2–5. Adm.: $1.25 (children 6–12, 25¢; under 6, free). All three sites closed Jan. 1, Thanksgiving, and Dec. 25. Library also closed on legal holidays.
Estate is known as Spiegel Grove. It contains Hayes' home, his tomb, and White House gates.

JAMES A. GARFIELD

Lawnfield: 8095 Mentor Ave., Mentor, Ohio 44060. Open: April 15–Nov. 15, Tues.-Sat. 9–5, Sun and hldys. 1–5. Adm. $2 (children 12–17, $1, under 12 with adult, free; over 65, $1).
Garfield's home and Lake County Historical Society Museum.

BENJAMIN HARRISON

Benjamin Harrison Memorial Home: 1230 North Delaware St., Indianapolis, Ind. 46202. Open: Mon.-Sat. 10–3:30, Sun. 12:30–3:30 (closed Jan. 1, Thanksgiving, Dec. 25). Adm. $1.50 (students, 75¢).
Harrison's home; completed in 1875.

THEODORE ROOSEVELT

Theodore Roosevelt Birthplace National Historic Site: 28 E. 20th St., New York, N.Y. 10003. Open: Wed.-Sun. 9–5 (closed Jan. 1, Thanksgiving, Dec.

25). Adm. 50¢. (children under 16 and persons 62 and over, free).
Sagamore Hill National Historic Site: 3 mi. east of Oyster Bay, L.I., N.Y. 11771, via E. Main St. Open: daily 9:30–4:30 (Oct.-April); 9:30–5:30 (May-Sept.); (closed Jan. 1, Thanksgiving, Dec. 25). Adm. 50¢ (children under 16 and persons 62 and over, free).
Roosevelt's home and rural estate.

WOODROW WILSON

Birthplace of Woodrow Wilson: Coalter and Frederick Sts., Staunton, Va. 24401. Open: daily 9–5 (closed Sun., Dec.-Feb.; Jan. 1, Thanksgiving, Dec. 25). Adm. $2 (senior citizens, students, and children 6–16, $1).
Woodrow Wilson House: 2340 S St. N.W., Washington, D.C. 20008. Open: Tues.-Fri. 10–2; Sat., Sun., hldys. 12–4 (closed Jan. 1, Thanksgiving, Dec. 25). Adm.: $2.00 (students and senior citizens, $1.00).
Wilson retired to this house after his second term and died here three years later in 1924.

WARREN G. HARDING

Warren G. Harding Home and Museum: 380 Mt. Vernon Ave., Marion, Ohio 43302. Open: Memorial Day weekend to Labor Day weekend, Wed.-Sat. 9:30–5; Sun. 1–5 (closed Mon., Tues.). Adm. $1 (children 6–12, 50¢).

CALVIN COOLIDGE

Calvin Coolidge Birthplace and Historic Plymouth Village: Route 100A, Plymouth, Vt. 05056. Open: mid-May to mid-Oct.—daily 9:30–5:30. Adm. $1 (children under 15 free).

HERBERT HOOVER

Herbert Hoover National Historic Site: ½ mi. north of I-80, exit 254, West Branch, Iowa 52358. Grounds open daily 8–5. (closed Jan. 1, Thanksgiving, Dec. 25). Free admission.
Restored two-room cottage where Hoover was born; replica of his father's blacksmith shop. Quaker meetinghouse, grave site.
Herbert Hoover Presidential Library–Museum: Interstate 80, West Branch, Iowa 52358. Open: Sept.–May, Mon.-Sat. 8–5, Sun. 12–5; Memorial Day–Labor Day, Mon.-Sat. 9–6, Sun. 10–6. (closed Jan. 1, Thanksgiving, Dec. 25). Adm. 75¢ (children under 16 free).
Exhibits portray Hoover as engineer, public servant, and humanitarian. Located in surrounding park are birthplace cottage, Quaker Meeting House, replica of Jesse Hoover's blacksmith shop, and graves of President and Mrs. Hoover.

FRANKLIN D. ROOSEVELT

Home of Franklin D. Roosevelt National Historic Site: on U.S. 9, south end of Hyde Park, N.Y. 12538. Open: daily 9–5 (closed Jan. 1, Dec. 25). Adm. $1.50 (children under 16 and adults over 62, free). Fee includes admission to Vanderbilt Mansion and the Library–Museum.
Franklin D. Roosevelt Library and Museum: 259 Albany Post Road, Hyde Park, N.Y. 12538. Open: daily 9–5; summer 9–6 (closed Jan. 1, Dec. 25). Adm. $1.50, includes admission to Roosevelt Home and Vanderbilt Mansion (children under 16 and adults over 62, free). Archives open Mon-Fri. 9–5 (closed natl. hldys).
Exhibits feature lives and special interests of Franklin D. and Eleanor Roosevelt. Archives contain historic papers of President and Mrs. Roosevelt and of prominent figures in his Administration. Near the Library are Roosevelt family home, which is open to public, and graves of President and Mrs. Roosevelt.

HARRY S. TRUMAN

Harry S. Truman Birthplace State Historic Site: Truman Ave. & 11th St., Lamar, Mo. 64759. Open: Mon.-Sat. 10–4; Sun. 12–5 (closed Jan. 1, Easter, Thanksgiving, Dec. 25). Free.

Harry S. Truman Library and Museum: U.S. Highway 24 and Delaware St., Independence, Mo. 64050. Open: daily, 9–5; Memorial Day weekend to Labor Day weekend, 9–7 (closed Jan. 1, Thanksgiving, Dec. 25). Adm 75¢ (children under 16 free).

Copy of Truman's White House office, United Nations Charter Table, state gifts and Japanese surrender documents. Film programs. Mural by Thomas Hart Benton decorates entrance hall. Truman's gravesite is in the courtyard.

DWIGHT D. EISENHOWER

Eisenhower Birthplace State Historical Site: 208 E. Day St., Denison, Tex. 75020. Open: June 1–Aug. 31, daily, 8–5; Sept. 1–May 31, daily, 10–12, 1–5 (closed Jan. 1, Thanksgiving, Dec. 25). Adm.: 50¢ (children under 12, 25¢; under 6, free).

Dwight D. Eisenhower Center: Kansas Highway 15, Abilene, Kan. 67410. Open: daily 9–4:45 (closed Jan. 1, Thanksgiving, Dec. 25). Adm., Library, free; museum, 75¢.

Exhibits of paintings and memorabilia relating to Eisenhower Administration are on display in Library and Museum. Place of Meditation, where Eisenhower is buried, and his boyhood home are nearby and are open to visitors.

JOHN F. KENNEDY

John F. Kennedy National Historic Site: 83 Beals St., Brookline, Mass. 02146. Open: daily 9–4:30 (closed Jan. 1, Thanksgiving, Dec. 25). Adm. 50¢ (children under 16 and senior citizens, free).

Kennedy's birthplace.

John Fitzgerald Kennedy Library: Columbia Point on Dorchester Bay, Boston, Mass. 02125. Open: Daily, 9–5 (closed Jan. 1, Thanksgiving, Dec. 25). Adm. 75¢.

Research rooms, exhibits and educational activities relating to Kennedy, his times and Administration.

LYNDON B. JOHNSON

Lyndon B. Johnson National Historical Park: P.O. Box 329, Johnson City, Tex. 78636. Open: daily 9–5 (closed Dec. 25). Free.

Site includes LBJ Ranch, birthplace and family cemetery at Stonewall (15 miles west of Johnson City) and his boyhood home and grandfather's ranch headquarters in Johnson City.

Lyndon Baines Johnson Library: 2313 Red River, Austin, Tex. 78705. Open daily 9–5 (closed Dec. 25). Free.

Documents, photographs, art objects, audio tapes, films, and memorabilia concerning the Presidency are exhibited. Audio tapes and film recreate four decades of U.S. history. Archives house 31 million documents. Replica of Oval Office during Johnson's Presidency is on view.

GERALD R. FORD

Gerald R. Ford Library: 1000 Beal Ave., Ann Arbor, Mich. 48109. Open: Mon.-Fri., 9–5 (closed Jan. 1, Washington's Birthday, Memorial Day, July 4, Labor Day, Columbus Day, Veterans Day, Thanksgiving, and Dec. 25). Free.

Documents and audio-visual materials of Ford's Presidency and service in House of Representatives.

Gerald R. Ford Museum: 303 Pearl St., N.W., Grand Rapids, Mich. 49504. Open: daily 9–4:45 (closed Jan.1, Thanksgiving, and Dec. 25) Adm. 75¢ (children under 16 and school groups, free).

Exhibits relating to Ford's career, the Presidency and American politics.

The Statue of Liberty

The Statue of Liberty ("Liberty Enlightening the World") is a 225-ton, steel-reinforced copper female figure, 152 ft in height, facing the ocean from Liberty[1] Island in New York Harbor. The right hand holds aloft a torch, and the left hand carries a tablet upon which is inscribed: "July IV MDCCLXXVI."

The statue was designed by Frédéric Auguste Bartholdi of Alsace as a gift to the United States from the people of France to memorialize the alliance of the two countries in the American Revolution and their abiding friendship. The French people contributed the $250,000 cost.

The 150-foot pedestal was designed by Richard M. Hunt and built by Gen. Charles P. Stone, both Americans. It contains steel underpinnings designed by Alexander Eiffel of France to support the statue. The $270,000 cost was borne by popular subscription in this country. President Grover Cleveland accepted the statue for the United States on Oct. 28, 1886.

On Sept. 26, 1972, President Richard M. Nixon

1. Called Bedloe's Island prior to 1956.

dedicated the American Museum of Immigration, housed in structural additions to the base of the statue. Some 200 exhibits memorialize the flow of immigrants into the United States, including as many as 5,000 a day on nearby Ellis Island.

On a tablet inside the pedestal is engraved the following sonnet, written by Emma Lazarus (1849–1887):

The New Colossus

Not like the brazen giant of Greek fame,
With conquering limbs astride from land to land;
Here at our sea-washed, sunset gates shall stand
A mighty woman with a torch, whose flame
Is the imprisoned lightning, and her name
Mother of Exiles. From her beacon-hand
Glows world-wide welcome; her mild eyes command
The air-bridged harbor that twin cities frame.
"Keep, ancient lands, your storied pomp!" cries she
With silent lips. "Give me your tired, your poor,
Your huddled masses yearning to breathe free,
The wretched refuse of your teeming shore.
Send these, the homeless, tempest-tost to me,
I lift my lamp beside the golden door!"

Automobile Recalls Decline Sharply

Recalls of motor vehicles dropped sharply in 1980. According to the Automotive Information Council, the total for that year was 5 million, compared with 9 million recalled in 1978 and 1979. A record 12.6 million cars were recalled by manufacturers in 1977.

Road Mileages Between U.S. Cities[1]

Cities	Birmingham	Boston	Buffalo	Chicago	Cleveland	Dallas	Denver
Birmingham, Ala.	—	1,194	947	657	734	653	1,318
Boston, Mass.	1,194	—	457	983	639	1,815	1,991
Buffalo, N.Y.	947	457	—	536	192	1,387	1,561
Chicago, Ill.	657	983	536	—	344	931	1,050
Cleveland, Ohio	734	639	192	344	—	1,205	1,369
Dallas, Tex.	653	1,815	1,387	931	1,205	—	801
Denver, Colo	1,318	1,991	1,561	1,050	1,369	801	—
Detroit, Mich.	754	702	252	279	175	1,167	1,301
El Paso, Tex.	1,278	2,358	1,928	1,439	1,746	625	652
Houston, Tex.	692	1,886	1,532	1,092	1,358	242	1,032
Indianapolis, Ind.	492	940	510	189	318	877	1,051
Kansas City, Mo.	703	1,427	997	503	815	508	616
Los Angeles, Calif.	2,078	3,036	2,606	2,112	2,424	1,425	1,174
Louisville, Ky.	378	996	571	305	379	865	1,135
Memphis, Tenn.	249	1,345	965	546	773	470	1,069
Miami, Fla.	777	1,539	1,445	1,390	1,325	1,332	2,094
Minneapolis, Minn.	1,067	1,402	955	411	763	969	867
New Orleans, La.	347	1,541	1,294	947	1,102	504	1,305
New York, N.Y.	983	213	436	840	514	1,604	1,780
Omaha, Neb.	907	1,458	1,011	493	819	661	559
Philadelphia, Pa.	894	304	383	758	432	1,515	1,698
Phoenix, Ariz.	1,680	2,664	2,234	1,729	2,052	1,027	836
Pittsburgh, Pa.	792	597	219	457	131	1,237	1,411
St. Louis, Mo.	508	1,179	749	293	567	638	871
Salt Lake City, Utah	1,805	2,425	1,978	1,458	1,786	1,239	512
San Francisco, Calif.	2,385	3,179	2,732	2,212	2,540	1,765	1,266
Seattle, Wash.	2,612	3,043	2,596	2,052	2,404	2,122	1,373
Washington, D.C.	751	440	386	695	369	1,372	1,635

Cities	Detroit	El Paso	Houston	Indianapolis	Kansas City	Los Angeles	Louisville
Birmingham, Ala.	754	1,278	692	492	703	2,078	378
Boston, Mass.	702	2,358	1,886	940	1,427	3,036	996
Buffalo, N.Y.	252	1,928	1,532	510	997	2,606	571
Chicago, Ill.	279	1,439	1,092	189	503	2,112	305
Cleveland, Ohio	175	1,746	1,358	318	815	2,424	379
Dallas, Tex.	1,167	625	242	877	508	1,425	865
Denver, Colo.	1,310	652	1,032	1,051	616	1,174	1,135
Detroit, Mich.	—	1,696	1,312	290	760	2,369	378
El Paso, Tex.	1,696	—	756	1,418	936	800	1,443
Houston, Tex.	1,312	756	—	1,022	750	1,556	981
Indianapolis, Ind.	290	1,418	1,022	—	487	2,096	114
Kansas City, Mo.	760	936	750	487	—	1,609	519
Los Angeles, Calif.	2,369	800	1,556	2,096	1,609	—	2,128
Louisville, Ky.	378	1,443	981	114	519	2,128	—
Memphis, Tenn.	756	1,095	586	466	454	1,847	396
Miami, Fla.	1,409	1,957	1,237	1,225	1,479	2,757	1,111
Minneapolis, Minn.	698	1,353	1,211	600	466	2,041	716
New Orleans, La.	1,101	1,121	365	839	839	1,921	725
New York, N.Y.	671	2,147	1,675	729	1,216	2,825	785
Omaha, Neb.	754	1,015	903	590	204	1,733	704
Philadelphia, Pa.	589	2,065	1,586	647	1,134	2,743	703
Phoenix, Ariz.	1,986	402	1,158	1,713	1,226	398	1,749
Pittsburgh, Pa.	288	1,778	1,395	360	847	2,456	416
St. Louis, Mo.	529	1,179	799	239	255	1,864	264
Salt Lake City, Utah	1,721	877	1,465	1,545	1,128	728	1,647
San Francisco, Calif.	2,475	1,202	1,958	2,299	1,882	403	2,401
Seattle, Wash.	2,339	1,760	2,348	2,241	1,909	1,150	2,355
Washington, D.C.	526	1,997	1,443	565	1,071	2,680	601

1. These figures represent estimates and are subject to change.

Road Mileages Between U.S. Cities

Cities	Memphis	Miami	Minne-apolis	New Orleans	New York	Omaha	Phila-delphia
Birmingham, Ala.	249	777	1,067	347	983	907	894
Boston, Mass.	1,345	1,539	1,402	1,541	213	1,458	304
Buffalo, N.Y.	965	1,445	955	1,294	436	1,011	383
Chicago, Ill.	546	1,390	411	947	840	493	758
Cleveland, Ohio	773	1,325	763	1,102	514	819	432
Dallas, Tex.	470	1,332	969	504	1,604	661	1,515
Denver, Colo.	1,069	2,094	867	1,305	1,780	559	1,698
Detroit, Mich.	756	1,409	698	1,101	671	754	589
El Paso, Tex.	1,095	1,957	1,353	1,121	2,147	1,015	2,065
Houston, Tex.	586	1,237	1,211	365	1,675	903	1,586
Indianapolis, Ind.	466	1,225	600	839	729	590	647
Kansas City, Mo.	454	1,479	466	839	1,216	204	1,134
Los Angeles, Calif.	1,847	2,757	2,041	1,921	2,825	1,733	2,743
Louisville, Ky.	396	1,111	716	725	785	704	703
Memphis, Tenn.	—	1,025	854	401	1,134	658	1,045
Miami, Fla.	1,025	—	1,801	892	1,328	1,683	1,239
Minneapolis, Minn.	854	1,801	—	1,255	1,259	373	1,177
New Orleans, La.	401	892	1,255	—	1,330	1,043	1,241
New York, N.Y.	1,134	1,328	1,259	1,330	—	1,315	93
Omaha, Neb.	658	1,683	373	1,043	1,315	—	1,233
Philadelphia, Pa.	1,045	1,239	1,177	1,241	93	1,233	—
Phoenix, Ariz.	1,464	2,359	1,644	1,523	2,442	1,305	2,360
Pittsburgh, Pa.	810	1,250	876	1,118	386	932	304
St. Louis, Mo.	295	1,241	559	696	968	459	886
Salt Lake City, Utah	1,556	2,571	1,243	1,743	2,282	967	2,200
San Francisco, Calif.	2,151	3,097	1,997	2,269	3,036	1,721	2,954
Seattle, Wash.	2,363	3,389	1,641	2,606	2,900	1,705	2,818
Washington, D.C.	902	1,101	1,114	1,098	229	1,170	140

Cities	Phoenix	Pitts-burgh	St. Louis	Salt Lake City	San Francisco	Seattle	Wash-ington
Birmingham, Ala.	1,680	792	508	1,805	2,385	2,612	751
Boston, Mass.	2,664	597	1,179	2,425	3,179	3,043	440
Buffalo, N.Y.	2,234	219	749	1,978	2,732	2,596	386
Chicago, Ill.	1,729	457	293	1,458	2,212	2,052	695
Cleveland, Ohio	2,052	131	567	1,786	2,540	2,404	369
Dallas, Tex.	1,027	1,237	638	1,239	1,765	2,122	1,372
Denver, Colo.	836	1,411	871	512	1,266	1,373	1,635
Detroit, Mich.	1,986	288	529	1,721	2,475	2,339	526
El Paso, Tex.	402	1,778	1,179	877	1,202	1,760	1,997
Houston, Tex.	1,158	1,395	799	1,465	1,958	2,348	1,443
Indianapolis, Ind.	1,713	360	239	1,545	2,299	2,241	565
Kansas City, Mo.	1,226	847	255	1,128	1,882	1,909	1,071
Los Angeles, Calif.	398	2,456	1,864	728	403	1,150	2,680
Louisville, Ky.	1,749	416	264	1,647	2,401	2,355	601
Memphis, Tenn.	1,464	810	295	1,556	2,151	2,363	902
Miami, Fla.	2,359	1,250	1,241	2,571	3,097	3,389	1,101
Minneapolis, Minn.	1,644	876	559	1,243	1,997	1,641	1,114
New Orleans, La.	1,523	1,118	696	1,743	2,269	2,626	1,098
New York, N.Y.	2,442	386	968	2,282	3,036	2,900	229
Omaha, Neb.	1,305	932	459	967	1,721	1,705	1,178
Philadelphia, Pa.	2,360	304	886	2,200	2,954	2,818	140
Phoenix, Ariz.	—	2,073	1,485	651	800	1,482	2,278
Pittsburgh, Pa.	2,073	—	599	1,899	2,653	2,517	241
St. Louis, Mo.	1,485	599	—	1,383	2,137	2,164	836
Salt Lake City, Utah	651	1,899	1,383	—	754	883	2,110
San Francisco, Calif.	800	2,653	2,137	754	—	817	2,864
Seattle, Wash.	1,482	2,517	2,164	883	817	—	2,755
Washington, D.C.	2,278	241	836	2,110	2,864	2,755	—

Air Distances Between U.S. Cities in Statute Miles

Cities	Birming-ham	Boston	Buffalo	Chicago	Cleveland	Dallas	Denver
Birmingham, Ala.	—	1,052	776	578	618	581	1,095
Boston, Mass.	1,052	—	400	851	551	1,551	1,769
Buffalo, N. Y.	776	400	—	454	173	1,198	1,370
Chicago, Ill.	578	851	454	—	308	803	920
Cleveland, Ohio	618	551	173	308	—	1,025	1,227
Dallas, Tex.	581	1,551	1,198	803	1,025	—	663
Denver, Colo.	1,095	1,769	1,370	920	1,227	663	—
Detroit, Mich.	641	613	216	238	90	999	1,156
El Paso, Tex.	1,152	2,072	1,692	1,252	1,525	572	557
Houston, Tex.	567	1,605	1,286	940	1,114	225	879
Indianapolis, Ind.	433	807	435	165	263	763	1,000
Kansas City, Mo.	579	1,251	861	414	700	451	558
Los Angeles, Calif.	1,802	2,596	2,198	1,745	2,049	1,240	831
Louisville, Ky.	331	826	483	269	311	726	1,038
Memphis, Tenn.	217	1,137	803	482	630	420	879
Miami, Fla.	665	1,255	1,181	1,188	1,087	1,111	1,726
Minneapolis, Minn.	862	1,123	731	355	630	862	700
New Orleans, La.	312	1,359	1,086	833	924	443	1,082
New York, N. Y.	864	188	292	713	405	1,374	1,631
Omaha, Neb.	732	1,282	883	432	739	586	488
Philadelphia, Pa.	783	271	279	666	360	1,299	1,579
Phoenix, Ariz.	1,456	2,300	1,906	1,453	1,749	887	586
Pittsburgh, Pa.	608	483	178	410	115	1,070	1,320
St. Louis, Mo.	400	1,038	662	262	492	547	796
Salt Lake City, Utah	1,466	2,099	1,699	1,260	1,568	999	371
San Francisco, Calif.	2,013	2,699	2,300	1,858	2,166	1,483	949
Seattle, Wash.	2,082	2,493	2,117	1,737	2,026	1,681	1,021
Washington, D.C.	661	393	292	597	306	1,185	1,494

Cities	Detroit	El Paso	Houston	Indian-apolis	Kansas City	Los Angeles	Louisville
Birmingham, Ala.	641	1,152	567	433	579	1,802	331
Boston, Mass.	613	2,072	1,605	807	1,251	2,596	826
Buffalo, N. Y.	216	1,692	1,286	435	861	2,198	483
Chicago, Ill.	238	1,252	940	165	414	1,745	269
Cleveland, Ohio	90	1,525	1,114	263	700	2,049	311
Dallas, Tex.	999	572	225	763	451	1,240	726
Denver, Colo.	1,156	557	879	1,000	558	831	1,038
Detroit, Mich.	—	1,479	1,105	240	645	1,983	316
El Paso, Tex.	1,479	—	676	1,264	839	701	1,254
Houston, Tex.	1,105	676	—	865	644	1,374	803
Indianapolis, Ind.	240	1,264	865	—	453	1,809	107
Kansas City, Mo.	645	839	644	453	—	1,356	480
Los Angeles, Calif.	1,983	701	1,374	1,809	1,356	—	1,829
Louisville, Ky.	316	1,254	803	107	480	1,829	—
Memphis, Tenn.	623	976	484	384	369	1,603	320
Miami, Fla.	1,152	1,643	968	1,024	1,241	2,339	919
Minneapolis, Minn.	543	1,157	1,056	511	413	1,524	605
New Orleans, La.	939	983	318	712	680	1,673	623
New York, N. Y.	482	1,905	1,420	646	1,097	2,451	652
Omaha, Neb.	669	878	794	525	166	1,315	580
Philadelphia, Pa.	443	1,836	1,341	585	1,038	2,394	582
Phoenix, Ariz.	1,690	346	1,017	1,499	1,049	357	1,508
Pittsburgh, Pa.	205	1,590	1,137	330	781	2,136	344
St. Louis, Mo.	455	1,034	679	231	238	1,589	242
Salt Lake City, Utah	1,492	689	1,200	1,356	925	579	1,402
San Francisco, Calif.	2,091	995	1,645	1,949	1,506	347	1,986
Seattle, Wash.	1,938	1,376	1,891	1,872	1,506	959	1,943
Washington, D.C.	396	1,728	1,220	494	945	2,300	476

Source: National Geodetic Survey.

Air Distances Between U.S. Cities in Statute Miles

Cities	Memphis	Miami	Minne-apolis	New Orleans	New York	Omaha	Phila-delphia
Birmingham, Ala.	217	665	862	312	864	732	783
Boston, Mass.	1,137	1,255	1,123	1,359	188	1,282	271
Buffalo, N. Y.	803	1,181	731	1,086	292	883	279
Chicago, Ill.	482	1,188	355	833	713	432	666
Cleveland, Ohio	630	1,087	630	924	405	739	360
Dallas, Tex.	420	1,111	862	443	1,374	586	1,299
Denver, Colo.	879	1,726	700	1,082	1,631	488	1,579
Detroit, Mich.	623	1,152	543	939	482	669	443
El Paso, Tex.	976	1,643	1,157	983	1,905	878	1,836
Houston, Tex.	484	968	1,056	318	1,420	794	1,341
Indianapolis, Ind.	384	1,024	511	712	646	525	585
Kansas City, Mo.	369	1,241	413	680	1,097	166	1,038
Los Angeles, Calif.	1,603	2,339	1,524	1,673	2,451	1,315	2,394
Louisville, Ky.	320	919	605	623	652	580	582
Memphis, Tenn.	—	872	699	358	957	529	881
Miami, Fla.	872	—	1,511	669	1,092	1,397	1,019
Minneapolis, Minn.	699	1,511	—	1,051	1,018	290	985
New Orleans, La.	358	669	1,051	—	1,171	847	1,089
New York, N. Y.	957	1,092	1,018	1,171	—	1,144	83
Omaha, Neb.	529	1,397	290	847	1,144	—	1,094
Philadelphia, Pa.	881	1,019	985	1,089	83	1,094	—
Phoenix, Ariz.	1,263	1,982	1,280	1,316	2,145	1,036	2,083
Pittsburgh, Pa.	660	1,010	743	919	317	836	259
St. Louis, Mo.	240	1,061	466	598	875	354	811
Salt Lake City, Utah	1,250	2,089	987	1,434	1,972	833	1,925
San Francisco, Calif.	1,802	2,594	1,584	1,926	2,571	1,429	2,523
Seattle, Wash.	1,867	2,734	1,395	2,101	2,408	1,369	2,380
Washington, D.C.	765	923	934	966	205	1,014	123

Cities	Phoenix	Pitts-burgh	St. Louis	Salt Lake City	San Francisco	Seattle	Wash-ington
Birmingham, Ala.	1,456	608	400	1,466	2,013	2,082	661
Boston, Mass.	2,300	483	1,038	2,099	2,699	2,493	393
Buffalo, N. Y.	1,906	178	662	1,699	2,300	2,117	292
Chicago, Ill.	1,453	410	262	1,260	1,858	1,737	597
Cleveland, Ohio	1,749	115	492	1,568	2,166	2,026	306
Dallas, Tex.	887	1,070	547	999	1,483	1,681	1,185
Denver, Colo.	586	1,320	796	371	949	1,021	1,494
Detroit, Mich.	1,690	205	455	1,492	2,091	1,938	396
El Paso, Tex.	346	1,590	1,034	689	995	1,376	1,728
Houston, Tex.	1,017	1,137	679	1,200	1,645	1,891	1,220
Indianapolis, Ind.	1,499	330	231	1,356	1,949	1,872	494
Kansas City, Mo.	1,049	781	238	925	1,506	1,506	945
Los Angeles, Calif.	357	2,136	1,589	579	347	959	2,300
Louisville, Ky.	1,508	344	242	1,402	1,986	1,943	476
Memphis, Tenn.	1,263	660	240	1,250	1,802	1,867	765
Miami, Fla.	1,982	1,010	1,061	2,089	2,594	2,734	923
Minneapolis, Minn.	1,280	743	466	987	1,584	1,395	934
New Orleans, La.	1,316	919	598	1,434	1,926	2,101	966
New York, N. Y.	2,145	317	875	1,972	2,571	2,408	205
Omaha, Neb.	1,036	836	354	833	1,429	1,369	1,014
Philadelphia, Pa.	2,083	259	811	1,925	2,523	2,380	123
Phoenix, Ariz.	—	1,828	1,272	504	653	1,114	1,983
Pittsburgh, Pa.	1,828	—	559	1,668	2,264	2,138	192
St. Louis, Mo.	1,272	559	—	1,162	1,744	1,724	712
Salt Lake City, Utah	504	1,668	1,162	—	600	701	1,848
San Francisco, Calif.	653	2,264	1,744	600	—	678	2,442
Seattle, Wash.	1,114	2,138	1,724	701	678	—	2,329
Washington, D.C.	1,983	192	712	1,848	2,442	2,329	—

Source: National Geodetic Survey.

Air Distances Between World Cities in Statute Miles

Cities	Berlin	Buenos Aires	Cairo	Calcutta	Cape Town	Caracas	Chicago
Berlin	—	7,402	1,795	4,368	5,981	5,247	4,405
Buenos Aires	7,402	—	7,345	10,265	4,269	3,168	5,598
Cairo	1,795	7,345	—	3,539	4,500	6,338	6,129
Calcutta	4,368	10,265	3,539	—	6,024	9,605	7,980
Cape Town, South Africa	5,981	4,269	4,500	6,024	—	6,365	8,494
Caracas, Venezuela	5,247	3,168	6,338	9,605	6,365	—	2,501
Chicago	4,405	5,598	6,129	7,980	8,494	2,501	—
Hong Kong	5,440	11,472	5,061	1,648	7,375	10,167	7,793
Honolulu, Hawaii	7,309	7,561	8,838	7,047	11,534	6,013	4,250
Istanbul	1,078	7,611	768	3,638	5,154	6,048	5,477
Lisbon	1,436	5,956	2,363	5,638	5,325	4,041	3,990
London	579	6,916	2,181	4,947	6,012	4,660	3,950
Los Angeles	5,724	6,170	7,520	8,090	9,992	3,632	1,745
Manila	6,132	11,051	5,704	2,203	7,486	10,620	8,143
Mexico City	6,047	4,592	7,688	9,492	8,517	2,232	1,691
Montreal	3,729	5,615	5,414	7,607	7,931	2,449	744
Moscow	1,004	8,376	1,803	3,321	6,300	6,173	4,974
New York	3,965	5,297	5,602	7,918	7,764	2,132	713
Paris	545	6,870	1,995	4,883	5,807	4,736	4,134
Rio de Janeiro	6,220	1,200	6,146	9,377	3,773	2,810	5,296
Rome	734	6,929	1,320	4,482	5,249	5,196	4,808
San Francisco	5,661	6,467	7,364	7,814	10,247	3,904	1,858
Shanghai, China	5,218	12,201	5,183	2,117	8,061	9,501	7,061
Stockholm	504	7,808	2,111	4,195	6,444	5,420	4,278
Sydney, Australia	10,006	7,330	8,952	5,685	6,843	9,513	9,272
Tokyo	5,540	11,408	5,935	3,194	9,156	8,799	6,299
Warsaw	320	7,662	1,630	4,048	5,958	5,517	4,667
Washington, D.C.	4,169	5,218	5,800	8,084	7,901	2,059	597

Cities	Hong Kong	Honolulu	Istanbul	Lisbon	London	Los Angeles	Manila
Berlin	5,440	7,309	1,078	1,436	579	5,724	6,132
Buenos Aires	11,472	7,561	7,611	5,956	6,916	6,170	11,051
Cairo	5,061	8,838	768	2,363	2,181	7,520	5,704
Calcutta	1,648	7,047	3,638	5,638	4,947	8,090	2,203
Cape Town, South Africa	7,375	11,534	5,154	5,325	6,012	9,992	7,486
Caracas, Venezuela	10,167	6,013	6,048	4,041	4,660	3,632	10,620
Chicago	7,793	4,250	5,477	3,990	3,950	1,745	8,143
Hong Kong	—	5,549	4,984	6,853	5,982	7,195	693
Honolulu, Hawaii	5,549	—	8,109	7,820	7,228	2,574	5,299
Istanbul	4,984	8,109	—	2,012	1,552	6,783	5,664
Lisbon	6,853	7,820	2,012	—	985	5,621	7,546
London	5,982	7,228	1,552	985	—	5,382	6,672
Los Angeles, Calif.	7,195	2,574	6,783	5,621	5,382	—	7,261
Manila	693	5,299	5,664	7,546	6,672	7,261	—
Mexico City	8,782	3,779	7,110	5,390	5,550	1,589	8,835
Montreal	7,729	4,910	4,789	3,246	3,282	2,427	8,186
Moscow	4,439	7,037	1,091	2,427	1,555	6,003	5,131
New York	8,054	4,964	4,975	3,364	3,458	2,451	8,498
Paris	5,985	7,438	1,400	904	213	5,588	6,677
Rio de Janeiro	11,021	8,285	6,389	4,796	5,766	6,331	11,259
Rome	5,768	8,022	843	1,161	887	6,732	6,457
San Francisco	6,897	2,393	6,703	5,666	5,357	347	6,967
Shanghai, China	764	4,941	4,962	6,654	5,715	6,438	1,150
Stockholm	5,113	6,862	1,348	1,856	890	5,454	5,797
Sydney, Australia	4,584	4,943	9,294	11,302	10,564	7,530	3,944
Tokyo	1,794	3,853	5,560	6,915	5,940	5,433	1,866
Warsaw	5,144	7,355	863	1,715	899	5,922	5,837
Washington, D.C.	8,147	4,519	5,215	3,562	3,663	2,300	8,562

Source: *Encyclopaedia Britannica.*

Air Distances Between World Cities in Statute Miles

Cities	Mexico City	Montreal	Moscow	New York	Paris	Rio de Janeiro	Rome
Berlin	6,047	3,729	1,004	3,965	545	6,220	734
Buenos Aires	4,592	5,615	8,376	5,297	6,870	1,200	6,929
Cairo	7,688	5,414	1,803	5,602	1,995	6,146	1,320
Calcutta	9,492	7,607	3,321	7,918	4,883	9,377	4,482
Cape Town, South Africa	8,517	7,931	6,300	7,764	5,807	3,773	5,249
Caracas, Venezuela	2,232	2,449	6,173	2,132	4,736	2,810	5,196
Chicago	1,691	744	4,974	713	4,134	5,296	4,808
Hong Kong	8,782	7,729	4,439	8,054	5,985	11,021	5,768
Honolulu	3,779	4,910	7,037	4,964	7,438	8,285	8,022
Istanbul	7,110	4,789	1,091	4,975	1,400	6,389	843
Lisbon	5,390	3,246	2,427	3,364	904	4,796	1,161
London	5,550	3,282	1,555	3,458	213	5,766	887
Los Angeles	1,589	2,427	6,003	2,451	5,588	6,331	6,732
Manila	8,835	8,186	5,131	8,498	6,677	11,259	6,457
Mexico City	—	2,318	6,663	2,094	5,716	4,771	6,366
Montreal	2,318	—	4,386	320	3,422	5,097	4,080
Moscow	6,663	4,386	—	4,665	1,544	7,175	1,474
New York	2,094	320	4,665	—	3,624	4,817	4,281
Paris	5,716	3,422	1,544	3,624	—	5,699	697
Rio de Janeiro	4,771	5,097	7,175	4,817	5,699	—	5,684
Rome	6,366	4,080	1,474	4,281	697	5,684	—
San Francisco	1,887	2,539	5,871	2,571	5,558	6,621	6,240
Shanghai, China	8,022	7,053	4,235	7,371	5,754	11,336	5,677
Stockholm	5,959	3,667	762	3,924	958	6,651	1,234
Sydney, Australia	8,052	9,954	9,012	9,933	10,544	8,306	10,136
Tokyo	7,021	6,383	4,647	6,740	6,034	11,533	6,135
Warsaw	6,365	4,009	715	4,344	849	6,467	817
Washington, D.C.	1,887	488	4,858	205	3,829	4,796	4,434

Cities	San Francisco	Shanghai	Stockholm	Sydney	Tokyo	Warsaw	Washington
Berlin	5,661	5,218	504	10,006	5,540	320	4,169
Buenos Aires	6,467	12,201	7,808	7,330	11,408	7,662	5,218
Cairo	7,364	5,183	2,111	8,952	5,935	1,630	5,800
Calcutta	7,814	2,117	4,195	5,685	3,194	4,048	8,084
Cape Town, South Africa	10,247	8,061	6,444	6,843	9,156	5,958	7,901
Caracas, Venezuela	3,904	9,501	5,420	9,513	8,799	5,517	2,059
Chicago	1,858	7,061	4,278	9,272	6,299	4,667	597
Hong Kong	6,897	764	5,113	4,584	1,794	5,144	8,147
Honolulu	2,393	4,941	6,862	4,943	3,853	7,355	4,519
Istanbul	6,703	4,962	1,348	9,294	5,560	863	5,215
Lisbon	5,666	6,654	1,856	11,302	6,915	1,715	3,562
London	5,357	5,715	890	10,564	5,940	899	3,663
Los Angeles	347	6,438	5,454	7,530	5,433	5,922	2,300
Manila	6,967	1,150	5,797	3,944	1,866	5,837	8,562
Mexico City	1,887	8,022	5,959	8,052	7,021	6,365	1,887
Montreal	2,539	7,053	3,667	9,954	6,383	4,009	488
Moscow	5,871	4,235	762	9,012	4,647	715	4,858
New York	2,571	7,371	3,924	9,933	6,740	4,344	205
Paris	5,558	5,754	958	10,544	6,034	849	3,829
Rio de Janeiro	6,621	11,336	6,651	8,306	11,533	6,467	4,796
Rome	6,240	5,677	1,234	10,136	6,135	817	4,434
San Francisco	—	6,140	5,361	7,416	5,135	5,841	2,442
Shanghai, China	6,140	—	4,825	4,899	1,097	4,951	7,448
Stockholm	5,361	4,825	—	9,696	5,051	501	4,123
Sydney, Australia	7,416	4,899	9,696	—	4,866	9,696	9,758
Tokyo	5,135	1,097	5,051	4,866	—	5,249	6,772
Warsaw	5,841	4,951	501	9,696	5,249	—	4,457
Washington, D.C.	2,442	7,448	4,123	9,758	6,772	4,457	—

Source: Encyclopedia Britannica.

STRUCTURES

The Seven Wonders of the World

(Not all classical writers list the same items as the Seven Wonders, but most of them agree on the following.)

The Pyramids of Egypt. A group of three pyramids, *Khufu, Khafra,* and *Menkaura* at Giza, outside modern Cairo, is often called the first wonder of the world. The largest pyramid, built by Khufu (Cheops), a king of the fourth Dynasty, had an original estimated height of 482 ft (now approximately 450 ft). The base has sides 755 ft long. It contains 2,300,000 blocks; the average weight of each is 2.5 tons. Estimated date of construction is 2800 B.C. Of all the Seven Wonders, the pyramids alone survive.

Hanging Gardens of Babylon. Often listed as the second wonder, these gardens were supposedly built by Nebuchadnezzar about 600 B.C. to please his queen, Amuhia. They are also associated with the mythical Assyrian Queen, Semiramis. Archeologists surmise that the gardens were laid out atop a vaulted building, with provisions for raising water. The terraces were said to rise from 75 to 300 ft.

The Walls of Babylon, also built by Nebuchadnezzar, are sometimes referred to as the second (or the seventh) wonder instead of the Hanging Gardens.

Statue of Zeus (Jupiter) at Olympia. The work of Phidias (5th century B.C.), this colossal figure in gold and ivory was reputedly 40 ft high. All trace of it is lost, except for reproductions on coins.

Temple of Artemis (Diana) at Ephesus. A beautiful structure, begun about 350 B.C. in honor of a non-Hellenic goddess who later became identified with the Greek goddess of the same name. The temple, with Ionic columns 60 ft high, was destroyed by invading Goths in A.D. 262.

Mausoleum at Halicarnassus. This famous monument was erected by Queen Artemisia in memory of her husband, King Mausolus of Caria in Asia Minor, who died in 353 B.C. Some remains of the structure are in the British Museum. This shrine is the source of the modern word "mausoleum."

Colossus at Rhodes. This bronze statue of Helios (Apollo), about 105 ft high, was the work of the sculptor Chares, who reputedly labored for 12 years before completing it in 280 B.C. It was destroyed during an earthquake in 224 B.C.

Pharos of Alexandria. The seventh wonder was the Pharos (lighthouse) of Alexandria, built by Sostratus of Cnidus during the 3rd century B.C. on the island of Pharos off the coast of Egypt. It was destroyed by an earthquake in the 13th century.

Famous Structures

Ancient

The *Great Sphinx of Egypt,* one of the wonders of ancient Egyptian architecture, adjoins the pyramids of Giza and has a length of 240 ft. It was built in the 4th dynasty.

Other Egyptian buildings of note include the *Temples of Karnak* and *Edfu* and the *Tombs at Beni Hassan.*

The *Parthenon of Greece,* built on the Acropolis in Athens, was the chief temple to the goddess Athena. It was believed to have been completed by 438 B.C. The present temple remained intact until the 5th century A.D. Today, though the Parthenon is in ruins, its majestic proportions are still discernible.

Other great structures of ancient Greece were the *Temples at Paestum* (about 540 and 420 B.C.); the *Temple of Poseidon* (about 460 B.C.); the *Temple of Apollo* at Corinth (about 540 B.C.); the *Temple of Apollo* at Bassae (about 450–420 B.C.); the famous *Erechtheum* atop the Acropolis (about 421–405 B.C.); the *Temple of Athena Niké* at Athens (about 426 B.C.); the *Olympieum* at Athens (174 B.C.–A.D. 131); the *Athenian Treasury* at Delphi (about 515 B.C.); the *Propylaea* of the Acropolis at Athens (437–432 B.C.); the *Theater of Dionysus* at Athens (about 350–325 B.C.); the *House of Cleopatra* at Delos (138 B.C.) and the *Theater* at Epidaurus (about 325 B.C.).

The *Colosseum (Flavian Amphitheater) of Rome,* the largest and most famous of the Roman amphitheaters, was opened for use A.D. 80. Elliptical in shape, it consisted of three stories and an upper gallery, rebuilt in stone in its present form in the third century A.D. Its seats rise in tiers, which in turn are buttressed by concrete vaults and stone piers. It could seat between 40,000 and 50,000 spectators. It was principally used for gladiatorial combat.

The *Pantheon* at Rome, begun by Agrippa in 27 B.C. as a temple, was rebuilt in its present circular form by Hadrian (A.D. 110–25). Literally the Pantheon was intended as a temple of "all the gods." It is remarkable for its perfect preservation today, and it has served continuously for 20 centuries as a place of worship.

Famous Roman arches include the *Arch of Constantine* (about A.D. 315) and the *Arch of Titus* (about A.D. 80).

Later European

St. Mark's Cathedral in Venice (1063–67), one of the great examples of Byzantine architecture, was begun in the 9th century. Partly destroyed by fire in 976, it was later rebuilt as a Byzantine edifice.

Other famous Byzantine examples of architecture are *St. Sophia* in Istanbul (A.D. 532–37); *San Vitale* in Ravenna (542); *St. Paul's Outside the Walls,* Rome (5th century); the *Kremlin* baptism and marriage church, Moscow (begun in 1397); and *St. Lorenzo Outside the Walls*, Rome, begun in 588.

The *Cathedral Group* at Pisa (1067–1173), one of the most celebrated groups of structures built in Romanesque style, consists of the cathedral, the cathedral's baptistery, and the *Leaning Tower*. This trio forms a group by itself in the northwest corner of the city. The cathedral and baptistery are built in varicolored marble. The campanile *(Leaning Tower)* is 179 ft. high and leans more than 16 ft out of the perpendicular. There is little reason to believe that the architects intended to have the tower lean.

Other examples of Romanesque architecture include the *Vézelay Abbey* in France (1130); the *Church of Notre-Dame-du-Port* at Clermont-Ferrand in France (1100); the *Church of San Zeno* (begun in 1138) at Verona, and *Durham Cathedral* in England.

The *Alhambra* (1248–1354), located in Granada, Spain, is universally esteemed as one of the greatest masterpieces of Moslem architecture. Designed as a palace and fortress for the Moorish monarchs of Granada, it is surrounded by a heavily fortified wall more than a mile in perimeter. The location of the Alhambra in the Sierra Nevada provides a magnificent setting for this jewel of Moorish Spain.

The *Tower of London* is a group of buildings and towers covering 13 acres along the north bank of the Thames. The central *White Tower*, begun in 1078 during the reign of William the Conqueror, was originally a fortress and royal residence, but was later used as a prison. The *Bloody Tower* is associated with Anne Boleyn and other notables.

Westminster Abbey, in London, was begun in 1045 and completed in 1065. It was rebuilt and enlarged in 1245–50.

Notre-Dame de Paris (begun in 1163), one of the great examples of Gothic architecture, is a twin-towered church with a steeple over the crossing and immense flying buttresses supporting the masonry at the rear of the church.

Other famous Gothic structures are *Chartres Cathedral* (12th century); *Sainte Chapelle*, Paris (1246–48); *Laon Cathedral*, France (1160–1205); *Reims Cathedral* (about 1210–50; rebuilt after its almost complete destruction in World War I); *Rouen Cathedral* (13th–16th centuries); *Amiens Cathedral* (1218–69); *Beauvais Cathedral* (begun 1247); *Salisbury Cathedral* (1220–60); *York Minster* or the *Cathedral of St. Peter* (begun in the 7th century); *Milan Cathedral* (begun 1386); and *Cologne Cathedral* (13th–19th centuries; badly damaged in World War II.

The Duomo (cathedral) in Florence was founded in 1298, completed by Brunelleschi and consecrated in 1436. The oval-shaped dome dominates the entire structure.

The *Vatican* is a group of buildings in Rome comprising the official residence of the Pope. The *Basilica of St. Peter*, the largest church in the Christian world, was begun in 1450. The *Sistine Chapel*, begun in 1473, is noted for the art masterpieces of Michelangelo, Botticelli, and others. The *Basilica of the Savior* (known as *St. John Lateran*) is the first-ranking Catholic Church in the world, for it is the cathedral of the Pope.

Other examples of Renaissance architecture are the *Palazzo Riccardi*, the *Palazzo Pitti* and the *Palazzo Strozzi* in Florence; the *Farnese Palace* in Rome; *Palazzo Grimani* (completed about 1550) in Venice; the *Escorial* (1563–93) near Madrid; the *Town Hall* of Seville (1527–32); the *Louvre*, Paris;

the *Château* at Blois, France; *St. Paul's Cathedral*, London (1675–1710; badly damaged in World War II); the *École Militaire*, Paris (1752); the *Pazzi Chapel*, Florence, designed by Brunelleschi (1429); the Palace of *Fontainebleau* and the *Château de Chambord* in France.

The *Palace of Versailles*, containing the famous Hall of Mirrors, was built during the reign of Louis XIV and served as the royal palace until 1793.

Outstanding European buildings of the 18th and 19th centuries are the *Superga* at Turin, the *Hôtel-Dieu* in Lyons, the *Belvedere Palace* at Vienna, the *Royal Palace* of Stockholm, the *Opera House* of Paris (1863–75); the *Bank of England*, the *British Museum*, the *University of London*, and the *Houses of Parliament*, all in London; the *Panthéon*, the *Church of the Madeleine*, the *Bourse*, and the *Palais de Justice* in Paris.

The *Eiffel Tower*, in Paris, was built for the Exposition of 1889 by Alexandre Eiffel. It is 984 ft high.[1]

1. 1,056 ft, including the television tower.

Asiatic and African

The *Taj Mahal* (1632–50), at Agra, India, built by Shah Jahan as a tomb for his wife, is considered by some as the most perfect example of the Mogul style and by others as the most beautiful building in the world. Four slim white minarets flank the building, which is topped by a white dome; the entire structure is of marble.

Other examples of Indian architecture are temples at Benares and Tanjore.

Among famed Moslem edifices are the *Dome of the Rock* or *Mosque of Omar*, Jerusalem (A.D. 691); the *Citadel* (1166), and the *Tombs of the Mamelukes* (15th century), in Cairo; the *Tomb of Humayun* in Delhi; the *Blue Mosque* (1468) at Tabriz, and the *Tamerlane Mausoleum* at Samarkand.

Angkor Wat, outside the city of Angkor Thom, Cambodia, is one of the most beautiful examples of Cambodian or Khmer architecture. The sanctuary was built during the 12th century.

Great Wall of China (228 B.C.?), designed specifically as a defense against nomadic tribes, has numerous large watch towers which could be called buildings. It was erected by Emperor Ch'in Shih Huang Ti and is 1,400 miles long. Built mainly of earth and stone, it varies in height between 18 and 30 ft.

Typical of Chinese architecture are the pagodas or temple towers. Among some of the better-known pagodas are the *Great Pagoda of the Wild Geese* at Sian (founded in 652); *Nan t'a* (11th century) at Fang Shan; the *Pagoda of Sung Yueh Ssu* (A.D. 523) at Sung Shan, Honan.

Other well-known Chinese buildings are the *Drum Tower* (1273), the *Three Great Halls* in the Purple Forbidden City (1627), *Buddha's Perfume Tower* (19th century), the *Porcelain Pagoda*, and the *Summer Palace*, all at Peking.

United States

Rockefeller Center, in New York City, extends from 5th Ave. to the Avenue of the Americas between 48th and 52nd Sts. (and halfway to 7th Ave. between 47th and 51st Sts.). It occupies more than 22 acres and has 19 buildings.

The Cathedral of St. John the Divine, at 112th St. and Amsterdam Ave. in New York City, was begun in 1892 and is now in the final stages of completion. When completed, it will be the largest cathedral in the world: 601 ft long, 146 ft wide at the nave, 320 ft wide at the transept. The east end is designed in

Romanesque-Byzantine style, and the nave and west end are Gothic.

St. Patrick's Cathedral, at Fifth Ave. and 50th St. in New York City, has a seating capacity of 2,500. The nave was opened in 1877, and the cathedral was dedicated in 1879.

Louisiana Superdome, in New Orleans, is the largest arena in the history of mankind. The main area can accommodate up to 95,000 people. It is the world's largest steel-constructed room. Unobstructed by posts, it covers 13 ac. and reaches 27 stories at its peak.

World Trade Center, in New York City, was dedicated in 1973. Its twin towers are 110 stories high (1,350 ft), and the complex contains over 9 million sq ft of office space. A restaurant is on the 107th floor of the No. Tower.

World's Highest Dams

Name	River	Maximum height feet	Maximum height meters	Reservoir capacity in acre-feet	Reservoir capacity in millions of cubic meters	Year completed
Rogunsky	Vakhsh, U.S.S.R.	1,066	325	9,485,000	11,700	UC
Nurek	Vakhsh, U.S.S.R.	1,040	317	8,424,000	10,400	UC
Grand Dixence	Dixence, Switzerland	935	285	325,000	401	1962
Inguri	Inguri, U.S.S.R.	892	272	801,000	1,100	UC
Vaiont	Vaiont, Italy	869	265	137,000	169	1961
Chicoasen	Grijalva, Mexico	869	265	1,346,000	1,660	UC
Mica	Columbia, Canada	794	242	20,000,000	24,670	1974
Sayanskaya	Yenesei, U.S.S.R.	794	242	25,353,000	31,300	UC
Chivor	Bata, Colombia	778	237	661,000	815	1975
Mauvoisin	Drance de Bagnes, Switzerland	777	237	148,000	182	1957
Oroville	Feather, California	770	235	3,538,000	4,299	1968
Chirkey	Sulak, U.S.S.R.	764	233	2,252,000	2,780	1975
Bhakra	Sutlej, India	742	226	8,000,000	9,868	1963
Hoover	Colorado, Arizona-Nevada	726	221	29,755,000	36,703	1936
Contra	Verzasca, Switzerland	722	220	86,000	106	1965
Piva (Mratinje)	Piva, Yugoslavia	722	220	713,000	880	1975
Dworshak	North Fork, Clearwater, Idaho	717	219	3,453,000	4,259	1974
Glen Canyon	Colorado, Arizona	710	216	27,000,000	33,305	1964
Daniel Johnson	Manicougan, Canada	703	214	115,000,000	141,852	1968
Toktogul	Naryn, U.S.S.R.	699	213	15,800,000	19,500	1978
Auburn	North Fork, California	685	209	2,300,000	2,837	UC
Luzzone	Brenno di Luzzone, Switzerland	682	208	71,000	88	1963
Keban	Firat, Turkey	679	207	25,110,000	31,000	1974
Dez	Dez, Iran	666	203	2,707,000	3,340	1963
Almendra	Turmes-Douro, Spain	662	202	2,148,000	2,649	1970
Karoun	Karoun, Iran	656	200	2,351,000	2,900	1975
Koelnbrein	Malta, Austria	656	200	162,000	200	1977
New Bullard's Bar	North Yuba, California	637	194	960,000	1,184	1970
New Melones	Stanislaus, California	625	191	2,400,000	2,960	1975
Kurobe No. 4	Kurobe, Japan	610	186	162,000	199	1964
Swift	Lewis, Washington	610	186	756,000	932	1958
Mossyrock	Cowlitz, Washington	605	184	1,300,000	1,603	1968
Shasta	Sacramento, California	602	183	4,552,000	5,615	1945
W.A.C. Bennett	Peace, Canada	600	183	57,006,000	70,309	1967
Tignes	Isere, France	591	180	186,000	230	1952
Amir Kabir (Karad)	Karadj, Iran	591	180	166,000	205	1962
Tachien (Techi)	Tachia, Taiwan	591	180	207,000	255	1974
Dartmouth	Mitta-Mitta, Australia	591	180	3,232,000	4,000	1978
Emosson	Barberine, Switzerland	590	180	184,000	227	1974
Don Pedro	Tuolume, California	585	178	2,030,000	2,504	1971
Alpa-Gera	Cormor, Italy	584	178	53,000	65	1965
Kopperston Tailings No. 3	Jones Branch, West Virginia	580	177	—	—	1963
Hungry Horse	South Fork, Flathead, Montana	564	172	3,468,000	4,278	1953
Idikki	Periyar, India	561	171	1,182,000	1,460	1974
Cabora Bassa	Zambezi, Mozambique	561	171	51,900,000	64,000	1974
Charvak	Chirchik, U.S.S.R.	551	168	1,620,000	2,000	1970
Grand Coulee	Columbia, Washington	550	168	9,724,000	11,795	1942
Vidraru	Arges-Danube, Romania	547	167	380,000	465	1966
Kremasta (King Paul)	Acheloos, Greece	541	165	3,850,000	4,750	1965
Ross	Skagit, Washington	540	165	1,435,000	1,770	1949
Trinity	Trinity, California	537	164	2,448,000	3,020	1962
Talbingo	Tumut, Australia	530	162	747,000	921	1971
Yellowtail	Bighorn, Montana	525	160	1,375,000	1,696	1966

Name	River	Maximum height feet	Maximum height meters	Reservoir capacity in acre-feet	Reservoir capacity in millions of cubic meters	Year completed
Gokcekaya	Sakarya, Turkey	525	160	737,000	910	1973
Cougar	South Fork, McKenzie, Oregon	519	158	219,000	270	1964
Curnera	Rein de Curnera, Switzerland	518	158	33,000	41	1966
Okutadami	Tadami, Japan	515	157	487,000	601	1961
Speccheri	Leno di Vallarsa, Italy	514	157	8,000	10	1957
Zeuzier	Lienne, Switzerland	512	156	41,000	51	1957
Sakuma	Tenryu, Japan	510	156	265,000	327	1956
Monteynard	Drac, France	509	155	195,000	240	1962
Nagawado	Azusa, Japan	509	155	99,000	123	1969
Göscheneralp	Göschenerreuss, Switzerland	508	155	62,000	76	1960
Bhumiphol (Yanhee)	Ping-Chao Phaya, Thailand	505	154	10,914,000	13,462	1964
Flaming Gorge	Green, Utah	502	153	3,789,000	4,674	1964
Place Moulin	Buthier, Italy	502	153	81,000	100	1965
Gepatsch	Faggenbach, Austria	500	153	113,000	139	1965
Santa Giustina	Noce-Adige, Italy	500	153	148,000	183	1950
Zervreila	Valserrhein, Switzerland	495	151	81,000	100	1957
Roselend	Doron-de-Beaufort, France	492	150	152,000	187	1961
Canelles	Noguera, Spain	492	150	549,000	678	1960

NOTE: UC = under construction in 1980. *Source:* Department of the Interior, Water and Power Resources Service.

World's Largest Hydroelectric Plants

Name of dam	Location	Rated capacity (Mw) Present	Rated capacity (Mw) Ultimate	Year of initial operation
Itaipu	Brazil–Paraguay	—	12,870	UC
Raul Leoni	Venezuela	2,100	10,100	1968
Grand Coulee	Washington	6,263[1]	10,080	1941
Guri	Venezuela	524	7,300	1967
Sayanskaya	U.S.S.R.	—	6,400	UC
Krasnoyarsk	U.S.S.R.	6,096	6,096	1968
La Grande 2	Canada	—	5,328	UC
Churchill Falls	Canada	5,225	5,225	1971
Bratsk	U.S.S.R.	4,100	4,600	1964
Sukhovo	U.S.S.R.	—	4,500	UC
Ust-Ipimsk	U.S.S.R.	720	4,320	1974
Cabora Bassa	Mozambique	2,425	4,150	1975
Paulo Afonso	Brazil	1,524	3,409	1955
Inga 1	Zaire	360	2,820	1974
John Day	Oregon–Washington	2,160	2,700	1968
Solteira	Brazil	2,650	2,650	1973
Volgograd—22nd Congress	U.S.S.R.	2,560	2,560	1958
Volga—V.I. Lenin (Kuibisher)	U.S.S.R.	2,300	2,300	1955
Iron Gates 1	Romania–Yugoslavia	2,300	2,300	1970
W.A.C. Bennett	Canada	2,116	2,270	1969
High Aswan (Sadd-el-Aali)	Egypt	2,100	2,100	1967
Tarbela	Pakistan	700	2,100	1977
Chief Joseph	Washington	1,879	2,069	1956
Robert Moses-Niagara	New York	1,950	1,950	1961
Salto Grande	Argentina—Uruguay	135	1,890	1979
Ludington	Michigan	1,872	1,872	1973
St. Lawrence Power Dam	United States—Canada	1,824	1,824	1958
The Dalles	Washington	1,807	1,807	1957
Kemano	Canada	813	1,670	1954
Beauharnois	Canada	1,021	1,574	1950
Kariba	Zimbabwe–Zambia	1,266	1,566	1959
Raccoon Mountain	Tennessee	1,530	1,530	1975
Tumut 3	Australia	1,500	1,500	1972
Jupia	Brazil	1,411	1,411	1966
McNary	Oregon	980	1,406	1953

1. Present dam being enlarged. NOTE: UC = under construction in 1980. *Source:* Department of the Interior, Water and Power Resources Service.

United States Tallest Buildings

City	Building	Stories	Height ft	Height m	City	Building	Stories	Height ft	Height m
Chicago	Sears Tower	110	1,454	443	Boston	John Hancock Tower	60	790	241
New York	World Trade Center	110	1,377	419	San Francisco	Bank of America	52	779	237
New York	Empire State	102	1,250	381	Minneapolis	IDS Tower	57	775	236
Chicago	Standard Oil (Indiana)	80	1,136	346	New York	One Liberty Plaza	54	775	236
Chicago	John Hancock Center	100	1,127	343	New York	One Penn Plaza	57	774	236
New York	Chrysler	77	1,046	319	Atlanta	Peachtree Plaza	73	754	230
New York	American International	66	952	290	New York	Exxon	54	750	229
New York	Citicorp Center	59	915	279	Boston	Prudential Tower	52	750	229
New York	40 Wall Tower	71	900	274	Detroit	Detroit Plaza Hotel	73	747	228
Chicago	Water Tower Place	74	859	262	Los Angeles	Security Pacific Plaza	55	743	226
Los Angeles	United California Bank	62	858	261	New York	One Astor Plaza	54	730	222
San Francisco	Transamerica Pyramid	61	853	260	New York	Marine Midland	52	724	221
Chicago	First National Bank	60	851	259	Houston	One Shell Plaza	50	714	218
New York	RCA	70	850	259	Dallas	First International	56	710	216
Pittsburgh	U.S. Steel Headquarters	64	841	256	Cleveland	Terminal Tower	52	708	216
New York	Chase Manhattan	60	813	248	New York	Union Carbide	52	707	215
New York	Pan Am	59	808	246	New York	General Motors	50	705	215
New York	Woolworth	55	792	241	New York	Metropolitan Life	50	700	213

NOTE: Does not include buildings under construction and not completed in 1981. Height does not include TV towers and antennas. *Source: Information Please* questionnaires to buildings.

Notable Tunnels

Railroad, excluding subways

Name	Location	Length mi.	Length km	Year completed
Seikan	Tsugara Strait, Japan	33.1	53.3	UC
Simplon (I and II)	Alps, Switzerland-Italy	12.3	19.8	1906 & 1922
Kammon Straits	Honshu to Kyoshu Islands, Japan	11.6	18.7	UC
Apennine	Genoa, Italy	11.5	18.5	1934
St. Gotthard	Swiss Alps	9.3	14.9	1881
Lötschberg	Swiss Alps	9.1	14.6	1911
Nakayama	Komochi Mountain, Japan	8.8	14.2	UC
Mont Cénis	French Alps	8.5[1]	13.7	1871
New Cascade	Cascade Mountains, Washington	7.8	12.6	1929
Vosges	Vosges, France	7.0	11.3	1940
Arlberg	Austrian Alps	6.3	10.1	1884
Moffat	Rocky Mountains, Colorado	6.2	9.9	1928
Shimuzu	Shimuzu, Japan	6.1	9.8	1931
Rimutaka	Wairarapa, New Zealand	5.5	8.9	1955

Vehicular

Name	Location	Length mi.	Length km	Year completed
St. Gotthard	Alps, Switzerland	10.2	16.4	1980
Mt. Blanc	Alps, France-Italy	7.5	12.1	1965
Mt. Ena	Japan Alps, Japan	5.3	8.5	1976[2]
Great St. Bernard	Alps, Switzerland-Italy	3.4	5.5	1964
Mount Royal	Montreal, Canada	3.2	5.1	1918
Lincoln	Hudson River, New York-New Jersey	2.5	4.0	1937
Queensway Road	Mersey River, Liverpool, England	2.2	3.5	1934
Brooklyn-Battery	East River, New York City	2.1	3.4	1950
Holland	Hudson River, New York-New Jersey	1.7	2.7	1927
Hampton Roads	Norfolk, Virginia	1.4	2.3	1957
Queens-Midtown	East River, New York City	1.3	2.1	1940
Liberty Tubes	Pittsburgh, Pennsylvania	1.2	1.9	1923
Baltimore Harbor	Baltimore, Maryland	1.2	1.9	1957
Allegheny Tunnels	Pennsylvania Turnpike	1.2	1.9	1940[3]

1. Lengthened to its present 8.5 miles in 1881. 2. Parallel tunnel begun in 1976. 3. Parallel tunnel built in 1965, twin tunnel in 1966. NOTE: UC = under construction. *Source:* American Society of Civil Engineers.

Notable Modern Bridges

Suspension

Name	Location	Length of main span, ft	m	Year completed
Humber	Hull, Britain	4,626	1,410	UC
Verrazano-Narrows	Lower New York Bay	4,260	1,298	1964
Golden Gate	San Francisco Bay	4,200	1,280	1937
Mackinac Straits	Michigan	3,800	1,158	1957
Bosporus	Istanbul	3,524	1,074	1973
George Washington	Hudson River at New York City	3,500	1,067	1931
Ponte 25 de Abril	Tagus River at Lisbon	3,323	1,013	1966
Forth Road	Queensferry, Scotland	3,300	1,006	1964
Severn	Severn River at Beachley, England	3,240	988	1966
Tacoma Narrows	Puget Sound at Tacoma, Wash.	2,800	853	1950
Kanmon Strait	Kyushu-Honshu, Japan	2,336	712	1973
Angostura	Orinoco River at Ciudad Bolívar, Venezuela	2,336	712	1967
Transbay (twin spans)	San Francisco Bay	2,310	704	1936
Bronx-Whitestone	East River, New York City	2,300	701	1939
Pierre Laporte	St. Lawrence River at Quebec, Canada	2,190	668	1970
Delaware Memorial (twin bridges)	Delaware River near Wilmington, Del.	2,150	655	1951, 1968
Seaway Skyway	St. Lawrence River at Ogdensburg, N.Y.	2,150	655	1960
Gas Pipe Line	Atchafalaya River, Louisiana	2,000	610	1951
Walt Whitman	Delaware River at Philadelphia	2,000	610	1957
Tancarville	Seine River at Tancarville, France	1,995	608	1959
Lillebaelt	Lillebaelt Strait, Denmark	1,969	600	1970
Ambassador International	Detroit River at Detroit	1,850	564	1929
Throgs Neck	East River, New York City	1,800	549	1961
Benjamin Franklin	Delaware River at Philadelphia	1,750	533	1926
Skjomen	Narvik, Norway	1,722	525	1972
Kvalsund	Hammerfest, Norway	1,722	525	1977
Kleve-Emmerich	Rhine River at Emmerich, West Germany	1,640	500	1965
Bear Mountain	Hudson River at Peekskill, N.Y.	1,632	497	1924
Wm. Preston Lane, Jr., Memorial (twin bridges)	Near Annapolis, Md.	1,600	488	1952, 1973
Williamsburg	East River, New York City	1,600	488	1903
Newport	Narragansett Bay at Newport, R.I.	1,600	488	1969
Brooklyn	East River, New York City	1,595	486	1883

Cantilever

Name	Location	ft	m	Year completed
Quebec Railway	St. Lawrence River at Quebec, Canada	1,800	549	1917
Forth Railway (twin spans)	Queensferry, Scotland	1,710	521	1890
Minato Ohashi	Osaka, Japan	1,673	510	1974
Commodore John Barry	Chester, Pa.	1,644	501	1974
Greater New Orleans	Mississippi River, Louisiana	1,576	480	1958
Howrah	Hooghly River at Calcutta	1,500	457	1943
Transbay Bridge	San Francisco Bay	1,400	427	1936
Baton Rouge	Mississippi River, Louisiana	1,235	376	1968
Tappan Zee	Hudson River at Tarrytown, N.Y.	1,212	369	1955
Longview	Columbia River at Longview, Wash.	1,200	366	1930
Patapsco River	Baltimore Outer Harbor Crossing	1,200	366	1976
Queensboro	East River, New York City	1,182	360	1909

Steel Arch

Name	Location	ft	m	Year completed
New River Gorge	Fayetteville, W. Va.	1,700	518	1977
Bayonne	Kill Van Kull at Bayonne, N.J.	1,675	510	1931
Sydney Harbor	Sydney, Australia	1,670	509	1932
Fremont	Portland, Ore.	1,255	383	1973
Zdákov	Vltava River, Czechoslovakia	1,244	380	1967
Port Mann	Fraser River at Vancouver, British Columbia	1,200	366	1964
Thatcher Ferry	Panama Canal, Panama	1,128	344	1962
Laviolette	St. Lawrence River, Trois Rivieres, Quebec	1,100	335	1967
Runcorn-Widnes	Mersey River, England	1,082	330	1961
Birchenough	Sabi River at Fort Victoria, Rhodesia	1,080	329	1935

Cable-Stayed

Name	Location	Length of main span, ft	m	Year completed
Second Hooghly	Calcutta	1,500	457	UC
St.-Nazaire	Loire River, St.-Nazaire, France	1,325	404	1975
Stretto di Rande	Spain	1,312	400	UC
Luling	Missipi River, Luling, La.	1,235	376	UC
Düsseldorf-Flehe	Rhine River, West Germany	1,205	367	UC
Yamatogawa	Osaka, Japan	1,165	355	UC
Duisburg-Neuenkamp	Duisburg, West Germany	1,148	350	1970
Mesopotamia	Corrientes, Argentina	1,116	340	1972
West Gate	Lower Yarra River at Melbourne, Australia	1,102	336	1970
Zárate	Paraná River, Argentina	1,083	330	1976
Brazo Largo	Paraná River, Argentina	1,083	330	1977
Köhlbrand	Hamburg, West Germany	1,066	325	1974
Kniebrücke	Rhine River at Düsseldorf, West Germany	1,050	320	1969
Brotonne[1]	Seine River, France	1,050	320	1976
Erskine	Clyde River at Glasgow, Scotland	1,000	305	1971

Continuous Truss

Name	Location	Length of main span, ft	m	Year completed
Astoria	Columbia River at Astoria, Oregon	1,232	376	1966
Oshima	Oshima Island, Japan	1,066	325	1976
Croton Reservoir	Croton, N.Y.	1,052	321	1970
Tenmon	Kumamoto, Japan	984	300	1966
Kuronoseto	Nagashima-Kyushu, Japan	984	300	1974
Ravenswood	Ohio River, Ravenswood, W. Va.	902	275	UC
Dubuque	Mississippi River at Dubuque, Iowa	845	258	1943
Braga Memorial	Taunton River at Somerset, Mass.	840	256	1966
Graf Spee	Germany	839	256	1936

Concrete Arch

Name	Location	Length of main span, ft	m	Year completed
KRK	Zagreb, Yugoslavia	1,280	390	1979
Gladesville	Parramatta River at Sydney, Australia	1,000	305	1964
Amizade	Paraná River at Foz do Iguassu, Brazil	951	290	1964
Arrábida	Porto, Portugal	886	270	1963
Sandö	Angerman River at Kramfors, Sweden	866	264	1943
Shibenik	Krka River, Yugoslavia	808	246	1966
Fiumarella	Catanzaro, Italy	758	231	1961
Zaporozhe	Old Dnepr River, U.S.S.R.	748	228	1952
Novi Sad	Danube River, Yugoslavia	692	211	1961

1. Concrete bridge. NOTE: UC = under construction. *Source: Encyclopaedia Britannica* and American Society of Civil Engineers.

Famous Ship Canals

Name	Location	Length (miles)[1]	Width (feet)	Depth (feet)	Locks	Year opened
Albert	Belgium	80.0	53.0	16.5	6	1939
Amsterdam–Rhine	Netherlands	45.0	164.0	41.0	3	1952
Beaumont–Port Arthur	United States	40.0	200.0	34.0	—	1916
Chesapeake and Delaware	United States	19.0	250.0	27.0	—	1927
Houston	United States	43.0	300.0	34.0	—	1914
Kiel (Nord-Ostsee Kanal)	Germany	61.3	144.0	36.0	4	1895
Panama	Canal Zone	50.7	110.0	41.0	12	1914
St. Lawrence Seaway	U.S. and Canada	2,400.0[2]	(3)	—	—	1959
Montreal to Prescott	U.S. and Canada	11.5	80.0	30.0	7	1959
Welland	Canada	27.5	80.0	27.0	8	1931
Sault Ste. Marie	Canada	1.2	60.0	16.8	1	1895
Sault Ste. Marie	United States	1.6	80.0	25.0	4	1915
Suez	Egypt	100.6[4]	197.0	36.0	—	1869

1. Statute miles. 2. From Montreal to Duluth. 3. 442–550 feet; there are 11.5 miles of locks, 80 feet wide and 30 feet deep. 4. From Port Said lighthouse to entrance channel in Suez roads. *Source:* American Society of Civil Engineers.

World's Largest Dams

Dam	Location	Volume (thousands)		Year completed
		Cubic meters	Cubic yards	
New Cornelia Tailings	Arizona	209,500	274,026	1973
Tarbela	Pakistan	121,000	158,268	1975
Fort Peck	Montana	96,034	125,612	1940
Raúl Leoni	Venezuela	78,000	102,014	(1)
Ataturk	Turkey	73,700	96,400	UC
Guri	Venezuela	70,762	92,557	UC
Oahe	South Dakota	70,343	92,008	1963
Oosterschelde	Netherlands	70,000	91,560	UC
Yacyreta-Apipe	Argentina–Paraguay	70,000	91,560	UC
Mangla	Pakistan	65,651	85,872	1967
Gardiner	Canada	65,440	85,596	1968
Afsluitdijk	Netherlands	63,400	82,927	1932
Oroville	California	59,639	78,008	1968
San Luis	California	59,378	77,666	1967
Nurek	U.S.S.R.	58,000	75,864	UC
Garrison	North Dakota	50,846	66,506	1956
Cochiti	New Mexico	49,417	64,631	1975
Tabka	Syria	46,000	60,168	1975
Kiev	U.S.S.R.	44,000	57,552	1964
W.A.C. Bennett	Canada	43,733	57,203	1967
High Aswan (Sadd-el-Aali)	Egypt	43,733	57,203	1970
Dantiwada Left Earthen Bank	India	41,040	53,680	1965
Saratov	U.S.S.R.	40,400	52,843	1967
Mission Tailings #2	Arizona	40,088	52,435	1973
Fort Randall	South Dakota	38,383	50,205	1956
Kanev	U.S.S.R.	37,860	49,520	1974
Kakhova	U.S.S.R.	35,640	46,617	1955
Tsimlyanska	U.S.S.R.	33,891	44,323	1952

1. Present dam being enlarged. NOTE: Based on total volume of dam structure. All dams listed are predominantly earth or rockfill and may contain masonry sections. UC = under construction in 1980. *Source:* Department of the Interior, Water and Power Resources Service.

Space Telescope Eagerly Awaited

There is a heavy anticipated demand for use of the Space Telescope, when the U.S. Space Shuttle brings the 10-ton satellite into a 500-kilometer (310.5-mile) high orbit in late 1983. The 2.4-meter (7-ft-10½-in.) Space Telescope is designed to last past the end of this century and is to be serviced about every two and a half years by Space Shuttle astronauts. It will be taken back to earth occasionally for overhaul and relaunching during its 20-year lifetime.

Energy-Saving Tips for Home Buyers

If you are considering buying a house, the U.S. government has published a booklet that can help you determine how energy efficient it is. The 60-page "The Energy-Wise Home Buyer," published by the Department of Housing and Urban Development, in cooperation with the Department of Energy, is available for $2 from the Superintendent of Documents, U.S. Government Printing Office, Department 32, Washington, D.C. 20402.

Tips on Buying Wood for Home Heating

Wood is usually sold by the cord or fraction thereof. There is a standard cord, face cord, short cord, long cord, a solid cord, and maybe others.

The standard cord should be specified when you order wood. It is a pile of wood measuring four feet high, eight feet wide, and four feet long. A face cord measures four feet high by eight feet wide but the pieces may be any length. So a face cord of stove-length (16 in.) wood would be only one third of a standard cord. The term "short cord" is another way of saying "face cord."

When buying cord, be sure that the pile you measure is tightly stacked with all the wood pieces lying in the same direction. Otherwise, you will pay for the air space instead of wood. Even piled carefully, a cord has only 80 cubic feet of solid wood in it, although its dimensions measure 128 cubic feet.

Pound for pound, most species of wood produce about the same amount of heat if the wood is dry. Some species of wood are lighter than others, so a cord of wood such as aspen will weigh about half as much as a cord of dry white oak and will therefore have about half the heat value.

Ask the seller how long the wood was "air-dried" and whether it was cut to length and split before drying. If the answers are "at least nine months" and "yes," respectively, you can assume that you'll get fair heat value for the weight.

UNITED NATIONS

The 154 Members of the United Nations

Country	Joined U.N.[1]	Country	Joined U.N.[1]	Country	Joined U.N.[1]
Afghanistan	1946	Ghana	1957	Papua New Guinea	1975
Albania	1955	Greece	1945	Paraguay	1945
Algeria	1962	Grenada	1974	Peru	1945
Angola	1976	Guatemala	1945	Philippines	1945
Argentina	1945	Guinea	1958	Poland	1945
Australia	1945	Guinea-Bissau	1974	Portugal	1955
Austria	1955	Guyana	1966	Qatar	1971
Bahamas	1973	Haiti	1945	Romania	1955
Bahrain	1971	Honduras	1945	Rwanda	1962
Bangladesh	1974	Hungary	1955	St. Lucia	1979
Barbados	1966	Iceland	1946	St. Vincent and the Grenadines	1980
Belgium	1945	India	1945	Sao Tomé and Principe	1975
Benin	1960	Indonesia	1950	Saudi Arabia	1945
Bhutan	1971	Iran	1945	Senegal	1960
Bolivia	1945	Iraq	1945	Seychelles	1976
Botswana	1966	Ireland	1955	Sierra Leone	1961
Brazil	1945	Israel	1949	Singapore	1965
Bulgaria	1955	Italy	1955	Solomon Islands	1978
Burma	1948	Ivory Coast	1960	Somalia	1960
Burundi	1962	Jamaica	1962	South Africa	1945
Byelorussian S.S.R.	1945	Japan	1956	Spain	1955
Cambodia	1955	Jordan	1955	Sri Lanka	1955
Cameroon	1960	Kenya	1963	Sudan	1956
Canada	1945	Kuwait	1963	Suriname	1975
Cape Verde	1975	Laos	1955	Swaziland	1968
Central African Republic	1960	Lebanon	1945	Sweden	1946
Chad	1960	Lesotho	1966	Syria	1945
Chile	1945	Liberia	1945	Tanzania	1961
China[2]	1945	Libya	1955	Thailand	1946
Colombia	1945	Luxembourg	1945	Togo	1960
Comoros	1975	Madagascar	1960	Trinidad and Tobago	1962
Congo	1960	Malawi	1964	Tunisia	1956
Costa Rica	1945	Malaysia	1957	Turkey	1945
Cuba	1945	Maldives	1965	Uganda	1962
Cyprus	1960	Mali	1960	Ukrainian S.S.R.	1945
Czechoslovakia	1945	Malta	1964	U.S.S.R.	1945
Denmark	1945	Mauritania	1961	United Arab Emirates	1971
Djibouti	1977	Mauritius	1968	United Kingdom	1945
Dominica	1978	Mexico	1945	United States	1945
Dominican Republic	1945	Mongolia	1961	Upper Volta	1960
Ecuador	1945	Morocco	1956	Uruguay	1945
Egypt	1945	Mozambique	1975	Venezuela	1945
El Salvador	1945	Nepal	1955	Vietnam	1977
Equatorial Guinea	1968	Netherlands	1945	Western Samoa	1976
Ethiopia	1945	New Zealand	1945	Yemen Arab Republic	1947
Fiji	1970	Nicaragua	1945	Yemen, People's Dem.	
Finland	1955	Niger	1960	Republic of	1967
France	1945	Nigeria	1960	Yugoslavia	1945
Gabon	1960	Norway	1945	Zaire	1960
Gambia	1965	Oman	1971	Zambia	1964
Germany, East	1973	Pakistan	1947	Zimbabwe	1980
Germany, West	1973	Panama	1945		

1. The U.N. officially came into existence on Oct. 24, 1945. 2. On Oct. 25, 1971, the U.N. voted membership to the People's Republic of China, which replaced the Republic of China (Taiwan) in the world body.

Iraqi Elected President of General Assembly for 1981–82

Ismat Kittani, a veteran Iraqi diplomat, will be president of the 36th General Assembly in 1981–82. He and his closest rival, Khwaja Mohammed Kaiser of Bangladesh, were tied in the voting. The winner was then picked by drawing a name out of a ballot box.

Member Countries' Assessments to U.N. Budget, 1981

Country	Total	Country	Total	Country	Total
Afghanistan	$ 57,128	Germany, West	$47,473,338	Pakistan	$ 399,896
Albania	57,128	Ghana	171,384	Panama	114,256
Algeria	685,535	Greece	1,999,479	Papua New Guinea	57,128
Angola	57,128	Grenada	57,128	Paraguay	57,128
Argentina	4,455,981	Guatemala	114,256	Peru	342,767
Australia	10,454,418	Guinea	57,128	Philippines	571,279
Austria	4,056,086	Guinea-Bissau	57,128	Poland	7,083,868
Bahamas	57,128	Guyana	57,128	Portugal	1,085,431
Bahrain	57,128	Haiti	57,128	Qatar	114,256
Bangladesh	228,511	Honduras	57,128	Romania	1,199,687
Barbados	57,128	Hungary	1,885,223	Rwanda	57,128
Belgium	6,969,612	Iceland	171,384	São Tomé and Príncipe	57,128
Benin	57,128	India	3,427,678	Saudi Arabia	3,313,422
Bhutan	57,128	Indonesia	914,047	Senegal	57,128
Bolivia	57,128	Iran	3,713,318	Seychelles	57,128
Botswana	57,128	Iraq	685,535	Sierra Leone	57,128
Brazil	7,255,252	Ireland	914,047	Singapore	457,023
Bulgaria	914,047	Israel	1,428,199	Solomon Islands	57,128
Burma	57,128	Italy	19,709,147	Somalia	57,128
Burundi	57,128	Ivory Coast	171,384	South Africa	2,399,375
Byelorussian S.S.R.	2,227,991	Jamaica	114,256	Spain	9,711,754
Cambodia	57,128	Japan	54,728,589	Sri Lanka	114,256
Cameroon	57,128	Jordan	57,128	St. Lucia	57,128
Canada	18,737,973	Kenya	57,128	Sudan	57,128
Cape Verde	57,128	Kuwait	1,142,560	Suriname	57,128
Central African Republic	57,128	Laos	57,128	Swaziland	57,128
Chad	57,128	Lebanon	171,384	Sweden	7,483,763
Chile	399,896	Lesotho	57,128	Syria	114,256
China	9,254,730	Liberia	57,128	Tanzania	57,128
Colombia	628,408	Libya	1,313,943	Thailand	571,279
Comoros	57,128	Luxembourg	285,639	Togo	57,128
Congo	57,128	Madagascar	57,128	Trinidad and Tobago	171,384
Costa Rica	114,256	Malawi	57,128	Tunisia	171,384
Cuba	628,408	Malaysia	514,151	Turkey	1,722,628
Cyprus	57,128	Maldives	57,128	Uganda	57,128
Czechoslovakia	4,741,621	Mali	57,128	Ukrainian S.S.R.	8,340,682
Denmark	4,227,469	Malta	57,128	U.S.S.R.	63,412,040
Djibouti	57,128	Mauritania	57,128	United Arab Emirates	571,279
Dominica	57,128	Mauritius	57,128	United Kingdom	25,479,071
Dominican Republic	171,384	Mexico	4,341,725	United States	167,347,460
Ecuador	114,256	Mongolia	57,128	Upper Volta	57,128
Egypt	399,896	Morocco	285,639	Uruguay	228,511
El Salvador	57,128	Mozambique	57,128	Venezuela	2,856,398
Equatorial Guinea	57,128	Nepal	57,128	Vietnam	171,384
Ethiopia	57,128	Netherlands	9,311,858	Western Samoa	57,128
Fiji	57,128	New Zealand	1,542,455	Yemen Arab Republic	57,128
Finland	2,742,142	Nicaragua	57,128	Yemen, People's Dem.	
France	35,762,106	Niger	57,128	Republic of	57,128
Gabon	114,256	Nigeria	914,047	Yugoslavia	2,399,375
Gambia	57,128	Norway	2,856,398	Zaire	114,256
Germany, East	7,940,788	Oman	57,128	Zambia	114,256

United Nations Headquarters

The first regular session of the General Assembly held at Central Hall, Westminster, London, voted that interim headquarters of the Organization should be located in New York. From London the U.N. moved to Hunter College in the Bronx. In August 1946, an interim headquarters was set up at Lake Success on Long Island, in a part of the Sperry Gyroscope Co.'s plant. The New York City building at Flushing Meadows, site of the 1939 World's Fair, was converted for the use of the General Assembly. The search for a permanent home ended in December 1946, when the General Assembly accepted an offer from John D. Rockefeller, Jr., of $8,500,000[1] for the purchase of the present Headquarters site—an 18-acre tract in Manhattan, alongside the East River. The U.S. Government lent the U.N. $65,000,000 interest free, which is being repaid in annual installments.

Architectural plans drawn up by an international Board of Design were approved by the Assembly, and construction began in September 1948. By mid-1950, the 39-story Secretariat Building was ready for occupancy, and in the spring of 1951 "United Nations, New York" became the Organization's permanent address. The other main structures are the Conference Building, the General Assembly Hall, and the Dag Hammarskjold Library. All are interconnected.

1. This amount paid for two-thirds of the land; New York City gave one-third.

Preamble of the United Nations Charter

The Charter of the United Nations was adopted at the San Francisco Conference of 1945. The complete text may be obtained by writing to the United Nations Sales Section, United Nations, New York, N.Y. 10017, and enclosing $1.

We the peoples of the United Nations determined to save succeeding generations from the scourge of war, which twice in our lifetime has brought untold sorrow to mankind, and

To reaffirm faith in fundamental human rights, in the dignity and worth of the human person, in the equal rights of men and women and of nations large and small, and

To establish conditions under which justice and respect for the obligations arising from treaties and other sources of international law can be maintained, and

To promote social progress and better standards of life in larger freedom, and for these ends

To practice tolerance and live together in peace with one another as good neighbors, and

To unite our strength to maintain international peace and security, and

To insure, by the acceptance of principles and the institution of methods, that armed force shall not be used, save in the common interest, and

To employ international machinery for the promotion of the economic and social advancement of all peoples, have resolved to combine our efforts to accomplish these aims.

Accordingly, our respective Governments, through representatives assembled in the city of San Francisco, who have exhibited their full powers found to be in good and due form, have agreed to the present Charter of the United Nations and do hereby establish an international organization to be known as the United Nations.

Principal Organs of the United Nations

Secretariat

This is the directorate on U.N. operations, apart from political decisions. All members contribute to its upkeep. Its staff of over 6,000 specialists is recruited from member nations on the basis of as wide a geographical distribution as possible. The staff works under the Secretary-General, whom it assists and advises.

Secretaries-General

Kurt Waldheim, Austria, Jan. 1, 1972.
U Thant, Burma, Nov. 3, 1961, to Dec. 31, 1971.
Dag Hammarskjöld, Sweden, April 11, 1953, to Sept. 17, 1961.
Trygve Lie, Norway, Feb. 1, 1946, to April 10, 1953.

General Assembly

The General Assembly is the world's forum for discussing matters affecting world peace and security, and for making recommendations concerning them. It has no power of its own to enforce decisions.

The Assembly is composed of the 51 original member nations and those admitted since, a total of 153. Each nation has one vote. On major questions involving international peace and security, a two-thirds majority of those present and voting is required. Decisions on other questions are made by a simple majority.

The Assembly's agenda can be as broad as the Charter. It can make recommendations to member nations, the Security Council, or both. Emphasis is given questions relating to international peace and security brought before it by any member, the Security Council, or nonmembers.

The Assembly also maintains a broad program of international cooperation in economic, social, cultural, educational, and health fields, and for assisting in human rights and freedoms.

Among other duties, the Assembly has functions relating to the trusteeship system, and considers and approves the U.N. Budget. Every member contributes to operating expenses according to its means.

Security Council

The Security Council is the primary instrument for establishing and maintaining international peace. Its main purpose is to prevent war by settling disputes between nations.

Under the Charter, the Council is permitted to dispatch a U.N. force to stop aggression. All member nations undertake to make available armed forces, assistance, and facilities to maintain international peace and security.

Any member may bring a dispute before the Security Council or the General Assembly. Any nonmember may do so if it accepts the charter obligations of pacific settlement.

The Security Council has 15 members. There are five permanent members: the United States, the Soviet Union, Britain, France, and China and 10 temporary members elected by the General Assembly for two-year terms, with different regions of the world rotating.

Voting on procedural matters requires a nine-vote majority to carry. However, on questions of substance, the vote of each of the five permanent members is required. Thus, any one of the five possess a veto.

Current temporary members are (term expires Dec. 31, 1981): East Germany, Mexico, Niger, Philippines, Tunisia; (term expires Dec. 31, 1982): Ireland, Japan, Panama, Spain, Uganda.

Economic and Social Council

This council is composed of 54 members elected by the General Assembly to 3-year terms. It works closely with the General Assembly as a link with groups formed within the U.N. to help peoples in such fields as education, health, and human rights. It insures that there is no overlapping and sets up commissions to deal with economic conditions and collect facts and figures on conditions over the world. It issues studies and reports and may make recommendations to the Assembly and specialized agencies.

Functional Commissions

Statistical Commission; Population Commission; Commission for Social Development; Commission on Human Rights; Commission on the Status of Women; Commission on Narcotic Drugs.

Regional Commissions

Economic Commission for Europe; Economic and Social Commission for Asia and the Pacific;

Economic Commission for Latin America; Economic Commission for Africa; Economic Commission for Western Asia.

Trusteeship Council

This council supervises territories administered by various nations and placed under an international trusteeship system by the United Nations. Each nation is charged with developing the self-government of the territory and preserving and advancing the cultural, political, economic, and other forms of welfare of the people.

The Trusteeship Council is currently composed of 5 members: 1 member—the United States—that administers a trust territory, and 4 members—China, France, the Soviet Union, and the United Kingdom—that are permanent members of the Security Council but do not administer trust territories.

The following countries ceased to be administering members because of the independence of territories they had administered: Italy and France in 1960, Belgium in 1962, New Zealand and the United Kingdom in 1968 and Australia in 1975. France and the U. K. became nonadministering members.

As of December 1980, there was only one trust territory: the Trust Territory of the Pacific Islands (administered by the United States).

International Court of Justice

The International Court of Justice sits at The Hague, the Netherlands. Its 15-judge bench was established to hear disputes among states, who must agree to accept its verdicts. Its judges, charged with administering justice under international law, deal with cases ranging from disputes over territory to those concerning rights of passage.

Following are the members of the Court and the years in which their terms expire:
President: Vacant.
Vice President: Taslim Olawale Elias, Nigeria (1985)
Isaac Forster, Senegal (1982)
André Gros, France (1982)
Nagendra Singh, India (1982)
José María Ruda, Argentina (1982)
Manfred Lachs, Poland (1985)
Hermann Mösler, West Germany (1985)
Shigeru Oda, Japan (1985)
Abdullah Fikri El-Khani, Syria (1985)
Platon D. Morozov, U.S.S.R. (1988)
Roberto Ago, Italy (1988)
Abdullah Ali El-Erian, Egypt (1988)
José Sette Câmara, Brazil (1988)
Stephen M. Schwebel, U.S. (1988)

Agencies of the United Nations

INTERNATIONAL ATOMIC ENERGY AGENCY (IAEA)

Established: Statute for IAEA, approved on Oct. 26, 1956, at a conference held at U.N. Headquarters, New York, came into force on July 29, 1957. The Agency is under the aegis of the U.N., but unlike the following, it is not a specialized agency.

Purpose: To promote the peaceful uses of atomic energy; to ensure that assistance provided by it or at its request or under its supervision or control is not used in such a way as to further any military purpose.

Headquarters: P.O. Box 100 A-1400, Vienna, Austria.

FOOD AND AGRICULTURE ORGANIZATION OF THE UNITED NATIONS (FAO)

Established: October 16, 1945, when constitution became effective.

Purpose: To raise nutrition levels and living standards; to secure improvements in production and distribution of food and agricultural products.

Headquarters: Via delle Terme di Caracalla, 00100, Rome, Italy.

GENERAL AGREEMENT ON TARIFFS AND TRADE (GATT)

Established: Jan. 1, 1948.

Purpose: An International Trade Organization (ITO) was planned when the U.N. Agencies were first set up. Although this agency has not materialized, some of its objectives have been embodied in an international commercial treaty, the General Agreement on Tariffs and Trade. Its purpose is to sponsor trade negotiations.

Headquarters: Centre William Rappard, 154 Rue de Lausanne, 1211 Geneva 21, Switzerland.

INTER-GOVERNMENTAL MARITIME CONSULTATIVE ORGANIZATION (IMCO)

Established: March 17, 1958.

Purpose: To give advisory and consultative help to promote international cooperation in maritime navigation and to encourage the highest standards of safety and navigation. Its aim is to bring about a uniform system of measuring ship tonnage; systems now vary widely in different parts of the world. Other activities include cooperation with other U.N. agencies on matters affecting the maritime field.

Headquarters: 101–104 Piccadilly, London, W1V 0AE, England.

INTERNATIONAL BANK FOR RECONSTRUCTION AND DEVELOPMENT (IBRD) (WORLD BANK)

Established: December 27, 1945, when Articles of Agreement drawn up at Bretton Woods Conference in July 1944 came into force. Began operations on June 25, 1946.

Purpose: To assist in reconstruction and development of economies of members by facilitating capital investment and by making loans to governments and furnishing technical advice.

Headquarters: 1818 H St., N.W., Washington, D.C. 20433.

INTERNATIONAL CIVIL AVIATION ORGANIZATION (ICAO)

Established: April 4, 1947, after working as a provisional organization since June 1945.

Purpose: To study problems of international civil aviation; to establish international standards and regulations; to promote safety measures, uniform regulations for operation, simpler procedures at international borders, and the use of new technical methods and equipment. It has evolved standards for meteorological services, traffic control, communications, radio beacons and ranges, search and rescue organization, and other facilities. It has brought about much simplification of customs, immigration, and public health regulations as they apply to international air transport. It drafts international air law conventions, and is concerned with economic aspects of air travel.

Headquarters: International Aviation Square, 1000 Sherbrooke St. West, Montreal, Quebec, H3A 2R2, Canada.

INTERNATIONAL DEVELOPMENT ASSOCIATION (IDA)
Established: Sept. 24, 1960. An affiliate of the World Bank, IDA has the same officers and staff as the Bank.
Purpose: To further economic development of its members by providing finance on terms which bear less heavily on balance of payments of members than those of conventional loans.
Headquarters: 1818 H St., N.W., Washington, D.C. 20433.

INTERNATIONAL FINANCE CORPORATION (IFC)
Established: Charter of IFC came into force on July 20, 1956. Although IFC is affiliated with the World Bank, it is a separate legal entity, and its funds are entirely separate from those of the Bank. However, membership in the Corporation is open only to Bank members.
Purpose: To further economic development by encouraging the growth of productive private enterprise in its member countries, particularly in the less developed areas; to invest in productive private enterprises in association with private investors, without government guarantee of repayment where sufficient private capital is not available on reasonable terms; to serve as a clearing house to bring together investment opportunities, private capital (both foreign and domestic), and experienced management.
Headquarters: 1818 H St., N.W., Washington, D.C. 20433.

INTERNATIONAL FUND FOR AGRICULTURAL DEVELOPMENT (IFAD)
Established: June 18,1976. Began operations in December 1977.
Purpose: To mobilize additional funds for agricultural and rural development in developing countries through projects and programs directly benefiting the poorest rural populations.
Headquarters: 107 Via del Serafico, 00142 Rome, Italy.

INTERNATIONAL LABOR ORGANIZATION (ILO)
Established: April 11, 1919, when constitution was adopted as Part XIII of Treaty of Versailles. Became specialized agency of U.N. in 1946.
Purpose: To contribute to establishment of lasting peace by promoting social justice; to improve labor conditions and living standards through international action; to promote economic and social stability. The U.S. withdrew from the ILO in 1977 and resumed membership in 1980.
Headquarters: 4 route des Morillons, CH-1211 Geneva 22, Switzerland.

INTERNATIONAL MONETARY FUND (IMF)
Established: Dec. 27, 1945, when Articles of Agreement drawn up at Bretton Woods Conference in July 1944 came into force. Fund began operations on March 1, 1947.
Purpose: To promote international monetary cooperation and expansion of international trade; to promote exchange stability; to assist in establishment of multilateral system of payments in respect of currency transactions between members.
Headquarters: 700 19th St., N.W., Washington, D.C. 20431.

INTERNATIONAL TELECOMMUNICATION UNION (ITU)
Established: 1865. Became specialized agency of U.N. in 1947.
Purpose: To extend technical assistance to help members keep up with present day telecommunication needs; to standardize communications equipment and procedures; to lower costs. It also works for orderly sharing of radio frequencies and makes studies and recommendations to benefit its members.
Headquarters: Place des Nations, 1211 Geneva 20, Switzerland.

UNITED NATIONS EDUCATIONAL, SCIENTIFIC, AND CULTURAL ORGANIZATION (UNESCO)
Established: Nov. 4, 1946, when twentieth signatory to constitution deposited instrument of acceptance with government of U.K.
Purpose: To promote collaboration among nations through education, science, and culture in order to further justice, rule of law, and human rights and freedoms without distinction of race, sex, language, or religion.
Headquarters: UNESCO House, 7 Place de Fontenoy, F 75700, Paris, France.

UNIVERSAL POSTAL UNION (UPU)
Established: Oct. 9, 1874. Became specialized agency of U.N. in 1947.
Purpose: To facilitate reciprocal exchange of correspondence by uniform procedures by all UPU members; to help governments modernize and speed up mailing procedures.
Headquarters: Weltpoststrasse 4, 3000 Berne 15, Switzerland.

WORLD HEALTH ORGANIZATION (WHO)
Established: April 7, 1948, when 26 members of the U.N. had accepted its constitution, adopted July 22, 1946, by the International Health Conference in New York City.
Purpose: To aid attainment by all people of highest possible level of health.
Headquarters: 20 Avenue Appia, 1211 Geneva, Switzerland.

WORLD INTELLECTUAL PROPERTY ORGANIZATION (WIPO)
Established: April 26, 1970, when its Convention came into force. Originated as International Bureau of Paris Union (1883) and Berne Union (1886), later succeeded by United International Bureau for the Protection of Intellectual Property (BIRPI). Became a specialized agency of the U.N. in December 1974.
Purpose: To promote legal protection of intellectual property, including artistic and scientific works, artistic performances, sound recordings, broadcasts, inventions, trademarks, industrial designs, and commercial names.
Headquarters: 32 Chemin des Colombettes, 1211 Geneva 20, Switzerland.

WORLD METEOROLOGICAL ORGANIZATION (WMO)
Established: March 23, 1950, succeeding the International Meteorological Organization, a nongovernmental organization founded in 1878.
Purpose: To promote international exchange of weather reports and maximum standardization of observations; to help developing countries establish weather services for their own economic needs; to fill gaps in observation stations; to promote meteorological investigations affecting jet aircraft, satellites, energy resources, etc.
Headquarters: 41 Avenue Giuseppe Motta, Geneva, Switzerland.

The Year in Energy—1981

Although the issue was in doubt for the past few years, it looked, during 1981, like the Law of Supply and Demand was still valid, after all. Nowhere could this have come as anything but the best of news than in the world's oil-consuming nations. After several years of steady increases, crude oil prices actually began to drop. As this issue went to press, a barrel of crude could command no more than $32 on some markets, and there were strong indications that the price would hold, if not actually fall still further. For the American consumer, this meant a return to gasoline at relatively "old-fashioned" prices approaching $1.20 per gallon in some parts of the country. There was no shortage of gasoline in sight: in fact, the reason for all the rejoicing was the growth of a world-wide oil glut, clearly the biggest energy news of the year.

Several factors contributed to the changing energy picture, but all could be seen as eventually lessening the influence of OPEC as the controlling force in petroleum markets. Most important among these factors were conservation, the growing impact of non-OPEC oil producers, and a shift to alternate sources of energy. Domestic energy consumption, for example, dropped by 6.4% from 1980 levels, more than anyone thought possible. Part of this decrease was attributable to generally depressed economic conditions, but conservation was rightfully given most of the credit. While the U.S. nuclear industry still appeared to be grounded on the shoals of Three Mile Island, the use of coal continued to rise, this despite a protracted strike by bituminous coal miners. Domestic crude oil production rose as well, due principally to Federal decontrol of "new" oil prices, which provided the needed shot in the arm to U.S. drilling and exploration efforts. Alaskan crude production increased, and there were new or expanded discoveries in the Gulf of Mexico, Michigan, and the Western area known as the Overthrust Belt. Thus, the country used less energy, it increased the use of coal, and it produced more of its own crude. The over-all result was a sharply reduced dependence on foreign oil, from 1980's 6.8 million barrels per day to 5.4 million barrels per day in 1981, a drop of just over 20%.

The worldwide picture changed also, and again, the shift was definitely not in OPEC's favor. Conservation led to a drop in demand (Germany, for example, cut back 8%). Supplies continued to rise, however, since oil prices were nevertheless high enough to prompt massive exploration and drilling programs around the world. This meant that more and more non-OPEC producers were getting into the business. Whereas OPEC still accounted for about one half of the world's petroleum supplies, non-OPEC sources were estimated to be growing at 5% per year. OPEC production itself dropped during 1981, and was running far below capacity by year's end.

An interesting sidelight on world oil flow was provided by, of all things, the Central Intelligence Agency. In earlier assessments, the CIA had projected that Russia would lose her oil self-sufficiency by the mid-1980s, forcing her to import as much as 3.5 million barrels per day from non-communist countries. Had this been true, it would have put considerable strain on Free World resources, thereby keeping prices high. However, in a decidedly more optimistic analysis released during 1981, the cloak-and-dagger folks revised their estimate of Soviet oil production capacity upward, maintaining that the U.S.S.R. and its satellites will remain self-sufficient until 1990. By that time, if current supply and demand patterns continue, more than a few sheiks will have had to trade in their Rolls-Royces for camels.

Barnyard Fuel

Not that the camels would have been so bad, at least from an energy standpoint. From the U.S. Meat Animal Research Center came reports that optimum conditions had been worked out for producing methane (the principal ingredient in natural gas) from animal dung. The new process relies on fermentation, taking place over three days at 140°F, to produce maximum amounts of the gaseous fuel. As an added benefit, the process yields a by-product containing 60% protein. Having an amino acid content similar to that of soy bean oil, the residue is usable as an animal feed supplement. The process would cost as little as $15 per animal per year when applied to feed lots containing 100,-000 or more head of cattle, but it would produce $20 worth of methane and $40 worth of protein per animal annually. There shouldn't be any shortage of raw materials: it is estimated that there are more than 26 million tons of animal dung lying around.

Cow pies aren't the only unconventional energy source being considered: 1981 also brought a new fermentation process that will turn cheese whey into an alcohol fuel for use in gasohol. The process relies on yeast plants immobilized on polymer beads to ferment lactose contained in the whey. The beauty of the new process is that it would turn a profit from a waste product that is expensive to get rid of. Cheese whey used to be dumped into streams, but it caused a serious pollution problem. Government-mandated settling ponds eliminated the pollution problem, but at added expense to producers and, inevitably, consumers.

The so-called biomass fuel supplies are, in fact, becoming important sooner than expected. In 1981, for example, wood surpassed nuclear power as an energy source in the U.S.. It could provide up to 20% of the nation's fuel supply by the year 2000, according to a report issued by the World-watch Institute, Washington, D.C. Should you, as millions of Americans already have, switch to a wood-burning stove as your primary source of heat? It depends on what you're switching from and on how much wood costs in your area. World-watch estimates that it already pays to switch from oil (now around $1.25 per gallon) if you can buy a cord of wood (four feet by four feet by eight feet) for less than $150. If you heat your house with natural gas, which is generally cheaper than oil, the cord would have to cost less than $70 to make the switch pay.

But an electrically heated home (power at the national average price of 5.8 cents per kilowatt-hour) can be converted economically even if a cord of wood costs $190. All this assumes that you're using a stove with an efficiency of 50%, and that you're burning good, dry hardwood with a heat value of 22.5 million Btus per cord. Three such cords will heat the average house for a winter, and a power saw will cut six of them (equivalent to $900 worth of fuel oil) on $10-$15 worth of gasoline. Chop-chop.

Fuel vs. Food

There has been an ongoing controversy over the morality of using biomass fuel supplies in cases where human foodstuffs are the medium being consumed or converted. Corn is the obvious example. It is a common food staple throughout the Western World, and every moonshiner knows it can be converted to ethanol without a lot of fuss. But what if a really big ethanol/gasohol program got under way? Would this mean less corn for the hungry, here and abroad? Would it raise the price of corn-fed beef and pork? Not likely, according to a 1981 symposium on future food vs. fuel conflicts. As reported in *Science News*, several speakers at the symposium claimed the U.S. could produce two billion gallons of ethanol from less farm acreage than was taken out of corn production in 1978. Two million acres of new land put into corn production would provide one billion gallons of ethanol, about 1% of current gasoline requirements. The ethanol would cost between $1.21 and $1.55 per gallon so the price of gasoline, now in that range, would have a major influence on the corn-fuel program's competitive viability.

New Energy Sources, New Technology

Solar energy continued to command attention, and it also attracted its share of controversy. A 1981 report put out by the Solar Energy Research Institute stated that massive investments in sun-sourced technology, plus increased emphasis on conservation, could make the U.S. nearly energy self-sufficient by the year 2000. Unfortunately, the report recommended that part of the $750-$800 billion needed should come from reduced government subsidies to traditional energy industries, so it was not very warmly received on the banks of the Potomac.

There were, however, several reports of significant progress in solar energy devices. Electricity was generated by a new type of photoelectrochemical cell in a way that is a step beyond photosynthesis, the process by which plants produce chemicals. Present efficiency of the new cells is only 1.7%, but if this could be increased by 5%, the new devices could compete with today's silicon photovoltaic cells. The source of the new cells, incidentally, were chloroplasts taken from spinach leaves. Maybe Popeye had something there, after all.

Photovoltaic cells made their own share of history in 1981: 15,000 of them were used to cover the wings and horizontal stabilizers of *Solar Challenger*, an experimental solar powered airplane. Stephen Ptacek, the plane's 130-pound pilot, successfully flew the 210-pound, U.S.-designed craft from Paris to the English coast. *Solar* looks a lot like *Gossamer Condor*, which flew across the Channel under human power. Both were designed and built by Dr. Paul MacCready, an American physicist. *Solar Challenger* has a little more pep than its pedal-powered predecessor: it ascends at about 150 feet per minute on a tiny 2.75 horsepower engine and cruises, between 6000 and 10,000 feet, at around 33 miles per hour. Top speed is 41 mph at 14,000 feet, where the Sun's rays are stronger.

Another new photocell was developed, this one using what are called liquid-junction cathodes to produce electricity from light. The materials used don't corrode when exposed to high-intensity sunlight so the cells should last longer in, for example, satellite power supplies. Unfortunately, present-day cathodes are made of indium phosphide, which is very, very expensive. The search is on for a cheaper material. A non-metallic, organic battery was also developed during 1981, and it may eventually have potential for use in electric cars. The battery relies on thin films of a simple polymer, polyacetylene, immersed in a solution of tetrabutylammonium in propylene carbonate. It is rechargeable and is said to have a very high energy density. Now if they can only make it easier to pronounce.

Konrad J.A. Kundig

Electric Cars Have a Long History

Electric cars are expected to be taking a share of the vehicle market after 1985. One new unit can power a car at 55 miles per hour for 150 miles before it has to be recharged. Also in the works are hybrids, which combine electric and gasoline power.

According to the Automotive Information Council (AIC), the first electric vehicle was built in 1839 by Robert Anderson of Aberdeen, Scotland, but the first practical use did not occur until 1886 when one was introduced as a taxicab in England. The battery had 28 bulky cells and the taxi had a top speed of eight miles per hour.

By 1904 electrics were somewhat common on U.S. city streets for short runs. The Electric Vehicle Co. in that year made 2,000 taxis, accounting for one third of the cabs used in New York, Chicago, and Boston.

By 1910 the use of electric vehicles had peaked. They quickly lost ground to the internal-combustion engine with its great improvements such as the self-starter, and the availability of inexpensive gasoline, plus the low price of gasoline-powered mass-assembled cars.

Gasohol Isn't New

Farmers knew they could make motor fuels long before the current energy crisis. So did Henry Ford. He built his Model T to run on gasoline, alcohol, or any mixture in between.

During the depression, farmers often raised more corn than they could eat, feed to livestock, or haul to markets. By fermenting the grain to get alcohol and feed, they found new ways to use their crops. Some burned the stuff in their "Tin Lizzies," trimming the gas bill at a time when the dollar was hard to come by.

World Production, Trade, and Consumption
of Commercial Energy, 1979
(in million metric tons of coal equivalent)

Activity	World	Developed countries[1]	Developing countries[2]	Centrally planned economic[3]	U.S.	U.S.S.R.	Saudi Arabia
Total primary energy production	9,560	3,428	2,969	3,164	2,088	1,884	706
Imports of commercial energy	3,429	2,586	602	241	653	34	3
Exports of commercial energy	3,448	604	2,433	410	75	320	666
Total energy consumption							
Solid fuel	2,738	1,137	138	1,462	557	497	—
Liquid fuels	3,834	2,456	627	751	1,115	500	16
Natural gas	1,846	1,158	126	562	763	445	9
Hydro/nuclear electricity	288	202	42	44	70	26	—
Total commercial energy							
in kg per capita	2,019	6,317	437	2,027	11,361	5,558	2,105

1. Australia, Canada, Israel, Japan, New Zealand, South Africa, U.S., Western Europe (incl. Yugoslovia). 2. Developing market economies of Africa, Caribbean, Middle East (incl. Turkey), Far East, etc. 3. Albania, Bulgaria, Czechoslovakia, East Germany, Hungary, Poland, Romania, U.S.S.R. *Source:* United Nations, *1979 Yearbook of World Energy Statistics* (Statistical Papers, Series J No. 23).

World's Ten Largest Electric Energy Producers, 1979
(in billion kilowatt hours)

Country	Production Hydro	Nuclear	Thermal	Total	Country	Production Hydro	Nuclear	Thermal	Total
United States	285,382[1][2]	255,376	1,783,028	2,323,806	China	73,000[1]	—	208,950[1]	281,950
U.S.S.R.	180,000[1]	45,000[1]	1,015,000	1,240,000	France	68,950[1]	37,908[1]	134,266[1]	241,124
Japan	85,431[1][2]	60,506[1]	435,504[1]	581,441	Italy	50,628[1][2]	2,700[1]	127,194[1]	180,522
West Germany	18,745[1]	41,795[1]	313,078[1]	373,618	Poland	2,460[1]	—	115,000[1]	117,460
Canada	243,041	33,275	75,988	352,304	Sub-total	1,013,101	512,474	4,466,590	5,992,185
United Kingdom	5,464	35,914[1]	258,582[1]	299,960	All others	718,122	90,457	1,165,600	1,974,159
					World total	**1,731,223[2]**	**602,931**	**5,632,190**	**7,966,344**

1. U.N. Statistical Office estimate. 2. Production from geothermal sources included. *Source:* United Nations, *1979 Yearbook of World Energy Statistics* (Statistical Papers, Series J No. 23).

Per Capita Electric Energy Consumption, 1979
(20 highest per capita consumers)

Country	kwh per capita[1]	Population (thousands)[2]	Production plus net imports[3]	Country	kwh per capita[1]	Population (thousands)[2]	Production plus net imports[3]
Norway	20,228	4,082	89,263	Finland	7,495	4,767	35,955
Panama Canal Zone	17,857	45	650	New Zealand	7,106	3,125	22,000
Canada	13,623	23,858	354,096	Turks & Caicos Islands	7,000	6	7
Iceland	12,746	227	2,906	U.S. Virgin Islands	6,952	120	730
Sweden	11,424	8,302	99,425	Netherlands Antilles	6,923	242	1,800
Luxembourg	11,085	358	4,272	Qatar	6,667	170	1,400
Christmas Island	11,000	1	33	Australia	6,381	14,476	92,000
United States	10,669	221,196	2,355,254	Switzerland	6,176	6,304	51,885
Guam	9,483	114	1,100	Kuwait	6,124	1,318	7,790
New Caledonia	8,394	142	1,150	West Germany	6,103	61,193	389,322
				World	**1,849**	**4,406,000**	**8,120,097**

1. Production plus net imports divided by total population. 2. Estimate. 3. In billion kilowatt hours. NOTE: Data on consumption are derived from the formula "production plus imports minus exports." Accordingly, apparent consumption may occasionally be only an indication of the magnitude of actual gross inland availability. Where relatively small populations are involved, large fluctuations in per capita consumption series may derive from small quantitative variations. *Source:* United Nations, *1979 Yearbook of World Energy Statistics* (Statistical Papers, Series J No. 23).

U.S. Energy Supply and Disposition
(in quadrillion Btus)

Activity and fuel	1960	1965	1970	1975	1977	1978	1979	1980[1]
SUPPLY								
Production								
Crude Oil and Lease Condensate	14.93	16.52	20.40	17.73	17.45	18.43	18.10	18.25
Natural Gas Plant Liquids	1.46	1.88	2.51	2.37	2.33	2.25	2.29	2.27
Natural Gas[2]	12.66	15.78	21.67	19.64	19.57	19.49	20.08	19.70
Coal[3]	11.12	13.38	15.05	15.19	15.83	15.04	17.65	18.88
Nuclear Power	0.01	0.04	0.24	1.90	2.70	2.98	2.75	2.70
Hydropower	1.60	2.06	2.63	3.15	2.34	2.96	2.95	2.91
Other[4]	(Z)	0.01	0.02	0.07	0.08	0.07	0.09	0.11
Total Production	41.78	49.67	62.51	60.06	60.30	61.21	63.91	64.82
Imports								
Crude Oil[5]	2.20	2.65	2.81	8.72	14.03	13.46	13.83	11.06
Refined Petroleum Products[6]	1.80	2.75	4.66	4.23	4.73	4.36	4.11	3.38
Natural Gas	0.16	0.47	0.85	0.98	1.04	0.99	1.30	1.03
Other[7]	0.07	0.04	0.07	0.19	0.30	0.44	0.39	0.28
Total Imports	4.23	5.92	8.39	14.11	20.09	19.26	19.62	15.75
Adjustments[8]	−0.44	−0.74	−1.41	−1.08	−1.91	−0.36	−1.66	−0.54
Total Supply	45.57	54.85	69.49	73.09	78.49	80.11	81.87	80.03
DISPOSITION								
Consumption								
Refined Petroleum Products[9]	19.92	23.25	29.52	32.73	37.18	37.97	37.12	34.25
Natural Gas[2]	12.39	15.77	21.79	19.95	19.93	20.00	20.67	20.44
Coal[5]	10.12	11.89	12.66	12.82	14.14	13.85	15.11	15.67
Nuclear Power	0.01	0.04	0.24	1.90	2.70	2.98	2.75	2.70
Hydropower[10]	1.65	2.06	2.65	3.22	2.52	3.17	3.17	3.13
Other	(Z)	0.01	0.02	0.07	0.08	0.07	0.09	0.11
Net Imports of Coal Coke	−0.01	−0.02	−0.06	0.01	0.02	0.13	0.07	−0.04
Total Consumption	44.08	52.99	66.83	70.71	76.56	78.15	78.97	76.27
Exports								
Coal[3]	1.02	1.38	1.94	1.79	1.47	1.10	1.78	2.47
Other[11]	0.46	0.48	0.73	0.60	0.63	0.85	1.12	1.29
Total Exports	1.48	1.86	2.66	2.39	2.10	1.95	2.90	3.76
Total Disposition	45.57	54.85	69.49	73.09	78.66	80.11	81.87	80.03

1. Preliminary. 2. Dry marketed gas. 3. Includes bituminous, lignite, and anthracite coal. 4. Geothermal, wood, refuse, and other vegetal fuels used for electricity generation at utilities. 5. Includes imports of crude oil for the Strategic Petroleum Reserve. 6. Also includes imports of unfinished oils and natural gas plant liquids. 7. Includes bituminous, lignite, and anthracite coal, as well as coke made from coal, and hydropower. 8. A balancing item. Includes stock changes, losses, gains, miscellaneous blending compounds, unaccounted for supply, and shipments of anthracite coal to U.S. Armed Forces in Europe. 9. Refined petroleum products supplied includes natural gas plant liquids and crude oil burned as fuel. 10. Includes industrial generation of hydropower and net imports. 11. Includes crude oil, refined petroleum products, natural gas, coke made from coal, and hydropower. (Z) = Less than 0.005 quadrillion Btu. NOTE: The sum of the components may not equal the total due to independent rounding. *Source:* Energy Information Administration, Annual Report to Congress 1980, Volume 2.

Comparing Energy Sources[1]
(converting energy sources into BTU equivalents)

One British Thermal Unit (BTU) = the amount of heat needed to increase the temperature of one pound of water by 1° F. (252 calories).

	BTU (in thousands)
Bituminous Coal and Lignite	
Production, average/short ton	23,500.0
Consumption, average/short ton	22,800.0
Electricity generation/short ton	21,630.0
Anthracite, short ton	25,400.0
Crude petroleum, barrel (42 gallons)	5,800.0
Natural gas, dry, cubic foot	1.021
Nuclear power, kilowatt-hour	10.66
Hydropower[2] kilowatt-hour	10.38

1. For helpful conversion factors, *see* the "Science" section of this *Almanac*. 2. Calculated from national average heat rates for fossil-fueled steam-electric plants.

Petroleum Imported Directly[1] from OPEC[2] Countries, 1970–1980
(thousand barrels per day)

Year	Saudi Arabia	Iran	Vene-zuela	Libya	Indo-nesia	United Arab Emirates	Algeria	Nigeria	Other OPEC[3]	Total OPEC
1970	30	39	989	47	70	63	8	50	38	1,334
1971	128	112	1,020	58	112	79	15	102	47	1,673
1972	190	142	960	123	164	73	92	251	68	2,063
1973	486	223	1,135	164	213	71	136	459	106	2,993
1974	461	469	979	4	300	74	190	713	88	3,280
1975	715	280	703	232	390	117	282	762	121	3,601
1976	1,230	299	700	453	539	254	432	1,025	134	5,066
1977	1,380	535	690	723	541	335	559	1,143	287	6,193
1978	1,144	555	645	654	573	385	649	919	226	5,751
1979	1,356	304	690	658	420	281	636	1,080	212	5,637
1980[4]	1,252	8	460	550	337	179	481	846	121	4,233

1. Excludes indirect imports from OPEC countries which refers to U.S. imports of refined petroleum products, primarily from Caribbean and West European areas, which were refined from crude oil produced in OPEC countries. 2. Organization of Petroleum Exporting Countries. 3. Includes Ecuador, Gabon, Iraq, Kuwait, and Qatar. 4. Preliminary. NOTE: Includes data for individual countries prior to their entrance into OPEC. Data include imports for Strategic Petroleum Reserve, which began in 1977. Sum of components may not equal total due to independent rounding. *Source:* 1960 through 1975—U.S. Dept. of the Interior, Bureau of Mines, *Mineral Industry Surveys*, "Petroleum Statement Annual"; 1976 through 1979—U.S. Dept. of Energy, Energy Information Administration, *Energy Data Reports*, "Petroleum Statement, Annual"; 1980—U.S. Dept. of Energy, Energy Information Administration, *Energy Data Reports*, "Petroleum Statement, Monthly."

Production of Crude Petroleum by Countries
(in thousands of 42-gallon barrels)

Area and country	1980	1979	Percent change	Area and country	1980	1979	Percent change
Western Hemisphere	5,681,955	5,584,135	+1.8	Sharjah[1]	3,650	4,745	−23.1
Argentina	177,755	170,455	+4.3	Syria	60,225	59,495	+1.2
Bolivia	10,950	10,950	—	Turkey	16,060	20,440	−21.4
Brazil	66,430	58,765	+13.0	Asia–Pacific	997,180	1,052,295	−5.2
Canada	515,380	546,040	−5.6	Australia	138,335	160,965	−14.1
Chile	10,585	8,395	+26.1	Brunei	83,950	93,440	−10.2
Colombia	45,625	45,260	+0.8	Burma	10,950	10,950	—
Ecuador	81,030	82,125	−1.3	India	66,430	89,425	−25.7
Guatemala	1,825	730	+150.00	Indonesia	575,240	582,175	−1.2
Mexico	597,140	533,265	+32.5	Japan	3,650	2,920	+25.0
Peru	69,715	71,175	−2.1	Malaysia	105,120	94,535	+11.2
Trinidad and Tobago	77,015	78,475	−1.9	New Zealand	2,555	3,285	−22.2
United States	3,127,685	3,118,560	+0.3	Pakistan	3,650	3,650	—
Venezuela	790,955	859,940	−8.0	Philippines	5,475	9,490	−42.3
Western Europe	902,645	828,550	+8.9	Taiwan	1,825	1,825	—
Austria	10,585	12,775	−17.1	Africa	2,201,680	2,422,505	−9.1
Denmark	2,190	2,920	−25.0	Algeria	370,840	428,875	−13.5
France	9,490	7,300	+30.0	Angola	16,425	16,425	+2.3
West Germany	32,850	34,310	−4.3	Cabinda[3]	38,325	37,595	+1.9
Italy	14,235	10,950	+30.0	Cameroon	21,170	12,410	+70.6
Netherlands	9,125	9,125	—	Congo	20,440	20,805	−1.8
Norway	192,720	147,095	+31.0	Egypt	217,540	191,990	+13.3
Spain	10,950	5,475	+100.0	Gabon	65,700	74,460	−11.8
United Kingdom	590,935	572,320	+3.3	Ghana	730	1,460	−50.0
Yugoslavia	29,200	25,550	+14.3	Ivory Coast	365		
Middle East	6,708,335	7,846,040	−14.5	Libya	652,525	754,090	−13.6
Abu Dhabi[1]	492,750	534,360	−7.8	Morocco	365	365	—
Bahrain	17,520	18,615	−5.9	Nigeria	750,805	840,595	−10.7
Dubai	127,385	129,210	−1.4	Tunisia	40,150	36,500	+10.0
Iran	535,455	1,134,785	−52.7	Zaire	7,300	7,665	−4.8
Iraq	962,870	1,253,410	−23.2	Communist bloc	5,288,120	5,192,855	+1.8
Israel	365	11,315	−96.8	China	773,435	786,575	−1.7
Kuwait	504,430	807,745	−37.6	Romania	91,250	94,900	−3.8
Neutral Zone[2]	197,100	206,955	−4.8	U.S.S.R.	4,383,650	4,271,595	+2.6
Oman	103,495	107,675	−4.1	Other	39,785	40,150	−0.9
Qatar	172,280	183,960	−4.1	World total	21,779,560	22,926,380	−5.0
Saudi Arabia	3,514,950	3,376,615	+4.1				

1. A state within the United Arab Emirates. 2. Shared by Kuwait and Saudi Arabia. 3. An enclave in West Africa on Atlantic coast between the Congo and Angola. *Source: Oil & Gas Journal*, Feb. 23, 1981.

Largest Nuclear Power Plants in the United States
(over a million kilowatts)

Location	Operating utility	Capacity (kilowatts)	Year operative
Daisy, Tenn. (Unit 1)	Tennessee Valley Authority	1,148,000	1980
Prescott, Ore. (Unit 1)	Portland General Electric Co.	1,130,000	1976
Bridgman, Mich. (Unit 2)	Indiana & Michigan Electric Co.	1,100,000	1978
Salem, N.J. (Unit 1)	Public Service Electric and Gas, N.J.	1,090,000	1977
Decatur, Ala. (Unit 1)	Tennessee Valley Authority	1,065,000	1974
Decatur, Ala. (Unit 2)	Tennessee Valley Authority	1,065,000	1975
Decatur, Ala. (Unit 3)	Tennessee Valley Authority	1,065,000	1977
Peach Bottom, Pa. (Unit 2)	Philadelphia Electric Co.	1,065,000	1974
Peach Bottom, Pa. (Unit 3)	Philadelphia Electric Co.	1,065,000	1974
Bridgman, Mich. (Unit 1)	Indiana & Michigan Electric Co.	1,054,000	1975
Zion, Ill. (Unit 1)	Commonwealth Edison Co.	1,040,000	1973
Zion, Ill. (Unit 2)	Commonwealth Edison Co.	1,040,000	1974

Source: Nuclear Regulatory Commission.

Radiation Doses

Radiation doses were originally measured in *roentgens,* (r), a unit of exposure to X-ray or gamma-ray radiation in the air. The roentgen drew its name from Wilhelm Conrad Roentgen (1845–1923), who discovered X-rays in 1895 and who received the first Nobel Prize in physics in 1901.

Today, the *rad* (ra) is the unit commonly used for measuring the amount of radiation to which the whole body, as contrasted with a single organ, is exposed.

The *millirad* is one-thousandth of a rad. Most scientists believe that a dose of a few millirads is safe, but there is significant controversy over the threshold at which a dose becomes hazardous.

The *rem* (for "roentgen equivalent, man") is a measure of ionizing radiation of the type that produces the same damage to human beings as one roentgen of approximately 200 kilowatts of X-radiation.

Millirem is the term used to describe the amount of absorption of radiation by humans. The average American is exposed to 100–200 millirems of radiation per year from man-made and natural sources. A normal chest X-ray exposes one to 20–30 millirems.

U.S. Motor Vehicle Fuel Consumption
(1979 estimate)

Type of vehicle	Total travel (million vehicle miles)	Number of registered vehicles (thousands)	Average miles traveled per vehicle	Fuel consumed (million gallons)	Average fuel consumption per vehicle (gallons)	Average miles per gallon
All passenger vehicles	1,168,633	126,270,807	9,255	81,255,937	644	14.38
Total personal passenger vehicles	1,162,528	125,750,440	9,245	80,232,937	638	14.49
Cars	1,140,518	120,247,990	9,485	79,792,751	664	14.29
Motorcycles	22,010	5,502,450	4,000	440,200	80	50.00
All buses	6,105	520,367	11,732	81,255,937	644	14.38
Commercial	3,125	105,250	29,691	618,000	5,872	5.06
School and other nonrevenue	2,980	415,117	7,179	405,000	976	7.36
All cargo vehicles	360,500	33,349,742	10,810	40,858,995	1,225	8.82
Single unit trucks	294,000	32,010,742	9,184	28,543,995	892	10.30
Combinations	66,500	1,339,000	49,664	12,315,000	9,197	5.40
All motor vehicles	1,529,133	159,620,549	9,580	122,114,932	765	12.52

Source: Department of Transportation, Federal Highway Administration.

Report Record Income from 1980 Mineral Operations

Preliminary estimates indicate that royalties including Windfall Profit Tax revenues collected in 1980 from production of oil, gas, coal, potash, phosphate, sodium, and other minerals on federal and Indian lands will exceed $2.8 billion, setting a new high and topping the previous record set in 1979 by $697 million. According to the U.S. Geological Survey, about $191 million represents oil Windfall Profit Tax revenue. The increases in revenue are due mainly to continued increases in oil and gas prices.

Royalties accruing from mineral and energy leases supervised by the U.S. Geological Survey are ultimately credited to the states, Indians, the Reclamation Fund, the Land and Water Conservation Fund, Historic Preservation Fund, and the U.S. Treasury.

Beware of Underinflated Tires

Survey after survey by tire companies and other sources show that up to 90% of the tires on the road are underinflated, many to the point of being not only wasteful of gas, but of being dangerous.

Improper air pressure not only cuts into gas mileage by about 5% but it also reduces the life of a tire because of heat build-up caused by too much sidewall flexing.

Some motorists try to guess the tire pressure by looking at the tires. That system won't work with radials, which have a natural appearance of being too low, so the car owner becomes accustomed to that look. But put one tire inflated to 24 pounds next to one with 16 pounds, a difference of one third, and the tires will look virtually the same. Therefore, it is important to check the air pressure with a gauge.

Annual Cost of Fuel
(Based on driving 10,000 miles per year)

MPG	Price Per Gallon						
	$1.60	$1.70	$1.80	$1.90	$2.00	$2.10	$2.20
50	320	340	360	380	400	420	440
45	355	377	400	422	444	466	488
40	400	425	450	475	500	525	550
35	458	486	515	543	572	601	629
30	533	566	599	633	666	699	733
25	640	680	720	760	800	840	880
20	800	850	900	950	1,000	1,050	1,100
15	1,067	1,134	1,201	1,267	1,334	1,401	1,467
10	1,600	1,700	1,800	1,900	2,000	2,100	2,200

Be Wary of Gas Gadgets

With most motorists concerned about getting more miles per gallon of gasoline, the promoters of "miracle" devices and additives are having a field day. But be wary of the claims, warns the Automotive Information Council (AIC), because most of them will do nothing for the car's mileage.

The auto manufacturers have used their best engineering know-how to gain maximum miles per gallon, not only for competitive but for regulatory reasons. If there was a product on the market which would increase the mileage, the car companies would be using it.

Buying Gasoline—Converting Liters to Gallons[1]
(Rounded-off Figures)

Liters	Gallons	Liters	Gallons	Liters	Gallons	Liters	Gallons
1	.3	26	6.9	51	13.5	76	20.1
2	.5	27	7.1	52	13.7	77	20.3
3	.8	28	7.4	53	14.0	78	20.6
4	1.1	29	7.7	54	14.3	79	20.9
5	1.3	30	7.9	55	14.5	80	21.1
6	1.6	31	8.2	56	14.8	81	21.4
7	1.8	32	8.5	57	15.0	82	21.7
8	2.1	33	8.7	58	15.3	83	21.9
9	2.4	34	9.0	59	15.6	84	22.2
10	2.6	35	9.2	60	15.9	85	22.5
11	2.9	36	9.5	61	16.1	86	22.7
12	3.2	37	9.8	62	16.4	87	23.0
13	3.4	38	10.0	63	16.6	88	23.2
14	3.7	39	10.3	64	16.9	89	23.5
15	4.0	40	10.6	65	17.2	90	23.8
16	4.2	41	10.8	66	17.4	91	24.0
17	4.5	42	11.1	67	17.7	92	24.3
18	4.8	43	11.4	68	18.0	93	24.6
19	5.0	44	11.6	69	18.2	94	24.8
20	5.3	45	11.9	70	18.5	95	25.1
21	5.5	46	12.2	71	18.8	96	25.4
22	5.8	47	12.4	72	19.0	97	25.6
23	6.1	48	12.7	73	19.3	98	25.9
24	6.3	49	12.9	74	19.6	99	26.1
25	6.6	50	13.2	75	19.8	100	26.4

1. For precise conversion: 1 liter = .2642 gallons. 1 gallon = 3.785 liters. Multiplying prices per liter by 3.785 gives price per gallon.

SCIENCE

The Year in Science—1981

The past year saw several major advances in genetic "engineering", the recently developed technology that permits scientists to grow organisms with the ability to produce useful products by implanting appropriate genes from other cells. The new cells are grown in specially prepared cultures and their chemical or pharmaceutical products extracted through conventional processes. In one such case, genetically engineered cells have been used to produce human insulin, which for the first time has been injected into diabetes patients. The new hormone is apparently just as effective as that traditionally extracted from livestock pancreas glands; in fact, it seems to be assimilated somewhat faster after being injected under the skin. Development of the new insulin production process promises to forestall the insulin shortage expected to arise within 15–20 years.

Researchers have also used bacteria to produce Human Growth Hormone (HGH), a defiency of which can cause a form of dwarfism. Natural HGH is found in the human pituitary gland, so the ability to produce the hormone outside the body is an obvious breakthrough. Genetic engineers have also produced a hybrid cell line by fusing human bone cancer cells with specially prepared human spleen cells. The hybrid cells produce antibodies which may eventually be useful in treating the disease. Veterinary medicine has benefitted from genetic engineering as well: 1981 saw the first production of a vaccine—for hoof-and-mouth disease—from genetically altered bacteria. The vaccine works, and promises to have a major beneficial impact on world food supplies.

Busy Bacteria

What happens when you mix cheese whey, which the U.S. alone produces in quantities exceeding 40 billion pounds per year and which has led to serious environmental pollution problems, with selected strains of yeast? You get a dry white wine perfectly acceptable for human consumption, at about one half the cost of that produced from grapes. Or, if you prefer, change the mix and the whey can be used to produce an alcohol fuel for use in automobile engines. Conversely, British chemists have brought on stream a huge fermenter (1300 cubic meter capacity, the world's largest) in which the bacteria *Methylophilus methylotrophus* converts methyl alcohol derived from North Sea crude oil refining into a high-protein animal feed. The only raw materials needed are methanol, ammonia, oxygen, and a few trace elements.

Synthetic Skin

A polymer engineer has teamed up with a surgeon to produce the first artificial skin usable in treating burn victims. The synthetic skin has a sandwich structure containing an outer layer of silicone and an inner layer composed of fiber collagen and a polysaccharide (glycosaminoglycan). It is flexible and porous enough to permit about the same moisture permeation as natural skin. So far, it has been used successfully to treat patients burned over 90% of their bodies, cases in which skin grafts from unburned areas would have been unavailable.

Run up your IQ

Everyone knows exercise is good for you, and many a pair of jogging shoes has been worn out in the pursuit of physical fitness. Now comes news that exercise appears to benefit your mental fitness, as well. It has been found that serial processing, a higher intellectual activity that takes place in the left lobe of the brain, improves significantly in middle-aged men who follow a moderate exercise program. About 1½ hours of exercise per day for four months was sufficient to produce the observed effects. In a related finding, it was noted that mice that are forced to jog experience far more remission in purposely initiated cancers than those that don't. The results of this investigation have not as yet been applied to human subjects, however.

Test-tube Twins?

In other genetic news, Australian researchers have successfully implanted fertile eggs in the uteri of two otherwise sterile women. The trick employed by the Australians, who had attempted implantation without success before, was to treat the women first with a fertility drug known to produce multiple ovae, remove the eggs thus produced from the women's ovaries, fertilize them with the fathers' sperm and re-implant more than one in each mother's uterus. The thinking was that with more than one egg present, chances for at least one surviving were better. The surprising result was that in both cases, both ovae "took", leading to the possibility that the women would give birth to non-identical twins. The joyous events were still pending at press time: stay tuned. The first successful implantation of a fertilized egg in the U.S. was also announced during 1981, but no further details were released.

It was, however, revealed that researchers at the University of Geneva had succeeded in cloning mice. There had been controversy over whether the Swiss experiments had actually produced clones, the first in a mammalian life-form, but tests of the offsprings' genetic material proved that cloning had in fact been achieved.

Deepest Simulated Dive

If man is to explore the ocean's depths, it becomes essential that the body's ability to withstand extremely high pressures first be established. Otherwise, oceanographers and deep-sea divers would be constrained by the need for massive pressure vessels or heavy diving suits. The pressure frontier was pushed back a bit farther in 1981 when three scientists at Duke University School of Medicine were subjected to pressures equivalent to an ocean depth of 2,250 feet. The men breathed a special mixture of oxygen, helium, and nitrogen. It took seven days to reach the simulated "depth," which the subjects endured for 24 hours without apparent ill effects. Depressurization was carried out over 31 days, the long, slow process being needed to avoid the often-fatal "bends."

Earth Sciences

Mt. St. Helens, whose violent eruption in 1980 left 60 dead, slipped into the relative obscurity of rebuilding. The volcano continues to exude lava, but at the more deliberate rate characteristic of this stage of its activity. By mid 1981, the mountain had formed a lava cone approximately 500 feet high and 1,200 feet long inside the huge crater left by its earlier explosion. The process now going on is expected to continue for several years. Sicily's Mt. Etna also erupted, on March 18 and 19, 1981, but, again, it was a case of lava oozing out of a fissure on the side of the 2.5-million-year-old mountain. The eruption was all over by March 22, and the nearby town of Randazzo was spared serious damage.

Volcanic activity is understood to be related to shifts in the Earth's crust, the same kind of activity that causes earthquakes. Tectonics, that branch of the geologic sciences which seeks to understand these crustal movements, now benefits from new techniques that enable researchers to fix the geographic orientation of a rock at the time it was formed. Called paleomagnetics, the technique is able to detect the alignment of a rock with respect to the Earth's magnetic field during formation. This development, in fact, has given rise to a new field, called microplate tectonics, which looks at the smaller chunks of continents formed when the larger tectonic plates crunch against each other. Alaska is an area now under intensive study by this new technology, since it now appears that portions of what is now our 51st state were once part of Mexico and Central America. The surprising result that the latest paleomagnetic measurements seem to indicate is the speed with which this continent-building takes place: parts of California, for example, have made a 750-mile trip in only 15 million years. In geologic terms, that's really zipping right along.

Jet Set Weather

Portions of the U.S. have undergone noticeable changes in seasonal weather patterns over the past 25 years, and meteorologists now think they understand the reason. The changes have apparently been brought about by jet contrails, those thin traces of exhaust gases made by high-flying commercial aircraft. Jets have been in widespread use since about the early 1960s (lower-flying piston powered aircraft don't create contrails) and scientists have been able to analyze weather data from before and since that time in areas where jet traffic is heavy. As one might expect, cloud cover in some of those areas has increased by up to 10% since 1955, and this could have had some influence on crop production. Not that the effects are necessarily bad, however. The most noticeable change has been a leveling of diurnal temperatures, meaning cooler days and warmer nights. That, in turn, could have reduced over-all energy consumption by lowering heating and air conditioning requirements.

Small Stuff

Sub-atomic particle physicists try to discover what it is that atoms themselves are made of. One of their problems has always been that they can never actually see the objects of their investiga-
tions: the particles are just too small. Mathematical theory is therefore used to predict the existence of a sub-atomic particle, along with the properties and effects such a particle should have. The trick then is to look for the property or effect under conditions where the particle should have been present, and if these can be observed, everything falls into place. Current thinking is that all matter is composed of combinations of six types of particles called quarks—plus six anti-quarks, to keep our universe symmetrical. The quarks are assembled into protons, neutrons, and electrons, which comprise atoms, and so forth. The difficulty now is that some of these little beasties aren't behaving the way theory predicts they should. Neutrinos, for example, may actually have a small rest mass (a mass when they aren't moving at the speed of light) and, worse yet, phonons, or "particles" of electromagnetic radiation, including visible light, may have one too. If that weren't bad enough, evidence is now mounting that electric charge may exist in fractions of the charge on a single electron. If this can be proven unambiguously, it would upset modern quark theory completely, perhaps suggesting the existence of "sub-quarks."

On the brighter side, researchers at the Swiss Institute for Nuclear Research (SIN) may have discovered a new, extremely light particle which may be the postulated but never-before-seen axion. Since the physicists running the experiments are from the University of Aachen (Germany), the new particles are tentatively being called "aachions." Also in Switzerland, enough anti-protons have been collected in the CERN Antiproton Accumulator to allow them to be accelerated and collided with ordinary protons, annihilating both particles and leaving nothing but energy. Results of the experiment are not in yet, but despite the 24-billion-electron-volt acceleration potential used, Geneva was still on the map.

Elsewhere, a second organic superconductor has been found: it is di(tetramethylselenafulvaenium)-hexafluorophosphate, or $(TMTSF)_2PF_6$, for short. Its technological significance lies in the fact that it can be made superconducting (that is, conduct electricity without resistance losses) simply by cooling it to 1–2 degrees Kelvin above absolute zero. The previously found organic superconductor required not only low temperature, but high pressure, as well, to achieve the same effect.

Oldies but Goodies

Anthropologists haven't been able to match 1980's discovery of *aegyptopithicus*, man's oldest ancestor, but 1980 saw the dawn of human-like behavior pushed back another half million years. Simple tools found in the Hadar of the Afar region of northeastern Ethiopia in 1977 have now been analyzed and their age, 2½ million years, makes them the oldest man-made objects found to date. It is still not known who made the tools.

A new genus and specie of early reptile has been discovered inside the rib cages of two 180-million-year-old fossil skeletons. It appears as though the two skeletons' original owners ate the smaller reptiles, then promptly died. It has therefore been suggested that *Malerisaurus robinsonae*, as the new creature has been named, may have been poisonous. The animal, incidentally, belongs to the group from which snakes and lizards are thought to have evolved.

Konrad J.A. Kundig

Table of Geological Periods

It is now generally assumed that planets are formed by the accretion of gas and dust in a cosmic cloud, but there is no way of estimating the length of this process. Our earth acquired its present size, more or less, between 4,000 and 5,000 million years ago. Life on earth originated about 2,000 million years ago, but there are no good fossil remains from periods earlier than the Cambrian, which began about 550 million years ago. The largely unknown past before the Cambrian Period is referred to as the Pre-Cambrian and is subdivided into the Lower (or older) and Upper (or younger) Pre-Cambrian—also called the Archaeozoic and Proterozoic Eras.

The known geological history of the earth since the beginning of the Cambrian Period is subdivided into three "eras," each of which comprises a number of "periods." They, in turn, are subdivided into "subperiods." In a subperiod, a certain section may be especially well known because of rich fossil finds. Such a section is called a "formation," and it is usually identified by a place name.

Paleozoic Era

This era began 550 million years ago and lasted for 355 million years. The name was compounded from Greek *palaios* (old) and *zoön* (animal).

Period	Duration[1]	Subperiods	Events
Cambrian (from *Cambria*, Latin name for Wales)	70	Lower Cambrian Middle Cambrian Upper Cambrian	Invertebrate sea life of many types, proliferating during this and the following period
Ordovician (from Latin *Ordovices*, people of early Britain)	85	Lower Ordovician Upper Ordovician	
Silurian (from Latin *Silures*, people of early Wales)	40	Lower Silurian Upper Silurian	First known fishes; gigantic sea scorpions
Devonian (from Devonshire in England)	50	Lower Devonian Upper Devonian	Proliferation of fishes and other forms of sea life; land still largely lifeless
Carboniferous (from Latin *carbo* = coal + *fero* = to bear)	85	Lower or Mississippian Upper or Pennsylvanian	Period of maximum coal formation in swampy forests; early insects and first known amphibians
Permian (from district of Perm in Russia)	25	Lower Permian Upper Permian	Early reptiles and mammals; earliest form of turtles

Mesozoic Era

This era began 195 million years ago and lasted for 135 million years. The name was compounded from Greek *mesos* (middle) and *zoön* (animal). Popular name: Age of Reptiles.

Period	Duration[1]	Subperiods	Events
Triassic (from *trias* = triad)	35	Lower or Buntsandstein (from German *bunt* = colorful + *Sandstein* = sandstone) Middle or Muschelkalk (from German *Muschel* = clam + *Kalk* = limestone) Upper or Keuper (old miners' term)	Early saurians
Jurassic (from Jura Mountains)	35	Lower or Black Jurassic, or Lias (from French *liais* = hard stone) Middle or Brown Jurassic, or Dogger (old provincial English for ironstone) Upper or White Jurassic, or Malm (Middle English for sand)	Many sea-going reptiles; early large dinosaurs; somewhat later, flying reptiles (pterosaurs), earliest known birds
Cretaceous (from Latin *creta* = chalk)	65	Lower Cretaceous Upper Cretaceous	Maximum development of dinosaurs; birds proliferating; oppossum-like mammals

Cenozoic Era

This era began 60 million years ago and includes the geological present. The name was compounded from Greek *kainos* (new) and *zoön* (animal). Popular name: Age of Mammals.

Period	Duration[1]	Subperiods	Events
Tertiary (originally thought to be the third of only three periods)	c. 60	Paleocene (from Greek *palaios* = old + *kainos* = new)	First mammals other than marsupials
		Eocene (from Greek *eos* = dawn + *kainos* = new)	Formation of amber; rich insect fauna; early bats
		Oligocene (from Greek *oligos* = few + *kainos* = new)	Steady increase of large mammals
		Miocene (from Greek *meios* = less + *kainos* = new)	
		Pliocene (from Greek *pleios* = more + *kainos* = new)	Mammals closely resembling present types; protohumans
Pleistocene (from Greek *pleistos* = most + *kainos* = new) (popular name: Ice Age)	1	Four major glaciations, named Günz, Mindel, Riss, and Würm, originally the names of rivers. Last glaciation ended 10,000 to 15,000 years ago	Various forms of early man
Holocene (from Greek *holos* = entire + *kainos* = new)		The present	The last 3,000 years are called "history"

1. In millions of years.

Chemical Elements

Element	Symbol	Atomic no.	Atomic weight	Specific gravity	Melting point °C	Boiling point °C	Number of isotopes[1]	Discoverer	Year
Actinium	Ac	89	227[2]	10.07[2]	1050	3200 ± 300	11	Debierne	1899
Aluminum	Al	13	26.9815	2.6989	660.37	2467	8	Wöhler	1827
Americium	Am	95	243[6]	13.67	994 ± 4	2607	13[3]	Seaborg et al.	1944
Antimony	Sb	51	121.75	6.691	630.74	1750	29	Early historic times	—
Argon	Ar	18	39.948	1.7837[4]	−189.2	−185.7	8	Rayleigh and Ramsay	1894
Arsenic (gray)	As	33	74.9216	5.73	817 (28 atm.)	613[5]	8	Albertus Magnus	1250?
Astatine	At	85	~210		302	337	14	Corson et al.	1940
Barium	Ba	56	137.34	3.5	725	1640	21	Davy	1808
Berkelium	Bk	97	247[6]	14.00[7]			25	Seaborg et al.	1949
Beryllium	Be	4	9.01218	1.848	1278 ± 5	2970 (5 mm.)	8[3]	Vauquelin	1798
							6		
Bismuth	Bi	83	208.9806	9.747	271.3	1560 ± 5	19	Geoffroy	1753
Boron	B	5	10.81	2.37[8]	2300	2550[5]	6	Gay-Lussac and Thénard; Davy	1808
Bromine	Br	35	79.904	3.12[4]	−7.2	58.78	19	Balard	1826
Cadmium	Cd	48	112.40	8.65	320.9	765	22	Stromeyer	1817
Calcium	Ca	20	40.08	1.55	839 ± 2	1484	14	Davy	1808
Californium	Cf	98	251[6]				12[3]	Seaborg et al.	1950
Carbon	C	6	12.011	1.8–3.5[9]	~3550	4827	7	Prehistoric	—
Cerium	Ce	58	140.12	6.771	798 ± 3	3257	19	Berzelius and Hisinger; Klaproth	1803
Cesium	Cs	55	132.9055	1.873	28.40	678.4	22	Bunsen and Kirchhoff	1860
Chlorine	Cl	17	35.453	1.56[4]	−100.98	−34.6	11	Scheele	1774
Chromium	Cr	24	51.996	7.18–7.20	1857 ± 20	2672	9	Vauquelin	1797
Cobalt	Co	27	58.9332	8.9	1495	2870	14	Brandt	c.1735
Copper	Cu	29	63.546	8.96	1083.4 ± 0.2	2567	11	Prehistoric	—
Curium	Cm	96	247[6]	13.51[2]	1340 ± 40		13[3]	Seaborg et al.	1944
Dysprosium	Dy	66	162.50	8.540	1409	2335	21	Boisbaudran	1886
Einsteinium	Es	99	254[6]				12[3]	Ghiorso et al	1952
Erbium	Er	68	167.26	9.045	1522	2510	16	Mosander	1843
Europium	Eu	63	151.96	5.283	822 ± 5	1597	21	Demarcay	1896
Fermium	Fm	100	257[6]				10[3]	Ghiorso et al	1953
Fluorine	F	9	18.9984	1.108[4]	−219.62	−188.14	6	Moissan	1886
Francium	Fr	87	223[6]		27[2]	677[2]	21	Perey	1939
Gadolinium	Gd	64	157.25	7.898	1311 ± 1	3233	17	Marignac	1880
Gallium	Ga	31	69.72	5.904	29.78	2403	14	Boisbaudran	1875
Germanium	Ge	32	72.59	5.323	937.4	2830	17	Winkler	1886
Gold	Au	79	196.9665	19.32	1064.43	2807	21	Prehistoric	—
Hafnium	Hf	72	178.49	13.31	2227 ± 20	4602	17	Coster and von Hevesy	1923
Helium	He	2	4.00260	0.1785[4]	−272.2 (26 atm.)	−268.934	5	Janssen	1868
Holmium	Ho	67	164.9303	8.781	1470	2720	29	Delafontaine and Soret	1878
Hydrogen	H	1	1.0080	0.070[4]	−259.14	−252.87	3	Cavendish	1766
Indium	In	49	114.82	7.31	156.61	2080	34	Reich and Richter	1863

Element	Symbol	Atomic no.	Atomic weight	Specific gravity	Melting point °C	Boiling point °C	Number of isotopes[1]	Discoverer	Year
Iodine	I	53	126.9045	4.93	113.5	184.35	24	Courtois	1811
Iridium	Ir	77	192.22	22.42	2410	4130	25	Tennant	1803
Iron	Fe	26	55.847	7.894	1535	2750	10	Prehistoric	—
Krypton	Kr	36	83.80	3.733[4]	−156.6	−152.30±0.10	23	Ramsay and Travers	1898
Lanthanum	La	57	138.9055	6.166	920±5	3454	19	Mosander	1839
Lawrencium	Lr	103	257[6]	—	—	—	20[3]	Ghiorso et al.	1961
Lead	Pb	82	207.2	11.35	327.502	1740	29	Prehistoric	—
Lithium	Li	3	6.941	0.534	180.54	1347	5	Arfvedson	1817
Lutetium	Lu	71	174.97	9.835	1656±5	3315	22	Urbain	1907
Magnesium	Mg	12	24.305	1.738	648.8±0.5	1090	8	Black	1755
Manganese	Mn	25	54.9380	7.21–7.44[10]	1244±3	1962	11	Gahn, Scheele, and Bergman	1774
Mendelevium	Md	101	256[6]	—	—	—	3[3]	Ghiorso et al.	1955
Mercury	Hg	80	200.59	13.546	−38.87	356.58	26	Prehistoric	—
Molybdenum	Mo	42	95.94	10.22	2617	4612	20	Scheele	1778
Neodymium	Nd	60	144.24	6.80 & 7.004[10]	1010	3127	16	von Welsbach	1885
Neon	Ne	10	20.179	0.89990 (g/1 0°C/1 atm)	−248.67	−246.048	8	Ramsay and Travers	1898
Neptunium	Np	93	237.0482	20.25	640±1	3902	15[3]	McMillan and Abelson	1940
Nickel	Ni	28	58.71	8.902	1453	2732	11	Cronstedt	1751
Niobium (Columbium)	Nb	41	92.9064	8.57	2468±10	4742	24	Hatchett	1801
Nitrogen	N	7	14.0067	0.808[4]	−209.86	−195.8	8	Rutherford	1772
Nobelium	No	102	254[6]	—	—	—	7[3]	Ghiorso et al.	1957
Osmium	Os	76	190.2	22.57	3045±30	5027±100	19	Tennant	1803
Oxygen	O	8	15.9994	1.14[4]	−218.4	−182.962	8	Priestley	1774
Palladium	Pd	46	106.4	12.02	1552	3140	21	Wollaston	1803
Phosphorus	P	15	30.9738	1.82 (white)	44.1	280	7	Brand	1669
Platinum	Pt	78	195.09	21.45	1772	3827±100	32	Ulloa	1735
Plutonium	Pu	94	244[6]	19.84	641	3232	16[3]	Seaborg et al.	1940
Polonium	Po	84	~210[6]	9.32	254	962	34	Curie	1898
Potassium	K	19	39.102	0.862	63.65	774	10	Davy	1807
Praseodymium	Pr	59	140.9077	6.772	931±4	3212	15	von Welsbach	1885
Promethium	Pm	61	145[6]	—	~1080	2460?	14	Marinsky et al.	1945
Protactinium	Pa	91	231.0359	15.37[2]	<1600	—	14	Hahn and Meitner	1917
Radium	Ra	88	226.0254	5.0?	700	1140	15	P. and M. Curie	1898
Radon	Rn	86	222[6]	4.4[4]	−71	−61.8	20	Dorn	1900
Rhenium	Re	75	186.2	21.02	3180	5627[7]	21	Noddack, Berg, and Tacke	1925
Rhodium	Rh	45	102.9055	12.41	1966±3	3727±100	20	Wollaston	1803
Rubidium	Rb	37	85.4678	1.532	38.89	688	20	Bunsen and Kirchoff	1861
Ruthenium	Ru	44	101.07	12.44	2310	3900	16	Klaus	1844
Samarium	Sm	62	150.4	7.536	1072±5	1778	17	Boisbaudran	1879
Scandium	Sc	21	44.9559	2.989	1539	2832	15	Nilson	1879
Selenium	Se	34	78.96	4.79 (gray)	217	684.9±1	20	Berzelius	1817
Silicon	Si	14	28.086	2.33	1410	2355	8	Berzelius	1824
Silver	Ag	47	107.868	10.50	961.93	2212	27	Prehistoric	—
Sodium	Na	11	22.9898	0.971	97.81±0.03	882.9	7	Davy	1807
Strontium	Sr	38	87.62	2.54	769	1384	18	Davy	1808
Sulfur	S	16	32.06	2.07[11]	112.8	444.674	10	Prehistoric	—
Tantalum	Ta	73	180.9479	16.654	2996	5425±100	19	Ekeberg	1801
Technetium	Tc	43	98.9062	11.50[2]	2172	4877	23	Perrier and Segrè	1937
Tellurium	Te	52	127.60	6.24	449.5±0.3	989.8±3.8	29	von Reichenstein	1782
Terbium	Tb	65	158.9254	8.234	1360±4	3041	24	Mosander	1843
Thallium	Tl	81	204.37	11.85	303.5	1457±10	28	Crookes	1861
Thorium	Th	90	232.0381	11.72	1750	~4790	12	Berzelius	1828
Thulium	Tm	69	168.9342	9.314	1545±15	1727	18	Cleve	1879
Tin	Sn	50	118.69	7.31 (white)	231.9681	2270	28	Prehistoric	—
Titanium	Ti	22	47.90	4.55	1660±10	3287	9	Gregor	1791
Tungsten (Wolfram)	W	74	183.85	19.3	3410±20	5660	22	J. and F. d'Elhuyar	1783
Uranium	U	92	238.029	~18.95	1132.3±0.8	3818	15	Peligot	1841
Vanadium	V	23	50.9414	6.11	1890±10	3380	9	del Rio	1801
Xenon	Xe	54	131.30	3.52[4]	−111.9	−107.1±3	31	Ramsay and Travers	1898
Ytterbium	Yb	70	173.04	6.972	824±5	1193	16	Marignac	1878
Yttrium	Y	39	88.9059	4.457	1523±8	3337	21	Gadolin	1794
Zinc	Zn	30	65.38	7.133	419.58	907	15	Prehistoric	—
Zirconium	Zr	40	91.22	6.506[2]	1852±2	4377	20	Klaproth	1789

1. Isotopes are different forms of the same element having the same atomic number but different atomic weights. 2. Calculated figure. 3. Artificially produced. 4. Liquid. 5. Sublimation point. 6. Mass number of the isotope of longest known life. 7. Estimated. 8. Amorphous. 9. Depending on whether amorphous, graphite or diamond. 10. Depending on allotropic form. 11. Rhombic. ~ Is approximately. < Is less than. NOTE: There is a dispute between groups at the Lawrence Berkeley Laboratory of the University of California and at the Dubna Laboratory in the Soviet Union concerning the discovery of elements 104, 105, and 106. The Lawrence Berkeley Laboratory claims that 104 and 105 were discovered in 1969 and 1970, respectively, by Ghiorso et al. and has suggested the names Rutherfordium and Hahnium. The U.S. laboratory claims also that Ghiorso et al. discovered element 106 in 1974. No name has yet been suggested for this element. Names will not be official until the controversy is resolved and they have been approved by the International Union for Pure and Applied Chemistry.

Atomic Energy

Just as the Space Age is said to have started with the orbiting of Sputnik I, the Atomic Age is said to have started with the explosion of a test bomb on July 16, 1945, near Alamogordo, N.M., at 5:30 A.M. local time. The bomb was placed on top of a steel tower, and observers were stationed in bunkers 10,000 yards away. The explosion vaporized the steel tower, produced a mushroom cloud rising to 40,000 feet, and melted the desert sand into glass for distances up to 800 yards from the tower.

The first operational use of an atom bomb took place only three weeks later, when a uranium bomb was exploded over Hiroshima, Japan, on Aug. 6, 1945. The bomb, cylindrical in shape, 10 feet long with a diameter of 2 feet 4 inches, weighed about 9,000 pounds. Its explosive force was equal to 20,000 tons of TNT, hence the term "20-kiloton bomb." Three days later another atomic bomb, this time of plutonium, was exploded over Nagasaki.

Of course, the Atomic Age did not begin with the explosion of the test bomb at Alamogordo, just as the Space Age did not begin with the orbiting of the first artificial satellite. In both cases these visible feats were just experiments which proved the theory that had been built up patiently over decades.

At the turn of the century, scientists began to wonder whether the atoms of the chemical elements might not be composed of smaller particles. This was actually a contradiction in terms, because the Greek word *atomos*, from which the word *atom* was derived, meant "indivisible." But there were some indications of particles smaller than an atom —the electrons. In 1905, Albert Einstein suggested that matter might just be "condensed energy" and gave the conversion formula $E = mc^2$, in which E represents the energy, m the mass, and c the velocity of light. If this formula was correct, a small piece of matter should represent enormous amounts of energy.

Fission and Fusion

As is now generally known, atomic energy can be released in two ways. One is the *fission* of elements with very heavy atoms, such as uranium and plutonium, which will split when struck by a neutron, a sub-atomic particle. The splitting of the heavy atom releases more neutrons, which are then available to split other atoms—the so-called chain reaction. The other way of obtaining atomic energy is *fusion;* four light atoms (hydrogen) are fused together into the next heavier element (helium). The fusion reaction requires enormous heat and very high pressures. These pressures, coupled with very high temperatures, can most easily be produced by exploding a fission bomb, which is the reason why it is often said that a fission bomb is the trigger for a fusion (hydrogen) bomb.

Interestingly enough, the fusion reaction was discovered first, though only on paper. For the period from, say, 1910 to 1930, most physicists believed that the release of atomic energy, if it could be done, would be of no practical value. They asserted that causing the release would require more energy than could be obtained. Most astronomers, on the other hand, were convinced that atomic energy was released in the sun and the other stars because there was no other way to account for the energy the stars radiated into space. Trying to account for the energy radiated by the stars led to theoretical papers predicting what we now call the fusion reaction. At the time (1930), atomic fission was still unknown; it was discovered first by Enrico Fermi in 1934. But nobody yet knew that the sudden bursts of energy observed in the experiments were due to the fission of the uranium-235 atom. This was established (by way of calculation) by Dr. Lise Meitner. Once it was known what happened, the way to a premeditated release of atomic energy was clear.

But nobody could be quite certain whether the release would take the form of an explosion or whether it would be slow enough to be used to generate power. American scientists proceeded under the assumption that the release would be sudden and violent (and the Alamogordo test proved them right), while Professor Heisenberg in Germany thought the slow release to be more likely, which is the reason why the Germans did not start a large-scale atomic energy project.

Atoms for Peace

The *peaceful* Atomic Age can be said to have been born in 1954, when the original U.S. Atomic Energy Act was amended to release many so-called "secrets" of nuclear energy so that nuclear power plants could be built and radioactive isotopes be used in medicine. The next year, the first International Conference on the Peaceful Uses of the Atom was convened at Geneva, bringing together scientists from all over the world to discuss what hitherto had been considered to be secret.

Actually there was little that was really secret about nuclear energy. When the results of the 1938 experiments were brought to the United States, scientists from different parts of the world openly stated that the possibility of atomic bombs was inherent in the scientific findings.

Once the veil of "secrecy" had been dispelled by revision of the Atomic Energy Act and the Geneva meeting, construction of plants to produce electricity by controlled fission of uranium atoms got under way in the United States and several other industrialized nations. Electric power was first produced as a result of nuclear fission in December 1951 at the National Reactor Testing Station in Idaho. When a reactor was connected to a generator, the nuclear power plant produced enough electricity for about 50 homes.

The Stages of Invention

Alexander von Humbolt (1769–1859), the German naturalist, said that an invention goes through three stages: doubt of its existence, denial of its importance, and, finally, credit for its discovery going to someone else.

One example of the truth in this perception is the invention of the "Pullman," the railroad sleeping car. The first sleeper was built by Richard Imlay of Philadelphia. It ran between Chambersburg and Harrisburg, Pa., in 1838. At least eight railroads advertised some kind of sleeping car before 1850. Pullman's first car was not built until 1859. George M. Pullman and his friend Ben Field patented the folding upper berth in 1864. Pullman seems to have been a better businessman and a better promoter.

Scientific Inventions, Discoveries, and Theories

Most inventions are the results of the discoveries, theories, experiments, and improvements of many people. This list tries to suggest the development of certain particularly important ideas. In some instances, it tries to connect the fundamental theory with the ultimate practical invention.

Abacus: *See* Calculating machine

Adding machine: *See* Calculating machine; Computer

Adrenaline: (isolation of) Jokichi Takamine, U.S., 1901

Air brake: George Westinghouse, U.S., 1868

Air conditioning: Willis Carrier, U.S., 1911

Airplane: (first powered, sustained, controlled flight) Orville and Wilbur Wright, U.S., 1903. *See also* Jet propulsion, aircraft

Airship: (non-rigid) Henri Giffard, France, 1852; (rigid) Ferdinand von Zeppelin, Germany, 1900

Aluminum manufacture: (by electrolytic action) Charles M. Hall, U.S., 1866

Anesthetic: (first use of anesthetic—ether—on man) Crawford W. Long, U.S., 1842

Antibiotics: (first demonstration of antibiotic effect) Louis Pasteur, Jules-François Joubert, France, 1887; (penicillin, first modern antibiotic) Alexander Fleming, England, 1928

Antiseptic: (surgery) Joseph Lister, England, 1867

Antitoxin, diphtheria: Emil von Behring, Germany, 1890

Atomic theory: (ancient) Leucippus, Democritus, Greece, c.500 B.C.; Lucretius, Rome, c.100 B.C.; (modern) John Dalton, England, 1808

Automobile: (first with internal combustion engine, 250 rpm) Karl Benz, Germany, 1885; (first with practical high-speed internal combustion engine, 900 rpm) Gottlieb Daimler, Germany, 1885; (first true automobile, not carriage with motor) René Panhard, Emile Lavassor, France, 1891; (carburetor, spray) Charles E. Duryea, U.S., 1892

Bacteria: Anton van Leeuwenhoek, The Netherlands, 1683

Bakelite: *See* Plastics

Balloon, hot-air: Joseph and Jacques Montgolfier, France, 1783

Ball-point pen: *See* Pen

Barometer: Evangelista Torricelli, Italy, 1643

Bicycle: Karl D. von Sauerbronn, Germany, 1816; (first modern model) James Starley, England, 1884

Bifocal lens: *See* Lens, bifocal

Blood, circulation of: William Harvey, England, 1628

Braille: Louis Braille, France, 1829

Bullet: (conical) Claude Minié, France, 1849

Calculating machine: (Abacus) China, c.190; (logarithms: made multiplying easier and thus calculators practical) John Napier, Scotland, 1614; (slide rule) William Oughtred, England, 1632; (digital calculator) Blaise Pascal, 1642; (multiplication machine) Gottfried Leibnitz, Germany, 1671; (important 19th-century contributors to modern machine) Frank S. Baldwin, Jay R. Monroe, Dorr E. Felt, W. T. Ohdner, William Burroughs, all U.S.; ("analytical engine" design, included concepts of programming, taping) Charles Babbage, England, 1835. *See also* Computer

Camera: (hand-held) George Eastman, U.S., 1888; (Polaroid Land) Edwin Land, U.S., 1948. *See also* Photography

Carburetor: *See* Automobile

Celanese: *See* Fibers, man-made

Celluloid: *See* Plastics

Classification of plants and animals: (by genera and species) Carolus Linnaeus, Sweden, 1737–53

Clock, pendulum: Christian Huygens, The Netherlands, 1656

Combustion: (nature of) Antoine Lavoisier, France, 1777

Computer: (differential analyzer, mechanically operated) Vannevar Bush, U.S., 1928; (Mark I, first information-processing digital computer) Howard Aiken, U.S., 1944; (ENIAC, Electronic Numerical Integrator and Calculator, first all-electronic) J. Presper Eckert, John W. Mauchly, U.S., 1946; (stored-program concept) John von Neumann, U.S., 1947

Conditioned reflex: Ivan Pavlov, Russia, c.1910

Converter, Bessemer: William Kelly, U.S., 1851

Cosmetics: Egypt, c.4000 B.C.

Cotton gin: Eli Whitney, U.S., 1793

Crossbow: China, c.300 B.C.

Cyclotron: Ernest O. Lawrence, U.S., 1931

Deuterium: (heavy hydrogen) Harold Urey, U.S., 1931

DNA: (deoxyribonucleic acid) Friedrich Meischer, Germany, 1869; (determination of double-helical structure) F. H. Crick, England, James D. Watson, U.S., 1953

Dynamite: Alfred Nobel, Sweden, 1867

Electric generator (dynamo): (laboratory model) Michael Faraday, England, 1832; Joseph Henry, U.S., c.1832; (hand-driven model) Hippolyte Pixii, France, 1833; (alternating-current generator) Nikola Tesla, U.S., 1892

Electric lamp: (arc lamp) Sir Humphrey Davy, England, 1801; (fluorescent lamp) A. E. Becquerel, France, 1867; (incandescent lamp) Sir Joseph Swann, England, Thomas A. Edison, U.S., contemporaneously, 1870s; (carbon arc street lamp) Charles F. Brush, U.S., 1879; (first widely marketed incandescent lamp) Thomas A. Edison, U.S., 1879; (mercury vapor lamp) Peter Cooper Hewitt, U.S., 1903; (neon lamp) Georges Claude, France, 1911; (tungsten filament) Irving Langmuir, U.S., 1915

Electric motor: *See* Motor

Electromagnet: William Sturgeon, England, 1823

Electron: Sir Joseph J. Thompson, England, 1897

Elevator, passenger: (safety device permitting use by passengers) Elisha G. Otis, U.S., 1852; (elevator utilizing safety device) 1857

E = mc²: (equivalence of mass and energy) Albert Einstein, Switzerland, 1905

Engine, internal combustion: No single inventor. Fundamental theory established by Sadi Carnot, France, 1824; (two-stroke) Étienne Lenoir, France, 1860; (ideal operating cycle for four-stroke) Alphonse Beau de Rochet, France, 1862; (operating four-stroke) Nikolaus Otto, Germany, 1876; (diesel) Rudolf Diesel, Germany, 1892; (rotary) Felix Wankel, Germany, 1956. *See also* Automobile

Engine, steam: *See* Steam engine

Evolution: (by natural selection) Charles Darwin, England, 1859

Falling bodies, law of: Galileo Galilei, Italy, 1590

Fermentation: (micro-organisms as cause of) Louis Pasteur, France, c.1860

Fibers, man-made: (nitrocellulose fibers treated to change flammable nitrocellulose to harmless cel-

lulose, precursor of rayon) Sir Joseph Swann, England, 1883; (rayon) Count Hilaire de Chardonnet, France, 1889; (Celanese) Henry and Camille Dreyfuss, U.S., England, 1921; (research on polyesters and polyamides, basis for modern man-made fibers) U.S., England, Germany, 1930s; (nylon) Wallace H. Carothers, U.S., 1935

Fountain pen: See Pen

Geometry, elements of: Euclid, Alexandria, Egypt, c.300 B.C.

Gravitation, law of: Sir Isaac Newton, England, c.1665 (published 1687)

Gunpowder: China, c.700

Gyrocompass: Elmer A. Sperry, U.S., 1905

Gyroscope: Léon Foucault, France, 1852

Helicopter: Igor Sikorsky, U.S., 1939

Helium first observed on sun: Sir Joseph Lockyer, England, 1868

Heredity, laws of: Gregor Mendel, Austria, 1865

Induction, electric: Joseph Henry, U.S., 1828

Insulin: Sir Frederick G. Banting, J. J. R. MacLeod, Canada, 1922

Intelligence testing: Alfred Binet, Theodore Simon, France, 1905

Isotopes: (concept of) Frederick Soddy, England, 1912; (stable isotopes) J. J. Thompson, England, 1913; (existence demonstrated by mass spectrography) Francis W. Ashton, 1919

Jet propulsion, aircraft: Sir Frank Whittle, England, 1930

Laser: (theoretical work on) Charles H. Townes, Arthur L. Schawlow, U.S., N. Basov, A. Prokhorov, U.S.S.R., 1958; (first working model) T. H. Maiman, U.S., 1960

Lens, bifocal: Benjamin Franklin, U.S., c.1760

Light, nature of: (wave theory) Christian Huygens, Denmark, 1678; (electromagnetic theory) James Clerk Maxwell, England, 1873

Light, speed of: (theory that light has finite velocity) Olaus Roemer, Denmark, 1675

Lightning rod: Benjamin Franklin, U.S., 1752

Linotype: See Printing

Lithography: See Printing

Locomotive: (steam-powered) Richard Trevithick, England, 1804; (first practical, due to multiple-fire-tube boiler) George Stephenson, England, 1829; (largest steam-powered) Union Pacific's "Big Boy," U.S., 1941

Logarithms: See Calculating machine

Loom: (horizontal, two-beamed) Egypt, c.4400 B.C.; (Jacquard drawloom, pattern controlled by punch cards) Jacques de Vaucanson, France, 1745, Joseph-Marie Jacquard, 1801; (flying shuttle) John Kay, England, 1733; (power-driven loom) Edmund Cartwright, England, 1785

Machine gun: James Puckle, England, 1718; Richard J. Gatling, U.S., 1861

Match: (phosphorus) François Derosne, France, 1816; (friction) Charles Sauria, France, 1831; (safety) J. E. Lundstrom, Sweden, 1855

Mendelian law: See Heredity

Microscope: (compound) Zacharias Janssen, The Netherlands, 1590; (electron) Vladimir Zworykin et al., U.S., Canada, Germany, 1932–1939

Motion pictures: Thomas A. Edison, U.S., 1893

Motion pictures, sound: Product of various inventions. First picture with synchronized musical score: Don Juan, 1926; with spoken dialogue: The Jazz Singer, 1927; both Warner Bros.

Motor, electric: Michael Faraday, England, 1822; (alternating-current) Nikola Tesla, U.S., 1892

Motor, gasoline: See Engine, internal combustion

Motorcycle: (motor tricycle) Edward Butler, England, 1884; (gasoline-engine motorcycle) Gottieb Daimier, Germany, 1885

Neptunium: (first transuranic element, synthesis of) Edward M. McMillan, Philip H. Abelson, U.S., 1940

Neutron: James Chadwick, England, 1932

Neutron-induced radiation: Enrico Fermi et al., Italy, 1934

Nitroglycerin: Ascanio Sobrero, Italy, 1846

Nuclear fission: Otto Hahn, Fritz Strassmann, Germany, 1938

Nuclear reactor: Enrico Fermi et al., U.S., 1942

Nylon: See Fibers, man-made

Ohm's law: (relationship between strength of electric current, electromotive force, and circuit resistance) Georg S. Ohm, Germany, 1827

Ozone: Christian Schönbein, Germany, 1839

Paper: China, c.100 B.C.

Parachute: Louis S. Lenormand, France, 1783

Pen: (fountain) Lewis E. Waterman, U.S., 1884; (ball-point, for marking on rough surfaces) John H. Loud, U.S., 1888; (ball-point, for handwriting) Lazlo Biro, Argentina, 1944

Penicillin: See Antibiotics

Periodic law: (that properties of elements are functions of their atomic weights) Dmitri Mendeleev, Russia, 1869

Periodic table: (arrangement of chemical elements based on periodic law) Dmitri Mendeleev, Russia, 1869

Phonograph: Thomas A. Edison, U.S., 1877

Photography: (first paper negative, first photograph, on metal) Joseph Nicéphore Niepce, France, 1816–1827; (discovery of fixative powers of hyposulfite of soda) Sir John Herschel, England, 1819; (first direct positive image on silver plate, the daguerreotype) Louis Daguerre, France, 1839; (first paper negative from which a number of positive prints could be made) William Talbot, England, 1841. Work of these four men, taken together, forms basis for all modern photography. (First color images) Alexandre Becquerel, Claude Niepce de Saint-Victor, France, 1848–60; (commercial color film with three emulsion layers, Kodachrome) U.S., 1935. See also Camera

Plastics: (first material, nitrocellulose softened by vegetable oil, camphor, precursor to Celluloid) Alexander Parkes, England, 1855; (Celluloid, involving recognition of vital effect of camphor) John W. Hyatt, U.S., 1869; (Bakelite, first completely synthetic plastic) Leo H. Baekeland, U.S., 1910; (theoretical background of macromolecules and process of polymerization on which modern plastics industry rests) Hermann Staudinger, Germany, 1922. See also Fibers, man-made

Plow, forked: Mesopotamia, before 3000 B.C.

Plutonium, synthesis of: Glenn T. Seaborg, Edwin M. McMillan, Arthur C. Wahl, Joseph W. Kennedy, U.S., 1941

Polaroid Land camera: See Camera

Polio, vaccine against: (vaccine made from dead virus strains) Jonas E. Salk, U.S., 1955; (vaccine made from live virus strains) Albert Sabin, U.S., 1960

Positron: Carl D. Anderson, U.S., 1932

Pressure cooker: (early version) Denis Papin, France, 1679

Printing: (block) Japan, c.700; (movable type) Korea, c.1400; Johann Gutenberg, Germany, c.1450 (lithography, offset) Aloys Senefelder, Germany, 1796; (rotary press) Richard Hoe, U.S., 1844; (linotype) Ottman Mergenthaler, U.S. 1884

Programming, information: *See* Calculating machine

Propeller, screw: Sir Francis P. Smith, England, 1836; John Ericsson, England, worked independently of and simultaneously with Smith, 1837

Proton: Ernest Rutherford, England, 1919

Psychoanalysis: Sigmund Freud, Austria, c.1904

Quantum theory: Max Planck, Germany, 1901

Rabies immunization: Louis Pasteur, France, 1885

Radar: (limited to one-mile range) Christian Hulsmeyer, Germany, 1904; (pulse modulation, used for measuring height of ionosphere) Gregory Breit, Merle Tuve, U.S., 1925; (first practical radar—radio detection and ranging) Sir Robert Watson-Watt, England, 1934–35

Radio: (electromagnetism, theory of) James Clerk Maxwell, England, 1873; (spark coil, generator of electromagnetic waves) Heinrich Hertz, Germany, 1886; (first practical system of wireless telegraphy) Gugliemo Marconi, Italy, 1895; (vacuum electron tube, basis for radio telephony) Sir John Fleming, England, 1904; (triode amplifying tube) Lee de Forest, U.S., 1906; (regenerative circuit, allowing long-distance sound reception) Edwin H. Armstrong, U.S., 1912; (frequency modulation—FM) Edwin H. Armstrong, U.S., 1933

Radioactivity: (X-rays) William K. Roentgen, Germany, 1895; (radioactivity of uranium) Henri Becquerel, France, 1896; (radioactive elements, radium and polonium in uranium ore) Marie Sklodowska-Curie, Pierre Curie, France, 1898; (classification of alpha and beta particle radiation) Pierre Curie, France, 1900; (gamma radiation) Paul-Ulrich Villard, France, 1900; (carbon dating) Willard F. Libby et al., U.S., 1955

Rayon: *See* Fibers, man-made

Reaper: Cyrus McCormick, U.S., 1834

Relativity: (special and general theories of) Albert Einstein, Switzerland, Germany, U.S., 1905–53

Revolver: Samuel Colt, U.S., 1835

Rifle: (muzzle-loaded) Italy, Germany, c.1475; (breech-loaded) England, France, Germany, U.S., c.1866; (bolt-action) Paul von Mauser, Germany, 1889; (automatic) John Browning, U.S., 1918

Roller bearing: (wooden for cartwheel) Germany or France, c.100 B.C.

Rubber: (vulcanization process) Charles Goodyear, U.S., 1839

Safety match: *See* Match

Solar system, universe: (sun-centered universe) Nicolaus Copernicus, Warsaw, 1543; (establishment of planetary orbits as elliptical) Johannes Kepler, Germany, 1609; (infinity of universe) Giordano Bruno, Italian monk, 1584

Spectrum: (heterogeneity of light) Sir Isaac Newton, England, 1665–66

Spermatozoa: Anton van Leeuwenhoek, The Netherlands, 1683

Spinning: (spinning wheel) India, introduced to Europe in Middle Ages; (Saxony wheel, continuous spinning of wool or cotton yarn) England, c.1500–1600; (spinning jenny) James Hargreaves, England, 1764; (spinning frame) Sir Richard Arkwright, England, 1769; (spinning mule, completed mechanization of spinning, permitting production of yarn to keep up with demands of modern looms) Samuel Crompton, England, 1779

Steam engine: (first commercial version based on principles of French physicist Denis Papin) Thomas Savery, England, 1639; (atmospheric steam engine) Thomas Newcomen, England, 1705; (steam engine for pumping water from collieries) Savery, Newcomen, 1725; (modern condensing, double-acting) James Watt, England, 1782

Steam engine, railroad: *See* Locomotive

Steamship: Claude de Jouffroy d'Abbans, France, 1783; James Rumsey, U.S., 1787; John Fitch, U.S., 1790. All preceded Robert Fulton, U.S., 1807, credited with launching first commercially successful steamship

Sulfa drugs: (parent compound, para-aminobenzenesulfanomide) Paul Gelmo, Austria, 1908; (antibacterial activity) Gerhard Domagk, Germany, 1935

Syphilis, test for: *See* Wassermann test

Tank, military: Sir Ernest Swinton, England, 1914

Telegraph: Samuel F. B. Morse, U.S., 1837

Telephone: Alexander Graham Bell, U.S., 1876

Telescope: Hans Lippershey, The Netherlands, 1608

Television: (mechanical disk-scanning method) successfully demonstrated by J. L. Baird, England, C. F. Jenkins, U.S., 1926; (electronic scanning method) Vladimir K. Zworykin, U.S., 1928; (color, all-electronic) Zworykin, 1925; (color, mechanical disk) Baird, 1928; (color, compatible with black and white) George Valensi, France, 1938; (color, sequential rotating filter) Peter Goldmark, U.S., first introduced, 1951; (color, compatible with black and white) commercially introduced in U.S., National Television Systems Committee, 1953

Thermometer: (open-column) Galileo Galilei, c.1593; (clinical) Santorio Santorio, Padua, c.1615; (mercury, also Fahrenheit scale) Gabriel D. Fahrenheit, Germany, 1714; (centigrade scale) Anders Celsius, Sweden, 1742; (absolute-temperature, or Kelvin, scale) William Thompson, Lord Kelvin, England, 1848

Tire, pneumatic: Robert W. Thompson, England, 1845; (bicycle tire) John B. Dunlop, Northern Ireland, 1888

Toilet, flush: Product of Minoan civilization, Crete, c.2000 B.C. Alleged invention by "Thomas Crapper" is untrue.

Tractor: Benjamin Holt, U.S., 1900

Transformer, electric: William Stanley, U.S., 1885

Transistor: John Bardeen, William Shockley, Walter Brattain, U.S., 1948

Uncertainty principle: (that position and velocity of an object cannot both be measured exactly, at the same time) Werner Heisenberg, Germany, 1927

Vaccination: Edward Jenner, England, 1796

Vacuum tube: *See* Radio

Van Allen (radiation) Belt: (around the earth) James Van Allen, U.S., 1958

Vitamins: (hypothesis of disease deficiency) Sir F. G. Hopkins, Casimir Funk, England, 1912; (vitamin A) Elmer V. McCollum, M. Davis, U.S., 1912–14; (vitamin B) Elmer V. McCollum, U.S., 1915–16; (thiamin, B_1) Casimir Funk, England, 1912; (riboflavin, B_2) D. T. Smith, E. G. Hendrick, U.S., 1926; (niacin) Conrad Elvehjem, U.S., 1937; (B_6) Paul Gyorgy, U.S., 1934; (vitamin C) C. A. Holst, T. Froelich, Norway, 1912; (vitamin D) Elmer V. McCollum, U.S., 1922; (folic acid) Lucy Wills, England, 1933

Wassermann test: (for syphilis) August von Wassermann, Germany, 1906

Weaving, cloth: *See* Loom

Wheel: (cart, solid wood) Mesopotamia, c.3800–3600 B.C.

Windmill: Persia, c.600

X-ray: *See* Radioactivity

Xerography: Chester Carlson, U.S., 1938

Zero: India, c.600; (absolute zero, cessation of all molecular energy) William Thompson, Lord Kelvin, England, 1848

WEIGHTS & MEASURES

Measures and Weights

Source: Department of Commerce, National Bureau of Standards.

The International System (Metric)

The International System of Units is a modernized version of the metric system, established by international agreement, i.e. provides a logical and interconnected framework for all measurements in science, industry, and commerce. The system is built on a foundation of seven basic units, and all other units are derived from them. (Use of metric weights and measures was legalized in the United States in 1866, and our customary units of weights and measures are defined in terms of the meter and kilogram.)

Length. Meter. The meter is defined as 1,650,763.73 wavelengths in vacuum of the orange-red line of the spectrum of krypton-86.

Time. Second. The second is defined as the duration of 9,192,631,770 cycles of the radiation associated with a specified transition of the cesium 133 atom.

Mass. Kilogram. The standard for the kilogram is a cylinder of platinum-iridium alloy kept by the International Bureau of Weights and Measures at Paris. A duplicate at the National Bureau of Standards serves as the mass standard for the United States. The kilogram is the only base unit still defined by a physical object.

Temperature. Kelvin. The kelvin is defined as the fraction 1/273.16 of the thermodynamic temperature of the triple point of water; that is, the point at which water forms an interface of solid, liquid and vapor. This is defined as 0.01°C on the Centigrade or Celsius scale and 32.02°F on the Fahrenheit scale. The temperature 0°K is called "absolute zero."

Electric Current. Ampere. The ampere is defined as that current that, if maintained in each of two long parallel wires separated by one meter in free space, would produce a force between the two wires (due to their magnetic fields) of 2×10^{-7} newton for each meter of length. (A newton is the unit of force which when applied to one kilogram mass would experience an acceleration of one meter per second per second.)

Luminous Intensity. Candela. The candela is defined as the luminous intensity of 1/600,000 of a square meter of a cavity at the temperature of freezing platinum (2,042K).

Amount of Substance. Mole. The mole is the amount of substance of a system that contains as many elementary entities as there are atoms in 0.012 kilograms of carbon-12.

Tables of Metric Weights and Measures

LINEAR MEASURE

10 millimeters (mm) = 1 centimeter (cm)
10 centimeters = 1 decimeter (dm) = 100 millimeters
10 decimeters = 1 meter (m) = 1,000 millimeters
10 meters = 1 dekameter (dam)
10 dekameters = 1 hectometer (hm) = 100 meters
10 hectometers = 1 kilometer (km) = 1,000 meters

AREA MEASURE

100 square millimeters (mm²) = 1 sq centimeter (cm²)
10,000 square centimeters = 1 sq meter (m²) = 1,000,000 sq millimeters
100 square meters = 1 are (a)
100 ares = 1 hectare (ha) = 10,000 sq meters
100 hectares = 1 sq kilometer (km²) = 1,000,000 sq meters

VOLUME MEASURE

10 milliliters (ml) = 1 centiliter (cl)
10 centiliters = 1 deciliter (dl) = 100 milliliters
10 deciliters = 1 liter (1) = 1,000 milliliters
10 liters = 1 dekaliter (dal)
10 dekaliters = 1 hectoliter (hl) = 100 liters
10 hectoliters = 1 kiloliter (kl) = 1,000 liters

CUBIC MEASURE

1,000 cubic millimeters (mm³) = 1 cu centimeter (cm³)
1,000 cubic centimeters = 1 cu decimeter (dm³) = 1,000,000 cu millimeters
1,000 cubic decimeters = 1 cu meter (m³) = 1 stere = 1,000,000 cu centimeters = 1,000,000,000 cu millimeters

WEIGHT

10 milligrams (mg) = 1 centigram (cg)
10 centigrams = 1 decigram (dg) = 100 milligrams
10 decigrams = 1 gram (g) = 1,000 milligrams
10 grams = 1 dekagram (dag)
10 dekagrams = 1 hectogram (hg) = 100 grams
10 hectograms = 1 kilogram (kg) = 1,000 grams
1,000 kilograms = 1 metric ton (t)

Tables of Customary U.S. Weights and Measures

LINEAR MEASURE

12 inches (in.) = 1 foot (ft)
3 feet = 1 yard (yd)
5 1/2 yards = 1 rod (rd), pole, or perch (16 1/2 ft)
40 rods = 1 furlong (fur) = 220 yds = 660 ft
8 furlongs = 1 statute mile (mi.) = 1,760 yds = 5,280 ft
3 land miles = 1 league
5,280 feet = 1 statute or land mile
6,076.11549 feet = 1 international nautical mile

AREA MEASURE

144 square inches = 1 sq ft
9 square feet = 1 sq yd = 1,296 sq in.
30 1/4 square yards = 1 sq rd = 272 1/4 sq ft
160 square rods = 1 acre = 4,840 sq yds = 43,560 sq ft
640 acres = 1 sq mi.
1 mile square = 1 section (of land)
6 miles square = 1 township = 36 sections = 36 sq mi.

CUBIC MEASURE

1,728 cubic inches = 1 cu ft
27 cubic feet = 1 cu yd

LIQUID MEASURE

When necessary to distinguish the liquid pint or quart from the dry pint or quart, the word "liquid" or the abbreviation "liq" should be used in combination with the name or abbreviation of the liquid unit.

4 gills (gi) = 1 pint (pt) (= 28.875 cu in.)
2 pints = 1 quart (qt) (= 57.75 cu in.)
4 quarts = 1 gallon (gal) (= 231 cu in.) = 8 pts = 32 gills

APOTHECARIES FLUID MEASURE

60 minims (min.) = 1 fluid dram (fl dr) (= 0.2256 cu in.)
8 fluid drams = 1 fluid ounce (fl oz) (= 1.8047 cu in.)
16 fluid ounces = 1 pt (= 28.875 cu in.) = 128 fl drs
2 pints = 1 qt (= 57.75 cu in.) = 32 fl oz = 256 fl drs
4 quarts = 1 gal (= 231 cu in.) = 128 fl oz = 1,024 fl drs

DRY MEASURE

When necessary to distinguish the dry pint or quart from the liquid pint or quart; the word "dry" should be used in combination with the name or abbreviation of the dry unit.

2 pints = 1 qt (=67.2006 cu in.)
8 quarts = 1 peck (pk) (=537.605 cu in.) = 16 pts
4 pecks = 1 bushel (bu) (= 2,150.42 cu in.) = 32 qts

AVOIRDUPOIS WEIGHT

When necessary to distinguish the avoirdupois dram from the apothecaries dram, or to distinguish the avoirdupois dram or ounce from the fluid dram or ounce, or to distinguish the avoirdupois ounce or pound from the troy or apothecaries ounce or pound, the word "avoirdupois" or the abbreviation "avdp" should be used in combination with the name or abbreviation of the avoirdupois unit.
(The "grain" is the same in avoirdupois, troy, and apothecaries weights.)

27 11/32 grains = 1 dram (dr)
16 drams = 1 oz = 437 1/2 grains
16 ounces = 1 lb = 256 drams = 7,000 grains
100 pounds = 1 hundredweight (cwt)[1]
20 hundredweights = 1 ton (tn) = 2,000 lbs[1]

In "gross" or "long" measure, the following values are recognized:

112 pounds = 1 gross or long cwt[1]
20 gross or long hundredweights = 1 gross or long ton = 2,240 lbs[1]

1. When the terms "hundredweight" and "ton" are used unmodified, they are commonly understood to mean the 100-pound hundredweight and the 2,000-pound ton, respectively; these units may be designated "net" or "short" when necessary to distinguish them from the corresponding units in gross or long measure.

UNITS OF CIRCULAR MEASURE

Second (″) = —
Minute (′) = 60 seconds
Degree (°) = 60 minutes
Right angle = 90 degrees
Straight angle = 180 degrees
Circle = 360 degrees

TROY WEIGHT

24 grains = 1 pennyweight (dwt)
20 pennyweights = 1 ounce troy (oz t) = 480 grains
12 ounces troy = 1 pound troy (lb t) = 240 pennyweights = 5,760 grains

APOTHECARIES WEIGHT

20 grains = 1 scruple (s ap)
3 scruples = 1 dram apothecaries (dr ap) = 60 grains
8 drams apothecaries = 1 ounce apothecaries (oz ap) = 24 scruples = 480 grains
12 ounces apothecaries = 1 pound apothecaries (lb ap) = 96 drams apothecaries = 288 scruples = 5,760 grains

GUNTER'S OR SURVEYOR'S CHAIN MEASURE

7.92 inches = 1 link (li)
100 links = 1 chain (ch) = 4 rods = 66 ft
80 chains = 1 statute mile = 320 rods = 5,280 ft

Metric and U.S. Equivalents

1 angstrom[1] (light wave measurement)	0.1 millimicron 0.000 1 micron 0.000 000 1 millimeter 0.000 000 004 inch	1 decimeter	3.937 inches
		1 dekameter	32.808 feet
1 cable's length	120 fathoms 720 feet 219.456 meters	1 fathom	6 feet 1.8288 meters
		1 foot	0.3048 meter
1 centimeter	0.3937 inch	1 furlong	10 chains (surveyor's) 660 feet 220 yards 1/8 statute mile 201.168 meters
1 chain (Gunter's or surveyor's)	66 feet 20.1168 meters		

1 inch	2.54 centimeters
1 kilometer	0.621 mile
1 league (land)	3 statute miles 4.828 kilometers
1 link (Gunter's or surveyor's)	7.92 inches 0.201 168 meter
1 meter	39.37 inches 1.094 yards
1 micron	0.001 millimeter 0.000 039 37 inch
1 mil	0.001 inch 0.025 4 millimeter
1 mile (statute or land)	5,280 feet 1.609 kilometers
1 mile (nautical international)	1.852 kilometers 1.151 statute miles 0.999 U.S. nautical miles
1 millimeter	0.03937 inch
1 millimicron (mμ)	0.001 micron 0.000 000 039 37 inch
1 nanometer	0.001 micrometer or 0.000 000 039 37 inch
1 point (typography)	0.013 837 inch 1/72 inch (approximately) 0.351 millimeter
1 rod, pole, or perch	16 1/2 feet 5.0292 meters
1 yard	0.9144 meter

AREAS OR SURFACES

1 acre	43,560 square feet 4,840 square yards 0.405 hectare
1 are	119.599 square yards 0.025 acre
1 hectare	2.471 acres
1 square centimeter	0.155 square inch
1 square decimeter	15.5 square inches
1 square foot	929.030 square centimeters
1 square inch	6.4516 square centimeters
1 square kilometer	0.386 square mile 247.105 acres
1 square meter	1.196 square yards 10.764 square feet
1 square mile	258.999 hectares
1 square millimeter	0.002 square inch
1 square rod, square pole or square perch	25.293 square meters
1 square yard	0.836 square meters

CAPACITIES OR VOLUMES

1 barrel, liquid	31 to 42 gallons[2]
1 barrel, standard for fruits, vegetables, and other dry commodities except cranberries	7,056 cubic inches 105 dry quarts 3.281 bushels, struck measure
1 barrel, standard, cranberry	5.286 cubic inches 86 45/64 dry quarts 2.709 bushels, struck measure
1 bushel (U.S.) struck measure	2,150.42 cubic inches 35.238 liters
1 bushel, heaped (U.S.)	2,747.715 cubic inches 1.278 bushels, struck measure[3]
1 cord (firewood)	128 cubic feet
1 cubic centimeter	0.061 cubic inches
1 cubic decimeter	61.024 cubic inches
1 cubic foot	7.481 gallons 28.316 cubic decimeters
1 cubic inch	0.554 fluid ounce 4.433 fluid drams 16.387 cubic centimeters
1 cubic meter	1.308 cubic yards
1 cubic yard	0.765 cubic meter
1 cup, measuring	8 fluid ounces 1/2 liquid pint
1 dram, fluid or liquid (U.S.)	1/8 fluid ounces 0.226 cubic inch 3.697 milliliters 1.041 British fluid drachms
1 dekaliter	2.642 gallons 1.135 pecks
1 gallon (U.S.)	231 cubic inches 3.785 liters 0.833 British gallon 128 U.S. fluid ounces
1 gallon (British Imperial)	277.42 cubic inches 1.201 U.S. gallons 4.546 liters 160 British fluid ounces
1 gill	7.219 cubic inches 4 fluid ounces 0.118 liter
1 hectoliter	26.418 gallons 2.838 bushels
1 liter	1.057 liquid quarts 0.908 dry quart 61.024 cubic inches
1 milliliter	0.271 fluid drams 16.231 minims 0.061 cubic inch
1 ounce, fluid or liquid (U.S.)	1.805 cubic inch 29.574 milliliters 1.041 British fluid ounces

1 peck	8.810 liters	1 hundredweight, net or short	100 pounds 45.359 kilograms
1 pint, dry	33.600 cubic inches 0.551 liter	1 kilogram	2.205 pounds
1 pint, liquid	28.875 cubic inches 0.473 liter	1 microgram [μg (the Greek letter mu in combination with the letter g)]	0.000 001 gram
1 quart, dry (U.S.)	67.201 cubic inches 1.101 liters 0.969 British quart	1 milligram	0.015 grain
1 quart, liquid (U.S.)	57.75 cubic inches 0.946 liter 0.833 British quart	1 ounce, avoirdupois	437.5 grains 0.911 troy or apothecaries ounce 28.350 grams
1 quart (British)	69.354 cubic inches 1.032 U.S. dry quarts 1.201 U.S. liquid quarts	1 ounce, troy or apothecaries	480 grains 1.097 avoirdupois ounces 31.103 grams
1 tablespoon, measuring	3 teaspoons 4 fluid drams 1/2 fluid ounce	1 pennyweight	1.555 grams
1 teaspoon, measuring	1/3 tablespoon 1 1/3 fluid drams	1 point	0.01 carat 2 milligrams
1 assay ton[4]	29.167 grams	1 pound, avoirdupois	7,000 grains 1.215 troy or apothecaries pounds 453.592 37 grams
1 carat	200 milligrams 3.086 grains	1 pound, troy or apothecaries	5,760 grains 0.823 avoirdupois pound 373.242 grams
1 dram, apothecaries	60 grains 3.888 grams	1 ton, gross or long[5]	2,240 pounds 1.12 net tons 1.016 metric tons
1 dram, avoirdupois	27 11/32 (=27.344) grains 1.772 grams	1 ton, metric	2,204.623 pounds 0.984 gross ton 1.102 net tons
1 grain	64.798 91 milligrams	1 ton, net or short	2,000 pounds 0.893 gross ton 0.907 metric ton
1 gram	15.432 grains 0.035 ounce, avoirdupois		
1 hundredweight, gross or long[5]	112 pounds 50.802 kilograms		

1. The angstrom is basically defined as 10^{-10} meter. 2. There is a variety of "barrels" established by law or usage. For example, federal taxes on fermented liquors are based on a barrel of 31 gallons; many state laws fix the "barrel for liquids" at 31 1/2 gallons; one state fixes a 36-gallon barrel for cistern measurement; federal law recognizes a 40-gallon barrel for "proof spirits"; by custom, 42 gallons comprise a barrel of crude oil or petroleum products for statistical purposes, and this equivalent is recognized "for liquids" by four states. 3. Frequently recognized as 1 1/4 bushels, struck measure. 4. Used in assaying. The assay ton bears the same relation to the milligram that a ton of 2,000 pounds avoirdupois bears to the ounce troy; hence the weight in milligrams of precious metal obtained from one assay ton of ore gives directly the number of troy ounces to the net ton. 5. The gross or long ton and hundredweight are used commercially in the United States to only a limited extent, usually in restricted industrial fields. These units are the same as the British "ton" and "hundredweight."

Miscellaneous Units of Measure

Acre: An area of 43,560 square feet. Originally, the area a yoke of oxen could plow in one day.

Agate: Originally a measurement of type size (5 1/2 points). Now equal to 1/14 inch. Used in printing for measuring column length.

Ampere: Unit of electric current. A potential difference of one volt across a resistance of one ohm produces a current of one ampere.

Astronomical Unit (A.U.): 93,000,000 miles, the average distance of the earth from the sun. Used in astronomy.

Bale: A large bundle of goods. In the U.S., the approximate weight of a bale of cotton is 500 pounds. The weight varies in other countries.

Board Foot (fbm): 144 cubic inches (12 in. x 12 in. x 1 in.). Used for lumber.

Bolt: 40 yards. Used for measuring cloth.

BTU: British thermal unit. Amount of heat needed to increase the temperature of one pound of water by one degree Fahrenheit (252 calories).

Carat (c): 200 milligrams or 3.086 grains troy.

Originally the weight of a seed of the carob tree in the Mediterranean region. Used for weighing precious stones. *See also* Karat.

Chain (ch): a chain 66 feet or one-tenth of a furlong in length, divided into 100 parts called links. One mile is equal to 80 chains. Used in surveying and sometimes called Gunter's or surveyor's chain.

Cubit: 18 inches or 45.72 cm. Derived from distance between elbow and tip of middle finger.

Decibel: Unit of relative loudness. One decibel is the smallest amount of change detectable by the human ear.

Ell, English: 1 1/4 yards or 1/32 bolt. Used for measuring cloth.

Freight Ton (also called Measurement Ton): 40 cubic feet of merchandise. Used for cargo freight.

Great Gross: 12 gross or 1728.

Gross: 12 dozen or 144.

Hand: 4 inches or 10.16 cm. Derived from the width of the hand. Used for measuring the height of horses at withers.

Hertz: Modern unit for measurement of electromagnetic wave frequencies (equivalent to "cycles per second").

Hogshead: (hhd): 2 liquid barrels or 14,653 cubic inches.

Horsepower: The power needed to lift 33,000 pounds a distance of one foot in one minute (about 1 1/2 times the power an average horse can exert). Used for measuring power of steam engines, etc.

Karat (kt): A measure of the purity of gold, indicating how many parts out of 24 are pure. For example, 18 karat gold is 3/4 pure. Sometimes spelled *carat.*

Knot: Not a distance, but the rate of speed of one nautical mile per hour. Used for measuring speed of ships.

League: Rather indefinite and varying measure, but usually estimated at 3 miles in English-speaking countries.

Light-Year: 5,880,000,000,000 miles, the distance light travels in a year at the rate of 186,281.7 miles per second. (If an astronomical unit were represented by one inch, a light-year would be represented by about one mile.) Used for measurements in interstellar space.

Magnum: Two-quart bottle. Used for measuring wine, etc.

Ohm: Unit of electrical resistance. A circuit in which a potential difference of one volt produces a current of one ampere has a resistance of one ohm.

Parsec: Approximately 3.26 light-years of 19.2 trillion miles. Term is combination of first syllables of *par*allax and *sec*ond, and distance is that of imaginary star when lines drawn from it to both earth and sun form a maximum angle or parallax of one second (1/3600 degree). Used for measuring interstellar distances.

Pi (π): 3.14159265+. The ratio of the circumference of a circle to its diameter. For practical purposes, the value is used to four decimal places: 3.1416.

Pica: 1/6 inch or 12 points. Used in printing for measuring column width, etc.

Pipe: 2 hogsheads. Used for measuring wine and other liquids.

Point: .013837 (approximately 1/72) inch or 1/12 pica. Used in printing for measuring type size.

Quintal: 100,000 grams or 220.46 pounds avoirdupois.

Quire: Used for measuring paper. Sometimes 24 sheets but more often 25. There are 20 quires in a ream.

Ream: Used for measuring paper. Sometimes 480 sheets, but more often 500 sheets.

Roentgen: Dosage unit of radiation exposure produced by X-rays.

Score: 20 units.

Sound, Speed of: Usually placed at 1,088 ft per second at 32°F at sea level. It varies at other temperatures and in different media.

Span: 9 inches or 22.86 cm. Derived from the distance between the end of the thumb and the end of the little finger when both are outstretched.

Square: 100 square feet. Used in building.

Stone: Legally 14 pounds avoirdupois in Great Britain.

Therm: 100,000 BTU's.

Township: U. S. land measurement of almost 36 square miles. The south border is 6 miles long. The east and west borders, also 6 miles long, follow the meridians, making the north border slightly less than 6 miles long. Used in surveying.

Tun: 252 gallons, but often larger. Used for measuring wine and other liquids.

Watt: Unit of power. The power used by a current of one ampere across a potential difference of one volt equals one watt.

Kelvin Scale

Absolute zero, −273.16° on the Celsius (Centigrade) scale, is 0° Kelvin. Thus, degrees Kelvin are equivalent to degrees Celsius plus 273.16. The freezing point of water, 0°C. and 32°F., is 273.16°K. The conversion formula is K° = C° + 273.16.

Conversion of Miles to Kilometers and Kilometers to Miles

Miles	Kilometers	Miles	Kilometers	Miles	Kilometers	Kilometers	Miles	Kilometers	Miles	Kilometers	Miles
1	1.6	8	12.8	60	96.5	1	0.6	8	4.9	60	37.2
2	3.2	9	14.4	70	112.6	2	1.2	9	5.5	70	43.4
3	4.8	10	16.0	80	128.7	3	1.8	10	6.2	80	49.7
4	6.4	20	32.1	90	144.8	4	2.4	20	12.4	90	55.9
5	8.0	30	48.2	100	160.9	5	3.1	30	18.6	100	62.1
6	9.6	40	64.3	1,000	1609	6	3.7	40	24.8	1,000	621
7	11.2	50	80.4			7	4.3	50	31.0		

Bolts and Screws: Conversion from Fractions of an Inch to Millimeters

Inch	mm	Inch	mm	Inch	mm	Inch	mm
1/64	0.40	17/64	6.75	33/64	13.10	49/64	19.45
1/32	0/79	9/32	7.14	17/32	13.50	25/32	19.84
3/64	1.19	19/64	7.54	35/64	13.90	51/64	20.24
1/16	1.59	5/16	7.94	9/16	14.29	13/16	20.64
5/64	1.98	21/64	8.33	37/64	14.69	53/64	21.03
3/32	2.38	11/32	8.73	19/32	15.08	27/32	21.43
7/64	2.78	23/64	9.13	39/64	15.48	55/64	21.83
1/8	3.18	3/8	9.53	5/8	15.88	7/8	22.23
9/64	3.57	25/64	9.92	41/64	16.27	57/64	22.62
5/32	3.97	13/32	10.32	21/32	16.67	29/32	23.02
11/64	4.37	27/64	10.72	43/64	17.06	59/64	23.42
3/16	4.76	7/16	11.11	11/64	17.46	15/16	23.81
13/64	5.16	29/64	11.51	45/64	17.86	61/64	24.21
7/32	5.56	15/32	11.91	23/32	18.26	31/32	24.61
15/64	5.95	31/64	12.30	47/64	18.65	63/64	25.00
1/4	6.35	1/2	12.70	3/4	19.05	1	25.40

U.S.—Metric Cooking Conversions

U.S. customary system				Metric			
Capacity		**Weight**		**Capacity**		**Weight**	
1/5 teaspoon	1 milliliter	1 fluid oz	30 milliliters	1 milliliter	1/5 teaspoon	1 gram	.035 ounce
1 teaspoon	5 ml		28 grams	5 ml	1 teaspoon	100 grams	3.5 ounces
1 tablespoon	15 ml	1 pound	454 grams	15 ml	1 tablespoon	500 grams	1.10 pounds
1/5 cup	50 ml			34 ml	1 fluid oz	1 kilogram	2.205 pounds
1 cup	240 ml			100 ml	3.4 fluid oz		35 oz
2 cups (1 pint)	470 ml			240 ml	1 cup		
4 cups (1 quart)	.95 liter			1 liter	34 fluid oz		
4 quarts (1 gal.)	3.8 liters				4.2 cups		
					2.1 pints		
					1.06 quarts		
					0.26 gallon		

Cooking Measurement Equivalents

16 tablespoons	= 1 cup	2 tablespoons	= 1/8 cup
12 tablespoons	= 3/4 cup	2 tablespoons + 2 teaspoons	= 1/6 cup
10 tablespoons + 2 teaspoons	= 2/3 cup	1 tablespoon	= 1/16 cup
8 tablespoons	= 1/2 cup	2 cups	= 1 pint
6 tablespoons	= 3/8 cup	2 pints	= 1 quart
5 tablespoons + 1 teaspoon	= 1/3 cup	3 teaspoons	= 1 tablespoon
4 tablespoons	= 1/4 cup	48 teaspoons	= 1 cup

Conversion Factors

To change	To	Multiply by	To change	To	Multiply by
acres	hectares	.4047	liters	pints (dry)	1.8162
acres	square feet	43,560	liters	pints (liquid)	2.1134
acres	square miles	.001562	liters	quarts (dry)	.9081
atmospheres	cms. of mercury	76	liters	quarts (liquid)	1.0567
BTU	horsepower-hour	.0003931	meters	feet	3.2808
BTU	kilowatt-hour	.0002928	meters	miles	.0006214
BTU/hour	watts	.2931	meters	yards	1.0936
bushels	cubic inches	2150.4	metric tons	tons (long)	.9842
bushels (U.S.)	hectoliters	.3524	metric tons	tons (short)	1.1023
centimeters	inches	.3937	miles	kilometers	1.6093
centimeters	feet	.03281	miles	feet	5280
circumference	radians	6.283	miles (nautical)	miles (statute)	1.1516
cubic feet	cubic meters	.0283	miles (statute)	miles (nautical)	.8684
cubic meters	cubic feet	35.3145	miles/hour	feet/minute	88
cubic meters	cubic yards	1.3079	millimeters	inches	.0394
cubic yards	cubic meters	.7646	ounces avdp.	grams	28.3495
degrees	radians	.01745	ounces	pounds	.0625
dynes	grams	.00102	ounces (troy)	ounces (avdp)	1.09714
fathoms	feet	6.0	pecks	liters	8.8096
feet	meters	.3048	pints (dry)	liters	.5506
feet	miles (nautical)	.0001645	pints (liquid)	liters	.4732
feet	miles (statute)	.0001894	pounds ap or t	kilograms	.3782
feet/second	miles/hour	.6818	pounds avdp	kilograms	.4536
furlongs	feet	660.0	pounds	ounces	16
furlongs	miles	.125	quarts (dry)	liters	1.1012
gallons (U.S.)	liters	3.7853	quarts (liquid)	liters	.9463
grains	grams	.0648	radians	degrees	57.30
grams	grains	15.4324	rods	meters	5.029
grams	ounces avdp	.0353	rods	feet	16.5
grams	pounds	.002205	square feet	square meters	.0929
hectares	acres	2.4710	square kilometers	square miles	.3861
hectoliters	bushels (U.S.)	2.8378	square meters	square feet	10.7639
horsepower	watts	745.7	square meters	square yards	1.1960
hours	days	.04167	square miles	square kilometers	2.5900
inches	millimeters	25.4000	square yards	square meters	.8361
inches	centimeters	2.5400	tons (long)	metric tons	1.1060
kilograms	pounds avdp or t	2.2046	tons (short)	metric tons	.9072
kilometers	miles	.6214	tons (long)	pounds	2240
kilowatts	horsepower	1.341	tons (short)	pounds	2000
knots	nautical miles/hour	1.0	watts	BTU/hour	3.4129
knots	statute miles/hour	1.151	watts	horsepower	.001341
liters	gallons (U.S.)	.2642	yards	meters	.9144
liters	pecks	.1135	yards	miles	.0005682

Fahrenheit and Celsius (Centigrade) Scales

Zero on the Fahrenheit scale represents the temperature produced by the mixing of equal weights of snow and common salt.

	F	C
Boiling point of water	212°	100°
Freezing point of water	32°	0°
Absolute zero	−459.6°	−273.1°

Absolute zero is theoretically the lowest possible temperature, the point at which all molecular motion would cease.

To convert Fahrenheit to Celsius (Centigrade), subtract 32 and multiply by 5/9.

To convert Celsius (Centigrade) to Fahrenheit, multiply by 9/5 and add 32.

° Centigrade	° Fahrenheit	° Centigrade	° Fahrenheit
−273.1	−459.6	30	86
−250	−418	35	95
−200	−328	40	104
−150	−238	45	113
−100	−148	50	122
−50	−58	55	131
−40	−40	60	140
−30	−22	65	149
−20	−4	70	158
−10	14	75	167
0	32	80	176
5	41	85	185
10	50	90	194
15	59	95	203
20	68	100	212
25	77		

Prefixes and Multiples

Prefix	Symbol	Equivalent	Multiple/submultiple	Prefix	Symbol	Equivalent	Multiple/submultiple
atto	a	quintillionth part	10^{-18}	deci	d	tenth part	10^{-1}
femto	f	quadrillionth part	10^{-15}	deka	da	tenfold	10
pico	p	trillionth part	10^{-12}	hecto	h	hundredfold	10^2
nano	n	billionth part	10^{-9}	kilo	k	thousandfold	10^3
micro	μ	millionth part	10^{-6}	mega	M	millionfold	10^6
milli	m	thousandth part	10^{-3}	giga	G	billionfold	10^9
centi	c	hundredth part	10^{-2}	tera	T	trillionfold	10^{12}

Common Formulas

Circumference

Circle: $C = \pi d$, in which π is 3.1416 and d the diameter.

Area

Triangle: $A = \dfrac{ab}{2}$, in which a is the base and b the height.

Square: $A = a^2$, in which a is one of the sides.

Rectangle: $A = ab$, in which a is the base and b the height.

Trapezoid: $A = \dfrac{h(a+b)}{2}$, in which h is the height, a the longer parallel side, and b the shorter.

Regular pentagon: $A = 1.720a^2$, in which a is one of the sides.

Regular hexagon: $A = 2.598a^2$, in which a is one of the sides.

Regular octagon: $A = 4.828a^2$, in which a is one of the sides.

Circle: $A = \pi r^2$, in which π is 3.1416 and r the radius.

Volume

Cube: $V = a^3$, in which a is one of the edges.

Rectangular prism: $V = abc$, in which a is the length, b the width, and c the depth.

Pyramid: $V = \dfrac{Ah}{3}$, in which A is the area of the base and h the height.

Cylinder: $V = \pi r^2 h$, in which π is 3.1416, r the radius of the base, and h the height.

Cone: $V = \dfrac{\pi r^2 h}{3}$, in which π is 3.1416, r the radius of the base, and h the height.

Sphere: $V = \dfrac{4\pi r^3}{3}$, in which π is 3.1416 and r the radius.

Miscellaneous

Speed per second acquired by falling body: $v = 32t$, in which t is the time in seconds.

Distance in feet traveled by falling body: $d = 16t^2$, in which t is the time in seconds.

Speed of sound in feet per second through any given temperature of air: $V = \dfrac{1087\sqrt{273+t}}{16.52}$, in which t is the temperature Centigrade.

Cost in cents of operation of electrical device: $C = \dfrac{Wtc}{1000}$, in which W is the number of watts, t the time in hours, and c the cost in cents per kilowatt-hour.

Conversion of matter into energy (Einstein's Theorem): $E = mc^2$, in which E is the energy in ergs, m the mass of the matter in grams, and c the speed of light in centimeters per second. ($c^2 = 9 \cdot 10^{20}$).

Decimal Equivalents of Common Fractions

1/2	.5000	1/10	.1000	2/7	.2857	3/11	.2727	5/9	.5556	7/11	.6364
1/3	.3333	1/11	.0909	2/9	.2222	4/5	.8000	5/11	.4545	7/12	.5833
1/4	.2500	1/12	.0833	2/11	.1818	4/7	.5714	5/12	.4167	8/9	.8889
1/5	.2000	1/16	.0625	3/4	.7500	4/9	.4444	6/7	.8571	8/11	.7273
1/6	.1667	1/32	.0313	3/5	.6000	4/11	.3636	6/11	.5455	9/10	.9000
1/7	.1429	1/64	.0156	3/7	.4286	5/6	.8333	7/8	.8750	9/11	.8182
1/8	.1250	2/3	.6667	3/8	.3750	5/7	.7143	7/9	.7778	10/11	.9091
1/9	.1111	2/5	.4000	3/10	.3000	5/8	.6250	7/10	.7000	11/12	.9167

Conversion Factors

To change	To	Multiply by	To change	To	Multiply by
acres	hectares	.4047	liters	pints (dry)	1.8162
acres	square feet	43,560	liters	pints (liquid)	2.1134
acres	square miles	.001562	liters	quarts (dry)	.9081
atmospheres	cms. of mercury	76	liters	quarts (liquid)	1.0567
BTU	horsepower-hour	.0003931	meters	feet	3.2808
BTU	kilowatt-hour	.0002928	meters	miles	.0006214
BTU/hour	watts	.2931	meters	yards	1.0936
bushels	cubic inches	2150.4	metric tons	tons (long)	.9842
bushels (U.S.)	hectoliters	.3524	metric tons	tons (short)	1.1023
centimeters	inches	.3937	miles	kilometers	1.6093
centimeters	feet	.03281	miles	feet	5280
circumference	radians	6.283	miles (nautical)	miles (statute)	1.1516
cubic feet	cubic meters	.0283	miles (statute)	miles (nautical)	.8684
cubic meters	cubic feet	35.3145	miles/hour	feet/minute	88
cubic meters	cubic yards	1.3079	millimeters	inches	.0394
cubic yards	cubic meters	.7646	ounces avdp.	grams	28.3495
degrees	radians	.01745	ounces	pounds	.0625
dynes	grams	.00102	ounces (troy)	ounces (avdp)	1.09714
fathoms	feet	6.0	pecks	liters	8.8096
feet	meters	.3048	pints (dry)	liters	.5506
feet	miles (nautical)	.0001645	pints (liquid)	liters	.4732
feet	miles (statute)	.0001894	pounds ap or t	kilograms	.3782
feet/second	miles/hour	.6818	pounds avdp	kilograms	.4536
furlongs	feet	660.0	pounds	ounces	16
furlongs	miles	.125	quarts (dry)	liters	1.1012
gallons (U.S.)	liters	3.7853	quarts (liquid)	liters	.9463
grains	grams	.0648	radians	degrees	57.30
grams	grains	15.4324	rods	meters	5.029
grams	ounces avdp	.0353	rods	feet	16.5
grams	pounds	.002205	square feet	square meters	.0929
hectares	acres	2.4710	square kilometers	square miles	.3861
hectoliters	bushels (U.S.)	2.8378	square meters	square feet	10.7639
horsepower	watts	745.7	square meters	square yards	1.1960
hours	days	.04167	square miles	square kilometers	2.5900
inches	millimeters	25.4000	square yards	square meters	.8361
inches	centimeters	2.5400	tons (long)	metric tons	1.1060
kilograms	pounds avdp or t	2.2046	tons (short)	metric tons	.9072
kilometers	miles	.6214	tons (long)	pounds	2240
kilowatts	horsepower	1.341	tons (short)	pounds	2000
knots	nautical miles/hour	1.0	watts	BTU/hour	3.4129
knots	statute miles/hour	1.151	watts	horsepower	.001341
liters	gallons (U.S.)	.2642	yards	meters	.9144
liters	pecks	.1135	yards	miles	.0005682

Fahrenheit and Celsius (Centigrade) Scales

Zero on the Fahrenheit scale represents the temperature produced by the mixing of equal weights of snow and common salt.

	F	C
Boiling point of water	212°	100°
Freezing point of water	32°	0°
Absolute zero	−459.6°	−273.1°

Absolute zero is theoretically the lowest possible temperature, the point at which all molecular motion would cease.

To convert Fahrenheit to Celsius (Centigrade), subtract 32 and multiply by 5/9.

To convert Celsius (Centigrade) to Fahrenheit, multiply by 9/5 and add 32.

° Centigrade	° Fahrenheit	° Centigrade	° Fahrenheit
−273.1	−459.6	30	86
−250	−418	35	95
−200	−328	40	104
−150	−238	45	113
−100	−148	50	122
− 50	− 58	55	131
− 40	− 40	60	140
− 30	− 22	65	149
− 20	− 4	70	158
− 10	14	75	167
0	32	80	176
5	41	85	185
10	50	90	194
15	59	95	203
20	68	100	212
25	77		

Prefixes and Multiples

Prefix	Symbol	Equivalent	Multiple/submultiple	Prefix	Symbol	Equivalent	Multiple/submultiple
atto	a	quintillionth part	10^{-18}	deci	d	tenth part	10^{-1}
femto	f	quadrillionth part	10^{-15}	deka	da	tenfold	10
pico	p	trillionth part	10^{-12}	hecto	h	hundredfold	10^2
nano	n	billionth part	10^{-9}	kilo	k	thousandfold	10^3
micro	μ	millionth part	10^{-6}	mega	M	millionfold	10^6
milli	m	thousandth part	10^{-3}	giga	G	billionfold	10^9
centi	c	hundredth part	10^{-2}	tera	T	trillionfold	10^{12}

Common Formulas

Circumference

Circle: $C = \pi d$, in which π is 3.1416 and d the diameter.

Area

Triangle: $A = \dfrac{ab}{2}$, in which a is the base and b the height.

Square: $A = a^2$, in which a is one of the sides.

Rectangle: $A = ab$, in which a is the base and b the height.

Trapezoid: $A = \dfrac{h(a+b)}{2}$, in which h is the height, a the longer parallel side, and b the shorter.

Regular pentagon: $A = 1.720a^2$, in which a is one of the sides.

Regular hexagon: $A = 2.598a^2$, in which a is one of the sides.

Regular octagon: $A = 4.828a^2$, in which a is one of the sides.

Circle: $A = \pi r^2$, in which π is 3.1416 and r the radius.

Volume

Cube: $V = a^3$, in which a is one of the edges.

Rectangular prism: $V = abc$, in which a is the length, b the width, and c the depth.

Pyramid: $V = \dfrac{Ah}{3}$, in which A is the area of the base and h the height.

Cylinder: $V = \pi r^2 h$, in which π is 3.1416, r the radius of the base, and h the height.

Cone: $V = \dfrac{\pi r^2 h}{3}$, in which π is 3.1416, r the radius of the base, and h the height.

Sphere: $V = \dfrac{4\pi r^3}{3}$, in which π is 3.1416 and r the radius.

Miscellaneous

Speed per second acquired by falling body: $v = 32t$, in which t is the time in seconds.

Distance in feet traveled by falling body: $d = 16t^2$, in which t is the time in seconds.

Speed of sound in feet per second through any given temperature of air: $V = \dfrac{1087\sqrt{273+t}}{16.52}$, in which t is the temperature Centigrade.

Cost in cents of operation of electrical device: $C = \dfrac{Wtc}{1000}$, in which W is the number of watts, t the time in hours, and c the cost in cents per kilowatt-hour.

Conversion of matter into energy (Einstein's Theorem): $E = mc^2$, in which E is the energy in ergs, m the mass of the matter in grams, and c the speed of light in centimeters per second. $(c^2 = 9 \cdot 10^{20})$.

Decimal Equivalents of Common Fractions

1/2	.5000	1/10	.1000	2/7	.2857	3/11	.2727	5/9	.5556	7/11	.6364
1/3	.3333	1/11	.0909	2/9	.2222	4/5	.8000	5/11	.4545	7/12	.5833
1/4	.2500	1/12	.0833	2/11	.1818	4/7	.5714	5/12	.4167	8/9	.8889
1/5	.2000	1/16	.0625	3/4	.7500	4/9	.4444	6/7	.8571	8/11	.7273
1/6	.1667	1/32	.0313	3/5	.6000	4/11	.3636	6/11	.5455	9/10	.9000
1/7	.1429	1/64	.0156	3/7	.4286	5/6	.8333	7/8	.8750	9/11	.8182
1/8	.1250	2/3	.6667	3/8	.3750	5/7	.7143	7/9	.7778	10/11	.9091
1/9	.1111	2/5	.4000	3/10	.3000	5/8	.6250	7/10	.7000	11/12	.9167

dromeda. It is somewhat larger than our own galaxy and is visible to the naked eye.

Recent developments in radio astronomy have revealed additional celestial objects that are still incompletely understood.

Quasars ("quasi-stellar" objects), originally thought to be peculiar stars in our own galaxy, are now believed to be the most remote objects in the Universe. Spectral studies of quasars indicate that some are 9 billion light years away and moving away from us at the incredible rate of 150,000 miles per second. Quasars emit tremendous amounts of light and microwave radiation. Although they appear to be far smaller than ordinary galaxies, some quasars emit as much as 100 times more energy. Some astronomers believe that quasars are the cores of violently exploding galaxies.

Pulsars are believed to be rapidly spinning neutron stars, so crushed by their own gravity that a million tons of their matter would hardly fill a thimble. Pulsars are so named because they emit bursts of radio energy at regular intervals. Some have pulse rates as rapid as 10 per second.

A *black hole* is the theoretical end-product of the total gravitational collapse of a massive star or group of stars. Crushed even smaller than an incredibly dense neutron star, such a body may become so dense that not even light can escape its gravitational field. It has been suggested that black holes may be detectable in proximity to normal stars when they draw matter away from their visi-

ble neighbors. Strong sources of X-rays in our galaxy and beyond may also indicate the presence of black holes. One possible black hole now being studied is the invisible companion to a supergiant star in the constellation Cygnus.

Origin of the Universe

Evidence uncovered in recent years tends to confirm that the universe began its existence about 15 billion years ago as a dense, hot globule of gas expanding rapidly outward. At that time, the universe contained nothing but hydrogen and a small amount of helium. There were no stars and no planets. The first stars probably began to condense out of the primordial hydrogen when the universe was about 100 million years old and continued to form as the universe aged. The Sun arose in this way 4.6 billion years ago. Many stars came into being before the Sun was formed; many others formed after the Sun appeared. This process continues, and through telescopes we can now see stars forming out of compressed pockets of hydrogen in outer space.

Birth and Death of a Star

When a star begins to form as a dense cloud of gas, the individual hydrogen atoms fall toward the center of the cloud under the force of the star's gravity. As they fall, they pick up speed, and their

The Brightest Stars

Star	Constellation	Mag.	Dist. (l.-y.)	Star	Constellation	Mag.	Dist. (l.-y.)
Sirius	Canis Major	−1.6	8	Antares	Scorpius	1.2	170
Canopus	Carina	−0.9	650	Fomalhaut	Piscis Austrinus	1.3	27
Alpha Centauri	Centaurus	+0.1	4	Deneb	Cygnus	1.3	465
Vega	Lyra	0.1	23	Regulus	Leo	1.3	70
Capella	Auriga	0.2	42	Beta Crucis	Crux	1.5	465
Arcturus	Boötes	0.2	32	Eta Carinae	Carina	1–7	—
Rigel	Orion	0.3	545	Alpha-one Crucis	Crux	1.6	150
Procyon	Canis Minor	0.5	10	Castor	Gemini	1.6	44
Achernar	Eridanus	0.6	70	Gamma Crucis	Crux	1.6	—
Beta Centari	Centaurus	0.9	130	Epsilon Canis Majoris	Canis Major	1.6	325
Altair	Aquila	0.9	18	Epsilon Ursae Majoris	Ursa Major	1.7	50
Betelgeuse	Orion	0.9	300	Bellatrix	Orion	1.7	215
Aldebaran	Taurus	1.1	54	Lambda Scorpii	Scorpius	1.7	205
Spica	Virgo	1.2	190	Epsilon Carinae	Carina	1.7	325
Pollux	Gemini	1.2	31	Mira	Cetus	2–10	250

Conversion of Universal Time (U. T.) to Civil Time

U.T.	E.D.T.[1]	E.S.T.[2]	C.S.T.[3]	M.S.T.[4]	P.S.T.[5]	U.T.	E.D.T.[1]	E.S.T.[2]	C.S.T.[3]	M.S.T.[4]	P.S.T.[5]
00	*8P	*7P	*6P	*5P	*4P	12	8A	7A	6A	5A	4A
01	*9P	*8P	*7P	*6P	*5P	13	9A	8A	7A	6A	5A
02	*10P	*9P	*8P	*7P	*6P	14	10A	9A	8A	7A	6A
03	*11P	*10P	*9P	*8P	*7P	15	11A	10A	9A	8A	7A
04	M	*11P	*10P	*9P	*8P	16	N	11A	10A	9A	8A
05	1A	M	*11P	*10P	*9P	17	1P	N	11A	10A	9A
06	2A	1A	M	*11P	*10P	18	2P	1P	N	11A	10A
07	3A	2A	1A	M	*11P	19	3P	2P	1P	N	11A
08	4A	3A	2A	1A	M	20	4P	3P	2P	1P	N
09	5A	4A	3A	2A	1A	21	5P	4P	3P	2P	1P
10	6A	5A	4A	3A	2A	22	6P	5P	4P	3P	2P
11	7A	6A	5A	4A	3A	23	7P	6P	5P	4P	3P

1. Eastern Daylight Time. 2. Eastern Standard Time, same as Central Daylight Time. 3. Central Standard Time, same as Mountain Daylight Time. 4. Mountain Standard Time, same as Pacific Daylight Time. 5. Pacific Standard Time. NOTES: *denotes previous day. N = noon. M = midnight.

Data for Sun, Moon, and Planets

	Mean distance from Sun in millions of miles	Period of revolution around the Sun	Eccentricity of orbit	Inclination to ecliptic ° '	Diameter (miles)	Period of rotation on axis	Inclination of equator to orbit plane °	Surface gravity (earth = 1)	Density H_2O = 1	Number of satellites	Mean velocity in orbit (mi./sec.)	Max. stellar mag.
Sun	—	—	—	—	865,400	24d.64²	7.2	28	1.4	0	—	−26.7
Moon	—	(27d.322)¹	0.05	5 8	2,160	27d.322	6.7	0.16	3.3	0	0.63	−12.6
Mercury	36.00	87d.969	0.21	7 0	3,100	58.66d	7	0.28	3.8	0	30	−1.2
Venus	67.27	224d.701	0.01	3 24	7,700	243.2d	—	0.85	5.1	0	22	−4.4
Earth	93.00	365d.256	0.02	0 0	7,927³	23h56m	23.4	1.00	5.5	1	18.5	—
Mars	141.71	1y.881	0.09	1 51	4,200	24h37m	25.2	0.38	4.0	2	15	−2.8
Jupiter	483.88	11y.862	0.05	1 18	88,700³	9h50m ²	3.1	2.6	1.3	16	8	−2.5
Saturn	887.14	29y.458	0.06	2 29	75,100³	16h39m ²	26.8	1.2	0.7	15	6	−0.4
Uranus	1783.98	84y.013	0.05	0 46	32,000	12.8h	98	1.1	1.3	5	4	+5.7
Neptune	2795.46	164y.794	0.01	1 46	27,700	15h.8	29	1.4	2.2	2	3	+7.8
Pluto	3675.27	248y.430	0.25	17 9	1,500(?)	6d8h(?)	—	—	>1.0	1	<3	+14

1. Period of revolution around the earth. 2. Voyager 1 and 2 data. 3. The equatorial diameters of the earth, Jupiter, and Saturn are given; polar diameters are: earth, 7,900.0 mi., Jupiter 82,789 mi., Saturn 67,170 mi. OTHER DATA ON THE EARTH: Equatorial circumference, 24,902.4 mi.; total area, 196,949,970 sq mi.; mass, 6.6 sextillion tons; mean diameter, 7,917.8

energy increases. The increase in energy heats the gas. When this process has continued for some millions of years, the temperature reaches about 20 million degrees Fahrenheit. At this temperature, the hydrogen within the star ignites and burns in a continuing series of nuclear reactions in which all the elements in the universe are manufactured from hydrogen and helium. The onset of these reactions marks the birth of a star. When a star begins to exhaust its hydrogen supply, its life nears an end. The first sign of old age is a swelling and reddening of its outer regions. Such an aging, swollen star is called a red giant. The Sun, a middle-aged star, will probably swell to a red giant in 5 billion years, vaporizing the earth and any creatures that may be left on its surface. When all its fuel has been exhausted, a star cannot generate sufficient pressure at its center to balance the crushing force of gravity. The star collapses under the force of its own weight; if it is a small star, it collapses gently and remains collapsed. Such a collapsed star, at its life's end, is called a white dwarf. The Sun will probably end its life in this way. A different fate awaits a large star. Its final collapse generates a violent explosion, blowing the innards of the star out into space. There, the materials of the exploded star mix with the primeval hydrogen of the universe. Later in the history of the galaxy, other stars are formed out of this mixture. The Sun is one of these stars. It contains the debris of countless other stars that exploded before the Sun was born.

Formation of the Solar System

The Sun, like other stars, seems to have been formed 4.6 billion years ago from a cloud of hydrogen mixed with small amounts of other substances that had been manufactured in the bodies of other stars before the Sun was born. This was the parent cloud of the solar system. The dense hot gas at the center of the cloud gave rise to the Sun; the outer regions of the cloud—cooler and less dense—gave birth to the planets.

Our solar system consists of one star (the Sun), nine planets and all their moons, several thousand minor planets called asteroids or planetoids, and an equally large number of comets.

The Sun

All the stars, including our Sun, are gigantic balls of superheated gas, kept hot by atomic reactions in their centers. In our Sun, this atomic reaction is hydrogen fusion: four hydrogen atoms are combined to form one helium atom. The temperature at the core of our Sun must be 20 million degrees centigrade, the surface temperature is around 6,000 degrees centigrade, or about 11,000 degrees Fahrenheit. The diameter of the sun is 865,400 miles, and its surface area is approximately 12,000 times that of the Earth. Compared with other stars, our Sun is just a bit below average in size and temperature. Its fuel supply (hydrogen) is estimated to last for another 5 billion years.

Our Sun is not motionless in space; in fact it has two proper motions. One is a seemingly straight-line motion in the direction of the constellation Hercules at the rate of about 12 miles per second. But since the Sun is a part of the Milky Way system and since the whole system rotates slowly around its own center, the Sun also moves at the rate of 175 miles per second as part of the rotating Milky Way system.

In addition to this motion, the Sun rotates on its axis. Observing the motion of sun spots (darkish areas which look like enormous whirling storms) and solar flares, which are usually associated with sun spots, has shown that the rotational period of our Sun is just short of 25 days. But this figure is valid for the Sun's equator only; the sections near the Sun's poles seem to have a rotational period of 34 days. Naturally, since the Sun generates its own heat and light, there is no temperature difference between poles and equator.

What we call the Sun's "surface" is technically known as the photosphere. Since the whole Sun is a ball of very hot gas, there is really no such thing as a surface; it is a question of visual impression. The next layer outside the photosphere is known as the chromosphere, which extends several thousand miles beyond the photosphere. It is in steady motion, and often enormous prominences can be seen to burst from it, extending as much as 100,000 miles into space. Outside the chromosphere is the corona. The corona consists of very tenuous gases (essentially hydrogen) and makes a magnificent sight when the Sun is eclipsed.

The Moon

Mercury and Venus do not have any moons. Therefore, the Earth is the planet nearest the Sun to be orbited by a moon.

The next planet farther out, Mars, has two very small moons. Jupiter has four major moons and twelve minor ones. Saturn, the ringed planet, has fifteen known moons, of which one (Titan) is larger than the planet Mercury. Uranus has five known moons (four of them large) as well as rings, while Neptune has one large and one small moon. Pluto has one moon, discovered in 1978. Some astronomers still consider Pluto to be a "runaway moon" of Neptune.

Our own Moon, with a diameter of 2,160 miles, is one of the larger moons in our solar system and is especially large when compared with the planet that it orbits. In fact, the common center of gravity of the Earth-Moon system is only about 1,000 miles below the Earth's surface. The closest our Moon can come to us (its perigee) is 221,463 miles; the farthest it can go away (its apogee) is 252,710 miles. The period of rotation of our Moon is equal to its period of revolution around the Earth. Hence from Earth we can see only one hemisphere of the Moon. Both periods are 27 days, 7 hours, 43 minutes and 11.47 seconds. But while the rotation of the Moon is constant, its velocity in its orbit is not, since it moves more slowly in apogee than in perigee. Consequently, some portions near the rim which are not normally visible will appear briefly. This phenomenon is called "libration," and by taking advantage of the librations, astronomers have succeeded in mapping approximately 59% of the lunar surface. The other 41% can never be seen from the earth but has been mapped by American and Russian Moon-orbiting spacecraft.

Though the Moon goes around the Earth in the time mentioned, the interval from new Moon to new Moon is 29 days, 12 hours, 44 minutes and 2.78 seconds. This delay of nearly two days is due to the fact that the Earth is moving around the Sun, so that the Moon needs two extra days to reach a spot in its orbit where no part is illuminated by the Sun, as seen from Earth.

If the plane of the Earth's orbit around the Sun (the ecliptic) and the plane of the Moon's orbit around the Earth were the same, the Moon would be eclipsed by the Earth every time it is full, and the Sun would be eclipsed by the Moon every time the Moon is "new" (it would be better to call it the "black Moon" when it is in this position). But because the two orbits do not coincide, the Moon's shadow normally misses the Earth and the Earth's shadow misses the Moon. The inclination of the two orbital planes to each other is 5 degrees. The tides are, of course, caused by the Moon with the help of the Sun, but in the open ocean they are surprisingly low, amounting to about one yard. The very high tides which can be observed near the shore in some places are due to funnelling effects of the shorelines. At new Moon and at full Moon the tides raised by the Moon are reinforced by the Sun; these are the "spring tides." If the Sun's tidal power acts at right angles to that of the Moon (quarter moons) we get the low "neap tides."

Our Planet Earth

The Earth, circling the Sun at an average distance of 93 million miles, is the fifth largest planet and the third from the Sun. It orbits the Sun at a speed of 67,000 miles per hour, making one revolution in 365 days, 5 hours, 48 minutes, and 45.51 seconds. The Earth completes one rotation on its axis every 23 hours, 56 minutes, and 4.09 seconds. Actually a bit pear-shaped rather than a true sphere, the Earth has a diameter of 7,927 miles at the Equator and a few miles less at the poles. It has an estimated mass of about 6.6 sextillion tons, with an average density of 5.52 grams per cubic centimeter. The Earth's surface area encompasses 196,-949,970 square miles, of which about three-fourths is water.

Origin of the Earth. The Earth, along with the other planets, is believed to have been born 4.5 billion years ago as a solidified cloud of dust and gases left over from the creation of the Sun. For perhaps 500 million years, the interior of the Earth stayed solid and relatively cool, perhaps 2000° F. The main ingredients, according to the best available evidence, were iron and silicates, with small amounts of other elements, some of them radioactive. As millions of years passed, energy released by radioactive decay —mostly of uranium, thorium, and potassium— gradually heated the Earth, melting some of its constituents. The iron melted before the silicates, and, being heavier, sank toward the center. This forced upward the silicates that it found there. After many years, the iron reached the center, almost 4,000 miles deep, and began to accumulate. No eyes were around at that time to view the turmoil which must have taken place on the face of the Earth—gigantic heaves and bubbling of the surface, exploding volcanoes, and flowing lava covering everything in sight. Finally, the iron in the center accumulated as the core. Around it, a thin but fairly stable crust of solid rock formed as the Earth cooled. Depressions in the crust were natural basins in which water, rising from the interior of the planet through volcanoes and fissures, collected to form the oceans. Slowly the Earth acquired its present appearance.

The Earth Today. As a result of radioactive heating over millions of years, the Earth's molten *core* is probably fairly hot today, around 11,000° F. By comparison, lead melts at around 800° F. Most of the Earth's 2,100-mile-thick core is liquid, but there is evidence that the center of the core is solid. The liquid outer portion, about 95% of the core, is constantly in motion, causing the Earth to have a magnetic field that makes compass needles point north and south. The details are not known, but the latest evidence suggests that planets which have a magnetic field probably have a solid core or a partially liquid one.

Outside the core is the Earth's *mantle,* 1,800 miles thick, and extending nearly to the surface. The mantle is composed of heavy silicate rock, similar to that brought up by volcanic eruptions. It is somewhere between liquid and solid, slightly yielding, and therefore contributing to an active, moving Earth. Most of the Earth's radioactive material is in the thin *crust* which covers the mantle, but some is in the mantle and continues to give off heat. The crust's thickness ranges from 5 to 25 miles.

Continental Drift. A great deal of recent evidence confirms the long-disputed theory that the continents of the Earth, made mostly of relatively light granite, float in the slightly yielding mantle, like logs in a pond. For many years it had been noticed that if North and South America could be pushed toward western and southern Europe and western Africa, they would fit like pieces in a jigsaw puzzle. Today, there is little question—the continents have drifted widely and continue to do so.

In 10 million years, the world as we know it may be unrecognizable, with California drifting out to sea, Florida joining South America, and Africa moving farther away from Europe and Asia.

The Earth's Atmosphere. The thin blanket of atmosphere that envelops the Earth extends several hundred miles into space. From sea level—the very bottom of the ocean of air—to a height of about 60 miles, the air in the atmosphere is made up of the same gases in the same ratio: about 78% nitrogen, 21% oxygen, and the remaining 1% being a mixture of argon, carbon dioxide, and tiny amounts of neon, helium, krypton, xenon, and other gases. The atmosphere becomes less dense with increasing altitude: more than three-fourths of the Earth's huge envelope is concentrated in the first 5 to 10 miles above the surface. At sea level, a cubic foot of the atmosphere weighs about an ounce and a quarter. The entire atmosphere weighs 5,700,000,000,000,-000 tons, and the force with which gravity holds it in place causes it to exert a pressure of nearly 15 pounds per square inch. Going out from the Earth's surface, the atmosphere is divided into five regions. The regions, and the heights to which they extend, are: *Troposphere,* 0 to 7 miles (at middle latitudes); *stratosphere,* 7 to 30 miles; *mesosphere,* 30 to 50 miles; *thermosphere,* 50 to 400 miles; and *exosphere,* above 400 miles. The boundaries between each of the regions are known respectively as the *tropopause, stratopause, mesopause,* and *thermopause.* Alternate terms often used for the layers above the troposphere are *ozonosphere* (for stratosphere) and *ionosphere* for the remaining upper layers.

The Seasons. Seasons are caused by the 23.4 degree tilt of the Earth's axis, which alternately turns the North and South Poles toward the Sun. Times when the Sun's apparent path crosses the Equator are known as *equinoxes.* Times when the Sun's apparent path is at the greatest distance from the Equator are known as *solstices.* The lengths of the days are most extreme at each solstice. If the Earth's axis were perpendicular to the plane of the Earth's orbit around the Sun, there would be no seasons, and the days always would be equal in length. Since the Earth's axis is at an angle, the Sun strikes the Earth directly at the Equator only twice a year: in March (vernal equinox) and September (autumnal equinox). In the Northern Hemisphere, spring begins at the vernal equinox, summer at the summer solstice, fall at the autumnal equinox, and winter at the winter solstice. The situation is reversed in the Southern Hemisphere.

Mercury

Mercury is the planet nearest the Sun. Appropriately named for the wing-footed Roman messenger of the gods, Mercury whizzes around the Sun at a speed of 30 miles per second, completing one circuit in 88 days. The planet rotates on its axis over a period of nearly 59 days. Daytime on cratered Mercury is hot, about 800 degrees F., although at night the temperature may fall to room temperature. Mercury has no moons, but it does have a trace of atmosphere and a weak magnetic field, according to findings of Mariner 10. Until this spacecraft flew by Mercury in 1974 and 1975, very little was known about the planet, primarily because of its short angular distance from the Sun as seen from Earth, which puts it too close to the Sun to be easily observed.

• Mercury is a naked eye object at morning or evening twilight when it is at greatest elongation.

Venus

Although Venus is Earth's nearest neighbor, little is known about this planet because it is permanently covered by thick clouds. In 1962, Soviet and American space probes, coupled with Earth-based radar and infrared spectroscopy, began slowly unraveling some of the mystery surrounding Venus. According to the latest results, Venus' atmosphere is about 96% carbon dioxide, exerting a pressure at the surface 90.5 times greater than Earth's. Walking on Venus would be as difficult as walking a half-mile beneath the ocean. Because of the thick blanket of carbon dioxide, a "greenhouse effect" exists on Venus: Venus intercepts twice as much of the Sun's light as does the Earth. The light enters freely through carbon dioxide gas and is changed to heat radiation in molecular collisions. But carbon dioxide prevents the heat from escaping. Consequently, the temperature of the surface of Venus is over 800 degrees F., hot enough to melt lead. The atmosphere appears to have five distinct layers and to flash almost continuously with lightning. Radar bounced off the planet recently revealed what appear to be large craters and an immense, 900-mile-long canyon. Venus rotates in retrograde motion for a reason not yet known.

• Venus is the brightest of all the planets and is often visible in the morning or evening, when it is frequently referred to as the Morning Star or Evening Star. At its brightest, it can sometimes be seen with the naked eye in full daylight, if one knows where to look.

Mars

Mars, on the other side of the Earth from Venus, is Venus' direct opposite in terms of physical properties. Its atmosphere is cold, thin, and transparent, and readily permits observation of the planet's features. We know more about Mars than any other planet except Earth. Mars is a forbidding, rugged planet with huge volcanoes and deep chasms. The largest volcano, Olympus Mons rises 78,000 feet above the surface, higher than Mount Everest. The plains of Mars are pockmarked by the hits of thousands of meteors over the years. Most of our information about Mars comes from the Mariner 9 spacecraft, which orbited the planet in 1971. Mariner 9, photographing 100% of the planet, uncovered spectacular geological formations, including a Martian Grand Canyon that dwarfs the one on Earth. The spacecraft's cameras also recorded what appeared to be dried riverbeds, suggesting the onetime presence of water on the planet. The latter idea gives encouragement to scientists looking for life on Mars, for where there is water, there may be life. However, by 1979, no evidence of life has been found. Temperatures near the equator range from −17 degrees F. in the daytime to −130 degrees F. at night. Mars rotates upon its axis in nearly the same period as Earth—24 hours, 37 minutes—so that a Mars day is almost identical to an Earth day. Mars takes 687 days to make one trip around the Sun. Because of its eccentric orbit Mars' distance from the Sun can vary by about 36 million miles. Its distance from Earth can vary by as much as 200 million miles. The atmosphere of Mars is much thinner than Earth's; atmospheric pressure is about 1% that of our planet. Its gravity is one-third of Earth's. Major constituents are carbon dioxide and nitrogen. Water vapor and oxygen are minor constituents. Mars' polar caps, composed mostly of carbon dioxide, recede and advance according to the Martian seasons. Mars was named for the Roman god of war, because when seen from Earth its distinct red color reminded the ancient people of blood. We know now that the reddish hue reflects the oxidized (rusted) iron in the surface material. The landing of two robot Viking spacecraft on the surface of Mars in 1976 provided more information about Mars in a few months than in all the time that has gone before.

Jupiter

Jupiter, with an equatorial diameter of 88,000 miles, is the largest of a group of planets which differ markedly from the terrestrial planets. The others in the group are Saturn, Uranus, and Neptune. All are large, with very dense atmospheres, and indeed may be giant balls of gas without any perceptible surfaces. They all whirl rapidly around their axes, but more slowly around the Sun, resulting in short days and long years. They have many moons. Majestic Jupiter, named for the king of the Roman gods, rotates so fast that it is greatly flattened at the poles. According to Pioneers 10 and 11, which flew past Jupiter in 1974 and 1975, this planet is a whirling ball of liquid hydrogen with perhaps an Earth-sized iron core. Other atmospheric constituents are helium, methane, and ammonia. Its clouds are probably ammonia ice crystals, becoming ammonia droplets deeper towards the "surface." Temperatures range from perhaps minus 300 degrees F. at the tops of the cloud decks to 100,000 degrees F. or more deep down at the center. The pressure at the center of the planet is estimated to be a crushing 10 million pounds per square inch. The Great Red Spot, a 13,000-mile-wide storm that may have been raging for thousands of years, was found by Voyagers 1 and 2 in 1979 to be cooler at the top than the surrounding clouds, indicating that the Red Spot may tower high above them. Jupiter has 16 satellites, more than any other planet. The four largest moons, called Galilean moons, are Europa, Ganymede, Io, and Callisto. *Voyagers 1 and 2* found them to be very different from each other in terms of surface relief, volcanic activity, and other characteristics.
    • Even when nearest the Earth, Jupiter is still almost 400 million miles away. But because of its size, it may rival Venus in brilliance when near. Jupiter's four large moons may be seen through field glasses, moving rapidly around Jupiter and changing their position from night to night.

Saturn

Saturn, the second largest planet in the solar system, is the least dense. It would float in an ocean if there were one big enough to hold it. Aside from its rings, Saturn is very similar to Jupiter except that it is probably colder, being twice as far from the Sun. Recent radar observations of Saturn's rings indicate that they are no more than 10 miles thick, and probably composed of chunks of rock and ice averaging a meter in size. Saturn's ring system begins about 7000 miles from the planet's disk, and extends out to about 35,000 miles. Recent observations have shown Saturn to have between 15 and 18 moons. The two *Voyager* probes that examined Jupiter in 1979 flew by Saturn in 1980 and 1981. *Voyager 2* will encounter Uranus in 1986.
    • Saturn is the last of the planets visible to the naked eye. Saturn is never an object of overwhelming brilliance, but it looks like a bright star. The rings can be seen with a small telescope.

Uranus and Neptune

Little is known about the distant giant planets Uranus and Neptune, but they are believed to be similar to Saturn and Jupiter. Being twice as far from the Sun as Saturn, Uranus must be a grim frozen world, and Neptune, 11 A.U. beyond Uranus, must be even colder and darker. The axis of Uranus is tilted at 98 degrees, so it goes around the Sun nearly lying on its side. In 1977, American astronomers made the startling discovery that Uranus has rings, like Saturn. The first Voyager to Uranus may take pictures of the rings in 1986. Uranus has five known moons; Neptune, two. Neptune's Triton, Jupiter's Ganymede and Callisto, and Saturn's Titan are the four largest moons in the solar system.
    • Uranus and Neptune can—on rare occasion —become bright enough to be seen with the naked eye, if one knows exactly where to look; normally, they are objects for good field glasses or small portable telescopes.

Pluto

Pluto, the outermost and smallest planet in the solar system, looks more like a terrestrial planet than a gaseous planet. But so little is known about it, that it is difficult to classify. Appropriately named for the Roman god of the underworld, it must be frozen, dark, and dead.
In 1978, light curve studies gave evidence of a moon revolving around Pluto with the same period as Pluto's rotation. Therefore, it stays over the same point on Pluto's surface. In addition, it keeps the same face toward the planet. The discovery of this moon of 500–600 miles in diameter reduces the previously estimated diameter of Pluto to little more than 1,500 miles, making the pair more like a double planet than any other in the solar system. Previously, the Earth-Moon system held this distinction. The density of Pluto is slightly greater than that of water.
Pluto was predicted by calculation when Percival Lowell noticed irregularities in the orbits of Uranus and Neptune. Clyde Tombaugh discovered the planet in 1930, precisely where Lowell predicted it would be. The name Pluto was chosen because the first two letters represent the initials of Percival Lowell.
    • Pluto has the most eccentric orbit in the solar system, bringing it at times closer to the Sun than Neptune. Pluto is now approaching the perihelion of its orbit, and for the rest of this century will be closer to the Sun than Neptune. Even then, it can be seen only with a large telescope.

The First Ten Minor Planets (Asteroids)

Name	Year of discovery	Mean distance from sun (millions of miles)	Orbital period (years)	Diameter (miles)	Magnitude
1. Ceres	1801	257.0	4.60	485	7.4
2. Pallas	1802	257.4	4.61	304	8.0
3. Juno	1804	247.8	4.36	118	8.7
4. Vesta	1807	219.3	3.63	243	6.5
5. Astraea	1845	239.3	4.14	50	9.9
6. Hebe	1847	225.2	3.78	121	8.5
7. Iris	1847	221.4	3.68	121	8.4
8. Flora	1847	204.4	3.27	56	8.9
9. Metis	1848	221.7	3.69	78	8.9
10. Hygeia	1849	292.6	5.59	40(?)	9.5

The Asteroids

Between the orbits of Mars and Jupiter are an estimated 30,000 pieces of rocky debris, known collectively as the asteroids, or planetoids. The first and, incidentally, the largest was discovered during the New Year's night of 1801 by the Italian astronomer Father Piazzi, and its orbit was calculated by the German mathematician Karl Friedrich Gauss. (Gauss invented a new method of calculating orbits on that occasion.) A German amateur astronomer, the physician Olbers, discovered the second asteroid. The number now known, catalogued, and named is around 1,600; the estimated total is about 20 times that figure. A few asteroids do not move in orbits beyond the orbit of Mars, but in orbits which cross the orbit of Mars. The first of them was named Eros because of this peculiar orbit. It had become the rule to bestow female names on the asteroids, but when it was found that Eros crossed the orbit of a major planet, it received a male name. Since then around two dozen orbit-crossers have been discovered, and they are often referred to as the "male asteroids." A few of them—Albert, Adonis, Apollo, Amor, and Icarus—cross the orbit of the Earth, and two of them may come closer than our Moon; but the crossing is like a bridge crossing a highway, not like two highways intersecting. Hence there is very little danger of collision from these bodies. They are all small, three to five miles in diameter, and therefore very difficult objects to identify, even when quite close. Some scientists believe the asteroids represent the remains of an exploded planet.

Comets

Comets, according to the noted astronomer, Fred L. Whipple, are enormous "snowballs" of frozen gases (mostly carbon dioxide, methane, and water vapor) and contain very little solid material. The whole behavior of comets can then be explained as the behavior of frozen gas being heated by the Sun. When the comet Kohoutek made its first appearance to man in 1973, its behavior seemed to confirm this Whipple theory of the make-up of comets.

Kohoutek will probably not appear in view for another 75,000 years. The next comet large and brilliant enough to be very easily seen is predicted for 1986, when Halley's comet will approach perihelion (the point of its orbit closest to the Sun) again.

But a large and brilliant comet is possible at any time. More than 1,000 comets are on the lists now, with several new ones being discovered every year. But while there is a comet visible to the unaided eye almost every year, none of them since the last appearance of Halley's comet in 1910–11 has been conspicuous to a casual watcher.

Since comets appear in the sky without any warning, people in classical times and especially during the Middle Ages believed that they had a special meaning, which, of course, was bad. Since a natural catastrophe of some sort or a military conflict occurs every year, it was quite simple to blame the comet that happened to be visible. But even in the past, there were some people who used logical reasoning. When, in Roman times, a comet was blamed for the loss of a battle and hence was called a "bad omen," a Roman writer observed that the victors in the battle probably did not think so.

Up until the middle of the sixteenth century, comets were believed to be phenomena of the upper atmosphere; they were usually "explained" as "burning vapors" which had risen from "distant

21 Famous Comets

Year and no.	Name of comet	Period (years)
1744	De Chéseaux's Comet	—
1806	Biela's Comet	6.7
1811 I	Great Comet of 1811	3000
1812	Di Vico's Comet	70.7
1815	Olbers' Comet	74.0
1819 I	Encke's Comet	3.3
1819	Pons-Winnecke Comet	6.0
1835 III	Halley's Comet	76.3
1843 I	Great Comet of 1843	512.4
1844 II	Great Comet of 1844	102,050
1858 VI	Donati's Comet	2,040(?)
1864 II	Great Comet of 1864	2,800,000
1871 III	Tuttle's Comet	13.8
1874 III	Coggia's Comet	6,000(?)
1879	Brorsen's Comet	5.6
1881 II	Tebbutt's Comet	
1889 II	Swift's 2nd Comet	7.0
1892 III	Holmes' Comet	6.9
1923	d'Arrest's Comet	6.6
1925 II	Comet Schwassmann-Wachmann	16.2
1973 I	Comet Kohoutek	75,000(?)

swamps." That nobody had ever actually seen burning vapors rise from a swamp did not matter.

But a large comet which appeared in 1577 was carefully observed by Tycho Brahe, a Danish astronomer who is often, and with the best of reasons, called "eccentric" but who insisted on precise measurements for everything. It was Tycho Brahe's accumulation of literally thousands of precise measurements which later enable his younger collaborator, Johannes Kepler, to discover the laws of planetary motion. Measuring the motion of the comet of 1577, Tycho Brahe could show that it had been far beyond the atmosphere, even though he could not give figures for the distance. Tycho Brahe's work proved that comets were astronomical and not meteorological phenomena.

In 1682, the second Astronomer Royal of Great Britain, Dr. Edmond Halley, checked the orbit of a bright comet that was in the sky then and compared it with earlier comet orbits which were known in part. Halley found that the comet of 1682 was the third to move through what appeared to be the same orbit. And the three appearances were roughly 76 years apart. Halley concluded that this was the same comet, moving around the Sun in a closed orbit, like the planets. He predicted that it would reappear in 1758 or 1759. Halley himself died in 1742, but a large comet appeared sixteen years after his death as predicted and was immediately referred to as "Halley's comet."

In the Spring of 1973, the discovery of comet Kohoutek, apparently headed for a close-Christmastime rendezvous with the Sun, created worldwide excitement. The comet was a visual disappointment, but turned out to be a treasure trove of information on these little-understood celestial objects. Given an unprecedented advance notice of nine months on the advent of the fiery object, scientists were able to study the comet in visible, ultraviolet and infrared light; with optical telescopes, radio telescopes, and radar. They observed it from the ground, from high-flying aircraft, with instruments aboard unmanned satellites, with sounding rockets, and telescopes and cameras on the Earth-orbiting Skylab space station.

Astronomers refer to comets as "periodic" or as "non-periodic" comets, but the latter term does not mean that these comets have no period; it merely

Important Meteor Showers

Approx. date	Name of meteor stream	Radiant in constellation
Jan. 1–4	Quadrantids	Boötes
Feb. 5–10	Alpha Aurigids	Auriga
March 10–12	Zeta Boötids	Boötes
April 19–23	Lyrids	Hercules
May 1–6	May Aquarids	Aquarius
May 30	Eta Pegasids	Pegasus
June 27–30	Pons-Winnecke meteors	Draco
July 14	Alpha Cygnids	Cygnus
July 26–31	Delta Aquarids	Aquarius
Aug. 10–14	Perseids	Cassiopeia
Aug. 10–20	Kappa Cygnids	Cygnus
Aug. 21–31	Zeta Draconids	Draco
Sept. 22	Alpha Aurigids	Auriga
Oct. 2	Quadrantids	Boötes
Oct. 9	Giacobinids	Draco
Oct. 18–23	Orionids	Orion
Nov. 14–18	Leonids	Leo
Dec. 10–13	Geminids	Gemini

means that their period is not known. The actual periods of comets run from 3.3 years (the shortest known) to many thousands of years. Their orbits are elliptical, like those of the planets, but they are very eccentric, long and narrow ellipses. Only comet Schwassmann-Wachmann has an orbit which has such a low eccentricity (for a cometary orbit) that it could be the orbit of a minor planet.

When a comet, coming from deep space, approaches the Sun, it is at first indistinguishable from a minor planet. Somewhere between the orbits of Mars and Jupiter its outline becomes fuzzy; it is said to develop a "coma" (the word used here is the Latin word *coma*, which means "hair," not the phonetically identical Greek word which means "deep sleep"). Then, near the orbit of Mars, the comet develops its tail, which at first trails behind. This grows steadily as the comet comes closer and closer to the Sun. As it rounds the Sun (as first noticed by Girolamo Fracastoro) the tail always points away from the Sun so that the comet, when moving away from the Sun, points its tail ahead like the landing lights of an airplane.

The reason for this behavior is that the tail is pushed in these directions by the radiation pressure of the Sun. It sometimes happens that a comet loses its tail at perihelion; it then grows another one. Although the tail is clearly visible against the black of the sky, it is very tenuous. It has been said that if the tail of Halley's comet could be compressed to the density of iron, it would fit into a small suitcase.

Although very low in mass, comets are among the largest members of the solar system. The nucleus of a comet may be up to 10,000 miles in diameter; its coma between 10,000 and 50,000 miles in diameter; and its tail as long as 28 million miles.

Meteors and Meteorites

The term "meteor" for what is usually called a "shooting star" bears an unfortunate resemblance to the term "meteorology," the science of weather and weather forecasting. This resemblance is due to an ancient misunderstanding which wrongly considered meteors an atmospheric phenomenon. Actually, the streak of light in the sky that scientists call a meteor is essentially an astronomical phenomenon: the entry of a small piece of cosmic matter into our atmosphere.

The distinction between "meteors" and "fireballs" (formerly also called "bolides") is merely one of convenience; a fireball is an unusually bright meteor. Incidentally, it also means that a fireball is larger than a faint meteor.

Bodies which enter our atmosphere become visible when they are about 60 miles above the ground. The fact that they grow hot enough to emit light is not due to the "friction" of the atmosphere, as one can often read. The phenomenon responsible for the heating is one of compression. Unconfined air cannot move faster than the speed of sound. Since the entering meteorite moves with 30 to 60 times the speed of sound, the air simply cannot get out of the way. Therefore, it is compressed like the air in the cylinder of a Diesel engine and is heated by compression. This heat—or part of it—is transferred to the moving body. The details of this process are now fairly well understood as a result of re-entry tests with ballistic-missile nose cones.

The average weight of a body producing a faint "shooting star" is only a small fraction of an ounce. Even a bright fireball may not weigh more than 2 or 3 pounds. Naturally, the smaller bodies are worn

The 88 Recognized Constellations

In astronomical works, the Latin names of the constellations are used. The letter N or S following the Latin name indicates whether the constellation is located to the north or south of the Zodiac. The letter Z indicates that the constellation is within the Zodiac.

Latin name	Letter	English version	Latin name	Letter	English version	Latin name	Letter	English version
Andromeda	N	Andromeda	Delphinus	N	Dolphin	Pavo	S	Peacock
Antlia	S	Airpump	Dorado	S	Swordfish (Goldfish)	Pegasus	N	Pegasus
Apus	S	Bird of Paradise	Draco	N	Dragon	Perseus	N	Perseus
Aquarius	Z	Water Bearer	Equuleus	N	Filly	Phoenix	S	Phoenix
Aquila	N	Eagle	Eridanus	S	Eridanus (river)	Pictor	S	Painter (or his Easel)
Ara	S	Altar	Fornax	S	Furnace	Pisces	Z	Fishes
Aries	Z	Ram	Gemini	Z	Twins	Piscis Austrinus	S	Southern Fish
Auriga	N	Charioteer	Grus	S	Crane	Puppis	S	Poop (of Argo)[1]
Boötes	N	Herdsmen	Hercules	N	Hercules	Pyxis	S	Mariner's Compass
Caelum	S	Sculptor's Tool	Horologium	S	Clock			
Camelopardalis	N	Giraffe	Hydra	N	Sea Serpent	Reticulum	S	Net
Cancer	Z	Crab	Hydrus	S	Water Snake	Sagitta	N	Arrow
Canes Venatici	N	Hunting Dogs	Indus	S	Indian	Sagittarius	Z	Archer
Canis Major	S	Great Dog	Lacerta	N	Lizard	Scorpius	Z	Scorpion
Canis Minor	S	Little Dog	Leo	Z	Lion	Sculptor	S	Sculptor
Capricornus	Z	Goat (or Sea-Goat)	Leo Minor	N	Little Lion	Scutum	N	Shield
Carina	S	Keel (of Argo)[1]	Lepus	S	Hare	Serpens	S	Serpent
Cassiopeia	N	Cassiopeia	Libra	Z	Scales	Sextans	S	Sextant
Centaurus	S	Centaur	Lupus	S	Wolf	Taurus	Z	Bull
Cepheus	N	Cepheus	Lynx	N	Lynx	Telescopium	S	Telescope
Cetus	S	Whale	Lyra	N	Lyre (Harp)	Triangulum	N	Triangle
Chamaeleon	S	Chameleon	Mensa	S	Table (mountain)	Triangulum Australe	S	Southern Triangle
Circinus	S	Compasses						
Columba	S	Dove	Microscopium	S	Microscope	Tucana	S	Toucan
Coma Berenices	N	Berenice's Hair	Monoceros	S	Unicorn	Ursa Major	N	Big Dipper
Corona Australis	S	Southern Crown	Musca	S	Southern Fly	Ursa Minor	N	Little Dipper
Corona Borealis	N	Northern Crown	Norma	S	Rule (straightedge)	Vela	S	Sail (of Argo)[1]
Corvus	S	Crow (Raven)				Virgo	Z	Virgin
Crater	S	Cup	Octans	S	Octant	Volans	S	Flying Fish
Crux	S	Southern Cross	Ophiuchus	N	Serpent-Bearer	Vulpecula	N	Fox
Cygnus	N	Swan	Orion	N	Orion			

1. The original constellation Argo Navis (the Ship Argo) has been divided into Carina, Puppis, and Vela. Normally the brightest star in each constellation is designated by alpha, the first letter of the Greek alphabet, the second brightest by beta, the second letter of the Greek alphabet, and so forth. But the Greek letters run through Carina, Puppis, and Vela as if it were still one constellation.

to dust by the passage through the atmosphere; only rather large ones reach the ground. Those that are found are called meteorites. (The "meteor," to repeat, is the term for the light streak in the sky.)

The largest meteorite known is still imbedded in the ground near Grootfontein in SW Africa and is estimated to weight 70 tons. The second largest known is the 34-ton Anighito (on exhibit in the Hayden Planetarium, New York), which was found by Admiral Peary at Cape York in Greenland. The largest meteorite found in the United States is the Willamette meteorite (found in Oregon, weight ca. 15 tons), but large portions of this meteorite weathered away before it was found. Its weight as it struck the ground may have been 20 tons.

All these are iron meteorites (an iron meteorite normally contains about 7% nickel), which form one class of meteorites. The other class consists of the stony meteorites, and between them there are the so-called "stony irons." The so-called "tektites" consist of glass similar to our volcanic glass obsidian, and because of the similarity, there is doubt in a number of cases whether the glass is of terrestrial or of extra-terrestrial origin.

Though no meteorite larger than the Grootfontein is actually known, we do know that the Earth has, on occasion, been struck by much larger bodies. Evidence for such hits are the meteorite craters, of which an especially good example is located near the Cañon Diablo in Arizona. Another meteor crater in the United States is a rather old crater near Odessa, Texas. A large number of others are known, especially in eastern Canada; and for many "probables," meteoric origin has now been proved.

The meteor showers are caused by multitudes of very small bodies travelling in swarms. The Earth travels in its orbit through these swarms like a car driving through falling snow. The point from which the meteors seem to emanate is called the *radiant* and is named for the constellation in that area. The Perseid meteor shower in August is the most spectacular of the year, boasting at peak roughly 60 meteors per hour under good atmospheric conditions. The presence of a bright moon diminishes the number of visible meteors.

The Constellations

Constellations are groupings of stars which form patterns that can be easily recognized and remembered, for example, Orion and the Big Dipper. Actually, the stars of the majority of all constellations do not "belong together." Usually they are at greatly varying distances from the Earth and just happen to lie more or less in the same line of sight as seen from our solar system. But in a few cases the stars of a constellation are actually associated; most of the bright stars of the Big Dipper travel together and form what astronomers call an open cluster.

If you observe a planet, say Mars, for one complete revolution, you will see that it passes successively through twelve constellations. All planets (except Pluto at certain times) can be observed only in these twelve constellations, which form the so-called Zodiac, and the Sun also moves through the signs of the Zodiac, though the Sun's apparent movement is actually caused by the movement of the Earth.

Although the constellations are due mainly to the optical accident of line of sight and have no real significance, astronomers have retained them as reference areas. It is much easier to speak of a star in Orion than to give its geometrical position in the sky. During the Astronomical Congress of 1928, it was decided to recognize 88 constellations. A description of their agreed-upon boundaries was published at Cambridge, England, in 1930, under the title *Atlas Céleste*.

The Auroras

The "northern lights" *(Aurora borealis)* as well as the "southern lights" *(Aurora australis)* are upper-atmosphere phenomena of astronomical origin. The auroras center around the magnetic (not the geographical) poles of the Earth, which explains why, in the Western Hemisphere, they have been seen as far to the south as New Orleans and Florida while the equivalent latitude in the Eastern Hemisphere never sees an aurora. The northern magnetic pole happens to be in the Western Hemisphere. The lower limit of an aurora is at about 50 miles. Upper limits have been estimated to be as high as 400 miles. Since about 1880, a connection between the auroras on Earth and the sun spots has been suspected and has gradually come to be accepted. It was said that the sun spots probably eject "particles" (later the word *electrons* was substituted) which on striking the Earth's atmosphere, cause the auroras. But this explanation suffered from certain difficulties. Sometimes a very large sun spot group on the Sun, with individual spots bigger than the Earth itself, would not cause an aurora. Moreover, even if a sun spot caused an aurora, the time that passed between the appearance of the one and the occurrence of the other was highly unpredictable.

This problem of the time lag is, in all probability, solved by the discovery of the Van Allen layer by artificial satellite *Explorer I*. The Van Allen layer is a double layer of charged sub-atomic particles around the Earth. The inner layer, with its center some 1,500 miles from the ground, reaches from about 40°N. to about 40°S. and does not touch the atmosphere. The outer layer, much larger and with its center several thousand miles from the ground, does touch the atmosphere in the vicinity of the magnetic poles.

It seems probable that the "leakage" of electrons from the outer Van Allen layer causes the auroras. A new burst of electrons from the Sun seems to be caught in the outer layer first. Under the assumption that all electrons are first caught in the outer layer, the time lag can be understood. There has to be an "overflow" from the outer layer to produce an aurora.

The Atmosphere

Astronomically speaking, the presence of our atmosphere is deplorable. Though reasonably transparent to visible light, the atmosphere may absorb as much as 60% of the visible and near-visible light. It is opaque to most other wave-lengths, except certain fairly short radio waves. In addition to absorbing much light, our atmosphere bends light rays entering at a slant (for a given observer) so that the true position of a star close to the horizon is not what it seems to be. One effect is that we see the Sun above the horizon before it actually is. And the unsteady movement of the atmosphere causes the "twinkling" of the stars, which may be romantic but is a nuisance when it comes to observing.

The composition of our atmosphere near the ground is 78% nitrogen and 21% oxygen, the remaining 1% consisting of other gases, most of it argon. The composition stays the same to an altitude of at least 70 miles (except that higher up two impurities, carbon dioxide and water vapor, are missing), but the pressure drops very fast. At 18,000 feet, half of the total mass of the atmosphere is below, and at 100,000 feet, 99% of the mass of the atmosphere is below. The upper limit of the atmosphere is usually given as 120 miles; no definitive figure is possible, since there is no boundary line between the incredibly attenuated gases 120 miles up and space.

Astronomical Telescopes

Optical telescopes used in astronomy are of two basic kinds: refracting and reflecting. In the *refractor telescope*, a lens is used to collect light from a distant object and bring it to a focus. A second lens, the eyepiece, then magnifies the image which may be examined visually or photographed directly. The *reflector telescope* uses a concave mirror instead of a lens, which reflects the light rays back toward the upper end of the telescope where they are magnified and observed or photographed. Most large optical telescopes now being built are reflectors.

Radio telescopes are used to study radio waves coming from outside the Earth's atmosphere. The waves are gathered by an antenna or "dish," which is a parabolic reflecting surface made of metal or finely meshed wire. Radio signals have been received from the Sun, Moon, and planets, and from the center of our galaxy and other galaxies. Radio signals are the means by which the distant and mysterious quasars and pulsars were recently discovered.

Symbols

☉ the sun	♀ Venus	♃ Jupiter	♆ Neptune	✓ occultation	☽ first quarter
☾ the moon	⊕ the earth	♄ Saturn	♇ Pluto	☍ opposition	○ full moon
☿ Mercury	♂ Mars	♅ Uranus	☌ conjunction	● new moon	☾ last quarter

Chinese Calendar

The Chinese lunar year is divided into 12 months of 29 or 30 days. The calendar is adjusted to the length of the solar year by the addition of extra months at regular intervals.

The years are arranged in major cycles of 60 years. Each successive year is named after one of 12 animals. These 12-year cycles are continuously repeated. The Chinese New Year is celebrated at the first new moon after the sun enters Aquarius— sometime between Jan. 21 and Feb. 19.

Rat	Ox	Tiger	Cat (Rabbit)	Dragon	Snake	Horse	Sheep (Goat)	Monkey	Rooster	Dog	Pig
1864	1865	1866	1867	1868	1869	1870	1871	1872	1873	1874	1875
1876	1877	1878	1879	1880	1881	1882	1883	1884	1885	1886	1887
1888	1889	1890	1891	1892	1893	1894	1895	1896	1897	1898	1899
1900	1901	1902	1903	1904	1905	1906	1907	1908	1909	1910	1911
1912	1913	1914	1915	1916	1917	1918	1919	1920	1921	1922	1923
1924	1925	1926	1927	1928	1929	1930	1931	1932	1933	1934	1935
1936	1937	1938	1939	1940	1941	1942	1943	1944	1945	1946	1947
1948	1949	1950	1951	1952	1953	1954	1955	1956	1957	1958	1959
1960	1961	1962	1963	1964	1965	1966	1967	1968	1969	1970	1971
1972	1973	1974	1975	1976	1977	1978	1979	1980	1981	1982	1983
1984	1985	1986	1987	1988	1989	1990	1991	1992	1993	1994	1995

Eclipses of the Sun and the Moon, 1982

January 9: Total eclipse of the Moon: The beginning of the umbral phase visible in Greenland, Europe, Africa except the extreme western part, Asia, Australia, the Indian Ocean, the Arctic regions, and extreme northwestern North America; the end visible in most of Asia, extreme western Australia, the Indian Ocean, Africa, Europe, extreme northeastern South America, the Atlantic Ocean, the Arctic regions, extreme northeastern North America, and Greenland.

January 25: Partial eclipse of the Sun. Visible in Antarctica, New Zealand except in the northern part.

June 21: Partial eclipse of the Sun. Visible in extreme southern part of Africa.

July 6: Total eclipse of the Moon. The beginning of the umbral phase visible in New Zealand, Antarctica, the Pacific Ocean, South America, North America except the northern part, the Atlantic Ocean, and extreme western Africa; the end visible in Australia except the extreme western part, New Zealand, the Pacific Ocean, Antarctica, North America except the northeastern part, and South America except the extreme northeastern part.

July 20: Partial eclipse of the Sun. Visible in extreme northern part of Asia, northwestern Europe, the northwestern part of North America, Greenland, Iceland, and arctic regions.

December 15: Partial eclipse of the Sun: Visible in Europe except extreme north, western Asia and extreme northeastern part of Africa.

December 30: Total eclipse of the Moon. The beginning of the umbral phase visible in eastern Australia, New Zealand, northeastern Asia, the Pacific Ocean, North America, the Arctic regions, northwestern South America, Greenland, and the western Atlantic Ocean; the end visible in North America, the Pacific Ocean, the Arctic regions, Australia, Asia except the western part, New Zealand, and extreme northeastern Europe.

Phenomena, 1982

Configurations of Sun, Moon, and Planets

JANUARY

d	h	
3	05	FIRST QUARTER
4	11	Earth at perihelion
8	06	Saturn 5° N of Spica
8	12	Moon at perigee
9	14	Mercury 5° S of Venus
9	20	FULL MOON (Eclipse)
15	19	Mars 3° S of Moon
16	12	Mercury greatest elong. E (19°)
16	13	Saturn 3° S of Moon
17	00	LAST QUARTER
17	20	Jupiter 4° S of Moon
20	01	Uranus 4° S of Moon
20	12	Moon at apogee
21	10	Venus in inferior conjunction
21	23	Neptune 1°.1 S of Moon
22	06	Vesta 0°.5 N of Moon
22	18	Mercury stationary
25	05	NEW MOON (Eclipse)

FEBRUARY

d	h	
1	04	Mercury in inferior conjunction
1	05	Saturn stationary
1	14	FIRST QUARTER
4	16	Pluto stationary
5	14	Moon at perigee
8	08	FULL MOON
10	14	Venus stationary
12	16	Mars 2° S of Moon
12	22	Saturn 3° S of Moon
12	22	Mercury stationary
14	09	Jupiter 4° S of Moon
15	20	LAST QUARTER
16	10	Uranus 4° S of Moon
17	08	Moon at apogee
18	09	Neptune 1°.0 S of Moon
20	16	Venus 7° N of Moon
21	05	Mars stationary
21	15	Mercury 2° N of Moon
23	21	NEW MOON

d	h	
24	14	Jupiter stationary
24	23	Pallas stationary
25	01	Venus greatest brilliancy
25	08	Saturn 5° N of Spica
26	11	Mercury greatest elong. W (27°)

MARCH

d	h	
2	22	FIRST QUARTER
4	05	Moon at perigee
9	20	Uranus stationary
9	21	FULL MOON
11	22	Mars 2° S of Moon
12	05	Saturn 3° S of Moon
13	17	Jupiter 4° S of Moon
15	19	Uranus 4° S of Moon
17	05	Moon at apogee
17	17	LAST QUARTER
17	18	Neptune 0°.7 S of Moon
20	23	Equinox
21	14	Venus 5° N of Moon

23 09	Ceres stationary
24 01	Mercury 2° N of Moon
25 10	NEW MOON
29 06	Moon at perigee
29 17	Neptune stationary
31 10	Mars at opposition

APRIL

1 05	FIRST QUARTER
1 18	Venus greatest elong. W (46°)
1 22	Pallas at opposition
5 07	Mars closest approach
7 13	Mars 2° S of Moon
8 10	FULL MOON
8 10	Saturn 2° S of Moon
9 02	Saturn at opposition
9 21	Jupiter 3° S of Moon
11 18	Mercury in superior conjunction
12 02	Uranus 3° S of Moon
14 00	Moon at apogee
14 02	Neptune 0°.4 S of Moon
15 21	Pluto at opposition
16 13	LAST QUARTER
20 06	Venus 4° N of Moon
23 20	NEW MOON
25 21	Moon at perigee
26 00	Jupiter at opposition
29 23	Juno stationary
30 12	FIRST QUARTER

MAY

4 05	Mars 3° S of Moon
5 13	Saturn 3° S of Moon
6 21	Jupiter 4° S of Moon
8 01	FULL MOON
9 00	Mercury greatest elong. E (21°)
9 07	Uranus 3° S of Moon
10 12	Ceres at opposition
10 14	Mercury 8° N of Aldebaran
11 08	Neptune 0°.3 S of Moon
11 15	Moon at apogee
13 05	Mars stationary
16 05	LAST QUARTER
20 02	Venus 3° N of Moon
21 10	Mercury stationary
22 00	Pallas stationary
23 05	NEW MOON
24 03	Moon at perigee
24 03	Uranus at opposition
29 20	FIRST QUARTER
31 13	Mars 5° S of Moon

JUNE

1 16	Saturn 3° S of Moon
1 20	Mercury in inferior conjunction
2 21	Jupiter 4° S of Moon
5 11	Uranus 3° S of Moon
6 16	FULL MOON
7 13	Neptune 0°.3 S of Moon
7 23	Moon at apogee
12 09	Vesta 0°.7 N of Moon
13 21	Mercury stationary
14 18	LAST QUARTER
17 05	Neptune at opposition
18 23	Venus 2° N of Moon
19 12	Saturn stationary
20 02	Mercury 1°.1 S of Moon
21 12	NEW MOON (Eclipse)
21 12	Moon at perigee

21 17	Solstice
23 03	Mercury 1°.7 N of Aldebaran
24 06	Juno at opposition
26 14	Mercury greatest elong. W (22°)
28 06	FIRST QUARTER
28 08	Jupiter stationary
28 12	Mars 6° S of Moon
28 21	Saturn 3° S of Moon
29 21	Vesta stationary
30 01	Jupiter 4° S of Moon

JULY

1 04	Ceres 0°.2 N of Moon
2 05	Ceres stationary
2 15	Uranus 4° S of Moon
4 01	Venus 4° N of Aldebaran
4 13	Earth at aphelion
4 17	Neptune 0°.3 S of Moon
5 01	Moon at apogee
6 08	FULL MOON (Eclipse)
10 00	Mars 3° S of Saturn
11 16	Pluto stationary
14 04	LAST QUARTER
18 19	Venus 0°.6 N of Moon
19 21	Moon at perigee
20 19	NEW MOON (Eclipse)
21 19	Mars 1°.6 N of Spica
25 08	Mercury in superior conjunction
26 07	Saturn 3° S of Moon
26 22	Mars 6° S of Moon
27 10	Jupiter 4° S of Moon
27 18	FIRST QUARTER
29 21	Uranus 4° S of Moon
31 23	Neptune 0°.4 S of Moon

AUGUST

1 10	Moon at apogee
4 23	FULL MOON
8 04	Mercury 1°.0 N of Regulus
9 12	Uranus stationary
9 16	Venus 7° S of Pollux
10 01	Mars 2° S of Jupiter
10 11	Vesta at opposition
12 11	LAST QUARTER
17 02	Moon at perigee
17 14	Venus 1°.4 S of Moon
19 03	NEW MOON
19 19	Juno stationary
20 15	Mercury 5° S of Moon
22 20	Saturn 3° S of Moon
24 01	Jupiter 4° S of Moon
24 15	Mars 6° S of Moon
26 04	Uranus 3° S of Moon
26 10	FIRST QUARTER
28 05	Neptune 0°.3 S of Moon
29 00	Moon at apogee

SEPTEMBER

3 12	FULL MOON
6 01	Neptune stationary
6 04	Mercury greatest elong. E (27°)
7 09	Venus 0°.7 N of Regulus
10 17	LAST QUARTER
13 18	Moon at perigee
17 12	NEW MOON
18 22	Mercury 10° S of Moon
19 07	Mercury stationary
19 10	Saturn 3° S of Moon
20 19	Jupiter 4° S of Moon

21 04	Saturn 5° N of Spica
22 13	Mars 1°.5 S of Uranus
22 14	Mars 5° S of Moon
22 14	Uranus 3° S of Moon
23 09	Equinox
23 13	Vesta stationary
24 13	Neptune 0°.07 S of Moon
25 04	FIRST QUARTER
25 19	Moon at apogee

OCTOBER

2 05	Mercury in inferior conjunction
3 01	FULL MOON
3 01	Mars 3° N of Antares
9 01	Moon at perigee
9 23	LAST QUARTER
10 13	Mercury stationary
15 11	Mercury 4° S of Moon
17 00	NEW MOON
17 18	Mercury greatest elong. W (18°)
18 15	Jupiter 3° S of Moon
18 21	Saturn in conjunction with Sun
20 01	Uranus 3° S of Moon
20 14	Pluto in conjunction with Sun
21 17	Mars 3° S of Moon
21 22	Neptune 0°.2 N of Moon
23 15	Moon at apogee
25 00	FIRST QUARTER
25 06	Mars 3° S of Neptune
29 04	Mercury 4° N of Spica

NOVEMBER

1 06	Mercury 0°.7 S of Saturn
1 13	FULL MOON
4 02	Venus in superior conjunction
4 10	Moon at perigee
8 07	LAST QUARTER
13 14	Jupiter in conjunction with Sun
13 15	Saturn 3° S of Moon
15 15	NEW MOON
18 08	Neptune 0°.4 N of Moon
19 18	Mercury in superior conjunction
19 21	Mars 0°.5 S of Moon
20 11	Moon at apogee
23 20	FIRST QUARTER
26 03	Pallas in conjunction with Sun
27 11	Uranus in conjunction with Sun

DECEMBER

1 00	FULL MOON
2 11	Moon at perigee
7 16	LAST QUARTER
8 13	Mercury 3° S of Neptune
11 02	Saturn 3° S of Moon
13 05	Jupiter 2° S of Moon
13 22	Uranus 2° S of Moon
15 09	NEW MOON (Eclipse)
18 02	Moon at apogee
19 00	Neptune in conjunction with Sun
19 01	Mars 1°.6 S of Moon
22 05	Solstice
23 14	FIRST QUARTER
29 23	Ceres in conjunction with Sun
30 12	FULL MOON (Eclipse)
30 19	Mercury greatest elong. E (20°)
30 22	Moon at perigee

NOTE: The hour listings are in Universal Time. For conversion to United States time zones, see conversion table in this section.

SPACE

The Year in Space

There was a lot of exciting news from space and astronomy during 1981: more rings around Saturn, another moon for Jupiter, pulsing white dwarf stars, a supersun thousands of times the size of our own, maybe even a tenth planet. But it all took a back seat a little after 7:00 on the morning of April 12th. While tens of millions of Americans sipped extra coffee and stared anxiously at their TV screens, the spaceship *Columbia* boomed off Kennedy Space Center's launch pad 39, heading straight for orbit and her rightful place in future history books. Exactly two days, six hours, 20 minutes, and 48 seconds later she was back on Earth, gliding to a textbook perfect landing at Edwards Air Force Base in California's Mojave Desert. Within minutes, even before debriefing physicians could complete their work, mission commander John Young popped out of the craft's hatch, trotted down the access ladder and, like a teenager who'd just taken his first car for a test drive, strode proudly around the still-warm ship, punching the air with obvious satisfaction and wearing a smile that seemed to be a whole continent wide. A few moments later, Young was joined by an equally jubilant *Columbia* captain Robert Crippen. Together with literally tens of thousands of scientists, engineers, and technicians, they had succeeded in putting America back in the manned spaceflight business after a wait of more than eleven and a half years.

The space shuttle was more than a continuation of the earlier *Apollo* Moon missions; with its many innovations, *Columbia* was really a new beginning: it made the first wheels-down landing of any spacecraft; it was the first spaceship to carry humans on its maiden voyage (all others had been tested by remote control first); it was the first one to ride to orbit piggyback on its own fuel tank; it had the first solid fuel boosters used in manned flight; it was the first winged spacecraft (wingspan 78 feet, total height 46.3 feet); and it was the first such craft designed specifically for re-use up to 100 times.

Columbia is only one of four or five crafts now built or in construction. Its main component is the delta-winged orbiter, 121 feet long, powered by three main ascent engines. It contains a crew compartment large enough to house seven astronauts, or up to ten persons, in the event of an emergency. Its cabin contains a normal sea-level atmosphere, so occupants are not encumbered by heavy space suits. Its cargo bay is large enough to carry 65,00 pounds in a volume big enough to hold a Greyhound bus. Cargo bay access is through two huge 60 foot by 15 foot doors, which must remain open during orbital flight to provide cooling for crew and equipment. The orbiter is equipped with five identical main computers, any one of which is capable of providing all necessary control functions. In case of disagreement, the computers "vote" to decide which one is most likely correct. The orbiter expends all its rocket power on the way to, and in, orbit, then lands in "dead-stick" fashion, either automatically or at the hands of its pilot.

The orbiter is pushed into orbit with the help of two solid-fuel booster rockets, each of which having more than twice the thrust of the three ascent rockets combined. The booster rockets fire for a little over two minutes, and burn for eight. They are jettisoned during ascent, and are parachuted into the ocean for recovery and re-use. The only expendable component on the way up is the enormous main fuel tank, 154 feet long and 15 feet in diameter. It carries liquid hydrogen and oxygen, and is separated from the orbiter 8.5 minutes into flight at an altitude of 70.6 miles. The fuel tank is equipped with a tumble system to insure its complete breakup during re-entry. Once in orbit, the shuttle makes use of two more rocket engines in the Orbital Maneuvering System, or OMS.

Columbia's maiden voyage was strictly a test flight; one observer stated that its mission was simply to "get up, get down." For cargo, it carried only test instrumentation to check the spacecraft's many systems, including the performance of the 30,922 insulating tiles needed to ward off the heat of re-entry. *Columbia* is scheduled for the first eight shuttle missions, including one and maybe two more during 1981. Astronauts Richard H. Truly and Joe H. Engle were designated as the crew for *Columbia*'s second flight. The second shuttle, designated *Challenger*, will be delivered to NASA in mid-1982 and flown sometime in 1983. The third shuttle *(Discovery)* is currently in early manufacturing stages and will be delivered in September 1983. Assembly of the fourth shuttle, *Atlantis*, is to begin in May 1983 with delivery in December 1984. The very first shuttle, named *Enterprise* to the delight of the Nation's "Trekkies," will not see orbit, but is used as a trainer.

Russian Shuttle, ESA Launcher

While America was the first country to develop and fly a shuttle, the U.S.S.R. is thought to be not far behind. The Russians have been very active in manned space flight during the 11½ year hiatus since the last *Apollo* Moon landing. In 1981, the U.S.S.R. launched over 100 payloads, about one quarter of which were manned or man-related. The Soviet shuttle is also a delta-winged craft, but is believed to be somewhat smaller than America's *Columbia*. It will probably not have the large cargo doors that give U.S. versions so much versatility. The Russian space ship will have one important advantage, however: it will be capable of landing, probably on skids, on most Russian airports. This operational flexibility is seen by observers as a distinct military plus. Possibly embarrassed by being beaten to the Moon, the Soviets have openly announced that their goal is to learn to live in space and perhaps shoot for a manned interplanetary mission within 10–15 years.

Other countries are getting into spaceflight as well, though not in manned orbiters. The European Space Agency (ESA), a consortium of 11 countries, successfully launched *Ariane 3* from Kourou, French Guiana, in 1981. This third launcher in the *Ariane* series was only the second to reach orbit. *Ariane 1* made it, but carried a dummy payload; *Ariane 2* failed to reach orbit and had to be aborted. *Ariane 3* carried a payload of 3740 pounds, consisting of the meteorological *Meteosat 2* and a geosynchronous communications satellite, for India, called *Apple*. The ESA launchsite, on the northern edge of South America, provides, because of its near-equatorial location, a 17% payload weight advantage over Cape Canaveral. Both the ESA and Japan plan probes to look at Halley's Comet in the mid-1980s. NASA budgets for similar missions have been cut back, but there is now a private "Halley Fund" to gather civilian money for such an effort.

Meanwhile, Back at the Solar System

Data from earlier interplanetary satellites continues to be analyzed, most of it coming from *Voyagers 1* and *2*. While *Voyager 2*'s fly-by of Saturn (August) came too late to be included here, there were nonetheless a few interesting surprises:

Saturn. Like Jupiter, Saturn was found to give off more energy than it receives from the Sun. The reason for this phenomenon was not clearly understood until *Voyager 1* data showed it came from separation of helium and hydrogen in the planet's atmosphere. A previously undetected high-atmosphere haze has been spotted on Saturn's limb, or edge. The haze is 37 miles thick and is located about 93 miles above the much denser layers below. *Voyager 1* also provided photos of the planet's curiously braided F ring, the structure of which may have been formed by the gravitational forces from two nearby moons. The main ring structure was also found to contain "spokes" which have yet to be explained. We now have more information about Saturn's moons (15 have been counted so far, but there may be more). Titan has a very dense atmosphere which blocks its surface from view. Dione is two-faced; one side has long, bright, wispy features, the other is cratered with some intervening plains. Dione shares its orbit with a smaller satellite, called Dione B. Tethys has two partners in its orbit, one in front and one behind. Tethys may be the iciest moon in the solar system, its density being very close to water. It contains at least one long groove, which may have been caused

by expansion and contraction. Mimas, with a diameter of 243 ± 6 miles the second smallest known Saturnian moon, is marked by a huge impact crater that gives it the appearance of a rocky pomegranate. *Voyager 2* is scheduled to take a closer look at Mimas, and at Hyperion (the smallest satellite), Enceladus and Iapetus. Cartographers have a problem mapping these small objects; they're not round, but often potato-shaped.

Jupiter. It appears that the Big Daddy of the Solar System has an even bigger magnetic tail, which may be wispy in shape. *Voyager 2* kept running into portions of it on its way to Saturn. The tail, an extension of Jupiter's magnetic field, may be up to 400 Jupiter radii (R_J) wide and 10,000 R_J long. The satellite count for Jupiter is now up to 16.

Uranus, Neptune. *Voyager 2* has now been cleared for a fly-by of Uranus, January 24, 1986. It could then go on to Neptune three years later. It seems that *Voyager 1* was so successful that version 2 didn't have to be reprogrammed to repeat earlier Saturn photos. Data gathered over the next few years could prove interesting: evidence is mounting that Neptune has another moon, and Uranus' rings may be warped. More startling still, however, is the fact that something seems to be disturbing Neptune's orbit. The mass of Pluto is too low to cause the observed irregularities; whatever—if anything—is out there would have to have a mass about four to five times that of the Earth. Darth Vader, where are you now?

Far Out

Two more (for a total of six, to date) 10-million-light-year-distant galaxies have been found. These have the highest red shifts ever observed for galaxies, making them the most distant—and oldest—known cosmic structures. The surprising finding, however, is that they seem to be quite mature, implying that both galaxy and star formation must have taken place within a mere two billion years after the birth of the universe, now pegged at about 18 billion years ago.

An enormous stellar mass has been found in the center of the Large Magellanic Cloud. Designated R136a, the object could be as big as 3000 times the mass of our Sun. Being so large, it is extremely unstable, as evidenced by the fact that it is losing one solar mass per century.

Quasars were in the news again in 1981. Astronomers have detected the possible existence of a quasar cluster near galaxy M82, and some "fuzzy" quasars have also been seen. If the quasar haze is real, it would give strength to the thought that quasars are galaxies that never developed. Analysis of the spectra from the double quasar 0957+561 re-

(Continued on page 377)

Lightning Caused by Cosmic Rays

Cosmic rays from space probably provide the extra electric potential that triggers a lightning stroke, according to a report made by Johns Hopkins scientists in the late seventies. Such rays, very high-energy particles moving at almost the speed of light, hit the upper atmosphere as an "air shower." When such a shower passes through a thunderhead, it releases electrons from oxygen and nitrogen atoms through ionization of the air. The free electrons are accelerated by the electric field already existing within the cloud, concentrating enough negative electric charge at the bottom of the cloud to generate a lightning stroke. The first stroke generated is a preliminary "leader stroke" of low luminosity. It travels the zigzag path of least electrical resistance to the ground. When the leader stroke is about 50 yards above the ground, an electric charge leaps up to meet it. These strokes complete the circuit between the cloud and the ground, clearing the way for the powerful return stroke, usually the first lightning seen. Often other strokes follow so quickly that they may seem to be one single stroke.

Major U.S. Space Projects

Scientific Satellites

Applications Technology Satellite (ATS). Series of spacecraft designed to test techniques and equipment in space for future communications, weather, and navigational systems. *ATS-1* was launched Dec. 6, 1966. *ATS-6,* the most powerful and versatile communications satellite ever developed, was launched on May 30, 1974. It is transmitting educational TV programs and health services to scores of isolated communities in Appalachia, the Rocky Mountains, and Alaska, as well as to school children and adults in 5,000 isolated villages and cities in India.

Biosatellite. Earth-orbiting biological laboratory, carrying a variety of plants and animals into space to determine effects of weightlessness (zero gravity). *Biosatellite 1,* launched Dec. 14, 1966, was unrecovered. *Biosatellite 2,* launched Sept. 7, 1967, was highly successful. The last in the series, *Biosatellite 3,* launched June 29, 1969, was returned to Earth because of the deteriorating condition of its primate passenger.

Explorer. Largest group of satellites in U.S. space program, used for a variety of scientific purposes in atmosphere, ionosphere and interplanetary space. *Explorer 1,* launched July 1, 1958, was America's first successful satellite. It confirmed the existence of the Van Allen radiation belts which girdle the Earth. First Explorer weighed about 18 lb; current spacecraft average about 100 lb, but some weigh as much as 500 lb. Orbits and design vary.

Geostationary Scientific Satellite (GEOS). A series of satellites designed to study the magnetosphere, that region of near-Earth space where the magnetic field of the Earth still plays a dominating role. GEOS-D, launched on Sept. 9, 1980, is the first to be able to take vertical readings of atmospheric moisture and temperature at various levels in the atmosphere.

Helios. A joint U.S.-German program to obtain new information on interplanetary space in the region close to the Sun. *Helios 1,* launched Dec. 10, 1974, flew within 28 million miles of the Sun—closer than any previous spacecraft—at times encountering temperatures hot enough to melt lead (700 degrees F). *Helios 2* was launched on Jan. 15, 1976.

High Energy Astronomy Observatory (HEAO). Series of space platforms designed for research in high-energy astrophysics—the domain of peculiar astronomical objects such as quasars, pulsars, and black holes in space. Weighing 2,200 lb, *HEAO-1* was launched into a 225-mile Earth orbit Aug. 12, 1977, to perform a detailed X-ray survey of the celestial sphere. After *HEAO-3,* 1979, HEAO scientific instruments will be carried into space by NASA's Space Shuttle.

Intelsat. Series of communications satellites launched by NASA on a reimbursable basis for the Communications Satellite Corporation (Comsat) to form a commercial, worldwide communications satellite system. Comsat is the U.S. member of the 102-nation consortium that owns the Intelsat network. *Early Bird,* launched April 6, 1965, was the world's first operational commercial communications satellite. The network now is composed of ten satellites, furnishing communications service including telecasts for North America, Europe, and Asia. The satellites are positioned about 22,000 miles above the Equator and, moving at the same speed as Earth, appear to hover permanently over one spot.

Landsat. Series of NASA satellites conducting a variety of earth resources observations (mineralogy, geography, mapping, land use) from space. *ERTS-1* (now called *Landsat* 1) was launched July 23, 1972, into a 570-mile circular polar-orbit around Earth. Weight: 1,800 lb. It was retired in 1978. *Landsat 3* was launched March 3, 1978. Orbiting Earth 14 times a day, Landsats scan a swath 115 miles wide in four bands of the spectrum that reveal much about Earth's natural resources that can be used to help manage them more wisely. The satellites pass over almost the entire globe every 18 days.

Laser Geodynamic Satellite (LAGEOS). Laser-carrying satellite designed to make detailed measurements of plate tectonic (continental drift) motions, regional fault motions, and the rotation and wobble of Earth. Weighing about 900 lb each, LAGEOS is a solid sphere fitted with 600 laser retroreflectors. Laser beams from ground stations are bounced off it and returned to Earth, permitting very accurate positioning of both ground station and satellite. The first *LAGEOS,* launched on May 4, 1976, is in a circular Earth orbit at 3,440 miles.

Large Space Telescope (LST). The LST program calls for the construction of a 10-ton telescope orbiting the Earth at a distance of 380 miles. This national facility, with a 2.4-meter (8-foot) aperture, would make possible astronomical observations 10 times deeper and with more detail than has ever been possible. It would be placed in orbit via the United States' Space Shuttle.

Marisat. Series of three satellites that make up the first Maritime Communications Satellite systems, owned by the Communications Satellite Corp. (Comsat). The first, *Marisat I,* was launched on Feb. 19, 1976, into a geosynchronous (appearing to hover over one spot on Earth) orbit.

Nimbus. Advanced meteorological satellites for detailed global weather and atmosphere soundings. Equipped with advanced television cameras and a high resolution infrared camera system, Nimbus can provide both day and night pictures of Earth's cloud cover. The first *Nimbus 1* was launched Aug. 28, 1964.

Orbiting Astronomical Observatory (OAO). Earth-orbiting observatory, operating above the obscuring effects of Earth's atmosphere, is able to study entire celestial sphere in electromagnetic wavelengths not easily accessible from the ground. *OAO-3* is one of the heaviest (4900 lb) U.S. unmanned satellites and carries 11 telescopes. It was launched Aug. 21, 1972, into a nearly circular, 740-mile Earth orbit.

Orbiting Geophysical Observatory (OGO). Large (1,000 lb) multipurpose space platforms designed to study Earth, Sun, and the interplanetary space in between. Carrying many scientific instruments, OGO has the advantage over smaller satellites of being able to observe numerous phenomena simultaneously over prolonged periods of time. *OGO 1* was launched Sept. 5, 1964, into a 13,910–92,845-mile orbit around Earth. The last *OGO* in the series was launched June 5, 1969

Orbiting Solar Observatory (OSO). Series of one-ton space platforms designed to study the Sun and phenomena such as solar flares above the obscuring effects of Earth's atmosphere. Most sophisticated version, *OSO-I*, was launched June 20, 1975. Carrying such instruments as X-ray and gamma-ray monitors, the OSO's have provided scientists with invaluable basic details about the functioning of the Sun. They orbit Earth at a distance of about 300 miles.

Pegasus. Among the heaviest (3,000 lb) of U.S. scientific satellites, with a wing-like structure spanning 96 feet. Designed to determine the frequency and depth of punctures by micrometeoroids (tiny particles of matter speeding through space faster than a bullet). Data from Pegasus helped prepare man for the Apollo lunar landing mission. *Pegasus I*, was launched Feb. 16, 1965.

Relay. Communications satellite system designed to demonstrate feasibility of intercontinental and transoceanic transmission of television and radio signals with a medium-altitude (up to 12,000 miles) radio-equipped satellite. *Relay I* was launched Dec. 13, 1962.

Small Astronomy Satellite (SAS). X-ray satellites designed to monitor the intensity of X-ray sources in our Galaxy and beyond. *SAS-1*, weighing about 400 lb, was launched Dec. 12, 1970.

Seasat. Series of satellites which are the first to study ocean data exclusively. *Seasat-A* was launched June 26, 1978. It circled the globe 14 times a day. Its mission was to determine if microwave instruments scanning the oceans from space can provide useful scientific data for oceanographers, meteorologists, and commercial users of the seas. The spacecraft sent back information on surface winds and temperatures, currents, wave heights, ice conditions, ocean topography, and coastal storm activity. On Oct. 9, 1978, it went dead in orbit, apparently from a short circuit.

Solar Maximum Mission (S.M.M.). Designed to study solar flares. The 5,100-lb spacecraft is the first to be built so that it could be repaired or retrieved by astronauts flying the space shuttle. The spacecraft, nicknamed Solar Max, was launched into a 356-mile high orbit on Feb. 14, 1980. In January 1981, mechanical failure resulted in the inability to point the craft's instruments precisely for observing solar events. However, much important information was already returned.

Synchronous Meteorological Satellite (SMS). Series of geostationary (hovering over same spot above Earth) satellites designed to keep continuous watch on fast-changing storms, such as hurricanes and tornadoes, sending back high resolution pictures every 30 minutes. *SMS-1* was launched May 17, 1974. With the launch of a second *SMS*, on Feb. 6, 1975, day-and-night surveillance is provided over the U.S. and adjacent ocean areas.

Syncom. First communications satellite to be placed in a synchronous Earth orbit for global communication. Three Syncom satellites were

launched between Feb. 14, 1963, and Aug. 19, 1964.

Telstar. Early experimental communications satellite system operated by American Telephone and Telegraph Co. *Telstar 1* was launched July 1, 1962, by NASA for AT&T on a reimbursable basis.

Tiros. Spectacularly successful early weather satellite system developed by NASA. *Tiros 1*, launched April 1, 1960, took more than 22,000 cloud-cover pictures in 78 days and transmitted them to ground stations. Operational system, called ITOS (Improved Tiros), is now handled by the National Oceanic and Atmospheric Administration (NOAA) of the Department of Commerce. Tiros stands for Television and Infrared Observation Satellite. Contributes significantly to early detection of hurricanes and other destructive storms. Provides weathermen with daily pictures of weather over the entire globe. Weight: Approximately 750 lb. Orbits Earth at distance of about 450 miles. *Tiros-N* was launched on Oct. 13, 1978.

Transit. Department of Defense navigational satellite system for military vessels. Consisting of four satellites, system is designed to allow ships to determine their precise position regardless of weather or time of day.

Vanguard. Earth-orbiting geodetic survey satellites. *Vanguard 1*, launched March 17, 1958, determined that Earth is slightly pear-shaped.

Westar. Domestic communications system developed by Western Union. Spacecraft are launched into a 200-by-19,500-mile Earth orbit. Program was begun in 1974, with the launch of *Westar 1* on April 13.

Unmanned Planetary and Lunar Programs

Lunar Orbiter. Series of spacecraft designed to orbit the Moon, taking pictures and obtaining data in support of the subsequent manned Apollo landings. The U.S. launched five *Lunar Orbiters* between Aug. 10, 1966 and Aug. 2, 1967.

Mariner. Designation for a series of spacecraft designed to fly past or orbit the planets, particularly Mercury, Venus, and Mars. *Mariners* provided the early information on Venus and Mars. *Mariner 9*, orbiting Mars in 1971, returned the most startling photographs of that planet to date, and helped pave the way for a *Viking* landing in 1976. *Mariner 10* explored Venus and Mercury in 1973 and was the first probe to use a planet's gravity to whip it toward another.

Pioneer. Designation for the United States' first series of sophisticated interplanetary spacecraft. *Pioneers 10* and *11* reached Jupiter in 1973 and 1974 and continued on to explore Saturn and the other outer planets. *Pioneer 11*, renamed *Pioneer Saturn*, examined the Saturn system in September 1979. Significant discoveries were the finding of a small new moon and a narrow new ring. In 1986, *Pioneer 10* will be the first man-made object to escape the solar system. *Pioneer Venus 1* and *2* reached Venus in 1978 and provided detailed information about that planet's surface and atmosphere.

Ranger. NASA's earliest moon exploration program. Spacecraft were designed for a crash landing on the Moon, taking pictures and returning scientific data up to the moment of impact. Provided the first closeup views of the lunar surface. The *Rangers* provided more than 17,000 closeup pictures, giving us more information about the Moon in a few years than in all the time that had gone before.

Surveyor. Series of unmanned spacecraft designed to land gently on the Moon and provide information on the surface in preparation for the manned lunar landings. Their legs were instrumented to return data on the surface hardness of the Moon. *Surveyor* dispelled the fear that Apollo spacecraft might sink several feet or more into the lunar dust.

Viking. Designation for two spacecraft designed to conduct detailed scientific examination of the planet Mars, including a search for life. *Viking 1* landed on July 20, 1976; *Viking 2*, Sept. 3, 1976. More was learned about the Red Planet in a few short months than in all the time that had gone before. But the question of life on Mars remains unresolved.

Voyager. Designation for two spacecraft designed to explore Jupiter and the other outer planets. *Voyager 1* and *Voyager 2* passed Jupiter in 1979 and sent back startling color TV images of that planet and its moons. They took a total of about 33,000 pictures. *Voyager 2* will continue on a trajectory that will take it to Uranus in 1986. *Voyager 1* passed Saturn November 1980 and *Voyager 2* passed Saturn August 1981.

Manned Space Flight Projects

Mercury. *Project Mercury,* America's first manned space program, was designed to further knowledge about man's capabilities in space. *Mercury 9,* with astronaut Gordon L. Cooper, was the longest flight. It proved conclusively that man can live and work in space for at least 34 hours, despite the high-gravity forces of launch and re-entry, and weightlessness.

Gemini. *Gemini* was an extension of *Project Mercury,* to determine the effects of prolonged space flight on man—two weeks or longer. "Walks in space" provided invaluable information for astronauts' later walks on the Moon. The *Gemini* spacecraft, twice as large as the *Mercury* capsule, accommodated two astronauts.

Apollo. *Apollo* was the designation for the United States' effort to land a man on the Moon and return him safely to Earth. The goal was successfully accomplished with *Apollo 11* on July 20, 1969, culminating eight years of rehearsal and centuries of

dreaming. Astronauts Neil A. Armstrong and Col. Edwin E. Aldrin, Jr., scooped up and brought back the first lunar rocks ever seen on Earth—about 47 pounds. Six *Apollo* flights followed, ending with Apollo 17 in December, 1972. The last three *Apollos* carried mechanized vehicles called lunar rovers for wide-ranging surface exploration of the Moon by astronauts. The rendezvous and docking of an *Apollo* spacecraft with a Russian *Soyuz* craft in Earth orbit on July 18, 1975, closed out the *Apollo* program.

Skylab. America's first Earth-orbiting space station. *Project Skylab* was designed to demonstrate that men can work and live in space for prolonged periods without ill effects. Originally the spent third stage of a Saturn 5 moon rocket, *Skylab* measured 118 feet from stem to stern, and carried the most varied assortment of experimental equipment ever assembled in a single spacecraft. Three three-man crews visited the space stations, spending more than 740 hours observing the Sun and bringing home more than 175,000 solar pictures. These were the first recordings of solar activity above Earth's obscuring atmosphere. *Skylab* also evaluated systems designed to gather information on Earth's resources and environmental conditions. *Skylab* biomedical findings indicated that man adapts well to space for at least a period of three months, provided he has a proper diet and adequately programmed exercise, sleep, work, and recreation periods. *Skylab* orbited Earth at a distance of about 300 miles. Five years after the last *Skylab* mission, the 77-ton space station's orbit began to deteriorate faster than expected, owing to unexpectedly high sunspot activity. On July 11, 1979, the parts of *Skylab* that did not burn up in the atmosphere came crashing down on parts of Australia and the Indian Ocean. No one was hurt.

Space Shuttle. The *Space Shuttle* is a new manned space transportation system developed by NASA to reduce the cost of using space for commercial, scientific, and defense needs. In effect, the *Shuttle* is a manned rocket which, after depositing its payload in space, can be flown back to Earth like a conventional airplane and be available for re-use. Because of its versatility and large cargo-carrying capacity, the *Space Shuttle* can combine missions. For example, on one trip to space the *Shuttle* might place a weather satellite and a scientific satellite into different orbits, and then retrieve a communications satellite and return it to Earth for servicing. Or, if the repairs required by the communications satellite were relatively simple, the *Shuttle* might carry technicians who would repair it in orbit. Although most of its cargoes will be unmanned, the *Shuttle* can serve as an inhabited Earth-orbiting laboratory for up to 30 days. The *Space Shuttle Columbia* was successfully launched on April 12, 1981.

How Old Is Man?

Paleoanthropologists (anthropologists who specialize in the study of fossil man) disagree on when humans first were differentiated from their pre-human ancestors. Estimates range from 2 to 3.8 million years ago, based on such criteria as brain size, knee joints indicating an ability to walk on two legs, and tool-making ability.

The oldest footprints of a human-like animal were found by Dr. Mary Leakey in 1979 in the Laetoli area of northern Tanzania, East Africa. The 3.6-million-year age of the footprints was determined by radioactive dating of the rock layer in which they were found.

The old concept of a single line of development from ape to man has been replaced by the generally accepted theory that there were at least three different forms of early man and near man in Africa, where most scientists agree humans first emerged.

Notable Unmanned Lunar and Interplanetary Probes

Spacecraft	Launch date	Destination	Remarks
Pioneer 1 (U.S.)	Oct. 11, 1958	Moon	Max. alt.: 71,300 mi. Flight duration: 43 h 17.5 min
Pioneer 3 (U.S.)	Dec. 6, 1958	Moon	Max. alt.: 66,654 mi. Discovered outer Van Allen layer.
Lunik 1 (U.S.S.R.)	Sept. 12, 1959	Moon	Landed in area of Mare Serenitatis.
Pioneer 5 (U.S.)	March 11, 1960	Inter-planetary	Orbited sun between Earth & Venus. Radio transmission over record distance of 20 million miles.
Ranger 4 (U.S.)	April 23, 1962	Moon	730-lb probe. Impacted on Moon's far side April 26. No transmission.
Mariner 2 (U.S.)	Aug. 27, 1962	Venus	Venus probe. Successful mid-course correction. Passed 21,648 mi. from Venus Dec. 14, 1962. Reported 800°F. surface temp. Contact lost Jan. 3, 1963 at 54 million mi.
Ranger 7 (U.S.)	July 28, 1964	Moon	Impacted near Crater Guericke 68.5 h after launch. Sent 4,316 pictures during last 15 min of flight as close as 1,000 ft above lunar surface.
Mariner 4 (U.S.)	Nov. 28, 1964	Mars	After mid-course correction, passed behind Mars July 14, 1965, taking 22 pictures from about 6,000 mi.
Ranger 8 (U.S.)	Feb. 17, 1965	Moon	809 lb. After 64.9 h, crashed into Mare Tranquilitatis, 2.59° N of lunar equator. Sent 7,137 pictures.
Ranger 9 (U.S.)	March 21, 1965	Moon	After 64.5 h, hit Crater Alphonsus. Sent 5,814 pictures.
Zond 3 (U.S.S.R.)	July 18, 1965	Moon	Sent close-ups of 3 million sq mi. of Moon. Now in solar orbit.
Venera 3 (U.S.S.R.)	Nov. 16, 1965	Venus	2,112 lb. Entered Venus atmosphere (March 1, 1966). No data sent.
Pioneer 6 (U.S.)	Dec. 16, 1965	Inter-planetary	Successfully orbiting Sun (every 311 days) to check space conditions between Earth & Venus. Perihelion: 75.6 million mi. Aphelion: 90.7 million mi.
Luna 9 (U.S.S.R.)	Jan. 31, 1966	Moon	3,428 lb. Instrument capsule of 220 lb soft-landed Feb. 3, 1966. Sent back about 30 pictures.
Luna 10 (U.S.S.R.)	March 31, 1966	Moon	540 lb. Orbit achieved April 2, 1966.
Surveyor 1 (U.S.)	May 30, 1966	Moon	Landed June 2, 1966. Sent almost 10,400 pictures, a number after surviving the 14-day lunar night.
Lunar Orbiter 1 (U.S.)	Aug. 10, 1966	Moon	Orbited Moon Aug. 14. 21 pictures sent.
Pioneer 7 (U.S.)	Aug. 17, 1966	Sun Orbit	Orbiting sun (400 days). Perihelion: 92 million mi. Aphelion: 102 million mi.
Luna 11 (U.S.S.R.)	Aug. 24, 1966	Moon	Moon orbit achieved Aug. 27.
Luna 12 (U.S.S.R.)	Oct. 22, 1966	Moon	Moon orbit achieved Oct. 25 for 3.5 h. Transmission difficulties.
Lunar Orbiter 2 (U.S.)	Nov. 7, 1966	Moon	Orbit achieved Nov. 10. Sent hundreds of excellent pictures.
Luna 13 (U.S.S.R.)	Dec. 21, 1966	Moon	Soft-landed 80 h after launch. Good pictures. Drove spike into Moon's surface.
Lunar Orbiter 3 (U.S.)	Feb. 4, 1967	Moon	Orbited Moon Feb. 8. Terminated Oct. 9, 1967. Excellent pictures.
Surveyor 3 (U.S.)	April 17, 1967	Moon	Soft-landed 65 h after launch on Oceanus Procellarum. Scooped and tested lunar soil.
Lunar Orbiter 4 (U.S.)	May 4, 1967	Moon	Achieved orbit May 7. Changed orbit on command.
Venera 4 (U.S.S.R.)	June 12, 1967	Venus	Arrived Oct. 17. Instrument capsule sent temperature and chemical data.
Mariner 5 (U.S.)	June 14, 1967	Venus	Fly-by Oct. 19, confirming Mariner 2 and Venera 4 findings
Surveyor 4 (U.S.)	July 14, 1967	Moon	Contact lost 2.5 min before landing
Explorer 35 (U.S.)	July 19, 1967	Moon	Orbit July 22. Perilune: 500 mi.; apolune: 4000 mi.
Lunar Orbiter 5 (U.S.)	Aug. 2, 1967	Moon	Orbited Aug. 5. Perilune: 125 mi.; apolune: 3,760 mi. Time 3 h 50 min. After filming, was crashed on Moon.
Surveyor 5 (U.S.)	Sept. 8, 1967	Moon	Landed near lunar equator Sept. 10. Radiological analysis of lunar soil. Mechanical claw for digging soil.
Surveyor 6 (U.S.)	Nov. 7, 1967	Moon	Landed in Sinus Medii Nov. 10. Jumped 8 ft to photograph original position. Sent back 11,524 pictures.
Pioneer 8 (U.S.)	Dec. 12, 1967	Sun Orbit	Achieved Solar orbit. Stopped functioning April 28, 1968.
Surveyor 7 (U.S.)	Jan. 6, 1968	Moon	Landed near Crater Tycho Jan. 10. Soil analysis. Sent 3,343 pictures.
Zond 4 (U.S.S.R.)	March 2, 1968	Unknown	Achieved parking orbit but was unable to leave. Re-entered March 3.
Zond 5 (U.S.S.R.)	Sept. 14, 1968	Moon	Circumlunar flight
Pioneer 9 (U.S.)	Nov. 8, 1968	Sun Orbit	Achieved orbit. Six experiments returned solar radiation data.
Zond 6 (U.S.S.R.)	Nov. 10, 1968	Moon	Circumlunar flight
Venera 5 (U.S.S.R.)	Jan. 5, 1969	Venus	Landed May 16, 1969. Returned atmospheric data.
Venera 6 (U.S.S.R.)	Jan. 10, 1969	Venus	Landed May 17, 1969. Sent data as Venera 5.
Mariner 6 (U.S.)	Feb. 24, 1969	Mars	Came within 2000 mi. of Mars July 31, 1969. Sent back data & TV pictures.
Mariner 7 (U.S.)	March 27, 1969	Mars	Came within 2000 mi. of Mars Aug. 5, 1969. Sent back data & TV pictures.

Spacecraft	Launch date	Destination	Remarks
Luna 15 (U.S.S.R.)	July 13, 1969	Moon	Lunar orbiter landed on Moon July 21, 1969 after completing varying orbits.
Zond 7 (U.S.S.R.)	Aug. 8, 1969	Moon	Circumlunar. Recovered Aug. 14, 1969.
Pioneer E (U.S.)	Aug. 27, 1969	Inter-planetary	To obtain data on particles and magnetic fields, but failed to achieve orbit.
Venera 7 (U.S.S.R.)	Aug. 17, 1970	Venus	Reached Venus Dec. 15, 1970. Sent data, apparently from surface, for 58 min.
Luna 16 (U.S.S.R.)	Sept. 12, 1970	Moon	Soft-landed Sept. 20, scooped up rock, returned to earth Sept. 24.
Zond 8 (U.S.S.R.)	Oct. 20, 1970	Moon	Circumlunar. Photographed Moon and Earth. Returned Oct. 27, 1970.
Luna 17 (U.S.S.R.)	Nov. 10, 1970	Moon	Soft-landed on Sea of Rains Nov. 17. Lunokhod 1, self-propelled vehicle, used for first time. Sent TV photos, made soil analysis, etc.
Mars 2 (U.S.S.R.)	May 19, 1971	Mars	Reached Mars Nov. 27. Dropped landing capsule on surface.
Mars 3 (U.S.S.R.)	May 28, 1971	Mars	Like Mars 2. Capsule landed Dec. 2. TV transmission cut short.
Mariner 9 (U.S.)	May 30, 1971	Mars	First craft to orbit Mars, Nov. 13. 7,300 pictures, 1st close-ups of Mars' moon. Transmission ended Oct. 27, 1972.
Luna 19 (U.S.S.R.)	Sept. 28, 1971	Moon	Orbited Moon, making measurements & taking photos. Soft-landed Feb. 21 in Sea of Fertility. Returned Feb. 25 with rock samples.
Pioneer 10 (U.S.)	March 3, 1972	Jupiter	620-million-mile flight path through asteroid belt passed Jupiter Dec. 3, 1973, to give man first close-up of planet. In 1986, will become first man-made object to escape solar system.
Venera 8 (U.S.S.R.)	March 27, 1972	Venus	Landed July 22. Sent signals for 50 min. Capsule burned or crushed because of surface heat and pressure. Sent data on atmosphere and surface.
Luna 21 (U.S.S.R.)	Jan. 8, 1973	Moon	Soft-landed Jan. 16. Lunokhod 2 (moon-car) scooped up soil samples, returned them to Earth Jan. 27.
Pioneer 11 (U.S.)	April 6, 1973	Jupiter	Flew by 25,000 mi. from Jupiter Dec. 3, 1974—3 times closer than Pioneer 10.
Mars 4 (U.S.S.R.)	July 21, 1973	Mars	Arrived Feb. 1974, briefly sending back photos
Mars 5 (U.S.S.R.)	July 25, 1973	Mars	Sister craft of Mars 4
Mariner 10 (U.S.)	Nov. 3, 1973	Venus, Mercury	Passed Venus Feb. 5, 1974. Arrived Mercury March 29, 1974, for man's first close-up look at planet. First time gravity of one planet (Venus) used to whip spacecraft toward another (Mercury).
Luna 22 (U.S.S.R.)	May 29, 1974	Moon	Orbited Moon June 2, 1974
Venera 9 (U.S.S.R.)	June 8, 1975	Venus	Soft-landed Oct. 25, 1976. Photographed surface of planet.
Venera 10 (U.S.S.R.)	June 14, 1975	Venus	(See Venera 9)
Viking 1 (U.S.)	Aug. 20, 1975	Mars	Carrying life-detection labs. Landed July 20, 1976, for detailed scientific research, including pictures.
Viking 2 (U.S.)	Sept. 9, 1975	Mars	Like Viking 1. Landed Sept. 3, 1976.
Luna 24 (U.S.S.R.)	Aug. 9, 1976	Moon	Soft-landed Aug. 18, 1976. Returned soil samples Aug. 22, 1976.
Voyager 1 (U.S.)	Sept. 5, 1977	Jupiter, Saturn, Uranus	Fly-by mission. Reached Jupiter in March 1979; passed Saturn Nov. 1980; to reach Uranus 1986.
Voyager 2 (U.S.)	Sept. 20, 1977	Jupiter, Saturn, Uranus	Like Voyager 1. Encountered Jupiter in July 1979; flew by Saturn Aug. 1981; to pass Uranus 1986; then perhaps Neptune.
Pioneer Venus 1 (U.S.)	May 20, 1978	Venus	Arrived Dec. 4 and orbited Venus, photographing surface and atmosphere.
Pioneer Venus 2 (U.S.)	Aug. 8, 1978	Venus	Four-part multi-probe, landed Dec. 9.
Venera 11 (U.S.S.R.)	Sept. 9, 1978	Venus	Soft-landed Dec. 25, 1978. Transmitted data for 95 minutes.
Venera 12 (U.S.S.R.)	Sept. 14, 1978	Venus	Like Venera 11. Landed Dec. 21 and transmitted data for 110 minutes.

Mars Photo Album Offered

"Images of Mars", an 8½- x 11-inch album, is a collection of photographs taken by the *Viking* spacecraft. The book contains 31 black and white pictures of the planet's craters, dunes, clouds, dust storms, volcanoes, and channels.

This spectacular photo album may be ordered from the Superintendent of Documents, U.S. Government Printing Office, Washington, D.C. 20402. Request NASA-SP-444. The price is $2.25.

Major Soviet Space Projects

Scientific Satellites

Cosmos. A designation that began in 1962 for many different kinds of Soviet satellites. *Cosmos 1* studied cosmic rays and other varieties of radiation. *Cosmos 936*, launched Aug. 3, 1977, performed biomedical experiments in cooperation with the U.S., France, and Communist bloc countries.

Elektron. Satellites launched in pairs to map radiation belts. Apogee: 40,000 miles; perigee: 4,000 miles. Four *Elektron* satellites were launched in 1964.

Intercosmos. Russian scientific satellites carrying experiments from other countries. The announced countries participating are from the Soviet bloc. *Intercosmos I* was launched October 14, 1969. *Intercosmos 17*, measuring charged particles and micrometeorites, was launched Sept. 26, 1977.

Oreol. Scientific satellites designed to study the upper atmosphere. Launched jointly with France. *Oreol I* was launched in 1971; *Oreol 2*, 1973.

Meteor. Designation for a series of about two dozen weather satellites, beginning with *Meteor 1* on March 26, 1969. In 1977, four *Meteors* were put in orbit, the last weighing over 3 tons.

Molniya. A communications satellite appearing in a highly elliptical orbit over the same portion of Earth each day on each of its climbs to apogee (the highest point), giving good coverage to the Soviet Union. *Molniya 1* and *2* were launched October 14, 1965. In 1975 and 1976, nine *Molniya* satellites were put in orbit.

Prognoz. A solar irradiation and magnetosphere satellite for the study of the solar wind. The last *Prognoz* was launched Dec. 22, 1975.

Polyot. Earth satellites incorporating on-board propulsion systems which enable them to change their orbits. Only two have been launched to date, in 1963 and 1964.

Sputnik. An early designation for Soviet unmanned spacecraft. *Sputnik 1*, launched October 4, 1957, was the world's first Earth-orbiting satellite, and is considered to have ushered in the Space Age.

Unmanned Planetary and Lunar Programs

Luna. Unmanned spacecraft launched to the Moon. These include lunar orbiters, lunar landers, and lunar lander return missions.

Mars. Unmanned spacecraft launched to explore the planet Mars. Three spacecraft, each weighing about 1,940 lb, were launched in 1962, but failed to reach their target. *Mars 4* was launched July 21, 1973, arriving at Mars in February, 1974, and briefly transmitting photographs of the planet back to Earth. *Mars 5, 6,* and *7* were launched between July 25 and August 9, 1974, but missed the planet.

Venera. Unmanned spacecraft launched to explore the planet Venus. The program was begun in 1961 but, out of 10 known tries, only four can be termed successful. *Venera 11* and *12* were twinned probes, launched Sept. 9 and Sept. 14, 1978, respectively. They soft-landed in late December and transmitted data to earth for 95 minutes and 110 minutes before failing under the intense heat and pressure of the Venusian atmosphere.

Zond. Soviet lunar and planetary probes not otherwise designated. *Zond* spacecraft have been launched to Venus, Mars, and the Moon.

Manned Space Flight Programs

Vostok. The Soviets' first manned capsule, roughly spherical, used to place the first six cosmonauts in Earth orbit (1961–65).

Voskhod. Adaptation of the *Vostok* capsule to accommodate two and three cosmonauts. *Voskhod 1* orbited three persons, and *Voskhod 2* orbited two persons performing the world's first manned extravehicular activity.

Soyuz. Late-model manned spacecraft with provisions for three cosmonauts and a "working compartment" accessible through a hatch. Soyuz is the Russian word for "union". Since 1973, all *Soyuz* spacecraft have carried two cosmonauts. *Soyuz 19*, launched July 15, 1975, docked with the American *Apollo* spacecraft. A new model of the spacecraft, *Soyuz-T2*, was launched in 1980.

Salyut. Earth-orbiting space station intended for prolonged occupancy and re-visitation by cosmonauts. They are usually launched by Soviet Proton rockets. *Salyut 1* was launched April 19, 1971, and was docked with by *Soyuz 10* and *11*. *Salyut 2*, launched April 3, 1973, malfunctioned in orbit and was never occupied. *Salyut 3*, visited by *Soyuz 14* and *16*, was launched June 25, 1974. *Salyut 4* was launched Dec. 26, 1974, and is still in orbit. It was visited by *Soyuz 17, 18,* and *20* (which was unmanned). *Salyut 5*, launched June 22, 1976, was docked with by *Soyuz 21* and *24*. *Salyut 6* was launched on Sept. 29, 1977. The crew of *Soyuz 35* visited *Salyut 6* and spent a record-breaking 185 days in space.

Old Magic and New Science

Over 1,000 years ago, certain "magic" stones protected people against many illnesses including arsenic poisoning—or so Persian pharmacists believed. These "bezoar" stones *(bezoar* meant "to protect against poison") were used by royalty, always afraid of poisoned wine. It is said that Queen Elizabeth I set these stones in her rings; other monarchs wore them on necklaces.

Bezoar stones are really bits of non-digestible hair and other substances, in the stomachs of cud-chewing animals, around which a mineral (sodium hydrogen phosphate) collects. The curative properties of these stones was considered yet another ancient myth—but recent research concerned with arsenic metabolism in the ocean at the Scripps Institution of Oceanography discovered that the partly digested animal hair really *did* absorb arsenite, one form of the poison, like a "chemical sponge." Earlier research at Scripps had discovered that the mineral accumulated in these stones switched phosphate for arsenate, another form of the poison, by means of ion exchange.

Notable Manned Space Flights

Designation and country	Date	Astronauts	Orbit: perigee/apogee (km)	Orbital period (min)	Number of orbits	Flight time (h/min)	Remarks
Vostok 1 (U.S.S.R.)	April 12, 1961	Yuri A. Gagarin	181/327	89.1	1	1/48	First manned orbital flight
MR III (U.S.)	May 5, 1961	Alan B. Shepard, Jr.	—	—	(*)	0/15	Range 486 km (302 mi.), peak 187 km (116.5 mi.); capsule recovered
MR IV (U.S.)	July 21, 1961	Virgil I. Grissom	—	—	(*)	0/16	Range 487 km, peak 190 km; capsule lost
Vostok 2 (U.S.S.R.)	Aug. 6–7, 1961	Gherman S. Titov	178/257	88.6	17.5	25/18	First long-duration flight
MA VI (U.S.)	Feb. 20, 1962	John H. Glenn, Jr.	161/261	88.5	3	4/55	First American in orbit
MA VII (U.S.)	May 24, 1962	M. Scott Carpenter	161/268	88.3	3	4/56	Overshot landing area; otherwise fine
Vostok 3 (U.S.S.R.)	Aug. 11–15, 1962	Andrian G. Nikolayev	173/221	88.1	64	94/22	Vostoks 3 and 4 approached within 5 km
MA VIII (U.S.)	Oct. 3, 1962	Walter M. Schirra, Jr.	161/283	88.5	6	9/13	First splashdown close to aiming point
MA IX (U.S.)	May 15–16, 1963	L. Gordon Cooper, Jr.	161/267	88.4	22	34/20	Longest Mercury flight
Vostok 5 (U.S.S.R.)	June 14–19, 1963	Valery F. Bykovsky	180/235	88.4	81	119/6	Longest Russian orbital flight to date
Vostok 6 (U.S.S.R.)	June 16–19, 1963	Valentina V. Tereshkova	183/233	88.3	48	70/50	First orbital flight by female cosmonaut
Voskhod 1 (U.S.S.R.)	Oct. 12, 1964	Vladimir M. Komarov; Konstantin P. Feoktistov; Boris G. Yegorov	177/409	90.1	16	24/17	First 3-man orbital flight; also first flight without space suits
Voskhod 2 (U.S.S.R.)	March 18, 1965	Alexei A. Leonov; Pavel I. Belyayev	174/495	90.9	17	26/2	First "space walk" (by Leonov), 10 min
GT III (U.S.)	March 23, 1965	Virgil I. Grissom; John W. Young	161/224	88.3	3	4/53	First manned test of Gemini spacecraft
GT IV (U.S.)	June 3–7, 1965	James A. McDivitt; Edward H. White 2d	161/282	89.0	62	97/48	First American "space walk" (by White), lasting slightly over 20 min
GT VI (U.S.)	Dec. 15–16, 1965	Walter M. Schirra, Jr.; Thomas P. Stafford	151/258	88.7	16	25/52	Orbit was extended to 298 km to make rendezvous with orbiting GT VII
GT VIII (U.S.)	March 16–17, 1966	Neil A. Armstrong; David R. Scott	160/270	88.8	6.5	10/42	Only Gemini flight cut short by malfunction: one thruster kept firing after rendezvous and docking with an orbiting Agena rocket had been accomplished
GT IX (U.S.)	June 3–6, 1966	Thomas P. Stafford; Eugene A. Cernan	167/169	90.0	44	72/21	Rendezvous (but no docking)
GT X (U.S.)	July 18–21, 1966	John W. Young; Michael Collins	165/274	88.8	43	70/47	Docking with orbiting Agena rocket
GT XI (U.S.)	Sept. 12–15, 1966	Charles Conrad, Jr.; Richard F. Gordon, Jr.	161/281	89.0	44	71/17	Docking with orbiting Agena on first orbit; apogee of orbit then extended to 1,368 km (850 mi.)
GT XII (U.S.)	Nov. 11–15, 1966	James A. Lovell, Jr.; Edwin E. Aldrin, Jr.	161/282	89.0	59	94/33	Docking with Agena visually, without computer; co-pilot outside spacecraft for total of 5½ hours
Soyuz 1 (U.S.S.R.)	April 23, 1967	Vladimir M. Komarov	201/224	88.6	17	26/40	First test of Soyuz spacecraft; crashed after re-entry, killing Komarov
Apollo 7 (U.S.)	Oct. 11–22, 1968	Walter M. Schirra, Jr.; Donn F. Eisele; R. Walter Cunningham	233/285	89.9	163	260/9	First manned test of Apollo command module; first live TV transmissions from orbit

Mission	Date	Crew					Remarks
Soyuz 3 (U.S.S.R.)	Oct. 26–30, 1968	Georgi T. Beregovoi	204/224	88.6	64	94/51	First manned rendezvous and possible docking by Soviet cosmonaut
Apollo 8 (U.S.)	Dec. 21–27, 1968	Frank Borman; James A. Lovell, Jr.; William A. Anders	—	—	10^3	147/00	First spacecraft in circumlunar orbit; TV transmissions from this orbit
Soyuz 5 (U.S.S.R.)	Jan. 15–18, 1969	Boris V. Volynov, Alexei S. Yeliseyev; Yevgeny V. Khrunov	208/232	88.8	49	72/46	Rendezvoused and docked with Soyuz 4; Khrunov and Yeliseyev perform EVA and transfer to Soyuz 4
Apollo 9 (U.S.)	Mar. 3–13, 1969	James A. McDivitt; David R. Scott; Russell L. Schweikart	197/508	91.5	151	241/1	First manned flight of Lunar Module
Apollo 10 (U.S.)	May 18–26, 1969	Thomas P. Stafford; Eugene A. Cernan; John W. Young	—	—	—	192/3	First descent to within 9 miles of Moon's surface by manned craft
Apollo 11 (U.S.)	July 16–24, 1969	Neil A. Armstrong; Edwin E. Aldrin, Jr.; Michael Collins	—	—	—	195/18	First manned landing and EVA on Moon; soil and rock samples collected; experiments left on lunar surface
Soyuz 6 (U.S.S.R.)	Oct. 11–16, 1969	Gorgiy Shonin; Valriy Kabasov	186/221	88.4	80	118/42	Three spacecraft and seven men put into earth orbit simultaneously for first time
Apollo 12 (U.S.)	Nov. 14–24, 1969	Charles Conrad, Jr.; Richard F. Gordon, Jr.; Alan Bean	—	—	—	244/36	Manned lunar landing mission; investigated Surveyor 3 spacecraft; collected lunar samples. EVA time: 15 h 30 min
Apollo 13 (U.S.)	April 11–17, 1970	James A. Lovell, Jr.; Fred W. Haise, Jr.; John L. Swigert, Jr.	—	—	—	142/54	Third manned lunar landing attempt; aborted due to pressure loss in liquid oxygen in service module and failure of fuel cells
Soyuz 9 (U.S.S.R.)	June 1–17, 1970	Andreiyan Nikolayev; Vitaly Sevastianov	236/249	89.3	287	424/59	Mission to test man's ability to withstand long periods of weightlessness
Apollo 14 (U.S.)	Jan. 31–Feb. 9, 1971	Alan B. Shepard; Stuart A. Roosa; Edgar D. Mitchell	—	—	—	216/42	Third manned lunar landing: returned largest amount of lunar material
Soyuz 10 (U.S.S.R.)	April 22–24, 1971	Vladimir A. Shatalov; Alexei S. Yeliseyev; Nikolai Rukavishnikov	208/246	88.9	—/	47/46	Linked up for 5½ hours with orbiting space station, Salyut 1
Soyuz 11 (U.S.S.R.)	June 6–30, 1971	Georgiy Tomofeyevich Dobrovolsky; Vladislav Nikolayevich Volkov; Viktor Ivanovich Patsyev	185/217	88.3	—	569/40	Linked up with first space station, Salyut 1. Astronauts died just before re-entry due to loss of pressurization in spacecraft
Apollo 15 (U.S.)	July 26–Aug. 7, 1971	David R. Scott; James B. Irwin; Alfred M. Worden	—	—	—	295/12	Fourth manned lunar landing; first use of Lunar Rover propelled by Scott and Irwin; first live pictures of LM lift-off from Moon; exploration time: 18 hours
Apollo 16 (U.S.)	April 16–27, 1972	John W. Young; Thomas K. Mattingly; Charles M. Duke, Jr.	—	—	—	265/51	Fifth manned lunar landing; second use of Lunar Rover, propelled by Young and Duke. Total exploration time on the Moon was 20 h 14 min, setting new record. Mattingly's in-flight "walk in space" was 1 h 23 min. Approximately 213 lb of lunar rock returned

Designation and country	Date	Astronauts	Orbit: perigee/apogee (km)	Orbital period (min)	Number of orbits	Flight time (h/min)	Remarks
Apollo 17 (U.S.)	Dec. 7–19, 1972	Eugene A. Cernan; Ronald E. Evans; Harrison H. Schmitt	—	—	—	301/51	Sixth and last manned lunar landing; third to carry lunar rover. Cernan and Schmitt, during three EVA's, completed total of 22 h 05 min 3 sec. USS Ticonderoga recovered crew and about 250 lbs of lunar samples.
Skylab SL-1 (U.S.)	May 14, 1973	—	423/440	93.4	—	—	Unmanned portion of Skylab comprised of Orbital Workshop (OWS), Airlock Module (AM), Multiple Docking Adapter (MDA), Apollo Telescope Mount (ATM), Instrument Unit (IU), and Payload Shroud (PS)
Skylab SL-2 (U.S.)	May 25–June 22, 1973	Charles Conrad, Jr.; Joseph P. Kerwin; Paul J. Weitz	401/424	93.2	—	672/50	First manned Skylab launch. Established Skylab Orbital Assembly and conducted scientific and medical experiments
Skylab SL-3 (U.S.)	July 28–Sept. 25, 1973	Alan L. Bean, Jr.; Jack R. Lousma; Owen K. Garriott	401/424	93.2	—	1427/9	Second manned Skylab launch. New crew remained in space for 59 days, continuing scientific and medical experiments and earth observations from orbit.
Skylab SL-4 (U.S.)	Nov. 16, 1973–Feb. 8, 1974	Gerald Carr; Edward Gibson; William Pogue	401/424	93.2	—	2017/16	Third manned Skylab launch; obtained medical data on crew for use in extending the duration of manned space flight; crews "walked in space" 4 times, totaling 44 h 40 min. Longest space mission yet—84 d 1 h 16 min. Splashdown in Pacific, Feb. 9, 1974.
Soyuz 12 (U.S.S.R.)	Sept. 27–29, 1973	Vasily G. Lazarev; Oleg K. Makarov	202/231	88.7	—	50/12	Two-day test flight. First Soviet manned flight since ill-fated Soyuz 11.
Soyuz 13 (U.S.S.R.)	Dec. 18–26, 1973	Pyotr Klimuk; Valentin Lebedev	188/246	88.9	—	188/55	Modified spacecraft to be used for rendezvous with U.S. spacemen in 1975
Soyuz 14 (U.S.S.R.)	July 3–19, 1974	Pavel Popovich; Yuri Artyukhin	201/338	89.9	—	377/29	Crewmen spent two weeks on board Soviet space station Salyut 3
Soyuz 17 (U.S.S.R.)	Jan. 11–Feb. 9, 1975	Col. Aleksey Gubarev; Georgi Grechko			—	709/20	Crew spent 30 days in Salyut 4 space station, which was launched Dec. 26, 1974 and placed in Earth orbit
Apollo/Soyuz Test Project (U.S. and U.S.S.R.)	July 15–24, 1975 (U.S.)	U.S.: Brig. Gen. Thomas P. Stafford, Vance D. Brand, Donald K. Slayton	152/166	87.7 89.0 (docked)	138 (docked)	216/05	World's first international manned rendezvous and docking in space; aimed at developing a space rescue capability. Apollo and Soyuz docked and crewmen exchanged visits on July 17, 1975. Mission duration for Soyuz: 142 h 31
(U.S.S.R.)	July 15–21, 1975 (U.S.S.R.)	U.S.S.R.: Col. A. A. Leonov, V. N. Kubasov	191/218	91.0 89.0 (docked)	138 (docked)	223/35	

THE YEAR IN SPACE

(Continued from page 336)

min. For Apollo: 217 h, 28 min.

Spacecraft	Date				Crew	Remarks
Soyuz 21 (U.S.S.R.)	July 6–Aug. 24, 1976	114/409	89.7	1218/24	Col. Boris Volynov; Lt. Col. Vitali Zholobov	Crew spent 50 days aboard Salyut 5 space station, which was launched June 22
Soyuz 24 (U.S.S.R.)	Feb. 7–25, 1977	173/323	89.5	425/23	Col. V. Gorbatko; Lt. Col. Yuri Glazkov	Docked and transferred to Salyut 5 on Feb. 8. Returned Feb. 25
Soyuz 31 (U.S.S.R.)	Aug. 26–Nov. 2, 1978	337/353	91.4	$1632/0^2$	Valery Bykovsky, Sigmund Jaehn	Docked with Salyut 6 and Soyuz 29; crew returned in Soyuz 29 on Sept. 3, 1978
Soyuz 33 (U.S.S.R.)	April 11–12, 1979	—	—	—	N. Rukavishnikov; G. Ivanov	Commander veteran of Soyuz 16
Soyuz 35 (U.S.S.R.)	April 9–Oct. 11, 1981	—	—	—	Valery Ryumin; Leonid Popov	Docked with Salyut 6; Crew set record of 185 days duration in space.
Soyuz T2 (U.S.S.R.)	June 5–9, 1980	—	—	—	Lt. Col. Yuri V. Mayyshev; Vladimir V. Aksenov	Docked with Salyut 6; tested new model spacecraft, T2
Columbia (U.S.)	April 12–14, 1981	54/20	—	—	Capt. Robert L. Crippen; John W. Young	Maiden voyage of *Space Shuttle*, the first spacecraft designed specifically for re-use up to 100 times.

1. Suborbital flight. 2. Approximate time. 3. Number of orbits around moon. NOTE: The letters MR stand for Mercury (capsule) and Redstone (rocket); MA, for Mercury and Atlas (rocket); GT, for Gemini (capsule) and Titan-II (rocket). The first astronaut listed in the Gemini and Apollo flights is the command pilot. The Mercury capsules had names: MR-III was *Freedom* 7, MR-IV was *Liberty Bell* 7, MA-VI was *Friendship* 7, MA-VII was *Aurora* 7, MA-VIII was *Sigma* 7, and MA-IX was *Faith* 7. The figure 7 referred to the fact that the first group of U.S. astronauts numbered seven men. Only one Gemini capsule had a name: GT-III was called *Molly Brown* (after the Broadway musical *The Unsinkable Molly Brown*); thereafter the practice of naming the capsules was discontinued.

veals that it is actually light from a single quasar that has been split by a gravitational lens. Einstein predicted that such a lens could produce this effect, but it has never before been seen. As yet unexplained is the observation that quasar 3C273 consists of two cores that appear to be separating at a speed 9.6 times that of light. Theory says that's impossible but a geometric optical illusion has already been ruled out, so the motion seems to be real. If it is, modern physics is in for a big shakeup.

Another theory is also in for revision. This one held that pulsars, which give out X-rays with a regular rhythm, should be associated with extremely dense neutron stars. Not necessarily, it turns out, for the constellation Aquarius contains a pulsar that has been definitely identified as having a white dwarf star as part of its (probably binary) make-up.

Asteroids and other Bits and Pieces

A new technique called speckle interferometry hints that even asteroids may have moons. Strongest evidence so far involves the asteroid Pallas, which may have a satellite approximately 110 miles in diameter. *Pioneer 6,* launched into solar orbit way back on December 6, 1965, is still functioning. Reason for its record-breaking longevity is that it relies on spin, rather than rocket power, to maintain stability: therefore, it has no fuel to run out of. Five of its six on-board instruments are still sending out data, but the satellite's solar panels are beginning to weaken. Further studies on a meteorite from Murchison, Australia, show that it contains more organic material than expected, including 18 kinds of amino acids and 17 types of fatty acids. Amino acids are the chemical building blocks of proteins, therefore life.

Finally, private space programs of sorts seem to be on the upswing. In addition to the Halley Fund mentioned above, a largely student group at Rensselaer Polytechnic Institute plans to build an Earth-orbiting astronomy satellite, whose images could be picked up by amateur-operated slow-scan TV monitors around the world. Not at all a NASA-scale operation, the students estimate they'll need $100,000 to build their satellite and a back-up spare (Independent Space Research Group, c/o John Ginder, 7 Sunset Terrace, Troy, NY 12180). The Viking Fund (357 Saratoga Avenue, Santa Clara, CA 95050) has already presented NASA with a check for $60,000. It took NASA officials a while to figure out how to accept the money—one can't just buy specific services from the government—but a plan has been worked out whereby the cash will pay for analysis of *Viking* lander data, from Mars, which NASA budget cutbacks would otherwise have ruled out. Contributions are tax deductible.

Konrad J.A. Kundig

Largest Single-Mirror Telescope

The 300-inch primary mirror for the proposed telescope for the University of Texas McDonald Observatory will have a 300-inch mirror of only four to five inches thick. If produced, the telescope would be the largest ground-based, single-mirror telescope in the world. It was estimated that the telescope will cost $45 million.

CALENDAR & HOLIDAYS

1982

JANUARY

S	M	T	W	T	F	S
–	–	–	–	–	1	2
3	4	5	6	7	8	9
10	11	12	13	14	15	16
17	18	19	20	21	22	23
24	25	26	27	28	29	30
31						

1– New Year's Day
6– Epiphany

FEBRUARY

S	M	T	W	T	F	S
–	1	2	3	4	5	6
7	8	9	10	11	12	13
14	15	16	17	18	19	20
21	22	23	24	25	26	27
28						

2– Groundhog Day
12– Lincoln's Birthday
14– St. Valentine's Day
15– Washington's Birthday
24– Ash Wednesday

MARCH

S	M	T	W	T	F	S
–	1	2	3	4	5	6
7	8	9	10	11	12	13
14	15	16	17	18	19	20
21	22	23	24	25	26	27
28	29	30	31			

9– Purim
17– St. Patrick's Day

APRIL

S	M	T	W	T	F	S
–	–	–	–	1	2	3
4	5	6	7	8	9	10
11	12	13	14	15	16	17
18	19	20	21	22	23	24
25	26	27	28	29	30	

4– Palm Sunday
8– 1st Day of Passover
9– Good Friday
11– Easter
25– Daylight Savings
　Time begins

MAY

S	M	T	W	T	F	S
–	–	–	–	–	–	1
2	3	4	5	6	7	8
9	10	11	12	13	14	15
16	17	18	19	20	21	22
23	24	25	26	27	28	29
30	31					

9– Mother's Day
20– Ascension Day
28– 1st Day of Shabuoth
30– Pentecost
31– Memorial Day

JUNE

S	M	T	W	T	F	S
–	–	1	2	3	4	5
6	7	8	9	10	11	12
13	14	15	16	17	18	19
20	21	22	23	24	25	26
27	28	29	30			

6– Trinity Sunday
14– Flag Day
20– Father's Day

JULY

S	M	T	W	T	F	S
–	–	–	–	1	2	3
4	5	6	7	8	9	10
11	12	13	14	15	16	17
18	19	20	21	22	23	24
25	26	27	28	29	30	31

4– Independence Day

AUGUST

S	M	T	W	T	F	S
1	2	3	4	5	6	7
8	9	10	11	12	13	14
15	16	17	18	19	20	21
22	23	24	25	26	27	28
29	30	31				

SEPTEMBER

S	M	T	W	T	F	S
–	–	–	1	2	3	4
5	6	7	8	9	10	11
12	13	14	15	16	17	18
19	20	21	22	23	24	25
26	27	28	29	30		

6– Labor Day
18– 1st Day of
　Rosh Hashana
27– Yom Kippur

OCTOBER

S	M	T	W	T	F	S
–	–	–	–	–	1	2
3	4	5	6	7	8	9
10	11	12	13	14	15	16
17	18	19	20	21	22	23
24	25	26	27	28	29	30
31						

2– 1st Day of Sukkoth
11– Columbus Day
31– Halloween
31– Daylight Savings
　Time ends

NOVEMBER

S	M	T	W	T	F	S
–	1	2	3	4	5	6
7	8	9	10	11	12	13
14	15	16	17	18	19	20
21	22	23	24	25	26	27
28	29	30				

1– All Saints' Day
2– Election Day
11– Veterans Day
25– Thanksgiving Day
28– 1st Sunday of Advent

DECEMBER

S	M	T	W	T	F	S
–	–	–	1	2	3	4
5	6	7	8	9	10	11
12	13	14	15	16	17	18
19	20	21	22	23	24	25
26	27	28	29	30	31	

11– 1st Day of Hanukkah
25– Christmas

Seasons for the Northern Hemisphere, 1982

Eastern Standard Time

March 20, 5:56 p.m., sun enters sign of Aries; spring begins

June 21, 12:23 p.m., sun enters sign of Cancer; summer begins

Sept. 23, 3:46 a.m., sun enters sign of Libra; fall begins

Dec. 21, 11:39 p.m., sun enters sign of Capricorn; winter begins

1981

JANUARY
```
S  M  T  W  T  F  S
-  -  -  -  1  2  3
4  5  6  7  8  9 10
11 12 13 14 15 16 17
18 19 20 21 22 23 24
25 26 27 28 29 30 31
```

FEBRUARY
```
S  M  T  W  T  F  S
1  2  3  4  5  6  7
8  9 10 11 12 13 14
15 16 17 18 19 20 21
22 23 24 25 26 27 28
```

MARCH
```
S  M  T  W  T  F  S
1  2  3  4  5  6  7
8  9 10 11 12 13 14
15 16 17 18 19 20 21
22 23 24 25 26 27 28
29 30 31
```

APRIL
```
S  M  T  W  T  F  S
-  -  -  1  2  3  4
5  6  7  8  9 10 11
12 13 14 15 16 17 18
19 20 21 22 23 24 25
26 27 28 29 30
```

MAY
```
S  M  T  W  T  F  S
-  -  -  -  -  1  2
3  4  5  6  7  8  9
10 11 12 13 14 15 16
17 18 19 20 21 22 23
24 25 26 27 28 29 30
31
```

JUNE
```
S  M  T  W  T  F  S
-  1  2  3  4  5  6
7  8  9 10 11 12 13
14 15 16 17 18 19 20
21 22 23 24 25 26 27
28 29 30
```

JULY
```
S  M  T  W  T  F  S
-  -  -  1  2  3  4
5  6  7  8  9 10 11
12 13 14 15 16 17 18
19 20 21 22 23 24 25
26 27 28 29 30 31
```

AUGUST
```
S  M  T  W  T  F  S
-  -  -  -  -  -  1
2  3  4  5  6  7  8
9 10 11 12 13 14 15
16 17 18 19 20 21 22
23 24 25 26 27 28 29
30 31
```

SEPTEMBER
```
S  M  T  W  T  F  S
-  -  1  2  3  4  5
6  7  8  9 10 11 12
13 14 15 16 17 18 19
20 21 22 23 24 25 26
27 28 29 30
```

OCTOBER
```
S  M  T  W  T  F  S
-  -  -  -  1  2  3
4  5  6  7  8  9 10
11 12 13 14 15 16 17
18 19 20 21 22 23 24
25 26 27 28 29 30 31
```

NOVEMBER
```
S  M  T  W  T  F  S
1  2  3  4  5  6  7
8  9 10 11 12 13 14
15 16 17 18 19 20 21
22 23 24 25 26 27 28
29 30
```

DECEMBER
```
S  M  T  W  T  F  S
-  -  1  2  3  4  5
6  7  8  9 10 11 12
13 14 15 16 17 18 19
20 21 22 23 24 25 26
27 28 29 30 31
```

1983

JANUARY
```
S  M  T  W  T  F  S
-  -  -  -  -  -  1
2  3  4  5  6  7  8
9 10 11 12 13 14 15
16 17 18 19 20 21 22
23 24 25 26 27 28 29
30 31
```

FEBRUARY
```
S  M  T  W  T  F  S
-  -  1  2  3  4  5
6  7  8  9 10 11 12
13 14 15 16 17 18 19
20 21 22 23 24 25 26
27 28
```

MARCH
```
S  M  T  W  T  F  S
-  -  1  2  3  4  5
6  7  8  9 10 11 12
13 14 15 16 17 18 19
20 21 22 23 24 25 26
27 28 29 30 31
```

APRIL
```
S  M  T  W  T  F  S
-  -  -  -  -  1  2
3  4  5  6  7  8  9
10 11 12 13 14 15 16
17 18 19 20 21 22 23
24 25 26 27 28 29 30
```

MAY
```
S  M  T  W  T  F  S
1  2  3  4  5  6  7
8  9 10 11 12 13 14
15 16 17 18 19 20 21
22 23 24 25 26 27 28
29 30 31
```

JUNE
```
S  M  T  W  T  F  S
-  -  -  1  2  3  4
5  6  7  8  9 10 11
12 13 14 15 16 17 18
19 20 21 22 23 24 25
26 27 28 29 30
```

JULY
```
S  M  T  W  T  F  S
-  -  -  -  -  1  2
3  4  5  6  7  8  9
10 11 12 13 14 15 16
17 18 19 20 21 22 23
24 25 26 27 28 29 30
31
```

AUGUST
```
S  M  T  W  T  F  S
-  1  2  3  4  5  6
7  8  9 10 11 12 13
14 15 16 17 18 19 20
21 22 23 24 25 26 27
28 29 30 31
```

SEPTEMBER
```
S  M  T  W  T  F  S
-  -  -  1  2  3
4  5  6  7  8  9 10
11 12 13 14 15 16 17
18 19 20 21 22 23 24
25 26 27 28 29 30
```

OCTOBER
```
S  M  T  W  T  F  S
-  -  -  -  -  -  1
2  3  4  5  6  7  8
9 10 11 12 13 14 15
16 17 18 19 20 21 22
23 24 25 26 27 28 29
30 31
```

NOVEMBER
```
S  M  T  W  T  F  S
-  -  1  2  3  4  5
6  7  8  9 10 11 12
13 14 15 16 17 18 19
20 21 22 23 24 25 26
27 28 29 30
```

DECEMBER
```
S  M  T  W  T  F  S
-  -  -  -  1  2  3
4  5  6  7  8  9 10
11 12 13 14 15 16 17
18 19 20 21 22 23 24
25 26 27 28 29 30 31
```

PERPETUAL CALENDAR

Year	No.	Year	No.	Year	No.	Year	No.	Year	No.	Year	No.
1800	4	1844	9	1888	8	1932	13	1976	12	2020	11
1801	5	1845	4	1889	3	1933	1	1977	7	2021	6
1802	6	1846	5	1890	4	1934	2	1978	1	2022	7
1803	7	1847	6	1891	5	1935	3	1979	2	2023	1
1804	8	1848	14	1892	13	1936	11	1980	10	2024	9
1805	3	1849	2	1893	1	1937	6	1981	5	2025	4
1806	4	1850	3	1894	2	1938	7	1982	6	2026	5
1807	5	1851	4	1895	3	1939	1	1983	7	2027	6
1808	13	1852	12	1896	11	1940	9	1984	8	2028	14
1809	1	1853	7	1897	6	1941	4	1985	3	2029	2
1810	2	1854	1	1898	7	1942	5	1986	4	2030	3
1811	3	1855	2	1899	1	1943	6	1987	5	2031	4
1812	11	1856	10	1900	2	1944	14	1988	13	2032	12
1813	6	1857	5	1901	3	1945	2	1989	1	2033	7
1814	7	1858	6	1902	4	1946	3	1990	2	2034	1
1815	1	1859	7	1903	5	1947	4	1991	3	2035	2
1816	9	1860	8	1904	13	1948	12	1992	11	2036	10
1817	4	1861	3	1905	1	1949	7	1993	6	2037	5
1818	5	1862	4	1906	2	1950	1	1994	7	2038	6
1819	6	1863	5	1907	3	1951	2	1995	1	2039	7
1820	14	1864	13	1908	11	1952	10	1996	9	2040	8
1821	2	1865	1	1909	6	1953	5	1997	4	2041	3
1822	3	1866	2	1910	7	1954	6	1998	5	2042	4
1823	4	1867	3	1911	1	1955	7	1999	6	2043	5
1824	12	1868	11	1912	9	1956	8	2000	14	2044	13
1825	7	1869	6	1913	4	1957	3	2001	2	2045	1
1826	1	1870	7	1914	5	1958	4	2002	3	2046	2
1827	2	1871	1	1915	6	1959	5	2003	4	2047	3
1828	10	1872	9	1916	14	1960	13	2004	12	2048	11
1829	5	1873	4	1917	2	1961	1	2005	7	2049	6
1830	6	1874	5	1918	3	1962	2	2006	1	2050	7
1831	7	1875	6	1919	4	1963	3	2007	2	2051	1
1832	8	1876	14	1920	12	1964	11	2008	10	2052	9
1833	3	1877	2	1921	7	1965	6	2009	5	2053	4
1834	4	1878	3	1922	1	1966	7	2010	6	2054	5
1835	5	1879	4	1923	2	1967	1	2011	7	2055	6
1836	13	1880	12	1924	10	1968	9	2012	8	2056	14
1837	1	1881	7	1925	5	1969	4	2013	3	2057	2
1838	2	1882	1	1926	6	1970	5	2014	4	2058	3
1839	3	1883	2	1927	7	1971	6	2015	5	2059	4
1840	11	1884	10	1928	8	1972	14	2016	13	2060	12
1841	6	1885	5	1929	3	1973	2	2017	1	2061	7
1842	7	1886	6	1930	4	1974	3	2018	2	2062	1
1843	1	1887	7	1931	5	1975	4	2019	3	2063	3

DIRECTIONS: The number given with each year in the key above is number of calendar to use for that year

Calendars numbered 1 through 6, each showing the twelve months (January–December) with S M T W T F S day-of-week columns.

7

JANUARY
S M T W T F S
          1
2 3 4 5 6 7 8
9 10 11 12 13 14 15
16 17 18 19 20 21 22
23 24 25 26 27 28 29
30 31

FEBRUARY
S M T W T F S
    1 2 3 4 5
6 7 8 9 10 11 12
13 14 15 16 17 18 19
20 21 22 23 24 25 26
27 28

MARCH
S M T W T F S
    1 2 3 4 5
6 7 8 9 10 11 12
13 14 15 16 17 18 19
20 21 22 23 24 25 26
27 28 29 30 31

APRIL
S M T W T F S
          1 2
3 4 5 6 7 8 9
10 11 12 13 14 15 16
17 18 19 20 21 22 23
24 25 26 27 28 29 30

MAY
S M T W T F S
1 2 3 4 5 6 7
8 9 10 11 12 13 14
15 16 17 18 19 20 21
22 23 24 25 26 27 28
29 30 31

JUNE
S M T W T F S
      1 2 3 4
5 6 7 8 9 10 11
12 13 14 15 16 17 18
19 20 21 22 23 24 25
26 27 28 29 30

JULY
S M T W T F S
          1 2
3 4 5 6 7 8 9
10 11 12 13 14 15 16
17 18 19 20 21 22 23
24 25 26 27 28 29 30
31

AUGUST
S M T W T F S
  1 2 3 4 5 6
7 8 9 10 11 12 13
14 15 16 17 18 19 20
21 22 23 24 25 26 27
28 29 30 31

SEPTEMBER
S M T W T F S
        1 2 3
4 5 6 7 8 9 10
11 12 13 14 15 16 17
18 19 20 21 22 23 24
25 26 27 28 29 30

OCTOBER
S M T W T F S
            1
2 3 4 5 6 7 8
9 10 11 12 13 14 15
16 17 18 19 20 21 22
23 24 25 26 27 28 29
30 31

NOVEMBER
S M T W T F S
    1 2 3 4 5
6 7 8 9 10 11 12
13 14 15 16 17 18 19
20 21 22 23 24 25 26
27 28 29 30

DECEMBER
S M T W T F S
        1 2 3
4 5 6 7 8 9 10
11 12 13 14 15 16 17
18 19 20 21 22 23 24
25 26 27 28 29 30 31

8

JANUARY
S M T W T F S
1 2 3 4 5 6 7
8 9 10 11 12 13 14
15 16 17 18 19 20 21
22 23 24 25 26 27 28
29 30 31

FEBRUARY
S M T W T F S
      1 2 3 4
5 6 7 8 9 10 11
12 13 14 15 16 17 18
19 20 21 22 23 24 25
26 27 28 29

MARCH
S M T W T F S
        1 2 3
4 5 6 7 8 9 10
11 12 13 14 15 16 17
18 19 20 21 22 23 24
25 26 27 28 29 30 31

APRIL
S M T W T F S
1 2 3 4 5 6 7
8 9 10 11 12 13 14
15 16 17 18 19 20 21
22 23 24 25 26 27 28
29 30

MAY
S M T W T F S
    1 2 3 4 5
6 7 8 9 10 11 12
13 14 15 16 17 18 19
20 21 22 23 24 25 26
27 28 29 30 31

JUNE
S M T W T F S
          1 2
3 4 5 6 7 8 9
10 11 12 13 14 15 16
17 18 19 20 21 22 23
24 25 26 27 28 29 30

JULY
S M T W T F S
1 2 3 4 5 6 7
8 9 10 11 12 13 14
15 16 17 18 19 20 21
22 23 24 25 26 27 28
29 30 31

AUGUST
S M T W T F S
      1 2 3 4
5 6 7 8 9 10 11
12 13 14 15 16 17 18
19 20 21 22 23 24 25
26 27 28 29 30 31

SEPTEMBER
S M T W T F S
            1
2 3 4 5 6 7 8
9 10 11 12 13 14 15
16 17 18 19 20 21 22
23 24 25 26 27 28 29
30

OCTOBER
S M T W T F S
  1 2 3 4 5 6
7 8 9 10 11 12 13
14 15 16 17 18 19 20
21 22 23 24 25 26 27
28 29 30 31

NOVEMBER
S M T W T F S
        1 2 3
4 5 6 7 8 9 10
11 12 13 14 15 16 17
18 19 20 21 22 23 24
25 26 27 28 29 30

DECEMBER
S M T W T F S
            1
2 3 4 5 6 7 8
9 10 11 12 13 14 15
16 17 18 19 20 21 22
23 24 25 26 27 28 29
30 31

9

JANUARY
S M T W T F S
  1 2 3 4 5 6
7 8 9 10 11 12 13
14 15 16 17 18 19 20
21 22 23 24 25 26 27
28 29 30 31

FEBRUARY
S M T W T F S
        1 2 3
4 5 6 7 8 9 10
11 12 13 14 15 16 17
18 19 20 21 22 23 24
25 26 27 28 29

MARCH
S M T W T F S
          1 2
3 4 5 6 7 8 9
10 11 12 13 14 15 16
17 18 19 20 21 22 23
24 25 26 27 28 29 30
31

APRIL
S M T W T F S
  1 2 3 4 5 6
7 8 9 10 11 12 13
14 15 16 17 18 19 20
21 22 23 24 25 26 27
28 29 30

MAY
S M T W T F S
      1 2 3 4
5 6 7 8 9 10 11
12 13 14 15 16 17 18
19 20 21 22 23 24 25
26 27 28 29 30 31

JUNE
S M T W T F S
            1
2 3 4 5 6 7 8
9 10 11 12 13 14 15
16 17 18 19 20 21 22
23 24 25 26 27 28 29
30

JULY
S M T W T F S
  1 2 3 4 5 6
7 8 9 10 11 12 13
14 15 16 17 18 19 20
21 22 23 24 25 26 27
28 29 30 31

AUGUST
S M T W T F S
        1 2 3
4 5 6 7 8 9 10
11 12 13 14 15 16 17
18 19 20 21 22 23 24
25 26 27 28 29 30 31

SEPTEMBER
S M T W T F S
1 2 3 4 5 6 7
8 9 10 11 12 13 14
15 16 17 18 19 20 21
22 23 24 25 26 27 28
29 30

OCTOBER
S M T W T F S
    1 2 3 4 5
6 7 8 9 10 11 12
13 14 15 16 17 18 19
20 21 22 23 24 25 26
27 28 29 30 31

NOVEMBER
S M T W T F S
          1 2
3 4 5 6 7 8 9
10 11 12 13 14 15 16
17 18 19 20 21 22 23
24 25 26 27 28 29 30

DECEMBER
S M T W T F S
1 2 3 4 5 6 7
8 9 10 11 12 13 14
15 16 17 18 19 20 21
22 23 24 25 26 27 28
29 30 31

10

JANUARY
S M T W T F S
    1 2 3 4 5
6 7 8 9 10 11 12
13 14 15 16 17 18 19
20 21 22 23 24 25 26
27 28 29 30 31

FEBRUARY
S M T W T F S
          1 2
3 4 5 6 7 8 9
10 11 12 13 14 15 16
17 18 19 20 21 22 23
24 25 26 27 28 29

MARCH
S M T W T F S
            1
2 3 4 5 6 7 8
9 10 11 12 13 14 15
16 17 18 19 20 21 22
23 24 25 26 27 28 29
30 31

APRIL
S M T W T F S
    1 2 3 4 5
6 7 8 9 10 11 12
13 14 15 16 17 18 19
20 21 22 23 24 25 26
27 28 29 30

MAY
S M T W T F S
        1 2 3
4 5 6 7 8 9 10
11 12 13 14 15 16 17
18 19 20 21 22 23 24
25 26 27 28 29 30 31

JUNE
S M T W T F S
1 2 3 4 5 6 7
8 9 10 11 12 13 14
15 16 17 18 19 20 21
22 23 24 25 26 27 28
29 30

JULY
S M T W T F S
    1 2 3 4 5
6 7 8 9 10 11 12
13 14 15 16 17 18 19
20 21 22 23 24 25 26
27 28 29 30 31

AUGUST
S M T W T F S
          1 2
3 4 5 6 7 8 9
10 11 12 13 14 15 16
17 18 19 20 21 22 23
24 25 26 27 28 29 30
31

SEPTEMBER
S M T W T F S
  1 2 3 4 5 6
7 8 9 10 11 12 13
14 15 16 17 18 19 20
21 22 23 24 25 26 27
28 29 30

OCTOBER
S M T W T F S
      1 2 3 4
5 6 7 8 9 10 11
12 13 14 15 16 17 18
19 20 21 22 23 24 25
26 27 28 29 30 31

NOVEMBER
S M T W T F S
            1
2 3 4 5 6 7 8
9 10 11 12 13 14 15
16 17 18 19 20 21 22
23 24 25 26 27 28 29
30

DECEMBER
S M T W T F S
  1 2 3 4 5 6
7 8 9 10 11 12 13
14 15 16 17 18 19 20
21 22 23 24 25 26 27
28 29 30 31

11

JANUARY
S M T W T F S
      1 2 3 4
5 6 7 8 9 10 11
12 13 14 15 16 17 18
19 20 21 22 23 24 25
26 27 28 29 30 31

FEBRUARY
S M T W T F S
            1
2 3 4 5 6 7 8
9 10 11 12 13 14 15
16 17 18 19 20 21 22
23 24 25 26 27 28 29

MARCH
S M T W T F S
1 2 3 4 5 6 7
8 9 10 11 12 13 14
15 16 17 18 19 20 21
22 23 24 25 26 27 28
29 30 31

APRIL
S M T W T F S
      1 2 3 4
5 6 7 8 9 10 11
12 13 14 15 16 17 18
19 20 21 22 23 24 25
26 27 28 29 30

MAY
S M T W T F S
          1 2
3 4 5 6 7 8 9
10 11 12 13 14 15 16
17 18 19 20 21 22 23
24 25 26 27 28 29 30
31

JUNE
S M T W T F S
  1 2 3 4 5 6
7 8 9 10 11 12 13
14 15 16 17 18 19 20
21 22 23 24 25 26 27
28 29 30

JULY
S M T W T F S
      1 2 3 4
5 6 7 8 9 10 11
12 13 14 15 16 17 18
19 20 21 22 23 24 25
26 27 28 29 30 31

AUGUST
S M T W T F S
            1
2 3 4 5 6 7 8
9 10 11 12 13 14 15
16 17 18 19 20 21 22
23 24 25 26 27 28 29
30 31

SEPTEMBER
S M T W T F S
    1 2 3 4 5
6 7 8 9 10 11 12
13 14 15 16 17 18 19
20 21 22 23 24 25 26
27 28 29 30

OCTOBER
S M T W T F S
        1 2 3
4 5 6 7 8 9 10
11 12 13 14 15 16 17
18 19 20 21 22 23 24
25 26 27 28 29 30 31

NOVEMBER
S M T W T F S
1 2 3 4 5 6 7
8 9 10 11 12 13 14
15 16 17 18 19 20 21
22 23 24 25 26 27 28
29 30

DECEMBER
S M T W T F S
    1 2 3 4 5
6 7 8 9 10 11 12
13 14 15 16 17 18 19
20 21 22 23 24 25 26
27 28 29 30 31

12

JANUARY
S M T W T F S
        1 2 3
4 5 6 7 8 9 10
11 12 13 14 15 16 17
18 19 20 21 22 23 24
25 26 27 28 29 30 31

FEBRUARY
S M T W T F S
1 2 3 4 5 6 7
8 9 10 11 12 13 14
15 16 17 18 19 20 21
22 23 24 25 26 27 28
29

MARCH
S M T W T F S
  1 2 3 4 5 6
7 8 9 10 11 12 13
14 15 16 17 18 19 20
21 22 23 24 25 26 27
28 29 30 31

APRIL
S M T W T F S
        1 2 3
4 5 6 7 8 9 10
11 12 13 14 15 16 17
18 19 20 21 22 23 24
25 26 27 28 29 30

MAY
S M T W T F S
            1
2 3 4 5 6 7 8
9 10 11 12 13 14 15
16 17 18 19 20 21 22
23 24 25 26 27 28 29
30 31

JUNE
S M T W T F S
    1 2 3 4 5
6 7 8 9 10 11 12
13 14 15 16 17 18 19
20 21 22 23 24 25 26
27 28 29 30

JULY
S M T W T F S
        1 2 3
4 5 6 7 8 9 10
11 12 13 14 15 16 17
18 19 20 21 22 23 24
25 26 27 28 29 30 31

AUGUST
S M T W T F S
1 2 3 4 5 6 7
8 9 10 11 12 13 14
15 16 17 18 19 20 21
22 23 24 25 26 27 28
29 30 31

SEPTEMBER
S M T W T F S
      1 2 3 4
5 6 7 8 9 10 11
12 13 14 15 16 17 18
19 20 21 22 23 24 25
26 27 28 29 30

OCTOBER
S M T W T F S
          1 2
3 4 5 6 7 8 9
10 11 12 13 14 15 16
17 18 19 20 21 22 23
24 25 26 27 28 29 30
31

NOVEMBER
S M T W T F S
  1 2 3 4 5 6
7 8 9 10 11 12 13
14 15 16 17 18 19 20
21 22 23 24 25 26 27
28 29 30

DECEMBER
S M T W T F S
      1 2 3 4
5 6 7 8 9 10 11
12 13 14 15 16 17 18
19 20 21 22 23 24 25
26 27 28 29 30 31

13

JANUARY
S M T W T F S
          1 2
3 4 5 6 7 8 9
10 11 12 13 14 15 16
17 18 19 20 21 22 23
24 25 26 27 28 29 30
31

FEBRUARY
S M T W T F S
  1 2 3 4 5 6
7 8 9 10 11 12 13
14 15 16 17 18 19 20
21 22 23 24 25 26 27
28 29

MARCH
S M T W T F S
    1 2 3 4 5
6 7 8 9 10 11 12
13 14 15 16 17 18 19
20 21 22 23 24 25 26
27 28 29 30 31

APRIL
S M T W T F S
          1 2
3 4 5 6 7 8 9
10 11 12 13 14 15 16
17 18 19 20 21 22 23
24 25 26 27 28 29 30

MAY
S M T W T F S
1 2 3 4 5 6 7
8 9 10 11 12 13 14
15 16 17 18 19 20 21
22 23 24 25 26 27 28
29 30 31

JUNE
S M T W T F S
      1 2 3 4
5 6 7 8 9 10 11
12 13 14 15 16 17 18
19 20 21 22 23 24 25
26 27 28 29 30

JULY
S M T W T F S
          1 2
3 4 5 6 7 8 9
10 11 12 13 14 15 16
17 18 19 20 21 22 23
24 25 26 27 28 29 30
31

AUGUST
S M T W T F S
  1 2 3 4 5 6
7 8 9 10 11 12 13
14 15 16 17 18 19 20
21 22 23 24 25 26 27
28 29 30 31

SEPTEMBER
S M T W T F S
        1 2 3
4 5 6 7 8 9 10
11 12 13 14 15 16 17
18 19 20 21 22 23 24
25 26 27 28 29 30

OCTOBER
S M T W T F S
            1
2 3 4 5 6 7 8
9 10 11 12 13 14 15
16 17 18 19 20 21 22
23 24 25 26 27 28 29
30 31

NOVEMBER
S M T W T F S
    1 2 3 4 5
6 7 8 9 10 11 12
13 14 15 16 17 18 19
20 21 22 23 24 25 26
27 28 29 30

DECEMBER
S M T W T F S
        1 2 3
4 5 6 7 8 9 10
11 12 13 14 15 16 17
18 19 20 21 22 23 24
25 26 27 28 29 30 31

14

JANUARY
S M T W T F S
            1
2 3 4 5 6 7 8
9 10 11 12 13 14 15
16 17 18 19 20 21 22
23 24 25 26 27 28 29
30 31

FEBRUARY
S M T W T F S
      1 2 3 4
5 6 7 8 9 10 11
12 13 14 15 16 17 18
19 20 21 22 23 24 25
26 27 28 29

MARCH
S M T W T F S
      1 2 3 4
5 6 7 8 9 10 11
12 13 14 15 16 17 18
19 20 21 22 23 24 25
26 27 28 29 30 31

APRIL
S M T W T F S
            1
2 3 4 5 6 7 8
9 10 11 12 13 14 15
16 17 18 19 20 21 22
23 24 25 26 27 28 29
30

MAY
S M T W T F S
  1 2 3 4 5 6
7 8 9 10 11 12 13
14 15 16 17 18 19 20
21 22 23 24 25 26 27
28 29 30 31

JUNE
S M T W T F S
        1 2 3
4 5 6 7 8 9 10
11 12 13 14 15 16 17
18 19 20 21 22 23 24
25 26 27 28 29 30

JULY
S M T W T F S
            1
2 3 4 5 6 7 8
9 10 11 12 13 14 15
16 17 18 19 20 21 22
23 24 25 26 27 28 29
30 31

AUGUST
S M T W T F S
      1 2 3 4
5 6 7 8 9 10 11
12 13 14 15 16 17 18
19 20 21 22 23 24 25
26 27 28 29 30 31

SEPTEMBER
S M T W T F S
          1 2
3 4 5 6 7 8 9
10 11 12 13 14 15 16
17 18 19 20 21 22 23
24 25 26 27 28 29 30

OCTOBER
S M T W T F S
1 2 3 4 5 6 7
8 9 10 11 12 13 14
15 16 17 18 19 20 21
22 23 24 25 26 27 28
29 30 31

NOVEMBER
S M T W T F S
      1 2 3 4
5 6 7 8 9 10 11
12 13 14 15 16 17 18
19 20 21 22 23 24 25
26 27 28 29 30

DECEMBER
S M T W T F S
          1 2
3 4 5 6 7 8 9
10 11 12 13 14 15 16
17 18 19 20 21 22 23
24 25 26 27 28 29 30
31

The Calendar

History of the Calendar

The purpose of a calendar is to reckon time in advance, to show how many days have to elapse until a certain event takes place—the harvest, a religious festival, or whatever. The earliest calendars, naturally, were crude, and they must have been strongly influenced by the geographical location of the people who made them. In the Scandinavian countries, for example, where the seasons are pronounced, the concept of the year was determined by the seasons, specifically by the end of winter. The Norsemen, before becoming Christians, are said to have had a calendar consisting of ten months of 30 days each.

But in warmer countries, where the seasons are less pronounced, the Moon became the basic unit for time reckoning; an old Jewish book actually makes the statement that "the Moon was created for the counting of the days." All the oldest calendars of which we have reliable information were lunar calendars, based on the time interval from one new moon to the next—a so-called "lunation." But even in a warm climate there are annual events that pay no attention to the phases of the Moon. In some areas it was a rainy season; in Egypt it was the annual flooding of the Nile. It was, therefore, necessary to regulate daily life and religious festivals by lunations, but to take care of the annual event in some other manner.

The calendar of the Assyrians was based on the phases of the Moon. The month began with the first appearance of the lunar crescent, and since this can best be observed in the evening, the day began with sunset. They knew that a lunation was $29\frac{1}{2}$ days long, so their lunar year had a duration of 354 days, falling eleven days short of the solar year.[1] After three years such a lunar calendar would be off by 33 days, or more than one lunation. We know that the Assyrians added an extra month from time to time, but we do not know whether they had developed a special rule for doing so or whether the priests proclaimed the necessity for an extra month from observation. If they made every third year a year of 13 lunations, their three-year period would cover $1,091\frac{1}{2}$ days (using their value of $29\frac{1}{2}$ days for one lunation), or just about four days too short. In one century this mistake would add up to 133 days by their reckoning (in reality closer to 134 days), requiring four extra lunations per century.

We now know that an eight-year period, consisting of five years with 12 months and three years with 13 months would lead to a difference of only 20 days per century, but we do not know whether such a calendar was actually used.

The best approximation that was possible in antiquity was a 19-year period, with seven of these 19 years having 13 months. This means that the period contained 235 months. This, still using the old value for a lunation, made a total of $6,932\frac{1}{2}$ days, while 19 solar years added up to 6,939.7 days, a difference of just one week per period and about five weeks per century. Even the 19-year period required constant adjustment, but it was the period that became the basis of the religious calendar of

the Jews. The Arabs used the same calendar at first, but Mohammed forbade shifting from 12 months to 13 months, so that the Islamic religious calendar, even today, has a lunar year of 354 days. As a result the Islamic religious festivals run through all the seasons of the year three times per century.

The Egyptians had a traditional calendar with 12 months of 30 days each. At one time they added five extra days at the end of every year. These turned into a five-day festival because it was thought to be unlucky to work during that time.

When Rome emerged as a world power, the difficulties of making a calendar were well known, but the Romans complicated their lives because of their superstition that even numbers were unlucky. Hence their months were 29 or 31 days long, with the exception of February, which had 28 days. However, four months of 31 days, seven months of 29 days, and one month of 28 days added up to only 355 days. Therefore, the Romans invented an extra month called Mercedonius of 22 or 23 days. It was added every second year.

Even with Mercedonius, the Roman calendar was so far off that Caesar, advised by the astronomer Sosigenes, ordered a sweeping reform in 45 B.C. One year, made 445 days long by imperial decree, brought the calendar back in step with the seasons. Then the solar year (with the value of 365 days and 6 hours) was made the basis of the calendar. The months were 30 or 31 days in length, and to take care of the six hours, every fourth year was made a 366-day year. Moreover, Caesar decreed, the year began with the first of January, not with the vernal equinox in late March.

This was the Julian calendar, named after Julius Caesar. It is still the calendar of the Eastern Orthodox churches.

However, the year is $11\frac{1}{2}$ minutes shorter than the figure written into Caesar's calendar by Sosigenes, and after a number of centuries, even $11\frac{1}{2}$ minutes add up, as the table below shows.

While Caesar could decree that the vernal equinox should not be used as the first day of the new year, the vernal equinox is still a fact of Nature that could not be disregarded. One of the first (as far as we know) to become alarmed about this was Roger Bacon. He sent a memorandum to Pope Clement IV, who apparently was not impressed. But Pope Sixtus IV (reigned 1471 to 1484) decided that another reform was needed and called the German astronomer Regiomontanus to Rome to advise him. Regiomontanus arrived in 1475, but one year later he died in an epidemic, one of the recurrent outbreaks of the plague. The Pope himself survived, but his reform plans died with Regiomontanus.

Less than a hundred years later, in 1545, the Council of Trent authorized the then Pope, Gregory XIII, to reform the calendar once more. Most of the mathematical and astronomical work was done by Father Christopher Clavius, S.J. The immediate correction, advised by Father Clavius and ordered by Pope Gregory XIII, was that Thursday, Oct. 4, 1582, was to be the last day of the Julian calendar. The next day was Friday, with the date of October 15. For long-range accuracy, a formula suggested by the Vatican librarian Aloysius Giglio (latinized into Lilius) was adopted: every fourth year is a leap year *unless* it is a century year like 1700 or 1800. Century years can be leap years *only* when they are divisible by 400 (e.g., 1600).

---

1. The correct figures are: lunation: 29 d, 12 h, 44 min, 2.8 sec (29.530585 d); solar year: 365 d, 5 h, 48 min, 46 sec (365.242216 d); 12 lunations: 354 d, 8 h, 48 min, 34 sec (354.3671 d).

Drift of the Vernal Equinox in the Julian Calendar

Date	Julian year	Date	Julian year	Date	Julian year
March 21	325 A.D.	March 17	837 A.D.	March 13	1349 A.D.
March 20	453 A.D.	March 16	965 A.D.	March 12	1477 A.D.
March 19	581 A.D.	March 15	1093 A.D.	March 11	1605 A.D.
March 18	709 A.D.	March 14	1221 A.D.		

This rule eliminates three leap years in four centuries, making the calendar sufficiently correct for all ordinary purposes.

Unfortunately, all the Protestant princes in 1582 chose to ignore the papal bull; they continued with the Julian calendar. It was not until 1698 that the German professor Erhard Weigel persuaded the Protestant rulers of Germany and of the Netherlands to change to the new calendar. In England the shift took place in 1752, and in Russia it needed the revolution to introduce the Gregorian calendar in 1918.

The average year of the Gregorian calendar, in spite of the leap year rule, is about 26 seconds longer than the earth's orbital period. But this discrepancy will need 3,323 years to build up to a single day.

Modern proposals for calendar reform do not aim at a "better" calendar, but at one that is more convenient to use, especially for commercial purposes. A 365-day year cannot be divided into equal halves or quarters; the number of days per month is haphazard; the months begin or end in the middle of a week; a holiday fixed by date (e.g., the Fourth of July) will wander through a week; a holiday fixed in another manner (e.g., Easter) can fall on thirty-five possible dates. The Gregorian calendar, admittedly, keeps the calendar dates in reasonable unison with astronomical events, but it still is full of minor annoyances. Moreover, you need a calendar every year to look up dates; an ideal calendar should be one that you can memorize for one year and that is valid for all other years, too.

In 1834 an Italian priest, Marco Mastrofini, suggested taking one day out of every year. It would be made a holiday and *not* be given the name of a weekday. That would make every year begin with January 1 as a Sunday. The leap-year day would be treated the same way, so that in leap years there would be two unnamed holidays at the end of the year.

About a decade later the philosopher Auguste Comte also suggested a 364-day calendar with an extra day, which he called Year Day.

Since then there have been other unsuccessful attempts at calendar reform.

Time and Calendar

The two natural cycles on which time measurements are based are the year and the day. The year is defined as the time required for the Earth to complete one revolution around the Sun, while the day is the time required for the Earth to complete one turn upon its axis. Unfortunately the Earth needs 365 days plus about six hours to go around the Sun once, so that the year does not consist of so and so many days; the fractional day has to be taken care of by an extra day every fourth year.

But because the Earth, while turning upon its axis, also moves around the Sun there are two kinds of days. A day may be defined as the interval between the highest point of the Sun in the sky on two successive days. This, averaged out over the year, produces the customary 24-hour day. But one might also define a day as the time interval between the moments when a certain point in the sky, say a conveniently located star, is directly overhead. This is called:

Sidereal time. Astronomers use a point which they call the "vernal equinox" for the actual determination. Such a sidereal day is somewhat shorter than the "solar day," namely by about 3 minutes and 56 seconds of so-called "mean solar time."

Apparent solar time is the time based directly on the Sun's position in the sky. In ordinary life the day runs from midnight to midnight. It begins when the Sun is invisible by being 12 hours from its zenith. Astronomers use the so-called "Julian Day," which runs from noon to noon; the concept was invented by the astronomer Joseph Scaliger, who named it after his father Julius. To avoid the problems caused by leap-year days and so forth, Scaliger picked a conveniently remote date in the past and suggested just counting days without regard to weeks, months, and years. The Julian Day 2,440,-225.5 is Jan. 1, 1969. The reason for having the Julian Day run from noon to noon is the practical one that astronomical observations usually extend across the midnight hour, which would require a change in date (or in the Julian Day number) if the astronomical day, like the civil day, ran from midnight to midnight.

Mean solar time, rather than apparent solar time, is what is actually used most of the time. The mean solar time is based on the position of a fictitious "mean sun." The reason why this fictitious sun has to be introduced is the following: The Earth turns on its axis regularly; it needs the same number of seconds regardless of the season. But the movement of the Earth around the Sun is not regular because the Earth's orbit is an ellipse. This has the result (as explained in the section The Seasons) that the Earth moves faster in January and slower in July. Though it is the Earth that changes velocity, it looks to us as if the Sun did. In January, when the Earth moves faster, the *apparent* movement of the Sun looks faster. The "mean sun" of time measurements, then, is a sun that moves regularly all year round; the real Sun will be either ahead of or behind the "mean sun." The difference between the real Sun and the fictitious mean sun is called the *equation of time.*

When the real Sun is west of the mean sun we have the "sun fast" condition, with the real Sun crossing the meridian ahead of the mean sun. The opposite is the "sun slow" situation when the real Sun crosses the meridian after the mean sun. Of course, what is observed is the real Sun. The equation of time is needed to establish mean solar time, kept by the reference clocks.

But if all clocks were actually set by mean solar time we would be plagued by a welter of time differences that would be "correct" but a major nuisance. A clock on Long Island, correctly showing mean solar time for its location (this would be *local*

The Names of the Days

Latin	Saxon	English	French	Italian	Spanish	German
Dies Solis	Sun's Day	Sunday	Dimanche	domenica	domingo	Sonntag
Dies Lunae	Moon's Day	Monday	Lundi	lunedì	lunes	Montag
Dies Martis	Tiw's Day	Tuesday	Mardi	martedì	martes	Dienstag
Dies Mercurii	Woden's Day	Wednesday	Mercredi	mercoledì	miércoles	Mittwoch
Dies Jovis	Thor's Day	Thursday	Jeudi	giovedì	jueves	Donnerstag
Dies Veneris	Frigg's Day	Friday	Vendredi	venerdì	viernes	Freitag
Dies Saturni	Seterne's Day	Saturday	Samedi	sabato	sábado	Sonnabend

NOTE: The Romans gave one day of the week to each planet known, the Sun and Moon being considered planets in this connection. The Saxon names are a kind of translation of the Roman names: Tiw was substituted for Mars, Woden (Wotan) for Mercury, Thor for Jupiter (Jove), Frigg for Venus, and Seterne for Saturn. The English names are adapted Saxon. The Spanish and Italian names, which are normally not capitalized, and the French are derived from the Latin. The German names follow the Saxon pattern with two exceptions: Wednesday is Mittwoch (Middle of the Week), and Saturday is Sonnabend (Sunday's Eve).

civil time), would be slightly ahead of a clock in Newark, N.J. The Newark clock would be slightly ahead of a clock in Trenton, N.J., which, in turn, would be ahead of a clock in Philadelphia. This condition actually prevailed in the past until 1883, when *standard time* was introduced. Standard time is the correct mean solar time for a designated meridian, and this time is used for a certain area to the east and west of this meridian. In the U.S. four meridians have been designated to supply standard times; they are 75°, 90°, 105°, and 120° west of Greenwich. The 75° meridian determines Eastern Standard Time. It happens to run through Camden, N.J., where standard time, therefore, is also mean solar time and local civil time. The 90° meridian (which happens to pass through the western part of Memphis, Tenn.) determines Central Standard Time, the 105° meridian (passing through Denver) determines Mountain Standard Time, and the 120° meridian (which runs through Lake Tahoe) determines Pacific Standard Time.

Canada, extending over more territory from west to east, adds one time zone on either side: Atlantic Standard Time (based on 60° west of Greenwich) for New Brunswick, Nova Scotia, and Quebec, and Yukon Standard Time (determined by the 135° meridian) for its extreme West. Alaska, extending still farther to the west, adds two more time zones, Alaska Standard Time (determined by the 150° meridian that passes through Anchorage) and Nome Standard Time, based on the 165° meridian just east of Nome.

In general the Earth is divided into 24 such time zones, which run one hour apart. For practical purposes the time zones sometimes show indentations, and there are a few "subzones" that differ from the neighboring zone by only half an hour, e.g., Newfoundland.

The date line. While the time zones are based on the natural event of the Sun crossing the meridian, the date must be an arbitrary decision. The meridians are traditionally counted from the meridian of the observatory of Greenwich in England, which is called the zero meridian. The logical place for changing the date is 12 hours, or 180° from Greenwich. Fortunately, the 180th meridian runs mostly through the open Pacific. The date line makes a zigzag in the north to incorporate the eastern tip of Siberia into the Siberian time system and then another one to incorporate a number of islands into the Alaska time system. In the south there is a similar zigzag for the purpose of tying a number of British-owned islands to the New Zealand time system. Otherwise the date line is the same as 180° from Greenwich. At points to the east of the date line the calendar is one day earlier than at points to the west of it. A traveller going eastward across the date line from one island to another would not have to re-set his watch because he would stay inside the time zone (provided he does so where the date line does *not* coincide with the 180° meridian), but it would be the same time of the previous day.

The Seasons

The seasons are caused by the tilt of the Earth's axis (23.4°) and not by the fact that the Earth's orbit around the Sun is an ellipse. The average distance of the Earth from the Sun is 93 million miles; the difference between aphelion (farthest away) and perihelion (closest to the Sun) is 3 million miles, so that perihelion is about 91.4 million miles from the Sun. The Earth goes through the perihelion point a few days after New Year, just when the northern hemisphere has winter. Aphelion is

The Names of the Months

January: named after Janus, protector of the gateway to heaven
February: named after Februalia, a time period when sacrifices were made to atone for sins
March: named after Mars, the god of war, presumably signifying that the campaigns interrupted by the winter could be resumed
April: from *aperire*, Latin for "to open" (buds)
May: named after Maia, the goddess of growth of

plants
June: from *juvenis*, Latin for "youth"
July: named after Julius Caesar
August: named after Augustus, the first Roman Emperor
September: from *septem*, Latin for "seven"
October: from *octo*, Latin for "eight"
November: from *novem*, Latin for "nine"
December: from *decem*, Latin for "ten"

NOTE: The earliest Latin calendar was a 10-month one; thus September was the seventh month, October, the eighth, etc. July was originally called Quintilis, as the fifth month; August was originally called Sextilis, as the sixth month.

passed during the first days in July. This by itself shows that the distance from the Sun is not important within these limits. What is important is that when the Earth passes through perihelion, the northern end of the Earth's axis happens to tilt away from the Sun, so that the areas beyond the Tropic of Cancer receive only slanting rays from a Sun low in the sky.

The tilt of the Earth's axis is responsible for four lines you find on every globe. When, say, the North Pole is tilted away from the Sun as much as possible, the farthest points in the North which can still be reached by the Sun's rays are $23^1/_2°$ from the pole. This is the Arctic Circle. The Antarctic Circle is the corresponding limit 23.4° from the South Pole; the Sun's rays cannot reach beyond this point when we have mid-summer in the North.

When the Sun is vertically above the equator, the day is of equal length all over the Earth. This hap-

pens twice a year, and these are the "equinoxes" in March and in September. After having been over the equator in March, the Sun will seem to move northward. The northernmost point where the Sun can be straight overhead is 23.4° north of the equator. This is the Tropic of Cancer; the Sun can never be vertically overhead to the north of this line. Similarly the Sun cannot be vertically overhead to the south of a line 23.4° south of the equator—the Tropic of Capricorn.

This explains the climatic zones. In the belt (the Greek word *zone* means "belt") between the Tropic of Cancer and the Tropic of Capricorn, the Sun can be straight overhead; this is the tropical zone. The two zones where the Sun cannot be overhead but will be above the horizon every day of the year are the two temperate zones; the two areas where the Sun will not rise at all for varying lengths of time are the two polar areas, Arctic and Antarctic.

Holidays

Religious and Secular, 1982

Since 1971, by federal law, Washington's Birthday, Memorial Day, Columbus Day, and Veterans' Day have been celebrated on Mondays to create three-day weekends for federal employees. Many states now observe these holidays on the same Mondays. (*See* page 388.) The dates given for the holidays listed below are the traditional ones.

New Year's Day, Friday, Jan. 1. A legal holiday in all states and the District of Columbia, New Year's Day has its origin in Roman times, when sacrifices were offered to Janus, the two-faced Roman deity who looked back on the past and forward to the future.

Epiphany, Wednesday, Jan. 6. Falls the twelfth day after Christmas and commemorates the manifestation of Jesus as the Son of God, as represented by the adoration of the Magi, the baptism of Jesus, and the miracle of the wine at the marriage feast at Cana. Epiphany originally marked the beginning of the carnival season preceding Lent, and the evening (sometimes the eve) is known as Twelfth Night.

Lincoln's Birthday, Friday, Feb. 12. A legal holiday in many states, this day was first formally observed in Washington, D.C., in 1866, when both houses of Congress gathered for a memorial address in tribute to the assassinated President.

St. Valentine's Day, Sunday, Feb. 14. This day is the festival of two third-century martyrs, both named St. Valentine. It is not known why this day is associated with lovers. It may derive from an old pagan festival about this time of year, or it may have been inspired by the belief that birds mate on this day.

Washington's Birthday, Monday, Feb. 22. The birthday of George Washington is celebrated as a legal holiday in every state of the Union, the District of Columbia, and all territories. The observance began in 1796.

Shrove Tuesday, Feb. 23. Falls the day before Ash Wednesday and marks the end of the carnival season, which once began on Epiphany but is now usually celebrated the last three days before Lent.

In France, the day is known as Mardi Gras (Fat Tuesday), and Mardi Gras celebrations are also held in several American cities, particularly in New Orleans. The day is sometimes called Pancake Tuesday by the English because fats, which were prohibited during Lent, had to be used up.

Ash Wednesday, Feb. 24. The first day of the Lenten season, which lasts 40 days. Having its origin sometime before A.D. 1000, it is a day of public penance and is marked in the Roman Catholic Church by the burning of the palms blessed on the previous year's Palm Sunday. With his thumb, the priest then marks a cross upon the forehead of each worshipper. The Anglican Church and a few Protestant groups in the United States also observe the day, but generally without the use of ashes.

Purim (Feast of Lots), Tuesday, March 9 (14 Adar). A day of joy and feasting celebrating deliverance of the Jews from a massacre planned by the Persian Minister Haman. The Jewish Queen Esther interceded with her husband, King Ahasuerus, to spare the life of her uncle, Mordecai, and Haman was hanged on the same gallows he had built for Mordecai. The holiday is marked by the reading of the Book of Esther (megillah), and by the exchange of gifts, donations to the poor, and the presentation of Purim plays.

St. Patrick's Day, Wednesday, March 17. St. Patrick, patron saint of Ireland, has been honored in America since the first days of the nation. There are many dinners and meetings but perhaps the most notable part of the observance is the annual St. Patrick's Day parade on Fifth Avenue in New York City.

Palm Sunday, April 4. Is observed the Sunday before Easter to commemorate the entry of Jesus into Jerusalem. The procession and the ceremonies introducing the benediction of palms probably had their origin in Jerusalem.

First Day of Passover (Pesach), Thursday, April 8 (15 Nisan). The Feast of the Passover, also called the Feast of Unleavened Bread, commemorates the escape of the Jews from Egypt. As the Jews fled they ate unleavened bread, and from that time the

Jews have allowed no leavening in the houses during Passover, bread being replaced by matzoth.

Good Friday, April 9. This day commemorates the Crucifixion, which is retold during services from the Gospel according to St. John. A feature in Roman Catholic churches is the Liturgy of the Passion; there is no Consecration, the Host having been consecrated the previous day. The eating of hot cross buns on this day is said to have started in England.

Easter Sunday, April 11. Observed in all Christian churches, Easter commemorates the Resurrection of Jesus. It is celebrated on the first Sunday after the full moon which occurs on or next after March 21 and is therefore celebrated between March 22 and April 25 inclusive. This date was fixed by the Council of Nicaea in A.D. 325. The Orthodox Church celebrates Easter on April 18, 1982.

Ascension Day, Thursday, May 20. Took place in the presence of His apostles 40 days after the Resurrection of Jesus. It is traditionally held to have occurred on Mount Olivet in Bethany.

First Day of Shavuot (Hebrew Pentecost), Friday, May 28 (6 Sivan). This festival, sometimes called the Feast of Weeks, or of Harvest, or of the First Fruits, falls 50 days after Passover and originally celebrated the end of the seven-week grain harvesting season. In later tradition, it also celebrated the giving of the Law to Moses on Mount Sinai.

Pentecost (Whitsunday), May 30. This day commemorates the descent of the Holy Ghost upon the apostles 50 days after the Resurrection. The sermon by the Apostle Peter, which led to the baptism of 3,000 who professed belief, originated the ceremonies that have since been followed. "Whitsunday" is believed to have come from "white Sunday" when, among the English, white robes were worn by those baptized on the day.

Memorial Day, Sunday, May 30. Also known as Decoration Day, Memorial Day is a legal holiday in most of the states and in the territories, and is also observed by the armed forces. In 1868, Gen. John A. Logan, Commander in Chief of the Grand Army of the Republic, issued an order designating the day as one in which the graves of soldiers would be decorated. The holiday was originally devoted to honoring the memory of those who fell in the Civil War, but is now also dedicated to the memory of all war dead.

Flag Day, Monday, June 14. This day commemorates the adoption by the Continental Congress on June 14, 1777, of the Stars and Stripes as the U.S. flag. Although it is a legal holiday only in Pennsylvania, President Truman, on Aug. 3, 1949, signed a bill requesting the President to call for its observance each year by proclamation.

Independence Day, Sunday, July 4. The day of the adoption of the Declaration of Independence in 1776, celebrated in all states and territories. The observance began the next year in Philadelphia.

Labor Day, Monday, Sept. 6. Observed the first Monday in September in all states and territories, Labor Day was first celebrated in New York in 1882 under the sponsorship of the Central Labor Union, following the suggestion of Peter J.

McGuire, of the Knights of Labor, that the day be set aside in honor of labor.

First Day of Rosh Hashana (Jewish New Year), Saturday, Sept. 18 (1 Tishri). This day marks the beginning of the Jewish year 5743 and opens the Ten Days of Penitence closing with Yom Kippur.

Yom Kippur (Day of Atonement), Monday, Sept. 27 (10 Tishri). This day marks the end of the Ten Days of Penitence that began with Rosh Hashana. It is described in *Leviticus* as a "Sabbath of rest," and synagogue services begin the preceding sundown, resume the following morning, and continue to sundown.

First Day of Sukkot (Feast of Tabernacles), Saturday, Oct. 2 (15 Tishri). This festival, also known as the Feast of the Ingathering, originally celebrated the fruit harvest, and the name comes from the booths or tabernacles in which the Jews lived during the harvest, although one tradition traces it to the shelters used by the Jews in their wandering through the wilderness. During the festival many Jews build small huts in their back yards or on the roofs of their houses.

Simhat Torah (Rejoicing of the Law), Sunday, Oct. 10 (23 Tishri). This joyous holiday falls on the eighth day of Sukkot. It marks the end of the year's reading of the Torah (Five Books of Moses) in the synagogue every Saturday and the beginning of the new cycle of reading.

Columbus Day, Tuesday, Oct. 12. A legal holiday in many states, commemorating the discovery of America by Columbus in 1492. Quite likely the first celebration of Columbus Day was that organized in 1792 by the Society of St. Tammany, or Columbian Order, more widely known as Tammany Hall.

Halloween, Sunday, Oct. 31. Eve of All Saints' Day, formerly called All Hallows and Hallowmass. Halloween is traditionally associated in some countries with old customs such as bonfires, masquerading, and the telling of ghost stories. These are old Celtic practices that marked the beginning of winter.

All Saints' Day, Monday, Nov. 1. A Roman Catholic and Anglican holiday celebrating all saints, known and unknown.

Election Day, (legal holiday in certain states), Tuesday, Nov. 2. Since 1845, by Act of Congress, the first Tuesday after the first Monday in November is the date for choosing Presidential electors. State elections are also generally held on this day.

Veterans Day, Thursday, Nov. 11. Armistice Day was established in 1926 to commemorate the signing in 1918 of the Armistice ending World War I. On June 1, 1954, the name was changed to Veterans Day to honor all men and women who have served America in its armed forces.

Thanksgiving, Thursday, Nov. 25. Observed nationally on the fourth Thursday in November by Act of Congress (1941), the first such national proclamation having been issued by President Lincoln in 1863, on the urging of Mrs. Sarah J. Hale, editor of *Godey's Lady's Book.* Most Americans believe that the holiday dates back to the day of thanks ordered by Governor Bradford of Plymouth Colony in New England in 1621, but scholars point out that days of thanks stem from ancient times.

First Sunday of Advent, Nov. 28. Advent is the season in which the faithful must prepare themselves for the advent of the Saviour on Christmas. The four Sundays before Christmas are marked by special church services.

First Day of Hanukkah (Festival of Lights), Saturday, Dec. 11 (25 Kislev). This festival was instituted by Judas Maccabaeus in 165 B.C. to celebrate the purification of the Temple of Jerusalem, which had been desecrated three years earlier by Antiochus Epiphanes, who set up a pagan altar and offered sacrifices to Zeus Olympius. In Jewish homes, a light is lighted on each night of the eight-day festival.

Christmas (Feast of the Nativity), Saturday, Dec. 25. The most widely celebrated holiday of the Christian year, Christmas is observed as the anniversary of the birth of Jesus. Christmas customs are centuries old. The mistletoe, for example, comes from the Druids, who, in hanging the mistletoe, hoped for peace and good fortune. Use of such plants as holly comes from the ancient belief that such plants blossomed at Christmas. Comparatively recent is the Christmas tree, first set up in Germany in the 17th century, and the use of candles on trees developed from the belief that candles appeared by miracle on the trees at Christmas. Colonial Manhattan Islanders introduced the name Santa Claus, a corruption of the Dutch name for the 4th-century Asia Minor St. Nicholas.

National Holidays Around the World, 1982

Afghanistan	Aug. 19	Grenada	Feb. 7	Papua New Guinea	Sept. 16
Albania	Nov. 29	Guatemala	Sept. 15	Paraguay	May 14
Algeria	Nov. 1	Guinea	Oct. 2	Peru	July 28
Angola	Nov. 11	Guinea-Bissau	Sept. 12	Philippines	June 12
Argentina	May 25	Guyana	Feb. 23	Poland	July 22
Australia	Jan. 26	Haiti	Jan. 1	Portugal	June 10
Austria	Oct. 26	Honduras	Sept. 15	Qatar	Sept. 3
Bahamas	July 10	Hungary	April 4	Romania	Aug. 23
Bahrain	Dec. 16	Iceland	June 17	Rwanda	July 1
Bangladesh	March 26	India	Jan. 26	St. Lucia	Dec. 13
Barbados	Nov. 30	Indonesia	Aug. 17	St. Vincent and	
Belgium	July 21	Iran	April 1	the Grenadines	Oct. 27
Benin	Nov. 30	Iraq	July 14	São Tomé and Príncipe	July 12
Bhutan	Dec. 17	Ireland	March 17	Saudi Arabia	Sept. 23
Bolivia	Aug. 6	Israel	April 28[1]	Senegal	April 4
Botswana	Sept. 30	Italy	June 2	Seychelles	June 5
Brazil	Sept. 7	Ivory Coast	Dec. 7	Sierra Leone	April 19
Bulgaria	Sept. 9	Jamaica	Aug. 2[2]	Singapore	Aug. 9
Burma	Jan. 4	Japan	April 29	Somalia	Oct. 21
Burundi	July 1	Jordan	May 25	South Africa	May 31
Cambodia	April 17	Kenya	Dec. 12	Spain	Oct. 12
Cameroon	May 20	Kuwait	Feb. 25	Sri Lanka	Feb. 4
Canada	July 1	Laos	Dec. 2	Sudan	Jan. 1
Cape Verde	Sept. 12	Lebanon	Nov. 22	Suriname	Nov. 25
Central African Republic	Dec. 1	Lesotho	Oct. 4	Swaziland	Sept. 6
Chad	April 13	Liberia	July 26	Sweden	April 30
Chile	Sept. 18	Libya	Sept. 1	Syria	April 17
China	Oct. 1	Luxembourg	June 23	Tanzania	April 26
Colombia	July 20	Madagascar	June 26	Thailand	Dec. 5
Congo	Aug. 15	Malawi	July 6	Togo	April 27
Costa Rica	Sept. 15	Malaysia	Aug. 31	Trinidad and Tobago	Aug. 31
Cuba	Jan. 1	Maldives	July 26	Tunisia	June 1
Cyprus	Oct. 1	Mali	Sept. 22	Turkey	Oct. 29
Czechoslovakia	May 9	Malta	March 31	Uganda	Oct. 9
Denmark	April 16	Mauritania	Nov. 28	U.S.S.R.	Nov. 7
Djibouti	June 27	Mauritius	March 12	United Arab Emirates	Dec. 2
Dominican Republic	Feb. 27	Mexico	Sept. 16	United States	July 4
Ecuador	Aug. 10	Mongolia	July 11	Upper Volta	Dec. 11
Egypt	July 23	Morocco	March 3	Uruguay	Aug. 25
El Salvador	Sept. 15	Mozambique	June 25	Venezuela	July 5
Equatorial Guinea	March 5	Nepal	Dec. 28	Vietnam	Sept. 2
Ethiopia	Sept. 12	Netherlands	April 30	Western Samoa	June 1
Fiji	Oct. 10	New Zealand	Feb. 6	Yemen, People's Dem.	
Finland	Dec. 6	Nicaragua	Sept. 15	Republic of	Oct. 14
France	July 14	Niger	Dec. 18	Yemen Arab Republic	Sept. 26
Gabon	Aug. 17	Nigeria	Oct. 1	Yugoslavia	Nov. 29
Gambia	Feb. 18	Norway	May 17	Zaire	June 30
Germany, East	Oct. 7	Oman	Nov. 18	Zambia	Oct. 24
Ghana	March 6	Pakistan	March 23	Zimbabwe	April 18
Greece	March 25	Panama	Nov. 3		

1. Changes yearly according to Hebrew calendar. 2. Celebrated on first Monday in August. *Source:* United Nations.

Legal Holidays in the 50 States, D.C., and Puerto Rico

HOLIDAYS WIDELY OBSERVED

January 1, New Year's Day: All states, D.C., Puerto Rico.

February 12, Lincoln's Birthday: Alaska, California, Colorado, Connecticut, Florida, Illinois, Indiana, Iowa, Kansas, Kentucky, Maryland, Missouri, Montana, Nebraska, New Jersey, New Mexico, New York, Utah, Vermont, Washington, West Virginia.

February (first Monday), Lincoln's Birthday: Delaware, Oregon.

February (second Monday), Lincoln Day: Arizona.

February (third Monday), Washington's Birthday: All states,[3] D.C., Puerto Rico. Called **Washington Day** in Arizona. Called **Presidents' Day** in Hawaii, Nebraska, Pennsylvania, South Dakota. Called **Founders Day** in Minnesota; **Washington-Lincoln Day** in Ohio, Wisconsin, Wyoming.

May 25, Memorial Day: New Mexico.

May 28, Memorial Day: Puerto Rico.

May 30, Memorial Day: Delaware,[2] Illinois, Maryland, New Hampshire, South Dakota, Vermont.

May (4th Monday), Memorial Day: West Virginia

May (last Monday), Memorial Day: All states,[3] D.C., except those listed above, and Alabama, Mississippi, South Carolina.

July 4, Independence Day: All states, D.C., Puerto Rico.

September (1st Monday), Labor Day: All states, D.C., Puerto Rico.

October 12, Columbus Day: Maryland, Puerto Rico.

October (2nd Monday), Columbus Day: All states,[2] D.C., except Alaska, Iowa, Maryland, Michigan, Mississippi, Nevada, North Carolina, North Dakota, Oregon, South Carolina, Washington, Puerto Rico. Also called **Fraternal Day** in Alabama. Called **Discoverers' Day** in Hawaii, **Farmers' Day** in Florida, **Pioneers' Day** in South Dakota.

November (4th Thursday), Thanksgiving Day: All states, D.C., Puerto Rico.

November, Day after Thanksgiving: Nebraska.

November (first Tuesday after the first Monday), Election Day: Arkansas, California, Colorado, D.C., Delaware, Florida, Hawaii, Idaho, Illinois, Indiana, Kentucky, Louisiana, Maryland, Missouri, Montana, New Hampshire, New Jersey, New York, Oklahoma, Pennsylvania, Rhode Island, South Carolina, Tennessee, Texas, Virginia, West Virginia, Wisconsin, Wyoming, Puerto Rico.

November 11, Veterans' Day: All states, D.C., Puerto Rico. Called **Armistice Day** and **Veterans' Day** in New Mexico.

December 25, Christmas: All states, D.C., Puerto Rico.

OTHER HOLIDAYS

January 6, Three Kings' Day: Puerto Rico.

January 8, Battle of New Orleans Day: Louisiana.

January 11, De Hostos's Day: Puerto Rico.

January 15, Martin Luther King Day: Connecticut, D.C., Florida, Illinois, Kentucky, Louisiana,[3] Maryland, Massachusetts, New Jersey, Pennsylvania, South Carolina.[1]

January 19, Robert E. Lee's Birthday: Arkansas, Florida, Georgia, Kentucky, Louisiana,[3] South Carolina.[1] Called **Confederate Heroes Day** in Texas, also in honor of Jefferson Davis and other Confederate heroes.

January (third Sunday), Martin Luther King Day: New York.

January (third Monday), Martin Luther King Day: Ohio.

January (third Monday), Robert E. Lee's Birthday: Alabama, Mississippi. **Lee-Jackson Day** in Virginia.

January 30, F. D. Roosevelt's Birthday: Kentucky.

February or March (1 day before Ash Wednesday), Mardi Gras (Shrove Tuesday): Alabama, Louisiana (in some parishes).

February 15, Susan B. Anthony's Birthday: Florida.

February 19, Robert E. Lee Day: Kentucky.

March (first Tuesday), Town Meeting Day: Vermont.

March 2, Texas Independence Day: Texas.

March 17, Evacuation Day: Massachusetts (in Suffolk Co. only).

March or April (2 days before Easter), Good Friday: Connecticut, Delaware, Florida, Hawaii, Indiana, Louisiana, Maryland, New Jersey, North Dakota, Pennsylvania, Tennessee, Wisconsin (11 a.m.-3 p.m.).

March or April (1 day after Easter), Easter Monday: North Carolina.

March 20, (First Day of Spring), Youth Day: Oklahoma.

March 22, Abolition Day: Puerto Rico.

March 25, Maryland Day: Maryland.

March 26, Prince Jonah Kuhio Kalanianaole Day: Hawaii.

March (last Monday), Seward's Day: Alaska.

April 2, Pascua Florida Day: Florida.

April 13, Thomas Jefferson's Birthday: Alabama, Oklahoma.

April 16, De Diego's Birthday: Puerto Rico.

April (third Monday), Patriots' Day: Maine, Mass.

April 21, San Jacinto Day: Texas.

April 22, Arbor Day: Nebraska.

April 22, Oklahoma Day: Oklahoma.

April 26, Confederate Memorial Day: Florida, Georgia.

April (4th Monday), Fast Day: New Hampshire.

April (last Monday), Arbor Day: Wyoming.

April (last Monday), Confederate Memorial Day: Alabama, Mississippi.

April (last Friday), Arbor Day: Utah.

May (1st Tuesday after the first Monday), Primary Election Day: Indiana.

May (2nd Sunday), Mother's Day: Arizona, Okla.

May 1, Bird Day: Oklahoma.

May 4, Rhode Island Independence Day: Rhode Island.

May 8, Truman Day: Missouri.

May 10, Confederate Memorial Day: South Carolina.[1]

May 20, Mecklenburg Independence Day: North Carolina.

June (first Monday), Jefferson Davis's Birthday: Alabama, Mississippi.

June (second Sunday), Flag Day: New York.

June (third Sunday), Father's Day: Arizona.

June 3, Jefferson Davis's Birthday: Florida, Georgia, South Carolina, also called **Confederate Memorial Day** in Kentucky and Louisiana.[3]

June 9, Senior Citizens Day: Oklahoma.

June 11, King Kamehameha I Day: Hawaii.

June 14, Flag Day: Pennsylvania.

June 15, Separation Day: Delaware.

June 17, Bunker Hill Day: Massachusetts (in Suffolk Co. only).

June 19, Emancipation Day: Texas.

June 20, West Virginia Day: West Virginia.

July 17, Muñoz Rivera's Birthday: Puerto Rico.

July 24, Pioneer Day: Utah.

---

1. Optional, two of three allowed. 2. In Delaware, actual date of observance has not yet been determined. 3. In Louisiana, observed only if proclaimed by governor.

July 25, Constitution Day: Puerto Rico.
July 27, Barbosa's Birthday: Puerto Rico.
August (first Sunday), American Family Day: Arizona.
August (first Monday), Colorado Day: Colo.
August (second Monday), Victory Day: Rhode Island.
August 16, Bennington Battle Day: Vermont.
August (third Friday), Admission Day: Hawaii.
August 27, Lyndon B. Johnson's Birthday: Texas.
August 30, Huey P. Long Day: Louisiana.[3]
September (first Tuesday), Primary Election Day: Wisconsin.
September, (second Tuesday), Primary Election Day: Wyoming.
September 9, Admission Day: California.
September 12, Defenders' Day: Maryland.

September 16, Cherokee Strip Day: Oklahoma.
September 23, Grito de Lares: Puerto Rico.
September (1st Saturday after full moon), Indian Day: Oklahoma.
October 10, Oklahoma Historical Day: Oklahoma.
October 18, Alaska Day: Alaska.
October 31, Nevada Day: Nevada.
November 1, All Saints' Day: Louisiana.[3]
November 4, Will Rogers Day: Oklahoma.
November (week of the 16th), Oklahoma Heritage Week: Oklahoma.
November 19, Discovery Day: Puerto Rico.
November 29, Nellie Tayloe Ross's Birthday: Wyoming.
December 7, Delaware Day: Delaware.
December 10, Wyoming Day: Wyoming.

Movable Holidays, 1982–1990
CHRISTIAN AND SECULAR

Year	Ash Wednesday	Easter	Pentecost	Labor Day	Election Day	Thanksgiving	1st Sun. Advent
1982	Feb. 24	April 11	May 30	Sept. 6	Nov. 2	Nov. 25	Nov. 28
1983	Feb. 16	April 3	May 22	Sept. 5	Nov. 8	Nov. 24	Nov. 27
1984	March 7	April 22	June 10	Sept. 3	Nov. 6	Nov. 22	Dec. 2
1985	Feb. 20	April 7	May 26	Sept. 2	Nov. 5	Nov. 28	Dec. 1
1986	Feb. 12	March 30	May 18	Sept. 1	Nov. 4	Nov. 27	Nov. 30
1987	March 4	April 19	June 7	Sept. 7	Nov. 3	Nov. 26	Nov. 29
1988	Feb. 17	April 3	May 22	Sept. 5	Nov. 8	Nov. 24	Nov. 27
1989	Feb. 8	March 26	May 14	Sept. 4	Nov. 7	Nov. 23	Dec. 3
1990	Feb. 28	April 15	June 3	Sept. 3	Nov. 6	Nov. 22	Dec. 2

Shrove Tuesday: 1 day before Ash Wednesday
Palm Sunday: 7 days before Easter
Maundy Thursday: 3 days before Easter
Good Friday: 2 days before Easter

Holy Saturday: 1 day before Easter
Ascension Day: 10 days before Pentecost
Trinity Sunday: 7 days after Pentecost
Corpus Christi: 11 days after Pentecost

NOTE: Easter is celebrated on April 18, 1982, by the Orthodox Church.

JEWISH

Year	Purim[1]	1st day Passover[2]	1st day Shavuot[3]	1st day Rosh Hashana[4]	Yom Kippur[5]	1st day Sukkot[6]	Simhat Torah[7]	1st day Hanukkah[8]
1982	March 9	April 8	May 28	Sept. 18	Sept. 27	Oct. 2	Oct. 10	Dec. 11
1983	Feb. 27	March 29	May 18	Sept. 8	Sept. 17	Sept. 22	Sept. 30	Dec. 1
1984	March 18	April 17	June 6	Sept. 27	Oct. 6	Oct. 11	Oct. 19	Dec. 19
1985	March 7	April 6	May 26	Sept. 16	Sept. 25	Sept. 30	Oct. 8	Dec. 8
1986	March 25	April 24	June 13	Oct. 4	Oct. 13	Oct. 18	Oct. 26	Dec. 27
1987	March 15	April 14	June 3	Sept. 24	Oct. 3	Oct. 8	Oct. 16	Dec. 16
1988	March 3	April 2	May 22	Sept. 12	Sept. 21	Sept. 26	Oct. 4	Dec. 4
1989	March 21	April 20	June 9	Sept. 30	Oct. 9	Oct. 14	Oct. 22	Dec. 23
1990	March 11	April 10	May 30	Sept. 20	Sept. 29	Oct. 4	Oct. 12	Dec. 12

1. Feast of Lots. 2. Feast of Unleavened Bread. 3. Hebrew Pentecost; or Feast of Weeks, or of Harvest, or of First Fruits. 4. Jewish New Year. 5. Day of Atonement. 6. Feast of Tabernacles, or of the Ingathering. 7. Rejoicing of the Law. 8. Festival of Lights.

Length of Jewish holidays (O=Orthodox, C=Conservative, R=Reform):

Passover: O & C, 8 days (holy days: first 2 and last 2); R, 7 days (holy days: first and last)
Shavuot: O & C, 2 days; R, 1 day
Rosh Hashana: O & C, 2 days; R, 1 day.
Yom Kippur: All groups, 1 day

Sukkot: All groups, 7 days (holy days: O & C, first 2; R, first only) O & C observe two additional days: Shemini Atseret (Eighth Day of the Feast) and Simhat Torah R observes Shemini Atseret but not Simhat Torah
Hanukkah: All groups, 8 days
NOTE: All holidays begin at sundown on the evening before the date given.

EPA Fuel Economy

EPA tests automobiles to make sure they meet federal emission standards and compiles information about the gas mileage consumers can expect from their automobiles.

Copies of a booklet on these gas mileage figures can be obtained from: Printing Management, Office (PM-215), Environmental Protection Agency, Washington, D.C. 20460.

MILITARY

Average Military Strength—Man Years[1]
(in thousands)

Year	Army	Air Force	Navy	Marine Corps	Total
1941	755	[2]	218	44	1,017
1942	1,992	[2]	416	89	2,498
1943	5,224	[2]	1,206	232	6,662
1944	7,507	[2]	2,386	398	10,290
1945	8,131	[2]	3,205	473	11,809
1946	4,816	[2]	2,394	336	7,545
1947	1,417	[2]	584	112	2,112
1948	585	345	444	87	1,460
1949	657	411	443	87	1,598
1950	632	415	412	80	1,539
1951	1,090	584	566	153	2,394
1952	1,597	899	789	219	3,504
1953	1,536	971	809	237	3,554
1954	1,477	939	767	242	3,425
1955	1,311	958	692	217	3,178
1960	871	828	617	173	2,489
1962	1,018	864	656	187	2,725
1965	966	844	669	190	2,668
1966	1,073	844	716	221	2,854
1969	1,510	886	759	311	3,465
1970	1,432	834	732	295	3,293
1971	1,238	763	656	234	2,891
1972	955	749	604	202	2,510
1973	839	706	580	198	2,323
1974	788	672	556	191	2,207
1975	779	628	545	193	2,145
1976	775	600	529	194	2,098
1977	779	577	527	190	2,073
1978	777	570	530	191	2,068
1979	765	565	527	188	2,045
1980	762	561	525	185	2,033

1. Data represent averages of month-end strengths including both current and preceding fiscal years' figures, each weighted one half. 2. Air Force data prior to June 30, 1948, included with Army data. NOTE: Detail may not add to totals due to rounding. *Source:* Department of Defense, Selected Manpower Statistics, Fiscal Year 1980.

History of the Armed Services
Source: Department of Defense.

U.S. Army

On June 14, 1775, the Continental Congress "adopted" the New England Army—a mixed force of militia and volunteers besieging the British in Boston—by appointing a committee to draft "Rules and regulations for the government of the Army" and voting to raise 10 rifle companies as a reinforcement. The next day, it appointed Washington commander-in-chief of the "Continental forces to be raised for the defense of liberty," and he took command at Boston on July 3, 1775. The Continental Army that fought the Revolution was our first national military organization, and hence the Army is the senior service. After the war, the Continental Army was radically reduced but enough survived to form a small Regular Army of about 700 men under the Constitution in 1789, a nucleus for expansion in the 1790s to successfully meet threats from the Indians and from France. From these humble beginnings, the U.S. Army has developed, normally expanding rapidly by absorbing citizen soldiers in wartime and contracting just as rapidly after each war.

U.S. Navy

The antecedents of the U.S. Navy go back to September 1775, when Gen. Washington commissioned 7 schooners and brigantines to prey on British supply vessels bound for the Colonies or Canada. On Oct. 13, 1775, a resolve of the Continental Congress called for the purchase of 2 vessels for the purpose of intercepting enemy transports. With its passage a Naval Committee of 7 men was formed, and they rapidly obtained passage of legislation calling for procurement of additional vessels. The Continental Navy was supplemented by privateers and ships operated as state navies, but soon after the British surrender it was disestablished.

In 1794, because of dissatisfaction with the payment of tribute to the Barbary pirates, Congress authorized construction of 6 frigates. The first,

United States, was launched May 10, 1797, but the Navy still remained under the control of the Secretary of War until April 1798, when the Navy Department was created under the Secretary of the Navy with Cabinet rank.

U.S. Air Force

Until creation of the National Military Establishment in September 1947, which united the services under one department, military aviation was a part of the U.S. Army. In the Army, aeronautical operations came under the Signal Corps from 1907 to 1918, when the Army Air Service was established. In 1926, the Army Air Corps came into being and remained until 1941, when the Army Air Forces succeeded it as the Army's air arm. On Sept. 18, 1947, the U.S. Air Force was established as an independent military service under the National Military Establishment. At that time, the name "Army Air Forces" was abolished.

U.S. Coast Guard

Our country's oldest continuous seagoing service, the U.S. Coast Guard, traces its history back to 1790, when the first Congress authorized the construction of ten vessels for the collection of revenue. Known first as the Revenue Marine, and later as the Revenue Cutter Service, the Coast Guard received its present name in 1915 under an act of Congress combining the Revenue Cutter Service with the Life-Saving Service. In 1939, the Lighthouse Service was also consolidated with this unit. The Bureau of Marine Inspection and Navigation was transferred temporarily to the Coast Guard in 1942, permanently in 1946. Through its antecedents, the Coast Guard is one of the oldest organizations under the federal government and, until the Navy Department was established in 1798, served as the only U.S. armed force afloat. In times of peace, it operates under the Department of Transportation, serving as the nation's primary agency for promoting marine safety and enforcing federal maritime laws. In times of war, or on direction of the President, it is attached to the Navy Department.

U.S. Marine Corps

Founded in 1775 and observing its official birthday on Nov. 10, the U.S. Marine Corps was developed to serve on land, on sea, and in the air.

Marines have fought in every U.S. war. From an initial two battalions in the Revolution, the Corps reached a peak strength of six divisions and five aircraft wings in World War II. Its present strength is three active divisions and aircraft wings and a Reserve division/aircraft wing team. In 1947, the National Security Act set Marine Corps strength at not less than three divisions and three aircraft wings.

Service Academies

U.S. Military Academy

Source: U.S. Military Academy.

Established in 1802 by an act of Congress, the U.S. Military Academy is located on the west bank of the Hudson River some 50 miles north of New York City. To gain admission a candidate must first secure a nomination from an authorized source. These sources, and the number of cadetships allocated to each, are:

Congressional

Representatives	5 each
Senators	5 each
Other: Vice Presidential	5
District of Columbia	5
Puerto Rico	6
Am. Samoa, Guam, Virgin Is.	1 each

Military-Service-Connected Nominations
(Each Class)

Presidential	100
Enlisted members of Army	85
Enlisted members of Army Reserve/ National Guard	85
Sons and daughters of deceased and disabled veterans (approximately)	10
Honor military, naval schools and ROTC	20
Sons and daughters of persons awarded the Medal of Honor	(unlimited)

Any number of applicants can meet the requirements for a *nomination* in these categories. *Appointments* (offers of admission), however, can only be made to the number of applicants shown above.

Candidates may be nominated for vacancies during the year preceding the day of admission, which occurs in early July. The best time to apply is during the junior year in high school.

Candidates must be citizens of the U.S., be unmarried, be at least 17 but not yet 22 years old on July 1 of the year admitted, have a secondary-school education or its equivalent, and be able to meet the academic, medical, and physical aptitude requirements. Academic qualification is determined by an analysis of entire scholastic record, and performance on either the American College Testing (ACT) Assessment Program Test or the College Entrance Examination Board Scholastic Aptitude Test (SAT). Entrance requirements and procedures for appointment are described in the Admissions Bulletin, available without charge from Admissions, U.S. Military Academy, West Point, N.Y. 10996.

Cadets are members of the Regular Army. As such they receive full scholarships and annual salaries from which they pay for their uniforms, textbooks, and incidental expenses. Upon successful completion of the four-year course, the graduate receives the degree of Bachelor of Science and is commissioned a second lieutenant in the Regular Army with a requirement to serve as an officer for a minimum of five years.

U.S. Naval Academy

Source: U.S. Naval Academy.

The Naval School, established in 1845 at Fort Severn, Annapolis, Md., was renamed the U.S. Naval Academy in 1850. A four-year course was adopted a year later.

The Superintendent is a rear admiral. A civilian academic dean heads the academic program. A captain heads the 4,500-man Brigade of Midshipmen and military, professional, and physical training. The faculty is half military and half civilian.

Graduates are awarded the Bachelor of Science or Bachelor of Science in Engineering and are commissioned as officers in the U.S. Navy or Marine Corps.

The primary avenues for selection for appointment as midshipmen follow. Congressmen, the Vice President, the Mayor of Washington, D. C., and the Resident Commissioner of Puerto Rico may each have 5 midshipmen at the Academy at any one time. Ten candidates may be nominated for each vacancy. Well over half of the more than 1,300 appointments as midshipmen made annually originate from these sources.

The President appoints the 65 best-qualified sons and daughters of deceased or disabled veterans, or sons and daughters of prisoners of war or servicemen missing in action, and the 100 best-qualified sons and daughters of officers and enlisted men in the regular Armed Services. He also appoints sons and daughters of Medal of Honor holders.

The Secretary of the Navy awards 170 (85 + 85) appointments to regular and reserve personnel of the Navy or Marine Corps; 150 to congressional alternate nominees, all on a competitive, best-qualified basis; and 20 outstanding graduates of NROTC or Honor Naval and Military Schools. He may also make additional appointments each year, to bring the Brigade up to authorized strength, from among qualified congressional and competitive nominees, again on a best-qualified basis. Three fourths of these additional appointments must, by law, be congressional nominees.

There are also limited numbers of appointments available from the Philippines, Canal Zone, Virgin Islands, Guam, American Samoa, and the American republics.

To have basic eligibility for admission, candidates must be citizens of the U.S., of good moral character, at least 17 and not more than 22 years of age on July 1 of their entering year, in the top 40% of their high school class, and unmarried.

In order to be considered for admission, a candidate must obtain a nomination from one of the sources of appointments listed above. The Admissions Board at the Naval Academy examines the candidate's school record, College Board or ACT scores, recommendations from school officials, extracurricular activities, and evidence from other sources concerning his or her character, leadership potential, academic preparation, and physical fitness. Qualification for admission is based on all of the above factors.

Tuition, board, lodging, and medical and dental care are provided. Midshipmen receive $420 a month for books, uniforms, and personal needs.

For a catalogue or answers to specific questions, write: Superintendent, U.S. Naval Academy, (Attention: Candidate Guidance SIC 88), Annapolis, Md. 21402.

U.S. Air Force Academy

Source: U.S. Air Force Academy.

The bill establishing the Air Force Academy was signed by President Eisenhower on April 1, 1954. The first class of 306 cadets was sworn in on July 11, 1955, at Lowry Air Force Base, Denver, the Academy's temporary location. The Cadet Wing moved into the Academy's permanent home north of Colorado Springs in 1958.

Cadets receive four years of academic, military, and physical education to prepare them for leadership as officers in the Air Force. The Academy is authorized a total of 4,544 cadets. Each new class averages 1,500. This includes approximately 1,300 men and 200 women. The candidates for the Academy must be at least 17 but less than 22 on July 1 of the year for which they seek admission, must be a United States citizen, be single, and be able to meet the mental and physical requirements. A candidate is required to take the following examinations and tests: (1) the Service Academies' Qualifying Medical Examination; (2) either the American College Testing (ACT) Assessment Program test or the College Entrance Examination Board Scholastic Aptitude Test (SAT), and (3) a Physical Aptitude Examination.

Cadets receive their entire education at government expense and, in addition, are paid $420 monthly. From this sum, they pay for their uniforms, textbooks, tailoring, laundry, entertainment tickets, etc. Upon completion of the four-year course, leading to a Bachelor of Science degree, a cadet who meets the physical qualifications is commissioned a second lieutenant in the regular U.S. Air Force. Many go on to pilot or navigator training. For details on admissions, write: Director of Cadet Admissions, USAF Academy, Colo. 80840.

U.S. Coast Guard Academy

Source: U.S. Coast Guard Academy.

The U.S. Coast Guard Academy, New London, Conn., was founded on July 31, 1876, to serve as the "School of Instruction" for the Revenue Cutter Service, predecessor to the Coast Guard.

The J.C. Dobbin, a converted schooner, housed the first Coast Guard Academy, and was succeeded in 1878 by the barque Chase, a ship built for cadet training. First winter quarters were in a sail loft at New Bedford, Mass. The school was moved in 1900 to Curtis Bay, Md., to provide a more technical education, and in 1910 was moved back to New England to Fort Trumbull, New London, Conn. In 1932 the Academy moved to its present location in New London.

The Academy today offers a four-year curriculum for the professional and academic training of cadets, which leads to a Bachelor of Science degree and a commission as ensign in the Coast Guard.

Cadets receive appointment through nationwide competition, which includes either the December administration of the College Entrance Examination Board tests, or the American College Testing (ACT) Program tests. Applications must be submitted to the Coast Guard not later than December 15 and to the College Entrance Examination Board, 30 days prior to the tests.

Women were admitted to the Coast Guard Academy for the first time during 1976 as members of the Class of 1980. Candidates must be between 17 and 22 years of age, physically sound, and unmarried. They must agree to remain unmarried until graduation and to serve at least five years on active duty. Cadets receive $4,140 per year to cover their uniform and incidental expenses and are furnished their rations and quarters. Applications may be made to Director of Admissions, U.S. Coast Guard Academy, New London, Conn. 06320.

U.S. Merchant Marine Academy

Source: U.S. Merchant Marine Academy.

The U.S. Merchant Marine Academy, situated at Kings Point, N.Y., on the north shore of Long Island, was dedicated Sept. 30, 1943. It is maintained by the Department of Commerce under direction of the Maritime Administration.

The Academy has a complement of approximately 1,100 men and women representing every state, D.C., the Canal Zone, Puerto Rico, Guam, American Samoa, and the Virgin Islands. It is also authorized to admit up to 12 candidates from the Western Hemisphere.

Candidates are nominated by Senators and members of the House of Representatives. Nominations to the Academy are governed by a state and territory quota system based on population and the results of the College Entrance Examination Board tests.

A candidate must be a citizen not less than 17 and not yet 22 years of age by July 1 of the year in which admission is sought. Fifteen high school credits, including 3 units in mathematics (from algebra, geometry and/or trigonometry), 1 unit in science (physics or chemistry) and 3 in English are required.

The course is four years and includes one year of practical training aboard a merchant ship. Study includes marine engineering including nuclear studies, navigation, satellite navigation and communications, electricity, ship construction, naval science and tactics, economics, business, languages, history, etc.

Upon completion of the course of study, a graduate receives a Bachelor of Science degree, a license as a merchant marine deck or engineering officer, and a commission as an ensign in the Naval Reserve.

The National Guard

Source: Departments of the Army and the Air Force, National Guard Bureau.

The National Guard of the U.S. originated with the Old North and East Regiments of the Colonial Militia in Massachusetts in 1636. It is the oldest military force in the country. Guardsmen have served overseas in every major conflict in which the U.S. has participated.

As of March 31, 1981, the Army and Air National Guard totaled about 478,000 men and women serving in 3,751 Army and Air Guard units in all 50 states, Puerto Rico, the Virgin Islands, and the District of Columbia. ANG units 326 (current Mar. 31, 1981), ARNG units, 3,425.

In peacetime, the National Guard is commanded by the governors of the respective states/territories and may be called to state active duty by the governor to assist in state emergencies, disasters, and civil disturbances. During a war or national emergency, the National Guard may be called to active duty by the President or Congress. The National Guard serves as the primary source of augmentation for the Army and the Air Force.

Budget requests for fiscal 1982 are $2.4 billion for the Army National Guard and $2.2 billion for the Air National Guard. Additional money is appropriated directly for the National Guard by the states. Substantial support is also provided by state, county, and municipal governments in land, police and fire protection, maintenance of roads, and the provision of direct county and municipal fiscal support to local units.

The Army National Guard provides 30% of the Army's entire organized structure and about 44% of its combat elements. That support consists of 8 combat divisions, 22 separate combat brigades, 4 armored cavalry units, 2 special forces groups, 1 infantry group arctic recon, 16 major command headquarters, and 1,022 other separate battalions, companies, headquarters, and detachments.

Army National Guard forces are an integral part of the nation's first-line defenses. For example, the 29th Infantry Brigade in the Hawaii National Guard is a round-out brigade for the active Army's 25th Infantry Division. Under the round-out concept, National Guard units work and train with the active Army unit to which they would be assigned upon mobilization. Under the total force policy, the program for increasing readiness is continually being improved. In 1981, 98 Army National Guard units will deploy overseas to participate in realistic contingency mission-oriented training. An addi-

tional four units will participate in an exchange with units from England and Norway, and selected individuals from other units with a NATO contingency mission will participate in orientation training in Germany. In order to improve readiness of the individual soldier, the Skill Qualification Training (Test) Program has been implemented. National Guard units take part in Joint Chiefs of Staff and Army exercises with the active forces to further develop the readiness of both units and individuals.

A totally new program implemented in the Army National Guard now provides opportunities for military personnel to seek full-time active duty careers in various duty positions with the Army National Guard. The new Full-Time Manning (FTM) program offers both officer and enlisted (male and female) personnel recurring tours of active duty in an Active Duty Guard/Reserve (AGR) status which could eventually lead to a 20-year active duty retirement identical to that authorized active Army personnel. Positions are located in all States at both State and local unit level. Duties encompass the areas of training, supply, administration, and maintenance. Applicants must be members of the Army National Guard to be considered for FTM positions, and generally qualified to perform the duties required of the position for which applying.

The Air National Guard has 91 flying units and 235 specialized ground support units which, upon mobilization, would be gained by one of seven major commands of the USAF. The gaining major commands are Tactical Air Command (TAC), Strategic Air Command (SAC), Military Airlift Command (MAC), Air Force Communications Service (AFCS), Pacific Air Forces (PACAF), Air Training Command (ATC), and Alaskan Air Command (AAC).

Air National Guard flying units support four mission areas; strategic with aerial refuelers in the offensive role and in the defensive role with interceptors and defense system evaluation; general purpose with tactical fighters, reconnaissance, electronic warfare and air support; mobility with tactical airlift; and defense wide with rescue and recovery. These are supported by communications, flight facilities, tactical air control, electronics installation, civil engineering, medical, and weather units.

The National Guard is administered by the National Guard Bureau, a joint Army and Air Force office in the Pentagon. Chief of the Bureau is Maj. Gen. LaVern E. Weber of Oklahoma.

The Army National Guard offers its young men and women a broad spectrum of educational opportunities. These not only include skill training associated with their military assignment, but in many instances embrace civilian occupations as well. The list of skills is not limited to those that are equipment oriented but includes management, medical, and other career fields. Some of these educational opportunities may even be pursued in civilian institutions, specifically that of the Clinical Specialist, which is compatible with a Licensed Practical Nurse or Licensed Vocational Nurse.

Participation in the military education system by Army National Guard personnel is not limited to initial entry-skill-level training. There are opportunities available to become a qualified aviator, improve managerial and leadership abilities through attendance at courses designed for middle managers, and, finally, there are the courses offered at the prestigious Senior Service Colleges that address the needs of personnel at the executive level and positions of greater responsibilities.

If openings exist, young men and women be-tween the ages of 17 and 35 may enlist for a period of six years. In certain circumstances the period of active participation may be less than six years. Upon enlistment, they serve a minimum of 12 weeks on active duty, training with the U.S. Army or the U.S. Air Force, depending upon which branch of the National Guard they choose. The remainder of their term of enlistment is spent in part-time training with their Guard unit.

A woman between the ages of 17 and 35 who has no previous military experience may also enlist in the National Guard for a period of six years. Women in the Army National Guard will receive basic training at either Fort McClellan, Ala., Fort Leonard Wood, Mo., or Fort Jackson, S.C.; women in the Air National Guard train at Lackland Air Force Base, Tex. Advanced individual training will be received at an appropriate training center.

A Guard member receives a full day's pay of his/her military rank for each unit assembly he attends. Additionally, he receives a day's pay of his military rank for each day of his 15 days of annual training, plus any other days on active duty for training at military schools or special assignments. All such training counts toward retirement eligibility at age 60 with 20 or more years of service.

Pay Grades of Enlisted Personnel

Army ranks[1]	Air Force ranks	Marine ranks	Navy and Coast Guard ranks	Pay grades
Command Sergeant Major and Staff Sergeant Major	Chief Master Sergeant	Sergeant Major and Master Gunnery Sergeant	Master Chief Petty Officer	E-9
1st Sergeant and Master Sergeant	Senior Master Sergeant	1st Sergeant and Master Sergeant	Senior Chief Petty Officer	E-8
Sergeant 1st Class	Master Sergeant	Gunnery Sergeant	Chief Petty Officer	E-7
Staff Sergeant	Technical Sergeant	Staff Sergeant	Petty Officer 1st Class	E-6
Sergeant	Staff Sergeant	Sergeant	Petty Officer 2nd Class	E-5
Corporal	Sergeant	Corporal	Petty Officer 3rd Class	E-4
Private 1st Class	Airman 1st Class	Lance Corporal	Seaman	E-3
Private	Airman	Private 1st Class	Seaman Apprentice	E-2
Private	Airman/Basic	Private	Seaman Recruit	E-1

1. Army specialist pay grades correspond to numbers: Specialist 4 (E-4), etc. *Source:* Department of Defense

Pay Grades of Commissioned Officers and Warrant Officers

	Rank		
Army, Air Force, and Marine Corps	Navy, Coast Guard, and National Oceanic and Atmospheric Adm. (NOAA)	Public Health Service	Pay grade
General	Admiral[1]	—	O–10
Lieutenant General	Vice Admiral	—	O–9
Major General	Rear Admiral (upper half)	Surgeon General; Deputy Surgeon General; Assistant Surgeon General	O–8
Brigadier General	Rear Admiral (lower half) and Commodore	Assistant Surgeon General	O–7
Colonel	Captain	Director Grade	O–6
Lieutenant Colonel	Commander	Senior Grade	O–5
Major	Lieutenant Commander	Full Grade	O–4
Captain	Lieutenant	Senior Assistant Grade	O–3
First Lieutenant	Lieutenant (junior grade)	Assistant Grade	O–2
Second Lieutenant	Ensign	Junior Assistant Grade	O–1
Chief Warrant Officer	Chief Warrant Officer[1]	—	W–4
Chief Warrant Officer	Warrant Officer[1]	—	W–3
Chief Warrant Officer	Warrant Officer[1]	—	W–2
Warrant Officer	Warrant Officer[1]	—	W–1

1. Not applicable to National Oceanic and Atmospheric Administration (NOAA). *Source:* Department of Defense.

Monthly Basic Pay and Allowance for Quarters Rates by Pay Grades, Effective Oct. 1980

Pay Grade	Pay rates														Allowance for quarters		
	Years of service														Without dependents		With dependents
	Under 2	2	3	4	6	8	10	12	14	16	18	20	22	26	Full rate[1]	Partial rate[2]	With dependents
COMMISSIONED OFFICERS																	
O-10	$3942.90	$4081.50	$4081.50	$4081.50	$4081.50	$4238.10	$4238.10	$4562.70	$4562.70	$4889.10	$4889.10	$5216.10	$5216.10	$5541.60	$427.80	$50.70	$535.20
O-9	3494.40	3586.20	3662.40	3662.40	3662.40	3755.70	3755.70	3911.70	3911.70	4238.10	4238.10	4562.70	4562.70	4889.10	427.80	50.70	535.20
O-8	3165.00	3259.80	3337.20	3337.20	3337.20	3586.20	3586.20	3755.70	3911.70	3911.70	4081.50	4238.10	4407.90	4407.90	427.80	50.70	535.20
O-7	2629.80	2808.90	2808.90	2808.90	2808.90	2934.60	3105.00	3105.00	3259.80	3586.20	3832.50	3832.50	3832.50	3832.50	427.80	50.70	535.20
O-6	1949.40	2142.00	2281.80	2281.80	2281.80	2281.80	2281.80	2281.80	2359.20	2732.70	2872.80	2934.60	3105.00	3367.50	384.00	39.60	468.60
O-5	1559.10	1830.90	1957.20	1957.20	1957.20	1957.20	2016.90	2124.90	2267.10	2436.90	2577.00	2654.70	2747.40	2747.40	354.00	33.00	426.30
O-4	1314.30	1599.90	1707.00	1707.00	1738.20	1815.60	1939.20	2048.40	2142.00	2235.60	2297.70	2297.70	2297.70	2297.70	315.30	26.70	380.40
O-3	1221.30	1365.30	1459.50	1614.90	1692.00	1753.20	1847.40	1939.20	1986.90	1986.90	1986.90	1986.90	1986.90	1986.90	277.20	22.20	342.00
O-2	1064.70	1163.10	1397.10	1444.20	1474.20	1474.20	1474.20	1474.20	1474.20	1474.20	1474.20	1474.20	1474.20	1474.20	240.60	17.70	304.50
O-1	924.30	962.10	1163.10	1163.10	1163.10	1163.10	1163.10	1163.10	1163.10	1163.10	1163.10	1163.10	1163.10	1163.10	187.80	13.20	244.50
COMMISSIONED OFFICERS WITH OVER 4 YEARS ACTIVE SERVICE AS ENLISTED MEMBERS																	
O-3	0.	0.	0.	0.	1692.00	1753.20	1847.40	1939.20	2016.90	2016.90	2016.90	2016.90	2016.90	2016.90	—	—	—
O-2	0.	0.	0.	0.	1474.20	1521.00	1599.90	1661.40	1707.00	1707.00	1707.00	1707.00	1707.00	1707.00	—	—	—
O-1	0.	0.	0.	0.	1242.30	1288.20	1334.70	1381.20	1444.20	1444.20	1444.20	1444.20	1444.20	1444.20	—	—	—
WARRANT OFFICERS																	
W-4	1244.10	1334.70	1334.70	1365.30	1427.40	1490.40	1552.80	1661.40	1738.20	1799.10	1847.40	1907.70	1971.60	2124.90	303.60	25.20	366.60
W-3	1131.00	1226.70	1226.70	1242.30	1257.00	1348.80	1427.40	1474.20	1521.00	1566.60	1614.90	1677.30	1738.20	1799.70	270.90	20.70	333.90
W-2	990.60	1071.30	1071.30	1102.50	1163.10	1226.70	1272.90	1319.70	1365.30	1413.00	1459.50	1505.70	1566.60	1566.60	235.50	15.90	299.70
W-1	825.30	946.20	946.20	1025.10	1071.30	1117.50	1163.10	1211.10	1257.00	1303.20	1348.80	1397.10	1397.10	1397.10	212.70	13.80	275.40
ENLISTED MEMBERS																	
E-9	0.	0.	0.	0.	0.	0.	1413.60	1445.60	1478.40	1512.60	1546.20	1576.20	1659.30	1820.40	229.20	18.60	322.50
E-8	0.	0.	0.	0.	0.	1185.90	1219.20	1251.60	1284.30	1317.90	1348.50	1381.50	1462.80	1626.00	211.20	15.30	297.90
E-7	828.00	893.70	927.00	959.10	992.10	1023.90	1056.30	1089.00	1138.20	1170.60	1203.60	1219.20	1301.10	1462.80	179.70	12.00	277.20
E-6	715.20	779.70	812.40	846.60	878.10	910.20	943.50	992.10	1023.30	1056.30	1072.20	1072.20	1072.20	1072.20	163.20	9.90	255.00
E-5	627.90	683.40	716.40	747.60	796.50	828.90	862.20	893.70	910.20	910.20	910.20	910.20	910.20	910.20	156.90	8.70	234.30
E-4	603.60	637.50	674.70	721.20	756.00	756.00	756.00	756.00	756.00	756.00	756.00	756.00	756.00	756.00	138.30	8.10	206.10
E-3	580.50	612.30	636.90	662.10	662.10	662.10	662.10	662.10	662.10	662.10	662.10	662.10	662.10	662.10	123.60	7.80	179.70
E-2	558.60	558.60	558.60	558.60	558.60	558.60	558.60	558.60	558.60	558.60	558.60	558.60	558.60	558.60	109.20	7.20	179.70
E-1	501.30	501.30	501.30	501.30	501.30	501.30	501.30	501.30	501.30	501.30	501.30	501.30	501.30	501.30	103.20	6.90	179.70

1. Payment of the full rate of basic allowance for quarters for members of the uniformed services at these rates to personnel without dependents is authorized by 37 U.S. Code 403 and Part IV of Executive Order 11157, as amended. 2. Payment of the partial rate of basic allowance for quarters at these rates to members of the uniformed services without dependents who, under 37 U.S. Code 403(b) or 403(c), are not entitled to the full rate of basic allowance for quarters, is authorized by 37 U.S. Code 1009(d) and Part IV of Executive Order 11157, as amended. The Chairman of the Joint Chiefs and the military heads of each service receive $4,176.04 a month. The senior enlisted person of the Air Force, Army, Coast Guard, Marine Corps and Navy each get $2,212.80 regardless of length of service. Note: Basic pay is limited to $4,176 by Level V of the executive schedule. Source: Department of Defense.

Extra Pay for Service During Hostilities

Act of March 3, 1847, during the Mexican War, provided for $2 a month extra pay for "distinguished service." This continued beyond the war and applied in the Civil War.

In the Spanish-American War, there was a 20% increase in enlisted men's pay for war service.

In World War I, additional incentive pay was offered for all types of services. Among these items was pay for certificate of merit of $2 a month. By the law passed in 1920, the reasons for additional pay had expanded. Recipients of the Medal of Honor, Distinguished Service Cross, and Distinguished Service Medal received $2 a month extra, while each bar in lieu of these medals also added another $2 a month. Added to this was a foreign service bonus of 20%.

Act of June 30, 1944, authorized $5 a month to enlisted men qualified as expert infantrymen and $10 to those qualified as combat infantrymen. Amounts were payable for the duration of war and 6 months thereafter.

By the Act of July 6, 1945, for the duration of war and for 6 months thereafter, enlisted men entitled to wear Medical Badges received additional pay of $10 a month.

Act of July 10, 1952, authorized $45 a month for each month beginning after May 31, 1950, for which the member was entitled to receive basic pay and during which he was a member of a combat unit in Korea.

The Combat Duty Pay Act of 1952 was repealed by the Uniformed Services Pay Act of 1963, which authorized special pay for duty subject to hostile fire under certain conditions at the rate of $55 (now $65) a month.

Family Separation Allowance

Military members with dependents in grades E-4 (over 4 years of service) and above are entitled to an allowance of $30 a month in addition to allowances or per diem when on a permanent change of station, with movement of dependents not authorized and dependents not residing near his station; or be on board ship or temporary duty for more than 30 days, with dependents not residing near the temporary duty station.

A second type of family separation allowance at the rate equal to the quarters allowance for a member in the same grade without dependents is payable to a member with dependents when assigned to permanent duty outside the United States or in Alaska when government quarters, or quarters under the jurisdiction of a uniformed service, are not available to the member. Further, the member's dependents must not be residing at or near his permanent duty station and are not authorized movement to or near the permanent duty station at Government expense.

Allowances for Subsistence

Officers receive $82.58 per month. Enlisted personnel receive allowances for subsistence under the following provisions: (1) when rations in kind are not available, $4.45 per day; (2) when on leave or authorized to mess separately, $3.94 per day; (3) when assigned to duty under emergency conditions where no messing facilities of the U.S. are available, $5.89 per day.

Veterans' Benefits

Although benefits of various kinds date back to Colonial days, veterans of World War I were the first to receive disability compensation, allotments for dependents, life insurance, medical care, and vocational rehabilitation. In 1940, these benefits were slowly broadened.

The following benefits available to veterans require certain minimum periods of active duty during qualifying periods of service and, except for service personnel, are applicable only to those whose discharges are not dishonorable.

Unemployment allowances. Every effort is being made to secure employment for Vietnam veterans. Unemployment benefits are administered by the U.S. Department of Labor.

Loans. GI loans are made for a variety of purposes, such as: to buy or build a home; to purchase a mobile home with or without a lot; and to refinance a home presently owned and occupied by the veteran. The VA will guarantee the lender against loss up to 60% of a home loan with a maximum of $25,000. On mobile home loans, the amount of the guaranty is 50% of the loan with a maximum of $17,500. The interest rate may not exceed the maximum rate set by the VA and in effect when the loan is made.

Compensation and rehabilitation benefits. These are available to those having some service-connected illness or disability.

Disability compensation. The VA pays from $44 to $809 per month, and for specific conditions up to $2,308 per month, plus allowances for dependents, where the disability is rated 50% or more.

Vocational rehabilitation. Necessary training expenses, special equipment, etc., toward a definite job objective are paid for, plus a monthly allowance of up to $241, with increased amounts for dependents, in addition to compensation.

Medical and dental care. This includes care in VA and, in certain instances, in non-VA, or other federal hospitals. It also covers outpatient treatment at a VA field facility or, in some cases, by an approved private physician or dentist. Full domiciliary care is also provided where necessary. Nursing home care may be provided at certain VA medical facilities or in approved community nursing homes. Hospital and other medical care may also be provided for the spouse and child dependents of a veteran who is permanently and totally disabled due to a service-connected disability; or for survivors of a veteran who dies from a service-connected disability; or for survivors of a veteran who at the time of death had a total disability, permanent in nature, resulting from a service-connected disability. These latter benefits are usually provided in non-federal facilities. Eligibility criteria for these benefits vary, and veterans and/or their dependents or survivors should always apply in advance. Contact the nearest VA medical facility.

Dependents' Educational Assistance. The VA pays $311 a month for up to 45 months of schooling to sons and daughters of veterans who died of service-connected causes or who were permanently and totally disabled from service-connected causes or while permanently and totally disabled or who are missing in action, captured in the line of duty, or forcibly detained or interned in line of duty by a foreign power for more than 90 days. Students must usually be between 18 and 26.

Spouses of veterans whose deaths are adjudged to be service-connected, and spouses of veterans who are permanently and totally disabled due to service-connected causes or who are prisoners of war or are missing in action are also eligible for this educational benefit.

Veterans readjustment education. Veterans who served on active duty for at least 181 days after Jan. 31, 1955, but before Jan. 1, 1977, may receive monthly educational assistance under the new GI Bill for post-Korean conflict veterans, varying from $311 for single full-time students to $422 for veterans with two dependents, plus $26 for each additional dependent. Veterans and servicepersons who initially entered the military on or after Jan. 1, 1977, may receive educational assistance under a contributory plan. Individuals contribute $50 to $75 from military pay, up to a maximum of $2,700. Participants receive monthly payments for the number of months they contributed, or for 36 months, whichever is less.

Pensions. The Veterans Pension Act of 1959, effective July 1, 1960, provides a sliding-scale formula for pension benefits for wartime veterans totally disabled from non-service-connected causes. These benefits are based on need. Surviving spouses and orphans of Mexican Border service, World War II, Korea, and Vietnam veterans have the same eligibility status.

Insurance. The VA life insurance programs have approximately 7.4 million policyholders with total coverage of about $86.1 billion. Detailed information on NSLI (National Service Life Insurance), USGLI (United States Government Life Insurance), and VMLI (Veterans Mortgage Life Insurance) may be obtained at any VA Office. Information regarding SGLI (Servicemen's Group Life Insurance) and VGLI (Veterans Group Life Insurance) may be obtained from the VA Center, P.O. Box 8079, Philadelphia, Pa. 19101, or the Office of Servicemen's Group Life Insurance, 212 Washington St., Newark, N.J. 07102

Women in the Armed Services
(In thousands except percent. As of June 30 except, beginning 1977, as of Sept. 30)

Item	1960	1965	1970	1974	1975	1976	1977	1978	1979
TOTAL MILITARY	2,476	2,655	3,066	2,162	2,128	2,082	2,074	2,062	2,027
Women	32	31	42	75	97	109	119	134	151
Percent	1.3	1.2	1.4	3.5	4.6	5.2	5.7	6.5	7.4
Officers, total	317	339	402	303	292	281	276	274	274
Women	11	11	13	13	14	14	15	17	19
Percent	3.4	3.1	3.3	4.3	4.6	5.0	5.4	6.2	6.9
Enlisted personnel	2,160	2,317	2,664	1,860	1,836	1,801	1,798	1,788	1,753
Women	21	20	28	62	83	95	104	117	132
Percent	1.0	.9	1.1	3.3	4.5	5.3	5.8	6.5	7.5

Source: U.S. Department of Defense.

Blacks in the Armed Forces
(As of Dec. 31, except 1977, June 30, and 1978 and 1979, Sept. 30[1])

Item	1965	1970	1975	1976	1977	1978	1979
Total Armed Forces (1,000)	2,816	2,861	2,071	2,059	2,063	2,048	2,013
Officers (1,000)	337	389	283	279	281	274	274
Enlisted (1,000)	2,478	2,472	1,788	1,780	1,782	1,774	1,739
Black personnel (1,000)	267	279	299	314	322	353	382
Officers (1,000)	6	8	9	10	11	12	13
Enlisted (1,000)	261	271	290	303	311	342	369
Percent Black							
Officers	1.9	2.2	3.2	3.6	3.9	4.3	4.7
Enlisted	10.5	11.0	16.2	17.1	17.4	19.3	21.2

1. Includes women. Officers include warrant officers. *Source:* U.S. Dept. of Defense, Office of Equal Opportunity. Through 1972, *The Black in the Armed Forces, Statistical Fact Book,* 1972; thereafter, unpublished data.

No More Spit-Shined Military Boots

By the end of the decade, most servicemen will be wearing a new nonshiny brown leather boot that they will not be permitted to polish. According to the Department of Defense, the spit-shined boots are being eliminated because soldiers wearing them are too easily spotted by enemies using infrared lenses.

The new boots will sport a rough leather outside, a steel toe, a fiber glass-protected sole, a high-traction tread, and a speed-lacing design.

Defense Budget by Major Programs
(Current millions of dollars)

Military programs	1980	1981	1982[2]	1981–82[2]
Strategic forces	11.1	13.2	17.4	+ 4.2
General purpose forces	52.4	68.8	89.5	+20.7
Intelligence and communications	9.1	11.4	14.5	+ 3.1
Airlift and sealift	2.1	3.0	4.4	+ 1.4
Guard and reserve forces	7.9	9.9	11.3	+ 1.4
Research and development	11.8	14.2	18.5	+ 4.3
Central supply and maintenance	15.3	17.7	20.1	+ 2.4
Training, medical, other general personnel activities	29.3	35.2	41.0	+ 5.8
Administrative and associated activities	2.5	3.5	4.2	+ 0.7
Support of other nations[1]	0.6	1.0	1.3	+ 0.3
Total	142.2	178.0	222.2	+44.2

1. Excluding Military Assistance Program. 2. Figures are latest available and are subject to change. NOTE: Figures represent Total Obligational Authority (TOA), that is, the value of the direct Defense program for each fiscal year regardless of the method of financing (which could include balances available from prior years or resources available from sale of items from inventory). *Source:* Department of Defense.

Budget Outlays for National Defense Functions
(in billions of dollars, except as indicated[6])

item	1980	1979	1978	1977	1976	1975	1974	1970
Defense Dept., military	127.4	115.0	103.0	95.7	88.0	85.0	77.6	77.2
Military personnel	30.6	28.4	27.1	25.7	25.1	25.0	23.7	23.0
Percent of military	24.0	24.7	26.3	26.9	28.5	29.4	30.6	29.9
Active forces	28.2	26.3	25.1	23.9	23.3	23.2	22.1	22.0
Reserve forces	2.4	2.1	2.0	1.9	1.8	1.7	1.6	1.1
Military retirees	11.9	10.3	9.2	8.2	7.3	6.2	5.1	2.8
Operation, maintenance	40.9	36.4	33.6	30.6	27.9	26.3	22.5	21.6
Procurement[2]	27.6	25.4	20.0	18.2	16.0	16.0	15.2	21.6
Army	5.0	4.5	3.2	2.6	1.4	2.5	2.6	5.2
Navy[3]	12.6	11.8	9.2	8.5	8.0	8.1	7.3	7.9
Air Force	9.7	8.9	7.3	6.9	6.5	5.3	5.4	8.4
Research and develop	12.9	11.2	10.5	9.8	8.9	8.9	8.6	7.2
Military construction	2.1	2.1	1.9	1.9	2.0	1.5	1.4	1.2
Family housing	1.6	1.5	1.4	1.4	1.2	1.1	.9	.6
Civil defense	(7)	(7)	(7)	.1	.1	.1	.1	.1
Other[4]	−.3	−.2	−.8	−.2	−.4	−.1	−.2	−1.0
Atomic energy activities[5]	3.0	2.5	2.1	1.9	1.6	1.5	1.5	1.4
Defense-related activities[7]	(1)	.1	.2	−.1	−.1	−.9	−1.3	—
Total	130.4	117.7	105.2	97.5	89.4	85.5	77.8	78.6

1. Less than $50 million. 2. Includes other defense agencies not shown separately. 3. Includes Marine Corps. 4. Revolving and management funds, trust funds, special foreign currency program, allowances, and offsetting receipts. 5. Defense activities only. 6. For years ending June 30 except, beginning 1977, ending Sept. 30. 1980 data are estimates. 7. After 1977, Civil Defense figures are included in Defense-related activities. *Source:* Office of Management and Budget.

Department of Defense Outlays by Branch of Service

	Outlays (in millions of dollars)					Percent distribution			
Year	Total	Army	Navy	Air Force	Other	Army	Navy	Air Force	Other
1965	47,098	11,552	13,339	18,146	4,061	24.5	28.3	38.5	8.6
1970	78,349	25,147	22,656	25,233	5,313	32.1	28.9	32.2	6.8
1975	84,988	23,678	28,299	26,709	6,303	27.9	33.3	31.4	7.4
1976	87,950	25,025	30,404	28,248	4,272	28.5	34.6	32.1	4.9
1977	94,810	24,231	31,287	28,356	10,936	25.6	33.0	29.9	11.5
1978	102,682	26,250	33,573	29,344	13,515	25.6	32.7	28.6	13.2
1979	113,464	29,068	37,951	32,506	13,939	25.6	33.4	28.6	12.3

Source: Department of the Treasury.

U.S. Military Actions Other Than Declared Wars

Hawaii (1893): U.S. Marines, ordered to land by U.S. Minister John L. Stevens, aided the revolutionary Committee of Safety in overthrowing the native government. Stevens then proclaimed Hawaii a U.S. protectorate. Annexation, resisted by the Democratic administration in Washington, was not formally accomplished until 1898.

China (1900): Boxers (a group of Chinese revolutionists) occupied Peking and laid siege to foreign legations. U.S. troops joined an international expedition which relieved the city.

Panama (1903): After Colombia had rejected a proposed agreement for relinquishing sovereignty over the Panama Canal Zone, revolution broke out, aided by promoters of the Panama Canal Co. Two U.S. warships were standing by to protect American privileges. The U.S. recognized the Republic of Panama on November 6.

Dominican Republic (1904): When the Dominican Republic failed to meet debts owed to the U.S. and foreign creditors, President Theodore Roosevelt declared the U.S. intention of exercising "international police power" in the Western Hemisphere whenever necessary. The U.S. accordingly administered customs and managed debt payments of the Dominican Republic from 1905 to 1907.

Nicaragua (1911): The possibility of foreign control over Nicaragua's canal route led to U.S. intervention and agreement. The U.S. landed Marines in Nicaragua (Aug. 14, 1912) to protect American interests there. A small detachment remained until 1933.

Mexico (1914): Mexican dictator Victoriano Huerta, opposed by President Woodrow Wilson, had the support of European governments. An incident involving unarmed U.S. sailors in Tampico led to the landing of U.S. forces on Mexican soil. Veracruz was bombarded by the Navy to prevent the landing of munitions from a German vessel. At the point of war, both powers agreed to mediation by Argentina, Brazil, and Chile. Huerta abdicated, and Venustiano Carranza succeeded to the presidency.

Haiti (1915): U.S. Marines imposed a military occupation. Haiti signed a treaty making it a virtual protectorate of the U.S. until troops were withdrawn in 1934.

Mexico (1916): Raids by Pancho Villa cost American lives on both sides of the border. President Carranza consented to a punitive expedition led by Gen. John J. Pershing, but antagonism grew in Mexico. Wilson withdrew the U.S. force when war with Germany became imminent.

Dominican Republic (1916): Renewed intervention in the Dominican Republic with internal administration by U.S. naval officers lasted until 1924.

Korea (1950): In this undeclared war, which terminated with the July 27, 1953, truce at Panmunjom and the establishment of a neutral nations' supervisory commission, the U.S. and 15 membernations of the U.N. came to the aid of the Republic of South Korea, whose 38th-parallel border was crossed by the invading Russian Communist-controlled North Koreans, who were later joined by the Chinese Communists.

Lebanon (1958): Fearful of the newly formed U.A.R. abetting the rebels of his politically and economically torn country, President Camille Chamoun appealed to the U.S. for military assistance. U.S. troops landed in Beirut in mid-July and left before the end of the year, after internal and external quiet were restored.

Dominican Republic (1965): On April 28, when a political coup-turned-civil war endangered the lives of American nationals, President Lyndon B. Johnson rushed 400 marines into Santo Domingo, the beginning of an eventual U.S. peak-commitment of 30,000 troops, constituting the preponderant military strength of the OAS-created Inter-American Peace Force, and 6,500 troops, including 5,000 Americans, remained until after the peaceful inauguration of President Joaquín Balaguer on July 1, 1966, and the entire force left the country on September 20.

Vietnam: This longest war in U.S. history began with economic and technical assistance after 1954 Geneva accords ending the Indochinese War. By 1964 it had escalated into a major conflict.

This involvement spanning the administrations of five Presidents led to domestic discontent in the late 1960s. By April 1969, U.S. troop strength reached a peak of 543,400. Peace negotiations began in Paris in 1968 but proved fruitless. Finally, on Jan. 27, 1973, a peace accord was signed in Paris by the U.S., North and South Vietnam, and the Vietcong. Within 60 days, U.S. POWs were returned, and the U.S. withdrew all military forces from South Vietnam.

U.S. Casualties in Major Wars

War	Branch of service	Numbers engaged	Battle deaths	Other deaths	Total deaths	Wounds not mortal	Total casualties[1]
Revolutionary War 1775 to 1783	Army	n.a.	4,044	n.a.	n.a.	6,004	n.a.
	Navy	n.a.	342	n.a.	n.a.	114	n.a.
	Marines	n.a.	49	n.a.	n.a.	70	n.a.
	Total	n.a.	4,435	n.a.	n.a.	6,188	n.a.
War of 1812 1812 to 1815	Army	n.a.	1,950	n.a.	n.a.	4,000	n.a.
	Navy	n.a.	265	n.a.	n.a.	439	n.a.
	Marines	n.a.	45	n.a.	n.a.	66	n.a.
	Total	286,730	2,260	n.a.	n.a.	4,505	n.a.

War	Branch of service	Numbers engaged	Battle deaths	Other deaths	Total deaths	Wounds not mortal	Total casualties[1]
Mexican War 1846 to 1848	Army	n.a.	1,721	11,550	13,271	4,102	17,373
	Navy	n.a.	1	n.a.	n.a.	3	n.a.
	Marines	n.a.	11	n.a.	n.a.	47	n.a.
	Total	**78,718**	**1,733**	**n.a.**	**n.a.**	**4,152**	**n.a.**
Civil War[2] 1861 to 1865	Army	2,128,948	138,154	221,374	359,528	280,040	639,568
	Navy	84,415	2,112	2,411	4,523	1,710	6,233
	Marines	148	148	312	460	131	591
	Total	**2,213,363**	**140,414**	**224,097**	**364,511**	**281,881**	**646,392**
Spanish-American War 1898	Army	280,564	369	2,061	2,430	1,594	4,024
	Navy	22,875	10	0	10	47	57
	Marines	3,321	6	0	6	21	27
	Total	**306,760**	**385**	**2,061**	**2,446**	**1,662**	**4,108**
World War I 1917 to 1918	Army	4,057,101	50,510	55,868	106,378	193,663	300,041
	Navy	599,051	431	6,856	7,287	819	8,106
	Marines	78,839	2,461	390	2,851	9,520	12,371
	Total	**4,734,991**	**53,402**	**63,114**	**116,516**	**204,002**	**320,518**
World War II 1941 to 1946	Army[3]	11,260,000	234,874	83,400	318,274	565,861	884,135
	Navy	4,183,466	36,950	25,664	62,614	37,778	100,392
	Marines	669,100	19,733	4,778	24,511	67,207	91,718
	Total	**16,112,566**	**291,557**	**113,842**	**405,399**	**670,846**	**1,076,245**
Korean War 1950 to 1953	Army	2,834,000	27,704	9,429	37,133	77,596	114,729
	Navy	1,177,000	458	4,043	4,501	1,576	6,077
	Marines	424,000	4,267	1,261	5,528	23,744	29,272
	Air Force	1,285,000	1,200	5,884	7,084	368	7,452
	Total	**5,720,000**	**33,629**	**20,617**	**54,246**	**103,284**	**157,530**
War in Southeast Asia[4]	Army	4,386,000	30,717	7,194	37,911	201,536	239,447
	Navy[5]	1,842,000	1,535	909	2,444	10,078	12,522
	Marines	794,000	13,025	1,680	14,705	88,633	103,338
	Air Force	1,740,000	1,339	603	1,942	3,457	5,399
	Total	**8,744,000**	**47,752**	**10,386**	**57,002**	**303,704**	**360,706**

1. Excludes captured or interned and missing in action who were subsequently returned to military control. 2. Union forces only. Totals should probably be somewhat larger as data or disposition of prisoners are far from complete. Final Confederate deaths, based on incomplete returns, were 133,821, to which should be added 26,000–31,000 personnel who died in Union prisons. 3. Army data include Air Force. 4. As of Sept. 30, 1977. 5. Includes a small number of Coast Guard. NOTE: All data are subject to revision. For wars before World War I, information represents best data from available records. However, due to incomplete records and possible difference in usage of terminology, reporting systems, etc., figures should be considered estimates. n.a. = not available. *Source:* Department of Defense.

Casualties in World War I

Country	Total mobilized forces	Killed or died[1]	Wounded	Prisoners or missing	Total casualties
Austria-Hungary	7,800,000	1,200,000	3,620,000	2,200,000	7,020,000
Belgium	267,000	13,716	44,686	34,659	93,061
British Empire[2]	8,904,467	908,371	2,090,212	191,652	3,190,235
Bulgaria	1,200,000	87,500	152,390	27,029	266,919
France[2]	8,410,000	1,357,800	4,266,000	537,000	6,160,800
Germany	11,000,000	1,773,700	4,216,058	1,152,800	7,142,558
Greece	230,000	5,000	21,000	1,000	27,000
Italy	5,615,000	650,000	947,000	600,000	2,197,000
Japan	800,000	300	907	3	1,210
Montenegro	50,000	3,000	10,000	7,000	20,000
Portugal	100,000	7,222	13,751	12,318	33,291
Romania	750,000	335,706	120,000	80,000	535,706
Russia	12,000,000	1,700,000	4,950,000	2,500,000	9,150,000
Serbia	707,343	45,000	133,148	152,958	331,106
Turkey	2,850,000	325,000	400,000	250,000	975,000
United States	4,734,991	116,516	204,002	—	320,518

1. Includes deaths from all causes. 2. Official figures. NOTE: For additional U.S. figures, *see* the table on U.S. Casualties in Major Wars in this section.

Casualties in World War II

Country	Men in war	Battle deaths	Wounded
Australia	1,000,000	26,976	180,864
Austria	800,000	280,000	350,117
Belgium	625,000	8,460	55,513[1]
Brazil[2]	40,334	943	4,222
Bulgaria	339,760	6,671	21,878
Canada	1,041,080	32,412	53,145
China[3]	17,250,521	1,324,516	1,762,006
Czechoslovakia	—	6,683[4]	8,017
Denmark	—	4,339	—
Finland	500,000	79,047	50,000
France	—	201,568	400,000
Germany	20,000,000	3,250,000[4]	7,250,000
Greece	—	17,024	47,290
Hungary	—	147,435	89,313
India	2,393,891	32,121	64,354
Italy	3,100,000	149,496[4]	66,716
Japan	9,700,000	1,270,000	140,000
Netherlands	280,000	6,500	2,860
New Zealand	194,000	11,625[4]	17,000
Norway	75,000	2,000	—
Poland	—	664,000	530,000
Romania	650,000[5]	350,000[6]	—
South Africa	410,056	2,473	—
U.S.S.R.	—	6,115,000[4]	14,012,000
United Kingdom	5,896,000	357,116[4]	369,267
United States	16,112,566	291,557	670,846
Yugoslavia	3,741,000	305,000	425,000

1. Civilians only. 2. Army and navy figures. 3. Figures cover period July 7, 1937–Sept. 2, 1945, and concern only Chinese regular troops. They do not include casualties suffered by guerrillas and local military corps. 4. Deaths from all causes. 5. Against Soviet Russia; 385,847 against Nazi Germany. 6. Against Soviet Russia; 169,822 against Nazi Germany. NOTE: The figures in this table are unofficial estimates obtained from various sources. For additional U.S. Figures, *see* the tables on U.S. Casualties in Major Wars in this section.

Highest Ranking Officers in the Armed Forces

ARMY[1]
Generals: Edward C. Meyer, Chief of Staff; Bernard W. Rogers, Supreme Allied Commander, Europe; Frederick J. Kroesen; John W. Vessey, Jr.; John R. Guthrie; Donn A. Starry; Robert M. Shoemaker; Volney F. Warner; John A. Wickham.

AIR FORCE
Generals: David C. Jones, Chairman, Joint Chiefs of Staff; Lew Allen, Jr.; Richard H. Ellis; Robert E. Huyser; James R. Allen; Wilbur L. Creech; Benny L. Davis; Robert C. Mathis; Bryce Poe II; William Y. Smith; Robert T. Marsh; Charles A. Gabiel; Richard L. Lawson.

NAVY
Admirals: Thomas B. Hayward, Chief of Naval Operations; Hyman G. Rickover; Bobby R. Inman; Robert L. J. Long; Donald C. Davis; Alfred J. Whittle, Jr.; Harry D. Train II; James D. Watkins; William J. Crowe, Jr.

MARINE CORPS
Generals: Robert H. Barrow, Commandant of the Marine Corps.
Lieutenant Generals: Richard E. Carey Adolph G. Schwenk; John H. Miller; William J. White; Edward J. Bronars; Paul X. Kelley.

COAST GUARD
Admiral: John B. Hayes, Commandant.
Vice Admirals: Robert H. Scarborough, Jr., Vice Commandant; Robert I. Price, Commander, Atlantic Area; James S. Gracey, Commander, Pacific Area.

1. On March 15, 1978, George Washington, the commander of the Continental Army in the American Revolution and our first President, was promoted to the newly-created rank of General of the Armies of the United States. Congress authorized this title two years ago to make it clear that Washington is the Army's senior general. *Source:* Department of Defense.

U.S. Navy Combatant Vessels, 1981

Type	Number	Type	Number
Carriers	12	Mine warfare	3
Destroyers	80	Patrol ships	3
Cruisers	27	Amphibious warfare	60
Frigates	73	Auxiliaries	78
Submarines[1]	118	Total	454

1. 5 conventional and 76 nuclear attack submarines; 36 nuclear missile submarines; and 1 other. NOTE: As of February 1981, exact figures are classified information. *Source:* Department of Navy.

U.S. Military Sales Deliveries to Foreign Governments
(in millions of dollars)

Country	1970-1979[1]	1979	1978	1977	1960-1969
Argentina	96.6	8.4	10.9	6.8	57.7
Australia	848.2	180.0	151.8	29.0	487.5
Austria	56.2	4.3	2.0	28.2	42.1
Belgium	231.9	147.6	27.8	5.8	76.4
Bolivia	1.0	(4)	.1	(4)	.5
Brazil	184.3	8.7	8.0	8.5	61.9
Canada	605.3	76.9	73.6	66.2	243.3
Chile	150.3	8.2	11.2	56.0	18.6
China (Taiwan)	991.0	201.3	130.0	139.4	29.1
Colombia	18.3	5.1	2.0	.9	2.6
Denmark	133.9	17.7	12.2	19.9	52.0
Dominican Republic	.6	(4)	.1	(4)	.9
Ecuador	35.4	12.8	7.8	8.9	2.7
Egypt	281.9	220.5	50.8	10.5	1.6
Ethiopia	90.5	—	—	65.5	.2
France	81.2	3.5	4.4	5.2	258.9
Germany	3,252.9	266.8	231.9	316.1	2,471.1
Greece	1,175.4	127.0	127.5	261.3	22.7
Guatemala	24.6	3.7	2.4	2.2	2.0
Honduras	8.1	.9	.5	.4	.2
India	12.8	1.3	1.2	1.4	19.3
Indonesia	57.8	6.3	6.3	25.4	.6
Iran[2]	9,502.6	924.5	1,907.4	2,424.7	237.8
Israel	5,587.4	415.5	864.5	860.2	156.2
Italy	395.0	35.5	28.7	38.1	322.8
Japan	299.4	43.0	41.7	26.4	179.6
Jordan	527.6	77.7	108.4	103.9	74.7
Kampuchea	—	—	—	—	—
Korea[3]	1,259.5	417.6	414.1	177.8	2.2
Kuwait	469.3	96.3	190.7	157.8	—
Laos[3]	—	—	—	—	—
Lebanon	24.4	5.3	8.4	.4	1.7
Liberia	3.0	.6	.1	.4	.4
Libya	12.3	—	(4)	—	17.3
Malaysia	56.6	3.5	3.4	2.3	3.9
Mexico	8.3	.4	.5	3.6	7.9
Morocco	297.4	133.1	88.4	31.8	9.8
Netherlands	284.0	92.9	53.4	20.2	74.3
New Zealand	73.6	6.0	4.3	3.2	53.0
Nicaragua	3.0	(4)	.8	.4	.6
Nigeria	23.0	5.9	5.9	2.0	.4
Norway	238.4	24.3	28.7	31.4	101.9
Pakistan	218.8	61.3	46.7	39.5	40.3
Panama	4.8	.3	.2	.2	(3)
Paraguay	.3	(4)	(4)	.2	(3)
Peru	110.0	11.9	13.7	26.1	16.4
Philippines[3]	122.7	26.7	34.6	32.3	3.5
Portugal	7.6	.9	1.2	.3	5.9
Saudi Arabia	8,449.1	2,521.1	2,369.2	1,501.5	126.6
Singapore	131.8	82.2	9.8	15.2	.8
South Vietnam	1.2	—	—	—	(3)
Spain	624.2	98.1	59.1	164.9	60.0
Sweden	39.3	3.5	4.5	18.1	29.7
Switzerland	494.9	310.7	48.7	45.1	50.5
Thailand[3]	273.8	89.5	95.3	17.7	.5
Tunisia	48.0	42.0	1.6	3.2	1.6
Turkey	553.2	132.8	159.6	35.0	1.5
U.K.	1,245.5	246.5	103.9	104.2	948.4
Uruguay	15.0	1.0	1.2	5.3	1.5
Venezuela	130.1	5.8	4.4	44.3	71.9
Yemen	124.8	74.6	27.3	20.9	—
Yugoslavia	2.7	.4	.2	1.4	8.9
Zaire	44.5	4.2	10.9	7.4	1.4
Other countries	120.9	68.4	87.8	1.8	19.7
International Organizations	305.4	34.4	40.3	47.7	166.5
Total	40,471.6	7,399.4	7,732.1	7,074.7	6,718.2

1. Includes transactions for the transition quarter, July-Sept. 1976. 2. Change between 1978 and 1979 reflects values adjusted for cancellation and program reductions agreed to by the governments of the United States and Iran. 3. Includes MAP and MASF programs for military assistance deliveries. 4. Less than $50,000.—Represents zero. *Source:* U.S. Defense Security Assistance Agency.

Strengths of Military Formations, 1980–1981

Type of unit	U.S.	U.S.S.R.	China	W. Germany	India	Egypt
Division: Armored						
Men	18,900	11,000	9,200	17,000	15,000	11,000
Tanks	324	335[1]	270	300	200	300
Mechanized						
Men	18,500	14,000	12,700[2]	17,500	17,500	12,000
Tanks	216	266[1]	30[2]	250	—	190
Airborne						
Men	16,500	7,000	9,000	8–9,000	—	—
Brigade: Armored						
Men	4,500	1,300[3]	1,200[3]	4,500	6,000	3,500
Tanks	108	95[3]	90[3]	110	150	96
Mechanized						
Men	4,800	2,300[3]	2,000	5,000	4,500	3,500
Tanks	54	40[3]	—	54	—	36
Squadron: Fighter Aircraft	18–24	12–15	9–10	15–21	12–20	10–12

1. Tank strengths are for Soviet division in Eastern Europe; other divisions have fewer. 2. Infantry division. 3. Strength of a regiment, which is equivalent formation in Soviet and Chinese command structures. Particularly in West European countries, "regiment" often describes a battalion-size unit. It is so used here. *Source:* International Institute for Strategic Studies.

Military Spending and Strengths of World Nations, 1980

Country	Expenditures				Total in armed forces	Manpower				Para-military forces
	Total (millions)	Per person	% of govt spending	% of GNP[1] (1979)		Army	Navy	Air Forces	Estimated reservists[2]	
United States	$142,700	$644	23.3	5.2	2,050,000	774,000	717,000[3]	555,100	817,900	n.a.
Canada	4,240	177	n.a.	1.7	78,600[4]	12,675	5,327	15,327	29,800	—
U.S.S.R.	133,000[5]	508[5]	n.a.	11–13	3,568,000	1,825,000	433,000	475,000	5,000,000	460,000
China	57	56	n.a.	9.0	4,450,000	3,600,000	360,000	490,000	—	9,000,000
NATO (not including U.S. and Canada)										
Belgium	3,735	378	n.a.	3.3	87,900	63,000	4,400	20,500	115,500	16,300
Britain	24,448	437	10.7	4.9	329,000	167,250	72,240	89,714	265,500	—
Denmark	1,404	274	6.4	2.0	35,100	21,000	6,200	7,850	154,500	—
France	20,220	374	n.a.	3.9	494,700	321,320	69,950	103,460	342,000	85,500
Germany, West[6]	25,120	410	22.2	3.3	495,000	335,200	36,500	106,000	750,000	—
Greece	1,770	236	19.8	n.a.	181,500	140,000	17,000	24,500	290,000	126,000
Italy	6,580	n.a.	n.a.	2.4	366,000	253,000	42,000	71,000	738,000	201,000
Luxembourg	49	134	3.3	1.0	660	660	—	—	—	1,000
Netherlands	5,239	374	7.3	3.4	115,000	75,000	16,580	19,000	171,000	8,000
Norway	1,570	383	n.a.	3.1	37,000	18,000	9,000	10,000	247,000	—
Portugal	699	71	n.a.	4.0	59,500	37,000	13,040	9,500	—	36,000
Turkey	2,591[7]	58[7]	15.6[7]	9.0[7]	567,000	470,000	45,000	52,000	425,000	120,000
WARSAW PACT[8] (not including U.S.S.R.)										
Bulgaria	1,140	128	6.0	2.1	149,000	105,000	10,000	34,000	240,000	189,000
Czechoslovakia	3,520	229	7.6	2.8	195,000	140,000	—	55,000	350,000	133,500
Germany, East	4,790	285	7.5	6.3	162,000	108,000	16,000	38,000	305,000	571,500
Hungary	1,080	101	3.8	2.1	93,000	72,000	—	21,000	143,000	75,000
Poland	4,670	131	6.0	2.4	317,500	210,000	22,500	85,000	605,000	445,000
Romania	1,470	66	4.0	1.4	184,500	140,000	10,500	34,000	502,000	737,000
OTHER EUROPEAN COUNTRIES										
Austria	915	122	4.1	1.3	50,300	46,000	—	4,300	870,000	11,300
Finland	656	142	5.4	1.4	39,900	34,400	2,500	3,000	700,000	4,000
Ireland	285	86	3.3	1.6	14,800	13,370	783	637	18,600	—
Spain	4,819[7]	90[7]	n.a.	2.9	342,000	255,000	49,000	38,000	1,085,000	104,000
Sweden	3,588	432	7.7	3.3	66,100	44,500	11,800	9,800	656,500	—
Switzerland	1,832	290	18.9	1.9	18,500	580,000	—	45,000	621,500	—
Yugoslavia	3,634	164	56.9	n.a.	264,000	190,000	30,000	44,000	500,000	1,016,000

Country										
MIDDLE EAST										
Algeria	705	36	5.3	1.9	101,000	90,000	4,000	7,000	100,000	10,000
Egypt	2,168[7]	54[7]	n.a.	13.2	367,000	320,000	20,000	27,000	535,000	49,000
Iran	4,200	110	12.3	n.a.	240,000	150,000	20,000	70,000	400,000	75,000
Iraq	2,328[7]	183[7]	30.1[7]	10.9	242,500	200,000	4,250	38,000	250,000	79,800
Israel	5,200	1,333	32.0	31.1	169,600	135,000	6,600	28,000	460,000	9,500
Jordan	380[7]	125[7]	22.2[7]	12.2[7]	67,000	60,000	200	7,000	30,000	10,000
Libya	448[9]	162[9]	19.5[9]	1.8[9]	53,200	45,000	4,000	4,000	—	—
Saudi Arabia	20,704	2,518	28.1	15.0	47,000	31,000	1,500	14,500	—	26,500
Syria	4,040	459	54.9	22.1	247,500	200,000	2,500	45,000	102,500	515,500
AFRICA										
Ethiopia	385	17	n.a.	n.a.	229,500	225,000[10]	1,500	3,000	20,000	169,000
Morocco	676	34	20.7	6.0	116,500	105,000	4,500	7,000	—	30,000
Nigeria	1,702	22	n.a.	n.a.	156,000	130,000	8,000	8,000	2,000	—
South Africa	2,556	89	n.a.	3.9	86,100	71,000	4,750	10,300	155,000	165,000
Sudan	237[5]	12[5]	10.4[5]	5.4[5]	68,000	65,000	1,500	1,500	—	3,500
Zimbabwe	444	6	22.0	n.a.	13,500	12,000	—	1,500	—	42,500
ASIA (not including People's Republic of China)										
Australia	3,900	272	9.7	2.8	71,000	31,010	16,930	22,071	27,400	100,000
China (Taiwan)	1,672[5]	95[5]	48.3[5]	8.3[5]	438,200	310,000	61,200[3]	67,000	1,160,000	300,000
India	4,406	7	n.a.	3.9	1,104,000	944,000	47,000	113,000	240,000	112,000
Indonesia	2,070	14	12.3	3.4	241,800	181,000	35,800	25,000	—	—
Japan	8,960	75	4.7	0.9	241,000	155,000	42,000	44,000	39,600	38,000
Korea, North	1,300	74	n.a.	11.2	678,000	600,000	31,000	47,000	300,000	300,000
Korea, South	3,460	91	36.0	5.5	600,600	520,000	48,000	32,600	1,240,000	2,800,000
Malaysia	1,465	108	14.3	n.a.	66,000	54,000	6,000	6,000	27,000	214,800
New Zealand	362[7]	137	n.a.	1.8[7]	12,600	5,666	2,755	4,219	6,000	—
Pakistan	1,050[7]	137	n.a.	7.2[7]	438,600	408,000	13,000	17,600	513,000	109,000
Philippines	962	20	13.0	n.a.	112,800	70,000	26,000	16,800	124,000	78,500
Singapore	574	239	n.a.	n.a.	42,000	35,000	3,000	4,000	50,000	37,500
Thailand	1,092	23	20.5	4.3	230,800	155,500	32,200	43,100	500,000	44,000
LATIN AMERICA										
Argentina	1,819[7]	105[7]	n.a.	0.9[7]	139,500	85,000	35,000	19,500	250,000	42,000
Brazil	2,088[7]	18[7]	8.9[7]	1.3[7]	272,600	182,750	47,000	42,800	560,000	185,000
Colombia	215[7]	8[7]	7.8[7]	0.8[7]	65,800	53,000	9,000	3,800	500,000	50,000
Cuba	1,126	114	n.a.	n.a.	206,000	180,000	10,000	16,000	90,000	118,000
Mexico	519[7]	77	1.1[7]	0.7[7]	107,000	83,000	20,000	4,000	250,000	—
Peru	430[7]	25[7]	n.a.	3.1[7]	95,500	75,000	10,500	10,000	—	25,000
Venezuela	804	53	n.a.	n.a.	40,500	27,000	9,000	4,500	—	15,000

1. Based on local currency, GNP estimated where official figures are unavailable. 2. Reservists with recent training. 3. Includes 45,000 not identified by service. 5. 1977 figure. 6. Includes aid to West Berlin. 7. 1979 figure. 8. This section is not directly comparable to others. Difficulty of calculating suitable exchange rates makes conversion to dollars impractical. 9. 1978 figure. 10. Includes 150,000 People's Militia. NOTE: n.a. = not available. *Source:* International Institute for Strategic Studies, London.

NATO and Warsaw Pact Military Balance, 1980–1981

Category	Northern and Central Europe[1]			Southern Europe[2]		
	NATO	Warsaw Pact	(of which) U.S.S.R.	NATO	Warsaw Pact	(of which) U.S.S.R.
Ground forces available in peacetime (division equivalents):						
Armored	10	23	13	5⅔	6	2
Infantry and mechanized	13	23	13	37⅔	15	2
Airborne	4	—	—	⅔	—	—
Main battle tanks available in peacetime	7,000	19,500	12,500	4,000	6,700	2,500
Tactical aircraft in operational service:						
Fighter/ground attack	1,602	1,350	930	612	325	70
Interceptors	386	2,050	1,000	202	1,000	400
Reconnaisance	263	550	300	106	200	125

Missile strength (all theaters)	Intercontinental ballistic missiles	Submarine launched ballistic missiles	Long-range bombers
United States[3]	1,054	656	338
Soviet Union[3]	1,398	1,028	156

1. On NATO side, excludes ground forces in Portugal, Britain, and West Berlin; French forces also not included. On Warsaw Pact side, includes forces of East Germany, Czechoslovakia, and Poland, and those Soviet units normally deployed in those countries in peacetime. 2. On NATO side, includes Italian, Greek, and Turkish land forces. On Warsaw Pact side, includes Bulgarian, Hungarian, and Romanian forces and such Soviet units stationed in Hungary. 3. 1980. *Source:* International Institute for Strategic Studies, London.

Insignia and Ranks of the Armed Forces

Army, Air Force, and Marines		Navy and Coast Guard		
Insignia	Rank	Insignia	Rank	Stripes[1]
Five silver stars	General of the Army, AF	Five silver stars	Fleet Admiral	1—4—0
Four silver stars	General	Four silver stars	Admiral	1—3—0
Three silver stars	Lieutenant General	Three silver stars	Vice Admiral	1—2—0
Two silver stars	Major General	Two silver stars	Rear Admiral	1—1—0
One silver star	Brigadier General	One silver star	Commodore Admiral[2]	1—0—0
Silver eagle	Colonel	Silver eagle	Captain	0—4—0
Silver oak leaf	Lieutenant Colonel	Silver oak leaf	Commander	0—3—0
Gold oak leaf	Major	Gold oak leaf	Lt. Commander	0—2—1
Two silver bars	Captain	Two silver bars	Lieutenant	0—2—0
One silver bar	First Lieutenant	One silver bar	Lieutenant (jg)	0—1—1
One gold bar	Second Lieutenant	One gold bar	Ensign	0—1—0
Silver bar with 4 enamel bands[3]	Chief Warrant Officer (W-4)	Silver bar with 3 enamel bands[3]	Chief Warrant Officer (W-4)	0—1—0[4]
Silver bar with 3 enamel bands[3]	Chief Warrant Officer (W-3)	Silver bar with 2 enamel bands[3]	Chief Warrant Officer (W-3)	0—1—0[5]
Silver bar with 2 enamel bands[3]	Chief Warrant Officer (W-2)	Gold bar with 3 enamel bands[3]	Chief Warrant Officer (W-2)	0—1—0[6]
Silver bar with 1 enamel band[3]	Warrant Officer (W-1)	Gold bar with 2 enamel bands[3]	Warrant Officer (W-1)	0—0—1[6]

1. Of gold embroidery; first figure is number of 2-in. stripes, second is number of ½-inch strips, third is number of ¼-in. stripes. 2. The Navy rank of Commodore Admiral became effective Sept. 15, 1981, although the first Navy officer will not be promoted to the rank until Fiscal Year 1983. Until Fiscal Year 1983, the Navy will retain its system of upper-half (O—8) and lower-half (O—7) Rear Admirals. The Coast Guard will continue to have Rear Admirals at both O—7 and O—8 grades. 3. Navy and Marine Corps use same size insignia as Army when worn on shoulder straps, but miniature size on shirt collars. Enamel bands are black for Army, scarlet for Marines, medium blue for Air Force, and blue for Navy and Coast Guard. 4. One break. 5. Two breaks. 6. Three breaks.

Soviet Sub Is World's Fastest

The Soviet Union has launched a new type of submarine which can travel almost an unprecedented 50 miles per hour under water. Dubbed the *"Alpha"* by the U.S. Navy, the submarine can also dive to more than 3,000 feet or three times deeper than an American submarine.

The Soviet sub's hull is made of titanium metal which is nonmagnetic and therefore helps it to avoid detection from the air. Titanium metal is also light in weight and has a very high tensile strength which contributes to the *Alpha's* deep-diving ability.

Arms Exports and Imports, Supplier and Recipient Countries
(in millions of constant 1977 dollars)

Country	1969-71	1972-75	1976	1977	1978
SUPPLIERS					
Canada	$ 881	$ 704	$ 127	$ 70	$ 74
China, Mainland	902	1,876	148	110	130
Czechoslovakia	523	1,550	465	600	744
France	885	3,789	1,058	1,300	1,256
Germany, West	646	1,374	687	850	814
Poland	723	924	243	240	325
U.S.S.R.	6,454	20,623	5,607	6,500	6,609
United Kingdom	711	2,719	820	950	1,024
United States	15,470	23,051	6,242	6,900	6,237
RECIPIENTS—Developed countries					
Australia	391	537	84	140	232
Canada	153	668	190	170	214
Czechoslovakia	370	1,471	317	250	102
Germany, East	602	2,231	581	500	270
Germany, West	1,179	3,155	555	470	269
Hungary	184	782	222	170	242
Italy	311	612	179	150	121
Japan	322	370	190	130	158
Poland	555	1,742	412	370	149
Romania	184	668	148	170	223
Soviet Union	925	1,221	402	525	768
United Kingdom	747	470	253	150	139
United States	870	752	116	120	111
RECIPIENTS—Developing countries					
Algeria	120	191	338	460	581
Brazil	184	428	190	140	148
Cambodia	173	1,019	5	10	37
China: Taiwan	1,074	509	169	180	176
Cuba	106	341	137	100	288
Egypt	1,696	2,579	158	220	214
Greece	870	618	555	480	279
India	733	969	518	725	260
Indonesia	75	102	84	60	83
Iran	1,074	3,996	2,221	2,400	1,955
Iraq	248	2,544	1,058	1,500	1,396
Israel	996	2,712	1,058	1,100	884
Jordan	263	257	148	120	158
Korea, North	357	833	84	110	18
Korea, South	1,252	1,013	359	290	512
Laos	366	529	.n.a.	40	n.a.
Libya	270	1,437	1,058	1,200	1,768
Nigeria	62	178	52	10	37
Pakistan	294	560	201	220	158
Peru	151	434	243	420	139
Saudi Arabia	204	953	497	925	930
Spain	287	557	190	290	102
Syria	334	3,559	555	775	768
Turkey	1,157	703	328	140	195
Vietnam, Socialist Rep.	1,282	2,325	42	5	—
Vietnam, South	4,105	7,559	(2)	(2)	(2)
World, total[1]	27,917	60,669	17,352	19,300	19,177

1. Includes countries, not shown separately. 2. Absorbed by Vietnam Socialist Republic in 1976. n.a. = Not available.—
Represents zero. *Source:* U.S. Arms Control and disarmament Agency, World Military Expenditures and Arms Transfers, annual.

New Battle Tank Honors Gen. Abrams

The XM-1 is the Army's new main battle tank. It has been named the Abrams tank in honor of the late Gen. Creighton W. Abrams, Army Chief of Staff.

The Abrams tank has a crew of four, a turbine engine, weighs 60 tons, and can travel at 45 miles per hour on a road and can go 30 miles per hour cross country. The top speed of the former main battle tank, the M-60, is 30 miles per hour.

At present, the XM-1 has a 105-millimeter gun. There are plans to replace this in 1984 with a new West German 120-millimeter gun now being developed. 7,058 of the new tanks are scheduled to be built in the next ten years.

Major Religions of the World

Judaism

The determining factors of Judaism are: descendance from Israel, the *Torah,* and Tradition.

The name Israel (Jacob, a patriarch) also signifies his descendants as a people. During the 15th–13th centuries B.C., Israelite tribes, coming from South and East, gradually settled in Palestine, then inhabited by Canaanites. They were held together by Moses, who gave them religious unity in the worship of *Jahweh,* the God who had chosen Israel to be his people.

Under Judges, the 12 tribes at first formed an amphictyonic covenant. Saul established kingship (circa 1050 B.C.), and under David, his successor (1000–960 B.C.), the State of Israel comprised all of Palestine with Jerusalem as religio-political center. A golden era followed under Solomon (965–926 B.C.), who built *Jahweh* a temple.

After Solomon's death, the kingdom separated into Israel in the North and Judah in the South. A period of conflicts ensued, which ended with the conquest of Israel by Assyria in 722 B.C. The Babylonians defeated Judah in 586 B.C., destroying Jerusalem and its temple, and deporting many to Babylon.

The era of the kings is significant also in that the great prophets worked in that time, emphasizing faith in *Jahweh* as both God of Israel and God of the universe, and stressing social justice.

When the Persians permitted the Jews to return from exile (539 B.C.), temple and cult were restored in Jerusalem. The Persian rulers were succeeded by the Seleucides. The Maccabaean revolt against these Hellenistic kings gave independence to the Jews in 128 B.C., which lasted till the Romans occupied the country.

Important groups that exerted influence during these times were the Sadducees, priests in the temple in Jerusalem; the Pharisees, teachers of the Law in the synagogues; Essenes, a religious order (from whom Dead Sea Scrolls, discovered in 1947, came); Apocalyptists, who were expecting the heavenly Messiah; and Zealots, who were prepared to fight for national independence.

When the latter turned against Rome in A.D. 66, Roman armies under Titus suppressed the revolt, destroying Jerusalem and its temple in A.D. 70. The Jews were scattered in the *diaspora* (Dispersion), subject to oppressions until the Age of the Enlightenment (18th century) brought their emancipation, although persecutions did not end entirely.

The fall of the Jerusalem temple was an important event in the religious life of the Jews, which now developed around *Torah* (Law) and synagogue. Around A.D. 100 the Sacred Scriptures were codified. Synagogue worship became central, with readings from *Torah* and prophets. Most important prayers are the *Shema* (Hear) and the Prayer of the 18 Benedictions.

Religious life is guided by the commandments contained in the *Torah:* circumcision and *Sabbath,* as well as other ethical and ceremonial commandments.

The *Talmud,* based on the *Mishnah* and its interpretations, took shape over many centuries in the Babylonian and Palestinian Schools. It was a strong binding force of Judaism in the Dispersion.

In the 12th century, Maimonides formulated his "13 Articles of Faith," which carried great authority. Fundamental in this creed are: belief in God and his oneness *(Shema),* belief in the changeless

Estimated Membership of the Principal Religions of the World

Statistics of the world's religions are only very rough approximations. Aside from Christianity, few religions, if any, attempt to keep statistical records; and even Protestants and Catholics employ different methods of counting members. All persons of whatever age who have received baptism in the Catholic Church are counted as members, while in most Protestant Churches only those who "join" the church are numbered. The compiling of statistics is further complicated by the fact that in China one may be at the same time a Confucian, a Taoist, and a Buddhist. In Japan, one may be both a Buddhist and a Shintoist.

Religion	North America[1]	South America	Europe	Asia	Africa	Oceania[2]	World
Total Christian	237,096,500	175,114,000	342,630,400	95,987,240	128,617,000	18,058,500	997,503,640
Roman Catholic	133,489,000	162,489,000	177,087,300	55,077,000	47,024,500	4,395,500	579,562,300
Eastern Orthodox	4,750,000	516,000	55,035,600	2,428,000	13,306,000	409,000	76,444,600
Protestant	98,857,500	12,109,000	110,507,500	38,482,240	68,286,500	13,254,000	341,496,740
Jewish[3]	6,250,340	595,800	4,045,120	3,192,860	176,400	76,000	14,336,520
Muslim	376,200	251,500	14,945,000	428,266,000	145,214,700	90,000	589,143,400
Zoroastrian	1,250	2,100	10,000	256,000	650	1,000	271,000
Shinto	60,000	90,000	—	57,003,000	1,200	—	57,154,200
Taoist	16,000	10,000	—	31,260,000	—	—	31,286,000
Confucian	97,100	70,000	—	155,887,500	1,500	14,000	156,070,100
Buddhist	185,250	193,200	193,000	254,241,000	20,000	35,000	254,867,450
Hindu	88,500	850,000	400,000	475,073,000	1,179,800	400,000	477,991,300
Totals	244,171,140	177,176,600	362,223,520	1,501,166,600	275,211,250	18,674,500	2,578,623,610

1. Includes Central America and West Indies. 2. Includes Australia and New Zealand, as well as islands of the South Pacific. 3. Includes total Jewish population, whether or not related to the synagogue. Source: *Britannica Book of the Year, 1981.*

Torah, in the words of Moses and the prophets, belief in reward and punishment, the coming of the Messiah, and the resurrection of the dead.

Judaism is divided into theological schools, the main divisions of which are Orthodox, Conservative, and Reform.

Christianity

Christianity is founded upon Jesus Christ, to whose life the New Testament writings testify. Jesus, a Jew, was born in about 7 B.C. and assumed his public life, after his 30th year, in Galilee. The Gospels tell of many extraordinary deeds that accompanied his ministry. He proclaimed the Kingdom of God, a future reality that is at the same time already present. Nationalistic-Jewish expectations of the Messiah he rejected. Rather, he referred to himself as the "Son of Man," the Christ, who has power to forgive sins now and who shall also come as Judge at the end of time. Jesus set forth the religio-ethical demands for participation in the Kingdom of God as change of heart and love of God and neighbor.

At the Last Supper he signified his death as a sacrifice, which would inaugurate the New Covenant, by which many would be saved. Circa A.D. 30 he died on a cross in Jerusalem. The early Church carried on Jesus' proclamation, the apostle Paul emphasizing his death and resurrection.

The person of Jesus is fundamental to the Christian faith since it is believed that in his life, death, and resurrection, God's revelation became historically tangible. He is seen as the turning point in history, and man's relationship to God as determined by his attitude to Jesus.

Historically Christianity thus arose out of Judaism, claiming fulfillment of the promises of the Old Testament in Jesus. The early Church designated itself as "the true Israel," which expected the speedy return of Jesus. The mother church was at Jerusalem, but churches were soon founded in many other places. The apostle Paul was instrumental in founding and extending a Gentile Christianity that was free from Jewish legalism.

The new religion spread rapidly throughout the eastern and western parts of the Roman Empire. In coming to terms with other religious movements within the Empire, Christianity began to take definite shape as an organization in its doctrine, liturgy, and ministry circa A.D. 200. In the 4th century the Catholic Church had taken root in countries stretching from Spain in the West to Persia and India in the East. Christians had been repeatedly subject to persecution by the Roman state, but finally gained tolerance under Constantine the Great (A.D. 313). Since that time, the Church became favored under his successors and in 380 the Emperor Theodosius proclaimed Christianity the State religion. Paganism was suppressed and public life was gradually molded in accordance with Christian ethical demands.

It was in these years also that the Church was able to achieve a certain unity of doctrine. Due to differences of interpretation of basic doctrines concerning Christ, which threatened to divide the Catholic Church, a standard Christian Creed was formulated by bishops at successive Ecumenical Councils, the first of which was held in A.D. 325 (Nicaea). The chief doctrines formulated concerned the doctrine of the Trinity, i.e., that there is one God in three persons: Father, Son, and Holy Spirit (Constantinople, A.D. 381); and the nature of

Christ as both divine and human (Chalcedon, A.D. 541).

Through differences and rivalry between East and West the unity of the Church was broken by schism in 1054. In 1517 a separation occurred in the Western Church with the Reformation. From the major Protestant denominations [Lutheran, Presbyterian, Anglican (Episcopalian)], many Free Churches separated themselves in an age of individualism.

In the 20th century, however, the direction is toward unity. The Ecumenical Movement led to the formation of the World Council of Churches in 1948 (Amsterdam), which has since been joined by many Protestant and Orthodox Churches.

Through its missionary activity Christianity has spread to most parts of the globe.

Eastern Orthodoxy

Eastern Orthodoxy comprises the faith and practice of Churches stemming from ancient Churches in the Eastern part of the Roman Empire. The term covers Orthodox Churches in communion with the See of Constantinople, Uniate Churches in communion with Rome, and Nestorian and Monophysite Churches.

The Orthodox, Catholic, Apostolic Church is the direct descendant of the Byzantine State Church and consists of a series of independent national churches that are united by Doctrine, Liturgy, and Hierarchical organization (deacons and priests, who may either be married or be monks before ordination, and bishops, who must be celibates). The heads of these Churches are patriarchs or metropolitans; the Patriarch of Constantinople is only "first among equals." Rivalry between the Pope of Rome and the Patriarch of Constantinople, aided by differences and misunderstandings that existed for centuries between the Eastern and Western parts of the Empire, led to a schism in 1054. Repeated attempts at reunion have failed in past centuries. The mutual excommunication pronounced in that year was lifted in 1965, however, and because of greater interaction in theology between Orthodox Churches and those in the West, a climate of better understanding has been created in the 20th century. First contacts were with Anglicans and Old Catholics. Orthodox Churches belong to the World Council of Churches.

The Eastern Orthodox Churches recognize only the canons of the seven Ecumenical Councils (325–787) as binding for faith and they reject doctrines that have been added in the West.

The central worship service is called the Liturgy, which is understood as representation of God's acts of salvation. Its center is the celebration of the Eucharist, or Lord's Supper.

In their worship *icons* (sacred pictures) are used that have a sacramental meaning as representation. The Mother of Christ, angels, and saints are highly venerated.

The number of sacraments in the Orthodox Church is the same as in the Western Catholic Church.

Orthodox Churches are found in the Balkans and the Soviet Union also, since the 20th century, in Western Europe and other parts of the world, particularly in America.

Eastern Orthodoxy also includes the Uniate Churches that recognize the authority of the Pope but keep their own traditional liturgies and those Churches dating back to the 5th century that emancipated themselves from the Byzantine State

Church; the Nestorian Church in the Near East and India with approximately half a million members and the Monophysite Churches with some 17 million members (Coptic, Ethiopian, Syrian, Armenian, and the Mar Thoma Church in India).

Roman Catholicism

Roman Catholicism comprises the belief and practice of the Roman Catholic Church. The Church stands under the authority of the Bishop of Rome, the Pope, and is ruled by him and bishops who are held to be, through ordination, successors of Peter and the Apostles, respectively. Fundamental to the structure of the Church is the juridical aspect: doctrine and sacraments are bound to the power of jurisdiction and consecration of the hierarchy. The Pope, as the head of the hierarchy of archbishops, bishops, priests, and deacons, has full ecclesiastical power, granted him by Christ, through Peter. As successor to Peter, he is the Vicar of Christ. The powers that others in the hierarchy possess are delegated.

Roman Catholics believe their Church to be the one, holy, catholic, and apostolic Church, possessing all the properties of the one, true Church of Christ.

The faith of the Church is understood to be identical with that taught by Christ and his Apostles and contained in Bible and Tradition, i.e. the original deposit of faith, to which nothing new may be added. New definitions of doctrines, such as the Immaculate Conception of Mary (1854) and the bodily Assumption of Mary (1950), have been declared by Popes, however, in accordance with the principle of development (implicit-explicit doctrine).

At Vatican Council I (1870) the Pope was proclaimed "endowed with infallibility, *ex cathedra*, i.e., when exercising the office of Pastor and Teacher of all Christians."

The center of Roman Catholic worship is the celebration of the Mass, the Eucharist, which is the commemoration of Christ's sacrificial death and of his resurrection. Other sacraments are Baptism, Confirmation, Confession, Matrimony, Ordination, and Extreme Unction, seven in all. The Virgin Mary and saints, and their relics, are highly venerated and prayers are made to them to intercede with God, in whose presence they are believed to dwell.

The Roman Catholic Church is the largest Christian organization in the world, found in most countries. Some 8 million belong to the Uniate rites, the vast majority to the Latin rite.

Since Vatican Council II (1962–65), and the effort to "update" the Church, many interesting changes and developments have been taking place.

Protestantism

Protestantism comprises the Christian churches that separated from Rome during the Reformation in the 16th century, initiated by an Augustinian monk, Martin Luther. "Protestant" was originally applied to followers of Luther, who protested at the Diet of Spires (1529) against the decree which prohibited all further ecclesiastical reforms. Subsequently, Protestantism came to mean rejection of attempts to tie God's revelation to earthly institutions, and a return to the Gospel and the Word of God as sole authority in matters of faith and practice. Central in the biblical message is the justification of the sinner by faith alone. The Church is understood as a fellowship and the priesthood of all believers stressed.

The Augsburg Confession (1530) was the principal statement of Lutheran faith and practice. It became a model for other Confessions of Faith, which in their turn had decisive influence on Church polity. Major Protestant denominations are the Lutheran, Reformed (Calvinist), Presbyterian, and Anglican (Episcopal). Smaller ones are the Mennonite, Schwenkfeldians, and Unitarians. In Great Britain and America there are the Congregationalists, Baptists, Quakers, Methodists, and other free church types of communities. (In regarding themselves as being faithful to original biblical Christianity, these Churches differ from such religious bodies as Unitarians, Mormons, Jehovah's Witnesses, and Christian Scientists, who either teach new doctrines or reject old ones.)

Since the latter part of the 19th century, national councils of churches have been established in many countries, e.g. the Federal Council of Churches of Christ in America in 1908. Denominations across countries joined in federations and world alliances, beginning with the Anglican Lambeth Conference in 1867.

Protestant missionary activity, particularly strong in the last century, resulted in the founding of many younger churches in Asia and Africa. The Ecumenical Movement, which originated with Protestant missions, aims at unity among Christians and churches.

Islam

Islam is the religion founded in Arabia by Mohammed between 610 and 632. Its more than 600 million adherents are found in countries stretching from Morocco in the West to Indonesia in the East.

Mohammed was born in A.D. 570 at Mecca and belonged to the Quraysh tribe, which was active in caravan trade. At the age of 25 he joined the caravan trade from Mecca to Syria in the employment of a rich widow, Khadiji, whom he married. Critical of the idolatry of the inhabitants of Mecca, he began to lead a contemplative life in the deserts. There he received a series of revelations. Encouraged by Khadiji, he gradually became convinced that he was given a God-appointed task to devote himself to the reform of religion and society. Idolatry was to be abandoned.

The *Hegira (Hijra)* (migration) of Mohammed from Mecca, where he was not honored, to Medina, where he was well received, occurred in 622 and marks the beginning of the Muslim era. In 630 he marched on Mecca and conquered it. He died at Medina in 632. His grave there has since been a place of pilgrimage.

Mohammed's followers, called Moslems, revered him as the prophet of *Allah* (God), beside whom there is no other God. Although he had no close knowledge of Judaism and Christianity, he considered himself succeeding and completing them as the seal of the Prophets. Sources of the Islamic faith are the *Qur'an*, regarded as the uncreated, eternal Word of God, and Tradition *(hadith)* regarding sayings and deeds of the prophet.

Islam means surrender to the will of *Allah*. He is the all-powerful, whose will is supreme and determines man's fate. Good deeds will be rewarded in paradise and evil deeds will be punished in hell.

The Five Pillars, primary duties, of Islam are: witness; confessing the oneness of God and of Mohammed, his prophet; prayer, to be performed five times a day; almsgiving to the poor and the mosque (house of worship); fasting during daylight hours in the month of Ramadan; and pilgrimage to Mecca at least once in the Moslem's lifetime.

The practice of Holy War *(jihad)*, at first responsible for the rapid growth of the new religion, could not be maintained. Mohammed curtailed the practice of polygamy by limiting it to four wives. In modern times the position of women has improved, due to Western influence. The eating of pork and drinking of intoxicants is forbidden.

Islam, upholding the law of brotherhood, succeeded in uniting an Arab world that had disintegrated into tribes and castes. Disagreements concerning the succession of the prophet caused a great division in Islam between *Sunnis* and *Shias*. Among these, other sects arose *(Wahhabi)*. Doctrinal issues also led to the rise of different schools of thought in theology. Nevertheless, since Arab armies turned against Syria and Palestine in 635, Islam has expanded successfully under Mohammed's successors. Its rapid conquests in Asia and Africa are unsurpassed in history. Turning against Europe, Moslems conquered Spain in 713. In 1453 Constantinople fell into their hands and in 1529 Moslem armies besieged Vienna. Since then, Islam has lost its foothold in Europe.

In modern times it has made great gains in Africa.

Hinduism

In India alone there are more than 300 million adherents of Hinduism. In contrast to other religions, it has no founder. Considered the oldest religion in the world, it dates back, perhaps, to prehistoric times.

Hinduism is hard to define, there being no common creed, no one doctrine to bind Hindus together. Intellectually there is complete freedom of belief, and one can be monotheist, polytheist, or atheist. What matters is the social system: a Hindu is one born into a caste.

As a religion, Hinduism is founded on the sacred scriptures, written in Sanskrit and called the *Vedas* (*Veda*-knowledge). There are four Vedic books, among which the *Rig Veda* is the most important. It speaks of many gods and also deals with questions concerning the universe and creation. The dates of these works are unknown (1000 B.C.?).

The *Upanishads* (dated 1000–300 B.C.), commentaries on the Vedic texts, have philosophical speculations on the origin of the universe, the nature of deity, of *atman* (the human soul), and its relationship to *Brahman* (the universal soul).

Brahman is the principle and source of the universe who can be indicated only by negatives. As the divine intelligence, he is the ground of the visible world, a presence that pervades all beings. Thus the many Hindu deities came to be understood as manifestations of the one *Brahman* from whom everything proceeds and to whom everything ultimately returns. The religio-social system of Hinduism is based on the concept of reincarnation and transmigration in which all living beings, from plants below to gods above, are caught in a cosmic system that is an everlasting cycle of becoming and perishing.

Life is determined by the law of *karma*, according to which rebirth is dependent on moral behavior in a previous phase of existence. The doctrine of transmigration thus provides a rationale for the caste system. In this view, life on earth is regarded

as transient *(maya)* and a burden. The goal of existence is liberation from the cycle of rebirth and redeath and entrance into the indescribable state of what in Buddhism is called *nirvana* (extinction of passion).

Further important sacred writings are the Epics *(puranas)*, which contain legendary stories about gods and men. They are the *Mahabharata* (composed between 200 B.C. and A.D. 200) and the *Ramayana*. The former includes the *Bhagavad-Gita* (Song of the Lord), its most famous part, that tells of devotion to *Krishna* (Lord), who appears as an *avatar* (incarnation) of the god *Vishnu*, and of the duty of obeying caste rules. The work begins with a praise of the *yoga* (discipline) system.

The practice of Hinduism consists of rites and ceremonies, performed within the framework of the caste system and centering on the main socioreligious occasions of birth, marriage, and death. There are many Hindu temples, which are dwelling places of the deities and to which people bring offerings. There are also places of pilgrimages, the chief one being Benares on the Ganges, most sacred among the rivers in India.

In modern times work has been done to reform and revive Hinduism. One of the outstanding reformers was Ramakrishna (1836–86), who inspired many followers, one of whom founded the Ramakrishna mission, which seeks to convert others to its religion. The mission is active both in India and in other countries.

Buddhism

Founded in the 6th century B.C. in northern India by Gautama Buddha, who was born in southern Nepal as son to a king. His birth is surrounded by many legends, but Western scholars agree that he lived from 563 to 483 B.C. Warned by a sage that his son would become an ascetic or a universal monarch, the king confined him to his home. He was able to escape and began the life of a homeless wanderer in search of peace, passing through many disappointments until he finally came to the Tree of Enlightenment, under which he lived in meditation till enlightenment came to him and he became a Buddha (enlightened one).

Now he understood the origin of suffering, summarized in the *Four Noble Truths*, which constitutes the foundation of Buddhism. The Four are the truth of suffering, which all living beings must endure; of the origin of suffering, which is craving and which leads to rebirth; that it can be destroyed; and of the way that leads to cessation of pain, i.e., the *Noble Eightfold Way*, which is the rule of practical Buddhism: right views, right intention, right speech, right action, right livelihood, right effort, right concentration, and right ecstasy.

Nirvana is the goal of all existence, the state of complete redemption, into which the redeemed enters. Buddha's insight can free every man from the law of reincarnation through complete emptying of the self.

The nucleus of Buddha's church or association was originally formed by monks and lay-brothers, whose houses gradually became monasteries used as places for religious instruction. The worship service consisted of a sermon, expounding of Scripture, meditation, and confession. At a later stage pilgrimages to the holy places associated with the Buddha came into being, as well as veneration of relics.

In the 3rd century B.C., King Ashoka made Buddhism the State religion of India but, as centuries passed, it gradually fell into decay through splits, persecutions, and the hostile Brahmans. Buddhism spread to countries outside India, however.

At the beginning of the Christian era, there occurred a split that gave rise to two main types: *Hinayana* (Little Vehicle), or southern Buddhism, and *Mahayana* (Great Vehicle), or northern Buddhism. The former type, more individualistic, survived in Ceylon and southern Asia. *Hinayana* retained more closely the original teachings of the Buddha, which did not know of a personal god or soul. *Mahayana*, more social, polytheistic, and developing a pluralistic pompous cult, was strong in the Himalayas, Tibet, Mongolia, China, Korea, and Japan.

In the present century, Buddhism has found believers also in the West and Buddhist associations have been established in Europe and the U. S.

Confucianism

Confucius (K'ung Fu-tzu), born in the state of Lu (northern China), lived from 551 to 479 B.C. Tradition, exaggerating the importance of Confucius in life, has depicted him as a great statesman but, in fact, he seems to have been a private teacher. Anthologies of ancient Chinese classics, along with his own Analects (*Lun Yu*), became the basis of Confucianism. These Analects were transmitted as a collection of his sayings as recorded by his students, with whom he discussed ethical and social problems. They developed into men of high moral standing, who served the State as administrators.

In his teachings, Confucius emphasized the importance of an old Chinese concept *(li)*, which has the connotation of proper conduct. There is some disagreement as to the religious ideas of Confucius, but he held high the concepts handed down from centuries before him. Thus he believed in Heaven *(T'ien)* and sacrificed to his ancestors. Ancestor worship he indeed encouraged as an expression of filial piety, which he considered the loftiest of virtues.

Piety to Confucius was the foundation of the family as well as the State. The family is the nucleus of the State, and the "five relations," between king and subject, father and son, man and wife, older and younger brother, and friend and friend, are determined by the virtues of love of fellow men, righteousness, and respect.

An extension of ancestor worship may be seen in the worship of Confucius, which became official in the 2nd century B.C. when the emperor, in recognition of Confucius' teachings as supporting the imperial rule, offered sacrifices at his tomb.

Mencius (Meng Tse), who lived around 400 B.C., did much to propagate and elaborate Confucianism in its concern with ordering society. Thus, for two millennia, Confucius' doctrine of State, with its emphasis on ethics and social morality, rooted in ancient Chinese tradition and developed and continued by his disciples, has been standard in China and the Far East.

With the revolution of 1911 in China, however, students, burning Confucius in effigy, called for the removal of "the old curiosity shop."

Shintoism

Shinto, the Chinese term for the Japanese *Kami no Michi*, i.e., the Way of the Gods, comprises the religious ideas and cult indigenous to Japan. *Kami*, or gods, considered divine forces of nature that are worshipped, may reside in rivers, trees, rocks, mountains, certain animals, or, particularly, in the sun and moon. The worship of ancestors, heroes, and deceased emperors was incorporated later.

After Buddhism had come from Korea, Japan's native religion at first resisted it. Then there followed a period of compromise and amalgamation with Buddhist beliefs and ceremonies, resulting, since the 9th century A.D., in a syncretistic religion, a Twofold Shinto. Buddhist deities came to be regarded as manifestations of Japanese deities and Buddhist priests took over most of the Shinto shrines.

In modern times Shinto regained independence from Buddhism. Under the reign of the Emperor Meiji (1868–1912) it became the official State religion, in which loyalty to the emperor was emphasized. The line of succession of emperors is traced back to the first Emperor Jimmu (660 B.C.) and beyond him to the Sun-goddess *Amaterasuomikami*.

The centers of worship are the shrines and temples in which the deities are believed to dwell and believers approach them through *torii* (gateways). Most important among the shrines is the imperial shrine of the Sun-goddess at Ise, where state ceremonies were once held in June and December. The *Yasukuni* shrine of the war dead in Tokyo is also well known.

Acts of worship consist of prayers, clapping of hands, acts of purification, and offerings. On feast days processions and performances of music and dancing take place and priests read prayers before the gods in the shrines, asking for good harvest, the well-being of people and emperor, etc. In Japanese homes there is a god-shelf, a small wooden shrine that contains the tablets bearing the names of ancestors. Offerings are made and candles lit before it.

After World War II the Allied Command ordered the disestablishment of State Shinto. To be distinguished from State Shinto is Sect Shinto, consisting of 13 recognized sects. These have arisen in modern times, gaining large followings. Most important among them is *Tenrikyo* in Tenri City (Nara), in which healing by faith plays a central role.

Taoism

Taoism, a religion of China, was, according to tradition, founded by Lao Tse, a Chinese philosopher, long considered one of the prominent religious leaders from the 6th century B.C.

Data about him are for the most part legendary, however, and the *Tao Te Ching* (the classic of the Way and of its Power), traditionally ascribed to him, is now believed by many scholars to have originated in the 3rd century B.C. The book is composed in short chapters, written in aphoristic rhymes. Central are the word *Tao*, which means way or path and, in a deeper sense, signifies the principle that underlies the reality of this world and manifests itself in nature and in the lives of men, and the word *Te* (power).

The virtuous man draws power from being absorbed in *Tao*, the ultimate reality within an ever-changing world. By non-action and keeping away from human striving it is possible for man to live in harmony with the principles that underlie and govern the universe. *Tao* cannot be comprehended by reason and knowledge, but only by inward quiet.

Besides the *Tao Te Ching*, dating from approximately the same period, there are two Taoist works, written by Chuang Tse and Lieh Tse.

Theoretical Taoism of this classical philosophical movement of the 4th and 3rd centuries B.C. in China differed from popular Taoism, into which it gradually degenerated. The standard of theoretical Taoism was maintained in the classics, of course, and among the upper classes it continued to be alive until modern times.

Religious Taoism is a form of religion dealing with deities and spirits, magic and soothsaying. In the 2nd century A.D. it was organized with temples, cult, priests, and monasteries and was able to hold its own in the competition with Buddhism that came up at the same time.

After the 7th century A.D., however, Taoist religion further declined. Split into numerous sects, which often operate like secret societies, it has become a syncretistic folk religion in which some of the old deities and saints live on.

History of Leading Religious Groups in the United States

(50,000 members or over)

Source: Yearbook of American and Canadian Churches, 1981.

BAPTIST

American Baptist Association: A group of independent Missionary Baptist Churches, mainly in the South, Southeast, and Southwest, organized in 1905. Members (1980): 1,500,000. Headquarters: 4605 N. State Line Ave., Texarkana, Tex. 75501.

American Baptist Churches in the U.S.A.: Formerly known as the Northern Baptist Convention and the American Baptist Convention, this body changed its name in 1973. Although national missionary organizational developments began in 1814 with the establishment of the American Baptist Foreign Mission Society, the Convention was not formed until 1907. Members (1978): 1,271,688. Headquarters: Valley Forge, Pa. 19481.

Baptist General Conference: Formerly known as the Swedish Baptist General Conference of America. It has operated as a general conference since 1879. Members (1979): 126,800. Headquarters: 2002 S. Arlington Heights Rd., Arlington Heights, Ill. 60005.

Baptist Missionary Association of America: Formerly called the North American Baptist Association. It was organized in 1950 in Little Rock, Ark. Members (1979): 226,290. Office of president: Rt. 2, Box 272, Corinth, Miss. 38834.

Conservative Baptist Association of America: Organized in 1947. Adherents regard the Bible as infallible. Local churches are independent, autonomous, and free from ecclesiastical or political authority. Members (1979): 225,000. Headquarters: Geneva Rd., Box 66, Wheaton, Ill. 60187.

Free Will Baptists: A body of evangelical Baptists, organized in 1727 in the South and 1780 in the North. Members (1979): 231,167. Headquarters: 1134 Murfreesboro Rd., Nashville, Tenn. 37217.

General Association of Regular Baptist Churches: Founded in 1932 in Chicago by a group of churches which had withdrawn from the Northern Baptist Convention (now the American Baptist Convention) because of doctrinal differences. Members (1980): 244,000. Headquarters: 1300 N. Meacham Rd., Schaumburg, Ill. 60195.

General Baptists (General Association of): An Arminian group of Baptists, organized in England in 1607 and transplanted to the colonies in 1714. It died out along the Seaboard, but revived in the Midwest in 1823. Members (1979): 73,046. Office of moderator: 100 Stinson Dr., Poplar Bluff, Mo. 63901.

National Baptist Convention, U.S.A.: The older and parent convention of Black Baptists. This body is to be distinguished from the National Baptist Convention of America, usually referred to as the "unincorporated" body. Members (1958): 5,500,000. Office of president: 405 E. 31st St., Chicago, Ill. 60616.

National Baptist Convention of America: This is a body usually referred to as the "unincorporated" convention, not to be confused with the "incorporated" National Baptist Convention, U.S.A., Inc., from which this body withdrew. Organized in 1880. Members (1956): 2,668,799. Office of president: 954 Kings Rd., Jacksonville, Fla. 32204.

National Primitive Baptist Convention: A group of Baptists having local associations and a National Convention. Organized in 1907. Members (1975): 250,000. Headquarters: Box 2355, Tallahassee, Fla.

North American Baptist Association: *See* Baptist Missionary Association of America.

Primitive Baptists: A large group of Baptists, largely through the South, who are opposed to all centralization and to modern missionary societies. Members (1960): 72,000. Headquarters: Cayce Publishing Co., S. Second St., Thornton, Ariz., 71766.

Progressive National Baptist Convention: A body that held its organizational meeting in Cincinnati in 1961 and its first annual session in Philadelphia in 1962. Members (1967): 521,692. Office of president: Savannah Grove Baptist Church, 312 S. Main St., Sumter, S.C. 29150.

U. S. Church Membership

Religious group	Members
Protestant bodies and others	72,814,971
Roman Catholics	49,812,178
Jewish congregations[1]	5,860,900
Eastern churches	3,821,655
Old Catholic, Polish National Catholic, Armenian churches	936,801
Buddhist Churches of America	60,000
Miscellaneous	163,185
Total[2]	133,469,690

1. Includes Orthodox, Conservative, and Reform. 2. As reported in the *1981 Yearbook* from statistics furnished by 219 religious bodies in the United States.

Southern Baptist Convention: In 1845, Southern Baptists withdrew from the General Missionary Convention over the question of slavery and other matters and formed the Southern Baptist Convention. Members (1979): 13,372,757. Office of recording secretary: 127 9th Ave. N., Nashville, Tenn. 37234.

United Free Will Baptist Church: A body which set up its organization in 1870. Members (1952): 100,000. Headquarters: Kinston College, 1000 University St., Kinston, N.C. 28501.

CATHOLIC AND ORTHODOX

American Carpatho-Russian Orthodox Greek Catholic Church: This church is a self-governing diocese in communion with the Ecumenical Patriarchate of Constantinople. On Sept. 19, 1938, the late Patriarch Benjamin I canonized the diocese in the name of the Orthodox Church of Christ. Members (1976): 100,000. Headquarters: Johnstown, Pa. 15906.

Antiochian Orthodox Christian Archdiocese of North America: Formed in 1975 by merger of the Antiochian Orthodox Christian Archdiocese of New York and All North America (formerly the Syrian Antiochian Orthodox Archdiocese of New York and North America) and the Antiochian Orthodox Archdiocese of Toledo, Ohio, and Dependencies in North America. The new Archdiocese is under the jurisdiction of the Patriarch of Antioch. Members (1977): 152,000. Headquarters: 358 Mountain Rd., Englewood, N.J. 07631.

Armenian Apostolic Church of America: The Armenian Church divided into two separate dioceses in 1933 because of a dispute regarding the political activities of the prelate at that time, and because of the status of the church in Soviet Armenia. Since 1956, this diocese has been under the jurisdiction of the Holy See of Cilicia, Beirut, Lebanon. Members (1972): 125,000. Headquarters: 138 E. 39th St., New York, N.Y. 10016.

Armenian Church of America, Diocese of the (including Diocese of California): The American branch of the Ancient Church of Armenia. Established in the U. S. in 1889. Diocesan organization is under the jurisdiction of the Holy See of Etchmiadzin, Armenia, U.S.S.R. Members (1979): 450,000. Headquarters: St. Vartan Cathedral, 630 Second Ave., New York, N.Y. 10016.

Bulgarian Eastern Orthodox Church (Diocese of North and South America and Australia): A Synod of the Bulgarian Eastern Orthodox Church, established as the Bulgarian Orthodox Mission in 1909. Became a canonical metropolitan archdiocese in 1947. Members (1971): 86,000. Headquarters: 312 W. 101st St., New York, N.Y. 10025; 1953 Stockbridge Rd., Akron, Ohio, 44313.

Coptic Orthodox Church: Part of the ancient Coptic Orthodox Church of Egypt. Egyptian immigrants have formed many parishes in the United States. Members (1980): 100,000. Office of correspondent: 427 West Side Ave., Jersey City, N.J. 07304.

Greek Orthodox Archdiocese of North and South America: Greek-speaking Orthodox Christians have parishes in the U. S., Canada, and South America. These are under the Ecumenical Patriarchate of Constantinople. Members (1977): 1,950,-000. Headquarters: 8–10 E. 79th St., New York, N.Y. 10021.

North American Old Roman Catholic Church: A body with the doctrine of the Old Catholics; identical with the Roman Catholic Church in most worship and discipline. It is not under Papal jurisdiction. Members (1979): 69,412. Office of presiding archbishop: 4200 N. Kedvale Ave., Chicago, Ill. 60641.

Orthodox Church in America (The Russian Orthodox Greek Catholic Church of America): This body entered Alaska in 1792. In 1872, its headquarters were moved from Sitka to San Francisco and, in 1905, to New York. Members (1978): 1,000,000. Office of primate: Box 675, Syosset, N.Y. 11791.

Polish National Catholic Church of America: After long dissatisfaction with Roman Catholic administration and ideology, this group was organized in 1897. Members. (1960): 282,411. Headquarters: 529 E. Locust St., Scranton, Pa. 18505.

Roman Catholic Church: The largest single group of Christians in the U. S., the Roman Catholic Church is under the spiritual leadership of the Pope. This group dates back to the priests who accompanied Columbus on his second voyage to the New World. A settlement, later discontinued, was made at St. Augustine, Fla. The continuous history of this Church in the colonies began at St. Mary's in 1634, in Maryland. Members (1979): 49,812,178. National Conference of Catholic Bishops, 1312 Massachusetts Ave., N.W., Washington, D.C. 20005.

Russian Orthodox Church in the U.S.A., Patriarchial Parishes of the: This autonomous body is the direct canonical successor of the Orthodox Catholic mission established in Alaska by the Russian Orthodox Church in 1793. It is under the spiritual jurisdiction of the Patriarch of Moscow and all Russia, His Holiness Pimen. In 1962 an administration was established for the Orthodox Mission in Puerto Rico and the Spanish-speaking people in the United States. Members (1975): 51,500. Headquarters: St. Nicholas Patriarchal Cathedral, 15 E. 97th St., New York, N.Y. 10029.

Russian Orthodox Church Outside Russia: The governing body was set up in Constantinople. In 1950, it came to the U. S. Members (1955): 55,000. Headquarters: 75 E. 93rd St., New York, N.Y. 10028.

Serbian Eastern Orthodox Church for the U.S.A. and Canada: This body of the Eastern Orthodox Church is autonomous. Members (1967): 65,000. Chancery: St. Sava Monastery, Box 519, Libertyville, Ill. 60048.

Syrian Antiochian Orthodox Archdiocese of New York and North America: *See* Antiochian Orthodox Christian Archdiocese of New York and All North America.

Ukrainian Orthodox Church in the U.S.A.: This church was organized in the U.S. in 1919. Members (1966): 87,745. Headquarters: South Bound Brook, N.J. 08880.

JEWISH

Jews arrived in the colonies before 1650. The first congregation is recorded in 1654, in New York City, the Shearith Israel (Remnant of Israel). Members (1979): 5,860,900.

Following are the major Jewish organizations:
Central Conference of American Rabbis (Reform): 790 Madison Ave., New York, N.Y. 10021
Rabbinical Alliance of America (Orthodox): 156 Fifth Ave., New York, N.Y. 10011
Rabbinical Assembly (Conservative): 3080 Broadway, New York, N.Y. 10027
Rabbinical Council of America (Orthodox): 1250 Broadway, New York, N.Y. 10001
Synagogue Council of America: 432 Park Ave. South, New York, N.Y. 10016
Union of American Hebrew Congregations (Reform): 838 Fifth Ave., New York, N.Y. 10021
Union of Orthodox Jewish Congregations of America: 116 E. 27th St., New York, N.Y. 10016
Union of Orthodox Rabbis of the United States and Canada: 235 E. Broadway, New York, N.Y. 10002
United Synagogue of America (Conservative): 155 Fifth Ave., New York, N.Y. 10010

LUTHERAN

American Lutheran Church: This church is the result of the merger in 1960 of the American Lutheran Church, the Evangelical Lutheran Church, and the United Evangelical Lutheran Church. In 1963, the Lutheran Free Church merged with The American Lutheran Church. Members (1979): 2,362,685. Headquarters: 422 S. Fifth St., Minneapolis, Minn. 55415.

Evangelical Lutheran Churches, Association of: Formed in 1976, this group is made up mainly of former affiliates of the Lutheran Church-Missouri Synod, plus some new and some formerly independent congregations. Its members have joined together to be in mission and ministry. Members (1979): 113,942. Headquarters: 12015 Manchester Rd., St. Louis, Mo. 63131.

Lutheran Church—Missouri Synod: This body, the largest constituent part of the Evangelical Lutheran Synodical Conference of North America, was organized in 1847. It is the leader in the conservative group among the Lutherans. Members (1979): 2,623,181. Headquarters: 500 N. Broadway, St. Louis, Mo. 63102.

Lutheran Church in America: This body was organized in 1962 by the consolidation of the American Evangelical Lutheran Church (1874), the Augustana Evangelical Lutheran Church (1860), the Finnish Evangelical Lutheran Church (1890), and the United Lutheran Church in America (1918). Members (1979): 2,921,090. Headquarters: 231 Madison Ave., New York, N.Y. 10016.

Wisconsin Evangelical Lutheran Synod: This body was organized in Wisconsin in 1850. Members (1979): 404,564. Office of president: 3512 W. North Ave., Milwaukee, Wis. 53208.

METHODIST

African Methodist Episcopal Church: This church began in 1787 in Philadelphia when persons in a Methodist Episcopal Church withdrew. In 1816, the denomination was started. Members (1979): 1,970,000. Office of senior bishop: 1002 Kirkwood Ave., Nashville, Tenn. 37203.

African Methodist Episcopal Zion Church: This group was organized in 1796, having withdrawn from the John Street Methodist Church, New York.

Members (1979): 1,125,176. Office of president: 6401 Sunset Lane, Indianapolis, Ind. 46260.

Christian Methodist Episcopal Church: In 1870, the General Conference of the M.E. Church, South, approved the request of its black membership for the formation of their conferences into a separate body. Members (1965): 466,718. Office of secretary: Box 74, Memphis, Tenn. 38101.

Free Methodist Church of North America: This body, organized in 1860, grew out of a movement in the Genesee Conference of the Methodist Episcopal Church about 1850 towards a more original Methodism. Members (1979): 67,394. Headquarters: 901 College Ave., Winona Lake, Ind. 46590.

United Methodist Church: The United Methodist Church was formed in April, 1968, by the union of the Methodist Church and the Evangelical United Brethren Church. The two churches shared a common historical and spiritual heritage. The Methodist Church resulted in 1939 from the unification of three branches of Methodism—the Methodist Episcopal Church; the Methodist Episcopal Church South; and the Methodist Protestant Church. The Methodist movement began in 18th-century England under the preaching of John Wesley, but the so-called Christmas Conference of 1784 in Baltimore is regarded as the date on which the organized Methodist Church was founded as an ecclesiastical organization. The Evangelical United Brethren Church was formed in 1946 with the merger of the Evangelical Church and the Church of the United Brethren in Christ, both of which had their beginnings in Pennsylvania in the evangelistic movement of the 18th and early 19th centuries. Members (1979): 9,653,711. Office of Secretary of General Conference, Perkins School of Theology, Southern Methodist University, Dallas, Tex. 75222.

PRESBYTERIAN

Cumberland Presbyterian Church: An outgrowth of the Great Revival of 1800, the Cumberland Presbytery was organized in 1810 in Tennessee. A union with the Presbyterian Church, U.S.A., in 1906, was only partially successful, and the Cumberland Presbyterian Church continued as a separate denomination. Members (1979): 94,574. Office of moderator: 907 E. Main, Murfreesboro, Tenn. 37130.

Presbyterian Church in America: Formed in Birmingham, Ala., in 1973 after separating from the Presbyterian Church in the United States, this body believes the Bible is the only infallible rule of faith and practice. It is committed to the Reformed Faith as set forth in the Westminster Confession and Catechisms. Members (1979): 86,885. Office of stated clerk: Box 312, Brevard, N.C. 28712.

Presbyterian Church in the United States: This body is a branch of the Presbyterian Church established in separate existence in 1861. Members (1979): 852,711. Headquarters: 341 Ponce de Leon Ave., NE, Atlanta, Ga. 30365.

United Presbyterian Church in the United States of America: This group was formed in 1958 by a merger of the Presbyterian Church in the U.S.A. (dating from 1706) and the United Presbyterian Church of North America (established in 1858). Members (1979): 2,477,364. Headquarters: 475 Riverside Dr., New York, N.Y. 10115.

OTHER RELIGIOUS BODIES

Apostolic Overcoming Holy Church of God: A black body incorporated in Alabama in 1919. It is evangelistic in purpose and emphasizes sanctification, holiness, and divine healing. Members (1956): 75,000. Office of secretary, 909 Jasper Rd. W., Birmingham, Ala. 35204.

Assemblies of God: A pentecostal, evangelical, missionary denomination which grew out of the spiritual revivals of the early 1900's. The organization is composed of self-governing churches. Founded in Arkansas in 1914. Members (1979): 1,629,014. Headquarters: 1445 Boonville Ave., Springfield, Mo. 65802.

Baháʼí Faith: Baháís are followers of Baháʼuʼlláh (1817–1892), whose religion upholds the basic principle of progressive revelation, religious unity and a new world order. There is a spiritual and administrative world center in Haifa, Israel. Headquarters, 536 Sheridan Rd., Wilmette, Ill. 60091.

Buddhist Churches of America: Organized in 1914 as the Buddhist Mission of North America, this body was incorporated in 1942 under the present name and represents the Jodo Shinshu Sect of Buddhism in this country. Members (1975): 60,000. Headquarters: 1710 Octavia St., San Francisco, Calif. 94109.

Christian and Missionary Alliance: An evangelical, evangelistic, and missionary movement organized in 1887. It stresses "the deeper Christian life and consecration to the Lord's service." Members (1979): 173,986. Headquarters: 350 N. Highland Ave., Nyack, N.Y. 10960.

Christian Congregation, The: Incorporated in 1887, denomination provides ministerial affiliation for independent clergymen. Members (1979): 83,199. Office of general superintendent: 804 W. Hemlock St., LaFollette, Tenn. 37766.

Christian Church (Disciples of Christ): In the revival period of the early nineteenth century, a movement resulted in the establishment of a fellowship called "Christians" or "Disciples." This movement calls for the reunion of the church on the basis of a return to New Testament faith and order. It is congregational in government. Members (1979): 1,213,061. Headquarters: 222 S. Downey Ave., Box 1986, Indianapolis, Ind. 46206.

Christian Churches and Churches of Christ: This fellowship, congregational in polity, has its origin in the movement to "restore the New Testament church in doctrine, ordinances and life." Members (1979): 1,054,266. North American Christian Convention, Box 39456, Cincinnati, Ohio 45231.

Christian Reformed Church in North America: A group of Dutch Calvinists which dissented from the Reformed Church in America in 1857 and which was strengthened by later accessions from the same source and by immigration. Members (1979): 212,700. Office of stated clerk: William P. Brink, 2850 Kalamazoo Ave., S.E., Grand Rapids, Mich. 49560.

Church of Christ, Scientist: Founded by Mary Baker Eddy in 1879 to reinstate the healing power of original Christianity. As defined by Mrs. Eddy, her religion is the scientific system of divine healing.[1]

Headquarters: Christian Science Church Center, Boston, Mass. 02115.

Church of God: Inaugurated by Bishop A. J. Tomlinson, who served as General Overseer 1903–43. Episcopal in administration. Members (1978): 75,890. Headquarters: 2504 Arrow Wood Dr., S.E., Huntsville, Ala. 35803.

Church of God (Anderson, Ind.): This group is one of the largest of the groups which have taken the name "Church of God." It originated about 1880 and emphasizes Christian unity. Members (1979): 175,113. Headquarters: Box 2420, Anderson, Ind. 46011.

Church of God (Cleveland, Tenn.): This church is one of the large groups which use the name "Church of God." Organized in 1886 in Tennessee as the Christian Union, it was reorganized in 1902 as the Holiness Church, and in 1907 under its present name. Members (1979): 411,385. Headquarters: Keith St. at 25th., N.W., Cleveland, Tenn. 37311.

Church of God in Christ: Organized in Arkansas in 1895, by C. P. Jones and C. H. Mason, who believed there was no salvation without holiness; incorporated 1897. Members (1965): 425,000. Headquarters: 938 Mason St., Memphis, Tenn. 38126.

Church of God in Christ, International: Organized in 1969 in Kansas City, Mo., by 14 bishops of the Church of God in Christ of Memphis, Tenn., after disagreement over polity and governmental authority. Church is Wesleyan in theology. Members (1971): 501,000. Headquarters: 170 Adelphi St., Brooklyn, N.Y. 11025.

Church of God of Prophecy: Organized in 1903 at Murphy, N. C. Doctrine stresses justification by faith and the second coming of Christ. Members (1979): 227,850. Headquarters: Bible Place, Cleveland, Tenn. 37311.

Church of the Brethren: German pietists from Krefeld, Germany, under the leadership of Peter Becker, entered the colonies in 1719, and settled at Germantown, Philadelphia, Pa. They hold to the principles of nonviolence, temperance, and the expression of religion through the good life. Members (1979): 172,115. Headquarters: 1451 Dundee Ave., Elgin, Ill. 60120.

Church of the Nazarene: One of the larger holiness bodies, organized in Pilot Point, Tex., in 1908. It is in general accord with the early doctrines of Methodism and emphasizes entire sanctification. Members (1979): 474,820. Headquarters: 6401 The Paseo, Kansas City, Mo. 64131.

Churches of Christ: This body is made up of a large group of churches, formerly reported with the Disciples of Christ but, since the religious census of 1906, reported separately. They are strictly congregational and have no organization larger than the local congregation. Members (1979): 1,600,000.

Community Churches, National Council of: This body was formed in 1946 by the merger of the

1. Membership figure not available. The manual of the church forbids "the numbering of people and the reporting of such statistics for publication."

Biennial Council of Community Churches, a black group, with white churches which had the name of the present Council. Its members are ecumenically minded, congregationally governed, non-creedal Protestant churches. Members (1979): 190,000. Headquarters: 89 E. Wilson Bridge Rd., Worthington, Ohio, 43085.

Congregational Christian Churches: See United Church of Christ.

Congregational Christian Churches, National Association of: Organized in Detroit, Mich., in 1955 to continue the Congregational way of faith and order in church life. It has no doctrinal requirements, and participation by member churches is voluntary. Members (1980): 100,000. Headquarters: Box 1620, Oak Creek, Wis. 53154.

Disciples of Christ: See Christian Church.

Episcopal Church, The: This group entered the colonies with the earliest settlers as the Church of England. It became autonomous, adopted its present name in 1789. It is an integral part of the Anglican Communion. In 1967, the General Convention adopted "The Episocal Church" as an alternate name. Members (1979): 2,841,350. Headquarters: 815 Second Ave., New York, N.Y. 10017.

Evangelical and Reformed Church: See United Church of Christ.

Evangelical Covenant Church of America: This church has its roots in historical Christianity as it emerged in the Protestant Reformation in the biblical instruction of the Lutheran State Church of Sweden. Organized in 1885 in Chicago. Prior to 1957, it was known as the Evangelical Mission Covenant Church of America. Members (1979): 76,092. Headquarters: 5101 N. Francisco Ave., Chicago, Ill. 60625.

Evangelical Free Church of America: Organized in the 1880's in Boone, Iowa, as the Swedish Evangelical Free Mission. Later the name was changed to the Evangelical Free Church of America. In 1950, the Evangelical Free Church Association merged with this group. Members (1979): 77,592. Headquarters: 1515 E. 66th St., Minneapolis, Minn. 55423.

Evangelical United Brethren Church: See United Methodist Church under Methodist Churches.

Friends United Meeting: The Five Years Meeting of Friends was formed in 1902 by 11 Yearly Meetings entering into a loose confederation. Since then, two of the original Yearly Meetings have withdrawn (Kansas and Oregon) and two American and three Yearly Meetings outside the U. S. have joined. In 1965, the name was changed to Friends United Meeting. Members (1979): 61,366. Office of presiding clerk: 101 Quaker Hill Dr., Richmond, Ind. 47374.

Independent Fundamental Churches of America: Organized in 1930 by representatives of various independent churches. Members (1980): 120,446. Headquarters: 1860 Mannheim Rd., Westchester, Ill. 60153.

International Church of the Foursquare Gospel: An evangelistic missionary body organized by Aimee Semple McPherson in 1927. The parent church is Angelus Temple, 1100 Glendale Blvd., Los Angeles, Calif. 90026. Members (1963): 89,215.

Jehovah's Witnesses: A group calling themselves primitive Christians. They believe that the Kingdom under Christ will replace all earthly governments. Members (1979): 526,961. Headquarters: 124 Columbia Heights, Brooklyn, N.Y. 11201.

Latter-day Saints, Church of Jesus Christ of: Organized in 1830. A group in which the Bible, the Book of Mormon, the Doctrine and Covenants, and the Pearl of Great Price are regarded as the word of God. Their belief is summed up in 13 Articles of Faith written by Joseph Smith. Members (1979): 2,706,000. Headquarters: 50 E. North Temple St., Salt Lake City, Utah, 84111.

Latter-day Saints, Reorganized Church of Jesus Christ of: A division among the Latter-day Saints (non-Mormon) occurred on the death of Joseph Smith in 1844. His son, Joseph Smith, became presiding officer of this group, which has headquarters at Independence, Mo. Members (1979): 188,580. Headquarters: the Auditorium, Box 1059, Auditorium, Independence, Mo. 64051.

Mennonite Church: The largest group of the Mennonites who began arriving in the U. S. in 1683, settling in Germantown, Pa. They derive their name from Menno Simons, born 1496. Members (1979): 98,027. Headquarters: 528 E. Madison St., Lombard, Ill. 60148.

Moravian Church in America (Unitas Fratrum): In 1735, Moravian missionaries of the pre-Reformation faith of John Hus came to Georgia, in 1740 to Pennsylvania, and in 1753 to North Carolina. Members: Northern Province (1979): 32,588. Headquarters: 69 W. Church St., P.O. Box 1245, Bethlehem, Pa. 18018; Southern Province (1979): 21,058. Headquarters: 459 S. Church St., Winston-Salem, N.C. 27108.

Old Order Amish Church: Members of this group worship in private homes and adhere to the older forms of worship and attire. Members (1979): 80,250.

Open Bible Standard Churches: An evangelical, full gospel denomination emphasizing evangelism, missions, and the message of the Open Bible. Members (1980): 60,000. Headquarters: 2020 Bell Ave., Des Moines, Iowa 50315.

Pentecostal Church of God: Organized in 1919 at Chicago, Ill. The first convention was held in October, 1933. Members (1977): 110,870. Headquarters: Messenger Plaza, 221 Main St., Joplin, Mo. 64801.

Pentecostal Holiness Church: This body grew out of the holiness movement in the South and Middle West from 1895 to 1900. Members (1977): 86,103. Headquarters: Box 12609, Oklahoma City, Okla. 73157.

Plymouth Brethren (also known as Christian Brethren): This orthodox and evangelical movement began in Britain in the 1820s and has since become worldwide. It is made of up two groups—the smaller "exclusive" branch, which stresses the interdependency of congregations, and the "open" branch, in which each assembly is guided by local elders. Members (1980): 79,000.

Reformed Church in America: This group was established by the earliest Dutch settlers of New York as the Reformed Protestant Dutch Church in 1628. Members (1979): 348,417. Headquarters: 475 Riverside Dr., New York, N.Y. 10115.

Salvation Army: An evangelistic organization, with a military government, first set up by General William Booth in England in 1865 and introduced into the U.S. in 1880. Members (1979): 414,659. Headquarters: 120–30 W. 14th St., New York, N.Y. 10011.

Seventh-day Adventists: This body developed out of an interdenominational movement in the early decades of the 19th century, but was not formally organized until 1863. Their two cardinal points of faith are belief in the personal, imminent, premillennial return of Christ and observance of the seventh day as the Sabbath. Members (1979): 553,089. Headquarters: 6840 Eastern Ave., N.W., Washington, D.C. 20012.

Triumph the Church and Kingdom of God in Christ (International): Organized by Elder E. D. Smith in Georgia in 1902. This group emphasizes the sanctification and the Second Coming of Christ. Members (1972): 54,307. Headquarters: 213 Farrington Ave., Atlanta, Ga. 30318.

Unitarian Universalist Association: This association is the result of a merger in 1961 of the American Unitarian Association, formed in 1825, and the Universalist Church in America, organized in the 1770's. Members (1979): 139,052. Headquarters, 25 Beacon St., Boston, Mass. 02108.

United Church of Christ: A merger in 1961 of the Evangelical and Reformed Church and the Congregational Christian Churches. Members (1979): 1,745,533. Headquarters: 105 Madison Ave., New York, N.Y. 10016.

United Pentecostal Church, International: Pentecostal Church, Inc., and Pentecostal Assemblies of Jesus Christ merged in 1945 at St. Louis. Members (1980): 465,000. Headquarters: 8855 Dunn Rd., Hazelwood, Mo. 63042.

Wesleyan Church: Originated through the uniting of the Pilgrim Holiness Church (1897) and the Wesleyan Methodist Church of America (1843) in 1968. Members (1979): 100,925. Headquarters: Box 2000, Marion, Ind. 46952.

Other Religious Groups

(1,000–50,000 members)

Advent Christian Church (1979: 29,535)
Albanian Orthodox Archdiocese in America (1978: 40,000)
Albanian Orthodox Diocese of America (1979: 5,250)
American Rescue Workers (1978: 2,140)
Anglican Orthodox Church (1972: 2,630)
Apostolic Christian Church (Nazarean) (1979: 2,497)
Apostolic Christian Churches of America (1980: 10,672)
Apostolic Faith (1979: 4,100)
Apostolic Lutheran Church of America (1974: 9,384)
Associate Reformed Presbyterian Church (General Synod) (1979: 31,984)
Beachy Amish Mennonite Church (1979: 4,846)
Berean Fundamental Church (1976: 4,269)
Bethel Ministerial Association (1971: 5,000)
Bible Church of Christ, (1979: 2,300)
Bible Protestant Church (1978: 2,077)
Bible Way Church of Our Lord Jesus Christ World Wide (1970: 30,000)
Brethren Church (Ashland, Ohio) (1978: 15,802)
Brethren in Christ Church (1979: 15,283)
Christ Catholic Church (1979: 1,415)
Christadelphians (1964: 15,800)
Christian Catholic Church (Evangelical-Protestant) (1980: 2,500)
Christian Church of North America, General Council (1980: 12,000)
Christian Nation Church U.S.A. (1976: 2,000)
Christian Union (1979: 5,463)
Church of Christ (1972: 2,400)
Church of God General Conference (Oregon, Ill.) (1979: 7,620)
Church of God (7th Day) (1960: 2,000)
Church of God (Seventh Day), Denver (1976: 8,000)
Church of God by Faith (1973: 4,500)
Church of God in Christ (Mennonite) (1979: 7,259)
Church of God of the Mountain Assembly (1977: 3,125)
Church of Illumination (1963: 9,000)
Church of Jesus Christ (Bickertonites) (1979: 2,567)
Church of Our Lord Jesus Christ of the Apostolic Faith (1954: 45,000)
Church of the Living God (1964: 45,320)
Church of the Lutheran Brethren of America (1979: 10,267)
Church of the Lutheran Confession (1979: 9,340)
Churches of Christ in Christian Union (1979: 10,703)
Churches of God; General Conference (1979: 34,874)
Congregational Holiness Church (1966: 4,859)

Conservative Congregational Christian Conference (1979: 23,751)
Duck River (and Kindred) Association of Baptists (1975: 8,632)
Elim Fellowship (1973: 5,000)
Estonian Evangelical Lutheran Church (1979: 8,481)
Ethical Culture Movement (1979: 5,000)
Evangelical Church of North America (1979: 12,581)
Evangelical Congregational Church (1980: 27,995)
Evangelical Friends Alliance (1975: 25,531)
Evangelical Lutheran Church in America (Eielsen Synod) (1957: 2,500)
Evangelical Lutheran Synod (1979: 20,044)
Evangelical Mennonite Brethren Conference (1979: 2,165)
Evangelical Mennonite Church (1979: 3,704)
Evangelical Methodist Church (1974: 10,502)
Free Christian Zion Church of Christ (1956: 22,260)
Free Lutheran Congregations, Association of (1980: 14,738)
Friends General Conference (1974: 26,184)
Full Gospel Assemblies, International (1979: 2,900)
General Church of the New Jerusalem (1971: 2,143)
General Conference of Mennonite Brethren Churches (1979: 16,165)
General Convention, The Swedenborgian Church (1977: 2,640)
General Conference of the Evangelical Baptist Church (1952: 2,200)
Grace Brethren Churches, Fellowship of (1978: 39,605)
Grace Gospel Fellowship (1979: 3,900)
Holy Apostolic and Catholic Church of the East (Assyrian) (1980: 29,100)
Holy Ukrainian Autocephalic Orthodox Church in Exile (1965: 4,800)
House of God, Which Is the Church of the Living God, the Pillar and Ground of the Truth (1956: 2,350)
Hungarian Reformed Church in America (1978: 10,500)
Hutterian Brethren (1979: 3,443)
International Pentecostal Church of Christ (1979: 4,997)
Latvian Evangelical Lutheran Church in America (1979: 14,294)
Liberal Catholic Church—Province of the United States of America (1973: 2,393)
Mennonite Church, The General Conference (1979: 36,775)
Metropolitan Community Churches, Universal Fellowship of (1980: 26,000)
Missionary Church, The (1972: 20,078)

National Spiritual Alliance of the U.S.A., The (1971: 3,230)
National Spiritualist Association of Churches (1976: 5,168)
Netherlands Reformed Congregations (1979: 4,876)
New Apostolic Church of North America (1979: 27,071)
North American Baptist Conference (1979: 42,779)
North American Old Roman Catholic Church (Archdiocese of New York) (1979: 5,600)
Old German Baptist Brethren (1979: 4,987)
Old Order (Wisler) Mennonite (1972: 8,000)
(Original) Church of God, The (1971: 20,000)
Orthodox Presbyterian Church, The (1979: 16,265)
Pentecostal Assemblies of the World (1960: 4,500)
Pentecostal Free-Will Baptist Church, The (1978: 12,272)
Pillar of Fire (1949: 5,100)
Primitive Methodist Church, U.S.A. (1979: 10,126)
Protestant Conference (Lutheran), The (1979: 1,950)
Protestant Reformed Churches in America (1979: 4,383)
Reformed Baptists (1980: 5,000)
Reformed Church in the United States (1977: 3,790)
Reformed Episcopal Church (1977: 6,211)
Reformed Methodist Union Episcopal Church (1976: 3,800)
Reformed Presbyterian Church, Evangelical Synod (1977: 25,448)
Reformed Presbyterian Church of North America (1977: 4.878)

Reformed Zion Union Apostolic Church (1965: 16,000)
Religious Society of Friends (Conservative) (1976: 1,728)
Religious Society of Friends (Unaffiliated Meetings) (1975: 5,696)
Romanian Orthodox Episcopate of America, The (1979: 40,000)
Schwenkfelder Church, The (1977: 2,748)
Second Cumberland Presbyterian Church in U.S. (1959: 30,000)
Separate Baptists in Christ (1972: 7,496)
Seventh-Day Baptist General Conference (1979: 5,125)
Social Brethren (1975: 1,784)
Southern Methodist Church (1979: 11,000)
Syrian Orthodox Church of Antioch (Archdiocese of the U.S.A. and Canada) (1978: 30,000)
Ukrainian Orthodox Church in America (Ecumenical Patriarchate) (1977: 25,000)
United Brethren in Christ (1976: 28,035)
United Holy Church of America (1960: 28,980)
Unity of the Brethren (1964: 6,142)
Vedanta Society of New York (1979: 1,000)
Volunteers of America (1978: 36,634)

Roman Catholic Pontiffs

St. Peter, of Bethsaida in Galilee, Prince of the Apostles, was the first Pope. He lived first in Antioch and then in Rome for 25 years. In AD 64 or 67, he was martyred. St. Linus became the second Pope.

Name	Birthplace	Reigned From	Reigned To	Name	Birthplace	Reigned From	Reigned To
St. Linus	Tuscia	67	76	St. Celestine I	Campania	422	432
St. Anacletus (Cletus)	Rome	76	88	St. Sixtus III	Rome	432	440
				St. Leo I (the Great)	Tuscany	440	461
St. Clement	Rome	88	97				
St. Evaristus	Greece	97	105	St. Hilary	Sardinia	461	468
St. Alexander I	Rome	105	115	St. Simplicius	Tivoli	468	483
St. Sixtus I	Rome	115	125	St. Felix III (II)[2]	Rome	483	492
St. Telesphorus	Greece	125	136	St. Gelasius I	Africa	492	496
St. Hyginus	Greece	136	140	Anastasius II	Rome	496	498
St. Pius I	Aquileia	140	155	St. Symmachus	Sardinia	498	514
St. Anicetus	Syria	155	166	St. Hormisdas	Frosinone	514	523
St. Soter	Campania	166	175	St. John I	Tuscany	523	526
St. Eleutherius	Epirus	175	189	St. Felix IV (III)	Samnium	526	530
St. Victor I	Africa	189	199	Boniface II	Rome	530	532
St. Zephyrinus	Rome	199	217	John II	Rome	533	535
St. Callistus I	Rome	217	222	St. Agapitus I	Rome	535	536
St. Urban I	Rome	222	230	St. Silverius	Campania	536	537
St. Pontian	Rome	230	235	Vigilius	Rome	537	555
St. Anterus	Greece	235	236	Pelagius I	Rome	556	561
St. Fabian	Rome	236	250	John III	Rome	561	574
St. Cornelius	Rome	251	253	Benedict I	Rome	575	579
St. Lucius I	Rome	253	254	Pelagius II	Rome	579	590
St. Stephen I	Rome	254	257	St. Gregory I (the Great)	Rome	590	604
St. Sixtus II	Greece	257	258				
St. Dionysius	Unknown	259	268	Sabinianus	Tuscany	604	606
St. Felix I	Rome	269	274	Boniface III	Rome	607	607
St. Eutychian	Luni	275	283	St. Boniface IV	Marsi	608	615
St. Caius	Dalmatia	283	296	St. Deusdedit (Adeodatus I)	Rome	615	618
St. Marcellinus	Rome	296	304				
St. Marcellus I	Rome	308	309	Boniface V	Naples	619	625
St. Eusebius	Greece	309[1]	309[1]	Honorius I	Campania	625	638
St. Meltiades	Africa	311	314	Severinus	Rome	640	640
St. Sylvester I	Rome	314	335	John IV	Dalmatia	640	642
St. Marcus	Rome	336	336	Theodore I	Greece	642	649
St. Julius I	Rome	337	352	St. Martin I	Todi	649	655
Liberius	Rome	352	366	St. Eugene I[3]	Rome	654	657
St. Damasus I	Spain	366	384	St. Vitalian	Segni	657	672
St. Siricius	Rome	384	399	Adeodatus II	Rome	672	676
St. Anastasius I	Rome	399	401	Donus	Rome	676	678
St. Innocent I	Albano	401	417	St. Agatho	Sicily	678	681
St. Zozimus	Greece	417	418	St. Leo II	Sicily	682	683
St. Boniface I	Rome	418	422	St. Benedict II	Rome	684	685

Name	Birthplace	Reigned From	Reigned To	Name	Birthplace	Reigned From	Reigned To
John V	Syria	685	686	Benedict IX (3rd time)	—	1047	1048
Conon	Unknown	686	687	Damasus II	Bavaria	1048	1048
St. Sergius I	Syria	687	701	St. Leo IX	Alsace	1049	1054
John VI	Greece	701	705	Victor II	Germany	1055	1057
John VII	Greece	705	707	Stephen IX (X)	Lorraine	1057	1058
Sisinnius	Syria	708	708	Nicholas II	Burgundy	1059	1061
Constantine	Syria	708	715	Alexander II	Milan	1061	1073
St. Gregory II	Rome	715	731	St. Gregory VII	Tuscany	1073	1085
St. Gregory III	Syria	731	741	Bl. Victor III	Benevento	1086	1087
St. Zachary	Greece	741	752	Bl. Urban II	France	1088	1099
Stephen II (III)[4]	Rome	752	757	Paschal II	Ravenna	1099	1118
St. Paul I	Rome	757	767	Gelasius II	Gaeta	1118	1119
Stephen III (IV)	Sicily	768	772	Callistus II	Burgundy	1119	1124
Adrian I	Rome	772	795	Honorius II	Fiagnano	1124	1130
St. Leo III	Rome	795	816	Innocent II	Rome	1130	1143
Stephen IV (V)	Rome	816	817	Celestine II	Città di Castello	1143	1144
St. Paschal I	Rome	817	824				
Eugene II	Rome	824	827	Lucius II	Bologna	1144	1145
Valentine	Rome	827	827	Bl. Eugene III	Pisa	1145	1153
Gregory IV	Rome	827	844	Anastasius IV	Rome	1153	1154
Sergius II	Rome	844	847	Adrian IV	England	1154	1159
St. Leo IV	Rome	847	855	Alexander III	Siena	1159	1181
Benedict III	Rome	855	858	Lucius III	Lucca	1181	1185
St. Nicholas I (the Great)	Rome	858	867	Urban III	Milan	1185	1187
Adrian II	Rome	867	872	Gregory VIII	Benevento	1187	1187
John VIII	Rome	872	882	Clement III	Rome	1187	1191
Marinus I	Gallese	882	884	Celestine III	Rome	1191	1198
St. Adrian III	Rome	884	885	Innocent III	Anagni	1198	1216
Stephen V (VI)	Rome	885	891	Honorius III	Rome	1216	1227
Formosus	Portus	891	896	Gregory IX	Anagni	1227	1241
Boniface VI	Rome	896	896	Celestine IV	Milan	1241	1241
Stephen VI (VII)	Rome	896	897	Innocent IV	Genoa	1243	1254
Romanus	Gallese	897	897	Alexander IV	Anagni	1254	1261
Theodore II	Rome	897	897	Urban IV	Troyes	1261	1264
John IX	Tivoli	898	900	Clement IV	France	1265	1268
Benedict IV	Rome	900	903	Bl. Gregory X	Piacenza	1271	1276
Leo V	Ardea	903	903	Bl. Innocent V	Savoy	1276	1276
Sergius III	Rome	904	911	Adrian V	Genoa	1276	1276
Anastasius III	Rome	911	913	John XXI[7]	Portugal	1276	1277
Landus	Sabina	913	914	Nicholas III	Rome	1277	1280
John X	Tossignano	914	928	Martin IV[8]	France	1281	1285
Leo VI	Rome	928	928	Honorius IV	Rome	1285	1287
Stephen VII (VIII)	Rome	928	931	Nicholas IV	Ascoli	1288	1292
John XI	Rome	931	935	St. Celestine V	Isernia	1294	1294
Leo VII	Rome	936	939	Boniface VIII	Anagni	1294	1303
Stephen VIII (IX)	Rome	939	942	Bl. Benedict XI	Treviso	1303	1304
Marinus II	Rome	942	946	Clement V	France	1305	1314
Agapitus II	Rome	946	955	John XXII	Cahors	1316	1334
John XII	Tusculum	955	964	Benedict XII	France	1334	1342
Leo VIII[5]	Rome	963	965	Clement VI	France	1342	1352
Benedict V[5]	Rome	964	966	Innocent VI	France	1352	1362
John XIII	Rome	965	972	Bl. Urban V	France	1362	1370
Benedict VI	Rome	973	974	Gregory XI	France	1370	1378
Benedict VII	Rome	974	983	Urban VI	Naples	1378	1389
John XIV	Pavia	983	984	Boniface IX	Naples	1389	1404
John XV	Rome	985	996	Innocent VII	Sulmona	1404	1406
Gregory V	Saxony	996	999	Gregory XII	Venice	1406	1415
Sylvester II	Auvergne	999	1003	Martin V	Rome	1417	1431
John XVII	Rome	1003	1003	Eugene IV	Venice	1431	1447
John XVIII	Rome	1004	1009	Nicholas V	Sarzana	1447	1455
Sergius IV	Rome	1009	1012	Callistus III	Jativa	1455	1458
Benedict VIII	Tusculum	1012	1024	Pius II	Siena	1458	1464
John XIX	Tusculum	1024	1032	Paul II	Venice	1464	1471
Benedict IX[6]	Tusculum	1032	1044	Sixtus IV	Savona	1471	1484
Sylvester III	Rome	1045	1045	Innocent VIII	Genoa	1484	1492
Benedict IX (2nd time)	—	1045	1045	Alexander VI	Jativa	1492	1503
				Pius III	Siena	1503	1503
Gregory VI	Rome	1045	1046	Julius II	Savona	1503	1513
Clement II	Saxony	1046	1047	Leo X	Florence	1513	1521

Name	Birthplace	Reigned From	Reigned To	Name	Birthplace	Reigned From	Reigned To
Adrian VI	Utrecht	1522	1523	Innocent XII	Spinazzola	1691	1700
Clement VII	Florence	1523	1534	Clement XI	Urbino	1700	1721
Paul III	Rome	1534	1549	Innocent XIII	Rome	1721	1724
Julius III	Rome	1550	1555	Benedict XIII	Gravina	1724	1730
Marcellus II	Montepulciano	1555	1555	Clement XII	Florence	1730	1740
Paul IV	Naples	1555	1559	Benedict XIV	Bologna	1740	1758
Pius IV	Milan	1559	1565	Clement XIII	Venice	1758	1769
St. Pius V	Bosco	1566	1572	Clement XIV	Rimini	1769	1774
Gregory XIII	Bologna	1572	1585	Pius VI	Cesena	1775	1799
Sixtus V	Grottammare	1585	1590	Pius VII	Cesena	1800	1823
Urban VII	Rome	1590	1590	Leo XII	Genga	1823	1829
Gregory XIV	Cremona	1590	1591	Pius VIII	Cingoli	1829	1830
Innocent IX	Bologna	1591	1591	Gregory XVI	Belluno	1831	1846
Clement VIII	Florence	1592	1605	Pius IX	Senegallia	1846	1878
Leo XI	Florence	1605	1605	Leo XIII	Carpineto	1878	1903
Paul V	Rome	1605	1621	St. Pius X	Riese	1903	1914
Gregory XV	Bologna	1621	1623	Benedict XV	Genoa	1914	1922
Urban VIII	Florence	1623	1644	Pius XI	Desio	1922	1939
Innocent X	Rome	1644	1655	Pius XII	Rome	1939	1958
Alexander VII	Siena	1655	1667	John XXIII	Sotto il Monte	1958	1963
Clement IX	Pistoia	1667	1669	Paul VI	Concesio	1963	1978
Clement X	Rome	1670	1676	John Paul I	Forno di Canale	1978	1978
Bl. Innocent XI	Como	1676	1689	John Paul II	Wadowice, Poland	1978	
Alexander VIII	Venice	1689	1691				

1. Or 310. 2. He should be called Felix II, and his successors of the same name should be numbered accordingly. The discrepancy was caused by the erroneous insertion in some lists of the name of St. Felix of Rome, Martyr. 3. He was elected during the exile of St. Martin I, who endorsed him as Pope. 4. After St. Zachary died, a Roman priest named Stephen was elected but died before his consecration as Bishop of Rome. His name is not included in all lists for this reason. In view of this historical confusion, the *National Catholic Almanac* lists the true Stephen II as Stephen II (III), the true Stephen III as Stephen III (IV), etc. 5. Confusion exists concerning the legitimacy of claims. If the deposition of John was invalid, Leo was an antipope until after the end of Benedict's reign. If the deposition of John was valid, Leo was the legitimate Pope and Benedict an antipope. 6. If the triple removal of Benedict IX was not valid, Sylvester III, Gregory VI, and Clement II were antipopes. 7. Elimination was made of the name of John XX in an effort to rectify the numerical designation of Popes named John. The error dates back to the time of John XV. 8. The names of Marinus I and Marinus II were construed as Martin. In view of these two pontificates and the earlier reign of St. Martin I, this pontiff was called Martin IV. *Source: National Catholic Almanac, from Annuarto Pontificio.*

Books of the Bible

OLD TESTAMENT — STANDARD VERSIONS

Genesis
Exodus
Leviticus
Numbers
Deuteronomy
Joshua
Judges
Ruth
I Samuel
II Samuel
I Kings
II Kings
I Chronicles
II Chronicles
Ezra
Nehemiah
Esther
Job
Psalms
Proverbs
Ecclesiastes
Song of Solomon
Isaiah
Jeremiah
Lamentations
Ezekiel
Daniel
Hosea
Joel
Amos
Obadiah
Jonah
Micah
Nahum
Habakkuk
Zephaniah
Haggai
Zechariah
Malachi

NEW TESTAMENT — STANDARD VERSIONS

Matthew
Mark
Luke
John
Acts
Romans
Corinthians
Galatians
Ephesians
Philippians
Colossians
Thessalonians
Timothy
Titus
Philemon
Hebrews
James
Peter
John
Jude
Revelation

OLD TESTAMENT — DOUAY VERSION[1]

Genesis
Exodus
Leviticus
Numbers
Deuteronomy
Josue
Judges
Ruth
I Kings
II Kings
III Kings
IV Kings
II Esdras
Tobias
Judith
Esther
Job
Psalms
Proverbs
Ecclesiastes
Canticle of Canticles
Wisdom
Ecclesiasticus
Isaias
Jeremias
Lamentations
Baruch
Ezechiel
Daniel
Osee
Joel
Amos
Abdias
Jonas
Micheas
Nahum
Habacuc
Sophonias
Aggeus
Zacharias
Malachias
I Machabees
II Machabees

1. In the Douay Version of the Bible, the books of the New Testament are the same as those of the Authorized (King James) Version, except that the Revelation of St. John is called the Apocalypse of St. John in the Douay Version.

WEATHER & CLIMATE

World and U.S. Extremes of Climate

Highest recorded temperature

	Place	Date	Degree Fahrenheit	Degree Centigrade
World (Africa)	El Azizia, Libya	Sept. 13, 1922	136	58
North America (U.S.)	Death Valley, Calif.	July 10, 1913	134	57
Asia	Tirat Tsvi, Israel	June 21, 1942	129	54
Australia	Cloncurry, Queensland	Jan. 16, 1889	128	53
Europe	Seville, Spain	Aug. 4, 1881	122	50
South America	Rivadavia, Argentina	Dec. 11, 1905	120	49
Antarctica	Esperanza, Palmer Peninsula	Oct. 20, 1956	58	14

Lowest recorded temperature

	Place	Date	Degree Fahrenheit	Degree Centigrade
World (Antarctica)	Vostok	Aug. 24, 1960	−127	−88
Asia	Verkhoyansk/Oimekon	Feb. 6, 1933	−90	−68
Greenland	Northice	Jan. 9, 1954	−87	−66
North America (excl. Greenland)	Snag, Yukon, Canada	Feb. 3, 1947	−81	−63
Europe	Ust 'Shchugor, U.S.S.R.	n.a.	−67	−55
South America	Sarmiento, Argentina	Jan. 1, 1907	−27	−33
Africa	Ifrane, Morocco	Feb. 11, 1935	−11	−24
Australia	Charlotte Pass, N.S.W.	July 22, 1947	−8	−22
United States	Prospect Creek, Alaska	Jan. 23, 1971	−80	−62

Greatest rainfalls

	Place	Date	Inches	Centimeters
1 minute (U.S.)	Unionville, Md.	—	1.23	3.1
20 minutes (Romania)	Curtea-de-Arges	—	8.1	20.6
42 minutes (U.S.)	Holt, Mo.	—	12	30
12 hours (Indian Ocean)	Belouve, La Réunion	—	53	135
24 hours (Indian Ocean)	Cilaos, La Réunion	—	74	188
5 days (Indian Ocean)	Cilaos, La Réunion	—	152	386
1 month (India)	Cherrapunji	—	366	930
1 month (U.S.)	Kukui, Maui, Hawaii	—	460	1,168
12 months (India)	Cherrapunji	—	1,042	2,647

Greatest snowfalls

	Place	Date	Inches	Centimeters
1 month (U.S.)	Tamarack, Calif.	Jan. 1911	390	991
24 hours (U.S.)	Silver Lake, Colo.	April 14–15, 1921	76	193
19 hours (France)	Bessans	—	68	173
1 storm (U.S.)	Mt. Shasta Ski Bowl, Calif.	—	189	480
1 season (U.S.)	Paradise Ranger Sta., Wash.	—	1,122	2,850

NOTE: n.a. = not available. *Source:* National Oceanic and Atmospheric Administration, Environmental Data Service.

Tropical Storms and Hurricanes, 1886–1980

	Jan.–April	May	June	July	Aug.	Sept.	Oct.	Nov.	Dec.	Total
Number of tropical storms (incl. hurricanes)	3	13	50	61	183	264	172	33	5	784
Number of tropical storms that reached hurricane intensity	1	3	21	32	134	172	85	17	2	467

Climate of Selected U.S. Cities, 1980

(T = trace)

Month	Temperature, °F				Precipitation			Percentage possible sunshine	Percentage relative humidity, afternoon
	Average daily maximum	Average daily minimum	Record high	Record low	Rainfall, inches	Snowfall, inches	Days with precipitation		
Bakersfield, California (Kern County Air Terminal): lat. 35° 25′ N, long. 119° 03′ W; elevation: 475 ft									
January	59.9	45.7	73	33	2.60	0.0	13	n.a.	74
April	74.8	50.5	94	44	0.66	0.0	4	n.a.	37
July	98.8	71.3	112	58	0.00	0.0	0	n.a.	25
October	85.7	57.4	103	44	0.03	0.0	1	n.a.	27
Annual	78.0	54.0	112	30	6.01	0.0	35	n.a.	39
Caribou, Maine (Municipal Airport): lat. 46° 52′ N, long. 68° 01′ W; elevation: 624 ft									
January	22.5	4.1	47	−7	1.55	7.9	12	n.a.	58
April	51.3	33.9	67	20	2.57	0.8	14	n.a.	56
July	74.7	54.8	86	46	5.42	0.0	18	n.a.	65
October	48.1	33.7	64	22	2.51	0.2	15	n.a.	60
Annual	48.0	29.3	89	−23	32.55	90.0	169	n.a.	59
Charleston, South Carolina (Municipal Airport): lat. 32° 54′ N, long. 80° 02′ W; elevation: 40 ft									
January	57.6	39.8	70	24	3.99	0.0	13	35	64
April	75.7	52.9	91	38	3.43	0.0	9	72	50
July	91.6	73.2	100	69	6.97	0.0	11	82	59
October	75.7	54.2	88	39	1.52	0.0	6	61	52
Annual	74.9	54.3	100	15	40.92	5.1	102	67	55
Chicago, Illinois (O'Hare International Airport): lat. 41° 59′ N, long. 87° 54′ W; elevation: 658 ft									
January	31.0	15.8	56	0	1.04	6.2	14	n.a.	70
April	56.4	36.6	91	24	3.41	4.2	16	n.a.	59
July	86.9	64.5	102	50	3.56	0.0	10	67	59
October	58.8	38.0	80	24	2.09	T	7	60	51
Annual	58.0	39.1	102	−8	38.66	51.5	145	n.a.	60
Dallas-Fort Worth, Texas (Regional Airport): lat. 32° 54′ N, long. 97° 02′ W; elevation: 551 ft									
January	54.5	36.5	71	25	2.52	0.0	8	50	67
April	75.9	50.3	92	41	2.23	0.0	4	70	48
July	105.3	78.7	110	72	0.71	0.0	1	92	30
October	77.7	53.0	89	29	1.08	0.0	4	69	44
Annual	78.5	55.1	113	15	22.08	1.6	56	69	50
Denver, Colorado (Stapleton International Airport): lat. 39° 45′ long. 104° 52′ W; elevation: 5,283 ft									
January	37.5	14.4	61	−4	0.64	12.3	10	64	57
April	59.4	35.9	81	23	2.54	10.0	6	75	33
July	89.8	62.9	97	54	2.93	0.0	10	81	29
October	67.0	37.8	82	25	0.10	1.5	1	78	23
Annual	65.3	39.0	100	−5	13.67	53.8	85	73	36
Duluth, Minnesota (International Airport): lat. 46° 50′ N, long. 92° 11′ W; elevation: 1,428 ft									
January	17.1	0.2	38	−24	1.55	21.9	10	50	68
April	52.1	30.7	80	20	0.41	1.5	8	64	51
July	79.5	55.6	95	42	3.94	0.0	10	70	54
October	46.7	31.1	80	15	1.64	1.3	10	42	62
Annual	47.7	28.9	95	−24	25.57	56.3	129	57	62

Month	Temperature, °F				Precipitation				
	Average daily maximum	Average daily minimum	Record high	Record low	Rainfall, inches	Snowfall, inches	Days with precipitation	Percentage possible sunshine	Percentage relative humidity, afternoon

Great Falls, Montana (International Airport): lat. 47° 29′ N, long. 111° 22′ W; elevation: 3,663 ft _____

January	25.8	4.5	52	−30	0.67	7.0	9	39	55
April	65.7	40.0	89	26	0.62	4.4	6	64	31
July	84.3	54.4	98	40	0.27	0.0	6	81	27
October	60.2	37.8	85	24	1.75	7.7	10	61	43
Annual	57.3	34.1	98	−30	16.22	43.9	104	54	43

Kansas City, Missouri (International Airport): lat. 39° 19′ N, long. 94° 43′ W; elevation: 973 ft _____

January	36.6	20.7	58	−8	1.60	5.4	10	47	60
April	66.2	42.9	90	29	1.02	0.0	7	68	45
July	97.4	72.9	106	60	1.99	0.0	8	80	46
October	66.4	41.7	89	23	4.13	T	8	79	48
Annual	64.8	43.9	106	−8	31.79	26.7	96	65	54

Los Angeles, California (International Airport): lat. 33° 56′ N, long. 118° 24′ W; elevation: 97 ft _____

January	66.4	52.9	79	43	6.97	0.0	15	n.a.	68
April	67.8	53.4	85	49	0.17	0.0	2	n.a.	62
July	75.5	61.8	91	59	0.00	0.0	0	n.a.	65
October	73.9	58.5	88	52	T	0.0	0	n.a.	62
Annual	70.8	56.0	98	43	21.60	0.0	40	n.a.	64

Miami, Florida (International Airport): lat. 25° 49′ N, long. 80° 17′ W; elevation: 7 ft _____

January	75.1	59.9	86	46	1.89	0.0	4	76	60
April	81.9	68.8	89	58	10.20	0.0	9	77	60
July	89.1	76.0	95	71	9.40	0.0	17	80	68
October	86.4	73.8	95	58	6.05	0.0	12	75	65
Annual	82.5	69.1	95	32	57.34	0.0	113	77	63

New Orleans, Louisiana (International Airport): lat. 29° 59′ N, long. 90° 15′ W; elevation: 4 ft _____

January	65.4	46.8	79	27	6.37	0.0	11	36	71
April	76.7	55.7	85	44	16.12	0.0	9	58	61
July	94.9	76.7	101	71	4.84	0.0	11	73	65
October	79.9	57.6	91	42	5.87	0.0	6	77	55
Annual	79.3	59.8	102	25	73.09	T	103	61	63

New York, New York (Central Park): lat. 40° 47′ N, long. 73° 58′ W; elevation: 132 ft _____

January	39.4	28.0	60	17	1.72	2.0	7	n.a.	48
April	62.7	46.3	76	32	8.26	T	12	n.a.	53
July	87.6	70.9	102	61	5.26	0.0	10	n.a.	49
October	62.6	47.8	79	37	3.86	0.0	8	n.a.	48
Annual	62.6	47.3	102	−1	44.55	12.1	104	n.a.	48

Phoenix, Arizona (Sky Harbor International Airport): lat. 33° 26′ N, long. 112° 01′ W; elevation: 1,110 ft _____

January	65.8	47.3	75	38	1.58	0.0	8	57	45
April	83.3	56.3	102	41	0.44	0.0	3	87	19
July	107.6	83.6	115	76	0.56	0.0	5	84	17
October	88.7	62.4	107	49	0.02	0.0	1	95	19
Annual	86.4	61.6	115	35	6.06	0.0	41	86	22

Salt Lake City, Utah (International Airport): lat. 40° 47′ N, long. 111° 57′ W; elevation: 4,221 ft _____

January	41.1	26.2	57	−4	2.87	24.5	14	44	70
April	64.8	40.5	85	30	0.89	1.2	6	81	33
July	92.2	63.0	101	56	1.34	0.0	8	88	24

Month	Temperature, °F				Precipitation			Percentage possible sunshine	Percentage relative humidity, afternoon
	Average daily maximum	Average daily minimum	Record high	Record low	Rainfall, inches	Snowfall, inches	Days with precipitation		
October	65.4	39.7	84	28	1.74	T	6	73	39
Annual	64.3	41.3	101	−4	17.19	55.7	100	71	44

San Francisco, California (International Airport): lat. 37° 37′ N, long. 122° 23′ W; elevation: 8 ft

Month	Average daily maximum	Average daily minimum	Record high	Record low	Rainfall, inches	Snowfall, inches	Days with precipitation	Percentage possible sunshine	Percentage relative humidity, afternoon
January	57.0	44.0	68	31	4.85	0.0	11	n.a.	67
April	64.7	47.0	80	40	0.90	0.0	5	n.a.	59
July	71.9	54.1	85	50	0.10	0.0	2	n.a.	62
October	71.9	50.4	97	44	0.10	0.0	4	n.a.	56
Annual	65.6	48.6	97	31	18.34	T	55	n.a.	60

Seattle, Washington (Seattle-Tacoma Airport): lat. 47° 27′ N, long. 122° 18′ W; elevation: 400 ft

Month	Average daily maximum	Average daily minimum	Record high	Record low	Rainfall, inches	Snowfall, inches	Days with precipitation	Percentage possible sunshine	Percentage relative humidity, afternoon
January	39.9	29.7	52	15	4.09	8.8	16	36	68
April	60.4	42.8	76	35	3.23	T	11	62	51
July	73.3	54.3	85	49	0.46	T	6	65	51
October	62.3	45.4	82	35	1.32	0.0	7	56	62
Annual	58.4	44.3	87	15	35.60	11.7	147	44	64

Washington, D.C. (National Airport): lat. 38° 51′ N, long. 77° 02′ W; elevation: 10 ft

Month	Average daily maximum	Average daily minimum	Record high	Record low	Rainfall, inches	Snowfall, inches	Days with precipitation	Percentage possible sunshine	Percentage relative humidity, afternoon
January	43.4	31.0	57	20	2.85	8.6	8	31	61
April	69.6	50.6	80	35	3.28	0.0	10	61	52
July	91.0	73.6	103	66	3.86	0.0	11	81	52
October	68.6	51.2	85	38	2.59	0.0	6	64	51
Annual	68.1	50.9	103	12	29.32	20.1	110	64	53

NOTE: n.a. = not available. *Source:* Department of Commerce, National Oceanic and Atmospheric Administration, Environmental Data Service.

Other Recorded Extremes

Highest average annual temperature (World): Dallol, Ethiopia (1960–66), 94°F (34.4°C). **(U.S.):** Key West, Fla. (30-year normal), 78.2°F (25.7°C).
Lowest average annual temperature (Antarctica): Plateau Station −70°F (−56.7°C). **(U.S.):** Barrow, Alaska (30-year normal), 9.3°F (−12.6°C).
Greatest average yearly rainfall (U.S.): Mt. Waialeale, Kauai, Hawaii (1912–58), 460 in. (1,168 cm). **(India):** Cherrapunji (74-year avg), 450 in. (1,143 cm).
Minimum average yearly rainfall (Chile): Arica (59-year avg), 0.03 in. (0.08 cm) (no rainfall for 14 consecutive years). **(U.S.):** Death Valley, Calif. (49-year avg), 1.63 in. (4.14 cm). (Bagdad, Calif. holds the U.S. record for the longest period with no measurable rain, 767 days, from Oct. 3, 1912 to Nov. 8, 1914).
Hottest summer avg in Western Hemisphere (U.S.): Death Valley, Calif., 98°F (36.7°C).
Longest hot spell (W. Australia): Marble Bar, 100°F (37.8°C) (or above) for 162 consecutive days.
Largest hailstone (U.S.): Potter, Neb., 1½ lb (.68 kg).

Wind Chill Factors

Wind speed (mph)	Thermometer reading (degrees Fahrenheit)																
	35	30	25	20	15	10	5	0	−5	−10	−15	−20	−25	−30	−35	−40	−45
5	33	27	21	19	12	7	0	−5	−10	−15	−21	−26	−31	−36	−42	−47	−52
10	22	16	10	3	−3	−9	−15	−22	−27	−34	−40	−46	−52	−58	−64	−71	−77
15	16	9	2	−5	−11	−18	−25	−31	−38	−45	−51	−58	−65	−72	−78	−85	−92
20	12	4	−3	−10	−17	−24	−31	−39	−46	−53	−60	−67	−74	−81	−88	−95	−103
25	8	1	−7	−15	−22	−29	−36	−44	−51	−59	−66	−74	−81	−88	−96	−103	−110
30	6	−2	−10	−18	−25	−33	−41	−49	−56	−64	−71	−79	−86	−93	−101	−109	−116
35	4	−4	−12	−20	−27	−35	−43	−52	−58	−67	−74	−82	−89	−97	−105	−113	−120
40	3	−5	−13	−21	−29	−37	−45	−53	−60	−69	−76	−84	−92	100	−107	−115	−123
45	2	−6	−14	−22	−30	−38	−46	−54	−62	−70	−78	−85	−93	−102	−109	−117	−125

NOTES: This chart gives equivalent temperatures for combinations of wind speed and temperatures. For example, the combination of a temperature of 10° Fahrenheit and a wind blowing at 10 mph has a cooling power equal to −9° F. Wind speeds of higher than 45 mph have little additional cooling effect.

Weather Glossary

blizzard: storm characterized by strong winds, low temperatures, and large amounts of snow.

cyclone: circulation of winds rotating counterclockwise in the northern hemisphere and clockwise in the southern hemisphere. Hurricanes and tornadoes are both examples of cyclones.

drizzle: uniform close precipitation of tiny drops with diameter of less than .02 inch.

flash flood: dangerous rapid rise of water levels in streams, rivers, or over land area.

gale warning: winds in the 33–48 knot (38–55 mph) range forecast.

heavy snow warnings: issued when 4 inches or more of snow are expected to fall in a 12-hour period or when 6 inches or more are anticipated in a 24-hour period.

hurricane: devastating cyclonic storm; winds over 74 mph near storm center; usually tropical in origin; called cyclone in Indian Ocean, typhoon in the Pacific.

hurricane warning: winds in excess of 64 knots (74 mph) in connection with hurricane.

snow flurries: snow falling for a short time at intermittent periods; accumulations are usually small.

snow squall: brief, intense falls of snow, usually accompanied by gusty winds.

storm warnings: winds greater than 48 knots (55 mph) are forecast.

temperature-humidity index (THI): measure of personal discomfort based on the combined effects of temperature and humidity. Most people are uncomfortable when the THI is 75. A THI of 80 produces acute discomfort for almost everyone.

tidal waves: series of ocean waves caused by earthquakes; can reach speeds of 600 mph; they grow in height as they reach shore and can crest as high as 100 feet.

thunder: the sound produced by the rapid expansion of air heated by lightning.

tornado: dangerous whirlwind associated with the cumulonimbus clouds of severe thunderstorms; winds up to 300 mph.

tornado warning: tornado has actually been detected by radar or sighted in designated area.

tornado watch: potential exists in the watch area for storms that could contain tornadoes.

tsunami: *see* tidal waves.

warning: the designated condition is imminent.

wind-chill factor: combined effect of temperature and wind speed as compared to equivalent temperature in calm air.

Tornadoes That Caused Outstanding Damage

Date	Number of tornadoes	Deaths	Property losses	States in which storms occurred
1884, Feb. 19	60	800	(1)	Mississippi, Alabama, North and South Carolina, Tennessee, Kentucky, Indiana
1917, May 26–27	(1)	249	$ 5,555,000	Illinois, Indiana, Arkansas, Kentucky, Tennessee, Alabama, Mississippi
1920, April 20	6	220	3,525,000	Mississippi, Alabama, Tennessee
1924, April 29–30	22	115	4,372,300	Oklahoma, Arkansas, Alabama, Georgia, Louisiana, North and South Carolina, Virginia
1924, June 28	4	96	13,050,000	Ohio and Pennsylvania
1925, March 18	8	792	17,872,000	Missouri, Illinois, Indiana, Kentucky, Tennessee, Alabama
1927, May 8–9	36	227	7,877,000	Texas, Louisiana, Missouri, Nebraska, Indiana, Michigan
1932, March 21	27	321	5,514,000	Alabama, Mississippi, Georgia, Tennessee
1936, April 5–6	22	498	21,800,000	Arkansas, Alabama, Tennessee, Georgia, South Carolina
1944, June 23	4	153	5,160,000	Pennsylvania, West Virginia, Maryland
1947, April 9–10	8	167	10,030,750	Texas, Oklahoma, Kansas
1952, March 21–22	31	343	15,327,100	Arkansas, Tennessee, Missouri, Mississippi, Alabama, Kentucky
1953, June 7–9	12	234	93,230,840	Michigan, Ohio, and New England states
1953, May 11	1	114	39,500,000	Texas
1955, May 25	13	102	11,747,500	Oklahoma and Kansas
1965, April 11–12	47	257	200,000,000	Iowa, Illinois, Wisconsin, Michigan, Indiana, Ohio
1968, May 15	7	63	65,000,000	Arkansas, Iowa, Illinois
1970, May 11	1	26	135,000,000	Texas
1971, Feb. 21	(1)	117	17,000,000	Louisiana, Mississippi
1973, March 31	2	9	115,000,000	Georgia, South Carolina
1973, May 26–28	96	22	(1)	Hawaii and 18 states in South, Southwest, Midwest, and East
1974, April 3–4	144	307	500,000,000 +	13 states in East, South, and Midwest
1975, May 6	3	3	400,000,000 +	Nebraska
1977, April 4	7	22	15,000,000	Alabama
1978, Dec. 3	13	4	100,000,000 +	Louisiana and Arkansas
1979, April 10	10	54	(1)	Texas and Oklahoma
1979, Oct. 3	1	3	200,000,000	Connecticut
1980, April 7	12	0	19,000,000 +	Arkansas
1980, May 13	1	5	40,000,000	Michigan
1980, Aug. 9–11	29	0	50,000,000 +	Texas

1. Not definitely known; believed to be large. NOTE: Additional storms may be listed in the *Current Events* section. *Source:* Data for 1884–1953, reprinted from *Tornadoes of the United States*, by S. D. Flora, copyright 1954, by University of Oklahoma Press. Used by permission. Also, Department of Commerce, National Oceanic and Atmospheric Administration.

Devastating North Atlantic Hurricanes of the 20th Century

The following is a selected list of North Atlantic hurricanes based on casualties, damage, and general public interest. Facts about each storm are taken from Weather records, although in some cases only estimates of wind speed are available. Data given in this list pertain only to U.S. land areas except where indicated otherwise.

Date	Areas hardest hit	Land stations with highest wind speed	Deaths (U.S. only)	Est. damage (millions)	Remarks
1900, Aug. 27-Sept. 15	Galveston, Tex.	Galveston, Tex. (120[1] mph)	6,000	$30	Damage due to both winds and storm wave. Galveston Is. inundated.
1909, Sept. 10-21	Louisiana and Mississippi	New Orleans, La. (53 mph)	350	5	Winds 50-75 mi. W of New Orleans, where deaths occurred, were stronger than 68 mph.
1915, Aug. 5-23	East Texas and Louisiana	Galveston, Tex. (120 mph)	275	50	Water 5-6 ft deep in Galveston business district. 90% of homes demolished. Warnings issued well ahead of time.
1915, Sept. 22-Oct. 1	Mid-Gulf Coast	Burrwood, La. (140 mph)	275	13	Many casualties due to persons insisting on staying in low-lying areas despite warnings.
1919, Sept. 2-15	Florida, Louisiana, and Texas	Sand Key, Fla. (84[1] mph)	287	22	488 persons drowned at sea.
1926, Sept. 11-22	Florida and Alabama	Miami, Fla. (138 mph)	243	112	Most deaths were in Miami area. Said to have been one of most destructive storms of century.
1928, Sept. 6-20	Southern Florida	Lake Okeechobee, Fla. (75[1] mph)	1,836	25	1,870 injured. Nearly all deaths were in Lake Okeechobee area. Winds estimated as high as 160 mph caused Lake to overflow into populated areas.
1935, Aug. 29-Sept. 10	Southern Florida	Tampa, Fla. (86 mph)	408	6	Sustained winds over Florida Keys est. 150-200 mph. Remembered as "Labor Day Storm."
1938, Sept. 10-22	Long Island and Southern New England	Blue Hills Obs., Mass. (183 mph)	600	306	Unusually destructive. Storm center moved as fast as 56 mph at times. 1,754 injured.
1944, Sept. 9-16	North Carolina to New England	Cape Henry, Va. (150[1] mph)	46	100	344 deaths at sea. Shipping lanes were crowded with war-time activity.
1944, Oct. 12-23	Florida	Dry Tortugas Is. (120 mph)	18	100	About 300 were killed in Cuba area before storm reached U.S. Evacuation of thousands from threatened areas in Fla. prevented higher toll.
1947, Sept. 4-21	Florida and Mid-Gulf Coast	Hillsboro Light, Fla. (155 mph)	51	110	Wind damage especially heavy Along Gulf Coast and Florida east coast.
1954, Aug. 25-31	North Carolina to New England	Block Island, R.I. (135 mph)	60	461	"CAROL"—more damage than any other single storm to this date. Water and high waves flooded low-lying areas; 1,000 injuries in Long Island-New England area.
1954, Sept. 2-14	New Jersey to New England	Block Island, R.I. (87 mph)	21	40	"EDNA"—New England again heavily hit. Gusts of 120 mph at Martha's Vineyard, Mass.
1954, Oct. 5-18	South Carolina to New York	New York, N.Y. (113 mph) (See Remarks)	95	252	"HAZEL"—several N.C. localities had winds of 130-150 mph with unusually heavy wave damage resulting. Est. 400-1,000 casualties in Haiti. In Canada there were 78 deaths, mostly due to flooding.
1955, Aug. 7-21	North Carolina to New England	Wilmington, N.C. (83 mph)	184	832	"DIANE"—worst floods in history in Southern New England. 16 in. of rain in Hartford area.
1957, June 25-28	Texas to Alabama	Sabine Pass, Tex. (100 mph)	390	150	"AUDREY"—gave an early start to the hurricane season and wiped out Cameron, La. Two

Date	Areas hardest hit	Land stations with highest wind speed	Deaths (U.S. only)	Est. damage (millions)	Remarks
1960, Aug. 29–Sept. 13	Florida to New England	Ft. Myers, Fla. (92 mph) Block Island, R.I. (130 mph) (See Remarks)	50	500	weeks later "BERTHA" struck same area. "DONNA"—hurricane winds from a single storm swept the entire Atlantic seaboard from Florida to New England for the first time in a 75-year record. Winds estimated near 140 mph with gusts 175–180 mph on Central Keys and lower southwest Florida coast. 115 deaths in Antilles, most from flash floods in Puerto Rico.
1961, Sept. 3–15	Texas coast	Port Lavaca, Tex. (145 mph)	46	408	"CARLA"—devastated Texas Gulf Coast Cities with 15-foot tides and 15-inch rains. Gusts to 175 mph at Port Lavaca.
1964, Aug. 20–Sept. 5	Southern Florida, Eastern Virginia	Miami, Fla. (110 mph)	3	129	"CLEO"—first hurricane in Miami area since 1950. Killed 214 in Caribbean Islands.
1964, Aug. 28–Sept. 16	Northeastern Florida, Southern Georgia	St. Augustine, Fla. (125 mph)	5	250	"DORA"—first storm of full hurricane force on record to move inland from east over northeastern Florida.
1965, Aug. 27–Sept. 12	Southern Florida and Louisiana	Port Sulphur, La. (136 mph)	75	1,420	"BETSY"—Damage in Louisiana, $1.2 billion. 27,000 homes destroyed, 17,500 injured or ill, 300,000 evacuated. Gusts of 165 mph at Pine Key, Fla.
1967, Sept. 5–22	Southern Texas	Brownsville, Texas (109 mph gust)	15	200	"BEULAH"—main damage was caused by torrential rains.
1969, Aug. 14–22	Mississippi, Louisiana, Alabama, Virginia, W. Virginia	Oil drilling rig east of Boothville, La. (172 mph)	256	1,420	"CAMILLE"—68 additional persons missing. One of most destructive killer storms ever to hit U.S.
1970, July 23–Aug. 5	Texas coast	Corpus Christi, Tex. (130 mph)	11	453.8	"CELIA"—Costliest storm in history to hit Texas coast. Gusts of 161 mph recorded.
1972, June 14–23	Florida to New York	Key West, Fla. (43 mph)	117	3,097	"AGNES"—Devastating floods with many record-breaking river crests. Pa. hardest hit, with 50 deaths.
1975, Sept. 13–24	Florida and Southern Alabama	Ozark, Ala. (104 mph)	21	490	"ELOISE"—Structures destroyed from Panama City Beach, Fla., to Ft. Walton Beach, Fla. Major flooding from rainfall.
1976, Aug. 6–10	New York, New Jersey, and Southern New England	Bridgeport, Conn. (77 mph gust)	5	100	"BELLE"—Crop damage in the Northeast. Considerable Inland stream and road flooding.
1979, Aug. 25–Sept. 7	Florida to New England	Fort Pierce, Fla. (95 mph gust)	5	320	"DAVID"—1200 deaths in the Dominican Republic. Homes 80 percent destroyed in Dominica.
1979, Aug. 29–Sept. 14	Alabama and Mississippi	Dauphin Island, Alabama (145 mph gust)	5	2300	"FREDERIC"— highest dollar dammage ever in the United States.
1980, Aug. 3–10	Caribbean Islands to Texas Gulf Coast	Port Mansfield, Texas (120 mph gust.)	28	300	"ALLEN"—Highest tides in 61 years. Over 200 killed in Caribbean Islands. Extensive crop damage in Caribbean.

1. Wind-measuring equipment disabled at speed indicated. NOTE: Additional hurricanes may be listed in *News Chronology*.
Source: Department of Commerce, National Oceanic and Atmospheric Administration.

Tornado Fatalities

In the 1970s, there were 8,573 tornadoes in the United States resulting in the deaths of 986 people. If the previous decades are any indication of the future, the National Oceanic and Atmospheric Administration forsees that there will be at least 7,000 tornadoes during the 1980s in which up to 1,000 Americans will be killed.

TAXES

History of the Income Tax in the United States

Source: Touche Ross & Co.

The nation had few taxes in its early history. From 1791 to 1802, the United States Government was supported by internal taxes on distilled spirits, carriages, refined sugar, tobacco and snuff, property sold at auction, corporate bonds, and slaves. The high cost of the War of 1812 brought about the nation's first sales taxes on gold, silverware, jewelry, and watches. In 1817, however, Congress did away with all internal taxes, relying on tariffs on imported goods to provide sufficient funds for running the Government.

In 1862, in order to support the Civil War effort, Congress enacted the nation's first income tax law. It was a forerunner of our modern income tax in that it was based on the principles of graduated, or progressive, taxation and of withholding income at the source. During the Civil War, a person earning from $600 to $10,000 per year paid tax at the rate of 3%. Those with incomes of more than $10,000 paid taxes at a higher rate. Additional sales and excise taxes were added, and an "inheritance" tax also made its debut. In 1866, internal revenue collections reached their highest point in the nation's 90-year history—more than $310 million, an amount not reached again until 1911.

The Act of 1862 established the office of Commissioner of Internal Revenue. The Commissioner was given the power to assess, levy, and collect taxes, and the right to enforce the tax laws through seizure of property and income and through prosecution. His powers and authority remain very much the same today.

In 1868, Congress again focused its taxation efforts on tobacco and distilled spirits and eliminated the income tax in 1872. It had a short-lived revival in 1894 and 1895. In the latter year, the U.S. Supreme Court decided that the income tax was unconstitutional because it was not apportioned among the states in conformity with the Constitution.

By 1913, with the 16th Amendment to the Constitution, the income tax had become a permanent fixture of the U.S. tax system. The amendment gave Congress legal authority to tax income and resulted in a revenue law that taxed incomes of both individuals and corporations. In fiscal year 1918, annual internal revenue collections for the first time passed the billion-dollar mark, rising to $5.4 billion by 1920. With the advent of World War II, employment increased, as did tax collections—to $7.3 billion. The withholding tax on wages was introduced in 1943 and was instrumental in increasing the number of taxpayers to 60 million and tax collections to $43 billion by 1945.

In 1981, Congress enacted the largest tax cut in U.S. history, including a 25% reduction in individual tax rates over a three-year period. The Economic Recovery Tax Act of 1981 has resulted in numerous changes in the tax law, including the reduction of total taxes for individuals and businesses by approximately $750 billion over a six-year period.

Internal Revenue Service

The Internal Revenue Service (IRS), a bureau of the U.S. Treasury Department, is the federal agency charged with the administration of the tax laws passed by Congress. The IRS functions through a national office in Washington, 7 regional offices, 58 district offices, and 10 service centers.

Operations involving most taxpayers are carried out in the district offices and service centers. District offices are organized into Resources Management, Examination, Collection, Taxpayer Service, and Criminal Investigation. All tax returns are filed with the service centers, where the IRS computer operations are located.

Auditing Tax Returns

Most taxpayers' contacts with IRS arise through the auditing of their tax returns. The Service has been empowered by Congress to inquire about all persons who may be liable for any tax and to obtain for review the books and/or records pertinent to those taxpayers' returns. A wide-ranging audit operation is carried out in the 58 district offices by some 14,000 field agents and 5,000 office auditors.

Selecting Returns for Audit

The primary method used by the IRS in selecting returns for audits is a computer program that measures the probability of tax error in each return. The data base (established by an in-depth audit of randomly selected returns in various income categories) consists of approximately 200–250 individual items of information taken from each return. These 200–250 variables individually or in combination are weighted as relative indicators of potential tax change. Returns are then scored according to the weights given the combinations of variables as they appear on each return. The higher the score, the greater the tax change potential. Other returns are selected for examination on the basis of claims for refund, multi-year audits, related return audits, and other audits initiated by the IRS as a result of informants' information, special compliance programs, and the information document matching program.

During 1980, the IRS initiated a new method to group individual returns for examination selection purposes. Total positive income, the sum of all positive income amounts appearing on a return, with losses treated as zero is the newly utilized factor. This new method replaces the adjusted gross income method of classifying returns. In a similar manner, total gross receipts is used for business returns.

Internal Revenue Service

	1980	1979	1978	1970	1960	1950
U.S. population (in thousands)	223,383	220,999	219,033	204,878	180,671	152,271
Number of IRS employees	87,464	86,630	85,329	68,098	50,199	55,551
Cost to govt. of collecting						
$100 in taxes	0.44	$0.46	$0.49	$0.45	$0.40	$0.59
Tax per capita	$2,325.04	$2,083.32	$1,827.00	$955.31	$507.96	$255.84
Collections by principal sources (in thousands of dollars)						
Total IRS collections	$519,375,273	$460,412,185	$399,776,389	$195,722,096	$91,744,803	$38,957,132
Income and profits taxes						
Individual	287,547,782	251,545,857	213,058,144	103,651,585	44,945,711	17,153,308
Corporation	72,379,610	71,447,876	65,380,145	35,036,983	22,179,414	10,854,351
Employment taxes	128,330,480	112,849,874	97,291,653	37,449,188	11,158,589	2,644,575
Estate and gift taxes	6,498,381	5,519,074	5,381,499	3,680,076	1,626,348	706,227
Alcohol taxes	5,704,768	5,647,924	5,612,715	4,746,382	3,193,714	2,219,202
Tobacco taxes	2,446,416	2,495,517	2,450,913	2,094,212	1,931,504	1,328,464
Manufacturers' excise taxes	6,487,421	7,057,612	6,555,681	6,683,061	4,735,129	1,836,053
All other taxes	9,980,417	3,848,450	4,045,639	2,380,609	2,004,394	2,214,951

NOTE: For fiscal year ending September 30th.

The Appeals Process

The IRS attempts to resolve tax disputes through an administrative appeals system. Taxpayers who, after audit of their tax returns, disagree with a proposed change in their tax liabilities are entitled to an independent review of their cases. Taxpayers are able to seek an immediate, informal appeal with the Appeals Office. If, however, the dispute arises from a field audit and the amount in question exceeds $2,500, a taxpayer must submit a written protest. Alternatively, the taxpayer can wait for the examiner's report and then request consideration by the Appeals Office and file a protest if necessary. Taxpayers may represent themselves or be represented by an attorney, accountant, or any other advisor authorized to practice before the IRS.

Taxpayers can forego their right to the above process and await receipt of a deficiency notice. At this juncture, taxpayers can either (1) not pay the deficiency and petition the Tax Court by a required deadline or (2) pay the deficiency and file a claim for refund with the District Director's office. If the claim is denied, a suit for refund may be brought either in the District Court or the Court of Claims within a specified period. A third option is to let the IRS assess the tax and then submit a compromise offer on Form 656. In 1980, 49,971 cases were disposed of by agreement through the administrative process. The Tax Court tried 1,227 cases, and the U.S. District Courts and the Court of Claims tried 898 cases.

Federal Individual Income Tax

The Federal individual income tax is levied on the world-wide income of U.S. citizens and resident aliens and on certain types of U.S. source income of non-residents. A new term, "tax table income," was introduced by the Tax Reduction and Simplification Act of 1977. For a non-itemizer, "tax table income" is adjusted gross income (*see* below) since the tax tables have been simplified to account for both the zero bracket amount and personal exemptions. If a taxpayer itemizes, tax table income is adjusted gross income minus excess itemized deductions. Excess itemized deductions are the excess of a taxpayer's itemized deductions on Schedule A, Form 1040, over the zero bracket amount. The zero bracket amount is $2,300 for unmarried individuals and heads of household; $3,400 for married individuals filing jointly and for surviving spouses; $1,700 for married individuals filing separately. The tax tables apply to taxpayers up to a set ceiling on tax table income and personal exemptions as shown in the accompanying table. Taxpayers who exceed the tax table limits will use the tax rate schedules and Schedule TC, Form 1040. For this purpose tax rates are graduated from

Tax table	Filing status	Ceiling Amount	Maximum exemptions
A	Single	$20,000	3
B	Married filing jointly and qualified widow(er)	40,000	9
C	Married, filing separately	20,000	3
D	Head of household	20,000	8

a minimum of 14% on the first $2,100 of taxable income above $3,400 (for joint returns) to a maximum of 70% of taxable income above $215,400. The maximum rate on earned income, however, is 50%. The Economic Recovery Tax Act of 1981 will eliminate the distinction between earned income and unearned income. The maximum tax rate on all income will be reduced from 70% to 50% effective January 1, 1982. In addition, the minimum rate of tax will be reduced from 14% to 12% for 1982.

Who Must File a Return[1]

You must file a return if you are:	and your gross income is at least:
Single (legally separated, divorced, or married living apart from spouse with dependent child) and are under 65	$3,300
Single (legally separated, divorced, or married living apart from spouse with dependent child) and are 65 or older	$4,300
A person who can be claimed as a dependent on your parent's return, and who has taxable dividends, interest, or other unearned income	$1,000
A qualifying widow(er) with a dependent child and under 65	$4,400
A qualifying widow(er) with a dependent child and are 65 or older	$5,400
Married, filing jointly, living together at end of year (or at date of death of spouse), and both are under 65	$5,400
Married, filing jointly, living together at end of year (or at date of death of spouse), and one is 65 or older	$6,400
Married, filing jointly, living together at end of year (or at date of death of spouse), and both are 65 or older	$7,400
Married, filing separate return, or married but not living together at end of year	$1,000
A person with income from sources within U.S. possessions	$1,000
Self-employed and your net earnings from self-employment were at least $400	
A person who received any advance earned income credit payments from their employer during 1980	
A person who owes minimum tax, individual retirement arrangement tax, investment credit recapture tax or social security tax on unreported tips	

1. In 1981.

Adjusted Gross Income

Gross income consists of wages and salaries, tips and gratuities, interest, dividends, annuities, rents and royalties, and certain other types of income. Among the items excluded from gross income, and thus not subject to tax, are social security payments, federal and state unemployment compensation (phased out above a base amount), public assistance benefits, interest on exempt securities (mostly state and local bonds), and 60 percent of net capital gains. Net capital gain is the excess of net long-term capital gain over the net short-term capital loss for the year. In addition, effective for 1981 only, the dividend exclusion is expanded to include interest income and is increased to $200 ($400 on a joint return). The maximum exclusion ($400) may be claimed on a joint return regardless of how the qualifying income is earned between the spouses. *Adjusted gross income* is determined by subtracting from gross income those business-type expenses considered necessary in earning income. Job-related moving expenses and alimony may also be deducted in arriving at adjusted gross income. Starting in 1982, a limited amount of charitable contributions will be allowed as deductions in arriving at adjusted gross income.

Deductions

Taxpayers may itemize deductions or, as previously discussed, take the benefit of the zero bracket amount incorporated in the tax tables and tax rate schedules. In itemizing deductions, the following are the major items that may be deducted (with limits, in some instances); interest payments; state and local general sales, income, and property taxes; medical expenses; charitable contributions; and casualty losses.

Personal Exemptions

Personal exemptions are available to the taxpayer, his spouse, and his dependents. The amount is $1,000 for each individual. Additional exemptions of $1,000 each are granted for persons 65 and over and for the blind.

Credits

For tax years beginning after 1978, the earned income credit became permanent. The Revenue Act of 1978 grants a refundable credit for certain lower-income households with dependent children, with a maximum credit of $500 on $5,000 of earned income. This maximum credit will be reduced if earned income or adjusted gross income exceeds $6,000 and the credit will be zero for families with incomes over $10,000.

The Tax Reform Act of 1976 provided for a credit for child or dependent care expense of 20% of employment-related expenses up to $2,000 for one qualifying individual in the taxpayer's household and up to $4,000 if there are two or more qualifying individuals, this credit increases after 1981.

The Revenue Act of 1978 extended the child care credit to include payments to grandparents for care of their grandchildren, provided that the parents are not also entitled to a dependency deduction for the grandparents.

The Tax Reform Act of 1976 also provided for a new expanded and simplified credit for the elderly. A credit (a reduction of tax owed) of as much as $375 (if single) or $562.50 (if married and filing jointly) may be claimed by persons 65 or older (or persons under age 65 and retired under a public retirement system) who have retirement income. This credit, however, phases out for married couples with adjusted gross income over $10,000 and single persons with adjusted gross income over $7,500. Taxpayer may, under certain conditions, elect to claim the retirement income credit as it existed under prior law.

Expenditures for insulation and other energy–conserving components and for renewable energy source equipment are eligible for residential energy credits. The residential insulation and energy conservation credit is 15% of the first $2,000 of qualifying expenditures, with a maximum $300 credit. The residential renewable energy source equipment credit is 40% of the first $10,000 of expenditures, with a maximum credit of $4,000.

Other tax credits available to taxpayers include the targeted jobs credit and contributions to candidates for public office credit.

Federal Individual Income Tax Rates
Effective January 1, 1981

**MARRIED INDIVIDUALS FILING JOINT RETURNS
AND SURVIVING SPOUSES:**

If the taxable income is:	The tax is:
Not over $3,400	No tax
Over $3,400 but not over $5,500	14% of the excess over $3,400
Over $5,500 but not over $7,600	$294, plus 16% of the excess over $5,500
Over $7,600 but not over $11,900	$630, plus 18% of the excess over $7,600
Over $11,900 but not over $16,000	$1,404, plus 21% of the excess over $11,900
Over $16,000 but not over $20,200	$2,265, plus 24% of the excess over $16,000
Over $20,200 but not over $24,600	$3,273, plus 28% of the excess over $20,200
Over $24,600 but not over $29,900	$4,505, plus 32% of the excess over $24,600
Over $29,900 but not over $35,200	$6,201, plus 37% of the excess over $29,900
Over $35,200 but not over $45,800	$8,162, plus 43% of the excess over $35,200
Over $45,800 but not over $60,000	$12,720, plus 49% of the excess over $45,800
Over $60,000 but not over $85,600	$19,678, plus 54% of the excess over $60,000
Over $85,600 but not over $109,400	$33,502, plus 59% of the excess over $85,600
Over $109,400 but not over $162,400	$47,544, plus 64% of the excess over $109,400
Over $162,400 but not over $215,400	$81,464, plus 68% of the excess over $162,400
Over $215,400	$117,504, plus 70% of the excess over $215,400

HEADS OF HOUSEHOLDS:

If the taxable income is:	The tax is:
Not over $2,300	No tax
Over $2,300 but not over $4,400	14% of the excess over $2,300
Over $4,400 but not over $6,500	$294, plus 16% of the excess over $4,400
Over $6,500 but not over $8,700	$630, plus 18% of the excess over $6,500
Over $8,700 but not over $11,800	$1,026, plus 22% of the excess over $8,700
Over $11,800 but not over $15,000	$1,708, plus 24% of the excess over $11,800
Over $15,000 but not over $18,200	$2,476, plus 26% of the excess over $15,000
Over $18,200 but not over $23,500	$3,308, plus 31% of the excess over $18,200
Over $23,500 but not over $28,800	$4,951, plus 36% of the excess over $23,500
Over $28,800 but not over $34,100	$6,859, plus 42% of the excess over $28,800
Over $34,100 but not over $44,700	$9,085, plus 46% of the excess over $34,100
Over $44,700 but not over $60,600	$13,961, plus 54% of the excess over $44,700
Over $60,600 but not over $81,800	$22,547, plus 59% of the excess over $60,600
Over $81,800 but not over $108,300	$35,055, plus 63% of the excess over $81,800
Over $108,300 but not over $161,300	$51,750, plus 68% of the excess over $108,300
Over $161,300	$87,790, plus 70% of the excess over $161,300

NOTE: A 1 1/4 % credit will be applied against tax liability to reflect the 5% tax reduction effective October 1, 1981.

Recent Legislation

1980 Tax Legislation. 1980 saw a rush of tax legislation during the recent "Lame Duck" session of Congress.

A major reform of installment sales reporting (the Installment Sales Revision Act of 1980) was enacted. Under the new law, for dispositions after October 19, 1980, virtually any sale where payment is deferred will automatically qualify for installment treatment. If installment reporting is not desired, an election of normal reporting is required.

Additional legislation passed included the Bankruptcy Tax Act of 1980 which provides new tax rules applicable to debt discharge both for bankrupt and insolvent debtors and for solvent debtors not in bankruptcy.

New legislation affecting estimated tax payments by large corporations is effective for taxable years beginning after December 31, 1980. The new law provides that a corporation which has incurred taxable income of $1,000,000 or more in any one of the three years preceding the taxable year involved cannot rely on certain exceptions, based on the preceding year's tax or taxable income using current year's tax rates unless the estimated tax payments equal at least 60% of the tax shown on the current corporate income tax return. As a result of 1981 tax legislation this minimum percentage payment is gradually increased to 80% over a three-year period.

Sales of U.S. real property after June 18, 1980 by non-resident aliens and foreign corporations are governed by the Foreign Investment in Real Property Tax Act of 1980. With few exceptions, this act attempts to prevent most foreign investors from obtaining tax-free capital gain treatment upon the disposal of U.S. real property interests.

Other significant legislation affects the use of allowable tax credits against the alternative minimum tax; amortization of business start-up costs; and prevention of abuse of certain employee

Federal Individual Income Tax Rates
Effective January 1, 1981

UNMARRIED INDIVIDUALS:

If the taxable income is:	The tax is:
Not over $2,300	No tax
Over $2,300 but not over $3,400	14% of the excess over $2,300
Over $3,400 but not over $4,400	$154, plus 16% of the excess over $3,400
Over $4,400 but not over $6,500	$314, plus 18% of the excess over $4,400
Over $6,500 but not over $8,500	$692, plus 19% of the excess over $6,500
Over $8,500 but not over $10,800	$1,072, plus 21% of the excess over $8,500
Over $10,800 but not over $12,900	$1,555, plus 24% of the excess over $10,800
Over $12,900 but not over $15,000	$2,059, plus 26% of the excess over $12,900
Over $15,000 but not over $18,200	$2,605, plus 30% of the excess over $15,000
Over $18,200 but not over $23,500	$3,565, plus 34% of the excess over $18,200
Over $23,500 but not over $28,800	$5,367, plus 39% of the excess over $23,500
Over $28,800 but not over $34,100	$7,434, plus 44% of the excess over $28,800
Over $34,100 but not over $41,500	$9,766, plus 49% of the excess over $34,100
Over $41,500 but not over $55,300	$13,392, plus 55% of the excess over $41,500
Over $55,300 but not over $81,800	$20,982, plus 63% of the excess over $55,300
Over $81,800 but not over $108,300	$37,677, plus 68% of the excess over $81,800
Over $108,300	$55,697, plus 70% of the excess over $108,300

MARRIED INDIVIDUALS FILING SEPARATE RETURNS:

If the taxable income is:	The tax is:
Not over $1,700	No tax
Over $1,700 but not over $2,750	14% of the excess over $1,700
Over $2,750 but not over $3,800	$147, plus 16% of the excess over $2,750
Over $3,800 but not over $5,950	$315, plus 18% of the excess over $3,800
Over $5,950 but not over $8,000	$702, plus 21% of the excess over $5,950
Over $8,000 but not over $10,100	$1,132.50, plus 24% of the excess over $8,000
Over $10,100 but not over $12,300	$1,636.50, plus 28% of the excess over $10,100
Over $12,300 but not over $14,950	$2,252.50, plus 32% of the excess over $12,300
Over $14,950 but not over $17,600	$3,100.50, plus 37% of the excess over $14,950
Over $17,600 but not over $22,900	$4,081, plus 43% of the excess over $17,600
Over $22,900 but not over $30,000	$6,360, plus 49% of the excess over $22,900
Over $30,000 but not over $42,800	$9,839, plus 54% of the excess over $30,000
Over $42,800 but not over $54,700	$16,751, plus 59% of the excess over $42,800
Over $54,700 but not over $81,200	$23,772, plus 64% of the excess over $54,700
Over $81,200 but not over $107,700	$40,732, plus 68% of the excess over $81,200
Over $107,700	$58,752, plus 70% of the excess over $107,700

NOTE: A $1\frac{1}{4}$% credit will be applied against tax liability to reflect the 5% tax reduction effective October 1, 1981.

benefit requirements through a device utilizing two or more professional corporations in a partnership structure.

Crude Oil Windfall Profit Tax Act of 1980. The Crude Oil Windfall Profit Tax of 1980 covers primarily the excise tax provisions affecting domestic oil producers. It is based on windfall profits, which equals the selling price of the oil less base price which is adjusted for inflation and less a limited deduction for state severance taxes on removal of crude oil from the ground. The tax is deductible in arriving at federal taxable income for the taxable year in which the tax is paid or accrued.

Also included in the Act are certain residential energy tax credits, business energy investment credits, an increase from $100 to $200 in the dividend exclusion for 1981 which is now broadened to include an interest exclusion, and certain other business income tax provisions. Of special significance is the repeal of carryover basis for inherited property so that property acquired from a decedent gets a "stepped up" basis to date of death (or alternate valuation date—6 months after death).

Economic Recovery Tax Act of 1981. The Economic Recovery Tax Act of 1981 enacted on August 13, 1981, has as its chief objective the stimulation of economic growth through the reduction of individual income taxes. The act seeks to encourage savings and provides investment incentives to both individuals and business.

In addition to reducing both the minimum and maximum marginal rates of tax for individuals, the act reduces the maximum tax on capital gains from 28% to 20% for sales or exchanges as of June 10, 1981. Starting in 1982, the act provides for a marriage tax offset deduction of 5% of the lower-paid spouse's salary up to $1,500 and permits an adjustment to gross income for contributions to Individual Retirement Accounts of up to $2,000 per working spouse regardless of pension coverage by an employer. It also exempts cumulative interest income of up to $1,000 ($2,000 joint return) on special one-year "All-Saver" certificates issued between October 1, 1981, and December 31, 1982. The act revived the stock option as a compensation technique by providing that qualified incentive stock options exercised after 1980 will not be taxed

Federal Income Tax Comparisons
Taxes at Selected Rate Brackets After Standard Deductions/Zero Bracket Amounts[2]

Adjusted gross income	Single return listing no dependents				Joint return listing[1] dependent			
	1980	1979	1972[1]	1967	1980	1979	1972[1]	1967
$ 3,000	$ 0	$ 0	$ 141	$ 333	$ −300[3]	$ −300[3]	$ 0	$ 4
5,000	250	250	495	667	$ −500[3]	−500[3]	102	286
10,000	1,177	1,177	1,545	1,742	374	374	901	1,114
15,000	2,345	2,345	2,703	3,334	1,242	1,242	1,820	2,172
20,000	3,837	3,837	4,255	5,350	2,265	2,265	3,010	3,428
25,000	5,562	5,562	6,090	7,730	3,497	3,497	4,380	4,892

1. A 2.5% surcharge was in effect. 2. For comparison purposes, tax rate schedules were used. 3. Refund based on Earned Income credit for families with dependent children ($400 maximum), earning up to $8,000 adjusted gross income.

Returns Filed and Examined
Internal Revenue Service

Category	Returns filed for calendar year 1979	Returns examined 1980	Percent coverage
Individual total	90,727,115	1,833,858	2.02
Under $10,000[2] (non-business)	38,538,636	438,150	1.14
$10,000–$15,000 (non-business)	12,631,046	255,975	2.03
$15,000–$50,000 (non-business)	27,270,309	725,465	2.66
$50,000 and over (non-business)	1,251,151	109,337	8.74
Under $10,000 (business)	3,696,353	117,394	3.18
$10,000–$30,000 (business)	5,465,678	97,731	1.79
$30,000 and over (business)	1,873,942	89,806	4.79
Fiduciary	1,820,708	9,875	.54
Partnership	1,289,315	23,041	1.79
Corporation, total	2,061,672	133,593	6.48
Assets not reported	125,622	5,790	4.61
Under $100,000[3]	1,006,189	36,520	3.63
$100,000–$1 million	746,767	51,953	6.96
$1 million–$10 million	151,663	27,636	18.22
$10 million–$100 million	26,302	7,756	29.49
$100 million and over	5,129	3,938	76.78
Form 1120S	504,366	10,457	2.07
Form 1120 DISC	6,756	1,635	24.20
Estate, total	156,392	28,414	18.17
Gross estate under $300,000	119,199	10,376	8.70
Gross estate $300,000 and over	37,193	18,038	48.50
Gift	205,191	8,327	4.06
Income, Estate and Gift, total[1]	96,771,515	2,049,200	2.12
Excise	1,065,175	79,604	7.47
Employment	26,429,842	49,966	.19

1. Does not add due to rounding. 2. Adjusted gross income. 3. Balance sheet assets.

Results of Criminal Action in Tax Fraud Cases
Internal Revenue Service

Action	Number of Defendants					
	1980	1979	1978	1977	1976	1975
Plea of guilty nolo contendere	1,337	1,270	1,189	1,229	977	1,046
Convicted after trial	264	342	225	247	216	173
Acquitted	80	86	70	55	77	83
Nol-prossed or dismissed	193	183	119	110	71	168
Total disposals	1,874	1,881	1,603	1,641	1,341	1,470
Indictments and Informations	1,832	1,820	1,724	1,636	1,331	1,495

to the employee until sold. Starting in 1982, individual income earned abroad will be allowed a flat $75,000 exclusion from gross income. In addition, reasonable housing expenses in excess of a base amount (currently $6,059) can also be excluded or deducted from gross income.

The act also increases the amount of depreciation deduction for real property acquired after 1980 by allowing an accelerated 15–year recovery period. The Accelerated Cost Recovery System section of the act provides for a faster writeoff of capital expenditures for property acquired or placed in service retroactive to January 1, 1981. For tangible personal property, assets are grouped into four classes with recovery periods of 3, 5, 10, and 15 years. As an incentive for research and experimentation, the act provides for a 25% tax credit for certain expenditures made after June 30, 1981.

In the Estate and Gift Tax area, the unified credit for post–1976 lifetime and death transfers is gradually increased from $47,000 in 1981 to 192,800 in 1987, the equivalent of a 600,000 exemption. The maximum rate of 70% on taxable transfers will be reduced 5% a year starting in 1982 to 50% in 1985 and thereafter.

Tax Errors

In 1980, 55.3 million taxpayers filed a Form 1040, a 1.4% increase over 1979. In 1980, 37.6 million taxpayers filed a Form 1040A, a rise of 4.3% over 1979. 40% of all individual taxpayers used the short form 1040A.

Error rates rose from 1979 to 1980:

1979	Form 1040	7.3%
1979	Form 1040A	5.5%
1980	Form 1040	7.5%
1980	Form 1040A	6.3%

Federal Corporation Taxes

For tax years beginning after 1978, the old corporate system of normal tax, surtax, and surtax exemption is replaced by a graduated tax rate structure that provides for tax reductions to stimulate the economy. The new rates are graduated over the first four $25,000 amounts of taxable income as follows:

1981

Taxable income	Tax	Percent over excess
$0 to $25,000[1]	$ 0	17% over $0
$25,000–50,000[1]	$ 4,250	20% over $25,000
$50,000–75,000	$ 9,250	30% over $50,000
$75,000–100,000	$16,750	40% over $75,000
$100,000 and over	$26,750	46% over $100,000

1. Rates will decrease after 1981.

The Tax Reform Act of 1976 made certain changes affecting the taxation of corporations. Foreign tax advantages are denied to companies that participate in international boycotts. The foreign tax credit, deferral of earnings of foreign subsidiaries, and benefits derived through Domestic International Sales Corporations (DISC) are denied in proportion to income attributable to boycott activity. The amount of any illegal payments to a foreign official may not be deducted.

DISC is exempt from all federal taxes, but DISC shareholders are deemed to have received as a dividend 50% of the corporation's net income every taxable year. Thus, use of a DISC permitted deferral of tax on one-half of DISC income. The 1976 Tax Reform Act reduced this deferral and permits DISC benefits only to the extent that gross export receipts exceed 67% of the average for a four-year base. Full DISC benefits are retained for those having taxable income of $100,000 or less for a taxable year, but phase out at $150,000.

The tax law provides for a credit for investments in depreciable personal property. The 10% credit as well as the $100,000 limitation on used property eligible for the credit has been made permanent by the Revenue Act of 1978. There is an additional 1% credit if the employer established an Employee Stock Ownership Plan (ESOP) meeting specified criteria. An additional half percent credit is available if employee contributions to an ESOP match the half percent. The tax liability credit limitation is increased over a transitional period. The 1978 Energy Tax Act provides for certain additional investment credits.

In 1978, the targeted jobs credit replaced the new jobs credit. The credit may be elected by employers who hire individuals from certain target groups. The credit is equal to 50% of the first $6,000 of qualified first-year wages and 25% of the first $6,000 of qualified second-year wages paid to each such individual. However, the qualified first-year wages for all such employees may not exceed 30% of the total unemployment insurance wages (FUTA) paid by the employer during the current year.

State Corporation Income and Franchise Taxes

All states but Nevada, South Dakota, Texas, Washington, and Wyoming impose a tax on corporation net income. The majority of states impose the tax at flat rates ranging from 3% to 12%. Several states have adopted a graduated basis of rates for corporations.

Nearly all states follow the federal law in defining net income. However, many states provide for varying exclusions and adjustments.

A state is empowered to tax all of the net income of its domestic corporations. With regard to nonresident corporations, however, it may only tax the net income on business carried on within its boundaries. Corporations are, therefore, required to apportion their incomes among the states where they do business and pay a tax to each of these states. Nearly all states provide an apportionment to their domestic corporations, too, in order that they not be unduly burdened.

Several states tax unincorporated businesses separately.

Federal Estate and Gift Taxes

A Federal Estate Tax Return must be filed for the estate of every U.S. citizen or resident whose gross estate, if the decedent died in 1981, exceeds $175,625. The gross estate filing requirement is increased and phased in from 1982 to 1987 from the present $175,625 to $600,000. An estate tax return must also be filed for the estate of a non-resident, not a citizen, if the value of his gross estate in the U.S. is more than $30,000 at the date of death. The estate tax return is due nine months after the date of death of the decedent, but a reasonable extension of time to file may be obtained for good reason. Tax due is to be paid when the return is filed. The executor of an estate with an interest in closely held business may pay estate tax attributable to the business in from two to ten equal annual installments. In 1981, to be eligible for this treatment, the interest in the closely held business (or businesses) represented at least 35% of the gross estate or 50% of the taxable estate. A 15-year extension for the payment of estate taxes may be exercised for that portion of the tax attributable to a closely held business whose value constitutes more than 65% of the decedent's adjusted gross estate.

Under the unified federal estate and gift tax structure, a gift tax return is required to be filed on a quarterly basis only when the sum of (1) the taxable gifts made during the calendar quarter plus (2) all other gifts made during the calendar year exceeds $25,000. If a return is required, it should be filed no later than one and one half months after the end of a calendar quarter. The gift tax is due at the same time the return is required to be filed. Effective for returns reporting gifts made in calendar year 1979 and thereafter, the filing of the fourth quarter gift tax return can be made on April 15 rather than February 15.

The Tax Reform Act of 1976 replaced the old $30,000 gift tax exemption and $60,000 estate tax exemption with a unified credit. This credit is used for both estate and gift taxes. Any part of the credit used to offset gift taxes is not available to offset estate taxes. As a result, although they are still taxable as gifts, lifetime transfers no longer cushion the impact of progressive estate tax rates. Lifetime transfers and transfers made at death are cumulated for estate tax rate purposes. Gift taxes are computed by applying the uniform rate schedule to lifetime taxable transfers (after deducting the unified credit) and subtracting the taxes payable for prior taxable periods. In general, estate taxes are computed by applying the uniform rate schedule to cumulated transfers and subtracting the gift taxes paid. An appropriate adjustment is made for taxes on lifetime transfers—such as gifts within three years of death—in a decedent's estate.

Among the deductions allowed in computing the amount of the estate subject to tax are funeral expenditures, administrative costs, claims and bequests to religious, charitable, and fraternal organizations or government welfare agencies, and state inheritance taxes. A marital deduction is also allowable for both estates and gifts. The Tax Reform Act of 1976 provides a maximum estate marital deduction of the greater of $250,000 or one-half of the decedent's adjusted gross estate. As a result, a decedent utilizing the maximum marital deduction will have no estate tax in 1981. The Tax Reform Act of 1976 provides for a gift marital deduction of $100,000 for the first $100,000 of lifetime gifts made to a spouse, no deduction for the next $100,000 of such gifts, and thereafter a deduction for one half of the aggregate lifetime gifts made to a spouse in excess of $200,000. For transfers made after 1981 during life or death, there will be an unlimited marital deduction. An annual gift tax exclusion is provided that permits tax-free gifts to each donee of $3,000 for each year. A husband and wife that agree to treat gifts to third persons as joint gifts can exclude up to $6,000 a year to each donee. Effective January 1, 1982, an individual will be permitted to make a tax free gift of up to $10,000 to each donee and a husband and wife may similarly gift $20,000 jointly to a third person. An unlimited exclusion for medical expenses and school tuition paid for the benefit of any donee is available after 1981.

Unified Credit— Estate & Gift Taxes

Year	Credit
1977	$30,000
1978	34,000
1979	38,000
1980	42,500
1981	47,000

The Erosion of Purchasing Power

In 1970, a $10,000-a-year family had $8,640 to spend after Federal income and Social Security taxes. In 1980, the same family needed a gross income of $20,187 to match its 1970 after-tax spending power. Taxes siphoned off $3,408 of income, while an additional $8,139 was needed to cover the rise in prices over the ten-year period.

Estimates indicate that the median family income for 1980 was $21,350, up from $9,867 in 1970. Despite this 116% rise in income, real purchasing power after taxes was only 7% greater than in 1970.

Federal Estate and Gift Taxes
Unified Rate Schedule, 1981[1]

If the net amount is:		Tentative tax is:		
From	To	Tax +	%	On excess over
$ 0	$ 10,000	$ 0	18	$ 0
$10,000	20,000	1,800	20	10,000
20,000	40,000	3,800	22	20,000
40,000	60,000	8,200	24	40,000
60,000	80,000	13,000	26	60,000
80,000	100,000	18,200	28	80,000
100,000	150,000	23,800	30	100,000
150,000	250,000	38,800	32	150,000
250,000	500,000	70,800	34	250,000
500,000	750,000	155,800	37	500,000
750,000	1,000,000	248,300	39	750,000
1,000,000	1,250,000	345,800	41	1,000,000
1,250,000	1,500,000	448,300	43	1,250,000
1,500,000	2,000,000	555,800	45	1,500,000
2,000,000	2,500,000	780,800	49	2,000,000
2,500,000	3,000,000	1,025,800	53	2,500,000
3,000,000	3,500,000	1,290,800	57	3,000,000
3,500,000	4,000,000	1,575,800	61	3,500,000
4,000,000	4,500,000	1,880,800	65	4,000,000
4,500,000	5,000,000	2,205,800	69	4,500,000
5,000,000	—	2,550,800	70	5,000,000

1. The estate and gift tax rates are combined in the single rate schedule effective for the estates of decedents dying, and for gifts made, after Dec. 31, 1976.

State General Sales and Use Taxes[1]
(as of August 1, 1981)

State	Percent rate	State	Percent rate	State	Percent rate
Alabama	4	Kentucky	5	Ohio	4
Arizona	4	Louisiana	3	Oklahoma	2
Arkansas	3	Maine	5	Pennsylvania	6
California	4.75	Maryland	5	Rhode Island	6
Colorado	3	Massachusetts	5	South Carolina	4
Connecticut	7.5	Michigan	4	South Dakota	4
D.C.	6	Minnesota	4	Tennessee[3]	4.5
Florida	4	Mississippi	5	Texas	4
Georgia	3	Missouri	3.125	Utah	4
Hawaii	4	Nebraska	3	Vermont	3
Idaho	3	Nevada	5.75	Virginia	3
Illinois[2]	4	New Jersey	5	Washington	4.5
Indiana	4	New Mexico	3.5	West Virginia[4]	5
Iowa	3	New York	4	Wisconsin	4
Kansas	3	North Carolina	3	Wyoming	3
		North Dakota	3		

1. Local and county taxes, if any, are additional. 2. 2% on food and drugs. 3. Continues temporary State Retail Sales Tax for one year at 4.5%. 4. 3% on mobile homes used as principal year-round residence. NOTE: Alaska, Delaware, Montana, New Hampshire and Oregon have no statewide sales and use taxes. *Source: Information Please Almanac* questionnaires to the states.

Income Tax Rates in Selected Cities
(Population exceeding 50,000)

City	Percent rate	Year begun	City	Percent rate	Year begun
Akron, Ohio	1.8	1962	Kettering, Ohio	1	1968
Allentown, Pa.	1	1958	Lakewood, Ohio	1	1968
Altoona, Pa.	1	1948	Lancaster, Pa.	0.5	1959
Baltimore	(1)	1966	Lansing, Mich.	1	1968
Bethlehem, Pa.	1	1957	Lexington, Ky.	2	1952
Birmingham, Ala.	1	1970	Lima, Ohio	1	1959
Canton, Ohio	1.5	1954	Lorain, Ohio	1	1967
Cincinnati	2	1954	Louisville, Ky.	2.2	1948
Cleveland	2	1967	Mansfield, Ohio	1	1966
Cleveland Heights, Ohio	2	1968	New York	0.9–4.3	1966
Columbus, Ohio	1.5	1947	Owensboro, Ky.	1	1960
Covington, Ky.	2.5	1956	Parma, Ohio	1	1967
Dayton, Ohio	1.75	1949	Philadelphia	4.3125	1939
Detroit	2	1965	Pontiac, Mich.	1	1968
District of Columbia	2–11	1947	Reading, Pa.	1	1969
Elyria, Ohio	1.5	1969	Saginaw, Mich.	1	1965
Erie, Pa.	1	1948	St. Louis	1	1948
Euclid, Ohio	1.5	1967	Scranton, Pa.	2.6	1948
Flint, Mich.	1	1965	Springfield, Ohio	2	1948
Gadsden, Ala.	2	1956	Toledo, Ohio	1.5	1946
Grand Rapids, Mich.	1	1967	Warren, Ohio	1	1952
Hamilton, Ohio	1.5	1960	Wilkes-Barre, Pa.	2	1966
Harrisburg, Pa.	1	1966	Wilmington, Del.	1	1970
Kansas City, Mo.	1	1964	York, Pa.	1	1965
			Youngstown, Ohio	1.5	1948

1. Tax is 50% of state income tax. NOTE: Rates are for residents only, except in Kentucky, Ohio, and Pennsylvania cities, where non-resident rate is the same. *Source:* Tax Foundation, Inc.

Sales Tax Rates in Selected Cities[1]

City	Percent rate	City	Percent rate	City	Percent rate
Amarillo, Tex.	1	Ithaca, N.Y.[2]	3	Richmond, Va.	1
Anaheim, Calif.[2]	1.25	Jefferson City, Mo.	1	Roanoke, Va.	1
Austin, Tex.	1	Lincoln, Neb.	1	Sacramento, Calif.[2]	1.25
Baton Rouge, La.[3]	3	Los Angeles[2]	1.25	St. Louis	1
Berkeley, Calif.[2][4]	1.75	Lynchburg, Va.	1	San Antonio, Tex.	1
Birmingham, Ala.	1	Mobile, Ala.	2	San Diego, Calif.[2]	1.25
Boulder, Colo.	2	Montgomery, Ala.	2	San Francisco[2][4]	1.75
Chicago[2]	2	New Orleans[3]	3	Seattle[2]	0.925
Dallas	1	New York	4	Shreveport, La.[3]	3
Denver	3	Nome, Alaska	3	Spokane, Wash.[2]	0.925
Duluth, Minn.	1	Norfolk, Va.	1	Springfield, Ill.[2]	2
El Paso	1	Oakland, Calif.[2][4]	1.75	Topeka, Kan.	0.5
Fort Worth	1	Oklahoma City	2	Troy, N.Y.[2]	3
Fresno, Calif.[2]	1.25	Omaha, Neb.	1.5	Tucson, Ariz.	2
Glendale, Calif.[2]	1.25	Pasadena, Calif.[2]	1.25	Tulsa, Okla.	3
Houston	1	Phoenix, Ariz.	1	Washington, D.C.	6
Huntsville, Ala.	2	Rapid City, S.D.	1.5	Yonkers, N.Y.[2]	4

1. Excludes state and county sales taxes unless otherwise indicated. 2. Combined city and county rate. 3. Includes Parish School Board tax. 4. Includes 0.5% imposed by San Francisco Bay Area Rapid Transit District. *Source: Information Please Almanac* questionnaires.

Tax Burden Highest in Large Cities

According to the Census Bureau, the tax burden in large cities is four times the rate in small cities. New York has the highest tax burden, $841.79 per person, and Houston has the lowest at $175.03. The national average is $201 per person in taxes collected by all communities and a per-capita burden of $108 in cities of less than 50,000 residents.

According to the study, which is based on fiscal year 1977–78, the predominant tax source was property which provided $16.3 billion in revenues.

AVIATION

Famous Firsts in Aviation

1782 First balloon flight. Jacques and Joseph Montgolfier of Annonay, France, sent up a small smoke-filled balloon about mid-November.

1783 First hydrogen-filled balloon flight. Jacques A. C. Charles, Paris physicist, supervised construction by A. J. and M. N. Robert of a 13-ft diameter balloon that was filled with hydrogen. It got up to about 3,000 ft and traveled about 16 mi. in a 45-min flight (Aug. 27).

First human balloon flights. A Frenchman, Jean Pilâtre de Rozier, made the first captive-balloon ascension (Oct. 15). With the Marquis d'Arlandes, Pilâtre de Rozier made the first free flight, reaching a peak altitude of about 500 ft, and traveling about 5½ mi. in 20 min (Nov. 21).

1784 First powered balloon. Gen. Jean Baptiste Marie Meusnier developed the first propeller-driven and elliptically-shaped balloon—the crew cranking three propellers on a common shaft to give the craft a speed of about 3 mph.

First woman to fly. Mme. Thible, a French opera singer (June 4).

1793 First balloon flight in America. Jean Pierre Blanchard, a French pilot, made it from Philadelphia to near Woodbury, Gloucester County, N.J., in a little over 45 min (Jan. 9).

1794 First military use of the balloon. Jean Marie Coutelle, using a balloon built for the French Army, made two 4-hr observation ascents. The military purpose of the ascents seems to have been to damage the enemy's morale.

1797 First parachute jump. André-Jacques Garnerin dropped from about 6,500 ft over Monceau Park in Paris in a 23-ft diameter parachute made of white canvas with a basket attached (Oct. 22).

1843 First air transport company. In London, William S. Henson and John Stringfellow filed articles of incorporation for the Aerial Transit Company (March 24). It failed

1852 First dirigible. Henri Giffard, a French engineer, flew in a controllable (more or less) steam-engine powered balloon, 144 ft long and 39 ft in diameter, inflated with 88,000 cu ft of coal gas. It reached 6.7 mph on a flight from Paris to Trappe (Sept. 24).

1860 First aerial photographers. Samuel Archer King and William Black made two photos of Boston, still in existence.

1872 First gas-engine powered dirigible. Paul Haenlein, a German engineer, flew in a semi-rigid-frame dirigible, powered by a 4-cylinder internal-combustion engine running on coal gas drawn from the supporting bag.

1873 First transatlantic attempt. *The New York Daily Graphic* sponsored the attempt with a 400,000 cu ft balloon carrying a lifeboat. A rip in the bag during inflation brought collapse of the balloon and the project.

1897 First successful metal dirigible. An all-metal dirigible, designed by David Schwarz, a Hungarian, took off from Berlin's Tempelhof Field and, powered by a 16-hp Daimler engine, got several miles before leaking gas caused it to crash (Nov. 13).

1900 First Zeppelin flight. Germany's Count Ferdinand von Zeppelin flew the first of his long series of rigid-frame airships. It attained a speed of 18 mi. per h and got 3½ mi. before its steering gear failed (July 2).

1903 First successful heavier-than-air machine flight. Aviation was really born on the sand dunes at Kitty Hawk, N.C., when Orville Wright crawled to his prone position between the wings of the biplane he and his brother Wilbur had built, opened the throttle of their homemade 12-hp engine and took to the air. He covered 120 ft in 12 sec. Later that day, in one of four flights, Wilbur stayed up 59 sec and covered 852 ft (Dec. 17).

1904 First airplane maneuvers. Orville Wright made the first turn with an airplane (Sept. 15); 5 days later his brother Wilbur made the first complete circle.

1905 First airplane flight over half an hour. Orville Wright kept his craft up 33 min 17 sec (Oct. 4).

1906 First European airplane flight. Alberto Santos-Dumont, a Brazilian, flew a heavier-than-air machine at Bagatelle Field, Paris (Sept. 13).

1908 First airplane fatality. Lt. Thomas E. Selfridge, U.S. Army Signal Corps, was in a group of officers evaluating the Wright plane at Fort Myer, Va. He was up about 75 ft with Orville Wright when the propeller hit a bracing wire and was broken, throwing the plane out of control, killing Selfridge and seriously injuring Wright (Sept. 17).

1910 First licensed woman pilot. Baroness Raymonde de la Roche of France, who learned to fly in 1909, received ticket No. 36 on March 8.

First flight from shipboard. Lt. Eugene Ely, USN, took a Curtiss plane off from the deck of cruiser *Birmingham* at Hampton Roads, Va., and flew to Norfolk (Nov. 14). The following January, he reversed the process, flying from Camp Selfridge to the deck of the armored cruiser *Pennsylvania* in San Francisco Bay (Jan. 18).

1911 First U.S. woman pilot. Harriet Quimby, a magazine writer, who got ticket No. 37.

1913 First multi-engined aircraft. Built and flown by Igor Ivan Sikorsky while still in his native Russia.

1914 First aerial combat. In August, Allied and German pilots and observers started shooting at each other with pistols and rifles—with negligible results.

1915 First air raids on England. German Zeppelins started dropping bombs on four English communities (Jan. 19).

1918 **First U.S. air squadron.** The U.S. Army Air Corps made its first independent raids over enemy lines, in DH-4 planes (British-designed) powered with 400-hp American-designed Liberty engines (April 8).

First regular airmail service. Operated for the Post Office Department by the Army, the first regular service was inaugurated with one round trip a day (except Sunday) between Washington, D.C., and New York City (May 15).

1919 **First transatlantic flight.** The NC-4, one of four Curtiss flying boats commanded by Lt. Comdr. Albert C. Read, reached Lisbon, Portugal, (May 27) after hops from Trepassy Bay, Newfoundland, to Horta, Azores (May 16–17), to Ponta Delgada (May 20). The Liberty-powered craft was piloted by Walter Hinton.

First nonstop transatlantic flight. Capt. John Alcock and Lt. Arthur Whitten Brown, British World War I flyers, made the 1,900 mi. from St. John's, Newfoundland, to Clifden, Ireland, in 16 h 12 min in a Vickers-Vimy bomber with two 350-hp Rolls-Royce engines (June 15–16).

First lighter-than-air transatlantic flight. The British dirigible R-34, commanded by Maj. George H. Scott, left Firth of Forth, Scotland, (July 2) and touched down at Mineola, L.I., 108 h later. The eastbound trip was made in 75 h (completed July 13).

First scheduled passenger service (using airplanes). Aircraft Travel and Transport inaugurated London-Paris service (Aug. 25). Later the company started the first trans-channel mail service on the same route (Nov. 10).

1921 **First naval vessel sunk by aircraft.** Two battleships being scrapped by treaty were sunk by bombs dropped from Army planes in demonstration put on by Brig. Gen. William S. Mitchell (July 21).

First helium balloon. The C-7, non-rigid Navy dirigible was first to use non-inflammable helium as lifting gas, making a flight from Hampton Roads, Va., to Washington, D.C. (Dec. 1).

1922 **First member of Caterpillar Club.** Lt. (later Maj. Gen.) Harold Harris bailed out of a crippled plane he was testing at McCook Field, Dayton, Ohio (Oct. 20), and became the first man to join the Caterpillar Club—those whose lives have been saved by parachute.

1923 **First nonstop transcontinental flight.** Lts. John A. Macready and Oakley Kelly flew a single-engine Fokker T-2 nonstop from New York to San Diego, a distance of just over 2,500 mi. in 26 h 50 min (May 2–3).

First autogyro flight. Juan de la Cierva, a brilliant Spanish mathematician, made the first successful flight in a rotary wing aircraft in Madrid (June 9).

1924 **First round-the-world flight.** Four Douglas Cruiser biplanes of the U.S. Army Air Corps took off from Seattle under command of Maj. Frederick Martin (April 6). 175 days later, two of the planes (Lt. Lowell Smith's and Lt. Erik Nelson's) landed in Seattle after a circuitous route—one source saying 26,345 mi., another saying 27,553 mi.

1926 **First polar flight.** Then-Lt. Cmdr. Richard E. Byrd, acting as navigator, and Floyd Bennett as pilot, flew a trimotor Fokker from Kings Bay, Spitsbergen, over the North Pole and back in 15½ h (May 8–9).

1927 **First solo transatlantic flight.** Charles Augustus Lindbergh lifted his Wright-powered Ryan monoplane, *Spirit of St. Louis*, from Roosevelt Field, L.I., to stay aloft 33 h 39 min and travel 3,600 mi. to Le Bourget Field outside Paris (May 20–21).

First transatlantic passenger. Charles A. Levine was piloted by Clarence D. Chamberlin from Roosevelt Field, L.I., to Eisleben, Germany, in a Wright-powered Bellanca (June 4–5).

1928 **First east-west transatlantic crossing.** Baron Guenther von Huenefeld, piloted by German Capt. Hermann Koehl and Irish Capt. James Fitzmaurice, left Dublin for New York City (April 12) in a single-engine all-metal Junkers monoplane. Some 37 h later, they crashed on Greely Island, Labrador. Rescued.

First U.S.-Australia flight. Sir Charles Kingsford-Smith and Capt. Charles T. P. Ulm, Australians, and two American navigators, Harry W. Lyon and James Warner, crossed the Pacific from Oakland to Brisbane. They went via Hawaii and the Fiji Islands in a trimotor Fokker (May 31–June 8).

First transarctic flight. Sir Hubert Wilkins, an Australian explorer and Carl Ben Eielson, who served as pilot, flew from Point Barrow, Alaska, to Spitsbergen (mid-April).

1929 **First of the endurance records.** With Air Corps Maj. Carl Spaatz in command and Capt. Ira Eaker as chief pilot, an Army Fokker, aided by refueling in the air, remained aloft 150 h 40 min at Los Angeles (Jan. 1–7).

First blind flight. James H. Doolittle proved the feasibility of instrument-guided flying when he took off and landed entirely on instruments (Sept. 24).

First rocket-engine flight. Fritz von Opel, a German auto maker, stayed aloft in his small rocket-powered craft for 75 sec, covering nearly 2 mi. (Sept. 30).

First South Pole flight. Comdr. Richard E. Byrd, with Bernt Balchen as pilot, Harold I. June, radio operator, and Capt. A. C. McKinley, photographer, flew a trimotor Fokker from the Bay of Whales, Little America, over the South Pole and back (Nov. 28–29).

1930 **First Paris–New York nonstop flight.** Dieudonné Coste and Maurice Bellonte, French pilots, flew a Hispano-powered Breguet biplane from Le Bourget Field to Valley Stream, L.I., in 37 h 18 min. (Sept. 2–3).

1931 **First flight into the stratosphere.** Auguste Piccard, a Swiss physicist, and Charles Knipfer, ascended in a balloon from Augsburg, Germany, and reached a height of 51,793 ft in a 17-h flight that terminated on a glacier near Innsbruck, Austria (May 27).

First nonstop transpacific flight. Hugh Herndon and Clyde Pangborn took off from Sabishiro Beach, Japan, dropped their landing gear, and flew 4,860 mi. to near Wenatchee, Wash., in 41 h 13 min. (Oct. 4–5).

1932 **First woman's transatlantic solo.** Amelia Earhart, flying a Pratt & Whitney Wasp-powered Lockheed Vega, flew alone from Harbor Grace, Newfoundland, to Ireland in approximately 15 h (May 20–21).

First westbound transatlantic solo. James A. Mollison, a British pilot, took a de Havilland Puss Moth from Portmarnock, Ireland, to Pennfield, N.B. (Aug. 18).

First woman airline pilot. Ruth Rowland Nichols, first woman to hold three international records at the same time—speed, distance, altitude—was employed by N.Y.-New England Airways.

1933 **First round-the-world solo.** Wiley Post took a Lockheed Vega, *Winnie Mae*, 15,596 mi. around the world in 7 d 18 h 49½ min (July 15–22).

1937 **First successful helicopter.** Hanna Reitsch, a German pilot, flew Dr. Heinrich Focke's FW-61 in free, fully-controlled flight at Bremen (July 4).

1939 **First turbojet flight.** Just before their invasion of Poland, the Germans flew a Heinkel He-178 plane powered by a Heinkel S3B turbojet (Aug. 27).

1942 **First American jet plane flight.** Robert Stanley, chief pilot for Bell Aircraft Corp., flew the Bell XP-59 *Airacomet* at Muroc Army Base, Calif. (Oct. 1).

1947 **First piloted supersonic flight in an airplane.** Capt. Charles E. Yeager, U.S. Air Force, flew the X-1 rocket-powered research plane built by Bell Aircraft Corp., faster than the speed of sound at Muroc Air Force Base, California (Oct. 14).

1949 **First round-the-world nonstop flight.** Capt. James Gallagher and USAF crew of 13 flew a Boeing B-50A Superfortress around the world nonstop from Ft. Worth, returning to same point: 23,452 mi. in 94 h 1 min, with 4 aerial refuelings enroute (Feb. 27–March 2).

1950 **First nonstop transatlantic jet flight.** Col. David C. Schilling (USAF) flew 3,300 mi. from England to Limestone, Maine, in 10 h 1 min (Sept. 22).

1951 **First solo across North Pole.** Charles F. Blair, Jr., flew a converted P-51 (May 29).

1952 **First jetliner service.** De Havilland Comet flight inaugurated by BOAC between London and Johannesburg, South Africa (May 2). Flight, including stops, took 23 h 38 min.

First transatlantic helicopter flight. Capt. Vincent H. McGovern and 1st Lt. Harold W. Moore piloted 2 Sikorsky H-19s from Westover, Mass., to Prestwick, Scotland (3,410 mi.). Trip was made in 5 steps, with flying time of 42 h 25 min (July 15–31).

First transatlantic round trip in same day. British Canberra twin-jet bomber flew from Aldergrove, Northern Ireland, to Gander, Newfoundland, and back in 7 h 59 min flying time (Aug. 26).

1955 **First transcontinental round trip in same day.** Lt. John M. Conroy piloted F-86 Sabrejet across U.S. (Los Angeles–New York) and back—5,085 mi.—in 11 h 33 min 27 sec (May 21).

1957 **First round-the-world, nonstop jet plane flight.** Maj. Gen. Archie J. Old, Jr., USAF, led a flight of 3 Boeing B-52 bombers, powered with 8 10,-000-lb. thrust Pratt & Whitney Aircraft J57 engines around the world in 45 h 19 min; distance 24,325 mi.; average speed 525 mph. (Completed Jan. 18.)

1958 **First transatlantic jet passenger service.** BOAC, New York to London (Oct. 4). Pan American started daily service, N.Y. to Paris (Oct. 26).

First domestic jet passenger service. National Airlines inaugurated service between New York and Miami (Dec. 10).

1976 **First regularly-scheduled commercial supersonic transport (SST) flights begin.** Air France and British Airways inaugurate service (January 21). Air France flies the Paris-Rio de Janeiro route; B.A., the London-Bahraine. Both airlines begin SST service to Washington, D.C. (May 24).

1977 **First successful man-powered aircraft.** Paul MacCready, an aeronautical engineer from Pasadena, Calif., was awarded the Kremer Prize for creating the world's first successful man-powered aircraft. The *Gossamer Condor* was flown by Bryan Allen over the required 3-mile course on Aug. 23.

1978 **First successful transatlantic balloon flight.** Three Albuquerque, N.M., men, Ben Abruzzo, Larry Newman, and Maxie Anderson, completed the crossing (Aug. 16. Landed, Aug. 17) in their hot air balloon, *Double Eagle II*.

1979 **First man-powered aircraft to fly across the English Channel.** The Kremer Prize for the Channel crossing was won by Bryan Allen who flew the *Gossamer Albatross* from Folkestone, England to Cape Gris-Nez, France, in 2 h 55 min (June 12).

1980 **First successful balloon flight over the North Pole.** Sidney Conn and his wife Eleanor, in hot-air balloon *Joy of Sound* (April 11).

First nonstop transcontinental balloon flight, and also record for longest overland voyage in a balloon. Maxie Anderson and his son, Kris, completed four-day flight from Fort Baker, Calif., to successful landing outside Matane, Quebec, on May 12 in their helium-filled balloon, *Kitty Hawk*.

First long-distance solar-powered flight. Janice Brown, 98-lb. former teacher, flew tiny experimental solar-powered aircraft, *Solar Challenger* six miles in 22-min near Marana, Ariz. (Dec. 3). The craft was powered by a 2.75-hp engine.

First solar-powered aircraft to fly across the English Channel. Stephen R. Ptacek flew the 210-lb *Solar Challenger* at the average speed of 30 mph from Cormeilles-en-Vexin near Paris to the Royal Manston Air Force Base on England's southeastern coast in 5h 30 min (July 7).

U. S. Airlines Transport Planes

Manufacturer	Type	Number of passengers	Maximum speed, mph	Typical gross weight, lbs	Wingspan, ft	Maximum length, ft
4-ENGINE						
Boeing	707–120B	100–181	600	258,000	142.4	145.1
Boeing	707–320, –402/Intercontinental	108–189	600	316,000	142.4	152.9
Boeing	707–320B, C/Intercontinental	145	600	336,000	145.8	152.9
Boeing	747–100B/Superjet	442	640	733,000	195.7	231.9
Boeing	747–200B, C/Superjet	442	640	785,000	195.7	231.9
Boeing	747SR/Superjet	512	640	600,000	195.7	231.9
Boeing	747SP/Superjet	321	640	696,000	195.7	184.7
Douglas	DC–6B	90–100	300	100,000	117.5	106.8
McDonnell Douglas	DC–8/Series 30,40	116–176	600+	315,000	142.3	150.5
McDonnell Douglas	DC–8/Series 50	116–189	600	325,000	142.3	150.5
McDonnell Douglas	DC–8/Super 61	259	600	325,000	142.3	187.4
McDonnell Douglas	DC–8/Super 62	189	600	325,000	148.4	157.4
McDonnell Douglas	DC–8/Super 63	259	600	350,000	148.4	187.4
DeHavilland	DHC–7	50	270	26,700	93.0	80.6
Lockheed	L–188	94	373	113,000	99.0	104.5
3-ENGINE						
Airbus Industries	A–300	269–345	600	347,100	147.1	175.1
Boeing	727–100	70–131	600+	170,000	108.0	133.1
Boeing	727–200/Advanced	145	600+	191,500	108.0	153.1
McDonnell Douglas	DC–10/Series 10	250–380	600+	455,000	155.3	182.3
McDonnell Douglas	DC–10/Series 30	250–380	600+	572,000	165.3	181.6
McDonnell Douglas	DC–10/Series 40	250–350	600+	572,000	165.3	182.3
Lockheed	L–1011–1/TriStar	240–400	620+	430,000	155.3	177.7
Lockheed	L–1011–100, –200/TriStar	250–400	620+	466,000	155.3	177.7
Lockheed	L–1011–500/TriStar	230–330	620+	496,000	155.3	164.2
2-ENGINE						
Beech	B–99	15	285	10,900	45.8	44.6
Boeing	737–100	112	586	111,000	93.0	94.0
Boeing	737–200/Advanced	115	586	116,000	93.0	100.2
Boeing	737–200/Advanced	115	586	125,000	93.0	100.2
Cessna	402	6–10	242	6,885	44.1	36.4
Convair	580	50	270	52,000	105.4	81.5
DeHavilland	DHC–6	20	210	12,500	65.0	51.7
Douglas	DC–3	21–30	200	24,800	95.0	64.5
McDonnell Douglas	DC–9/Series 10	90	576	90,700	89.4	104.4
McDonnell Douglas	DC–9/Series 20	90	576	98,000	93.4	104.4
McDonnell Douglas	DC–9 Series 30	115	576	121,000	93.4	119.3
McDonnell Douglas	DC–9/Series 40	125	576	121,000	93.4	125.6
McDonnell Douglas	DC–9/Series 50	139	576	122,000	93.4	133.6
McDonnell Douglas	DC–9/Series 80	167	576	140,000	107.8	149.9
Marcel Dassault	Falcon–10	4–7	600+	10,760	42.9	45.5
Piper	PA–23	6	247	5,200	37.3	31.2
Piper	PA–31	6	247	6,500	40.7	32.6
Short Brothers Harland	SH–330	30	228	22,600	74.7	58.0
Swearingen	SA–226TC	20	300	12,500	46.4	59.4

NOTE: Data show the most-used manufacturers' type and model aircraft used by air carriers and commercial operators as of April 1980. *Source:* Federal Aviation Administration.

Active Pilot Certificates Held
(as of January 1)

Year	Total[1]	Airline transport	Commercial	Private
1970	720,028	31,442	176,585	299,491
1975	733,728	41,002	192,425	305,848
1980	814,667	63,652	182,097	343,276
1981	827,071	69,569	183,442	357,479

1. Includes other pilot categories—helicopter, glider and lighter-than-air (1981: 16,748); and students (1981: 199,833). *Source:* Department of Transportation, Federal Aviation Administration.

Important American Aircraft Types (U.S. Air Force)

Abbreviations: GA—Garrett AiResearch; All—Detroit Diesel Allison Div. of General Motors; Con—Continental; GD—General Dynamics; GE—General Electric; Lyc—Lycoming; RI—Rockwell International; P&W—Pratt & Whitney; PWC—Pratt & Whitney Aircraft of Canada, Ltd; Wr—Curtiss Wright; kt—knots.

Type	Manufacturer	Popular name	Power plant	Crew	Wing-span ft/in.	Length, ft/in.	Height, ft/in.	Gross weight, lb	Speed, mph
ATTACK									
A-7D	LTV Aerospace	Corsair II	1 All TF41-A-1	1	38/9	46/1	16/0	42,000	698
A-10A	Fairchild Hiller	Thunderbolt II	2 GE TF34-GE-100	1	57/5	53/3	14/6	46,038	449
A-37B	Cessna	Dragonfly	2 GE J85-GE-17A	1	35/8	29/3	8/9	14,000	507
BOMBERS									
B-52D	Boeing	Stratofortress	8 P&W J57-P-29W	6	185/0	156/6	48/4	450,000	650
B-52G	Boeing	Stratofortress	8 P&W J57-P-43W	6	185/0	161/11	40/8	488,000	650
B-52H	Boeing	Stratofortress	8 P&W TF33-P-3	6	185/0	159/3	40/8	488,000	650
FB-111A	GD/Ft. Worth	—	2 P&W TF30-P-7	2	70/0[3]	73/6	17/0	114,000	Mach 2+
FIGHTERS									
F-4D/E	McDonnell Douglas	Phantom II	2 GEJ79-GE-17	2	38/7	63/0	16/5	61,975	Mach 2.2
F-15A/B/C	McDonnell Douglas	Eagle	2 P&W F100-PW-100	1/2	42/8	63/8	18/6	56,000	Mach 2.5
F-5E/F	Northrop	Tiger II	2 J85-GE-21A	1/2	25/3	47/2	13/2	24,676	Mach 1.6
F-16A	GD/Ft. Worth	—	1 P&W F100-PW-200	1	31/0	47/6	16/4	22,000	Mach 2
F-106A	GD/Convair	Delta Dart	1 P&W J75-P-17	1/2	38/3	70/8	20/3	36,000	Mach 2.3
F-111	GD/Ft. Worth	—	2 P&W TF30-P-3/100(F)	2	63/0[4]	73/6	17/0	100,000	Mach 2.5
F-101B	McDonnell Douglas	Voodoo	2 P&W J57-P-55	2	39/8	67/4	18/0	46,500	Mach 1.85
RECONNAISSANCE									
RF-4C	McDonnell Douglas	Phantom II	2 GE J79-GE-17	2	38/7	63/0	16/5	61,795	Mach 2.2
SR-71	Lockheed/Calif.	—	2 P&W J58	2	55/6	107/4	18/5	170,000	Mach 3
U/WU-2	Lockheed/Calif.	—	1 P &W J75	1	80/0	49/6	13/0	19,850	400 kt
OBSERVATION									
0-2A	Cessna		2 Con 10-360-D	2	38/0	29/2	9/5	5,400	199
OV-10A[1]	RI/Columbus	Bronco	2 T76-G-416/417	2	40/0	39/7	15/1	14,466	281
EARLY WARNING COMMAND, CONTROL AND COMMUNICATIONS									
E-3A	Boeing		4 P&W TF33-P-100/A	17	145/9	152/1	42/0	325,000	530
E-4A/B	Boeing	—	4 GE CF6-50E	5	195/7	231/3	63/5	803,000	—
CARGO/TRANSPORT									
C-5A	Lockheed/Georgia	Galaxy	4 GE TF39-GE-1C	7	222/8	245/9	65/1	764,500	550
C-9A	McDonnell Douglas	Nightingale	2 P&W JT8D-9	2–7	93/3	119/3	27/5	108,000	570
C-12A[2]	Beech		2 PWC PT6A-38	2	54/5	43/6	14/6	12,500	260 kt
C-130E/H	Lockheed/Georgia	Hercules	4 All T56-A-7/-15(H)	5	132/6	99/5	38/4	155,000	360
C-140A	Lockheed/Georgia	Jetstar	4 P&W J60-P-5	5	54/4	60/4	20/4	40,921	525
C-141A	Lockheed/Georgia	Starlifter	4 P&W TF33-P-7	4–9	160/7	145/0	39/3	325,000	505
KC-135A	Boeing	Stratotanker	4 P&W J57-P-59W	4	130/9	136/3	38/4	297,000	530
C-137C	Boeing	Stratoliner	4 P&W JT3D-3B	4	145/9	152/9	42/5	328,000	627
CT-39	RI/General Aviation	Sabreliner	2 P&W J60-P-3	2	44/5	43/8	15/9	18,650	595
TRAINERS									
T-33A	Lockheed/Calif.	Shooting Star	1 All J33-A-35	2	38/9	37/7	11/7	15,100	505
T-37B	Cessna	Tweet	2 CAE J69-T-25	2	33/8	29/3	9/2	6,575	425
T-38A	Northrop	Talon	2 GE J85-5	2	25/3	46/4	12/1	12,500	Mach 1.2
T-41B/C	Cessna	Mescalero	1 CON 10-360-D	2	36/2	26/5	8/9	2,550	142
T-43A	Boeing	—	2 P&W JT8D-9	2	93/0	100/0	37/0	115,500	Mach .7

1. Air Force/Marines. 2. Air Force/Army. 3. Wing extended; 34 ft fully swept. 4. Wing extended; 31.11 ft fully swept. *Source:* Department of the Air Force.

Lower Ozone Levels for Air Passengers

Ozone in airplanes has been linked with respiratory and skin problems. Air passengers usually encounter high ozone levels in aircraft cabins during transoceanic or high-altitude flights. According to new regulations, the ozone levels within an airplane cannot exceed 0.3 parts per million.

Ozone is a gaseous allotrope of oxygen and is a powerful bleaching, poisonous, oxidizing agent with a pungent, irritating odor. It is used commercially to purify and deodorize air, to sterilize water, and as a bleach.

Helicopter Records

Source: National Aeronautic Association.

Distance in Straight Line
International: 2,213.04 mi., 3,561.55 km.
Robert G. Ferry (U.S.) in Hughes YOH-
6A helicopter powered by Allison T-63-A-5 engine;
from Culver City, Calif., to Daytona Beach, Fla.,
April 6–7, 1966.
Distance, Closed Circuit
International: 1,739.96 mi; 2,800.20 km.
Jack Schweibold (U.S.) in Hughes YOH-
6A helicopter powered by Allison T-62-A-5 engine;
Edwards Air Force Base, Calif., March 26, 1966.
Altitude
International: 40,820 ft; 12,442 m.
Jean Boulet (France) in Alouette SA 315–
001 "Lama" powered by Artouste IIIB 735 KW
engine; Istres, France, June 21, 1972.
Maximum Speed
International: 228.91 mph; 368.4 kph.

Gourguen Karapetyan (U.S.S.R.) in A-10
helicopter powered by 2 TB-3-117 engines;
Podmoskovnoye, U.S.S.R., Sept. 21, 1978.
Speed for 100 Km (Closed Circuit)
International: 211.35 mph; 340.15 kph.
Boris Galitsky (U.S.S.R.) in MI-6 heli-
copter powered by 2 TB-2BM turbine engines;
Podmoskovnoye, U.S.S.R., Aug. 26, 1964.
Speed for 500 Km (Closed Circuit)
International: 205.688 mph; 331.023 kph.
Galina Rastorgoueva (U.S.S.R.) in A-10
helicopter powered by 2 TV2 117A engines;
Ramenskoye, U.S.S.R., Aug. 1, 1975.
Speed for 1,000 Km (Closed Circuit)
International: 200.48 mph; 322.646 kph.
Galina Rastorgoueva (U.S.S.R.) in A-10
helicopter powered by 2 TV2 117A engines; Aug.
13, 1975.
Speed for 2,000 Km (Closed Circuit)
International: 146.09 mph; 235.119 kph.
Inna Kopets (U.S.S.R.) in MI-8 helicopter; Sept. 14,
1967.

Average Hours and Earnings in Aircraft Industries

Hours and earnings	1980	1979	1978	1977	1975	1970	1965	1960	1955
Average weekly hours									
Aircraft industries	41.8	42.8	42.1	42.7	40.4	41.0	41.2	40.6	41.4
Engines and parts industries	41.8	42.3	41.7	42.0	41.4	40.5	42.1	41.1	40.6
Average weekly earnings									
Aircraft industries	$404.21	$357.86	$324.17	$310	$250	$171	$130	$110	$90
Engines and parts industries	$393.76	$360.82	$325.26	$315	$249	$166	$133	$112	$86
Average hourly earnings									
Aircraft industries	$9.67	$8.46	$7.70	$7.27	$6.20	$4.17	$3.16	$2.71	$2.17
Engines and parts industries	$9.42	$8.53	$7.80	$7.50	$6.03	$4.10	$3.17	$2.73	$2.13

NOTE: Figures are latest available. *Source:* Department of Transportation, Federal Aviation Administration.

Concorde Fuel Consumption Costly

At peak efficiency, the 1,350-miles-per-hour supersonic Concorde uses four times as much fuel on a transoceanic trip as a Boeing 747.

Airline Safety at Record High

Major U.S. air carriers were involved in 20 accidents and 14 deaths during 1980, a record low. This compares sharply with a yearly average of 258 deaths in the 1970s. Commuter airlines had 36 accidents and 23 deaths in 1980, much lower than the previous year's total of 57 accidents and 65 deaths.

Modern Wedding Anniversary Gift List

Anniversary	Gift	Anniversary	Gift	Anniversary	Gift
1st	Clock	10th	Diamond jewelry	19th	Bronze
2nd	China	11th	Fashion jewelry and	20th	Platinum
3rd	Crystal, glass		accessories	25th	Sterling Silver Jubilee
4th	Electrical Appliances	12th	Pearls or colored gems	30th	Diamond
5th	Silverware	13th	Textiles, furs	35th	Jade
6th	Wood	14th	Gold jewelry	40th	Ruby
7th	Desk sets, pen and pencil	15th	Watches	45th	Sapphire
	sets	16th	Silver hollow ware	50th	Golden Jubilee
8th	Linens, laces	17th	Furniture	55th	Emerald
9th	Leather	18th	Porcelain	60th	Diamond Jubilee

Source: Jewelry Industry Council

MEDIA

Major U.S. Daily Newspapers[1]

City and newspaper	Net paid circulation		
	Morning[2]	Evening[2]	Sunday
Akron, Ohio: *Beacon Journal*	—	162,607	221,344
Albany, N.Y.: *Times–Union* (M & S); *Knickerbocker News* (E)	82,195	47,799[4]	149,644
Albuquerque, N.M.: *Journal* (M & S); *Tribune* (E)	87,707[4]	44,688[4]	130,141[4]
Allentown, Pa.: *Call*	118,348[4][5]		155,373[4]
Asbury Park, N.J.: *Press*	—	109,313	139,787
Atlanta: *Constitution* (M); *Journal* (E);			
Journal and Constitution (S)	215,684	193,916	499,341
Augusta, Ga.: *Chronicle* (M); *Herald* (E);			
Chronicle–Herald (S)	58,372	18,692	85,235
Austin, Tex.; *American–Statesman*	132,163[5]		152,712
Bakersfield, Calif.: *Californian*	70,178[4]	—	78,497[4]
Baltimore: *Sun*	178,515[3]	169,944[3]	375,644
News American	—	142,119[3]	204,052
Baton Rouge, La.: *Advocate* (M & S); *State–Times* (E)	76,488	39,480	118,573
Bergen County (Hackensack), N.J.:			
Record (E); *Sunday Record*	—	149,593[4]	211,554[4]
Beaumont, Tex.: *Enterprise* (M); *Journal*			
(E); *Enterprise–Journal* (S)	64,761[3]	13,034[3]	79,793
Binghamton, N.Y.: *Press* (E & S); *Sun–Bulletin* (M)	27,805[3]	66,820[3]	83,364
Birmingham, Ala.: *News* (E & S); *Post–Herald* (M)	67,293[3]	167,321[3]	214,295
Boston: *Globe*	502,920[5]		741,614
Herald–American	209,128	—	246,298
Christian Science Monitor	164,311[3]	—	—
Bridgeport, Conn.: *Telegram* (M); *Post* (E); *Sunday Post*	17,714[3][4]	73,257[3][4]	94,301[4]
Buffalo, N.Y.: *Evening News*	—	268,928[3]	177,288
Courier–Express	131,990	—	263,584
Camden, N.J.: *Courier–Post*	—	119,879[4]	100,546[4]
Canton, Ohio: *Repository*	—	62,770	76,956
Cedar Rapids, Iowa: *Gazette*	—	67,812	75,676
Charleston, W.Va.: *Gazette* (M); *Daily Mail* (E);			
Gazette–Mail (S)	54,956	55,018	105,820
Charlotte, N.C.: *Observer* (M & S); *News* (E)	167,964	47,964	246,327
Chattanooga, Tenn.: *News–Free Press* (E & S); *Times* (M)	46,998[3]	59,376[3]	109,321
Chicago: *Tribune*	790,475[3][5]		1,150,540
Sun–Times	661,531[3]	—	715,892
Wall Street Journal (Midwest edition)	545,075[3]	—	—
Cincinnati: *Enquirer* (M & S); *Post* (E)	194,469	147,018	293,710
Cleveland: *Plain Dealer* (M & S); *Press* (E)	406,444	302,410	468,541
Cocoa, Fla.: *Today*	70,183	—	85,490
Colorado Springs, Colo.: *Gazette Telegraph*	28,924	50,624	84,134
Sun	30,607[3]	—	31,732
Columbia, S.C.: *State* (M & S); *Record* (E)	106,836	31,232	131,153
Columbus, Ohio: *Dispatch* (E & S); *Citizen–Journal* (M)	114,899	202,209	343,721
Corpus Christi, Tex.: *Caller* (M & S); *Times* (E)	63,311[3][4]	24,403[3][4]	90,603[4]
Dallas: *News*			
Times Herald			
Wall Street Journal (Southwest edition)	218,044[3]	—	—
Davenport, Iowa: *Quad City Times*	64,752[5]		84,175
Dayton, Ohio: *Daily News* (S & S); *Journal Herald* (M)	101,629	139,022	219,268
Daytona Beach, Fla.: *Journal* (M); *News* (E);			
News–Journal (S)	54,669	31,572[3]	75,868
Denver: *Post*	—	276,389[3]	357,157
Rocky Mountain News	288,410	—	306,627
Des Moines, Iowa: *Register* (M & S); *Tribune* (E)	210,465	80,114	391,421
Detroit: *News*	617,879[5]		819,992
Free Press	613,311[3]	—	737,119
Duluth, Minn.: *News–Tribune* (M & S); *Herald* (E)	50,342	19,591[3]	81,576
Erie, Pa.: *News* (M); *Times* (E); *Times–News* (S)	24,013[3]	49,938[3]	94,319
El Paso, Tex.: *Times* (M & S); *Herald–Post* (E)	56,676[4]	33,346[3][4]	87,786[4]
Evansville, Ind.: *Courier* (M); *Press* (E); *Courier & Press* (S)	63,552	44,476	117,127
Flint, Mich.: *Journal*	—	107,778[4]	110,135[4]

City and newspaper	Net paid circulation		
	Morning[2]	Evening[2]	Sunday
Fort Lauderdale, Fla.: *Sun–Sentinel* (M); *News* (E);			
News & Sun–Sentinel (S)	81,098[3]	99,234[3]	218,941
Fort Myers, Fla.: *News–Press*	76,715	—	90,914
Fort Wayne, Ind.: *Journal–Gazette* (M & S);			
News–Sentinel (E)	60,257[4]	70,945[4]	105,836[4]
Fort Worth: *Star–Telegram*	100,007[3]	129,467[3]	256,663
Fresno, Calif.: *Bee*	134,777	—	152,993
Gary, Ind.: *Post–Tribune*	—	81,954	89,388
Grand Rapids, Mich.: *Press*	—	127,550	152,289
Greensboro, N.C.: *News* (M & S); *Record* (E)	83,330	30,760	113,694
Greenville, S.C.: *Piedmont* (E & S); *News* (M)	86,086[3]	23,956[3]	109,939
Hammond–East Chicago, Ind.: *Times*	—	70,042[3]	79,002
Harrisburg, Pa.: *Patriot* (M); *Evening News;*			
Patriot–News (S)	47,030[3]	61,184[3]	151,611
Hartford, Conn.: *Courant*	212,032	—	290,167
Honolulu: *Advertiser* (M); *Star–Bulletin*			
Star–Bulletin & Advertiser (S)	85,137	116,777	202,887
Houston: *Chronicle*	367,782[5]		453,036
Post	347,921	—	419,308
Indianapolis: *Star* (M & S); *News* (E)	220,292[4]	140,576[4]	363,201[4]
Jackson, Miss.: *Clarion–Ledger* (M); *Daily News* (E);			
Clarion–Ledger–Daily News (S)	65,220	40,127	102,343
Jacksonville, Fla.: *Florida–Times Union* (M & S); *Journal* (E)	157,776	45,475	203,725
Kansas City, Mo.: *Star* (E & S); *Times* (M)	297,406	253,046[3]	404,424
Knoxville, Tenn.: *News–Sentinel* (E & S); *Journal* (M)	56,208	100,646	158,654
Lancaster, Pa.: *Intelligencer–Journal* (M);			
New Era (E); *News* (S)	40,643[4]	59,162[4]	134,877[4]
Lansing, Mich.: *State–Journal*	—	74,677	82,012
Las Vegas, Nev.: *Review–Journal*	—	89,079[3]	97,767
Sun	59,494[3]		62,510
Lexington, Ky.: *Herald* (M); *Leader* (E); *Herald–Leader* (S)	72,029[3]	33,878[3]	114,484
Little Rock, Ark.: *Arkansas Gazette*	128,740	—	154,875
Arkansas Democrat	67,511	—	121,997
Long Beach, Calif.: *Independent* (M); *Press–Telegram* (E);			
Independent Press–Telegram (S)	68,652[3]	68,481[3]	138,336
Long Island (Garden City), N.Y.: *Newsday*	—	503,336[3]	573,726
Los Angeles: *Times*	1,026,092[3]		1,271,603
Herald–Examiner	—	285,099[3]	303,724
Louisville, Ky.: *Courier–Journal* (M & S); *Times* (E)	186,348	149,423	327,565
Lubbock, Tex.: *Avalanche–Journal*	58,114[3]	14,147[3]	80,187
Macon, Ga.: *Telegraph* (M); *News* (E); *Telegraph and News* (S)	51,781[3]	19,282[3]	85,859
Madison, Wis.: *State Journal* (M & S); *Capital Times* (E)	77,811	33,881	130,732
Memphis, Tenn.: *Commercial Appeal* (M & S);			
Press Scimitar (E)	203,920	95,553	281,978
Miami, Fla.: *Herald* (M & S); *News* (E)	444,860	60,028	545,898
Milwaukee: *Journal* (E & S); *Sentinel* (M)	173,264	318,203	519,365
Minneapolis: *Tribune* (M & S); *Star* (E)	231,759[3]	192,508[3]	587,255
Mobile, Ala.: *Register* (M); *Press* (E); *Press–Register* (S)	50,784[4]	51,443[4]	96,254[4]
Modesto, Calif.: *Bee*	69,511	—	75,008
Nashville, Tenn.: *Tennesseean* (M & S); *Banner* (E)	132,146	79,556	244,204
New Haven, Conn.: *Register* (E & S); *Journal–Courier* (E)	37,837	96,526	140,372
New Orleans: *Times–Picayune/States–Item*	281,546[3 4 5]		323,731[4]
New York City: *News*	1,491,556	—	1,995,702
Times	930,546[3]	—	1,479,263
Post	732,158[3 5]		470,359[6]
Wall Street Journal (Eastern edition)	780,662[3]	—	—
National edition	1,948,121[3]	—	—
Staten Island Advance	—	73,785	81,140
Women's Wear Daily	63,060[3]	—	—
Newark, N.J.: *Star–Ledger*	403,798[3 4]	—	585,174[4]
Newport News–Hampton, Va.: *Daily Press* (M & S);			
Times Herald (E)	57,407[4]	43,208[4]	102,544[4]
Norfolk–Portsmouth–Virginia Beach–Chesapeake, Va.:			
Virginian Pilot (M); *Ledger–Star* (E);			
Virginian Pilot/Ledger–Star (S)	129,022[4]	95,500[4]	206,752[4]
Oakland, Calif.: *Tribune* (E & S); *Eastbay Today* (M)	71,432[3]	134,489[3]	179,206
Oklahoma City: *Daily Oklahoman* (M); *Times* (E);			
Sunday Oklahoman	194,119[3]	90,531[3]	304,552
Omaha, Neb.: *World–Herald*	121,741[3]	107,303[3]	281,045
Orange County (Santa Ana), Calif.: *Register*	238,757[3 5]		272,369

City and newspaper	Morning[2]	Evening[2]	Sunday
Orlando, Fla.: *Sentinel Star*	207,621[3][5]		248,282
Palo Alto, Calif.: *Wall Street Journal* (Western edition)	404,340[3]	—	—
Peoria, Ill.; *Journal Star*	103,097[5]		121,374
Philadelphia: *Inquirer*	428,862[3]	—	851,964
Bulletin	—	412,268[3]	466,409
Daily News	—	232,190[3]	—
Phoenix, Ariz.: *Republic* (M & S); *Gazette* (E)	272,173[4]	113,329[4]	411,156[4]
Pittsburgh: *Post–Gazette, Sun Telegraph* (M); *Press* (E & S)	180,375[3]	268,490[3]	637,435
Portland, Me.: *Press–Herald* (M); *Express* (E);			
Maine Sunday Telegram	55,939	30,371	120,136
Portland, Ore.: *Oregonian* (M & S); *Oregon Journal* (E)	247,811	109,199[3]	420,688
Providence, R.I.: *Journal* (M & S); *Bulletin* (E)	79,739	139,305	233,813
Quincy, Mass.: *Patriot–Ledger*	—	87,605[3][4]	
Raleigh, N.C.: *News & Observer* (M & S); *Times* (E)	129,044[4]	33,872[4]	166,501[4]
Reading, Pa.: *Eagle* (E & S); *Times* (M)	43,032	42,695	102,411
Richmond, Va.: *Times–Dispatch* (M & S); *News–Leader* (E)	136,385	114,412	222,273
Riverside, Calif.: *Enterprise* (M); *Press* (E);			
Press–Enterprise (S)	72,396[3]	34,166[3]	112,468
Roanoke, Va.: *Times & World News*	70,072[3]	48,204[3]	120,413
Rochester, N.Y.: *Democrat & Chronicle* (M & S);			
Times–Union (E)	128,539[3]	116,144[3]	233,343
Rockford, Ill.: *Register Star*	77,127	—	86,244
Sacramento, Calif.: *Bee*	214,021	—	238,854
Union	103,701	—	105,220
St. Louis: *Post–Dispatch*	—	244,599[3]	436,298
Globe–Democrat	256,226[3]	—	250,815[7]
St. Paul: *Pioneer Press* (M & S); *Dispatch* (E)	109,199[3]	118,737[3]	251,320
St. Petersburg, Fla.: *Times* (M & S); *Independent* (E)	244,226	41,895	304,039
Salt Lake City, Utah: *Tribune* (M & S); *Deseret News* (E)	110,998	71,430	178,299
San Antonio: *Express* (M); *News* (E); *Express–News* (S)	81,112[3]	73,954[3]	186,815
Light	—	115,172[3]	181,778
San Bernardino, Calif.: *Sun*	79,420	—	83,455
San Diego, Calif.: *Union* (M & S); *Tribune* (E)	207,171[4]	127,271[4]	329,820[4]
San Francisco: *Chronicle* (M); *Examiner* (E);			
Examiner & Chronicle (S)	515,453[3]	154,099[3]	665,887
San Jose, Calif.: *Mercury* (M); *News* (E);			
Mercury–News (S)	154,750	65,772	269,351
Sarasota, Fla.: *Herald–Tribune* (M & S); *Journal* (E)	98,432[4]	5,560[3][4]	108,996[4]
Seattle: *Post–Intelligencer*	185,962[3]	—	211,876
Times	261,432[3][5]		344,724
Shreveport, La.: *Times* (M & S); *Journal* (E)	86,093[4]	32,659[4]	123,558[4]
South Bend–Mishawaka, Ind.: *Tribune*	—	106,211	126,044
Spokane, Wash.: *Spokesman–Review* (M & S); *Chronicle* (E)	77,818	59,026	125,898
Springfield, Mass.: *Union* (M); *News* (E); *Republican* (S)	72,360	75,715	144,219
Syracuse, N.Y.: *Post–Standard* (M); *Herald–Journal* (E); *Herald–American* (S)	81,696	112,140	233,220
Tacoma, Wash.: *News-Tribune* (E); *News–Tribune* &			
Ledger (S)	—	107,169	111,211
Tampa, Fla.: *Tribune* (M & S); *Times* (E)	198,489	23,824	246,271
Toledo, Ohio: *Blade*	—	167,028	211,721
Topeka, Kan.: *Capital–Journal*	67,896[3][5][7]		74,379
Trenton, N.J.: *Times* (E); *Times–Advertiser* (S)	—	65,266[3]	77,622
Trentonian	65,515	—	58,611
Tucson, Ariz.: *Daily Star* (M & S); *Citizen* (E)	75,452[4]	66,156[4]	138,094[4]
Tulsa, Okla.: *World* (M & S); *Tribune* (E)	128,587[4]	77,772[4]	222,755[4]
Washington, D.C.: *Post*	618,111[3]	—	845,176
Star[9]	—	322,827[3]	294,086
West Palm Beach, Fla.: *Post* (M); *Times* (E);			
Post–Times (S)	95,474[3]	29,296[3]	148,072
Wichita, Kan.: *Eagle* (M); *Eagle and Beacon* (S)	124,984	—	173,591
Wilmington, Del.: *News* (M); *News Journal* (E);			
Sunday News Journal	52,552[4]	75,710[4]	113,621[4]
Winston–Salem, N.C.: *Journal* (M & S); *Sentinel* (E)	72,106[4]	36,646[4]	96,852[4]
Worcester, Mass.: *Telegram* (M & S); *Gazette* (E)	54,916[4]	89,159[4]	111,689[4]
Youngstown, Ohio: *Vindicator*	—	102,319[4]	155,159[4]

1. Listing is of cities in which any one edition of a newspaper exceeds an average net paid circulation of 75,000; newspapers of smaller circulation in those cities are also included. 2. Unless otherwise indicated, figures are average Monday-through-Saturday circulation for six-month period ending March 31, 1981. 3. Average Monday-through-Friday circulation. 4. Three-month average for period ending March 31, 1981. 5. All-day newspaper. 6. Published on Saturday. 7. Week-end edition. 8. For three-month period ending Dec. 31, 1980. 9. Ceased publication Aug. 7, 1981. *Source:* Audit Bureau of Circulations.

Leading Magazines: United States and Canada

Magazine	Circulation[1]	Magazine	Circulation[1]
AARP News Bulletin	6,762,921	1,001 Decorating Ideas	1,106,394
American Legion Magazine, The	2,599,187	Organic Gardening	1,335,699
Better Homes and Gardens	8,052,693	Outdoor Life	1,733,692
Bon Appetit	1,190,001	Parents	1,515,707
Boys' Life	1,462,745	Penthouse	4,330,949
Changing Times, the Kiplinger Magazine	1,407,690	People Weekly	2,499,573
Chatelaine	1,034,161	Playboy	5,011,099
Cosmopolitan	2,837,325	Popular Mechanics	1,677,303
D C Comics Group	5,637,970	Popular Science	1,933,262
Discovery	1,004,939	Prevention	2,429,439
Ebony	1,287,670	Psychology Today	1,171,347
Elks Magazine, The	1,651,862	Reader's Digest	17,898,681
Family Circle	7,529,734	Reader's Digest (Canadian English Edition)	1,288,435
Family Handyman	1,018,380	Redbook Magazine	4,353,745
Farm Journal	1,221,387	Scholastic Magazines	3,397,261
Field and Stream	2,021,599	Senior Scholastic Unit	2,529,206
Glamour	1,935,636	Seventeen	1,552,884
Globe	1,802,988	Smithsonian	1,904,515
Golf Digest	1,016,161	Southern Living	1,783,152
Good Housekeeping	5,290,833	Sport	1,222,718
House and Garden	1,126,114	Sports Illustrated	2,265,760
Hustler	1,420,678	Star, The	3,508,558
Ladies' Home Journal	5,601,449	Sunset, The Magazine of Western Living	1,417,304
Life	1,338,026	'Teen	1,058,870
McCall's	6,218,169	Time, The Weekly Magazine	4,358,911
Mademoiselle	1,096,558	Today's Education	1,651,783
Marvel Comics Group	10,597,780	True Story	1,432,900
Mechanix Illustrated	1,626,182	TV Guide	17,981,657
Modern Maturity	6,748,925	U.S. News and World Report	2,055,993
Mother Earth News	1,043,774	Us	1,103,404
National Enquirer	5,051,496	V.F.W. Magazine	1,844,891
National Geographic Magazine, The	10,711,886	Vogue (incl. Vanity Fair)	1,101,451
Nation's Business	1,265,555	Woman's Day	7,748,069
Newsweek	2,964,279	Workbasket, The	1,472,139
New Woman	1,251,595		

1. Average total paid circulation for the six-month period ending December 31, 1980. The table lists magazines of over 1,000,000 circulation. *Source:* Audit Bureau of Circulations. Publishers' Statements for six-month period ending December 31, 1980.

English Language Daily and Sunday U.S. Newspapers
(number of newspapers as of Feb. 1, 1981; circulation as reported for Sept. 30, 1980)

State	Morning papers	and circulation	Evening papers	and circulation	Total M and E	and circulation	Sunday papers	and circulation
Alabama	8	204,934	20	539,780	28	744,714	21	685,383
Alaska	2	30,559	6	76,732	8	107,291	1	58,532
Arizona	3	336,140	16	285,044	19	621,184	8	578,281
Arkansas[1]	6	245,094	28	234,428	33	479,522	17	481,599
California[1]	29	3,352,470	95	2,661,321	122	6,013,791	50	5,568,875
Colorado	4	371,788	23	530,502	27	902,290	10	926,995
Connecticut	6	366,256	19	540,662	25	906,918	7	677,065
Delaware	1	50,970	2	105,338	3	156,308	2	139,455
District of Columbia	1	584,500	1	329,489	2	913,989	2	1,124,607
Florida[1]	21	1,899,297	32	734,089	52	2,633,386	33	2,717,426
Georgia	9	455,320	27	581,729	36	1,037,049	15	1,011,528
Hawaii	1	82,305	4	155,444	5	237,749	2	219,616
Idaho	5	111,438	9	97,888	14	209,326	7	190,256
Illinois[1]	12	1,409,618	69	1,428,901	77	2,838,519	24	2,795,859
Indiana	7	442,742	71	1,188,631	78	1,631,373	18	1,190,390
Iowa[1]	4	302,940	38	581,147	41	884,087	9	742,768
Kansas[1]	6	217,341	44	379,455	48	596,796	18	487,076
Kentucky	6	312,037	21	444,475	27	756,512	11	602,255
Louisiana[1]	6	393,152	20	418,695	25	811,847	14	806,130
Maine	5	218,191	4	71,578	9	289,769	1	148,298
Maryland	6	262,992	8	439,837	14	702,829	4	648,930

State	Morning papers and circulation		Evening papers and circulation		Total M and E and circulation		Sunday papers and circulation	
Massachusetts[1]	7	806,858	42	1,216,976	48	2,023,834	9	1,483,018
Michigan[1]	9	957,484	44	1,490,047	52	2,447,531	15	2,360,899
Minnesota	7	421,565	23	597,014	30	1,018,579	11	1,016,849
Mississippi	6	129,847	19	268,582	25	398,429	13	319,537
Missouri	10	701,105	43	847,021	53	1,548,126	18	1,149,397
Montana	5	151,907	6	45,038	11	196,945	8	198,209
Nebraska	4	188,003	15	298,636	19	486,639	6	411,225
Nevada	3	99,004	6	123,040	9	222,044	5	220,697
New Hampshire[1]	1	32,584	9	163,369	9	195,953	2	77,744
New Jersey	7	673,097	20	1,020,038	27	1,693,135	16	1,591,759
New Mexico	1	83,357	19	189,691	20	273,048	14	250,638
New York[1]	23	5,258,983	58	2,625,906	79	7,884,889	33	5,995,335
North Carolina	10	613,362	45	764,484	55	1,377,846	24	1,131,121
North Dakota[1]	2	38,047	9	157,568	10	195,615	3	106,662
Ohio[1]	11	906,923	85	2,382,924	95	3,289,847	28	2,532,017
Oklahoma	7	380,420	47	457,436	54	837,856	44	861,937
Oregon	3	317,367	18	385,096	21	702,463	6	618,093
Pennsylvania[1]	34	1,613,135	73	2,244,311	101	3,857,446	19	3,088,454
Rhode Island	1	77,527	6	238,185	7	315,712	2	238,970
South Carolina	8	403,995	12	199,025	20	603,020	8	497,385
South Dakota	2	47,601	10	125,963	12	173,564	4	125,525
Tennesse	8	458,346	23	622,355	31	1,080,701	16	1,004,275
Texas[1]	27	1,644,265	94	1,794,648	118	3,438,913	97	3,934,811
Utah	1	107,538	5	170,285	6	277,823	5	273,954
Vermont	2	71,371	6	46,256	8	117,627	3	75,969
Virginia	12	516,407	23	575,083	35	1,091,490	15	854,387
Washington[1]	9	486,334	19	700,931	26	1,187,265	16	1,103,252
West Virginia	9	242,486	16	228,653	25	471,139	9	391,950
Wisconsin	4	269,074	32	952,966	36	1,222,040	10	926,842
Wyoming	6	65,960	4	31,112	10	97,072	3	63,938
Total	387	29,414,036	1,388	32,787,804	1,745	62,201,840	736	54,676,173
Total U.S., Sept. 30, 1979	382	28,574,879	1,405	33,648,161	1,763	62,223,040	720	54,379,923
Total U.S., Sept. 30, 1978	355	27,656,739	1,419	34,333,258	1,756	61,989,997	696	53,990,033
Total U.S., Sept. 30, 1977	352	26,742,318	1,435	34,752,822	1,753	61,495,140	668	52,429,234
Total U.S., Sept. 30, 1976	346	25,858,386	1,435	35,118,625	1,762	60,977,011	650	51,565,334
Total U.S., Sept. 30, 1975	339	25,490,186	1,436	35,165,245	1,756	60,655,431	639	51,096,323
Total U.S., Sept. 30, 1974	340	26,144,966	1,449	35,732,231	1,768	61,877,197	641	51,678,726
Total U.S., Sept. 30, 1972	337	26,078,386	1,441	36,431,856	1,761	65,510,242	605	50,000,669
Total U.S., Sept. 30, 1970	334	25,933,783	1,429	36,173,744	1,748	62,107,527	586	49,216,602

1. "All-day" newspapers are listed in morning and evening columns but only once in the total, and their circulations are divided between morning and evening figures. Adjustments have been made in state and U.S. total figures. *Source: Editor and Publisher Yearbook, 1981.*

See the Entertainment and Culture section for additional Media information.

"Go West, Young Man"

It was not Horace Greeley but John Babsone Lane Soule, editor of the Terre Haute (Indiana) *Express* who gave this advice in 1851. As 100,000 pioneers moved west to Oregon and California in the 1840s, Greeley called their trek "an aspect of insanity."

From 1840 to 1870, about 254,000 emigrants traveled from the Missouri River to the Pacific; 43,000 more stopped in Utah.

In this 30-year period, only 342 emigrants were killed by Indians, while 426 Indians were killed by whites, reports Charles D. Unruh in *The Plains Across* (1979). Nine out of 10 deaths on the trail came from disease; almost as many died from drowning as from Indian action.

"Junk" Mail

If you want to unclutter your mailbox of unwanted advertising mail or if you want more mail, the Direct Mail Marketing Association Inc. offers a free service allowing consumers to have their names added or deleted from national advertising lists.

Copies of a booklet, "How Did They Get My Name?" which explains consumer mailing lists, are available without charge from DMMA, Dept. M, 6 E. 43rd St., New York, N.Y. 10017.

Reference Books And Other Sources

This cannot be a complete record of all the thousands of available sources of information. Nevertheless, these selected references will enable the reader to locate additional facts about many subjects covered in the *Information Please Almanac*. The editors have chosen sources that they believe will be most helpful to the general reader.

General References

Encyclopedias are a unique category, since they attempt to cover most subjects quite thoroughly. Two most valuable multivolume encyclopedias are the **Encyclopaedia Britannica** and the **Encyclopedia Americana.** Useful one-volume encyclopedias are the **New Columbia Encyclopedia** and the **Random House Encyclopedia.**

Dictionaries and similar "word books" are also unique: **Webster's New International Dictionary** (third edition, unabridged). **Random House Dictionary. Merriam Webster's Collegiate Dictionary** (eighth edition, abridged). **Oxford English Dictionary. Bartlett's Familiar Quotations. Roget's Thesaurus. Modern American Usage.**

There are a number of useful **atlases: New York Times Atlas of the World,** a number of historical atlases (Penguin Books), **Oxford Economic Atlas of the World, Atlas of the Universe** (Rand McNally), **Atlas of the Historical Geography of the U.S.** (Carnegie Institution of Washington and the American Geographical Society), and contemporary road atlases of the U.S. (Rand McNally).

A source of information on virtually all subjects is the United States Government Printing Office. For information write: Superintendent of Documents, Washington, D.C. 20402.

For help on any subject, consult: **Subject Guide to Books in Print, The New York Times Index,** and the **Reader's Guide to Periodical Literature** in your library.

Specific References

America Votes (Congressional Quarterly, Inc.)
American Indian, Reference Encyclopedia of the (Todd Publications)
Antiques, Collectors Encyclopedia of (Crown)
Architecture, Encyclopedia of World (Facts on File)
Art, Encyclopedia of World (McGraw-Hill)
Art, History of (Prentice-Hall)
Art, Oxford Companion to (Oxford University Press)
Art, Who's Who in American (R.R. Bowker)
Art Directory, American (R.R. Bowker)
Authors, 1000–1900, European (H.W. Wilson)
Authors, 1600–1900, American (H.W. Wilson)
Authors, Twentieth Century (H.W. Wilson)
Authors Before 1800 (H.W. Wilson)
Authors of the Nineteenth Century, British (H.W. Wilson)
Auto Racing (Morrow)
Banking and Finance, Encyclopedia of (Bankers Publishing Co.)
Baseball Encyclopedia (Information Concepts/Macmillan)

(Baseball) **World Series Records** (The Sporting News)
Basketball, Modern Encyclopedia of (Four Winds Press)
Biographical Dictionary, Chambers (St. Martin's Press)
Biographical Dictionary, Webster's (G. & C. Merriam)
Biography Yearbook, Current (H.W. Wilson)
Birds of America (Audubon)
Book Review Digest, 1905— (H.W. Wilson)
Business Almanac, Dow Jones-Irwin (Dow Jones-Irwin)
Catholic Encyclopedia, New (Publishers Guild/McGraw-Hill)
CB: Citizens Band Radio Service Rules (Government Printing Office)
Chemistry, Encyclopedia of (Van Nostrand Reinhold)
Chemistry and Physics, Handbook of (Chemical Rubber Co.)
Christian Church, Oxford Dictionary of the (Oxford University Press)
Church Annual, Episcopal (Morehouse-Barlow)
Churches, Yearbook of American and Canadian (Abingdon Press)
Climate and Man (U.S. Department of Agriculture)
Communist Affairs, Yearbook on International (Hoover Institution Press)
Composers, Great, 1300–1900; A Biographical and Critical Guide (H.W. Wilson)
Composers Since 1900; A Biographical and Critical Guide (H.W. Wilson)
Congressional Quarterly Directory (Congressional Quarterly, Inc.)
(Consumer) **Agriculture, Yearbook of: Gardening for Food and Fun** (Government Printing Office)
(Consumer) **HELP: The Indispensable Almanac of Consumer Information 1980** (Everest House)
Consumer Sourcebook (Gale Research Co.)
Consumer Reports (Consumers Union)
Dance Encyclopedia (Simon & Schuster)
Drama, Crowell's Handbook of Classical (Crowell)
Ecology Information and Organizations, Guide to (H.W. Wilson)
Energy Factbook 1980–81 (McGraw)
Environment, Living With Our (Government Printing Office)
Environmental Quality Report (Council on Environmental Quality)
Environmental Science (Holt, Rinehart & Winston)
Europa Year Book (Europa Publications)
Facts, Famous First (H.W. Wilson)
Facts on File (Facts on File, Inc.)
Film, Oxford Companion to (Oxford University Press)
Filmgoer's Companion (Hill & Wang)
Fishing: An Encyclopedic Guide to Tackle and Tactics for Fresh and Salt Water (Dutton)
Football, Encyclopedia of (A.S. Barnes & Co.)
Foreign Terms, Dictionary of (Crowell)
Game, Rules of the (Bantam Books)
Geographical Dictionary, Webster's New (G. & C. Merriam)

Geography, Dictionary of (Penguin Books)
Government Manual, U.S. (U.S. Office of the Federal Register)
History, Album of American (Charles Scribner's)
History, Atlas of American (Oxford University Press)
History, Dictionary of American (Charles Scribner's)
History, Documents of American (Appleton-Century-Crofts)
History, Encyclopedia of Latin American (Bobbs-Merrill)
History, Encyclopedia of World (Houghton-Mifflin)
History, Timetables of (Simon & Schuster)
History and Literature, Oxford Companion to Canadian (Oxford University Press)
Ice Hockey A to Z (Lothrop)
Investments, American and Foreign, Manual of (Moody's Investors Service)
Jazz in the Seventies, Encyclopedia of (Horizon)
Jewish Concepts, Encyclopedia of (Hebrew Publishers)
Job Outlook in Brief, The (Government Printing Office)
Libraries, World Guide to (K.G. Saur)
Library Directory, American (R.R. Bowker)
Literary History of the United States (Macmillan)
Literature, Oxford Companion to American (Oxford University Press)
Literature, Oxford Companion to Classical (Oxford University Press)
Literature, Oxford Companion to English (Oxford University Press)
Literature, Reader's Adviser to the Best in (R.R. Bowker)
Literature, Reader's Encyclopedia of American (Crowell)
Medical Adviser, Modern Home (Doubleday)
Museums, Directory of World (Columbia University Press)
Music and Musicians, Handbook of American (Free Press, Div. of Macmillan)
(Music) ASCAP. Biographical Dictionary (American Society of Authors, Composers, and Publishers)
Music, Concise Oxford Dictionary of (Oxford University Press)
Music, Harvard Dictionary of (Harvard University Press)
Musical Terms, Dictionary of (Gordon Press)
Mythology, (Larousse) Greek and Roman (McGraw)
Nations, Handbook of New (Crowell)
Nations, Worldmark Encyclopedia of the (Harper & Row)
Newspapers and Periodicals, Ayer Directory of (Ayer Press)

Pain, Coping With Chronic (Crown Publishers)
Pocket Data Book, U.S.A. (Bureau of Census)
Poetry, Granger's Index to (Columbia University Press)
Politics, Almanac of American (Gambit, Inc.)
Politics, Who's Who in American (R.R. Bowker)
Private Schools, Handbook of (Porter Sargent)
Robert's Rules of Order (Morrow & Co.)
Science, American Men and Women of (R.R. Bowker)
Science and Technology, Asimov's Biographical Encyclopedia of (Doubleday)
Scientific Encyclopedia, Van Nostrand's (Van Nostrand Reinhold)
Sports Dictionary, Webster's (G. & C. Merriam Co.)
Sports, Encyclopedia of (A.S. Barnes & Co.)
States, Book of (Council of State Governments)
Statesman's Yearbook (Burke's Peerage, Ltd.)
Tennis, Encyclopedia of (Viking Press)
Theater, Oxford Companion to the (Oxford University Press)
Theater, Who's Who in the (Gale Research Co.)
United Nations, Demographic Yearbook (U.N. Publishing Service)
United States, Historical Statistics of the (U.S. Department of Commerce)
United States, Statistical Abstract of the (Government Printing Office)
United Nations, Statistical Yearbook of the (U.N. Publishing Service)
Washington Information Directory (Congressional Quarterly, Inc.)
Way Things Work (Simon & Schuster)
Weather Almanac (Gale Research Co.)
Wildlife, Atlas of World (Rand McNally)
Women, Notable American, 1607–1950 (Belknap Press)
Who's Who (British), (St. Martin's Press)
Who's Who in America (Marquis)
World, Harper Encyclopedia of the Modern (Harper & Row)
Zip Code and Post Office Directory, National (Government Printing Office)

See the full range of publications of Dun & Bradstreet and Standard & Poor's for corporate financial and stockholder information.

For detailed information on American colleges and universities, see the many publications of the **American Council on Education.**

Also see the many specialized **Who's Who** volumes issued by Marquis for biographies of famous contemporaries in many fields.

Most Years Are Actually Longer—By One Leap Second

June 1981 lasted one second longer than usual due to the discrepancy between the average spin rate of the earth and the internationally agreed length of the second. Those concerned about accuracy should have set their clocks back one second at midnight on June 30, 1981.

According to the international agreement of 1967 establishing Coordinated Universal Time, the second is defined as equal to 9,192,631,770 oscillations of the cesium atom. This number was agreed upon because it equalled the length of the second as derived from the measured length of a full year in 1900.

However, since then, sun time has been getting

out of phase with atomic time due to a number of factors that slow the earth and therefore lengthen the day. The most significant of these are lunar gravity, the slight wobble in the earth's spin, solar eruptions, and severe changes in wind patterns and surface features.

T.V. broadcasters, seismologists, and power companies all rely on time precise to within billionths of a second in order to function accurately and efficiently.

There have been other leap seconds—except for 1980, there has been one leap second added to the end of every year since 1972. In addition, another leap second was added in June 1972.

GEOGRAPHY

World Geography

Explorations and Discoveries
(All years are A.D. unless B.C. is specified.)

Country or place	Event	Explorer or discoverer	Date
AFRICA			
Sierra Leone	Visited	Hanno, Carthaginian seaman	c. 520 B.C.
Congo River	Mouth discovered	Diogo Cão, Portuguese	c. 1484
Cape of Good Hope	Rounded	Bartolomeu Diaz, Portuguese	1488
Gambia River	Explored	Mungo Park, Scottish explorer	1795
Sahara	Crossed	Dixon Denham and Hugh Clapperton, English explorers	1822–23
Zambezi River	Discovered	David Livingstone, Scottish explorer	1851
Sudan	Explored	Heinrich Barth, German explorer	1852–55
Victoria Falls	Discovered	Livingstone	1855
Lake Tanganyika	Discovered	Richard Burton and John Speke, British explorers	1858
Congo River	Traced	Sir Henry M. Stanley, British explorer	1877
ASIA			
Punjab (India)	Visited	Alexander the Great	327 B.C.
China	Visited	Marco Polo, Italian traveler	c. 1272
Tibet	Visited	Odoric of Pordenone, Italian monk	c. 1325
Southern China	Explored	Niccolò dei Conti, Venetian traveler	c. 1440
India	Visited (Cape route)	Vasco da Gama, Portuguese navigator	1498
Japan	Visited	St. Francis Xavier of Spain	1549
Arabia	Explored	Carsten Niebuhr, German explorer	1762
China	Explored	Ferdinand Richthofen, German scientist	1868
Mongolia	Explored	Nikolai M. Przhevalsky, Russian explorer	1870–73
Central Asia	Explored	Sven Hedin, Swedish scientist	1890–1908
EUROPE			
Shetland Islands	Visited	Pytheas of Massilia (Marseille)	c. 325 B.C.
North Cape	Rounded	Ottar, Norwegian explorer	c. 870
Iceland	Colonized	Norwegian noblemen	c. 890–900
NORTH AMERICA			
Greenland	Colonized	Eric the Red, Norwegian	c. 985
Labrador; Nova Scotia (?)	Discovered	Leif Ericson, Norse explorer	1000
West Indies	Discovered	Christopher Columbus, Italian	1492
North America	Coast discovered	Giovanni Caboto (John Cabot), for British	1497
Pacific Ocean	Discovered	Vasco Núñez de Balboa, Spanish explorer	1513
Florida	Explored	Ponce de León, Spanish explorer	1513
Mexico	Conquered	Hernando Cortés, Spanish adventurer	1519–21
St. Lawrence River	Discovered	Jacques Cartier, French navigator	1534
Southwest U. S.	Explored	Francisco Coronado, Spanish explorer	1540–42
Colorado River	Discovered	Hernando de Alarcón, Spanish explorer	1540
Mississippi River	Discovered	Hernando de Soto, Spanish explorer	1541
Frobisher Bay	Discovered	Martin Frobisher, English seaman	1576

Country or place	Event	Explorer or discoverer	Date
Maine Coast	Explored	Samuel de Champlain, French explorer	1604
Jamestown, Va.	Settled	John Smith, English colonist	1607
Hudson River	Explored	Henry Hudson, English navigator	1609
Hudson Bay (Canada)	Discovered	Henry Hudson	1610
Baffin Bay	Discovered	William Baffin, English navigator	1616
Lake Michigan	Navigated	Jean Nicolet, French explorer	1634
Arkansas River	Discovered	Jacques Marquette and Louis Jolliet, French explorers	1673
Mississippi River	Explored	Sieur de La Salle, French explorer	1682
Bering Strait	Discovered	Vitus Bering, Danish explorer	1728
Alaska	Discovered	Vitus Bering	1741
Mackenzie River (Canada)	Discovered	Sir Alexander Mackenzie, Scottish-Canadian explorer	1789
Northwest U. S.	Explored	Meriwether Lewis and William Clark	1804–06
Northeast Passage (Arctic Ocean)	Navigated	Nils Nordenskjöld, Swedish explorer	1879
Greenland	Explored	Robert Peary, American explorer	1892
Northwest Passage	Navigated	Roald Amundsen, Norwegian explorer	1906
SOUTH AMERICA			
Continent	Visited	Columbus, Italian	1498
Brazil	Discovered	Pedro Alvarez Cabral, Portuguese	1500
Peru	Conquered	Francisco Pizarro, Spanish explorer	1532–33
Amazon River	Explored	Francisco Orellana, Spanish explorer	1541
Cape Horn	Discovered	Willem C. Schouten, Dutch navigator	1615
OCEANIA			
New Guinea	Visited	Jorge de Menezes, Portuguese explorer	1526
Australia	Visited	Abel Janszoon Tasman, Dutch navigator	1642
Tasmania	Discovered		
Australia	Explored	John McDouall Stuart, English explorer	1828
Australia	Explored	Robert Burke and William Wills, Australian explorers	1861
New Zealand	Sighted (and named)	Abel Janszoon Tasman	1642
New Zealand	Visited	James Cook, English navigator	1769
ARCTIC, ANTARCTIC, AND MISCELLANEOUS			
Ocean exploration	Expedition	Magellan's ships circled globe	1519–22
Galápagos Islands	Visited	Diego de Rivadeneira, Spanish captain	1535
Spitsbergen	Visited	Willem Barents, Dutch navigator	1596
Antarctic Circle	Crossed	James Cook, English navigator	1773
Antarctica	Discovered	Nathaniel Palmer, U. S. whaler (archipelago) and Fabian Gottlieb von Bellingshausen, Russian admiral (mainland)	1820–21
Antarctica	Explored	Charles Wilkes, American explorer	1840
North Pole	Reached	Robert E. Peary, American explorer	1909
South Pole	Reached	Roald Amundsen, Norwegian explorer	1911

The Continents

A continent is defined as a large unbroken land mass completely surrounded by water, although in some cases continents are (or were in part) connected by land bridges.

The hypothesis first suggested late in the 19th century was that the continents consist of lighter rocks that rest on heavier crustal material in about the same manner that icebergs float on water. That the rocks forming the continents are lighter than the material below them and under the ocean bot-

toms is now established. As a consequence of this fact, Alfred Wegener (for the first time in 1912) suggested that the continents are slowly moving, at a rate of about one yard per century, so that their relative positions are not rigidly fixed. Many geologists that were originally skeptical have come to accept this theory of Continental Drift.

When describing a continent, it is important to remember that there is a fundamental difference between a deep ocean, like the Atlantic, and shallow seas, like the Baltic and most of the North Sea, which are merely flooded portions of a continent. Another and entirely different point to remember is that political considerations have often overridden geographical facts when it came to naming continents.

Geographically speaking, Europe, including the British Isles, is a large western peninsula of the continent of Asia; and many geographers, when referring to Europe and Asia, speak of the Eurasian Continent. But traditionally, Europe is counted as a separate continent, with the Ural and the Caucasus mountains forming the line of demarcation between Europe and Asia.

To the south of Europe, Asia has an odd-shaped peninsula jutting westward, which has a large number of political subdivisions. The northern section is taken up by Turkey; to the south of Turkey there are Syria, Iraq, Israel, Jordan, Saudi Arabia, and a number of smaller Arab countries. All this is part of Asia. Traditionally, the island of Cyprus in the Mediterranean is also considered to be part of Asia, while the island of Crete is counted as European.

The large islands of Java, Borneo, and Sumatra and the smaller islands near them are counted as part of "tropical Asia," while New Guinea is counted as related to Australia. In the case of the Americas, the problem arises as to whether they should be considered one or two continents. There are good arguments on both sides, but since there is now a land bridge between North and South America (in the past it was often flooded) and since no part of the sea east of the land bridge is deep ocean, it is more logical to consider the Americas as one continent.

Politically, based mainly on history, the Americas are divided into North America (from the Arctic to the Mexican border), Central America (from Mexico to Panama, with the Caribbean islands), and South America. Greenland is considered a section of North America, while Iceland is traditionally counted as a European island because of its political ties with the Scandinavian countries.

The island groups in the Pacific are often called "Oceania," but this name does *not* imply that scientists consider them the remains of a continent.

Volcanoes of the World

About 500 volcanoes have had recorded eruptions within historical times. Almost two thirds of these are in the Northern Hemisphere. Most volcanoes occur at the boundaries of the earth's crustal plates, such as the famous "Ring of Fire" that surrounds the Pacific Ocean plate. Of the world's active volcanoes, about 60% are along the perimeter of the Pacific, about 17% on mid-oceanic islands, about 14% in an arc along the south of the Indonesian islands, and about 9% in the Mediterranean area, Africa, and Asia Minor. Many of the world's volcanoes are submarine and have unrecorded eruptions.

Pacific "Ring of Fire"

NORTHWEST
Japan: At least 33 active vents.

Aso (5,223 ft; 1,592 m), on Kyushu, has one of the largest craters in the world.

Asama (over 8,300 ft; 2,530 m), on Honshu, is continuously active; violent eruption in 1783.

Azuma (nearly 7,700 ft; 2,347 m), on Honshu, erupted in 1900.

Chokai (7,300 ft; 2,225 m), on Honshu, erupted in 1974 after having been quiescent since 1861.

Fujiyama (Fujisan) (12,385 ft; 3,775 m), on Honshu, southwest of Tokyo. Symmetrical in outline, snow-covered. Regarded as a sacred mountain.

On-take (3,668 ft; 1,118 m), on peninsula of Kyushu. Strong smoke emissions and explosions began November 1973 and continued through 1974.

U.S.S.R.: Kamchatka peninsula, 14–18 active volcanoes. Klyuchevskaya (Kluchev) (15,500 ft; 4,724 m) reported active in 1974.

Kuril Islands: At least 13 active volcanoes and several submarine outbreaks.

SOUTHWEST
New Zealand: Mount Tarawera (3,645 ft; 1,112 m), on North Island, had a severe eruption in 1886 that destroyed the famous Pink and White sinter terraces of Rotomahana, a hot lake.

Ngauruhoe (7,515 ft; 2,291 m), on North Island,

emits steam and vapor constantly. Erupted 1974.
Papua New Guinea: Karkar Island (4,920 ft; 1,500 m). Mild eruptions 1974.
Philippine Islands: About 100 eruptive centers; Hibok Hibok, on Camiguin, erupted September 1950 and again in December 1951, when about 750 were reported killed or missing; eruptions continued during 1952–53.

Taal (4,752 ft; 1,448 m), on Luzon. Major eruption in 1965 killed 190; erupted again, 1968.
Volcano Islands: Mount Suribachi (546 ft; 166 m), on Iwo Jima. A sulfurous steaming volcano. Raising of U.S. flag over Mount Suribachi was one of the dramatic episodes of World War II.

NORTHEAST
Alaska: Mount Wrangell (14,163 ft; 4,317 m) and Mount Katmai (about 6,700 ft; 2,042 m). On June 6, 1912, a violent eruption (Nova Rupta) of Mount Katmai occurred, during which the "Valley of Ten Thousand Smokes" was formed.
Aleutian Islands: There are 32 active vents known and numerous inactive cones. Akutan Island (over 4,000 ft; 1,220 m) erupted in 1974, with ash and debris rising over 300 ft.

Great Sitkin (5,741 ft; 1,750 m). Explosive activity February-September 1974, accompanied by earthquake originating at volcano that registered 2.3 on Richter scale.
California, Oregon, Washington: Lassen Peak (10,453 ft; 3,186 m) in California is one of two observed active volcanoes in the U.S. outside Alaska and Hawaii. The last period of activity was 1914–17. Mt. St. Helens (9,677 ft; 2,950 m) in the Cascade Range of southwest Washington became active on March 27, 1980, and erupted on May 18. It last erupted in 1857. Other mountains of volcanic origin include Mount Shasta (California), Mount Hood (Oregon), Mount Mazama (Oregon)—the mountain containing Crater Lake, Mount Rainier (Washington), and Mount Baker (Washington), which has been steaming since October 1975, but gives no sign of an impending eruption.

SOUTHEAST

Chile and Argentina: About 25 active or potentially active.

Colombia: Huila (nearly 18,900 ft; 5,760 m), a vapor-emitting volcano, and Tolima (nearly 18,500 ft; 5,640 m). Eruption of Puracé (15,600 ft; 4,755 m) in 1949 killed 17 people.

Ecuador: Cayambe (nearly 19,000 ft; 5,791 m). Almost on the equator.

Cotopaxi (19,344 ft; 5,896 m). Perhaps highest active volcano in the world. Possesses a beautifully formed cone.

Reventador (11,434 ft; 3,485 m). Observed in active state in late 1973.

El Salvador: Izalco ("beacon of Central America") (7,830 ft; 2,387 m) first appeared in 1770 and is still growing (erupted in 1950, 1956; last erupted in October-November 1966). San Salvador (6,187 ft; 1,886 m) had a violent eruption in 1923. Conchagua (about 4100 ft; 1250 m) erupted with considerable damage early in 1947.

Guatemala: Santa Maria Quezaltenango (12,361 ft; 3,768 m). Frequent activity between 1902–08 and 1922–28 after centuries of quiescence. Most dangerously active vent of Central America. Other volcanoes include Tajumulco (13,814 ft; 4,211 m) and Atitlán (11,633 ft; 3,546 m).

Mexico: Boquerón ("Big Mouth"), on San Benedicto, about 250 mi. south of Lower California. Newest volcano in Western Hemisphere, discovered September 1952.

Colima (about 14,000 ft; 4,270 m), in group that has had frequent eruptions.

Orizaba (Citlaltépetl) (18,701 ft; 5,700 m).

Parícutin (7,450 ft; 2,270 m). First appeared in February 1943. In less than a week, a cone over 140 ft high developed with a crater one quarter mile in circumference. Cone grew more than 1,500 ft (457 m) in 1943. Erupted 1952.

Popocatépetl (17,887 ft; 5,452 m). Large, deep, bell-shaped crater. Not entirely extinct; steam still escapes.

Nicaragua: Volcanoes include Telica, Coseguina, and Momotombo. Between Momotombo on the west shore of Lake Managua and Coseguina overlooking the Gulf of Fonseca, there is a string of more than 20 cones, many still active. One of these, Cerro Negro, erupted in July 1947, with considerable damage and loss of life, and again in 1971.

Concepción (5,100 ft; 1,555 m). Ash eruptions 1973–74.

Mid-oceanic Islands

Canary Islands: Pico de Teide (12,192 ft; 3,716 m), on Tenerife.

Cape Verde Islands: Fogo (nearly 9,300 ft; 2,835 m). Severe eruption in 1857; quiescent until 1951.

Caribbean: La Soufrière (4,813 ft; 1,467 m), on Basse-Terre, Guadeloupe. Also called La Grande Soufrière. Violent activity in July-August 1976 caused evacuation of 73,000 people; renewed activity in April 1977 again caused thousands to flee their homes.

La Soufrière (4,048 ft; 1,234 m), on St. Vincent. Major eruption in 1902 killed over 1,000 people.

Comoros: One volcano, Karthala (nearly 8,000 ft; 2,440 m), is visible for over 100 miles. Last erupted in 1904.

Hawaii: Mauna Loa ("Long Mountain") (13,680 ft; 4,170 m), on Hawaii, discharges from its high side vents more lava than any other volcano. Largest volcanic mountain in the world in cubic content. Area of crater is 3.7 sq mi. Violent eruption in June 1950, with lava pouring 25 miles into the ocean. Last major eruption in July 1975.

Mauna Kea (13,796 ft; 4,205 m), on Hawaii. Highest mountain in state.

Kilauea (4,090 ft; 1,247 m) is a vent in the side of Mauna Loa, but its eruptions are apparently independent. One of the most spectacular and active craters. Crater has an area of 4.14 sq mi. Earthquake in July 1975 caused major eruption. Eruptions began in September 1977 and reached a height of 980 ft (300 m). Activity ended Oct. 1.

Iceland: At least 25 volcanoes active in historical times. Very similar to Hawaiian volcanoes. Askja (over 4,700 ft; 1,433 m) is the largest.

Lesser Antilles (West Indian Islands): Mount Pelée (over 4,500 ft; 1,370 m), northwestern Martinique. Eruption in 1902 destroyed town of St. Pierre and killed approximately 40,000 people.

Réunion Island (east of Madagascar): Piton de la Fournaise (Le Volcan) (8,610 ft; 2,624 m). Large lava flows. Last erupted in 1972.

Samoan archipelago: Savai'i Island had an eruption in 1905 that caused considerable damage. Niuafoo (Tin Can), in the Tonga Islands, has a crater that extends 6,000 feet below and 600 feet above water.

Indonesia

Sumatra: Ninety volcanoes have been discovered; 12 are now active. The most famous, Krakatau, is a small volcanic island in the Sunda Strait. Numerous volcanic discharges occurred in 1883. One extremely violent explosion caused the disappearance of the highest peak and the northern part of the island. Fine dust was carried around the world in the upper atmosphere. Over 36,000 persons lost their lives in resultant tidal waves that were felt as far away as Cape Horn. Active in 1972.

Mediterranean Area

Italy: Mount Etna (10,902 ft; 3,323 m), eastern Sicily. Two new craters formed in eruptions of February-March 1947. Worst eruption in 50 years occurred November 1950-Jaunary 1951. Erupted again in 1974, 1975, 1977, 1978, and 1979.

Stromboli (about 3,000 ft; 914 m), Lipari Islands (north of Sicily). Called "Lighthouse of the Mediterranean." Reported active in 1971.

Mount Vesuvius (4,200 ft; 1,280 m), southeast of Naples. Only active volcano on European mainland. Pompeii buried by an eruption, A.D. 79.

Measuring Earthquakes

Earthquakes are generally measured on the scale developed by Charles F. Richter in 1935. The scale is logarithmic—the release of energy increases about 10 times with each whole number of the scale. A quake whose magnitude is less than 2 will not be noticed by humans; there are thousands of such tremors per year. Earthquakes whose magnitude is more than 4.5 can cause damage; 6.5 indicates a serious and hazardous quake. At a magnitude of about 8, great damage can occur. The San Francisco earthquake of 1906 has been variously estimated at 7.8 to 8.3. The April 1979 quake in Yugoslavia was measured at magnitude 7.2; it caused heavy casualties because it occurred in a densely populated area.

World Population, Land Areas, and Elevations

Area	Estimated population, 1978	Approximate Land area sq mi.	Percent of total land area	Population density per sq mi.	Elevation, feet Highest	Elevation, feet Lowest	Dimensions, miles East-West	Dimensions, miles North-South
WORLD	4,258,000,000	58,451,000	100.0	81.2[1]	Mt. Everest, Asia, 29,028	Dead Sea, Asia, 1,290 below sea level	24,902	24,860
ASIA, incl. Philippines, Indonesia, and European Turkey and Asiatic Turkey, excl. Asiatic U.S.S.R.	2,461,000,000	10,678,000	18.2	230.5	Mt. Everest, Tibet-Nepal, 29,028	Dead Sea, Israel-Jordan, 1,290 below sea level	5,400[2]	5,300[2]
AFRICA	442,000,000	11,714,000	20.0	37.7	Mt. Kilimanjaro, Tanzania, 19,340	Lake Assal, Djibouti, 571 below sea level	4,600	5,000
NORTH AMERICA, including Hawaii, Central America, and Caribbean region	359,000,000	9,363,000	16.0	38.3	Mt. McKinley, Alaska, 20,320	Death Valley, Calif., 282 below sea level	3,200[5]	4,000[5]
SOUTH AMERICA	233,000,000	6,885,000	11.8	33.8	Mt. Aconcagua, Arg.-Chile, 23,034	Valdes Peninsula, 131 below sea level	3,200	4,600
ANTARCTICA	—	6,000,000	10.3	—	Vinson Massif, Sentinel Range, 16,863	Sea level	—	—
EUROPE, incl. Iceland; excl. European U.S.S.R. and European Turkey	480,000,000	1,906,000	3.3	251.8	Mont Blanc, France, 15,781	Sea level	3,300[3]	2,400[3]
OCEANIA, incl. Australia, New Zealand, Melanesia, Micronesia, and Polynesia[4]	22,100,000	3,286,000	5.6	6.7	Mauna Kea, Hawaii, 13,796	Lake Eyre, Australia, 38 below sea level	—	—
U.S.S.R., both European and Asiatic	262,000,000	8,649,000	14.8	30.3	Communism Peak, Pamir, 24,547	Caspian Sea, 96 below sea level	5,000	2,500

1. In computing density per square mile, the area of Antarctica is omitted. 2. Including Asiatic U.S.S.R. 3. Including European U.S.S.R. 4. Although Hawaii is geographically part of Oceania, its population is included in the population figure for North America. 5. Excludes Hawaii. Source: United Nations Demographic Yearbook, 1978.

Some Countries With High Population Densities (per square mile)

Monaco	41,095.9	Lebanon	805.4	India	556.0
Singapore	10,168.1	West Germany	640.8	Jamaica	504.4
Bangladesh	1,645.3	United Kingdom	593.1	Israel	500.5
China, Rep. of	1,324.3	Sri Lanka	592.1	Italy	491.4

Netherlands	1,040.4
South Korea	1,020.2
Belgium	837.8
Japan	819.4

Longitude and Latitude of Foreign Cities
(and time corresponding to 12:00 noon, eastern standard time)

City	Long. ° '	Lat. ° '	Time	City	Long. ° '	Lat. ° '	Time
Aberdeen, Scotland	2 9 w	57 9 n	5:00 p.m.	La Paz, Bolivia	68 22 w	16 27 s	1:00 p.m.
Adelaide, Australia	138 36 e	34 55 s	2:30 a.m.[1]	Leeds, England	1 30 w	53 45 n	5:00 p.m.
Algiers	3 0 e	36 50 n	6:00 p.m.	Leningrad	30 18 e	59 56 n	8:00 p.m.
Amsterdam	4 53 e	52 22 n	6:00 p.m.	Lima, Peru	77 2 w	12 0 s	12:00 noon
Ankara, Turkey	32 55 e	39 55 n	7:00 p.m.	Lisbon	9 9 w	38 44 n	5:00 p.m.
Asunción, Paraguay	57 40 w	25 15 s	1:00 p.m.	Liverpool, England	3 0 w	53 25 n	5:00 p.m.
Athens	23 43 e	37 58 n	7:00 p.m.	London	0 5 w	51 32 n	5:00 p.m.
Auckland, New Zeland	174 45 e	36 52 s	5:00 a.m.[1]	Lyons, France	4 50 e	45 45 n	6:00 p.m.
Bangkok, Thailand	100 30 e	13 45 n	midnight[1]	Madrid	3 42 w	40 26 n	6:00 p.m.
Barcelona	2 9 e	41 23 n	6:00 p.m.	Manchester, England	2 15 w	53 30 n	5:00 p.m.
Belém, Brazil	48 29 w	1 28 s	2:00 p.m.	Manila	120 57 e	14 35 n	1:00 a.m.[1]
Belfast, Northern Ireland	5 56 w	54 37 n	5:00 p.m.	Marseilles, France	5 20 e	43 20 n	6:00 p.m.
				Mazatlán, Mexico	106 25 w	23 12 n	10:00 a.m.
Belgrade, Yugoslavia	20 32 e	44 52 n	6:00 p.m.	Mecca, Saudi Arabia	39 45 e	21 29 n	8:00 p.m.
Berlin	13 25 e	52 30 n	6:00 p.m.	Melbourne	144 58 e	37 47 s	3:00 a.m.[1]
Birmingham, England	1 55 w	52 25 n	5:00 p.m.	Mexico City	99 7 w	19 26 n	11:00 a.m.
Bogotá, Colombia	74 15 w	4 32 n	12:00 noon	Milan, Italy	9 10 e	45 27 n	6:00 p.m.
Bombay	72 48 e	19 0 n	10:30 p.m.	Montevideo, Uruguay	56 10 w	34 53 s	2:00 p.m.
Bordeaux, France	0 31 w	44 50 n	6:00 p.m.	Moscow	37 36 e	55 45 n	8:00 p.m.
Bremen, Germany	8 49 e	53 5 n	6:00 p.m.	Munich, Germany	11 35 e	48 8 n	6:00 p.m.
Brisbane, Australia	153 8 e	27 29 s	3:00 a.m.[1]	Nagasaki, Japan	129 57 e	32 48 n	2:00 a.m.[1]
Bristol, England	2 35 w	51 28 n	5:00 p.m.	Nagoya, Japan	136 56 e	35 7 n	2:00 a.m.[1]
Brussels	4 22 e	50 52 n	6:00 p.m.	Nairobi, Kenya	36 55 e	1 25 s	8:00 p.m.
Bucharest	26 7 e	44 25 n	7:00 p.m.	Nanjing (Nanking), China	118 53 e	32 3 n	1:00 a.m.[1]
Budapest	19 5 e	47 30 n	6:00 p.m.	Naples, Italy	14 15 e	40 50 n	6:00 p.m.
Buenos Aires	58 22 w	34 35 s	2:00 p.m.	Newcastle-on-Tyne, Eng.	1 37 w	54 58 n	5:00 p.m.
Cairo	31 21 e	30 2 n	7:00 p.m.	Odessa, U.S.S.R.	30 48 e	46 27 n	8:00 p.m.
Calcutta	88 24 e	22 34 n	10:30 p.m.	Osaka, Japan	135 30 e	34 32 n	2:00 a.m.[1]
Canton, China	113 15 e	23 7 n	1:00 a.m.[1]	Oslo	10 42 e	59 57 n	6:00 p.m.
Cape Town, South Africa	18 22 e	33 55 s	7:00 p.m.	Panama City, Panama	79 32 w	8 58 n	12:00 noon
				Paramaribo, Surinam	55 15 w	5 45 n	1:30 p.m.
Caracas, Venezuela	67 2 w	10 28 n	12:30 p.m.	Paris	2 20 e	48 48 n	6:00 p.m.
Cayenne, French Guiana	52 18 w	4 49 n	1:00 p.m.	Peking	116 25 e	39 55 n	1:00 a.m.[1]
Chihuahua, Mexico	106 5 w	28 37 n	11:00 a.m.	Perth, Australia	115 52 e	31 57 s	1:00 a.m.[1]
Chongqing, China	106 34 e	29 46 n	1:00 a.m.[1]	Plymouth, England	4 5 w	50 25 n	5:00 p.m.
Copenhagen	12 34 e	55 40 n	6:00 p.m.	Port Moresby, Papua New Guinea	147 8 e	9 25 s	3:00 a.m.[1]
Córdoba, Argentina	64 10 w	31 28 s	2:00 p.m.	Prague	14 26 e	50 5 n	6:00 p.m.
Dakar, Senegal	17 28 w	14 40 n	5:00 p.m.	Rangoon, Burma	96 0 e	16 50 n	11:30 p.m.
Darwin, Australia	130 51 e	12 28 s	2:30 a.m.[1]	Reykjavik, Iceland	21 58 w	64 4 n	4:00 p.m.
Djibouti	43 3 e	11 30 n	8:00 p.m.	Rio de Janeiro	43 12 w	22 57 s	2:00 p.m.
Dublin	6 15 w	53 20 n	5:00 p.m.	Rome	12 27 e	41 54 n	6:00 p.m.
Durban, South Africa	30 53 e	29 53 s	7:00 p.m.	Salvador, Brazil	38 27 w	12 56 s	2:00 p.m.
Edinburgh, Scotland	3 10 w	55 55 n	5:00 p.m.	Santiago, Chile	70 45 w	33 28 s	1:00 p.m.
Frankfurt	8 41 e	50 7 n	6:00 p.m.	Sao Paulo, Brazil	46 31 w	23 31 s	2:00 p.m.
Georgetown, Guyana	58 15 w	6 45 n	1:15 p.m.	Shanghai, China	121 28 e	31 10 n	1:00 a.m.[1]
Glasgow, Scotland	4 15 w	55 50 n	5:00 p.m.	Singapore	103 55 e	1 14 n	0:30 a.m.[1]
Guatemala City, Guatemala	90 31 w	14 37 n	11:00 a.m.	Sofia, Bulgaria	23 20 e	42 40 n	7:00 p.m.
Guayaquil, Ecuador	79 56 w	2 10 s	12:00 noon	Stockholm	18 3 e	59 17 n	6:00 p.m.
Hamburg	10 2 e	53 33 n	6:00 p.m.	Sydney, Australia	151 0 e	34 0 s	3:00 a.m.[1]
Hammerfest, Norway	23 38 e	70 38 n	6:00 p.m.	Tananarive, Madagascar	47 33 e	18 50 s	8:00 p.m.
Havana	82 23 w	23 8 n	12:00 noon	Teheran, Iran	51 45 e	35 45 n	8:30 p.m.
Helsinki, Finland	25 0 e	60 10 n	7:00 p.m.	Tokyo	139 45 e	35 40 n	2:00 a.m.[1]
Hobart, Tasmania	147 19 e	42 52 s	3:00 a.m.[1]	Tripoli, Libya	13 12 e	32 57 n	7:00 p.m.
Iquique, Chile	70 7 w	20 10 s	1:00 p.m.	Venice	12 20 e	45 26 n	6:00 p.m.
Irkutsk, U.S.S.R.	104 20 e	52 30 n	1:00 a.m.[1]	Veracruz, Mexico	96 10 w	19 10 n	11:00 a.m.
Jakarta, Indonesia	106 48 e	6 16 s	0:30 a.m.[1]	Vienna	16 20 e	48 14 n	6:00 p.m.
Johannesburg, South Africa	28 4 e	26 12 s	7:00 p.m.	Vladivostok, U.S.S.R.	132 0 e	43 10 n	3:00 a.m.[1]
				Warsaw	21 0 e	52 14 n	6:00 p.m.
Kingston, Jamaica	76 49 w	17 59 n	12:00 noon	Wellington, New Zealand	174 47 e	41 17 s	5:00 a.m.[1]
Kinshasa, Zaire	15 17 e	4 18 s	6:00 p.m.	Zürich	8 31 e	47 21 n	6:00 p.m.

1. On the following day.

WORLD TIME ZONES

U.S.S.R. Standard Times are one hour in advance of Zone Times.

When crossing the date line going east, the date is set back one day.

When crossing the date line going west, the date is set forward one day.

= Fractional deviation from standard time or no legal time.

Highest Mountain Peaks of the World
(For U.S. peaks, see Index)

Mountain peak	Range	Location	Height feet	Height meters
Everest[1]	Himalayas	Nepal-Tibet	29,028	8,848
Godwin Austen (K-2)	Karakoram	India	28,741	8,750
Kanchenjunga	Himalayas	Nepal-Sikkim	28,208	8,598
Lhotse	Himalayas	Nepal-Tibet	27,890	8,501
Makalu	Himalayas	Tibet-Nepal	27,790	8,470
Dhaulagiri I	Himalayas	Nepal	26,810	8,172
Manaslu	Himalayas	Nepal	26,760	8,156
Cho Oyu	Himalayas	Nepal	26,750	8,153
Nanga Parbat	Himalayas	India	26,660	8,126
Annapurna I	Himalayas	Nepal	26,504	8,078
Gasherbrum I	Karakoram	India	26,470	8,068
Broad Peak	Karakoram	India	26,400	8,047
Gasherbrum II	Karakoram	India	26,360	8,033
Gosainthan	Himalayas	Tibet	26,291	8,013
Gasherbrum III	Karakoram	India	26,090	7,952
Annapurna II	Himalayas	Nepal	26,041	7,937
Gasherbrum IV	Karakoram	India	26,000	7,925
Kangbachen	Himalayas	Nepal	25,925	7,902
Gyachung Kang	Himalayas	Nepal	25,910	7,897
Himal Chuli	Himalayas	Nepal	25,895	7,893
Disteghil Sar	Karakoram	India	25,868	7,885
Nuptse	Himalayas	Nepal	25,850	7,829
Kunyang Kish	Karakoram	India	25,760	7,852
Dakum (Peak 29)	Himalayas	Nepal	25,760	7,852
Masherbrum	Karakoram	India	25,660	7,821
Nanda Devi	Himalayas	India	25,645	7,817
Chomolonzo	Himalayas	Nepal-Tibet	25,640	7,815
Rakaposhi	Karakoram	India	25,550	7,788
Batura	Karakoram	India	25,540	7,785
Kanjut Sar	Karakoram	India	25,460	7,760
Kamet	Himalayas	India-Tibet	25,447	7,756
Namche Barwa	Himalayas	Tibet	25,445	7,756
Dhaulagiri II	Himalayas	Nepal	25,427	7,750
Saltoro Kangri	Karakoram	India	25,400	7,742
Gurla Mandhata	Himalayas	Tibet	25,355	7,728
Ulugh Muztagh	Kunlun	Tibet	25,341	7,724
Trivor	Karakoram	India	25,330	7,721
Jannu	Himalayas	Nepal	25,294	7,710
Saser Kangri	Karakoram	India	25,170	7,672
Makalu II	Himalayas	Nepal	25,130	7,660
Chogolisa	Karakoram	India	25,110	7,654
Dhaulagiri IV	Himalayas	Nepal	25,064	7,639
Fang	Himalayas	Nepal	25,013	7,624
Kula Gangri	Himalayas	Tibet	24,783	7,554
Changtse	Himalayas	Tibet	24,780	7,553
Muztagh Ata	Muztagh Ata	China	24,757	7,546
Skyang Kangri	Himalayas	Kashmir	24,750	7,544
Communism Peak	Pamir	U.S.S.R.	24,547	7,482
Victory Peak	Pamir	U.S.S.R.	24,406	7,439
Sia Kangri	Himalayas	Kashmir	24,340	7,419
Chamlang	Himalayas	Nepal	24,012	7,319
Alung Gangri	Himalayas	Tibet	23,999	7,315
Chomo Lhari	Himalayas	Tibet-Bhutan	23,996	7,314
Muztagh (K-5)	Kunlun	China	23,891	7,282
Amne Machin	Kunlun	China	23,490	7,160
Gaurisankar	Himalayas	Nepal-Tibet	23,440	7,145
Lenin Peak	Pamir	U.S.S.R.	23,405	7,134
Korzhenevski Peak	Pamir	U.S.S.R.	23,310	7,105
Kangto	Himalayas	Tibet	23,260	7,090
Dunagiri	Himalayas	India	23,184	7,066
Pauhunri	Himalayas	India-Tibet	23,180	7,065
Aconcagua	Andes	Argentina-Chile	23,034	7,021
Revolution Peak	Pamir	U.S.S.R.	22,880	6,974
Kangchenjhan	Himalayas	India	22,700	6,919
Siniolchu	Himalayas	India	22,620	6,895
Ojos des Salado	Andes	Argentina-Chile	22,588	6,885

Mountain peak	Range	Location	Height feet	Height meters
Bonete	Andes	Argentina-Chile	22,546	6,872
Simvuo	Himalayas	India	22,346	6,811
Tup	Andes	Argentina	22,309	6,800
Kungpu	Himalayas	Bhutan	22,300	6,797
Falso-Azufre	Andes	Argentina-Chile	22,277	6,790
Moscow Peak	Pamir	U.S.S.R.	22,260	6,785
Veladero	Andes	Argentina	22,244	6,780
Pissis	Andes	Argentina	22,241	6,779
Mercedario	Andes	Argentina-Chile	22,211	6,770
Huascarán	Andes	Peru	22,198	6,766
Tocorpuri	Andes	Bolivia-Chile	22,162	6,755
Karl Marx Peak	Pamir	U.S.S.R.	22,067	6,726
Llullaillaco	Andes	Argentina-Chile	22,057	6,723
Libertador	Andes	Argentina	22,047	6,720
Kailas	Himalayas	Tibet	22,027	6,714
Lingtren	Himalayas	Nepal-Tibet	21,972	6,697
Incahuasi	Andes	Argentina-Chile	21,719	6,620
Carnicero	Andes	Peru	21,689	6,611
Kurumda	Pamir	U.S.S.R.	21,686	6,610
Garmo Peak	Pamir	U.S.S.R.	21,637	6,595
Sajama	Andes	Bolivia	21,555	6,570
Ancohuma	Andes	Bolivia	21,490	6,550
El Muerto	Andes	Argentina-Chile	21,456	6,540
Nacimiento	Andes	Argentina	21,302	6,493
Illimani	Andes	Bolivia	21,184	6,457
Antofalla	Andes	Argentina-Chile	21,129	6,440
Coropuña	Andes	Peru	21,079	6,425
Cuzco (Ausangate)	Andes	Peru	20,995	6,399
Toro	Andes	Argentina-Chile	20,932	6,380
Parinacota	Andes	Bolivia-Chile	20,768	6,330
Chimboraso	Andes	Ecuador	20,702	6,310
Salcantay	Andes	Peru	20,575	6,271
General Manuel Belgrano	Andes	Argentina	20,505	6,250
Chañi	Andes	Argentina	20,341	6,200
Caca Aca	Andes	Bolivia	20,328	6,196
McKinley	Alaska	Alaska	20,320	6,194
Vudor Peak	Pamir	U.S.S.R.	20,118	6,132
Condoriri	Andes	Bolivia	20,095	6,125
Solimana	Andes	Peru	20,069	6,117
Nevada	Andes	Argentina	20,023	6,103

1. The U. S. Air Force Planning Charts list the height of Mt. Everest as 29,141 ft.

Oceans and Seas

Name	Area sq mi.	Area sq km	Average depth feet	Average depth meters	Greatest known depth feet	Greatest known depth meters	Place greatest known depth
Pacific Ocean	64,000,000	165,760,000	13,215	4,028	37,782	11,516	Mindanao Deep
Atlantic Ocean	31,815,000	82,400,000	12,880	3,926	30,246	9,219	Puerto Rico Trough
Indian Ocean	25,300,000	65,526,700	13,002	3,963	24,460	7,455	Sunda Trench
Arctic Ocean	5,440,200	14,090,000	3,953	1,205	18,456	5,625	77° 45′ N; 175° W
Mediterranean Sea[1]	1,145,100	2,965,800	4,688	1,429	15,197	4,632	Off Cape Matapan, Greece
Caribbean Sea	1,049,500	2,718,200	8,685	2,647	22,788	6,946	Off Cayman Islands
South China Sea	895,400	2,319,000	5,419	1,652	16,456	5,016	West of Luzon
Bering Sea	884,900	2,291,900	5,075	1,547	15,659	4,773	Off Buldir Island
Gulf of Mexico	615,000	1,592,800	4,874	1,486	12,425	3,787	Sigsbee Deep
Okhotsk Sea	613,800	1,589,700	2,749	838	12,001	3,658	146° 10′ E; 46° 50′ N
East China Sea	482,300	1,249,200	617	188	9,126	2,782	25° 16′ N; 125° E
Hudson Bay	475,800	1,232,300	420	128	600	183	Near entrance
Japan Sea	389,100	1,007,800	4,429	1,350	12,276	3,742	Central Basin
Andaman Sea	308,100	797,700	2,854	870	12,392	3,777	Off Car Nicobar Island
North Sea	222,100	575,200	308	94	2,165	660	Skagerrak
Red Sea	169,100	438,000	1,611	491	7,254	2,211	Off Port Sudan
Baltic Sea	163,000	422,200	180	55	1,380	421	Off Gotland

1. Includes Black Sea and Sea of Azov. NOTE: For Caspian Sea, *see* Large Lakes of World elsewhere in this section.

World's Greatest Man-Made Lakes[1]

Name of dam	Location	Millions of cubic meters	Thousands of acre-feet	Year completed
Owen Falls	Uganda	204,800	166,000	1954
Bratsk	U.S.S.R.	169,270	137,220	1964
High Aswan	Egypt	169,000	137,000	1970
Kariba	Zambia–Zimbabwe	160,368	130,000	1959
Akosombo	Ghana	148,000	120,000	1965
Daniel Johnson	Canada	141,852	115,000	1968
Raul Leoni	Venezuela	136,000	110,257	UC
Krasnoyarsk	U.S.S.R.	73,300	59,425	1972
W. A. C. Bennett	Canada	70,309	57,006	1967
Zeya	U.S.S.R.	68,400	55,452	1975
Cabora Bassa	Mozambique	64,000	51,900	1974
LaGrande	Canada	62,260	50,475	UC
Ust–Ilimsk	U.S.S.R.	59,300	48,100	UC
Volga-V. I. Lenin	U.S.S.R.	58,000	47,020	1955
Bukhtarma	U.S.S.R.	53,000	42,970	1960
Ataturk	Turkey	48,700	39,481	UC
Irkutsk	U.S.S.R.	46,000	37,290	1956
Hoover	Nevada-Arizona	36,703	29,755	1936
Vilyui	U.S.S.R.	35,900	29,104	1967
Sobradinho	Brazil	34,200	27,700	1978
Tucurui	Brazil	34,000	27,564	UC
Volgograd-22nd Congress	U.S.S.R.	33,500	27,160	1958
Glen Canyon	Arizona	33,305	27,000	1964
Keban	Turkey	31,000	25,110	1974
Garrison	North Dakota	30,000	24,321	1956
Iroquois	U.S.-Canada	29,960	24,288	1958
Oahe	South Dakota	29,100	23,591	1963

1. Formed by construction of dams. NOTE: UC means under construction in 1980. *Source:* Department of the Interior, Water and Power Resources Service.

Large Lakes of the World

Name and location	Area		Length		Maximum depth	
	sq mi.	sq km	mi.	km	feet	meters
Caspian Sea, U.S.S.R.-Iran[1]	152,239	394,299	745	1,199	3,104	946
Superior, U.S.-Canada	31,820	82,414	383	616	1,333	406
Victoria, Tanzania–Uganda	26,828	69,485	200	322	270	82
Aral, U.S.S.R.	25,659	66,457	266	428	223	68
Huron, U.S.-Canada	23,010	59,596	247	397	750	229
Michigan, U.S.	22,400	58,016	321	517	923	281
Tanganyika, Tanzania-Zaire	12,700	32,893	420	676	4,708	1,435
Baikal, U.S.S.R.	12,162	31,500	395	636	5,712	1,741
Great Bear, Canada	12,000	31,080	232	373	270	82
Nyasa, Malawi-Mozambique-Tanzania	11,600	30,044	360	579	2,316	706
Great Slave, Canada	11,170	28,930	298	480	2,015	614
Chad,[2] Chad-Niger-Nigeria	9,946	25,760	—	—	23	7
Erie, U.S.-Canada	9,930	25,719	241	388	210	64
Winnipeg, Canada	9,094	23,553	264	425	204	62
Ontario, U.S.-Canada	7,520	19,477	193	311	778	237
Balkash, U.S.S.R.	7,115	18,428	376	605	87	27
Ladoga, U.S.S.R.	7,000	18,130	124	200	738	225
Onega, U.S.S.R.	3,819	9,891	154	248	361	110
Titicaca, Bolivia-Peru	3,141	8,135	110	177	1,214	370
Nicaragua, Nicaragua	3,089	8,001	110	177	230	70
Athabaska, Canada	3,058	7,920	208	335	407	124
Rudolf, Kenya	2,473	6,405	154	248	—	—
Reindeer, Canada	2,444	6,330	152	245	—	—
Eyre, South Australia	2,400[3]	6,216	130	209	varies	varies
Issyk-Kul, U.S.S.R.	2,394	6,200	113	182	2,297	700
Urmia,[2] Iran	2,317	6,001	81	130	49	15
Torrens, South Australia	2,200	5,698	130	209	—	—
Vänern, Sweden	2,141	5,545	87	140	322	98

Name and location	Area		Length		Maximum depth	
	sq mi.	sq km	mi.	km	feet	meters
Winnipegosis, Canada	2,086	5,403	152	245	59	18
Mobutu Sese Seko, Uganda	2,046	5,299	100	161	180	55
Nettilling, Baffin Island, Canada	1,950	5,051	70	113	—	—
Nipigon, Canada	1,870	4,843	72	116	—	—
Manitoba, Canada	1,817	4,706	140	225	22	7
Great Salt, U.S.	1,800	4,662	75	121	15/25	5/8
Kioga, Uganda	1,700	4,403	50	80	about 30	9
Koko-Nor, China	1,630	4,222	66	106	—	—

1. The Caspian Sea is called "sea" because the Romans, finding it salty, named it *Mare Caspium*. Many geographers, however, consider it a lake because it is land-locked. 2. Figures represent high-water data. 3. Varies with the rainfall of the wet season. It has been reported to dry up almost completely on occasion.

Principal Rivers of the World
(For other U.S. rivers, see Index)

River	Source	Outflow	Approx. length	
			miles	km
Nile	Tributaries of Lake Victoria, Africa	Mediterranean Sea	4,180	6,690
Amazon	Glacier-fed lakes, Peru	Atlantic Ocean	3,912	6,296
Mississippi-Missouri-Red Rock	Source of Red Rock, Montana	Gulf of Mexico	3,741	6,020
Yangtze Kiang	Tibetan plateau, China	China Sea	3,602	5,797
Ob	Altai Mts., U.S.S.R.	Gulf of Ob	3,459	5,567
Yellow (Hwang Ho)	Eastern part of Kunlan Mts., west China	Gulf of Chihli	2,900	4,667
Yenisei	Tannu-Ola Mts., western Tuva, U.S.S.R.	Arctic Ocean	2,800	4,506
Paraná	Confluence of Paranaiba and Grande rivers	Río de la Plata	2,795	4,498
Irtish	Altai Mts., U.S.S.R.	Ob River	2,758	4,438
Congo	Confluence of Lualaba and Luapula rivers, Zaire	Atlantic Ocean	2,716	4,371
Amur	Confluence of Shilka (U.S.S.R.) and Argun (Manchuria) rivers	Tatar Strait	2,704	4,352
Lena	Baikal Mts., U.S.S.R.	Arctic Ocean	2,652	4,268
Mackenzie	Head of Finlay River, British Columbia, Canada	Beaufort Sea (Arctic Ocean)	2,635	4,241
Niger	Guinea	Gulf of Guinea	2,600	4,184
Mekong	Tibetan highlands	South China Sea	2,500	4,023
Mississippi	Lake Itasca, Minnesota	Gulf of Mexico	2,348	3,779
Missouri	Confluence of Jefferson, Gallatin, and Madison rivers, Montana	Mississippi River	2,315	3,726
Volga	Valdai plateau, U.S.S.R.	Caspian Sea	2,291	3,687
Madeira	Confluence of Beni and Maumoré rivers, Bolivia-Brazil boundary	Amazon River	2,012	3,238
Purus	Peruvian Andes	Amazon River	1,993	3,207
São Francisco	Southwest Minas Gerais, Brazil	Atlantic Ocean	1,987	3,198
St. Lawrence	Lake Ontario	Gulf of St. Lawrence	1,900	3,058
Yukon	Junction of Lewes and Pelly rivers, Yukon Territory, Canada	Bering Sea	1,900	3,058
Rio Grande	San Juan Mts., Colorado	Gulf of Mexico	1,885	3,034
Brahmaputra	Himalayas	Ganges River	1,800	2,897
Indus	Himalayas	Arabian Sea	1,800	2,897
Danube	Black Forest, W. Germany	Black Sea	1,766	2,842

River	Source	Outflow	Approx. length	
			miles	km
Euphrates	Confluence of Murat Nehri and Kara Su rivers, Turkey	Shatt-al-Arab	1,739	2,799
Darling	Central part of Eastern Highlands, Australia	Murray River	1,702	2,739
Zambezi	11°21'S, 24°22'E, Zambia	Mozambique Channel	1,700	2,736
Tocantins	Goiás, Brazil	Pará River	1,677	2,699
Murray	Australian Alps, New South Wales	Indian Ocean	1,609	2,589
Nelson	Head of Bow River, western Alberta, Canada	Hudson Bay	1,600	2,575
Paraguay	Mato Grosso, Brazil	Paraná River	1,584	2,549
Ural	Southern Ural Mts., U.S.S.R.	Caspian Sea	1,574	2,533
Ganges	Himalayas	Bay of Bengal	1,557	2,506
Amu Darya (Oxus)	Nicholas Range, Pamir Mts., U.S.S.R.	Aral Sea	1,500	2,414
Japurá	Andes, Colombia	Amazon River	1,500	2,414
Salween	Tibet, south of Kunlun Mts.	Gulf of Martaban	1,500	2,414
Arkansas	Central Colorado	Mississippi River	1,450	2,333
Colorado	Grand County, Colorado	Gulf of California	1,450	2,333
Dnieper	Valdai Hills, U.S.S.R.	Black Sea	1,419	2,284
Ohio-Allegheny	Potter County, Pennsylvania	Mississippi River	1,306	2,102
Irrawaddy	Confluence of Nmai and Mali rivers, northeast Burma	Bay of Bengal	1,300	2,092
Orange	Lesotho	Atlantic Ocean	1,300	2,092
Orinoco	Serra Parima Mts., Venezuela	Atlantic Ocean	1,281	2,062
Pilcomayo	Andes Mts., Bolivia	Paraguay River	1,242	1,999
Xi Jiang (Si Kiang)	Eastern Yunnan Province, China	China Sea	1,236	1,989
Columbia	Columbia Lake, British Columbia, Canada	Pacific Ocean	1,232	1,983
Don	Tula, R.S.F.S.R., U.S.S.R.	Sea of Azov	1,223	1,968
Sungari	China-North Korea boundary	Amur River	1,215	1,955
Saskatchewan	Canadian Rocky Mts.	Lake Winnipeg	1,205	1,939
Peace	Stikine Mts., British Columbia, Canada	Great Slave River	1,195	1,923
Tigris	Taurus Mts., Turkey	Shatt-al-Arab	1,180	1,899

Highest Waterfalls of the World

Waterfall	Location	River	Height	
			feet	meters
Angel	Venezuela	Tributary of Caroní	3,281	1,000
Tugela	Natal, South Africa	Tugela	3,000	914
Cuquenán	Venezuela	Cuquenán	2,000	610
Sutnerland	South Island, N.Z.	Arthur	1,904	580
Takkakaw	British Columbia	Tributary of Yoho	1,650	503
Ribbon (Yosemite)	California	Creek flowing into Yosemite	1,612	491
Upper Yosemite	California	Yosemite Creek, tributary of Merced	1,430	436
Gavarnie	Southwest France	Gave de Pau	1,384	422
Vettisfoss	Norway	Mörkedola	1,200	366
Widows' Tears (Yosemite)	California	Tributary of Merced	1,170	357
Staubbach	Switzerland	Staubbach (Lauterbrunnen Valley)	984	300

Interesting Caves and Caverns of the World

Aggtelek. In village of same name, northern Hungary. Large stalactitic cavern about 5 miles long.

Altamira Cave. Near Santander, Spain. Contains animal paintings (Old Stone Age art) on roof and walls.

Antiparos. On island of same name in the Grecian Archipelago. Some stalactites are 20 ft long. Brilliant colors and fantastic shapes.

Blue Grotto. On island of Capri, Italy. Cavern hollowed out in limestone by constant wave action. Now half filled with water because of sinking coast. Name derived from unusual blue light permeating the cave. Source of light is a submerged opening, light passing through the water.

Carlsbad Caverns. Southeast New Mexico. Largest underground labyrinth yet discovered. Three levels: 754, 900, and 1,320 ft below the surface.

Fingal's Cave. On island of Staffa off coast of western Scotland. Penetrates about 200 ft inland. Contains basaltic columns almost 40 ft high.

Ice Cave. Near Dobsina, Czechoslovakia. Noted for its beautiful crystal effects.

Jenolan Caves. In Blue Mountain plateau, New South Wales, Australia. Beautiful stalactitic formations.

Kent's Cavern. Near Torquay, England. Source of much information on Paleolithic man.

Luray Cavern. Near Luray, Va. Has large stalactitic and stalagmitic columns of many colors.

Mammoth Cave. Limestone cavern in central Kentucky. Cave area is about 10 miles in diameter but has at least 150 miles of irregular subterranean passageways at various levels. Temperature remains fairly constant at 54°F.

Peak Cavern or **Devil's Hole.** Derbyshire, England. About 2,250 ft into a mountain. Lowest part is about 600 ft below the surface.

Postojna (Postumia) Grotto. Near Postumia in Julian Alps, about 25 miles northeast of Trieste. Stalactitic cavern, largest in Europe. Piuca (Pivka) River flows through part of it. Caves have numerous beautiful stalactites.

Singing Cave. Iceland. A lava cave; name derived from echoes of people singing in it.

Wind Cave. In Black Hills of South Dakota. Limestone caverns with stalactites and stalagmites almost entirely missing. Variety of crystal formations called "boxwork."

Wyandotte Cave. In Crawford County, southern Indiana. A limestone cavern with five levels of passages; one of the largest in North America. "Monumental Mountain," approximately 135 ft high, is believed to be one of the world's largest underground "mountains."

U.S. Geography

Miscellaneous Data for the United States

Source: Department of the Interior, U.S. Geological Survey.

Highest point: Mount McKinley, Alaska	20,320 ft (6,193 m)
Lowest point: Death Valley, Calif.	282 ft (86 m) below sea level
Approximate mean altitude	2,500 ft (762 m)
Points farthest apart (50 states):	
Log Point, Elliot Key, Fla., and Kure Island, Hawaii	5,852 mi. (9,418 km)
Geographic center (50 states):	
In Butte County, S.D. (west of Castle Rock)	44° 58′ N. lat. 103° 46′ W. long.
Geographic center (48 conterminous states):	
In Smith County, Kan. (near Lebanon)	39° 50′ N. lat. 98° 35′ W. long.
Boundaries:	
Between Alaska and Canada	1,538 mi. (2,475 km)
Between the 48 conterminous states and Canada (incl. Great Lakes)	3,987 mi. (6,416 km)
Between the United States and Mexico	1,933 mi. (3,111 km)

Extreme Points of the United States (50 States)

Extreme point	Latitude	Longitude	Distance[1] mi.	km
Northernmost point: Point Barrow, Alaska	71°23′ N	156°29′ W	2,502	4,027
Easternmost point: West Quoddy Head, Me.	44°49′ N	66°57′ W	1,785	2,873
Southernmost point: Ka Lae (South Cape), Hawaii	18°56′ N	155°41′ W	3,456	5,562
Westernmost point: Cape Wrangell, Alaska (Attu Island)	52°55′ N	172°27′ E	3,620	5,826

1. From geographic center of United States (incl. Alaska and Hawaii), west of Castle Rock, S.D., 44°58′ N. lat., 103°46′ W long.

Highest, Lowest, and Mean Altitudes in the United States

State	Altitude, ft[1]	Highest point	Altitude, ft	Lowest point	Altitude, ft
Alabama	500	Cheaha Mountain	2,407	Gulf of Mexico	Sea level
Alaska	1,900	Mount McKinley	20,320	Pacific Ocean	Sea level
Arizona	4,100	Humphreys Peak	12,633	Colorado River	70
Arkansas	650	Magazine Mountain	2,753	Ouachita River	55
California	2,900	Mount Whitney	14,494	Death Valley	282[2]
Colorado	6,800	Mount Elbert	14,433	Arkansas River	3,350
Connecticut	500	Mount Frissell, on south slope	2,380	Long Island Sound	Sea level
Delaware	60	On Ebright Road	442	Atlantic Ocean	Sea level
D. C.	150	Tenleytown, northwest part	410	Potomac River	1
Florida	100	Sec. 30, T6N, R20W[3]	345	Atlantic Ocean	Sea level
Georgia	600	Brasstown Bald	4,784	Atlantic Ocean	Sea level
Hawaii	3,030	Mauna Kea	13,796	Pacific Ocean	Sea level
Idaho	5,000	Borah Peak	12,662	Snake River	710
Illinois	600	Charles Mound	1,235	Mississippi River	279
Indiana	700	Franklin Township, Wayne County	1,257	Ohio River	320
Iowa	1,100	Sec. 29, T100N, R41W[4]	1,670	Mississippi River	480
Kansas	2,000	Mount Sunflower	4,039	Verdigris River	680
Kentucky	750	Black Mountain	4,145	Mississippi River	257
Louisiana	100	Driskill Mountain	535	New Orleans	5[2]
Maine	600	Mount Katahdin	5,268	Atlantic Ocean	Sea level
Maryland	350	Backbone Mountain	3,360	Atlantic Ocean	Sea level
Massachusetts	500	Mount Greylock	3,491	Atlantic Ocean	Sea level
Michigan	900	Mount Curwood	1,980	Lake Erie	572
Minnesota	1,200	Eagle Mountain	2,301	Lake Superior	602
Mississippi	300	Woodall Mountain	806	Gulf of Mexico	Sea level
Missouri	800	Taum Sauk Mountain	1,772	St. Francis River	230
Montana	3,400	Granite Peak	12,799	Kootenai River	1,800
Nebraska	2,600	Johnson Township, Kimball County	5,426	Southeast corner of state	840
Nevada	5,500	Boundary Peak	13,143	Colorado River	470
New Hampshire	1,000	Mount Washington	6,288	Atlantic Ocean	Sea level
New Jersey	250	High Point	1,803	Atlantic Ocean	Sea level
New Mexico	5,700	Wheeler Peak	13,161	Red Bluff Reservoir	2,817
New York	1,000	Mount Marcy	5,344	Atlantic Ocean	Sea level
North Carolina	700	Mount Mitchell	6,684	Atlantic Ocean	Sea level
North Dakota	1,900	White Butte	3,506	Red River	750
Ohio	850	Campbell Hill	1,550	Ohio River	433
Oklahoma	1,300	Black Mesa	4,973	Little River	287
Oregon	3,300	Mount Hood	11,239	Pacific Ocean	Sea level
Pennsylvania	1,100	Mount Davis	3,213	Delaware River	Sea level
Rhode Island	200	Jerimoth Hill	812	Atlantic Ocean	Sea level
South Carolina	350	Sassafras Mountain	3,560	Atlantic Ocean	Sea level
South Dakota	2,200	Harney Peak	7,242	Big Stone Lake	962
Tennessee	900	Clingmans Dome	6,643	Mississippi River	182
Texas	1,700	Guadalupe Peak	8,749	Gulf of Mexico	Sea level
Utah	6,100	Kings Peak	13,528	Beaverdam Creek	2,000
Vermont	1,000	Mount Mansfield	4,393	Lake Champlain	95
Virginia	950	Mount Rogers	5,729	Atlantic Ocean	Sea level
Washington	1,700	Mount Rainier	14,410	Pacific Ocean	Sea level
West Virginia	1,500	Spruce Knob	4,863	Potomac River	240
Wisconsin	1,050	Timms Hill	1,952	Lake Michigan	581
Wyoming	6,700	Gannett Peak	13,804	Belle Fourche River	3,100
United States	2,500	Mount McKinley (Alaska)	20,320	Death Valley (California)	282[2]

1. Approximate mean altitude. 2. Below sea level. 3. Walton County. 4. Osceola County. *Source:* Department of the Interior, U.S. Geological Survey.

Mason and Dixon's Line

Mason and Dixon's Line (often called the Mason-Dixon Line) is the boundary between Pennsylvania and Maryland, running at a north latitude of 39°43'19.11". The greater part of it was surveyed from 1763–67 by Charles Mason and Jeremiah Dixon, English astronomers who had been appointed to settle a dispute between the colonies. As the line was partly the boundary between the free and the slave states, it has come to signify the division between the North and the South.

Named Summits in the U. S. Over 14,000 Feet Above Sea Level

Name	State	Height	Name	State	Height	Name	State	Height
Mt. McKinley	Alaska	20,320	Mt. Antero	Colo.	14,269	Windom Peak	Colo.	14,087
Mt. St. Elias	Alaska	18,008	Torreys Peak	Colo.	14,267	Mt. Russell	Calif.	14,086
Mt. Foraker	Alaska	17,400	Castle Peak	Colo.	14,265	Mt. Eolus	Colo.	14,084
Mt. Bona	Alaska	16,421	Quandary Peak	Colo.	14,265	Mt. Columbia	Colo.	14,073
Mt. Blackburn	Alaska	16,390	Mt. Evans	Colo.	14,264	Mt. Augusta	Alaska	14,070
Mt. Sanford	Alaska	16,237	Longs Peak	Colo.	14,255	Missouri Mtn.	Colo.	14,067
South Buttress	Alaska	15,885	Mt. Wilson	Colo.	14,246	Humboldt Peak	Colo.	14,064
Mt. Vancouver	Alaska	15,700	White Mtn.	Calif.	14,246	Mt. Bierstadt	Colo.	14,060
Mt. Churchill	Alaska	15,638	North Palisade	Calif.	14,242	Sunlight Peak	Colo.	14,059
Mt. Fairweather	Alaska	15,300	Shavano Peak	Colo.	14,229	Split Mtn.	Calif.	14,058
Mt. Hubbard	Alaska	15,015	Crestone Needle	Colo.	14,197	Handies Peak	Colo.	14,048
Mt. Bear	Alaska	14,831	Mt. Belford	Colo.	14,197	Culebra Peak	Colo.	14,047
East Buttress	Alaska	14,730	Mt. Princeton	Colo.	14,197	Mt. Lindsey	Colo.	14,042
Mt. Hunter	Alaska	14,573	Mt. Yale	Colo.	14,196	Middle Palisade	Calif.	14,040
Mt. Alverstone	Alaska	14,565	Mt. Bross	Colo.	14,172	Little Bear Peak	Colo.	14,037
Browne Tower	Alaska	14,530	Kit Carson Mtn.	Colo.	14,165	Mt. Sherman	Colo.	14,036
Mt. Whitney	Calif.	14,494	Mt. Wrangell	Alaska	14,163	Redcloud Peak	Colo.	14,034
Mt. Elbert	Colo.	14,433	Mt. Shasta	Calif.	14,162	Mt. Langley	Calif.	14,028
Mt. Massive	Colo.	14,421	Mt. Sill	Calif.	14,162	Mt. Tyndall	Calif.	14,018
Mt. Harvard	Colo.	14,420	El Diente Peak	Colo.	14,159	Pyramid Peak	Colo.	14,018
Mt. Rainier	Wash.	14,410	Maroon Peak	Colo.	14,156	Wilson Peak	Colo.	14,017
Mt. Williamson	Calif.	14,375	Tabeguache Mtn.	Colo.	14,155	Mt. Muir	Calif.	14,015
Blanca Peak	Colo.	14,345	Mt. Oxford	Colo.	14,153	Wetterhorn Peak	Colo.	14,015
La Plata Peak	Colo.	14,336	Mt. Sneffels	Colo.	14,150	No. Maroon Pk.	Colo.	14,014
Uncompahgre Pk.	Colo.	14,309	Mt. Democrat	Colo.	14,148	San Luis Peak	Colo.	14,014
Crestone Peak	Colo.	14,294	Capitol Peak	Colo.	14,130	Huron Peak	Colo.	14,005
Mt. Lincoln	Colo.	14,286	Pikes Peak	Colo.	14,110	Mt. of the Holy Cross	Colo.	14,005
Grays Peak	Colo.	14,270	Snowmass Mtn.	Colo.	14,092	Sunshine Peak	Colo.	14,001

Source: Department of the Interior, U.S. Geological Survey.

Post-Eruption Map of Mount St. Helens for Sale

A post-eruption map of Mount St. Helens and vicinity that includes color photographs of the major eruption and aftereffects has been published by the U.S. Geological Survey.

The 30- x 40-inch topographical map shows how the area appears in the wake of the violent eruption of May 18, 1980. Presented at a scale of 1:100,000 (one inch equals about 1.68 miles), the map denotes land managed by federal and state agencies and includes numerical designations for roads within the Gifford Pinchot National Forest, viewpoints, campgrounds, picnic areas, visitor centers and points of interest.

On the reverse side of the map, the Forest Service has prepared a text and color photographs providing a narrative of recent Mount St. Helens volcanic activities.

The map, "Mount St. Helens and Vicinity, March 1981," may be purchased by mail for $1.00 each, from the Branch of Distribution, U.S. Geological Survey, Box 25286, Federal Center, Denver, Colo. 80225. Map orders *must* specify the correct title given here, and a check or money order made payable to the U.S. Geological Survey must be included with your order.

Rivers of the United States

(350 or more miles long)

Alabama (735 mi.; 1,183 km): From junction of Tallapoosa R. and Coosa R. in Alabama to Mobile R.
Altamaha-Ocmulgee (392 mi.; 631 km): From junction of Yellow R. and South R., Newton Co. in Georgia to Atlantic Ocean.
Apalachicola-Chattahoochee (524 mi.; 843 km): From Towns Co. in Georgia to Gulf of Mexico in Florida.
Arkansas (1,459 mi.; 2,348 km): From Lake Co. in Colorado to Mississippi R. in Arkansas.
Brazos (870 mi.; 1,400 km): From junction of Salt Fork and Double Mountain Fork in Texas to Gulf of Mexico.
Canadian (906 mi.; 1,458 km): From Las Animas Co. in Colorado to Arkansas R. in Oklahoma.
Cimarron (600 mi.; 966 km): From Colfax Co. in New Mexico to Arkansas R. in Oklahoma.
Clark Fork-Pend Oreille (505 mi.; 813 km): From Silver Bow Co. in Montana to Columbia R. in British Columbia.
Colorado (1,450 mi.; 2,333 km): From Rocky Mountain National Park in Colorado to Gulf of California in Mexico.
Colorado (840 mi.; 1,352 km): From Borden Co. in Texas to Matagorda Bay.
Columbia (1,243 mi.; 2,000 km): From Columbia Lake in British Columbia to Pacific Ocean (entering between Oregon and Washington).
Colville (350 mi.; 563 km): From Brooks Range in Alaska to Beaufort Sea.
Connecticut (407 mi.; 655 km): From Third Connecticut Lake in New Hampshire to Long Island Sound in Connecticut.
Cumberland (720 mi.; 1,159 km): From junction of Poor and Clover Forks in Harlan Co. in Kentucky to Ohio R.

Delaware (390 mi.; 628 km): From Schoharie County in New York to Liston Point, Delaware Bay.
Gila (630 mi.; 1,014 km): From Catron Co. in New Mexico to Colorado R. in Arizona.
Green (360 mi.; 579 km): From Lincoln Co. in Kentucky to Ohio R. in Kentucky.
Green (730 mi.; 1,175 km): From Sublette Co. in Wyoming to Colorado R. in Utah.
Illinois (420 mi.; 676 km): From St. Joseph Co. in Indiana to Mississippi R. at Grafton in Illinois.
James (sometimes called *Dakota*) (710 mi.; 1,143 km): From Wells Co. in North Dakota to Missouri R. in South Dakota.
Kanawha-New (352 mi.; 566 km): From junction of North and South Forks of New R. in North Carolina, through Virginia and West Virginia (New River becoming Kanawha River), to Ohio River.
Koyukuk (470 mi.; 756 km): From Brooks Range in Alaska to Yukon R.
Kuskokwim (680 mi.; 1,094 km): From Alaska Range in Alaska to Kuskokwim Bay.
Licking (350 mi.; 563 km): From Magoffin Co. in Kentucky to Ohio R. at Cincinnati in Ohio.
Little Missouri (560 mi.; 901 km): From Crook Co. in Wyoming to Missouri R. in North Dakota.
Milk (625 mi.; 1,006 km): From junction of forks in Alberta Province to Missouri R.
Mississippi (2,348 mi.; 3,779 km): From Lake Itasca in Minnesota to mouth of Southwest Pass in Louisiana.
Mississippi-Missouri-Red Rock (3,710 mi.; 5,971 km): From source of Red Rock R. in Montana to mouth of Southwest Pass in Louisiana.
Missouri (2,315 mi.; 3,726 km): From junction of Jefferson R., Gallatin R., and Madison R. in Montana to Mississippi R. near St. Louis.
Missouri-Red Rock (2,533 mi.; 4,076 km): From source of Red Rock R. in Montana to Mississippi R. near St. Louis.
Mobile-Alabama-Coosa (780 mi.; 1,255 km): From junction of Etowah R. and Oostanaula R. in Georgia to Mobile Bay.
Neosho (460 mi.; 740 km): From Morris Co. in Kansas to Arkansas R. in Oklahoma.
Niobrara (431 mi.; 694 km): From Niobrara Co. in Wyoming to Missouri R. in Nebraska.
Noatak (350 mi.; 563 km): From Brooks Range in Alaska to Kotzebue Sound.
North Canadian (760 mi.; 1,223 km): From Union Co. in New Mexico to Canadian R. in Oklahoma.
North Platte (618 mi.; 995 km): From Jackson Co. in Colorado to junction with So. Platte R. in Nebraska to form Platte R.
Ohio (981 mi.; 1,579 km): From junction of Allegheny R. and Monongahela R. at Pittsburgh to Mississippi R. between Illinois and Kentucky.
Ohio-Allegheny (1,306 mi.; 2,102 km): From Potter Co. in Pennsylvania to Mississippi R. at Cairo in Illinois.
Osage (500 mi.; 805 km): From east-central Kansas to Missouri R. near Jefferson City in Missouri.
Ouachita (605 mi.; 974 km): From Polk Co. in Arkansas to Red R. in Louisiana.
Pearl (411 mi.; 661 km): From Neshoba County in Mississippi to Gulf of Mexico (Mississippi-Louisiana).
Pecos (735 mi.; 1,183 km): From Mora Co. in New Mexico to Rio Grande in Texas.
Pee Dee-Yadkin (435 mi.; 700 km): From Watauga Co. in North Carolina to Winyah Bay in South Carolina.
Pend Oreille (490 mi.; 789 km): Near Butte in Montana to Columbia R. on Washington-Canada border.
Porcupine (460 mi.; 740 km): From Yukon Territory, Canada, to Yukon R. in Alaska.
Potomac (383 mi.; 616 km): From Garrett Co. in Maryland to Chesapeake Bay at Point Lookout in Maryland.
Powder (375 mi.; 603 km): From junction of forks in Johnson Co. in Wyoming to Yellowstone R. in Montana.
Red (1,270 mi.; 2,044 km): From junction of forks in Harmon Co. in Oklahoma to Mississippi R. in Louisiana.
Red (officially called *Red River of the North*) (545 mi.; 877 km): From junction of Otter Tail R. and Bois de Sioux R. in Minnesota to Lake Winnipeg in Manitoba.
Republican (445 mi.; 716 km): From junction of North Fork and Arikaree R. in Nebraska to junction with Smoky Hill R. in Kansas to form Kansas R.
Rio Grande (1,885 mi.; 3,034 km): From San Juan Co. in Colorado to Gulf of Mexico.
Roanoke (380 mi.; 612 km): From junction of forks in Montgomery Co. in Virginia to Albemarle Sound in North Carolina.
Sabine (380 mi.; 612 km): From junction of forks in Hunt Co. in Texas to Sabine Lake between Texas and Louisiana.
Sacramento (377 mi.; 607 km): From Siskiyou Co. in California to Suisun Bay.
Saint Francis (425 mi.; 684 km): From Iron Co. in Missouri to Mississippi R. in Arkansas.
Salmon (420 mi.; 676 km): From Custer Co. in Idaho to Snake R.
San Joaquin (350 mi.; 563 km): From junction of forks in Madera Co. in California to Suisun Bay.
San Juan (360 mi.; 579 km): From Archuleta Co. in Colorado to Colorado R. in Utah.
Santee-Wateree-Catawba (538 mi.; 866 km): From McDowell Co. in North Carolina to Atlantic Ocean in South Carolina.
Smoky Hill (540 mi.; 869 km): From Cheyenne Co. in Colorado to junction with Republican R. in Kansas to form Kansas R.
Snake (1,038 mi.; 1,670 km): From Ocean Plateau in Wyoming to Columbia R. in Washington.
South Platte (424 mi.; 682 km): From Park Co. in Colorado to junction with North Platte R. in Nebraska to form Platte R.
Susquehanna (444 mi.; 715 km): From Otsego Lake in New York to Chesapeake Bay in Maryland.
Tanana (620 mi.; 998 km): From Wrangell Mts. in Yukon Territory, Canada, to Yukon R. in Alaska.
Tennessee (652 mi.; 1,049 km): From junction of Holston R. and French Broad R. in Tennessee to Ohio R. in Kentucky.
Tennessee-French Broad (900 mi.; 1,448 km): From Bland Co. in Virginia to Ohio R. at Paducah in Kentucky.
Tombigbee (525 mi.; 845 km): From junction of forks in Itawamba Co. in Mississippi to Mobile R. in Alabama.
Trinity (360 mi.; 579 km): From junction of forks in Dallas Co. in Texas to Galveston Bay.
Wabash (529 mi.; 851 km): From Darke Co. in Ohio to Ohio R. between Illinois and Indiana.
Washita (500 mi.; 805 km): From Hemphill Co. in Texas to Red R. in Oklahoma.
White (720 mi.; 1,159 km): From Madison Co. in Arkansas to Mississippi R.
Wisconsin (430 mi.; 692 km): From Vilas Co. in Wisconsin to Mississippi R.
Yellowstone (671 mi.; 1,080 km): From Park Co. in Wyoming to Missouri R. in North Dakota.
Yukon (1,770 mi.; 2,848 km): From junction of Lewes R. and Pelly R. in Yukon Territory, Canada, to Bering Sea in Alaska.

Rules for Correct Punctuation, Capitalization, Abbreviation

Blanche Ormont

Punctuation

Period (.) Use a period: (1) After a statement or command: *Panama is roughly the size of South Carolina. Go to the head of the line.*

(2) After most abbreviations: C.O.D., Ms., U.S. (In familiar abbreviations, where the letters themselves are usually spoken, the period is often omitted: *CIO, NBC, SPCA.*)

(3) With decimals and in dollars and cents: *.05, 22.5, $12.95.* Do not use a period after *percent,* as in *twenty percent;* if cents is written out or the cents sign is used, as in *27 cents, 27¢;* or after Roman numerals, *XXIII, Act III,* except when numbering or listing.

Question Mark (?) Use the question mark after a direct question: *Do you know why the world's climate is changing?* Do not use the question mark after an indirect question or request: *The teacher asked him if he knew the capital of South Dakota. Will you please return this book as soon as possible.*

Exclamation Point (!) Use an exclamation point after an emphatic statement or after a sentence, phrase, or word expressing strong feeling: *You're absolutely wrong! Ouch! That hurts!*

Comma (,) The comma is the most commonly used (and misused) punctuation mark. It indicates a slight separation between words or groups of words and should serve primarily to make the writer's meaning clear. Too many commas may cause the reader to separate words that should be grouped together, or they may unnecessarily slow the movement of a sentence. Too few commas, or misplaced commas, may seriously distort the writer's meaning. Although one should always use good judgment in deciding when and where to use commas, the following rules are generally applicable. Use a comma:

(1) To separate words, phrases, or clauses (a clause is a group of words that has a subject and a predicate) in a series of three or more items: *Tuition, board, lodging, and medical and dental care are provided.* (Note that the comma before the second *and* has been omitted because *medical and dental care* is considered a single unit. However, in some cases it is necessary to insert the comma before *and* to avoid misreading: *The course includes navigation, electricity, ship construction, marine biology, and engineering.*)

Commas are used between two or more adjectives preceding a noun if each separately could modify the noun and if switching the order of the adjectives does not alter the sense: *It was a cold, bleak, rainy day.* Do not use commas if the first adjective qualifies the entire expression following

it: *Their constitution established a strong central government.*

Use a comma after *etc.* (abbreviation of *et cetera*) when it is the last of a series within a sentence: *Books, papers, cartons, etc., lay scattered about the room.*

(2) Between independent clauses (clauses that could stand alone as complete sentences) joined by *and, but, for, or, nor: Pluto has the most eccentric orbit in the solar system, and at times it comes closer to the sun than Neptune. A huge fireball appeared in the sky, but the natives were not afraid.* In a short compound sentence—a sentence made up of two or more independent clauses—the comma is often omitted: *The canoe turned over and everyone fell into the water*

(3) To set off introductory words, phrases, or clauses: *Outraged, he slammed the door behind him. During the wars that followed the French Revolution, Belgium was occupied and later annexed to France. Because Bolivia has no access to the sea, foreign trade must pass through free ports in Chile and river ports on the Amazon.*

If the introductory phrase or clause is very short, or if it is the subject of the sentence, do not use a comma: *Because of its beaches the state is a popular resort area. To cross the sea in ancient times was an extraordinary feat.*

Such introductory transitional words as *yes, no, still, nevertheless, moreover, however, therefore, besides, furthermore,* and weak exclamations like *well, oh,* and *why* should be followed by a comma: *No, I cannot go with you. Well, that's a long story. Why, how nice!*

(4) To set off nonessential elements—words, phrases, or clauses that are not closely related to the rest of the sentence and could be left out without drastically changing its meaning: *Hinduism dates back, perhaps, to prehistoric times. The emperor, in recognition of Confucius' teachings, offered sacrifices at his tomb. Gold, which was responsible for California's settlement boom, is still found in that state.*

To determine whether a modifying expression is restrictive or nonrestrictive (essential or nonessential), see if it can be omitted without significantly changing the meaning. If it is essential to the meaning of the sentence, commas are not used: *Delhi residents who would not limit their families were denied government assistance.* The clause "who would not limit their families" is clearly restrictive; if it were removed, the sentence would indicate that *all* Delhi residents were denied government assistance.

Use the comma before *for, although, though, as, since,* and *because* when these words introduce nonrestrictive clauses or phrases: *The Age of Enlightenment brought about the Jews' emancipation, although persecutions did not end entirely.* But: *The famous Dutch dikes are requisite to the use of much land because half of the country's area is below sea level.* (No comma before *because*, which introduces a restrictive clause.)

Appositives are words or phrases that directly follow a noun or pronoun and identify or explain it. If an appositive is nonrestrictive, it is set off by commas: *The fur-bearing chinchilla, a native of the colder plateau regions, is also raised.* If it is restrictive, no commas are used: *The phrase "hot line" refers to the emergency communications link between Washington and Moscow.*

Contrasting expressions introduced by such words and phrases as *not, but not,* and *though not* are usually nonrestrictive and are therefore set off by commas: *Venus, not Mars, is Earth's nearest neighbor.*

When nonrestrictive words, phrases, or clauses occur within a sentence, they must be set off by two commas—one before the expression and one after.

(5) In certain conventional places: (a) To separate items in addresses and dates: *He wrote to his aunt at 94 Birch Road, Omaha, Nebraska, on June 12, 1924.* (b) With numbers greater than three figures: *1,422, 12,498,620.* (c) In letters, after salutations (in informal letters) and after the complimentary close: *Dear Aunt Mary, Sincerely yours,.* (d) To set off the name of a person addressed: *John, please close the door. Listen carefully, Sarah, because this is important.* (e) To separate degrees and titles from names: *Margaret Harrison, M.D., Ph.D. Frank Simmons, Treasurer.* (f) To set off direct quotations: *"Happiness," someone said, "is a warm puppy."* With exclamations or very short quotations, no comma is necessary: *"Hi there!" she called. He constantly said "like" and "you know."*

(6) Whenever necessary to avoid misunderstanding: *Several months after, he saw his father.* (Without the comma the sentence changes meaning, turning into the clause *Several months after he saw his father.)*

Semicolon (;) The semicolon is a mark of separation that functions like a weak period or a strong comma. Use a semicolon:

(1) Between two independent clauses which are not joined by a conjunction: *The soil is generally poor; high crop yields are dependent upon large-scale use of fertilizers.*

(2) Between two independent clauses containing one or more commas even if a conjunction is used: *After members of the committee have debated the bill, a vote is taken; and if the vote is favorable, the bill is sent back to the floor of the house.*

(3) Between two main clauses linked by such connecting words as *therefore, however, finally, thus, otherwise, nevertheless,* and by such phrases as *for example, in fact, on the contrary: The first game of lawn tennis in the United States was played in 1874; however, it was not until 1880 that standard measurements for the court were established.*

(4) Between items in a series if one or more are subdivided by commas: *Among the great libraries of the world are the British Museum, with more than 6,000,000 printed volumes; the National Diet Library in Tokyo, containing more than 4,100,000 volumes; and, of course, the United States Library of Congress, whose extensive collections total over 72,466,000 volumes.*

Colon (:) The colon is a mark of anticipation introducing material that follows it. Use a colon:

(1) To introduce a long quotation, explanatory statement, or question: *The Declaration of Independence states: "We hold these truths to be self-evident, that all men are created equal, that they are endowed by their Creator with certain unalienable Rights, that among these are Life, Liberty, and the Pursuit of Happiness." In 1976, the World Health Organization accomplished a major goal: It virtually eliminated one of mankind's most ancient enemies—smallpox. The question we discussed was: What are the real differences between Socialism and Communism?*

(2) To introduce a list of items. The colon here is frequently, though not always, preceded by such phrases as *the following* or *as follows: Among the great Gothic structures of Europe are the following: Chartres Cathedral, Notre Dame de Paris, Milan Cathedral, and Cologne Cathedral.*

(3) In these customary places: (Note preceding use of colon.) After a formal salutation in a letter: *Dear Sir:;* between hours and minutes: *10:15 a.m.;* between volume and page in formal footnotes and bibliography: *The Dictionary of Dates 2:120–142;* between chapter and verse in the Bible: *Genesis 1:10;* between numerical elements in ratios: *4:2;* after the name of a speaker in a play: *Lady Macbeth: Out, damned spot!*

Quotation Marks (" ") Use quotation marks:
(1) To enclose a direct quotation: *"Life," said Julia Ward Howe, who lived to be ninety-one, "is like a cup of tea; the sugar is all at the bottom."*

Quotation marks are always used in *pairs,* before the quoted material and after it. However, if you quote two or more paragraphs, place quotation marks at the beginning of each paragraph and at the end of the entire quotation.

Single marks are used to enclose a quotation within a quotation. *"His constant use of such words as 'cool' and 'far out' has become very tiresome," the teacher remarked.*

(2) To enclose the title of a short literary work—a chapter, article, essay, poem, or short story—and titles of paintings, short musical compositions, and radio and television programs. The titles of longer works should be italicized. (Joyce's collection of short stories *Dubliners* includes the famous story "The Dead.")

(3) To enclose all words or phrases that are borrowed, that the writer does not wish to claim as his own, or that he uses ironically: *The term "the chain of being" was for centuries a descriptive name for the universe. For many of the world's poor, "home" is a tarpaper shack or a large old pipe.*

(4) To enclose words or phrases which themselves are being discussed: *Many women now prefer the term "feminism" to the earlier phrase "women's lib."*

(5) When quotation marks are used with other punctuation, they appear as follows:
Outside a comma or period. *"I'm tired," she said. "It's been a long day."*
Inside the semicolon or colon: *A foreign phrase commonly misused to describe aristocracy is "hoi polloi"; actually, it means "the common people."*
Outside a question mark or exclamation point if either is part of the quotation—otherwise, inside. *"Get out of here!" she shrieked. Who wrote "The Unfinished Symphony"?*

Apostrophe (') Use an apostrophe:
(1) In contractions to indicate the omission of a letter: *haven't.*
(2) Before an *s* to form the plural of figures and

letters: *Two size 12's. Cross your t's and dot your i's.*

(3) To form possessives: *Mary's house, men's clothing.* If a plural ends in *s*, add only the apostrophe: *girls' sports, hostesses' duties.* If a singular ends in *s*, add the apostrophe and *s: James's car.* However, the second *s* may be omitted, especially if the word would become more difficult to pronounce: *Socrates' teachings.* Be sure never to use the apostrophe with the possessive pronouns *his, hers, its, yours, ours, theirs.*

Hyphen (-) Use a hyphen:

(1) To link many compound words—two or more words considered as a single unit: *secretary-treasurer, bull's-eye, heavy-hearted, cease-fire.* Do not use a hyphen if a compound modifier follows the noun: *This scientist is well known.* (But note use of hyphen in *a well-known scientist.*) Do not use a hyphen in a compound modifier that includes an adverb ending in *-ly* even if it precedes the noun: *richly deserved praise.*

(2) With certain prefixes and suffixes: *self-support, ex-wife, anti-American, co-worker, president-elect, husband-to-be.* When the parts have become merged in general use, the hyphen may be unnecessary: *midsummer, prehistoric, nonaligned.* (Since usage here is often inconsistent, it is wise, when in doubt, to consult a dictionary.)

(3) In compound numbers from twenty-one to ninety-nine and in fractions: *twenty-five, one-third.*

(4) To divide a word *between syllables* at the end of a line.

(5) Wherever misreading might occur, as in *a navy-blue uniform,* or if a prefix ends with a vowel and the root word begins with the same vowel: *re-elected, anti-inflationary, semi-independent.*

Dash (—) The dash indicates greater separation than a comma but lesser separation than parentheses. Use the dash:

(1) To indicate a sudden change in thought or sentence structure: *We rescheduled the picnic for the following Sunday—we hoped it would be a nice day—but it rained again.*

(2) To emphasize parenthetic, appositive, or explanatory matter. *Imagine a device that is only a cubic foot in size—the size of a hat box—containing 40,000 electronic parts!*

(3) To set off a parenthetic or appositive expression that is itself broken by commas: *She was beset by fears—of heights, open spaces, animals, traffic, strangers—and, as a result, she never left her home.*

Parentheses (()) Generally speaking, dashes add emphasis to the material they enclose, while parentheses tend to subordinate it. Use parentheses:

(1) To enclose incidental or explanatory material that may be relevant but is not strictly necessary: *The rivers, lakes, and surrounding seas (except the Black Sea) are rich in fish. During the reign of Henry VIII (1509–47), the Church of England asserted its independence from the Roman Catholic Church.*

(2) Around figures or letters to enumerate items in a series: *Three qualities of good writing are (1) clarity, (2) consistency, and (3) coherence.*

Parenthetical statements within a sentence begin with a small letter and have no end punctuation, except a question mark or exclamation point if needed. If a comma, semicolon, or colon are necessary after the parenthetical material within a sentence, they are placed outside the closing curve. A complete parenthetic sentence within a paragraph but not within another sentence has an initial capital and end punctuation placed within the closing curve: *Although Nigeria was the world's sixth largest oil producer (its 1974 oil revenues totaled $8 billion), the country's per capita income was only $120 per year. (Even so, it remained black Africa's wealthiest nation.) This problem contributed to continuing government instability.*

Brackets ([]) Use brackets to enclose parenthetic comments inserted in a quotation by the person using the quotation: *In his Nobel Lecture, Martin Luther King said, "In a dark, confused world [where war, poverty, and racism exist] the kingdom of God may yet reign in the hearts of men."*

Capitalization

The use of capital letters is quite standardized in general English. Avoid unnecessary capitals, and when in doubt consult a dictionary. As a rule, capitalize the following:

(1) The first word of a complete sentence: *The modern museum originated during the Renaissance.;* of a quoted sentence: *Freud said, "What does a woman want?";* of each line of poetry:

> *Had we but world enough, and time,*
> *This coyness, lady, were no crime.*—Andrew Marvell

(2) Proper names. A proper name is the name of a *particular* person, place, or thing. Capitalize all proper names including adjectives and abbreviations derived from proper names. Among the proper names to be capitalized are the names of specific persons or places: *John F. Kennedy, Vermont, China, Central Park;* organizations, institutions, buildings, and monuments: *the Republican Party, the Bank of America, Harvard University, the Museum of Modern Art, the Lincoln Memorial;* peoples, languages, religions, and political groups: *Africans, Indians, French, Caucasian, Methodist, Communist;* days of the week, months, holidays: *Tuesday, August, New Year's Day, Easter;* historical periods, events, or documents: *the Dark Ages, the Renaissance, the Holocaust, the Civil War, the Magna Carta, the Social Security Act;* geographical names and regions: *Yellowstone National Park, Lake Huron, the South Pole, the Northeast* (when words like *south* and *north* refer to directions rather than regions, they are not capitalized); names of departments of government and of institutions: *Department of Commerce, Police Department, the City Council, the English Department, the Graduate School;* stars, planets, constellations, satellites, except the sun, earth, and moon: *Sirius, Venus, Orion, Viking I, Halley's Comet;* words referring to the Deity, the Bible, and other sacred writings: *Jehovah, the Messiah, the Virgin, Genesis, Lamentations, the Koran.*

(3) Titles preceding proper names and titles of high rank used without the name: *Professor Cohen, Mayor Daley, Sergeant Jones, Aunt Ellen, the Pope, the President, the Secretary of State, the Queen Mother.*

(4) First and last words and all other words, except the articles *a, an, the,* conjunctions, and prepositions in titles of books, plays, poems, articles, movies, etc.: *Wild Animals of the World, Ode to the West Wind, All in the Family, Porgy and Bess.*

(5) The pronoun *I* and the exclamation *O: If I forget thee, O Jerusalem, let my right hand forget her cunning.*—Psalms

492 *Writer's Guide*

Abbreviations

Abbreviations are useful and appropriate in notetaking, in reference works, in statistical tables, and in certain other situations where speed and space-saving are important. In general writing, however, abbreviations should be avoided. A few standard abbreviations that are correct in all writing are the following:

(1) Titles and names: *Mr., Messrs., Mrs., Dr., Esq., Sr., Jr., Ph.D., M.D., LL.D.* Do not use a title both before and after a name: *Mr. James T. Smith* or *James T. Smith, Ph.D.*, not *Mr. James T. Smith, Ph.D.*

Do not abbreviate civil, professional (except *Dr.*), military, or political titles, except when the person's first name or initials are used: *Professor Downey* or *Prof. Charles Downey, General Marshall* or *Gen. G. C. Marshall*, never *Prof. Downey* or *Gen. Marshall.*

First names should, as a rule, be spelled out: *William Shakespeare*, not *Wm. Shakespeare.*

(2) Certain units of measurements: *a.m., p.m., A.D., B.C., mph*, when used with figures, as in *50 mph; No.* with numbers expressed in figures, as in *No. 8.* Write out other expressions for time, weight, and size, as in *three ounces, two miles, four hours,* unless such expressions appear in directions, recipes, or technical writing: *½ tsp salt, 10 ft 2 in.*

(3) Names of organizations, governmental agencies, scientific words, trade names, and other expressions that are familiar to most people and are frequently referred to by their initials: *YMCA, AFL-CIO, FCC, CIA, FBI, NASA, DDT, DNA, CBS, MGM.* Generally no period is used. (Exceptions: *C.O.D., F.O.B.*) Abbreviations like *Co., Inc., Ltd.*, or *Corp.* are correct when they are part of the company name: *Jones Publishing, Inc.*

(4) Certain literary abbreviations: *i.e.* (that is); *e.g.* (for example); *ibid.* (in the same place); *etc.* (and so forth).

In ordinary usage, write out: names of states, countries, months, days of the week; words like *street, road, square* when they are used as part of a proper name: *Maple Street;* and numbers that can be expressed in not more than one or two words: *twenty books, four hundred miles* (but *$3,560.23, 60,211 miles*).

> These are "general" rules of punctuation, capitalization, and abbreviation designed to make writing as clear and "correct" as possible. There are no absolutes. Many publications have modifications of these basic rules that reflect their own special needs.

Forms of Address[1]

By permission, From Webster's New Collegiate Dictionary, © 1981 by G. & C. Merriam Co., Publishers of the Merriam-Webster Dictionaries.

Abbot. *Address:* The Right Reverend _____, O.S.B. (or other initials of the order), Abbot of _____. *Begin:* Right Reverend and Dear Father.

Ambassador (U.S.). *Address:* The Honorable _____, American Ambassador; **(to the U.S.):** His Excellency _____, Ambassador of _____. *Begin:* Sir; *or* Dear Mr. Ambassador.

Archbishop. *Address:* The Most Reverend Archbishop of _____; *or* The Most Reverend _____, Archbishop of _____. *Begin:* Your Excellency; *or* Dear Archbishop _____.

Archdeacon. *Address:* The Venerable the Archdeacon of _____. *Begin:* Venerable Sir.

Armed Forces (U.S.). See *Military and Naval Officers.*

Assemblyman. *Address:* The Honorable _____, The Assembly, State Capitol. *Begin:* Dear Mr. _____.

Associate Justice (Supreme Court). *Address:* Mr. Justice _____, The Supreme Court of the United States. *Begin:* Dear Mr. Justice.

Attorney. *Address:* Mr. _____, Attorney-at-Law; *or* _____, Esq. *Begin:* Dear Mr. _____.

Bishop (Episcopal). *Address:* The Right Reverend _____, Bishop of _____. *Begin:* Right Reverend Sir; *or* Dear Bishop _____.

Bishop (Roman Catholic). *Address:* The Most Reverend _____, Bishop of _____. *Begin:* Your Excellency; *or* Dear Bishop _____.

Bishop (other denominations). *Address:* The Reverend _____. *Begin:* Reverend Sir; *or* Dear Bishop _____.

Brother (Roman Catholic). *Address:* Brother _____ (first name followed by initials of the order). *Begin:* Dear Brother _____.

Cabinet Officer (U.S.). *Address:* The Honorable _____, Secretary of State (or other department); *or* The Honorable _____, Attorney General of the United States. *Begin:* Dear Sir.

Cardinal. *Address:* His Eminence John Cardinal Smith. *Begin:* Your Eminence; *or* Dear Cardinal _____.

Chargé d'Affaires (U.S.). *Address:* _____, Esq., American Chargé d'Affaires. *Begin:* Dear Sir.

Chief Justice (Supreme Court). *Address:* The Chief Justice of the United States. *Begin:* Dear Mr. Chief Justice.

Clergyman (Protestant). *Address:* The Reverend _____; *or* (if a Doctor of Divinity) The Reverend Dr. _____; *Begin:* Dear Sir; *or* Dear Mr. _____; *or* Dear Dr. _____.

Commissioner (of a Department or Bureau). *Address:* The Honorable _____. *Begin:* Dear Mr. _____.

Consul. *Address:* _____, Esq., American Consul. *Begin:* Dear Sir.

Dean (of a Cathedral). *Address:* The Very Reverend _____; *or* Dean _____. *Begin:*

1. Since the relationship between correspondents affects the form of address used in letters, no rigid guidelines can be set down for all occasions. When two salutations are shown, it is to be understood that the formal styling precedes the informal. In salutations where the addressee is a woman, it is to be understood that in formal address Madam may be substituted for Sir, and in informal address Mrs. or Miss or Ms. may be substituted for Mr. 2. From Webster's Eighth New Collegiate Dictionary. NOTE: Forms of Address for foreign dignitaries may be obtained from their United Nations missions in New York City.

Very Reverend Sir; *or* Dear Dean _____.

Dean (of a College or University). *Address:* Dean _____ _____. *Begin:* Dear Dean _____.

Dentist. *Address:* _____ _____, D.D.S. (office address); *or* Dr. _____ _____ (home address). *Begin:* Dear Dr. _____.

Divorced Woman. *Address:* Ordinarily use *Mrs.* with her maiden name as a prename. Some divorced women prefer to resume the *Miss.*[2]

Doctor of Divinity. See *Clergyman.*

Doctor of Philosophy, Laws, etc. *Address:* _____ _____, Ph.D. (LL.D.) (or other degree). *Begin:* Dear Sir; *or* Dear Dr. _____.

Governor. *Address:* The Honorable _____ _____, Governor of _____. *Begin:* Dear Governor _____.

Governor-General of Canada. *Address:* His Excellency The Right Honourable _____ _____ (plus personal rank or title, if any). *Begin:* My Lord; *or* Sir (according to rank).[2]

Governor-General's Wife. *Address:* Her Excellency _____ _____ (plus personal rank or title, if any). *Begin:* Madam.[2]

Judge (Federal). *Address:* The Honorable _____ _____, United States District Judge. *Begin:* Dear Judge _____.

Judge (State or Local). *Address:* The Honorable _____ _____, Judge of the Court of Appeals (or other court). *Begin:* Dear Judge _____.

King. *Address:* The King's Most Excellent Majesty; *or* His Most Gracious Majesty, King _____. *Begin:* Sir; *or* May It Please Your Majesty.[2]

Lieutenant Governor. *Address:* The Honorable _____ _____, Lieutenant Governor of _____. *Begin:* Dear Mr. _____.

Mayor (in Canadian Cities and Towns, and English Boroughs and Cities). *Address:* The Right Worshipful the Mayor of _____ (English cities only); His Worship, The Mayor of _____ (other). *Begin:* Sir.[2]

Mayor (U.S.). *Address:* The Honorable _____ _____, Mayor of _____. *Begin:* Dear Mayor _____.

Member of Parliament (or of a Legislative Council). The ordinary form of address followed by M.P. (or M.L.C.).[2]

Military and Naval Officers (U.S.): *Address:* (full rank) _____ _____, U.S.N. (or U.S.A., U.S.A.F., U.S.M.C., U.S.C.G.). *Begin:* Sir (admirals and generals only); *or* Dear (full rank) _____ (other officers, including admirals and generals); *or* Dear Mr. _____ (lieutenant commander, lieutenant, ensign only).

Minister (to U.S.). *Address:* The Honorable _____ _____, Minister of _____. *Begin:* Sir; *or* Dear Mr. Minister.

Minister of Religion. See *Clergyman, Priest, Rabbi.*

Monsignor. *Address:* The Right Reverend Monsignor _____. *Begin:* Dear Monsignor _____.

Mother Superior of a Sisterhood. *Address:* The Reverend Mother Superior, O.S.F. (or other initials of the order); *Begin:* Reverend Mother; or Dear Reverend Mother.

Nun. See *Sister of a Religious Order.*

Papal Nuncio or Internuncio or Apostolic Delegate. *Address:* His Excellency, The Papal Nuncio (*or* Internuncio *or* Apostolic Delegate) to _____. *Begin:* Your Excellency.[2]

Patriarch (Eastern Church). *Address:* His Beatitude the Patriarch of _____. *Begin:* Most Reverend Lord.

Physician. *Address:* _____ _____, M.D. (office address); *or* Dr. _____ _____ (home address). *Begin:* Dear Dr. _____.

Pope. *Address:* His Holiness Pope _____; *or* His Holiness the Pope. *Begin:* Your Holiness; *or* Most Holy Father.

President of a College or University. *Address:* President _____ _____. *Begin:* Dear President _____.

President of a State Senate. *Address:* The Honorable _____ _____, President of the Senate of _____. *Begin:* Dear Senator _____.[2]

President of the U.S. *Address:* The President. *Begin:* Dear Mr. President.

President of the U.S. (Former). *Address:* The Honorable _____ _____. *Begin:* Dear Mr. _____.

Priest (Roman Catholic). *Address:* The Reverend Father _____; *or* The Reverend _____ _____. *Begin:* Dear Father _____; *or* Dear Father.

Prime Minister of Canada. *Address:* The Right Honourable _____ _____, P.C., Prime Minister of Canada. *Begin:* Sir.[2]

Privy Councillor (of Canada). *Address:* The Honourable _____ _____. *Begin:* Sir.[2]

Professor at a College or University. *Address:* Professor _____ _____. *Begin:* Dear Professor _____.

Queen. *Address:* The Queen's Most Excellent Majesty; *or* Her Gracious Majesty, The Queen. *Begin:* Madam; *or* May It Please Your Majesty.[2]

Rabbi. *Address:* Rabbi _____; *or* Rabbi _____ _____, D.D. (if a Doctor of Divinity). *Begin:* Dear Rabbi _____; *or* Dear Dr. _____.

Representative (State). *Address:* The Honorable _____ _____, House of Representatives, State Capitol. *Begin:* Dear Mr. _____.

Representative (U.S.). *Address:* The Honorable _____ _____, The United States House of Representatives. *Begin:* Dear Mr. _____.

Secretary-General of the U.N. *Address:* His Excellency _____ _____, Secretary-General of the United Nations. *Begin:* Excellency; *or* Dear Mr. Secretary-General; *or* Dear Mr. _____.

Senator (State). *Address:* The Honorable _____ _____, The State Senate, State Capitol. *Begin:* Dear Senator _____.

Senator (U.S.). *Address:* The Honorable _____ _____, United States Senate. *Begin:* Dear Senator _____.

Sister of a Religious Order. *Address:* Sister _____ _____, S.C. (or other initials of the order). *Begin:* Dear Sister _____ _____; *or* Dear Sister.

Speaker of the House of Commons (Canada). *Address:* The Honourable _____ _____, The Speaker of the House of Commons. *Begin:* Dear Mr. Speaker.[2]

Speaker of the House of Representatives (U.S.). *Address:* The Honorable _____ _____, Speaker of the House of Representatives. *Begin:* Dear Mr. Speaker.

Superior of a Brotherhood. *Address:* Brother _____ (first name followed by initials of the order), Superior. *Begin:* Dear Brother _____.

United Nations Representative (Foreign). *Address:* His Excellency _____ _____, Representative of _____ to the United Nations. *Begin:* Excellency; *or* Dear Mr. Ambassador.[2]

United Nations Representative (U.S.). *Address:* The Honorable _____ _____, United States Representative to the United Nations. *Begin:* Sir; *or* Dear Mr. Ambassador.[2]

Veterinarian. *Address:* _____ _____, D.V.M. (office address); or Dr. _____ _____ (home address). *Begin:* Dear Dr. _____.

Vice President of the U.S. *Address:* The Vice President, United States Senate. *Begin:* Dear Mr. Vice President.

Widow. Ordinarily addressed by her former title: as, Mrs. John Doe, not Mrs. Jane Doe, unless the latter form is preferred by the person herself.[2]

Foreign Words and Phrases

(The English meanings given are not necessarily literal translations.)

ab ovo: from the beginning
à bon marché: good bargain; cheap
à deux: for two; between two
a priori: from something previous
à votre santé: to your health
ad infinitum: to infinity; with no end
ad valorem: according to its value
al fresco: outdoors
alma mater: one's college or school
alter ego: other self
amicus curiae: friend of the court
ancien regime: the old order
anno Domini: year of our Lord
ante bellum: before the war
au contraire: on the contrary
au courant: current; up-to-date
auf Wiedersehen: goodbye
bête noire: particular nemesis
bienvenue: welcome
bon mot: a funny or witty saying
bon vivant: a gourmet, an epicure
bona fide: in good faith; genuine; honest
carpe diem: enjoy today; seize the day
carte blanche: unlimited authority
cause célèbre: a cause that generates wide interest
caveat emptor: buy at your own risk; let the buyer beware
circa: about; approximately
chacun à son goût: each to his own taste
combien: how much?
corpus delicti: fundamental fact or facts about the commission of a crime
coup de grâce: finishing blow
cum grano salis: with a grain of salt
d'accord: in accord; agreement
de facto: as a matter of fact; actual
de profundis: out of the depths
Deo gratias: thanks be to God
Deo volente: God willing
dernier cri: the last word
deus ex machina: artificially produced to bring a solution to some extreme difficulty
dramatis personae: characters in a play
ecce homo: this is the man
en masse: all together
en passant: in passing
fait accompli: an accomplished fact
faux pas: a false step; a mistake
flagrante delicto: caught in the act
Gesundheit: good health (God bless you)
habeas corpus: common-law writ to bring a person before a court or judge

hoi polloi: the common people
honi soit qui mal y pense: evil to him who thinks evil of it
hors d'oeuvre: appetizer
idée fixe: fixed idea; obsession
in loco parentis: in place of a parent
ipso facto: by the very fact
je ne sais quoi: I don't know what; an elusive quality
jeunesse dorée: gilded youth
laissez faire: noninterference
l'chaim: to life
maven: an expert; connoisseur
mea culpa: I am to blame
mirabile dictu: wonderful to relate
modus operandi: method of operation; way of working
nom de plume: pen name
non compos mentis: not of sound mind
non sequitur: it does not follow
O tempora! O mores!: What sad times and customs
omnia vincit amor: love conquers all
per annum: by the year
per capita: by the head; individually
per diem: by the day; daily
persona non grata: an unwelcome or unacceptable person
plus ça change, plus c'est le même chose: the more things change, the more they remain the same
post mortem: after death
pro bono publico: for the public good
pro tempore (pro tem): for the time being; temporary
quid pro quo: something done or given in exchange for something else
repondez s'il vous plait: please reply; please answer (abbr. R.S.V.P.)
requiescat in pace: rest in peace
sans souci: without worry or care
savoir faire: know-how; manners for all occasions
semper fidelis: always faithful
shalom: peace
sic transit gloria mundi: so passes the glory of the world
s'il vous plait: if you please; please
sine die: with no day set for the next meeting
sine qua non: indispensable
status (in) quo: state in which anything is
sui generis: in a class by itself
tempus fugit: time flies
tout de suite: immediately
veni, vidi, vici: I came, I saw, I conquered
vis-à-vis: face-to-face

Carbon 14 Dating Technique

The old method for determining the age of a fossil by carbon 14 dating usually required samples so large that the fossil being analyzed was often destroyed. The latest technique developed by the University of Rochester uses a special high-voltage generator to directly measure the carbon 14 remaining in the sample. The advantage of this technique is that it requires only a one-milligram sample for testing.

Copyrights

Source: Library of Congress, Copyright Office.

The copyright law (Title 17 of the United States Code) has been amended by the enactment of a statute for its general revision, Public Law 94-553 (90 Stat. 2541), which was signed by the President on October 19, 1976. The new law superseded the copyright act of 1909, as amended, which remained effective until the new enactment took effect on January 1, 1978.

Under the new law, all copyrightable works, whether published or unpublished, are subject to a single system of statutory protection which gives a copyright owner the exclusive right to reproduce the copyrighted work in copies or phonorecords and distribute them to the public by sale, rental, lease, or lending. Among the other rights given to the owner of a copyright are the exclusive rights to prepare derivative works based upon the copyrighted work, to perform the work publicly if it be literary, musical, dramatic, choreographic, a pantomime, motion picture, or other audiovisual work, and in the case of literary, musical, dramatic, and choreographic works, pantomimes, and pictorial, graphic, or sculptural works, including the individual images of a motion picture or other audiovisual work, to display the copyrighted work publicly. All of these rights are subject to certain exceptions, including the principle of "fair use" which the new statute specifically recognizes.

Special provisions are included which permit compulsory licensing for the recording of musical compositions, noncommercial transmissions by public broadcasters of published musical and graphic works, performances of copyrighted music by jukeboxes, and the secondary transmission of copyrighted works on cable television systems.

Copyright protection under the new law extends to original works of authorship fixed in any tangible medium of expression, now known or later developed, from which they can be perceived, reproduced, or otherwise communicated, either directly or with the aid of a machine or device. Works of authorship include books, periodicals and other literary works, musical compositions with accompanying lyrics, dramas and dramatico-musical compositions, pantomimes and choreographic works, motion pictures and other audiovisual works, and sound recordings.

As a mandatory condition of copyright protection under the law in effect before 1978, all published copies of a work were required to bear a copyright notice. The 1976 Act provides for a notice on published copies, but omission or errors will not immediately result in forfeiture of the copyright, and can be corrected within certain time limits. Innocent infringers misled by the omission or error will be shielded from liability.

Registration in the Copyright Office is not a condition of copyright protection but will be a prerequisite to bringing an action in a court of law for infringement. With certain exceptions, the remedies of statutory damages and attorney's fees will not be available for infringements occurring before registration. Copies or phonorecords published in the United States with notice of copyright are required to be deposited for the collections of the Library of Congress, not as a condition of copyright protection, but under provisions of the law subjecting the copyright owner to certain penalties for failure to deposit after a demand by the Register of Copyrights. Registration is permissive, but may be made either at the time the depository requirements are satisfied or at any other time during the subsistence of the copyright.

For works already under statutory protection, the new law retains the present term of copyright of 28 years from first publication (or from registration in some cases), renewable by certain persons for a second period of protection, but it increases the length of the second period to 47 years. Copyrights in their first term on January 1, 1978, must still be renewed during the last (28th) year of the original copyright term to receive the maximum statutory term of 75 years (a first term of 28 years plus a renewal term of 47 years).

Copyrights in their second term on January 1, 1978, are automatically extended up to a maximum of 75 years, without the need for further renewal. Unpublished works that are already in existence on January 1, 1978, but are not protected by statutory copyright and have not yet gone into the public domain, will generally obtain automatic Federal copyright protection for the author's life, plus an additional 50 years after the author's death, but in any event, for a minimal term of 25 years (that is, until December 31, 2002), and if the work is published before that date, then for an additional term of 25 years, through the end of 2027.

For works created on or after January 1, 1978, the new law provides a term lasting for the author's life, plus an additional 50 years after the author's death. For works made for hire, and for anonymous and pseudonymous works (unless the author's identity is revealed in Copyright Office records), the new term will be 75 years from publication or 100 years from creation, whichever is shorter. The new law provides that all terms of copyright will run through the end of the calendar year in which they would otherwise expire. This will not only affect the duration of copyrights, but also the time-limits for renewal registrations.

Works already in the public domain cannot be protected under the new law. The 1976 Act provides no procedure for restoring protection to works in which copyright has been lost for any reason. In general, works published before September 19, 1906, are not under copyright protection in the United States, at least insofar as any version published before that date is concerned.

The new law requires that all visually perceptible copies published in the United States or elsewhere bear a notice of copyright affixed in such manner and location as to give reasonable notice of the claim of copyright. The notice consists of the symbol © (the letter C in a circle), the word "Copyright," or the abbreviation "Copr.," and the year of first publication of the work, and the name of the owner of copyright in the work. EXAMPLE: © *1982 John Doe.*

The notice of copyright prescribed for sound recordings consists of the symbol ℗ (the letter P in a circle), the year of first publication of the sound recording, and the name of the owner of copyright in the sound recording, placed on the surface of the phonorecord, or on the phonorecord label or container, in such manner and location as to give reasonable notice of the claim of copyright. EXAMPLE: ℗ *1982 Doe Records, Inc.*

A work by a U.S. citizen may obtain copyright protection in all countries that are members of the Universal Copyright Convention (UCC), provided the copyright notice appearing on all copies from the date of first publication includes the symbol ©, together with the name of the copyright owner and the year date of publication. EXAMPLE: © *John Doe 1978.*

Further information and application forms may be obtained free of charge upon request from the Copyright Office, Library of Congress, Washington, D.C. 20559.

Patents

Source: Department of Commerce, Patent and Trademark Office.

A patent, in the most general sense, is a document issued by a government, conferring some special right or privilege. The term is now restricted mainly to patents for inventions; occasionally, land patents.

The grant of a patent for an invention gives the inventor the privilege, for a limited period of time, of excluding others from making, using, or selling a certain article. However, it does not give him the right to make, use, or sell his own invention if it is an improvement on some unexpired patent whose claims are infringed thereby.

In the U.S., the law provides that a patent may be granted, for a term of 17 years, to any person who has invented or discovered any new and useful art, machine, manufacture, or composition of matter, as well as any new and useful improvements thereof. A patent may also be granted to a person who has invented or discovered and asexually reproduced a new and distinct variety of plant (other than a tuber-propagated one) or has invented a new, original and ornamental design for an article of manufacture.

A patent is granted only upon a regularly filed application, complete in all respects; upon payment of the fees; and upon determination that the

disclosure is complete and that the invention is new, useful, and, in view of the prior art, unobvious to one skilled in the art. The disclosure must be of such nature as to enable others to reproduce the invention.

A complete application, which must be addressed to the Commissioner of Patents and Trademarks, Washington, D.C. 20231, consists of a specification with one or more claims; oath or declaration; drawing (whenever the nature of the case admits of it); and a basic filing fee of $65, plus certain additional charges for claims. The filing fee is not returned to the applicant if the patent is refused. If the patent is allowed, another fee of $100, plus additional printing charges, is required before the patent is issued. The fees for design patents vary.

Applications are ordinarily considered in the order in which they are received. Patents are not granted for printed matter, for methods of doing business, or for devices for which claims contrary to natural laws are made. Applications for a perpetual-motion machine have been made from time to time, but until a working model is presented that actually fulfills the claim, no patent will be issued.

Trademarks

Source: Department of Commerce, Patent and Trademark Office.

A trademark may be defined as a word, letter, device, or symbol, as well as some combination of these, which is used in connection with merchandise and which points distinctly to the origin of the goods.

Certificates of registration of trademarks are issued under the seal of the Patent and Trademark Office and may be registered by the owner if he is engaged in interstate or foreign commerce, since any Federal jurisdiction over trademarks arises under the commerce clause of the Constitution. Trademarks may be registered by foreign owners who comply with our law, as well as by citizens of foreign countries with which the U.S. has treaties relating to trademarks. American citizens may register trademarks in foreign countries by complying

with the laws of those countries. The right to registration and protection of trademarks in many foreign countries is guaranteed by treaties.

General jurisdiction in trademark cases involving Federal Registrations is given to Federal courts. Adverse decisions of examiners on applications for registration are appealable to the Trademark Trial and Appeal Board, whose affirmances, and decisions in *inter partes* proceedings, are subject to court review. Before adopting a trademark, a person should make a search of prior marks to avoid infringing unwittingly upon them.

The duration of a trademark registration is 20 years, but it may be renewed indefinitely for 20-year periods, provided the trademark is still in use at the time of expiration.

Birthstones

Month	Stone	Month	Stone
January	Garnet	July	Ruby or Star Ruby
February	Amethyst	August	Peridot or Sardonyx
March	Aquamarine or Bloodstone	September	Sapphire or Star Sapphire
April	Diamond	October	Opal or Tourmaline
May	Emerald	November	Topaz
June	Pearl, Alexandrite, or Moonstone	December	Turquoise or Zircon

Source: Jewelry Industry Council.

Nobel Prizes

The Nobel prizes are awarded under the will of Alfred Bernhard Nobel, Swedish chemist and engineer, who died in 1896. The interest of the fund is divided annually among the persons who have made the most outstanding contributions in the fields of physics, chemistry, and physiology or medicine, who have produced the most distinguished literary work of an idealist tendency, and who have contributed most toward world peace.

In 1968, a Nobel Prize of economic sciences was established by Riksbank, the Swedish bank, in celebration of its 300th anniversary. The prize was awarded for the first time in 1969.

The prizes for physics and chemistry are awarded by the Swedish Academy of Science in Stockholm, the one for physiology or medicine by the Caroline Medical Institute in Stockholm, that for literature by the academy in Stockholm, and that for peace by a committee of five elected by the Norwegian Storting. The distribution of prizes was begun on December 10, 1901, the anniversary of Nobel's death. The amount of each prize varies with the income from the fund and currently is about $210,000. No Nobel prizes were awarded for 1940, 1941, and 1942; prizes for Literature were not awarded for 1914, 1918, and 1943.

PEACE

1901	Henri Dunant (Switzerland); Frederick Passy (France)
1902	Elie Ducommun and Albert Gobat (Switzerland)
1903	Sir William R. Cremer (England)
1904	Institut de Droit International (Belgium)
1905	Bertha von Suttner (Austria)
1906	Theodore Roosevelt (U.S.)
1907	Ernesto T. Moneta (Italy) and Louis Renault (France)
1908	Klas P. Arnoldson (Sweden) and Frederik Bajer (Denmark)
1909	Auguste M. F. Beernaert (Belgium) and Baron Paul H. B. B. d'Estournelles de Constant de Rebecque (France)
1910	Bureau International Permanent de la Paix (Switzerland)
1911	Tobias M. C. Asser (Holland) and Alfred H. Fried (Austria)
1912	Elihu Root (U.S.)
1913	Henri La Fontaine (Belgium)
1915	No award
1916	No award
1917	International Red Cross
1919	Woodrow Wilson (U.S.)
1920	Léon Bourgeois (France)
1921	Karl H. Branting (Sweden) and Christian L. Lange (Norway)
1922	Fridtjof Nansen (Norway)
1923	No award
1924	No award
1925	Sir Austen Chamberlain (England) and Charles G. Dawes (U.S.)
1926	Aristide Briand (France) and Gustav Stresemann (Germany)
1927	Ferdinand Buisson (France) and Ludwig Quidde (Germany)
1928	No award
1929	Frank B. Kellogg (U.S.)
1930	Lars O. J. Söderblom (Sweden)
1931	Jane Addams and Nicholas M. Butler (U.S.)
1932	No award
1933	Sir Norman Angell (England)
1934	Arthur Henderson (England)
1935	Karl von Ossietzky (Germany)
1936	Carlos de S. Lamas (Argentina)
1937	Lord Cecil of Chelwood (England)
1938	Office International Nansen pour les Réfugiés (Switzerland)
1939	No award
1944	International Red Cross
1945	Cordell Hull (U.S.)
1946	Emily G. Balch and John R. Mott (U.S.)
1947	American Friends Service Committee (U.S.) and British Society of Friends' Service Council (England)
1948	No award
1949	Lord John Boyd Orr (Scotland)
1950	Ralph J. Bunche (U.S.)
1951	Léon Jouhaux (France)
1952	Albert Schweitzer (French Equatorial Africa)
1953	George C. Marshall (U.S.)
1954	Office of U.N. High Commissioner for Refugees
1955	No award
1956	No award
1957	Lester B. Pearson (Canada)
1958	Rev. Dominique Georges Henri Pire (Belgium)
1959	Philip John Noel-Baker (England)
1960	Albert John Luthuli (South Africa)
1961	Dag Hammarskjöld (Sweden)
1962	Linus Pauling (U.S.)
1963	Intl. Comm. of Red Cross; League of Red Cross Societies (both Geneva)
1964	Rev. Dr. Martin Luther King, Jr. (U.S.)
1965	UNICEF (United Nations Children's Fund)
1966	No award
1967	No award
1968	René Cassin (France)
1969	International Labour Organization
1970	Norman E. Borlaug (U.S.)
1971	Willy Brandt (West Germany)
1972	No award
1973	Henry A. Kissinger (U.S.); Le Duc Tho (North Vietnam)[1]
1974	Eisaku Sato (Japan); Sean MacBride (Ireland)
1975	Andrei D. Sakharov (U.S.S.R.)
1976	Mairead Corrigan and Betty Williams (both Northern Ireland)
1977	Amnesty International
1978	Menachem Begin (Israel) and Anwar el-Sadat (Egypt)
1979	Mother Teresa of Calcutta (Albania)
1980	Adolfo Pérez Esquivel (Argentina)

1. Le Duc Tho refused prize, charging that peace had not yet been really established in South Vietnam.

LITERATURE

1901	René F. A. Sully Prudhomme (France)
1902	Theodor Mommsen (Germany)
1903	Björnstjerne Björnson (Norway)
1904	Frédéric Mistral (France) and José Echegaray (Spain)
1905	Henryk Sienkiewicz (Poland)
1906	Giosuè Carducci (Italy)

1907	Rudyard Kipling (England)
1908	Rudolf Eucken (Germany)
1909	Selma Lagerlöf (Sweden)
1910	Paul von Heyse (Germany)
1911	Maurice Maeterlinck (Belgium)
1912	Gerhart Hauptmann (Germany)
1913	Rabindranath Tagore (India)
1915	Romain Rolland (France)
1916	Verner von Heidenstam (Sweden)
1917	Karl Gjellerup (Denmark) and Henrik Pontoppidan (Denmark)
1919	Carl Spitteler (Switzerland)
1920	Knut Hamsun (Norway)
1921	Anatole France (France)
1922	Jacinto Benavente (Spain)
1923	William B. Yeats (Ireland)
1924	Wladyslaw Reymont (Poland)
1925	George Bernard Shaw (England)
1926	Grazia Deledda (Italy)
1927	Henri Bergson (France)
1928	Sigrid Undset (Norway)
1929	Thomas Mann (Germany)
1930	Sinclair Lewis (U.S.)
1931	Erik A. Karlfeldt (Sweden)
1932	John Galsworthy (England)
1933	Ivan G. Bunin (Russia)
1934	Luigi Pirandello (Italy)
1935	No award
1936	Eugene O'Neill (U.S.)
1937	Roger Martin du Gard (France)
1938	Pearl S. Buck (U.S.)
1939	Frans Eemil Sillanpää (Finland)
1944	Johannes V. Jensen (Denmark)
1945	Gabriela Mistral (Chile)
1946	Hermann Hesse (Switzerland)
1947	André Gide (France)
1948	Thomas Stearns Eliot (England)
1949	William Faulkner (U.S.)
1950	Bertrand Russell (England)
1951	Pär Lagerkvist (Sweden)
1952	François Mauriac (France)
1953	Sir Winston Churchill (England)
1954	Ernest Hemingway (U.S.)
1955	Halldór Kiljan Laxness (Iceland)
1956	Juan Ramón Jiménez (Spain)
1957	Albert Camus (France)
1958	Boris Pasternak (U.S.S.R.) (declined)
1959	Salvatore Quasimodo (Italy)
1960	St.-John Perse (Alexis St.-Léger Léger) (France)
1961	Ivo Andric (Yugoslavia)
1962	John Steinbeck (U.S.)
1963	Giorgios Seferis (Seferiades) (Greece)
1964	Jean-Paul Sartre (France) (declined)
1965	Mikhail Sholokhov (U.S.S.R.)
1966	Shmuel Yosef Agnon (Israel) and Nelly Sachs (Sweden)
1967	Miguel Angel Asturias (Guatemala)
1968	Yasunari Kawabata (Japan)
1969	Samuel Beckett (France)
1970	Aleksandr Solzhenitsyn (U.S.S.R.)
1971	Pablo Neruda (Chile)
1972	Heinrich Böll (Germany)
1973	Patrick White (Australia)
1974	Eyvind Johnson and Harry Martinson (both Sweden)
1975	Eugenio Montale (Italy)
1976	Saul Bellow (U.S.)
1977	Vicente Aleixandre (Spain)
1978	Isaac Bashevis Singer (U.S.)
1979	Odysseus Elytis (Greece)
1980	Czeslaw Milosz (U.S.)

PHYSICS

1901	Wilhelm K. Roentgen (Germany), for discovery of Roentgen rays
1902	Hendrik A. Lorentz and Pieter Zeeman (Netherlands), for work on influence of magnetism upon radiation
1903	A. Henri Becquerel (France), for work on spontaneous radioactivity; and Pierre and Marie Curie (France), for study of radiation
1904	John Strutt (Lord Rayleigh) (England), for discovery of argon in investigating gas density
1905	Philipp Lenard (Germany), for work with cathode rays
1906	Sir Joseph Thomson (England), for investigations on passage of electricity through gases
1907	Albert A. Michelson (U.S.), for spectroscopic and metrologic investigations
1908	Gabriel Lippmann (France), for method of reproducing colors by photography
1909	Guglielmo Marconi (Italy) and Ferdinand Braun (Germany), for development of wireless
1910	Johannes D. van der Waals (Netherlands), for work with the equation of state for gases and liquids
1911	Wilhelm Wien (Germany), for his laws governing the radiation of heat
1912	Gustaf Dalén (Sweden), for discovery of automatic regulators used in lighting lighthouses and light buoys
1913	Heike Kamerlingh-Onnes (Netherlands), for work leading to production of liquid helium
1914	Max von Laue (Germany), for discovery of diffraction of Roentgen rays passing through crystals
1915	Sir William Bragg and William L. Bragg (England), for analysis of crystal structure by X rays
1916	No award
1917	Charles G. Barkla (England), for discovery of Roentgen radiation of the elements
1918	Max Planck (Germany), discoveries in connection with quantum theory
1919	Johannes Stark (Germany), discovery of Doppler effect in Canal rays and decomposition of spectrum lines by electric fields
1920	Charles E. Guillaume (Switzerland), for discoveries of anomalies in nickel steel alloys
1921	Albert Einstein (Germany), for discovery of the law of the photoelectric effect
1922	Niels Bohr (Denmark), for investigation of structure of atoms and radiations emanating from them
1923	Robert A. Millikan (U.S.), for work on elementary charge of electricity and photoelectric phenomena
1924	Karl M. G. Siegbahn (Sweden), for investigations in X-ray spectroscopy
1925	James Franck and Gustav Hertz (Germany), for discovery of laws governing impact of electrons upon atoms
1926	Jean B. Perrin (France), for work on discontinous structure of matter and discovery of the equilibrium of sedimentation
1927	Arthur H. Compton (U.S.), for discovery of Compton phenomenon; and Charles T. R. Wilson (England), for method of perceiving paths taken by electrically charged particles
1928	In 1929, the 1928 prize was awarded to Sir Owen Richardson (England), for work on the phenomenon of thermionics and discovery of the Richardson Law
1929	Prince Louis Victor de Broglie (France), for discovery of the wave character of electrons
1930	Sir Chandrasekhara Raman (India), for work on

diffusion of light and discovery of the Raman effect

1931 No award

1932 In 1933, the prize for 1932 was awarded to Werner Heisenberg (Germany), for creation of the quantum mechanics

1933 Erwin Schrödinger (Austria) and Paul A. M. Dirac (England), for discovery of new fertile forms of the atomic theory

1934 No award

1935 James Chadwick (England), for discovery of the neutron

1936 Victor F. Hess (Austria), for discovery of cosmic radiation; and Carl D. Anderson (U.S.), for discovery of the positron

1937 Clinton J. Davisson (U.S.) and George P. Thomson (England), for discovery of diffraction of electrons by crystals

1938 Enrico Fermi (Italy), for identification of new radioactivity elements and discovery of nuclear reactions effected by slow neutrons

1939 Ernest Orlando Lawrence (U.S.), for development of the cyclotron

1943 Otto Stern (U.S.), for detection of magnetic momentum of protons

1944 Isidor Isaac Rabi (U.S.), for work on magnetic movements of atomic particles

1945 Wolfgang Pauli (Austria), for work on atomic fissions

1946 Percy Williams Bridgman (U.S.), for studies and inventions in high-pressure physics

1947 Sir Edward Appleton (England), for discovery of layer which reflects radio short waves in the ionosphere

1948 Patrick M. S. Blackett (England), for improvement on Wilson chamber and discoveries in cosmic radiation

1949 Hideki Yukawa (Japan), for mathematical prediction, in 1935, of the meson

1950 Cecil Frank Powell (England), for method of photographic study of atom nucleus, and for discoveries about mesons

1951 Sir John Douglas Cockcroft (England) and Ernest T. S. Walton (Ireland), for work in 1932 on transmutation of atomic nuclei

1952 Edward Mills Purcell and Felix Bloch (U.S.), for work in measurement of magnetic fields in atomic nuclei

1953 Fritz Zernike (Netherlands), for development of "phase contrast" microscope

1954 Max Born (England), for work in quantum mechanics; and Walther Bothe (Germany), for work in cosmic radiation

1955 Polykarp Kusch and Willis E. Lamb, Jr. (U.S.), for atomic measurements

1956 William Shockley, Walter H. Brattain, and John Bardeen (U.S.), for developing electronic transistor

1957 Tsung Dao Lee and Chen Ning Yang (China), for disproving principle of conservation of parity

1958 Pavel A. Cherenkov, Ilya M. Frank, and Igor E. Tamm (U.S.S.R.), for work resulting in development of cosmic-ray counter

1959 Emilio Segre and Owen Chamberlain (U.S.), for demonstrating the existence of the anti-proton

1960 Donald A. Glaser (U.S.), for invention of "bubble chamber" to study subatomic particles

1961 Robert Hofstadter (U.S.), for determination of shape and size of atomic nucleus; Rudolf Mössbauer (Germany), for method of producing and measuring recoil-free gamma rays

1962 Lev D. Landau (U.S.S.R.), for his theories about condensed matter

1963 Eugene Paul Wigner, Maria Goeppert Mayer (both U.S.), and J. Hans D. Jensen (Germany), for research on structure of atom and its nucleus

1964 Charles Hard Townes (U.S.), Nikolai G. Basov, and Aleksandr M. Prochorov (both U.S.S.R.), for developing maser and laser principle of producing high-intensity radiation

1965 Richard P. Feynman, Julian S. Schwinger (both U.S.), and Shinichero Tomonaga (Japan), for research in quantum electrodynamics

1966 Alfred Kastler (France), for work on energy levels inside atom

1967 Hans A. Bethe (U.S.), for work on energy production of stars

1968 Luis Walter Alvarez (U.S.), for study of subatomic particles

1969 Murray Gell-Mann (U.S.), for study of subatomic particles

1970 Hannes Alfvén (Sweden), for theories in plasma physics; and Louis Néel (France), for discoveries in antiferromagnetism and ferrimagnetism

1971 Dennis Gabor (England), for invention of holographic method of three-dimensional imagery

1972 John Bardeen, Leon N. Cooper, and John Robert Schrieffer (all U.S.), for theory of superconductivity, where electrical resistance in certain metals vanishes above absolute zero temperature

1973 Ivar Giaever (U.S.), Leo Esaki (Japan), and Brian D. Josephson (U.K.), for theories that have advanced and expanded the field of miniature electronics

1974 Antony Hewish (England), for discovery of pulsars; Martin Ryle (England), for using radiotelescopes to probe outer space with high degree of precision

1975 James Rainwater (U.S.) and Ben Mottelson and Aage N. Bohr (both Denmark), for showing that the atomic nucleus is asymmetrical

1976 Burton Richter and Samuel C. C. Ting (U.S.), for discovery of subatomic particles known as J and psi

1977 Philip W. Anderson and John H. Van Vleck (both U.S.), and Nevill F. Mott (U.K.), for work underlying computer memories and electronic devices

1978 Arno A. Penzias and Robert W. Wilson (both U.S.), for work in cosmic microwave radiation; Piotr L. Kapitsa (U.S.S.R.), for basic inventions and discoveries in low-temperature physics

1979 Steven Weinberg and Sheldon L. Glashow (both U.S.) and Abdus Salam (Pakistan), for developing theory that electromagnetism and the "weak" force, which causes radioactive decay in some atomic nuclei, are facets of the same phenomenon

1980 James W. Cronin and Val L. Fitch (both U.S.), for work concerning the asymmetry of subatomic particles

CHEMISTRY

1901 Jacobus H. van't Hoff (Netherlands), for laws of chemical dynamics and osmotic pressure in solutions

1902 Emil Fischer (Germany), for experiments in sugar and purin groups of substances

1903 Svante A. Arrhenius (Sweden), for his electrolytic theory of dissociation

1904 Sir William Ramsay (England), for discovery and determination of place of inert gaseous elements in air

Year	Award
1905	Adolf von Baeyer (Germany), for work on organic dyes and hydroaromatic combinations
1906	Henri Moissan (France), for isolation of fluorine, and introduction of electric furnace
1907	Eduard Buchner (Germany), discovery of cell-less fermentation and investigations in biological chemistry
1908	Sir Ernest Rutherford (England), for investigations into disintegration of elements
1909	Wilhelm Ostwald (Germany), for work on catalysis and investigations into chemical equilibrium and reaction rates
1910	Otto Wallach (Germany), for work in the field of alicyclic compounds
1911	Marie Curie (France), for discovery of elements radium and polonium
1912	Victor Grignard (France), for reagent discovered by him; and Paul Sabatier (France), for methods of hydrogenating organic compounds
1913	Alfred Werner (Switzerland), for linking up atoms within the molecule
1914	Theodore W. Richards (U.S.), for determining atomic weight of many chemical elements
1915	Richard Willstätter (Germany), for research into coloring matter of plants, especially chlorophyll
1916	No award
1917	No award
1918	Fritz Haber (Germany), for synthetic production of ammonia
1919	No award
1920	Walther Nernst (Germany), for work in thermochemistry
1921	Frederick Soddy (England), for investigations into origin and nature of isotopes
1922	Francis W. Aston (England), for discovery of isotopes in nonradioactive elements and for discovery of the whole number rule
1923	Fritz Pregl (Austria), for method of microanalysis of organic substances discovered by him
1924	No award
1925	In 1926, the 1925 prize was awarded to Richard Zsigmondy (Germany), for work on the heterogeneous nature of colloid solutions
1926	Theodor Svedberg (Sweden), for work on disperse systems
1927	In 1928 the 1927 prize was awarded to Heinrich Wieland (Germany), for investigations of bile acids and kindred substances
1928	Adolf Windaus (Germany), for investigations on constitution of the sterols and their connection with vitamins
1929	Sir Arthur Harden (England) and Hans K. A. S. von Euler-Chelpin (Sweden), for research of fermentation of sugars
1930	Hans Fischer (Germany), for work on coloring matter of blood and leaves and for his synthesis of hemin
1931	Karl Bosch and Friedrich Bergius (Germany), for invention and development of chemical high-pressure methods
1932	Irving Langmuir (U.S.), for work in realm of surface chemistry
1933	No award
1934	Harold C. Urey (U.S.), for discovery of heavy hydrogen
1935	Frédéric and Irène Joliot-Curie (France), for synthesis of new radioactive elements
1936	Peter J. W. Debye (Netherlands), for investigations on dipole moments and diffraction of X rays and electrons in gases
1937	Walter N. Haworth (England), for research on carbohydrates and Vitamin C; and Paul Karrer (Switzerland), for work on carotenoids, flavins, and Vitamins A and B
1938	Richard Kuhn (Germany), for carotinoid study and vitamin research (declined the prize)
1939	Adolf Butenandt (Germany), for work on sexual hormones (declined the prize); and Leopold Ruzicka (Switzerland), for work with polymethylenes
1943	Georg Hevesy De Heves (Hungary), for work on use of isotopes as indicators
1944	Otto Hahn (Germany), for work on atomic fission
1945	Artturi Ilmari Virtanen (Finland), for research in the field of conservation of fodder
1946	James B. Sumner (U.S.), for crystallizing enzymes; John H. Northrop and Wendell M. Stanley (U.S.), for preparing enzymes and virus proteins in pure form
1947	Sir Robert Robinson (England), for research in plant substances
1948	Arne Tiselius (Sweden), for biochemical discoveries and isolation of mouse paralysis virus
1949	William Francis Giauque (U.S.), for research in thermodynamics, especially effects of low temperature
1950	Otto Diels and Kurt Alder (Germany), for discovery of diene synthesis enabling scientists to study structure of organic matter
1951	Glenn T. Seaborg and Edwin H. McMillan (U.S.), for discovery of plutonium
1952	Archer John Porter Martin and Richard Laurence Millington Synge (England), for development of partition chromatography
1953	Hermann Staudinger (Germany), for research in giant molecules
1954	Linus C. Pauling (U.S.), for study of forces holding together protein and other molecules
1955	Vincent du Vigneaud (U.S.), for work on pituitary hormones
1956	Sir Cyril Hinshelwood (England) and Nikolai N. Semenov (U.S.S.R.), for parallel research on chemical reaction kinetics
1957	Sir Alexander Todd (England), for research with chemical compounds that are factors in heredity
1958	Frederick Sanger (England), for determining molecular structure of insulin
1959	Jaroslav Heyrovsky (Czechoslovakia), for development of polarography, an electrochemical method of analysis
1960	Willard F. Libby (U.S.), for "atomic time clock" to measure age of objects by measuring their radioactivity
1961	Melvin Calvin (U.S.), for establishing chemical steps during photosynthesis
1962	Max F. Perutz and John C. Kendrew (England), for mapping protein molecules with X rays
1963	Carl Ziegler (Germany) and Giulio Natta (Italy), for work in uniting simple hydrocarbons into large molecule substances
1964	Dorothy Mary Crowfoot Hodgkin (England), for determining structure of compounds needed in combating pernicious anemia
1965	Robert B. Woodward (U.S.), for work in synthesizing complicated organic compounds
1966	Robert Sanderson Mulliken (U.S.), for research on bond holding atoms together in molecule
1967	Manfred Eigen (Germany), Ronald G. W. Norrish, and George Porter (both England), for work in high-speed chemical reactions
1968	Lars Onsager (U.S.), for development of system of equations in thermodynamics
1969	Derek H. R. Barton (England) and Odd Hassel (Norway), for study of organic molecules

1970 Luis F. Leloir (Argentina), for discovery of sugar nucleotides and their role in biosynthesis of carbohydrates

1971 Gerhard Herzberg (Canada), for contributions to knowledge of electronic structure and geometry of molecules, particularly free radicals

1972 Christian Boehmer Anfinsen, Stanford Moore, and William Howard Stein (all U.S.), for pioneering studies in enzymes

1973 Ernst Otto Fischer (W. Germany) and Geoffrey Wilkinson (U.K.), for work that could solve problem of automobile exhaust pollution

1974 Paul J. Flory (U.S.), for developing analytic methods to study properties and molecular structure of long-chain molecules

1975 John W. Cornforth (Australia) and Vladimir Prelog (Switzerland), for research on structure of biological molecules such as antibiotics and cholesterol

1976 William N. Lipscomb, Jr. (U.S.), for work on the structure and bonding mechanisms of boranes

1977 Ilya Prigogine (Belgium), for contributions to nonequilibrium thermodynamics, particularly the theory of dissipative structures

1978 Peter Mitchell (U.K.), for contributions to the understanding of biological energy transfer

1979 Herbert C. Brown (U.S.) and Georg Wittig (West Germany), for developing a group of substances that facilitate very difficult chemical reactions

1980 Paul Berg and Walter Gilbert (both U.S.) and Frederick Sanger (England), for developing methods to map the structure and function of DNA, the substance that controls the activity of the cell

PHYSIOLOGY OR MEDICINE

1901 Emil A. von Behring (Germany), for work on serum therapy against diphtheria

1902 Sir Ronald Ross (England), for work on malaria

1903 Niels R. Finsen (Denmark), for his treatment of lupus vulgaris with concentrated light rays

1904 Ivan P. Pavlov (U.S.S.R.), for work on the physiology of digestion

1905 Robert Koch (Germany), for work on tuberculosis

1906 Camillo Golgi (Italy) and Santiago Ramón y Cajal (Spain), for work on structure of the nervous system

1907 Charles L. A. Laveran (France), for work with protozoa in the generation of disease

1908 Paul Ehrlich (Germany), and Elie Metchnikoff (U.S.S.R.), for work on immunity

1909 Theodor Kocher (Switzerland), for work on the thyroid gland

1910 Albrecht Kossel (Germany), for achievements in the chemistry of the cell

1911 Allvar Gullstrand (Sweden), for work on the dioptrics of the eye

1912 Alexis Carrel (France), for work on vascular ligature and grafting of blood vessels and organs

1913 Charles Richet (France), for work on anaphylaxy

1914 Robert Bárány (Austria), for work on physiology and pathology of the vestibular system

1915 No award
1916 No award
1917 No award
1918 No award

1919 Jules Bordet (Belgium), for discoveries in connection with immunity

1920 August Krogh (Denmark), for discovery of regulation of capillaries' motor mechanism

1921 No award

1922 In 1923, the 1922 prize was shared by Archibald V. Hill (England), for discovery relating to heat-production in muscles; and Otto Meyerhof (Germany), for correlation between consumption of oxygen and production of lactic acid in muscles

1923 Sir Frederick Banting (Canada) and John J. R. Macleod (Scotland), for discovery of insulin

1924 Willem Einthoven (Netherlands), for discovery of the mechanism of the electrocardiogram

1925 No award

1926 Johannes Fibiger (Denmark), for discovery of the Spiroptera carcinoma

1927 Julius Wagner-Jauregg (Austria), for use of malaria inoculation in treatment of dementia paralytica

1928 Charles Nicolle (France), for work on typhus exanthematicus

1929 Christiaan Eijkman (Netherlands), for discovery of the antineuritic vitamins; and Sir Frederick Hopkins (England), for discovery of growth-promoting vitamins

1930 Karl Landsteiner (U.S.), for discovery of human blood groups

1931 Otto H. Warburg (Germany), for discovery of the character and mode of action of the respiratory ferment

1932 Sir Charles Sherrington (England) and Edgar D. Adrian (U.S.), for discoveries of the function of the neuron

1933 Thomas H. Morgan (U.S.), for discoveries on hereditary function of the chromosomes

1934 George H. Whipple, George R. Minot, and William P. Murphy (all U.S.), for discovery of liver therapy against anemias

1935 Hans Spemann (Germany), for discovery of the organizer-effect in embryonic development

1936 Sir Henry Dale (England) and Otto Loewi (Germany), for discoveries on chemical transmission of nerve impulses

1937 Albert Szent-Györgyi von Nagyrapolt (Hungary), for discoveries on biological combustion

1938 Corneille Heymans (Belgium), for determining importance of sinus and aorta mechanisms in the regulation of respiration

1939 Gerhard Domagk (Germany), for antibacterial effect of prontocilate

1943 Henrik Dam (Denmark) and Edward A. Doisy (U.S.), for analysis of Vitamin K

1944 Joseph Erlanger and Herbert Spencer Gasser (U.S.), for work on functions of the nerve threads

1945 Sir Alexander Fleming, Ernst Boris Chain, and Sir Howard Florey (England), for discovery of penicillin

1946 Herman J. Muller (U.S.), for hereditary effects of X rays on genes

1947 Carl F. and Gerty T. Cori (U.S.), for work on animal starch metabolism; Bernardo A. Houssay (Argentina), for study of pituitary

1948 Paul Mueller (Switzerland), for discovery of insect-killing properties of DDT

1949 Walter Rudolf Hess (Switzerland), for research on brain control of body; and Antonio Caetano de Abreu Freire Egas Moniz (Portugal), for development of brain operation

1950 Philip S. Hench, Edward C. Kendall (both U.S.), and Tadeus Reichstein (Switzerland), for discoveries about hormones of adrenal cortex

1951 Max Theiler (South Africa), for development of anti-yellow-fever vaccine

1952 Selman A. Waksman (U.S.), for co-discovery of

streptomycin

1953 Fritz A. Lipmann (Germany-U.S.) and Hans Adolph Krebs (Germany-England), for studies of living cells

1954 John F. Enders, Thomas H. Weller, and Frederick C. Robbins (U.S.), for work with cultivation of polio virus

1955 Hugo Theorell (Sweden), for work on oxidation enzymes

1956 Dickinson W. Richards, Jr., André F. Cournand (both U.S.), and Werner Forssmann (Germany), for new techniques in treating heart disease

1957 Daniel Bovet (Italy), for development of drugs to relieve allergies and relax muscles during surgery

1958 Joshua Lederberg (U.S.), for work with genetic mechanisms; George W. Beadle and Edward L. Tatum (U.S.), for discovering how genes transmit hereditary characteristics

1959 Severo Ochoa and Arthur Kornberg (U.S.), for discoveries related to compounds within chromosomes, which play a vital role in heredity

1960 Sir Macfarlane Burnet (Australia) and Peter Brian Medawar (England), for discovery of acquired immunological tolerance

1961 Georg von Bekesy (U.S.), for discoveries about physical mechanisms of stimulation within cochlea

1962 James D. Watson (U.S.), Maurice H. F. Wilkins, and Francis H. C. Crick (England), for determining structure of deoxyribonucleic acid (DNA)

1963 Alan Lloyd Hodgkin, Andrew Fielding Huxley (both England), and Sir John Carew Eccles (Australia), for research on nerve cells

1964 Konrad E. Bloch (U.S.) and Feodor Lynen (Germany), for research on mechanism and regulation of cholesterol and fatty acid metabolism

1965 François Jacob, André Lwolff, and Jacques Monod (France), for study of regulatory activities in body cells

1966 Charles Brenton Huggins (U.S.), for studies in hormone treatment of cancer of prostate; Francis Peyton Rous (U.S.), for discovery of tumor-producing viruses

1967 Haldan K. Hartline, George Wald, and Ragnar Granit (U.S.), for work on human eye

1968 Robert W. Holley, Har Gobind Khorana, and Marshall W. Nirenberg (U.S.), for studies of genetic code

1969 Max Delbruck, Alfred D. Hershey, and Salvador E. Luria (U.S.), for study of mechanism of virus infection in living cells

1970 Julius Axelrod (U.S.), Ulf S. von Euler (Sweden), and Sir Bernard Katz (England), for studies of how nerve impulses are transmitted within the body

1971 Earl W. Sutherland, Jr., (U.S.), for research on how hormones work

1972 Gerald M. Edelman (U.S.), and Rodney R. Porter (U.K.), for research on the chemical structure and nature of antibodies

1973 Karl von Frisch and Konrad Lorenz (Austria), and Nikolaas Tinbergen (Netherlands), for their studies of individual and social behavior patterns

1974 George E. Palade and Christian de Duve (both U.S.) and Albert Claude (Belgium), for contributions to understanding inner workings of living cells

1975 David Baltimore, Howard M. Temin and Renato Dulbecco (all U.S.), for work in interaction between tumor viruses and genetic material of the cell

1976 Baruch S. Blumberg and D. Carleton Gajdusek (U.S.), for discoveries concerning new mechanisms for the origin and dissemination of infectious diseases

1977 Rosalyn S. Yalow, Roger C. L. Guillemin, and Andrew V. Schally (all U.S.), for research in role of hormones in chemistry of the body

1978 Daniel Nathans and Hamilton Smith (both U.S.) and Werner Arber (Switzerland), for discovery of restriction enzymes and their application to problems of molecular genetics

1979 Allan McLeod Cormack (U.S.) and Godfrey Newbold Hounsfield (England), for developing computed axial tomography (CAT scan) X-ray technique

1980 Baruj Benacerraf and George D. Snell (both U.S.) and Jean Dausset (France), for discoveries that explain how the structure of cells relates to organ transplants and diseases

ECONOMIC SCIENCE

1969 Ragnar Frisch (Norway) and Jan Tinbergen (Netherlands), for work in econometrics (application of mathematics and statistical methods to economic theories and problems)

1970 Paul A. Samuelson (U.S.), for efforts to raise the level of scientific analysis in economic theory

1971 Simon Kuznets (U.S.), for developing concept of using a country's gross national product to determine its economic growth

1972 Kenneth J. Arrow (U.S.) and Sir John R. Hicks (U.K.), for theories that help to assess business risk and government economic and welfare policies

1973 Wassily Leontief (U.S.), for devising the input-output technique to determine how different sectors of an economy interact

1974 Gunnar Myrdal (Sweden) and Friedrich A. von Hayek (Austria), for pioneering analysis of the interdependence of economic, social and institutional phenomena

1975 Leonid V. Kantorovich (U.S.S.R.) and Tjalling C. Koopmans (U.S.), for work on the theory of optimum allocation of resources

1976 Milton Friedman (U.S.), for work in consumption analysis and monetary history and theory, and for demonstration of complexity of stabilization policy

1977 Bertil Ohlin (Sweden) and James E. Meade (U.K.), for contributions to theory of international trade and international capital movements

1978 Herbert A. Simon (U.S.), for research into the decision-making process within economic organizations

1979 Sir Arthur Lewis (England) and Theodore Schultz (U.S.), for work on economic problems of developing nations

1980 Lawrence R. Klein (U.S.), for developing models for forecasting economic trends and shaping policies to deal with them

Major Grammy Awards for Recording in 1980

Source: National Academy of Recording Arts and Sciences.

Record: "Sailing," Christopher Cross (Warner Bros.)

Album: "Christopher Cross," Christopher Cross (Warner Bros.)

Song: "Sailing," Christopher Cross

New Artist: Christopher Cross (Warner Bros.)

Pop Vocalists Bette Midler, "The Rose" (Atlantic); Kenny Loggins, "This Is It" (Columbia)

Pop Duo: Barbra Streisand and Barry Gibb, "Guilty" (Columbia)

Pop Instrumentalists: Bob James and Earl Klugh, "One on One" (Columbia)

Rock Vocalists: Pat Benatar, "Crimes of Passion" (Chrysalis); Billy Joel, "Glass Houses" (Columbia)

Rock Group: Bob Seger and the Silver Bullet Band, "Against the Wind" (Capitol)

Rock Instrumentalists: Police, "Reggatta De Blanc" (A&M)

Country Vocalists: Anne Murray, "Could I Have This Dance" (Capitol); George Jones, "He Stopped Loving Her Today" (Epic)

Country Duo: Roy Orbison and Emmylou Harris, "That Lovin' You Feelin' Again" (Warner Bros.)

Country Instrumentalists: Gilley's "Urban Cowboy" Band, "Orange Blossom Special/Hoedown" (Full Moon/Asylum)

Country Song: "On the Road Again," Willie Nelson

Rhythm and Blues Vocalists: Stephanie Mills, "Never Knew Love Like This Before" (20th Century); George Benson, "Give Me the Night" (Warner Bros./QWest)

Rhythm and Blues Group: Manhattans, "Shining Star" (Columbia)

Rhythm and Blues Instrumentalist: George Benson, "Off Broadway" (Warner Bros./QWest)

Rhythm and Blues Song: "Never Knew Love Like This Before," Reggie Lucas and James Mtume

Jazz Vocalists: Ella Fitzgerald, "A Perfect Match/Ella and Basie"; (Pablo) George Benson, "Moody's Mood" (Warner Bros./QWest)

Jazz Instrumentalist: Bill Evans, "I Will Say Goodbye" (Fantasy)

Jazz Instrumental Group: Bill Evans, "We Will Meet Again" (Warner Bros.)

Jazz, Big Band: Count Basie, "On the Road" (Pablo)

Jazz Fusion: Manhattan Transfer, "Birdland" (Atlantic)

Gospel Inspirational: Reba Rambo, Dony McGuire, B.J. Thomas, Andrae Crouch, The Archers, Walter and Tramaine Hawkins and Cynthia Clawson, "The Lord's Prayer" (Light)

Gospel, Traditional: Blackwood Brothers, "We Come to Worship" (Voice Box)

Soul Gospel, Contemporary: Shirley Caesar, "Rejoice" (Myrrh)

Soul Gospel, Traditional: James Cleveland and the Charles Fold Singers, "Lord, Let Me Be an Instrument" (Savoy)

Inspirational: Debby Boone, "With My Song I Will Praise Him" (Lamb & Lion)

Ethnic or Traditional: "Rare Blues," Norman Dayron, producer (Takoma)

Latin: Cal Tjader, "La Onda Va Bien" (Concert Jazz)

For Children: "In Harmony/A Sesame Street Record," Lucy Simon and David Levine, producers (Sesame St./Warner Bros.)

Comedy: Rodney Dangerfield, "No Respect" (Casablanca)

Spoken Word: Pat Carroll, "Gertrude Stein, Gertrude Stein, Gertrude Stein" (Caedmon)

Instrumental Composition: "The Empire Strikes Back," John Williams

Instrumental Arrangement: "Dinorah, Dinorah," Quincy Jones and Jerry Hey

Motion Picture Score: "The Empire Strikes Back," John Williams

Cast Show Album: "Evita—Premier American Recording," Andrew Lloyd Weber and Tim Rice (MCA)

Classical Album: "Lulu (Complete Version)," Alban Berg; Pierre Boulez, conducting Orchestre de l'Opera de Paris (Deutsche Grammophon)

Classical, Orchestral Recording: Symphony No. 6, Bruckner; Sir Georg Solti, conducting Chicago Symphony Orchestra (London)

Classical, Soloist Without Orchestra: Itzhak Perlman, "The Spanish Album" (Angel)

Classical, Soloist With Orchestra: Itzhak Perlman, Concerto for Violin and Orchestra, Berg/Concerto in D for Violin and Orchestra, Stravinsky; with Seiji Ozawa conducting Boston Symphony Orchestra (Deutsche Grammophon) Itzhak Perlman and Mstislav Rostropovich, Concerto in A Minor for Violin and Cello (Double Concerto), Brahms with Bernard Haitink conducting Concertgebouw Orchestra (Angel)

Chamber Music: Itzhak Perlman and Pinchas Zukerman, "Music for Two Violins (Suite for Two Violins, Moszkowski/Duets, Shostakovich/Sonata for Two Violins, Prokofiev) (Angel)

Classical, Vocal Soloist: Leontyne Price, "Prima Donna, Volume 5—Great Soprano Arias From Handel to Britten" with Henry Lewis conducting Philharmonia Orchestra (RCA)

Classical, Choral: Requiem, Mozart; Carlo Maria Giulini, conductor; Norbert Balatsch, chorusmaster, Philharmonia Chorus & Orchestra (Angel)

Opera: "Lulu" (Complete Version), Berg; Pierre Boulez, conducting Orchestre de l'Opera de Paris (Deutsche Grammophon)

Poets Laureate of England

Edmund Spenser	1591–1599	Nicholas Rowe	1715–1718	William Wordsworth	1843–1850
Samuel Daniel	1599–1619	Laurence Eusden	1718–1730	Alfred Lord Tennyson	1850–1892
Ben Jonson	1619–1637	Colley Cibber	1730–1757	Alfred Austin	1896–1913
William Davenant	1638–1668	William Whitehead	1757–1785	Robert Bridges	1913–1930
John Dryden[1]	1670–1689	Thomas Warton	1785–1790	John Masefield	1930–1967
Thomas Shadwell	1689–1692	Henry James Pye	1790–1813	C. Day Lewis	1967–1972
Nahum Tate	1692–1715	Robert Southey	1813–1843	Sir John Betjeman	1972–

1. First to bear the title officially. *Source: Encyclopaedia Britannica.*

Motion Picture Academy Awards (Oscars)

	Picture	Director	Actress
1928	*Wings,* Paramount	Frank Borzage, *Seventh Heaven;* Lewis Milestone, *Two Arabian Nights*	Janet Gaynor, *Seventh Heaven, Street Angel, Sunrise*
1929	*The Broadway Melody,* M-G-M	Frank Lloyd, *The Divine Lady*	Mary Pickford, *Coquette*
1930	*All Quiet on the Western Front,* Universal	Lewis Milestone, *All Quiet on the Western Front*	Norma Shearer, *The Divorcee*
1931	*Cimarron,* RKO Radio	Norman Taurog, *Skippy*	Marie Dressler, *Min and Bill*
1932	*Grand Hotel,* M-G-M	Frank Borzage, *Bad Girl*	Helen Hayes, *The Sin of Madelon Claudet*
1933	*Cavalcade,* Fox	Frank Lloyd, *Cavalcade*	Katharine Hepburn, *Morning Glory*
1934	*It Happened One Night,* Columbia	Frank Capra, *It Happened One Night*	Claudette Colbert *It Happened One Night*
1935	*Mutiny on the Bounty,* M-G-M	John Ford, *The Informer*	Bette Davis, *Dangerous*
1936	*The Great Ziegfeld,* M-G-M	Frank Capra, *Mr. Deeds Goes to Town*	Luise Rainer, *The Great Ziegfeld*
1937	*The Life of Emile Zola,* Warner Bros.	Leo McCarey, *The Awful Truth*	Luise Rainer, *The Good Earth*
1938	*You Can't Take It with You,* Columbia	Frank Capra, *You Can't Take It with You*	Bette Davis, *Jezebel*
1939	*Gone with the Wind,* Selznick-M-G-M	Victor Fleming, *Gone with the Wind*	Vivien Leigh, *Gone with the Wind*
1940	*Rebecca,* Selznick-UA	John Ford, *The Grapes of Wrath*	Ginger Rogers, *Kitty Foyle*
1941	*How Green Was My Valley,* 20th Century-Fox	John Ford, *How Green Was My Valley*	Joan Fontaine, *Suspicion*
1942	*Mrs. Miniver,* M-G-M	William Wyler, *Mrs. Miniver*	Greer Garson, *Mrs. Miniver*
1943	*Casablanca,* Warner Bros.	Michael Curtiz, *Casablanca*	Jennifer Jones, *The Song of Bernadette*
1944	*Going My Way,* Paramount	Leo McCarey, *Going My Way*	Ingrid Bergman, *Gaslight*
1945	*The Lost Weekend,* Paramount	Billy Wilder, *The Lost Weekend*	Joan Crawford, *Mildred Pierce*
1946	*The Best Years of Our Lives,* Goldwyn-RKO Radio	William Wyler, *The Best Years of Our Lives*	Olivia de Havilland, *To Each His Own*
1947	*Gentleman's Agreement,* 20th Century-Fox	Elia Kazan, *Gentleman's Agreement*	Loretta Young, *The Farmer's Daughter*
1948	*Hamlet,* Rank-Two Cities-U-I	John Houston, *Treasure of Sierra Madre*	Jane Wyman, *Johnny Belinda*
1949	*All the King's Men,* Rossen-Columbia	Joseph L. Mankiewicz, *A Letter to Three Wives*	Olivia de Havilland, *The Heiress*
1950	*All About Eve,* 20th Century-Fox	Joseph L. Mankiewicz, *All About Eve*	Judy Holliday, *Born Yesterday*
1951	*An American in Paris,* M-G-M	George Stevens, *A Place in the Sun*	Vivien Leigh, *A Streetcar Named Desire*
1952	*The Greatest Show on Earth,* DeMille-Paramount	John Ford, *The Quiet Man*	Shirley Booth, *Come Back, Little Sheba*
1953	*From Here to Eternity,* Columbia	Fred Zinnemann, *From Here to Eternity*	Audrey Hepburn, *Roman Holiday*
1954	*On the Waterfront,* Horizon-American Corp., Columbia	Elia Kazan, *On the Waterfront*	Grace Kelley, *The Country Girl*
1955	*Marty,* Hecht and Lancaster, United Artists	Delbert Mann, *Marty*	Anna Magnani, *The Rose Tattoo*
1956	*Around the World in 80 Days,* Michael Todd Co., Inc.-UA	George Stevens, *Giant*	Ingrid Bergman, *Anastasia*
1957	*The Bridge on the River Kwai,* Horizon Picture, Columbia	David Lean, *The Bridge on the River Kwai*	Joanne Woodward, *The Three Faces of Eve*
1958	*Gigi,* Arthur Freed Productions, Inc., M-G-M	Vincente Minnelli, *Gigi*	Susan Hayward, *I Want to Live!*
1959	*Ben-Hur,* M-G-M	William Wyler, *Ben-Hur*	Simone Signoret, *Room at the Top*
1960	*The Apartment,* Mirisch Co., Inc., United Artists	Billy Wilder, *The Apartment*	Elizabeth Taylor, *Butterfield 8*
1961	*West Side Story,* Mirisch Pictures, Inc., and B and P Enterprises, Inc., United Artists	Robert Wise and Jerome Robbins, *West Side Story*	Sophia Loren, *Two Women*

Actor	Supporting Actress	Supporting Actor	
Emil Jannings, *The Way of All Flesh, The Last Command*	—	—	1928
Warner Baxter, *In Old Arizona*	—	—	1929
George Arliss, *Disraeli*	—	—	1930
Lionel Barrymore, *A Free Soul*	—	—	1931
Fredric March, *Dr. Jekyll and Mr. Hyde,* and Wallace Beery, *The Champ*	—	—	1932
Charles Laughton, *The Private Life of Henry VIII*	—	—	1933
Clark Gable, *It Happened One Night*	—	—	1934
Victor McLaglen, *The Informer*	—	—	1935
Paul Muni, *The Story of Louis Pasteur*	Gale Sondergaard, *Anthony Adverse*	Walter Brennan, *Come and Get It*	1936
Spencer Tracy, *Captains Courageous*	Alice Brady, *In Old Chicago*	Joseph Schildkraut, *The Life of Emile Zola*	1937
Spencer Tracy, *Boys Town*	Fay Bainter, *Jezebel*	Walter Brennan, *Kentucky*	1938
Robert Donat, *Goodbye, Mr. Chips*	Hattie McDaniel, *Gone with the Wind*	Thomas Mitchell, *Stagecoach*	1939
James Stewart, *The Philadelphia Story*	Jane Darwell, *The Grapes of Wrath*	Walter Brennan, *The Westerner*	1940
Gary Cooper, *Sergeant York*	Mary Astor, *The Great Lie*	Donald Crisp, *How Green Was My Valley*	1941
James Cagney, *Yankee Doodle Dandy*	Teresa Wright, *Mrs. Miniver*	Van Heflin, *Johnny Eager*	1942
Paul Lukas, *Watch on the Rhine*	Katina Paxinou, *For Whom the Bell Tolls*	Charles Coburn, *The More the Merrier*	1943
Bing Crosby, *Going My Way*	Ethel Barrymore, *None But the Lonely Heart*	Barry Fitzgerald, *Going My Way*	1944
Ray Milland, *The Lost Weekend*	Anne Revere, *National Velvet*	James Dunn, *A Tree Grows in Brooklyn*	1945
Fredric March, *The Best Years of Our Lives*	Anne Baxter, *The Razor's Edge*	Harold Russell, *The Best Years of Our Lives*	1946
Ronald Colman, *A Double Life*	Celeste Holm, *Gentleman's Agreement*	Edmund Gwenn, *Miracle on 34th Street*	1947
Laurence Olivier, *Hamlet*	Claire Trevor, *Key Largo*	Walter Huston, *Treasure of Sierra Madre*	1948
Broderick Crawford, *All the King's Men*	Mercedes McCambridge, *All the King's Men*	Dean Jagger, *Twelve O'Clock High*	1949
José Ferrer, *Cyrano de Bergerac*	Josephine Hull, *Harvey*	George Sanders, *All About Eve*	1950
Humphrey Bogart, *The African Queen*	Kim Hunter, *A Streetcar Named Desire*	Karl Malden, *A Streetcar Named Desire*	1951
Gary Cooper, *High Noon*	Gloria Grahame, *The Bad and the Beautiful*	Anthony Quinn, *Viva Zapata!*	1952
William Holden, *Stalag 17*	Donna Reed, *From Here to Eternity*	Frank Sinatra, *From Here to Eternity*	1953
Marlon Brando, *On the Waterfront*	Eva Marie Saint, *On the Waterfront*	Edmond O'Brien, *The Barefoot Contessa*	1954
Ernest Borgnine, *Marty*	Jo Van Fleet, *East of Eden*	Jack Lemmon, *Mister Roberts*	1955
Yul Brynner, *The King and I*	Dorothy Malone, *Written on the Wind*	Anthony Quinn, *Lust for Life*	1956
Alec Guinness, *The Bridge on the River Kwai*	Miyoshi Umeki, *Sayonara*	Red Buttons, *Sayonara*	1957
David Niven, *Separate Tables*	Wendy Hiller, *Separate Tables*	Burl Ives, *The Big Country*	1958
Charlton Heston, *Ben-Hur*	Shelley Winters, *The Diary of Anne Frank*	Hugh Griffith, *Ben-Hur*	1959
Burt Lancaster, *Elmer Gantry*	Shirley Jones, *Elmer Gantry*	Peter Ustinov, *Spartacus*	1960
Maximilian Schell, *Judgment at Nuremberg*	Rita Moreno, *West Side Story*	George Chakiris, *West Side Story*	1961

	Picture	Director	Actress
1962	*Lawrence of Arabia,* Horizon Pictures, Ltd.-Columbia	David Lean, *Lawrence of Arabia*	Anne Bancroft, *The Miracle Worker*
1963	*Tom Jones,* A Woodfall Production, UA-Lopert Pictures	Tony Richardson, *Tom Jones*	Patricia Neal, *Hud*
1964	*My Fair Lady,* Warner Bros.	George Cukor, *My Fair Lady*	Julie Andrews, *Mary Poppins*
1965	*The Sound of Music,* Argyle Enterprises Production, 20th Century-Fox	Robert Wise, *The Sound of Music*	Julie Christie, *Darling*
1966	*A Man for All Seasons,* Highland Films, Ltd., Production, Columbia	Fred Zinnemann, *A Man for All Seasons*	Elizabeth Taylor, *Who's Afraid of Virginia Woolf?*
1967	*In the Heat of the Night,* Mirisch Corp. Production, United Artists	Mike Nichols, *The Graduate*	Katharine Hepburn, *Guess Who's Coming to Dinner*
1968	*Oliver!,* Columbia Pictures	Sir Carol Reed, *Oliver!*	Katharine Hepburn, *The Lion in Winter,* and Barbara Streisand, *Funny Girl*
1969	*Midnight Cowboy,* Jerome Hellman-John Schlesinger Production, United Artists	John Schlesinger, *Midnight Cowboy*	Maggie Smith, *The Prime of Miss Jean Brodie*
1970	*Patton,* Frank McCarthy-Franklin J. Schaffner Production, 20th Century-Fox	Franklin J. Schaffner, *Patton*	Glenda Jackson, *Women in Love*
1971	*The French Connection,* D'Antoni Productions, 20th Century-Fox	William Friedkin, *The French Connection*	Jane Fonda, *Klute*
1972	*The Godfather,* Albert S. Ruddy Production, Paramount	Bob Fosse, *Cabaret*	Liza Minnelli, *Cabaret*
1973	*The Sting,* Universal-Bill-Phillips-George Roy Hill Production, Universal	George Roy Hill, *The Sting*	Glenda Jackson, *A Touch of Class*
1974	*The Godfather, Part II,* Coppola Co. Production, Paramount	Francis Ford Coppola, *The Godfather, Part II*	Ellen Burstyn, *Alice Doesn't Live Here Anymore*
1975	*One Flew Over the Cuckoo's Nest,* Fantasy Films Production, United Artists	Milos Forman, *One Flew Over the Cuckoo's Nest*	Louise Fletcher, *One Flew Over the Cuckoo's Nest*
1976	*Rocky,* Robert Chartoff-Irwin Winkler Production, United Artists	John G. Avildsen, *Rocky*	Faye Dunaway *Network*
1977	*Annie Hall,* Jack Rollins-Charles H. Joffe Production, United Artists	Woody Allen, *Annie Hall*	Diane Keaton, *Annie Hall*
1978	*The Deer Hunter,* Michael Cimino Film Production, Universal	Michael Cimino, *The Deer Hunter*	Jane Fonda, *Coming Home*
1979	*Kramer vs. Kramer,* Stanley Jaffe Production, Columbia Pictures	Robert Benton, *Kramer vs. Kramer*	Sally Field, *Norma Rae*
1980	*Ordinary People,* Wildwood Enterprises Production, Paramount	Robert Redford, *Ordinary People*	Sissy Spacek, *Coal Miner's Daughter*

Other Academy Awards for 1980

Art direction: Pierre Guffroy and Jack Stephens, *Tess*

Cinematography: Geoffrey Unsworth (deceased) and Ghislain Cloquet, *Tess*

Costume design: Anthony Powell, *Tess*

Documentary (feature): *From Mao to Mozart: Isaac Stern in China;* **short subject:** *Karl Hess: Toward Liberty*

Editing: Thelma Schoonmaker, *Raging Bull*

Foreign-language film: *Moscow Does Not Believe in Tears,* U.S.S.R.

Music (original score): Michael Gore, *Fame*

Screenplay (original): Bo Goldman, *Melvin and How-*ard; **adaptation:** Alvin Sargent, *Ordinary People*

Short subject (animated): *The Fly;* **dramatic:** *The Dollar Bottom*

Song: "Fame," by Michael Gore and Dean Pitchford, from *Fame*

Sound: Bill Varney, Steve Maslow, Gregg Landaker and Peter Sutton, *The Empire Strikes Back*

SPECIAL AWARDS

Special Achievement for Visual Effects: *The Empire Strikes Back*

Technical Achievement: Acme-Dunn Optical Printer

Honorary: Henry Fonda

"Oscar"

In 1928, the Academy of Motion Picture Arts and Sciences began the annual presentation of its awards for motion picture excellence. The "Oscar" was originally sketched by Cedric Gibbons. The statue is 10 inches tall, weighs 7 pounds, and is made of gold plate over bronze. When Margaret Harrick, the Academy's first executive director, saw the statue, she remarked that it looked like her Uncle Oscar. The nickname stuck, and today the "Oscar" is the most important and sought after of film awards.

Actor	Supporting Actress	Supporting Actor	
Gregory Peck, *To Kill a Mockingbird*	Patty Duke, *The Miracle Worker*	Ed Begley, *Sweet Bird of Youth*	1962
Sidney Poitier, *Lilies of the Field*	Margaret Rutherford, *The V.I.P.s*	Melvyn Douglas, *Hud*	1963
Rex Harrison, *My Fair Lady*	Lila Kedrova, *Zorba the Greek*	Peter Ustinov, *Topkapi*	1964
Lee Marvin, *Cat Ballou*	Shelley Winters, *A Patch of Blue*	Martin Balsam, *A Thousand Clowns*	1965
Paul Scofield, *A Man for All Seasons*	Sandy Dennis, *Who's Afraid of Virginia Woolf?*	Walter Matthau, *The Fortune Cookie*	1966
Rod Steiger, *In the Heat of the Night*	Estelle Parsons, *Bonnie and Clyde*	George Kennedy, *Cool Hand Luke*	1967
Cliff Robertson, *Charly*	Ruth Gordon, *Rosemary's Baby*	Jack Albertson, *The Subject Was Roses*	1968
John Wayne, *True Grit*	Goldie Hawn, *Cactus Flower*	Gig Young, *They Shoot Horses, Don't They?*	1969
George C. Scott, *Patton*	Helen Hayes, *Airport*	John Mills, *Ryan's Daughter*	1970
Gene Hackman, *The French Connection*	Cloris Leachman, *The Last Picture Show*	Ben Johnson, *The Last Picture Show*	1971
Marlon Brando, *The Godfather*	Eileen Heckart, *Butterflies Are Free*	Joel Grey, *Cabaret*	1972
Jack Lemmon, *Save the Tiger*	Tatum O'Neal, *Paper Moon*	John Houseman, *The Paper Chase*	1973
Art Carney, *Harry and Tonto*	Ingrid Bergman, *Murder on the Orient Express*	Robert De Niro, *The Godfather, Part II*	1974
Jack Nicholson, *One Flew Over the Cuckoo's Nest*	Lee Grant, *Shampoo*	George Burns, *The Sunshine Boys*	1975
Peter Finch, *Network*	Beatrice Straight, *Network*	Jason Robards, *All the President's Men*	1976
Richard Dreyfuss, *The Goodbye Girl*	Vanessa Redgrave, *Julia*	Jason Robards, *Julia*	1977
Jon Voight, *Coming Home*	Maggie Smith, *California Suite*	Christopher Walken, *The Deer Hunter*	1978
Dustin Hoffman, *Kramer vs. Kramer*	Meryl Streep, *Kramer vs. Kramer*	Melvyn Douglas, *Being There*	1979
Robert De Niro, *Raging Bull*	Mary Steenburgen, *Melvin and Howard*	Timothy Hutton, *Ordinary People*	1980

Major American Book Awards, 1981

Established by Association of American Publishers

Fiction: *Plains Song,* by Wright Morris (Harper & Row)

First novel: *Sister Wolf,* by Ann Arensberg (Alfred A. Knopf)

General nonfiction: *China Men,* by Maxine Hong Kingston (Alfred A. Knopf)

History: *Christianity, Social Tolerance and Homosexuality,* by John Boswell (University of Chicago)

Biography/Autobiography: *Walt Whitman,* by Justin Kaplan (Simon & Schuster)

Science: *The Panda's Thumb,* by Stephen Jay Gould (W.W. Norton)

Poetry: *The Need to Hold Still,* by Lisel Mueller (Louisiana State University)

Translation: Francis Steegmuller for *The Letters of Gustave Flaubert, 1830–1857* (Belknap Press of Harvard University) and John E. Wood for *Evening Edged in Gold,* by Arno Schmidt (Harcourt Brace Jovanovich)

Children's fiction: *The Night Swimmers,* by Betsy Byars (Delacorte Press)

Children's nonfiction: *Oh, Boy! Babies,* by Alison Cragin Herzig and Jane Lawrence Mali (Little, Brown)

Book design, pictorial: *In China,* photographed by Eve Arnold; designed by R.D. Scudellari (Alfred A. Knopf)

Book design typographical: *Saul Bellow, Drumlin Woodchuck,* Richard Hendel (University of Georgia)

Book illustration: *The Lost Museum,* by Robert M. Adams; designed by Michael Shroyer (Viking Press Studio Book)

Jacket design: *In China,* R.D. Scudellari (Alfred A. Knopf)

National Medal for Literature: Kenneth Burke

Pulitzer Prize Awards

(For years not listed, no award was made.)

Source: Columbia University.

Pulitzer Prizes in Journalism

MERITORIOUS PUBLIC SERVICE

1918 *New York Times;* also special award to Minna Lewinson and Henry Beetle Hough
1919 *Milwaukee Journal*
1921 *Boston Post*
1922 *New York World*
1923 *Memphis Commercial Appeal*
1924 *New York World*
1926 *Columbus* (Ga.) *Enquirer Sun*
1927 *Canton* (Ohio) *Daily News*
1928 *Indianapolis Times*
1929 *New York Evening World*
1931 *Atlanta Constitution*
1932 *Indianapolis News*
1933 *New York World-Telegram*
1934 *Medford* (Ore.) *Mail Tribune*
1935 *Sacramento Bee*
1936 *Cedar Rapids* (Iowa) *Gazette*
1937 *St. Louis Post-Dispatch*
1938 *Bismarck* (N.D.) *Tribune*
1939 *Miami Daily News*
1940 *Waterbury* (Conn.) *Republican* and *American*
1941 *St. Louis Post-Dispatch*
1942 *Los Angeles Times*
1943 *Omaha World-Herald*
1944 *New York Times*
1945 *Detroit Free Press*
1946 *Scranton* (Pa.) *Times*
1947 *Baltimore Sun*
1948 *St. Louis Post-Dispatch*
1949 *(Lincoln) Nebraska State Journal*
1950 *Chicago Daily News;* and *St. Louis Post-Dispatch*
1951 *Miami Herald;* and *Brooklyn Eagle*
1952 *St. Louis Post-Dispatch*
1953 *Whiteville* (N.C.) *News Reporter;* and *Tabor City* (N.C.) *Tribune*
1954 *Newsday* (Garden City, L.I.)
1955 *Columbus* (Ga.) *Ledger* and *Sunday Ledger-Enquirer*
1956 *Watsonville* (Calif.) *Register-Pajaronian*
1957 *Chicago Daily News*
1958 *(Little Rock) Arkansas Gazette*
1959 *Utica* (N.Y.) *Observer Dispatch* and *Utica Daily Press*
1960 *Los Angeles Times*
1961 *Amarillo* (Tex.) *Globe-Times*
1962 *Panama City* (Fla.) *News-Herald*
1963 *Chicago Daily News*
1964 *St. Petersburg* (Fla.) *Times*
1965 *Hutchinson* (Kan.) *News*
1966 *Boston Globe*
1967 *Louisville Courier-Journal* and *Milwaukee Journal*
1968 *Riverside* (Calif.) *Press-Enterprise*
1969 *Los Angeles Times*
1970 *Newsday* (Garden City, L.I.)
1971 *Winston-Salem* (N.C.) *Journal and Sentinel*
1972 *New York Times*
1973 *Washington Post*
1974 *Newsday* (Garden City, L.I.)
1975 *Boston Globe*
1976 *Anchorage* (Alaska) *Daily News*
1977 *Lufkin* (Tex.) *News*
1978 *Philadelphia Inquirer*
1979 *Point Reyes* (Calif.) *Light*
1980 *Boston Globe*
1981 *Charlotte* (N.C.) *Observer*

EDITORIAL

1917 *New York Tribune*
1918 *Louisville Courier-Journal*
1920 Harvey E. Newbranch *(Omaha Evening World-Herald)*
1922 Frank M. O'Brien *(New York Herald)*
1923 William Allen White *(Emporia* [Kan.] *Gazette)*
1924 *Boston Herald* (Frank Buxton); special prize: Frank I. Cobb *(New York World)*
1925 *Charleston* (S.C.) *News and Courier*
1926 *New York Times* (Edward M. Kingsbury)
1927 *Boston Herald* (F. Lauriston Bullard)
1928 Grover Cleveland Hall *(Montgomery* [Ala.] *Advertiser)*
1929 Louis Isaac Jaffe *(Norfolk Virginian-Pilot)*
1931 Charles S. Ryckman *(Fremont* [Neb.] *Tribune)*
1933 *Kansas City* (Mo.) *Star*
1934 E. P. Chase *(Atlantic* [Iowa] *News Telegraph)*
1936 Felix Morley *(Washington Post);* George B. Parker (Scripps-Howard Newspapers)
1937 John W. Owens *(Baltimore Sun)*
1938 W. W. Waymack *(Des Moines Register and Tribune)*
1939 Ronald G. Callvert *(Portland Oregonian)*
1940 Bart Howard *(St. Louis Post-Dispatch)*
1941 Reuben Maury *(New York Daily News)*
1942 Geoffrey Parsons *(New York Herald Tribune)*
1943 Forrest W. Seymour *(Des Moines Register and Tribune)*
1944 *Kansas City* (Mo.) *Star* (Henry J. Haskell)
1945 George W. Potter *(Providence* [R.I.] *Journal-Bulletin)*
1946 Hodding Carter *([Greenville, Miss.] Delta Democrat-Times)*
1947 William H. Grimes *(Wall Street Journal)*
1948 Virginius Dabney *(Richmond Times-Dispatch)*
1949 John H. Crider *(Boston Herald);* Herbert Elliston *(Washington Post)*
1950 Carl M. Saunders *(Jackson* [Mich.] *Citizen Patriot)*
1951 William H. Fitzpatrick *(New Orleans States)*
1952 Louis LaCoss *(St. Louis Globe-Democrat)*
1953 Vermont C. Royster *(Wall Street Journal)*
1954 *Boston Herald* (Don Murray)
1955 *Detroit Free Press* (Royce Howes)
1956 Lauren K. Soth *(Des Moines Register and Tribune)*
1957 Buford Boone *Tuscaloosa* ([Ala.] *News)*
1958 Harry S. Ashmore *(Arkansas Gazette)*
1959 Ralph McGill *(Atlanta Constitution)*
1960 Lenoir Chambers *(Virginian-Pilot)*
1961 William J. Dorvillier *(San Juan* [P.R.] *Star)*
1962 Thomas M. Storke *(Santa Barbara* [Calif.] *News-Press)*
1963 Ira B. Harkey, Jr. *(Pascagoula* [Miss.] *Chronicle)*
1964 Hazel Brannon Smith *(Lexington* [Miss.] *Advertiser)*
1965 John R. Harrison *(Gainesville* [Fla.] *Daily Sun)*

1966 Robert Lasch (St. Louis Post-Dispatch)
1967 Eugene Patterson (Atlanta Constitution)
1968 John S. Knight (Knight Newspapers)
1969 Paul Greenberg (Pine Bluff [Ark.] Commercial)
1970 Philip L. Geyelin (Washington Post)
1971 Horance G. Davis, Jr. (Gainesville [Fla.] Sun)
1972 John Strohmeyer (Bethlehem [Pa.] Globe Times)
1973 Roger Bourne Linscott (Berkshire Eagle [Pittsfield, Mass.])
1974 F. Gilman Spencer (Trenton [N.J.] Trentonian)
1975 John Daniell Maurice (Charleston [W. Va] Daily Mail)
1976 Philip P. Kerby (Los Angeles Times)
1977 Warren L. Lerude, Foster Church and Norman F. Cardoza (Reno [Nev.] Gazette and Nevada State Journal)
1978 Meg Greenfield (Washington Post)
1979 Edwin M. Yoder, Jr. (Washington Star)
1980 Robert L. Bartley (Wall Street Journal)
1981 Not awarded

CORRESPONDENCE

1929 Paul Scott Mowrer (Chicago Daily News)
1930 Leland Stowe (New York Herald Tribune)
1931 H. R. Knickerbocker (Philadelphia Public Ledger and New York Evening Post)
1932 Walter Duranty (New York Times); Charles G. Ross (St. Louis Post-Dispatch)
1933 Edgar Ansel Mowrer (Chicago Daily News)
1934 Frederick T. Birchall (New York Times)
1935 Arthur Krock (New York Times)
1936 Wilfred C. Barber (Chicago Tribune)
1937 Anne O'Hare McCormick (New York Times)
1938 Arthur Krock (New York Times)
1939 Louis P. Lochner (Associated Press)
1940 Otto D. Tolischus (New York Times)
1941 Group award[1]
1942 Carlos P. Romulo (Philippines Herald)
1943 Hanson W. Baldwin (New York Times)
1944 Ernie Pyle (Scripps-Howard Newspaper Alliance)
1945 Harold V. (Hal) Boyle (Associated Press)
1946 Arnaldo Cortesi (New York Times)
1947 Brooks Atkinson (New York Times)
1948 Discontinued

CARTOON

1922 Rollin Kirby (New York World)
1924 Jay Norwood Darling (New York Tribune)
1925 Rollin Kirby (New York World)
1926 D. R. Fitzpatrick (St. Louis Post-Dispatch)
1927 Nelson Harding (Brooklyn Eagle)
1928 Nelson Harding (Brooklyn Eagle)
1929 Rollin Kirby (New York World)
1930 Charles R. Macauley (Brooklyn Eagle)
1931 Edmund Duffy (Baltimore Sun)
1932 John T. McCutcheon (Chicago Tribune)
1933 H. M. Talburt (Washington Daily News)
1934 Edmund Duffy (Baltimore Sun)
1935 Ross A. Lewis (Milwaukee Journal)
1937 C. D. Batchelor (New York Daily News)
1938 Vaughn Shoemaker (Chicago Daily News)
1939 Charles G. Werner (Daily Oklahoman [Oklahoma City])
1940 Edmund Duffy (Baltimore Sun)
1941 Jacob Burck (Chicago Times)
1942 Herbert L. Block (NEA Service)
1943 Jay Norwood Darling (New York Herald Tribune)

1. For the public services and the individual achievements of American news reporters in the war zones.

1944 Clifford K. Berryman (Washington Evening Star)
1945 Bill Mauldin (United Features Syndicate)
1946 Bruce Alexander Russell (Los Angeles Times)
1947 Vaughn Shoemaker (Chicago Daily News)
1948 Reuben L. Goldberg (New York Sun)
1949 Lute Pease (Newark Evening News)
1950 James T. Berryman (Washington Evening Star)
1951 Reg (Reginald W.) Manning (Arizona Republic [Phoenix])
1952 Fred L. Packer (New York Mirror)
1953 Edward D. Kuekes (Cleveland Plain Dealer)
1954 Herbert L. Block (Washington Post and Times-Herald)
1955 Daniel R. Fitzpatrick (St. Louis Post-Dispatch)
1956 Robert York (Louisville Times)
1957 Tom Little (Nashville Tennessean)
1958 Bruce M. Shanks (Buffalo Evening News)
1959 Bill Mauldin (St. Louis Post-Dispatch)
1961 Carey Orr (Chicago Tribune)
1962 Edmund S. Valtman (Hartford Times)
1963 Frank Miller (Des Moines Register)
1964 Paul Conrad (formerly of Denver Post, later on Los Angeles Times)
1966 Don Wright (Miami News)
1967 Patrick B. Oliphant (Denver Post)
1968 Eugene Gray Payne (Charlotte [N.C.] Observer)
1969 John Fischetti (Chicago Daily News)
1970 Thomas F. Darcy (Newsday [Garden City, L.I.])
1971 Paul Conrad (Los Angeles Times)
1972 Jeffrey K. MacNelly (Richmond [Va.] News Leader)
1974 Paul Szep (Boston Globe)
1975 Garry Trudeau (Universal Press Syndicate)
1976 Tony Auth (Philadelphia Inquirer)
1977 Paul Szep (Boston Globe)
1978 Jeffrey K. MacNelly (Richmond [Va.] News Leader)
1979 Herbert L. Block (Washington Post)
1980 Don Wright (Miami News)
1981 Mike Peters (Dayton [Ohio] Daily News)

NEWS PHOTOGRAPHY

1942 Milton Brooks (Detroit News)
1943 Frank Noel (Associated Press)
1944 Frank Filan (Associated Press); Earle L. Bunker (Omaha World-Herald)
1945 Joe Rosenthal (Associated Press)
1947 Arnold Hardy
1948 Frank Cushing (Boston Traveler)
1949 Nat Fein (New York Herald Tribune)
1950 Bill Crouch (Oakland Tribune)
1951 Max Desfor (Associated Press)
1952 John Robinson and Don Ultang (Des Moines Register & Tribune)
1953 William M. Gallagher (Flint [Mich.] Journal)
1954 Mrs. Walter M. Schau
1955 John L. Gaunt, Jr. (Los Angeles Times)
1956 New York Daily News
1957 Harry A. Trask (Boston Traveler)
1958 William C. Beall (Washington Daily News)
1959 William Seaman (Minneapolis Star)
1960 Andrew Lopez (United Press International)
1961 Yasushi Nagao (Mainichi Newspapers, Tokyo)
1962 Paul Vathis (Harrisburg [Pa.] bureau of Associated Press)
1963 Hector Rondon (La Republica, Caracas, Venezuela)
1964 Robert H. Jackson (Dallas Times Herald)
1965 Horst Faas (Associated Press)

1966 Kyoichi Sawada (United Press International)
1967 Jack R. Thornell (Associated Press)
1968 News: Rocco Morabito *(Jacksonville* [Fla.] *Journal);* features: Toshio Sakai (United Press International)
1969 Spot news: Edward T. Adams (Associated Press); features: Moneta Sleet, Jr.
1970 Spot news: Steve Starr (Associated Press); features: Dallas Kinney *(Palm Beach Post)*
1971 Spot news: John Paul Filo *(Valley Daily News and Daily Dispatch* [Tarentum and New Kensington, Pa.]); features: Jack Dykinga *(Chicago Sun-Times)*
1972 Spot news: Horst Faas and Michel Laurent (Associated Press); features: Dave Kennerly (United Press International)
1973 Spot News: Huynh Cong Ut *(Associated Press);* features: Brian Lanker *(Topeka Capital-Journal)*
1974 Spot news: Anthony K. Roberts (Associated Press); features: Slava Veder (Associated Press)
1975 Spot news: Gerald H. Gay *(Seattle Times);* features: Matthew Lewis *(Washington Post)*
1976 Spot news: Stanley J. Forman *(Boston Herald-American);* features: photographic staff of *Louisville Courier-Journal* and *Times)*
1977 Spot news: Neal Ulevich (Associated Press) and Stanley J. Forman *(Boston Herald-American);* features: Robin Hood *(Chattanooga News-Free Press)*
1978 Spot news: John Blair, freelance, Evansville, Ind.; features: J. Ross Baughman (Associated Press)
1979 Spot news: Thomas J. Kelly, 3rd *(Pottstown* [Pa.] *Mercury);* features: photographic staff of *Boston Herald American*
1980 Features: Erwin H. Hagler *(Dallas Times Herald)*
1981 Spot news: Larry C. Price *(Fort Worth Star-Telegram);* features: Taro M. Yamasaki *(Detroit Free Press)*

NATIONAL TELEGRAPHIC REPORTING

1942 Louis Stark *(New York Times)*
1944 Dewey L. Fleming *(Baltimore Sun)*
1945 James Reston *(New York Times)*
1946 Edward A. Harris *(St. Louis Post-Dispatch)*
1947 Edward T. Folliard *(Washington Post)*

NATIONAL REPORTING

1948 Bert Andrews *(New York Herald Tribune);* Nat S. Finney *(Minneapolis Tribune)*
1949 C. P. Trussel *(New York Times)*
1950 Edwin O. Guthman *(Seattle Times)*
1952 Anthony Leviero *(New York Times)*
1953 Don Whitehead (Associated Press)
1954 Richard Wilson (Cowles Newspapers)
1955 Anthony Lewis *(Washington Daily News)*
1956 Charles L. Bartlett *(Chattanooga Times)*
1957 James Reston *(New York Times)*
1958 Relman Morin (Associated Press) and Clark Mollenhoff *(Des Moines Register & Tribune)*
1959 Howard Van Smith *(Miami News)*
1960 Vance Trimble (Scripps-Howard Newspaper Alliance)
1961 Edward R. Cony *(Wall Street Journal)*
1962 Nathan G. Caldwell and Gene S. Graham *(Nashville Tennessean)*
1963 Anthony Lewis *(New York Times)*
1964 Merriman Smith (United Press International)
1965 Louis M. Kohlmeier *(Wall Street Journal)*
1966 Haynes Johnson *(Washington Evening Star)*
1967 Stanley Penn and Monroe Karmin *(Wall Street Journal)*

1968 Howard James *(Christian Science Monitor);* Nathan K. (Nick) Kotz *(Des Moines Register* and *Minneapolis Tribune)*
1969 Robert Cahn *(Christian Science Monitor)*
1970 William J. Eaton *(Chicago Daily News)*
1971 Lucinda Franks and Thomas Powers (United Press International)
1972 Jack Anderson *(United Feature Syndicate)*
1973 Robert Boyd and Clark Hoyt *(Knight Newspapers)*
1974 Jack White *(Providence* [R.I.] *Journal-Bulletin);* and James R. Polk *(Washington Star-News)*
1975 Donald L. Barlett and James B. Steele *(Philadelphia Inquirer)*
1976 James Risser *(Des Moines Register)*
1977 Walter Mears (Associated Press)
1978 Gaylord D. Shaw *(Los Angeles Times)*
1979 James Risser *(Des Moines Register)*
1980 Bette Swenson Orsini and Charles Stafford *(St. Petersburg Times)*
1981 John M. Crewdson *(New York Times)*

INTERNATIONAL TELEGRAPHIC REPORTING

1942 Laurence Edmund Allen (Associated Press)
1943 Ira Wolfert (North American Newspaper Alliance, Inc.)
1944 Daniel De Luce (Associated Press)
1945 Mark S. Watson *(Baltimore Sun)*
1946 Homer W. Bigart *(New York Herald Tribune)*
1947 Eddy Gilmore (Associated Press)

INTERNATIONAL REPORTING

1948 Paul W. Ward *(Baltimore Sun)*
1949 Price Day *(Baltimore Sun)*
1950 Edmund Stevens *(Christian Science Monitor)*
1951 Keyes Beech and Fred Sparks *(Chicago Daily News);* Homer Bigart and Marguerite Higgins *(New York Herald Tribune);* Relman Morin and Don Whitehead (Associated Press)
1952 John M. Hightower (Associated Press)
1953 Austin C. Wehrwein *(Milwaukee Journal)*
1954 Jim G. Lucas (Scripps-Howard Newspapers)
1955 Harrison E. Salisbury *(New York Times)*
1956 William Randolph Hearst, Jr., and Frank Conniff (Hearst newspapers) and Kingsbury Smith (INS)
1957 Russell Jones (United Press)
1958 *New York Times*
1959 Joseph Martin and Philip Santora *(New York Daily News)*
1960 A. M. Rosenthal *(New York Times)*
1961 Lynn Heinzerling (Associated Press)
1962 Walter Lippmann (New York Herald Tribune Syndicate)
1963 Hal Hendrix *(Miami News)*
1964 Malcolm W. Browne (Associated Press) and David Halberstam *(New York Times)*
1965 J. A. Livingston *(Philadelphia Bulletin)*
1966 Peter Arnett (Associated Press)
1967 R. John Hughes *(Christian Science Monitor)*
1968 Alfred Friendly *(Washington Post)*
1969 William Tuohy *(Los Angeles Times)*
1970 Seymour M. Hersh (Dispatch News Service)
1971 Jimmie Lee Hoagland *(Washington Post)*
1972 Peter R. Kann *(Wall Street Journal)*
1973 Max Frankel *(New York Times)*
1974 Hedrick Smith *(New York Times)*
1975 William Mullen and Ovie Carter *(Chicago Tribune)*
1976 Sydney H. Schanberg *(New York Times)*
1978 Henry Kamm *(New York Times)*

1979 Richard Ben Cramer *(Philadelphia Inquirer)*
1980 Joel Brinkley and Jay Mather *(Louisville Courier-Journal)*
1981 Shirley Christian *(Miami Herald)*

REPORTING

1917 Herbert B. Swope *(New York World)*
1918 Harold A. Littledale *(New York Evening Post)*
1920 John J. Leary, Jr. *(New York World)*
1921 Louis Seibold *(New York World)*
1922 Kirke L. Simpson (Associated Press)
1923 Alva Johnston *(New York Times)*
1924 Magner White *(San Diego Sun)*
1925 James W. Mulroy and Alvin H. Goldstein *(Chicago Daily News)*
1926 William Burke Miller *(Louisville Courier-Journal)*
1927 John T. Rogers *(St. Louis Post-Dispatch)*
1929 Paul Y. Anderson *(St. Louis Post-Dispatch)*
1930 Russell D. Owen *(New York Times)*; special award: W. O. Dapping *(Auburn* [N.Y.] *Citizen)*
1931 A. B. MacDonald *(Kansas City* [Mo.] *Star)*
1932 W. C. Richards, D. D. Martin, J. S. Pooler, F. D. Webb, J. N. W. Sloan (all of *Detroit Free Press)*
1933 Francis A. Jamieson (Associated Press)
1934 Royce Brier *(San Francisco Chronicle)*
1935 William H. Taylor *(New York Herald Tribune)*
1936 Lauren D. Lyman *(New York Times)*
1937 John J. O'Neill *(New York Herald Tribune)*, William Leonard Laurence *(New York Times)*, Howard W. Blakeslee (Associated Press), Gobind Behari Lal (Universal Service), David Dietz (Scripps-Howard Newspapers)
1938 Raymond Sprigle *(Pittsburg Post-Gazette)*
1939 Thomas L. Stokes *(New York World-Telegram)*
1940 S. Burton Heath *(New York World-Telegram)*
1941 Westbrook Pegler *(New York World-Telegram)*
1942 Stanton Delaplane *(San Francisco Chronicle)*
1943 George Weller *(Chicago Daily News)*
1944 Paul Schoenstein and associates *(New York Journal-American)*
1945 Jack S. McDowell *(San Francisco Call-Bulletin)*
1946 William Leonard Laurence *(New York Times)*
1947 Frederick Woltman *(New York World-Telegram)*
1948 George E. Goodwin *(Atlanta Journal)*
1949 Malcolm Johnson *(New York Sun)*
1950 Meyer Berger *(New York Times)*
1951 Edward S. Montgomery *(San Francisco Examiner)*
1952 George de Carvalho *(San Francisco Chronicle)*
1953 Editorial staff *(Providence Journal and Evening Bulletin)*;[1] Edward J. Mowery *(New York World-Telegram and Sun)*[2]
1954 *Vicksburg* (Miss.) *Sunday Post-Herald*;[1] Alvin Scott McCoy *(Kansas City* [Mo.] *Star)*[2]
1955 Mrs. Caro Brown *(Alice* [Tex.] *Daily Echo)*;[1] Roland Kenneth Towery *(Cuero* [Tex.] *Record)*[2]
1956 Lee Hills *(Detroit Free Press)*;[1] Arthur Daley *(New York Times)*[2]
1957 *Salt Lake Tribune*;[1] Wallace Turner and William Lambert *(Portland Oregonian)*[2]
1958 *Fargo* [N.D.] *Forum*;[1] George Beveridge *(Washington* [D.C.] *Evening Star)*[2]
1959 Mary Lou Werner *(Washington* [D.C.] *Evening*

1. Reporting under pressure of edition deadlines. 2. Reporting not under pressure of edition deadlines.

Star);[1] John Harold Brislin *(Scranton* [Pa.] *Tribune & Scrantonian)*[2]
1960 Jack Nelson *(Atlanta Constitution)*;[1] Miriam Ottenberg *(Washington Evening Star)*[2]
1961 Sanche de Gramont *(New York Herald Tribune)*;[1] Edgar May *(Buffalo Evening News)*[2]
1962 Robert D. Mullins *(Deseret News,* Salt Lake City);[1] George Bliss *(Chicago Tribune)*[2]
1963 Sylvan Fox, Anthony Shannon, and William Longgood *(New York World-Telegram and Sun)*;[1] Oscar Griffin, Jr. (former editor of *Pecos* [Tex.] *Independent and Enterprise,* now on staff of *Houston Chronicle)*[2]

GENERAL LOCAL REPORTING

1964 Norman C. Miller *(Wall Street Journal)*
1965 Melvin H. Ruder *(Hungry Horse News,* Columbia Falls, Mont.)
1966 Staff of *Los Angeles Times*
1967 Robert V. Cox *(Chambersburg* [Pa.] *Public Opinion)*
1968 Staff of *Detroit Free Press*
1969 John Fetterman *(Louisville Times* and *Courier-Journal)*
1970 Thomas Fitzpatrick *(Chicago Sun-Times)*
1971 Staff of *Akron* (Ohio) *Beacon*
1972 Richard Cooper and John Machacek *(Rochester* [N.Y.] *Times-Union)*
1973 *Chicago Tribune*
1974 Arthur M. Petacque and Hugh F. Hough *(Chicago Sun-Times)*
1975 *Xenia* (Ohio) *Daily Gazette*
1976 Gene Miller *(Miami Herald)*
1977 Margo Huston *(Milwaukee Journal)*
1978 Richard Whitt *(Louisville Courier-Journal)*
1979 Staff of *San Diego* (Calif.) *Evening Tribune*
1980 Staff of *Philadelphia Inquirer*
1981 *Longview* (Wash.) *Daily News*

SPECIAL LOCAL REPORTING

1964 James V. Magee, Albert V. Gaudiosi, and Frederick A. Meyer *(Philadelphia Bulletin)*
1965 Gene Goltz *(Houston Post)*
1966 John A. Frasca *(Tampa Tribune)*
1967 Gene Miller *(Miami Herald)*
1968 J. Anthony Lukas *(New York Times)*
1969 Albert L. Delugach and Denny Walsh *(St. Louis Globe-Democrat)*
1970 Harold Eugene Martin *(Montgomery Advertiser)*
1971 William Hugh Jones *(Chicago Tribune)*
1972 Timothy Leland, Gerard N. O'Neill, Stephen A. Kurkjian, and Ann DeSantis *(Boston Globe)*
1973 Sun Newspapers of Omaha, Neb.
1974 William Sherman *(New York Daily News)*
1975 *Indianapolis Star*
1976 *Chicago Tribune*
1977 Acel Moore and Wendell Rawls, Jr. *(Philadelphia Inquirer)*
1978 Anthony R. Dolan *(Stamford* [Conn.] *Advocate)*
1979 Gilbert M. Gaul and Elliot G. Jaspin *(Pottsville* Pa. *Republican)*
1980 Nils J. Bruzelius, Alexander B. Hawes, Jr., Stephen A. Kurkjian, and Joan Vennochi *(Boston Globe)*
1981 Clark Hallas and Robert B. Lowe *(Arizona Daily Star,* Tucson)

FEATURE WRITING

1979 Jon D. Franklin *(Baltimore Evening Sun)*

1980 Madeleine Blais *(Miami Herald)*
1981 Teresa Carpenter (*Village Voice*, New York)

COMMENTARY

1970 Marquis W. Childs *(St. Louis Post-Dispatch)*
1971 William A. Caldwell (*Record* [Hackensack, N.J.])
1972 Mike Royko *(Chicago Daily News)*
1973 David S. Broder *(Washington Post)*
1974 Edwin A. Roberts, Jr. *(National Observer)*
1975 Mary McGrory *(Washington Star)*
1976 Walter W. (Red) Smith *(New York Times)*
1977 George F. Will (*Washington Post* Writers Group)
1978 William Safire *(New York Times)*
1979 Russell Baker *(New York Times)*
1980 Ellen H. Goodman *(Boston Globe)*
1981 Dave Anderson *(New York Times)*

CRITICISM

1970 Ada Louise Huxtable *(New York Times)*
1971 Harold C. Schonberg *(New York Times)*
1972 Frank Peters, Jr. *(St. Louis Post-Dispatch)*
1973 Ronald Powers *(Chicago Sun-Times)*
1974 Emily Genauer (Newsday Syndicate)
1975 Roger Ebert *(Chicago Sun-Times)*
1976 Alan M. Kriegsman *(Washington Post)*
1977 William McPherson *(Washington Post)*
1978 Walter Kerr *(New York Times)*
1979 Paul Gapp *(Chicago Tribune)*
1980 William A. Henry 3rd *(Boston Globe)*
1981 Jonathan Yardley *(Washington Star)*

SPECIAL CITATIONS

1938 Edmonton (Alberta) *Journal,* special bronze plaque for editorial leadership in defense of freedom of press in Province of Alberta.
1941 *New York Times* for the public educational value of its foreign news report.
1944 Byron Price, Director of the Office of Censorship, for the creation and administration of the newspaper and radio codes. Mrs. William Allen White, for her husband's interest and services during the past seven years as a member of the Advisory Board of the Graduate School of Journalism, Columbia University. Richard

Rodgers and Oscar Hammerstein II for their musical *Oklahoma!*
1945 The cartographers of the American press for their war maps.
1947 (Pulitzer centennial year.) Columbia University and the Graduate School of Journalism, for their efforts to maintain and advance the high standards governing the Pulitzer Prize awards. The *St. Louis Post-Dispatch,* for its unswerving adherence to the public and professional ideals of its founder and its leadership in American journalism.
1948 Dr. Frank D. Fackenthal, for his interest and service.
1951 Cyrus L. Sulzberger *(New York Times)* for his exclusive interview with Archbishop Stepinac in a Yugoslav prison.
1952 *Kansas City Star* for coverage of 1951 floods; Max Kase *(New York Journal-American)* for exposures of bribery in college basketball.
1953 *New York Times* for its 17-year publication of "News of the Week in Review"; and Lester Markel, its founder.
1957 Kenneth Roberts for his historical novels.
1958 Walter Lippmann *(New York Herald Tribune)* for his "wisdom, perception and high sense of responsibility" in his commentary on national and international affairs.
1960 Garrett Mattingly, for *The Armada.*
1961 *American Heritage Picture History of the Civil War,* as distinguished example of American book publishing.
1964 Gannett Newspapers, Rochester, N.Y.
1973 James Thomas Flexner for his biography *George Washington.*
1974 Roger Sessions, for his "life's work in music."
1976 John Hohenberg for "services for 22 years as administrator of the Pulitzer Prizes." Scott Joplin for his contributions to American music.
1977 Alex Haley for his novel, *Roots*
1978 E.B.White of *New Yorker* magazine and Richard L. Strout of *Christian Science Monitor*

Pulitzer Prizes in Letters

FICTION[1]

1918 *His Family.* Ernest Poole
1919 *The Magnificent Ambersons.* Booth Tarkington
1921 *The Age of Innocence.* Edith Wharton
1922 *Alice Adams.* Booth Tarkington
1923 *One of Ours.* Willa Cather
1924 *The Able McLaughlins.* Margaret Wilson
1925 *So Big.* Edna Ferber
1926 *Arrowsmith.* Sinclair Lewis
1927 *Early Autumn.* Louis Bromfield
1928 *The Bridge of San Luis Rey.* Thornton Wilder
1929 *Scarlet Sister Mary.* Julia Peterkin
1930 *Laughing Boy.* Oliver La Farge
1931 *Years of Grace.* Margaret Ayer Barnes
1932 *The Good Earth.* Pearl S. Buck
1933 *The Store.* T. S. Stribling
1934 *Lamb in His Bosom.* Caroline Miller
1935 *Now in November.* Josephine Winslow Johnson
1936 *Honey in the Horn.* Harold L. Davis

1. Before 1948, award was for novels only.

1937 *Gone with the Wind.* Margaret Mitchell
1938 *The Late George Apley.* John Phillips Marquand
1939 *The Yearling.* Marjorie Kinnan Rawlings
1940 *The Grapes of Wrath.* John Steinbeck
1942 *In This Our Life.* Ellen Glasgow
1943 *Dragon's Teeth.* Upton Sinclair
1944 *Journey in the Dark.* Martin Flavin
1945 *A Bell for Adano.* John Hersey
1947 *All the King's Men.* Robert Penn Warren
1948 *Tales of the South Pacific.* James A. Michener
1949 *Guard of Honor.* James Gould Cozzens
1950 *The Way West.* A. B. Guthrie, Jr.
1951 *The Town.* Conrad Richter
1952 *The Caine Mutiny.* Herman Wouk
1953 *The Old Man and the Sea.* Ernest Hemingway
1955 *A Fable.* William Faulkner
1956 *Andersonville.* MacKinlay Kantor
1958 *A Death in the Family.* James Agee
1959 *The Travels of Jaimie McPheeters.* Robert

Lewis Taylor

1960 *Advise and Consent.* Allen Drury
1961 *To Kill a Mockingbird.* Harper Lee
1962 *The Edge of Sadness.* Edwin O'Connor
1963 *The Reivers.* William Faulkner
1965 *The Keepers of the House.* Shirley Ann Grau
1966 *Collected Stories of Katherine Anne Porter.* Katherine Anne Porter
1967 *The Fixer.* Bernard Malamud
1968 *The Confessions of Nat Turner.* William Styron
1969 *House Made of Dawn.* N. Scott Momaday
1970 *Collected Stories.* Jean Stafford
1972 *Angle of Repose.* Wallace Stegner
1973 *The Optimist's Daughter.* Eudora Welty
1975 *The Killer Angels.* Michael Shaara
1976 *Humboldt's Gift.* Saul Bellow
1978 *Elbow Room.* James Alan McPherson
1979 *The Stories of John Cheever.* John Cheever
1980 *The Executioner's Song.* Norman Mailer
1981 *A Confederacy of Dunces.* John Kennedy Toole

DRAMA

1918 *Why Marry?* Jesse Lynch Williams
1920 *Beyond the Horizon.* Eugene O'Neill
1921 *Miss Lulu Bett.* Zona Gale
1922 *Anna Christie.* Eugene O'Neill
1923 *Icebound.* Owen Davis
1924 *Hell-Bent Fer Heaven.* Hatcher Hughes
1925 *They Knew What They Wanted.* Sidney Howard
1926 *Craig's Wife.* George Kelly
1927 *In Abraham's Bosom.* Paul Green
1928 *Strange Interlude.* Eugene O'Neill
1929 *Street Scene.* Elmer L. Rice
1930 *The Green Pastures.* Marc Connelly
1931 *Alison's House.* Susan Glaspell
1932 *Of Thee I Sing.* George S. Kaufman, Morrie Ryskind, and Ira Gershwin
1933 *Both Your Houses.* Maxwell Anderson
1934 *Men in White.* Sidney Kingsley
1935 *The Old Maid.* Zöe Akins
1936 *Idiot's Delight.* Robert E. Sherwood
1937 *You Can't Take It with You.* Moss Hart and George S. Kaufman
1938 *Our Town.* Thornton Wilder
1939 *Abe Lincoln in Illinois.* Robert E. Sherwood
1940 *The Time of Your Life.* William Saroyan
1941 *There Shall Be No Night.* Robert E. Sherwood
1943 *The Skin of Our Teeth.* Thornton Wilder
1945 *Harvey.* Mary Chase
1946 *State of the Union.* Russel Crouse and Howard Lindsay
1948 *A Streetcar Named Desire.* Tennessee Williams
1949 *Death of a Salesman.* Arthur Miller
1950 *South Pacific.* Richard Rodgers, Oscar Hammerstein II, and Joshua Logan
1952 *The Shrike.* Joseph Kramm
1953 *Picnic.* By William Inge
1954 *The Teahouse of the August Moon.* John Patrick
1955 *Cat on a Hot Tin Roof.* Tennessee Williams
1956 *The Diary of Anne Frank.* Frances Goodrich and Albert Hackett
1957 *Long Day's Journey Into Night.* Eugene O'Neill
1958 *Look Homeward, Angel.* Ketti Frings
1959 *J.B.* Archibald MacLeish
1960 *Fiorello!* George Abbott, Jerome Weidman, Jerry Bock, and Sheldon Harnick
1961 *All the Way Home.* Tad Mosel
1962 *How to Succeed in Business Without Really*

Trying. Frank Loesser and Abe Burrows
1965 *The Subject Was Roses.* Frank D. Gilroy
1967 *A Delicate Balance.* Edward Albee
1969 *The Great White Hope.* Howard Sackler
1970 *No Place to Be Somebody.* Charles Gordone
1971 *The Effect of Gamma Rays on Man-in-the-Moon Marigolds.* Paul Zindel
1973 *That Championship Season.* Jason Miller
1975 *Seascape.* Edward Albee
1976 *A Chorus Line.* Conceived by Michael Bennett
1977 *The Shadow Box.* Michael Cristofer
1978 *The Gin Game.* Donald L. Coburn
1979 *Buried Child.* Sam Shepard
1980 *Talley's Folly.* Lanford Wilson
1981 *Crimes of the Heart.* Beth Henley

HISTORY OF UNITED STATES

1917 *With Americans of Past and Present Days.* J. J. Jusserand, Ambassador of France to United States
1918 *A History of the Civil War, 1861–1865.* James Ford Rhodes
1920 *The War with Mexico.* Justin H. Smith
1921 *The Victory at Sea.* William Sowden Sims in collaboration with Burton J. Hendrick
1922 *The Founding of New England.* James Truslow Adams
1923 *The Supreme Court in United States History.* Charles Warren
1924 *The American Revolution—A Constitutional Interpretation.* Charles Howard McIlwain
1925 *A History of the American Frontier.* Frederic L. Paxson
1926 *The History of the United States.* Edward Channing
1927 *Pinckney's Treaty.* Samuel Flagg Bemis
1928 *Main Currents in American Thought.* Vernon Louis Parrington
1929 *The Organization and Administration of the Union Army, 1861–1865.* Fred Albert Shannon
1930 *The War of Independence.* Claude H. Van Tyne
1931 *The Coming of the War: 1914.* Bernadotte E. Schmitt
1932 *My Experiences in the World War.* John J. Pershing
1933 *The Significance of Sections in American History.* Frederick J. Turner
1934 *The People's Choice.* Herbert Agar
1935 *The Colonial Period of American History.* Charles McLean Andrews
1936 *The Constitutional History of the United States.* Andrew C. McLaughlin
1937 *The Flowering of New England.* Van Wyck Brooks
1938 *The Road to Reunion, 1865–1900.* Paul Herman Buck
1939 *A History of American Magazines.* Frank Luther Mott
1940 *Abraham Lincoln: The War Years.* Carl Sandburg
1941 *The Atlantic Migration, 1607–1860.* Marcus Lee Hansen
1942 *Reveille in Washington.* Margaret Leech
1943 *Paul Revere and the World He Lived In.* Esther Forbes
1944 *The Growth of American Thought.* Merle Curti
1945 *Unfinished Business.* Stephen Bonsal
1946 *The Age of Jackson.* Arthur M. Schlesinger, Jr.

1947	*Scientists Against Time.* James Phinney Baxter, 3rd
1948	*Across the Wide Missouri.* Bernard DeVoto
1949	*The Disruption of American Democracy.* Roy Franklin Nichols
1950	*Art and Life in America.* Oliver W. Larkin
1951	*The Old Northwest, Pioneer Period 1815–1840.* R. Carlyle Buley
1952	*The Uprooted.* Oscar Handlin
1953	*The Era of Good Feelings.* George Dangerfield
1954	*A Stillness at Appomattox.* Bruce Catton
1955	*Great River: The Rio Grande in North American History.* Paul Horgan
1956	*The Age of Reform.* Richard Hofstadter
1957	*Russia Leaves the War: Soviet-American Relations, 1917–1920.* George F. Kennan
1958	*Banks and Politics in America: From the Revolution to the Civil War.* Bray Hammond
1959	*The Republican Era: 1869–1901.* Leonard D. White, assisted by Jean Schneider
1960	*In the Days of McKinley.* Margaret Leech
1961	*Between War and Peace: The Potsdam Conference.* Herbert Feis
1962	*The Triumphant Empire, Thunder-Clouds Gather in the West.* Lawrence H. Gipson
1963	*Washington, Village and Capital, 1800–1878.* Constance McLaughlin Green
1964	*Puritan Village: The Formation of a New England Town.* Sumner Chilton Powell
1965	*The Greenback Era.* Irwin Unger
1966	*Life of the Mind in America.* Perry Miller
1967	*Exploration and Empire: The Explorer and Scientist in the Winning of the American West.* William H. Goetzmann
1968	*The Ideological Origins of the American Revolution.* Bernard Bailyn
1969	*Origins of the Fifth Amendment.* Leonard W. Levy
1970	*Present at the Creation: My Years in the State Department.* Dean Acheson
1971	*Roosevelt: The Soldier of Freedom.* James McGregor Burns
1972	*Neither Black Nor White. Slavery and Race Relations in Brazil and the United States.* Carl N. Degler
1973	*People of Paradox: An Inquiry Concerning the Origin of American Civilization.* Michael Kammen
1974	*The Americans: The Democratic Experience, Vol. 3.* Daniel J. Boorstin
1975	*Jefferson and His Time.* Dumas Malone
1976	*Lamy of Santa Fe.* Paul Horgan
1977	*The Impending Crisis: 1841–1861.* David M. Potter (posth)
1978	*The Invisible Hand: The Managerial Revolution in American Business.* Alfred D. Chandler Jr.
1979	*The Dred Scott Case: Its Significance in Law and Politics.* Don E. Fehrenbacher
1980	*Been in the Storm So Long.* Leon F. Litwack
1981	*American Education: The National Experience 1783–1876.* Lawrence A. Cremin

BIOGRAPHY OR AUTOBIOGRAPHY

1917	*Julia Ward Howe.* Laura E. Richards and Maude Howe Elliott, assisted by Florence Howe Hall
1918	*Benjamin Franklin, Self-Revealed.* William Cabell Bruce
1919	*The Education of Henry Adams.* Henry Adams
1920	*The Life of John Marshall.* Albert J. Beveridge
1921	*The Americanization of Edward Bok.* Edward Bok
1922	*A Daughter of the Middle Border.* Hamlin Garland
1923	*The Life and Letters of Walter H. Page.* Burton J. Hendrick
1924	*From Immigrant to Inventor.* Michael Idvorsky Pupin
1925	*Barrett Wendell and His Letters.* M. A. DeWolfe Howe
1926	*The Life of Sir William Osler.* Harvey Cushing
1927	*Whitman.* Emory Holloway
1928	*The American Orchestra and Theodore Thomas.* Charles Edward Russell
1929	*The Training of an American. The Earlier Life and Letters of Walter H. Page.* Burton J. Hendrick
1930	*The Raven.* Marquis James
1931	*Charles W. Eliot.* Henry James
1932	*Theodore Roosevelt.* Henry F. Pringle
1933	*Grover Cleveland.* Allan Nevins
1934	*John Hay.* Tyler Dennett
1935	*R. E. Lee.* Douglas S. Freeman
1936	*The Thought and Character of William James.* Ralph Barton Perry
1937	*Hamilton Fish.* Allan Nevins
1938	*Pedlar's Progress.* Odell Shepard. *Andrew Jackson.* Marquis James
1939	*Benjamin Franklin.* Carl Van Doren
1940	*Woodrow Wilson. Life and Letters,* Vols. VII and VIII. Ray Stannard Baker
1941	*Jonathan Edwards.* Ola E. Winslow
1942	*Crusader in Crinoline.* Forrest Wilson
1943	*Admiral of the Ocean Sea.* Samuel Eliot Morison
1944	*The American Leonardo: The Life of Samuel F. B. Morse.* Carleton Mabee
1945	*George Bancroft: Brahmin Rebel.* Russel Blaine Nye
1946	*Son of the Wilderness.* Linnie Marsh Wolfe
1947	*The Autobiography of William Allen White*
1948	*Forgotten First Citizen: John Bigelow.* Margaret Clapp
1949	*Roosevelt and Hopkins.* Robert E. Sherwood
1950	*John Quincy Adams and the Foundations of American Foreign Policy.* Samuel Flagg Bemis
1951	*John C. Calhoun: American Portrait.* Margaret Louise Coit
1952	*Charles Evans Hughes.* Merlo J. Pusey
1953	*Edmund Pendleton 1721–1803.* David J. Mays
1954	*The Spirit of St. Louis.* Charles A. Lindbergh
1955	*The Taft Story.* William S. White
1956	*Benjamin Henry Latrobe.* Talbot F. Hamlin
1957	*Profiles in Courage.* John F. Kennedy
1958	*George Washington.* Douglas Southall Freeman (Vols. 1–6) and John Alexander Carroll and Mary Wells Ashworth (Vol. 7)
1959	*Woodrow Wilson, American Prophet.* Arthur Walworth
1960	*John Paul Jones.* Samuel Eliot Morison
1961	*Charles Sumner and the Coming of the Civil War.* David Donald
1963	*Henry James: Vol. II, The Conquest of London, 1870–1881; Vol. III, The Middle Years, 1881–1895.* Leon Edel
1964	*John Keats.* Walter Jackson Bate
1965	*Henry Adams* (3 vols.). Ernest Samuels
1966	*A Thousand Days.* Arthur M. Schlesinger, Jr.
1967	*Mr. Clemens and Mark Twain.* Justin Kaplan
1968	*Memoirs, 1925–1950.* George F. Kennan
1969	*The Man from New York.* B. L. Reid
1970	*Huey Long.* T. Harry Williams

1971 *Robert Frost: The Years of Triumph, 1915–1938.* Lawrance Thompson
1972 *Eleanor and Franklin: The Story of Their Relationship Based on Eleanor Roosevelt's Private Papers.* Joseph P. Lash
1973 *Luce and His Empire.* W. A. Swanberg
1974 *O'Neill, Son and Artist.* Louis Sheaffer
1975 *The Power Broker: Robert Moses and the Fall of New York.* Robert A. Caro
1976 *Edith Wharton: A Biography.* Richard W. B. Lewis
1977 *A Prince of Our Disorder.* John E. Mack
1978 *Samuel Johnson.* Walter Jackson Bate
1979 *Days of Sorrow and Pain: Leo Baeck and the Berlin Jews.* Leonard Baker
1980 *The Rise of Theodore Roosevelt.* Edmund Morris
1981 *Peter the Great.* Robert K. Massie

POETRY[1]

1918 *Love Songs.* Sara Teasdale
1919 *Old Road to Paradise.* Margaret Widdemer; *Corn Huskers.* Carl Sandburg
1922 *Collected Poems.* Edwin Arlington Robinson
1923 *The Ballad of the Harp-Weaver; A Few Figs from Thistles;* eight sonnets in *American Poetry, 1922, A Miscellany.* Edna St. Vincent Millay
1924 *New Hampshire: A Poem with Notes and Grace Notes.* Robert Frost
1925 *The Man Who Died Twice.* Edwin Arlington Robinson
1926 *What's O'Clock.* Amy Lowell
1927 *Fiddler's Farewell.* Leonora Speyer
1928 *Tristram.* Edwin Arlington Robinson
1929 *John Brown's Body.* Stephen Vincent Benét
1930 *Selected Poems.* Conrad Aiken
1931 *Collected Poems.* Robert Frost
1932 *The Flowering Stone.* George Dillon
1933 *Conquistador.* Archibald MacLeish
1934 *Collected Verse.* Robert Hillyer
1935 *Bright Ambush.* Audrey Wurdemann
1936 *Strange Holiness.* Robert P. T. Coffin
1937 *A Further Range.* Robert Frost
1938 *Cold Morning Sky.* Marya Zaturenska
1939 *Selected Poems.* John Gould Fletcher
1940 *Collected Poems.* Mark Van Doren
1941 *Sunderland Capture.* Leonard Bacon
1942 *The Dust Which Is God.* William Rose Benét
1943 *A Witness Tree.* Robert Frost
1944 *Western Star.* Stephen Vincent Benét
1945 *V-Letter and Other Poems.* Karl Shapiro
1947 *Lord Weary's Castle.* Robert Lowell
1948 *The Age of Anxiety.* W. H. Auden
1949 *Terror and Decorum.* Peter Viereck
1950 *Annie Allen.* Gwendolyn Brooks
1951 *Complete Poems.* Carl Sandburg
1952 *Collected Poems.* Marianne Moore
1953 *Collected Poems 1917–1952.* Archibald MacLeish
1954 *The Waking.* Theodore Roethke
1955 *Collected Poems.* Wallace Stevens
1956 *Poems—North & South.* Elizabeth Bishop
1957 *Things of This World.* Richard Wilbur
1958 *Promises: Poems 1954–1956.* Robert Penn Warren
1959 *Selected Poems, 1928–1958.* Stanley Kunitz
1960 *Heart's Needle.* William Snodgrass
1961 *Times Three: Selected Verse from Three Decades.* Phyllis McGinley

1. This prize was established in 1922. The 1918 and 1919 awards were made from gifts provided by the Poetry Society.

1962 *Poems.* Alan Dugan
1963 *Pictures from Breughel.* William Carlos Williams
1964 *At the End of the Open Road.* Louis Simpson
1965 *77 Dream Songs.* John Berryman
1966 *Selected Poems.* Richard Eberhart
1967 *Live or Die.* Anne Sexton
1968 *The Hard Hours.* Anthony Hecht
1969 *Of Being Numerous.* George Oppen
1970 *Untitled Subjects.* Richard Howard
1971 *The Carrier of Ladders.* William S. Merwin
1972 *Collected Poems.* James Wright
1973 *Up Country.* Maxine Winokur Kumin
1974 *The Dolphin.* Robert Lowell
1975 *Turtle Island.* Gary Snyder
1976 *Self-Portrait in a Convex Mirror.* John Ashbery
1977 *Divine Comedies.* James Merrill
1978 *Collected Poems.* Howard Nemerov: *Poems 1976–1978.*
1979 *Now and Then* Robert Penn Warren.
1980 *Selected Poems.* Donald Rodney Justice
1981 *The Morning of the Poem.* James Schuyler

GENERAL NONFICTION

1962 *The Making of the President 1960.* Theodore H. White
1963 *The Guns of August.* Barbara W. Tuchman
1964 *Anti-intellectualism in American Life.* Richard Hofstadter
1965 *O Strange New World.* Howard Mumford Jones
1966 *Wandering Through Winter.* Edwin Way Teale
1967 *The Problem of Slavery in Western Culture.* David Brion Davis
1968 *Rousseau and Revolution.* Will and Ariel Durant
1969 *So Human an Animal.* Rene Jules Dubos *The Armies of the Night.* Norman Mailer
1970 *Gandhi's Truth.* Erik H. Erikson
1971 *The Rising Sun.* John Toland
1972 *Stilwell and the American Experience in China, 1911–1945.* Barbara W. Tuchman
1973 *Fire in the Lake: The Vietnamese and the Americans in Vietnam.* Frances FitzGerald; and *Children of Crisis* (Vols. 1 and 2). Robert M. Coles
1974 *The Denial of Death.* Ernest Becker
1975 *Pilgrim at Tinker Creek.* Annie Dillard
1976 *Why Survive? Being Old in America.* Robert N. Butler
1977 *Beautiful Swimmers: Watermen, Crabs and the Chesapeake Bay.* William W. Warner
1978 *The Dragons of Eden.* Carl Sagan
1979 *On Human Nature.* Edward O. Wilson
1980 *Gödel, Escher, Bach: An Eternal Golden Braid.* Douglas R. Hofstadter
1981 *Fin-de-Siècle Vienna: Politics and Culture.* Carl E. Schorske

Pulitzer Prizes in Music

1943 *Secular Cantata No. 2, A Free Song.* William Schuman
1944 *Symphony No. 4* (Op. 34). Howard Hanson
1945 *Appalachian Spring.* Aaron Copland
1946 *The Canticle of the Sun.* Leo Sowerby
1947 *Symphony No. 3.* Charles Ives
1948 *Symphony No. 3.* Walter Piston
1949 *Louisiana Story* music. Virgil Thomson
1950 *The Consul.* Gian Carlo Menotti

1951 Music for opera *Giants in the Earth*. Douglas Stuart Moore
1952 *Symphony Concertante*. Gail Kubik
1954 *Concerto for Two Pianos and Orchestra.* Quincy Porter
1955 *The Saint of Bleecker Street*. Gian Carlo Menotti
1956 *Symphony No. 3*. Ernst Toch
1957 *Meditations on Ecclesiastes*. Norman Dello Joio
1958 *Vanessa*. Samuel Barber
1959 *Concerto for Piano and Orchestra*. John La Montaine
1960 *Second String Quartet*. Elliott Carter
1961 *Symphony No. 7*. Walter Piston
1962 *The Crucible*. Robert Ward
1963 *Piano Concerto No. 1*. Samuel Barber
1966 *Variations for Orchestra*. Leslie Bassett
1967 *Quartet No. 3*. Leon Kirchner
1968 *Echoes of Time and the River*. George Crumb

1969 *String Quartet No. 3*. Karel Husa
1970 *Time's Encomium*. Charles Wuorinen
1971 *Synchronisms No. 6 for Piano and Electronic Sound*. Mario Davidowsky
1972 *Windows*. Jacob Druckman
1973 *String Quartet No. 3*. Elliott Carter
1974 *Notturno*. Donald Martino
1975 *From the Diary of Virginia Woolf*. Dominick Argento
1976 *Air Music*. Ned Rorem
1977 *Visions of Terror and Wonder*. Richard Wernick
1978 *Déjà Vu for Percussion Quartet and Orchestra*. Michael Colgrass
1979 *Aftertones of Infinity*. Joseph Schwantner
1980 *In Memory of a Summer Day*. David Del Tredici
1981 Not awarded

Antoinette Perry (Tony) Awards, 1981

Dramatic play: *Amadeus*, by Peter Shaffer
Musical: *42nd Street*
Actor (play): Ian McKellen, *Amadeus*
Actress (play): Jane Lapotaire, *Piaf*
Actor (musical): Kevin Kline, *The Pirates of Penzance*
Actress (musical): Lauren Bacall, *Woman of the Year*
Actor, featured (play): Brian Backer, *The Floating Light Bulb*
Actress, featured (play): Swoosie Kurtz, *Fifth of July*
Actor, featured (musical): Hinton Battle, *Sophisticated Ladies*
Actress, featured (musical): Marilyn Cooper, *Woman of the Year*

Director (play): Peter Hall, *Amadeus*
Director (musical): Wilford Leach, *The Pirates of Penzance*
Score: John Kander and Fred Ebb, *Woman of the Year*
Musical book: Peter Stone, *Woman of the Year*
Choreography: Gower Champion, *42nd Street*
Scenic design: John Bury, *Amadeus*
Costumes: Willa Kim, *Sophisticated Ladies*
Lighting: John Bury, *Amadeus*
Special Awards: Lena Horne and Trinity Square Repertory Company of Providence, R.I.

Sigma Delta Chi Journalism Awards, 1980

General reporting: News staff of *Longview* (Wash.) *Daily News*
Editorial writing: Louis J. Salome, William Hallstrom, and Betsy Poller, *Miami News*
Washington correspondence: Joseph Albright, Cox Newspapers
Foreign correspondence: Edward Girardet, *Christian Science Monitor*
News photography: Giovanni Foggia, Associated Press
Editorial cartoon: Paul Conrad, *Los Angeles Times*
Public service in newspaper journalism: *Long Beach* (Calif.) *Independent* and *Press-Telegram*

Magazine reporting: Penny Lernoux, *The Nation*
Public service in magazine journalism: *Philadelphia Magazine*
Radio reporting: WHDH News, Boston
Public service in radio journalism: WIND, Chicago
Editorializing on radio: Lesley Crosson, WEEI, Boston
Television reporting: Bill Blakemore and Greg Dobbs, ABC
Public service in television journalism: KSL, Salt Lake City
Editorializing on television: Bill Moyers, WNET, New York
Research about journalism: John Lofton, St. Louis

Enrico Fermi Award

Named in honor of Enrico Fermi, the atomic pioneer, the $25,000 award is given in recognition of "exceptional and altogether outstanding" scientific and technical achievement in atomic energy.

1954	Enrico Fermi	1963	J. Robert Oppenheimer	1971	Shields Warren and Stafford L. Warren
1956	John von Neumann	1964	Hyman G. Rickover		
1957	Ernest O. Lawrence	1966	Otto Hahn, Lise Meitner, and Fritz Strassman	1972	Manson Benedict
1958	Eugene P. Wigner			1976	William L. Russell
1959	Glenn T. Seaborg	1968	John A. Wheeler	1978	Harold M. Agnew and Wolfgang K. H. Panofsky
1961	Hans A. Bethe	1969	Walter H. Zinn		
1962	Edward Teller	1970	Norris E. Bradbury		

New York Drama Critics' Circle Awards

1935–36
Winterset, Maxwell Anderson
1936–37
High Tor, Maxwell Anderson
1937–38
Of Mice and Men, John Steinbeck
Shadow and Substance, Paul Vincent Carroll[1]
1938–39
(No award) *The White Steed*, Paul Vincent Carroll[1]
1939–40
The Time of Your Life, William Saroyan
1940–41
Watch on the Rhine, Lillian Hellman
The Corn Is Green, Emlyn Williams[1]
1941–42
(No award) *Blithe Spirit*, Noel Coward[1]
1942–43
The Patriots, Sidney Kingsley
1943–44
(No award) *Jacobowsky and the Colonel*. Franz Werfel and S. N. Behrman[1]
1944–45
The Glass Menagerie, Tennessee Williams
1945–46
(No award) *Carousel*, Richard Rodgers and Oscar Hammerstein II[2]
1946–47
All My Sons, Arthur Miller
No Exit, Jean-Paul Sartre[1]
Brigadoon, Alan Jay Lerner and Frederick Loewe[2]
1947–48
A Streetcar Named Desire, Tennessee Williams
The Winslow Boy, Terence Rattigan[1]
1948–49
Death of a Salesman, Arthur Miller
The Madwoman of Chaillot, Jean Giraudoux and Maurice Valency[1]
South Pacific, Richard Rodgers, Oscar Hammerstein II, and Joshua Logan[2]
1949–50
The Member of the Wedding, Carson McCullers
The Cocktail Party, T. S. Eliot[1]
The Consul, Gian Carlo Menotti[2]
1950–51
Darkness at Noon, Sidney Kingsley[3]
The Lady's Not for Burning, Christopher Fry[1]
Guys and Dolls, Abe Burrows, Jo Swerling and Frank Loesser[2]
1951–52
I Am a Camera, John Van Druten[4]
Venus Observed, Christopher Fry[1]
Pal Joey, Richard Rodgers, Lorenz Hart, and John O'Hara[2]
Don Juan in Hell, George B. Shaw[5]
1952–53
Picnic, William Inge
The Love of Four Colonels, by Peter Ustinov[1]
Wonderful Town, Joseph Fields, Jerome Chodorov, Betty Comden, Adolph Green, and Leonard Bernstein[2]
1953–54
The Teahouse of the August Moon, John Patrick
Ondine, Jean Giraudoux[1]
The Golden Apple, John Latouche and Jerome Moross[2]
1954–55
Cat on a Hot Tin Roof, Tennessee Williams
Witness for the Prosecution, Agatha Christie[1]
The Saint of Bleecker Street, Gian Carlo Menotti[2]

1955–56
The Diary of Anne Frank, Frances Goodrich and Albert Hackett
Tiger at the Gates, Jean Giraudoux and Christopher Fry[1]
My Fair Lady, Frederick Loewe and Alan Jay Lerner[2]
1956–57
Long Day's Journey Into Night, Eugene O'Neill
Waltz of the Toreadors, Jean Anouilh[1]
The Most Happy Fella, Frank Loesser[2] [6]
1957–58
Look Homeward, Angel, Ketti Frings[7]
Look Back in Anger, John Osborne[1]
The Music Man, Meredith Willson[2]
1958–59
A Raisin in the Sun, Lorraine Hansberry
The Visit, Friedrich Duerrenmatt–Maurice Valency[1]
La Plume de ma Tante, Robert Dhery and Gerard Calvi[2]
1959–60
Toys in the Attic, Lillian Hellman
Five Finger Exercise, Peter Shaffer[1]
Fiorello!, Jerome Weidman, George Abbott, Jerry Bock, and Sheldon Harnick[2]
1960–61
All the Way Home, Tad Mosel[8]
A Taste of Honey, Shelagh Delaney[1]
Carnival, Michael Stewart[2]
1961–62
The Night of the Iguana, Tennessee Williams
A Man for All Seasons, Robert Bolt[1]
How to Succeed in Business Without Really Trying, Abe Burrows, Jack Weinstock, Willie Gilbert, and Frank Loesser[2] [9]
1962–63
Who's Afraid of Virginia Woolf?, Edward Albee
Beyond the Fringe, Alan Bennett, Peter Cook, Jonathan Miller, and Dudley Moore[10]
1963–64
Luther, John Osborne
Hello, Dolly!, Michael Stewart and Jerry Herman[2] [11]
The Trojan Women, Euripides[10] [12]
1964–65
The Subject Was Roses, Frank D. Gilroy
Fiddler on the Roof, Joseph Stein, Jerry Bock, and Sheldon Harnick[2] [13]
1965–66
The Persecution and Assassination of Marat as Performed by the Inmates of the Asylum of Charenton under the Direction of the Marquis de Sade, Peter Weiss
The Man of La Mancha, Dale Wasserman, Mitch Leigh, and Joe Darion
1966–67
The Homecoming, Harold Pinter
Cabaret, Joe Masteroff, John Kander, and Fred Ebb[2] [14]
1967–68
Rosencrantz and Guildenstern Are Dead, Tom Stoppard
Your Own Thing, Donald Driver, Hal Hester, and Danny Apolinar[2]
1968–69
The Great White Hope, Howard Sackler
1776, Sherman Edwards and Peter Stone[2]
1969–70
Borstal Boy, Frank McMahon[15]
The Effect of Gamma Rays on Man-in-the-Moon Marigolds, Paul Zindel[16]

Company, George Furth and Stephen Sondheim[2]
1970–71
Home, David Storey
The House of Blue Leaves, John Guare[16]
Follies, James Goldman and Stephen Sondheim[2]
1971–72
That Championship Season, Jason Miller
Two Gentlemen of Verona, adapted by John Guare and Mel Shapiro[2]
The Screens, Jean Genet[1]
1972–73
The Changing Room, David Storey
The Hot l Baltimore, by Lanford Wilson[16]
A Little Night Music, Hugh Wheeler and Stephen Sondheim[2]
1973–74
The Contractors, David Storey
Short Eyes, Miguel Piñero[16]
Candide, Leonard Bernstein, Hugh Wheeler, and Richard Wilbur[2]
1974–75
Equus, Peter Shaffer
The Taking of Miss Janie, Ed Bullins[16]
A Chorus Line, James Kirkwood and Nicholas Dante[2]
1975–76
Travesties, Tom Stoppard
Streamers, David Rabe[16]
Pacific Overtures, Stephen Sondheim, John Weidman, and Hugh Wheeler[2]
1976–77
Otherwise Engaged, Simon Gray

American Buffalo, David Mamet[16]
Annie, Thomas Meehan, Charles Strouse, and Martin Charnin[2]
1977–78
Da, Hugh Leonard
Ain't Misbehavin', conceived by Richard Maltby, Jr.[2]
1978–79
The Elephant Man, Bernard Pomerance
Sweeney Todd, Hugh Wheeler and Stephen Sondheim[2]
1979–80
Talley's Folly, Lanford Wilson
Evita,[2] Andrew Lloyd Webber and Tim Rice
Betrayal, Harold Pinter[1]
1980–81
A Lesson From Aloes, Athol Fugard
Crimes of the Heart, Beth Henley[16]

1. Citation for best foreign play. 2. Citation for best musical. 3. Based on a novel by Arthur Koestler. 4. Based on Christopher Isherwood's *Berlin Stories.* 5. For "distinguished and original contribution to the theater." 6. Based on Sidney Howard's *They Knew What They Wanted.* 7. Based on a novel by Thomas Wolfe. 8. Based on James Agee's *A Death in the Family.* 9. Based on a book by Shepherd Mead. 10. Special citation. 11. Based on Thornton Wilder's *The Matchmaker.* 12. Translated by Edith Hamilton. 13. Based on Sholem Aleichem's Tevye stories, translated by Arnold Perl. 14. Based on John Van Druten's *I Am a Camera,* which won the award for the best play in 1951–52. 15. Based on Brendan Behan's autobiography. 16. Citation for best American play.

American Library Association Awards for Children's Books, 1981

John Newbery Medal for best book: *Jacob Have I Loved,* by Katherine Paterson (Thomas Y. Crowell)
Newbery Honor Books: *The Fledgling,* by Jane Langton (Harper & Row); *A Ring of Endless Light,* by Madeleine L'Engle (Farrar, Straus & Giroux)
Randolph Caldecott Medal for best picture book: *Fables,* by Arnold Lobel (Harper & Row)

Caldecott Honor Books: *Truck,* by Donald Crews (Greenwillow Books/William Morrow); *The Grey Lady and the Strawberry Snatcher,* by Molly Bang (Four Winds Press); *Mice Twice,* by Joseph Low (Margaret McElderry Book/Atheneum); *The Bremen-Town Musicians,* by Ilse Plume (Doubleday)

George Foster Peabody Awards for Broadcasting, 1980

Radio
NBC: *The Hallelujah Caucus*
Minnesota Public Radio: *A Prairie Home Companion*
WNCN, New York: Overall station performance as exemplified by *Conversations With Horowitz*
National Public Radio: *Jazz Alive!*
Canadian Broadcasting Corporation: *Peniel,* from Hornby Collection series; and *The Wonderful World of Science*
San Francisco Opera: San Francisco Opera broadcasts
WFMT, Chicago: Studs Terkel

Television
CBS News: Walter Cronkite and *Universe*
WTVJ, Miami, Fla.: Mary Nissenson for *Poland: Changing Nation*
CBS Entertainment: *Gideon's Trumpet* and *Playing for Time*
NBC and Paramount Television: *Shogun*
Broadcasting magazine: Sol Taishoff, editor
Public Broadcasting Service: Robert Geller for *The American Short Story*

ABC: *IBM Presents Baryshnikov on Broadway* and *Amber Waves*
WCPO, Cincinnati: Elaine Green for *Hoskins Interview*
British Broadcasting Corporation: *All Creatures Great and Small*
CBS: Carroll O'Connor for *Edith's Death* episode of *Archie Bunker's Place*
KCET, Los Angeles: Adrian Malone and Carl Sagan for *Cosmos*
Maryland Instructional Television: *Terra: Our World*
WQED, Pittsburgh and National Geographic Society: *Mysteries of the Mind, The Superliners, Twilight of an Era, The Invisible World* and other specials
KTEH, San Jose, Calif: Carol Mon Pere and Sandra Nichols for *The Battle of Westlands*
NBC: Phil Donahue: *The Phil Donahue Show*
KQED, San Francisco: *Broken Arrow: Can a Nuclear Weapons Accident Happen Here?*
KUED, Salt Lake City, Utah; and WNET, New York: *The MX Debate,* a special edition of *Bill Moyers' Journal*

Presidential Medal of Freedom

The nation's highest civilian award, the Presidential Medal of Freedom, was established in 1963 by President John F. Kennedy to continue and expand Presidential recognition of meritorious service which, since 1945, had been granted as the Medal of Freedom. NOTE: An asterisk following a year denotes a posthumous award.

AWARDED BY PRESIDENT KENNEDY

Marian Anderson (contralto)	1963
Ralph J. Bunche (statesman)	1963
Ellsworth Bunker (diplomat)	1963
Pablo Casals (cellist)	1963
Genevieve Caulfield (educator)	1963
James B. Conant (educator)	1963
John F. Enders (bacteriologist)	1963
Felix Frankfurter (jurist)	1963
Karl Horton (youth authority)	1963
John XXIII (Pope)	1963*
Robert J. Kiphuth (athletic director)	1963
Edwin H. Land (inventor)	1963
Herbert H. Lehman (statesman)	1963*
Robert A. Lovett (statesman)	1963
J. Clifford MacDonald (educator)	1963*
John J. McCloy (banker and statesman)	1963
George Meany (labor leader)	1963
Alexander Meiklejohn (philosopher)	1963
Ludwig Mies van der Rohe (architect)	1963
Jean Monnet (European statesman)	1963
Luis Muñoz-Marín (Governor of Puerto Rico)	1963
Clarence B. Randall (industrialist)	1963
Rudolf Serkin (pianist)	1963
Edward Steichen (photographer)	1963
George W. Taylor (educator)	1963
Alan T. Waterman (scientist)	1963
Mark S. Watson (journalist)	1963
Annie D. Wauneka (public health worker)	1963
E. B. White (author)	1963
Thornton N. Wilder (author)	1963
Edmund Wilson (author and critic)	1963
Andrew Wyeth (artist)	1963

AWARDED BY PRESIDENT JOHNSON

Dean G. Acheson (statesman)	1964
Eugene R. Black (banker)	1969
Detlev W. Bronk (neurophysiologist)	1964
McGeorge Bundy (government service)	1969
Ellsworth Bunker (diplomat)	1968
Clark Clifford (statesman)	1969
Aaron Copland (composer)	1964
Michael E. DeBakey (surgeon)	1969
Willem de Kooning (artist)	1964
Walt Disney (cartoon film producer)	1964
J. Frank Dobie (author)	1964
David Dubinsky (labor leader)	1969
Lena F. Edwards (physician and humanitarian)	1964
Thomas Stearns Eliot (poet)	1964
Ralph Ellison (author)	1969
Lynn Fontanne (actress)	1964
Henry Ford II (industrialist)	1969
John W. Gardner (educator)	1964
W. Averell Harriman (statesman)	1969
Rev. Theodore M. Hesburgh (educator)	1964
Bob Hope (comedian)	1969
Clarence L. Johnson (aircraft engineer)	1964
Edgar F. Kaiser (industrialist)	1969
Frederick R. Kappel (telecommunications executive)	1964
Helen A. Keller (educator)	1964
John Fitzgerald Kennedy (U.S. President)	1963*
Robert W. Komer (government service)	1968
Mary Lasker (philanthropist)	1969
John L. Lewis (labor leader)	1964
Walter Lippmann (journalist)	1964
Eugene M. Locke (diplomat)	1968
Alfred Lunt (actor)	1964

John W. Macy, Jr. (government service)	1969
Ralph McGill (journalist)	1964
Robert S. McNamara (government service)	1968
Samuel Eliot Morison (historian)	1964
Lewis Mumford (urban planner and critic)	1964
Edward R. Murrow (radio-TV commentator)	1964
Reinhold Niebuhr (theologian)	1964
Gregory Peck (actor)	1969
Leontyne Price (soprano)	1964
A. Philip Randolph (labor leader)	1964
Laurance S. Rockefeller (conservationist)	1969
Walt Whitman Rostow (government service)	1969
Deak Rusk (statesman)	1969
Carl Sandburg (poet and biographer)	1964
Merriman Smith (journalist)	1969
John Steinbeck (author)	1964
Helen B. Taussig (pediatrician)	1964
Cyrus R. Vance (government service)	1969
Carl Vinson (legislator)	1964
Thomas J. Watson, Jr. (industrialist)	1964
James E. Webb (NASA administrator)	1968
Paul Dudley White (physician)	1964
William S. White (journalist)	1969
Roy Wilkins (social welfare executive)	1969
Whitney M. Young, Jr. (social welfare executive)	1969

AWARDED BY PRESIDENT NIXON

Edwin E. Aldrin (astronaut)	1969
Apollo 13 Mission Operations Team	1970
Neil A. Armstrong (astronaut)	1969
Earl Charles Behrens (journalist)	1970
Manlio Brosio (NATO secretary general)	1971
Michael Collins (astronaut)	1969
Edward K. "Duke" Ellington (musician)	1969
Edward T. Folliard (journalist)	1970
John Ford (film director)	1973
Samuel Goldwyn (film producer)	1971
Fred Wallace Haise, Jr. (astronaut)	1970
William M. Henry (journalist)	1970*
Paul G. Hoffman (statesman)	1974
William J. Hopkins (White House service)	1971
Arthur Krock (journalist)	1970
Melvin R. Laird (government service)	1974
David Lawrence (journalist)	1970
George Gould Lincoln (journalist)	1970
James A. Lovell, Jr. (astronaut)	1970
Dr. Charles L. Lowman (orthopedist)	1974
Raymond Moley (journalist)	1970
Eugene Ormandy (conductor)	1970
William P. Rogers (diplomat)	1973
Adela Rogers St. Johns (journalist)	1970
John Leonard Swigert, Jr. (astronaut)	1970
John Paul Vann (adviser, Vietnam war)	1972*
DeWitt and Lila Wallace (founders, Reader's Digest)	1972

AWARDED BY PRESIDENT FORD

I. W. Abel (labor leader)	1977
John Bardeen (physicist)	1977
Irving Berlin (composer)	1977
Norman Borlaug (agricultural scientist)	1977
Omar N. Bradley (national security)	1977
David K. E. Bruce (diplomat)	1976
Arleigh Burke (national security)	1977
Alexander Calder (sculptor)	1977*
Bruce Catton (historian)	1977
Joseph P. DiMaggio (baseball star)	1977

Ariel Durant (author)	1977	Lucia Chase (ballet director)	1980
Will Durant (author)	1977	Warren M. Christopher (government service)	1981
Arthur Fiedler (conductor)	1977	Walter Cronkite (TV newscaster)	1981
Henry J. Friendly (jurist)	1977	Kirk Douglas (actor)	1981
Martha Graham (dancer-choreographer)	1976	Arthur J. Goldberg (government service)	1978
Claudia "Lady Bird" Johnson (service to U.S.		Hubert H. Humphrey (government service)	1980*
scenic beauty)	1977	Archbishop Iakovos (churchman)	1980
Henry A. Kissinger (statesman)	1977	Lyndon B. Johnson (U.S. President)	1980*
Archibald MacLeish (poet)	1977	Rev. Dr. Martin Luther King, Jr. (civil rights leader)	1977*
James A. Michener (author)	1977	Margaret Craig McNamara (educator)	1981
Georgia O'Keeffe (artist)	1977	Margaret Mead (anthropologist)	1979*
Jesse Owens (track champion)	1976	Karl Menninger (psychiatrist)	1981
Nelson A. Rockefeller (government service)	1977	Clarence Mitchell, Jr. (civil rights leader)	1980
Norman Rockwell (illustrator)	1977	Edmund S. Muskie (government service)	1981
Artur Rubinstein (pianist)	1976	Esther Peterson (government service)	1981
Donald H. Rumsfeld (government service)	1977	Roger Tory Peterson (ornithologist)	1980
Katherine Filene Shouse (service to the		Adm. Hyman Rickover (national security)	1980
performing arts)	1977	Jonas Salk (medical research)	1977
Lowell Thomas (radio-TV commentator)	1977	Beverly Sills (opera singer)	1980
James D. Watson (biochemist)	1977	Gerard C. Smith (government service)	1981
		Robert S. Strauss (government service)	1981
AWARDED BY PRESIDENT CARTER		Elbert Parr Tuttle (government service)	1981
Ansel Adams (photographer)	1980	Earl Warren (government service)	1981*
Horace M. Albright (government service)	1980	Robert Penn Warren (author and poet)	1980
Roger Baldwin (civil libertarian)	1981	John Wayne (actor)	1980*
Harold Brown (government service)	1981	Eudora Welty (author)	1980
Zbigniew Brzezinski (government service)	1981	Tennessee Williams (playwright)	1980
Rachel Carson (author)	1980*	Andrew M. Young (government service)	1981

Winners of Bollingen Prize in Poetry

($5,000 award is given biennially. It is administered by Yale University and the Bollingen Foundation.)

1949	Ezra Pound	1961	Yvor Winters
1950	Wallace Stevens	1962	John Hall Wheelock and Richard Eberhart
1951	John Crowe Ransom	1963	Robert Frost
1952	Marianne Moore	1965	Horace Gregory
1953	Archibald MacLeish and William Carlos Williams	1967	Robert Penn Warren
1954	W. H. Auden	1969	John Berryman and Karl Shapiro
1955	Léonie Adams and Louise Bogan	1971	Richard Wilbur and Mona Van Duyn
1956	Conrad Aiken	1973	James Merrill
1957	Allen Tate	1975	Archie Randolph Ammons
1958	E.E. Cummings	1977	David Ignatow
1959	Theodore Roethke	1979	W. S. Merwin
1960	Delmore Schwartz	1981	Howard Nemerov and May Swenson

National Book Critics Circle Awards, 1981

Fiction: *The Transit of Venus*, by Shirley Hazzard (Viking/Penguin)

General nonfiction: *Walter Lippmann and the American Century*, by Ronald Steel (Atlantic/Little, Brown)

Poetry: *Sunrise*, by Frederick Seidel (Viking/Penguin)

Criticism: *Part of Nature, Part of Us: Modern American Poets*, by Helen Vendler (Harvard University Press)

Selected CB 10-Codes

10–1	Receiving poorly	10–21	Call by phone	10–51	Wrecker needed at . . .
10–2	Receiving well	10–23	Stand by	10–52	Ambulance needed at . . .
10–3	Stop transmitting	10–25	Can you contact?	10–53	Road blocked
10–4	OK, message received	10–26	Disregard last information	10–59	Convoy or escort
10–5	Relay message	10–27	I am moving to channel . . .	10–62	Unable to copy, use phone
10–6	Stand by	10–28	Identify your station	10–66	Message cancellation
10–7	Out of service	10–29	I am leaving this location	10–70	Fire at . . .
10–8	In service	10–30	Does not conform to FCC rules	10–73	Speed Trap at . . .
10–9	Repeat message	10–32	Radio check	10–75	You are causing interference
10–10	Transmission completed,	10–33	Emergency traffic at this station	10–77	ETA (estimated time of arrival
	standing by	10–34	Trouble here, help needed	10–82	Reserve lodging
10–11	Speak more slowly	10–36	Correct time is . . .	10–91	Talk closer to mike
10–12	Visitors present	10–39	Your message delivered	10–92	Have your transmitter checked
10–13	Report road conditions, weather	10–44	I have a message for . . .	10–93	Check my frequency
10–17	Urgent business	10–45	All units please report	10–94	Give me a long count
10–20	Location . . .	10–46	Assist motorist	10–200	Police needed at . . .
		10–50	Accident at . . .		

PEOPLE

Many public figures not listed here may be found elsewhere in the *Information Please Almanac.*

675 Governors
583 Presidents
585 Presidents' Wives
606 Senators

801 Sports Personalities
603 Supreme Court Justices
583 Vice Presidents

A name in parentheses is the original name or form of name. Localities are places of birth. Dates of birth appear as day/month/year. **Boldface** years in parentheses are dates of **(birth-death).** Information has been gathered from many sources, including the individuals themselves. However, the *Information Please Almanac* cannot guarantee the accuracy of every individual item.

A

Aalto, Alvar (architect); Kuortane, Finland **(1898–1976)**
Abbott, Bud (William) (comedian); Asbury Park, N.J. **(1898–1974)**
Abbott, George (stage producer); Forestville, N.Y., 6/25/1887
Abel, Walter (actor); St. Paul, 6/6/1898
Abernathy, Ralph (civil rights leader); Linden, Ala., 3/11/1926
Acheson, Dean (statesman); Middletown, Conn. **(1893–1971)**
Acuff, Roy Claxton (musician); nr. Maynardsville, Tenn. 9/15/1903
Adams, Charles Francis (diplomat); Boston **(1807–1886)**
Adams, Don (actor); New York City, 4/19/1927
Adams, Edie (actress); Kingston, Pa., 4/16/1929
Adams, Franklin Pierce (columnist and author); Chicago **(1881–1960)**
Adams, Henry Brooks (historian); Boston **(1838–1918)**
Adams, Joey (comedian); New York City, 1/6/1911
Adams, Maude (Maude Kiskadden) (actress); Salt Lake City, **(1872–1953)**
Adams, Samuel (American Revolutionary patriot); Boston **(1722–1803)**
Adamson, Joy (naturalist); Troppau, Silesia **(1910–1980)**
Addams, Charles (cartoonist); Westfield, N.J., 1/7/1912
Addams, Jane (social worker); Cedarville, Ill. **(1860–1935)**
Adderley, Julian "Cannonball" (jazz saxophonist); Tampa, Fla. **(1928–1975)**
Ade, George (humorist); Kentland, Ind. **(1866–1944)**
Adenauer, Konrad (statesman); Cologne, Germany **(1876–1967)**
Adler, Alfred (psychoanalyst); Vienna **(1870–1937)**
Adler, Larry (musician); Baltimore, 2/10/1914
Adler, Richard (songwriter); New York City, 8/3/1921
Adoree, Renée (Renée La Fonte) (actress); Lille, France **(1898–1933)**
Aeschylus (dramatist); Eleusis (Greece) **(525–456 B.C.)**
Aesop (fabulist); birthplace unknown (lived c. 600 B.C.)
Aherne, Brian (actor); King's Norton, England, 5/2/1902
Aiken, Conrad (poet); Savannah, Ga. **(1889–1973)**
Ailey, Alvin (choreographer); Rogers, Tex., 1/5/1931
Aimée, Anouk (actress); Paris, 4/27/1934
Albanese, Licia (operatic soprano); Bari, Italy, 7/22/1913
Albee, Edward (playwright); Washington, D.C., 3/12/1928
Albers, Josef (painter); Bottrop, Germany **(1888–1976)**
Albert, Eddie (Edward Albert Heimberger) (actor); Rock Island, Ill., 4/22/1908
Albertson, Jack (actor); Malden, Mass., 6/16/1910(?)
Albright, Lola (actress); Akron, Ohio, 7/20/1925
Alcott, Louisa May (novelist); Germantown, Pa. **(1832–1888)**
Alda, Alan (actor); New York City, 1/28/1936
Alda, Robert (Alphonso d'Abruzzo) (actor); New York City, 2/26/1914
Alden, John (American Pilgrim); England **(1599?–1687)**
Alexander the Great (monarch and conqueror); Pella, Macedonia (now Greece) **(356–323 B.C.)**
Alger, Horatio (author); Revere, Mass. **(1834–1899)**
Algren, Nelson (novelist); Detroit **(1909–1981)**
Allen, Ethan (American Revolutionary soldier); Litchfield, Conn. **(1738–1789)**
Allen, Fred (John Florence Sullivan) (comedian); Cambridge, Mass. **(1894–1956)**
Allen, Gracie (Grace Ethel Cecile Rosalie Allen) (comedienne); San Francisco **(1906–1964)**
Allen, Mel (Melvin Israel) (sportscaster); Birmingham, Ala., 2/14/1913
Allen, Steve (TV entertainer); New York City, 12/26/1921
Allen, Woody (Allen Stewart Konigsberg) (actor, writer, and director); Brooklyn, N.Y., 12/1/1935
Allison, Fran (actress); LaPorte City, Iowa, 1924(?)
Allman, Gregg (singer); Nashville, Tenn., 12/8/1947
Allyson, June (Jan Allyson) (actress); New York City, 10/7/1923

Alonso, Alicia (ballerina); Havana, 12/21/1921(?)
Alpert, Herb (band leader); Los Angeles, 3/31/1935(?)
Alsop, Joseph W., Jr. (journalist); Avon, Conn., 10/11/1910
Alsop, Stewart (journalist); Avon, Conn. **(1914–1974)**
Altman, Robert (film director); Kansas City, Mo., 2/20/1925
Ambler, Eric (suspense writer); London, 6/28/1909
Ameche, Don (Dominic Amici) (actor); Kenosha, Wis., 5/31/1908
Amis, Kingsley (novelist); London, 4/16/1922
Amory, Cleveland (writer and conservationist); Nahant, Mass., 9/2/1917
Amos (Freeman F. Gosden) (radio comedian); Richmond, Va., 5/5/1899
Amsterdam, Morey (actor); Chicago, 12/14/1914
Andersen, Hans Christian (author of fairy-tales); Odense, Denmark **(1805–1875)**
Anderson, Eddie. *See* Rochester
Anderson, Jack (journalist); Long Beach, Calif., 10/19/1922
Anderson, Dame Judith (actress); Adelaide, Australia, 2/10/1898
Anderson, Lindsay (Gordon) (director); Bangalore, India, 4/17/1923
Anderson, Lynn (singer); Grand Forks, N.D., 9/26/1947
Anderson, Marian (contralto); Philadelphia, 2/17/1902
Anderson, Maxwell (dramatist); Atlantic, Pa. **(1888–1959)**
Anderson, Robert (playwright); New York City, 4/28/1917
Andersson, Bibi (actress); Stockholm, 11/11/1935
Andress, Ursula (actress); Switzerland, 3/19/1938
Andrews, Dana (actor); Collins, Miss., 1/1/1909
Andrews, Julie (Julia Wells) (actress and singer); Walton-on-Thames, England, 10/1/1935
Andrews, La Verne (singer); Minneapolis **(1916–1967)**
Andrews, Maxene (singer); Minneapolis, 1/3/1918
Andrews, Patti (singer); Minneapolis, 2/16/1920
Andy (Charles J. Correll) (radio comedian); Peoria, Ill. **(1890–1972)**
Angeles, Victoria de los (Victoria Gamez Cima) (operatic soprano); Barcelona, 11/1/1924
Anka, Paul (singer and composer); Ottawa, 7/30/1941
Ann-Margret (Ann-Margret Olsson) (actress); Valsjobyn, Sweden, 4/28/1941
Annabella (actress); Paris, 1912
Anouilh, Jean (playwright); Bordeaux, France, 6/23/1910
Anthony, Susan Brownell (woman suffragist); Adams, Mass. **(1820–1906)**
Antonioni, Michelangelo (director); Ferrara, Italy, 9/29/1912
Antony, Mark (Marcus Antonius) (statesman); Rome **(83?–30 B.C.)**
Anuszkiewicz, Richard (painter); Erie, Pa., 5/23/1930
Aquinas, St. Thomas (philosopher); nr. Aquino (Italy) **(1225? –1274)**
Arbuckle, Roscoe "Fatty" (actor and director); San Jose, Calif. **(1887–1933)**
Archimedes (physicist and mathematician); Syracuse, Sicily **(287?–212 B.C.)**
Archipenko, Alexandre (sculptor); Kiev, Russia **(1887–1964)**
Arden, Elizabeth (Florence Nightingale Graham) (cosmetics executive); Woodbridge, Canada **(1891–1966)**
Arden, Eve (Eunice Quedens) (actress); Mill Valley, Calif., 4/30/1912
Arendt, Hannah (historian); Hannover, Germany **(1906–1975)**
Aristophanes (dramatist); Athens **(448?–38 B.C.)**
Aristotle (philosopher); Stagirus, Macedonia **(384–322 B.C.)**
Arkin, Alan (actor and director); New York City, 3/26/1934
Arledge, Roone (TV executive); Forest Hills, N.Y., 7/8/1931
Arlen, Harold (Hyman Arluck) (composer); Buffalo, N.Y., 2/15/1905
Arlen, Richard (actor); Charlottesville, Va. **(1900–1976)**
Arliss, George (actor); London **(1868–1946)**
Armstrong, Louis "Satchmo" (musician); New Orleans **(1900–1971)**
Armstrong-Jones, Anthony. *See* Snowden, Earl of
Arnaz, Desi (Desiderio) (actor and producer); Santiago, Cuba, 3/2/1917
Arness, James (James Aurness) (TV actor); Minneapolis, 5/26/1923
Arno, Peter (cartoonist); New York City **(1904–1968)**

Arnold, Benedict (American Revolutionary War General, convicted of treason); Norwich, Conn. (1741–1801)

Arnold, Eddy (singer); Henderson, Tenn., 5/15/1918

Arnold, Edward (actor); New York City (1890–1956)

Arnold, Matthew (poet and critic); Laleham, England (1822–1888)

Arp, Jean (sculptor and painter); Strasbourg (France) (1887–1966)

Arquette, Cliff ("Charley Weaver") (actor); Toledo, Ohio (1905–1974)

Arrau, Claudio (pianist); Chillán, Chile, 2/6/1903

Arthur, Bea (Bernice Frankel) (actress); New York City, 5/13/1926(?)

Arthur, Jean (Gladys Greene) (actress); New York City, 10/17/1905

Asch, Sholem (novelist); Kutno, Poland (1880–1957)

Ashkenazy, Vladimir (concert pianist); Gorki, U.S.S.R., 7/6/1937

Ashley, Elizabeth (actress); Ocala, Fla., 8/30/1939

Asimov, Isaac (author); Petrovichi, Russia, 1/2/1920

Asner, Edward (actor); Kansas City, Mo., 11/15/1929

Astaire, Fred (Frederick Austerlitz) (dancer and actor); Omaha, Neb., 5/10/1899

Astor, John Jacob (financier); Waldorf (Germany) (1763–1848)

Astor, Mary (Lucile Langhanke) (actress); Quincy, Ill., 5/3/1906

Atkins, Chet (guitarist); nr. Luttrell, Tenn., 6/20/1924

Atkinson, Brooks (drama critic); Melrose, Mass., 11/28/1894

Attenborough, Richard (actor); Cambridge, England, 8/29/1923

Attila (King of Huns, called "Scourge of God") (406?–453)

Attlee, Clement Richard (statesman); London (1883–1967)

Auchincloss, Louis (author); Lawrence, N.Y., 9/27/1917

Auden, W(ystan) H(ugh) (poet); York, England (1907–1973)

Audubon, John James (naturalist and painter); Haiti (1785–1851)

Auer, Leopold (violinist and teacher); Veszprém, Hungary (1845–1930)

Auer, Mischa (actor); St. Petersburg, Russia (1905–1967)

Augustine, Saint (Aurelius Augustinus) (philosopher); Numidia (Algeria) (354–430)

Augustus (Gaius Octavius) (Roman emperor); Rome (63 B.C.-A.D. 14)

Aumont, Jean-Pierre (actor); Paris, 1/5/1913

Austen, Jane (novelist); Steventon, England (1775–1817)

Autry, Gene (singer and actor); Tioga, Tex., 9/29/1907

Avalon, Frankie (singer); Philadelphia, 9/18/1940

Avedon, Richard (photographer); New York City, 5/15/1923

Avery, Milton (painter); Altmar, N.Y. (1893–1965)

Axelrod, George (playwright); New York City, 6/9/1922

Ayckbourn Alan (playwright); London, 4/12/1939

Ayres, Lew (actor); Minneapolis, 12/28/1908

B

Bacall, Lauren (Betty Joan Perske) (actress); New York City, 9/16/1924

Bach, Johann Sebastian (composer); Eisenach (Germany) (1685–1750)

Bacharach, Burt (songwriter); Kansas City, Mo., 5/12/1929

Backus, Jim (actor); Cleveland, 2/25/1913

Bacon, Francis (painter); Dublin, 1910

Bacon, Francis (philosopher and essayist); London (1561–1626)

Bacon, Roger (philosopher and scientist); Ilchester, England (1214?–1294)

Baedeker, Karl (travel-guidebook publisher); Essen (Germany) (1801–1859)

Baez, Joan (folk singer); Staten Island, N.Y., 1/9/1941

Bagnold, Enid (novelist); Rochester, England (1889–1981)

Bailey, F. Lee (lawyer); Waltham, Mass., 6/10/1933

Bailey, Pearl (singer); Newport News, Va., 3/29/1918

Bainter, Fay (actress); Los Angeles (1891–1968)

Baird, Bil (William B.) (puppeteer); Grand Island, Neb., 8/15/1904

Baker, Carroll (actress); Johnstown, Pa., 5/28/1931

Baker, Josephine (singer and dancer); St. Louis (1906–1975)

Baker, Kenny (singer and actor); Monrovia, Calif., 9/30/1912

Baker, Russell (columnist); Loudoun County, Va., 8/14/1925

Balanchine, George (choreographer); St. Petersburg, Russia, 1/9/1904

Balboa, Vasco Nuñez de (explorer); Jerez de los Caballeros (Spain) (1475–1517)

Baldwin, Faith (novelist); New Rochelle, N.Y. (1893–1978)

Baldwin, James (novelist); New York City, 8/2/1924

Balenciaga, Cristóbal (fashion designer); Guetaria, Spain (1895–1972)

Ball, Lucille (actress and producer); Celoron (nr. Jamestown), N.Y., 8/6/1911

Ballard, Kaye (Catherine Gloria Balotta) (actress); Cleveland, 11/20/1926

Balmain, Pierre (fashion designer); St.-Jean-de-Maurienne, France, 5/18/1914

Balsam, Martin (actor); New York City, 11/4/1919

Balzac, Honoré de (novelist); Tours, France (1799–1850)

Bancroft, Anne (Annemarie Italiano) (actress); New York City, 9/17/1931

Bancroft, George (actor); Philadelphia (1882–1956)

Bankhead, Tallulah (actress); Huntsville, Ala. (1903–1968)

Banneker, Benjamin (almanacker and mathematician-astronomer on District of Columbia site survey); Ellicott, Md. (1731–1806)

Bara, Theda (Theodosia Goodman) (actress); Cincinnati (1890–1955)

Barber, Red (Walter Lanier) (sportscaster); Columbus, Miss., 2/17/1908

Barber, Samuel (composer); West Chester, Pa. (1910–1981)

Bardot, Brigitte (actress); Paris, 1935

Barenboim, Daniel (concert pianist and conductor); Buenos Aires, 11/15/1942

Barnard, Christiaan N. (heart surgeon); Beauford West, South Africa, 1923

Barnum, Phineas Taylor (showman); Bethel, Conn. (1810–1891)

Barrie, Sir James Matthew (author); Kirriemuir, Scotland (1860–1937)

Barrie, Wendy (actress); Hong Kong (1913–1978)

Barry, Gene (Eugene Klass) (actor); New York City, 6/4/1922

Barry, John (naval officer); County Wexford, Ireland (1745–1803)

Barrymore, Diana (actress); New York City (1921–1960)

Barrymore, Ethel (Ethel Blythe) (actress); Philadelphia (1879–1959)

Barrymore, Georgiana Drew (actress); Philadelphia (1856–1893)

Barrymore, John (John Blythe) (actor); Philadelphia (1882–1942)

Barrymore, John, Jr. (John Drew Barrymore) (actor); Beverly Hills, Calif., 1932

Barrymore, Lionel (Lionel Blythe) (actor); Philadelphia (1878–1954)

Barrymore, Maurice (Herbert Blythe) (actor and playwright); Agra, India (1847–1905)

Barthelme, Donald (novelist); Philadelphia, 4/7/1931

Barthelmess, Richard (actor); New York City (1897–1963)

Bartholomew, Freddie (actor); London, 3/28/1924

Bartók, Béla (composer); Nagyszentmiklos (Romania) (1881–1945)

Barton, Clara (founder of American Red Cross); Oxford, Mass. (1821–1912)

Baruch, Bernard Mannes (statesman); Camden, S.C. (1870–1965)

Baryshnikov, Mikhail Nikolayevich (ballet dancer); Riga, Latvia, 1/27/1948

Basehart, Richard (actor); Zanesville, Ohio, 8/31/1919

Basie, Count (William) (band leader); Red Bank, N.J., 8/21/1904

Bassey, Shirley (singer); Cardiff, Wales, 1/8/1937

Batchelor, Clarence Daniel (political cartoonist); Osage City, Kan. (1888–1977)

Bates, Alan (actor); Allestree, England, 2/17/1934

Baudelaire, Charles Pierre (poet); Paris (1821–1867)

Baudouin (King); Palace of Laeken, Belgium, 9/7/1930

Baxter, Anne (actress); Michigan City, Ind., 5/7/1923

Baxter, Warner (actor); Columbus, Ohio (1891–1951)

Bean, Orson (Dallas Frederick Burrows) (actor); Burlington, Vt., 7/22/1928

Beardsley, Aubrey Vincent (illustrator); Brighton, England (1872–1898)

Beaton, Cecil (photographer and designer); London (1904–1980)

Beatty, Warren (actor and producer); Richmond, Va., 3/30/1937

Becket, Thomas à (Archbishop of Canterbury); London (1118?–1170)

Beckett, Samuel (playwright); Dublin, 4/13/1906

Beckmann, Max (painter); Leipzig, Germany (1884–1950)

Bede, Saint ("The Venerable Bede") (scholar); Monkwearmouth, England (673–735)

Beecham, Sir Thomas (conductor); St. Helens, England (1879–1961)

Beecher, Henry Ward (clergyman); Litchfield, Conn. (1813–1887)

Beerbohm, Sir Max (author); London (1872–1956)

Beery, Noah, Jr. (actor); New York City, 8/10/1916

Beery, Wallace (actor); Kansas City, Mo. (1886–1949)

Beethoven, Ludwig van (composer); Bonn (Germany) (1770–1827)

Begley, Ed (actor); Hartford, Conn. (1901–1970)

Belafonte, Harry (singer and actor); New York City, 3/1/1927

Belasco, David (dramatist and producer); San Francisco (1854–1931)

Bell, Alexander Graham (inventor); Edinburgh, Scotland (1847–1922)

Bellamy, Edward (author); Chicopee Falls, Mass. (1850–1898)

Bellamy, Ralph (actor); Chicago, 6/17/1904

Bellini, Giovanni (painter); Venice (c.1430–1516)

Bellow, Saul (novelist); Lachine, Quebec, Canada, 7/10/1915

Bellows, George Wesley (painter and lithographer); Columbus, Ohio (1882–1925)

Belmondo, Jean-Paul (actor); Neuilly-sur-Seine, France, 4/9/1933

Belushi, John (comedian, actor); Chicago, 1/24/1949

Benchley, Peter Bradford (novelist); New York City, 5/8/1940

Benchley, Robert Charles (humorist); Worcester, Mass. (1889–1945)

Bendix, William (actor); New York City (1906–1964)

Benes, Eduard (statesman); Kozlany (Czechoslovakia) (1884–1948)

Benét, Stephen Vincent (poet and story writer); Bethlehem, Pa. (1898–1943)

Benét, William Rose (poet and novelist); Ft. Hamilton, Brooklyn, N.Y. (1886–1950)

Ben-Gurion, David (David Green) (statesman); Plónsk (Poland) (1886–1973)

Benjamin, Richard (actor); New York City, 5/22/1938

Bennett, Constance (actress); New York City (1905–1965)

Bennett, Enoch Arnold (novelist and dramatist); Hanley, England (1867–1931)

Bennett, James Gordon (editor); Keith, Scotland (1795–1872)

Bennett, Joan (actress); Palisades, N.J., 2/27/1910

Bennett, Robert Russell (composer); Kansas City, Mo. (1894–1981)

Bennett, Tony (Anthony Benedetto) (singer); Astoria, Queens, N.Y., 8/3/1926

Benny, Jack (Benjamin Kubelsky) (comedian); Chicago (**1894–1974**)

Benton, Thomas Hart (painter); Neosho, Mo. (**1889–1975**)

Berg, Gertrude (writer and actress); New York City (**1899–1966**)

Bergen, Candice (actress); Beverly Hills, Calif., 5/9/1946

Bergen, Edgar (ventriloquist); Chicago, (**1903–1978**)

Bergen, Polly (actress and singer); Knoxville, Tenn., 7/14/1930

Bergman, Ingmar (film director); Uppsala, Sweden, 7/14/1918

Bergman, Ingrid (actress); Stockholm, 8/29/1917

Berle, Milton (Milton Berlinger) (comedian); New York City, 7/12/1908

Berlin, Irving (Israel Baline) (songwriter); Temum, Russia, 5/11/1888

Berlioz, Louis Hector (composer); La Côte-Saint-André, France (**1803–1869**)

Berman, Lazar (concert pianist); Leningrad, 1930.

Berman, Shelley (Sheldon) (comedian); Chicago, 2/3/1926

Bernardi, Herschel (actor); New York City, 1923

Bernhardt, Sarah (Rosine Bernard) (actress); Paris (**1844–1923**)

Bernini, Gian Lorenzo (sculptor and painter); Naples (Italy) (**1598–1680**)

Bernstein, Leonard (conductor); Lawrence, Mass., 8/25/1918

Berry, Chuck (Charles Edward Berry) (singer); San Jose, Calif., 1/15/1926

Betjeman, Sir John (Poet Laureate); London, 8/28/1906

Bickford, Charles (actor); Cambridge, Mass. (**1889–1967**)

Bierce, Ambrose Gwinnett (journalist); Meigs County, Ohio (**1842–1914?**)

Bikel, Theodore (actor and folk singer); Vienna, 5/2/1924

Bing, Sir Rudolf (opera manager); Vienna, 1/9/1902

Bingham, George Caleb (painter); Augusta Co., Va. (**1811–1879**)

Bishop, Joey (Joseph Gottlieb) (comedian); New York City, 2/3/1919

Bismarck-Schönhausen, Prince Otto Eduard Leopold von (statesman); Schönhausen (Germany) (**1815–1898**)

Bisset, Jacqueline (actress); Weybridge, England, 9/13/1944

Bixby, Bill (actor); San Francisco, 1/22/1934

Bizet, Georges (Alexandre César Léopold Bizet) (composer); Paris (**1838–1875**)

Black, Cilla (singer and actress); Liverpool, England, 5/27/1943

Black, Karen (actress); Park Ridge, Ill., 7/1/1942

Black, Shirley Temple (former actress); Santa Monica, Calif., 4/23/1928

Blackman, Honor (actress); London, 8/22/1929

Blackmer, Sidney (actor); Salisbury, N.C. (**1898–1973**)

Blackstone, Sir William (jurist); London (**1723–1780**)

Blaine, Vivian (actress and singer); Newark, N.J., 11/21/1924

Blair, Janet (actress); Altoona, Pa., 4/23/1921

Blake, Amanda (Beverly Louise Neall) (actress); Buffalo, N.Y., 1931

Blake, Eubie (James Hubert) (pianist); Baltimore, 2/7/1883

Blake, Robert (Michael Gubitosi) (actor); Nutley, N.J., 9/18/1933

Blake, William (poet and artist); London (**1757–1827**)

Blanc, Mel(vin Jerome) (actor and voice specialist); San Francisco, 5/30/1908

Blass, Bill (fashion designer); Fort Wayne, Ind., 6/22/1922

Bloch, Ernest (composer); Geneva (**1880–1959**)

Blondell, Joan (actress); New York City (**1909–1979**)

Bloom, Claire (actress); London, 2/15/1931

Bloomgarden, Kermit (producer); Brooklyn, N.Y. (**1904–1976**)

Blue, Monte (actor); Indianapolis (**1890–1963**)

Blyth, Ann (actress); New York City, 8/16/1928

Boccaccio, Giovanni (author); Paris (**1313–1375**)

Boccioni, Umberto (painter and sculptor); Reggio di Calabria, Italy (**1882–1916**)

Bock, Jerry (composer); New Haven, Conn., 11/23/1928

Bogarde, Dirk (Derek Van den Bogaerde) (film actor and director); London, 3/28/1921

Bogart, Humphrey DeForest (actor); New York City (**1899–1957**)

Bogdanovich, Peter (producer and director); Kingston, N.Y., 7/30/1939

Bohlen, Charles E. (diplomat); Clayton, N.Y. (**1904–1974**)

Bohr, Niels (atomic physicist); Copenhagen (**1885–1962**)

Bolger, Ray (dancer and actor); Dorchester, Mass., 1/10/1904

Bolivar, Simón (South American liberator); Caracas, Venezuela (**1783–1830**)

Bologna, Giovanni da (sculptor); Douai (France) (**1529–1608**)

Bombeck, Erma (author, columnist); Dayton, Ohio 2/21/1927

Bonaparte, Napoleon (Emperor of the French); Ajaccio, Corsica (France) (**1769–1821**)

Bond, Julian (Georgia legislator); Nashville, Tenn., 1/14/1940

Bondi, Beulah (actress); Chicago (**1888–1981**)

Bonnard, Pierre (painter); Fontenayaux-Roses, France (**1867–1947**)

Bono, Sonny (Salvatore) (singer); Detroit, 2/16/1935

Boone, Daniel (frontiersman); nr. Reading, Pa. (**1734–1820**)

Boone, Pat (Charles) (singer); Jacksonville, Fla., 6/1/1934

Boone, Richard (actor); Los Angeles (**1917–1981**)

Booth, Edwin Thomas (actor); Bel Air, Md. (**1833–1893**)

Booth, Evangeline Cory (religious leader); London (**1865–1950**)

Booth, John Wilkes (actor; assassin of Lincoln); Harford County, Md. (**1838–1865**)

Booth, Shirley (Thelma Booth Ford) (actress); New York City, 8/30/1907

Bordoni, Irene (actress); Ajaccio (France) (**1895–1953**)

Borge, Victor (pianist and comedian); Copenhagen, 1/3/1909

Borgia, Cesare (nobleman and soldier); Rome (**1475?–1507**)

Borgia, Lucrezia (Duchess of Ferrara); Rome (**1480–1519**)

Borgnine, Ernest (actor); Hamden, Conn., 1/24/1917

Borromini, Francesco (architect); Bissone (Italy) (**1599–1667**)

Bosch, Hieronymus (Hieronymus van Aeken) (painter); Hertogenbosch (Netherlands) (c.**1450–1516**)

Bosley, Tom (actor); Chicago, 10/1/1927

Boswell, Connee (singer); New Orleans (**1907–1976**)

Boswell, James (diarist and biographer); Edinburgh, Scotland (**1740–1795**)

Botticelli, Sandro (Alessandro di Mariano dei Filipepi) (painter); Florence (Italy) (**1444?–1510**)

Boulez, Pierre (conductor); Montbrison, France, 3/26/1925

Bow, Clara (actress); Brooklyn, N.Y. (**1905–1965**)

Bowen, Catherine Drinker (biographer); Haverford, Pa. (**1897–1973**)

Bowie, David (David Robert Jones) (actor and musician); London, 1/8/1947(?)

Bowie, James (soldier); Burke County, Ga. (**1799–1836**)

Bowles, Chester (diplomat); Springfield, Mass. 4/5/1901

Bowman, Lee (actor); Cincinnati (**1914–1979**)

Boyd, Bill (William) ("Hopalong Cassidy") (actor); Cambridge, Ohio (**1898–1972**)

Boyd, Stephen (Stephen Millar) (actor); Belfast, Northern Ireland (**1928–1977**)

Boyer, Charles (actor); Figeac, France (**1899–1978**)

Bracken, Eddie (actor); Astoria, Queens, N.Y., 2/7/1920

Bradbury, Ray Douglas (science-fiction writer); Waukegan, Ill., 8/22/1920

Bradlee, Benjamin C. (editor); Boston, 8/26/1921

Bradley, Omar N. (5-star general); Clark, Mo. (**1893–1981**)

Bradley, Thomas (Mayor of Los Angeles); Calvert, Tex., 12/29/1917

Brady, Scott (actor); Brooklyn, N.Y., 9/13/1924

Brahms, Johannes (composer); Hamburg (**1833–1897**)

Braille, Louis (teacher of blind); Coupvray, France (**1809–1862**)

Brailowsky, Alexander (pianist); Kiev, Russia (**1896–1976**)

Bramante, Donato D'Agnolo (architect); Monte Asdrualdo (now Fermignano, Italy) (**1444–1514**)

Brancusi, Constantin (sculptor); Pestisansi, Romania (**1876–1957**)

Brando, Marlon (actor); Omaha, Neb., 4/3/1924

Brandt, Willy (Herbert Frahm) (ex-Chancellor); Lübeck, Germany, 12/18/1913

Braque, Georges (painter); Argenteuil, France (**1882–1963**)

Braun, Wernher von (rocket scientist); Wirsitz, Germany (**1912–1977**)

Brazzi, Rossano (actor); Bologna, Italy, 9/18/1916

Brecht, Bertolt (dramatist and poet); Augsburg, Bavaria (**1898–1956**)

Brel, Jacques (singer and composer); Brussels, (**1929–1978**)

Brennan, Walter (actor); Lynn, Mass. (**1894–1974**)

Brent, George (actor); Dublin (**1904–1979**)

Breslin, Jimmy (journalist); Jamaica, Queens, N.Y., 10/17/1930

Breuer, Marcel (architect and designer); Pécs, Hungary (**1902–1981**)

Brewer, Teresa (singer); Toledo, Ohio, 5/7/1931

Brewster, Kingman, Jr. (ex-president of Yale); Longmeadow, Mass., 6/17/1919

Brezhnev, Leonid I. (Communist Party Secretary); Dneprodzerzhinsk, Ukraine, 12/19/1906

Brice, Fanny (Fannie Borach) (comedienne); New York City (**1892–1951**)

Bridges, Beau (actor); Los Angeles, 12/9/1941

Bridges, Lloyd (actor); San Leandro, Calif. 1/15/1913

Brinkley, David (TV newscaster); Wilmington, N.C., 7/10/1920

Britt, May (Maybritt Wilkins) (actress); Sweden, 3/22/1936

Britten, Benjamin (composer); Lowestoft, England (**1913–1976**)

Britton, Barbara (actress); Long Beach, Calif. (**1920–1980**)

Bromfield, Louis (novelist); Mansfield, Ohio (**1896–1956**)

Bronson, Charles (Charles Buchinsky) (actor); Ehrenfield, Pa., 11/3/1922(?)

Brontë, Charlotte (novelist); Thornton, England (**1816–1855**)

Brontë, Emily Jane (novelist); Thornton, England (**1818–1848**)

Bronzino, Agnolo (painter); Monticelli (Italy) (**1503–1572**)

Brook, Peter (director); London, 3/21/1925

Brooke, Rupert (poet); Rugby, England (**1887–1915**)

Brooks, Geraldine (Geraldine Stroock) (actress); New York City (**1925–1977**)

Brooks, Gwendolyn (poet); Topeka, Kan., 6/7/1917

Brooks, Mel (Melvin Kaminsky) (writer and film director); Brooklyn, N.Y., 1926(?)

Broun, Matthew Heywood Campbell (journalist); Brooklyn, N.Y. (**1888–1939**)

Brown, Helen Gurley (author); Green Forest, Ark., 2/18/1922

Brown, James (singer); Augusta, Ga., 5/3/1934

Brown, Joe E. (comedian); Holgate, Ohio (**1892–1973**)

Brown, John (abolitionist); Torrington, Conn. (**1800–1859**)

Brown, John Mason (critic); Louisville, Ky. (**1900–1969**)

Brown, Les (band leader); Reinerton, Pa., 1912

Brown, Pamela (actress); London (**1918–1975**)

Brown, Vanessa (Smylla Brind) (actress); Vienna, 3/24/1928

Browne, Jackson (singer and guitarist); Heidelberg, Germany, 10/9/late 1940s
Browning, Elizabeth Barrett (poet); Durham, England **(1806–1861)**
Browning, Robert (poet); London **(1812–1889)**
Brubeck, Dave (musician); Concord, Calif., 12/6/1920
Bruce, Lenny (comedian); Long Island, N.Y. **(1926–1966)**
Brueghel, Pieter (painter); nr. Breda, Flanders (Netherlands) **(1520?–1569)**
Bruhn, Erik (Belton Evers) (ballet dancer); Copenhagen, 10/3/1928
Brunelleschi, Filippo (architect); Florence (Italy) **(1377–1446)**
Brutus, Marcus Junius (Roman politician); (85?–42 B.C.)
Bryan, William Jennings (orator and politician); Salem, Ill. **(1860–1925)**
Bryant, Anita (singer); Barnsdall, Okla., 3/25/1940
Bryant, William Cullen (poet and editor); Cummington, Mass. **(1794–1878)**
Brynner, Yul (Taidje Khan) (actor); Sakhalin Island, Russia, 7/11/1920
Brzezinski, Zbigniew (ex-presidential adviser); Warsaw, 3/28/1928
Buber, Martin (philosopher and theologian); Vienna **(1878–1965)**
Buchanan, Edgar (actor); Humansville, Mo., **(1903–1979)**
Buchholz, Horst (actor); Berlin, 12/4/1933
Buchwald, Art (Arthur) (columnist); Mount Vernon, N.Y., 10/20/1925
Buck, Pearl S(ydenstricker) (author); Hillsboro, W. Va. **(1892–1973)**
Buckley, William F., Jr. (journalist); New York City, 11/24/1925
Buddha. *See* Gautama Buddha
Buffalo Bill (William Frederick Cody) (scout); Scott County, Iowa **(1846–1917)**
Bujold, Genevieve (actress); Montreal, 7/1/1942
Bujones, Fernando (ballet dancer); Miami, Fla., 3/9/1955
Bullins, Ed (playwright); Philadelphia, 7/2/1935
Bumbry, Grace (mezzo-soprano); St. Louis, 1/4/1937
Bunche, Ralph J. (statesman); Detroit **(1904–1971)**
Bundy, McGeorge (educator); Boston, 3/30/1919
Bundy, William Putnam (editor); Washington, D.C., 9/24/1917
Buñuel, Luis (film director); Calanda, Spain, 2/22/1900
Bunyan, John (preacher and author); Elstow, England **(1628–1688)**
Burbank, Luther (horticulturist); Lancaster, Mass. **(1849–1926)**
Burke, Adm. Arleigh A. (ex-Chief of Naval Operations); Boulder, Colo., 10/19/1901
Burke, Billie (comedienne); Washington, D.C. **(1885–1970)**
Burke, Edmund (statesman); Dublin **(1729–1797)**
Burne-Jones, Edward Coley (painter); Birmingham, England **(1833–1898)**
Burnett, Carol (comedienne); San Antonio, 4/26/1936
Burns, George (Nathan Birnbaum) (comedian); New York City, 1/20/1896
Burns, Robert (poet); Alloway, Scotland **(1759–1796)**
Burr, Aaron (political leader); Newark, N.J. **(1756–1836)**
Burr, Raymond (William Stacey Burr) (actor); New Westminster, British Columbia, Canada, 5/21/1917
Burroughs, Edgar Rice (novelist); Chicago **(1875–1950)**
Burrows, Abe (playwright and director); New York City, 12/18/1910
Burstyn, Ellen (Edna Rae Gillooly) (actress); Detroit, 12/7/1932
Burton, Richard (Richard Jenkins) (actor); Pontrhydfen, Wales, 11/10/1925
Bush, Vannevar (scientist); Everett, Mass. **(1890–1974)**
Bushman, Francis X. (actor); Baltimore **(1883–1966)**
Butler, Samuel (author); Langar, England **(1835–1902)**
Buttons, Red (Aaron Chwatt) (actor); New York City, 2/5/1919
Buzzi, Ruth (comedienne); Wequetequock, Conn., 7/24/1936
Byrd, Richard Evelyn (polar explorer); Winchester, Va. **(1888–1957)**
Byrne, Jane (Mayor of Chicago); Chicago, 5/24/1934
Byron, George Gordon (6th Baron Byron) (poet); London **(1788–1824)**

C

Caan, James (actor); The Bronx, N.Y., 3/26/1939
Cabot, John (Giovanni Caboto) (navigator); Genoa (?) **(1450–1498)**
Cabot, Sebastian (navigator); Venice **(1476?–1557)**
Cadmus, Paul (painter and etcher); New York City, 12/17/1904
Caesar, Gaius Julius (statesman); Rome **(100?–44 B.C.)**
Caesar, Sid (comedian); Yonkers, N.Y., 9/8/1922
Cagney, James (actor); New York City, 7/17/1899
Cahn, Sammy (songwriter); New York City, 6/18/1913
Caine, Michael (Maurice J. Micklewhite) (actor); London, 3/14/1933
Calder, Alexander (sculptor); Lawnton, Pa. **(1898–1976)**
Caldwell, Erskine (novelist); White Oak, Ga., 12/17/1903
Caldwell, Sarah (opera director and conductor); Maryville, Mo., 1928
Caldwell, Taylor (novelist); Manchester, England, 9/7/1900
Caldwell, Zoe (actress); Hawthorn, Australia, 9/14/1933
Calhern, Louis (Carl Henry Vogt) (actor); Brooklyn, N.Y. **(1895–1956)**
Calhoun, John Caldwell (statesman); nr. Calhoun Mills, S.C. **(1782–1850)**
Calisher, Hortense (novelist); New York City, 12/20/1911
Callas, Maria (Maria Calogeropoulos) (dramatic soprano); New York City **(1923–1977)**
Calloway, Cab (Cabell) (band leader); Rochester, N.Y., 12/25/1907
Calvet, Corinne (actress); Paris, 4/30/1926

Calvin, John (Jean Chauvin) (religious reformer); Noyon, Picardy **(1509–1564)**
Cambridge, Godfrey (comedian); New York City **(1933–1976)**
Cameron, Rod (Rod Cox) (actor); Calgary, Alberta, Canada, 12/7/1912
Campbell, Glen (singer); nr. Delight, Ark., 4/22/1938
Camus, Albert (author); Mondovi, Algeria **(1913–1960)**
Caniff, Milton (cartoonist); Hillsboro, Ohio, 2/28/1907
Cannon, Dyan (actress); Tacoma, Wash., 1/4/1937
Canova, Judy (comedienne); Jacksonville, Fla., 11/20/1916
Cantinflas (Mario Moreno) (comedian); Mexico City, 8/12/1911
Cantor, Eddie (Edward Iskowitz) (actor); New York City **(1892–1964)**
Cantrell, Lana (singer); Sydney, Australia, 1944
Capote, Truman (novelist); New Orleans, 9/30/1924
Capp, Al (Alfred Gerald Caplin) (cartoonist); New Haven, Conn. **(1909–1979)**
Capra, Frank (film producer, director); Palermo, Italy, 5/18/1897
Caravaggio, Michelangelo Merisi da (painter); Caravaggio (Italy) **(1573–1610)**
Cardin, Pierre (fashion designer); nr. Venice, 7/7/1922
Cardinale, Claudia (actress); Tunis, Tunisia, 1939
Carey, Harry (actor); New York City **(1878–1947)**
Carey, Macdonald (actor); Sioux City, Iowa, 3/15/1913
Carlisle, Kitty (singer and actress); New Orleans, 9/3/1915
Carlson, Richard (actor); Albert Lea, Minn., **(1912–1977)**
Carlyle, Thomas (essayist and historian); Ecclefechan, Scotland **(1795–1881)**
Carmichael, Hoagy (Hoagland Howard) (songwriter); Bloomington, Ind., 11/22/1899
Carne, Judy (Joyce Botterill) (singer); Northampton, England, 1939
Carnegie, Andrew (industrialist); Dunfermline, Scotland **(1835–1919)**
Carney, Art (actor); Mt. Vernon, N.Y., 11/4/1918
Carnovsky, Morris (actor); St. Louis, 9/5/1897
Caron, Leslie (actress); Paris, 7/1/1931
Carr, Vikki (singer); El Paso, 7/19/1942
Carracci, Annibale (painter); Bologna (Italy) **(1560–1609)**
Carracci, Lodovico (painter); Bologna (Italy) **(1555–1619)**
Carradine, David (actor); Hollywood, Calif., 12/8/1936
Carradine, John (actor); New York City, 2/5/1906
Carrillo, Leo (actor); Los Angeles **(1881–1961)**
Carroll, Diahann (Carol Diahann Johnson) (singer and actress); Bronx, N.Y., 7/17/1935
Carroll, Leo G. (actor); Weedon, England **(1892–1972)**
Carroll, Lewis (Charles Lutwidge Dodgson) (author and mathematician); Daresbury, England **(1832–1898)**
Carroll, Madeleine (actress); West Bromwich, England, 2/26/1909
Carroll, Pat (comedienne); Shreveport, La., 5/5/1927
Carson, Johnny (TV entertainer); Corning, Iowa, 10/23/1925
Carson, Kit (Christopher) (scout); Madison County, Ky. **(1809–1868)**
Carson, Rachel (biologist and author); Springdale, Pa. **(1907–1964)**
Carter, (Bessie) Lillian (President's mother); Richland, Ga., 8/15/1898
Carter, Jack (comedian); New York City, 1923
Cartier-Brisson, Henri (photographer); Chanteloup, France, 8/22/1908
Cartland, Barbara (author); England, 7/9/1901
Caruso, Enrico (Errico) (tenor); Naples, Italy **(1873–1921)**
Carver, George Washington (botanist); Missouri **(1864–1943)**
Cary, Arthur Joyce Lunel (novelist); Londonderry, Ireland **(1888–1957)**
Casals, Pablo (cellist); Vendrell, Spain **(1876–1973)**
Casanova de Seingalt, Giovanni Jacopo (adventurer); Venice **(1725–1798)**
Cash, Johnny (singer); nr. Kingsland, Ark., 2/26/1932
Cass, Peggy (comedienne); Boston, 5/21/1924
Cassatt, Mary (painter); Allegheny, Pa. **(1844–1926)**
Cassavetes, John (actor and director); New York City, 12/9/1929
Cassidy, David (singer); New York City, 4/12/1950
Cassidy, Jack (actor); Richmond Hill, Queens, N.Y. **(1927–1976)**
Cassini, Oleg (Oleg Lolewski-Cassini) (fashion designer); Paris, 4/11/1913
Castagno, Andrea del (painter); San Martino a Corella (Italy) (c.1421–1457)
Castellano, Richard (actor); New York City, 9/2/1934
Castle, Irene (Irene Foote) (actress and dancer); New Rochelle, N.Y. **(1893–1969)**
Castle, Vernon Blythe (dancer and aviator); Norwich, England **(1887–1918)**
Castro Ruz, Fidel (Premier); Mayari, Oriente, Cuba, 8/13/1926
Cather, Willa Sibert (novelist); Winchester, Va. **(1876–1947)**
Cato, Marcus Porcius (called Cato the Elder) (statesman); Tusculum (Italy) **(234–149 B.C.)**
Catt, Carrie Chapman Lane (woman suffragist); Ripon, Wis. **(1859–1947)**
Catton, Bruce (historian); Petoskey, Mich. **(1899–1978)**
Cavallaro, Carmen (band leader); New York City, 1913
Cavett, Dick (Richard) (TV entertainer); Gibbon, Neb., 11/19/1936
Cellini, Benvenuto (goldsmith and sculptor); Florence (Italy) **(1500–1571)**
Cervantes Saavedra, Miguel de (novelist); Alcalá de Henares, Spain **(1547–1616)**
Cézanne, Paul (painter); Aix-en-Provence, France **(1839–1906)**
Chagall, Marc (painter); Vitebsk, Russia, 7/7/1887

Chaliapin, Feodor Ivanovitch (operatic basso); Kazan, Russia **(1873–1938)**

Chamberlain, Arthur Neville (statesman); Edgbaston, England **(1869–1940)**

Chamberlain, Richard (actor); Los Angeles, 3/31/1935(?)

Champion, Gower (choreographer); Geneva, Ill. **(1921–1980)**

Champion, Marge (actress and dancer); Los Angeles, 9/2/1923

Champlain, Samuel de (explorer); nr. Rochefort, France **(1567?–1635)**

Chancellor, John (TV commentator); Chicago, 7/14/1927

Chandler, Raymond (writer); Chicago **(1888–1959)**

Chanel, "Coco" (Gabriel Bonheur) (fashion designer); Issoire, France **(1883–1971)**

Chaney, Lon (actor); Colorado Springs, Colo. **(1883–1930)**

Channing, Carol (actress); Seattle, 1/31/1923

Chaplin, Geraldine (actress); Santa Monica, Calif., 7/31/1944

Chaplin, Sir Charles (actor); London **(1889–1977)**

Charisse, Cyd (Tula Finklea) (dancer and actress); Amarillo, Tex., 3/8/1923

Charlemagne (Holy Roman Emperor); birthplace unknown **(742–814)**

Charles, Ray (Ray Charles Robinson) (pianist, singer, and songwriter); Albany Ga., 9/23/1930

Chase, Chevy (Cornelius Crane Chase) (comedian); New York City, 10/8/1943

Chase, Ilka (author and actress); New York City **(1905–1978)**

Chase, Lucia (ballet company manager); Waterbury, Conn., 3/24/1907

Chatterton, Ruth (actress); New York City **(1893–1961)**

Chaucer, Geoffrey (poet); London **(1340?–1400)**

Chávez, Carlos (composer); nr. Mexico City **(1899–1978)**

Chavez, Cesar (labor leader); nr. Yuma, Ariz., 3/31/1927

Chayefsky, Paddy (Sidney) (playwright); New York City, **(1923–1981)**

Checker, Chubby (Ernest Evans) (performer); Philadelphia, 10/3/1941

Cheever, John (novelist); Quincy, Mass., 5/27/1912

Chekhov, Anton Pavlovich (dramatist and short-story writer); Taganrog, Russia **(1860–1904)**

Cher (Cherilyn LaPiere) (singer); El Centro, Calif., 5/20/1946

Chesterton, Gilbert Keith (author); Kensington, England **(1874–1936)**

Chevalier, Maurice (entertainer); Paris **(1888–1972)**

Chiang Ch'ing (political leader); Chucheng, China, 1913(?)

Chiang Kai-shek (Chief of State); Feng-hwa, China **(1887–1975)**

Child, Julia (food expert); Pasadena, Calif., 8/15/1912

Chippendale, Thomas (cabinet-maker); Otley, England **(1718?–1779)**

Chirico, Giorgio de (painter); Vólos, Greece, **(1888–1978)**

Chisholm, Shirley (Representative); Brooklyn, N.Y., 11/30/1924

Chopin, Frédéric François (composer); nr. Warsaw **(1810–1849)**

Chou En-lai. *See* Zhou Enlai

Christian, Linda (Blanca Rosa Welter) (actress); Tampico, Mexico, 11/13/1924

Christie, Agatha (mystery writer); Torquay, England, **(1890–1976)**

Christie, Julie (actress); Chukua, India, 4/14/1941

Christopher, Jordon (actor and musician); Youngstown, Ohio, 1941

Christy, June (singer); Springfield, Ill., 1925

Churchill, Sarah (actress); London, 10/7/1914

Churchill, Sir Winston Leonard Spencer (statesman); Blenheim Palace, Oxfordshire, England **(1874–1965)**

Cicero, Marcus Tullius (orator and statesman); Arpinum (Italy) **(106–43 B.C.)**

Cilento, Diane (actress); Queensland, Australia, 10/5/1933

Cimabue, Giovanni (painter); Florence (Italy) **(c.1240–c.1302)**

Cimino, Michael (film director); New York City, 1943(?)

Clair, René (René Chomette) (film director); Paris **(1898–1981)**

Claire, Ina (Ina Fagan) (actress); Washington, D.C., 10/15/1895

Clapton, Eric (singer and guitarist); Ripley, England, 3/30/1945

Clark, Dane (Barney Zanville) (actor); New York City, 2/18/1915

Clark, Dick (TV personality); Mt. Vernon, N.Y., 11/30/1929

Clark, Mark W. (general); Madison Barracks, N.Y., 5/1/1896

Clark, Petula (singer); Epsom, England, 11/15/1934

Clark, Roy (country music artist); Meherrin, Va., 4/15/1933

Clark, William (explorer); Caroline County, Va. **(1770–1838)**

Claude Lorrain (Claude Gellée) (painter); Champagne, France **(1600–1682)**

Clay, Henry (statesman); Hanover County, Va. **(1777–1852)**

Clay, Lucius D. (banker, ex-general); Marietta, Ga. **(1897–1978)**

Clayburgh, Jill (actress); New York City, 4/30/1944

Clemenceau, Georges (statesman); Mouilleron-en-Pareds, Vendée, France **(1841–1929)**

Clemens, Samuel L. *See* Mark Twain

Cleopatra (Queen of Egypt); Alexandria, Egypt **(69–30 B.C.)**

Cliburn, Van (Harvey Lavan Cliburn, Jr.) (concert pianist); Shreveport, La., 7/12/1934

Clifford, Clark M. (ex-Secretary of Defense); Ft. Scott, Kan., 12/25/1906

Clift, Montgomery (actor); Omaha, Neb. **(1920–1966)**

Clooney, Rosemary (singer); Maysville, Ky., 5/23/1928

Clurman, Harold (stage producer); New York City **(1901–1980)**

Cobb, Irvin Shrewsbury (humorist); Paducah, Ky. **(1876–1944)**

Cobb, Lee J. (Leo Jacob) (actor); New York City **(1911–1976)**

Coburn, Charles Douville (actor); Savannah, Ga. **(1877–1961)**

Coburn, James (actor): Laurel, Neb., 8/31/1928

Coca, Imogene (comedienne); Philadelphia, 11/18/1908

Cocker, Joe (John Robert Cocker) (singer); Sheffield, England, 5/20/1944

Coco, James (actor); New York City, 3/21/1929

Cocteau, Jean (author); Maison-Lafitte, France **(1891–1963)**

Cody, W. F. *See* Buffalo Bill

Cohan, George Michael (actor and dramatist); Providence, R.I. **(1878–1942)**

Cohen, Leonard (singer and songwriter); Montreal, 1935

Colbert, Claudette (Lily Chauchoin) (actress); Paris, 9/13/1903

Colby, William E. (ex-Director of CIA); St. Paul, 1/4/1920

Cole, Nat "King" (singer); Montgomery, Ala. **(1919–1965)**

Cole, Natalie (singer); Los Angeles, 2/6/1950

Cole, Thomas (painter); Lancashire, England **(1801–1848)**

Coleridge, Samuel Taylor (poet); Ottery St. Mary, England **(1772–1834)**

Colette (Sidonie-Gabrielle Colette) (novelist); St.-Sauveur, France **c.1873–1954)**

Collingwood, Charles (TV commentator); Three Rivers, Mich., 6/4/1917

Collins, Dorothy (Marjorie Chandler) (singer); Windsor, Ontario, Canada, 11/18/1926

Collins, Joan (actress); London, 1933

Collins, Judy (singer); Seattle, 5/1/1939

Colman, Ronald (actor); Richmond, England **(1891–1958)**

Colonna, Jerry (comedian); Boston, 1905

Columbus, Christopher (Cristoforo Colombo) (discoverer of America); Genoa (Italy) **(1451–1506)**

Comden, Betty (writer); New York City, 5/3/1919

Commager, Henry Steele (historian); Pittsburgh, 10/25/1902

Como, Perry (Pierino) (singer); Canonsburg, Pa., 5/18/1913

Compton, Karl Taylor (physicist); Wooster, Ohio **(1887–1954)**

Conant, James B. (educator and statesman); Dorchester, Mass. **(1893–1978)**

Condon, Eddie (jazz musician); Goodland, Ind. **(1905–1973)**

Confucius (K'ung Fu-tzu) (philosopher); Shantung province, China **(c.551–479 B.C.)**

Congreve, William (dramatist); nr. Leeds, England **(1670–1729)**

Connelly, Marc (playwright); McKeesport, Pa. **(1890–1980)**

Connery, Sean (actor); Edinburgh, Scotland, 8/25/1930

Conniff, Ray (band leader); Attleboro, Mass., 11/6/1916

Connors, Chuck (actor); Brooklyn, N.Y., 4/10/1921

Connors, Mike (Krekor Ohanian) (actor); Fresno, Calif., 8/15/1925

Conrad, Joseph (Teodor Jozef Konrad Korzeniowski) (novelist); Berdichev, Ukraine **(1857–1924)**

Conrad, Robert (actor); Chicago, 1935

Conrad, William (actor); Louisville, Ky., 9/27/1920

Conried, Hans (Frank Foster) (actor); Baltimore, 1917

Constable, John (painter); East Bergholt, Suffolk, England **(1776–1837)**

Constantine II (ex-king); Athens, 6/2/1940

Conte, Richard (actor); New York City **(1916–1975)**

Converse, Frank (actor); St. Louis, 1938

Conway, Tim (actor); Chagrin Falls, Ohio, 12/15/1933

Coogan, Jackie (actor); Los Angeles, 10/26/1914

Cooke, Alistair (Alfred Alistair); (TV narrator and journalist); Manchester, England, 11/20/1908

Cooley, Denton A(rthur) (heart surgeon); Houston, Tex., 8/22/1920

Coolidge, Rita (singer); Nashville, Tenn., 1944

Cooper, Alice (Vincent Furnier) (rock musician); Detroit, 2/4/1948

Cooper, Gary (Frank James Cooper) (actor); Helena, Mont. **(1901–1961)**

Cooper, Jackie (actor and director); Los Angeles, 9/15/1922

Cooper, James Fenimore (novelist); Burlington, N.J. **(1789–1851)**

Cooper, Peter (industrialist and philanthropist); New York City **(1791–1883)**

Copernicus, Nicolaus (Mikolaj Kopernik) (astronomer); Thorn, Poland **(1473–1543)**

Copland, Aaron (composer); Brooklyn, N.Y., 11/14/1900

Copley, John Singleton (painter); Boston, Mass. **(1738–1815)**

Coppola, Francis Ford (film director); Detroit, 4/7/1939

Corelli, Franco (operatic tenor); Ancona, Italy, 4/8/1923

Corneille, Pierre (dramatist); Rouen, France **(1606–1684)**

Cornell, Katharine (actress); Berlin **(1893–1974)**

Corot, Jean Baptiste Camille (painter); Paris **(1796–1875)**

Correggio, Antonio Allegri da (painter); Correggio (Italy) **(1494–1534)**

Corsaro, Frank (opera director); New York harbor, 12/22/1924

Cortés (or Cortez), Hernando (explorer); Medellín, Spain **(1485–1547)**

Cosby, Bill (actor); Philadelphia, 7/12/1937

Cosell, Howard (Howard Cohen) (sportscaster); Winston-Salem, N.C., 3/25/1920

Costa-Gavras, Henri (Kostantinos Gavras) (film director); Athens, 1933

Costello, Lou (comedian); Paterson, N.J. **(1908–1959)**

Cotten, Joseph (actor); Petersburg, Va., 5/15/1905

Courbet, Gustave (painter); Ornans, France **(1819–1877)**

Courrèges, André (fashion designer); Pau, France, 3/9/1923

Courtenay, Tom (actor); Hull, England, 2/25/1937

Cousins, Norman (publisher); Union Hill, N.J., 6/24/1915

Cousteau, Jacques-Yves (marine explorer); St. André-de-Cubzac, France, 6/11/1910

Coward, Sir Noel (playwright and actor); Teddington, England (1899–1973)
Cowles, Gardner (newspaper publisher); Algona, Iowa, 1/31/1903
Cowper, William (poet); Great Berkhamstead, England (1731–1800)
Cozzens, James Gould (novelist); Chicago (1903–1978)
Crabbe, Buster (Clarence) (actor); Oakland, Calif., 2/7/1908
Crain, Jeanne (actress); Barstow, Calif., 5/25/1925
Cranach, Lucas, the elder (painter); Kronach (Germany) (1472–1553)
Crane, Hart (poet); Garrettsville, Ohio (1899–1932)
Crane, Stephen (novelist and poet); Newark, N.J. (1871–1900)
Crawford, Broderick (actor); Philadelphia, 12/9/1911
Crawford, Cheryl (stage producer); Akron, Ohio, 9/24/1902
Crawford, Joan (Lucille LeSueur) (actress and business executive); San Antonio (1908–1977)
Crenna, Richard (actor); Los Angeles, 11/30/1927
Crespin, Régine (operatic soprano); Marseilles, France, 2/23/1929
Crichton, (John) Michael (novelist); Chicago, 10/23/1942
Crisp, Donald (actor); London (1880–1974)
Croce, Benedetto (philosopher); Pescasseroli, Aquila, Italy (1866–1952)
Croce, Jim (singer); Philadelphia (1942–1973)
Crockett, Davy (David) (frontiersman); Greene County, Tenn. (1786–1836)
Cromwell, Oliver (statesman); Huntingdon, England (1599–1658)
Cronin, A. J. (Archibald J. Cronin) (novelist); Cardross, Scotland (1896–1981)
Cronkite, Walter (TV newscaster); St. Joseph, Mo., 11/4/1916
Cronyn, Hume (actor); London, Ontario, Canada, 7/18/1911
Crosby, Bing (Harry Lillis) (singer, actor); Tacoma, Wash. (1904–1977)
Crosby, Bob (musician); Spokane, Wash., 8/23/1913
Crosby, David (singer); Los Angeles, 8/14/1941
Cross, Milton (opera commentator); New York City (1897–1975)
Crouse, Russel (playwright); Findlay, Ohio (1893–1966)
Cugat, Xavier (band leader); Barcelona, Spain, 1/1/1900
Cukor, George (film director); New York City, 7/7/1899
Cullen, Bill (William Lawrence Cullen) (radio and TV entertainer); Pittsburgh, 2/18/1920
Culp, Robert (actor); Berkeley, Calif., 8/16/1930
Cummings, E. E. (Edward Estlin Cummings) (poet); Cambridge, Mass. (1894–1962)
Cummings, Robert (actor); Joplin, Mo., 6/9/1910
Curie, Marie (Marja Sklodowska) (physical chemist); Warsaw (1867–1934)
Curtin, Phyllis (soprano); Clarksburg, W.Va., 12/3/1927
Curtis, Tony (Bernard Schwartz) (actor); Bronx, N.Y., 6/3/1925
Curzon, Clifford (concert pianist); London, 5/18/1907
Custer, George Armstrong (army officer); New Rumley, Ohio (1839–1876)

D

Daché, Lilly (fashion designer); Bèigles, France
Dahl, Arlene (actress); Minneapolis, 8/11/1928
Dailey, Dan (actor and dancer); New York City, (1917–1978)
Daley, Richard J. (ex-Mayor of Chicago); Chicago (1902–1976)
Dali, Salvador (painter); Figueras, Spain, 5/11/1904
Daly, James (actor); Wisconsin Rapids, Wis. (1918–1978)
Daly, John (radio and TV news analyst); Johannesburg, South Africa, 2/20/1914
d'Amboise, Jacques (ballet dancer); Dedham, Mass., 7/28/1934
Damone, Vic (Vito Farinola) (singer); Brooklyn, N.Y., 6/12/1928
Damrosch, Walter Johannes (orchestra conductor); Breslau (Poland) (1862–1950)
Dana, Charles Anderson (editor); Hinsdale, N.H. (1819–1897)
Dandridge, Dorothy (actress); Cleveland (1923–1965)
Dangerfield, Rodney (comedian); Babylon, L.I., N.Y., 1921
Daniels, Bebe (Virginia Daniels) (actress); Dallas (1901–1971)
Danilova, Alexandra (ballerina); Peterhof, Russia, 11/20/1904
Danner, Blythe (actress); Philadelphia, 1944(?)
D'Annunzio, Gabriele (soldier and author); Francaville al Mare, Pescara, Italy (1863–1938)
Dante (or Durante) Alighieri (poet); Florence (Italy) (1265–1321)
Danton, Georges Jacques (French Revolutionary leader); Arcis-sur-Aube, France (1759–1794)
Darnell, Linda (actress); Dallas (1921–1965)
Darren, James (actor); Philadelphia, 6/8/1936
Darrieux, Danielle (actress); Bordeaux, France, 5/1/1917
Darrow, Clarence Seward (lawyer); Kinsman, Ohio (1857–1938)
Darwin, Charles Robert (naturalist); Shrewsbury, England (1809–1882)
daSilva, Howard (actor); Cleveland, 5/4/1909
Dassin, Jules (film director); Middletown, Conn., 12/18/1911
Daumier, Honoré (caricaturist); Marseilles, France (1808–1879)
Dauphin, Claude (actor); Corbeil, France (1903–1978)
David, Jacques-Louis (painter); Paris (1748–1825)
David (King of Israel and Judah) (died c. 973 B.C.)
Davidson, John (singer and actor); Pittsburgh, 12/13/1941
Davies, Marion (Marion Douras) (actress); New York City (1898?–1961)

da Vinci, Leonardo (painter and scientist); Vinci, Tuscany (Italy) (1452–1519)
Davis, Bette (actress); Lowell, Mass., 4/5/1908
Davis, Elmer Holmes (radio commentator); Aurora, Ind. (1890–1958)
Davis, Jefferson (President of the Confederacy); Christian (now Todd) County, Ky. (1808–1889)
Davis, Mac (singer); Lubbock, Tex.
Davis, Miles (jazz trumpeter); Alton, Ill., 5/25/1926
Davis, Ossie (actor and writer); Cogdell, Ga., 12/18/1917
Davis, Sammy, Jr. (actor and singer); New York City, 12/8/1925
Davis, Skeeter (Mary Francis Penick) (singer); Dry Ridge, Ky., 12/30/1931
Davis, Stuart (painter); Philadelphia (1894–1964)
Day, Dennis (singer); New York City, 5/21/1917
Day, Doris (Doris von Kappelhoff) (singer and actress); Cincinnati, 4/3/1924
Day, Laraine (La Raine Johnson) (actress); Roosevelt, Utah, 10/13/1920
Dayan, Moshe (ex-Defense Minister of Israel); Dagania, Palestine (Jordan), 5/20/1915
Dean, James (actor); Marion, Ind. (1931–1955)
Dean, Jimmy (singer); Seth Ward, nr. Plainview, Tex., 8/10/1928
De Bakey, Michael E. (heart surgeon); Lake Charles, La., 9/7/1908
de Beauvoir, Simone (novelist and philosopher); Paris, 1/9/1908
Debs, Eugene Victor (Socialist leader); Terre Haute, Ind. (1855–1926)
Debussy, Claude Achille (composer); St. Germain-en-Laye, France (1862–1918)
De Carlo, Yvonne (Peggy Yvonne Middleton) (actress); Vancouver, B.C., Canada, 9/1/1924
de Chirico, Giorgio (painter); Volos, Greece, (1888–1978)
Dee, Ruby (Ruby Ann Wallace) (actress); Cleveland, 10/27/1924(?)
Dee, Sandra (Alexandra Zuck) (actress); Bayonne, N.J., 4/23/1942
Defoe, Daniel (novelist); London (1659?–1731)
Degas, Hilaire Germain Edgar (painter); Paris (1834–1917)
De Gaulle, Charles André Joseph Marie (soldier and statesman); Lille, France (1890–1970)
DeHaven, Gloria (actress); Los Angeles, 7/23/1925
de Havilland, Olivia (actress); Tokyo, 7/1/1916
Dekker, Albert (actor); Brooklyn, N.Y. (1904–1968)
De Kooning, Willem (painter); Rotterdam, 4/24/1904
Delacroix, Eugène (painter); Charenton-St. Maurice, France (1798–1863)
de la Renta, Oscar (fashion designer); Santo Domingo, Dominican Republic, 7/22/1932
Delaunay, Robert (painter); Paris (1885–1941)
De Laurentiis, Dino (film producer); Torre Annunziata, Bay of Naples, Italy, 8/8/1919
Delon, Alain (actor); Sceaux, France, 11/8/1935
Del Rio, Dolores (actress); Durango, Mexico, 8/3/1905
DeLuise, Dom (comedian); Brooklyn, N.Y., 8/1/1933
Demarest, William (actor); St. Paul, 2/27/1892
de Mille, Agnes (choreographer); New York City
De Mille, Cecil Blount (film director); Ashfield, Mass. (1881–1959)
Demosthenes (orator); Athens (385?–322 B.C.)
Deneuve, Catherine (actress); Paris, 10/22/1943
De Niro, Robert (actor); New York City, 8/17/1943
Dennis, Sandy (actress); Hastings, Neb., 4/27/1937
Denver, John (Henry John Deutschendorf, Jr.) (singer); Roswell, N.M., 12/31/1943
Derain, André (painter); Chatou, Seine-et-Oise, France (1880–1954)
Dern, Bruce (actor); Chicago, 6/4/1936
Descartes, René (philosopher and mathematician); La Haye, France (1596–1650)
De Seversky, Alexander P. (aviator); Tiflis, Russia (1894–1974)
De Sica, Vittorio (film director); Sora, Italy (1901–1974)
Desmond, Johnny (composer); Detroit, 11/14/1921
Desmond, William (actor); Dublin (1878–1949)
De Soto, Hernando (explorer); Barcarrota, Spain (1500?–1542)
De Valera, Eamon (ex-President of Ireland); New York City (1882–1975)
Devine, Andy (actor); Flagstaff, Ariz. (1905–1977)
De Vries, Peter (novelist); Chicago, 2/27/1910
Dewey, George (admiral); Montpelier, Vt. (1837–1917)
Dewey, John (philosopher and educator); Burlington, Vt. (1859–1952)
Dewey, Thomas E. (politician); Owosso, Mich. (1902–1971)
Dewhurst, Colleen (actress); Montreal, 1926(?)
Diamond, Neil (singer); Brooklyn, N.Y., 1/24/1941
Dickens, Charles John Huffam (novelist); Portsea, England (1812–1870)
Dickey, James (poet); Atlanta, 2/2/1923
Dickinson, Angie (Angeline Brown) (actress); Kulm, N.D., 9/30/1932
Dickinson, Emily Elizabeth (poet); Amherst, Mass. (1830–1886)
Diddley, Bo (Elias McDaniel) (guitarist); McComb, Miss., 12/30/1928
Diefenbaker, John G. (ex-Prime Minister); Grey County, Ontario, Canada (1895–1979)
Dietrich, Marlene (Maria Magdalena von Losch) (actress); Berlin, 12/27/1901
Diggs, Dudley (actor); Dublin (1879–1947)
Diller, Phyllis (Phyllis Driver) (comedienne); Lima, Ohio, 7/17/1917
Dillinger, John (American bank robber); prob. Indianapolis (1902–1934)

Dillman, Bradford (actor); San Francisco, 4/14/1930
Dine, Jim (painter); Cincinnati, 6/16/1935
Diogenes (philosopher); Sinope (Turkey) **(412?–323** B.C.)
Dion (Dion DiMucci) (singer); Bronx, N.Y., 7/18/1939
Dior, Christian (fashion designer); Granville, France **(1905–1957)**
Disney, Walt(er) Elias (film animator and producer); Chicago **(1901–1966)**
Disraeli, Benjamin (Earl of Beaconsfield) (statesman); London **(1804–1881)**
Dix, Dorothea (civil rights reformer); Hampden, Me. **(1802–1887)**
Dix, Richard (Ernest Carlton Brimmer) (actor); St. Paul **(1894–1949)**
Dixon, Jeane (Jeane Pinckert) (seer); Medford, Wis., 1918
Doctorow, E.L. (Edgar Laurence) (novelist); New York City, 1/6/1931
Dodgson, C. L. *See* Carroll, Lewis.
Dolin, Anton (dancer); Slinfold, England, 7/27/1904
Domingo, Placido (tenor); Madrid, 1/21/1941
Domino, Fats (Antoine) (musician); New Orleans, 2/26/1928
Donahue, Phil (television personality); Cleveland, 12/21/1935
Donahue, Troy (Merle Johnson) (actor); New York City, 1/27/1938
Donat, Robert (actor); Withington, England **(1905–1958)**
Donatello (Donato Niccolò di Betto Bardi) (sculptor); Florence (Italy) (c.1386–1466)
Donne, John (poet); London **(1573–1631)**
Donovan (Donovan Leitch) (singer and songwriter); Glasgow, Scotland, 2/10/1946
Doolittle, James H. (ex-Air Force general); Alameda, Calif., 12/14/1896
Dorati, Antal (orchestra conductor); Budapest, 4/9/1906
Dors, Diana (Diana Fluck) (actress); Swondon, England, 10/23/1931
Dos Passos, John (author); Chicago **(1896–1970)**
Dostoevski, Fyodor Mikhailovich (novelist); Moscow **(1821–1881)**
Douglas, Helen Gahagan (ex-Representative); Boonton, N.J. **(1900–1980)**
Douglas, Kirk (Issur Danielovitch) (actor); Amsterdam, N.Y., 12/9/1916
Douglas, Melvyn (Melvyn Hesselberg) (actor); Macon, Ga., **(1901–1981)**
Douglas, Mike (Michael D. Dowd, Jr.) (TV personality); Chicago, 8/11/1925
Douglas, Paul (actor); Philadelphia **(1907–1959)**
Douglas, Stephen Arnold (politician); Brandon, Vt. **(1813–1861)**
Dowling, Eddie (Edward Goucher) (actor and stage producer); Woonsocket, R.I., **(1894–1976)**
Downs, Hugh (TV entertainer); Akron, Ohio, 2/14/1921
Doyle, Sir Arthur Conan (novelist and spiritualist); Edinburgh, Scotland **(1859–1930)**
Drake, Alfred (singer and actor); New York City, 10/7/1914
Drake, Sir Francis (navigator); Tavistock, England **(1545–1596)**
Dreiser, Theodore (writer); Terre Haute, Ind. **(1871–1945)**
Dressler, Marie (Leila Koeber) (actress); Cobourg, Ontario, Canada **(1869–1934)**
Dreyfus, Alfred (French army officer); Mulhouse (France) **(1859–1935)**
Dreyfuss, Richard (actor); Brooklyn, N.Y., 10/29/1947
Drury, Allen (novelist); Houston, 9/2/1918
Dryden, John (poet); Northamptonshire, England **(1631–1700)**
Dubček, Alexander (ex-President of Czechoslovakia); Uhroved (Czechoslovakia), 11/27/1921
Dubinsky, David (David Dobnievski) (labor leader); Brest-Litovsk (U.S.S.R.), 2/22/1892
Duchamp, Marcel (painter); Blainville, France **(1887–1968)**
Duchin, Peter (pianist and band leader); New York City, 7/28/1937
Duff, Howard (actor); Bremerton, Wash., 11/24/1917
Dufy, Raoul (painter); Le Havre, France **(1877–1953)**
Duke, James B. (industrialist); nr. Durham, N.C. **(1856–1925)**
Duke, Patty (Anna Marie Duke) (actress); New York City, 12/14/1946
Dullea, Keir (actor); Cleveland, 5/30/1936(?)
Dulles, Allen Welsh (ex-Director of CIA); Watertown, N.Y. **(1893-1969)**
Dulles, John Foster (statesman); Washington, D.C. **(1888–1959)**
Dumas, Alexandre (called Dumas fils) (novelist); Paris **(1824–1895)**
Dumas, Alexandre (called Dumas père) (novelist); Villers-Cotterets, France **(1802–1870)**
Du Maurier, Daphne (novelist); London, 5/13/1907
Du Maurier, George Louis Palmella Busson (novelist); Paris **(1834–1896)**
Dumont, Margaret (actress); **(1889–1965)**
Dunaway, Faye (actress); Bascom, Fla., 1/14/1941
Duncan, Isadora (dancer); San Francisco **(1878–1927)**
Duncan, Sandy (actress); Henderson, Tex., 2/20/1946
Dunn, James (actor); Santa Monica, Calif. **(1905–1967)**
Dunne, Irene (actress); Louisville, Ky., 12/20/1904
Dunnock, Mildred (actress); Baltimore, 1/25/(?)
Du Pont, Pierre S. (economist); Paris **(1739–1817)**
Durante, Jimmy (comedian); New York City **(1893–1980)**
Durbin, Deanna (Edna Mae) (actress); Winnipeg, Canada, 12/4/1922
Dürer, Albrecht (painter and engraver); Nürnberg (Germany) **(1471–1528)**
Durrell, Lawrence George (novelist); Julundur, India, 2/27/1912
Duse, Eleonora (actress); Chioggia, Italy **(1859–1924)**
Duvalier, Jean-Claude (President; son of "Papa Doc"); Port-au-Prince, Haiti, 7/3/1951
Duvall, Robert (actor); San Diego, Calif., 1931

Dvořák, Antonín (composer); Nelahozeves (Czechoslovakia) **(1841–1904)**
Dylan, Bob (Robert Zimmerman) (folk singer and composer); Duluth, Minn., 5/24/1941

E

Eagels, Jeanne (actress); Kansas City, Mo. **(1894–1929)**
Eakins, Thomas (painter and sculptor); Philadelphia, **(1844–1916)**
Earhart, Amelia (aviator); Atchison, Kan. **(1898–1937)**
Eastman, George (inventor); Waterville, N.Y. **(1854–1932)**
Eastwood, Clint (actor); San Francisco, 5/31/1931(?)
Ebsen, Buddy (Christian Ebsen, Jr.) (actor); Belleville, Ill., 4/2/1908
Eckstine, Billy (singer); Pittsburgh, 7/8/1914
Eddy, Duane (band leader); Corning, N.Y., 4/26/1938
Eddy, Mary Baker (founder of Christian Science Church); Bow, N.H. **(1821–1910)**
Eddy, Nelson (baritone and actor); Providence, R.I. **(1901–1967)**
Eden, Sir Anthony (Earl of Avon) (ex-Prime Minister); Durham, England **(1897–1977)**
Eden, Barbara (Barbara Huffman) (actress); Tucson, Ariz., 1934
Edison, Thomas Alva (inventor); Milan, Ohio **(1847–1931)**
Edwards, Ralph (TV and radio producer); Merino, Colo., 1913
Edwards, Vincent (actor); Brooklyn, N.Y., 7/7/1928
Egan, Richard (actor); San Francisco, 7/29/1923
Eggar, Samantha (actress); London, 5/3/1939
Eglevsky, André (ballet dancer); Moscow **(1917–1977)**
Ehrlich, Paul (bacteriologist); Strzelin (Poland) **(1854–1915)**
Einstein, Albert (physicist); Ulm, Germany **(1879–1955)**
Eisenhower, Milton S. (educator); Abilene, Kan., 9/15/1899
Eisenstaedt, Alfred (photographer and photojournalist); Dirschau (Poland), 12/6/1898
Ekberg, Anita (actress); Malmö, Sweden, 9/29/1931
Eldridge, Florence (Florence McKechnie) (actress); Brooklyn, N.Y., 9/5/1901
Elgar, Sir Edward (composer); Worcester, England **(1857–1934)**
Elgart, Larry (band leader); New London, Conn., 3/20/1922
El Greco (Domenicos Theotocopoulos) (painter); Candia, Crete (Greece) **(c.1541–1614)**
Eliot, George (Mary Ann Evans) (novelist); Chilvers Coton, England **(1819–1880)**
Eliot, Thomas Stearns (poet); St. Louis **(1888–1965)**
Ellington, Duke (Edward Kennedy) (jazz musician); Washington, D.C. **(1899–1974)**
Elliot, "Mama" Cass (Ellen Naomi Cohen) (singer); Baltimore **(1941–1974)**
Elman, Mischa (violinist); Stalnoye, Ukraine **(1891–1967)**
Emerson, Ralph Waldo (philosopher and poet); Boston **(1803–1882)**
Enesco, Georges (composer); Dorohoi, Romania **(1881–1955)**
Engels, Friedrich (Socialist writer); Barmen (Germany) **(1820–1895)**
Entremont, Philippe (concert pianist); Rheims, France, 6/7/1934
Epicurus (philosopher); Samos (Greece) **(341–270** B.C.)
Epstein, Sir Jacob (sculptor); New York City **(1880–1959)**
Erasmus, Desiderius (Gerhard Gerhards) (scholar); Rotterdam **(1466?–1536)**
Erhard, Ludwig (ex-Chancellor); Furth, Germany **(1897–1977)**
Erickson, Leif (actor); Alameda, Calif., 10/27/1911
Ericson, Leif (navigator); (c. 10th century A.D.)
Erikson, Erik H. (psychoanalyst); Frankfurt, Germany, 6/15/1902
Ernst, Max (painter); Bruhl, Germany **(1891–1976)**
Euclid (mathematician); Megara (Greece) **(c. 300** B.C.)
Euripides (dramatist); Salamis (Greece) **(c.484–407** B.C.)
Evans, Dale (Frances Butts) (actress and singer); Uvalde, Tex., 10/31/1912
Evans, Dame Edith (actress); London **(1888–1976)**
Evans, Maurice (actor); Dorchester, England, 6/3/1901
Everett, Chad (actor); South Bend, Ind., 1937
Evers, Charles (civil rights leader); Decatur, Miss., 9/14/1923(?)
Evers, Medgar (civil rights leader); Decatur, Miss. **(1925–1963)**
Ewell, Tom (Yewell Tompkins) (actor); Owensboro, Ky., 4/29/1909

F

Fabian (Fabian Anthony Forte) (singer); Philadelphia, 2/6/1943
Fabray, Nanette (Nanette Fabares) (actress); San Diego, Calif., 10/27/1922
Fadiman, Clifton (literary critic); Brooklyn, N.Y., 5/15/1904
Fairbanks, Douglas (Julius Ullman) (actor); Denver **(1883–1939)**
Fairbanks, Douglas, Jr. (actor); New York City, 12/9/1909
Faith, Percy (conductor); Toronto **(1908–1976)**
Falk, Peter (actor); New York City, 9/16/1927
Falla, Manuel de (composer); Cadiz, Spain **(1876–1946)**
Faraday, Michael (physicist); Newington, England **(1791–1867)**
Farber, Barry (radio broadcaster); Baltimore, Md., 1930
Farentino, James (actor); Brooklyn, N.Y., 2/24/1938

Farmer, James (civil rights leader); Marshall, Tex., 1/12/1920
Farnum, William (actor); Boston **(1876–1953)**
Farrell, Charles (actor); Onset Bay, Mass., 1901
Farrell, Eileen (operatic soprano); Willimantic, Conn., 2/13/1920
Farrell, Glenda (actress); Enid, Okla. **(1904–1971)**
Farrell, James T. (novelist); Chicago **(1904–1979)**
Farrell, Suzanne (Roberta Sue Ficker) (ballerina); Cincinnati, 8/16/1945
Farrow, Mia (actress); Los Angeles, 2/9/1946
Fasanella, Ralph (painter); New York City, 9/2/1914
Fassbinder, Rainer Werner (film and stage director); Bad Worishofen, West Germany, 5/31/1946
Fast, Howard (novelist); New York City, 11/11/1914
Faulkner, William (novelist); New Albany, Miss. **(1897–1962)**
Fawcett, Farrah (actress); Corpus Christi, Tex., 2/2/1947(?)
Faye, Alice (Ann Leppert) (actress); New York City, 5/5/1915
Feiffer, Jules (cartoonist); New York City, 1/26/1929
Feininger, Lyonel (painter); New York City **(1871–1956)**
Feldon, Barbara (actress); Pittsburgh, 3/12/1941
Feliciano, José (singer); Larez, Puerto Rico, 9/10/1945
Felker, Clay S. (editor and publisher); St. Louis, 10/2/1925(?)
Fellini, Federico (film director); Rimini, Italy, 1/20/1920
Fender, Freddie (Baldemar Huerta) (singer); San Benito, Tex., 1937
Ferber, Edna (novelist); Kalamazoo, Mich. **(1885–1968)**
Ferguson, Maynard (jazz trumpeter); Verdun, Quebec, Canada, 5/4/1928
Fermi, Enrico (atomic physicist); Rome **(1901–1954)**
Fernandel (Fernand Joseph Desire Contandin) (actor); Marseilles, France **(1903–1971)**
Ferrer, José (actor and director); Santurce, Puerto Rico, 1/8/1912
Ferrer, Mel (actor); Elberon, N.J., 8/25/1917
Fetchit, Stepin (comedian); Key West, Fla., 1902
Fiedler, Arthur (conductor); Boston **(1894–1979)**
Field, Eugene (poet); St. Louis **(1850–1895)**
Field, Marshall (merchant); nr. Conway, Mass. **(1834–1906)**
Field, Sally (actress); Pasadena, Calif., 11/6/1946
Fielding, Henry (novelist); nr. Glastonbury, England **(1707–1754)**
Fields, Gracie (comedienne); Rochdale, England **(1898–1979)**
Fields, Totie (comedienne); Hartford, Conn. **(1931–1978)**
Fields, W. C. (William Claude Dukenfield) (comedian); Philadelphia **(1880–1946)**
Filene, Edward A. (merchant); **(1860–1937)**
Finch, Peter (actor); Kensington, England **(1916–1977)**
Finney, Albert (actor); Salford, England, 5/9/1936
Firkusny, Rudolf (pianist); Napajedla (Czechoslovakia), 2/11/1912
Fischer-Dieskau, Dietrich (baritone); Berlin, 5/28/1925
Fisher, Eddie (Edwin) (singer); Philadelphia, 8/10/1928
Fitzgerald, Barry (William Joseph Shields) (actor); Dublin **(1888–1961)**
Fitzgerald, Edward (radio broadcaster); Troy, N.Y., 1898(?)
Fitzgerald, Ella (singer); Newport News, Va., 4/25/1918
Fitzgerald, F. Scott (Francis Scott Key) (novelist); St. Paul, Minn. **(1896–1940)**
Fitzgerald, Geraldine (actress); Dublin, 11/24/1914
Fitzgerald, Pegeen (radio broadcaster); Norcatur, Kan., 1910
Flack, Roberta (singer); Black Mountain, N.C., 2/10/1940
Flagstad, Kirsten (Wagnerian soprano); Hamar, Norway **(1895–1962)**
Flatt, Lester Raymond (bluegrass musician); Overton County, Tenn. **(1914–1979)**
Flaubert, Gustave (novelist); Rouen, France **(1821–1880)**
Fleming, Sir Alexander (bacteriologist); Lochfield, Scotland **(1881–1955)**
Fleming, Rhonda (Marilyn Louis) (actress); Los Angeles, 8/10/1923
Flynn, Errol (actor); Hobart, Tasmania **(1909–1959)**
Foch, Nina (actress); Leyden, Netherlands, 4/20/1924
Fodor, Eugene (violinist); Turkey Creek, Colo., 3/5/1950
Fonda, Henry (actor); Grand Island, Neb., 5/16/1905
Fonda, Jane (actress); New York City, 12/21/1937
Fonda, Peter (actor); New York City, 2/23/1939
Fontaine, Frank (singer and comedian); Cambridge, Mass. **(1920–1979)**
Fontaine, Joan (Joan de Havilland) (actress); Tokyo, 10/22/1917
Fontanne, Lynn (actress); London, 12/6/1887(?)
Fonteyn, Dame Margot (Margaret Hookham) (ballerina); Reigate, England, 5/18/1919
Forbes, Malcolm S(tevenson) (publisher and sportsman); Brooklyn, N.Y., 8/19/1919
Ford, Glenn (Gwyllyn Ford) (actor); Quebec, 5/1/1916
Ford, Henry (industrialist); Greenfield, Mich. **(1863–1947)**
Ford, Henry, II (auto maker); Detroit, 9/4/1917
Ford, John (film director); Cape Elizabeth, Me. **(1895–1973)**
Ford, Paul (actor); Baltimore **(1901–1976)**
Ford, Tennessee Ernie (Ernie Jennings Ford) (singer); Bristol, Tenn., 2/13/1919
Forsythe, John (actor); Carney's Point, N.J., 1/29/1918
Fosdick, Harry Emerson (clergyman); Buffalo, N.Y. **(1878–1968)**
Fosse, Bob (Robert Louis) (choreographer and director); Chicago, 6/23/1927
Foster, Jodie (actress); Los Angeles, 1962
Foster, Stephen Collins (composer); nr. Pittsburgh **(1826–1864)**

Foxx, Redd (John Elroy Sanford) (actor and comedian); St. Louis, 12/9/1922
Foy, Eddie, Jr. (dancer and actor); New Rochelle, N.Y., 2/4/1905
Fra Angelico (Giovanni da Fiesole) (painter); Vicchio in the Mugello, Tuscany (Italy) **(c.1387–1455)**
Fracci, Carla (ballerina); Milan, Italy, 8/20/1936
Fragonard, Jean Honoré (painter); Grasse, France **(1732–1806)**
Frampton, Peter (rock musician); Beckenham, England, 4/20/1950
France, Anatole (Jacques Anatole François Thibault) (author); Paris **(1844–1924)**
Francescatti, Zino (violinist); Marseilles, France, 8/9/1905
Franciosa, Anthony (Anthony Papaleo) (actor); New York City, 10/25/1928
Francis, Arlene (Arlene Francis Kazanjian) (actress); Boston, 10/20/1908
Francis, Connie (Concetta Franconero) (singer); Newark, N.J., 12/12/1938
Francis, Kay (Katherine Edwina Gibbs) (actress); Oklahoma City **(1903–1968)**
Franciscus, James (actor); Clayton, Mo., 1/31/1934
Franck, César Auguste (composer); Liège (Belgium) **(1822–1890)**
Franco Bahamonde, Francisco (Chief of State); El Ferrol, Spain **(1892–1975)**
Franklin, Aretha (singer); Memphis, Tenn., 3/25/1942
Franklin, Benjamin (statesman and scientist); Boston **(1706–1790)**
Frazer, Sir James George (anthropologist); Glasgow, Scotland **(1854–1941)**
Freud, Sigmund (psychoanalyst); Moravia (Czechoslovakia) **(1856–1939)**
Friedan, Betty (Betty Noami Goldstein) (feminist); Peoria, Ill., 2/4/1921
Fromm, Erich (psychoanalyst); Frankfurt-am-Main, Germany **(1900–1980)**
Frost, David (TV entertainer); Tenterden, England, 4/7/1939
Frost, Robert Lee (poet); San Francisco **(1874–1963)**
Fry, Christopher (playwright); Bristol, England, 12/18/1907
Frye, David (impressionist); Brooklyn, N.Y., 1934
Fuller, R(ichard) Buckminster (Jr.) (architect and educator); Milton, Mass., 7/12/1895
Fulton, Robert (inventor); Lancaster County, Pa. **(1765–1815)**
Funt, Allen (TV producer); Brooklyn, N.Y., 9/16/1914
Furness, Betty (Elizabeth) (ex-actress and consumer advocate); New York City, 1/3/1916

G

Gabel, Martin (actor and producer); Philadelphia, 1912
Gabin, Jean (actor); Paris **(1904–1976)**
Gable, (William) Clark (actor); Cadiz, Ohio **(1901–1960)**
Gabo, Naum (sculptor); Briansk, Russia **(1890–1977)**
Gabor, Eva (actress); Budapest, 2/11/1926(?)
Gabor, Zsa Zsa (Sari) (actress); Budapest, 2/6/1923
Gainsborough, Thomas (painter); Sudbury, Suffolk, England **(1727–1788)**
Galbraith, John Kenneth (economist); Iona Station, Ontario, Canada, 10/15/1908
Galilei, Galileo (astronomer and physicist); Pisa (Italy) **(1564–1642)**
Gallico, Paul (novelist); New York City **(1897–1976)**
Gallup, George H. (poll taker); Jefferson, Iowa, 11/18/1901
Galsworthy, John (novelist and dramatist); Coombe, England **(1867–1933)**
Galway, James (flutist); Belfast, Northern Ireland, 12/8/1939
Gambling, John A. (radio broadcaster); New York City, 1930
Gandhi, Indira (Indira Nehru) (Prime Minister); Allahabad, India, 11/19/1917
Gandhi, Mohandas Karamchand (called Mahatma Gandhi) (Hindu leader); Porbandar, India **(1869–1948)**
Gannett, Frank E. (editor and publisher); **(1876–1957)**
Garagiola, Joe (Joseph Henry) (sportscaster); St. Louis, 2/12/1926
Garbo, Greta (Greta Gustafsson) (actress); Stockholm, 9/18/1905
Gardner, Ava (Lucy Johnson) (actress); Smithfield, N.C., 12/24/1922
Gardner, Erle Stanley (novelist); Malden, Mass. **(1889–1970)**
Garfield, John (Jules Garfinkle) (actor); New York City **(1913–1952)**
Garfunkel, Art (Arthur) (singer); Newark, N.J., 11/5/1941
Gargan, William (actor); Brooklyn, N.Y., **(1905–1979)**
Garibaldi, Giuseppe (Italian nationalist leader); Nice, France **(1807–1882)**
Garland, Judy (Frances Gumm) (actress and singer); Grand Rapids, Minn. **(1922–1969)**
Garner, Erroll (jazz pianist); Pittsburgh **(1921–1977)**
Garner, James (James Bumgarner) (actor); Norman, Okla., 4/7/1928
Garner, Peggy Ann (actress); Canton, Ohio, 2/3/1932
Garrett, Betty (actress); St. Joseph, Mo., 5/23/1919
Garrick, David (actor); Hereford, England **(1717–1779)**
Garrison, William Lloyd (abolitionist); Newburyport, Mass. **(1805–1879)**
Garroway, Dave (TV host); Schenectady, N.Y., 7/13/1913
Garson, Greer (actress); County Down, Northern Ireland, 9/29/1912(?)
Gary, John (singer); Watertown, N.Y., 11/29/1932
Gassman, Vittorio (film actor and director); Genoa, Italy, 9/1/1922
Gaudí, Antonio (architect); Reus, Spain **(1852–1926)**

Gauguin, Eugène Henri Paul (painter); Paris (1848-1903)
Gautama Buddha (Prince Siddhartha) (philosopher); Kapilavastu (India) (563?-?483 B.C.)
Gavin, John (actor); Los Angeles, 4/8/1935
Gayle, Crystal (Brenda Gayle Webb) (singer); Paintsville, Ky., 1951
Gaynor, Janet (actress); Philadelphia, 10/6/1906
Gaynor, Mitzi (Francesca Mitzi Marlene de Czanyi von Gerber) (actress); Chicago, 9/4/1931
Gazzara, Ben (Biago Anthony Gazzara) (actor); New York City, 8/28/1930
Gebel-Williams, Gunther (animal trainer); Schweidnitz (Poland), 1934
Geddes, Barbara Bel (actress); New York City, 10/31/1922
Genet, Jean (playwright); Paris, 12/19/1910
Genghis Khan (Temujin) (conqueror); nr. Lake Baikal (U.S.S.R.) (1162-1227)
Genn, Leo (actor); London (1905-1978)
Gentry, Bobbie (Roberta Streeter) (singer); Chickasaw Co., Miss., 7/27/1944
Gericault, Jean Louis (painter); Rouen, France (1791-1824)
Gernreich, Rudi (fashion designer); Vienna, 8/8/1922
Geronimo (Goyathlay) (Apache chieftain); Arizona (1829-1909)
Gershwin, George (composer); Brooklyn, N.Y. (1898-1937)
Gershwin, Ira (lyricist); New York City, 12/6/1896
Getty, J. Paul (oil executive); Minneapolis (1892-1976)
Getz, Stan (saxophonist); Philadelphia, 2/2/1927
Ghiberti, Lorenzo (goldsmith and sculptor); Florence (1378-1455)
Giacometti, Alberto (sculptor); Switzerland (1901-1966)
Giannini, Giancarlo (actor); La Spezia, Italy, 8/1/1942
Gibbon, Edward (historian); Putney, England (1737-1794)
Gibson, Charles Dana (illustrator); Roxbury, Mass. (1867-1944)
Gibson, Hoot (Edward) (actor); Tememah, Neb. (1892-1962)
Gide, André (author); Paris (1869-1951)
Gielgud, Sir John (actor); London, 4/14/1904
Gilbert, John (movie actor); Logan, Utah (1897-1936)
Gilbert, Sir William Schwenck (librettist); London (1836-1911)
Gilels, Emil (concert pianist); Odessa, Ukraine, 1916
Gillespie, Dizzy (John Birks Gillespie) (jazz trumpeter); Cheraw, S.C., 10/21/1917
Gimbel, Bernard F. (merchant); Vincennes, Ind. (1885-1966)
Gingold, Hermione (actress and comedienne); London, 12/9/1897
Ginsberg, Allen (poet); Newark, N.J., 6/3/1926
Giorgione (painter); Castelfranco, (Italy) (c.1477-1510)
Giotto di Bondone (painter); Vespignamo (Italy) (c.1266-1337)
Giovanni, Nikki (poet); Knoxville, Tenn., 6/7/1943
Giroud, Françoise (French government official); Geneva, 9/21/1916
Gish, Dorothy (actress); Massillon, Ohio (1898-1968)
Gish, Lillian (Lillian de Guiche) (actress); Springfield, Ohio, 10/14/1896(?)
Givenchy, Hubert (fashion designer); Beauvais, France, 2/21/1927
Gladstone, William Ewart (statesman); Liverpool, England (1809-1898)
Gleason, Jackie (comedian); Brooklyn, N.Y., 2/26/1916
Gleason, James (actor); New York City (1886-1959)
Gluck, Christoph Willibald (composer); Erasbach (Germany) (1714-1787)
Gobel, George (comedian); Chicago, 5/20/1920
Godard, Jean Luc (film director); Paris, 12/3/1930
Goddard, Paulette (Marion Levy) (actress); Great Neck, N.Y., 6/3/1911
Godfrey, Arthur (entertainer); New York City, 8/31/1903
Goebbels, Joseph Paul (Nazi leader); Rheydt, Germany (1897-1945)
Goering, Hermann (Nazi leader); Rosenheim, Germany (1893-1946)
Goethals, George Washington (engineer); Brooklyn, N.Y. (1858-1928)
Goethe, Johann Wolfgang von (poet); Frankfurt am Main, Germany (1749-1832)
Gogol, Nikolai Vasilievich (novelist); nr. Mirgorod, Ukraine (1809-1852)
Goldberg, Rube (cartoonist); San Francisco (1883-1970)
Golden, Harry (Harry Goldhurst) (author); New York City, 5/6/1902
Goldsmith, Oliver (dramatist and poet); County Longford, Ireland (1728-1774)
Goldwyn, Samuel (Samuel Goldfish) (film producer); Warsaw (1882-1974)
Golenpaul, Dan (creator of Information Please radio show and editor of almanac of same name); New York City (1900-1974)
Gompers, Samuel (labor leader); London (1850-1924)
Goodall, Jane (Baroness van Lawick-Goodall) (ethologist); London, 4/3/1934
Goodman, Benny (clarinetist); Chicago, 5/30/1909
Goodyear, Charles (inventor); New Haven, Conn. (1800-1860)
Gordimer, Nadine (novelist and short-story writer); Springs, South Africa, 12/20/1923
Gordon, Max (stage producer); New York City; (1892-1978)
Gordon, Ruth (actress); Wollaston, Mass., 10/30/1896
Gordy, Berry, Jr. (record company executive); Detroit, 11/28/1929
Gore, Lesley (singer); Tenafly, N.J., 1946
Goren, Charles H. (bridge expert); Philadelphia, 3/4/1901
Gorki, Maxim (Alexei Maximovich Peshkov) (author); Nizhni Novgorod, Russia (1868-1936)
Gorky, Arshile (painter); Armenia (1904-1948)
Gorme, Eydie (singer); Bronx, N.Y., 8/16/1932

Gorshin, Frank (actor); Pittsburgh, 4/5/1934
Gosden, Freeman F. See Amos
Gould, Chester (cartoonist); Pawnee, Okla., 11/20/1900
Gould, Elliott (Elliott Goldstein) (actor); Brooklyn, N.Y., 8/29/1938
Gould, Glenn (concert pianist); Toronto, 9/25/1932
Gould, Morton (composer); Richmond Hill, Queens, N.Y., 12/10/1913
Goulet, Robert (singer); Lawrence, Mass., 11/26/1933
Gounod, Charles François (composer); Paris (1818-1893)
Goya y Lucientes, Francisco José de (painter); Fuendetodos, Spain (1746-1828)
Grable, Betty (actress); St. Louis (1916-1973)
Graham, Bill (Wolfgang Grajonca) (rock impresario); Berlin, 1931
Graham, Billy (William F.) (evangelist); Charlotte, N.C., 11/7/1918
Graham, Katharine Meyer (newspaper publisher); New York City, 6/16/1917
Graham, Martha (choreographer); Pittsburgh, 5/11/1894(?)
Grahame, Gloria (Gloria Hallwood) (actress); Los Angeles, 11/28/1929
Gramm, Donald (bass-baritone); Milwaukee, 2/26/1927
Granger, Farley (actor); San Jose, Calif., 7/1/1925
Granger, Stewart (James Stewart) (actor); London, 5/6/1913
Grant, Cary (Alexander Archibald Leach) (actor); Bristol, England, 1/18/1904
Grant, Kathryn (actress); Houston, Tex., 1933
Grant, Lee (Lyova Haskell Rosenthal) (actress); New York City, 10/31/1930
Granville, Bonita (actress and producer); New York City, 1923
Grass, Günter (novelist); Danzig (Poland), 10/16/1927
Grauer, Ben (radio and TV announcer); New York City (1908-1977)
Graves, Peter (Peter Arness) (actor); Minneapolis, 3/18/1926
Graves, Robert (writer); London, 7/24/1895
Gray, Barry (Bernard Yaroslaw) (radio interviewer); Atlantic City, N.J., 7/2/1916
Gray, Dolores (singer and actress); Chicago, 6/7/1930
Gray, Thomas (poet); London (1716-1771)
Grayson, Kathryn (Zelma Hednick) (singer and actress); Winston-Salem, N.C., 2/9/1923
Greco, Buddy (singer); Philadelphia, 8/14/1926
Greco, José (dancer); Montorio nei Frentani, Italy, 12/23/1918
Greeley, Horace (journalist and politician); Amherst, N.H. (1811-1872)
Green, Adolph (actor and lyricist); New York City, 12/2/1915
Green, Al (singer); Forrest City, Ark., 4/13/1946
Greene, Graham (novelist); Berkhamsted, England, 10/2/1904
Greene, Lorne (actor); Ottawa, 2/12/1915
Greene, Martyn (actor); London (1899-1975)
Greenstreet, Sydney (actor); Sandwich, England (1879-1954)
Greenwood, Joan (actress and director); London, 3/4/1921
Greer, Germaine (feminist); Melbourne, 1/29/1939
Gregory, Cynthia (ballerina); Los Angeles, 7/8/1946
Gregory, Dick (comedian); St. Louis, 1932
Greuze, Jean-Baptiste (painter); Tournus, France (1725-1805)
Grey, Joel (Joel Katz) (actor); Cleveland, 4/11/1932
Grey, Zane (author); Zanesville, Ohio (1875-1939)
Grieg, Edvard Hagerup (composer); Bergen, Norway (1843-1907)
Grier, Roosevelt (entertainer and former athlete); Cuthbert, Ga., 7/14/1932
Griffin, Merv (TV entertainer); San Mateo, Calif., 7/6/1925
Griffith, Andy (actor); Mount Airy, N.C., 6/1/1926
Griffith, David Lewelyn Wark (film producer); La Grange, Ky. (1875-1948)
Grigorovich, Yuri (choreographer); Leningrad, 1/1/1927
Grimes, Tammy (actress); Lynn, Mass., 1/30/1934
Grimm, Jacob (author of fairy tales); Hanau (Germany) (1785-1863)
Grimm, Wilhelm (author of fairy tales); Hanau (Germany) (1786-1859)
Gris, Juan (José Victoriano González) (painter); Madrid (1887-1927)
Grizzard, George (actor); Roanoke Rapids, N.C., 4/1/1928
Gromyko, Andrei A. (diplomat); Starye Gromyki, Russia, 7/5/1909
Gropius, Walter (architect); Berlin (1883-1969)
Gropper, William (painter, illustrator); New York City (1897-1977)
Grosz, George (painter); Germany (1893-1959)
Guardino, Harry (actor); New York City, 12/23/1925
Guggenheim, Meyer (capitalist); Langnau, Switzerland (1828-1905)
Guinness, Sir Alec (actor); London, 4/2/1914
Guitry, Sacha (Alexandre) (actor and film director); St. Petersburg, Russia (1885-1957)
Gunther, John (author); Chicago (1901-1970)
Gutenberg, Johann (printer); Mainz (Germany) (1400?-?1468)
Guthrie, Arlo (singer); New York City, 7/10/1947
Guthrie, Woody (folk singer and composer); Okemah, Okla. (1912-1967)
Gwenn, Edmund (actor); London (1875-1959)

H

Hackett, Bobby (trumpeter); Providence, R.I. (1915-1976)
Hackett, Buddy (Leonard Hacker) (comedian and actor); Brooklyn, N.Y., 8/31/1924
Hackman, Gene (actor); San Bernardino, Calif., 1/30/1931

Hagen, Uta (actress); Göttingen, Germany, 6/12/1919
Haggard, Merle (songwriter); Bakersfield, Calif., 4/6/1937
Hagman, Larry (actor); Weatherford, Tex., 1931
Haig, Alexander Meigs, Jr. (Secretary of State and ex-general); Bala-Cynwyd, Pa., 12/2/1924
Haile Selassie (Ras Tafari Makonnen) (ex-Emperor); Ethiopia (1892–1975)
Hailey, Arthur (novelist); Luton, England, 4/5/1920
Halberstam, David (journalist); New York City, 4/10/1934
Hale, Edward Everett (clergyman and author); Boston (1822–1909)
Hale, Nathan (American Revolutionary officer); Coventry, Conn. (1755–1776)
Haley, Alex (writer); Ithaca, N.Y., 8/11/1921
Hall, Monty (TV personality); Winnipeg, Canada, 1923
Hals, Frans (painter); Antwerp (Netherlands) (1580?–1666)
Halsey, William Frederick, Jr. (naval officer); Elizabeth, N.J. (1882–1959)
Hamill, Pete (journalist); Brooklyn, N.Y., 6/24/1935
Hamilton, Alexander (statesman); Nevis Island (West Indies Associated States) (1757?–1804)
Hamilton, George (actor); Memphis, Tenn., 8/12/1939
Hamilton, Margaret (actress); Cleveland, 9/12/1902
Hamlisch, Marvin (composer and pianist); New York City, 6/2/1944
Hammarskjøld, Dag (U.N. Secretary-General); Jönköping, Sweden (1905–1961)
Hammerstein, Oscar, II (librettist and stage producer); New York City (1895–1960)
Hampden, Walter (Walter Hampden Dougherty) (actor); Brooklyn, N.Y. (1879–1955)
Hampton, James (actor); Oklahoma City, 7/9/1936
Hampton, Lionel (vibraharpist and band leader); Birmingham, Ala., 4/20/1914
Hancock, John (statesman); Braintree, Mass. (1737–1793)
Hand, Learned (jurist); Albany, N.Y. (1872–1961)
Handel, George Frederick (Georg Friedrich Händel) (composer); Halle (Germany) (1685–1759)
Handy, William Christopher (blues composer); Florence, Ala. (1873–1958)
Hannibal (Carthaginian general); North Africa (247–182 B.C.)
Hanson, Howard (conductor); Wahoo, Neb., (1896–1981)
Harburg, E. Y. "Yip" (songwriter); New York City, 4/8/1896
Harding, Ann (actress); San Antonio, Tex. (1902–1981)
Hardwicke, Sir Cedric (actor); Stourbridge, England (1893–1964)
Hardy, Oliver (comedian); Atlanta (1892–1957)
Hardy, Thomas (novelist); Dorsetshire, England (1840–1928)
Harkness, Edward S. (capitalist); Cleveland (1874–1940)
Harlow, Jean (Harlean Carpentier) (actress); Kansas City, Mo. (1911–1937)
Harnick, Sheldon (lyricist); Chicago, 4/30/1924
Harper, Valerie (actress); Suffern, N.Y., 8/22/1940(?)
Harriman, W. (William) Averell (ex-Governor of New York); New York City, 11/15/1891
Harris, Barbara (actress); Evanston, Ill., 1935
Harris, Emmylou (singer); Birmingham, Ala., 1949
Harris, Julie (actress); Grosse Pointe Park, Mich., 12/2/1925
Harris, Phil (actor and band leader); Linton, Ind., 6/24/1906
Harris, Richard (actor); Limerick, Ireland, 10/1/1933
Harris, Rosemary (actress); Ashby, England, 9/19/1930
Harris, Roy (composer); Lincoln County, Olka. (1898–1979)
Harrison, George (singer and songwriter); Liverpool, England, 2/25/1943
Harrison, Noel (singer and actor); London, 1/29/1936
Harrison, Rex (Reginald Carey) (actor); Huyton, England, 3/5/1908
Hart, Lorenz (lyricist); New York (1895–1943)
Hart, Moss (playwright); New York City (1904–1961)
Hart, William S. (actor); Newburgh, N.Y. (1862–1946)
Harte, Bret (Francis Brett Harte) (author); Albany, N.Y. (1836–1902)
Hartford, Huntington (George Huntington Hartford II) (A.&P. heir); New York City, 4/18/1911
Hartford, John (singer and banjoist); New York City, 12/30/1937
Hartman, Elizabeth (actress); Youngstown, Ohio, 12/23/1941
Harvey, Laurence (Larushka Skikne) (actor); Joniskis, Lithuania (1928–1973)
Harvey, William (physician); Folkestone, England (1578–1657)
Hasso, Signe (actress); Stockholm, 8/15/1915
Haver, June (actress); Rock Island, Ill., 6/10/1926
Havoc, June (June Hovick) (actress); Seattle, 1916
Hawkins, Jack (actor); London (1910–1973)
Hawn, Goldie (actress); Washington, D.C., 11/21/1945
Haworth, Jill (actress); Sussex, England, 1945
Hawthorne, Nathaniel (novelist); Salem, Mass. (1804–1864)
Hay, John Milton (statesman); Salem, Ind. (1838–1905)
Hayakawa, Sessue (actor); Honshu, Japan (1890–1973)
Hayden, Melissa (ballerina); Toronto, 4/25/1923
Hayden, Sterling (Sterling Relyea Walter) (actor and writer); Montclair, N.J., 3/26/1916
Haydn, Franz Joseph (composer); Rohrau (Austria) (1732–1809)
Hayes, Helen (Helen Hayes Brown) (actress); Washington, D.C., 10/10/1900
Hayes, Isaac (composer); Covington, Tenn., 8/20/1942

Hayward, Louis (actor); Johannesburg, South Africa, 1909
Hayward, Susan (Edythe Marrener) (actress); Brooklyn, N.Y. (1919?–1975)
Hayworth, Rita (Margarita Cansino) (actress); New York City, 10/17/1918
Head, Edith (costume designer); Los Angeles, 10/28/1907
Hearst, William Randolph (publisher); San Francisco (1863–1951)
Hearst, William Randolph, Jr. (publisher); New York City, 1/27/1908
Heath, Edward (ex-Prime Minister); Broadstairs, England, 7/9/1916
Heatherton, Joey (actress); Rockville Centre, N.Y., 9/14/1944
Hecht, Ben (author); New York City (1894–1964)
Heckart, Eileen (actress); Columbus, Ohio, 3/29/1919
Heflin, Van (Emmet Evan Heflin) (actor); Walters, Okla. (1910–1971)
Hefner, Hugh (publisher); Chicago, 4/9/1926
Hegel, Georg Wilhelm Friedrich (philosopher); Stuttgart (Germany) (1770–1831)
Heifetz, Jascha (concert violinist); Vilna, Russia, 2/2/1901
Heine, Heinrich (Harry) (poet); Düsseldorf (Germany) (1797–1856)
Heinemann, Gustav (ex-President of Germany); Schweim, Germany (1899–1976)
Heller, Joseph (novelist); Brooklyn, N.Y., 5/1/1923
Hellman, Lillian (playwright); New Orleans, 6/20/1905
Hemingway, Ernest Miller (novelist); Oak Park, Ill. (1899–1961)
Hemmings, David (actor); Guilford, England, 11/2/1941
Henderson, Florence (actress); Dale, Ind., 2/14/1934
Henderson, Skitch (Lyle Russell Cedric) (conductor and pianist); Birmingham, England(?), 1/27/1918
Hendrix, Jimi (James Marshall Hendrix) (guitarist); Seattle (1942–1970)
Henning, Doug (magician and actor); Winnipeg, Canada, 1947(?)
Henreid, Paul (actor); Trieste, 1/10/1908
Henri, Robert (painter); Cincinnati (1865–1926)
Henry, O. (William Sidney Porter) (story writer); Greensboro, N.C. (1862–1910)
Henry, Patrick (statesman); Hanover County, Va. (1736–1799)
Henson, Jim (puppeteer); Greenville, Miss., 9/24/1936
Hepburn, Audrey (actress); Brussels, Belgium, 5/4/1929
Hepburn, Katharine (actress); Hartford, Conn., 11/8/1909
Hepplewhite, George (furniture designer); England (?–1786)
Hepworth, Barbara (sculptor); Wakefield, England (1903–1975)
Herbert, Victor (composer); Dublin (1859–1924)
Herblock (Herbert L. Block) (political cartoonist); Chicago, 10/13/1909
Herman, Woody (Woodrow Charles) (band leader); Milwaukee, 5/16/1913
Herod (Herodes) (called Herod the Great) (King of Judea) (73?–4 B.C.)
Herodotus (historian); Halicarnassus (Turkey) (c. 484–425 B.C.)
Hershfield, Harry (humorist and raconteur); Cedar Rapids, Iowa (1885–1974)
Hersholt, Jean (actor); Copenhagen (1886–1956)
Heston, Charlton (actor); Evanston, Ill., 10/4/1924
Heyerdahl, Thor (ethnologist and explorer); Larvik, Norway, 10/6/1914
Hildegarde (Hildegarde Loretta Sell) (singer); Adell, Wis., 2/1/1906
Hill, Arthur (actor); Melfort, Canada, 8/1/1922
Hillary, Sir Edmund (mountain climber); New Zealand, 7/20/1919
Hiller, Wendy (actress); Bramhall, England, 8/15/1912
Hilliard, Harriet. *See* Nelson, Harriet
Hindemith, Paul (composer); Hanau, Germany (1895–1963)
Hindenburg, Paul von (statesman); Posen (Poland) (1847–1934)
Hines, Earl "Fatha" (jazz pianist); Duquesne, Pa., 12/28/1905
Hines, Jérome (Jerome Heinz) (basso); Los Angeles, 11/8/1921
Hingle, Pat (actor); Denver, 7/19/1924
Hippocrates (physician); Cos, Greece (c. 460–c. 377 B.C.)
Hirohito (Emperor); Tokyo, 4/29/1901
Hirschfeld, Al (Albert) (cartoonist); St. Louis, 6/21/1903
Hirschhorn, Joseph Herman (financier, speculator, and art collector); Mitau, Latvia (1899–1981)
Hirt, Al (trumpeter); New Orleans, 11/7/1922
Hitchcock, Alfred J. (film director); London (1899–1980)
Hitler, Adolf (Adolf Schicklgruber) (German dictator); Braunau, Austria (1889–1945)
Hitzig, William Maxwell (physician); Austria, 12/15/1904
Hobson, Laura Z. (Laura K. Zametkin) (novelist); New York City, 1900(?)
Hodges, Eddie (actor); Hattiesburg, Miss., 3/5/1947
Hoffa James R(iddle) (labor leader); Brazil, Ind., 2/14/1913 (presumed dead, 1977)
Hoffman, Dustin (film actor and director); Los Angeles, 8/8/1937
Hofmann, Hans (painter); Germany (1880–1966)
Hogarth, William (painter and engraver); London (1697–1764)
Holbein, Hans (the Elder) (painter); Augsburg (Germany) (1465?–1524)
Holbein, Hans (the Younger) (painter); Augsburg (Germany) (1497?–1543)
Holbrook, Hal (actor); Cleveland, 2/17/1925
Holden, William (William Franklin Beedle, Jr.) (actor); O'Fallon, Ill., 4/17/1918
Holder, Geoffrey (dancer); Port-of-Spain, Trinidad, 8/1/1930
Holiday, Billie (Eleanora Fagan) (jazz-blues singer); Baltimore (1915–1959)
Holliday, Judy (Judith Tuvim) (comedienne); New York City (1922–1965)

Holloway, Stanley (actor); London, 10/1/1890
Holloway, Sterling (actor); Cedartown, Ga., 1905
Holm, Celeste (actress); New York City, 4/29/1919
Holmes, Oliver Wendell (author); Cambridge, Mass. **(1809–1894)**
Holt, Jack (actor); Winchester, Va. **(1888–1951)**
Holtz, Lou (comedian); San Francisco **(1898–1980)**
Home, Lord (Alexander Frederick Douglas-Home) (diplomat); London, 7/2/1903
Homeier, Skip (actor); Chicago, 1930
Homer, Winslow (painter); Boston, Mass. **(1836–1910)**
Homer (Greek poet) **(c.850** B.C.**?)**
Homolka, Oscar (actor); Vienna **(1898–1978)**
Honegger, Arthur (composer); Le Havre, France **(1892–1955)**
Hook, Sidney (philosopher); New York City, 12/20/1902
Hoover, J. Edgar (FBI director); Washington, D.C. **(1895–1972)**
Hope, Bob (Leslie Townes Hope) (comedian); London, 5/29/1903
Hopkins, Anthony (actor); Port Talbot, Wales, 12/31/1937
Hopkins, Johns (financier); Anne Arundel County, Md. **(1795–1873)**
Hopkins, Miriam (actress); Bainbridge, Ga. **(1902–1972)**
Hopper, Dennis (actor); Dodge City, Kan., 5/17/1936
Hopper, Edward (painter); Nyack, N.Y. **(1882–1967)**
Horace (Quintus Horatius Flaccus) (poet); Venosa (Italy) **(65–8** B.C.**)**
Horne, Lena (singer); Brooklyn, N.Y., 6/30/1917
Horne, Marilyn (mezzo-soprano); Bradford, Pa., 1/16/1934
Horowitz, Vladimir (pianist); Kiev, Russia, 10/1/1904
Horton, Edward Everett (comedian); Brooklyn, N.Y. **(1887–1970)**
Houdini, Harry (Ehrich Weiss) (magician); Appleton, Wis. **(1874–1926)**
Houseman, John (John Haussmann) (producer, director, and actor); Bucharest, 9/22/1902
Housman, Alfred Edward (poet); Fockburg, England **(1859–1936)**
Houston, Samuel (political leader); Rockbridge County, Va. **(1793–1863)**
Howard, Leslie (Leslie Stainer) (actor); London **(1893–1943)**
Howard, Trevor (actor); Kent, England, 9/29/1916
Howe, Elias (inventor); Spencer, Mass. **(1819–1867)**
Howe, Irving (literary critic); New York City, 6/11/1920
Howe, Julia Ward (actress and reformer); New York City **(1819–1910)**
Howes, Sally Ann (actress); London, 7/20/1934
Hudson, Henry (English navigator); **(?–1611)**
Hudson, Rock (born Roy Scherer, Jr.; took Roy Fitzgerald as legal name) (actor); Winnetka, Ill., 11/17/1925
Hughes, Charles Evans (jurist); Glens Falls, N.Y. **(1862–1948)**
Hughes, Howard (industrialist and film producer); Houston **(1905–1976)**
Hughes, Langston (poet); Joplin, Mo. **(1902–1967)**
Hugo, Victor Marie (author); Besançon, France **(1802–1885)**
Hume, David (philosopher); Edinburgh, Scotland **(1711–1776)**
Humperdinck, Engelbert (Arnold Dorsey) (singer); Madras, India, 5/2/1936
Humperdinck, Engelbert (composer); Siegburg (Germany) **(1854–1921)**
Hunt, H. L. (industrialist); nr. Vandalia, Ill. **(1889–1974)**
Hunt, Marsha (actress); Chicago, 10/17/1917
Hunter, Kim (Janet Cole) (actress); Detroit, 11/12/1922
Hunter, Tab (Arthur Andrew Gelien) (actor); New York City, 7/11/1931
Huntley, Chet (TV newscaster); Cardwell, Mont. **(1911–1974)**
Hurok, Sol (Solomon) (impresario); Pogar, Russia **(1884–1974)**
Hurst, Fannie (novelist); Hamilton, Ohio **(1889–1968)**
Hussein I (King); Jordan, 11/14/1935
Huston, John (film director and writer); Nevada, Mo., 8/5/1906
Huston, Walter (Walter Houghston) (actor); Toronto **(1884–1950)**
Hutchins, Robert M. (educator); Brooklyn, N.Y. **(1899–1977)**
Hutton, Barbara (Woolworth heiress); New York City **(1912–1979)**
Hutton, Betty (Betty Thornburg) (actress); Battle Creek, Mich., 2/26/1921
Hutton, Lauren (model and actress); Charleston, S.C., 1944
Huxley, Aldous (author); Godalming, England **(1894–1963)**
Huxley, Sir Julian S. (biologist and author); London **(1887–1975)**
Huxley, Thomas Henry (biologist); Ealing, England **(1825–1895)**

I

Ian, Janis (singer); New York City, 5/7/1951
Ibsen, Henrik (dramatist); Skien, Norway **(1828–1906)**
Inge, William (playwright); Independence, Kan. **(1913–1973)**
Ingres, Jean Auguste Dominique (painter); Montauban, France **(1780–1867)**
Inness, George (painter); nr. Newburgh, N.Y. **(1825–1894)**
Ionesco, Eugène (playwright); Slatina, Romania, 11/26/1912
Ireland, John (actor); Vancouver, B.C., Canada, 1/30/1915
Irving, Washington (author); New York City **(1783–1859)**
Isherwood, Christopher (novelist and playwright); nr. Dilsey and High Lane, England, 8/26/1904
Iturbi, José (concert pianist); Valencia, Spain **(1895–1980)**
Ives, Burl (Icle Ivanhoe) (singer); Hunt, Ill., 6/14/1909
Ives, Charles E(dward) (composer); Danbury, Conn. **(1874–1954)**

J

Jackson, Anne (actress); Millvale, Pa., 9/3/1926
Jackson, Glenda (actress); Hoylake, England, 1937(?)
Jackson, Rev. Jesse (civil rights leader); Greenville, S.C., 10/8/1941
Jackson, Kate (actress); Alabama, 1949
Jackson, Mahalia (gospel singer); New Orleans **(1912–1972)**
Jackson, Thomas Jonathan ("Stonewall") (general); Clarksburg, Va. (now W. Va.) **(1824–1863)**
Jacobi, Lou (actor); Toronto, 12/28/1913
Jacobs, Jane (urbanologist); Scranton, Pa., 5/1/1916
Jaffe, Sam (actor); New York City, 3/8/1893
Jagger, Dean (actor); Lima, Ohio, 11/7/1903
Jagger, Mick (Michael Philip) (singer); Dartford, England, 7/26/1944
James, Harry (trumpeter); Albany, Ga., 3/15/1916
James, Henry (novelist); New York City **(1843–1916)**
James, Jesse Woodson (outlaw); Clay County, Mo. **(1847–1882)**
James, William (psychologist); New York City **(1842–1910)**
Jameson, (Margaret) Storm (novelist); Whitby, England, 1897
Janis, Byron (pianist); McKeesport, Pa., 3/24/1928
Jannings, Emil (actor); Brooklyn, N.Y. **(1886–1950)**
Janssen, David (David Meyer) (actor); Naponee, Neb. **(1930–1980)**
Jay, John (statesman and jurist); New York City **(1745–1829)**
Jeanmaire, Renée (dancer); Paris, 4/29/1924
Jenner, Edward (physician); Berkeley, England **(1749–1823)**
Jennings, Waylon (singer); Littlefield, Tex., 1937
Jessel, George (entertainer); New York City **(1898–1981)**
Jessup, Philip C. (jurist); New York City, 1/5/1897
Joan of Arc (Jeanne d'Arc) (saint and patriot); Domremy-la-Pucelle, France **(1412–1431)**
Joffrey, Robert (Abdullah Jaffa Bey Khan) (choreographer); Seattle, 12/24/1930
John, Elton (Reginald Kenneth Dwight) (singer and pianist); Pinner, England, 3/25/1947
Johns, Glynis (actress); Pretoria, South Africa, 10/5/1923
Johns, Jasper (painter and sculptor); Augusta, Ga., 5/15/1930
Johnson, James Weldon (author and educator); Jacksonville, Fla. **(1871–1938)**
Johnson, Philip Cortelyou (architect); Cleveland, Ohio, 7/8/1906
Johnson, Samuel (lexicographer and author); Lichfield, England **(1709–1784)**
Johnson, Van (actor); Newport, R.I., 8/20/1916
Joliot-Curie, Frédéric (physicist); Paris **(1900–1958)**
Joliot-Curie, Irène (Irène Curie) (physicist); France **(1897–1956)**
Jolliet (or Joliet), Louis (explorer); Beaupré, Canada **(1645–1700)**
Jolson, Al (Asa Yoelson) (actor and singer); St. Petersburg, Russia **(1886–1950)**
Jones, Carolyn (singer and actress); Amarillo, Tex., 4/28/1933
Jones, Dean (actor); Morgan County, Ala., 1/25/1935
Jones, George (singer); Saratoga, Tex., 9/12/1931
Jones, Inigo (architect); London **(1573–1652)**
Jones, James (novelist); Robinson, Ill. **(1921–1977)**
Jones, James Earl (actor); Arkabutla, Miss., 1/17/1931
Jones, Jennifer (Phyllis Isley) (actress); Tulsa, Okla., 3/2/1919
Jones, John Paul (John Paul) (naval officer); Scotland **(1747–1792)**
Jones, Quincy (composer); Chicago, 3/14/1933
Jones, Shirley (singer and actress); Smithtown, Pa., 3/31/1934
Jones, Tom (Thomas Jones Woodward) (singer); Pontypridd, Wales, 6/7/1940
Jong, Erica (writer); New York City, 3/26/1942
Jonson, Ben (Benjamin) (poet and dramatist); Westminster, England **(1572–1637)**
Joplin, Janis (singer); Port Arthur, Tex. **(1943–1970)**
Jory, Victor (actor); Dawson City, Yukon, Canada, 11/23/1902
Jourdan, Louis (Louis Gendre) (actor); Marseilles, France, 6/19/1920
Joyce, James (novelist); Dublin **(1882–1941)**
Juárez, Benito Pablo (statesman); Guelatao, Mexico **(1806–1872)**
Juliana (Queen); The Hague, Netherlands, 4/30/1909
Jung, Carl Gustav (psychoanalyst); Basel, Switzerland **(1875–1961)**
Jurado, Katy (actress); Guadalajara, Mexico, 1927

K

Kabalevsky, Dmitri (composer); St. Petersburg, Russia, 12/30/1904
Kádár, János (Communist Party leader); Hungary, 1912
Kahn, Gus (songwriter); Coblenz, Germany **(1886–1941)**
Kahn, Louis I. (architect); Oesel Island, Estonia **(1901–1974)**
Kahn, Madeline (actress); Boston, 9/29/1942
Kaminska, Ida (actress); Odessa, Russia **(1899–1980)**
Kandinsky, Wassily (painter); Moscow **(1866–1944)**
Kanin, Garson (playwright); Rochester, N.Y., 11/24/1912
Kant, Immanuel (philosopher); Königsberg (Germany) **(1724–1804)**
Kantor, MacKinlay (novelist); Webster City, Iowa **(1904–1977)**

Kaplan, Gabe (actor); Brooklyn, N.Y., 1945
Karloff, Boris (William Henry Pratt) (actor); London **(1887–1969)**
Kaufman, George S. (playwright); Pittsburgh **(1889–1961)**
Kaye, Danny (David Daniel Kominski) (comedian); Brooklyn, N.Y., 1/18/1913
Kaye, Sammy (band leader); Cleveland, 3/13/1910
Kazan, Elia (director); Constantinople, Turkey, 9/7/1909
Kazan, Lainie (singer); New York City, 1940
Keach, Stacy (actor); Savannah, Ga., 6/2/1941
Keaton, Buster (Joseph Frank Keaton) (comedian); Piqua, Kan. **(1896–1966)**
Keaton, Diane (actress); Los Angeles, 1/5/1946
Keats, John (poet); London **(1795–1821)**
Keel, Howard (singer and actor); Gillespie, Ill., 4/13/1919
Keeler, Ruby (Lehy Keeler) (actress and dancer); Halifax, Nova Scotia, Canada, 8/25/1910
Kefauver, Estes (legislator); Madisonville, Tenn. **(1903–1963)**
Keith, Brian (actor); Bayonne, N.J., 11/14/1921
Keller, Helen Adams (author and educator); Tuscumbia, Ala. **(1880–1968)**
Kellerman, Sally (actress); Long Beach, Calif., 6/2/1938
Kelly, Emmett (clown); Sedan, Kan., **(1898–1979)**
Kelly, Gene (dancer and actor); Pittsburgh, 8/23/1912
Kelly, Grace (Princess Grace of Monaco) (former actress); Philadelphia, 11/12/1929
Kelly, Patsy (actress and comedienne); Brooklyn, N.Y., 1/12/1910
Kelly, Walt (cartoonist); Philadelphia **(1913–1973)**
Kemal Ataturk (Mustafa Kemal) (Turkish soldier and statesman); Salonika (Greece) **(1881–1938)**
Kennan, George F. (diplomat); Milwaukee, 2/16/1904
Kennedy, Arthur (actor); Worcester, Mass., 2/17/1914
Kennedy, George (actor); New York City, 2/18/1925
Kennedy, Jacqueline. *See* Onassis, Jacqueline
Kennedy, Joseph P. (financier); Boston **(1888–1969)**
Kennedy, Robert Francis (legislator); Brookline, Mass. **(1925–1968)**
Kennedy, Rose Fitzgerald (President's mother); Boston, 7/22/1890
Kent, Rockwell (painter); Tarrytown Heights, N.Y. **(1882–1971)**
Kenton, Stan (Stanley Newcomb) (jazz musician); Wichita, Kan. **(1912–1979)**
Kepler, Johannes (astronomer); Weil (Germany) **(1571–1630)**
Kerensky, Alexander Fedorovich (statesman); Simbirks, Russia **(1881–1970)**
Kern, Jerome David (composer); New York City **(1885–1945)**
Kerr, Deborah (actress); Helensburgh, Scotland, 9/30/1921
Kesey, Ken (novelist); La Junta, Colo., 9/17/1935
Kettering, Charles F. (engineer and inventor); nr. Loudonville, Ohio **(1876–1958)**
Key, Francis Scott (lawyer and author of national anthem); Frederick (now Carroll) County, Md. **(1779–1843)**
Keyes, Frances Parkinson (novelist); Charlottesville, Va. **(1885–1970)**
Keynes (1st Baron of Tilton) (John Maynard Keynes) (economist); Cambridge, England **(1883–1946)**
Khachaturian, Aram (composer); Tiflis, Russia **(1903–1978)**
Khrushchev, Nikita S. (Soviet leader); Kalinovka, nr. Kursk, Ukraine **(1894–1971)**
Kibbee, Guy (actor); El Paso **(1886–1956)**
Kidd, Michael (choreographer); Brooklyn, N.Y., 1917
Kidd, William (called Captain Kidd) (pirate); Greenock, Scotland **(1645?–1701)**
Kieran, John (writer); New York City, 8/2/1892
Kiesinger, Kurt Georg (diplomat); Ebingen, Germany, 4/6/1904
Kiley, Richard (actor and singer); Chicago, 3/31/1922
Kilmer, Alfred Joyce (poet); New Brunswick, N.J. **(1886–1918)**
King, Alan (Irwin Alan Kniberg) (entertainer); Brooklyn, N.Y., 12/26/1927
King, B.B. (Riley King) (guitarist); Itta Bena, Miss., 9/16/1925
King, Carole (singer and songwriter); Brooklyn, N.Y., 2/9/1941
King, Coretta Scott (civil rights leader); Marion, Ala., 4/27/1927
King, Martin Luther, Jr. (civil rights leader); Atlanta **(1929–1968)**
King, Pee Wee (Frank) (singer); Abrams, Wis., 2/18/1914
Kingsley, Sidney (Sidney Kirschner) (playwright); New York City, 10/18/1906
Kipling, Rudyard (author); Bombay **(1865–1936)**
Kipnis, Alexander (basso); Ukraine, **(1891–1978)**
Kirby, George (comedian); Chicago, 1923(?)
Kirk, Grayson (educator); Jeffersonville, Ohio, 10/12/1903
Kirk, Lisa (actress and singer); Charleroi, Pa., 1925
Kirk, Phyllis (actress); Plainfield, N.J., 9/18/1930
Kirkland, Gelsey (ballerina); Bethelhem, Pa., 12/29/1952
Kirkpatrick, Ralph (harpsichordist); Leominster, Mass., 6/10/1911
Kirkwood, James (actor); Grand Rapids, Mich. **(1883–1963)**
Kirsten, Dorothy (soprano); Montclair, N.J., 7/6/1919
Kissinger, Henry (Heinz Alfred Kissinger) (ex-Secretary of State); Furth, Germany, 5/27/1923
Kitt, Eartha (singer); North, S.C., 1/26/1928
Klee, Paul (painter); Münchenbuchsee, nr. Bern, Switzerland **(1879–1940)**
Klein, Calvin (fashion designer); Bronx, N.Y., 11/19/1942

Klein, Robert (comedian); Bronx, N.Y., 2/8/1942
Klemperer, Otto (conductor); Breslau (Poland) **(1885–1973)**
Klemperer, Werner (actor); Cologne, Germany, 3/22/1920
Klugman, Jack (actor); Philadelphia, 4/27/1922
Knievel, Evel (Robert Craig) (daredevil motorcyclist); Butte, Mont., 10/17/1938
Knight, Gladys (singer); Atlanta, 5/28/1944
Knight, John S. (publisher); Bluefield, W. Va. **(1894–1981)**
Knopf, Alfred A. (publisher); New York City, 9/12/1892
Knotts, Don (actor); Morgantown, W.Va., 7/21/1924
Knox, John (religious reformer); Haddington, East Lothian, Scotland **(1505–1572)**
Koch, Robert (physician); Klausthal (Germany) **(1843–1910)**
Koestler, Arthur (novelist); Budapest, 9/5/1905
Kokoschka, Oskar (painter); Póchlarn Austria **(1886–1980)**
Kooper, Al (singer and pianist); Brooklyn, N.Y., 2/5/1944
Korman, Harvey (actor); Chicago, 2/15/1927
Kosciusko, Thaddeus (Tadeusz Andrzej Bonawentura Kosciuszko) (military officer); Grand Duchy of Lithuania **(1746–1817)**
Kostelanetz, André (orchestra conductor); St. Petersburg, Russia **(1901–1980)**
Kosygin, Aleksei N. (Premier); St. Petersburg, Russia **(1904–1980)**
Koussevitzky, Serge (Sergei) Alexandrovitch (orchestra conductor); Vishni Volochek, Tver, Russia **(1874–1951)**
Kovacs, Ernie (comedian); Trenton, N.J. **(1919–1962)**
Kramer, Stanley E. (film producer and director); New York City, 9/29/1913
Kraus, Lili (pianist); Budapest, 3/4/1905(?)
Kreisler, Fritz (violinist and composer); Vienna **(1875–1962)**
Kresge, S. S. (merchant); Bald Mount, Pa. **(1867–1966)**
Krips, Josef (orchestra conductor); Vienna **(1902–1974)**
Kristofferson, Kris (singer); Brownsville, Tex., 6/22/1936
Kruger, Otto (actor); Toledo, Ohio **(1885–1974)**
Krupa, Gene (drummer); Chicago **(1909–1973)**
Kubelik, Rafael (conductor); Bychory (Czechoslovakia), 6/29/1914
Kublai Khan (Mongol conqueror) **(1216–1294)**
Kubrick, Stanley (producer and director); New York City, 7/26/1928
Kuralt, Charles (TV journalist); North Carolina, 1934
Kurosawa, Akira (film director); Tokyo, 3/23/1910
Kurtz, Efrem (conductor); St. Petersburg, Russia, 11/7/1900
Ky, Nguyen Cao (ex-Vice President of South Vietnam); Son Tay (Vietnam), 9/8/1930

L

Ladd, Alan (actor); Hot Springs, Ark. **(1913–1964)**
Ladd, Cheryl (actress); Huron, S.D., 4/2/(?)
Lafayette, Marquis de (Marie Joseph Paul Yves Roch Gilbert du Motier) (military officer); Auvergne, France **(1757–1834)**
La Follette, Robert Marin (politician); Primrose, Wis. **(1855–1925)**
La Guardia, Fiorello Henry (Mayor of New York); New York City **(1882–1947)**
Lahr, Bert (Irving Lahrheim) (comedian); New York City **(1895–1967)**
Laine, Frankie (Frank Paul LoVecchio) (singer); Chicago, 3/30/1913
Laird, Melvin (ex-Secretary of Defense); Omaha, Neb., 9/1/1922
Lamarck, Chevalier de (Jean Baptiste Pierre Antoine de Monet) (naturalist); Bazantin, France **(1744–1829)**
Lamarr, Hedy (Hedwig Kiesler) (actress); Vienna, 1915
Lamas, Fernando (actor); Buenos Aires, 1/9/1915
Lamb, Charles (Elia) (essayist); London **(1775–1834)**
Lamour, Dorothy (Dorothy Kaumeyer) (actress); New Orleans, 10/10/1914
Lancaster, Burt (actor); New York City, 11/2/1913
Lanchester, Elsa (Elsa Sullivan) (actress); London, 10/28/1902
Landau, Martin (actor); Brooklyn, N.Y. 1925(?)
Landers, Ann (columnist); Sioux City, Iowa, 7/4/1918
Landon, Michael (Michael Orowitz) (actor); Forest Hills, Queens, N.Y., 10/31/1936(?)
Lane, Abbe (singer); New York City, 1933
Lang, Fritz (film director); Vienna **(1890–1976)**
Lang, Paul Henry (music critic); Budapest, 8/28/1901
Lange, Hope (actress); Redding Ridge, Conn., 11/28/1933
Langella, Frank (actor); Bayonne, N.J., 1/1/1940
Langford, Frances (singer); Lakeland, Fla., 4/4/1913
Langmuir, Irving (chemist); Brooklyn, N.Y. **(1881–1957)**
Langtry, Lily (Emily le Breton) (actress); Island of Jersey **(1852–1929)**
Lansbury, Angela (actress); London, 10/16/1925
Lansing, Robert (actor); San Diego, Calif., 6/5/1929
Lanza, Mario (Alfred Arnold Cocozza) (singer and actor); Philadelphia **(1925–1959)**
Lao-Tzu (or Lao-Tse) (Li Erh) (philosopher); Honan Province, China (c. 604–531 B.C.)
Lardner, Ring (Ringgold Wilmer Lardner) (story writer); Niles, Mich. **(1885–1933)**

La Salle, Sieur de (Robert Cavelier) (explorer); Rouen, France (1643–1687)
Lasser, Louise (actress); New York City, 1940(?)
Lauder, Sir Harry (Harry MacLennan) (singer); Portobello, Scotland (1870–1950)
Laughton, Charles (actor); Scarborough, England (1899–1962)
Laurel, Stan (Arthur Jefferson) (comedian); Ulverston, England (1890–1965)
Laurents, Arthur (playwright); New York City, 7/14/1918
Laurie, Piper (Rosetta Jacobs) (actress); Detroit, 1/22/1932
Lavoisier, Antoine-Laurent (chemist); Paris (1743–1794)
Lawford, Peter (actor); London, 9/7/1923
Lawrence, Carol (Carol Maria Laraia) (dancer and actress); Melrose Park, Ill., 9/5/1932
Lawrence, David Herbert (novelist); Nottingham, England (1885–1930)
Lawrence, Gertrude (Gertrud Klasen) (actress); London (1900–1952)
Lawrence, Marjorie (singer); Deans Marsh, Australia (1908–1979)
Lawrence, Steve (Sidney Leibowitz) (singer); Brooklyn, N.Y., 7/8/1935
Lawrence, Vicki (actress); Inglewood, Calif., 1949
Lawrence of Arabia (Thomas Edward Lawrence, later changed to Shaw) (author and soldier); Tremadoc, Wales (1888–1935)
Leachman, Cloris (actress); Des Moines, Iowa, 4/30/1926(?)
Lean, David (film director); Croydon, England, 3/25/1908
Lear, Edward (nonsense poet); London (1812–1888)
le Carré, John (David John Moore Cornwell) (novelist); Poole, England, 10/19/1931
Le Corbusier (Charles Edouard Jeanneret) (architect); La Chaux-de-Fonds, Switzerland (1887–1965)
Lederer, Francis (actor); Prague, 11/6/1906
Lee, Christopher (actor); London, 5/27/1922
Lee, Gypsy Rose (Rose Louise Hovick) (entertainer); Seattle (1919–1970)
Lee, Peggy (Norma Engstrom) (singer); Jamestown, N.D., 5/26/1920
Lee, Robert Edward (Confederate general); Stratford Estate, Va. (1807–1870)
Leek, Sybil (Sybil Falk) (astrologer); Staffordshire, England, 1923
Le Gallienne, Eva (actress); London, 1/11/1899
Lehár, Franz (composer); Komárom (Czechoslovakia) (1870–1948)
Lehman, Herbert H. (Governor and Senator); New York City (1878–1963)
Lehmann, Lotte (soprano); Perleberg (Germany) (1888–1976)
Leigh, Janet (Jeanette Morrison) (actress); Merced, Calif., 7/6/1927
Leigh, Vivien (Vivien Mary Hartley) (actress); Darjeeling, India (1913–1967)
Leighton, Margaret (actress); nr. Birmingham, England (1922–1976)
Leinsdorf, Erich (conductor); Vienna, 2/4/1912
Lemmon, Jack (actor); Boston, 2/8/1925
Lenin, Nicolai (Vladimir Ilich Ulyanov) (Soviet leader); Simbirsk, Russia (1870–1924)
Lennon, John (singer and songwriter); Liverpool, England (1940–1980)
Lenya, Lotte (Karoline Balmauer) (singer and actress); Hitzing, Austria, 1905
Leonard, Sheldon (actor and director); New York City, 2/22/1907
Lerner, Alan Jay (lyricist); New York City, 8/31/1918
Lerner, Max (columnist); Minsk, Russia, 12/20/1902
Le Roy, Mervyn (film producer); San Francisco, 10/15/1900
Leslie, Joan (actress); Detroit, 1/26/1925
Lessing, Doris (novelist); Kermanshah, Iran, 10/22/1919
Lester, Mark (actor); Richmond, England, 1958
Letterman, David (TV personality); Indianapolis, 1944
Levant, Oscar (pianist); Pittsburgh (1906–1972)
Levene, Sam (actor); New York City (1905–1980)
Levenson, Sam (humorist); New York City (1911–1980)
Levi, Carlo (novelist); Turin, Italy (1902–1975)
Levine, James (music director, Metropolitan Opera); Cincinnati, 6/23/1943
Levine, Joseph E. (film producer); Boston, 9/9/1905
Lewis, Jerry (Joseph Levitch) (comedian and film director); Newark, N.J., 3/16/1926
Lewis, Jerry Lee (singer); Ferriday, La., 9/29/1935
Lewis, John Llewellyn (labor leader); Lucas, Iowa (1880–1969)
Lewis, Meriwether (explorer); Albemarle Co., Va. (1774–1809)
Lewis, Shari (Shari Hurwitz) (puppeteer); New York City, 1/17/1934
Lewis, Sinclair (novelist); Sauk Centre, Minn. (1885–1951)
Lewis, Ted (entertainer); Circleville, Ohio (1891–1971)
Ley, Willy (science writer); Berlin (1906–1969)
Liberace (Wladziu Liberace) (pianist); West Allis, Wis., 5/16/1919
Lichtenstein, Roy (painter); New York City, 10/27/1923
Lie, Trygve Halvdan (first U.N. Secretary-General); Oslo (1896–1968)
Lightfoot, Gordon (singer and songwriter); Orillia, Ontario, Canada, 11/17/1938
Lillie, Beatrice (Lady Peel) (actress and comedienne); Toronto, 5/29/1898
Lin Yutang (author); Changchow, China (1895–1976)
Lind, Jenny (Johanna Maria Lind) (soprano); Stockholm (1820–1887)
Lindbergh, Anne Morrow (author); Englewood, N.J., 6/22/1906
Lindbergh, Charles A. (aviator); Detroit (1902–1974)

Linden, Hal (actor); New York City, 3/20/1931
Lindfors, Viveca (actress); Uppsala, Sweden, 12/29/1920
Lindsay, Howard (dramatist); Waterford, N.Y. (1889–1968)
Lindsay, John Vliet (ex-Mayor of New York City); New York City, 11/24/1921
Lindstrom, Pia (TV newscaster); Stockholm, 11/?/1938
Linkletter, Art (radio-TV personality); Moose Jaw, Saskatchewan, Canada, 7/17/1912
Lipchitz, Jacques (sculptor); Druskieniki, Latvia (1891–1973)
Lippmann, Walter (columnist, author, and political analyst); New York City (1889–1974)
Lister, (1st Baron of Lyme Regis) (Joseph Lister) (surgeon); Upton, England (1827–1912)
Liszt, Franz (composer and pianist); Raiding (Hungary) (1811–1886)
Little, Cleavon (actor and comedian); Chickasha, Okla., 6/1/1939
Little, Rich (impressionist); Ottawa, 11/26/1938
Livesey, Roger (actor); Barry, Wales (1906–1976)
Livingstone, David (missionary and explorer); Lanarkshire, Scotland (1813–1873)
Livingstone, Mary (Sadye Marks) (comedienne); Seattle, 1909
Llewellyn, Richard (novelist); St. David's, Wales
Lloyd, Harold (comedian); Burchard, Neb. (1894–1971)
Lloyd George, David (Earl of Dwyfor) (statesman); Manchester, England (1863–1945)
Locke, John (philosopher); Somersetshire, England (1632–1704)
Lockhart, Gene (actor); London, Ontario, Canada (1891–1957)
Lockhart, June (actress); New York City, 6/25/1925
Lockwood, Margaret (actress); Karachi (Pakistan), 9/15/1916
Lodge, Henry Cabot (legislator); Boston (1850–1924)
Lodge, Henry Cabot, Jr. (diplomat); Nahant, Mass., 7/5/1902
Loesser, Frank (composer); New York City (1910–1969)
Loewe, Frederick (composer); Vienna, 6/10/1904
Logan, Joshua (director and producer); Texarkana, Tex., 10/5/1908
Lollobrigida, Gina (actress); Subiaco, Italy, 1928
Lombard, Carole (Carol Jane Peters) (actress); Ft. Wayne, Ind. (1908–1942)
Lombardo, Guy (band leader); London, Ontario, Canada (1902–1977)
London, George (baritone); Montreal, 5/30/1920
London, Jack (John Griffith London) (novelist); San Francisco (1876–1916)
London, Julie (Julie Peck) (singer and actress); Santa Rosa, Calif., 9/26/1926
Long, Huey Pierce (politician); Winnfield, La. (1893–1935)
Longfellow, Henry Wadsworth (poet); Portland, Me. (1807–1882)
Longworth, Alice Roosevelt (social figure); New York City (1884–1980)
Loos, Anita (novelist); Sissons, Calif. (1888–1981)
Lopez, Trini (Trinidad Lopez III) (singer); Dallas, 5/15/1937
Lopez, Vincent (band leader); Brooklyn, N.Y. (1895–1975)
Lord, Jack (actor); New York City, 12/30/1930
Loren, Sophia (Sofia Scicolone) (actress); Rome, 9/20/1934
Lorre, Peter (Laszlo Löewenstein) (actor); Rosenberg (Czechoslovakia) (1904–1964)
Louise, Tina (actress); New York City, 2/11/1937
Lowell, Amy (poet); Brookline, Mass. (1874–1925)
Lowell, James Russell (poet); Cambridge, Mass. (1819–1891)
Lowell, Robert (poet); Boston (1917–1977)
Loy, Myrna (Myrna Williams) (actress); nr. Helena, Mont., 8/2/1905
Loyola, St. Ignatius of (Iñigo de Oñez y Loyola) (founder of Jesuits); Güipuzcoa Province, Spain (1491–1556)
Lubitsch, Ernst (film director); Berlin (1892–1947)
Luce, Clare Boothe (playwright and former Ambassador); New York City, 4/10/1903
Luce, Henry Robinson (editor and publisher); Tengchow, China (1898–1967)
Lugosi, Bela (Bela Lugosi Blasko) (actor); Logos, Hungary (1888–1956)
Lukas, Paul (actor); Budapest (1895–1971)
Lumet, Sidney (film and TV director); Philadelphia, 6/25/1924
Lunt, Alfred (actor); Milwaukee (1892–1977)
Lupino, Ida (actress and director); London, 2/4/1918
Luther, Martin (religious reformer); Eisleben (Germany) (1483–1546)
Lynde, Paul (comedian); Mt. Vernon, Ohio, 6/13/1926
Lynley, Carol (actress); New York City, 2/13/1942
Lynn, Jeffrey (actor); Auburn, Mass., 1909
Lynn, Loretta (singer); Butcher's Hollow, Ky., 4/14/1935

M

Maazel, Lorin (conductor); Neuilly, France, 3/5/1930
MacArthur, Charles (playwright); Scranton, Pa. (1895–1956)
MacArthur, Douglas (five-star general); Little Rock Barracks, Ark. (1880–1964)
MacArthur, James (actor); Los Angeles, 12/8/1937
Macaulay, Thomas Babington (author); Rothley Temple, England (1800–1859)
MacDermot, Galt (composer); Montreal, 12/19/1928

MacDonald, James Ramsay (statesman); Lossiemouth, Scotland **(1866–1937)**

MacDonald, Jeanette (actress and soprano); Philadelphia **(1907–1965)**

Macdonald, Ross (Kenneth Millar) (mystery writer); Los Gatos, Calif., 12/13/1915

MacDowell, Edward Alexander (composer); New York City **(1861–1908)**

Macfadden, Bernarr (physical culturist); nr. Mill Spring, Mo. **(1868–1955)**

MacGraw, Ali (actress); New York City, 4/1/1939

Machiavelli, Niccolò (political philosopher); Florence (Italy) **(1469–1527)**

Mack, Ted (TV personality); Greeley, Colo. **(1904–1976)**

MacKenzie, Gisele (Marie Marguerite Louise Gisele LaFleche) (singer and actress); Winnipeg, Manitoba, Canada, 1/10/1927

MacLaine, Shirley (Shirley MacLean Beaty) (actress); Richmond, Va., 4/24/1934

MacLeish, Archibald (poet); Glencoe, Ill., 5/7/1892

Macmillan, Harold (ex-Prime Minister); London, 2/10/1894

MacMurray, Fred (actor); Kankakee, Ill., 8/30/1908

MacNeil, Cornell (baritone); Minneapolis, 1925

MacRae, Gordon (singer); East Orange, N.J., 3/12/1921

MacRae, Sheila (comedienne); London, 9/24/1924

Madison, Guy (Robert Moseley) (actor); Bakersfield, Calif., 1/19/1922

Maeterlinck, Count Maurice (author); Ghent, Belgium **(1862–1949)**

Magellan, Ferdinand (Fernando de Magalhaes) (navigator); Sabrosa, Portugal **(1480?–1521)**

Magnani, Anna (actress); Rome **(1908–1973)**

Magritte, René (painter); Belgium **(1898–1967)**

Magsaysay, Ramón (statesman); Iba, Luzon, Philippines **(1907–1957)**

Mahan, Alfred Thayer (naval historian); West Point, N.Y. **(1840–1914)**

Mahler, Gustav (composer and conductor); Kalischt (Czechoslovakia) **(1860–1911)**

Mailer, Norman (novelist); Long Branch, N.J., 1/31/1923

Maillol, Aristide (sculptor); Banyuls-sur-Mer, Rousillon, France **(1861–1944)**

Main, Marjorie (Mary Tomlinson Krebs) (actress); Acton, Ind. **(1890–1975)**

Mainbocher (Main Rousseau Bocher) (fashion designer); Chicago **(1891–1976)**

Majors, Lee (actor); Wyandotte, Mich., 1942

Makarova, Natalia (ballerina); Leningrad, 11/21/1940

Makeba, Miriam (singer); Johannesburg, South Africa, 3/4/1932

Malamud, Bernard (novelist); Brooklyn, N.Y., 4/26/1914

Malden, Karl (Mladen Sekulovich) (actor); Chicago, 3/22/1913

Malone, Dorothy (actress); Chicago, 1/30/1925

Malraux, André (author); Paris **(1901–1976)**

Manchester, Melissa (singer); Bronx, N.Y., 2/15/1951

Manchester, William (writer); Attleboro, Mass., 4/1/1922

Mancini, Henry (composer and conductor); Cleveland, 4/16/1924

Manet, Edouard (painter); Paris **(1832–1883)**

Mangano, Silvana (actress); Rome, 4/21/1930

Mangione, Chuck (hornist, pianist, and composer); Rochester, N.Y., 11/29/1940

Manilow, Barry (singer); Brooklyn, N.Y., 6/17/1946

Mankiewicz, Frank F. (columnist); New York City, 5/16/1924

Mankiewicz, Joseph L. (film writer and director); Wilkes-Barre, Pa., 2/11/1909

Mann, Horace (educator); Franklin, Mass. **(1796–1859)**

Mann, Thomas (novelist); Lübeck, Germany **(1875–1955)**

Mannes, Marya (writer); New York City, 11/14/1904

Mansfield, Jayne (Jayne Palmer) (actress); Bryn Mawr, Pa. **(1932–1967)**

Mansfield, Katherine (story writer); Wellington, New Zealand **(1888–1923)**

Mantovani, Annunzio (conductor); Venice **(1905–1980)**

Mao Zedong (Tse-tung) (Chinese leader); Shao Shan, China **(1893–1976)**

Marat, Jean Paul (French revolutionist); Boudry, Neuchâtel, Switzerland **(1743–1793)**

Marceau, Marcel (mime); Strasbourg, France, 3/22/1923

March, Fredric (Frederick Bickel) (actor); Racine, Wis. **(1897–1975)**

Marconi, Guglielmo (inventor); Bologna, Italy **(1874–1937)**

Marcus Aurelius (Marcus Annius Verus) (Roman emperor); Rome **(121–180)**

Marcuse, Herbert (philosopher); Berlin **(1898–1979)**

Margaret Rose (Princess); Glamis Castle, Angus, Scotland, 8/21/1930

Margrethe II (Queen); Copenhagen, 4/16/1940

Marie Antoinette (Josèphe Jeanne Marie Antoinette) (Queen of France); Vienna **(1755–1793)**

Marisol (sculptor); Venezuela, 1930

Markham, Edwin (poet); Oregon City, Ore. **(1852–1940)**

Markova, Dame Alicia (Lilian Alice Marks) (ballerina); London, 12/1/1910

Marley, Bob (reggae singer and songwriter); Kingston, Jamaica **(1945–1981)**

Marlowe, Christopher (dramatist); Canterbury, England **(1564–1593)**

Marlowe, Julia (Sarah Frances Frost) (actress); Cumberlandshire, England **(1866–1950)**

Marquand, John Phillips (novelist); Wilmington, Del. **(1893–1960)**

Marquette, Jacques (missionary and explorer); Laon, France **(1637–1675)**

Marriner, Neville (conductor); Lincoln, England, 4/15/1924

Marsh, Jean (actress); Stoke Newington, England, 7/1/1934

Marshall, E.G. (actor); Owatonna, Minn., 6/18/1910

Marshall, George Catlett (general); Uniontown, Pa. **(1880–1959)**

Marshall, Herbert (actor); London **(1890–1968)**

Marshall, John (jurist); nr. Germantown, Va. **(1755–1835)**

Marshall, Penny (actress); New York City, 10/15/1942

Martin, Dean (Dino Crocetti) (singer and actor); Steubenville, Ohio, 6/17/1917

Martin, Dick (actor and comedian); Battle Creek, Mich., 1/30/1922

Martin, Mary (singer and actress); Weatherford, Tex., 12/1/1913

Martin, Steve (comedian); prob. Waco, Tex., 1945(?)

Martin, Tony (Alvin Morris) (singer); San Francisco, 12/25/1913

Martin, William McChesney, Jr. (ex-chairman of Federal Reserve Board); St. Louis, 12/17/1906

Martinelli, Giovanni (tenor); Montagnana, Italy **(1885–1969)**

Marvin, Lee (actor); New York City, 2/19/1924

Marx, Chico (Leonard) (comedian); New York City **(1891–1961)**

Marx, Groucho (Julius) (comedian); New York City **(1890–1977)**

Marx, Harpo (Arthur) (comedian); New York City **(1893–1964)**

Marx, Karl (Socialist writer); Treves (Germany) **(1818–1883)**

Marx, Zeppo (Herbert) (comedian); New York City **(1901–1979)**

Mary Stuart (Queen of Scotland); Linlithgow, Scotland **(1542–1587)**

Masaryk, Jan Garrigue (statesman); Prague (Czechoslovakia) **(1886–1948)**

Masaryk, Thomas Garrigue (statesman); Hodonin (Czechoslovakia) **(1850–1937)**

Masefield, John (poet); Ledbury, England **(1878–1967)**

Masekela, Hugh (trumpeter); Wilbank, South Africa, 4/4/1939

Mason, James (actor); Huddersfield, England, 5/15/1909

Massenet, Jules Emile Frédéric (composer); Montaud, France **(1842–1912)**

Massey, Raymond (actor); Toronto, 8/30/1896

Massine, Léonide (choreographer); Moscow, **(1895–1979)**

Masters, Edgar Lee (poet); Garnett, Kan. **(1869–1950)**

Mastroianni, Marcello (actor); Fontana Liri, Italy, 9/28/1924

Mathis, Johnny (singer); San Francisco, 9/30/1935

Matisse, Henri (painter); Le Cateau, France **(1869–1954)**

Matthau, Walter (Walter Matuschanskayasky) (actor); New York City, 10/1/1920

Mature, Victor (actor); Louisville, Ky., 1/19/1916

Maugham, (William) Somerset (author); Paris **(1874–1965)**

Mauldin, Bill (political cartoonist); Mountain Park, N.M., 10/29/1921

Maupassant, Henri René Albert Guy de (story writer); Normandy, France **(1850–1893)**

Maurois, André (Emile Herzog) (author); Elbeuf, France **(1885–1967)**

Maximilian (Ferdinand Maximilian Joseph) (Emperor of Mexico); Vienna **(1832–1867)**

Maxwell, James Clerk (physicist); Edinburgh, Scotland **(1831–1879)**

May, Elaine (entertainer); Philadelphia, 4/21/1932

May, Rollo (psychologist); Ada, Ohio, 4/21/1909

Mayall, John (singer and songwriter); Manchester, England, 11/29/1933

Mayo, Charles H. (surgeon); Rochester, Minn. **(1865–1939)**

Mayo, Charles W. (surgeon); Rochester, Minn. **(1898–1968)**

Mayo, Virginia (actress); St. Louis, 1920

Mayo, William J. (surgeon); Le Sueur, Minn. **(1861–1939)**

McBride, Mary Margaret (radio personality); Paris, Mo. **(1899–1976)**

McBride, Patricia (ballerina); Teaneck, N.J., 8/23/1942

McCallum, David (actor); Glasgow, Scotland, 9/19/1933

McCambridge, Mercedes (actress); Joliet, Ill., 3/17/1918

McCarthy, Eugene J. (ex-Senator); Watkins, Minn., 3/29/1916

McCarthy, Joseph Raymond (Senator); Grand Chute, Wis. **(1908–1957)**

McCarthy, Kevin (actor); Seattle, 1915

McCarthy, Mary (novelist); Seattle, 6/21/1912

McCartney, Paul (singer and songwriter); Liverpool, England, 6/18/1942

McClellan, George Brinton (general); Philadelphia **(1826–1885)**

McCloy, John J. (lawyer and banker); Philadelphia, 3/31/1895

McClure, Doug (actor); Glendale, Calif., 5/11/1938

McCormack, John (tenor); Athlone, Ireland **(1884–1945)**

McCormack, John W. (ex-Speaker of House); Boston **(1891–1980)**

McCormack, Patty (actress); New York City, 8/21/1945

McCormick, Cyrus Hall (inventor); Rockbridge County, Va. **(1809–1884)**

McCoy, Col. Tim (actor); Saginaw, Mich. **(1891–1978)**

McCracken, James (dramatic tenor); Gary, Ind., 12/16/1926

McCrea, Joel (actor); Los Angeles, 11/5/1905

McCullers, Carson (novelist); Columbus, Ga. **(1917–1967)**

McDowall, Roddy (actor); London, 9/17/1928

McDowell, Malcolm (actor); Leeds, England, 6/19/1943

McGavin, Darren (actor); San Joaquin, Calif., 5/7/1922

McGinley, Phyllis (poet and writer); Ontario, Ore. **(1905–1978)**

McGoohan, Patrick (actor); Astoria, Queens, N.Y., 1928

McGuire, Dorothy (actress); Omaha, Neb., 6/14/1919

McKenna, Siobhan (actress); Belfast, Northern Ireland, 5/24/1923

McKuen, Rod (singer and composer); Oakland, Calif., 4/29/1933

McLaglen, Victor (actor); Tunbridge Wells, Kent, England **(1886–1959)**

McLaughlin, John (guitarist); Yorkshire, England, 1942

McLean, Don (singer and songwriter); New Rochelle, N.Y., 10/2/1945
McLuhan, Marshall (Herbert Marshall) (communications writer); Edmonton, Canada (1911–1980)
McMahon, Ed (TV personality); Detroit, 3/6/1923
McNamara, Robert S. (former president of World Bank); San Francisco, 6/9/1916
McQueen, Steve (Terence Stephen McQueen) (actor); Indianapolis (1930–1980)
Mead, Margaret (anthropologist); Philadelphia, (1901–1978)
Meadows, Audrey (actress); Wu Chang, China, 1922(?)
Meadows, Jayne (actress); Wu Chang, China 9/27/1926
Meany, George (labor leader); New York City (1894–1980)
Meara, Anne (actress); New York City, 1929
Medici, Lorenzo de' (called Lorenzo the Magnificent) (Florentine ruler); Florence (Italy) (1449–1492)
Meeker, Ralph (Ralph Rathgeber) (actor); Minneapolis, 11/21/1920
Mehta, Zubin (conductor); Bombay, 4/29/1936
Meir, Golda (Golda Myerson, nee Mabovitz) (ex-Premier of Israel); Kiev, Russia (1898–1978)
Melanie (Melanie Safka) (singer and songwriter); New York City, 2/3/1947
Melba, Dame Nellie (Helen Porter Mitchell) (soprano); nr. Melbourne (1861–1931)
Melchior, Lauritz (Lebrecht Hommel) (heroic tenor); Copenhagen (1890–1973)
Mellon, Andrew William (financier); Pittsburgh (1855–1937)
Melville, Herman (novelist); New York City (1819–1891)
Mencken, Henry Louis (writer); Baltimore (1880–1956)
Mendel, Gregor Johann (geneticist); Heinzendorf, Austrian Silesia (1822–1884)
Mendeleyev, Dmitri Ivanovich (chemist); Tobolsk, Russia (1834–1907)
Mendelssohn-Bartholdy, Jakob Ludwig Felix (composer); Hamburg (1809–1847)
Mendès-France, Pierre (ex-Premier); Paris, 1/11/1905
Menjou, Adolphe (actor); Pittsburgh (1890–1963)
Mennin, Peter (Peter Mennini) (composer); Erie, Pa., 5/17/1923
Menninger, William C. (psychiatrist); Topeka, Kan. (1899–1966)
Menotti, Gian Carlo (composer); Cadegliano, Italy, 7/7/1911
Menuhin, Yehudi (violinist and conductor); New York City, 4/22/1916
Menzies, Robert Gordon (ex-Prime Minister); Jeparit, Australia (1894–1978)
Mercer, Johnny (songwriter); Savannah, Ga. (1909–1976)
Mercer, Mabel (singer); Burton-on-Trent, England, 1/?/1900
Mercouri, Melina (actress); Athens, 10/18/1925
Meredith, Burgess (actor); Cleveland, 11/16/1908
Merkel, Una (actress); Covington, Ky., 12/10/1903
Merman, Ethel (Ethel Zimmerman) (singer and actress); Astoria, Queens, N.Y., 1/16/1909
Merrick, David (David Margulois) (stage producer); St. Louis, 11/27/1912
Merrill, Dina (actress); New York City, 12/9/1925
Merrill, Gary (actor); Hartford, Conn., 8/2/1914
Merrill, Robert (baritone); Brooklyn, N.Y., 6/4/1919
Merton, Thomas (clergyman and writer); France (1915–1968)
Mesmer, Franz Anton (physician); Itzmang, nr. Constance (Germany) (1733–1815)
Mesta, Perle (social figure); Sturgis, Mich. (1889–1975)
Metternich, Prince Klemens Wenzel Nepomuk Lothar von (statesman); Coblenz (Germany) (1773–1859)
Michelangelo Buonarroti (painter, sculptor, and architect); Caprese (Italy) (1475–1564)
Michener, James A. (novelist); New York City, 2/3/1907
Midler, Bette (singer); Honolulu, 1945
Mielziner, Jo (stage designer); Paris (1901–1976)
Mies van der Rohe, Ludwig (architect and designer); Aachen, Germany (1886–1969)
Mikoyan, Anastas I. (diplomat); Sanain, Armenia, (1895–1978)
Miles, Sarah (actress); Essex, England, 12/31/1943
Miles, Sylvia (actress); New York City, 9/9/1932
Miles, Vera (Vera Ralston) (actress); nr. Boise City, Okla., 8/23/1930
Milhaud, Darius (composer); Aix-en-Provence, France (1892–1974)
Mill, John Stuart (philosopher); London, (1806–1873)
Milland, Ray (Reginald Truscott-Jones) (actor); Neath, Wales, 1/3/1907
Millay, Edna St. Vincent (poet); Rockland, Me. (1892–1950)
Miller, Ann (Lucille Ann Collier) (dancer and actress); Cherino, Tex., 4/12/1923
Miller, Arthur (playwright); New York City, 10/17/1915
Miller, Glenn (band leader); Clarinda, Iowa (1909?–1944)
Miller, Henry (novelist); New York City (1891–1980)
Miller, Jason (John Miller) (playwright); New York City, 1939(?)
Miller, Mitch (Mitchell) (musician); Rochester, N.Y., 7/4/1911
Miller, Roger (singer); Fort Worth, 1/2/1936
Millet, Jean François (painter); Gruchy, France (1814–1875)
Millett, Kate (feminist); St. Paul, 9/14/1934
Mills, Hayley (actress); London, 4/18/1946
Mills, John (actor); Felixstowe, England, 2/22/1908

Milne, A(lan) A(lexander) (author); London (1882–1956)
Milstein, Nathan (concert violinist); Odessa, Russia, 12/31/1904
Milton, John (poet); London (1608–1674)
Mimieux, Yvette (actress); Hollywood, Calif., 1/8/1941
Mineo, Sal (actor); New York City (1939–1976)
Minnelli, Liza (singer and actress); Hollywood, Calif., 3/12/1946
Minnelli, Vincente (film director); Chicago, 2/28/1913
Minuit, Peter (Governor of New Amsterdam); Wesel (Germany) (1580–1638)
Miranda, Carmen (Maria do Carmo da Cunha) (singer and dancer); Lisbon (1913–1955)
Miró, Joan (painter); Barcelona, 4/20/1893
Mitchell, Cameron (actor); Dallastown, Pa., 4/11/1918
Mitchell, Guy (actor); Detroit, 2/27/1927
Mitchell, John N. (former Attorney General); Detroit, 9/15/1913
Mitchell, Joni (Roberta Joan Anderson) (singer and songwriter); Ft. MacCleod, Canada, 11/7/1943
Mitchell, Margaret (novelist); Atlanta (1900–1949)
Mitchum, Robert (actor); Bridgeport, Conn., 8/6/1917
Mitropoulos, Dimitri (orchestra conductor); Athens (1896–1960)
Mix, Tom (actor); Mix Run, Pa. (1880–1940)
Modigliani, Amedeo (painter); Leghorn, Italy (1884–1920)
Moffo, Anna (soprano); Wayne, Pa., 6/27/1934
Mohammed (prophet); Mecca (Saudi Arabia) (570–632)
Molière (Jean Baptiste Poquelin) (dramatist); Paris (1622–1673)
Molnar, Ferenc (dramatist); Budapest (1878–1952)
Molotov, Vyacheslav M. (V. M. Skryabin) (diplomat); Kukarka, Russia, 3/9/1890
Mondrian, Piet (painter); Amersfoort, Netherlands (1872–1944)
Monet, Claude (painter); Paris (1840–1926)
Monk, Thelonious (pianist); Rocky Mount, N.C., 10/10/1918
Monroe, Marilyn (Norma Jean Mortenson or Baker) (actress); Los Angeles (1926–1962)
Monroe, Vaughn (Wilton) (band leader); Akron, Ohio (1912–1973)
Monsarrat, Nicholas (novelist); Liverpool, England, (1910–1979)
Montaigne, Michel Eyquem de (essayist); nr. Bordeaux, France (1533–1592)
Montalban, Ricardo (actor); Mexico City, 11/25/1920
Montand, Yves (Yves Montand Livi) (actor and singer); Mansummano, Italy, 10/13/1921
Montez, Maria (actress); Dominican Republic (1918–1951)
Montezuma II (Aztec emperor); Mexico (1480?–1520)
Montgomery, Elizabeth (actress); Hollywood, Calif., 4/15/1933
Montgomery, George (George Letz) (actor); Brady, Mont., 1929
Montgomery, Robert (Henry Jr.) (actor); Beacon, N.Y., 5/21/1904
Montgomery of Alamein, 1st Viscount of Hindhead (Sir Bernard Law Montgomery) (military leader); London (1887–1976)
Montoya, Carlos (guitarist); Madrid, 12/13/1903
Moore, Clement Clarke (author); New York City (1779–1863)
Moore, Garry (Thomas Garrison Morfit) (TV personality); Baltimore, 1/31/1915
Moore, Grace (soprano); Jellico, Tenn. (1901–1947)
Moore, Henry (sculptor); Castleford, England, 7/30/1898
Moore, Marianne (poet); Kirkwood, Mo. (1887–1972)
Moore, Mary Tyler (actress); Brooklyn, N.Y., 12/29/1937
Moore, Melba (Beatrice) (singer and actress); New York City, 10/27/1945
Moore, Roger (actor); London, 10/14/1927(?)
Moore, Thomas (poet); Dublin (1779–1852)
Moore, Victor (actor); Hammonton, N.J. (1876–1962)
Moorehead, Agnes (actress); Clinton, Mass. (1906–1974)
More, Sir Thomas (statesman and author); London (1478–1535)
Moreau, Jeanne (actress); Paris, 1/23/1928
Moreno, Rita (Rosita Dolores Alverio) (actress); Humacao, Puerto Rico, 12/11/1931
Morgan, Dennis (actor); Prentice, Wis., 12/10/1920
Morgan, Helen (singer); Danville, Ohio (1900?–1941)
Morgan, Henry (comedian); New York City, 3/31/1915
Morgan, Jane (Florence Currier) (singer); Boston, 1920
Morgan, John Pierpont (financier); Hartford, Conn. (1837–1913)
Moriarty, Michael (actor); Detroit, 4/5/1941
Morini, Erica (concert violinist); Vienna, 1/5/1910
Morison, Samuel Eliot (historian); Boston (1887–1976)
Morley, Christopher Darlington (novelist); Haverford, Pa. (1890–1957)
Morley, Robert (actor); Semley, England, 5/26/1908
Morrison, Jim (James Douglas Morrison) (singer and songwriter); Melbourne, Fla. (1943–1971)
Morse, Marston (mathematician); Waterville, Me. (1892–1977)
Morse, Robert (actor); Newton, Mass., 5/18/1931
Morse, Samuel Finley Breese (painter and inventor); Charlestown, Mass. (1791–1872)
Moses, Grandma (Mrs. Anna Mary Robertson Moses) (painter); Greenwich, N.Y. (1860–1961)
Moses, Robert (urban planner); New Haven, Conn., (1888–1981)
Mostel, Zero (Samuel Joel Mostel) (actor); Brooklyn, N.Y. (1915–1977)
Moussorgsky, Modest Petrovich (composer); Karev, Russia (1839–1881)

Moyers, Bill D. (Billy Don) (journalist); Hugo, Okla., 6/5/1934
Moynihan, Daniel Patrick (New York Senator); Tulsa, Okla., 3/16/1927
Mozart, Wolfgang Amadeus (Johannes Chrysostomus Wolfgangus Theophilus Mozart) (composer); Salzburg (Austria) **(1756–1791)**
Mudd, Roger (TV newscaster); Washington, D.C., 2/9/1928
Muggeridge, Malcolm (Thomas) (writer); Croydon, England, 3/24/1903
Muhammad, Elijah (Elijah Poole) (religious leader); Sandersville, Ga. **(1897–1975)**
Mulhare, Edward (actor); Ireland, 1923
Mumford, Lewis (cultural historian and city planner); Flushing, Queens, N.Y., 10/19/1895
Munch, Edvard (painter); Löten, Norway **(1863–1944)**
Muni, Paul (Muni Weisenfreund) (actor); Lemburg (Ukraine) **(1895–1967)**
Munsel, Patrice (soprano); Spokane, Wash., 5/14/1925
Murdoch, Iris (novelist); Dublin, 7/15/1919
Murdoch, Rupert (publisher); Melbourne, 3/11/1931
Murillo, Bartolomé Esteban (painter); Seville, Spain **(1617–1682)**
Murphy, Audie (actor and war hero); Kingston, Tex. **(1924–1971)**
Murphy, George (actor, dancer, and ex-Senator); New Haven, Conn., 7/4/1902
Murray, Arthur (dance teacher); New York City, 4/4/1895
Murray, Kathryn (dance teacher); Jersey City, N.J., 1906
Murray, Ken (Don Court) (producer); New York City, 7/14/1903
Murray, Mae (Marie Adrienne Koenig) (actress); Portsmouth, Va. **(1890–1965)**
Murrow, Edward R. (commentator and government official); Greensboro, N.C. **(1908–1965)**
Mussolini, Benito (Italian dictator); Dovia, Forli, Italy **(1883–1945)**
Myerson, Bess (consumer advocate); Bronx, N.Y., 1924
Myrdal, Gunnar (sociologist and economist); Gustaf Parish, Sweden, 12/6/1898

N

Nabokov, Vladimir (novelist); St. Petersburg, Russia **(1899–1977)**
Nabors, Jim (actor and singer); Sylacauga, Ala., 6/12/1932
Nader, Ralph (consumer advocate); Winsted, Conn., 2/27/1934
Nagel, Conrad (actor); Keokuk, Iowa **(1897–1970)**
Naish, J. Carrol (actor); New York City **(1900–1973)**
Naldi, Nita (Anita Donna Dooley) (actress); New York City **(1899–1961)**
Napoleon Bonaparte. *See* Bonaparte, Napoleon
Nash, Graham (singer); Blackpool, England, 1942
Nash, Ogden (poet); Rye, N.Y. **(1902–1971)**
Nasser, Gamal Abdel (statesman); Beni Mor, Egypt **(1918–1970)**
Nast, Thomas (cartoonist); Landau (Germany) **(1840–1902)**
Nation, Carry Amelia (temperance leader); Garrard County, Ky. **(1846–1911)**
Natwick, Mildred (actress); Baltimore, 6/19/1908
Nazimova, Alla (actress); Yalta, Crimea, Russia **(1879–1945)**
Neagle, Anna (Marjorie Robertson) (actress); London, 10/20/1908
Neal, Patricia (actress); Packard, Ky., 1/20/1926
Neff, Hildegarde (actress); Ulm, Germany, 12/28/1925
Negri, Pola (Appolina Chapulez) (actress); Bromberg (Poland), c. 1897
Nehru, Jawaharlal (first Prime Minister of India); Allahabad, India **(1889–1964)**
Nelson, Barry (actor); San Francisco, 1920
Nelson, David (actor); New York City, 10/24/1936
Nelson, Harriet Hilliard (Peggy Lou Snyder) (actress); Des Moines, Iowa, 1914
Nelson, Ozzie (Oswald) (actor); Jersey City, N.J. **(1907–1975)**
Nelson, Ricky (Eric) (singer and actor); Teaneck, N.J., 5/8/1940
Nelson, Viscount Horatio (naval officer); Burnham Thorpe, England **(1758–1805)**
Nenni, Pietro (Socialist leader); Faenza, Italy **(1891–1980)**
Nero (Nero Claudius Caesar Drusus Germanicus) (Roman emperor); Antium (Italy) **(37–68)**
Nero, Peter (pianist); New York City, 5/22/1934
Nesbitt, Cathleen (actress); Cheshire, England, 1889
Nevelson, Louise (sculptor); Kiev, Russia, 9/23/1900
Newhart, Bob (entertainer); Chicago, 9/5/1929
Newhouse, Samuel I. (publisher); New York City **(1895–1979)**
Newley, Anthony (actor and song writer); London, 9/24/1931
Newman, Edwin (news commentator); New York City, 1/25/1919
Newman, Paul (actor and director); Cleveland, 1/26/1925
Newman, Randy (singer); Los Angeles, 11/28/1943
Newton, Huey (black activist); New Orleans, 2/17/1942
Newton, Sir Isaac (mathematician and scientist); nr. Grantham, England **(1642–1727)**
Newton, Wayne (singer); Norfolk, Va., 4/3/1942
Newton-John, Olivia (singer); Cambridge, England, 9/26/1948
Nichols, Mike (Michael Peschkowsky) (stage and film director); Berlin, 11/6/1931
Nicholson, Jack (actor); Neptune, N.J., 4/22/1937

Nietzsche, Friedrich Wilhelm (philosopher); nr. Lützen (Germany) **(1844–1900)**
Nightingale, Florence (nurse); Florence (Italy) **(1820–1910)**
Nijinsky, Waslaw (ballet dancer); Warsaw **(1890–1950)**
Nilsson, Birgit (soprano); West Karup, Sweden, 5/17/1923
Nilsson, Harry (singer and songwriter); Brooklyn, N.Y., 6/15/1941
Nimitz, Chester W. (naval officer); Fredericksburg, Tex. **(1885–1966)**
Nimoy, Leonard (actor); Boston, 3/26/1931
Nin, Anais (author and diarist); Neuilly, France **(1903–1977)**
Niven, David (actor); Kirriemuir, Scotland, 3/1/1910
Nizer, Louis (lawyer and author); London, 2/6/1902
Nobel, Alfred Bernhard (industrialist); Stockholm **(1833–1896)**
Noguchi, Isamu (sculptor); Los Angeles, 11/7/1904
Nolan, Lloyd (actor); San Francisco, 8/11/1902
Nolte, Nick (actor); Omaha, Neb., 1942
Norell, Norman (Norman Levinson) (fashion designer); Noblesville, Ind. **(1900–1972)**
Norstad, Gen. Lauris (ex-commander of NATO forces); Minneapolis, 3/24/1907
North, John Ringling (circus director); Baraboo, Wis., 8/14/1903
North, Sheree (actress); Los Angeles, 1/17/1933
Norton, Eleanor Holmes (New York City government official, lawyer); Washington, D.C., 6/13/1937
Nostradamus (Michel de Notredame) (astrologer); St. Rémy, France **(1503–1566)**
Novaes, Guiomar (pianist); Sao Joao de Boa Vista, Brazil **(1895–1979)**
Novak, Kim (Marilyn Novak) (actress); Chicago, 2/13/1933
Novarro, Ramon (Ramon Samaniegoes) (actor); Durango, Mexico **(1899–1968)**
Nugent, Elliott (actor and director); Dover, Ohio, **(1899–1980)**
Nureyev, Rudolf (ballet dancer); U.S.S.R., 3/17/1938
Nuyen, France (actress); Marseilles, France, 7/31/1939
Nyro, Laura (singer and songwriter); Bronx, N.Y., 1947

O

Oakie, Jack (actor); Sedalia, Mo. **(1903–1978)**
Oates, Joyce Carol (novelist); Lockport, N.Y., 6/16/1938
Oberon, Merle (Estelle Merle O'Brien Thompson) (actress); Tasmania **(1911–1979)**
O'Brian, Hugh (Hugh J. Krampe) (actor); Rochester, N.Y., 4/19/1930
O'Brien, Edmond (actor); New York City, 9/10/1915
O'Brien, Margaret (Angela Maxine O'Brien) (actress); San Diego, Calif., 1/15/1937
O'Brien, Pat (William Joseph O'Brien, Jr.) (actor); Milwaukee, 11/11/1899
O'Casey, Sean (playwright); Dublin **(1881–1964)**
Ochs, Adolph Simon (publisher); Cincinnati **(1858–1935)**
O'Connor, Carroll (actor); New York City, 8/2/1924
O'Connor, Donald (actor); Chicago, 8/28/1925
Odets, Clifford (playwright); Philadelphia **(1906–1963)**
Odetta (Odetta Holmes) (folk singer and actress); Brimingham, Ala., 12/31/1930
Offenbach, Jacques (composer); Cologne, Germany **(1819–1880)**
O'Hara, John (novelist); Pottsville, Pa. **(1905–1970)**
O'Hara, Maureen (Maureen FitzSimons) (actress); Dublin, 8/17/1921
Oistrakh, David (concert violinist); Odessa, Russia **(1908–1974)**
O'Keeffe, Georgia (painter); Sun Prairie, Wis., 11/15/1887
Oland, Warner (actor); Umea, Sweden **(1880–1938)**
Olav V (King of Norway); Sandringham, England, 7/2/1903
Oldenburg, Claes (painter); Stockholm, Sweden, 1/28/1929
Olivier, Lord (Laurence) (actor); Dorking, England, 5/22/1907
Olmsted, Frederick Law (landscape architect); Hartford, Conn. **(1822–1903)**
Olsen, Ole (John Sigvard Olsen) (comedian); Peru, Ind. **(1892–1963)**
Omar Khayyam (poet and astronomer); Nishapur (Iran) **(died c. 1123)**
Onassis, Aristotle (shipping executive); Smyrna, Turkey **(1906–1975)**
Onassis, Christina (shipping executive); New York City, 12/11/1950
Onassis, Jacqueline Kennedy (Jacqueline Bouvier) (President's widow); Southampton, N.Y., 7/28/1929
O'Neal, Ryan (Patrick) (actor); Los Angeles, 4/20/1941
O'Neal, Tatum (actress); Los Angeles, Calif., 1963
O'Neill, Eugene Gladstone (playwright); New York City **(1888–1953)**
O'Neill, Jennifer (actress); Rio de Janeiro, 2/20/1949
Oppenheimer, J. Robert (nuclear physicist); New York City **(1904–1967)**
Orff, Carl (composer); Munich, Germany, 7/10/1895
Orlando, Tony (singer); New York City, 1944
Ormandy, Eugene (conductor); Budapest, 11/18/1899
Orozco, José Clemente (painter); Zapotlán, Jalisco, Mexico **(1883–1949)**
Orwell, George (Eric Arthur Blair) (British author); Motihari, India **(1903–1950)**
Osborn, Paul (playwright); Evansville, Ind., 9/4/1901
Osborne, John (playwright); London, 12/12/1929
Osler, Sir William (physician); Bondhead, Ontario, Canada **(1849–1919)**

Osmond, Donny (singer); Ogden, Utah, 12/9/1957
Osmond, Marie (singer); Ogden, Utah, 1959
O'Sullivan, Maureen (actress); County Roscommon, Ireland, 5/17/1911
Otis, Elisha (inventor); Halifax, Vt. **(1811–1861)**
O'Toole, Peter (actor); Connemara, Ireland, 8/2/1933
Ovid (Publius Ovidius Naso) (poet); Sulmona (Italy) **(43** B.C.–? A.D. **17)**
Owens, Buck (Alvis Edgar Owens) (singer); Sherman, Tex., 8/12/1929

P

Paar, Jack (TV personality); Canton, Ohio, 5/1/1918
Pacino, Al (Alfred) (actor); New York City, 4/25/1940
Packard, Vance (author); Granville Summit, Pa., 5/22/1914
Paderewski, Ignace Jan (pianist and statesman); Kurylowka, Russian Podolia **(1860–1941)**
Paganini, Nicolò (violinist); Genoa (Italy) **(1782–1840)**
Page, Geraldine (actress); Kirksville, Mo., 11/22/1924
Page, Patti (Clara Ann Fowler) (singer and entertainer); Claremore, Okla., 11/8/1927
Paige, Janis (actress); Tacoma, Wash., 9/16/1922
Paine, Thomas (political philosopher); Thetford, England **(1737–1809)**
Palance, Jack (Walter Palanuik) (actor); Lattimer, Pa., 2/18/1920
Paley, William S. (broadcasting executive); Chicago, 9/28/1901
Palladio, Andrea (architect); Padua or Vicenza (Italy) **(1508–1580)**
Palmer, Betsy (actress); East Chicago, Ind., 1929
Palmer, Lilli (actress); Posen (Poland), 5/24/1914
Palmerston, Henry John Templeton (3rd Viscount) (statesman); Broadlands, England **(1784–1865)**
Papanicolaou, George N. (physician); Coumi, Greece **(1883–1962)**
Papas, Irene (actress); Chiliomodion, Greece, 1929
Papp, Joseph (Joseph Papirofsky) (stage producer and director); Brooklyn, N.Y., 6/22/1921
Park, Chung Hee (President of South Korea); Sangmo-ri, Korea **(1917–1979)**
Parker, Dorothy (Dorothy Rothschild) (author); West End, N.J. **(1893–1967)**
Parker, Eleanor (actress); Cedarville, Ohio, 6/26/1922
Parker, Fess (actor); Fort Worth, Tex., 1925
Parker, Suzy (model and actress); San Antonio, 10/28/1933
Parkinson, C. (Cyril) Northcote (historian); Durham, England, 7/30/1909
Parks, Bert (Bert Jacobson) (entertainer); Atlanta, 12/30/1914
Parks, Gordon (film director); Ft. Scott, Kan., 11/30/1912
Parnell, Charles Stewart (statesman); Avondale, Ireland **(1846–1891)**
Parnis, Mollie (Mollie Parnis Livingston) (fashion designer); New York City, 3/18/1905
Parsons, Estelle (actress); Marblehead, Mass., 11/20/1927
Parton, Dolly (singer); Locust Ridge, Tenn. 1/19/1946
Pascal, Blaise (philosopher); Clermont, France **(1623–1662)**
Pasternak, Boris Leonidovich (author); Moscow **(1890–1960)**
Pasternak, Joseph (film producer); Silagy-Somlyo, Romania, 9/19/1901
Pasteur, Louis (chemist); Dôle, France **(1822–1895)**
Patton, George Smith, Jr. (general); San Gabriel, Calif., **(1885–1945)**
Paul, Les (Lester William Polfus) (guitarist); Waukesha, Wis., 6/9/1915
Paul VI (Giovanni Battista Montini) (Pope); Concesio, nr. Brescia, Italy **(1897–1978)**
Pauling, Linus Carl (chemist); Portland, Ore., 2/28/1901
Pavarotti, Luciano (tenor); Modena, Italy, 10/12/1935
Pavlov, Ivan Petrovich (physiologist); Ryazan district, Russia **(1849–1936)**
Pavlova, Anna (ballerina); St. Petersburg, Russia **(1885–1931)**
Payne, John (actor); Roanoke, Va., 1912
Peale, Norman Vincent (clergyman); Bowersville, Ohio, 5/31/1898
Pearl, Minnie (Sarah Ophelia Colley Cannon) (comedienne and singer); Centerville, Tenn., 10/25/1912
Pears, Peter (tenor); Farnham, England, 6/22/1910
Pearson, Drew (Andrew Russel Pearson) (columnist); Evanston, Ill. **(1897–1969)**
Pearson, Lester B. (statesman); Toronto **(1897–1972)**
Peary, Robert Edwin (explorer); Cresson, Pa. **(1856–1920)**
Peck, Gregory (actor); La Jolla, Calif., 4/5/1916
Peckinpah, Sam (film director); Fresno, Calif., 2/21/1925
Peerce, Jan (tenor); New York City, 1904
Pegler, (James) Westbrook (columnist); Minneapolis, **(1894–1969)**
Pei, I. M. (architect); Canton, China, 4/26/1917
Penn, Arthur (stage and film director); Philadelphia, 9/27/1922
Penn, William (American colonist); London **(1644–1718)**
Penney, James C. (merchant); Hamilton, Mo. **(1875–1971)**
Peppard, George (actor); Detroit, 10/1/1928
Pepys, Samuel (diarist); Bampton, England **(1633–1703)**
Perelman, S. J. (Sidney J.) (humorist); Brooklyn, N.Y. **(1904–1979)**
Pericles (statesman); Athens (died 429 B.C.)
Perkins, Osgood (actor); West Newton, Mass. **(1892–1937)**
Perkins, Tony (Anthony) (actor); New York City, 4/14/1932
Perlman, Itzhak (violinist); Tel Aviv, Israel, 8/31/1945
Perón, Isabel (María Estela Martínez Cartas) (former chief of state); La

Rioja, Argentina, 2/4/1931
Perón, Juan D. (statesman); nr. Lobos, Argentina **(1895–1974)**
Perón, Maria Eva Duarte de (political leader); Los Toldos, Argentina **(1919–1952)**
Perrine, Valerie (actress and dancer); Galveston, Tex., 9/3/1943
Pershing, John Joseph (general); Linn County, Mo. **(1860–1948)**
Peters, Bernadette (actress); New York City, 1944
Peters, Jean (actress); Canton, Ohio, 10/15/1926
Peters, Roberta (Roberta Peterman) (soprano); New York City, 5/4/1930
Petrarch (Francesco Petrarca) (poet); Arezzo (Italy) **(1304–1374)**
Philip (Philip Mountbatten) (Duke of Edinburgh); Corfu, Greece, 6/10/1921
Piaf, Edith (Edith Gassion) (chanteuse); Paris **(1916–1963)**
Piatigorsky, Gregor (cellist); Ekaterinoslav, Russia **(1903–1976)**
Piazza, Ben (actor); Little Rock, Ark., 7/30/1934
Piazza, Marguerite (soprano); New Orleans, 5/6/1926
Picasso, Pablo (painter and sculptor); Málaga, Spain **(1881–1973)**
Pickford, Jack (Jack Smith) (actor); Toronto **(1896–1933)**
Pickford, Mary (Gladys Mary Smith) (actress); Toronto **(1893–1979)**
Picon, Molly (actress); New York City, 6/1/1898
Pidgeon, Walter (actor); East St. John, New Brunswick, Canada, 9/23/1898
Pinter, Harold (playwright); London, 10/10/1930
Pinza, Ezio (basso); Rome **(1892–1957)**
Pirandello, Luigi (dramatist and novelist); nr. Girgenti, Italy **(1867–1936)**
Pissaro, Camille Jacob (painter); St. Thomas (U.S. Virgin Islands) **(1830–1903)**
Piston, Walter (composer); Rockland, Me. **(1894–1976)**
Pitman, Sir (Isaac) James (educator and publisher); Bath, England, 8/14/1901
Pitt, William ("Younger Pitt") (statesman); nr. Bromley, England **(1759–1806)**
Pitts, ZaSu (actress); Parsons, Kan. **(1898–1963)**
Pius XII (Eugenio Pacelli) (Pope); Rome **(1876–1958)**
Pizarro, Francisco (explorer); Trujillo, Spain **(1470?–1541)**
Plato (Aristocles) (philosopher); Athens (?) **(4277–347** B.C.)
Pleasence, Donald (actor); Worksop, England, 10/5/1919
Pleshette, Suzanne (actress); New York City, 1/31/1937
Plimpton, George (author); New York City, 3/18/1927
Plisetskaya, Maya (ballerina); Moscow, 11/20/1925
Plowright, Joan (actress); Brigg, England, 10/28/1929
Plummer, Christopher (actor); Toronto, 12/13/1929
Plutarch (biographer); Chaeronea (Greece) **(46?–?120)**
Pocahontas (Matoaka) (American Indian princess); Virginia (?) **(1595?–1617)**
Podhoretz, Norman (author); Brooklyn, N.Y., 1/16/1930
Poe, Edgar Allan (poet and story writer); Boston, Mass. **(1809–1849)**
Poitier, Sidney (film actor and director); Miami, Fla., 2/20/1927
Polanski, Roman (film director); Paris, 8/18/1933
Pollard, Michael J. (actor); Passaic, N.J., 5/30/1939
Pollock, Jackson (painter); Cody, Wyo. **(1912–1956)**
Polo, Marco (traveler); Venice **(1254?–?1324)**
Pompey (Gnaeus Pompeius Magnus) (general); Rome (?) **(106–48** B.C.)
Ponce de León, Juan (explorer); Servas, Spain **(1460?–1521)**
Pons, Lily (coloratura soprano); Cannes, France **(1904–1976)**
Ponti, Carlo (director; Milan, Italy, 12/11/1913
Pope, Alexander (poet); London **(1688–1744)**
Porter, Cole (songwriter); Peru, Ind. **(1892–1964)**
Porter, Katherine Anne (novelist); Indian Creek, Tex. **(1891–1980)**
Post, Wiley (aviator); Grand Plain, Tex. **(1900–1935)**
Poston, Tom (actor); Columbus, Ohio, 10/17/1927
Potok, Chaim (author); New York City, 2/17/1929
Pound, Ezra (poet); Hailey, Idaho **(1885–1972)**
Powell, Adam Clayton, Jr. (Congressman); New Haven, Conn. **(1908–1972)**
Powell, Dick (actor); Mt. View, Ark. **(1904–1963)**
Powell, Eleanor (actress); Springfield, Mass., 11/21/1912
Powell, Jane (Suzanne Burce) (actress and singer); Portland, Ore., 4/1/1929
Powell, William (actor); Pittsburgh, 7/29/1892
Power, Tyrone (actor); Cincinnati, Ohio **(1914–1958)**
Powers, Stephanie (Taffy Paul) (actress); Hollywood, Calif., 11/12/1942
Praxiteles (sculptor); Athens (c.370–c.330 B.C.)
Preminger, Otto (film director and producer); Vienna, 12/5/1906
Prentiss, Paula (Paula Ragusa) (actress); San Antonio, 1939
Presley, Elvis (singer and actor); Tupelo, Miss. **(1935–1977)**
Preston, Robert (Robert Preston Meservey) (actor); Newton Highlands, Mass., 6/8/1918
Previn, André (conductor); Berlin, 4/6/1929
Previn, Dory (singer); Rahway, N.J., 10/22/1929(?)
Price, Leontyne (Mary) (soprano); Laurel, Miss., 2/10/1927
Price, Ray (country music artist); Perryville, Tex., 1/12/1926
Price, Vincent (actor); St. Louis, 5/27/1911
Pride, Charley (singer); Sledge, Miss., 3/18/1938(?)
Priestley, J. B. (John B.) (author); Bradford, England, 9/13/1894
Priestley, Joseph (chemist); nr. Leeds, England **(1733–1804)**

Primrose, William (violist); Glasgow, Scotland, 8/23/1904
Prince, Harold (stage producer); New York City, 1/30/1928
Prinze, Freddie (actor); New York City (1954–1977)
Pritchett, V(ictor) S(awdon) (literary critic); Ipswich, England, 12/16/1900
Procter, William (scientist); Cincinnati (1872–1951)
Prokofieff, Sergei Sergeevich (composer); St. Petersburg, Russia (1891–1953)
Proust, Marcel (novelist); Paris (1871–1922)
Provine, Dorothy (actress); Deadwood, S. Dak., 1/20/1937
Prowse, Juliet (actress); Bombay, 9/25/1936
Pryor, Richard (comedian); Peoria, Ill., 12/1/1940
Ptolemy (Claudius Ptolemaeus) (astronomer and geographer); Ptolemais Hermii (Egypt) (2nd century A.D.)
Pucci, Emilio (Marchese di Barsento) (fashion designer); Naples, Italy, 11/20/1914
Puccini, Giacomo (composer); Lucca, Italy (1858–1924)
Puente, Tito (band leader); New York City, 4/20/1923
Pulaski, Casimir (military officer); Podolia, Poland (1748–1779)
Pulitzer, Joseph (publisher); Makó (Hungary) (1847–1911)
Pullman, George (inventor); Brockton, N.Y. (1831–1897)
Pusey, Nathan M. (educator); Council Bluffs, Iowa, 4/4/1907
Pushkin, Alexander Sergeevich (poet and dramatist); Moscow (1799–1837)
Puzo, Mario (novelist); New York City, 10/15/1921
Pyle, Ernest Taylor (journalist); Dana, Ind. (1900–1945)
Pythagoras (mathematician and philosopher); Samos (Greece) (6th century B.C.)

Q

Quayle, Anthony (actor); Ainsdale, England, 9/7/1913
Queen, Ellery: pen name of Frederic Dannay and the late Manfred B. Lee.
Quinn, Anthony (actor); Chihuahua, Mexico, 4/21/1916

R

Rabe, David (playwright); Dubuque, Iowa, 3/10/1940
Rabelais, François (satirist); nr. Chinon, France (1494?–1553)
Rabi, I. I. (Isidor Isaac) (physicist); Rymanow (Poland), 7/29/1898
Rachmaninoff, Sergei Wassilievitch (pianist and composer); Oneg Estate, Novgorod, Russia (1873–1943)
Racine, Jean Baptiste (dramatist); La Ferté-Milon, France (1639–1699)
Radner, Gilda (comedienne); Detroit, 6/28/1946
Raft, George (actor); New York City (1895–1980)
Rainer, Luise (actress); Vienna, 1912
Raines, Ella (actress); Snoqualmie Falls, Wash., 8/6/1921
Rainier III (Prince); Monaco, 5/31/1923
Rains, Claude (actor); London (1889–1967)
Raitt, Bonnie (singer); Los Angeles, 1950
Raleigh, Sir Walter (courtier and navigator); London (1552?–1618)
Randall, Tony (Leonard Rosenberg) (actor); Tulsa, Okla., 2/26/1920
Randolph, Asa Philip (labor leader); Crescent City, Fla. (1889–1979)
Raphael (Raffaello Santi) (painter and architect); Urbino (Italy) (1483–1520)
Rasputin, Grigori Efimovich (monk); Tobolsk Province, Russia (1871?–1916)
Rathbone, Basil (actor); Johannesburg, South Africa (1892–1967)
Rather, Dan (TV newscaster); Wharton, Tex., 10/31/1931
Ratoff, Gregory (film director); St. Petersburg, Russia (1897–1960)
Rattigan, Terence (playwright); London (1911–1977)
Rauschenberg, Robert (painter); Port Arthur, Tex., 1925
Ravel, Maurice Joseph (composer); Ciboure, France (1875–1937)
Rawls, Lou (singer); Chicago, 12/1/1935
Ray, Man (painter); Philadelphia (1890–1976)
Ray, Satyajat (film director); Calcutta, 5/2/1922
Rayburn, Gene (TV personality); Christopher, Ill., 12/22/1917
Raye, Martha (Margie Yvonne Reed) (comedienne and actress); Butte, Mont., 8/27/1916
Raymond, Gene (actor); New York City, 8/13/1908
Reasoner, Harry (TV commentator); Dakota City, Iowa, 4/17/1923
Redding, Otis (singer); Dawson, Ga. (1941–1967)
Reddy, Helen (singer); Melbourne, 10/25/1941
Redford, Robert (Charles Robert Redford, Jr.) (actor); Santa Monica, Calif., 8/18/1937
Redgrave, Lynn (actress); London, 3/8/1943
Redgrave, Sir Michael (actor); Bristol, England, 3/20/1908
Redgrave, Vanessa (actress); London, 1/30/1937
Reed, Donna (actress); Denison, Iowa, 1/27/1921
Reed, Rex (critic); Ft. Worth, 10/2/1940
Reed, Walter (army surgeon); Belroi, Va. (1851–1902)
Reese, Della (Deloreese Patricia Early) (singer); Detroit, 7/6/1932
Reeves, Jim (singer); Panola County, Tex. (1923–1964)
Reid, Wallace (actor); St. Louis (1891–1923)

Reiner, Carl (actor); New York City, 3/20/1922
Reiner, Fritz (conductor); Budapest (1888–1963)
Reiner, Robert (actor); Bronx, N.Y., 1945
Reinhardt, Max (Max Goldmann) (theater producer); nr. Vienna (1873–1943)
Remarque, Erich Maria (novelist); Osnabruk, Germany (1898–1970)
Rembrandt (Rembrandt Harmensz van Rijn) (painter); Leyden (Netherlands) (1606–1669)
Remick, Lee (Ann) (actress); Boston, 12/14/1935
Rennert, Günther (opera director and producer); Essen, Germany, 4/1/1911
Rennie, Michael (actor); Bradford, England (1909–1971)
Renoir, Jean (film director and writer); Paris, (1894–1979)
Renoir, Pierre Auguste (painter); Limoges, France (1841–1919)
Resnais, Alain (film director); Vannes, France, 6/3/1922
Resnik, Regina (mezzo-soprano); New York City, 8/30/1922
Respighi, Ottorino (composer); Bologna, Italy (1879–1936)
Reston, James (journalist); Clydebank, Scotland, 11/3/1909
Reuther, Walter (labor leader); Wheeling, W. Va. (1907–1970)
Revere, Paul (silversmith and hero of famous ride); Boston (1735–1818)
Revson, Charles (business executive); Boston (1906–1975)
Reynolds, Burt (actor); Waycross, Ga., 2/11/1936
Renolds, Debbie (Marie Frances Reynolds) (actress); El Paso, 4/1/1932
Reynolds, Sir Joshua (painter); nr. Plymouth, England (1723–1792)
Rhodes, Cecil John (South African statesman); Bishop Stortford, England (1853–1902)
Rice, Elmer (playwright); New York City (1892–1967)
Rice, Grantland (sports writer); Murfreesboro, Tenn. (1880–1954)
Rich, Buddy (Bernard) (drummer); Brooklyn, N.Y., 6/30/1917
Rich, Charlie (singer); Colt, Ark., 12/14/1932
Richardson, Elliot L. (ex-Cabinet member); Boston, 7/20/1920
Richardson, Sir Ralph (actor); Cheltenham, England, 12/19/1902
Richardson, Tony (director); Shipley, England, 6/5/1928
Richelieu, Duc de (Armand Jean du Plessis) (cardinal); Paris (1585–1642)
Richter, Charles Francis (seismologist); Hamilton, Canada, 4/26/1900
Richter, Sviatoslav (pianist); Zhitomir, Ukraine, 3/20/1914
Rickenbacker, Edward V. (aviator); Columbus, Ohio (1890–1973)
Rickles, Don (comedian); New York City, 5/8/1926
Rickover, Vice Admiral Hyman G. (atomic energy expert); Russia, 1/27/1900
Riddle, Nelson (composer); Hackensack, N.J., 6/1/1921
Ridgway, General Matthew B. (ex-Army Chief of Staff); Ft. Monroe, Va., 3/3/1895
Rigg, Diana (actress); Doncaster, England, 7/20/1938
Riley, James Whitcomb (poet); Greenfield, Ind. (1849–1916)
Rimsky-Korsakov, Nikolai Andreevich (composer); Tikhvin, Russia (1844–1908)
Rinehart, Mary (née Roberts) (novelist); Pittsburgh (1876–1958)
Ritchard, Cyril (actor and director); Sydney, Australia (1898–1977)
Ritter, John (Jonathan) (actor); Burbank, Calif., 9/17/1948
Ritter, Tex (Woodward Maurice Ritter) (singer); Panola County, Tex., (1905–1973)
Ritz, Al (Al Joachim) (comedian); Newark, N.J. (1901–1965)
Rivera, Diego (painter); Guanajuato, Mexico (1886–1957)
Rivera, Geraldo (Miguel) (TV newscaster); New York City, 7/3/1943
Rivers, Joan (comedienne); Brooklyn, N.Y., 1935(?)
Rivers, Larry (Yitzroch Loiza Grossberg) (painter); New York City, 8/17/1923
Robards, Jason, Jr. (actor); Chicago, 7/26/1922
Robards, Jason, Sr. (actor); Hillsdale, Mich. (1892–1963)
Robbins, Harold (Harold Rubin) (novelist); New York City, 5/21/1916
Robbins, Jerome (Jerome Rabinowitz) (choreographer); New York City, 10/11/1918
Robbins, Marty (singer); Glendale, Ariz., 12/26/1925
Roberts, (Granville) Oral (evangelist and publisher); nr. Ada, Okla., 1/24/1918
Robertson, Cliff (actor); La Jolla, Calif., 9/9/1925
Robertson, Dale (actor); Oklahoma City, 1923
Robeson, Paul (singer and actor); Princeton, N.J., (1898–1976)
Robespierre, Maximilien François Marie Isidore de (French Revolutionist); Arras, France (1758–1794)
Robinson, Bill "Bojangles" (Luther) (dancer); Richmond, Va. (1878–1949)
Robinson, Edward G. (Emanuel Goldenberg) (actor); Bucharest (1893–1973)
Robinson, Edwin Arlington (poet); Head Tide, Me. (1869–1935)
Robson, Dame Flora (actress); South Shields, England, 3/28/1902
Rochester (Eddie Anderson) (actor); Oakland, Calif. (1905–1977)
Rockefeller, David (banker); New York City, 6/12/1915
Rockefeller, John Davison (capitalist); Richford, N.Y. (1839–1937)
Rockefeller, John Davison, Jr. (industrialist); Cleveland (1874–1960)
Rockefeller, John D., 3rd (philanthropist); New York City (1906–1978)
Rockefeller, Laurance S. (conservationist); New York City, 5/26/1910
Rockwell, Norman (painter and illustrator); New York City, (1894–1978)
Rodgers, Jimmie (singer); Meridian, Miss. (1897–1933)
Rodgers, Richard (composer); New York City (1902–1979)

Rodin, François Auguste René (sculptor); Paris **(1840–1917)**

Roentgen, Wilhelm Konrad (physicist); Lennep, Prussia **(1845–1923)**

Rogers, Buddy (Charles) (actor); Olathe, Kan., 8/13/1904

Rogers, Ginger (Virginia McMath) (dancer and actress); Independence, Mo., 7/16/1911

Rogers, Kenny (singer); Houston, 1939(?)

Rogers, Roy (Leonard Slye) (actor); Cincinnati, 11/5/1912

Rogers, Will (William Penn Adair Rogers) (humorist); Oologah, Okla. **(1879–1935)**

Rogers, Will, Jr. (actor); New York City, 10/20/1911

Rogers, William P. (ex-Secretary of State); Norfolk, N.Y., 6/23/1913

Roland, Gilbert (actor); Juarez, Mexico, 12/11/1905

Rolland, Romain (author); Clamecy, France **(1866–1944)**

Rollins, Sonny (saxophonist); New York City, 9/7/1930

Romberg, Sigmund (composer); Szeged (Hungary) **(1887–1951)**

Rome, Harold (composer); Hartford, Conn., 5/27/1908

Romero, Cesar (actor); New York City, 2/15/1907

Romney, George W. (ex-Secretary of HUD); Chihuahua, Mexico, 7/8/1907

Romulo, Carlos P. (diplomat and educator); Manila, 1/14/1899

Ronstadt, Linda (singer); Tucson, Ariz., 7/30/1946

Rooney, Mickey (Joe Yule, Jr.) (actor); Brooklyn, N.Y., 9/23/1920

Roosevelt, Anna Eleanor (reformer and humanitarian); New York City **(1884–1962)**

Rose, Billy (showman); New York City **(1899–1966)**

Rose, Leonard (concert cellist); Washington, D.C., 7/27/1918

Ross, Diana (singer); Detroit, 3/26/1944

Ross, Katharine (actress); Hollywood, Calif., 1/29/1943

Rossellini, Roberto (film director); Rome **(1906–1977)**

Rossetti, Dante Gabriel (painter and poet); London **(1828–1882)**

Rossini, Gioacchino Antonio (composer); Pesaro (Italy) **(1792–1868)**

Rostand, Edmond (dramatist); Marseilles, France **(1868–1918)**

Rostow, Walt Whitman (economist); New York City, 10/7/1916

Rostropovich, Mstislav (cellist and conductor); Baku, U.S.S.R., 8/12/1927

Roth, Lillian (singer); Boston **(1910–1980)**

Roth, Philip (novelist); Newark, N.J., 3/19/1933

Rothko, Mark (Marcus Rothkovich) (painter); Russia **(1903–1970)**

Rouault, Georges (painter); Paris, France **(1871–1958)**

Roundtree, Richard (actor); New Rochelle, N.Y., 9/7/1942

Rousseau, Henri (painter); Laval, France **(1844–1910)**

Rousseau, Jean Jacques (philosopher); Geneva **(1712–1778)**

Rovere, Richard H. (journalist); Jersey City, N.J., 5/5/1915

Rowan, Dan (comedian); Beggs, Okla., 7/2/1922

Rowlands, Gena (actress); Cambria, Wis., 6/19/1936(?)

Rubens, Sir Peter Paul (painter); Siegen (Germany) **(1577–1640)**

Rubenstein, Arthur (concert pianist); Lódz (Poland), 1/28/1887

Rubinstein, Helena (cosmetics executive); Kraków (Poland) **(1882?–1965)**

Rudel, Julius (conductor); Vienna, 3/6/1921

Ruggles, Charles (actor); Los Angeles **(1892–1970)**

Rule, Janice (actress); Norwood, Ohio, 8/15/1931

Runcie, Robert (Archbishop of Canterbury); Liverpool, England, **(1882–1921)**

Runyon, (Alfred) Damon (journalist); Manhattan, Kan. **(1884–1946)**

Rusk, Dean (ex-Sec. of State); Cherokee County, Ga., 2/9/1909

Ruskin, John (art critic); London **(1819–1900)**

Russell, Lord Bertrand (Arthur William) (mathematician and philosopher); Trelleck, Wales **(1872–1970)**

Russell, Jane (actress); Bemidji, Minn., 6/21/1921

Russell, Leon (pianist and singer); Lawton, Okla., 4/2/1941

Russell, Lillian (Helen Louise Leonard) (soprano); Clinton, Iowa **(1861–1922)**

Russell, Nipsy (comedian); Atlanta, 1924(?)

Russell, Rosalind (actress); Waterbury, Conn. **(1912–1976)**

Rustin, Bayard (civil rights leader); West Chester, Pa., 1910

Rutherford, Dame Margaret (actress); London, England **(1892–1972)**

Ryan, Robert (actor); Chicago **(1909–1973)**

Rydell, Bobby (singer); Philadelphia, 1942

Rysanek, Leonie (dramatic soprano); Vienna, 11/14/1928

S

Saarinen, Eero (architect); Finland **(1910–1961)**

Sabin, Albert B. (polio researcher); Bialystok (Poland), 8/26/1906

Sadat, Anwar el- (President); Egypt, 12/25/1918

Sagan, Françoise (novelist); Cajarc, France, 6/21/1935

Sahl, Mort (Morton Lyon Sahl) (comedian); Montreal, 5/11/1927

Saint, Eva Marie (actress); Newark, N.J., 7/4/1924

Saint-Gaudens, Augustus (sculptor); Dublin **(1848–1907)**

St. James, Susan (actress); Los Angeles, 1946

St. John, Jill (actress); Los Angeles, 8/19/1940

St. Johns, Adela Rogers (journalist and author); Los Angeles, 5/20/1894

Saint-Laurent, Yves (Henri Donat Mathieu) (fashion designer); Oran, Algeria, 8/1/1936

Saint-Saëns, Charles Camille (composer); Paris **(1835–1921)**

Sainte-Marie, Buffy (Beverly) (folk singer); Craven, Saskatchewan, Canada, 2/20/1942(?)

Salinger, J. D. (Jerome David) (novelist); New York City, 1/1/1919

Salisbury, Harrison E. (journalist); Minneapolis, 11/14/1908

Salk, Jonas (polio researcher); New York City, 10/28/1914

Salk, Lee (psychologist); New York City, 1926

Salomon, Haym (American Revolution financier); Leszno, Poland **(1740–1785)**

Sand, George (Amandine Lucille Aurore Dudevant, née Dupin) (novelist); Paris **(1804–1876)**

Sandburg, Carl (poet and biographer); Galesburg, Ill. **(1878–1967)**

Sanders, George (actor); St. Petersburg, Russia **(1906–1972)**

Sands, Tommy (singer); Chicago, 8/27/1937

Sanger, Margaret (birth control leader); Corning, N.Y. **(1883–1966)**

Santayana, George (philosopher); Madrid **(1863–1952)**

Sappho (poet); Lesbos (Greece) (lived c. 600 B.C.)

Sargent, John Singer (painter); Florence, Italy **(1856–1925)**

Sarnoff, David (radio executive); Minsk, Russia **(1891–1971)**

Saroyan, William (novelist); Fresno, Calif. **(1908–1981)**

Sarrazin, Michael (actor); Quebec, 5/22/1940

Sarto, Andrea del (Andrea Domenico d'Agnolo di Francesco) (painter); Florence (Italy) **(1486–1531)**

Sartre, Jean-Paul (existentialist writer); Paris **(1905–1980)**

Sassoon, Vidal (hair stylist); London, 1/(?)/1928

Saul (King of Israel) (11th century B.C.)

Savalas, Telly (Aristoteles) (actor); Garden City, N.Y., 1/21/1924(?)

Sayao, Bidú (soprano); Rio de Janeiro, 5/11/1902

Scaasi, Arnold (Arnold Isaacs) (fashion designer); Montreal

Schary, Dore (producer and writer); Newark, N.J. **(1905–1980)**

Schell, Maria (actress); Vienna, 1/15/1926

Schell, Maximilian (actor); Vienna, 12/8/1930

Schiaparelli, Elsa (fashion designer); Rome **(1890?–1973)**

Schiff, Dorothy (newspaper publisher); New York City, 3/11/1903

Schildkraut, Joseph (actor); Vienna **(1896–1964)**

Schiller, Johann Christoph Friedrich von (dramatist and poet); Marbach (Germany) **(1759–1805)**

Schippers, Thomas (conductor); Kalamazoo, Mich. **(1930–1977)**

Schlesinger, Arthur M., Jr. (historian); Columbus, Ohio, 10/15/1917

Schneider, Romy (Rose-Marie Albach) (actress); Vienna, 9/23/1938

Schoenberg, Arnold (composer); Vienna **(1874–1951)**

Schopenhauer, Arthur (philosopher); Danzig (Poland) **(1788–1860)**

Schubert, Franz Peter (composer); Vienna **(1797–1828)**

Schulberg, Budd (novelist); New York City, 3/27/1914

Schulz, Charles M. (cartoonist); Minneapolis, 11/26/1922

Schuman, Robert (statesman); Luxembourg **(1886–1963)**

Schuman, William (composer); New York City, 8/4/1910

Schumann, Robert Alexander (composer); Zwickau (Germany) **(1810–1856)**

Schwartz, Arthur (song writer); Brooklyn, N.Y., 11/25/1900

Schwartz, Maurice (actor); Russia **(1891–1960)**

Schwarzkopf, Elisabeth (soprano); Jarotschin, Poznán (Poland), 12/9/1915

Schweitzer, Albert (humanitarian); Kaysersburg, Upper Alsace **(1875–1965)**

Scofield, Paul (actor); Hurstpierpoint, England, 1/21/1922

Scorsese, Martin (film director); Flushing, N.Y., 11/17/1942

Scott, George C. (actor); Wise, Va., 10/18/1927

Scott, Lizabeth (Emma Matso) (actress); Scranton, Pa., 1923

Scott, Martha (actress); Jamesport, Mo., 9/22/1914

Scott, Randolph (Randolph Crane) (actor); Orange County, Va., 1/23/1903

Scott, Robert Falcon (explorer); Devonport, England **(1868–1912)**

Scott, Sir Walter (novelist); Edinburgh, Scotland **(1771–1832)**

Scott, Zachary (actor); Austin, Tex. **(1914–1965)**

Scotto, Renata (operatic soprano); Savona, Italy, 2/?/1936?

Scruggs, Earl Eugene (bluegrass musician); Cleveland County, N.C., 1/6/1924

Sebastian, John (composer); New York City, 3/17/1944

Seberg, Jean (actress); Marshalltown, Iowa **(1938–1979)**

Sedaka, Neil (singer); Brooklyn, N.Y., 3/13/1939

Seeger, Pete (folk singer); New York City, 5/3/1919

Segal, Erich (novelist); Brooklyn, N.Y., 6/16/1937

Segal, George (actor); New York City, 2/13/1936

Segovia, Andrés (guitarist); Linares, Spain, 2/21/1893

Sellers, Peter (actor); Southsea, England **(1925–1980)**

Selye, Hans (physician); Vienna, 1/26/1907

Selznick, David O. (film producer); Pittsburgh **(1902–1965)**

Sendak, Maurice (Bernard) (children's book author and illustrator); Brooklyn, N.Y., 6/10/1928

Sennett, Mack (Michael Sinnott) (film producer); Richmond, Quebec, Canada **(1880–1960)**

Serkin, Rudolf (pianist); Eger (Hungary), 3/28/1903

Serling, Rod (story writer); Syracuse, N.Y. **(1924–1975)**

Sessions, Roger (composer); Brooklyn, N.Y., 12/28/1896

Seurat, Georges (painter); Paris **(1859–1891)**

Seuss, Dr. (Theodor Seuss Geisel) (author and illustrator); Springfield, Mass., 3/2/1904
Sevareid, Eric (TV commentator); Velva, N.D., 11/26/1912
Severinsen, Doc (band leader); Arlington, Ore., 1927
Sexton, Anne (poet); Newton, Mass. **(1928–1974)**
Shahn, Ben(jamin) (painter); Kaunas, Lithuania **(1898–1969)**
Shakespeare, William (dramatist); Stratford on Avon, England **(1564–1616)**
Shankar, Ravi (sitar player); Benares, India, 4/7/1920
Shanker, Albert (labor leader); New York City, 9/14/1928
Sharif, Omar (Michael Shalhoub) (actor); Alexandria, Egypt, 4/10/1932
Shatner, William (actor); Montreal, 3/22/1931
Shaw, Artie (Arthur Arshawsky) (band leader); New York City, 5/23/1910
Shaw, George Bernard (dramatist); Dublin, **(1856–1950)**
Shaw, Irwin (novelist); Brooklyn, N.Y., 2/27/1913
Shaw, Robert (actor); Lancashire, England **(1927–1978)**
Shaw, Robert (chorale conductor); Red Bluff, Calif., 4/30/1916
Shearer, Moira (ballerina); Dunfermline, Scotland, 1/17/1926
Shearer, Norma (actress); Montreal, 1904
Shearing, George (pianist); London, 8/13/1920
Sheen, Fulton J. (Peter Sheen) (Roman Catholic bishop); El Paso, Ill. **(1895–1979)**
Sheen, Martin (Ramon Estevez) (actor); Dayton, Ohio, 8/3/1940
Shelley, Percy Bysshe (poet); nr. Horsham, England **(1792–1822)**
Shepard, Sam (playwright); Ft. Sheridan, Ill. 11/5/1943
Sheraton, Thomas (furniture designer); Stockton-on-Tees, England **(1751–1806)**
Sheridan, Ann (actress); Denton, Tex. **(1915–1967)**
Sheridan, Philip (army officer); Albany, N.Y. **(1831–1888)**
Sheridan, Richard Brinsley (dramatist); Dublin, **(1751–1816)**
Sherman, William Tecumseh (army officer); Lancaster, Ohio **(1820–1891)**
Sherwood, Robert Emmet (playwright); New Rochelle, N.Y. **(1896–1955)**
Shirer, William L. (journalist and historian); Chicago, 2/23/1904
Sholokhov, Mikhail (novelist); Veshenskaya, Russia, 5/24/1905
Shore, Dinah (Frances Rose Shore) (singer); Winchester, Tenn., 3/1/1917(?)
Short, Bobby (Robert Waltrip Short) (singer and pianist); Danville, Ill., 9/15/1924
Shostakovich, Dmitri (composer); St. Petersburg, Russia **(1906–1975)**
Shriver, Sargent (Robert Sargent Shriver, Jr.) (business executive); Westminster, Md., 11/9/1915
Shulman, Max (novelist); St. Paul, 3/14/1919
Sibelius, Jean (Johann Julius Christian Sibelius) (composer); Tavastehus (Finland) **(1865–1957)**
Sidney, Sylvia (actress); New York City, 8/8/1910
Siepi, Cesare (basso); Milan, Italy, 2/10/1923
Signoret, Simone (Simone Kaminker) (actress); Wiesbaden, Germany, 3/25/1921
Sikorsky, Igor I. (inventor); Kiev, Russia **(1889–1972)**
Sills, Beverly (Belle Silverman) (soprano); Brooklyn, N.Y., 5/25/1929
Silone, Ignazio (Secondo Tranquilli) (novelist); Pescina del Marsi, Italy **(1900–1978)**
Silverman, Fred (broadcasting executive); New York City, 9/13/1937
Silvers, Phil (Philip Silversmith) (comedian); Brooklyn, N.Y., 5/11/1912
Sim, Alastair (actor); Edinburgh, Scotland **(1900–1976)**
Simenon, Georges (Georges Sim) (mystery writer); Liège, Belgium, 2/13/1903
Simmons, Jean (actress); Crouch Hill, London, 1/31/1929
Simon, Carly (singer and songwriter); New York City, 6/25/1945
Simon, Neil (playwright); Bronx, N.Y., 7/4/1927
Simon, Norton (business executive); Portland, Ore., 2/5/1907
Simon, Paul (singer and songwriter); Newark, N.J., 11/5/1942
Simon, Simone (actress); Marseilles, France, 4/23/1914
Simone, Nina (Eunice Kathleen Waymon) (singer and pianist); Tryon, N.C., 2/21/1933
Simpson, Adele (Adele Smithline) (fashion designer); New York City, 12/8/1903
Sinatra, Frank (singer and actor); Hoboken, N.J., 12/12/1915
Sinclair, Upton Beall (novelist); Baltimore **(1878–1968)**
Singer, Isaac Bashevis (novelist); Radzymin (Poland), 7/14/1904
Siqueiros, David (painter); Chihuahua, Mexico **(1896–1974)**
Sisley, Alfred (painter); Paris **(1839–1899)**
Sitting Bull (Prairie Sioux Indian Chief); on Grand River, S.D. (c. 1835–1890)
Skelton, Red (Richard) (comedian); Vincennes, Ind., 7/18/1913
Skinner, B. F. (Burrhus Frederic) (psychologist); Susquehanna, Pa., 3/20/1904
Skinner, Cornelia Otis (writer and actress); Chicago, **(1901–1979)**
Skinner, Otis (actor); Cambridge, Mass. **(1858–1942)**
Slezak, Walter (actor); Vienna, 5/3/1902
Sloan, Alfred P., Jr. (industrialist); New Haven, Conn. **(1875–1966)**
Sloan, John (painter); Lock Haven, Pa. **(1871–1951)**
Smetana, Bedrich (composer); Litomysl (Czechoslovakia) **(1824–1884)**
Smith, Adam (economist); Kirkaldy, Scotland **(1723–1790)**
Smith, Alexis (actress); Penticon, Canada, 6/8/1921

Smith, Alfred Emanuel (politician); New York City **(1873–1944)**
Smith, David (sculptor); Decatur, Ind. **(1906–1965)**
Smith, H. Allen (humorist); McLeansboro, Ill. **(1907–1976)**
Smith, Howard K. (TV commentator); Ferriday, La., 5/12/1914
Smith, Jaclyn (actress); Houston, 10/26/(?)
Smith, John (American colonist); Willoughby, Lincolnshire, England **(1580–1631)**
Smith, Joseph (religious leader); Sharon, Vt. **(1805–1844)**
Smith, Kate (Kathryn) (singer); Greenville, Va., 5/1/1909
Smith, Maggie (actress); Ilford, England, 12/28/1934
Smith, Red (Walter) (sports columnist); Green Bay, Wis., 9/25/1905
Smothers, Dick (Richard) (comedian); Governors Island, New York City, 11/20/1939
Smothers, Tom (Thomas) (comedian); Governors Island, New York City, 2/2/1937
Snow, Lord (Charles Percy) (author); Leicester, England **(1905–1980)**
Snowden, Earl of (Anthony Armstrong-Jones) (photographer); London, 3/7/1930
Snyder, Tom (TV personality); Milwaukee, 5/12/1936
Socrates (philosopher); Athens **(469–399 B.C.)**
Solomon (King of Israel); Jerusalem (?) **(died c. 933 B.C.)**
Solon (lawgiver); Salamis (Greece) **(638?–7559 B.C.)**
Solti, Sir Georg (conductor); Budapest, 10/21/1912
Solzhenitsyn, Aleksandr (novelist); Kislovodsk, Russia, 12/11/1918
Sommer, Elke (Elke Schletz) (actress); Berlin, 11/5/1942
Sondheim, Stephen (composer); New York City, 3/22/1930
Sontag, Susan (author and film director); New York City, 1/28/1933
Sophocles (dramatist); nr. Athens **(496?–406 B.C.)**
Sothern, Ann (Harriette Lake) (actress); Valley City, N.D., 1/22/1912
Soul, David (David Solberg) (actor); Chicago, 8/28/(?)
Sousa, John Philip (composer); Washington, D.C. **(1854–1932)**
Soyer, Raphael (painter); Borisoglebsk, Russia, 12/25/1899
Spaak, Paul-Henri (statesman); Brussels **(1899–1972)**
Spacek, Sissy (Mary Elizabeth) (actress); Quitman, Tex., 12/25/1949
Spark, Muriel (novelist); Edinburgh, Scotland, 2/1/1918
Spector, Phil (rock producer); Bronx, N.Y., 12/25/1940
Spencer, Herbert (philosopher); Derby, England **(1820–1903)**
Spender, Stephen (poet); nr. London, 2/28/1909
Spengler, Oswald (philosopher); Blankenburg, Germany **(1880–1936)**
Spenser, Edmund (poet); London **(1552?–1599)**
Spewack, Bella (playwright); Hungary, 1899
Spiegel, Sam (producer); Jaroslaw (Poland), 11/11/1901
Spielberg, Steven (film director); Cincinnati, 12/18/1947
Spillane, Mickey (Frank Spillane) (mystery writer); Brooklyn, N.Y., 3/9/1918
Spinoza, Baruch (philosopher); Amsterdam (Netherlands) **(1632–1677)**
Spivak, Lawrence (TV producer); Brooklyn, N.Y., 1900
Spock, Benjamin (pediatrician); New Haven, Conn., 5/2/1903
Springsteen, Bruce (singer and songwriter); Freehold, N.J., 9/23/1949
Sproul, Robert G. (educator); San Francisco **(1891–1975)**
Stack, Robert (actor); Los Angeles, 1/13/1919
Stafford, Jo (singer); Coalinga, Calif., 1918
Stalin, Joseph Vissarionovich (Iosif V. Dzhugashvili) (Soviet leader); nr. Tiflis, Russia **(1879–1953)**
Stalina, Svetlana Alliluyeva (Stalin's daughter); Moscow, 2/28/1926
Stallone, Sylvester (actor and writer); New York City, 7/6/1946
Stamp, Terrence (actor); London, 1940
Stang, Arnold (comedian); Chelsea, Mass., 1925
Stanislavski (Konstantin Sergeevich Alekseev) (stage producer); Moscow **(1863–1938)**
Stanley, Sir Henry Morton (John Rowlands) (explorer); Denbigh, Wales **(1841–1904)**
Stanley, Kim (Patricia Reid) (actress); Tularosa, N.M., 2/11/1925
Stans, Maurice H. (ex-Secretary of Commerce); Shakope, Minn., 3/22/1908
Stanton, Frank (broadcasting executive); Muskegon, Mich., 3/20/1908
Stanwyck, Barbara (Ruby Stevens) (actress); Brooklyn, N.Y., 7/16/1907
Stapleton, Jean (Jeanne Murray) (actress); New York City, 1/19/1923
Stapleton, Maureen (actress); Troy, N.Y., 6/21/1925
Starker, János (cellist); Budapest 7/5/1926
Starr, Kay (Starks) (singer); Dougherty, Okla., 7/21/1922
Starr, Ringo (Richard Starkey) (singer and songwriter); Liverpool, England, 7/7/1940
Stassen, Harold E. (ex-government official); West St. Paul, Minn., 4/13/1907
Steegmuller, Francis (biographer); New Haven, Conn., 7/3/1906
Steele, Tommy (singer); London, 12/17/1936
Stegner, Wallace (Earle) (novelist and critic); Lake Mills, Iowa, 2/18/1909
Steiger, Rod (Rodney) (actor); Westhampton, N.Y., 4/14/1925
Stein, Gertrude (author); Allegheny, Pa. **(1874–1946)**
Steinbeck, John Ernst (novelist); Salinas, Calif. **(1902–1968)**
Steinberg, William (conductor); Cologne, Germany **(1899–1978)**
Steinem, Gloria (feminist); Toledo, Ohio, 3/25/1935(?)
Steinmetz, Charles (electrical engineer); Breslau (Poland) **(1865–1923)**
Stendhal (Marie Henri Beyle) (novelist); Grenoble, France **(1783–1842)**

Sterling, Jan (actress); New York City, 4/3/1923
Stern, Isaac (concert violinist); Kreminiecz, Russia, 7/21/1920
Sterne, Laurence (novelist); Clonmel, Ireland **(1713–1768)**
Stevens, Cat (Steven Georgiou) (singer and songwriter); London, 7/?/1947
Stevens, Connie (Concetta Ingolia) (singer); Brooklyn, N.Y., 8/8/1938
Stevens, George (film director); Oakland, Calif. **(1905–1975)**
Stevens, Risë (mezzo-soprano); New York City, 6/11/1913
Stevens, Stella (actress); Yazoo City, Miss., 10/1/1936
Stevenson, Adlai Ewing (statesman); Los Angeles **(1900–1965)**
Stevenson, McLean (actor); Bloomington, Ind., 11/14/1929(?)
Stevenson, Robert Louis Balfour (novelist and poet); Edinburgh, Scotland **(1850–1894)**
Stewart, James (actor); Indiana, Pa., 5/20/1908
Stewart, Rod (Roderick David) (singer); London, 1/10/1945
Stickney, Dorothy (actress); Dickinson, N.D. 6/21/1903
Stills, Stephen (singer and songwriter); Dallas, 1/3/1945
Stokes, Carl (TV newscaster); Cleveland, 6/21/1927
Stokowski, Leopold (conductor); London **(1882–1977)**
Stone, Edward Durell (architect); Fayetteville, Ark. **(1902–1978)**
Stone, Ezra (actor and producer); New Bedford, Mass., 12/2/1917
Stone, I. F. (Isidor Feinstein Stone) (journalist); Philadelphia, 12/24/1907
Stone, Irving (Irving Tennenbaum) (novelist); San Francisco, 7/14/1903
Stone, Lewis (actor); Worcester, Mass. **(1879–1953)**
Stone, Lucy (woman suffragist); nr. West Brookfield, Mass. **(1818–1893)**
Stone, Sly (Sylvester) (rock musician); 1944
Storm, Gale (actress); Bloomington, Tex., 1922
Stout, Rex (mystery writer); Noblesville, Ind. **(1886–1975)**
Stowe, Harriet Elizabeth Beecher (novelist); Litchfield, Conn. **(1811–1896)**
Stradivari, Antonio (violinmaker); Cremona (Italy) **(1644–1737)**
Strasberg, Lee (stage director); Budanov, Austria, 11/17/1901
Strasberg, Susan (actress); New York City, 5/22/1938
Straus, Oskar (composer); Vienna **(1870–1954)**
Strauss, Johann (composer); Vienna **(1825–1899)**
Strauss, Lewis L. (naval officer and scientist); Charleston, W. Va. **(1896–1974)**
Strauss, Richard (composer); Munich, Germany **(1864–1949)**
Stravinsky, Igor (composer); Orienbaum, Russia **(1882–1971)**
Streep, Meryl (Mary Louise) (actress); Summit, N.J., 6/22/1949
Streisand, Barbra (singer and actress); Brooklyn, N.Y., 4/24/1942
Stritch, Elaine (actress); Detroit, 2/2/1928
Struthers, Sally Ann (actress); Portland, Ore., 7/28/1948
Stuart, Gilbert Charles (painter); Rhode Island **(1755–1828)**
Stuart, James Ewell Brown (known as Jeb) (Confederate army officer); Patrick County, Va. **(1833–1864)**
Stuyvesant, Peter (Governor of New Amsterdam); West Friesland (Netherlands) **(1592–1672)**
Styron, William (William Clark Styron, Jr.) (novelist); Newport News, Va., 6/11/1925
Sullavan, Margaret Brooke (actress); Norfolk, Va. **(1911–1960)**
Sullivan, Sir Arthur Seymour (composer); London **(1842–1900)**
Sullivan, Barry (Patrick Barry) (actor); New York City, 8/29/1912
Sullivan, Ed (columnist and TV personality); New York City **(1901–1974)**
Sullivan, Francis Loftus (actor); London **(1903–1956)**
Sullivan, Frank (Francis John) (humorist); Saratoga Springs, N.Y. **(1892–1976)**
Sullivan, Louis Henry (architect); Boston, Mass. **(1856–1924)**
Sulzberger, Arthur Ochs (newspaper publisher); New York City, 2/5/1926
Sumac, Yma (singer); Ichocan, Peru, 9/10/1927
Summer, Donna (singer); Boston, 12/31/1948
Sun Yat-sen (statesman); nr. Macao, China **(1866–1925)**
Susann, Jacqueline (novelist); Philadelphia **(1926?–1974)**
Susskind, David (TV producer); New York City, 12/19/1920
Sutherland, Joan (soprano); Sydney, Australia, 11/7/1926
Suzuki, Pat (actress); Cressey, Calif., 1931
Swados, Elizabeth (composer, playwright); Buffalo, N.Y., 2/5/1951
Swanson, Gloria (Josephine Swenson) (actress); Chicago, 3/27/1899
Swarthout, Gladys (soprano); Deepwater, Mo. **(1904–1969)**
Swayze, John Cameron (news commentator); Wichita, Kan., 4/4/1906
Swift, Jonathan (satirist); Dublin **(1667–1745)**
Swinburne, Algernon Charles (poet); London **(1837–1909)**
Swope, Herbert Bayard (journalist); St. Louis **(1882–1958)**
Sydow, von, Max (Carl Adolf von Sydow) (actor); Lund, Sweden, 4/10/1929
Synge, John Millington (dramatist); nr. Dublin **(1871–1909)**
Szilard, Leo (physicist); Budapest **(1898–1964)**

T

Taft, Robert Alphonso (legislator); Cincinnati **(1889–1953)**
Tagore, Sir Rabindranath (poet); Calcutta **(1861–1941)**
Tallchief, Maria (ballerina); Fairfax, Okla., 1/24/1925
Talleyrand-Périgord, Charles Maurice de (statesman); Paris **(1754–1838)**
Talmadge, Norma (actress); Niagara Falls, N.Y. **(1897–1957)**

Tamerlane (Timur) (Mongol conqueror); nr. Samarkand (U.S.S.R.) **(1336?–1405)**
Tandy, Jessica (actress); London, 6/7/1909
Tarkington, (Newton) Booth (novelist); Indianapolis **(1869–1946)**
Tate, Allen (John Orley) (poet and critic); Winchester, Ky., **(1899–1979)**
Tate, Sharon (actress); Dallas **(1943–1969)**
Tati, Jacques (Jacques Tatischeff) (actor); Pecq, France, 10/9/1908
Taylor, Elizabeth (actress); London, 2/27/1932
Taylor, Estelle (actress); Wilmington, Del. **(1899–1958)**
Taylor, Harold (educator); Toronto, 9/28/1914
Taylor, James (singer and songwriter); Boston, 3/12/1948
Taylor, (Joseph) Deems (composer); New York City **(1885–1966)**
Taylor, Laurette (Laurette Cooney) (actress); New York City **(1884–1946)**
Taylor, Gen. Maxwell D. (former Army Chief of Staff); Keytesville, Mo., 8/26/1901
Taylor, Robert (Spangler Arlington Brugh) (actor); Filley, Neb. **(1911–1969)**
Taylor, Rod (actor); Sydney, Australia, 1/11/1930
Tchaikovsky, Peter (Pëtr) Ilich (composer); Votkinsk, Russia **(1840–1893)**
Teasdale, Sara (poet); St. Louis **(1884–1933)**
Tebaldi, Renata (lyric soprano); Pesaro, Italy, 1/2/1922
Tecumseh (Shawnee Indian chief); nr. Springfield, Ohio **(1768?–1813)**
Teller, Edward (atomic physicist); Budapest, 1/15/1908
Temple, Shirley. See Black, Shirley Temple
Tennyson, Alfred (1st Baron Tennyson) (poet); Somersby, England **(1809–1892)**
Terhune, Albert Payson (novelist and journalist); Newark, N.J. **(1872–1942)**
Terry, Ellen Alicia (actress); Coventry, England **(1848–1928)**
Terry-Thomas (Thomas Terry Hoar Stevens) (actor); London, 7/14/1911
Tesla, Nikola (electrician and inventor); Smiljan (Yugoslavia) **(1856–1943)**
Thackeray, William Makepeace (novelist); Calcutta **(1811–1863)**
Thant, U (U.N. statesman); Pantanaw (Burma) **(1909–1974)**
Tharp, Twyla (dancer and choreographer); Portland, Ind., 7/1/1941(?)
Thatcher, Margaret (Prime Minister); Grantham, England, 10/13/1925
Thaxter, Phyllis (actress); Portland, Me., 1921
Thebom, Blanche (mezzo-soprano); Monessen, Pa., 9/19/1919
Theodorakis, Mikis (composer); Chios, Greece, 7/29/1925
Thieu, Nguyen Van (ex-President of South Vietnam); Trithuy (Vietnam) 4/5/1923
Thomas, Danny (Amos Jacobs) (entertainer and TV producer); Deerfield, Mich., 1/6/1914
Thomas, Dylan Marlais (poet); Carmarthenshire, Wales **(1914–1953)**
Thomas, Lowell (explorer, commentator); Woodington, Ohio **(1892–1981)**
Thomas, Marlo (actress); Detroit, 11/21/1943
Thomas, Michael Tilson (conductor); Hollywood, Calif., 12/21/1944
Thomas, Norman Mattoon (Socialist leader); Marion, Ohio **(1884–1968)**
Thomas, Richard (actor); New York City, 6/13/1951
Thompson, Dorothy (writer); Lancaster, N.Y. **(1894–1961)**
Thompson, Sada (actress); Des Moines, Iowa, 9/27/1929
Thoreau, Henry David (naturalist and author); Concord, Mass. **(1817–1862)**
Thorndike, Dame Sybil (actress); Gainsborough, England **(1882–1976)**
Thurber, James Grover (author and cartoonist); Columbus, Ohio **(1894–1961)**
Tibbett, Lawrence (baritone); Bakersfield, Calif. **(1896–1960)**
Tierney, Gene (actress); Brooklyn, N.Y., 11/20/1920
Tiffin, Pamela (actress); Oklahoma City, 10/13/1942
Tillstrom, Burr (puppeteer); Chicago, 10/13/1917
Tintoretto, Il (Jacopo Robusti) (painter); Venice **(1518–1594)**
Tiny Tim (Herbert Khaury) (entertainer); New York City, 1923(?)
Tiomkin, Dmitri (composer); St. Petersburg, Russia **(1894–1979)**
Titian (Tiziano Vecelli) (painter); Pieve di Cadore (Italy) **(1477–1576)**
Tito (Josip Broz or Brozovich) (President of Yugoslavia); Croatia (Yugoslavia) **(1892–1980)**
Tocqueville, Alexis de (writer); Verneuil, France **(1805–1859)**
Todd, Thelma (actress); Lawrence, Mass. **(1905–1935)**
Tolstoi, Count Leo (Lev) Nikolaevich (novelist); Tula Province, Russia **(1828–1910)**
Tomlin, Lily (comedienne); Detroit, 1939(?)
Tone, Franchot (actor); Niagara Falls, N.Y. **(1905–1968)**
Torme, Mel (Melvin) (singer); Chicago, 9/13/1925
Torn, Rip (Elmore Torn, Jr.) (actor and director); Temple, Tex., 2/6/1931
Toscanini, Arturo (orchestra conductor); Parma, Italy **(1867–1957)**
Toulouse-Lautrec (Henri Marie Raymond de Toulouse-Lautrec Monfa) (painter); Albi, France **(1864–1901)**
Toynbee, Arnold J. (historian); London **(1889–1975)**
Tracy, Spencer (actor); Milwaukee **(1900–1967)**
Traubel, Helen (Wagnerian soprano); St. Louis **(1903–1972)**
Travolta, John (actor); Englewood, N.J., 2/18/1954
Treacher, Arthur (actor); Brighton, England **(1894–1975)**
Trevor, Claire (actress); New York City, 1911
Trigère, Pauline (fashion designer); Paris, 11/4/1912

Trilling, Lionel (author and educator); New York City (1905–1975)
Trotsky, Leon (Lev Davidovich Bronstein) (statesman); Elisavetgrad, Russia (1879–1940)
Trudeau, Pierre Elliott (Prime Minister); Montreal, 10/18/1919
Truffaut, François (film director); Paris, 2/6/1932
Trujillo y Molina, Rafael Leonidas (Dominican Republic dictator); San Cristóbal, Dominican Republic (1891–1961)
Truman, Margaret (author); Independence, Mo., 2/17/1924
Tryon, Thomas (actor and novelist); Hartford, Conn., 1/14/1926
Tucker, Forrest (actor); Plainfield, Ind., 2/12/1919
Tucker, Richard (tenor); New York City (1914–1975)
Tucker, Sophie (Sophie Abuza) (singer); Boston (1884?–1966)
Tudor, Antony (choreographer); London, 4/4/1909
Turgenev, Ivan Sergeevich (novelist); Orel, Russia (1818–1883)
Turner, Ike (singer); Clarksdale, Miss., 11/?/1931
Turner, Joseph M.W. (painter); London (1775–1851)
Turner, Lana (Julia Jean Mildred Frances Turner) (actress); Wallace, Idaho, 2/8/1920
Turner, Nat (civil rights leader); Southampton County, Va. (1800–1831)
Turner, Tina (Annie Mae Bullock) (singer); Brownsville, Tex., 1939
Turpin, Ben (comedian); New Orleans (1874–1940)
Tushingham, Rita (actress); Liverpool, England, 3/14/1942
Twain, Mark (Samuel Langhorne Clemens) (author); Florida, Mo. (1835–1910)
Tweed, William Marcy (politician); New York City (1823–1878)
Twiggy (Leslie Hornby) (model); London, 9/19/1949
Twining, Gen. Nathan F. (former Air Force Chief of Staff); Monroe, Wis., 10/11/1897
Twitty, Conway (Harold Lloyd Jenkins) (singer and guitarist); Friars Point, Miss., 9/1/1933
Tyson, Cicely (actress); New York City, 12/19/1939(?)

U

Udall, Stewart L. (ex-Secretary of the Interior); St. Johns, Ariz., 1/31/1920
Uggams, Leslie (singer and actress); New York City, 5/25/1943
Ulanova, Galina (ballerina); St. Petersburg, Russia, 1/10/1910
Ullmann, Liv (actress); Tokyo, 12/16/1939
Ulric, Lenore (actress); New Ulm, Minn. (1894–1970)
Untermeyer, Louis (anthologist and poet); New York City (1885–1977)
Updike, John (novelist); Shillington, Pa., 3/18/1932
Urey, Harold C. (physicist); Walkerton, Ind. (1893–1981)
Uris, Leon (novelist); Baltimore, 8/3/1924
Ustinov, Peter (actor and producer); London, 4/16/1921
Utrillo, Maurice (painter); Paris (1883–1955)

V

Vaccaro, Brenda (actress); Brooklyn, N.Y., 11/18/1939
Valentine, Karen (actress); Santa Rosa, Calif., 1947
Valentino, Rudolph (Rodolpho d'Antonguolla) (actor); Castellaneta, Italy (1895–1926)
Valentino (Valentino Garavani) (fashion designer); nr. Milan, Italy, 5/11/1932
Vallee, Rudy (Hubert Vallée) (band leader and singer); Island Pond, Vt., 7/28/1901
Van Allen, James Alfred (space physicist); Mt. Pleasant, Iowa, 9/7/1914
Van Buren, Abigail (Mrs. Morton Phillips) (columnist); Sioux City, Iowa, 7/4/1918
Vance, Vivian (actress); Cherryvale, Kan. (1912–1979)
Vanderbilt, Alfred G. (sportsman); London, 9/22/1912
Vanderbilt, Cornelius (financier); Port Richmond, N.Y. (1794–1877)
Vanderbilt, Gloria (artist and heiress); New York City, 2/20/1924
Van Doren, Carl (writer and educator); Hope, Ill. (1885–1950)
Van Doren, Mamie (actress); Rowena, S.D., 2/6/1933
Van Dyke, Dick (actor); West Plains, Mo., 12/13/1925
Vandyke (or Van Dyck), Sir Anthony (painter); Antwerp (Belgium) (1599–1641)
Van Eyck, Jan (painter); Maeseyck (Belgium) (c.1390–1441)
van Gogh, Vincent (painter); Groot Zundert, Brabant (1853–1890)
van Hamel, Martine (ballerina); Brussels, 11/16/1945
Van Heusen, Jimmy (Edward Chester Babcock) (songwriter); Syracuse, N.Y., 1/26/1913
Van Peebles, Melvin (playwright); Chicago, 9/21/1932
Vaughan, Sarah (singer); Newark, N.J., 3/27/1924
Vaughan Williams, Ralph (composer); Down Ampney, England (1872–1958)
Vaughn, Robert (actor); New York City, 11/22/1932
Velázquez, Diego Rodriguez de Silva y (painter); Seville, Spain (1599–1660)
Velez, Lupe (Guadelupe Velez de Villalobos) (actress); San Luis Potosi, Mexico (1908–1944)
Venturi, Robert (Charles) (architect); Philadelphia, 6/25/1925

Verdi, Giuseppe (composer); Roncole (Italy) (1813–1901)
Verdon, Gwen (actress); Culver City, Calif., 1/13/1925
Vereen, Ben (actor and singer); Miami, Fla., 10/10/1946
Vermeer, Jan (or Jan van der Meer van Delft) (painter); Delft (Netherlands) (1632–1675)
Verne, Jules (author); Nantes, France (1828–1905)
Verrazano, Giovanni da (navigator); Florence (Italy) (1485?–1528)
Verrett, Shirley (mezzo-soprano); New Orleans, 5/31/1933
Vespucci, Amerigo (navigator); Florence (Italy) (1454–1512)
Vickers, Jon (tenor); Prince Albert, Sask., Canada, 10/29/1926
Vidal, Gore (novelist); West Point, N.Y., 10/3/1925
Vidor, King (film director and producer); Galveston, Tex., 2/8/1895
Villa, Pancho (Doroteo Arango) (bandit); Rio Grande, Mexico (1877–1923)
Villella, Edward (ballet dancer); Bayside, Queens, N.Y., 10/1/1936
Villon, François (François de Montcorbier) (poet); Paris (1431–1463)
Vinton, Bobby (singer); Canonsburg, Pa., 4/16/1935(?)
Virgil (or Vergil) (Publius Vergilius Maro) (poet); nr. Mantua (Italy) (70–19 B.C.)
Vishnevskaya, Galina (soprano); Leningrad, 10/25/1926
Vlaminck, Maurice de (painter); Paris (1876–1958)
Voight, Jon (actor); Yonkers, N.Y., 12/29/1938
Voltaire (François Marie Arouet) (author); Paris (1694–1778)
Von Braun. *See* Braun
von Furstenberg, Betsy (actress); Neiheim-Heusen, Germany, 8/16/1935
von Fürstenberg, Diane (Diane Simone Michelle Halfin) (fashion designer); Brussels, 12/31/1946
von Karajan, Herbert (conductor); Salzburg (Austria), 4/5/1908
Vonnegut, Kurt, Jr. (novelist); Indianapolis, 11/11/1922
Von Stroheim, Erich Oswald Hans Carl Maria von Nordenwall (film actor and director); Vienna (1885–1957)
Vorster, Balthazar Johannes (Prime Minister); Jamestown, Cape Province, South Africa, 12/13/1915
Vreeland, Diana (Diana Dalziel) (fashion journalist and museum consultant); Paris, 1903(?)

W

Wagner, Lindsay (actress); Los Angeles, 1949
Wagner, Robert (actor); Detroit, 2/10/1930
Wagner, Robert F. (ex-Mayor of New York City); New York City, 4/20/1910
Wagner, Wilhelm Richard (composer); Leipzig (Germany) (1813–1883)
Waldheim, Kurt (U.N. Secretary-General); St. Andrae-Wörden, Austria, 12/21/1918
Walker, Clint (actor); Hartford, Ill., 5/30/1927
Walker, Nancy (Ann Myrtle Swoyer); (actress and comedienne); Philadelphia, 5/10/1922
Wallace, DeWitt (publisher); St. Paul (1889–1981)
Wallace, George C. (ex-Governor); Clio, Ala., 8/25/1919
Wallace, Irving (novelist); Chicago, 3/19/1916
Wallace, Mike (Myron Wallace) (TV interviewer and commentator); Brookline, Mass., 5/9/1918
Wallach, Eli (actor); Brooklyn, N.Y., 12/7/1915
Waller, Thomas "Fats" (pianist); New York City (1904–1943)
Wallis, Hal (film producer); Chicago, 9/14/1899
Waltari, Mika (novelist); Helsinki, Finland, (1908–1979)
Walter, Bruno (Bruno Walter Schlesinger) (orchestra conductor); Berlin (1876–1962)
Walters, Barbara (TV commentator); Boston, 9/25/1931
Walton, Izaak (author); Stafford, England (1593–1683)
Wambaugh, Joseph (author and screenwriter); East Pittsburgh, Pa., 1/22/1937
Wanamaker, John (merchant); Philadelphia (1838–1922)
Ward, Barbara (economist); York, England (1914–1981)
Warhol, Andy (artist and producer); Cleveland, 8/8/1930(?)
Waring, Fred (band leader); Tyrone, Pa., 6/9/1900
Warner, H. B. (Henry Bryan Warner Lickford) (actor); London (1876–1958)
Warren, Earl (Chief Justice of the U.S.); Los Angeles (1891–1974)
Warren, Robert Penn (novelist); Guthrie, Ky., 4/24/1905
Warwicke, Dionne (singer); East Orange, N.J., 1941
Washington, Booker Taliaferro (educator); Franklin County, Va. (1856–1915)
Waters, Ethel (actress and singer); Chester, Pa. (1896–1977)
Waters, Muddy (McKinley Morganfield) (singer and guitarist); Rolling Fork, Miss., 4/4/1915
Watson, Thomas John (industrialist); Campbell, N.Y. (1874–1956)
Watt, James (inventor); Greenock, Scotland (1736–1819)
Watteau, Jean-Antoine (painter); Valenciennes, France (1684–1721)
Watts, André (concert pianist); Nuremberg, Germany, 6/20/1946
Waugh, Alec (Alexander Raban Waugh) (novelist); London (1898–1981)
Waugh, Evelyn (satirist); London (1903–1966)
Wayne, Anthony (military officer); Waynesboro (family farm), nr. Paoli, Pa. (1745–1796)

Wayne, David (David McMeakan) (actor); Traverse City, Mich., 1/30/1914
Wayne, John (Marion Michael Morrison) (actor); Winterset, Iowa, **(1907–1979)**
Weaver, Dennis (actor); Joplin, Mo., 6/4/1925
Weaver, Fritz (actor); Pittsburgh, 1/19/1926
Webb, Clifton (Webb Parmelee Hollenbeck) (actor); Indianapolis **(1893–1966)**
Webb, Jack (film actor and producer); Santa Monica, Calif., 4/2/1920
Weber, Karl Maria Friedrich Ernst von (composer); nr. Lübeck (Germany) **(1786–1826)**
Webster, Daniel (statesman); Salisbury, N.H. **(1782–1852)**
Webster, Noah (lexicographer); West Hartford, Conn. **(1758–1843)**
Weill, Kurt (composer); Dessau, Germany **(1900–1950)**
Weizmann, Chaim (statesman); Grodno Province, Russia **(1874–1952)**
Welch, Raquel (Raquel Tejada) (actress); Chicago, 9/5/1942
Weld, Tuesday (Susan) (actress); New York City, 8/27/1943
Welk, Lawrence (band leader); Strasburg, N.D., 3/11/1903
Welles, Orson (actor and producer); Kenosha, Wis., 5/6/1915
Wellington, Duke of (Arthur Wellesley) (statesman); Ireland **(1769–1852)**
Wells, H(erbert) G(eorge) (author); Bromley, England **(1866–1946)**
Welty, Eudora (novelist); Jackson, Miss., 4/13/1909
Werfel, Franz (novelist); Prague **(1890–1945)**
Werner, Oskar (Josef Schliessmayer) (film actor and director); Vienna, 11/13/1922
Wertmuller, Lina (film director); Rome, 1926(?)
Wesley, John (religious leader); Epworth Rectory, Lincolnshire, England **(1703–1791)**
West, Dame Rebecca (Cicily Fairchild) (novelist); County Kerry, Ireland, 12/25/1892
West, Jessamyn (novelist); nr. North Vernon, Ind., 7/18/1902
West, Mae (actress); Brooklyn, N.Y. **(1893–1980)**
West, Nathanael (Nathan Weinstein) (novelist); New York City **(1902–1940)**
Westinghouse, George (inventor); Central Bridge, N.Y. **(1846–1914)**
Westmoreland, William Childs (ex-Army Chief of Staff); Saxon, S.C., 3/26/1914
Wharton, Edith Newbold (née Jones) (novelist); New York City **(1862–1937)**
Wheeler, Bert (Albert Jerome Wheeler) (comedian); Paterson, N.J. **(1895–1968)**
Whistler, James Abbott McNeill (painter and etcher); Lowell, Mass. **(1834–1903)**
White, E. B. (Elwyn Brooks White) (author); Mt. Vernon, N.Y., 7/11/1899
White, Stanford (architect); New York City **(1853–1906)**
White, Theodore H. (historian); Boston, 5/6/1915
White, William Allen (journalist); Emporia, Kan. **(1868–1944)**
Whitehead, Alfred North (mathematician and philosopher); Isle of Thanet, England **(1861–1947)**
Whiteman, Paul (band leader); Denver **(1891–1967)**
Whitman, Walt (Walter) (poet); West Hills, N.Y. **(1819–1892)**
Whitmore, James (actor); White Plains, N.Y., 10/1/1921
Whitney, Cornelius Vanderbilt (sportsman); New York City, 2/20/1899
Whitney, Eli (inventor); Westboro, Mass. **(1765–1825)**
Whitney, John Hay (publisher); Ellsworth, Me., 8/17/1904
Whittier, John Greenleaf (poet); Haverhill, Mass. **(1807–1892)**
Widmark, Richard (actor); Sunrise, Minn., 12/26/1914
Wiesel, Elie (Eliezer) (author); Sighet, Romania, 9/30/1928
Wilbur, Richard (poet); New York City, 3/1/1921
Wilde, Cornel (film actor and producer); New York City, 10/13/1918
Wilde, Oscar Fingal O'Flahertie Wills (author); Dublin **(1854–1900)**
Wilder, Billy (film producer and director); Vienna, 6/22/1906
Wilder, Gene (Jerome Silberman) (actor); Milwaukee, 6/11/1935(?)
Wilder, Thornton (author); Madison, Wis. **(1897–1975)**
Wilding, Michael (actor); Westcliff, England **(1912–1979)**
Wilkins, Roy (civil rights leader); St. Louis **(1901–1981)**
Williams, Andy (singer); Wall Lake, Iowa, 12/3/1930
Williams, Cindy (actress); Van Nuys, Calif., 8/22/(?)
Williams, Edward Bennett (lawyer); Hartford, Conn., 5/31/1920
Williams, Emlyn (actor and playwright); Mostyn, Wales, 11/26/1905
Williams, Esther (actress); Los Angeles, 8/8/1923
Williams, Gluyas (cartoonist); San Francisco, 7/23/1888
Williams, Hank, Sr. (Hiram King Williams) (singer); Georgiana, Ala. **(1923–1953)**
Williams, Robin (comedian); Chicago, 7/?/1952
Williams, Roger (clergyman); London **(1603?–1683)**
Williams, Tennessee (Thomas L. Williams) (playwright); Columbus, Miss., 3/26/1911
Willkie, Wendell Lewis (lawyer); Elwood, Ind. **(1892–1944)**
Willson, Meredith (composer); Mason City, Iowa, 5/18/1902
Wilson, Don (radio and TV announcer); Lincoln, Neb., 9/1/1900
Wilson, Flip (Clerow) (comedian); Jersey City, N.J., 12/8/1933
Wilson, Harold (ex-Prime Minister); Huddersfield, England, 3/11/1916
Wilson, Nancy (singer); Chillicothe, Ohio, 2/20/1937

Wilson, Sloan (novelist); Norwalk, Conn., 5/8/1920
Winchell, Walter (columnist); New York City **(1897–1972)**
Windsor, Duchess of (Bessie Wallis Warfield); Blue Ridge Summit, Pa., 6/19/1896
Windsor, Duke of (formerly King Edward VIII of England); Richmond Park, England **(1894–1972)**
Winkler, Henry (actor); New York City, 10/30/1945
Winter, Johnny (guitarist); Leland, Miss., 2/23/1944
Winters, Jonathan (comedian); Dayton, Ohio, 11/11/1925
Winters, Shelley (Shirley Schrift) (actress); East St. Louis, Ill., 8/18/1922
Winthrop, John (first Governor, Massachusetts Bay Colony); Suffolk, England **(1588–1649)**
Wise, Stephen Samuel (rabbi); Budapest **(1874–1949)**
Withers, Jane (actress); Atlanta, 1927
Wittgenstein, Ludwig (Josef Johann) (philosopher); Vienna **(1889–1951)**
Wodehouse, P(elham) G(renville) (novelist); Guildford, England **(1881–1975)**
Wolfe, Thomas Clayton (novelist); Asheville, N.C. **(1900–1938)**
Wolfe, Tom (journalist); Richmond, Va., 3/2/1931
Wolsey, Thomas (prelate and statesman); Ipswich, England **(1475?–1530)**
Wonder, Stevie (Steveland Judkins, later Steveland Morris) (singer and songwriter); Saginaw, Mich., 5/13/1950
Wong, Anna May (Lu Tsong Wong) (actress); Los Angeles **(1907–1961)**
Wood, Grant (painter); Anamosa, Iowa **(1892–1942)**
Wood, Natalie (Natasha Gurdin) (film actress); San Francisco, 7/20/1938
Woodward, Joanne (film actress); Thomasville, Ga., 2/27/1930
Woolf, Adeline Virginia (née Stephens) (novelist); London **(1882–1941)**
Woollcott, Alexander (author); Phalanx, N.J. **(1887–1943)**
Woolley, Monty (Edgar Montillion Woolley) (actor); New York City **(1888–1963)**
Woolworth, Frank (merchant); Rodman, N.Y. **(1852–1919)**
Wordsworth, William (poet); Cockermouth, England **(1770–1850)**
Worley, Jo Anne (actress and singer); Lowell, Ind., 9/6/1937
Wouk, Herman (novelist); New York City, 5/27/1915
Wray, Fay (actress); Alberta, Canada, 1907
Wren, Sir Christopher (architect); East Knoyle, England **(1632–1723)**
Wright, Frank Lloyd (architect); Richland Center, Wis. **(1869–1959)**
Wright, Orville (inventor); Dayton, Ohio **(1871–1948)**
Wright, Richard (novelist); nr. Natchez, Miss. **(1908–1960)**
Wright, Teresa (actress); New York City, 10/27/1918
Wright, Wilbur (inventor); Millville, Ind. **(1867–1912)**
Wyatt, Jane (film actress); Campgaw, N.J., 8/12/1912
Wyeth, Andrew (painter); Chadds Ford, Pa., 7/12/1917
Wyler, William (film director); Mulhouse (France), **(1902–1981)**
Wyman, Jane (Sarah Jane Fulks) (actress); St. Joseph, Mo., 1/4/1914
Wynette, Tammy (Wynette Pugh) (singer); Tupelo, Miss. 5/5/1942
Wynn, Ed (Isaiah Edwin Leopold) (comedian); Philadelphia **(1886–1966)**
Wynn, Keenan (actor); New York City, 7/27/1916
Wynter, Dana (actress); London, 6/8/1930

Y

Yeats, William Butler (poet); nr. Dublin **(1865–1939)**
Yevtushenko, Yevgeny (poet); Zima, U.S.S.R., 7/18/1933
York, Michael (actor); Fulmer, England, 3/27/1942
York, Susannah (Fletcher) (actress); London, 1/9/1942
Yorty, Samuel W. (ex-Mayor of Los Angeles); Lincoln, Neb., 10/1/1909
Young, Alan (actor); North Shield, England, 11/19/1919
Young, Brigham (religious leader); Whitingham, Vt. **(1801–1877)**
Young, Gig (Byron Barr) (actor); St. Cloud, Minn. **(1917–1978)**
Young, Loretta (Gretchen Young) (actress); Salt Lake City, Utah, 1/6/1913
Young, Neil (singer and songwriter); Toronto, 11/12/1945
Young, Robert (actor); Chicago, 2/22/1907
Youngman, Henny (comedian); England, 1906

Z

Zanuck, Darryl F. (film producer); Wahoo, Neb. **(1902–1979)**
Zappa, Frank (Francis Vincent Zappa, Jr.) (singer and songwriter); Baltimore, 12/21/1940
Zeffirelli, Franco (director); Florence, Italy, 2/12/1923
Zhou Enlai (Premier); Hualyin, China **(1898–1976)**
Ziegfeld, Florenz (theatrical producer); Chicago **(1869–1932)**
Zimbalist, Efrem (concert violinist); Rostov-on-Don, Russia, 4/9/1889
Zimbalist, Efrem, Jr. (actor); New York City, 11/30/1923
Zola, Emile (novelist); Paris **(1840–1902)**
Zoroaster (religious leader); Persian Empire **(c. 6th century** B.C.)
Zukerman, Pinchas (violinist); Tel Aviv, Israel 7/16/1948
Zweig, Stefan (author); Vienna **(1881–1942)**

Firsts in America

This selection is based on our editorial judgment. Other sources may list different firsts.

Admiral in U.S. Navy: David Glasgow Farragut, 1866.

Air-mail route, first transcontinental: Between New York City and San Francisco, 1920.

Assembly, representative: House of Burgesses, founded in Virginia, 1619.

Bank established: Bank of North America, Philadelphia, 1781.

Birth in America to English parents: Virginia Dare, born Roanoke Island, N.C., 1587.

Botanic garden: Established by John Bartram in Philadelphia, 1728. (Oldest still existing was established in Cambridge, Mass., in 1807.)

Cartoon, colored: "The Yellow Kid," by Richard Outcault, in *New York World,* 1895.

College: Harvard, founded 1636.

College to confer degrees on women: Oberlin (Ohio) College, 1841.

College to establish coeducation: Oberlin (Ohio) College, 1833.

Electrocution of a criminal: William Kemmler in Auburn Prison, Auburn, N.Y., Aug. 6, 1890.

Five and Ten Cents Store: Founded by Frank Woolworth, Utica, N.Y., 1879 (moved to Lancaster, Pa., same year).

Fraternity: Phi Beta Kappa; founded Dec. 5, 1776, at College of William and Mary.

Law to be declared unconstitutional by U.S. Supreme Court: Judiciary Act of 1789. Case: *Marbury v. Madison,* 1803.

Library, circulating: Philadelphia, 1731.

Newspaper, illustrated daily: *New York Daily Graphic,* 1873.

Newspaper published daily: *Pennsylvania Packet and General Advertiser,* Philadelphia, Sept., 1784.

Newspaper published over a continuous period: *The Boston News-Letter,* April, 1704.

Newsreel: Pathé Frères of Paris, in 1910, circulated a weekly issue of their *Pathé Journal.*

Oil well, commercial: Titusville, Pa., 1859.

Panel quiz show on radio: *Information Please,* May 17, 1938.

Postage stamps issued: 1847.

Railroad, transcontinental: Central Pacific and Union Pacific railroads, joined at Promontory, Utah, May 10, 1869.

Savings bank: The Provident Institute for Savings, Boston, 1816.

Science museum: Founded by Charleston (S.C.) Library Society, 1773.

Skyscraper: Home Insurance Co., Chicago, 1885 (10 floors, 2 added later).

Slaves brought into America: At Jamestown, Va., 1619, from a Dutch ship.

Sorority: Kappa Alpha Theta, at De Pauw University, 1870.

State to abolish capital punishment: Michigan, 1847.

State to enter Union after original 13: Vermont, 1791.

Steam-heated building: Eastern Hotel, Boston, 1845.

Steam railroad (carried passengers and freight): Baltimore & Ohio, 1830.

Strike on record by union: Journeymen Printers, New York City, 1776.

Subway: Opened in Boston, 1897.

"Tabloid" picture newspaper: *The Illustrated Daily News* (now *The Daily News*), New York City, 1919.

Vaudeville theater: Gaiety Museum, Boston, 1883.

Woman cabinet member: Frances Perkins, Secretary of Labor, 1933.

Woman candidate for President: Victoria Claflin Woodhull, nominated by National Woman's Suffrage Assn. on ticket of Nation Radical Reformers, 1872.

Woman doctor of medicine: Elizabeth Blackwell, M.D. from Geneva Medical College of Western New York, 1849.

Woman elected governor of a state: Mrs. Nellie Tayloe Ross, Wyoming, 1925.

Woman elected to U.S. Senate: Mrs. Hattie Caraway, Arkansas; elected Nov., 1932.

Woman graduate of law school: Mrs. Ada H. Kepley, Union College of Law, Chicago, 1870.

Woman member of U.S. House of Representatives: Jeannette Rankin; elected Nov., 1916.

Woman member of U.S. Senate: Mrs. Rebecca Latimer Felton of Georgia; appointed Oct. 3, 1922.

Woman member of U.S. Supreme Court: Mrs. Sandra Day O'Connor; appointed July 1981.

Woman suffrage granted: Wyoming Territory, 1869.

Written constitution: *Fundamental Orders of Connecticut,* 1639.

Figures and Legends in American Folklore

Appleseed, Johnny (John Chapman, 1774–1847): Massachusetts-born nurseryman; reputed to have spread seeds and seedlings from which rose orchards of the Midwest.

Billy the Kid (William H. Bonney, 1859–1881): New York-born desperado; killed his first man before he reached his teens; after short life of crime in Wild West, was gunned down by Sheriff Pat Garrett; symbol of lawless West.

Boone, Daniel (1734–1820): Frontiersman and Indian fighter, about whom legends of early America have been built; figured in Byron's *Don Juan*.

Brodie, Steve (1863–1901): Reputed to have dived off Brooklyn Bridge on July 23, 1886. (Whether he actually did so has never been proved.)

Buffalo Bill (William F. Cody, 1846–1917): Buffalo hunter and Indian scout; much of legend about him and Wild West stems from his own Wild West show, which he operated in late 19th century.

Bunyan, Paul: Mythical lumberjack; subject of tall tales throughout timber country (that he dug Grand Canyon, for example).

Crockett, David (1786–1836): Frontiersman and member of U.S. Congress, about whom legends have been built of heroic feats; died in defense of Alamo.

Fritchie (or Frietchie), Barbara: Symbol of patriotism; in ballad by John Greenleaf Whittier, 90-year-old Barbara Fritchie defiantly waves Stars and Stripes as "Stonewall" Jackson's Confederate troops march through Frederick, Md.

James, Jesse (1847–1882): Bank and train robber; folklore has given him quality of American Robin Hood.

Jones, Casey (John Luther Jones, 1863–1900): Example of heroic locomotive engineer given to feats of prowess; died in wreck with his hand on brake lever when his Illinois Central "Cannonball" express hit freight train at Vaughan, Miss.

Ross, Betsy (1752–1836): Member of Philadelphia flag-making family; reported to have designed and sewn first American flag. (Report is without confirmation.)

Uncle Sam: Personification of United States and its people; origin uncertain; may be based on inspector of government supplies in Revolutionary War and War of 1812.

Assassinations and Attempts in U. S. Since 1865

Cermak, Anton J. (Mayor of Chicago): Shot Feb. 15, 1933, in Miami by Giuseppe Zangara, who attempted to assassinate Franklin D. Roosevelt; Cermak died March 6.

Ford, Gerald R. (President of U.S.): Escaped assassination attempt Sept. 5, 1975, in Sacramento, Calif., by Lynette Alice (Squeaky) Fromm, who pointed but did not fire .45-caliber pistol.

Ford, Gerald R. (President of U.S.): Escaped assassination attempt in San Francisco, Calif., Sept. 22, 1975, by Sara Jane Moore, who fired one shot from a .38-caliber pistol that was deflected.

Garfield, James A. (President of U.S.): Shot July 2, 1881, in Washington, D.C., by Charles J. Guiteau; died Sept. 19.

Jordan, Vernon E., Jr. (civil rights leader): Shot and critically wounded in assassination attempt May 29, 1980, in Fort Wayne, Ind.

Kennedy, John F. (President of U.S.): Shot Nov. 22, 1963, in Dallas, Tex., allegedly by Lee Harvey Oswald; died same day. Injured was Gov. John B. Connally of Texas. Oswald was shot and killed two days later by Jack Ruby.

Kennedy, Robert F. (U.S. Senator from New York): Shot June 5, 1968, in Los Angeles by Sirhan Bishara Sirhan; died June 6.

King, Martin Luther, Jr. (civil rights leader): Shot April 4, 1968, in Memphis by James Earl Ray; died same day.

Lincoln, Abraham (President of U.S.): Shot April 14, 1865, in Washington, D.C., by John Wilkes Booth; died April 15.

Long, Huey P. (U.S. Senator from Louisiana): Shot Sept. 8, 1935, in Baton Rouge by Dr. Carl A. Weiss; died Sept. 10.

McKinley, William (President of U.S.): Shot Sept. 6, 1901, in Buffalo by Leon Czolgosz; died Sept. 14.

Roosevelt, Franklin D. (President-elect of U.S.): Escaped assassination unhurt Feb. 15, 1933, in Miami. *See* Cermak.

Roosevelt, Theodore (ex-President of U.S.): Escaped assassination (though shot) Oct. 14, 1912, in Milwaukee while campaigning for President.

Seward, William H. (Secretary of State): Escaped assassination (though injured) April 14, 1865, in Washington, D.C., by Lewis Powell (or Paine), accomplice of John Wilkes Booth.

Truman, Harry S. (President of U.S.): Escaped assassination unhurt Nov. 1, 1950, in Washington, D.C., as 2 Puerto Rican nationalists attempted to shoot their way into Blair House.

Wallace, George C. (Governor of Alabama): Shot and critically wounded in assassination attempt May 15, 1972, at Laurel, Md., by Arthur Herman Bremer. Wallace paralyzed from waist down.

Reagan, Ronald (President of U.S.): Shot in left lung in Washington by John W. Hinckley, Jr., on March 30, 1981; three others also wounded.

THE DECLARATION OF INDEPENDENCE
In Congress, July 4, 1776

The unanimous Declaration of the thirteen united States of America.

When in the Course of human events it becomes necessary for one people to dissolve the political bands which have connected them with another, and to assume among the powers of the earth, the separate and equal station to which the Laws of Nature and of Nature's God entitle them, a decent respect to the opinions of mankind requires that they should declare the causes which impel them to the separation.

We hold these truths to be self-evident, that all men are created equal, that they are endowed by their Creator with certain unalienable Rights, that among these are Life, Liberty and the pursuit of Happiness.—That to secure these rights, Governments are instituted among Men, deriving their just powers from the consent of the governed,—That whenever any Form of Government becomes destructive of these ends, it is the Right of the People to alter or to abolish it, and to institute new Government, laying its foundation on such principles and organizing its powers in such form, as to them shall seem most likely to effect their Safety and Happiness. Prudence, indeed, will dictate that Governments long established should not be changed for light and transient causes; and accordingly all experience hath shewn that mankind are more disposed to suffer, while evils are sufferable, than to right themselves by abolishing the forms to which they are accustomed. But when a long train of abuses and usurpations, pursuing invariably the same Object evinces a design to reduce them under absolute Despotism, it is their right, it is their duty, to throw off such Government, and to provide new Guards for their future security.—Such has been the patient sufferance of these Colonies; and such is now the necessity which constrains them to alter their former Systems of Government. The history of the present King of Great Britain is a history of repeated injuries and usurpations, all having in direct object the establishment of an absolute Tyranny over these States. To prove this, let Facts be submitted to a candid world.

He has refused his Assent to Laws, the most wholesome and necessary for the public good.

He has forbidden his Governors to pass Laws of immediate and pressing importance, unless suspended in their operation till his Assent should be obtained; and when so suspended, he has utterly neglected to attend to them.

He has refused to pass other Laws for the accommodation of large districts of people, unless those people would relinquish the right of Representation in the Legislature, a right inestimable to them and formidable to tyrants only.

He has called together legislative bodies at places unusual, uncomfortable, and distant from the depository of their Public Records, for the sole purpose of fatiguing them into compliance with his measures.

He has dissolved Representative Houses repeatedly, for opposing with manly firmness his invasions on the rights of the people.

He has refused for a long time, after such dissolutions, to cause others to be elected; whereby the Legislative Powers, incapable of Annihilation, have returned to the People at large for their exercise; the State remaining in the mean time exposed to all the dangers of invasion from without, and convulsions within.

He has endeavoured to prevent the population of these States; for that purpose obstructing the Laws for Naturalization of Foreigners; refusing to pass others to encourage their migrations hither, and raising the conditions of new Appropriations of Lands.

He has obstructed the Administration of Justice, by refusing his Assent to Laws for establishing Judiciary Powers.

He has made Judges dependent on his Will alone, for the tenure of their offices, and the amount and payment of their salaries.

He has erected a multitude of New Offices, and sent hither swarms of Officers to harass our people, and eat out their substance.

He has kept among us, in times of peace, Standing Armies without the Consent of our legislatures.

He has affected to render the Military independent of and superior to the Civil Power.

He has combined with others to subject us to a jurisdiction foreign to our constitution, and unacknowledged by our laws; giving his Assent to their Acts of pretended Legislation:

For quartering large bodies of armed troops among us:

For protecting them, by a mock Trial, from punishment for any Murders which they should commit on the Inhabitants of these States:

For cutting off our Trade with all parts of the

NOTE: On April 12, 1776, the legislature of North Carolina authorized its delegates to the Continental Congress to join with others in a declaration of separation from Great Britain; the first colony to instruct its delegates to take the actual initiative was Virginia on May 15. On June 7, 1776, Richard Henry Lee of Virginia offered a resolution to the Congress to the effect "that these United Colonies are, and of right ought to be, free and independent States. . . ." A committee, consisting of Thomas Jefferson, John Adams, Benjamin Franklin, Robert R. Livingston, and Roger Sherman was organized to "prepare a declaration to the effect of the said first resolution." The Declaration of Independence was adopted on July 4, 1776.

Most delegates signed the Declaration August 2, but George Wythe (Va.) signed August 27; Richard Henry Lee (Va.), Elbridge Gerry (Mass.), and Oliver Wolcott (Conn.) in September; Matthew Thornton (N. H.), not a delegate until September, in November; and Thomas McKean (Del.), although present on July 4, not until 1781 by special permission, having served in the army in the interim.

world:

For imposing Taxes on us without our Consent:

For depriving us in many cases, of the benefits of Trial by Jury:

For transporting us beyond Seas to be tried for pretended offences:

For abolishing the free System of English Laws in a neighbouring Province, establishing therein an Arbitrary government, and enlarging its Boundaries so as to render it at once an example and fit instrument for introducing the same absolute rule into these Colonies:

For taking away our Charters, abolishing our most valuable Laws and altering fundamentally the Forms of our Governments:

For suspending our own Legislatures, and declaring themselves invested with power to legislate for us in all cases whatsoever.

He has abdicated Government here, by declaring us out of his Protection and waging War against us.

He has plundered our seas, ravaged our Coasts, burnt our towns, and destroyed the lives of our people.

He is at this time transporting large Armies of foreign Mercenaries to compleat the works of death, desolation, and tyranny, already begun with circumstances of Cruelty & Perfidy scarcely paralleled in the most barbarous ages, and totally unworthy the Head of a civilized nation.

He has constrained our fellow Citizens taken Captive on the high Seas to bear Arms against their Country, to become the executioners of their friends and Brethren, or to fall themselves by their Hands.

He has excited domestic insurrections amongst us, and has endeavoured to bring on the inhabitants of our frontiers, the merciless Indian Savages, whose known rule of warfare, is an undistinguished destruction of all ages, sexes and conditions.

In every stage of these Oppressions We have Petitioned for Redress in the most humble terms: Our repeated Petitions have been answered only by repeated injury. A Prince, whose character is thus marked by every act which may define a Tyrant, is unfit to be the ruler of a free people.

Nor have We been wanting in attentions to our Brittish brethren. We have warned them from time to time of attempts by their legislature to extend an unwarrantable jurisdiction over us. We have reminded them of the circumstances of our emigration and settlement here. We have appealed to their native justice and magnanimity, and we have conjured them by the ties of our common kindred to disavow these usurpations, which would inevitably interrupt our connections and correspondence. They too have been deaf to the voice of justice and of consanguinity. We must, therefore, acquiesce in the necessity, which denounces our Separation, and hold them, as we hold the rest of mankind, Enemies in War, in Peace Friends.

We, therefore, the Representatives of the United States of America, in General Congress, Assembled, appealing to the Supreme Judge of the world for the rectitude of our intentions, do, in the Name, and by Authority of the good People of these Colonies, solemnly publish and declare, That these United Colonies are, and of Right ought to be Free and Independent States; that they are Absolved from all Allegiance to the British Crown, and that all political connection between them and the State of Great Britain, is and ought to be totally dissolved; and that as Free and Independent States, they have full Power to levy War, conclude Peace, contract Alliances, establish Commerce, and to do all other Acts and Things which Independent States may of right do.—And for the support of this Declaration, with a firm reliance on the protection of Divine Providence, we mutually pledge to each other our Lives, our Fortunes and our sacred Honor.

John Hancock

New Hampshire
Josiah Bartlett
Wm. Whipple
Matthew Thornton

Rhode Island
Step. Hopkins
William Ellery

Connecticut
Roger Sherman
Sam'el Huntington
Wm. Williams
Oliver Wolcott

New York
Wm. Floyd
Phil. Livingston
Frans. Lewis
Lewis Morris

New Jersey
Richd. Stockton
Jno. Witherspoon
Fras. Hopkinson
John Hart
Abra. Clark

Pennsylvania
Robt. Morris
Benjamin Rush
Benj. Franklin
John Morton
Geo. Clymer
Jas. Smith
Geo. Taylor
James Wilson
Geo. Ross

Massachusetts-Bay
Saml. Adams
John Adams
Robt. Treat Paine
Elbridge Gerry

Delaware
Caesar Rodney
Geo. Read
Tho. M'Kean

Maryland
Samuel Chase
Wm. Paca
Thos. Stone
Charles Carroll of Carrollton

Virginia
George Wythe
Richard Henry Lee
Th. Jefferson
Benj. Harrison
Ths. Nelson, Jr.
Francis Lightfoot Lee
Carter Braxton

North Carolina
Wm. Hooper
Joseph Hewes
John Penn

South Carolina
Edward Rutledge
Thos. Heyward, Junr.
Thomas Lynch, Junr.
Arthur Middleton

Georgia
Button Gwinnett
Lyman Hall
Geo. Walton

Constitution of the United States of America

(Historical text has been edited to conform to contemporary American usage.
The bracketed words are designations for your convenience; they are not part of the Constitution.)

The oldest federal constitution in existence was framed by a convention of delegates from twelve of the thirteen original states in Philadelphia in May, 1787, Rhode Island failing to send a delegate. George Washington presided over the session, which lasted until September 17, 1787. The draft (originally a preamble and seven Articles) was submitted to all thirteen states and was to become effective when ratified by nine states. It went into effect on the first Wednesday in March, 1789, having been ratified by New Hampshire, the ninth state to approve, on June 21, 1788. The states ratified the Constitution in the following order:

Delaware	December 7, 1787	South Carolina	May 23, 1788
Pennsylvania	December 12, 1787	New Hampshire	June 21, 1788
New Jersey	December 18, 1787	Virginia	June 25, 1788
Georgia	January 2, 1788	New York	July 26, 1788
Connecticut	January 9, 1788	North Carolina	November 21, 1789
Massachusetts	February 6, 1788	Rhode Island	May 29, 1790
Maryland	April 28, 1788		

[Preamble]

We the people of the United States, in order to form a more perfect Union, establish justice, insure domestic tranquility, provide for the common defence, promote the general welfare, and secure the blessings of liberty to ourselves and our posterity, do ordain and establish this Constitution for the United States of America.

Article I

Section 1

[Legislative powers vested in Congress.] All legislative powers herein granted shall be vested in a Congress of the United States, which shall consist of a Senate and House of Representatives.

Section 2

[Composition of the House of Representatives.—1.] The House of Representatives shall be composed of members chosen every second year by the people of the several States, and the electors in each State shall have the qualifications requisite for electors of the most numerous branch of the State Legislature.

[Qualifications of Representatives.—2.] No Person shall be a Representative who shall not have attained to the age of twenty-five years, and been seven years a citizen of the United States, and who shall not, when elected, be an inhabitant of that State in which he shall be chosen.

[Apportionment of Representatives and direct taxes—census.[1]—3.] (Representatives and direct taxes shall be apportioned among the several States which may be included within this Union, according to their respective numbers, which shall be determined by adding to the whole number of free persons, including those bound to service for a term of years, and excluding Indians not taxed, three fifths of all other persons.) The actual enumeration shall be made within three years after the first meeting of the Congress of the United States, and within every subsequent term of ten years, in such manner as they shall by law direct. The number of Representatives shall not exceed one for every thirty thousand, but each State shall have at least one Representative; and until such enumeration shall be made, the State of New Hampshire shall be entitled to choose three, Massachusetts

eight, Rhode-Island and Providence Plantations one, Connecticut five, New York six, New Jersey four, Pennsylvania eight, Delaware one, Maryland six, Virginia ten, North Carolina five, South Carolina five, and Georgia three.

[Filling of vacancies in representation.—4.] When vacancies happen in the representation from any State, the Executive Authority thereof shall issue writs of election to fill such vacancies.

[Selection of officers; power of impeachment.—5.] The House of Representatives shall choose their Speaker and other officers; and shall have the sole power of impeachment.

Section 3[2]

[The Senate.—1.] The Senate of the United States shall be composed of two Senators from each State, chosen by the Legislature thereof, for six years; and each Senator shall have one vote.

[Classification of Senators; filling of vacancies.—2.] Immediately after they shall be assembled in consequence of the first election, they shall be divided as equally as may be into three classes. The seats of the Senators of the first class shall be vacated at the expiration of the second year, of the second class at the expiration of the fourth year, and of the third class at the expiration of the sixth year, so that one-third may be chosen every second year; and if vacancies happen by resignation, or otherwise, during the recess of the Legislature of any State, the Executive thereof may make temporary appointments (until the next meeting of the Legislature, which shall then fill such vacancies).

[Qualification of Senators.—3.] No person shall be a Senator who shall not have attained to the age of thirty years, and been nine years a citizen of the United States, and who shall not, when elected, be an inhabitant of that State for which he shall be chosen.

[Vice President to be President of Senate.—4.] The Vice President of the United States shall be President of the Senate, but shall have no vote, unless they be equally divided.

[Selection of Senate officers; President pro tempore.—5.] The Senate shall choose their other officers, and also a President pro tempore, in the absence of the Vice President, or when he shall exercise the office of President of the United States.

[Senate to try impeachments.—6.] The Senate

shall have the sole power to try all impeachments. When sitting for that purpose, they shall be on oath or affirmation. When the President of the United States is tried, the Chief Justice shall preside: and no person shall be convicted without the concurrence of two thirds of the members present.

[Judgment in cases of Impeachment.—7.] Judgment in cases of impeachment shall not extend further than to removal from office, and disqualification to hold and enjoy any office of honor, trust, or profit under the United States: but the party convicted shall nevertheless be liable and subject to indictment, trial, judgment and punishment, according to Law.

Section 4

[Control of congressional elections.—1.] The times, places, and manner of holding elections for Senators and Representatives, shall be prescribed in each State by the Legislature thereof; but the Congress may at any time by law make or alter such regulations, except as to the places of choosing Senators.

[Time for assembling of Congress.³—2.] The Congress shall assemble at least once in every year, and such meeting shall be on the first Monday in December, unless they shall by law appoint a different day.

Section 5

[Each house to be the judge of the election and qualifications of its members; regulations as to quorum.—1.] Each House shall be the judge of the elections, returns, and qualifications of its own members, and a majority of each shall constitute a quorum to do business; but a smaller number may adjourn from day to day, and may be authorized to compel the attendance of absent members, in such manner, and under such penalties as each House may provide.

[Each house to determine its own rules.—2.] Each House may determine the rules of its proceedings, punish its members for disorderly behavior, and, with the concurrence of two thirds, expel a member.

[Journals and yeas and nays.—3.] Each House shall keep a journal of its proceedings, and from time to time publish the same, excepting such parts as may in their judgment require secrecy; and the yeas and nays of the members of either House on any question shall, at the desire of one fifth of those present, be entered on the journal.

[Adjournment.—4.] Neither House, during the session of Congress, shall, without the consent of the other, adjourn for more than three days, nor to any other place than that in which the two Houses shall be sitting.

Section 6

[Compensation and privileges of members of Congress.—1.] The Senators and Representatives shall receive a compensation for their services, to be ascertained by law, and paid out of the Treasury of the United States. They shall in all cases, except treason, felony, and breach of the peace, be privileged from arrest during their attendance at the session of their respective Houses, and in going to and returning from the same; and for any speech or debate in either House, they shall not be questioned in any other place.

[Incompatible offices; exclusions.—2.] No Senator or Representative shall, during the time for which he was elected, be appointed to any civil office under the authority of the United States, which shall have been created, or the emoluments whereof shall have been increased during such time; and no person holding any office under the United States shall be a member of either House during his continuance in office.

Section 7

[Revenue bills to originate in House.—1.] All bills for raising revenue shall originate in the House of Representatives; but the Senate may propose or concur with amendments as on other bills.

[Manner of passing bills; veto power of President.—2.] Every bill which shall have passed the House of Representatives and the Senate, shall, before it becomes a law, be presented to the President of the United States; if he approve he shall sign it, but if not he shall return it, with his objections to that House in which it shall have originated, who shall enter the objections at large on their journal, and proceed to reconsider it. If after such reconsideration two thirds of that House shall agree to pass the bill, it shall be sent, together with the objections, to the other House, by which it shall likewise be reconsidered, and if approved by two thirds of that House, it shall become a law. But in all such cases the votes of both Houses shall be determined by yeas and nays, and the names of the persons voting for and against the bill shall be entered on the journal of each house, respectively. If any bill shall not be returned by the President within ten days (Sundays excepted) after it shall have been presented to him, the same shall be a law, in like manner as if he had signed it, unless the Congress by their adjournment prevent its return, in which case it shall not be a law.

[Concurrent orders or resolutions, to be passed by President.—3.] Every order, resolution, or vote to which the concurrence of the Senate and House of Representatives may be necessary (except on a question of adjournment) shall be presented to the President of the United States; and before the same shall take effect, shall be approved by him, or being disapproved by him, shall be repassed by two thirds of the Senate and House of Representatives, according to the rules and limitations prescribed in the case of a bill.

Section 8

[General powers of Congress.⁴]
[Taxes, duties, imposts, and excises.—1.] The Congress shall have power to lay and collect taxes, duties, imposts and excises, to pay the debts and provide for the common defense and general welfare of the United States; but all duties, imposts and excises shall be uniform throughout the United States;

[Borrowing of money.—2.] To borrow money on the credit of the United States;

[Regulation of commerce.—3.] To regulate commerce with foreign nations, and among the several States, and with the Indian tribes;

[Naturalization and bankruptcy.—4.] To establish a uniform rule of naturalization, and uniform laws on the subject of bankruptcies throughout the United States;

[Money, weights and measures.—5.] To coin money, regulate the value thereof, and of foreign coin, and fix the standard of weights and measures;

[Counterfeiting.—6.] To provide for the punishment of counterfeiting the securities and current coin of the United States;

[Post offices.—7.] To establish post offices and post roads;

[Patents and copyrights.—8.] To promote the

progress of science and useful arts, by securing for limited times to authors and inventors the exclusive right to their respective writings and discoveries;

[**Inferior courts.—9.**] To constitute tribunals inferior to the Supreme Court;

[**Piracies and felonies.—10.**] To define and punish piracies and felonies commited on the high seas, and offences against the law of nations;

[**War; marque and reprisal.—11.**] To declare war, grant letters of marque and reprisal, and make rules concerning captures on land and water;

[**Armies.—12.**] To raise and support armies, but no appropriation of money to that use shall be for a longer term than two years;

[**Navy.—13.**] To provide and maintain a navy;

[**Land and naval forces.—14.**] To make rules for the government and regulation of the land and naval forces;

[**Calling out militia.—15.**] To provide for calling forth the militia to execute the laws of the Union, suppress insurrections, and repel invasions.

[**Organizing, arming, and disciplining militia.—16.**] To provide for organizing, arming, and disciplining, the militia, and for governing such part of them as may be employed in the service of the United States, reserving to the States, respectively, the appointment of the officers, and the authority of training the militia according to the discipline prescribed by Congress;

[**Exclusive legislation over District of Columbia.—17.**] To exercise exclusive legislation in all cases whatsoever, over such district (not exceeding ten miles square) as may, by cession of particular States, and the acceptance of Congress,become the seat of the Government of the United States, and to exercise like authority over all places purchased by the consent of the Legislature of the State in which the same shall be, for the erection of forts, magazines, arsenals, dock-yards, and other needful buildings; —And

[**To enact laws necessary to enforce Constitution.—18.**] To make all laws which shall be necessary and proper for carrying into execution the foregoing powers, and all other powers vested by this Constitution in the Government of the United States, or in any department or officer thereof.

Section 9

[**Migration or importation of certain persons not to be prohibited before 1808.—1.**] The migration or importation of such persons as any of the States now existing shall think proper to admit, shall not be prohibited by the Congress prior to the year one thousand eight hundred and eight, but a tax or duty may be imposed on such importation, not exceeding ten dollars for each person.

[**Writ of habeas corpus not to be suspended; exception.—2.**] The privilege of the writ of habeas corpus shall not be suspended, unless when in cases of rebellion or invasion the public safety may require it.

[**Bills of attainder and ex post facto laws prohibited.—3.**] No bill of attainder or ex post facto law shall be passed.

[**Capitation and other direct taxes.—4.**] No capitation, or other direct, tax shall be laid, unless in proportion to the census or enumeration herein before directed to be taken.[5]

[**Exports not to be taxed.—5.**] No tax or duty shall be laid on articles exported from any State.

[**No preference to be given to ports of any State; interstate shipping.—6.**] No preference shall be given by any regulation of commerce or revenue to the ports of one State over those of another: nor shall vessels bound to, or from, one State, be obliged to enter, clear, or pay duties in another.

[**Money, how drawn from treasury; financial statements to be published.—7.**] No money shall be drawn from the Treasury, but in consequence of appropriations made by law; and a regular statement and account of the receipts and expenditures of all public money shall be published from time to time.

[**Titles of nobility not to be granted; acceptance by government officers of favors from foreign powers.—8.**] No title of nobility shall be granted by the United States: and no person holding any office of profit or trust under them, shall, without the consent of the Congress, accept of any present, emolument, office, or title, of any kind whatever, from any king, prince, or foreign state.

Section 10

[**Limitations of the powers of the several States.—1.**] No State shall enter into any treaty, alliance, or confederation; grant letters of marque and reprisal; coin money; emit bills of credit; make any thing but gold and silver coin a tender in payment of debts; pass any bill of attainder, ex post facto law, or law impairing the obligation of contracts, or grant any title of nobility.

[**State imposts and duties.—2.**] No State shall, without the consent of the Congress, lay any imposts or duties on imports or exports, except what may be absolutely necessary for executing its inspection laws: and the net produce of all duties and imposts, laid by any State on imports or exports, shall be for the use of the Treasury of the United States; and all such laws shall be subject to the revision and control of the Congress.

[**Further restrictions on powers of States.—3.**] No State shall, without the consent of Congress, lay any duty of tonnage, keep troops, or ships of war in time of peace, enter into any agreement or compact with another state, or with a foreign power, or engage in war, unless actually invaded, or in such imminent danger as will not admit of delay.

Article II

Section 1

[**The President; the executive power.—1.**] The executive power shall be vested in a President of the United States of America. He shall hold his office during the term of four years, and, together with the Vice President, chosen for the same term, be elected, as follows

[**Appointment and qualifications of presidential electors.—2.**] Each State shall appoint, in such manner as the Legislature thereof may direct, a number of electors, equal to the whole number of Senators and Representatives to which the State may be entitled in the Congress: but no Senator or Representative, or person holding an office of trust or profit under the United States, shall be appointed an elector.

[**Original method of electing the President and Vice President.[6]**] (The electors shall meet in their respective States, and vote by ballot for two persons, of whom one at least shall not be an inhabitant of the same State with themselves. And they shall make a list of all the persons voted for, and of the number of votes for each; which list they shall sign and certify, and transmit sealed to the seat of the Government of the United States, directed to the President of the Senate. The President of the Senate shall, in the presence of the Senate and House of Representatives, open all the certificates, and the votes shall then be counted. The person having the greatest number of votes shall be the President, if such number be a majority of the whole number of electors appointed; and if there be more than one who have such majority, and have an equal number of votes, then the House of Representatives shall immediately choose by ballot one of them for President; and if no person have a majority, then from the five highest on the list the said House shall in like manner choose the President. But in choosing the President, the votes shall be taken by States, the representation from each State having one vote; A quorum for this purpose shall consist of a member or members from two thirds of the States, and a majority of all the states shall be necessary to a choice. In every case, after the choice of the President, the person having the greatest number of votes of the electors shall be the Vice President. But if there should remain two or more who have equal votes, the Senate should choose from them by ballot the Vice President.)

[Congress may determine time of choosing electors and day for casting their votes.—3.] The Congress may determine the time of choosing the electors, and the day on which they shall give their votes; which day shall be the same throughout the United States.

[Qualifications for the office of President.[7]—4.] No person except a natural born citizen, or a citizen of the United States, at the time of the adoption of this Constitution, shall be eligible to the office of President; neither shall any person be eligible to that office who shall not have attained to the age of thirty-five years, and been fourteen years a resident within the United States.

[Filling vacancy in the office of President.[8]—5.] In case of the removal of the President from office, or of his death, resignation, or inability to discharge the powers and duties of the said office, the same shall devolve on the Vice President, and the Congress may by law provide for the case of removal, death, resignation or inability, both of the President and Vice President, declaring what officer shall then act as President, and such officer shall act accordingly, until the disability be removed, or a President shall be elected.

[Compensation of the President.—6.] The President shall, at stated times, receive for his services, a compensation, which shall neither be increased nor diminished during the period for which he shall have been elected, and he shall not receive within that period any other emolument from the United States, or any of them.

[Oath to be taken by the President.—7.] Before he enter on the execution of his office, he shall take the following oath or affirmation:—"I do solemnly swear (or affirm) that I will faithfully excute the office of President of the United States, and will to the best of my ability, preserve, protect, and defend the Constitution of the United States."

Section 2
[The President to be commander in chief of army and navy and head of executive departments; may grant reprieves and pardons.—1.] The President shall be Commander in Chief of the Army and Navy of the United States, and of the militia of the several States, when called into the actual service of the United States; he may require the opinion, in writing, of the principal officer in each of the executive departments, upon any subject relating to the duties of their respective offices, and he shall have power to grant reprieves and pardons for offences against the United States, except in cases of impeachment.

[President may, with concurrence of Senate, make treaties, appoint ambassadors, etc.; appointment of inferior officers, authority of Congress over.—2.] He shall have power, by and with the advice and consent of the Senate, to make treaties, provided two thirds of the Senators present concur; and he shall nominate, and by and with the advice and consent of the Senate, shall appoint ambassadors, other public ministers and consuls, judges of the Supreme Court, and all other officers of the United States, whose appointments are not herein otherwise provided for, and which shall be established by law: but the Congress may by law vest the appointment of such inferior officers, as they think proper, in the President alone, in the courts of law, or in the heads of departments.

[President may fill vacancies in office during recess of Senate.—3.] The President shall have power to fill up all vacancies that may happen during the recess of the Senate, by granting commissions which shall expire at the end of their session.

Section 3
[President to give advice to Congress; may convene or adjourn it on certain occasions; to receive ambassadors, etc.; have laws executed and commission all officers.] He shall from time to time give to the Congress information of the state of the Union, and recommend to their consideration such measures as he shall judge necessary and expedient; he may, on extraordinary occasions, convene both Houses, or either of them, and in case of disagreement between them, with respect to the time of adjournment, he may adjourn them to such time as he shall think proper; he shall receive ambassadors and other public ministers: he shall take care that the laws be faithfully executed, and shall commission all the officers of the United States.

Section 4
[All civil officers removable by impeachment.] The President, Vice President, and all civil officers of the United States shall be removed from office on impeachment for, and conviction of, treason, bribery, or other high crimes and misdemeanors.

Article III
Section 1
[Judicial powers; how vested; term of office and compensation of judges.] The judicial Power of the United States, shall be vested in one Supreme Court, and in such inferior courts as the Congress may from time to time ordain and establish. The judges, both of the supreme and inferior courts, shall hold their offices during good behavior, and shall, at stated times, receive for their services, a compensation, which shall not be diminished during their continuance in office.

Section 2
[Jurisdiction of Federal courts.[9]—1.] The judicial power shall extend to all cases, in law and equity, arising under this Constitution, the laws of the United States, and treaties made, or which shall be made, under their authority; to all cases affecting ambassadors, other public ministers and consuls; to all cases of admiralty and maritime jurisdiction; to controversies to which the United States, shall be a party; to controversies between two or more States; between a State and citizens of another State; between citizens of different States, between

citizens of the same State claiming lands under grants of different states, and between a State, or the citizens thereof, and foreign states, citizens, or subjects.

[**Original and appellate jurisdiction of Supreme Court.—2.**] In all cases affecting ambassadors, other public ministers and consuls, and those in which a State shall be party, the Supreme Court shall have original jurisdiction. In all the other cases before mentioned, the Supreme Court shall have appellate jurisdiction, both as to law and fact, with such exceptions, and under such regulations, as the Congress shall make.

[**Trial of all crimes, except impeachment, to be by jury.—3.**] The trial of all crimes, except in cases of impeachment, shall be by jury; and such trial shall be held in the State where the said crimes shall have been committed; but when not committed within any State, the trial shall be at such place or places as the Congress may by law have directed.

Section 3

[**Treason defined; conviction of.—1.**] Treason against the United States, shall consist only in levying war against them, or, in adhering to their enemies, giving them aid and comfort. No person shall be convicted of treason unless on the testimony of two witnesses to the same overt act, or on confession in open court.

[**Congress to declare punishment for treason; proviso.—2.**] The Congress shall have power to declare the punishment of treason, but no attainder of treason shall work corruption of blood, or forfeiture except during the life of the person attainted.

Article IV

Section 1

[**Each State to give full faith and credit to the public acts and records of other States.**] Full faith and credit shall be given in each State to the public acts, records, and judicial proceedings of every other State. And the Congress may by general laws prescribe the manner in which such acts, records, and proceedings shall be proved, and the effect thereof.

Section 2

[**Privileges of citizens.—1.**] The citizens of each State shall be entitled to all privileges and immunities of citizens in the several States.

[**Extradition between the several States.—2.**] A person charged in any State with treason, felony, or other crime, who shall flee from justice, and be found in another State, shall on demand of the Executive authority of the State from which he fled, be delivered up, to be removed to the State having jurisdiction of the crime.

[**Persons held to labor or service in one State, fleeing to another, to be returned.—3.**] No person held to service or labor in one State, under the laws thereof, escaping into another, shall, in consequence of any law or regulation therein, be discharged from such service or labor, but shall be delivered up on claim of the party to whom such service or labor may be due.

Section 3

[**New States.—1.**] New States may be admitted by the Congress into this Union; but no new State shall be formed or erected within the jurisdiction of any other State; nor any State be formed by the junction of two or more States, or parts of States, without the consent of the Legislatures of the States concerned as well as of the Congress.

[**Regulations concerning territory.—2.**] The Congress shall have power to dispose of and make all needful rules and regulations respecting the territory or other property belonging to the United States; and nothing in this Constitution shall be so construed as to prejudice any claims of the United States, or of any particular State.

Section 4

[**Republican form of government and protection guaranteed the several States.**] The United States shall guarantee to every State in this Union a Republican form of government, and shall protect each of them against invasion; and on application of the Legislature, or of the Executive (when the Legislature cannot be convened) against domestic violence.

Article V

[**Ways in which the Constitution can be amended.**] The Congress, whenever two thirds of both Houses shall deem it necessary, shall propose amendments to this Constitution, or, on the application of the Legislatures of two thirds of the several States shall call a convention for proposing amendments, which, in either case, shall be valid to all intents and purposes, as part of this Constitution, when ratified by the Legislatures of three fourths of the several States, or by conventions in three fourths thereof, as the one or the other mode of ratification may be proposed by the Congress; provided that no amendment which may be made prior to the year one thousand eight hundred and eight shall in any manner affect the first and fourth clauses in the ninth Section of the first Article; and that no State, without its consent, shall be deprived of its equal suffrage in the Senate.

Article VI

[**Debts contracted under the confederation secured.—1.**] All debts contracted and engagements entered into, before the adoption of this Constitution, shall be as valid against the United States under this Constitution, as under the Confederation.

[**Constitution, laws, and treaties of the United States to be supreme.—2.**] This Constituion, and the laws of the United States which shall be made in pursuance thereof; and all treaties made, or which shall be made, under the authority of the United States, shall be the supreme law of the land; and the judges in every State shall be bound thereby, any thing in the Constitution or laws of any State to the contrary notwithstanding.

[**Who shall take constitutional oath; no religious test as to official qualification.—3.**] The Senators and Representatives before mentioned, and the

---

1. The clause included in parentheses is amended by the 14th Amendment, Section 2. 2. The first paragraph of this section and the part of the second paragraph included in parentheses are amended by the 17th Amendment. 3. Amended by the 20th Amendment, Section 2. 4. By the 16th Amendment, Congress is given the power to lay and collect taxes on income. 5. See the 16th Amendment. 6. This clause has been superseded by the 12th Amendment. 7. For qualifications of the Vice President, see 12th Amendment. 8. Amended by the 20th Amendment, Sections 3 and 4. 9. This section is abridged by the 11th Amendment. 10. See the 13th Amendment.

members of the several State Legislatures, and all executive and judicial officers, both of the United States and of the several States, shall be bound by oath or affirmation, to support this Constitution; but no religious test shall ever be required as a qualification to any office or public trust under the United States.

Article VII

[**Constitution to be considered adopted when ratified by nine States.**] The ratification of the conventions of nine States shall be sufficient for the establishment of this Constitution between the States so ratifying the same.

Done in convention by the unanimous consent of the States present the seventeenth day of September in the year of our Lord one thousand seven hundred and eighty-seven and of the independence of the United States of America the Twelfth. In witness whereof we have hereunto subscribed our names.

GEORGE WASHINGTON
President and Deputy from Virginia

NEW HAMPSHIRE
John Langdon   Nicholas Gilman

MASSACHUSETTS
Nathaniel Gorham   Rufus King

CONNECTICUT
Wm. Saml. Johnson   Roger Sherman

NEW YORK
Alexander Hamilton

NEW JERSEY
Wil. Livingston   Wm. Paterson
David Brearley   Jona. Dayton

PENNSYLVANIA
B. Franklin   Thomas Mifflin
Robt. Morris   Geo. Clymer
Thos. FitzSimons   Jared Ingersoll
James Wilson   Gouv. Morris

DELAWARE
Geo. Read   Gunning Bedford Jun.
John Dickinson   Richard Bassett
Jaco. Broom

MARYLAND
James McHenry   Dan. of St. Thos. Jenifer
Danl. Carroll

VIRGINIA
John Blair   James Madison, Jr.

NORTH CAROLINA
Wm. Blount   Richd Dobbs Spaight
Hu. Williamson

SOUTH CAROLINA
J. Rutledge   Charles Cotesworth
Charles Pinckney   Pinckney
                                 Pierce Butler

GEORGIA
William Few   Abr. Baldwin
Attest: William Jackson, Secretary

Amendments to the Constitution
of the United States

(Amendments I to X inclusive, popularly known as the Bill of Rights, were proposed and sent to the states by the first session of the First Congress. They were ratified Dec. 15, 1791.)

Article I

[**Freedom of religion, speech, of the press, and right of petition.**] Congress shall make no law respecting an establishment of religion, or prohibiting the free exercise thereof; or abridging the freedom of speech, or of the press; or the right of the people peaceably to assemble, and to petition the Government for a redress of grievances.

Article II

[**Right of people to bear arms not to be infringed.**] A well regulated militia, being necessary to the security of a free State, the right of the people to keep and bear arms, shall not be infringed.

Article III

[**Quartering of troops.**] No soldier shall, in time of peace be quartered in any house, without the consent of the owner, nor in time of war, but in a manner to be prescribed by law.

Article IV

[**Persons and houses to be secure from unreasonable searches and seizures.**] The right of the people to be secure in their persons, houses, papers, and effects, against unreasonable searches and seizures, shall not be violated, and no warrants shall issue, but upon probable cause, supported by oath or affirmation, and particularly describing the place to be searched, and the persons or things to be seized.

Article V

[**Trials for crimes; just compensation for private property taken for public use.**] No person shall be held to answer for a capital, or otherwise infamous crime, unless on a presentment or indictment of a Grand Jury, except in cases arising in the land or naval forces, or in the militia, when in actual service in time of war or public danger; nor shall any person be subject for the same offence to be twice put in jeopardy of life or limb; nor shall be compelled in any criminal case to be a witness, against himself, nor be deprived of life, liberty, or property, without due process of law; nor shall private property be taken for public use, without just compensation.

Article VI

[**Civil rights in trials for crimes enumerated.**] In all criminal prosecutions, the accused shall enjoy the right to a speedy and public trial, by an impartial jury of the State and district wherein the crime shall have been committed, which district shall have been previously ascertained by law, and to be informed of the nature and cause of the accusation;

554 *U.S. Constitution*

to be confronted with the witnesses against him; to have compulsory process for obtaining witnesses in his favor, and to have the assistance of counsel for his defense.

Article VII

[**Civil rights in civil suits.**] In suits at common law, where the value in controversy shall exceed twenty dollars, the right of trial by jury shall be preserved, and no fact tried by a jury, shall be otherwise re-examined in any court of the United States, than according to the rules of the common law.

Article VIII

[**Excessive bail, fines, and punishments prohibited.**] Excessive bail shall not be required, nor excessive fines imposed, nor cruel and unusual punishments inflicted.

Article IX

[**Reserved rights of people.**] The enumeration in the Constitution, of certain rights, shall not be construed to deny or disparage others retained by the people.

Article X

[**Powers not delegated, reserved to states and people respectively.**] The powers not delegated to the United States by the Constitution, nor prohibited by it to the States, are reserved to the States, respectively, or to the people.

Article XI

(The proposed amendment was sent to the states Mar. 5, 1794, by the Third Congress. It was ratified Feb. 7, 1795.)

[**Judicial power of United States not to extend to suits against a State.**] The judicial power of the United States shall not be construed to extend to any suit in law or equity, commenced or prosecuted against one of the United States by citizens of another State, or by citizens or subjects of any foreign state.

Article XII

(The proposed amendment was sent to the states Dec. 12, 1803, by the Eighth Congress. It was ratified July 27, 1804.)

[**Present mode of electing President and Vice-President by electors.[1]**] The electors shall meet in their respective states, and vote by ballot for President and Vice President, one of whom, at least, shall not be an inhabitant of the same state with themselves; they shall name in their ballots the person voted for as President, and in distinct ballots the person voted for as Vice President, and they shall make distinct lists of all persons voted for as President, and of all persons voted for as Vice President, and of the number of votes for each, which lists they shall sign and certify, and transmit sealed to the seat of the government of the United States, directed to the President of the Senate; the President of the Senate shall, in the presence of the Senate and House of Representatives, open all the certificates and the votes shall then be counted; the person having the greatest number of votes for President, shall be the President, if such number be a majority of the whole number of electors appoint-

ed; and if no person have such majority, then from the persons having the highest numbers not exceeding three on the list of those voted for as President, the House of Representatives shall choose immediately, by ballot, the President. But in choosing the President, the votes shall be taken by states, the representation from each State having one vote; a quorum for this purpose shall consist of a member or members from two thirds of the states, and a majority of all the states shall be necessary to a choice. And if the House of Representatives shall not choose a President whenever the right of choice shall devolve upon them, before the fourth day of March next following, then the Vice President shall act as President, as in the case of the death or other constitutional disability of the President. The person having the greatest number of votes as Vice President, shall be the Vice President, if such number be a majority of the whole number of electors appointed, and if no person have a majority, then from the two highest numbers on the list, the Senate shall choose the Vice President; a quorum for the purpose shall consist of two thirds of the whole number of Senators, and a majority of the whole number shall be necessary to a choice. But no person constitutionally ineligible to the office of President shall be eligible to that of Vice President of the United States.

Article XIII

(The proposed amendment was sent to the states Feb. 1, 1865, by the Thirty-eighth Congress. It was ratified Dec. 6, 1865.)

Section 1

[**Slavery prohibited.**] Neither slavery nor involuntary servitude, except as a punishment for crime whereof the party shall have been duly convicted, shall exist within the United States, or any place subject to their jurisdiction.

Section 2

[**Congress given power to enforce this article.**] Congress shall have power to enforce this article by appropriate legislation.

Article XIV

(The proposed amendment was sent to the states June 16, 1866, by the Thirty-ninth Congress. It was ratified July 9, 1868.)

Section 1

[**Citizenship defined; privileges of citizens.**] All persons born or naturalized in the United States, and subject to the jurisdiction thereof, are citizens of the United States and of the State wherein they reside. No State shall make or enforce any law which shall abridge the privileges or immunities of citizens of the United States; nor shall any State deprive any person of life, liberty, or property, without due process of law; nor deny to any person within its jurisdiction the equal protection of the laws.

Section 2

[**Apportionment of Representatives.**] Representatives shall be apportioned among the several States according to their respective numbers, counting the whole number of persons in each State, excluding Indians not taxed. But when the right to vote at any election for the choice of electors for President and Vice President of the United

States, Representatives in Congress, the executive and judicial officers of a State, or the members of the Legislature thereof, is denied to any of the male inhabitants of such State, being twenty-one years of age, and citizens of the United States, or in any way abridged, except for participation in rebellion, or other crime, the basis of representation therein shall be reduced in the proportion which the number of such male citizens shall bear to the whole number of male citizens twenty-one years of age in such State.

Section 3

[**Disqualification for office; removal of disability.**] No person shall be a Senator or Representative in Congress, or elector of President and Vice President, or hold any office, civil or military, under the United States, or under any State, who, having previously taken an oath, as a member of Congress, or as an officer of the United States, or as a member of any State Legislature, or as an executive or judicial officer of any State, to support the Constitution of the United States, shall have engaged in insurrection or rebellion against the same, or given aid or comfort to the enemies thereof. But Congress may by a vote of two thirds of each House, remove such disability.

Section 4

[**Public debt not to be questioned; payment of debts and claims incurred in aid of rebellion forbidden.**] The validity of the public debt of the United States, authorized by law, including debts incurred for payment of pensions and bounties for services in suppressing insurrection or rebellion, shall not be questioned. But neither the United States nor any State shall assume or pay any debt or obligation incurred in aid of insurrection or rebellion against the United States, or any claim for the loss or emancipation of any slave; but all such debts, obligations, and claims shall be held illegal and void.

Section 5

[**Congress given power to enforce this article.**] The Congress shall have power to enforce, by appropriate legislation, the provisions of this article.

Article XV

(The proposed amendment was sent to the states Feb. 27, 1869, by the Fortieth Congress. It was ratified Feb. 3, 1870.)

Section 1

[**Right of certain citizens to vote established.**] The right of citizens of the United States to vote shall not be denied or abridged by the United States or by any State on account of race, color, or previous condition of servitude.

Section 2

[**Congress given power to enforce this article.**] The Congress shall have power to enforce this article by appropriate legislation.

Article XVI

(The proposed amendment was sent to the states July 12, 1909, by the Sixty-first Congress. It was ratified Feb. 3, 1913.)

[**Taxes on income; Congress given power to lay and collect.**] The Congress shall have power to lay and collect taxes on incomes, from whatever source derived, without apportionment among the several States, and without regard to any census or enumeration.

Article XVII

(The proposed amendment was sent to the states May 16, 1912, by the Sixty-second Congress. It was ratified April 8, 1913.)

[**Election of United States Senators; filling of vacancies; qualifications of electors.**] The Senate of the United States shall be composed of two Senators from each State, elected by the people thereof, for six years; and each Senator shall have one vote. The electors in each State shall have the qualifications requisite for electors of the most numerous branch of the State Legislatures.

When vacancies happen in the representation of any State in the Senate, the executive authority of such State shall issue writs of election to fill such vacancies: Provided, that the legislature of any State may empower the executive thereof to make temporary appointment until the people fill the vacancies by election as the legislature may direct.

This amendment shall not be so construed as to affect the election or term of any Senator chosen before it becomes valid as part of the Constitution.

Article XVIII[2]

(The proposed amendment was sent to the states Dec. 18, 1917, by the Sixty-fifth Congress. It was ratified by three quarters of the states by Jan. 16, 1919, and became effective Jan. 16, 1920.)

Section 1

[**Manufacture, sale, or transportation of intoxicating liquors, for beverage purposes, prohibited.**] After one year from the ratification of this article the manufacture, sale, or transportation of intoxicating liquors within, the importation thereof into, or the exportation thereof from the United States and all territory subject to the jurisdiction thereof for beverage purposes is hereby prohibited.

Section 2

[**Congress and the several States given concurrent power to pass appropriate legislation to enforce this article.**] The Congress and the several States shall have concurrent power to enforce this article by appropriate legislation.

Section 3

[**Provisions of article to become operative, when adopted by three fourths of the States.**] This article shall be inoperative unless it shall have been ratified as an amendment to the Constitution by the legislatures of the several States, as provided in the Constitution, within seven years from the date of the submission hereof to the States by Congress.

Article XIX

(The proposed amendment was sent to the states June 4, 1919, by the Sixty-sixth Congress. It was ratified Aug. 18, 1920.)

[**The right of citizens to vote shall not be denied because of sex.**] The right of citizens of the United States to vote shall not be denied or abridged by the United States or by any State on account of sex.

[**Congress given power to enforce this article.**] Congress shall have power to enforce this article by appropriate legislation.

Article XX

(The proposed amendment, sometimes called the "Lame Duck Amendment," was sent to the states Mar. 3, 1932, by the Seventy-second Congress. It was ratified Jan. 23, 1933; but, in accordance with Section 5, Sections 1 and 2 did not go into effect until Oct. 15, 1933.)

Section 1

[Terms of President, Vice President, Senators, and Representatives.] The terms of the President and Vice President shall end at noon on the twentieth day of January, and the terms of Senators and Representatives at noon on the third day of January, of the years in which such terms would have ended if this article had not been ratified; and the terms of their successors shall then begin.

Section 2

[Time of assembling Congress.] The Congress shall assemble at least once in every year, and such meeting shall begin at noon on the third day of January, unless they shall by law appoint a different day.

Section 3

[Filling vacancy in office of President.] If, at the time fixed for the beginning of the term of the President, the President-elect shall have died, the Vice President-elect shall become President. If a President shall not have been chosen before the time fixed for the beginning of his term, or if the President-elect shall have failed to qualify, then the Vice President-elect shall have qualified; and the Congress may by law provide for the case wherein neither a President-elect nor a Vice President-elect shall have qualified, declaring who shall then act as President, or the manner in which one who is to act shall be selected, and such person shall act accordingly until a President or Vice President shall have qualified.

Section 4

[Power of Congress in Presidential succession.] The Congress may by law provide for the case of the death of any of the persons from whom the House of Representatives may choose a President whenever the right of choice shall have devolved upon them, and for the case of the death of any of the persons from whom the Senate may choose a Vice President whenever the right of choice shall have devolved upon them.

Section 5

[Time of taking effect.] Sections 1 and 2 shall take effect on the 15th day of October following the ratification of this article.

Section 6

[Ratification.] This article shall be inoperative unless it shall have been ratified as an amendment to the Constitution by the legislatures of three fourths of the several States within seven years from the date of its submission.

Article XXI

(The proposed amendment was sent to the states Feb. 20, 1933, by the Seventy-second Congress. It was ratified Dec. 5, 1933.)

Section 1

[Repeal of Prohibition Amendment.] The eighteenth article of amendment to the Constitution of the United States is hereby repealed.

Section 2

[Transportation of intoxicating liquors.] The transportation or importation into any State, territory, or possession of the United States for delivery or use therein of intoxicating liquors, in violation of the laws thereof, is hereby prohibited.

Section 3

[Ratification.] This article shall be inoperative unless it shall have been ratified as an amendment to the Constitution by convention in the several States, as provided in the Constitution, within seven years from the date of the submission thereof to the States by the Congress.

Article XXII

(The proposed amendment was sent to the states Mar. 21, 1947, by the Eightieth Congress. It was ratified Feb. 27, 1951.)

Section 1

[Limit to number of terms a President may serve.] No person shall be elected to the office of the President more than twice, and no person who has held the office of President, or acted as President, for more than two years of a term to which some other person was elected President shall be elected to the office of the President more than once. But this article shall not apply to any person holding the office of President when this article was proposed by the Congress, and shall not prevent any person who may be holding the office of President, or acting as President, during the term within which this article becomes operative from holding the office of President or acting as President during the remainder of such term.

Section 2

[Ratification.] This article shall be inoperative unless it shall have been ratified as an amendment to the Constitution by the legislatures of three fourths of the several States within seven years from the date of its submission to the States by the Congress.

Article XXIII

(The proposed amendment was sent to the states June 16, 1960, by the Eighty-sixth Congress. It was ratified March 29, 1961.)

Section 1

[Electors for the District of Columbia.] The District constituting the seat of Government of the United States shall appoint in such manner as the Congress may direct:

A number of electors of President and Vice President equal to the whole number of Senators and Representatives in Congress to which the District would be entitled if it were a State, but in no event more than the least populous State; they shall be in addition to those appointed by the States, but they shall be considered, for the purposes of the election of President and Vice President, to be electors appointed by a State; and they shall meet in the District and perform such duties as provided by the twelfth article of amendment.

Section 2

[Congress given power to enforce this article.] The Congress shall have the power to enforce this article by appropriate legislation.

Article XXIV

(The proposed amendment was sent to the states Aug. 27, 1962, by the Eighty-seventh Congress. It was ratified Jan. 23, 1964.)

Section 1

[Payment of poll tax or other taxes not to be prerequisite for voting in federal elections.] The right of citizens of the United States to vote in any primary or other election for President or Vice President, for electors for President or Vice President, or for Senator or Representative in Congress, shall not be denied or abridged by the United States or any State by reasons of failure to pay any poll tax or other tax.

Section 2

[Congress given power to enforce this article.] The Congress shall have the power to enforce this article by appropriate legislation.

Article XXV

(The proposed amendment was sent to the states July 6, 1965, by the Eighty-ninth Congress. It was ratified Feb. 10, 1967.)

Section 1

[Succession of Vice President to Presidency.] In case of the removal of the President from office or of his death or resignation, the Vice President shall become President.

Section 2

[Vacancy in office of Vice President.] Whenever there is a vacancy in the office of the Vice President, the President shall nominate a Vice President who shall take office upon confirmation by a majority vote of both Houses of Congress.

Section 3

[Vice President as Acting President.] Whenever the President transmits to the President pro tempore of the Senate and the Speaker of the House of Representatives his written declaration that he is unable to discharge the powers and duties of his office, and until he transmits to them a written declaration to the contrary, such powers and duties shall be discharged by the Vice President as Acting President.

Section 4

[Vice President as Acting President.] Whenever the Vice President and a majority of either the principal officers of the executive departments or of such other body as Congress may by law provide, transmit to the President pro tempore of the Senate and the Speaker of the House of Representatives their written declaration that the President is unable to discharge the powers and duties of his office, the Vice President shall immediately assume the powers and duties of the office as Acting President.

Thereafter, when the President transmits to the President pro tempore of the Senate and the Speaker of the House of Representatives his written declaration that no inability exists, he shall resume the powers and duties of his office unless the Vice President and a majority of either the principal officers of the executive department or of such other body as Congress may by law provide, transmit within four days to the President pro tempore of the Senate and the Speaker of the House of Representatives their written declaration that the President is unable to discharge the powers and duties of his office. Thereupon Congress shall decide the issue, assembling within forty-eight hours for that purpose if not in session. If the Congress, within twenty-one days after receipt of the latter written declaration, or, if Congress is not in session, within twenty-one days after Congress is required to assemble, determines by two thirds vote of both Houses that the President is unable to discharge the powers and duties of his office, the Vice President shall continue to discharge the same as Acting President; otherwise, the President shall resume the powers and duties of his office.

Article XXVI

(The proposed amendment was sent to the states Mar. 23, 1971, by the Ninety-second Congress. It was ratified July 1, 1971.)

Section 1

[Voting for 18-year-olds.] The right of citizens of the United States, who are 18 years of age or older, to vote shall not be denied or abridged by the United States or by any state on account of age.

Section 2

[Congress given power to enforce this article.] The Congress shall have power to enforce this article by appropriate legislation.

1. Amended by the 20th Amendment, Sections 3 and 4. 2. Repealed by the 21st Amendment.

The White House

Source: Department of the Interior, U.S. National Park Service.

The White House, the official residence of the President, is at 1600 Pennsylvania Avenue in Washington, D.C. The site, covering about 18 acres, was selected by President Washington and Pierre Charles L'Enfant, and the architect was James Hoban. The design of the residence is said to have been suggested by the Duke of Leinster's house in Ireland. The cornerstone was laid Oct. 13, 1792, and the first residents were President and Mrs. John Adams in November 1800. The building was fired by the British in 1814. The sandstone exterior was painted white during the course of the reconstruction.

From December 1948 to March 1952, the interior of the White House was rebuilt, and the outer walls were strengthened.

The rooms for public functions are on the first floor; on the second and third are the President's apartments. The most celebrated public room is the East Room, where formal receptions take place. Other public rooms are the Red Room, the Green Room, and the Blue Room. The State Dining Room is used for formal dinners. There are 132 rooms.

The Mayflower Compact

On Sept. 6, 1620, the *Mayflower*, a sailing vessel of about 180 tons, started her memorable voyage from Plymouth, England, with about 100[1] pilgrims aboard, bound for Virginia to establish a private permanent colony in North America. Arriving at what is now Provincetown, Mass., on Nov. 11 (Nov. 21, new style calendar), 41 of the passengers signed the famous "Mayflower Compact" as the boat lay at anchor in that Cape Cod harbor. A small detail of the pilgrims, led by William Bradford, assigned to select a place for permanent settlement landed at what is now Plymouth, Mass., on Dec. 21 (n.s.).

The text of the compact follows:

In the name of God, Amen. We, whose names are underwritten, the Loyal Subjects of our dread Sovereign Lord, King *James*, by the Grace of God, of *Great Britain, France* and *Ireland*, King, *Defender of the Faith,* &,
Having undertaken for the Glory of God, and Advancement of the Christian Faith, and the Honour of our King and Country, a voyage to plant the first colony in the northern Parts of Virginia; do by these Presents, solemnly and mutually in the Presence of God and one of another, covenant and combine ourselves together into a civil Body Politick, for our better Ordering and Preservation, and Furtherance of the Ends aforesaid; And by Virtue hereof to enact, constitute, and frame, such just and equal Laws, Ordinances, Acts, Constitutions and Offices, from time to time, as shall be thought most meet and convenient for the General good of the Colony; unto which we promise all due Submission and Obedience.
In Witness whereof we have hereunto subscribed our names at *Cape Cod* the eleventh of *November,* in the Reign of our Sovereign Lord, King *James* of *England, France* and *Ireland,* the eighteenth, and of *Scotland* the fifty-fourth. *Anno Domini,* 1620

John Carver	William Mullins	John Billington	Peter Brown
Digery Priest	Thomas English	Thomas Tinker	John Turner
William Brewster	John Howland	Samuel Fuller	Edward Tilly
Edmund Margesson	Stephen Hopkins	Richard Clark	John Craxton
John Alden	Edward Winslow	John Allerton	Thomas Rogers
George Soule	Gilbert Winslow	Richard Warren	John Goodman
James Chilton	Miles Standish	Edward Liester	Edward Fuller
Francis Cooke	Richard Bitteridge	William Bradford	Richard Gardiner
Moses Fletcher	Francis Eaton	Thomas Williams	William White
John Ridgate	John Tilly	Isaac Allerton	Edward Doten
Christopher Martin			

1. Historians differ as to whether 100, 101, or 102 passengers were aboard.

The Monroe Doctrine

The Monroe Doctrine was announced in President James Monroe's message to Congress, during his second term on Dec. 2, 1823, in part as follows:

"In the discussions to which this interest has given rise, and in the arrangements by which they may terminate, the occasion has been deemed proper for asserting as a principle in which rights and interests of the United States are involved, that the American continents, by the free and independent condition which they have assumed and maintain, are henceforth not to be considered as subjects for future colonization by any European power. . . . We owe it, therefore, to candor and to the amicable relations existing between the United States and those powers to declare that we should consider any attempt on their part to extend their system to any portion of this hemisphere as dangerous to our peace and safety. With the existing colonies or dependencies of any European power we have not interfered and shall not interfere. But with the governments who have declared their independence and maintain it, and whose independence we have, on great consideration and on just principles, acknowledged, we could not view any interposition for the purpose of oppressing them or controlling in any other manner their destiny by any European power in any other light than as the manifestation of an unfriendly disposition toward the United States."

Order of Presidential Succession

1. The Vice President
2. Speaker of the House
3. President pro tempore of the Senate
4. Secretary of State
5. Secretary of the Treasury
6. Secretary of Defense
7. Attorney General
8. Secretary of the Interior
9. Secretary of Agriculture
10. Secretary of Commerce
11. Secretary of Labor
12. Secretary of Health and Human Services
13. Secretary of Housing and Urban Development
14. Secretary of Transportation
15. Secretary of Energy
16. Secretary of Education

NOTE: An official cannot succeed to the Presidency unless that person meets the Constitutional requirements.

The Star-Spangled Banner

Francis Scott Key, 1814

O say, can you see, by the dawn's early light,
What so proudly we hail'd at the twilight's last gleaming?
Whose broad stripes and bright stars, thro' the perilous fight,
O'er the ramparts we watch'd, were so gallantly streaming?
And the rockets' red glare, the bombs bursting in air,
Gave proof thro' the night that our flag was still there.
O say, does that star-spangled banner yet wave
O'er the land of the free and the home of the brave?

On the shore dimly seen thro' the mists of the deep,
Where the foe's haughty host in dread silence reposes,
What is that which the breeze, o'er the towering steep,
As it fitfully blows, half conceals, half discloses?
Now it catches the gleam of the morning's first beam,
In full glory reflected, now shines on the stream:
'T is the star-spangled banner: O, long may it wave
O'er the land of the free and the home of the brave!

And where is that band who so vauntingly swore
That the havoc of war and the battle's confusion,
A home and a country should leave us no more?
Their blood has wash'd out their foul footsteps' pollution.
No refuge could save the hireling and slave
From the terror of flight or the gloom of the grave:
And the star-spangled banner in triumph doth wave
O'er the land of the free and the home of the brave.

O thus be it ever when free-men shall stand
Between their lov'd home and the war's desolation;
Blest with vict'ry and peace, may the heav'n-rescued land
Praise the Pow'r that hath made and preserv'd us a nation!
Then conquer we must, when our cause it is just,
And this be our motto: "In God is our trust!"
And the star-spangled banner in triumph shall wave
O'er the land of the free and the home of the brave!

On Sept. 13, 1814, Francis Scott Key visited the British fleet in Chesapeake Bay to secure the release of Dr. William Beanes, who had been captured after the burning of Washington, D.C. The release was secured, but Key was detained on ship overnight during the shelling of Fort McHenry, one of the forts defending Baltimore. In the morning, he was so delighted to see the American flag still flying over the fort that he began a poem to commemorate the occasion. First published under the title "Defense of Fort M'Henry," and later as "The Star-Spangled Banner," the poem soon attained wide popularity as sung to the tune "To Anacreon in Heaven." The origin of this tune is obscure, but it may have been written by John Stafford Smith, a British composer born in 1750. "The Star-Spangled Banner" was officially made the National Anthem by Congress in 1931, although it had been already adopted as such by the Army and the Navy.

The Emancipation Proclamation

January 1, 1863

By the President of the United States of America:

A Proclamation.

Whereas on the 22d day of September, A.D. 1862, a proclamation was issued by the President of the United States, containing, among other things, the following, to wit:

"That on the 1st day of January, A.D. 1863, all persons held as slaves within any State or designated part of a State the people whereof shall then be in rebellion against the United States shall be then, thenceforward, and forever free; and the executive government of the United States, including the military and naval authority thereof, will recognize and maintain the freedom of such persons and will do no act or acts to repress such persons, or any of them, in any efforts they may make for their actual freedom.

"That the executive will on the 1st day of January aforesaid, by proclamation, designate the States and parts of States, if any, in which the people thereof, respectively, shall then be in rebellion against the United States; and the fact that any State or the people thereof shall on that day be in good faith represented in the Congress of the United States by members chosen thereto at elections wherein a majority of the qualified voters of such States shall have participated shall, in the absence of strong countervailing testimony, be deemed conclusive evidence that such State and the people thereof are not then in rebellion against the United States."

Now, therefore, I, Abraham Lincoln, President

of the United States, by virtue of the power in me vested as Commander-in-Chief of the Army and Navy of the United States in time of actual armed rebellion against the authority and government of the United States, and as a fit and necessary war measure for suppressing said rebellion, do, on this 1st day of January, A.D. 1863, and in accordance with my purpose so to do, publicly proclaimed for the full period of one hundred days from the first day above mentioned, order and designate as the States and parts of States wherein the people thereof, respectively, are this day in rebellion against the United States the following, to wit:

Arkansas, Texas, Louisiana (except the parishes of St. Bernard, Plaquemines, Jefferson, St. John, St. Charles, St. James, Ascension, Assumption, Terrebonne, Lafourche, St. Mary, St. Martin, and Orleans, including the city of New Orleans), Mississippi, Alabama, Florida, Georgia, South Carolina, North Carolina, and Virginia (except the forty-eight counties designated as West Virginia, and also the counties of Berkeley, Accomac, Northhampton, Elizabeth City, York, Princess Anne, and Norfolk, including the cities of Norfolk and Portsmouth), and which excepted parts are for the present left precisely as if this proclamation were not issued.

And by virtue of the power and for the purpose aforesaid, I do order and declare that all persons held as slaves within said designated States and parts of States are, and henceforward shall be, free; and that the Executive Government of the United States, including the military and naval authorities thereof, will recognize and maintain the freedom of said persons.

And I hereby enjoin upon the people so declared to be free to abstain from all violence, unless in necessary self-defense; and I recommend to them that, in all cases when allowed, they labor faithfully for reasonable wages.

And I further declare and make known that such persons of suitable condition will be received into the armed service of the United States to garrison forts, positions, stations, and other places, and to man vessels of all sorts in said service.

And upon this act, sincerely believed to be an act of justice, warranted by the Constitution upon military necessity, I invoke the considerate judgment of mankind and the gracious favor of Almighty God.

The Confederate States of America

State	Seceded from Union	Readmitted to Union[1]	State	Seceded from Union	Readmitted to Union[1]
1. South Carolina	Dec. 20, 1860	July 9, 1868	7. Texas	March 2, 1861	March 30, 1870
2. Mississippi	Jan. 9, 1861	Feb. 23, 1870	8. Virginia	April 17, 1861	Jan. 26, 1870
3. Florida	Jan. 10, 1861	June 25, 1868	9. Arkansas	May 6, 1861	June 22, 1868
4. Alabama	Jan. 11, 1861	July 13, 1868	10. North Carolina	May 20, 1861	July 4, 1868
5. Georgia	Jan. 19, 1861	July 15, 1870[2]	11. Tennessee	June 8, 1861	July 24, 1866
6. Louisiana	Jan. 26, 1861	July 9, 1868			

1. Date of readmission to representation in U.S. House of Representatives. 2. Second readmission date. First date was July 21, 1868, but the representatives were unseated March 5, 1869. NOTE: Four other slave states—Delaware, Kentucky, Maryland, and Missouri—remained in the Union.

Lincoln's Gettysburg Address

The Battle of Gettysburg, one of the most noted battles of the Civil War, was fought on July 1, 2, and 3, 1863. On Nov. 19, 1863, the field was dedicated as a national cemetery by President Lincoln in a two-minute speech that was to become immortal. At the time of its delivery the speech was relegated to the inside pages of the papers, while a two-hour address by Edward Everett, the leading orator of the time, caught the headlines.

The following is the text of the address revised by President Lincoln from his own notes:

Fourscore and seven years ago our fathers brought forth on this continent a new nation conceived in liberty and dedicated to the proposition that all men are created equal. Now we are engaged in a great civil war testing whether that nation, or any nation so conceived and so dedicated, can long endure. We are met on a great battlefield of that war. We have come to dedicate a portion of that field as a final resting-place for those who here gave their lives that that nation might live. It is altogether fitting and proper that we should do this. But, in a larger sense, we cannot dedicate, we cannot consecrate, we cannot hallow this ground. The brave men, living and dead, who struggled here have consecrated it far above our poor power to add or detract. The world will little note nor long remember what we say here, but it can never forget what they did here. It is for us the living rather to be dedicated here to the unfinished work which they who fought here have thus far so nobly advanced. It is rather for us to be here dedicated to the great task remaining before us—that from these honored dead we take increased devotion to that cause for which they gave the last full measure of devotion—that we here highly resolve that these dead shall not have died in vain, that this nation under God shall have a new birth of freedom, and that government of the people, by the people, for the people shall not perish from the earth.

The Early Congresses

At the urging of Massachusetts and Virginia, the First Continental Congress met in Philadelphia on Sept. 5, 1774, and was attended by representatives of all the colonies except Georgia. Patrick Henry of Virginia declared: "The distinctions between Pennsylvanians, New Yorkers and New Englanders are no more. I am not a Virginian but an American." This Congress, which adjourned Oct. 26, 1774, passed intercolonial resolutions calling for extensive boycott by the colonies against British trade.

The following year, most of the delegates from the colonies were chosen by popular election to attend the Second Continental Congress, which assembled in Philadelphia on May 10. As war had already begun between the colonies and England, the chief problems before the Congress were the procuring of military supplies, the establishment of an army and proper defenses, the issuing of continental bills of credit, etc. On June 15, 1775, George Washington was elected to command the Conti-

nental army. Congress adjourned Dec. 12, 1776.

Other Continental Congresses were held in Baltimore (1776–77), Philadelphia (1777), Lancaster, Pa. (1777), York, Pa. (1777–78), and Philadelphia (1778–81).

In 1781, the Articles of Confederation, although establishing a league of the thirteen states rather than a strong central government, provided for the continuance of Congress. Known thereafter as the Congress of the Confederation, it held sessions in Philadelphia (1781–83), Princeton, N.J. (1783), Annapolis, Md. (1783–84), and Trenton, N.J. (1784). Five sessions were held in New York City between the years 1785 and 1789.

The Congress of the United States, established by the ratification of the Constitution, held its first meeting on March 4, 1789, in New York City. Several sessions of Congress were held in Philadelphia, and the first meeting in Washington, D.C., was on Nov. 17, 1800.

Presidents of the Continental Congresses

Name	Elected	Born	Died
Peyton Randolph, Va.	Sept. 5, 1774	c.1721	1775
Henry Middleton, S.C.	Oct. 22, 1774	1717	1784
Peyton Randolph, Va.	May 10, 1775	c.1721	1775
John Hancock, Mass.	May 24, 1775	1737	1793
Henry Laurens, S.C.	Nov. 1, 1777	1724	1792
John Jay, N.Y.	Dec. 10, 1778	1745	1829
Samuel Huntington, Conn.	Sept. 28, 1779	1731	1796
Thomas McKean, Del.	July 10, 1781	1734	1817
John Hanson, Md.	Nov. 5, 1781	1715	1783
Elias Boudinot, N.J.	Nov. 4, 1782	1740	1821
Thomas Mifflin, Pa.	Nov. 3, 1783	1744	1800
Richard Henry Lee, Va.	Nov. 30, 1784	1732	1794
John Hancock, Mass.[1]	Nov. 23, 1785	1737	1793
Nathaniel Gorham, Mass.	June 6, 1786	1738	1796
Arthur St. Clair, Pa.	Feb. 2, 1787	1734	1818
Cyrus Griffin, Va.	Jan. 22, 1788	1748	1810

1. Resigned May 29, 1786, never having served, because of continued illness.

The Great Seal of the U.S.

On July 4, 1776, the Continental Congress appointed a committee consisting of Benjamin Franklin, John Adams, and Thomas Jefferson "to bring in a device for a seal of the United States of America." After many delays, a verbal description of a design by William Barton was finally approved by Congress on June 20, 1782. The seal shows an Ameri-

can bald eagle with a ribbon in its mouth bearing the device *E pluribus unum* (One out of many). In its talons are the arrows of war and an olive branch of peace. On the reverse side it shows an unfinished pyramid with an eye (the eye of Providence) above it.

Statistical History of The United States

There are many ways of looking at American history—at the growth of the United States, its people, and its economy. One of the most interesting is to examine certain aspects of American life "by the numbers." This "Statistical History" makes such an examination possible. The data below—stripped of the men and women, events, and technological changes that have shaped American society—reveal much that is often hidden in the complex folds of the fabric of history.

This section includes over 1,100 entries in over

100 categories, from population to the price of steak. Teachers, writers, and editors will find these data particularly useful as they seek to make events of a particular era more understandable.

History buffs should discover that this material can add significantly to their knowledge of the past. And browsers in *Information Please* will find that this "Statistical History" is a counterpoint to the "Headline History" that appears elsewhere in this book.

Item	Unit	1975	1970	1960	1950	1940
1. Population estimates[1]	thousands	213,540	204,879	180,671[2]	151,684	132,122
2. Land area	sq miles	3,536,855	3,536,855	3,540,911[2]	2,974,726	2,977,128
3. Population per sq mile[3]		60.2	57.5	50.6[2]	50.7	44.2
4. Median age of population	years	28.8	28.1	29.5[2]	30.2	29.0
5. Number of households	thousands	71,120	63,401	52,799[2]	43,554	34,949
6. Average household size		2.94	3.14	3.33[2]	3.37	3.67
7. Homicides		21,310	16,848	8,464[2]	7,942	8,329
8. Rate per 100,000 population		10.0	8.3	4.7[2]	5.3	6.3
9. Suicides		27,063	23,480	19,041[2]	17,145	18,907
10. Rate per 100,000 population		12.7	11.6	10.6[2]	11.4	14.4
11. Number of immigrants		386,200	373,326	265,398	249,187	70,756
Immigrants by selected occupations						
12. Professional[4]		38,500	46,151	21,940	20,502	6,802
13. Farmers[4][5]		900	3,839	3,050	17,642	847
14. Skilled[4][6]		38,500	46,622	34,135	41,450	5,710
15. Laborers[4][7]		13,000	14,148	12,838	5,693	2,120
16. Total Gross National Product— Current prices	billion dollars	1,516.3	977.1	503.7[2]	284.8	99.7
17. Per capita Gross National Product—Current prices	dollars	7,016	4,808	2,788[2]	1,877	754
Retail prices of selected foods in U.S. cities						
18. Flour—5 lb	¢/unit shown	99.5	58.9	55.4	49.1	21.5
19. Bread—1 lb	¢/unit shown	36.0	24.3	20.3	14.3	8.0
20. Round steak—1 lb	¢/unit shown	188.5	130.2	105.5	93.6	36.4
21. Butter—1 lb	¢/unit shown	102.5	86.6	74.9	72.9	36.0
22. Potatoes—10 lb	¢/unit shown	134.0	89.7	71.8	46.1	23.9
23. Sugar—5 lb	¢/unit shown	186.0	64.8	58.2	48.7	26.0
24. Total labor force[10]	thousands 16 years and over	94,793	82,049	69,877[2][11]	59,643[11]	53,011[11]
25. Percent of population		61.8	59.0	56.1[2][11]	54.1[11]	52.9[11]
26. Percent of civilian labor force unemployed[13]	10 years and over	8.5	4.9	5.5[2]	5.3	14.6
Physical output of selected manufactured commodities						
27. Wheat flour	mil. bbl	—	129.1	130.4	115.4	110.9
28. Beer	thou. bbl	158,000	134,654	94,548	88,807	54,892
29. Cigarettes	millions	627,000	562,154	506,127	391,956	189,373
30. Total raw steel	thou. short tons	116,642	131,514	99,282	96,836	66,983
31. Total value of new construction put in place	mil. dollars	132,043	94,855	54,738	33,575	8,682
32. Total concerns in business	thousands	2,679	2,442	2,708	2,687	2,156
33. Business failure rate	per 10,000 listed enterprises	43	44	57	34	63
34. Average annual earnings of employees	dollars	10,434[17]	7,564	4,743	2,992	1,299
Average annual earnings per full time employee in selected industries						
35. Services[19]	current $	8,141[20]	5,946	3,513	2,183	953
36. Agriculture, Forestry, and Fisheries	current $	5,756[20]	3,063	1,658	1,282	407
37. Manufacturing	current $	10,834[20]	8,150	5,352	3,302	1,432
38. Mining[21]	current $	12,935[20]	9,262	5,676	3,460	1,388
39. Construction	current $	12,206[20]	9,293	5,443	3,333	1,330
40. Transportation	current $	12,616[20]	9,928	6,185	3,714	1,756
41. Communications and public utilities	current $	12,353[20]	8,897	5,681	3,346	1,717
42. Wholesale and retail trade	current $	8,749[20]	6,886	4,597	3,045	1,382
43. Finance, insurance, and real estate	current $	9,854[20]	8,026	5,030	3,223	1,725
44. Government	current $	10,632[20]	7,965	4,676	3,014	1,344
45. Total farm population	thousands	8,864	9,712	15,635	23,048	30,547
46. Number of farms	thousands	2,808	2,954	3,962	5,388	6,102
47. Total land in farms	mil. acres	1,086.0	1,102.8	1,176.9	1,161.4	1,065.1
48. Total value of all farm property	mil. dollars	—	265,744	167,564	101,117[22]	41,829
49. Average value per farm of land and buildings	dollars	—	70,485	32,854	14,005	5,532
50. Farm wages, per day, with room and board	dollars	16.13[17]	10.70	6.50	4.45	1.30

1930	1920	1910	1900	1890	1880	1870	1860	1850	1840	
123,188	106,461	92,407	76,094	63,056	50,262	39,905	31,513	23,261	17,120	1.
2,977,128	2,969,451	2,969,565	2,969,834	2,969,640	2,969,640	2,969,640	2,969,640	2,940,042	1,749,462	2.
41.2	35.6	31.0	25.6	21.2	16.9	13.4	10.6	7.9	9.8	3.
26.5	25.3	24.1	22.9	22.0	20.9	20.2	19.4	18.9	17.8	4.
29,905	24,352	20,256	15,964	12,690	9,946	7,579	5,211	3,598	—	5.
4.11	4.34	4.54	4.76	4.93	5.04	5.09	5.28	5.55	—	6.
10,331	5,815	2,161	230	—	—	—	—	—	—	7.
8.8	6.8	4.6	1.2	—	—	—	—	—	—	8.
18,323	8,790	7,283	2,036	—	—	—	—	—	—	9.
15.6	10.2	15.3	10.2	—	—	—	—	—	—	10.
241,700	430,001	1,041,570	448,572	455,302	457,257	387,203	179,691	315,337	92,207	11.
8,585	10,540	9,689	2,392	3,236	1,773	1,831	792	918	481	12.
8,375	12,192	11,793	5,433	29,296	47,204	35,656	21,742	42,873	18,476	13.
32,474	55,991	121,847	54,793	44,540	49,929	35,698	19,342	26,369	10,811	14.
18,080	83,496	216,909	164,261	139,365	105,012	84,577	31,268	46,640	9,640	15.
90.4	91.5	35.3	18.7	13.1	11.2[8]	7.4[9]	—	—	—	16.
734	860	382	246	208	205[8]	170[9]	—	—	—	17.
23.0	40.5	18.0	12.5	14.5	—	—	—	—	—	18.
8.6	11.5	—			—	—	—	—	—	19.
42.6	39.5	17.4	13.2	12.3	—	—	—	—	—	20.
46.4	70.1	35.9	26.1	25.5	—	—	—	—	—	21.
36.0	63.0	17.0	14.0	16.0	—	—	—	—	—	22.
30.5	97.0	30.0	30.5	34.5	—	—	—	—	—	23.
48,830[12]	41,614[12]	38,167[12]	29,073[12]	23,318[12]	17,392[12]	12,506[12]	—	—	—	24.
49.5[12]	50.3[12]	53.3[12]	50.2[12]	49.2[12]	47.3[12]	44.3[12]	—	—	—	25.
8.7	5.2	5.9	5.0	4.0	—	—	—	—	—	26.
123.6[14]	130.4	107.2	105.8	83.3	64.3	47.9	39.8	—	—	27.
3,681	9,200	59,500	39,500	27,600	13,300	6,600	—	—	—	28.
124,193	48,091	9,782	3,870	2,505	533	16	—	—	—	29.
44,591	46,183	28,330	11,227	—	—	—	—	—	—	30.
8,741	6,749	3,262	—	—	—	—	—	—	—	31.
2,183	1,821	1,515	1,174	1,111	747	427	230[15]	—	—	32.
122[16]	48	84	92	99	63	83	170[15]	—	—	33.
1,368	1,236[18]	517[18]	375[18]	—	—	—	—	—	—	34.
1,066	912	447	340	—	—	—	—	—	—	35.
388	528	223	178	—	—	—	—	—	—	36.
1,488	1,532	651	487	—	—	—	—	—	—	37.
1,424	1,684	668	479	—	—	—	—	—	—	38.
1,526	1,710	804	593	—	—	—	—	—	—	39.
1,610	1,645	607	505	—	—	—	—	—	—	40.
1,499	1,238	516	470	—	—	—	—	—	—	41.
1,569	1,270	630	508	—	—	—	—	—	—	42.
1,973	1,758	1,301	1,040	—	—	—	—	—	—	43.
1,553	1,245	725	584	—	—	—	—	—	—	44.
30,529	31,974	32,077	29,875	24,771	21,973	—	—	—	—	45.
6,295	6,454	6,366	5,740	4,565	4,009	2,660	2,044	1,449	—	46.
990.1	958.7	881.4	841.2	623.2	536.1	407.7	407.2	293.6	—	47.
57,689	78,386	40,959	20,365	16,439	12,404	9,412	7,980	3,967	—	48.
7,624	10,295	5,480	2,895	2,909	2,544	2,799	3,251	2,258	—	49.
1.80	2.80	1.05	.75[23]	.70	.65	.65[24]	—	—	—	50.

(continued)

Item	Unit	1830	1820	1810	1800	1790
1. Population estimates[1]	thousands	12,901	9,618	7,224	5,297	3,929
2. Land area	sq miles	1,749,462	1,749,462	1,681,828	864,746	864,746
3. Population per sq mile[3]		7.4	5.5	4.3	6.1	4.5
4. Median age of population	years	17.2	16.7	—	—	—
5. Number of households	thousands	—	—	—	—	—
6. Average household size		—	—	—	—	5.79
7. Homicides		—	—	—	—	—
8. Rate per 100,000 population		—	—	—	—	—
9. Suicides		—	—	—	—	—
10. Rate per 100,000 population		—	—	—	—	—
11. Number of immigrants		24,837	10,311	—	—	—
Immigrants by selected occupations						
12. Professional[4]		136	105	—	—	—
13. Farmers[4][5]		1,424	874	—	—	—
14. Skilled[4][6]		1,745	1,090	—	—	—
15. Laborers[4][7]		720	334	—	—	—
16. Total Gross National Product— Current prices	billion dollars	—	—	—	—	—
17. Per capita Gross National Product—Current prices	dollars	—	—	—	—	—
Retail prices of selected foods in U.S. cities						
18. Flour—5 lb	¢/unit shown	—	—	—	—	—
19. Bread—1 lb	¢/unit shown	—	—	—	—	—
20. Round steak—1 lb	¢/unit shown	—	—	—	—	—
21. Butter—1 lb	¢/unit shown	—	—	—	—	—
22. Potatoes—10 lb	¢/unit shown	—	—	—	—	—
23. Sugar—5 lb	¢/unit shown	—	—	—	—	—
24. Total labor force[10]	thousands 16 years and over	—	—	—	—	—
25. Percent of population		—	—	—	—	—
26. Percent of civilian labor force unemployed[13]	10 years and over	—	—	—	—	—
Physical output of selected manufactured commodities						
27. Wheat flour	mil. bbl	—	—	—	—	—
28. Beer	thou. bbl	—	—	—	—	—
29. Cigarettes	millions	—	—	—	—	—
30. Total raw steel	thou. short tons	—	—	—	—	—
31. Total value of new construction put in place	mil. dollars	—	—	—	—	—
32. Total concerns in business	thousands	—	—	—	—	—
33. Business failure rate	per 10,000 listed enterprises	—	—	—	—	—
34. Average annual earnings of employees	dollars	—	—	—	—	—
Average annual earnings per full time employee in selected industries						
35. Services[19]	current $	—	—	—	—	—
36. Agriculture, Forestry, and Fisheries	current $	—	—	—	—	—
37. Manufacturing	current $	—	—	—	—	—
38. Mining[21]	current $	—	—	—	—	—
39. Construction	current $	—	—	—	—	—
40. Transportation	current $	—	—	—	—	—
41. Communications and public utilities	current $	—	—	—	—	—
42. Wholesale and retail trade	current $	—	—	—	—	—
43. Finance, insurance, and real estate	current $	—	—	—	—	—
44. Government	current $	—	—	—	—	—
45. Total farm population	thousands	—	—	—	—	—
46. Number of farms	thousands	—	—	—	—	—
47. Total land in farms	mil. acres	—	—	—	—	—
48. Total value of all farm property	mil. dollars	—	—	—	—	—
49. Average value per farm of land and buildings	dollars	—	—	—	—	—
50. Farm wages, per day, with room and board	dollars	—	—	—	—	—

Item	Unit	1975	1970	1960	1950	1940
Farm Productivity						
51. Wheat—yield per acre	bushels	31.0	31.0	25.2[25]	17.3[26]	17.1[27]
52. Wheat—man-hours	100 bushels	9	9	12[25]	27[26]	44[27]
53. Cotton—yield per acre	pounds	473	438	475[25]	296[26]	260[27]
54. Cotton—man-hours	bale	23	26	47[25]	107[26]	182[27]
55. Potatoes—yield per acre	cwt	239.0	229.0	194.9[25]	151.2[26]	82.1[27]
56. Potatoes—man-hours	ton	4	4	5[25]	8[26]	17[27]
57. Tobacco—yield per acre	pounds	2,000	2,121	1,879[25]	1,292[26]	1,026[27]
58. Tobacco—man-hours	100 pounds	14	23	26[25]	36[26]	43[27]
59. Milk cows—milk per cow	pounds	10,200.0	9,385.0	7,507.0[25]	5,440.0[26]	4,653.0[27]
60. Milk cows—man-hours	cwt of milk	0.6	0.7	1.2[25]	2.2[26]	3.1[27]
61. Total use of electrical energy	mil. kwh	—	1,641,731	848,723[2]	396,346	181,706
62. Residential	mil. kwh	—	453,015	196,296[2]	72,200	24,068
63. Commercial	mil. kwh	—	295,057	121,437[2]	52,091	22,373
64. Industrial	mil. kwh	—	685,693	415,699[2]	194,835	92,390
65. Value of exports	mil. dollars	107,591	43,265	20,603	10,816	4,030
66. Value of imports	mil. dollars	96,940	40,189	15,046	9,125	7,433
67. Passenger car factory sales	thousands	6,713.0	6,546.8	6,674.7	6,665.8	3,717.3
68. Total motor vehicle registrations	millions	133.7	108.4	73.9	49.2	32.4
69. Miles of travel by motor vehicles	mil. miles	1,300,100	1,120,705	718,845	458,246	302,188
70. Number of operating railroads		341[20]	351	407[2]	471	574
71. Railroad passengers	thousands	275,000[20]	289,469	327,172[2]	488,019	456,088
Air transportation						
72. Number of operators		30	33	42	52	19
73. Aircraft in service		2,267	2,437	1,594	960	369
74. Revenue passengers carried	thousands	189,000[34]	153,408[34]	56,352[34]	17,345[34]	2,523[34]
75. Total school enrollments—elementary and secondary	thousands	50,562[20]	51,319	41,762[2]	28,492	28,045
76. High school graduates	thousands	3,139[17]	2,906	1,864	1,200	1,221
77. Percent of persons 17 years old	percent	74.3[17]	75.6	63.4	57.4	49.0
78. Total institutions of higher education		2,747	2,525	1,959[2]	1,863	1,708
79. Bachelor's or first professional degrees conferred		944,000[17]	827,234	389,183	432,058	186,500
Radio and television						
80. Radio sets produced	thousands	—	16,406	17,127	13,468	11,831
81. Households with radio sets	thousands	—	62,000	50,193	40,700	28,500
82. Television sets produced	thousands	—	4,852	5,708	7,464	—
83. Households with television sets	thousands	—	59,550	45,750	3,875	—
84. Books published		39,372	36,071	15,012	11,022	11,328
85. Daily newspapers—number		1,756	1,748	1,763	1,772	1,878
86. Daily newspapers—circulation	thousands	60,655	62,108	58,882	53,829	41,132
87. Telephones per 1,000 population		695.0	583.4	407.8	280.9	165.1
88. Average number of daily telephone conversations	thousands	633,000	485,200	285,386	170,623	98,783
89. Patents issued for inventions		71,994	64,427	47,170	43,040	42,238
90. Currency in circulation	mil. dollars	92,095.0	54,351.0	32,064.6	27,156.3	7,847.5
91. Total social welfare expenditures under public programs	mil. dollars	286,547[38]	145,893	52,293	23,508	8,795
92. Percent of GNP	percent	19.9[38]	15.3	10.6	8.9	9.2
93. Percent of all government expenditures	percent	58.4[38]	47.8	38.0	37.6	49.0
94. Per capita (actual prices)	dollars	1,319[38]	701	286	153	66
95. Per capita health expenditure	dollars	484.73[20]	343.44	146.30	81.86	29.62
96. Number of physicians		394,000[20]	348,328	274,833[2]	191,947	165,989
97. Rate per 100,000 population		186	166	148[2]	128	126
Summary of federal government finances						
98. Receipts	mil. dollars	281,000.0	193,700.0	92,500.0	40,900.0	6,900.0
99. Outlays	mil. dollars	324,600.0	196,600.0	92,200.0	43,100.0	9,600.0
100. Total public debt	mil. dollars	533,200.0	370,918.7	286,300.8	257,357.4	42,967.5
101. Per capita public debt	dollars	2,496	1,811	1,585	1,697	325
102. Paid civilian employees of the federal government		2,896,944	2,981,574	2,398,704	1,960,708	1,042,420
103. Military personnel on active duty[54]		2,127,000[55]	3,066,294[55]	2,476,435	1,460,261	458,365[56]

(continued)

Item	Unit	1930	1920	1910	1900
Farm Productivity					
51. Wheat—yield per acre	bushels	13.5[28]	13.8[29]	14.4[30]	13.9
52. Wheat—man-hours	100 bushels	70[28]	90[29]	106[30]	108
53. Cotton—yield per acre	pounds	184[28]	155[29]	201[30]'	189
54. Cotton—man-hours	bale	252[28]	296[29]	276[30]	284
55. Potatoes—yield per acre	cwt	64.6[28]	64.6[29]	59.8[30]	—
56. Potatoes—man-hours	ton	21[28]	23[29]	25[30]	—
57. Tobacco—yield per acre	pounds	784[28]	773[29]	816[30]	—
58. Tobacco—man-hours	100 pounds	47[28]	46[29]	44[30]	—
59. Milk cows—milk per cow	pounds	4,289.0[28]	4,000.0[29]	3,842.0[30]	—
60. Milk cows—man-hours	cwt of milk	3.4[28]	3.6[29]	3.8[30]	—
61. Total use of electrical energy	mil. kwh	115,783	57,125	14,262[31]	6,029[32]
62. Residential	mil. kwh	11,018	3,190	—	—
63. Commercial	mil. kwh	13,944	6,150	—	—
64. Industrial	mil. kwh	61,023	31,500	—	—
65. Value of exports	mil. dollars	4,013	8,664	1,919	1,499
66. Value of imports	mil. dollars	3,500	5,784	1,646	930
67. Passenger car factory sales	thousands	2,787.4	1,905.5	181.0	4.1
68. Total motor vehicle registrations	millions	26.7	9.2	.5	.008
69. Miles of travel by motor vehicles	mil. miles	206,320	55,027[33]	—	—
70. Number of operating railroads		775	1,085	1,306	1,224
71. Railroad passengers	thousands	707,987	1,269,913	971,683	576,831
Air transportation					
72. Number of operators		43	—	—	—
73. Aircraft in service		497	—	—	—
74. Revenue passengers carried	thousands	385[35]	—	—	—
75. Total school enrollments— elementary and secondary	thousands	28,329	23,278	19,372	16,885
76. High school graduates	thousands	667	311	156	95
77. Percent of persons 17 years old	percent	28.8	16.3	8.6	6.3
78. Total institutions of higher education		1,409	1,041	951	977
79. Bachelor's or first professional degrees conferred		122,484	48,622	37,199	27,410
Radio and television					
80. Radio sets produced	thousands	3,789	100[37]	—	—
81. Households with radio sets	thousands	13,750	60[37]	—	—
82. Television sets produced	thousands	—	—	—	—
83. Households with television sets	thousands	—	—	—	—
84. Books published		10,027	8,422	13,470	6,356
85. Daily newspapers—number		1,942	2,042	—	—
86. Daily newspapers—circulation	thousands	39,589	27,791	—	—
87. Telephones per 1,000 population		162.6	123.4	82.0	17.6
88. Average number of daily telephone conversations	thousands	83,520	51,814	36,161	7,882
89. Patents issued for inventions		45,226	37,060	35,141	24,644
90. Currency in circulation	mil. dollars	4,521.0	5,467.6	3,148.7	2,081.2
91. Total social welfare expenditures under public programs	mil. dollars	4,085	—	1,000[39]	—
92. Percent of GNP	percent	4.2	—	2.5[39]	—
93. Percent of all government expenditures	percent	—	—	34.0[39]	—
94. Per capita (actual prices)	dollars	33	—	—	—
95. Per capita health expenditure	dollars	29.49[14]	—	—	—
96. Number of physicians		153,803	144,977	151,132	132,002
97. Rate per 100,000 population		125	137	164	173
Summary of federal government finances					
98. Receipts	mil. dollars	4,057.9	6,648.9	675.5	567.2
99. Outlays	mil. dollars	3,320.2	6,357.7	693.6	520.9
100. Total public debt	mil. dollars	16,185.3	24,299.3	1,146.9	1,263.4
101. Per capita public debt	dollars	132	228	12	17
102. Paid civilian employees of the federal government		601,319	655,265	388,708	239,476[44]
103. Military personnel on active duty[54]		255,648	343,302	139,344[57]	125,923

1890	1880	1870	1860	1850	1840	1830	1820	1810	1800	1790	
—	13.2	—	—	—	15.0	—	—	—	15.0	—	51.
—	152	—	—	—	233	—	—	—	373	—	52.
—	188	—	—	—	147	—	—	—	147	—	53.
—	303	—	—	—	438	—	—	—	601	—	54.
—	—	—	—	—	—	—	—	—	—	—	55.
—	—	—	—	—	—	—	—	—	—	—	56.
—	—	—	—	—	—	—	—	—	—	—	57.
—	—	—	—	—	—	—	—	—	—	—	58.
—	—	—	—	—	—	—	—	—	—	—	59.
—	—	—	—	—	—	—	—	—	—	—	60.
—	—	—	—	—	—	—	—	—	—	—	61.
—	—	—	—	—	—	—	—	—	—	—	62.
—	—	—	—	—	—	—	—	—	—	—	63.
910	853	451	400	152	132	74	70	67	71	—	64.
823	761	462	362	178	107	71	74	85	91	20	65.
—	—	—	—	—	—	—	—	—	—	23	66.
—	—	—	—	—	—	—	—	—	—	—	67.
—	—	—	—	—	—	—	—	—	—	—	68.
—	—	—	—	—	—	—	—	—	—	—	69.
1,013	—	—	—	—	—	—	—	—	—	—	70.
492,431	—	—	—	—	—	—	—	—	—	—	71.
—	—	—	—	—	—	—	—	—	—	—	72.
—	—	—	—	—	—	—	—	—	—	—	73.
—	—	—	—	—	—	—	—	—	—	—	74.
14,479	9,868[36]	6,872[36]	—	—	—	—	—	—	—	—	75.
44	24	16	—	—	—	—	—	—	—	—	76.
3.5	2.5	2.0	—	—	—	—	—	—	—	—	77.
998	811	563	—	—	—	—	—	—	—	—	78.
15,539	12,896	—	—	—	—	—	—	—	—	—	79.
—	—	—	—	—	—	—	—	—	—	—	80.
—	—	—	—	—	—	—	—	—	—	—	81.
—	—	—	—	—	—	—	—	—	—	—	82.
4,559	2,076	—	—	—	—	—	—	—	—	—	83.
—	—	—	—	—	—	—	—	—	—	—	84.
—	—	—	—	—	—	—	—	—	—	—	85.
3.6	0.9	—	—	—	—	—	—	—	—	—	86.
—	—	—	—	—	—	—	—	—	—	—	87.
1,448	239	—	—	—	—	—	—	—	—	—	88.
25,313	12,903	12,137	4,357	883	458	544	155	223	41	3	89.
1,429.3	973.4	775.0	435.4	278.8	186.3	87.3	67.1	55.0	26.5	—	90.
318	—	—	—	—	—	—	—	—	—	—	91.
2.4	—	—	—	—	—	—	—	—	—	—	92.
38.0	—	—	—	—	—	—	—	—	—	—	93.
—	—	—	—	—	—	—	—	—	—	—	94.
104,805	85,671	64,414	55,055	40,755	—	—	—	—	—	—	95.
166	171	162	175	176	—	—	—	—	—	—	96.
—	—	—	—	—	—	—	—	—	—	—	97.
403.1	333.5	411.3	56.1	43.6	19.5	24.8	17.9	9.4	10.8	4.4[41]	98.
318.0	267.6	309.7	63.1	39.5	24.3	15.1	18.3	8.2	10.8	4.3[41]	99.
1,222.4	2,090.9	2,436.5	64.8	63.5	3.6	48.6	91.0	53.2	83.0	75.5[42]	100.
18	42	61	2	3[43]	—	—	—	—	—	—	101.
157,442[45]	100,020[46]	51,020[47]	36,672[48]	26,274[49]	18,038[50]	11,491[51]	6,914[52]	4,837[53]	—	—	102.
38,666	37,894	50,348	27,958[58]	20,824	21,616	11,942	15,113	11,554	7,108[59]	718[60]	103.

Statistical History Table—Footnotes

1. Total, including Armed Forces overseas, as of July 1. For population during Colonial years (1610–1780), *see* table of Colonial Population Estimates. 2. Beginning with 1960, figures include Alaska and Hawaii. 3. Based on resident population figures, excluding Armed Forces overseas. 4. Like occupations have been grouped as closely as possible to allow for changing definitions over the years. *See* source for definitions and further explanation. 5. For 1900–75, includes "Farmers and Farm Managers." 6. For 1900–75, includes craftsmen, foremen, operatives, and kindred workers; for 1820–90, includes those occupations requiring special training of a manual rather than mental nature. 7. For 1900–75, excludes farm and mine laborers. 8. Decade average; 1879–88. 9. Decade average; 1869–78. 10. 1940–75, includes Armed Forces. 11. Data for persons 14 years old and over. 12. Data for persons 10 years old and over reporting a gainful occupation. 13. Prior to 1950, figures are for persons 14 years old and over. Annual averages. Unemployment percentages for the Depression years as follows: 1931, 15.9%; 1932, 23.6%; 1933, 24.9%; 1934, 21.7%; 1935, 20.1%; 1936, 16.9%; 1937, 14.3%; 1938, 19.0%; 1939, 17.2%. 14. Figure is for 1929. 15. Figure is for 1859. 16. In 1932, the rate reached a high of 154. 17. Estimate. 18. After deduction for unemployment. 19. Includes workers in personal, medical, and other health services, domestic, nonprofit, educational service industries. 20. Figure is for 1974. 21. Includes workers in anthracite coal, bituminous coal, and metal mining. 22. Figure is for 1949. 23. Figure is for 1899. 24. Figure is for 1869. 25. Figures are annual averages for 1960–64. 26. Figures are annual averages for 1950–54. 27. Figures are annual averages for 1940–44. 28. Figures are annual averages 1930–34. 29. Figures are annual averages for 1920–24. 30. Figures are annual averages for 1910–14. 31. Figure is for 1907. 32. Figure is for 1902. 33. Figure is for 1921. 34. Duplication has been eliminated where the same passengers were carried on more than one route of an air carrier, but still exists where the same passengers were carried by more than one air carrier. 35. Includes nonrevenue passengers. 36. Figure for public day schools only. 37. Figure is for 1922. 38. Preliminary figures. 39. Figure is for 1913. 40. Includes hospital care, professional services, drugs and sundries, eyeglasses and appliances, nursing home care, expenses for prepayment and administration, government public health activities, other health services, and research and medical facilities construction. 41. Figure is for 1789–91, 42. Figure is for 1791. 43. Figure is for 1851. 44. Figure is for 1901. 45. Figure is for 1891. 46. Figure is for 1881. 47. Figure is for 1871. 48. Figure is for 1861. 49. Figure is for 1851. 50. Figure is for 1841. 51. Figure is for 1831. 52. Figure is for 1821. 53. Figure is for 1816. 54. Excludes Coast Guard. 55. Estimated. 56. In 1945, 12,123,455 people were on active military duty. 57. In 1918, 2,897,167 people were on active military duty. 58. In 1865, 1,062,848 people were on active military duty. 59. Figure is for 1801. 60. Figure is for 1789.
Source: Historical Statistics of the U.S., Department of Commerce, Bureau of the Census.

U.S. Capitol

When the French architect and engineer Maj. Pierre L'Enfant first began to lay out the plans for a new Federal city (now Washington, D.C.), he noted that Jenkins' Hill, overlooking the area, seemed to be "a pedestal waiting for a monument." It was here that the U.S. Capitol would be built. The basic structure as we know it today evolved over a period of more than 150 years. In 1792 a competition was held for the design of a capitol building. Dr. William Thornton, a physician and amateur architect, submitted the winning plan, a simple, low-lying structure of classical proportions with a shallow dome. Later, internal modifications were made by Benjamin Henry Latrobe. After the building was burned by the British in 1814, Latrobe and architect Charles Bulfinch were responsible for its reconstruction. Finally, under Thomas Walter, who was Architect of the Capitol from 1851 to 1865, the House and Senate wings and the imposing cast iron dome topped with the Statue of Freedom were added, and the Capitol assumed the form we see today. It was in the old Senate chamber that Daniel Webster cried out, "Liberty and Union, now and forever, one and inseparable!" In Statuary Hall, which used to be the old House chamber, a small disk on the floor marks the spot where John Quincy Adams was fatally stricken after more than 50 years of service to his country. A whisper from one side of this room can be heard across the vast space of the hall. Visitors can see the original Supreme Court chamber a floor below the Rotunda.

In addition to its historical association, the Capitol Building is also a vast artistic treasure house. The works of such famous artists as Gilbert Stuart, Rembrandt Peale, and John Trumbull are displayed on the walls. The Great Rotunda, with its 180-foot- (54.9-m-) high dome, is decorated with a massive fresco by Constantino Brumidi, which extends some 300 feet (90 m) in circumference. Throughout the building are many paintings of events in U.S. history and sculptures of outstanding Americans. The Capitol itself is situated on a 68-acre (27.5-ha) park designed by the 19th-century landscape architect Frederick Law Olmsted. There are free guided tours of the Capitol, which include admission to the House and Senate galleries. Those who wish to visit the visitors' gallery in either wing without taking the tour may obtain passes from their Senators or Congressmen. Visitors may ride on the monorail subway that joins the House and Senate wings of the Capitol with the Congressional office buildings.

Washington Monument

Construction of this magnificent Washington, D.C., monument, which draws some two million visitors a year, took nearly a century of planning, building, and controversy. Provision for a large equestrian statue of George Washington was made in the original city plan, but the project was soon dropped. After Washington's death it was taken up again, and a number of false starts and changes of design were made. Finally, in 1848, work was begun on the monument that stands today. The design, by architect Robert Mills, then featured an ornate base. In 1854, however, political squabbling and a lack of money brought construction to a halt. Work was resumed in 1880, and the monument was completed in 1884 and opened to the public in 1888. The tapered shaft, faced with white marble and rising from walls 15 feet thick (4.6 m) at the base was modeled after the obelisks of ancient Egypt. The monument, one of the tallest masonry constructions in the world, stands just over 555 feet (169 m). Memorial stones from the 50 States, foreign countries, and organizations line the interior walls. The top, reached only by elevator, commands a panoramic view of the city.

History of the Flag

Source: Encyclopaedia Britannica.

The first official American flag, the Continental or Grand Union flag, was displayed on Prospect Hill, Jan. 1, 1776, in the American lines besieging Boston. It had 13 alternate red and white stripes, with the British Union Jack in the upper left corner.

On June 14, 1777, the Continental Congress adopted the design for a new flag, which actually was the Continental flag with the red cross of St. George and the white cross of St. Andrew replaced on the blue field by 13 stars, one for each state. No rule was made as to the arrangement of the stars, and while they were usually shown in a circle, there were various other designs. It is uncertain when the new flag was first flown, but its first official announcement is believed to have been on Sept. 3, 1777.

The first public assertion that Betsy Ross made the first Stars and Stripes appeared in a paper read before the Historical Society of Pennsylvania on March 14, 1870, by William J. Canby, a grandson. However, Mr. Canby on later investigation found no official documents of any action by Congress on the flag before June 14, 1777. Betsy Ross's own story, according to her daughter, was that Washington, Robert Morris, and George Ross, as representatives of Congress, visited her in Philadelphia in June 1776, showing her a rough draft of the flag and asking her if she could make one. However, the only actual record of the manufacture of flags by Betsy Ross is a voucher in Harrisburg, Pa., for 14 pounds and some shillings for flags for the Pennsylvania navy.

On Jan. 13, 1794, Congress voted to add two stars and two stripes to the flag in recognition of the admission of Vermont and Kentucky to the Union. By 1818, there were 20 states in the Union, and as it was obvious that the flag would soon become unwieldly, Congress voted April 18 to return to the original 13 stripes and to indicate the admission of a new state simply by the addition of a star following July 4. The 49th star, for Alaska, was added July 4, 1959; and the 50th star, for Hawaii, was added July 4, 1960.

The first Confederate flag, adopted in 1861 by the Confederate convention in Montgomery, Ala., was called the Stars and Bars; but because of its similarity in colors to the American flag, there was much confusion in the Battle of Bull Run. To remedy this situation, Gen. G. T. Beauregard suggested a battle flag, which was used by the Southern armies throughout the war. The flag consisted of a red field on which was placed a blue cross of St. Andrew separated from the field by a white fillet and adorned with 13[1] white stars for the Confederate states. In May 1863, at Richmond, an official flag was adopted by the Confederate Congress. This flag was white and twice as long as wide; the union, two-thirds the width of the flag, contained the battle flag designed for Gen. Beauregard. A broad transverse stripe of red was added Feb. 4, 1865, so that the flag might not be mistaken for a signal of truce.

1. 11 states formally seceded, and unofficial groups in Kentucky and Missouri adopted ordinances of secession. On this basis, these two states were admitted to the Confederacy, although the official state governments remained in the Union.

The Pledge of Allegiance[1] to the Flag

"I pledge allegiance to the Flag of the United States of America, and to the Republic for which it stands, one Nation under God,[2] indivisible, with liberty and justice for all."

1. The original pledge was published in the Sept. 8, 1892, issue of *The Youth's Companion* in Boston. For years, the authorship was in dispute between James B. Upham and Francis Bellamy of the magazine's staff. In 1939, after a study of the controversy, the United States Flag Association decided that authorship be credited to Bellamy. 2. The phrase "under God" was added to the pledge on June 14, 1954.

Arlington National Cemetery

Arlington National Cemetery occupies 612 acres in Virginia on the Potomac River, directly opposite Washington. This land was part of the estate of John Parke Custis, Martha Washington's son, who built the mansion which later became the home of Robert E. Lee. In 1864, Arlington became a military cemetery. Over 182,000 persons, including many thousands of soldiers as well as hundreds of distinguished Americans, are buried there. Expansion of the cemetery began in fiscal year 1965, using a 180-acre tract of land directly east of the present site.

In 1921, an Unknown American Soldier of World War I was buried in a temporary crypt in the cemetery; the completed Tomb was opened to the public without ceremony in 1932. Two additional Unknowns, one from World War II and one from the Korean War, were buried May 30, 1958. The inscription carved on the side of the Tomb of the Unknown Soldier reads:

HERE RESTS IN
HONORED GLORY
AN AMERICAN
SOLDIER
KNOWN BUT TO GOD

Biographies of the Presidents

GEORGE WASHINGTON was born on Feb. 22, 1732 (Feb. 11, 1731/2, old style) in Westmoreland County, Va. While in his teens, he trained as a surveyor, and at the age of 20 he was appointed adjutant in the Virginia militia. For the next three years, he fought in the wars against the French and Indians, serving as Gen. Edward Braddock's aide in the disastrous campaign against Fort Duquesne. In 1759, he resigned from the militia, married Martha Dandridge Custis, a widow, and settled down as a gentleman farmer at Mount Vernon, Va.

As a militiaman, Washington had been exposed to the arrogance of the British officers, and his experience as a planter with British commercial restrictions increased his anti-British sentiment. He opposed the Stamp Act of 1765 and after 1770 became increasingly prominent in organizing resistance. A delegate to the Continental Congress, Washington was selected as commander in chief of the Continental Army and took command at Cambridge, Mass., on July 3, 1775.

Inadequately supported and sometimes covertly sabotaged by the Congress, in charge of troops who were inexperienced, badly equipped, and impatient of discipline, Washington conducted the war on the policy of avoiding major engagements with the British and wearing them down by harassing tactics. His able generalship, along with the French alliance and the growing weariness within Britain, brought the war to a conclusion with the surrender of Cornwallis at Yorktown, Va., on Oct. 19, 1781.

The chaotic years under the Articles of Confederation led Washington to return to public life in the hope of promoting the formation of a strong central government. He presided over the Constitutional Convention and yielded to the universal demand that he serve as first President. He was inaugurated on April 30, 1789, in New York, the first national capital. In office, he sought to unite the nation and establish the authority of the new government at home and abroad. Greatly distressed by the emergence of the Hamilton-Jefferson rivalry, Washington worked to maintain neutrality but actually sympathized more with Hamilton. Following his unanimous re-election in 1792, his second term was dominated by the Federalists. His Farewell Address on Sept. 17, 1796 (published but never delivered) rebuked party spirit and warned against "permanent alliances" with foreign powers.

He died at Mount Vernon on Dec. 14, 1799.

JOHN ADAMS was born on Oct. 30 (Oct. 19, old style), 1735, at Braintree (now Quincy), Mass. A Harvard graduate, he considered teaching and the ministry but finally turned to law and was admitted to the bar in 1758. Six years later, he married Abigail Smith. He opposed the Stamp Act, served as lawyer for patriots indicted by the British, and by the time of the Continental Congresses, was in the vanguard of the movement for independence. In 1778, he went to France as commissioner. Subsequently he helped negotiate the peace treaty with Britain, and in 1785 became envoy to London. Resigning in 1788, he was elected Vice President under Washington and was re-elected in 1792.

Though a Federalist, Adams did not get along with Hamilton, who sought to prevent his election to the presidency in 1796 and thereafter intrigued against his administration. In 1798, Adams's inde-

pendent policy averted a war with France but completed the break with Hamilton and the right-wing Federalists; at the same time, the enactment of the Alien and Sedition Acts, directed against foreigners and against critics of the government, exasperated the Jeffersonian opposition. The split between Adams and Hamilton resulted in Jefferson's becoming the next President. Adams retired to his home in Quincy. He and Jefferson died on the same day, July 4, 1826, the 50th anniversary of the signing of the Declaration of Independence.

His *Defence of the Constitutions of Government of the United States* (1787) contains original and striking, if conservative, political ideas.

THOMAS JEFFERSON was born on April 13 (April 2, old style), 1743, at Shadwell in Goochland (now Albemarle) County, Va. A William and Mary graduate, he studied law, but from the start showed an interest in science and philosophy. His literary skill and political clarity brought him to the forefront of the revolutionary movement in Virginia. As delegate to the Continental Congress, he drafted the Declaration of Independence. In 1776, he entered the Virginia House of Delegates and initiated a comprehensive reform program for the abolition of feudal survivals in land tenure and the separation of church and state.

In 1779, he became governor, but constitutional limitations on his power, combined with his own lack of executive energy, caused an unsatisfactory administration, culminating in Jefferson's virtual abdication when the British invaded Virginia in 1781. He retired to his beautiful home at Monticello, Va., to his family. His wife, Martha Wayles Skelton, whom he married in 1772, died in 1782.

Jefferson's *Notes on Virginia* (1784–85) illustrate his many-faceted interests, his limitless intellectual curiosity, his deep faith in agrarian democracy. Sent to Congress in 1783, he helped lay down the decimal system and drafted basic reports on the organization of the western lands. In 1785 he was appointed minister to France, where the Anglo-Saxon liberalism he had drawn from John Locke, the British philosopher, was stimulated by contact with the thought that would soon ferment in the French Revolution. In 1789, Washington appointed him Secretary of State. While favoring the Constitution and a strengthened central government, Jefferson came to believe that Hamilton contemplated the establishment of a monarchy. Growing differences resulted in Jefferson's resignation on Dec. 31, 1793.

Elected vice president in 1796, Jefferson continued to serve as spiritual leader of the opposition to Federalism, particularly to the repressive Alien and Sedition Acts. He was elected President in 1801 by the House of Representatives as a result of Hamilton's decision to throw the Federalist votes to him rather than to Aaron Burr, who had tied him in electoral votes. He was the first President to be inaugurated in Washington, which he had helped to design.

The purchase of Louisiana from France in 1803, though in violation of Jefferson's earlier constitutional scruples, was the most notable act of his administration. Re-elected in 1804, with the Federalist Charles C. Pinckney opposing him, Jefferson tried desperately to keep the United States out of the Napoleonic Wars in Europe, employing to this end the unpopular embargo policy.

After his retirement to Monticello in 1809, he developed his interest in education, founding the University of Virginia and watching its development with never-flagging interest. He died at Monticello on July 4, 1826. Jefferson had an enormous variety of interests and skills, ranging from education and science to architecture and music.

JAMES MADISON was born in Port Conway, Va., on March 16, 1751 (March 5, 1750/1, old style). A Princeton graduate, he joined the struggle for independence on his return to Virginia in 1771. In the 1770s and 1780s he was active in state politics, where he championed the Jefferson reform program, and in the Continental Congress. Madison was influential in the Constitutional Convention as leader of the group favoring a strong central government and as recorder of the debates; and he subsequently wrote, in collaboration with Alexander Hamilton and John Jay, the *Federalist* papers to aid the campaign for the adoption of the Constitution.

Serving in the new Congress, Madison soon emerged as the leader in the House of the men who opposed Hamilton's financial program and his pro-British leanings in foreign policy. Retiring from Congress in 1797, he continued to be active in Virginia and drafted the Virginia Resolution protesting the Alien and Sedition Acts. His intimacy with Jefferson made him the natural choice for Secretary of State in 1801.

In 1809, Madison succeeded Jefferson as President, defeating Charles C. Pinckney. His attractive wife, Dolley Payne Todd, whom he married in 1794, brought a new social sparkle to the executive mansion. In the meantime, increasing tension with Britain culminated in the War of 1812—a war for which the United States was unprepared and for which Madison lacked the executive talent to clear out incompetence and mobilize the nation's energies. Madison was re-elected in 1812, running against the Federalist De Witt Clinton. In 1814, the British actually captured Washington and forced Madison to flee to Virginia.

Madison's domestic program capitulated to the Hamiltonian policies that he had resisted 20 years before and he now signed bills to establish a United States Bank and a higher tariff.

After his presidency, he remained in retirement in Virginia until his death on June 28, 1836.

JAMES MONROE was born on April 28, 1758, in Westmoreland County, Va. A William and Mary graduate, he served in the army during the first years of the Revolution and was wounded at Trenton. He then entered Virginia politics and later national politics under the sponsorship of Jefferson. In 1786, he married Elizabeth (Eliza) Kortright.

Fearing centralization, Monroe opposed the adoption of the Constitution and, as senator from Virginia, was highly critical of the Hamiltonian program. In 1794, he was appointed minister to France, where his ardent sympathies with the Revolution exceeded the wishes of the State Department. His troubled diplomatic career ended with his recall in 1796. From 1799 to 1802, he was governor of Virginia. In 1803, Jefferson sent him to France to help negotiate the Louisiana Purchase and for the next few years he was active in various negotiations on the Continent.

In 1808, Monroe flirted with the radical wing of the Republican Party, which opposed Madison's candidacy; but the presidential boom came to naught and, after a brief term as governor of Virginia in 1811, Monroe accepted Madison's offer to become Secretary of State. During the War of 1812, he vainly sought a field command and instead served as Secretary of War from September 1814 to March 1815.

Elected President in 1816 over the Federalist Rufus King, and re-elected without opposition in 1820, Monroe, the last of the Virginia dynasty, pursued the course of systematic tranquilization that won for his administrations the name "the era of good feeling." He continued Madison's surrender to the Hamiltonian domestic program, signed the Missouri Compromise, acquired Florida, and with the able assistance of his Secretary of State, John Quincy Adams, promulgated the Monroe Doctrine in 1823, declaring against foreign colonization or intervention in the Americas. He died in New York City on July 4, 1831, the third president to die on the anniversary of Independence.

JOHN QUINCY ADAMS was born on July 11, 1767, at Braintree (now Quincy), Mass., the son of John Adams, the second President. He spent his early years in Europe with his father, graduated from Harvard, and entered law practice. His anti-Jeffersonian newspaper articles won him political attention. In 1794, he became minister to the Netherlands, the first of several diplomatic posts that occupied him until his return to Boston in 1801. In 1797, he married Louisa Catherine Johnson.

In 1803, Adams was elected to the Senate, nominally as a Federalist, but his repeated displays of independence on such issues as the Louisiana Purchase and the embargo caused his party to demand his resignation and ostracize him socially. In 1809, Madison rewarded him for his support of Jefferson by appointing him minister to St. Petersburg. He helped negotiate the Treaty of Ghent in 1814, and in 1815 became minister to London. In 1817 Monroe appointed him Secretary of State where he served with great distinction, gaining Florida from Spain without hostilities and playing an equal part with Monroe in formulating the Monroe Doctrine.

When no presidential candidate received a majority of electoral votes in 1824, Adams, with the support of Henry Clay, was elected by the House in 1825 over Andrew Jackson, who had the original plurality. Adams had ambitious plans of government activity to foster internal improvements and promote the arts and sciences, but congressional obstructionism, combined with his own unwillingness or inability to play the role of a politician, resulted in little being accomplished. After being defeated for re-election by Jackson in 1828, he successfully ran for the House of Representatives in 1830. There though nominally a Whig, he pursued as ever an independent course. He led the fight to force Congress to receive antislavery petitions and fathered the Smithsonian Institution.

Stricken on the floor of the House, he died on Feb. 23, 1848. His long and detailed *Diary* gives a unique picture of the personalities and politics of the times.

ANDREW JACKSON was born on March 15, 1767, in what is now generally agreed to be Waxhaw, S.C. After a turbulent boyhood as an orphan and a British prisoner, he moved west to Tennessee, where he soon qualified for law practice but found time for such frontier pleasures as horse racing, cockfighting, and dueling. His marriage to Rachel Donelson Robards in 1791 was complicated by subsequent legal uncertainties about the status of her divorce. During the 1790s, Jackson served in the Tennessee Constitutional Convention, the United States House of Representatives and Senate, and on the Tennessee Supreme Court.

After some years as a country gentleman, living at the Hermitage near Nashville, Jackson in 1812 was given command of Tennessee troops sent against the Creeks. He defeated the Indians at Horseshoe Bend in 1814; subsequently he became a major general and won the Battle of New Orleans over veteran British troops, though after the treaty of peace had been signed at Ghent. In 1818, Jackson invaded Florida, captured Pensacola, and hanged two Englishmen named Arbuthnot and Ambrister, creating an international incident. A presidential boom began for him in 1821, and to foster it, he returned to the Senate (1823–25). Though he won a plurality of electoral votes in 1824, he lost in the House when Clay threw his strength to Adams. Four years later, he easily defeated Adams.

As President, Jackson greatly expanded the power and prestige of the presidential office and carried through an unprecedented program of domestic reform, vetoing the bill to extend the United States Bank, moving toward a hard-money currency policy, and checking the program of federal internal improvements. He also vindicated federal authority against South Carolina with its doctrine of nullification and against France on the question of debts. The support given his policies by the workingmen of the East as well as by the farmers of the East, West, and South resulted in his triumphant re-election in 1832 over Clay.

After watching the inauguration of his hand-picked successor, Martin Van Buren, Jackson retired to the Hermitage, where he maintained a lively interest in national affairs until his death on June 8, 1845.

MARTIN VAN BUREN was born on Dec. 5, 1782, at Kinderhook, N.Y. After graduating from the village school, he became a law clerk, entered practice in 1803, and soon became active in state politics as state senator and attorney general. In 1820, he was elected to the United States Senate. He threw the support of his efficient political organization, known as the Albany Regency, to William H. Crawford in 1824 and to Jackson in 1828. After leading the opposition to Adams's administration in the Senate, he served briefly as governor of New York (1828–29) and resigned to become Jackson's Secretary of State. He was soon on close personal terms with Jackson and played an important part in the Jacksonian program.

In 1832, Van Buren became vice president; in 1836, President. The Panic of 1837 overshadowed his term. He attributed it to the overexpansion of the credit and favored the establishment of an independent treasury as repository for the federal funds. In 1840, he established a 10-hour day on public works. Defeated by Harrison in 1840, he was the leading contender for the Democratic nomination in 1844 until he publicly opposed immediate annexation of Texas, and was subsequently beaten by the Southern delegations at the Baltimore convention. This incident increased his growing misgivings about the slave power.

After working behind the scenes among the antislavery Democrats, Van Buren joined in the movement that led to the Free-Soil Party and became its candidate for President in 1848. He subsequently returned to the Democratic Party while continuing to object to its pro-Southern policy. He died in

Kinderhook on July 24, 1862. His *Autobiography* throws valuable sidelights on the political history of the times.

His wife, Hannah Hoes, whom he married in 1807, died in 1819.

WILLIAM HENRY HARRISON was born in Charles City County, Va., on Feb. 9, 1773. Joining the army in 1791, he was active in Indian fighting in the Northwest, became secretary of the Northwest Territory in 1798 and governor of Indiana in 1800. He married Anna Symmes in 1795. Growing discontent over white encroachments on Indian lands led to the formation of an Indian alliance under Tecumseh to resist further aggressions. In 1811, Harrison won a nominal victory over the Indians at Tippecanoe and in 1813 a more decisive one at the Battle of the Thames, where Tecumseh was killed.

After resigning from the army in 1814, Harrison had an obscure career in politics and diplomacy, ending up 20 years later as a county recorder in Ohio. Nominated for President in 1835 as a military hero whom the conservative politicians hoped to be able to control, he ran surprisingly well against Van Buren in 1836. Four years later, he defeated Van Buren but caught pneumonia and died in Washington on April 4, 1841, a month after his inauguration. Harrison was the first president to die in office.

JOHN TYLER was born in Charles City County, Va., on March 29, 1790. A William and Mary graduate, he entered law practice and politics, serving in the House of Representatives (1817–21), as governor of Virginia (1825–27), and as senator (1827–36). A strict constructionist, he supported Crawford in 1824 and Jackson in 1828, but broke with Jackson over his United States Bank policy and became a member of the Southern state-rights group that cooperated with the Whigs. In 1836, he resigned from the Senate rather than follow instructions from the Virginia legislature to vote for a resolution expunging censure of Jackson from the Senate record.

Elected vice president on the Whig ticket in 1840, Tyler succeeded to the presidency on Harrison's death. His strict-constructionist views soon caused a split with the Henry Clay wing of the Whig party and a stalemate on domestic questions. Tyler's more considerable achievements were his support of the Webster-Ashburton Treaty with Britain and his success in bringing about the annexation of Texas.

After his presidency he lived in retirement in Virginia until the outbreak of the Civil War, when he emerged briefly as chairman of a peace convention and then as delegate to the provisional Congress of the Confederacy. He died on Jan. 18, 1862. He married Letitia Christian in 1813 and, two years after her death in 1842, Julia Gardiner.

JAMES KNOX POLK was born in Mecklenburg County, N.C., on Nov. 2, 1795. A graduate of the University of North Carolina, he moved west to Tennessee, was admitted to the bar, and soon became prominent in state politics. In 1825, he was elected to the House of Representatives, where he opposed Adams and, after 1829, became Jackson's floor leader in the fight against the Bank. In 1835, he became Speaker of the House. Four years later, he was elected governor of Tennessee, but was beaten in tries for re-election in 1841 and 1843.

The supporters of Van Buren for the Democratic

nomination in 1844 counted on Polk as his running mate; but, when Van Buren's stand on Texas alienated Southern support, the convention swung to Polk on the ninth ballot. He was elected over Henry Clay, the Whig candidate. Rapidly disillusioning those who thought that he would not run his own administration, Polk proceeded steadily and precisely to achieve four major objectives—the acquisition of California, the settlement of the Oregon question, the reduction of the tariff, and the establishment of the independent treasury. He also enlarged the Monroe Doctrine to exclude all non-American intervention in American affairs, whether forcible or not, and he forced Mexico into a war that he waged to a successful conclusion.

His wife, Sarah Childress, whom he married in 1824, was a woman of charm and ability. Polk died in Nashville, Tenn., on June 15, 1849.

ZACHARY TAYLOR was born at Montebello, Orange County, Va., on Nov. 24, 1784. Embarking on a military career in 1808, Taylor fought in the War of 1812, the Black Hawk War, and the Seminole War, meanwhile holding garrison jobs on the frontier or desk jobs in Washington. A brigadier general as a result of his victory over the Seminoles at Lake Okeechobee (1837), Taylor held a succession of Southwestern commands and in 1846 established a base on the Rio Grande, where his forces engaged in hostilities that precipitated the war with Mexico. He captured Monterrey in September 1846 and, disregarding Polk's orders to stay on the defensive, defeated Santa Anna at Buena Vista in February 1847, ending the war in the northern provinces.

Though Taylor had never cast a vote for president, his party affiliations were Whiggish and his availability was increased by his difficulties with Polk. He was elected president over the Democrat Lewis Cass. During the revival of the slavery controversy, which was to result in the Compromise of 1850, Taylor began to take an increasingly firm stand against appeasing the South; but he died in Washington on July 9, 1850, during the fight over the Compromise. He married Margaret Mackall Smith in 1810. His bluff and simple soldierly qualities won him the name Old Rough and Ready.

MILLARD FILLMORE was born at Locke, Cayuga County, N.Y., on Jan. 7, 1800. A lawyer, he entered politics with the Anti-Masonic Party under the sponsorship of Thurlow Weed, editor and party boss, and subsequently followed Weed into the Whig Party. He served in the House of Representatives (1833–35 and 1837–43) and played a leading role in writing the tariff of 1842. Defeated for governor of New York in 1844, he became State comptroller in 1848, was put on the Whig ticket with Taylor as a concession to the Clay wing of the party, and became president upon Taylor's death in 1850.

As president, Fillmore broke with Weed and William H. Seward and associated himself with the pro-Southern Whigs, supporting the Compromise of 1850. Defeated for the Whig nomination in 1852, he ran for president in 1856 as candidate of the American, or Know-Nothing Party, which sought to unite the country against foreigners in the alleged hope of diverting it from the explosive slavery issue. Fillmore opposed Lincoln during the Civil War. He died in Buffalo on March 8, 1874.

He was married in 1826 to Abigail Powers, who died in 1853, and in 1858 to Caroline Carmichael McIntosh.

FRANKLIN PIERCE was born at Hillsboro, N.H., on Nov. 23, 1804. A Bowdoin graduate, lawyer, and Jacksonian Democrat, he won rapid political advancement in the party, in part because of the prestige of his father, Gov. Benjamin Pierce. By 1831 he was Speaker of the New Hampshire House of Representatives; from 1833 to 1837, he served in the federal House and from 1837 to 1842 in the Senate. His wife, Jane Means Appleton, whom he married in 1834, disliked Washington and the somewhat dissipated life led by Pierce; in 1842 Pierce resigned from the Senate and began a successful law practice in Concord, N.H. During the Mexican War, he was a brigadier general.

Thereafter Pierce continued to oppose antislavery tendencies within the Democratic Party. As a result, he was the Southern choice to break the deadlock at the Democratic convention of 1852 and was nominated on the 49th ballot. In the election, Pierce overwhelmed Gen. Winfield Scott, the Whig candidate.

As president, Pierce followed a course of appeasing the South at home and of playing with schemes of territorial expansion abroad. The failure of his foreign and domestic policies prevented his renomination; and he died in Concord on Oct. 8, 1869, in relative obscurity.

JAMES BUCHANAN was born near Mercersburg, Pa., on April 23, 1791. A Dickinson graduate and a lawyer, he entered Pennsylvania politics as a Federalist. With the disappearance of the Federalist Party, he became a Jacksonian Democrat. He served with ability in the House (1821–31), as minister to St. Petersburg (1832–33), and in the Senate (1834–45), and in 1845 became Polk's Secretary of State. In 1853, Pierce appointed Buchanan minister to Britain, where he participated with other American diplomats in Europe in drafting the expansionist Ostend Manifesto.

He was elected president in 1856, defeating John C. Frémont, the Republican candidate, and former President Millard Fillmore of the American Party. The growing crisis over slavery presented Buchanan with problems he lacked the will to tackle. His appeasement of the South alienated the Stephen Douglas wing of the Democratic Party without reducing Southern militancy on slavery issues. While denying the right of secession, Buchanan also denied that the federal government could do anything about it. He supported the administration during the Civil War and died in Lancaster, Pa., on June 1, 1868.

The only president to remain a bachelor throughout his term, Buchanan used his charming niece, Harriet Lane, as White House hostess.

ABRAHAM LINCOLN was born in Hardin (now Larue) County, Ky., on Feb. 12, 1809. His family moved to Indiana and then to Illinois, and Lincoln gained what education he could along the way. While reading law, he worked in a store, managed a mill, surveyed, and split rails. In 1834, he went to the Illinois legislature as a Whig and became the party's floor leader. For the next 20 years he practiced law in Springfield, except for a single term (1847–49) in Congress, where he denounced the Mexican War. In 1855, he was a candidate for senator and the next year he joined the new Republican Party.

A leading but unsuccessful candidate for the vice-presidential nomination with Frémont, Lincoln gained national attention in 1858 when, as

Republican candidate for senator from Illinois, he engaged in a series of debates with Stephen A. Douglas, the Democratic candidate. He lost the election, but continued to prepare the way for the 1860 Republican convention and was rewarded with the presidential nomination on the third ballot. He won the election over three opponents.

From the start, Lincoln made clear that, unlike Buchanan, he believed the national government had the power to crush the rebellion. Not an abolitionist, he held the slavery issue subordinate to that of preserving the Union, but soon perceived that the war could not be brought to a successful conclusion without freeing the slaves. His administration was hampered by the incompetence of many Union generals, the inexperience of the troops, and the harassing political tactics both of the Republican Radicals, who favored a hard policy toward the South, and the Democratic Copperheads, who desired a negotiated peace. The Gettysburg Address of Nov. 19, 1863, marks the high point in the record of American eloquence. Lincoln's long search for a winning combination finally brought Generals Ulysses S. Grant and William T. Sherman to the top; and their series of victories in 1864 dispelled the mutterings from both Radicals and Peace Democrats that at one time seemed to threaten Lincoln's re-election. He was re-elected in 1864, defeating Gen. George B. McClellan, the Democratic candidate. His inaugural address urged leniency toward the South: "With malice toward none, with charity for all . . . let us strive on to finish the work we are in; to bind up the nation's wounds . . . " This policy aroused growing opposition on the part of the Republican Radicals, but before the matter could be put to the test, Lincoln was shot by the actor John Wilkes Booth at Ford's Theater, Washington, on April 14, 1865. He died the next morning.

Lincoln's marriage to Mary Todd in 1842 was often unhappy and turbulent, in part because of his wife's pronounced instability.

ANDREW JOHNSON was born at Raleigh, N.C., on Dec. 29, 1808. Self-educated, he became a tailor in Greeneville, Tenn., but soon went into politics, where he rose steadily. He served in the House of Representatives (1843–54), as governor of Tennessee (1853–57), and as a senator (1857–62). Politically he was a Jacksonian Democrat and his specialty was the fight for a more equitable land policy. Alone among the Southern Senators, he stood by the Union during the Civil War. In 1862, he became war governor of Tennessee and carried out a thankless and difficult job with great courage. Johnson became Lincoln's running mate in 1864 as a result of an attempt to give the ticket a nonpartisan and nonsectional character. Succeeding to the presidency on Lincoln's death, Johnson sought to carry out Lincoln's policy, but without his political skill. The result was a hopeless conflict with the Radical Republicans who dominated Congress, passed measures over Johnson's vetoes, and attempted to limit the power of the executive concerning appointments and removals. The conflict culminated with Johnson's impeachment for attempting to remove his disloyal Secretary of War in defiance of the Tenure of Office Act which required senatorial concurrence for such dismissals. The opposition failed by one vote to get the two thirds necessary for conviction.

After his presidency, Johnson maintained an interest in politics and in 1875 was again elected to the Senate. He died near Carter Station, Tenn., on July 31, 1875. He married Eliza McCardle in 1827.

ULYSSES SIMPSON GRANT was born (as Hiram Ulysses Grant) at Point Pleasant, Ohio, on April 27, 1822. He graduated from West Point in 1843 and served without particular distinction in the Mexican War. In 1848 he married Julia Dent. He resigned from the army in 1854, after warnings from his commanding officer about his drinking habits, and for the next six years held a wide variety of jobs in the Middle West. With the outbreak of the Civil War, he sought a command and soon, to his surprise, was made a brigadier general. His continuing successes in the western theaters, culminating in the capture of Vicksburg, Miss., in 1863, brought him national fame and soon the command of all the Union armies. Grant's dogged, implacable policy of concentrating on dividing and destroying the Confederate armies brought the war to an end in 1865. The next year, he was made full general.

In 1868, as Republican candidate for president, Grant was elected over the Democrat, Horatio Seymour. From the start, Grant showed his unfitness for the office. His Cabinet was weak, his domestic policy was confused, many of his intimate associates were corrupt. The notable achievement in foreign affairs was the settlement of controversies with Great Britain in the Treaty of London (1871), negotiated by his able Secretary of State, Hamilton Fish.

Running for re-election in 1872, he defeated Horace Greeley, the Democratic and Liberal Republican candidate. The Panic of 1873 graft scandals close to the presidency created difficulties for his second term.

After retiring from office, Grant toured Europe for two years and returned in time to accede to a third-term boom, but was beaten in the convention of 1880. Illness and bad business judgment darkened his last years, but he worked steadily at the *Personal Memoirs*, which were to be so successful when published after his death at Mount McGregor, near Saratoga, N.Y., on July 23, 1885.

RUTHERFORD BIRCHARD HAYES was born in Delaware, Ohio, on Oct. 4, 1822. A graduate of Kenyon College and the Harvard Law School, he practiced law in Lower Sandusky (now Fremont) and then in Cincinnati. In 1852 he married Lucy Webb. A Whig, he joined the Republican party in 1855. During the Civil War he rose to major general. He served in the House of Representatives from 1865 to 1867 and then confirmed a reputation for honesty and efficiency in two terms as Governor of Ohio (1868–72). His election to a third term in 1875 made him the logical candidate for those Republicans who wished to stop James G. Blaine in 1876, and he was nominated.

The result of the election was in doubt for some time and hinged upon disputed returns from South Carolina, Louisiana, Florida, and Oregon. Samuel J. Tilden, the Democrat, had the larger popular vote but was adjudged by the strictly partisan decisions of the Electoral Commission to have one fewer electoral vote, 185 to 184. The national acceptance of this result was due in part to the general understanding that Hayes would pursue a conciliatory policy toward the South. He withdrew the troops from the South, took a conservative position on financial and labor issues, and urged civil service reform.

Hayes served only one term by his own wish and

spent the rest of his life in various humanitarian endeavors. He died in Fremont on Jan. 17, 1893.

JAMES ABRAM GARFIELD, the last president to be born in a log cabin, was born in Cuyahoga County, Ohio, on Nov. 19, 1831. A Williams graduate, he taught school for a time and entered Republican politics in Ohio. In 1858, he married Lucretia Rudolph. During the Civil War, he had a promising career, rising to major general of volunteers; but he resigned in 1863, having been elected to the House of Representatives, where he served until 1880. His oratorical and parliamentary abilities soon made him the leading Republican in the House, though his record was marred by his unorthodox acceptance of a fee in the DeGolyer paving contract case and by suspicions of his complicity in the Crédit Mobilier scandal.

In 1880, Garfield was elected to the Senate, but instead became the presidential candidate on the 36th ballot as a result of a deadlock in the Republican convention. In the election, he defeated Gen. Winfield Scott Hancock, the Democratic candidate. Garfield's administration was barely under way when he was shot by Charles J. Guiteau, a disappointed office seeker, in Washington on July 2, 1881. He died in Elberon, N.J., on Sept. 19.

CHESTER ALAN ARTHUR was born at Fairfield, Vt., on Oct. 5, 1830. A graduate of Union College, he became a successful New York lawyer. In 1859, he married Ellen Herndon. During the Civil War, he held administrative jobs in the Republican state administration and in 1871 was appointed collector of the Port of New York by Grant. This post gave him control over considerable patronage. Though not personally corrupt, Arthur managed his power in the interests of the New York machine so openly that President Hayes in 1877 called for an investigation and the next year Arthur was suspended.

In 1880 Arthur was nominated for vice president in the hope of conciliating the followers of Grant and the powerful New York machine. As president upon Garfield's death, Arthur, stepping out of his familiar role as spoilsman, backed civil service reform, reorganized the Cabinet, and prosecuted political associates accused of post office graft. Losing machine support and failing to gain the reformers, he was not renominated for a full term in 1884. He died in New York City on Nov. 18, 1886.

STEPHEN GROVER CLEVELAND was born at Caldwell, N.J., on March 18, 1837. He was admitted to the bar in Buffalo, N.Y., in 1859 and lived there as a lawyer, with occasional incursions into Democratic politics, for more than 20 years. He did not participate in the Civil War. As mayor of Buffalo in 1881, he carried through a reform program so ably that the Democrats ran him successfully for governor in 1882. In 1884 he won the Democratic nomination for President. The campaign contrasted Cleveland's spotless public career with the uncertain record of James G. Blaine, the Republican candidate, and Cleveland received enough Mugwump (independent Republican) support to win.

As president, Cleveland pushed civil service reform, opposed the pension grab and attacked the high tariff rates. While in the White House, he married Frances Folsom in 1886. Renominated in 1888, Cleveland was defeated by Benjamin Harrison, polling more popular but fewer electoral votes.

In 1892, he was elected over Harrison. When the Panic of 1893 burst upon the country, Cleveland's attempts to solve it by sound-money measures alienated the free-silver wing of the party, while his tariff policy alienated the protectionists. In 1894, he sent troops to break the Pullman strike. In foreign affairs, his firmness caused Great Britain to back down in the Venezuela border dispute.

In his last years Cleveland was an active and much-respected public figure. He died in Princeton, N.J., on June 24, 1908.

BENJAMIN HARRISON was born in North Bend, Ohio, on Aug. 20, 1833, the grandson of William Henry Harrison, the ninth president. A graduate of Miami University in Ohio, he took up the law in Indiana and became active in Republican politics. In 1853, he married Caroline Lavinia Scott. During the Civil War, he rose to brigadier general. A sound-money Republican, he was elected senator from Indiana in 1880. In 1888, he received the Republican nomination for President on the eighth ballot. Though behind on the popular vote, he won over Grover Cleveland in the electoral college by 233 to 168.

As President, Harrison failed to please either the bosses or the reform element in the party. In foreign affairs he backed Secretary of State Blaine, whose policy foreshadowed later American imperialism. Harrison was renominated in 1892 but lost to Cleveland. His wife died in the White House in 1892 and Harrison married her niece, Mary Scott (Lord) Dimmick, in 1896. After his presidency, he resumed law practice. He died in Indianapolis on March 13, 1901.

WILLIAM McKINLEY was born in Niles, Ohio, on Jan. 29, 1843. He taught school, then served in the Civil War, rising from the ranks to become a major. Subsequently he opened a law office in Canton, Ohio, and in 1871 married Ida Saxton. Elected to Congress in 1876, he served there until 1891, except for 1883–85. His faithful advocacy of business interests culminated in the passage of the highly protective McKinley Tariff of 1890. With the support of Mark Hanna, a shrewd Cleveland businessman interested in safeguarding tariff protection, McKinley became governor of Ohio in 1892 and Republican presidential candidate in 1896. The business community, alarmed by the progressivism of William Jennings Bryan, the Democratic candidate, spent considerable money to assure McKinley's victory.

The chief event of McKinley's administration was the war with Spain, which resulted in our acquisition of the Philippines and other islands. With imperialism an issue, McKinley defeated Bryan again in 1900. On Sept. 6, 1901, he was shot at Buffalo, N.Y., by Leon F. Czolgosz, an anarchist, and he died there eight days later.

THEODORE ROOSEVELT was born in New York City on Oct. 27, 1858. A Harvard graduate, he was early interested in ranching, in politics, and in writing picturesque historical narratives. He was a Republican member of the New York Assembly in 1882–84, an unsuccessful candidate for mayor of New York in 1886, a U.S. Civil Service Commissioner under Benjamin Harrison, Police Commissioner of New York City in 1895, and Assistant Secretary of the Navy under McKinley in 1897. He resigned in 1898 to help organize a volunteer regiment, the Rough Riders, and take a more direct part in the war with Spain. He was elected governor of New York in 1898 and vice president in 1900, in spite of lack of enthusiasm on the part of the bosses.

Assuming the presidency of the assassinated McKinley in 1901, Roosevelt embarked on a wide-ranging program of government reform and conservation of natural resources. He ordered antitrust suits against several large corporations, threatened to intervene in the anthracite coal strike of 1902, which prompted the operators to accept arbitration, and, in general, championed the rights of the "little man" and fought the "malefactors of great wealth." He was also responsible for such progressive legislation as the Elkins Act of 1901, which outlawed freight rebates by railroads; the bill establishing the Department of Commerce and Labor; the Hepburn Act, which gave the I.C.C. greater control over the railroads; the Meat Inspection Act; and the Pure Food and Drug Act.

In foreign affairs, Roosevelt pursued a strong policy, permitting the instigation of a revolt in Panama to dispose of Colombian objections to the Panama Canal and helping to maintain the balance of power in the East by bringing the Russo-Japanese War to an end, for which he won the Nobel Peace Prize, the first American to achieve a Nobel prize in any category. In 1904, he decisively defeated Alton B. Parker, his conservative Democratic opponent.

Roosevelt's increasing coldness toward his successor, William Howard Taft, led him to overlook his earlier disclaimer of third-term ambitions and to re-enter politics. Defeated by the machine in the Republican convention of 1912, he organized the Progressive Party (Bull Moose) and polled more votes than Taft, though the split brought about the election of Woodrow Wilson. From 1915 on, Roosevelt strongly favored intervention in the European war. He became deeply embittered at Wilson's refusal to allow him to raise a volunteer division. He died in Oyster Bay, N.Y., on Jan. 6, 1919. He was married twice: in 1880 to Alice Hathaway Lee, who died in 1884, and in 1886 to Edith Kermit Carow.

WILLIAM HOWARD TAFT was born in Cincinnati on Sept. 15, 1857. A Yale graduate, he entered Ohio Republican politics in the 1880s. In 1886 he married Helen Herron. From 1887 to 1890, he served on the Ohio Superior Court; 1890–92, as solicitor general of the United States; 1892–1900, on the federal circuit court. In 1900 McKinley appointed him president of the Philippine Commission and in 1901 governor general. Taft had great success in pacifying the Filipinos, solving the problem of the church lands, improving economic conditions, and establishing limited self-government. His period as Secretary of War (1904–08) further demonstrated his capacity as administrator and conciliator, and he was Roosevelt's hand-picked successor in 1908. In the election, he polled 321 electoral votes to 162 for William Jennings Bryan, who was running for the presidency for the third time.

Though he carried on many of Roosevelt's policies, Taft got into increasing trouble with the progressive wing of the party and displayed mounting irritability and indecision. After his defeat in 1912, he became professor of constitutional law at Yale. In 1921 he was appointed Chief Justice

of the United States. He died in Washington on March 8, 1930.

THOMAS WOODROW WILSON was born in Staunton, Va., on Dec. 28, 1856. A Princeton graduate, he turned from law practice to post-graduate work in political science at Johns Hopkins University, receiving his Ph.D. in 1886. He taught at Bryn Mawr, Wesleyan, and Princeton, and in 1902 was made president of Princeton. After an unsuccessful attempt to democratize the social life of the university, he welcomed an invitation in 1910 to be the Democratic gubernatorial candidate in New Jersey, and was elected. His success in fighting the machine and putting through a reform program attracted national attention.

In 1912, at the Democratic convention in Baltimore, Wilson won the nomination on the 46th ballot and went on to defeat Roosevelt and Taft in the election. Wilson proceeded under the standard of the New Freedom to enact a program of domestic reform, including the Federal Reserve Act, the Clayton Antitrust Act, the establishment of the Federal Trade Commission, and other measures designed to restore competition in the face of the great monopolies. In foreign affairs, while privately sympathetic with the Allies, he strove to maintain neutrality in the European war and warned both sides against encroachments on American interests.

Re-elected in 1916 as a peace candidate, he tried to mediate between the warring nations; but when the Germans resumed unrestricted submarine warfare in 1917, Wilson brought the United States into what he now believed was a war to make the world safe for democracy. He supplied the classic formulations of Allied war aims and the armistice of Nov. 11, 1918 was negotiated on the basis of Wilson's Fourteen Points. In 1919 he strove at Versailles to lay the foundations for enduring peace. He accepted the imperfections of the Versailles Treaty in the expectation that they could be remedied by action within the League of Nations. He probably could have secured ratification of the treaty by the Senate if he had adopted a more conciliatory attitude toward the mild reservationists; but his insistence on all or nothing eventually caused the diehard isolationists and diehard Wilsonites to unite in rejecting a compromise.

In September 1919 Wilson suffered a paralytic stroke that limited his activity. After leaving the presidency he lived on in retirement in Washington, dying on Feb. 3, 1924. He was married twice—in 1885 to Ellen Louise Axson, who died in 1914, and in 1915 to Edith Bolling Galt.

WARREN GAMALIEL HARDING was born in Morrow County, Ohio, on Nov. 2, 1865. After attending Ohio Central College, Harding became interested in journalism and in 1884 bought the *Marion* (Ohio) *Star.* In 1891 he married a wealthy widow, Florence Kling De Wolfe. As his paper prospered, he entered Republican politics, serving as state senator (1899–1903) and as lieutenant governor (1904–06). In 1910, he was defeated for governor, but in 1914 was elected to the Senate. His reputation as an orator made him the keynoter at the 1916 Republican convention.

When the 1920 convention was deadlocked between Leonard Wood and Frank O. Lowden, Harding became the dark-horse nominee on his solemn affirmation that there was no reason in his past that he should not be. Straddling the League question, Harding was easily elected over James M. Cox, his Democratic opponent. His Cabinet contained some able men, but also some manifestly unfit for public office. Harding's own intimates were mediocre when they were not corrupt. The impending disclosure of the Teapot Dome scandal in the Interior Department and illegal practices in the Justice Department and Veterans' Bureau, as well as political setbacks, profoundly worried him. On his return from Alaska in 1923, he died unexpectedly in San Francisco on Aug. 2.

JOHN CALVIN COOLIDGE was born in Plymouth, Vt., on July 4, 1872. An Amherst graduate, he went into law practice at Northampton, Mass., in 1897. He married Grace Anna Goodhue in 1905. He entered Republican state politics, becoming successively mayor of Northampton, state senator, lieutenant governor and, in 1919, governor. His use of the state militia to end the Boston police strike in 1919 won him a somewhat undeserved reputation for decisive action and brought him the Republican vice-presidential nomination in 1920. After Harding's death Coolidge handled the Washington scandals with care and finally managed to save the Republican Party from public blame for the widespread corruption.

In 1924, Coolidge was elected without difficulty, defeating the Democrat, John W. Davis, and Robert M. La Follette running on the Progressive ticket. His second term, like his first, was characterized by a general satisfaction with the existing economic order. He stated that he did not choose to run in 1928.

After his presidency, Coolidge lived quietly in Northampton, writing an unilluminating *Autobiography* and conducting a syndicated column. He died there on Jan. 5, 1933.

HERBERT CLARK HOOVER was born at West Branch, Iowa, on Aug. 10, 1874, the first president to be born west of the Mississippi. A Stanford graduate, he worked from 1895 to 1913 as a mining engineer and consultant throughout the world. In 1899, he married Lou Henry. During World War I, he served with distinction as chairman of the American Relief Committee in London, as chairman of the Commission for Relief in Belgium, and as U.S. Food Administrator. His political affiliations were still too indeterminate for him to be mentioned as a possibility for either the Republican or Democratic nomination in 1920, but after the election he served Harding and Coolidge as Secretary of Commerce.

In the election of 1928, Hoover overwhelmed Gov. Alfred E. Smith of New York, the Democratic candidate and the first Roman Catholic to run for the presidency. He soon faced the worst depression in the nation's history, but his attacks upon it were hampered by his devotion to the theory that the forces that brought the crisis would soon bring the revival and then by his belief that there were too many areas in which the federal government had no power to act. In a succession of vetoes, he struck down measures proposing a national employment system and a national relief, he reduced income tax rates, and only at the end of his term did he yield to popular pressure and set up agencies such as the Reconstruction Finance Corporation to make emergency loans to assist business.

After his 1932 defeat, Hoover returned to pri-

vate business. In 1946, President Truman charged him with various world food missions; and from 1947 to 1949 and 1953 to 1955, he was head of the Commission on Organization of the Executive Branch of the Government. He died in New York City on Oct. 20, 1964.

FRANKLIN DELANO ROOSEVELT was born in Hyde Park, N.Y., on Jan. 30, 1882. A Harvard graduate, he attended Columbia Law School and was admitted to the New York bar. In 1910, he was elected to the New York State Senate as a Democrat. Re-elected in 1912, he was appointed Assistant Secretary of the Navy by Woodrow Wilson the next year. In 1920, his radiant personality and his war service resulted in his nomination for vice president as James M. Cox's running mate. After his defeat, he returned to law practice in New York. In August 1921, Roosevelt was stricken with infantile paralysis while on vacation at Campobello, New Brunswick. After a long and gallant fight, he recovered partial use of his legs. In 1924 and 1928, he led the fight at the Democratic national conventions for the nomination of Gov. Alfred E. Smith of New York, and in 1928 Roosevelt was himself induced to run for governor of New York. He was elected, and was re-elected in 1930.

In 1932, Roosevelt received the Democratic nomination for president and immediately launched a campaign that brought new spirit to a weary and discouraged nation. He defeated Hoover by a wide margin. His first term was characterized by an unfolding of the New Deal program, with greater benefits for labor, the farmers, and the unemployed, and the progressive estrangement of most of the business community.

At an early stage, Roosevelt became aware of the menace to world peace posed by totalitarian fascism, and from 1937 on he tried to focus public attention on the trend of events in Europe and Asia. As a result, he was widely denounced as a warmonger. He was re-elected in 1936 over Gov. Alfred M. Landon of Kansas by the overwhelming electoral margin of 523 to 8, and the gathering international crisis prompted him to run for an unprecedented third term in 1940. He defeated Wendell L. Willkie.

Roosevelt's program to bring maximum aid to Britain and, after June 1941, to Russia was opposed, until the Japanese attack on Pearl Harbor restored national unity. During the war, Roosevelt shelved the New Deal in the interests of conciliating the business community, both in order to get full production during the war and to prepare the way for a united acceptance of the peace settlements after the war. A series of conferences with Winston Churchill and Joseph Stalin laid down the bases for the postwar world. In 1944 he was elected to a fourth term, running against Gov. Thomas E. Dewey of New York.

On April 12, 1945, Roosevelt died of a cerebral hemorrhage at Warm Springs, Ga., shortly after his return from the Yalta Conference. His wife, Anna Eleanor Roosevelt, whom he married in 1905, was a woman of great ability who made significant contributions to her husband's policies.

HARRY S. TRUMAN was born on a farm near Lamar, Mo., on May 8, 1884. During World War I, he served in France as a captain with the 129th Field Artillery. He married Bess Wallace in 1919. After engaging briefly and unsuccessfully in the haberdashery business in Kansas City, Mo., Truman entered local politics. Under the sponsorship of Thomas Pendergast, Democratic boss of Missouri, he held a number of local offices, preserving his personal honesty in the midst of a notoriously corrupt political machine. In 1934, he was elected to the Senate and was re-elected in 1940. During his first term he was a loyal but quiet supporter of the New Deal, but in his second term, an appointment as head of a Senate committee to investigate war production brought out his special qualities of honesty, common sense, and hard work, and he won widespread respect.

Elected vice president in 1944, Truman became president upon Roosevelt's sudden death in April 1945 and was immediately faced with the problems of winding down the war against the Axis and preparing the nation for postwar adjustment.

The years 1947–48 were distinguished by civil-rights proposals, the Truman Doctrine to contain the spread of Communism, and the Marshall Plan to aid in the economic reconstruction of war-ravaged nations. Truman's general record, highlighted by a vigorous Fair Deal campaign, brought about his unexpected election in 1948 over the heavily favored Thomas E. Dewey.

Truman's second term was primarily concerned with the Cold War with the Soviet Union, the implementing of the North Atlantic Pact, the United Nations police action in Korea, and the vast rearmament program with its accompanying problems of economic stabilization.

On March 29, 1952, Truman announced that he would not run again for the presidency. After leaving the White House, he returned to his home in Independence, Mo., to write his memoirs. He further busied himself with the Harry S. Truman Library there. He died in Kansas City, Mo., on Dec. 26, 1972.

DWIGHT DAVID EISENHOWER was born in Denison, Tex., on Oct. 14, 1890. His ancestors lived in Germany and emigrated to America, settling in Pennsylvania, early in the 18th century. His father, David, had a general store in Hope, Kan., which failed. After a brief time in Texas, the family moved to Abilene, Kan.

After graduating from Abilene High School in 1909, Eisenhower did odd jobs for almost two years. He won an appointment to the Naval Academy at Annapolis, but was too old for admittance. Then he received an appointment in 1910 to West Point, from which he graduated as a second lieutenant in 1915.

He did not see service in World War I, having been stationed at Fort Sam Houston, Tex. There he met Mamie Geneva Doud, whom he married in Denver on July 1, 1916, and by whom he had two sons: Doud Dwight (died in infancy) and John Sheldon Doud.

Eisenhower served in the Philippines from 1935 to 1939 with Gen. Douglas MacArthur. Afterward, Gen. George C. Marshall, the Army Chief of Staff, brought him into the War Department's General Staff and in 1942 placed him in command of the invasion of North Africa. In 1944, he was made Supreme Allied Commander for the invasion of Europe.

After the war, Eisenhower served as Army Chief of Staff from November 1945 until February 1948, when he was appointed president of Columbia University.

In December 1950, President Truman recalled Eisenhower to active duty to command the North Atlantic Treaty Organization forces in Europe. He held this post until the end of May 1952.

At the Republican convention of 1952 in Chicago, Eisenhower won the presidential nomination on the first ballot in a close race with Senator Robert A. Taft of Ohio. In the election, he defeated Gov. Adlai E. Stevenson of Illinois.

Through two terms, Eisenhower hewed to moderate domestic policies. He sought peace through Free World strength in an era of new nationalisms, nuclear missiles, and space exploration. He fostered alliances pledging the United States to resist Red aggression in Europe, Asia, and Latin America. The Eisenhower Doctrine of 1957 extended commitments to the Middle East.

At home, the popular president lacked Republican Congressional majorities after 1954, but he was re-elected in 1956 by 457 electoral votes to 73 for Stevenson.

While retaining most Fair Deal programs, he stressed "fiscal responsibility" in domestic affairs. A moderate in civil rights, he sent troops to Little Rock, Ark., to enforce court-ordered school integration.

With his wartime rank restored by Congress, Eisenhower returned to private life and the role of elder statesman, with his vigor hardly impaired by a heart attack, an ileitis operation, and a mild stroke suffered while in office. He died in Washington on March 28, 1969.

JOHN FITZGERALD KENNEDY was born in Brookline, Mass., on May 29, 1917. His father, Joseph P. Kennedy, was Ambassador to Great Britain from 1937 to 1940.

Kennedy was graduated from Harvard University in 1940 and joined the Navy the next year. He became skipper of a PT boat that was sunk in the Pacific by a Japanese destroyer. Although given up for lost, he swam to a safe island, towing an injured enlisted man.

After recovering from a war-aggravated spinal injury, Kennedy entered politics in 1946 and was elected to Congress. In 1952, he ran against Senator Henry Cabot Lodge, Jr., of Massachusetts, and won.

Kennedy was married on Sept. 12, 1953, to Jacqueline Lee Bouvier, by whom he had three children: Caroline, John Fitzgerald, Jr., and Patrick Bouvier (died in infancy).

In 1957 Kennedy won the Pulitzer Prize for a book he had written earlier, *Profiles in Courage*.

After strenuous primary battles, Kennedy won the Democratic presidential nomination on the first ballot at the 1960 Los Angeles convention. With a plurality of only 118,574 votes, he carried the election over Vice President Richard M. Nixon and became the first Roman Catholic president.

Kennedy brought to the White House the dynamic idea of a "New Frontier" approach in dealing with problems at home, abroad, and in the dimensions of space. Out of his leadership in his first few months in office came the 10-year Alliance for Progress to aid Latin America, the Peace Corps, and accelerated programs that brought the first Americans into orbit in the race in space.

Failure of the U.S.-supported Cuban invasion in April 1961 led to the entrenchment of the Communist-backed Castro regime, only 90 miles from United States soil. When it became known that Soviet offensive missiles were being installed in Cuba in 1962, Kennedy ordered a naval "quarantine" of the island and moved troops into position to eliminate this threat to U.S. security. The world seemed on the brink of a nuclear war until Soviet Premier Khrushchev ordered the removal of the missiles.

A sudden "thaw," or the appearance of one, in the cold war came with the agreement with the Soviet Union on a limited test-ban treaty signed in Moscow on Aug. 6, 1963.

In his domestic policies, Kennedy's proposals for medical care for the aged, expanded area redevelopment, and aid to education were defeated, but on minimum wage, trade legislation, and other measures he won important victories.

Widespread racial disorders and demonstrations led to Kennedy's proposing sweeping civil rights legislation. As his third year in office drew to a close, he also recommended an $11-billion tax cut to bolster the economy. Both measures were pending in Congress when Kennedy, looking forward to a second term, journeyed to Texas for a series of speeches.

While riding in a procession in Dallas on Nov. 22, 1963, he was shot to death by an assassin firing from an upper floor of a building. The alleged assassin, Lee Harvey Oswald, was killed two days later in the Dallas city jail by Jack Ruby, owner of a strip-tease place.

At 46 years of age, Kennedy became the fourth president to be assassinated and the eighth to die in office.

LYNDON BAINES JOHNSON was born in Stonewall, Tex., on Aug. 27, 1908. On both sides of his family he had a political heritage mingled with a Baptist background of preachers and teachers. Both his father and his paternal grandfather served in the Texas House of Representatives.

After his graduation from Southwest Texas State Teachers College, Johnson taught school for two years. He went to Washington in 1932 as secretary to Rep. Richard M. Kleberg. During this time, he married Claudia Alta Taylor, known as "Lady Bird." They had two children: Lynda Bird (Robb) and Luci Baines (Nugent).

In 1935, Johnson became Texas administrator for the National Youth Administration. Two years later, he was elected to Congress as an all-out supporter of Franklin D. Roosevelt, and served until 1949. He was the first member of Congress to enlist in the armed forces after the attack on Pearl Harbor. He served in the Navy in the Pacific and won a Silver Star.

Johnson was elected to the Senate in 1948 after he had captured the Democratic nomination by only 87 votes. He was 40 years old. He became the Senate Democratic leader in 1953. A heart attack in 1955 threatened to end his political career, but he recovered fully and resumed his duties.

At the height of his power as Senate leader, Johnson sought the Democratic nomination for president in 1960. When he lost to John F. Kennedy, he surprised even some of his closest associates by accepting second place on the ticket.

Johnson was riding in another car in the motorcade when Kennedy was assassinated in Dallas on Nov. 22, 1963. He took the oath of office in the presidential jet on the Dallas airfield.

With Johnson's insistent backing, Congress finally adopted a far-reaching civil-rights bill, a voting-rights bill, a Medicare program for the aged, and measures to improve education and conservation. Congress also began what Johnson described as "an all-out war" on poverty.

Amassing a record-breaking majority of nearly 16 million votes, Johnson was elected president in his own right in 1964, defeating Senator Barry Goldwater of Arizona.

The double tragedy of a war in Southeast Asia and urban riots at home marked Johnson's last two years in office. Faced with disunity in the nation and challenges within his own party, Johnson surprised the country on March 31, 1968, with the announcement that he would not be a candidate for re-election. He died of a heart attack suffered at his LBJ Ranch on Jan. 22, 1973.

RICHARD MILHOUS NIXON was born in Yorba Linda, Calif., on Jan. 9, 1913, to Midwestern-bred parents, Francis A. and Hannah Milhous Nixon, who raised their five sons as Quakers.

Nixon was a high school debater and was undergraduate president at Whittier College in California, where he was graduated in 1934. As a scholarship student at Duke University Law School in North Carolina, he graduated third in his class in 1937.

After five years as a lawyer, Nixon joined the Navy in August 1942. He was an air transport officer in the South Pacific and a legal officer stateside before his discharge in 1946 as a lieutenant commander.

Running for Congress in California as a Republican in 1946, Nixon defeated Rep. Jerry Voorhis. As a member of the House Un-American Activities Committee, he made a name as an investigator of Alger Hiss, a former high State Department official, who was later jailed for perjury. In 1950, Nixon defeated Rep. Helen Gahagan Douglas, a Democrat, for the Senate. He was criticized for portraying her as a Communist dupe.

Nixon's anti-Communism, his Western base, and his youth figured in his selection in 1952 to run for vice president on the ticket headed by Dwight D. Eisenhower. Demands for Nixon's withdrawal followed disclosure that California businessmen had paid some of his Senate office expenses. He televised rebuttal, known as "the Checkers speech" (named for a cocker spaniel given to the Nixons), brought him support from the public and from Eisenhower. The ticket won easily in 1952 and again in 1956.

Eisenhower gave Nixon substantive assignments, including missions to 56 countries. In Moscow in 1959, Nixon won acclaim for his defense of U.S. interests in an impromptu "kitchen debate" with Soviet Premier Nikita S. Khrushchev.

Nixon lost the 1960 race for the presidency to John F. Kennedy.

In 1962, Nixon failed in a bid for California's governorship and seemed to be finished as a national candidate. He became a Wall Street lawyer, but kept his old party ties and developed new ones through constant travels to speak for Republicans.

Nixon won the 1968 Republican presidential nomination after a shrewd primary campaign, then made Gov. Spiro T. Agnew of Maryland his surprise choice for vice president. In the election, they edged out the Democratic ticket headed by Vice President Hubert H. Humphrey by 510,314 votes out of 73,212,065 cast.

Committed to wind down the U.S. role in the Vietnamese War, Nixon pursued "Vietnamization" —training and equipping South Vietnamese to do their own fighting. American ground combat forces in Vietnam fell steadily from 540,000 when Nixon took office to none in 1973 when the military draft was ended. But there was heavy continuing use of U.S. air power.

Nixon improved relations with Moscow and reopened the long-closed door to mainland China with a good-will trip there in February 1972. In May of that year, he visited Moscow and signed agreements on arms limitation and trade expansion and approved plans for a joint U.S.-Soviet space mission in 1975.

Inflation was a campaign issue for Nixon, but he failed to master it as president. On Aug. 15, 1971, with unemployment edging up, Nixon abruptly announced a new economic policy: a 90-day wage-price freeze, stimulative tax cuts, a temporary 10% tariff, and spending cuts. A second phase, imposing guidelines on wage, price and rent boosts, was announced October 7.

The economy responded in time for the 1972 campaign, in which Nixon played up his foreign-policy achievements. Played down was the burglary on June 17, 1972, of Democratic national headquarters in the Watergate apartment complex in Washington. The Nixon-Agnew re-election campaign cost a record $60 million and swamped the Democratic ticket headed by Senator George McGovern of South Dakota with a plurality of 17,-999,528 out of 77,718,554 votes. Only Massachusetts, with 14 electoral votes, and the District of Columbia, with 3, went for McGovern.

In January 1973, hints of a cover-up emerged at the trial of six men found guilty of the Watergate burglary. With a Senate investigation under way, Nixon announced on April 30 the resignations of his top aides, H. R. Haldeman and John D. Ehrlichman, and the dismissal of White House counsel John Dean III. Dean was the star witness at televised Senate hearings that exposed both a White House cover-up of Watergate and massive illegalities in Republican fund-raising in 1972.

The hearings also disclosed that Nixon had routinely tape-recorded his office meetings and telephone conversations.

On Oct. 10, 1973, Agnew resigned as vice president, then pleaded no-contest to a negotiated federal charge of evading income taxes on alleged bribes. Two days later, Nixon nominated the House minority leader, Rep. Gerald R. Ford of Michigan, as the new vice president. Congress confirmed Ford on Dec. 6, 1973.

In June 1974, Nixon visited Israel and four Arab nations. Then he met in Moscow with Soviet leader Leonid I. Brezhnev and reached preliminary nuclear arms limitation agreements.

But, in the month after his return, Watergate ended the Nixon regime. On July 24 the Supreme Court ordered Nixon to surrender subpoenaed tapes. On July 30, the Judiciary Committee referred three impeachment articles to the full membership. On August 5, Nixon bowed to the Supreme Court and released tapes showing he halted an FBI probe of the Watergate burglary six days after it occurred. It was in effect an admission of obstruction of justice, and impeachment appeared inevitable.

Nixon resigned on Aug. 9, 1974, the first president ever to do so. A month later, President Ford issued an unconditional pardon for any offenses Nixon might have committed as president, thus forestalling possible prosecution.

In 1940, Nixon married Thelma Catherine (Pat) Ryan. They had two daughters, Patricia (Tricia) Cox and Julie, who married Dwight David Eisenhower II, grandson of the former president.

GERALD RUDOLPH FORD was born in Omaha, Neb., on July 14, 1913, the only child of Leslie and Dorothy Gardner King. His parents were divorced in 1915. His mother moved to Grand Rapids, Mich., and married Gerald R. Ford. The boy was renamed for his stepfather.

Ford captained his high school football team in Grand Rapids, and a football scholarship took him to the University of Michigan, where he starred as varsity center before his graduation in 1935. A job as assistant football coach at Yale gave him an opportunity to attend Yale Law School, from which he graduated in the top third of his class in 1941.

He returned to Grand Rapids to practice law, but entered the Navy in April 1942. He saw wartime service in the Pacific on the light aircraft carrier *Monterey* and was a lieutenant commander when he returned to Grand Rapids early in 1946 to resume law practice and dabble in politics.

Ford was elected to Congress in 1948 for the first of his 13 terms in the House. He was soon assigned to the influential Appropriations Committee and rose to become the ranking Republican on the subcommittee on Defense Department appropriations and an expert in the field.

As a legislator, Ford described himself as "a moderate on domestic issues, a conservative in fiscal affairs, and a dyed-in-the-wool internationalist." He carried the ball for Pentagon appropriations, was a hawk on the war in Vietnam, and kept a low profile on civil-rights issues.

He was also dependable and hard-working and popular with his colleagues. In 1963, he was elected chairman of the House Republican Conference. He served in 1963–64 as a member of the Warren Commission that investigated the assassination of John F. Kennedy in 1965 made him minority leader.

Ford shelved his hopes for the Speakership on Oct. 12, 1973, when Nixon nominated him to fill the vice presidency left vacant by Agnew's resignation under fire. It was the first use of the procedures for filling vacancies in the vice presidency laid down in the 25th Amendment to the Constitution, which Ford had helped enact.

Congress confirmed Ford as vice president on Dec. 6, 1973. Once in office, he said he did not believe Nixon had been involved in the Watergate scandals, but criticized his stubborn court battle against releasing tape recordings of Watergate-related conversations for use as evidence.

The scandals led to Nixon's unprecedented resignation on Aug. 9, 1974, and Ford was sworn in immediately as the 38th president, the first to enter the White House without winning a national election.

Ford assured the nation when he took office that "our long national nightmare is over" and pledged "openness and candor" in all his actions. He won a warm response from the Democratic 93rd Congress when he said he wanted "a good marriage" rather than a honeymoon with his former colleagues. In December 1974 Congressional majorities backed his choice of former New York Gov. Nelson A. Rockefeller as his successor in the again-vacant vice presidency.

The cordiality was chilled by Ford's announcement on Sept. 8, 1974, that he had granted an unconditional pardon to Nixon for any crimes he might have committed as president. Although no formal charges were pending, Ford said he feared "ugly passions" would be aroused if Nixon were brought to trial. The pardon was widely criticized.

To fight inflation, the new president first proposed fiscal restraints and spending curbs and a 5% tax surcharge that got nowhere in the Senate and House. Congress again rebuffed Ford in the spring of 1975 when he appealed for emergency military aid to help the governments of South Vietnam and Cambodia resist massive Communist offensives.

In November 1974, Ford visited Japan, South Korea, and the Soviet Union, where he and Soviet leader Leonid I. Brezhnev conferred in Vladivostok and reached a tentative agreement to limit the number of strategic offensive nuclear weapons. It was Ford's first meeting as president with Brezhnev, who planned a return visit to Washington in the fall of 1975.

Politically, Ford's fortunes improved steadily in the first half of 1975. Badly divided Democrats in Congress were unable to muster votes to override his vetoes of spending bills that exceeded his budget. He faced some right-wing opposition in his own party, but moved to pre-empt it with an early announcement—on July 8, 1975—of his intention to be a candidate in 1976.

Early state primaries in 1976 suggested an easy victory for Ford despite Ronald Reagan's bitter attacks on administration foreign policy and defense programs. But later Reagan primary successes threatened the President's lead. At the Kansas City convention, Ford was nominated by the narrow margin of 1,187 to 1,070. But Reagan had moved the party to the right, and Ford himself was regarded as a caretaker president lacking in strength and vision. He was defeated in November by Jimmy Carter.

In 1948, Ford married Elizabeth Anne (Betty) Bloomer. They had four children, Michael Gerald, John Gardner, Steven Meigs, and Susan Elizabeth.

JAMES EARL CARTER, JR., was born in the tiny village of Plains, Ga., Oct. 1, 1924, and grew up on the family farm at nearby Archery. Both parents were fifth-generation Georgians. His father, James Earl Carter, was known as a segregationist, but treated his black and white workers equally. Carter's mother, Lillian Gordy, was a matriarchal presence in home and community and opposed the then-prevailing code of racial inequality. The future President was baptized in 1935 in the conservative Southern Baptist Church and spoke often of being a "born again" Christian, although committed to the separation of church and state.

Carter married Rosalynn Smith, a neighbor, in 1946. Their first child, John William, was born a year later in Portsmouth, Va. Their other children are James Earl III, born in Honolulu in 1950; Donnel Jeffrey, born in New London, Conn., in 1952, and Amy Lynn, born in Plains in 1967.

In 1946 Carter was graduated from the U.S. Naval Academy at Annapolis and served in the nuclear-submarine program under Adm. Hyman G. Rickover. In 1954, after his father's death, he resigned from the Navy to take over the family's flourishing warehouse and cotton gin, with several thousand acres for growing seed peanuts.

Carter was elected to the Georgia Senate in 1962. In 1966 he lost the race for Governor, but was elected in 1970. His term brought a state government reorganization, sharply reduced agencies, increased economy and efficiency, and new social programs, all with no general tax increase. In 1972 the peanut farmer-politician set his sights on the Presidency and in 1974 built a base for himself as

he criss-crossed the country as chairman of the Democratic Campaign Committee, appealing for revival and reform. In 1975 his image as a typical Southern white was erased when he won support of most of the old Southern civil-rights coalition after endorsement by Rep. Andrew Young, black Democrat from Atlanta, who had been the closest aide to the Rev. Martin Luther King, Jr. At Carter's 1971 inauguration as Governor he had called for an end to all forms of racial discrimination.

In the 1976 spring primaries, he won 19 out of 31 with a broad appeal to conservatives and liberals, black and white, poor and well-to-do. Throughout his campaigning Carter set forth his policies in his soft Southern voice, and with his electric-blue stare faced down skeptics who joked about "Jimmy Who?" His toothy smile became his trademark. He was nominated on the first roll-call vote of the 1976 Bicentennial Democratic National Convention in New York, and defeated Gerald R. Ford in November. Likewise, in 1980 he was renominated on the first ballot after vanquishing Senator Edward M. Kennedy of Massachusetts in the primaries. At the convention he defeated the Kennedy forces in their attempt to block a party rule that bound a large majority of pledged delegates to vote for Carter. In the election campaign, Carter attacked his rivals, Ronald Reagan and John B. Anderson, independent, with the warning that a Reagan Republican victory would heighten the risk of war and impede civil rights and economic opportunity. In November Carter lost to Reagan, who won 489 Electoral College votes and 51% of the popular tally, to 49 electoral votes and 41% for Carter.

In his one term, Carter fought hard for his programs against resistance from an independent-minded Democratic Congress that frustrated many pet projects although it overrode only two vetoes. Many of his difficulties were traced to his aides' brusqueness in dealing with Capitol Hill and insensitivity to Congressional feelings and tradition. Observers generally viewed public dissatisfaction with the "stagflation" economy as a principal factor in his defeat. Others included his jittery performance in the debate Oct. 28 with Reagan and the final uncertainties in the negotiations for freeing the Iranians' hostages, along with earlier staff problems, friction with Congress, long gasoline lines, and the months-long Iranian crisis, including the abortive sally in April 1980 to free the hostages. The President, however, did deflect criticism resulting from the activities of his brother, Billy. Yet, assessments of his record noted many positive elements. There was, for one thing, peace throughout his term, with no American combat deaths and with a brake on the advocates of force. Regarded as perhaps his greatest personal achievements were the Camp David accords between Israel and Egypt and the resulting treaty—the first between Israel and an Arab neighbor. The treaty with China and the Panama Canal treaties were also major achievements. Carter worked for nuclear-arms control. His concern for international human rights was credited with saving lives and reducing torture, and he supported the British policy that ended internecine warfare in Rhodesia, now Zimbabwe. Domestically, his environmental record was a major accomplishment. His judicial appointments won acclaim; the Southerner who had forsworn racism made 265 choices for the Federal bench that included minority members and women. On energy, he ended by price decontrols the practice of holding U.S. petroleum prices far below world levels. He broke with outmoded liberal ideas to begin the deregulation of airlines, trucks, and banking.

In his final days, the agreement that resulted in freeing the Iranians' hostages was a crowning achievement, although Carter was no longer the President to welcome them on their return. Instead, he traveled to Germany to meet the freed captives as the special envoy of his successor.

—*A.P.R.*

RONALD REAGAN, actor turned politician, New Dealer turned conservative, came to the films and politics from a thoroughly middle-American background—middle class, Middle West, and small town. He was born in Tampico, Ill., Feb. 6, 1911, the second son of John Edward Reagan and Nelle Wilson Reagan, and the family later moved to Dixon, Ill. The father, of Irish descent, was a shop clerk and merchant with Democratic sympathies. It was an impoverished family; Ronald sold homemade popcorn at highschool games and worked as a lifeguard to earn money for his college tuition. When the father got a New Deal WPA job, the future President became an ardent Roosevelt Democrat.

Reagan won his B.A. degree in 1932 from Eureka (Ill.) College, where a photographic memory aided in his studies and in debating and college theatricals. In a Depression year, he was making $100 a week as a sports announcer for radio station WHO in Des Moines, Iowa, from 1932 to 1937. His career as a film and TV actor stretched from 1937 to 1966, and his salary climbed to $3,500 a week. As a World War II captain in an Army film studio, Reagan recoiled from what he saw as the laziness of Civil Service workers and soon moved to the Right. As president of the Screen Actors Guild, he resisted what he considered a Communist plot to subvert the film industry. With advancing age, Reagan was eased out of leading-man roles and became a television spokesman for the General Electric Company at $150,000 a year, giving countless speeches on the "mashed potato" circuit. Eight years later he had become a nationally known conservative commentator and herald of the old-fashioned virtues; he was pro-business to a point where a skittish G.E. tried to cut down on his speaking engagements and he left the company.

With oratorical skill his trademark, Reagan became an active Republican, and in 1964 made a dramatic speech supporting Senator Barry Goldwater, who became the party's Presidential nominee. At the behest of a small group of conservative Southern California businessmen, he ran for Governor with a pledge to cut spending, and was elected by almost a million votes over the political veteran, Democratic Gov. Edmund G. Brown, father of the later Governor. But, bowing to the reality of a depleted state treasury, Reagan sponsored a billion-dollar tax increase, then the largest state tax rise in U.S. history. He later rebated $6 billion in property taxes, although there was a net increase of $15 billion in additional taxes from individuals and businesses in his eight years in office. At the end of his second term in 1974, the state budget had grown by $6 billion.

Thus his public career evinced a shrewd tempering of rightist principles to welfare-state realities. Indeed, his first campaign for Governor saw the start of a gradual move from the hard-line right wing to the ideological center, although Reagan remained friendly with his original conservative supporters.

In 1968 Reagan was nosed out by Richard M. Nixon for the G.O.P. presidential nomination and in 1976 by Gerald Ford. In 1980 Reagan won the nomination after a more aggressively conservative campaign.

In the election battle against Jimmy Carter, Reagan rode a tide of resurgent right-wing sentiment among an electorate battered by the winds of unwanted change, longing for a distant, simpler era. Broadening his appeal by espousing moderate policies, Reagan gained much of his success from crossover votes from disaffected Democrats and blue-collar workers. This was reflected by his winning of Hispanic and blue-collar votes in the California campaigns. In a conciliatory convention speech, he expressed a concern for the poor and urged an end to discrimination against women. His selection of George Bush for Vice President and his overtures to Gerald Ford were viewed as tokens of his outreach to a wider audience, as was his campaign appeal to blacks. In general, the Reagan camp made Carter's record the issue and capitalized on the issues of the economy, energy, and public spending. The candidate fared particularly well in the televised debate with President Carter on Oct. 28.

The incoming Administration immediately set out to "turn the Government around" with a new economic program. In a few months that program had become reality. Despite strenuous opposition in Congress, Reagan triumphed on the major elements of his "supply side" theory to stimulate production and control inflation through tax cuts and sharp reductions in Government spending. Through adroit and daring maneuvering and the exercise of personal charm in television appeals to the public and direct contacts with Congressmen, he won over the converts needed for massive victories. Thus, he achieved the largest budget and tax cuts in recent United States history; many compared the "Reagan revolution" to the early New Deal of Franklin D. Roosevelt. (*See* "Current Events" for details of tax and budget measures.)

The President won high acclaim for his nomination of Sandra Day O'Connor of the Arizona Court of Appeals to be the first woman on the Supreme Court. But the choice encountered some opposition from extreme conservatives over her reported stands on abortion and the equal rights amendment. Critics on the Left questioned her judicial fitness.

Barely three months in office, Reagan was the target of an assassin's bullet. On Monday, March 30, he was shot in the chest by a gunman as he walked to his limousine after addressing a meeting at the Washington Hilton Hotel. James S. Brady, the White House press secretary, and two law officers were also wounded. Surgeons removed a .22-caliber bullet that had penetrated Reagan's left lung three inches. The President made a good recovery, and by April he was meeting key aides and working on a limited schedule. On April 11 he walked out of the hospital.

Reagan is devoted to his wife, Nancy, whom he married after his divorce from the screen actress Jane Wyman. The Reagans spend much time together at the White House and Camp David and at their California home and ranch when Presidential duties permit. Reagan enjoys horseback riding and is a connoisseur of fine wines. The children of the first marriage are Maureen, his daughter by Miss Wyman, and Michael, an adopted son. In the present marriage, the children are Patricia and Ronald.

—*A.P.R.*

Presidents

Name and (party)[1]	Term	State of birth	Born	Died	Religion	Age at inaug.	Age at death
1. Washington (F)[2]	1789–1797	Va.	2/22/1732	12/14/1799	Episcopalian	57	67
2. J. Adams (F)	1797–1801	Mass.	10/30/1735	7/4/1826	Unitarian	61	90
3. Jefferson (DR)	1801–1809	Va.	4/13/1743	7/4/1826	Deist	57	83
4. Madison (DR)	1809–1817	Va.	3/16/1751	6/28/1836	Episcopalian	57	85
5. Monroe (DR)	1817–1825	Va.	4/28/1758	7/4/1831	Episcopalian	58	73
6. J. Q. Adams (DR)	1825–1829	Mass.	7/11/1767	2/23/1848	Unitarian	57	80
7. Jackson (D)	1829–1837	S.C.	3/15/1767	6/8/1845	Presbyterian	61	78
8. Van Buren (D)	1837–1841	N.Y.	12/5/1782	7/24/1862	Reformed Dutch	54	79
9. W. H. Harrison (W)[3]	1841	Va.	2/9/1773	4/4/1841	Episcopalian	68	68
10. Tyler (W)	1841–1845	Va.	3/29/1790	1/18/1862	Episcopalian	51	71
11. Polk (D)	1845–1849	N.C.	11/2/1795	6/15/1849	Methodist	49	53
12. Taylor (W)[3]	1849–1850	Va.	11/24/1784	7/9/1850	Episcopalian	64	65
13. Fillmore (W)	1850–1853	N.Y.	1/7/1800	3/8/1874	Unitarian	50	74
14. Pierce (D)	1853–1857	N.H.	11/23/1804	10/8/1869	Episcopalian	48	64
15. Buchanan (D)	1857–1861	Pa.	4/23/1791	6/1/1868	Presbyterian	65	77
16. Lincoln (R)[4]	1861–1865	Ky.	2/12/1809	4/15/1865	Liberal	52	56
17. A. Johnson (U)[5]	1865–1869	N.C.	12/29/1808	7/31/1875	(6)	56	66
18. Grant (R)	1869–1877	Ohio	4/27/1822	7/23/1885	Methodist	46	63
19. Hayes (R)	1877–1881	Ohio	10/4/1822	1/17/1893	Methodist	54	70
20. Garfield (R)[4]	1881	Ohio	11/19/1831	9/19/1881	Disciples of Christ	49	49
21. Arthur (R)	1881–1885	Vt.	10/5/1830	11/18/1886	Episcopalian	50	56
22. Cleveland (D)	1885–1889	N.J.	3/18/1837	6/24/1908	Presbyterian	47	71
23. B. Harrison (R)	1889–1893	Ohio	8/20/1833	3/13/1901	Presbyterian	55	67
24. Cleveland (D)[7]	1893–1897	—	—	—	—	55	—
25. McKinley (R)[4]	1897–1901	Ohio	1/29/1843	9/14/1901	Methodist	54	58
26. T. Roosevelt (R)	1901–1909	N.Y.	10/27/1858	1/6/1919	Reformed Dutch	42	60
27. Taft (R)	1909–1913	Ohio	9/15/1857	3/8/1930	Unitarian	51	72
28. Wilson (D)	1913–1921	Va.	12/28/1856	2/3/1924	Presbyterian	56	67
29. Harding (R)[3]	1921–1923	Ohio	11/2/1865	8/2/1923	Baptist	55	57
30. Coolidge (R)	1923–1929	Vt.	7/4/1872	1/5/1933	Congregationalist	51	60
31. Hoover (R)	1929–1933	Iowa	8/10/1874	10/20/1964	Quaker	54	90
32. F. D. Roosevelt (D)[3]	1933–1945	N.Y.	1/30/1882	4/12/1945	Episcopalian	51	63
33. Truman (D)	1945–1953	Mo.	5/8/1884	12/26/1972	Baptist	60	88
34. Eisenhower (R)	1953–1961	Tex.	10/14/1890	3/28/1969	Presbyterian	62	78
35. Kennedy (D)[4]	1961–1963	Mass.	5/29/1917	11/22/1963	Roman Catholic	43	46
36. L. B. Johnson (D)	1963–1969	Tex.	8/27/1908	1/22/1973	Disciples of Christ	55	64
37. Nixon (R)[8]	1969–1974	Calif.	1/9/1913	—	Quaker	56	—
38. Ford (R)	1974–1977	Neb.	7/14/1913	—	Episcopalian	61	—
39. Carter (D)	1977–1981	Ga.	10/1/1924	—	Southern Baptist	52	—
40. Reagan (R)	1981–	Ill.	2/6/1911	—	Disciples of Christ	69	—

1. F—Federalist; DR—Democratic-Republican; D—Democratic; W—Whig; R—Republican; U—Union. 2. No party for first election. The party system in the U.S. made its appearance during Washington's first term. 3. Died in office. 4. Assassinated in office. 5. The Republican National Convention of 1864 adopted the name Union Party. It renominated Lincoln for President; for Vice President it nominated Johnson, a War Democrat. Although frequently listed as a Republican Vice President and President, Johnson undoubtedly considered himself strictly a member of the Union Party. When that party broke apart after 1868, he returned to the Democratic Party. 6. Johnson was not a professed church member; however, he admired the Baptist principles of church government. 7. Second nonconsecutive term. 8. Resigned Aug. 9, 1974.

Vice Presidents

Name and (party)[1]	Term	State of birth	Birth and death dates	President served under
1. John Adams (F)[2]	1789–1797	Massachusetts	1735–1826	Washington
2. Thomas Jefferson (DR)	1797–1801	Virginia	1743–1826	J. Adams
3. Aaron Burr (DR)	1801–1805	New Jersey	1756–1836	Jefferson
4. George Clinton (DR)[3]	1805–1812	New York	1739–1812	Jefferson and Madison
5. Elbridge Gerry (DR)[3]	1813–1814	Massachusetts	1744–1814	Madison
6. Daniel D. Tompkins (DR)	1817–1825	New York	1774–1825	Monroe
7. John C. Calhoun[4]	1825–1832	South Carolina	1782–1850	J. Q. Adams and Jackson
8. Martin Van Buren (D)	1833–1837	New York	1782–1862	Jackson
9. Richard M. Johnson (D)	1837–1841	Kentucky	1780–1850	Van Buren
10. John Tyler (W)[5]	1841	Virginia	1790–1862	W. H. Harrison
11. George M. Dallas (D)	1845–1849	Pennsylvania	1792–1864	Polk
12. Millard Fillmore (W)[5]	1849–1850	New York	1800–1874	Taylor
13. William R. King (D)[3]	1853	North Carolina	1786–1853	Pierce
14. John C. Breckinridge (D)	1857–1861	Kentucky	1821–1875	Buchanan

Name and (party)[1]	Term	State of birth	Birth and death dates	President served under
15. Hannibal Hamlin (R)	1861–1865	Maine	1809–1891	Lincoln
16. Andrew Johnson (U)[5]	1865	North Carolina	1808–1875	Lincoln
17. Schuyler Colfax (R)	1869–1873	New York	1823–1885	Grant
18. Henry Wilson (R)[3]	1873–1875	New Hampshire	1812–1875	Grant
19. William A. Wheeler (R)	1877–1881	New York	1819–1887	Hayes
20. Chester A. Arthur(R)[5]	1881	Vermont	1830–1886	Garfield
21. Thomas A. Hendricks (D)[3]	1885	Ohio	1819–1885	Cleveland
22. Levi P. Morton (R)	1889–1893	Vermont	1824–1920	B. Harrison
23. Adlai E. Stevenson (D)	1893–1897	Kentucky	1835–1914	Cleveland
24. Garrett A. Hobart (R)[3]	1897–1899	New Jersey	1844–1899	McKinley
25. Theodore Roosevelt (R)[5]	1901	New York	1858–1919	McKinley
26. Charles W. Fairbanks (R)	1905–1909	Ohio	1852–1918	T. Roosevelt
27. James S. Sherman (R)[3]	1909–1912	New York	1855–1912	Taft
28. Thomas R. Marshall (D)	1913–1921	Indiana	1854–1925	Wilson
29. Calvin Coolidge (R)[5]	1921–1923	Vermont	1872–1933	Harding
30. Charles G. Dawes (R)	1925–1929	Ohio	1865–1951	Coolidge
31. Charles Curtis (R)	1929–1933	Kansas	1860–1936	Hoover
32. John N. Garner (D)	1933–1941	Texas	1868–1967	F. D. Roosevelt
33. Henry A. Wallace (D)	1941–1945	Iowa	1888–1965	F. D. Roosevelt
34. Harry S. Truman (D)[5]	1945	Missouri	1884–1972	F. D. Roosevelt
35. Alben W. Barkley (D)	1949–1953	Kentucky	1877–1956	Truman
36. Richard M. Nixon (R)	1953–1961	California	1913–	Eisenhower
37. Lyndon B. Johnson (D)[5]	1961–1963	Texas	1908–1973	Kennedy
38. Hubert H. Humphrey (D)	1965–1969	South Dakota	1911–1978	Johnson
39. Spiro T. Agnew (R)[6]	1969–1973	Maryland	1918–	Nixon
40. Gerald R. Ford (R)[7]	1973–1974	Nebraska	1913–	Nixon
41. Nelson A. Rockefeller (R)[8]	1974–1977	Maine	1908–1979	Ford
42. Walter F. Mondale (D)	1977–1981	Minnesota	1928–	Carter
43. George Bush (R)	1981–	Massachusetts	1924–	Reagan

1. F—Federalist; DR—Democratic-Republican; D—Democratic; W—Whig; R—Republican; U—Union. 2. No party for first election. The party system in the U.S. made its appearance during Washington's first term as President. 3. Died in office. 4. Democratic-Republican with J. Q. Adams; Democratic with Jackson. Calhoun resigned in 1832 to become a U.S. Senator. 5. Succeeded to presidency on death of President. 6. Resigned Oct. 10, 1973, after pleading no contest to Federal income tax evasion charges. 7. Nominated by Nixon on Oct. 12, 1973, under provisions of 25th Amendment. Confirmed by Congress on Dec. 6, 1973, and was sworn in same day. He became President Aug. 9, 1974, upon Nixon's resignation. 8. Nominated by Ford Aug. 20, 1974; confirmed by Congress on Dec. 19, 1974, and was sworn in same day.

Burial Places of the Presidents

President	Burial place	President	Burial place
Washington	Mt. Vernon, Va.	Grant	New York City
J. Adams	Quincy, Mass.	Hayes	Fremont, Ohio
Jefferson	Charlottesville, Va.	Garfield	Cleveland, Ohio
Madison	Montpelier Station, Va.	Arthur	Albany, N.Y.
Monroe	Richmond, Va.	Cleveland	Princeton, N.J.
J. Q. Adams	Quincy, Mass.	B. Harrison	Indianapolis
Jackson	The Hermitage, nr. Nashville, Tenn.	McKinley	Canton, Ohio
Van Buren	Kinderhook, N.Y.	T. Roosevelt	Oyster Bay, N.Y.
W. H. Harrison	North Bend, Ohio	Taft	Arlington National Cemetery
Tyler	Richmond, Va.	Wilson	Washington National Cathedral
Polk	Nashville, Tenn.	Harding	Marion, Ohio
Taylor	Louisville, Ky.	Coolidge	Plymouth, Vt.
Fillmore	Buffalo, N.Y.	Hoover	West Branch, Iowa
Pierce	Concord, N.H.	F. D. Roosevelt	Hyde Park, N.Y.
Buchanan	Lancaster, Pa.	Truman	Independence, Mo.
Lincoln	Springfield, Ill.	Eisenhower	Abilene, Kan.
A. Johnson	Greeneville, Tenn.	Kennedy	Arlington National Cemetery
		L. B. Johnson	Stonewall, Tex.

The Liberty Bell

The Liberty Bell was cast in England in 1752 for the Pennsylvania Statehouse (now named Independence Hall) in Philadelphia. It was recast in Philadelphia in 1753. It is inscribed with the words, "Proclaim liberty throughout all the land unto all the inhabitants thereof" (Lev. 25:10). The bell was rung on July 8, 1776, for the first public reading of the Declaration of Independence. Hidden in Allentown during the British occupation of Philadelphia, it was replaced in Independence Hall in 1778. The bell cracked on July 8, 1835, while tolling the death of Chief Justice John Marshall. In 1976 the Liberty Bell was moved to a special exhibition building near Independence Hall.

Wives and Children of the Presidents

President	Wife's name	Year and place of wife's birth	Married	Wife died	Children of President[1]	
					Sons	Daughters
Washington	Mrs. Martha Dandridge Custis	1732, Va.	1759	1802	—	—
John Adams	Abigail Smith	1744, Mass.	1764	1818	3	2
Jefferson	Mrs. Martha Wayles Skelton	1748, Va.	1772	1782	1	5
Madison	Mrs. Dorothy "Dolley" Payne Todd	1768, N.C.	1794	1849	—	—
Monroe	Elizabeth "Eliza" Kortright	1768, N.Y.	1786	1830	—	2
J. Q. Adams	Louisa Catherine Johnson	1775, England	1797	1852	3	1
Jackson	Mrs. Rachel Donelson Robards	1767, Va.	1791	1828	—	—
Van Buren	Hannah Hoes	1788, N.Y.	1807	1819	4	—
W. H. Harrison	Anna Symmes	1775, N.J.	1795	1864	6	4
Tyler	Letitia Christian	1790, Va.	1813	1842	3	4
	Julia Gardiner	1820, N.Y.	1844	1889	5	2
Polk	Sarah Childress	1803, Tenn.	1824	1891	—	—
Taylor	Margaret Smith	1788, Md.	1810	1852	1	5
Fillmore	Abigail Powers	1798, N.Y.	1826	1853	1	1
	Mrs. Caroline Carmichael McIntosh	1813, N.J.	1858	1881	—	—
Pierce	Jane Means Appleton	1806, N.H.	1834	1863	3	—
Buchanan	(Unmarried)	—	—	—	—	—
Lincoln	Mary Todd	1818, Ky.	1842	1882	4	—
A. Johnson	Eliza McCardle	1810, Tenn.	1827	1876	3	2
Grant	Julia Dent	1826, Mo.	1848	1902	3	1
Hayes	Lucy Ware Webb	1831, Ohio	1852	1889	7	1
Garfield	Lucretia Rudolph	1832, Ohio	1858	1918	5	2
Arthur	Ellen Lewis Herndon	1837, Va.	1859	1880	2	1
Cleveland	Frances Folsom	1864, N.Y.	1886	1947	2	3
B. Harrison	Caroline Lavinia Scott	1832, Ohio	1853	1892	1	1
	Mrs. Mary Scott Lord Dimmick	1858, Pa.	1896	1948	—	1
McKinley	Ida Saxton	1847, Ohio	1871	1907	—	2
T. Roosevelt	Alice Hathaway Lee	1861, Mass.	1880	1884	—	1
	Edith Kermit Carow	1861, Conn.	1886	1948	4	1
Taft	Helen Herron	1861, Ohio	1886	1943	2	1
Wilson	Ellen Louise Axson	1860, Ga.	1885	1914	—	3
	Mrs. Edith Bolling Galt	1872, Va.	1915	1961	—	—
Harding	Mrs. Florence Kling DeWolfe	1860, Ohio	1891	1924	—	—
Coolidge	Grace Anna Goodhue	1879, Vt.	1905	1957	2	—
Hoover	Lou Henry	1875, Iowa	1899	1944	2	—
F. D. Roosevelt	Anna Eleanor Roosevelt	1884, N.Y.	1905	1962	5	1
Truman	Bess Wallace	1885, Mo.	1919	—	—	1
Eisenhower	Mamie Geneva Doud	1896, Iowa	1916	1979	2	—
Kennedy	Jacqueline Lee Bouvier	1929, N.Y.	1953	—	2	1
L. B. Johnson	Claudia Alta "Lady Bird" Taylor	1912, Tex.	1934	—	—	2
Nixon	Thelma Catherine "Pat" Ryan	1912, Nev.	1940	—	—	2
Ford	Mrs. Elizabeth "Betty" Bloomer Warren	1918, Ill.	1948	—	3	1
Carter	Rosalynn Smith	1928, Ga.	1946	—	3	1
Reagan	Jane Wyman	1914, Mo.	1940[2]	—	1[3]	1
	Nancy Davis	1923, N.Y.	1952	—	1	1

1. Includes children who died in infancy. 2. Divorced in 1948. 3. Adopted.

How the House of Representatives Elects a President

Should no candidate receive a majority—270 or more—of the electoral votes for President on January 6th, then the members of the House of Representatives would meet immediately to choose a President from among the three highest candidates.

Each state would have only one vote, and a majority of 26 or more votes would be needed to elect a President. If the House of Representatives is unable to elect a winner by Inauguration Day, January 20th, then the Vice-President-elect serves as acting President until the House can decide.

The new Vice-President would be elected separately by the Senate from among the two running-mate candidates who received the most electoral votes. The senators would vote as individuals, with only one vote each.

Should neither the House nor Senate agree on the new President or Vice-President, then the Speaker of the House acts as President until one of them can decide.

Elections

How a President is Nominated and Elected

The National Conventions of both major parties are held during the summer of a presidential-election year. Earlier, each party selects delegates by primaries, conventions, committees, etc.

For their 1980 National Convention, the Republicans allowed each state a base of 6 delegates at large; the District of Columbia, 14; Puerto Rico, 14; Guam and the Virgin Islands, 4 each. In addition, each state received 3 district delegates for each of its Representatives in the House. This did not apply to the District of Columbia, Puerto Rico, Guam and the Virgin Islands.

Each state was awarded additional delegates at large on the basis of having supported the Republican candidate for President in 1976 and electing Republican candidates for Senator, Governor, and U.S. Representative in the 1976 and 1978 elections.

The number of delegates at the 1980 convention, held in Detroit starting July 14, was 1,997.

Following was the apportionment of delegates:

Ala.	27	Fla.	51	Ky.	27	Mont.	20	Ohio	77	Tex.	80
Alaska	19	Ga.	36	La.	31	Neb.	25	Okla	34	Utah	21
Ariz.	28	Guam	4	Me.	21	Nev.	17	Ore.	29	Vt.	19
Ark.	19	Hawaii	14	Md.	30	N.H.	22	Pa.	83	Va.	51
Calif.	168	Idaho	21	Mass.	42	N.J.	66	P.R.	14	V.I.	4
Colo.	31	Ill.	102	Mich.	82	N.M.	22	R.I.	13	Wash.	37
Conn.	35	Ind.	54	Minn.	34	N.Y.	123	S.C.	25	W. Va.	18
Del.	12	Iowa	37	Miss.	22	N.C.	40	S.D.	22	Wis.	34
D.C.	14	Kan.	32	Mo.	37	N.D.	17	Tenn.	32	Wyo.	19

The Democrats also based the number of delegates on a state's showing in the 1976 and 1978 elections. At the 1980 convention, held in New York City starting Aug. 11, there were 3,331[1] delegates casting votes. Following was the apportionment:

Ala.	45	Fla.	100	Ky.	50	Mont.	19	Ohio	161	Tex.	152
Alaska	11	Ga.	63	La.	51	Neb.	24	Okla.	42	Utah	20
Ariz.	29	Guam	4	Me.	22	Nev.	12	Ore.	39	Vt.	12
Ark.	33	Hawaii	19	Md.	59	N.H.	19	Pa.	185	V.I.	4
Calif.	306	Idaho	17	Mass.	111	N.J.	113	P.R.	41	Va.	64
Canal Zone	4	Ill.	179	Mich.	141	N.M.	20	R.I.	23	Wash.	58
Colo.	40	Ind.	80	Minn.	75	N.Y.	282	S.C.	37	W.Va.	35
Conn.	54	Iowa	50	Miss.	32	N.C.	69	S.D.	19	Wis.	75
Del.	14	Kan.	37	Mo.	77	N.D.	14	Tenn.	55	Wyo.	11
D.C.	19										

1. Includes three votes for Democrats abroad.

The Conventions

At each convention, a temporary chairman is chosen. After a credentials committee seats the delegates, a permanent chairman is elected. The convention then votes on a platform, drawn up by the platform committee.

By the third or fourth day, presidential nominations begin. The chairman calls the roll of states alphabetically. A state may place a candidate in nomination or yield to another state.

Voting, again alphabetically by roll call of states, begins after all nominations have been made and seconded. A simple majority is required in each party, although this may require many ballots.

Finally, the vice-presidential candidate is selected. Although there is no law saying that the candidates *must* come from different states, it is, practically, necessary for this to be the case. Otherwise, according to the Constitution (*see* Amendment XII), electors from that state could vote for only one of the candidates and would have to cast their other vote for some person of another state. This could result in a presidential candidate's receiving a majority electoral vote and his running mate's failing to.

The Electoral College

The next step in the process is the nomination of electors in each state, according to its laws. These electors must not be Federal office holders. In the November election, the voters cast their votes for electors, not for President. In some states, the ballots include only the names of the presidential and vice-presidential candidates; in others, they include only names of the electors. Nowadays, it is rare for electors to be split between parties. The last such occurrence was in North Carolina in 1968[1]; the last before that, in Tennessee in 1948. On three occasions (1824, 1876, and 1888), the presidential candidate with the largest popular vote failed to obtain an electoral-vote majority.

Each state has as many electors as it has Senators and Representatives. For the 1976 election, the total electors were 538, based on 100 Senators, 435 Representatives, plus 3 electoral votes from the District of Columbia as a result of the 23rd Amendment to the Constitution.

On the first Monday after the second Wednesday in December, the electors cast their votes in their respective state capitols. Constitutionally they may vote for someone other than the party candidate but usually they do not since they are pledged to one party and its candidate on the ballot. Should the presidential or vice-presidential candidate die between the November election and the December meetings, the electors pledged to vote for him could vote for whomever they pleased. However, it seems certain that the national committee would attempt to get an agreement among the state party leaders for a replacement candidate.

The votes of the electors, certified by the states, are sent to Congress, where the president of the Senate opens the certificates and has them counted in the presence of both Houses on January 6. The new President is inaugurated at noon on January 20.

Should no candidate receive a majority of the electoral vote for President, the House of Representatives chooses a President from among the three highest candidates, voting, not as individuals, but as states, with a majority (now 26) needed to elect. Should no vice-presidential candidate obtain the majority, the Senate, voting as individuals, chooses from the highest two.

1. In 1956, 1 of Alabama's 11 electoral votes was cast for Walter B. Jones. In 1960, 6 of Alabama's 11 electoral votes and 1 of Oklahoma's 8 electoral votes were cast for Harry Flood Byrd. (Byrd also received all 8 of Mississippi's electoral votes.)

National Political Conventions Since 1856

Opening date	Party	Where held	Opening date	Party	Where held
June 17, 1856	Republican	Philadelphia	June 28, 1920	Democratic	San Francisco
June 2, 1856	Democratic	Cincinnati	June 10, 1924	Republican	Cleveland
May 16, 1860	Republican	Chicago	June 24, 1924[2]	Democratic	New York City
April 23, 1860	Democratic	Charleston and Baltimore	June 12, 1928	Republican	Kansas City
June 7, 1864	Republican[1]	Baltimore	June 26, 1928	Democratic	Houston
Aug. 29, 1864	Democratic	Chicago	June 14, 1932	Republican	Chicago
May 20, 1868	Republican	Chicago	June 27, 1932	Democratic	Chicago
July 4, 1868	Democratic	New York City	June 9, 1936	Republican	Cleveland
June 5, 1872	Republican	Philadelphia	June 23, 1936	Democratic	Philadelphia
June 9, 1872	Democratic	Baltimore	June 24, 1940	Republican	Philadelphia
June 14, 1876	Republican	Cincinnati	July 15, 1940	Democratic	Chicago
June 28, 1876	Democratic	St. Louis	June 26, 1944	Republican	Chicago
June 2, 1880	Republican	Chicago	July 19, 1944	Democratic	Chicago
June 23, 1880	Democratic	Cincinnati	June 21, 1948	Republican	Philadelphia
June 3, 1884	Republican	Chicago	July 12, 1948	Democratic	Philadelphia
July 11, 1884	Democratic	Chicago	July 17, 1948	(3)	Birmingham
June 19, 1888	Republican	Chicago	July 22, 1948	Progressive	Philadelphia
June 6, 1888	Democratic	St. Louis	July 7, 1952	Republican	Chicago
June 7, 1892	Republican	Minneapolis	July 21, 1952	Democratic	Chicago
June 21, 1892	Democratic	Chicago	Aug. 20, 1956	Republican	San Francisco
June 16, 1896	Republican	St. Louis	Aug. 13, 1956	Democratic	Chicago
July 7, 1896	Democratic	Chicago	July 25, 1960	Republican	Chicago
June 19, 1900	Republican	Philadelphia	July 11, 1960	Democratic	Los Angeles
July 4, 1900	Democratic	Kansas City	July 13, 1964	Republican	San Francisco
June 21, 1904	Republican	Chicago	Aug. 24, 1964	Democratic	Atlantic City
July 6, 1904	Democratic	St. Louis	Aug. 5, 1968	Republican	Miami Beach
June 16, 1908	Republican	Chicago	Aug. 26, 1968	Democratic	Chicago
July 7, 1908	Democratic	Denver	July 10, 1972	Democratic	Miami Beach
June 18, 1912	Republican	Chicago	Aug. 21, 1972	Republican	Miami Beach
June 25, 1912	Democratic	Baltimore	July 12, 1976	Democratic	New York City
June 7, 1916	Republican	Chicago	Aug. 16, 1976	Republican	Kansas City, Mo.
June 14, 1916	Democratic	St. Louis	Aug. 11, 1980	Democratic	New York City
June 8, 1920	Republican	Chicago	July 14, 1980	Republican	Detroit

1. The Convention adopted name Union party to attract War Democrats and others favoring prosecution of war. 2. In session until July 10, 1924. 3. States' Rights delegates from 13 Southern states.

Plurality and Majority

In order to win a plurality, a candidate must receive a greater number of votes than anyone running against him. If he receives 50 votes, for example, and two other candidates receive 49 and 2, he will have a plurality of one vote over his closest opponent.

However, a candidate does not have a majority unless he receives more than 50% of the total votes cast. In the example above, the candidate does not have a majority, because his 50 votes are less than 50% of the 101 votes cast.

Presidential Elections, 1789 to 1980

For the original method of electing the President and the Vice President (elections of 1789, 1792, 1796, and 1800), see Article II, Section 1, of the Constitution. The election of 1804 was the first one in which the electors voted for President and Vice President on separate ballots. (See Amendment XII to the Constitution.)

Year	Presidential candidates	Party	Electoral vote	Year	Presidential candidates	Party	Electoral vote
1789[1]	George Washington	(no party)	69	1796	John Adams	Federalist	71
	John Adams	(no party)	34		Thomas Jefferson	Dem.-Rep.	68
	Scattering	(no party)	35		Thomas Pinckney	Federalist	59
	Votes not cast		8		Aaron Burr	Dem.-Rep.	30
					Scattering		48
1792	George Washington	Federalist	132				
	John Adams	Federalist	77	1800[2]	Thomas Jefferson	Dem.-Rep.	73
	George Clinton	Anti-Federalist	50		Aaron Burr	Dem.-Rep.	73
	Thomas Jefferson	Anti-Federalist	4		John Adams	Federalist	65
	Aaron Burr	Anti-Federalist	1		Charles C. Pinckney	Federalist	64
	Votes not cast		6		John Jay	Federalist	1

Year	Presidential candidates	Party	Electoral vote	Vice-presidential candidates	Party	Electoral vote
1804	Thomas Jefferson	Dem.-Rep.	162	George Clinton	Dem.-Rep.	162
	Charles C. Pinckney	Federalist	14	Rufus King	Federalist	14
1808	James Madison	Dem.-Rep.	122	George Clinton	Dem.-Rep.	113
	Charles C. Pinckney	Federalist	47	Rufus King	Federalist	47
	George Clinton	Dem.-Rep.	6	John Langdon	Ind. (no party)	9
	Votes not cast		1	James Madison	Dem.-Rep.	3
				James Monroe	Dem.-Rep.	3
				Votes not cast		1
1812	James Madison	Dem.-Rep.	128	Elbridge Gerry	Dem.-Rep.	131
	De Witt Clinton	Federalist	89	Jared Ingersoll	Federalist	86
	Votes not cast		1	Votes not cast		1
1816	James Monroe	Dem.-Rep.	183	Daniel D. Tompkins	Dem.-Rep.	183
	Rufus King	Federalist	34	John E. Howard	Federalist	22
	Votes not cast		4	James Ross	Ind. (no party)	5
				John Marshall	Federalist	4
				Robert G. Harper	Ind. (no party)	3
				Votes not cast		4
1820	James Monroe	Dem-Rep	231	Daniel D. Tompkins	Dem.-Rep.	218
	John Quincy Adams	Ind. (no party)	1	Richard Stockton	Ind. (no party)	8
	Votes not cast		3	Daniel Rodney	Ind. (no party)	4
				Richard Rush	Ind. (no party)	1
				Robert G. Harper	Ind. (no party)	1
				Votes not cast		3
1824[3]	John Quincy Adams	(no party)	84	John C. Calhoun	(no party)	182
	Andrew Jackson	(no party)	99	Nathan Sanford	(no party)	30
	William H. Crawford	(no party)	41	Nathaniel Macon	(no party)	24
	Henry Clay	(no party)	37	Andrew Jackson	(no party)	13
				Martin Van Buren	(no party)	9
				Henry Clay	(no party)	2
				Votes not cast		1
1828	Andrew Jackson	Democratic	178	John C. Calhoun	Democratic	171
	John Quincy Adams	Natl. Rep.	83	Richard Rush	Natl. Rep.	83
				William Smith	Democratic	7
1832	Andrew Jackson	Democratic	219	Martin Van Buren	Democratic	189
	Henry Clay	Natl. Rep.	49	John Sergeant	Natl. Rep.	49
	John Floyd	Ind. (no party)	11	Henry Lee	Ind. (no party)	11
	William Wirt	Antimasonic[4]	7	Amos Ellmaker	Antimasonic	7
	Votes not cast		2	William Wilkins	Ind. (no party)	30
				Votes not cast		2

Year	Presidential candidates	Party	Electoral vote	Vice-presidential candidates	Party	Electoral vote
1836	Martin Van Buren	Democratic	170	Richard M. Johnson[5]	Democratic	147
	William H. Harrison	Whig	73	Francis Granger	Whig	77
	Hugh L. White	Whig	26	John Tyler	Whig	47
	Daniel Webster	Whig	14	William Smith	Ind. (no party)	23
	W. P. Mangum	Ind. (no party)	11			
1840	William H. Harrison[6]	Whig	234	John Tyler	Whig	234
	Martin Van Buren	Democratic	60	Richard M. Johnson	Democratic	48
				L. W. Tazewell	Ind. (no party)	11
				James K. Polk	Democratic	1
1844	James K. Polk	Democratic	170	George M. Dallas	Democratic	170
	Henry Clay	Whig	105	Theo. Frelinghuysen	Whig	105
1848	Zachary Taylor[7]	Whig	163	Millard Fillmore	Whig	163
	Lewis Cass	Democratic	127	William O. Butler	Democratic	127
1852	Franklin Pierce	Democratic	254	William R. King	Democratic	254
	Winfield Scott	Whig	42	William A. Graham	Whig	42
1856	James Buchanan	Democratic	174	John C. Breckinridge	Democratic	174
	John C. Frémont	Republican	114	William L. Dayton	Republican	114
	Millard Fillmore	American[8]	8	A. J. Donelson	American[8]	8
1860	Abraham Lincoln	Republican	180	Hannibal Hamlin	Republican	180
	John C. Breckinridge	Democratic	72	Joseph Lane	Democratic	72
	John Bell	Const. Union	39	Edward Everett	Const. Union	39
	Stephen A. Douglas	Democratic	12	H. V. Johnson	Democratic	12
1864	Abraham Lincoln[9]	Union[10]	212	Andrew Johnson	Union[15]	212
	George B. McClellan	Democratic	21	G. H. Pendleton	Democratic	21
1868	Ulysses S. Grant	Republican	214	Schuyler Colfax	Republican	214
	Horatio Seymour	Democratic	80	Francis P. Blair, Jr.	Democratic	80
	Votes not counted[11]		23	Votes not counted[11]		23

Year	Presidential candidates	Party	Electoral vote	Popular vote	Vice-presidential candidates and party
1872	Ulysses S. Grant	Republican	286	3,597,132	Henry Wilson—R
	Horace Greeley	Dem., Liberal Rep.	(12)	2,834,125	B. Gratz Brown—D, LR—(47)
	Thomas A. Hendricks	Democratic	42		Scattering—(19)
	B. Gratz Brown	Dem., Liberal Rep.	18		Votes not counted—(14)
	Charles J. Jenkins	Democratic	2		
	David Davis	Democratic	1		
	Votes not counted		17		
1876[13]	Rutherford B. Hayes	Republican	185	4,033,768	William A. Wheeler—R
	Samuel J. Tilden	Democratic	184	4,285,992	Thomas A. Hendricks—D
	Peter Cooper	Greenback	0	81,737	Samuel F. Cary—G
1880	James A. Garfield[14]	Republican	214	4,449,053	Chester A. Arthur—R
	Winfield S. Hancock	Democratic	155	4,442,035	William H. English—D
	James B. Weaver	Greenback	0	308,578	B. J. Chambers—G
1884	Grover Cleveland	Democratic	219	4,911,017	Thomas A. Hendricks—D
	James G. Blaine	Republican	182	4,848,334	John A. Logan—R
	Benjamin F. Butler	Greenback	0	175,370	A. M. West—G
	John P. St. John	Prohibition	0	150,369	William Daniel—P
1888	Benjamin Harrison	Republican	233	5,440,216	Levi P. Morton—R
	Grover Cleveland	Democratic	168	5,538,233	A. G. Thurman—D
	Clinton B. Fisk	Prohibition	0	249,506	John A. Brooks—P
	Alson J. Streeter	Union Labor	0	146,935	Charles E. Cunningham—UL
1892	Grover Cleveland	Democratic	277	5,556,918	Adlai E. Stevenson—D
	Benjamin Harrison	Republican	145	5,176,108	Whitelaw Reid—R
	James B. Weaver	People's[15]	22	1,041,028	James G. Field—Peo
	John Bidwell	Prohibition	0	264,133	James B. Cranfill—P

Year	Presidential candidates	Party	Electoral vote	Popular vote	Vice-presidential candidates and party
1896	William McKinley	Republican	271	7,035,638	Garret A. Hobart—R
	William J. Bryan	Dem., People's[15]	176	6,467,946	Arthur Sewall—D—(149)
					Thomas E. Watson—Peo—(27)
	John M. Palmer	Natl. Dem.	0	133,148	Simon B. Buckner—ND
	Joshua Levering	Prohibition	0	132,007	Hale Johnson—P
1900	William McKinley[16]	Republican	292	7,219,530	Theodore Roosevelt—R
	William J. Bryan	Dem., People's[15]	155	6,358,071	Adlai E. Stevenson—D, Peo
	Eugene V. Debs	Social Democratic	0	94,768	Job Harriman—SD
1904	Theodore Roosevelt	Republican	336	7,628,834	Charles W. Fairbanks—R
	Alton B. Parker	Democratic	140	5,084,491	Henry G. Davis—D
	Eugene V. Debs	Socialist	0	402,400	Benjamin Hanford—S
1908	William H. Taft	Republican	321	7,679,006	James S. Sherman—R
	William J. Bryan	Democratic	162	6,409,106	John W. Kern—D
	Eugene V. Debs	Socialist	0	402,820	Benjamin Hanford—S
1912	Woodrow Wilson	Democratic	435	6,286,214	Thomas R. Marshall—D
	Theodore Roosevelt	Progressive	88	4,126,020	Hiram Johnson—Prog
	William H. Taft	Republican	8	3,483,922	Nicholas M. Butler—R[17]
	Eugene V. Debs	Socialist	0	897,011	Emil Seidel—S
1916	Woodrow Wilson	Democratic	277	9,129,606	Thomas R. Marshall—D
	Charles E. Hughes	Republican	254	8,538,221	Charles W. Fairbanks—R
	A. L. Benson	Socialist	0	585,113	G. R. Kirkpatrick—S
1920	Warren G. Harding[18]	Republican	404	16,152,200	Calvin Coolidge—R
	James M. Cox	Democratic	127	9,147,353	Franklin D. Roosevelt—D
	Eugene V. Debs	Socialist	0	917,799	Seymour Stedman—S
1924	Calvin Coolidge	Republican	382	15,725,016	Charles G. Dawes—R
	John W. Davis	Democratic	136	8,385,586	Charles W. Bryan—D
	Robert M. LaFollette	Progressive, Socialist	13	4,822,856	Burton K. Wheeler—Prog S
1928	Herbert Hoover	Republican	444	21,392,190	Charles Curtis—R
	Alfred E. Smith	Democratic	87	15,016,443	Joseph T. Robinson—D
	Norman Thomas	Socialist	0	267,420	James H. Maurer—S
1932	Franklin D. Roosevelt	Democratic	472	22,821,857	John N. Garner—D
	Herbert Hoover	Republican	59	15,761,841	Charles Curtis—R
	Norman Thomas	Socialist	0	884,781	James H. Maurer—S
1936	Franklin D. Roosevelt	Democratic	523	27,751,597	John N. Garner—D
	Alfred M. Landon	Republican	8	16,679,583	Frank Knox—R
	Norman Thomas	Socialist	0	187,720	George Nelson—S
1940	Franklin D. Roosevelt	Democratic	449	27,244,160	Henry A. Wallace—D
	Wendell L. Willkie	Republican	82	22,305,198	Charles L. McNary—R
	Norman Thomas	Socialist	0	99,557	Maynard C. Krueger—S
1944	Franklin D. Roosevelt[19]	Democratic	432	25,602,504	Harry S. Truman—D
	Thomas E. Dewey	Republican	99	22,006,285	John W. Bricker—R
	Norman Thomas	Socialist	0	80,518	Darlington Hoopes—S
1948	Harry S. Truman	Democratic	303	24,179,345	Alben W. Barkley—D
	Thomas E. Dewey	Republican	189	21,991,291	Earl Warren—R
	J. Strom Thurmond	States' Rights Dem.	39	1,176,125	Fielding L. Wright—SR
	Henry A. Wallace	Progressive	0	1,157,326	Glen Taylor—Prog
	Norman Thomas	Socialist	0	139,572	Tucker P. Smith—S
1952	Dwight D. Eisenhower	Republican	442	33,936,234	Richard M. Nixon—R
	Adlai E. Stevenson	Democratic	89	27,314,992	John J. Sparkman—D
1956[20]	Dwight D. Eisenhower	Republican	457	35,590,472	Richard M. Nixon—R
	Adlai E. Stevenson	Democratic	73	26,022,752	Estes Kefauver—D
1960	John F. Kennedy[22]	Democratic	303	34,226,731	Lyndon B. Johnson—D
	Richard M. Nixon	Republican	219	34,108,157	Henry Cabot Lodge—R

Year	Presidential candidates	Party	Electoral vote	Popular vote	Vice-presidential candidates and party
1964	Lyndon B. Johnson	Democratic	486	43,129,484	Hubert H. Humphrey—D
	Barry M. Goldwater	Republican	52	27,178,188	William E. Miller—R
1968	Richard M. Nixon	Republican	301	31,785,480	Spiro T. Agnew—R
	Hubert H. Humphrey	Democratic	191	31,275,166	Edmund S. Muskie—D
	George C. Wallace	American Independent	46	9,906,473	Curtis F. LeMay—AI
1972	Richard M. Nixon[23]	Republican	520[24]	47,169,911	Spiro T. Agnew—R
	George McGovern	Democratic	17	29,170,383	Sargent Shriver—D
	John G. Schmitz	American	0	1,099,482	Thomas J. Anderson—A
1976	Jimmy Carter	Democratic	297	40,830,763	Walter F. Mondale—D
	Gerald R. Ford	Republican	240[25]	39,147,973	Robert J. Dole—R
	Eugene J. McCarthy	Independent	0	756,631	None
1980	Ronald Reagan	Republican	489	43,899,248	George Bush—R
	Jimmy Carter	Democratic	49	36,481,435	Walter F. Mondale—D
	John B. Anderson	Independent	0	5,719,437	Patrick J. Lucey—I

1. Only 10 states participated in the election. The New York legislature chose no electors, and North Carolina and Rhode Island had not yet ratified the Constitution. 2. As Jefferson and Burr were tied, the House of Representatives chose the President. In a vote by states, 10 votes were cast for Jefferson, 4 for Burr; 2 votes were not cast. 3. As no candidate had an electoral-vote majority, the House of Representatives chose the President from the first three. In a vote by states, 13 votes were cast for Adams, 7 for Jackson, and 4 for Crawford. 4. The Antimasonic Party on Sept. 26, 1831, was the first party to hold a nominating convention to choose candidates for President and Vice-President. 5. As Johnson did not have an electoral-vote majority, the Senate chose him 33–14 over Granger, the others being legally out of the race. 6. Harrison died April 4, 1841, and Tyler succeeded him April 6. 7. Taylor died July 9, 1850, and Fillmore succeeded him July 10. 8. Also known as the Know-Nothing Party. 9. Lincoln died April 15, 1865, and Johnson succeeded him the same day. 10. Name adopted by the Republican National Convention of 1864. Johnson was a War Democrat. 11. 23 Southern electoral votes were excluded. 12. See Election of 1872 in *Unusual Voting Results* under Elections, Presidential, in Index. 13. See Election of 1876 in *Unusual Voting Results* under Elections, Presidential, in Index. 14. Garfield died Sept. 19, 1881, and Arthur succeeded him Sept. 20. 15. Members of People's Party were called Populists. 16. McKinley died Sept. 14, 1901, and Roosevelt succeeded him the same day. 17. James S. Sherman, Republican candidate for Vice President, died Oct. 30, 1912, and the Republican electoral votes were cast for Butler. 18. Harding died Aug. 2, 1923, and Coolidge succeeded him Aug. 3. 19. Roosevelt died April 12, 1945, and Truman succeeded him the same day. 20. One electoral vote from Alabama was cast for Walter B. Jones. 21. Sen. Harry F. Byrd received 15 electoral votes. 22. Kennedy died Nov. 22, 1963, and Johnson succeeded him the same day. 23. Nixon resigned Aug. 9, 1974, and Gerald R. Ford succeeded him the same day. 24. One electoral vote from Virginia was cast for John Hospers, Libertarian Party. 25. One electoral vote from Washington was cast for Ronald Reagan.

National Committee Chairmen Since 1932

Chairman and (state)	Term	Chairman and (state)	Term
REPUBLICAN		**DEMOCRATIC**	
Everett Sanders (Ind.)	1932–34	James A. Farley (N.Y.)	1932–40
Henry P. Fletcher (Pa.)	1934–36	Edward J. Flynn (N.Y.)	1940–43
John Hamilton (Kan.)	1936–40	Frank C. Walker (Mont.)	1943–44
Joseph W. Martin, Jr. (Mass.)	1940–42	Robert E. Hannegan (Mo.)	1944–47
Harrison E. Spangler (Iowa)	1942–44	J. Howard McGrath (R.I.)	1947–49
Herbert Brownell, Jr. (N.Y.)	1944–46	William M. Boyle, Jr. (Mo.)	1949–51
Carroll Reece (Tenn.)	1946–48	Frank E. McKinney (Ind.)	1951–52
Hugh D. Scott, Jr. (Pa.)	1948–49	Stephen A. Mitchell (Ill.)	1952–54
Guy G. Gabrielson (N.J.)	1949–52	Paul M. Butler (Ind.)	1955–60
Arthur E. Summerfield (Mich.)	1952–53	Henry M. Jackson (Wash.)	1960–61
Wesley Roberts (Kan.)	1953–	John M. Bailey (Conn.)	1961–68
Leonard W. Hall (N.Y.)	1953–57	Lawrence F. O'Brien (Mass.)	1968–69
Meade Alcorn (Conn.)	1957–59	Fred R. Harris (Okla.)	1969–70
Thruston B. Morton (Ky.)	1959–61	Lawrence F. O'Brien (Mass.)	1970–72
William E. Miller (N.Y.)	1961–64	Jean Westwood (Utah)	1972–
Dean Burch (Ariz.)	1964–65	Robert S. Strauss (Tex.)	1972–77
Ray C. Bliss (Ohio)	1965–69	Kenneth M. Curtis (Me.)	1977–
Rogers C. B. Morton (Md.)	1969–71	John C. White (Tex.)	1977–81
Robert Dole (Kan.)	1971–73	Charles T. Manatt (Calif.)	1981–
George H. Bush (Tex.)	1973–74		
Mary Louise Smith (Iowa)	1974–77		
William E. Brock III (Tenn.)	1977–81		
Richard Richards (Utah)	1981–		

Republican National Committee: 310 First St., S.E., Washington, D. C. 20003.
Democratic National Committee: 1625 Massachusetts Ave., N.W., Washington, D.C. 20036.

Presidential Election of 1968

Principal Candidates for President and Vice President
Republican: Richard M. Nixon; Spiro T. Agnew
Democratic: Hubert H. Humphrey; Edmund S. Muskie
American Independent Party: George C. Wallace; Curtis E. LeMay

State	Total	Nixon Rep.	Humphrey Dem.	Wallace Am. Ind.	Plurality	Electoral Vote R	D	A	Votes at Natl. Convs. Dem.	Rep.
Alabama	1,049,922	146,923	196,579[1]	691,425[2]	494,846 A	—	—	10	32	26
Alaska	83,035	37,600	35,411	10,024	2,189 R	3	—	—	22	12
Arizona	486,936	266,721	170,514	46,573	96,207 R	5	—	—	19	16
Arkansas	619,969	190,759	188,228	240,982	50,223 A	—	—	6	33	18
California	7,251,587	3,467,664	3,244,318	487,270	223,346 R	40	—	—	174	86
Colorado	811,199	409,345	335,174	60,813	74,171 R	6	—	—	35	18
Connecticut	1,256,232	556,721	621,561	76,650	64,840 D	—	8	—	44	16
Delaware	214,367	96,714	89,194	28,459	7,520 R	3	—	—	22	12
D.C.	170,578	31,012	139,566	—	108,554 D	—	3	—	23	9
Florida	2,187,805	886,804	676,794	624,207	210,010 R	14	—	—	63	34
Georgia	1,250,266	380,111	334,440	535,550	155,439 A	—	—	12	43	30
Hawaii	236,218	91,425	141,324	3,469	49,899 D	—	4	—	26	14
Idaho	291,183	165,369	89,273	36,541	76,096 R	4	—	—	25	14
Illinois	4,619,749	2,174,774	2,039,814	390,958	134,960 R	26	—	—	118	58
Indiana	2,123,597	1,067,885	806,659	243,108	261,226 R	13	—	—	63	26
Iowa	1,167,931	619,106	476,699	66,422	142,407 R	9	—	—	46	24
Kansas	872,783	478,674	302,996	88,921	175,678 R	7	—	—	38	20
Kentucky	1,055,893	462,411	397,541	193,098	64,870 R	9	—	—	46	24
Louisiana	1,097,450	257,535	309,615	530,300	220,685 A	—	—	10	36	26
Maine	392,936	169,254	217,312	6,370	48,058 D	—	4	—	27	14
Maryland	1,235,039	517,995	538,310	178,734	20,315 D	—	10	—	49	26
Massachusetts	2,331,752	766,844	1,469,218	87,088	702,374 D	—	14	—	72	34
Michigan	3,306,250	1,370,665	1,593,082	331,968	222,417 D	—	21	—	96	48
Minnesota	1,588,506	658,643	857,738	68,931	199,095 D	—	10	—	52	26
Mississippi	654,509	88,516	150,644	415,349	264,705 A	—	—	7	24	20
Missouri	1,809,502	811,932	791,444	206,126	20,488 R	12	—	—	60	24
Montana	274,404	138,835	114,117	20,015	24,718 R	4	—	—	26	14
Nebraska	536,851	321,163	170,784	44,904	150,379 R	5	—	—	30	16
Nevada	154,218	73,188	60,598	20,432	12,590 R	3	—	—	22	12
New Hampshire	297,298	154,903	130,589	11,173	24,314 R	4	—	—	26	8
New Jersey	2,875,395	1,325,467	1,264,206	262,187	61,261 R	17	—	—	82	40
New Mexico	327,350	169,692	130,081	25,737	39,611 R	4	—	—	26	14
New York	6,791,688	3,007,932	3,378,470[3]	358,864	370,538 D	—	43	—	190	92
North Carolina	1,587,493	627,192	464,113	496,188	131,004 R	12	—	1	59	26
North Dakota	247,882	138,669	94,769	14,244	43,900 R	4	—	—	25	8
Ohio	3,959,698	1,791,014	1,700,586	467,495	90,428 R	26	—	—	115	58
Oklahoma	943,086	449,697	301,658	191,731	148,039 R	8	—	—	41	22
Oregon	819,622	408,433	358,866	49,683	49,567 R	6	—	—	35	18
Pennsylvania	4,747,928	2,090,017	2,259,405	378,582	169,388 D	—	29	—	130	64
Rhode Island	385,000	122,359	246,518	15,678	124,159 D	—	4	—	27	14
South Carolina	666,978	254,062	197,486	215,430	38,632 R	8	—	—	28	22
South Dakota	281,264	149,841	118,023	13,400	31,818 R	4	—	—	26	14
Tennessee	1,248,617	472,592	351,233	424,792	47,800 R	11	—	—	51	28
Texas	3,079,406	1,227,844	1,266,804	584,269	38,960 D	—	25	—	104	56
Utah	422,568	238,728	156,665	26,906	82,063 R	4	—	—	26	8
Vermont	161,404	85,142	70,255	5,104	14,887 R	3	—	—	22	12
Virginia	1,361,491	590,319	442,387	321,833	147,932 R	12	—	—	54	24
Washington	1,304,281	588,510	616,037	96,990	27,527 D	—	9	—	47	24
West Virginia	754,206	307,555	374,091	72,560	66,536 D	—	7	—	38	14
Wisconsin	1,691,538	809,997	748,804	127,835	61,193 R	12	—	—	59	30
Wyoming	127,205	70,927	45,173	11,105	25,754 R	3	—	—	22	12
Total	73,212,065	31,785,480	31,275,166	9,906,473	510,314 R	301	191	46	2,622[4]	1,333[5]

1. This vote, cast for Humphrey, is a combination of National Democratic (54,144) and Independent Democratic (142,435).
2. This vote for Wallace was cast as Democratic in Alabama. 3. Contains 3,066,840 Democratic and 311,622 Liberal votes.
4. Includes 23 votes allocated to U.S. territories. 5. Includes 8 votes allocated to U.S. territories.
OTHER CANDIDATES FOR PRESIDENT: New Party, Dick Gregory; Peace and Freedom Party, Eldridge Cleaver; Prohibition Party,
E. Harold Munn; Socialist Labor Party, Hennings Blomen; Socialist Workers Party, Fred Halstead.
NATIONAL TOTAL OF OTHER VOTES: 244,946, from 30 states.
Source: America Votes, compiled and edited by Richard M. Scammon.

Presidential Election of 1972

Principal Candidates for President and Vice President
Republican: Richard M. Nixon; Spiro T. Agnew
Democratic: George McGovern; Sargent Shriver
American Party[1]: John G. Schmitz; Thomas J. Anderson

State	Total	Nixon Republican	McGovern Democratic	Schmitz American	Plurality	R	D	A	Votes at Natl. Convs. Dem.	Rep.
Alabama	1,006,111	728,701	256,923	11,928	471,778 R	9	—	—	37	17
Alaska	95,219	55,349	•32,967	6,903	22,382 R	3	—	—	10	12
Arizona	622,926	402,812	198,540	21,208	204,272 R	6	—	—	25	18
Arkansas	651,320	448,541	199,892	2,887	248,649 R	6	—	—	27	18
California	8,367,862	4,602,096	3,475,847	232,554	1,126,249 R	45	—	—	271	96
Colorado	953,884	597,189	329,980	17,269	267,209 R	7	—	—	36	20
Connecticut	1,384,277	810,763	555,498	17,239	255,265 R	8	—	—	51	22
Delaware	235,516	140,357	92,283	2,638	48,074 R	3	—	—	13	12
D.C.	163,421	35,226	127,627	—	92,401 D	—	3	—	15	9
Florida	2,583,283	1,857,759	718,117	—	1,139,642 R	17	—	—	81	40
Georgia	1,174,772	881,496	289,529	812	591,967 R	12	—	—	53	24
Hawaii	270,274	168,865	101,409	—	67,456 R	4	—	—	17	14
Idaho	310,379	199,384	80,826	28,869	118,558 R	4	—	—	17	14
Illinois	4,723,236	2,788,179	1,913,472	2,471	874,707 R	26	—	—	170	58
Indiana	2,125,529	1,405,154	708,568	—	696,586 R	13	—	—	76	32
Iowa	1,225,944	706,207	496,206	22,056	210,001 R	8	—	—	46	20
Kansas	916,095	619,812	270,287	21,808	349,525 R	7	—	—	35	24
Kentucky	1,067,499	676,446	371,159	17,627	305,287 R	9	—	—	47	20
Louisiana	1,051,491	686,852	298,142	52,099	388,710 R	10	—	—	44	8
Maine	417,042	256,458	160,584	—	95,874 R	4	—	—	20	26
Maryland	1,353,812	829,305	505,781	18,726	323,524 R	10	—	—	53	34
Massachusetts	2,458,756	1,112,078	1,332,540	2,877	220,462 D	—	14	—	102	48
Michigan	3,489,727	1,961,721	1,459,435	63,321	502,286 R	21	—	—	132	26
Minnesota	1,741,652	898,269	802,346	31,407	95,923 R	10	—	—	64	26
Mississippi	645,963	505,125	126,782	11,598	378,343 R	7	—	—	25	13
Missouri	1,855,803	1,153,852	697,147	—	456,705 R	12	—	—	73	30
Montana	317,603	183,976	120,197	13,430	63,779 R	4	—	—	17	14
Nebraska	576,289	406,298	169,991	—	236,307 R	5	—	—	24	16
Nevada	181,766	115,750	66,016	—	49,734 R	3	—	—	11	12
New Hampshire	334,055	213,724	116,435	3,386	97,289 R	4	—	—	18	14
New Jersey	2,997,229	1,845,502	1,102,211	34,378	743,291 R	17	—	—	109	40
New Mexico	386,241	235,606	141,084	8,767	94,522 R	4	—	—	18	14
New York	7,165,919	4,192,778	2,951,084	—	1,241,694 R	41	—	—	278	88
North Carolina	1,518,612	1,054,889	438,705	25,018	616,184 R	13	—	—	64	32
North Dakota	280,514	174,109	100,384	5,646	73,725 R	3	—	—	14	12
Ohio	4,094,787	2,441,827	1,558,889	80,067	882,938 R	25	—	—	153	56
Oklahoma	1,029,900	759,025	247,147	23,728	511,878 R	8	—	—	39	22
Oregon	927,946	486,686	392,760	46,211	93,926 R	6	—	—	34	18
Pennsylvania	4,592,106	2,714,521	1,796,951	70,593	917,570 R	27	—	—	182	60
Rhode Island	415,808	220,383	194,645	25	25,738 R	4	—	—	22	8
South Carolina	673,960	477,044	186,824	10,075	290,220 R	8	—	—	32	22
South Dakota	307,415	166,476	139,945	—	26,531 R	4	—	—	17	14
Tennessee	1,201,182	813,147	357,293	30,373	455,854 R	10	—	—	49	26
Texas	3,471,281	2,298,896	1,154,289	6,039	1,144,607 R	26	—	—	130	52
Utah	478,476	323,643	126,284	28,549	197,359 R	4	—	—	19	14
Vermont	186,947	117,149	68,174	—	48,975 R	3	—	—	12	12
Virginia	1,457,019	988,493	438,887	19,721	549,606 R	11[2]	—	—	53	30
Washington	1,470,847	837,135	568,334	58,906	268,801 R	9	—	—	52	24
West Virginia	762,399	484,964	277,435	—	207,529 R	6	—	—	35	18
Wisconsin	1,852,890	989,430	810,174	47,525	179,256 R	11	—	—	67	18
Wyoming	145,570	100,464	44,358	748	56,106 R	3	—	—	11	12
Total	77,718,554	47,169,911	29,170,383	1,099,482	17,999,528 R	520	17	0	3,016[3]	1,346[4]

1. Known as American Independent Party and by other names in some states. 2. One Virginia elector cast vote for Libertarian Party. 3. Includes 16 votes allocated to U.S. territories. 4. Includes 11 votes allocated to U.S. territories.
OTHER CANDIDATES FOR PRESIDENT: Communist, Gus Hall; Libertarian Party, John Hospers; People's Party, Benjamin Spock; Prohibition Party, Earle H. Munn; Socialist Labor Party, Louis Fisher; Socialist Workers Party, Linda Jenness.
NATIONAL TOTALS OF OTHER VOTES: People's, 78,756; Social Workers, 66,677; Socialist Labor, 53,814; Communist, 25,595; Prohibition, 13,505; others and scattered, 40,431.
Source: America Votes 10, compiled and edited by Richard M. Scammon.

Presidential Election of 1976
Principal Candidates for President and Vice President
Democratic: Jimmy Carter; Walter F. Mondale
Republican: Gerald R. Ford; Robert J. Dole
Independent: Eugene J. McCarthy

State	Total	Carter Dem.	Ford Rep.	McCarthy Ind.	Plurality	Electoral vote D	Electoral vote R	Votes at Natl. Convs. Dem.	Votes at Natl. Convs. Rep.
Alabama	1,182,850	659,170	504,070	99	155,100 D	9	—	35	37
Alaska	123,574	44,058	71,555	—	27,497 R	—	3	10	19
Arizona	742,719	295,602	418,642	19,229	123,040 R	—	6	25	29
Arkansas	767,535	498,604	267,903	639	230,701 D	6	—	26	27
California	7,867,117	3,742,284	3,882,244	58,412	139,960 R	—	45	280	167
Colorado	1,081,554	460,801	584,278	26,047	123,477 R	—	7	35	31
Connecticut	1,381,526	647,895	719,261	3,759	71,366 R	—	8	51	35
Delaware	235,834	122,596	109,831	2,437	12,765 D	3	—	12	17
D.C.	168,830	137,818	27,873	—	109,945 D	3	—	17	14
Florida	3,150,631	1,636,000	1,469,531	23,643	166,469 D	17	—	81	66
Georgia	1,467,458	979,409	483,743	991	495,666 D	12	—	50	48
Hawaii	291,301	147,375	140,003	—	7,372 D	4	—	17	19
Idaho	344,071	126,549	204,151	1,194	77,602 R	—	4	16	21
Illinois	4,718,914	2,271,295	2,364,269	55,939	92,974 R	—	26	169	101
Indiana	2,220,362	1,014,714	1,183,958	—	169,244 R	—	13	75	54
Iowa	1,279,306	619,931	632,863	20,051	12,932 R	—	8	47	36
Kansas	957,845	430,421	502,752	13,185	72,331 R	—	7	34	34
Kentucky	1,167,142	615,717	531,852	6,837	83,865 D	9	—	46	37
Louisiana	1,278,439	661,365	587,446	6,588	73,919 D	10	—	41	41
Maine	483,216	232,279	236,320	10,874	4,041 R	—	4	20	20
Maryland	1,439,897	759,612	672,661	4,541	86,951 D	10	—	53	43
Massachusetts	2,547,558	1,429,475	1,030,276	65,637	399,199 D	14	—	104	43
Michigan	3,653,749	1,696,714	1,893,742	47,905	197,028 R	—	21	133	84
Minnesota	1,949,931	1,070,440	819,395	35,490	251,045 D	10	—	65	42
Mississippi	769,361	381,309	366,846	4,074	14,463 D	7	—	24	30
Missouri	1,953,600	998,387	927,443	24,029	70,944 D	12	—	71	49
Montana	328,734	149,259	173,703	—	24,444 R	—	4	17	20
Nebraska	607,668	233,293	359,219	9,409	125,926 R	—	5	23	25
Nevada	201,876	92,479	101,273	—	8,794 R	—	3	11	18
New Hampshire	339,618	147,645	185,935	4,095	38,290 R	—	4	17	21
New Jersey	3,014,472	1,444,653	1,509,688	32,717	65,035 R	—	17	108	67
New Mexico	418,409	201,148	211,419	1,161	10,271 R	—	4	18	21
New York	6,534,170	3,389,558	3,100,791	4,303	288,767 D	41	—	274	154
North Carolina	1,678,914	927,365	741,960	780	185,405 D	13	—	61	54
North Dakota	297,188	136,078	153,470	2,952	17,392 R	—	3	13	18
Ohio	4,111,873	2,011,621	2,000,505	58,258	11,116 D	25	—	152	97
Oklahoma	1,092,251	532,442	545,708	14,101	13,266 R	—	8	37	36
Oregon	1,029,876	490,407	492,120	40,207	1,713 R	—	6	34	30
Pennsylvania	4,620,787	2,328,677	2,205,604	50,584	123,073 D	27	—	178	103
Rhode Island	411,170	227,636	181,249	479	46,387 D	4	—	22	19
South Carolina	802,583	450,807	346,149	289	104,658 D	8	—	31	36
South Dakota	300,678	147,068	151,505	—	4,437 R	—	4	17	20
Tennessee	1,476,345	825,879	633,969	5,004	191,910 D	10	—	46	43
Texas	4,071,884	2,082,319	1,953,300	20,118	129,019 D	26	—	130	100
Utah	541,198	182,110	337,908	3,907	155,798 R	—	4	18	20
Vermont	187,765	78,789	100,387	4,001	21,598 R	—	3	12	18
Virginia	1,697,094	813,896	836,554	—	22,658 R	—	12	54	51
Washington	1,555,534	717,323	777,732	36,986	60,409 R	—	8[1]	53	38
West Virginia	750,964	435,914	314,760	113	121,154 D	6	—	33	28
Wisconsin	2,104,175	1,040,232	1,004,987	34,943	35,245 D	11	—	68	45
Wyoming	156,343	62,239	92,717	624	30,478 R	—	3	10	17
Total	81,555,889	40,830,763	39,147,793	756,631	1,682,970 D	297	240	3,008[2]	2,259[3]

1. Ninth Washington elector cast vote for Ronald Reagan. 2. Includes 34 votes allocated to U.S. territories and Democrats abroad. 3. Includes 16 votes allocated to U.S. territories.
OTHER CANDIDATES FOR PRESIDENT: Roger L. MacBride, Libertarian; Lester G. Maddox, American Independent; Thomas J. Anderson, American; Peter Camejo, Socialist Workers; Gus Hall, Communist; Margaret Wright, People's; Lyndon LaRouche, United States Labor; Benjamin C. Bubar, Prohibition; Julius Levin, Socialist Labor; Frank P. Zeidler, Socialist.
NATIONAL TOTALS OF OTHER VOTES: Libertarian, 173,011; American Independent, 170,531; American, 160,773; Socialist Workers, 91,314; Communist, 58,992; People's, 49,024; United States Labor, 40,043; Prohibition, 15,934; Socialist Labor, 9,616; Socialist, 6,038; others and scattered, 45,366.
Source: America Votes 12, compiled and edited by Richard M. Scammon and Alice V. McGillivray.

Presidential Election of 1980

Principal Candidates for President and Vice President
Democratic: Jimmy Carter; Walter F. Mondale
Republican: Ronald Reagan; George Bush
Independent: John B. Anderson; Patrick J. Lucey

State	Total	Carter Dem.	Per-cent	Reagan Rep.	Per-cent	Anderson Independent	Per-cent	Plurality		Electoral vote D	R	I
Alabama	1,341,929	636,730	47	654,192	49	16,481	1	17,462	R	—	9	—
Alaska	157,589	41,842	27	86,112	55	11,156	7	44,270	R	—	3	—
Arizona	873,945	246,843	28	529,688	61	76,952	9	282,845	R	—	6	—
Arkansas	837,582	398,041	48	403,164	48	22,468	3	5,123	R	—	6	—
California	8,585,789	3,083,652	36	4,524,835	53	739,832	9	1,441,183	R	—	45	—
Colorado	1,184,450	368,009	31	652,264	55	130,633	11	284,255	R	—	7	—
Connecticut	1,406,285	541,732	39	677,210	48	171,807	12	135,478	R	—	8	—
Delaware	235,723	105,754	45	111,252	47	16,288	7	5,498	R	—	3	—
D.C.	173,889	130,231	75	23,313	13	16,131	9	106,918	D	3	—	—
Florida	3,686,926	1,419,475	39	2,046,951	56	189,692	5	734,394	R	—	17	—
Georgia	1,596,582	890,733	56	654,168	41	36,055	2	236,565	D	12	—	—
Hawaii	303,287	135,879	45	130,112	43	32,021	11	5,767	D	4	—	—
Idaho	437,431	110,192	25	290,699	67	27,058	6	180,507	R	—	4	—
Illinois	4,749,766	1,981,413	42	2,358,094	50	346,754	7	376,681	R	—	26	—
Indiana	2,242,033	844,197	38	1,255,656	56	111,639	5	411,459	R	—	13	—
Iowa	1,317,661	508,672	39	676,026	51	115,633	9	167,354	R	—	8	—
Kansas	979,786	326,150	33	566,812	58	68,231	7	240,662	R	—	7	—
Kentucky	1,295,627	617,417	48	635,274	49	31,127	2	17,857	R	—	9	—
Louisiana	1,548,591	708,453	46	792,853	51	26,345	2	84,400	R	—	10	—
Maine	523,134	220,974	42	238,522	46	53,450	10	17,548	R	—	4	—
Maryland	1,540,496	726,161	47	680,606	44	119,537	8	45,555	R	10	—	—
Massachusetts	2,524,630	1,053,802	42	1,056,233	42	382,539	15	2,421	R	—	14	—
Michigan	3,909,725	1,661,532	43	1,915,225	49	275,223	7	253,393	R	—	21	—
Minnesota	2,045,780	954,173	47	873,268	43	174,997	9	80,905	D	10	—	—
Mississippi	892,620	429,281	48	441,089	49	12,036	1	11,808	R	—	7	—
Missouri	2,099,824	931,182	44	1,074,181	51	77,920	4	142,999	R	—	12	—
Montana	363,952	118,032	32	206,814	57	29,281	8	88,782	R	—	4	—
Nebraska	639,533	166,424	26	419,214	66	44,854	7	252,790	R	—	5	—
Nevada	243,692	66,666	27	155,017	64	17,651	7	177,026	R	—	3	—
New Hampshire	383,999	108,864	28	221,705	58	49,693	13	112,841	R	—	4	—
New Jersey	2,975,684	1,147,364	39	1,546,557	52	234,632	8	399,193	R	—	17	—
New Mexico	456,237	167,832	37	250,770	55	29,459	6	82,938	R	—	4	—
New York	6,201,959	2,728,372	44	2,893,831	47	467,801	8	165,459	R	—	41	—
North Carolina	1,855,833	875,635	47	915,018	49	52,800	3	39,383	R	—	13	—
North Dakota	301,545	79,189	26	193,695	64	23,640	8	114,506	R	—	3	—
Ohio	4,283,603	1,752,414	41	2,206,545	52	254,472	6	454,131	R	—	25	—
Oklahoma	1,149,708	402,026	35	695,570	60	38,284	3	293,544	R	—	8	—
Oregon	1,181,516	456,890	39	571,044	48	112,389	10	114,154	R	—	6	—
Pennsylvania	4,561,501	1,937,540	42	2,261,872	50	292,921	6	324,332	R	—	27	—
Rhode Island	415,967	198,342	48	154,793	37	59,819	14	43,549	D	4	—	—
South Carolina	893,190	28,220	48	39,277	49	13,868	2	11,456	R	—	8	—
South Dakota	327,703	103,855	32	198,343	61	21,431	7	94,488	R	—	4	—
Tennessee	1,617,616	783,051	48	787,761	49	35,991	2	4,710	R	—	10	—
Texas	4,541,636	1,881,147	41	2,510,705	55	111,613	2	629,558	R	—	26	—
Utah	604,152	124,266	21	439,687	73	30,284	5	315,421	R	—	4	—
Vermont	213,299	81,952	38	94,628	44	31,761	15	12,676	R	—	3	—
Virginia	1,866,032	752,174	40	989,609	53	95,418	5	237,435	R	—	12	—
Washington	1,742,394	650,193	37	865,244	50	185,073	11	215,051	R	—	9	—
West Virginia	737,715	367,462	50	334,206	45	31,691	4	33,256	D	6	—	—
Wisconsin	2,273,221	981,584	43	1,088,845	48	160,657	7	107,261	R	—	11	—
Wyoming	176,713	49,427	28	110,700	63	12,072	7	61,273	R	—	8	—
Total	86,495,678	35,481,435	41	43,899,248	51	5,719,437	6	8,417,813	R	49	489	—

NATIONAL TOTALS OF OTHER CANDIDATES FOR PRESIDENT: Ed Clark, Libertarian, 920,859; Barry Commoner, Citizens, 230,377; Gus Hall, Communist, 43,871; John Rarick, American Independent, 41,172; Clifton DeBerry, Socialist Workers, 40,105; Ellen McCormack, Respect for Life, 32,319; Margaret Smith, Peace and Freedom, 18,117; Deirdre Griswold, Workers' World, 13,211; others and write-ins, 55,527. *Source:* Federal Election Commission.

1980 Election Had Lowest Voter Turnout in 32 Years

According to the Federal Election Commission, only 53.95% of the eligible voters in the country cast their ballots in the 1980 presidential election. This was the lowest since the Truman-Dewey election of 1948 when only 51.1% of the voters went to the polls.

The highest voter turnout in the last 50 years was in the Kennedy-Nixon contest of 1960 with 62.8% of the electorate participating.

Qualifications for Voting

The Supreme Court decision of March 21, 1972, declared lengthy requirements for voting in state and local elections unconstitutional and suggested that 30 days was an ample period. Most of the states have changed or eliminated their durational residency requirements to comply with the ruling, as shown.

NO DURATIONAL RESIDENCY REQUIREMENT

Alabama, Arkansas, California, Connecticut,[14] Delaware,[13] District of Columbia,[2] Florida,[5] Georgia,[2] Hawaii,[2] Idaho, Iowa,[6] Louisiana,[2] Maine, Maryland, Massachusetts,[8] Nebraska,[9] New Hampshire, New Mexico,[7] North Carolina, Oklahoma, South Carolina,[2] South Dakota,[10] Tennessee,[12] Texas, Utah,[2] Virginia, West Virginia,[2] Wyoming[2]

30-DAY RESIDENCY REQUIREMENT

Alaska, Arizona,[11] Illinois, Indiana, Kentucky,[2] Michigan, Minnesota,[16] Mississippi, Montana, Nevada, New Jersey, New York, North Dakota,[3] Ohio, Pennsylvania, Rhode Island, Washington

OTHER

Colorado,[1] Kansas, Oregon, 20 days; Missouri,[4] 6 months; Vermont, 17 days;[15] Wisconsin, 10 days

1. 29-day for Presidential elections, 32 for all other. 2. 30-day registration requirement. 3. 10-day for Presidential elections; 45-day for state elections. 6. 10-day registration requirement. 7. 42-day registration requirement. 8. Registration deadline 28 days prior to primary or state elections. 9. Registration requirement, 2nd Friday prior to elections. 10. 15-day registration requirement. 11. 50-day for state. 12. 20-day registration requirement. 13. Must reside in Delaware and register by the last day that the books are open for registration. 14. 21-day registration requirement for elections; 14-day for primaries. 15. Administrative cut-off date for processing applications. 16. Must also be U.S. citizen for 3 months. *Source: Information Please* questionnaires to the states.

Unusual Voting Results

Election of 1872

The presidential and vice-presidential candidates of the Liberal Republicans and the northern Democrats in 1872 were Horace Greeley and B. Gratz Brown. Greeley died Nov. 29, 1872, before his 66 electors voted. In the electoral balloting for President, 63 of Greeley's votes were scattered among four other men, including Brown.

Election of 1876

In the election of 1876 Samuel J. Tilden, the Democratic candidate, received a popular majority but lacked one undisputed electoral vote to carry a clear majority of the electoral college. The crux of the problem was in the 22 electoral votes which were in dispute because Florida, Louisiana, South Carolina, and Oregon each sent in two sets of election returns. In the three southern states, Republican election boards threw out enough Democratic votes to certify the Republican candidate, Hayes. In Oregon, the Democratic governor disqualified a Republican elector, replacing him with a Democrat. Since the Senate was Republican and the House of Representatives Democratic, it seemed useless to refer the disputed returns to the two houses for solution. Instead Congress appointed an Electoral Commission with five representatives each from the Senate, the House, and the Supreme Court. All but one Justice was named, giving the Commission seven Republican and seven Democratic members. The naming of the fifth Justice was left to the other four. He was a Republican who first favored Tilden but, under pressure from his party, switched to Hayes, ensuring his election by the Commission voting 8 to 7 on party lines.

Minority Presidents

Fifteen candidates have become President of the United States with a popular vote less than 50% of the total cast. It should be noted, however, that in elections before 1872, presidential electors were not chosen by popular vote in all states. Adams' election in 1824 was by the House of Representatives, which chose him over Jackson, who had a plurality of both electoral and popular votes, but not a majority in the electoral college.

Besides Jackson in 1824, only two other candidates receiving the largest popular vote have failed to gain a majority in the electoral college—Samuel J. Tilden (D) in 1876 and Grover Cleveland (D) in 1888.

The "minority" Presidents follow:

Vote Received by Minority Presidents

Year	President	Electoral Percent	Popular vote Percent
1824	John Q. Adams	31.8	29.8
1844	James K. Polk (D)	61.8	49.3
1848	Zachary Taylor (W)	56.2	47.3
1856	James Buchanan (D)	58.7	45.3
1860	Abraham Lincoln (R)	59.4	39.9
1876	Rutherford B. Hayes (R)	50.1	47.9
1880	James A. Garfield (R)	57.9	48.3
1884	Grover Cleveland (D)	54.6	48.8
1888	Benjamin Harrison (R)	58.1	47.8
1892	Grover Cleveland (D)	62.4	46.0
1912	Woodrow Wilson (D)	81.9	41.8
1916	Woodrow Wilson (D)	52.1	49.3
1948	Harry S. Truman (D)	57.1	49.5
1960	John F. Kennedy (D)	56.4	49.7
1968	Richard M. Nixon (R)	56.1	43.4

Government Officials
Cabinet Members With Dates of Appointment

Although the Constitution made no provision for a President's advisory group, the heads of the three executive departments (State, Treasury, and War) and the Attorney General were organized by Washington into such a group; and by about 1793, the name "Cabinet" was applied to it. With the exception of the Attorney General up to 1870 and the Postmaster General from 1829 to 1872, Cabinet members have been heads of executive departments.

A Cabinet member is appointed by the President, subject to the confirmation of the Senate; and as his term is not fixed, he may be replaced at any time by the President. At a change in Administration, it is customary for him to tender his resignation, but he remains in office until a successor is appointed.

The table of Cabinet members lists only those members who actually served after being duly commissioned.

The dates shown are those of appointment. "Cont." indicates that the term continued from the previous Administration for a substantial amount of time.

With the creation of the Department of Transportation in 1966, the Cabinet consisted of 12 members. This figure was reduced to 11 when the Post Office Department became an independent agency in 1970 but, with the establishment in 1977 of a Department of Energy, became 12 again. Creation of the Department of Education in 1980 raised the number to 13.

WASHINGTON

Secretary of State	Thomas Jefferson 1789
	Edmund Randolph 1794
	Timothy Pickering 1795
Secretary of the Treasury	Alexander Hamilton 1789
	Oliver Wolcott, Jr. 1795
Secretary of War	Henry Knox 1789
	Timothy Pickering 1795
	James McHenry 1796
Attorney General	Edmund Randolph 1789
	William Bradford 1794
	Charles Lee 1795

J. ADAMS

Secretary of State	Timothy Pickering (Cont.)
	John Marshall 1800
Secretary of the Treasury	Oliver Wolcott, Jr. (Cont.)
	Samuel Dexter 1801
Secretary of War	James McHenry (Cont.)
	Samuel Dexter 1800
Attorney General	Charles Lee (Cont.)
Secretary of the Navy	Benjamin Stoddert 1798

JEFFERSON

Secretary of State	James Madison 1801
Secretary of the Treasury	Samuel Dexter (Cont.)
	Albert Gallatin 1801
Secretary of War	Henry Dearborn 1801
Attorney General	Levi Lincoln 1801
	Robert Smith 1805
	John Breckinridge 1805
	Caesar A. Rodney 1807
Secretary of the Navy	Benjamin Stoddert (Cont.)
	Robert Smith 1801

MADISON

Secretary of State	Robert Smith 1809
	James Monroe 1811
Secretary of the Treasury	Albert Gallatin (Cont.)
	George W. Campbell 1814
	Alexander J. Dallas 1814
	William H. Crawford 1816
Secretary of War	William Eustis 1809
	John Armstrong 1813
	James Monroe 1814
	William H. Crawford 1815
Attorney General	Caesar A. Rodney (Cont.)
	William Pinckney 1811
	Richard Rush 1814
Secretary of the Navy	Paul Hamilton 1809
	William Jones 1813
	B. W. Crowninshield 1814

MONROE

Secretary of State	John Quincy Adams 1817
Secretary of the Treasury	William H. Crawford (Cont.)
Secretary of War	John C. Calhoun 1817
Attorney General	Richard Rush (Cont.)

	William Wirt 1817
Secretary of the Navy	B. W. Crowninshield (Cont.)
	Smith Thompson 1818
	Samuel L. Southard 1823

J. Q. ADAMS

Secretary of State	Henry Clay 1825
Secretary of the Treasury	Richard Rush 1825
Secretary of War	James Barbour 1825
	Peter B. Porter 1828
Attorney General	William Wirt (Cont.)
Secretary of the Navy	Samuel L. Southard (Cont.)

JACKSON

Secretary of State	Martin Van Buren 1829
	Edward Livingston 1831
	Louis McLane 1833
	John Forsyth 1834
Secretary of the Treasury	Samuel D. Ingham 1829
	Louis McLane 1831
	William J. Duane 1833
	Roger B. Taney[3] 1833
	Levi Woodbury 1834
Secretary of War	John H. Eaton 1829
	Lewis Cass 1831
Attorney General	John M. Berrien 1829
	Roger B. Taney 1831
	Benjamin F. Butler 1833
Postmaster General[1]	William T. Barry 1829
	Amos Kendall 1835
Secretary of the Navy	John Branch 1829
	Levi Woodbury 1831
	Mahlon Dickerson 1834

VAN BUREN

Secretary of State	John Forsyth (Cont.)
Secretary of the Treasury	Levi Woodbury (Cont.)
Secretary of War	Joel R. Poinsett 1837
Attorney General	Benjamin F. Butler (Cont.)
	Felix Grundy 1838
	Henry D. Gilpin 1840
Postmaster General	Amos Kendall (Cont.)
	John M. Niles 1840
Secretary of the Navy	Mahlon Dickerson (Cont.)
	James K. Paulding 1838

W. H. HARRISON

Secretary of State	Daniel Webster 1841
Secretary of the Treasury	Thomas Ewing 1841
Secretary of War	John Bell 1841
Attorney General	John J. Crittenden 1841
Postmaster General	Francis Granger 1841
Secretary of the Navy	George E. Badger 1841

TYLER

Secretary of State	Daniel Webster (Cont.)
	Abel P. Upshur 1843
	John C. Calhoun 1844
Secretary of the Treasury	Thomas Ewing (Cont.)

Secretary of War	Walter Forward 1841
	John C. Spencer[3] 1843
	George M. Bibb 1844
	John Bell (Cont.)
	John C. Spencer 1841
	James M. Porter[3] 1843
	William Wilkins 1844
Attorney General	John J. Crittenden (Cont.)
	Hugh S. Legaré 1841
	John Nelson 1843
Postmaster General	Francis Granger (Cont.)
	Charles A. Wickliffe 1841
Secretary of the Navy	George E. Badger (Cont.)
	Abel P. Upshur 1841
	David Henshaw[3] 1843
	Thomas W. Gilmer 1844
	John Y. Mason 1844

POLK

Secretary of State	James Buchanan 1845
Secretary of the Treasury	Robert J. Walker 1845
Secretary of War	William L. Marcy 1845
Attorney General	John Y. Mason 1845
	Nathan Clifford 1846
	Isaac Toucey 1848
Postmaster General	Cave Johnson 1845
Secretary of the Navy	George Bancroft 1845
	John Y. Mason 1846

TAYLOR

Secretary of State	John M. Clayton 1849
Secretary of the Treasury	William M. Meredith 1849
Secretary of War	George W. Crawford 1849
Attorney General	Reverdy Johnson 1849
Postmaster General	Jacob Collamer 1849
Secretary of the Navy	William B. Preston 1849
Secretary of the Interior	Thomas Ewing 1849

FILLMORE

Secretary of State	Daniel Webster 1850
	Edward Everett 1852
Secretary of the Treasury	Thomas Corwin 1850
Secretary of War	Charles M. Conrad 1850
Attorney General	John J. Crittenden 1850
Postmaster General	Nathan K. Hall 1850
	Samuel D. Hubbard 1852
Secretary of the Navy	William A. Graham 1850
	John P. Kennedy 1852
Secretary of the Interior	Thos. M. T. McKennan 1850
	Alex. H. H. Stuart 1850

PIERCE

Secretary of State	William L. Marcy 1853
Secretary of the Treasury	James Guthrie 1853
Secretary of War	Jefferson Davis 1853
Attorney General	Caleb Cushing 1853
Postmaster General	James Campbell 1853
Secretary of the Navy	James C. Dobbin 1853
Secretary of the Interior	Robert McClelland 1853

BUCHANAN

Secretary of State	Lewis Cass 1857
	Jeremiah S. Black 1860
Secretary of the Treasury	Howell Cobb 1857
	Philip F. Thomas 1860
	John A. Dix 1861
Secretary of War	John B. Floyd 1857
	Joseph Holt 1861
Attorney General	Jeremiah S. Black 1857
	Edwin M. Stanton 1860
Postmaster General	Aaron V. Brown 1857
	Joseph Holt 1859
	Horatio King 1861
Secretary of the Navy	Isaac Toucey 1857
Secretary of the Interior	Jacob Thompson 1857

LINCOLN

Secretary of State	William H. Seward 1861
Secretary of the Treasury	Salmon P. Chase 1861
	William P. Fessenden 1864
	Hugh McCulloch 1865
Secretary of War	Simon Cameron 1861
	Edwin M. Stanton 1862

Attorney General	Edward Bates 1861
	James Speed 1864
Postmaster General	Montgomery Blair 1861
	William Dennison 1864
Secretary of the Navy	Gideon Welles 1861
Secretary of the Interior	Caleb B. Smith 1861
	John P. Usher 1863

A. JOHNSON

Secretary of State	William H. Seward (Cont.)
Secretary of the Treasury	Hugh McCulloch (Cont.)
Secretary of War	Edwin M. Stanton (Cont.)
	John M. Schofield 1868
Attorney General	James Speed (Cont.)
	Henry Stanbery 1866
	William M. Evarts 1868
Postmaster General	William Dennison (Cont.)
	Alexander W. Randall 1866
Secretary of the Navy	Gideon Welles (Cont.)
Secretary of the Interior	John P. Usher (Cont.)
	James Harlan 1865
	Orville H. Browning 1866

GRANT

Secretary of State	Elihu B. Washburne 1869
	Hamilton Fish 1869
Secretary of the Treasury	George S. Boutwell 1869
	William A. Richardson 1873
	Benjamin H. Bristow 1874
	Lot M. Morrill 1876
Secretary of War	John A. Rawlins 1869
	William W. Belknap 1869
	Alphonso Taft 1876
	James D. Cameron 1876
Attorney General	Ebenezer R. Hoar 1869
	Amos T. Akerman 1870
	George H. Williams 1871
	Edwards Pierrepont 1875
	Alphonso Taft 1876
Postmaster General	John A. J. Creswell 1869
	Marshall Jewell 1874
	James N. Tyner 1876
Secretary of the Navy	Adolph E. Borie 1869
	George M. Robeson 1869
Secretary of the Interior	Jacob D. Cox 1869
	Columbus Delano 1870
	Zachariah Chandler 1875

HAYES

Secretary of State	William M. Evarts 1877
Secretary of the Treasury	John Sherman 1877
Secretary of War	George W. McCrary 1877
	Alexander Ramsey 1879
Attorney General	Charles Devens 1877
Postmaster General	David M. Key 1877
	Horace Maynard 1880
Secretary of the Navy	Richard W. Thompson 1877
	Nathan Goff, Jr. 1881
Secretary of the Interior	Carl Schurz 1877

GARFIELD

Secretary of State	James G. Blaine 1881
Secretary of the Treasury	William Windom 1881
Secretary of War	Robert T. Lincoln 1881
Attorney General	Wayne MacVeagh 1881
Postmaster General	Thomas L. James 1881
Secretary of the Navy	William H. Hunt 1881
Secretary of the Interior	Samuel J. Kirkwood 1881

ARTHUR

Secretary of State	James G. Blaine (Cont.)
	F. T. Frelinghuysen 1881
Secretary of the Treasury	William Windom (Cont.)
	Charles J. Folger 1881
	Walter Q. Gresham 1884
	Hugh McCulloch 1884
Secretary of War	Robert T. Lincoln (Cont.)
Attorney General	Wayne MacVeagh (Cont.)
	Benjamin H. Brewster 1881
Postmaster General	Thomas L. James (Cont.)
	Timothy O. Howe 1881
	Walter Q. Gresham 1883
	Frank Hatton 1884
Secretary of the Navy	William H. Hunt (Cont.)

Secretary of the Interior	William E. Chandler 1882
	Samuel J. Kirkwood (Cont.)
	Henry M. Teller 1882

CLEVELAND

Secretary of State	Thomas F. Bayard 1885
Secretary of the Treasury	Daniel Manning 1885
	Charles S. Fairchild 1887
Secretary of War	William C. Endicott 1885
Attorney General	Augustus H. Garland 1885
Postmaster General	William F. Vilas 1885
	Don M. Dickinson 1888
Secretary of the Navy	William C. Whitney 1885
Secretary of the Interior	Lucius Q. C. Lamar 1885
	William F. Vilas 1888
Secretary of Agriculture	Norman J. Colman 1889

B. HARRISON

Secretary of State	James G. Blaine 1889
	John W. Foster 1892
Secretary of the Treasury	William Windom 1889
	Charles Foster 1891
Secretary of War	Redfield Proctor 1889
	Stephen B. Elkins 1891
Attorney General	William H. H. Miller 1889
Postmaster General	John Wanamaker 1889
Secretary of the Navy	Benjamin F. Tracy 1889
Secretary of the Interior	John W. Noble 1889
Secretary of Agriculture	Jeremiah M. Rusk 1889

CLEVELAND

Secretary of State	Walter Q. Gresham 1893
	Richard Olney 1895
Secretary of the Treasury	John G. Carlisle 1893
Secretary of War	Daniel S. Lamont 1893
Attorney General	Richard Olney 1893
	Judson Harmon 1895
Postmaster General	Wilson S. Bissell 1893
	William L. Wilson 1895
Secretary of the Navy	Hilary A. Herbert 1893
Secretary of the Interior	Hoke Smith 1893
	David R. Francis 1896
Secretary of Agriculture	Julius Sterling Morton 1893

McKINLEY

Secretary of State	John Sherman 1897
	William R. Day 1898
	John Hay 1898
Secretary of the Treasury	Lyman J. Gage 1897
Secretary of War	Russell A. Alger 1897
	Elihu Root 1899
Attorney General	Joseph McKenna 1897
	John W. Griggs 1898
	Philander C. Knox 1901
Postmaster General	James A. Gary 1897
	Charles E. Smith 1898
Secretary of the Navy	John D. Long 1897
Secretary of the Interior	Cornelius N. Bliss 1897
	Ethan A. Hitchcock 1898
Secretary of Agriculture	James Wilson 1897

T. ROOSEVELT

Secretary of State	John Hay (Cont.)
	Elihu Root 1905
	Robert Bacon 1909
Secretary of the Treasury	Lyman J. Gage (Cont.)
	Leslie M. Shaw 1902
	George B. Cortelyou 1907
Secretary of War	Elihu Root (Cont.)
	William H. Taft 1904
	Luke E. Wright 1908
Attorney General	Philander C. Knox (Cont.)
	William H. Moody 1904
	Charles J. Bonaparte 1906
Postmaster General	Charles E. Smith (Cont.)
	Henry C. Payne 1902
	Robert J. Wynne 1904
	George B. Cortelyou 1905
	George von L. Meyer 1907
Secretary of the Navy	John D. Long (Cont.)
	William H. Moody 1902
	Paul Morton 1904
	Charles J. Bonaparte 1905
	Victor H. Metcalf 1906

Secretary of the Interior	Truman H. Newberry 1908
	Ethan A. Hitchcock (Cont.)
	James R. Garfield 1907
Secretary of Agriculture	James Wilson (Cont.)
Secretary of Commerce and Labor	George B. Cortelyou 1903
	Victor H. Metcalf 1904
	Oscar S. Straus 1906

TAFT

Secretary of State	Philander C. Knox 1909
Secretary of the Treasury	Franklin MacVeagh 1909
Secretary of War	Jacob M. Dickinson 1909
	Henry L. Stimson 1911
Attorney General	George W. Wickersham 1909
Postmaster General	Frank H. Hitchcock 1909
Secretary of the Navy	George von L. Meyer 1909
Secretary of the Interior	Richard A. Ballinger 1909
	Walter L. Fisher 1911
Secretary of Agriculture	James Wilson (Cont.)
Secretary of Commerce and Labor	Charles Nagel 1909

WILSON

Secretary of State	William J. Bryan 1913
	Robert Lansing 1915
	Bainbridge Colby 1920
Secretary of the Treasury	William G. McAdoo 1913
	Carter Glass 1918
	David F. Houston 1920
Secretary of War	Lindley M. Garrison 1913
	Newton D. Baker 1916
Attorney General	James C. McReynolds 1913
	Thomas W. Gregory 1914
	A. Mitchell Palmer 1919
Postmaster General	Albert S. Burleson 1913
Secretary of the Navy	Josephus Daniels 1913
Secretary of the Interior	Franklin K. Lane 1913
	John B. Payne 1920
Secretary of Agriculture	David F. Houston 1913
	Edwin T. Meredith 1920
Secretary of Commerce	William C. Redfield 1913
	Joshua W. Alexander 1919
Secretary of Labor	William B. Wilson 1913

HARDING

Secretary of State	Charles E. Hughes 1921
Secretary of the Treasury	Andrew W. Mellon 1921
Secretary of War	John W. Weeks 1921
Attorney General	Harry M. Daugherty 1921
Postmaster General	Will H. Hays 1921
	Hubert Work 1922
	Harry S. New 1923
Secretary of the Navy	Edwin Denby 1921
Secretary of the Interior	Albert B. Fall 1921
	Hubert Work 1923
Secretary of Agriculture	Henry C. Wallace 1921
Secretary of Commerce	Herbert Hoover 1921
Secretary of Labor	James J. Davis 1921

COOLIDGE

Secretary of State	Charles E. Hughes (Cont.)
	Frank B. Kellogg 1925
Secretary of the Treasury	Andrew W. Mellon (Cont.)
Secretary of War	John W. Weeks (Cont.)
	Dwight F. Davis 1925
Attorney General	Harry M. Daugherty (Cont.)
	Harlan F. Stone 1924
	John G. Sargent 1925
Postmaster General	Harry S. New (Cont.)
Secretary of the Navy	Edwin Denby (Cont.)
	Curtis D. Wilbur 1924
Secretary of the Interior	Hubert Work (Cont.)
	Roy O. West 1928
Secretary of Agriculture	Henry C. Wallace (Cont.)
	Howard M. Gore 1924
	William M. Jardine 1925
Secretary of Commerce	Herbert Hoover (Cont.)
	William F. Whiting 1928
Secretary of Labor	James J. Davis (Cont.)

HOOVER

Secretary of State	Frank B. Kellogg (Cont.)

Secretary of the Treasury	Henry L. Stimson 1929
	Andrew W. Mellon (Cont.)
	Ogden L. Mills 1932
Secretary of War	James W. Good 1929
	Patrick J. Hurley 1929
Attorney General	William D. Mitchell 1929
Postmaster General	Walter F. Brown 1929
Secretary of the Navy	Charles F. Adams 1929
Secretary of the Interior	Ray Lyman Wilbur 1929
Secretary of Agriculture	Arthur M. Hyde 1929
Secretary of Commerce	Robert P. Lamont 1929
	Roy D. Chapin 1932
Secretary of Labor	James J. Davis (Cont.)
	William N. Doak 1930

F. D. ROOSEVELT

Secretary of State	Cordell Hull 1933
	E. R. Stettinius, Jr. 1944
Secretary of the Treasury	William H. Woodin 1933
	Henry Morgenthau, Jr. 1934
Secretary of War	George H. Dern 1933
	Harry H. Woodring 1936
	Henry L. Stimson 1940
Attorney General	Homer S. Cummings 1933
	Frank Murphy 1939
	Robert H. Jackson 1940
	Francis Biddle 1941
Postmaster General	James A. Farley 1933
	Frank C. Walker 1940
Secretary of the Navy	Claude A. Swanson 1933
	Charles Edison 1940
	Frank Knox 1940
	James Forrestal 1944
Secretary of the Interior	Harold L. Ickes 1933
Secretary of Agriculture	Henry A. Wallace 1933
	Claude R. Wickard 1940
Secretary of Commerce	Daniel C. Roper 1933
	Harry L. Hopkins 1938
	Jesse H. Jones 1940
	Henry A. Wallace 1945
Secretary of Labor	Frances Perkins 1933

TRUMAN

Secretary of State	E. R. Stettinius, Jr. (Cont.)
	James F. Byrnes 1945
	George C. Marshall 1947
	Dean Acheson 1949
Secretary of the Treasury	Henry Morgenthau, Jr. (Cont.)
	Frederick M. Vinson 1945
	John W. Snyder 1946
Secretary of Defense	James Forrestal 1947
	Louis A. Johnson 1949
	George C. Marshall 1950
	Robert A. Lovett 1951
Attorney General	Francis Biddle (Cont.)
	Tom C. Clark 1945
	J. Howard McGrath 1949
	James P. McGranery 1952
Postmaster General	Frank C. Walker (Cont.)
	Robert E. Hannegan 1945
	Jesse M. Donaldson 1947
Secretary of the Interior	Harold L. Ickes (Cont.)
	Julius A. Krug 1946
	Oscar L. Chapman 1949
Secretary of Agriculture	Claude R. Wickard (Cont.)
	Clinton P. Anderson 1945
	Charles F. Brannan 1948
Secretary of Commerce	Henry A. Wallace (Cont.)
	W. Averell Harriman 1946
	Charles Sawyer 1948
Secretary of Labor	Frances Perkins (Cont.)
	Lewis B. Schwellenbach 1945
	Maurice J. Tobin 1948
Secretary of War[2]	Henry L. Stimson (Cont.)
	Robert P. Patterson 1945
	Kenneth C. Royall 1947
Secretary of the Navy[2]	James Forrestal (Cont.)

EISENHOWER

Secretary of State	John Foster Dulles 1953
	Christian A. Herter 1959
Secretary of the Treasury	George M. Humphrey 1953
	Robert B. Anderson 1957

Secretary of Defense	Charles E. Wilson 1953
	Neil H. McElroy 1957
	Thomas S. Gates, Jr. 1959
Attorney General	Herbert Brownell, Jr. 1953
	William P. Rogers 1958
Postmaster General	Arthur E. Summerfield 1953
Secretary of the Interior	Douglas McKay 1953
	Frederick A. Seaton 1956
Secretary of Agriculture	Ezra Taft Benson 1953
Secretary of Commerce	Sinclair Weeks 1953
	Lewis L. Strauss[3] 1958
	Frederick H. Mueller 1959
Secretary of Labor	Martin P. Durkin 1953
	James P. Mitchell 1953
Secretary of Health, Education, and Welfare	Oveta Culp Hobby 1953
	Marion B. Folsom 1955
	Arthur S. Flemming 1958

KENNEDY

Secretary of State	Dean Rusk 1961
Secretary of the Treasury	C. Douglas Dillon 1961
Secretary of Defense	Robert S. McNamara 1961
Attorney General	Robert F. Kennedy 1961
Postmaster General	J. Edward Day 1961
	John A. Gronouski 1963
Secretary of the Interior	Stewart L. Udall 1961
Secretary of Agriculture	Orville L. Freeman 1961
Secretary of Commerce	Luther H. Hodges 1961
Secretary of Labor	Arthur J. Goldberg 1961
	W. Willard Wirtz 1962
Secretary of Health, Education, and Welfare	Abraham A. Ribicoff 1961
	Anthony J. Celebrezze 1962

L. B. JOHNSON

Secretary of State	Dean Rusk (Cont.)
Secretary of the Treasury	C. Douglas Dillon (Cont.)
	Henry H. Fowler 1965
	Joseph W. Barr[4] 1968
Secretary of Defense	Robert S. McNamara (Cont.)
	Clark M. Clifford 1968
Attorney General	Robert F. Kennedy (Cont.)
	N. de B. Katzenbach 1965
	Ramsey Clark 1967
Postmaster General	John A. Gronouski (Cont.)
	Lawrence F. O'Brien 1965
	W. Marvin Watson 1968
Secretary of the Interior	Stewart L. Udall (Cont.)
Secretary of Agriculture	Orville L. Freeman (Cont.)
Secretary of Commerce	Luther H. Hodges (Cont.)
	John T. Connor 1964
	A. B. Trowbridge 1967
	C. R. Smith 1968
Secretary of Labor	W. Willard Wirtz (Cont.)
Secretary of Health, Education, and Welfare	Anthony J. Celebrezze (Cont.)
	John W. Gardner 1965
	Wilbur J. Cohen 1968
Secretary of Housing and Urban Development	Robert C. Weaver 1966
	Robert C. Wood[4] 1969
Secretary of Transportation	Alan S. Boyd 1966

NIXON

Secretary of State	William P. Rogers 1969
	Henry A. Kissinger 1973
Secretary of the Treasury	David M. Kennedy 1969
	John B. Connally 1971
	George P. Shultz 1972
	William E. Simon 1974
Secretary of Defense	Melvin R. Laird 1969
	Elliot L. Richardson 1973
	James R. Schlesinger 1973
Attorney General	John N. Mitchell 1969
	Richard G. Kleindienst 1972
	Elliot L. Richardson 1973
	William B. Saxbe 1974
Postmaster General[5]	William M. Blount 1969
Secretary of the Interior	Walter J. Hickel 1969
	Rogers C. B. Morton 1971
Secretary of Agriculture	Clifford M. Hardin 1969
	Earl L. Butz 1971
Secretary of Commerce	Maurice H. Stans 1969
	Peter G. Peterson 1972

Secretary of Labor	Frederick B. Dent 1973
	George P. Shultz 1969
	James D. Hodgson 1970
	Peter J. Brennan 1973
Secretary of Health, Education, and Welfare	Robert H. Finch 1969
	Elliot L. Richardson 1970
	Caspar W. Weinberger 1973
Secretary of Housing and Urban Development	George Romney 1969
	James T. Lynn 1973
Secretary of Transportation	John A. Volpe 1969
	Claude S. Brinegar 1973

FORD

Secretary of State	Henry A. Kissinger (Cont.)
Secretary of the Treasury	William E. Simon (Cont.)
Secretary of Defense	James R. Schlesinger (Cont.)
	Donald H. Rumsfeld 1975
Attorney General	William B. Saxbe (Cont.)
	Edward H. Levi 1975
Secretary of the Interior	Rogers C. B. Morton (Cont.)
	Stanley K. Hathaway 1975
	Thomas S. Kleppe 1975
Secretary of Agriculture	Earl L. Butz (Cont.)
	John Knebel 1976
Secretary of Commerce	Frederick B. Dent (Cont.)
	Rogers C. B. Morton 1975
	Elliot L. Richardson 1976
Secretary of Labor	Peter J. Brennan (Cont.)
	John T. Dunlop 1975
	William J. Usery, Jr. 1976
Secretary of Health, Education and Welfare	Caspar W. Weinberger (Cont.)
	F. David Mathews 1975
Secretary of Housing and Urban Development	James T. Lynn (Cont.)
	Carla A. Hills 1975
Secretary of Transportation	Claude S. Brinegar (Cont.)
	William T. Coleman, Jr. 1975

CARTER

Secretary of State	Cyrus R. Vance 1977
	Edmund S. Muskie 1980
Secretary of the Treasury	W. Michael Blumenthal 1977
	G. William Miller 1979
Secretary of Defense	Harold Brown 1977
Attorney General	Griffin B. Bell 1977
	Benjamin R. Civiletti 1979
Secretary of the Interior	Cecil D. Andrus 1977
Secretary of Agriculture	Bob S. Bergland 1977
Secretary of Commerce	Juanita M. Kreps 1977
	Philip M. Klutznick 1979
Secretary of Labor	F. Ray Marshall 1977
Secretary of Health and Human Services[6]	Joseph A. Califano, Jr. 1977
	Patricia Roberts Harris 1979
Secretary of Housing and Urban Development	Patricia Roberts Harris 1977
	Moon Landrieu 1979
Secretary of Transportation	Brock Adams 1977
	Neil E. Goldschmidt 1979
Secretary of Energy	James R. Schlesinger 1977
	Charles W. Duncan, Jr. 1979
Secretary of Education	Shirley Mount Hufstedler 1979

REAGAN

Secretary of State	Alexander M. Haig, Jr. 1981
Secretary of the Treasury	Donald T. Regan 1981
Secretary of Defense	Caspar W. Weinberger 1981
Attorney General	William French Smith 1981
Secretary of the Interior	James G. Watt 1981
Secretary of Agriculture	John R. Block 1981
Secretary of Commerce	Malcolm Baldrige 1981
Secretary of Labor	Raymond J. Donovan 1981
Secretary of Health and Human Services	Richard S. Schweiker 1981
Secretary of Housing and Urban Development	Samuel R. Pierce, Jr. 1981
Secretary of Transportation	Andrew L. Lewis, Jr. 1981
Secretary of Energy	James B. Edwards 1981
Secretary of Education	T. H. Bell 1981

1. The Postmaster General did not become a Cabinet member until 1829. Earlier Postmasters General were: Samuel Osgood (1789), Timothy Pickering (1791), Joseph Habersham (1795), Gideon Granger (1801), Return J. Meigs, Jr. (1814), and John McLean (1823). 2. On July 26, 1947, the Departments of War and of the Navy were incorporated into the Department of Defense. 3. Not confirmed by the Senate. 4. Recess appointment. 5. The Postmaster General is no longer a Cabinet member. 6. Known as Department of Health, Education, and Welfare until May 1980.

How a Bill Becomes a Law

When a Senator or a Representative introduces a bill, he sends it to the clerk of his house, who gives it a number and title. This is the *first reading*, and the bill is referred to the proper committee.

The committee may decide the bill is unwise or unnecessary and *table* it, thus killing it at once. Or it may decide the bill is worthwhile and hold hearings to listen to facts and opinions presented by experts and other interested persons. After members of the committee have debated the bill and perhaps offered amendments, a vote is taken; and if the vote is favorable, the bill is sent back to the floor of the house.

The clerk reads the bill sentence by sentence to the house, and this is known as the *second reading*. Members may then debate the bill and offer amendments. In the House of Representatives, the time for debate is limited by a *cloture rule*, but there is no such restriction in the Senate for cloture, where 60 votes are required. This makes possible a *filibuster*, in which one or more opponents hold the floor to defeat the bill.

The *third reading* is by title only, and the bill is put to a vote, which may be by voice or roll call, depending on the circumstances and parliamentary rules. Members who must be absent at the time but who wish to record their vote may be paired if each negative vote has a balancing affirmative one.

The bill then goes to the other house of Congress, where it may be defeated, or passed with or without amendments. If the bill is defeated, it dies. If it is passed with amendments, a joint Congressional committee must be appointed by both houses to iron out the differences.

After its final passage by both houses, the bill is sent to the President. If he approves, he signs it, and the bill becomes a law. However, if he disapproves, he *vetoes* the bill by refusing to sign it and sending it back to the house of origin with his reasons for the veto. The objections are read and debated, and a roll-call vote is taken. If the bill receives less than a two-thirds vote, it is defeated and goes no farther. But if it receives a two-thirds vote or greater, it is sent to the other house for a vote. If that house also passes it by a two-thirds vote, the President's veto is *overridden*, and the bill becomes a law.

Should the President desire neither to sign nor to veto the bill, he may retain it for ten days, Sundays excepted, after which time it automatically becomes a law without signature. However, if Congress has adjourned within those ten days, the bill is automatically killed, that process of indirect rejection being known as a *pocket veto*.

Federal Judiciary
Source: Administrative Office of the United States Courts.

SUPREME COURT OF THE U.S.

(Washington, D.C. 20543)
Chief Justice: Warren E. Burger

Associate Justices:
William J. Brennan, Jr.
Byron R. White
Thurgood Marshall
Harry A. Blackmun
Lewis F. Powell, Jr.
William H. Rehnquist
John Paul Stevens
Sandra Day O'Connor

U.S. COURTS OF APPEALS

(CJ indicates Chief Judge)

District of Columbia: Spottswood W. Robinson III, CJ, J.Skelly Wright, Carl McGowan, Edward Allen Tamm, Patricia M. Wald, Abner J. Mikva, Roger Robb, George E. MacKinnon, Malcolm R. Wilkey, Harry T. Edwards, Ruth Bader Ginsburg, all Washington.

First Circuit (Me., Mass., N.H., R.I., Puerto Rico): Frank M. Coffin, CJ, Portland, Me.; Levin H. Campbell, Stephen G. Bryer, both Boston; Hugh H. Bownes, Concord, N.H.

Second Circuit (Conn., N.Y., Vt.): Wilfred Feinbert, CJ, Irving R. Kaufman, Walter R. Mansfield, Amalya Lyle Kearse, all New York City; Ellsworth A. Van Graafeiland, Rochester, N.Y.; James L. Oakes, Brattleboro, Vt.; Thomas J. Meskill, New Britain, Conn; Jon O. Newman, Hartford, Conn.

Third Circuit (Del., N.J., Pa., Virgin Is.): Collins J. Seitz, CJ, Wilmington, Del.; Arlin M. Adams, Dolores K. Sloviter, Philadelphia; Ruggero J. Aldisert, Joseph F. Weis, Jr., both Pittsburgh; John J. Gibbons, Leonard I. Garth, both Newark, N.J.; James Hunger, III, Camden, N.J.; A. Leon Higginbotham, Jr., Philadelphia.

Fourth Circuit (Md., N.C., S.C., Va., W. Va.): Harrison L. Winter, CJ, Francis D. Murnaghan, Jr., both Baltimore, Md.; John D. Butzner, Jr., Richmond, Va.; Donald Stuart Russell, Spartanburg, S.C.; H. Emory Widener, Jr., Abingdon, Va.; Kenneth K. Hall, James M. Sprouse, both Charleston, W. Va.; James Dickson Phillips, Jr., Durham, N.C.; Sam J. Ervin III, Morganton, N.C.

Fifth Circuit (Ala., Fla., Ga., La., Miss., Tex., Canal Zone): John C. Godbold, CJ, Montgomery, Ala.; James P. Coleman, Ackerman, Miss.; John R. Brown, Carolyn D. Randall, both Houston; Robert A. Ainsworth, Albert Tate, Jr., both New Orleans; Alvin B. Rubin, Baton Rouge, La.; Thomas G. Gee, Thomas M. Reavley, Samuel D. Johnson, Jerre S. Williams, all Austin, Tex.; Irving L. Goldberg, Dallas; Frank M. Johnson, Montgomery, Ala.; Charles Clark, Jackson, Miss.; Paul H. Roney, St. Petersburg, Fla.; Gerald B. Tjoflat, Jacksonville, Fla.; James C. Hill, Atlanta; Peter T. Fay, Miami, Fla.; Robert S. Vance, Birmingham, Ala.; Phyllis A. Kravitch, Albert J. Henderson, Jr., both Atlanta; Reynaldo G. Garza, Brownsville, Tex.; Joseph W. Hatchett, Tallahassee, Fla.; Henry A. Politz, Shreveport, La.; R. Lanier Anderson, Macon, Ga.; Thomas A. Clark, Tampa, Fla.

Sixth Circuit (Ky., Mich., Ohio, Tenn.): George Clifton Edwards, Jr., CJ, Cincinnati; Ohio; Nathaniel R. Jones, Cleveland, Ohio; Gilbert S. Merritt, Nashville, Tenn.; Paul C. Weick, Akron, Ohio; Albert J. Engel, Grand Rapids, Mich.; Pierce Lively, Danville, Ky.; Damon J. Keith, Cornelia G.

Kennedy, both Detroit, Mich.; Bailey Brown, Memphis, Tenn.; Boyce F. Martin, Jr., Louisville, Ky.

Seventh Circuit (Ill., Ind., Wis.): Thomas E. Fairchild, CJ, Luther M. Swygert, Walter J. Cummings, Wilbur F. Pell, Jr., Robert A. Sprecher, William J. Bauer, Harlington Wood, Jr., Richard D. Cudahy, all Chicago.

Eighth Circuit (Ark., Iowa, Minn., Mo., Neb., N.D., S.D.): Donald P. Lay, CJ, Donald R. Ross, both Omaha, Neb.; Gerald W. Heaney, Duluth, Minn.; Myron H. Bright, Fargo, N.D.; Roy L. Stephenson, Des Moines, Iowa; J. Smith Henley, Harrison, Ark.; Theodore McMillian, St. Louis; Richard Sheppard Arnold, Little Rock, Ark.

Ninth Circuit (Ariz., Calif., Idaho, Mont., Nev., Ore., Wash., Alaska, Hawaii, Guam): James R. Browning, CJ, Joseph T. Sneed, Cecil F. Poole, all San Francisco; Harry Pregerson, Arthur L. Alarcon, Warren J. Ferguson, Dorothy W. Nelson, William A. Norris, Stephen Reinhardt, all Los Angeles; J. Clifford Wallace, San Diego, Calif.; Eugene A. Wright, Jerome Farris, Betty B. Fletcher, all Seattle; Thomas Tang, Mary M. Schroeder, William C. Canby, all Phoenix, Ariz.; Herbert Y. C. Choy, Honolulu; Alfred T. Goodwin, Otto R. Skopil, Jr., both Portland, Ore.; Anthony M. Kennedy, Sacramento, Calif.; J. Blaine Anderson, Boise, Idaho; Procter Hug, Jr., Reno, Nev.; Robert Boochever, Juneau, Alaska.

Tenth Circuit (Colo., Kan., N.M., Okla., Utah, Wyo.): Oliver Seth, CJ, Santa Fe, N.M.; William J. Holloway, Jr., Oklahoma City; Robert H. McWilliams, William E. Doyle, both Denver; James E. Barrett, Cheyenne, Wyo.; James K. Logan, Olathe, Kan.; Monroe G. McKay, Salt Lake City, Utah; Stephanie K. Seymour.

U.S. COURT OF CLAIMS

(Washington, D.C. 20005)
Chief Judge: Daniel M. Friedman.
Associate Judges: Oscar H. Davis, Philip Nichols, Jr., Shiro Kashiwa, Robert L. Kunzig, Marion T. Bennett, Edward S. Smith.

U.S. COURT OF CUSTOMS AND PATENT APPEALS

(Washington, D.C. 20439)
Chief Judge: Howard T. Markey.
Associate Judges: Giles S. Rich, Phillip B. Baldwin, Jack R. Miller, Helen W. Nies.

U.S. CUSTOMS COURT

(One Federal Plaza, New York, N.Y. 10007)
Chief Judge: Edward D. Re.
Judges: Paul P. Rao, Morgan Ford, Scovel Richardson, Frederick Landis, James L. Watson, Herbert N. Maletz, Bernard Newman, Nils A. Boe.

U.S. TAX COURT

(Washington, D.C. 20217)
Chief Judge: Theodore Tannenwald, Jr.
Judges: William M. Drennen, Irene F. Scott, William M. Fay, Howard A. Dawson, Jr., Charles R. Simpson, C. Moxley Featherston, Leo H. Irwin, Samuel B. Sterrett, William A. Goffe, Cynthia H. Hall, Darrell D. Wiles, Richard C. Wilbur, Herbert L. Chabot, Arthur L. Nims, III, Edna G. Parker, Sheldon V. Ekman, J. Gregory Bruce, Norman O. Tietjens, Bruce M. Forrester, Arnold Raum, William M. Drennen.

NOTE: To keep abreast of changes see *United States Court Directory 1982.*

The Growth of Social Security Taxes

A worker who entered the Social Security system in 1937 and paid the maximum tax each year would have contributed only $2,673.60 if he retired 30 years later in 1967. A worker who joined the system in 1968 and continues to pay the maximum rate will pay $27,512.25 after only 20 years assuming that the scheduled tax rate and wage base are not changed.

The initial Social Security tax rate which went into effect in 1937 was 1%. By 1990, this will have risen to 7.65%.

Members of the Supreme Court of the United States

Name	Birth Place	Birth Date	Religious affiliation (Source: Library of Congress)	Appointment From	Appointment President	Oath taken Date	Oath taken Age	Service terminated Date	Service terminated Cause	Service terminated Years served	Service terminated Age	Death Date	Death Age
CHIEF JUSTICES													
John Jay	N.Y.	1745	Episcopal	N.Y.	Washington	1789	44	1795	resigned	5	49	1829	83
John Rutledge	S.C.	1739	Church of England	S.C.	Washington	1795	55	1795	rejected	0	56	1800	60
Oliver Ellsworth	Conn.	1745	Congregational	Conn.	Washington	1796	50	1800	resigned	4	55	1807	62
John Marshall	Va.	1755	Episcopal	Va.	J. Adams	1801	45	1835	death	34	79	1835	79
Roger B. Taney	Md.	1777	Roman Catholic	Md.	Jackson	1836	59	1864	death	28	87	1864	87
Salmon P. Chase	N.H.	1808	Episcopal	Ohio	Lincoln	1864	56	1873	death	8	65	1873	65
Morrison R. Waite	Conn	1816	Episcopal	Ohio	Grant	1874	57	1888	death	14	71	1888	71
Melville W. Fuller	Me.	1833	Episcopal	Ill.	Cleveland	1888	55	1910	death	21	77	1910	77
Edward D. White	La.	1845	Roman Catholic	La.	Taft	1910	65	1921	death	10	75	1921	75
William H. Taft	Ohio	1857	Unitarian	Conn.	Harding	1921	63	1930	retired	8	72	1930	72
Charles E. Hughes	N.Y.	1862	Baptist	N.Y.	Hoover	1930	67	1941	retired	11	79	1948	86
Harlan F. Stone	N.H.	1872	Episcopal	N.Y.	F. Roosevelt	1941	68	1946	death	4	73	1946	73
Frederick M. Vinson	Ky.	1890	Methodist	Ky.	Truman	1946	56	1953	death	7	63	1953	63
Earl Warren	Calif.	1891	Protestant	Calif.	Eisenhower	1953	62	1969	retired	15	78	1974	83
Warren E. Burger	Minn.	1907	Presbyterian	Va.	Nixon	1969	61						
ASSOCIATE JUSTICES													
James Wilson	Scotland	1742	Episcopal	Pa.	Washington	1789	47	1798	death	8	55	1798	55
John Rutledge	S.C.	1739	Church of England	S.C.	Washington	1790	50	1791	resigned	1	51	1800	60
William Cushing	Mass.	1732	Unitarian	Mass.	Washington	1790	57	1810	death	20	78	1810	78
John Blair	Va.	1732	Presbyterian	Va.	Washington	1790	58	1796	resigned	5	64	1800	68
James Iredell	England	1751	Episcopal	N.C.	Washington	1790	38	1799	death	9	48	1799	48
Thomas Johnson	Md.	1732	Episcopal	Md.	Washington	1792	59	1793	resigned	0	60	1819	86
William Paterson	Ireland	1745	Protestant	N.J.	Washington	1793	47	1806	death	13	60	1806	60
Samuel Chase	Md.	1741	Episcopal	Md.	Washington	1796	54	1811	death	15	70	1811	70
Bushrod Washington	Va.	1762	Episcopal	Va.	Washington	1799	36	1829	death	30	67	1829	67
Alfred Moore	N.C.	1755	Episcopal	N.C.	J. Adams	1800	45	1804	resigned	3	48	1810	55
William Johnson	S.C.	1771	Presbyterian	S.C.	Jefferson	1804	32	1834	death	30	62	1834	62
Brockholst Livingston	N.Y.	1757	Presbyterian	N.Y.	Jefferson	1807	49	1823	death	16	65	1823	65
Thomas Todd	Va.	1765	Presbyterian	Ky.	Jefferson	1807	42	1826	death	18	61	1826	61
Gabriel Duval	Md.	1752	French Protestant	Md.	Madison	1811	58	1835	resigned	23	82	1844	91
Joseph Story	Mass.	1779	Unitarian	Mass.	Madison	1812	32	1845	death	33	65	1845	65
Smith Thompson	N.Y.	1768	Presbyterian	N.Y.	Monroe	1823	55	1843	death	20	75	1843	75
Robert Trimble	Va.	1777	Protestant	Ky.	J. Q. Adams	1826	49	1828	death	2	51	1828	51
John McLean	N.J.	1785	Methodist-Epis.	Ohio	Jackson	1830	44	1861	death	31	76	1861	76
Henry Baldwin	Conn.	1780	Trinity Church	Pa.	Jackson	1830	50	1844	death	14	64	1844	64
James M. Wayne	Ga.	1790	Protestant	Ga.	Jackson	1835	45	1867	death	32	77	1867	77
Philip P. Barbour	Va.	1783	Episcopal	Va.	Jackson	1836	52	1841	death	4	57	1841	57
John Catron	Pa.	1786	Presbyterian	Tenn.	Jackson	1837	51	1865	death	28	79	1865	79

Name	Birth Place	Birth Date	Religious affiliation (Source: Library of Congress)	Appointment From	President	Oath taken Date	Oath taken Age	Service terminated Date	Cause	Years served	Age	Death Date	Death Age
John McKinley	Va	1780	Protestant	Ala.	Van Buren	1837	57	1852	death	14	72	1852	72
Peter V. Daniel	Va.	1784	Episcopal	Va.	Van Buren	1841	57	1860	death	18	76	1860	76
Samuel Nelson	N.Y.	1792	Protestant	N.Y.	Tyler	1845	52	1872	retired	27	80	1873	81
Levi Woodbury	N.H.	1789	Protestant	N.H.	Polk	1845	55	1851	death	5	61	1851	61
Robert C. Grier	Pa.	1794	Presbyterian	Pa.	Polk	1846	52	1870	retired	23	75	1870	76
Benjamin R. Curtis	Mass.	1809	(?)	Mass.	Fillmore	1851	41	1857	resigned	5	47	1874	64
John A. Campbell	Ga.	1811	Episcopal	Ala.	Pierce	1853	41	1861	resigned	8	49	1889	77
Nathan Clifford	N.H.	1803		Maine	Buchanan	1858	54	1881	death	23	77	1881	77
Noah H. Swayne	Va.	1804	(?)	Ohio	Lincoln	1862	57	1881	retired	18	76	1884	79
Samuel F. Miller	Ky.	1816	Quaker	Iowa	Lincoln	1862	46	1890	death	28	74	1890	74
David Davis	Md.	1815	Unitarian	Ill.	Lincoln	1862	47	1877	resigned	14	61	1886	71
Stephen J. Field	Conn.	1816	(?)	Calif.	Lincoln	1863	46	1897	retired	34	81	1899	82
William Strong	Conn.	1808	Episcopal	Pa.	Grant	1870	61	1880	retired	10	72	1895	87
Joseph P. Bradley	N.Y.	1813	Presbyterian	N.J.	Grant	1870	57	1892	death	21	78	1892	78
Ward Hunt	N.Y.	1810	Presbyterian	N.Y.	Grant	1872	62	1882	disabled	9	71	1886	75
John M. Harlan	Ky.	1833	Episcopal	Ky.	Hayes	1877	44	1911	death	33	78	1911	78
William B. Woods	Ohio	1824	Presbyterian	Ga.	Hayes	1880	56	1887	death	6	62	1887	62
Stanley Matthews	Ohio	1824	Protestant	Ohio	Garfield	1881	56	1889	death	7	64	1889	64
Horace Gray	Mass.	1828	Presbyterian	Mass.	Arthur	1882	53	1902	death	20	73	1902	74
Samuel Blatchford	N.Y.	1820	(?)	N.Y.	Arthur	1882	62	1893	death	11	67	1893	73
Lucius Q. C. Lamar	Ga.	1825	Presbyterian	Miss.	Cleveland	1888	62	1893	death	5	72	1893	67
David J. Brewer	Asia Minor	1837	Methodist	Kan.	Harrison	1889	52	1910	death	20	70	1910	72
Henry B. Brown	Mass.	1836	Protestant	Mich.	Harrison	1890	54	1906	retired	15	70	1913	77
George Shiras, Jr.	Pa.	1832	Presbyterian	Pa.	Harrison	1892	60	1903	retired	10	71	1924	92
Howell E. Jackson	Tenn.	1832	Baptist	Tenn.	Harrison	1893	60	1895	death	2	63	1895	63
Edward D. White	La.	1845	Roman Catholic	La.	Cleveland	1894	48	1910	promoted	16	65	1921	75
Rufus W. Peckham	N.Y.	1838	Episcopal	N.Y.	Cleveland	1895	57	1909	death	13	70	1909	70
Joseph McKenna	Pa.	1843	Roman Catholic	Calif.	McKinley	1898	54	1925	retired	26	81	1926	83
Oliver W. Holmes	Mass.	1841	Unitarian	Mass.	T. Roosevelt	1902	61	1932	retired	29	90	1935	93
William R. Day	Ohio	1849	Protestant	Ohio	T. Roosevelt	1903	53	1922	retired	19	73	1923	74
William H. Moody	Mass.	1853	Episcopal	Mass.	T. Roosevelt	1906	52	1910	disabled	3	56	1917	63
Horace H. Lurton	Ky.	1844	Episcopal	Tenn.	Taft	1909	65	1914	death	4	70	1914	70
Charles E. Hughes	N.Y.	1862	Baptist	N.Y.	Taft	1910	48	1916	resigned	5	54	1948	86
Willis Van Devanter	Ind.	1859	Episcopal	Wyo.	Taft	1910	51	1937	retired	26	78	1941	81
Joseph R. Lamar	Ga.	1857	Ch. of Disciples	Ga.	Taft	1910	53	1916	death	4	58	1916	58
Mahlon Pitney	N.J.	1858	Presbyterian	N.J.	Taft	1912	54	1922	disabled	10	64	1924	66
James C. McReynolds	Tenn.	1862	Disciples of Christ	Tenn.	Wilson	1914	52	1941	retired	26	78	1946	84
Louis D. Brandeis	Ky.	1856	Jewish	Mass.	Wilson	1916	59	1939	retired	22	82	1941	84
John H. Clarke	Ohio	1857	Protestant	Ohio	Wilson	1916	59	1922	resigned	5	65	1945	87
George Sutherland	England	1862	Episcopal	Utah	Harding	1922	60	1938	retired	15	75	1942	80
Pierce Butler	Minn.	1866	Roman Catholic	Minn.	Harding	1923	56	1939	death	16	73	1939	73
Edward T. Sanford	Tenn.	1865	Episcopal	Tenn.	Harding	1923	57	1930	death	7	64	1930	64

Harlan F. Stone	N.H.	1872	Episcopal	1925	52	Coolidge	promoted	1941	16	68	1946	73
Owen J. Roberts	Pa.	1875	Episcopal	1930	55	Hoover	resigned	1945	15	70	1955	80
Benjamin N. Cardozo	N.Y.	1870	Jewish	1932	61	Hoover	death	1938	6	68	1938	68
Hugo L. Black	Ala.	1886	Baptist	1937	51	F. Roosevelt	retired	1971	34	85	1971	85
Stanley F. Reed	Ky.	1884	Protestant	1938	53	F. Roosevelt	retired	1957	19	72	1980	95
Felix Frankfurter	Austria	1882	Jewish	1939	56	F. Roosevelt	retired	1962	23	79	1965	82
William O. Douglas	Minn.	1898	Presbyterian	1939	40	F. Roosevelt	retired	1975	36	77	1980	81
Frank Murphy	Mich.	1890	Roman Catholic	1940	49	F. Roosevelt	death	1949	9	59	1949	59
James F. Byrnes	S.C.	1879	Episcopal	1941	62	F. Roosevelt	resigned	1942	1	63	1972	92
Robert H. Jackson	N.Y.	1892	Episcopal	1941	49	F. Roosevelt	death	1954	13	62	1954	62
Wiley B. Rutledge	Ky.	1894	Unitarian	1943	48	F. Roosevelt	death	1949	6	55	1949	55
Harold H. Burton	Mass.	1888	Unitarian	1945	57	Truman	retired	1958	13	67	1964	76
Tom C. Clark	Tex.	1899	Presbyterian	1949	49	Truman	retired	1967	17	70	1977	78
Sherman Minton	Ind.	1890	Roman Catholic	1949	58	Truman	retired	1956	7	65	1965	74
John M. Harlan	Ill.	1899	Presbyterian	1955	55	Eisenhower	retired	1971	16	72	1971	72
William J. Brennan, Jr.	N.J.	1906	Roman Catholic	1956	50	Eisenhower	—	—	—	—	—	—
Charles E. Whittaker	Kan.	1901	Methodist	1957	56	Eisenhower	disabled	1962	5	61	1973	73
Potter Stewart	Mich.	1915	Episcopal	1958	43	Eisenhower	retired	1981	23	66	—	—
Byron R. White	Colo.	1917	Episcopal	1962	44	Kennedy	—	—	—	—	—	—
Arthur J. Goldberg	Ill.	1908	Jewish	1962	54	Kennedy	resigned	1965	2	56	—	—
Abe Fortas	Tenn.	1910	Jewish	1965	55	Johnson	resigned	1969	3	58	—	—
Thurgood Marshall	Md.	1908	Episcopalian	1967	59	Johnson	—	—	—	—	—	—
Harry A. Blackmun	Ill.	1908	Methodist	1970	61	Nixon	—	—	—	—	—	—
Lewis F. Powell, Jr.	Va.	1907	Presbyterian	1972	64	Nixon	—	—	—	—	—	—
William H. Rehnquist	Wis.	1924	Lutheran	1972	47	Nixon	—	—	—	—	—	—
John Paul Stevens	Ill.	1920	Protestant	1975	55	Ford	—	—	—	—	—	—
Sandra Day O'Connor	Tex.	1930	Episcopal	1981	51	Reagan	—	—	—	—	—	—

1. Congregationalist; later Unitarian; then Episcopal. 2. Unitarian. 3. Unitarian or Congregational. 4. Not a member of any church.

Impeachments of Federal Officials

Source: Congressional Directory

The procedure for the impeachment of Federal officials is detailed in Article I, Section 3, of the Constitution. See Index.

The Senate has sat as a court of impeachment in the following cases:

William Blount, Senator from Tennessee; charges dismissed for want of jurisdiction, January 14, 1799.

John Pickering, judge of the U.S. District Court for New Hampshire; removed from office March 12, 1804.

Samuel Chase, Associate Justice of the Supreme Court; acquitted March 1, 1805.

James H. Peck, judge of the U.S. District Court for Missouri; acquitted Jan. 31, 1831.

West H. Humphreys, judge of the U.S. District Court for the middle, eastern, and western districts of Tennessee; removed from office June 26, 1862.

Andrew Johnson, President of the United States; acquitted May 26, 1868.

William W. Belknap, Secretary of War; acquitted Aug. 1, 1876.

Charles Swayne, judge of the U.S. District Court for the northern district of Florida; acquitted Feb. 27, 1905.

Robert W. Archbald, Associate Judge, U.S. Commerce Court; removed Jan. 13, 1913.

George W. English, judge of the U.S. District Court for eastern district of Illinois; resigned Nov. 4, 1926; proceedings dismissed.

Harold Louderback, judge of the U.S. District Court for the northern district of California; acquitted May 24, 1933.

Halsted L. Ritter, judge of the southern district of Florida; removed from office April 17, 1936.

The Ninety-Seventh Congress

Composition of 96th and 97th Congresses

	96th Congress				97th Congress			
	Dem.	Rep.	Male	Female	Dem.	Rep.	Male	Female
Senate	59[1]	41	99	1	47[1]	53	98	2
House	276	159	418	16	243[2]	191	415	19

1. Includes one Independent (Byrd of Virginia). 2. Includes one unaffiliated (Foglietta of Pennsylvania), and one independent (Smith of Pennsylvania). There is one vacancy—in Connecticut. NOTE: There are 17 black members in the House.

The Senate

Senior Senator is listed first. The dates in the first column indicate period of service. The date given in parentheses after the Senator's name is year of birth. All terms are for six years and expire in January. Mailing address of Senators: The Senate, Washington, D.C. 20510.

ALABAMA
1979–85   Howell T. Heflin, D (1921)
1981–87   Jeremiah A. Denton, Jr., R (1924)
ALASKA
1968–85   Ted Stevens, R[1] (1923)
1981–87   Frank H. Murkowski, R (1933)
ARIZONA
1969–87   Barry Goldwater, R (1909)
1977–83   Dennis DeConcini, D (1937)
ARKANSAS
1975–87   Dale Bumpers, D (1925)
1979–85   David H. Pryor, D (1934)
CALIFORNIA
1969–87   Alan Cranston, D[2] (1914)
1977–83   S. I. Hayakawa, R (1906)
COLORADO
1975–87   Gary Hart, D (1937)
1979–85   William L. Armstrong, R (1937)
CONNECTICUT
1971–83   Lowell P. Weicker, Jr., R (1931)
1981–87   Christopher J. Dodd, D (1944)
DELAWARE
1971–83   William V. Roth, Jr., R (1921)
1973–85   Joseph R. Biden, Jr., D (1942)
FLORIDA
1971–83   Lawton Chiles, D (1930)
1981–87   Paula Hawkins, R (1927)
GEORGIA
1973–85   Sam Nunn, D (1938)
1981–87   Mack Mattingly, R (1931)
HAWAII
1963–87   Daniel K. Inouye, D (1924)
1977–83   Spark M. Matsunaga, D (1916)
IDAHO
1973–85   James A. McClure, R (1924)
1981–87   Steven D. Symms, R (1938)
ILLINOIS
1967–85   Charles H. Percy, R (1919)
1981–87   Alan J. Dixon, D (1927)
INDIANA
1977–83   Richard G. Lugar, R (1932)
1981–87   Dan Quayle, R (1947)
IOWA
1979–85   Roger W. Jepsen, R (1928)
1981–87   Charles E. Grassley, R (1933)
KANSAS
1969–87   Robert J. Dole, R (1923)
1979–85   Nancy Landon Kassebaum, R (1932)
KENTUCKY
1973–85   Walter Huddleston, D (1926)
1975–87   Wendell H. Ford, D (1924)
LOUISIANA
1948–87   Russell B. Long, D (1918)
1973–85   J. Bennett Johnston, D (1932)

MAINE
1979–85   William S. Cohen, R (1940)
1980–83   George J. Mitchell, D (1933)
MARYLAND
1969–87   Charles McC. Mathias, Jr., R (1922)
1977–83   Paul S. Sarbanes, D (1933)
MASSACHUSETTS
1962–83   Edward M. Kennedy, D (1932)
1979–85   Paul E. Tsongas, D (1941)
MICHIGAN
1977–83   Donald W. Riegle, Jr., D (1938)
1979–85   Carl Levin, D (1934)
MINNESOTA
1978–83   David F. Durenberger, R (1934)
1979–85   Rudy Boschwitz, R (1930)
MISSISSIPPI
1947–83   John C. Stennis, D (1901)
1978–85   Thad Cochran, R (1937)
MISSOURI
1968–87   Thomas F. Eagleton, D (1929)
1977–83   John C. Danforth, R (1936)
MONTANA
1977–83   John Melcher, D (1924)
1979–85   Max Baucus, D (1941)
NEBRASKA
1977–83   Edward Zorinsky, D (1928)
1979–85   J. James Exon, D (1921)
NEVADA
1959–83   Howard W. Cannon, D (1912)
1975–87   Paul Laxalt, R (1922)
NEW HAMPSHIRE
1979–85   Gordon J. Humphrey, R (1940)
1981–87   Warren Rudman, R (1930)
NEW JERSEY
1959–83   Harrison A. Williams, Jr., D (1919)
1979–85   Bill Bradley, D (1943)
NEW MEXICO
1973–85   Pete V. Domenici, R (1932)
1977–83   Harrison H. Schmitt, R (1935)
NEW YORK
1977–83   Daniel P. Moynihan, D (1927)
1981–87   Alfonse M. D'Amato, R (1937)
NORTH CAROLINA
1973–85   Jesse Helms, R (1921)
1981–87   John P. East, R (1931)
NORTH DAKOTA
1960–83   Quentin N. Burdick, D (1908)
1981–87   Mark Andrews, R (1926)
OHIO
1975–87   John H. Glenn, Jr., D (1921)
1977–83   Howard M. Metzenbaum, D (1917)
OKLAHOMA
1979–85   David L. Boren, D (1941)
1981–87   Don Nickles, R (1948)

OREGON
1967–85   Mark O. Hatfield, R (1922)
1969–87   Bob Packwood, R (1932)
PENNSYLVANIA
1977–83   John Heinz, R (1938)
1981–87   Arlen Specter, R (1930)
RHODE ISLAND
1961–85   Claiborne Pell, D (1918)
1977–83   John H. Chafee, R (1922)
SOUTH CAROLINA
1956–85   Strom Thurmond, R[3] (1902)
1966–87   Ernest F. Hollings, D (1922)
SOUTH DAKOTA
1979–85   Larry Pressler, R (1942)
1981–87   James Abdnor, R (1923)
TENNESSEE
1967–85   Howard H. Baker, Jr., R[4] (1925)
1977–83   James R. Sasser, D (1936)
TEXAS
1961–85   John G. Tower, R (1925)
1971–83   Lloyd M. Bentsen, D (1921)

UTAH
1975–87   E. J. (Jake) Garn, R (1932)
1977–83   Orrin G. Hatch, R (1934)
VERMONT
1971–83   Robert T. Stafford, R (1913)
1975–87   Patrick J. Leahy, D (1940)
VIRGINIA
1965–83   Harry F. Byrd, Jr., I[5] (1914)
1979–85   John W. Warner, R (1927)
WASHINGTON
1953–83   Henry M. Jackson, D (1912)
1981–87   Slade Gorton, R (1928)
WEST VIRGINIA
1958–85   Jennings Randolph, D (1902)
1959–83   Robert C. Byrd, D[6] (1918)
WISCONSIN
1957–83   William Proxmire, D (1915)
1981–87   Robert W. Kasten, Jr., R (1942)
WYOMING
1977–83   Malcolm Wallop, R (1933)
1979–85   Alan K. Simpson, R (1931)

1. Assistant majority leader (whip). 2. Assistant minority leader (whip). 3. President pro tempore. 4. Majority leader. 5. Minority leader. 6. Independent.

Facts About Elections

Candidate with highest popular vote: Nixon (1972), 47,169,911.
Candidate with highest electoral vote: F. D. Roosevelt (1936), 523.
Candidate carrying most states: Nixon (1972), 49.

Candidate running most times: Norman Thomas, 6 (1928, 1932, 1936, 1940, 1944, 1948).
Candidate elected, defeated, then reelected: Cleveland (1884, 1888, 1892).

A Voting Majority Never Elected a President

In the 1964 election, Lyndon B. Johnson became the only President to almost succeed in receiving a majority of votes. He got 43,130,000 votes or 37.8% of those who were eligible to vote. The number of Americans of voting age who did not vote that year was 43,445,000 or 38.1%.

The President who received the smallest share of votes from eligible Americans was Martin Van Buren, who obtained 11.4% of the ballots from voting-age Americans.

Since universal suffrage was enacted, Calvin Coolidge claimed the smallest percentage by receiving only 23.7% of the ballots from voting-age citizens.

The House of Representatives

The numerals indicate the Congressional Districts of the states; the designation AL means At-Large. All terms end January 1983. Mailing address of Representatives: House of Representatives, Washington, D.C. 20515.

ALABAMA
(7 Representatives)
1. Jack Edwards, R
2. William L. Dickinson, R
3. William Nichols, D
4. Tom Bevill, D
5. Ronnie G. Flippo, D
6. Albert L. Smith, Jr., R
7. Richard C. Shelby, D

ALASKA
(1 Representative)
AL Don Young, R

ARIZONA
(4 Representatives)
1. John J. Rhodes, R
2. Morris K. Udall, D
3. Bob Stump, D
4. Eldon Rudd, R

ARKANSAS
(4 Representatives)
1. Bill Alexander, D
2. Ed Bethune, R
3. John P. Hammerschmidt, R
4. Beryl F. Anthony, Jr., D

CALIFORNIA
(43 Representatives)
1. Eugene A. Chappie, R
2. Don H. Clausen, R
3. Robert T. Matsui, D
4. Vic Fazio, D
5. John L. Burton, D
6. Phillip Burton, D
7. George Miller, D
8. Ronald V. Dellums, D
9. Fortney H. Stark, D
10. Don Edwards, D
11. Tom Lantos, D

12. Paul N. McCloskey, Jr., R
13. Norman Y. Mineta, D
14. Norman D. Shumway, R
15. Tony Coelho, D
16. Leon E. Panetta, D
17. Charles Pashayan, Jr., R
18. William M. Thomas, R
19. Robert J. Lagomarsino, R
20. Barry M. Goldwater, Jr., R
21. Bobbi Fiedler, R
22. Carlos J. Moorhead, R
23. Anthony C. Beilenson, D
24. Henry A. Waxman, D
25. Edward R. Roybal, D
26. John H. Rousselot, R
27. Robert K. Dornan, R
28. Julian C. Dixon, D
29. Augustus F. Hawkins, D
30. George E. Danielson, D
31. Mervyn M. Dymally, D

32. Glenn M. Anderson, D
33. Wayne R. Grisham, R
34. Dan E. Lungren, R
35. Dave Dreier, R
36. George E. Brown, Jr., D
37. Jerry Lewis, R
38. Jerry M. Patterson, D
39. William E. Dannemeyer, R
40. Robert E. Badham, R
41. William Lowery, R
42. Duncan L. Hunter, R
43. Clair W. Burgener, R

COLORADO
(5 Representatives)
1. Patricia Schroeder, D
2. Timothy E. Wirth, D
3. Raymond P. Kogovsek, D
4. Hank Brown, R
5. Kenneth B. Kramer, R

CONNECTICUT
(6 Representatives)
1. Vacant
2. Samuel Gejdenson, D
3. Lawrence J. DeNardis, R
4. Stewart B. McKinney, R
5. William R. Ratchford, D
6. Toby Moffett, D

DELAWARE
(1 Representative)
AL Thomas B. Evans, Jr., R

FLORIDA
(15 Representatives)
1. Earl D. Hutto, D
2. Don Fuqua, D
3. Charles E. Bennett, D
4. William V. Chappell, Jr., D
5. Bill McCollum, R
6. C. W. Bill Young, R
7. Sam M. Gibbons, D
8. Andy Ireland, D
9. Bill Nelson, D
10. Louis A. Bafalis, R
11. Daniel A. Mica, D
12. Clay Shaw, R
13. William Lehman, D
14. Claude D. Pepper, D
15. Dante B. Fascell, D

GEORGIA
(10 Representatives)
1. Bo Ginn, D
2. Charles F. Hatcher, D
3. Jack T. Brinkley, D
4. Elliott H. Levitas, D
5. Wyche Fowler, Jr., D
6. Newt Gingrich, R
7. Lawrence P. McDonald, D
8. Billy Lee Evans, D
9. Edgar L. Jenkins, D
10. Doug Barnard, Jr., D

HAWAII
(2 Representatives)
1. Cecil Heftel, D
2. Daniel K. Akaka, D

IDAHO
(2 Representatives)
1. Larry E. Craig, R
2. George V. Hansen, R

ILLINOIS
(24 Representatives)
1. Harold Washington, D
2. Gus Savage, D
3. Marty Russo, D
4. Edward J. Derwinski, R
5. John G. Fary, D
6. Henry J. Hyde, R
7. Cardiss Collins, D
8. Dan Rostenkowski, D
9. Sidney R. Yates, D
10. John E. Porter, R
11. Frank Annunzio, D
12. Philip M. Crane, R
13. Robert McClory, R
14. John N. Erlenborn, R
15. Tom Corcoran, R
16. Lynn M. Martin, R
17. George M. O'Brien, R
18. Robert H. Michel, R[1]
19. Tom Railsback, R
20. Paul Findley, R
21. Edward R. Madigan, R
22. Daniel B. Crane, R
23. Melvin Price, D
24. Paul Simon, D

INDIANA
(11 Representatives)
1. Adam Benjamin, Jr., D
2. Floyd J. Fithian, D
3. John P. Hiler, R
4. Daniel R. Coats, R
5. Elwood H. Hillis, R
6. David W. Evans, D
7. John T. Myers, R
8. Joel Deckard, R
9. Lee H. Hamilton, D
10. Philip R. Sharp, D
11. Andrew Jacobs, Jr., D

IOWA
(6 Representatives)
1. Jim Leach, R
2. Thomas J. Tauke, R
3. Cooper Evans, R
4. Neal Smith, D
5. Thomas R. Harkin, D
6. Berkley W. Bedell, D

KANSAS
(5 Representatives)
1. Pat Roberts, R
2. Jim Jeffries, R
3. Larry Winn, Jr., R
4. Dan Glickman, D
5. Bob Whittaker, R

KENTUCKY
(7 Representatives)
1. Carroll Hubbard, Jr., D
2. William H. Natcher, D
3. Romano L. Mazzoli, D
4. Gene Snyder, R
5. Harold D. Rogers, R
6. Larry J. Hopkins, R
7. Carl D. Perkins, D

LOUISIANA
(8 Representatives)
1. Robert L. Livingston, Jr., R

2. Corinne C. (Lindy) Boggs, D
3. W. J. (Billy) Tauzin, D
4. Buddy Roemer, R
5. Thomas J. Huckaby, D
6. W. Henson Moore, R
7. John B. Breaux, D
8. Gillis W. Long, D

MAINE
(2 Representatives)
1. David F. Emery, R
2. Olympia J. Snowe, R

MARYLAND
(8 Representatives)
1. Roy P. Dyson, D
2. Clarence D. Long, D
3. Barbara A. Mikulski, D
4. Marjorie S. Holt, R
5. Steny H. Hoyer, D
6. Beverly B. Byron, D
7. Parren J. Mitchell, D
8. Michael D. Barnes, D

MASSACHUSETTS
(12 Representatives)
1. Silvio O. Conte, R
2. Edward P. Boland, D
3. Joseph D. Early, D
4. Barney Frank, D
5. James M. Shannon, D
6. Nicholas Mavroules, D
7. Edward J. Markey, D
8. Thomas P. O'Neill, Jr., D[2]
9. John J. Moakley, D
10. Margaret M. Heckler, R
11. Brian J. Donnelly, D
12. Gerry E. Studds, D

MICHIGAN
(19 Representatives)
1. John Conyers, Jr., D
2. Carl D. Pursell, R
3. Howard E. Wolpe, D
4. Mark Siljander, R
5. Harold S. Sawyer, R
6. Jim Dunn, R
7. Dale E. Kildee, D
8. Bob Traxler, D
9. Guy Vander Jagt, R
10. Donald J. Albosta, D
11. Robert W. Davis, R
12. David E. Bonior, D
13. George W. Crockett, Jr., D
14. Dennis M. Hertel, D
15. William D. Ford, D
16. John D. Dingell, D
17. William M. Brodhead, D
18. James J. Blanchard, D
19. William S. Broomfield, R

MINNESOTA
(8 Representatives)
1. Arlen Erdahl, R
2. Thomas M. Hagedorn, R

3. Bill Frenzel, R
4. Bruce F. Vento, D
5. Martin Olav Sabo, D
6. Vin Weber, R
7. Arlan Stangeland, R
8. James L. Oberstar, D

MISSISSIPPI
(5 Representatives)
1. Jamie L. Whitten, D
2. David R. Bowen, D
3. G. V. (Sonny) Montgomery, D
4. Wayne Dowdy, D
5. Trent Lott, R[3]

MISSOURI
(10 Representatives)
1. William L. Clay, D
2. Robert A. Young, D
3. Richard A. Gephardt, D
4. Ike Skelton, D
5. Richard Bolling, D
6. E. Thomas Coleman, R
7. Gene Taylor, R
8. Wendell Bailey, R
9. Harold L. Volkmer, D
10. William Emerson, R

MONTANA
(2 Representatives)
1. Pat Williams, D
2. Ron Marlenee, R

NEBRASKA
(3 Representatives)
1. Douglas K. Bereuter, R
2. Hal Daub, R
3. Virginia Smith, R

NEVADA
(1 Representative)
AL James D. Santini, D

NEW HAMPSHIRE
(2 Representatives)
1. Norman E. D'Amours, D
2. Judd Gregg, R

NEW JERSEY
(15 Representatives)
1. James J. Florio, D
2. William J. Hughes, D
3. James J. Howard, D
4. Christopher H. Smith, R
5. Millicent Fenwick, R
6. Edwin B. Forsythe, R
7. Marge Roukema, R
8. Robert A. Roe, D
9. Harold C. Hollenbeck, R
10. Peter W. Rodino, Jr., D

11. Joseph G. Minish, D
12. Matthew J. Rinaldo, R
13. James A. Courter, R
14. Frank J. Guarini, D
15. Bernard J. Dwyer, D

NEW MEXICO
(2 Representatives)
1. Manuel Lujan, Jr., R
2. Joseph R. Skeen, R

NEW YORK
(39 Representatives)
1. William Carney, R
2. Thomas J. Downey, D
3. Gregory W. Carman, R
4. Norman F. Lent, R
5. Raymond J. McGrath, R
6. John LeBoutillier, R
7. Joseph P. Addabbo, D
8. Benjamin S. Rosenthal, D
9. Geraldine A. Ferraro, D
10. Mario Biaggi, D
11. James H. Scheuer, D
12. Shirley A. Chisholm, D
13. Stephen J. Solarz, D
14. Frederick W. Richmond, D
15. Leo C. Zeferetti, D
16. Charles E. Schumer, D
17. Guy Molinari, R
18. Bill Green, R
19. Charles B. Rangel, D
20. Ted Weiss, D
21. Robert Garcia, D
22. Jonathan B. Bingham, D
23. Peter A. Peyser, D
24. Richard L. Ottinger, D
25. Hamilton Fish, Jr., R
26. Benjamin A. Gilman, R
27. Matthew F. McHugh, D
28. Samuel S. Stratton, D
29. Gerald B. Solomon, R
30. David O'B. Martin, R
31. Donald J. Mitchell, R
32. George C. Wortley, R
33. Gary A. Lee, R
34. Frank Horton, R
35. Barber B. Conable, Jr., R
36. John J. LaFalce, D
37. Henry J. Nowak, D
38. Jack Kemp, R
39. Stanley N. Lundine, D

NORTH CAROLINA
(11 Representatives)
1. Walter B. Jones, D
2. L. H. Fountain, D
3. Charles O. Whitley, D
4. Ike F. Andrews, D
5. Stephen L. Neal, D
6. Eugene Johnston, R
7. Charlie Rose, D
8. W. G. Hefner, D
9. James G. Martin, R
10. James T. Broyhill, R
11. Bill Hendon, R

NORTH DAKOTA
(1 Representative)
AL Byron L. Dorgan, D

OHIO
(23 Representatives)
1. Willis D. Gradison, Jr., R
2. Thomas A. Luken, D
3. Tony P. Hall, D
4. Michael G. Oxley, R
5. Delbert L. Latta, R
6. Bob McEwen, R
7. Clarence J. Brown, R
8. Thomas N. Kindness, R
9. Edward F. Weber, R
10. Clarence E. Miller, R
11. J. William Stanton, R
12. Robert N. Shamansky, D
13. Donald J. Pease, D
14. John F. Seiberling, D
15. Chalmers P. Wylie, R
16. Ralph Regula, R
17. John M. Ashbrook, R
18. Douglas Applegate, D
19. Lyle Williams, R
20. Mary Rose Oakar, D
21. Louis Stokes, D
22. Dennis E. Eckart, D
23. Ronald M. Mottl, D

OKLAHOMA
(6 Representatives)
1. James R. Jones, D
2. Mike Synar, D
3. Wesley W. Watkins, D
4. Dave McCurdy, D
5. Mickey Edwards, R
6. Glenn English, D

OREGON
(4 Representatives)
1. Les AuCoin, D
2. Denny Smith, R
3. Ronald L. Wyden, D
4. Jim Weaver, D

PENNSYLVANIA
(25 Representatives)
1. Thomas M. Foglietta[4]
2. William H. Gray III, D
3. Joseph Smith, I
4. Charles F. Dougherty, R
5. Richard T. Schulze, R
6. Gus Yatron, D
7. Bob Edgar, D
8. James K. Coyne, R
9. Bud Shuster, R
10. Joseph M. McDade, R
11. James L. Nelligan, R
12. John P. Murtha, D
13. Lawrence Coughlin, R
14. William J. Coyne, D
15. Donald L. Ritter, R
16. Robert S. Walker, R
17. Allen E. Ertel, D
18. Doug Walgren, D
19. William F. Goodling, R
20. Joseph M. Gaydos, D
21. Don Bailey, D
22. Austin J. Murphy, D
23. William F. Clinger, Jr., R

24. Marc L. Marks, R
25. Eugene V. Atkinson, D

RHODE ISLAND
(2 Representatives)
1. Fernand J. St. Germain, D
2. Claudine Schneider, R

SOUTH CAROLINA
(6 Representatives)
1. Thomas F. Hartnett, R
2. Floyd D. Spence, R
3. Butler C. Derrick, Jr., D
4. Carroll A. Campbell, Jr., R
5. Ken Holland, D
6. John L. Napier, R

SOUTH DAKOTA
(2 Representatives)
1. Thomas A. Daschle, D
2. Clint Roberts, R

TENNESSEE
(8 Representatives)
1. James H. Quillen, R
2. John J. Duncan, R
3. Marilyn Lloyd Bouquard, D
4. Albert Gore, Jr., D
5. William H. Boner, D
6. Robin L. Beard, R
7. Ed Jones, D
8. Harold Ford, D

TEXAS
(24 Representatives)
1. Sam B. Hall, Jr., D
2. Charles Wilson, D

3. James M. Collins, R
4. Ralph M. Hall, D
5. James A. Mattox, D
6. Phil Gramm, D
7. Bill Archer, R
8. Jack M. Fields, R
9. Jack Brooks, D
10. J. J. (Jake) Pickle, D
11. Marvin Leath, D
12. Jim Wright, D[5]
13. Jack E. Hightower, D
14. William Patman, D
15. E. (Kika) de la Garza, D
16. Richard C. White, D
17. Charles W. Stenholm, D
18. George T. (Mickey) Leland, D
19. Kent R. Hance, D
20. Henry B. Gonzalez, D
21. Tom Loeffler, R
22. Ron Paul, R
23. Abraham Kazen, Jr., D
24. Martin Frost, D

UTAH
(2 Representatives)
1. James V. Hansen, R
2. David D. Marriott, R

VERMONT
(1 Representative)
AL James M. Jeffords, R

VIRGINIA
(10 Representatives)
1. Paul S. Trible, Jr., R
2. G. William Whitehurst, R
3. Thomas J. Bliley, Jr., R
4. Robert W. Daniel, Jr., R

5. Dan Daniel, D
6. M. Caldwell Butler, R
7. J. Kenneth Robinson, R
8. Stan Parris, R
9. William C. Wampler, R
10. Frank R. Wolf, R

WASHINGTON
(7 Representatives)
1. Joel Pritchard, R
2. Al Swift, D
3. Don L. Bonker, D
4. Sid W. Morrison, R
5. Thomas S. Foley, D[6]
6. Norman Dicks, D
7. Mike Lowry, D

WEST VIRGINIA
(4 Representatives)
1. Robert H. Mollohan, D
2. Cleveland K. Benedict, R
3. David Michael Staton, R
4. Nick J. Rahall II, D

WISCONSIN
(9 Representatives)
1. Les Aspin, D
2. Robert W. Kastenmeier, D
3. Steven C. Gunderson, R
4. Clement J. Zablocki, D
5. Henry S. Reuss, D
6. Thomas E. Petri, R
7. David R. Obey, D
8. Toby Roth, R
9. F. James Sensenbrenner, Jr., R

WYOMING
(1 Representative)
AL Dick Cheney, R

1. Minority leader. 2. Speaker. 3. Assistant minority leader (whip). 4. Not affiliated with any party. 5. Majority leader. 6. Assistant majority leader (whip). NOTE: The District of Columbia is represented by a non-voting delegate. Puerto Rico has a resident commissioner in the House and Guam and the Virgin Islands have one delegate each.

Senate and House Standing Committees, 97th Congress

Committees of the Senate

Agriculture, Nutrition, and Forestry (17 members)
Chairman: Jesse Helms (N.C.)
Ranking Dem.: Walter D. Huddleston (Ky.)
Appropriations (29 members)
Chairman: Mark O. Hatfield (Ore.)
Ranking Dem.: William Proxmire (Wis.)
Armed Services (17 members)
Chairman: John Tower (Tex.)
Ranking Dem.: John C. Stennis (Miss.)
Banking, Housing, and Urban Affairs (15 members)
Chairman: E.J. (Jake) Garn (Utah)
Ranking Dem.: Harrison A. Williams, Jr. (N.J.)
Budget (22 members)
Chairman: Pete V. Domenici (N.M.)
Ranking Dem.: Ernest F. Hollings (S.C.)
Commerce, Science, and Transportation (17 members)
Chairman: Bob Packwood (Ore.)

Ranking Dem.: Howard W. Cannon (Nev.)
Energy and Natural Resources (20 members)
Chairman: James A. McClure (Idaho)
Ranking Dem.: Henry M. Jackson (Wash.)
Environment and Public Works (16 members)
Chairman: Robert T. Stafford (Vt.)
Ranking Dem.: Jennings Randolph (W.Va.)
Finance (20 members)
Chairman: Robert J. Dole (Kan.)
Ranking Dem.: Russell B. Long (La.)
Foreign Relations (17 members)
Chairman: Charles H. Percy (Ill.)
Ranking Dem.: Claiborne Pell (R.I.)
Governmental Affairs (17 members)
Chairman: William V. Roth, Jr. (Del.)
Ranking Dem.: Thomas F. Eagleton (Mo.)
Judiciary (18 members)
Chairman: Strom Thurmond (S.C.)
Ranking Dem.: Joseph R. Biden, Jr. (Del.)
Labor and Human Resources (16 members)
Chairman: Orrin G. Hatch (Utah)
Ranking Dem.: Edward M. Kennedy (Mass.)

Rules and Administration (12 members)
Chairman: Charles McC. Mathias, Jr. (Md.)
Ranking Dem.: Wendell H. Ford (Ky.)
Small Business (17 members)
Chairman: Lowell P. Weicker, Jr. (Conn.)
Ranking Dem.: Sam Nunn (Ga.)
Veterans' Affairs (12 members)
Chairman: Alan K. Simpson (Wyo.)
Ranking Dem.: Alan Cranston (Calif.)

Select and Special Committees

Aging (15 members)
Chairman: John Heinz (Pa.)
Ranking Dem.: Lawton Chiles (Fla.)
Ethics (6 members)
Chairman: Malcolm Wallop (Wyo.)
Vice Chairman: Howell T. Heflin (Ala.)
Indian Affairs (7 members)
Chairman: William S. Cohen (Me.)
Ranking Dem.: John Melcher (Mont.)
Intelligence (15 members)
Chairman: Barry Goldwater (Ariz.)
Ranking Dem.: Daniel Patrick Moynihan (N.Y.)

Committees of the House

Agriculture (43 members)
Chairman: E. (Kika) de la Garza (Tex.)
Ranking Repub.: William C. Wampler (Va.)
Appropriations (55 members)
Chairman: Jamie L. Whitten (Miss.)
Ranking Repub.: Silvio O. Conte (Mass.)
Armed Services (44 members)
Chairman: Melvin Price (Ill.)
Ranking Repub.: William L. Dickinson (Ala.)
Banking, Finance, and Urban Affairs (44 members)
Chairman: Fernand J. St. Germain (R.I.)
Ranking Repub.: J. William Stanton (Ohio)
Budget (30 members)
Chairman: James R. Jones (Okla.)
Ranking Repub.: Delbert L. Latta (Ohio)
District of Columbia (15 members)
Chairman: Ronald V. Dellums (Calif.)
Ranking Repub.: Stewart B. McKinney (Conn.)
Education and Labor (33 members)
Chairman: Carl D. Perkins (Ky.)
Ranking Repub.: John M. Ashbrook (Ohio)
Energy and Commerce (42 members)
Chairman: John D. Dingell (Mich.)
Ranking Repub.: James T. Broyhill (N.C.)
Foreign Affairs (37 members)
Chairman: Clement J. Zablocki (Wis.)
Ranking Repub.: William S. Broomfield (Mich.)
Government Operations (40 members)
Chairman: Jack Brooks (Tex.)
Ranking Repub.: Frank Horton (N.Y.)
House Administration (20 members)
Chairman: Augustus F. Hawkins (Calif.)
Ranking Repub.: Bill Frenzel (Minn.)
Interior and Insular Affairs (40 members)
Chairman: Morris K. Udall (Ariz.)
Ranking Repub.: Manuel Lujan, Jr. (N.M.)
Judiciary (28 members)
Chairman: Peter W. Rodino, Jr. (N.J.)
Ranking Repub.: Robert McClory (Ill.)
Merchant Marine and Fisheries (35 members)
Chairman: Walter B. Jones (N.C.)
Ranking Repub.: Gene Snyder (Ky.)
Post Office and Civil Service (24 members)
Chairman: William D. Ford (Mich.)
Ranking Repub.: Edward J. Derwinski (Ill.)
Public Works and Transportation (44 members)
Chairman: James J. Howard (N.J.)
Ranking Repub.: Don H. Clausen (Calif.)
Rules (16 members)
Chairman: Richard Bolling (Mo.)
Ranking Repub.: James H. Quillen (Tenn.)
Science and Technology (40 members)
Chairman: Don Fuqua (Fla.)
Ranking Repub.: Larry Winn, Jr. (Kan.)
Small Business (40 members)
Chairman: Parren J. Mitchell (Md.)
Ranking Repub.: Joseph M. McDade (Pa.)
Standards of Official Conduct (12 members)
Chairman: Louis Stokes (Ohio)
Ranking Repub.: Floyd D. Spence (S.C.)
Veterans' Affairs (31 members)
Chairman: G.V. (Sonny) Montgomery (Miss.)
Ranking Repub.: John P. Hammerschmidt (Ark.)
Ways and Means (35 members)
Chairman: Dan Rostenkowski (Ill.)
Ranking Repub.: Barber B. Conable, Jr. (N.Y.)

Select Committees

Aging (54 members)
Chairman: Claude Pepper (Fla.)
Ranking Repub.: Matthew J. Rinaldo (N.J.)
Intelligence (14 members)
Chairman: Edward P. Boland (Mass.)
Ranking Repub.: J. Kenneth Robinson (Va.)
Narcotics Abuse and Control (19 members)
Chairman: Leo C. Zeferetti (N.Y.)
Ranking Repub.: Tom Railsback (Ill.)

"In God We Trust"

"In God We Trust" first appeared on U.S. coins after April 22, 1864, when Congress passed an act authorizing the coinage of a 2-cent piece bearing this motto. Thereafter, Congress extended its use to other coins. On July 30, 1956, it became the national motto.

The American's Creed

William Tyler Page

"I believe in the United States of America as a government of the people, by the people, for the people; whose just powers are derived from the consent of the governed; a democracy in a republic; a sovereign Nation of many sovereign States; a perfect union, one and inseparable; established upon those principles of freedom, equality, justice, and humanity for which American patriots sacrificed their lives and fortunes.

"I therefore believe it is my duty to my country to love it, to support its Constitution, to obey its laws, to respect its flag, and to defend it against all enemies."

NOTE: William Tyler Page, Clerk of the U.S. House of Representatives, wrote "The American's Creed" in 1917. It was accepted by the House on behalf of the American people on April 3, 1918.

Speakers of the House of Representatives

Dates served	Congress	Name and state	Dates served	Congress	Name and state
1789–1791	1	Frederick A. C. Muhlenberg (Pa.)	1863–1869	38–40	Schuyler Colfax (Ind.)
1791–1793	2	Jonathan Trumbull (Conn.)	1869–1869	40	Theodore M. Pomeroy (N.Y.)[5]
1793–1795	3	Frederick A. C. Muhlenberg (Pa.)	1869–1875	41–43	James G. Blaine (Me.)
1795–1799	4–5	Jonathan Dayton (N.J.)[1]	1875–1876	44	Michael C. Kerr (Ind.)[6]
1799–1801	6	Theodore Sedgwick (Mass.)	1876–1881	44–46	Samuel J. Randall (Pa.)
1801–1807	7–9	Nathaniel Macon (N.C.)	1881–1883	47	J. Warren Keifer (Ohio)
1807–1811	10–11	Joseph B. Varnum (Mass.)	1883–1889	48–50	John G. Carlisle (Ky.)
1811–1814	12–13	Henry Clay (Ky.)[2]	1889–1891	51	Thomas B. Reed (Me.)
1814–1815	13	Langdon Cheves (S.C.)	1891–1895	52–53	Charles F. Crisp (Ga.)
1815–1820	14–16	Henry Clay (Ky.)[3]	1895–1899	54–55	Thomas B. Reed (Me.)
1820–1821	16	John W. Taylor (N.Y.)	1899–1903	56–57	David B. Henderson (Iowa)
1821–1823	17	Philip P. Barbour (Va.)	1903–1911	58–61	Joseph G. Cannon (Ill.)
1823–1825	18	Henry Clay (Ky.)	1911–1919	62–65	Champ Clark (Mo.)
1825–1827	19	John W. Taylor (N.Y.)	1919–1925	66–68	Frederick H. Gillett (Mass.)
1827–1834	20–23	Andrew Stevenson (Va.)[4]	1925–1931	69–71	Nicholas Longworth (Ohio)
1834–1835	23	John Bell (Tenn.)	1931–1933	72	John N. Garner (Tex.)
1835–1839	24–25	James K. Polk (Tenn.)	1933–1934	73	Henry T. Rainey (Ill.)[7]
1839–1841	26	Robert M. T. Hunter (Va.)	1935–1936	74	Joseph W. Byrns (Tenn.)[8]
1841–1843	27	John White (Ky.)	1936–1940	74–76	William B. Bankhead (Ala.)[9]
1843–1845	28	John W. Jones (Va.)	1940–1947	76–79	Sam Rayburn (Tex.)
1845–1847	29	John W. Davis (Ind.)	1947–1949	80	Joseph W. Martin, Jr. (Mass.)
1847–1849	30	Robert C. Winthrop (Mass.)	1949–1953	81–82	Sam Rayburn (Tex.)
1849–1851	31	Howell Cobb (Ga.)	1953–1955	83	Joseph W. Martin, Jr. (Mass.)
1851–1855	32–33	Linn Boyd (Ky.)	1955–1961	84–87	Sam Rayburn (Tex.)[10]
1855–1857	34	Nathaniel P. Banks (Mass.)	1962–1971	87–91	John W. McCormack (Mass.)[11]
1857–1859	35	James L. Orr (S.C.)	1971–1977	92–94	Carl Albert (Okla.)[12]
1859–1861	36	Wm. Pennington (N.J.)	1977–	95–	Thomas P. O'Neill, Jr. (Mass.)
1861–1863	37	Galusha A. Grow (Pa.)			

1. George Dent (Md.) was elected Speaker pro tempore for April 20 and May 28, 1798. 2. Resigned during second session of 13th Congress. 3. Resigned between first and second sessions of 16th Congress. 4. Resigned during first session of 23rd Congress. 5. Elected Speaker and served the day of adjournment. 6. Died between first and second sessions of 44th Congress. During first session, there were two Speakers pro tempore: Samuel S. Cox (N.Y.), appointed for Feb. 17, May 12, and June 19, 1876, and Milton Sayler (Ohio), appointed for June 4, 1876. 7. Died in 1934 after adjournment of second session of 73rd Congress. 8. Died during second session of 74th Congress. 9. Died during third session of 76th Congress. 10. Died between first and second sessions of 87th Congress. 11. Not a candidate in 1970 election. 12. Not a candidate in 1976 election. *Source:* Congressional Directory.

Floor Leaders of the Senate

Democratic	Republican
Gilbert M. Hitchcock, Neb. (Min. 1919–20)	Charles Curtis, Kan. (Maj. 1925–29)
Oscar W. Underwood, Ala. (Min. 1920–23)	James E. Watson, Ind. (Maj. 1929–33)
Joseph T. Robinson, Ark. (Min. 1923–33, Maj. 1933–37)	Charles L. McNary, Ore. (Min. 1933–44)
Alben W. Barkley, Ky. (Maj. 1937–46, Min. 1947–48)	Wallace H. White, Jr., Me. (Min. 1944–47, Maj. 1947–48)
Scott W. Lucas, Ill. (Maj. 1949–50)	Kenneth S. Wherry, Neb. (Min. 1949–51)
Ernest W. McFarland, Ariz. (Maj. 1951–52)	Styles Bridges, N. H. (Min. 1951–52)
Lyndon B. Johnson, Tex. (Min. 1953–54, Maj. 1955–60)	Robert A. Taft, Ohio (Maj. 1953)
Mike Mansfield, Mont. (Maj. 1961–77)	William F. Knowland, Calif. (Maj. 1953–54, Min. 1955–58)
Robert C. Byrd, W. Va. (Maj. 1977–81, Min. 1981–)	Everett M. Dirksen, Ill. (Min. 1959–69)
	Hugh Scott, Pa. (Min. 1969–1977)
	Howard H. Baker, Jr., Tenn. (Min. 1977–81, Maj. 1981–)

NOTE: Min. = Minority Leader; Maj. = Majority Leader. *Source:* United States Senate, Secretary for the Majority.

Annual Salaries of Federal Officials

President of the U.S.	$200,000[1]	Secretaries of the Army, Navy, Air Force	$60,662
Vice President of the U.S.	79,125[2]	Senators and Representatives	60,662
Cabinet members	69,630	President Pro Tempore of Senate	68,575
Under secretaries of executive departments	55,387	Speaker of the House	79,125
Deputy Secretaries of State, Defense, Treasury	60,662	Majority and Minority Leader of the Senate	68,575
Deputy Attorney General	60,662	Majority and Minority Leader of the House	68,575
Under Secretary of Transportation	60,662	Chief Justice of the United States	75,000
		Associate Justices of the Supreme Court	72,000

1. Plus taxable $50,000 for expenses and a nontaxable sum (not to exceed $100,000 a year) for travel expenses. 2. Plus taxable $10,000 for expenses. NOTE: All salaries shown above are taxable.

Executive Departments and Agencies

Source: U.S. Government Organization Manual.

Unless otherwise indicated, addresses shown are in Washington, D.C.

CENTRAL INTELLIGENCE AGENCY (CIA)
Washington, D.C. (20505)
Established: 1947.
Director: William J. Casey.
Activities: Coordinates intelligence activities of certain government departments and agencies by making recommendations to the National Security Council; correlates and evaluates intelligence and disseminates the results; performs certain additional services for existing intelligence agencies when the National Security Council determines that these can be more efficiently accomplished centrally.

COUNCIL OF ECONOMIC ADVISERS (CEA)
Executive Office Bldg. (20506).
Members: 3.
Established: Feb. 20, 1946.
Chairman: Murray L. Weidenbaum.
Activities: Assists President in preparation of economic reports to Congress; studies economic trends; appraises government activities on nation's economy; recommends economic policies.

COUNCIL ON ENVIRONMENTAL QUALITY
722 Jackson Pl., N.W. (20006).
Members: 3.
Established: 1969.
Chairman: Malcolm F. Baldwin (acting).
Activities: Develops and recommends to President national policies that promote environmental quality.

NATIONAL SECURITY COUNCIL (NSC)
Old Executive Office Bldg. (20506).
Members: 4.
Established: July 26, 1947.
Chairman: The President.
Other members: Vice President; Secretary of State; Secretary of Defense.
Activities: Assesses and appraises objectives, commitments and risks of United States in relation to our actual and potential military power.

OFFICE OF ADMINISTRATION
Executive Office of the President (20500).
Established: Dec. 12, 1977.
Director: John F. W. Rogers.
Activities: Provides the common services for the Executive Office of the President such as mail, payroll, dataprocessing and messengers.

OFFICE OF MANAGEMENT AND BUDGET
Executive Office Bldg. (20503).
Established: July 1, 1970.
Director: David A. Stockman.
Activities: Assists President in preparing budget and formulating fiscal program; supervises administration of budget; coordinates advice on proposed legislation; plans improvements in statistical services; keeps President informed of progress of activities by government agencies so that Congressional appropriations are spent most economically.

OFFICE OF SCIENCE AND TECHNOLOGY POLICY
Executive Office Building (20500).
Established: June 8, 1962.
Director: Benjamin Huberman (acting).
Activities: Advises the President on scientific, engineering, and technological aspects of issues requiring his attention.

OFFICE OF THE UNITED STATES TRADE REPRESENTATIVE
1800 G St., N.W. (20506).
Established: Jan. 15, 1963.
Special Representative: Bill Brock.
Activities: Advises the President on the administration and carrying out of the trade agreements program and on non-tariff barriers to international trade and international commodity agreements; chairs the Trade Expansion Act Advisory Committee.

WHITE HOUSE OFFICE OF POLICY DEVELOPMENT
The White House (20500)
Established: Jan. 21, 1981.
Director: Edwin J. Gray.
Activities: Formulates and coordinates domestic policy recommendations for the President.

Executive Departments

DEPARTMENT OF STATE
2201 C St., N.W. (20520).
Established: 1781 as Department of Foreign Affairs; reconstituted, 1789, following adoption of Constitution; name changed to Department of State Sept. 15, 1789.
Secretary: Alexander M. Haig, Jr.
Deputy Secretary: William P. Clark.
Chief delegate to U.N.: Jeane J. Kirkpatrick.
Activities: Determines government policy in relation to international problems; formulates measures for promoting friendship with other countries; develops policies and programs for U.S. participation in U.N. and other international organizations; conducts correspondence with our representatives abroad and accredited foreign representatives here; administers Foreign Service, Agency for International Development.

DEPARTMENT OF THE TREASURY
15th St. & Pennsylvania Ave., N.W. (20220).
Established: Sept. 2, 1789.
Secretary: Donald T. Regan.
Deputy Secretary: Richard McNamar.
Treasurer of the U.S.: Angela M. Buchanan.
Comptroller of the Currency: John G. Heimann.
Activities: Manages national finances; grants warrants for money drawn from Treasury pursuant to legal appropriations; handles collection of revenue; keeps and renders public accounts; prepares plans for improvement of revenue and for support of public credit; controls coinage and printing of money; administers Secret Service, Customs Service, Internal Revenue Service, Bureau of Engraving and Printing, Bureau of the Mint, Bureau of Alcohol, Tobacco and Firearms, Federal Law Enforcement Training Center, Bureau of the Public Debt.

DEPARTMENT OF DEFENSE
The Pentagon (20301).

Established: July 26, 1947, as National Department Establishment; name changed to Department of Defense on Aug. 10, 1949. Subordinate to Secretary of Defense are Secretaries of Army, Navy, Air Force.

Secretary: Caspar W. Weinberger.
Deputy Secretary: Frank C. Carlucci.
Secretary of Army: John O. Marsh, Jr.
Secretary of Navy: John F. Lehman, Jr.
Secretary of Air Force: Verne Orr.
Commandant of Marine Corps: Gen. Robert H. Barrow.
Joint Chiefs of Staff:[1] Gen. David C. Jones, Chairman; Adm. Thomas B. Hayward, Jr., Navy; Gen. Lew Allen, Jr., Air Force: Gen. Edward C. Meyer, Army; Gen. Robert H. Barrow, Marine Corps.

Activities: Provides for security of U.S. by establishing integrated policies and procedures; co-ordinates and directs the activities of three separately administered military departments (Army, Navy, and Air Force).

1. Consisting of chairman and chiefs of each service.

DEPARTMENT OF JUSTICE
Constitution Ave. between 9th & 10th Sts., N.W. (20530).

Established: Office of Attorney General was created Sept. 24, 1789. Although he was one of original Cabinet members, he was not executive department head until June 22, 1870, when Department of Justice was established.

Attorney General: William French Smith.
Deputy Attorney General: Edward C. Schmults.
Solicitor General: Rex E. Lee.
Director of FBI: William H. Webster.

Activities: Provides means for enforcing federal laws; investigates and detects violations; represents U.S. in legal matters generally and gives advice and opinions when requested by President or heads of executive departments; directs FBI, Bureau of Prisons, Immigration and Naturalization Service, Drug Enforcement Administration, Marshals Service.

DEPARTMENT OF THE INTERIOR
C St. between 18th & 19th Sts., N.W. (20240).

Established: March 3, 1849.
Secretary: James G. Watt.
Under Secretary: Donald P. Hodel.

Activities: Develops and conserves natural resources of U.S. and territories; supervises public business relating to such offices as Bureau of Land Management, Geological Survey, Bureau of Indian Affairs, National Park Service, Bureau of Mines, Fish and Wildlife Service, Bureau of Land Management, Heritage Conservation and Recreation Service, Water and Power Resources Service.

DEPARTMENT OF AGRICULTURE
Independence Ave. between 12th & 14th Sts., S.W. (20250).

Established: May 15, 1862. Administered by Commissioner of Agriculture until 1889, when it was made executive department.
Secretary: John R. Block.
Deputy Secretary: Richard E. Lyng.

Activities: Conducts comprehensive research and educational program relating to agriculture; provides crop reports, commodity standards, meat inspection and other marketing services; administers national forests; aids in flood control; administers price-support and production-adjustment programs; makes loans to farmers; supervises Farmers Home Administration, Agricultural Marketing Service, Rural Electrification Administration, Federal Grain Inspection Service, Animal and Plant Inspection Service, Food and Nutrition Service, Food Safety and Quality Service, Commodity Credit Corporation, Federal Crop Insurance Corporation, Science and Education Administration, Soil Conservation Service, Office of Environmental Quality, Forest Service, Foreign Agricultural Service, Agricultural Stabilization and Conservation Service, Office of International Cooperation and Development, Rural Telephone Bank.

DEPARTMENT OF COMMERCE
14th St. between Constitution Ave. & E St., N.W. (20230).

Established: Department of Commerce and Labor was created Feb. 14, 1903. On March 4, 1913, all labor activities were transferred out of Department of Commerce and Labor and it was renamed Department of Commerce.
Secretary: Malcolm Baldrige.
Under Secretary: Joseph R. Wright, Jr.

Activities: Fosters and develops foreign and domestic commerce of U.S.; maintains Bureau of the Census, International Trade Administration, Economic Development Administration, Bureau of Economic Analysis, Office of Minority Business Enterprise, Patent and Trademark Office, National Oceanic and Atmospheric Administration (including National Weather Service), National Technical Information Service, National Telecommunications and Information Service, Travel Service, Maritime Administration, National Bureau of Standards, Minority Business Development Agency, Office of Product Technology and Innovation, Office of Industrial Economics.

DEPARTMENT OF LABOR
Frances Perkins Building, 200 Constitution Ave., N.W. (20210).

Established: Bureau of Labor was created in 1884 under Department of the Interior; later became independent department without executive rank. Returned to bureau status in Department of Commerce and Labor, but on March 4, 1913, became independent executive department under its present name.
Secretary: Raymond J. Donovan.
Under Secretary: Vacant.

Activities: Promotes welfare of wage earners of U.S., improving working conditions and advancing opportunities for profitable employment; directs collection and collation of statistics concerning labor conditions; promulgates and enforces certain maximum-hour, minimum-wage, child-labor, safety and health standards. Maintains Employment and Training Administration, Labor-Management Services Administration, Employment Standards Administration, Occupational Safety and Health Administration, Bureau of Labor Statistics, Women's Bureau, Mine Safety and Health Administration.

DEPARTMENT OF HEALTH AND HUMAN SERVICES[1]
200 Independence Ave., S.W. (20201).
Established: April 11, 1953, replacing Federal Security Agency created in 1939.[1]
Secretary: Richard S. Schweiker.
Under Secretary: David B. Swoap.
Activities: Supervises and coordinates various organizations within the department. Organizations are: Food and Drug Administration, Office of Human Development Services, Public Health Service, Social Security Administration, Alcohol, Drug Abuse and Mental Health Administration, National Institutes of Health, Center for Disease Control, Health Care Financing Administration, Office of Child Support Enforcement, Health Resources Administration.
1. Originally Department of Health, Education and welfare. Name changed in May 1980 when Department of Education was activated.

DEPARTMENT OF HOUSING AND URBAN DEVELOPMENT
451 7th St., S.W. (20410).
Established: 1965, replacing Housing and Home Finance Agency created in 1947.
Secretary: Samuel R. Pierce, Jr.
Under Secretary: Donald I. Hovde.
Activities: Supervises and coordinates New Community Development Corporation, Government National Mortgage Association.

DEPARTMENT OF TRANSPORTATION
400 7th St., S.W. (20590).
Established: Oct. 15, 1966, as result of Department of Transportation Act, which became effective April 1, 1967.
Secretary: Drew Lewis.
Deputy Secretary: Darrell M. Trent.
Activities: Supervises and coordinates activities of Coast Guard, Federal Aviation Administration, Federal Highway Administration, Federal Railroad Administration, St. Lawrence Seaway Development Corporation, National Highway Traffic Safety Administration, Urban Mass Transportation Administration.

DEPARTMENT OF ENERGY
1000 Independence Ave., S.W. (20585).
Established: August 1977.
Secretary: James B. Edwards.
Deputy Secretary: Kenneth Davis.
Activities: Takes over the Federal Energy Administration, the Federal Power Commission, the Energy Research and Development Administration, and functions of other government agencies concerned with energy. Has management responsibility for such projects as Bonneville Dam, the Energy Information Administration, the Energy Regulatory Commission, Economic Regulatory Administration.

DEPARTMENT OF EDUCATION
400 Maryland Avenue, S.W. (20202)
Established: May 4, 1980
Secretary: T. H. Bell.
Under Secretary: William C. Clohan, Jr.
Activities: Administers federally mandated education programs that pertain to elementary and secondary education, post-secondary, vocational and adult education, and special education and rehabilitative services. Supervises National Institute of Education, Fund for the Improvement of Postsecondary Education, Institute of Museum Services, and National Center for Educational Statistics.

Independent Agencies

(Titles and addresses of independent agencies not described below follow on page 618)

ACTION
806 Connecticut Ave., N.W. (20525).
Established: July 1, 1971.
Director: Thomas Weir Pauken.
Activities: Coordinates a system of volunteer services to people in need at home and abroad; administers Peace Corps and VISTA (Volunteers in Service to America).

CIVIL AERONAUTICS BOARD (CAB)
1825 Connecticut Ave., N.W. (20428)
Members: 5.
Established: June 30, 1940.
Chairman: Marvin S. Cohen.
Activities: Regulates economic aspects of U.S. air carrier operation; assists in development of international air transportation; promotes safety in civil aviation.

COMMUNITY SERVICES ADMINISTRATION
1200 19th St., N.W. (20506).
Established: 1974.
Director: William W. Allison (acting).
Activities: Assists low-income individuals and persons of limited English-speaking ability to attain the skills, knowledge, and opportunities to become self-sufficient.

CONSUMER PRODUCT SAFETY COMMISSION
1111 18th St., N.W. (20207).
Members: 5.
Established: May 14, 1973.
Chairman: Stuart M. Statler (acting).
Activities. Protects the public against unreasonable risks of injury associated with consumer products; assists consumers to evaluate the comparative safety of products; develops uniform safety standards for products; promotes research into causes and prevention of product-related deaths, illnesses, and injuries.

ENVIRONMENTAL PROTECTION AGENCY (EPA)
401 M St., S.W. (20460).
Established: Dec. 2, 1970.
Administrator: Anne M. Gorsuch.
Activities: Coordinates governmental action to assure protection of the environment by abating and controlling pollution.

EQUAL EMPLOYMENT OPPORTUNITY COMMISSION (EEOC)
2401 E St., N.W. (20506).
Members: 5.
Established: July 2, 1965.
Chairman: J. Clay Smith, Jr. (acting).
Activities: Prohibits employment discrimination based on race, color, religion, sex, or national origin.

FARM CREDIT ADMINISTRATION (FCA)
490 L'Enfant Plaza East, S.W. (20578).
  Members: 13.
  Established: July 17, 1916.
  Chairman of Federal Farm Credit Board: William Dale Nix.
  Activities: Supervises and coordinates cooperative credit system for agriculture; provides long- and short-term credit to farmers and their cooperative marketing, purchasing, and business service organizations.

FEDERAL COMMUNICATIONS COMMISSION (FCC)
1919 M St., N.W. (20554).
  Members: 7.
  Established: 1934.
  Chairman: Mark S. Fowler.
  Activities: Regulates interstate and foreign communications by wire and radio, including amateur radio and TV; regulates operator's licenses; classifies radio stations and prescribes their services.

FEDERAL DEPOSIT INSURANCE CORPORATION (FDIC)
550 17th St., N.W. (20429)
  Members: 3.
  Established: June 16, 1933.
  Chairman: Irvine H. Sprague.
  Activities: Insures (up to $40,000) deposits in national banks, state banks that are members of the Federal Reserve System, and other state banks that qualify for Federal Deposit Insurance.

FEDERAL ELECTION COMMISSION (FEC)
1325 K St., N.W. (20463).
  Members: 6.
  Established: 1974.
  Chairman: John W. McGarry.
  Activities: Certifies distribution of public funding of federal elections; regulates compliance with Federal Election Campaign Act; makes available to the public copies of reports filed with the commission.

FEDERAL MARITIME COMMISSION
1100 L St., N.W. (20573).
  Members: 5.
  Established: Aug. 12, 1961.
  Chairman: Leslie L. Kanuk.
  Activities: Regulates waterborne shipping in foreign and domestic offshore commerce of U.S.

FEDERAL MEDIATION AND CONCILIATION SERVICE (FMCS)
2100 K St., N.W. (20427).
  Established: 1947.
  Director: Kenneth E. Moffett (acting).
  Activities: Assists in labor-management disputes in industries affecting interstate commerce to reach settlements by mediation or conciliation.

FEDERAL RESERVE SYSTEM (FRS), BOARD OF GOVERNORS OF
20th St. & Constitution Ave., N.W. (20551).
  Members: 7.
  Established: Dec. 23, 1913.
  Chairman: Paul A. Volcker.
  Activities: Supervises the 12 Federal Reserve banks, 24 branches and member commercial banks; determines country's monetary policy, including setting maximum interest paid by member banks, amount of credit extended for purchase of securities and discount rates charged by members; handles Government deposits and debt issue; regulates open-market operations; issues Federal Reserve notes.

FEDERAL TRADE COMMISSION (FTC)
Pennsylvania Ave. at 6th St., N.W. (20580).
  Members: 5.
  Established: Sept. 26, 1914.
  Chairman: James C. Miller, 3rd.
  Activities: Prevents unfair competition, deceptive practices, false advertising, price discrimination, monopolies.

GENERAL SERVICES ADMINISTRATION (GSA)
18th and F Sts., N.W. (20405).
  Established: July 1, 1949.
  Administrator: Gerald P. Carmen.
  Activities: Establishes policy and provides efficient system for management of the government's property and records, including construction and operation of buildings, procurement and distribution of supplies, stockpiling of strategic materials and utilization and disposal of property. Directs National Archives and Records Service, Federal Supply Service, Public Buildings Service, Federal Preparedness Agency, Automated Data and Telecommunications Service.

INTERNATIONAL COMMUNICATION AGENCY
1750 Pennsylvania Ave., N.W. (20547).
  Established: April 1, 1978.
  Director: John W. Shirley (acting).
  Activities: Conducts international communication, educational, cultural, and exchange programs with other peoples of the world.

INTERSTATE COMMERCE COMMISSION (ICC)
12th St. & Constitution Ave., N.W. (20423).
  Members: 11.
  Established: Feb. 4, 1887.
  Chairman: Marcus Alexis (acting).
  Activities: Regulates railroads, motor carriers, water carriers, and freight forwarders as to rates, through-routes, services, and bills of lading; authorizes mergers or consolidations; authorizes issue of securities by carriers.

NATIONAL AERONAUTICS AND SPACE ADMINISTRATION (NASA)
400 Maryland Ave., S.W. (20546).
  Established: 1958.
  Administrator: Alan M. Lovelace (acting).
  Activities: Conducts research into problems of flight within and outside earth's atmosphere.

NATIONAL FOUNDATION ON THE ARTS AND THE HUMANITIES
2401 E St., N.W. (20506).
  Established: 1965.
  Chairman: National Endowment for the Arts, Francis S. M. Hodsoll (designate); National Endowment for the Humanities, Joseph D. Duffey.
  Activities: Encourages and supports national progress in the humanities and the arts. Also includes National Councils on the Arts and the Humanities, which coordinates activities of the two endowments and related programs of other agencies.

NATIONAL LABOR RELATIONS BOARD (NLRB)
1717 Pennsylvania Ave., N.W. (20570).
Members: 5.
Established: July 5, 1935.
Chairman: John H. Fanning.
Activities: Prevents unfair labor practices by employers or labor organizations; conducts secret ballots among employees to determine bargaining representatives.

NATIONAL SCIENCE FOUNDATION (NSF)
1800 G St., N.W. (20550).
Established: 1950.
Director: John B. Slaughter.
Activities: Awards grants and contracts to support research in the sciences. Encourages research in areas that can lead to improvements in economic growth, productivity, and environmental quality. Administered by 25-member National Science Board.

NATIONAL TRANSPORTATION SAFETY BOARD
800 Independence Ave., S.W. (20594).
Members: 5.
Established: April 1, 1975.
Chairman: James B. King.
Activities: Conducts investigations into accidents, assesses techniques of accident investigation and recommends safety-improvement measures.

NUCLEAR REGULATORY COMMISSION (NRC)
1717 H St., N.W. (20555) and Bethesda, Md. (20014).
Members: 5.
Established: Jan. 19, 1975.
Chairman: Nunzio J. Palladino.
Activities: Regulates civilian nuclear facilities to assure protection of public health and safety and the environment, and safeguarding of nuclear materials and facilities.

OFFICE OF PERSONNEL MANAGEMENT (OPM)
1900 E St., N.W. (20415).
Member: 3.
Established: Jan. 16, 1883.
Director: Donald J. Devine.
Activities: Provides examinations to test fitness of applicants for positions in competitive service; provides personnel in response to requests from appointing officers; investigates applicants for national security purposes; classifies positions; provides leadership to Federal agencies in personnel matters.

SECURITIES AND EXCHANGE COMMISSION (SEC)
500 N. Capitol St., N.W. (20549).
Members: 5.
Established: June 6, 1934.
Chairman: Harold M. Williams.
Activities: Registers and issues regulations for securities and exchanges; registers securities offered for public sale; penalizes violators of regulations subject to appeal to U.S. Court of Appeals.

SELECTIVE SERVICE SYSTEM (SSS)
600 E. St., N.W. (20435).
Established: Sept. 16, 1940
Director: Bernard D. Rostker.
Activities: Authorizes registration of male citizens and all other male persons, except aliens in certain categories, for military service. (Authority to induct registrants expired July 1, 1973.)

SMALL BUSINESS ADMINISTRATION (SBA)
1441 L St., N.W. (20416).
Established: July 30, 1953.
Administrator: Michael Cardenas.
Activities: Aids and assists the interests of small business firms to insure a fair share of total government contracts; makes loans to small firms and victims of flood and disaster.

TENNESSEE VALLEY AUTHORITY (TVA)
400 Commerce Ave., Knoxville, Tenn. (37902). Washington office: Woodward Bldg., 15th & H Sts., N.W. (20444).
Members of Board of Directors: 3.
Established: May 18, 1933.
Chairman: S. David Freeman.
Activities: Provides navigable channel and flood control of Tennessee River and some of its larger tributaries; disposes of surplus electric power, improves, increases, and cheapens fertilizer production.

U.S. ARMS CONTROL AND DISARMAMENT AGENCY
Department of State Building (20451).
Established: Sept. 26, 1961.
Director: Eugene V. Rostow.
Chief Arms Control Negotiator: Edward L. Rowny.
Activities: Conducts studies and provides advice relating to arms control and disarmament policy fomulation; prepares for and manages U.S. participation in international negotiations in arms control and disarmament; prepares for, operates, or as needed, directs U.S. participation in international control systems.

U.S. COMMISSION ON CIVIL RIGHTS
1121 Vermont Avenue, N.W. (20425).
Members: 6.
Established: 1957.
Chairman: Arthur S. Flemming.
Activities: Collects and studies information concerning discrimination or denial of equal protection of the nation's laws because of race, color, religion, sex, age, handicap, or national origin. Complaints about denials of rights are usually referred to the appropriate Federal agencies for action.

U.S. INTERNATIONAL DEVELOPMENT COOPERATION AGENCY
320 21st. St., N.W. (20523)
Established: Oct. 1, 1979.
Director: M. Peter McPherson.
Activities: Plans and coordinates policy for economic matters affecting relations with developing countries. Administers Agency for International Development, Institute for Scientific & Technological Cooperation, and Overseas Private Investment Corporation.

U.S. INTERNATIONAL TRADE COMMISSION
701 E St., N.W. (20436).
Members: 6.
Established: Sept. 8, 1916.
Chairman: Bill Alberger.
Activities: Investigates customs laws, unfair competition, and foreign and domestic manufacturing costs; advises the President on duty rates.

U.S. POSTAL SERVICE
475 L'Enfant Plaza West, S.W. (20260).
   Postmaster General: William F. Bolger.
   Deputy Postmaster General: C. Neil Benson.
   Activities: Maintains postal system of U.S.
   Established: Office of Postmaster General and temporary post office system created in 1789. Act of Feb. 20, 1792, made detailed provisions for Post Office Department. Postmaster General became Cabinet member in 1829, and Department received executive status in 1872. In 1970 became independent agency headed by 11-member board of governors. Postmaster General, no longer Cabinet member, is chosen by nine governors, who, with Postmaster General, choose Deputy Postmaster General.

VETERANS ADMINISTRATION (VA)
810 Vermont Ave., N.W. (20420).
   Established: July 21, 1930.
   Administrator: Robert Nimmo.
   Activities: Administers laws authorizing benefits for veterans and dependents or beneficiaries. Included are hospitals, pensions, insurance, loans, education, etc.

Other Independent Agencies

Administrative Conference of the United States— 2120 L St., N.W. (20037).
American Battle Monuments Commission— 20 Massachusetts Ave., S.W. (20314).
Appalachian Regional Commission— 1666 Connecticut Ave., N.W. (20235).
Board for International Broadcasting— 1030 15th St., N.W. (20005).
Commission of Fine Arts— 708 Jackson Place, N.W. (20006).
Commodity Futures Trading Commission— 2033 K St., N.W. (20581).
Export-Import Bank of the United States— 811 Vermont Ave., N.W. (20571).
Federal Council on the Aging— 330 Independence Ave. S.W. (20201)
Federal Emergency Management Agency— 1725 I St., N.W. (20472).
Federal Home Loan Bank Board— 1700 G St., N.W. (20552).
Federal Labor Relations Authority— 1900 E St., N.W. (20424).
Inter-American Foundation— 1515 Wilson Blvd., Rosslyn, Va. (22209).
Merit Systems Protection Board— 1717 H St., N.W. (20419).
National Center for the Prevention and Control of Rape— 5600 Fishers Lane, Rockville, Md. (20857).
National Commission on Libraries and Information Science— 1717 K St. (20036).
National Credit Union Administration— 1776 G St., N.W. (20456).
National Mediation Board— 1425 K St., N.W. (20572).
Occupational Safety and Health Review Commission —1825 K St., N.W. (20006).
Panama Canal Commission— 425 13th St., N.W. (20004).
Pension Benefit Guaranty Corporation— 2020 K St., N.W. (20006).
Postal Rate Commission— 2000 L St., N.W. (20268).
President's Committee on Employment of the Handicapped— 1111 20th St., N.W. (20210).
President's Council on Physical Fitness and Sports

—400 6th St., S.W. (20201).
Railroad Retirement Board (RRB)— 844 Rush St., Chicago, Ill. (60611). Washington Liaison Office: Room 444, 425 13th St., N.W. (20004).
U.S. Metric Board— 1600 Wilson Blvd., Arlington, Va. (22209).

Legislative Department
ARCHITECT OF THE CAPITOL
U.S. Capitol Building (20515).
   Established: First Architect of the Capitol was appointed in 1793; office has been continuous since 1851.
   Architect of Capitol: George M. White.
   Activities: Architect of the Capitol has charge of structural and mechanical care of Capitol Building and various other government buildings in Washington.

GENERAL ACCOUNTING OFFICE (GAO)
441 G Street, N.W. (20548).
   Established: 1921.
   Comptroller General: Charles A. Bowsher (designate).
   Deputy Comptroller General: Vacant.
   Activities: Assists Congress in providing legislative control over receipt, disbursement, and application of public funds.

GOVERNMENT PRINTING OFFICE (GPO)
North Capitol & H Sts., N.W. (20401).
   Established: June 23, 1860.
   Public Printer: Samuel L. Saylor (acting).
   Superintendent of Documents: Carl A. LaBarre.
   Activities: Executes printing and binding orders for Congress and federal agencies; distributes government publications.

LIBRARY OF CONGRESS
10 First St., S.E. (20540).
   Established: April 24, 1800.
   Librarian of Congress: Daniel J. Boorstin.
   Activities: Extends services to members of government and offers facilities for persons engaged in scholarly research.

OFFICE OF TECHNOLOGY ASSESSMENT
600 Pennsylvania Ave., S.E. (20510).
   Established: 1972.
   Director: John H. Gibbons.
   Activities: Helps Congress anticipate and plan for the consequences of the uses of technology.

UNITED STATES BOTANIC GARDEN
Office of Director, 245 First St., S.W. (20024).
   Established: 1820.
   Director: George M. White (acting).
   Activities: Collects, cultivates, and grows various vegetable products for exhibition and study.

Quasi-Official Agencies
American National Red Cross— 17th & D Sts., N.W. (20006).
Legal Services Corporation— 733 15th St., N.W. (20005).
National Academy of Sciences, National Academy of Engineering, National Research Council, Institute of Medicine— 2101 Constitution Ave., N.W. (20418).
National Railroad Passenger Corporation (Amtrak) —400 N. Capitol St., N.W. (20001).
Smithsonian Institution— 1000 Jefferson Dr., S.W. (20560).
U.S. Railway Association— 955 L'Enfant Plaza North, S.W. (20595).

U.S. SOCIETIES&ASSOCIATIONS

Source: Information Please questionnaires to organizations.

Names are listed alphabetically according to key word in title; figure in parentheses is year of founding; other figure is membership.

Abortion Federation, National (1976): 110 E. 59th St., New York, N.Y. 10022. Uta Landy, Executive Director.

Abortion Rights Action League, National (1969): 825 15th St., N.W., Washington, D.C. 20005. 100,000; Karen Mulhauser, Executive Director.

Accountants, American Institute of Certified Public (1887): 1211 Avenue of the Americas, New York, N.Y. 10036. 170,000; Philip B. Chenok, President.

Accountants, National Association of (1919): 919 Third Ave., New York, N.Y. 10022. 94,000; Robert L. Shultis, Executive Director.

Actors' Equity Association (1913): 165 W. 46th St., New York, N.Y. 10036. 30,000; Willard Swire, Executive Secretary.

Aeronautic Association, National (1905): 821 15th St., N.W., Washington, D.C. 20005. 160,000; Ev Langworthy, Executive Director.

Aeronautics and Astronautics, American Institute of (1932): 1290 Avenue of the Americas, New York, N.Y. 10104. 27,000; James J. Harford, Executive Secretary.

African-American Institute, The (1953): 833 United Nations Plaza, New York, N.Y. 10017. Donald B. Easum, President.

AFS International/Intercultural Programs (1947): 313 E. 43rd St., New York, N.Y. 10017. 164,000; William M. Dyal, Jr., President.

Air Force Association (1946): 1750 Pennsylvania Ave., N.W., Washington, D.C. 20006. 156,000; Russell E. Dougherty, Executive Director.

Air Line Pilots Association (1931): 1625 Massachusetts Ave., N.W., Washington, D.C. 20036. 33,000; John J. O'Donnell, President.

Air Pollution Control Association (1907): P.O. Box 2861, Pittsburgh, Pa. 15230. 8,000; William G. Hamlin, Executive Vice President.

Alcohol Problems, American Council on (1900): 6955 University Ave., Des Moines, Iowa 50311. 2,000; William N. Plymat, Executive Director.

Alcoholics Anonymous (1935): P.O. Box 459, Grand Central Station, New York, N.Y. 10163. 1,000,000. Address communications to General Service Office.

America-Mideast Educational and Training Services (1951): 1717 Massachusetts Ave., N.W., Washington, D.C. 20036. 350; Orin D. Parker, President.

American Federation of Labor and Congress of Industrial Organizations (AFL-CIO) (1955): 815 16th St., N.W., Washington, D.C. 20006. 13,600,000; Saul Miller, Director of Information.

American Friends Service Committee (1917): 1501 Cherry St., Philadelphia, Pa. 19102. Paul E. Brink, Director of Information.

American Indian Affairs, National Association on (1923): 432 Park Ave. S., New York, N.Y. 10016. 50,000; Steven Unger, Executive Director.

American Legion (1919): P.O. Box 1055, Indianapolis, Ind. 46206. 2,500,000; Frank C. Momsen, National Adjutant.

American Legion Auxiliary (1919): 777 N. Meridian St., Indianapolis, Ind. 46204. 940,000; Miriam Junge, National Secretary.

Americans for Democratic Action (1947): 1411 K St., N.W., Washington, D.C. 20005. 75,000; Leon Shull, National Director.

AMVETS (American Veterans of World War II, Korea, and Vietnam) (1944): 4647 Forbes Blvd., Lanham, Md. 20801. 200,000; Leon Sanchez, National Executive Director.

AMVETS National Auxiliary (1946): Saco Rd., Old Orchard Beach, Me. 04064. 60,000. Rita J. Potvin, Executive Secretary.

Animals, The American Society for the Prevention of Cruelty to (1866): 441 E. 92nd St., New York, N.Y. 10028. 23,000; John F. Kullberg, Executive Director.

Animals, Fund For (1967): 140 W. 57th St., New York, N.Y. 10019. 175,000; Cleveland Amory, President.

Anti-Defamation League of B'nai B'rith (1913): 823 United Nations Plaza, New York, N.Y. 10017. Nathan Perlmutter, National Director.

Anti-Vivisection Society, The American (1883): Suite 204, Noble Plaza, 801 Old York Rd., Jenkintown, Pa. 19046. 15,000; William A. Cave, President.

Arbitration Association, American (1926): 140 W. 51st St., New York, N.Y. 10020. 4,337; E. W. Dippold, Corporate Secretary.

Architects, American Institute of (1857): 1735 New York Ave., N.W., Washington, D.C. 20006. 34,000; David O. Meeker, Jr., Executive Vice President.

Army, Association of the United States (1950): 2425 Wilson Blvd., Arlington, Va. 22201. 117,800; Robert F. Cocklin, Executive Vice President.

Arthritis Foundation (1948): 3400 Peachtree Rd., N.E., Atlanta, Ga. 30326. 71 local chapters; Clifford M. Clarke, President.

Arts and Letters, American Academy and Institute of (1904): 633 W. 155th St., New York, N.Y. 10032. 250; Margaret M. Mills, Executive Director.

Astronomical Society, American (1899): Louisiana State University, Box BK, LSU Observatory, Baton Rouge, La. 70803. 3,700; Arlo U. Landolt, Secretary.

Audubon Society, National (1905): 950 Third Ave., New York, N.Y. 10022. 430,000; Andrew Bihun, Conservation Information.

Authors League of America (1912): 234 W. 44th St., New York, N.Y. 10036. 10,000; Helen A. Stephenson, Administrative Assistant.

Automobile Association, American (1902): 8111 Gatehouse Rd., Falls Church, Va. 22047. 21,000,000; J. B. Creal, President.

Automobile Club, National (1924): One Market Plaza, San Francisco, Calif. 94105. 427,780; Gene Halliburton, President.

Bar Association, American (1898): 1155 E. 60th St., Chicago, Ill. 60637. 263,000; Bert H. Early, Executive Director.

Barber Shop Quartet Singing in America, Society for the Preservation and Encouragement of (1938): Box 575, Kenosha, Wis. 53141. 36,000; Hugh Ingraham, Executive Director.

Bible Society, American (1816): 1865 Broadway, New York, N.Y. 10023. 328,000; Charles W. Baas, Alice E. Ball, John D. Erickson, General Officers.

Big Brothers/Big Sisters of America (1977): 117 S. 17th St., Suite 1200, Philadelphia, Pa. 19103. Betty Larkin, Manager, Information and Liaison.

Blind, National Federation of the (1940): 1800 Johnson St., Baltimore, Md. 21230. 50,000; Kenneth Jernigan, President.

Blindness, National Society to Prevent (1908): 79 Madison Ave., New York, N.Y. 10016. 26 affiliates; Virginia Boyce, Executive Director.

Blue Shield Association (1946): 676 St. Clair, Chicago, Ill. 60611. 69 affiliates; Tom K. Mura, Vice President, Advertising.

B'nai B'rith (1843): 1640 Rhode Island Ave., N.W., Washington, D.C. 20036. 500,000; Hank Siegel, Press Officer.

Boy Scouts of America (1910): P.O. Box 61030, Dallas-Fort Worth Airport, Tex. 75261. 4,493,491.

Boys Clubs of America (1906): 771 First Ave., New York, N.Y. 10017. 1,000,000; Joan R. Licursi, Director of Communications Services.

Brookings Institution, The (1927): 1775 Massachusetts Ave., N.W., Washington, D.C. 20036. James D. Farrell, Information Editor.

Camp Fire, Inc. (1910): 4601 Madison Ave., Kansas City, Mo. 64112. 500,000; Roberta van der Voort, National Executive Director.

Campers & Hikers Association, National (1949): 7172 Transit Rd., Buffalo, N.Y. 14221. 45,000 families. Fran Opela, National Office Manager.

Camping Association, The American (1910): Bradford Woods, Martinsville, Ind. 46151. 6,000; Armand Ball, Executive Vice President.

Cancer Society, American (1913): 777 Third Ave., New York, N.Y. 10017. 2,300,000 volunteers; Lane W. Adams, Executive Vice President.

CARE (Cooperative for American Relief Everywhere) (1945): 660 First Ave., New York, N.Y. 10016. 26 agencies; Philip Johnston, Executive Director.

Catholic Bishops, National Conference of (1966): 1312 Massachusetts Ave., N.W., Washington, D.C. 20005. 340; Most Rev. John R. Roach, President.

Catholic Charities, National Conference of (1910): 1346 Connecticut Ave., N.W., Washington, D.C. 20036. 2,735 individuals, 824 agencies and institutions; Rev. Msgr. Lawrence Corcoran, Executive Director.

Catholic Conference, United States (1966): 1312 Massachusetts Ave., N.W., Washington, D.C. 20005. Bishop Thomas C. Kelly, O.P., General Secretary.

Catholic Daughters of the Americas (1903): 10 W. 71st St., New York, N.Y. 10023. 175,000; Lorraine McMahon, Executive Secretary.

Catholic War Veterans of the U.S.A. (1935): 2 Massachusetts Ave., N.W., Washington, D.C. 20001. 75,000; Walter W. Stachacz, National Commander.

Cerebral Palsy Associations, Inc., United (1949): 66 E. 34th St., New York, N.Y. 10016. 250 affiliates; Earl H. Cunerd, Executive Director.

Chamber of Commerce of the U.S. (1912): 1615 H St., N.W., Washington, D.C. 20062. 125,000; Richard L. Lesher, President.

Chartered Life Underwriters, American Society of (1929): 270 Bryn Mawr Ave., Bryn Mawr, Pa. 19010. 27,000; John R. Driskill, Executive Vice President.

Chemical Engineers, American Institute of (1908): 345 E. 47th St., New York, N.Y. 10017. 51,000; J. Charles Forman, Executive Director and Secretary.

Chemical Society, American (1876): 1155 16th St., N.W., Washington, D.C. 20036. 120,000; Raymond P. Mariella, Executive Director.

Chess Federation, United States (1939): 186 Rt. 9W, New Windsor, N.Y. 12550. 50,000; Gerard J. Dullea, Executive Director.

Child Welfare League of America (1920): 67 Irving Pl., New York, N.Y. 10003. Edwin F. Watson, Executive Director.

Chiropractic Association, American (1963): 1635 De Sales St., N.W., Washington, D.C. 20036. 15,-000; G.M. Brassard, Executive Vice President.

Christians and Jews, National Conference of (1928): 43 W. 57th St., New York, N.Y. 10019. 200,000; David Hyatt, President.

Churches, National Council of (1950): 475 Riverside Drive, New York, N.Y. 10115. 32 Protestant and Orthodox communions; Claire Randall, General Secretary.

Civil Engineers, American Society of (1852): 345 E. 47th St., New York, N.Y. 10017. 78,000; Eugene Zwoyer, Executive Director.

Civil Liberties Union, American (1920): 132 W. 43rd St., New York, N.Y. 10036. 200,000; Alan Reitman, Associate Director.

Colleges, Association of American (1915): 1818 R St., N.W., Washington, D.C. 20009. 600 institutions; Mark H. Curtis, President.

Colored Women's Clubs, National Association of (1896): 5808 16th St., N.W., Washington, D.C. 20011. 40,000; Mrs. Otelia E. Champion, National President.

Common Cause (1970): 2030 M St., N.W., Washington, D.C. 20036. 225,000; Archibald Cox, Chairman.

Composers, Authors, and Publishers, American Society of (ASCAP) (1914): One Lincoln Plaza, New York, N.Y. 10023. 30,000; Hal David, President.

Congress of Racial Equality (CORE) (1942): 1916–38 Park Ave., New York, N.Y. 10037. Nationwide network of chapters; Roy Innis, National Director.

Conscientious Objectors, Central Committee for (1948): 2208 South St., Philadelphia, Pa. 19146.

Consumer Federation of America (1968): 1413 14th St., N.W., Washington, D.C. 20005. 220 member organizations; Stephen Brobeck, Executive Director.

Consumers Union (1936): 256 Washington St., Mt. Vernon, N.Y. 10550. 2,950,000 subscribers to *Consumer Reports;* Rhoda H. Karpatkin, Executive Director.

Contract Bridge League, American (1927): 2200 Democrat Rd., Memphis, Tenn. 38116. 200,000; Richard L. Goldberg, Executive Secretary.

Cooperative League of the U.S.A. (1916): 1828 L St., N.W., Washington, D.C. 20036. 30,000,000 families; E. Morgan Williams, President.

Country Music Association (1958): Box 22299, Nashville, Tenn. 37202. 5,500; Jo Walker, Executive Director.

Crime and Delinquency, National Council on (1907): Continental Plaza, Hackensack, N.J. 07601. Nationwide membership; Milton G. Rector, President.

Daughters of the American Revolution, National Society (1890): 1776 D St., N.W., Washington, D.C. 20006. 208,000; Mrs. Richard Denny Shelby, President General.

Daughters of the Confederacy, United (1894): 328 N. Boulevard, Richmond, Va. 23220. 26,000.

Deaf, National Association of the (1880): 814 Thayer Ave., Silver Spring, Md. 20910. Albert T. Pimentel, Executive Director.

Defense Preparedness Association, American (1919): 1700 N. Moore St., Arlington, Va. 22209. 34,000; H.A. Miley, Jr., President.

Democratic Club, National (1834): Chemists Club, 52 E. 41st St., New York, N.Y. 10017. 500; John G. Treacy, Secretary.

Dental Association, American (1859): 211 E. Chicago Ave., Chicago, Ill. 60611. 138,000; John M. Coady, Executive Director.

Diabetes Association, American (1940): 2 Park Ave., New York, N.Y. 10016. Robert S. Bolan, Executive Vice President.

Dignity (1969): 1500 Massachusetts Ave., N.W., Washington, D.C. 20005. 5,000; Frank Scheuren, President.

Disabled American Veterans (1922): P.O. Box 14301, Cincinnati, Ohio 45214. 700,000; Richard M. Wilson, Assistant National Adjutant for Public Relations.

Ducks Unlimited (1937): Box 66300, Chicago, Ill. 60666. 365,600; Dale E. Whitesell, Executive Vice President.

Eagles, Fraternal Order of (1898): 2401 W. Wisconsin Ave., Milwaukee, Wis. 53233. 850,000; Art Ehrmann, Publications Editor.

Easter Seal Society, The National (1921): 2023 W. Ogden Ave., Chicago, Ill. 60612. 50 affiliated state societies; John R. Garrison, Executive Director.

Eastern Star, Order of the, General Grand Chapter (1876): 1618 New Hampshire Ave., N.W., Washington, D.C. 20009. 3,000,000; Thelma R. Bailey, Most Worthy Grand Matron.

Education Association, National (1857): 1201 16th St., N.W., Washington, D.C. 20036. 1,600,000; Terry Herndon, Executive Director.

Electrochemical Society, The (1902): 10 S. Main St., Pennington, N.J. 08534. 4,476; Donna N. Kimberlin, Administrative Assistant.

Elks of the U.S.A., Benevolent and Protective Order of the (1868): 2750 Lake View Ave., Chicago, Ill. 60614. 1,650,000; Stanley F. Kocur, Grand Secretary.

English-Speaking Union of the United States (1920): 16 E. 69th St., New York, N.Y. 10021. 32,000; John D. Walker, Executive Director.

Euthanasia Foundation, American (1972): 95 N. Birch Rd., Fort Lauderdale, Fla. 33304. Vincent F. Sullivan, Executive Director.

Exploration Geophysicists, Society of (1930): P.O. Box 3098, Tulsa, Okla. 74101. 15,000; John Hyden, Executive Director.

Family Service Association of America (1911): 44 E. 23rd St., New York, N.Y. 10010. 275 member agencies; W. Keith Daugherty, General Director.

Farm Bureau Federation, American (1919): 225 Touhy Ave., Park Ridge, Ill. 60068. 3,297,224 member families; J. Patrick Batts, Director of Information.

Fleet Reserve Association (1924): 1303 New Hampshire Ave., N.W., Washington, D.C. 20036. 149,000; Robert W. Nolan, National Executive Secretary.

Foreign Policy Association (1918): 205 Lexington Ave., New York, N.Y. 10016. Thetis Reavis, Vice President for Public Affairs.

Foreign Relations, Council on (1921): 58 E. 68th St., New York, N.Y. 10021. 2,039; Winston Lord, President.

Foreign Study, American Institute for (1965): 102 Greenwich Ave., Greenwich, Conn. 06830. 250,000; Henry C. Kahn, President.

Foreign Trade Council, Inc., National (1914): 10 Rockefeller Plaza, New York, N.Y. 10020. Over 650 companies; Richard W. Roberts, President.

Foster Parents Plan International (1937): Box 400, Warwick, R.I. 02887. George W. Ross, International Executive Director.

4-H Program (early 1900s): Room 5035S, U.S. Department of Agriculture, Washington, D.C. 20250. 5,200,00; Eugene Williams, Deputy Administrator.

Future Farmers of America (1928): 5632 Mt. Vernon Hgwy, Alexandria, Va. 22309. 494,394; Byron F. Rawls, National Advisor.

Future Homemakers of America (1945): 2010 Massachusetts Ave., N.W., Washington, D.C. 20036. 400,000; Mildred Reel, Executive Director.

Gamblers Anonymous Fellowship: Box 17173, Los Angeles, Calif. 90017. 7,000; Jim Z., National Executive Secretary.

Geographic Society, National (1888): 17th and M Sts., N.W., Washington, D.C. 20036. 10,700,000; Gilbert M. Grosvenor, President.

Geriatrics Society, American (1942): 10 Columbus Circle, New York, N.Y. 10019. 8,000; Kathryn S. Henderson, Executive Director.

Gideons International, The (1889): 2900 Lebanon Rd., Nashville, Tenn. 37214. 66,000; M.A. Henderson, Executive Director.

Girl Scouts of the U.S.A. (1912): 830 Third Ave., New York, N.Y. 10022. 2,784,000; Rhoda Pauley, Communications Services.

Girls Clubs of America (1945): 205 Lexington Ave., New York, N.Y. 10016. 220,000; Edith B. Phelps, National Executive Director.

Hadassah, The Women's Zionist Organization of America (1912): 50 W. 58th St., New York, N.Y. 10019. 370,000; Aline Kaplan, Executive Director.

Health, Physical Education, Recreation, and Dance, American Alliance for (1885): 1900 Association Dr., Reston, Va. 22091. 50,000; Ray Ciszek, Executive Vice President.

Hearing and Speech Action, National Association for (1919): 6110 Executive Blvd., Rockville, Md. 20852. 153 agencies.

Heart Association, American (1924): 7320 Greenville Ave., Dallas, Tex. 75231. 115,000; Dudley Hafner, Executive Vice President.

Hemispheric Affairs, Council on (1975): 1201 16th St., N.W., Washington, D.C. 20036. Laurence R. Birns, Director.

Historical Association, American (1884): 400 A St., S.E., Washington, D.C. 20003. 15,000; Samuel R. Gammon, Executive Director.

Home Economics Association, American (1909): 2010 Massachusetts Ave., N.W., Washington, D.C. 20036. 32,000; Kinsey Green, Executive Director.

Horticultural Society, American (1922): Mt. Vernon, Va. 22121. 35,000; Thomas W. Richards, Executive Vice President.

Hospital Association, American (1898): 840 N. Lake Shore Dr., Chicago, Ill. 60611. 6,165 institutions; J. Alexander McMahon, President.

Humane Association, American (1877): 9725 E. Hampden, Denver, Colo. 80231.

Humane Society of the United States (1954): 2100 L St., N.W., Washington, D.C. 20037. 130,500; Patrick B. Parkes, Vice President for Field Services.

Indian Rights Association (1882): 1505 Race St., Philadelphia, Pa. 19102. 1,400; Sandra L. Cadwalader, Executive Director.

Interfraternity Conference, National (1909): 3901 W. 86th St., Indianapolis, Ind. 46268. 55; Jack L. Anson, Executive Director.

Jaycees, The United States (1920): 4 W. 21st St., Tulsa, Okla. 74121. 300,000; Arthur Boutiette, Executive Vice President.

Jewish Appeal, United (1939): 1290 Avenue of the Americas, New York, N.Y. 10019. Irving Bernstein, Executive Vice Chairman.

Jewish Committee, American (1906): 165 E. 56th St., New York, N.Y. 10022. 40,000; Morton Yarmon, Director of Public Relations.

Jewish Community Centers, World Confederation of (1946): 15 E. 26th St., New York, N.Y. 10010. Herbert Millman, Executive Director.

Jewish War Veterans of the U.S.A. (1896): 1712 New Hampshire Ave., N.W., Washington, D.C. 20009.

JWB (National Jewish Welfare Board) (1917): 15 E. 26th St., New York, N.Y. 10010. 275 affiliated community centers and YM–YWHAs; Arthur Rotman, Executive Vice President.

Jewish Women, National Council of (1893): 15 E. 26th St., New York, N.Y. 10010. Shirley I. Leviton, National President.

John Birch Society (1958): 395 Concord Ave., Belmont, Mass. 02178. 100,000; Ellen Sproul, Clerk of Corporation.

Journalists, Society of Professional, Sigma Delta Chi (1909): 840 N. Lake Shore Dr., Chicago, Ill. 60611. 30,000; Russell C. Tornabene, Executive Officer.

Judaism, American Council for (1943): 307 Fifth Ave., New York, N.Y. 10016. 10,000; Clarence L. Coleman, Jr., President.

Junior Achievement (1919): 550 Summer St., Stamford, Conn. 06901. 5,000,000; Glenn V. Gardinier, National Public Relations Director.

Junior Leagues, Association of (1921): 825 Third Ave., New York, N.Y. 10022. 130,000.

Kennel Club, American (1884): 51 Madison Ave., New York, N.Y. 10010. 420 member clubs; Mark T. Mooty, Secretary.

Kiwanis International (1915): 101 E. Erie, Chicago, Ill. 60611. 300,000; R. P. Merridew, International Secretary.

Knights of Columbus (1882): One Columbus Plaza, New Haven, Conn. 06507. 1,349,507; Virgil Dechant, Supreme Knight.

Knights of Pythias, Supreme Lodge (1864): 47 N. Grant St., Stockton, Calif. 95202. 130,645; Jule O. Pritchard, Supreme Secretary.

Knights Templar, Grand Encampment of (1816): 14 E. Jackson Blvd., Suite 1700, Chicago, Ill. 60604. 360,000; Paul C. Rodenhauser, Grand Recorder.

La Leche League International (1956): 9616 Minneapolis Ave., Franklin Park, Ill. 60131. 53,543; Betty Wagner, Chief Executive Officer.

Library Association, American (1876): 50 E. Huron St., Chicago, Ill. 60611. 35,257; Robert Wedgeworth, Executive Director.

Life Underwriters, National Association of (1890): 1922 F St., N.W., Washington, D.C. 20006. Jack E. Bobo, Executive Vice President.

Lions Clubs, The International Association of (1917): 300 22nd St., Oak Brook, Ill. 60570. 1,303,850; Roy Schaetzel, Executive Administrator.

Lupus Foundation of America (1976): 11673 Holly Spring Drive., St. Louis, Mo. 63141. 60 chapters; Virginia Masters, Executive Secretary.

Management Associations, American (1923): 135 W. 50th St., New York, N.Y. 10020. 85,000; Joseph P. Keyes, Vice President Public Relations.

Manufacturers, National Association of (1895): 1776 F St., N.W., Washington, D.C. 20006. 13,000; Edmund W. Haskins, Secretary.

March of Dimes Birth Defects Foundation (1938): 1275 Mamaroneck Ave., White Plains, N.Y. 10605. 756 chapters; Charles L. Massey, President.

Marine Corps League (1923): 933 N. Kenmore St., Arlington, Va. 22201. 20,000; F. B. Starr, National Adjutant Paymaster.

Masons, Ancient and Accepted Scottish Rite, Northern Masonic Jurisdiction, Supreme Council 33° (1867): 33 Marrett Rd., Lexington, Mass. 02173. 502,114; Laurence E. Eaton, Grand Secretary General.

Masons, Ancient and Accepted Scottish Rite, Southern Jurisdiction, Supreme Council (1801): 1733 16th St., N.W., Washington, D.C. 20009. 659,500; C. Fred Kleinknecht, Grand Secretary General.

Masons, Royal Arch, International General Grand Chapter (1797): Box 5320, Lexington, Ky. 40505. 450,000; Charles K.A. McGaughey, General Grand Secretary.

Mathematical Society, American (1888): 201 Charles St., Providence, R.I. 02940. 19,994; William J. LeVeque, Executive Director.

Mayflower Descendants, General Society of (1897): 4 Winslow St., P.O. Box 297, Plymouth, Mass. 02361. 20,000; Anne Borden Harding, Historian General.

Mechanical Engineers, American Society of (1880): 345 E. 47th St., New York, N.Y. 10017. 101,162; Rogers Finch, Executive Director.

Medical Association, American (1847): 535 N. Dearborn St., Chicago, Ill. 60610.

Mental Health Association, National (1909): 1800 N. Kent St., Arlington, Va. 22209. 1,000,000; Lynn Schultz-Writsel, Acting Director, Public Information and Education.

Mining, Metallurgical and Petroleum Engineers, American Institute of (1871): 345 E. 47th St., New York, N.Y. 10017. 81,733; Joe B. Alford, Executive Director.

Modern Language Association of America (1883): 62 Fifth Avenue., New York, N.Y. 10011. 30,000.

Modern Woodmen of America (1883): Mississippi River at 17th St., Rock Island, Ill. 61201. 500,000; W.B. Foster, President.

Moose, Loyal Order of (1888): Mooseheart, Ill. 60539. 1,746,773; Carl A. Weis, Supreme Secretary.

Motion Picture Arts & Sciences, Academy of (1927): 8949 Wilshire Blvd., Beverly Hills, Calif. 90211. James M. Roberts, Executive Director.

Multiple Sclerosis Society, National (1946): 205 E. 42nd St., New York, N.Y. 10017. Sylvia Lawry, Executive Director.

Muscular Dystrophy Association (1950): 810 Seventh Ave., New York, N.Y. 10019. 1,800,000 volunteers. Jerry Lewis, National Chairman.

Museums, American Association of (1906): 1055 Thomas Jefferson St., N.W., Washington, D.C. 20007. 7,500; Lawrence Reger, Director.

Musicians, American Federation of (1896): 1500 Broadway, New York, N.Y. 10036. 300,000; Victor W. Fuentealba, President.

National Association for the Advancement of Col-

ored People (1909): 1790 Broadway, New York, N.Y. 10019. 450,000; Benjamin L. Hooks, Executive Director.

National Grange, The (1867): 1616 H St., N.W., Washington, D.C. 20006. 460,000; Edward Andersen, Master.

National PTA (National Congress of Parents and Teachers) (1897): 700 N. Rush St., Chicago, Ill. 60611. 6,170,027; Ronald L. Smith, Executive Director.

Negro College Fund, Inc., United (1944): 500 E. 62nd St., New York, N.Y. 10021. 41 institutions; Christopher F. Edley, Executive Director.

Newspaper Publishers Association, American (1887): The Newspaper Center, P.O. Box 17407, Dulles International Airport, Washington, D.C. 20041. 1,422; Jerry W. Friedheim, Executive Vice President and General Manager.

Nurses' Association, American (1896): 1030 15th St., N.W. Washington, D.C. 20005. 170,000.

Odd Fellows, Independent Order of (1819): 16 W. Chase St., Baltimore, Md. 21201. 1,200,000; Edward T. Rogers, Sovereign Grand Secretary.

Olympic Committee, United States (1921): 1750 Boulder St., Colorado Springs, Colo. 80909. Bob Paul, Director of Communications.

Organization of American States, General Secretariat (1890): 1889 F St., N.W., Washington, D.C. 20006. 28 member nations.

ORT Federation, American (1922): 817 Broadway, New York, N.Y. 10003. 160,000; Donald H. Klein, Executive Vice President.

Overeaters Anonymous (1960): 2190 190th St., Torrance, Calif. 90504. 100,000.

Parents Without Partners, Inc. (1957): 7910 Woodmont Ave., N.W., Washington, D.C. 20014. 196,500; Virginia L. Martin, Executive Director.

Parks and Conservation Association, National (1919): 1701 18th St., N.W., Washington, D.C. 20009. 35,000; Paul C. Pritchard, Executive Director.

Philatelic Society, American (1886): P.O. Box 800, State College, Pa. 16801. 53,000; Keith A. Wagner, Executive Director.

Philosophical Society, American (1743): 104 S. 5th St., Philadelphia, Pa. 19106. 600; W. J. Bell, Jr., Executive Officer.

Photographic Society of America (1933): 2005 Walnut St., Philadelphia, Pa. 19103. 17,500; Harold J. Vermes, Executive Director.

Physical Society, American (1899): 335 E. 45th St., New York, N.Y. 10017. 30,000; W. W. Havens, Jr., Executive Secretary.

Physics, American Institute of (1931): 335 E. 45th St., New York, N.Y. 10017. 56,000; H. William Koch, Director.

Planned Parenthood Federation of America (1916): 810 Seventh Ave., New York, N.Y. 10019. 187 affiliates.

Political Science, Academy of (1880): 619 W. 114th St., Suite 500, New York, N.Y. 10025. 10,500; Robert H. Connery, President.

Professional Engineers, National Society of (1934): 2029 K St., N.W., Washington, D.C. 20006. 80,000; Donald G. Weinert, Executive Director.

Psychiatric Association, American (1844): 1700 18th St., N.W., Washington, D.C. 20009. 26,000; Daniel X. Freedman, M.D., President.

Psychological Association, American (1892): 1200 17th St., N.W., Washington, D.C. 20036. 50,000; Michael S. Pallak, Executive Officer.

Public Health Association, American (1872): 1015 15th St., N.W., Washington, D.C. 20005. 30,201;

William H. McBeath, M.D., Executive Director.

Puppeteers of America (1937): 5 Cricklewood Path, Pasadena, Calif. 91107. Gayle Schluter, Treasurer.

Red Cross, American (1881): 17th and D Sts., N.W., Washington, D.C. 20006. 3,000 chapters; George M. Elsey, President.

Rehabilitation Association, National (1925): 633 S. Washington St., Alexandria, Va. 22314. 20,000; David L. Mills, Executive Director.

Reserve Officers Association of the United States (1922): 1 Constitution Ave., N.E., Washington, D.C. 20002. 130,000; J. Milnor Roberts, Executive Director.

Retarded Citizens, Association for (1950): 2501 Avenue J, Arlington, Tex. 76011. 1,900 units; Philip Roos, National Executive Director.

Retired Federal Employees, National Association of (1921): 1533 New Hampshire Ave., N.W., Washington, D.C. 20036. 313,000; Michael C. Nave, President.

Retired Persons, American Association of (1958): 1909 K St., N.W., Washington, D.C. 20049. 12,041,639; Cyril F. Brickfield, Executive Director.

Retired Teachers Association, National (1947): 1909 K St., N.W., Washington, D.C. 20049. 530,897; Cyril F. Brickfield, Executive Director.

Rifle Association of America, National (1871): 1600 Rhode Island Ave., N.W., Washington, D.C. 20036. 1,900,000; Harlon B. Carter, Executive Vice President.

Right to Life, National Committee (1973): 529 14th St., N.W., Washington, D.C. 20045. Iris Ruegg, Office Manager.

Rotary International (1905): 1600 Ridge Ave., Evanston, Ill. 60201. 880,000; Herbert A. Pigman, General Secretary.

Safety Council, National (1913): 444 N. Michigan Ave., Chicago, Ill. 60611. Charles C. Vance, Director of Public Relations.

Salvation Army, The (1865): 120 W. 14th St., New York, N.Y. 10011. 414,659; Col. G.E. Murray, National Chief Secretary.

Save-the-Redwoods League (1918): 114 Sansome St., San Francisco, Calif. 94104. 55,000; John B. Dewitt, Executive Director.

Science, American Association for the Advancement of (1848): 1515 Massachusetts Ave., N.W., Washington, D.C. 20005. 135,000; Carol L. Rogers, Public Information.

Screen Actors Guild (1933): 7750 Sunset Blvd., Hollywood, Calif. 90046. 46,000; Kim Fellner, Information Director.

Seeing Eye (1929): Morristown, N.J. 07960. Stuart Grout, Executive Vice President.

Shrine of North America (Shriners Hospitals) (1872): Box 25356, Tampa, Fla. 33622. 932,744; Charles G. Cumpstone, Jr., Executive Secretary of Fraternal Affairs.

Sierra Club (1892): 530 Bush St., San Francisco, Calif. 94108. 200,000; Michael McCloskey, Executive Director.

Small Business Association, National (1937): 1604 K St., N.W., Washington, D.C. 20006. 40,000; Herbert Liebenson, President.

Social Welfare, National Conference on (1873): 1730 M St., N.W., Washington, D.C. 20036. 4,000; John E. Hansan, Executive Director.

Social Workers, National Association of (1955): 1425 H St., N.W., Washington, D.C. 20005. 85,000; Chauncey A. Alexander, Executive Director.

Sons of Italy in America, Order (1905): 219 E St., N.E., Washington, D.C. 20002. 2,700 lodges; Frank J. Montemuro, National President.

Sons of the American Revolution, National Society of the (1889): 1000 S. 4th St., Louisville, Ky. 40203. 23,000; John C. Davis, Assistant to President General.

Soroptimist International of the Americas (1921): 1616 Walnut St., Philadelphia, Pa. 19103. 36,000; Mary Helen Madden, Executive Director.

Southern Christian Leadership Conference (1957): 334 Auburn Ave., N.E., Atlanta, Ga. 30303. 1,000,000; 350 chapters, 260 affiliated organizations; Dr. Joseph E. Lowery, President.

Speech-Language-Hearing Association, American (1925): 10801 Rockville Pike, Rockville, Md. 20852. 35,000; Frederick T. Spahr, Executive Director.

Sports Car Club of America (1944): 6750 S. Emporia, Englewood, Colo. 80112. 23,000; Mac DeMere, News Department Manager.

Student Association, United States (1947): 1220 G St., S.E., Washington, D.C. 20003. Frank X. Viggiano, Executive Director.

Surgeons, American College of (1913): 55 E. Erie, St., Chicago, Ill. 60611. 42,000; C. Rollins Hanlon, Director.

Teachers, American Federation of (1916): 11 Dupont Circle, N.W., Washington, D.C. 20036. 550,000; Albert Shanker, President.

Travel Agents, American Society of (ASTA) (1931): 711 Fifth Ave., New York, N.Y. 10022. 16,000; Joseph R. Stone, Chairman.

Travelers Aid Society of New York (1905): 204 E. 39th St., New York, N.Y. 10016. Elizabeth P. Anderson, General Director.

University Women, American Association of (1881): 2401 Virginia Ave., N.W., Washington, D.C. 20037. 190,000; Quincalee Brown, Executive Director.

Urban League, National (1910): 500 E. 62nd St., New York, N.Y. 10021. 116; James D. Williams, Director of Communications.

Veterans Committee, American (AVC) (1944): 1346 Connecticut Ave., N.W., Suite 930, Washington, D.C. 20036. 25,000; June A. Willenz, Executive Director.

Veterans of Foreign Wars of the U.S. (1899): V.F.W. Bldg., 34th and Broadway, Kansas City, Mo. 64111. V.F.W. and Auxiliary, 2,600,000; Howard E. Vander Clute, Jr., Adjutant General.

Veterinary Medical Association, American (1863): 930 N. Meacham Rd., Schaumburg, Ill. 60196. 32,000; Dr. D. A. Price, Executive Vice President.

Wildlife Federation, National (1936): 1412 16th St., N.W., Washington, D.C. 20036. 4,600,000; Jay D. Hair, Executive Vice President.

Woman's Christian Temperance Union, National (1874): 1730 Chicago Ave., Evanston, Ill. 60201. 250,000; Martha G. Edgar, President.

Women Voters of the U.S., League of (1920): 1730 M St., N.W., Washington, D.C. 20036. 115,000; Harriet Hentges, Executive Director.

Women's American ORT (1927): 1250 Broadway, New York, N.Y. 10001. 145,000; Nathan Gould, National Executive Director.

Women's Clubs, General Federation of (1890): 1734 N St., N.W., Washington, D.C. 20036. 600,000; Mildred Baptista, Executive Director.

Young Men's Christian Associations, National Council of (1844): 101 N. Wacker Dr., Chicago, Ill. 60606. 10,000,000; Solon B. Cousins, Executive Director.

Young Women's Christian Association of the U.S.A. (1858 in U.S.A., 1855 in England): 600 Lexington Ave., New York, N.Y. 10022. 2,471,000; Jane Pinkerton, Director of Communications.

Youth Hostels, American (1934): National Campus, 1332 I St., N.W., Washington, D.C. 20005. 100,000.

Zionist Organization of America (1897): ZOA House, 4 E. 34th St., New York, N.Y. 10016. 120,000; Paul I. Flacks, National Executive Director.

Getting Uncle Sam to Enforce Your Civil Rights

Do you know what to do if you believe you have been discriminated against on the basis of race, color, religion, sex, national origin, age, or handicap? One option available to you is to file a complaint with the federal government.

Single copies of the 44-page booklet, "Getting Uncle Sam to Enforce your Civil Rights," are available free from the Publications Division, U.S. Commission on Civil Rights, Washington, D.C. 20425.

This handy booklet can help you to decide whether to file your complaint at the federal level, or whether to seek help from your state or local government.

Department of Defense Hotline for Preventing Waste and Fraud

The Department of Defense operates a toll-free "Defense Hotline" for citizens to report suspected cases of fraud and waste involving the Department of Defense. The nationwide, toll-free number is 800–424–9098. It is operated in Washington, D.C., between 8 a.m. and 4:30 p.m. The Defense Investigative Service operates the hotline with assurance that the anonymity of any caller will be respected.

Federal Government Hotlines

Toll-free phone information is available to the public from selected government agencies. These are "live," not recorded.

Cancer: For information on all aspects of cancer, call 800–638–6694.

Consumer product safety: Call 800–638–2666.

Federal Taxes: Call 800–555–1212 for the toll-free IRS number in your areas.

Auto Safety: Call 800–424–9393 for information on auto safety problems, recalls, and complaints about specific makes and models.

Flood insurance: Call 800–424–8872 for information on federally subsidized flood insurance in hazardous areas.

POSTAL REGULATIONS

Domestic Mail Service

First Class

First-class consists of letters and written and sealed matter. The rate is 18¢ for the first oz; 17¢ for each additional oz, or fraction of an oz, up to 12 oz. Pieces over 12 oz are subject to priority-mail (heavy pieces) rates. Single postcards, 12¢; double postcards, 24¢ (12¢ for each half). The post office sells prestamped single and double postal cards. Consult your postmaster for information on business-reply mail and presort rates.

The weight limit for first-class mail is 70 lb, and the maximum size is 100 in. in combined length and girth.

Weight	Rates
First oz	$ .18
Over 1 oz, but not over 2	.35
Over 2 oz, but not over 3	.52
Over 3 oz, but not over 4	.69
Over 4 oz, but not over 5	.86
Over 5 oz, but not over 6	1.03
Over 6 oz, but not over 7	1.20
Over 7 oz, but not over 8	1.37
Over 8 oz, but not over 9	1.54
Over 9 oz, but not over 10	1.71
Over 10 oz, but not over 11	1.88
Over 11 oz, but not over 12	2.25
Over 12 oz, *see* Priority Mail	

Priority Mail (over 12 oz to 70 lb)

The zone rate applies to mailable matter over 12 oz of any class carried by air. Such matter shall not exceed 100 in. in length and girth combined. Your local post office will supply free official zone tables appropriate to your location.

Airmail

First-class and priority mail receive airmail service.

Express Mail

Express Mail Service is available for any mailable article up to 70 lb, and guarantees next day delivery between major U.S. cities or your money back.

Articles received by 5 p.m. at a postal facility offering Express Mail Service will be delivered by 3 p.m. the next day or, if you prefer, your shipment can be picked up as early as 10 a.m. the next business day. Rates include Insurance, Shipment Receipt, and Record of Delivery at the destination post office.

Consult Postmaster for other Express Mail Services and rates.

The Postal Service will refund, upon application to originating office, the postage for any Express Mail shipments not meeting the service standard except for those delayed by strike or work stoppage.

Second Class

Second-class mail is used primarily by newspapers, magazines, and other periodicals with second-class mailing privileges. For copies mailed by the public, the rate is:

Weight	Rates	Weight	Rates
0 to 1 oz	$.15	Over 4 to 5 oz	$.69
Over 1 to 2 oz	.33	Over 5 to 6 oz	.79
Over 2 to 3 oz	.49	Over 6 to 7 oz	.89
Over 3 to 4 oz	.59	Over 7 to 8 oz	.99
Each additional two ounces over 8 oz, add $ .10			

Third Class (under 16 oz)

Third-class mail is used for circulars, books, printed matter, and all other mailable matter not in first or second class. There are two rate structures for this class, a single-piece and a bulk rate.

Many community organizations, as well as businesses, find it economical to use this service. Because of the number of categories of third-class mail, you should consult your postmaster for the one best suited to your needs.

Third-Class, Single-Piece Rates

Weight	Rates	Weight	Rates
0 to 1 oz	$ .18	Over 8 to 10 oz	$1.14
Over 1 to 2 oz	.35	Over 10 to 12 oz	1.36
Over 2 to 3 oz	.52	Over 12 to 14 oz	1.58
Over 3 to 4 oz	.69	Over 14 but less	
Over 4 to 6 oz	.70	than 16 oz	1.81
Over 6 to 8 oz	.92		

Fourth Class (Parcel Post— 16 oz and over)

Fourth-class mail is used for merchandise, books, printed matter, and all other mailable matter not in first, second, or third class. Special fourth-class rates apply to books, library books, publications or records for the blind, and certain controlled-circulation publications.

Packages should be taken to your local post office, where the postage will be determined according to the weight of the package and the distance it is being sent. Information on weight and size limits for fourth-class mail may be obtained there.

Special Fourth-Class Rate

The special fourth-class rate is restricted specifically to books; 16-mm or narrower width films and catalogs of such films (except when mailed to or from commercial theaters); printed music, printed objective-test materials, sound recordings, and playscripts and manuscripts for books, periodicals, and music; printed educational reference charts permanently processed for preservation; looseleaf pages, and binders therefor, consisting of medical information for distribution to doctors, hospitals, medical schools, and medical students. The rate is 63¢ for the first lb or fraction, plus 23¢ for each additional lb or fraction through 7 lb, 14¢ for each additional lb or fraction over 7 lb.

Consult your postmaster for information on the Library Rate which allows certain restricted educational materials to be sent at a lower rate if mailed by or to certain educational institutions.

Special Services

Registered Mail. When you use registered mail service, you are buying security—the safest way to send valuables. The full value of your mailing must be declared when mailed. You receive a receipt and the movement of your mail is controlled throughout the postal system. For an additional fee, a return receipt showing to whom, when, and where delivered may be obtained.

Fees for articles (in addition to postage)

Value			with Insurance	without Insurance
0.00	to	$ 100	$3.30	$3.25
100.00	to	500	3.60	3.55
500.01	to	1,000	3.90	3.85
1,000.01	to	2,000	4.20	4.10
2,000.01	to	3,000	4.50	4.35
3,000.01	to	4,000	4.80	4.60
4,000.01	to	5,000	5.10	4.85
5,000.01	to	6,000	5.40	5.10
6,000.01	to	7,000	5.70	5.35
7,000.01	to	8,000	6.00	5.60
8,000.01	to	9,000	6.30	5.85
9,000.01	to	10,000	6.60	6.10
10,000.01	to	11,000[1]	6.90	6.35

1. Consult your postmaster for registry fees for values over $11,000.

Additional services. COD collection charge (max. amt. collectible is $400): Extra fee is $1.20; Restricted delivery: $1.00.

Certified Mail. Certified mail service provides for a receipt to the sender and a record of delivery at the post office of address. No record is kept at the post office where mailed. It is handled in the ordinary mails and no insurance coverage is provided.

Any mail prepaid at the first-class rate having no intrinsic value will be accepted as certified mail. Return-receipt service, requested at the time of mailing only, and special-delivery service are available.

Fee in addition to postage, 75¢; restricted delivery (additional fee), $1.00.

Return Receipts. Requested at time of mailing:

Showing to whom and date delivered	$ .60
Showing to whom, date, and address where delivered	.70
Requested after mailing:	
Showing to whom and date delivered	3.75

C.O.D. Mail. Consult your postmaster for fees and conditions of mailing.

Insured Mail. Fees, in addition to postage, for coverage against loss or damage:

Liability			Fees
$ .01	to	$20	$ .45
$ 20.01	to	$50	.85
$ 50.01	to	$100	1.25
$100.01	to	$150	1.70
$150.01	to	$200	2.05
$200.01	to	$300	3.45
$300.01	to	$400[1]	4.70

1. Liability for insured mail is limited to $400.

Special Delivery. The payment of the special-delivery fee entitles mail to the most expeditious transportation and delivery. The fee is in addition to the regular postage.

	Weight/Fees		
		More than 2 lb	
Class of mail	Not more than 2 lb	but not more than 10 lb	More than 10 lb
First-class and priority mail	$2.10	$2.35	$3.00
All other classes	2.35	3.00	3.40

Special Handling. Payment of the special-handling fee entitles third- and fourth-class matter to the most expeditious handling and transportation, but not special delivery. The fee is in addition to the regular postage.

Weight	Fees
Not more than 10 lb	$ .75
More than 10 lb	1.30

Money Orders. Money orders are used for the safe transmission of money.

Amount of money order			Fees
$ .01	to	$25	$ .75
$25.01	to	$50	1.10
$50.01	to	$500	1.55

Adhesive Stamps Available

Purpose	Form	Denomination and prices
Ordinary postage	Single or sheet	1, 2, 3, 4, 5, 6, 10, 11, 12, 13, 14, 15, 16, 17, 18, 20, 25, 28, 30, 40, and 50¢, $1 and $5.
	Book	6 at 18¢ + 2 at 6¢=$1.20 20 at 18¢=$3.60
	Coil of 100[1]	18¢
	Coil of 500	1, 2, 3, 5, 6, 9, 10, 12, 13, 15, 16, and $1.
	Coil of 3,000	1, 2, 3, 5, 6, 9, 10, 15, 16, and 25¢
International airmail postage	Single or sheet	28, 35, and 40¢

1. Dispenser to hold coil of 100 stamps may be purchased for 10¢.

Minimum Mail Sizes

All mail must be at least 0.007 in. thick and mail that is $1/4$ in. or less in thickness must be at least 3 $1/2$ in. in height, at least 5 in. long, and rectangular in shape.

As of March 22, 1981, there is a surcharge of 9¢ applied to first-class mail weighing one ounce or less and single-piece third-class mail weighing one ounce or less that is more than $6^1/8$ inches high or $11^1/2$ inches long or $1/4$ inch thick. Also subject to the surcharge are pieces with a length less than 1.3 times the height or more than 2.5 times the height.

International Mail Service

Canada and Mexico—Surface Rates

Weight	Letter mail	Printed matter and small packets
1 oz	$ .18	$ .18
2 oz	.35	.35
3 oz	.52	.52
4 oz	.69	.69
6 oz	1.03	.70
8 oz	1.37	.92
10 oz	1.71	1.14
12 oz	2.05	1.36
14 oz	—	1.58
16 oz	2.42	1.81
Postcards	.10	—

Consult your postmaster for rates for heavier items.

International Airmail

Destination	Letters and letter packages[1]	Post-cards	Air letter sheets[2]
Central America Colombia, Venezuela, Caribbean Islands, Bahamas, Bermuda, St. Pierre and Miquelon	35¢ per half oz through 2 oz 30¢ each additional half oz or fraction	28¢	30¢
All other countries	40¢ per half oz through 2 oz 35¢ each additional half oz or fraction	28¢	30¢

1. Weight limit, 4 lb. 2. No enclosures permitted.

For Canada and Mexico, *see* Surface Rates.

International Money Order Fees

Amount of money order	Fees
$ .01 to $25	$ .75
$25.01 to $50	1.10
$50.01 to $300	1.55

Countries Other Than Canada and Mexico—Surface Rates

Ounces	Letter mail	Printed matter	Small packets
1	$ .30	$ .23	$ .23
2	.47	.35	.35
4	.81	.72	.72
8	1.49	1.14	1.14
16	2.76	1.81	1.81
32	4.80	2.76	2.76
64	7.80	3.86	—
Each additional 32 oz		.96	—

International Surface Parcel Post

Weight through lb	Canada, Mexico, Central America, Caribbean Islands, Bahamas, Bermuda, St. Pierre and Miquelon	All other countries
2	$ 3.10	$ 3.25
3	4.10	4.30
4	5.10	5.35
5	6.10	6.40
6	7.10	7.45
7	8.10	8.50
8	9.10	9.55
9	10.10	10.60
10	11.10	11.65
	$1.00 each additional lb or fraction	$1.05 each additional lb or fraction

Consult your postmaster for weight and size limits.

For other international services and rates consult your local postmaster.

United Nations Stamps

United Nations stamps are issued in three different currencies, namely, U.S. dollars, Swiss francs, and Austrian schillings. Stamps in all three currencies are available at face value at each of the U.N. Postal Administration offices in New York, Geneva, and Vienna. They may be purchased over the counter, by mail, or by opening a Customer Deposit Account.

Mail orders for mint (unused) stamps and postal stationery may be sent to the U.N. Postal Administration in New York, Geneva, and Vienna. A special order form, listing all available mint issues, is available on request. Write to: United Nations Postal Administration, P.O. Box 5900, Grand Central Station, New York, N.Y. 10017. All mint stamps and postal stationery are sold by the U.N. Postal Administration at face value.

Authorized 2-Letter State Abbreviations

When the Post Office instituted the ZIP Code for mail in 1963, it also drew up a list of two-letter abbreviations for the states which would gradually replace the traditional ones in use. Following is the official list, including the District of Columbia, Guam, Puerto Rico, and the Virgin Islands (note that only capital letters are used):

State	Abbr.	State	Abbr.	State	Abbr.
Alabama	AL	Kentucky	KY	Ohio	OH
Alaska	AK	Louisiana	LA	Oklahoma	OK
Arizona	AZ	Maine	ME	Oregon	OR
Arkansas	AR	Maryland	MD	Pennsylvania	PA
California	CA	Massachusetts	MA	Puerto Rico	PR
Colorado	CO	Michigan	MI	Rhode Island	RI
Connecticut	CT	Minnesota	MN	South Carolina	SC
Delaware	DE	Mississippi	MS	South Dakota	SD
Dist. of Columbia	DC	Missouri	MO	Tennessee	TN
Florida	FL	Montana	MT	Texas	TX
Georgia	GA	Nebraska	NE	Utah	UT
Guam	GU	Nevada	NV	Vermont	VT
Hawaii	HI	New Hampshire	NH	Virginia	VA
Idaho	ID	New Jersey	NJ	Virgin Islands	VI
Illinois	IL	New Mexico	NM	Washington	WA
Indiana	IN	New York	NY	West Virginia	WV
Iowa	IA	North Carolina	NC	Wisconsin	WI
Kansas	KS	North Dakota	ND	Wyoming	WY

Consider Unordered Mail Merchandise a Gift

Have you ever received something in the mail you did not order? If so, you may consider it a gift and keep it without paying for it.

Only two kinds of merchandise can be sent legally through the mails without a consumer's prior consent: (1) free samples, clearly marked as such, and (2) merchandise mailed by a charitable organization for contributions. Even though unordered merchandise from charitable organizations can legally be sent to your house, the same rule applies: you don't have to pay for it.

It's illegal for the sender to pressure you to return unordered merchandise or to send you a bill for it.

The Mail Order Merchandise Rule

The mail order rule adopted by the Federal Trade Commission in October 1975 provides that when you order by mail:

You must receive the merchandise when the seller says you will.

If you are not promised delivery within a certain time period, the seller must ship the merchandise to you no later than 30 days after your order comes in.

If you don't receive it shortly after that 30-day period, you can cancel your order and get your money back.

How the Rule Works

The seller must notify you if the promised delivery date (or the 30-day limit) cannot be met. The seller must also tell you what the new shipping date will be and give you the option to cancel the order and receive a full refund or agree to the new shipping date. The seller must also give you a free way to send back your answer, such as a stamped envelope or a postage-paid postcard. *If you don't answer, it means that you agree to the shipping delay.*

The seller must tell you if the shipping delay is going to be more than 30 days. You then can agree to the delay or, if you do not agree, the seller must return your money by the end of the first 30 days of the delay.

If you cancel a prepaid order, the seller must mail you the refund within seven business days. Where there is a credit sale, the seller must adjust your account within one billing cycle.

It would be impossible, however, for one rule to apply uniformly to such a varied field as mail order merchandising. For example, the rule does not apply to mail order photo finishing, magazine subscriptions, and other serial deliveries (except for the initial shipment); to mail order seeds and growing plants; to COD orders; or to credit orders where the buyer's account is not charged prior to shipment of the merchandise.

The Pony Express

Established in April 1860, the Pony Express provided fast mail service between St. Joseph, Mo., the westernmost extent of the U.S. telegraph line, and Sacramento, Calif. The freighting and stagecoach firm of Russell, Majors & Waddell hired expert riders to ride fleet horses in relays over the 1,838-mile distance. Along the route, there were 157 stations, spaced about 12 miles apart, at which the riders changed horses. Each man changed horses about six times before being replaced by another. The route, which was covered in about ten days, passed through hostile Indian territory, and, during the Paiute War in the summer of 1860, Indians burned a number of stations and killed the occupants. October 24, 1861, the day the first telegram to San Francisco was transmitted, marked the downfall of the Pony Express. No longer the crucial link to the West, the Pony Express was discontinued. Though a financial failure, it remains one of the most colorful episodes of American history.

ENVIRONMENT

1981 Environmental Quality Index

Source: Copyright 1981 by the National Wildlife Federation.
Reprinted from the February-March issue of *National Wildlife* Magazine.

National Wildlife's annual Environmental Quality Index is a subjective analysis of the state of the nation's natural resources. The judgments on resource trends represent the collective thinking of editors and the National Wildlife Federation staff.

Wildlife: Worse. The land and water wildlife needs to survive are still going down the drain, but now conservationists have a new tool to help stem the flow: a hard-won law promising broader programs, fresh sources of funds. In 1979 America's wildlife enjoyed its best year in more than a decade. In 1980 the long downward slide resumed. The main reason: habitat loss. The U.S. Environmental Protection Agency reports that up to 2 million acres will disappear annually between now and the year 2000. To make matters worse, there is a growing resistance in some parts of the country to "bureaucratic regulations" and other environmental constraints aimed at slowing the habitat drain. However, there were some habitat victories. North Dakota lost ground in its long court fight against U.S. wetlands protection. Farther south, three new waterfowl refuges were created in Mississippi, Louisiana, and Alabama. Another bright spot was the passage of a bill authorizing up to $5 million annually to help states pay for nongame and other wildlife conservation plans.

Air: Same. Air quality is not deteriorating in many of the nation's cities, but pollution in some rural areas is getting worse as a result of a rapidly increasing phenomenon: acid rainfall. Prospects for further progress are clouded by political problems. The EPA has been rolling back deadlines in the face of mounting efforts to soften rules. It delayed three exhaust standards for the auto industry and gave Ohio's utilities more time to burn high sulfur coal without installing costly scrubbers. This despite evidence that acid rain has increased fiftyfold in the last 25 years over the eastern half of the country. For now, at least, deterioration of air quality in many cities has been halted. "As a holding action, the Clean Air Act has been successful," says David Hawkins, an EPA official. "There are more cars and industries every year but the air is not appreciably worse." Despite this solid evidence of progress, industrial lobbyists continue to press for relaxation of air-pollution rules.

Minerals: Same. Uncle Sam has embarked on a costly "Synthetic fuels" program to produce more oil, but millions of Americans are stressing conservation and taking a hard look at alternative energy sources. Oil dominated the minerals scene in 1980 as it has since the 1973 Arab embargo. There were disquieting signs that many Americans were committed to one energy path while their government was emphasizing another—the "Synthetic fuels" program. Most environmentalists insist it is the wrong way to go. At the other end of the spectrum millions of Americans continued to make conservation an important part of their daily lives. Some experts think conservation could reduce U.S. energy needs by as much as 40%, but conservation alone is not enough. More and more people are turning to alternative energy sources: solar, biomass, hydroelectric, and wind power. On balance there was enough evidence in 1980 that the country was slowly turning in the right energy direction to level off the EQ mineral trend for the first time in 12 years.

Water: Worse. Over much of the country, polluters have stopped dumping wastes directly into rivers and lakes, but now there's an appalling new threat: Toxic dumps are contaminating the nation's ground water supplies. Since the Clean Water Act was passed nine years ago many U.S. rivers and lakes have become swimmable and fishable again. However, unable to dump their toxic wastes into waterways, many industrial polluters have illegally buried or stored them on land. This has increased the flow of dangerous chemicals into the earth. As a result, pollution of the ground water people use in their homes has gotten worse. In some parts of the U.S. ground water depletion, rather than pollution, is the problem. In Arizona, where ground water is being consumed eight times faster than nature can replenish it, one of the country's most ambitious water management laws was passed in 1980.

Forests: Same. Wood demand is down for now, but there's mounting pressure to tap more riches on our national forests. Although a depressed U.S. construction industry is keeping domestic demand low for now, consumption is expected to leap from 13.3 billion cubic feet in 1976 to 28.3 billion in 2030. Some ominous signs for conservationists: more interest in wood as a fuel increased fears of overcutting and air pollution. Tight government budgets could mean less emphasis on recreation, wildlife, and watershed protection on public forests. However, there were some heartening developments. The federal government proposed to reserve about 15.4 million acres of national forest as wilderness, with possible future addition of as much as another 10.6 million acres. The government also pledged its support for less dependence on national forests for commercial timber, more incentive to increase production on private forests.

Soil: Worse. The U.S. is losing a million acres of farmland annually to development, and despite some holding action in a few states, cropland protection remains almost nonexistent throughout most of America. In the last 50 years, the country has paved over the equivalent of all the cropland in Ohio. In the next two decades, the nation may pave over another section of agricultural lands equal to the size of Indiana. Losses to development are temporarily offset by gains elsewhere. About 1.3 million acres of new cropland are brought into production annually in this country by draining swamps, irrigating deserts, and clearing woodlands. However, these new lands are subject to more serious erosion losses than prime acreage. What's being done? Most states are belatedly attempting to protect rural lands, but thus far, only a handful have adopted meaningful controls on development. On the erosion front many U.S. farmers have shifted from conventional plowing practices that hasten erosion to minimum tillage techniques that can halt soil loss. But minimum tillage requires large amounts of chemical herbicides, which may contribute to pollution runoff.

Living space: Worse. A mutiny for the bounty on public western lands could challenge U.S. jurisdiction nationwide. A grass-roots movement out West against land-use controls on about 400 million acres of public western lands is a cause of concern to conservationists. Its aim is the transfer of federal lands to state ownership. "The states would find the cost of properly managing the land unbearable," says Tom Kimball, the National Wildlife Federation's executive vice president. U.S. living space declined further in both quality and quantity. The National Park Service reports that already overburdened parks are deteriorating because of overcrowding and pollution. Meanwhile, wasteful water projects continue to destroy pristine areas. Encouraging events were passage of two significant acts: an Alaska lands bill and a Coastal Management Improvement Act. The former reserves 104.3 million acres of Alaska as public land. The latter budgets $71 million in incentives for states to protect coastlines.

Some Endangered Species of the World[1]

Common name	Scientific name	Range
MAMMALS		
Anteater, scaly	*Manis temmincki*	Africa
Bear, brown	*Ursus arctos pruinosus*	China (Tibet)
Bear, brown or grizzly	*Ursus arctos horribilis*	Canada, Western U.S.
Cat, leopard	*Felis bengalensis bengalensis*	Eastern Asia
Cat, tiger	*Felis tigrina*	Costa Rica to northern South America
Cheetah	*Acinonyx jubatus*	Africa to India
Chimpanzee	*Pan troglodytes*	Western and central Africa
Chinchilla	*Chinchilla brevicaudata boliviana*	Bolivia
Deer, Columbian white-tailed	*Odocoileus virginianus leucurus*	U.S. (Ore., Wash.)
Deer, marsh	*Blastocerus dichotomus*	Argentina, Uruguay, Paraguay, Brazil
Deer, musk	*Moschus moschiferus moschiferus*	Southcentral Asia
Elephant, Asian	*Elephas maximus*	Southcentral and Southeast Asia
Gazelle, Clark's (Dibatag)	*Ammordorcas clarkei*	Somalia, Ethiopia
Gazelle, slender-horned (Rhim)	*Gazella leptoceros*	Sudan, Algeria, Egypt, Libya
Gorilla	*Gorilla gorilla*	Central and western Africa
Ibex, Walia	*Capra walie*	Ethiopia
Jaguar	*Panthera onca*	Central and South America, U.S. (Texas, N.M., Ariz.)
Kangaroo, red	*Megaleia rufa*	Australia
Leopard	*Panthera pardus*	Africa, S.E. Asia and India
Leopard, snow	*Panthera uncia*	Central Asia
Lion, Asiatic	*Panthera leo persica*	India
Mandrill	*Papio sphinx*	Western Iran to Equatorial west Africa
Monkey, black howler	*Alouatta pigra*	Mexico, Guatemala, Belize
Ocelot	*Felis pardalis*	Central and South America, Southwest U.S.
Orangutan	*Pongo pygmaeus*	Borneo, Sumatra
Otter, Southern Sea	*Enhydra lutris nereis*	West coast U.S. (Wash.), south to Mexico (Baja Calif.)
Panther, Florida	*Felis concolor coryi*	U.S. (La. and Ariz., east to S.C. and Fla.)
Prairie Dog, Utah	*Cynomys parvidens*	U.S. (Utah)
Pronghorn, Sonoran	*Antilocapra americana sonoriensis*	U.S. (Ariz.), Mexico
Rat, Morro Bay kangaroo	*Dipodomys heermanni*	U.S. (Calif.)
Rhinoceros, great Indian	*Rhinoceros unicornis*	India, Nepal
Sloth, Brazilian three-toed	*Bradypus torquatus*	Brazil
Tiger	*Panthera tigris*	Temperate and tropical Asia
Whale, humpback	*Megaptera novaeangliae*	Oceanic
Wolf, gray	*Canis lupus*	U.S., Mexico
Zebra, mountain	*Equus zebra zebra*	Southern Africa
BIRDS		
Albatross, short-tailed	*Diomedea albatrus*	North Pacific Ocean: Japan, USSR, U.S. (Ark., Calif., Hawaii, Ore., Wash.)

Common name	Scientific name	Range
Condor, Andean	Vultur gryphus	Colombia to Chile and Argentina
Eagle, bald	Haliaeetus leucocephalus	U.S.
Falcon, Eurasian peregrine	Falco peregrinus peregrinus	Europe, Eurasia south to Africa and Mideast
Parakeet, paradise	Psephotus pulcherrimus	Australia
Pelican, brown	Pelecanus occidentalis	U.S., (Carolinas to Texas, Calif., West Indies, Central and South America, coastal.)
Penguin, Galápagos	Spheniscus mendiculus	Ecuador (Galápagos Islands)
Stork, white oriental	Ciconia ciconia boyciana	China, Japan, Korea, U.S.S.R.
REPTILES		
Alligator, American	Alligator mississippiensis	Southeastern U.S.
Crocodile, American	Crocodylus acutus	U.S. (Fla.), Mexico, South America, Central America, Caribbean
Iguana, Anegada ground	Cyclura pinquis	West Indies, British Virgin Is. (Anegada Is.)
Python, Indian	Python molurus molurus	Sri Lanka, India
Snake, Atlantic salt-marsh	Nerodia fasciata taeniata	U.S. (Fla.)
Tortoise, Indian flap-shell	Lissemys punctata punctata	India, Pakistan, Bangladesh
AMPHIBIANS		
Frog, Israel painted	Discoglossus nigriventer	Israel
Toads, African viviparous	Nectophrynoides sps.	Tanzania, Guinea
Treefrog, Pine Barrens	Hyla andersonii	U.S. (Fla.)
FISH		
Catfish, giant	Pangasianodon gigas	Thailand
Pike, blue	Stizostedion vitreum glaucum	U.S. and Canada (Lakes Erie and Ontario)
Trout, greenback cutthroat	Salmo clarki stomias	U.S. (Colo.)

1. Due to space limitations, does not include clams, crustaceans, insects, and plants. *Source:* Department of the Interior, Fish and Wildlife Service.

Sources of Information

Source: Brooklyn Botanic Garden, *Handbook on The Environment and The Home Gardener.*

Advice on various aspects of conservation programs and problems is available from national, state, and local organizations. Dr. Richard H. Pough, President of the Natural Area Council, has compiled a list of membership organizations that are happy to help smaller groups get started on worthwhile projects in conservation.

America the Beautiful Fund, Inc. 219 Shoreham Building, Washington, D.C. 20005
American Forestry Association, 1319 18th St., N.W., Washington, D.C. 20036
Defenders of Wildlife, 1244 19th St., N.W., Washington, D.C. 20036
Environmental Defense Fund, Inc., 444 Park Ave. South, New York, N.Y. 10016
Friends of the Earth, 72 Jane St., New York, N.Y. 10014
Izaak Walton League of America, 1800 N. Kent St., Suite 806, Arlington, VA. 22209

National Audubon Society, 950 Third Ave., New York, N.Y. 10022
National Park and Conservation Association, 1701 18th St., N.W., Washington, D.C. 20009
National Trust for Historic Preservation, 748 Jackson Place, N.W., Washington, D.C. 20006
National Wildlife Federation, 1412 16th St., N.W., Washington, D.C. 20036
Natural Science for Youth Foundation, 763 Silvermine Rd., New Canaan, Conn. 06840
The Nature Conservancy, 1800 N. Kent St., Suite 800, Arlington, Va. 22209
Open Space Institute, Inc., Room 4500, 122 East 42nd St., New York, N.Y. 10168
Sierra Club, 530 Bush St., San Francisco, Calif. 94108
The Wilderness Society, 1901 Pennsylvania Ave., N.W., Washington, D.C. 20006
World Wildlife Fund, 1319 18th St., N.W., Washington, D.C. 20036

U.S. Soil Resources Threatened by Erosion

Erosion causes an annual loss of 5.5 billion tons of soil in this country. That amounts to enough soil to cover the state of Iowa with a layer an inch thick each year. Fortunately, the United States has the know-how to bring soil erosion under control.

Modern conservation methods and advanced agricultural technology can prevent another Dust Bowl. Many farmers and ranchers are aware of this and are taking appropriate action. However, on land that has no conservation measures, erosion continues.

Air Pollutant Emissions, by Source
(estimates)

Year and pollutant	Total emissions[1]	Transportation		Fuel combustion[2]		Industrial processes	Solid waste disposal	Misc. uncontrollable[1]
		Total	Road vehicles	Total	Electric utilities			
1970								
Carbon monoxide	112.7	88.7	78.2	1.4	.2	8.8	6.8	6.8
Sulfur oxides	32.8	.8	.3	24.9	17.5	6.9	.1	.1
Hydrocarbons	32.5	13.4	11.7	1.7	.1	9.5	1.9	6.1
Particulates[3]	24.5	1.3	.8	7.8	4.5	13.1	1.2	1.0
Nitrogen oxides	21.6	8.2	5.8	12.2	5.7	.7	.3	.2
1975								
Carbon monoxide	106.8	90.4	81.3	1.2	.3	8.0	3.2	4.0
Sulfur oxides	28.8	.8	.3	22.9	18.5	5.1	—	—
Hydrocarbons	29.7	12.5	10.8	1.5	.1	10.1	.9	4.6
Particulates[3]	15.1	1.2	.9	5.5	4.1	7.2	.6	.7
Nitrogen oxides	23.1	9.5	7.1	12.7	6.8	.8	.1	.1
1978								
Carbon monoxide	112.5	94.2	85.0	1.3	n.a.	8.4	3.0	5.6
Sulfur oxides	29.8	.9	.4	24.4	19.4	4.5	—	—
Hydrocarbons	30.6	11.8	10.2	.3	n.a.	15.0	.9	2.6
Particulates[3]	13.8	1.4	1.0	4.2	2.8	6.8	.6	.8
Nitrogen oxides	25.7	10.4	7.4	14.2	7.9	.9	.1	.1

1. In millions of tons. 2. Stationary. 3. Suspended particulate matter (particles of smoke or dust, fumes, and droplets of viscous liquid remaining in the air for varying periods of time and ranging from less than 1 micron [1/25,000 in.] to 100 microns). n.a. = not available — represents zero. *Source:* Environmental Protection Agency.

Estimated Total Pollution Abatement and Environmental Quality Expenditures, 1979–88
(billions of 1979 dollars)

	1979			1988			Cumulative (1979–88)		
	Operation and maintenance	Annual capital costs	Total annual costs	Operation and maintenance	Annual capital costs[1]	Total annual costs	Operation and maintenance	Capital costs	Total costs
Air Pollution									
Public	1.7	.4	2.1	2.8	.7	3.5	22.5	5.3	27.8
Private									
Mobile	3.2	4.9	8.1	3.7	11.0	14.7	32.1	83.7	115.8
Industrial	2.5	2.9	5.4	3.9	5.1	9.0	32.5	41.5	74.0
Electric Utilities	6.3	3.5	9.8	8.5	6.5	15.0	71.1	50.1	121.2
Subtotal	13.7	11.7	25.4	18.9	23.3	42.2	158.2	180.6	338.8
Water Pollution									
Public	3.7	8.2	11.9	5.4	14.2	19.6	45.4	99.7	145.1
Private									
Industrial	4.4	3.2	7.6	6.4	5.1	11.5	52.4	41.1	93.5
Electric Utilities	.4	.5	.9	.4	1.1	1.5	3.6	7.8	11.4
Subtotal	8.5	11.9	20.4	12.2	20.4	32.6	101.4	148.6	250.0
Solid waste									
Public	1.7	.3	2.0	2.5	.6	3.1	21.8	5.3	27.1
Private	4.5	.7	5.2	7.5	1.6	9.1	61.3	12.5	73.8
Subtotal	6.2	1.0	7.2	10.0	2.2	12.2	83.1	17.8	100.9
Toxic Substances	.1	.2	.3	.5	.6	1.1	3.6	4.6	8.2
Drinking Water	.3	.4	.7	.5	.8	1.3	5.3	5.2	10.5
Noise	<.05	.1	.1	.6	1.0	1.6	2.6	4.3	6.9
Pesticides	.1	<.05	.1	.1	<.05	.1	1.6	.1	1.7
Land Reclamation	.4	1.3	1.7	.4	1.4	1.8	4.5	13.5	18.0
Total	29.3	26.6	55.9	43.2	49.7	92.9	360.3	374.7	735.0

1. Interest and depreciation. *Source: Environmental Quality—1980,* Council on Environmental Quality.

Water Supply of the World[1]

The Antarctic Icecap is the largest supply of fresh water, nearly 2 percent of the world's total of fresh and salt water. As can be seen from the table below, the amount of water in our atmosphere is over ten times as large as the water in all the rivers taken together. The fresh water actually available for human use in lakes and rivers and the accessible ground water amounts to only about one third of one percent of the world's total water supply.

	Surface area (square miles)	Volume (cubic miles)	Percentage of total
Salt Water			
The oceans	139,500,000	317,000,000	97.2
Inland seas and saline lakes	270,000	25,000	0.008
Fresh Water			
Freshwater lakes	330,000	30,000	0.009
All rivers (average level)	—	300	0.0001
Antarctic Icecap	6,000,000	6,300,000	1.9
Arctic Icecap and glaciers	900,000	680,000	0.21
Water in the atmosphere	197,000,000	3,100	0.001
Ground water within half a mile from surface	—	1,000,000	0.31
Deep-lying ground water	—	1,000,000	0.31
Total (rounded)	—	326,000,000	100.00

1. All figures are estimated. *Source:* Department of the Interior, Geological Survey.

Speed of Animals

Most of the following measurements are for maximum speeds over approximate quarter-mile distances. Exceptions—which are included to give a wide range of animals—are the lion and elephant, whose speeds were clocked in the act of charging; the whippet, which was timed over a 200-yard course; the cheetah over a 100-yard distance; man for a 15-yard segment of a 100-yard run; and the black mamba, six-lined race runner, spider, giant tortoise, three-toed sloth, and garden snail, which were measured over various small distances.

Animal	Speed mph	Animal	Speed mph	Animal	Speed mph
Cheetah	70	Mongolian wild ass	40	Man	27.89
Pronghorn antelope	61	Greyhound	39.35	Elephant	25
Wildebeest	50	Whippet	35.5	Black mamba snake	20
Lion	50	Rabbit (domestic)	35	Six-line race runner	18
Thomson's gazelle	50	Mule deer	35	Squirrel	12
Quarter horse	47.5	Jackal	35	Pig (domestic)	11
Elk	45	Reindeer	32	Chicken	9
Cape hunting dog	45	Giraffe	32	Spider (Tegenearia atrica)	1.17
Coyote	43	White-tailed deer	30	Giant tortoise	0.17
Gray fox	42	Wart hog	30	Three-toed sloth	0.15
Hyena	40	Grizzly bear	30	Garden snail	0.03
Zebra	40	Cat (domestic)	30		

Source: Natural History Magazine, March 1974, copyright 1974, The American Museum of Natural History; and James Doherty, Curator of Mammals, N.Y. Zoological Society.

Animal Names: Male, Female, and Young

Animal	Male	Female	Young	Animal	Male	Female	Young	Animal	Male	Female	Young
Ass	Jack	Jenny	Foal	Duck	Drake	Duck	Duckling	Sheep	Ram	Ewe	Lamb
Bear	Boar	Sow	Cub	Elephant	Bull	Cow	Calf	Swan	Cob	Pen	Cygnet
Cat	Tom	Queen	Kitten	Fox	Dog	Vixen	Cub	Swine	Boar	Sow	Piglet
Cattle	Bull	Cow	Calf	Goose	Gander	Goose	Gosling	Tiger	Tiger	Tigress	Cub
Chicken	Rooster	Hen	Chick	Horse	Stallion	Mare	Foal	Whale	Bull	Cow	Calf
Deer	Buck	Doe	Fawn	Lion	Lion	Lioness	Cub	Wolf	Dog	Bitch	Pup
Dog	Dog	Bitch	Pup	Rabbit	Buck	Doe	Bunny				

Source: James Doherty, Curator of Mammals, N.Y. Zoological Society.

Animal Group Terminology

Source: James Doherty, Curator of Mammals, N.Y. Zoological Society, and *Information Please* data.

ants: colony
bears: sleuth, sloth
bees: grist, hive, swarm
birds: flight, volery
cattle: drove
cats: clutter, clowder
chicks: brood, clutch
clams: bed
cranes: sedge, seige
crows: murder
doves: dule
ducks: brace, team
elephants: herd
elks: gang
finches: charm
fish: school, shoal, draught
foxes: leash, skulk
geese: flock, gaggle, skein
gnats: cloud, horde
goats: trip

gorillas: band
hares: down, husk
hawks: cast
hens: brood
hogs: drift
horses: pair, team
hounds: cry, mute, pack
kangaroos: troop
kittens: kindle, litter
larks: exaltation
lions: pride
locusts: plague
magpies: tidings
mules: span
nightingales: watch
oxen: yoke
oysters: bed
parrots: company
partridges: covey

peacocks: muster, ostentation
pheasants: nest, bouquet
pigs: litter
ponies: string
quail: bevy, covey
rabbits: nest
seals: pod
sheep: drove, flock
sparrows: host
storks: mustering
swans: bevy, wedge
swine: sounder
toads: knot
turkeys: rafter
turtles: bale
vipers: nest
whales: gam, pod
wolves: pack, route
woodcocks: fall

Gestation, Incubation, and Longevity of Certain Animals

Animal	Gestation or incubation, in days & (average)	Longevity, in years & (record exceptions)	Animal	Gestation or incubation, in days & (average)	Longevity, in years & (record exceptions)
Ass	365	18–20 (63)	Horse	329–345 (336)	20–25 (50+)
Bear	180–240[1]	15–30 (47)	Kangaroo	32–39[1]	4–6 (23)
Cat	52–69 (63)	10–12 (26+)	Lion	105–113 (108)	10 (29)
Chicken	22	7–8 (14)	Man	253–303	(2)
Cow	c. 280	9–12 (39)	Monkey	139–270[1]	12–15[1](29)
Deer	197–300[1]	10–15 (26)	Mouse	19–31[1]	1–3 (4)
Dog	53–71 (63)	10–12 (24)	Parakeet (Budgerigar)	17–20 (18)	8 (12+)
Duck	21–35[1](28)	10 (15)	Pig	101–130 (115)	10 (22)
Elephant	510–730 (624)[1]	30–40 (71)	Pigeon	11–19	10–12 (39)
Fox	51–63[1]	8–10 (14)	Rabbit	30–35 (31)	6–8 (15)
Goat	136–160 (151)	12 (17)	Rat	21	3 (5)
Groundhog	31–32	4–9	Sheep	144–152 (151)[1]	12 (16)
Guinea pig	58–75 (68)	3 (6)	Squirrel	44	8–9 (15)
Hamster, golden	15–17	2 (8)	Whale	365–547[1]	
Hippopotamus	220–255 (240)	30 (49+)	Wolf	60–63	10–12 (16)

1. Depending on kind. 2. For life expectancy charts, *see* Index. *Source:* James Doherty, Curator of Mammals, N.Y. Zoological Society.

Zoological Gardens

North America has more than 30 major zoos, in the United States, Canada, and Mexico. The *Quebec Zoological Society's* collection is made up of Canadian species; Toronto has many exotic species.

The first zoological garden in the United States was established in Philadelphia in 1874. Since that time nearly every large city in the country has acquired a zoo. Among the largest are San Diego's on the West Coast; Chicago's Brookfield Zoo and those of St. Louis and Kansas City in the Middle West; and, in the East, the New York Zoological Society's park in the Bronx. The *National Zoological Park* in Washington, D.C., in a beautiful setting of hills, woods, and streams, was established in 1890 by an act of Congress. The major U.S. zoos now have created large natural-habitat areas for their collections.

In Europe, zoological gardens have long been popular public institutions. The *Jardin d'Acclimatation*, in the Bois de Boulogne, Paris, is the oldest and largest. Others are located at Clères, Ermenonville, Lyons, Marseilles, Maubeuge, Mulhouse, and Nancy.

Germany had about 20 zoological gardens, many of which were developed in the peacetime years between World Wars I and II. Large zoos were located in Berlin and Frankfurt am Main. In Munich, the animals were grouped according to the continent of their origin. At Stellingen near Hamburg, the *Hagenback Garden* became an outstanding show place and distributing center for animals. The *Schönbrunn* at Vienna is one of the oldest zoos in Europe. The Budapest zoological gardens house a fine collection of European birds. At Antwerp, the *Royal Zoological Society* founded a large menagerie in 1843. It was seriously damaged by German bombs during World War II.

In the British Isles, a popular zoo is in the garden of the *London Zoological Society* in Regent's Park. Although this zoo received a number of direct bomb hits in 1940–41 and again in 1944, it remained open throughout World War II; visitors during this period numbered 6,500,000. Manchester and Clifton have smaller gardens, and the one at Edinburgh is famous for its collection of penguins. The *Dublin Zoo* is noted for its lions, many of which were born there.

The Amsterdam zoo, with its East Indian collec-tion and its aquarium, and the Rotterdam gardens are the two best known in the Netherlands. Built on a high elevation, the *Skansen Zoo* in Stockholm exhibits north European specimens. The most important gardens in the U.S.S.R. are found in Moscow, where northern as well as exotic species are collected. The zoo at Rome has part of its collection confined in barless pits. At Lisbon there is a small zoological garden, and in Madrid a part of the original royal menagerie.

Notable American Zoos

Source: *Information Please* questionnaires to the zoos.

Atlanta Zoological Park: 800 Cherokee Ave., S.E., Atlanta, Ga. 30315

Audubon Park and Zoological Garden: St. Charles Ave. between Magazine St. and Mississippi River, New Orleans, La. 70118

Baltimore Zoo: Druid Hill Park, Baltimore, Md. 21217

Belle Isle Aquarium and Zoo: Detroit, Mich. Mailing address: Box 39, Royal Oak, Mich. 48068

Bronx Zoo. See New York Zoological Park

Buffalo Zoological Gardens: Delaware Park, Buffalo, N.Y. 14214

Burnet Park Zoo: Coleridge and Wilbur Ave., Syracuse, N.Y. 13204

Central Park Zoo: 830 Fifth Ave. at 64th St., New York, N.Y. 10021

Cheyenne Mountain Zoological Park: Cheyenne Mountain Hwy., P.O. Box 158, Colorado Springs, Colo. 80901

Chicago Zoological Park (Brookfield Zoo): First Ave. and 31st St., Brookfield, Ill. 60513

Cincinnati, Zoological Society of: 3400 Vine St., Cincinnati, Ohio 45220

Cleveland Metroparks Zoo: Brookside Park, Cleveland, Ohio 44109

Columbus Zoo: 9990 Riverside Drive, Powell, Ohio 43065

Dallas Zoo: 621 East Clarendon Drive, Dallas, Tex. 75203

Denver Zoological Gardens: City Park, Denver, Colo. 80205

Detroit Zoological Park: Woodward and Ten Mile Road, Royal Oak, Mich. 48068

El Paso Zoological Park: Evergreen and Paisano, El Paso, Tex. 79905

Fort Worth Zoological Park: 2727 Zoological Park Drive, Fort Worth, Tex. 76110

Franklin Park Zoological Gardens: Boston, Mass. 02121

Hogle Zoological Gardens: 2600 East Sunnyside Ave., Salt Lake City, Utah 84108

Houston Zoological Gardens: Hermann Park, P.O. Box 1562, Houston, Tex. 77001

Jacksonville Zoological Park: 8605 Zoo Road, Jacksonville, Fla. 32218

Kansas City Zoo: Swope Park, Kansas City, Mo. 64132

Lincoln Municipal Zoo: 1300 South 27th St., Lincoln, Neb. 68502

Lincoln Park Zoological Gardens: 2200 N. Cannon Drive, Chicago, Ill. 60614

Los Angeles Zoo: 5333 Zoo Drive, Los Angeles, Calif. 90027

Memphis Zoo and Aquarium: Overton Park, Memphis, Tenn. 38112

Mesker Park Zoo: Bement Ave., Evansville, Ind. 47712

Milwaukee County Zoo: 10001 West Bluemound Road, Milwaukee, Wis. 53226

National Zoological Park: 3000 block of Connecticut Ave. N.W., Washington, D.C. 20008

New York Zoological Park (Bronx Zoo): Fordham Rd., Southern Blvd., Bronx, N.Y. 10460

Oakland Zoo: Golf Links Road, off Freeway 580, Oakland, Calif. 94605

Oklahoma City Zoo: 2101 N.E. 50th St., Oklahoma City, Okla. 73111

Philadelphia Zoo: 34th St. and Girard Ave., Philadelphia, Pa. 19104

Pittsburgh Zoo: Highland Park, P.O. Box 5250, Pittsburgh, Pa. 15206

Rio Grande Zoological Park: 903 Tenth St., S.W., Albuquerque, N.M. 87102

St. Louis Zoological Park: Forest Park, St. Louis, Mo. 63110

St. Paul's Como Zoo: Midway Pkwy. and Kaufman Drive, St. Paul, Minn. 55103

San Diego Zoo: Park Blvd. and Zoo Place, P.O. Box 551, San Diego, Calif. 92112

San Francisco Zoo: Sloat Blvd. at Pacific Ocean, San Francisco, Calif., 94132

Seneca Park Zoo: 2222 St. Paul St., Rochester, N.Y. 14621

Staten Island Zoo: 614 Broadway, W. Brighton, Staten Island, New York 10310

Toledo Zoological Gardens: 2700 Broadway, Toledo, Ohio 43609

Washington Park Zoo: 4001 S.W. Canyon Road, Portland, Ore. 97221

Woodland Park Zoological Gardens: 5500 Phinney Ave. N., Seattle, Wash. 98103

The National Park System

Source: Department of the Interior, National Park Service.

The National Park System of the United States is administered by the National Park Service, a bureau of the Department of the Interior. Started with the establishment of Yellowstone National Park in 1872, the system includes not only the most extraordinary and spectacular scenic exhibits in the United States but also a large number of sites distinguished either for their historic or prehistoric importance or scientific interest, or for their superior recreational assets. The number and extent of the various types of areas that make up the system follow.

Type of area	Number	Total acreage[1]
National Parks	48	46,737,056.91
National Monuments	78	4,598,883.09
National Preserves	12	19,640,550.00
National Lakeshores	4	196,406.30
National Rivers[4]	10	525,443.33
National Seashores	10	598,089.29
National Historic Sites	63	17,738.19
National Memorials	23	8,262.19
National Military Parks	10	34,469.09
National Battlefield Parks	3	6,685.18
National Battlefields	10	10,572.37

Type of area	Number	Total acreage[1]
National Battlefield Site	1	12.36
National Historical Parks	26	143,012.58
National Recreation Areas	17	3,661,664.79
National Parkways	4	160,854.45
National Trail[5]	1	52,034.25
Other Parks[2]	10	32,016.97
National Capital Parks[3]	1	6,468.82
White House	1	18.07
National Mall	1	146.35
National Visitor Center	1	0.00
Affiliated Areas	23	1,045,815.65
Total	357	77,476,187.84

1. Acreage as of January 1, 1980, for most areas. New areas reflect data available at time of authorization. Ten national cemeteries administered by the National Park Service are administered in conjunction with associated historical units and are not listed separately. 2. Parks without national designation. 3. Comprises 346 units within the District of Columbia, Maryland, and Virginia. 4. Includes Wild and Scenic Rivers and Riverways. 5. Includes scenic and historic trails.

National Parks

Name, location, and year authorized	Acreage	Outstanding characteristics
Acadia (Maine), 1919	38,631.86	Rugged seashore on Mt. Desert Island and adjacent mainland
Arches (Utah), 1971	73,378.98	Unusual stone arches, windows, pedestals caused by erosion
Badlands (S.D.), 1978	243,302.33	Arid land of fossils, prairie, bison, deer, bighorn, antelope
Big Bend (Tex.), 1935	708,118.40	Mountains and desert bordering the Rio Grande
Biscayne (Fla.), 1980	180,128	Aquatic, coral reef park south of Miami was a national monument, 1968–80
Bryce Canyon (Utah), 1924	38,835.08	Area of grotesque eroded rocks brilliantly colored
Canyonlands (Utah), 1964	377,570.43	Colorful wilderness with impressive red-rock canyons, spires, arches
Capitol Reef (Utah), 1971	241,904.26	Highly colored sedimentary rock formations in high, narrow gorges
Carlsbad Caverns (N.M.), 1930	46,755.33	The world's largest known caves
Channel Islands (Calif.) 1980	124,740	Area is rich in marine mammals, sea birds, endangered species and archeology
Crater Lake (Ore.), 1902	160,290.33	Deep blue lake in heart of inactive volcano
Denali (Alaska), 1917	4,065,593	Mt. McKinley National Park was renamed and enlarged by Act. of Dec. 2, 1980. Contains Mt. McKinley, N. America's highest mountain (20,320 ft)
Everglades (Fla.), 1934	1,398,800.00	Subtropical area with abundant bird and animal life
Gates of the Arctic (Alaska), 1980	7,052,000	Diverse north central wilderness contains part of Brooks Range
Glacier (Mont.), 1910	1,013,594.67	Rocky Mountain scenery with many glaciers and lakes
Glacier Bay (Alaska), 1980	3,878,269	Park was a national monument (1925–1980) popular for wildlife, whale-watching, glacier-calving, and scenery
Grand Canyon (Ariz.), 1919	1,218,375.24	Mile-deep gorge, 4 to 18 miles wide, 217 miles long
Grand Teton (Wyo.), 1929	310,515.89	Picturesque range of high mountain peaks
Great Smoky Mts. (N.C.-Tenn), 1926	517,368.61	Highest mountain range east of Black Hills; luxuriant plant life
Guadalupe Mountains (Tex.), 1966	76,293.06	Contains highest point in Texas: Guadalupe Peak (8,751 ft)
Haleakala (Hawaii), 1960	28,655.25	World-famous 10,023-ft Haleakala volcano (dormant)
Hawaii Volcanoes (Hawaii), 1916	229,177.03	Spectacular volcanic area; luxuriant vegetation at lower levels
Hot Springs (Ark.), 1921	5,826.26	47 mineral hot springs said to have therapeutic value
Isle Royale (Mich.), 1931	571,796.18	Largest wilderness island in Lake Superior; moose, wolves, lakes
Katmai (Alaska), 1980	4,430,125	Expansion may assure brown bear's preservation. Park was national monument 1918–80; is known for fishing, 1912 eruption, bears
Kenai Fjords (Alaska), 1980	567,000	Mountain goats, marine mammals, birdlife are features at this seacoast park near Seward
Kings Canyon (Calif.), 1940	460,136.20	Huge canyons; high mountains; giant sequoias
Kobuk Valley (Alaska), 1980	1,710,000	Native culture and anthropology center around the broad Kobuk River in northwest Alaska
Lake Clark (Alaska), 1980	2,439,000	Park provides scenic and wilderness recreation across Cook Inlet from Anchorage
Lassen Volcanic (Calif.), 1916	106,372.36	Exhibits of impressive volcanic phenomena
Mammoth Cave (Ky.), 1926	52,452.22	Vast limestone labyrinth with underground river

Name, location, and year authorized	Acreage	Outstanding characteristics
Mesa Verde (Colo.), 1906	52,085.14	Best-preserved prehistoric cliff dwellings in United States
Mount Rainier (Wash.), 1899	235,404.00	Single-peak glacial system; dense forests, flowered meadows
North Cascades (Wash.), 1968	504,780.94	Roadless Alpine landscape; jagged peaks; mountain lakes; glaciers
Olympic (Wash.), 1938	908,781.42	Finest Pacific Northwest rain forest; scenic mountain park
Petrified Forest (Ariz.), 1962	93,492.57	Extensive natural exhibit of petrified wood
Redwood (Calif.), 1968	109,027.04	Coastal redwood forests; contains world's tallest known tree (369.2 ft)
Rocky Mountain (Colo.), 1915	263,808.71	Section of the Rocky Mountains; 107 named peaks over 10,000 ft
Sequoia (Calif.), 1890	403,023.00	Giant sequoias; magnificent High Sierra scenery, including Mt. Whitney
Shenandoah (Va.), 1926	194,826.30	Tree-covered mountains; scenic Skyline Drive
Theodore Roosevelt (N.D.), 1978	70,416.39	Scenic valley of Little Missouri River; T.R. Ranch; Wildlife
Virgin Islands (U.S. V.I.), 1956	14,695.37	Beaches; lush hills; prehistoric Carib Indian relics
Voyageurs (Minn.), 1971	219,128.00	Wildlife, canoeing, fishing, and hiking
Wind Cave (S.D.), 1903	28,292.08	Limestone caverns in Black Hills; buffalo herd
Wrangell-St. Elias (Alaska), 1980	8,147,000	Largest Park System area has abundant wildlife, second highest peak in U.S. (Mt. St. Elias); adjoins Canadian park
Yellowstone (Wyo.-Mont.-Idaho), 1872	2,219,822.70	World's greatest geyser area; abundant falls, wildlife, and canyons
Yosemite (Calif.), 1890	760,917.18	Mountains; inspiring gorges and waterfalls; giant sequoias
Zion (Utah), 1919	146,551.10	Multicolored gorge in heart of southern Utah desert

NATIONAL HISTORICAL PARKS

Name and location	Total acreage
Appomattox Court House (Va.)	1,318.70
Boston (Mass.)	40.17
Chaco Culture (N.M.)	33,189
Chesapeake and Ohio Canal (Md.-W.Va.-D.C.)	20,781.00
Colonial (Va.)	9,462.37
Cumberland Gap (Ky.-Tenn.-Va.)	20,350.90
George Rogers Clark (Ind.)	24.30
Harpers Ferry (W.Va.-Md.)	1,909.47
Independence (Pa.)	37.10
Jean Lafitte (La.)	20,000
Kalaupapa (Hawaii)	5,000
Klondike Goldrush (Alaska)	13,270.49
Koloko-Honokohau (Hawaii)	1,250.24
Lowell (Mass.)	134.00
Lyndon B. Johnson (Tex.)	236
Minute Man (Mass.)	752.35
Morristown (N.J.)	1,677.65
Nez Perce (Idaho)	2,109.06
Puuhonua o Honaunau (Hawaii)	181,80
San Antonio Missions (Tex.)	2,500
San Juan Island (Wash.)	1,751.99
Saratoga (N.Y.)	2,455.11
Sitka (Alaska)	107.71
Valley Forge (Pa.)	2,551.04
War in the Pacific (Guam)	1,919.68
Women's Rights (N.Y.)	2.45

Name and location	Total acreage
Chiricahua (Ariz.)	11,088.25
Colorado (Colo.)	20,457.25
Congaree Swamp (S.C.)	15,200.00
Craters of the Moon (Idaho)	53,545.05
Custer Battlefield (Mont.)	765.34
Death Valley (Calif.-Nev.)	2,067,795.06
Devils Postpile (Calif.)	798.46
Devils Tower (Wyo.)	1,346.91
Dinosaur (Utah-Colo.)	211,058.37
Effigy Mounds (Iowa)	1,474.63
El Morro (N.M.)	1,278.72
Florissant Fossil Beds (Colo.)	5,998.09
Fort Frederica (Ga.)	213.72
Fort Jefferson (Fla.)	47,125.00
Fort Matanzas (Fla.)	298.51
Fort McHenry (Md.)	43.26
Fort Pulaski (Ga.)	5,615.50
Fort Stanwix (N.Y.)	15.52
Fort Sumter (S.C.)	64.27
Fort Union (N.M.)	720.60
Fossil Butte (Wyo.)	8,198.00
George Washington Birthplace (Va.)	538.23
George Washington Carver (Mo.)	210.00
Gila Cliff Dwellings (N.M.)	533.13
Grand Portage (Minn.)	709.97
Great Sand Dunes (Colo.)	38,951.50
Hohokam Pima (Ariz.)	1,690.00
Homestead (Neb.)	194.57
Hovenweep (Utah-Colo.)	785.43
Jewel Cave (S.D.)	1,274.56
John Day Fossil Beds (Ore.)	14,044.28
Joshua Tree (Calif.)	559,959.50
Lava Beds (Calif.)	46,821.33
Lehman Caves (Nev.)	640.00
Montezuma Castle (Ariz.)	857.69
Mound City Group (Ohio)	67.50
Muir Woods (Calif.)	553.55
Natural Bridges (Utah)	7,779.14
Navajo (Ariz.)	360.00
Ocmulgee (Ga.)	683.48
Oregon Caves (Ore.)	473.80
Organ Pipe Cactus (Ariz.)	330,688.86
Pecos (N.M.)	364.80
Pinnacles (Calif.)	16,221.77
Pipe Spring (Ariz.)	40.00
Pipestone (Minn.)	281.78

NATIONAL MONUMENTS

Name and location	Total acreage
Agate Fossil Beds (Neb.)	3,055.22
Alibates Flint Quarries (Tex.)	1,332.56
Aniakchak (Alaska)	138,000.00
Aztec Ruins (N.M.)	27.14
Bandelier (N.M.)	36,971.20
Black Canyon (Colo.)	13,672.13
Booker T. Washington (Va.)	223.92
Buck Island Reef (U.S. V.I.)	880.00
Cabrillo (Calif.)	143.94
Canyon de Chelly (Ariz.)	83,840.00
Cape Krusenstern (Alaska)	560,000.00
Capulin Mountain (N.M.)	775.38
Casa Grande (Ariz.)	472.50
Castillo de San Marcos (Fla.)	20.49
Castle Clinton (N.Y.)	1.00
Cedar Breaks (Utah)	6,154.60

Name and location	Total acreage
Rainbow Bridge (Utah)	160.00
Russell Cave (Ala.)	310.45
Saguaro (Ariz.)	83,576.07
St. Croix Island (Me.)	35.39
Salinas (N.M.)	1,113.00
Scotts Bluff (Neb.)	2,987.97
Statue of Liberty (N.Y.-N.J.)	58.38
Sunset Crater (Ariz.)	3,040.00
Timpanogos Cave (Utah)	250.00
Tonto (Ariz.)	1,120.00
Tumacacori (Ariz.)	16.65
Tuzigoot (Ariz.)	848.78
Walnut Canyon (Ariz.)	2,249.46
White Sands (N.M.)	144,458.24
Wupatki (Ariz.)	35,253.24
Yucca House (Colo.)	10.00

NATIONAL PRESERVES

Aniakchak (Alaska)	376,000.00
Bering Land Bridge (Alaska)	2,457,000.00
Big Cypress (Fla.)	570,000.00
Big Thicket (Tex.)	84,550.00
Denali (Alaska)	1,330,000.00
Gates of the Arctic (Alaska)	900,000.00
Glacier Bay (Alaska)	57,000.00
Katmai (Alaska)	308,000.00
Lake Clark (Alaska)	1,214,000.00
Noatak (Alaska)	6,460,000.00
Wrangell-St. Elias (Alaska)	4,171,000.00
Yukon-Charley Rivers (Alaska)	1,713,000.00

NATIONAL MILITARY PARKS

Chickamauga and Chattanooga (Ga.-Tenn.)	8,098.21
Fort Donelson (Tenn.)	536.09
Fredericksburg and Spotsylvania (Va.)	5,888.56
Gettysburg (Pa.)	3,862.06
Guilford Courthouse (N.C.)	220.25
Horseshoe Bend (Ala.)	2,040.00
Kings Mountain (S.C.)	3,945.29
Pea Ridge (Ark.)	4,300.35
Shiloh (Tenn.)	3,837.50
Vicksburg (Miss.)	1,740.78

NATIONAL BATTLEFIELDS

Antietam (Md.)	3,249.63
Big Hole (Mont.)	655.61
Cowpens (S.C.)	841.04
Fort Necessity (Pa.)	900.97
Monocacy (Md.)	1,220.31
Moores Creek (N.C.)	86.78
Petersburg (Va.)	1,536.26
Stones River (Tenn.)	330.86
Tupelo (Miss.)	1.00
Wilson's Creek (Mo.)	1,749.91

NATIONAL BATTLEFIELD PARKS

Kennesaw Mountain (Ga.)	2,884.38
Manassas (Va.)	3,031.67
Richmond (Va.)	769.13

NATIONAL BATTLEFIELD SITE

Brices Crossroads (Miss.)	1.00

NATIONAL HISTORIC SITES

Abraham Lincoln Birthplace (Ky.)	116.50
Adams (Mass.)	9.17
Allegheny Portage Railroad (Pa.)	1,476.00
Andersonville (Ga.)	475.70
Andrew Johnson (Tenn.)	16.68
Bent's Old Fort (Colo.)	800.00
Boston African American (Mass.)	2.00
Carl Sandburg Home (N.C.)	247.37
Christiansted (V.I.)	27.15

Name and location	Total acreage
Clara Barton (Md.)	8.59
Edgar Allan Poe (Pa.)	0.51
Edison (N.J.)	21.25
Eisenhower (Pa.)	690.46
Eleanor Roosevelt (N.Y.)	180.50
Eugene O'Neill (Calif.)	14.00
Ford's Theatre (Lincoln Museum) (D.C.)	0.29
Fort Bowie (Ariz.)	1,000.00
Fort Davis (Tex.)	460.00
Fort Laramie (Wyo.)	840.52
Fort Larned (Kan.)	718.39
Fort Point (Calif.)	29.00
Fort Raleigh (N.C.)	157.40
Fort Scott (Kan.)	16.86
Fort Smith (Ark.-Okla.)	63.04
Fort Union Trading Post (N.D.-Mont.)	436.45
Fort Vancouver (Wash.)	208.89
Frederick Law Olmsted (Mass.)	1.75
Friendship Hill (Pa.)	675.00
Georgia O'Keeffe (N.M.)	3.50
Golden Spike (Utah)	2,203.20
Grant-Kohrs Ranch (Mont.)	1,527.69
Hampton (Md.)	59.44
Herbert Hoover (Iowa)	186.80
Home of F. D. Roosevelt (N.Y.)	263.89
Hopewell Village (Pa.)	848.06
Hubbell Trading Post (Ariz.)	160.09
James A. Garfield (Ohio)	7.60
Jefferson National Expansion Memorial (Mo.)	90.96
John F. Kennedy (Mass.)	0.09
John Muir (Calif.)	8.90
Knife River Indian Villages (N.D.)	1,293.35
Lincoln Home (Ill.)	12.28
Longfellow (Mass.)	1.98
Maggie L. Walker (Va.)	1.29
Martin Luther King, Jr. (Ga.)	23.50
Martin Van Buren (N.Y.)	39.59
Ninety Six (S.C.)	1,115.08
Palo Alto Battlefield (Tex.)	50.00
Puukohola Heiau (Hawaii)	76.57
Sagamore Hill (N.Y.)	78.00
Saint-Gaudens (N.H.)	149.31
Salem Maritime (Mass.)	9.10
San Juan (P.R.)	53.20
Saugus Iron Works (Mass.)	8.51
Sewall-Belmont House (D.C.)	0.35
Springfield Armory (Mass.)	54.98
Theodore Roosevelt Birthplace (N.Y.)	0.11
Theodore Roosevelt Inaugural (N.Y.)	1.03
Thomas Stone (Md.)	328.25
Tuskegee Institute (Ala.)	74.39
Vanderbilt Mansion (N.Y.)	211.65
Whitman Mission (Wash.)	98.15
William Howard Taft (Ohio)	3.83

NATIONAL MEMORIALS

Arkansas Post (Ark.)	389.18
Arlington House, the Robert E. Lee Memorial (Va.)	27.91
Chamizal (Tex.)	54.90
Coronado (Ariz.)	4,976.77
Desoto (Fla.)	30.00
Federal Hall (N.Y.)	0.45
Fort Caroline (Fla.)	138.88
Fort Clatsop (Ore.)	130.00
General Grant (N.Y.)	0.76
Hamilton Grange (N.Y.)	0.71
John F. Kennedy Center for Performing Arts (D.C.)	17.50
Johnstown Flood (Pa.)	175.60
Lincoln Boyhood (Ind.)	197.60
Lincoln Memorial (D.C.)	163.63

Name and location	Total acreage
Lyndon Baines Johnson Memorial Grove on the Potomac (D.C.)	17.00
Mount Rushmore (S.D.)	1,278.45
Roger Williams (R.I.)	4.56
Thaddeus Kosciuszko (Pa.)	0.02
Theodore Roosevelt Island (D.C.)	88.50
Thomas Jefferson Memorial (D.C.)	18.36
USS Arizona Memorial (Hawaii)	14.00
Washington Monument (D.C.)	106.01
Wright Brothers (N.C.)	431.40

NATIONAL CEMETERIES[1]

Antietam (Md.)	11.36
Battleground (D.C.)	1.03
Fort Donelson (Tenn.)	15.34
Fredericksburg (Va.)	12.00
Gettysburg (Pa.)	20.58
Poplar Grove (Va.)	8.72
Shiloh (Tenn.)	10.05
Stones River (Tenn.)	20.09
Vicksburg (Miss.)	116.28
Yorktown (Va.)	2.91

NATIONAL SEASHORES

Assateague Island (Md.-Va.)	39,630.93
Canaveral (Fla.)	57,627.07
Cape Cod (Mass.)	44,596.43
Cape Hatteras (N.C.)	30,318.63
Cape Lookout (N.C.)	28,400.00
Cumberland Island (Ga.)	36,978.28
Fire Island (N.Y.)	19,578.55
Gulf Islands (Fla.-Miss.)	139,775.46
Padre Island (Tex.)	133,918.72
Point Reyes (Calif.)	67,265.22

NATIONAL PARKWAYS

Blue Ridge (Va.-N.C.)	81,561.56
George Washington Memorial (Va.-Md.)	7,141.63
John D. Rockefeller, Jr., Memorial (Wyo.)	23,777.22
Natchez Trace (Miss.-Tenn.-Ala.)	48,374.04

NATIONAL LAKESHORES

Apostle Islands (Wis.)	42,009.20
Indiana Dunes (Ind.)	12,534.82
Pictured Rocks (Mich.)	70,757.28
Sleeping Bear Dunes (Mich.)	71,105.00

NATIONAL SCENIC RIVERS AND RIVERWAYS

Big South Fork National River & Recreation Area (Ky.-Tenn.)	122,960.00
Buffalo (Ark.)	94,146.00
Delaware (N.Y.-N.J.-Pa.)	2,750.00
Lower St. Croix (Minn.-Wis.)	8,716.13
New River Gorge (W. Va.)	62,024.00
Obed Wild & Scenic River (Tenn.)	5,250.00
Ozark (Mo.)	82,301.29
Rio Grande Wild & Scenic (Tex.)	9,600.00
St. Croix (Minn.-Wis.)	62,695.91
Upper Delaware (N.Y., N.J.-Pa.)	75,000.00

NATIONAL CAPITAL PARKS

National Capital Parks (D.C.-Va.-Md.)	6,467.79

WHITE HOUSE

White House (D.C.)	18.07

OTHER PARKS

Catoctin Mountain (Md.)	5,768.90
Fort Benton (Mont.)	0.0

1. The National Cemeteries are not independent areas of the National Park System; each is part of a military park, battlefield, etc., except Battleground. Their acreage is kept separately. Arlington National Cemetery is under the Department of the Army. See Index.

Name and location	Total acreage
Fort Washington Park (Md.)	341.00
Frederick Douglass Home (D.C.)	8.08
Greenbelt Park (Md.)	1,166.56
Perry's Victory and International Peace Memorial (Ohio)	25.38
Piscataway (Md.)	4,250.85
Prince William Forest (Va.)	18,571.55
Rock Creek Park (D.C.)	1,754.37
Wolf Trap Farm Park for the Performing Arts (Va.)	130.28

NATIONAL RECREATION AREAS

Amistad (Tex.)	62,451.74
Bighorn Canyon (Wyo.-Mont.)	120,279.97
Chattahoochee River (Ga.)	8,514.57
Chickasaw (Okla.)	9,500.06
Coulee Dam (Wash.)	100,059.00
Curecanti (Colo.)	42,114.47
Cuyahoga Valley (Ohio)	32,460.19
Delaware Water Gap (Pa.-N.J.)	71,000.00
Gateway (N.Y.-N.J.)	26,172.00
Glen Canyon (Ariz.-Utah)	1,236,880.00
Golden Gate (Calif.)	38,676.59
Lake Chelan (Wash.)	61,889.84
Lake Mead (Ariz.-Nev.)	1,496,600.52
Lake Meredith (Tex.)	44,994.30
Ross Lake (Wash.)	117,574.09
Santa Monica Mountains (Calif.)	150,000.00
Whiskeytown-Shasta-Trinity (Calif.)	42,497.45

NATIONAL SCENIC TRAIL

Appalachian (Maine, N.H. Vt., Mass., Conn., N.Y., N.J., Pa., Md., W.Va., Va., N.C., Tenn., Ga.)	52,034.25

NATIONAL MALL

National Mall (D.C.)	146.35

NATIONAL VISITOR CENTER

National Visitor Center (D.C.)	0.00

AFFILIATED AREAS

(National Historic Sites unless otherwise noted.)

American Memorial Park (N. Mariana Is.)	0.00
Benjamin Franklin (Pa.)[1]	0.00
Cherokee Strip Living Museum (Kan.)	6.00
Chicago Portage (Ill.)	91.20
Chimney Rock (Neb.)	83.36
David Burger (Ohio)[1]	
Ebey's Landing (Wash.)	8,000.00
Father Marquette (Mich.)	52.00
Gloria Dei Church (Pa.)	3.71
Ice Age (Wis.)[2]	32,500.00
Iditarod National Historic Trail (Alaska)	
International Peace Garden (N.D.)	2,330.30
Jamestown (Va.)*	20.63
Lewis & Clark Natl. Historic Trail (Ill., Mo., Kan., Neb., Iowa, Idaho, S.D., N.D., Mont., Ore., Wash.)	
McLoughlin House (Ore.)	0.63
Mormon Pioneer Natl. Historic Trail (Ill., Iowa, Neb., Wyo., Utah)	—
North Country Nat'l Scenic Trail (N.Y., Pa., Ohio, Mich., Wis., Minn., N.D.)	—
Oregon Natl. Historic Trail (Mo., Kan., Neb., Wyo., Idaho, Ore., Wash.)	—
Pennsylvania Avenue (D.C.)	0.00
Pinelands Natl. Reserve (N.J.)	1,000,000.00
Roosevelt-Campobello International Park (Canada)	
St. Paul's Church (N.Y.)	2,721.50
Touro Synagogue (R.I.)	6.09
	0.23

1. National Memorial. 2. National Scientific Reserve.

Environmental Glossary

Source: Environmental Protection Agency

abatement: the reduction in degree or intensity of pollution.

acclimation: the physiological and behavioral adjustments of an organism to changes in the environment.

adaptation: a change in structure or habit of an organism that produces better adjustment to its surroundings.

adulterants: chemical impurities or substances that by law do not belong in a food, plant, animal, or pesticide formulation.

aeration: to circulate oxygen through a substance, as in waste water treatment where it aids in purification.

agricultural pollution: the liquid and solid wastes from farming, including: runoff from pesticides, fertilizers, and feedlots; erosion and dust from plowing; animal manure and carcasses, crop residues, and debris.

air pollution: the presence of contaminant substances in the air that do not disperse properly and interfere with human health.

air quality standards: the level of pollutants prescribed by law that cannot be exceeded during a specified time in a defined area.

ambient air: any unconfined portion of the atmosphere; open air.

asbestos: a mineral fiber that can pollute air or water and cause cancer if inhaled or ingested.

A-scale sound level: a measurement of sound approximating the sensitivity of the human ear, used to note the intensity or annoyance of sounds.

attractant: a chemical or agent that lures insects or other pests by stimulating their sense of smell.

biodegradable: any substance that decomposes quickly through the action of microorganisms.

breeder: a nuclear reactor that produces more fuel than it consumes.

carcinogenic: cancer-producing.

catalytic converter: an air pollution abatement device that removes organic contaminants by oxidizing them into carbon dioxide and water.

chilling effect: the lowering of the earth's temperature because of increased particles in the air blocking the sun's rays.

chlorination: the application of chlorine to drinking water, sewage, or industrial waste to disinfect or oxidize undesirable compounds.

combined sewers: a system that carries both sewage and storm water runoff. In dry weather all flow goes to the waste treatment plant. During a storm, only part of the flow is intercepted due to overloading. The remaining mixture of sewage and storm water overflows untreated into the receiving stream.

desalinization: removing salt from ocean or brackish water.

ecological impact: the total effect of an environmental change, natural or man-made, on the community of living things.

ecology: the relationships of living things to one another and to their environment, or the study of such relationships.

effluent: treated or untreated waste material discharged into the environment. Generally refers to water pollution.

emission standard: the maximum amount of discharge legally allowed from a single source, mobile or stationary.

environment: the sum of all external conditions affecting the life, development, and survival of an organism.

fluorocarbons: a gas used as a propellant in aerosols, thought to be modifying the ozone layer in the stratosphere, thereby allowing more harmful solar radiation to reach the earth's surface.

fossil fuels: combustibles—like coal, oil, and natural gas—derived from the remains of ancient plants and animals.

greenhouse effect: the warming of our atmosphere caused by build-up of carbon dioxide, which allows light from the sun's rays to heat the earth, but prevents loss of the heat.

groundwater: the supply of fresh water under the earth's surface that forms a natural reservoir.

habitat: the sum of environmental conditions in a specific place that is occupied by an organism, population, or community.

herbicide: a chemical that controls or destroys undesirable plants.

inversion: an atmospheric condition caused by a layer of warm air preventing the rise of cool air trapped beneath it. This holds down pollutants that might otherwise be dispersed, and can cause an air pollution episode.

nuclear power plant: a device that converts atomic energy into usable power; heat produced by a reactor makes steam to drive electricity-generating turbines.

oil spill: accidental discharge into bodies of water, can be controlled by chemical dispersion, combustion, mechanical containment, and absorption.

organic: referring to or derived from living organisms. In chemistry, any compound containing carbon.

pesticide: any substance used to control pests ranging from rats, weeds, and insects to algae and fungi. Pesticides can accumulate in the food chain and can contaminate the environment if misused.

pollutant: any introduced substance that adversely affects the usefulness of a resource.

pollution: the presence of matter or energy whose nature, location, or quantity produces undesired environmental effects.

radiation: the emission of particles or rays by the nucleus of an atom.

radiation standards: regulations that govern exposure to permissible concentrations of and transportation of radioactive materials.

radioactive: substances that emit rays either naturally or as a result of scientific manipulation.

recycling: converting solid waste into new products by using the resources contained in discarded materials.

refuge, wildlife: an area designated for the protection of wild animals, within which hunting and fishing are either prohibited or strictly controlled.

runoff: water from rain, snow melt, or irrigation that flows over the ground surface and returns to streams. It can collect pollutants from air or land and carry them to the receiving waters.

sanitary landfill, landfilling: protecting the environment when disposing of solid waste. Waste is spread in thin layers, compacted by heavy machinery, and covered with soil daily.

thermal pollution: discharge of heated water from industrial processes that can affect the life processes of aquatic plants and animals.

water pollution: the addition of enough harmful or objectionable material to damage water quality.

(For later disasters, see Current Events of 1981).

Earthquakes and Volcanic Eruptions

A.D. 79 Aug. 24, Italy: eruption of Mt. Vesuvius buried cities of Pompeii and Herculaneum, killing thousands.

1556 Jan. 24, Shaanxi (Shensi) Province, China: most deadly earthquake in history; 830,000 killed.

1755 Nov. 1, Portugal: one of the most severe of recorded earthquakes leveled Lisbon and was felt as far away as southern France and North Africa; 10,000–20,000 killed in Lisbon.

1883 Aug. 26–28, Netherlands Indies: eruption of Krakatau; violent explosions destroyed two thirds of island. Sea waves occurred as far away as Cape Horn, and possibly England. Estimated 36,000 dead.

1902 May 8, Martinique, West Indies: Mt. Pelée erupted and wiped out city of St. Pierre; 40,000 dead.

1906 April 18, San Francisco: earthquake accompanied by fire razed more than 4 sq mi.; more than 500 dead or missing; property damage about $250–300 million.

1908 Dec. 28, Messina, Sicily: about 85,000 killed and city totally destroyed.

1920 Dec. 16, Gansu (Kansu) Province, China: earthquake killed 200,000.

1923 Sept. 1, Japan: earthquake destroyed third of Tokyo and most of Yokohama; more than 140,000 killed.

1933 March 10, Long Beach, Calif.: 117 left dead by earthquake.

1935 May 31, India: earthquake at Quetta killed an estimated 50,000.

1939 Jan. 24, Chile: earthquake razed 50,000 sq mi.; about 30,000 killed.

Dec. 27, Northern Turkey: severe quakes destroyed city of Erzingan; about 100,000 casualties.

1946 April 1, Alaska, Hawaii, West Coast: earthquake and tsunami (tidal wave) left 173 dead in Hawaii.

1950 Aug. 15, India: earthquake affected 30,000 sq mi. in Assam; 20,000–30,000 believed killed.

1963 July 26, Skoplje, Yugoslavia: four fifths of city destroyed; 1,011 dead, 3,350 injured.

1964 March 27, Alaska: strongest earthquake ever to strike North America hit 80 miles east of Anchorage; followed by seismic wave 50 feet high that traveled 8,445 miles at 450 miles per hour; 117 killed and damage in Alaska and West Coast $500–750 million.

1970 May 31, Peru: earthquake left 50,000 dead, 17,000 missing.

1971 Feb. 9, Los Angeles: earthquake rocked San Fernando Valley. Death toll 64; damage $1 billion.

1972 April 10, Iran: 5,000 killed in earthquake 600 miles south of Teheran.

Dec. 22, Managua, Nicaragua: earthquake devastated city, leaving up to 6,000 dead.

1976 Feb. 4, Guatemala: earthquake left over 23,000 dead.

June 26, Irian-Jaya, Indonesia: earthquake and landslides killed over 3,000, with another 3,000 missing.

July 28, Tangshan, China: earthquake devastated 20-sq-mi. area of city leaving estimated 242,000 dead.

Aug. 17, Mindanao, Philippines: earthquake and tidal wave left up to 8,000 dead or missing.

1977 March 4, Bucharest: earthquake razed most of downtown Bucharest; 1,541 reported dead, over 11,000 injured.

1978 Sept. 16, Tabas, Iran: earthquake destroyed city in eastern Iran, leaving 25,000 dead.

1980 Nov. 23, Naples, Italy: 3,000 killed when earthquake struck southern Italy.

Floods, Avalanches, and Tidal Waves

1228 Holland: 100,000 persons reputedly drowned by sea flood in Friesland.

1642 China: rebels destroyed Kaifeng seawall; 300,000 drowned.

1889 May 31, Johnstown, Pa.: more than 2,200 died in flood.

1896 June 15, Sanriku, Japan: earthquake and tidal wave killed 27,000.

1928 March 12, Santa Paula, Calif.: collapse of St. Francis Dam left 450 dead.

1953 Northwest Europe: storm followed by floods devastated North Sea coastal areas. Netherlands was hardest hit with 1,794 dead.

1959 Dec. 2, Frejus, France: flood caused by collapse of Malpasset Dam left 412 dead.

1960 Agadir, Morocco: 10,000–12,000 dead as earthquake set off tidal wave and fire, destroying most of city.

1962 Jan. 10, Peru: avalanche down Huascaran, extinct Andean volcano, killed more than 3,000 persons.

1963 Oct. 9, Italy: landslide into the Vaiont Dam; flood killed about 2,000.

1966 Oct. 21, Aberfan, Wales: avalanche of coal, waste, mud, and rocks killed 144 persons, including 116 children in school.

1969 Jan. 18–26, Southern California: floods and mudslides from heavy rains caused widespread property damage; at least 100 dead. Another downpour (Feb. 23–26) caused further floods and mudslides; at least 18 dead.

1970 Nov. 13, East Pakistan: 200,000 killed by cyclone-driven tidal wave from Bay of Bengal. Over 100,000 missing.

1971 Sept. 29, Orissa State, India: cyclone and tidal wave off Bay of Bengal killed as many as 10,000.

1972 Feb. 26, Man, W. Va.: more than 118 died when slag-pile dam collapsed under pressure of torrential rains and flooded 17-mile valley.

June 9–10, Rapid City, S.D.: flash flood caused 237 deaths and $160 million in damage.

June 20, Eastern Seaboard: tropical storm Agnes, in 10-day rampage, caused widespread flash floods. Death toll was 129, 115,000 were left homeless, and damage estimated at $3.5 billion.

1976 Aug. 1, Loveland, Colo.: Flash flood along Route 34 in Big Thompson Canyon left 139 dead.

1977 Nov. 6, Toccoa, Ga.: rupture of Kelly Barnes Dam left 39 dead.

Nov. 19, Andhra Pradesh State, India: cyclone and flood from Bay of Bengal left 7,000–10,000 dead.

Storms and Weather

(For U.S. tornadoes and hurricanes, see Index)

1864 **Oct. 5, India:** most of Calcutta denuded by cyclone; 70,000 killed.

1930 **Sept. 3, Santo Domingo:** hurricane killed about 2,000 and injured 6,000.

1934 **Sept. 21, Japan:** hurricane killed more than 4,000 on Honshu.

1942 **Oct. 16, India:** cyclone devastated Bengal; about 40,000 lives lost.

1963 **May 28–29, East Pakistan:** cyclone killed about 22,000 along coast.

Oct. 2–7, Caribbean: Hurricane Flora killed up to 7,000 in Haiti and Cuba.

1965 **May 11–12 and June 1–2, East Pakistan:** cyclones killed about 47,000.

Dec. 15, Karachi, Pakistan: cyclone killed about 10,000.

1974 **Sept. 20, Honduras:** Hurricane Fifi struck northern section of country, leaving 8,000 dead, 100,000 homeless.

Dec. 25, Darwin, Australia: cyclone destroyed nearly the entire city, causing mass evacuation.

1977 **Nov. 19, India:** cyclone struck state of Andhra Pradesh, killing 10,000.

Fires and Explosions

1666 **Sept. 2, England:** "Great Fire of London" destroyed St. Paul's Church, etc. Damage £10 million.

1835 **Dec. 16, New York City:** 530 buildings destroyed by fire.

1871 **Oct. 8, Chicago:** the "Chicago Fire" burned 17,-450 buildings, killed 250 persons; $196 million damage.

Oct. 8, Peshtigo, Wis.: 1,152 lives lost; 2 billion trees burned.

1872 **Nov. 9, Boston:** fire destroyed 800 buildings; $75-million damage.

1876 **Dec. 5, New York City:** fire in Brooklyn Theater killed more than 300.

1881 **Dec. 8, Vienna:** at least 620 died in fire at Ring Theatre.

1894 **Sept. 1, Minnesota:** forest fire over 480-square-mile area destroyed six towns and killed 480 people.

1900 **May 1, Scofield, Utah:** explosion of blasting powder in coal mine killed 200.

June 30, Hoboken, N.J.: piers of North German Lloyd Steamship line burned; 326 dead.

1903 **Dec. 30, Chicago:** Iroquois Theatre fire killed 602.

1904 **Feb. 7, Baltimore:** business section burned; estimated $125-million damage.

1906 **March 10, France:** explosion in coal mine in Courrières killed 1,060.

1907 **Dec. 6, Monongha, W. Va.:** coal mine explosion killed 361.

Dec. 19, Jacobs Creek, Pa.: explosion in coal mine left 239 dead.

1909 **Nov. 13, Cherry, Ill.:** explosion in coal mine killed 259.

1911 **March 25, New York City:** fire in Triangle Shirtwaist Factory fatal to 145.

1913 **Oct. 22, Dawson, N.M.:** coal mine explosion left 263 dead.

1917 **April 10, Eddystone, Pa.:** explosion in munitions plant killed 133.

Dec. 6, Canada: explosion and fire at Halifax when ammunition ship collided with a vessel; 1,500 dead.

1930 **April 21, Columbus, Ohio:** fire in Ohio State Penitentiary killed 320 convicts.

1937 **March 18, New London, Tex.:** explosion destroyed schoolhouse; 294 killed.

1942 **April 26, Manchuria:** explosion in Honkeiko Colliery killed 1,549.

Nov. 28, Boston: Cocoanut Grove nightclub fire killed 491.

1943 **Sept. 7, Houston:** fire in Gulf Hotel left 55 dead.

1944 **July 6, Hartford, Conn.:** fire and ensuing stampede in main tent of Ringling Brothers Circus killed 168, injured 487.

July 17, Port Chicago, Calif.: 322 killed as ammunition ships explode.

Oct. 20, Cleveland: liquid-gas tanks exploded, killing 130.

1946 **June 5, Chicago:** fire in La Salle hotel fatal to 61.

Dec. 7, Atlanta: fire in Winecoff Hotel killed 119.

1947 **April 16–18, Texas City, Tex.:** most of city destroyed, 561 dead following explosion on ship.

1949 **Sept. 2, China:** fire on Chongqing (Chungking) waterfront killed 1,700.

1953 **Oct. 16, Boston:** explosion and fire aboard U.S.S. *Leyte* killed 37.

1954 **May 26, off Quonset Point, R.I.:** explosion and fire aboard aircraft *Bennington* killed 103 crewmen.

1955 **June 11, France:** crash and explosion of racing car into crowd during Grand Prix race, Le Mans, killed 82.

1956 **Aug. 7, Colombia:** about 1,100 reported killed when seven army ammunition trucks exploded at Cali.

Aug. 8, Belgium: 262 died in coal mine fire at Marcinelle.

1958 **Dec. 1, Chicago:** fire at Our Lady of the Angels school killed 95.

1960 **Jan. 21, Coalbrook, South Africa:** coal mine explosion killed 437.

Nov. 13, Syria: 152 children killed in moviehouse fire.

Dec. 19, Brooklyn, N.Y.: blaze on aircraft carrier *Constellation* killed 49 workmen.

1961 **Dec. 17, Niteroi, Brazil:** circus fire fatal to 323.

1962 **Feb. 7, Saarland, West Germany:** coal mine gas explosion killed 298.

1963 **Nov. 9, Japan:** explosion in coal mine at Omuta killed 447.

1965 **May 28, India:** coal mine fire in state of Bihar killed 375.

June 1, near Fukuoka, Japan: coal mine explosion killed 236.

1966 **Oct. 17, New York City:** 12 firemen killed in sudden collapse of burning building.

Oct. 26, off South Vietnam: fire on U.S. carrier *Oriskany* killed 43.

1967 **May 22, Brussels:** fire in L'Innovation, major department store, left 322 dead.

July 29, off North Vietnam: fire on U.S. carrier *Forrestal* killed 134.

1969 **Jan. 14, Pearl Harbor, Hawaii:** nuclear aircraft carrier *Enterprise* ripped by explosions; 27 dead, 82 injured.

April 6, New Orleans: Taiwanese freighter and string of oil-loaded barges collided in fiery explosion on Mississippi River; 25 dead.

1970 **Nov. 1, Saint-Laurent-du-Pont, France:** fire in dance hall killed 146 young people.

Dec. 30, Wooten, Ky.: coal-dust explosion in coal mine killed 38.

1972 **May 2, Kellogg, Idaho:** fire in Sunshine silver mine killed 91 miners; two men survived.

May 13, Osaka, Japan: 118 people died in fire in nightclub on top floor of Sennichi department store.

June 6, Wankie, Rhodesia: explosion in coal mine killed 427.

1973 **Nov. 29, Kumamoto, Japan:** fire in Taiyo department store killed 101.

1974 **Feb. 1, Sao Paulo, Brazil:** fire in upper stories of bank building killed 189 persons, many of whom leaped to death.

1975 **Dec. 27, Dhanbad, India:** explosion in coal mine followed by flooding from nearby reservoir left 372 dead.

1977 **Feb. 25, Moscow:** fire in 6,000-bed Hotel Rossiya fatal to at least 45 guests.

May 28, Southgate, Ky.: fire in Beverly Hills Supper Club; 167 dead.

June 26, Columbia, Tenn.: fire believed set by inmate was fatal to 42 prisoners and visitors at Maury County Jail.

Dec. 22, Westwego, La.: explosion destroyed Continental Grain Company plant, killing 36.

1978 **July 11, Tarragona, Spain:** 140 killed at coastal campsite when tank truck carrying liquid gas overturned and exploded.

Aug. 20, Abadan, Iran: nearly 400 killed when arsonists set fire to crowded theater.

1979 **July 12, Saragossa, Spain:** fire in 10-story Hotel Corona de Aragon killed more than 72 guests when a pastry machine exploded.

Dec. 31, Chapais, Quebec, Canada: fire at Opemiska Club fatal to 45 New Year's Eve partygoers.

1980 **Oct. 23, Ortuella, Spain:** explosion leveled elementary school, killing 48, nearly all of them children.

Nov. 21, Las Vegas, Nev.: fire in MGM Grand Hotel left 84 dead.

Dec. 4, Harrison, N.Y.: fire in a Stouffer's Inn conference center fatal to 26, most of them corporation executives.

Shipwrecks

1833 **May 11, *Lady of the Lake:*** bound from England to Quebec, struck iceberg; 215 perished.

1853 **Sept. 29 *Annie Jane:*** emigrant vessel off coast of Scotland; 348 died.

1865 **April 27, *Sultana:*** boiler explosion on Mississippi River steamboat near Memphis, 1,547 killed.

1898 **Nov. 26, *City of Portland:*** Loss of 157 off Cape Cod.

1904 **June 15, *General Slocum:*** excursion steamer burned in East River, New York; 1,021 perished.

1912 **March 5, *Principe de Asturias:*** Spanish steamer struck rock off Sebastien Point; 500 drowned.

April 15, *Titanic:* sank after colliding with iceberg; 1,513 died.

1914 **May 29, *Empress of Ireland:*** sank after collision in St. Lawrence River; 1,024 died.

1915 **July 24, *Eastland:*** Great Lakes excursion steamer overturned in Chicago River; 812 died.

1928 **Nov. 12, *Vestris:*** British steamer sank in gale off Virginia; 110 died.

1931 **June 14:** French excursion steamer overturned in gale off St. Nazaire; approximately 450 died.

1934 **Sept. 8, *Morro Castle:*** 134 killed in fire off Asbury Park, N.J.

1939 **May 23, *Squalus:*** submarine with 59 men sank off Hampton Beach, N.H.; 33 saved.

June 1, Submarine *Thetis:* sank in Liverpool Bay, England; 99 perished.

1942 **Oct. 2, *Queen Mary:*** rammed and sank a British cruiser; 338 aboard the cruiser died.

1945 **April 9:** U.S. ship, loaded with aerial bombs, exploded at Bari, Italy; at least 360 killed.

1948 **Dec. 3, *Kiangya:*** Chinese refugee ship wrecked in explosion; about 1,000 believed dead.

1949 **Sept. 17, *Noronic:*** Canadian Great Lakes cruise ship burned at Toronto dock; about 130 died.

1951 **April 16, *Affray:*** British submarine sank in English Channel; 75 dead.

1952 **April 26, *Hobson:*** minesweeper collided with aircraft carrier *Wasp* and sank during night maneuvers in mid-Atlantic; 176 persons lost.

1953 **Jan. 9, *Chang Tyong-Ho:*** South Korean ferry foundered off Pusan; 249 reported dead.

Jan. 31, *Princess Victoria:* British ferry sank in Irish Sea; 133 lost.

1956 **July 25, *Andrea Doria:*** Italian liner collided with Swedish liner *Stockholm* off Nantucket Island, Mass., sinking next day; 52, mostly passengers on Italian ship, dead or unaccounted for; over 1,600 rescued.

1962 **April 8, *Dara,*** British liner, exploded and sank in Persian Gulf; 236 persons dead. Caused by time bomb.

1963 **April 10, *Thresher:*** atomic-powered submarine sank in North Atlantic; 129 dead.

May 4: U.A.R. ferry capsized and sank in upper Nile; over 200 died.

1965 **Nov. 13, *Yarmouth Castle:*** cruise ship burned and sank 60 miles northeast of Nassau en route from Miami to Bahamas; 90 dead.

1968 **Late May, *Scorpion:*** nuclear submarine sank in Atlantic 400 miles S.W. of Azores; 99 dead. (Located Oct. 31.)

1970 **Dec. 15:** ferry in Korean Strait capsized; 261 lost.

1976 **Oct. 20, Luling, La.:** *George Prince,* Mississippi River ferry, rammed by Norwegian tanker *Frosta;* 77 dead.

1980 **Jan. 28, *Blackthorn:*** *Coast Guard cutter and Tanker Capricorn* collided under Sunshine Skyway near Tampa, Fla. 23 members of cutter's crew lost.

Aircraft Accidents

1921 **Aug. 24, England:** *ZR-2* British dirigible, broke in two on trial trip near Hull; 62 died.

1925 **Sept. 3, Caldwell, Ohio:** U.S. dirigible *Shenandoah* broke apart; 14 dead.

1930 **Oct. 5, Beauvais, France:** British dirigible R 101 crashed, killing 47.

1933 **April 4, New Jersey Coast:** U.S. dirigible *Akron* crashed; 73 died.

1937 **May 6, Lakehurst, N.J.:** German zeppelin *Hindenburg* destroyed by fire at tower mooring; 36 killed.

1945 **July 28, New York City:** U.S. Army bomber crashed into Empire State Building; 13 dead.

1946 **May 20, New York City:** U.S. Army plane crashed into Manhattan Company building; five dead.

1949 **Nov. 1, Washington, D.C.:** fighter plane rammed airliner, killing 55.

1951 **Dec. 16, Elizabeth, N.J.:** nonscheduled airliner crash killed 56.

1952 **Jan. 22, Elizabeth, N.J.:** 29 killed, including former Secretary of War Robert P. Patterson, when airliner hit apartments; seven of dead were on ground.

Feb. 11, Elizabeth, N.J.: third major air disaster in Elizabeth within two months fatally injured 33.

1953 **June 18, near Tokyo:** crash of U.S. Air Force "Globemaster" killed 129 servicemen.

1955 **Nov. 1, near Longmont, Colo.:** time bomb hidden in luggage destroyed airliner in flight, killing 44.

1956 **June 30, Grand Canyon, Ariz.:** 128 died in collision of TWA Super Constellation and United Airlines DC-7.

1957 **March 17, near Cebu City, Philippines:** President Ramón Magsaysay and 24 others killed in crash.

1959 **Feb. 3, New York City:** American Airlines Lockheed Electra turboprop plane crashed in East River; 65 dead.

1960 **Feb. 25, Rio de Janeiro:** U.S. Navy plane, flying Navy musicians to perform at dinner given by visiting President Eisenhower, collided with Brazilian airliner, killing 61.
Sept. 19, near Guam: crash shortly after take-off of World Airways plane took 78 lives.
Dec. 16, New York City: United and Trans World planes collided in fog, crashed in two boroughs, killing 134 in air and on ground.

1961 **Feb. 15, near Brussels:** 72 on board and farmer on ground killed in crash of Sabena plane; U.S. figure skating team wiped out.

1962 **March 1, New York City:** American Airlines jetliner crashed into Jamaica Bay, near Idlewild Airport, killing all 95 on board.
June 3, Paris: chartered Air France Boeing Jet 707 crashed at Orly Airport; 130 dead.

1965 **Feb. 8, New York City:** Eastern Airlines DC-7B went down in Atlantic shortly after take-off from Kennedy International Airport; 84 dead.

1966 **Jan. 24, Mont Blanc:** Indian airliner crashed into mountain in fog; 117 dead.
March 5, Japan: British airliner caught fire and crashed into Mt. Fuji; 124 dead.
Dec. 24, Binh Thai, South Vietnam: crash of military-chartered plane into village killed 129.

1967 **April 20, Nicosia, Cyprus:** crash of chartered Swiss Turboprop killed 126.
July 19, near Hendersonville, N.C.: Piedmont Airlines Boeing 727 collided with private plane; 82 dead.

1968 **May 3, near Dawson, Tex.:** Braniff airliner crashed; 85 dead.

1969 **March 16, Maracaibo, Venezuela:** Venezuelan jetliner crashed and exploded; 84 crew members and passengers died and 71 were killed on ground.
Sept. 9, Shelbyville, Ind.: Allegheny Airlines jetliner and single-engine plane flown by student pilot collided in air and crashed; 83 dead.
Dec. 8, Keratea, Greece: rain and hurricane winds caused Greek airliner to crash into 2,000-foot mountain while approaching Athens; 90 dead.

1970 **Feb. 15, Santo Domingo, Dominican Republic:** Dominican Republic jetliner plunged into Caribbean on takeoff; 102 dead.
July 4, Arbucias, Spain: British Comet crashed into mountains while coming in for landing at Barcelona; 112 dead.
July 5, Toronto: Canadian jetliner crashed on landing approach; 109 dead.
Aug. 9, Cuzco, Peru: Peruvian turboprop, with 51 teen-age U.S. students among passengers, crashed shortly after takeoff; 99 dead.
Nov. 14, Huntington, W. Va.: chartered plane carrying 43 players and coaches of Marshall University football team crashed; 75 dead.

1971 **June 6, near Los Angeles:** Air West DC-9 and Navy F-4 fighter collided over San Gabriel Canyon; 49 killed; one Navy crewman parachuted to safety.
July 30, Morioka, Japan: Japanese Boeing 727 and F-86 fighter collided in mid-air; toll was 162.
Sept. 4, near Juneau, Alaska: Alaska Airlines Boeing 727 crashed into Chilkoot Mountains; 111 killed.

1972 **June 18, London:** B.E.A. Trident jetliner plunged into field minutes after take-off from Heathrow Airport; all 118 aboard dead.
Aug. 14, East Berlin, East Germany: Soviet-built East German Ilyushin plane crashed, killing 156.
Oct. 13, Moscow: 176 died when Soviet Ilyushin airliner crashed.
Dec. 3, Santa Cruz de Tenerife, Canary Islands: Spanish charter jet carrying West German tourists crashed on take-off; all 155 aboard killed.
Dec. 30, Miami, Fla.: Eastern Airlines Lockheed 1011 TriStar Jumbo jet crashed into Everglades; 101 killed, 75 survived.

1973 **Jan. 22, Kano, Nigeria:** 171 Nigerian Moslems returning from Mecca and five crewmen died in crash.
April 10, Hochwald, Switzerland: British airliner carrying tourists to Swiss fair crashed in blizzard; 106 dead.
July 11, Paris: Boeing 707 of Varig Airlines, en route to Rio de Janeiro, crashed near airport, killing 122 of 134 passengers.
July 31, Boston: Delta Airlines jet crashed in heavy fog in landing at Logan International Airport killing 88 of 89 aboard.

1974 **Jan. 31, Pago Pago, Samoa:** Pan American 707 crashed while landing; 97 of 101 persons aboard killed.
March 3, Paris: Turkish DC-10 jumbo jet crashed in forest shortly after take-off; all 346 passengers and crew killed in worst single-plane disaster to date.
Dec. 1, Berryville, Va.: all 92 aboard killed in crash of TWA 727 into wooded area.
Dec. 4, Colombo, Sri Lanka: Dutch DC-8 carrying Moslems to Mecca crashed on landing approach, killing all 191 persons aboard.

1975 **April 4, near Saigon, Vietnam:** Air Force Galaxy C-5A crashed after take-off, killing 172, mostly Vietnamese children.
June 24, New York City: Eastern Airlines Boeing 727, arriving from New Orleans, crashed at Kennedy International Airport, killing 113.
Aug. 3, Agadir, Morocco: Chartered Boeing 707, returning Moroccan workers home after vacation in France, plunged into mountainside; all 188 aboard killed.
Aug. 20, Damascus, Syria: Czech airliner crashed while landing, killing 126 of 128 persons aboard.

1976 **Sept. 10, Zagreb, Yugoslavia:** midair collision between British Airways Trident and Yugoslav charter DC-9 fatal to all 176 persons aboard; worst mid-air collision on record.

1977 **March 27, Santa Cruz de Tenerife, Canary Islands:** Pan American and KLM Boeing 747s collided on runway. All 249 on KLM plane and 333 of 394 aboard Pan Am jet killed. Total of 582 is highest for any type of aviation disaster.

1978 **Jan. 1, Bombay:** Air India 747 with 213 aboard exploded and plunged into sea minutes after takeoff.
Sept. 25, San Diego, Calif.: Pacific Southwest

plane collided in midair with Cessna. All 135 on airliner, 2 in Cessna, and 7 on ground killed for total of 144.

Nov. 15, Colombo, Sri Lanka: Chartered Icelandic Airlines DC-8, carrying 249 Moslem pilgrims from Mecca, crashed in thunderstorm during landing approach; 183 killed.

1979   **May 26, Chicago:** American Airlines DC-10 lost left engine upon take-off and crashed seconds later, killing all 272 persons aboard and three on the ground, in worst U.S. air disaster.

Aug. 15, Ukraine, U.S.S.R.: Two planes collided in mid-air; 150 killed.

Oct. 15, Mexico City: Western Airlines DC-10 crashed on landing, killing 73.

Nov. 26, Jidda, Saudi Arabia: Pakistan International Airlines 707 carrying pilgrims returning from Mecca crashed on take-off; all 156 aboard killed.

Nov. 28, Mt. Erebus, Antarctica: Air New Zealand DC-10 crashed on sightseeing flight; 257 killed.

1980   **Jan. 21, near Laskgarak, Iran:** Iran Air Boeing 727 crashed into mountains, killing all 128 aboard.

March 14, Warsaw: LOT Polish Airlines Ilyushin 62 crashed while attempting landing; 22 boxers and officials of a U.S. amateur boxing team killed along with 65 others.

April 25, Santa Cruz de Tenerife, Canary Islands: Chartered Boeing 727 carrying 138 British vacationers and crew of 8 crashed into mountain while approaching for landing; all killed.

Aug. 19, Riyadh, Saudi Arabia: all 301 aboard Saudi Arabian jet killed when burning plane made safe landing but passengers were unable to escape.

Railroad Accidents

1904   **Aug. 7, Eden, Colo.:** Two-train collision killed 96.

1910   **March 1, Wellington, Wash.:** two trains swept into canyon by avalanche; 96 dead.

1915   **May 22, Gretna, Scotland:** two passenger trains and troop train collided; 227 killed.

1917   **Dec. 12, Modane, France:** nearly 550 killed in derailment of troop train near mouth of Mt. Cenis tunnel.

1918   **Nov. 1, New York City:** derailment of subway train in Malbone St. tunnel in Brooklyn left 92 dead.

1939   **Dec. 22, near Magdeburg, Germany:** more than 125 killed in collision; 99 killed in another wreck near Friedrichshafen.

1943   **Dec. 16, near Rennert, N.C.:** 72 killed in derailment and collision of two Atlantic Coast Line trains.

1944   **March 2, near Salerno, Italy:** 521 suffocated when Italian train stalled in tunnel.

Dec. 31, near Ogden, Utah: 48 killed in collision of two sections of Southern Pacific's Pacific Limited.

1946   **April 25, Naperville, Ill.:** at least 47 killed in collision of two trains of Burlington Railroad.

1949   **Oct. 22, near Nowy Dwor, Poland:** more than 200 reported killed in derailment of Danzig-Warsaw express.

1950   **Feb. 17, Rockville Centre, N.Y.:** head-on crash of two Long Island Rail Road commuter trains killed 30.

Nov. 22, Richmond Hill, N.Y.: 79 died when one Long Island Rail Road commuter train

crashed into rear of another.

1951   **Feb. 6, Woodbridge, N.J.:** 85 died when Pennsylvania Railroad commuter train plunged through temporary overpass.

1952   **Oct. 8, Harrow-Wealdstone, England:** two express trains crashed into commuter train; 112 dead.

1953   **Dec. 24, near Sakvice, Czechoslovakia:** two trains crashed; over 100 dead.

1956   **Sept. 2, near Mahbubnagar, India:** at least 120 killed when bridge collapsed under train.

1957   **Sept. 1, near Kendal, Jamaica:** about 175 killed when train plunged into ravine.

Sept. 29, near Montgomery, West Pakistan: express train crashed into standing oil train; nearly 300 killed.

Dec. 4, St. John's, England: 92 killed, 187 injured as one commuter train crashed into another in fog.

1958   **Sept. 15, near Bayonne, N.J.:** over 40 killed when Central Railroad of New Jersey train went through open drawbridge.

1960   **Nov. 14, Pardubice, Czechoslovakia:** two trains collided; 110 dead, 106 injured.

1962   **May 3, near Tokyo:** 163 killed and 400 injured when train crashed into wreckage of collision between inbound freight train and outbound commuter train.

1963   **Nov. 9, near Yokohama, Japan:** two passenger trains crashed into derailed freight, killing 162.

1964   **July 26, Custoias, Portugal:** passenger train derailed; 94 dead.

1970   **Feb. 4, near Buenos Aires:** 236 killed when express train crashed into standing commuter train.

1972   **July 21, Seville, Spain:** head-on crash of two passenger trains killed 76.

Oct. 6, near Saltillo, Mexico: train carrying religious pilgrims derailed and caught fire, killing 204 and injuring over 1,000.

Oct. 30, Chicago: two Illinois Central commuter trains collided during morning rush hour; 45 dead and over 200 injured.

1974   **Aug. 30, Zagreb, Yugoslavia:** train entering station derailed, killing 153 and injuring over 60.

1977   **Feb. 4, Chicago:** 11 killed and over 180 injured when elevated train hit rear of another, sending two cars to street.

Miscellaneous

1955   **June 11, Le Mans, France:** Racing car in Grand Prix hurtled into grandstand, killing 82 spectators.

1967   **Aug. 27, Huron, Ohio:** Sky divers jumping through overcast from off-course plane landed in Lake Erie; 16 killed.

1978   **April 27, St. Mary's, W. Va.:** Scaffolding in power-plant cooling tower under construction collapsed; killing 57 workmen.

Aug. 4, Lac d'Argent, Quebec: Bus carrying handicapped theatergoers plunged into lake, killing 40.

1980   **Jan. 20, Sincelejo, Colombia:** Bleachers at a bullring collapsed, leaving 222 dead.

March 30, Stavanger, Norway: Floating hotel in North Sea collapsed, killing 123 oil workers.

May 9, St. Petersburg, Fla.: *Summit Venture,* 606-foot phosphate carrier, struck Sunshine Skyway Bridge in blinding rain squall; 1,300-foot section of roadway fell into Tampa Bay, taking with it several passenger cars and a Greyhound bus; 35 killed.

States and Territories

State flower, bird, etc., are official unless otherwise indicated; dates in parentheses are those of adoption. Largest cities include incorporated places only. Land areas for 1980 are revised figures. For secession and readmission dates of the former Confederate states, *see* Index. For lists of Governors, Senators, and Representatives, *see* Index. For additional state information, *see* the sections on "Business and the Economy," "Taxes," and "U.S. Statistics."

ALABAMA

Capital: Montgomery
Governor: Forrest H. James, Jr., D (to Jan. 1983)
Lieut. Governor: George McMillan, D (to Jan. 1983)
Secy. of State: Don Seigleman, D (to Jan. 1983)
Comptroller: J.T. Brassell
Atty. General: Charles A. Graddick, D (to Jan. 1983)
Organized as territory: March 3, 1817
Entered Union & (rank): Dec. 14, 1819 (22)
Present constitution adopted: 1901
Motto: *Audemus jura nostra defendere* (We dare defend our rights)
State flower: Camellia (1959)
State bird: Yellowhammer (1927)
State song: "Alabama" (1931)
State tree: Southern pine (longleaf) (1949)
Nickname: Yellowhammer State
Origin of name: May come from Choctaw meaning "thicket-clearers" or "vegetation-gatherers"
1970 population & (rank): 3,444,354 (21)
1980 population (1980 census) & (rank): 3,890,061 (22)
1980 land area & (rank): 50,708 sq mi. (131,334 sq km) (28)
Geographic center: In Chilton Co., 12 mi. SW of Clanton
Number of counties: 67
Largest cities (1980 census): Birmingham, 284,413; Mobile, 200,452; Montgomery, 178,157; Huntsville, 142,513; Tuscaloosa, 75,143; Gadsden, 47,565
State forests: 8 (14,248.58 ac.)
State parks: 22 (45,614 ac.)
Gross receipts (1979–80): $7,772,332,819
Net receipts (1979–80): $6,248,660,289
Net disbursements (1979–80): $6,275,128,639

Spanish explorers are believed to have arrived at Mobile Bay in 1519, and the territory was visited in 1540 by the explorer Hernando de Soto. The first permanent European settlement in Alabama was founded by the French at Fort Louis in 1702. The British gained control of the area in 1763 by the Treaty of Paris, but had to cede almost all the Alabama region to the U.S. after the American Revolution. The Confederacy was founded at Montgomery in February 1861 and, for a time, the city was the Confederate capital.

During the last part of the 19th century, the economy of the state slowly improved. At Tuskegee Institute, founded in 1881 by Booker T. Washington, Dr. George Washington Carver carried out his famous agricultural research.

In the 1950s and '60s, Alabama was the site of such landmark civil-rights actions as the bus boycott in Montgomery (1955–56) and the "Freedom March" from Selma to Birmingham (1965).

Today, Alabama is the leading heavy-industry state in the South. Textiles, iron, and steel lead its manufacturing, which centers around Birmingham, the "Pittsburgh of the South." Industry is growing rapidly in other areas, including the Tennessee River Valley, with its great Muscle Shoals power plant. Manufacturing also includes cement, feed, fertilizer, chemical, rubber, and aluminum products. The state ranks high in the output of poultry, cotton, cattle, hogs, corn, potatoes, peanuts, and fruit.

Points of interest include the George C. Marshall Space Flight Center at Huntsville, Russell Cave National Monument near Bridgeport, and the White House of the Confederacy in Montgomery.

ALASKA

Capital: Juneau
Governor: Jay S. Hammond, R (to Dec. 1982)
Lieut. Governor: Terry Miller, R (to Dec. 1982)
Commissioner of Administration: W. R. Hudson, R (to Dec. 1982)
Atty. General: Wilson L. Condon, D (apptd. by Governor)
Organized as territory: 1912
Entered Union & (rank): Jan. 3, 1959 (49)
Constitution ratified: April 24, 1956
Motto: North to the Future
State flower: Forget-me-not
State tree: Sitka spruce
State bird: Willow ptarmigan
State fish: King salmon
State song: "Alaska's Flag"
Nickname: The state is commonly called "The Last Frontier" or "Land of the Midnight Sun"
Origin of name: Corruption of Aleut word meaning "great land" or "that which the sea breaks against"
1970 population & (rank): 302,583 (50)
1980 population (1980 census) & (rank): 400,481 (50)
1980 land area & (rank): 566,432 sq mi. (1,467,059 sq km) (1)
Geographic center: 60 mi. NW of Mt. McKinley
Number of boroughs: 10
Largest cities (1980 census): Anchorage, 173,017; Fairbanks, 22,645; Juneau, 19,528; Sitka, 7,803; Ketchikan, 7,198; Kodiak, 4,756; Bethel, 3,576
State forests: None
State parks: 5; 59 waysides and areas (3.3 million ac.)
General revenue (1979–80): $2,840,159,521
General expenditures (1979–80): $1,527,221,087

Vitus Bering, a Dane working for the Russians, and Alexei Chirikov discovered the Alaskan mainland and the Aleutian Islands in 1741. The tremendous land mass of Alaska—equal to one fifth of the continental U.S.—was unexplored in 1867 when Secretary of State William Seward arranged for its purchase from the Russians for $7,200,000. The transfer of the territory took place on Oct. 18, 1867. Despite a price of about two cents an acre, the purchase was widely ridiculed as "Seward's Folly." The first official census (1880) reported a total of 33,426 Alaskans, all but 430 being of aboriginal stock. The Gold Rush of 1898 resulted in a mass influx of more than 30,000 people. Since then, Alaska has returned billions of dollars' worth of products to the U.S.

In 1968, a large oil and gas reservoir near Prudhoe Bay on the Arctic Coast was found. The Prudhoe Bay reservoir, with an estimated recoverable 10 billion barrels of oil and 27 trillion cubic feet of gas, is twice as large as any other oil field in North America. The Trans-Alaska pipeline was completed in 1977 at a cost of $7.7 billion. On June 20, oil started flowing through the 800-mile-long pipeline from Prudhoe Bay to the port of Valdez.

Other industries important to Alaska's economy are fisheries, wood and wood products, and furs.

Denali National Park (Mount McKinley National Park) and Mendenhall Glacier in North Tongass National Forest are of interest, as is the large totem pole collection at Sitka National Historical Park. The Katmai National Park includes the "Valley of Ten Thousand Smokes," an area of active volcanoes.

ARIZONA

Capital: Phoenix
Governor: Bruce Babbitt, D (to Jan. 1983)
Secy. of State: Rose Mofford, D (to Jan. 1983)
Atty. General: Bob Corbin, R (to Jan. 1983)
State Treasurer: Clark Dierks, R (to Jan. 1983)
Organized as territory: Feb. 24, 1863
Entered Union & (rank): Feb. 14, 1912 (48)
Present constitution adopted: 1911
Motto: *Ditat Deus* (God enriches)
State flower: Flower of saguaro cactus (1931)
State bird: Cactus wren (1931)
State colors: Blue and old gold (1915)
State song: "Arizona," a march song (1919)
State tree: Paloverde (1957)
Nickname: Grand Canyon State
Origin of name: From the Indian "Arizonac," meaning "little spring"
1970 population & (rank): 1,775,399 (33)
1980 population (1980 census) & (rank): 2,717,866 (29)
1980 land area & (rank): 113,417 sq mi. (293,750 sq km) (6)
Geographic center: In Yavapai Co., 55 mi. ESE of Prescott
Number of counties: 14
Largest cities (1980 census): Phoenix, 764,911; Tucson, 330,537; Mesa, 152,453; Tempe, 106,743; Glendale, 96,988; Scottsdale, 88,364; Yuma, 42,433
State forests: None
State parks: 16
State revenue (1979): $1,703,804,605
State expenditure (1979): $1,612,986,610

Marcos de Niza, a Spanish Franciscan friar, was the first European to explore Arizona. He entered the area in 1539 in search of the mythical Seven Cities of Gold. Although he was followed a year later by another gold seeker, Francisco Vásquez de Coronado, most of the early settlement was for missionary purposes. In 1776 the Spanish established Fort Tucson. In 1848, after the Mexican War, most of the Arizona territory became part of the U.S., and the southern portion of the territory was added by the Gadsden Purchase in 1853.

In 1973 the world's biggest dam, the New Cornelia Tailings, was completed near Ajo.

Arizona history is rich in legends of America's Old West. It was here that the great Indian chiefs Geronimo and Cochise led their people against the frontiersmen. Tombstone, Ariz., was the site of the West's most famous shoot-out—the gunfight at the O.K. Corral. Today, Arizona has the largest U.S. Indian population; more than 14 tribes are represented on 19 reservations.

Manufacturing has become Arizona's most important industry. Principal products include electrical, communications, and aeronautical items. The state produces over half the country's copper. Agriculture is also important to the state's economy.

State attractions include such famous scenery as the Grand Canyon, the Petrified Forest, and the Painted Desert. Hoover Dam, Lake Mead, Fort Apache, and the reconstructed London Bridge at Lake Havasu City are of particular interest.

ARKANSAS

Capital: Little Rock
Governor: Frank White, R (to Jan. 1983)
Lieut. Governor: Winston Bryant, D (to Jan. 1983)
Secy. of State: Paul Reviere, D (to Jan. 1983)
Atty. General: Steve Clark (to Jan. 1983)
Auditor of State: Julia Highes Jones, D (to Jan. 1983)
Treasurer of State: Jimmie Lou Fisher, D (to Jan. 1983)
Land Commissioner: Bill McCuen, D (to Jan. 1983)
Organized as territory: March 2, 1819
Entered Union & (rank): June 15, 1836 (25)
Present constitution adopted: 1874
Motto: *Regnat populus* (The people rule)
State flower: Apple Blossom (1901)
State tree: Pine (1939)
State bird: Mockingbird (1929)
State insect: Honeybee
State song: "Arkansas" (1963)
Nickname: Land of Opportunity
Origin of name: From the Quapaw Indians
1970 population & (rank): 1,923,322 (32)
1980 population (1980 census) & (rank): 2,285,513 (33)
1980 land area & (rank): 51,945 sq mi. (134,538 sq km) (27)
Geographic center: In Pulaski Co., 12 mi. NW of Little Rock
Number of counties: 75
Largest cities (1980 census): Little Rock, 158,461; Fort Smith, 71,384; North Little Rock, 64,419; Pine Bluff, 56,576; Fayetteville, 36,604; Hot Springs, 35,166
State forests: None
State parks: 43
State tax receipts (1980): $1,221,168,664
Taxes from all sources (1980): $2,132,181,091
State general expenditure (1980): $2,134,312,457

Hernando de Soto, in 1541, was among the early European explorers to visit the territory. It was a Frenchman, Henri de Tonty, who in 1686 founded the first permanent white settlement—the Arkansas Post. In 1803 the area was acquired by the U.S. as part of the Louisiana Purchase.

Food products are the state's largest employing sector, with lumber and wood products a close second. Arkansas is also a leader in the production of cotton, rice, and soybeans. The state produces 97% of the nation's high-grade domestic bauxite ore—the source of aluminum. It also has the country's only active diamond mine; located near Murfreesboro, it is operated as a tourist attraction.

Hot Springs National Park is a major state attraction. Its 47 curative springs flow at an average temperature of 147°F year round. Blanchard Springs Caverns, the Arkansas Territorial Capitol Restoration at Little Rock, and Dogpatch U.S.A. near Harrison are of interest. There are two large national forests in Arkansas—the Ouachita and the Ozark—and one of the nation's smallest—the St. Francis.

CALIFORNIA

Capital: Sacramento
Governor: Edmund G. Brown, Jr., D (to Jan. 1983)
Lieut. Governor: Mike Curb, R (to Jan. 1983)
Secy. of State: March Fong Eu, D (to Jan. 1983)
Controller: Ken Cory, D (to Jan. 1983)
Atty. General: George Deukmejian, R (to Jan. 1983)
Treasurer: Jesse M. Unruh, D (to Jan. 1983)
Entered Union & (rank): Sept. 9, 1850 (31)
Present constitution adopted: 1879
Motto: *Eureka* (I have found it)
State flower: Golden poppy (1903)
State tree: California redwoods *(Sequoia sempervirens & Sequoia gigantea)* (1937 & 1953)
State bird: California valley quail (1931)
State animal: California grizzly bear (1953)
State fish: California golden trout (1947)
State insect: California dog-face butterfly (1972)
State colors: Blue and gold (1951)
State song: "I Love You, California" (1951)
Nickname: Golden State
Origin of name: From a book, *Las Sergas de Esplandián,* by Garcia Ordóñez de Montalvo, c. 1500
1970 population & (rank): 19,953,134 (1)
1980 population (1980 census) & (rank): 23,668,562 (1)
1980 land area & (rank): 156,361 sq mi. (404,975 sq km) (3)
Geographic center: In Madera Co., 35 mi. NE of Madera
Number of counties: 58
Largest cities (1980 census): Los Angeles, 2,966,763; San Diego, 875,504; San Francisco, 678,974; San Jose, 636,550; Long Beach, 361,334; Oakland, 339,288
State forests: 8 (70,283 ac.)
State parks and beaches: 180 (723,000 ac.)
State general revenue (1979–80): $17,548,663,021
State general expenditure (1979–80): $17,613,869,011

Although California was sighted by Spanish navigator Juan Rodríguez Cabrillo in 1542, its first Spanish mission (at San Diego) was not established until 1769. California became a U.S. Territory in 1847 when Mexico surrendered it to John C. Frémont. On Jan. 24, 1848, James W. Marshall discovered gold at Sutter's Mill, starting the California Gold Rush and bringing settlers to the state in large numbers.

In 1964, the U.S. Census Bureau estimated that California had become the most populous state, surpassing New York. California also leads the country in personal income and consumer expenditures.

Leading industries include manufacturing (transportation equipment, machinery, and electronic equipment), agriculture, and tourism. Principal natural resources include petroleum, cement, and natural gas.

The Bank of America National Trust and Savings Association, founded by the Giannini family, ranks first or second in the world.

Death Valley, in the southeast, is 282 feet below sea level, the lowest point in the nation; and Mt. Whitney (14,495 ft) is the highest point in the contiguous 48 states. Lassen Peak is one of two active U.S. volcanos outside of Alaska and Hawaii; its last eruptions were recorded in 1917. The General Sherman Tree in Sequoia National Park is estimated to be about 3,500 years old and a stand of bristlecone pine trees in the White Mountains may be over 4,000 years old.

Other points of interest include Yosemite National Park, Disneyland, Hollywood, the Golden Gate bridge, San Simeon State Park, and Point Reyes National Seashore.

COLORADO

Capital: Denver
Governor: Richard D. Lamm, D (to Jan. 1983)
Lieut. Governor: Nancy E. Dick, D (to Jan. 1983)
Secy. of State: Mary Estill Buchanan, R (to Jan. 1983)
Treasurer: Roy Romer, D (to Jan. 1983)
Controller: Dan S. Whittemore
Atty. General: J. D. MacFarlane, D (to Jan. 1983)
Organized as territory: Feb. 28, 1861
Entered Union & (rank): Aug. 1, 1876 (38)
Present constitution adopted: 1876
Motto: *Nil sine Numine* (Nothing without Providence)
State flower: Rocky Mountain columbine (1899)
State tree: Colorado blue spruce (1939)
State bird: Lark bunting (1931)
State animal: Rocky Mountain bighorn sheep
State colors: Blue and white (1911)
State gemstone: Aquamarine (1971)
State song: "Where the Columbines Grow" (1915)
Nickname: Centennial State
Origin of name: From the Spanish, meaning "ruddy" or "red"
1970 population & (rank): 2,209,596 (30)
1980 population (1980 census) & (rank): 2,888,834 (28)
1980 land area & (rank): 103,766 sq mi. (268,754 sq km) (8)
Geographic center: In Park Co., 30 mi. NW of Pikes Peak
Number of counties: 63
Largest cities (1980 census): Denver, 491,396; Colorado Springs, 215,150; Aurora, 158,588; Lakewood, 112,848; Pueblo, 101,686; Arvada, 84,576; Boulder, 76,685
State forests: 1 (71,000 ac.)
Total state revenue (1979–80): $3,575,662,953
Total state expenditure (1979–80): $3,438,061,669

First visited by Spanish explorers in the 1500s, the territory was claimed for Spain by Juan de Ulibarri in 1706. The U.S. obtained eastern Colorado as part of the Louisiana Purchase in 1803, the central portion in 1845 with the admission of Texas as a state, and the western part in 1848 as a result of the Mexican War.

Colorado has the highest mean elevation of any state, with more than 1,000 Rocky Mountain peaks over 10,000 feet high and 54 towering above 14,-000 feet. Pikes Peak, the most famous of these mountains, was discovered by U.S. Army Lieut. Zebulon M. Pike in 1806.

Gold was first discovered near present-day Denver in 1858 and at Cripple Creek in 1891. Rich silver deposits were also found in 1875.

Once primarily a mining and agricultural state, today Colorado draws the largest segment of its income from manufacturing. Denver is a leader in electronics and space-age industry. Pueblo, the "Pittsburgh of the West," makes iron, steel, brick, tile, and foundry products.

Rich in natural resources, Colorado now produces most of the world's molybdenum. Uranium, vanadium, gold, silver, lead, tin, zinc, and other minerals are also mined. Colorado's highly developed irrigation system promotes farming of wheat, hay, beans, sugar beets, corn, potatoes, barley, and truck vegetables. Cattle and sheep raising is also important.

Tourism has developed into a major industry largely because of Colorado's magnificent scenery. Among the major attractions are Rocky Mountain National Park, Garden of the Gods, Great Sand Dunes and Dinosaur National Monuments, Pikes Peak and Mt. Evans Highways, and Mesa Verde National Park (prehistoric cliff dwellings).

Colorado Springs, with the nearby U.S. Air Force Academy, is probably the most popular tourist center in the Rocky Mountains, while Aspen and Vail have become leading ski resorts.

CONNECTICUT

Capital: Hartford
Governor: William A. O'Neill, D (to Jan. 1983)
Lieut. Governor: Joseph J. Fauliso, D (to Jan. 1983)
Secy. of State: Barbara B. Kennelly, D (to Jan. 1983)
Comptroller: J. Edward Caldwell, D (to Jan. 1983)
Treasurer: Henry E. Parker, D (to Jan. 1983)
Atty. General: Carl R. Ajello, D (to Jan. 1983)
Entered Union & (rank): Jan. 9, 1788 (5)
Present constitution adopted: Dec. 30, 1965
Motto: *Qui transtulit sustinet* (He who transplanted still sustains)
State flower: Mountain laurel (1907)
State tree: White Oak (1947)
State animal: Sperm whale (1975)
State bird: American robin (1943)
State insect: Praying mantis (1977)
State mineral: Garnet (1977)
State song: "Yankee Doodle" (1978)
Official designation: *Constitution State* (1959)
Nickname: Nutmeg State
Origin of name: From an Indian word (Quinnehtukqut) meaning "beside the long tidal river"
1970 population & (rank): 3,032,217 (24)
1980 population (1980 census) & (rank): 3,107,576 (24)
1980 land area & (rank): 4,862 sq mi. (12,593 sq km) (48)
Geographic center: In Hartford Co., at East Berlin
Number of counties: 8
Largest cities (1980 census): Bridgeport, 142,546; Hartford, 136,392; New Haven, 126,109; Waterbury, 103,266; Stamford, 102,453; Norwalk, 77,767
State forests: 30 (134,461 ac.)
State parks: 88 (30,316 ac.)
State and local general revenue (1979–80): $4,179,000,000
State and local general expenditure (1979–80): $4,294,000,000

The Dutch navigator, Adriaen Block, was the first European of record to explore the area, sailing up the Connecticut River in 1614. In 1633, Dutch colonists built a fort and trading post near present-day Hartford, but soon lost control to English Puritans migrating south from the Massachusetts Bay Colony.

English settlements, established in the 1630s at Windsor, Wethersfield, and Hartford, united in 1639 to form the Connecticut Colony and adopted the *Fundamental Orders*, considered the world's first written constitution.

The colony's royal charter of 1682 was exceptionally liberal. When Gov. Edmund Andros tried to seize it in 1687, it was hidden in the Hartford Oak, commemorated in Charter Oak Place.

Connecticut played a prominent role in the Revolutionary War, serving as the Continental Army's major supplier. Sometimes called the "Arsenal of the Nation," the state became one of the most industrialized in the nation. Its early business and industrial pioneers included Eli Whitney, Samuel Colt, and Charles Goodyear.

Today, Connecticut factories produce weapons, sewing machines, jet engines, helicopters, motors, hardware and tools, cutlery, clocks, locks, ball bearings, silverware, and submarines. Hartford, which has the oldest U.S. newspaper still being published —the *Courant*, established 1764— is the insurance capital of the nation.

Poultry, fruit, and dairy products account for the largest portion of farm income, and Connecticut shade-grown tobacco is acknowledged to be the nation's most valuable crop, per acre.

Connecticut is a popular resort area with its 250-mile Long Island Sound shoreline and many inland lakes. Among the major points of interest are the American Shakespeare Theatre in Stratford, Yale University's Gallery of Fine Arts and Peabody Museum. Other famous museums include the P.T. Barnum, Winchester Gun, and American Clock and Watch. The town of Mystic features a recreated 19th-century New England seaport and the Mystic Marinelife Aquarium.

DELAWARE

Capital: Dover
Governor: Pierre S. du Pont IV, R (to Jan. 1985)
Lieut. Governor: Michael N. Castle (to Jan. 1985)
Secy. of State: Glenn C. Kenton, R (Pleasure of Governor)
State Treasurer: Thomas R. Carper, D (to Jan. 1983)
Atty. General: Richard S. Gebelein (to Jan. 1983)
Entered Union & (rank): Dec. 7, 1787 (1)
Present constitution adopted: 1897
Motto: Liberty and independence
State colors: Colonial blue and buff
State flower: Peach blossom
State tree: American holly
State bird: Blue Hen chicken
State insect: Ladybug
State song: "Our Delaware"
Nicknames: Diamond State; First State
Origin of name: From Delaware River and Bay; named in turn for Sir Thomas West, Lord De La Warr
1970 population & (rank): 548,104 (46)
1980 population (1980 census) & (rank): 595,225 (47)
1980 land area & (rank): 1,982 sq mi. (5,133 sq km) (49)
Geographic center: In Kent Co., 11 mi. S of Dover
Number of counties: 3
Largest cities (1980 census): Wilmington, 70,195; Newark, 25,247; Dover, 23,512; Elsmere, 6,493; Milford, 5,356; Seaford, 5,256; New Castle, 4,709; Lewes, 2,197
State forests: 3 (6,149 ac.)
State parks: 10
State receipts (1980): $599,732,291[1]
State disbursements (1980): $590,434,368[1]

1. General Funds, do not include Federal funds.

Henry Hudson, sailing under the Dutch flag, is credited with Delaware's discovery in 1609. The following year, Capt. Samuel Argall of Virginia named Delaware for his colony's governor, Thomas West, Baron De La Warr. An attempted Dutch settlement failed in 1631. Swedish colonization began at Fort Christina (now Wilmington) in 1638, but New Sweden fell to Dutch forces led by New Netherlands' Gov. Peter Stuyvesant in 1655.

England took over the area in 1664 and it was transferred to William Penn as the southern Three Counties in 1682. Semiautonomous after 1704, Delaware fought as a separate state in the American Revolution and became the first state to ratify the constitution in 1787.

During the Civil War, although a slave state, Delaware did not secede from the Union.

In 1802, Éleuthère Irénée du Pont established a gunpowder mill near Wilmington that laid the foundation for Delaware's huge chemical industry. Delaware's manufactured products now also include vulcanized fiber, glazed kid and morocco leathers, textiles, paper, dental supplies, metal products, machinery, machine tools, and automobiles.

Delaware also grows a great variety of fruits and vegetables and is a U.S. pioneer in the food-canning industry. Corn, soybeans, potatoes, and hay are important crops. Delaware's broiler chicken farms supply the big Eastern markets, and fishing is another major industry.

Points of interest include the Fort Christina Monument, Hagley Museum, Holy Trinity Church (erected in 1698, the oldest Protestant church in the United States still in use), and Winterthur Museum, in and near Wilmington; central New Castle, an almost unchanged late 18th-century capital; and the Delaware Museum of Natural History.

Popular recreation areas include Cape Henlopen, Delaware Seashore, Trapp Pond State Park, and Rehoboth Beach.

DISTRICT OF COLUMBIA

See listing at end of *50 Largest Cities of the United States.*

FLORIDA

Capital: Tallahassee
Governor: Bob Graham, D (to Jan. 1983)
Lieut. Governor: Wayne Mixson, D (to Jan. 1983)
Secy. of State: George Firestone, D (to Jan. 1983)
Comptroller: Gerald Lewis, D (to Jan. 1983)
Commissioner of Agriculture: Doyle Connor, D (to Jan. 1983)
Atty. General: Jim Smith, D (to Jan. 1983)
Organized as territory: March 30, 1822
Entered Union & (rank): March 3, 1845 (27)
Present constitution adopted: 1969
Motto: In God we trust (1868)
State flower: Orange blossom (1909)
State bird: Mockingbird (1927)
State song: "Suwannee River" (1935)
Nickname: Sunshine State (1970)
Origin of name: From the Spanish, meaning "feast of flowers" (Easter)
1970 population & (rank): 6,791,418 (9)
1980 population (1980 census) & (rank): 9,739,992 (7)
1980 land area & (rank): 54,090 sq mi. (140,093 sq km) (26)
Geographic center: In Hernando Co., 12 mi. NNW of Brooksville
Number of counties: 67
Largest cities (1980 census): Jacksonville, 540,898; Miami, 346,931; Tampa, 271,523; St. Petersburg, 236,893; Fort Lauderdale, 153,256; Hialeah, 145,254
State forests: 4 (306,881 ac.)
State parks: 88 (215,820 ac.)
State tax receipts (1979–80): $4,752,940,345
Other state revenue (1979–80): $8,729,065,111
State expenditures (1979–80): $13,395,271,035

In 1513, Ponce de Leon, seeking the mythical "Fountain of Youth," named Florida and claimed it for Spain. Later, Florida would be held at different times by Spain, France, and England until Spain finally sold it to the United States in 1819.

Florida's early 19th-century history as a U.S. territory was scarred by savage wars with the Seminole Indians that did not end until 1842.

One of the nation's fastest-growing states, Florida's population has gone from 2.8 million in 1950 to more than 9.5 million today.

Florida's economy rests on a solid base of tourism, manufacturing, and agriculture. The state entertained more than 35.9 million visitors, who spent about $16.5 billion, in 1979.

Oranges and grapefruit lead Florida's crop list, followed by sugarcane, tomatoes, beans, celery, potatoes, field corn, honey, watermelons, limes, and mangoes. Forestry, truck gardening, commercial fishing, and cattle raising are leading industries. Deep-sea fishing for sport is a leading tourist industry.

Florida is expanding in all industrial areas with the greatest development taking place in the research-oriented Space Age manufacturing. The state produces 80% of the nation's phosphate.

Major tourist attractions are Miami Beach, Palm Beach, St. Augustine (founded in 1565 and the oldest permanent city in the U.S.), Daytona Beach, and Fort Lauderdale, on the East Coast. West Coast resorts include Sarasota, Tampa, Key West, and St. Petersburg. Disney World, located on a 27,000-acre site near Orlando, is a popular attraction.

The John F. Kennedy Space Center at Cape Canaveral, and Everglades National Park, a 5,000-square-mile preserve, also draw many visitors.

GEORGIA

Capital: Atlanta
Governor: George Busbee, D (to Jan. 1983)
Lieut. Governor: Zell Miller, D (to Jan. 1983)
Secy. of State: David Poythress, D (to Jan. 1983)
Comptroller General: Johnnie Caldwell, D (to Jan. 1983)
Atty. General: Arthur K. Bolton, D (to Jan. 1983)
Entered Union & (rank): Jan. 2, 1788 (4)
Present constitution adopted: 1977
Motto: Wisdom, justice, and moderation
State flower: Cherokee rose (1916)
State tree: Live oak (1937)
State bird: Brown thrasher (1935)
State song: "Georgia on my Mind" (1922)
Nicknames: Peach State, Empire State of the South
Origin of name: In honor of George II of England
1970 population & (rank): 4,587,930 (15)
1980 population (1980 census) & (rank): 5,464,265 (13)
1980 land area & (rank): 58,073 sq mi. (150,409 sq km) (21)
Geographic center: In Twiggs Co., 18 mi. SE of Macon
Number of counties: 159
Largest cities (1980 census): Atlanta, 425,022; Columbus, 169,441; Savannah, 141,634; Macon, 116,860; Albany, 73,934; Augusta, 47,532; Athens, 42,549; Warner Robins, 39,893
State forests: 25,258,000 ac. (67% of total state area)
State parks: 53 (42,600 ac.)
State revenue receipts (1980): $2,809,997,680
State revenue distribution (1980): $2,809,997,680

Hernando de Soto, the Spanish explorer, first traveled parts of Georgia in 1540. British claims later conflicted with those of Spain. After obtaining a royal charter, Gen. James Oglethorpe established the first permanent settlement in Georgia in 1733 as a refuge for English debtors. In 1742, Oglethorpe defeated Spanish invaders in the Battle of Bloody Marsh.

A Confederate stronghold, Georgia was the

scene of extensive military action during the Civil War. Union General William T. Sherman burned Atlanta and destroyed a 60-mile wide path to the coast where he captured Savannah in 1864.

The largest state east of the Mississippi, Georgia is typical of the changing South with an ever-increasing industrial development. Atlanta, largest city in the state, is the communications and transportation center for the Southeast and the area's chief distributor of goods.

Georgia leads the nation in the production of paper and board, tufted textile products, and processed chicken. Other major manufactured products are transportation equipment, food products, apparel, and chemicals.

Important agricultural products are corn, cotton, tobacco, soybeans, eggs, and peaches. Georgia produces twice as many peanuts as the next leading state. From its vast stands of pine come more than half the world's resins and turpentine and 74.4% of the U.S. supply. Georgia is also a leader in the production of marble, kaolin, barite, and bauxite.

Principal tourist attractions in Georgia include the Okefenokee National Wildlife Refuge, Andersonville Prison Park and National Cemetery, Chickamauga and Chattanooga National Military Park, the Little White House at Warm Springs where Pres. Franklin D. Roosevelt died in 1945, Sea Island, the enormous Confederate Memorial at Stone Mountain, Kennesaw Mountain National Battlefield Park, and Cumberland Island National Seashore.

sugar industry (pineapple came after 1898) meant increasing U.S. business and political involvement. In 1893, Queen Liliuokalani was deposed and a year later the Republic of Hawaii was established with Sanford B. Dole as president. Then, following its annexation in 1898, Hawaii became a U.S. Territory in 1900.

The Japanese attack on the naval base at Pearl Harbor on Dec. 7, 1941, was directly responsible for U.S. entry into World War II.

Hawaii, 2,100 miles west-southwest of San Francisco, is a 1,600-mile chain of islets and eight main islands—Hawaii, Kahoolawe, Maui, Lanai, Molokai, Oahu, Kauai, and Niihau. Kure (Ocean) Atoll, an islet in the Northwestern Hawaiian Islands, is administratively part of Hawaii.

The temperature is mild and Hawaii's soil is fertile for tropical fruits and vegetables. Cane sugar and pineapple are the chief products. Hawaii also grows coffee, bananas and nuts. The tourist business is Hawaii's largest source of outside income.

Hawaii's highest peak is Mauna Kea (13,796 ft.). Mauna Loa (13,677 ft.) is the largest volcanic mountain in the world in cubic content.

Among the major points of interest are Hawaii Volcanoes National Park (Hawaii), Haleakala National Park (Maui), Puuhonua o Honaunau National Historical Park (Hawaii), Polynesian Cultural Center (Oahu), the U.S.S. *Arizona* Memorial at Pearl Harbor, and Iolani Palace (the only royal palace in the U.S.), Bishop Museum, and Waikiki Beach (all in Honolulu).

HAWAII

Capital: Honolulu (on Oahu)
Governor: George R. Ariyoshi, D (to Dec. 1982)
Lieut. Governor: Jean King, D (to Dec. 1982)
Comptroller: Hideo Murakami, (to Dec. 1982)
Atty. General: Tany S. Hong, (to Dec. 1982)
Organized as territory: 1900
Entered Union & (rank): Aug. 21, 1959 (50)
Motto: *Ua Mau Ke Ea O Ka Aina I Ka Pono* (The life of the land is perpetuated in righteousness)
State flower: Hibiscus
State song: "Hawaii Ponoi"
State bird: Nene (Hawaiian goose)
Nickname: Aloha State
Origin of name: Uncertain. The islands may have been named by Hawaii Loa, their traditional discoverer. Or they may have been named after Hawaii or Hawaiki, the traditional home of the Polynesians.
1970 population & (rank): 769,913 (40)
1980 population (1980 census) & (rank): 965,000 (39)
1980 land area & (rank): 6,425 sq mi. (16,641 sq km) (47)
Geographic center: In Hawaii Co., off Maui Island
Number of counties: 4
Largest cities (1980 census): Honolulu, 365,048; Hilo, 37,017[1]
State parks and historic sites: 65
Total state government revenues (1978–79): $1,670,028,000
Total state government expenditures (1978–79): $1,524,074,000

1. There are no political boundaries to Honolulu or any other place, but statistical boundaries are assigned under state law.

First settled by Polynesians sailing from other Pacific islands in the 6th century, Hawaii was visited in 1778 by British Captain James Cook who called the group the Sandwich Islands.

Hawaii was a native kingdom throughout most of the 19th century when the expansion of the vital

IDAHO

Capital: Boise
Governor: John V. Evans, D (to Jan. 1983)
Lieut. Governor: Phil Batt, R (to Jan. 1983)
Secy. of State: Pete T. Cenarrusa, R (to Jan. 1983)
State Auditor: Joe R. Williams, D (to Jan. 1983)
Atty. General: David Leroy, R (to Jan. 1983)
Organized as territory: March 3, 1863
Entered Union & (rank): July 3, 1890 (43)
Present constitution adopted: 1890
Motto: *Esto perpetua* (May you last forever)
State flower: Syringa (1931)
State tree: White pine (1935)
State bird: Mountain bluebird (1931)
State horse: Appaloosa (1975)
State gem: Star garnet (1967)
State song: "Here We Have Idaho"
Nicknames: Gem State; Spud State; Panhandle State
Origin of name: Means "Gem of the Mountains"
1970 population & (rank): 713,015 (42)
1980 population (1980 census) & (rank): 943,935 (41)
1980 land area & (rank): 82,677 sq mi. (214,133 sq km) (11)
Geographic center: In Custer Co., at Custer, SW of Challis
Number of counties: 44, plus small part of Yellowstone National Park
Largest cities (1980 census): Boise, 102,451; Pocatello, 46,340; Idaho Falls, 39,590; Lewiston, 27,986; Twin Falls, 26,209; Nampa, 25,112
State forests: 881,000 ac.
State parks: 21 (38,487) ac.
State revenue (1979–80): $356,284,100
State expenditure (1979–80): $360,218,700

After its acquisition by the U.S. as part of the Louisiana Purchase in 1803, the region was explored by Meriwether Lewis and William Clark in 1805–06. Northwest boundary disputes with Great

Britain were settled by the Oregon Treaty in 1846 and the first permanent U.S. settlement in Idaho was established by the Mormons at Franklin in 1860.

After gold was discovered on Orofino Creek in 1860, prospectors swarmed into the territory, but left little more than a number of ghost towns.

In the 1870s, growing white occupation of Indian lands led to a series of battles between U.S. forces and the Nez Percé, Bannock, and Sheepeater tribes.

Mining, lumbering, and irrigation farming have been important for years. Idaho produces more than one third of all the silver mined in the U.S. It also ranks high among the states in antimony, lead, cobalt, garnet, phosphate rock, vanadium, zinc, and mercury.

Idaho's most impressive growth began when World War II military needs made processing agricultural products a big industry, particularly the dehydrating and freezing of potatoes. The state produces about one fourth of the nation's potato crop, as well as wheat, apples, corn, barley, sugar beets, and hops. More money is made from livestock in the state than from all agricultural products.

With the growth of winter sports, tourism now outranks mining in dollar revenue. Idaho's many streams and lakes provide fishing, camping, and boating sites. The nation's largest elk herds draw hunters from all over the world and the famed Sun Valley resort attracts thousands of visitors to its swimming and skiing facilities.

Other points of interest are the Craters of the Moon National Monument; Nez Percé National Historic Park, which includes many sites visited by Lewis and Clark; and the State Historical Museum in Boise.

ILLINOIS

Capital: Springfield
Governor: James R. Thompson, R (to Jan. 1983)
Lieut. Governor: Dave O'Neal, R (to Jan. 1983)
Secy. of State: Jim Edgar, R (to Jan. 1983)
Comptroller: Roland J. Burris, D (to Jan. 1983)
Atty. General: Tyrone C. Fahner, R (to Jan. 1983)
Treasurer: Jerry Cosentino, D (to Jan. 1983)
Organized as territory: Feb. 3, 1809
Entered Union & (rank): Dec. 3, 1818 (21)
Present constitution adopted: 1970
Motto: State sovereignty, national union
State flower: Violet (1908)
State tree: White oak (1973)
State bird: Cardinal (1929)
State insect: Monarch butterfly
State song: "Illinois" (1925)
State slogan: Land of Lincoln
State mineral: Fluorite (1965)
Nickname: Prairie State
Origin of name: From an Indian word and French suffix meaning "tribe of superior men"
1970 population & (rank): 11,110,285 (5)
1980 population (1980 census) & (rank): 11,418,461 (5)
1980 land area & (rank): 56,400 sq mi. (146,076 sq km) (23)
Geographic center: In St. Clair County near Mascoutah
Number of counties: 102
Largest cities (1980 census): Chicago, 3,005,072; Rockford, 139,712; Peoria, 124,160; Springfield, 99,637; Decatur, 94,081; Aurora, 81,293; Joliet, 77,956
Public use areas: 187 (275,000 ac.), incl. state parks, memorials, forests and conservation areas

Total state revenue, all appropriated funds, all sources (fiscal 1980): $10,953,200,000
Total state expenditure, all appropriated funds (fiscal 1980): $11,102,884,000

French explorers Marquette and Joliet, in 1673, were the first Europeans of record to visit the region. In 1699 French settlers established the first permanent settlement at Cahokia, near present-day East St. Louis.

Great Britain obtained the region at the end of the French and Indian War in 1763. The area figured prominently in frontier struggles during the Revolutionary War and in Indian wars during the early 19th century.

Significant episodes in the state's early history include the growing migration of Eastern settlers following the opening of the Erie Canal in 1825; the Black Hawk War, which virtually ended the Indian troubles in the area; and the rise of Abraham Lincoln from farm laborer to President-elect.

Today, Illinois stands high in manufacturing, coal mining, agriculture, and oil production. The sprawling Chicago district (including a slice of Indiana) is a great iron and steel producer, meat packer, grain exchange, and railroad center. Chicago is also famous as a busy long-flight airport city and Great Lakes port.

Illinois ranks first in the nation in export of agricultural products and second in hog production. An important dairying state, Illinois is also a leader in corn, oats, wheat, barley, rye, truck vegetables, and nursery products.

The state manufactures a great variety of industrial and consumer products: railroad cars, clothing, furniture, tractors, liquor, watches, and farm implements are just some of the items made in its factories and plants.

Central Illinois is noted for shrines and memorials associated with the life of Abraham Lincoln. In Springfield are the Lincoln Home, the Lincoln Tomb, and the restored Old State Capitol. Other points of interest are the home of Mormon leader Joseph Smith in Nauvoo and, in Chicago: the Art Institute, Field Museum, Museum of Science and Industry, Shedd Aquarium, Adler Planetarium, Merchandise Mart, and Chicago Portage National Historic Site.

INDIANA

Capital: Indianapolis
Governor: Robert D. Orr, R (to Jan. 1985)
Lieut. Governor: John M. Muntz, R (to Jan. 1985)
Secy. of State: Edwin J. Simcox, R (to Dec. 1982)
Treasurer: Julian L. Ridlen, R (to Feb. 1983)
Atty. General: Linley E. Pearson, R (to Jan. 1985)
Auditor: Charles D. Loos, R (to Dec. 1982)
Organized as territory: May 7, 1800
Entered Union & (rank): Dec. 11, 1816 (19)
Present constitution adopted: 1851
Motto: The Crossroads of America
State flower: Peony (1957)
State tree: Tulip tree (1931)
State bird: Cardinal (1933)
State song: "On the Banks of the Wabash, Far Away" (1913)
Nickname: Hoosier State
Origin of name: Meaning "land of Indians"
1970 population & (rank): 5,195,392 (11)
1980 population (1980 census) & (rank): 5,490,179 (12)

1980 land area & (rank): 36,097 sq mi. (93,491 sq km) (38)
Geographic center: In Boone Co., 14 mi. NNW of Indianapolis
Number of Counties: 92
Largest cities (1980 census): Indianapolis, 700,807; Fort Wayne, 172,196; Gary, 151,953; Evansville, 130,496; South Bend, 109,727; Hammond, 93,714; Muncie, 77,216
State parks: 19 (54,126 ac.)
State memorials: 16 (941.977 ac.)
State general revenue (1978–79): $4,612,299,000
State general expenditure (1978–79): $4,088,514,000

First explored for France by La Salle in 1679–80, the region figured importantly in the Franco-British struggle for North America that culminated with British victory in 1763.

George Rogers Clark led American forces against the British in the area during the Revolutionary War and, prior to becoming a state, Indiana was the scene of frequent Indian uprisings until the victory of Gen. William Henry Harrison at Tippecanoe in 1811.

Indiana's 41-mile Lake Michigan waterfront—one of the world's great industrial centers—turns out iron, steel, and oil products. Products include automobile parts and accessories, mobile homes and recreational vehicles, truck and bus bodies, aircraft engines, farm machinery, and fabricated structural steel. Phonograph records, wood office furniture, and pharmaceuticals are also manufactured.

The state is a leader in agriculture with corn the principal crop. Hogs, soybeans, wheat, oats, rye, tomatoes, onions, and poultry also contribute heavily to Indiana's agricultural output. Much of the building limestone used in the U.S. is quarried in Indiana which is also a large producer of coal.

Wyandotte Cave, one of the largest in the U.S., is located in Crawford County in southern Indiana and West Baden and French Lick are well known for their mineral springs. Other attractions include Indiana Dunes National Lakeshore, Indianapolis Motor Speedway, Lincoln Boyhood National Memorial, and the George Rogers Clark National Historical Park.

Geographic center: In Story Co., 5 mi. NE of Ames
Number of counties: 99
Largest cities (1980 census): Des Moines, 191,003; Cedar Rapids, 110,243; Davenport, 103,264; Sioux City 82,003; Waterloo, 75,985; Dubuque, 62,321; Council Bluffs, 56,449; Iowa City, 50,508; Ames, 45,775
State forests: 5 (28,000 ac.)
State parks: 95 (49,237)
Total revenue (1980): $1,929,680,000
Total expenditures (1980): $1,608,950,814

The first Europeans to visit the area were the French explorers, Father Jacques Marquette and Louis Jolliet in 1673. The U.S. obtained control of the area in 1803 as part of the Louisiana Purchase.

During the first half of the 19th century, there was heavy fighting between white settlers and Indians. Lands were taken from the Indians after the Black Hawk War in 1832 and again in 1836 and 1837.

When Iowa became a state in 1846, its capital was Iowa City; the more centrally located Des Moines became the new capital in 1857. At that time, the state's present boundaries were also drawn.

Although Iowa produces a tenth of the nation's food supply, the value of Iowa's manufactured products is almost 2½ times that of its agriculture. Major industries are food and associated products, non-electrical machinery, electrical equipment, printing and publishing, and fabricated products.

Iowa stands in a class by itself as an agricultural state. Its farms sell over $9 billion worth of crops and livestock annually. Iowa leads the nation in all livestock and hog marketings, with about 25% of the pork supply and 12% of the grain-fed cattle. Iowa's forests produce hardwood lumber, particularly walnut, and its mineral products include cement, limestone, sand, gravel, gypsum, and coal.

Tourist attractions include the Herbert Hoover birthplace and library near West Branch; the Amana Colonies; Fort Dodge Historical Museum, Fort, and Stockade; the Iowa State Fair at Des Moines in August; and the Effigy Mounds National Monument at Marquette, a prehistoric Indian burial site.

IOWA

Capital: Des Moines
Governor: Robert D. Ray, R (to Jan. 1983)
Lieut. Governor: Terry Branstad, R (to Jan. 1983)
Secy. of State: Mary Jane Odell, R (to Jan. 1983)
Treasurer: Maurice E. Baringer, R (to Jan. 1983)
Atty. General: Tom Miller, D (to Jan. 1983)
Organized as territory: June 12, 1838
Entered Union & (rank): Dec. 28, 1846 (29)
Present constitution adopted: 1857
Motto: Our liberties we prize and our rights we will maintain
State flower: Wild rose (1897)
State bird: Eastern goldfinch (1933)
State colors: Red, white, and blue (in state flag)
State song: "Song of Iowa"
Nickname: Hawkeye State
Origin of name: Probably from an Indian word meaning "I-o-w-a, this is the place," or "The Beautiful Land"
1970 population & (rank): 2,825,368 (25)
1980 population (1980 census) & (rank): 2,913,387 (27)
1980 land area & (rank): 55,491 sq mi. (144,887 sq km) (24)

KANSAS

Capital: Topeka
Governor: John W. Carlin, D (to Jan. 1983)
Lieut. Governor: Paul V. Dugan, D (to Jan. 1983)
Secy. of State: Jack H. Brier, R (to Jan. 1983)
Treasurer: Joan Finney, D (to Jan. 1983)
Atty. General: Robert T. Stephan, R (to Jan. 1983)
Organized as territory: May 30, 1854
Entered Union & (rank): Jan. 29, 1861 (34)
Present constitution adopted: 1859
Motto: *Ad astra per aspera* (To the stars through difficulties)
State flower: Sunflower (1903)
State tree: Cottonwood (1937)
State bird: Western meadow lark (1937)
State animal: Buffalo (1955)
State song: "Home on the Range" (1947)
State march: "The Kansas March" (1935)
Nicknames: Sunflower State; Jayhawk State
Origin of name: From a Siouan word meaning "people of the south wind"
1970 population & (rank): 2,249,071 (28)
1980 population (1980 census) & (rank): 2,363,208 (32)

1980 land area & (rank): 81,787 sq mi. (211,828 sq km) (13)
Geographic center: In Barton Co., 15 mi. NE of Great Bend
Number of counties: 105
Largest cities (1980 census): Wichita, 279,272; Kansas City, 161,087; Topeka, 115,266; Overland Park, 81,784; Lawrence, 52,738; Salina, 41,843; Hutchinson, 40,284
State parks: 22 (14,394 ac.)
State operating revenue (1979–80): $2,405,717,000
State operating expenditure (1979–80): $2,382,020,000

Spanish explorer Francisco de Coronado, in 1541, is considered the first European to have traveled this region. La Salle's extensive land claims for France (1682) included present-day Kansas. Ceded to Spain by France in 1763, the territory reverted back to France in 1800 and was sold to the U.S. as part of the Louisiana Purchase in 1803.

Lewis and Clark, Zebulon Pike, and Stephen H. Long explored the region between 1803 and 1819. The first permanent settlements in Kansas were outposts—Fort Leavenworth (1827), Fort Scott (1842), and Fort Riley (1853)—established to protect travelers along the Santa Fe and Oregon Trails.

Just before the Civil War, the conflict between the pro- and anti-slavery forces earned the region the grim title "Bleeding Kansas."

Today, wheat fields, oil well derricks, herds of cattle, and grain storage elevators are chief features of the Kansas landscape. A leading wheat-growing state, Kansas also raises corn, sorghums, oats, barley, soy beans, and potatoes. Kansas stands high in petroleum production and mines zinc, coal, salt, and lead. It is also the nation's leading producer of helium.

Wichita is one of the nation's leading aircraft manufacturing centers, ranking first in production of private aircraft. Kansas City is an important transportation, milling, and meat-packing center.

Points of interest include the Kansas State Historical Society Museum at Topeka, the Eisenhower boyhood home and the new Eisenhower Memorial Museum and Presidential Library at Abilene, John Brown's cabin at Osawatomie, recreated Front Street in Dodge City, Fort Larned (once the most important military post on the Santa Fe Trail), and Fort Leavenworth and Fort Riley, still active military posts.

KENTUCKY

Capital: Frankfort
Governor: John Y. Brown, Jr., D (to Dec. 1983)
Lieut. Governor: Martha Layne Collins, D (to Dec. 1983)
Secy. of the Commonwealth: Francis Jones Mills, D (to Jan. 1984)
State Treasurer: Drexell Davis, D (to Jan. 1984)
State Auditor: James B. Graham, D (to Jan. 1984)
Atty. General: Steven L. Beshear, D (to Jan. 1984)
Entered Union & (rank): June 1, 1792 (15)
Present constitution adopted: 1891
Motto: United we stand, divided we fall
State tree: Coffeetree
State flower: Goldenrod
State bird: Kentucky cardinal
State song: "My Old Kentucky Home"
Nickname: Bluegrass State
Origin of name: From an Iroquoian word "Ken-tah-ten" meaning "land of tomorrow"
1970 population & (rank): 3,220,711 (23)
1980 population (1980 census) & (rank): 3,661,433 (23)
1980 land area & (rank): 39,650 sq mi. (102,694 sq km) (37)

Geographic center: In Marion Co., 3 mi. NNW of Lebanon
Number of counties: 120
Largest cities (1980 census): Louisville, 298,451; Lexington, 204,165; Owensboro, 54,450; Covington, 49,013; Bowling Green, 40,450; Paducah, 29,315; Hopkinsville, 27,318
State forests: 9 (44,173 ac.)
State parks: 43 (40,574 ac.)
Total state revenue (1979–80): $4,230,818,614[2]
Total state expenditure (1979–1980): $3,913,108,000[1]

1. Figures taken from Kentucky's Financial Report for fiscal year ending June 30, 1980. 2. Five operating funds only.

Kentucky was the first region west of the Allegheny Mountains settled by American pioneers. James Harrod established the first permanent settlement at Harrodsburg in 1774; the following year Daniel Boone, who had explored the area in 1767, blazed the Wilderness Trail and founded Boonesboro.

Politically, the Kentucky region was originally part of Virginia, but early statehood was gained in 1792.

During the Civil War, as a slaveholding state with a considerable abolitionist population, Kentucky was caught in the middle of the conflict, supplying both Union and Confederate forces with thousands of troops.

In recent years, manufacturing has shown important gains, but agriculture and mining are still vital to Kentucky's economy. Kentucky prides itself on producing some of the nation's best tobacco, horses, and whiskey. Corn, soybeans, wheat, fruit, hogs, cattle, and dairy farming are also important.

Among the manufactured items produced in the state are furniture, aluminum ware, brooms, shoes, lumber products, machinery, textiles, and iron and steel products. Kentucky also produces significant amounts of petroleum, natural gas, fluorspar, clay, and stone. However, coal accounts for 90% of the total mineral income.

Louisville, the largest city, famed for the Kentucky Derby at Churchill Downs, is also the location of a large state university, whiskey distilleries, and cigarette factories. The Bluegrass country around Lexington is the home of some of the world's finest race horses. Other attractions are Mammoth Cave, the George S. Patton, Jr., Military Museum at Fort Knox, and Old Fort Harrod State Park.

LOUISIANA

Capital: Baton Rouge
Governor: David C. Treen, R (to March 1984)
Lieut. Governor: Robert L. Freeman, D (to March 1984)
Secy. of State: James H. Brown, Jr., D (to March 1984)
Treasurer: Mary Evelyn Parker, D (to March 1984)
Atty. General: William J. Guste, Jr., D (to March 1984)
Organized as territory: March 26, 1804
Entered Union & (rank): April 30, 1812 (18)
Present constitution adopted: 1974
Motto: Union, justice, and confidence
State flower: Magnolia (1900)
State tree: Bald cypress
State bird: Pelican
State song: "Give Me Louisiana," and "You Are My Sunshine"
Nicknames: Pelican State; Sportsman's Paradise; Creole State; Sugar State
Origin of name: In honor of Louis XIV of France
1970 population & (rank): 3,644,637 (20)
1980 population (1980 census) & (rank): 4,203,972 (18)

1980 land area & (rank): 44,930 sq mi. (116,369 sq km) (33)
Geographic center: In Avoyelles Parish, 3 mi. SE of Marksville
Number of parishes (counties): 64
Largest cities (1980 census): New Orleans, 557,482; Baton Rouge, 219,486; Shreveport, 205,815; Lafayette, 81,961; Lake Charles, 75,051; Monroe, 57,597; Alexandria, 51,565
State forests: 1 (8,000 ac.)
State parks: 30 (13,932 ac.)
State general revenue (1980–81 est.): $3,889,745,744
  Federal Grants: $1,419,048,091
State general expenditure (1980–81 est.): $5,599,275,956

Louisiana has a rich, colorful historical background. Early Spanish explorers were Piñeda, 1519; Cabeza de Vaca, 1528; and de Soto in 1541. La Salle reached the mouth of the Mississippi and claimed all the land drained by it and its tributaries for Louis XIV of France in 1682.

Louisiana became a French crown colony in 1731, was ceded to Spain in 1763, returned to France in 1800, and sold by Napoleon to the U.S. as part of the Louisiana Purchase (with large territories to the north and northwest) in 1803.

In 1815, Gen. Andrew Jackson's troops defeated a larger British army in the Battle of New Orleans, neither side aware that the treaty ending the War of 1812 had been signed.

As to total value of its mineral output, Louisiana is a leader in natural gas, salt, petroleum, and sulfur production. Much of the oil and sulfur comes from offshore deposits. The state also produces large crops of sweet potatoes, rice, sugarcane, pecans, soybeans, corn, and cotton.

Leading manufactures include chemicals, processed food, petroleum and coal products, paper, lumber and wood products, transportation equipment, and apparel.

Louisiana marshes supply most of the nation's muskrat fur as well as that of opossum, raccoon, mink, and otter, and large numbers of game birds.

Major points of interest include New Orleans with its French Quarter and Superdome, plantation homes near Natchitoches and New Iberia, Cajun country in the Mississippi delta region, Chalmette National Historical Park, and the state capital at Baton Rouge.

MAINE

Capital: Augusta
Governor: Joseph E. Brennan, D (to Jan. 1983)
Secy. of State: Rodney F. Quinn, D (to Jan. 1983)
Controller: Donald A. Brown (term indefinite)
Atty. General: James Tierney, D (to Jan. 1983)
Entered Union & (rank): March 15, 1820 (23)
Present constitution adopted: 1820
Motto: *Dirigo* (I direct)
State flower: White pine cone and tassel (1895)
State tree: White pine tree (1945)
State bird: Chickadee (1927)
State fish: Landlocked salmon (1969)
State mineral: Tourmaline (1971)
State song: "State of Maine Song" (1937)
Nickname: Pine Tree State
Origin of name: First used to distinguish the mainland from the offshore islands. It has been considered a compliment to Henrietta Maria, Queen of Charles I of England. She was said to have owned the province of Mayne in France.
1970 population & (rank): 993,722 (38)
1980 population (1980 census) & (rank): 1,124,660 (38)

1980 land area & (rank): 30,920 sq mi. (80,083 sq km) (39)
Geographic center: In Piscataquis Co., 18 mi. N of Dover-Foxcroft
Number of counties: 16
Largest cities (1980 census): Portland, 61,572; Lewiston, 40,481; Bangor, 31,643; Auburn, 23,128; South Portland, 22,712; Augusta, 21,819; Biddeford, 19,638
State forests: 1 (21,000 ac.)
State parks: 26 (247,627 ac.)
State historic sites: 18 (403 ac.)
State total revenue (1980): $1,130,949,281
State total expenditure (1980): $1,139,884,453

John Cabot and his son, Sebastian, are believed to have visited the Maine coast in 1498. However, the first permanent English settlements were not established until more than a century later, in 1623.

The first naval action of the Revolutionary War occurred in 1775 when colonials captured the British sloop *Margaretta* off Machias on the Maine coast. In that same year, the British burned Falmouth (now Portland).

Long governed by Massachusetts, Maine became the 23rd state as part of the Missouri Compromise in 1820.

Maine produced 24.9 million hundred weight of potatoes or 9.4% of the national production in 1980 and 95% of the nation's low-bush blueberries. Farm income is also derived from apples, sweet corn, peas, and beans, with poultry and eggs the largest items.

The state is one of the world's largest pulp-paper producers. It ranks fifth in boot-and-shoe manufacturing. With more than 90% of its area forested, Maine turns out wood products from boats to toothpicks.

Maine leads the world in the production of the familiar flat tins of sardines, producing more than 100 million of them annually. Lobstermen normally catch 80–90% of the nation's true total of lobsters.

A scenic seacoast, beaches, lakes, mountains, and resorts make Maine a popular vacationland. There are more than 2,500 lakes and 5,000 streams, plus 26 state parks, to attract hunters, fishermen, skiers, and campers.

Major points of interest are: Bar Harbor, Allagash National Wilderness Waterway, the Wadsworth-Longfellow House in Portland, Roosevelt Campobello International Park, and the St. Croix Island National Monument.

MARYLAND

Capital: Annapolis
Governor: Harry Hughes, D (to Jan. 1983)
Lieut. Gov.: Samuel W. Bogley, D (to Jan. 1983)
Secy. of State: Fred L. Wineland, D (appointed by governor)
Comptroller of the Treasury: Louis L. Goldstein, D (to Jan. 1983)
Treasurer: William S. James, D (to Jan. 1983)
Atty. General: Stephen H. Sachs, D (to Jan. 1983)
Entered Union & (rank): April 28, 1788 (7)
Present constitution adopted: 1867
Motto: *Fatti maschii, parole femine* (Manly deeds, womanly words)
State flower: Black-eyed susan (1918)
State tree: White oak (1941)
State bird: Baltimore oriole (1947)
State dog: Chesapeake Bay retriever (1964)
State fish: Rockfish (1965)

State insect: Baltimore checkerspot butterfly (1973)
State sport: Jousting (1962)
State song: "Maryland! My Maryland!" (1939)
Nicknames: Free State; Old Line State
Origin of name: In honor of Henrietta Maria (Queen of Charles I of England)
1970 population & (rank): 3,923,897 (18)
1980 population (1980 census) & (rank): 4,216,446 (19)
1980 land area & (rank): 9,891 sq mi. (25,618 sq km) (42)
Geographic center: In Prince Georges Co., 4½ mi. NW of Davidsonville
Number of counties: 23, and 1 independent city
Largest cities (1980 census): Baltimore, 786,775; Rockville, 43,811; Hagerstown, 34,132; Bowie, 33,695; Annapolis, 31,740; Frederick, 27,557; Gaithersburg, 26,424
State forests: 10 (120,921 ac.)
State parks: 42 (70,302 ac.)
State general revenue (1981 est.): $2,653,326,000
State general expenditure (1981 est.): $2,837,605,750

In 1608, Chesapeake Bay was explored by Capt. John Smith. Charles I granted a royal charter to Cecil Calvert, Lord Baltimore, in 1632 and English Roman Catholics landed on St. Clement's (now Blakistone Island) in 1634. Religious freedom, granted all Christians in the Toleration act passed by the Maryland assembly in 1649, was ended by a Puritan revolt, 1654–58.

In 1814, when the British unsuccessfully tried to capture Baltimore, the bombardment of Fort McHenry inspired Francis Scott Key to write *The Star Spangled Banner.*

Maryland is almost cut in two by the Chesapeake Bay, and the many estuaries and rivers create one of the longest waterfronts of any state. The Bay produces more seafood—oysters, crabs, clams, fin fish—than any comparable body of water. Important agricultural products, in order of cash value, are chickens, dairy products, corn, cattle, tobacco, and vegetables. Maryland is a leader in vegetable canning. Sand, gravel, lime and cement, stone, coal, and clay are the chief mineral products.

Manufacturing industries produce missiles, airplanes, steel, clothing, and chemicals. Baltimore, home of The Johns Hopkins University and Hospital, ranks as the nation's second port in foreign tonnage. Annapolis, site of the U.S. Naval Academy, has one of the earliest state houses (1772–79) still in regular use by a State government.

Among the popular attractions in Maryland are the Fort McHenry National Monument, Harpers Ferry and Chesapeake and Ohio Canal National Historical Parks, St. Marys City restoration near Leonardtown, USS *Constellation* at Baltimore, U.S. Naval Academy in Annapolis, Assateague Island National Seashore, and Catoctin Mountain and Piscataway parks.

MASSACHUSETTS

Capital: Boston
Governor: Edward King, D (to Jan. 1983)
Lieut. Governor: Thomas P. O'Neill III, D (to Jan. 1983)
Secy. of the Commonwealth: Michael Joseph Connolly, D (to Jan. 1983)
Treasurer & Receiver-General: Robert Q. Crane, D (to Jan. 1983)
Auditor of the Commonwealth: John J. Finnegan, D (to Jan. 1983)
Atty. General: Francis X. Bellotti (to Jan. 1983)
Entered Union & (rank): Feb. 6, 1788 (6)

Motto: *Ense petit placidam sub libertate quietem* (By the sword we seek peace, but peace only under liberty)
State flower: Mayflower (1918)
State tree: American elm (1941)
State bird: Chickadee (1941)
State colors: Blue and gold
State song: "All Hail to Massachusetts" (1966)
State beverage: Cranberry juice (1970)
State horse: Morgan horse (1970)
State insect: Ladybug (1974)
Nicknames: Bay State; Old Colony State
Origin of name: From two Indian words meaning "Great mountain place"
1970 population & (rank): 5,689,170 (10)
1980 population (1980 census) & (rank): 5,737,037 (11)
1980 land area & (rank): 7,826 sq mi. (20,269 sq km) (45)
Geographic center: In Worcester Co., in S part of city of Worcester
Number of counties: 14
Largest cities (1980 census): Boston, 562,994; Worcester, 161,799; Springfield, 152,319; New Bedford, 98,478; Cambridge, 95,322; Brockton, 95,172; Fall River, 94,574
State forests and parks: 129 (242,000 ac.)
State general revenue (1979–80): $6,464,453,235
State general expenditure (1979–80): $6,786,663,007

1. The Metropolitan District Commission, an agency of the Commonwealth serving municipalities in the Boston area, has about 14,000 acres of parkways and reservations under its jurisdiction.

Massachusetts has played a significant role in American history since the Pilgrims, seeking religious freedom, founded Plymouth Colony in 1620.

As one of the most important of the 13 colonies, Massachusetts became a leader in resisting British oppression. In 1773, the Boston Tea Party protested unjust taxation. The Minutemen started the American Revolution by battling British troops at Lexington and Concord on April 19, 1775.

During the 19th century, Massachusetts was famous for the vigorous intellectual activity of famous writers and educators and for its expanding commercial fishing, shipping, and manufacturing interests.

Massachusetts pioneered in the manufacture of textiles and shoes. Today, these industries have been replaced in importance by activity in the electronics and communications equipment fields.

The state's cranberry crop is the nation's largest. Also important are dairy and poultry products, nursery and greenhouse produce, vegetables, and fruit.

Tourism has become an important factor in the economy of the state because of its numerous recreational areas and historical landmarks.

Cape Cod has summer theaters, water sports, and an artists' colony at Provincetown. Tanglewood, in the Berkshires, features the summer concerts of the Boston Symphony.

Among the many other points of interest are Old Sturbridge Village, Minute Man National Historical Park between Lexington and Concord, and, in Boston: Old North Church, Old State House, Faneuil Hall, the USS *Constitution* and the John F. Kennedy Library.

MICHIGAN

Capital: Lansing
Governor: William C. Milliken, R (to Jan. 1983)
Lieut. Governor: James H. Brickley, R (to Jan. 1983)

Secy. of State: Richard H. Austin, D (to Jan. 1983)
Atty. General: Frank J. Kelley, D (to Jan. 1983)
Organized as territory: Jan. 11, 1805
Entered Union & (rank): Jan. 26, 1837 (26)
Present constitution adopted: April 1, 1963, (effective Jan. 1, 1964)
Motto: *Si quaeris peninsulam amoenam circumspice* (If you seek a pleasant peninsula, look around you)
State flower: Apple blossom (1897)
State bird: Robin
State fish: Brook trout (1965)
State gem: Isle Royal Greenstone (Chlorastrolite) (1972)
State stone: Petoskey stone (1965)
Nickname: Wolverine State
Origin of name: From two Indian words meaning "great lake"
1970 population & (rank): 8,881,826 (7)
1980 population (1980 census) & (rank): 9,258,344 (8)
1980 land area & (rank): 56,817 sq mi. (147,156 sq km) (22)
Geographic center: In Wexford Co., 5 mi. NNW of Cadillac
Number of counties: 83
Largest cities (1980 census): Detroit, 1,203,339; Grand Rapids, 181,843; Flint, 159,611; Lansing, 130,414; Ann Arbor, 107,316; Livonia, 104,814
State forests: 33 (3,762,184 ac.)
State parks and recreation areas: 92 (216,857 ac.)
State general revenue (1979): $9,798,730,000
State general expenditure (1979): $9,442,455,000

Indian tribes were living in the Michigan region when the first European, Étienne Brulé of France, arrived in 1618. Other French explorers, including Marquette, Jolliet, and La Salle, followed, and the first permanent settlement was established in 1668 at Sault Ste. Marie. France was ousted from the territory by Great Britain in 1763, following the French and Indian War.

After the Revolutionary War, the U.S. acquired most of the region, which remained the scene of constant conflict between the British and U.S. forces and their respective Indian allies through the War of 1812.

Bordering on four of the five Great Lakes, Michigan is divided into Upper and Lower Peninsulas by the Straits of Mackinac, which link Lakes Michigan and Huron. The two parts of the state are connected by the Mackinac Bridge, one of the world's longest suspension bridges. To the north, connecting Lakes Superior and Huron are the busy Sault Ste. Marie Canals.

While Michigan ranks first among the states in production of motor vehicles and parts, it is also a leader in many other manufacturing and processing lines including prepared cereals, machine tools, airplane parts, refrigerators, hardware, steel springs, and furniture.

The state produces important amounts of iron, copper, iodine, gypsum, bromine, salt, lime, gravel, and cement. Michigan's farms grow apples, cherries, pears, grapes, potatoes, and sugar beets and the annual value of its forest products is estimated at $2 billion. With over 36,000 miles of streams, some 11,000 lakes, and a 2,000 mile shoreline, Michigan is a prime area for both commercial and sport fishing.

Points of interest are the automobile plants in Dearborn, Detroit, Flint, Lansing, and Pontiac; Mackinac Island; Pictured Rocks and Sleeping Bear Dunes National Lakeshores, Greenfield Village near Dearborn; and the many summer resorts along both the inland and Great Lakes.

MINNESOTA

Capital: St. Paul
Governor: Albert H. Quie, R (to Jan. 1983)
Lieut. Governor: Lou Wangberg, R (to Jan. 1983)
Secy. of State: Joan Grow (to Jan. 1983)
State Auditor: Arne Carlson, R (to Jan. 1983)
Atty. General: Warren Spannus, D (to Jan. 1983)
State Treasurer: Jim Lord (to Jan. 1983)
Organized as territory: March 3, 1849
Entered Union & (rank): May 11, 1858 (32)
Present constitution adopted: 1858
Motto: L'Etoile du Nord (The North Star)
State flower: Showy lady slipper (1902)
State tree: Red (or Norway) pine
State bird: Common loon (also called Great Northern Diver)
State song: "Hail Minnesota"
Nicknames: North Star State; Gopher State; Land of 10,000 Lakes
Origin of name: From a Dakota Indian word meaning "sky-tinted water"
1970 population & (rank): 3,806,103 (19)
1980 population (1980 census) & (rank): 4,077,148 (21)
1980 land area & (rank): 79,289 sq mi. (205,359 sq km) (14)
Geographic center: In Crow Wing Co., 10 mi. SW of Brainerd
Number of counties: 87
Largest cities (1980 census): Minneapolis, 370,951; St. Paul, 270,230; Duluth, 92,811; Bloomington, 81,831; Rochester, 57,855; Edina, 46,073; St. Cloud, 42,566
State forests: 55 (2,984,000 ac.)
State parks: 92 (202,205 ac.)
Total revenue (Fiscal 1980): $3,681,811,300
Total expenditures (Fiscal 1980): $3,560,901,300

Following the visits of several French explorers, fur traders, and missionaries, including Marquette and Jolliet and La Salle, the region was claimed for Louis XIV by Daniel Greysolon, Sieur Duluth, in 1679.

The U.S. acquired eastern Minnesota from Great Britain after the Revolutionary War and 20 years later bought the western part from France in the Louisiana Purchase of 1803. Much of the region was explored by U.S. Army Lt. Zebulon M. Pike before cession of the northern strip of Minnesota bordering Canada by Britain in 1818.

The state is rich in natural resources. A few square miles of land in the north in the Mesabi, Cuyuna, and Vermillion ranges, produce more than 60% of the nation's iron ore. The state's farms rank high in yields of corn, wheat, rye, alfalfa, and sugar beets. Other leading farm products include butter, eggs, milk, potatoes, green peas, barley, and livestock.

Minnesota's factory production includes non-electrical machinery, fabricated metals, flour-mill products, plastics, electronic computers, scientific instruments, and processed foods.

Minneapolis is the trade center of the Northwest; St. Paul is the nation's biggest publisher of calendars and law books. These "twin cities" are the nation's third largest trucking center. Duluth has the nation's largest inland harbor and now handles a significant amount of foreign trade. Rochester is the home of the Mayo Clinic, an internationally famous medical center.

Today, tourism is a major revenue producer in Minnesota, with fishing, hunting, water sports, and winter sports bringing in millions of visitors each year.

Among the most popular attractions are the St.

Paul Winter Carnival; the Tyrone Guthrie Theatre, the Institute of Arts, Walker Art Center, and Minnehaha Park, in Minneapolis; Voyageurs National Park; North Shore Drive; and the Minnesota Zoological Gardens.

Battlefield Site, Tupelo National Battlefield, and part of Natchez Trace National Parkway. Pre-Civil War mansions are the special pride of Natchez, Oxford, Hattiesburg, and Jackson.

MISSISSIPPI

Capital: Jackson
Governor: William F. Winter, D (to Jan. 1984)
Lieut. Governor: Brad Dye, D (to Jan. 1984)
Secy. of State: Edwin Lloyd Pittman, D (to Jan. 1984)
Treasurer: Bill Cole, D (to Jan. 1984)
Atty. General: William A. (Bill) Allain (to Jan. 1984)
Organized as Territory: April 7, 1798
Entered Union & (rank): Dec. 10, 1817 (20)
Present constitution adopted: 1890
Motto: *Virtute es armis* (By valor and arms)
State flower: Flower or bloom of the magnolia or evergreen magnolia (1952)
State tree: Magnolia (1938)
State bird: Mockingbird (1944)
State song: "Go, Mississippi" (1962)
Nickname: Magnolia State
Origin of name: From an Indian word meaning "Father of Waters"
1970 population & (rank): 2,216,994 (29)
1980 population (1980 census) & (rank): 2,520,638 (31)
1980 land area & (rank): 47,296 sq mi. (122,497 sq km) (31)
Geographic center: In Leake Co., 9 mi. WNW of Carthage
Number of counties: 82
Largest cities (1980 census): Jackson, 202,895; Biloxi, 49,311; Hattiesburg, 40,829; Greenville, 40,613; Gulfport, 39,676; Pascagoula, 29,318
State forests: 1 (1,760 ac.)
State parks: 27 (16,763 ac.)
State general and special revenue (1980): $919,558,778
State general and special expenditure (1980): $976,989,649

First explored for Spain by Hernando de Soto who discovered the Mississippi River in 1540, the region was later claimed by France. In 1699, a French group under Sieur d'Iberville established the first permanent settlement near present-day Biloxi.

Great Britain took over the area in 1763 after the French and Indian War, ceding it to the U.S. in 1783 after the Revolution. Spain did not relinquish its claims until 1798, and in 1810 the U.S. annexed West Florida from Spain, including what is now southern Mississippi.

Mississippi, the stronghold of the Old South, has until the past decade been one of the least industrialized states, with more than half its population making a living from the soil. However, a recent industrialization program has attracted manufacturing industries such as lumber, furniture, paper, food processing, apparel, chemicals, transportation equipment, and machinery.

Cotton, nevertheless, is still king with the state ranking second to Texas in cotton production, though soybeans have become Mississippi's largest crop. Other important farm products are corn, peanuts, pecans, rice, sugarcane, sweet potatoes, and hay. Poultry and eggs are also important.

The state abounds in historical landmarks and is the home of the Vicksburg National Military Park where visitors may see the remains of forts, trenches, and other military relics used in the 1863 Union-army siege of the city. Other National Park Service areas are Brices Cross Roads National

MISSOURI

Capital: Jefferson City
Governor: Christopher S. Bond, R (to Jan. 1985)
Lieut. Governor: Kenneth J. Rothman, D (to Jan. 1985)
Secy. of State: James C. Kirkpatrick, D (to Jan. 1985)
Auditor: James F. Antonio, R (to Jan. 1983)
Treasurer: Mel Carnahan, D (to Jan. 1985)
Atty. General: John D. Ashcroft, R (to Jan. 1985)
Organized as territory: June 4, 1812
Entered Union & (rank): Aug. 10, 1821 (24)
Present constitution adopted: 1945
Motto: *Salus populi suprema lex esto* (The welfare of the people shall be the supreme law)
State flower: Hawthorn (1923)
State bird: Bluebird (1927)
State colors: Red, white, and blue (1913)
State song: "Missouri Waltz" (1949)
State rock: Mozarkite (1967)
State mineral: Galena (1967)
Nickname: Show-me State
Origin of name: Named after a tribe called Missouri Indians. "Missouri" means "town of the large canoes."
1970 population & (rank): 4,677,623 (13)
1980 population (1980 census) & (rank): 4,917,444 (15)
1980 land area & (rank): 68,995 sq mi. (178,697 sq km) (18)
Geographic center: In Miller Co., 20 mi. SW of Jefferson City
Number of counties: 114, plus 1 independent city
Largest cities (1980 census): St. Louis, 453,085; Kansas City, 448,159; Springfield, 133,116; Independence, 111,806; Columbia, 62,061; Florissant, 55,372
State forests and Tower sites: 93 (265,000 ac.)
State parks: 68 (98,422 ac.)[1]
State cash receipts (1980): $3,493,741,780
State general expenditure (1980): $3,518,774,574

---

1. Includes 19 historic sites and 1 archaeological site.

De Soto visited the Missouri area in 1541. France's claim to the entire region was based on La Salle's travels in 1682. French fur traders established Ste. Genevieve in 1735 and St. Louis was first settled in 1764.

The U.S. gained Missouri from France as part of the Louisiana Purchase in 1803, and the territory was admitted as a state following the Missouri Compromise of 1820. Throughout the pre-Civil War period and during the war, Missourians were sharply divided in their opinions about slavery and in their allegiances, supplying both Union and Confederate forces with troops. However, the state itself remained in the Union.

Historically, Missouri played a leading role as a gateway to the West, St. Joseph being the eastern starting point of the Pony Express, while the much-traveled Santa Fe and Oregon Trails began in Independence. Now a popular vacationland, Missouri has 11 major lakes and numerous fishing streams, springs, and caves. Bagnell Dam, across the Osage River in the Ozarks, completed in 1931, created one of the largest man-made lakes in the world, covering 65,000 acres of surface area.

Manufacturing, paced by the aerospace industry, provides more income and jobs than any other segment of the economy. Missouri is also a leading producer of transportation equipment, shoes, lead, and beer. Among the major crops are corn, soybeans, wheat, oats, barley, potatoes, tobacco, and cotton.

Points of interest include Mark Twain's boyhood home and Mark Twain Cave (Hannibal), the Harry S. Truman Library and Museum (Independence), the house where Jesse James was killed in St. Joseph, Jefferson National Expansion Memorial (St. Louis), and the Ozark National Scenic Riverway.

MONTANA

Capital: Helena
Governor: Ted Schwinden, D (to Jan. 1984)
Lieut. Governor: George Turman, D (to Jan. 1984)
Secy. of State: Jim Waltermire, R (to Jan. 1984)
Auditor: E. V. "Sonny" Omholt, R (to Jan. 1981)
Atty. General: Michael Greely, D (to Jan. 1981)
Organized as territory: May 26, 1864
Entered Union & (rank): Nov. 8, 1889 (41)
Present constitution adopted: 1972
Motto: *Oro y plata* (Gold and silver)
State flower: Bitterroot (1895)
State tree: Ponderosa pine (1949)
State stones: Sapphire and agate (1969)
State bird: Western meadow lark (1931)
State song: "Montana" (1945)
Nickname: Treasure State
Origin of name: Chosen from Latin dictionary by J. M. Ashley. It is a Latinized Spanish word.
1970 population & (rank): 694,409 (43)
1980 population (1980 census) & (rank): 786,690 (44)
1980 land area & (rank): 145,587 sq mi. (377,070 sq km) (4)
Geographic center: In Fergus Co., 12 mi. W of Lewistown
Number of counties: 56, plus small part of Yellowstone National Park
Largest cities (1980 census): Billings, 66,798; Great Falls, 56,725; Butte-Silver Bow, 37,205; Missoula, 33,388; Helena, 23,938; Bozeman, 21,645; Havre, 10,891
State forests: 7 (214,000 ac.)
State parks and recreation areas: 68 (18,273 ac.)
State general revenue (1979–80): $248,131,743
State general expenditure (1979–80): $236,116,548

First explored for France by François and Louis-Joseph Verendrye in the early 1740s, much of the region was acquired by the U.S. from France as part of the Louisiana Purchase in 1803. Before western Montana was obtained from Great Britain in the Oregon Treaty of 1846, American trading posts and forts had been established in the territory.

The major Indian wars (1867–1877) included the famous 1876 Battle of the Little Big Horn, better known as "Custer's Last Stand," in which Cheyennes and Sioux killed George A. Custer and more than 200 of his men in southeastern Montana.

Much of Montana's early history was concerned with mining with copper, lead, zinc, silver, coal, and oil as principal products.

Butte, sitting on the "richest hill in the world," is the center of the area that once supplied half of the U.S. copper.

Fields of grain cover much of Montana's plains; it ranks high among the states in wheat and barley, with rye, oats, flaxseed, sugar beets, and potatoes other important crops. Sheep and cattle raising make significant contributions to the state's economy.

Tourist attractions include hunting, fishing, skiing, and dude ranching. Glacier National Park, on the Continental Divide, is a scenic and vacation wonderland with 60 glaciers, 200 lakes, and many streams with good trout fishing.

Other major points of interest include the Custer Battlefield National Monument, Virginia City, Yellowstone National Park, Museum of the Plains Indians at Browning, and the Fort Union Trading Post and Grant-Kohr's Ranch National Historic Sites.

NEBRASKA

Capital: Lincoln
Governor: Charles Thone, R (to Jan. 1983)
Lieut. Governor: Roland Luedtke, R (to Jan. 1983)
Secy. of State: Allen J. Beermann, R (to Jan. 1983)
Atty. General: Paul L. Douglas, R (to Jan. 1983)
Auditor: Ray A. C. Johnson, R (to Jan. 1983)
Treasurer: Frank Marsh, R (to Jan. 1983)
Organized as territory: May 30, 1854
Entered Union & (rank): March 1, 1867 (37)
Present constitution adopted: Nov. 1, 1875 (extensively amended 1919–20)
Motto: Equality before the law
State flower: Goldenrod (1895)
State tree: Cottonwood (1972)
State bird: Western meadow lark (1929)
State insect: Honey Bee (1975)
State gem stone: Blue agate (1967)
State rock: Prairie agate (1967)
State fossil: Mammoth (1967)
State song: "Beautiful Nebraska" (1967)
Nicknames: Cornhusker State; Beef State; Tree Planters State
Origin of name: From an Oto Indian word meaning "flat water"
1970 population & (rank): 1,485,333 (35)
1980 population (1980 census) & (rank): 1,570,006 (35)
1980 land area & (rank): 76,483 sq mi. (198,091 sq km) (15)
Geographic center: In Custer Co., 10 mi. NW of Broken Bow
Number of counties: 93
Largest cities (1980 census): Omaha, 311,681; Lincoln, 171,932; Grand Island, 33,180; North Platte, 24,479; Fremont, 23,979; Hastings, 23,045; Bellevue, 21,813
State forests: None
State parks: 93 areas, 4 categories, 5 major areas
State general revenue (1979–80): $714,784,346
State general expenditure (1979–80): $660,810,784

French fur traders first visited Nebraska in the early 1700s. Part of the Louisiana Purchase in 1803, Nebraska was explored by Lewis and Clark in 1804–06.

Robert Stuart pioneered the Oregon Trail across Nebraska in 1812–13 and the first permanent settlement was established at Bellevue in 1823. Western Nebraska was acquired by treaty following the Mexican War in 1848. The Union Pacific began its transcontinental railroad at Omaha in 1865. In 1937, Nebraska became the only state in the Union to have a unicameral (one-house) legislature. Members are elected to it without party designation.

Nebraska is a leading grain-producer with bumper crops of rye, corn, and wheat. More varieties of grass, valuable for forage, grow in this state than in any other in the nation.

The state's sizable cattle and hog industries make Omaha with its surrounding area the nation's largest meat-packing center and the second-largest cattle market in the world.

Manufacturing has become diversified in Nebraska, strengthening the state's economic base. Firms making electronic components, auto accessories, pharmaceuticals, and mobile homes have joined such older industries as clothing, farm machinery, chemicals, and transportation equipment. Oil was discovered in 1939 and natural gas in 1949.

Among the principal attractions are Agate Fossil Beds, Homestead, and Scotts Bluff National Monuments; Chimney Rock National Historic Site; a recreated pioneer village at Minden; the Union stockyards in Omaha; the Stuhr Museum of the Prairie Pioneer with 57 original 19th-century buildings near Grand Island; and the Sheldon Memorial Art Gallery at the University of Nebraska in Lincoln.

NEVADA

Capital: Carson City
Governor: Robert F. List, R (to Jan. 1983)
Lieut. Governor: Myron E. Leavitt, D (to Jan. 1983)
Secy. of State: Wm. D. Swackhamer, D (to Jan. 1983)
State Treasurer: Stan Colton, D (to Jan. 1983)
Controller: Wilson McGowan, R (to Jan. 1983)
Atty. General: Richard H. Bryan, D (to Jan. 1983)
Organized as territory: March 2, 1861
Entered Union & (rank): Oct. 31, 1864 (36)
Present constitution adopted: 1864
Motto: All for Our Country
State flower: Sagebrush (1967)
State tree: Single-leaf pinon (1953)
State bird: Mountain bluebird (1967)
State animal: Desert bighorn sheep (1973)
State colors: Silver and blue (unofficial)
State song: "Home Means Nevada" (1933)
Nicknames: Sagebrush State; Silver State; Battle-born State
Origin of name: Spanish: "snowcapped"
1970 population & (rank): 488,738 (47)
1980 population (1980 census) & (rank): 799,184 (43)
1980 land area & (rank): 109,889 sq mi. (284,613 sq km) (7)
Geographic center: In Lander Co., 26 mi. SE of Austin
Number of counties: 16, plus 1 independent city
Largest cities (1980 census): Las Vegas, 164,674; Reno, 100,756; North Las Vegas, 42,739; Sparks, 40,780; Carson City, 32,022; Henderson, 24,363; Boulder City, 9,590
State forests: None
State parks: 20 (150,000 ac., including leased lands)
General fund revenue (1979–80): $332,000,000
General fund expenditure (1979–80): $354,000,000, made possible by surpluses from previous years.

Trappers and traders, including Jedediah Smith and Peter Skene Ogden, entered the Nevada area in the 1820s. In 1843–45, John C. Fremont and Kit Carson explored the Great Basin and Sierra Nevada.

In 1848 following the Mexican War, the U.S. obtained the region and the first permanent settlement was a Mormon trading post near present-day Genoa.

The driest state in the nation with an average annual rainfall of only 3.73 inches, much of Nevada is uninhabited, sagebrush-covered desert.

Nevada was made famous by the discovery of the fabulous Comstock Lode in 1859 and its mines have produced large quantities of gold, silver, cop-

per, lead, zinc, mercury, barite, and tungsten. Oil was discovered in 1954. Copper now far exceeds all other minerals in value of production.

In 1931, the state created two industries, divorce and gambling. For many years, Reno and Las Vegas were the "divorce capitals of the nation." More liberal divorce laws in many states have ended this distinction, but Nevada is the gambling and entertainment capital of the U.S. State gambling taxes account for 45% of tax revenues. Although Nevada leads the nation in per capita gambling revenue, it ranks only fourth in total gambling revenue.

Near Las Vegas, on the Colorado River, stands Hoover Dam, which impounds the waters of Lake Mead, one of the world's largest artificial lakes.

The state's agricultural crop consists mainly of hay, alfalfa seed, barley, and wheat.

Nevada manufactures gaming devices, chemicals, forest products, suntan lotion, and stone-clay-glass products.

Major resort areas flourish in Lake Tahoe, Reno, and Las Vegas. Recreation areas include those at Pyramid Lake, Lake Tahoe, and Lake Mead and Lake Mohave, both in Lake Mead National Recreation Area. Among the other attractions are Hoover Dam, Virginia City, and Lehman Caves National Monument.

NEW HAMPSHIRE

Capital: Concord
Governor: Hugh Gallen, D (to Jan. 1983)
Secy. of State: William M. Gardner, D (to Jan. 1983)
Comptroller: Arthur H. Fowler
Atty. General: Gregory Smith
Entered Union & (rank): June 21, 1788 (9)
Present constitution adopted: 1784
Motto: Live free or die
State flower: Purple lilac (1919)
State tree: White birch (1947)
State bird: Purple finch (1957)
State songs: "Old New Hampshire" (1949) and "New Hampshire, My New Hampshire" (1963)
Nickname: Granite State
Origin of name: From the English county of Hampshire
1970 population & (rank): 737,681 (41)
1980 population (1980 census) & (rank): 920,610 (42)
1980 land area & (rank): 9,027 sq mi. (23,380 sq km) (44)
Geographic center: In Belknap Co., 3 mi. E of Ashland
Number of counties: 10
Largest cities (1980 census): Manchester, 90,936; Nashua, 67,865; Concord, 30,400; Portsmouth, 26,254; Dover, 22,377; Rochester, 21,560; Keene, 21,449
State forests & parks: 175 (96,975 ac.)
State revenue (1980): $612,359,356
State expenditure (1980): $682,945,560

Under an English land grant, Capt. John Smith sent settlers to establish a fishing colony at the mouth of the Piscataqua River, near present-day Rye and Dover, in 1623. Capt. John Mason, who participated in the founding of Portsmouth in 1630, gave New Hampshire its name.

After a 38-year period of union with Massachusetts, New Hampshire was made a separate royal colony in 1679. As leaders in the revolutionary cause, New Hampshire delegates received the honor of being the first to vote for the Declaration of Independence on July 4, 1776. New Hampshire is the only state that ever played host at the formal conclusion of a foreign war when, in 1905, Portsmouth was the scene of the treaty ending the Russo-Japanese War.

Abundant water power early turned New Hampshire into an industrial state and manufacturing is the principal source of income in the state. The most important industrial products are leather goods, electrical and other machinery, textiles, and pulp and paper products.

Dairy and poultry farming and growing fruit, truck vegetables, corn, potatoes, and hay are the major agricultural pursuits.

Tourism, because of New Hampshire's scenic and recreational resources, now brings over $400 million into the state annually.

Vacation attractions include Lake Winnipesaukee, largest of 1,300 lakes and ponds; the 724,000-acre White Mountain National Forest; Daniel Webster's birthplace near Franklin; Strawberry Banke, restored building of the original settlement at Portsmouth; and the famous "Old Man of the Mountain" granite head profile, the state's official emblem, at Franconia.

NEW JERSEY

Capital: Trenton
Governor: Brendan T. Byrne, D (to Jan. 1982)
Secy. of State: Donald Lan (to Jan. 1982) (apptd. by Governor)
Treasurer: Clifford A. Goldman, D (to Jan. 1982) (apptd. by Governor)
Atty. General: James Zazzali, D (to Jan. 1982)
Entered Union & (rank): Dec. 18, 1787 (3)
Present constitution adopted: 1947
Motto: Liberty and prosperity
State flower: Purple violet (1913)
State bird: Eastern goldfinch (1935)
State insect: Honeybee
State tree: Red oak (1950)
State animal: Horse (1977)
State colors: Buff and blue (1965)
State song: None
Nickname: Garden State
Origin of name: From the Channel Isle of Jersey
1970 population & (rank): 7,171,112 (8)
1980 population (1980 census) & (rank): 7,364,158 (9)
1980 land area & (rank): 7,521 sq mi. (19,479 sq km) (46)
Geographic center: In Mercer Co., 5 mi. SE of Trenton
Number of counties: 21
Largest cities (1980 census): Newark, 329,248; Jersey City, 223,532; Paterson, 137,970; Elizabeth, 106,201; Trenton, 92,124; Camden, 84,910; Clifton, 74,388
State forests: 11
State parks: 40 (73,483 ac.)
State general revenue (1979–80): $3,504,516,143
State appropriations (1979–80): $4,655,547,361

New Jersey's early colonial history was involved with that of New York (New Netherlands), of which it was a part. One year after the Dutch surrender to England in 1664, New Jersey was organized as an English colony under Gov. Philip Carteret.

In the late 1600s the colony was divided between Carteret and William Penn; later it would be administered by the royal governor of New York. Finally, in 1738, New Jersey was separated from New York under its own royal governor, Lewis Morris.

Because of its key location between New York City and Philadelphia, New Jersey saw much fighting during the American Revolution.

Today, New Jersey, an area of wide industrial diversification, is known as the Crossroads of the East. Products from over 15,000 factories can be delivered overnight to almost 60 million people, representing 12 states and the District of Columbia. The greatest single industry is chemicals and New Jersey is one of the foremost research centers in the world. Many large oil refineries are located in northern New Jersey and other important manufactures are pharmaceuticals, instruments, machinery, electrical goods, and apparel.

Of the total land area, 43% is forested and about 24% is devoted to agriculture. The state ranks high in production of almost all garden vegetables. Tomatoes, asparagus, corn, and blueberries are important crops, and poultry farming and dairying make significant contributions to the state's economy.

Tourism is the second largest industry in New Jersey. The state has numerous resort areas on 127 miles of Atlantic coastline. In 1977, New Jersey voters approved legislation allowing legalized casino gambling in Atlantic City. Points of interest include the Walt Whitman House in Camden, the Delaware Water Gap, the Edison National Historic Site in West Orange, and Princeton University.

NEW MEXICO

Capital: Santa Fe
Governor: Bruce King, D (to Jan. 1983)
Lieut. Governor: Roberto A. Mondragon, D (to Jan. 1983)
Secy. of State: Shirley Hooper, D (to Jan. 1983)
Atty. General: Jeff Bingaman, D (to Jan. 1983)
State Auditor: Alvino E. Castillo, D (to Jan. 1983)
State Treasurer: Jan Alan Hartke, D (to Jan. 1983)
Commissioner of Public Lands: Alex J. Armijo, D (to Jan. 1983)
Organized as territory: Sept. 9, 1850
Entered Union & (rank): Jan. 6, 1912 (47)
Present constitution adopted: 1911
Motto: *Crescit eundo* (It grows as it goes)
State flower: Yucca (1927)
State tree: Pinon (1949)
State animal: Black bear (1963)
State bird: Roadrunner (1949)
State fish: Cutthroat trout (1955)
State vegetables: Chile and frijol (1965)
State gem: Turquoise (1967)
State colors: Red and yellow of old Spain (1925)
State song: "O Fair New Mexico" (1917)
Spanish language state song: "Asi Es Nuevo Mejico" (1971)
Nicknames: Land of Enchantment; Sunshine State
Origin of name: From the country of Mexico
1970 population & (rank): 1,017,055 (37)
1980 population (1980 census) & (rank): 1,299,968 (37)
1980 land area & (rank): 121,412 sq mi. (314,457 sq km) (5)
Geographic center: In Torrance Co., 12 mi. SSW of Willard
Number of counties: 33
Largest cities (1980 census): Albuquerque, 331,767; Santa Fe, 48,899; Las Cruces, 45,086; Roswell, 39,676; Clovis, 31,194; Farmington, 30,729; Hobbs, 28,794
State-owned forested land: 933,000 ac.
State parks: 29 (105,012 ac.)
State general revenue (1982 est.): $1,247,665,000
State general expenditure (1982 est.): $1,073,832,271

Francisco Vásquez de Coronado, Spanish explorer searching for gold, traveled the region that became New Mexico in 1540–42. In 1598 the first Spanish settlement was established on the Rio Grande River by Juan de Onate and in 1610 Santa Fe was founded and made the capital of New Mexico.

The U.S. acquired most of New Mexico in 1848, as a result of the Mexican War, and the remainder in the 1853 Gadsden Purchase. Union troops captured the territory from the Confederates during the Civil War. With the surrender of Geronimo in 1886, the Apache Wars and most of the Indian troubles in the area were ended.

Since 1945, New Mexico has been a leader in energy research and development with extensive experiments conducted at Los Alamos Scientific Laboratory and Sandia Laboratories in the nuclear, solar, and geothermal areas.

Minerals are the state's richest natural resource and New Mexico leads the U.S. in output of uranium and potassium salts. Petroleum, natural gas, copper, gold, silver, zinc, lead, and molybdenum also contribute heavily to the state's income.

The principal manufacturing industries include food products, chemicals, transportation equipment, lumber, electrical machinery, and stone-clay-glass products. More than two thirds of New Mexico's farm income comes from livestock products, especially sheep. Cotton, pecans, and sorghum are the most important field crops. Corn, peanuts, beans, onions, and lettuce are also grown.

Tourist attractions in New Mexico include the Carlsbad Caverns National Park, Inscription Rock at El Morro National Monument, the ruins at Fort Union, Billy the Kid mementos at Lincoln, and the White Sands and Gila Cliff Dwellings National Monuments.

NEW YORK

Capital: Albany
Governor: Hugh L. Carey, D (to Jan. 1983)
Lieut. Governor: Mario M. Cuomo, D (to Jan. 1983)
Secy. of State: Basil A. Paterson, D (to Jan. 1983)
Comptroller: Edward V. Regan, R (to Jan. 1983)
Atty. General: Robert Abrams, D (to Jan. 1983)
Entered Union & (rank): July 26, 1788 (11)
Present constitution adopted: 1777 (last revised 1938)
Motto: *Excelsior* (Ever upward)
State animal: Beaver (1975)
State fish: Brook trout (1975)
State gem: Garnet (1969)
State flower: Rose (1955)
State tree: Sugar maple (1956)
State bird: Bluebird
State song: None
Nickname: Empire State
Origin of name: In honor of the English Duke of York
1970 population & (rank): 18,241,391 (2)
1980 population (1980 census) & (rank): 17,557,288 (2)
1980 land area & (rank): 47,831 sq mi. (123,882 sq km) (30)
Geographic center: In Madison Co., 12 mi. S of Oneida and 26 mi. SW of Utica
Number of counties: 62
Largest cities (1980 census): New York, 7,071,030; Buffalo, 357,870; Rochester, 241,741; Yonkers, 195,351; Syracuse, 170,105; Albany, 101,727; Utica, 75,632
State forest preserves: Adirondacks, 2,500,000 ac., Catskills, 250,000 ac.
State parks: 145 (more than 220,000 ac.)
State general fund income (1981–82): $15,196,000
State general fund outgo (1981–82): $15,196,000

Giovanni da Verrazano, Italian-born navigator sailing for France, discovered New York Bay in 1524. Henry Hudson, an Englishman employed by the Dutch, reached the bay and sailed up the river now bearing his name in 1609, the same year that northern New York was explored and claimed for France by Samuel de Champlain.

In 1624 the first permanent Dutch settlement was established at Fort Orange (now Albany); one year later Peter Minuit is said to have purchased Manhattan Island from the Indians for trinkets worth about $24 and founded the Dutch colony of New Amsterdam (now New York City), which was surrendered to the English in 1664.

For a short time, New York City was the U.S. capital and George Washington was inaugurated there as first President on April 30, 1789.

New York's extremely rapid commercial growth may be partly attributed to Governor De Witt Clinton, who pushed through the construction of the Erie Canal (Buffalo to Albany), which was opened in 1825. Today, the 559-mile Governor Thomas E. Dewey Thruway connects New York City with Buffalo and with Connecticut, Massachusetts, and Pennsylvania express highways. Two toll-free superhighways, the Adirondack Northway (linking Albany with the Canadian border) and the North-South-Expressway (crossing central New York from the Pennsylvania border to the Thousand Islands) have been opened.

New York, with the great metropolis of New York City, is the spectacular nerve center of the nation. It is a leader in manufacturing, foreign trade, commercial and financial transactions, book and magazine publishing, and theatrical production.

New York City is not only a national but an international leader. A leading seaport, its John F. Kennedy International Airport is one of the busiest airports in the world. The largest manufacturing center in the country, it had, in 1977, over 21,000 manufacturing establishments employing 610,000 persons and reported $14.6 billion of value added by manufacture. The apparel industry is the city's largest manufacturing employer, with printing and publishing second.

Nearly all the rest of the state's manufacturing is done on Long Island, along the Hudson River north to Albany and through the Mohawk Valley, Central New York, and Southern Tier regions to Buffalo. The St. Lawrence seaway and power projects have opened the North Country to industrial expansion and have given the state a second seacoast. In 1962, the Niagara power development was completed, giving the state the largest hydroelectric installation in the free world.

The state ranks second in the nation in manufacturing with 1,509,900 employees and $44.3 billion in value added by manufacture in 1977. The principal industries are machinery, printing and publishing, instruments, apparel, and food.

The convention and tourist business is one of the state's most important sources of income.

New York farms are famous for dairying, truck gardening, and the raising of potatoes, onions, cabbage, fruits, and poultry. The state is a leading wine producer.

Among the major points of interest are Castle Clinton, Fort Stanwix, and Statue of Liberty National Monuments; Niagara Falls; U.S. Military Academy at West Point; National Historic Sites that include homes of Franklin D. Roosevelt at Hyde Park and Theodore Roosevelt in Oyster Bay and New York City; National Memorials, including Grant's Tomb and Federal Hall in New York City; Fort Ticonderoga; the Baseball Hall of Fame in Cooperstown; and the United Nations, skyscrapers, museums, theaters, and parks in New York City.

NORTH CAROLINA

Capital: Raleigh
Governor: James B. Hunt, Jr., D (to Jan. 1985)
Lieut. Governor: James C. Greene (to Jan. 1985)
Secy. of State: Thad Eure, D (to Jan. 1985)
Treasurer: Harlan E. Boyles (to Jan. 1985)
Auditor: Edward Renfrow, D (to Jan. 1985)
Atty. General: Rufus Edmisten, D (to Jan. 1985)
Entered Union & (rank): Nov. 21, 1789 (12)
Present constitution adopted: 1971
Motto: *Esse quam videri* (To be rather than to seem)
State flower: Dogwood (1941)
State tree: Pine (1963)
State bird: Cardinal (1943)
State mammal: Gray Squirrel (1969)
State insect: Honeybee (1973)
State Reptile: Turtle (1979)
State gem stone: Emerald (1973)
State shell: Scotch bonnet (1965)
State song: "The Old North State" (1927)
State colors: Red and blue (1945)
Nickname: Tar Heel State
Origin of name: In honor of Charles I of England
1970 population & (rank): 5,084,411 (12)
1980 population (1980 census) & (rank): 5,874,429 (10)
1980 land area & (rank): 48,798 sq mi. (126,387 sq km) (29)
Geographic center: In Chatham Co., 10 mi. NW of Sanford
Number of counties: 100
Largest cities (1980 census): Charlotte, 314,447; Greensboro, 155,642; Raleigh, 149,771; Winston–Salem, 131,885; Durham, 100,831; High Point, 64,107
State forests: 1
State parks: 26 (115,051 ac.)
State revenues (1979–80): $3,736,734,141[1]
State expenditure (1979–80): $3,665,096,845[2]

1. Excludes all Federal revenues and expenditures. 2. All expenditures: operating, and capital improvements.

English colonists, sent by Sir Walter Raleigh, unsuccessfully attempted to settle Roanoke Island in 1585 and 1587. Virginia Dare, born there in 1587, was the first child of English parentage born in America.

In 1653 the first permanent settlements were established by English colonists from Virginia near the Roanoke and Chowan Rivers.

The region was established as an English proprietary colony in 1663–65 and its early history was the scene of Culpepper's Rebellion (1677), the Quaker-led Cary Rebellion of 1708, the Tuscarora Indian War in 1711–13, and many pirate raids.

During the American Revolution, there was relatively little fighting within the state, but many North Carolinians saw action elsewhere. Despite considerable pro-Union, anti-slavery sentiment, North Carolina joined the Confederacy.

North Carolina is the nation's largest furniture, tobacco, brick, and textile producer. It holds second place in the Southeast in population and first place in the value of its industrial and agricultural production. This production is highly diversified, with metalworking, chemicals, and paper constituting enormous industries. Tobacco, corn, cotton, hay, peanuts, and truck and vegetable crops are of major importance. It is the country's leading producer of mica and lithium.

Tourism is also important, with travelers and va-

cationers spending more than $1 billion annually in North Carolina. Sports include year-round golfing, skiing at mountain resorts, both fresh and salt water fishing, and hunting.

Among the major attractions are the Great Smoky Mountains, the Blue Ridge National Parkway, the Cape Hatteras and Cape Lookout National Seashores, the Wright Brothers National Memorial at Kitty Hawk, Guilford Courthouse and Moores Creek National Military Parks, Carl Sandburg's home near Hendersonville, and the Old Salem Restoration in Winston–Salem.

NORTH DAKOTA

Capital: Bismarck
Governor: Allen I. Olson, R (to Jan. 1985)
Lieut. Governor: Ernest M. Sands, R (to Jan. 1985)
Secy. of State: Ben Meier, R (to Jan. 1985)
Auditor: Robert W. Peterson, R (to Jan. 1985)
State Treasurer: John Lesmeister, R (to Jan. 1985)
Atty. General: Bob Wefald, R (to Jan. 1985)
Organized as territory: March 2, 1861
Entered Union & (rank): Nov. 2, 1889 (39)
Present constitution adopted: 1889
Motto: Liberty and union, now and forever: one and inseparable
State tree: American Elm (1947)
State bird: Western meadow lark (1947)
State song: "North Dakota Hymn" (1947)
Nickname: Sioux State; Flickertail State
Origin of name: From the Dakotah tribe, meaning "allies"
1970 population & (rank): 617,792 (45)
1980 population (1980 census) & (rank): 652,695 (46)
1980 land area & (rank): 69,273 sq mi (179,417 sq km) (17)
Geographic center: In Sheridan Co., 5 mi. SW of McClusky
Number of counties: 53
Largest cities (1980 census): Fargo, 61,308; Bismarck, 44,485; Grand Forks, 43,765; Minot, 32,843; Jamestown, 16,280; Dickinson, 15,924; Mandan, 15,513
State forests: None
State parks: 14 (14,922.6 ac.)
Total state collections (1980): $292,245,022
Total state disbursements (1980): $293,943,061

North Dakota was explored in 1738–40 by French Canadians led by Vérendrye. In 1803, the U.S. acquired most of North Dakota from France in the Louisiana Purchase. Lewis and Clark explored the region in 1804–06 and the first settlements were made at Pembina in 1812 by Scottish and Irish families while this area was still in dispute between the U.S. and Great Britian.

In 1818, the U.S. obtained the northeastern part of North Dakota by treaty with Great Britain and took possession of Pembina in 1823.

North Dakota is the most rural of all the states, with farms covering more than 90% of the land. Only Kansas produces more wheat and the state's coal and oil reserves are plentiful.

Other agricultural products include barley, rye, oats and flaxseed, sugar beets, and hay; beef cattle, sheep, and hogs are also important to the state's economy.

Recently, manufacturing industries have grown, especially food processing and farm equipment. The state also produces natural gas, lignite, salt, clay, sand, and gravel.

The Garrison Dam on the Missouri River provides extensive irrigation and produces 400,000 kilowatts of electricity for the Missouri Basin areas.

Known for its waterfowl, grouse, and deer hunting and bass, trout, and northern pike fishing, North Dakota has 20 state parks and recreation areas. Points of interest include the International Peace Garden near Dunseith, Fort Union Trading Post National Historic Site, the State Capitol at Bismarck, the Badlands, and Fort Lincoln, now a state park, from which Gen. George Custer set out on his last campaign in 1876.

OHIO

Capital: Columbus
Governor: James A. Rhodes, R (to Jan. 1983)
Lieut. Governor: (Vacant)
Secy. of State: Anthony J. Celebrezze, Jr., R (to Jan. 1983)
Auditor: Thomas E. Ferguson (to Jan. 1983)
Treasurer: Gertrude W. Donahey, D (to Jan. 1983)
Atty. General: William J. Brown, D (to Jan. 1983)
Entered Union & (rank): March 1, 1803 (17)
Present constitution adopted: 1851
Motto: With God, all things are possible
State flower: Scarlet carnation (1904)
State tree: Buckeye (1953)
State bird: Cardinal (1933)
State insect: Ladybug (1975)
State gem stone: Flint (1965)
State song: "Beautiful Ohio"
State drink: Tomato juice (1965)
Nickname: Buckeye State
Origin of name: From an Iroquoian word meaning "great river"
1970 population & (rank): 10,657,423 (6)
1980 population (1980 census) & (rank): 10,797,419 (6)
1980 land area & (rank): 40,975 sq mi. (106,125 sq km) (35)
Geographic center: In Delaware Co., 25 mi. NNE of Columbus
Number of counties: 88
Largest cities (1980 census): Cleveland, 573,822; Columbus, 564,871; Cincinnati, 385,457; Toledo, 354,635; Akron, 237,177; Dayton, 203,588; Youngstown, 115,436
State forests: 19 (172,744 ac.)
State parks: 71 (198,027 ac.)
State actual revenue (1979–80): $7,938,890,332
State actual expenditure (1979–80): $8,339,544,015

First explored for France by La Salle in 1669, the Ohio region became British property after the French and Indian War. Ohio was acquired by the U.S. after the Revolutionary War in 1783 and, in 1788, the first permanent settlement was established at Marietta, capital of the Northwest Territory.

The 1790s saw severe fighting with the Indians in Ohio; a major battle was won by Maj. Gen. Anthony Wayne at Fallen Timbers in 1794. In the War of 1812, Commodore Oliver H. Perry defeated the British in the Battle of Lake Erie on Sept. 10, 1813.

Ohio is one of the nation's industrial leaders, ranking third in the value of manufactured products. Important manufacturing centers are located in or near Ohio's major cities. Akron is known for rubber; Canton for roller bearings; Cincinnati for jet engines and machine tools; Cleveland for auto assembly and parts, refining, and steel; Dayton for office machines, refrigeration, and heating and auto equipment; Youngstown and Steubenville for steel; and Toledo for glass and auto parts.

The state's thousands of factories almost overshadow its importance in agriculture and mining. Its fertile soil produces soybeans, corn, oats, grapes, and clover. More than half of Ohio's farm receipts come from dairying and sheep and hog raising. Ohio is the top state in lime production and among the leaders in coal, clay, salt, sand, and gravel. Petroleum, gypsum, cement, and natural gas are also important.

Tourism is a valuable revenue producer, bringing in over $3 billion annually. Attractions include the Indian burial grounds at Mound City Group National Monument, Perry's Victory International Peace Memorial, the Pro Football Hall of Fame at Canton, and the homes of Presidents Grant, Taft, Hayes, Harding, and Garfield.

OKLAHOMA

Capital: Oklahoma City
Governor: George P. Nigh, D (to Jan. 1983)
Lieut. Governor: Spencer Bernard, D (to Jan. 1983)
Secy. of State: Jeannette Edmondson, D (to Jan. 1983)
Treasurer: Leo Winters, D (to Jan. 1983)
Atty. General: Jan Eric Cartwright, D (to Jan. 1983)
Organized as territory: May 2, 1890
Entered Union & (rank): Nov. 16, 1907 (46)
Present constitution adopted: 1907
Motto: *Labor omnia vincit* (Labor conquers all things)
State flower: Mistletoe (1893)
State tree: Redbud (1937)
State bird: Scissor-tailed flycatcher (1951)
State animal: Bison (1972)
State reptile: Mountain boomer lizard (1969)
State stone: Rose Rock (barite rose) (1968)
State colors: Green and white (1915)
State song: "Oklahoma" (1953)
Nickname: Sooner State
Origin of name: From two Choctaw Indian words meaning "red people"
1970 population & (rank): 2,559,463 (27)
1980 population (1980 census) & (rank): 3,025,266 (26)
1980 land area & (rank): 68,782 sq mi. (178,145 sq km) (19)
Geographic center: In Oklahoma Co., 8 mi. N of Oklahoma City
Number of counties: 77
Largest cities (1980 census): Oklahoma City, 403,213; Tulsa, 360,919; Lawton, 80,054; Norman, 68,020; Enid, 50,363; Midwest City, 49,559; Muskogee, 40,011
State forests: None
State parks: 28 (88,959 ac.)
Total state revenue (1980): $3,353,159,871
Total state expenditure (1980): $3,277,386,901

Francisco Vásquez de Coronado first explored the region for Spain in 1541. The U.S. acquired most of Oklahoma in 1803 in the Louisiana Purchase from France; the Western Panhandle region became U.S. territory with the annexation of Texas in 1845.

In 1834, Oklahoma was set aside as Indian Territory. It remained so until April 22, 1889, when it was opened to homestead settlement. On that one day 50,000 people swarmed in and the term "Sooners" was applied to those who tried to beat the noon starting gun. Other Oklahoma "Land Rushes" took place through 1901.

Oil has made Oklahoma a rich state and Tulsa one of the world's wealthiest cities per capita. Oil refining, meat packing, food processing, and machinery manufacturing (especially construction and oil equipment) are important industries.

Other minerals produced in Oklahoma include natural gas, helium, gypsum, zinc, cement, coal, copper, and silver.

Oklahoma's rich plains produce bumper yields of wheat, as well as large crops of sorghum, corn, cotton, and peanuts. Its beef cattle herd is among the largest in the nation; more than half of Oklahoma's annual farm receipts are contributed by livestock products.

Tourist attractions include the National Cowboy Hall of Fame in Oklahoma City, the Will Rogers Memorial in Claremore, the Cherokee Cultural Center with a restored Cherokee village, the restored Fort Gibson Stockade near Muskogee, and the Lake Texoma recreation area.

OREGON

Capital: Salem
Governor: Victor G. Atiyeh, R (to Jan. 1983)
Secy. of State: Norma Paulus, R (to Jan. 1985)
Treasurer: Clay Myers, R (to Jan. 1985)
Atty. General: David B. Frohnmayer, R (to Jan. 1985)
Organized as territory: Aug. 14, 1848
Entered Union & (rank): Feb. 14, 1859 (33)
Present constitution adopted: 1859
Motto: The Union (1957)
State flower: Oregon grape (1899)
State tree: Douglas fir (1939)
State animal: Beaver (1969)
State bird: Western meadow lark (1927)
State fish: Chinook salmon (1961)
State rock: Thunderegg (1965)
State colors: Navy blue and gold (1959)
State song: "Oregon, My Oregon" (1927)
Nickname: Beaver State
Origin of name: Unknown. However, it is generally accepted that the name, first used by Jonathan Carver in 1778, was taken from the writings of Maj. Robert Rogers, an English army officer.
1970 population & (rank): 2,091,533 (31)
1980 population (1980 census) & (rank): 2,632,663 (30)
1980 land area & (rank): 96,184 sq mi. (249,117 sq km) (10)
Geographic center: In Crook Co., 25 mi. SSE of Prineville
Number of counties: 36
Largest cities (1980 census): Portland, 366,383; Eugene, 105,624; Salem, 89,233; Springfield, 41,621; Corvallis, 40,960; Medford, 39,603; Gresham, 33,005
State forests: 820,000 ac.
State parks: 240 (93,330 ac.)
State general revenue (1981–83 est.): $3,223,380,057
State general expenditure (1981–83 est.): $3,227,816,067

Spanish and English sailors are believed to have sighted the Oregon coast in the 1500s and 1600s. Capt. James Cook, seeking the Northwest Passage, charted some of the coastline in 1778. In 1792, Capt. Robert Gray, in the *Columbia*, discovered the river named after his ship and claimed the area for the U.S.

In 1805 the Lewis and Clark expedition explored the area and John Jacob Astor's fur depot, Astoria, was founded in 1811. Disputes for control of Oregon between American settlers and the Hudson Bay Company were finally resolved in the 1846 Oregon Treaty in which Great Britain gave up claims to the region.

Oregon, with the greatest U.S. reserve of standing timber, has a five-billion-dollar wood processing industry. Its salmon-fishing industry, centered at Astoria at the mouth of the Columbia, is one of the world's largest.

In agriculture, the state leads in growing peppermint, winter pears, fresh plums, prunes, blackber-

ries, boysenberries, filberts, Blue Lake beans, and cover seed crops, and also raises strawberries, hops, wheat and other grains, sugar beets, potatoes, green peas, fiber flax, dairy products, livestock and poultry, apples, pears, and cherries. Oregon is the source of all the nickel produced in the U.S.

With the low-cost electric power provided by Bonneville Dam, McNary Dam, and other dams in the Pacific Northwest, Oregon has developed steadily as a manufacturing state. Leading manufactures are lumber and plywood, metalwork, machinery, aluminum, chemicals, paper, food packing, and electronic equipment.

Crater Lake National Park, Mount Hood, and Bonneville Dam on the Columbia are major tourist attractions. Oregon Dunes National Recreation Area has been established near Florence. Other points of interest include the Oregon Caves National Monument, Cape Perpetua in Siuslaw National Forest, Columbia River Gorge between The Dalles and Troutdale, and Hells Canyon.

PENNSYLVANIA

Capital: Harrisburg
Governor: Richard L. Thornburgh, R (to Jan. 1983)
Lieut. Governor: William W. Scranton III, R (to Jan. 1983)
Secy. of the Commonwealth: William R. Davis (to Jan. 1983)
Auditor General: Al Benedict, D (to Jan. 1985)
Atty. General: Leroy S. Zimmerman, R (to Jan. 1985)
Entered Union & (rank): Dec. 12, 1787 (2)
Present constitution adopted: 1874
Motto: Virtue, liberty, and independence
State flower: Mountain laurel (1933)
State tree: Hemlock (1931)
State bird: Ruffed grouse (1931)
State insect: Firefly (1974)
State dog: Great Dane (1965)
State colors: Blue and gold
State song: None
Nickname: Keystone State
Origin of name: In honor of Adm. Sir. William Penn, father of William Penn. It means "Penn's Woodland."
1970 population & (rank): 11,800,766 (3)
1980 population (1980 census) & (rank): 11,866,728 (4)
1980 land area & (rank): 44,966 sq mi. (116,462 sq km) (32)
Geographic center: In Centre Co., 2½ mi. SW of Bellefonte
Number of counties: 67
Largest cities (1980 census): Philadelphia, 1,688,210; Pittsburgh, 423,938; Erie, 119,123; Scranton, 88,117; Reading, 78,686; Bethlehem, 70,419
State forests: 1,930,108 ac.
State parks: 120 (297,438 ac.)
Total estimated revenue subject to general appropriations (1981–82): $7,197,045,000
Total est. appropriations (1981–82): $7,196,236,000

Rich in historic lore, Pennsylvania territory was disputed in the early 1600s among the Dutch, the Swedes, and the English. England acquired the region in 1664 with the capture of New York and in 1681 Pennsylvania was granted to William Penn, a Quaker, by King Charles II.

Philadelphia was the seat of the federal government almost continuously from 1776 to 1800; there the Declaration of Independence was signed in 1776 and the U.S. Constitution drawn up in 1787. Valley Forge, of Revolutionary War fame, and Gettysburg, the turning-point of the Civil War, are both in Pennsylvania. The Liberty Bell is located in Independence Hall in Philadelphia.

Approximately 23% of all American pig iron steel is made in Pennsylvania, which ranks first among the states in steel wire and structural metal production. Other manufactures include machinery, chemicals, storage batteries, motor vehicles and trailers, computers, textiles and apparel, shoes, plastics, and explosives. Pennsylvania produces almost all the nation's anthracite coal. Also important are bituminous coal, cement, stone, petroleum, natural gas, lime, clays, zinc, and iron.

Prosperous farms brought in total receipts of more than $1.3 billion in 1973. The state ranked high in milk cows, chickens, and turkeys. Agricultural products include apples, peaches, potatoes, corn, wheat, barley, buckwheat, and mushrooms.

Tourists now spend approximately $6 billion in Pennsylvania annually. Among the chief attractions: the Gettysburg National Military Park, Valley Forge National Historical Park, Independence National Historical Park in Philadelphia, the Pennsylvania Dutch region, the Eisenhower farm near Gettysburg, and the Delaware Water Gap National Recreation Area.

RHODE ISLAND

Capital: Providence
Governor: J. Joseph Garrahy, D (to Jan. 1983)
Lieut. Governor: Thomas R. Di Luglio, D (to Jan. 1983)
Secy. of State: Robert F. Burns, D (to Jan. 1983)
Controller: James A. Carter (civil service)
Atty. General: Dennis J. Roberts II, D (to Jan. 1983)
Entered Union & (rank): May 29, 1790 (13)
Present constitution adopted: 1843
Motto: Hope
State flower: Violet (unofficial)
State tree: Red maple (official)
State bird: Rhode Island Red (official)
State colors: Blue, white, and gold (in state flag)
State song: "Rhode Island" (1946)
Nickname: The Ocean State
Origin of name: From the Greek island of Rhodes
1970 population & (rank): 949,723 (39)
1980 population (1980 census) & (rank): 947,154 (40)
1980 land area & (rank): 1,049 sq mi. (2,717 sq km) (50)
Geographic center: In Kent Co., 1 mi. SSW of Crompton
Number of counties: 5
Largest cities (1980 census): Providence, 156,804; Warwick, 87,123; Cranston, 71,992; Pawtucket, 71,204; East Providence, 50,980; Woonsocket, 45,914
State forests: 11 (20,900 ac.)
State parks: 17 (8,200 ac.)
State general revenue (1979–80): $950,883,014
State general expenditure (1979–80): $965,643,375

From its beginnings, Rhode Island has been distinguished by its support for freedom of conscience and action, started by Roger Williams, exiled by the Massachusetts Bay Colony Puritans in 1636, and the founder of the present state capital, Providence. Williams was followed by other religious exiles who founded Pocasset, now Portsmouth, in 1638 and Newport in 1639.

The first Baptist church in the U.S. was established in Providence in 1638 and Rhode Island provided a haven for Quakers in 1657 and for Jews from Holland in 1659.

Rhode Island's rebellious, authority-defying nature was further demonstrated by the burnings of the British revenue cutters *Liberty* and *Gaspee*

prior to the Revolution, by its early declaration of independence from Great Britain in May 1776, its refusal to participate actively in the War of 1812, and by Dorr's Rebellion of 1842, which protested property requirements for voting.

Rhode Island, smallest of the 50 states, is densely populated and highly industrialized. The state pioneered in the manufacture of jewelry and silverware and still retains first place in the U.S. Other leading industries are primary metal processing, metal products, machinery, rubber and plastics, food processing, chemicals, transportation equipment and electronic equipment.

With more than eight tenths of the population living in urban areas, adjacent areas of the state are involved in dairying and poultry and truck farming. Nursery and greenhouse products, potatoes, corn, apples, oats, and hay lead the crop list.

Newport became famous as the summer capital of society in the mid-19th century. Touro Synagogue (1763) is the oldest in the U.S. Other points of interest include the Roger Williams National Memorial in Providence, Samuel Slater's Mill in Pawtucket, the General Nathaniel Greene Homestead in Coventry, Block Island, and Narragansett Pier.

SOUTH CAROLINA

Capital: Columbia
Governor: Richard W. Riley, D (to Jan. 1983)
Lieut. Governor: Nancy Stevenson, D (to Jan. 1983)
Secy. of State: John T. Campbell, D (to Jan. 1983)
Comptroller General: Earl E. Morris, Jr. (to Jan. 1983)
Atty. General: Daniel R. McLeod, D (to Jan. 1983)
Entered Union & (rank): May 23, 1788 (8)
Present constitution adopted: 1895
Mottoes: *Animis opibusque parati* (Prepared in mind and resources) and *Dum spiro spero* (While I breathe, I hope)
State flower: Carolina yellow jessamine (1924)
State tree: Palmetto tree (1939)
State bird: Carolina wren (1948)
State song: "Carolina" (1911)
Nickname: Palmetto State
Origin of name: In honor of Charles I of England
1970 population & (rank): 2,590,713 (26)
1980 population (1980 census) & (rank): 3,119,208 (25)
1980 land area & (rank): 30,225 sq mi. (78,283 sq km) (40)
Geographic center: In Richland Co., 13 mi. SE of Columbia
Number of counties: 46
Largest cities (1980 census): Columbia, 99,296; Charleston, 69,510; North Charleston, 65,630; Greenville, 58,242; Spartanburg, 43,968; Rock Hill, 35,344
State forests: 4 (124,052 ac.)
State parks: 50 (61,726 ac.)
State general fund revenue (1980–81 est.): $1,727,026,566[1]
State general expenditures (1980–81 est.): $1,727,025,707[1]

1. Highway Department has separate funding and expenditures.

Following exploration of the coast in 1521 by De Gordillo, the Spanish tried unsuccessfully to establish a colony near present-day Georgetown in 1526 and the French also failed to colonize Parris Island near Fort Royal in 1562.

The first English settlement was made in 1670 at Albemarle Point on the Ashley River, but poor conditions drove the settlers to the site of Charleston (originally called Charles Town). South Carolina, officially separated from North Carolina in 1729, was the scene of extensive military action during the Revolution and again during the Civil War. The

Civil War began in 1861 as South Carolina troops fired on federal Fort Sumter in Charleston Harbor and the state was the first to secede from the Union.

Once primarily agricultural, South Carolina has built so many large textile and other mills that today its factories produce eight times the output of its farms in cash value. Charleston makes asbestos, wood, pulp, and steel products; chemicals, machinery, and apparel are also important.

Farms have become fewer but larger in recent years. South Carolina grows more peaches than any other state except California; it ranks fourth in tobacco. Other farm products include cotton, peanuts, sweet potatoes, soybeans, corn, and oats. Poultry and dairy products are also important revenue producers.

Points of interest include Fort Sumter National Monument, Fort Moultrie, Fort Johnson, and aircraft carrier USS *Yorktown* in Charleston Harbor; the Middleton, Magnolia, and Cypress Gardens in Charleston; Cowpens National Battlefield; and the Hilton Head resorts.

SOUTH DAKOTA

Capital: Pierre
Governor: William J. Janklow, R (to Jan. 1983)
Lieut. Governor: Lowell C. Hansen II, R (to Jan. 1983)
Atty. General: Mark Meirhenry, R (to Jan. 1983)
Secy. of State: Alice Kundert, R (to Jan. 1983)
State Auditor: Vern Larson, R (to Jan. 1983)
State Treasurer: David L. Volk, R (to Jan. 1983)
Organized as territory: March 2, 1861
Entered Union & (rank): Nov. 2, 1889 (40)
Present constitution adopted: 1889
Motto: Under God the people rule
State flower: American pasqueflower (1903)
State grass: Western wheat grass (1970)
State tree: Black Hills spruce (1947)
State bird: Ring-necked pheasant (1943)
State insect: Honeybee (1978)
State animal: Coyote (1949)
State mineral stone: Rose quartz (1966)
State gem stone: Fairburn agate (1966)
State colors: Blue and gold (in state flag)
State song: "Hail! South Dakota" (1943)
Nicknames: Sunshine State; Coyote State
Origin of name: Same as for North Dakota
1970 population & (rank): 666,257 (44)
1980 population (1980 census) & (rank): 690,178 (45)
1980 land area & (rank): 75,955 sq mi. (196,723 sq km) (16)
Geographic center: In Hughes Co., 8 mi. NE of Pierre
Number of counties: 67 (64 county governments)
Largest cities (1980 census): Sioux Falls, 81,343; Rapid City, 46,492; Aberdeen, 25,956; Watertown, 15,694; Brookings, 14,951; Mitchell, 13,916; Huron, 13,000
State forests: None[1]
State parks: 13 plus 39 recreational areas (87,269 ac.)[2]
State general revenue (1980): $521,631,300
State general expenditure (1980): $450,207,386

1. No designated state forests; about 13,000 ac. of state land is forestland. 2. Acreage includes 39 recreation areas and 80 roadside parks, in addition to 12 state parks.

Exploration of this area began in 1743 when Louis-Joseph and François Verendrye came from France in search of a route to the Pacific.

The U.S. acquired the region as part of the Louisiana Purchase in 1803 and it was explored by Lewis and Clark in 1804–06. Fort Pierre, the first permanent settlement, was established in 1817

and, in 1831, the first Missouri River steamboat reached the fort.

Settlement of South Dakota did not begin in earnest until the arrival of the railroad in 1873 and the discovery of gold in the Black Hills the following year.

Agriculture is South Dakota's basic industry today. It normally ranks first in the U.S. in the size of its rye crop and high in spring wheat, flaxseed, oats, and barley. In 1974 South Dakota had 5 million cattle, almost a million sheep, and 2 million hogs.

South Dakota is the nation's second leading producer of gold (Nevada ranks first) and the Homestake Mine is the richest in the U.S. Other minerals produced include berylium, bentonite, granite, silver, petroleum, and uranium.

Processing of foods produced by farms and ranches is the largest South Dakota manufacturing industry, followed by lumber, wood products, and machinery, including farm equipment.

The Black Hills, a great tourist attraction, are the highest mountains east of the Rockies. Mt. Rushmore, in this group, is famous for the likenesses of Washington, Jefferson, Lincoln, and Theodore Roosevelt, which were carved in granite by Gutzon Borglum. The Badlands offer scenic masses of bare rock and clay unrelieved by any vegetation. Other points of interest are Deadwood, where Wild Bill Hickok was killed in 1876; the Crazy Horse Memorial near Custer; and the Corn Palace in Mitchell.

TENNESSEE

Capital: Nashville
Governor: Lamar Alexander, R (to Jan. 1983)
Lieut. Governor: John S. Wilder, D (to Jan. 1985)
Secy. of State: Gentry Crowell, D (to Jan. 1985)
Atty. General: Brooks McLemore, D (to Sept. 1982)
State Treasurer: Harlan Matthews, D (to Jan. 1983)
Entered Union & (rank): June 1, 1796 (16)
Present constitution adopted: 1870; amended 1953, 1960, 1965 and 1973
Motto: "Tennessee—America at its best" (1965)
State flower: Iris (1933)
State tree: Tulip poplar (1947)
State bird: Mockingbird (1933)
State horse: Tennessee walking horse
State animal: Raccoon
State wild flower: Passion flower
State song: "Tennessee Waltz" (1965)
Nickname: Volunteer State
Origin of name: Of Cherokee origin; the exact meaning is unknown
1970 population & (rank): 3,926,018 (17)
1980 population (1980 census) & (rank): 4,590,750 (17)
1980 land area & (rank): 41,328 sq mi. (107,040 sq km) (34)
Geographic center: In Rutherford Co., 5 mi. NE of Murfreesboro
Number of counties: 95
Largest cities (1980 census): Memphis, 646,356; Nashville-Davidson, 455,651; Knoxville, 183,139; Clarksville, 54,777; Jackson, 49,131; Johnson City, 39,459; Kingsport, 32,027
State forests: 14 (155,752 ac.)
State parks: 21 (130,000 ac.)
State general revenue (1979): $3,614,601
State general expenditure (1979): $3,360,630

First visited by the Spanish explorer de Soto in 1541, the Tennessee area would later be claimed by both France and England as a result of the 1670s and 1680s explorations of Marquette and Jolliet, La Salle, and the Englishmen James Needham and Gabriel Arthur.

Great Britain obtained the region following the French and Indian War in 1763 and it was rapidly occupied by settlers moving in from Virginia and the Carolinas.

During 1784–87, the settlers formed the "state" of Franklin, which was disbanded when the region was allowed to send representatives to the North Carolina legislature. In 1790 Congress organized the territory south of the Ohio River and Tennessee joined the Union in 1796.

Although Tennessee joined the Confederacy during the Civil War, there was much pro-Union sentiment in the state, which was the scene of extensive military action.

The state is now predominantly industrial; in 1970, 58.8% of its population lived in urban areas. Among the most important products are chemicals, textiles, apparel, electrical machinery, furniture, and leather goods. Other lines include food processing, lumber, primary metals, and metal products. The state is known as the U.S. hardwood-flooring center and ranks first in the production of marble, zinc, pyrite, and ball clay.

Tennessee is one of the leading tobacco-producing states in the nation and its farming income is also derived from livestock and dairy products as well as corn, cotton, and soybeans.

With six other states, Tennessee shares the extensive federal reservoir developments on the Tennessee and Cumberland River systems. The Tennessee Valley Authority operates a number of dams and reservoirs in the state.

Among the major points of interest: the Andrew Johnson National Historic Site at Greenville, American Museum of Atomic Energy at Oak Ridge, Great Smoky Mountains National Park, The Hermitage (home of Andrew Jackson near Nashville), Rock City Gardens near Chattanooga, and three National Military Parks.

TEXAS

Capital: Austin
Governor: Bill Clements, R (to Jan. 1983)
Lieut. Governor: William P. Hobby, D (to Jan. 1981)
Secy. of State: George Strake, Jr., R (to Jan. 1983)
Comptroller: Bob Bullock (to Jan. 1983)
Atty. General: Mark White, D (to Jan. 1983)
Entered Union & (rank): Dec. 29, 1845 (28)
Present constitution adopted: 1876
Motto: Friendship
State flower: Bluebonnet (1901)
State tree: Pecan (1919)
State bird: Mockingbird (1927)
State song: "Texas, Our Texas" (1930)
Nickname: Lone Star State
Origin of name: From an Indian word meaning "friends"
1970 population & (rank): 11,198,655 (4)
1980 population (1980 census) & (rank): 14,228,383 (3)
1980 land area & (rank): 262,134 sq mi. (678,927 sq km) (2)
Geographic center: In McCulloch Co., 15 mi. NE of Brady
Number of counties: 254
Largest cities (1980 census): Houston, 1,594,086; Dallas, 904,078; San Antonio, 785,410; El Paso, 425,259; Fort Worth, 385,141; Austin, 345,496
State forests: 4 (6,306 ac.)
State parks: 83 (64 developed)

State revenue receipts (1978–79): $10,884,709,348
State government cost (1978–79): $10,807,466,326
Total net revenue: (1979–80): $11,181,462,060
Total net expenditures (1979–80): $10,210,907,514

Spanish explorers, including Cabeza de Vaca and Coronado, were the first to visit the region in the 16th and 17th centuries, settling at Ysleta near present-day El Paso in 1682. In 1685, La Salle established a short-lived French colony at Matagorda Bay.

Americans, led by Stephen F. Austin, began to settle along the Brazos River in 1821 when Texas was controlled by Mexico, recently independent from Spain. In 1836, following a brief war between the American settlers in Texas and the Mexican government, and famous for the battles of the Alamo and San Jacinto, the Independent Republic of Texas was proclaimed with Sam Houston as president.

After Texas became the 28th U.S. state in 1845, border disputes led to the Mexican War of 1846–48.

Today, Texas, second only to Alaska in land area, leads all other states in such categories as oil, cattle, sheep, and cotton. Possessing enormous natural resources, Texas is a major agricultural state and an industrial giant.

Sulfur, salt, helium asphalt, graphite, bromine, natural gas, cement, and clays give Texas first place in mineral production—nearly $8 billion in 1973. Chemicals, oil refining, food processing, machinery, and transportation equipment are among the major Texas manfacturing industries.

Texas ranches and farms produce beef cattle, poultry, rice, pecans, peanuts, sorghum, and an extensive variety of fruits and vegetables.

Millions of tourists spend well over $2 billion annually visiting more than 70 state parks, recreations areas, and points of interest such as the Gulf Coast resort area, the Lyndon B. Johnson Space Center in Houston, the Alamo in San Antonio, the state capital in Austin, and the Big Bend and Guadalupe Mountains National Parks.

UTAH

Capital: Salt Lake City
Governor: Scott M. Matheson, D (to Jan. 1984)
Lieut. Governor/Secretary of State: David S. Monson, R (to Jan. 1984)
Atty. General: David Wilkison, R (to Jan. 1984)
Organized as territory: Sept. 9, 1850
Entered Union & (rank): Jan. 4, 1896 (45)
Present constitution adopted: 1896
Motto: Industry
State flower: Sego lily (1911)
State tree: Blue spruce (1933)
State bird: Seagull (1955)
State emblem: Beehive
State song: "Utah, We Love Thee"
Nickname: Beehive State
Origin of name: From the Ute tribe, meaning "people of the mountains"
1970 population & (rank): 1,059,273 (36)
1980 population (1980 census) & (rank): 1,461,037 (36)
1980 land area & (rank): 82,096 sq mi. (212,629 sq km) (12)
Geographic center: In Sanpete Co., 3 mi. N. of Manti
Number of counties: 29
Largest cities (1980 census): Salt Lake City, 163,033; Provo, 73,907; Ogden, 64,407; Orem, 52,399; Sandy City,

51,022; Bountiful, 32,877; Logan, 26,844; Murray, 25,750
State forests: None
State parks: 35 (64,097 ac.)
Total state receipt (1980): $1,410,038,000
Total state disbursements (1980): $1,446,038,000
Cash balance—Unappropriated general fund balance (1980): $8,677,000

The region was first explored for Spain by Franciscan friars, Escalante and Dominguez in 1776. In 1824 the famous American frontiersman Jim Bridger discovered the Great Salt Lake.

Fleeing the religious persecution encountered in eastern and middle-western states, the Mormons reached the Great Salt Lake in 1847 and began to build Salt Lake City. The U.S. acquired the Utah region in the treaty ending the Mexican War in 1848 and the first transcontinental railroad was completed with the driving of a golden spike at Promontory Point in 1869.

Mormon difficulties with the federal government about polygamy did not end until the Mormon Church renounced the practice in 1890, six years before Utah became a state.

In recent years, manufacturing has become Utah's most important industry, ahead of mining, agriculture, and tourism. The state's factories produce transportation equipment, food products, machinery, metal products, and electrical equipment. Utah has also become an important aerospace research and production center and is a leading warehousing and distribution point for much of the western U.S.

Rich in natural resources, Utah has long been a leading producer of copper, gold, silver, lead, zinc, and molybdenum. Oil has also become a major product; with Colorado and Wyoming, Utah shares what have been called the world's richest oil shale deposits.

Ranked eighth among the states in number of sheep in 1973, Utah also produces large crops of apricots and cherries as well as sugar beets, potatoes, onions, alfalfa, winter wheat, and beans. Utah's farmlands and crops require extensive irrigation.

Utah is a great vacationland with 11,000 miles of fishing streams and 147,000 acres of lakes and reservoirs. Among the many tourist attractions are Arches, Bryce Canyon, Canyonlands, Capitol Reef, and Zion National Parks; Dinosaur, Natural Bridges, and Rainbow Bridge National Monuments; the Mormon Tabernacle in Salt Lake City; and Monument Valley.

VERMONT

Capital: Montpelier
Governor: Richard A. Snelling, R (to Jan. 1983)
Lieut. Governor: Madeleine M. Kunin (to Jan. 1983)
Secy. of State: James H. Douglas (to Jan. 1983)
Treasurer: Emory A. Hebard, R (to Jan. 1983)
Auditor of Accounts: Alexander V. Acebo (to Jan. 1983)
Atty. General: John J. Easton, Jr. (to Jan. 1983)
Entered Union & (rank): March 4, 1791 (14)
Present constitution adopted: 1793
Motto: Vermont, Freedom, and Unity
State flower: Red clover (1894)
State tree: Sugar maple (1949)
State bird: Hermit thrush (1941)
State animal: Morgan horse (1961)
State insect: Honeybee (1978)

State song: "Hail, Vermont!" (1938)
Nickname: Green Mountain State
Origin of name: From the French "vert mont," meaning "green mountain"
1970 population & (rank): 444,732 (48)
1980 population (1980 census) & (rank): 511,456 (48)
1980 land area & (rank): 9,276 sq mi. (24,025 sq km) (43)
Geographic center: In Washington Co., 3 mi. E of Roxbury
Number of counties: 14
Largest cities (1980 census): Burlington, 37,712; Rutland, 18,436; South Burlington, 10,679; Barre, 9,824; Montpelier, 8,241; St. Albans, 7,308; Winooski, 6,318
State forests: 34 (113,953 ac.)
State parks: 45 (31,325 ac.)
State receipts (1980): $544,495,539
State disbursements (1980): $579,047,519

The Vermont region was explored and claimed for France by Samuel de Champlain in 1609 and the first French settlement was established at Fort Ste. Anne in 1666. The first English settlers moved into the area in 1724 and built Fort Drummer on the site of present-day Brattleboro. England gained control of the area in 1763 after the French and Indian War.

First organized to drive settlers from New York out of Vermont, the Green Mountain Boys, led by Ethan Allen, won fame by capturing Fort Ticonderoga from the British on May 10, 1775, in the early days of the Revolution.

In 1777 Vermont adopted its first constitution abolishing slavery and providing for universal male suffrage without property qualifications. In 1791 Vermont became the first state after the original 13 to join the Union.

Vermont leads the nation in the production of monument granite, marble, and maple syrup. It is also a leader in the production of asbestos and talc.

In ratio to population, Vermont keeps more dairy cows than any other state. Vermont's soil is devoted to dairying, truck farming, and fruit growing because the rugged, rocky terrain discourages extensive farming.

Principal manufactured goods are machine tools, computer components, stone and clay products, lumber, furniture, and paper.

Tourism is a major industry in Vermont. Vermont's many famous ski areas include Stowe, Killington, Mt. Snow, Bromley, Jay Peak, and Sugarbush. Hunting and fishing also attract many visitors to Vermont each year. Among the many points of interest are the Green Mountain National Forest, Bennington Battle Monument, the Calvin Coolidge Homestead at Plymouth, and the Marble Exhibit in Proctor.

VIRGINIA

Capital: Richmond
Governor: John N. Dalton, R (to Jan. 1982)
Lieut. Governor: Charles S. Robb, D (to Jan. 1982)
Secy. of the Commonwealth: Frederick T. Gray, D (apptd. by Governor)
Acting Comptroller: Vincent Pross, Jr. (apptd. by Governor)
Atty. General: J. Marshall Coleman, R (to Jan. 1982)
Entered Union & (rank): June 25, 1788 (10)
Present constitution adopted: 1970
Motto: *Sic semper tyrannis* (Thus always to tyrants)
State flower: American dogwood (1918)
State bird: Cardinal (1950)
State dog: American foxhound (1966)

State shell: Oyster shell
State song: "Carry Me Back to Old Virginia" (1940)
Nicknames: The Old Dominion; Mother of Presidents
Origin of name: In honor of Elizabeth "Virgin Queen" of England
1970 population & (rank): 4,651,448 (14)
1980 population (1980 census) & (rank): 5,346,279 (14)
1980 land area & (rank): 39,780 sq mi. (103,030 sq km) (36)
Geographic center: In Buckingham Co., 5 mi. SW of Buckingham
Number of counties: 95, plus 41 independent cities
Largest cities (1980 census): Norfolk, 266,979; Virginia Beach, 262,199; Richmond, 219,214; Newport News, 144,903; Hampton, 122,617; Chesapeake, 114,226
State forests: 8 (49,566 ac.)
State parks and recreational parks: 22, plus 3 in process of acquisition and/or development (42,722 ac.)[1]
State revenue (1979–80): $5,170,300,000
State expenditure (1979–80): $5,252,100,000

1. Does not include portion of Breaks Interstate Park (Va.-Ky., 1,200 ac.) which lies in Virginia.

The history of America is closely tied to that of Virginia, particularly in the Colonial period. Jamestown, founded in 1607, was the first permanent English settlement in North America and slavery was introduced there in 1619. The surrenders ending both the American Revolution (Yorktown) and the Civil War (Appomattox) occurred in Virginia. The state is called the "Mother of Presidents" because eight chief executives of the United States were born there.

Today, Virginia has a large number of diversified manufacturing industries including chemicals, textiles, food products, and clothing. Other important lines are lumber, paper, furniture, cigarettes, electrical machinery, transportation equipment, and stone-glass-clay products.

Agriculture remains an important sector in the Virginia economy and the state ranks among the leaders in the U.S. in tobacco, peanuts, apples, and sweet potatoes. Other crops include corn, vegetables, barley, and peaches. Famous for its turkeys and Smithfield hams, Virginia also has a large dairy industry.

Coal mining accounts for roughly 70% of Virginia's mineral output, and lime, zinc, and stone are also mined.

Points of interest include Mt. Vernon and other places associated with George Washington; Monticello, home of Thomas Jefferson; Stratford, home of the Lees; Richmond, capital of the Confederacy and of Virginia; and Williamsburg, the restored Colonial capital.

The Chesapeake Bay Bridge-Tunnel spans the mouth of Chesapeake Bay, connecting Cape Charles with Norfolk. Consisting of a series of low trestles, two bridges and two mile-long tunnels, the complex is 18 miles (29 km) long. It was opened in 1964.

Other attractions are the Shenandoah National Park, Fredericksburg and Spotsylvania National Military Park, the Booker T. Washington birthplace near Roanoke, Arlington House (the Robert E. Lee Memorial), the Skyline Drive, and the Blue Ridge National Parkway.

WASHINGTON

Capital: Olympia
Governor: John Spellman (to Jan. 1985)
Lieut. Governor: John A. Cherberg, (to Jan. 1985)

Secy. of State: Ralph Munro (to Jan. 1985)
State Treasurer: Robert S. O'Brien (to Jan. 1985)
Atty. General: Kenneth O. Eikenberry (to Jan. 1985)
Organized as territory: March 2, 1853
Entered Union & (rank): Nov. 11, 1889 (42)
Present constitution adopted: 1889
Motto: *Al-Ki* (Indian word meaning "by and by")
State flower: Rhododendron (1949)
State tree: Western hemlock (1947)
State bird: Willow goldfinch (1951)
State fish: Steelhead trout (1969)
State gem: Petrified wood (1975)
State colors: Green and gold (1925)
State song: "Washington, My Home" (1959)
State dance: Square dance (1979)
Nicknames: Evergreen State; Chinook State
Origin of name: In honor of George Washington
1970 population & (rank): 3,413,244 (22)
1980 population (1980 census) & (rank): 4,130,163 (20)
1980 land area & (rank): 66,570 sq mi (172,416 sq km) (20)
Geographic center: In Chelan Co., 10 mi. WSW of Wenatchee
Number of counties: 39
Largest cities (1980 census): Seattle, 493,846; Spokane, 171,300; Tacoma, 158,501; Bellevue, 73,903; Everett, 54,413; Yakima, 49,826; Bellingham, 45,794
State forest lands: 1,922,880 ac.
State parks: 202 (171,700 ac.)[1]
State revenue (1981–83 projected): $13,386,100,000
State expenditure (1981–83 projected): $14,244,800,000

1. Parks and undeveloped areas administered by Parks and Recreation Dept. Game Dept. administers wildlife and recreation areas totaling 762,895 acres.

As part of the vast Oregon Country, Washington territory was visited by Spanish, American, and British explorers—Bruno Heceta for Spain in 1775, the American Capt. Robert Gray in 1792, and Capt. George Vancouver for Britain in 1792–94. Lewis and Clark explored the Columbia River region and coastal areas for the U.S. in 1805–06.

Rival American and British settlers and conflicting territorial claims threatened war in the early 1840s. However, in 1846 the Oregon Treaty set the boundary at the 49th parallel and war was averted.

Washington is a leading lumber producer. Its rugged surface is rich in stands of Douglas fir, hemlock, ponderosa and white pine, spruce, larch, and cedar. The state holds first place in apples, blueberries, hops, and red raspberries and it ranks high in potatoes, winter wheat, pears, grapes, apricots, and strawberries. Livestock and livestock products make important contributions to total farm revenue and the commercial fishing catch of salmon, halibut, and bottomfish makes a significant contribution to the state's economy.

Manufacturing industries in Washington include aircraft and missiles, shipbuilding and other transportation equipment, lumber, food processing, metals and metal products, chemicals, and machinery.

The Columbia River contains one third of the potential water power in the U.S., harnessed by such dams as the Grand Coulee, one of the greatest power producers in the world. Washington has 90 dams throughout the state built for irrigation, power, flood control, and water storage. Its abundance of electrical power makes Washington the nation's largest producer of refined aluminum.

Among the major points of interest: Mt. Rainier, Olympic, and North Cascades. In 1980, Mount St. Helens, a peak in the Cascade Range in Southwest-

ern Washington erupted on May 18th. Also of interest are National Parks; Whitman Mission and Fort Vancouver National Historic Sites; and the Pacific Science Center and Space Needle in Seattle.

WEST VIRGINIA

Capital: Charleston
Governor: John D. Rockefeller IV, D (to Jan. 1985)
Secy. of State: James A. Manchin, D (to Jan. 1985)
State Auditor: Glen Gainer (to Jan. 1985)
Atty. General: Chauncey H. Browning, Jr., D (to Jan. 1985)
Entered Union & (rank): June 20, 1863 (35)
Present constitution adopted: 1872
Motto: *Montani semper liberi* (Mountaineers are always free)
State flower: Rhododendron (1903)
State tree: Sugar maple (1949)
State bird: Cardinal (1949)
State animal: Black bear
State colors: Blue and gold (unofficial)
State songs: "West Virginia, My Home Sweet Home," "The West Virginia Hills," and "This Is My West Virginia" (adopted by Legislature in 1947, 1961 and 1963 as official state songs)
Nickname: Mountain State
Origin of name: Same as for Virginia
1970 population & (rank): 1,744,237 (34)
1980 population (1980 census) & (rank): 1,949,644 (34)
1980 land area & (rank): 24,070 sq mi. (62,341 sq km) (41)

Geographic center: In Braxton Co., 4 mi. E of Sutton
Number of counties: 55
Largest cities (1980 census): Charleston, 63,968; Huntington, 63,684; Wheeling, 43,070; Parkersburg, 39,967; Morgantown, 27,605; Weirton, 24,736
State forests: 9 (77,000 ac.)
State parks: 34 (65,861 ac.)
Total state revenue (1979–80): $3,608,262,063
Total state expenditure (1979–80): $3,638,672,449

West Virginia's early history from 1609 until 1863 is largely shared with Virginia, of which it was a part until Virginia seceded from the Union in 1861. Then the delegates of 40 western counties formed their own government, which was granted statehood in 1863.

First permanent settlement dates from 1731 when Morgan Morgan founded Mill Creek. In 1742 coal was discovered on the Coal River, an event that would be of great significance in determining West Virginia's future.

The state usually ranks first in bituminous coal production with about 20% of the U.S. total. It also is a leader in steel, glass, aluminum, and chemical manufactures; natural gas, oil, quarry products, and hardwood lumber.

Poultry, dairy products, cattle, and sheep account for the major portion of farm receipts. Apples, peaches, wheat, corn, and hay are profitable crops. More than 75% of West Virginia is covered with forests.

Tourism is increasingly popular in mountainous West Virginia and visitors spend over $750 million annually. More than a million acres have been set aside in 34 state parks and recreation areas and in 9 state forests.

Major points of interest include Harpers Ferry and Chesapeake and Ohio Canal National Historical Parks, White Sulphur Springs and Berkeley Springs resorts, the scenic railroad at Cass, and the historic homes at Charles Town.

WISCONSIN

Capital: Madison
Governor: Lee Sherman Dreyfus, R (to Jan. 1983)
Lieut. Governor: Russell A. Olson, R (to Jan. 1983)
Secy. of State: Vel R. Phillips, D (to Jan. 1983)
State Treasurer: Charles P. Smith, D (to Jan. 1983)
Atty. General: Bronson C. La Follette, D (to Jan. 1983)
Superintendent of Public Instruction: Herbert J. Grover, Nonpartisan (to July 1985)
Organized as territory: July 4, 1836
Entered Union & (rank): May 29, 1848 (30)
Present constitution adopted: 1848
Motto: Forward
State flower: Wood violet
State tree: Sugar maple
State bird: Robin
State animal: Badger; "wild life" animal: white-tailed deer; "domestic" animal: dairy cow
State insect: Honeybee (1977)
State fish: Musky (Muskellunge)
State song: "On Wisconsin"
State mineral: Galena (1971)
State rock: Red Granite (1971)
Nickname: Badger State
Origin of name: French corruption of an Indian word whose meaning is disputed
1970 population & (rank): 4,417,821 (16)
1980 population (1980 census) & (rank): 4,705,335 (16)
1980 land area & (rank): 54,464 sq mi. (141,062 sq km) (25)

Geographic center: In Wood Co., 9 mi. SE of Marshfield
Number of counties: 72
Largest cities (1980 census): Milwaukee, 636,212; Madison, 170,616; Green Bay, 87,899; Racine, 85,725; Kenosha, 77,685; West Allis, 63,982; Appleton, 59,032
State forests: 8 (449,486 ac.)
State parks & scenic trails: 55 parks, 8 trails (61,340 ac.)
State revenue (1979–80): $7,381,599,086
State expenditure (1979–80): $6,836,970,173

The Wisconsin region was first explored for France by Jean Nicolet who landed at Green Bay in 1634. In 1660 a French trading post and Roman Catholic mission were established near present-day Ashland.

Great Britain obtained the region in settlement of the French and Indian War in 1763; the U.S. acquired it in 1783 after the Revolutionary War. However, Great Britain retained actual control until after the War of 1812. The region was successively governed as part of the territories of Indiana, Illinois, and Michigan between 1800 and 1836, when it became a separate territory.

Wisconsin leads the nation in milk and cheese production. In 1979, the state ranked first in the number of milk cows (1,813,000), and produced nearly 18% of the nation's total output of milk. Other important farm products are peas, beets, corn, potatoes, cabbage, maple sugar, and cranberries.

The chief industrial products of the state are automobiles, machinery, furniture, paper, beer, and processed foods. Wisconsin ranks second among the 47 paper-producing states. Tourism also ranks among the major industries.

Wisconsin pioneered in social legislation, providing pensions for the blind (1907), aid to dependent children (1913), and old-age assistance (1925). In 1932 it was the first state to enact an unemployment compensation law. In labor legislation, the state has also pioneered in important laws, among them the first workmen's compensation law actually to take effect. Wisconsin had the first state-wide primary-election law and the first successful income-tax law.

The state has over 8,500 lakes, of which Winnebago is the largest. Water sports, ice-boating, and fishing are popular, as are skiing and hunting. Public parks and forests take up one seventh of the land, with 55 state parks, 8 state forests, and 2 national forests.

Among the many points of interest are the Apostle Islands National Lakeshore; Ice Age National Scientific Reserve; the Circus World Museum at Baraboo; the Wolf, St. Croix, and Lower St. Croix national scenic riverways; and the Wisconsin Dells.

WYOMING

Capital: Cheyenne
Governor: Ed Herschler, D (to Jan. 1983)
Secy. of State: Thyra G. Thomson, R (to Jan. 1983)
Auditor: James B. Griffith, Jr., R (to Jan. 1983)
Treasurer: Shirley Wittler, D (to Jan. 1983)
Atty. General: Steven F. Freudenthal, D (apptd. by Governor)
Organized as territory: May 19, 1869
Entered Union & (rank): July 10, 1890 (44)
Present constitution adopted: 1890
Motto: Equal rights (1955)
State flower: Indian paintbrush (1917)
State tree: Cottonwood (1947)
State bird: Meadow lark (1927)
State gemstone: Jade (1967)
State insignia: Bucking horse (unofficial)
State song: "Wyoming" (1955)
Nickname: Equality State
Origin of name: From the Delaware Indian word, meaning "mountains and valleys alternating"; the same as the Wyoming Valley in Pennsylvania
1970 population & (rank): 332,416 (49)
1980 population (1980 census) & (rank): 470,816 (49)
1980 land area & (rank): 97,203 sq mi. (251,756 sq km) (9)
Geographic center: In Fremont Co., 58 mi. ENE of Lander
Number of counties: 23, plus Yellowstone National Park
Largest cities (1980 census): Casper, 51,016; Cheyenne,

47,283; Laramie, 24,410; Rock Springs, 19,458; Sheridan, 15,146; Green River, 12,807; Gillette, 12,134
State forests: None
State parks: 9 (44,732 ac.)
Estimated income (1980–82): $816,225,862
Estimated expenditure (1980–82): $533,345,366

The U.S. acquired the territory from France as part of the Louisiana Purchase in 1803. John Colter, a fur-trapper, is the first white man known to have entered present Wyoming. In 1807 he explored the Yellowstone area and brought back news of its geysers and hot springs.

Robert Stuart pioneered the Oregon Trail across Wyoming in 1812–13 and, in 1834, Fort Laramie, the first permanent trading post in Wyoming, was built. Western Wyoming was obtained by the U.S. in the 1846 Oregon Treaty with Great Britain and as a result of the treaty ending the Mexican War in 1848.

When the Wyoming Territory was organized in 1869 Wyoming women became the first in the nation to obtain the right to vote. In 1925 Mrs. Nellie Tayloe Ross was elected first woman governor in the United States.

Wyoming's towering mountains and vast plains provide spectacular scenery, grazing lands for sheep and cattle, and rich mineral deposits.

Mining, particularly oil and natural gas, is the most important industry. In January 1981, Wyoming led the nation in sodium carbonate (natrona) and bentonite production, and was second in uranium.

Wyoming ranks second among the states in wool production. In January 1981, its sheep numbered 1,110,000, exceeded only by Texas and California; it also had 1,350,000 cattle. Principal crops include wheat, oats, sugar beets, corn, potatoes, barley, and alfalfa.

Second in mean elevation to Colorado, Wyoming has many attractions for the tourist trade, notably Yellowstone National Park. Cheyenne is famous for its annual "Frontier Days" celebration. Flaming Gorge, the Fort Laramie National Historic Site, and Devils Tower and Fossil Butte National Monuments are other National points of interest.

Self-Governing Areas

PUERTO RICO

Capital: San Juan
Governor: Carlos Romero Barceló, New Progressive Party (to Jan. 1985)
Song: "La Borinqueña"
1970 population: 2,712,033
1980 est. population: 3,300,000
1980 land area: 3,421 sq mi. (8,860 sq km)
Largest cities (1976): San Juan (516,500); Ponce (198,600); Caguas (117,600); Mayagüez (102,500)

Puerto Rico is an island about 100 miles long and 35 miles wide at the northeastern end of the Caribbean Sea. It is a self-governing Commonwealth freely and voluntarily associated with the U.S. Under its Constitution, a Governor and a Legislative Assembly are elected by direct vote for a four-year period. The judiciary is vested in a Supreme Court and lower courts established by law. The people elect a Resident Commissioner to the U.S. House of Representatives, where he has a voice but

no vote. The island was formerly an unincorporated territory of the U.S. after being ceded by Spain as a result of the Spanish-American War.

The Commonwealth, established in 1952, has one of the highest standards of living in Latin America. Featuring Puerto Rican economic development is Operation Bootstrap. This program has established over 2,300 new factories and has greatly increased agricultural production, transportation and communications facilities, electric power, housing, and other industries.

The island's chief exports are chemicals, textiles, fish products and petroleum products.

Columbus discovered the island on his second voyage to America in 1493.

GUAM

Capital: Agaña
Governor: Paul M. Calvo
1950 population: 59,498
1960 population: 67,044

1970 population: 84,996
1980 population: 105,816
1980 land area: 212 sq mi. (549 sq km)

Guam, the largest of the Mariana Islands, is independent of the trusteeship assigned to the U.S. in 1947. It was acquired by the U.S. from Spain in 1898 (occupied 1899) and was placed under the Navy Department.

In World War II, Guam was seized by the Japanese on Dec. 11, 1941; but on July 21, 1944, it was once more in U. S. hands.

On Aug. 1, 1950, President Truman signed a bill which granted U.S. citizenship to the people of Guam and established self-government. However, the people do not vote in national elections. In 1972 Guam elected its first delegate to the U.S. Congress. The Executive Branch of the Guam government is under the general supervision of the U.S. Secretary of the Interior. In November 1970, Guam elected its first Governor.

Military installations and tourism are important factors in Guam's economy.

Non-Self-Governing Territories

AMERICAN SAMOA

Capital: Fagatogo (on Tutuila Island)
Governor: Peter Tali Coleman
Lieut. Governor: Tufele Liá
1950 population: 18,937
1960 population: 20,051
1980 est. population: 33,506
1970 land area: 76 sq mi. (197 sq km)

American Samoa, a group of five volcanic islands and two coral atolls located some 2,600 miles south of Hawaii in the South Pacific Ocean, is an unincorporated, unorganized territory of the U.S., administered by the Department of the Interior.

By the Treaty of Berlin, signed Dec. 2, 1899, and ratified Feb. 16, 1900, the U.S. was internationally acknowledged to have rights extending over all the islands of the Samoa group east of longitude 171° west of Greenwich. On April 17, 1900, the chiefs of Tutuila and Aunu'u ceded those islands to the U.S. In 1904, the King and chiefs of Manu'a ceded the islands of Ofu, Olosega and Tau (composing the Manu'a group) to the U.S. Swains Island, some 214 miles north of Samoa, was included as part of the territory by Act of Congress March 4, 1925; and on Feb. 20, 1929, Congress formally accepted sovereignty over the entire group and placed the responsibility for administration in the hands of the President. From 1900 to 1951, by Presidential direction, the Department of the Navy governed the territory. On July 1, 1951, administration was transferred to the Department of the Interior. The first Constitution for the territory was signed on April 27, 1960, and became effective on Oct. 17, 1960. It was revised in 1967.

Congress has provided for a non-voting delegate to sit in the House of Representatives in 1981.

The principal products are canned tuna, pet food, fish meal, mats, and handicrafts.

BAKER, HOWLAND, AND JARVIS ISLANDS

These Pacific islands were not to play a role in the extraterritorial plans of the U.S. until May 13, 1936. President F. D. Roosevelt, at that time, placed them under the control and jurisdiction of the Secretary of the Interior for administration purposes.

Baker Island is a saucer-shaped atoll with an area of approximately one square mile. It is about 1,650 miles from Hawaii.

Howland Island, 36 miles to the northeast, is approximately one and a half miles long and half a mile wide.

Jarvis Island is several hundred miles to the east and is approximately two miles long by one and an eighth miles wide.

Baker, Howland, and Jarvis have been uninhabited since 1942. In 1974, these islands became part of the National Wildlife Refuge System, administered by the U.S. Fish & Wildlife Service, Department of The Interior.

CANTON AND ENDERBURY ISLANDS

Canton and Enderbury islands, the largest of the Phoenix group, are jointly administered by the U.S. and Great Britain after an agreement signed April 6, 1939. The status of Canton and Enderbury was the subject of negotiations between the U.S., U.K., and Gilbert Islands Governments in 1979. The negotiations resulted in the signing on September 20, 1979, of a Treaty of Friendship between the U.S. and the Republic of Kiribati, which, once ratified by the U.S. Senate, will formally renounce the U.S. claim to Canton and Enderbury. The Republic of Kiribati declared its independence on July 12, 1979.

Canton is triangular in shape and the largest of the eight islands of this group. It lies about 1,600 miles southwest of Hawaii and was discovered at the turn of the 18th century by U.S. whalers. After World War II it served as an aviation support facility, and later as a missile tracking station. Since 1967, the island has been utilized by the U.S. Air Force Space and Missile Test Center.

Enderbury is rectangular in shape and is 3.5 miles long by 1.5 miles wide. It is unpopulated and lies about 32 miles southeast of Canton.

JOHNSTON ATOLL

Johnston is a coral atoll about 700 miles southwest of Hawaii. It consists of four small islands—Johnston Island, Sand Island, Hikina Island, and Akau Island—which lie on a reef about 9 miles long in a northeast-southwest direction.

The atoll was discovered by Capt. Charles James Johnston of *H.M.S. Cornwallis* in 1807. In 1858 it was claimed by Hawaii, and later became a U.S. possession.

Johnston Atoll is a Naval Defense Sea Area and Airspace Reservation and is closed to the public. The administration of Johnston Atoll is under the jurisdiction of the Defense Nuclear Agency, Commander, Johnston Atoll (FGDNA), APO San Francisco, CA 96305.

KINGMAN REEF

Kingman Reef, located about 1,000 miles south of Hawaii, was discovered by Capt. E. Fanning in 1798, but named for Capt. W. E. Kingman, who rediscovered it in 1853. The reef, drying only on its northeast, east and southeast edges, is of atoll character. A small islet, 3 feet high, lies on its east side. The reef is triangular in shape, with its apex northward; it is about 9.5 miles long, east and west, and 5 miles wide, north and south, within the 100-fathom curve.

A United States possession, Kingman Reef is a Defense Sea Area and Airspace Reservation, and is closed to the public. The Airspace Entry Control has been suspended, but is subject to immediate reinstatement without notice. No vessel or aircraft, except those authorized by the Secretary of the Navy, shall be navigated in or above the area within the 3-mile limit.

MIDWAY ISLANDS

Midway Islands, lying about 1,200 miles westnorthwest of Hawaii, were discovered by Captain N. C. Brooks of the Hawaiian bark *Gambia* on July 5, 1859, in the name of the United States. The atoll was formally declared a U.S. possession in 1867, and in 1903 Theodore Roosevelt made it a naval reservation.

Midway Islands consist of a circular atoll, 6 miles in diameter, and enclosing two islands. Eastern Island, on its southeast side, is triangular in shape, and about 1.2 miles long. Sand Island on its south side, is about 2 miles long in a northeast-southwest direction.

The Midway Islands are within a naval defensive sea area. The Navy Department maintains an installation and has jurisdiction over the atoll. Permission to enter the Naval Defense Sea Area must be obtained in advance from the Commanding Officer, Naval Air Facility, Midway Islands, FPO San Francisco, CA 96614.

SWAN ISLANDS

The Swan Islands are two small islands, Great Swan and Little Swan, in the Caribbean Sea, 98 miles north of Honduras. They were claimed by the U.S. in 1863, but Honduras also claimed them on the basis of their discovery by the Spanish. After years of dispute, the U.S. in 1971 signed a treaty recognizing Honduran sovereignty over the islands. The treaty ratifications were exchanged on Sept. 1, 1972.

U.S. VIRGIN ISLANDS

Capital: Charlotte Amalie (on St. Thomas)
Governor: Juan Luis
1950 population: 26,665
1960 population: 32,099
1970 population: 62,468 (St. Thomas, 28,960; St. Croix, 31,779; St. John, 1,729)
1980 est. population: 95,214 (St. Croix, 48,916; St. Thomas, 43,828; St. John, 2,470)

1980 land area: 136 sq mi. (352 sq km) (St. Croix, 84 [218 sq km]; St. Thomas, 32 [83 sq km]; St. John, 20 [52 sq km])

The Virgin Islands, consisting of nine main islands and some 75 islets, were discovered by Columbus in 1493. Since 1666, England has held six of the main islands; the other three (St. Croix, St. Thomas, and St. John), as well as about 50 of the islets, were eventually acquired by Denmark, which named them the Danish West Indies. In 1917, these islands were purchased by the U.S. from Denmark for $25 million.

Congress granted U.S. citizenship to Virgin Islanders in 1927; and, in 1931, administration was transferred from the Navy to the Department of the Interior. Universal suffrage was given in 1936 to all persons who could read and write the English language. The Governor was elected by popular vote for the first time in 1970; previously he had been appointed by the President of the U.S. A unicameral 15-man legislature serves the Virgin Islands, and recent Congressional legislation gave the islands a non-voting Representative in Congress.

The "Constitution" of the Virgin Islands is the Revised Organic Act. of 1954 in which the U.S. Congress defines the three branches of the territorial government, i.e., the Executive Branch, the Legislative Branch, and the Judicial Branch. Residents of the islands substantially enjoy the same rights as those enjoyed by mainlanders with one important exception: citizens of the U.S. who are residents may not vote in presidential elections.

About 80% of the population is black, and there is limited farming, fishing, and cattle raising. Industrial products include rum, watches, costume jewelry, clothing, alumina, pharmaceuticals, and petroleum products. Tourism is the principal industry.

WAKE ISLAND

Wake Island, about halfway between Midway and Guam, is an atoll comprising the three islets of Wilkes, Peale, and Wake. They were discovered by the British in 1796 and annexed by the U.S. in 1898. The entire area comprises 3 square miles and has no native population. In 1938, Pan American Airways established a seaplane base and Wake Island has been used as a commercial base since then. On Dec. 8, 1941, it was attacked by the Japanese, who finally took possession on Dec. 23. It was surrendered by the Japanese on Sept. 4, 1945.

The Federal Aviation Administration maintained a station on Wake Island until June 1972, when civil administration of the island was taken over by the U.S. Air Force. In 1962, the area was placed under the jurisdiction of the Department of the Interior.

Trust Territory of the Pacific Islands (Micronesia)

In 1885, Germany assumed a protectorate over the Marshall Islands; and, in 1899, she purchased the Northern Mariana and Caroline Islands from Spain. These islands were occupied by the Japanese in 1914 and were mandated to Japan by the League of Nations in 1919. On April 2, 1947, the U. N. Security Council approved a trusteeship agreement proposed by the U.S. under which the Northern Mariana, Caroline, and Marshall Islands became a Strategic Trust Territory under the administration of the U.S. The measure was approved by the President, with the agreement of Congress, on July 18, 1947. Administration was transferred from the Navy to the Department of the Interior on July 1, 1951. However, during 1953, administration of the islands of the Northern Marianas, except Rota, was transferred back to the Navy. The Department of the Interior again took over administration of these islands in July, 1962.

In February 1975 a covenant was signed by the

U.S. and the Marianas Political Status Commission that would make the 17 islands in the Northern Marianas a commonwealth under American sovereignty. The covenant was overwhelmingly ratified by the people of the islands and was approved by President Ford on March 24, 1976.

On April 9, 1978, in Hilo, Hawaii, the heads of the three Micronesian political status commissions and the U.S. negotiator signed a statement of agreed principles which is intended to form the basis of a free association relationship between the U.S. and Micronesia. A draft Compact of Free Association was initialled by the U.S. and the respective Micronesian commissions in late 1980, and the U.S. currently has the agreement under review.

The entire group comprises more than 2,000 islands, but the total land area is only 717 square miles, many of the islands being only tiny coral reefs. The Micronesians are the main ethnic group; however, the inhabitants of two outlying islands, Kapingamarangi and Nukuoro, are Polynesian. The population of the Trust Territory in 1977 was estimated to be 126,440.

MARIANA ISLANDS

The Mariana Islands, east of the Philippines and south of Japan, include the islands of Guam, Rota, Saipan, Tinian, Pagan, Guguan, Agrihan, and Aguijan. Guam, the largest, is independent of the trusteeship, having been acquired by the U.S. from Spain in 1898. (For more information, *see* the entry on Guam in this section.)

Chief crops are copra and fresh fruits and vegetables.

CAROLINE ISLANDS

The Caroline Islands, east of the Philippines and south of the Marianas, include the Yap, Truk, and the Palau groups and the islands of Ponape and Kosrae, as well as many coral atolls.

The islands are composed chiefly of volcanic rock, and their peaks rise 2,000 to 3,000 feet above sea level. Chief exports of the islands are copra, fish products, and handicrafts.

MARSHALL ISLANDS

The Marshall Islands, east of the Carolines, are divided into two chains: the western or Ralik group, including the atolls Jaluit, Kwajalein, Wotho, Bikini, and Enewetak; and the eastern or Ratak group, including the atolls Mili, Majuro, Maloelap, Wotje, and Likiep.

The islands are of the coral-reef type and rise only a few feet above sea level. The chief crop is coconuts; exports include copra, tortoise shell, mother-of-pearl, etc.

Bikini and Enewetak were the scene of several atom-bomb tests after World War II. Enewetak was returned to Trust Territory administration in August 1976. In April 1977, some 55 original inhabitants, the forerunner of 450 returnees, were resettled after an absence of 30 years.

The Governors of the Fifty States

State	Governor	Year of birth	Current term[1]	State	Governor	Year of birth	Current term[1]
Ala.	Forrest James, Jr., D	1936	1979–83	Mont.	Ted Schwinden, D	1925	1981–85
Alaska	Jay S. Hammond, R	1922	1978–82[2]	Neb.	Charles Thone, R	1924	1979–83
Ariz.	Bruce E. Babbitt, D	1938	1979–83	Nev.	Robert F. List, R	1936	1979–83
Ark.	Frank D. White, R	1934	1981–83	N.H.	Hugh J. Gallen, D	1924	1981–83
Calif.	Edmund G. Brown, Jr., D	1938	1979–83	N.J.	Brendan T. Byrne, D	1924	1978–82
Colo.	Richard D. Lamm, D	1935	1979–83	N.M.	Bruce King, D	1924	1979–83
Conn.	William A. O'Neill, D	1930	1980–83	N.Y.	Hugh L. Carey, D	1919	1979–83
Del.	Pierre S. du Pont, IV, R	1935	1981–85	N.C.	James B. Hunt, Jr., D	1937	1981–85
Fla.	Robert Graham, D	1936	1979–83	N.D.	Allen I. Olson, R	1938	1981–85
Ga.	George Busbee, D	1927	1979–83	Ohio	James A. Rhodes, R	1909	1979–83
Hawaii	George R. Ariyoshi, D	1926	1978–82[2]	Okla.	George P. Nigh, D	1927	1979–83
Idaho	John V. Evans, D	1925	1979–83	Ore.	Victor G. Atiyeh, R	1923	1979–83
Ill.	James R. Thompson, R	1936	1979–83	Pa.	Richard L. Thornburgh, R	1932	1979–83
Ind.	Robert D. Orr, R	1917	1981–85	R.I.	J. Joseph Garrahy, D	1931	1981–83
Iowa	Robert D. Ray, R	1928	1979–83	S.C.	Richard W. Riley, D	1933	1979–83
Kan.	John W. Carlin, D	1940	1979–83	S.D.	William J. Janklow, R	1939	1979–83
Ky.	John Y. Brown, Jr., D	1934	1979–83[2]	Tenn.	Lamar Alexander, R	1940	1979–83
La.	David C. Treen, R	1928	1980–84[3]	Tex.	Bill Clements, R	1917	1979–83
Me.	Joseph E. Brennan, D	1934	1979–83	Utah	Scott M. Matheson, D	1929	1981–85
Md.	Harry R. Hughes, D	1926	1979–83	Vt.	Richard A. Snelling, R	1928	1981–83
Mass.	Edward J. King, D	1925	1979–83	Va.	John N. Dalton, R	1931	1978–82
Mich.	William G. Milliken, R	1922	1979–83	Wash.	John Spellman, R	1927	1981–85
Minn.	Albert H. Quie, R	1923	1979–83	W.Va.	John D. Rockefeller IV, D	1937	1981–85
Miss.	William F. Winter, D	1923	1980–84	Wis.	Lee Sherman Dreyfus, R	1926	1979–83
Mo.	Christopher S. Bond, R	1939	1981–85	Wyo.	Ed C. Herschler, D	1918	1979–83

1. Except where indicated, all terms begin in January. 2. December. 3. March.

Tabulated Data on State Governments

State	Governor Term, years	Governor Annual salary	Legislature[1] Membership U[3]	Legislature[1] Membership L[4]	Legislature[1] Term, yrs. U[3]	Legislature[1] Term, yrs. L[4]	Legislature[1] Salaries of members[5]	Highest Court[2] Members	Highest Court[2] Term, years	Highest Court[2] Annual salary[6]
Alabama	4[10]	$50,000[16]	35	105	4	4	$6,800 per annum[16]	9	6	$39,500
Alaska	4	74,196	20	40	4	2	18,768 per annum	5	(8)	74,196
Arizona	4	50,000	30	60	2	2	15,000 per annum	5	6	47,500
Arkansas	2	35,000	35	100	4	2	7,500 per annum[26]	7	8	46,214
California	4	49,100	40	80	4	2	28,110 per annum	7	12	62,935[26]
Colorado	4	50,000	35	65	4	2	14,000 per annum[27]	7	10	50,000
Connecticut	4	42,000	36	151	2	2	17,000 per biennium	6	8	46,600
Delaware	4[9]	35,000	21	41	4	2	10,545 per annum	5	12	46,000
Florida	4[10]	60,498	40	120	4	2	12,000 per annum	7	6	60,453
Georgia	4[9]	65,934	56	180	2	2	7,200 per annum	7	6	53,325
Hawaii	4	50,000	25	51	4	2	13,650 per session	5	10	45,000
Idaho	4	33,000	35	70	2	2	4,200 per annum	5	6	38,000
Illinois	4	58,000	59	118	4-2	2	28,000 per annum	7	10	58,000
Indiana	4[10]	48,000	50	100	4	2	9,600 per annum	5	(25)	42,000
Iowa	4	60,000	50	100	4	2	12,000 per annum	9	8	49,000
Kansas	4	45,000	40	125	4	2	42 per diem[22]	7	6	47,500
Kentucky	4[7]	50,000	38	100	4	2	50 per diem[22]	7	8	49,000
Louisiana	4	52,400	39	105	4	4	75 per diem[23 16]	7	10	56,200
Maine	4	35,000	33	151	2	2	7,000 per biennium[16]	7	7	36,637
Maryland	4[10]	60,000	47	141	4	4	18,500 per annum	7	10	56,200
Massachusetts	4	60,000	40	160	2	2	20,335 per annum	7	Life	50,000
Michigan	4	61,500	38	110	4	2	27,000 per annum	7	8	56,500
Minnesota	4	58,000	67	134	4	2	18,500 per annum[16]	9	6	56,000
Mississippi	4[7]	53,000	52	122	4	4	8,100 per session	9	8	46,000
Missouri	4[10]	55,000	34	163	4	2	15,000 per annum[5]	7	12	50,000
Montana	4	37,500	50	100	4	2	40 per diem[16]	7	8	43,360[28]
Nebraska	4[10]	40,000	49[11]	—	4[11]	—	4,800 per annum	7	6	48,315
Nevada	4	50,000	20	40	4	2	4,800 per biennium	5	6	47,250
New Hampshire	2	47,550	24	(12)	2	2	200 per biennium	5	(13)	45,280
New Jersey	4[10]	65,000	40	80	4[14]	2	18,000 per annum	7	7[15]	63,000
New Mexico	4[7]	50,000	42	70	4	2	40 per diem	5	8	49,500
New York	4	85,000	60	150	2	2	23,500 per annum	7	14	69,352
North Carolina	4[9]	55,104	50	120	2	2	6,936 per annum[16]	7	8	55,440
North Dakota	4	47,000[16]	50	100	4	2	5 per diem[16 24]	5	10	49,900[29]
Ohio	4	50,000	33	99	4	2	22,500 per annum	7	6	51,000
Oklahoma	4	48,000	48	101	4	2	18,000 per annum	(19)	6	48,000
Oregon	4[10]	55,423	30	60	4	2	8,400 per annum	7	6	53,308
Pennsylvania	4[10]	66,000	50	203	4	2	25,000 per annum	7	10	64,500
Rhode Island	2	42,500	50	100	2	2	5 per diem[17]	5	(18)	48,788
South Carolina	4[7]	60,000	46	124	4	2	10,000 per annum	5	10	47,000
South Dakota	4[10]	46,750	35	70	2	2	6,000 per biennium	5	8	43,000
Tennessee	4	68,226	33	99	4	2	8,308 per annum	(20)	8	62,616
Texas	4	78,700	31	150	4	2	7,200 per annum	(20)	6	65,700
Utah	4	48,000	29	75	4	2	800 per session	5	10	46,500
Vermont	2	44,850	30	150	2	2	250 per week[21]	5	6	37,630
Virginia	4[7]	75,000	40	100	4	2	8,000 per annum	7	12	58,000
Washington	4	63,000	49	98	4	2	11,200 per annum	9	6	51,500
West Virginia	4	60,000	34	100	4	2	5,136 per annum	5	12	49,000
Wisconsin	4	65,801	33	99	4	2	22,638 per annum	7	10	56,009
Wyoming	4	55,000	30	62	4	2	30 per diem[16]	5	8	55,775

1. General Assembly in Ark., Colo., Conn., Del., Ga., Ind., Ky., Md., Mo., N.C., Ohio, Pa., R.I., S.C., Tenn., Vt., Va.; Legislative Assembly in N.D., Ore.; General Court in Mass., N.H.; Legislature in other states. Meets biennially in Calif., Ky., Me., Mont., Nev., N.H., N.J., N.C., N.D., Ore., Pa., Texas, Wash. and Wyo.; meets annually in other states. 2. Court of Appeals in Md., N.Y., Supreme Court of Virginia in Va., Supreme Judicial Court in Me., Mass.; Supreme Court in other states. 3. Upper house: Senate in all states. 4. Lower house: Assembly in Calif., Nev., N.Y., Wis.; House of Delegates in Md., Va., W.Va.; General Assembly in N.J.; House of Representatives in other states. 5. Does not include additional payments for expenses, mileage, special sessions, etc., or additional per diem payments beyond salary shown. 6. In some states, Chief Justice receives a higher salary. 7. Cannot succeed himself. 8. Appointed for 3 years; thereafter subject to approval or rejection on a nonpartisan ballot for 10-year term. 9. May serve only 2 terms, consecutive or otherwise. 10. May not serve 3rd consecutive term. 11. Unicameral legislature. 12. Constitutional number: 375–400. 13. Until 70 years old. 14. When term begins in Jan. of 2nd year following U.S. census, term shall be 2 years. 15. 2nd term receive tenure, mandatory retirement at 70. 16. Plus additional expenses. 17. For 60 days only. 18. Term of good behavior. 19. 9 members in Supreme Court, highest in civil cases; 3 in Court of Criminal Appeals. 20. 9 members in Supreme Court, highest in civil cases; 9 in Court of Criminal Appeals. 21. To limit of $7,500 per biennium; $2,000 for special session. 22. When in session. 23. $1,000 per month when not in session. 24. Plus $180 per month. 25. Appointed for 2 years; thereafter elected popularly for 10-year term. 26. To receive cost of living increase not to exceed 10% in the two year period. 27. Those elected before 1980 receive $12,000 until re-elected. 28. $47,023 after June 30, 1982. 29. $53,900 after June 30, 1982. *Source: Information Please* questionnaires to the states.

50 Largest Cities of the United States

Source of population and land area: Bureau of the Census. Television households apply to county or counties in which a city is located, except for independent cities; source: the Arbitron Company. Telephones; source: American Telephone & Telegraph Co. Other data were supplied by the cities in response to *Information Please* questionnaires.

ALBUQUERQUE, N.M.

Incorporated as city: 1891
Mayor: David Rusk (to Dec. 1981)
1970 population & (rank): 244,501 (58)
1980 population (1980 census) & (rank): 331,767 (45)
1970–80 population change: +35.7%
1980 land area: 95.2 sq mi.
Altitude: 4,958 ft.
Location: Central part of state on Rio Grande River
County: Bernalillo
Churches: 211
City-owned parks: 135
Telephones (Jan. 1, 1979): 308,271
Television households (Jan. 1, 1980): 141,600 (98%)
Radio stations: 14
Television stations: 5
Assessed valuation (1980): $1,318,049,290
City tax rate (1981): $22.02 per $1,000
Bonded debt (1981): $113,930,000
Revenue (1981): $86,080,200
Expenditures (1981): $91,778,547
Chamber of Commerce: Albuquerque Chamber of Commerce, 401 2nd St., N.W., Albuquerque, N.M. 87102. Hispanic Chamber of Commerce 407 Rio Grande Blvd., N.W. Albuquerque, N.M. 87104

ATLANTA, GA.

Incorporated as city: 1847
Mayor: Maynard Jackson (to Jan. 1982)
1970 population & (rank): 495,039 (27)
1980 population (1980 census) & (rank): 425,022 (29)
1970–80 population change: −14.1%
1980 city land area: 136 sq mi.
Altitude: Highest, 1,050 ft; lowest, 940
Location: In northwest central part of state, near Chattahoochee River
Counties: Fulton and De Kalb
Churches (5-county area): 1,500
City-owned parks: 20 (3,000 ac.)
Telephones (Jan. 1, 1979): 907,830
Television households (Jan. 1980): 366,900 (98%)
Radio stations (15-county area): AM, 26; FM, 10; educational, 5
Television stations (15-county area): 6 commercial; 2 educational
Gross assessed valuation (city, 1980): $3,703,819,629
City tax rate (1980): $43.15 per $1,000
Total bonded debt (1980): $177,903,225
Revenue (1980, incl. General Fund, Airport Revenue, Water/Sewer Fund): $259,718,307
Expenditures (1980): $235,052,908
Chamber of Commerce: Atlanta Chamber of Commerce, 1300 N Omni International, Atlanta, Ga. 30303
Information is gathered on 3 geographic areas: City of Atlanta, 5-county metro area, 15-county SMSA

AUSTIN, TEX.

Incorporated as city: 1839
Mayor: Carole Keeton McClellan (to May, 1983)
1970 population & (rank): 253,539 (56)
1980 population (1980 census) & (rank): 345,496 (42)
1970–80 population change: +36.3%
1976 city land area: 101.0 sq mi.
Altitude: Highest, 425 ft
Location: In south central part of state, on the Colorado River
County: Seat of Travis Co.
Churches: Protestant, 230; Roman Catholic, 19; Jewish, 2
City-owned parks and playgrounds: 137
Telephones (Jan. 1, 1979): 324,658
Television households (Jan. 1980): 133,300 (98%)
Radio stations: AM, 4; FM, 9
Television stations: 3 commercial; 1 educational
Assessed valuation (1980–81): $6,680,634,190
Tax rate (1980–81): $5.70 per $1,000 at 100% assessed valuation
Bonded debt (1980–81): $132,270,000
Revenue (1980–81): $98,806,248
Expenditures (1980–81): $102,843,197
Chamber of Commerce: Austin Chamber of Commerce, 901 W Riverside Dr., Austin, Tex. 78701

BALTIMORE, MD.

Incorporated as city: 1797
Mayor: William D. Schaefer (to Dec. 1983)
1970 population & (rank): 905,787 (7)
1980 population (1980 census) & (rank): 786,775 (9)
1970–80 population change: −13.1%
1980 land area: 78.3 sq mi.
Altitude: Highest, 490 ft; lowest, sea level
Location: On Patapsco River, about 12 mi. from Chesapeake Bay
County: Independent city
Churches: Roman Catholic, 72; Jewish, 50; Protestant and others, 344
City-owned parks: 347 park areas and tracts (6,314 ac.)
Telephones (Jan. 1, 1979): 1,400,808
Television households (Jan. 1981): 273,100 (99%)
Radio stations: AM, 11; FM, 9
Television stations: 5
Assessed valuation (1980–81): $2,933,326,000
City tax rate (1979–80): $5.95 per $100
Net bonded debt (April 1981): $471,078,000
Revenue (1981): $1,944,000
Expenditures (1980): $1,731,154,967
Chamber of Commerce: Greater Baltimore Committee, 2 Hopkins Plaza, Baltimore, Md. 21201

BIRMINGHAM, ALA.

Incorporated as city: 1871
Mayor: Richard Arrington, Jr. (to Nov. 1983)
1970 population & (rank): 300,910 (48)
1980 population (1980 census) & (rank): 284,413 (50)
1970–80 population change: −5.5%
1980 land area: 90 sq mi.
Altitude: Highest, 1,200 ft.; lowest, 583
Location: In north central part of state in Jones Valley
County: Seat of Jefferson Co.
Churches: 1,100
City-owned parks and playgrounds: 100 (1,684 ac.)
Telephones (Jan. 1, 1979): 466,176
Television households (Jan. 1981): 240,000 (99%)

Radio stations: AM, 11; FM, 4
Television stations: 4
Assessed valuation (1980): $321,562,942
City tax rate (1981): ad valorem tax, $29.00 per $1000 assessed value
Bonded debt (April 1981): $132,765,819
Revenue (1980): $78,785,516
Expenditures (1980): $77,491,191
Chamber of Commerce: Chamber of Commerce, 1st Ave. and 21st St., Birmingham, Ala.

BOSTON, MASS.

Incorporated as city: 1822
Mayor: Kevin H. White (to Jan. 1984)
1970 population & (rank): 641,071 (16)
1980 population (1980 census) & (rank): 562,994 (20)
1970–80 population change: −12.2%
1980 land area: 46.0 sq mi.
Altitude: Highest, 330 ft; lowest, sea level
Location: On Massachusetts Bay, at mouths of Charles and Mystic Rivers
County: Seat of Suffolk Co.
Churches: Protestant, 187; Roman Catholic, 73; Jewish, 28; others, 100
City-owned parks, playgrounds, etc.: 2,276.36 ac.
Telephones (Jan. 1, 1979): 534,287
Television households (Jan. 1981): 251,000 (96%)
Radio stations: AM, 9; FM, 8
Television stations: 7
Assessed valuation (1980): $1,902,000,000
City tax rate (1980): $270.90 per $1,000
Gross direct bonded debt (July 1, 1981): $487,590,000
Revenue (1978–79)[1]: $759,297,234
Expenditures (1978–79)[1]: $735,216,414
Chamber of Commerce: Boston Chamber of Commerce, 125 High St., Boston, Mass. 02110
1. Figures are latest available.

BUFFALO, N.Y.

Incorporated as city: 1832
Mayor: James Griffin (to Dec. 1981)
1970 population & (rank): 462,768 (28)
1980 population (1980 census) & (rank): 357,870 (39)
1970–80 population change: −22.7%
1980 land area: 41.3 sq mi.
Altitude: Highest, 698 ft; lowest, 571
Location: At east end of Lake Erie, on Niagara River
County: Seat of Erie Co.
Churches: 60 denominations, with over 1,100 churches
County-owned parks: 9 public parks (3,000 ac.)
Telephones (Jan. 1, 1979): 409,914
Television households (Jan. 1980): 375,000 (98%)
Radio stations: AM, 13; FM, 14
Television stations: 5 (plus reception from 4 Canadian stations)
Assessed valuation (1979–80): $1,014,912,000
City tax rate (1979–80): $81.56 per $1,000
Total funded debt (long-term, June 30, 1980): $128,308,000
Revenue (general fund, 1979–80): $199,214,000
Expenditures (1979–80): $134,929,000
Chamber of Commerce: Buffalo Area Chamber of Commerce, 107 Delaware Ave., Buffalo, N.Y. 14202

CHARLOTTE, N.C.

Incorporated as city: 1768
Mayor: H. Edward Knox (to Nov. 1981)
1970 population & (rank): 241,420 (60)
1980 population (1980 census) & (rank): 314,447 (47)

1970–80 population change: +30.2%
1980 city land area: 138.0 sq mi.
Altitude: 765 ft
Location: In the southern part of state near the border of South Carolina
County: Seat of Mecklenburg Co.
Churches: Protestant, over 400; Roman Catholic, 8; Jewish, 3; Greek Orthodox, 1
City-owned parks and parkways: 87
Telephones (Jan. 1, 1979): 366,246
Television households (Jan. 1981): 136,700 (98%)
Radio stations: AM, 8; FM, 4
Television stations: 4 commercial; 2 educational
Assessed valuation (1980–81): $6,396,251,605
City tax rate (includes county, 1980–81): $17.45 per $1,000
Bonded debt (June 30, 1980): $167,160,000
Revenue (1980–81): $77,991,088
Expenditures (1980–81): $77,461,526
Chamber of Commerce: Greater Charlotte Chamber of Commerce, P.O. Box 32785, Charlotte, N.C., 28232

CHICAGO, ILL.

Incorporated as city: 1837
Mayor: Jane M. Byrne (to April 1983)
1970 population & (rank): 3,369,357 (2)
1980 population (1980 census) & (rank): 3,005,061 (2)
1970–80 population change: −10.8%
1980 land area: 222.8 sq mi.
Altitude: Highest, 672 ft; lowest, 578.5
Location: On lower west shore of Lake Michigan
County: Seat of Cook Co.
Churches: Protestant, 850; Roman Catholic, 263; Jewish, 65
City-owned parks: 580
Telephones (Jan. 1, 1979): 2,639,826
Television households (Jan. 1980): 1,882,300 (98%)
Radio stations: AM, 15; FM, 17
Television stations: 8
Assessed valuation (1979): $10,488,594,902
Total Chicago tax rate (1979): $98.19 per $1,000
Total gross bonded debt (1979): $246,880,000
Revenue (est. 1981): $1,631,937,451
Expenditures (est. 1981): $1,617,083,124
Chamber of Commerce: Chicago Association of Commerce & Industry, 130 S Michigan Ave., Chicago, Ill. 60603

CINCINNATI, OHIO

Incorporated as city: 1819
Mayor: David S. Mann (to Dec. 1981)
City Manager: Sylvester Murray
1970 population & (rank): 453,514 (30)
1980 population (1980 census) & (rank): 385,457 (32)
1970–80 population change: −15.0%
1980 land area: 78.1 sq mi.
Altitude: Highest, 960 ft; lowest, 441
Location: In southwestern corner of state on Ohio River
County: Seat of Hamilton Co.
Churches: 850
City-owned parks: 96 (4,345 ac.)
Telephones (Jan. 1, 1979): 961,410
Television households (Jan. 1980): 312,300 (98%)
Radio stations: AM, 9; FM, 12 (Greater Cincinnati)
Television stations: 6
Assessed valuation (1980): $2,363,921,460
City tax rate (1980): $11.12 per $1,000
Bonded debt (1980): $168,001,210
Revenue (general fund, 1980): $124,960,324
Expenditures (general fund, 1980): $119,691,554
Chamber of Commerce: Cincinnati Chamber of Commerce, 120 W Fifth St., Cincinnati, Ohio 45202

CLEVELAND, OHIO

Incorporated as city: 1836
Mayor: George V. Voinovich (to Dec. 1981)
1970 population & (rank): 750,879 (10)
1980 population (1980 census) & (rank): 573,822 (18)
1970–80 population change: −23.6%
1980 land area: 75.9 sq. mi.
Altitude: Highest, 865 ft.; lowest, 573
Location: On Lake Erie at mouth of Cuyahoga River
County: Seat of Cuyahoga Co.
Churches: [1] Protestant, 717; Roman Catholic, 162; Jewish, 23; Eastern Orthodox, 18
City-owned parks: 41 (1,930 ac.)
Telephones (Jan. 1, 1979): 924,277
Television households (Jan. 1981): 548,600 (98%)
Radio stations: AM, 13; FM, 14
Television stations: 7
Assessed valuation (1981): $3,460,974,116
City tax rate (1980): $69.80 per $1,000
Bonded debt (March 31, 1980): $429,622,000
Revenue (est. 1981): $211,585,294
Expenditures (est. 1981): $210,936,241
Chamber of Commerce: Greater Cleveland Growth Association, 690 Union Commerce Building, Cleveland, Ohio 44115
1. 100-mile area.

COLUMBUS, OHIO

Incorporated as city: 1834
Mayor: Tom Moody (to Jan. 1984)
1970 population & (rank): 540,025 (21)
1980 population (1980 census) & (rank): 564,871 (19)
1970–80 population change: +4.6%
1981 land area: 183.1 sq. mi.
Altitude: Highest, 902 ft; lowest, 702
Location: In central part of state, on Scioto River
County: Seat of Franklin Co.
Churches: Protestant, 412; Roman Catholic, 43; Jewish, 5
City-owned parks: 135 (10,931 ac.)
Telephones (Jan. 1, 1979): 484,446
Television households (Jan. 1981): 319,100 (98%)
Radio stations: AM, 8; FM, 6
Television stations: 3 commercial, 2 educational
Assessed valuation (1980): $3,661,440,000
City tax rate (1980): $41.20 per $1,000
Bonded debt (Dec. 31, 1980): $392,178,909
Revenue (1980): $959,816,362
Expenditures (1980): $1,076,883,096
Chamber of Commerce: Columbus Area Chamber of Commerce, P.O. Box 1527, Columbus, Ohio 43216

DALLAS, TEX.

Incorporated as city: 1856
Mayor: Jack Evans (to April 1983)
City Manager: George Schrader (apptd. Dec. 1972)
1970 population & (rank): 844,401 (8)
1980 population (1980 census) & (rank): 904,078 (7)
1970–80 population change: +7.1%
1980 land area: 309.3 sq. mi.
Altitude: Highest, 750 ft; lowest, 375
Location: In northeastern part of state, on Trinity River
County: Seat of Dallas Co.
Churches: 1,200 (in Dallas Co.)
City-owned parks: 272 (23,434 ac.)
Telephones (Jan. 1, 1979): 838,735
Television households (Jan. 1980): 524,900 (98%)
Radio stations: AM, 14; FM, 15
Television stations: 7
Assessed valuation (1980–81): $26,051,000,000

City tax rate (1980–81): $5.66 per $1,000 (at 100% valuation)
Net revenue bond debt (Sept. 30, 1980): $247,546,750
Net tax supported debt (Sept. 30, 1980): $379,069,336
Revenue (est. 1980–81): $280,797,184
Expenditures (est. 1980–81): $486,500,395
Chamber of Commerce: Dallas Chamber of Commerce. 1507 Pacific, Dallas, Tex. 75201

DENVER, COLO.

Incorporated as city: 1861
Mayor: William H. McNichols, Jr. (to July 1, 1983)
1970 population & (rank): 514,678 (24)
1980 population (1980 census) & (rank): 491,396 (24)
1970–80 population change: −4.5%
1980 land area: 113.6 sq. mi.
Altitude: Highest, 5,470 ft; lowest, 5,130
Location: In northeast central part of state, on South Platte River
County: Coextensive with Denver Co.
Churches: Protestant, 815; Roman Catholic, 63; Jewish, 13[1]
City-owned parks: 155 (3,600 ac.)
City-owned mountain parks: 40 (13,448 ac.)
Telephones (Jan. 1, 1979): 1,354,374
Television households (Jan. 1980): 204,200 (97%)
Radio stations: AM, 18; FM, 13[1]
Television stations: 5
Assessed valuation (1979): $2,197,976,100
City tax rate (1979): $28.34 per $1,000[2]
Bonded debt (1979): $330,903,000[2]
Revenue (1979): $478,562,100[2]
Expenditures (1979): $452,973,000[2]
Chamber of Commerce: Denver Chamber of Commerce, 1301 Welton, Denver, Colo. 80204
1. Metropolitan area. 2. Excluding school district.

DETROIT, MICH.

Incorporated as city: 1815
Mayor: Coleman A. Young (to Jan. 1982)
1970 population & (rank): 1,514,063 (5)
1980 population (1980 census) & (rank): 1,203,339 (6)
1970–80 population change: −20.5%
1980 land area: 138.0 sq. mi.
Altitude: Highest, 685 ft; lowest, 574
Location: In southeastern part of state, on Detroit River
County: Seat of Wayne Co.
Churches: [1] Protestant, 2,204; Roman Catholic, 333; Jewish, 40
City-owned parks: 60 parks (3,843 ac.); 388 sites (5,838 ac.)
Telephones (Jan. 1, 1979): 1,509,894
Television households (Jan. 1980): 817,600 (98%)
Radio stations: AM, 17; FM, 37 (7-county area)
Television stations: 8 (incl. Windsor, Ontario, Canada)[1]
Assessed valuation (1981): $5,227,447,000,000
City tax rate (1981–82): $33.78 per $1,000[2]
Net bonded debt (June 1980): General obligations, (net): $417,106,280; revenue and self-supported debt (gross): $299,040,000
Revenue (1980–81): $1,468,393,329[3]
Expenditures (1980–81): $1,468,393,329[3]
Chamber of Commerce: Greater Detroit Chamber of Commerce, 150 Michigan Ave., Detroit, Mich. 48226
1. Six-county metropolitan area. 2. Excludes school system and county tax. 3. Includes utilities.

EL PASO, TEX.

Incorporated as city: 1873
Mayor: Jonathan Rogers (to April 1983)

1970 population & (rank): 322,261 (45)
1980 population (1980 census) & (rank): 425,259 (28)
1970–80 population change: +32.0%
1980 land area: 161.1 sq mi.
Altitude: 4,000 ft
Location: In far western part of state, on Rio Grande
County: Seat of El Paso Co.
Churches: Protestant, 212; Roman Catholic, 36; Jewish, 2; others, 13
City-owned parks: 83 (4,694 ac.)
Telephones (Jan. 1, 1979): 259,609
Television households (Jan. 1980): 132,600 (98%)
Radio stations: AM, 9; FM, 5
Television stations: 5
Assessed valuation (1981): $6,573,536,568
City tax rate (1980): $53.12 per $1,000, city; $6.56, El Paso Independent School District: $7.30, Ysleta Independent School District.
Bonded debt (1980): $41,790,000
Revenue (1980): -$68,306,043
Expenditures (1980): $66,909,481
Chamber of Commerce: El Paso Chamber of Commerce, 10 Civic Center Plaza, El Paso, Tex. 79944

FORT WORTH, TEX.

Incorporated as city: 1873
Mayor: Woodie Woods (to April 1983)
City Manager: Robert L. Herchert
1970 population & (rank): 393,455 (33)
1980 population (1980 census) & (rank): 385,141 (33)
1970–80 population change: −21.1%
1980 land area: 230.1 sq mi.
Altitude: Highest, 780 ft; lowest, 520
Location: In north central part of state, on Trinity River
County: Seat of Tarrant Co.
Churches: Protestant, 392; Roman Catholic, 16; Jewish, 2
City-owned parks: 126 (7,817 ac.; 3,500 ac. in Nature Center)
Telephones (Jan. 1, 1979): 365,150
Television households (Jan. 1980): 276,800 (98%)
Radio stations: AM, 6; FM, 8
Television stations: 6 (2 local)
Assessed valuation (1980–81): $2,797,200,770
City tax rate (1980–81): $14.89 per $1,000
Bonded debt (1980–81): $154,667,000
Revenue (1980–81 tax-supported funds): $109,449,832
Expenditures (1980–81 tax-supported funds): $109,449,832
Chamber of Commerce: Fort Worth Chamber of Commerce, 700 Throckmorton, Fort Worth, Tex. 76102

HONOLULU, HAWAII

Incorporated as city and county: 1907
Mayor: Eileen R. Anderson (to Jan. 1985)
1970 population & (rank): 324,871 (44)
1980 population (1980 census) & (rank): 365,048[1] (36)
1970–1980 population change: +12.4%
1980 land area of city and county: 604 sq mi.
Altitude: Highest, 4,025 ft; lowest, sea level
Location: The city and county government's jurisdiction includes the entire island of Oahu
Churches: Roman Catholic, 33; Buddhist, 32; Jewish, 2; Protestant and others, 325
City-owned parks: 4,556 ac.
Telephones (Jan. 1, 1979): 375,858
Television households (Sept. 1976): 204,200 (97%)
Radio stations: AM, 19; FM, 7
Television stations: 5
Assessed valuation (1980): $9,404,212,382 (60% of market value.)
City and county tax rate (1980): $15.23 per $1,000

Bonded debt (June 1980): $163,163,745
Net revenue (1979–80): $253,834,454
Net expenditures (1979–80): $219,635,064; capital improvement budget, $37,763,869
Chamber of Commerce: Chamber of Commerce of Hawaii, 735 Bishop St., Honolulu, Hawaii 96813
1. City and county area.

HOUSTON, TEX.

Incorporated as city: 1837
Mayor: Jim McConn (to Dec. 1981)
1970 population & (rank): 1,233,535 (6)
1980 population (1980 census) & (rank): 1,594,086 (5)
1970–80 population change: +29.2%
1980 land area: 489.2 sq mi.
Altitude: Highest, 120 ft; lowest, sea level
Location: In southeastern part of state, near Gulf of Mexico
County: Seat of Harris Co.
Churches: 1,750[2]
City-owned parks: 259 (5,742 ac., not including parkways)
Telephones (Jan. 1, 1979): 1,436,358
Television households (Jan. 1980): 816,400 (98%)
Radio stations: AM, 14; FM, 16[1]
Television stations: 6
Assessed valuation (1980): $27,014,920,000
City tax rate (1980): $8.40 per $1,000
Bonded debt (1980): $1,637,934,000
Revenue (1980): $452,331,000
Expenditures (1980): $455,390,000
Chamber of Commerce: Houston Chamber of Commerce, 1100 Milam Building, Houston, Tex. 77002
1. Includes annexations since 1970. 2. Metropolitan area (Harris County).

INDIANAPOLIS, IND.

Incorporated as city: 1832 (reincorporated 1838)
Mayor: William H. Hudnut III (to Jan. 1984)
1970 population & (rank): 736,856 (11)
1980 population (1980 census) & (rank): 700,807 (12)
1970–80 population change: −4.9%
1980 land area: 375.2 sq mi.
Altitude: Highest, 840 ft; lowest, 700
Location: In central part of the state, on West Fork of White River
County: Seat of Marion Co.
Churches: 1,200[1]
City-owned parks: 188 (8,992 ac.)
Telephones (Jan. 1, 1979): 680,183
Television households (Jan. 1981): 266,500 (98%)
Radio stations: AM, 9; FM, 13[1]
Television stations: 6[1]
Assessed valuation (1980): (consolidated city), $3,256,968,999; (Marion County) $3,496,065,239
City tax rate (Center Township, 1980): $125.60 per $1,000
Gross debt (consolidated city, Dec. 31, 1980): $223,009,003
Revenue (1980): $281,257,295
Expenditures (1980): $216,563,849
Chamber of Commerce: Indianapolis Chamber of Commerce, 320 N Meridian St., Indianapolis, Ind. 46202
1. Marion County.

JACKSONVILLE, FLA.

Incorporated as city: 1822
Mayor: Jake M. Godbold (to July 1, 1983)
1970 population & (rank): 504,265 (26)
1980 population (1980 census) & (rank): 540,898 (22)
1970–80 population change: +7.3%

1980 land area: 765.7 sq mi.
Altitude: Highest, 71 ft; lowest, sea level
Location: On St. Johns River, 20 miles from Atlantic Ocean
County: Duval
Churches: Protestant, 725; Roman Catholic, 24; Jewish, 4; others, 7
City-owned parks and playgrounds: 138 (1,522 ac.)
Telephones (Jan. 1, 1979): 431,204
Television households (Jan. 1980): 198,700 (98%)
Radio stations: AM, 15; FM, 10
Television stations: 6 commercial, 1 educational
Assessed valuation (1980): $6,941,421,687
City tax rate (1980–81): $19.69 per $1,000 (old city area); $20.49 (old county area)
Bonded debt (1980): $55,048,048
Revenue (1980–81): $1,027,077,885
Expenditures (1980–81): $1,027,077,885
Chamber of Commerce: Jacksonville Area Chamber of Commerce, Jacksonville, Fla. 32202

KANSAS CITY, MO.

Incorporated as city: 1850
Mayor: Richard L. Berkley (to April 1983)
City Manager: Robert A. Kipp (apptd. Jan. 1974)
1970 population & (rank): 507,330 (25)
1980 population (1980 census) & (rank): 448,159 (27)
1970–80 population change: −11.7%
1980 land area: 316.3 sq mi.
Altitude: Highest, 1,014 ft; lowest, 722
Location: In western part of state, at juncture of Missouri and Kansas Rivers
County: Located in Jackson, Clay, and Platte Co.
Churches: 1,100 churches of all denominations
City-owned parks and playgrounds: 157 (7,320 ac.)
Telephones (Jan. 1, 1979): 351,494
Television households (Jan. 1980): 303,300 (98%)
Radio stations: AM, 14; FM, 13[1]
Television stations: 6[1]
Assessed valuation (1979–80): $1,801,361,743
City tax rate (1979–80): $15.20 per $1,000
Bonded debt (1979–80): $75,010,000
Revenue (1979–80): $271,908,088
Expenditures (1979–80): $271,560,261
Budget (gross total, 1980–81): $302,373,472
Chamber of Commerce: Chamber of Commerce of Greater Kansas City, 920 Main St., Kansas City, Mo. 64105
1. Metropolitan area.

LONG BEACH, CALIF.

Founded: 1881
Mayor: Eunice N. Sato (to July 1982)
City Manager: John E. Dever (Jan. 1, 1977)
1970 population & (rank): 358,879 (40)
1980 population (1980 census) & (rank): 361,334 (37)
1970–80 population change: +0.7%
1980 land area: 50.1 sq mi.
Altitude: Highest, 170 ft; lowest, sea level
Location: On San Pedro Bay, south of Los Angeles
County: In Los Angeles Co.
Churches: 236
City-owned parks: 43 (1,620 ac.)
Telephones: (included in Los Angeles area)
Television households: (included in Los Angeles area)
Radio stations: AM, 2; FM, 6
Television stations: 1 (cable)
Assessed valuation (1981): $2,127,848,550
City tax rate (1980–81): none; county, $40 per $1,000
Bonded debt (June 1980): $4,275,000
Revenue (1980–81): $838,505,875
Expenditures (1980–81): $979,032,446

Chamber of Commerce: Long Beach Chamber of Commerce, 50 Oceangate Plaza, Long Beach, Calif. 90802

LOS ANGELES, CALIF.

Incorporated as city: 1850
Mayor: Tom Bradley (to June 1985)
1970 population & (rank): 2,811,801 (3)
1980 population (1980 census) & (rank): 2,966,763 (3)
1970–80 population change: +5.5%
1980 land area: 463.9 sq mi.
Altitude: Highest, sea level
Location: In southwestern part of state, on Pacific Ocean
County: Seat of Los Angeles Co.
Churches: 1,963 of all denominations
City-owned parks: 296 (14,489 ac.)
Telephones (extended area, Jan. 1, 1979): 6,096,663[1]
Television households (Jan. 1980): 2,701,700 (96%)[1]
Radio stations: AM, 32; FM, 40
Television stations: 18
Assessed valuation (1980–81): $16,173,770,308
City tax rate (1980–81): $1.31 per $1,000 (25% ratio)[2]
Gross debt (June 30, 1980): general obligation bonds, $95,915,000; revenue bonds, $2,532,087,000
Revenue (1980–81): $3,410,743,828
Expenditures (1980–81): $3,410,743,828
Chamber of Commerce: Los Angeles Chamber of Commerce, 404 S Bixel St., Los Angeles, Calif. 90017
1. Includes Long Beach, Calif. 2. City rate for indebtedness. City also receives 33.5% of revenues collected within the county at rate of $40 per $1,000 of assessed value.

LOUISVILLE, KY.

Incorporated as city: 1828
Mayor: William B. Stansbury (to Dec. 1981)
1970 population & (rank): 361,706 (38)
1980 population (1980 census) & (rank): 298,451 (49)
1970–80 population change: −17.5%
1980 land area: 60.0 sq mi.
Altitude: Highest, 565 ft; lowest, 477
Location: In north central part of state, on Ohio River
County: Seat of Jefferson Co.
Churches: 678[1]
City-owned parks and playgrounds: 166 (over 7,000 ac.)
Telephones (Jan. 1, 1979): 576,756
Television households (Jan. 1980): 236,100 (99%)
Radio stations: 16
Television stations: 5
Assessed valuation (1980): $3,367,958,345
City tax rate (1980–81): $5.66 per $1,000 (city purposes only; exclusive of schools)
Net bonded debt (Jan. 1, 1981): $37,854,000
Revenue (1979–80): $100,663,887
Expenditures (1979–80): $107,907,705
Chamber of Commerce: Louisville Area Chamber of Commerce, 300 W Liberty St., Louisville, Ky. 40202
1. Metropolitan area.

MEMPHIS, TENN.

Incorporated as city: 1826
Mayor: Wyeth Chandler (to Dec. 1984)
1970 population & (rank): 623,988 (17)
1980 population (1980 census) & (rank): 646,356 (14)
1970–80 population change: +3.6%
1980 land area: 280.1 sq mi.
Altitude: Highest, 331 ft
Location: In southwestern corner of state, on Mississippi River
County: Seat of Shelby Co.
Churches: 1,000

Parks and playgrounds: 155 (5,300 ac.)
Telephones (Jan. 1979): 621,276
Television households (Jan. 1, 1980): 256,000 (98%)
Radio stations: AM, 13; FM, 8
Television stations: 5
Assessed valuation (1980): $1,944,007,833
City tax rate (1980): $37.40 per $1,000
Bonded debt (June 30, 1980): $483,385,000
Revenue (1980): $407,849,417
Expenditures (1980): $372,322,652
Chamber of Commerce: Memphis Area Chamber of Commerce, P.O. Box 224, Memphis, Tenn. 38103

MIAMI, FLA.

Incorporated as city: 1896
Mayor: Maurice A. Ferre (to Nov. 1981)
City manager: Joseph R. Grassie (apptd. May 1976)
1970 population & (rank): 334,859 (42)
1980 population (1980 census) & (rank): 346,931 (41)
1970–80 population change: +3.6%
1980 land area: 34.3 sq mi.
Altitude: Average, 12 ft
Location: In southeastern part of state, on Biscayne Bay
County: Seat of Dade Co.
Churches: Protestant, 592; Roman Catholic, 53; Jewish, 48
City-owned parks: 94
Telephones (Jan. 1, 1979): 1,066,918
Television households (Jan. 1981): 564,600 (98%)
Radio stations: AM, 18; FM, 20; educational, 1
Television stations: 5 commercial, 2 educational
Assessed valuation (1980–81): $6,234,404,089
City tax rate (1980–81): $11.98 per $1,000
Bonded debt (1980–81): $136,320,000
Revenue (1980–81): $187,515,709
Expenditures (1980–81): $187,515,709
Chamber of Commerce: Greater Miami Chamber of Commerce, 391 N.E. 15th St., Miami, Fla. 33132

MILWAUKEE, WIS.

Incorporated as city: 1846
Mayor: Henry W. Maier (to April 1984)
1970 population & (rank): 717,372 (12)
1980 population (1980 census) & (rank): 636,212 (17)
1970–80 population change: −11.3%
1980 land area: 95.0 sq mi.
Altitude: 580.60 ft
Location: In southeastern part of state, on Lake Michigan
County: Seat of Milwaukee Co.
Churches: 411
County-owned parks: 14,061 ac.
Telephones (Jan. 1, 1979): 862,735
Television households (Jan. 1980): 353,200 (98%)
Radio stations: AM, 9; FM, 12
Television stations: 7
Assessed valuation (1981): $7,680,526,589
City tax rate (1981): $32.73 per $1,000
Gross debt (1980): $181,536,600
Revenue (1980): $434,930,565
Expenditures (1980): $413,678,267
Chamber of Commerce: Metropolitan Milwaukee Association of Commerce, 828 N. Broadway, Milwaukee, Wis. 53202

MINNEAPOLIS, MINN.

Incorporated as city: 1867
Mayor: Donald M. Fraser (to Jan. 1982)
1970 population & (rank): 434,400 (31)
1980 population (1980 census) & (rank): 370,951 (34)

1970–80 population change: −14.6%
1980 land area: 55.5 sq mi.
Altitude: Highest, 945 ft; lowest, 695
Location: In southeast central part of state, on Mississippi River
County: Seat of Hennepin Co.
Churches: 419
City-owned parks: 153
Telephones (incl. St. Paul, Jan. 1, 1979): 1,610,700
Television households (Jan. 1981): 334,200 (98%)
Radio stations: AM, 17; FM, 15 (metro area)
Television stations: 6 (metro area)
Assessed valuation (1980): $2,083,266,920[1]
City tax rate (1980): $103.12 per $1,000
Net debt (Dec. 31, 1980): $280,385,000
Revenue (1980): $278,955,049
Expenditures (1980): $311,782,349
Chamber of Commerce: Greater Minneapolis Chamber of Commerce, 15 S Fifth Street, Minneapolis, Minn. 55402
1. Assessed valuations on majority of properties now range from 16% (homesteads) to 43% (commercial, industrial) of actual market value.

NASHVILLE, TENN.

Incorporated as city: 1806
Mayor: Richard H. Fulton (to Sept. 1983)
1970 population & (rank): 426,029 (32)
1980 population (1980 census) & (rank): 455,651 (25)
1970–80 population change: +7.0%
1980 land area: 532.0 sq mi.
Altitude: Highest, 1,100 ft; lowest, approx. 400 ft
Location: In north central part of state, on Cumberland River
County: Davidson
Churches: Protestant, 739; Roman Catholic, 16; Jewish, 3
City-owned parks: 68 (6,500 ac.)
Telephones (Jan. 1, 1979): 420,995
Television households (Jan. 1981): 167,700 (99%)
Radio stations: AM, 11; FM, 8
Television stations: 5
Assessed valuation (1980): $1,934,376,256
City tax rate (1980): $68.30 per $1,000
Bonded debt (June 1980): $209,297,000
Revenue (1980): $290,072,208
Expenditures (1980): $292,850,865
Chamber of Commerce: Nashville Area Chamber of Commerce, 161 Fourth Ave. North, Nashville, Tenn. 37219

NEWARK, N.J.

Incorporated as city: 1836
Mayor: Kenneth A. Gibson (to July 1982)
1970 population & (rank): 381,930 (35)
1980 population (1980 census) & (rank): 329,248 (46)
1970–80 population change: −13.8%
1980 land area: 23.5 sq mi.
Altitude: Highest, 273.4 ft; lowest, sea level
Location: In northeastern part of state, on Passaic River and Newark Bay
County: Seat of Essex Co.
Churches: Roman Catholic, 32; Jewish, 4; Protestant and others, 250
City-owned parks: 40 (and 20 mini parks); (39.3 ac.)
County-governed parks in city: 7 (743.97 ac.)
Telephones (Jan. 1, 1979): 329,254
Television households (Jan. 1980): 290,400 (98%)
Radio stations: AM, 2; FM, 4
Television stations: UHF, 1; VHF, 1
Assessed valuation (1981): $1,043,197,000
City tax rate (1981): $101.80 per $1,000
Net bonded debt (1981): $54,963,000

Revenue (est. 1981): $295,188,001
Expenditures (est. 1981): $295,188,001
Chamber of Commerce: Greater Newark Chamber of
Commerce, 50 Park Place, Newark, N.J. 07102

NEW ORLEANS, LA.

Incorporated as city: 1805
Mayor: Ernest N. Morial (to May 1982)
1970 population & (rank): 593,471 (19)
1980 population (1980 census) & (rank): 557,482 (21)
1970–80 population change: −6.1%
1980 land area: 197.1 sq mi.
Altitude: Highest, 15 ft; lowest, −4
Location: In southeastern part of state, between
Mississippi River and Lake Ponchartrain
Parish: Seat of Orleans Parish
Churches: 644
City-owned parks: 69 (21,000 ac.)
Telephones (Jan. 1, 1979): 754,517
Television households (Jan. 1980): 203,800 (98%)
Radio stations: AM, 12; FM, 5
Television stations: 5
Assessed valuation (1981): $698,915,044
City tax rate (1980): $93.57 per $1,000
Bonded debt (Jan. 1981): $150,783,000
Revenue (est. 1981): $280,014,718
Expenditures (est. 1981): $280,014,718
Chamber of Commerce: New Orleans and the River Region
Chamber of Commerce, 301 Camp Street, New Orleans,
La. 70130.

NEW YORK, N.Y.

Chartered as "Greater New York": 1898
Mayor: Edward Koch (to Dec. 31, 1981)
Borough Presidents: Bronx, Stanley Simon; Brooklyn,
Howard Golden; Manhattan, Andrew Stein; Queens,
Donald R. Manes; Staten Island, Anthony Gaeta
1970 population & (rank): 7,895,563 (1)[1]
1980 population (1980 census) & (rank): 7,071,030 (1)[1]
1970–80 population change: −10.4%
1980 land area: 303.7 sq mi. (Queens, 109.6; Brooklyn,
72.8; Staten Island, 55.8; Bronx, 42.5; Manhattan, 23.0)
Altitude: Highest, 410 ft; lowest, sea level
Location: In south of state, at mouth of Hudson River
(also known as the North River as it passes Manhattan)
Counties: Consists of 5 counties: Bronx, Kings (Brooklyn),
New York (Manhattan), Queens, Richmond (Staten
Island)
Churches: Protestant, 1,766; Jewish, 1,256; Roman Catholic
437; Orthodox, 66
City-owned parks: 1,588 (37,372 ac.)
Telephones (Jan. 1, 1979): 5,847,731
Television households (Jan. 1981): 2,825,200 (97%)
Radio stations: AM and FM, 7; AM only, 10; FM only, 12
Television stations: 6 commercial
Assessed valuation (1980–81): $39,495,654,887[2]
City tax rate: (1980–81) $89.50 per $1,000
Total funded debt (June 30, 1979): $6,968,192,000
Revenue (1980): $13,210,849,029
Expenditures (1981): $13,901,070,326
Chamber of Commerce: New York Chamber of Commerce
and Industry, 65 Liberty St., New York, N.Y. 10005
1. For population of boroughs, see Index. 2. Taxable property
only.

OAKLAND, CALIF.

Incorporated as city: 1854
Mayor: Lionel J. Wilson (to June 30, 1985)

City Manager: Henry L. Gardner (apptd. June 1981)
1970 population & (rank): 361,561 (39)
1980 population (1980 census) & (rank): 339,288 (43)
1970–80 population change: −6.2%
1980 land area: 53.4 sq mi.
Altitude: Highest, 1,700 ft; lowest, sea level
Location: In west central part of state, on east side of
San Francisco Bay
County: Seat of Alameda Co.
Churches: 374, representing over 78 denominations in the
City; over 500 churches in Alameda County
City-owned parks: 2,196 ac.
Telephones (Jan. 1, 1979): 589,155[1]
Television households: (included in San Francisco area)
Radio stations: AM, 3; FM, 2
Television stations: 9 commercial; 3 educational
Assessed valuation (1979–80): $1,553,886,787 (25% of
appraised value)
City tax rate (1979–80): $48.25 per $1,000
Bonded debt (est. June 1980): $5,265,000
Revenue (1979–80): $160,228,000
Expenditures (1979–80): $165,665,610
Chamber of Commerce: Oakland Chamber of Commerce,
1939 Harrison St., Suite 400, Oakland, Calif. 94612
1. In East Bay Exchange, which includes Oakland.

OKLAHOMA CITY, OKLA.

Incorporated as city: 1890
Mayor: Mrs. Patience Latting (to April 1983)
City Manager: James J. Cook (apptd. April 3, 1976)
1970 population & (rank): 368,164 (37)
1980 population (1980 census) & (rank): 403,213 (31)
1970–80 population change: +9.5%
1980 land area: 635.7 sq mi.
Altitude: Highest, 1,320 ft; lowest, 1,140
Location: In central part of state, on North Canadian River
County: Seat of Oklahoma Co.
Churches: Roman Catholic, 15; Jewish, 2; Protestant and
others, 741
City-owned parks: 132 (3,934 ac.)
Telephones (Jan. 1, 1979): 641,434
Television households (Jan. 1980): 207,100 (98%)
Television stations: 6
Radio stations: AM, 10; FM, 14
Assessed valuation (1980–81): $1,041,290,383
City tax rate (1980–81): $26.89 per $1,000
Bonded debt (1980–81): $241,353,670
Revenue (general fund, 1980–81): $124,440,448
Expenditures (general fund, 1980–81): $124,440,448
Chamber of Commerce: Oklahoma City Chamber of
Commerce, 1 Santa Fe Plaza, Oklahoma City, Okla. 73102

OMAHA, NEB.

Incorporated as city: 1857
Mayor: Mike Boyle (to June 1985)
1970 population & (rank): 346,929 (41)
1980 population (1980 census) & (rank): 311,681 (48)
1970–80 population change: −10.2%
1980 land area: 81.7 sq mi.
Altitude: Highest, 1,270 ft
Location: In eastern part of state, on Missouri River
County: Seat of Douglas Co.
Churches: Protestant, 246; Roman Catholic, 44; Jewish, 4
City-owned parks: 99 (3,671.6 ac.)
Telephones (Jan. 1, 1979): 469,200
Television households (Jan. 1981): 145,600 (98%)
Radio stations: AM, 7; FM, 6
Television stations: 4
Assessed valuation (1981): $1,792,540,615
City tax rate (1981): $19.70 per $1,000

Bonded debt (1980): $77,169,000
Revenue (1981): $73,087,361
Expenditures (1981): $72,522,890
Chamber of Commerce: Omaha Chamber of Commerce, 1620 Dodge St., Omaha, Neb. 68102

PHILADELPHIA, PA.

First charter as city: 1701
Mayor: William J. Green (to Jan. 1984)
1970 population & (rank): 1,949,996 (4)
1980 population (1980 census) & rank: 1,688,210 (4)
1970—80 population change: —13.4%
1980 land area: 128.5 sq mi.
Altitude: Highest, 440 ft; lowest, sea level
Location: In southeastern part of state, at junction of Schuylkill and Delaware Rivers
County: Seat of Philadelphia Co. (coterminous)
Churches: Roman Catholic, 139; Jewish, 70; Protestant and others, 830
City-owned parks: 219 (9,160 ac.)
Telephones (Jan. 1, 1979): 1,706,199
Television households (Jan. 1980): 633,400 (97%)
Radio stations: AM, 20; FM, 22
Television stations: 8
Assessed valuation (1981): $5,855,000,000
City and school district tax rate (1979): $61.75 per $1,000
Net bonded debt (June 30, 1980): $1,722,200,000 (incl. revenue bonds of $442,500,000 for water and sewer; $201,800,000 for gas works; $71,400,000 for airport)
Revenue (1980): $1,062,542,388
Expenditures (1980): $1,071,804,282
Chamber of Commerce: Greater Philadelphia Chamber of Commerce, 1617 John F. Kennedy Blvd., Philadelphia, Pa. 19103

PHOENIX, ARIZ.

Incorporated as city: 1881
Mayor: Margaret T. Hance (to Jan. 1982)
City Manager: Marvin A. Andrews (appt. Oct. 1976)
1970 population & (rank): 584,303 (20)
1980 population (1980 census) & (rank): 764,911 (11)
1970—80 population change: +30.9%
1980 land area: 329.3 sq mi.
Altitude: Highest, 2,740 ft.; lowest, 1,017
Location: In center of state, on Salt River
County: Seat of Maricopa Co.
City-owned parks: 130 (25,841 ac.)
Telephones (Jan. 1, 1979): 1,089,327
Television households (Jan. 1981): 492,400 (97%)
Radio stations: AM, 19; FM, 15
Television stations: 8 commercial; 1 educational
Assessed valuation (est. 1981–82): $1,892,658,297
City tax rate (1981–82): $17.90 per $1,000
Bonded debt (May 1980): $494,182,000
Revenues (est. 1981–82): $435,823,000
Expenditures (est. 1981–82): $423,265,000
Chamber of Commerce: Phoenix Chamber of Commerce, 805 N Second St., Phoenix, Ariz. 85004

PITTSBURGH, PA.

Incorporated as city: 1816
Mayor: Richard S. Caliguiri (to Jan. 1982)
1970 population & (rank): 520,089 (23)
1980 population (1980 census) & (rank): 423,938 (30)
1970—80 population change: —18%
1980 land area: 55.2 sq mi.
Altitude: Highest, 1,240 ft; lowest, 715
Location: In southwestern part of state, at beginning of Ohio River

County: Seat of Allegheny Co.
Churches: Protestant, 348; Roman Catholic, 86; Jewish, 28; Orthodox, 26
City-owned parks and playgrounds: 88 (2,471 ac.)
Telephones (Jan. 1, 1979): 821,039
Television households (Jan. 1980): 518,600 (98%)
Radio stations: AM, 18; FM, 9
Television stations: 4
Assessed valuation (1981): land, $381,157,486; buildings, $1,107,779,406
City tax rate (1981): $125.50 per $1,000 buildings; $24.75 per $1,000 land
Net bonded debt (March 1981): $144,065,706
Revenue (1980): $266,938,258
Expenditures (1980): $256,288,412
Chamber of Commerce: The Chamber of Commerce of Greater Pittsburgh, 411 Seventh Ave., Pittsburgh, Pa. 15222

PORTLAND, ORE.

Incorporated as city: 1851
Mayor: Francis Ivancie (to Jan. 1984)
1970 population & (rank): 379,967 (36)
1980 population (1980 census) & (rank): 366,383 (35)
1970—80 population change: —3.6%
1980 land area: 94.3 sq mi.
Altitude: Highest, 1,073 ft; lowest, sea level
Location: In northwestern part of state, on Willamette River
County: Seat of Multnomah Co.
Churches: Protestant, 332; Roman Catholic, 27; Jewish, 4; Buddhist, 4; Vedanta Society, 1
City-owned parks: 228 (8,718 ac.)
Telephones (Jan. 1, 1979): 511,223
Television households (Jan. 1981): 209,600 (95%)
Radio stations: AM, 12; FM, 12
Television stations: 5
Assessed valuation (1980–81): $9,504,166,045 (at 100% of cash value)
City tax rate (1980–81): $6.29 per $1,000
Bonded debt (est. July 1, 1982): $237,990,888
Revenue (est. 1981–82): $251,847,278
Expenditures (est. 1981–82): $273,026,902
Chamber of Commerce: Portland Chamber of Commerce, 824 SW Fifth Ave., Portland, Ore. 97204

ST. LOUIS, MO.

Incorporated as city: 1822
Mayor: Vincent Schoemehl, Jr. (to April 1985)
1970 population & (rank): 622,236 (18)
1980 population (1980 census) & (rank): 453,085 (26)
1970—80 population change: —27.2%
1980 land area: 61.2 sq mi.
Altitude: Highest, 616 ft; lowest, 413
Location: In east central part of state, on Mississippi River
County: Independent city
Churches: 900[1]
City-owned parks: 89 (2,639 ac.)
Telephones (Jan. 1, 1979): 586,830
Television households (Jan. 1981): 182,000 (98%)
Radio stations: AM, 18; FM, 20[1]
Television stations: 5 commercial; 1 educational
Assessed valuation (1979): $1,109,450,960
City tax rate (1980): $62.50 per $1,000
Bonded debt (1980–81): $48,464,000
Revenue (1980): $218,337,930
Expenditures (1980): $228,833,784
Chamber of Commerce: St. Louis Regional Commerce and Growth Association, 10 Broadway, St. Louis, Mo. 63102.
1. Metropolitan area.

SAN ANTONIO, TEX.

Incorporated as city: 1837
Mayor: Henry Cisneros (to May 1983)
City Manager: Thomas E. Huebner (apptd. Jan. 1977)
1970 population & (rank): 654,153 (15)
1980 population (1980 census) & (rank): 785,410 (10)
1970–80 population change: +20.1%
1980 land area: 267.1 sq mi.
Altitude: 700 ft
Location: In south central part of state, on San Antonio River
County: Seat of Bexar Co.
City-owned parks: Approximately 5,881 ac.
Telephones (Jan. 1, 1979): 428,249
Television households, (Jan. 1981): 306,400 (98%)
Radio stations: AM, 13; FM, 12
Television stations: 5
Assessed valuation (1979): $2,870,534,350
City tax rate (1980): $16.50 per $1,000
Net funded debt (1980): $100,230,240
Revenue (est. 1980–81): $253,135,536
Expenditures (est. 1980–81): $254,505,180
Chamber of Commerce: Greater San Antonio Chamber of Commerce, P.O. Box 1628, 602 E Commerce, San Antonio, Tex. 78296

SAN DIEGO, CALIF.

Incorporated as city: 1850
Mayor: Pete Wilson (to Dec. 1984)
City Manager: Ray T. Blair, Jr. (apptd. May 1978)
1970 population & (rank): 697,471 (14)
1980 population (1980 census) & (rank): 875,504 (8)
1970–80 population change: +25.5%
1980 land area: 322.9 sq mi.
Altitude: Highest, 1,591 ft; lowest, sea level
Location: In southwesternmost part of state, on San Diego Bay
County: Seat of San Diego Co.
Churches: Roman Catholic, 80; Jewish, 8; Protestant 334; Eastern Orthodox, 7; other, 6
City park and recreation facilities: 200 (16,499 ac.)
Telephones (Jan. 1, 1979): 1,101,169[1]
Television households (Jan. 1980): 675,100 (96%)
Radio stations: AM, 10; FM, 19
Television stations: 4
Assessed valuation (1981): $4,881,167,478
City tax rate (1981): $40.90 per $1,000 (includes city and county school district)
Bonded debt (1981): $30,380,000
Revenue (est. 1982): $371,781,617
Expenditures (est. 1982): $371,781,617
Chamber of Commerce: San Diego Chamber of Commerce, 110 W. C St., Suite 1600, San Diego, Calif. 92101
1. Metropolitan area.

SAN FRANCISCO, CALIF.

Incorporated as city: 1850
Mayor: Dianne Feinstein (to Jan. 1984)
1970 population & (rank): 715,674 (13)
1980 population (1980 census) & (rank): 678,974 (13)
1970–80 population change: −5.1%
1980 land area: 45.4 sq mi.
Altitude: Highest, 925 ft; lowest, sea level
Location: In northern part of state between Pacific Ocean and San Francisco Bay
County: Coextensive with San Francisco Co.
Churches: 540 of all denominations
City-owned parks and squares: 120
Telephones (Jan. 1, 1979): 845,547
Television households (Jan. 1981): 290,900 (92%)
Radio stations: 22
Television stations: 7
Assessed valuation (1980–81): $4,587,646,023
City and county tax rate (1980–81): $47.20 per $1,000
Bonded debt (April 1981): $485,482,000
Revenue (1978–79): $890,249,357
Expenditures (1978–79): $883,018,915
Chamber of Commerce: Greater San Francisco Chamber of Commerce, 465 California St., San Francisco, Calif. 94104

SAN JOSE, CALIF.

Incorporated as city: 1897
Mayor: Janet Gray Hayes (to Dec. 31, 1982)
1970 population & (rank): 459,913 (29)
1980 population (1980 census) & (rank): 636,550 (16)
1970–80 population change: +38.4%
1980 land area: 149.3 sq mi.
Altitude: 80 ft
Location: In northern part of state, on south San Francisco Bay, 50 miles from San Francisco
County: Santa Clara
Churches: Protestant, 195; Roman Catholic, 29; Jewish, 4; others, 24
City-owned parks and playgrounds: 148 (2,993 ac.)[1]
Telephones (Jan. 1, 1979): 638,121
Television households (Jan. 1980): 496,700 (95%)[2]
Radio stations: AM, 5; FM, 6
Television stations: 2 commercial; 1 educational
Assessed valuation (1980–81): $3,121,497,142
City tax rate (1980–81): $6.07 per $1,000
Bonded debt (March 1980): $39,388,000
Revenue (1980–81): $394,535,000
Expenditures (1980–81): $394,535,000
Chamber of Commerce: San Jose Chamber of Commerce, One Paseo de San Antonio, San Jose, Calif. 95113
1. Includes undeveloped sites. 2. County total.

SEATTLE, WASH.

Incorporated as city: 1869
Mayor: Charles Royer (to Nov. 1981)
1970 population & (rank): 530,831 (22)
1980 population (1980 census) & (rank): 493,846 (23)
1970–80 population change: −7.0%
1980 land area: 83.6 sq mi.
Altitude: Highest, 540 ft; lowest, sea level
Location: In west central part of state, on Puget Sound
County: Seat of King Co.
Churches: Roman Catholic, 36; Jewish, 13; Protestant and others, 535
City-owned parks, playgrounds, etc.: 278 (4,773.4 ac.)
Telephones (Jan. 1, 1979): 660,792
Television households (Jan. 1981): 465,300 (95%)
Radio stations: AM, 22; FM, 26
Television stations: 3 commercial; 1 educational
Assessed valuation (1981): $18,257,783,972
City tax rate (1981): $8.93 per $1,000
Bonded debt (1980): $464,601,000
Revenue (1980): $278,300,123
Expenditures (1980): $278,317,024
Chamber of Commerce: Seattle Chamber of Commerce, 215 Columbia Street, Seattle, Wash. 98104

TOLEDO, OHIO

Incorporated as city: 1837
Mayor: Doug DeGood (to Dec. 1981)
City Manager: J. Michael Porter (apptd. Feb. 1979)
1970 population & (rank): 383,062 (34)
1980 population (1980 census) & (rank): 354,635 (40)
1970–80 population change: −7.4%

1980 land area: 81.2 sq mi.
Altitude: 630 ft
Location: In northwestern part of state, on Maumee River at Lake Erie
County: Seat of Lucas Co.
Churches: Protestant, 301; Roman Catholic, 55; Jewish, 4; others, 98
City-owned parks and playgrounds: 134 (2,650.90 ac.)
Telephones (Jan. 1, 1979): 315,797
Television households (Jan. 1981): 173,100 (99%)
Radio stations: AM, 8; FM, 8
Television stations: 4
Assessed valuation (1980): $2,406,890,022
City tax rate (1980): $57.50 per $1,000
Bonded debt (1980): $163,639,100
Revenue (est. 1981): $155,301,770
Expenditures (est. 1981): $152,111,070
Chamber of Commerce: Toledo Area Chamber of Commerce, 218 Huron St., Toledo, Ohio 43604

TUCSON, ARIZ.

Incorporated as city: 1877
Mayor: Lewis C. Murphy (to Dec. 1983)
1970 population & (rank): 262,933 (53)
1980 population (1980 census) & (rank): 330,537 (44)
1970–80 population change: +25.7%
1980 city land area: 91.7 sq mi.
Altitude: 2,500 ft
Location: In southeastern part of state, on the Santa Cruz River
County: Seat of Pima Co.
Churches: Protestant, 181; Roman Catholic, 24; other, 136
City-owned parks and parkways: (2,001.75 ac.)
Telephones (Jan. 1, 1979): 335,032
Television households (Jan. 1981): 172,000 (97%)
Radio stations: AM, 12; FM, 6
Television stations: 3 commercial; 1 educational; 1 other
Assessed valuation (1981): $680,386,981
City tax rate (1981): $9.80 per $1,000
Net bonded debt (1981): $45,017,037
Revenue (1981): $146,548,057
Expenditures (1981): $142,341,697
Chamber of Commerce: Tucson Chamber of Commerce, P.O. Box 991, Tucson, Ariz., 85702

TULSA, OKLA.

Incorporated as city: 1898
Mayor: James Inhofe (to May 1982)
1970 population & (rank): 330,350 (43)
1980 population (1980 census) & (rank): 360,919 (38)
1970–80 population change: +9.3%
1980 land area: 177.3 sq mi.
Altitude: 674 ft
Location: In northeastern part of state, on Arkansas River
County: Seat of Tulsa Co.
Churches: Protestant, 593; Roman Catholic, 32; Jewish, 2; others, 4
City parks and playgrounds: 107 (4,811 ac.)
Telephones (Jan. 1, 1979): 412,906
Television households (Jan. 1981): 176,400 (99%)
Radio stations: AM, 9; FM, 6
Television stations: 3 commercial; 1 educational
Assessed valuation (1980–81): $1,113,654,036
City tax rate (1980–81): $75.88 per $1,000
Bonded debt (June 1980): $112,595,000
Revenue (1979–80): $153,606,004
Expenditures (1979–80): $160,804,702
Chamber of Commerce: Metropolitan Tulsa Chamber of Commerce, 616 S Boston, Tulsa, Okla. 74119

WASHINGTON, D.C.

Land ceded to Congress: 1788 by Maryland; 1789 by Virginia (retroceded to Virginia Sept. 7, 1846)
Seat of government transferred to D. C.: Dec. 1, 1800
Created municipal corporation: Feb. 21, 1871
Mayor: Marion S. Barry, Jr. (to Jan. 1983)
Motto: *Justitia omnibus* (Justice to all)
Flower: American beauty rose
Tree: Scarlet oak
Origin of name: In honor of Columbus
1970 population & (rank): 756,668 (9)
1980 population (1980 census) & (rank): 637,651 (15)
1970–80 population change: −15.7%
1980 land area: 61.4 sq mi.
Geographic center: Near corner of Fourth and L Sts., NW
Altitude: Highest, 420 ft; lowest, sea level
Location: Between Virginia and Maryland, on Potomac River
Churches: Protestant, 446; Roman Catholic, 23; Jewish, 10; others, 23
City parks: 753 (7,725 ac.)
Telephones (Jan. 1, 1979): 1,056,076
Television households (Jan. 1981): 271,800 (98%)
Radio stations: AM, 15; FM, 16
Television stations: 6 (including 2 UHF stations)
Assessed valuation (1980): $12,400,776,662[1]
City tax rate (1978–79): $18.30 per $1,000; $12.20 per $1,000 single-family rate.
Bonded debt: None
Revenue (est. 1980): $906,353,000
Expenditures (est. 1980): $1,734,652,000
Chamber of Commerce: D.C. Chamber of Commerce, 1319 F St., NW, Washington, D.C. 20004
1. On taxable property only. More than 50% of all land in District of Columbia is owned by the Federal government and tax-exempt organizations, and therefore is nontaxable.

The District of Columbia—identical with the City of Washington—is the capital of the United States and the first carefully planned capital in the world.

D.C. history began in 1790 when Congress directed selection of a new capital site, 10 miles square, along the Potomac. When the site was determined, it included 30.75 square miles on the Virginia side of the river. In 1846, however, Congress returned that area to Virginia.

The city was planned and partly laid out by Major Pierre Charles L.'Enfant, a French engineer. This work was perfected and completed by Major Andrew Ellicott. In 1814, during the War of 1812, a British force fired the capital, and it was from the white paint applied to cover fire damage that the President's home was called the White House.

Until Nov. 3, 1967, the District of Columbia was administered by three commissioners appointed by the President. On that day, a government consisting of a mayor-commissioner and a 9-member Council, all appointed by the President with the approval of the Senate, took office. On May 7, 1974, the citizens of the District of Columbia approved the Home Rule Charter, giving them their first form of elected government in over 100 years. The District also has one non-voting member in the House of Representatives.

On Aug. 22, 1978, the Senate passed a proposed constitutional amendment to give Washington, D.C., voting representation in the Congress. The House had approved the legislation in the spring. The amendment must be ratified by at least 38 state legislatures within the next seven years to become effective.

Tabulated Data on City Governments

City	Mayor Term, years	Mayor Salary[1]	City manager's salary[2]	Council or Commission Name	Members	Term, years	Salary[3]
Albuquerque, N.M.	4	$39,000	$43,500[4]	Council	9	4	$ 3,900
Atlanta	4	50,000	—	Council	19	4	13,500
Austin, Tex.	2	18,312	64,451	Council	6	2	16,300
Baltimore	4	47,000	—	Council	19	4	19,500
Birmingham, Ala.	4	52,500	—	Council	9	4	6,900
Boston	4	40,000	—	Council	9	2	20,000
Buffalo, N.Y.	4	41,500	—	Council	15	2[5]	20,000
Charlotte, N.C.	2	11,000	51,900	Council	11	2	5,700
Chicago	4	60,000	—	Council	50	4	25,760
Cincinnati	2	27,875	60,000	Council	9	2	24,375
Cleveland	2	50,000	—	Council	33	2	18,000
Columbus, Ohio	4	40,000	—	Council	7	4	10,000
Dallas	2	50[6]	89,380	Council	11	2	50[6]
Denver	4	50,000	—	Council	13	4	18,675
Detroit	4	69,927	—	Council	9	4	37,926
El Paso	2	9,600	—	Council	7[7]	2	4,800
Fort Worth	2	10[8]	63,690	Council	9	2	10[8]
Honolulu	4	55,908	50,820	Council	9	4	17,500[9]
Houston	2	81,560	—	Council	14	2	21,750
Indianapolis	4	40,664	—	Council	29	4	3,700[10]
Jacksonville, Fla.	4	40,000	32,000[11]	Council	19	4	10,000
Kansas City, Mo.	4	35,000	62,440	Council	13[7]	4	9,600
Long Beach, Calif.	2	638[12]	65,949	Council	9[13]	4	638[12]
Los Angeles	4	66,550	78,949	Council	15	4	39,930
Louisville, Ky.	4	34,081	—	Board of Aldermen	12	2	13,348
Memphis, Tenn.	4	40,000[14]	41,000	Council	13	4	6,000
Miami, Fla.	2	6,000[15]	62,920	Commission	8	4	6,000
Milwaukee	4	58,964	—	Council	16	4	24,880
Minneapolis	2	36,250	52,000	Council	13	2	27,985
Nashville, Tenn.	4	50,000	—	Council	41	4	5,400
New Orleans	4	59,868	—	Council	7	4	15,000
New York	4	80,000	64,584[16]	Council	43	4	35,000
Newark, N.J.	4	52,500	47,270[17]	Council	9	4	24,500
Oakland, Calif.	4	15,000	59,500	Council	9[7]	4	(18)
Oklahoma City	4	2,000	58,500	Council	8	4	20[19]
Omaha, Neb.	4	38,520	—	Council	7	4	10,272
Philadelphia	4	65,000	50,000[20]	Council	17	4	35,000
Phoenix, Ariz.	2	25,000	64,000	Council	7[7]	2	15,000
Pittsburgh	4	45,000	—	Council	9	4	(21)
Portland, Ore.	4	50,822	—	Commission	4	4	40,737
St. Louis	4	25,000	—	Board of Aldermen	29	4	12,500
San Antonio	2	3,000[22]	71,500	Council	11[7]	2	20[23]
San Diego, Calif.	4	31,250	60,187	Council	8	4	21,500
San Francisco	4	62,710	54,131[24]	Board of Supervisors	11	4	9,600
San Jose, Calif.	4	7,200	68,619	Council	10	4	4,800
Seattle	4	75,237	—	Council	9	4	49,643
Toledo, Ohio	2	23,350	48,000	Council	9[13]	2	7,800
Tucson, Ariz.	4	14,000	45,000	Council	7	4	7,200
Tulsa, Okla.	2	42,500	—	Commission	4	2	31,875
Washington, D.C.	4	64,200	52,800	Council	13	4	35,000[25]

1. Annual salary unless otherwise indicated. 2. Annual salary. City Manager's term is indefinite and at will of Council. 3. Annual salary unless otherwise indicated. In some cities, President of Council receives a higher salary. 4. City Administrative Officer appointed by Mayor, approved by Council. 5. For 9 District Councilmen; 4 years for 5 Councilmen-at-Large. 6. Per Council meeting; not over $2,600 per year. 7. Including Mayor. 8. Per week and per Council meeting. 9. Managing Director appointed by Mayor; no Council approval required. 10. Plus $30 per meeting for three meetings a month. 11. Chief Administrative Officer appointed by Mayor; not subject to Council confirmation. 12. Per month. 13. Including Mayor and Vice-Mayor. 14. Plus $5,000 expense account. 15. Plus $2,500 expense account. 16. No City Manager; salary is for Deputy Mayor. 17. Business Administrator, appointed by Mayor and confirmed by Council. 18. Flat $500 per month, or $6,000 annually. 19. Per Council meeting; not to exceed 5 meetings a month. 20. Appointed by Mayor, with title of Managing Director. 21. 4 members at $22,500; 5 members at $27,500. 22. Plus Council pay. 23. Per Council meeting; not over $1,040 per year. 24. Chief Administrative Officer; appointed by Mayor for 10-year term. 25. $10,000 additional for Chairman. Source: *Information Please* questionnaires to the cities.

GUIDE TO GROWING OLDER

Aging Children, Elderly Parents—And the Challenges of Growing Old Together

Barry Robinson

American Association of Retired Persons

After suffering a mild heart attack, a 76-year-old man was rushed to a nearby hospital where doctors observed that he also appeared to be somewhat disoriented. He became rational again, however, as soon as his heart function was stabilized. Still, he kept insisting that his "mommy" would soon come and drive him home—an insistence which left his physicians a bit concerned about his over-all mental state.

Once his physical condition had improved to the point where he could be discharged, the doctors decided that he should be kept in the hospital a while longer for psychological observation. A few days later, the medical staff was more than slightly surprised—and undoubtedly a bit relieved—when the man's 95-year-old mother drove to the hospital from a town a hundred miles away, fully prepared to drive her son home.

Don't laugh too hard—it could happen to you! Sooner or later, depending upon your age now, you could find that you have become either the parent or child in this little anecdote. The most rapid population growth is at present taking place among people over 75 because relatively fewer people than ever before in that age group are dying.

In 1971, the Census Bureau was estimating that, in the year 2000, there would be 28.8 million persons over age 65. By 1975, that estimate had been revised upward to 30.6, and then a couple of years later adjusted upward once more to 31.8 million.

Of particular significance is the fact that more than half of these additional older Americans will be at least 80 years old. Where there are now nearly five million people who are 80 or older, there will by the turn of the century be at least eight million—and probably more if the present trend continues as expected.

Thus, there are going to be more and more 76-year-old men and women with 95-year-old mothers and/or fathers, and not all of them are going to be as healthy and self-reliant as the mother in our little story. Hence the inescapable question of who is going to be responsible for their care.

"Can we," asks industrial gerontologist Harold L. Sheppard, "really expect an increasing proportion of Americans in their early 60s to take care of their elderly relatives, especially if they themselves are retired? They might have more time to provide such care, but what about the expenses involved—particularly in relation to retirement income?"

And what happens when the younger, "responsible" relatives are in their 60s, or in their 70s, or even 80s?

Then, too, as a result of the lowered birthrates which prevailed through much of the 20th Century, warns demographer Jacob S. Siegel, "elderly persons in the future will have fewer brothers and sisters and fewer children than in the past to provide needed or desirable economic or psychological support."

As a result, we may soon be seeing a redefining of relationships between generations of middle-aged and older adults. According to a new life cycle grid promulgated a few years ago in an effort to relate changing social roles to the increasingly prevalent longer human lifespan, middle age now encompasses the years between 35 and 55. People between the ages of 55 and 75 are now the young-old, and those over 75 are the old-old—and it is the old-old whose population is expanding so rapidly.

Large numbers of people are now living long enough to be able to watch their children growing old along with them. It is no longer unusual, in fact, for people to reach at least the beginnings of old age while one or both of their parents are still alive. While this can be—and often is—a joyful and rewarding experience, it is often accompanied by the distressing intimations of one's own mortality that stem from seeing a parent grown suddenly old.

For anyone unprepared to deal with this new situation, few experiences can be more disconcerting than having to deal with a family crisis involving one's elderly parents who have now grown dependent on an adult child to resolve their problems in the same way the child once depended upon them. Unfortunately, some disturbing manifestations of what can happen when this changing relationship doesn't work are becoming visible.

One end result of this process is a syndrome called "battered parents," which usually involves old people who move in with, are perhaps overly dependent upon, and are physically abused by

Barry Robinson is communication counsel for the American Association of Retired Persons and its sister organization, the National Retired Teachers Association, which—with a combined membership of more than thirteen million—comprise the largest association of older people in the world today. He is the author of *Options for Older Americans*, published for the 1971 White House Conference on Aging; *On the Beat: Policemen at Work*, and the forthcoming *Visual Acuity and Aging*.

Founded in 1947 and 1958, respectively, NRTA and AARP are nonprofit, nonpartisan organizations providing older Americans with a wide range of membership programs and services, including legislative representation at both federal and state levels.

their adult children. Little is known about the exact dimensions of this emerging problem. We don't know, for instance, whether the battering of elderly parents is a temporary social quirk typical of the troubled times in which we live or a long-term trend with profoundly frightening implications for the future. We also don't know much about the socio-cultural and economic backgrounds of the battered parents, or even how many elderly parents are abused each year. All we know for sure, at this point, is that it happens.

"The battered elderly often refuse to report the abuse for fear of retaliation, lack of alternative shelter, or fear of the unknown," explains Suzanne K. Steinmetz, the University of Delaware professor who first called a Congressional committee's attention to this ugly phenomenon several years ago.

"Besides," comments Eloise Rathbone-McCuan of St. Louis' Washington University, "think of the stigma. What parents would want other people to know that their children beat them?"

What emerges from the case studies cited by Drs. Steinmetz and Rathbone-McCuan is a series of tragic situations in which both parent and child are victims—frequently of circumstances with which neither can cope. For the most part, battered parents tend to be those who are no longer capable of fending for themselves. Unable to function on their own, they are essentially forced to move in with one of their children, an arrangement which neither they nor their children really want, and which results in more stress than either can handle.

"Each family," observes Steinmetz, "has only *x* amount of resources or capacities to deal with stress. The bottom line is that, if you increase the stress on family members without adding supports to help them cope with it, you increase the likelihood of violence because a person and a family can handle only so much."

At this point, it should be noted that this happens only when the relationships between elderly parents and their aging adult children don't work, and that for every relationship that fails, there are literally hundreds—maybe even thousands or tens of thousands—that do indeed work. There are, after all, millions of middle-aged and older people whose lives flow like an unrippled stream until the end.

Nonetheless, old age will probably always be a time of continual loss. The longer one survives, the more one loses in terms of friends, spouses, siblings, pets, social standing, familiar surroundings, etc. Perhaps the most tragic of these losses is the loss of an adult child.

After people reach a certain age, their anticipation of bereavement is usually associated with the probable loss of their spouses or siblings. Thus, the blow is even more crushing when the natural order is reversed and an adult son or daughter dies unexpectedly.

Around the country, there are many self-help and mutual support programs for widowed persons of all ages and for parents whose children die during childhood or adolescence. However, there are few, if any, programs to help older parents who have the tragic misfortune to outlive one or all of their adult children. Because this is a social and psychological phenomenon about which comparatively little research has been done, there is no substantial body of accumulated knowledge to which one can refer when trying to help bereaved parents cope with their distress.

You have probably noticed that throughout this essay there have been frequent references to what is not known. The constantly changing relationship between aging adult children and their elderly parents is a relatively new phenomenon about which there are not yet—and may never be—any hard and fast rules. What there are, however, are observations and lessons learned from first-hand experience which those of us who have dealt—or are dealing—with these situations can share with each other.

Know What You're Getting Into. Taking an ailing elderly parent into your home is an immense undertaking and a full-time job—usually for the wife whose career frequently becomes the first casualty. If you need a second salary to keep your household running smoothly, this could represent a serious financial hardship which, if possible, should be considered in advance.

Caring for a parent in your home for more than a brief period is becoming the economic equivalent of putting someone through college and, not only are there no scholarships available for those embarking on this mission of mercy, but you don't even receive a diploma of accomplishment. Then, too, you may be part of the "sandwich generation" whose members are literally surrounded by obligations—for the nurturing of their children on one side, the care of their elderly parents on the other, and their own preparations for their later years—and thus have to balance carefully their responsibilities lest none of them be met. If you are not an only child, there may be sibling rivalries over who cares—or escapes—from the chores of caring—for the parent-in-need.

Realize now that your lifestyle may be in for some very drastic changes as you attempt to accommodate your parent's needs or desires. Your work habits and schedule may be disrupted, your personal productivity may decline as you begin spending time (which you might otherwise devote to work brought home from the office) on resolving his

U.S. Population by Age
(in millions)

Age		2000[1]	Percent	1980	Percent	1900	Percent
Under 19		100.9	35	70.5	32	33.7	44
20–34		55.6	19	57.1	26	19.4	26
35–44	Middle age	41.3	14	25.7	11	9.2	12
45–54		35.8	12	22.6	10	6.4	8
55–64	Young-old	22.9	8	21.1	10	4.0	5
65–74		17.1	6	15.4	7	2.2	3
75 & over	Old-old	13.5	5	9.4	4	.9[2]	1

1. Projected. 2. 899,000. NOTE: Percentages are approximate and because of rounding may not add to 100%.

or her problems. There are thus emotional costs which you should expect and be prepared to bear.

Know Why You're Doing What You're Doing. In *The Best Friend You'll Ever Have*, a tragi-comic memoir of his family's experiences during the final months of his mother's life, Bernard Sloan confesses that, although he and his mother had not had a good relationship for years, he brought her into his home because "we were positive she would relinquish her prejudices in exchange for love and care." If you're thinking about striking such an unspoken bargain (he never bothered to discuss this with his mother), forget it! Sloan's mother didn't change under the circumstances, and it's doubtful if any parent would. Unresolved differences don't usually lend themselves to being resolved in the crucible of family crisis; if such differences are to be breached, they should have been breached long ago instead of being held hostage to a parent's health and well-being.

Don't Be Afraid To Ask for Help. Like most professionals in the field of aging, I have a conceptual understanding of our nation's aging services network, but when it came to seeking assistance in dealing with my father's problems, my wife and I did what any member of the public should do—we asked his doctor for help and advice. The doctor put us in touch with the local Visiting Nurses Association, which provided still more information. The most important word on the subject of seeking assistance is ask—and keep asking until you get the answers or the help you need. This can often include psychological counseling for you and/or your family since you are undergoing something of an emotional trauma; such counseling may be one of

the best ways to prevent parents and their children from becoming battered by life-crushing circumstances.

Read and Heed. A great source of help is the printed word to be found in a steadily growing selection of books about aging child/elderly parent relationships. My personal favorites are *You and Your Aging Parent* by Barbara Silverstone and Helen Kandel Hyman, *When Your Parents Grow Old* by Jane Otten and Florence D. Shelley, and *Aging Parents* by Pauline K. Ragan. Also worth perusing are *Understanding Aging Parents* by Andrew D. and Judith L. Lester, *Your Aging Parents: When and How to Help* by Margaret J. Anderson, and *Caring for Your Aged Parents* by Earl A. and Sharon Hya Grollman.

Don't Expect Miracles. If you do, you and your parent are going to be terribly disappointed. To a great extent, you're going to be fighting a holding action against further deterioration, and trying to make your parent as happy and comfortable as he or she can be under the circumstances. Each case is different so your goal should be established in consultation with a physician (hopefully one with a background in geriatric medicine) and related professionals. If you even get near your goal, you'll be doing well.

Know When To Bail Out. There comes a point when your parent's physical and/or psychological condition may be such that the situation has become potentially damaging for both you and your parent and presumably anyone else who is involved intimately. If you continue, you'll probably end up sacrificing yourself, but without saving your parent.

Characteristics of Persons 65 Years Old and Over
(in percentages)

Characteristic	1979 Male	1979 Female	1978 Male	1978 Female	1975 Male	1975 Female	1970 Male	1970 Female
Marital status:[1]								
Single	5.4	6.1	5.4	6.2	4.7	5.8	7.5	7.7
Married	77.1	38.5	77.5	38.6	79.3	39.1	73.1	35.6
Spouse present	74.6	36.9	74.8	36.7	77.3	37.6	69.9	33.9
Spouse absent	2.6	1.6	2.7	1.8	2.0	1.5	3.2	1.7
Widowed	14.1	52.2	14.2	52.0	13.6	52.5	17.1	54.4
Divorced	3.3	3.3	2.9	3.2	2.5	2.6	2.3	2.3
Family status:[1]								
In families	82.3	56.5	82.1	57.3	83.3	59.3	79.2	58.5
Primary individuals	16.0	42.3	16.3	41.6	15.4	39.4	14.9	35.2
Secondary individuals	1.8	1.1	1.6	1.1	1.2	1.3	2.4	1.9
Residents of institutions[1]	n.a.	n.a.	n.a.	n.a.	n.a.	n.a.	3.6	4.4
Labor force participation:								
Employed	19.0	8.3	18.1	8.1	21.1	7.8	26.2	10.0
Unemployed	.9	.4	1.1	.3	1.2	.4	1.0	.3
Not in labor force	80.1	91.3	80.1	91.6	77.7	91.8	72.8	89.7
Living arrangements:[1]								
Living in household	99.8	99.8	99.7	99.7	99.8	99.8	95.5	95.0
Living alone	15.4	41.1	15.7	40.3	14.8	38.0	14.1	33.8
Spouse present	74.6	36.9	74.8	36.7	77.3	37.6	69.9	33.9
Living with someone else	9.8	21.9	9.3	22.6	7.7	24.2	11.5	27.4
Not in household[2]	.2	.2	.3	.3	.2	.2	4.5	5.0

1. Resident population as of March of year indicated. Beginning 1975, excludes institutional population. 2. In institutions and other group quarters. NOTE: n.a. = not available. *Source:* Department of Commerce, Bureau of the Census.

People may tell you you're a saint for what you're doing, but remember that sainthood is usually preceded by martyrdom. It may sound callous, but you have to be realistic at some point, or all of you will go under. Once your parent is out of your home —and, to some extent, off your hands—you may experience some form of decompression, a sort of postpartum depression or after-the-battle fatigue. Such reactions are normal, but if they linger too long or interfere with your functioning in any way, don't hesitate to seek professional help.

Anticipation Adds Alternatives. One way of avoiding—or at least alleviating—crisis situations, such as those involving elderly parents, is to find out in advance what they would prefer to have you do if and when they should become incapable of deciding for themselves. For that matter, this is probably a good time for you to begin thinking about your own alternatives should such a situation befall you in the near or distant future.

Perhaps the best key to planning for one's later life is to ignore wholeheartedly the old line about "crossing that bridge when you come to it." Consider the possibility that the bridge may no longer be there upon your arrival, and that you could be stranded on the wrong side of the river unless alternatives are available, having been considered in advance.

Anticipate and plan, but be flexible in expectations. Try to avoid locking yourself into a single lifestyle which illness or external events can cancel. If enough options aren't kept open at any age, people may eventually end up on that apocryphal park bench, posturing for the pigeons after the parade has passed.

The Facts of Later Life

Income

Most economists estimate that for retirees to maintain their pre-retirement lifestyle within reasonable limits, they need a retirement income equal to 60–70% of their earnings immediately preceding retirement, plus occasional adjustments for inflation.

Even with recent improvements in Social Security benefits, this is a goal beyond the reach of most older Americans who, on average, have half the income of their younger counterparts.

One-seventh of the over-65 population now lives below the poverty level—an improvement over 1970 when a full quarter of all older Americans did. Poverty most often afflicts women and minority aged. While there are, of course, many well-off older persons, most tend to fall economically somewhere between poverty and affluence.

Most of the aged poor did not become poor until they retired, and their income dropped by 50–66%. These are essentially middle-class working people, and it is probably harder for them to cope with their newfound poverty than it is for people who have been poor all their lives.

The economic situation of almost all older Americans, however, is complicated by years of continually escalating inflation, which steadily saps the purchasing power of people living on fixed incomes. Since the elderly do not generally possess the ability to increase their income in response to inflationary pressures, they are perenially attempting to cut back and catch up with little hope of ever breaking even again.

Even with annual Social Security increments, which are supposed to offset inflation, retirees continue to fall farther and farther behind. This is due to the increments coming at least a year after the fact of a cost-of-living increase and thus never compensating fully for inflation's inroads.

Health

Although generally healthier than previous generations of elders, today's older people are still more subject to chronic illness and disability than younger persons. On average, they visit physicians 50% more often, and have health care and medication costs nearly four times those of younger individuals.

Comprising only 11% of the nation's population, older people account for 29% of total personal health care expenditures ($49.4 billion out of $167.9 billion). Yet, most older Americans regard themselves as being comparatively healthy and capable of caring for themselves well enough to continue living independently.

In a 1975 survey, 69% of the older persons questioned described their health as good or excellent in comparison with others of their own age, and 22% said their health was fair. Those describing their health as being chronically poor reported suffering from arthritis (38%), hearing loss (29%), and vision impairment, hypertension, and heart disease (20% each). Many suffered from several of these conditions simultaneously.

A 1978 study found that 82% of the older persons polled had not been hospitalized during the previous year. And most persons entering nursing homes returned later to their own residences.

Employment

In 1900, 67% of men and 8% of women over 65 were actively working. By 1979, only 20% of older men remained employed, while the percentage of women in the workforce had slipped back to eight after rising to ten in 1974. In general, they are working today at part-time jobs, agricultural labor, or self-employment.

Once unemployed, however, older workers usually experience greater difficulty finding new jobs and have longer average periods of unemployment than younger workers. This tendency begins in the mid-to-late 40s and increases with the worker's age.

Marital Status

In 1979, 77% of all older men were married. Among older women, 52% were widows, a figure which rises to 70% after age 75. It is almost predictable: If the husband is five years younger than his wife, the chances of widowhood are 50%; if the husband and wife are the same age, the chances are two out of three; if the husband is five years older than his wife, the chances are three out of four.

Widows outnumber widowers by 5.3 to 1. Men, however, experience greater difficulty adjusting to the loss of a mate—most likely because they don't expect their wives to die before they do.

In 1977, there were 16,760 brides and 30,721 grooms over 65. For approximately 904 of these older brides and 1,438 older grooms, it was a first marriage. For the rest, remarriage came mostly after widowhood rather than divorce. Interestingly, the actual number of marriages involving people over 65 has decreased in the last few years.

Marriage rates for older men in 1977 were seven times those for older women. The number of older men entering into first marriages was 2.5 times that of older women, while the number of older men remarrying was 8.6 times greater than that of older women.

Living Arrangements

While most older persons live in a family setting —with a husband, wife or other relatives—this frequently decreases with advancing age.

More than a third of older Americans—52% of all older women, but only 23% of all older men—live alone or with non-relatives. One reason for this disparity is that women live longer than men, and thus eventually outnumber them in later life.

The majority of older women are widows or divorcees (or, in some cases, both) without adequate means of support and little, if any, preparation for living alone—a circumstance which may in time give rise to new forms of communal living.

Pensions

The newer the retiree, the greater the chances of participation in a company or union pension—and the greater the likelihood of collecting on that pension, thanks to the Employee Retirement Income Security Act (ERISA) of 1974 which regulates pension plans and insures the worker's stake in them.

Prior to that, many workers participated in plans but were unable to collect pensions upon retirement. Thus, most older retirees do not receive private pension payments, but live instead solely on Social Security and whatever savings they have managed to accumulate; some must also depend upon Supplemental Security Income (SSI) payments to assist them in making ends meet.

Of today's active workers, however, it is estimated that nearly half are covered by pension plans.

Transportation

Most public transportation systems are designed primarily to satisfy the needs of the commuting worker. Older people (whose needs are usually quite different) are thus forced either to rely upon automobiles—which are becoming increasingly expensive to own and maintain—or to surrender their mobility and settle for whatever is within walking distance, no matter how inferior it may be.

Some communities have attempted to provide special transportation services at reduced rates for their older residents, but many of these subsidized systems have fallen victim to their own success. The more they are utilized, the more they cost to operate, and the growing cost often exceeds a community's ability to sustain them. In this age of energy scarcity, this looms large as a major problem.

Crime

While violent crimes against the elderly have been increasing lately and have thus received the most news coverage, they are not nearly as prevalent as "bunco" offenses, in which the victim is defrauded of whatever savings he or she may have managed to accumulate over the course of a lifetime.

Older victims tend to suffer more intensely. A younger victim can recoup a monetary loss by accumulating future earnings, but older victims no longer have that opportunity. Similarly, older victims wounded in crimes of violence require longer to heal, leading to prolonged loss of mobility and the increased possibility of medical complications.

Coping

When You Need Help or Information

Whether your concern is for your own later years or for someone you know with problems, the basic approaches to seeking help or information are essentially the same. In general, your primary sources of information are your local telephone directory and your community's public library.

A good way to begin is to take stock of your resources relating to the problem. This doesn't necessarily mean financial resources, although they can be undeniably important. There are, however, other resources which you may have built up over a lifetime of activity without really being aware of them.

Did you, for instance, serve in the nation's military services? If so, check with the Veterans Administration (listed in the phonebook under "U.S. Government") to see if it can help.

Are you a union member? Then, contact your nearest local and find out if the union has any programs to help retirees with your particular problem. This also applies to any civic or fraternal organizations to which you may belong.

Don't forget the many local and national organizations for older people; being a member of one or more of them can prove helpful. These are the major national ones:

American Association of Retired Persons/National Retired Teachers Association (AARP/NRTA), 1909 K Street N.W., Washington, D.C. 20049

National Council of Senior Citizens (NCSC), 1511 K Street N.W., Washington, D.C. 20005

National Association of Retired Federal Employees (NARFE), 1533 New Hampshire Avenue N.W., Washington, D.C. 20036

Gray Panthers, 3700 Chestnut Street, Philadelphia, Pa. 19104

Older Women's League Educational Fund, 3800 Harrison Street, Oakland, Calif. 94611 For ages 50–64:

Action for Independent Maturity (AIM), 1909 K Street N.W., Washington, D.C. 20049

There are also organizations of professionals who work with and on behalf of the elderly: National Council on the Aging (NCOA), 600 Maryland Avenue, S.W., Washington, D.C. 20024; The Gerontological Society, 1835 K Street N.W., Washington, D.C. 20006; American Geriatric Society, 10 Columbus Circle, New York, N.Y. 10019.

When You Have a Problem . . .

For just about every problem today, there is a private public service organization or government program trying to solve it. The trick is for you to get in touch with the right one.

In this *Almanac (see* Index), there is a listing of U.S. Societies and Associations in which you might find the name of an organization dealing with your particular problem. Look in your telephone directory to see if there is a branch office in your area; if not, contact the organization's national headquarters at the address given.

To find government agencies that might be able to help, start with your local government (city, town, or village) and move on to county, state, and federal levels only as necessary. Often, the agency nearest home will be the most help. Again, your telephone directory can be your best source of information; if you can't find exactly what you're looking for there, try phoning the municipal or country clerk's office for more specific guidance.

Keys to Finding Help

A few of the sources of assistance or information to which you might turn when dealing with a specific problem are given below. (Unless an address is given, look in your phonebook for the key-word indicated.)

Aging. Administration on Aging, U.S. Department of Health and Human Services, Washington, D.C. 20201. Locally, try state **Offices, Commissions, Departments,** or **Bureaus** on **Aging** or **Senior Citizens Affairs;** look for county or municipal agencies with similar titles, and for regional **Area Agencies on Aging.**

Career Considerations: If you're unhappy in your present work situation, and are trying to decide whether to stick with it until you can retire gracefully or to attempt to start anew in middle age, these books might provide some helpful insights. *Overcoming Executive Mid-Life Crisis* by Homer R. Figler; *Second Chance: Blueprints for Change* by Herbert B. Livesey; *What Color Is Your Parachute?* by Richard N. Bolles; *The Three Boxes of Life and How to Get Out of Them* by Richard N. Bolles; *The Women's Guide to Re-Entry Employment* by Mary Zimmeth; *What To Do With the Rest of Your Life* by the Catalyst staff.

Federal Government. Your tie-line and guide to the federal bureaucracy is the **Federal Information Center,** listed in the phonebook under "U.S. Government." If nothing else works, try phoning your Congressional representative's local office; his or her staff can sometimes cut through a lot of red tape.

Food. The key words here are **Food Stamps, Meals on Wheels, National Nutrition Program for the Elderly.** If none of these is listed in your phonebook, check with the agencies listed under Aging.

Health Care. Don't overlook your local **health department.** If your problem involves a hospital, there is probably a staff social worker to whom you can turn. Also, try local medical and dental societies and schools—the latter frequently provide quality care at relatively low cost. For information about health care at home, contact the National Council for Homemaker-Home Health Aide Service, 67 Irving Place, New York, N.Y. 10003.

Housing. The key agency here is the U.S. Department of Housing and Urban Development; check your phonebook for a local office, or write to HUD, Washington, D.C. 20410. If you live in a rural area, contact your agricultural extension agent or write directly to Farmers Home Administration, U.S. Department of Agriculture, 14th Street and Independence Avenue S.W., Washington, D.C. 20250. Your local **housing authority** can also prove helpful.

Legal Problems. Many communities have special legal counseling programs for older residents. Try your local **Aging** agency, or write to National Senior Citizens Law Center, 1709 West 8th Street, Los

Aging: Myths and Truths

Myth: You can't teach an old dog new tricks.
Truth: A smart dog can learn new tricks at any age, and so can most people. Research has shown that older people do not necessarily lose their ability to learn, but sometimes learn differently than when younger. Their speed of comprehension, for instance, may decrease somewhat, but their retention and interpretation of new information may improve. Contrary to common belief, senility is not a state of mind that invariably accompanies old age. Rather, it is a serious and complex illness which, in many cases, can be alleviated through proper medical diagnosis and treatment.

Myth: Sex doesn't exist after age 60, and anyone who thinks it does is a "dirty old man" (or woman).
Truth: Normal sexual activity continues well into later life—sometimes even into the 90s—although frequency may decrease somewhat over the years.

Myth: When you grow old, you end up in a nursing home or some other institution.
Truth: Less than 5% of people 65 and over are institutionalized; the rest maintain their independence in a variety of residential situations. The majority of people who enter nursing homes usually do so following a period of hospitalization and eventually return to their homes.

Myth: Like birds in winter, people head south as soon as they retire.
Truth: While some do move south, most don't. Approximately 82.7% of the 65-plus population still live in the same house in which they lived before retiring. Of those who have moved, most moved a relatively short distance—frequently to a smaller residence more suited to their needs—while only 3.6% moved to different states, such as Florida, Arizona, and Nevada.

Angeles, Calif. 90017. Information is also available from the National Resource Center for Consumers of Legal Services, 1302 18th Street N.W., Washington, D.C. 20036.

Middle Age. The processes, problems, and potentials of adult development in the middle years are explored in authoritative depth in two recent books, *The Seasons of a Man's Life* by Daniel Levinson and *Transformations* by Roger Gould. The original research and theories of both of these psychiatrists served as a basis for Gail Sheehy's bestselling *Passages.*

Money. Information about **Social Security** and **Supplemental Security Income** may be found in this *Almanac* or from the **Social Security Administration** office nearest you. Also helpful in special circumstances are the U.S. Office of Personnel Management, Compensation Group, Bureau of Retirement, 1900 E Street N.W., Washington, D.C. 20415; and the U.S. Railroad Retirement Board, Headquarters office, 844 Rush Street, Chicago, Ill. 60611.

Nursing Homes. Check with your local **health department,** hospital social worker, or the nearest branches of the American Nursing Home Association and the American Association of Homes for the Aging. Some state **Aging** agencies have a **Nursing Home Ombudsman.** Write for the free pamphlet *Thinking About a Nursing Home* to the American Health Care Association, 1200 15th Street N.W., Washington, D.C. 20005.

Research. If you want to read more about growing older, look in your local library catalog under **aging, gerontology, geriatrics, retirement.**

Volunteering. If you're interested in working as a volunteer, check with your local **hospitals, nonprofit nursing homes, social service agencies,** and **civic organizations.** Or write to: National Center for Citizen Involvement, 1214 16th Street, N.W., Washington, D.C. 20036, ACTION, Older Americans Volunteer Programs, Washington, D.C. 20525; Service Corps of Retired Executives (SCORE), Small Business Administration, 1441 L Street N.W., Washington, D.C. 20416.

Social Security

The original Social Security Act was passed in 1935 and amended in 1939, 1946, 1950, 1952, 1954, 1956, 1958, 1960, 1961, 1965, 1967, 1969, 1972, 1974, 1977, and 1980.

The act is administered by the Social Security Administration and the Health Care Financing Administration, and other agencies within the Department of Health and Human Services.

For purposes of clarity, the explanations given below will describe the provisions of the act as amended.

Old Age, Disability, and Survivors Insurance

Practically everyone who works fairly regularly is covered by social security. Many state and local government employees are covered under voluntary agreements between states and the Secretary of Health and Human Services. Workers not covered include most federal civilian employees, career railroad workers, and a few other exceptions.

Cash tips count for social security if they amount to $20 or more in a month from employment with a single employer.

To qualify for benefits or make payments possible for your survivors, you must be in work covered by the law for a certain number of "quarters of coverage." Before 1978, a quarter of coverage was earned if a worker was paid $50 or more wages in a 3-month calendar quarter. A self-employed person got 4 "quarters of coverage" for a year in which his net earnings were $400 or more.

In 1978, a worker, whether employed or self-employed, received one quarter of coverage for each $250 of covered annual earnings up to a maximum of four for a year. The quarter of coverage measure was increased to $260 in 1979 and $290 in 1980 and will increase automatically in future years to keep pace with increases in average wages. The number of quarters needed differs for different persons and depends on the date of your birth; in general, it is related to the number of years after 1950, or after the year you reach 21, if later,

and up to the year you reach 62, become disabled, or die. One "quarter of coverage" is required for each such year in order for you or your family to get benefits. No one will need more than 40 quarters. Your local social security office can tell you how long you need to work.

Who Pays for the Insurance?

Both workers and their employers pay for the workers' insurance. Self-employed persons pay their own social security contributions annually along with their income tax. The rates include the

Social Security Contribution and Rate Schedule
(percent of covered earnings)

Year	Retirement, survivors, and disability insurance	Hospital insurance	Total
EMPLOYERS AND EMPLOYEES			
1978	4.95%	1.10%	6.05%
1979–80	5.08	1.05	6.13
1981	5.35	1.30	6.65
1982–84	5.40	1.30	6.70
1985	5.70	1.35	7.05
1986–89	5.70	1.45	7.15
1990 & later	6.20	1.45	7.65
SELF-EMPLOYED			
1978	7.00%	1.10%	8.10%
1979–80	7.05	1.05	8.10
1981	8.00	1.30	9.30
1982–84	8.05	1.30	9.35
1985	8.55	1.35	9.90
1986–89	8.55	1.45	10.00
1990 & later	9.30	1.45	10.75

cost of Medicare hospital insurance. The contribution and benefit base is $29,700 for 1981, and will increase automatically in future years as earnings levels rise. The contribution rate schedules under present law are shown in a table in this section.

The separate payroll contribution to finance hospital insurance is placed in a separate trust fund in the U.S. Treasury. In addition, the medical insurance premiums, currently $9.60 a month, and the government's shares go into another separate trust fund.

How to Apply for Benefits

You apply for benefits by filing a claim either in person, by mail, or by telephone at any social security office. You can get the address either from the post office or from the phone book under the listing, United States Government—Department of Health and Human Services—Social Security Administration. You will need certain kinds of proof, depending upon the type of benefit you are claiming. If it is a retirement benefit, you should provide a birth or baptismal certificate. If you are unable to get these documents, other old documents showing your age or date of birth—such as census records, school records, early naturalization certificate, etc. —may be acceptable. A widow, or widower, 60 or older who is claiming widow's benefits based on his or her spouse's earnings should have both proof of age and a copy of the marriage certificate. If formal proof is not available, the social security office will tell you what kinds of information will be acceptable.

What Does Social Security Offer?

The social security contribution you pay gives you four different kinds of protection: (1) retirement benefits, (2) survivors' benefits, (3) disability benefits, and (4) Medicare hospital insurance benefits.

Retirement benefits A worker becomes eligible for the full amount of his retirement benefits at age 65, if he has retired under the definition in the law. A worker may retire at 62 and get 80% of his full benefit. The closer he is to age 65 when he starts collecting his benefit, the larger is the fraction of his full benefit that he will get.

The amount of the retirement benefit you are entitled to at 65 is the key to all other benefits under the program. The retirement benefit is based on covered earnings, generally those after 1950. Your covered earnings will be updated (indexed) to the second year before you reach age 62, become disabled, or die, and will reflect the increases in average wages that have occurred since the earnings were paid.

A worker who delays his retirement past age 65, or who does not receive a benefit for some months after age 65 because of high earnings will get a special credit that can mean a larger benefit. The credit adds to a worker's benefits 1% (3% for workers age 62 after 1978) for each year (1/12 of 1% for each month) from age 65 to age 72 for which he did not get benefits.

The law provides a special minimum benefit at retirement for people who worked under social security for many years. The provision will help people who had low incomes, but above a specific level, in their working years. The amount of the special minimum depends on the number of years of coverage. For a worker retiring at 65 in January

1981 with 30 or more years of coverage, the special minimum benefit would be $289.00 (effective June 1980). These benefits are reduced if a worker is under 65 and are increased automatically for increases in the cost of living.

If you retired at age 65 in January 1981 with average earnings, you would get a benefit of $532.80.

If your spouse is also 65, then he or she will get a spouse's benefit that is equal to half your benefit. So if your benefit is $532.80, your spouse gets $266.40.

If your spouse is between ages 62 and 65, he or she can draw a reduced benefit; the amount depends on the number of months before 65 that he or she starts getting checks. If he or she draws his or her benefit when he or she is 62, he or she will get about ³/₈ of your basic benefit, or $199.80. (He or she will get this amount for the rest of his or her life, unless you should die first; then he or she can start getting widow's, or widower's, benefits, described below.)

If the spouse is entitled to a worker's retirement benefit on his or her own earnings, he or she can draw whichever amount is larger. If the spouse is entitled to a retirement benefit which is less than the spouse's benefit, he or she will receive his or her own retirement benefit plus the difference between the retirement benefit and the spouse's benefit.

If you have children under 18 or a child in school aged 18 up to 22 or a son or daughter who became totally disabled prior to reaching age 22, when you retire they will get a benefit equal to half your full retirement benefits (subject to maximum payments that can be made to a family). If your spouse is caring for a child who is under 18 or who became disabled before 22 (and getting benefits too), he or she is eligible for benefits, even if he or she is under 62.

In general, the highest retirement check that can be paid to a worker who retired at 65 in January 1981 is about $677.00 a month. Maximum payment to the family of this retired worker is about $1,184.70 in January 1981. When your children reach age 18, their benefits will stop except for children in school aged 18 up to 22, and except for a benefit that is going to a son or daughter who became totally disabled before attaining age 22. Such a person can continue to get his benefits as long as his disability meets the definition in the law.

If you are divorced, you can get social security benefits (the same as a spouse or widow, or widower,) based on your ex-spouse's earnings record if you were married at least 10 years and if your ex-spouse has retired, become disabled, or died.

Survivor benefits. This feature of the social security program gives your family valuable life insurance protection—in some cases benefits to a family could amount to $100,000 or more over a period of years. The amount of protection is again geared to what the worker would be entitled to if he had been age 65 when he died. Your survivors could get:

1. A cash payment to help cover your burial expenses. This "lump-sum death payment" is $255.
2. A benefit for each child until he reaches 18, or 22 if the child is in school, or at any age if disabled before 22. Each eligible child receives 75% of the basic benefit (subject to reduction for the family maximum). (A disabled child can continue to collect benefits after age 22.) If certain conditions are

met, dependent grandchildren of insured workers can receive survivor or dependent benefits.

3. A benefit for your widow, or widower, if she has children under 18 or disabled in her care. Her benefit is also 75% of the basic benefit. She can collect this as long as she has a child under 18 or disabled in her care. Payments stop then (they will start again upon application when she is 60 at a slightly lower amount).

Total family survivor benefits are estimated to be as high as $1,125.20 a month, in 1981.

4. If there are no children either under 18 or disabled, your spouse can get a widow's, or widower's, benefit starting at age 60. This would come to 71½% of the basic amount at age 60. A widow, or widower, who first becomes entitled at 65 or later may get 100% of his or her deceased spouse's basic amount (provided neither he nor she ever drew reduced benefits).

5. Dependent parents can sometimes collect survivors' benefits. They are usually eligible if: (a) they were getting at least half their support from the deceased worker at (1) the time of the worker's death if the worker did not qualify for disability benefits before death, or (2) if the worker had been entitled to disability benefits which had not been terminated before death either at the beginning of the period of disability or at the time of death; (b) they have reached 62; and (c) they are not eligible for a greater retirement benefit based on their own earnings. A single surviving parent can then get 82½% of the basic benefit. If two parents are eligible, each would get 75%.

Here is an example of survivors' benefits in one family situation: John Jones died at age 29 in June 1980 leaving a wife and two children aged one and three. He had average covered earnings under social security. Family survivors' benefits would include: (1) a cash lump-sum death payment of $255,000, and (2) a total monthly benefit of $804.40 for the family. When the children reach 18, their benefits stop unless they are attending school full-time, in which case payments continue up to age 22. When the older child no longer collects benefits, the widow and younger child continue to get benefits until that child is 18. If he continues in school, he will still get a benefit, but Mrs. Jones' checks will stop. When Mrs. Jones becomes 60 (assuming she has not remarried), she will be able to get a reduced widow's benefit if she so chooses, or she can wait until age 65 to get a full benefit.

If in addition to your social security benefit as a wife, husband, widow, or widower you receive a pension based on your work in public employment not covered by social security, your benefit as a dependent or survivor will be reduced by the amount of that pension. Under an exception in the law, your government pension will not affect your dependent's or survivor's benefit if you became eligible for that pension before December 1982 and if, at the time you apply or become entitled to your social security benefit as a dependent or survivor, you could have qualified for that benefit if the law in effect in January 1977 had remained in effect. (At that time, men had to prove they were dependent upon their wives for support to be eligible for benefits as a dependent or survivor.) Your government pension, however, will not affect any social security benefit based on your own work covered by social security.

Disability Benefits. Disability benefits can be paid to several groups of people:

Disabled workers under 65 and their families.

Persons disabled before 22 who continue to be disabled. These benefits are payable as early as 18 when a parent (or grandparent under certain circumstances) receives social security retirement or disability benefits or when an insured parent dies.

Disabled widows and widowers and (under certain conditions) disabled surviving divorced spouses of workers who were insured at death. These benefits are payable as early as 50.

A disabled person is eligible for Medicare after being entitled to disability payments for 24 months.

If you are a worker and become severely disabled, you will be eligible for monthly benefits if you have worked under social security long enough and recently enough. The amount of work you will need depends on your age when you become disabled:

Before 24: You need credit for 1½ years of work in the 3-year period ending when your disability begins.

24 through 30: You need credit for having worked half the time between 21 and the time you become disabled.

31 or older: All workers disabled at 31 or older—except the blind—need the amount of credit shown in the chart below:

Work Credit for Disability Benefits

Born after 1929, become disabled at age	Born before 1930, become disabled before 62 in	Years of work credit you need
42 or younger	1971	5
44	1973	5½
46	1975	6
48	1977	6½
50	1979	7
51	1980	7¼
52	1981	7½
54	1983	8
56	1985	8½
58	1987	9
60	1989	9½
62 or older	1991 or later	10

NOTE: Five years of this credit must have been earned in the 10 years ending when you became disabled; years need not be continuous or in units of full years.

To be considered disabled under the social security law you must have a physical or mental condition which: (1) prevents you from doing any substantial gainful work; and (2) is expected to last (or has lasted) for at least 12 months, or is expected to result in death.

If you meet these conditions, you may be able to get payments even if your recovery from the disability is expected.

The medical evidence from your physician or other sources will show the severity of your condition and the extent to which it prevents you from doing substantial gainful work. Your age, education, training, and work experience also may be considered in deciding whether you are able to work.

If you can't do your regular work but can do other substantial gainful work, you will not be considered disabled. A person whose vision is no better than 20/200 even with glasses, or who has a limited visual field of 20 degrees or less, is considered "blind" under the social security law.

While you are receiving benefits as a disabled worker, payments can also be made to certain members of your family. These family members include:

Your unmarried children under 18.

Your children 18–22 if they are unmarried and attending school full time.

Your unmarried children 18 or older who were disabled before reaching 22 and continue to be disabled.

Your wife at any age if she has in her care a child who is under 18 or disabled and who is getting benefits based on your social security record.

Your wife 62 or older even if there are no children entitled to benefits.

Your husband 62 or older.

A child may be eligible on a grandparent's social security record only if the child's parents are disabled or deceased and the child was living with and dependent upon the grandparent at the time the grandparent qualified for benefits.

Benefits begin after a waiting period of 5 full calendar months. No benefits can be paid for these first 5 months of disability; therefore, the first payment is for the 6th full month. If you are disabled more than 6 full months before you apply, back benefits may be payable, but not before the 6th full month of disability. It is important to apply soon after the disability starts because back payments are limited to the 12 months preceding the month you apply.

Certain disabled people under 65 are eligible for Medicare. They include disabled workers at any age, persons who became disabled before age 22, and disabled widows and widowers age 50 or over who have been entitled to disability checks for 2 years or more.

Medicare protection generally ends when monthly disability benefits end, and can continue an additional 3 years after benefits stop because an individual returns to gainful work.

If a person becomes entitled to disability benefits again, Medicare coverage starts at the same time if a worker becomes disabled again within 5 years after benefits end (or within 7 years for a disabled widow, widower, or person disabled before age 22).

Benefits to workers disabled after 1978 and their dependents are based, in part, on earnings that have been adjusted to take account of increases in average wages since they were earned. The adjusted earnings are averaged together and a formula is applied to the adjusted average to figure the benefit rate.

Monthly benefits in July 1980 or later range from $139.50 to $647 for a worker and as high as $970.50 for a worker with a family. Once a person starts receiving benefits, the amount will increase automatically in future years to keep pace with the rising cost of living.

If you receive benefits as a disabled worker, an adult disabled since childhood, or a disabled widow or widower, you are not subject to the general rule under which some benefits are withheld if you have substantial earnings. There are special rules, which include medical considerations, for determining how any work you do might affect your disability payments.

If one of your dependents who is under 65 and who is not disabled works and earns more than $3,720 in 1980, some of the dependent's benefits may be withheld. In general, $1 in benefits is withheld for each $2 over $3,720. Different rules apply to your dependents who are 65 or over.

The amount a person can earn without having any benefits withheld will increase in future years as the level of average wages rises.

If you are receiving disability benefits, you are required by law to let the Social Security Administration know if your condition improves or if you return to work no matter how little you earn.

If at any time medical evidence shows that you no longer meet the requirements for entitlement to disability benefits, you will still receive benefits for a 3-month period of adjustment. Benefits will then be stopped.

Whether or not you report a return to work or that your condition has improved, social security will review your claim periodically to see if you continue to meet the requirements for benefits.

If you are a disabled worker or a person disabled in childhood and you return to work in spite of a severe condition, your benefits may continue to be paid during a trial work period of up to 9 months—not necessarily consecutive months. This will give you a chance to test your ability to work. If after 9 months it is decided that you are able to do substantial gainful work, your benefits will be paid for an adjustment period of 3 additional months.

Thus, if you go to work in spite of your disability, you may continue to receive disability benefits for up to 12 months, even though the work is substantial gainful work. If it is decided that the work you are able to do is not substantial and gainful, you may continue to receive benefits. Of course, should you no longer meet the requirements for entitlement your benefits would be stopped after a 3-month adjustment period even though your trial work period might not be over.

Disabled widows and widowers also can have a trial work period. If your benefits are stopped because you return to work and you become unable to continue working within the next 12 months, your benefits can be restarted automatically. You do not have to file a new disability application.

You Can Earn Income Without Losing Benefits

If you are 72 or over, you can earn any amount and still get all your benefits if your earnings do not exceed the annual exempt amount. The annual amount for 1980 is $5,000 for people 65 or over and $3,720 for people under 65.

If your earnings go over the annual amount, $1 in benefits is withheld for each $2 of earnings above the limit.

The monthly measure used for 1977 and earlier years to determine whether benefits could be paid for any month during which they earned 1/12 or less of the annual exempt amount and did no substantial work in their business has been eliminated. A person can now use the monthly test only in the first year that he or she has a month in which earnings do not exceed 1/12 of the annual exempt amount or does not perform substantial services in self-employment. If such a month occurs in 1980, a benefit can be paid for any month in which you earn $417 or less (if 65 or older) or $310 (if under 65) and don't perform substantial services in self-employment even though your total yearly earnings exceed the annual amount.

For people 65 or over, the annual exempt amount will increase to $5,500 for 1981, and to $6,000 for 1982. After that, the limit will increase automatically as the level of average wages rises. The limit for people under 65 will also continue to increase.

If a worker's earnings exceed the exempt amount, social security benefits to his dependents may be reduced. However, a dependent's benefits will not be reduced if another dependent has excess earnings.

Anyone earning over the annual exempt amount a year while receiving benefits (and under age 72) must report these earnings to the Social Security Administration. If you continue to work after you have applied for social security, your additional earnings may increase the amount of your monthly payment. This will be done automatically by the Social Security Administration. You need not ask for it.

Medicare

The Medicare program is administered by the Health Care Financing Administration.

Most people 65 and over and many under 65 who have been entitled to disability checks for at least 2 years have Medicare protection. So do insured people and their dependents who need a kidney transplant or dialysis treatment because of permanent kidney failure.

The hospital insurance part of Medicare helps pay the cost of inpatient hospital care and certain kinds of follow-up care. The medical insurance part helps pay for the cost of doctors' services, outpatient hospital services, and for certain other medical items and services.

A person who is eligible for monthly benefits at 65 gets hospital insurance automatically and does not have to pay a premium. He does pay a monthly premium for medical insurance.

Supplemental Security Income

The supplemental security income program started January 1974. These federal payments assure a minimum level of income for aged, blind, and disabled people who have limited income and resources.

This program is administered by the Social Security Administration, but it is financed from general revenues, not from social security contributions. Before 1974, payments to these people were made by state and local public assistance agencies.

Payments of up to $264.70 a month for an individual and up to $397.00 for a couple can be made and States may supplement the federal payments. Further information is available from any social security office.

How to Protect Your Social Security Record

Always show your social security card when you start a new job. In that way you will be sure that your earnings will be credited to *your* social security record and not someone else's. If you lose your social security card, apply for a new one at any social security office. When a woman marries, she should apply for a new card showing her married name (and the same number).

Public Assistance

The Federal government makes grants to the states to help them provide financial assistance, medical care, and social services to certain persons in need, including children dependent because of the death, absence from home, incapacity, or (in some states) unemployment of a parent. In addition, some help is provided from only state and/or local funds to some other needy persons.

Federal sharing in state cash assistance expenditures made in accordance with the Social Security Act is based on formulas which are set forth in the Act. The Social Security Act gives the states the option of using one of two formulas, whichever is to its benefit. One formula limits the amount of assistance payment in which there is federal sharing. The other formula permits federal sharing without a limit on the amount of assistance payment. Administrative costs in all the programs are shared equally by the federal and state governments.

Within these and other general patterns set by the requirements of the Social Security Act and their administrative interpretations, each state initiates and administers its own public assistance programs, including the determination of who is eligible to receive assistance, and how much can be granted and under what conditions. Assistance is in the form of cash payments made to recipients, except that direct payments are used for medical care, and restricted payments may be used in cases of mismanagement. Other social services are provided, in some instances, to help assistance recipients increase their capacity for self-care and self-support or to strengthen family life.

In the medical assistance Medicaid program, federal funds pay 50% to 83% of the costs for medical care. If it is to a state's benefit, it may use the Medicaid formula for federal sharing for its money payment programs, ignoring the maximum on dollar amounts per recipient.

Unemployment Insurance

Unemployment insurance is managed jointly by the states and the federal government. Most states began paying benefits in 1938 and 1939.

Under What Conditions Can the Worker Collect?

The laws vary from state to state. In general, a waiting period of one week is required after a claim is filed before collecting unemployment insurance; the worker must be able to work, must not have quit

without good cause or have been discharged for misconduct; he must not be involved in a labor dispute; above all, he must be ready and willing to work. He may be disqualified if he refuses, without good cause, to accept a job which is suitable for him in terms of his qualifications and experience, unless the wages, hours and working conditions offered are substantially less favorable than those prevailing for similar jobs in the community.

The unemployed worker must go to the local state employment security office and register for work. If that office has a suitable opening available, he must accept it or lose his unemployment payments, unless he has good cause for the refusal. If a worker moves out of his own state, he can still collect at his new residence; the state in which he is now located will act as agent for the other state, which will pay his benefits.

Benefits are paid only to unemployed workers who have had at least a certain amount of recent past employment or earnings in a job covered by the state law. The amount of employment or earnings, and the period used to measure them, vary from state to state, but the intent of the various laws is to limit benefits to workers whose recent records indicate that they are members of the labor force. The amount of benefits an unemployed worker may receive for any week is also determined by application to his past wages of a formula specified in the law. The general objective is to provide a weekly benefit which is about half the worker's customary weekly wages, up to a maximum set by the law (see table). In a majority of states, the total benefits a worker may receive in a 12-month period is limited to a fraction of his total wages in a prior 12-month period, as well as to a stated number of weeks. Thus, not all workers in a state are entitled to benefits for the number of weeks shown in the table.

Who Pays for the Insurance?

The total cost is borne by the employer in all but three states. Each state has a sliding scale of rates. The standard rate is set at 2.7% of taxable payroll in most states. But employers with records of less unemployment (that is, with fewer unemployment benefits paid to their former workers) are rewarded with rates lower than the standard 2.7%. The estimated average rate for employers in 1980 was 2.3% of taxable wages or 1.0% of total wages. Contributions for 1981 are required on wages up to $6,000 in all states except Pa., $6,300; Ill., $6,500; Ala., $6,600; W. Va., $6,600; Ark., $6,900; N.J., $7,500; Mont., $7,800; R.I., $7,800; Iowa, Minn., and N. Mex., $8,000; Nev. and N.D., $8,400; Or., $10,000; Wash., $10,200; Idaho and Utah, $12,000; Hawaii, $12,200; Alaska, $13,300; P.R., all wages. Employees as well as employers pay a tax in Alaska ranging from 0.3% to 1.0% in accordance with their employer's tax; in N.J., employees pay 0.5% for unemployment insurance. In Ala., employees pay contributions of 0.5% only when the fund is below a specified amount.

Employers pay an additional unemployment tax to the federal government—0.7% of the first $6,000 paid to each employee. This money is used for the federal and state costs of administering the employment security program, including both unemployment insurance and the employment service. Any amount over these costs, up to the greater of $550 million or 0.125% of total wages subject to contributions under the state unemployment compensation laws for the calendar year, is put in a special fund on which the states draw when the benefit payment funds are low. Any remaining excess is distributed to the states in proportion to their taxable payrolls. These excess funds may be used for benefit payments, or may be used for administrative expenses if so appropriated by the state legislature.

Requirements vary from state to state, but all states cover firms having at least one employee for 20 weeks or a quarterly payroll of $1,500 in the current or preceding calendar year. In some states, firms with one employee at any time are covered.

State Unemployment Compensation Maximums, 1981

State	Weekly benefit[1]	Maximum duration, weeks	State	Weekly benefit[1]	Maximum duration, weeks
Alabama	$90	26	Montana	145	26
Alaska	150–222	26	Nebraska	106	26
Arizona	95	26	Nevada	136	26
Arkansas	136	26	New Hampshire	114	26
California	130	26	New Jersey	133	26
Colorado	160	26	New Mexico	117	26
Connecticut	140–190	26	New York	125	26
Delaware	150	26	North Carolina	139	26
D. C.	196	34	North Dakota	156	26
Florida	105	26	Ohio	136–215	26
Georgia	115	26	Oklahoma	176	26
Hawaii	157	26	Oregon	150	26
Idaho	145	26	Pennsylvania	175–183	30
Illinois	148–198	26	Puerto Rico	84	20
Indiana	84–141	26	Rhode Island	143–163	26
Iowa	146–176	26	South Carolina	114	26
Kansas	149	26	South Dakota	129	26
Kentucky	140	26	Tennessee	110	26
Louisiana	164	28	Texas	126	26
Maine	115–173	26	Utah	166	36
Maryland	140	26	Vermont	135	26
Massachusetts	142–213	30	Virginia	138	26
Michigan	182–221	26	Washington	163	30
Minnesota	177	26	West Virginia	194	28
Mississippi	90	26	Wisconsin	175	34
Missouri	105	26	Wyoming	165	26

1. Maximum amounts. When two amounts are shown, higher includes dependents' allowances. *Source:* Department of Labor, Employment and Training Administration.

Certain classes of workers are specifically excluded under some or all state laws—members of the employer's family, insurance agents on commission, student nurses, internes, casual labor, and the self-employed.

During periods of high unemployment on either a state or national level, federal-state extended benefits are available to workers who have exhausted their regular benefits. An unemployed worker may receive benefits equal to the weekly benefit he received under the state program for one half the weeks of his basic entitlement to benefits up to a maximum (including regular benefits) of 39 weeks.

Federal Unemployment Insurance Programs

Amendments to the Social Security Act provided unemployment insurance for Federal civilian employees (1954) and for ex-servicemen (1958). Benefits under these programs are paid by state employment security agencies as agents of the federal government under agreements with the Secre-

tary of Labor. Eligibility for benefits and the amount of benefits paid are determined according to the terms and conditions of the applicable state unemployment insurance law. Thus, federal civilian employees and ex-servicemen are subject to the same eligibility, disqualification, and benefit payment provisions as are claimants for benefits under the state unemployment insurance system.

Railroad Workers

These are covered by the federal Railroad Retirement Act which provides retirement and survivor annuities and lump-sum death benefits for aged or disabled employees and their families. Railroad workers are also covered by the Railroad Unemployment Insurance Act, which provides unemployment and sickness benefits as well as a placement service. Both acts are administered by the U.S. Railroad Retirement Board. Those covered by the railroad retirement system also participate in the health insurance program (Medicare) provided by the Social Security Act.

Medicare Program

The Medicare program is a federal health-insurance program for persons 65 and over, disabled people under 65 who have been entitled to social security disability benefits at least 24 months, and insured workers and their dependents who need dialysis treatment or a kidney transplant because of permanent kidney failure.

Enacted under the Social Security Amendments of 1965, Medicare's official name is Title XVIII of the Social Security Act. These amendments also carried Title XIX, providing federal assistance to state medical-aid programs, which has come to be known as Medicaid.

Medicare

It will be helpful to your understanding of the Medicare program if you keep the following points in mind:

• The federal health-insurance program does not of itself offer medical services. It helps pay hospital, doctor, and other medical bills. You choose your own doctor, who prescribes your treatment and place of treatment. But, you should always make sure that health care facilities or persons who provide you with treatment or services are participating in Medicare. Usually, Medicare cannot pay for care from non-participating health care organizations.

• There are two parts of the program:
(1) The hospital insurance part for the payment of most of the cost of covered care provided by participating hospitals, skilled nursing facilities, and home health agencies.
(2) The medical insurance part which helps pay doctors' bills and certain other expenses.

• Another important point to remember: While Medicare pays the major share of the costs of many illnesses requiring hospitalization, it does not offer adequate protection for long-term illness or mental illness.

• Therefore, it may be advisable not to cancel any private health insurance you now carry. You may wish to cancel a policy whose benefits are duplicated by the federal program, and consider a

new policy that will provide for the payment of costs not covered by the federal program. Private insurance companies offer policies supplementing the protection offered by the federal program.

If you want help in deciding whether to buy private supplemental insurance, ask at any social security office for the pamphlet, *Guide to health insurance for people with Medicare.* This free pamphlet describes the various types of supplemental insurance available.

Do You Qualify for Hospital Insurance?

If you're entitled to monthly social security or railroad retirement checks (as a worker, dependent, or survivor), you have hospital insurance protection automatically when you're 65. Disabled people will have hospital insurance automatically after they have been entitled to social security disability benefits for 24 months. (Disabled people who get railroad annuities must meet special requirements.) People 65 or older who are not entitled to monthly benefits need credit for some work under social security to get hospital insurance without paying a monthly premium. If they do not have enough work, they can buy hospital insurance. The premium is $89 a month for the 12-month period starting July 1, 1981.

To be sure your protection will start the month you reach 65, apply for Medicare insurance 3 months before reaching 65, even if you don't plan to retire.

Do You Qualify for Voluntary Medical Insurance?

The voluntary medical insurance plan is a vital supplement to the hospital plan. It helps pay for doctors' and other medical services. Many people have not been able to obtain such insurance from private companies because they could not afford it or because of their medical histories.

Medicaid Services by State
(as of December 1, 1980[1])

Basic required Medicaid services: Every Medicaid program must cover at least these services for at least everyone receiving federally supported financial assistance: inpatient hospital care; outpatient hospital services; other laboratory and X-ray services; skilled nursing facility services and home health services for individuals 21 and older; early and periodic screening, diagnosis, and treatment for individuals under 21; family planning; and physician services. Federal financial participation is also available to states electing to expand their Medicaid programs by covering additional services and/or by including people eligible for medical but not for financial assistance. For the latter group, states may offer the services required for financial assistance recipients or may substitute a combination of seven services. Services provided only under the Medicare buy-in or the screening and treatment program for individuals under 21 are not shown on this chart.

NOTE: O = Offered for people receiving federally supported financial assistance. X = Offered also for people in public assistance[2] and SSI[3] categories who are financially eligible for medical but not for financial assistance. Definitions and limitations on eligibility and services vary from state to state. Details are available from local welfare offices and state Medicaid agencies.

Additional services for which federal financial participation is available to states under Medicaid

States	Basic required Medicaid services	Clinic services	Prescribed drugs	Dental services	Prosthetic devices	Eyeglasses	Private-duty nursing	Physical therapy and/or related services[4]	Other diagnostic, screening, preventive, and rehabilitative services	Emergency hospital services	Skilled nursing facility services for patients under 21	Optometrists' services	Podiatrists' services	Chiropractors' services	Care for patients 65 or older in institutions for mental diseases[5]	Care for patients 65 or older in institutions for tuberculosis[5]	Care for patients under 22 in psychiatric hospitals	Institutional services in intermediate care facilities[6]
Alabama	O	—	O	—	O	O	—	—	—	O	O	O	—	—	O	O	O	O
Alaska	O	O	—	—	—	O	—	O	—	O	O	O	—	—	O	O	O	O
Arizona	—	—	—	—	—	—	—	—	—	O	O	O	—	—	O	—	O	O
Arkansas	X	X	X	X	X	X	—	—	—	X	O	X	O	—	X	O	O	O
California	X	X	X	X	X	X	—	X	X	X	X	X	X	X	X	O	O	X
Colorado	O	O	O	O	—	O	—	—	—	O	O	O	—	O	O	X	X	X
Connecticut	X	X	X	X	X	X	X	X	X	X	X	O	O	—	X	X	X	X
Delaware	O	O	O	—	X	O	—	X	X	X	X	O	O	—	X	—	—	X
D.C.	X	X	X	—	X	X	—	X	X	X	O	O	O	—	X	—	—	X
Florida	O	—	O	O	—	O	—	X	X	X	X	O	O	—	X	X	X	X
Georgia	O	O	—	O	—	O	—	—	—	O	O	O	—	O	O	O	O	O
Guam	X	X	X	X	X	X	—	X	—	X	—	O	—	O	O	O	—	O
Hawaii	X	X	X	X	X	X	—	X	X	X	X	O	O	—	X	X	—	X
Idaho	O	O	O	—	—	O	—	—	O	O	O	X	O	—	X	—	—	O
Illinois	X	X	X	X	X	X	X	X	X	X	X	X	X	—	X	X	X	X
Indiana	O	O	O	O	O	O	O	O	O	O	O	O	O	O	O	O	O	O
Iowa	O	—	O	O	O	O	O	O	O	O	O	O	O	O	O	O	O	O
Kansas	X	X	X	X	X	X	X	X	X	X	X	X	X	X	X	X	X	X
Kentucky	X	X	X	X	X	X	X	X	—	X	X	X	X	—	X	X	X	X
Louisiana	X	X	X	—	X	X	—	X	—	X	O	—	—	X	X	O	O	X
Maine	X	X	X	—	X	—	—	X	X	X	O	—	—	X	X	O	O	X
Maryland	X	X	X	X	X	—	X	X	X	X	X	—	—	—	X	—	X	X
Massachusetts	X	X	X	X	X	X	X	X	X	X	X	—	—	X	—	X	—	X
Michigan	X	X	X	X	X	X	X	X	X	X	X	X	X	—	X	X	—	X
Minnesota	X	X	X	X	X	X	—	X	X	X	X	X	X	X	X	X	X	X
Mississippi	O	—	O	O	—	—	—	—	—	O	—	—	—	O	—	X	X	X
Missouri	O	—	O	O	—	O	—	O	—	O	O	O	—	O	O	O	O	O
Montana	X	X	X	X	X	X	X	X	—	X	X	—	O	—	O	O	O	O
Nebraska	X	X	X	X	X	X	X	X	X	X	X	X	X	X	X	—	X	X
Nevada	O	O	O	—	O	O	O	O	O	O	O	O	O	O	O	O	O	O
New Hampshire	X	X	X	X	X	X	X	X	—	X	X	X	O	O	O	O	O	O
New Jersey	O	O	O	O	O	O	O	O	O	O	O	O	O	O	O	—	O	O
New Mexico	O	O	O	O	O	O	O	O	O	O	O	O	O	O	O	O	—	O
New York	X	X	X	X	X	X	X	—	X	X	X	X	X	—	X	—	—	O
North Carolina	X	X	X	X	X	—	—	X	X	X	—	O	—	—	X	X	X	X
North Dakota	X	X	X	X	X	X	—	X	X	X	X	X	—	—	X	X	X	X
N. Mariana Islands	X	X	X	X	X	X	—	X	—	X	—	O	—	—	O	—	—	X
Ohio	O	O	O	O	O	O	—	O	O	O	O	O	O	—	O	X	X	X
Oklahoma	X	—	X	X	X	—	—	—	—	O	O	O	O	—	O	O	O	O
Oregon	O	O	O	O	O	O	O	O	O	O	O	O	O	—	O	O	O	X
Pennsylvania	X	X	O	O	O	—	—	—	—	X	X	O	O	X	X	—	—	X

States	Basic required Medicaid services	Clinic services	Prescribed drugs	Dental services	Prosthetic devices	Eyeglasses	Private-duty nursing	Physical therapy and/or related services[4]	Other diagnostic, screening, preventive, and rehabilitative services	Emergency hospital services	Skilled nursing facility services for patients under 21	Optometrists' services	Podiatrists' services	Chiropractors' services	Care for patients 65 or older in institutions for mental diseases[3]	Care for patients 65 or older in institutions for tuberculosis[5]	Care for patients under 22 in psychiatric hospitals	Institutional services in intermediate care facilities[6]
Puerto Rico	X	X	X	X	—	—	—	X	X	X	—	—	—	—	X	—	—	O
Rhode Island	X	—	X	X	X	X	—	—	—	—	X	X	X	—	X	—	—	O
South Carolina	0	—	0	—	0	—	—	—	—	0	0	—	0	0	0	0	0	0
South Dakota	0	0	0	0.	0	—	—	0	0	0	0	—	—	0	0	0	—	0
Tennessee	X	X	X	—	—	—	—	—	X	—	—	—	—	—	X	X	X	O
Texas	0	—	0	—	0	0	—	—	0	—	0	0	0	0	—	0	—	O
Utah	X	X	X	—	X	X	X	—	X	—	X	X	X	—	X	—	X	X
Vermont	X	X	X	—	X	X	—	—	X	—	X	X	X	—	X	—	X	X
Virgin Islands	X	X	X	X	X	—	X	—	—	—	—	—	—	—	X	—	—	X
Virginia	X	X	X	—	X	—	X	—	X	—	X	X	X	—	X	X	—	X
Washington	X	X	X	X	X	X	X	X	X	—	X	X	X	X	X	X	O	X
West Virginia	X	X	X	—	X	—	X	—	X	—	X	X	X	X	X	—	X	X
Wisconsin	X	X	X	X	X	X	X	X	X	—	X	X	X	X	X	—	X	X
Wyoming	0	—	—	—	0	—	—	—	0	0	—	—	—	—	0	—	—	O

1. Data from Regional Office reports of characteristics of state programs and state plan amendments. 2. People qualifying as members of families with dependent children (usually families with at least one parent absent or incapacitated). 3. People qualifying as aged, blind, or disabled under the Supplemental Security Income program. 4. Includes therapy in speech, hearing, and language disorder. 5. In some states, services for age 65 and older may include inpatient hospital services, and/or skilled nursing facilities services, and/or intermediate care facilities services. 6. Including intermediate care facilities services in institutions for the mentally retarded. *Source:* Department of Health and Human Services, Health Care Financing Administration.

One difference between the hospital insurance plan and the medical insurance plan is that you do not have to be under the social security or railroad retirement systems to enroll in the medical plan. Anyone who is 65 or older or who is eligible for hospital insurance can enroll in medical insurance.

People who get social security benefits or retirement benefits under the railroad retirement system will be enrolled automatically for medical insurance—unless they say they don't want it—when they become entitled to hospital insurance. Automatic enrollment does not apply to people who plan to continue working past 65, who are disabled widows or widowers between 50 and 65 who aren't getting disability checks, who are 65 but have not worked long enough to be eligible for hospital insurance, who have permanent kidney failure, or who live in Puerto Rico or foreign countries. These people have to apply for medical insurance if they want it. People who have medical insurance pay a monthly premium covering part of the cost of this protection. The other part is paid from general federal revenues. The basic premium for enrollees is $11 a month for the 12-month period starting July 1, 1981.

Is Other Insurance Necessary?

As already indicated, Medicare provides only partial reimbursement. Therefore, you should know how much medical cost you can bear and perhaps arrange for other insurance.

In 1981, for the first 60 days of inpatient hospital care in each benefit period, hospital insurance pays for all covered services except for the first $204. For the 61st through 90th day of a covered inpatient hospital stay, hospital insurance pays for all covered services except for $51 a day. People who need to be in a hospital for more than 90 days in a benefit period can use their 60 inpatient hospital reserve days. Hospital insurance pays for all covered services except for $102 a day for each reserve day used. Hospital insurance also does not pay the full cost of an inpatient stay in a skilled nursing facility.

Under medical insurance, the patient must meet an annual deductible of $60. After the patient has $60 in approved amounts for covered services each year, medical insurance generally pays 80% of the approved amounts for any additional covered services the patient receives during the rest of the year.

How You Obtain Coverage

If you are receiving social security or railroad retirement monthly benefits, you will receive from the government information concerning Medicare about 3 months before you become entitled to hospital insurance.

If you are not receiving benefits or are not covered under social security, contact any social security office to find out how you can get Medicare. People who have permanent kidney failure also should contact a social security office to apply for Medicare.

EDUCATION

Special Education in the 1980s

Prepared by Educational Testing Service*

For the nation's public schools, the impact of Public Law 94–142, the Education for All Handicapped Children Act of 1975, was nearly as profound, if not as dramatic, as the U.S. Supreme Court's decision to outlaw school segregation.

Essentially a civil rights package, the bill, signed into law by President Ford in 1975 and scheduled to apply this year to handicapped children ages 5 to 21, was the culmination of a "quiet revolution" in policy that had begun a decade earlier. Like the historic Brown vs. the Board of Education (of Topeka) decision mandating the inclusion of racial minorities into the educational mainstream, PL 94–142 articulated a fundamental notion: Free education is a right for all, rather than a privilege for some.

Educating the Exceptional

Although Americans have long supported the concept of free public schooling for all, frequently the "all" has not included a portion of the 10–12% of school-age children who are "exceptional." These are the sight, hearing, speech, or orthopedically impaired; the intellectually gifted or limited; the emotionally disturbed; and the learning disabled.

The judgment of how or if to educate this population was traditionally—like much of education policy—left up to individual states. As a result, some children were denied access to schooling entirely, others were placed in institutions where the emphasis was on day-care rather than learning, and still others—frequently minorities—were labeled "educable mentally retarded" on the basis of IQ tests many consider culturally biased.

By the time PL 94–142 became law:

Over 1.75 million American children were being excluded entirely from school solely on the basis of their handicaps.

More than half the estimated eight million handicapped children in the nation were not receiving appropriate educational services they either needed or were entitled to.

Almost three times as many black and culturally different children as white children were being placed in classes for the "educable mentally retarded." Many school districts, according to recent congressional testimony by the Office for Civil Rights, "placed children with English language difficulties or cultural differences in special education programs without properly evaluating their skills."

Since PL 94–142 became law, the share of the nation's school-age handicapped children receiving special education has jumped from less than 50 to nearly 75%. Institutionalized, incarcerated, and rural handicapped children who never received an education are now being served. And the philosophy of special education has shifted from confining

exceptional children to classes of their peers toward "mainstreaming" them into regular classrooms.

Despite these gains, most educators agree there remains a chasm between reality and the dream of full educational opportunity for the exceptional. Part of the gap undoubtedly results from lingering societal attitudes about the handicapped—that they're "weak," "a burden on society," and "incapable of participating in life." Some believe such myths have affected the practice of special education itself. "Special education is one area where what's practiced in the classroom is 10 years behind what's been proven in the laboratory," one research scientist was heard to say.

Closing the Gap

By 1975, special educators were reacting to the successes of behaviorists who demonstrated that, contrary to popular opinion, handicapped people can be taught very complex skills and be stable and dependable employees when adequately prepared for entrance into the job market. PL 94–142 mandated the change in educational practice that was presaged by scientific findings. There was a rush to revise out-of-date curriculums, update archaic means of assessment, and locate children who had not been receiving an education because of their handicaps.

One result has been an increasing awareness of rights among parents of exceptional learners. Rather than being content with a limited education for their children, parents are filing suits aimed at forcing school districts to acknowledge that the rights of handicapped children are as inalienable as those of any American.

The Institute for the Study of Exceptional Children

Considerable basic research into the early detection, assessment, and treatment of young handicapped children, as well as the development of educational programs for both the handicapped and the gifted, is being conducted by the Institute for the Study of Exceptional Children (ISEC). The institute is an interdisciplinary, collaborative effort of two research-service organizations: the Infant Laboratory of Educational Testing Service (ETS) and the pediatrics department of St. Luke-Roosevelt Hospital Center in New York City.

Under the direction of Michael Lewis, the institute's researchers are conducting a three-year longitudinal study comparing premature infants with their normal peers. Data gathered by contrasting the developmental competencies of sick-term, healthy-term, sick-premature, and healthy-premature infants are being examined in hope of finding new means for the early detection of handicaps in "at risk" infants, those most likely to develop handicaps later in life.

*This article was excerpted from FOCUS: New Vistas in Special Education, copyright © 1980, Educational Testing Service. All rights reserved. Reprinted by permission.

Some believe that early conditions such as anoxia, prenatal and birth trauma, low birth weight, and drug addiction translate later into cognitive defects. Others say that, because the central nervous system readily adapts to early trauma, these complications may—if the infants' environment is supportive—barely affect later behavior. ISEC researchers take the latter view and operate from the theoretical assumption that the identified developmental dysfunction is a result of the interaction between the infant's early trauma and his or her environment.

In exploring this interaction, the researchers assess the four different domains of development: the physical, socioemotional, perceptual-cognitive, and communicative-linguistic. As these affect one another in complex ways, the aim is to pinpoint the nature of these relationships and pursue their implications for the course of development.

The Interactive Nature of Development

ISEC's belief that the social environment is a crucial component of development is rooted in the history of the psychological research on exceptional children.

To understand physical and cognitive growth, one must know how these are affected by the social environment, ISEC scientists believe. Toward this end, they have developed ways to assess the total environment in which the exceptional infant lives.

This philosophy has been incorporated into the Infant Assessment Battery (IAB), an array of assessment tools for exceptional learners developed in 1977 by Infant Lab researchers Lewis and Jeanne Brooks-Gunn. More than 100 children, ages one to four and with different handicaps, have been given the IAB, and a broad base of information on their skills has been compiled.

One social index the battery assesses is the infant's relationship with his or her mother, through which the child learns cognitive as well as emotional skills. There appear to be several basic differences between the ways mothers interact with handicapped infants and normal ones. For example, at one year, normal children are more likely to cry than handicapped children when their mothers leave the room; mothers of handicapped children are more likely to use non-verbal cues, such as touching, holding, and gesturing, than mothers of normal children.

By giving parents feedback on how they relate to their handicapped infants, ISEC researchers hope to influence them to change inappropriate home interactive styles. The results of the battery, the Infant Assessment Profile, will also give educators a picture of each child's strengths and weaknesses and is useful in curriculum design and child evaluation.

The IQ Test Controversy

An underlying assumption uniting the work of ISEC scientists with others involved in the development of new, holistic means of assessing exceptionality is the notion that no single test can serve as a decisive indicator of a child's subsequent performance. This concern—addressed in PL 94–142—is relatively recent as regards the second largest class of exceptionality—the mentally retarded.

For years, the judgment of who was "intellectually inadequate" was made by educators and psychologists who, in many cases, had only one guide—performance on an IQ test. Originally designed as an objective means of determining which children needed special class placement because of limited ability, IQ scores too often have been the sole determinants of children's academic fates. In recent years, this use of IQ scores has come under increasing attack.

But the sharpest attacks on intelligence testing have stemmed from their alleged cultural and linguistic bias—a bias many believe responsible for the assignment of disproportionate numbers of minority children to special education classes.

IQ testing also affects the group of learners who are exceptional in the most positive sense—the gifted. Just as the misuse of IQ tests has apparently led to the overinclusion of minorities in special education classes, it may have also tended to exclude them from classes for the gifted. The sole use of IQ tests to determine high aptitude places some culturally different children in a "Catch-22" situation: To be classified gifted, they often have to excel on tests based on the definitions of giftedness of the mainstream culture, standards that are difficult for culturally different learners to achieve because they are not of that culture.

Somewhat typical is the case of the Flint, Michigan, Community Schools. In 1977, 62% of the students in the Flint system were black, but blacks made up only 26% of those classified as "gifted." Flint administrators asked ETS to design a test for determining giftedness which would be as free of cultural biases as possible. The aim was to eliminate reliance on academic records and traditional IQ tests for determining giftedness, to broaden the definitions of giftedness, and, reflecting that broadening, to identify the gifted by new means.

ETS' Midwestern Regional Office (worked) with Flint school administrators, teachers, psychologists, and students' parents, to determine what kinds of giftedness to measure. They decided on creativity, intellectual potential, learning ability, motivation, leadership and social self-awareness, and exceptional academic achievement.

Standards of admissibility were then determined. Flint Community Schools' representatives determined that students had to fall into one of three categories: They had to have scored two years above grade level on the reading or math portions of the SRA Achievement tests, they had to be nominated in one of the six areas of giftedness by a faculty member, or they had to place at or above the 90th percentile in their school and grade on a questionnaire of behavioral indicators answered by their parents.

Once a pupil was designated eligible, a detailed behavioral checklist of his or her capacities was completed by the classroom teacher. The instructors forwarded their lists, prepared in a way to guarantee candidates' anonymity, to a final selection committee comprised of community representatives.

Panel members rated students and ratings were combined to form composite scores. If the panel decided it had insufficient information, it could refer a candidate for further testing. Administrators then were able to decide which of the highest-ranking pupils would be included in the giftedness program.

Initially implemented on a pilot basis in five schools, the basic concept behind the Flint "culturally fair" method of identifying gifted children was expanded in 1979 to include all the system's schools. By that time, minority participation was up to 44%—much more in line with the school system's racial composition. Initial comparisons showed statistically insignificant differences between performances of children selected by the old and new procedures. Students chosen by the old process, however, tended to have slightly higher reading scores—a result which might have been expected.

The Long Road Ahead

Funded by the Bureau of Education for the Handicapped (BEH) and coordinated by the ETS Berkeley Office, the first National Needs Assessment of Educational Media and Materials for the Handicapped illustrated several of the problems still confronting special education. And there are other issues that are equally as serious:

A recent report by the U.S. Department of Health, Education, and Welfare (HEW) found that three out of four teachers, administrators, parents, and students said that there are unserved handicapped children in the schools.

The head of the BEH recently informed Congress that approximately 14,000 handicapped in New York City alone are awaiting evaluation or placement. Some had been waiting for as long as two years.

A recent study by the Office of Civil Rights (OCR) reported that at least 6,000 children in residential institutions throughout the country were receiving no education of any kind.

According to a recent BEH report, national level private school officials, particularly the U.S. Catholic Conference, are saying that public schools in many districts are not providing needed services to private school students.

Perhaps, the "mainstreaming" of the exceptional child into the "normal" world represents the last and most elusive index of a society's commitment to equal rights. We've come a long way since the days when the handicapped were banished from society and the gifted were ignored. But there's a long road ahead.

EDITOR'S NOTE: Copies of the full 20-page report, *FOCUS: New Vistas in Special Education,* are available upon request from the Information Division, ETS, Princeton, N.J. 08541. In ordering, please reference the *Information Please Almanac.*

Purposes of Institutional Accreditation

Institutional accreditation of the postsecondary level is a means used by the accrediting commissions for the purposes of: fostering excellence in postsecondary education through the development of criteria and guidelines for assessing educational effectiveness; encouraging institutional improvement of educational endeavors through continuous self-study and evaluation; assuring the educational community, the general public, and other agencies or organizations that an institution has clearly defined and appropriate objectives, has established conditions under which their achievement can reasonably be expected, appears in fact to be accomplishing them substantially, and is so organized, staffed, and supported that it can be expected to continue to do so; providing counsel and assistance to established and developing institutions; protecting institutions against encroachments which might jeopardize their educational effectiveness or academic freedom.

Accreditation is attained through a process of evaluation and periodic review of total institutions conducted by the commission in accord with policies and procedures approved by the Council on Postsecondary Accreditation.

Federal Grants and Loans for Education, Fiscal Year 1979

Type of support, level, and program area	Amount in millions[1]	Type of support, level, and program area	Amount in millions[1]
Grants, total	$24,392	and traineeships	$925
Elementary-secondary education	7,090[2]	Facilities and equipment	100
School assistance in federally affected areas	619	Other institutional support	577
Economic opportunity programs	4,648[3]	Other student assistance	5,012
Supporting services	364	Vocational-technical and continuing education	7,563
Teacher corps	13	Vocational-technical & work training	7,051
Vocational education	423	Veterans' education	274
Dependents' schools abroad	358	General continuing education	196
Public lands revenue for schools	319	Training state and local personnel	42
Assistance in special areas	67	Loans, total (higher education)	1,226
Emergency school assistance	234	Student loan program, National Defense Education Act	1,246
Higher education	9,739	College facilities loans	−20
Basic research	2,642	**Total grants and loans**	**25,618**
Research facilities	482		
Training grants, fellowships			

1. Estimated outlay for fiscal year 1980. 2. Includes other outlays not shown separately. 3. Includes assistance for educationally deprived. NOTE: The table lists the federal funds that support education in educational institutions. Excluded are certain other federal funds for education and related activities. *Source:* Department of Education, National Center for Educational Statistics.

School Enrollment, October 1980
(in thousands)

Age	White Enrolled	White Percent	Black Enrolled	Black Percent	Spanish origin[1] Enrolled	Spanish origin[1] Percent	All races Enrolled	All races Percent
3 and 4 years	1,844	36.3	371	38.2	172	28.5	2,280	36.7
5 and 6 years	4,781	95.8	904	95.4	491	94.5	5,853	95.7
7 to 9 years	7,973	99.0	1,507	99.4	847	98.4	9,735	99.1
10 to 13 years	11,612	99.4	2,091	99.4	1,162	99.7	14,016	99.4
14 and 15 years	6,038	98.3	1,088	97.9	568	94.3	7,282	98.2
16 and 17 years	5,937	88.6	1,047	90.6	454	81.8	7,129	89.0
18 and 19 years	3,199	46.3	494	45.7	226	37.8	3,788	46.4
20 and 21 years	2,206	31.9	242	23.4	111	19.5	2,515	31.0
22 to 24 years	1,669	16.4	196	13.6	93	11.7	1,931	16.3
25 to 29 years	1,473	9.2	187	8.8	84	6.9	1,714	9.3
30 to 34 years	942	6.3	124	6.8	54	5.1	1,105	6.4
Total	47,673	48.9	8,251	53.9	4,263	49.8	57,348	49.7

1. Persons of Spanish origin may be of any race. NOTE: Figures include persons enrolled in nursery school, kindergarten, elementary school, high school, and college. *Source:* Department of Commerce, Bureau of the Census.

Persons Not Enrolled in School, October 1980
(in thousands)

Age	Population	Total not enrolled Number	Total not enrolled Percent	High school graduate Number	High school graduate Percent	Not high school graduate (dropouts)[1] Number	Not high school graduate (dropouts)[1] Percent
14 and 15 years	7,414	132	1.8	5	0.1	127	1.7
16 and 17 years	8,013	884	11.0	175	2.2	709	8.8
18 and 19 years	8,160	4,372	53.6	3,088	37.8	1,284	15.7
20 and 21 years	8,112	5,597	69.0	4,303	53.0	1,294	15.9
22 to 24 years	11,858	9,927	83.7	8,128	68.5	1,798	15.2

1. Persons who are not enrolled in school and who are not high school graduates are considered dropouts. *Source:* Department of Commerce, Bureau of the Census.

School Enrollment by Grade, Control, and Race
(in thousands)

Grade level and type of control	White Oct. 1980	White Oct. 1979	White Oct. 1970	Black Oct. 1980	Black Oct. 1979	Black Oct. 1970	All races[1] Oct. 1980	All races[1] Oct. 1979	All races[1] Oct. 1970
Nursery school: Public	432	428	198	180	185	129	633	636	333
Private	1,205	1,110	695	115	93	49	1,354	1,233	763
Kindergarten: Public	2,172	2,069	2,233	440	443	374	2,690	2,593	2,674
Private	423	368	473	50	54	53	486	432	536
Grades 1–8: Public	19,743	20,174	24,923	4,058	4,053	4,668	24,398	24,756	30,001
Private	2,768	2,785	3,715	202	243	200	3,051	3,109	3,949
Grades 9–12: Public	12,056[2]	11,549	11,599	2,200[2]	2,171	1,794	14,556[2]	13,994	13,545
Private	—	1,033	1,124	—	74	41	—	1,122	1,170
College: Public	8,875[2]	6,672	5,168	1,007[2]	814	422	10,180[2]	7,699	5,699
Private	—	2,037	1,591	—	188	100	—	2,280	1,714
Total: Public	—	40,892	44,121	—	7,666	7,387	—	49,679	52,225
Private	—	7,333	7,598	—	651	443	—	8,176	8,132
Grand total	47,673	48,225	51,719	8,251	8,317	7,830	57,348	57,854	60,357

1. Includes persons of Spanish origin. 2. Total public and private. Breakdown not available. *Source:* Department of Commerce, Bureau of the Census.

Foreign Study

Young people who want to study in Western Europe will find useful information in a guidebook published by the European Common Market. It lists school fees, entrance requirements, etc., mainly for Common Market countries. *The Handbook for Students* costs $6.15 and it can be obtained from the European Community Information Service, 2100 M Street, N.W., Suite 707, Washington, D.C. 20037.

State Compulsory School Attendance Laws

State	Enactment[1]	Age limits	State	Enactment[1]	Age limits
Alabama	1915	7–16	Montana	1883	7–16
Alaska	1929	7–16	Nebraska	1887	7–16
Arizona	1899	8–16	Nevada	1873	7–17
Arkansas	1909	7–15	New Hampshire	1871	6–16
California	1874	6–16	New Jersey	1875	6–16
Colorado	1889	7–16	New Mexico	1891	6–17
Connecticut	1872	7–16	New York	1874	6–16
Delaware	1907	6–16	North Carolina	1907	7–16
D. C.	1864	7–16	North Dakota	1883	7–16
Florida	1915	7–16	Ohio	1877	6–18
Georgia	1916	7–16	Oklahoma	1907	8–16
Hawaii	1896	6–18	Oregon	1889	7–18
Idaho	1887	7–16	Pennsylvania	1895	8–17
Illinois	1883	7–16	Rhode Island	1883	7–16
Indiana	1897	7–16	South Carolina	1915	7–16
Iowa	1902	7–16	South Dakota	1883	7–16
Kansas	1874	7–16	Tennessee	1905	7–16
Kentucky	1896	7–16	Texas	1915[2]	7–17
Louisiana	1910	7–15	Utah	1890	6–18
Maine	1875	7–15	Vermont	1867	7–16
Maryland	1902	6–16	Virginia	1908	6–17
Massachusetts	1852	6–16	Washington	1871	8–15
Michigan	1871	6–16	West Virginia	1897	7–16
Minnesota	1885	7–16	Wisconsin	1879	6–16
Mississippi	1918	7–13	Wyoming	1876	7–16
Missouri	1905	7–16			

1. Date of enactment of first compulsory attendance law. 2. A compulsory school attendance law was contained in a law of 1873 establishing free public schools. However, the provision was omitted in superseding legislation passed in 1876. *Source:* Department of Education, National Center for Educational Statistics.

High School and College Graduates

Year of graduation	High School			College[1]		
	Men	Women	Total	Men	Women	Total
1900	38,075	56,808	94,883	22,173	5,237	27,410
1910	63,676	92,753	156,429	28,762	8,437	37,199
1920	123,684	187,582	311,266	31,980	16,642	48,622
1929–30	300,376	366,528	666,904	73,615	48,869	122,484
1939–40	578,718	642,757	1,221,475	109,546	76,954	186,500
1949–50	570,700	629,000	1,199,700	328,841	103,217	432,058
1957–58	727,500	780,400	1,505,900	241,560	121,942	363,502
1959–60	898,000	966,000	1,864,000	254,063	138,377	392,440
1960–61	958,000	1,013,000	1,971,000	254,215	144,495	398,710
1961–62	941,000	984,000	1,925,000	260,531	157,315	417,846
1962–63	959,000	991,000	1,950,000	273,169	174,453	447,622
1963–64	1,121,000	1,169,000	2,290,000	296,676	197,477	494,153
1964–65	1,314,000	1,351,000	2,665,000	316,286	213,717	530,003
1965–66	1,308,000	1,324,000	2,632,000	328,853	222,194	551,047
1966–67	1,332,000	1,348,000	2,679,000	353,349	237,198	590,547
1967–68	1,341,000	1,361,000	2,702,000	390,507	276,203	666,710
1968–69	1,402,000	1,427,000	2,829,000	444,380	319,805	764,185
1969–70	1,433,000	1,463,000	2,896,000	484,174	343,060	827,234
1970–71	1,456,000	1,487,000	2,943,000	511,138	366,538	877,676
1971–72	1,490,000	1,516,000	3,006,000	541,313	389,371	930,684
1972–73	1,501,000	1,536,000	3,037,000	564,680	407,700	972,380
1973–74	1,515,000	1,565,000	3,080,000	575,843	423,749	999,592
1974–75	1,541,000	1,599,000	3,140,000	533,797	425,052	978,849
1975–76	1,554,000	1,600,000	3,154,000	557,817	430,578	988,395
1976–77	1,548,000	1,606,000	3,154,000	547,919	435,989	983,908
1977–78	1,540,000	1,607,000	3,147,000	487,000	434,000	921,000

1. Includes bachelor's and first-professional degrees through 1960; thereafter bachelor's degree only. NOTE: Includes graduates from public and private schools. Beginning in 1959–60, figures include Alaska and Hawaii. Because of rounding, details may not add to totals. Most recent data available. *Source:* Department of Education, National Center for Education Statistics.

Enrollment in Educational Institutions
(in thousands)

Type of School	1970	1972	1973	1974	1975	1976	1977	1978	1979
Kindergarten[1]									
Public	2,601	2,483	2,502	2,639	2,784	2,945	2,919	2,766	2,642
Nonpublic	200[3]	180[3]	190[3]	180[3]	200[3]	200[3]	200[3]	200[3]	200[3]
Total kindergarten	2,821	2,683	2,710	2,838	3,002	3,164	3,138	2,985	2,861
Grades 1–8[2]									
Public	29,996	29,782	29,342	28,694	28,137	27,542	27,087	26,450	25,813
Nonpublic	4,000[3]	3,720[3]	3,510[3]	3,420[3]	3,700[3]	3,400[3]	3,400[3]	3,400[3]	3,400[3]
Residential schools for exceptional children[4]	87[3]	87[3]	} 182[2 3]	} 85[3]	85[3]	83[3]	83[3]	81[3]	79[3]
Federal schools:									
For Indians	34	34		33	31	29	29	29[3]	28
On Federal installations	33[3]	33[3]		25[3]	25	23	24	24[3]	23
Total grades 1–8	34,190	33,697	33,034	32,297	32,019	31,118	30,664	30,182	29,381
Grades 9–12[2]									
Public high schools	13,022	13,816	13,909	14,076	14,132	14,304	14,310	14,233	14,156
Nonpublic high schools	1,300[3]	1,300[3]	1,300[3]	1,250[3]	1,400[3]	1,400[3]	1,400[3]	1,400[3]	1,400[3]
Residential schools for exceptional children[4]	37[3]	39[3]	} 100[2 3]	} 41[3]	41[3]	41[3]	41[3]	41[3]	41[3]
Federal schools:									
For Indians	12	12[3]		11	11	11	11	10[3]	10
On Federal installations	3[3]	3[3]		4	4	3	3	3[3]	3
Total grades 9–12	14,418	15,214	15,309	15,427	15,633	15,804	15,810	15,766	15,654
Higher education[5]									
Publicly controlled	5,112	5,745	6,159	6,389	6,838	7,426	7,275[3]	7,415[3]	7,363[3]
Privately controlled	2,024	2,055	2,106	2,130	2,185	2,306	2,314[3]	2,392[3]	2,427[3]
Total higher education	7,136	7,800	8,265	8,518	9,023	9,731	9,589[3]	9,807[3]	9,790[3]
Total all levels	**58,566**	**59,394**	**59,318**	**59,080**	**59,677**	**59,817**	**59,201**	**58,740**	**57,686**

1. Includes subcollegiate departments of institutions of higher education, residential schools for exceptional children, and Federal schools, not shown separately. 2. Includes subcollegiate departments of institutions of higher education, not shown separately. 3. Estimated. 4. Schools for blind, deaf, mentally deficient, epileptic, and delinquent. 5. Excludes subcollegiate departments of institutions of higher education. Degree-credit enrollment only. *Source:* Department of Education, National Center for Education Statistics.

Major U.S. College and University Libraries
(over 1.75 million volumes)

Institution	Volumes	Microforms[1]	Institution	Volumes	Microforms[1]
Harvard	10,082,663	2,101,575	U of Arizona	2,540,839	1,750,874
Yale	7,401,953	1,294,923	U of Virginia	2,431,322	2,487,650
U of Illinois	5,936,823	1,552,446	Johns Hopkins	2,321,935	1,089,875
U of California, Berkeley	5,753,731	1,569,956	U of Iowa	2,295,266	1,502,000
U of Michigan	5,234,380	1,786,069	U of Pittsburgh	2,246,371	1,235,358
Columbia	5,016,460	2,135,332	Rutgers	2,216,843	1,512,086
Stanford	4,694,769	2,678,740	U of Florida	2,162,982	1,657,092
U of Texas	4,547,508	2,211,079	Pennsylvania State	2,149,603	2,198,360
U of Chicago	4,310,824	743,893	U of Kansas	2,148,451	979,944
U of California, Los Angeles	4,234,835	1,806,105	U of Southern California	2,035,570	1,246,952
Cornell	4,216,915	2,239,135	U of Missouri	2,016,647	2,209,010
U of Washington	3,877,238	3,019,186	U of Utah	1,990,000	1,386,143
U of Minnesota	3,807,570	1,229,743	U of Georgia	1,985,646	1,859,981
Indiana	3,759,203	980,060	SUNY, Buffalo	1,936,437	1,876,285
U of Wisconsin	3,631,669	1,829,367	Syracuse	1,888,312	1,849,080
Ohio State	3,529,985	1,602,962	U of Colorado	1,852,904	1,983,890
Princeton	3,260,396	1,396,298	Wayne State	1,839,429	905,543
Duke	3,085,654	739,291	Louisiana State	1,822,626	1,073,997
U of Pennsylvania	2,938,890	1,230,767	U of South Carolina	1,819,230	1,699,611
New York	2,869,122	1,456,577	U of Oklahoma	1,808,276	1,303,431
Northwestern	2,806,320	944,804	Washington, St. Louis	1,798,711	952,974
Michigan State	2,613,447	1,117,363	Massachusetts Inst. of Tech.	1,797,623	947,593
North Carolina	2,604,404	1,447,865	U of Kentucky	1,792,048	2,010,756

1. Includes reels of microfilm and number of microcards, microprint sheets, and microfiches. *Source:* Association of Research Libraries.

College and University Endowments, 1979-80

(in millions)

Institution	Endowment (market value)	Voluntary support[1]	Expenditures[2]	Institution	Endowment (market value)	Voluntary support[1]	Expenditures[2]
Harvard U	$1,491.0	$ 76.2	$ n.a.	Trinity U	$ 108.9	$ 6.8	$ 18.5
Yale U	676.4	59.6	244.8	U of Minnesota	106.2	40.6	437.9
Stanford U	642.6	60.1	318.4	U of Pittsburgh	104.2	10.7	203.1
Massachusetts Inst. of Tech.	550.9	38.1	268.3	Southern Methodist U	103.0	20.8	50.1
Princeton U	547.8	32.7	98.1	Princeton Theol. Sem.	97.1	16.5	6.0
Columbia U	533.0	38.1	302.1	Williams C	96.8	7.2	17.3
U of California	417.5	75.0	2,221.1	Rensselaer Poly. Inst.	93.6	5.7	53.3
U of Rochester	376.4	13.6	127.7	Swarthmore C	91.6	5.3	12.1
U of Chicago	343.0	33.7	291.1	Berea C	86.5	4.8	9.0
Rice U	342.0	11.2	39.9	Vassar C	86.4	3.3	18.1
Northwestern U	329.9	31.0	184.6	Loyola U of Chicago	81.9	14.4	65.8
Cornell U	328.7	46.3	299.7	Amherst C	81.9	4.1	17.0
New York U	280.8	27.6	389.7	Ohio State U	76.3	13.1	328.4
Emory U	266.5	115.6	91.9	Baylor U	71.8	16.8	33.8
Washington U (St. Louis)	245.6	22.4	171.7	U of Washington	70.3	25.0	329.5
Johns Hopkins U	236.5	29.0	205.4	Brandeis U	67.0	15.1	46.3
Rockefeller U	228.6	17.2	39.9	U of Wisconsin (Madison)	66.8	31.1	352.9
U of Pennsylvania	224.5	49.1	395.2	Wake Forest U	65.5	8.6	68.7
Dartmouth C	215.5	31.6	84.9	Texas Christian U	63.1	10.6	29.8
California Inst. of Tech.	193.4	15.5	76.3	Middlebury C	62.0	3.3	13.7
U of Notre Dame	172.2	22.0	63.4	Lehigh U	61.9	10.0	44.3
U of Virginia	160.2	9.1	n.a.	Loyola U	60.0	1.2	16.5
U of So. California	154.3	42.2	252.0	Rochester Inst. of Tech.	59.5	3.5	66.7
Duke U	142.0	27.0	145.0	Pomona C	58.9	7.1	9.7
Wellesley College	139.9	8.1	22.6	U of Texas (Austin)	57.6	23.1	235.8
Case Western Reserve U	130.8	29.2	103.7	Georgetown U	56.6	9.8	101.4
U of Michigan	129.1	33.9	400.1	Tulane U	56.5	12.2	86.3
Brown U	123.4	13.6	69.0	Wabash C	54.8	2.8	8.5
U of Kansas	120.7	8.4	213.1	Carleton C	54.0	2.3	12.9
Carnegie-Mellon U	119.2	14.2	63.2	Syracuse U	52.3	9.0	109.4
Wesleyan U	117.6	2.4	25.8	St. Louis U	51.7	6.0	66.1
U of Delaware	113.1	7.4	92.4	Texas A&M U	50.8	26.8	231.1
Smith C	111.2	15.5	27.6	State U of N.Y. (Buffalo)	50.0	1.4	130.5

1. Gifts from business, alumni, religious denominations, and others. 2. Figure represents about 80% of typical operating budget. Does not include auxiliary enterprises and capital outlays. NOTE: C = College; U = University; n.a. = not available. *Source:* Council for Financial Aid to Education.

Degrees Conferred by Institutions of Higher Education, 1978

Field of study	Bachelor's[1]	Master's	Doctorate	Field of study	Bachelor's[1]	Master's	Doctorate
Agriculture and natural resources	22.7	4,023	971	Library sciences	.7	6,914	67
Architecture and environmental design	9.3	3,115	73	Mathematics	12.6	3,373	805
Area studies	2.9	925	145	Military sciences	.4	45	—
Biological sciences	51.5	6,806	3,309	Physical sciences	23.0	5,561	3,133
Business and management	161.3	48,484	867	Psychology	44.6	8,160	2,587
Communications	25.4	3,296	191	Public affairs and services	37.2	19,953	395
Computer and information sciences	7.2	3,038	196	Social sciences	113.2	14,634	3,583
Education	136.1	118,582	7,586	Theology	6.3	3,329	1,160
Engineering	55.7	16,398	2,440	Interdisciplinary studies	35.6	4,487	301
Fine and applied arts	41.0	9,036	708	Total	921.2	311,620	32,131
Foreign languages	12.7	2,726	649	First-professional degrees:			
Health professions	59.4	14,325	654	Dentistry (D.D.S. or D.M.D.)	5,189	—	—
Home economics	17.6	2,613	203	Law (LL.B. or J.D.)	34,402	—	—
Law	.7	1,786	39	Medicine (M.D.)	14,279	—	—
Letters	44.3	10,011	2,069	Theological professions (B.D., M. Div., Rabbi)	6,367	—	—
				Total first-professional	60,237	—	—

1. In thousands (except for first-professional degrees); total may not add because of rounding. *Source:* Department of Education, National Center for Educational Statistics.

Community, Junior, and Technical Colleges

An asterisk indicates tuition and required fees of $600 or less for the full academic year 1979–80; where applicable, the costs are for students living within the state and within the institutional district.

ALABAMA

Publicly controlled

Alabama Aviation and Tech. College*	Ozark
Alabama Technical College*	East Gadsden
Alexander City State Junior College*	Alexander City
Atmore State Technical Institute*	Atmore
Bessemer State Technical College*	Bessemer
Brewer State Junior College*	Fayette
Carver State Tech. College*	Mobile
Chattahoochee Valley State Comm. Coll.*	Phenix City
Community College of the Air Force	Maxwell AFB
Douglas MacArthur St. Tech. Coll.*	Opp
Enterprise State Junior College*	Enterprise
Gadsden State Junior College*	East Gadsden
Gadsden State Technical Institute*	Gadsden
George C. Wallace State Comm. Coll.*	Dothan
George C. Wallace State Comm. College*	Hanceville
George Corley Wallace St. Comm. Coll.*	Selma
Harry M. Ayers State Tech. College*	Anniston
Hobson State Technical College*	Thomasville
J. F. Drake State Technical College*	Huntsville
James H. Faulkner State Junior College*	Bay Minette
Jefferson Davis State Junior College*	Brewton
Jefferson State Junior College*	Birmingham
John C. Calhoun State Comm. College*	Decatur
John M. Patterson State Tech. College*	Montgomery
Lawson State Community College*	Birmingham
Lurleen B. Wallace State Junior College*	Andalusia
Muscle Shoals State Tech. College*	Muscle Shoals
N.F. Nunneley St. Tech. College*	Childersburg
Northeast Alabama State Junior College*	Rainsville
Northwest Alabama State Junior College*	Phil Campbell
Northwest Alabama State Tech. College*	Hamilton
Patrick Henry State Junior College*	Monroeville
Reid State Technical College*	Evergreen
S. D. Bishop State Junior College*	Mobile
Shelton State Technical College*	Tuscaloosa
Snead State Junior College*	Boaz
Southern Union State Junior College*	Wadley
Southwest State Technical College*	Mobile
Trenholm State Technical College*	Montgomery
Walker State Technical College*	Sumiton

Privately controlled

Alabama Christian College	Montgomery
Alabama Lutheran College—Academy	Selma
Marion Military Institute	Marion
Selma University	Selma
Walker College	Jasper

ALASKA

Publicly controlled

Univ. of Alaska Community Colleges	Fairbanks
Anchorage Community College*	Anchorage
Chukchi Community College*	Kotzebue
Juneau-Douglas Community College*	Juneau
Kenai Peninsula Community College*	Soldotna
Ketchikan Community College*	Ketchikan
Kodiak Community College*	Kodiak
Kuskokwim Community College*	Bethel
Matanuska Susitna Community College*	Palmer
Northwest Community College*	Nome
Prince William Sound Comm. Coll.*	Valdez
Sitka Community College*	Sitka
Tanana Valley Community College*	Fairbanks

Privately controlled

Sheldon Jackson College	Sitka

ARIZONA

Publicly controlled

Arizona Western College	Yuma
Central Arizona Coll. District*	Coolidge
Aravaipa Campus*	Winkleman
Signal Peak Campus*	Coolidge
Cochise College*	Douglas
Eastern Arizona College*	Thatcher
Maricopa County Comm. Coll. District	Phoenix
Glendale Community College*	Glendale
Maricopa Technical Community Coll.*	Phoenix
Mesa Community College*	Mesa
Phoenix College*	Phoenix
Rio Salado Community College*	Phoenix
Scottsdale Community College*	Scottsdale
South Mountain Comm. College*	Phoenix
Mohave Community College*	Kingman
Navajo Community College	Tsaile
Northland Pioneer College*	Holbrook
Pima Community College*	Tucson
Community Campus	Tucson
Downtown Campus	Tucson
East Campus	Tucson
West Campus	Tucson
Yavapai College	Prescott

Privately controlled

Ganado, College of	Ganado

ARKANSAS

Publicly controlled

Arkansas State Univ.—Beebe Branch*	Beebe
East Arkansas Community College*	Forrest City
Garland County Community College*	Hot Springs
Mississippi County Community College*	Blytheville
North Arkansas Community College*	Harrison
Phillips County Community College*	Helena
Southern Arkansas University	Magnolia
El Dorado Branch*	El Dorado
Technical Branch*	East Camden
Westark Community College*	Fort Smith

Privately controlled

Crowley's Ridge College	Paragould
Shorter College	North Little Rock
Southern Baptist College	Walnut Ridge

CALIFORNIA

Publicly controlled

Allan Hancock College*	Santa Maria
Antelope Valley College*	Lancaster
Barstow Community College	Barstow
Butte College*	Oroville
Cabrillo College*	Aptos
Canyons, College of the*	Valencia
Cerritos College	Norwalk
Chabot College	Hayward
Chaffey College*	Alta Loma
Citrus College*	Azusa
Coast Community College District	Costa Mesa
Coastline Community College	Fountain Valley
Golden West College*	Huntington Beach
Orange Coast College*	Costa Mesa
Compton Community College*	Compton
Contra Costa Community Coll. District	Martinez
Contra Costa College	San Pablo
Diablo Valley College	Pleasant Hill
Los Medanos College*	Pittsburg

Cuesta College*	San Luis Obispo	San Joaquin Delta College*	Stockton
Desert, College of the*	Palm Desert	San Jose Community College District	San Jose
El Camino College	Via Torrance	Evergreen Valley College*	San Jose
Foothill-Deanza Comm. Coll. District	Los Altos Hills	San Jose City College*	San Jose
De Anza College*	Cupertino	San Mateo County Comm. Coll. District	San Mateo
Foothill College*	Los Altos Hills	Canada College*	Redwood City
Gavilan College*	Gilroy	San Mateo, College of*	San Mateo
Glendale Community College	Glendale	Skyline College*	San Bruno
Grossmont Community College District	El Cajon	Santa Ana College*	Santa Ana
Cuyamaca College*	El Cajon	Santa Barbara City College*	Santa Barbara
Grossmont College*	El Cajon	Santa Monica College*	Santa Monica
Hartnell College	Salinas	Santa Rosa Junior College*	Santa Rosa
Imperial Valley College*	Imperial	Shasta College*	Redding
Kern Community College District	Bakersfield	Sequoias, College of the*	Visalia
Bakersfield College	Bakersfield	Sierra College*	Rocklin
Cerro Coso Community College*	Ridgecrest	Siskiyous, College of the*	Weed
Porterville College*	Porterville	Solano Community College*	Suisun City
Lake Tahoe Community College*	South Lake Tahoe	Southwestern College*	Chula Vista
		State Center Community College District	Fresno
Lassen College*	Susanville	Fresno City College*	Fresno
Long Beach City College	Long Beach	Kings River Comm. Coll.*	Reedley
Los Angeles Community College District	Los Angeles	Taft College	Taft
East Los Angeles College	Monterey Park	Ventura County Community Coll. District	Ventura
Los Angeles City College	Los Angeles	Moorpark College*	Moorpark
Los Angeles Harbor College	Wilmington	Oxnard College*	Oxnard
Los Angeles Mission College	San Fernando	Ventura College*	Ventura
Los Angeles Pierce College	Woodland Hills	Victor Valley College*	Victorville
Los Angeles Southwest College	Los Angeles	West Hills Community College*	Coalinga
Los Angeles Trade-Technical College	Los Angeles	West Valley Joint Comm. Coll. District*	Saratoga
Los Angeles Valley College	Van Nuys	Mission College*	Santa Clara
West Los Angeles College	Culver City	West Valley College*	Saratoga
Los Rios Community College District	Sacramento	Yosemite Community College District	Modesto
American River College	Sacramento	Columbia College*	Columbia
Cosumnes River College	Sacramento	Modesto Junior College*	Modesto
Sacramento City College	Sacramento	Yuba College*	Marysville
Marin County Community Coll. District	Kentfield	*Privately controlled*	
Indian Valley Colleges*	Novato	Brooks College	Long Beach
Marin, College of*	Kentfield	Deep Springs College	Via Dyer, Nevada
Mendocino College*	Ukiah		
Merced College*	Merced	Don Bosco Technical Institute	Rosemead
Mira Costa College*	Oceanside	Fashion Inst. of Design/Merch.	Los Angeles
Monterey Peninsula College*	Monterey	Heald Inst. of Technology	Santa Clara
Mt. San Antonio College*	Walnut	Humphreys College	Stockton
Mt. San Jacinto College*	San Jacinto	Marymount Palos Verdes College	Rancho Palos Verdes
Napa College	Napa		
North Orange County Comm. Coll. District	Fullerton	Nairobi College	East Palo Alto
Cypress College*	Cypress	Queen of the Holy Rosary College	Mission San Jose
Fullerton College*	Fullerton		
Ohlone College*	Fremont		
Palo Verde College	Blythe		
Palomar College*	San Marcos	**COLORADO**	
Pasadena City College*	Pasadena	*Publicly controlled*	
Peralta Community College District	Oakland	Aims Community College*	Greeley
Alameda, College of*	Alameda	Arapahoe Community College*	Littleton
Feather River College*	Quincy	Colorado Mountain College	Glenwood Springs
Laney College*	Oakland		
Merritt College*	Oakland	Community Education Unit*	Glenwood Springs
Vista College	Berkeley		
Redwoods, College of the	Eureka	East Campus*	Leadville
Rio Hondo College	Whittier	West Campus*	Glenwood Springs
Riverside City College*	Riverside		
Saddleback College	Mission Viejo	Colorado Northwestern Comm. College*	Rangely
San Bernardino Community Coll. District	San Bernardino	Community College of Denver	Denver
Crafton Hills College*	Yucaipa	Auraria Campus*	Denver
San Bernardino Valley College*	San Bernardino	North Campus*	Westminster
San Diego Community College District	San Diego	Red Rocks Campus*	Golden
San Diego City College*	San Diego	Lamar Community College	Lamar
San Diego Evening College	San Diego	Morgan Community College*	Fort Morgan
San Diego Mesa College*	San Diego	Northeastern Junior College	Sterling
San Diego Miramar College*	San Diego	Otero Junior College	La Junta
San Francisco Community Coll. District	San Francisco	Pikes Peak Community Coll.*	Colorado Springs
San Francisco, City College of	San Francisco	Pueblo Vocational Community College*	Pueblo
Community College Centers	San Francisco	Trinidad State Junior College*	Trinidad

CONNECTICUT

Publicly controlled

Asnuntuck Community College*	Enfield
Greater Hartford Community College*	Hartford
Greater New Haven State Tech. Coll.*	North Haven
Hartford State Technical College*	Hartford
Housatonic Community College*	Bridgeport
Manchester Community College*	Manchester
Mattatuck Community College*	Waterbury
Middlesex Community College*	Middletown
Mohegan Community College*	Norwich
Northwestern Connecticut Comm. College*	Winsted
Norwalk Community College*	Norwalk
Norwalk State Technical College*	Norwalk
Quinebaug Valley Community College*	Danielson
South Central Community College*	New Haven
Thames Valley State Technical College*	Norwich
Tunxis Community College*	Farmington
Waterbury State Technical College*	Waterbury

Privately controlled

Hartford College for Women	Hartford
Mitchell College	New London
Mount Sacred Heart College	Hamden

DELAWARE

Publicly controlled

Delaware Technical and Comm. College	Dover
Southern Campus*	Georgetown
Stanton/Wilmington Campuses*	Wilmington
Terry Campus*	Dover

Privately controlled

Brandywine College	Wilmington

FLORIDA

Publicly controlled

Brevard Community College*	Cocoa
Broward Community College*	Ft. Lauderdale
Central Florida Community College*	Ocala
Chipola Junior College*	Marianna
Daytona Beach Community College*	Daytona Beach
Edison Community College*	Ft. Myers
Florida Junior Coll. at Jacksonville*	Jacksonville
Downtown Campus*	Jacksonville
Fred H. Kent Campus*	Jacksonville
North Campus*	Jacksonville
South Campus*	Jacksonville
Florida Keys Community College*	Key West
Gulf Coast Community College*	Panama City
Hillsborough Community College*	Tampa
Indian River Community College*	Ft. Pierce
Lake City Community College*	Lake City
Lake-Sumter Community College*	Leesburg
Manatee Junior College*	Bradenton
Miami-Dade Community College*	Miami
Medical Center Campus*	Miami
New World Center Campus*	Miami
North Campus*	Miami
South Campus*	Miami
North Florida Junior College*	Madison
Okaloosa-Walton Junior College*	Niceville
Palm Beach Junior College*	Lake Worth
Pasco-Hernando Community College*	Dade City
Pensacola Junior College*	Pensacola
Polk Community College*	Winter Haven
St. Johns River Community College*	Palatka
St. Petersburg Junior College*	St. Petersburg
Santa Fe Community College*	Gainesville
Seminole Community College*	Sanford
South Florida Junior College*	Avon Park
Tallahassee Community College*	Tallahassee
Valencia Community College*	Orlando

Privately controlled

Bauder Fashion College	Miami

Florida College	Temple Terrace
International Fine Arts College	Miami
Webber College	Babson Park

GEORGIA

Publicly controlled

Abraham Baldwin Agriculture College*	Tifton
Albany Junior College*	Albany
Atlanta Junior College*	Atlanta
Bainbridge Junior College*	Bainbridge
Brunswick Junior College*	Brunswick
Clayton Junior College*	Morrow
Dalton Junior College*	Dalton
DeKalb Community College*	Clarkston
Emanuel County Junior College*	Swainsboro
Floyd Junior College*	Rome
Gainesville Junior College*	Gainesville
Gordon Junior College*	Barnesville
Macon Junior College*	Macon
Middle Georgia College*	Cochran
South Georgia College*	Douglas
Waycross Junior College*	Waycross

Privately controlled

Andrew College	Cuthbert
Brewton-Parker College	Mt. Vernon
Emmanuel College	Franklin Springs
Georgia Military College	Milledgeville
Oxford College of Emory University	Oxford
Reinhardt College	Waleska
Truett-McConnell College	Cleveland
Young Harris College	Young Harris

HAWAII

Publicly controlled

Univ. of Hawaii Community Coll. System	Honolulu
Hawaii Community College*	Hilo
Honolulu Community College*	Honolulu
Kapiolani Community College*	Honolulu
Kauai Community College*	Lihue Kauai
Leeward Community College*	Pearl City
Maui Community College*	Kahului
Windward Community College*	Kaneohe

IDAHO

Publicly controlled

North Idaho College*	Coeur d'Alene
Southern Idaho, College of*	Twin Falls

Privately controlled

Ricks College	Rexburg

ILLINOIS

Publicly controlled

Belleville Area College*	Belleville
Black Hawk College	Moline
East Campus	Kewanee
Quad Cities Campus	Moline
Carl Sandburg College*	Galesburg
Chicago, City Colleges of	Chicago
Chicago City-Wide College*	Chicago
Chicago Urban Skills Institute	Chicago
Kennedy-King College*	Chicago
Loop College, The*	Chicago
Malcolm X College*	Chicago
Olive Harvey College*	Chicago
Richard J. Daley College*	Chicago
Truman College*	Chicago
Wilbur Wright College*	Chicago
Danville Area Community College*	Danville
DuPage, College of	Glen Ellyn
Dupage Open College	Glen Ellyn
Main Campus	Glen Ellyn
Elgin Community College*	Elgin

Highland Community College*	Freeport
Illinois Central College*	East Peoria
Illinois Eastern Community Colleges	Olney
Frontier Community College*	Fairfield
Lincoln Trail College*	Robinson
Olney Central College*	Olney
Wabash Valley College*	Mt. Carmel
Illinois Valley Community College*	Oglesby
John A. Logan College*	Carterville
John Wood Community College*	Quincy
Joliet Junior College*	Joliet
Kankakee Community College*	Kankakee
Kaskaskia College*	Centralia
Kishwaukee College*	Malta
Lake County, College of*	Grayslake
Lake Land College*	Mattoon
Lewis and Clark Community College*	Godfrey
Lincoln Land Community College*	Springfield
McHenry County College*	Crystal Lake
Moraine Valley Community College*	Palos Hills
Morton College*	Cicero
Oakton Community College*	Des Plaines
Parkland College*	Champaign
Prairie State College*	Chicago Heights
Rend Lake College*	Ina
Richland Community College*	Decatur
Rock Valley College*	Rockford
Sauk Valley College	Dixon
Shawnee Community College*	Ullin
Southeastern Illinois College*	Harrisburg
Spoon River College*	Canton
State Comm. College of East St. Louis*	East St. Louis
Thornton Community College	South Holland
Triton College*	River Grove
Waubonsee Community College*	Sugar Grove
William Rainey Harper College*	Palatine

Privately controlled

Central YMCA Community College	Chicago
Felician College	Chicago
Lincoln College	Lincoln
MacCormac College	Chicago
Mallinckrodt College	Wilmette
Springfield College in Illinois	Springfield

INDIANA

Publicly controlled

Indiana Vocational Technical College	Indianapolis
Central Indiana Region	Indianapolis
Columbus Technical Inst.	Columbus
East Central Tech. Inst.	Muncie
Kokomo Technical Inst.	Kokomo
Lafayette Technical Inst.	Lafayette
North Central Tech. Inst.	South Bend
Northeast Technical Inst.	Fort Wayne
Northwest Region	Gary
South Central Tech. Inst.	Sellersburg
Southeast Region	Madison
Southwest Technical Inst.	Evansville
Wabash Valley Region	Terre Haute
Whitewater Technical Inst.	Richmond
Vincennes University	Vincennes

Privately controlled

Ancilla College	Donaldson
Holy Cross Junior College	Notre Dame

IOWA

Publicly controlled

Des Moines Area Community College*	Ankeny
Ankeny Campus	Ankeny
Boone Campus	Boone
Eastern Iowa Community Coll. District	Davenport
Clinton Community College	Clinton
Muscatine Community College	Muscatine
Scott Community College*	Bettendorf
Hawkeye Institute of Technology*	Waterloo
Indian Hills Community College*	Ottumwa
Centerville Campus	Centerville
Ottumwa Airport Campus	Ottumwa
Ottumwa Heights Campus	Ottumwa
Iowa Central Community College*	Fort Dodge
Iowa Lakes Community College*	Estherville
Iowa Valley Community Coll. District	Marshalltown
Ellsworth Community College	Iowa Falls
Marshalltown Community College*	Marshalltown
Iowa Western Community College	Council Bluffs
Kirkwood Community College*	Cedar Rapids
North Iowa Area Community College*	Mason City
Northeast Iowa Technical Institute*	Calmar
Northwest Iowa Technical College	Sheldon
Southeastern Community College*	West Burlington
North Campus	West Burlington
South Campus	Keokuk
Southwestern Community College*	Creston
Western Iowa Tech. Community College	Sioux City

Privately controlled

Sioux Empire College	Hawarden
Waldorf College	Forest City

KANSAS

Publicly controlled

Allen County Community College*	Iola
Barton County Community Junior Coll.*	Great Bend
Butler County Community College*	El Dorado
Cloud County Community College*	Concordia
Coffeyville Community College*	Coffeyville
Colby Community Junior College*	Colby
Cowley County Community Junior Coll.*	Arkansas City
Dodge City Community Junior College*	Dodge City
Fort Scott Community College*	Fort Scott
Garden City Community Junior College*	Garden City
Haskell Indian Junior College	Lawrence
Highland Community Junior College*	Highland
Hutchinson Community College*	Hutchinson
Independence Community College*	Independence
Johnson County Community Junior Coll.*	Overland Park
Kansas City, Kan., Community Coll.*	Kansas City
Kansas Technical Institute*	Salina
Labette Community College*	Parsons
Neosho County Community College*	Chanute
Pratt Community Junior College*	Pratt
Seward County Community Junior Coll.*	Liberal

Privately controlled

Brown Mackie College, The	Salina
Central College	McPherson
Donnelly College	Kansas City
Hesston College	Hesston
St. John's College	Winfield

KENTUCKY

Publicly controlled

Eastern Kentucky Univ.—Office of Community College Programs*	Richmond
Kentucky, Univ. of, Comm. Coll. System	Lexington
Ashland Community College*	Ashland
Elizabethtown Community College*	Elizabethtown
Hazard Community College*	Hazard
Henderson Community College*	Henderson
Hopkinsville Community College*	Hopkinsville
Jefferson Community College*	Louisville
Lexington Technical Institute	Lexington
Madisonville Community College*	Madisonville
Maysville Community College*	Maysville
Paducah Community College*	Paducah

Prestonsburg Community College*	Prestonsburg
Somerset Community College	Somerset
Southeast Community College*	Cumberland
Privately controlled	
Alice Lloyd College	Pippa Passes
Lees Junior College	Jackson
Lindsey Wilson College	Columbia
Midway College	Midway
St. Catharine College	St. Catharine
Sue Bennett College	London

LOUISIANA

Publicly controlled

Bossier Parish Community College*	Bossier City
Delgado Community College*	New Orleans
Louisiana State University	Baton Rouge
Alexandria Campus*	Alexandria
Eunice Campus*	Eunice
Southern University at Shreveport*	Shreveport

MAINE

Publicly controlled

Central Maine Vocational Tech. Inst.*	Auburn
Eastern Maine Vocational Tech. Inst.	Bangor
Kennebec Valley Vocational Tech. Inst.	Waterville
Maine, University of	Bangor
Augusta Branch	Augusta
Bangor Community College	Bangor
Northern Maine Vocational Tech. Inst.*	Presque Isle
Southern Maine Vocational Tech. Inst.*	South Portland
Washington County Voc. Tech. Inst.*	Calais

MARYLAND

Publicly controlled

Allegany Community College*	Cumberland
Anne Arundel Community College*	Arnold
Catonsville Community College*	Baltimore
Cecil Community College*	North East
Charles County Community College*	La Plata
Chesapeake College*	Wye Mills
Community College of Baltimore*	Baltimore
Dundalk Community College*	Dundalk
Essex Community College*	Baltimore Co.
Frederick Community College*	Frederick
Garrett Community College*	McHenry
Hagerstown Junior College	Hagerstown
Harford Community College*	Bel Air
Howard Community College*	Columbia
Montgomery College	Rockville
Germantown Campus	Germantown
Rockville Campus	Rockville
Takoma Park Campus	Takoma Park
Prince George's Community College*	Largo
Wor-Wic Tech. Community College*	Salisbury
Privately controlled	
Villa Julie College	Stevenson

MASSACHUSETTS

Publicly controlled

Berkshire Community College*	Pittsfield
Blue Hills Regional Tech. Institute*	Canton
Bristol Community College*	Fall River
Bunker Hill Community College*	Boston
Cape Cod Community College*	W. Barnstable
Greenfield Community College*	Greenfield
Holyoke Community College*	Holyoke
Massachusetts Bay Community College*	Wellesley
Massasoit Community College*	Brockton
Middlesex Community College*	Bedford
Mount Wachusett Community College*	Gardner
North Shore Community College*	Beverly
Northern Essex Community College*	Haverhill
Quincy Junior College	Quincy
Quinsigamond Community College*	Worcester

Roxbury Community College*	Roxbury
Springfield Technical Community Coll.*	Springfield
Privately controlled	
Aquinas Junior College	Milton
Bay Path Junior College	Longmeadow
Becker Junior College	Worcester
Leicester Campus	Leicester
Chamberlayne Junior College	Boston
Dean Junior College	Franklin
Endicott College	Beverly
Fisher Junior College	Boston
Franklin Inst. of Boston	Boston
Laboure Junior College	Boston
Lasell Junior College	Newton
Mount Ida Junior College	Newton Centre
Newbury Junior College	Boston
Worcester Junior College	Worcester

MICHIGAN

Publicly controlled

Alpena Community College*	Alpena
Bay de Noc Community College*	Escanaba
Charles Stewart Mott Community Coll.*	Flint
Delta College*	University Center
Glen Oaks Community College*	Centreville
Gogebic Community College	Ironwood
Grand Rapids Junior College*	Grand Rapids
Henry Ford Community College*	Dearborn
Highland Park Community College*	Highland Park
Jackson Community College	Jackson
Kalamazoo Valley Community College*	Kalamazoo
Kellogg Community College*	Battle Creek
Kirtland Community College*	Roscommon
Lake Michigan College*	Benton Harbor
Lansing Community College*	Lansing
Macomb County Community College	Warren
Center Campus*	Mt. Clemens
South Campus*	Warren
Mid Michigan Community College*	Harrison
Monroe County Community College*	Monroe
Montcalm Community College*	Sidney
Muskegon Community College*	Muskegon
North Central Michigan College	Petoskey
Northwestern Michigan College*	Traverse City
Oakland Community College*	Bloomfield Hills
Auburn Hills Campus	Auburn Heights
Highland Lakes Campus	Union Lake
Orchard Ridge Campus	Farmington
Southeast Campus	Oak Park
St. Clair County Community College*	Port Huron
Schoolcraft College*	Livonia
Southwestern Michigan College*	Dowagiac
Washtenaw Community College*	Ann Arbor
Wayne County Community College*	Detroit
West Shore Community College*	Scottville
Privately controlled	
Davenport College of Business	Grand Rapids
Suomi College	Hancock

MINNESOTA

Publicly controlled

Alexandria Vocational Tech. Inst.	Alexandria
Anoka-Ramsey Community College*	Coon Rapids
Austin Community College	Austin
Brainerd Community College*	Brainerd
Fergus Falls Community College	Fergus Falls
Hibbing Community College	Hibbing
Inver Hills Community College*	Inver Grove Heights
Itasca Community College*	Grand Rapids
Lakewood Community College	White Bear Lake
Mesabi Community College	Virginia

Minneapolis Community College	Minneapolis
Minnesota, Univ. of, Technical Coll.	Minneapolis
Crookston Campus	Crookston
Waseca Campus	Waseca
Normandale Community College	Bloomington
North Hennepin Community College*	Brooklyn Park
Northland Community College	Thief River Falls
Rainy River Community College	International Falls
Rochester Community College*	Rochester
Vermilion Community College*	Ely
Willmar Area Technical Institute*	Willmar
Willmar Community College	Willmar
Worthington Community College	Worthington

Privately controlled

Bethany Lutheran College	Mankato
Crosier Seminary Junior College	Onamia
Golden Valley Lutheran College	Minneapolis
St. Mary's Junior College	Minneapolis

MISSISSIPPI

Publicly controlled

Coahoma Junior College*	Clarksdale
Copiah-Lincoln Junior College*	Wesson
East Central Junior College*	Decatur
East Mississippi Junior College*	Scooba
Hinds Junior College*	Raymond
Holmes Junior College*	Goodman
Itawamba Junior College*	Fulton
Jones County Junior College*	Ellisville
Meridian Junior College*	Meridian
Mississippi Delta Junior College*	Moorhead
Mississippi Gulf Coast Junior College	Perkinston
Jackson County Campus*	Gautier
Jefferson Davis Campus*	Gulfport
Perkinston Campus*	Perkinston
Northeast Mississippi Junior College*	Booneville
Northwest Mississippi Junior College*	Senatobia
Pearl River Junior College*	Poplarville
Southwest Mississippi Junior College*	Summit
Utica Junior College*	Utica

Privately controlled

Clarke College	Newton
Mary Holmes College	West Point
Wood Junior College	Mathiston

MISSOURI

Publicly controlled

Crowder College*	Neosho
East Central College*	Union
Jefferson College*	Hillsboro
Metropolitan Community Colleges, The	Kansas City
Longview Community College*	Lee's Summit
Maple Woods Community College*	Kansas City
Penn Valley Community College*	Kansas City
Pioneer Community College*	Kansas City
Mineral Area College*	Flat River
Moberly Junior College*	Moberly
St. Louis Community College	St. Louis
St. Louis C.C.—Florissant Valley*	St. Louis
St. Louis C.C. at Forest Park*	St. Louis
St. Louis C.C.—Meramec*	St. Louis
State Fair Community College*	Sedalia
Three Rivers Community College*	Poplar Bluff
Trenton Junior College*	Trenton

Privately controlled

Cottey College	Nevada
Kemper Military School and College	Boonville
St. Mary's College of O'Fallon	O'Fallon
St. Paul's College	Concordia
Wentworth Military Academy	Lexington

MONTANA

Publicly controlled

Dawson College*	Glendive
Flathead Valley Community College*	Kalispell
Miles Community College*	Miles City

NEBRASKA

Publicly controlled

Central Technical Comm. Coll. Area	Grand Island
Central Technical Community Coll.*	Hastings
Grand Island Education Center*	Grand Island
Platte Technical Community Coll.*	Columbus
Metropolitan Technical Community Coll.*	Omaha
Mid-Plains Technical Comm. Coll. Area	North Platte
McCook Community College*	McCook
Mid-Plains Community College*	North Platte
Nebraska, Univ. of, Sch. of Tech. Agri.	Curtis
Northeast Technical Community College*	Norfolk
Southeast Community College*	Lincoln
Fairbury/Beatrice Campus*	Fairbury
Lincoln Campus	Lincoln
Milford Campus*	Milford
Western Technical Comm. Coll. Area	Scottsbluff
Nebraska Western College*	Scottsbluff
Western Nebraska Technical Coll.*	Sidney

Privately controlled

York College	York

NEVADA

Publicly controlled

Nevada, Univ. of, Comm. Coll. System	Reno
Clark County Community College*	North Las Vegas
Northern Nevada Community College*	Elko
Truckee Meadows Community College*	Sparks
Western Nevada Community College*	Carson City

NEW HAMPSHIRE

Publicly controlled

New Hampshire Technical Institute	Concord
New Hampshire Vocational Technical Coll.	Berlin
Berlin Campus	Berlin
Claremont Campus	Claremont
Laconia Campus	Laconia
Manchester Campus	Manchester
Nashua Campus	Nashua
Portsmouth Campus	Portsmouth

Privately controlled

Daniel Webster College	Nashua
White Pines College	Chester

NEW JERSEY

Publicly controlled

Atlantic Community College	Mays Landing
Bergen Community College	Paramus
Brookdale Community College*	Lincroft
Burlington County College	Pemberton
Camden County College*	Blackwood
County College of Morris*	Dover
Cumberland County College*	Vineland
Essex County College	Newark
Gloucester County College*	Sewell
Hudson County Comm. Coll. Commission*	Jersey City
Mercer County Community College*	Trenton
Middlesex County College*	Edison
Ocean County College	Toms River
Passaic County Community College*	Paterson
Salem Community College	Penns Grove
Somerset County College	Somerville

Privately controlled

Edward Williams College	Hackensack
Union College	Cranford

NEW MEXICO

Publicly controlled

Albuquerque Tech. Voc. Inst.*	Albuquerque
Eastern New Mexico University	Portales
Clovis Campus*	Clovis
Roswell Campus*	Roswell
Inst. of American Indian Arts	Santa Fe
Luna Vocational Technical Institute*	Las Vegas
New Mexico, University of	Albuquerque
Gallup Campus*	Gallup
New Mexico Junior College*	Hobbs
New Mexico Military Institute	Roswell
New Mexico State University	Las Cruces
Alamogordo Campus*	Alamogordo
Carlsbad Campus*	Carlsbad
Dona Ana Branch	Las Cruces
Grants Campus*	Grants
San Juan Campus*	Farmington
Northern New Mexico Community Coll.*	El Rito

NEW YORK

Publicly controlled

Adirondack Community College	Glens Falls
Borough of Manhattan Community Coll.	New York
Bronx Community College	Bronx
Broome Community College	Binghamton
Cayuga County Community College	Auburn
Clinton Community College	Plattsburgh
Columbia-Greene Community College	Hudson
Comm. Coll. of the Finger Lakes	Canandaigua
Corning Community College	Corning
Dutchess Community College	Poughkeepsie
Erie Community College	Buffalo
City Campus	Buffalo
North Campus	Williamsville
South Campus	Orchard Park
Fashion Institute of Technology	New York
Fulton-Montgomery Community College	Johnstown
Genesee Community College	Batavia
Herkimer County Community College	Herkimer
Hostos Community College	Bronx
Hudson Valley Community College	Troy
Jamestown Community College	Jamestown
Jefferson Community College	Watertown
Kingsborough Community College	Brooklyn
Laguardia Community College	Long Island City
Mohawk Valley Community College	Utica
Monroe Community College	Rochester
Nassau Community College	Garden City
New York City Community College	Brooklyn
Niagara County Community College	Sanborn
North Country Community College	Saranac Lake
Onondaga Community College	Syracuse
Orange County Community College	Middletown
Queensborough Community College	Bayside
Rockland Community College	Suffern
Schenectady County Community College	Schenectady
SUNY Agricultural & Technical Colleges	
Alfred Campus	Alfred
Canton Campus	Canton
Cobleskill Campus	Cobleskill
Delhi Campus	Delhi
Farmingdale Campus	Farmingdale
Morrisville Campus	Morrisville
Suffolk County Community College	Selden
Sullivan County Community College	Loch Sheldrake
Tompkins-Cortland Community College	Dryden
Ulster County Community College	Stoneridge
Westchester Community College	Valhalla
Privately controlled	
Aeronautics, Academy of	Flushing
Albany, Junior College of	Albany

Bramson Ort Technical Institute	New York
Cazenovia College	Cazenovia
Elizabeth Seton College	Yonkers
Harriman College	Harriman
Hilbert College	Hamburg
Human Services, College for	New York
Lab Inst. of Merchandising	New York City
Maria College	Albany
Maria Regina College	Syracuse
Mater Dei College	Ogdensburg
Paul Smith's Coll. of Arts & Science	Paul Smiths
Trocaire College	Buffalo
Villa Maria College of Buffalo	Buffalo
Wood School, The	New York City

NORTH CAROLINA

Publicly controlled

Albemarle, College of the*	Elizabeth City
Anson Technical Institute*	Ansonville
Asheville-Buncombe Technical Institute*	Asheville
Beaufort County Technical Institute*	Washington
Bladen Technical Institute*	Dublin
Blue Ridge Technical College*	Flat Rock
Caldwell Comm. Coll. and Tech. Inst.*	Hudson
Cape Fear Technical Institute*	Wilmington
Carteret Technical Institute*	Morehead City
Catawba Valley Technical College*	Hickory
Central Carolina Technical College*	Sanford
Central Piedmont Community College*	Charlotte
Cleveland Technical College*	Shelby
Coastal Carolina Community College*	Jacksonville
Craven Community College*	New Bern
Davidson County Community College*	Lexington
Durham Technical Institute*	Durham
Edgecombe Technical College*	Tarboro
Fayetteville Technical Institute*	Fayetteville
Forsyth Technical Institute*	Winston Salem
Gaston College*	Dallas
Guilford Technical Institute*	Jamestown
Halifax Community College*	Weldon
Haywood Technical Institute*	Clyde
Isothermal Community College*	Spindale
James Sprunt Technical College*	Kenansville
Johnston Technical College*	Smithfield
Lenoir Community College*	Kinston
Martin Community College*	Williamston
Mayland Technical College*	Spruce Pine
McDowell Technical College*	Marion
Mitchell Community College*	Statesville
Montgomery Technical Institute*	Troy
Nash Technical Institute*	Rocky Mount
Pamlico Technical College*	Grantsboro
Piedmont Technical College*	Roxboro
Pitt Community College*	Greenville
Randolph Technical College*	Asheboro
Richmond Technical College*	Hamlet
Roanoke-Chowan Technical Institute	Ahoskie
Robeson Technical College*	Lumberton
Rockingham Community College*	Wentworth
Rowan Technical College*	Salisbury
Sampson Technical College*	Clinton
Sandhills Community College*	Carthage
Southeastern Community College*	Whiteville
Southwestern Technical College*	Sylva
Stanly Technical Institute*	Albemarle
Surry Community College*	Dobson
Technical College of Alamance*	Haw River
Tri-County Community College*	Murphy
Vance-Granville Community College*	Henderson
Wake Technical College*	Raleigh
Wayne Community College*	Goldsboro
Western Piedmont Community College*	Morganton
Wilkes Community College*	Wilkesboro

Wilson County Technical Institute*	Wilson
Privately controlled	
Brevard College	Brevard
Chowan College	Murfreesboro
Lees-McRae College	Banner Elk
Louisburg College	Louisburg
Montreat-Anderson College	Montreat
Mount Olive College	Mount Olive
Peace College	Raleigh
St. Mary's College	Raleigh

NORTH DAKOTA

Publicly controlled	
Bismarck Junior College	Bismarck
Lake Region Junior College	Devils Lake
North Dakota, Univ. of—Williston	Williston
North Dakota State School of Science*	Wahpeton
North Dakota State Univ.—Bottineau*	Bottineau
Turtle Mountain Comm. College*	Belcourt
Privately controlled	
Standing Rock Comm. College	Fort Yates

OHIO

Publicly controlled	
Akron, Univ. of, Comm. and Tech. Coll.	Akron
Wayne General & Technical Coll.	Orrville
Belmont Technical College	St. Clairsville
Bowling Green Univ.–Firelands Campus	Huron
Central Ohio Technical College	Newark
Cincinnati, University of	Cincinnati
Clermont General & Technical Coll.	Batavia
Ohio College of Applied Science	Cincinnati
Raymond Walters Gen. & Tech. Coll.	Cincinnati
University College	Cincinnati
Cincinnati Technical College	Cincinnati
Clark Technical College	Springfield
Coll. of Applied Science & Technology	Youngstown
Columbus Technical Institute	Columbus
Cuyahoga Community College District*	Cleveland
Eastern Campus	Warrensville Twnsp.
Metropolitan Campus	Cleveland
Western Campus	Parma
Edison State Community College	Piqua
Hocking Technical College	Nelsonville
Jefferson Technical College*	Steubenville
Kent State University	Kent
Ashtabula Campus	Ashtabula
East Liverpool Regional Campus	East Liverpool
Geauga Campus	Burton
Salem Campus	Salem
Stark Regional Campus	Canton
Trumbull Campus	Warren
Tuscarawas Campus	New Philadelphia
Lakeland Community College*	Mentor
Lima Technical College	Lima
Lorain County Community College	Elyria
Marion Technical College	Marion
Miami University	Oxford
Hamilton Campus	Hamilton
Middletown Campus	Middletown
Michael J. Owens Technical College	Toledo
Muskingum Area Technical College	Zanesville
North Central Technical College	Mansfield
Northwest Technical College	Archbold
Ohio State University	Columbus
Agricultural Technical Institute	Wooster
Lima Campus	Lima
Mansfield Campus	Mansfield
Marion Campus	Marion
Newark Campus	Newark
Ohio University	Athens
Belmont County Campus	St. Clairsville

Chillicothe Campus	Chillicothe
Ironton Campus	Ironton
Lancaster Campus	Lancaster
Zanesville Campus	Zanesville
Rio Grande Community College*	Rio Grande
Shawnee State Community College	Portsmouth
Sinclair Community College*	Dayton
Southern State Community College	Wilmington
Stark Technical College	Canton
Terra Technical College	Fremont
Toledo, Univ. of, Comm. & Tech. Coll.	Toledo
Washington Technical College*	Marietta
Wright State Univ.—Western Branch	Celina
Privately controlled	
Chatfield College	St. Martin
Kettering College of Medical Arts	Kettering
Lourdes College	Sylvania

OKLAHOMA

Publicly controlled	
Carl Albert Junior College*	Poteau
Claremore Junior College*	Claremore
Connors State College*	Warner
Eastern Oklahoma State College	Wilburton
El Reno Junior College*	El Reno
Murray State College*	Tishomingo
Northeastern Oklahoma A&M College*	Miami
Northern Oklahoma College*	Tonkawa
Oklahoma State U. Technical Institute*	Oklahoma City
Oscar Rose Junior College*	Midwest City
Sayre Junior College*	Sayre
Seminole Junior College*	Seminole
South Oklahoma City Junior College*	Oklahoma City
Tulsa Junior College*	Tulsa
Western Oklahoma State College*	Altus
Privately controlled	
Bacone College	Muskogee
Hillsdale Free Will Baptist	Moore
St. Gregory's College	Shawnee

OREGON

Publicly controlled	
Blue Mountain Community College*	Pendleton
Central Oregon Community College*	Bend
Chemeketa Community College*	Salem
Clackamas Community College*	Oregon City
Clatsop Community College*	Astoria
Lane Community College*	Eugene
Linn-Benton Community College*	Albany
Mt. Hood Community College*	Gresham
Portland Community College*	Portland
Rogue Community College*	Grants Pass
Southwestern Oregon Community Coll.*	Coos Bay
Treasure Valley Community College*	Ontario
Umpqua Community College*	Roseburg
Privately controlled	
Bassist College	Portland

PENNSYLVANIA

Publicly controlled	
Bucks County Community College	Newtown
Butler County Community College	Butler
Community Coll. of Allegheny County	Pittsburgh
Allegheny Campus	Pittsburgh
Boyce Campus	Monroeville
College Center—North	Pittsburgh
South Campus	West Mifflin
Community College of Beaver County	Monaca
Comm. College of Philadelphia	Philadelphia
Delaware County Community College	Media
Harrisburg Area Community College	Harrisburg
Lehigh County Community College	Schnecksville
Luzerne County Community College	Nanticoke
Montgomery County Community College	Blue Bell

Northhampton County Area Comm. Coll.	Bethlehem
Reading Area Community College	Reading
Westmoreland County Community Coll.	Youngwood
Williamsport Area Community College	Williamsport
Privately controlled	
Center for Degree Studies	Scranton
Central Penn. Business School	Summerdale
Harcum Junior College	Bryn Mawr
Keystone Junior College	La Plume
Lackawanna Junior College	Scranton
Manor Junior College	Jenkintown
Mount Aloysius Junior College	Cresson
Northeastern Christian Junior College	Villanova
Peirce Junior College	Philadelphia
Pennsylvania Institute of Technology	Upper Darby
Pinebrook Junior College	Coopersburg
Valley Forge Military Junior College	Wayne
Wheeler School	Pittsburgh

PUERTO RICO

Publicly controlled	
Puerto Rico, Univ. of, Regional Colleges	Rio Piedras
Aguadilla Regional College*	Aguadilla
Arecibo Regional College*	Arecibo
Bayamon U. Technological Coll.*	Bayamon
Carolina Regional College*	Carolina
Ponce Regional College*	Ponce
Privately controlled	
Catholic University of Puerto Rico	Ponce
Aguadilla Center	Aguadilla
Arecibo Center	Arecibo
Guayama Center	Guayama
Ponce Center	Ponce
ICPR Junior College	Hato Rey
Interamerican University of Puerto Rico	San Juan
Aguadilla Regional College	Aguadilla
Arecibo Regional College	Arecibo
Barranquitas Regional College	Barranquitas
Fajardo Regional Campus	Fajardo
Guayama Regional College	Guayama
Ponce Regional College	Ponce
Puerto Rico Junior College	Rio Piedras
Ramirez Coll. of Business Tech.	Santurce
U. of the Sacred Heart Junior Coll.	Santurce

RHODE ISLAND

Publicly controlled	
Community Coll. of Rhode Island*	Warwick

SOUTH CAROLINA

Publicly controlled	
State System of Technical Colleges:	Columbia
Aiken Technical College*	Aiken
Beaufort Technical College*	Beaufort
Chesterfield-Marlboro Technical Coll.*	Cheraw
Denmark Technical College*	Denmark
Florence-Darlington Technical Coll.*	Florence
Greenville Technical College*	Greenville
Horry-Georgetown Technical College*	Conway
Midlands Technical College*	Columbia
Airport Campus	West Columbia
Beltline Campus	Columbia
Orangeburg-Calhoun Technical College*	Orangeburg
Piedmont Technical College*	Greenwood
South Carolina, University of	Columbia
Beaufort Regional Campus	Beaufort
Lancaster Regional Campus	Lancaster
Salkehatchie Regional Campus	Allendale
Sumter Regional Campus	Sumter
Union Campus	Union
Spartanburg Technical College*	Spartanburg
Sumter Area Technical College*	Sumter
Tri-County Technical College*	Pendleton

Trident Technical College*	No. Charleston
North Campus	No. Charleston
Palmer Campus*	Charleston
Williamsburg Technical College*	Kingstree
York Technical College*	Rock Hill
Privately controlled	
Anderson College	Anderson
Clinton Junior College	Rock Hill
Friendship College	Rock Hill
North Greenville College	Tigerville
Spartanburg Methodist College	Spartanburg

SOUTH DAKOTA

Privately controlled	
Freeman Junior College	Freeman
Oglala Sioux Community College*	Pine Ridge
Presentation College	Aberdeen
Sinte Gleska College Center*	Rosebud

TENNESSEE

Publicly controlled	
Chattanooga State Tech. Comm. Coll.*	Chattanooga
Cleveland State Community College*	Cleveland
Columbia State Community College*	Columbia
Dyersburg State Community College*	Dyersburg
Jackson State Community College*	Jackson
Motlow State Community College*	Tullahoma
Nashville State Technical Institute*	Nashville
Roane State Community College*	Harriman
Shelby State Community College*	Memphis
State Technical Inst. at Memphis*	Memphis
Volunteer State Community College*	Gallatin
Walters State Community College*	Morristown
Privately controlled	
Aquinas Junior College	Nashville
Cumberland College of Tennessee	Lebanon
Hiwassee College	Madisonville
John A. Gupton College	Nashville
Martin College	Pulaski
Morristown College	Morristown
State Technical Inst. at Knoxville*	Knoxville
Tomlinson College	Cleveland

TEXAS

Publicly controlled	
Alvin Community College*	Alvin
Amarillo College*	Amarillo
Angelina College*	Lufkin
Austin Community College*	Austin
Bee County College*	Beeville
Blinn College*	Brenham
Brazosport College*	Lake Jackson
Central Texas College*	Killeen
Cisco Junior College*	Cisco
Clarendon College*	Clarendon
Cooke County College*	Gainesville
Dallas County Community Coll. District	Dallas
Brookhaven College*	Farmers Branch
Cedar Valley College*	Lancaster
Eastfield College*	Mesquite
El Centro College*	Dallas
Mountain View College*	Dallas
North Lake College*	Irving
Richland College*	Dallas
Del Mar College*	Corpus Christi
El Paso County Comm. Coll. District*	El Paso
Rio Grande Campus*	El Paso
Transmountain Campus*	El Paso
Valle Verde Campus*	El Paso
Frank Phillips College*	Borger
Galveston College*	Galveston
Grayson County Junior College*	Denison

Henderson County Junior College*	Athens
Hill Junior College*	Hillsboro
Houston Community College*	Houston
Howard College at Big Spring*	Big Spring
Kilgore College*	Kilgore
Lamar University	Beaumont
Orange County Center*	Orange
Port Arthur Branch*	Port Arthur
Laredo Junior College*	Laredo
Lee College*	Baytown
Mainland, College of the*	Texas City
McLennan Community College*	Waco
Midland College*	Midland
Navarro College*	Corsicana
North Harris County College*	Houston
Odessa College*	Odessa
Panola Junior College*	Carthage
Paris Junior College*	Paris
Ranger Junior College*	Ranger
San Antonio Community Coll. District	San Antonio
St. Philip's College*	San Antonio
San Antonio College*	San Antonio
San Jacinto College	Pasadena
Central Campus*	Pasadena
North Campus*	Houston
South Campus*	Houston
South Plains College*	Levelland
Southwest Texas Junior College*	Uvalde
Tarrant County Junior Coll. District	Fort Worth
Northeast Campus*	Hurst
Northwest Campus*	Fort Worth
South Campus*	Fort Worth
Temple Junior College*	Temple
Texarkana Community College*	Texarkana
Texas Southmost College*	Brownsville
Texas State Technical Institute	Waco
Harlingen Campus*	Harlingen
Mid-Continent Campus*	Amarillo
Sweetwater Campus*	Sweetwater
Waco Campus*	Waco
Tyler Junior College*	Tyler
Vernon Regional Junior College*	Vernon
Victoria College*	Victoria
Weatherford College*	Weatherford
Western Texas College*	Snyder
Wharton County Junior College*	Wharton
Privately controlled	
Jacksonville College	Jacksonville
Lon Morris College	Jacksonville
Schreiner College	Kerrville
Southwestern Christian College	Terrell
Southwestern Junior College	Waxahachie

UTAH

Publicly controlled

Dixie College*	St. George
Eastern Utah, College of*	Price
Snow College*	Ephraim
Utah Technical College at Provo*	Provo
Utah Technical College at Salt Lake*	Salt Lake City

VERMONT

Publicly controlled

Community College of Vermont	Montpelier
Vermont Technical College	Randolph Center

Privately controlled

Burlington College	Burlington
Champlain College	Burlington
Ethan Allen Community College	Manchester Center
Vermont College of Norwich University	Montpelier

VIRGINIA

Publicly controlled

Blue Ridge Community College*	Weyers Cave
Central Virginia Community College*	Lynchburg
Dabney S. Lancaster Community Coll.*	Clifton Forge
Danville Community College*	Danville
Eastern Shore Community College*	Melfa
Germanna Community College*	Locust Grove
J. Sargeant Reynolds Community Coll.*	Richmond
Downtown Campus	Richmond
Parham Road Campus	Richmond
Western Campus	Richmond
John Tyler Community College*	Chester
Lord Fairfax Community College*	Middletown
Mountain Empire Community College*	Big Stone Gap
New River Community College*	Dublin
Northern Virginia Community College*	Annandale
Alexandria Campus	Alexandria
Annandale Campus	Annandale
Loudoun Campus	Sterling
Manassas Campus	Manassas
Woodbridge Campus	Woodbridge
Patrick Henry Community College*	Martinsville
Paul D. Camp Community College*	Franklin
Piedmont Virginia Community College*	Charlottesville
Rappahannock Community College*	Glenns
North Campus*	Warsaw
South Campus	Glenns
Richard Bland College*	Petersburg
Southside Virginia Community College*	Alberta
Christanna Campus	Alberta
John H. Daniel Campus	Keysville
Southwest Virginia Community College*	Richlands
Thomas Nelson Community College*	Hampton
Tidewater Community College	Portsmouth
Chesapeake Campus*	Chesapeake
Frederick Campus*	Portsmouth
Virginia Beach Campus*	Virginia Beach
Virginia Highlands Community College*	Abingdon
Virginia Western Community College*	Roanoke
Wytheville Community College*	Wytheville
Privately controlled	
Southern Seminary Junior College	Buena Vista

WASHINGTON

Publicly controlled

Bellevue Community College*	Bellevue
Big Bend Community College*	Moses Lake
Centralia College*	Centralia
Clark College*	Vancouver
Columbia Basin College*	Pasco
Community College District VI	Seattle
North Seattle Community College*	Seattle
Seattle Central Community College*	Seattle
South Seattle Community College*	Seattle
Community College District XVII	Spokane
Spokane Community College*	Spokane
Spokane Falls Community College*	Spokane
Fort Steilacoom Community College*	Tacoma
Grays Harbor College*	Aberdeen
Green River Community College*	Auburn
Highline Community College*	Midway
Lower Columbia College*	Longview
Olympia Technical Community College*	Olympia
Olympic College*	Bremerton
Peninsula College*	Port Angeles
Shoreline Community College*	Seattle
Skagit Valley College*	Mount Vernon
Snohomish County Comm. Colleges	Everett
Edmonds Community College*	Lynnwood
Everett Community College*	Everett

Tacoma Community College*	Tacoma
Walla Walla Community College	Walla Walla
Wenatchee Valley College*	Wenatchee
Whatcom Community College*	Bellingham
Yakima Valley College*	Yakima

WEST VIRGINIA

Publicly controlled

Fairmont Community College*	Fairmont
Marshall Univ.—Community College*	Huntington
Parkersburg Community College*	Parkersburg
Shepherd College—Community College Component*	Shepherdstown
Southern West Virginia Comm. College*	Logan
Logan Campus	Logan
Williamson Campus	Williamson
West Virginia Institute of Technology—Community and Technical College*	Montgomery
West Virginia Northern Comm. College*	Wheeling
West Virginia State Comm. College	Institute
West Virginia University—Potomac State College*	Keyser

Privately controlled

Beckley College	Beckley
Ohio Valley College	Parkersburg

WISCONSIN

Publicly controlled

University Center System	Madison
Baraboo-Sauk County Campus	Baraboo
Barron County Campus	Rice Lake
Fond du Lac Campus	Fond du Lac
Fox Valley Campus	Menasha
Manitowoc County Campus	Manitowoc
Marathon County Campus	Wausau
Marinette County Campus	Marinette
Marshfield-Wood County Campus	Marshfield
Medford Campus	Medford
Richland Campus	Richland Center
Rock County Campus	Janesville
Sheboygan Campus	Sheboygan
Washington County Campus	West Bend
Waukesha County Campus	Waukesha
Vocational Tech. & Adult Education Sys.	Madison
Blackhawk Technical Institute*	Janesville
District One Technical Institute*	Eau Claire
Fox Valley Technical Institute*	Appleton
Appleton Campus	Appleton
Oshkosh Campus	Oshkosh
Gateway Technical Institute*	Kenosha
Elkhorn Campus	Elkhorn
Kenosha Campus	Kenosha
Racine Campus	Racine
Lakeshore Technical Institute*	Cleveland
Madison Area Technical Coll.*	Madison
Mid-State Technical Institute*	Wisconsin Rapids
Marshfield Campus*	Marshfield
Stevens Point Campus*	Stevens Point
Wisconsin Rapids Campus*	Wisconsin Rapids
Milwaukee Area Technical College	Milwaukee
Central Campus*	Milwaukee
North Campus*	Mequon
South Campus*	Oak Creek
West Campus*	West Allis
Moraine Park Technical Institute*	Fond du Lac
Beaver Dam Campus	Beaver Dam

Fond du Lac Campus	Fond du Lac
West Bend Campus	West Bend
Nicolet College and Tech. Institute*	Rhinelander
North Central Technical Institute*	Wausau
Antigo Campus	Antigo
Wausau Campus	Wausau
Northeast Wisconsin Technical Inst.	Green Bay
Green Bay Campus*	Green Bay
Marinette Campus*	Marinette
Sturgeon Bay Campus	Sturgeon Bay
Southwest Wisconsin Technical Inst.*	Fennimore
Waukesha County Technical Institute*	Pewaukee
Western Wisconsin Technical Institute*	La Crosse
Wisconsin Indianhead VTAE District	Shell Lake
Ashland Campus*	Ashland
New Richmond Campus	New Richmond
Rice Lake Campus*	Rice Lake
Superior Campus*	Superior

Privately controlled

Milwaukee School of Engineering	Milwaukee

WYOMING

Publicly controlled

Casper College*	Casper
Central Wyoming College*	Riverton
Eastern Wyoming College*	Torrington
Laramie County Community College*	Cheyenne
Northern Wyoming Community College*	Sheridan
Northwest Community College*	Powell
Western Wyoming Community College*	Rock Springs

AMERICAN SAMOA

Publicly controlled

American Samoa Community College*	Pago Pago

CANADA

Publicly controlled

Fraser Valley College*	Mission, B.C.
Grant MacEwan Community College*	Edmonton, Alberta
Keyano College*	Alberta
Lambton College*	Sarnia, Ont.
Medicine Hat College*	Medicine Hat, Alberta
Mount Royal College*	Calgary, Albta.
Red Deer College	Alberta

GUAM

Publicly controlled

Guam Community College*	Guam

MICRONESIA

Publicly controlled

Community Coll. of Micronesia	East Caroline Isl.

PANAMA

Privately controlled

Panama Canal College*	APO Miami

OTHER COUNTRIES

Publicly Controlled

St. Johns College*	British Honduras

Privately controlled

American College of Switzerland	Leysin, Switz.
Schiller International Univ.	Heidelberg, W. Ger.

Record Personal Bankruptcies Filed

It has been estimated that almost 355,000 Americans filed for bankruptcy in 1980. This was 120,000 more persons than in 1975 when the previous record was set.

Accredited U.S. Senior Colleges and Universities, Spring 1981

Source: Information Please questionnaires to Colleges and Universities.

Schools listed are those that offer at least a Bachelor's degree, and are fully accredited by one of the institutional and professional accrediting associations recognized by the Council on Postsecondary Accreditation. The number of students is for matriculated undergraduate and graduate students who are working for a degree.

Tuition, room, and board listed are average annual figures, subject to fluctuation, covering two semesters, two out of three trimesters, or three out of four quarters, depending on school calendar.

For further information, write to the Registrar of the school concerned.

NOTE: An asterisk (*) indicates that the college has not supplied up-to-date information. A dash (—) means the information does not apply. n.a. = information not available.

Abbreviations used for controls:

AB	American Baptist	L	Lutheran
AC	Advent Christian	LCA	Lutheran Church of America
AG	Assembly of God	LDS	Latter Day Saints
AL	American Lutheran	M	Methodist
AME	African Methodist Episcopal	MB	Mennonite Brethren
B	Baptist	MC	Missionary Church
BC	Brethren in Christ	Men	Mennonite
CB	Church of Brethren	Mor	Moravian
CC	Church of Christ	Mun	Municipal
CG	Church of God	Naz	Nazarene
ChC	Christian Church	ND	Non-denominational
CMA	Christian & Missionary Alliance	OBS	Open Bible Standard
CME	Christian Methodist Episcopal	P	Private
Cong	Congregationist	PH	Pentecostal Holiness
CP	Cumberland Presbyterian	Pres	Presbyterian
CR	Christian Reformed	Pub	Public
DC	Disciples of Christ	PUS	Presbyterian, U.S.
E	Episcopalian	RC	Roman Catholic
EC	Evangelical Covenant	RCA	Reformed Church in America
ECh	Evangelical Christian		
EFC	Evangelical Free Church	RP	Reformed Presbyterian
EL	Evangelical Lutheran	S	State
Fed	Federal	SB	Southern Baptist
FGB	Fellowship of Grace Brethren Churches	SDA	Seventh Day Adventist
		SOF	Society of Friends
FM	Free Methodist	Sw	Swedenborgian
FWB	Free Will Baptist	UCC	United Church of Christ
GGF	Grace Gospel Fellowship	UM	United Methodist
ID	Interdenominational	UP	United Presbyterian
Ind	Independent	W	Wesleyan

Institution and location	Enrollment				Tuition		
	Male	Female	Faculty	Control	Res.	Nonres.	Rm/Bd
Abilene Christian University; Abilene, Tex. 79699	1,956[1]	1,860[1]	171	P	$2,460	$2,460	$2,290
Adams State College; Alamosa, Colo. 81102	950	1,000	110	S	754	3,050	2,000
Adelphi University; Garden City, N.Y. 11530	1,395	3,069	375	P	3,840	3,840	2,362
Adrian College; Adrian, Mich. 49221	509	519	62	UM	3,760	3,760	1,800
Agnes Scott College; Decatur, Ga. 30030	—	541[1]	72	P	4,300	4,300	1,700
Akron, The University of; Akron, Ohio 44313	12,417[1]	12,215[1]	942	S	1,190	2,566	1,980
Alabama, The University of; University, Ala. 35486	8,699[1]	8,220[1]	836	S	994	2,119	1,687
Alabama, The University of, in Birmingham; Birmingham, Ala. 35294							
Alabama, The University of, in Huntsville; Huntsville, Ala. 35899	6,593[1]	7,261[1]	1,313	S	1,040	2,080	—
Alabama A&M University; Normal, Ala. 35762	1,426[1]	1,438[1]	195	S	780	1,560[6]	2,240
Alabama State University; Montgomery, Ala. 36195	2,275[1]	2,104[1]	269	S	560	840	1,360
Alaska, University of, Anchorage; Anchorage, Alaska 99504	1,470	2,106	194	S	600	1,200	1,200
Alaska, University of, Fairbanks; Fairbanks, Alaska 99701	1,297	2,287	128	S	681	1,851	
Albany College of Pharmacy; Albany, N.Y. 12208	1,238[1]	977[1]	353	S	572	1,352	2,080[1]
	262	302	30	P	2,500	2,500	2,250
Albany Law School; Albany, N.Y. 12208	435[1]	253[1]	27	P	5,000	5,000	1,000
Albany Medical College; Albany, N.Y. 12208	380[1]	134[1]	281	P	1,200	1,200	920[2]
Albany State College; Albany, Ga. 31705	791	960	125[1]	S	699	1,017	1,545
Albertus Magnus College*; New Haven, Conn. 06511	2	388	27	P/RC	3,600	3,600	2,260
Albion College; Albion, Mich. 49224	947	867	119	P/UM	4,716	4,716	2,272
Albright College; Reading, Pa. 19603	618	701	86	P	4,180	4,180	1,690

Institution and location	Enrollment		Faculty	Control	Tuition		Rm/Bd
	Male	Female			Res.	Nonres.	
Albuquerque, University of*; Albuquerque, N.M. 87140	912	1,085	75	P	936	936	n.a.
Alcorn State University; Lorman, Miss. 39096	995[1]	1,346[1]	150	S	384	1,234	566
Alderson–Broaddus College; Philippi, W. Va. 26416	271[1]	475[1]	64	P/AB	3,300	3,300	1,400
Alfred Adler Institute of Chicago[3]; Chicago, Ill. 60601	19	57	27	P	1,200	1,200	—
Alfred University[4]; Alfred, N.Y. 14802	1,146[1]	1,119[1]	140	P/S	5,650	5,650	2,270
Allegheny College; Meadville, Pa. 16335	937	914	130	P	4,300	4,300	810
Allentown College of St. Francis de Sales; Center Valley, Pa. 18034	321	303	40	P/RC	3,670	3,670	2,180
Alliance College; Cambridge Springs, Pa. 16403	129	78	17	P	2,600	2,600	2,210
Alma College; Alma, Mich. 48801	546	553	72	P	4,144	4,144	1,956
Alvernia College; Reading, Pa. 19607	115	167	76	P/RC	2,050	2,050	1,700
Alverno College; Milwaukee, Wis. 53215	—	1,363[1]	75	P/RC	3,400	3,400	1,550
American Baptist College; Nashville, Tenn. 37207	141	20	16	P/B	920	920	880
American College, The; Bryn Mawr, Pa. 19010	14,336	2,370	31	P	220	220	—
American College in Paris; Paris, France 75007	242	333	20	P	3,800	3,800	4,500
American Conservatory of Music; Chicago, Ill. 60603	106[1]	66[1]	14	P	3,600	3,600	—
American Grad. School of Intl. Mgt.; Glendale, Ariz. 85306	695	298	64	P	6,065[5]	6,065[5]	2,860[5]
American International College; Springfield, Mass. 01109	773[6]	563[6]	76[7]	P	3,630	3,630	2,116
American Technological University; Killeen, Tex. 76541	578	186	15	P	(8)	(8)	5,175[9]
American University, The; Washington, D.C. 20016	12,500[1]		400	P/M	5,240	5,240	2,704
Americas, University of the*; Puebla, Mexico	1,650		55	P	1,377	1,733	n.a.
Amherst College; Amherst, Mass. 01002	959[1]	603[1]	147	P	7,250	7,250	2,550
Ana G. Méndez Educational Foundation*; Rio Piedras, P.R. 00928	n.a.	n.a.	n.a.	P	n.a.	n.a.	n.a.
Colegio Universitario Metropolitano*; Cupey, P.R. 00928	2,200	n.a.	n.a.	P	n.a.	n.a.	n.a.
Turabo University College*; Caguas, P.R. 00625	2,172	2,460	n.a.	P	n.a.	n.a.	n.a.
Anderson College; Anderson, Ind. 46012	776[1]	916[1]	109	P/CG	3,560	3,560	1,430
Andrews University; Berrien Springs, Mich. 49104	1,407[1]	1,028[1]	228	P/SDA	4,485	4,485	2,400
Angelo State University; San Angelo, Tex. 76909	2,803[1]	2,902[1]	191	S	120	1,200	1,920
Anna Maria College; Paxton, Mass. 01612	91[6]	493[6]	26	P/RC	3,600	3,600	2,360
Antillian College; Mayaguez, P.R. 00619	295	431	43	P/SDA	896	896	830
Antioch School of Law; Washington, D.C. 20009	222	172	n.a.	P	5,040	5,040	—
Antioch University; Yellow Springs, Ohio 45387	1,241	2,254	194	P	(10)	(10)	—
Appalachian Bible College; Bradley, W. Va. 25818	134	109	12	P/Ind	2,000	2,000	1,550
Appalachian State University. See North Carolina, University System of							
Aquinas College*; Grand Rapids, Mich. 49506	495	668	n.a.	P/RC	n.a.	n.a.	n.a.
Arizona, University of; Tucson, Ariz. 85721	12,849[1]	11,394[1]	1,426	S	650	2,950	1,870
Arizona State University; Tempe, Ariz. 85281	19,599[1]	18,229[1]	1,566	S	650	2,300	1,511
Arkansas, Univ. of, at Fayetteville; Fayetteville, Ark. 72701	9,152[1]	6,452[1]	n.a.	S	600	1,430	1,540
Arkansas, Univ. of, at Little Rock; Little Rock, Ark. 72204	2,161[1]	2,358[1]	356	S	600	1,245	—
Arkansas, Univ. of, at Monticello; Monticello, Ark. 71655	885	1,017	96	S	900	1,730	1,618
Arkansas, Univ. of, at Pine Bluff; Pine Bluff, Ark. 71601	1,314	1,683	170	S	600	1,430	1,280
Arkansas College; Batesville, Ark. 72501	171[1]	219[1]	36	P/Pres	2,200	2,200	1,422
Arkansas State University; State University, Ark. 72467	2,900[1]	3,051[1]	289	S	660	1,050	1,200
Arkansas Tech. University; Russellville, Ark. 72801	1,550	1,400	140	S	750	1,584	1,440
Armstrong College; Berkeley, Calif. 94704	298[1]	154[1]	40	P	2,160	2,160	2,700
Armstrong State College; Savannah, Ga. 31406	928	1,486	185	P	640	1,500	—
Art Academy of Cincinnati; Cincinnati, Ohio 45202	103[6]	123[6]	15	P	2,797	2,797	—
Art Center College of Design; Pasadena, Calif. 91103	719	467	45	P	3,580	3,580	3,200
Arthur D. Little Management Education Institute; Cambridge, Mass. 02140	59	3	26[11]	P	—	8,580	—
Art Institute of Chicago, School of the*; Chicago, Ill. 60603	446	528	70	P	3,420	3,420	2,500
Asbury College; Wilmore, Ky. 40390	536	581	114	P	2,690	2,690	1,796
Ashland College; Ashland, Ohio 44805	827[1]	646[1]	124	P	4,626	4,626	2,030
Assemblies of God Graduate School; Springfield, Mo. 65802	269	40	12	P/AG	(12)	(12)	—
Associated Arts, School of the; St. Paul, Minn. 55102	51[1]	53[1]	n.a.	P	2,700	2,700	2,800
Assumption College*; Worcester, Mass. 01609	702	769	75	P/RC	3,750	3,750	2,075
Athens State College; Athens, Ala. 35611	265[1]	226[1]	39	S	675	1,350	1,000
Atlanta Christian College; East Point, Ga. 30344	94	66	12	P/ChC	1,344	1,344	1,400
Atlanta College of Art; Atlanta, Ga. 30309	132	135	30	P	2,975	2,975	2,700
Atlanta University; Atlanta, Ga. 30314	424	438	127	P	(13)	(13)	910
Atlantic, College of the; Bar Harbor, Maine 04609	83	106	22	P	4,300	4,300	2,000
Atlantic Christian College; Wilson, N.C. 27893	587[1]	959[1]	111	P/DC	2,500	2,500	1,400
Atlantic Union College; South Lancaster, Mass. 01561	230	320	56	P/SDA	4,600	4,600	2,200
Auburn University; Auburn, Ala. 36849	9,501[1]	6,864[1]	1,045	S	720	1,440	1,635
Auburn University at Montgomery*; Montgomery, Ala. 36117	1,718	1,793	n.a.	S	n.a.	n.a.	n.a.

Institution and location	Enrollment Male	Enrollment Female	Faculty	Control	Tuition Res.	Tuition Nonres.	Rm/Bd
Augsburg College*; Minneapolis, Minn. 55454	661	801	94	P/AL	3,660	3,660	1,837
Augusta College*; Augusta, Ga. 30910	1,619	2,083	157	S	609	1,563	—
Augustana College; Rock Island, Ill. 61201	1,076[1]	1,199[1]	117	P/LCA	3,540	3,540	1,722
Augustana College; Sioux Falls, S.D. 57197	645	1,061	142	P/AL	4,100	4,100	1,500
Aurora College; Aurora, Ill. 60507	596	497	47	P	3,600[14]	3,600[14]	2,160[14]
Austin College*; Sherman, Tex. 75090	633	497	82	P/PUS	3,300	3,300	1,600
Austin Peay State University*; Clarksville, Tenn. 37040[15]	2,724	2,746	195	S	495	1,497	900
Averett College; Danville, Va. 24541	254[1]	511[1]	52	P/B	2,400	2,400	1,800
Avila College; Kansas City, Mo. 64145	203	684	72	P/RC	2,500	2,500	1,600
Azusa Pacific College; Azusa, Calif. 91702	911[1]	1,135[1]	94	P/ID	3,888	3,888	1,924
Babson College*; Babson Park, Mass. 02157	917	362	n.a.	P	4,670	4,670	2,400
Baker University; Baldwin City, Kan. 66006	418[1]	418[1]	65	P/UM	2,950[6]	2,950[6]	1,670[6]
Baldwin–Wallace College; Berea, Ohio 44017	866	875	135	P/UM	4,545[14]	4,545[14]	2,595[14]
Ball State University; Muncie, Ind. 47306	8,264	10,236	850	S	1,116	2,460	1,719
Baltimore, University of; Baltimore, Md. 21201	2,941	1,891	135	S	990	1,990	—
Baltimore Hebrew College; Baltimore, Md. 21215	62[1]	142[1]	16	P	970	970	—
Bank Street College of Education; New York, N.Y. 10025	46	352	54	P	([16])	([16])	—
Baptist Bible College*; Springfield, Mo. 65802	995	774	59	P/B	416	416	1,200
Baptist College at Charleston; Charleston, S.C. 29411	1,065[1]	1,305[1]	80	P/B	3,404	3,404	2,410
Barat College; Lake Forest, Ill. 60045	—	376[1]	43	P	4,200	4,200	2,100
Barber–Scotia College; Concord, N.C. 28025	135	186	17	P/Pres	2,000	2,000	895
Bard College; Annandale–on–Hudson, N.Y. 12504	325	428	52	P	7,450	7,450	2,555
Barnard College. *See* Columbia University							
Barrington College; Barrington, R.I. 02806	183	250	25	P/ECh	3,450	3,450	2,000
Barry College; Miami, Fla. 33161	323[1]	1,084[1]	110	P/RC	4,050	4,050	n.a.
Bartlesville Wesleyan College; Bartlesville, Okla. 74003	177	205	24	P/W	2,400	2,400	1,780
Bates College; Lewiston, Maine 04240	725	700	126	P	5,720	5,720	1,880
Bayamón Central University; Bayamón, P.R. 00619	562	711	24	P/RC	1,700	1,700	1,560
Bayamón Technological University College. *See* Puerto Rico, Univ. of							
Baylor College of Dentistry*; Dallas, Tex. 75246	395	125	110	P	510	3,000	—
Baylor College of Medicine*; Houston, Tex. 77030	614	240	n.a.	P	n.a.	n.a.	n.a.
Baylor University; Waco, Tex. 76798	4,553[1]	4,964[1]	476	P/SB	2,560	2,560	1,940
Beaver College; Glenside, Pa. 19038	130[1]	584[1]	58	P	4,850	4,850	2,350
Behrend College. *See* Pennsylvania State University							
Belhaven College; Jackson, Miss. 39202	379	550	30	Pres	2,500	2,500	1,450
Bellarmine College; Louisville, Ky. 40205	946	1,334	92	P/RC	2,800	2,800	1,600
Bellevue College; Bellevue, Neb. 68005	1,278[1]	1,102[1]	32	P	([17])	([17])	—
Belmont Abbey College; Belmont, N.C. 28012	473	325	32	RC	4,270	4,820	1,570
Belmont College; Nashville, Tenn. 37203	739	839	88	P/B	2,300	2,300	1,670
Beloit College; Beloit, Wis. 53511	548[1]	463[1]	73	P	5,070	5,070	1,750
Bemidji State Univ. *See* Minnesota State College System							
Benedict College; Columbia, S.C. 29204	518	861	98	P/B	2,200	2,200	1,600
Benedictine College*; Atchison, Kan. 66002	507	457	63	P	2,800	2,800	1,701
Benjamin Franklin University*; Washington, D.C. 20036	321		n.a.	P	n.a.	n.a.	n.a.
Bennett College; Greensboro, N.C. 27420	—	600	n.a.	P/UM	2,300	2,300	1,300
Bennington College; Bennington, Vt. 05201	176	374	54	P	8,260	8,260	2,300
Bentley College*; Waltham, Mass. 02154	2,249	1,191	137	P	3,970	3,970	2,320
Berea College; Berea, Ky. 40404	631[1]	810[1]	106	P	—	—	1,575
Berklee College of Music; Boston, Mass. 02215	2,284[1]	359[1]	140	P	3,140	3,140	2,230
Berkshire Christian College; Lenox, Mass. 01240	66	57	13	P/AC	2,650	2,650	2,520
Bernard M. Baruch Coll. *See* New York, City Univ. of							
Berry College; Mount Berry, Ga. 30149	537	752	97	P	2,310	2,310	1,560
Bethany Bible College*; Santa Cruz, Calif. 95066	278	247	27	P/AG	1,900	1,900	1,660
Bethany College; Bethany, W. Va. 26032	494	359	59	P/DC	4,480	4,480	1,765
Bethany College; Lindsborg, Kan. 67456	417[1]	403[1]	62	P/LCA	2,740[6]	2,740[6]	1,655[6]
Bethany Nazarene College; Bethany, Okla. 73008	497[1]	599[1]	62	Naz	2,180	2,180	1,660
Bethel College; McKenzie, Tenn. 38201	190	178	24	P/CP	1,980	1,980	1,500
Bethel College; Mishawaka, Ind. 46544	204	239	26	P/MC	2,790[6]	2,790[6]	1,600
Bethel College; North Newton, Kan. 67117	314[1]	342[1]	55	P/Men	3,012[14]	3,012[14]	1,856
Bethel College; St. Paul, Minn. 55112	826	999	97	P/B	3,925	3,925	1,872
Bethune–Cookman College*; Daytona Beach, Fla. 32015	690	1,046	114	P/M	2,728	2,728	1,806
Biola University; La Mirada, Calif. 90639	753	1,068	105	P/ND	3,634	3,634	2,148
Birmingham–Southern College; Birmingham, Ala. 35254	736[1]	707[1]	75	P/M	2,900	2,900	1,700
Biscayne College; Miami, Fla. 33054	1,532	1,427	45	P/RC	3,700	3,700	2,400
Bishop College; Dallas, Tex. 75241	654	260	52	P/B	2,400	2,400	1,580
Blackburn College; Carlinville, Ill. 62626	201	232	37	P/UP	2,880	2,880	1,075[18]
Black Hills State College; Spearfish, S.D. 57783	814	994	93	S	882	1,662	1,255
Bloomfield College; Bloomfield, N.J. 07003	464	731	49	P/Pres	3,960	3,960	2,200
Bloomsburg State College; Bloomsburg, Pa. 17815	1,975	2,944	334	S	1,120	1,950	1,198

Institution and location	Enrollment Male	Female	Faculty	Control	Tuition Res.	Nonres.	Rm/Bd
Bluefield College; Bluefield, Va. 24605	212[1]	173[1]	23	P/B	1,760[14]	1,760[14]	1,780[14]
Bluefield State College; Bluefield, W. Va. 24701	600	617	100	S	380	1,320	—
Blue Mountain College; Blue Mountain, Miss. 38610	81	215	25	P/B	1,440	1,440	1,280
Bluffton College; Bluffton, Ohio 45817	288[1]	309[1]	43	P/Men	3,510	3,510	1,470
Boise State University; Boise, Idaho 83725	3,140	2,683	620	S	678[14]	2,378[14]	1,750
Borromeo College of Ohio; Wickliffe, Ohio 44092	75		14	RC	2,375	2,375	1,200
Boston College; Chestnut Hill, Mass. 02167	4,921[1]	6,088[1]	550	P/RC	5,180	5,180	3,000
Boston Conservatory of Music*; Boston, Mass. 02215	142	296	30	P	3,100	3,100	1,800
Boston State College; Boston, Mass. 02115	2,662[1]	2,569[1]	284	S	600	2,100	—
Boston University; Boston, Mass. 02215	8,512	9,267	1,496	P	6,300	6,300	2,970
Bowdoin College; Brunswick, Maine 04011	757	531	100	P	6,800[6]	6,800[6]	*2,670[6]
Bowie State College*; Bowie, Md. 20715	1,243	1,636	109	S	870	1,825	1,590
Bowling Green State University; Bowling Green, Ohio 43403	7,530	9,323	737	S	1,206	2,733	1,611
Bradford College; Bradford, Mass. 01830	111	202	26	P	5,050	5,050	7,800
Bradley University; Peoria, Ill. 61625	2,766	1,847	284	P	4,080	4,080	1,898
Brandeis University; Waltham, Mass. 02254	1,684	1,303	400	P	6,700	6,700	2,975
Brenau College; Gainesville, Ga. 30501	356	1,005	75	P	2,400	2,400	2,600
Brescia College; Owensboro, Ky. 42301	183	268	54	P	(19)	(19)	1,620
Briar Cliff College; Sioux City, Iowa 51104	343[6]	595[6]	55	P/RC	2,760	2,760	1,380
Bridgeport, University of; Bridgeport, Conn. 06602	3,413[1]	3,392[1]	285	P	5,090	5,090	2,775
Bridgeport Engineering Institute; Bridgeport, Conn. 06606	720	45	93	P	1,480	1,480	—
Bridgewater College; Bridgewater, Va. 22812	469[1]	464[1]	60	P	3,100[14]	3,100[14]	1,950[14]
Bridgewater State College; Bridgewater, Mass. 02324	1,538	2,695	282	S	600	2,100	1,775
Brigham Young University; Provo, Utah 84602	14,692	13,080	1,168	P/LDS	1,100[20]	1,650[21]	1,640
Hawaii Campus; Laie, Hawaii 96762	730[1]	1,042[1]	78	P/LDS	820[20]	1,300[21]	1,500
Brooklyn Center. See Long Island Univ. Center							
Brooklyn College. See New York, City University of							
Brooklyn Law School; Brooklyn, N.Y. 11201	694	486	34	P	4,500	4,500	—
Brooks Institute of Photography; Santa Barbara, Calif. 93108	612	198	36	P	4,050	4,050	—
Brown University; Providence, R.I. 02912	2,755	2,555	460	P	7,120	7,120	3,110
Bryan College; Dayton, Tenn. 37321	258[1]	312[1]	37	P/ID	2,500	2,500	2,200
Bryant College; Smithfield, R.I. 02917	3,420	2,455	90	P	3,325	3,325	2,375
Bryn Mawr College; Bryn Mawr, Pa. 19010		1,784	n.a.	P	5,930	5,930	2,650
Bucknell University; Lewisburg, Pa. 17837	1,657	1,496	223	P	6,400[14]	6,400[14]	1,850[14]
Buena Vista College; Storm Lake, Iowa 50588	596[1]	543[1]	n.a.	P/Pres	4,270	4,270	1,690
Butler University; Indianapolis, Ind. 46208	883	1,216	n.a.	P	3,850[14]	3,850[14]	1,850
Cabrini College; Radnor, Pa. 19087	85	401	31	P/RC	3,100	3,100	2,100
Caldwell College; Caldwell, N.J. 07006	—	555	42	P/RC	3,100	3,100	1,800
California, University of; Berkeley, Calif. 94720							
UC, Berkeley; Berkeley, Calif. 94720	18,076[1]	12,807[1]	1,494	S	805	3,685	5,496
UC, Davis; Davis, Calif. 95616	9,937[6]	8,563[6]	1,400	P	800	3,200	1,990
UC, Hastings College of Law*; San Francisco; Calif. 94102	898	572	n.a.	S	n.a.	n.a.	n.a.
UC, Irvine; Irvine, Calif. 92717	4,942	4,748	377	S	768	2,400	2,434
UC, Los Angeles; Los Angeles, Calif. 90024	17,564	15,118	2,100	S	798	3,678	2,000
UC, San Diego; La Jolla, Calif. 92121	6,564	4,550	825	S	741	3,620	2,600
UC, Riverside; Riverside, Calif. 92521	2,336[1]	2,037[1]	318	S	813	3,654	1,995
UC, San Francisco*; San Francisco, Calif. 94143	2,205	1,606	n.a.	S	n.a.	n.a.	n.a.
UC, Santa Barbara*; Santa Barbara, Calif. 93106	7,248	6,983	1,051	S	—	2,400	1,835
UC, Santa Cruz; Santa Cruz, Calif. 95060	3,400[1]	3,072[1]	347	S	831	3,231	3,336
California Baptist College; Riverside, Calif. 92504	342	319	36	P/SB	3,064	3,064	1,600
California College of Arts and Crafts; Oakland, Calif. 94618	329[6]	634[6]	70	P	4,260[25]	4,260[25]	925[2]
California College of Podiatric Medicine; San Francisco, Calif. 94120	345[1]	52[1]	195	P	7,890	7,890	2,600
California Institute of Technology; Pasadena, Calif. 91125	1,494[1]	216[1]	740	P	5,229	5,229	2,500
California Institute of the Arts; Valencia, Calif. 91355	455[1]	342[1]	73	P	5,000	5,000	3,700
California Lutheran College; Thousand Oaks, Calif. 91360	1,100	1,402	n.a.	P	3,900	3,900	2,100
California Maritime Academy*; Vallejo, Calif. 94590	470	15	30	S	645	1,290	2,100
California Polytechnic State University; San Luis Obispo, Calif. 93407	9,269	6,594	820	S	(24)	(24)	n.a.
California School of Professional Psychology—Berkeley*; Berkeley, Calif. 94704	97	133	17	P	5,500	5,500	3,750[9]
California School of Professional Psychology—Fresno; Fresno, Calif. 93721	109	43	7	P	6,250	6,250	4,140
California School of Professional Psychology—Los Angeles; Los Angeles, Calif. 90004	96	172	20	P	5,445	5,445	—
California School of Professional Psychology—San Diego; San Diego, Calif. 92121	123	105	18	P	6,250	6,250	4,100

Institution and location	Enrollment		Faculty	Control	Tuition		Rm/Bd
	Male	Female			Res.	Nonres.	
California State College; California, Pa. 15419							
California State College, Bakersfield; Bakersfield, Calif. 93309[22]	2,209[1]	2,199[1]	295	S	1,250	1,250	1,550
California State College, San Bernardino; San Bernardino, Calif. 92407[22]	1,032[1]	1,355[1]	137	S	206	2,366	2,100
	1,410	1,890	165	S	243	2,400	1,800
California State Coll., Stanislaus; Turlock, Calif. 95380[22]	729	1,041	181	S	245	2,376	2,000
California State Polytechnic University, Pomona; Pomona, Calif. 91768[22]	7,429	4,953	667	S	249	2,160	2,424
California State University and Colleges, Consortium of the*; Long Beach, Calif. 90802	170		80	S	495	495	—
California State Univ., Chico; Chico, Calif. 95929[22]	6,795[1]	7,134[1]	808	S	239	2,160	2,200
California St. Univ., Dominguez Hills; Carson, Calif. 90747[22]	1,902[6]	2,650[6]	200	S	225	2,385	3,000[9]
California State Univ., Fresno; Fresno, Calif. 93740[22]	7,792	8,112	710	S	281	2,160	2,000
California State Univ., Fullerton; Fullerton, Calif. 92634[22]	10,759[1]	11,711[1]	676	S	235	2,160	3,000
California State Univ., Hayward; Hayward, Calif. 94542[22]	4,787[1]	5,879[1]	476	S	212	2,160	1,648
California State University, Long Beach; Long Beach, Calif. 90840[22]	7,639	8,310	1,700	S	256	2,416	2,500
California State University, Los Angeles; Los Angeles, Calif. 90032[22]	9,083	11,404	810	S	300	3,185	—
California State University, Northridge; Northridge, Calif. 91330[22]	12,026	14,423	908	S	232	2,392	3,330
California State University, Sacramento; Sacramento, Calif. 95819[22]	6,656	6,815	828	S	245	3,080	2,000
California Western School of Law; San Diego, Calif. 92101	534	162	24	P	5,190	5,190	3,300
Calumet College; Whiting, Ind. 46394	203[1]	224[1]	30	P/RC	1,673	1,673	—
Calvary Bible College; Kansas City, Mo. 64147	186	168	20	ND	1,600	1,600	1,592
Calvin College; Grand Rapids, Mich. 49506	1,797[1]	1,987[1]	204	P/CR	3,000	3,000	1,520
Cameron University; Lawton, Okla. 73505	1,234	1,431	175	S	450	1,200	1,552
Campbellsville College; Campbellsville, Ky. 42718	276	315	43	P/SB	2,440	2,440	1,770
Campbell University; Buie's Creek, N.C. 27506	1,203[1]	905[1]	103	P/SB	3,002	3,027	762
Canisius College; Buffalo, N.Y. 14208	1,746[1]	1,122[1]	151	P	3,050	3,050	1,850
Capital University; Columbus, Ohio 43209	1,351	1,156	119	P/AL	4,720	4,720	2,018
Capitol Institute of Technology; Kensington, Md. 20795	639	51	13	P	2,628	2,628	—
Cardinal Stritch College; Milwaukee, Wis. 53217	98	382	52	P	3,200	3,200	1,800
Caribbean Center for Advanced Studies, Santurce, P.R. 00940	92	142	6	P	(26)	(26)	—
Caribbean University College; Bayamón, P.R. 00619	432	174	36	P	1,470	1,470	—
Carleton College; Northfield, Minn. 55057	923	901	142	P	4,885	4,885	6,940
Carlow College; Pittsburgh, Pa. 15213	25	631	45	P/RC	4,140	1,140	2,280
Carnegie–Mellon University; Pittsburgh, Pa. 15213	3,381[1]	1,444[1]	432	P	5,400[14]	5,400[14]	2,530[14]
Carroll College; Helena, Mont. 59601	550[1]	776[1]	75	P/RC	2,060	2,060	1,600
Carroll College; Waukesha, Wis. 53186	500	576	75	P/UP	4,710[14]	4,710[14]	1,680
Carson–Newman College; Jefferson City, Tenn. 37760	833[1]	836[1]	96	P/SB	2,200	2,200	1,500
Carthage College, Kenosha, Wis. 53141	541	512	79	P/LCA	1,825	1,825	775
Case Western Reserve University; Cleveland, Ohio 44106	3,849	1,989	1,150	P	5,400	5,400	2,700
Castleton State College*; Castleton, Vt. 05701	560	703	88	S	1,120	2,760	2,100
Catawba College; Salisbury, N.C. 28144	480	428	64	P/UCC	2,850	2,850	1,360
Cathedral College of the Immaculate Conception*; Douglaston, N.Y. 11362	—	135	31	RC	2,600	2,600	2,000
Catholic University of America, The; Washington, D.C. 20064	2,239[1]	2,322[1]	448	P/RC	5,200	5,200	4,000
Catholic University of Puerto Rico*; Ponce, P.R. 00731	3,048	5,524	n.a.	P/RC	n.a.	n.a.	n.a.
Cayey University College. *See* Puerto Rico, University of							
Cedar Crest College; Allentown, Pa. 18104	1[1]	742[1]	52	P	4,500[6]	4,500[6]	2,100
Cedarville College; Cedarville, Ohio 45314	626	719	62	P/B	2,400	2,400	1,794
Centenary College; Hackettstown, N.J. 07840	—	593	48	P	6,200[27]	6,200[27]	—
Center for Early Education, Coll. of the; Los Angeles, Calif. 90048	3	58	—	P	1,800	1,800	5,400
Centenary College of Louisiana; Shreveport, La. 71104	492	468	66	P/M	2,700	2,700	1,000
Central Arkansas, University of; Conway, Ark. 72032	2,078	3,113	267	S	740	1,450	1,500
Central Baptist College*; Conway, Ark. 72032	98	70	12	B	720	720	1,040
Central Bible College; Springfield, Mo. 65802	676	420	50	P/AG	1,716	1,716	1,490
Central Connecticut State College; New Britain, Conn. 06050	3,562	3,023	414	S	830	1,770	2,129
Central Florida, University of; Orlando, Fla. 32816	4,142[1]	3,548[1]	459	S	708	2,013	1,596
Central Methodist College; Fayette, Mo. 65248	317[1]	331[1]	60	P/M	3,450	3,450	1,600
Central Michigan University; Mt. Pleasant, Mich. 48859	6,030	7,455	617	S	1,145	2,840	1,998
Central Missouri State University; Warrensburg, Mo. 64093	4,864	5,125	441	S	525	1,600	1,650
Central New England College of Technology*; Worcester, Mass. 01610	895	310	22	P	2,400	2,400	1,600

Institution and location	Enrollment Male	Female	Faculty	Control	Tuition Res.	Nonres.	Rm/Bd
Central State University; Edmond, Okla. 73034	3,903	4,767	336	S	410	840	1,136
Central State University*; Wilberforce, Ohio 45384	1,212	1,160	112	S	882	1,107	1,182
Central University of Iowa; Pella, Iowa 50219	620	764	73	P/RCA	4,110	4,110	1,644
Central Washington University; Ellensburg, Wash. 98926	3,399	3,998	321	S	618	1,833	2,000
Central Wesleyan College; Central, S.C. 29630	186	214	30	P/W	3,200	3,200	1,750
Centre College of Kentucky; Danville, Ky. 40422	422[1]	327[1]	65	P	4,600[14]	4,600[14]	2,100[14]
Chadron State College; Chadron, Neb. 69337	636	672	77	S	664	1,114	1,360
Chaminade University of Honolulu; Honolulu, Hawaii 96816	1,474	831	55	P/RC	2,660	2,660	2,335
Chapman College; Orange, Calif. 92666	530	534	95	P/DC	4,970[14]	4,970[14]	2,200[14]
Charleston, The College of; Charleston, S.C. 29401	1,643[1]	2,570[1]	185	S	850	1,750	1,560
Charleston, University of; Charleston, W. Va. 25304	361[1]	492[1]	72	P	2,700	2,700	2,280
Chatham College; Pittsburgh, Pa. 15232	—	555[1]	56	P	4,425	4,425	2,175
Chestnut Hill College; Philadelphia, Pa. 19118	—	621	45	RC	2,850	2,850	2,000
Cheyney State College*; Cheyney, Pa. 19319	1,100	1,257	178	S	1,210	2,040	1,250
Chicago, The University of*; Chicago, Ill. 60637	1,800	900	1,020	P	5,100	5,100	3,000
Chicago College of Osteopathic Medicine; Chicago, Ill. 60615	316	71	270	P	7,500	7,500	4,200
Chicago Conservatory College*; Chicago, Ill. 60605	23	25	19	P	2,380	2,380	—
Chicago State University; Chicago, Ill. 60628	1,157	1,982	265	S	788	2,168	—
Christian Brothers College; Memphis, Tenn. 38104	691	413	75	P/RC	3,050	3,050	2,024
Christopher Newport College; Newport News, Va. 23606	717	903	112	S	1,110	1,443	—
Cincinnati, University of; Cincinnati, Ohio 45221	12,850[1]	10,214[1]	1,779	S	1,154	2,723	2,076
Circleville Bible College; Circleville, Ohio 43113	136	101	16	P/CC	2,186	2,186	1,398
Citadel, The*; Charleston, S.C. 29409	2,568	817	200	S	125	385	1,420
City College; Seattle, Wash. 98104	1,185[1]	763[1]	6[28]	P	n.a.	n.a.	—
City College (NYC). See New York, City University of							
Claflin College*; Orangeburg, S.C. 29115	286	580	62	P/UM	1,850	1,850	1,125
Claremont Colleges:							
Claremont Graduate School*; Claremont, Calif. 91711	433	186	58	P	4,050	4,050	—
Claremont Men's College; Claremont, Calif. 91711	601	197	73	P	5,450	5,450	2,240
Harvey Mudd College; Claremont, Calif. 91711	401	70	64	P	6,200[14]	6,200[14]	2,700
Pitzer College; Claremont, Calif. 91711	286	394	55	P	5,370	5,370	2,052
Pomona College; Claremont, Calif. 91711	650[1]	650[1]	n.a.	P	6,250	6,250	2,650
Scripps College; Claremont, Calif. 91711	—	545	49	P	5,176	5,176	2,500
Clarion State College; Clarion, Pa. 16214	2,273	2,693	309	S	1,320	2,130	1,360
Clark College; Atlanta, Ga. 30314	659	1,363	129	P/UM	2,700	2,700	1,600
Clarke College; Dubuque, Iowa 52001	46	451	46	P/RC	3,475	3,475	1,695
Clarkson College of Technology; Potsdam, N.Y. 13676	3,016[1]	686[1]	190	P	5,100[14]	5,100[14]	2,415[14]
Clark University; Worcester, Mass. 01610	998[1]	963[1]	135	P	6,300	6,300	2,100
Cleary College; Ypsilanti, Mich. 48197	150	457	16	P	(29)	(29)	—
Clemson University; Clemson, S.C. 29631	6,599[1]	4,292[1]	718	S	1,210	2,488	1,520
Cleveland Institute of Art, The; Cleveland, Ohio 44106	246[6]	266[6]	45	P	3,575	3,575	2,550
Cleveland Institute of Music*; Cleveland, Ohio 44106	120	124	n.a.	P	n.a.	n.a.	n.a.
Cleveland State University; Cleveland, Ohio 44115	10,588	8,662	550	S	1,089	2,978	1,830
Clinch Valley College. See Virginia, University of							
Coe College; Cedar Rapids, Iowa 52402	572	502	85	P	3,890	3,890	1,500
Cogswell College; San Francisco, Calif. 94108	387[6]	51[6]	25	P	3,000	4,000	—
Coker College; Hartsville, S.C. 29550	100[1]	213[1]	38	P	3,030	3,030	1,680
Colby College; Waterville, Me. 04901	883[1]	780[1]	120	P	6,210	6,210	2,550
Colby–Sawyer College; New London, N.H. 03257	4	518	n.a.	P	4,683	4,683	1,992
Colegio Universitario Metropolitano. See Ana G. Méndez Educational Foundation							
Colgate University; Hamilton, N.Y. 13346	1,342	1,008	219	P	6,345	6,345	2,425
College Misericordia; Dallas, Pa. 18612	131[1]	719[1]	103	P/RC	2,880	2,880	1,750
Colorado, University of; Boulder, Colo. 80302							
U. of Colorado at Boulder; Boulder, Colo. 80309	11,251	9,402	1,000	S	900	3,200	1,700
U. of Colorado at Colorado Springs; Colorado Springs, Colo. 80907	2,233	2,594	117	S	600	2,600	—
U. of Colorado at Denver; Denver, Colo. 80202	1,222	1,075	246	S	666	2,530	—
Colorado College, The; Colorado Springs, Colo. 80903	991	963	136	P	5,500	5,500	1,800
Colorado School of Mines; Golden, Colo. 80401	2,018	377	175	S	1,282	4,564	1,800
Colorado State University; Fort Collins, Colo. 80523	9,556[1]	8,527[1]	950	S	828	2,930	2,000
Colorado Technical College; Colorado Springs, Colo. 80907	310	72	40	P	2,475	2,475	—
Colorado Women's College; Denver, Colo. 80220	—	509[1]	12	P	(30)	(30)	2,150
Columbia Christian College; Portland, Ore. 97220	127	136	14	P/CC	2,452	2,452	1,785
Columbia College; Chicago, Ill. 60605	1,214[1]	1,151[1]	60	P	2,970[14]	2,970[14]	n.a.
Columbia College; Columbia, Mo. 65201	345	441	50	P/ChC	3,725	3,725	1,950
Columbia College; Columbia, S.C. 29203	—	964[1]	68	P/M	3,300	3,300	1,900
Columbia College; Los Angeles, Calif. 90038	237	63	36	P	3,520	3,520	—
Columbia Union College; Takoma Park, Md. 20012	342[1]	530[1]	65	P/SDA	4,000	4,000	2,100
Columbia University*; New York, N.Y. 10027	9,379	4,706	1,530	P	6,010	6,010	2,920

Institution and location	Enrollment Male	Enrollment Female	Faculty	Control	Tuition Res.	Tuition Nonres.	Rm/Bd
Barnard College*; New York, N.Y. 10027	—	2,441	149	P	5,120	5,120	2,320
Teachers College; New York, N.Y. 10027	600	1,100	150	P	4,560	4,560	[31]
Columbus College; Columbus, Ga. 31993	997	1,241	196	S	540	1,512	—
Columbus College of Art and Design, The; Columbus, Ohio 43215	359[1]	386[1]	41	P	3,350	3,350	900[2]
Concord College; Athens, W. Va. 24712	750[1]	966[1]	86	S	472	1,412	1,885
Concordia College; Ann Arbor, Mich. 48105	288	236	45	L	2,274	2,274	1,830
Concordia College; Bronxville, N.Y. 10708	159[1]	198[1]	33	P/L	2,870	2,870	2,120
Concordia College; Milwaukee, Wis. 53208	188[1]	177[1]	28	P/L	3,050	3,050	1,700
Concordia College; Moorhead, Minn. 56560	1,134[1]	1,491[1]	147	P/AL	3,635	3,635	1,325
Concordia College; River Forest, Ill. 60305	408[1]	789[1]	88	L	2,650	2,650	1,850
Concordia College; St. Paul, Minn. 55104	316	298	54	P/L	2,790	2,790	1,470
Concordia Teachers College, Seward, Neb. 68434	442[1]	583[1]	90	L	2,750	2,750	1,570
Connecticut, University of*; Storrs, Conn. 06268	8,642	7,857	1,544	S	540	1,230	1,930
Connecticut College; New London, Conn. 06320	638	1,058	139	P	6,850	6,850	2,450
Conservatory of Music of Puerto Rico; Hato Rey, P.R. 00918	145[1]	40[1]	25	S	210	210	
Converse College; Spartanburg, S.C. 29301	3[1]	745[1]	82	P	4,000	4,000	2,250
Cooper Union, The; New York, N.Y. 10003	620[1]	250[1]	49	P			
Coppin State College; Baltimore, Md. 21216	435	1,260	142	S	1,045	1,995	—
Cornell College; Mt. Vernon, Iowa 52314	488[1]	445[1]	70	P	5,112	5,112	1,866
Cornell University[32]; Ithaca, N.Y. 14853	10,480[1]	7,085[1]	1,850	P	7,000[14]	7,000[14]	2,885
Cornish Institute of Allied Arts*; Seattle, Wash. 98102	128	162	30	P	2,520	2,520	—
Corpus Christi State Univ. See South Texas, Univ. System of							
Covenant College; Lookout Mountain, Tenn./Ga. 37350	259[1]	229[1]	31	P/RP	3,760	3,760	1,990
Cranbrook Academy of Art; Bloomfield Hills, Mich. 48013	77	72	9	P	3,750	3,750	2,600
Creative Studies, Center for; Detroit, Mich. 48202	306	263	42	P	3,900	3,900	—
Creighton University; Omaha, Neb. 68178	2,968[1]	1,977[1]	465	P	3,700	3,700	1,892
Criswell Bible College*; Dallas, Tex. 75201	180	17	n.a.	P/B	n.a.	n.a.	n.a.
Culver–Stockton College; Canton, Mo. 63435	236	226	35	P/DC	3,350	3,350	1,750
Cumberland College; Williamsburg, Ky. 40769	776[1]	928[1]	99	P/B	1,823	1,823	1,224
Curry College; Milton, Mass. 02186	388	381	56	P	4,950	4,950	2,900
Curtis Institute of Music, The; Philadelphia, Pa. 19103	77	80	69[11]	P	—	—	—
C.W. Post Center. See Long Island Univ. Center							
Daemen College; Amherst, N.Y. 14226	382[1]	805[1]	76	P	3,250	3,250	1,750
Dakota State College; Madison, S.D. 57042	368[1]	485[1]	51	S	748	1,552	1,380
Dakota Wesleyan University*; Mitchell, S.D. 57301	203	364	40	P/UM	2,765	2,765	1,806
Dallas, University of; Irving, Tex. 75061	1,738[1]	950[1]	87	RC	3,000	3,000	2,050
Dallas Baptist College; Dallas, Tex. 75211	1,182		53	P/B	(19)	(19)	1,490
Dallas Bible College; Dallas, Tex. 75228	149	77	10	P	2,200	2,200	1,600
Dallas Christian College; Dallas, Tex. 75234	66	42	11	ChC	1,264	1,264	1,708
Dana College; Blair, Neb. 68008	275[1]	289[1]	35	P/AL	3,000	3,000	1,355
Daniel Webster College*; Nashua, N.H. 03060	565	155	18	P	3,980	3,980	2,000
Dartmouth College; Hanover, N.H. 03755	3,235	1,469	552	P	6,075	6,075	1,350
David Lipscomb College; Nashville, Tenn. 37203	1,012	1,101	104	P	2,000	2,000	1,500
Davidson College; Davidson, N.C. 28036	910	478	109	P/Pres	4,900[14]	4,900[14]	1,975[14]
Davis and Elkins College; Elkins, W. Va. 26241	500[1]	480[1]	81	P/Pres	3,600	3,600	1,800
Dayton, University of; Dayton, Ohio 45469	4,914	3,745	355	P/RC	3,200	3,200	1,820
Defiance College, The; Defiance, Ohio 43512	306	311	48	P	3,970	3,970	1,870
Delaware, University of; Newark, Del. 19711	8,715[1]	10,543[1]	n.a.	Pub[33]	1,160	2,900	2,168
Delaware Law School of Widener University; Wilmington, Del. 19803	593	171	28	P	4,100	4,100	—
Delaware State College; Dover, Del. 19901	722	895	150	S	570	1,470	1,650
Delaware Valley College of Science and Agriculture; Doylestown, Pa. 18901	840	450	80	P	3,820	3,820	1,805
Delta State University*; Cleveland, Miss. 38733	1,011	1,183	157	S	554	1,329	912
Denison University; Granville, Ohio 43023	1,047	1,049	149	P	5,670[14]	5,670[14]	2,065[14]
Denver, University of; Denver, Colo. 80208	2,925[1]	2,670[1]	485	P	4,530	4,530	1,875
DePaul University; Chicago, Ill. 60604	4,157[1]	3,513[1]	398	P	3,588[14]	3,588[14]	2,474[14]
Goodman School of Drama*; Chicago, Ill. 60614	100	100	20	P	3,600	3,600	2,000
DePauw University; Greencastle, Ind. 46135	1,095	1,312	147	P/M	5,482	5,482	2,300
Detroit, University of; Detroit, Mich. 48221	2,100[1]	1,400[1]	251	P/RC	4,230	4,230	2,100
Detroit Bible College*; Detroit, Mich. 48018	64	43	13	P/ID	1,970	1,970	800
Detroit College of Business; Dearborn, Mich. 48126	438[1]	1,001[1]	17	P	2,496[14]	2,496[14]	—
Branch Campus*; Flint, Mich. 48504	n.a.	n.a.	n.a.	P	n.a.	n.a.	n.a.
Detroit College of Law; Detroit, Mich. 48201	616	253	28	P	3,450	3,450	—
Detroit Institute of Technology, The*; Detroit, Mich. 48201	331	136	27	P	2,100	2,100	—
DeVry Institute of Technology*; Atlanta, Ga. 30308	668	51	n.a.	P	n.a.	n.a.	n.a.
DeVry Institute of Technology*; Chicago, Ill. 60618	2,313	184	44	P	2,425	2,425	—
DeVry Institute of Technology*; Dallas, Tex. 75235	774	37	15	P	2,425	2,425	—

Institution and location	Enrollment Male	Enrollment Female	Faculty	Control	Tuition Res.	Tuition Nonres.	Rm/Bd
DeVry Institute of Technology*; Phoenix, Ariz. 85016	2,386	181	36	P	2,425	2,425	—
Dickinson College; Carlisle, Pa. 17013	783	936	114	P	5,840	5,840	2,150
Dickinson School of Law; Carlisle, Pa. 17013	337	163	18	P	3,100	3,100	1,700
Dickinson State College*; Dickinson, N.D. 58601	449	613	74	S	471	1,032	1,200
Dillard University; New Orleans, La. 70122	306[1]	902[1]	92	P	2,200	2,200	1,700
District of Columbia, University of the*; Washington, D.C. 20004	2,073	2,091	668	S	165	1,415	2,925
Georgia Ave.–Harvard St. Campus*; Washington, D.C. 20009	n.a.	n.a.	n.a.	S	n.a.	n.a.	n.a.
Mount Vernon Square Campus*; Washington, D.C. 20005	n.a.	n.a.	n.a.	S	n.a.	n.a.	n.a.
Van Ness Campus*; Washington, D.C. 20008	n.a.	n.a.	n.a.	S	n.a.	n.a.	n.a.
Divine Word College*; Epworth, Iowa 52045	88	—	20	P/RC	2,600	2,600	1,100
Doane College; Crete, Neb. 68333	301[1]	335[1]	45	P	3,750[14]	3,750[14]	1,450[14]
Dr. Martin Luther College; New Ulm, Minn. 56073	220	536	72	EL	1,460	1,460	1,152
Dominican College of Blauvelt; Orangeburg, N.Y. 10962	12	38	61	P	2,250	2,250	—
Dominican College of San Rafael; San Rafael, Calif. 94901	121	421	58	P/RC	3,950	3,950	2,850
Dordt College; Sioux Center, Iowa 51250	533[14]	627[14]	70	P	3,400	3,400	1,410
Dowling College; Oakdale, N.Y. 11769	2,070		70	P	3,960	3,960	1,300[2]
Drake University; Des Moines, Iowa 50311	3,167[1]	3,425[1]	250	P	4,590[6]	4,590[6]	2,120[6]
Drew University*; Madison, N.J. 07940	779	853	130	P/UM	4,700	4,700	1,820
Drexel University; Philadelphia, Pa. 19104	5,030	2,139	330	P	4,011	4,011	n.a.
Dropsie University, The; Philadelphia, Pa. 19132	59	6	12	P	4,200	4,200	—
Drury College; Springfield, Mo. 65802	520	592	67	P	3,150	3,150	1,700
Dubuque, University of; Dubuque, Iowa 52001	556	483	50	P	3,650	3,650	1,550
Duke University; Durham, N.C. 27706	5,230[1]	3,721[1]	1,412	P	5,400	5,400	2,863
Duquesne University; Pittsburgh, Pa. 15282	3,102	3,345	294	P	4,175	4,175	2,013
Dyke College; Cleveland, Ohio 44114	450	1,000	25	P	1,800	1,800	—
D'Youville College; Buffalo, N.Y. 14201	197[1]	1,331[1]	80	P	3,440	3,440	1,950
Earlham College; Richmond, Ind. 47374	453	524	78	P/SOF	5,658	5,658	1,950
East Carolina Univ. See North Carolina, Univ. System of							
East Central Oklahoma State University; Ada, Okla. 74820	1,269	1,572	147	S	350	900	1,270
Eastern College; St. Davids, Pa. 19151	192	333	36	P/AB	3,500	3,500	1,900
Eastern Connecticut State College; Willimantic, Conn. 06226	997	1,155	116	S	440	1,030	1,931
Eastern Illinois University; Charleston, Ill. 61920	4,186	5,227	672	S	995	2,327	1,771
Eastern Kentucky University; Richmond, Ky. 40475	4,531[1]	5,633[1]	602	S	787	2,030	1,837
Eastern Mennonite College; Harrisonburg, Va. 22801	369	554	63	P/Men	3,360	3,360	1,566
Eastern Michigan University; Ypsilanti, Mich. 48197	8,888[1]	12,401[1]	606	S	999	2,394	1,643
Eastern Montana College; Billings, Mont. 59101	979[1]	1,566[1]	150	S	624	1,632	1,900
Eastern Nazarene College; Quincy, Mass. 02170	357[1]	475[1]	58	P/Naz	2,520	2,520	1,630
Eastern New Mexico University; Portales, N.M. 88130	1,394[1]	1,462[1]	150	S	678	1,792	1,500
Eastern Oregon State College; La Grande, Ore. 97850	856	1,006	100	S	1,035	1,035	1,995
Eastern Virginia Medical School; Norfolk, Va. 23501	189	86	142	P	7,000[14]	9,000[14]	4,200
Eastern Washington University; Cheney, Wash. 99004	3,177	3,032	375	S	618	1,983	1,680
East Stroudsburg State College; East Stroudsburg, Pa. 18301	1,612[1]	1,945[1]	240	S	1,360	2,300	1,426
East Tennessee State University[34]; Johnson City, Tenn. 37614	4,113[1]	5,040[1]	530	S	680	2,160	1,410
East Texas Baptist College; Marshall, Tex. 75670	468[1]	452[1]	45	P/B	1,652	1,652	1,630
East Texas State University; Commerce, Tex. 75428	3,887	4,181	341	S	456	1,536	1,600
East Texas State University at Texarkana; Texarkana, Tex. 75501	462[1]	786[1]	32	S	300	690	—
Eckerd College; St. Petersburg, Fla. 33733	543	463	70	P/Pres	5,095	5,095	2,145
Edgewood College; Madison, Wis. 53711	97	361	48	P/RC	3,100	3,100	1,660
Edinboro State College*; Edinboro, Pa. 16444	2,337	3,259	390	S	1,100	1,930	1,170
Edward Waters College; Jacksonville, Fla. 32209	277	625	n.a.	P	n.a.	n.a.	n.a.
Eisenhower College of Rochester Institute of Technology; Seneca Falls, N.Y. 13148	305	220	50	P	4,383	4,383	2,566
Elizabeth City State University. See North Carolina, University System of							
Elizabethtown College; Elizabethtown, Pa. 17022	539	877	100	P/CB	3,825	3,825	1,875
Elmhurst College; Elmhurst, Ill. 60126	1,590		98[1]	P/UCC	3,988[1]	3,988[1]	2,060[1]
Elmira College; Elmira, N.Y. 14901	458[1]	716[1]	65	P	4,100	4,100	1,875
Elon College; Elon College, N.C. 27244	1,368[1]	1,208[1]	84	P	2,230	2,230	1,371
Embry–Riddle Aeronautical University; Daytona Beach, Fla. 32014	4,588[1]	272[1]	200	P	2,600	2,600	4,500
Emerson College*; Boston, Mass. 02116	670	794	78	P	4,360	4,360	2,825
Emmanuel College; Boston, Mass. 02115	4[1]	702[1]	61	P/RC	4,700	4,700	2,600
Emory and Henry College; Emory, Va. 24327	378	342	58	P/UM	2,874	2,874	1,626
Emory University; Atlanta, Ga. 30322	3,811	2,735	1,195	P/UM	5,400	5,400	1,830

Institution and location	Enrollment				Tuition		Rm/Bd
	Male	Female	Faculty	Control	Res.	Nonres.	
Emporia State University; Emporia, Kan. 66801	2,364	3,258	242	S	609	1,259	1,730
Erskine College; Due West, S.C. 29639	322	319	49	P/RP	3,350	3,350	1,650
Eureka College; Eureka, Ill. 61530	231[1]	219[1]	43	P/DC	3,375	3,375	1,920
Evangel College; Springfield, Mo. 65802	764	1,021	73	P	1,940	1,940	1,590
Evansville, University of; Evansville, Ind. 47702	1,429[1]	1,749[1]	200	P/UM	3,705	3,705	1,935
Evergreen State College, The; Olympia, Wash. 98505	1,155	1,317	206	S	618	1,983	1,900
Fairfield University; Fairfield, Conn. 06430	1,485[1]	1,565[1]	171	P/RC	4,450[14]	4,450[14]	2,500[14]
Fairleigh Dickinson University; Rutherford, N.J. 07070	3,757[1]	3,205[1]	531	P	4,032	4,032	2,066
Florham–Madison Campus*; Madison, N.J. 07940	n.a.	n.a.	n.a.	P	n.a.	n.a.	n.a.
Rutherford Campus*; Rutherford, N.J. 07070	n.a.	n.a.	n.a.	P	n.a.	n.a.	n.a.
Teaneck–Hackensack Campus*; Teaneck, N.J. 07666	n.a.	n.a.	n.a.	P	n.a.	n.a.	n.a.
Fairmont State College; Fairmont, W. Va. 26554	1,603[1]	1,687[1]	151	S	365	1,304	1,824
Faith Baptist Bible College; Ankeny, Iowa 50021	219	202	19	P/B	1,800	1,800	1,690
Fashion Institute of Technology[35]; New York, N.Y. 10001	593[1]	2,971[1]	180	S	900	1,800	2,350
Fayetteville State U. See North Carolina, U. System of							
Felician College; Lodi, N.J. 07644	17	689	52	P	2,100	2,100	
Ferris State College; Big Rapids, Mich. 49307	6,588[1]	4,524[1]	500	S	1,209	2,775	2,067
Ferrum College; Ferrum, Va. 24088	847	568	75	P/UM	2,040	2,040	1,200
Findlay College; Findlay, Ohio 45840	355[1]	346[1]	55	P/CG	3,992[14]	3,992[14]	1,800
Fisk University; Nashville, Tenn. 37203	287	614	66	P	3,750	3,750	1,935
Fitchburg State College; Fitchburg, Mass. 01420	1,487[1]	2,287[1]	207	S	750	2,538	1,728
Flagler College; St. Augustine, Fla. 32084	316	488	33	P	2,450	2,450	3,990
Florida, University of; Gainesville, Fla. 32611	16,955[1]	11,729[1]	2,833	S	750	2,350	2,400
Florida A&M University; Tallahassee, Fla. 32308	2,451	2,585	372	S	n.a.	n.a.	n.a.
Florida Atlantic University; Boca Raton, Fla. 33431	1,650	1,733	351	S	800	2,350	2,145
Florida Institute of Technology; Melbourne, Fla. 32901	3,414	847	155	P	2,268	2,268	2,205
Florida International University*; Miami, Fla. 33199	1,739	1,594	343	S	n.a.	n.a.	n.a.
Florida Memorial College*; Miami, Fla. 33054	400	432	44	P/B	1,440	1,440	1,320
Florida Southern College*; Lakeland, Fla. 33802	762	916	84	P/UM	2,430	2,430	1,850
Florida State University; Tallahassee, Fla. 32306	8,500[1]	9,479[1]	1,100	S	735	1,770	2,205
Fontbonne College; St. Louis, Mo. 63105	866		60	P/RC	3,550	3,550	925
Fordham University; Bronx, N.Y. 10458	7,078[1]	7,575[1]	499	P/RC	4,250	4,250	2,300
Fort Hays State University; Hays, Kan. 67601	2,543[1]	3,320[1]	316	S	690	1,343	1,552
Fort Lauderdale College; Fort Lauderdale, Fla. 33301	554	362	7	P	([36])	([36])	—
Fort Lewis College; Durango, Colo. 81301	1,788[1]	1,472[1]	150	S	483	2,123	1,422
Fort Valley State College, The*; Fort Valley, Ga. 31030	730	843	152	S	624	1,410	1,215
Fort Wayne Bible College; Fort Wayne, Ind. 46807	211	198	27	P/MC	2,400	2,400	1,520
Framingham State College; Framingham, Mass. 01701	1,020	2,062	155	S	600	2,100	1,502
Francis Marion College; Florence, S.C. 29501	1,254[1]	1,720[1]	104	S	680[14]	1,320[14]	1,900
Franklin and Marshall College; Lancaster, Pa. 17604	1,162[1]	916[1]	138	P	4,950	4,950	1,800
Franklin College of Indiana; Franklin, Ind. 46131	280	285	50	P	4,340	4,340	1,930
Franklin Pierce College; Rindge, N.H. 03461	493	388	65	P	4,490	4,490	2,625
Franklin University; Columbus, Ohio 43215	797	899	48	P	n.a.	n.a.	
Freed-Hardeman College; Henderson, Tenn. 38340	662	731	68	P/CC	2,450	2,450	1,610
Free Will Baptist Bible College; Nashville, Tenn. 37205	238	176	22	P/FWB	1,600	1,600	1,730
Fresno Pacific College; Fresno, Calif. 93702	331[1]	403[1]	32	P/MB	3,400	3,400	1,900
Friends Bible College; Haviland, Kan. 67059	64[6]	43[6]	10	P/SOF	1,400	1,400	2,800
Friends University; Wichita, Kan. 67213	433	404	50	P/SOF	3,200	3,200	1,540
Frostburg State College; Frostburg, Md. 21532	1,485	1,465	203	S	870	1,820	1,830
Furman University; Greenville, S.C. 29613	1,303	1,244	147	B	3,360	3,360	2,192
Gallaudet College*; Washington, D.C. 20002	510	706	175	P	684	684	1,725
Gannon University; Erie, Pa. 16541	1,393	979	125	P/RC	2,930	2,930	1,650
Gardner–Webb College; Boiling Springs, N.C. 28017	690[1]	736[1]	69	P/SB	2,960	2,960	1,695
General Motors Institute; Flint, Mich. 48502	1,606[1]	721[1]	148	P	1,344	1,344	1,210
Geneva College; Beaver Falls, Pa. 15010	589	482	62	RP	3,230	3,230	1,720
George Fox College; Newberg, Ore. 97132	294[1]	452[1]	43	P/SOF	3,600	3,600	1,770
George Mason University; Fairfax, Va. 22030	2,881[1]	3,446[1]	439	S	1,008	1,872	1,450
Georgetown College; Georgetown, Ky. 40324	514	546	62	P/SB	2,960	2,960	1,950
Georgetown University; Washington, D.C. 20057	6,718[1]	5,223[1]	929	P/RC	2,485	2,485	n.a.
George Washington University, The; Washington, D.C. 20052	4,898[1]	4,024[1]	1,090	P	4,100	4,100	2,940
George Williams College; Downers Grove, Ill. 60515	394	730	60	P	3,975	3,975	1,866
Georgia, University of; Athens, Ga. 30602	9,313[1]	9,031[1]	1,418	S	708	2,052	1,515
Georgia College; Milledgeville, Ga. 31061	1,464[1]	1,872[1]	144	S	645	1,602	1,260
Georgia Institute of Technology; Atlanta, Ga. 30332	8,405	2,050	685	S	1,000	2,585	2,250
Southern Technical Institute; Marietta, Ga. 30060	2,360[1]	223[1]	101	S	633	1,587	2,350
Georgian Court College; Lakewood, N.J. 08701	4	576	56	P/RC	2,700	2,700	1,700
Georgia Southern College; Statesboro, Ga. 30460	2,037[1]	2,532[1]	312	S	672	1,626	1,380
Georgia Southwestern College; Americus, Ga. 31709	639[1]	963[1]	114	S	666	1,620	1,650
Georgia State University; Atlanta, Ga. 30303	8,897[1]	11,436[1]	842	S	747	2,356	—

Institution and location	Enrollment Male	Enrollment Female	Faculty	Control	Tuition Res.	Tuition Nonres.	Rm/Bd
Germain School of Photography*; New York, N.Y. 10007	110	59	n.a.	P	n.a.	n.a.	n.a.
Gettysburg College; Gettysburg, Pa. 17325	963[1]	974[1]	132	P/L	5,300	5,300	1,900
Glassboro State College; Glassboro, N.J. 08028	2,574	3,354	387	S	963	1,603	1,930
Glenville State College; Glenville, W. Va. 26351	581	621	78	S	400	3,000	2,000
Golden Gate University; San Francisco, Calif. 94105	6,582[1]	3,669[1]	39[37]	P	3,210	3,210	—
Goldey Beacom College; Wilmington, Del. 19808	250	500	26	P	2,400	2,400	1,450[2]
Gonzaga University; Spokane, Wash. 99258	1,663	1,004	163	P/RC	4,040	4,040	2,110
Gordon College; Wenham, Mass. 01984	476[1]	596[1]	57	P	3,825	3,825	1,893
Goshen College; Goshen, Ind. 46526	485[1]	670[1]	108	P/Men	3,325	3,325	845
Goucher College; Towson, Baltimore, Md. 21204	3[1]	898[1]	70	P	5,400	5,400	2,900
Governors State University; Park Forest South, Ill. 60466	353[1]	397[1]	168	S	606	1,818	—
Grace Bible College; Grand Rapids, Mich. 49509	80[1]	60[1]	8	P/GGF	1,300	1,300	1,900
Grace College; Winona Lake, Ind. 46590	389	504	47	P/FGB	(38)	(38)	1,742
Grace College of the Bible; Omaha, Neb. 68108	238	196	25	P/ID	2,250	2,250	1,650
Graceland College; Lamoni, Iowa 50140	574[1]	594[1]	80	P/LDS	3,245	3,245	1,475
Graduate School and University Center (NYC). *See* New York, City University of							
Grambling State University; Grambling, La. 71245	1,643[1]	1,628[1]	184	S	442	442	1,360
Grand Canyon College; Phoenix, Ariz. 85017	418	456	34	P/SB	2,080	2,080	1,785
Grand Rapids Baptist College; Grand Rapids, Mich. 49505	464[1]	505[1]	40	P/B	2,650	2,650	1,950
Grand Valley State Colleges; Allendale, Mich. 49401		3,605	217	S	1,200	2,730	2,120
Grand View College; Des Moines, Iowa 50316	433[1]	487[1]	53	P/LCA	2,890[14]	2,890[14]	1,600
Gratz College; Philadelphia, Pa. 19141	25	55	7	P	375	375	—
Great Falls, College of; Great Falls, Mont. 59405	544	432	36	P/RC	2,850	2,850	1,550
Great Lakes Bible College; Lansing, Mich. 48901	91	67	13	P/CC	1,575	1,575	1,830
Green Mountain College; Poultney, Vt. 05764		386	27	P	4,050	4,050	2,550
Greensboro College; Greensboro, N.C. 27420	207	383	37	P/M	2,500	2,500	1,600
Greenville College; Greenville, Ill. 62246	344[1]	431[1]	46	P/FM	3,696	3,696	1,920
Grinnell College; Grinnell, Iowa 50112	641	546	105	P	5,785[6]	5,785[6]	1,765
Grove City College; Grove City, Pa. 16127	1,172[1]	1,055[2]	100	P	2,370[14]	2,370[14]	790
Guam, University of; Agana, Guam 96913	674	828	173	S	360	672	2,200
Guilford College; Greensboro, N.C. 27410	778[1]	660[1]	83	P/SOF	3,310	3,860	1,810
Gustavus Adolphus College; St. Peter, Minn. 56082	996[1]	1,391[1]	141	P/LCA	5,700[27]	5,700[27]	—
Gwynedd–Mercy College; Gwynedd Valley, Pa. 19437	194	1,502	92	RC	2,600	2,600	1,800
Hahnemann Medical College; Philadelphia, Pa. 19102	774	926	535	P	8,000	8,000	—
Hamilton College; Clinton, N.Y. 13323	1,011[1]	629[1]	135	P	6,150	6,150	1,950
Hamline University; St. Paul, Minn. 55104	929	648	87	P/UM	4,150	4,150	1,700
Hampden–Sydney College; Hampden–Sydney, Va. 23943	680	—	52	P/Pres	5,040	5,040	1,525
Hampshire College; Amherst, Mass. 01002	550	650	103	P	6,300	6,300	2,000
Hampton Institute; Hampton, Va. 23668	1,205[1]	1,745[1]	205	P	2,935[14]	2,935[14]	1,410[14]
Hannibal–LaGrange College; Hannibal, Mo. 63401	277	142	18	P/SB	2,200	2,200	1,320
Hanover College; Hanover, Ind. 47243	494[1]	518[1]	69	P/Pres	3,090[14]	3,090[14]	1,690[14]
Harding University; Searcy, Ark. 72143	1,278	1,352	175	P/CC	2,600	2,600	1,600
Hardin–Simmons University; Abilene, Tex. 79698	972[1]	997[1]	94	P/B	2,160	2,160	1,700
Harris–Stowe State College; St. Louis, Mo. 63103	343[1]	832[1]	32	S	450	955	—
Hartford, University of; West Hartford, Conn. 06117	2,600[1]	2,042[1]	310	P	5,000	5,000	3,200
Hartford Graduate Center, The*; Hartford, Conn. 06120	1,108	264	18	P	n.a.	n.a.	—
Hartwick College; Oneonta, N.Y. 13820	548	822	102	P	4,900	4,900	2,040
Harvard University; Cambridge, Mass. 02138	10,457[1]	5,675[1]	2,114	P	6,930[14]	6,930[14]	3,610[14]
Radcliffe College*; Cambridge, Mass. 02138	—	2,246	n.a.	P	5,300	5,300	2,840
Harvey Mudd College. *See* Claremont Colleges							
Hastings College; Hastings, Neb. 68901	356[1]	476[1]	54	P/Pres	2,850	2,850	810
Haverford College; Haverford, Pa. 19041	917	123	81	P	7,150	7,150	2,510
Hawaii, University of, at Hilo; Hilo, Hawaii 96720[39]	1,215	1,242	170	S	300	900	1,500
Hawaii, University of, at Manoa; Honolulu, Hawaii 96822[39]	7,910[1]	8,496[1]	1,586	S	450	1,125	2,965
Hawaii Loa College; Kaneohe, Hawaii 96744	161	137	26	P[40]	2,800	2,800	2,600
Hawaii Pacific College; Honolulu, Hawaii 96813	417[1]	233[1]	19	P	2,000	2,000	3,000
Hebrew College; Brookline, Mass. 02146	45	42	11	P	800	800	—
Heidelberg College; Tiffin, Ohio 44883	316	309	54	P	4,410	4,410	1,800
Henderson State University; Arkadelphia, Ark. 71923	1,100[1]	1,393[1]	165	S	790	1,510	1,500
Hendrix College; Conway, Ark. 72032	534	503	57	P	2,400	2,400	1,230
Herbert H. Lehman College. *See* New York, City University of							
High Point College; High Point, N.C. 27262	695[1]	745[1]	61	P/UM	2,700	2,700	1,690
Hillsdale College; Hillsdale, Mich. 49242	553[1]	453[1]	67	P	4,140	4,140	2,140
Hiram College; Hiram, Ohio 44234	469	413	75	P	4,659	4,659	1,525
Hobart and William Smith Colleges; Geneva, N.Y. 14456	1,088	727	131	P	6,300[14]	6,300[14]	2,335[14]
Hofstra University; Hempstead, N.Y. 11550	3,702	3,060	411	P	3,700	3,700	2,200
Hollins College; Hollins College, Va. 24020	—	920	76	P	5,300	5,300	2,600
Holy Apostles College; Cromwell, Conn. 06416	86	2	n.a.	P/RC	1,800	1,800	2,000

Institution and location	Enrollment		Faculty	Control	Tuition		Rm/Bd
	Male	Female			Res.	Nonres.	
Holy Cross, College of the; Worcester, Mass. 01610	1,319	1,199	172	P/RC	5,400	5,400	2,650
Holy Family College*; Mission San Jose, Calif. 94538	—	66	n.a.	P/RC	n.a.	n.a.	n.a.
Holy Family College; Philadelphia, Pa. 19114	66[1]	470[1]	40	P	2,650	2,650	—
Holy Names College; Oakland, Calif. 94619	174	218	51	P/RC	3,370	3,370	2,050
Holy Redeemer College; Waterford, Wis. 53185	42[1]	—	15	P/RC	1,740[14]	1,740[14]	1,620[14]
Hood College; Frederick, Md. 21701	21	820	107	P	4,135	4,135	2,125
Hope College; Holland, Mich. 49423	1,213[1]	1,251[1]	140	P/RCA	4,490	4,490	2,100
Houghton College; Houghton, N.Y. 14744	510[1]	752[1]	76	P/W	3,720[14]	3,720[14]	1,850[14]
Houston, University of, System:							
Central Campus*; Houston, Tex. 77004	15,637	12,777	955	S	400	1,260	2,025
Downtown College; Houston, Tex. 77002	1,156[1]	964[1]	97	S	380	1,240	
U. of Houston at Clear Lake City; Houston, Tex. 77058	2,700[1]	2,900[1]	n.a.	S	400	1,700	—
U. of Houston at Victoria; Victoria, Tex. 77901	40	120	25	S	356	1,618	—
Houston Baptist University; Houston, Tex. 77074	602	726	102	P/SB	3,135	3,135	1,715
Howard Payne University; Brownwood, Tex. 76801	456	432	78	P/SB	(8)	(8)	1,670
Howard University; Washington, D.C. 20059	4,285	4,456	1,096	P	1,965	1,965	2,109
Humacao University College. See Univ. of Puerto Rico							
Humboldt State University*; Arcata, Calif. 95521[22]	4,208	3,383	450	S	208	2,368	2,250
Hunter College. See New York, City University of							
Huntingdon College; Montgomery, Ala. 36106	227[1]	262[1]	40	P/UM	2,500[14]	2,500[14]	1,950[14]
Huntington College; Huntington, Ind. 46750	252	226	44	P/BC	3,600	3,600	1,820
Huron College; Huron, S.D. 57350	140	129	24[14]	P/Pres	2,970[14]	2,970[14]	1,820[14]
Husson College; Bangor, Me. 04401	335	372	35	P	3,360	3,360	2,050
Huston–Tillotson College; Austin, Tex. 78702	408	274	35	P	1,400	1,400	1,240
Idaho, The College of; Caldwell, Idaho 83605	278[1]	250[1]	37	P	3,950	3,950	1,800
Idaho, University of; Moscow, Idaho 83843	4,370[1]	2,496[1]	496	S	690	2,490	1,800
Idaho State University; Pocatello, Idaho 83209	2,665[1]	2,129[1]	314	S	680	2,380	1,840
Illinois, University of; Urbana, Ill. 61801							
Univ. of Illinois at Chicago Circle; Chicago, Ill. 60680	8,690[1]	6,697[1]	1,056	S	747	2,241	—
Univ. of Illinois at the Medical Center; Chicago, Ill. 60612	2,636[1]	2,276[1]	1,233	S	681	2,043	3,348
Univ. of Illinois at Urbana–Champaign, Urbana, Ill. 61801	19,401	13,761	3,076	S	682	2,046	2,128
Illinois Benedictine College; Lisle, Ill. 60532	755	692	100	P/RC	3,328	3,328	1,800
Illinois College; Jacksonville, Ill. 62650	428[1]	356[5]	45	P/UCC	2,820	2,820	1,730
Illinois College of Optometry; Chicago, Ill. 60616	507[1]	91[1]	73	P	5,500	5,500	3,000
Illinois College of Podiatric Medicine; Chicago, Ill. 60610	560	63	25	P	6,600	6,600	7,500
Illinois Institute of Technology; Chicago, Ill. 60616	3,491	819	256	P	4,970[14]	4,970[14]	2,380[14]
Illinois State University; Normal, Ill. 61761	6,899	8,529	960	S	680	2,040	1,998
Illinois Wesleyan University; Bloomington, Ill. 61701	723	941	125	P	4,815	4,815	2,070
Immaculata College; Immaculata, Pa. 19345	—	533	52	P/RC	2,700	2,700	1,850
Incarnate Word College; San Antonio, Tex. 78209	201	736	115	P/RC	2,760	2,760	1,474
Indiana Central University; Indianapolis, Ind. 46227	421	659	87	P	3,200	3,200	1,640
Indiana Institute of Technology; Fort Wayne, Ind. 46803	613[1]	151[1]	29	P	3,240	3,240	2,175
Indiana State University; Terre Haute, Ind. 47809	4,823[1]	4,595[1]	665	S	1,007	2,247	1,411
Evansville Campus; Evansville, Ind. 47712	1,544[1]	1,707[1]	94	S	992	2,248	
Indiana University; Bloomington, Ind. 47405	16,359[1]	15,518[1]	1,380	S	(41)	(42)	1,850
Indiana Univ. at Kokomo*; Kokomo, Ind. 46901	500	554	64	Mun	780	1,770	—
Indiana Univ.–Bloomington*; Bloomington, Ind. 47401	13,776	12,635	n.a.	S	n.a.	n.a.	n.a.
Indiana Univ. at South Bend; South Bend, Ind. 46615	825	969	157[43]	S	975	2,280	—
Indiana University Northwest*; Gary, Ind. 46408	501	904	115	S	780	1,020	—
Indiana University Southeast; New Albany, Ind. 47150	824[1]	1,044[1]	90	S	(44)	(45)	—
I.U.–Purdue U. at Fort Wayne; Fort Wayne, Ind. 46805	1,819	1,723	300	S	900	2,700	—
I.U.–Purdue U. at Indianapolis; Indianapolis, Ind. 46202	4,569	4,359	1,239	S	696	1,632	—
Indiana University of Pennsylvania; Indiana, Pa. 15705	4,493[6]	6,079[6]	606	S	1,100	1,930	680
Instituto Tecnológico*; Monterrey, Mexico	1,879	6,521	223	P	2,000	2,000	2,000
Insurance, The College of; New York, N.Y. 10038	235[1]	93[1]	33	P	4,000	4,000	1,500[2]
Inter American University of Puerto Rico; Santurce, P.R. 00910							
Arecibo Regional College*; Arecibo, P.R. 00612	532[1]	285[1]	28	P	(46)	(46)	—
Metropolitan Campus; Hato Rey, P.R. 00919	n.a.	n.a.	n.a.	P	n.a.	n.a.	n.a.
San Germán Campus; San Germán, P.R. 00753	1,982	5,223	232	P	1,082	1,082	—
San Juan Campus*; San Juan, P.R. 00919	2,094[1]	3,089[1]	145	P	1,500	1,500	1,240
School of Law*; Santurce, P.R. 00910	3,979	4,865	191	P	n.a.	n.a.	—
International Correspondence Institute*; Brussels, Belgium	586	256	25	P	3,000	3,000	—
International Institute of the Americas*; Hato Rey, P.R. 00917	n.a.	n.a.	n.a.	P	n.a.	n.a.	n.a.
International Training, The School for; Brattleboro, Vt. 05301	1,816	2,117	n.a.	P	n.a.	n.a.	n.a.
	207[1]	292[1]	31	P	5,655[14]	5,655[14]	2,925[14]

Institution and location	Enrollment		Faculty	Control	Tuition		Rm/Bd
	Male	Female			Res.	Nonres.	
Iona College*; New Rochelle, N.Y. 10801	3,285	2,297	170	P	3,280	3,280	2,100
Iowa, University of; Iowa City, Iowa 52242	10,699¹	9,178¹	1,337	S	950	2,350	1,834
Iowa State University; Ames, Iowa 50011	14,744¹	9,524¹	1,796	S	950	2,350	1,640
Iowa Wesleyan College; Mount Pleasant, Iowa 52641	244¹	371¹	50	P/UM	4,060¹⁴	4,060¹⁴	1,520¹⁴
Ithaca College; Ithaca, N.Y. 14850	1,957¹	2,310¹	289	P	5,000	5,000	2,276
Jackson College for Women. See Tufts University							
Jackson State University; Jackson, Miss. 39217	1,928	2,676	307	S	750	850	1,266
Jacksonville State University; Jacksonville, Ala. 36265	2,775¹	3,192¹	264	S	700	1,050	1,390
Jacksonville University; Jacksonville, Fla. 32211	1,145¹	878¹	94	P	3,390	3,390	2,286
James Madison University; Harrisonburg, Va. 22807	3,457¹	4,064¹	441	S	1,210	1,930	2,010
Jamestown College; Jamestown, N.D. 58401	304¹	333¹	n.a.	P/Pres	3,900¹⁴	3,900¹⁴	1,575¹⁴
Jarvis Christian College; Hawkins, Tex. 75765	262	293	41	P/DC	2,250	2,250	1,584
Jersey City State College; Jersey City, N.J. 07305	1,891	2,141	300	S	1,012	1,652	—
John Brown University; Siloam Springs, Ark. 72761	400¹	403¹	47	P/ID	2,300	2,300	1,700
John Carroll University; Cleveland, Ohio 44118	1,453¹	1,169¹	179	P/RC	3,500	3,500	2,000
John F. Kennedy University; Orinda, Calif. 94598	200¹	342¹	4	P	2,770	2,770	5,320
John Jay College of Criminal Justice. See New York, City University of							
John Marshall Law School, The; Chicago, Ill. 60604	724¹	255¹	45	P	3,920	3,920	n.a.
Johns Hopkins University, The; Baltimore, Md. 21218	5,773¹	4,080¹	1,322	P	5,850¹⁴	5,850¹⁴	2,665¹⁴
Johnson and Wales College; Providence, R.I. 02903	2,717		108	P	2,985	2,985	1,695
Johnson Bible College*; Knoxville, Tenn. 37920	202	160	n.a.	P/CC	n.a.	n.a.	n.a.
Johnson C. Smith University; Charlotte, N.C. 28216	625	715	78	P	1,840	1,840	1,326
Johnson State College; Johnson, Vt. 05656	379	348	58	S	1,120	2,760	2,100
Johnston College, Calif. See Redlands, University of							
Jones College; Jacksonville, Fla. 32211	648	531	18	P	1,620	1,620	—
Branch Campus*; Fort Pierce, Fla. 33450	809	345	n.a.	P	n.a.	n.a.	n.a.
Jones College*; Orlando, Fla. 32803	1,288		9	P	1,093	1,093	—
Judge Advocate General's School, U.S. Army*; Charlottesville, Va. 22901	58	2	n.a.	Pub	n.a.	n.a.	n.a.
Judson College; Elgin, Ill. 60120	165	172	22	P/AB	3,783	3,783	2,865
Judson College; Marion, Ala. 36756	—	501	n.a.	P/B	1,760	1,760	1,280
Juilliard School, The; New York, N.Y. 10023	489¹	367¹	159	P	3,500	3,500	—
Juniata College; Huntingdon, Pa. 16652	703¹	590¹	73	P	4,740¹⁴	4,740¹⁴	2,055¹⁴
Kalamazoo College; Kalamazoo, Mich. 49007	765¹	687¹	86	P/B	5,529	5,529	2,169
Kansas, University of; Lawrence, Kan. 66045	26,000		2,200	S	918	2,234	1,880
Kansas City Art Institute; Kansas City, Mo. 64111	308¹	280¹	44	P	4,740	4,740	1,030²
Kansas City College of Osteopathic Medicine; Kansas City, Mo. 64124	534	88	59	P	9,250	9,250	—
Kansas Newman College*; Wichita, Kan. 67213	219	239	26	P/RC	2,340	2,340	1,490
Kansas State University; Manhattan, Kan. 66506	10,450	7,884	1,544	S	764	1,844	1,450
Kansas Wesleyan University; Salina, Kan. 67401	227	185	32	P/UM	3,158	3,158	1,823
Kean College of New Jersey; Union, N.J. 07083	4,915	8,264	368¹	S	750	1,350	1,885
Kearney State College; Kearney, Neb. 68847	2,146¹	2,619¹	236	S	608	1,088	1,206
Keene State College; Keene, N.H. 03431	1,492	2,190	175	S	1,100	3,000	1,980
Keller Graduate School of Management; Chicago, Ill. 60606	1,100		70	P	(47)	(47)	—
Kendall College; Evanston, Ill. 60201	145	208	28	P	3,434	3,434	2,982
Kent State University; Kent, Ohio 44242	8,981¹	9,955¹	800	S	874	2,074	1,744
Kentucky, University of; Lexington, Ky. 40506	12,115¹	10,898¹	1,477	S	682	2,032	1,878
Kentucky Christian College; Grayson, Ky. 41143	196	195	18	P	646	646	1,624
Kentucky State University; Frankfort, Ky. 40601	654¹	547¹	101	S	700	1,800	1,500
Kentucky Wesleyan College; Owensboro, Ky. 42301	296	359	49	P/M	2,880	2,880	1,630
Kenyon College; Gambier, Ohio 43022	807¹	640¹	91	P	5,190	5,190	2,075
Keuka College; Keuka Park, N.Y. 14478	4	496	52	P	4,890	4,890	1,820
King College; Bristol, Tenn. 37620	138	104	26	P	2,850	2,850	1,650
King's College; Wilkes-Barre, Pa. 18711	967	711	100	P	1,830	1,830	990
King's College, The; Briarcliff Manor, N.Y. 10510	329¹	499¹	47	P/ND	4,050	4,050	1,650
Kirksville College of Osteopathic Medicine; Kirksville, Mo. 63501	426	74	85	P	11,500	11,500	4,230
Knox College; Galesburg, Ill. 61401	475	422	87	P	5,500¹⁴	5,500¹⁴	2,070¹⁴
Knoxville College*; Knoxville, Tenn. 37921	335	265	38	P/UP	2,400	2,400	1,635
Kutztown State College; Kutztown, Pa. 19530	1,648	2,215	320	S	1,250	2,190	1,480
Lafayette College; Easton, Pa. 18042	1,235¹	845¹	158	P	6,000	6,000	2,275
LaGrange College; LaGrange, Ga. 30240	425¹	525¹	52	P/UM	1,890	1,890	1,485
Lake Erie College; Painesville, Ohio 44077	102¹	407¹	46	P	5,365	5,365	2,085
Lake Forest College; Lake Forest, Ill. 60045	500	461	79	P	5,240	5,240	1,850
Lake Forest School of Management*; Lake Forest, Ill. 60045	252	77	25	P	1,700	1,700	—
Lakeland College; Sheboygan, Wis. 53081	250	212	35	P/UCC	3,640	3,640	2,030

Institution and location	Enrollment				Tuition		
	Male	Female	Faculty	Control	Res.	Nonres.	Rm/Bd
Lake Superior State College; Sault Ste. Marie, Mich. 49783	1,082[1]	886[1]	104	S	1,059	2,067	2,050
Lamar University; Beaumont, Tex. 77710	6,800	6,600	485	S	440	1,200	1,350
Lambuth College; Jackson, Tenn. 38301	216	360	53	P/UM	2,600	2,600	1,470
Lander College; Greenwood, S.C. 29646	512[1]	863[1]	84	S	1,050	1,050	1,650
Lane College; Jackson, Tenn. 38301	335	371	45	P/CME	2,064	2,064	1,405
Langston University; Langston, Okla. 73050	721	468	76	S	260	604	785
Laredo State Univ. *See* South Texas, Univ. System of							
La Roche College, Pittsburgh, Pa. 15237	515	934	34	P	2,750	2,750	2,050
LaSalle Extension University*; Chicago, Ill. 60605	n.a.	n.a.	n.a.	P	n.a.	n.a.	n.a.
U.S. School of Music, Inc.*; Chicago Ill. 60605	n.a.	n.a.	n.a.	P	n.a.	n.a.	n.a.
Washington School of Art*; Chicago, Ill. 60605	n.a.	n.a.	n.a.	P	n.a.	n.a.	n.a.
Wayne School*; Chicago, Ill. 60605	n.a.	n.a.	n.a.	P	n.a.	n.a.	n.a.
La Salle College; Philadelphia, Pa. 19141	2,574[1]	1,848[1]	205	P/RC	3,700	3,700	2,470
La Verne, University of; La Verne, Calif. 91750	1,155[1]		85	P	4,500	4,500	2,200
Lawrence Institute of Technology; Southfield, Mich. 48075	4,367	893	250	P	1,725	1,725	—
Lawrence University; Appleton, Wis. 54912	558[1]	549[1]	120	P	5,256	5,256	1,569
L.D.S. Business College*; Salt Lake City, Utah 84111	253	321	n.a.	P/LDS	n.a.	n.a.	n.a.
Lebanon Valley College; Annville, Pa. 17003	431	428	77	P/UM	4,650[14]	4,650[14]	2,185[14]
Lee College; Cleveland, Tenn. 37311	698[1]	632[1]	65	P	1,980	1,980	1,480
Lehigh University; Bethlehem, Pa. 18015	3,656[1]	1,312[1]	344	P	6,100[14]	6,100[14]	2,370[14]
Le Moyne College*; Syracuse, N.Y. 13214	1,012	838	n.a.	P	n.a.	n.a.	n.a.
LeMoyne-Owen College; Memphis, Tenn. 38126	336	594	64	P	930	1,000	n.a.
Lenoir–Rhyne College; Hickory, N.C. 28603	468[1]	701[1]	82	P/LCA	3,230[14]	3,230[14]	1,585[14]
Lesley College; Cambridge, Mass. 02238	28	1,012	45	P	4,800	4,800	2,830
LeTourneau College; Longview, Tex. 75607	875[1]	97[1]	65	P	3,150	3,150	1,630
Lewis and Clark College*; Portland, Ore. 97219	852	1,035	124	P/Pres	4,306	4,306	1,694
Lewis-Clark State College*; Lewiston, Idaho 83501	633	821	85	S	380	1,430	1,850
Lewis University; Romeoville, Ill. 60441	1,598[1]	1,215[1]	104	P/RC	3,840	3,840	1,800
Limestone College; Gaffney, S.C. 29340	139[1]	243[1]	31	P	3,170	3,170	1,660
Lincoln Christian College; Lincoln, Ill. 62656	188	167	21	P/ChC	1,958	1,958	1,150
Lincoln Memorial University; Harrogate, Tenn. 37752	443	637	40	P	2,025	2,025	1,575
Lincoln University; Jefferson City, Mo. 65101	1,454	1,189	143	S	450	850	1,140
Lincoln University; Lincoln University, Pa. 19352	614[1]	642[1]	72	P	1,430	1,930	1,650
Lindenwood Colleges, The; St. Charles, Mo. 63301	787[1]	1,182[1]	50	P	4,100	4,100	3,200
Linfield College; McMinnville, Ore. 97128	588[1]	654[1]	75	P	4,410	4,410	1,920
Livingstone College; Salisbury, N.C. 28144	508[1]	348[1]	53	P/AME	2,400	2,400	1,596
Livingston University; Livingston, Ala. 35470	441[1]	394[1]	74	S	723	723	1,332
Lock Haven State College; Lock Haven, Pa. 17745	1,119[1]	1,240[1]	170	S	1,250	2,190	1,312
Logan College of Chiropractic; Chesterfield, Mo. 63017	517	129	30	P	4,020	4,020	3,960
Loma Linda University; Loma Linda, Calif. 92350	2,688[1]	2,663[1]	943	SDA	4,725	4,725	n.a.
Long Island University Center*; Greenvale, N.Y. 11548	n.a.	n.a.	n.a.	P	n.a.	n.a.	n.a.
Arnold and Marie Schwartz College of Pharmacy and Health Sciences; Brooklyn, N.Y. 11581	500	300	40	P	4,000	4,000	1,300
Brooklyn Center; Brooklyn, N.Y. 11201	2,959	3,910	250	P	3,200	3,200	1,400
C.W. Post Center; Greenvale, N.Y. 11548	4,564[1]	4,802[1]	384	P	4,400	4,400	2,560
Southampton College; Southampton, N.Y. 11968	648[1]	588[1]	68	P	3,950	3,950	2,400
Longwood College; Farmville, Va. 23901	559	1,614	174	S	725	1,225	1,595
Loras College; Dubuque, Iowa 52001	882	575	103	P	3,550	3,550	5,300
Loretto Heights College*; Denver, Colo. 80236	161	652	75	P	3,900	3,900	2,170
Los Angeles Baptist College; Newhall, Calif. 91322	185[1]	164[1]	25	P/B	4,110	4,110	1,600
Los Angeles College of Chiropractic; Glendale, Calif. 91205	401	110	43	P	5,232	5,232	—
Louisiana College; Pineville, La. 71360	341	420	57	P/SB	1,350	1,350	1,300
Louisiana State University*; Baton Rouge, La. 70803	12,651	11,157	1,069	S	281	746	670
LSU and A&M College; Baton Rouge, La. 70803	12,201[1]	10,094[1]	1,325	S	664	1,596	1,908
LSU in Shreveport; Shreveport, La. 71112	1,617	1,846	139	S	290	805	
LSU Medical Center at New Orleans; New Orleans, La. 70112	1,359	1,067	800	S	(50)	(51)	1,500
Louisiana Tech University; Ruston, La. 71272	4,666[1]	3,143[1]	400	S	651	1,281	1,755
Louisville, University of; Louisville, Ky. 40292	6,290[1]	4,876[1]	923	S	670	2,000	1,405
Lowell, University of; Lowell, Mass. 01854	13,000		550	S	842	2,900	1,522
Loyola College; Baltimore, Md. 21210	3,123	2,851	125	P/RC	3,250	3,250	1,975
Loyola Marymount University; Los Angeles, Calif. 90045	3,204[1]	3,130[1]	282	P/RC	4,526	4,526	2,450
Loyola University, New Orleans; New Orleans, La. 70118	2,174[1]	2,442[1]	196	P/RC	3,200	3,200	2,200
Loyola University of Chicago; Chicago, Ill. 60611	4,186[1]	4,359[1]	666	P/RC	3,780	3,780	2,400
Lubbock Christian College; Lubbock, Tex. 79407	629	545	64	P/CC	2,400	2,400	1,370
Lutheran Bible Institute of Seattle; Issaquah, Wash. 98027	137	149	17	P/L	1,938	1,938	2,100
Luther College; Decorah, Iowa 52101	853	1,154	127	P/AL	4,750	4,750	1,450
Lycoming College; Williamsport, Pa. 17701	603[1]	457[1]	60	P/UM	3,720	3,720	1,770
Lynchburg College; Lynchburg, Va. 24501	745[6]	941[6]	114	P	4,200	4,200	2,100
Lyndon State College; Lyndonville, Vt. 05851	486	386	65	S	1,120	2,760	2,100

Institution and location	Enrollment Male	Enrollment Female	Faculty	Control	Tuition Res.	Tuition Nonres.	Rm/Bd
Macalester College; St. Paul, Minn. 55105	816	816	132	P	5,425	5,425	1,900
MacMurray College; Jacksonville, Ill. 62650	103[1]	531[1]	53	P/UM	3,990	3,990	1,800
Madonna College; Livonia, Mich. 48150	814	2,310	79	P	1,748	1,748	1,860
Maharishi International Univ.*; Fairfield, Iowa 52556	421	265	n.a.	P	n.a.	n.a.	n.a.
Maine, Univ. of, at Farmington; Farmington, Me. 04938	521[1]	1,446[1]	84	S	1,170	3,270	2,110
Maine, Univ. of, at Fort Kent; Fort Kent, Me. 04743	312	280	21	S	970	2,900	1,500
Maine, Univ. of, at Machias; Machias, Me. 04654	185	235	40	S	930	2,900	1,950
Maine, Univ. of, at Orono; Orono, Me. 04469	5,321	4,308	800	S	540	1,450	1,077
Maine, Univ. of, at Presque Isle; Presque Isle, Maine 04769	408	484	60	Pub	930	2,900	1,887
Maine Maritime Academy; Castine, Me. 04421	622[1]	24[1]	50	S	1,620	2,920	2,220
Malone College; Canton, Ohio 44709	360[1]	416[1]	40	P/SOF	3,934	3,934	1,875
Manchester College; North Manchester, Inc. 46962	536	580	77	P/CB	3,200	3,200	1,520
Manhattan Christian College; Manhattan, Kan. 66502	85	58	14	P/ChC	1,520	1,520	1,875
Manhattan College; Riverdale, Bronx, N.Y. 10471	3,409	1,496	220	P	3,450	3,450	2,600
Manhattan School of Music; New York, N.Y. 10027	277	283	—	P	4,000	4,000	3,375
Manhattanville College; Purchase, N.Y. 10577	264[1]	657[1]	74	P	5,750	5,750	2,950
Mankato State University. *See* Minnesota State College System							
Mannes College of Music*; New York, N.Y. 10021	116	81	100[11]	P	3,200	3,200	—
Mansfield State College; Mansfield, Pa. 16933	993	1,148	200	S	1,100	1,930	708
Marian College; Indianapolis, Ind. 46222	270[1]	575[1]	54	P/RC	2,920	2,920	2,020
Marian College of Fond du Lac; Fond du Lac, Wis. 54935	61	456	45	P/RC	2,900	2,900	1,500
Marietta College; Marietta, Ohio 45750	788	437	93	P	5,500	5,500	825
Marion College; Marion, Ind. 46952	335	437	62	P/W	2,880	2,880	1,642
Marist College; Poughkeepsie, N.Y. 12601	1,092	835	85	P	3,450	3,450	2,250
Marlboro College; Marlboro, Vt. 05344	96[1]	109[1]	22	P	5,680	5,680	2,800
Marquette University; Milwaukee, Wis. 53233	5,408[1]	3,993[1]	545	P/RC	4,010	4,010	2,100
Marshall University; Huntington, W. Va. 25701	5,308[1]	6,575[1]	373	S	392	1,382	2,090
Mars Hill College; Mars Hill, N.C. 28754	758[1]	1,104[1]	100	P/SB	2,960	2,960	1,355
Mary Baldwin College; Staunton, Va. 24401	—	785	54	P/Pres	3,900	3,900	2,465
Mary College; Bismarck, N.D. 58501	318[1]	670[1]	56	P/RC	2,430	2,430	1,390
Marycrest College; Davenport, Iowa 52804	124[1]	573[1]	60	P	3,225	3,225	1,570
Marygrove College; Detroit, Mich. 48221	147[1]	630[1]	47	P/RC	3,360	3,360	1,950
Mary Hardin–Baylor, University of*; Belton, Tex. 76513	318	689	62	P/B	2,016	2,016	1,330
Maryland, University of (System); College Park, Md. 20742							
UM, Baltimore County (UMBC)*; Catonsville, Md. 21228	2,550	2,650	330	S	860	2,536	2,000
UM University College (UMUC); College Park, Md. 20742	5,520[1]	5,763[1]	11	S	(52)	(52)	—
UM at Baltimore (UMAB)*; Baltimore, Md. 21201	1,820	2,007	721	S	705	2,550	855
UM–College Park (UMCP); College Park, Md. 20742	18,371	16,972	1,801	S	1,073	2,998	2,650
UM Eastern Shore (UMES); Princess Anne, Md. 21853	507	524	69	S	859	2,448	2,200
Maryland Institute College of Art; Baltimore, Md. 21217	371[1]	537[1]	45	P	3,750	3,750	2,800
Marylhurst College for Lifelong Learning; Marylhurst, Ore. 97036	223	573	28	P	1,944	1,944	—
Marymount College of Kansas; Salina, Kan. 67401	271	507	50	P/RC	2,400	2,400	1,486
Marymount College; Tarrytown, N.Y. 10591	48[1]	971[1]	55	P	4,250	4,250	2,860
Marymount College of Virginia; Arlington, Va. 22101	7[1]	817[1]	52	P/RC	3,700	3,700	2,300
Marymount Manhattan College; New York, N.Y. 10021	44[1]	872[1]	52	P	3,540	3,540	2,590
Maryville College; Maryville, Tenn. 37801	301[1]	302[1]	50	P/UP	3,125	3,125	1,565
Maryville College; St. Louis, Mo. 63141	187	558	60	P	3,650	3,650	1,960
Mary Washington College; Fredericksburg, Va. 22401	552[1]	2,076[1]	127	S	788	1,633	1,955
Marywood College; Scranton, Pa. 18509	667[1]	2,494[1]	185	P/RC	2,624[14]	2,624[14]	1,850
Massachusetts at Amherst, Univ. of; Amherst, Mass. 01003	11,600[1]	10,044[1]	1,204	S	750	2,750	1,875
Massachusetts at Boston, Univ. of; Boston, Mass. 02125	4,138[1]	4,322[1]	444	S	625	2,150	—
Massachusetts College of Art; Boston, Mass. 02215	390	696	44	S	600	2,100	—
Massachusetts College of Optometry. *See* New England College of Optometry							
Massachusetts College of Pharmacy*; Boston, Mass. 02115	771	544	n.a.	P	n.a.	n.a.	n.a.
Massachusetts Institute of Technology; Cambridge, Mass. 02139	7,169	1,601	1,041	P	7,400	7,400	3,200
Massachusetts Maritime Academy; Buzzards Bay, Mass. 02532	872	31	55	S/Fed	600	600	2,252
Mayo Medical School; Rochester, Minn. 55901[53]	120	42	25	P	5,000	5,000	4,500
Mayville State College; Mayville, N.D. 58257	239	286	43	S	602	1,163	1,200
McKendree College; Lebanon, Ill. 62254	243	243	32	P	3,360	3,360	1,750
McMurry College; Abilene, Tex. 79697	761	630	59	M	2,370	2,370	1,380
McNeese State University; Lake Charles, La. 70609	1,216	1,913	214	S	552	1,182	1,280
McPherson College; McPherson, Kan. 67460	291	251	31	P/CB	2,800	2,800	1,590
Medaille College; Buffalo, N.Y. 14214	258	358	41	P	1,329	1,329	—

Institution and location	Male	Female	Faculty	Control	Res.	Nonres.	Rm/Bd
Medical College of Georgia; Augusta, Ga. 30912	892	832	571	S	1,175	2,254	700
Medical College of Wisconsin, The; Milwaukee, Wis. 53226	564[1]	194[1]	510	P	6,325	10,450	n.a.
Medical Univ. of South Carolina; Charleston, S.C. 29425	1,355[1]	1,209[1]	722	S	1,024	2,048	1,950
Medicine and Dentistry, College of, of New Jersey; Newark, N.J. 07103							
New Jersey Dental School; Newark, N.J. 07103	1,268[1]	552[1]	725	S	5,000	5,000	—
New Jersey Medical School*; Newark, N.J. 07103	266	62	40	S	5,000	6,250	—
New Jersey School of Osteopathic Medicine; Camden, N.J. 08103	441	150	301	S	4,500	5,625	—
Rutgers Medical School; Piscataway, N.J. 08854	96	21	55	S	5,000	6,250	—
	300	123	264	S	5,000	5,625	3,440
Meharry Medical College; Nashville, Tenn. 37208	583[1]	434[1]	220	P	5,500	5,500	3,800
Memphis Academy of Arts, The*; Memphis, Tenn. 38112	111	76	17	P	1,900	1,900	1,600
Memphis State University[15]; Memphis, Tenn. 38152	9,594[1]	11,062[1]	798	S	556	1,224	2,100
Menlo College; Menlo Park, Calif. 94025	419	187	35	P	3,750	3,750	1,245
Mercer University; Macon, Ga. 31207	2665[1]	2,290[1]	250	P/B	3,669	3,669	1,785
Mercer University in Atlanta*; Atlanta, Ga. 30319	779	664	56	P/B	2,394	2,394	—
Southern School of Pharmacy; Atlanta, Ga. 30312	224	131	35	P	3,300	3,300	—
Mercy College; Dobbs Ferry, N.Y. 10522	2,684	3,219	152	P	2,550	2,550	—
Mercy College of Detroit; Detroit, Mich. 48219	-354[1]	1,544[1]	138	P/RC	3,000[6]	3,000[6]	1,400
Mercyhurst College; Erie, Pa. 16546	500[6]	600[6]	70	P/RC	3,650[6]	3,650[6]	1,775
Meredith College; Raleigh, N.C. 27611	31	1,521	74	P/SB	2,750	2,750	1,250
Meredith Manor School of Horsemanship; Waverly, W. Va. 26184	21	120	n.a.	P	6,852	6,852	1,764
Merrimack College; North Andover, Mass. 01845	1,304[1]	973[1]	119	P/RC	4,260	4,260	2,700
Mesa College; Grand Junction, Colo. 81501	1,434	1,194	123	S	716	2,500	1,796
Messiah College; Grantham, Pa. 17027	462	723	70	P/BC	3,640	3,640	1,940
Methodist College; Fayetteville, N.C. 28301	371	344	46	P/M	2,500	2,500	1,650
Metropolitan State College; Denver, Colo. 80209	3,268	2,731	315	S	590	2,470	—
Metropolitan State University; Minn. *See* Minnesota State University System							
Miami, University of*; Coral Gables, Fla. 33124	10,606	7,883	1,215	P	4,530	4,530	2,017
Miami University; Oxford, Ohio 45056	6,726	7,390	n.a.	S	665	800	795
Univ. of Michigan—Dearborn; Dearborn, Mich. 48128	18,022[1]	13,046[1]	2,255	S	1,668	2,188	2,281
Univ. of Michigan—Flint; Flint, Mich. 48503	1,845	1,327	336	S	1,088	3,344	—
Michigan State University; East Lansing, Mich. 48824	1,772	2,160	123	S	1,000	3,236	—
Michigan Technological University; Houghton, Mich. 49931	19,082[6]	18,322[6]	3,432	S	1,474[14]	3,041[14]	1,882
Mid-America Nazarene College; Olathe, Kan. 66061	6,081	1,784	374	S	1,272	3,006	2,073
	651[6]	703[6]	67	P/Naz	1,908	1,908	1,590
Middlebury College; Middlebury, Vt. 05753	1,000	904	147	P	9,300[27]	9,300[27]	—
Middle Tennessee State Univ.[15]; Murfreesboro, Tenn. 37132	4,162[1]	4,254[1]	400	S	550	1,774	1,152
Midland Lutheran College*; Fremont, Neb. 68025	370	460	61	P	3,200	3,200	1,460
Mid-South Bible College; Memphis, Tenn. 38112	105	44	8	P	1,824	1,824	1,570
Midwest Christian College; Oklahoma City, Okla. 73111	56	63	10	P	1,354	1,354	1,500
Midwest College of Engineering*; Lombard, Ill. 60148	27	1	n.a.	P	n.a.	n.a.	n.a.
Midwestern State University; Wichita Falls, Tex. 76308	1,044	1,124	143	S	405	1,485	1,020
Miles College; Birmingham, Ala. 35208	430	405	n.a.	CME	1,000	1,000	1,450
Millersville State College; Millersville, Pa. 17551	2,040[1]	2,455[1]	310	S	1,100	1,800	1,400
Milligan College; Milligan College, Tenn. 37682	348[1]	406[1]	39	P/CC	2,522	2,522	1,750
Millikin University; Decatur, Ill. 62522	701[1]	703[1]	105	P/UP	3,925	3,925	1,655
Millsaps College; Jackson, Miss. 39210	466[1]	396[1]	n.a.	P/M	3,099	3,099	1,240
Mills College; Oakland, Calif. 94613	32[1]	900[1]	56	P	5,550	5,550	2,850
Milton College; Milton, Wis. 53563	233	98	30	P	3,300	3,300	1,750
Milwaukee School of Engineering*; Milwaukee, Wis. 53201	1,330	70	108	P	3,600	3,600	1,500
Minneapolis College of Art and Design; Minneapolis, Minn. 55404	233	301	32	P	3,700	3,700	1,800
Minnesota, The University of; Minneapolis, Minn. 55455	28,444	23,599	5,603	S	1,135	2,758	2,030
Univ. of Minnesota, Duluth; Duluth, Minn. 55812	3,865[1]	3,528[1]	425	S	1,008	2,652	1,950
Univ. of Minnesota, Morris; Morris, Minn. 56267	813[1]	811[1]	105	S	927	2,550	1,716
Minnesota Bible College; Rochester, Minn. 55901	54[6]	48[6]	10	CC	1,650	1,650	1,435
Minnesota State University System; St. Paul, Minn. 55101							
Bemidji State University; Bemidji, Minn. 56601	2,120[1]	1,889[1]	198	S	586	1,164	1,265
Mankato State University; Mankato, Minn. 56001	4,544[1]	4,791[1]	476	S	730	1,308	1,313
Metropolitan State University; St. Paul, Minn. 55101	923[1]	1,223[1]	20	S	800	1,600	—
Moorhead State University; Moorhead, Minn. 56560	2,643[6]	3,044[6]	287	S	655	1,303	1,266
St. Cloud State University; St. Cloud, Minn. 56301	4,212	4,240	573	S	585	1,164	1,245
Southwest State University; Marshall, Minn. 56258	970	764	104	S	850	1,350	1,500
Winona State University; Winona, Minn. 55987	1,639[1]	2,306[1]	200	S	585	1,164	1,236
Minot State College; Minot, N.D. 58701	900[1]	1,600[1]	120	S	687	1,245	1,200

Institution and location	Enrollment Male	Female	Faculty	Control	Tuition Res.	Nonres.	Rm/Bd
Mississippi, The University of; University, Miss. 38677	5,124	4,483	500	S	1,054[14]	1,904[14]	1,725[14]
Medical Center; Jackson, Miss. 39216	938	632	n.a.	S	905[54]	1,831	2,472
Mississippi College*; Clinton, Miss. 39058	1,483	1,534	n.a.	P/B	1,800	1,800	1,270
Mississippi State University; Mississippi State, Miss. 39762	5,853	3,808	710	S	930	1,805	1,700
Mississippi University for Women; Columbus, Miss. 39701	—	2,070[1]	161	S	674	1,524	1,564
Mississippi Valley State University; Itta Bena, Miss. 38941	1,030[1]	1,233[1]	151	S	750	1,200	1,223
Missouri, University of; Columbia, Mo. 65201							
Univ. of Missouri—Columbia; Columbia, Mo. 65211	12,255	10,743	n.a.	S	870	2,610	1,525
Univ. of Missouri—Kansas City; Kansas City, Mo. 64110	3,313[1]	2,744[1]	625	S	952	2,692	2,100
Univ. of Missouri—Rolla; Rolla, Mo. 65401	4,512[1]	950[1]	377	S	1,015	2,010	1,735
Univ. of Missouri—St. Louis; St. Louis, Mo. 63121	3,313[1]	2,856[1]	410	S	870	1,740	—
Missouri Baptist College; St. Louis, Mo. 63141	194	217	20	P/SB	2,000	2,000	1,750
Missouri Institute of Technology; Kansas City, Mo. 64114	1,321	91	27	P	1,280	1,280	2,800
Missouri Southern State College; Joplin, Mo. 64801	1,238[6]	1,270[6]	180	S	470	940	1,300
Missouri Valley College; Marshall, Mo. 65340	290[1]	167[1]	35	P/Pres	3,050	3,050	1,750
Missouri Western State College; St. Joseph, Mo. 64507	1,972[1]	2,089[1]	149	S	580	1,084	1,344
Mobile College; Mobile, Ala. 36613	339[1]	738[1]	50	P	([55])	([55])	820
Molloy College; Rockville Centre, N.Y. 11570	27	1,068	105	P/RC	3,050	3,050	—
Monmouth College; Monmouth, Ill. 61462	309	334	50	P/UP	3,675	3,675	1,830
Monmouth College*; West Long Branch, N.J. 07764	952	964	165	P	3,830	3,830	920
Montana, University of; Missoula, Mont. 59812	3,931	3,347	384	S	657	2,025	1,726
Montana College of Mineral Science and Technology; Butte, Mont. 59701	900	350	75	S	560	1,930	1,950
Montana State University; Bozeman, Mont. 59717	6,095[1]	4,650[1]	500	S	674	2,042	1,900
Montclair State College; Upper Montclair, N.J. 07043	3,224	4,665	473	S	800	1,600	1,800
Monterey Institute of International Studies; Monterey, Calif. 93940	160	235	32	P	4,590	4,590	n.a.
Montevallo, University of; Montevallo, Ala. 35115	729[1]	1,346[1]	156	S	728	1,148	1,420
Moody Bible Institute; Chicago, Ill. 60610	751	586	86	P/ND	—	—	2,250
Moore College of Art; Philadelphia, Pa. 19103	—	527[1]	42	P	4,300	4,300	2,150
Moorhead State University. See Minnesota State University System							
Moravian College*; Bethlehem, Pa. 18018	647	634	85	P/Mor	3,900	3,900	1,700
Morehead State University*; Morehead, Ky. 40351	3,061	3,968	300	S	480	820	1,610
Morehouse College*; Atlanta, Ga. 30314	1,756	—	98	P	2,602	2,602	1,746
Morgan State University; Baltimore, Md. 21239	1,593	2,063	375	S	1,111	2,146	2,430
Morningside College; Sioux City, Iowa 51106	1,038		66	P	4,076	4,076	1,470
Morris Brown College; Atlanta, Ga. 30314	638	963	98	P	2,700	2,700	2,321
Morris College; Sumter, S.C. 29150	254	372	45	P/B	2,207[14]	2,207[14]	1,502[14]
Mount Holyoke College; South Hadley, Mass. 01075	—	1,850[1]	171	P	6,530[14]	6,530[14]	2,870
Mount Marty College; Yankton, S.D. 57078	122	366	50	P/RC	2,900	2,900	1,590
Mount Mary College; Milwaukee, Wis. 53222	—	720	84	P/RC	2,900	2,900	1,730
Mount Mercy College; Cedar Rapids, Iowa 52402	203[1]	686[1]	52	P/RC	3,145	3,145	1,600
Mount Saint Clare College; Clinton, Iowa 52732	133[1]	259[1]	8	P	1,650	1,650	1,610
Mount St. Joseph on the Ohio, College of*; Mount St. Joseph, Ohio 45051	39	756	53	P/RC	2,624	2,624	1,720
Mount Saint Mary College; Newburgh, N.Y. 12550	82	727	53	P	3,000	3,000	1,850
Mount Saint Mary's College; Emmitsburg, Md. 21727	769	684	91	P	3,650	3,650	1,850
Mount St. Mary's College; Los Angeles, Calif. 90049	9[1]	895[1]	77	P/RC	3,900	3,900	2,275
Mount Saint Vincent, College of; Riverdale, N.Y. 10471	50	1,200	75	P	3,650	3,650	2,410
Mount Senario College; Ladysmith, Wis. 54848	163[1]	181[1]	34	P	3,520	3,520	1,930
Mount Sinai School of Medicine. See New York, City University of							
Mount Union College; Alliance, Ohio 44601	540	461	73	P/UM	4,200	4,200	1,575
Mount Vernon College; Washington, D.C. 20007	—	429	25	P	4,200	4,200	3,000
Mount Vernon Nazarene College*; Mount Vernon, Ohio 43050	416	473	50	P/Naz	2,200	2,200	1,460
Muhlenberg College; Allentown, Pa. 18104	822[1]	724[1]	106	P/L	4,495	4,495	1,625
Multnomah School of the Bible; Portland, Ore. 97220	410	307	41	P	2,760[14]	2,760[14]	1,550[14]
Mundelein College; Chicago, Ill. 60660	40[1]	800[1]	77	P	3,840	3,840	1,980
Murray State University; Murray, Ky. 42071	2,748[1]	3,000[1]	350	S	626	1,780	1,460
Museum Art School; Portland, Ore. 97034	51[1]	116[1]	16	P	2,650	2,650	—
Muskingum College; New Concord, Ohio 43762	528[1]	449[1]	69	P/Pres	4,337	4,337	1,668
Nasson College; Springvale, Me. 04083	317	196	41	P	4,680	4,680	2,220
Nathaniel Hawthorne College; Antrim, N.H. 03440	331	80	20	P	4,400	4,400	1,650
National College; Rapid City, S.D. 57701	400[1]	677[1]	45	P	3,525	3,525	3,045
National College of Education; Evanston, Ill. 60201	346	1,154	79	P	3,795	3,795	2,445
National University[48]; San Diego, Calif. 92108	4,130[1]	1,802[1]	35[56]	P	3,840	3,840	—

Institution and location	Enrollment		Faculty	Control	Tuition		Rm/Bd
	Male	Female			Res.	Nonres.	
Naval Postgraduate School; Monterey, Calif. 93940	1,009	39	231	Fed	—	—	—
Nazareth College at Kalamazoo; Nazareth, Mich. 49074	95[1]	436[1]	32	P/RC	4,240	4,240	2,120
Nazareth College of Rochester; Rochester, N.Y. 14610	247[1]	1,104[1]	112	P	3,780	3,780	2,250
Nebraska, University of; Lincoln, Neb. 68588	10,958[1]	7,739[1]	1,071	S	940	2,305	1,555
Univ. of Nebraska at Omaha; Omaha, Neb. 68182	3,595	2,967	570	S	1,000	2,500	
Univ. of Nebraska Medical Center; Omaha, Neb. 68105	858[1]	870[1]	539	S	2,000	4,000	6,360[9]
Nebraska Wesleyan University; Lincoln, Neb. 68504	446	515	91	P	3,050	3,050	1,524
Neumann College; Aston, Pa. 19014[57]	83	617	32	P	2,500	2,500	
Nevada, University of; Reno, Nev. 89557:							
Univ. of Nevada, Las Legas; Las Vegas, Nev. 89154	5,093	5,443	308	S	672	2,000	2,150
Univ. of Nevada—Reno; Reno, Nev. 89557	2,886	2,349	332	S	768	2,268	1,756
Newberry College; Newberry, S.C. 29108	479[1]	320[1]	54	P/LCA	3,665[27]	3,665[27]	
New Church College, Academy of the; Bryn Athyn, Pa. 19009	77	64	24	P/Sw	1,236	1,236	1,476
Newcomb College. *See* Tulane University							
New College of California; San Francisco, Calif. 94110	190[1]	226[1]	4	P	2,700	2,700	—
New England, University of; Biddeford, Me. 04005:							
College of Osteopathic Medicine; Biddeford, Me. 04005	139	22	11	P	11,000	11,000	2,010
Saint Francis College; Biddeford, Me. 04005	206	173	25	P	4,300	4,300	2,420
New England College*; Henniker, N.H. 03242	835	685	n.a.	P	4,680	4,680	1,800
New England College of Optometry; Boston, Mass. 02115	270	90	50	P	8,970	8,970	
New England Conservatory of Music; Boston, Me. 02115	341	271	55	P	5,500	5,500	3,125
New England School of Law; Boston, Mass. 02116	674	340	26	P	4,200	4,200	
New Hampshire, University of; Durham, N.H. 03824	4,949[1]	5,305[1]	514	S	1,150	3,700	1,769
New Hampshire College; Manchester, N.H. 03104	1,968[1]	1,405[1]	57	P	4,870	4,870	2,872
New Haven, University of; West Haven, Conn. 06516	1,644	1,011	146	P	3,496	3,496	1,900
New Jersey Institute of Technology; Newark, N.J. 07102	5,591[1]	610[1]	247	S	1,110	2,220	2,090
New Mexico, The University of; Albuquerque, N.M. 87131	7,257[1]	6,776[1]	1,030	S	720[14]	2,232[14]	1,750[14]
New Mexico Highlands University; Las Vegas, N.M. 87701	1,082	1,257	121	S	453	1,430	1,360
New Mexico Institute of Mining and Technology; Socorro, N.M. 87801	882	343	81	S	400	1,912	2,348
New Mexico State University; Las Cruces, N.M. 88001	6,188	5,205	664	S	708	2,082	1,294
New Orleans, University of; New Orleans, La. 70122[58]	3,696	3,501	589	S	624	1,654	1,360
Newport College, The—Salve Regina; Newport, R.I. 02840	137[1]	885[1]	76	P/RC	3,950	3,950	2,300
New Rochelle, College of*; New Rochelle, N.Y. 10801	258	3,002	100	P	3,150	3,150	2,320
New School for Social Research; New York, N.Y. 10011	295[1]	319[1]	58	P	4,500[14]	4,500[14]	3,340
Parsons School of Design; New York, N.Y. 10011	632[1]	1,063[1]	36	P	4,980[14]	4,980[14]	3,340
New School of Music, The; Philadelphia, Pa. 19103	33	49	4	P	3,400	3,400	2,350
New York, City University of; New York, N.Y. 10021	48,508	61,527	6,871	Mun/S	925	1,425	—
Bernard M. Baruch College; New York, N.Y. 10010	4,047[1]	4,491[1]	481	Mun	925	1,425	—
Brooklyn College; Brooklyn, N.Y. 11210	5,820	7,605	750	Mun	925	1,425	—
City College; New York, N.Y. 10031	4,868	3,145	604	Mun	925	1,425	—
College of Staten Island; Staten Island, N.Y. 10301	4,858[1]	5,750[1]	300	S	925	1,425	—
Graduate School and University Center; New York, N.Y. 10036	1,511[1]	1,460[1]	1,351	Mun	1,616	2,116	4,000
Herbert H. Lehman College; Bronx, N.Y. 10468	3,191	6,056	442	Mun	935	1,500	—
Hunter College; New York, N.Y. 10021	4,246[1]	13,263[1]	715	Mun/S	925	1,425	—
John Jay College of Criminal Justice; New York, N.Y. 10019	2,157[1]	1,838[1]	268	Mun/S	925	1,425	—
Medgar Evers College; Brooklyn, N.Y. 11225	762	2,039	171	Mun	925	1,425	—
Mount Sinai School of Medicine*; New York, N.Y. 10029	309	144	968	P	7,500	7,500	3,000
Queens College; Flushing, N.Y. 11367	5,013	5,918	840	Mun/S	935	1,425	—
York College; Jamaica, N.Y. 11451	412[1]	938[1]	220	Mun	925	1,425	—
New York, State University of; Albany, N.Y. 12246:							
SUNY at Albany; Albany, N.Y. 12222	6,025[1]	5,847[1]	715	S	1,050	1,750	2,020
SUNY at Binghamton*; Binghamton, N.Y. 13901	5,276	5,360	477	S	900	1,500	1,875
SUNY at Buffalo; Buffalo, N.Y. 14214	11,524[6]	7,542[6]	1,404	S	1,050	1,750	2,282
SUNY at Stony Brook; Stony Brook, N.Y. 11794	6,195	4,819	n.a.	S	1,800	3,000	3,940
SUNY College at Brockport; Brockport, N.Y. 14420	3,107[1]	3,234[1]	433	S	1,050	1,750	1,970
SUNY College at Buffalo; Buffalo, N.Y. 14222	11,408		500	S	1,050	1,750	2,200
SUNY College at Cortland; Cortland, N.Y. 13045	2,343[1]	3,737[1]	295	S	1,050	1,750	1,904
SUNY College at Fredonia; Fredonia, N.Y. 14063	2,163[1]	2,073[1]	260	S	1,800	3,000	1,600
SUNY College at Geneseo; Geneseo, N.Y. 14454	1,724[1]	3,207[1]	263	S	900	1,500	1,830
SUNY College at New Paltz; New Paltz; N.Y. 12561	3,058[1]	4,146[1]	325	S	1,050	1,750	2,050
SUNY College at Old Westbury; Old Westbury, N.Y. 11568	1,270	1,795	135	S	1,100	1,800	2,000
SUNY College at Oneonta; Oneonta, N.Y. 13820	2,443[1]	3,203[1]	352	S	900	1,200	1,800
SUNY College at Oswego; Oswego, N.Y. 13126	3,444[1]	3,170[1]	375	S	1,050	1,750	2,080
SUNY College at Plattsburgh; Plattsburgh, N.Y. 12901	2,416[6]	3,071[6]	375	S	1,005	1,500	1,897
SUNY College at Potsdam; Potsdam, N.Y. 13676	1,789[1]	2,046[1]	289	S	1,050	1,750	2,040

Institution and location	Enrollment		Faculty	Control	Tuition		Rm/Bd
	Male	Female			Res.	Nonres.	
SUNY College at Purchase; Purchase, N.Y. 10577	898[1]	1,308[1]	153	S	1,005	1,605	1,714
SUNY College of Environmental Science and Forestry; Syracuse, N.Y. 13210	1,206	367	107	S	900	1,500	2,450
SUNY College of Optometry; New York, N.Y. 10010	170	90	37	S	4,300	6,300	—
SUNY College of Technology; Utica, N.Y. 13502	588[1]	586[1]	70	S	900	1,500	2,200
SUNY Downstate Medical Center; Brooklyn, N.Y. 11203	838	594	700	S	3,300	4,840	3,000
SUNY Empire State College; Saratoga Springs, N.Y. 12866	447[1]	744[1]	119	S	1,050[6]	1,750[6]	—
SUNY Maritime College; Fort Schuyler, Bronx, N.Y. 10465	845[1]	54[1]	66	S	1,050	1,750	2,150
SUNY Upstate Medical Center; Syracuse, N.Y. 13210	516	351	236	S	900	1,500	2,400
New York, University of the State of, Regents External Degree Program; Albany, N.Y. 12230	10,867	10,172	200	P	200[59]	200[59]	—
New York Chiropractic College*; Glen Head, N.Y. 11545	520	130	50	P	3,750	3,750	—
New York College of Podiatric Medicine*; New York, N.Y. 10035	405	48	25	P	7,095	7,095	n.a.
New York Institute of Technology; Old Westbury, N.Y. 11568	2,880[1]	990[1]	205	P	3,026	3,026	—
New York Law School; New York, N.Y. 10013	879	463	38	P	5,000	5,000	—
New York Medical College*; Valhalla, N.Y. 10595	578	223	527	P	9,100	9,100	—
New York University; New York, N.Y. 10003	8,968[1]	8,740[1]	n.a.	P	5,516[14]	5,516[14]	2,984[14]
Niagara University; Niagara University, N.Y. 14109	1,397	1,605	174	P/RC	3,690	3,690	2,450
Nicholls State University; Thibodaux, La. 70301	2,339[1]	2,428[1]	233	S	541	1,171	1,300
Nichols College; Dudley, Mass. 01570	585	142	50	P	4,845	4,845	2,300
Norfolk State University*; Norfolk, Va. 23504	2,202	3,163	406	S	550	975	1,448
North Adams State College; North Adams, Mass. 01247	974[1]	1,164[1]	98	S	725	2,538	2,015
North Alabama, University of; Florence, Ala. 35630	2,327[1]	2,941[1]	181	S	750	1,500	1,526
North Carolina, University System of; Chapel Hill, N.C. 27514:							
Appalachian State University; Boone, N.C. 28608	3,928[1]	4,325[1]	350	S	614	2,334	1,410
East Carolina University; Greenville, N.C. 27834	4,710[1]	5,936[1]	763	S	310	2,030	1,590
Elizabeth City State University*; Elizabeth City, N.C. 27909	681	843	100	S	250	1,734	1,370
Fayetteville State University; Fayetteville, N.C. 28301	999	1,398	146	S	612	2,114	1,300
North Carolina Agricultural and Technical State University; Greensboro, N.C. 27411	2,936	2,374	345	S	367	1,219	684
North Carolina Central University; Durham, N.C. 27707	1,897[1]	3,013[1]	250	S	310	2,048	1,418
North Carolina School of the Arts; Winston-Salem, N.C. 27107	304[1]	333[1]	77	S	568	2,020	1,796[1]
N.C. State Univ. at Raleigh; Raleigh, N.C. 27607	13,867[1]	7,358[1]	1,700	S	648	2,410	710[2]
Pembroke State University; Pembroke, N.C. 28372	957[6]	1,344[6]	118	S	270	1,760	1,210
Univ. of N.C. at Asheville; Asheville, N.C. 28814	926	1,173	85	S	500	2,270	1,760
Univ. of N.C. at Chapel Hill; Chapel Hill, N.C. 27514	10,020[1]	11,445[1]	1,887	S	598	2,308	1,650
Univ. of N.C. at Charlotte; Charlotte, N.C. 28223	3,475[1]	2,931[1]	424	S	560	2,292	1,544
Univ. of N.C. at Greensboro; Greensboro, N.C. 27412	2,962	6,833	616	S	625	2,082	1,570
Univ. of N.C. at Wilmington; Wilmington, N.C. 28403	1,853[1]	1,899[1]	209	S	582	2,337	1,815
Western Carolina University; Cullowhee, N.C. 28723	2,579[1]	2,448[1]	322	S	590	2,328	1,360
Winston-Salem State University; Winston-Salem, N.C. 27102	880	1,293	170	S	2,187[27]	3,716[27]	—
North Carolina Wesleyan College; Rocky Mount, N.C. 27801	434	433	41	P	2,760	2,760	1,530
North Central Bible College; Minneapolis, Minn. 55404	399	298	n.a.	P/AG	1,680	1,680	1,520
North Central College; Naperville, Ill. 60566	575	542	55	P/UM	4,209	4,209	2,115
North Dakota, University of*; Grand Forks, N.D. 58202	5,180	4,528	485	S	660	1,428	1,290
North Dakota State University; Fargo, N.D. 58105	4,745[1]	3,191[1]	380	S	633	1,401	n.a.
Northeastern Bible College*; Essex Fells, N.J. 07021	141	89	18	P/ID	2,592	2,592	1,669
Northeastern Illinois University; Chicago, Ill. 60625	2,080[1]	2,822[1]	355	S	666	1,998	⊥
Northeastern Oklahoma State University; Tahlequah, Okla. 74464	1,327	1,758	266	S	555	1,350	1,472
Northeastern University*; Boston, Mass. 02115	11,100	6,400	777	P	3,637	3,637	2,505
Northeast Louisiana University; Monroe, La. 71209	4,151	5,483	353	S	527	1,157	1,564
Northeast Missouri State University; Kirksville, Mo. 63501	2,335	2,832	240	S	390	850	1,264
Northern Arizona University; Flagstaff, Ariz. 86011	6,050[6]	6,045[6]	393	S	625	2,500	1,600
Northern Colorado, University of; Greeley, Colo. 80639	3,961[1]	5,613[1]	623	S	606	2,658	1,665
Northern Illinois University; DeKalb, Ill. 60115	7,968[6]	9,415[6]	1,110	S	895	2,087	2,040
Northern Iowa, University of; Cedar Falls, Iowa 50613	3,343	4,216	559	S	900	1,860	1,528
Northern Kentucky University; Highland Heights, Ky. 41076	3,933[1]	4,439[1]	264	S	626	1,780	—
Northern Michigan University; Marquette, Mich. 49855	4,059[1]	3,600[1]	325	S	1,040	2,400	1,920
Northern Montana College; Havre, Mont. 59501	636[1]	461[1]	72	S	461	1,469	1,685
Northern State College; Aberdeen, S.D. 57401	857	1,073	112	S	768	1,572	1,318

Institution and location	Enrollment		Faculty	Control	Tuition		Rm/Bd
	Male	Female			Res.	Nonres.	
North Florida, University of; Jacksonville, Fla. 32216	650	783	180	S	(60)	(61)	—
North Georgia College; Dahlonega, Ga. 30597	495[1]	558[1]	102	S	666	1,620	1,335
Northland College; Ashland, Wis. 54806	337	253	35	P	3,650	3,650	1,970
North Park College; Chicago, Ill. 60625	550	650	80	P/EC	3,960	3,960	2,028
Northrop University[62]; Inglewood, Calif. 90306	1,341[1]	111[1]	n.a.	P	4,725	4,725	2,952
North Texas State University; Denton, Tex. 76201	7,761	8,164	704	S	436	1,516	1,928
Northwest Bible College; Minot, N.D. 58701	88	56	9	P/CG	1,200	1,200	1,270
Northwest Christian College; Eugene, Ore. 97401	123	81	12	P	2,970	2,970	1,755
Northwest College*; Kirkland, Wash. 98033	362	272	21	P/AG	1,740	1,740	1,427
Northwestern College; Orange City, Iowa 51041	422	533	54	P/RCA	3,645[14]	3,645[14]	1,505
Northwestern College; Roseville, Minn. 55113	332	312	34	P/Ind	3,000	3,000	1,710
Northwestern Coll. of Chiropractic; St. Paul, Minn. 55116	319	64	27	P	3,230	3,230	—
Northwestern Oklahoma State University; Alva, Okla. 73717	780	840	n.a.	S	260	1,175	1,130
Northwestern State University of Louisiana; Natchitoches, La. 71457	1,263	1,746	n.a.	S	668	1,298	1,280
Northwestern University; Evanston, Ill. 60201	5,269	3,874	2,100	P	6,885[14]	6,885[14]	2,794[14]
Northwest Missouri State University; Maryville, Mo. 64468	2,407[1]	2,568[1]	247	S	530	930	n.a.
Northwest Nazarene College; Nampa, Idaho 83651	570[1]	675[1]	82	P/Naz	3,165	3,165	1,695
Northwood Institute; Midland, Mich. 48640		1,945	45	P	2,820	2,820	1,710
Norwich University; Northfield, Vt. 05663	1,295[1]	169[1]	167	P	7,790[27]	7,790[27]	—
Vermont College; Montpelier, Vt. 05602	81	432	140	P	6,900[27]	6,900[27]	—
Notre Dame, College of; Belmont, Calif. 94002	309	501	64	P/RC	3,600	3,600	2,100
Notre Dame, University of; Notre Dame, Ind. 46556	6,608[1]	2,317[1]	695	P	5,250[14]	5,250[14]	3,530[14]
Notre Dame College; Manchester, N.H. 03104	89[1]	681[1]	38	P/RC	2,700	2,700	1,800
Notre Dame College of Ohio; Cleveland, Ohio 44121	—	384[1]	34	P/RC	2,825	2,825	1,800
Notre Dame of Maryland, College of; Baltimore, Md. 21210	—	517	50	P	3,400	3,400	2,300
Nova University; Ft. Lauderdale, Fla. 33314	1,912[1]	1,741[1]	57	P	n.a.	n.a.	n.a.
Nyack College; Nyack N.Y. 10960	240	317	22	P/CMA	3,150	3,150	1,924
Oakland City College; Oakland City, Ind. 47660	334	206	29	P/B	2,400	2,400	1,437
Oakland University; Rochester, Mich. 48063	4,564[1]	7,442[1]	470	S	1,216	3,152	2,480
Oakwood College; Huntsville, Ala. 35805	459	579	71	P/SDA	3,360	3,360	1,175
Oberlin College; Oberlin, Ohio 44074	1,217[1]	1,420[1]	207	P	6,440	6,440	2,570
Occidental College; Los Angeles, Calif. 90041	840[1]	812[1]	115	P	5,340	5,340	2,200
Oglethorpe University; Atlanta, Ga. 30319	503[1]	650[1]	35	P	3,100	3,100	1,750
Ohio College of Podiatric Medicine; Cleveland, Ohio 44106	537[1]	52[1]	70	P	6,385	6,385	
Ohio Dominican College; Columbus, Ohio 43219	226[1]	397[1]	44	P/RC	3,620	3,620	2,050
Ohio Institute of Technology; Columbus, Ohio 43209	2,518	210	46	P	2,740	2,740	—
Ohio Northern University; Ada, Ohio 45810	1,618[1]	1,064[1]	164	P/UM	4,125	4,125	1,755
Ohio State University, The; Columbus, Ohio 43210	28,643	22,262	3,028	S	1,155	2,520	2,037
Columbus Campus; Columbus, Ohio 43210	26,578	20,432	2,865	S	1,155	2,520	2,037
Lima Campus; Lima, Ohio 45804	381	403	36	S	1,110	2,475	2,052
Mansfield Campus; Mansfield, Ohio 44906	447	438	38	S	1,110	2,475	2,052
Marion Campus; Marion, Ohio 43302	311	306	26	S	1,110	2,475	2,052
Newark Campus; Newark, Ohio 43055	435	441	28	S	1,110	2,475	2,052
Ohio University; Athens, Ohio 45701	7,149[1]	5,840[1]	727	S	1,206	2,781	2,019
Ohio Wesleyan University; Delaware, Ohio 43015	1,102	1,083	160	P/M	5,550	5,550	2,110
Oklahoma, University of; Norman, Okla. 73019	9,827[1]	6,943[1]	782	S	643	1,712	1,670
Oklahoma, University of Science and Arts of; Chickasha, Okla. 73018	258	391	55	S	448	1,152	1,400
Oklahoma Baptist University; Shawnee, Okla. 74801	620	767	96	P/SB	1,050	1,150	1,505
Oklahoma Christian College; Oklahoma City, Okla. 73111	641[1]	792[1]	60	P/CC	2,000	2,000	1,500
Oklahoma City Southwestern Coll. See Southwestern Coll. of Christian Ministries							
Oklahoma City University; Oklahoma City, Okla. 73106	785[1]	585[1]	87	P/UM	2,360	2,360	1,830
Oklahoma College of Osteopathic Medicine and Surgery; Tulsa, Okla. 74101	212	38	30	S	2,500	2,500	—
Oklahoma Panhandle State University*; Goodwell, Okla. 73939	503	329	n.a.	S	n.a.	n.a.	n.a.
Oklahoma State University; Stillwater, Okla. 74078	11,045[1]	7,842[1]	879	S	600	1,650	1,300
Old Dominion University*; Norfolk, Va. 23508	4,762	4,461	581	S	840	1,440	1,690
Olivet College; Olivet, Mich. 49076		610	40	P	3,990[14]	3,990[14]	1,900[14]
Olivet Nazarene College; Kankakee, Ill. 60901	753[1]	1,037[1]	95	P/Naz	2,790	2,790	1,716
Open Bible College; Des Moines, Iowa 50321	54	36	10	P/OBS	1,800	1,800	2,150
Oral Roberts University; Tulsa, Okla. 74171	2,099[1]	1,646[1]	300	P	3,300	3,300	2,067
Oregon, University of; Eugene, Ore. 97403	7,547[1]	6,952[1]	673	S	969	3,282	n.a.
Oregon Coll. of Education. See Western Oregon Coll. of Education							
Oregon Graduate Center; Beaverton, Ore. 97006	34	2	21	P	4,000	4,000	—
Otis Art Institute of Parsons School of Design; Los Angeles, Calif. 90057	98[1]	188[1]	11	P	3,350	3,350	1,850[2]

Institution and location	Enrollment			Control	Tuition		Rm/Bd
	Male	Female	Faculty		Res.	Nonres.	
Ottawa University; Ottawa, Kan. 66067	273	202	25	P/AB	2,842	2,842	1,600
Otterbein College; Westerville, Ohio 43081	500	657	93	P/UM	4,428	4,428	1,683
Ouachita Baptist University; Arkadelphia, Ark. 71923	727	782	109	P/SB	2,210	2,210	1,500
Our Lady of Angels College. *See* Neumann College							
Our Lady of Holy Cross College; New Orleans, La. 70114	81	190	30	P/RC	1,900	1,900	—
Our Lady of the Elms, College of; Chicopee, Mass. 01013	—	527	48	P/RC	3,500	3,500	2,000
Our Lady of the Lake University of San Antonio; San Antonio, Tex. 78285	424[1]	873[1]	82	P/RC	2,700	2,700	1,900
Ozarks, The College of; Clarksville, Ark. 72830	303[1]	253[1]	37	P/Pres	1,175	1,175	1,350
Ozarks, The School of the; Point Lookout, Mo. 65726	600	600	81	P	(63)	(63)	(63)
Pace University*; New York, N.Y. 10038	**2,024**	**2,003**	**772**	**P**	**3,264**	**3,264**	**2,225**
College of White Plains of Pace University; White Plains, N.Y. 10603	244	398	36	P	3,848[6]	3,848[6]	2,700
Pace University, Pleasantville/Briarcliff; Pleasantville, N.Y. 10570	1,151	1,324	125	P	3,648	3,648	2,700
Pacific, University of the; Stockton, Calif. 95211	2,007[1]	2,136[1]	275	P	5,877	5,877	2,522
Pacific Christian College; Fullerton, Calif. 92631	193	270	15	P/CC	2,600	2,600	2,200
Pacific Lutheran University; Tacoma, Wash. 98447	1,109[1]	1,544[1]	204	P/L	4,672	4,672	2,090
Pacific Oaks College; Pasadena, Calif. 91103	27	234	20	P	3,360	3,360	—
Pacific Union College; Angwin, Calif. 94508	936	975	115	P	4,125	4,125	2,145
Pacific University; Forest Grove, Ore. 97116	622[1]	425[1]	82	P/UCC	4,900	4,900	2,150
Paine College; Augusta, Ga. 30910	270	488	66	P/M	2,175	2,175	1,365
Palm Beach Atlantic College; West Palm Beach, Fla. 33401	282	359	27	P/SB	1,700	1,700	1,600
Pan American University; Edinburg, Tex. 78539	4,004	5,446	430	S	390	1,850	1,555
Paper Chemistry, The Institute of; Appleton, Wis. 54911	70	10	45	P	3,000	3,000	1,647
Park College; Parkville, Mo. 64152	222	177	28	P/LDS	3,290	3,290	1,700
Parks College of Saint Louis University; Cahokia, Ill. 62206	865	87	44	P/RC	2,920	2,920	1,930
Parsons School of Design. *See* New School for Social Research							
Patten College; Oakland, Calif. 94601	55	67	17	P	1,926	1,926	1,930
Paul Quinn College*; Waco, Tex. 76704	537		n.a.	P/AME	1,350	n.a.	1,600
Peabody Institute of the Johns Hopkins University, Conservatory of Music; Baltimore, Md. 21202	152[1]	157[1]	45	P	4,950	4,950	2,630
Pembroke State University. *See* North Carolina, University System of							
Pennsylvania, University of; Philadelphia, Pa. 19104	10,575[1]	6,875[1]	6,298	P	6,900[14]	6,900[14]	3,091[14]
Pennsylvania College of Optometry*; Philadelphia, Pa. 19141	481	106	n.a.	P	n.a.	n.a.	n.a.
Pennsylvania College of Podiatric Medicine; Philadelphia, Pa. 19107	409	61	35	P	6,950	6,950	6,000
Pennsylvania State University, The; University Park, Pa. 16802	30,252[1]	19,681[1]	3,004	S	1,641	3,297	2,037
Behrend College; Erie, Pa. 16563	1,092	558	100	S	1,416	3,270	1,955
Capitol Campus*; Middletown, Pa. 17057	1,197	520	130	S	1,233	2,748	1,566
Radnor Center for Graduate Studies*; Radnor, Pa. 19087	204	154	6	S	n.a.	n.a.	—
The Milton S. Hershey Medical Center*; Hershey, Pa. 17033	364	183	n.a.	S	n.a.	n.a.	n.a.
Pepperdine University; Malibu, Calif. 90265	4,196	2,905	208	P/CC	5,888	5,888	2,780
Peru State College; Peru, Neb. 68421	313[1]	313[1]	47	S	630	1,020	1,682
Pfeiffer College; Misenheimer, N.C. 28109	428[1]	386[1]	56	P/UM	2,580	2,580	1,565
Philadelphia College of Art*; Philadelphia, Pa. 19102	468	670	70	P	4,500	4,500	2,050
Philadelphia College of Bible; Langhorne, Pa. 19047	231	218	40	P	2,800	2,800	1,900
Philadelphia College of Osteopathic Medicine; Philadelphia, Pa. 19131	665	156	94	P	7,600	7,900	n.a.
Philadelphia College of Pharmacy and Science; Philadelphia, Pa. 19104	574[1]	508[1]	101	P	4,000	4,000	2,600
Philadelphia College of Textiles and Science; Philadelphia, Pa. 19144	626	892	87	P	3,600	3,600	1,250
Philadelphia College of the Performing Arts; Philadelphia, Pa. 19102	136	156	13	P	4,400	4,400	—
Philander Smith College*; Little Rock, Ark. 72203	351	259	n.a.	UM	1,000	1,000	1,475
Phillips University; Enid, Okla. 73701	714[1]	585[1]	71	P/CC	2,720	2,720	1,760
Phoenix, University of; Phoenix, Ariz. 85004	1,000		82[11]	P	3,000	3,000	—
Piedmont Bible College; Winston-Salem, N.C. 27101	239	147	18	P/B	1,570	1,570	1,090
Piedmont College; Demorest, Ga. 30535	200	178	20	P/Cong	900	1,575	2,085
Pikeville College; Pikeville, Ky. 41501	273[1]	343[1]	45	P/PUS	2,550	2,550	4,160
Pine Manor College*; Chestnut Hill, Mass. 02167	—	471	25	P	4,280	4,280	2,675
Pittsburgh, University of; Pittsburgh, Pa. 15260	15,098[1]	14,217[1]	2,104	P/S	1,790	3,580	2,184
U. of Pittsburgh at Bradford*; Bradford, Pa. 16701	400	310	42	P/S	1,520	2,970	1,850
U. of Pittsburgh at Johnstown*; Johnstown, Pa. 15904	1,301	889	150	P/S	1,410	2,820	1,440

Institution and location	Enrollment		Faculty	Control	Tuition		Rm/Bd
	Male	Female			Res.	Nonres.	
Pittsburg State University; Pittsburg, Kan. 66762	1,770	1,496	219	S	300	625	1,588
Pitzer College. *See* Claremont Colleges							
Plymouth State College; Plymouth, N.H. 03264	1,386[1]	1,383[1]	142	S	800	2,700	1,725
Point Loma College; San Diego, Calif. 92106	721	858	73	P/Naz	3,120	3,120	1,445
Point Park College; Pittsburgh, Pa. 15222	630[1]	570[1]	70	P	3,920	3,920	2,000
Polytechnic Institute of New York*; Brooklyn, N.Y. 11201							
Pomona College. *See* Claremont Colleges	4,271	423	180	P	4,800	4,800	1,050
Portland, University of; Portland, Ore. 97203							
Portland School of Art; Portland, Me. 04101	998[1]	887[1]	110	P	3,900	3,900	1,780
Portland State University; Portland, Ore. 97207	95	165	12	P	3,550	3,550	—
	8,068[1]	8,662[1]	567	S	947	3,233	2,475
Post College; Waterbury, Conn. 06708	280[1]	537[1]	33	P	3,300[6]	3,300[6]	2,200[6]
Prairie View A&M University; Prairie View, Tex. 77445	2,367	2,557	225	S	136	1,360	1,862
Pratt Institute; Brooklyn, N.Y. 11205	2,194[1]	1,544[1]	136	P	5,118	5,118	1,595[2]
Presbyterian College; Clinton, S.C. 29325	486	413	53	P/PUS	3,705	3,705	1,835
Princeton University; Princeton, N.J. 08544	3,866[1]	2,103[1]	730	P	7,250	7,250	2,744
Principia College*; Elsah, Ill. 62028	391	477	45	P	4,239	4,239	2,400
Providence College; Providence, R.I. 02918	1,748	1,764	240	P/RC	4,628	4,628	2,900
Puerto Rico, University of; Río Piedras, P.R. 00931:							
Bayamón Technological University College; Bayamón, P.R. 00619							
Cayey University College; Cayey, P.R. 00633	1,470	1,780	174	S	([64])	n.a.	—
Humacao University College*; Humacao, P.R. 00661	990	1,528	123	S	1,900	1,900	1,200
Mayaguez Campus*; Mayaguez, P.R. 00708	3,868		252	S	205	205	n.a.
Medical Sciences Campus; San Juan, P.R. 00936	4,969	3,370	479	S	212	212	—
	942	1,576	702	S	150	n.a.	—
Río Piedras Campus; Río Piedras, P.R. 00931	5,558[1]	9,751[1]	1,106	S	200	2,077	902
Puget Sound, University of; Tacoma, Wash. 98416	1,702[1]	1,599[1]	193	P/M	4,800	4,800	2,260
Puget Sound College of the Bible; Edmonds, Wash. 98020	84	69	9	P/CC	1,800	1,800	1,755
Purdue University; West Lafayette, Ind. 47907	18,052	12,401	1,779	S	1,008	2,600	1,870
Calumet Campus; Hammond, Ind. 46323	1,396	1,209	202	S	1,007	2,065	
Indiana University–Purdue University at Indianapolis. *See* Indiana University							
Queens College; Charlotte, N.C. 28274	—	555	43	P/Pres	3,750	3,750	2,110
Queens College (NYC). *See* New York, City University of							
Quincy College; Quincy, Ill. 62301	419	421	67	P/RC	3,600	3,600	1,800
Quinnipiac College; Hamden, Conn. 06518	788	1,377	150	P	4,500	4,500	1,000
Radcliffe College. *See* Harvard University							
Radford University; Radford, Va. 24142	1,423[1]	3,427[1]	284	S	1,035	1,635	2,016
Ramapo College of New Jersey; Mahwah, N.J. 07430	2,567		140	S	([65])	([36])	1,250[2]
Rand Graduate Institute; Santa Monica, Calif. 90406							
Randolph–Macon College; Ashland, Va. 23005	42[1]	7[1]	—	P	4,500	4,500	—
Randolph–Macon Woman's College; Lynchburg, Va. 24503	518	374	65	P	4,450[14]	4,450[14]	1,970[14]
	—	715	65	P/UM	5,100[14]	5,100[14]	2,200[14]
Redlands, University of; Redlands, Calif. 92373	1,549	1,201	115	P	5,000	5,000	2,100
Reed College; Portland, Ore. 97202	621	448	87	P	6,400	6,400	2,350
Reformed Bible College; Grand Rapids, Mich. 49506	124	89	17	P	1,800	1,800	1,450
Regis College; Denver, Colo. 80221	582[1]	470[1]	79	P/RC	4,460	4,460	2,624
Regis College; Weston, Mass. 02193	—	908[1]	55	P/RC	4,025[14]	4,025[14]	2,630[14]
Rensselaer Polytechnic Institute; Troy, N.Y. 12181	4,723[1]	976[1]	370	P	6,500	6,500	2,453
Rhode Island, University of; Kingston, R.I. 02881	5,393	5,175	900	S	934	2,960	2,181
Rhode Island College*; Providence, R.I. 02908	1,053	2,306	350	S	820	2,420	2,015
Rhode Island School of Design; Providence, R.I. 02903	669	899	82	P	5,900	5,900	2,510
Rice University*; Houston, Tex. 77001	2,253	1,215	463	P	2,900	2,900	2,520
Richmond, University of; Richmond, Va. 23173	1,636	1,221	200	P/B	4,845	4,845	1,920
Rider College; Lawrenceville, N.J. 08638	1,758[1]	1,646[1]	188	P	3,600	3,600	2,004
Ringling School of Art*; Sarasota, Fla. 33580	203	262	n.a.	P	n.a.	n.a.	n.a.
Rio Grande College; Rio Grande, Ohio 45674	392	483	62	P	675	2,700	1,920
Ripon College; Ripon, Wis. 54971	526[1]	404[1]	72	P	5,316	5,316	1,700
Rivier College; Nashua, N.H. 03060	523	1,204	40	P/RC	3,000	3,000	2,000
Roanoke Bible College*; Elizabeth City, N.C. 27909	62	48	n.a.	P/ChC	n.a.	n.a.	n.a.
Roanoke College; Salem, Va. 24153	565	591	72	P/L	4,100	4,100	2,000
Robert Morris College; Coraopolis, Pa. 15108	1,292	1,347	92	P	2,460	2,460	1,500
Roberts Wesleyan College; Rochester, N.Y. 14624	170	381	60	P/FM	3,200	3,200	1,650
Rochester, The University of; Rochester, N.Y. 14627	4,967[1]	3,512[1]	1,129	P	5,300	5,300	2,473
Rochester Institute of Technology*; Rochester, N.Y. 14623	4,834	2,005	560	P	3,879	3,879	2,368
Rockford College; Rockford, Ill. 61101	255	360	60	P	3,890	3,890	1,875
Rockhurst College; Kansas City, Mo. 64110	763	646	84	P/RC	3,360	3,360	2,050
Rocky Mountain College; Billings, Mont. 59102	201	191	35	P[66]	2,790	2,790	1,755
Roger Williams College*; Bristol, R.I. 02809	1,248	642	82	P	3,100	3,100	2,000

Institution and location	Enrollment Male	Enrollment Female	Faculty	Control	Tuition Res.	Tuition Nonres.	Rm/Bd
Rollins College; Winter Park, Fla. 32789	634	658	107	P	5,010	5,010	2,630
Roosevelt University*; Chicago, Ill. 60605	1,767	2,385	248	P	3,000	3,000	n.a.
Rosary College; River Forest, Ill. 60305	157[1]	628[1]	68	P/RC	3,850	3,850	2,250
Rose-Hulman Institute of Technology; Terre Haute, Ind. 47803	1,196	—	90	P	4,140	4,140	1,995
Rosemont College*; Rosemont, Pa. 19010	—	585	29	P/RC	3,800	3,800	2,400
Rush University; Chicago, Ill. 60612	426[1]	525[1]	636	P	3,450	3,450	3,135
Russell Sage College; Troy, N.Y. 12180	—	1,303	133	P	4,100	4,100	2,250
Rust College; Holly Springs, Miss. 38635	246	378	40	P/UM	2,125	2,125	1,110
Rutgers University; New Brunswick, N.J. 08903	16,101[1]	15,879[1]	2,625	S	940	1,880	1,844
Sacred Heart, Univ. of the; Santurce, P.R. 00914	2,306	3,932	100	P/RC	1,408	1,408	900
Sacred Heart College; Belmont, N.C. 28012	107[1]	299[1]	21	P/RC	2,900	2,900	1,793
Sacred Heart University; Bridgeport, Conn. 06606	625	793	n.a.	P	3,040	3,040	—
Saginaw Valley State College; University Center, Mich. 48710	1,019	966	110	S	990	2,175	1,050
St. Ambrose College; Davenport, Iowa 52803	675[1]	505[1]	75	P/RC	3,750	3,750	2,110
St. Andrews Presbyterian College; Laurinburg, N.C. 28352	373[1]	348[1]	50	P/Pres	3,350	3,350	1,770
St. Anselm College; Manchester, N.H. 03102	918[1]	738[1]	104	P/RC	3,600	3,600	1,880
St. Augustine's College; Raleigh, N.C. 27611	786[1]	975[1]	67	P/E	1,600	1,600	1,200
St. Benedict, College of; St. Joseph, Minn. 56374	—	1,715[1]	92	P	3,690[14]	3,690[14]	1,610
St. Bonaventure University; St. Bonaventure, N.Y. 14778	1,208	1,180	149	P	3,300	3,300	1,950
St. Catherine, The College of; St. Paul Minn. 55105	10[1]	1,815[1]	132	P/RC	3,780	3,780	1,900
St. Cloud State University. See Minnesota State College System							
St. Edward's University; Austin, Tex. 78704	980	670	71	P/RC	2,750	2,750	2,300
St. Elizabeth, College of; Convent Station, N.J. 07961	3[1]	522[1]	48	P/RC	3,400	3,400	2,000
St. Francis, College of; Joliet, Ill. 60435	228[1]	385[1]	46	P/RC	3,300	3,300	1,930
St. Francis College; Brooklyn, N.Y. 11201	1,024	772	69	P	3,020	3,020	—
St. Francis College; Fort Wayne, Ind. 46808	150[1]	281[1]	37	RC	(67)	(67)	1,900
St. Francis College; Loretto, Pa. 15940	626[1]	498[1]	64	P/RC	3,520	3,520	2,000
St. Francis de Sales College*; Milwaukee, Wis. 53207	55	1	16	P/RC	700	700	500
St. John Fisher College; Rochester, N.Y. 14618	878	680	80	P	4,166[6]	4,166[6]	2,363[6]
St. John's College; Annapolis, Md. 21404	205	170	42	P	6,000	6,000	2,400
St. John's College; Santa Fe, N.M. 87501	184	151	35	P	6,000	6,000	2,400
Saint John's University; Collegeville, Minn. 56321	1,890[1]	21[1]	92	P	3,895[14]	3,895[14]	1,940[14]
St. John's University; Jamaica, N.Y. 11439	10,226[1]	7,719[1]	542	P/RC	3,050[14]	3,050[14]	—
St. Joseph College; West Hartford, Conn. 06117	1	771	75	P/RC	3,450	3,450	2,000
St. Joseph's College; Brooklyn, N.Y. 11205	195[1]	957[1]	267	P	2,400	2,400	—
St. Joseph's College; North Windham, Me. 04062	111[6]	386[6]	37	P/RC	2,800	2,800	1,700
St. Joseph's College; Rensselaer, Ind. 47978	570	374	52	RC	3,520[14]	3,520[14]	995
St. Joseph's University; Philadelphia, Pa. 19131	1,486	1,065	129	P/RC	3,250	3,250	2,160
St. Joseph the Provider, College of; Rutland, Vt. 05701	40	140	10	P/RC	2,825	2,825	1,775
St. Lawrence University; Canton, N.Y. 13617	1,159	1,076	152	P	5,745	5,745	2,165
St. Leo College; St. Leo, Fla. 33574	600[1]	400[1]	53	P/RC	3,000	3,000	1,800
St. Louis Christian College; Florissant, Mo. 63033	88	68	12	P/CC	1,400	1,400	1,260
St. Louis College of Pharmacy; St. Louis, Mo. 63110	381[1]	303[1]	29	P	2,300[68]	2,300[68]	1,900
St. Louis Conservatory of Music*; St. Louis, Mo. 63130	30	25	5	P	2,700	2,700	—
St. Louis University; St. Louis, Mo. 63103	3,858	2,640	1,865	P	4,220	4,220	2,000
St. Martin's College*; Lacey, Wash. 98503	228	172	40	P/RC	3,422	3,422	1,800
St. Mary, College of; Omaha, Neb. 68124	84	666	38	P/RC	(69)	(69)	1,576
St. Mary College; Leavenworth, Kan. 66048	240[1]	610[1]	42	P/RC	2,510	2,510	1,540
St. Mary of the Plains College; Dodge City, Kan. 67801	223	475	61	P/RC	2,800	2,800	1,800
St. Mary-of-the-Woods College; St. Mary-of-the-Woods, Ind. 47876	—	529	56	P/RC	3,540	3,540	1,735
St. Mary's College; Notre Dame, Ind. 46556	14	1,709	114	P/RC	4,420[14]	4,420[14]	2,266
St. Mary's College; Orchard Lake, Mich. 48033	116	95	21	P/RC	1,900	1,900	900
St. Mary's College*; Winona, Minn. 55987	634	595	72	P/RC	3,379	3,379	1,830
St. Mary's College of California; Moraga, Calif. 94575	1,143[1]	1,292[1]	75	P/RC	4,471	4,471	2,431
St. Mary's College of Maryland; St. Mary's City, Md. 20686	442	581	70	S	675	1,650	1,950
St. Mary's Dominican College; New Orleans, La. 70118	19	378	n.a.	P/RC	2,900	2,900	1,830
St. Mary's University; San Antonio, Tex. 78284	1,872	1,398	125	RC	1,350	1,350	950
St. Michael's College; Winooski, Vt. 05404	942	769	89	P/RC	4,525	4,525	2,170
St. Norbert College; De Pere, Wis. 54115	818[1]	811[1]	90	P/RC	3,950	3,950	2,000
St. Olaf College; Northfield, Minn. 55057	1,412[1]	1,579[1]	190	P/AL	4,710	4,710	1,740
St. Patrick's College; Mountain View Calif. 94042	68	—	12	P/RC	1,800	1,800	700
St. Paul's College; Lawrenceville, Va. 23868	343	350	41	P/E	2,180	2,180	1,660
St. Peter's College; Jersey City, N.J. 07306	1,908[1]	2,182[1]	138	P/RC	3,400	3,400	—
St. Rose, The College of*; Albany, N.Y. 12203	217	926	105	P	2,500	2,500	1,600

Institution and location	Male	Female	Faculty	Control	Res.	Nonres.	Rm/Bd
St. Scholastica, College of; Duluth, Minn. 55811	210	852	73	P/RC	3,606	3,606	1,890
St. Teresa, College of; Winona, Minn. 55987	20	700	65	P/RC	3,960[14]	3,960[14]	1,800
St. Thomas, College of; St. Paul, Minn. 55105	1,991	1,121	159	P/RC	3,520	3,520	1,875
St. Thomas, University of; Houston, Tex. 77006	658[1]	1,166[1]	126	P/RC	2,500	2,500	1,500
St. Thomas Aquinas College*; Sparkill, N.Y. 10976	500	650	50	P	2,375	2,375	825[2]
St. Xavier College; Chicago, Ill. 60655	365	898	185	P/RC	3,638	3,638	2,350
Salem College; Salem, W. Va. 26426	440	439	59	P	1,600	1,600	1,000
Salem College; Winston–Salem, N.C. 27108	1	544	56	P/Mor	3,865	3,865	2,310
Salem State College; Salem, Mass. 01970	1,977	2,970	280	S	600	2,000	1,600
Salisbury State College; Salisbury, Md. 21801	1,211	1,516	184	S	680	1,650	1,940
Salve Regina College. *See* Newport College							
Samford University*; Birmingham, Ala. 35229	1,791	1,588	218	P/B	2,464	2,560	1,600
Sam Houston State University; Huntsville, Tex. 77341	4,670	4,861	333	S	592	2,102	2,512
San Diego, University of*; San Diego, Calif. 92110	1,070	1,383	175	P/RC	4,050	4,050	2,500
San Diego State University; San Diego, Calif. 9218[22]	9,974	10,773	1,029	S	—	2,538	2,250
San Francisco, University of; San Francisco, Calif. 94117	3,035	3,114	575	P/RC	4,430	4,430	2,606
San Francisco Art Institute; San Francisco, Calif. 94133	352	330	53	P	4,250	4,250	—
San Francisco Conservatory of Music, The; San Francisco, Calif. 94122	81[1]	98[1]	12[70]	P	4,600	4,600	—
San Francisco State Univ.; San Francisco, Calif. 94132[22]	10,153	13,293	827	S	266	2,160	2,196
Sangamon State University; Springfield, Ill. 62708	558	452	179	S	632	1,824	1,440
San Jose Bible College*; San Jose, Calif. 95108	87	40	7	P/ND	1,680	1,680	1,260
San Jose State University; San Jose, Calif. 95192[22]	12,609	1,675	984	S	—	2,160	2,110
Santa Clara, University of; Santa Clara, Calif. 95053	2,319	1,989	253	P/RC	4,593	4,593	2,385
Santa Fe, College of; Santa Fe, N.M. 87501	416	601	60	P/RC	3,000	3,000	2,200
Sarah Lawrence College; Bronxville, N.Y. 10708	215[1]	845[1]	60	P	7,200	7,200	3,200
Savannah State College; Savannah, Ga. 31404	866	1,016	139	S	699	1,653	1,371
Scranton, University of; Scranton, Pa. 18510	2,500	1,800	200	P/RC	3,104	4,044	1,830
Scripps College. *See* Claremont Colleges							
Seattle Pacific University; Seattle, Wash. 98119	1,008	1,524	199	P/FM	4,002	4,002	2,190
Seattle University; Seattle, Wash. 98122	1,221[1]	1,376[1]	186	P/RC	4,275	4,275	2,275
Seton Hall University*; South Orange, N.J. 07079	3,615	3,381	n.a.	P/RC	n.a.	n.a.	n.a.
Seton Hill College; Greensburg, Pa. 15601	—	747[1]	47	P	3,550	3,550	2,000
Shaw University*; Raleigh, N.C. 27611	736	594	57	P/B	2,500	2,500	1,300
Sheldon Jackson College; Sitka, Alaska 99835	70	57	17	P	2,700	2,700	2,700
Shepherd College; Shepherdstown, W. Va. 25443	1,250[1]	1,751[1]	106	S	370	1,310	1,380
Sherwood Music School; Chicago, Ill. 60605	24	26	10	P	2,100	2,100	2,600
Shimer College; Waukegan, Ill. 60085	19[6]	21[6]	12	P	3,500	3,500	2,300
Shippensburg State College; Shippensburg, Pa. 17257	2,222[1]	2,464[1]	266	S	1,250	2,190	1,470
Shorter College; Rome, Ga. 30161	314[1]	458[1]	53	P/SB	2,350	2,350	1,500
Siena College; Loudonville, N.Y. 12211	1,339	1,033	130	P	3,625	3,625	2,350
Siena Heights College; Adrian, Mich. 49221	251	447	55	P/RC	2,940	2,940	1,900
Sierra Nevada College; Incline Village, Nev. 89450	56	50	32[11]	P	2,000	2,000	—
Silver Lake College; Manitowoc, Wis. 54220	52[1]	192[1]	40	P/RC	3,200	3,200	1,980
Simmons College; Boston, Mass. 02115	—	1,653	150	P	5,728	5,728	2,806
Simon's Rock of Bard College; Great Barrington, Mass. 01230	165	135	30	P	5,265	5,265	1,025
Simpson College; Indianola, Iowa 50125	411[1]	337[1]	60	P/UM	4,480	4,480	1,630
Simpson College; San Francisco, Calif. 94134	121[1]	105[1]	13	P/CMA	2,400	2,400	1,700
Sioux Falls College; Sioux Falls, S.D. 57101	245	328	42	P/B	2,650	2,650	1,585
Skidmore College; Saratoga Springs, N.Y. 12866	488	1,590	163	P	6,390[14]	6,390[14]	3,010[14]
Slippery Rock State College; Slippery Rock, Pa. 16057	2,612[1]	3,078[1]	307	S	1,250	2,190	1,350
Smith College; Northampton, Mass. 01060	—	2,867[1]	247	P	5,900	5,900	2,300
Sonoma State University; Rohnert Park, Calif. 94928[22]	2,268	3,181	261	S	238	2,398	2,410
South, The University of the; Sewanee, Tenn. 37375	607	454	116	P/E	5,680	5,680	1,590
South Alabama, University of; Mobile, Ala. 36688	3,848[1]	4,132[1]	349	S	1,026	1,176	1,596
Southampton College. *See* Long Island Univ. Center							
South Carolina, University of; Columbia, S.C. 29208	7,257	6,754	1,005	S	1,040	2,220	1,520
USC at Aiken; Aiken, S.C. 29801	1,148		58	S	770	1,760	
USC at Spartanburg; Spartanburg, S.C. 29303	720[1]	872[1]	130	S	770	1,760	—
USC–Coastal Carolina; Conway, S.C. 29526	1,164[1]	1,088[1]	115	S	770	1,760	—
South Carolina State College; Orangeburg, S.C. 29117	1,737	2,192	240	S	790	1,390	1,300
South Dakota, University of; Vermillion, S.D. 57069	2,684[1]	2,390[1]	327	S	783	1,728	1,440
University of South Dakota at Springfield; Springfield, S.D. 57062	658	194	62	S	748	1,100	1,600
South Dakota School of Mines and Technology; Rapid City, S.D. 57701	1,500[1]	387[1]	109	S	732	1,836	1,722
South Dakota State University; Brookings, S.D. 57007	3,342[1]	2,724[1]	413	S	783[14]	1,728[14]	1,475[14]
Southeastern Bible College*; Birmingham, Ala. 35205	170	139	20	P/Ind	2,240	2,240	1,740
Southeastern College of the Assemblies of God; Lakeland, Fla. 33801	743[1]	510[1]	n.a.	P/AG	([71])	([71])	1,200

Institution and location	Enrollment Male	Female	Faculty	Control	Tuition Res.	Nonres.	Rm/Bd
Southeastern Louisiana University; Hammond, La. 70402	3,207[1]	4,500[1]	265	S	618	1,248	1,242
Southeastern Massachusetts University; North Dartmouth, Mass. 02740	2,753[1]	2,760[1]	300	S	664	2,400	2,700
Southeastern Oklahoma State Univ.; Durant, Okla. 74701	2,040	2,056	143	S	384	954	1,300
Southeastern University; Washington, D.C. 20024	378	176	n.a.	P	2,160	2,160	—
Southeast Missouri State University; Cape Girardeau, Mo. 63701	3,645[1]	4,418[1]	396	S	390	640	1,370
Southern Arkansas University; Magnolia, Ark. 71753	929[1]	1,058[1]	104	S	660	1,050	1,330
Southern Bible College; Houston, Tex. 77015	81	56	7	P/CG	1,660	1,660	1,600
Southern California, Univ. of; Los Angeles, Calif. 90007	10,541[1]	7,051[1]	1,610	P	6,150	6,150	2,822
Southern California College*; Costa Mesa, Calif. 92626	358	318	32	P/AG	1,990	1,990	1,745
Southern California College of Optometry; Fullerton, Calif. 92631	273	90	45	P	5,925	5,925	—
Southern California Institute of Architecture; Santa Monica, Calif. 90404	260	90	30	P	3,230	3,230	—
Southern College of Optometry; Memphis, Tenn. 38104	524	56	50	P	4,760	8,760	3,283
Southern Colorado, University of; Pueblo, Colo. 81001	2,088	1,541	205	S	581	2,555	1,840
Southern Connecticut State College; New Haven, Conn. 06515	2,626[1]	4,373[1]	422	S	792	1,732	2,242
Southern Illinois University at Carbondale; Carbondale, Ill. 62901	12,378[1]	7,170[1]	1,889	S	703	2,109	n.a.
Southern Illinois University at Edwardsville; Edwardsville, Ill. 62026	4,711	5,121	600	S	952	2,338	2,100
Southern Maine, University of*; Portland, Me. 04103	1,731	2,223	n.a.	Pub	n.a.	n.a.	n.a.
Southern Methodist University; Dallas, Tex. 75275	3,355	3,030	433	P	4,350	4,350	2,752
Southern Missionary College; Collegedale, Tenn. 37315	916[1]	1,175[1]	106	P/SDA	3,390	3,390	1,800
Southern Mississippi, Univ. of; Hattiesburg, Miss. 39401	3,945[1]	4,453[1]	425	S	916	1,842	1,415
Southern Oregon State College; Ashland, Ore. 97520	2,184[1]	2,515[1]	250	S	942	2,946	1,850
Southern University and A&M College System; Baton Rouge, La. 70813:							
Southern University and A&M College; Baton Rouge, La. 70813	3,989[1]	4,415[1]	394	S	538	1,168	1,870
Southern University in New Orleans; New Orleans, La. 70126	755	1,402	n.a.	S	500	1,130	—
Southern Utah State College; Cedar City, Utah 84720	894[1]	812[1]	106	S	684	1,722	2,226
Southern Vermont College; Bennington, Vt. 05201	159[1]	198[1]	15	P	2,940	2,940	2,510
South Florida, The University of; Tampa, Fla. 33620	12,042[1]	13,011[1]	1,095	S	803	2,311	1,730
New College Campus; Sarasota, Fla. 33580	250	250	50	S	960	2,920	1,700
St. Petersburg Campus*; St. Petersburg, Fla. 33701	980	1,123	30	S	792	2,184	—
South Texas, University System of:							
Corpus Christi State Univ.; Corpus Christi, Tex. 78412	1,209	1,606	108	S	364	1,440	600
Laredo State University; Laredo, Tex. 78040	128	176	25	S	100	960	—
Texas A&I University; Kingsville, Tex. 78363	2,226[1]	1,678[1]	236	S	363	1,443	1,394
South Texas College of Law; Houston, Tex. 77002	819	379	19	P	3,482	3,482	5,041[9]
Southwest Baptist College; Bolivar, Mo. 65613	593	668	72	P/B	2,620	2,620	1,260
Southwestern Adventist College; Keene, Tex. 76059	333[1]	367[1]	50	SDA	4,084	4,084	2,074
Southwestern Assemblies of God College of the Bible; Waxahachie, Tex. 75165	327	287	21	P/AG	1,500	1,500	1,890
Southwestern at Memphis; Memphis, Tenn. 38112	532	504	86	P/PUS	4,000	4,000	1,970
Southwestern Baptist Bible College; Phoenix, Ariz. 85032	86	54	10	P/B	1,920	1,920	1,850
Southwestern College; Winfield, Kan. 67156	248	245	45	P/UM	2,400	2,400	1,566
Southwestern College of Christian Ministries[12]; Oklahoma City, Okla. 73127	138	56	8	PH	1,580	1,580	1,440
Southwestern Louisiana, University of; Lafayette, La. 70504	5,477[1]	5,053[1]	601	S	550	1,200	2,000
Southwestern Oklahoma State University; Weatherford, Okla. 73096	1,758[6]	1,945[6]	218	S	480	1,240	1,130
Southwestern University; Georgetown, Tex. 78626	466[1]	563[1]	53	M	3,000	3,000	2,200
Southwestern University School of Law*; Los Angeles, Calif. 90005	730	317	51	P	n.a.	n.a.	—
Southwest Missouri State Univ.; Springfield, Mo. 65802	5,178[1]	5,214[1]	514	S	520	1,040	1,290
Southwest Texas State Univ.; San Marcos, Tex. 78666	6,140[1]	6,606[1]	561	S	426	1,506	1,755
Spalding College; Louisville, Ky. 40203	101	811	62	P/RC	2,400	2,400	1,600
Spelman College; Atlanta, Ga. 30314	—	1,367[6]	86	P	2,350	2,350	1,850
Spertus College of Judaica; Chicago, Ill. 60605	150	250	10	P	4,050	4,050	—
Spring Arbor College; Spring Arbor, Mich. 49283	336[1]	388[1]	40	P/FM	3,900	3,900	1,700
Springfield College; Springfield, Mass. 01109	1,021[1]	1,090[1]	145	P	3,366	3,366	1,866
Spring Garden College; Philadelphia, Pa. 19118	601[6]	129[6]	60	P	3,550	3,550	2,000
Spring Hill College; Mobile, Ala. 36608	450[1]	383[1]	52	P/RC	3,800	3,800	2,280
Stanford University; Stanford, Calif. 94305	7,373[1]	4,152[1]	1,652	P	6,285	6,285	2,636

Institution and location	Male	Female	Faculty	Control	Res.	Nonres.	Rm/Bd
					Enrollment		Tuition

Institution and location	Male	Female	Faculty	Control	Res.	Nonres.	Rm/Bd
Staten Island, College of (NYC). *See* New York, City University of							
Steed College; Johnson City, Tenn. 37601	202	206	17	P	2,160	2,160	—
Stephen F. Austin State Univ.; Nacogdoches, Tex. 75962	4,005	4,895	420	S	350	1,222	1,700
Stephens College; Columbia, Mo. 65215	22[1]	1,264[1]	119	P	4,675	4,675	2,100
Sterling College; Sterling, Kan. 67579	247[1]	242[1]	36	P/UP	3,100	3,100	1,600
Stetson University; DeLand, Fla. 32720	1,298[1]	1,111[1]	129	P/B	3,700	3,700	1,760
Stetson Univ. College of Law; St. Petersburg, Fla. 33707	296	160	20	P	4,000	4,000	2,062
Steubenville, University of; Steubenville, Ohio 43952	300[1]	350[1]	40	P/RC	3,630	3,630	2,178
Stevens Institute of Technology; Hoboken, N.J. 07030	1,328	230	125	P	5,500	5,500	2,810
Stillman College*; Tuscaloosa, Ala. 35403	245	390	38	P	1,800	1,800	1,825
Stockton State College*; Pomona, N.J. 08241	1,992	1,516	163	S	736	1,440	1,464
Stonehill College; North Easton, Mass. 02356	856[1]	884[1]	81	P/RC	4,275	4,275	2,500
Suffolk University*; Boston, Mass. 02114	1,298	1,164	103	P	2,900	2,900	—
Sul Ross State University; Alpine, Tex. 79830	841	589	70	S	392	1,444	1,520
Susquehanna University; Selinsgrove, Pa. 17870	817[1]	677[1]	103	P/LCA	4,600	4,600	2,122
Swarthmore College; Swarthmore, Pa. 19081	697	589	133	P	6,250	6,250	2,650
Sweet Briar College; Sweet Briar, Va. 24595	—	669	74	P	4,010	4,010	1,940
Syracuse University; Syracuse, N.Y. 13210	7,830[1]	6,552[1]	1,304	P	5,000	5,000	1,500
Tabor College; Hillsboro, Kan. 67063	215	218	31	MB	2,560	2,560	1,671
Talladega College*; Talladega, Ala. 35160	214	428	49	P	1,615	1,615	1,360
Tampa, The University of; Tampa, Fla. 33606	969[1]	721[1]	88	P	4,356	4,356	2,030
Tampa College*; Tampa, Fla. 33607		1,000	10	P	1,458	1,458	—
Tarkio College; Tarkio, Mo. 64491	126	110	28	P/Pres	2,825	2,825	1,475
Tarleton State University[73]; Stephenville, Tex. 76402	1,700	1,900	144	S	564	1,644	n.a.
Taylor University; Upland, Ind. 46989	619	765	84	P/ND	4,179	4,179	1,925
Temple University; Philadelphia, Pa. 19122	16,899	16,254	n.a.	S	2,068	3,854	1,870
Tennessee State University[15]; Nashville, Tenn. 37203	2,480	2,638	428	S	726	2,256	1,826
Tennessee System, University of; Knoxville, Tenn. 37916:							
U. of Tennessee at Chattanooga; Chattanooga, Tenn. 37402	2,373[1]	2,288[1]	246	S	620	1,840	695[2]
U. of Tennessee at Knoxville; Knoxville, Tenn. 37916	16,486[1]	13,796[1]	1,285	S	624	1,848	1,631
U. of Tennessee at Martin; Martin, Tenn. 38238	2,135	2,221	218	S	750	1,560	1,647
U. of Tennessee Center for the Health Sciences*; Memphis, Tenn. 38163	1,324	746	n.a.	S	1,095	1,995	2,025
Tennessee Technological Univ.[15]; Cookeville, Tenn. 38501	3,320	2,267	356	S	561	1,785	n.a.
Tennessee Wesleyan College; Athens, Tenn. 37303	252[1]	206[1]	30	P/UM	2,400	2,400	1,710
Texas, University of, System; Austin, Tex. 78701:							
U. of Texas at Arlington; Arlington, Tex. 76019	10,999	7,681	850	S	442	1,522	n.a.
U. of Texas at Austin; Austin, Tex. 78712	25,355[1]	20,793[1]	1,800	S	452	1,532	2,096
U. of Texas at Dallas; Richardson, Tex. 75080	1,035[1]	1,004[1]	200	S	382	1,242	—
U. of Texas at El Paso; El Paso, Tex. 79968	8,169	7,581	475	S	304	1,164	1,370
U. of Texas at San Antonio; San Antonio, Tex. 78285	4,472	4,906	223	S	120	1,200	—
U. of Texas at Tyler; Tyler, Tex. 75701	278	429	69	S	360	1,368	—
U. of Texas Health Science Center at Dallas; Dallas, Tex. 75235	849	473	531	S	300	900	—
U. of Texas Health Science Center at Houston; Houston, Tex. 77025	1,439[1]	1,295[1]	799	S	132	1,280	4,500
U. of Texas Health Science Center at San Antonio*; San Antonio, Tex. 78284	1,145	873	490	S	400	1,200	—
U. of Texas Medical Branch at Galveston; Galveston, Tex. 77550	598[1]	578[1]	450	S	400	1,200	—
U. of Texas of the Permian Basin; Odessa, Tex. 79762	718	834	67	S	220	1,200	([74])
Texas A&I Univ. *See* South Texas, Univ. System of							
Texas A&M University; College Station, Tex. 77843	20,031	11,412	1,621	S	120	1,200	2,000
Texas A&M Univ. at Galveston*; Galveston, Tex. 77553	444	133	n.a.	S	180	1,440	1,863
Texas Chiropractic College; Pasadena, Tex. 77505	362[1]	68[1]	28	P	3,185	3,185	—
Texas Christian University; Fort Worth, Tex. 76129	2,875[1]	3,408[1]	300	P/ChC	3,520	3,520	2,000
Texas College; Tyler, Tex. 75702	266	221	43	P/CME	1,800	1,800	1,954
Texas Coll. of Osteopathic Medicine; Fort Worth, Tex. 76107	246	73	200	S	400	900	5,496
Texas Lutheran College; Seguin, Tex. 78155	495[1]	467[1]	76	P/AL	2,550	2,550	1,525
Texas Southern University*; Houston, Tex. 77004	4,552	4,274	450	S	400	1,600	1,600
Texas Tech University; Lubbock, Tex. 79409	9,670	7,161	781	S	621	2,231	2,096
Texas Wesleyan College; Fort Worth, Tex. 76105	716[1]	951[1]	83	P/M	2,800	2,800	1,950
Texas Woman's University; Denton, Tex. 76204	500	7,500	485	S	128	1,280	2,300
Thiel College; Greenville, Pa. 16125	420	431	61	P/LCA	3,884	3,884	1,821
Thomas Aquinas College; Santa Paula, Calif. 93060	54	54	13	P/RC	4,290	4,290	2,290
Thomas College; Waterville, Me. 04901	199[1]	255[1]	25	P	4,000	4,000	2,200
Thomas Jefferson University; Philadelphia, Pa. 19107		1,416	363	P	4,400	4,400	n.a.
Thomas M. Cooley Law School; Lansing, Mich. 48933	747[1]	253[1]	20	P	3,000	3,000	n.a.

Institution and location	Enrollment Male	Female	Faculty	Control	Tuition Res.	Nonres.	Rm/Bd
Thomas More College; Fort Mitchell, Ky. 41017	388[1]	337[1]	63	P/RC	3,168	3,168	2,080
Tiffin University; Tiffin, Ohio 44883	178[1]	185[1]	11	P	2,160	2,160	1,400
Tift College; Forsyth, Ga. 31029	104	599	33	P/B	1,800	1,800	1,500
Toccoa Falls College; Toccoa Falls, Ga. 30598	281[1]	237[1]	28	P/ID	2,270	2,270	1,800
Toledo, The University of; Toledo, Ohio 43606	10,391[1]	9,879[1]	652	S	1,107	2,562	1,995
Tougaloo College*; Tougaloo, Miss. 39174	279	468	65	P	2,025	2,025	1,225
Touro College; New York, N.Y. 10036	787	1,199	220	P	3,200[14]	3,200[14]	1,200
Towson State University; Towson, Md. 21204	4,224[6]	5,376[6]	485	S	827	2,437	1,640
Transylvania University; Lexington, Ky. 40508	405[1]	405[1]	810	P	4,600	4,600	1,900
Trenton State College; Trenton, N.J. 08625	2,220	3,231	375	S	1,033	1,673	2,150
Trevecca Nazarene College; Nashville, Tenn. 37210	428[1]	492[1]	50	P/Naz	2,607	2,607	1,728
Tri-College University*; Moorhead, Minn. 56560	89		n.a.	P	n.a.	n.a.	n.a.
Trinity Christian College; Palos Heights, Ill. 60463	160[1]	200[1]	25	P/CR	3,350[14]	3,350[14]	1,875
Trinity College; Burlington, Vt. 05401	137	646	41	P	3,540	3,540	2,220
Trinity College; Deerfield, Ill. 60015	289	351	35	P/EFC	3,900	3,900	2,000
Trinity College; Hartford, Conn. 06106	887	746	135	P	6,300[14]	6,300[14]	2,550[14]
Trinity College; Washington, D.C. 20017	50[1]	950[1]	50	P/RC	4,700	4,700	2,900
Trinity University; San Antonio, Tex. 78284	1,284[1]	1,410[1]	220	P	3,622	3,622	1,800
Tri-State University; Angola, Ind. 46703	1,200[1]	400[1]	95	P	(75)	(75)	1,710
Troy State University; Troy, Ala. 36082	2,307[1]	2,038[1]	225	S	750	1,080	1,425
Tufts University*; Medford, Mass. 02155	3,465[1]	2,791[1]	413	P	5,850	5,850	3,031
Jackson College for Women*; Medford, Mass. 02155	n.a.	n.a.	n.a.	P	n.a.	n.a.	n.a.
Tulane University; New Orleans, La. 70118	5,218	2,902	985	P	5,056	5,056	1,450
Newcomb College for Women; New Orleans, La. 70118	—	1,623	125	P	5,706	5,706	1,230
Tulsa, The University of; Tulsa, Okla. 74104	2,304[1]	1,879[1]	311	P	2,700	2,700	1,412
Tusculum College; Greeneville, Tenn. 37743	353		28	P/Pres	2,700	2,700	1,990
Tuskegee Institute; Tuskegee Institute, Ala. 36088	1,822	1,899	329	P	2,500	2,500	1,750
Union College*; Barbourville, Ky. 40906	133	185	48	P	2,700	2,700	1,390
Union College; Lincoln, Neb. 68516	427[1]	461[1]	84	P/SDA	4,290	4,290	1,850
Union College; Schenectady, N.Y. 12308	1,433[1]	775[1]	139	P	5,520	5,520	2,030
Union University; Jackson, Tenn. 38301	375	560	68	SB	1,900	1,900	1,100
U.S. Air Force Academy; USAF Academy, Colo. 80840	3,614	450	555	Fed	—	—	—
U.S. Army Command and General Staff College*; Fort Leavenworth, Kan. 66027	753	14	n.a.	Fed	n.a.	n.a.	n.a.
U.S. Coast Guard Academy; New London, Conn. 06320	922	132	112	Fed	—	—	—
U.S. International University; San Diego, Calif. 92131	1,249[1]	647[1]	88	P	4,320	4,320	2,520
U.S. Merchant Marine Academy; Kings Point, N.Y. 11024	1,021	79	83	Fed	—	—	—
U.S. Military Academy*; West Point, N.Y. 10996	3,749	313	639	Fed	—	—	—
U.S. Naval Academy; Annapolis, Md. 21402	4,119	276	550	Fed	—	—	—
U.S. School of Music, Inc. *See* LaSalle Extension Univ.							
Unity College; Unity, Me. 04988	234[1]	78[1]	25	P	3,800[14]	3,800[14]	2,200[14]
Upper Iowa University; Fayette, Iowa 52142	205	217	35	P	3,100	3,100	1,500
Upsala College; East Orange, N.J. 07019	673	423	74	P/L	4,212	4,212	2,000
Urbana College; Urbana, Ohio 43078	455[1]	213[1]	25	P/Sw	2,895	2,895	1,890
Ursinus College; Collegeville, Pa. 19426	675[1]	484[1]	75	P	4,450	4,450	2,000
Ursuline College; Cleveland, Ohio 44124	38[1]	467[1]	44	P/RC	2,830	2,830	1,900
Utah, University of; Salt Lake City, Utah 84112	13,406[1]	9,564[1]	3,000	S	690	1,815	1,885
Utah State University; Logan, Utah 84322	5,744[1]	4,195[1]	462	S	786	1,203	1,900
Utica College of Syracuse University; Utica, N.Y. 13502	614	720	90	P	4,400[14]	4,400[14]	2,000
Valdosta State College; Valdosta, Ga. 31698	2,108[1]	2,793[1]	250	S	663	1,620	1,200
Valley City State College; Valley City, N.D. 58072	399	499	55	S	572	1,133	1,230
Valley Forge Christian College; Phoenixville, Pa. 19460	314[1]	221[1]	18	P/AG	2,200	2,200	1,897
Valparaiso University; Valparaiso, Ind. 46383	1,802	1,979	268	P/L	3,900	3,900	2,090
Vanderbilt University; Nashville, Tenn. 37240	4,450	3,865	1,160	P	5,300	5,300	2,540
VanderCook College of Music*; Chicago, Ill. 60616	73	17	14	P	2,780	2,780	2,000
Vassar College; Poughkeepsie, N.Y. 12601	1,290	957	187	P	6,400	6,400	2,800
Vennard College; University Park, Iowa 52595	95	85	11	P/ID	1,838	1,838	1,604
Vermont, University of; Burlington, Vt. 05405	4,113[1]	5,126[1]	742	S	1,650	4,560	1,996
Vermont College. *See* Norwich University							
Villa Maria College*; Erie, Pa. 16505	3	428	49	P/RC	3,000	3,000	1,750
Villanova University; Villanova, Pa. 19085	3,553	2,648	431	P/RC	4,290[6]	4,290[6]	2,772[6]
Virginia, University of; Charlottesville, Va. 22906	9,017[1]	7,435[1]	1,429	S	1,044	2,404	1,852
Clinch Valley College; Wise, Va. 24293	342[1]	375[1]	43	S	720	1,020	528
Virginia Commonwealth University; Richmond, Va. 23284	8,423[1]	11,394[1]	1,408	S	920	1,890	2,074
Virginia Intermont College; Bristol, Va. 24201	87	497	42	P/B	3,050	3,050	1,925
Virginia Military Institute; Lexington, Va. 24450	1,271[1]	—	94	S	720	1,970	1,365
Virginia Polytechnic Institute and State University; Blacksburg, Va. 24061	13,191	7,878	1,900	S	972	1,917	1,296

Institution and location	Enrollment		Faculty	Control	Tuition		Rm/Bd
	Male	Female			Res.	Nonres.	
Virginia State University; Petersburg, Va. 23803	1,647[1]	1,985[1]	200	S	979	1,554	2,054
Virginia Union University*; Richmond, Va. 23220	544	568	81	P/B	2,390	2,390	1,600
Virginia Wesleyan College; Norfolk, Va. 23502	381[1]	453[1]	40	P/UM	3,700	3,700	1,950
Virgin Islands, College of the; St. Thomas, V.I. 00801	167	416	66	S	400	1,200	1,770
Visual Arts, School of; New York, N.Y. 10010	1,197	1,079	n.a.	P	4,200	4,200	—
Viterbo College; La Crosse, Wis. 54601	306[6]	807[6]	65	P/RC	2,970	2,970	1,800
Voorhees College; Denmark, S.C. 29042	223[1]	390[1]	44	P	2,329	2,329	1,862
Wabash College; Crawfordsville, Ind. 47933	790[1]	—	69	P	4,100	4,100	1,950
Wagner College; Staten Island, N.Y. 10301	848	1,044	83	P	4,212	4,212	2,576
Wake Forest University; Winston–Salem, N.C. 27109	3,063	1,848	1,048	P/B	4,100	4,100	1,200
Walla Walla College; College Place, Wash. 99324	984[1]	921[1]	130	P/SDA	4,650	4,650	2,100
Walsh College; Canton, Ohio 44720	320	235	32	P	3,200	3,200	1,800
Walsh College; Troy, Mich. 48084	42	38	8	P	1,908	1,908	—
Warner Pacific College; Portland, Ore. 97215	233	189	28	CG	3,000	3,000	1,500
Warner Southern College; Lake Wales, Fla. 33853	145[1]	140[1]	23	P/CG	2,700	2,700	1,500
Warren Wilson College; Swannanoa, N.C. 28778	222[1]	274[1]	37	P/UP	2,800	2,800	1,500
Wartburg College; Waverly, Iowa 50677	475[1]	603[1]	72	P/AL	3,574	3,574	1,552
Washburn University of Topeka; Topeka, Kan. 66621	1,746[1]	1,546[1]	180	Mun	950	1,660	1,700
Washington, University of; Seattle, Wash. 98105	13,085	11,162	2,005	S	1,059	3,048	2,000
Washington and Jefferson College*; Washington, Pa. 15301	655	343	89	P	4,055	4,055	1,550
Washington and Lee University; Lexington, Va. 24450	1,522[1]	92[1]	154	P	4,800	4,800	1,800
Washington Bible College; Lanham, Md. 20801	251	137	26	P	2,000	2,000	2,000
Washington College; Chestertown, Md. 21620	359[1]	305[1]	64	P	3,350	3,350	1,025
Washington School of Art. *See* LaSalle Extension Univ.							
Washington State University; Pullman, Wash. 99164	10,007[1]	7,461[1]	1,000	S	1,060[6]	3,048[6]	2,004[6]
Washington University in St. Louis; St. Louis, Mo. 63130	5,089[1]	3,310[1]	1,299	P	6,250	6,250	2,745
Wayland Baptist College*; Plainview, Tex. 79072	279	264	49	SB	1,700	1,700	1,730
Waynesburg College; Waynesburg, Pa. 15370	474	353	54	P/Pres	4,200	4,200	1,950
Wayne School. *See* LaSalle Extension Univ.							
Wayne State College; Wayne, Neb. 68787	781[1]	1,044[1]	108	S	796	1,276	1,528
Wayne State University; Detroit, Mich. 48202	15,108	15,688	1,400	S	1,350	2,750	1,500[2]
Webb Institute of Naval Architecture; Glen Cove, N.Y. 11542	64	3	10	P	—	—	2,400
Weber State College; Ogden, Utah 84408	5,655[1]	4,410[1]	345	S	705	1,785	2,540
Webster College; St. Louis, Mo. 63119	952[1]	682[1]	70	P	3,600	3,600	1,900
Wellesley College; Wellesley, Mass. 02181	—	2,092[1]	222	P	6,450	6,450	3,180
Wells College; Aurora, N.Y. 13026	1[1]	520[1]	50	P	5,900	5,900	2,200
Wentworth Institute of Technology; Boston, Mass. 02115	2,550	150	144	P	3,475	3,475	2,550
Wesleyan College; Macon, Ga. 31297	3[1]	420[1]	42	P/M	2,800	3,600	1,800
Wesleyan University; Middletown, Conn. 06457	2,600[6]		235	P	6,950	6,950	2,770
Wesley College; Dover, Del. 19901	572	647	51	P/UM	3,850	3,850	1,930
Wesley College; Florence, Miss. 39073	29	37	7	P/M	1,090	1,090	1,210
Westbrook College; Portland, Me. 04103	185[1]	735[1]	45	P	3,825	3,825	1,970
West Chester State College; West Chester, Pa. 19380	3,580	5,320	503	S	1,100	1,930	1,400
West Coast Bible College*; Fresno, Calif. 93710	116	74	n.a.	P/CG	n.a.	n.a.	n.a.
West Coast University[62]; Los Angeles, Calif. 90020	1,005[1]	199[1]	47	P	2,256	2,256	—
Western Baptist College; Salem, Ore. 97302	217[6]	200[6]	17	P/B	3,100[14]	3,100[14]	1,935[14]
Western Bible College; Morrison, Colo. 80209	121[1]	82[1]	11	P/ID	1,920	1,920	1,520
Western Carolina University. *See* North Carolina, University System of							
Western Connecticut State College; Danbury, Conn. 06810	1,174[1]	1,563[1]	175	S	775	1,765	1,918
Western Illinois University; Macomb, Ill. 61455	5,699[1]	4,993[1]	624	S	667	2,001	1,798
Western Kentucky University; Bowling Green, Ky. 42101	4,510[1]	4,849[1]	697	S	626	1,780	1,798
Western Maryland College; Westminster, Md. 21157	610	744	88	P	4,500	4,500	1,925
Western Michigan University; Kalamazoo, Mich. 49008	7,992[1]	7,444[1]	860	S	1,200	2,900	2,011
Western Montana College; Dillon, Mont. 59725	404[1]	548[1]	38	S	579	1,587	1,925
Western New England College; Springfield, Mass. 01095	1,356	777	95	P	3,600	3,600	2,130
Western New Mexico University; Silver City, N.M. 88061	637	839	65	S	306	1,095	1,408
Western Oregon State College[76]; Monmouth, Ore. 97361	874[1]	1,560[1]	180	S	921	2,925	1,795
Western State College of Colorado; Gunnison, Colo. 81230	1,810[1]	1,290[1]	159	S	524	2,280	1,594
Western State University College of Law of Orange County*; Fullerton, Calif. 92631	1,221	525	61	P	2,490	2,490	3,875
Western State University College of Law of San Diego; San Diego, Calif. 92101	516	283	13	P	3,420	3,420	—
Western Washington University; Bellingham, Wash. 98225	4,511[1]	4,830[1]	429	S	618	1,983	1,680
Westfield State College; Westfield, Mass. 01086	1,027	1,563	155	S	725	2,538	1,687
West Florida, The University of*; Pensacola, Fla. 32504	2,538	2,647	232	S	n.a.	n.a.	1,570
West Georgia College; Carrollton, Ga. 30118	1,952	2,930	238	S	708	1,662	1,500

Institution and location	Enrollment			Control	Tuition		Rm/Bd
	Male	Female	Faculty		Res.	Nonrès.	
West Liberty State College; West Liberty, W. Va. 26074	993[1]	1,086[1]	133	S	390	1,330	1,615
Westmar College; LeMars, Iowa 51031	292	250	35	P/UM	3,600	3,600	1,720
Westminster Choir College; Princeton, N.J. 08540	200[1]	238[1]	46	P	4,100	4,100	1,975
Westminster College; Fulton, Mo. 65251	563[1]	79[1]	49	P	3,900[14]	3,900[14]	1,950
Westminster College; New Wilmington, Pa. 16142	710	791	116	P/UP	4,376	4,376	1,824
Westminster College; Salt Lake City, Utah 84105	554	678	67	P	2,860	2,860	1,800
Westmont College; Santa Barbara, Calif. 93108	487[1]	566[1]	60	P/ID	4,960	4,960	2,500
West Texas State University; Canyon, Tex. 79016	2,929	3,292	265	S	120	1,200	1,500
West Virginia College of Graduate Studies; Institute, W. Va. 25112	1,177[1]	2,146[1]	60	S	250	1,270	—
West Virginia Institute of Technology; Montgomery, W. Va. 25136	1,563[1]	632[1]	145	S	372	1,312	1,837
West Virginia School of Osteopathic Medicine; Lewisburg, W. Va. 24901	181	48	32	S	285	785	—
West Virginia State College; Institute, W. Va. 25112	1,179	961	131	S	415	1,355	1,840
West Virginia University; Morgantown, W. Va. 26506	9,259[1]	6,398[1]	1,312	S	492	1,512	1,864
West Virginia Wesleyan College; Buckhannon, W. Va. 26201	691[1]	991[1]	103	P/UM	3,275	3,275	2,075
Wheaton College*; Norton, Mass. 02766	—	1,206	90	P	6,040	6,040	2,400
Wheaton College; Wheaton, Ill. 60187	1,165	1,193	145	P	4,084	4,084	2,358
Wheeling College; Wheeling, W. Va. 26003	491[1]	535[1]	58	P	3,800[14]	3,800[14]	2,150[14]
Wheelock College; Boston, Mass. 02215	8[1]	568[1]	59	P	4,240	4,240	2,100
Whitman College; Walla Walla, Wash. 99362	587	553	85	P	5,150	5,150	1,360
Whittier College*; Whittier, Calif. 90602	544	614	85	P	4,250	4,250	1,885
Whitworth College; Spokane, Wash. 99251	586[1]	639[1]	69	P/Pres	4,450[14]	4,450[14]	2,000
Wichita State University; Wichita, Kan. 67208	3,303	3,091	516	S	880	2,130	1,900
Widener University; Chester, Pa. 19013	1,275[1]	1,000[1]	136	P	4,475	4,475	2,400
Wilberforce University; Wilberforce, Ohio 45384	523[6]	553[6]	50	P/AME	3,840	3,840	2,100
Wiley College; Marshall, Tex. 75670	269	312	34	UM	897	897	1,666
Wilkes College; Wilkes-Barre, Pa. 18766	1,020	901	155	P	4,200[14]	4,200[14]	2,100[14]
Willamette University; Salem, Ore. 97301	1,012[1]	784[1]	117	P	4,860	4,860	2,150
William and Mary, College of; Williamsburg, Va. 23185	3,010	3,364	355	S	1,334	3,368	2,345
William Carey College; Hattiesburg, Miss. 39401	563[1]	1,140[1]	81	P/SB	2,010	2,010	1,450
William Jewell College; Liberty, Mo. 64068	800	600	91	P	3,170	3,170	1,620
William Mitchell College of Law; St. Paul, Minn. 55105	741	416	30	P	2,770	2,770	
William Paterson Coll. of New Jersey; Wayne, N.J. 07470	2,825	3,208	393	S	975	1,575	1,150
William Penn College; Oskaloosa, Iowa 52577	365[1]	206[1]	34	P/SOF	4,490	4,490	1,420
Williams College; Williamstown, Mass. 01267	1,100[1]	900[1]	160	P	5,950	5,950	2,330
William Smith College. See Hobart and William Smith Colleges							
William Woods College; Fulton, Mo. 65251	—	926[1]	75	P	4,160	4,160	1,790
Wilmington College; New Castle, Del. 19720	161	213	10	P	(26)	(26)	1,000
Wilmington College; Wilmington, Ohio 45177	490[1]	250[1]	75	P/SOF	3,570[77]	3,570[77]	705
Wilson College; Chambersburg, Pa. 17201	—	167	30	P/Pres	4,880	4,880	2,000
Wingate College; Wingate, N.C. 28174	800	734	63	P/B	1,850	1,850	1,200
Winona State Univ. See Minnesota State Univ. System							
Winston–Salem State University. See North Carolina, University System of							
Winthrop College; Rock Hill, S.C. 29733	1,352	3,479	258[78]	S	1,012[14]	1,800[14]	1,372
Wisconsin, University of*; Madison, Wis. 53706	21,986	18,247	2,350	S	1,006	3,491	1,475
U. of Wisconsin—Eau Claire; Eau Claire, Wis. 54701	4,702[6]	6,352[6]	502	S	447	1,522	1,500
U. of Wisconsin—Green Bay; Green Bay, Wis. 54302	1,827[1]	2,337[1]	n.a.	S	860	2,954	1,990
U. of Wisconsin—La Crosse; La Crosse, Wis. 54601	3,174	3,843	370	S	913	3,062	1,480
U. of Wisconsin—Madison; Madison, Wis. 53706	22,579[1]	18,770[1]	2,350	S	947	3,432	2,095[14]
U. of Wisconsin—Milwaukee; Milwaukee, Wis. 53201	7,044[1]	6,794[1]	904	S	1,003	3,488	1,997
U. of Wisconsin—Oshkosh; Oshkosh, Wis. 54901	4,825	5,375	450	S	950	3,100	1,550
U. of Wisconsin—Parkside; Kenosha, Wis. 53141	2,766[1]	2,602[1]	182	S	866	3,015	—
U. of Wisconsin—Platteville; Platteville, Wis. 53818	2,923	1,653	260	S	721	2,870	1,500
U. of Wisconsin—River Falls; River Falls, Wis. 54022	2,668[1]	2,564[1]	325	S	921	3,070	1,700
U. of Wisconsin—Stevens Point; Stevens Point, Wis. 54481	4,168	4,294	394	S	972	3,121	1,694
U. of Wisconsin—Stout; Menomonie, Wis. 54751	3,405[1]	3,375[1]	315	S	959	3,108	1,730
U. of Wisconsin—Superior*; Superior, Wis. 54880	885	654	145	S	895	3,050	1,895
U. of Wisconsin—Whitewater; Whitewater, Wis. 53190	4,093[1]	4,357[1]	516	S	904	3,053	1,952
Wittenberg University; Springfield, Ohio 45501	1,054[1]	1,165[1]	136	P/LCA	5,259	5,259	2,130
Wofford College; Spartanburg, S.C. 29301	750[1]	251[1]	60	P/UM	3,440	3,440	1,910
Woodbury University*; Los Angeles, Calif. 90017[62]	697	512	42	P	3,048	3,048	n.a.
Wooster, The College of; Wooster, Ohio 44691	931[1]	812[1]	140	P/Pres	7,930[27]	7,930[27]	
Worcester Polytechnic Institute; Worcester, Mass. 01609	2,138[1]	391[1]	186	P	4,950	4,950	2,170
Worcester State College; Worcester, Mass. 01602	1,182[1]	1,550[1]	179	S	600	2,250	1,742
Wright Institute*; Berkeley, Calif. 94704	3,135	3,092	575	P	960	1,950	n.a.
Wright State University; Dayton, Ohio 45435	7,580[1]	8,055[1]	650	S	1,278	2,448	1,600

Institution and location	Enrollment				Tuition		
	Male	Female	Faculty	Control	Res.	Nonres.	Rm/Bd
Wyoming, University of; Laramie, Wyo. 82071	5,051[1]	3,962[1]	806	S	592	1,878	1,887
Xavier University; Cincinnati, Ohio 45207	7,157		184	P/RC	3,400	3,400	2,000
Xavier University of Louisiana; New Orleans, La. 70125	671	1,286	140	P/RC	1,300	1,300	925
Yale University; New Haven, Conn. 06520	9,700		1,300	P	6,210	6,210	2,900
Yankton College; Yankton, S.D. 57078	128	105	30	P/UCC	3,580[6]	3,580[6]	1,690
Yeshiva University; New York, N.Y. 10033	3,479[1]	2,121[1]	1,200	P	4,500[14]	4,500[14]	2,180[14]
York College (NYC). See New York, City University of							
York College of Pennsylvania; York, Pa. 17405	1,621[1]	2,206[1]	102	P	2,472	2,472	1,708
Youngstown State Univ.; Youngstown, Ohio 44555	5,513[1]	4,709[1]	405	S	915	1,635	1,605

1. Fall 1980. 2. Room only. 3. Part-time school. 4. Includes SUNY College of Ceramics. 5. Includes summer 1982. 6. Fall 1981. 7. Plus 29 part time. 8. $60 per credit hour. 9. Off campus. 10. From $1,700 to $6,400, depending on branch. 11. Part time. 12. $70 per hour. 13. $100 per semester hour. 14. 1981-82. 15. Member of State University and Community College System. 16. $150 per credit. 17. $35 per hour. 18. Plus 15 hours of work each week. 19. $80 per semester hour. 20. LDS members. 21. Non-LDS members. 22. Member California State University and Colleges. 23. Fees: $266 for 6 or less units; $306 for more than 6. 24. $40 or $48 per unit or to a maximum of $600 or $720 plus registration fees. 25. Entering students; continuing students, $3,790. 26. $90 per credit. 27. Comprehensive fee covering tuition, room, and board. 28. Plus 150 adjunct faculty. 29. $48 per credit hour. 30. $145 per credit hour. 31. $550 per month. 32. Includes SUNY statutory colleges and medical college in New York City. 33. State assisted. 34. Member of State University and Community College System. 35. Under SUNY supervision. 36. $45 per credit. 37. Plus 1,135 part-time teacher-practitioners. 38. $96 per credit hour. 39. Member University of Hawaii System. 40. Protestant. 41. $33.50 per credit hour. 42. $87.50 per credit hour. 43. Plus 180 part time. 44. $28.25 per credit hour. 45. $64 per credit hour. 46. $150 per credit hour. 47. $325 per course. 48. Accreditation Probation/Show Cause. 49. Includes La Sierra Campus in Riverside. 50. $570-$1,600. 51. $1,500-$6,350. 52. $51 per credit hour. 53. Affiliated academically with the University of Minnesota. 54. Undergraduate; medical and dental, $2,000. 55. $62 per semester hour. 56. Plus 590 adjunct faculty. 57. Formerly Our Lady of Angels College. 58. Part of Louisiana State University System. 59. Fees. 60. $16.50 per credit hour. 61. $51.50 per credit hour. 62. Accreditation on probation. 63. Tuition, room, and board paid for by required campus employment and scholarships. 64. $5 per credit. 65. $25 per credit. 66. UM/UP/UCC. 67. $82 per semester hour. 68. Year 1; years 2-5, $3,300. 69. $108 per credit hour. 70. Plus 45 part time. 71. $47.00 per credit hour. 72. Formerly Oklahoma City Southwestern College. 73. Member Texas A&M System. 74. Room only, $100 per month. 75. From 1 to 14 credit hours, $77 per credit hour. 76. Formerly Oregon College of Education. 77. 1982. 78. Fall 1982.

Institutions of Higher Education—Faculty and Enrollment Characteristics and Projections to 1985

(in thousands except for institutions)

Item	1985	1980	1978[2]	1977[2]	1976[2]	1975	1974	1973	1972	1971
Institutions	n.a.	n.a.	2,871	2,826	2,785	2,765	2,747	2,720	2,665	2,606
4-year	n.a.	n.a.	1,816	1,808	1,783	1,767	1,744	1,717	1,701	1,675
2-year	n.a.	n.a.	1,055	1,018	1,002	998	1,003	1,003	964	931
Resident instructional staff	696	730	809	812	793	670	622	599	590	590
ENROLLMENT										
Degree credit	11,000	11,142	n.a.	n.a.	n.a.	9,731	9,023	8,518	8,265	8,116
Male	5,621	5,876	5,641	5,789	5,811	5,321	4,969	4,771	4,701	4,717
Female	5,379	5,266	5,619	5,497	5,201	4,410	4,055	3,747	3,564	3,399
4-year institutions	7,530	7,896	7,232	7,243	7,129	7,223	6,825	6,597	6,473	6,391
2-year institutions	3,470	3,246	4,027	4,043	3,883	2,508	2,198	1,921	1,792	1,725
Full-time	6,139	6,585	6,668	6,793	6,717	6,147	5,817	5,683	5,647	5,676
Part-time	4,861	4,557	4,592	4,493	4,295	3,584	3,206	2,835	2,618	2,440
Public	8,756	8,721	8,786	8,847	8,653	7,426	6,838	6,389	6,159	6,014
Private	2,244	2,421	2,474	2,439	2,359	2,306	2,185	2,130	2,106	2,102
Graduate	1,456	1,468	1,081	1,085	1,085	1,263	1,190	1,123	1,066	1,012
Undergraduate[1]	9,544	9,674	10,179	10,201	9,927	8,468	7,833	7,395	7,199	7,104
Male	4,915	5,114	5,057	5,193	5,209	4,621	4,306	4,124	4,074	4,102
Female	4,629	4,560	5,122	5,008	4,719	3,847	3,527	3,271	3,125	3,002
4-year institutions	6,074	6,428	6,152	6,158	6,045	5,960	5,635	5,474	5,407	5,379
Full-time	4,421	4,830	4,678	4,703	4,622	4,619	4,429	4,350	4,350	4,358
Part-time	1,653	1,598	1,474	1,456	1,423	1,341	1,206	1,124	1,057	1,021
2-year institutions	3,470	3,246	4,028	4,043	3,883	2,508	2,198	1,921	1,792	1,725
Public	7,704	7,663	8,083	8,128	7,924	6,520	5,986	5,589	5,401	5,302
Private	1,840	2,011	2,096	2,073	2,003	1,948	1,847	1,806	1,799	1,802
1st time enrolled	1,709	1,936	2,422	2,432	2,377	1,910	1,854	1,757	1,740	1,766
Nondegree credit	2,360	2,072	n.a.	n.a.	n.a.	1,453	1,200	1,084	950	833
Total	13,360	13,214	11,260	11,286	11,012	11,184	10,223	9,602	9,215	8,949

1. Includes first-professional enrollment. 2. Total enrollment, degree and nondegree credit. NOTE: As of fall. Covers universities, colleges, professional schools, junior and teachers colleges, and normal schools, both publicly and privately controlled, regular session, n.a. = not available. Source: Department of Education, National Center for Educational Statistics.

U.S. STATISTICS

Population
Colonial Population Estimates (in round numbers)

Year	Population	Year	Population	Year	Population	Year	Population
1610	350	1660	75,100	1710	331,700	1760	1,593,600
1620	2,300	1670	111,900	1720	466,200	1770	2,148,100
1630	4,600	1680	151,500	1730	629,400	1780	2,780,400
1640	26,600	1690	210,400	1740	905,600		
1650	50,400	1700	250,900	1750	1,170,800		

National Censuses[1]

Year	Resident population[2]	Land area, sq mi.	Pop. per sq mi.	Year	Resident population[2]	Land area, sq mi.	Pop. per sq mi.
1790	3,929,214	864,746	4.5	1890	62,947,714	2,969,640	21.2
1800	5,308,483	864,746	6.1	1900	75,994,575	2,969,834	25.6
1810	7,239,881	1,681,828	4.3	1910	91,972,266	2,969,565	31.0
1820	9,638,453	1,749,462	5.5	1920	105,710,620	2,969,451	35.6
1830	12,866,020	1,749,462	7.4	1930	122,775,046	2,977,128	41.2
1840	17,069,453	1,749,462	9.8	1940	131,669,275	2,977,128	44.2
1850	23,191,876	2,940,042	7.9	1950	150,697,361	2,974,726	50.7
1860	31,443,321	2,969,640	10.6	1960	179,323,175	3,540,911	50.6
1870	39,818,449	2,969,640	13.4	1970	203,302,031	3,540,023	57.4
1880	50,155,783	2,969,640	16.9	1980	226,504,825	n.a.	62.7[3]

1. Beginning with 1960, figures include Alaska and Hawaii. 2. Excludes armed forces overseas. 3. Based on 1970 area. NOTE: n.a. = not available. *Source:* Department of Commerce, Bureau of the Census.

Population Distribution by Age, Race, Nativity, and Sex

Year	Total	Age					Race and nativity				
		Under 5	5–19	20–44	45–64	65 and over	White[1] Total	Native born	Foreign born	Black	Other races[1]
PERCENT DISTRIBUTION											
1860[2]	100.0	15.4	35.8	35.7	10.4	2.7	85.6	72.6	13.0	14.1	0.3
1870[2]	100.0	14.3	35.4	35.4	11.9	3.0	87.1	72.9	14.2	12.7	0.2
1880[2]	100.0	13.8	34.3	35.9	12.6	3.4	86.5	73.4	13.1	13.1	0.3
1890[3]	100.0	12.2	33.9	36.9	13.1	3.9	87.5	73.0	14.5	11.9	0.3
1900	100.0	12.1	32.3	37.7	13.7	4.1	87.9	74.5	13.4	11.6	0.5
1910	100.0	11.6	30.4	39.0	14.6	4.3	88.9	74.4	14.5	10.7	0.4
1920	100.0	10.9	29.8	38.4	16.1	4.7	89.7	76.7	13.0	9.9	0.4
1930	100.0	9.3	29.5	38.3	17.4	5.4	89.8	78.4	11.4	9.7	0.5
1940	100.0	8.0	26.4	38.9	19.8	6.8	89.8	81.1	8.7	9.8	0.4
1950[4]	100.0	10.7	23.2	37.6	20.3	8.1	89.5	82.8	6.7	10.0	0.5
1960[4]	100.0	11.3	27.1	32.2	20.1	9.2	88.6	83.4	5.2	10.5	0.9
1970[4]	100.0	8.4	29.5	31.7	20.6	9.8	87.6	83.4	4.3	11.1	1.4
1979[5]	100.0	7.1	25.2	36.6	19.9	11.2	86.3	n.a.	n.a.	11.8	1.9
1980[5]	100.0	7.2	24.8	37.1	19.6	11.3	83.2	n.a.	n.a.	11.7	5.2
MALES PER 100 FEMALES											
1860[2]	104.7	102.4	101.2	107.9	111.5	98.3	105.3	103.7	115.1	99.6	260.8
1870[2]	102.2	102.9	101.2	99.2	114.5	100.5	102.8	100.6	115.3	96.2	400.7
1880[2]	103.6	103.0	101.3	104.0	110.2	101.4	104.0	102.1	115.9	97.8	362.2
1890[3]	105.0	103.6	101.4	107.3	108.3	104.2	105.4	102.9	118.7	99.5	165.2
1900	104.4	102.1	100.9	105.8	110.7	102.0	104.9	102.8	117.4	98.6	185.2
1910	106.0	102.5	101.3	108.1	114.4	101.1	106.6	102.7	129.2	98.9	185.6
1920	104.0	102.5	100.8	102.8	115.2	101.3	104.4	101.7	121.7	99.2	156.6
1930	102.5	103.0	101.4	100.5	109.1	100.5	102.9	101.1	115.8	97.0	150.6
1940	100.7	103.2	102.0	98.1	105.2	95.5	101.2	100.1	111.1	95.0	140.5
1950[4]	98.6	103.9	102.5	96.2	100.1	89.6	99.0	98.8	102.0	93.7	129.7

Year	Total	Under 5	5–19	20–44	45–64	65 and over	White[1] Total	Native born	Foreign born	Black	Other races[1]
1960[4]	97.1	103.4	102.7	95.6	95.7	82.8	97.4	97.6	94.2	93.3	109.7
1970[4]	94.8	104.0	103.3	95.1	91.6	72.1	95.3	95.9	83.8	90.8	100.2
1979[5]	94.6	104.7	103.7	97.5	92.1	68.4	95.2	n.a.	n.a.	90.6	92.6
1980[5]	94.5	104.7	104.0	98.1	90.7	67.6	94.8	n.a.	n.a.	89.6	100.3

1. The 1980 census data for White and other races categories are not directly comparable to those shown for the preceding years because of changes in the way some persons reported their race, as well as changes in 1980 procedures relating to the racial classification. 2. Excludes Indians in Indian territory and on Indian reservations. 3. The age figures exclude all persons residing on Indian reservations; these persons are included in the race and nativity distributions. 4. Data by age and race include, and data by nativity exclude, Armed Forces overseas and other persons abroad. 5. Total population including Armed Forces overseas. NOTE: In 1860, the data in the census reports at ages 40–49 and 60–69 are published in 10-year age groupings; these were subdivided into 5-year groupings by the author. Beginning 1960, includes Alaska and Hawaii. n.a. = not available. *Source:* Mortimer Spiegelman, *Introduction to Demography;* Department of Commerce, Bureau of the Census.

Population and Rank of Large Metropolitan Areas, 1970–1980
(over 150,000)

Standard metropolitan statistical area	1980 Census Number	Rank	1970 Census Number	Rank	Change, 1970–80 Number	%
Akron, Ohio	660,328	57	679,239	52	−18,911	−2.7
Albany–Schenectady–Troy, N.Y.	795,019	50	777,977	43	17,042	2.2
Albuquerque, N.M.	454,499	86	333,266	102	121,233	36.4
Alexandria, La.	151,985	205	131,749	203	20,236	15.4
Allentown–Bethlehem–Easton, Pa.–N.J.	636,714	62	594,382	60	42,332	7.2
Amarillo, Tex.	173,699	188	144,396	192	29,303	20.3
Anaheim–Santa Ana–Garden Grove, Calif.	1,931,570	18	1,421,233	20	510,337	36.0
Anchorage, Alaska	173,017	191	126,385	211	46,632	36.9
Ann Arbor, Mich.	264,748	145	234,103	141	30,645	13.1
Appleton–Oshkosh, Wis.	291,325	129	276,948	121	14,377	5.2
Asheville, N.C.	177,761	184	161,059	181	16,702	10.4
Atlanta	2,029,618	16	1,595,517	18	434,101	27.3
Atlantic City, N.J.	194,119	171	175,043	168	19,076	10.9
Augusta, Ga.–S.C.	327,372	113	275,787	122	51,585	18.8
Austin, Tex.	536,450	70	360,463	93	175,987	48.9
Bakersfield, Calif.	403,089	97	330,234	104	72,855	22.1
Baltimore	2,174,023	14	2,071,016	13	103,007	5.0
Baton Rouge, La.	493,973	80	375,628	87	118,345	31.6
Battle Creek, Mich.	187,338	177	180,129	164	7,209	4.1
Beaumont–Port Arthur, Tex.	375,497	104	347,568	97	27,929	8.1
Biloxi–Gulfport, Miss.	191,918	174	160,070	183	31,848	19.9
Binghamton, N.Y.–Pa.	301,336	126	302,672	111	−1,336	−0.4
Birmingham, Ala.	847,360	45	767,230	44	80,130	10.5
Boise, Idaho	173,036	190	112,230	232	60,806	54.2
Boston	2,763,357	10	2,899,101	8	−135,744	−4.6
Bridgeport, Conn.	395,455	98	401,752	82	−6,297	−1.5
Brockton, Mass.	169,374	196	150,416	186	18,958	12.7
Brownsville–Harlingen–San Benito, Tex.	209,680	164	140,368	194	69,312	49.4
Buffalo, N.Y.	1,242,573	31	1,349,211	24	−106,638	−7.9
Canton, Ohio	404,421	96	393,789	83	10,632	2.7
Cedar Rapids, Iowa	169,775	194	163,213	179	6,562	4.1
Champaign–Urbana–Rantoul, Ill.	168,392	197	163,281	178	5,111	3.2
Charleston–North Charleston, S.C.	430,301	91	336,036	100	94,265	28.1
Charleston, W. Va.	269,595	142	257,140	133	12,455	4.9
Charlotte–Gastonia, N.C.	637,218	61	557,785	62	79,433	14.3
Chattanooga, Tenn.–Ga.	426,540	92	370,857	90	55,683	15.1
Chicago	7,102,328	3	6,974,755	3	127,573	1.9
Cincinnati, Ohio–Ky.–Ind.	1,401,403	27	1,387,207	22	14,196	1.1
Clarksville–Hopkinsville, Tenn.–Ky.	150,220	209	118,945	220	31,275	26.3
Cleveland	1,898,720	19	2,063,729	14	−165,009	−7.9
Colorado Springs, Colo.	317,458	120	239,288	139	78,170	32.7
Columbia, S.C.	408,176	95	322,880	107	85,296	26.5
Columbus, Ga.–Ala.	239,196	154	238,584	140	612	0.3
Columbus, Ohio	1,093,293	35	1,017,847	33	75,446	7.5
Corpus Christi, Tex.	326,228	114	284,832	118	41,396	14.6

Standard metropolitan statistical area	1980 Census Number	1980 Census Rank	1970 Census Number	1970 Census Rank	Change, 1970–80 Number	Change, 1970–80 %
Dallas–Fort Worth	2,974,878	8	2,377,623	12	597,255	25.2
Davenport–Rock Island–Moline, Iowa–Ill.	383,958	100	362,638	91	21,320	5.9
Dayton, Ohio	830,070	47	852,531	40	−22,461	−2.6
Daytona Beach, Fla.	258,762	148	169,487	174	89,275	52.7
Denver–Boulder, Colo.	1,619,921	22	1,239,545	27	380,376	30.7
Des Moines, Iowa	338,048	111	313,562	109	24,486	7.9
Detroit	4,352,762	5	4,435,051	5	−82,289	−1.8
Duluth–Superior, Minn.–Wis.	266,650	143	265,350	126	1,300	0.5
El Paso	479,899	82	359,291	94	120,608	33.6
Erie, Pa.	279,780	135	263,654	128	16,126	6.2
Eugene–Springfield, Ore.	275,226	138	215,401	151	59,825	27.8
Evansville, Ind.–Ky.	309,408	123	284,959	117	24,449	8.6
Fall River, Mass.–R.I.	176,831	185	169,549	173	7,282	4.3
Fayetteville–Springdale, Ark.	177,850	183	127,846	208	50,004	39.2
Fayetteville, N.C.	247,160	152	212,042	152	35,118	16.6
Flint, Mich.	521,589	77	508,664	69	12,925	2.6
Fort Lauderdale–Hollywood, Fla.	1,014,043	37	620,100	58	393,943	63.6
Fort Myers–Cape Coral, Fla.	205,266	166	105,216	238	100,050	95.1
Fort Smith, Ark.–Okla.	203,269	167	160,421	182	42,848	26.8
Fort Wayne, Ind.	382,961	101	361,984	92	20,977	5.8
Fresno, Calif.	515,013	78	413,329	77	101,684	24.7
Gainesville, Fla.	151,348	208	104,764	239	46,584	44.5
Galveston–Texas City, Tex.	195,940	170	169,812	172	26,128	15.4
Gary–Hammond–East Chicago, Ind.	642,781	58	633,367	54	9,414	1.5
Grand Rapids, Mich.	601,680	64	539,225	67	62,455	11.6
Green Bay, Wis.	175,280	187	158,244	185	17,036	10.8
Greensboro–Winston-Salem–High Point, N.C.	827,385	48	724,129	47	103,256	14.3
Greenville–Spartanburg, S.C.	568,758	68	473,454	71	95,304	20.2
Hamilton–Middletown, Ohio	258,787	147	226,207	145	32,580	14.5
Harrisburg, Pa.	446,072	88	410,505	80	35,567	8.7
Hartford, Conn.	726,114	54	720,581	48	5,533	0.8
Honolulu	762,874	52	630,528	55	132,346	21.0
Houston	2,905,350	9	1,999,316	16	906,034	45.4
Huntington–Ashland, W. Va.–Ky.–Ohio	311,350	122	286,935	116	24,415	8.6
Huntsville, Ala.	308,593	124	282,450	119	26,143	9.3
Indianapolis	1,166,929	34	1,111,352	29	55,577	5.1
Jackson, Mich.	151,495	207	143,274	193	8,221	5.8
Jackson, Miss.	320,425	117	258,906	130	61,519	23.8
Jacksonville, Fla.	737,519	53	621,827	57	115,692	18.7
Jersey City, N.J.	556,972	69	607,839	59	−50,867	−8.3
Johnson Cty–Kingsport–Bristol, Tenn.–Va.	433,638	90	373,591	88	60,047	16.1
Johnstown, Pa.	264,506	146	262,822	129	1,684	0.7
Kalamazoo–Portage, Mich.	279,192	137	257,723	132	21,469	8.4
Kansas City, Mo.–Kan.	1,327,020	29	1,273,926	25	53,094	4.2
Killeen–Temple, Tex.	214,656	162	159,794	184	54,862	34.4
Knoxville, Tenn.	476,517	83	409,409	81	67,108	16.4
Lafayette, La.	150,017	210	111,643	233	38,374	34.4
Lake Charles, La.	167,048	198	145,415	189	21,633	14.9
Lakeland–Winter Haven, Fla.	321,652	116	228,515	143	93,137	40.8
Lancaster, Pa.	362,346	108	320,079	108	42,267	13.3
Lansing–East Lansing, Mich.	468,482	84	424,271	75	44,211	10.5
Las Vegas, Nev.	461,816	85	273,288	123	188,528	69.0
Lawrence–Haverhill, Mass.–N.H.	281,981	133	258,564	131	23,417	9.1
Lexington–Fayette, Ky.	318,136	119	266,701	125	51,435	19.3
Lima, Ohio	218,244	160	210,074	153	8,170	3.9
Lincoln, Neb.	192,884	173	167,972	176	24,912	14.9
Little Rock–North Little Rock, Ark.	393,494	99	323,296	106	70,198	21.8
Long Branch–Asbury Park, N.J.	503,173	79	461,849	72	41,324	9.0
Longview–Marshall, Tex.	151,752	206	120,770	217	30,982	25.7
Lorain–Elyria, Ohio	274,909	139	256,843	134	18,066	7.1
Los Angeles–Long Beach, Calif.	7,477,657	2	7,041,980	2	435,677	6.2
Louisville, Ky.–Ind.	906,240	43	867,330	39	38,910	4.5
Lowell, Mass.–N.H.	233,410	155	218,268	149	15,142	7.0
Lubbock, Tex.	211,651	163	179,295	165	32,356	18.1
Lynchburg, Va.	153,260	204	134,744	198	18,516	13.8
Macon, Ga.	254,623	149	226,782	144	27,841	12.3
Madison, Wis.	323,545	115	290,272	114	33,273	11.5
Manchester, N.H.	160,767	202	132,512	201	28,255	21.4
McAllen–Pharr–Edinburg, Tex.	283,229	132	181,535	162	101,694	56.1

Standard metropolitan statistical area	1980 Census		1970 Census		Change, 1970–80	
	Number	Rank	Number	Rank	Number	%
Melbourne–Titusville–Cocoa, Fla.	272,959	140	230,006	142	42,953	18.7
Memphis, Tenn.–Ark.–Miss.	912,887	42	834,103	41	78,784	9.5
Miami, Fla.	1,625,979	21	1,267,792	26	358,187	28.3
Milwaukee	1,397,143	28	1,403,884	21	−6,741	−0.4
Minneapolis–St. Paul	2,114,256	15	1,965,391	17	148,865	7.6
Mobile, Ala.	442,819	89	376,690	86	66,129	17.6
Modesto, Calif.	265,902	144	194,506	158	71,396	36.8
Montgomery, Ala.	272,687	141	225,911	146	46,776	20.8
Muskegon–Norton Shores–Muskegon Heights, Mich.	179,591	182	175,410	166	4,181	2.4
Nashville–Davidson, Tenn.	850,505	44	699,271	50	151,234	21.7
Nassau–Suffolk, N.Y.	2,605,813	11	2,555,868	9	49,945	2.0
Newark, N.J.	1,965,304	17	2,057,468	15	−92,164	−4.4
New Bedford, Mass.	169,425	195	161,288	180	8,137	5.1
New Brunswick–Perth Amboy– Sayreville, N.J.	595,893	65	583,813	61	12,080	2.1
New Haven–West Haven, Conn.	417,592	93	411,287	79	6,305	1.6
New London–Norwich, Conn.–R.I.	248,554	151	241,862	138	6,692	2.8
New Orleans	1,186,725	33	1,046,470	32	140,255	13.5
Newport News–Hampton, Va.	364,449	107	333,140	103	31,309	9.4
New York, N.Y.–N.J.	9,119,737	1	9,973,716	1	−853,979	−8.5
Norfolk–Virginia Beach– Portsmouth, Va.–N.C.	806,691	49	732,600	46	74,091	10.2
Northeast Pennsylvania	640,396	60	621,882	56	18,514	3.0
Oklahoma City	834,088	46	699,092	51	134,996	19.4
Omaha, Neb.–Iowa	570,399	67	542,646	65	27,753	5.2
Orlando, Fla.	700,699	55	453,270	74	247,429	54.6
Oxnard–Simi Valley–Ventura, Calif.	529,899	75	378,497	85	151,402	40.1
Parkersburg–Marietta, W. Va.–Ohio	162,836	201	148,132	187	14,704	10.0
Paterson–Clifton–Passaic, N.J.	447,585	87	460,782	73	−13,197	−2.8
Pensacola, Fla.	289,782	131	243,075	137	46,707	19.3
Peoria, Ill.	365,864	106	341,979	98	23,885	7.0
Philadelphia, Pa.–N.J.	4,716,818	4	4,824,110	4	−107,292	−2.2
Phoenix, Ariz.	1,508,030	26	971,228	35	536,802	55.3
Pittsburgh	2,263,894	13	2,401,362	11	−137,468	−5.7
Portland, Me.	183,625	181	170,081	171	13,544	8.0
Portland, Ore.–Wash.	1,242,187	32	1,007,131	34	235,057	23.4
Poughkeepsie, N.Y.	245,055	153	222,295	147	22,760	10.3
Providence–Warwick–Pawtucket, R.I.–Mass.	919,216	41	908,887	37	10,329	1.2
Provo–Orem, Utah	218,106	161	137,776	196	80,330	58.4
Racine, Wis.	173,132	189	170,838	170	2,294	1.4
Raleigh–Durham, N.C.	530,673	73	419,254	76	111,419	26.6
Reading, Pa.	312,509	121	296,382	112	16,127	5.5
Reno, Nev.	193,623	172	121,068	216	72,555	60.0
Richmond, Va.	632,015	63	547,542	64	84,473	15.5
Riverside–San Bernardino–Ontario, Calif.	1,557,080	25	1,139,149	28	417,931	36.7
Roanoke, Va.	224,548	159	203,153	157	21,395	10.6
Rochester, N.Y.	971,879	39	961,516	36	10,363	1.1
Rockford, Ill.	279,514	136	272,063	124	7,451	2.8
Sacramento, Calif.	1,014,002	38	803,793	42	210,209	26.2
Saginaw, Mich.	228,059	158	219,743	148	8,316	3.8
St. Cloud, Minn.	163,256	199	134,585	199	28,671	21.4
St. Louis, Mo.–Ill.	2,355,276	12	2,410,884	10	−55,608	−2.3
Salem, Ore.	249,895	150	186,658	160	63,237	33.9
Salinas–Seaside–Monterey–Calif.	290,444	130	247,450	136	42,994	17.4
Salt Lake City–Ogden, Utah	936,255	40	705,458	49	230,797	32.8
San Antonio	1,071,954	36	888,179	38	183,775	20.7
San Diego, Calif.	1,861,846	20	1,357,854	23	503,992	37.2
San Francisco–Oakland, Calif.	3,252,721	6	3,109,249	6	143,472	4.7
San Jose, Calif.	1,295,071	30	1,065,313	31	229,758	21.6
Santa Barbara–Santa Maria–Lompoc, Calif.	298,660	128	264,324	127	34,336	13.0
Santa Cruz, Calif.	188,141	175	123,790	213	64,351	52.0
Santa Rosa, Calif.	299,827	127	204,885	156	94,942	46.4
Sarasota, Fla.	202,251	168	120,413	218	81,838	68.0
Savannah, Ga.	230,728	156	207,987	154	22,741	11.0
Seattle–Everett, Wash.	1,606,765	23	1,424,605	19	182,160	12.8
Shreveport, La.	376,646	103	336,000	101	40,646	12.1
South Bend, Ind.	280,772	134	279,813	120	959	0.4
Spokane, Wash.	341,835	110	287,487	115	54,348	19.0
Springfield, Ill.	187,789	176	171,020	169	16,769	9.9

Standard metropolitan statistical area	1980 Census Number	1980 Census Rank	1970 Census Number	1970 Census Rank	Change, 1970–80 Number	Change, 1970–80 %
Springfield–Chicopee–Holyoke, Mass.–Conn.	530,668	74	541,752	66	−11,084	−2.0
Springfield, Mo.	207,704	165	168,053	175	39,651	23.6
Springfield, Ohio	183,885	180	187,606	159	−3,721	−1.9
Stamford, Conn.	198,854	169	206,340	155	−7,486	−3.6
Steubenville–Weirton, Ohio–W. Va.	163,099	200	166,385	177	−3,286	−1.9
Stockton, Calif.	347,342	109	291,073	113	56,269	19.4
Syracuse, N.Y.	642,375	59	636,596	53	5,779	1.0
Tacoma, Wash.	485,643	81	412,344	78	73,299	17.8
Tallahassee, Fla.	159,542	203	109,355	235	50,187	45.9
Tampa–St. Petersburg, Fla.	1,569,492	24	1,088,549	30	480,943	44.2
Terre Haute, Ind.	176,583	186	175,143	167	1,440	0.9
Toledo, Ohio–Mich.	791,599	51	762,658	45	28,941	3.8
Topeka, Kan.	185,442	179	180,619	163	4,823	2.7
Trenton, N.J.	307,863	125	304,116	110	3,747	1.3
Tucson, Ariz.	531,263	72	351,667	95	179,596	51.1
Tulsa, Okla.	689,628	56	549,154	63	140,474	25.6
Utica–Rome, N.Y.	320,180	118	340,477	99	−20,297	−5.9
Vallejo–Fairfield–Napa, Calif.	334,402	112	251,129	135	83,273	33.2
Waco, Tex.	170,755	193	147,553	188	23,202	15.8
Washington, D.C.–Md.–Va.	3,060,240	7	2,910,111	7	150,129	5.2
Waterbury, Conn.	228,178	157	216,808	150	11,370	5.3
West Palm Beach–Boca Raton, Fla.	573,125	66	348,993	96	224,132	64.3
Wheeling, W. Va.–Ohio	185,566	178	181,954	161	3,612	2.0
Wichita, Kan.	411,313	94	389,352	84	21,961	5.7
Wilmington, Del.–N.J.–Md.	524,108	76	499,493	70	24,615	5.0
Worcester, Mass.	372,940	105	372,144	89	796	0.3
Yakima, Wash.	172,508	192	145,212	191	27,296	18.8
York, Pa.	381,255	102	329,540	105	51,715	15.7
Youngstown–Warren, Ohio	531,350	71	537,124	68	−5,774	−1.0

NOTE: The general concept of a standard metropolitan statistical area (SMSA) is one of a large population nucleus together with adjacent communities that have a high degree of economic and social integration with that nucleus. *Source:* Department of Commerce, Bureau of the Census.

Population by Age, Sex, Race, and Spanish Origin, 1980
(in thousands)

Age	White Male	White Female	Black Male	Black Female	Spanish origin Male	Spanish origin Female	Other races Male	Other races Female	All persons Male	All persons Female
Under 5	6,483	6,148	1,228	1,208	848	815	650	627	8,360	7,984
5–9	6,684	6,347	1,255	1,235	783	754	598	578	8,538	8,159
10–14	7,408	7,053	1,344	1,329	747	728	563	544	9,315	8,926
15–19	8,631	8,326	1,488	1,495	826	779	632	588	10,752	10,410
20–24	8,680	8,603	1,300	1,424	819	766	680	625	10,660	10,652
25–29	8,004	7,978	1,084	1,237	697	678	615	599	9,703	9,814
30–34	7,299	7,344	871	1,017	558	570	506	521	8,676	8,882
35–39	5,830	5,929	662	795	416	438	368	378	6,860	7,103
40–44	4,849	4,976	566	684	345	367	292	300	5,708	5,961
45–49	4,638	4,818	515	627	300	321	234	255	5,388	5,701
50–54	4,918	5,239	504	624	270	294	198	226	5,620	6,089
55–59	4,852	5,385	466	570	217	237	163	178	5,481	6,133
60–64	4,173	4,801	385	486	147	174	111	130	4,669	5,416
65–69	3,481	4,330	331	445	116	148	90	104	3,902	4,879
70–74	2,552	3,542	234	329	85	109	67	72	2,853	3,944
75–79	1,650	2,659	153	235	59	77	45	52	1,847	2,945
80–84	923	1,762	75	125	27	39	21	28	1,019	1,915
85 and over	614	1,430	53	106	19	30	14	23	681	1,558
All ages	91,670	96,671	12,516	13,972	7,278	7,328	5,847	5,829	110,032	116,473
15 and over	71,095	77,124	8,689	10,200	4,901	5,030	4,035	4,080	83,819	91,404
20 and over	62,463	68,798	7,345	8,871	4,153	4,302	3,450	3,492	74,504	82,478
65 and over	9,220	13,724	846	1,240	305	404	236	277	10,302	15,242
Median age	30.0	32.6	23.6	26.2	22.7	23.8	24.1	25.7	28.8	31.1

NOTE: Figures represent resident population of the 50 states and the District of Columbia plus Armed Forces overseas.

Population by State

State	1980	Percent change, 1970–80	Pop. per sq. mi. 1980	Pop. rank, 1980	1970	1950	1900	1790
Alabama	3,890,061	+12.9	76.7	22	3,444,354	3,061,743	1,828,697	—
Alaska	400,481	+32.4	0.7	50	302,583	128,643	63,592	—
Arizona	2,717,866	+53.1	24.0	29	1,775,399	749,587	122,931	—
Arkansas	2,285,513	+18.8	44.0	33	1,923,322	1,909,511	1,311,564	—
California	23,668,562	+18.5	151.4	1	19,971,069	10,586,223	1,485,053	—
Colorado	2,888,834	+30.7	27.8	28	2,209,596	1,325,089	539,700	—
Connecticut	3,107,576	+ 2.5	639.2	24	3,032,217	2,007,280	908,420	237,946
Delaware	595,225	+ 8.6	300.3	47	548,104	318,085	184,735	59,096
D.C.	637,651	−15.7	10,385.2	—	756,668	802,178	278,718	—
Florida	9,739,992	+43.4	180.1	7	6,791,418	2,771,305	528,542	—
Georgia	5,464,265	+19.1	94.1	13	4,587,930	3,444,578	2,216,331	82,548
Hawaii	965,000	+25.3	150.2	39	769,913	499,794	154,001	—
Idaho	943,935	+32.4	11.4	41	713,015	588,637	161,772	—
Illinois	11,418,461	+ 2.8	202.5	5	11,110,285	8,712,176	4,821,550	—
Indiana	5,490,179	+ 5.7	152.1	12	5,195,392	3,934,224	2,516,462	—
Iowa	2,913,387	+ 3.1	52.5	27	2,825,368	2,621,073	2,231,853	—
Kansas	2,363,208	+ 5.1	28.9	32	2,249,071	1,905,299	1,470,495	—
Kentucky	3,661,433	+13.7	92.3	23	3,220,711	2,944,806	2,147,174	73,677
Louisiana	4,203,972	+15.3	93.6	18	3,644,637	2,683,516	1,381,625	—
Maine	1,124,660	+13.2	36.4	38	993,722	913,774	694,466	96,540
Maryland	4,216,446	+ 7.5	426.3	19	3,923,897	2,343,001	1,188,044	319,728
Massachusetts	5,737,037	+ 0.8	733.1	11	5,689,170	4,690,514	2,805,346	378,787
Michigan	9,258,344	+ 4.2	162.95	8	8,881,826	6,371,766	2,420,982	—
Minnesota	4,077,148	+ 7.1	51.4	21	3,806,103	2,982,483	1,751,394	—
Mississippi	2,520,638	+13.7	53.3	31	2,216,994	2,178,914	1,551,270	—
Missouri	4,917,444	+ 5.1	71.3	15	4,677,623	3,954,653	3,106,665	—
Montana	786,690	+13.3	5.4	44	694,409	591,024	243,329	—
Nebraska	1,570,006	+ 5.7	20.5	35	1,485,333	1,325,510	1,066,300	—
Nevada	799,184	+63.5	7.3	43	488,738	160,083	42,335	—
New Hampshire	920,610	+24.8	102.0	42	737,681	533,242	411,588	141,885
New Jersey	7,364,158	+ 2.7	979.2	9	7,171,112	4,835,329	1,883,669	184,139
New Mexico	1,299,968	+27.8	10.7	37	1,017,055	681,187	195,310	—
New York	17,557,288	− 3.8	367.1	2	18,241,391	14,830,192	7,268,894	340,120
North Carolina	5,874,429	+15.5	120.4	10	5,084,411	4,061,929	1,893,810	393,751
North Dakota	652,695	+ 5.6	9.4	46	617,792	619,636	319,146	—
Ohio	10,797,419	+ 1.3	263.5	6	10,657,423	7,946,627	4,157,545	—
Oklahoma	3,025,266	+18.2	44.0	26	2,559,463	2,233,351	790,391[1]	—
Oregon	2,632,663	+25.9	27.4	30	2,091,533	1,521,341	413,536	—
Pennsylvania	11,866,728	+ 0.6	263.9	4	11,800,766	10,498,012	6,302,115	434,373
Rhode Island	947,154	− 0.3	902.9	40	949,723	791,896	428,556	68,825
South Carolina	3,119,208	+20.4	103.2	25	2,590,713	2,117,027	1,340,316	249,073
South Dakota	690,178	+ 3.6	9.1	45	666,257	652,740	401,570	—
Tennessee	4,590,750	+16.9	111.1	17	3,926,018	3,291,718	2,020,616	35,691
Texas	14,228,383	+27.1	54.3	3	11,198,655	7,711,194	3,048,710	—
Utah	1,461,037	+37.9	17.8	36	1,059,273	688,862	276,749	—
Vermont	511,456	+15.0	55.1	48	444,732	377,747	343,641	85,425
Virginia	5,346,279	+14.9	134.4	14	4,651,448	3,318,680	1,854,184	747,610[2]
Washington	4,130,163	+21.0	62.0	20	3,413,244	2,378,963	518,103	—
West Virginia	1,949,644	+11.8	81.0	34	1,744,237	2,005,552	958,800	—
Wisconsin	4,705,335	+ 6.5	86.4	16	4,417,821	3,434,575	2,069,042	—
Wyoming	470,816	+41.6	4.8	49	332,416	290,529	92,531	—
Total U.S.	226,504,825	+10.9	62.7	—	203,302,031	151,325,798	76,212,168	3,929,214

1. Includes population of Indian Territory: 1900, 392,960. 2. Until 1863, Virginia included what is now West Virginia. Source: Department of Commerce, Bureau of the Census.

Population Center Moves West Again

As a result of the 1980 census findings, DeSoto, Mo., has become the center of population in the United States, the first time it has moved west of the Mississippi River. In the first census in 1790 the center was 23 miles east of Baltimore. Over the years it moved westward along the 39th parallel through Maryland, West Virginia, Ohio, Indiana, and Illinois. By 1950 it began to veer a little to the south in its westward progress until it almost reached the 38th parallel at DeSoto. Located 30 miles southwest of St. Louis's Gateway Arch, DeSoto is a town of 5,993 people.

The Census Bureau defines the population center as the point at which an imaginary flat, weightless, and rigid map of the United States would balance if weights of identical value, each representing the location of one person, were placed on it.

Incorporated Places Over 25,000 Population

Asterisk denotes more than one ZIP code for a city and refers to Postmaster. To find the ZIP code for a particular address, consult the ZIP code directory available in every post office. For latest population figures of many cities, see listing for individual states in The United States section.

City and major ZIP code	1980 census	1970 census	City and major ZIP code	1980 census	1970 census
Aberdeen, SD (57401)	25,956	26,476	Bellingham, WA (98225)	45,794	39,375
Abilene, TX (79604*)	98,315	89,653	Beloit, WI (53511)	35,207	35,729
Addison, IL (60101)	28,836	24,482	Bergenfield, NJ (07621)	25,568	29,000
Akron, OH (44309*)	237,177	275,425	Berkeley, CA (94704*)	103,328	114,091
Alameda, CA (94501)	63,852	70,968	Berwyn, IL (60402)	46,849	52,502
Albany, GA (31706*)	73,934	72,623	Bessemer, AL (35020)	31,729	33,428
Albany, NY (12212*)	101,727	115,781	Bethel Park, PA (15102)	34,755	34,758
Albany, OR (97321)	26,546	18,181	Bethlehem, PA (18016*)	70,419	72,686
Albuquerque, NM (87101*)	331,767	244,501	Bettendorf, IA (52722)	27,381	22,126
Alexandria, LA (71301)	51,565	41,811	Beverly, MA (01915)	37,655	38,348
Alexandria, VA (22313*)	103,217	110,927	Beverly Hills, CA (90213*)	32,367	33,416
Alhambra, CA (91802*)	64,615	62,125	Billings, MT (59101*)	66,798	61,581
Allen Park, MI (48101)	34,196	40,747	Biloxi, MS (39530*)	49,311	48,486
Allentown, PA (18101*)	103,758	109,871	Binghamton, NY (13902*)	55,860	64,123
Alton, IL (62002)	34,171	39,700	Birmingham, AL (35203*)	284,413	300,910
Altoona, PA (16603*)	57,078	63,115	Bismarck, ND (58501)	44,485	34,703
Amarillo, TX (79120*)	149,230	127,010	Blacksburg, VA (24060)	30,638	9,384
Ames, IA (50010)	45,775	39,505	Blaine, MN (55433)	28,558	20,573
Anaheim, CA (92803*)	221,847	166,408	Bloomfield, NJ (07003)	47,792	52,029
Anchorage, AK (99502*)	173,017	48,081	Bloomington, IL (61701)	44,189	39,992
Anderson, IN (46011*)	64,695	70,787	Bloomington, IN (47401)	51,646	43,262
Anderson, SC (29621*)	27,313	27,556	Bloomington, MN (55420)	81,831	81,970
Annapolis, MD (21401*)	31,740	30,095	Blue Springs, MO (64015)	25,927	6,779
Ann Arbor, MI (48106*)	107,316	100,035	Boca Raton, FL (33432*)	49,505	28,506
Anniston, AL (36201*)	29,523	31,533	Boise, ID (83708*)	102,451	74,990
Antioch, CA (94509)	47,559	28,060	Bolingbrook, IL (60439)	37,261	7,651
Appleton, WI (54911*)	59,032	56,377	Bossier City, LA (71111*)	49,969	43,769
Arcadia, CA (91006)	45,994	45,138	Boston, MA (02109*)	562,994	641,071
Arlington, TX (76010*)	160,123	90,229	Boulder, CO (80302*)	76,685	66,870
Arlington Heights, IL (60004*)	66,116	65,058	Bountiful, UT (84010)	32,877	27,751
Arvada, CO (80001*)	84,576	49,844	Bowie, MD (20715)	33,695	35,028
Asheville, NC (28810*)	53,281	57,820	Bowling Green, KY (42101)	40,450	36,705
Ashland, KY (41101)	27,064	29,245	Bowling Green, OH (43402)	25,728	14,656
Athens, GA (30603*)	42,549	44,342	Boynton Beach, FL (33435*)	35,624	18,115
Atlanta, GA (30304*)	425,022	495,039	Bradenton, FL (33506*)	30,170	21,040
Atlantic City, NJ (08401*)	40,199	47,859	Brea, CA (92621)	27,913	18,447
Attleboro, MA (02703)	34,196	32,907	Bremerton, WA (98310)	36,208	35,307
Auburn, AL (36830)	28,471	22,767	Bridgeport, CT (06602*)	142,546	156,542
Auburn, NY (13021)	32,548	34,599	Bristol, CT (06010)	57,370	55,487
Auburn, WA (98002)	26,417	21,653	Brockton, MA (02403*)	95,172	89,040
Augusta, GA (30901*)	47,532	59,864	Broken Arrow, OK (74012)	35,761	11,018
Aurora, CO (80010*)	158,588	74,974	Brookfield, WI (53005)	34,035	31,761
Aurora, IL (60507*)	81,293	74,389	Brooklyn Center, MN (55429)	31,230	35,173
Austin, TX (78710*)	345,496	253,539	Brooklyn Park, MN (55429)	43,332	26,230
Azusa, CA (91702)	29,380	25,217	Brook Park, OH (44142)	26,195	30,774
Bakersfield, CA (93302*)	105,611	69,515	Brownsville, TX (78520*)	84,997	52,522
Baldwin Park, CA (91706)	50,554	47,285	Brunswick, OH (44212)	27,689	15,852
Baltimore, MD (21233*)	786,775	905,787	Bryan, TX (77801)	44,337	33,719
Bangor, ME (04401)	31,643	33,168	Buena Park, CA (90622*)	64,165	63,646
Barberton, OH (44203)	29,751	33,052	Buffalo, NY (14240*)	357,870	462,768
Bartlesville, OK (74003)	34,568	29,683	Burbank, CA (91505*)	84,625	88,871
Baton Rouge, LA (70821*)	219,486	165,921	Burbank, IL (60459)	28,462	—
Battle Creek, MI (49016*)	35,724	38,931	Burlingame, CA (94010)	26,173	27,320
Bay City, MI (48706)	41,593	49,449	Burlington, IA (52601)	29,529	32,366
Bayonne, NJ (07002)	65,047	72,743	Burlington, NC (27215)	37,266	35,930
Baytown, TX (77520*)	56,923	43,980	Burlington, VT (05401)	37,712	38,633
Beaumont, TX (77704*)	118,102	117,548	Burnsville, MN (55337)	35,674	19,940
Beavercreek, OH (45401)	31,589	—	Burton, MI (48502)	29,976	—
Beaverton, OR (97005*)	30,582	18,577	Butte, MT (59701)	37,205	23,368
Bell, CA (90201)	25,450	21,836	Calumet City, IL (60409)	39,673	33,107
Belleville, IL (62220*)	42,150	41,223	Camarillo, CA (93010)	37,732	19,219
Belleville, NJ (07109)	35,367	37,629	Cambridge, MA (02140)	95,322	100,361
Bellevue, WA (98009*)	73,903	61,196	Camden, NJ (08101*)	84,910	102,551
Bellflower, CA (90706)	53,441	52,334	Campbell, CA (95008)	27,067	23,797
Bell Gardens, CA (90201)	34,117	29,308	Canton, OH (44711*)	94,730	110,053

City and major ZIP code	1980 census	1970 census
Cape Coral, FL (33904)	32,103	—
Cape Girardeau, MO (63701)	34,361	31,282
Carbondale, IL (62901)	27,194	22,816
Carlsbad, CA (92008)	35,490	14,944
Carlsbad, NM (88220)	25,496	21,297
Carrollton, TX (75006*)	40,591	13,855
Carson, CA (90749)	81,221	71,150
Carson City, NV (89701)	32,022	15,468
Casper, WY (82601)	51,016	39,361
Cedar Falls, IA (50613)	36,322	29,597
Cedar Rapids, IA (52401*)	110,243	110,642
Cerritos, CA (90701)	52,756	15,856
Champaign, IL (61820)	58,133	56,837
Chandler, AZ (85224)	29,673	13,763
Chapel Hill, NC (27514)	32,421	26,199
Charleston, SC (29401*)	69,510	66,945
Charleston, WV (25301*)	63,968	71,505
Charlotte, NC (28228*)	314,447	241,420
Charlottesville, VA (22906*)	45,010	38,880
Chattanooga, TN (37401*)	169,565	119,923
Chelsea, MA (02150)	25,431	30,625
Chesapeake, VA (23320*)	114,226	89,580
Chester, PA (19013*)	45,794	56,331
Cheyenne, WY (82001)	47,283	41,254
Chicago, IL (60607*)	3,005,072	3,369,357
Chicago Heights, IL (60411)	37,026	40,900
Chico, CA (95926)	26,601	19,580
Chicopee, MA (01021*)	55,112	66,676
Chino, CA (91710)	40,165	20,411
Chula Vista, CA (91010*)	83,927	67,901
Cicero, IL (60650)	61,232	67,058
Cincinnati, OH (45234*)	385,457	453,514
Claremont, CA (91711)	30,950	24,776
Clarksville, TN (37040)	54,777	31,719
Clearwater, FL (33515*)	85,450	52,074
Cleveland, OH (44101*)	573,822	750,879
Cleveland, TN (37311)	26,415	21,446
Cleveland Heights, OH (44118)	56,438	60,767
Clifton, NJ (07015*)	74,388	82,437
Clinton, IA (52732)	32,828	34,719
Clovis, CA (93612)	33,021	13,856
Clovis, NM (88101)	31,194	28,495
College Station, TX (77840)	37,272	17,676
Colorado Springs, CO (80901*)	215,150	135,517
Colton, CA (92324)	27,419	20,016
Columbia, MO (65201)	62,061	58,812
Columbia, SC (29201*)	99,296	113,542
Columbia, TN (38401)	25,767	21,471
Columbus, GA (31908*)	169,441	155,028
Columbus, IN (47201)	30,292	26,457
Columbus, MS (39701)	27,383	25,795
Columbus, OH (43216*)	564,871	540,025
Compton, CA (90220*)	81,286	78,547
Concord, CA (94520*)	103,251	85,164
Concord, NH (03301*)	30,400	30,022
Coon Rapids, MN (55433)	35,826	30,505
Coral Gables, FL (33134)	43,241	42,494
Coral Springs, FL (33065)	37,349	1,489
Corona, CA (91720)	37,791	27,519
Corpus Christi, TX (78408*)	231,999	204,525
Corvallis, OR (97330)	40,960	35,056
Costa Mesa, CA (92626*)	82,291	72,660
Council Bluffs, IA (51501)	56,449	60,348
Covina, CA (91722*)	33,751	30,395
Covington, KY (41011*)	49,013	52,535
Cranston, RI (02910)	71,992	74,287
Crystal, MN (55428)	25,543	30,925
Culver City, CA (90230)	38,139	34,451
Cumberland, MD (21502)	25,933	29,724
Cupertino, CA (95014)	25,770	17,895
Cuyahoga Falls, OH (44222*)	43,710	49,815
Cypress, CA (90630)	40,391	31,569
Dallas, TX (75260*)	904,078	844,401
Daly City, CA (94015*)	78,519	66,922
Danbury, CT (06810)	60,470	50,781
Danville, IL (61832)	38,985	42,570
Danville, VA (24541)	45,642	46,391
Davenport, IA (52802*)	103,264	98,469
Davis, CA (95616)	36,640	23,488
Dayton, OH (45401*)	203,588	243,023
Daytona Beach, FL (32015*)	54,176	45,327
Dearborn, MI (48120*)	90,660	104,199
Dearborn Heights, MI (48127)	67,706	80,069
Decatur, AL (35602*)	42,002	38,044
Decatur, IL (62521*)	94,081	90,397
Deerfield Beach, FL (33441)	39,193	16,662
De Kalb, IL (60115)	33,099	32,949
Del City, OK (73115)	28,424	27,133
Delray Beach, FL (33444*)	34,325	19,915
Del Rio, TX (78840)	30,034	21,330
Denton, TX (76201)	47,063	39,874
Denver, CO (80202*)	491,396	514,678
Des Moines, IA (50318*)	191,003	201,404
Des Plaines, IL (60018*)	53,568	57,239
Detroit, MI (48233*)	1,203,339	1,514,063
Dothan, AL (36303*)	48,750	36,733
Downers Grove, IL (60515*)	39,274	32,544
Downey, CA (90241*)	82,602	88,573
Dubuque, IA (52001)	62,321	62,309
Duluth, MN (55806*)	92,811	100,578
Duncanville, TX (75116*)	27,781	14,105
Dunedin, FL (33528)	30,203	17,639
Durham, NC (27701*)	100,831	95,438
East Chicago, IN (46312)	39,786	49,982
East Cleveland, OH (44112)	36,957	39,660
East Detroit, MI (48021)	38,280	45,920
East Lansing, MI (48823)	48,309	47,540
Easton, PA (18042)	26,027	29,450
East Orange, NJ (07019*)	77,025	75,471
East Point, GA (30364)	37,486	39,315
East Providence, RI (02914)	50,980	48,207
East St. Louis, IL (62201*)	55,200	70,169
Eau Claire, WI (54701)	51,509	44,619
Edina, MN (55424)	46,073	44,046
Edmond, OK (73034)	34,637	16,633
Edmonds, WA (98020)	27,526	23,684
El Cajon, CA (92020*)	73,892	52,273
El Dorado, AR (71730)	26,685	25,283
Elgin, IL (60120)	63,798	55,691
Elizabeth, NJ (07207*)	106,201	112,654
Elk Grove, IL (60007)	28,907	20,346
Elkhart, IN (46515*)	41,305	43,152
Elmhurst, IL (60126)	44,251	46,392
Elmira, NY (14901*)	35,327	39,945
El Monte, CA (91734*)	79,494	69,892
El Paso, TX (79910*)	425,259	322,261
Elyria, OH (44035*)	57,504	53,427
Emporia, KN (66801)	25,287	23,327
Englewood, CO (80110*)	30,021	33,695
Enid, OK (73701)	50,363	44,986
Erie, PA (16501*)	119,123	129,265
Escondido, CA (92025*)	62,480	36,792
Euclid, OH (44117)	59,999	71,552
Eugene, OR (97401*)	105,624	79,028
Evanston, IL (60204*)	73,706	80,113
Evansville, IN (47708*)	130,496	138,764
Everett, MA (02149)	37,195	42,485
Everett, WA (98201*)	54,413	53,622
Fairborn, OH (45324)	29,702	32,267
Fairfield, CA (94533)	58,099	44,146
Fairfield, OH (45014)	30,777	14,680
Fair Lawn, NJ (07401)	32,229	38,040

City and major ZIP code	1980 census	1970 census
Fall River, MA (02722*)	92,574	96,898
Fargo, ND (58102*)	61,308	53,365
Farmington, NM (87401)	30,729	21,979
Farmington Hills, MI (48024*)	58,056	—
Fayetteville, AR (72701)	36,604	30,729
Fayetteville, NC (28302*)	59,507	53,510
Ferndale, MI (48220)	26,227	30,850
Findlay, OH (45840)	35,594	35,800
Fitchburg, MA (01420)	39,580	43,343
Flagstaff, AZ (86001)	34,641	26,117
Flint, MI (48502*)	159,611	193,317
Florence, AL (35631*)	37,029	34,031
Florence, SC (29501)	30,062	25,997
Florissant, MO (63033*)	55,372	65,908
Fond du Lac, WI (54935)	35,863	35,515
Fontana, CA (92335)	37,109	20,673
Fort Collins, CO (80521*)	64,632	43,337
Fort Dodge, IA (50501)	29,423	31,263
Fort Lauderdale, FL (33310*)	153,256	139,590
Fort Lee, NJ (07024)	32,449	30,631
Fort Pierce, FL (33454*)	33,802	29,721
Fort Smith, AR (72901*)	71,384	62,802
Fort Wayne, IN (46802*)	172,196	178,269
Fort Worth, TX (76101*)	385,141	393,455
Fountain Valley, CA (92708)	55,080	31,886
Frankfort, KY (40601)	25,973	21,902
Frederick, MD (21701)	27,557	23,641
Freeport, IL (61032)	26,406	27,736
Freeport, NY (11520)	38,272	40,374
Fremont, CA (94538*)	131,945	100,869
Fresno, CA (93706*)	218,202	165,655
Fridley, MN (55432)	30,228	29,233
Fullerton, CA (92631*)	102,034	85,987
Gadsden, AL (35901*)	47,565	53,928
Gainesville, FL (32601*)	81,371	64,510
Gaithersburg, MD (20760)	26,424	8,344
Galesburg, IL (61401)	35,305	36,290
Galveston, TX (77553*)	61,902	61,809
Gardena, CA (90247*)	45,165	41,021
Garden City, MI (48135)	35,640	41,864
Garden Grove, CA (92640*)	123,351	121,155
Garfield, NJ (07026)	26,803	30,797
Garfield Heights, OH (44125)	33,380	41,417
Garland, TX (75040*)	138,857	81,437
Gary, IN (46401*)	151,953	175,415
Gastonia, NC (28052)	47,333	47,322
Glendale, AZ (85301*)	96,988	36,228
Glendale, CA (91209*)	139,060	132,664
Glendora, CA (91740)	38,654	32,143
Glenview, IL (60025)	30,842	24,880
Gloucester, MA (01930)	27,768	27,941
Goldsboro, NC (27530)	31,871	26,960
Grand Forks, ND (58201)	43,765	39,008
Grand Island, NE (68801)	33,180	32,358
Grand Junction, CO (81501*)	28,144	20,170
Grand Prairie, TX (75051*)	71,462	50,904
Grand Rapids, MI (49501*)	181,843	197,649
Granite City, IL (62040)	36,815	40,685
Great Falls, MT (59403*)	56,725	60,091
Greeley, CO (80631)	53,006	38,902
Green Bay, WI (54305*)	87,899	87,809
Greenfield, WI (53220)	31,467	24,424
Greensboro, NC (27420*)	155,642	144,076
Greenville, MS (38701)	40,613	39,648
Greenville, NC (27834)	35,740	29,063
Greenville, SC (29602*)	58,242	61,436
Gresham, OR (97030)	33,005	10,030
Gulfport, MS (39503*)	39,676	40,791
Hackensack, NJ (07602*)	36,039	36,008
Hagerstown, MD (21740)	34,132	35,862
Hallandale, FL (33009)	36,517	23,849
Haltom City, TX (76117)	29,014	28,127
Hamilton, OH (45012*)	63,189	67,865
Hammond, IN (46320*)	93,714	107,983
Hampton, VA (23669*)	122,617	120,779
Hanover Park, IL (60103)	28,850	11,735
Harlingen, TX (78550)	43,543	33,503
Harrisburg, PA (17105*)	53,264	68,061
Hartford, CT (06101*)	136,392	158,017
Harvey, IL (60426)	35,810	34,636
Hattiesburg, MS (39401)	40,829	38,277
Haverhill, MA (01830)	46,865	46,120
Hawthorne, CA (90250)	56,447	53,304
Hayward, CA (94544*)	94,167	93,058
Hazleton, PA (18201)	27,318	30,426
Hempstead, NY (11551*)	40,404	39,411
Hendersonville, TN (37075)	26,561	412
Hialeah, FL (33010*)	145,254	102,452
Highland, IN (46322)	25,935	24,947
Highland Park, IL (60035)	30,611	32,263
Highland Park, MI (48203)	27,909	35,444
High Point, NC (27260*)	64,107	63,229
Hillsboro, OR (97123)	27,664	14,675
Hilo, HI (96720)	37,017	28,412
Hobbs, NM (88240)	28,794	26,025
Hoboken, NJ (07030)	42,460	45,380
Hoffman Estates, IL (60195)	38,258	22,238
Holland, MI (49423)	26,281	26,479
Hollywood, FL (33022*)	117,188	106,873
Holyoke, MA (01040)	44,678	50,112
Honolulu, HI (96820*)	365,048	324,871
Hopkinsville, KY (42240)	27,318	21,395
Hot Springs, AR (71901)	35,166	35,631
Houma, LA (70360)	32,602	30,922
Houston, TX (77201*)	1,594,086	1,233,535
Huntington, WV (25704*)	63,684	74,315
Huntington Beach, CA (92647*)	170,505	115,960
Huntington Park, CA (90255)	46,223	33,744
Huntsville, AL (35804*)	142,513	139,282
Hurst, TX (76053)	31,420	27,215
Hutchinson, KN (67501)	40,284	36,885
Idaho Falls, ID (83401)	39,590	35,776
Independence, MO (64051*)	111,806	111,630
Indianapolis, IN (46206*)	700,807	736,856
Inglewood, CA (90311*)	94,245	89,985
Inkster, MI (48141)	35,190	38,595
Iowa City, IA (52240)	50,508	46,850
Irvine, CA (92713)	62,134	—
Irving, TX (75061*)	109,943	97,260
Irvington, NJ (07111)	61,493	59,743
Ithaca, NY (14850)	28,732	26,226
Jackson, MI (49201*)	39,739	45,484
Jackson, MS (39205*)	202,895	153,968
Jackson, TN (38301)	49,131	39,996
Jacksonville, AR (72076)	27,589	19,832
Jacksonville, FL (33203*)	540,898	504,265
Jamestown, NY (14701)	35,775	39,795
Janesville, WI (53545*)	51,071	46,426
Jefferson City, MO (65101)	33,619	32,407
Jersey City, NJ (07303*)	223,532	260,350
Johnson City, TN (37601)	39,753	33,770
Johnstown, PA (15901*)	35,496	42,476
Joliet, IL (60431*)	77,956	78,827
Jonesboro, AR (72401)	31,530	27,050
Joplin, MO (64801)	38,893	39,256
Kalamazoo, MI (49001*)	79,722	85,555
Kankakee, IL (60901)	30,141	30,944
Kansas City, KN (66110*)	161,087	168,213
Kansas City, MO (64108*)	448,159	507,330
Kearney, NJ (07032)	35,735	37,585
Kenner, LA (70062)	66,382	29,858
Kennewick, WA (99336)	34,397	15,212
Kenosha, WI (53141*)	77,685	78,805
Kent, OH (44240)	26,164	28,183

City and major ZIP code¹	1980 census	1970 census
Kentwood, MI (49508)	30,438	20,310
Kettering, OH (45429)	61,186	71,864
Killeen, TX (76541*)	46,296	35,507
Kingsport, TN (37662*)	32,027	31,938
Kingsville, TX (78363)	28,808	28,915
Kinston, NC (28501)	25,234	23,020
Kirkwood, MO (63122)	27,987	31,679
Knoxville, TN (37901*)	183,139	174,587
Kokomo, IN (46901)	47,808	44,042
La Crosse, WI (54601)	48,347	50,286
Lafayette, IN (47901*)	43,011	44,955
Lafayette, LA (70501*)	81,961	68,908
La Habra, CA (90631)	45,232	41,350
Lake Charles, LA (70601*)	75,051	77,998
Lakeland, FL (33802*)	47,406	42,803
Lakewood, CA (90714*)	74,654	83,025
Lakewood, CO (80215)	112,848	92,743
Lakewood, OH (44107)	61,963	70,173
Lake Worth, FL (33461*)	27,048	23,714
La Mesa, CA (92041)	50,342	39,178
La Mirada, CA (90638)	40,986	30,808
Lancaster, CA (93534)	48,027	—
Lancaster, OH (43130)	34,953	32,911
Lancaster, PA (17604*)	54,725	57,690
Lansing, IL (60438)	29,039	25,805
Lansing, MI (48924*)	130,414	131,403
La Puente, CA (91747*)	30,882	31,092
Laredo, TX (78041*)	91,449	69,024
Largo, FL (33540*)	58,977	24,230
Las Cruces, NM (88001)	45,086	37,857
Las Vegas, NV (89114*)	164,674	125,787
Lauderdale Lakes, FL (33313)	25,426	10.577
Lauderhill, FL (33313)	37,271	8,465
Lawrence, IN (46226)	25,591	16,353
Lawrence, KN (66044)	52,738	45,698
Lawrence, MA (01842*)	63,175	66,915
Lawton, OK (73501*)	80,054	74,470
Leavenworth, KN (66048)	33,656	25,147
Lebanon, PA (17042)	25,711	28,572
Lee's Summit, MO (64063)	28,741	16,230
Leominster, MA (01453)	34,508	32,939
Lewiston, ID (83501)	27,986	26,068
Lewiston, ME (04240)	40,481	41,779
Lexington, KY (40511*)	204,165	108,137
Lima, OH (45802*)	47,381	53,734
Lincoln, NE (68501*)	171,932	149,518
Lincoln Park, MI (48146)	45,105	52,984
Linden, NJ (07036)	37,836	41,409
Lindenhurst, NY (11757)	26,919	28,359
Little Rock, AR (72201*)	158,461	132,483
Littleton, CO (80120*)	28,631	26,466
Livermore, CA (94550)	48,349	37,703
Livonia, MI (48150*)	104,814	110,109
Lodi, CA (95240)	35,221	28,691
Logan, UT (84321)	26,844	22,333
Lombard, IL (60148)	37,295	34,043
Lompoc, CA (93436)	26,267	25,284
Long Beach, CA (90801*)	361,334	358,879
Long Branch, NJ (11561)	34,073	33,127
Long Branch, NJ (07740)	29,819	31,774
Longmont, CO (80501)	42,942	23,209
Longview, TX (75602*)	62,762	45,547
Longview, WA (98632)	31,052	28,373
Lorain, OH (44052*)	75,416	78,185
Los Altos, CA (94022)	25,769	25,062
Los Angeles, CA (90052*)	2,966,763	2,811,801
Los Gatos, CA (95030)	26,593	22,613
Louisville, KY (40231*)	298,451	361,706
Loveland, CO (80537)	30,244	16,220
Lowell, MA (01853*)	92,418	94,239
Lubbock, TX (79408*)	173,979	149,101
Lufkin, TX (75901)	28,562	23,049

City and major ZIP code	1980 census	1970 census
Lynchburg, VA (24505*)	66,743	54,083
Lynn, MA (01901*)	78,471	90,294
Lynwood, CA (90262)	48,548	43,354
Macon, GA (31203*)	116,860	122,423
Madison, WI (53707*)	170,616	171,809
Madison Heights, MI (48071)	35,375	38,599
Malden, MA (02148)	53,386	56,127
Manchester, NH (03103*)	90,936	87,754
Manhattan, KN (66502)	32,644	27,575
Manhattan Beach, CA (90266)	31,542	35,352
Manitowoc, WI (54220)	32,547	33,430
Mankato, MN (56001)	28,651	30,895
Mansfield, OH (44901*)	53,927	55,047
Maple Heights, OH (44137)	29,735	34,093
Maplewood, MN (55109)	26,990	25,186
Margate, FL (33063)	36,044	8,867
Marietta, GA (30060*)	30,805	27,216
Marion, IN (46952)	35,874	39,607
Marion, OH (43302)	37,040	38,646
Marlborough, MA (01752)	30,617	27,936
Marshalltown, IA (50158)	26,938	26,219
Mason City, IA (50401)	30,144	30,279
Massillon, OH (44646)	30,557	32,539
Maywood, IL (60153)	27,998	29,019
McAllen, TX (78501)	67,042	37,636
McKeesport, PA (15134*)	31,012	37,977
Medford, MA (02155)	58,076	64,397
Medford, OR (97501)	39,603	28,973
Melbourne, FL (32901*)	46,536	40,236
Melrose, MA (02176)	30,055	33,180
Memphis, TN (38101*)	646,356	623,988
Menlo Park, CA (94025)	25,673	26,826
Menomonee Falls, WI (53051)	27,845	31,697
Mentor, OH (44060)	42,065	36,912
Merced, CA (95340)	36,499	22,670
Meriden, CT (06450)	57,118	55,959
Meridian, MS (39301)	46,577	45,083
Merrillville, IN (46410)	27,677	—
Mesa, AZ (85201*)	152,453	63,049
Mesquite, TX (75149*)	67,053	55,131
Miami, FL (33152*)	346,931	334,859
Miami Beach, FL (33139)	96,298	87,072
Michigan City, IN (46360)	36,850	39,369
Middletown, CT (06457)	39,040	36,924
Middletown, OH (45042)	43,719	48,767
Midland, MI (48640)	37,250	35,176
Midland, TX (79702*)	70,525	59,463
Midwest City, OK (73140)	49,559	48,212
Milford, CT (06460)	49,101	50,858
Milpitas, CA (95035)	37,820	26,561
Milwaukee, WI (53201*)	636,212	717,372
Minneapolis, MN (55401*)	370,951	434,400
Minnetonka, MN (55343)	38,683	35,776
Minot, ND (58701)	32,843	32,290
Miramar, FL (33023)	32,813	23,997
Mishawaka, IN (46544)	40,224	36,060
Missoula, MT (59801)	33,388	29,497
Mobile, AL (36601*)	200,452	190,026
Modesto, CA (95350*)	106,105	61,712
Moline, IL (61265)	45,709	46,237
Monroe, LA (71203*)	57,597	56,374
Monroeville, PA (15146)	30,977	29,011
Monrovia, CA (91016)	30,531	30,562
Montclair, NJ (07042*)	38,321	44,043
Montebello, CA (90640)	52,929	42,807
Monterey, CA (93940)	27,558	26,302
Monterey Park, CA (91754)	54,338	49,166
Montgomery, AL (36116*)	178,157	133,386
Moore, OK (73153)	35,063	18,761
Moorhead, MN (56560)	29,998	29,687
Morgantown, WV (26505)	27,605	29,431
Mountain View, CA (94042*)	58,655	54.132

City and major ZIP code	1980 census	1970 census	City and major ZIP code	1980 census	1970 census
Mount Prospect, IL (60056)	52,634	34,995	Oceanside, CA (92054)	76,698	40,494
Mount Vernon, NY (10551*)	66,713	72,778	Odessa, TX (79760*)	90,027	78,380
Muncie, IN (47302*)	77,216	69,082	Ogden, UT (84401*)	64,407	69,478
Murfreesboro, TN (37130)	32,845	26,360	Oklahoma City, OK (73125*)	403,213	368,164
Murray, UT (84107)	25,750	21,206	Olathe, KN (66061*)	37,258	17,917
Muskegon, MI (49440*)	40,823	44,631	Olympia, WA (98501*)	27,447	23,296
Muskogee, OK (74401)	40,011	37,331	Omaha, NE (68108*)	311,681	346,929
Nacogdoches, TX (75961)	27,149	22,544	Ontario, CA (91761*)	88,820	64,118
Nampa, ID (83651)	25,112	20,768	Orange, CA (92667*)	91,788	77,365
Napa, CA (94558)	50,879	36,103	Orange, NJ (07050*)	31,136	32,566
Naperville, IL (60566*)	42,330	22,794	Orem, UT (84057)	52,399	25,729
Nashua, NH (03061*)	67,865	55,820	Orlando, FL (32802*)	128,394	99,006
Nashville, TN (37202*)	455,651	426,029	Oshkosh, WI (54901)	49,678	53,082
National City, CA (92050)	48,772	43,184	Ottumwa, IA (52501)	27,381	29,610
Naugatuck, CT (06770)	26,456	23,034	Overland Park, KN (66204)	81,784	77,934
New Albany, IN (47150)	37,103	38,402	Owensboro, KY (42301)	54,450	50,329
Newark, CA (94560)	32,126	27,153	Oxnard, CA (93030*)	108,195	71,225
Newark, DE (19711*)	25,247	21,298	Pacifica, CA (94044)	36,866	36,020
Newark, OH (43055)	41,200	41,836	Paducah, KY (42001)	29,315	31,627
Newark, NJ (07102*)	329,248	381,930	Palatine, IL (60067)	32,166	26,050
New Bedford, MA (02741*)	98,478	101,777	Palm Springs, CA (92263*)	32,271	20,936
New Berlin, WI (53151)	30,529	26,910	Palo Alto, CA (94303*)	55,225	56,040
New Britain, CT (06050*)	73,840	83,441	Panama City, FL (32401*)	33,346	32,096
New Brunswick, NJ (08901*)	41,442	41,885	Paramount, CA (90723)	36,407	34,734
New Castle, PA (16101*)	33,621	38,559	Paramus, NJ (07652)	26,474	28,381
New Haven, CT (06511*)	126,109	137,707	Paris, TX (75460)	25,498	23,441
New Iberia, LA (70560)	32,766	30,147	Parkersburg, WV (26101)	39,967	44,208
New London, CT (06320)	28,842	31,630	Park Forest, IL (60466)	26,222	30,638
New Orleans, LA (70113*)	557,482	593,471	Park Ridge, IL (60068)	38,704	42,614
Newport, RI (02840)	29,259	34,562	Parma, OH (44129)	92,548	100,216
Newport Beach, CA (92660*)	63,475	49,582	Pasadena, CA (91109*)	119,374	112,951
Newport News, VA (23607*)	144,903	138,177	Pasadena, TX (77501*)	112,560	89,957
New Rochelle, NY (10802*)	70,794	75,385	Pascagoula, MS (39567)	29,318	27,264
Newton, MA (02158)	83,622	91,263	Passaic, NJ (07055)	52,463	55,124
New York, NY (10001*)	7,071,030	7,895,563	Paterson, NJ (07510*)	137,970	144,824
Bronx borough (10451*)	1,169,115	1,471,701	Pawtucket, RI (02860*)	71,204	76,984
Brooklyn borough (11201*)	2,230,936	2,602,012	Peabody, MA (01960)	45,976	48,080
Manhattan borough (10001*)	1,427,533	1,539,233	Pekin, IL (61554)	33,967	31,375
Queens borough[1]	1,891,325	1,987,174	Pembroke Pines, FL (33024*)	35,776	15,496
Staten Island borough (10314*)	352,121	295,443	Pensacola, FL (32501*)	57,619	59,507
Niagara Falls, NY (14302*)	71,384	85,615	Peoria, IL (61601*)	124,160	126,963
Niles, IL (60648)	30,363	31,432	Perth Amboy, NJ (08861*)	38,951	38,798
Norfolk, VA (23501*)	266,979	307,951	Petaluma, CA (94952)	33,834	24,870
Normal, IL (61761)	35,672	26,396	Petersburg, VA (23803)	41,055	36,103
Norman, OK (73070*)	68,020	52,117	Phenix City, AL (36867)	26,928	25,281
Norristown, PA (19401*)	34,684	38,169	Philadelphia, PA (19104*)	1,688,210	1,949,996
Northampton, MA (01060)	29,286	29,664	Phoenix, AZ (85026*)	764,911	584,303
Northbrook, IL (60062)	30,735	25,422	Pico Rivera, CA (90660)	53,459	54,170
North Charleston, SC (29406)	65,630	—	Pine Bluff, AR (71601*)	56,576	57,389
North Chicago, IL (60064)	38,774	47,275	Pinellas Park, FL (33565)	32,811	22,287
Northglenn, CO (80233)	29,847	27,785	Pittsburg, CA (94565)	33,034	21,423
North Las Vegas, NV (89030)	42,739	46,067	Pittsburgh, PA (15219*)	423,938	520,089
North Little Rock, AR (72114*)	64,419	60,040	Pittsfield, MA (01201)	51,974	57,020
North Miami, FL (33161)	42,566	34,767	Placentia, CA (92670)	35,041	21,948
North Miami Beach, FL (33160)	36,481	30,544	Plainfield, NJ (07061*)	45,555	46,862
North Olmsted, OH (44070)	36,486	34,861	Plano, TX (75074*)	72,331	17,872
North Richland Hills, TX (76118)	30,592	16,514	Plantation, FL (33318)	48,501	23,523
North Tonawanda, NY (14120)	35,760	36,012	Pleasant Hill, CA (94523)	25,124	24,610
Norwalk, CA (90650)	85,232	90,164	Pleasanton, CA (94566)	35,160	18,328
Norwalk, CT (06856*)	76,767	79,288	Plum, PA (15239)	25,390	21,932
Norwich, CT (06360)	38,074	41,739	Plymouth, MN (55447)	31,615	18,077
Norwood, OH (45212)	26,342	30,420	Pocatello, ID (83201)	46,340	40,036
Novato, CA (94947)	43,916	31,006	Pomona, CA (91766*)	92,742	87,384
Nutley, NJ (07110)	28,998	31,913	Pompano Beach, FL (33060*)	52,618	38,587
Oak Forest, IL (60452)	26,096	19,271	Ponca City, OK (74601)	26,238	25,940
Oakland, CA (94615*)	339,288	361,561	Pontiac, MI (48056*)	76,715	85,279
Oak Lawn, IL (60454*)	60,590	60,305	Portage, IN (46368)	27,409	19,127
Oak Park, IL (60301*)	54,887	62,511	Portage, MI (49081)	38,157	33,590
Oak Park, MI (48237)	31,537	36,762	Port Arthur, TX (77640)	61,195	57,371
Oak Ridge, TN (37830)	27,662	28,319	Port Huron, MI (48060)	33,981	35,794
Ocala, FL (32670*)	37,170	22,583	Portland, ME (04101*)	61,572	65,116

City and major ZIP code	1980 census	1970 census
Portland, OR (97208*)	366,383	379,967
Portsmouth, NH (03801)	26,254	25,717
Portsmouth, OH (45662)	25,943	27,633
Portsmouth, VA (23705*)	104,577	110,963
Poughkeepsie, NY (12601*)	29,757	32,029
Prichard, AL (36610)	39,541	41,578
Providence, RI (02940*)	156,804	179,116
Provo, UT (84601)	73,907	53,131
Pueblo, CO (81003*)	101,686	97,774
Quincy, IL (62301)	42,352	45,288
Quincy, MA (02269)	84,743	87,966
Racine, WI (53401*)	85,725	95,162
Rahway, NJ (07065*)	26,723	29,114
Raleigh, NC (27611*)	149,771	122,830
Rancho Cucamonga, CA (91730)	55,250	—
Rancho Palos Verdes, CA (90274)	35,227	—
Rapid City, SD (57701)	46,492	43,836
Raytown, MO (64133)	31,759	33,306
Reading, PA (19603*)	78,686	87,643
Redding, CA (96001*)	41,995	16,659
Redlands, CA (92373)	43,619	36,355
Redondo Beach, CA (90277*)	57,102	57,451
Redwood City, CA (94064*)	54,965	55,686
Reno, NV (89510*)	100,756	72,863
Renton, WA (98055)	30,612	25,878
Revere, MA (02151)	42,423	43,159
Rialto, CA (92376)	35,615	28,370
Richardson, TX (75080*)	72,496	48,405
Richfield, MN (55423)	37,851	47,231
Richland, WA (99352)	33,578	26,290
Richmond, CA (94802*)	74,676	79,043
Richmond, IN (47374)	41,349	43,999
Richmond, VA (23232*)	219,214	249,332
Ridgewood, NJ (07451*)	25,208	27,547
Riverside, CA (92507*)	170,876	140,089
Riviera Beach, FL (33404)	26,596	21,401
Roanoke, VA (24022*)	100,427	92,115
Rochester, MN (55901)	57,855	53,766
Rochester, NY (14692*)	241,741	295,011
Rockford, IL (61125*)	139,712	147,370
Rock Hill, SC (29730)	35,344	33,846
Rock Island, IL (61201)	47,036	50,166
Rockville, MD (20850*)	43,811	42,739
Rockville Centre, NY (11570)	25,405	27,444
Rocky Mount, NC (27801)	41,283	34,284
Rome, GA (30161)	29,654	30,759
Rome, NY (13440)	43,826	50,148
Rosemead, CA (91770)	42,604	40,972
Roseville, MI (48066)	54,311	60,529
Roseville, MN (55113)	35,820	34,438
Roswell, NM (88201)	39,676	33,908
Royal Oak, MI (48068*)	70,893	86,238
Sacramento, CA (95813*)	275,741	257,105
Saginaw, MI (48605*)	77,508	91,849
St. Charles, MO (63301)	37,379	31,834
St. Clair Shores, MI (48080*)	76,210	88,093
St. Cloud, MN (56301)	42,566	39,691
St. Joseph, MO (64501*)	76,691	72,748
St. Louis, MO (63155*)	453,085	622,236
St. Louis Park, MN (55426)	42,931	48,883
St. Paul, MN (55101*)	270,230	309,866
St. Petersburg, FL (33730*)	236,893	216,159
Salem, MA (01970)	38,220	40,556
Salem, OR (97301*)	89,233	68,725
Salina, KN (67401)	41,843	37,714
Salinas, CA (93901*)	80,479	58,896
Salt Lake City, UT (84119*)	163,033	175,885
San Angelo, TX (76902*)	73,240	63,884
San Antonio, TX (78284*)	785,410	654,153
San Bernardino, CA (92403*)	118,057	106,869
San Bruno, CA (94066)	35,417	36,254
San Buenaventura (Ventura), CA (93002*)	74,474	57,964

City and major ZIP code	1980 census	1970 census
San Clemente, CA (92672)	27,325	17,063
San Diego, CA (92199*)	875,504	697,471
Sandusky, OH (44870)	31,360	32,674
Sandy City, UT (84070)	51,022	6,438
San Francisco, CA (94101*)	678,974	715,674
San Gabriel, CA (91776*)	30,072	29,336
San Jose, CA (95101*)	636,550	459,913
San Leandro, CA (94577*)	63,952	68,698
San Luis Obispo, CA (93401)	34,252	28,036
San Mateo, CA (94402*)	77,561	78,991
San Rafael, CA (94901*)	44,700	38,977
Santa Ana, CA (92711*)	203,713	155,710
Santa Barbara, CA (93102*)	74,542	70,215
Santa Clara, CA (95050*)	87,746	86,118
Santa Cruz, CA (95060*)	41,483	32,076
Santa Fe, NM (87501)	48,899	41,167
Santa Maria, CA (93456*)	39,685	32,749
Santa Monica, CA (90406*)	88,314	88,289
Santa Rosa, CA (95402*)	83,205	50,006
Sarasota, FL (33578*)	48,868	40,237
Saratoga, CA (95070)	29,261	26,810
Savannah, GA (31401*)	141,634	118,349
Sayreville, NJ (08872)	29,969	32,508
Schaumburg, IL (60194)	52,319	18,531
Schenectady, NY (12301*)	67,972	77,958
Scottsdale, AZ (85251*)	88,364	67,823
Scranton, PA (18503*)	88,117	102,696
Seal Beach, CA (90740)	25,975	24,441
Seaside, CA (93955)	36,567	36,883
Seattle, WA (98109*)	493,846	530,831
Selma, AL (36701)	26,684	27,379
Shaker Heights, OH (44120)	32,487	36,306
Shawnee, KN (66203)	29,653	20,946
Shawnee, OK (74801)	26,506	25,075
Sheboygan, WI (53081)	48,085	48,484
Shelton, CT (06484)	31,314	27,165
Sherman, TX (75090)	30,413	29,061
Shreveport, LA (71102*)	205,815	182,064
Sierra Vista, AZ (85635)	25,968	6,689
Simi Valley, CA (93065*)	77,500	59,832
Sioux City, IA (51101*)	82,003	85,925
Sioux Falls, SD (57101*)	81,343	72,488
Skokie, IL (60076*)	60,278	68,322
Slidell, LA (70458)	26,718	16,101
Somerville, MA (02143)	77,372	88,779
South Bend, IN (46624*)	109,727	125,580
South Euclid, OH (44121)	25,713	29,579
Southfield, MI (48034*)	75,568	69,285
South Gate, CA (90280)	66,784	56,909
Southgate, MI (48195)	32,058	33,909
South San Francisco, CA (94080)	49,393	46,646
Sparks, NV (89431)	40,780	24,187
Spartanburg, SC (29301*)	43,968	44,546
Spokane, WA (99210*)	171,300	170,516
Springfield, IL (62703*)	99,637	91,753
Springfield, MA (01101*)	152,319	163,905
Springfield, MO (65801*)	133,116	120,096
Springfield, OH (45501*)	72,563	81,941
Springfield, OR (97477)	41,621	26,874
Stamford, CT (06904*)	102,453	108,798
State College, PA (16801)	36,130	32,833
Sterling Heights, MI (48077)	108,999	61,365
Steubenville, OH (43952)	26,400	30,771
Stillwater, OK (74074)	38,268	31,126
Stockton, CA (95208*)	149,779	109,963
Stow, OH (44224)	25,303	20,061
Strongsville, OH (44136)	28,577	15,182
Suffolk, VA (23434*)	47,621	9,858
Sunnyvale, CA (94086*)	106,618	95,976
Sunrise, FL (33338)	39,681	7,403
Superior, WI (54880)	29,571	32,237
Syracuse, NY (13220*)	170,105	197,297
Tacoma, WA (98413*)	158,501	154,407

City and major ZIP code	1980 census	1970 census	City and major ZIP code	1980 census	1970 census
Tallahassee, FL (32301*)	81,548	72,624	Warren, MI (48089*)	161,134	179,260
Tamarac, FL (33320)	29,142	5,193	Warren, OH (44481*)	56,629	63,494
Tampa, FL (33602*)	271,523	277,714	Warwick, RI (02887*)	87,123	83,694
Taunton, MA (02780)	45,001	43,756	Washington, DC (20013*)	637,651	756,668
Taylor, MI (48180)	77,568	70,020	Waterbury, CT (06701*)	103,266	108,033
Texarkana, TX (75501*)	31,271	30,497	Waterloo, IA (50701*)	75,985	75,533
Texas City, TX (77590*)	41,403	38,908	Watertown, NY (13601)	27,861	30,787
Tempe, AZ (85282*)	106,743	63,550	Waukegan, IL (60085)	67,653	65,134
Temple, TX (76501*)	42,483	33,431	Waukesha, WI (53186)	50,319	39,695
Temple City, CA (91780)	28,972	31,034	Wausau, WI (54401)	32,426	32,806
Terre Haute, IN (47808*)	61,125	70,335	Wauwatosa, WI (53213)	51,308	58,676
Thornton, CO (80229)	40,343	13,326	West Allis, WI (53214)	63,982	71,649
Thousand Oaks, CA (91360*)	77,797	35,873	West Covina, CA (91793*)	80,094	68,034
Tinley Park, IL (60477)	26,171	12,572	Westfield, MA (01085)	36,465	31,433
Titusville, FL (32780)	31,910	30,515	West Haven, CT (06516)	53,184	52,851
Toledo, OH (43601*)	354,635	383,062	West Jordan, UT (84084)	26,794	4,221
Topeka, KN (66603*)	115,266	125,011	Westland, MI (48185)	84,603	86,749
Torrance, CA (90510*)	131,497	134,968	West Memphis, AR (72301)	28,138	26,070
Torrington, CT (06790)	30,987	31,952	West Mifflin, PA (15122)	26,279	28,070
Trenton, NJ (08650*)	92,124	104,786	Westminster, CA (92683)	71,133	60,076
Troy, MI (48099*)	67,102	39,419	Westminster, CO (80030*)	50,211	19,512
Troy, NY (12180*)	56,638	62,918	West New York, NJ (07093)	39,194	40,627
Tucson, AZ (85726*)	330,537	262,933	West Orange, NJ (07052)	39,510	43,715
Tulsa, OK (74101*)	360,919	330,350	West Palm Beach, FL (33401*)	62,530	57,375
Turlock, CA (95380)	26,291	13,992	Wheaton, IL (60187)	43,043	31,138
Tuscaloosa, AL (35403*)	75,143	65,773	Wheat Ridge, CO (80033)	30,293	29,778
Tustin, CA (92680)	32,073	22,313	Wheeling, WV (26003)	43,070	48,188
Twin Falls, ID (83301)	26,209	21,914	White Plains, NY (10602*)	46,999	50,346
Tyler, TX (75702*)	70,508	57,770	Whittier, CA (90605*)	68,872	72,863
Union City, CA (94587)	39,406	14,724	Wichita, KN (67276*)	279,272	276,554
Union City, NJ (07087)	55,593	57,305	Wichita Falls, TX (76307*)	94,201	96,265
University City, MO (63130)	42,738	47,527	Wilkes-Barre, PA (18701*)	51,551	58,856
Upland, CA (91786)	47,647	32,551	Williamsport, PA (17701)	33,401	37,918
Upper Arlington, OH (43221)	35,648	38,727	Wilmette, IL (60091)	28,229	32,134
Urbana, IL (61801)	35,978	33,976	Wilmington, DE (19850*)	70,195	80,386
Utica, NY (13503*)	75,632	91,373	Wilmington, NC (28402*)	44,000	46,169
Vacaville, CA (95688)	43,367	21,690	Wilson, NC (27893)	34,424	29,347
Valdosta, GA (31601)	37,596	32,303	Winona, MN (55987)	25,075	26,438
Vallejo, CA (94590)	80,188	71,710	Winston-Salem, NC (27102*)	131,885	133,683
Valley Stream, NY (11580*)	35,769	40,413	Woburn, MA (01801)	36,626	37,406
Vancouver, WA (98660*)	42,834	41,859	Woodland, CA (95695)	30,235	20,677
Vicksburg, MS (39180)	25,434	25,478	Woonsocket, RI (02895)	45,914	46,820
Victoria, TX (77901)	50,695	41,349	Worcester, MA (01613*)	161,799	176,572
Vineland, NJ (08360)	53,753	47,399	Wyandotte, MI (48192)	34,006	41,061
Virginia Beach, VA (23458*)	262,199	172,106	Wyoming, MI (49509)	59,616	56,560
Visalia, CA (93277)	49,729	27,130	Yakima, WA (98903*)	49,826	45,588
Vista, CA (92083)	35,834	24,688	Yonkers, NY (10701*)	195,351	204,297
Waco, TX (76701*)	101,261	95,326	Yorba Linda, CA (92686)	28,254	11,856
Walla Walla, WA (99362)	25,618	23,619	York, PA (17405*)	44,619	50,335
Walnut Creek, CA (94596*)	53,643	39,844	Youngstown, OH (44501*)	115,436	140,909
Waltham, MA (02154)	58,200	61,582	Yuma, AZ (85364)	42,433	29,007
Warner Robins, GA (31093)	39,893	33,491	Zanesville, OH (43701)	28,655	33,045

1. Queens has four major ZIP codes: 11690*—Far Rockaway; 11351*—Flushing; 11431*—Jamaica; 11101*—Long Island City. *Sources:* Department of Commerce, Bureau of the Census; *1981 National ZIP Code & Post Office Directory.*

Persons Naturalized Since 1907

Period[1]	Civilian	Military	Total	Period[1]	Civilian	Military	Total
1907–30	2,713,389	300,506	3,013,895	1976	136,873	5,631	142,504
1931–40	1,498,573	19,891	1,518,464	1976, TQ[2]	46,705	1,513	48,218
1941–50	1,837,229	149,799	1,987,028	1977[3]	154,568	5,305	159,873
1951–60	1,148,241	41,705	1,189,946	1978	168,409	5,126	173,535
1961–70	1,084,195	36,068	1,120,263	1979	158,276	5,874	164,150
1971–75	579,672	38,882	618,554	1907–79	9,526,130	610,300	10,136,430

1. Fiscal year ending June 30, except as noted. 2. Transition Quarter, July–Sept. 1976. 3. Fiscal year, Oct. 1976–Sept. 1977. *Source:* Department of Justice, Immigration and Naturalization Service. NOTE: Data are latest available.

Territorial Expansion

Accession	Date	Area[1]
United States		
Territory in 1790	—	3,615,122
Louisiana Purchase	—	888,685
Florida	1803	827,192
By treaty with Spain	1819	58,560
Texas	1819	13,443
Oregon	1845	390,143
Mexican Cession	1846	285,580
Gadsden Purchase	1848	529,017
Alaska	1853	29,640
Hawaii	1867	586,412
Other territory	1898	6,450
	—	12,944
Philippines	1898	115,600[2]
Puerto Rico	1899	3,435
Guam	1899	212
American Samoa	1900	76
Canal Zone[4]	1904	553
Corn Islands[3]	1914	4
Virgin Islands of U.S.	1917	133
Trust Territory of Pacific Islands	1947	8,489
All other	—	42
Total, 1970	—	**3,628,066**

1. Total land and water area in square miles. 2. Became independent in 1946; area not included in total. 3. Leased from Nicaragua for 99 years in 1914, but returned April 25, 1971; area included in total. 4. Reverted to Panama. *Source:* Department of Commerce, Bureau of the Census.

Total Population

Area	1960	1970	1980
50 states of U.S.	179,323,175	203,235,298	226,504,825
48 coterminous	178,464,236	202,163,212	225,139,344
Alaska	226,167	302,173	400,841
Hawaii	632,772	769,913	965,000
American Samoa	20,051	27,159	32,395
Canal Zone	42,122	44,198	(1)
Canton Island	320	n.a.	—
Corn Islands	1,872	(2)	—
Guam	67,044	84,996	105,821
Johnston Island	156	1,007	n.a.
Midway	2,356	2,220	n.a.
Puerto Rico	2,349,544	2,712,033	3,187,570
Swan Islands	28	22	n.a.
Trust Ter. of Pac. Is.	70,724	90,940	n.a.
Virgin Is. of U.S.	32,099	62,468	95,591
Wake Island	1,097	1,647	n.a.
Population abroad	1,374,421	1,737,836	(3)
Armed forces	609,720	1,057,776	515,000
Other[4]	n.a.	n.a.	n.a.
Total	**183,285,009**	**207,999,824**	**230,458,062**

1. Granted independence on Oct. 1, 1979. 2. Returned to Nicaragua April 25, 1971. 3. Not enumerated in 1980 census. 4. Includes Baker Island, Enderbury Island, Howland Island, and Jarvis Island, all uninhabited. NOTE: n.a. = unavailable. *Source:* Department of Commerce, Bureau of the Census.

Population by Race, 1980 Census

State	White	Black	Spanish origin	Other	State	White	Black	Spanish origin	Other
Ala.	2,869,688	995,623	33,100	24,750	Mont.	740,148	1,786	9,974	44,756
Alaska	308,455	13,619	9,497	78,407	Neb.	1,490,569	48,389	28,020	31,048
Ariz.	2,240,033	75,034	440,915	402,799	Nev.	699,377	50,791	53,786	49,016
Ark.	1,890,002	373,192	17,873	22,319	N.H.	910,099	3,990	5,587	6,521
Calif.	18,031,689	1,819,282	4,543,770	3,817,591	N.J.	6,127,090	924,786	491,867	312,282
Colo.	2,570,596	101,702	339,300	216,517	N.M.	976,465	24,042	476,089	299,461
Conn.	2,799,420	217,433	124,499	90,723	N.Y.	13,961,106	2,401,842	1,659,245	1,194,340
Del.	488,543	95,971	9,671	10,711	N.C.	4,453,010	1,316,050	56,607	105,369
D.C.	171,796	488,229	17,652	17,626	N.D.	625,536	2,568	3,903	24,591
Fla.	8,178,387	1,342,478	857,898	219,127	Ohio	9,597,266	1,076,734	119,880	123,419
Ga.	3,948,007	1,465,457	61,261	50,801	Okla.	2,597,783	204,658	57,413	222,825
Hawaii	318,608	17,352	71,479	629,040	Ore.	2,490,192	37,059	65,833	105,412
Idaho	901,641	2,716	36,615	39,578	Pa.	10,654,325	1,047,609	154,004	164,794
Ill.	9,225,575	1,675,229	635,525	517,657	R.I.	896,692	27,584	19,707	22,878
Ind.	5,004,567	414,732	87,020	70,880	S.C.	2,145,122	948,146	33,414	25,940
Iowa	2,838,805	41,700	25,536	32,882	S.D.	638,955	2,144	4,028	49,079
Kan.	2,167,752	126,127	63,333	69,329	Tenn.	3,835,078	725,949	34,081	22,295
Ky.	3,379,648	259,490	27,403	22,295	Tex.	11,197,663	1,710,250	2,985,643	1,320,470
La.	2,911,243	1,237,263	99,105	55,466	Utah	1,382,550	9,225	60,302	69,262
Me.	1,109,850	3,128	5,005	11,682	Vt.	506,736	1,135	3,304	3,585
Md.	3,158,412	958,050	64,740	99,984	Va.	4,229,734	1,008,311	79,873	108,234
Mass.	5,362,836	221,279	141,043	152,922	Wash.	3,777,296	105,544	119,986	247,323
Mich.	7,868,956	1,198,710	162,388	190,678	W. Va.	1,874,751	65,051	12,707	9,842
Minn.	3,936,948	53,342	32,124	86,858	Wis.	4,442,598	182,593	62,981	80,144
Miss.	1,615,190	887,206	24,731	18,242	Wyo.	447,716	3,364	24,499	19,736
Mo.	4,346,267	514,274	51,667	56,903	**Total**	**188,340,790**	**26,488,218**	**14,605,883**	**11,675,817**

Source: Department of Commerce, Bureau of the Census.

American Workers Have Shortest Workweek

According to the International Labor Organization, Geneva, the United States has the shortest workweek. The American average is 35.6 hours, followed by Sweden, 35.7; Belgium, 35.8; and New Zealand with 37.6 hours. The rest of the world's workers put in a workweek of over 40 hours. The ILO stated that, worldwide, Egypt has the longest workweek, averaging 56 hours, and that among Western countries Switzerland leads with an average of 44.5 hours.

Immigration to U.S. by Country of Origin

(Figures are totals, not annual averages, and were tabulated as follows: 1820–67, alien passengers arrived; 1868–91 and 1895–97, immigrant aliens arrived; 1892–94 and 1898 to present, immigrant aliens admitted. Data before 1906 relate to country whence alien came; since 1906, to country of last permanent residence.)

Countries	1979	1820–1979	1961–70	1951–60	1941–50	1931–40	1921–30	1820–1920
Europe: Albania[1]	25	2,608	98	59	85	2,040	—	—
Austria[2]	507	4,315,486	20,621	67,106	24,860	3,563	32,868	3,626,110
Belgium	646	202,892	9,192	18,575	12,189	4,817	15,846	137,542
Bulgaria[3]	127	68,021	619	104	375	938	2,945	61,973
Czechoslovakia[1]	494	137,829	3,273	918	8,347	14,393	102,194	3,426
Denmark	378	364,548	9,201	10,984	5,393	2,559	32,430	300,036
Estonia[1]	9	1,148	163	185	212	506	—	—
Finland[1]	284	33,770	4,192	4,925	2,503	2,146	16,691	756
France	2,905	752,432	45,237	51,121	38,809	12,623	49,610	532,765
Germany[2]	7,166	6,984,081	190,796	477,765	226,578	114,058	412,202	5,495,691
Great Britain: England	14,336	3,189,988	174,452	156,171	112,252	21,756	157,420	2,462,015
Scotland	803	821,369	29,849	32,854	16,131	6,887	159,781	567,106
Wales	128	95,332	2,052	2,589	3,209	735	13,012	72,647
Not specified[4]	270	805,238	3,675	3,884	—	—	—	793,741
Greece	5,942	660,869	85,969	47,608	8,973	9,119	51,084	370,405
Hungary[2]	528	—	5,401	36,637	3,469	7,861	30,680	442,693
Ireland	808	4,724,609	37,461	57,332	26,967	13,167	220,591	4,358,350
Italy	5,969	5,300,770	214,111	185,491	57,661	68,028	455,315	4,195,880
Latvia[1]	13	2,604	510	352	361	1,192	—	—
Lithuania[1]	23	3,938	562	242	683	2,201	—	—
Luxembourg[1]	42	2,906	556	684	820	565	—	—
Netherlands	1,184	360,796	30,606	52,277	14,860	7,150	26,948	219,661
Norway[5]	438	856,907	15,484	22,935	10,100	4,740	68,531	731,584
Poland[6]	3,863	518,917	53,539	9,985	7,571	17,026	227,734	169,995
Portugal	7,068	452,350	76,065	19,588	7,423	3,329	29,994	222,721
Romania[7]	1,180	172,480	2,531	1,039	1,076	3,871	67,646	85,428
Spain	3,285	260,867	44,659	7,894	2,898	3,258	28,958	137,907
Sweden[5]	764	1,272,683	17,116	21,697	10,665	3,960	97,249	1,116,239
Switzerland	774	349,723	18,453	17,675	10,547	5,512	29,676	260,492
U.S.S.R.[8]	1,919	3,375,717	2,336	584	548	1,356	61,742	3,280,249
Yugoslavia[3]	1,861	115,804	20,381	8,225	1,576	5,835	49,064	1,888
Other Europe	434	56,027	4,203	8,155	3,983	2,361	22,983	10,716
Total Europe	64,173	36,264,178	1,123,363	1,325,640	621,124	347,552	2,463,194	29,658,016
Asia: China[9]	2,944	537,531	34,764	9,657	16,709	4,928	29,907	347,338
India	18,625	183,931	27,189	1,973	1,761	496	1,886	7,491
Japan[10]	4,496	410,444	39,988	46,250	1,555	1,948	33,462	242,181
Turkey	1,306	387,417	10,142	3,519	798	1,065	33,824	326,347
Other Asia	155,599	1,523,587	315,688	88,707	11,537	7,644	12,980	22,915
Total Asia[11]	182,970	3,042,910	427,771	150,106	32,360	16,081	112,059	946,272
America: Canada and Newfoundland[12]	20,181	4,118,406	413,310	377,952	171,718	108,527	924,515	1,972,686
Central America	17,709	330,244	101,330	44,751	21,665	5,861	15,769	27,524
Mexico[13]	52,479	2,175,891	453,937	299,811	60,589	22,319	459,287	296,649
South America	35,715	748,423	257,954	91,628	21,831	7,803	42,215	71,284
West Indies	71,029	1,761,474	470,213	123,091	49,725	15,502	74,899	356,570
Other America[13]	10	109,468	19,630	59,711	29,276	25	31	—
Total America	197,123	9,243,906	1,716,374	996,944	354,804	160,037	1,516,716	2,724,713
Africa	11,212	144,459	28,954	14,092	7,367	1,750	6,286	18,024
Australia and New Zealand	2,476	120,503	19,562	11,506	13,805	2,231	8,299	44,002
Pacific Islands[14]	135	24,706	1,769	4,698	5,437	780	427	9,938
Countries not specified[15]	2,259	284,651	3,884	12,493	142	—	228	253,838
Total all countries	460,348	49,125,313	3,321,677	2,515,479	1,035,039	528,431	4,107,209	33,654,803

1. Countries established since beginning of World War I are included with countries to which they belonged. 2. Data for Austria-Hungary not reported until 1861. Austria and Hungary recorded separately after 1905. Austria included with Germany 1938–45. 3. Bulgaria, Serbia, Montenegro first reported in 1899. Bulgaria reported separately since 1920. In 1920, separate enumeration for Kingdom of Serbs, Croats, Slovenes; since 1922, recorded as Yugoslavia. 4. United Kingdom not specified; for 1901–51, included in "Other Europe." 5. Norway included with Sweden 1820–68. 6. Included with Austria-Hungary, Germany, and Russia 1899–1919. 7. No record of immigration until 1880. 8. From 1931–63, the U.S.S.R. was broken down into European U.S.S.R. and Asian U.S.S.R. Since 1964, total U.S.S.R. has been reported in Europe. 9. Beginning in 1957, China includes Taiwan. 10. No record of immigration until 1861. 11. From 1952, Asia included Philippines. From 1934–51, Philippines were included in Pacific Islands; before 1934, recorded in separate tables as insular travel. 12. Includes all British North American possessions, 1820–98. 13. No record of immigration, 1886–93. 14. Included with "Countries not specified" prior to 1925. 15. Includes 32,897 persons returning in 1906 to their homes in U.S. *Source:* Department of Justice, Immigration and Naturalization Service. NOTE: Data are latest available.

Immigrant and Nonimmigrant Aliens Admitted to U.S.

Period[1]	Immigrants	Non-immigrants	Total	Period[1]	Immigrants	Non-immigrants	Total
1901–10	8,795,386	1,007,909	9,803,295	1966–70	1,871,365	16,227,660	18,099,025
1911–20	5,735,811	1,376,271	7,112,082	1971–75	1,936,281	29,545,190	31,481,471
1921–30	4,107,209	1,774,896	5,882,090	1976	398,613	7,654,491	8,053,104
1931–40	528,431	1,574,071	2,102,502	1976, TQ[2]	103,676	2,673,652	2,777,328
1941–50	1,035,039	2,461,359	3,496,398	1977[3]	462,315	8,036,916	8,499,231
1951–55	1,087,638	2,654,461	3,742,009	1978	601,442	9,343,710	9,945,152
1956–60	1,427,841	4,458,562	5,886,403	1979	460,348	n.a.	n.a.
1961–65	1,450,312	7,879,564	9,329,876				

1. Fiscal year ending June 30, except as noted. 2. Transition Quarter, July–Sept. 1976. 3. Starting 1977, for fiscal year ending Sept. 30. n.a. = not available. *Source:* Department of Justice, Immigration and Naturalization Service. NOTE: Nonimmigrant aliens include visitors for business or pleasure, students, foreign government officials, and others temporarily in the U.S.

Population of Largest Indian Reservations, 1979

Navajo (Ariz., N.M., Utah)	159,124	Papago (Ariz.)	16,033	Standing Rock (N.D., S.D.)	7,838
Creek (Okla.)[1]	28,224	Osage (Okla.)[1]	10,144	Chickasaw (Okla.)[1]	7,700
Cherokee (Okla.)[1]	25,300	Yakima (Wash.)	8,444	Wind River (Wyo.)	6,926
Southern Pueblos (N.M.)	21,433	Gila River (Ariz.)	9,219	Blackfeet (Mont.)	6,272
Choctaw (Okla.)[1]	18,171	Turtle Mountain (N.D.)	8,160	Zuni (N.M.)	6,602
Pine Ridge (S.D.)	16,000	Fort Apache (Ariz.)	8,020	San Carlos (N.M.)	6,041
Rosebud (S.D.)	9,143	Hopi (Ariz.)	8,072		

1. Includes Indians living in former reservation areas. NOTE: The Bureau of Indian Affairs lists 681,213 Indians residing on or near Federal reservations. *Source:* Department of the Interior, Bureau of Indian Affairs. NOTE: Figures are latest available.

Income of Households by Age of Head, 1979

Age of head	House-holds (thousands)	Income (per cent)						Total
		Under $5,000	$5,000 to $7,499	$7,500 to $9,999	$10,000 to $14,999	$15,000 to $24,999	$25,000 and over	
15–24 years	6,398	9.8	10.7	12.9	11.7	8.5	2.7	8.1
25–34 years	17,900	12.4	15.9	19.0	25.5	30.6	21.4	22.6
35–44 years	13,904	7.4	9.2	10.6	14.6	20.3	26.0	17.6
45–54 years	12,581	8.2	9.5	9.7	11.5	15.9	25.7	15.9
55–64 years	12,177	14.4	13.2	13.1	15.2	14.6	18.0	15.4
65 years and over	16,149	47.9	41.4	34.7	21.5	10.1	6.2	20.4
Total	79,108	100.0	100.0	100.0	100.0	100.0	100.0	100.0

Source: Department of Commerce, Bureau of the Census.

Household Size Declines

Since 1970 the size of the American household has fallen sharply, according to 1980 census figures. While the number of households increased by 27% since 1970, the number of persons living in them increased by only 12%. From the 1970 census to April 1980, the average number of persons per household declined from 3.11 to 2.75, while the total number of households increased from 63.4 million to 80.4 million.

These figures reflect a change in how Americans live. In 1930 when families were larger and aging relatives were more likely to be cared for at home, the average size of households was 4.11 persons.

Since then there has been a steady decline with the greatest percentage taking place in the 1970s when adults began living alone in record numbers.

According to a Census Bureau analysis, a considerable factor in the shrinking of average households has been a declining birth rate which it attributes to changed attitudes about childbearing coupled with the pursuit of educational and career goals. The increase in the number of people living alone is accounted for by wives outliving husbands and more young adults establishing homes before marriage or after separation or divorce.

Marriage and Divorce

Marriages and Divorces

Year	Marriage Number	Marriage Rate[2]	Divorce[1] Number	Divorce[1] Rate[2]	Year	Marriage Number	Marriage Rate[2]	Divorce[1] Number	Divorce[1] Rate[2]
1900	709,000	9.3	55,751	.7	1957	1,518,000	8.9	381,000	2.2
1905	842,000	10.0	67,976	.8	1958	1,451,000	8.4	368,000	2.1
1910	948,166	10.3	83,045	.9	1959	1,494,000	8.5	395,000	2.2
1915	1,007,595	10.0	104,298	1.0	1960	1,523,000	8.5	393,000	2.2
1920	1,274,476	12.0	170,505	1.6	1961	1,548,000	8.5	414,000	2.3
1925	1,188,334	10.3	175,449	1.5	1962	1,577,000	8.5	413,000	2.2
1930	1,126,856	9.2	195,961	1.6	1963	1,654,000	8.8	428,000	2.3
1935	1,327,000	10.4	218,000	1.7	1964	1,725,000	9.0	450,000	2.4
1940	1,595,879	12.1	264,000	2.0	1965	1,800,000	9.3	479,000	2.5
1942	1,772,132	13.2	321,000	2.4	1966	1,857,000	9.5	499,000	2.5
1943	1,577,050	11.7	359,000	2.6	1967	1,927,000	9.7	523,000	2.6
1944	1,452,394	10.9	400,000	2.9	1968	2,069,258	10.4	584,000	2.9
1945	1,612,992	12.2	485,000	3.5	1969	2,145,438	10.6	639,000	3.2
1946	2,291,045	16.4	610,000	4.3	1970	2,158,802	10.6	708,000	3.5
1947	1,991,878	13.9	483,000	3.4	1971	2,190,481	10.6	773,000	3.7
1948	1,811,155	12.4	408,000	2.8	1972	2,282,154	11.0	845,000	4.1
1949	1,579,798	10.6	397,000	2.7	1973	2,284,108	10.9	915,000	4.4
1950	1,667,231	11.1	385,144	2.6	1974	2,229,667	10.5	977,000	4.6
1951	1,594,694	10.4	381,000	2.5	1975	2,152,662	10.1	1,036,000	4.9
1952	1,539,318	9.9	392,000	2.5	1976	2,154,807	10.0	1,083,000	5.0
1953	1,546,000	9.8	390,000	2.5	1977	2,178,367	10.1	1,091,000	5.0
1954	1,490,000	9.2	379,000	2.4	1978	2,282,272	10.5	1,130,000	5.2
1955	1,531,000	9.3	377,000	2.3	1979	2,331,337	10.6	1,181,000	5.4
1956	1,585,000	9.5	382,000	2.3	1980[3]	2,413,000	10.9	1,182,000	5.3

1. Includes annulments. 2. Per 1,000 population. Divorce rates for 1941–46 are based on population including armed forces overseas. Marriage rates are based on population excluding armed forces overseas. 3. Provisional. NOTE: Marriage and divorce figures for most years include some estimated data. Alaska is included beginning 1959, Hawaii beginning 1960. *Source:* Department of Health and Human Services, National Center for Health Statistics.

Percent of Population Ever Married

Age group, years[1]	1980	1975	1970	1960	1950	1940	1930	1920	1910	1900
Males: 15 to 19	2.7	2.7	2.6	3.3	2.9	1.5	1.5	1.8	1.0	0.9
20 to 24	31.4	40.1	45.3	46.9	41.0	27.8	29.0	29.1	24.7	22.2
25 to 29	67.6	77.7	80.9	79.2	76.2	64.0	63.2	60.5	57.1	54.1
30 to 34	84.3	88.9	90.6	88.1	86.8	79.3	78.8	75.8	73.9	72.3
35 to 44	92.6	92.1	93.3	91.9	90.4	86.0	85.7	83.8	83.3	83.0
45 to 54	93.1	93.7	92.5	92.6	91.5	88.9	88.6	88.0	88.8	89.7
Females: 15 to 19	8.9	9.3	9.7	13.5	14.4	10.0	10.9	10.8	9.8	9.4
20 to 24	49.8	59.7	64.2	71.6	67.7	52.8	53.9	54.4	51.5	48.4
25 to 29	79.2	86.2	89.5	89.5	86.7	77.2	78.3	76.9	75.0	72.4
30 to 34	90.5	92.5	93.8	93.1	90.7	85.3	86.8	85.1	83.8	83.4
35 to 44	94.4	95.1	94.8	93.9	91.7	89.6	90.0	88.6	88.6	88.9
45 to 54	95.3	95.4	95.1	93.0	92.2	91.3	90.9	90.4	91.4	92.2

1. 1980: 15 years and over; previous years: 14 and older. *Source:* Department of Commerce, Bureau of the Census.

Households Headed by Women Are Fastest Growing

According to a recent Census Bureau report, households headed by women were the fastest-growing family type in the United States during the 1970s. While the number of families grew by 12% between 1970 and 1979, the number headed by women increased by 51%.

Among whites 12% of all families were maintained by women, while 20% of Hispanic families and 41% of black families were headed by women. However, in 1978 the median income of families headed by women was less than half the median income of all families.

Marriage Information by State

State	Legal minimum marriage age				Blood test required	Waiting period[1]		Marriages[2]	
	With parental consent[3]		Without parental consent			Before license	After license	1980[4]	1979
	M	F	M	F					
Alabama	14	14	18	18	yes	none	none	49,006	48,807
Alaska	16	16	18	18	yes	3 d	none	5,286	5,071
Arizona	18	18	18	18	yes	none	none	30,230	29,549
Arkansas	18	16	18	18	yes	3 d	none	25,197	24,947
California	18	16	18	18	yes	none	none	218,385	201,133
Colorado	16[19]	16[19]	18	18	yes[17]	none	none	34,078	31,889
Connecticut	16	16	18	18	yes	4 d	none	25,761	24,675
Delaware	18[25]	16[25]	18	18	yes[11]	none	24 h[5]	4,423	4,418
D. C.	16–17[7]	16–17[7]	18	18	yes	5 d[6]	none	5,128	4,974
Florida	18	16	18	18	yes	3 d	none	110,575	103,406
Georgia	16[25]	16[25]	18	18[25]	yes[21]	3 d	none	69,416	65,898
Hawaii	16	16	18	18	yes	none	none	11,670	11,658
Idaho	18	16	18	18	yes	3 d[24]	none	13,084	13,568
Illinois	16	16	18	18	yes	none	1 d	110,667	108,443
Indiana	17	17[20]	18	18	yes	3 d	none	57,852	59,613
Iowa	16	16	18	18	yes	3 d	none	27,527	27,731
Kansas	(23)	(23)	18	18	yes	3 d	none	24,928	24,867
Kentucky	(18)	(18)	18	18	yes	3 d	none	34,291	36,513
Louisiana	18	16	18	18	yes	none	72 h	41,658	41,861
Maine	16	16	18	18	no	5 d	none	14,351	11,944
Maryland	16[15]	16[15]	18	18	no	48 h	none	45,967	45,903
Massachusetts	14–17[12]	12–15[12]	18	18	yes	3 d	none	49,058	46,652
Michigan	18	16[8]	18	18	yes	3 d	none	89,606	86,660
Minnesota	16	16	21	18	no	5 d	none	37,825	36,298
Mississippi	17	15	21	21	yes	3 d	none	28,043	26,718
Missouri	15[12]	15[12]	18	18	yes	3 d	none	55,518	52,336
Montana	18	18	16[22]	16[22]	yes	5 d	3 d	8,367	8,246
Nebraska	17	17	19	19	yes	2 d	none	14,189	14,032
Nevada	16	16	18	18	no	none	none	115,411	121,874
New Hampshire	14[12 15]	13[12 15]	18	18	yes[11]	5 d	none	9,298	9,175
New Jersey	18	18	18	18	yes	72 h	none	54,956	54,844
New Mexico	16	16	18	18	yes	none	none	16,324	16,785
New York	16	14[9]	21	18	yes	none	(10)	141,299	141,350
North Carolina	16	16	18	18	yes	none	none	46,341	45,233
North Dakota	16	16	18	18	yes	none	none	6,139	5,977
Ohio	18	16	18	18	yes	5 d	none	99,522	102,539
Oklahoma	16[19]	16[19]	18	18	yes	none[14]	none	46,509	44,452
Oregon	17	17	18	18	yes	3 d	none	23,115	21,907
Pennsylvania	16	16	18	18	yes	3 d	none	95,394	89,417
Rhode Island	18	16[9]	18	18	yes	none	none	7,120	7,350
South Carolina	16	14	18	18	no	24 h	none	53,923	53,968
South Dakota	16	16	18	18	yes	none	none	8,929	9,098
Tennessee	16	16	18	18	yes	none[14]	none	58,751	59,407
Texas	16[13]	16[13]	18	18	yes	none	none	187,118	174,743
Utah	14	14	16	16	yes	none	none	17,074	16,823
Vermont	14[19]	14[19]	18	18	yes	none	3 d[16]	5,187	5,228
Virginia	16	16	18	18	yes	none	none	60,193	58,739
Washington	17	17	18	18	no	3 d	none	46,617	45,809
West Virginia	18	16	18	18	yes	3 d	none	17,451	17,733
Wisconsin	16	16	18	18	yes	5 d	none	40,953	39,551
Wyoming	16[19]	16[19]	19	19	yes	none	none	6,825	6,032

1. In some states, waiting period may be waived or reduced by court order. 2. By place of occurrence. 3. In most states, persons younger than the age shown may be married by court permission. 4. Provisional figures; data represent marriages reported, marriage intentions filed, or marriage licenses issued. 5. 96 hours if nonresidents. 6. Day of application and day of pickup are included in 5-day waiting period. 7. No exceptions granted under this age. 8. Consent of one parent or guardian necessary for female only. 9. Females 14 to 16 years old must also have consent of judge of Family Court. 10. Marriage may not be solemnized within 3 days from date on which specimen was taken for serological test, and not until 24 hours after issuance of marriage license. Waiting period may be waived by court order. 11. Blood test may be waived by court order. 12. Need court order. 13. Parent must appear in person or provide doctor's affidavit of his or her illness. 14. 3 days if either party is under legal age. 15. If pregnant. 16. After date on which marriage application has been filed with town clerk, excluding date of filing. 17. Blood test for rubella and RH type not required of females over 45 years or found by physician to be incapable of bearing children. 18. No age limit. 19. If under 16 need court order. 20. 15 for pregnancy or maternity. 21. Prior to issuance of license, a medical examination for rubella is required. 22. With judicial approval. 23. Under 18 with parental consent only. 24. Only for those under 18. 25. May marry at any age with proof of pregnancy signed by physician or if marrying father of child born out of wedlock. *Sources:* Legal information, *Information Please* questionnaires to states; marriage statistics, Department of Health and Human Services, National Center for Health Statistics.

Median Age at First Marriage

Year	Males	Females	Year	Males	Females	Year	Males	Females	Year	Males	Females
1890	26.1	22.0	1920	24.6	21.2	1950	22.8	20.3	1975	23.5	21.1
1900	25.9	21.9	1930	24.3	21.3	1960	22.8	20.3	1979	24.4	22.1
1910	25.1	21.6	1940	24.3	21.5	1970	23.2	20.8	1980	24.6	22.1

Source: Department of Commerce, Bureau of the Census.

Marriage Prospects of Single Men and Women

Age	Percent of population single[1] Male	Female	Percent who ever marry[2] Male	Female	Age	Percent of population single[1] Male	Female	Percent who ever marry[2] Male	Female
15	99.4	97.6	95.8	97.4	33	10.9	6.3	63.5	49.7
16	99.0	94.3	95.9	97.4	34	10.3	6.4	60.2	46.0
17	98.1	87.9	96.0	97.3	35	9.9	6.4	57.2	42.9
18	94.6	75.5	96.0	97.0	36	9.0	6.1	54.1	40.0
19	87.3	59.6	95.9	96.4	37	8.7	6.0	51.0	37.3
20	75.8	45.8	95.6	95.5	38	8.1	5.7	48.0	34.7
21	63.3	35.1	95.0	94.2	39	8.1	6.2	45.1	32.2
22	51.4	25.8	94.1	92.2	40	7.6	6.1	42.3	29.9
23	40.5	19.4	92.8	89.4	41	7.5	6.0	39.7	27.6
24	33.5	15.6	91.1	86.1	42	6.9	5.9	37.2	25.5
25	27.8	13.1	89.1	82.5	43	7.1	6.0	34.8	23.6
26	23.9	11.5	86.6	78.4	44	7.4	6.5	32.7	21.7
27	19.6	9.9	83.6	74.2	45	7.1	6.1	30.6	20.0
28	17.3	9.3	80.3	70.3	50	7.6	7.4	21.6	12.8
29	15.9	8.7	77.3	65.7	55	7.9	7.9	13.9	7.7
30	14.2	7.9	73.8	61.2	60	8.0	7.8	8.2	4.4
31	12.9	7.2	70.4	57.3	65 and over	7.7	8.5	—	—
32	11.7	6.6	67.1	53.3					

1. Percent single within specified year of age in 1960, in 5% sample of population (latest available data). 2. Percent of white persons single at beginning of year of age who marry during that year and all later years, based on data for 1958-60. NOTE: "Single" excludes widowed and divorced. *Source:* Department of Commerce, Bureau of the Census.

Persons Living Alone, by Sex and Age
(numbers in thousands)

Sex and age[1]	1980 Number	Percent	1975 Number	Percent	1970 Number	Percent	1965 Number	Percent	1960 Number	Percent
BOTH SEXES										
15 to 24 years	1,670	9.4	1,111	8.0	556	5.1	305	3.5	234	3.3
25 to 44 years	4,607	25.9	2,744	19.7	1,604	14.8	1,281	14.9	1,212	17.2
45 to 64 years	4,398	24.7	4,076	29.2	3,622	33.4	3,073	35.7	2,720	38.5
65 years and over	7,140	40.1	6,008	43.1	5,071	46.7	3,943	45.8	2,898	41.0
Total, 15 years and over	17,816	100.0	13,939	100.0	10,851	100.0	8,602	100.0	7,063	100.0
MALE										
15 to 24 years	919	5.2	610	4.4	274	2.5	141	1.6	124	1.8
25 to 44 years	2,848	16.0	1,689	12.1	933	8.6	737	8.6	686	9.7
45 to 64 years	1,589	8.9	1,329	9.5	1,152	10.6	1,013	11.8	965	13.7
65 years and over	1,437	8.1	1,290	9.3	1,174	10.8	1,033	12.0	853	12.1
Total, 15 years and over	6,793	38.1	4,918	35.3	3,532	32.5	2,923	34.0	2,628	37.2
FEMALE										
15 to 24 years	751	4.2	501	3.6	282	2.6	164	1.9	110	1.6
25 to 44 years	1,759	9.9	1,055	7.6	671	6.2	544	6.3	526	7.4
45 to 64 years	2,809	15.8	2,747	19.7	2,470	22.8	2,060	23.9	1,755	24.8
65 years and over	5,703	32.0	4,718	33.8	3,897	35.9	2,910	33.8	2,045	29.0
Total, 15 years and over	11,022	61.9	9,021	64.7	7,319	67.5	5,679	66.0	4,436	62.8

Source: Department of Commerce, Bureau of the Census. 1. 1980: 15 years and older; previous years: 14 and older.

Divorce Information by State

State	Residence for divorce	Period before parties may remarry		Divorce rate		
		Plaintiff	Defendant	1979	1978	1977
Alabama	6 mo	60 d	60 d	7.0	6.7	6.4
Alaska	(25)	none	none	8.6	8.4	8.8
Arizona	90 d	none	none	8.2	7.3	7.2
Arkansas	90 d	none	none	9.3[2]	9.2	9.0[2]
California	6 mo	none	none	6.1	6.0	6.0
Colorado	90 d[20]	none	none	6.0	6.9	7.8
Connecticut	1 yr	none	none	4.5	4.1	3.9
Delaware	1 yr[20]	none[12]	none[12]	5.3	5.7	5.2
D.C.	6 mo	60 d	60	6.8	5.1	4.6
Florida	6 mo	none	none	7.9	7.6	7.4
Georgia	6 mo	none	none	6.5	6.2	6.1
Hawaii	6 mo	none	none	5.5	5.4	5.1
Idaho	6 wk	none	none	7.1	7.2	7.0
Illinois	1 yr	none	none	4.6	4.5	4.4
Indiana	6 mo[4][6]	none	none	7.7	7.5	6.3[2]
Iowa	1 yr[11]	1 yr	1 yr	3.9	3.8	3.8
Kansas	60 d	30 d	30 d	5.4	5.4	5.4
Kentucky	6 mo[4][23]	none	none	4.5[2]	3.9[2]	4.5
Louisiana	1 yr	none[8]	none[8]	3.8	3.3	n.a.
Maine	6 mo	none	none	5.6	5.7	5.2
Maryland	1 yr[24]	none	none	4.1	4.0	4.0
Massachusetts	1 yr	none	none	3.0	2.8	2.9
Michigan	1 yr	none	none	4.8	4.9	4.7
Minnesota	1 yr	6 mo	6 mo	3.7[3]	3.6	3.5
Mississippi	6 mo	(10)	(10)	5.6[3]	5.5	5.3
Missouri	90 d	none	none	5.7	5.4	5.3
Montana	1 yr	none	none	6.5	6.3	6.2
Nebraska	1 yr[5]	none	none	4.0	3.9	3.9
Nevada	6 wk	none	none	16.8	16.8	16.2
New Hampshire	1 yr	none	none	5.9	5.4	5.2
New Jersey	1 yr	none	none	3.2	3.6	2.8
New Mexico	6 mo[13]	none	none	8.0	7.9	7.7
New York	(14)	none	none	3.7	3.3	3.1
North Carolina	6 mo	none	none	4.9	4.8	4.5
North Dakota	1 yr	(9)	(9)	3.2	3.2	3.0
Ohio	6 mo[6]	none	none	5.5	5.5	5.4
Oklahoma	6 mo[22]	6 mo[21]	6 mo[21]	7.9	7.9	7.8
Oregon	6 mo	60 d	60 d	7.0	6.9	6.9
Pennsylvania	6 mo	none	none[15]	3.4	3.3	3.2
Rhode Island	2 yr	none	none	3.9	3.7	3.7
South Carolina	1 yr	none	none	4.7	4.1	3.7
South Dakota	(7)	none	none	3.9	3.5	3.5
Tennessee	1 yr	none[16]	none[16]	6.8	6.6	6.4
Texas	6 mo	30 d[16]	30 d[16]	6.9	6.6	6.4
Utah	3 mo	3 mo[12]	3 mo[12]	5.6	5.4	5.5
Vermont	6 mo[19]	none	none	4.6	4.2	4.4
Virginia	6 mo	none	none	4.5	4.4	4.2
Washington	none[20]	none	none	6.9	7.0	7.3
West Virginia	1 yr[17]	(18)	(18)	5.3	5.2	5.2
Wisconsin	6 mo	6 mo	6 mo	3.6	3.4	3.1
Wyoming	60 d	none	none	7.8	7.4	7.6

1. By place of occurrence, including reported annulments. 2. Incomplete. 3. Estimated. 4. Only one party must have resided in the state for 180 days. 5. Decree not final until 6 months after trial and decision. 6. 6-month residence in county. 7. Physical presence plus intent to make state the place of residence. 8. In case of adultery, guilty party cannot marry correspondent. 9. At discretion of court. 10. Until court that grants the divorce is adjourned. 11. No time required if both parties are residents of state and intend to make state their place of residence. 12. 30 days between first and final judgment. 13. Servicemen acquire residence by being continuously stationed at military base in state for 6 months. 14. Action for divorce may be maintained only where (1) parties were married in the state and either has been a resident for one year preceding the action; (2) parties have resided in the state as husband and wife and either has been a resident for one year preceding the action; (3) cause for divorce occurred in the state and either party has been a resident for one year preceding the action; (4) cause for divorce occurred in the state and both parties are residents at time of the action; (5) either party is a resident for at least 2 years preceding the action. 15. Party guilty of adultery may not marry the correspondent during lifetime of former spouse. 16. Parties may remarry each other at any time. 17. 2 years if residence is acquired after cause of divorce action arose. 18. Court can lengthen waiting period if desired. 19. Court must find resumption of marital relations not reasonably probable. 20. Must be domiciled in state. 21. 30 days from date of judgment of appeal. 22. 5 years if on grounds of insanity and insane spouse is in institution. 23. No decree shall be entered until parties have lived apart for 60 days. 24. When cause for divorce occurred out of state. 25. No residency requirement but action will not be heard by court until 30 days after filing for divorce. NOTE: n.a. = not available. *Sources:* Legal information, *Information Please* questionnaires to states; divorce statistics, Department of Health and Human Services, National Center for Health Statistics.

Grounds for Divorce

State	Adultery	Cruelty	Desertion	Alcoholism	Impotence	Felony conviction	Neglect to provide	Insanity	Pregnancy at marriage[1]	Bigamy	Separation	Indignities	Drug addiction	Violence	Fraudulent contract	Others
Alabama	yes	yes	yes[2]	yes	yes	yes[16]	yes[3]	yes[6]	yes[1]	—	—	yes[3]	—	yes	yes	—	(27 29 34)
Alaska	yes	yes	yes[2]	yes	yes	yes	yes	yes[9]	—	—	—	—	yes	yes	yes	—	(29)
Arizona	—	—	—	—	—	—	—	—	—	—	—	—	—	—	yes	yes	(12 31 48)
Arkansas	yes	yes	yes[2]	yes	yes	yes	yes	yes	—	yes	yes[4]	yes	—	—	yes	yes	(28)
California	—	—	—	—	—	—	—	—	—	—	—	—	—	—	—	—	(29 52)
Colorado	—	—	—	—	—	—	—	—	—	—	—	—	—	—	—	yes	(13 23 30 42 46)
Connecticut	yes	yes	yes[2]	yes	—	yes[20]	—	yes[6]	—	—	yes[9]	—	—	—	—	—	(27 68)
Delaware	yes	yes	yes[2]	yes[3]	—	yes	yes	yes[6]	—	yes	yes[9]	—	—	—	—	—	(63)
D.C.	yes	yes[53]	—	—	—	—	—	—	—	—	yes[2]	—	—	—	—	—	(49 52)
Florida	—	—	—	—	—	—	—	—	—	—	—	—	—	—	—	—	(27 31 44 49)
Georgia	yes	yes	yes[2]	yes	yes	yes[15]	yes	yes	yes	—	yes	yes	yes	yes	yes	yes	(29)
Hawaii	—	—	—	—	—	—	—	—	—	—	yes[3]	—	—	—	—	—	(26 28 42)
Idaho	yes	yes	yes	—	—	yes	yes	yes[4]	—	yes	—	—	—	—	—	—	(32 37 56)
Illinois	yes	yes	yes[2]	yes[3]	yes	yes	—	—	—	—	yes[51]	—	—	yes[3]	yes	—	(29 33 52)
Indiana	—	—	—	—	yes	—	—	yes[3]	—	—	—	—	—	—	—	—	(49)
Iowa	—	—	—	—	—	—	—	—	—	—	—	—	—	—	—	yes	(31 48)
Kansas	yes	yes	yes[2]	yes	—	yes	yes	yes[6]	—	—	—	—	—	—	—	yes	(49)
Kentucky	—	—	—	—	—	—	—	—	—	—	—	—	—	—	—	—	(37 58)
Louisiana	yes	yes	yes	—	—	yes	yes	—	—	yes	yes[3]	—	yes	yes	—	—	(28)
Maine	yes	yes	yes	yes	yes	yes[20]	yes	yes[36]	—	—	—	—	—	yes	—	—	(28 35 67)
Maryland[65]	yes	—	—	—	yes	yes[18]	—	yes[66]	—	—	—	—	—	—	—	—	(29 49)
Massachusetts	yes	yes	yes[2]	yes	yes	yes[19]	yes	—	—	—	—	—	—	yes	—	—	(29)
Michigan	—	—	—	—	—	—	—	—	—	—	—	—	—	—	—	—	(49)
Minnesota	—	—	—	—	—	—	—	—	—	—	—	—	—	—	—	—	(10 28 31 49)
Mississippi	yes	yes	yes	yes	yes	yes[22]	—	yes[47]	yes	yes	yes[2]	yes	—	yes	yes	—	(10 30 32 52)
Missouri	yes	yes	yes	yes	yes	yes	—	yes	yes	—	yes	yes	—	—	—	—	(29)
Montana	—	—	—	—	—	—	—	—	—	—	—	—	—	—	—	—	(49)
Nebraska	—	—	—	—	—	—	—	—	—	—	—	—	—	—	—	—	(27)
Nevada	—	—	—	—	—	—	—	yes[3]	—	—	yes[2]	—	—	—	—	—	(25 28 40 57 60)
New Hampshire	yes	yes	yes[3]	yes[3]	yes	yes[14]	yes[3]	—	—	—	—	—	—	yes	—	—	(34 49)
New Jersey	yes	yes	yes[2]	yes[2]	yes[51]	yes[44]	—	yes[3]	—	—	yes[51]	yes[9]	—	yes[2]	—	yes[51]	(27)
New Mexico	yes	yes	yes	—	—	—	—	—	—	—	—	—	—	—	—	—	
New York	yes	yes	yes[2]	—	—	yes[17]	—	—	—	—	yes[2]	—	—	—	—	—	(34)
North Carolina	yes	—	—	—	yes	—	—	yes	yes	—	yes[2]	—	—	—	—	—	(28)
North Dakota	yes	yes	yes[2]	yes[2]	—	yes	yes[2]	yes[6]	—	—	—	—	—	—	—	yes	(12 24 41 55)
Ohio	yes	yes	yes	yes[4]	yes	yes	yes	yes[5]	—	yes	yes[3]	—	—	—	—	yes	(27 41 55)
Oklahoma	yes	yes	yes[2]	yes	yes	yes[21]	yes	yes[6]	—	—	—	—	—	—	—	yes	(49)
Oregon	—	—	—	—	—	—	—	—	—	—	—	—	—	—	—	—	(29 31)
Pennsylvania	yes	yes	yes[2]	—	yes[45]	yes[15]	—	yes	—	yes	yes[4]	yes	—	yes	yes	—	(13 38)
Rhode Island	yes	yes	yes[6]	yes	yes	yes[7]	yes[2]	yes[48]	—	yes	yes[3]	—	yes	yes	yes	—	(50)
South Carolina	yes	yes[39]	yes[2]	yes	—	—	—	—	—	—	yes[2]	—	yes	—	—	yes[61]	
South Dakota	yes	yes	yes[2]	yes[2]	—	yes	yes[2]	yes[6]	—	—	yes[61]	—	—	—	—	yes[61]	(28 32 37 59)
Tennessee	yes	yes	yes[2]	yes[43]	yes	yes	yes	yes	—	yes	yes	—	yes	—	—	—	(28)
Texas	yes	yes	yes[2]	—	—	yes[54]	—	yes[4]	—	—	yes[4]	yes	—	—	—	—	
Utah	yes	yes	yes[2]	yes	yes	yes	yes	yes	—	—	yes[4]	yes	—	—	—	—	(29)
Vermont	yes	yes	yes[7]	—	—	yes[17]	yes	yes[6]	—	—	yes[8]	—	—	—	—	—	
Virginia	yes	yes	yes[2]	—	yes[51]	yes	—	—	—	yes[51]	yes[51]	yes[2]	—	—	yes[51]		(29)
Washington	—	—	—	—	—	—	—	—	—	—	—	—	—	—	—	—	(62)
West Virginia	yes	yes	yes[8]	yes	—	yes	yes	yes	—	—	yes[3]	—	yes	yes	—		(29 64)
Wisconsin	—	—	—	—	—	—	—	—	—	—	—	—	—	—	—	—	
Wyoming	yes	yes	yes[2]	yes	yes	yes	yes[2]	yes[3]	yes	—	yes[3]	—	yes	—	—	—	(11 25 28)

1. If unknown to husband. 2. 1 year. 3. 2 years. 4. 3 years. 5. 4 years. 6. 5 years. 7. 7 years. 8. 6 months. 9. 18 months. 10. Absence of 1 year. 11. Absence of 1 year voluntarily, or under legal separation judgment. 12. Absence of 3 years. 13. Absence of one spouse; presumption of death. 14. With imprisonment of 1 year. 15. With imprisonment of 2 years. 16. With imprisonment for life. 17. With imprisonment of 3 years. 18. With imprisonment of three years, or an indeterminate sentence, twelve months of which have been served. 19. With imprisonment of 5 years. 20. With imprisonment for life. 21. Imprisonment of other party in state or federal penal institution under sentence thereto for commission of felony at time the petition is filed. 22. Unless pardoned before beginning sentence. 23. Noncohabitation for 18 months. 24. Court of Common Pleas may grant a dissolution of marriage—6 months residency required. 25. Noncohabitation for 2 years. 26. Noncohabitation for 5 years. 27. Incompatibility. 28. Irreconcilable differences. 29. Irretrievable breakdown of marriage relationship. 30. Irretrievably broken upon proof, decree of dissolution. 31. Relationship within prohibited degree. 32. Infamous crime. 33. Infamous crime subsequent to marriage. 34. Crime against nature. 35. Excessively vicious conduct; any cause which, by laws of state, renders marriage null and void at its inception. 36. Requiring confinement in mental institution for at least 7 years prior to commencement of action. 37. Attempt by one party on life of other. 38. Any other gross misbehavior or wickedness. 39. Physical cruelty only. 40. Treatment such as to injure health or endanger reason. 41. Gross neglect of duty.

42. Habitual intemperance. 43. Habitual drunkenness contracted after marriage. 44 With imprisonment of 18 months. 45 If at time of marriage and incurable. 46. Infamous crime involving violation of conjugal duty and punishable by imprisonmer of more than 1 year. 47. Incurable, regardless when it occurs. 48. Insanity at time of marriage. 49. No-fault divorce. 50. No-fau divorce after 1 year's separation. 51. Grounds for nullity. 52. The term divorce is no longer used. The term now used i Dissolution of Marriage. 53. Limited divorce; may be enlarged into absolute divorce after separation of 1 year. 54. Suit fo divorce cannot be sustained until 12 months after final judgment of conviction. Divorce cannot be obtained if plaintiff's testimony contributed toward conviction. 55. Defendant obtained divorce from plaintiff in any other state or country. 56. Infected othe party with communicable venereal disease. 57. Joining a religious cult disbelieving in marriage. 58. Public defamation. 59 Wife's refusal to remove with husband to this state and willfully absenting herself for 2 years. 60. Wife gone to reside outsid state and absent 10 years. 61. Annulment. 62. Abuse of a child. 63. Modified "no-fault" law enacted April 6, 1977. 64 Voluntary noncohabitation for 1 year. 65. Maryland grants two types of divorce—vinculo and mensa. The information her applies to vinculo divorce. 66. Only after confined 3 years, plus other requirements. 67. Abandonment after 12 months, o living separately for 3 years. 68. If wife was under 16 or husband was under 18 at time of marriage, unless marriage wa confirmed by each after arriving at such age. *Source: Information Please* questionnaires to the states.

Households, Families, and Married Couples

Date	Households		Families		Married couples
	Number	Average population per household	Number	Average population per family	Number
June 1890	12,690,000	4.93	—	—	—
April 1930	29,905,000	4.11	—	—	25,174,000
April 1940	34,949,000	3.67	32,166,000	3.76	28,517,000
April 1950	43,554,000	3.37	39,303,000	3.54	36,091,000
April 1955	47,874,000	3.33	41,951,000	3.59	37,556,000
March 1960[1]	52,799,000	3.33	45,111,000	3.67	40,200,000
March 1965	57,436,000	3.29	47,956,000	3.70	42,478,000
March 1970	63,401,000	3.14	51,586,000	3.58	45,373,000
March 1975	71,120,000	2.94	55,712,000	3.42	47,547,000
March 1978	76,030,000	2.81	57,215,000	3.33	47,920,000
March 1979	77,330,000	2.78	57,804,000	3.31	48,258,000
March 1980	79,108,000	2.75	52,426,000	3.28	48,765,000

1. First year in which figures for Alaska and Hawaii are included. *Source:* Department of Commerce, Bureau of the Census.

Families Maintained by Women
(numbers in thousands)

	1980		1975		1970		1965		1960	
	Number	Percent	Number	Percent	Number	Percent	Number	Percent	Number	Percent
Age of women:										
Under 35 years	2,907	34.0	2,356	32.5	1,364	24.4	958	19.1	796	17.7
35 to 44 years	1,925	22.5	1,510	20.9	1,074	19.2	1,146	22.9	940	20.9
45 to 64 years	2,469	28.9	2,266	31.3	2,021	36.1	1,813	36.2	1,731	38.5
65 years and over	1,240	14.5	1,108	15.3	1,131	20.2	1,091	21.8	1,027	22.9
Median age	41.8	—	43.4	—	48.5	—	49.0	—	50.1	—
Presence of children:										
No own children under 18 years	3,200	37.5	2,838	39.2	2,665	47.7	2,527	50.5	2,397	53.3
With own children under 18 years	5,340	62.5	4,404	60.8	2,926	52.3	2,480	49.5	2,097	46.7
Total own children under 18 years	9,962	—	9,227	—	6,694	—	6,007	—	4,674	—
Average per family	1.17	—	1.27	—	1.20	—	1.20	—	1.04	—
Average per family with children	1.87	—	2.10	—	2.29	—	2.42	—	2.24	—
Race:										
White	5,963	69.8	5,212	72.0	4,165	74.5	3,882	77.5	3,547	78.9
Black[1]	2,429	28.4	1,940	26.8	1,382	24.7	1,125	22.5	947	21.1
Other	148	1.7	90	1.2	44	0.8	n.a.	n.a.	n.a.	n.a.
Marital status:										
Married, husband absent	1,733	20.3	1,647	22.7	1,326	23.7	1,392	27.8	1,099	24.5
Widowed	2,518	29.5	2,559	35.3	2,396	42.9	2,307	46.1	2,325	51.7
Divorced	2,961	34.7	2,110	29.1	1,259	22.5	903	18.0	694	15.4
Single	1,328	15.6	926	12.8	610	10.9	404	8.1	376	8.4
Total families maintained by women	8,540	100.0	7,242	100.0	5,591	100.0	5,006	100.0	4,494	100.0

1. Includes other races in 1960 and 1965. NOTE: n.a. = not available. *Source:* Department of Commerce, Bureau of the Census.

Selected Family Characteristics

Characteristics	1979 Number (thousands)	Median income	Characteristics	1979 Number (thousands)	Median income
ALL RACES			Service workers	3,580	15,629
All families	58,426	$19,661	Private household workers	129	7,534
Type of residence			Service Workers, exc. private household	3,451	16,019
Nonfarm	56,760	19,754	Farm workers	1,419	14,770
Farm	1,666	16,357	Farmers and farm managers	1,064	16,481
Location of residence			Farm lab. and supervisors	355	11,570
Inside metropolitan areas	39,049	21,074	Householder unemployed	2,020	14,182
1,000,000 or more	21,858	22,096	Householder not in civilian labor force	13,871	10,400
Inside central cities	7,826	17,481	Tenure status		
Outside central cities	14,032	24,675	Owner occupied	44,116	22,076
Under 1,000,000	17,190	19,870	Renter occupied	13,406	12,664
Inside central cities	7,680	18,524	Occupier paid no cash rent	904	12,059
Outside central cities	9,510	20,901	Educational attainment of householder		
Outside metropolitan areas	19,377	16,975	Elementary	9,488	11,504
Region			High school	26,671	19,184
Northeast	12,850	20,643	College	18,542	26,559
North Central	15,568	20,601	1 to 3 years	8,145	22,929
South	19,367	17,623	4 Years or more	10,398	30,024
West	10,641	20,751	4 Years	5,533	28,070
Type of family			5 Years or more	4,865	32,417
Married-couple family	48,180	21,503	Total, 25 years and over	54,701	20,254
Wife in paid labor force	23,763	24,957			
Wife not in paid labor force	24,416	17,750	**WHITE**		
Male householder, no wife present	1,706	16,867	All families	51,389	20,502
Female householder, no husband present	8,540	9,927	Type of residence		
Number of earners[1]	57,702	19,715	Nonfarm	49,790	20,609
No earners	7,421	7,648	Farm	1,598	16,684
1 Earner	17,833	15,607	Location of residence		
2 Earners	23,938	22,687	Inside metropolitan areas	33,551	22,079
3 Earners	5,669	29,472	1,000,000 or more	18,349	23,486
4 Earners or more	2,841	36,002	Inside central cities	5,417	19,731
Size of family			Outside central cities	12,932	25,135
2 Persons	22,913	15,802	Under 1,000,000	15,202	20,697
3 Persons	13,332	20,141	Inside central cities	6,283	20,013
4 Persons	12,180	22,579	Outside central cities	8,919	21,163
5 Persons	5,871	23,456	Outside metropolitan areas	17,838	17,551
6 Persons	2,439	22,843	Region		
7 Persons or more	1,691	22,599	Northeast	11,548	21,349
Employment status and occupation of householder[2]			North Central	14,200	21,120
Householder in civilian labor force	44,555	22,305	South	16,143	18,960
Householder employed	42,535	22,679	West	9,499	21,113
White-collar workers	20,336	26,614	Type of family		
Professional, technical and kindred workers	7,066	28,754	Married-couple families	44,008	21,824
Salaried	6,388	28,231	Wife in paid labor force	21,313	25,313
Self-employed	678	38,863	Wife not in paid labor force	22,695	18,204
Managers and administrators, except farm	6,811	29,592	Male householder, no wife present	1,418	17,700
Salaried	5,650	30,762	Female householder, no husband present	5,963	11,452
Self-employed	1,161	21,532	Number of earners[1]	50,787	20,552
Sales workers	2,469	24,708	No earners	6,255	8,494
Clerical & kindred workers	3,990	20,048	1 Earner	15,482	16,721
Blue-collar workers	17,200	20,951	2 Earners	21,367	23,122
Craft and kindred workers	8,608	22,686	3 Earners	5,118	29,999
Operatives, incl. transport	6,751	19,686	4 Earners or more	2,565	36,833
Operatives, exc. transport	4,530	19,199	**BLACK**		
Transport equip. oper.	2,221	20,761	All families	6,042	11,644
Laborers, except farm	1,841	17,174	Type of residence		
			Nonfarm	5,995	11,689

Characteristics	1979 Number (thousands)	1979 Median income	Characteristics	1979 Number (thousands)	1979 Median income
Farm	47	5,688	Type of residence		
Location of residence			Nonfarm	3,079	14,588
Inside metropolitan areas	4,726	12,350	Farm	20	13,080
1,000,000 or more	2,998	12,975	Location of residence		
Inside central cities	2,149	11,861	Inside metropolitan areas	2,587	14,800
Outside central cities	849	16,505	1,000,000 or more	1,668	14,703
Under 1,000,000	1,728	11,552	Inside central cities	913	11,892
Inside central cities	1,282	11,202	Outside central cities	755	18,223
Outside central cities	446	12,957	Under 1,000,000	919	14,964
Outside metropolitan areas	1,316	9,267	Inside central cities	583	14,979
Region			Outside central cities	336	14,937
Northeast	1,159	12,097	Outside metropolitan areas	512	13,237
North Central	1,253	13,108	Region		
South	3,072	10,789	Northeast	606	11,419
West	558	13,201	North Central	241	15,987
Type of family			South	935	14,017
Married-couple families	3,355	16,887	West	1,319	16,180
Wife in paid labor force	1,984	20,705	Type of family		
Wife not in paid labor force	1,372	11,603	Married-couple families	2,373	16,836
Male householder, no			Wife in paid labor force	1,121	20,512
wife present	257	12,491	Wife not in paid labor force	1,251	13,085
Female householder, no			Male householder, no		
husband present	2,429	6,906	wife present	133	14,566
Number of earners[1]	5,937	11,580	Female householder, no		
No earners	1,065	4,325	husband present	594	6,639
1 Earner	2,087	9,127	Number of earners[1]	3,066	14,569
2 Earners	2,145	18,344	No earners	379	4,765
3 Earners	437	23,038	1 Earner	1,000	10,944
4 Earners or more	202	27,807	2 Earners	1,223	18,038
			3 Earners	300	23,534
SPANISH ORIGIN OF HOUSEHOLDER[3]			4 Earners or more	166	32,551
All families	3,100	14,569			

1. Excludes families with members in Armed Forces. 2. Employment status and occupation of householder as of March 1980. 3. Persons of Spanish origin may be of any race. *Source:* Department of Commerce, Bureau of the Census.

Births

Live Births and Birth Rates

Year	Births[1]	Rate[2]	Year	Births[1]	Rate[2]	Year	Births[1]	Rate[2]
1910	2,777,000	30.1	1949	3,649,000	24.5	1965[3]	3,760,358	19.4
1915	2,965,000	29.5	1950	3,632,000	24.1	1966[3]	3,606,274	18.4
1920	2,950,000	27.7	1951[3]	3,823,000	24.9	1967	3,520,959	17.8
1925	2,909,000	25.1	1952[3]	3,913,000	25.1	1968	3,501,564	17.5
1930	2,618,000	21.3	1953[3]	3,965,000	25.1	1969	3,600,206	17.8
1935	2,377,000	18.7	1954[3]	4,078,000	25.3	1970	3,731,386	18.4
1938	2,496,000	19.2	1955	4,104,000	25.0	1971	3,555,970	17.2
1939	2,466,000	18.8	1956[3]	4,218,000	25.2	1972	3,258,411	15.6
1940	2,559,000	19.4	1957[3]	4,308,000	25.3	1973	3,136,965	14.9
1942	2,989,000	22.2	1958[3]	4,255,000	24.5	1974	3,159,958	14.9
1943	3,104,000	22.7	1959[3]	4,295,000	24.3	1975	3,144,198	14.8
1944	2,939,000	21.2	1960[3]	4,257,850	23.7	1976	3,167,788	14.8
1945	2,858,000	20.4	1961[3]	4,268,326	23.3	1977	3,326,632	15.4
1946	3,411,000	24.1	1962[3]	4,167,362	22.4	1978	3,333,279	15.3
1947	3,817,000	26.6	1963[3]	4,098,020	21.7	1979[4]	3,473,000	15.8
1948	3,637,000	24.9	1964[3]	4,027,490	21.0	1980[4]	3,598,000	16.2

1. Figures through 1959 include adjustment for underregistration; beginning 1960, figures represent number registered. For comparison, the 1959 registered count was 4,245,000. 2. Rates are per 1,000 population estimated as of July 1 for each year except 1940, 1950, 1960, and 1970, which are as of April 1, the census date; for 1942–46 based on population including armed forces overseas. 3. Based on 50% sample of births. 4. Provisional. NOTE: Alaska is included beginning 1959; Hawaii beginning 1960. Since 1972, based on 100% of births in selected states and on 50% sample in all other states. *Sources:* Department of Commerce, Bureau of the Census; and Department of Health and Human Services, National Center for Health Statistics.

Live Births by Age of Mother

Year[1] and race	Total	Under 15 yr	15–19 yr	20–24 yr	25–29 yr	30–34 yr	35–39 yr	40–44 yr	45 yr and over
					Age of mother				
1940	2,558,647	3,865	332,667	799,537	693,268	431,468	222,015	68,269	7,558
1945	2,858,449	4,028	298,868	832,746	785,299	554,906	296,852	78,853	6,897
1950	3,631,512	5,413	432,911	1,155,167	1,041,360	610,816	302,780	77,743	5,322
1955	4,014,112	6,181	493,770	1,290,939	1,133,155	732,540	352,320	89,777	5,430
1960	4,257,850	6,780	586,966	1,426,912	1,092,816	687,722	359,908	91,564	5,182
1965	3,760,358	7,768	590,894	1,337,350	925,732	529,376	282,908	81,716	4,614
1970	3,731,386	11,752	644,708	1,418,874	994,904	427,806	180,244	49,952	3,146
1972	3,258,411	12,082	616,280	1,174,183	900,392	375,001	141,328	36,861	2,284
1974	3,159,958	12,529	595,449	1,108,051	923,318	372,907	118,115	27,878	1,711
1975	3,144,198	12,642	582,238	1,093,676	936,786	375,500	115,409	26,319	1,628
1976	3,167,788	11,928	558,744	1,091,602	972,130	391,896	115,662	24,383	1,443
1977	3,326,632	11,455	559,154	1,146,491	1,016,231	446,939	120,900	24,117	1,345
1978	3,333,279	10,772	543,407	1,139,524	1,015,183	474,318	126,196	22,627	1,252
White	2,681,116	4,512	380,060	914,772	860,209	401,221	101,880	17,521	941
Black	551,540	6,068	151,001	196,731	121,613	53,491	18,340	4,048	248
Other	100,623	192	12,346	28,021	33,361	19,606	5,976	1,058	63

1. Data for 1940–55 are adjusted for underregistration. Beginning 1960, registered births only are shown. Data for 1960–70 based on a 50% sample of births. Since 1972, based on 100% of births in selected states and on 50% sample in all other states. Beginning 1960, including Alaska and Hawaii. NOTE: Data refer only to births occurring within the U.S. Figures are shown to the last digit as computed for convenience in summation. They are not assumed to be accurate to the last digit. Figures for age of mother not stated are distributed. *Sources:* Department of Commerce, Bureau of the Census; and Department of Health and Human Services, National Center for Health Statistics. NOTE: Data are latest available.

Births to Unmarried Women
(in thousands, except as indicated)

Age and race	1978	1975	1970	1965	1960	1955	1950	1945	1940
By age of mother:									
Under 15 years	9.4	11.0	9.5	6.1	4.6	3.9	3.2	2.5	2.1
15–19 years	239.7	222.5	190.4	123.1	87.1	68.9	56.0	49.2	40.5
20–24 years	186.5	134.0	126.7	90.7	68.0	55.7	43.1	39.3	27.2
25–29 years	70.0	50.2	40.6	36.8	32.1	28.0	20.9	14.1	10.5
30–34 years	26.5	19.8	19.1	19.6	18.9	16.1	10.8	7.1	5.2
35–39 years	9.4	8.1	9.4	11.4	10.6	8.3	6.0	4.0	3.0
40 years and over	2.3	2.3	3.0	3.7	3.0	2.4	1.7	1.2	1.0
By race:									
White	233.6	186.4	175.1	123.7	82.5	64.2	53.5	56.4	40.3
Black and other	310.2	261.6	223.6	167.5	141.8	119.2	88.1	60.9	49.2
Total of above births	543.9	447.9	398.7	291.2	224.3	183.4	141.6	117.3	89.5
Percent of all births[1]	16.3	14.2	10.7	7.7	5.3	4.5	3.9	4.1	3.5
Rate[2]	26.2	24.8	26.4	23.4	21.8	19.3	14.1	10.1	7.1

1. Through 1955, based on data adjusted for underregistration; thereafter, registered births. 2. Rate per 1,000 unmarried (never married, widowed, and divorced) women, 15–44 years old. *Sources:* Department of Commerce, Bureau of the Census; and Department of Health and Human Services, National Center for Health Statistics. NOTE: Data are latest available.

Legal Abortions—Estimated Number, 1975–1978
(Refers to women 15–44 years old at time of abortion)

Item	1975 White	1975 Black[1]	1976 White	1976 Black[1]	1977 White	1977 Black[1]	1978 White	1978 Black[1]
Total women, 15–44 years old (1,000)	40,485	6,633	41,254	6,855	42,022	7,071	42,741	7,288
No. of abortions (1,000)	701.2	333.0	784.9	394.4	891.2	429.1	969.4	440.2
Annual percent change	n.a.	n.a.	11.9	18.4	13.5	8.8	8.8	2.6
Abortion rate per 1,000 women	17.3	50.2	19.0	57.5	21.2	60.7	22.7	60.4
Annual percent change	n.a.	n.a.	9.8	14.5	11.5	5.6	7.1	− .5
Abortion ratio per 1,000 live births	276	566	296	630	334	681	356	665
Annual percent change	n.a.	n.a.	7.2	11.3	12.8	8.1	6.6	−2.3

1. Includes other races. n.a. = Not applicable. *Source:* Alan Guttmacher Institute, unpublished data. Includes data from Department of Commerce, Bureau of the Census, Department of Health and Human Services, National Center for Health Statistics and Center for Disease Control.

Live Births and Birth Rates

State	1980[1] number	1980[1] rate	1979[1] number	1979[1] rate	State	1980[1] number	1980[1] rate	1979[1] number	1979[1] rate
Alabama	62,814	16.6	60,628	16.1	Montana	13,928	17.7	13,803	17.6
Alaska	9,368	23.0	8,912	22.0	Nebraska	27,851	17.6	26,093	16.6
Arizona	50,173	19.7	45,707	18.7	Nevada	13,156	17.9	11,830	16.9
Arkansas	36,863	16.7	35,008	16.1	New Hampshire	13,647	15.2	12,830	14.5
California	401,581	17.4	363,463	16.0	New Jersey	91,047	12.4	91,896	12.5
Colorado	50,279	17.8	47,813	17.2	New Mexico	25,661	20.0	25,570	20.6
Connecticut	34,069	10.9	36,959	11.9	New York	232,491	13.2	231,787	13.1
Delaware	9,544	16.5	9,123	15.7	North Carolina	85,123	15.0	84,388	15.1
D.C.	17,835	28.0	20,334	31.0	North Dakota	12,939	19.7	12,769	19.4
Florida	131,923	14.3	120,839	13.6	Ohio	169,359	15.8	164,111	15.3
Georgia	95,980	18.4	89,446	17.5	Oklahoma	50,681	17.2	47,514	16.3
Hawaii	18,277	19.5	17,429	19.0	Oregon	43,998	17.1	42,984	17.0
Idaho	19,495	21.3	19,686	21.8	Pennsylvania	161,025	13.7	157,783	13.5
Illinois	186,576	16.7	181,218	16.1	Rhode Island	12,512	13.6	12,235	13.2
Indiana	87,906	16.2	87,452	16.2	South Carolina	49,805	16.8	49,956	17.0
Iowa	48,050	16.5	47,083	16.2	South Dakota	13,013	18.8	12,623	18.3
Kansas	39,330	16.5	37,100	15.7	Tennessee	73,500	16.5	72,261	16.5
Kentucky	60,778	17.2	60,182	17.1	Texas	268,717	19.6	265,066	19.8
Louisiana	79,202	19.3	79,413	19.8	Utah	43,708	31.0	42,304	30.9
Maine	16,095	14.6	15,755	14.4	Vermont	7,640	15.3	7,396	15.0
Maryland	52,284	12.6	50,043	12.1	Virginia	75,042	14.3	73,812	14.2
Massachusetts	73,355	12.7	73,104	12.7	Washington	67,972	16.9	55,077	14.0
Michigan	143,007	15.5	142,127	15.4	West Virginia	29,923	15.9	30,263	16.1
Minnesota	68,233	16.6	64,939	16.0	Wisconsin	74,470	15.6	72,818	15.4
Mississippi	47,538	19.5	45,913	18.9	Wyoming	9,539	20.4	8,946	19.9
Missouri	79,623	16.3	78,506	16.1	Total	3,586,925	n.a.	3,463,996	n.a.

1. Provisional. NOTE: Based on 100% of births in selected states and 50% sample in others. Rates are per 1,000 population.
Source: Department of Health and Human Services, National Center for Health Statistics.

Live Births and Birth Rates by Race

Race	Births 1978[1]	Rates 1978	Rates 1950	Rates 1940	Race	Births 1978[1]	Rates 1978	Rates 1950	Rates 1940
White	2,681,116	14.2	23.0	18.6	Chinese	11,224	n.a.	43.9	14.5
Black	551,540	21.6	33.1	26.5	Filipino	13,753	n.a.	n.a.	n.a.
Indian	33,160	n.a.	45.8	42.0	Other	30,559	n.a.	19.1	22.0
Japanese	8,094	n.a.	24.5	15.0	All races	3,333,279	15.3	24.1	19.4

1. Based on all births in selected states and on a 50% sample of births in all other states. NOTES: Rates per 1,000 population in each specified group. Rates for 1940 and 1950 based on births adjusted for under-registration; n.a. = not available; Data are latest available. *Source:* Department of Health and Human Services, National Center for Health Statistics.

Live Births by Sex and Sex Ratio[1]

Year	Total[2] Male	Total[2] Female	Total[2] Males per 1,000 females	White Male	White Female	White Males per 1,000 females	Black Male	Black Female	Black Males per 1,000 females
1970[3]	1,915,378	1,816,008	1,055	1,590,140	1,501,124	1,059	290,508	281,854	1,031
1971[3]	1,822,910	1,733,060	1,052	1,499,958	1,419,788	1,056	286,430	278,530	1,028
1972[4]	1,669,927	1,588,484	1,051	1,364,578	1,290,980	1,057	268,842	262,487	1,024
1973[4]	1,608,326	1,528,639	1,052	1,311,032	1,239,998	1,057	259,877	252,720	1,028
1974[4]	1,622,114	1,537,844	1,055	1,325,019	1,250,773	1,059	257,277	249,885	1,030
1975[4]	1,613,135	1,531,063	1,054	1,312,308	1,239,688	1,059	259,610	251,971	1,030
1976[4]	1,624,436	1,543,352	1,053	1,319,717	1,247,897	1,058	260,661	253,818	1,027
1977[4]	1,705,916	1,620,716	1,053	1,383,440	1,307,630	1,058	275,556	268,665	1,026
1978[4]	1,709,394	1,623,885	1,053	1,378,222	1,302,894	1,058	279,598	271,942	1,028

1. Excludes births to nonresidents of U.S. 2. Includes races other than white and black. 3. Based on 50% sample of births. 4. Based on 100% of births for selected states and 50% sample in all others. *Source:* Department of Health and Human Services, National Center for Health Statistics. NOTE: Data are latest available.

Mortality

Death Rates for Selected Causes

Cause of death	Death rates per 100,000						
	1980	1979	1950	1945–49	1940–44	1920–24	1900–04
Typhoid fever	0.0	0.0	0.1	0.2	0.6	7.3	26.7
Communicable diseases of childhood	0.0	0.0	1.3	2.3	4.6	33.8	65.2
Measles	0.0	0.0	0.3	0.6	1.1	7.3	10.0
Scarlet fever	0.0	0.0	0.2	0.1	0.4	4.0	11.8
Whooping cough	0.0	0.0	0.7	1.0	2.2	8.9	10.7
Diphtheria	0.0	0.0	0.3	0.7	1.0	13.7	32.7
Enteritis and other diarrheal diseases	n.a.	n.a.	5.1	6.5	9.8	42.8	115.3
Pneumonia and influenza	23.6	20.0	31.3	41.3	63.7	140.3	184.3
Influenza	1.2	0.3	4.4	5.0	13.0	34.8	22.8
Pneumonia	22.5	19.7	26.9	37.2	50.7	105.5	161.5
Tuberculosis	0.8	0.9	22.5	33.3	43.4	96.7	184.7
Cancer	186.3	183.5	139.8	134.0	123.1	86.9	67.7
Diabetes mellitus	15.4	15.0	16.2	24.1	26.2	17.1	12.2
Major cardiovascular diseases	443.7	431.6	510.8	493.1	490.4	369.9	359.5
Diseases of the heart	342.3	330.4	356.8	325.1	303.2	169.8	153.0
Cerebrovascular diseases	76.2	76.5	104.0	93.8	91.7	93.5	106.3
Nephritis and nephrosis	7.8	7.3	16.4	48.4	72.1	81.5	84.3
Syphilis	0.1	0.1	5.0	8.4	12.7	17.6	12.9
Appendicitis	0.3	0.3	2.0	3.5	7.2	14.0	9.4
Accidents, all forms	47.0	47.0	60.6	67.6	73.0	70.8	79.2
Motor vehicle accidents	23.5	23.6	23.1	22.3	22.7	12.9	n.a.
Infant mortality[1]	12.5	13.0	29.2	33.3	42.4	76.7	n.a.
Neonatal mortality[1]	8.4	8.7	20.5	22.9	26.2	39.7	n.a.
Fetal mortality[1]	n.a.	n.a.	22.9	24.3	28.5	39.2[2]	n.a.
Maternal mortality[1]	n.a.	n.a.	0.8	1.4	2.8	6.9	n.a.
All causes	892.6	866.2	963.8	1,003.3	1,062.0	1,196.6	1,621.6

1. Rates per 1,000 live births. 2. 1922–24. NOTE: Includes only deaths occurring within the registration areas. Beginning with 1940, area includes the entire United States; beginning with 1960, Alaska and Hawaii are included. Rates per 100,000 population residing in areas, enumerated as of April 1 for 1940 and 1950 and estimated as of July 1 for all other years. Due to changes in statistical methods, death rates are not strictly comparable. n.a. = not available. *Source:* Department of Health and Human Services, National Center for Health Statistics.

Transportation-Accident Death Rates

	1979			1977–79 average death rate[1]
Kind of transportation	Passenger miles	Passenger deaths	Death rate[1]	
Passenger automobiles and taxis[2]	2,220,000,000,000	29,100	1.31	1.30
Passenger automobiles on turnpikes[2]	46,800,000,000	340	0.73	0.69
Buses	80,400,000,000	120	0.15	0.15
Intercity buses	17,300,000,000	3	0.02	0.02
Railroad passenger trains	11,300,000,000	6	0.05	0.07
Scheduled air transport planes (domestic)	223,800,000,000	262	0.12	0.06

1. Per 100 million passenger miles. 2. Drivers of passenger automobiles are considered passengers. *Source:* National Safety Council. NOTE: Figures are latest available.

Accident Rates, 1979

(twelve accidental deaths every hour)

Class of accident		One every		Class of accident		One every	
All accidents	Deaths	5	minutes	Workers off-job	Deaths	12	minutes
	Injuries	3	seconds		Injuries	10	seconds
Motor-vehicle	Deaths	9	minutes	Home	Deaths	24	minutes
	Injuries	16	seconds		Injuries	10	seconds
Work	Deaths	40	minutes	Public non-motor-vehicle	Deaths	25	minutes
	Injuries	14	seconds		Injuries	12	seconds

Source: National Safety Council. NOTE: Data are latest available.

Motor-Vehicle Deaths by Type of Accident

Year	Pedes-trians	Other motor vehicles	Railroad trains	Street cars	Pedalcycles	Animal-drawn vehicle or animal	Fixed objects	Deaths from non-collision accidents	Total deaths[1]
1937	15,500	10,320	1,810	264	700	200	1,160	9,690	39,643
1939	12,400	8,700	1,330	150	710	200	1,000	7,900	32,386
1941	13,550	12,500	1,840	118	910	250	1,350	9,450	39,969
1943	9,900	5,300	1,448	171	450	160	700	5,690	23,823
1945	11,000	7,150	1,703	163	500	130	800	6,600	28,076
1947	10,450	9,900	1,736	102	550	150	1,000	8,800	32,697
1949	8,800	10,500	1,452	56	550	140	1,100	9,100	31,701
1951	9,150	13,100	1,573	46	390	100	1,400	11,200	36,996
1953	8,750	13,400	1,506	26	420	120	1,500	12,200	37,955
1955	8,200	14,500	1,490	15	410	90	1,600	12,100	38,426
1957	7,850	15,400	1,376	13	460	80	1,700	11,800	38,702
1959	7,850	14,900	1,202	6	480	70	1,600	11,800	37,910
1961	7,650	14,700	1,267	5	490	80	1,700	12,200	38,091
1963	8,200	17,600	1,385	10	580	80	1,900	13,800	43,564
1965	8,900	20,800	1,556	5	680	120	2,200	14,900	49,163
1967	9,400	22,000	1,620	3	750	100	2,350	16,700	52,924
1969	10,100	23,700	1,495	2	800	100	3,900	15,700	55,791
1971	9,900	23,100	1,378	2	800	100	3,800	15,300	54,381
1973	10,200	23,600	1,194	2	1,000	100	3,800	15,600	55,511
1974	8,500	19,700	1,209	1	1,000	100	3,100	12,800	46,402
1975	8,400	19,550	979	1	1,000	100	3,130	12,700	45,853
1976	8,600	20,100	1,033	2	1,000	100	3,200	13,000	47,038
1977	9,100	21,200	902	3	1,100	100	3,400	13,700	49,510
1978	9,300	22,900	1,100	—	1,000	100	3,500	13,600	51,500
1979	9,400	22,700	900	—	1,000	100	3,500	14,300	51,900

1. Yearly totals do not quite equal sums of various types because totals for most types are estimated, and these have been made to nearest 10 deaths for some types and to nearest 50 deaths for others. *Source:* National Safety Council. NOTE: Figures are latest available.

Deaths and Death Rates

State	Total deaths[1] 1980 number	1980 rate	1979 rate	Motor vehicle[2] traffic deaths 1979 rate	State	Total deaths[1] 1980 number	1980 rate	1979 rate	Motor vehicle[2] traffic deaths 1979 rate
Alabama	35,386	9.4	9.1	3.7	Montana	6,592	8.4	8.2	4.9
Alaska	1,692	4.1	4.0	3.1	Nebraska	14,681	9.3	9.0	2.7
Arizona	21,609	8.5	8.3	5.1	Nevada	6,408	8.7	8.3	6.3
Arkansas	22,565	10.2	9.9	3.5	New Hampshire	7,547	8.4	8.2	3.0
California	190,247	8.2	7.5	3.4	New Jersey	64,727	8.8	8.7	2.1
Colorado	19,503	6.9	6.9	3.4	New Mexico	9,080	7.1	6.9	5.6
Connecticut	26,597	8.5	8.4	2.9	New York	167,769	9.5	9.1	3.8
Delaware	5,201	9.0	8.7	3.1	North Carolina	49,059	8.6	8.4	3.6
D.C.	9,165	4.4	13.8	1.6	North Dakota	5,850	8.9	8.5	3.5
Florida	106,815	11.6	11.4	3.5	Ohio	97,779	9.1	8.7	3.1
Georgia	43,519	8.3	8.3	3.3	Oklahoma	28,308	9.6	9.4	3.3
Hawaii	5,190	5.5	5.6	4.0	Oregon	21,793	8.5	8.3	3.5
Idaho	6,431	7.0	6.7	4.4	Pennsylvania	123,400	10.5	10.0	3.0
Illinois	100,450	9.0	8.9	3.1	Rhode Island	9,553	10.4	10.0	1.9
Indiana	46,721	8.6	8.7	3.0	South Carolina	24,337	8.2	8.1	3.8
Iowa	26,714	9.2	9.0	3.1	South Dakota	6,462	9.3	9.1	3.8
Kansas	21,399	9.0	8.7	3.4	Tennessee	43,205	9.7	9.4	3.2
Kentucky	33,268	9.4	9.2	3.2	Texas	108,586	7.9	8.0	4.1
Louisiana	35,626	8.7	8.7	4.8	Utah	8,556	6.1	6.3	3.5
Maine	10,857	9.9	9.5	3.3	Vermont	4,312	8.6	8.9	4.4
Maryland	33,337	8.0	7.7	2.4	Virginia	41,889	8.0	7.7	2.6
Massachusetts	54,773	9.5	9.1	2.8	Washington	32,495	8.1	7.5	3.5
Michigan	74,002	8.0	7.9	2.9	West Virginia	19,120	10.2	10.2	4.8
Minnesota	33,048	8.0	8.0	3.0	Wisconsin	40,972	8.6	8.2	3.0
Mississippi	22,911	9.4	9.4	4.3	Wyoming	3,062	6.6	6.5	5.3
Missouri	49,881	10.2	10.0	3.4					

1. Provisional. By place of occurrence. 2. Per 100 million vehicle-miles. NOTE: Rates for total deaths are per 1,000 population in each area. *Sources:* Department of Health and Human Services, National Center for Health Statistics; National Safety Council.

Death Rates

Year	Rate	Year	Rate	Year	Deaths	Rate
1900	17.2	1937	11.3	1959	1,656,814	9.4
1905	15.9	1938	10.6	1960	1,711,982	9.5
1910	14.7	1939	10.6	1961	1,701,522	9.3
1915	13.2	1940	10.8	1962	1,756,720	9.5
1918	18.1[1]	1941	10.5	1963	1,813,549	9.6
1920	13.0	1942	10.3	1964	1,798,051	9.4
1921	11.5	1943	10.9	1965	1,828,136	9.4
1922	11.7	1944	10.6	1966	1,863,149	9.5
1923	12.1	1945	10.6	1967	1,851,323	9.4
1924	11.6	1946	10.0	1968	1,930,082	9.7
1925	11.7	1947	10.1	1969	1,921,990	9.5
1926	12.1	1948	9.9	1970[2]	1,921,031	9.5
1927	11.3	1949	9.7	1971	1,927,542	9.3
1928	12.0	1950	9.6	1972	1,963,944	9.4
1929	11.9	1951	9.7	1973	1,973,003	9.4
1930	11.3	1952	9.6	1974	1,934,388	9.2
1931	11.1	1953	9.6	1975	1,892,879	8.9
1932	10.9	1954	9.2	1976	1,909,440	8.9
1933	10.7	1955	9.3	1977	1,899,597	8.8
1934	11.1	1956	9.4	1978	1,927,788	8.8
1935	10.9	1957	9.6	1979[3]	1,906,000	8.7
1936	11.6	1958	9.5	1980[3]	1,986,000	8.9

1. Year of influenza epidemic. 2. First year for which deaths of nonresidents are excluded. 3. Provisional. NOTE: Includes only deaths occurring within the registration area. Beginning with 1933, area includes entire U.S.; with 1959 includes Alaska, and with 1960 includes Hawaii. Excludes fetal deaths. Rates per 1,000 population residing in area, as of April 1 for 1940, 1950, 1960, and 1970, and estimated as of July 1 for all other years. *Sources:* Department of Commerce, Bureau of the Census; and Department of Health and Human Services, National Center for Health Statistics.

Death Rates by Age, Color, and Sex

Age	1980[1]	1975[2]	1970[2]	1960	1940	1920	1980[1]	1975[2]	1970[2]	1960	1940	1920
	White males						White females					
Under 1 year	12.5	15.9	21.1	26.9	56.7	98.1	9.7	12.2	16.1	20.1	43.6	76.1
1–4	0.7	0.7	0.8	1.0	2.8	9.8	0.5	0.6	0.8	0.9	2.4	9.0
5–14	0.4	0.4	0.5	0.5	1.1	2.7	0.3	0.3	0.3	0.3	0.8	2.3
15–24	1.7	1.7	1.7	1.4	2.0	4.2	0.6	0.6	0.6	0.5	1.4	4.3
25–34	1.8	1.7	1.8	1.6	2.8	5.9	0.7	0.7	0.8	0.9	2.2	6.5
35–44	2.6	3.0	3.4	3.3	5.1	7.7	1.3	1.6	1.9	1.9	3.7	7.3
45–54	7.2	7.9	8.8	9.3	11.4	12.0	3.7	4.1	4.6	4.6	7.5	10.9
55–64	17.5	19.5	22.0	22.3	25.2	24.2	9.0	9.4	10.1	10.8	16.8	21.7
65–74	40.2	43.6	48.1	48.5	54.0	54.2	20.4	21.5	24.7	27.8	41.5	49.9
75–84	93.6	96.1	101.0	103.0	122.0	122.5	51.5	60.3	67.0	77.0	104.8	116.4
85 and over	178.2	182.6	185.5	217.5	251.4	253.6	140.4	144.9	159.8	194.8	235.0	247.0
	All other males						All other females					
Under 1 year	23.9	30.0	40.2	51.9	101.2	167.7	20.2	25.2	31.7	40.7	77.4	131.1
1–4	1.0	1.1	1.4	2.1	5.3	15.0	0.8	0.9	1.2	1.7	4.4	14.2
5–14	0.5	0.6	0.6	0.8	1.6	3.7	0.3	0.3	0.4	0.5	1.4	3.9
15–24	2.1	2.4	3.0	2.1	5.0	9.9	0.7	0.9	1.1	1.1	5.0	10.8
25–34	3.9	4.5	5.0	3.9	8.5	12.2	1.4	1.6	2.2	2.6	7.4	13.5
35–44	6.1	7.4	8.7	7.3	13.2	14.4	2.8	3.6	4.9	5.5	11.7	16.0
45–54	12.5	14.2	16.5	15.5	24.5	20.1	7.0	7.8	9.8	11.4	21.1	23.4
55–64	27.4	28.1	30.5	31.5	37.1[3]	31.1	15.5	16.4	18.9	24.1	33.2[3]	35.8
65–74	44.7	49.7	54.7	56.6	62.8[3]	60.2	28.5	31.7	36.8	39.8	52.3[3]	60.4
75–84	97.9	86.0	89.8	86.6	108.8	116.0	68.9	59.8	63.9	67.1	84.1	106.4
85 and over	102.2	116.9	114.1	152.4	199.7	247.1	79.3	91.8	102.9	128.7	159.7	221.2

1. Provisional. 2. Excludes deaths of nonresidents of U.S. 3. Based on enumerated population adjusted for age bias in nonwhite population at ages 55–69 years. NOTE: For 1920, data are from only 10 selected states and the District of Columbia; for 1940, from D.C. and the former 48 states; for 1960, from D.C. and all 50 states. Excludes fetal deaths. Rates are per 1,000 population in each group, enumerated as of April 1 for 1940, 1950, and 1960, and estimated as of July 1 for all other years. *Sources:* Department of Commerce, Bureau of the Census; and Department of Health and Human Services, National Center for Health Statistics.

Expectation of Life

Expectation of Life in the United States

Calendar period	Age								
	0	10	20	30	40	50	60	70	80
WHITE MALES									
1850[1]	38.3	48.0	40.1	34.0	27.9	21.6	15.6	10.2	5.9
1890[1]	42.50	48.45	40.66	34.05	27.37	20.72	14.73	9.35	5.40
1900–1902[2]	48.23	50.59	42.19	34.88	27.74	20.76	14.35	9.03	5.10
1909–1911[2]	50.23	51.32	42.71	34.87	27.43	20.39	13.98	8.83	5.09
1919–1921[3]	56.34	54.15	45.60	37.65	29.86	22.22	15.25	9.51	5.47
1929–1931	59.12	54.96	46.02	37.54	29.22	21.51	14.72	9.20	5.26
1939–1941	62.81	57.03	47.76	38.80	30.03	21.96	15.05	9.42	5.38
1949–1951	66.31	58.98	49.52	40.29	31.17	22.83	15.76	10.07	5.88
1959–1961	67.55	59.78	50.25	40.98	31.73	23.22	16.01	10.29	5.89
1969–1971	67.94	59.69	50.22	41.07	31.87	23.34	16.07	10.38	6.18
1977	70.0	61.3	51.9	42.7	33.4	24.7	17.1	11.1	6.8
1978	70.2	61.5	52.0	42.8	33.6	24.8	17.2	11.1	6.7
WHITE FEMALES									
1850[1]	40.5	47.2	40.2	35.4	29.8	23.5	17.0	11.3	6.4
1890[1]	44.46	49.62	42.03	35.36	28.76	22.09	15.70	10.15	5.75
1900–1902[2]	51.08	52.15	43.77	36.42	29.17	21.89	15.23	9.59	5.50
1909–1911[2]	53.62	53.57	44.88	36.96	29.26	21.74	14.92	9.38	5.35
1919–1921[3]	58.53	55.17	46.46	38.72	30.94	23.12	15.93	9.94	5.70
1929–1931	62.67	57.65	48.52	39.99	31.52	23.41	16.05	9.98	5.63
1939–1941	67.29	60.85	51.38	42.21	33.25	24.72	17.00	10.50	5.88
1949–1951	72.03	64.26	54.56	45.00	35.64	26.76	18.64	11.68	6.59
1959–1961	74.19	66.05	56.29	46.63	37.13	28.08	19.69	12.38	6.67
1969–1971	75.49	66.97	57.24	47.60	38.12	29.11	20.79	13.37	7.59
1977	77.7	68.8	59.1	49.4	39.8	30.7	22.3	14.8	8.8
1978	77.8	68.9	59.1	49.5	39.9	30.7	22.3	14.8	8.8
ALL OTHER MALES[4]									
1900–1902[2]	32.54	41.90	35.11	29.25	23.12	17.34	12.62	8.33	5.12
1909–1911[2]	34.05	40.65	33.46	27.33	21.57	16.21	11.67	8.00	5.53
1919–1921[3]	47.14	45.99	38.36	32.51	26.53	20.47	14.74	9.58	5.83
1929–1931	47.55	44.27	35.95	29.45	23.36	17.92	13.15	8.78	5.42
1939–1941	52.33	48.54	39.74	32.25	25.23	19.18	14.38	10.06	6.46
1949–1951	58.91	52.96	43.73	35.31	27.29	20.25	14.91	10.74	7.07
1959–1961	61.48	55.19	45.78	37.05	28.72	21.28	15.29	10.81	6.87
1969–1971	60.98	53.67	44.37	36.20	28.29	21.24	15.35	10.68	7.57
1977	64.6	56.6	47.2	38.6	30.2	22.7	16.5	11.4	8.7
1978	65.0	57.0	47.4	38.8	30.4	22.8	16.5	11.6	8.8
ALL OTHER FEMALES[4]									
1900–1902[2]	35.04	43.02	36.89	30.70	24.37	18.67	13.60	9.62	6.48
1909–1911[2]	37.67	42.84	36.14	29.61	23.34	17.65	12.78	9.22	6.05
1919–1921[3]	46.92	44.54	37.15	31.48	25.60	19.76	14.69	10.25	6.58
1929–1931	49.51	45.33	37.22	30.67	24.30	18.60	14.22	10.38	6.90
1939–1941	55.51	50.83	42.14	34.52	27.31	21.04	16.14	11.81	8.00
1949–1951	62.70	56.17	46.77	38.02	29.82	22.67	16.95	12.29	8.15
1959–1961	66.47	59.72	50.07	40.83	32.16	24.31	17.83	12.46	7.66
1969–1971	69.05	61.49	51.85	42.61	33.87	25.97	19.02	13.30	9.01
1977	73.1	65.0	55.2	45.8	36.7	28.3	21.0	14.5	11.3
1978	73.6	65.4	55.6	46.2	37.0	28.5	21.2	14.8	11.5

1. Massachusetts only; white and nonwhite combined, the latter being about 1% of the total. 2. Original Death Registration States. 3. Death Registration States of 1920. 4. Data for periods 1900–1902 to 1929–1931 relate to blacks only. *Sources:* Metropolitan Life Insurance Company; Department of Health and Human Services, National Center for Health Statistics; Department of Commerce, Bureau of the Census. NOTE: Data are latest available.

What Are Parents' Legal Rights?

Do parents have a legal right to spank their children? That and many other questions are posed and answered in a paperback book "The Rights of Parents" published as an American Civil Liberties Union handbook at $2.50. In an increasingly legal-istic society, where children are suing their parents for "parental malpractice," this handbook, written by two lawyers, Alan N. Sussman and Martin Guggenheim, is a useful guide to legal problems today's parents may face.

Expectation of Life and Mortality Probabilities, 1978

Age	Total persons	White Male	White Female	All other Male	All other Female	Total Persons	White Male	White Female	All other Male	All other Female
		Expectation of life in years					Mortality probability per 1,000			
0	73.3	70.2	77.8	65.0	73.6	13.8	13.4	10.6	23.3	19.0
1	73.3	70.1	77.6	65.5	74.0	0.9	1.0	0.7	1.4	1.2
2	72.4	69.2	76.7	64.6	73.1	0.7	0.8	0.6	1.1	1.0
3	71.5	68.3	75.7	63.7	72.1	0.6	0.6	0.5	0.9	0.8
4	70.5	67.3	74.8	62.8	71.2	0.5	0.5	0.4	0.8	0.6
5	69.5	66.3	73.8	61.8	70.2	0.4	0.4	0.3	0.7	0.5
6	68.6	65.4	72.8	60.8	69.3	0.4	0.4	0.3	0.6	0.4
7	67.6	64.4	71.8	59.9	68.3	0.3	0.4	0.3	0.5	0.3
8	66.6	63.4	70.8	58.9	67.3	0.3	0.3	0.2	0.4	0.3
9	65.6	62.4	69.9	57.9	66.3	0.3	0.3	0.2	0.4	0.3
10	64.6	61.5	68.9	57.0	65.4	0.2	0.2	0.2	0.4	0.2
11	63.7	60.5	67.9	56.0	64.4	0.2	0.2	0.2	0.4	0.3
12	62.7	59.5	66.9	55.0	63.4	0.3	0.3	0.2	0.5	0.3
13	61.7	58.5	65.9	54.0	62.4	0.4	0.5	0.3	0.6	0.3
14	60.7	57.5	64.9	53.1	61.4	0.6	0.8	0.3	0.8	0.4
15	59.7	56.6	64.0	52.1	60.4	0.7	1.1	0.4	0.9	0.4
16	58.8	55.6	63.0	51.1	59.5	0.9	1.3	0.5	1.1	0.5
17	57.8	54.7	62.0	50.2	58.5	1.1	1.6	0.6	1.3	0.6
18	56.9	53.8	61.1	49.3	57.5	1.2	1.7	0.6	1.6	0.6
19	56.0	52.9	60.1	48.3	56.6	1.2	1.8	0.6	1.9	0.7
20	55.0	52.0	59.1	47.4	55.6	1.3	1.9	0.6	2.3	0.8
21	54.1	51.1	58.2	46.5	54.7	1.3	1.9	0.6	2.6	0.9
22	53.2	50.2	57.2	45.7	53.7	1.4	2.0	0.6	2.9	1.0
23	52.2	49.3	56.2	44.8	52.8	1.4	1.9	0.6	3.1	1.1
24	51.3	48.4	55.3	43.9	51.8	1.4	1.9	0.6	3.2	1.1
25	50.4	47.5	54.3	43.1	50.9	1.3	1.8	0.6	3.4	1.2
26	49.5	46.5	53.3	42.2	49.9	1.3	1.7	0.6	3.5	1.2
27	48.5	45.6	52.4	41.4	49.0	1.3	1.7	0.6	3.6	1.3
28	47.6	44.7	51.4	40.5	48.1	1.3	1.6	0.6	3.7	1.3
29	46.6	43.8	50.4	39.7	47.1	1.3	1.6	0.7	3.7	1.4
30	45.7	42.8	49.5	38.8	46.2	1.3	1.6	0.7	3.8	1.4
31	44.8	41.9	48.5	37.9	45.2	1.3	1.6	0.7	3.8	1.5
32	43.8	41.0	47.5	37.1	44.3	1.4	1.6	0.8	4.0	1.6
33	42.9	40.0	46.6	36.2	43.4	1.4	1.7	0.8	4.2	1.7
34	41.9	39.1	45.6	35.4	42.5	1.5	1.8	0.9	4.4	1.9
35	41.0	38.2	44.6	34.5	41.5	1.6	1.9	0.9	4.7	2.0
36	40.1	37.2	43.7	33.7	40.6	1.7	2.0	1.0	5.1	2.2
37	39.1	36.3	42.7	32.9	39.7	1.9	2.1	1.1	5.4	2.4
38	38.2	35.4	41.8	32.0	38.8	2.0	2.3	1.2	5.9	2.7
39	37.3	34.5	40.8	31.2	37.9	2.2	2.5	1.3	6.3	2.9
40	36.4	33.6	39.9	30.4	37.0	2.4	2.7	1.5	6.9	3.2
41	35.5	32.6	38.9	29.6	36.1	2.7	2.9	1.7	7.4	3.5
42	34.6	31.7	38.0	28.9	35.3	2.9	3.2	1.9	7.9	3.8
43	33.7	30.8	37.1	28.1	34.4	3.2	3.6	2.1	8.3	4.1
44	32.8	29.9	36.1	27.3	33.5	3.5	4.0	2.3	8.6	4.5
45	31.9	29.1	35.2	26.5	32.7	3.9	4.4	2.5	8.9	4.8
46	31.0	28.2	34.3	25.8	31.8	4.3	4.9	2.8	9.2	5.2
47	30.1	27.3	33.4	25.0	31.0	4.7	5.5	3.1	9.9	5.6
48	29.3	26.5	32.5	24.3	30.2	5.1	6.1	3.3	10.9	6.2
49	28.4	25.6	31.6	23.5	29.3	5.6	6.7	3.7	12.1	6.8
50	27.6	24.8	30.7	22.8	28.5	6.2	7.5	4.0	13.5	7.4
51	26.7	24.0	29.8	22.1	27.8	6.8	8.3	4.4	14.9	8.1
52	25.9	23.2	29.0	21.4	27.0	7.4	9.1	4.7	16.2	8.8
53	25.1	22.4	28.1	20.8	26.2	8.0	9.9	5.1	17.3	9.5
54	24.3	21.6	27.3	20.1	25.5	8.7	10.7	5.5	18.4	10.2
55	23.5	20.8	26.4	19.5	24.7	9.3	11.5	5.9	19.4	10.8
56	22.7	20.1	25.6	18.9	24.0	10.0	12.5	6.4	20.6	11.6
57	22.0	19.3	24.7	18.3	23.3	10.9	13.7	7.0	22.1	12.5
58	21.2	18.6	23.9	17.7	22.5	12.1	15.3	7.8	24.0	13.6
59	20.5	17.9	23.1	17.1	21.8	13.4	17.1	8.6	26.4	15.0
60	19.7	17.2	22.3	16.5	21.2	14.9	19.1	9.6	29.1	16.5
61	19.0	16.5	21.5	16.0	20.5	16.4	21.1	10.6	31.8	18.1
62	18.3	15.8	20.7	15.5	19.9	17.9	23.2	11.5	33.9	19.2
63	17.6	15.2	19.9	15.1	19.3	19.1	25.0	12.3	34.9	19.6
64	17.0	14.6	19.2	14.6	18.6	20.1	26.9	13.1	35.2	19.5
65	16.3	14.0	18.4	14.1	18.0	21.2	28.8	13.8	34.9	19.1

| | | Expectation of life in years | | | | | Mortality probability per 1,000 | | | |
| | Total persons | White | | All other | | Total Persons | White | | All other | |
Age		Male	Female	Male	Female		Male	Female	Male	Female
66	15.7	13.4	17.7	13.6	17.3	22.5	30.8	14.8	34.9	19.0
67	15.0	12.8	16.9	13.1	16.7	24.1	33.2	16.0	36.1	20.0
68	14.4	12.2	16.2	12.5	16.0	26.1	36.0	17.4	39.0	22.5
69	13.7	11.6	15.5	12.0	15.4	28.5	39.2	19.1	43.3	26.2
70	13.1	11.1	14.8	11.6	14.8	31.1	42.6	20.9	48.4	30.3
71	12.5	10.6	14.1	11.1	14.2	33.9	46.3	22.9	52.5	34.4
72	12.0	10.1	13.4	10.7	13.7	37.0	50.3	25.4	59.8	39.0
73	11.4	9.6	12.7	10.4	13.2	40.6	54.8	28.2	63.9	44.0
74	10.9	9.1	12.1	10.0	12.8	44.7	59.8	32.0	68.9	49.5
75	10.4	8.6	11.5	9.8	12.5	49.2	65.3	36.0	73.9	55.0
76	9.9	8.2	10.9	9.5	12.2	54.0	71.1	40.3	79.1	60.6
77	9.4	7.8	10.3	9.3	11.9	59.0	77.4	44.9	84.4	65.7
78	9.0	7.4	9.8	9.1	11.7	64.1	84.0	49.6	89.8	70.0
79	8.5	7.1	9.3	8.9	11.6	69.5	91.0	54.7	94.8	73.1
80	8.1	6.7	8.8	8.8	11.5	75.1	98.3	60.2	98.6	74.3
81	7.8	6.4	8.3	8.7	11.3	80.9	105.9	66.3	100.0	72.8
82	7.4	6.1	7.9	8.6	11.1	86.9	113.7	73.3	97.3	67.3
83	7.1	5.8	7.5	8.5	10.9	93.1	121.3	81.3	87.9	56.8
84	6.7	5.5	7.1	8.2	10.5	99.4	128.4	90.8	68.9	40.0
85	6.4	5.3	6.7	7.8	9.9	1000.0	1000.0	1000.0	1000.0	1000.0

Sources: Metropolitan Life Insurance Company; Department of Health and Human Services, National Center for Health Statistics. NOTE: Data are latest available.

Law Enforcement and Crime

Full-Time Law Enforcement Employees, 1979

City	Officers	Civilians	Total	Percent change 78–79	City	Officers	Civilians	Total	Percent change 78–79
Atlanta	1,116	331	1,447	+4.9	Minneapolis	745	93	838	−3.7
Baltimore	3,171	555	3,726	−4.8	New Orleans	1,482	502	1,984	+4.5
Birmingham, Ala.	684	185	869	−1.5	New York	23,310	4,702	28,012	−4.9
Boston	2,187	277	2,464	−16.0	Newark, N.J.	1,198	256	1,454	−15.6
Buffalo, N.Y.	1,107	140	1,247	+3.1	Norfolk, Va.	588	133	721	+1.8
Chicago	13,293	1,949	15,242	−6.4	Oakland, Calif.	621	296	917	+4.2
Cincinnati	945	155	1,100	+4.4	Oklahoma City	707	186	893	+2.3
Cleveland	1,864	134	1,998	−3.1	Omaha, Neb.	553	155	708	+4.6
Columbus, Ohio	914	289	1,203	+5.5	Philadelphia	7,903	845	8,748	−5.5
Dallas	2,031	562	2,593	+0.7	Phoenix, Ariz.	1,597	570	2,167	+5.7
Denver	1,403	283	1,686	+1.2	Pittsburgh	1,366	40	1,406	−1.7
Detroit	5,006	607	5,613	−11.9	Portland, Ore.	653	183	836	−6.1
El Paso	680	163	843	+2.4	Rochester, N.Y.	638	190	828	+9.4
Fort Worth	677	260	937	+5.5	St. Louis	2,002	595	2,597	+0.3
Honolulu	1,475	308	1,783	−3.0	St. Paul	547	128	675	−0.4
Houston	3,012	819	3,831	−1.1	San Antonio	1,138	231	1,369	−1.2
Indianapolis	996	334	1,330	+1.5	San Diego, Calif.	1,306	355	1,661	+6.7
Jacksonville, Fla.	955	634	1,589	−1.2	San Francisco	1,554	567	2,121	+12.5
Kansas City, Mo.	1,192	517	1,709	+3.1	San Jose, Calif.	762	243	1,005	+3.0
Long Beach, Calif.	616	227	843	+6.0	Seattle	966	334	1,300	+0.9
Los Angeles	6,699	2,299	8,998	−6.7	Tampa, Fla.	582	203	785	−1.0
Louisville, Ky.	672	201	873	−4.7	Toledo, Ohio	702	79	781	+15.4
Memphis, Tenn.	1,265	388	1,653	0.0	Tucson, Ariz.	546	191	737	+2.9
Miami, Fla.	674	219	893	−11.8	Tulsa, Okla.	677	134	811	+3.8
Milwaukee	2,029	252	2,281	+0.8	Washington, D.C.	4,034	549	4,583	−1.5

NOTE: As of Oct. 31, 1979. *Source:* Department of Justice, Federal Bureau of Investigation. *Uniform Crime Reports for the United States, 1979.*

Total Estimated Arrests, 1979[1]

Murder and non-negligent manslaughter	19,590	Weapons—carrying, possession, etc.	164,200
Forcible rape	31,470	Prostitution and commercial vice	89,400
Robbery	140,640	Sex offenses, except forcible rape	
Aggravated assault	276,000	and prostitution	67,400
Total violent crimes	467,700	Drug abuse violations	558,600
Burglary	503,600	Gambling	54,800
Larceny—theft	1,181,500	Offenses against family and children	57,400
Motor vehicle theft	154,500	Driving under the influence	1,324,800
Arson	19,800	Liquor laws	416,200
Total property crime	1,895,200	Drunkenness	1,172,700
Other assaults	485,500	Disorderly conduct	765,500
Forgery and counterfeiting	76,400	Vagrancy	37,200
Fraud	261,900	All other offenses, except traffic	1,716,600
Embezzlement	8,600	Curfew and loitering law violations	84,100
Stolen property—buying, receiving, possessing	115,800	Total	**10,205,800**
Vandalism	257,300		

1. Arrest totals based on all reporting agencies and estimates for unreported areas. _Source:_ Department of Justice, Federal Bureau of Investigation, _Uniform Crime Reports for the United States, 1979._

Number of Arrests by Sex and Age

	Male				Female			
	Total		Under 18		Total		Under 18	
Offense	1979	1978	1979	1978	1979	1978	1979	1978
---	---:	---:	---:	---:	---:	---:	---:	---:
Murder[1]	14,784	14,405	1,446	1,396	2,373	2,418	163	153
Forcible rape	27,477	25,218	4,254	3,876	210	214	55	77
Robbery	116,348	113,808	36,851	36,973	9,321	8,791	2,731	2,687
Aggravated assault	216,624	204,952	32,493	31,416	30,772	29,859	5,617	5,403
Total violent crimes	375,233	358,383	75,044	73,661	42,676	41,282	8,566	8,320
Burglary	241,651	423,519	205,514	220,623	28,613	28,115	14,355	14,426
Larceny—theft	739,565	695,675	314,530	309,847	322,425	326,265	116,142	122,456
Motor vehicle theft	126,261	127,829	61,503	64,805	12,410	12,012	6,998	7,029
Arson	15,656	14,774	7,865	7,473	1,997	2,018	835	785
Total property crime	1,303,133	1,261,797	589,412	602,748	365,445	368,410	138,330	144,696
Other assaults	375,353	360,361	64,761	62,162	59,302	57,349	16,545	15,632
Forgery and counterfeiting	47,081	47,362	6,835	6,683	21,175	20,648	2,808	2,767
Fraud	138,519	134,664	5,933	6,122	93,331	84,113	2,120	1,965
Embezzlement	5,728	5,365	739	643	1,950	1,832	223	221
Stolen property—buying, receiving, possessing	91,502	90,293	31,034	31,312	10,996	11,550	3,030	3,139
Vandalism	211,372	192,970	115,415	111,939	19,453	17,664	9,872	9,181
Weapons—carrying, possession, etc.	135,235	126,818	22,537	20,479	10,758	10,661	1,430	1,288
Prostitution and commercialized vice	25,239	25,746	1,121	1,330	53,919	55,981	2,057	2,282
Sex offenses, except forcible rape and prostitution	56,306	55,746	10,240	10,089	4,779	4,963	805	1,003
Drug abuse violations	451,637	480,530	92,383	111,673	67,452	76,933	18,155	22,323
Gambling	45,605	47,393	1,997	1,863	4,755	4,512	85	98
Offenses against family and children	46,279	46,863	1,592	1,800	5,057	5,353	906	992
Driving under the influence	1,082,191	1,053,559	25,712	23,847	103,022	97,433	2,770	2,541
Liquor laws	316,558	283,314	105,685	94,157	54,743	49,085	29,248	26,238
Drunkenness	978,775	1,005,815	38,156	36,211	77,288	80,647	6,006	5,824
Disorderly conduct	583,932	548,029	101,022	98,118	106,433	105,729	20,809	20,484
Vagrancy	26,262	28,122	3,842	5,007	7,410	12,510	813	953
All other offenses except traffic	1,290,898	1,338,732	229,160	242,067	225,201	230,133	55,777	61,887
Curfew and loitering law violations	59,096	60,306	59,096	60,306	16,596	16,538	16,596	16,538
Runaways	60,819	68,721	60,819	68,721	85,626	93,561	85,626	93,561
Total	7,706,753	7,620,862	1,642,535	1,670,938	1,437,361	1,446,887	422,577	441,933

1. Includes non-negligent manslaughter. NOTE: 1979 figures represent arrests reported by 11,239 agencies with a total 1979 population of 197,679,000 as estimated by FBI. _Source:_ Department of Justice, Federal Bureau of Investigation, _Uniform Crime Reports for the United States, 1979._

Arrests by Race, 1979
(in thousands)

Offense	White	Black	Other	Total	Offense	White	Black	Other	Total
Murder[1]	9.0	8.7	0.5	18.2	Prostitution and commercial vice	37.8	43.7	1.5	83.0
Forcible rape	14.6	13.9	0.6	29.1	Sex offenses, except forcible rape and prostitution	48.3	12.6	1.5	62.4
Robbery	53.5	74.3	2.8	130.6					
Aggravated assault	155.8	94.6	5.5	256.0					
Total violent crimes	232.9	191.5	9.5	433.9	Drug abuse violations	396.1	112.7	7.3	516.1
Burglary	322.5	133.0	8.6	464.1	Gambling	14.1	34.5	2.2	50.8
Larceny—theft	735.7	330.3	28.0	1,094.0	Offenses against family and children	33.5	18.7	0.9	53.0
Motor vehicle theft	100.2	38.9	4.1	143.2					
Arson	14.5	3.5	0.3	18.3	Driving under the influence	1,048.2	151.2	24.8	1,224.1
Total property crimes	1,172.8	505.8	41.1	1,719.6	Liquor laws	347.4	25.3	13.0	385.7
Other assaults	293.8	144.3	10.8	488.9	Drunkenness	876.1	181.5	32.4	1,090.0
Forgery and counterfeiting	47.0	22.6	0.8	70.5	Disorderly conduct	466.7	210.7	32.5	709.9
Fraud	164.2	75.0	2.5	241.7	Vagrancy	21.4	12.3	0.9	34.6
Embezzlement	5.9	1.9	0.1	7.9	All other offenses, except traffic	1,083.0	430.5	77.4	1,590.9
Stolen property— buying, receiving, possessing	70.9	34.3	1.6	106.7	Curfew and loitering law violations	59.8	16.9	1.4	78.1
Vandalism	196.0	36.8	4.8	237.6	Runaways	128.4	19.3	4.3	152.0
Weapons—carrying, possession, etc.	92.9	55.0	4.3	152.1	Total	6,837.2	2,337.2	275.2	9,449.5

1. Includes non-negligent manslaughter. NOTE: Figures represent arrests reported by 11,689 agencies with a total 1979 population of 204,363,000 estimated by FBI. *Source:* Department of Justice, Federal Bureau of Investigation, *Uniform Crime Reports for the United States, 1979.*

Total Arrests, by Age Groups, 1979

Age	Arrests	Age	Arrests	Age	Arrests	Age	Arrests	Age	Arrests
Under 15	662,043	18	595,798	22	425,099	30–34	827,300	50–54	271,102
15	407,152	19	550,079	23	382,882	35–39	564,716	55 and over	385,107
16	515,979	20	504,901	24	353,421	40–44	418,477	Not known	9,528
17	558,195	21	466,326	25–29	1,279,025	45–49	329,217	Total	9,506,347

NOTE: Based on reports furnished to the FBI by 11,758 agencies covering a 1979 estimated population of 204,622,000. *Source:* Department of Justice, Federal Bureau of Investigation. *Uniform Crime Reports for the United States, 1979.*

National Crime, Rate, and Percent Change

Crime index offenses	Estimated crime 1979		Percent change over 1978		Percent change over 1975		Percent change over 1970	
	Number	Rate per 100,000 inhabitants	Number	Rate	Number	Rate	Number	Rate
Murder	21,460	9.7	+9.7	+7.8	+4.6	+1.0	+34.1	+22.8
Forcible rape	75,990	34.5	+13.2	+12.0	+35.5	+31.2	+100.0	+84.5
Robbery	466,880	212.1	+12.0	+10.9	+.4	−2.8	+33.4	+23.2
Aggravated assault	614,210	279.1	+10.1	+9.1	+26.7	+22.7	+83.4	+69.4
Total violent crimes	1,178,540	535.5	+11.0	+10.0	+14.8	+11.2	+59.5	+47.3
Burglary	3,299,500	1,499.1	+6.3	+5.3	+1.5	−1.8	+49.6	+38.2
Larceny-theft	6,577,500	2,988.4	+9.9	+8.9	+10.0	+6.5	+55.7	+43.7
Motor vehicle theft	1,097,200	498.5	+10.6	+9.6	+9.7	+6.2	+18.2	+9.1
Arson								
Total property crimes	10,974,200	4,986.0	+8.9	+7.9	+7.3	+3.9	+49.1	+37.7
Total all crimes[1]	12,152,700	5,521.5	+9.1	+8.1	+8.0	+4.5	+50.1	+38.6

1. Because of rounding, offenses may not add up to totals. *Source:* Department of Justice, Federal Bureau of Investigation, *Uniform Crime Reports for the United States, 1979.*

Crime Rates for Population Groups and Selected Cities, 1979
(offenses known to the police per 100,000 population)

Group and city	Mur-der	Violent crime — Forc-ible rape	Rob-bery	Aggra-vated assault	Total	Property crime — Burglary—break-ing or enter-ing	Lar-ceny—theft	Motor vehicle theft	Total	Total all crimes
Cities over 250,000	23.1	71	668	475	1,238	2,336	3,828	1,054	7,218	8,456
100,000–249,999	11.4	50	282	358	701	2,114	4,356	655	7,125	7,827
50,000–99,999	7.2	37	194	288	525	1,773	3,769	594	6,135	6,661
25,000–49,999	5.8	27	134	254	420	1,477	3,607	459	5,543	5,963
10,000–24,999	4.5	18	78	216	315	1,187	3,139	349	4,674	4,990
Under 10,000	4.0	15	47	212	279	1,021	2,939	266	4,225	4,504
Total, 8,454 cities	11.2	41	294	323	668	1,725	3,601	627	5,954	6,622
Suburbs, 5,163 agencies[1]	5.6	25	99	225	356	1,303	2,794	381	4,477	4,833
Rural areas, 2,838 agencies	7.6	16	23	148	194	803	1,130	143	2,076	2,270
Total, 12,329 agencies	10.1	36	223	286	555	1,539	3,052	514	5,105	5,660
Selected cities:										
San Francisco	17.0	101	1,016	542	1,675	2,618	5,149	1,290	9,057	10,732
Dallas	34.8	111	505	647	1,298	2,997	5,443	890	9,330	10,628
Baltimore	31.0	71	1,072	788	1,963	2,139	4,367	856	7,361	9,324
Los Angeles	27.4	88	714	685	1,515	2,596	3,549	1,373	7,518	9,032
Detroit	35.9	109	907	619	1,670	2,598	2,820	1,708	7,125	8,795
Houston	40.4	91	575	171	878	3,022	3,335	1,517	7,874	8,752
New York	24.4	55	1,161	622	1,862	2,506	3,106	1,262	6,874	8,736
San Diego	11.6	40	348	256	656	2,406	4,730	902	8,038	8,693
Cleveland	45.6	102	958	514	1,619	2,412	2,364	2,251	7027	8,646
Washington, D.C.	27.4	75	1,055	452	1,609	2,051	4,393	550	6,993	8,602
Indianapolis	17.9	85	400	310	813	1,664	3,683	672	6,018	6,831
San Antonio	20.6	44	204	224	493	1,990	3,588	560	6,138	6,631
Chicago	28.0	54	473	354	909	1,091	3,074	1,027	5,192	6,101
Milwaukee	9.8	44	247	171	471	1,325	3,498	655	5,477	5,948
Philadelphia	21.9	48	503	255	827	1,193	1,927	752	3,872	4,699
CRIME INDEX TRENDS										
(percent change, 1979–80)										
Cities over 1,000,000 (total population 17,670,000)	+ 9	0	+28	+ 3	+17	+16	+12	+11	+13	+14
Cities 500,000 to 999,999 (total population, 12,422,000)	+ 3	+ 6	+13	+ 7	+10	+13	+ 8	− 1	+ 9	+ 9
Cities 250,000 to 499,999 (total population 11,314,000)	+ 9	+10	+17	+12	+14	+15	+10	− 1	+10	+11
Cities 100,000 to 249,999 (total population 16,130,000)	+ 7	+13	+17	+13	+14	+15	+ 9	0	+10	+10
Cities 50,000 to 99,999 (total population 19,557,000)	+ 7	+ 9	+17	+11	+13	+12	+ 5	0	+ 7	+ 7
Cities 25,000 to 49,999 (total population 21,019,000)	+ 7	+11	+17	+ 8	+11	+14	+ 7	0	+ 8	+ 9
Cities 10,000 to 24,999 (total population 23,839,000)	+11	+13	+19	+ 7	+11	+12	+ 7	− 3	+ 7	+ 7
Cities under 10,000 (total population 21,896,000)	+ 9	+10	+15	+ 7	+ 9	+12	+ 9	− 1	+ 9	+ 9
Suburban areas (total population 34,772,000)	+ 7	+14	+21	+ 7	+11	+16	+ 8	+ 3	+10	+10
Rural areas (total population 29,173,000)	+ 3	+12	+10	+ 3	+ 5	+13	+13	+ 2	+12	+12
All areas (total population 207,791,000)	+ 7	+ 9	+20	+ 8	+13	+14	+ 8	+ 2	+ 9	+10

1. Agencies also included in other city groups. NOTE: Population in 1979 as estimated by FBI. *Sources:* Department of Justice, Federal Bureau of Investigation, *Uniform Crime Reports for the United States, 1979* and *1980 Preliminary Annual Release.*

Domestic Production and Imports of Civilian Firearms
(in thousands)

Item	1980	1979	1978	1977	1976	1975	1974	1970	1965	1960
Domestic production	5,646	5,323	4,866	5,016	5,225	5,768	5,639	n.a.	2,355	1,508
Handguns	2,371	2,126	1,889	1,868	1,833	2,024	1,715	n.a.	666	475
Rifles	1,936	1,878	1,781	1,923	2,091	2,123	2,099	n.a.	790	469
Shotguns	1,339	1,319	1,196	1,225	1,301	1,621	1,825	n.a.	899	564
Imports for consumption	754	886	869	782	895	1,084	903	826	766	655
Handguns	299	271	273	316	270	462	259	227	347	128
Rifles	182	257	223	170	157	166	188	237	245	402
Shotguns	273	358	373	296	468	457	456	363	174	125
Total	6,400	6,209	5,735	5,798	6,120	6,852	6,542	n.a.	3,121	2,163

NOTE: Beginning 1972, fiscal-year data. Includes firearms sold under civilian marksmanship program of Department of Defense. n.a.=not available. *Source:* 1960–1970, Department of Commerce, Bureau of the Census; beginning 1972, Department of the Treasury, Bureau of Alcohol, Tobacco, and Firearms.

Prisoners Under Sentence of Death

Characteristic	1979	1978	1977	Characteristic	1979	1978	1977
White	344	261	244	Marital status:			
Black and other	223	184	199	Never married	208	187	192
Under 20 years	11	22	16	Married	190	136	143
20–24 years	145	113	135	Divorced or separated[1]	169	122	108
25–34 years	276	210	199	Time elapsed since sentencing:			
35–54 years	128	97	88	6 months or less }			
55 years and over	7	3	5	7–12 months }	158	162	123
Schooling completed:				1–3 years	309	237	314
7 years or less	55	55	49	4–8 years	100	46	6
8 years	55	46	46	More than 8 years	0	0	0
9–11 years	187	158	137	Legal status at arrest:			
12 years	121	99	88	Not under sentence	324	277	253
More than 12 years	39	28	25	On parole or probation	88	60	60
Unknown	110	59	98	In prison or escaped	38	35	20
				Unknown	117	73	110
				Total	**567**	**445**	**443**

1. Includes widows, widowers, and unknown. NOTE: As of Dec. 31. Excludes prisoners under sentence of death confined in local correctional systems pending appeal or who had not been committed to prison. *Source:* Department of Justice, Law Enforcement Assistance Administration; after 1978 U.S. Bureau of Justice Statistics, *Capital Punishment,* annual.

Methods of Execution[1]

State	Method	State	Method
Alabama[2]	Electrocution	Nevada[2]	Lethal gas
Alaska	No death penalty	New Hampshire[2]	Hanging
Arizona[2]	Lethal gas	New Jersey[5]	No death penalty
Arkansas[2]	Electrocution	New Mexico	Lethal injection
California	Lethal gas	New York	No death penalty
Colorado[2]	Lethal gas	North Carolina[2]	Lethal gas
Connecticut[2]	Electrocution	North Dakota	No death penalty
Delaware	Hanging	Ohio[2]	Electrocution
D.C.	No death penalty	Oklahoma	Lethal injection
Florida	Electrocution	Oregon	Lethal gas[6]
Georgia[2]	Electrocution	Pennsylvania[2]	Electrocution
Hawaii	No death penalty	Rhode Island[2]	(3)
Idaho[2]	Lethal injection	South Carolina[2]	Electrocution
Illinois	Electrocution	South Dakota	Electrocution
Indiana[2]	Electrocution	Tennessee[2]	Electrocution
Iowa	No death penalty	Texas[2]	Lethal injection
Kansas	No death penalty	Utah[2]	Shooting
Kentucky[2]	Electrocution	Vermont	Electrocution
Louisiana[2]	Electrocution	Virginia	Electrocution
Maine	No death penalty	Washington[2]	Hanging
Maryland[2]	Lethal gas	West Virginia	No death penalty
Massachusetts	No death penalty	Wisconsin	No death penalty
Michigan	No death penalty	Wyoming	Lethal gas
Minnesota	No death penalty	U.S. (Fed. Govt.)	(4)
Mississippi[2]	Lethal gas	American Samoa	(5)
Missouri	Lethal gas	Guam	No death penalty
Montana[2]	Hanging	Puerto Rico	No death penalty
Nebraska[2]	Electrocution	Virgin Islands	No death penalty

1. On July 1, 1976, by a 7–2 decision, the U.S. Supreme Court upheld the death penalty as not being "cruel or unusual." However, in another ruling the same day, the Court, by a 5–4 vote, stated that states may not impose "mandatory" capital punishment on every person convicted of murder. These decisions left uncertain the fate of condemned persons throughout the U.S. On Oct. 4, the Court refused to reconsider its July ruling, which allows some states to proceed with executions of condemned prisoners. The first execution in this country since 1967 was in Utah on Jan. 17, 1977. Gary Mark Gilmore was executed by shooting. 2. Voted to restore death penalty after June 29, 1972, Supreme Court decision ruling capital punishment unconstitutional. 3. Person shall be executed by gas if he commits murder while serving a prison term. 4. Method shall be that used by state in which sentence is imposed. If state does not have death penalty, federal judge shall prescribe method for carrying out sentence. 5. New criminal code re-establishes death penalty but at this time prescribes no method. 6. Death penalty overturned by the Oregon Supreme Court; status currently under review by the Oregon Legislature. *Source: Information Please* questionnaires to the states.

Motor Vehicle Laws, 1981

State	Date new license plates can be used	Age for driver's license[1] Regular	Learner's	Restrictive	State gasoline tax	Percent state tax[2]	Annual inspection required
Alabama	On issue	16	15[5]	14[15]	$.11	1½	no[19]
Alaska	On issue	18		16[3]	.08	—	no[19]
Arizona	On issue	18	15 & 7 mos.[3,5]	16[3]	.08	4	no[23]
Arkansas	On issue	18	(5)	14[3]	.095	3	yes
California	On issue	18	15[4,10]	16[4]	.07	6[23]	no[19]
Colorado	On issue	21	15½[5]	16[4]	.07	3	yes
Connecticut	On issue	18		16[4]	.11	7½[6]	no[24]
Delaware	On issue	18	(5)	16[4]	.09	(18)	yes
D. C.	On issue	18	(5)	16[3]	.10	(21)	yes
Florida	30 days before exp. of old	16	(5)	15[3]	.08	4	yes
Georgia	Jan. 1	18	15	16[3]	.075	3	yes
Hawaii	Jan. 1	18	(5)	15[3]	(8)	(9)	yes[12]
Idaho	On issue	16	(5)	14[4]	.115	3	no
Illinois	administratively determined	18	(5)	16[3,4]	.075	4	no
Indiana	On issue	18	15[20]	16 & 1 mo.[3,4]	(30)	4	no
Iowa	Jan. 1	18	14	16[4]	.085	3	(7)
Kansas	On issue	16	(5)	14	.08	3	no
Kentucky	On issue	18	(5)	16[3]	(31)	5	no
Louisiana	On issue	17		15[11]	.08	3	yes
Maine	On issue	17	(5)	15[4]	.09	5	6 mos.
Maryland	Mar. 1	18	(5)	16	.09	5	no[26]
Massachusetts	On issue	18	(5)	16½[3,4]	(32)	5	6 mos.
Michigan	On issue	18		16[3,4]	.11	4	no[19]
Minnesota	On issue	18	(5)	16[4]	.09	4	no[19]
Mississippi	On issue	15	(5)		.09	3	yes
Missouri	On issue	16		15[4]	.07	3	yes
Montana	On issue	18	(5)	15[3,4]	.09	1½[13]	no
Nebraska	On issue	16	15[5]	14	.139	3	yes
Nevada	On issue	18	15½[5]	16[3]	.06	2[14]	no
New Hampshire	On issue	18		16[4]	.11	—	6 mos.
New Jersey	On issue	17		16	.08	5	yes
New Mexico	Dec. 15	16	15	14[33]	.09	2	no
New York	On issue	17[4]		16[3]	.08[34]	4	yes
North Carolina	On issue	18		15[3,4]	.09	2[16]	yes
North Dakota	Apr. 1	16	(5)	14[3,4]	.08	3	no[19]
Ohio	1st day/mo. of exp.	18	16[3,5]	14[27]	.07	4	no[19]
Oklahoma	On issue	16		15½[4]	.0658	2	yes
Oregon	On issue	16	15[5]	14	.07	—	no[19]
Pennsylvania	On issue	17[4]	(5)	16[3]	.11	6	6 mos.
Rhode Island	Mar. 1	18	(5)	16[4]	.10	6	yes
South Carolina	On issue	16	15[35]	15	.11	4	yes
South Dakota	Jan. 1	16	(5)	14	.13	3[17]	no
Tennessee	On issue	16	(5)	15	.08	4½[28]	no
Texas	On issue	16[4]	15	15	.05	4	yes
Utah	On issue	16[4]	(5)		.09	4¾	yes
Vermont	On issue	18	15[5]	16	.09	4	6 mos.
Virginia	On issue	18	15 & 8 mos.[3,5]	16[3,4]	.09	2	6 mos.
Washington	On issue	18	15[20]	16[4]	(22)	4.5	no[19]
West Virginia	On issue	18	(5)	16[3]	.105	5	yes
Wisconsin	On issue	18	(5)	16[4]	.09	4	no
Wyoming	Jan. 1	18	15[3,10]	16[3]	.08	3	no

1. Full driving privileges at age given in "Regular" column. A license restricted or qualified in some manner may be obtained at age given in "Restricted" column. 2. Applicable to car sales (local and county sales taxes extra where applicable). 3. Guardian's or parent's consent required. 4. Must have completed approved Driver Education course. 5. Learner's Permit required. 6. Sales or use tax on first registration of new or used cars. 7. Prior to first registration and transfers. 8. 8.5.—13.5¢ varies by county. 9. 4% on cars purchased out of state only. 10. Driver with Learner's Permit must be accompanied by locally licensed operator 18 years or older. 11. All persons under 17 are prohibited from operating vehicles between 11 p.m. and 5 a.m. 12. If car is 10 years or older, every 6 months. 13. Periodic reductions for cars purchased later in year. 14. Plus 1% school support tax and 1/2% city and county relief tax in selected counties. 15. Restricted to Mopeds. 16. $120 maximum. 17. Tax on first registration. 18. Document fee of 2% of cost of car. 19. State troopers are authorized to inspect at their discretion. 20. Must be enrolled in a Driver Education course. 21. 4–7%, depending on weight of car. 22. Variable. Based on the average weighted retail sales price of fuel, the rate may be adjusted to not less than 12¢ per gallon, nor increased by more than 2¢ per gallon per year. 23. Arizona emission inspection, fee $5. 24. 6½% in some special districts. 25. Used motor vehicles being registered in Connecticut from out-of-state are required to be inspected and approved and Connecticut cars 10 years old or more must be inspected upon being sold or transferred. 26. Used passenger cars upon resale or transfer. 27. Upon proof of hardship. 28. Some counties have an additional 1 to 1¾% county tax. 29. Trucks and buses only. 30. 8% of retail price plus 4% sales tax. 31. 9% of average (per gallon) wholesale price, adjusted quarterly, with a 9¢ floor and 13.5¢ ceiling. 32. 10% of wholesale price. 33. For use while enrolled in driver education course. Must be accompanied by instructor.

34. New York City leaded gasoline tax 1¢ extra per gallon. 35. Driver with Learner's Permit must be accompanied by locally licensed operator 21 years or older. NOTES: A driver's license is required in every state. The national speed limit is 55 miles per hour. All states have an *implied consent* Chemical Test Law for alcohol. *Source:* American Automobile Association.

Law Enforcement Officers Killed in Line of Duty
(beginning 1972, includes federal officers)

Area	1979	1978	1977	1976	1975	1974	1973	1972	1970	1965	1960
New England	—	3	2	4	4	2	7	2	2	3	3
Middle Atlantic	13	9	12	15	24	18	21	22	29	10	7
East North Central	13	5	10	19	32	43	21	23	38	10	9
West North Central	3	5	14	11	8	8	6	12	6	3	3
South Atlantic	23	15	31	34	31	42	37	38	23	15	13
East South Central	15	13	11	14	18	12	13	12	5	9	2
West South Central	11	19	21	21	22	23	30	27	15	14	6
Mountain	8	5	3	4	14	9	16	7	4	7	0
Pacific	15	15	15	13	22	18	21	12	24	12	5
Puerto Rico	3	4	1	4	8	4	4	2	n.a.	n.a.	n.a.
CAUSE											
By felons	106[4]	93	93[3]	111	129[1]	132	134	116	100	53	n.a.
In accidents	56	53	30[3]	29	56	47	42	41	46	30	n.a.
Total	162[4]	146	123[3]	140[2]	185[1]	179	176	157	146	83	48

1. Includes one officer each in Virgin Islands and Guam. 2. Includes one officer killed in Bogota, Colombia. 3. Includes one officer killed in Virgin Islands and two FBI agents accidentally killed. 4. Includes two killed on Guam. NOTE: n.a. = not available. *Source:* Department of Justice, Federal Bureau of Investigation, *Uniform Crime Reports for the United States, 1979.*

Murder Victims by Weapons Used

Year	Murder victims, total	Guns Total	Guns Percent	Cutting or stabbing	Blunt object[1]	Strangulation and hands, fists, feet	Drownings, arson, etc.	All other[2]
1965	8,773	5,015	57.2	2,021	505	894	226	112
1966	9,552	5,660	59.3	2,134	516	896	203	143
1967	11,114	6,998	63.0	2,200	589	957	211	159
1968	12,503	8,105	64.8	2,317	713	936	294	138
1969	13,575	8,876	65.4	2,534	613	1,039	322	191
1970	13,649	9,039	66.2	2,424	604	1,031	353	198
1971	16,183	10,712	66.2	3,017	645	1,295	314	200
1972	15,832	10,379	65.6	2,974	672	1,291	331	185
1973	17,123	11,249	65.7	2,985	848	1,445	173[3]	423
1974	18,632	12,474	66.9	3,228	976	1,417	153[3]	384
1975	18,642	12,061	64.7	3,245	1,001	1,646	193[3]	496
1976	16,605	10,592	63.8	2,956	806	1,330	227[3]	694
1977	18,033	11,274	62.5	3,440	849	1,431	252[3]	787
1978	18,714	11,910	63.6	3,526	896	1,422	255[3]	705
1979	20,591	13,040	63.3	3,954	997	1,557	276[3]	767

1. Refers to club, hammer, etc. 2. Includes poison, explosives, unknown, and not stated; for 1973 to 1976, includes drowning. 3. Arson only. *Source:* Department of Justice, Federal Bureau of Investigation, *Uniform Crime Reports for the United States, 1979.*

Southern States Account for Most Death-Row Prisoners

Three Southern states accounted for more than half of the 714 prisoners awaiting execution at the end of 1980. They were Florida, Texas, and Georgia. The South as a whole had more than three quarters of the condemned prisoners in the United States.

At the end of 1980 there were more prisoners on death row than at any time since record keeping began in 1930. The total of 714 was 136 more than in the previous year.

Minimum Legal Age for Purchase of Liquor, Wine, and Beer

State	Liquor	Wine	Beer	State	Liquor	Wine	Beer
Alabama	19	19	19	Montana	19	19	19
Alaska	19	19	19	Nebraska	20	20	20
Arizona	19	19	19	Nevada	21	21	21
Arkansas	21	21	21	New Hampshire	20	20	20
California	21	21	21	New Jersey	19	19	19
Colorado	21	21	21[1]	New Mexico	21	21	21
Connecticut	18	18	18	New York	18	18	18
Delaware	20	20	20	North Carolina	21	21[2]	18
D.C.	21	21[2]	18	North Dakota	21	21	21
Florida	19	19	19	Ohio	21	21	21[1]
Georgia	19	19	19	Oklahoma	21	21	21[4]
Hawaii	18	18	18	Oregon	21	21	21
Idaho	19	19	19	Pennsylvania	21	21	21
Illinois	21	21	21	Rhode Island	19	19	19
Indiana	21	21	21	South Carolina	21	18	18
Iowa	19	19	19	South Dakota	21	21	21[1]
Kansas	21	21	21[1]	Tennessee	19	19	19
Kentucky	21	21	21	Texas	18	18	18
Louisiana	18	18	18	Utah	21	21	21
Maine	20	20	20	Vermont	18	18	18
Maryland	21	21[2]	18	Virginia	21	21	18[5]
Massachusetts	20	20	20	Washington	21	21	21
Michigan	21	21	21	West Virginia	18	18	18
Minnesota	19	19	19	Wisconsin	18	18	18
Mississippi	21	21[2]	21[3]	Wyoming	19	19	19
Missouri	21	21	21				

1. 3.2 beer: 18. 2. Light wine: 18. 3. Up to 4% alcohol by weight: 18. 4. 3.2 beer; 18 for off-premises consumption. 5. 19 for off-premises consumption. *Source:* Distilled Spirits Council of the United States.

Professional Misconduct
What to do when you are treated dishonestly or incompetently by a professional

Most people know that they should go to their bar association if they have a complaint about an attorney's misconduct. But where do you turn when you believe that you are being treated dishonestly or incompetently by a person with a license to practice another profession?

Most states have a specific agency to which you can complain. If the professional has been dishonest or incompetent or is guilty of other kinds of misconduct, his license to practice his profession in that state may be revoked or suspended—or he may be fined as much as $10,000 in some states for each instance of misconduct.

In most states, the licensed professions include: Medicine, Chiropractic, Engineering, Nursing, Pharmacy, Podiatry, Veterinary Medicine, Architecture, Dentistry, Land Surveying, Optometry, Occupational Therapy, Public Accountancy.

Though no states have identical regulations, a professional may be judged guilty of misconduct if he or she: practices the profession fraudulently; practices beyond the profession's authorized scope; practices negligently or incompetently; practices while impaired by alcohol, drugs, or physical or mental disability.

The professional may also be considered guilty of misconduct if habitually drunk or dependent on drugs; convicted of a crime; or has refused to provide the professional service because of a person's race, creed, or color.

You probably will never suffer at the hands of a licensed professional, but if you do, your state probably has an agency that can help you. You can obtain a state-by-state listing of where to go for help by writing: William L. Wood, Jr., Executive Director, New York State Office of Professional Discipline, 622 Third Avenue, New York, N.Y. 10017. Please include a self-addressed, stamped envelope.

National Earthquake Council

The National Earthquake Prediction Evaluation Council was established to aid the director of the U.S. Geological Survey in issuing any formal predictions of earthquakes.

The Council is expected to focus its efforts on potentially destructive earthquakes, which generally are those of a magnitude of 5.5 or greater on the Richter Scale. Data for smaller earthquakes will also be reviewed to establish a "track record" for prediction techniques.

Under terms of the charter, a prediction is defined to mean a statement on the time of occurrence, location, and magnitude of a future significant earthquake based on qualification or evaluation of the uncertainty of those factors.

If the USGS director decides to issue a prediction, or an advisory or negative evaluation of a prediction, the first people to be notified are the director of the Federal Emergency Management Agency, the Secretary of the Department of the Interior, and the governors of states affected by the predicted earthquake.

ENTERTAINMENT&CULTURE

Notable Books, 1980

This list has been compiled by the Notable Books Council of the American Library Association for use by the general reader and by librarians who work with adult readers. The titles were selected for their significant contribution to the expansion of knowledge or for the pleasure they can provide to adult readers. Criteria include wide general appeal and literary merit..

American Folk Painters of Three Centuries, edited by Jean Lipman and Tom Armstrong, Hudson Hills Press

Arnold, Eve, **In China,** Knopf

Atwood, Margaret, **Life Before Man,** Simon & Schuster

Bogan, Louise, **Journey around My Room: The Autobiography of Louise Bogan,** Viking

Calvino, Italo, compiler, **Italian Folktales,** Helen and Kurt Wolff/Harcourt

Desai, Anita, **Clear Light of Day,** Harper

Drabble, Margaret, **The Middle Ground,** Knopf

Flaubert, Gustave, **The Letters of Gustave Flaubert, 1830–1857,** Belknap Press/Harvard University Press

Gibson, Margaret, **The Butterfly Ward,** Vanguard

Gould, Stephen Jay, **The Panda's Thumb: More Reflections in Natural History,** Norton

Kaplan, Justin, **Walt Whitman: A Life,** Simon & Schuster

Keneally, Thomas, **Confederates,** Harper

Kiely, Benedict, **The State of Ireland: A Novella and Seventeen Stories,** Godine

Kingston, Maxine Hong, **China Men,** Knopf

Kramer, Jane, **Unsettling Europe,** Random

Lanes, Selma G., **The Art of Maurice Sendak,** Abrams

Lash, Joseph P., **Helen and Teacher: The Story of Helen Keller and Anne Sullivan Macy,** Delacorte/Seymour Lawrence

Manchester, William, **Goodbye, Darkness: A Memoir of the Pacific War,** Little, Brown

Massie, Robert K., **Peter the Great: His Life and World,** Knopf

Meredith, William, **The Cheer,** Knopf

Morris, Wright, **Plains Song: For Female Voices,** Harper

Pablo Picasso: A Retrospective, edited by William Rubin, Museum of Modern Art

Percy, Walker, **The Second Coming,** Farrar

Pym, Barbara, **A Glass of Blessings,** Dutton

Silk, Leonard, and Mark Silk, **The American Establishment,** Basic

Steel, Ronald, **Walter Lippmann and the American Century,** Atlantic Monthly Press/Little, Brown

Strand, Mark, **Selected Poems,** Atheneum

Strouse, Jean, **Alice James: A Biography,** Houghton

Toole, John Kennedy, **A Confederacy of Dunces,** Louisiana State University Press

Troyat, Henri, **Catherine the Great,** Dutton

Vendler, Helen, **Part of Nature, Part of Us: Modern American Poets,** Harvard University Press

Watt, Ian, **Conrad in the Nineteenth Century,** University of California Press

Welty, Eudora, **The Collected Stories of Eudora Welty,** Harcourt

Source: Reprinted by permission of the American Library Association. Issued as a pamphlet by ALA, 50 E. Huron St., Chicago, Ill. 60611, annually in the spring for the preceding year.

Major U.S. Symphony Orchestras and Their Music Directors

Source: American Symphony Orchestra League.

Atlanta Symphony: Robert Shaw
Baltimore Symphony: Sergiu Comissiona
Boston Symphony: Seiji Ozawa
Buffalo Philharmonic: Julius Rudel
Chicago Symphony: Georg Solti
Cincinnati Symphony: Michael Gielen
Cleveland Orchestra: Lorin Maazel
Dallas Symphony: Eduardo Mata
Denver Symphony: Gaetano Delogu
Detroit Symphony: Gary Bertini[2]
Honolulu Symphony: Donald Johanos
Houston Symphony: Sergiu Comissiona[1]
Indianapolis Symphony: John Nelson
Kansas City Philharmonic: Thomas Michalak[2]
Los Angeles Philharmonic: Carlo Maria Giulini
Milwaukee Symphony: Lukas Foss
Minnesota Orchestra: Neville Marriner

National Symphony (Washington, D.C.): Mstislav Rostropovich
New Jersey Symphony: Thomas Michalak
New Orleans Philharmonic Symphony Orchestra: Philippe Entremont
New York Philharmonic: Zubin Mehta
North Carolina Symphony: Lawrence Smith[3]
Philadelphia Orchestra: Riccardo Muti
Pittsburgh Symphony: André Previn
Rochester Philharmonic: David Zinman
Saint Louis Symphony: Leonard Slatkin
San Antonio Symphony: Lawrence Smith
San Diego Symphony: David Atherton
San Francisco Symphony: Edo de Waart
Seattle Symphony: Rainer Miedel
Syracuse Symphony: Christopher Keene
Utah Symphony: Varujan Kojian

1. Artistic Advisor. 2. Musical Advisor. 3. Artistic Advisor and Principal Guest Conductor.

Labors of Hercules

Hercules, hero and strong man, was the son of Zeus and Alcmene. He performed twelve labors or deeds to be free from bondage under Eurystheus. After his death, he became immortal. His twelve mythological labors were: (1) killing the Nemean Lion; (2) killing the Lernaean Hydra; (3) capturing the Cerynean Stag; (4) capturing the Erymanthian Boar; (5) cleaning the Augean Stables; (6) killing the Stymphalian Birds; (7) capturing the Cretan Bull; (8) capturing the Mares of Diomedes; (9) procuring the Girdle of Hippolyta; (10) capturing the Cattle of Geryon; (11) procuring the golden Apples of Hesperides; (12) bringing Cerberus up from Hades.

NOTE: List varies but the 12 given here represent widely accepted tradition.

Major Public Libraries

City (branches)	Volumes	Circulation	Budget (in millions)	City (branches)	Volumes	Circulation	Budget (in millions)
Akron, Ohio (18)	971,001	2,091,196	$ 4.3	Madison, Wis. (7)	543,954	2,018,813	$ 3.3
Albuquerque, N.M. (6)	351,506	1,493,342	2.0	Memphis, Tenn. (21)	1,608,845	2,593,506	6.1
Annapolis, Md. (12)	845,417	3,420,672	4.2	Miami, Fla. (20)	1,229,648	3,626,395	14.3
Atlanta (27)	1,054,996	3,540,533	6.2	Milwaukee (12)	2,296,784	3,303,140	9.5
Austin, Tex. (15)	681,530	1,919,884	4.3	Minneapolis (14)	1,578,166	2,396,398	9.5
Baltimore (34)	2,157,077	2,214,845	10.2	Nashville, Tenn. (15)	519,717	1,821,855	3.8
Baton Rouge, La. (8)	381,164	1,180,355	1.8	New Orleans (11)	747,135	1,143,420	3.2
Birmingham, Ala. (18)	1,016,892	2,040,626	4.1	New York City (83)	3,572,056	8,600,017	34.7
Boston (25)	4,829,050	1,950,492	9.3	Research	6,419,959	—	21.0
Buffalo, N.Y. (60)	3,267,472	5,671,596	12.9	Brooklyn (58)	3,743,828	6,983,217	17.4
Charleston, W.Va. (11)	516,002	1,058,854	1.8	Queens (58)	4,116,109	5,829,145	18.2
Charlotte, N.C. (15)	715,580	1,837,038	3.8	Newark, N.J. (12)	1,187,479	1,790,291	4.2
Chicago (88)	4,198,612	7,229,063	32.1	Norfolk, Va. (11)	656,867	1,043,663	2.5
Cincinnati (39)	3,265,163	5,845,093	9.6	Oklahoma City (10)	597,235	1,732,101	2.7
Cleveland (33)	2,418,323	3,118,006	17.8	Omaha, Neb. (9)	555,527	1,739,512	2.8
Columbus, Ohio (21)	1,233,587	3,307,731	7.7	Philadelphia (52)	2,930,607	4,903,301	21.3
Dallas (18)	1,912,317	3,743,104	8.7	Phoenix, Ariz. (9)	1,177,889	3,369,231	5.5
Dayton, Ohio (19)	1,381,400	4,441,967	6.2	Pittsburgh (21)	1,963,207	2,908,157	7.6
Des Moines, Iowa (5)	427,445	1,140,531	2.0	Portland, Ore. (16)	1,129,743	3,042,654	5.2
Denver (21)	1,728,650	2,922,046	8.7	Providence, R.I. (9)	699,110	612,966	2.5
Detroit (26)	2,512,917	1,921,921	14.9	Richmond, Va. (6)	632,095	1,082,516	1.7
D.C. (28)	1,425,820	1,466,623	11.2	Rochester, N.Y. (11)	932,000	1,567,594	5.1
El Paso (8)	460,950	1,430,625	2.4	Sacramento, Calif. (26)	1,075,000	3,428,680	6.7
Erie, Pa. (6)	383,644	1,138,535	1.3	St. Louis (14)	1,372,562	1,426,693	4.9
Evansville, Ind. (7)	501,806	1,596,806	2.1	St. Paul (10)	759,289	1,757,377	3.5
Fort Wayne, Ind. (12)	1,647,134	1,763,271	3.9	St. Petersburg, Fla. (4)	431,706	1,164,877	1.4
Fort Worth (7)	760,506	2,427,673	2.9	Salt Lake City, Utah (13)	742,086	2,727,097	4.1
Grand Rapids, Mich. (5)	600,708	823,775	2.5	San Antonio (9)	1,082,475	2,197,592	3.3
Greenville, S.C. (10)	445,545	1,129,131	2.3	San Diego, Calif. (29)	1,645,912	4,102,386	5.7
Honolulu (21)	1,348,108	3,466,401	5.4	San Francisco (26)	1,701,815	2,346,539	8.4
Houston (30)	2,446,943	5,753,205	13.4	San Jose, Calif. (16)	1,119,000	2,687,000	4.7
Independence, Mo. (23)	1,129,106	3,098,606	4.2	Seattle (22)	1,525,636	4,461,688	10.5
Indianapolis (24)	1,367,307	3,855,992	7.2	Springfield, Mass. (8)	709,707	962,920	2.5
Jackson, Miss. (37)	810,644	1,393,843	2.3	Tampa, Fla. (14)	940,797	2,048,563	4.5
Jacksonville, Fla. (11)	1,170,012	2,177,556	3.2	Tucson, Ariz. (15)	800,000	3,400,000	5.5
Kansas City, Mo. (13)	1,222,644	769,726	3.9	Tulsa, Okla. (20)	854,640	1,695,987	4.1
Knoxville, Tenn. (19)	607,557	1,643,064	2.6	Wichita, Kan. (11)	431,110	1,201,563	2.2
Lincoln, Neb. (10)	437,944	1,059,462	1.8	Winston-Salem, N.C. (8)	316,522	1,425,058	2.4
Long Beach, Calif. (10)	776,200	1,950,000	6.6	Worcester, Mass. (6)	913,992	824,041	2.3
Los Angeles	4,000,214	9,200,000	25.3	Youngstown, Ohio (23)	688,970	1,138,048	3.5
Louisville, Ky. (20)	1,009,220	2,214,707	5.2				

Source: Information Please questionnaires to the libraries.

Glossary of Art Movements

Abstract Expressionism. American art movement of the 1940s that emphasized form and color within a nonrepresentational framework. Jackson Pollock initiated the revolutionary technique of splattering the paint directly on canvas to achieve the subconscious interpretation of the artist's inner vision of reality.

Art Deco. A 1920s style characterized by setbacks, zigzag forms, and the use of chrome and plastic ornamentation. New York's Chrysler Building is an architectural example of the style.

Art Nouveau. An 1890s style in architecture, graphic arts, and interior decoration characterized by writhing forms, curving lines, and asymmetrical organization. Some critics regard the style as the first stage of modern architecture.

Ashcan School. A group of New York realist artists, formed in 1908, who abandoned decorous subject matter and portrayed the more common as well as the sordid aspects of city life.

Assemblage (Collage). Forms of modern sculpture and painting utilizing readymades, found objects, and pasted fragments to form an abstract composition. Louise Nevelson's boxlike enclosures, each with its own composition of assembled objects, illustrate the style in sculpture. Pablo Picasso developed the technique of cutting and pasting natural or manufactured materials to a painted or unpainted surface.

Barbizon School (Landscape Painting). A group of painters who, around the middle of the 19th century, reacted against classical landscape and advocated a direct study of nature. They were influenced by English and Dutch landscape masters. Theodore Rousseau, one of the principal figures of the group, led the fight for outdoor painting. In this respect, the school was a forerunner of Impressionism.

Baroque. European art and architecture of the 17th and 18th centuries. Giovanni Bernini, a major exponent of the style, believed in the union of the arts of architecture, painting, and sculpture to overwhelm the spectator with ornate and highly dramatized themes. Although the style originated in Rome as the instrument of the Church, it spread throughout Europe in such monumental creations as the Palace of Versailles.

Beaux Arts. Elaborate and formal architectural style characterized by symmetry and an abundance of sculptured ornamentation. New York's old Custom House at Bowling Green is an example of the style.

Black or Afro-American Art. The work of American artists of African descent produced in various styles characterized by a mood of protest and a search for identity and historical roots.

Classicism. A form of art derived from the study of Greek and Roman styles characterized by harmony, balance, and serenity. In contrast, the Romantic Movement gave free rein to the artist's imagination and to the love of the exotic.

Constructivism. A form of sculpture using wood, metal, glass, and modern industrial materials expressing the technological society. The mobiles of Alexander Calder are examples of the movement.

Cubism. Early 20th-century French movement marked by a revolutionary departure from representational art. Pablo Picasso and Georges Bracque penetrated the surface of objects, stressing basic abstract geometric forms that presented the object from many angles simultaneously.

Dada. A product of the turbulent and cynical post-World War I period, this anti-art movement extolled the irrational, the absurd, the nihilistic, and the nonsensical. The reproduction of *Mona Lisa* adorned with a mustache is a famous example. The movement is regarded as a precursor of Surrealism. Some critics regard HAPPENINGS as a recent development of Dada. This movement incorporates environment and spectators as active and important ingredients in the production of random events.

Expressionism. A 20th-century European art movement that stresses the expression of emotion and the inner vision of the artist rather than the exact representation of nature. Distorted lines and shapes and exaggerated colors are used for emotional impact. Vincent Van Gogh is regarded as the precursor of this movement.

Fauvism. The name "wild beasts" was given to this group of early 20th-century French painters because their work was characterized by distortion and violent colors. Henri Matisse and Georges Rouault were leaders of this group.

Futurism. This early 20th-century movement originating in Italy glorified the machine age and attempted to represent machines and figures in motion. The aesthetics of Futurism affirmed the beauty of technological society.

Genre. This French word meaning "type" now refers to paintings that depict scenes of everyday life without any attempt at idealization. Genre paintings can be found in all ages, but the Dutch productions of peasant and tavern scenes are typical.

Impressionism. Late 19th-century French school dedicated to defining transitory visual impressions painted directly from nature, with light and color of primary importance. If the atmosphere changed, a totally different picture would emerge. It was not the object or event that counted but the visual impression as caught at a certain time of day under a certain light. Claude Monet and Camille Pissarro were leaders of the movement.

Mannerism. A 17th-century movement, Italian in origin, although El Greco was a major practitioner of the style. The human figure, distorted and elongated, was the most frequent subject.

Neoclassicism. An 18th-century reaction to the excesses of Baroque and Rococo, this European art movement tried to recreate the art of Greece and Rome by imitating the ancient classics both in style and subject matter.

Op Art. The 1960s movement known as Optical Painting is characterized by geometrical forms that create an optical illusion in which the eye is required to blend the colors at a certain distance.

Pop Art. In this return to representational art, the artist returns to the world of tangible objects in a reaction against abstraction. Materials are drawn from the everyday world of popular culture—comic strips, canned goods, and science fiction.

Rococo. A French style of interior decoration developed during the reign of Louis XV consisting mainly of asymmetrical arrangements of curves in paneling, porcelain, and gold and silver objects. The characteristics of ornate curves, prettiness, and gaiety can also be found in the painting and sculpture of the period.

Surrealism. A further development of Collage, Cubism, and Dada, this 20th-century movement stresses the weird, the fantastic, and the dream-world of the subconscious. Salvador Dali's distorted timepiece in the desert is typical.

Search for Alexander

On the first leg of its U.S. tour, the exhibit *The Search for Alexander* was seen by 397,000 people at the National Gallery of Art in Washington, D.C. Before the tour ends in New York at the Metropolitan Museum, it will have visited Chicago, Boston, San Francisco, and New Orleans.

Top 10 Classical Albums, 1980

1. **O Solo Mio: Neopolitan Songs,** Luciano Pavarotti (London)
2. **Annie's Song,** James Galway, National Philharmonic Association, (Gerhardt), (RCA)
3. **Bravo Pavarotti,** Luciano Pavarotti (London)
4. **Pachelbel: Kanon,** Paillard Chamber Orchestra (RCA)
5. **Hits from Lincoln Center,** Luciano Pavarotti (London)
6. **Tchaikovsky: Violin Concerto,** Itzhak Perlman, Philadelphia Orchestra, (Ormandy), (Angel)
7. **Song of the Seashore,** James Galway (RCA)
8. **Tchaikovsky: 1812 Overture,** Cincinnati Orchestra, (Kunzel), (Telarc Digital)
9. **Brahms: Four Symphonies,** Chicago Symphony, (Solti), (London)
10. **Pavarotti's Greatest Hits,** Luciano Pavarotti (London)

Source: Billboard. © Billboard Publications, Inc., 1980. Dec. 20, 1980. Reprinted by permission.

Top 10 Pop Albums, 1980

1. **The Wall,** Pink Floyd (Columbia)
2. **The Long Run,** The Eagles (Asylum)
3. **Off the Wall,** Michael Jackson (Epic)
4. **Glass Houses,** Billy Joel (Columbia)
5. **Damn the Torpedoes,** Tom Petty & the Heartbreakers (Backstreet)
6. **Against the Wind,** Bob Seger & Silver Bullet Band (Capitol)
7. **In the Heat of the Night,** Pat Benatar (Chrysalis)
8. **Eat to the Beat,** Blondie (Chrysalis)
9. **In Through the Out Door,** Led Zeppelin (Swan Song)
10. **Kenny,** Kenny Rogers (United Artists)

Source: Billboard. © Billboard Publications, Inc., 1980. Dec. 20, 1980. Reprinted by permission.

Artists of the Year, 1980

Based on combined singles and albums chart performance—through sales and radio play—during the year.

Single of the Year: Call Me, Blondie
Album of the Year: The Wall, Pink Floyd
Female Artist of the Year: Donna Summer
Male Artist of the Year: Kenny Rogers
Group of the Year: Pink Floyd
New Artist of the Year: Christopher Cross
Country Artist of the Year: Kenny Rogers
Disco Artist of the Year: Change
Adult Contemporary Artist of the Year: Anne Murray
Jazz Artist of the Year: Spyro Gyra
Soundtrack of the Year: The Rose (Atlantic)

Source: Billboard. © Billboard Publications, Inc., 1980. Dec. 20, 1980. Reprinted by permission.

Top 10 Country Single Recordings, 1980

1. **My Heart/Silent Night (After the Fight),** Ronnie Milsap (RCA)
2. **One Day at a Time,** Cristy Lane (United Artists)
3. **He Stopped Loving Her Today,** George Jones (Epic)
4. **Dancin' Cowboys,** Bellamy Brothers (Warner/Curb)
5. **Tennessee River,** Alabama (RCA)
6. **Bar Room Buddies,** Merle Haggard & Clint Eastwood (Elektra)
7. **True Love Ways,** Mickey Gilley (Epic)
8. **Coward of the County,** Kenny Rogers (United Artists)
9. **Cowboys and Clowns,** Ronnie Milsap (RCA)
10. **Stand by Me,** Mickey Gilley (Asylum)

Source: Billboard. © Billboard Publications, Inc., 1980. Dec. 20, 1980. Reprinted by permission.

Top 10 Pop Single Recordings, 1980

1. **Call Me,** Blondie (Chrysalis)
2. **Another Brick in the Wall,** Pink Floyd (Columbia)
3. **Magic,** Olivia Newton-John (MCA)
4. **Rock with You,** Michael Jackson (Epic)
5. **Do That to Me One More Time,** Captain & Tennille (Casablanca)
6. **Crazy Little Thing Called Love,** Queen (Elektra)
7. **Coming Up,** Paul McCartney (Columbia)
8. **Funkytown,** Lipps Inc. (Casablanca)
9. **It's Still Rock & Roll to Me,** Billy Joel (Columbia)
10. **The Rose,** Bette Midler (Atlantic)

Source: Billboard. © Billboard Publications, Inc., 1980. Dec. 20, 1980. Reprinted by permission.

Manufacturers' Dollar Shipments of Phonograph Records

(in millions)

Year	Singles		Albums	
	Units	Dollars[1]	Units	Dollars[1]
1974	204	$194	276	$1,356
1975	164	212	257	1,485
1976	190	245	273	1,663
1977	190	245	344	2,195
1978	190	260	341	2,473
1979	212	354	290	2,058
1980	157	250	308	2,200

1. List price value. *Source:* Recording Industry Association of America, Inc.

Irresponsible Pet Owners Create Problems

More than 13 million dogs and cats are destroyed each year in animal shelters in the United States, representing the bulk of about 20 million pets no longer wanted by their owners. An estimated 5 million are just abandoned and presumably die from starvation, disease, or under the wheels of a car. Only some 2 million strays brought to shelters can be returned to their owners or placed in new homes. The bulk of these unwanted pets are the result of uncontrolled breeding. Pet owners should consider spaying to be one of the costs of owning a pet.

Audience Composition of Selected Prime Time Program Types

	General drama	Suspense and mystery drama	Situation comedy	Feature films	All regular network programs 7–11 p.m.
Women (18 years old and over)	17,750,000	11,240,000	14,190,000	10,550,000	11,920,000
Men (18 and over)	11,240,000	8,660,000	9,680,000	8,890,000	9,890,000
Teens (12–17)	3,000,000	2,290,000	3,150,000	2,440,000	2,570,000
Children (2–11)	3,920,000	1,150,000	4,750,000	2,200,000	3,140,000
Total	35,910,000	23,340,000	31,770,000	24,080,000	27,520,000

1. All figures are estimated for the period November 1980. *Source:* A. C. Nielsen Company, Nielsen Television Index Audience Estimates.

Top 15 Regular Prime Time TV Programs of 1980–81[1]

Rank	Program name (network)	Total percent of TV households
1.	Dallas (CBS)	34.9
2.	60 Minutes (CBS)	28.3
3.	Dukes of Hazzard (CBS)	26.7
4.	Love Boat (ABC)	25.7
5.	Alice (CBS)	25.6
6.	One Day at a Time (CBS)	25.2
7.	Jeffersons (CBS)	25.2
8.	Happy Days (ABC)	24.4
9.	Archie Bunker's Place (CBS)	24.2
10.	Three's Company (ABC)	23.3
11.	Laverne & Shirley (ABC)	23.0
12.	NBC Tuesday Night Movie (NBC)	22.6
13.	Too Close for Comfort (ABC)	22.1
14.	Little House on the Prairie (NBC)	22.1
15.	M*A*S*H (CBS)	22.0
	Total U.S. TV households	77,800,000

1. Oct. 27, 1980 through Nov. 23, 1980. NOTE: Percentages are calculated from average audience viewings, 15 minutes or longer and 4 or more telecasts. *Source:* A. C. Nielsen Company, Nielsen Television Index Audience Estimates.

Television Network Addresses

American Broadcasting Companies (ABC)
1330 Avenue of the Americas
New York, N.Y. 10019

Canadian Broadcasting Corporation (CBC)
1500 Bronson Avenue
Ottawa, Ontario, Canada K1G 3J5

Columbia Broadcasting System (CBS)
51 W. 52nd Street
New York, N.Y. 10019

Metromedia, Inc. (WNEW)
655 3rd Avenue
New York, N.Y. 10017

National Broadcasting Company (NBC)
30 Rockefeller Plaza
New York, N.Y. 10020

Public Broadcasting Service (PBS)
475 L'Enfant Plaza West, S.W.
Washington, D.C. 20024

Westinghouse Broadcasting (Group W)
90 Park Avenue
New York, N.Y. 10016

Source of Household Viewing—Prime Time
Pay Cable, Basic Cable, and Non-Cable Households

	July 1980			Nov. 1980			Feb. 1981		
	Pay cable	Basic cable	Non-cable	Pay cable	Basic cable	Non-cable	Pay cable	Basic cable	Non-cable
% TV Usage[1]	58.4	51.8	47.9	73.2	65.6	62.2	71.8	67.5	63.7
Pay Cable	13.2	—	—	10.9	—	—	11.8	—	—
Cable-originated programming	2.8	2.0	—	2.9	2.2	—	2.8	1.7	—
Other-on-Air stations	12.8	10.7	8.2	12.1	11.4	8.7	11.6	11.9	9.2
Network affiliated stations	32.5	40.2	40.4	50.9	53.8	54.7	49.7	55.3	55.7
Network Share[2]	(53)	(76)	(83)	(66)	(80)	(86)	(65)	(80)	(86)

1. May be less than sum of reception sources because of simultaneous viewing. 2. Percent Network/Sum of Sources. *Source:* A. C. Nielsen Company, Nielsen Television Index Estimates.

Weekly TV Viewing by Age
(in hours and minutes)

	Time per week	
	1980	1979
Women 18–34 years old	29 h 44 min	30 h 59 min
Women 35–54	33 h 31 min	35 h 21 min
Women 55 and over	38 h 26 min	40 h 28 min
Men 18–34	25 h 24 min	23 h 53 min
Men 35–54	27 h 28 min	27 h 06 min
Men 55 and over	35 h 39 min	35 h 35 min
Female Teens	22 h 19 min	24 h 11 min
Male Teens	23 h 40 min	24 h 03 min
Children 6–11	25 h 44 min	29 h 03 min
Children 2–5	29 h 14 min	32 h 47 min
Total Persons	29 h 46 min	31 h 19 min

NOTE: All figures are estimates based on National Audience Demographics Report, February 1979 and November 1980. *Source:* A. C. Nielsen Company, Nielsen Television Index Audience Estimates.

Persons Viewing Nightly Prime Time TV[1]
(in millions)

	Total persons[2]
Monday	90.1
Tuesday	93.8
Wednesday	90.2
Thursday	85.2
Friday	92.5
Saturday	89.2
Sunday	103.5
Total average	92.1

1. Average minute audiences. 2. Based on National Demographics Report (November 1980). NOTE: Prime time is 8-11 p.m. (EST), except 7-11 p.m. Sunday. *Source:* A. C. Nielsen Company, Nielsen Television Index Audience Estimates.

Average Hours of Household TV Usage
(in hours and minutes per day)

	Yearly average	February	July
1979–80	6 h 35 min	7 h 22 min	5 h 48 min
1978–79	6 h 26 min	7 h 11 min	5 h 46 min
1977–78	6 h 13 min	7 h 00 min	5 h 32 min
1976–77	6 h 13 min	6 h 55 min	5 h 13 min
1975–76	6 h 11 min	6 h 49 min	5 h 33 min
1970–71	6 h 01 min	6 h 53 min	5 h 08 min
1965–66	5 h 30 min	6 h 28 min	4 h 23 min

NOTE: Estimates are based on total U.S. TV households,-excluding unusual days. *Source:* A. C. Nielsen Company, Nielsen Television Index Audience Estimates.

Top 10 Syndicated TV Programs of 1980–81

Rank	Program	Rating (% U.S.)[1]
1.	M*A*S*H	12.8
2.	Muppets	12.0
3.	Hee Haw	9.9
4.	Family Feud (P.M.)	9.7
5.	Happy Days, Again	9.3
6.	Tic Tac Dough	8.9
7.	Lawrence Welk	8.8
8.	PM Magazine	8.7
9.	Donahue Show	6.6
10.	Sanford & Son	6.3

1. During November 1980. Ranked on the basis of average 15-minute audience ratings. *Source:* A.C. Nielsen Company, Nielsen Television Index Audience Estimates.

TOP RENTAL FILMS OF 1980

1.	The Empire Strikes Back (20th Century-Fox)	$120,000,000
2.	Kramer vs. Kramer (Columbia)	60,528,000
3.	The Jerk (Universal)	43,000,000
4.	Airplane (Paramount)	38,000,000
5.	Smokey and the Bandit II (Universal)	37,600,000
6.	Coal Miner's Daughter (Universal)	36,000,000
7.	Private Benjamin (Warner Bros.)	33,500,000
8.	The Blues Brothers (Universal)	31,000,000
9.	The Electric Horseman (Columbia)	30,917,000
10.	The Shining (Warner Bros.)	30,200,000
11.	The Blue Lagoon (Columbia)	28,456,000
12.	The Black Hole (Buena Vista)	25,000,000
13.	1941 (Universal)	23,400,000
14.	Urban Cowboy (Paramount)	22,700,000
15.	Cheech and Chong's Next Movie (Universal)	21,000,000
16.	All That Jazz (20th Century-Fox)	20,000,000
17.	Caddyshack (Warner Bros.)	20,000,000
18.	Brubaker (20th Century-Fox)	19,000,000
19.	Little Darlings (Paramount)	16,700,000
20.	Friday the 13th (Paramount)	16,500,000
21.	The Black Stallion (United Artists)	15,765,000
22.	Chapter Two (Columbia)	15,250,000
23.	Dressed to Kill (Filmways)	15,000,000
24.	Bronco Billy (Warner Bros.)	14,100,000
25.	Going in Style (Warner Bros.)	13,900,000

NOTE: United States and Canada only. *Source: Variety.*

1982 World's Fair To Be Held in Knoxville, Tenn.

Knoxville, Tenn. will be the host of the 1982 World's Fair, which will be open every day and evening from May 1 through October 31, 1982. The theme of this World's Fair, which has met the criteria of the Bureau of International Expositions in Paris, is "Energy Turns The World." Already signed up to build exhibits are Italy, France, West Germany, Britain, the European Economic Community, and Japan.

For additional information, write: The 1982 World's Fair, P.O. Box 1982, Knoxville, Tenn., U.S.A. Telephone (615)–971–1539. TWX/Telex No. 810–583–0582. For information on nearby accommodations and attractions, contact: KnoxVisit Convention and Tourist Bureau, Box 15012, Knoxville, Tenn. 37901.

Major U.S. Fairs and Expositions

1853 Crystal Palace Exposition, New York City: modeled on similar fair held in London.

1876 Centennial Exposition, Philadelphia: celebrating 100th year of independence.

1893 World's Columbian Exposition, Chicago: commemorating 400th anniversary of Columbus' voyage to America.

1894 Midwinter International Exposition, San Francisco: promoting business revival after Depression of 1893.

1898 Trans-Mississippi and International Exposition, Omaha, Neb.: exhibiting products, resources, industries, and civilization of states and territories west of the Mississippi River.

1901 Pan-American Exposition, Buffalo, N.Y.: promoting social and commercial interest of Western Hemisphere nations.

1904 Louisiana Purchase Exposition, St. Louis: marking 100th anniversary of major land acquisition from France and opening up of the West.

1905 Lewis and Clark Centennial Exposition, Portland, Ore.: commemorating 100th anniversary of exploration of a land route to the Pacific.

1907 Jamestown Ter Centennial Exposition, Hampton Roads, Va.: marking 300th anniversary of first permanent English settlement in America.

1909 Alaska-Yukon-Pacific Exposition, Seattle: celebrating growth of the Puget Sound area.

1915–16 Panama-Pacific International Exposition, San Francisco: celebrating opening of the Panama Canal.

1915–16 Panama-California Exposition, San Diego: promoting resources and opportunities for development and commerce of the Western states.

1926 Sesquicentennial Exposition, Philadelphia: marking 150th year of independence.

1933–34 Century of Progress International Exposition, Chicago: celebrating 100th anniversary of incorporation of Chicago as a city.

1935 California Pacific International Exposition, San Diego: marking 400 years of progress since the first Spaniard landed on the West Coast.

1939–40 New York World's Fair, New York City: "The World of Tomorrow," symbolized by Trylon and Perisphere. Officially commemorating 150th anniversary of inauguration of George Washington as President in New York.

1939–40 Golden Gate International Exposition, Treasure Island, San Francisco: celebrating new Golden Gate Bridge and Oakland Bay Bridge.

1962 The Century 21 Exposition, Seattle: "Man in the Space Age," symbolized by 600-foot steel space needle.

1964–65 New York World's Fair, New York City: "Peace Through Understanding."

1974 Expo '74, Spokane: "Tomorrow's Fresh, New Environment."

1982 World's Fair, Knoxville, Tenn.: "Energy Turns the World," symbolized by the bronze-globed Sunsphere.

For 1981 Emmy Awards see Current Events page 31

Plays and Movies

LONGEST BROADWAY RUNS[1]

1. Grease (M) (1972–80)	3,388
2. Fiddler on the Roof (M) (1964–72)	3,242
3. Life With Father (1939–47)	3,224
4. Tobacco Road (1933–41)	3,182
5. Hello, Dolly! (M) (1964–71)	2,844
6. My Fair Lady (M) (1956–62)	2,717
7. A Chorus Line (M) (1975–)	2,445
8. Man of La Mancha (M) (1965–71)	2,329
9. Abie's Irish Rose (1922–27)	2,327
10. Oklahoma! (M) (1943–48)	2,212
11. South Pacific (M) (1949–54)	1,925
12. Pippin (M) (1971–77)	1,908
13. Annie (M) (1977–)	1,860
14. The Magic Show (M) (1974–78)	1,859
15. Harvey (1944–49)	1,775
16. Hair (M) (1968–72)	1,742
17. The Wiz (M) (1975–79)	1,672
18. Born Yesterday (1946–49)	1,642
19. Mary, Mary (1961–64)	1,572
20. Voice of the Turtle (1943–48)	1,557
21. Barefoot in the Park (1963–67)	1,532
22. Deathtrap (1978–)	1,505
23. Mame (M) (1966–70)	1,503
24. Dancin' (M) (1978–)	1,471
25. Same Time, Next Year (1975–78)	1,444
25. Arsenic and Old Lace (1941–44)	1,444

TOP MONEY-MAKING FILMS[2]

1. Star Wars (1977)	$175,685,000
2. Jaws (1975)	133,435,000
3. The Empire Strikes Back (1980)	120,000,000
4. Grease (1978)	96,300,000
5. The Exorcist (1973)	88,500,000
6. The Godfather (1972)	86,275,000
7. Superman (1978)	82,500,000
8. The Sound of Music (1965)	79,748,000
9. The Sting (1973)	78,963,000
10. Close Encounters of the Third Kind (1977)	77,000,000
11. Gone With the Wind (1939)	76,700,000
12. Saturday Night Fever (1977)	74,100,000
13. National Lampoon's Animal House (1978)	74,000,000
14. Smokey and the Bandit (1977)	61,055,000
15. Kramer vs. Kramer (1979)	60,528,000
16. One Flew Over the Cuckoo's Nest (1975)	59,000,000
17. Star Trek (1979)	56,000,000
18. American Graffiti (1973)	55,886,000
19. Jaws II (1978)	55,608,000
20. Rocky (1976)	54,000,000
21. Every Which Way But Loose (1978)	51,800,000
22. Love Story (1970)	50,000,000
23. The Towering Inferno (1975)	49,400,000
24. Heaven Can Wait (1978)	49,400,000
25. The Graduate (1965)	49,078,000

1. As of Oct. 4, 1981. M = musical. Years are those of opening and closing. 2. Figures are rentals collected by film distributors in the U.S. and Canada as of Dec. 31, 1980. *Source: Variety.*

Museums of the United States

Source: Information Please questionnaires to museums

New York City

American Academy and Institute of Arts and Letters: 633 W. 155th St., NYC 10032. Open: Tues.-Sun. 1–4 during exhibitions (closed Mon. and natl. hldys.). Free.

Annual exhibitions of work of recipients of awards and honors, and paintings eligible for purchase under Hassam and Speicher Funds. Memorial exhibition of work of deceased members.

American Museum of Natural History: Central Park West at 79th St., NYC 10024. Open: Mon., Tues., Thurs., Fri. 10–4:45, Wed. 10–8, Sat., Sun., and hldys. 10–5. Suggested adm.: $2.50 (children, $1.50).

All branches of natural sciences with exhibits including astronomy at American Museum-Hayden Planetarium.

Brooklyn Museum, The: 188 Eastern Pkwy., Brooklyn, N.Y. 11238. Open: Wed.-Sat. 10–5, Sun. 12–5, hldys. 1–5 (closed Jan. 1, Dec. 25). Suggested voluntary admission fee, $1.50; children under 12 and senior citizens, free.

Egyptian and classical art, American and European paintings, decorative arts and period rooms, prints, drawings, costumes, and textiles. Arts of Africa, Oceania, Orient, Middle East, Islam, and New World. Two reference libraries, sculpture garden.

Cloisters, The: Ft. Tryon Pk., NYC 10040. Open: Tues.-Sat. 10–4:45; Sun. and hldys. 1–4:45 (May-Sept. 12–4:45) (closed Mon.).Suggested adm.: $3 (students and senior citizens, $1.50).

Cloisters, chapel, chapter house, apse. The various cloisters are reconstituted from elements of 12–15th-century French cloisters. Apse has been relocated here in its entirety. Frescoes, polychromed statues, stained glass, tapestries, paintings, ivories, precious metalwork. Medieval branch of The Metropolitan Museum of Art.

Cooper-Hewitt Museum, the Smithsonian Institution's National Museum of Design: 2 E. 91st St., NYC 10028. Open: Tues. 10–9, Wed.-Sat. 10–5, Sun. 12–5 (closed Mon.; also Jan. 1, July 4, Thanksgiving, Dec. 25). Adm. $1.50 (free on Tues. after 5:30).

Over 300,000 decorative arts objects and related library housed in 64-room former Carnegie mansion.

Frick Collection: 1 E. 70th St., NYC 10021. Open: Sept.-May—Tues.-Sat. 10–6, Sun. and most hldys. 1–6 (closed Mon.; also Jan. 1, Thanksgiving, Dec. 24–25); June-Aug.—Sun. 1–6, Wed.-Sat. 10–6 (closed Mon. and Tues.; also July 4). Adm. Tues.-Sat. $1 (students and senior citizens, 50¢); Sun. $2. Children under 10 not admitted.

Paintings, prints, drawings of 14th to 19th centuries, Italian Renaissance and French sculpture and furniture. Chinese and French porcelain. Concerts, lectures.

Guggenheim Museum, The Solomon R.: 1071 Fifth Ave. at 88th St., NYC 10028. Open: Tues. 11–8; Wed.-Sun. and hldys. 11–5 (closed Mon., except hldys., and Dec. 25). Adm. $2 (children under 7, free). Tues. 5–8 free. College students with ID's, and senior citizens, $1.25; school children in groups of 10 with a teacher, 75¢.

Works of leading 20th-century foreign and American painters and sculptors.

Hayden Planetarium. *See* American Museum of Natural History.

Hispanic Society of America, The (Museum and Library): Broadway and W. 155th St., NYC 10032. Museum open: Tues.-Sat. 10–4:30, Sun. 1–4 (closed Mon.; also Jan. 1, Feb. 12, Feb. 22, Good Friday, Easter, May 30, July 4, Oct. 12, Thanksgiving, Dec. 25). During Christmas Week, museum is open for three consecutive days from Dec. 26 through Dec. 31. Library open: Tues.-Fri. 1–4:30, Sat. 10:30–4:30 (closed Sun., Mon.; also hldys., Good Friday, month of Aug., and for two weeks beginning Tues. before Christmas Eve). Free.

Paintings, sculpture, decorative arts, manuscripts, and incunabula, representative of Hispanic culture. Works on Hispanic art, history, literature.

Jewish Museum, The: 1109 Fifth Ave. at 92nd St., NYC 10028. Open: Mon.-Thurs., 12–5, Sun. 11–6 (closed Fri. and Sat., major Jewish hldys. and certain legal hldys.). Adm. $2 (children 6–16 and students with ID's, $1). Members, free; senior citizens, pay what you wish.

Former Warburg mansion and adjoining Albert A. List building house most extensive collection of Jewish ceremonial objects in Western Hemisphere. Changing exhibitions of sculpture, paintings, photography and architecture illuminate Jewish experience, culture, and tradition. Also family and school programs.

Metropolitan Museum of Art, The: Fifth Ave. at 82nd St., NYC 10028. Open: Tues. 10–8:45, Wed.-Sat. 10–4:45, Sun. and hldys. 11–4:45 (closed Mon.). Discretionary admission fee.

Comprehensive collection of European and American paintings, drawings, sculpture, decorative arts, prints. Egyptian, Greek, Roman, Islamic, and Near and Far Eastern art. Musical instruments, arms and armor. European period rooms. Costumes and textiles. See also Cloisters.

Museum of the American Indian, Heye Foundation: Broadway at 155th St., NYC 10032. Open: Tues.-Sat. 10–5; Sun. 1–5 (closed Mon., also Jan. 1, Easter, July 4, Thanksgiving, Dec. 25). Adm. $1.50 (students and senior citizens, 75¢); groups of 10 or more, 25¢ per person.

Archeology, ethnology, and primitive-to-20th-century arts and artifacts of North, Central, and South America.

Museum of the City of New York: 1220 Fifth Ave. at 103rd St., NYC 10029. Open: Tues.-Sat. 10–5, Sun. and hldys. 1–5 (closed Mon.; also Dec. 25). Free.

History and life of New York City. Period costumes, furniture, miniature scenes, portraits, paintings, prints, manuscripts, theater and music collection, silver, dolls and doll houses.

Museum of Modern Art, The: 11 W. 53rd St., NYC 10019. Open: Mon., Tues., Fri., Sat. and Sun. 11–6, Thurs. 11–9 (closed Wed.; also Dec. 25). Adm. $2.50 (full-time students with ID's, $1.50; children and senior citizens, 75¢; members, free). Tuesday, pay what you wish.

Founded 1929 to help people enjoy and understand the art of our times. Changing exhibitions of contemporary painting, sculpture, drawings, prints, photography, architecture, industrial and graphic design, films, video.

National Academy of Design: 1083 Fifth Ave. at 89th St., NYC 10028. Open: Tues.-Sun. 12–5.

Exhibitions from permanent collection of Ameri

can paintings, sculptures and graphics; exhibitions of contemporary art.

New-York Historical Society: 170 Central Park West at 77th St., NYC 10024. Museum open; Tues.-Fri. 11-5, Sat. 10-5, Sun. 1-5. Library open to adults: Tues.-Sat. 10-5. (Both closed Mon.; also Jan. 1, July 4, Thanksgiving, Dec. 25). Library adm. $1 to nonmembers; museum, discretionary fee of $1.50 for adults, 75¢ for children.

New York city and state historical exhibits. Early American paintings and portraits. Period rooms. Audubon watercolors. Gallery of American silver.

Pierpont Morgan Library: 29 E. 36th St. NYC 10016. Open: Tues.-Sat. 10:30-5, Sun. 1-5 (closed Mon.; also legal hldys., Sundays in July, and month of August).

Medieval and Renaissance illuminated manuscripts, rare books, music and autograph manuscripts, old master drawings, bindings, early children's books, ancient written records.

Whitney Museum of American Art: 945 Madison Ave. at 75th St., NYC 10021. Open: Wed.-Sat. 11-6, Tues. 11-8 (free 5-8), Sun. and hldys. 12-6 (closed Mon.; also Dec. 25). Adm. $2 (senior citizens, college students with ID, and children under 12 accompanied by an adult, free).

Sculpture, paintings, watercolors, drawings, and prints by 20th-century American artists. Exhibitions of contemporary and historical American art. Daily film and video showings; occasional performing arts programs.

Chicago

Art Institute of Chicago, The: Michigan Ave. at Adams St., Chicago, Ill. 60603. Open: Mon.-Wed. and Fri. 10:30-4:30, Thurs. 10:30-8, Sat. 10-5, Sun. and hldys. 12-5 (Closed Dec. 25). Voluntary admission fee.

Paintings, sculpture, prints, drawings, textiles, photography. Oriental arts; European, American decorative arts; primitive art. Thorne Miniature Rooms. Junior Museum. Goodman Theatre, School of Art.

Beverly Art Center: 2153 W. 111th St., Chicago, Ill. 60643. Open: daily 9 a.m.-10 p.m.

Exhibitions change monthly.

Chicago Academy of Sciences, Museum of Ecology: Lincoln Park—2001 North Clark St., Chicago, Ill. 60614. Open: daily 10-5 (closed Dec. 25). Free.

Exhibits of ecology of animal and plant life, minerals and fossils of Great Lakes region. Walk-through coal forest, cave, and canyon. Lectures, field trips, movies.

Chicago Historical Society: Clark St. and North Ave., Chicago, Ill. 60614. Open: Mon.-Sat. 9:30-4:30, Sun. 12-5 (closed Jan. 1, Thanksgiving, Dec. 25). Adults, $1; children 6-17, 50¢; senior citizens, 25¢. Free admission Monday. Research collection open Tues.-Sat. 9:30-4:30.

Exhibits and collections relating to Chicago and Illinois history, Illinois pioneer crafts, American history, Lincoln, Civil War.

Field Museum of Natural History: Roosevelt Rd. at Lake Shore Dr., Chicago, Ill. 60605. Open: Daily at 9 a.m. to as early as 4 p.m. in winter and as late as 9 p.m. in summer (closed Jan. 1, Dec. 25). Adm: families, $4; adults, $2; children (6-17) and students with ID's, $1; senior citizens, 50¢. Free on Fri. (9-9). Free at all times to members, teachers, members of the armed forces, and children under 6.

Dioramas of plants, animals and fossils, rocks and geological fragments, and artifacts of early civilizations.

Museum of Science and Industry: 57th St. and Lake Shore Dr., Chicago, Ill. 60637. Open: Memorial Day-Labor Day 9:30-5:30; rest of year, Mon.-Fri. 9:30-4, Sat., Sun. and hldys. 9:30-5:30 (closed Dec. 25). Free (small fee to four exhibits).

Operating coal mine, captured German submarine, giant heart, Paul Bunyan house, Colleen Moore's Fairy Castle, The Farm, the Apollo 8 spacecraft, Sears' Cinema Circus, computerized "Food for Life," historic and advanced forms of planes, ships, trains, and cars.

Oriental Institute Museum of the University of Chicago: 1155 E. 58th St., Chicago, Ill. 60637. Open: Tues.-Sat. 10-4, Sun. 12-4 (closed Mon. and hldys.). Free.

Ancient Near Eastern objects, including 40-ton human-headed winged bull from Khorsabad in Assyria, 16-ft. statue of Tutankhamen from Egypt, colossal bull's head from Persepolis; glyptic, bronze, and ivory artifacts.

Vanderpoel (John H.) Memorial Art Gallery: 2135 W. 111th St., Chicago, Ill. 60643. Open: Tues.-Thurs. and Sun. 1-4 (closed Mon., Fri., Sat. and hldys.).

Paintings, watercolors, etchings, scuplture contributed by the artists in tribute to Mr. Vanderpoel.

Washington, D.C.

Anacostia Neighborhood Museum, Smithsonian Institution: 2405 Martin Luther King, Jr., Ave. SE, Washington, D.C. 20020. Open: Mon.-Fri. 10-6, Sat. and Sun. 1-6 (closed Dec. 25). Free.

Exhibits on Afro-American history, urban problems, art. Programs for children.

Arts and Industries Building, Smithsonian Institution: 900 Jefferson Dr. SW, Washington, D.C. 20560. Open: daily 10-5:30; summer 10-9 (closed Dec. 25). Free.

Constructed to house exhibits from 1876 Centennial Exhibition, building has been restored as nearly as possible to original appearance.

Corcoran Gallery of Art: 17th St. and New York Ave. NW, Washington, D.C. 20006. Open: Tues.-Sun. 10-4:30, until 9 on Thurs. (closed Mon.; also Jan. 1, July 4, Thanksgiving, Dec. 25). Free.

Comprehensive collection of American paintings, sculpture, graphics. Choice selection of European art.

Freer Gallery of Art, Smithsonian Institution: Jefferson Dr. at 12th St. SW, Washington, D.C. 20560. Open: daily 10-5:30 (closed Dec. 25). Free.

Oriental paintings, sculpture, bronzes, pottery, and metal work. Early Christian manuscripts. One of largest Whistler collections.

Hirshhorn Museum and Sculpture Garden, Smithsonian Institution: Eighth St. at Independence Ave. SW, Washington, D.C. 20560. Open: daily, 10-5:30; summer, 10-9 (closed Dec. 25). Free.

More than 7,000 works tracing development of modern painting and sculpture since 19th century. Rodin, Moore, Picasso, Calder, Miró, and Matisse among those represented.

Museum of African Art, Smithsonian Institution: 324 A St. NE, Washington, D.C. 20560. Open: Mon.-Fri. 11-5; Sat. and Sun. 12-5 (closed Dec. 25). Free.

Creative Heritage of Africa displayed and studied through collection of over 8,000 objects.

National Air and Space Museum, Smithsonian Institution: Independence Ave. bet. 4th and 7th Sts. SW, Washington, D.C. 20560. Open: daily 10-5:30, summer 10-9 (closed Dec. 25). Free.

Exhibits on aviation and space age; Wright Broth-

ers' Kitty Hawk Flyer, *Lindbergh's* Spirit of St. Louis.

National Gallery of Art: Constitution Ave. bet. 3rd and 7th Sts. NW, Washington, D.C. 20565. Open: Mon.-Sat. 10–5, Sun. 12–9[1] (closed Jan. 1, Dec. 25). Free.
> *Paintings, sculpture, drawings, prints, decorative arts given by Mellon, Kress, Widener, Rosenwald, Dale, Harriman, and others. Index of American Design.*

National Museum of American Art, Smithsonian Institution: Eighth and G Sts. NW, Washington, D.C. 20560. Open: daily 10–5:30 (closed Dec. 25). Free.
> *Collections survey 300 years of American art. Over 23,000 paintings, sculptures, and graphics.*

National Museum of American History, Smithsonian Institution: 14th St. and Constitution Ave. NW, Washington, D.C. 20560. Open: daily 10–5:30, summer 10–9 (closed Dec. 25). Free.
> *Exhibits showing scientific, technological, and cultural development feature original Star-Spangled Banner, costumes and furnishings, gowns of First Ladies, inventions, stamps, coins, musical instruments, ceramics, and crafts.*

National Museum of Natural History and National Museum of Man, Smithsonian Institution: 10th St. and Constitution Ave. NW, Washington, D.C. 20560. Open: daily 10–5:30, summer 10–9. (closed Dec. 25). Free.
> *Origin, development, and physical characteristics of man. Dioramas of peoples and animals in natural settings. Land and sea mammals, birds, fish, reptiles, and gems, minerals, meteorites, volcanoes, prehistoric animals, fossils. Hope Diamond. Insect Zoo.*

National Portrait Gallery, Smithsonian Institution: Eighth and F Sts. NW, Washington, D.C. 20560. Open: daily 10–5:30 (closed Dec. 25). Free.
> *Only major museum in hemisphere devoted exclusively to portraiture. Exhibits likenesses in all media of persons who have made significant contributions to U.S. history, development, and culture.*

Renwick Gallery, Smithsonian Institution: 17th St. and Pennsylvania Ave. NW, Washington, D.C. 20560. Open: daily 10–5:30 (closed Dec. 25). Free.
> *American crafts, decorative arts, and design, housed in a mid-19th-century building restored to its original appearance.*

Smithsonian Institution Building: 1000 Jefferson Dr. SW, Washington, D.C. 20560. Open: daily 10–5:30, summer 10–9 (closed Dec. 25). Free.
> *Information center and James Smithson's tomb are in original building. Institution maintains the museums and art galleries indicated above; also Cooper-Hewitt Museum in New York City, National Zoological Park in Washington, D.C., and research facilities elsewhere.*

Philadelphia

Academy of Natural Sciences of Philadelphia: 19th St. and the Parkway, Philadelphia, Pa. 19103. Natural History Museum open: daily 10–4 (closed Jan. 1, Thanksgiving, Dec. 25). Adm. $2.25 (students, senior citizens, military personnel, $2; children $1.75).
> *Exhibits on dinosaurs and extinct species; animal, bird, and gem displays. Live animal shows daily.*

Franklin Institute, The: 20th St. and the Parkway, Philadelphia, Pa. 19103. Open: Mon.-Sat. 10–5, Sun. 12–5 (closed Jan. 1, Memorial Day, July 4,

Thanksgiving, Dec. 24–25). Adm: $3.50; (senior citizens, $1.50; students, $2.50; children 4–11, $2; children under 4, free.)
> *Nonprofit educational and research institution operating science museum, planetarium, library, and research laboratories.*

Pennsylvania Academy of the Fine Arts: Broad and Cherry Sts., Philadelphia, Pa. 19102. Open: Tues.-Sat. 10–5, Sun. 1–5 (closed Jan. 1, Dec. 25). Adm. $1 (children under 12, students and senior citizens, 50¢).
> *Oldest art museum and school in U.S. Collection devoted to American art. Lectures, concerts. Multi-media exhibitions.*

Philadelphia Museum of Art: 26th St. and the Parkway, Philadelphia, Pa. 19130. Open: Wed.-Sun. 10–5 (closed major hldys.). Adm. $2 (children and senior citizens, $1), (free Sun. 10–1).
> *Paintings, drawings, prints, from old masters to present. Sculpture, decorative arts, period rooms and armor. Oriental collections. New American Wing open. Rodin Museum at Parkway and 22nd St. Colonial Houses in Fairmount Park. Samuel S. Fleisher Art Memorial, 715–19 Catharine St.*

Museums In Other Cities

Addison Gallery of American Art: Phillips Academy, Andover, Mass. 01810. Open: Tues.-Sat. 10–5, Sun. 2:30–5 (closed Mon.; also natl. hldys.). Free.
> *Paintings, sculpture, graphics, photographs of 18th, 19th, and 20th centuries. Changing contemporary exhibitions.*

Alabama, Museum of Natural History of: Smith Hall, on campus of U. of Alabama, Tuscaloosa, Ala. 35486. Open: Mon.-Fri. 8–5. Free.
> *All phases of natural history. See also Mound State Monument Museum.*

Albright-Knox Art Gallery: 1285 Elmwood Ave., Buffalo, N.Y. 14222. Open: Tues.-Sat. 10–5; Sun. 12–5 (closed Mon.; also Jan. 1, Thanksgiving, Dec. 25). Voluntary admission fee.
> *Comprehensive collection of contemporary paintings; 18th-19th-century English, French, and American paintings. Sculpture since 3000 B.C.*

Atomic Energy, American Museum of: *See* Science and Energy, American Museum of.

Baltimore Museum of Art: Art Museum Dr., Baltimore, Md. 21218. Open: Tues.-Sat. 11–5, Thurs. evening 7–10 (except in summer). Sun. 1–5 (closed Mon.). Free.
> *Paintings, sculpture, graphics, 2nd-6th-century mosaics from Antioch. Concerts, dance recitals, educational programs for all ages.*

Baseball Hall of Fame and Museum, National: Main St., Cooperstown, N.Y. 13326. Open: May-Oct. 9–9, Nov.-Apr. 9–5 (closed Jan. 1, Thanksgiving, Dec. 25). Adm. $3.50 (children 7–15, $1.50).
> *Memorabilia, pictures, documents of baseball history. Bronze plaques of game's immortals. Baseball movies shown daily. See also Hall of Fame in index.*

Berkshire Museum, The: 39 South St., Pittsfield, Mass. 01201. Open: Tues.-Sat. 10–5, Sun. 1–5 (closed Mon.; also Jan. 1, July 4, Thanksgiving, Dec 25). Open Mon. in July and Aug. Free.
> *Painting, sculpture, decorative arts—ancient to modern. Loan exhibits. Galleries on biology, birds, man, minerals, and American history. Live exhibits. Junior Department. Movies, lectures.*

Birmingham Museum of Art: 2000 Eighth Ave North, Birmingham, Ala. 35203. Open: Tues.-Wed. Fri. and Sat. 10–5, Thurs. 10–9, Sun. 2–6 (closed

Mondays; also Jan. 1, Dec. 25). Free.

Kress Collection of Italian art; 17th-century Dutch, Flemish, and English paintings; 19th-century American paintings; Beeson Wedgwood Collection; art of Old West, including Remington bronzes; modern American paintings; silver, porcelain; Oriental art.

(Boston) Museum of Fine Arts: Huntington Ave., Boston, Mass. 02115. Open: (entire museum): Tues. and Thurs.-Sun. 10–5; Wed. 10–10; (West Wing only): Thurs. and Fri. 5–10 (closed Mon.; also Jan. 1, July 4, Labor Day, Thanksgiving, and Dec. 24–25). Adm. $3; senior citizens, $2; members and children 16 and under, free.

European and American paintings, sculpture, furniture, interiors, tapestries, textiles, silver, costumes, musical instruments. Prints, drawings, watercolors. Egyptian, Asiatic, contemporary collections.

Buffalo Museum of Science: Humboldt Parkway, Buffalo, N.Y. 14211. Open: Mon.-Thurs. and Sat. 10–5; Fri. 10–10; Sun. and hldys. 10–5 (Jan. 1 and July 4, 1–5) (closed Dec. 25). Free.

Exhibits of astronomy, geology, zoology, botany, anthropology. Kellogg Observatory.

California Academy of Sciences: Golden Gate Park, San Francisco, Calif. 94118. Open: daily 10–5. Adm. $1 (children 12–17, 50¢; under 12 and senior citizens, 25¢). Free adm. first Wed. of month.

North American and African habitat groups. Astronomical exhibits, clocks, watches, lamps, minerals, fossils, plants. Steinhart Aquarium, Morrison Planetarium, Wattis Hall of Man.

California Palace of the Legion of Honor: 34th Ave. and Clement St., Lincoln Park, San Francisco, Calif. 94121. Open: Wed.-Sun. 10–5. Adm. $1.50 (youths 6–18 and senior citizens, 50¢; under 6, free). Free adm. first Wed. of month.

Devoted to arts of France: paintings, sculpture, and decorative arts; prints and drawings of all periods.

Carnegie Institute: 4400 Forbes Ave., Pittsburgh, Pa. 15213. Open: Tues.-Sat. 10–5, Sun. 1–5 (closed Mon. and major hldys.). Suggested contributions: Adults, $1.50; children and students, 75¢. Sat. free.

Museum of Art: European and American paintings, sculpture, and decorative arts. Carnegie Museum of Natural History. Hillman Hall of Minerals and Gems.

Cincinnati Art Museum: Eden Park, Cincinnati, Ohio 45202. Open: wkdys. 10–5, Sun. and hldys. 1–5 (closed Mon. and major hldys.). Adm. $1.25 (children 12–18, 50¢; 11 and under, free). Free to everyone on Sat.

European and American painting, prints, photographs, decorative arts, sculpture, costumes. Egyptian, Greco-Roman, Medieval, Near and Far Eastern arts. Ancient musical instruments.

Clark (Sterling and Francine) Art Institute: Williamstown, Mass. 01267. Open: daily except Monday, 10–5 (closed Jan. 1, Thanksgiving, Dec. 25). Free.

Paintings from 14th to 19th centuries, including works by Corot, Renoir, Degas, Toulouse-Lautrec, Homer; sculpture, antique silver, prints and drawings.

Cleveland Museum of Art: 11150 East Boulevard, Cleveland, Ohio 44106. Open: Tues. 10–6, Wed. 10 –10, Thurs. and Fri. 10–6, Sat. 9–5, Sun. 1–6 (closed Mon.; also Jan. 1, July 4, Thanksgiving, Dec. 25). Free.

Paintings, sculpture, graphic arts, furniture, silver, gold, arms, armor, textiles, ceramics from all cultures and periods.

Cleveland Museum of Natural History: Wade Oval,

University Circle, Cleveland, Ohio 44106. Open: Mon.-Sat. 10–5, Sun. 1–5:30 (closed Jan. 1, Memorial Day, July 4, Labor Day, Thanksgiving, Dec. 24–25). Adm. $2 (children 6–18 and senior citizens, 50¢). Free Tues. after 1.

Dinosaurs, area fossils, minerals, birds, mammals, insects, reptiles, plants. American Indian and Eskimo displays. Planetarium, observatory. Hall of Man's Ecology, Hall of Earth Science.

Colonial Williamsburg: Williamsburg, Va. 23185. Open: daily. Adm. $9 and $13; children 6–12 half price; under 6 free.

Restored 18th-century capital of Colonial Virginia; 173 acres of colonial city with more than 40 exhibition homes, craft shops, and public buildings; 90 acres of gardens; outdoor events; colonial lodging and dining.

Colorado Springs Fine Arts Center: 30 W. Dale St., Colorado Springs, Colo. 80903. Open: Tues.-Sat. 10–5; Sun. 1:30–5 (closed Mon.; also selected hldys.). Free.

Art produced within limits of U.S. from prehistoric to contemporary, including decorative and fine arts. Survey of arts of world. Drama, dance, and music programs.

Columbus Museum of Art: 480 E. Broad St., Columbus, Ohio 43215. Open: Tues., Thurs., Fri., and Sun. 11–5; Wed. 11–8:30; Sat. 10–5 (closed Mon.). Adm. $1.50 (children 6–17, students, and senior citizens, 50¢). Tues. free.

European paintings from 16th to 20th century; 19th- and 20th-century American and European paintings, sculpture, and works on paper. Chinese and Japanese ceramics. European and American decorative arts. Sculpture Park and Garden.

Corning Glass Center: Dept. IP, Corning, N.Y. 14831. Open daily 9–5 (closed Jan. 1, Thanksgiving, Dec. 24–25). Adm.: $2; youths 6–17, $1; children with adult free; family maximum, $5.

New museum building has comprehensive collection of glass dating from 1500 B.C. Demonstrations of making of glass and its uses in Hall of Science and Industry. Artisans handcraft and engrave crystal in Steuben factory.

Currier Gallery of Art, The: 192 Orange St., Manchester, N.H. 03104. Open: Tues., Wed., Fri., and Sat. 10–4; Sun. 2–5; Thurs. 10–10 (closed Mon. and major hldys.). Free.

European and American paintings, 13th-20th century. American decorative arts, 18th-19th century, including New England furniture, silver, pewter, and early glass.

Delaware Art Museum, The: 2301 Kentmere Pkwy., Wilmington, Del. 19806. Open: Mon.-Sat. 10–5, Sun. 1–5. Adm.: $1 (youths 12–18 and students, 50¢; children under 12, members, and senior citizens, free).

English pre-Raphaelite; 19th- and 20th-century American art; complete set of John Sloan's graphic work; Paintings by Wyeth, Homer and Hooper; American photography. Art reference library.

Denver Art Museum, The: 100 W. 14th Ave. Parkway, Denver, Colo. 80204. Open: Tues.-Sat. 9–5, Sun. 1–5; also Wed. 9–9 p.m.

Art from nearly every culture and period.

Denver Museum of Natural History: City Park, Denver, Colo. 80205. Open: Mon.-Sat. 9–4:30, Sun. and hldys. 12–4:30 (closed Jan. 1, Thanksgiving, Dec. 24–25, Dec. 31). Free.

Sixty-six life-size ecological habitat dioramas. Animals from four continents, earth-science exhibits, dinosaurs, displays of fossil mammals and historic native Americans. Planetarium (small charge).

Des Moines Art Center: Greenwood Park, 45th St. and Grand Ave., Des Moines, Iowa 50312. Open: Tues.-Sat. 11–5, Sun. 12–5. Free.

Permanent collection includes Calder, Rodin, Arp, Bellows, Johns, Hopper, Giacometti, David Smith, and Morris Louis, among others.

Detroit Historical Museum: 5401 Woodward Ave., Detroit, Mich. 48202. Open: Tues., Thurs., Fri., Sat. 9:30–5; Wed. 1–9; Sun. 1–5 (closed Mon. and legal hldys.).

"Streets of Old Detroit" recreates periods of 1840, 1870, and 1905; historic fashions, period rooms, automobile collection. Marine exhibits at Dossin Great Lakes Museum on Belle Isle; military history exhibits at historic Ft. Wayne, West Jefferson at foot of Livernois.

Detroit Institute of Arts, The: 5200 Woodward Ave., Detroit, Mich. 48202. Open: Tues.-Sun. 9:30–5:30 (closed Mon.; also legal hldys.). Voluntary admission fee.

Paintings, sculpture, decorative arts from ancient times to modern.

Dickson Mounds Museum: off Route 97–78 near Lewistown, Ill. 61542. Open: Daily 8:30–5 (closed Jan. 1, Easter, Thanksgiving, Dec. 25). Free.

Museum of anthropology with exhibits relating to prehistoric American Indian.

Farmers' Museum: Lake Rd., Route 80, Cooperstown, N.Y. 13326. Open: summer season, daily. 9–5; winter season, Tues.-Sat. 9–5, Sun. 1–5 (closed Mon.; also Jan. 1, Thanksgiving, Dec. 25). Adm. $3.50³ (children $1.50).

Re-created village crossroads. Early farm and handicraft tools. School house, country store, smithy, print shop, doctor's and lawyer's offices, pharmacy, tavern, church, farm unit. Cardiff Giant. Operated by New York State Historical Association.

Fenimore House: Lake Rd., Route 80, Cooperstown, N.Y. 13326. Open: summer season, daily 9–5; Nov., Dec., and April, Tues.-Sat. 9–5, Sun. 1–5 (closed Mon.; also Jan., Feb., March, Dec. 25). Adm: $3³ (children $1.25).

American portraits, genre paintings. Browere life masks of Founding Fathers. James Fenimore Cooper memorabilia. Folk art. Library. Operated by New York State Historical Association.

Florida State Museum, University of Florida: Museum Road, Gainesville, Fla. 32611. Open: Mon.-Fri. 9–5, Sat. 9–5, Sun. 1–5 (closed Dec. 25). Free.

State and University museum with research and exhibition emphasis on natural and anthropological history of Florida, southeastern United States, and Caribbean area.

Fogg Art Museum: Harvard University, 32 Quincy St., Cambridge, Mass. 02138. Open: Mon.-Fri. 9–5, Sat. 10–5, Sun. 2–5 (closed weekends from July 1 to Labor Day; also natl. hldys.). Free.

Collections illustrate evolution of Eastern and Western art from ancient to modern times. Chinese sculpture and bronzes; Romanesque sculpture; Italian primitives; French 19th-century paintings; European drawings and prints.

Gardner (Isabella Stewart) Museum: 2 Palace Road, Boston, Mass. 02115. Open: Tues., 1–9:30, Wed.-Sun. 1–5:30. July-Aug., Tues.-Sun. 1–5:30 (closed natl. hldys.). Adm.: Suggested contribution, $1, lesser amount acceptable.

Paintings, 14th-20th centuries, in building of Venetian palace style. Sculpture, tapestries, furniture. Flowering courtyard. Free tours on Thursday at 2:30 p.m.

Getty (J. Paul) Museum, The: 17985 Pacific Coast

Hgwy., Malibu, Calif. 90265. Open: Mon.-Fri. 10–5 (June-Sept.), Tues.-Sat. 10–5 (Oct.-May), (closed Jan. 1, Feb. 22, Memorial Day, July 4, Labor Day, Thanksgiving, Dec. 25). Free. Parking reservations for guaranteed admission are required (213 454–6541).

Re-creation of Roman seaside villa destroyed by Vesuvius in 79 A.D. Greek and Roman antiquities, Western European paintings, 18th-century French decorative arts. Research library.

Heard Museum: 22 East Monte Vista Rd., Phoenix, Ariz. 85004. Open: Mon.-Sat. 10–5, Sun. 1–5 (closed hldys.). Adm.: $1.50; (senior citizens, $1; children and students, 50¢).

Anthropology and primitive arts, with emphasis on rich heritage of Southwest.

High Museum of Art, The: 1280 Peachtree St. NE, Atlanta, Ga. 30309. Open: Tues.-Sat. 10–5, Sun. 12–5 (closed Mon.; natl. hldys.). Free.

Paintings and sculpture from 14th to 18th century in Samuel H. Kress Collection. Ralph K. Uhry Print Collection; decorative arts; Richman Collection of African Art; 18th-century European porcelains; photography, contemporary art.

(Houston) Museum of Fine Arts, The: 1001 Bissonnet at Main, Houston, Tex. 77005. Open: Tues.-Sat. 10–5, Sun. 12–6 (closed Mon.; also Jan. 1, July 4, Thanksgiving, Dec. 25). Free.

American and European art through 20th century; Southwest American Indian art and artifacts; early American furniture and decorative arts; pre-Columbian and Far Eastern art; native arts from Africa, Australia, South Pacific. Impressionist and post-Impressionist paintings. 20th-century photography.

Huntington Library, Art Gallery, and Botanical Gardens: 1151 Oxford Rd., San Marino, Calif. 91108. Open: Tues.-Sun. 1–4:30; (reservations required on Sun.) (closed Mon.; also month of Oct., Jan. 1, Easter, Memorial Day, July 4, Labor Day, Thanksgiving, Dec. 25). Free.

18th-century British and European paintings, including Gainsborough's "Blue Boy" and Lawrence's "Pinkie." Manuscript and rare-book exhibits include Gutenberg Bible, Franklin's Autobiography in his handwriting. Botanical gardens. Research library.

Illinois State Museum: Spring and Edwards Sts., Springfield, Ill. 62706. Open: Mon.-Sat. 8:30–5, Sun. 1:30–5 (closed Jan. 1, Easter, Thanksgiving, Dec. 25). Free.

Museum of natural history, anthropology, and art with emphasis on wild-life and early inhabitants of Illinois; Fine and decorative arts; works by 19th- and 20th-century Illinois artists.

Indianapolis Museum of Art: 1200 W. 38th St., Indianapolis, Ind. 46208. Krannert and Clowes Pavilions open: Tues.-Sun. and hldys. 11–5 (closed Mon.; also Jan. 1, Thanksgiving, Dec. 25). Free. Lilly Pavilion of Decorative Arts open Tues.-Sun. 1–4 (closed Mon. and major hldys.). Free.

Pre-Columbian through contemporary art in all media. British and American paintings of 19th century; J.M.W. Turner collection. Dutch and Flemish paintings of 17th century; textiles, decorative arts of 18th-century Germany, England, France, and Italy. Oriental collection. Clowes Fund Collection of old masters.

Los Angeles County Museum of Art: 5905 Wilshire Blvd., Los Angeles, Calif. 90036. Open: Tues.-Fri. 10–5; Sat.-Sun. 10–6 (closed Mon.; also Jan. 1, Thanksgiving, Dec. 25). Adm.: $1 (members free; students with ID, senior citizens, and children 5–17, 50¢). Free to all second Tues. of month.

Ahmanson Gallery houses permanent collections covering entire range of history of art. Special Exhibitions Gallery.

(Los Angeles County) Natural History Museum: Exposition Park, 900 Exposition Blvd., Los Angeles, Calif. 90007. Open: Tues.-Sun. 10–5 (closed Mon.; also Jan. 1, Thanksgiving, Dec. 25). Adm.: $1 (children 5–17, 50¢). Free to all first Tues. of month.

Exhibits in Pre-Columbian archeology, Pacific Islands and African ethnology, Southern California botany, evolution of life, marine biology, insects, mineralogy. Dinosaur and Cenozoic fossil reconstructions. North American and African animal habitat groups. U.S., California, Western, Plains, and West Coast Indian history. Rancho La Brea tar pits, a designated natural history landmark, are at 5801 Wilshire Blvd., Hancock Park, with satellite George C. Page Museum of La Brea. Pleistocene fossil reconstructions. Open: same as parent museum. Free to all second Tues. of month.

Milwaukee Art Museum: Milwaukee County War Memorial Bldg., 750 North Lincoln Memorial Dr., Milwaukee, Wis. 53202. Open: Tues., Wed., Fri., and Sat. 10–5; Thurs. 12–9; Sun. 1–6 (closed Mon.). Adm. $1 (students, senior citizens, 50¢; children under 12, free).

Paintings, sculpture, graphics, and decorative arts from ancient to modern; Bradley Collection of 19th- and 20th-century American art. Villa Terrace, Branch Museum for Decorative Arts, 2220 North Terrace Ave.; seasonal hours.

Milwaukee Public Museum: 800 W. Wells St., Milwaukee, Wis. 53233. Open: daily 9–5 (closed Jan. 1, Thanksgiving, Dec. 25). Adm.: $1.50 (children under 18, 75¢).

American Indian and West African art, pre-Columbian collections. Natural history and history displays that include Streets of Old Milwaukee, the Urban Habitat, and European Village.

Minneapolis, Institute of Arts, The: 2400 Third Ave. South, Minneapolis Minn. 55404. Open: Tues., Wed., Fri., Sat. 10–5; Thurs. 10–9; Sun. 12–5 (closed Mon.; also Dec. 25). Adm. $2 (Thurs. 5–9, free) (students 12–18, $1; senior citizens, and children under 12, free).

European and American paintings, sculpture, decorative arts, period rooms, prints and drawings, photography; Oriental, African, Oceanic, ancient and native North and South American arts.

Mint Museum, Art Museum: 501 Hempstead Pl., Charlotte, N.C. 28207. Open: Tues.-Fri. 10–5, Sat.-Sun. 2–5 (closed Mon. and hldys.). Free.

Paintings, sculpture, decorative arts, prints (Renaissance-20th century), pre-Columbian Collection, Delhom Gallery and Institute for Study and Research in Ceramics. Coins and artifacts from 19th-century Charlotte branch of U.S. Mint.

Mound State Monument Archaeological Museum: Rte. 69, Moundville, Ala. 35474. Open: daily 9–5 (closed Dec. 25). Adm. $2 (children $1).

Twenty prehistoric Indian mounds, excavated artifacts, re-created temple and village of Moundville Indians. Trailer and tent campgrounds. Operated by Alabama Museum of Natural History, The University of Alabama.

Mystic Seaport: Mystic, Conn. 06355. Open: daily. Dec.-March 10–4, April-Nov. 9–5 (mid-May to mid-Sept. open until 8) (closed Dec. 25). Adm. Dec.-March $6 (children 5–15, $3); April-Nov. $7.50 (children, $3.75). Two-day tickets and group rates available.

Maritime museum emphasizing Age of Sail. Tall ships, including Charles W. Morgan, 1841 whaling ship. Waterfront village with working craftsmen and demonstrations of maritime skills. Small boat collection and exhibits of figureheads and marine art. Working shipyard; planetarium. Summer steamboat rides at additional charge.

Nelson (William Rockhill) Gallery—Atkins Museum of Fine Arts: 4525 Oak St., Kansas City, Mo. 64111. Open: Tues.-Sat. 10–5, Sun. 2–6 (closed Mon.; also Jan. 1, Memorial Day, July 4, Thanksgiving, Dec. 25). Adm. $1.50 (children 6–12, 75¢). Free on Sun.

Egyptian, Oriental, classic, and European art. American paintings and decorative arts; five Early American rooms. Pre-Columbian and Indian art. Children's Museum, lectures, films, musical programs.

New Mexico, Museum of: Admin. bldg. at 113 Lincoln St., P.O. Box 2087, Santa Fe, N.M. 87503. Museum of Fine Arts, Museum of International Folk Art, Palace of the Governors. Open: daily 9–4:45 (closed Mon. Oct. 15-March 15; also state hldys). Laboratory of Anthropology. Open: Mon.-Fri. 9–4:45 (closed Sat., Sun., and hldys.).

Exhibits of fine arts, folk arts; history of Southwest and of American Indian; archeology; ethnology.

New Orleans Museum of Art: Lelong Ave., City Park, New Orleans, La. 70179. Open: Tues.-Sun. 10–5 (closed Mon.).

Old master paintings from 14th to 19th centuries, including Kress Collection of Italian Art; 20th-century European and American art; African, Oriental and pre-Columbian collections; Latin American Colonial painting and sculpture; prints and photographs.

New York State Historical Association; Lake Rd., Rte. 80, Cooperstown, N.Y. 13326.

Administers Farmers' Museum and Fenimore House. See those entries. Also, Cooperstown Graduate Program in history museum studies and art conservation.

Newark Museum: 49 Washington St., Newark, N.J. 07101. Open: daily 12–5 (closed Jan. 1, July 4, Thanksgiving, Dec. 25). Free.

Collections: American painting, sculpture; Tibetan, Chinese, Japanese arts; decorative arts, ancient glass and ceramics; natural science, ethnology. Planetarium. Ballantine House restoration. Fire Museum. Sculpture garden. Junior Museum. Newark's oldest schoolhouse (1784).

Norton Simon Museum of Art at Pasadena: Colorado Blvd. at Orange Grove, Pasadena, Calif. 91105. Open: Thurs.-Sun. 12–6. Adm. Thurs.-Sat. $2 (students and senior citizens, 75¢; children under 12, free); Sun. $3 for all.

Paintings by old masters and from Italian Renaissance; Dutch 17th-century school; paintings and sculpture by Impressionist and early 20th-century masters; Southeast Asian stone sculptures and bronzes.

Putnam Museum: 1717 W. 12th St., Davenport, Iowa 52804. Open: Tues.-Sat. 9–5, Sun. 1–5 (closed Mon.; also Jan. 1, Easter, Memorial Day, July 4, Labor Day, Thanksgiving, Dec. 25). Adm. $1 (students 13–18, 50¢; children 5–12, 25¢); free Sat. 9–12.

Art, history and natural history; ethnology; archaeology; botany; paleontology; anthropology. Arts of Asia, Africa, Oceania, the American Indian and pre-Columbian era.

Ringling Museums: P.O. Box 1838, Sarasota, Fla. 33578. John and Mable Ringling Museum of Art, Asolo Theater, Ringling Residence, Museum of the

Circus. Open: Mon.-Fri. 9 a.m.-10 p.m., Sat. 9–5, Sun. 11–6. Adm.: $3.50 (groups, $3; children under 12, free).

Extensive collection of Rubens and Baroque art. Asolo is only 18th-century Italian theater in America. Circus Museum contains gilded wagons and memorabilia.

Rosicrucian Egyptian Museum and Art Gallery: Park and Naglee Aves., San Jose, Calif. 95191. Open: Tues.-Fri. 9–5, Sat.-Mon. 12–5 (closed Jan. 1, July 4, Aug. 2, Thanksgiving, Dec. 25). Free.

Egyptian and Oriental antiquities. Mummies, statuary, jewelry, utensils, clothing. Reproduction of Egyptian rock tomb. Babylonian collection. Art gallery.

St. Louis Art Museum: Forest Park, St. Louis, Mo. 63110. Open: Tues. 2:30–9:30, Wed.-Sun. 10–5 (closed Mon.; also Jan. 1, Dec. 25). Free.

American, European, and Asian painting, sculpture, and decorative arts. African, Oceanic, pre-Columbian, and American Indian arts.

San Diego Museum of Art: Balboa Park, San Diego, Calif. 92101. Open: Tues.-Sun. 10–5 (closed Mon.; also Jan. 1, Thanksgiving, Dec. 25). Adm.: $2. Free on Tuesday.

European paintings, Renaissance to 20th century; American paintings and decorative arts. Oriental arts, including Indian and Persian miniatures. Contemporary sculpture.

San Diego Museum of Man: 1350 El Prado, Balboa Park, San Diego, Calif. 92101. Open: daily 10–4:30 (closed Jan. 1, Thanksgiving, Dec. 25). Adm. $1.50 (children 6–16, 25¢; under 6, free). Free adm. on Wed.

Exhibits on Man of the Western Americas, early man, Indians' life style, and Mayan civilization.

San Diego Society of Natural History—Natural History Museum: Balboa Park, San Diego, Calif. 92112. Open: wkdys. and Sun. 10–4:30 (closed Jan. 1, Dec. 25). Adm. $2 (children, free).

Mammals, birds, fossils, shells, plants, insects, minerals, marine biology. Emphasis on Southwestern U.S., Sonora, and Lower California.

San Francisco, The Fine Arts Museums of, M.H. de Young Memorial Museum: Kennedy Dr. and Eighth Ave., Golden Gate Park, San Francisco, Calif. 94118. Open: Wed.-Sun. 10–5. Adm. $1.50 (children 6–18 and senior citizens, 50¢). Free to all first Wed. of month.

Art of Europe, America, Ancient Egypt, Greece, and Rome; traditional arts of Africa, Oceania, and the Americas. Paintings, sculpture, and decorative arts. See also California Palace of the Legion of Honor.

San Francisco Museum of Modern Art: Van Ness at McAllister, San Francisco, Calif. 94102. Open: Tues., Wed., and Fri. 10–6, Thurs. 10–10, Sat. and Sun. 10–5 (closed Mon.; also Jan. 1, Easter Sunday, Memorial Day, July 4, Labor Day, Thanksgiving, Dec. 25). Adm. $2 (senior citizens and children under 16, $1).

Contemporary American and international paintings, sculpture, graphics, photography, and ceramics.

Science and Energy, American Museum of: 300 South Tulane, Oak Ridge, Tenn. 37830. Open: Sept-May, Mon.-Sat. 9–5, Sun. 12:30–5; June-Aug., Mon.-Sat. 9–6, Sun. 12:30–6 (closed Jan. 1, Thanksgiving, Dec. 25). Free.

Demonstrations, exhibits, motion pictures, models, etc., relating to all forms of energy. Traveling exhibits available free to qualified exhibitors in U.S.[2]

Seattle Art Museum: Volunteer Park, Seattle, Wash. 98112 and the Pavilion at Seattle Center, Seattle,

Wash. 98109. Both open: Tues.-Sat. 10–5 (Thurs. to 9), Sun. 12–5 (closed Mon.; also Jan. 1, Thanksgiving, Dec. 25). Adm. $1 (50¢ for students and senior citizens; children under 12 with adult, free). Free on Thurs.

Asian art and jade; Greek and Roman art; Samuel H. Kress Collection of 14th-18th-century European painting and sculpture. European and American modern art.

Southwest Museum: Marmion Way at Museum Dr., Highland Pk., Los Angeles, Calif. 90065. Open: Tues.-Sun. 1–4:45 (closed mid-Aug.-mid-Sept., Mon., Jan. 1, Easter, July 4, Thanksgiving, Dec. 25). Free.

American Indian exhibits, ancient and modern. Research library. Casa de Adobe, reproduction of adobe hacienda, at 4605 N. Figueroa St.; open Wed., Sat., and Sun. 1–4:45 (closed same as Southwest Museum).

Toledo Museum of Art, The: Monroe St. at Scottwood Ave., Toledo, Ohio 43697. Open: Tues.-Sat. 9–5, Sun. 1–5 (closed Mon. and legal hldys.). Free.

European and American paintings and decorative arts. Ancient and medieval art; books, manuscripts, prints, graphics. Ancient and American glass.

Virginia Museum of Fine Arts: Boulevard and Grove Ave., Richmond, Va. 23221. Open: Tues.-Sat. 11–5, Sun. 1–5 (closed Mon.; also Jan. 1, July 4, Thanksgiving, Dec. 25). Adm. Suggested donation of 50¢.

World art of all periods, Lillian Thomas Pratt Collection of Fabergé jewelry, Art Nouveau Gallery.

Wadsworth Atheneum: 600 Main St., Hartford, Conn. 06103. Open: Tues.-Fri. 11–3 (Thurs. to 8), Sat. and Sun. 11–5 (closed Mon.; also Jan. 1, July 4, Thanksgiving, Dec. 25). Adm.: $2 (students 13–18 and senior citizens, $1; children under 13, free). Free to all on Thurs.

European and American paintings and drawings. Sculpture. Bronzes, silver, porcelain, American period furniture, firearms.

Walker Art Center: Vineland Pl., Minneapolis, Minn. 55403. Open: Tues.-Sat. 10–5 (special exhibition galleries, 5–8), Sun. 11–5 (closed Mon.; also major hldys.). Free.

Collection of major 20th-century paintings, sculpture, drawings, and prints. Music, dance, film, theater, and educational programs.

Walters Art Gallery: 600 North Charles St., Baltimore, Md. 21201. Open: Mon. 1–5, Tues.-Sat. 11–5 (July-Aug. Mon. 1–4, Tues.-Sat. 11–4), Sun. and hldys. 2–5 (closed Jan. 1, July 4, Thanksgiving, Dec. 24–25). Free.

Art from ancient empires through 19th-century Europe. Collections of paintings, sculpture, decorative arts, and manuscripts.

Wheelwright Museum, The: 704 Camino Lejo, Santa Fe, N.M. 87502. Open: May-Oct., Mon.-Sat. 10–5, Sun. 1–5; Nov.-April, same as above except closed Mon. (closed Jan. 1, Thanksgiving, Dec. 25). Free.

Baskets, textiles, pottery, jewelry. Historic and contemporary Indian art. (Formerly the Museum of Navajo Ceremonial Art.)

Worcester Art Museum: 55 Salisbury St., Worcester, Mass. 01608. Open: Tues.-Sat. 10–5, Sun. 2–5 (closed Mon.; also Jan. 1, July 4, Thanksgiving, Dec. 25). Adm. $1.50 (children 10–14 and senior citizens, $1; under 10, free). Free to all on Wed.

Art from Egyptian to modern times, with emphasis on painting and sculpture.

1. Summer hours (April 1-Labor Day), Mon.-Sat. 10–9, Sun. 12–9. 2. Send inquiries to Museum Division, Oak Ridge Associated Universities, P.O. Box 117, Oak Ridge, Tenn. 37830. 3. Combination rates are available for Farmers' Museum and Fenimore House.

NEW HOME ENTERTAINMENT

The All-Seeing Eye
The Video Revolution

Theodore B. Dolmatch

We are two years into a new decade. If we didn't already know it, the 1980s have proven, yet again, that time changes everything—from the way we behave to, indeed, the way we are.

What we are has been affected for over a generation by television, both obviously and in ways so subtle that they can only be guessed at. An increasing number of serious critics propose that TV has not always improved us. Whether television has affected us for good or evil we may not be able to determine now. One thing is clear: it will continue to change us even more as the years go by.

We are now entering a period of accelerated technological change in the electronic media. New products, new concepts, and new ways of doing things are upon us. The companies that are developing these wonders are looking directly into our homes—hitting us, as it were, right where we live.

If certain highbrows mutter, "I hope it doesn't work," they should be reminded that was almost exactly what the horse said when he first saw the automobile.

Whether or not the critics approve, a lot is happening. To find out what—and to try to forecast what might happen before we turn around (and certainly before we know the new media's long-term implications) let's first establish where we are right now.

Television Today

In the United States, there are now more TV sets than bathtubs, automobiles, or telephones—150 million sets in all. Over 98% of all American homes have at least one TV set; 85% of them have two or more sets.

They are working about six and a half hours every day! That's about 45 hours a week, almost 2400 hours a year. One hundred 24-hour days. (As this Almanac notes elsewhere, there are only 365 of them usually available.) Since all those sets can't be on to scare away burglars, someone has to be watching, investing a considerable portion of his or her lifetime in the glowing screen.

What glows there increasingly reaches all those homes by cable, rather than through an antenna. Twenty million homes (almost twice as many as five years ago) receive their pictures by cable. Nine million of those homes now pay for at least some of their programs (*twenty* times as many as five years ago). And they pay enough to make cable TV a growing, $2 billion industry.

Video home recording has come of age. The first video recorders appeared in the stores in 1975; by 1977, there were 160,000 video cassette recorders sold annually. To indicate how fast video home recording is growing, however, one need only report sales in 1981: 1.5 million units!

A new industry has been born to supply all those home recorders, since not every program can be lifted off the air: Over four million prerecorded video cassettes will have been sold in 1981, and cassette sales are climbing at a frenetic rate.

There seems to be no stop to it. While sales of automobiles and appliances slump, sales of TV sets rise. About 11 million color sets will be sold in 1981; almost 7 million black-and-white sets. Small screens? Sales of nine-inch, five-inch, even two- and three-inch sets are rising fast. Large screens? Almost 100,000 sets with screens larger than 50 inches were sold in 1981. Sets for homes, cars, boats, airplanes—the market seems insatiable.

Yet More Hardware to Come

So much for the past—at least in terms of the *hardware*—the machines, electronics, the highly sophisticated gadgets. The technology of the future should be even more exciting. We can glimpse what is ahead by examining what has just come on the market, and what is being tested or in the pilot stage.

Video Recording: Two non-compatible methods of video tape recording (the Beta and VHS video cassette systems) are already on the market. Their sales have grown enormously, as noted above.

With the introduction in 1981 of a new video *disc* recording system, we now have two, also non-compatible, alternatives to cassette recording. The Magnavox/Pioneer Laserdisk—very flexible and high quality and high priced—has now been challenged by RCA's Videodisk, less flexible and also less expensive. It is reported that 1981 sales of the Videodisk system have been disappointing, but after about $200 million of development costs, no one should expect RCA to give up on the video recording market without a titanic struggle.

Television Sets: Late in 1981, several TV manufacturers announced "cable-ready" TV sets, capable of receiving over 120 channels directly—standard VHF and UHF, plus almost 60 cable channels.

The industry expects that projection TV sets

with large screens will begin to sell really well very soon. The estimate is that about five times as many sets as in 1981, costing about $3000 each, will be sold annually within the next few years.

By the end of the decade, those projection sets should be competing with four-inch thick panels that will hang on (or be built into) our walls and also display a very large TV picture. But despite the frequent reports in the popular science magazines, the arrival of these wall sets is not imminent.

Sharper Images: In 1981, Sony and Matsushita announced a remarkable new high-definition TV system that produces very sharp images. Its immediate users, in the next three years, are likely to be motion picture producers, who will use high-definition video tape instead of film. Eventually, it is possible that motion pictures could be sent by satellite directly into movie theaters. The first showings are likely to be of sporting events, like today's closed-circuit TV boxing matches.

Interactive Television (QUBE): For some time now, people in Columbus, Ohio, have been able to "talk back" to their television sets, thanks to a small, hand-held terminal which feeds back into a computer. The viewer can indicate his special preferences, choose programs, and even with some additional hook-ups, purchase things as they are being advertised or demonstrated. New QUBE systems are now being constructed in Pittsburgh, Dallas, Houston, and St. Louis.

*   *   *

The technology changes so quickly, however, that it is reasonable, even now, to ask if cable might not be obsolete before its full potential is achieved. We already have the capability for direct-broadcast satellites to beam a picture into our own homes. It is possible that we could soon have small microwave antennas in our window boxes.

Software

Though the technology grabs our attention—if only because of all the advertising and promotion by manufacturers who want to sell their products—any truly significant changes that occur require more than hardware.

New products were originally created to better satisfy *old*, established needs. If they do this successfully, they then also create new needs, which have the power to change the way we live in ways no forecaster can predict.

All the new media exist to carry (transmit, send, deliver, provide, communicate—choose the word) information, entertainment, and education. That is, *ideas*. And ideas are what really affect us. So changes in the "software"—the *messages* carried by the new media forms—are much more important than the media themselves.

For example, the result of transmitting television by cable is a great increase in the viewer's options. Until a few short years ago, all we had was the three

networks and a few local stations—the choice of perhaps a half dozen or fewer programs. UHF added a few more. But cable will give us another ninety or a hundred!

Today, when a program reaches only (!) ten million homes, it is a commercial failure—to be avoided by advertisers at any cost. Given the limited number of channels available, advertisers always looked for the largest possible audiences—*mass* markets. This means that the programmers search for content with the broadest possible appeal.

Almost inevitably, such programs must be aimed at the "lowest common denominator." As Fred Friendly remarked, "because television can make so much money doing its worst, it often cannot afford to do its best."

But 120 channels is another story. *They* require different programming—searching for specialized audiences, for stratified groups of consumers. Thus, "broadcasting" becomes "narrowcasting"—and programmers must create for those specialized audiences.

The eventual catalog of videotapes and videodiscs will also reflect the same kind of specialization. Home video will be more like book publishing than like commercial TV. The potential for education and dissemination of information is enormous. We already have 24-hour news programs on cable. At some point, some programmer will think of increasing the depth of its coverage as well as the program length. Or news programming will be varied, because of the number of outlets available, and we'll have tabloid news formats and, let us hope, a "news program of record," which covers more than merely a local mugging. The program's motivation may not be exemplary; it may be simply to fill the space and time available. Nature abhors a vacuum.

Cable and home video recording create the need for much greater diversity in programming. Inevitably, such diversity must increase the mobility of ideas. The technology gives us an opportunity to communicate concepts—intellectual, aesthetic, social—that have long been buried under the weight of large, simple, *mass* ideas. Will we seize this opportunity—or will we simply continue to trivialize everything?

But we have to look beyond the programming changes, the new problems faced by advertisers, the new relationships between performers and writers and the distribution of their work. We must peer into the murky future of a world transformed by these electronic marvels. *Government?* Will politics be drastically changed because interactive TV allows—encourages—immediate feedback to a politician's presentation on the screen? *Retailing?* People can already order directly and conveniently, pressing buttons in front of their television screen. *Information?* We already are experimenting with electronic mail and electronic newspapers. How will they transform our homes and offices?

Television is destined to have an even more profound effect on the way we live than it has had in the past. While we can't anticipate all that will happen, we ought to start thinking about it—right now.

VIDEO GLOSSARY
What the New Terms Mean

Beta: Videocassette system employed by Sony and other manufacturers including Toshiba, Sanyo, Nippon Electric Co., General, and Fisher.

Broadband distribution: Permits the distribution of many television, sound, or data channels through a single transmission system.

Cable television: The technology of distributing television signals to homes by wire instead of over the air.

Capacitance electronic disc system: RCA SelectaVision is one example of the CED system, which attaches to a television set and places a diamond stylus to the surface of a grooved videodisc to generate picture and sound. RCA will be joined by compatible players from Zenith and others.

CATV: Community antenna television, developed in the late 1940s to improve television reception in mountainous areas.

Communications satellites: These orbit the earth as repeaters and amplifiers of signals beamed to them from the ground.

Compuserve: Two-way telephone computer system which will transmit to users' homes the editorial content of papers around the country.

Courseware: Computer programming designed for educational use in schools and colleges.

CRT: cathode-ray tube. In the context of video, it is simply the TV picture tube.

Freeze frame: Stops the program at any point to let the operator closely examine the picture on the screen.

Home video recorders: Videotape recording and playback devices that can record off the air up to six hours of programming for later viewing.

Interactive program: A conversational program, usually dependent upon computer capabilities, in which the user and the software communicate in a dialogue. User responses determine the course of the program.

Lasers: Specialized devices that generate pure, high-intensity light beams.

Microwave: Broadband communications systems that use ultrahigh frequency (UHF) radio signals to transmit data, telephone communications, and television signals.

Narrowcasting: Directing a medium to a segment of the mass market, a medium especially created to address the special interests of a particular group.

Pay-cable: Pay-television by means of cable, which essentially provides subscribers with new movies, sporting events, and special variety programs.

QUBE: Trade name for a form of two-way cable whose special feature is the union of a cable with a system of polling computers; offers subscribers a pay-per-view option for programs ranging from opera to self-help and children's shows.

Reflective laser optical system: A videodisc system employing a laser beam to read and play back on a television screen the visual and audio components embedded in tiny pits on a grooveless disc. Pioneer and Magnavox market compatible laser systems.

Teletext: A one-way (noninteractive) medium transmitting information through regular or cable TV broadcast signals.

Telidon: A type of sophisticated technology being developed by Canada for both viewdata and teletext applications.

Two-way cable: Cable installations in which two wires are used, one carrying signals from the transmission center, the other taking signals from the television set.

VCR: Videocassette recorder. This abbreviation, however, is used not only as a generic term for all such equipment; it is also employed by Philips and Grundig for their own systems.

VHS: Video home system. Videocassette system employed by Matsushita, JVC, Akai, Hitachi, Matsubishi, and Sharp.

Videocassette: The video counterpart of the audio tape cassette; a self-contained program on videotape designed to play in any one of the incompatible videocassette recorders (VCRs) on the market.

Videodisc: The video counterpart of the phonograph record; it stores visual and audio matter that can be displayed on the television set through a special turntable. Being developed in three different, incompatible formats: LV (Laservision—MCA/Philips' reflective laser optical system), CED (RCA's capacitance electronic disc), and VHD (the Japanese video high density system).

Viewdata: A two-way (interactive), easy-to-operate medium linking computer databases to TVs through telephone or cable television lines. Also trademark of Knight-Ridder's subsidiary involved in experimental Viewtron.

Viewtron: Knight-Ridder Newspapers' videotex system being tested in Coral Gables, Fla. Information providers include Associated Press, Universal Press Syndicate, Congressional Quarterly, Consumers Union, and Macmillan.

Prepared by William N. Farlie, Jr.

Basic Differences of Video Disc Systems

The RCA SelectaVision system uses a stylus that moves in the grooves of the disc. Friction caused by the stylus tracking in the disc will cause gradual wear of both. SelectaVision is lower priced than the other systems.

The JVC VHD (Video High Density) system uses a stylus that glides along the recorded surface of a grooveless disc. Thus, disc and stylus wear is greatly minimized.

The Philips-MCA Laser system uses a laser instead of a stylus to read the recorded information on the disc. Because the scanner does not touch the disc at all, the disc does not wear out. The Laserdisc is the most expensive system.

None of the above systems allows one to record.

SPORTS

Sports Personalities

A name in parentheses is the original name or form of name. Localities are places of birth. Dates of birth appear as month/day/year. **Boldface** years in parentheses are dates of **(birth-death)**.
Information has been gathered from many sources, including the individuals themselves. However, the *Information Please Almanac* cannot guarantee the accuracy of every individual item.

Aaron, Hank (Henry) (baseball); Mobile, Ala., 2/5/1934
Abdul-Jabbar, Kareem (Lewis Ferdinand Alcindor, Jr.) (basketball); New York City, 4/16/1947
Adderly, Herbert A. (football); Philadelphia, 6/8/1939
Alcindor, Lew. See Abdul-Jabbar
Ali, Muhammad (Cassius Clay) (boxing); Louisville, Ky., 1/18/1942
Allen, Dick (Richard Anthony) (baseball); Wampum, Pa., 3/8/1942
Allison, Bobby (Robert Arthur) (auto racing); Hueytown, Ala., 12/3/1937
Alworth, Lance (football); Houston, 8/3/1940
Anderson, Donny (Gary Donny) (football); Brooklyn, N.Y., 4/3/1949
Anderson, Ken (football); Batavia, Ill., 2/15/1949
Anderson, Sparky (George) (baseball); Bridgewater, S.D., 2/22/1934
Andretti, Mario (auto racing); Montona, Trieste, Italy, 2/28/1940
Anthony, Earl (bowling); Kent, Wash., 4/27/1938
Arcaro, Eddie (George Edward) (jockey); Cincinnati, 2/19/1916
Arfons, Arthur Eugene (auto racing); Akron, Ohio, 2/3/1926
Ashe, Arthur (tennis); Richmond, Va., 7/10/1943
Austin, Tracy (tennis); Rolling Hills, Calif., 12/2/1962
Babashoff, Shirley (swimming); Whittier, Calif., 1/31/1957
Baer, Max (boxer); Omaha, Neb. **(1909–1959)**
Bakken, Jim (James Leroy) (football); Madison, Wis., 11/2/1940
Ball, Catherine (Catie) (swimming); Jacksonville, Fla., 9/30/1951
Banks, Ernie (baseball); Dallas, 1/31/1931
Bannister, Roger (runner); Harrow, England, 3/24/1929
Barry, Rick (Richard) (basketball); Elizabeth, N.J., 3/28/1944
Bauer, Hank (Henry) (baseball); East St. Louis, Ill., 7/31/1922
Baugh, Sammy (football); Temple, Tex., 3/17/1914
Bayi, Filbert (runner); Karratu, Tanganyika, 6/23/1953
Baylor, Elgin (basketball); Washington, D.C., 9/16/1934
Beamon, Bob (long jumper); New York City, 8/2/1946
Beard, Frank (golf); Dallas, 5/1/1939
Beliveau, Jean (hockey); Three Rivers, Quebec, Canada, 8/31/1931
Beman, Deane (golf); Washington, D.C., 4/22/1938
Bench, Johnny (Johnny Lee) (baseball); Oklahoma City, 12/7/1947
Berg, Patty (Patricia Jane) (golf); Minneapolis, 2/13/1918
Berning, Susie Maxwell (golf); Pasadena, Calif., 7/22/1941
Berra, Yogi (Lawrence) (baseball); St. Louis, 5/12/1925
Biletnikoff, Frederick (football); Erie, Pa., 2/23/1943
Bird, Larry (basketball); French Lick, Ind., 12/7/1956
Blaik, Earl H. (football); Detroit, 2/15/1897
Blanda, George Frederick (football); Youngwood, Pa., 9/17/1927
Blue, Vida (baseball); Mansfield, La., 7/28/1949
Borg, Björn (tennis); Stockholm, 6/6/1956
Boros, Julius (golf); Fairfield, Conn., 3/3/1920
Bossy, Mike (hockey); Montreal, 1/22/1957
Boston, Ralph (long jumper); Laurel, Miss., 5/9/1939
Bradley, Bill (William Warren) (basketball); Crystal City, Mo., 7/28/1943
Bradshaw, Terry (football); Shreveport, La., 9/2/1948
Breedlove, Craig (Norman) (speed driving); Los Angeles, 3/23/1938
Brett, George (baseball); Glendale, W. Va., 5/15/1953
Brock, Louis Clark (baseball); El Dorado, Ark., 6/18/1939
Brown, Jimmy (football); St. Simon Island, Ga., 2/17/1936
Brown, Larry (football); Clairton, Pa., 9/19/1947
Brumel, Valeri (high jumper); Tolbuzino, Siberia, 4/14/1942
Bryant, Rosalyn Evette (track); Chicago, 1/7/1956
Burton, Michael (swimming); Des Moines, Iowa, 7/3/1947
Butkus, Dick (Richard Marvin) (football); Chicago, 12/9/1942
Campanella, Roy (baseball); Homestead, Pa., 11/19/1921
Campbell, Earl (football); Tyler, Tex., 3/29/1955
Caponi, Donna Maria (golf); Detroit, 1/29/1945
Cappelletti, Gino (football); Keewatin, Minn., 3/26/1934
Carew, Rod (Rodney Cline) (baseball); Gatun, Panama, 10/1/1945
Carlos, John (sprinter); New York City, 6/5/1945
Carlton, Steven Norman (baseball); Miami, Fla., 12/22/1944
Carner, Joanne Gunderson (Mrs. Don) (golf); Kirkland, Wash., 3/4/1939
Casals, Rosemary (tennis); San Francisco, 9/16/1948
Casper, Billy (golf); San Diego, Calif., 6/24/1931
Caulkins, Tracy (swimming); Wimona, Minn., 1/11/63
Cauthen, Steve (jockey); Covington, Ky., 5/1/1960
Cawley, Evonne; see Goolagong
Chamberlain, Wilt (Wilton) (basketball); Philadelphia, 8/21/1936
Chapot, Frank (equestrian); Camden, N.J., 2/24/1934
Chinaglia, Giorgio (soccer); Carrara, Italy 1/24/1947

Clarke, Bobby (Robert Earle) (hockey); Flin Flon, Manitoba, Canada, 8/13/1949
Clay, Cassius. See Ali, Muhammad
Clemente, Roberto Walker (baseball); Carolina, Puerto Rico **(1934–1972)**
Cobb, Tyrus Raymond (Ty) (baseball); Narrows, Ga. **(1886–1961)**
Cochran, Barbara Ann (skiing); Claremont, N.H., 1/4/1951
Cochran, Marilyn (skiing); Burlington, Vt., 2/7/1950
Cochran, Robert (skiing); Claremont, N.H., 12/11/1951
Coe, Sebastian Newbold (track); London, England, 9/29/1956
Colavito, Rocky (Rocco Domenico) (baseball); New York City, 8/10/1933
Comaneci, Nadia (gymnast); Onesti, Romania, 11/12/1961
Connors, Jimmy (James Scott) (tennis); East St. Louis, Ill., 9/2/1952
Cordero, Angel (jockey); Santurce, Puerto Rico, 5/8/1942
Cournoyer, Yvan Serge (hockey); Drummondville, Quebec, Canada, 11/22/1943
Court, Margaret Smith (tennis); Albury, New South Wales, Australia, 7/16/1942
Cousy, Bob (basketball); New York City, 8/9/1928
Crenshaw, Ben (golf); Austin, Tex., 1/11/1952
Cronin, Joe (baseball executive); San Francisco, 10/12/1906
Cruyff, Johan (soccer); Amsterdam, Netherlands, 4/25/47
Csonka, Larry (Lawrence Richard) (football); Stow, Ohio, 12/25/1946
Dancer, Stanley (harness racing); New Egypt, N.J., 7/25/1927
Dark, Alvin (baseball); Comanche, Okla., 1/7/1922
Davenport, Willie (track); Troy, Ala., 6/6/1943
Dawson, Leonard Ray (football); Alliance, Ohio, 6/20/1935
Dean, Dizzy (Jay Hanna) (baseball); Lucas, Ark. **(1911–1974)**
DeBusschere, Dave (basketball); Detroit, 10/16/1940
Delvecchio, Alex Peter (hockey); Fort William, Ontario, Canada, 12/4/1931
Demaret, Jim (golf); Houston, 5/10/1910
Dempsey, Jack (William H.) (boxing); Manassa, Colo., 6/24/1895
DeVicenzo, Roberto (golf); Buenos Aires, 4/14/1923
Dibbs, Edward George (tennis); Brooklyn, N.Y., 2/23/1951
Dietz, James W. (rowing); New York, N.Y., 1/12/1949
DiMaggio, Joe (baseball); Martinez, Calif., 11/25/1914
Dionne, Marcel (hockey); Drummondville, Quebec, Canada, 8/3/1951
Dominguín, Luis Miguel (matador); Madrid, 12/9/1926
Dorsett, Tony (football); Rochester, Pa., 4/7/1954
Dryden, Kenneth (hockey); Hamilton, Ontario, Canada, 8/4/1947
Drysdale, Don (baseball); Van Nuys, Calif., 7/23/1936
Duran, Roberto (boxing); Panama City 6/16/1951
Durocher, Leo (baseball); West Springfield, Mass., 7/27/1906
Durr, François (tennis); Algiers, Algeria, 12/25/1942
El Cordobés, (Manuel Benítez Pérez) (matador); Palma del Río, Córdoba, Spain, 5/4/1936(?)
Elder, Lee (golf); Dallas, 7/14/1934
Emerson, Roy (tennis); Kingsway, Australia, 11/3/1936
Ender, Kornelia (swimming); Plauen, East Germany, 10/25/1958
Erving, Julius (Dr. J) (basketball); Roosevelt, N.Y., 2/22/1950
Esposito, Phil (Philip Anthony) (hockey); Sault Ste. Marie, Ontario, Canada, 2/20/1942
Evans, Lee (runner); Mandena, Calif., 2/25/1947
Evert, Chris; see Lloyd, Christ Evert
Ewbank, Weeb (football); Richmond, Ind., 5/6/1907
Feller, Robert (Bobby) (baseball); Van Meter, Iowa, 11/3/1918
Feuerbach, Allan Dean (track); Preston, Iowa, 1/12/1948
Finley, Charles O. (sportsman); Ensley, Ala., 2/22/1918
Fischer, Bobby (chess); Chicago, 3/9/1943
Fittipaldi, Emerson (auto racer); São Paulo, Brazil, 12/12/1946
Fitzsimmons, Bob (Robert Prometheus) (boxer); Cornwall, England **(1862–1917)**
Fleming, Peggy Gale (ice skating); San Jose, Calif., 7/27/1948
Ford, Whitey (Edward) (baseball); New York City, 10/21/1928
Foreman, George (boxing); Marshall, Tex., 1/10/1949
Fosbury, Richard (high jumper); Portland, Ore., 3/6/1947
Fox, Nellie (Jacob Nelson) (baseball); St. Thomas, Pa. **(1927–1975)**
Foxx, James Emory (baseball); Sudlersville, Md. **(1907–1967)**
Foyt, A. J. (auto racing); Houston, 1/16/1935
Francis, Emile (hockey); North Battleford, Sask., 9/13/1926
Fratianne, Linda (figure skating); Los Angeles, 8/2/1960
Frazier, Joe (boxing); Beauford, S.C., 1/17/1944
Frazier, Walt (basketball); Atlanta, 3/29/1945

Frick, Ford C. (baseball); Wawaka, Ind., **(1894–1978)**
Furniss, Bruce (swimming); Fresno, Calif., 5/27/1957
Gable, Dan (wrestling); Waterloo, Iowa; 10/25/1945
Gabriel, Roman (football); Wilmington, N.C., 8/5/1940
Gallagher, Michael Donald (skiing); Yonkers, N.Y., 10/3/1941
Gehrig, Lou (Henry Louis Gehrig) (baseball); New York City **(1903–1941)**
Gehringer, Charlie (baseball); Fowlerville, Mich., 5/11/1903
Geoffrion, Bernie (Boom Boom) (hockey); Montreal, 2/14/1931
Gerulaitis, Vitas (tennis); Brooklyn, N.Y., 7/26/1954
Giacomin, Ed (hockey); Sudbury, Ontario, Canada, 6/6/1939
Gibson, Bob (baseball); Omaha, Neb., 11/9/1935
Gifford, Frank (football); Santa Monica, Calif., 8/16/1930
Gilbert, Rod (Rodrique) (hockey); Montreal, 7/1/1941
Giles, Warren (baseball executive); Tiskilwa, Ill., **(1896–1979)**
Gilmore, Artis (basketball); Chipley, Fla., 9/21/1949
Glance, Harvey (track); Phenix City, Ala., 3/28/1957
Gonzalez, Pancho (tennis); Los Angeles, 5/9/1928
Goodell, Brian Stuart (swimming); Stockton, Calif., 4/2/1959
Goodrich, Gail (basketball); Los Angeles, 4/23/1943
Goolagong Cawley, Evonne (tennis); Griffith, Australia, 7/31/1951
Gottfried, Brian (tennis); Baltimore, Md., 1/27/1952
Graham, David (golf); Windsor, Australia; 5/23/1946
Graham, Otto Everett (football); Waukegan, Ill., 12/6/1921
Grange, Red (Harold) (football); Forksville, Pa., 6/13/1904
Green, Hubert (golf); Birmingham, Ala., 12/28/1946
Greene, Charles E. (sprinter); Pine Bluff, Ark., 3/21/1945
Gretzky, Wayne (hockey); Brantford, Ont., 1/26/1961
Griese, Bob (Robert Allen) (football); Evansville, Ind., 2/3/1945
Grove, Lefty (Robert Moses) (baseball); Lonaconing, Md., **(1900–1975)**
Groza, Lou (football); Martins Ferry, Ohio, 1/25/1924
Guidry, Ronald Ames (baseball); Lafayette, La., 8/28/1950
Gunter, Nancy Richey (tennis); San Angelo, Tex., 8/23/1942
Halas, George (football); Chicago, 2/2/1895
Hall, Gary (swimming); Fayetteville, N.C., 8/7/1951
Hamill, Dorothy (figure skater); Chicago, 1956(?)
Hammond, Kathy (runner); Sacramento, Calif., 11/2/1951
Harris, Franco (football); Ft. Dix, N.J., 3/7/1950
Hartack, William, Jr. (jockey); Colver, Pa., 12/9/1932
Haughton, William (harness racing); Gloversville, N.Y., 11/2/1923
Havlicek, John (basketball); Martins Ferry, Ohio, 4/8/1940
Hayes, Elvin (basketball); Rayville, La., 11/17/1945
Haynie, Sandra (golf); Fort Worth, 6/4/1943
Heiden, Eric (speed skating); Madison, Wis., 6/14/1958
Hencken, John (swimming); Culver City, Calif., 5/29/1954
Henie, Sonja (ice skater); Oslo **(1912–1969)**
Hickcox, Charles (swimming); Phoenix, Ariz., 2/6/1947
Hines, James (sprinter); Dumas, Ark., 9/10/1946
Hodges, Gil (baseball); Princeton, Ind. **(1924–1972)**
Hogan, Ben (golf); Dublin, Tex., 8/13/1912
Holmes, Larry (boxing); Cuthert, Ga., 11/3/1949
Hornsby, Rogers (baseball); Winters, Tex. **(1896–1963)**
Hornung, Paul (football); Louisville, Ky., 12/23/1935
Houk, Ralph (baseball); Lawrence, Kan., 8/9/1919
Howard, Elston (baseball); St. Louis **(1929–1980)**
Howe, Gordon (hockey); Floral, Sask., Canada, 3/31/1928
Howell, Jim Lee (football); Lonoke, Ark., 9/27/1914
Hubbell, Carl (baseball); Carthage, Mo., 6/22/1903
Huff, Sam (Robert Lee) (football); Morgantown, W. Va., 10/4/1934
Hull, Bobby (hockey); Point Anne, Ontario, Canada, 1/3/1939
Hunter, Jim (Catfish) (baseball); Hertford, N.C., 4/8/1946
Huntley, Joni (track); McMinnville, Ore., 8/4/1956
Hutson, Donald (football); Pine Bluff, Ark., 1/31/1913
Insko, Del (harness racing); Amboy, Minn., 7/10/1931
Irwin, Hale (golf); Joplin, Mo., 6/3/1945
Jackson, Reggie (baseball); Wyncote, Pa., 5/18/1946
Jeffries, James J. (boxer); Carroll, Ohio **(1875–1953)**
Jenkins, Ferguson Arthur (baseball); Chatham, Ontario, Canada, 12/13/1943
Jenner, (W.) Bruce (track); Mt. Kisco, N.Y., 10/28/1949
Jezek, Linda (swimming); Palo Alto, Calif., 3/10/1960
Johnson, Earvin (Magic) (basketball); E. Lansing, Mich., 8/14/1959
Johnson, Anthony (rowing); Washington, D.C., 11/6/1940
Johnson, Jack (John Arthur Johnson) (boxer); Galveston, Tex. **(1876–1946)**
Johnson, Rafer (decathlon); Hillsboro, Tex., 8/18/1935
Jones, Deacon (David) (football); Eatonville, Fla., 12/9/1938
Juantoreno, Alberto (runner); Santiago, Cuba, 12/3/1951
Jurgensen, Sonny (football); Wilmington, N.C., 8/23/1934
Kaline, Al (Albert) (baseball); Baltimore, 12/19/1934
Keino, Kipchoge (runner); Kapchemoiymo, Kenya, 1/?/1940
Kelly, Leroy (football); Philadelphia, 5/20/1942
Kelly, Red (Leonard Patrick) (hockey); Simcoe, Ontario, Canada, 7/9/1927
Killebrew, Harmon (baseball); Payette, Idaho, 6/29/1936
Killy, Jean-Claude (skiing); Saint-Cloud, France, 8/30/1943
Kilmer, Bill (William Orland) (football); Topeka, Kan., 9/5/1939

King, Billie Jean (Billie Jean Moffitt) (tennis); Long Beach, Calif., 11/22/1943
Kinsella, John (swimming); Oak Park, Ill., 8/26/1952
Kodes, Jan (tennis); Prague, 3/1/1946
Kolb, Claudia (swimming); Hayward, Calif., 12/19/1949
Koosman, Jerry Martin (baseball); Appleton, Minn., 12/23/1942
Korbut, Olga (gymnast); Grodno, Byelorussia, U.S.S.R., 5/16/1955
Koufax, Sandy (Sanford) (baseball); Brooklyn, N.Y., 12/30/1935
Kramer, Jack (tennis); Las Vegas, Nev., 8/1/1921
Kramer, Jerry (football); Jordan, Mont., 1/23/1936
Kuhn, Bowie Kent (baseball); Takoma Park, Md., 10/28/1926
Kwalik, Ted (Thaddeus John) (football); McKees Rocks, Pa., 4/15/1947
Lafleur, Guy Damien (hockey); Thurson, Quebec, Canada, 8/20/1951
Laird, Ronald (walker); Louisville, Ky., 5/31/1938
Lamonica, Daryle (football); Fresno, Calif., 7/17/1941
Landis, Kenesaw Mountain (1st baseball commissioner); Millville, Ohio **(1866–1944)**
Landry, Tom (football); Mission, Tex., 9/11/1924
Landy, John (runner); Australia, 4/4/1930
Larrieu, Francie (track); Palo Alto, Calif., 11/28/1952
Laver, Rod (tennis); Rockhampton, Australia, 8/9/1938
Leonard, Benny (Benjamin Leiner) (boxer); New York City **(1896–1947)**
Leonard, Sugar Ray (boxing); Wilmington, N.C., 5/17/1956
Linehan, Kim (swimming); Bronxville, N.Y., 12/11/1962
Liquori, Marty (runner); Montclair, N.J., 9/11/1949
Little, Floyd Douglas (football); New Haven, Conn., 7/4/1942
Little, Lou (football); Leominster, Mass., **(1893–1979)**
Littler, Gene (golf); San Diego, Calif., 11/16/1920
Lloyd, Chris Evert (Christine Marie) (tennis); Fort Lauderdale, Fla., 12/21/1954
Lombardi, Vince (football); Brooklyn, N.Y. **(1913–1970)**
Longden, Johnny (horse racing); Wakefield, England, 2/14/1907
Lopez, Al (baseball); Tampa, Fla., 8/20/1908
Lopez, Nancy (golf); Torrance, Calif., 1/6/1957
Louis, Joe (Joe Louis Barrow) (boxing); Lexington, Ala. **(1914–1981)**
Lynn, Frederic Michael (baseball); Chicago, Ill., 2/3/1952
Lynn, Janet (figure skating); Rockford, Ill., 4/6/1953
Mack, Connie (Cornelius Alexander McGillicuddy) (baseball executive); East Brookfield, Mass. **(1862–1956)**
Mackey, John (football); New York City, 9/24/1941
Mahovlich, Frank (Francis William) (hockey); Timmins, Ontario, Canada, 1/10/1938
Mann, Carol (golf); Buffalo, N.Y., 2/3/1941
Manning, Madeline (runner); Cleveland, 1/11/1948
Mantle, Mickey Charles (baseball); Spavinaw, Okla., 10/20/1931
Marciano, Rocky (boxing); Brockton, Mass. **(1923–1969)**
Marichal, Juan (baseball); Laguna Verde, Montecristi, Dominican Republic, 10/20/1937
Maris, Roger (baseball); Hibbing, Minn., 9/10/1934
Martin, Billy (Alfred Manuel) (baseball); Berkeley, Calif., 5/16/1928
Martin, Rick (Richard Lionel) (hockey); Verdun, Quebec, Canada, 7/26/1951
Mathews, Ed (Edwin) (baseball); Texarkana, Tex., 10/13/1931
Matson, Randy (shot putter); Kilgore, Tex., 3/5/1945
Mays, Willie (baseball); Westfield, Ala., 5/6/1931
McAdoo, Bob (basketball); Greensboro, N.C., 9/25/1951
McCarthy, Joe (Joseph Vincent) (baseball); Philadelphia **(1887–1978)**
McCovey, Willie Lee (baseball); Mobile, Ala., 1/10/1938
McEnroe, John Patrick, Jr. (tennis); Wiesbaden, Germany, 2/16/1959
McGraw, John Joseph (baseball); Truxton, N.Y. **(1873–1934)**
McIngvale, Cynthia Potter (diving); Houston, 8/27/1950
McLain, Dennis (baseball); Chicago, 3/24/1944
McMillan, Kathy Laverne (track); Raeford, N.C., 11/7/1957
Melton–Lopez, Nancy; See Lopez, Nancy
Merrill, Janice (runner); New London, Conn., 6/18/1962
Meyer, Deborah (swimming); Haddonfield, N.J., 8/14/1952
Middlecoff, Cary (golf); Halls, Tenn., 1/6/1921
Mikita, Stan (hockey); Sokolce, Czechoslovakia, 5/20/1940
Milburn, Rodney, Jr. (hurdler); Opelousas, La., 5/18/1950
Miller, Johnny (golf); San Francisco, 4/29/1947
Montgomery, Jim (swimming); Madison, Wis., 1/24/1955
Moore, Archie (boxing); Benoit, Miss., 12/13/1916
Morgan, Joe Leonard (baseball); Bonham, Tex., 9/19/1943
Morrall, Earl (football); Muskegon, Mich., 5/17/1934
Morris, Mercury (Eugene) (football); Pittsburgh, 1/5/1947
Morton, Craig L. (football); Flint, Mich., 2/5/1943
Mosconi, Willie (pocket billiards); Philadelphia, 6/27/1913
Moser, Annemarie. See Proell, Annemarie
Moses, Edward Corley (track); Dayton, Ohio, 8/31/1958
Munson, Thurman (baseball); Akron, Ohio, **(1947–1979)**
Murphy, Calvin (basketball); Norwalk, Conn., 5/9/1948
Musial, Stan (baseball); Donora, Pa., 11/21/1920
Myers, Linda (archery); York, Pa., 6/19/1947
Naber, John (swimming); Evanston, Ill., 1/20/1956
Namath, Joe (Joseph William) (football); Beaver Falls, Pa., 5/31/1943
Nastase, Ilie (tennis); Bucharest, 7/19/1946

Navratilova, Martina (tennis); Prague, 10/10/1956
Nehemiah, Renaldo (track); Newark, N.J., 3/24/1959
Nelson, Cindy (skiing); Lutsen, Minn. 8/19/1955
Newcombe, John (tennis); Sydney, Australia, 5/23/1943
Nicklaus, Jack (golf); Columbus, Ohio, 1/21/1940
North, Lowell (yachting); Springfield, Mo., 12/2/1929
Oerter, Al (discus thrower); New York City, 9/19/1936
Okker, Tom (tennis); Amsterdam, 2/22/1944
Oldfield, Barney (racing driver); Fulton County, Ohio (1878–1946)
Oliva, Tony (Pedro) (baseball); Pinar Del Rio, Cuba, 7/20/1940
Olsen, Merlin Jay (football); Logan, Utah, 9/15/1940
O'Malley, Walter (baseball executive); New York City (1903–1979)
Orantes, Manuel (tennis); Granada, Spain, 2/6/1949
Orr, Bobby (hockey); Parry Sound, Ontario, Canada, 3/20/1948
Ovett, Steve (track); Brighton, England, 10/9/1955
Owens, Jesse (track); Decatur, Ala. (1914–1980)
Pace, Darrell (archery); Cincinnati, 10/23/1956
Paige, Satchel (Leroy) (baseball); Mobile, Ala., 7/7/1906
Palmer, Arnold (golf); Latrobe, Pa., 9/10/1929
Palmer, James Alvin (baseball); New York City, 10/15/1945
Parent, Bernard Marcel (hockey); Montreal, 4/3/1945
Park, Brad (Douglas Bradford) (hockey); Toronto, Ontario, Canada, 7/6/1948
Parseghian, Ara (football); Akron, Ohio, 5/21/1923
Pasarell, Charles (tennis); San Juan, Puerto Rico, 2/12/1944
Patterson, Floyd (boxing); Waco, N.C., 1/4/1935
Pearson, David Gene (auto racing); 12/22/1934
Pelé (Edson Arantes do Nascimento) (soccer); Tres Coracoes, Brazil, 10/23/1940
Perry, Gaylord (baseball); Williamston, N.C., 9/13/1938
Pettit, Bob (basketball); Baton Rouge, La., 12/12/1932
Petty, Richard Lee (auto racing); Randleman, N.C., 7/2/1937
Pincay, Laffit, Jr. (jockey); Panama City, Panama, 12/29/1946
Plante, Jacques (hockey); Shawinigan Falls, Quebec, Canada, 1/17/1929
Player, Gary (golf); Johannesburg, South Africa, 11/1/1935
Plunkett, Jim (football); San Jose, Calif., 12/5/1947
Potter, Cynthia. See McIngvale
Potvin, Denis Charles (hockey); Hull, Quebec, Canada, 10/29/1953
Powell, Boog (John) (baseball); Lakeland, Fla., 8/17/1941
Prefontaine, Steve Roland (runner); Coos Bay, Ore. (1951–1975)
Proell, Annemarie Moser (Alpine skier); Kleinarl, Austria, 3/27/1953
Ralston, Dennis (tennis); Bakersfield, Calif., 7/27/1942
Rankin, Judy Torluemke (golf); St. Louis, Mo., 2/18/1945
Ratelle, Jean (Joseph Gilbert Yvon Jean) (hockey); St. Jean, Quebec, Canada, 10/29/1953
Rawls, Betsy (Elizabeth Earle) (golf); Spartanburg, S.C., 5/4/1928
Reed, Willis (basketball); Hico, La., 6/25/1942
Reese, Pee Wee (Harold) (baseball); Ekron, Ky., 7/23/1919
Reid, Kerry Melville (tennis); Mosman, Australia, 8/7/1947
Richard, Maurice (hockey); Montreal, 8/14/1924
Riessen, Martin (tennis); Hinsdale, Ill., 12/4/1941
Rigney, William (baseball); Alameda, Calif., 1/29/1918
Rizzuto, Phil (baseball); New York City, 9/25/1918
Roark, Helen Wills Moody (tennis); Centerville, Calif., 10/6/1906
Robertson, Oscar (basketball); Charlotte, Tenn., 11/24/1938
Robinson, Arnie (track); San Diego, Calif., 4/7/1948
Robinson, Brooks (baseball); Little Rock, Ark., 5/18/1937
Robinson, Frank (baseball); Beaumont, Tex., 8/31/1935
Robinson, Jackie (baseball); Cairo, Ga. (1919–1972)
Robinson, Larry Clark (hockey); Marvelville, Ontario, Canada, 6/2/1951
Robinson, (Sugar) Ray (boxing); Detroit, 5/3/1920
Rockne, Knute Kenneth (football); Voss, Norway (1888–1931)
Rockwell, Martha (skiing); Providence, R.I., 4/26/1944
Rono, Harry (track); Kiptaragon, Kenya, 2/12/1952
Rose, Pete (Peter Edward) (baseball); Cincinnati, 4/14/1942
Rosenbloom, Maxie (boxing); New York City (1904–1976)
Rosewall, Ken (tennis); Sydney, Australia, 11/2/1934
Rote, Kyle (football); San Antonio, 10/27/1928
Rozelle, Pete (Alvin Ray) (commissioner of National Football League); South Gate, Calif., 3/1/1926
Rudolph, Wilma Glodean (sprinter); St. Bethlehem, Tenn., 6/23/1940
Russell, Bill (basketball); Monroe, La., 2/12/1934
Ruth, Babe (George Herman Ruth) (baseball); Baltimore (1895–1948)
Rutherford, Johnny (auto racing); Fort Worth, 3/12/1938
Ryan, Nolan (Lynn Nolan, Jr.) (baseball); Refugio, Tex., 1/31/1947
Ryon, Luann (archery); Long Beach, Calif., 1/13/1953
Ryun, Jim (runner); Wichita, Kan., 4/29/1947
Santana, Manuel (Manuel Santana Martinez) (tennis); Chamartin, Spain, 5/10/1938
Sayers, Gale (football); Wichita, Kan., 5/30/1943
Schoendienst, Al (Albert) (baseball); Germantown, Ill., 2/2/1923
Schollander, Donald (swimming); Charlotte, N.C., 4/30/1946
Seagren, Bob (Robert Lloyd) (pole vaulter); Pomona, Calif., 10/17/1946
Seaver, Tom (baseball); Fresno, Calif., 11/17/1944
Seidler, Maren (track); Brooklyn, N.Y., 6/11/1962
Sherman, Allie (football); Brooklyn, N.Y., 2/10/1923

Shoemaker, Willie (jockey); Fabens, Tex., 8/19/1931
Shorter, Frank (runner); Munich, Germany, 10/31/1947
Shula, Don (Donald Francis) (football); Grand River, Ohio, 1/4/1930
Silvester, Jay (discus thrower); Tremonton, Utah, 2/27/1937
Simpson, O. J. (Orenthal James) (football); San Francisco, 7/9/1947
Sims, Billy (football); St. Louis, 9/18/1955
Smith, Bubba (Charles Aaron) (football); Orange, Tex., 2/28/1945
Smith, Ronnie Ray (sprinter); Los Angeles, 3/28/1949
Smith, Stanley Roger (tennis); Pasadena, Calif., 12/14/1946
Smith, Tommie (sprinter); Clarksville, Tex., 6/5/1944
Smoke, Marcia Jones (canoeing); Oklahoma City, 7/18/1941
Snead, Sam (golf); Hot Springs, Va., 5/27/1912
Sneva, Tom (auto racing); Spokane, Wash., 6/1/1948
Snider, Duke (Edwin) (baseball); Los Angeles, 9/19/1926
Solomon, Harold (tennis); Washington, D.C., 9/17/1952
Spahn, Warren (baseball); Buffalo, N.Y., 4/23/1921
Spassky, Boris (chess); Leningrad, 1/30/1937
Speaker, Tristram (baseball); Hubbard City, Tex. (1888–1958)
Spinks, Leon (boxing); St. Louis, 7/11/1953
Spitz, Mark (swimming); Modesto, Calif., 2/10/1950
Stabler, Kenneth (football); Foley, Ala., 12/25/1945
Stagg, Amos Alonzo (football); West Orange, N.J. (1862–1965)
Stapleton, Pat (hockey); Sarnia, Ontario, Canada, 7/4/1940
Stargell, Willie (Wilver Dornell) (baseball); Earlsboro, Okla., 3/6/1941
Starr, Bart (football); Montgomery, Ala., 1/9/1934
Staubach, Roger (football); Cincinnati, 2/5/1942
Steinkraus, William C. (equestrian); Cleveland, 10/12/1925
Stenerud, Jan (football); Fetsund, Norway, 11/26/1942
Stengel, Casey (Charles Dillon) (baseball); Kansas City, Mo. (1891–1975)
Stenmark, Ingemar (Alpine skier); Tarnaby, Sweden, 3/18/1956
Stockton, Richard LaClede (tennis); New York City, 2/18/1951
Stones, Dwight Edwin (track); Los Angeles, 12/6/1953
Sullivan, John Lawrence (boxer); Boston (1858–1918)
Sutton, Don (Donald Howard) (baseball); Clio, Ala., 4/2/1945
Tanner, Leonard Roscoe III (tennis); Chattanooga, Tenn., 10/15/1951
Tarkenton, Fran (Francis) (football); Richmond, Va., 2/3/1940
Tebbetts, Birdie (George R.) (baseball); Nashua, N.H., 11/10/1914
Thoeni, Gustavo (Alpine skier); Trafoi, Italy, 2/28/1951
Thompson, David (basketball); Shelby, N.C., 7/13/1954
Thorpe, Jim (James Francis Thorpe) (all-around athlete); nr. Prague, Okla. (1888–1953)
Tilden, William Tatem II (tennis); Philadelphia (1893–1953)
Tittle, Y. A. (Yelberton Abraham) (football); Marshall, Tex., 10/24/1926
Toomey, William (decathlon); Philadelphia, 1/10/1939
Trevino, Lee (golf); Dallas, 12/1/1939
Tunney, Gene (James J.) (boxing); New York City (1898–1978)
Tyus, Wyomia (runner); Griffin, Ga., 8/29/1945
Unitas, John (football); Pittsburgh, 5/7/1933
Unser, Al (auto racing); Albuquerque, N. Mex., 5/29/1939
Unser, Bobby (auto racing); Albuquerque N. Mex., 2/20/1934
Van Brocklin, Norm (football); Eagle Butte, S. Dak., 3/15/1926
Vilas, Guillermo (tennis); Mar del Plata, Argentina, 8/17/1952
Viren, Lasse (track); Myrskyla, Finland, 7/12/1949
Wade, Virginia (tennis); Bournemouth, England, 7/10/1945
Wagner, Honus (John Peter Honus) (baseball); Carnegie, Pa. (1867–1955)
Walcott, Jersey Joe (Arnold Cream) (boxing); Merchantville, N.J., 1/31/1914
Walton, Bill (basketball); La Mesa, Calif., 11/5/1952
Watson, Martha Rae (track); Long Beach, Calif., 8/19/1946
Watson, Tom (golf); Kansas City, Mo., 9/4/1949
Weaver, Earl (baseball); St. Louis, 8/14/1930
Webster, Alex (football); Kearny, N.J., 4/19/1931
Weiskopf, Tom (golf); Massillon, Ohio, 11/9/1942
Weiss, George (baseball executive); New Haven, Conn. (1895–1972)
Weissmuller, Johnny (swimmer and actor); Windber, Pa., 6/2/1904
West, Jerry (basketball); Cheylan, W. Va., 5/28/1938
White, Willye B. (long jumper); Money, Miss., 1/1/1936
Whitworth, Kathy (golf); Monahans, Tex., 9/27/1939
Wilkens, Mac Maurice (track); Eugene, Ore., 11/15/1950
Wilkins, Lennie (basketball); 11/25/1937
Wilkinson, Bud (football); Minneapolis, 4/23/1916
Williams, Dick (baseball); St. Louis, 5/7/1929
Williams, Ted (baseball); San Diego, Calif., 8/30/1918
Wills, Maury (baseball); Washington, D.C., 10/2/1932
Winfield, Dave (baseball); St. Paul, Minn., 10/3/1951
Wohlhuter, Richard C. (runner); Geneva, Ill. 12/23/1945
Woodhead, Cynthia (swimming); Riverside, Calif., 2/7/1964
Wottle, David James (runner); Canton, Ohio, 8/7/1950
Wright, Mickey (Mary Kathryn) (golf); San Diego, Calif., 2/14/1935
Yarborough, Cale (William Caleb) (auto racing); Timmonsville, S.C., 3/27/1939
Yastrzemski, Carl (baseball); Southampton, N.Y., 8/22/1939
Young, Cy (Denton True Young) (baseball); Gilmore, Ohio (1867–1955)
Young, Sheila (speed skater, bicycle racer); Detroit, 10/14/1950

THE OLYMPIC GAMES

(W)—Site of Winter Games. (S)—Site of Summer Games

1896	Athens	1932	Los Angeles (S)	1964	Tokyo (S)
1900	Paris	1936	Garmisch-Partenkirchen (W)	1968	Grenoble, France (W)
1904	St. Louis	1936	Berlin (S)	1968	Mexico City (S)
1906	Athens	1948	St. Moritz (W)	1972	Sapporo, Japan (W)
1908	London	1948	London (S)	1972	Munich (S)
1912	Stockholm	1952	Oslo (W)	1976	Innsbruck, Austria (W)
1920	Antwerp	1952	Helsinki (S)	1976	Montreal (S)
1924	Chamonix (W)	1956	Cortina d'Ampezzo, Italy (W)	1980	Lake Placid (W)
1924	Paris (S)	1956	Melbourne (S)	1980	Moscow (S)
1928	St. Moritz (W)	1960	Squaw Valley, Calif. (W)	1984	Sarajevo, Yugoslavia (W)
1928	Amsterdam (S)	1960	Rome (S)	1984	Los Angeles (S)
1932	Lake Placid (W)	1964	Innsbruck, Austria (W)		

The first Olympic Games of which there is record occurred in 776 B.C. and consisted of one event, a great foot race of about 200 yards held on a plain by the River Alpheus (now the Ruphia) just outside the little town of Olympia in Greece. It was from that date that the Greeks began to keep their calendar by "Olympiads," the four-year spans between the celebrations of the famous games.

The modern Olympic Games, which started in Athens in 1896, are the result of the devotion of a French educator, Baron Pierre de Coubertin, to the idea that, since young people and athletics have gone together down the ages, education and athletics might well go hand-in-hand toward a better international understanding.

At the top of the organization responsible for the Olympic movement and the staging of the Games every four years is the International Olympic Committee (IOC). Other important roles are played by National Olympic Committees in each participating country, international sports federations, and the Organizing Committee of the host city.

In 1979, the IOC consisted of 89 members, elected by the IOC itself. Its headquarters are in Lausanne, Switzerland. The president of the IOC is Juan Antonio Samaranch of Spain.

The Olympic motto is "Citius, Altius, Fortius"—"Faster, Higher, Stronger." The Olympic symbol is five interlocking circles colored blue, yellow, black, green, and red, on a white background, representing the five continents. At least one of these colors appears in the national flag of every country.

Summer Games

TRACK AND FIELD—MEN

100-Meter Dash

1896	Thomas Burke, United States	12s
1900	Francis W. Jarvis, United States	10.8s
1904	Archie Hahn, United States	11s
1906	Archie Hahn, United States	11.2s
1908	Reginald Walker, South Africa	10.8s
1912	Ralph Craig, United States	10.8s
1920	Charles Paddock, United States	10.8s
1924	Harold Abrahams, Great Britain	10.6s
1928	Percy Williams, Canada	10.8s
1932	Eddie Tolan, United States	10.3s
1936	Jesse Owens, United States	10.3s[1]
1948	Harrison Dillard, United States	10.3s
1952	Lindy Remigino, United States	10.4s
1956	Bobby Morrow, United States	10.5s
1960	Armin Hary, Germany	10.2s
1964	Robert Hayes, United States	10s
1968	James Hines, United States	9.9s
1972	Valery Borzov, U.S.S.R.	10.14s
1976	Hasely Crawford, Trinidad and Tebago	10.06s
1980	Allan Wells, Britain	10.25s

1. Wind assisted.

200-Meter Dash

1900	John Tewksbury, United States	22.2s
1904	Archie Hahn, United States	21.6s
1908	Robert Kerr, Canada	22.6s
1912	Ralph Craig, United States	21.7s
1920	Allan Woodring, United States	22s
1924	Jackson Scholz, United States	21.6s
1928	Percy Williams, Canada	21.8s
1932	Eddie Tolan, United States	21.2s
1936	Jesse Owens, United States	20.7s
1948	Melvin E. Patton, United States	21.1s
1952	Andrew Stanfield, United States	20.7s
1956	Bobby Morrow, United States	20.6s
1960	Livio Berruti, Italy	20.5s
1964	Henry Carr, United States	20.3s
1968	Tommie Smith, United States	19.8s
1972	Valery Borzov, U.S.S.R.	20s
1976	Don Quarrie, Jamaica	20.23s
1980	Pietro Mennea, Italy	20.19s

400-Meter Dash

1896	Thomas Burke, United States	54.2s
1900	Maxwell Long, United States	49.4s
1904	Harry Hillman, United States	49.2s
1906	Paul Pilgrim, United States	53.2s
1908	Wyndham Halswelle, Great Britain (walkover)	50s
1912	Charles Reidpath, United States	48.2s
1920	Bevil Rudd, South Africa	49.6s
1924	Eric Liddell, Great Britain	47.6s
1928	Ray Barbuti, United States	47.8s
1932	William Carr, United States	46.2s
1936	Archie Williams, United States	46.5s
1948	Arthur Wint, Jamaica, B.W.I.	46.2s
1952	George Rhoden, Jamaica, B.W.I.	45.9s
1956	Charles Jenkins, United States	46.7s
1960	Otis Davis, United States	44.9s
1964	Mike Larrabee, United States	45.1s
1968	Lee Evans, United States	43.8s
1972	Vincent Matthews, United States	44.66s
1976	Alberto Juantorena, Cuba	44.26s
1980	Viktor Markin, U.S.S.R.	44.60s

800-Meter Run

1896	Edwin Flack, Australia	2m11s
1900	Alfred Tysoe, Great Britain	2m1.4s
1904	James Lightbody, United States	1m56s
1906	Paul Pilgrim, United States	2m1.2s
1908	Mel Sheppard, United States	1m52.8s
1912	Ted Meredith, United States	1m51.9s

1920	Albert Hill, Great Britain	1m53.4s
1924	Douglas Lowe, Great Britain	1m52.4s
1928	Douglas Lowe, Great Britain	1m51.8s
1932	Thomas Hampson, Great Britain	1m49.8s
1936	John Woodruff, United States	1m52.9s
1948	Malvin Whitfield, United States	1m49.2s
1952	Malvin Whitfield, United States	1m49.2s
1956	Tom Courtney, United States	1m47.7s
1960	Peter Snell, New Zealand	1m46.3s
1964	Peter Snell, New Zealand	1m45.1s
1968	Ralph Doubell, Australia	1m44.3s
1972	David Wottle, United States	1m45.9s
1976	Alberto Juantorena, Cuba	1m43.5s
1980	Steve Ovett, Britain	1m45.4s

1,500-Meter Run

1896	Edwin Flack, Australia	4m33.2s
1900	Charles Bennett, Great Britain	4m6s
1904	James Lightbody, United States	4m5.4s
1906	James Lightbody, United States	4m12s
1908	Mel Sheppard, United States	4m3.4s
1912	Arnold Jackson, Great Britain	3m56.8s
1920	Albert Hill, Great Britain	4m1.8s
1924	Paavo Nurmi, Finland	3m53.6s
1928	Harry Larva, Finland	3m53.2s
1932	Luigi Beccali, Italy	3m51.2s
1936	Jack Lovelock, New Zealand	3m47.8s
1948	Henri Eriksson, Sweden	3m49.8s
1952	Joseph Barthel, Luxembourg	3m45.2s
1956	Ron Delany, Ireland	3m41.2s
1960	Herb Elliott, Australia	3m35.6s
1964	Peter Snell, New Zealand	3m38.1s
1968	Kipchoge Keino, Kenya	3m34.9s
1972	Pekka Vasala, Finland	3m36.3s
1976	John Walker, New Zealand	3m39.17s
1980	Sebastian Coe, Britain	3m38.4s

5,000-Meter Run

1912	Hannes Kolehmainen, Finland	14m36.6s
1920	Joseph Guillemot, France	14m55.6s
1924	Paavo Nurmi, Finland	14m31.2s
1928	Willie Ritola, Finland	14m38s
1932	Lauri Lehtinen, Finland	14m30s
1936	Gunnar Hockert, Finland	14m22.2s
1948	Gaston Reiff, Belgium	14m17.6s
1952	Emil Zatopek, Czechoslovakia	14m6.6s
1956	Vladimir Kuts, U.S.S.R.	13m39.6s
1960	Murray Halberg, New Zealand	13m43,4s
1964	Bob Schul, United States	13m48.8s
1968	Mohamed Gammoudi, Tunisia	14m.05s
1972	Lasse Viren, Finland	13m26.4s
1976	Lasse Viren, Finland	13m24.76s
1980	Miruts Yifter, Ethiopia	13m21s

5-Mile Run

1906	H. Hawtrey, Great Britain	26m26.2s
1908	Emil Voigt, Great Britain	25m11.2s

10,000-Meter Run

1912	Hannes Kolehmainen, Finland	31m20.8s
1920	Paavo Nurmi, Finland	31m45.8s
1924	Willie Ritola, Finland	30m23.2s
1928	Paavo Nurmi, Finland	30m18.8s
1932	Janusz Kusocinski, Poland	30m11.4s
1936	Ilmari Salminen, Finland	30m15.4s
1948	Emil Zatopek, Czechoslovakia	29m59.6s
1952	Emil Zatopek, Czechoslovakia	29m17s
1956	Vladimir Kuts, U.S.S.R.	28m45.6s
1960	Peter Bolotnikov, U.S.S.R.	28m32.2s
1964	Billy Mills, United States	28m24.4s
1968	Naftali Temu, Kenya	29m27.4s
1972	Lasse Viren, Finland	27m38.4s
1976	Lasse Viren, Finland	27m40.38s

1980	Miruts Yifter, Ethiopia	27m42.7s

Marathon

1896	Spiridon Loues, Greece	2h58m50s
1900	Michel Teato, France	2h59m45s
1904	Thomas Hicks, United States	3h28m53s
1906	William J. Sherring, Canada	2h51m23.65s
1908	John J. Hayes, United States	2h55m18.4s
1912	Kenneth McArthur, South Africa	2h36m54.8s
1920	Hannes Kolehmainen, Finland	2h32m35.8s
1924	Albin Stenroos, Finland	2h41m22.6s
1928	A. B. El Ouafi, France	2h32m57s
1932	Juan Zabala, Argentina	2h31m36s
1936	Kitei Son, Japan	2h29m19.2s
1948	Delfo Cabrera, Argentina	2h34m51.6s
1952	Emil Zatopek, Czechoslovakia	2h23m3.2s
1956	Alain Mimoun, France	2h25m
1960	Abebe Bikila, Ethiopia	2h15m16.2s
1964	Abebe Bikila, Ethiopia	2h12m11.2s
1968	Mamo Wold, Ethiopia	2h20m26.4s
1972	Frank Shorter, United States	2h12m19.8s
1976	Walter Cierpinski, East Germany	2h09m55s
1980	Walter Cierpinski, East Germany	2h11m3s

110-Meter Hurdles

1896	Thomas Curtis, United States	17.6s
1900	Alvin Kraenzlein, United States	15.4s
1904	Frederick Schule, United States	16s
1906	R. G. Leavitt, United States	16.2s
1908	Forrest Smithson, United States	15s
1912	Frederick Kelly, United States	15.1s
1920	Earl Thomson, Canada	14.8s
1924	Daniel Kinsey, United States	15s
1928	Sydney Atkinson, South Africa	14.8s
1932	George Saling, United States	14.6s
1936	Forrest Towns, United States	14.2s
1948	William Porter, United States	13.9s
1952	Harrison Dillard, United States	13.7s
1956	Lee Calhoun, United States	13.5s
1960	Lee Calhoun, United States	13.8s
1964	Hayes Jones, United States	13.6s
1968	Willie Davenport, United States	13.3s
1972	Rodney Milburn, United States	13.24s
1976	Guy Drut, France	13.30s
1980	Thomas Munkelt, East Germany	13.39s

200-Meter Hurdles

1900	Alvin Kraenzlein, United States	25.4s
1904	Harry Hillman, United States	24.6s

400-Meter Hurdles

1900	John Tewksbury, United States	57.6s
1904	Harry Hillman, United States	53s
1908	Charles Bacon, United States	55s
1920	Frank Loomis, United States	54s
1924	F. Morgan Taylor, United States	52.6s
1928	Lord David Burghley, Great Britain	53.4s
1932	Robert Tisdall, Ireland	51.8s[1]
1936	Glenn Hardin, United States	52.4s
1948	Roy Cochran, United States	51.1s
1952	Charles Moore, United States	50.8s
1956	Glenn Davis, United States	50.1s
1960	Glenn Davis, United States	49.3s
1964	Rex Cawley, United States	49.6s
1968	David Hemery, Great Britain	48.1s
1972	John Akii-Bua, Uganda	47.8s
1976	Edwin Moses, United States	47.64
1980	Volker Beck, East Germany	48.70s

1. Record not allowed.

2,500-Meter Steeplechase

1900	George Orton, United States	7m34s
1904	James Lightbody, United States	7m39.6s

3,000-Meter Steeplechase

1920	Percy Hodge, Great Britain	10m0.4s
1924	Willie Ritola, Finland	9m33.6s
1928	Toivo Loukola, Finland	9m21.8s
1932	Volmari Iso-Hollo, Finland	10m33.4s[1]
1936	Volmari Iso-Hollo, Finland	9m3.8s
1948	Thure Sjoestrand, Sweden	9m4.6s
1952	Horace Ashenfelter, United States	8m45.4s
1956	Chris Brasher, Great Britain	8m41.2s
1960	Zdzislaw Krzyskowiak, Poland	8m34.2s
1964	Gaston Roelants, Belgium	8m30.8s
1968	Amos Biwott, Kenya	8m51s
1972	Kipchoge Keino, Kenya	8m23.6s
1976	Anders Gardervd, Sweden	8m08.02s
1980	Bronislaw Malinowski, Poland	8m9.7s

1. About 3,450 meters—extra lap by error.

Cross-Country

1912	Hannes Kolehmainen, Finland (8,000 meters)	45m11.6s
1920	Paavo Nurmi, Finland (10,000 meters)	27m15s
1924	Paavo Nurmi, Finland (10,000 meters)	32m54.8s

Cross-Country Team Races

		Pts.
1912	Sweden (8,000 meters)	10
1920	Finland (10,000 meters)	10
1924	Finland (10,000 meters)	11

1,500-Meter Walk

1906	George V. Bonhag, United States	7m12.6s

3,000-Meter Walk

1920	Ugo Frigerio, Italy	13m14.2s

10,000-Meter Walk

1912	George Goulding, Canada	46m28.4s
1920	Ugo Frigerio, Italy	48m6.2s
1924	Ugo Frigerio, Italy	47m49s
1948	John Mikaelsson, Sweden	45m13.2s
1952	John Mikaelsson, Sweden	45m2.8s

20,000-Meter Walk

1956	Leonid Spirin, U.S.S.R.	1h31m27.4s
1960	Vladimir Golubnichy, U.S.S.R.	1h34m7.2s
1964	Ken Mathews, Great Britain	1h29m34s
1968	Vladimir Golubnichy, U.S.S.R.	1h33m58.4s
1972	Peter Frenkel, East Germany	1h26m42.4s
1976	Daniel Bautista, Mexico	1h24m40.6s
1980	Maurizio Damiliano, Italy	1h23m35.5s

50,000-Meter Walk

1932	Thomas W. Green, Great Britain	4h50m10s
1936	Harold Whitlock, Great Britain	4h30m41.1s
1948	John Ljunggren, Sweden	4h41m52s
1952	Giuseppe Dordoni, Italy	4h28m7.8s
1956	Norman Read, New Zealand	4h30m42.8s
1960	Donald Thompson, Great Britain	4h25m30s
1964	Abdon Pamich, Italy	4h11m12.4s
1968	Christoph Hohne, East Germany	4h20m13.6s
1972	Bern Kannernberg, West Germany	3h56m11.6s
1980	Hartwig Gauder, East Germany	3h49m24s

400-Meter Relay (4 x 100)

1912	Great Britain	42.4s
1920	United States	42.2s
1924	United States	41s
1928	United States	41s
1932	United States	40s
1936	United States	39.8s
1948	United States	40.6s
1952	United States	40.1s
1956	United States	39.5s
1960	Germany	39.5s
1964	United States	39s
1968	United States	38.2s
1972	United States	38.19s
1976	United States	38.33s
1980	U.S.S.R.	38.26s

1,600-Meter Relay (200–200–400–800)

1908	United States	3m29.4s

1,600-Meter Relay (4 x 400)

1912	United States	3m16.6s
1920	Great Britain	3m22.2s
1924	United States	3m16s
1928	United States	3m14.2s
1932	United States	3m8.2s
1936	Great Britain	3m9s
1948	United States	3m10.4s
1952	Jamaica, B.W.I.	3m3.9s
1956	United States	3m4.8s
1960	United States	3m2.2s
1964	United States	3m0.7s
1968	United States	2m56.1s
1972	Kenya	2m59.8s
1976	United States	2m58.65s
1980	U.S.S.R.	3m01.1s

Team Race

		Pts.
1900	Great Britain (5,000 meters)	26
1904	United States (4 miles)	27
1908	Great Britain (3 miles)	6
1912	United States (3,000 meters)	9
1920	United States (3,000 meters)	10
1924	Finland (3,000 meters)	9

Standing High Jump

1900	Ray Ewry, United States	5 ft 5 in.
1904	Ray Ewry, United States	4 ft 11 in.
1906	Ray Ewry, United States	5 ft 1⅝ in.
1908	Ray Ewry, United States	5 ft 2 in.
1912	Platt Adams, United States	5 ft 4⅛ in.

Running High Jump

1896	Ellery Clark, United States	5 ft 11¼ in.
1900	Irving Baxter, United States	6 ft 2¾ in.
1904	Samuel Jones, United States	5 ft 11 in.
1906	Con Leahy, Ireland	5 ft 9⅞ in.
1908	Harry Porter, United States	6 ft 3 in.
1912	Alma Richards, United States	6 ft 4 in.
1920	Richmond Landon, United States	6 ft 4¼ in.
1924	Harold Osborn, United States	6 ft 5¹⁵⁄₁₆ in.
1928	Robert W. King, United States	6 ft 4¾ in.
1932	Duncan McNaughton, Canada	6 ft 5⅝ in.
1936	Cornelius Johnson, United States	6 ft 7¹⁵⁄₁₆ in.
1948	John Winter, Australia	6 ft 6 in.
1952	Walter Davis, United States	6 ft 8⁹⁄₁₆ in.
1956	Charles Dumas, United States	6 ft 11¼ in.
1960	Robert Shavlakadze, U.S.S.R.	7 ft 1 in.
1964	Valeri Brumel, U.S.S.R.	7 ft 1¾ in.
1968	Dick Fosbury, United States	7 ft 4¼ in.
1972	Yuri Tarmak, U.S.S.R.	7 ft 3¾ in.
1976	Jacek Wszola, Poland	(2.25m) 7 ft 4½ in.
1980	Gerd Wessig, East Germany	7ft 8¾ in.

Standing Long Jump

1900	Ray Ewry, United States	10 ft 6⅖ in.
1904	Ray Ewry, United States	11 ft 4⅞ in.
1906	Ray Ewry, United States	10 ft 10 in.
1908	Ray Ewry, United States	10 ft 11¼ in.
1912	Constantin Tsicilitiras, Greece	11 ft ¼ in.

Long Jump

1896	Ellery Clark, United States	20 ft 9¾ in.
1900	Alvin Kraenzlein, United States	23 ft 6⅞ in.
1904	Myer Prinstein, United States	24 ft 1 in.
1906	Myer Prinstein, United States	23 ft 7½ in.
1908	Frank Irons, United States	24 ft 6½ in.
1912	Albert Gutterson, United States	24 ft 11¼ in.
1920	William Petterssen, Sweden	23 ft 5½ in.
1924	DeHart Hubbard, United States	24 ft 5⅛ in.
1928	Edward B. Hamm, United States	25 ft 4¾ in.
1932	Edward Gordon, United States	25 ft ¾ in.
1936	Jesse Owens, United States	26 ft 5⁵/₁₆ in.
1948	Willie Steele, United States	25 ft 8 in.
1952	Jerome Biffle, United States	24 ft 10 in.
1956	Gregory Bell, United States	25 ft 8¼ in.
1960	Ralph Boston, United States	26 ft 7¾ in.
1964	Lynn Davies, Great Britain	26 ft 5¾ in.
1968	Bob Beamon, United States	29 ft 2½ in.
1972	Randy Williams, United States	27 ft ½ in.
1976	Arnie Robinson, United States	(8.35m) 24 ft 7¾ in.
1980	Lutz Dombrowski, Poland	28 ft ¼ in.

Standing Triple Jump

1900	Ray Ewry, United States	34 ft 8½ in.
1904	Ray Ewry, United States	34 ft 7¼ in.

Triple Jump

1896	James B. Connolly, United States	45 ft
1900	Myer Prinstein, United States	47 ft 4¼ in.
1904	Myer Prinstein, United States	47 ft
1906	P. G. O'Connor, Ireland	46 ft 2 in.
1908	Timothy Ahearne, Great Britain	48 ft 11¼ in.
1912	Gustaf Lindblom, Sweden	48 ft 5⅛ in.
1920	Vilho Tuulos, Finland	47 ft 6⅞ in.
1924	Archie Winter, Australia	50 ft 11⅛ in.
1928	Mikio Oda, Japan	49 ft 10¹³/₁₆ in.
1932	Chuhei Nambu, Japan	51 ft 7 in.
1936	Naoto Tajima, Japan	52 ft 5⅞ in.
1948	Arne Ahman, Sweden	50 ft 6¼ in.
1952	Adhemar da Silva, Brazil	53 ft 2½ in.
1956	Adhemar da Silva, Brazil	53 ft 7½ in.
1960	Jozef Schmidt, Poland	55 ft 1¾ in.
1964	Jozef Schmidt, Poland	55 ft 3¼ in.
1968	Viktor Saneyev, U.S.S.R.	57 ft ¾ in.
1972	Viktor Saneyev, U.S.S.R.	56 ft 11 in.
1976	Viktor Saneyev, U.S.S.R.	(17.29m) 56 ft 8¾ in.
1980	Jaak Uudmae, U.S.S.R.	56 ft 11⅛ in.

Pole Vault

1896	William Hoyt, United States	10 ft 9¾ in.
1900	Irving Baxter, United States	10 ft 9⅞ in.
1904	Charles Dvorak, United States	11 ft 6 in.
1906	Fernand Gouder, France	11 ft 6 in.
1908	Alfred Gilbert, United States, and Edward Cook, United States (tie)	12 ft 2 in.
1912	Harry Babcock, United States	12 ft 11½ in.
1920	Frank Foss, United States	13 ft 5⁹/₁₆ in.
1924	Lee Barnes, United States	12 ft 11½ in.
1928	Sabin W. Carr, United States	13 ft 9¾ in.
1932	William Miller, United States	14 ft 1⅞ in.
1936	Earle Meadows, United States	14 ft 3¼ in.
1948	Guinn Smith, United States	14 ft 1¼ in.
1952	Robert Richards, United States	14 ft 11⅛ in.
1956	Robert Richards, United States	14 ft 11½ in.
1960	Don Bragg, United States	15 ft 5⅛ in.
1964	Fred Hansen, United States	16 ft 8¾ in.
1968	Bob Seagren, United States	17 ft 8½ in.
1972	Wolfgang Nordwig, East Germany	18 ft ½ in.
1976	Tadeusz Slusarski, Poland	(5.50m) 18 ft ½ in.
1980	Wladyslaw Kozakiewicz, Poland	18 ft 11½ in.

16-lb Shot-Put

1896	Robert Garrett, United States	36 ft 9¾ in.
1900	Richard Sheldon, United States	46 ft 3⅛ in.
1904	Ralph Rose, United States	48 ft 7 in.
1906	Martin Sheridan, United States	40 ft 4⅘ in.
1908	Ralph Rose, United States	46 ft 7½ in.
1912	Pat McDonald, United States	50 ft 4 in.
1920	Ville Porhola, Finland	48 ft 7⅛ in.
1924	Clarence Houser, United States	49 ft 2½ in.
1928	John Kuck, United States	52 ft 11¹¹/₁₆ in.
1932	Leo Sexton, United States	52 ft 6³/₁₆ in.
1936	Hans Woellke, Germany	53 ft 1¾ in.
1948	Wilbur Thompson, United States	56 ft 2 in.
1952	Parry O'Brien, United States	57 ft 1½ in.
1956	Parry O'Brien, United States	60 ft 11 in.
1960	Bill Nieder, United States	64 ft 6¾ in.
1964	Dallas Long, United States	66 ft 8¼ in.
1968	Randy Matson, United States	67 ft 4¾ in.
1972	Wladyslaw Komar, Poland	69 ft 6 in.
1976	Udo Beyer, East Germany	(21.05m) 69 ft ¾ in.
1980	Vladimir Kiselyov, U.S.S.R.	70 ft ½ in.

16-lb Shot-Put (Both Hands)

1912	Ralph Rose, United States	90 ft 5⅜ in.

Discus Throw

1896	Robert Garrett, United States	95 ft 7½ in.
1900	Rudolf Bauer, Hungary	118 ft 2⅞ in.
1904	Martin Sheridan, United States	128 ft 10½ in.
1906	Martin Sheridan, United States	136 ft ⅓ in.
1908	Martin Sheridan, United States	134 ft 2 in.
1912	Armas Taipale, Finland	145 ft ⁹/₁₆ in.
1920	Elmer Niklander, Finland	146 ft 7 in.
1924	Clarence Houser, United States	151 ft 5¼ in.
1928	Clarence Houser, United States	155 ft 2⅘ in.
1932	John Anderson, United States	162 ft 4⅞ in.
1936	Ken Carpenter, United States	165 ft 7⅜ in.
1948	Adolfo Consolini, Italy	173 ft 2 in.
1952	Simeon Iness, United States	180 ft 6½ in.
1956	Al Oerter, United States	184 ft 10½ in.
1960	Al Oerter, United States	194 ft 2 in.
1964	Al Oerter, United States	200 ft 1½ in.
1968	Al Oerter, United States	212 ft 6 in.
1972	Ludvik Danek, Czechoslovakia	211 ft 3 in.
1976	Mac Wilkins, United States	(67.5m) 221 ft 5 in.
1980	Viktor Rashchupkin, U.S.S.R.	218 ft 8 in.

Discus Throw—Greek Style

1906	Werner Jaervinen, Finland	115 ft 4 in.
1908	Martin Sheridan, United States	124 ft 8 in.

Discus Throw (Both Hands)

1912	Armas Taipale, Finland	271 ft 10⅛ in.

Javelin Throw

1906	Eric Lemming, Sweden	175 ft 6 in.
1908	Eric Lemming, Sweden	179 ft 10½ in.
1912	Eric Lemming, Sweden	198 ft 11¼ in.
1920	Jonni Myyra, Finland	215 ft 9¾ in.
1924	Jonni Myyra, Finland	206 ft 6¾ in.
1928	Eric Lundquist, Sweden	218 ft 6½ in.
1932	Matti Jarvinen, Finland	238 ft 7 in.
1936	Gerhard Stoeck, Germany	235 ft 8⁵/₁₆ in.
1948	Kaj Rautavaara, Finland	228 ft 10½ in.
1952	Cy Young, United States	242 ft ¾ in.
1956	Egil Danielsen, Norway	281 ft 2¼ in.
1960	Viktor Tsibulenko, U.S.S.R.	277 ft 8⅜ in.
1964	Pauli Nevala, Finland	271 ft 2¼ in.
1968	Janis Lusis, U.S.S.R.	295 ft 7 in.
1972	Klaus Wolfermann, West Germany	296 ft 10 in.
1976	Miklos Nemeth, Hungary	(94.58m) 310 ft 4 in.
1980	Dainis Kula, U.S.S.R.	299 ft 2⅜ in.

Javelin Throw—Free Style

1908	Eric Lemming, Sweden	178 ft 7½ in.

Javelin Throw (Both Hands)

1912	Julius Saaristo, Finland	358 ft 11½ in.

16-lb Hammer Throw

1900	John Flanagan, United States	167 ft 4 in.
1904	John Flanagan, United States	168 ft 1 in.
1908	John Flanagan, United States	170 ft 4¼ in.
1912	Matt McGrath, United States	179 ft 7⅛ in.
1920	Pat Ryan, United States	173 ft 5⅝ in.
1924	Fred Tootell, United States	174 ft 10¼ in.
1928	Patrick O'Callaghan, Ireland	168 ft 7½ in.
1932	Patrick O'Callaghan, Ireland	176 ft 11⅛ in.
1936	Karl Hein, Germany	185 ft 4 in.
1948	Imre Nemeth, Hungary	183 ft 11½ in.
1952	Jozsef Csermak, Hungary	197 ft 11⁹⁄₁₆ in.
1956	Harold Connolly, United States	207 ft 2¾ in.
1960	Vasily Rudenkov, U.S.S.R.	220 ft 1⅝ in.
1964	Romuald Klim, U.S.S.R.	228 ft 9½ in.
1968	Gyula Zsivotzky, Hungary	240 ft 8 in.
1972	Anatoly Bondarchuk, U.S.S.R.	247 ft 8½ in.
1976	Yuri Sedykh, U.S.S.R.	(77.52m) 254 ft 4 in.
1980	Yuri Sedykh, U.S.S.R.	(81.80m) 268 ft 4½ in.

Throwing the Stone (14 lbs.)

1906	Nicolas Georgantas, Greece	65 ft 4⅕ in.

56-lb Weight Throw

1904	Etienne Desmarteau, Canada	34 ft 4 in.
1920	Pat McDonald, United States	36 ft 11⅝ in.

All-Around

1904	Thomas Kiely, Great Britain	6,036 pts.

Pentathlon

1906	H. Mellander, Sweden	24 pts.
1912	Ferdinand Bie, Norway	21 pts.
1920	Eero Lehtonen, Finland	14 pts.
1924	Eero Lehtonen, Finland	16 pts.

Decathlon

1912	Hugo Wieslander, Sweden	7,724.495 pts.
1920	Helge Lovland, Norway	6,804.35 pts.
1924	Harold Osborn, United States	7,710.775 pts.
1928	Paavo Yrjola, Finland	8,053.29 pts.
1932	James Bausch, United States	8,462.23 pts.
1936	Glenn Morris, United States	7,900 pts.[1]
1948	Robert B. Mathias, United States	7,139 pts.
1952	Robert B. Mathias, United States	7,887 pts.
1956	Milton Campbell, United States	7,937 pts.
1960	Rafer Johnson, United States	8,392 pts.
1964	Willi Holdorf, Germany	7,887 pts.[1]
1968	Bill Toomey, United States	8,193 pts.
1972	Nikolai Avilov, U.S.S.R.	8,454 pts.
1976	Bruce Jenner, United States	8,618 pts.
1980	Daley Thompson, Britain	8,495 pts.

1. Point system revised.

Tug of War

1904	United States		1912	Sweden
1906	Germany		1920	Great Britain
1908	Great Britain			

TRACK AND FIELD—WOMEN

100-Meter Dash

1928	Elizabeth Robinson, United States	12.2s
1932	Stella Walsh, Poland	11.9s
1936	Helen Stephens, United States	11.5s
1948	Fanny Blankers-Koen, Netherlands	11.9s
1952	Marjorie Jackson, Australia	11.5s
1956	Betty Cuthbert, Australia	11.5s
1960	Wilma Rudolph, United States	11s
1964	Wyomia Tyus, United States	11.4s
1968	Wyomia Tyus, United States	11s
1972	Renate Stecher, East Germany	11.07s
1976	Annegret Richter, West Germany	11.08s
1980	Lyudmila Kondratyeva, U.S.S.R.	11.06s

200-Meter Dash

1948	Fanny Blankers-Koen, Netherlands	24.4s
1952	Marjorie Jackson, Australia	23.7s
1956	Betty Cuthbert, Australia	23.4s
1960	Wilma Rudolph, United States	24s
1964	Edith McGuire, United States	23s
1968	Irena Szewinska, Poland	22.5s
1972	Renate Stecher, East Germany	22.4s
1976	Baerbel Eckert, East Germany	22.37s
1980	Barbara Wockel, East Germany	22.03s

400-Meter Dash

1964	Betty Cuthbert, Australia	52s
1968	Colette Besson, France	52s
1972	Monika Zehrt, East Germany	51.08s
1976	Irena Szewinska, Poland	49.29s
1980	Marita Koch, East Germany	48.88s

800-Meter Run

1928	Lina Radke, Germany	2m16.8s
1960	Ljudmila Shevcova, U.S.S.R.	2m4.3s
1964	Ann Packer, Great Britain	2m1.1s
1968	Madeline Manning, United States	2m0.9s
1972	Hildegard Falck, West Germany	1m58.6s
1976	Tatiana Kazankina, U.S.S.R.	1m54.94s
1980	Nadezhda Olizarenko, U.S.S.R.	1m53.5s

1,500-Meter Run

1972	Ludmila Bragina, U.S.S.R.	4m01.4s
1976	Tatiana Kazankina, U.S.S.R.	4m05.48s

80-Meter Hurdles

1932	Mildred Didrikson, United States	11.7s
1936	Trebisonda Valla, Italy	11.7s
1948	Fanny Blankers-Koen, Netherlands	11.2s
1952	Shirley S. de la Hunty, Australia	10.9s
1956	Shirley S. de la Hunty, Australia	10.7s
1960	Irina Press, U.S.S.R.	10.8s
1964	Karin Balzer, Germany	10.5s[1]
1968	Maureen Caird, Australia	10.3s

1. Wind assisted.

100-Meter Hurdles

1972	Annelie Ehrhardt, East Germany	12.59s
1976	Johanna Schaller, East Germany	12.77s
1980	Vera Komisova, U.S.S.R.	12.56s

400-Meter Relay

1928	Canada	48.4s
1932	United States	47s
1936	United States	46.9s
1948	Netherlands	47.5s
1952	United States	45.9s
1956	Australia	44.5s
1960	United States	44.5s
1964	Poland	43.6s
1968	United States	42.8s
1972	West Germany	42.81s
1976	East Germany	42.55s
1980	East Germany	41.60s

1,600-Meter Relay

1972	East Germany	3m23s
1976	East Germany	3m19.23s
1980	U.S.S.R.	3m20.2s

Running High Jump

1928	Ethel Catherwood, Canada	5 ft 3 in.
1932	Jean Shiley, United States	5 ft 5¼ in.
1936	Ibolya Csak, Hungary	5 ft 3 in.
1948	Alice Coachman, United States	5 ft 6⅛ in.
1952	Ester Brand, South Africa	5 ft 5¾ in.
1956	Mildred McDaniel, United States	5 ft 9¼ in.
1960	Iolanda Balas, Romania	6 ft ¾ in.
1964	Iolanda Balas, U.S.S.R.	6 ft 2¾ in.
1968	Miloslava Rezkova, Czechoslovakia	5 ft 11¾ in.
1972	Ulrike Meyfarth, West Germany	6 ft 3⅜ in.
1976	Rosemarie Ackerman, E. Germany (1.93m)	6 ft 4 in.
1980	Sara Simeoni, Italy	6 ft 5½ in.

Long Jump

1948	Olga Gyarmati, Hungary	18 ft 8¼ in.
1952	Yvette Williams, New Zealand	20 ft 5¾ in.
1956	Elzbieta Krzesinska, Poland	20 ft 9¾ in.
1960	Vera Krepkina, U.S.S.R.	20 ft 10¾ in.
1964	Mary Rand, Great Britain	22 ft 2 in.
1968	Viorica Ciscopoleanu, Romania	22 ft 4½ in.
1972	Heidemarie Rosendahl, West Germany	22 ft 3 in.
1976	Angela Voigt, East Germany (6.72m)	22 ft ½ in.
1980	Tatiana Kolpakova, U.S.S.R.	23 ft 2 in.

Shot-Put

1948	Micheline Ostermeyer, France	45 ft 1½ in.
1952	Galina Zybina, U.S.S.R.	50 ft 1½ in.
1956	Tamara Tishkyevich, U.S.S.R.	54 ft 5 in.
1960	Tamara Press, U.S.S.R.	56 ft 9⅞ in.
1964	Tamara Press, U.S.S.R.	59 ft 6 in.
1968	Margitta Gummel, East Germany	64 ft 4 in.
1972	Nadezhda Chizhova, U.S.S.R.	69 ft
1976	Ivanka Christova, Bulgaria (21.16m)	69 ft 5 in.
1980	Ilona Sluplanek, East Germany	73 ft 6 in.

Discus Throw

1928	Helena Konopacka, Poland	129 ft 11⅞ in.
1932	Lillian Copeland, United States	133 ft 2 in.
1936	Gisela Mauermayer, Germany	156 ft 3³/₁₆ in.
1948	Micheline Ostermeyer, France	137 ft 6½ in.
1952	Nina Romaschkova, U.S.S.R.	168 ft 8⁷/₁₆ in.
1956	Olga Fikotova, Czechoslovakia	176 ft 1½ in.
1960	Nina Ponomareva, U.S.S.R.	180 ft 8¼ in.
1964	Tamara Press, U.S.S.R.	187 ft 10¾ in.
1968	Lia Manoliu, Romania	191 ft 2½ in.
1972	Faina Melnik, U.S.S.R.	218 ft 7 in.
1976	Evelin Schlaak, East Germany (69.0m)	226 ft 4 in.
1980	Evelin Jahl, East Germany	229 ft 6½ in.

Javelin Throw

1932	Mildred Didrikson, United States	143 ft 4 in.
1936	Tilly Fleischer, Germany	148 ft 2¾ in.
1948	Herma Bauma, Austria	149 ft 6 in.
1952	Dana Zatopek, Czechoslovakia	165 ft 7 in.
1956	Inessa Janzeme, U.S.S.R.	176 ft 8 in.
1960	Elvira Ozolina, U.S.S.R.	183 ft 8 in.
1964	Mihaela Penes, Romania	198 ft 7½ in.
1968	Angela Nemeth, Hungary	198 ft 0 in.
1972	Ruth Fuchs, East Germany	209 ft 7 in.
1976	Ruth Fuchs, East Germany (65.94m)	216 ft 4 in.
1980	Maria Colon, Cuba	224 ft 5 in.

Pentathlon

1964	Irina Press, U.S.S.R.	5,246 pts.
1968	Ingrid Becker, West Germany	5,098 pts.
1972	Mary Peters, Britain	4,801 pts.
1976	Siegrun Siegl, East Germany	4,745 pts.
1980	Nadyezhda Tkachenko, U.S.S.R.	5,083 pts.

SWIMMING—MEN

50-Yard Freestyle

1904	Zoltan de Halmay, Hungary	28s

100 Meters Freestyle

1896	Alfred Hajos, Hungary	1m22.2s
1904	Zoltan de Halmay, Hungary	1m2.8s[1]
1906	Charles Daniels, United States	1m13s
1908	Charles Daniels, United States	1m5.6s
1912	Duke P. Kahanamoku, United States	1m3.4s
1920	Duke P. Kahanamoku, United States	1m1.4s
1924	John Weissmuller, United States	59s
1928	John Weissmuller, United States	58.6s
1932	Yasuji Miyazaki, Japan	58.2s
1936	Ferenc Csik, Hungary	57.6s
1948	Walter Ris, United States	57.3s
1952	Clarke Scholes, United States	57.4s
1956	Jon Henricks, Australia	55.4s
1960	John Devitt, Australia	55.2s
1964	Don Schollander, United States	53.4s
1968	Michael Wenden, Australia	52.2s
1972	Mark Spitz, United States	51.22s
1976	Jim Montgomery, United States	49.99s
1980	Jorg Woithe, East Germany	50.40s

1. 100 yards.

200-Meter Freestyle

1900	Frederick Lane, Australia	2m25.2s
1904	Charles Daniels, United States	2m44.2s[1]
1968	Michael Wenden, Australia	1m55.2s
1972	Mark Spitz, United States	1m52.78s
1976	Bruce Furniss, United States	1m50.29s
1980	Sergei Kopliakov, U.S.S.R.	1m49.81s

1. 220 yards.

400-Meter Freestyle

1896	Paul Neumann, Austria	8m12.6s[1]
1904	Charles Daniels, United States	6m16.2s[2]
1906	Otto Sheff, Austria	6m23.8s
1908	Henry Taylor, Great Britain	5m36.8s
1912	George Hodgson, Canada	5m24.4s
1920	Norman Ross, United States	5m26.8s
1926	Jonn Weissmuller, United States	5m4.2s
1928	Albert Zorilla, Argentina	5m1.6s
1932	Clarence Crabbe, United States	4m48.4s
1936	Jack Medica, United States	4m44.5s
1948	William Smith, United States	4m41s
1952	Jean Boiteux, France	4m30.7s
1956	Murray Rose, Australia	4m27.3s
1960	Murray Rose, Australia	4m18.3s
1964	Don Schollander, United States	4m12.2s
1968	Mike Burton, United States	4m9s
1972	Bradford Cooper, Australia[3]	4m00.27s
1976	Brian Goodell, United States	3m51.93s
1980	Vladimir Salnikov, U.S.S.R.	3m51.31s

1. 500 meters. 2. 440 yards. 3. Rick DeMont, United States, won but was disqualified following day for medical reasons.

1,200-Meter Freestyle

1896	Alfred Hajos, Hungary	18m22.2s

1,500 Meters Freestyle

1904	Emil Rausch, Germany	27m18.2s[1]
1906	Henry Taylor, Great Britain	28m28s[2]
1908	Henry Taylor, Great Britain	22m48.4s
1912	George Hodgson, Canada	22m
1920	Norman Ross, United States	22m23.2s
1924	Andrew Charlton, Australia	20m6.6s
1928	Arne Borg, Sweden	19m51.8s
1932	Kusuo Kitamura, Japan	19m12.4s
1936	Noboru Terada, Japan	19m13.7s

1948	James McLane, United States	19m18.5s
1952	Ford Konno, United States	18m30s
1956	Murray Rose, Australia	17m58.9s
1960	Jon Konrads, Australia	17m19.6s
1964	Robert Windle, Australia	17m1.7s
1968	Michael Burton, United States	16m38.9s
1972	Mike Burton, United States	15m52.58s
1976	Brian Goodell, United States	15m02.4s
1980	Vladimir Salnikov, U.S.S.R.	14m58.27s

1. One mile. 2. 1,600 meters.

4,000-Meter Freestyle

1900	John Jarvis, Great Britain	58m24s

100-Meter Backstroke

1904	Walter Brack, Germany	1m16.8s[1]
1908	Arno Bieberstein, Germany	1m24.6s
1912	Harry Hebner, United States	1m21.2s
1920	Warren Kealoha, United States	1m15.2s
1924	Warren Kealoha, United States	1m13.2s
1928	George Kojac, United States	1m8.2s
1932	Masaji Kiyokawa, Japan	1m8.6s
1936	Adolph Kiefer, United States	1m5.9s
1948	Allen Stack, United States	1m6.4s
1952	Yoshinobu Oyakawa, United States	1m5.4s
1956	David Thiele, Australia	1m2.2s
1960	David Thiele, Australia	1m1.9s
1968	Roland Matthes, East Germany	58.7s
1972	Roland Matthes, East Germany	56.58s
1976	John Naber, United States	55.49s
1980	Bengt Baron, Sweden	56.53s

1. 100 yards

200-Meter Backstroke

1900	Ernst Hoppenberg, Germany	2m47s
1964	Jed Graef, United States	2m10.3s
1968	Roland Matthes, East Germany	2m9.6s
1972	Roland Matthes, East Germany	2m2.82s
1976	John Naber, United States	1m59.19s
1980	Sandor Wladar, Hungary	2:01.93s

100-Meter Breaststroke

1968	Donald McKenzie, United States	1m7.7s
1972	Nobutaka Taguchi, Japan	1m4.94s
1976	John Hencken, United States	1m03.11s
1980	Duncan Goodhew, Britain	1m03.34s

200-Meter Breaststroke

1908	Frederick Holman, Great Britain	3m9.2s
1912	Walter Bathe, Germany	3m1.8s
1920	Haken Malmroth, Sweden	3m4.4s
1924	Robert Skelton, United States	2m56.6s
1928	Yoshiyuki Tsuruta, Japan	2m48.8s
1932	Yoshiyuki Tsuruta, Japan	2m45.4s
1936	Tetsuo Hamuro, Japan	2m41.5s
1948	Joseph Verdeur, United States	2m39.3s
1952	John Davies, Australia	2m34.4s
1956	Masura Furukawa, Japan	2m34.7s
1960	Bill Mulliken, United States	2m37.4s
1964	Ian O'Brien, Australia	2m27.8s
1968	Felipe Munoz, Mexico	2m28.7s
1972	John Hencken, United States	2m21.55s
1976	David Willkie, Britain	2m15.11s
1980	Robertas Zulpa, U.S.S.R.	2m15.85s

400-Meter Breaststroke

1904	Georg Zacharias, Germany	7m23.6s[1]
1912	Walter Bathe, Germany	6m29.6s
1920	Haken Malmroth, Sweden	6m31.8s

1. 440 yards

100-Meter Butterfly

1968	Douglas Russell, United States	55.9s
1972	Mark Spitz, United States	54.27s
1976	Matt Vogel, United States	54.35s
1980	Par Arvidsson, Sweden	54.92s

200-Meter Butterfly

1956	Bill Yorzyk, United States	2m19.3s
1960	Mike Troy, United States	2m12.8s
1964	Kevin Berry, Australia	2m6.6s
1968	Carl Robie, United States	2m8.7s
1972	Mark Spitz, United States	2m00.7s
1976	Mike Bruner, United States	1m59.23s
1980	Sergei Fesenko, U.S.S.R.	1m59.76s

200-Meter Individual Medley

1968	Charles Hickcox, United States	2m12s
1972	Gunnar Larsson, Sweden	2m7.17s

400-Meter Individual Medley

1964	Dick Roth, United States	4m45.4s
1968	Charles Hickcox, United States	4m48.4s
1972	Gunnar Larsson, Sweden	4m31.98s
1976	Rod Strachan, United States	4m23.68s
1980	Aleksandr Sidorenko, U.S.S.R.	4m22.8s

60-Meter Underwater

1900	de Vaudeville, France	1m53.4s

200-Meter Obstacle

1900	Frederick Lane, Australia	2m38.4s

Relays

1900	Germany (200 meters, 5 men)	32 pts.
1904	United States (200 yards)	2m4.6s
1906	Hungary (1,000 meters)	16m52.4s

400-Meter Freestyle Relay

1964	United States	3m32.2s
1968	United States	3m31.7s
1972	United States	3m26.42s

800-Meter Freestyle Relay

1908	Great Britain	10m55.6s
1912	Australia	10m11.2s
1920	United States	10m4.4s
1924	United States	9m53.4s
1928	United States	9m36.2s
1932	Japan	8m58.4s
1936	Japan	8m51.5s
1948	United States	8m46s
1952	United States	8m31.1s
1956	Australia	8m23.6s
1960	United States	8m10.2s
1964	United States	7m52.1s
1968	United States	7m52.3s
1972	United States	7m35.78s
1976	United States	7m23.22s
1980	U.S.S.R.	7m23.50s

400-Meter Medley Relay

1960	United States	4m5.4s
1964	United States	3m58.4s
1968	United States	3m54.9s
1972	United States	3m48.16s
1976	United States	3m42.22s
1980	Australia	3m45.70s

Springboard Dive

		Points
1908	Albert Zuerner, Germany	85.5

1912	Paul Guenther, Germany	79.23
1920	Louis Kuehn, United States	675
1924	Albert White, United States	696.4
1928	Pete Desjardins, United States	185.04
1932	Michael Galitzen, United States	161.38
1936	Richard Degener, United States	163.57
1948	Bruce Harlan, United States	163.64
1952	David Browning, United States	205.59
1956	Robert Clotworthy, United States	159.56
1960	Gary Tobian, United States	170.00
1964	Ken Sitzberger, United States	159.90
1968	Bernard Wrightson, United States	170.15
1972	Vladimir Vasin, U.S.S.R.	594.09
1976	Phil Boggs, United States	619.05
1980	Alexsandr Portnov, U.S.S.R.	905.02

Platform Dive

		Points
1904	G. E. Sheldon, United States	12.75
1906	Gottlob Walz, Germany	156
1908	Hjalmar Johansson, Sweden	83.75
1912	Erik Adlerz, Sweden	73.94
1920	Clarence Pinkston, United States	100.67
1924	Albert White, United States	487.3
1928	Pete Desjardins, United States	98.74
1932	Harold Smith, United States	124.80
1936	Marshall Wayne, United States	113.58
1948	Samuel Lee, United States	130.05
1952	Samuel Lee, United States	156.28
1956	Joaquin Capilla, Mexico	152.44
1960	Bob Webster, United States	165.56
1964	Bob Webster, United States	148.58
1968	Klaus Dibiasi, Italy	164.18
1972	Klaus Dibiasi, Italy	504.12
1976	Klaus Dibiasi, Italy	600.51
1980	Falk Hoffman, E. Germany	835.65

Plain High Dive

		Points
1912	Erik Adlerz, Sweden	40
1920	Arvid Wallman, Sweden	7
1924	Richard Eve, Australia	160

Plunge for Distance
1904	W. E. Dickey, United States	62 ft 6 in.

SWIMMING—WOMEN

100 Meters Freestyle

1912	Fanny Durack, Australia	1m22.2s
1920	Ethelda Bleibtrey, United States	1m13.6s
1924	Ethel Lackie, United States	1m12.4s
1928	Albina Osipowich, United States	1m11s
1932	Helene Madison, United States	1m6.8s
1936	Hendrika Mastenbroek, Netherlands	1m5.9s
1948	Greta Andersen, Denmark	1m6.3s
1952	Katalin Szoke, Hungary	1m6.8s
1956	Dawn Fraser, Australia	1m2s
1960	Dawn Fraser, Australia	1m1.2s
1964	Dawn Fraser, Australia	59.5s
1968	Marge Jan Henne, United States	1m
1972	Sandra Neilson, United States	58.59s
1976	Kornelia Ender, East Germany	55.65s
1980	Barbara Krause, East Germany	54.79s

200-Meter Freestyle

1968	Debbie Meyer, United States	2m10.5s
1972	Shane Gould, Australia	2m3.56s
1976	Kornelia Ender, East Germany	1m59.26s
1980	Barbara Krause, East Germany	1m58.33s

400-Meter Freestyle
1920	Ethelda Bleibtrey, United States	4m34s[1]

1924	Martha Norelius, United States	6m2.2s
1928	Martha Norelius, United States	5m42.8s
1932	Helene Madison, United States	5m28.5s
1936	Hendrika Mastenbroek, Netherlands	5m26.4s
1948	Ann Curtis, United States	5m17.8s
1952	Valerie Gyenge, Hungary	5m12.1s
1956	Lorraine Crapp, Australia	4m54.6s
1960	Chris von Saltza, United States	4m50.6s
1964	Ginny Duenkel, United States	4m43.3s
1968	Debbie Meyer, United States	4m31.8s
1972	Shane Gould, Australia	4m19.04s
1976	Petra Thumer, East Germany	4m09.89s
1980	Ines Diers, East Germany	4m08.76s

1. 300 meters.

800-Meter Freestyle

1968	Debbie Meyer, United States	9m24s
1972	Keena Rothhammer, United States	8m53.68s
1976	Petra Thumer, East Germany	8m37.14s
1980	Michelle Ford, Australia	8m28.90s

100-Meter Backstroke

1924	Sybil Bauer, United States	1m23.2s
1928	Marie Braun, Netherlands	1m22s
1932	Eleanor Holm, United States	1m19.4s
1936	Dina Senff, Netherlands	1m18.9s
1948	Karen Harup, Denmark	1m14.4s
1952	Joan Harrison, South Africa	1m14.3s
1956	Judy Grinham, Great Britain	1m12.9s
1960	Lynn Burke, United States	1m9.3s
1964	Cathy Ferguson, United States	1m7.7s
1968	Kaye Hall, United States	1m6.2s
1972	Melissa Belote, United States	1m5.78s
1976	Ulrike Richter, East Germany	1m01.83s
1980	Rica Reinisch, East Germany	1m00.86s

200-Meter Backstroke

1968	Pokey Watson, United States	2m24.8s
1972	Melissa Belote, United States	2m19.19s
1976	Ulrike Richter, East Germany	2m13.43s
1980	Rica Reinisch, East Germany	2m11.77s

100-Meter Breaststroke

1968	Djurdjica Bjedov, Yugoslavia	1m15.8s
1972	Catherine Carr, United States	1m13.58s
1976	Hannelore Anke, East Germany	1m11.16s
1980	Ute Geweniger, East Germany	1m10.22s

200-Meter Breaststroke

1924	Lucy Morton, Great Britain	3m33.2s
1928	Hilde Schrader, Germany	3m12.6s
1932	Clare Dennis, Australia	3m6.3s
1936	Hideko Maehata, Japan	3m3.6s
1948	Nel van Vliet, Netherlands	2m57.2s
1952	Eva Szekely, Hungary	2m51.7s
1956	Ursala Happe, Germany	2m53.1s
1960	Anita Lonsbrough, Great Britain	2m49.5s
1964	Galina Prozumenschikova, U.S.S.R.	2m46.4s
1968	Sharon Wichman, United States	2m44.4s
1972	Beverly Whitfield, Australia	2m41.71s
1976	Marina Koshevaia, U.S.S.R.	2m33.35s
1980	Lina Kachushite, U.S.S.R.	2m29.54s

100-Meter Butterfly

1956	Shelley Mann, United States	1m11s
1960	Carolyn Schuler, United States	1m9.5s
1964	Sharon Stouder, United States	1m4.7s
1968	Lynn McClements, Australia	1m5.5s
1972	Mayumi Aoki, Japan	1m3.34s
1976	Kornelia Ender, East Germany	1m00.13s
1980	Caren Metschuck, East Germany	1m00.42s

200-Meter Butterfly

1968	Ada Kok, Netherlands	2m24.7s
1972	Karen Moe, United States	2m15.57s
1976	Andrea Pollack, East Germany	2m11.41s
1980	Ines Geissler, East Germany	2m10.44s

200-Meter Individual Medley

1968	Claudia Kolb, United States	2m24.7s
1972	Shane Gould, Australia	2m23.07s

400-Meter Individual Medley

1964	Donna de Varona, United States	5m18.7s
1968	Claudia Kolb, United States	5m8.5s
1972	Gail Neall, Australia	5m2.97s
1976	Ulrike Tauber, East Germany	4m42.77s
1980	Petra Schneider, East Germany	4m36.29s

400-Meter Freestyle Relay

1912	Great Britain	5m52.8s
1920	United States	5m11.6s
1924	United States	4m58.8s
1928	United States	4m47.6s
1932	United States	4m38s
1936	Netherlands	4m36s
1948	United States	4m29.2s
1952	Hungary	4m24.4s
1956	Australia	4m17.1s
1960	United States	4m8.9s
1964	United States	4m3.8s
1968	United States	4m2.5s
1972	United States	3m55.19s
1976	United States	3m44.82s
1980	East Germany	3m42.71s

400-Meter Medley Relay

1960	United States	4m41.1s
1964	United States	4m33.9s
1968	United States	4m28.3s
1972	United States	4m20.75s
1976	East Germany	4m07.95s
1980	East Germany	4m06.67s

Springboard Dive

		Points
1920	Aileen Riggin, United States	539.90
1924	Elizabeth Becker, United States	474.5
1928	Helen Meany, United States	78.62
1932	Georgia Coleman, United States	87.52
1936	Marjorie Gestring, United States	89.27
1948	Victoria M. Draves, United States	108.74
1952	Patricia McCormick, United States	147.30
1956	Patricia McCormick, United States	142.36
1960	Ingrid Kramer, Germany	155.81
1964	Ingrid Kramer Engel, Germany	145.00
1968	Sue Gossick, United States	150.77
1972	Micki King, United States	450.03
1976	Jennifer Chandler, United States	506.19
1980	Irina Kalinina, U.S.S.R.	725.91

Platform Dive

		Points
1912	Greta Johansson, Sweden	39.9
1920	Stefani Fryland, Denmark	34.60
1924	Caroline Smith, United States	166
1928	Elizabeth B. Pinkston, United States	31.60
1932	Dorothy Poynton, United States	40.26
1936	Dorothy Poynton Hill, United States	33.92
1948	Victoria M. Draves, United States	68.87
1952	Patricia McCormick, United States	79.37
1956	Patricia McCormick, United States	84.85
1960	Ingrid Kramer, Germany	91.28

DISTRIBUTION OF MEDALS
1980 SUMMER GAMES

	Gold	Silver	Bronze	Total
Soviet Union	80	70	47	197
East Germany	47	36	43	126
Bulgaria	8	16	16	40
Hungary	7	10	15	32
Poland	3	14	14	31
Romania	6	6	13	25
Britain	5	7	9	21
Cuba	8	7	5	20
Italy	8	3	4	15
France	6	5	3	14
Czechoslovakia	2	2	9	13
Sweden	3	3	6	12
Australia	2	2	5	9
Yugoslavia	2	3	4	9
Finland	3	1	4	8
Spain	1	3	2	6
Denmark	2	1	2	5
Austria	1	3	1	5
North Korea	0	3	2	5
Brazil	2	0	2	4
Ethiopia	2	0	2	4
Mongolia	0	2	2	4
Netherlands	0	1	3	4
Mexico	0	1	3	4
Greece	1	0	2	3
Jamaica	0	0	3	3
Switzerland	2	0	0	2
Tanzania	0	2	0	2
Ireland	0	1	1	2
Belgium	1	0	1	2
India	1	0	0	1
Zimbabwe	1	0	0	1
Venezuela	1	0	0	1
Uganda	0	1	0	1
Guyana	0	0	1	1
Lebanon	0	0	1	1

1964	Lesley Bush, United States	99.80
1968	Milena Duchkova, Czechoslovakia	109.59
1972	Ulrika Knape, Sweden	390.00
1976	Elena Vaytsekhovskaia, U.S.S.R.	406.59
1980	Martina Jaschke, East Germany	596.25

BOXING
(U.S. winners only)
(U.S. boycotted Olympics in 1980)

Flyweight—112 Pounds (51 kilograms)

1904	George V. Finnegan	1952	Nate Brooks
1920	Frank De Genaro	1976	Leo Randolph
1924	Fidel La Barba		

Bantamweight—119 pounds (54 kg)
1904 O.L. Kirk

Featherweight—126 pounds (57 kg)

1904	O.L. Kirk	1924	Jackie Fields

Lightweight—132 Pounds (60 kg)

1904	H.J. Spanger	1968	Ronnie Harris
1920	Samuel Mosberg	1976	Howard Davis

Light Welterweight—140 Pounds (63.5 kg)

1952	Charles Adkins	1976	Ray Leonard
1972	Ray Seales		

Welterweight—148 Pounds (67 kg)

1904	Al Young	1932	Edward Flynn

Light Middleweight—157 Pounds (71 kg)

1960	Wilbert McClure

Middleweight—165 Pounds (75 kg)

1904	Charles Mayer	1960	Eddie Crook
1932	Carmen Barth	1976	Mike Spinks
1952	Floyd Patterson		

Light Heavyweight—179 Pounds (81 kg)

1920	Edward Eagan	1960	Cassius Clay
1952	Norvel Lee	1976	Leon Spinks
1956	James Boyd		

Heavyweight (unlimited)

1904	Sam Berger	1964	Joe Frazier
1952	Edward Sanders	1968	George Foreman
1956	Pete Rademacher		

BASKETBALL—MEN

1904	United States	1960	United States
1936	United States	1964	United States
1948	United States	1968	United States
1952	United States	1972	U.S.S.R.
1956	United States	1976	United States
		1980	Yugoslavia

BASKETBALL—WOMEN

1976	U.S.S.R.
1980	U.S.S.R.

Winter Games

FIGURE SKATING—MEN

1908	Ulrich Salchow, Sweden
1920	Gillis Grafstrom, Sweden
1924	Gillis Grafstrom, Sweden
1928	Gillis Grafstrom, Sweden
1932	Karl Schaefer, Austria
1936	Karl Schaefer, Austria
1948	Richard Button, United States
1952	Richard Button, United States
1956	Hayes Alan Jenkins, United States
1960	David Jenkins, United States
1964	Manfred Schnelldorfer, Germany
1968	Wolfgang Schwartz, Austria
1972	Ondrej Nepela, Czechoslovakia
1976	John Curry, Great Britain
1980	Robin Cousins, Great Britain

FIGURE SKATING—WOMEN

1908	Madge Syers, Britain
1920	Magda Julin–Maurey, Sweden
1924	Herma Szabo-Planck, Austria
1928	Sonja Henie, Norway
1932	Sonja Henie, Norway
1936	Sonja Henie, Norway
1948	Barbara Ann Scott, Canada
1952	Jeannette Altwegg, Great Britain
1956	Tenley Albright, United States
1960	Carol Heiss, United States
1964	Sjoukje Dijkstra, Netherlands
1968	Peggy Fleming, United States
1972	Beatrix Schuba, Austria
1976	Dorothy Hamill, United States
1980	Anett Poetzsch, East Germany

SPEED SKATING—MEN
(U.S. winners only)

500 Meters

1924	Charles Jewtraw	44.0
1932	John A. Shea	43.4
1952	Kenneth Henry	43.2
1964	Terrence McDermott	40.1
1980	Eric Heiden	38.03

1,000 Meters

1976	Peter Mueller	1:19.32
1980	Eric Heiden	1:15.18

1,500 Meters

1932	John A. Shea	2:57.5
1980	Eric Heiden	1:55.44

5,000 Meters

1932	Irving Jaffee	9:40.8
1980	Eric Heiden	7:02.29

10,000 Meters

1932	Irving Jaffee	19:13.6
1980	Eric Heiden	14:28.13

SPEED SKATING—WOMEN

500 Meters

1972	Anne Henning	43.33
1976	Sheila Young	42.76

1,500 Meters

1972	Dianne Holum	2:20.85

HEIDEN FIRST ATHLETE TO WIN 5 GOLD MEDALS IN WINTER GAMES

Eric Heiden of Madison, Wis., became the first athlete to win five gold medals in the Winter Olympics when he swept the 1980 speed skating events at Lake Placid, N.Y. The 21-year-old Heiden captured the 500-, 1,000-, 1,500-, 5,000-, and 10,000-meter events. He set an Olympic record in each event and capped his performance on Feb. 23 with a world record of 14 minutes 28.13 seconds in the 10,000-meter race, breaking the mark set in 1977 by Viktor Leskin of the Soviet Union by 16.20 seconds.

Lydia Skoblikova of the Soviet Union was the only other athlete to sweep an Olympic speed skating program. She captured all four female events in the 1964 Winter Games at Innsbruck, Austria.

The weekend after his gold-medal sweep, Heiden failed in his attempt to win a fourth straight world title, at Heerenveen, the Netherlands. He was dethroned by 22-year-old Hilbert van der Duim of the host country.

SKIING, ALPINE—MEN

Downhill

1948	Henri Oreiller, France	2m55.0s
1952	Zeno Colo, Italy	2m30.8s
1956	Anton Sailer, Austria	2m52.2s
1960	Jean Vuarnet, France	2m06.2s
1964	Egon Zimmermann, Austria	2m18.16s
1968	Jean-Claude Killy, France	1m59.85s
1972	Bernhard Russi, Switzerland	1m51.43s
1976	Franz Klammer, Austria	1m45.72s
1980	Leonhard Stock, Austria	1m45.50s

Slalom

1948	Edi Reinalter, Switzerland	2m10.3s
1952	Othmar Schneider, Austria	2m00.0s
1956	Anton Sailer, Austria	194.7 pts.
1960	Ernst Hinterseer, Austria	2m08.9s
1964	Josef Stiegler, Austria	2m10.13
1968	Jean-Claude Killy, France	1m39.73s
1972	Francisco Fernandez Ochoa, Spain	1m49.27s
1976	Piero Gros, Italy	2m03.29s
1980	Ingemar Stenmark, Sweden	1m44.26s

Giant Slalom

1952	Stein Eriksen, Norway	2m25.0s
1956	Anton Sailer, Austria	3m00.1s
1960	Roger Staub, Switzerland	1m48.3s
1964	Francois Bonlieu, France	1m46.71s
1968	Jean-Claude Killy, France	3m29.28s
1972	Gustavo Thoeni, Italy	3m09.52s
1976	Heini Hemmi, Switzerland	3m26.97s
1980	Ingemar Stenmark, Sweden	2m40.74s

SKIING, ALPINE—WOMEN

Downhill

1948	Hedi Schlunegger, Switzerland	2m28.3s
1952	Trude Jochum-Beiser, Austria	1m47.1s
1956	Madeleine Berthod, Switzerland	1m40.1s
1960	Heidi Biebl, Germany	1m37.6s
1964	Christl Haas, Austria	1m55.39s
1968	Olga Pall, Austria	1m40.87s
1972	Marie-Therese Nadig, Switzerland	1m36.68s
1976	Rosi Mittermeier, West Germany	1m46.16s
1980	Annemarie Proell Moser, Austria	1m37.52s

Slalom

1948	Gretchen Fraser, United States	1m57.2s
1952	Andrea Mead Lawrence, United States	2m10.6s
1956	Renee Colliard, Switzerland	112.3 pts.
1960	Anne Heggtveigt, Canada	1m49.6s
1964	Christine Goitschel, France	1m29.86s
1968	Marielle Goitschel, France	1m25.86s
1972	Barbara Cochran, United States	1m31.24s
1976	Rosi Mittermeier, West Germany	1m30.54s
1980	Hanni Wenzel, Liechtenstein	1m25.09s

Giant Slalom

1952	Andrea M. Lawrence, United States	2m06.8s
1956	Ossi Reichert, Germany	1m56.5s
1960	Yvonne Ruegg, Switzerland	1m39.9s
1964	Marielle Goitschel, France	1m52.24s
1968	Nancy Greene, Canada	1m51.97s
1972	Marie-Therese Nadig, Switzerland	1m29.90s
1976	Kathy Kreiner, Canada	1m29.13s
1980	Hanni Wenzel, Liechtenstein	2m41.66s

ICE HOCKEY

1920	Canada		1956	U.S.S.R.
1924	Canada		1960	United States
1928	Canada		1964	U.S.S.R.
1932	Canada		1968	U.S.S.R.
1936	Great Britain		1972	U.S.S.R.
1948	Canada		1976	U.S.S.R.
1952	Canada		1980	United States

SKIING, NORDIC, JUMPING

90-Meter Hill

		Points
1924	Jacob T. Thams, Norway	227.5
1928	Alfred Andersen, Norway	230.5
1932	Birger Ruud, Norway	228.0
1936	Birger Ruud, Norway	232.0
1948	Peter Hugsted, Norway	228.1
1952	A. Bergmann, Norway	226.0
1956	Antti Hyvarinen, Finland	227.0
1960	Helmut Recknagel, Germany	227.2
1964	Toralf Engan, Norway	230.7
1968	Vladimir Beloussov, U.S.S.R.	231.3
1972	Wojciech Fortuna, Poland	219.9
1976	Karl Schnabl, Austria	234.8
1980	Jouko Tormanen, Finland	271.0

Small Hill (70 meters)

1964	Veikko Kankkonen, Finland	229.9
1968	Jiri Raska, Czechoslovakia	216.5
1972	Yukio Kasaya, Japan	244.2
1976	Hans-Georg Aschenbach, East Germany	252.0
1980	Anton Innauer, Austria	266.3

AMERICAN HOCKEY TEAM SCORES BIGGEST UPSET IN GAMES

The United States hockey team, made up of college and minor-league players, stunned the hockey world and stirred patriotic fervor among Americans everywhere with a 4–3 upset triumph in the Winter Olympics over the Soviet Union, considered by experts as the finest hockey team in the world—amateur or professional.

The Soviet team was heavily favored to win the Olympic gold medal at Lake Placid, N.Y., for a fifth straight time. The Americans were rated seventh among the 12 national teams and were given virtually no chance of gaining the final round. The 20-man American squad was coached by Herb Brooks, the coach of the University of Minnesota team. He instituted a new style for the Americans, stressing speed and puck control, tactics generally employed by European teams. The Americans opened their unbeaten streak with a 2–2 tie against Sweden in the first round, then stormed to victories over Romania, Czechoslovakia, West Germany, and Norway. Their upset of the Russians came in the first game of the final round on a goal by Mike Eruzione, the team captain from Winthrop, Mass.

They captured the gold medal with a 4–2 victory over Finland and touched off a national celebration and a surge of patriotism seldom seen in American sports. The triumph came at a time when the Olympic movement was under fire and the United States threatened to boycott the Summer Games in Moscow because of the Soviet invasion of Afghanistan. Only once before, in 1960 at Squaw Valley, Calif., had an American team won an Olympic hockey gold medal.

HOW U.S. HOCKEY ADVANCED TO OLYMPIC TITLE
FINAL STANDING

	W	L	T	Pts	GF	GA
United States	2	0	1	5	10	7
Soviet Union	2	1	0	4	16	8
Sweden	0	2	2	2	7	14
Finland	0	2	1	1	7	11

(The top two teams in the Red Division and the two top teams in the Blue Division of the preliminary round-robin advanced to the final, where the Red Division teams played the Blue Division teams. The records of the teams who played each other in their own divisions were counted in the final standing.)

Results of Final Round Games

United States 4, Soviet Union 3
Sweden 3, Finland 3
United States 4, Finland 2
Soviet Union 9, Sweden 2

Consolation for Fifth Place

Czechoslovakia 6, Canada 1

PRELIMINARY ROUND STANDING
Red Division

	W	L	T	Pts	GF	GA
Soviet Union	5	0	0	10	51	11
Finland	3	2	0	6	26	18
Canada	3	2	0	6	28	12
Poland	2	3	0	4	15	23
Holland	1	3	1	3	16	43
Japan	0	4	1	1	7	36

Blue Division

	W	L	T	Pts	GF	GA
Sweden	4	0	1	9	26	7
United States	4	0	1	9	25	10
Czechoslovakia	3	2	0	6	34	16
Romania	1	3	1	3	13	29
West Germany	1	4	0	2	21	30
Norway	0	4	1	1	9	36

(Top two teams in each division advanced to final round. Third place teams played for fifth.)

Results of Preliminary Round Games Involving U.S.

United States 2, Sweden 2
United States 7, Czechoslovakia 3
United States 5, Norway 1
United States 7, Romania 2
United States 4, West Germany 2

DISTRIBUTION OF MEDALS
1980 WINTER GAMES

	Gold	Silver	Bronze	Total
Soviet Union	10	6	6	22
East Germany	9	7	7	23
United States	6	4	2	12
Norway	1	3	6	10
Finland	1	5	3	9
Austria	3	2	2	7
West Germany	0	2	3	5
Switzerland	1	1	3	5
Liechtenstein	2	2	0	4
Netherlands	1	2	1	4
Sweden	3	0	1	4
Italy	0	2	0	2
Canada	0	1	1	2
Britain	1	0	0	1
Hungary	0	1	0	1
Japan	0	1	0	1
Bulgaria	0	0	1	1
Czechoslovakia	0	0	1	1
France	0	0	1	1

Total countries competing: 37.

Scoring of U.S. Victory Over Soviet Union

United States	2	0	2	—	4
Soviet Union	2	1	0	—	3

FIRST PERIOD—1, Soviet Union, Krutov (Kasatonov), 9:12; 2, United States, Schneider (Pavelich), 14:03; 3, Soviet Union, Makarov (A. Golikov), 17:34; 4, United States, Johnson (Christian, Silk), 19:59
SECOND PERIOD—5, Soviet Union, Maltsev (Krutiv), power-play goal, 2:18
THIRD PERIOD—6, United States, Johnson (Silk), power-play goal, 8:39; 7, United States, Eruzione (Pavelich, Harrington), 10:00
SHOTS ON GOAL—United States on Tretiak, Myshkin, 8, 2, 6—16. Soviet Union on Craig, 18, 12, 9—39

Scoring of U.S. Gold Medal Victory Over Finland

United States	0	1	3	—	4
Finland	1	1	0	—	2

FIRST PERIOD—1, Finland, Porvari (Leinonen, Litma), 9:20
SECOND PERIOD—2, United States, Christoff (unassisted), 4:39; 3, Finland, Leinonen (Haapalainen, Kimalainen), power-play goal, 6:30
THIRD PERIOD—4, United States, Verchota (Christian), 2:25; 5, McClanahan (Johnson, Christian), 6:05; 6, United States, Johnson, (Christoff), shorthanded goal, 16:25
SHOTS ON GOAL—United States on Valtonen, 14, 8, 7—29. Finland on Craig, 7, 6, 10—23.

AMERICAN SWIMMERS RACE AGAINST OLYMPIC CLOCK

Forty-eight hours after the Olympic swimming competition in Moscow ended, United States swimmers, who had boycotted the Games, protesting the Soviet intervention in Afghanistan, took to the water at Irvine, Calif., hoping to shatter records in the United States Championships and Olympic Trials. Organizers erected a huge scoreboard showing the Olympic times in each event so swimmers and spectators could make comparisons as to how the Americans would have fared had they chosen to go to Moscow.

In a sport they usually dominated, the Americans registered three world records, and on a basis of comparative times, showed they would have won six of 11 gold medals in men's events and four of 11 in women's events had they competed in the Olympics. The world records shattered at Irvine were by Craig Beardsley of Gainesville, Fla., in the 200-meter butterfly (1:58.46); Bill Barrett of Alpharetta, Ga., in the 200 individual medley (2:03.24); and Mary T. Meagher, a 15-year-old from Cincinnati, in the 200 butterfly (2:06.37).

Other 1980 Olympic Games Champions

SUMMER

Archery
Men—Tomi Polkolainen, Finland
Women—Keto Losaberodze, U.S.S.R.

Boxing
106 lb—Shamil Sabyrov, U.S.S.R.
112 lb—Petar Lessov, U.S.S.R.
119 lb—Juan Hernandez, Cuba
126 lb—Rudi Fink, E. Ger.
132 lb—Angel Herrera, Cuba
140 lb—Patrizio Oliva, Italy
148 lb—Andres Aldama, Cuba
157 lb—Armando Martinez, Cuba
165 lb—Jose Gomez, Cuba
179 lb—Slobodan Kacar, Yugoslavia
Heavyweight—Teofilo Stevenson, Cuba

Canadian Canoeing
500 m—Sergei Postrekhin, U.S.S.R.
1,000 m—Lubomir Lubenov, Bulgaria
500–m pairs—Laszlo Foltan and Istvan Vaskutl, Hungary
1,000–m pairs—Ivan Potzalchin and Toma Simionov, Romania

Kayak—Men
500 m—Vladimir Parfenovich, U.S.S.R.
1,000 m—Rudiger Helm, E. Ger.
500–m pairs—Vladimir Parfenovich and Sergei Chukhrai, U.S.S.R.
1,000–m pairs—Vladimir Parfenovich and Sergei Chukhrai, U.S.S.R.
1,000–m fours—E. Ger.

Kayak—Women
500 m—Birgit Fischer, E. Ger.
500–m pairs—Carsta Genauss and Martina Dischof, E. Ger.

Cycling
1,000 m—Lothar Thoms, E. Ger.
Sprint—Lutz Hesslich, E. Ger.
Pursuit—Robert Dill–Bondi, Switzerland
Team pursuit—U.S.S.R.
Road Race—Sergei Soukhoroutchenkov, U.S.S.R.
Team road race—U.S.S.R.

Equestrian
Dressage—Elisabeth Theurer, Austria
Dressage team—U.S.S.R.
Jumping—Jan Kowalczky, Poland
Team jumping—U.S.S.R.
3–Day event—Federico Euro Roman, Italy
Team 3–day event—U.S.S.R. (Aleksandr Blinov, Yuri Salnikov, Valeri Volkov)

Fencing
Foil—Vladimir Smirnov, U.S.S.R.
Team foil—France
Epee—Johan Harmenberg, Sweden
Team epee—France
Saber—Viktor Krovopuskov, U.S.S.R.
Team saber—U.S.S.R.
Women's foil—Pascale Trinquet, France
Women's team foil—France

Gymnastics—Men
All–around—Aleksandr Dityatin, U.S.S.R.
Floor exercises—Roland Bruckner, E. Ger.
Horizontal bar—Stoyan Deltchev, Bulgaria
Parallel bars—Aleksandr Tkachyov, U.S.S.R.
Pommel horse—Zoltan Magyar, Hungary
Rings—Aleksandr Dityatin, U.S.S.R.
Vault—Nikolai Andrianov, U.S.S.R.
Team all–around—U.S.S.R.

Gymnastics—Women
All–around—Yelena Davydova, U.S.S.R.
Balance beam—Nadia Comaneci, Romania
Floor exercises—Nelli Kim, U.S.S.R., and Nadia Comaneci, Romania, tie
Uneven bars—Maxi Gnauck, E. Ger.
Vault—Natalya Shaposhnikova, U.S.S.R.
Team all–round—U.S.S.R.

Judo
132 lb—Thierry Rey, France
143 lb—Nikolai Solodukhin, U.S.S.R.
157 lb—Ezio Gamba, Italy
172 lb—Shota Khabarell, U.S.S.R.
190 lb—Juerg Roethilsberger, Switzerland
209 lb—Robert Van De Walle, Belgium
Over 209 lb—Angelo Parisi, France
Open—Dietmar Lorenz, East Germany

Modern Pentathlon
Individual—Anatoly Starostin, U.S.S.R.
Team—U.S.S.R.

Rowing—Men
Singles—Pertti Karppinen, Finland
Doubles—Joachim Dreifke and Klaus Kroppelien, E. Ger.
Pairs—Bernd and Jorg Landvoigt, E. Ger.
Pairs with coxswain—Harald Jahrling–Friedrich-Wilhelm Ulrich–Georg Spohr, E. Ger.
Fours—Jurgen Thiele–Andreas Decker–Stefan Semmier–Siegfried Brietzke, E. Ger.
Fours with coxswains—Dieter Wemdisch–Ullrich Diessner–Walter Diessner–Gottfried Dohn–Andreas Gregor, E. Ger.
Quadruple sculls—Frank Dunba–Karstn Bunk–Uwe Heppner–Martin Winter, E. Ger.
Eights—Bernd Krauss–Hans-Peter Koppe–Ulrich Kons–Jorg Friedrich–Jens Doberschutz–Ulrich Karnatz–Uwe Duhring–Bernd Hoing–Klaus-Dieter Ludwig, E. Ger.

Rowing—Women
Singles—Sanda Toma, Romania
Doubles—Yelena Khloptseva and Larisa Popova, U.S.S.R.
Pairs—Ute Steindorf and Cornelia Klier, E. Ger.
Fours with coxswains—Romona Kapheim–Silvia Frohlich–Angelika Noack–Romy Saalfeld–Kirsten Wenzel, E. Ger.
Quadruple sculls—Sybille Reinhardt–Jutta Ploch–Jutta Lau–Roswietha Zobelt–Liane Buhr, E. Ger.
Eights—Martina Boesler–Kersten Neisser–Christiane Kopke–Brigit Schutz–Gabriele Kuhn–Ilona Richter–Marita Sandig–Karin Metze–Marina Wilke, E. Ger.

Shooting
Free pistol—Aleksandr Melentev, U.S.S.R.
Rapid–fire pistol—Corneliu Ion, Romania
Small–bore rifle, prone—Karoly Varga, Hungary
Small–bore rifle, 3 positions—Viktor Vlasov, U.S.S.R.
Rifle, running game target—Igor Sokolov, U.S.S.R.
Trap—Luciano Giovannetti, Italy
Skeet—Hans Kjeld Rasmussen, Denmark

Weight Lifting
114 lb—Kanybek Osmonalieu, U.S.S.R.
123 lb—Daniel Nunez, Cuba
132 lb—Viktor Mazin, U.S.S.R.
149 lb—Yanko Roussev, Bulgaria
165 lb—Assen Zlatev, Bulgaria
182 lb—Yurik Vardanyan, U.S.S.R.
198 lb—Peter Baczako, Hungary
220 lb—Ata Zaremba, Czechoslovakia
242 lb—Leonid Taranenko, U.S.S.R.

Wrestling—Freestyle
106 lb—Claudio Pollio, Italy
115 lb—Anatoly Belogiazov, U.S.S.R.
126 lb—Sergei Belogiazov, U.S.S.R.
137 lb—Magomrdgasan Abushev, U.S.S.R.
149 lb—Salpulla Absaidov, U.S.S.R.
163 lb—Valentin Raitchev, Bulgaria
181 lb—Ismail Abilov, Bulgaria
198 lb—Sanasar Oganesyan, U.S.S.R.
220 lb—Ilya Mate, U.S.S.R.
Over 220 lb—Sosian Andlev, U.S.S.R.

Wrestling—Greco-Roman
106 lb—Saksylik Ushkempirov, U.S.S.R.
114 lb—Vakhtang Blagidze, U.S.S.R.
125 lb—Shamil Sherikov, U.S.S.R.
136 lb—Stillanos Migiakis, Greece
150 lb—Stefan Rusu, Romania
163 lb—Ferenc Kocsis, Hungary
180 lb—Gennady Korban, U.S.S.R.
198 lb—Norbert Nottny, Hungary
220 lb—Gheorghi Raikov, Bulgaria
Over 220 lb—Aleksandr Kolchinsky, U.S.S.R.

Yachting
Finn—Esko Rechardt, Finland
Flying Dutchman—Alesandro Abascal and Miguel Noguer, Spain
470 Class—Marcos Soares and Eduardo Penido, Brazil
Soling—Poul Richard, Erik Hansen and

Valdemar Bandolowski, Denmark
Star—Valentin Mankin and Aleksandr
  Muzyschenko, U.S.S.R.
Tornado—Alexandre Welter and Lars
  Bjorkstrom, Brazil

Team Champions

Field hockey, men—India
Field hockey, women—Zimbabwe
Handball, men—E. Ger.
Handball, women—U.S.S.R.

Soccer—Czechoslovakia
Volleyball, men—U.S.S.R.
Volleyball, women—U.S.S.R.
Water polo—U.S.S.R.

WINTER

Biathlon

Individual—(10 km): Frank Ullrich, East Germany (20 km):
  Anatoly Alabyev, Soviet Union
Relay—Soviet Union (Vladimir Aliken, Aleksandr Tikhonov,
  Vladimir Barnaschov, and Anatoly Alabyev)

Bobsledding

2–Man—Erich Schaerer and Josef Benz, Switzerland
4–Man—East Germany (Meinhard Nehmer, Bogdan Musiol,
  Bernhard Germeshausen, and Hans Jurgen Gerhardt)

Figure Skating

Men—Robin Cousins, Great Britain
Women—Anett Poetzsch, East Germany
Pairs—Irina Rodnina and Aleksandr Zaitsev, Soviet Union
Dance—Natalya Linichuk and Gennadi Karponosov, Soviet
  Union

Speed Skating—Men

500 m—Eric Heiden, Madison, Wis.
1,000 m—Eric Heiden, Madison, Wis.
1,500 m—Eric Heiden, Madison, Wis.
5,000 m—Eric Heiden, Madison, Wis.
10,000 m—Eric Heiden, Madison, Wis.

Speed Skating—Women

500 m—Karin Enke, East Germany
1,000 m—Natalya Petruseva, Soviet Union

1,500 m—Annie Borckink, Netherlands
3,000 m—Bjoerg Eva Jensen, Norway

Hockey

Team—United States

Luge

Men—Bernhard Glass, East Germany
Doubles—Hans Rinn and Norbert Hahn, East Germany
Women—Vera Zozulya, Soviet Union

Skiing, Nordic—Men

Combined—Ulrich Wehling, East Germany
70–m jump—Anton Innauer, Austria
90–m jump—Jouko Tormanen, Finland

Cross–Country Skiing—Men

15 km—Thomas Wassberg, Sweden
30 km—Nikolai Zimyatov, Soviet Union
50 km—Nikolai Zimyatov, Soviet Union
40–km relay—Soviet Union (Vasily Rochev, Nikolai Bazhukov,
  Yevgeny Beliaev, and Nikolai Zimyatov)

Cross–Country Skiing—Women

5 km—Raisa Smetanina, Soviet Union
10 km—Barbara Petzold, East Germany
20–km relay—East Germany (Marlies Rostock, Carola Anding,
  Veronika Hesse, and Barbara Petzold)

JAMES E. SULLIVAN MEMORIAL AWARD WINNERS

(Amateur Athlete of Year Chosen in Amateur Athletic Union Poll)

1930	Robert Tyre Jones, Jr.	Golf
1931	Bernard E. Berlinger	Track and field
1932	James A. Bausch	Track and field
1933	Glenn Cunningham	Track and field
1934	William R. Bonthron	Track and field
1935	W. Lawson Little, Jr.	Golf
1936	Glenn Morris	Track and field
1937	J. Donald Budge	Tennis
1938	Donald R. Lash	Track and field
1939	Joseph W. Burk	Rowing
1940	J. Gregory Rice	Track and field
1941	Leslie MacMitchell	Track and field
1942	Cornelius Warmerdam	Track and field
1943	Gilbert L. Dodds	Track and field
1944	Ann Curtis	Swimming
1945	Felix (Doc) Blanchard	Football
1946	Y. Arnold Tucker	Football
1947	John B. Kelly, Jr.	Rowing
1948	Robert B. Mathias	Track and field
1949	Richard T. Button	Figure skating
1950	Fred Wilt	Track and field
1951	Robert E. Richards	Track and field
1952	Horace Ashenfelter	Track and field
1953	Major Sammy Lee	Diving
1954	Malvin Whitfield	Track and field
1955	Harrison Dillard	Track and field
1956	Patricia McCormick	Diving
1957	Bobby Jo Morrow	Track and field
1958	Glenn Davis	Track and field
1959	Parry O'Brien	Track and field
1960	Rafer Johnson	Track and field
1961	Wilma Rudolph Ward	Track and field
1962	Jim Beatty	Track and field
1963	John Pennel	Track and field
1964	Don Schollander	Swimming
1965	Bill Bradley	Basketball
1966	Jim Ryun	Track and field
1967	Randy Matson	Track and field
1968	Debbie Meyer	Swimming
1969	Bill Toomey	Decathlon
1970	John Kinsella	Swimming
1971	Mark Spitz	Swimming
1972	Frank Shorter	Marathon
1973	Bill Walton	Basketball
1974	Rick Wohlhuter	Track
1975	Tim Shaw	Swimming
1976	Bruce Jenner	Track and field
1977	John Naber	Swimming
1978	Tracy Caulkins	Swimming
1979	Kurt Thomas	Gymnastics
1980	Eric Heiden	Speed skating

FOOTBALL

The pastime of kicking around a ball goes back beyond the limits of recorded history. Ancient savage tribes played football of a primitive kind. There was a ball-kicking game played by Athenians, Spartans, and Corinthians 2500 years ago, which the Greeks called *Episkuros*. The Romans had a somewhat similar game called *Harpastum* and are supposed to have carried the game with them when they invaded the British Isles in the First Century, B.C.

Undoubtedly the game known in the United Stated as Football traces directly to the English game of Rugby, though the modifications have been many. Informal football was played on college lawns well over a century ago, and an annual Freshman-Sophomore series of "scrimmages" began at Yale in 1840. The first formal intercollegiate football game was the Princeton-Rutgers contest at New Brunswick, N.J., on Nov. 6, 1869, with Rutgers winning by 6 goals to 4.

In those days, games were played with 25, 20, 15, or 11 men on a side. In 1880, there was a convention at which Walter Camp of Yale persuaded the delegates to agree to a rule calling for 11 players on a side. The game grew so rough that it was attacked as brutal, and some colleges abandoned the sport. Conditions were so bad in 1906 that President Theodore Roosevelt called a meeting of Yale, Harvard, and Princeton representatives at the White House in the hope of reforming and improving the game. The outcome was that the game, with the forward pass introduced and some other modifications of the rules inserted, became faster and cleaner.

The first professional game was played in 1895 at Latrobe, Pa. The National Football League was founded in 1921. The All-American Conference went into action in 1946. At the end of the 1949 season the two circuits merged, retaining the name of the older league. In 1960, the American Football League, began operations. In 1970, the leagues merged.

College Football

NATIONAL COLLEGE FOOTBALL CHAMPIONS

The "National Collegiate A. A. Football Guide" recognizes as unofficial national champion the team selected each year by press association polls. Where The Associated Press poll (of writers) does not agree with the United Press International poll (of coaches), the guide lists both teams selected.

1937	Pittsburgh	1947	Notre Dame	1956	Oklahoma	1965	Alabama and	1973	Notre Dame
1938	Texas Christian	1948	Michigan	1957	Auburn and		Michigan State	1974	Oklahoma and
1939	Texas A & M	1949	Notre Dame		Ohio State	1966	Notre Dame		So. California
1940	Minnesota	1950	Oklahoma	1958	Louisiana State	1967	So. California	1975	Oklahoma
1941	Minnesota	1951	Tennessee	1959	Syracuse	1968	Ohio State	1976	Pittsburgh
1942	Ohio State	1952	Michigan State	1960	Minnesota	1969	Texas	1977	Notre Dame
1943	Notre Dame	1953	Maryland	1961	Alabama	1970	Texas and Nebraska	1978	Alabama and
1944	Army	1954	Ohio State and	1962	So. California				So. California
1945	Army		U.C.L.A.	1963	Texas	1971	Nebraska	1979	Alabama
1946	Notre Dame	1955	Oklahoma	1964	Alabama	1972	So. California	1980	Georgia

ARMY-NAVY SERIES RECORD SINCE 1962

1962	Navy 34, Army 14	1969	Army 27, Navy 0	1974	Navy 19, Army 0
1963	Navy 21, Army 15	1970	Navy 11, Army 7	1975	Navy 30, Army 6
1964	Army 11, Navy 8	1971	Army 24, Navy 23	1976	Navy 38, Army 10
1965	Army 7, Navy 7	1972	Army 23, Navy 15	1977	Army 17, Navy 14
1966	Army 20, Navy 7	1973	Navy 51, Army 0	1978	Navy 28, Army 0
1967	Navy 19, Army 14			1979	Navy 31, Army 7
1968	Army 21, Navy 14			1980	Navy 33, Army 6

RECORD OF ANNUAL MAJOR BOWL COLLEGE FOOTBALL GAMES

Rose Bowl

(At Pasadena, Calif.)

1902	Michigan 49, Stanford 0	1925	Notre Dame 27, Stanford 10	1940	So. California 14, Tennessee 0
1916	Washington State 14, Brown 0	1926	Alabama 20, Washington 19	1941	Stanford 21, Nebraska 13
1917	Oregon 14, Pennsylvania 0	1927	Alabama 7, Stanford 7	1942	Oregon State 20, Duke 16[1]
1918	Mare Island Marines 19, Camp Lewis 7	1928	Stanford 7, Pittsburgh 6	1943	Georgia 9, U.C.L.A. 0
		1929	Georgia Tech 8, California 7	1944	So. California 29, Washington 0
1919	Great Lakes 17, Mare Island Marines 0	1930	So. California 47, Pittsburgh 14	1945	So. California 25, Tennessee 0
		1931	Alabama 24, Washington State 0	1946	Alabama 34, So. California 14
1920	Harvard 7, Oregon 6	1932	So. California 21, Tulane 12	1947	Illinois 45, U.C.L.A. 14
1921	California 28, Ohio State 0	1933	So. California 35, Pittsburgh 0	1948	Michigan 49, So. California 0
1922	Washington and Jefferson 0, California 0	1934	Columbia 7, Stanford 0	1949	Northwestern 20, California 14
		1935	Alabama 29, Stanford 13	1950	Ohio State 17, California 14
1923	So. California 14, Penn State 3	1936	Stanford 7, So. Methodist 0	1951	Michigan 14, California 6
1924	Navy 14, Washington 14	1937	Pittsburgh 21, Washington 0	1952	Illinois 40, Stanford 7
		1938	California 13, Alabama 0	1953	So. California 7, Wisconsin 0
		1939	So. California 7, Duke 3	1954	Michigan State 28, U.C.L.A. 20

1955	Ohio State 20, So. California 7
1956	Michigan State 17, U.C.L.A. 14
1957	Iowa 35, Oregon State 19
1958	Ohio State 10, Oregon 7
1959	Iowa 38, California 12
1960	Washington 44, Wisconsin 8
1961	Washington 17, Minnesota 7
1962	Minnesota 21, U.C.L.A. 3
1963	So. California 42, Wisconsin 37
1964	Illinois 17, Washington 7
1965	Michigan 34, Oregon State 7
1966	U.C.L.A. 14, Michigan State 12
1967	Purdue 14, So. California 13
1968	So. California 14, Indiana 3
1969	Ohio State 27, So. California 16
1970	So. California 10, Michigan 3
1971	Stanford 27, Ohio State 17
1972	Stanford 13, Michigan 12
1973	So. California 42, Ohio State 17
1974	Ohio State 42, So. California 21
1975	So. California 18, Ohio State 17
1976	U.C.L.A. 23, Ohio State 10
1977	So. California 14, Michigan 6
1978	Washington 27, Michigan 20
1979	So. California 17, Michigan 10
1980	So. California 17, Ohio State 16
1981	Michigan 23, Washington 6

1. Played at Durham, N.C.

Orange Bowl

(At Miami)

1933	Miami (Fla.) 7, Manhattan 0
1934	Duquesne 33, Miami (Fla.) 7
1935	Bucknell 26, Miami (Fla.) 0
1936	Catholic 20, Mississippi 19
1937	Duquesne 13, Mississippi State 12
1938	Auburn 6, Michigan State 0
1939	Tennessee 17, Oklahoma 0
1940	Georgia Tech 21, Missouri 7
1941	Mississippi State 14, Georgetown 7
1942	Georgia 40, Texas Christian 26
1943	Alabama 37, Boston College 21
1944	Louisiana State 19, Texas A&M 14
1945	Tulsa 26, Georgia Tech 12
1946	Miami (Fla.) 13, Holy Cross 6
1947	Rice 8, Tennessee 0
1948	Georgia Tech 20, Kansas 14
1949	Texas 41, Georgia 28
1950	Santa Clara 21, Kentucky 13
1951	Clemson 15, Miami (Fla.) 14
1952	Georgia Tech 17, Baylor 14
1953	Alabama 61, Syracuse 6
1954	Oklahoma 7, Maryland 0
1955	Duke 34, Nebraska 7
1956	Oklahoma 20, Maryland 6
1957	Colorado 27, Clemson 21
1958	Oklahoma 48, Duke 21
1959	Oklahoma 21, Syracuse 6
1960	Georgia 14, Missouri 0
1961	Missouri 21, Navy 14
1962	Louisiana State 25, Colorado 7
1963	Alabama 17, Oklahoma 0
1964	Nebraska 13, Auburn 7
1965	Texas 21, Alabama 17
1966	Alabama 39, Nebraska 28
1967	Florida 27, Georgia Tech 12
1968	Oklahoma 26, Tennessee 24
1969	Penn State 15, Kansas 14
1970	Penn State 10, Missouri 3
1971	Nebraska 17, Louisiana State 12
1972	Nebraska 38, Alabama 6
1973	Nebraska 40, Notre Dame 6

1974	Penn State 16, Louisiana State 9
1975	Notre Dame 13, Alabama 11
1976	Oklahoma 14, Michigan 6
1977	Ohio State 27, Colorado 10
1978	Arkansas 31, Oklahoma 6
1979	Oklahoma 31, Nebraska 24
1980	Oklahoma 24, Florida State 7
1981	Oklahoma 18, Florida State 17

Sugar Bowl

(At New Orleans)

1935	Tulane 20, Temple 14
1936	Texas Christian 3, Louisiana State 2
1937	Santa Clara 21, Louisiana State 14
1938	Santa Clara 6, Louisiana State 0
1939	Texas Christian 15, Carnegie Tech 7
1940	Texas A & M 14, Tulane 13
1941	Boston College 19, Tennessee 13
1942	Fordham 2, Missouri 0
1943	Tennessee 14, Tulsa 7
1944	Georgia Tech 20, Tulsa 18
1945	Duke 29, Alabama 26
1946	Oklahoma A & M 33, St. Mary's (Calif.) 13
1947	Georgia 20, North Carolina 10
1948	Texas 27, Alabama 7
1949	Oklahoma 14, North Carolina 6
1950	Oklahoma 35, Louisiana State 0
1951	Kentucky 13, Oklahoma 7
1952	Maryland 28, Tennessee 13
1953	Georgia Tech 24, Mississippi 7
1954	Georgia Tech 42, West Virginia 19
1955	Navy 21, Mississippi 0
1956	Georgia Tech 7, Pittsburgh 0
1957	Baylor 13, Tennessee 7
1958	Mississippi 39, Texas 7
1959	Louisiana State 7, Clemson 0
1960	Mississippi 21, Louisiana State 0
1961	Mississippi 14, Rice 6
1962	Alabama 10, Arkansas 3
1963	Mississippi 17, Arkansas 13
1964	Alabama 12, Mississippi 7
1965	Louisiana State 13, Syracuse 10
1966	Missouri 20, Florida 18
1967	Alabama 34, Nebraska 7
1968	Louisiana State 20, Wyoming 13
1969	Arkansas 16, Georgia 2
1970	Mississippi 27, Arkansas 22
1971	Tennessee 34, Air Force Academy 13
1972	Oklahoma 40, Auburn 22
1973	Oklahoma 14, Penn State 0
1974	Notre Dame 24, Alabama 23
1975	Nebraska 13, Florida 10
1976	Alabama 13, Penn State 6
1977	Pittsburgh 27, Georgia 3
1978	Alabama 35, Ohio State 6
1979	Alabama 14, Penn State 7
1980	Alabama 24, Arkansas 9
1981	Georgia 17, Notre Dame 10

Cotton Bowl

(At Dallas)

1937	Texas Christian 16, Marquette 6
1938	Rice 28, Colorado 14
1939	St. Mary's (Calif.) 20, Texas Tech. 13
1940	Clemson 6, Boston College 3
1941	Texas A & M 13, Fordham 12
1942	Alabama 29, Texas A & M 21
1943	Texas 14, Georgia Tech 7

1944	Randolph Field 7, Texas 7
1945	Oklahoma A & M 34, Texas Christian 0
1946	Texas 40, Missouri 27
1947	Louisiana State 0, Arkansas 0
1948	So. Methodist 13, Penn State 13
1949	So. Methodist 21, Oregon 13
1950	Rice 27, North Carolina 13
1951	Tennessee 20, Texas 14
1952	Kentucky 20, Texas Christian 7
1953	Texas 16, Tennessee 0
1954	Rice 28, Alabama 6
1955	Georgia Tech 14, Arkansas 6
1956	Mississippi 14, Texas Christian 13
1957	Texas Christian 28, Syracuse 27
1958	Navy 20, Rice 7
1959	Air Force 0, Texas Christian 0
1960	Syracuse 23, Texas 14
1961	Duke 7, Arkansas 6
1962	Texas 12, Mississippi 7
1963	Louisiana State 13, Texas 0
1964	Texas 28, Navy 6
1965	Arkansas 10, Nebraska 7
1966	Louisiana State 14, Arkansas 7
1967	Georgia 24, So. Methodist 9
1968	Texas A & M 20, Alabama 16
1969	Texas 36, Tennessee 13
1970	Texas 21, Notre Dame 17
1971	Notre Dame 24, Texas 11
1972	Penn State 30, Texas 6
1973	Texas 17, Alabama 13
1974	Nebraska 19, Texas 3
1975	Penn State 41, Baylor 20
1976	Arkansas 31, Georgia 10
1977	Houston 30, Maryland 21
1978	Notre Dame 38, Texas 10
1979	Notre Dame 35, Houston 34
1980	Houston 17, Nebraska 14
1981	Alabama 30, Baylor 2

Gator Bowl

(At Jacksonville, Fla. Played on Saturday nearest New Year's Day of year indicated)

1953	Florida 14, Tulsa 13
1954	Texas Tech 35, Auburn 13
1955	Auburn 33, Baylor 13
1956	Vanderbilt 25, Auburn 13
1957	Georgia Tech 21, Pittsburgh 14
1958	Tennessee 3, Texas A & M 0
1959	Mississippi 7, Florida 3
1960	Arkansas 14, Georgia Tech 7
1961	Florida 13, Baylor 12
1962	Penn State 30, Georgia Tech 15
1963	Florida 17, Penn State 7
1964	No. Carolina 35, Air Force 0
1965	Florida State 36, Oklahoma 19
1966	Georgia Tech 31, Texas Tech 21
1967	Tennessee 18, Syracuse 12
1968	Penn State 17, Florida State 17
1969	Missouri 35, Alabama 10
1970	Florida 14, Tennessee 13
1971	Auburn 35, Mississippi 28
1972	Georgia 7, North Carolina 3
1973	Auburn 24, Colorado 3
1974	Texas Tech 28, Tennessee 19
1975	Auburn 27, Texas 3
1976	Maryland 13, Florida 0
1977	Notre Dame 20, Penn State 9
1978	Pittsburgh 34, Clemson 3
1979	Clemson 17, Ohio State 15
1980	North Carolina 17, Michigan 15
1981	Pittsburgh 37, South Carolina 9

RESULTS OF OTHER 1980 SEASON BOWL GAMES

Bluebonnet (Houston)—North Carolina 16, Texas 7

Fiesta (Tempe, Ariz.)—Penn State 31, Ohio State 19

Hall of Fame (Birmingham, Ala.)—Arkansas 34, Tulane 15

Holiday (San Diego)—Brigham Young 46, Southern Methodist 45

Independence (Shreveport, La.)—Southern Mississippi 16, McNeese State 14

Liberty (Memphis)—Purdue 28, Missouri 25

Garden State (East Rutherford, N.J.)—Houston 35, Navy 0

Peach (Atlanta)—Miami (Fla.) 20, Virginia Tech 10

Sun (El Paso)—Nebraska 31, Mississippi State 17

Tangerine (Orlando, Fla.)—Florida 35, Maryland 20

HEISMAN MEMORIAL TROPHY WINNERS

The Heisman Memorial Trophy is presented annually by the Downtown Athletic Club of New York City to the nation's outstanding college football player, as determined by a poll of sportswriters and sportscasters.

1935	Jay Berwanger, Chicago	1952	Billy Vessels, Oklahoma	1968	O. J. Simpson, Southern California
1936	Larry Kelley, Yale	1953	Johnny Lattner, Notre Dame		
1937	Clinton Frank, Yale	1954	Alan Ameche, Wisconsin	1969	Steve Owens, Oklahoma
1938	Davey O'Brien, Texas Christian	1955	Howard Cassady, Ohio State	1970	Jim Plunkett, Stanford
1939	Nile Kinnick, Iowa	1956	Paul Hornung, Notre Dame	1971	Pat Sullivan, Auburn
1940	Tom Harmon, Michigan	1957	John Crow, Texas A & M	1972	Johnny Rodgers, Nebraska
1941	Bruce Smith, Minnesota	1958	Pete Dawkins, Army	1973	John Cappelletti, Penn State
1942	Frank Sinkwich, Georgia	1959	Billy Cannon, Louisiana State	1974–75	Archie Griffin, Ohio State
1943	Angelo Bertelli, Notre Dame	1960	Joe Bellino, Navy	1976	Tony Dorsett, Pittsburgh
1944	Leslie Horvath, Ohio State	1961	Ernie Davis, Syracuse	1977	Earl Campbell, Texas
1945	Felix Blanchard, Army	1962	Terry Baker, Oregon State	1978	Billy Sims, Oklahoma
1946	Glenn Davis, Army	1963	Roger Staubach, Navy	1979	Charles White, Southern California
1947	Johnny Lujack, Notre Dame	1964	John Huarte, Notre Dame		
1948	Doak Walker, So. Methodist	1965	Mike Garrett, Southern California	1980	George Rogers, South Carolina
1949	Leon Hart, Notre Dame				
1950	Vic Janowicz, Ohio State	1966	Steve Spurrier, Florida		
1951	Dick Kazmaier, Princeton	1967	Gary Beban, U.C.L.A.		

COLLEGE FOOTBALL HALL OF FAME

(Kings Island, Interstate 71, Kings Mills, Ohio)

(Date given is player's last year of competition)

Players

Abell, Earl—Colgate, 1915
Agase, Alex—Purdue/Illinois, 1946
Agganis, Harry—Boston Univ., 1952
Albert, Frank—Stanford, 1941
Aldrich, Chas. (Ki)—T.C.U., 1938
Aldrich, Malcolm—Yale, 1921
Alexander, John—Syracuse, 1920
Ameche, Alan (Horse)—Wisconsin, 1954
Anderson, H. (Hunk)—Notre Dame, 1921
Bacon, C. Everett—Wesleyan, 1912
Bagnell, Francis (Reds)—Penn, 1950
Baker, Hobart (Hobey)—Princeton, 1913
Ballin, Harold—Princeton, 1914
Banker, Bill—Tulane, 1929
Barnes, Stanley—S. California, 1921
Barrett, Charles—Cornell, 1915
Baston, Bert—Minnesota, 1916
Battles, Cliff—W. Va. Wesleyan, 1931
Baugh, Sammy—Texas Christian U., 1936
Bausch, James—Kansas, 1930
Beckett, John—Oregon, 1913
Bednarik, Chuck—Pennsylvania, 1948
Bellini, Joe—Navy, 1960
Benbrook, A.—Michigan, 1911
Bertelli, A.—Notre Dame, 1943
Berry, Charlie—Lafayette, 1924
Berwanger, John (Jay)—Chicago, 1935
Bettencourt, Larry—St. Mary's, 1927
Blanchard, Felix (Doc)—Army, 1946
Bock, Ed—Iowa State, 1938
Bomar, Lynn—Vanderbilt, 1924
Bomeisler, Doug (Bo)—Yale, 1913
Booth, Albie—Yale, 1931
Borries, Fred—Navy, 1934
Bottari, Vic—California, 1939
Boynton, Ben—Williams, 1920
Brewer, Charles—Harvard, 1895
Brooke, George—Pennsylvania, 1895

Brown, Gordon—Yale, 1900
Brown, John, Jr.—Navy, 1913
Brown, Johnny Mack—Alabama, 1925
Brown, Raymond (Tay)—So. California, 1932
Bunker, Paul—Army, 1902
Butler, Robert—Wisconsin, 1912
Cafego, George—Tennessee, 1939
Cagle, Chris—SW La./Army, 1929
Cain, John—Alabama, 1932
Cameron, Eddie—Wash. & Lee, 1924
Campbell, David C.—Harvard, 1901
Cannon, Jack—Notre Dame, 1929
Carideo, Frank—Notre Dame, 1930
Caroline, J.C.—Illinois, 1954
Carney, Charles—Illinois, 1921
Carpenter, C. Hunter—VPI, 1905
Carroll, Charles—Washington, 1928
Casey, Edward L.—Harvard, 1919
Cassady, Howard—Ohio State, 1955
Chamberlain, Guy—Nebraska, 1915
Christman, Paul—Missouri, 1940
Clark, Earl (Dutch)—Colo. College, 1929
Clevenger, Zora—Indiana, 1903
Cochran, Gary—Princeton, 1895
Cody, Josh—Vanderbilt, 1920
Coleman, Don—Mich. State, 1951
Conerly, Chuck—Mississippi, 1947
Connor, George—Notre Dame, 1947
Corbin, W.—Yale, 1888
Corbus, William—Stanford, 1933
Cowan, Hector—Princeton, 1889
Coy, Edward H. (Tad)—Yale, 1909
Crawford, Fred—Duke, 1933
Crow, John D.—Texas A&M, 1957
Crowley, James—Notre Dame, 1924
Cutter, Slade—Navy, 1934
Czarobski, Ziggie—Notre Dame, 1947
Dalrymple, Gerald—Tulane, 1931

Daniell, James—Ohio State, 1941
Dawkins, Pete—Army, 1958
Dalton, John—Navy, 1912
Daly, Charles—Harvard/Army, 1902
Daniell, Averell—Pittsburgh, 1936
Davies, Tom—Pittsburgh, 1921
Davis, Ernest—Syracuse, 1961
Davis, Glenn—Army, 1946
Davis, Robert T.—Georgia Tech, 1947
DesJardien, Paul—Chicago, 1914
Devine, Aubrey—Iowa, 1921
DeWitt, John—Princeton, 1903
Dobbs, Glenn—Tulsa, 1942
Dodd, Bobby—Tennessee, 1930
Donchess, Joseph—Pittsburgh, 1929
Dougherty, Nathan—Tennessee, 1909
Drahos, Nick—Cornell, 1940
Driscoll, Paddy—Northwestern, 1917
Drury, Morley—So. California, 1927
Dudley, William (Bill)—Virginia, 1941
Eckersall, Walter—Chicago, 1906
Edwards, Turk—Washington State, 1931
Edwards, William—Princeton, 1900
Eichenlaub, R.—Notre Dame, 1913
Evans, Ray—Kansas, 1947
Exendine, Albert—Carlisle, 1908
Falaschi, Nello—Santa Clara, 1937
Fears, Tom—Santa Clara/UCLA, 1947
Feathers, Beattie—Tennessee, 1933
Fenimore, Robert—Oklahoma State, 1947
Fenton, G.E. (Doc)—La. State U., 1910
Ferraro, John—So. California, 1944
Fesler, Wesley—Ohio State, 1930
Fincher, Bill—Georgia Tech, 1920
Fish, Hamilton—Harvard, 1909
Fisher, Robert—Harvard, 1911
Flowers, Abe—Georgia Tech, 1920
Fortmann, Daniel—Colgate, 1935
Francis, Sam—Nebraska, 1936

Franco, Edmund (Ed)—Fordham, 1937
Frank, Clint—Yale, 1937
Franz, Rodney—California, 1949
Friedman, Benny—Michigan, 1926
Gain, Bob—Kentucky, 1950
Garbisch, Edgar—Army, 1924
Gelbert, Charles—Pennsylvania, 1896
Geyer, Forest—Oklahoma, 1915
Giel, Paul—Minnesota, 1953
Gifford, Frank—So. California, 1951
Gilbert, Walter—Auburn, 1936
Gipp, George—Notre Dame, 1920
Gladchuk, Chet—Boston College, 1940
Goldberg, Marshall—Pittsburgh, 1938
Gordon, Walter—California, 1918
Graham, Otto—Northwestern, 1943
Grange, Harold (Red)—Illinois, 1925
Grayson, Robert—Stanford, 1935
Gulick, Merel—Hobart, 1929
Guyon, Joe—Georgia Tech, 1919
Hale, Edwin—Mississippi Col, 1921
Hamilton, Robert (Bones)—Stanford, 1935
Hamilton, Tom—Navy, 1925
Hanson, Vic—Syracuse, 1926
Hardwick, H. (Tack)—Harvard, 1914
Hare, T. Truxton—Pennsylvania, 1900
Harley, Chick—Ohio State, 1919
Harmon, Tom—Michigan, 1940
Harpster, Howard—Carnegie Tech, 1928
Hart, Edward J.—Princeton, 1911
Hart, Leon—Notre Dame, 1949
Hazel, Homer—Rutgers, 1924
Healey, Ed—Dartmouth, 1916
Heffelfinger, W. (Pudge)—Yale, 1891
Hein, Mel—Washington State, 1930
Henry, Wilber—Wash. & Jefferson, 1919
Herschberger, Clarence—Chicago, 1899
Herwig, Robert—California, 1937
Heston, Willie—Michigan, 1904
Hickman, Herman—Tennessee, 1931
Hickok, William—Yale, 1895
Hill, Dan—Duke, 1938
Hillebrand, A.R. (Doc)—Princeton, 1900
Hinkey, Frank—Yale, 1894
Hinkle, Carl—Vanderbilt, 1937
Hinkle, Clark—Bucknell, 1932
Hirsch, Elroy—Wis./Mich., 1943
Hitchcock, James—Auburn, 1932
Hoffman, Frank—Notre Dame, 1931
Hogan, James J.—Yale, 1904
Holland, Jerome (Brud)—Cornell, 1938
Hollenbeck, William—Penn., 1908
Holovak, Michael—Boston College, 1942
Horrell, Edwin—California, 1924
Horvath, Les—Ohio State, 1944
Howe, Arthur—Yale, 1911
Howell, Millard (Dixie)—Alabama, 1934
Hubbard, Cal—Centenary, 1926
Hubbard, John—Amherst, 1906
Hubert, Allison—Alabama, 1925
Huff, Robert Lee (Sam)—W. Va., 1955
Humble, Weldon G.—Rice, 1946
Hunt, Joel—Texas A&M, 1927
Huntington, Ellery—Colgate, 1914
Hutson, Don—Alabama, 1934
Ingram, James—Navy, 1906
Isbell, Cecil—Purdue, 1937
Jablonsky, Harvey—Wash. U./Army, 1933
Janowicz, Vic—Ohio State, 1951
Jenkins, Darold—Missouri, 1941
Joesting, Herbert—Minnesota, 1927
Johnson, James—Carlisle, 1903
Jones, Calvin—Iowa, 1955
Jones, Gomer—Ohio State, 1935

Juhan, Frank—Univ. of South, 1910
Justice, Charlie—North Carolina, 1949
Kaer, Mort—So. California, 1926
Kavanaugh, Kenneth—La. State U., 1939
Kaw, Edgar—Cornell, 1922
Kazmaier, Richard—Princeton, 1951
Keck, James—Princeton, 1921
Kelley, Larry—Yale, 1936
Kelly, William—Montana, 1926
Ketcham, Henry—Yale, 1913
Killinger, William—Penn State, 1922
Kimbrough, John—Texas A&M, 1940
Kinard, Frank—Mississippi, 1937
King, Phillip—Princeton, 1893
Kinnick, Nile—Iowa, 1939
Kipke, Harry—Michigan, 1923
Kirkpatrick, John Reed—Yale, 1910
Kitzmiller, John—Oregon, 1929
Koch, Barton—Baylor, 1931
Kitner, Malcolm—Texas, 1942
Kramer, Ron—Michigan, 1956
Lach, Steve—Duke, 1941
Lane, Myles—Dartmouth, 1927
Lattner, Joseph J.—Notre Dame, 1953
Lauricella, Hank—Tennessee, 1952
Lautenschlaeger—Tulane, 1925
Layden, Elmer—Notre Dame, 1924
Layne, Bobby—Texas, 1947
Lea, Langdon—Princeton, 1895
LeBaron, Eddie—Univ. of Pacific, 1949
Leech, James—Va. Mil. Inst., 1920
Lilly, Bob—Texas Christian, 1960
Lio, Augie—Georgetown, 1940
Locke, Gordon—Iowa, 1922
Lourie, Don—Princeton, 1921
Luckman, Sid—Columbia, 1938
Lujack, John—Notre Dame, 1947
Lund, J.L. (Pug)—Minnesota, 1934
Macomber, Bart—Illinois, 1915
MacLeod, Robert—Dartmouth, 1938
Maegle, Dick—Rice, 1954
Mahan, Edward W.—Harvard, 1915
Mallory, William—Yale, 1893
Mann, Gerald—So. Methodist, 1927
Markov, Vic—Washington, 1937
Marshall, Robert—Minnesota, 1907
Matson, Ollie—San Fran. U., 1952
Matthews, Ray—Texas Christ. U., 1928
Maulbetsch, John—Michigan, 1914
Mauthe, J.L. (Pete)—Penn State 1912
Maxwell, Robert—Chi./Swarthmore, 1906
McAfee, George—Duke, 1939
McColl, William F.—Stanford, 1951
McCormick, James B.—Princeton, 1907
McDowall, Jack—No. Car. State, 1927
McElhenny, Hugh—Washington, 1951
McEver, Gene—Tennessee, 1931
McEwan, John—Minn./Army, 1916
McFadden, J.B.—Clemson, 1939
McClung, Thomas L.—Yale, 1891
McGinley, Edward—Pennsylvania, 1924
McGovern, J.—Minnesota, 1910
McGraw, Thurman—Colorado State, 1949
McLaren, George—Pittsburgh, 1918
McMillan, Dan—U.S.C./Calif., 1922
McMillin, A.N. (Bo)—Centre, 1921
McWhorter, Robert—Georgia, 1913
Mercer, Leroy—Pennsylvania, 1912
Mickal, Abe—La. State U., 1935
Miller, Creighton—Notre Dame, 1943
Miller, Don—Notre Dame, 1925
Miller, Edgar (Rip)—Notre Dame, 1924
Miller, Eugene—Penn State, 1913

Milstead, Century—Wabash, Yale 1923
Minds, John—Pennsylvania, 1897
Moffatt, Alex—Princeton, 1884
Montgomery, Cliff—Columbia, 1933
Moomaw, Donn—U.C.L.A., 1952
Morley, William—Columbia, 1903
Morris, George—Georgia Tech, 1952
Morton, William—Dartmouth, 1931
Muller, Harold (Brick)—Calif., 1922
Nagurski, Bronko—Minnesota, 1929
Nevers, Ernie—Stanford, 1925
Newell, Marshall—Harvard, 1893
Newman, Harry—Michigan, 1932
Nobis, Tommy—Texas, 1965
Nomellini, Leo—Minnesota, 1949
Oberlander, Andrew—Dartmouth, 1925
O'Brien, Davey—Texas Christ. U., 1938
O'Dea, Pat—Wisconsin, 1899
O'Hearn, J.—Cornell, 1915
Oliphant, Elmer—Purdue/Army, 1917
Olsen, Merlin—Utah State, 1961
Oosterbaan, Ben—Michigan, 1927
O'Rourke, Charles—Boston College, 1940
Osgood, W.D.—Cornell/Penn, 1895
Osmanski, William—Holy Cross, 1938
Parker, Clarence (Ace)—Duke, 1936
Parker, Jackie—Miss. State, 1953
Parker, James—Ohio State, 1956
Pazzetti, V.J.—Wes./Lehigh, 1912
Peabody, Endicott—Harvard, 1941
Peck, Robert—Pittsburgh, 1916
Pennock, Stanley B.—Harvard, 1914
Pfann, George—Cornell, 1923
Phillips, H.D.—U. of South, 1904
Pingel, John—Michigan State, 1938
Pihos, Pete—Indiana, 1945
Pinckert, Ernie—So. California, 1931
Poe, Arthur—Princeton, 1899
Pollard, Fritz—Brown, 1916
Poole, Barney—Miss./Army, 1947
Pund, Henry—Georgia Tech, 1928
Ramsey, Gerrard—Wm. & Mary, 1942
Reeds, Claude—Oklahoma, 1913
Reid, William—Harvard, 1900
Rentner, Ernest—Northwestern, 1932
Reynolds, Robert—Stanford, 1935
Rinehart, Charles—Lafayette, 1897
Rodgers, Ira—West Virginia, 1919
Rogers, Edward L.—Minnesota, 1903
Rosenberg, Aaron—So. California, 1934
Rote, Kyle—So. Methodist, 1950
Routt, Joe—Texas A&M., 1937
Salmon, Louis—Notre Dame, 1904
Sauer, George—Nebraska, 1933
Sayers, Gale—Kansas, 1964
Scarlett, Hunter—Pennsylvania, 1909
Schoonover, Wear—Arkansas, 1929
Schreiner, Dave—Wisconsin, 1942
Schultz, Adolf (Germany)—Mich., 1908
Schwab, Frank—Lafayette, 1922
Schwartz, Marchmont—Notre Dame, 1931
Schwegler, Paul—Washington, 1931
Scott, Clyde—Arkansas, 1949
Scott, Tom—Virgina, 1953
Seibels, Henry—Sewanee, 1899
Shelton, Murray—Cornell, 1915
Shevlin, Tom—Yale, 1905
Simons, Claude—Tulane, 1934
Sington, Fred—Alabama, 1930
Sinkwich, Frank—Georgia, 1942
Skladany, Joe—Pittsburgh, 1933
Slater, F.F. (Duke)—Iowa, 1921
Smith, Bruce—Minnesota, 1941
Smith, Ernie—So. California, 1932

Smith, Harry—So. California, 1939
Smith, John (Clipper)—Notre Dame, 1927
Smith, Vernon—Georgia, 1931
Snow, Neil—Michigan, 1901
Spears, Clarence W.—Dartmouth, 1915
Spears, W.D.—Vanderbilt, 1927
Sprackling, William—Brown, 1911
Sprague, M. (Bud)—Texas/Army, 1928
Stafford, Harrison—Texas, 1932
Stagg, Amos Alonzo—Yale, 1889
Staubach, Roger—Navy, 1963
Steffen, Walter—Chicago, 1908
Stein, Herbert—Pittsburgh, 1921
Steuber, Robert—Missouri, 1943
Stevens, Mal—Yale, 1923
Stinchcomb, Gaylord—Ohio State, 1920
Stevenson, Vincent—Pennsylvania, 1905
Strong, Ken—New York Univ., 1928
Strupper, George—Georgia Tech, 1917
Stuhldreher, Harry—Notre Dame, 1924
Stydahar, Joe—West Virginia, 1935
Suffridge, Robert—Tennessee, 1940
Sundstrom, Frank—Cornell, 1923
Swanson, Clarence—Nebraska, 1921
Swiacki, Bill—Holy Cross/Colombia. 1947
Swink, Jim—Texas Christian, 1956
Taliafarro, George—Indiana, 1948
Thompson, Joe—Pittsburgh, 1907
Thorne, Samuel B.—Yale, 1906

Thorpe, Jim—Carlisle, 1912
Ticknor, Ben—Harvard, 1930
Tigert, John—Vanderbilt, 1904
Tinsley, Gaynell—La. State U., 1936
Tipton, Eric—Duke, 1938
Tonnemaker, Clayton—Minnesota, 1949
Torrey, Robert—Pennsylvania, 1906
Travis, Ed Tarkio—Missouri, 1920
Trippi, Charles—Georgia, 1946
Tryon, J. Edward—Colgate, 1925
Utay, Joe—Texas A&M, 1907
Van Brocklin, Norm—Oregon, 1948
Van Sickel, Dale—Florida, 1929
Van Surdam, Henderson—Wesleyan, 1905
Very, Dexter—Penn State, 1912
Vessels, Billy—Oklahoma, 1931
Wagner, Huber—Pittsburgh, 1913
Walker, Doak—So. Methodist, 1949
Wallace, Bill—Rice, 1935
Walsh, Adam—Notre Dame, 1924
Warburton, I. (Cotton)—So. Calif., 1934
Ward, Robert (Bob)—Maryland, 1951
Warner, William—Cornell, 1903
Washington, Ken—U.C.L.A., 1939
Wedemeyer, Herman J.—St. Mary's, 1947
Weekes, Harold—Columbia, 1902
Weir, Ed—Nebraska, 1925
Welch, Gus—Carlisle, 1914

Weller, John—Princeton, 1935
Wendell, Percy—Harvard, 1913
West, D. Belford—Colgate, 1919
Weyand, Alex—Army, 1915
Wharton, Charles—Pennsylvania, 1896
Wheeler, Arthur—Princeton, 1894
White, Byron (Whizzer)—Colorado, 1937
Whitmire, Don—Alabama/Navy, 1944
Wickhorst, Frank—Navy, 1926
Widseth, Ed—Minnesota, 1936
Wildung, Richard—Minnesota, 1942
Williams, James—Rice, 1949
Willis, William—Ohio State, 1945
Wilson, George—Washington, 1925
Wilson, Harry—Penn State/Army, 1923
Wistert, Albert A.—Michigan, 1942
Wistert, Al—Michigan, 1949
Wistert, Frank (Whitey)—Mich., 1933
Wood, Barry—Harvard, 1931
Wojciechowicz, Alex—Fordham, 1936
Wyant, Andrew—Bucknell/Chicago, 1894
Wyatt, Bowden—Tennessee, 1938
Wyckoff, Clint—Cornell, 1896
Young, Claude (Buddy)—Illinois, 1946
Young, Harry—Wash. & Lee, 1916
Zarnas, Gus—Ohio State, 1937

Coaches

Bill Alexander
Dr. Ed Anderson
Ike Armstrong
Matty Bell
Hugo Bezdek
Dana X. Bible
Bernie Bierman
Earl (Red) Blaik
Charles W. Caldwell
Walter Camp
Len Casanova
Frank Cavanaugh
Fritz Crisler
Gil Dobie
Michael Donohue
Gus Dorais
Charles (Rip) Engle

Don Faurot
Jake Gaither
Ernest Godfrey
Jack Harding
Edward K. Hall
Richard Harlow
Jesse Harper
Percy Haughton
John W. Heisman
R. A. (Bob) Higgins
Orin E. Hollingberry
William Ingram
Morley Jennings
Howard Jones
L. (Biff) Jones
Thomas (Tad) Jones
Andy Kerr

Frank Leahy
George E. Little
Lou Little
El (Slip) Madigan
Herbert McCracken
Daniel McGugin
DeOrmond (Tuss) McLaughry
L. R. (Dutch) Meyer
Bernie Moore
Scrappy Moore
Ray Morrison
George A. Munger
Clarence Munn
William Murray
Ed (Hooks) Mylin
Earle (Greasy) Neale
Jess Neely

Robert Neyland
Homer Norton
Frank (Buck) O'Neill
Bennie Owen
Ara Parseghian
James Phalea
Knute Rockne
E. L. (Dick) Romney
William W. Roper
George F. Sanford
Francis A. Schmidt
Clark Shaughnessy
Buck Shaw
Andrew L. Smith
Carl Snavely
Amos A. Stagg

Jock Sutherland
Frank W. Thomas
John H. Vaught
Wallace Wade
Lynn Waldorf
Glenn (Pop) Warner
E. E. (Tad) Wieman
John W. Wilce
Bud Wilkinson
Henry L. Williams
George W. Woodruff
Fielding H. Yost
Robert Zuppke

MAJOR COLLEGE FOOTBALL RECORDS (1940–1979)
(Opposing teams are listed in parentheses. *Source:* National Collegiate Sports Services)

LONGEST PLAYS
Rushing

	Yards
Kelsey Finch, Tennessee (Florida) 1977	99
Ralph Thompson, W. Tex. State (Wichita State) 1970	99
Max Anderson, Arizona State (Wyoming) 1967	99
Gale Sayers, Kansas (Nebraska) 1963	99
Granville Amos, Virginia M. I. (Wm. & Mary) 1964	98
Jim Thacker, Davidson (George Washington) 1952	98
Bill Powell, California (Oregon State) 1951	98
Al Yannelli, Bucknell (Delaware) 1946	98
Meredith Warner, Iowa State (Iowa Pre-Flight) 1943	98
Stanley Howell, Miss. State (Southern Miss.) 1979	98
Mark Malone, Arizona State (Utah State) 1979	98

Passing

	Yards
Chris Collingsworth–Derrick Gaffney, Florida (Rice) 1977	99

	Yards
Terry Peel–Robert Ford, Houston (San Diego St.) 1972	99
Terry Peel–Robert Ford, Houston (Syracuse) 1970	99
Colin Clapton–Eddie Jenkins, Holy Cross (Boston U.) 1970	99
Bo Burris–Warren McVea, Houston (Wash. St.) 1966	99
Fred Owens–Jack Ford, Portland (St. Mary's) 1947	99
Jeff Martin–Mark Flaker, Drake (N.M. State) 1976	98
Pete Woods–Joe Stewart, Missouri (Nebraska) 1976	98
Dan Hagemann–Jack Steptoe, Utah (New Mexico) 1976	98
Bruce Shaw–Pat Kenny, N.C. State (Penn State) 1972	98
Jerry Rhome–Jeff Jordan, Tulsa (Wichita State) 1963	98
Bob Dean–Norman Dawson, Cornell (Navy) 1947	98

Punt Returns

	Yards
Jimmy Campagna, Georgia (Vanderbilt) 1952	100
Hugh McElhenny, Washington (So. Cal.) 1951	100
Frank Brady, Navy (Maryland) 1951	100

Bert Rechichar, Tennessee (Wash. & Lee) 1950   100
Eddie Macon, Pacific (Boston U.) 1950   100
Richie Luzzi, Clemson (Georgia) 1968   100[1]
Don Guest, California (Washington State) 1966   100[1]
1. Return of a field goal attempt.

Punts

	Yards
Pat Brady, Nevada (Loyola, L. A.) 1950	99
George O'Brien, Wisconsin (Iowa) 1952	96
John Hadl, Kansas (Oklahoma) 1959	94
Carl Knox, Texas Christian (Oklahoma State) 1947	94
Preston Johnson, SMU (Pittsburgh) 1940	94

Field Goals

	Yards
Joe Williams, Wichita State (So. Illinois) 1978	67
Steve Little, Arkansas (Texas) 1977	67
Russell Erxleben, Texas (Rice) 1977	67
Tony Franklin, Texas A&M (Baylor) 1976	65
Russell Erxleben, Texas (Oklahoma) 1977	64
Tony Franklin, Texas A&M (Baylor) 1976	64
Clark Kemble, Colorado State (Arizona) 1975	63
Dan Christopulos, Wyoming (Colorado State) 1977	62
Iseed Khoury, North Texas State (Richmond) 1977	62
Dave Lawson, Air Force Academy (Iowa State) 1975	62
Steve Little, Arkansas (Tulsa) 1976	61
Wayne Latimer, Virginia Tech (Florida State) 1975	61
Ray Guy, Southern Mississippi (Utah State) 1972	61

BEST SINGLE-GAME PERFORMANCES

Most yards, rushing—356, Eddie Lee Ivery, Georgia Tech (Air Force) 1978
Most yards, total offense—599, Virgil Carter, Brigham Young (Texas–El Paso) 1966
Most yards, passing—621, Dave Wilson, Illinois (Ohio State) 1980
Most yards, pass receiving—349, Chuck Hughes, Texas–El Paso (North Texas State) 1965
Most points scored—43, Jim Brown, Syracuse (Colgate) 1956
Most passes attempted—69, Chuck Hixson, Southern Methodist (Ohio State) 1968 and Dave Wilson, Illinois (Ohio State) 1980
Most passes completed—43, Dave Wilson, Illinois (Ohio State) 1980 and Rich Campbell, California (Florida) 1980
Most passes caught—22, Jay Miller, Brigham Young (New Mexico) 1973

CAREER LEADERS
Rushing

	Years	Plays	Yds	Avg
Tony Dorsett, Pittsburgh	1973–76	1,074[1]	6,082[1]	5.66
Charles White, So. Calif.	1976–79	1,023	5,598	5.47
Archie Griffin, Ohio State	1972–75	845	5,177	6.13
George Rogers, So. Calif.	1977–80	902	4,958	5.50
Ed Marinaro, Cornell	1969–71	918	4,715	5.14
Ted Brown, No. Carolina State	1975–78	860	4,602	5.35
Terry Miller, Oklahoma State	1974–77	847	4,582	5.41
Earl Campbell, Texas	1974–77	765	4,443	5.81
Amos Lawrence, North Carolina	1977–80	881	4,391	4.98
Jerome Persell, Western Mich.	1976–78	842	4,190	4.98
Stump Mitchell, Citadel	1977–80	756	4,062	5.37
Charles Alexander, L.S.U.	1975–78	855	4,035	4.72

1. Record.

Passing

	Years	Cmp	Pct	Yds	Td
Mark Herrmann, Purdue	1977–80	717[1]	.589	9,188[1]	62
Chuck Hixson, Southern Methodist	1968–70	642	.576	7,179	40
Joe Adams, Tennessee State	1977–80	604	.549	8,649	81[1]
John Reaves, Florida	1969–71	603	.535	7,549	54
Jack Thompson, Washington State	1975–78	601	.553	7,818	53
Ed Luther, San Jose State	1976–79	600	.537	7,190	47
Rich Campbell, California	1977–80	574	.644[1]	6,933	33
Randy Hertel, Rice	1977–80	561	.500	6,161	38
Gene Swick, Toledo	1972–75	556	.593	7,267	44
Marc Wilson, Brigham Young	1977–79	535	.571	7,637	61
Jim Plunkett, Stanford	1968–70	530	.551	7,544	52
Tommy Kramer, Rice	1973–76	507	.489	6,197	37

1. Record.

Total Offense

	Years	Plays	Yds	Tdr[1]
Mark Herrmann, Purdue	1977–80	1,354	8,444[2]	63
Gene Swick, Toledo	1972–75	1,579[2]	8,074	63
Joe Adams, Tennessee State	1977–80	1,256	7,972	86[2]
Jim Plunkett, Stanford	1968–70	1,174	7,887	62
Jack Thompson, Washington State	1975–78	1,345	7,698	63
Marc Wilson, Brigham Young	1977–79	1,183	7,602	68
Jean Reaves, Florida	1969–71	1,258	7,283	58
Steve Brown, Appalachian State	1977–80	1,160	7,129	49
Ed Luther, San Jose State	1976–79	1,230	6,981	55
Chuck Hixson, Southern Methodist	1968–70	1,358	6,884	50
Pat Sullivan, Auburn	1969–71	968	6,884	71

1. Touchdowns responsible for—scored or passed for. 2. Record.

Pass Receiving

	Years	Rec	Yds	Td
Howard Twilley, Tulsa	1963–65	261[1]	3,343	32
Ron Sellers, Florida State	1966–68	212	3,598	23
Gerald Harp, Western Carolina	1977–80	197	3,305	26
Phil Odle, Brigham Young	1965–67	181	2,548	25
Tim Delaney, San Diego State	1968–70	180	2,535	22

1. Record.

Scoring

	Years	Td	Pat	Fg	Pts
Tony Dorsett, Pittsburgh	1973–76	59[1]	2	0	356[1]
Glenn Davis, Army	1943–46	59[1]	0	0	354
Art Luppino, Arizona	1953–56	48	49	0	337
Steve Owens, Oklahoma	1967–69	56	0	0	336
Wilford White, Arizona State	1947–50	48	27	4	327
Ed Marinaro, Cornell	1969–71	52	6	0	318
Pete Johnson, Ohio State	1973–76	53	0	0	318
Ted Brown, North Carolina State	1975–78	51	6	0	312
Eddie Talboom, Wyoming	1948–50	34	99	0	303

1. Record.

N.C.A.A. DIVISION II AND III FOOTBALL RECORDS (1942–80)

LONGEST PLAYS
Rushing

	Yards
Kevin Doherty, Mass. Maritime (New Haven) 1980	99
Fred Deutsch, Springfield (Wagner) 1977	99
Sam Hallston, Albany State, N.Y. (Norwich) 1977	99
Sammy Croom, San Diego (Azusa Pacific) 1972	99
John Stenger, Swarthmore (Widener) 1970	99
Jed Knuttila, Hamline (St. Thomas) 1968	99
Dave Lanoha, Colorado College (Texas Lutheran) 1967	99
Tom Pabst, Cal–Riverside (Cal. Tech) 1965	99
George Phillips, Concord (Davis and Elkins) 1961	99
Gerry White, Connecticut (Rhode Island) 1960	99
Leo Williams, St. Augustine's (Morris) 1960	99
George Phelps, Cornell College (Monmouth) 1959	99
Mark Lydon, Tufts (Bowdoin) 1958	99
David Wells, Tufts (Williams) 1956	99
Jack Moskal, Western Reserve (Case Tech) 1954	99
Lou Mariano, Kent State (Western Reserve) 1954	99
Ron Temple, Chico State (Southern Oregon) 1963	99
Ellis Horton, Eureka, (Rose–Hulman) 1952	99
Pat Abbruzzi, Rhode Island (New Hampshire) 1951	99

Field Goals

Joe Duren, Arkansas State (McNeese State) 1974	63
Dom Antonini, Glassboro State (Salisbury State) 1976	62
Mike Flater, Colorado Mines (Western State) 1973	62
Duane Christian, Cameron (Southwestern Oklahoma) 1976	61
Mike Wood, Southeast Missouri (Lincoln) 1975	61
Bill Shear, Cortland State (Hobart) 1966	61

Passing

	Yards
John Guercio–Tom Bennett, C.W. Post (Juniata) 1980	99
Mike Moroski–Calvin Ellison, California-Davis (Puget Sound) 1978	99
Rich Boling–Lewis Borsellino, DePauw (Valparaiso) 1976	99
John Wicinski–Donnell Lipford, John Carroll (Allegheny) 1975	99
Jack Berry–Mercer West, Washington and Lee (Hampden–Sydney) 1974	99
Gary Shope–Rick Rudolph, Juniata (Moravian) 1973	99
Gary Dusenberg–Harvey King, North Park (Illinois Wesleyan) 1970	99
Bob Janesko–Frank Stankiewicz, Emporia (Pittsburg State) 1969	99
John Williams–Bill Carter, N.M. Highlands (North Colorado) 1964	99
Carl Meyers–Roger Sayers, Nebraska-Omaha (Drake) 1963	99

Punts

Earl Hurst, Emporia State (Central Missouri) 1964	97
Gary Frens, Hope (Olivet) 1966	96
Jim Jarrett, North Dakota (South Dakota) 1957	96
Elliot Mills, Carleton (Monmouth) 1970	93
Kaspar Fitins, Taylor (Georgetown, Ky.) 1966	93
Leeroy Sweeney, Pomona (Cal–Riverside) 1960	93

CAREER LEADERS
Rushing

	Years	Plays	Yds	Avg
Chris Cobb, Eastern Illinois	1976–79	930	5,042[1]	5.42
Jerry Linton, Panhandle State	1959–62	648	4,839	7.47
John VanWagner, Mich. Tech.	1973–76	958	4,788	5.00
Rich Kowalski, Hobart	1972–75	907	4,631	5.11
Don Aleksiewicz, Hobart	1969–72	819	4,525	5.53
Dale Mills, NE Missouri	1957–60	751	4,502	5.99
Leo Lewis, Lincoln (Mo.)	1951–54	623	4,458	7.16
Bernie Peeters, Luther	1968–71	1,072	4,435	4.14
Larry Schreiber, Tenn. Tech.	1966–69	878	4,421	5.04
Brad Rowland, McMurry	1947–50	683	4,347	6.36
Vincent Allen, Indiana State	1973–77	832	4,335	5.21
Bill Rhodes, Colorado Western	1953–56	506	4,294	8.49[1]
Lem Harkey, Col. of Emporia	1951–54	502	4,232	8.43

1. Record

Scoring

	Years	Td	Pat	Fg	Pts
Walter Payton, Jackson State	1971–74	66[1]	53	5	464[1]
Dale Mills, NE Missouri	1957–60	64	23	0	407
Garney Henley, Huron	1956–59	63	16	0	394
Leo Lewis, Lincoln (Mo.)	1951–54	64	0	0	384
Billy Johnson, Widener	1971–73	62	0	0	372
Tank Younger, Grambling	1945–48	60	9	0	369

1. Record

Passing

	Years	Cmp	Pct	Yds	Td
Jim Lindsey, Abilene Chr.	1967–70	642[1]	.519	8,521[1]	61
Bob Caress, Bradley	1962–65	610	.528	7,115	64
Dan Miles, So. Oregon	1964–67	577	.662[1]	6,531	52
George Bork, N. Illinois	1960–63	577	.640	6,782	60
Craig Soloman, Southwestern Tennessee	1975–78	542	.530	7,314	71
Ron Meehan, Towson State	1977–80	529	.527	6,164	31
Kim McQuilken, Lehigh	1971–73	516	.558	6,996	37
Tim Von Dulm, Portland St.	1969–70	500	.541	5,967	51
Greg Cavanaugh, St. Norbert	1977–80	489	.499	5,442	37
Doug Williams, Grambling	1974–77	484	.480	8,411	99[1]

1. Record.

Pass Receiving

	Years	Rec	Yards	Td
Chris Myers, Kenyon	1967–70	253[1]	3,897	33
Bruce Cerone, Yankton–Emporia St.	1966–67 1968–1969	241[1]	4,354[1]	49[1]
Harold Roberts, Austin Peay	1967–70	232	3,005	31
Jerry Hendren, Idaho	1967–69	230	3,435	27
Terry Fredenberg, Wis.–Milwaukee	1965–68	206	2,789	24
Rick Fry, Occidental	1974–77	200	3,073	18
Jay True, DePauw	1977–80	195	2,567	12
Bill Wick, Carroll (Wis.)	1966–69	190	2,967	20
Don Hutt, Boise State	1971–73	187	2,716	30

1. Record.

Total Offense

	Years	Plays	Yds
Jim Lindsey, Abilene Christian	1967–70	1,510[1]	8,385[1]
Doug Williams, Grambling	1974–77	1,072	8,195
Donald Smith, Langston	1958–61	998	7,376
Bruce Upstill, Coll. Emporia	1960–63	922	7,122
Craig Solomon, SW Tennessee	1975–78	1,261	7,055
Clay Sampson, Denison	1977–80	1,225	6,920
Kim McQuilken, Lehigh	1971–73	991	6,878
Bob Caress, Bradley	1962–65	1,361	6,757

1. Record.

MOST POINTS IN SEASON

	Yards	Tds	PAT	Fg	Pts
Terry Metcalf, Long Beach St.	1971	29[1]	4	0	178
Jim Switzer, Coll. Emporia	1963	28	0	0	168
Carl Herakovich, Rose Polytech	1958	25	18	0	168
Ted Scown, Sul Ross State	1948	28	0	0	168
Eddie McGovern, Rose Polytech	1942	23	27	0	165
Leon Burns, Long Beach State	1969	27	2	0	164

1. Record.

N.C.A.A. 1980 CHAMPIONSHIP PLAYOFFS

DIVISION I-AA
Semifinals

Boise State 14, Grambling 9
Eastern Kentucky 23, Lehigh 20

Championship

Boise State 31, Eastern Kentucky 29

DIVISION II
First Round

Northern Alabama 17, Virginia Union 8
Eastern Illinois 21, Northern Colorado 14
Santa Clara 27, Northern Michigan 26

Semifinals

Eastern Illinois 56, Northern Alabama 31
Cal Poly-San Luis Obispo 38, Santa Clara 14

Championship

Cal Poly-San Luis Obispo 21, Eastern Illinois 13

DIVISION III
Semifinals

Dayton 28, Widener 24
Ithaca 36, Minnesota Morris 0

Championship

Dayton 63, Ithaca 0

NATIONAL ASSOCIATION OF INTERCOLLEGIATE ATHLETICS 1980 CHAMPIONSHIPS

DIVISION I
First Round

Northeastern Oklahoma 10, Angelo State 3
Elon (N.C.) 17, Concord College 14
Kearney (Neb.) State 9, Mars Hill (N.C.) 3
East Texas State 27, Central Arkansas 21

Semifinals

Elon 14, East Texas State 6
Northeastern Oklahoma 14, Kearney State 0

Championship

Elon 17, Northeastern Oklahoma 10

DIVISION II
Championship

Pacific Lutheran 38, Wilmington (Oh.) 10

Professional Football

NATIONAL FOOTBALL LEAGUE FINAL STANDING 1980

AMERICAN CONFERENCE
Eastern Division

	W	L	T	Pct	Pts	OP
Buffalo	11	5	0	.688	320	260
New England	10	6	0	.625	441	325
Miami	8	8	0	.500	266	305
Baltimore	7	9	0	.438	355	387
New York Jets	4	12	0	.250	302	395

Central Division

	W	L	T	Pct	Pts	OP
Cleveland	11	5	0	.688	357	310
Houston[1]	11	5	0	.688	295	251
Pittsburgh	9	7	0	.563	352	313
Cincinnati	6	10	0	.375	244	312

Western Division

	W	L	T	Pct	Pts	OP
San Diego	11	5	0	.688	418	327
Oakland[1]	11	5	0	.688	364	306
Kansas City	8	8	0	.500	319	336
Denver	8	8	0	.500	310	323
Seattle	4	12	0	.250	291	408

NATIONAL CONFERENCE
Eastern Division

	W	L	T	Pct	Pts	OP
Philadelphia	12	4	0	.750	384	222
Dallas[1]	12	4	0	.750	454	311
Washington	6	10	0	.375	261	293
St. Louis	5	11	0	.313	299	350
New York Giants	4	12	0	.250	249	425

Central Division

	W	L	T	Pct	Pts	OP
Minnesota	9	7	0	.563	317	308
Detroit	9	7	0	.563	334	272
Chicago	7	9	0	.438	304	264
Tampa Bay	5	10	1	.344	271	341
Green Bay	5	10	1	.344	231	371

Western Division

	W	L	T	Pct	Pts	OP
Atlanta	12	4	0	.750	405	272
Los Angeles[1]	11	5	0	.688	424	289
San Francisco	6	10	0	.375	320	415
New Orleans	1	15	0	.063	291	487

1. Wild card qualifier for playoffs.
Playoffs: Oakland 27, Houston 7; San Diego 20, Buffalo 14; Oakland 14, Cleveland 12.
Conference championship: Oakland 34, San Diego 27.

1. Wild card qualifier for playoffs.
Playoffs: Dallas 34, Los Angeles 13; Philadelphia 31, Minnesota 16; Dallas 30, Atlanta 27.
Conference championship: Philadelphia 20, Dallas 7.

LEAGUE CHAMPIONSHIP—SUPER BOWL XV

(Jan. 25, 1981; at Superdome, New Orleans; Attendance 75,500)

Scoring

	1st Q	2nd Q	3rd Q	4th Q	Final
Oakland Raiders (AFC)	14	0	10	3	27
Philadelphia Eagles (NFC)	0	3	0	7	10

Scoring—Oakland: Touchdowns: Branch, 2-yard pass from Plunkett; King, 80-yard pass from Plunkett; Branch, 29-yard pass from Plunkett. Conversions: Bahr 3 (kicks). Field Goals: Bahr 2, 46 yards and 35 yards. Philadelphia: Touchdown: Krepfle, 8-yard pass from Jaworski. Conversion: Franklin (kick). Field goal: Franklin, 30 yards.

Statistics of the Game

	Oakland	Philadelphia
First downs	17	19
Yards gained rushing	117	69
Yards gained passing	261	291
Passes completed	13	18
Passes intercepted by	3	0
Punts	3–42	3–37
Ball lost, fumbles	0	1
Yards penalized	37	57

SUPER BOWLS I–XV[1]

Game	Date	Winner	Loser	Site	Attendance
XV	Jan. 25, 1981	Oakland (AFC) 27	Philadelphia (NFC) 10	Superdome, New Orleans	75,500
XIV	Jan. 20, 1980	Pittsburgh (AFC) 31	Los Angeles (NFC) 19	Rose Bowl, Pasadena	103,985
XIII	Jan. 21, 1979	Pittsburgh (AFC) 35	Dallas (NFC) 31	Orange Bowl, Miami	79,484
XII	Jan. 15, 1978	Dallas (NFC) 27	Denver (AFC) 10	Superdome, New Orleans	75,583
XI	Jan. 9, 1977	Oakland (AFC) 32	Minnesota (NFC) 14	Rose Bowl, Pasadena	103,424
X	Jan. 18, 1976	Pittsburgh (AFC) 21	Dallas (NFC) 17	Orange Bowl, Miami	80,187
IX	Jan. 12, 1975	Pittsburgh (AFC) 16	Minnesota (NFC) 6	Tulane Stadium, New Orleans	80,997
VIII	Jan. 13, 1974	Miami (AFC) 24	Minnesota (NFC) 7	Rice Stadium, Houston	71,882
VII	Jan. 14, 1973	Miami (AFC) 14	Washington (NFC) 7	Memorial Coliseum, Los Angeles	90,182
VI	Jan. 16, 1972	Dallas (NFC) 24	Miami (AFC) 3	Tulane Stadium, New Orleans	81,591
V	Jan. 17, 1971	Baltimore (AFC) 16	Dallas (NFC) 13	Orange Bowl, Miami	79,204
IV	Jan. 11, 1970	Kansas City (AFL) 23	Minnesota (NFL) 7	Tulane Stadium, New Orleans	80,562
III	Jan. 12, 1969	New York (AFL) 16	Baltimore (NFL) 7	Orange Bowl, Miami	75,389
II	Jan. 14, 1968	Green Bay (NFL) 33	Oakland (AFL) 14	Orange Bowl, Miami	75,546
I	Jan. 15, 1967	Green Bay (NFL) 35	Kansas City (AFL) 10	Memorial Coliseum, Los Angeles	61,946

1. Super Bowls I to IV were played before the American Football League and National Football League merged into the NFL, which was divided into two conferences, the NFC and AFC.

NATIONAL LEAGUE CHAMPIONS

Year	Champion (W-L-T)
1921	Chicago Bears (Staley's) (10–1–1)
1922	Canton Bulldogs (10–0–2)
1923	Canton Bulldogs (11–0–1)
1924	Cleveland Indians (7–1–1)
1925	Chicago Cardinals (11–2–1)
1926	Frankford Yellow Jackets (14–1–1)
1927	New York Giants (11–1–1)
1928	Providence Steamrollers (8–1–2)
1929	Green Bay Packers (12–0–1)
1930	Green Bay Packers (10–3–1)
1931	Green Bay Packers (12–2–0)
1932	Chicago Bears (7–1–6)

Eastern

Year	Conference winners (W-L-T)	Western Conference winners (W-L-T)	League champion playoff results
1933	New York Giants (11–3–0)	Chicago Bears (10–2–1)	Chicago Bears 23, New York 21
1934	New York Giants (8–5–0)	Chicago Bears (13–0–0)	New York 30, Chicago Bears 13
1935	New York Giants (9–3–0)	Detroit Lions (7–3–2)	Detroit 26, New York 7
1936	Boston Redskins (7–5–0)	Green Bay Packers (10–1–1)	Green Bay 21, Boston 6
1937	Washington Redskins (8–3–0)	Chicago Bears (9–1–1)	Washington 28, Chicago Bears 21
1938	New York Giants (8–2–1)	Green Bay Packers (8–3–0)	New York 23, Green Bay 17
1939	New York Giants (9–1–1)	Green Bay Packers (9–2–0)	Green Bay 27, New York 0
1940	Washington Redskins (9–2–0)	Chicago Bears (8–3–0)	Chicago Bears 73, Washington 0
1941	New York Giants (7–3–1)	Chicago Bears (10–1–1)[2]	Chicago Bears 37, New York 9
1942	Washington Redskins (10–1–1)	Chicago Bears (11–0–0)	Washington 14, Chicago Bears 6
1943	Washington Redskins (6–3–1)[2]	Chicago Bears (8–1–1)	Chicago Bears 41, Washington 21
1944	New York Giants (8–1–1)	Green Bay Packers (8–2–0)	Green Bay 14, New York 7
1945	Washington Redskins (8–2–0)	Cleveland Rams (9–1–0)	Cleveland 15, Washington 14
1946	New York Giants (7–3–1)	Chicago Bears (8–2–1)	Chicago Bears 24, New York 14
1947	Philadelphia Eagles (8–4–0)[2]	Chicago Cardinals (9–3–0)	Chicago Cardinals 28, Philadelphia 21
1948	Philadelphia Eagles (9–2–1)	Chicago Cardinals (11–1–0)	Philadelphia 7, Chicago Cardinals 0
1949	Philadelphia Eagles (11–1–0)	Los Angeles Rams (8–2–2)	Philadelphia 14, Los Angeles 0
1950[1]	Cleveland Browns (10–2–0)[2]	Los Angeles Rams (9–3–0)[2]	Cleveland 30, Los Angeles 28
1951[1]	Cleveland Browns (11–1–0)	Los Angeles Rams (8–4–0)	Los Angeles 24, Cleveland 17
1952[1]	Cleveland Browns (8–4–0)	Detroit Lions (9–3–0)[2]	Detroit 17, Cleveland 7
1953	Cleveland Browns (11–1–0)	Detroit Lions (10–2–0)	Detroit 17, Cleveland 16

1954	Cleveland Browns (9–3–0)	Detroit Lions (9–2–1)	Cleveland 56, Detroit 10
1955	Cleveland Browns (9–2–1)	Los Angeles Rams (8–3–1)	Cleveland 38, Los Angeles 14
1956	New York Giants (8–3–1)	Chicago Bears (9–2–1)	New York 47, Chicago Bears 7
1957	Cleveland Browns (9–2–1)	Detroit Lions (8–4–0)[3]	Detroit 59, Cleveland 14
1958	New York Giants (9–3–0)[2]	Baltimore Colts (9–3–0)	Baltimore 23, New York 17[3]
1959	New York Giants (10–2–0)	Baltimore Colts (9–3–0)	Baltimore 31, New York 16
1960	Philadelphia Eagles (10–2–0)	Green Bay Packers (8–4–0)	Philadelphia 17, Green Bay 13
1961	New York Giants (10–3–1)	Green Bay Packers (11–3–0)	Green Bay 37, New York 0
1962	New York Giants (12–2–0)	Green Bay Packers (13–1–0)	Green Bay 16, New York 7
1963	New York Giants (11–3–0)	Chicago Bears (11–1–2)	Chicago 14, New York 10
1964	Cleveland Browns (10–3–1)	Baltimore Colts (12–2–0)	Cleveland 27, Baltimore 0
1965	Cleveland Browns (11–3–0)	Green Bay Packers (11–3–1)[2]	Green Bay 23, Cleveland 12
1966	Dallas Cowboys (10–3–1)	Green Bay Packers (12–2–0)	Green Bay 34, Dallas 27
1967	Dallas Cowboys (9–5–0)[2]	Green Bay Packers (9–4–1)[2]	Green Bay 21, Dallas 17
1968	Cleveland Browns (10–4–0)[2]	Baltimore Colts (13–1–0)[2]	Baltimore 34, Cleveland 0
1969	Cleveland Browns (10–3–1)[2]	Minnesota Vikings (12–2–0)[2]	Minnesota 27, Cleveland 7

1. League was divided into American and National Conferences, 1950–52 and again in 1970, when leagues merged. 2. Won divisional playoff. 3. Won at 8:15 of sudden death overtime period.

NATIONAL CONFERENCE CHAMPIONS

Year	Eastern Division	Central Division	Western Division	Champion
1970	Dallas Cowboys (10–4–0)	Minnesota Vikings (12–2–0)	San Francisco 49ers (10–3–1)	Dallas
1971	Dallas Cowboys (11–3–0)	Minnesota Vikings (11–3–0)	San Francisco 49ers (9–5–0)	Dallas
1972	Washington Redskins (11–3–0)	Green Bay Packers (10–4–0)	San Francisco 49ers (8–5–1)	Washington
1973	Dallas Cowboys (10–4–0)	Minnesota Vikings (12–2–0)	Los Angeles Rams (12–2–0)	Minnesota
1974	St. Louis Cardinals (10–4–0)	Minnesota Vikings (10–4–0)	Los Angeles Rams (10–4–0)	Minnesota
1975	St. Louis Cardinals (11–3–0)	Minnesota Vikings (12–2–0)	Los Angeles Rams (12–2–0)	Dallas
1976	Dallas Cowboys (11–3–0)	Minnesota Vikings (11–2–1)	Los Angeles Rams (10–3–1)	Minnesota
1977	Dallas Cowboys (12–2–0)	Minnesota Vikings (9–5–0)	Los Angeles Rams (10–4–0)	Dallas
1978	Dallas Cowboys (12–4–0)	Minnesota Vikings (8–7–1)	Los Angeles Rams (12–4–0)	Dallas
1979	Dallas Cowboys (11–5–0)	Tampa Bay Buccaneers (10–6–0)	Los Angeles Rams (9–7–0)	Los Angeles
1980	Philadelphia Eagles (12–4–0)	Minnesota Vikings (9–7–0)	Atlanta Falcons (12–4–0)	Philadelphia

AMERICAN CONFERENCE CHAMPIONS

Year	Eastern Division	Central Division	Western Division	Champion
1970	Baltimore Colts (11–2–1)	Cincinnati Bengals (8–6–0)	Oakland Raiders (8–4–2)	Baltimore
1971	Miami Dolphins (10–3–1)	Cleveland Browns (9–5–0)	Kansas City Chiefs (10–3–1)	Miami
1972	Miami Dolphins (14–0–0)	Pittsburgh Steelers (11–3–0)	Oakland Raiders (10–3–1)	Miami
1973	Miami Dolphins (12–2–0)	Cincinnati Bengals (10–4–0)	Oakland Raiders (9–4–1)	Miami
1974	Miami Dolphins (11–3–0)	Pittsburgh Steelers (10–3–1)	Oakland Raiders (12–2–0)	Pittsburgh
1975	Baltimore Colts (10–4–0)	Pittsburgh Steelers (12–2–0)	Oakland Raiders (11–3–0)	Pittsburgh
1976	Baltimore Colts (11–3–0)	Pittsburgh Steelers (10–4–0)	Oakland Raiders (13–1–0)	Oakland
1977	Baltimore Colts (10–4–0)	Pittsburgh Steelers (9–5–0)	Denver Broncos (12–2–0)	Denver
1978	New England Patriots (11–5–0)	Pittsburgh Steelers (14–2–0)	Denver Broncos (10–6–0)	Pittsburgh
1979	Miami Dolphins (10–6–0)	Pittsburgh Steelers (12–4–0)	San Diego Chargers (12–4–0)	Pittsburgh
1980	Buffalo Bills (11–5–0)	Cleveland Browns (11–5–0)	San Diego Chargers (11–5–0)	Oakland

AMERICAN LEAGUE CHAMPIONS

Year	Eastern Division (W-L-T)	Western Division (W-L-T)	League champion, playoffs results
1960	Houston Oilers (10–4–0)	Los Angeles Chargers (10–4–0)	Houston 24, Los Angeles 16
1961	Houston Oilers (10–3–1)	San Diego Chargers (12–2–0)	Houston 10, San Diego 3
1962	Houston Oilers (11–3–0)	Dallas Texans (11–3–0)	Dallas 20, Houston 17[1]
1963	Boston Patriots (8–6–1)[2]	San Diego Chargers (11–3–0)	San Diego 51, Boston 10
1964	Buffalo Bills (12–2–0)	San Diego Chargers (8–5–1)	Buffalo 20, San Diego 7
1965	Buffalo Bills (10–3–1)	San Diego Chargers (9–2–3)	Buffalo 23, San Diego 0
1966	Buffalo Bills (9–4–1)	Kansas City Chiefs (11–2–1)	Kansas City 31, Buffalo 7
1967	Houston Oilers (9–4–1)	Oakland Raiders (13–1–0)	Oakland 40, Houston 7
1968	New York Jets (11–3–0)	Oakland Raiders (12–2–0)[2]	New York 27, Oakland 23
1969	New York Jets (10–4–0)	Oakland Raiders (12–1–1)	Kansas City 17, Oakland 7[3]

1. Won at 2:45 of second sudden death overtime period. 2. Won divisional playoff. 3. Kansas City defeated New York, 13–6, and Oakland defeated Houston, 56–7, in interdivisional playoffs.

NATIONAL FOOTBALL LEAGUE GOVERNMENT

Commissioner's Office: Pete Rozelle, commissioner; Don Weiss, executive director; Bill Ray, treasurer; Jay Moyer, counsel to commissioner; Jan Van Duser, director of operations; Jim Heffernan, director of public relations; Joe Browne, director of information; Warren Welsh, director of security; Charles R. Jackson, assistant director of security; Joel Bussert, director of personnel; Art McNally, supervisor of officials; Peter Hadhazy, administrative coordinator; Val Pinchbeck, Jr., director of broadcasting.

American Conference: Lamar Hunt, president; Al Ward, assistant to the president; Fran Connors, director of information.

National Conference: George Halas, president; Joe Rhein, assistant to the president; Dick Maxwell, director of information.

PRO FOOTBALL HALL OF FAME

(National Football Museum, Canton, Ohio)

Teams named are those with which player is best identified; figures in parentheses indicate number of playing seasons.

Adderley, Herb, defensive back, Packers, Cowboys (12)	1961–72
Alworth, Lance, wide receiver, Chargers, Cowboys (11)	1962–72
Badgro, Morris, end, N.Y. Yankees, Giants, Bklyn. Dodgers (8)	1927, 1930–36
Battles, Cliff, back, Redskins (6)	1932–37
Baugh, Sammy, quarterback, Redskins (16)	1937–52
Bednarik, Chuck, center-linebacker, Eagles (14)	1949–62
Bell, Bert, N.F.L. founder, owner Eagles and Steelers, N.F.L. Commissioner	
Berry, Raymond, end, Colts (13)	1946–59
Bidwell, Charles W., owner Chicago Cardinals	1955–67
Blanda, George, quarterback–kicker, Bears, Oilers, Raiders (27)	1933–47
Brown, Jim, fullback, Browns (9)	1949–75
Brown, Paul E., coach, Browns (1946–62), Bengals (1968–75)	1957–65
Brown, Roosevelt, tackle, Giants (13)	1946–75
Butkus, Dick, linebacker, Bears (9)	1953–65
Canadeo, Tony, back, Packers (11)	1965–73
Carr, Joe, president N.F.L. (18)	1941–52
Chamberlin, Guy, end 4 teams (9)	1921–39
Christiansen, Jack, defensive back, Lions (8)	1919–27
Clark, Earl (Dutch), Qback, Spartans, Lions (7)	1951–58
Connor, George, tackle, linebacker, Bears (8)	1931–38
Conzelman, Jimmy, Qback 5 teams (10), owner	1948–55
Davis, Willie, defensive end, Packers (10)	1921–48
Donovan, Art, defensive tackle, Colts (12)	1960–69
Driscoll, John (Paddy), Qback, Cards, Bears (11)	1950–61
Dudley, Bill, back, Steelers, Lions, Redskins (9)	1919–29
Edwards, Albert Glen (Turk), tackle, Redskins (9)	1942–53
Ewbank, Weeb, coach Colts, Jets (20)	1932–40
Fears, Tom, end, Rams (9); coach, Saints	1954–73
Flaherty, Ray, end, Yankees, Giants (9); coach, Redskins, Yankees (14)	1948–56
Ford, Len, end, def. end, Browns, Packers (11)	1928–49
Fortmann, Daniel J., guard, Bears (8)	1948–58
George, Bill, linebacker, Bears, Rams (15)	1936–43
Gifford, Frank, back, Giants (12)	1952–66
Graham, Otto, quarterback, Browns (10)	1952–64
Grange, Harold (Red), back, Bears, Yankees (9)	1946–55
Gregg, Forrest, tackle, Packers (15)	1925–34
Groza, Lou, place-kicker, tackle, Browns (21)	1956–71
Guyon, Joe, back, 6 teams (8)	1946–67
Halas, George, N.F.L. founder, owner and coach, Staleys and Bears, end (11)	1919–27
Healey, Ed, tackle, Bears (8)	1919–67
Hein, Mel, center, Giants (15)	1920–27
Henry, Wilbur (Pete), tackle, Bulldogs, Giants (8)	1931–45
Herber, Arnie, Qback, Packers, Giants (13)	1920–28
Hewitt, Bill, end, Bears, Eagles (9)	1930–45
Hinkle, Clarke, fullback, Packers (10)	1932–43
Hirsch, Elroy (Crazy Legs), back, end, Rams (12)	1932–41
Hubbard, R. (Cal), tackle, Giants, Packers (9)	1946–57
Hunt, Lamar, Founder A.F.L., owner Texans, Chiefs	1927–36
Hutson, Don, end, Packers (11)	1959—
Jones, David (Deacon), defensive end, Rams, Chargers, Redskins (14)	1935–45
Kiesling, Walt, guard 6 teams (13)	1961–74
Kinard, Frank (Bruiser), tackle, Dodgers (9)	1926–38
	1938–47
Lambeau, Earl (Curly), N.F.L. founder, coach, end, back, Packers (11)	1919–53
Lane, Richard (Night Train), defensive back, Rams, Cardinals, Lions (14)	1952–65
Lary, Yale, defensive back, punter, Lions (11)	1952–64
Lavelli, Dante, end, Browns (11)	1946–56
Layne, Bobby, Qback, Bears, Lions, Steelers (15)	1948–62
Leemans, Alphonse (Tuffy), back, Giants (8)	1936–43
Lilly, Bob, defensive tackle, Cowboys (14)	1961–74
Lombardi, Vince, coach, Packers, Redskins (11)	1959–70
Luckman, Sid, quarterback, Bears (12)	1939–50
Lyman, Roy (Link), tackle, Bulldogs, Bears (11)	1922–34
Mara, Tim, N.F.L. founder, owner Giants	1925–59
Marchetti, Gino, defensive end, Colts (14)	1952–66
Marshall, George P., N.F.L. founder, owner Redskins	1932–65
Matson, Ollie, back, Cardinals, Rams, Lions, Eagles (14)	1952–66
McAfee, George, back, Bears (8)	1940–50
McElhenny, Hugh, back, 49ers, Vikings, Giants (13)	1952–64
McNally, John (Blood), back, 7 teams (15)	1925–39
Michalske, August, guard, Yankees, Packers (11)	1926–37
Millner, Wayne, end, Redskins (7)	1936–45
Mix, Ron, tackle, Chargers (11)	1960–71
Moore, Lenny, back, Colts (12)	1956–67
Motley, Marion, fullback, Browns, Steelers (9)	1946–55
Nagurski, Bronko, fullback, Bears (9)	1930–43
Neale, Earle (Greasy), coach, Eagles	1941–50
Nevers, Ernie, fullback, Chicago Cardinals (5)	1926–31
Nitschke, Ray, linebacker, Packers (15)	1958–72
Nomellini, Leo, defensive tackle, 49ers (14)	1950–63
Otto, Jim, center, Raiders (15)	1960–74
Owen, Steve, tackle, Giants (9), coach, Giants (13)	1924–53
Parker, Clarence (Ace), quarterback, Dodgers (7)	1937–46
Parker, Jim, guard, tackle, Colts (11)	1957–67
Perry, Joe, fullback, 49ers, Colts (16)	1948–63
Pihos, Pete, end, Eagles (9)	1947–55
Ray, Hugh, Shorty, N.F.L. advisor	1938–52
Reeves, Dan, owner Rams	1941–71
Ringo, Jim, center, Packers (15)	1953–67
Robustelli, Andy, def. end, Rams, Giants (14)	1951–64
Rooney, Art, N.F.L. founder, owner Steelers	1933—
Sayers, Gale, back, Bears (7)	1965–71
Schmidt, Joe, linebacker, Lions (13)	1953–65
Starr, Bart, quarterback, coach, Packers (16)	1956–71
Stautner, Ernie, defensive tackle, Steelers (14)	1950–63
Strong, Ken, back, Giants, Yankees (14)	1929–47
Stydahar, Joe, tackle, Bears (9); coach, Rams, Cardinals (5)	1936–54
Taylor, Jim, fullback, Packers, Saints (10)	1958–67
Thorpe, Jim, back, 7 teams (12)	1915–28
Tittle, Y. A., Qback, Colts, 49ers, Giants (17)	1948–64
Trafton, George, center, Bears (13)	1920–32
Trippi, Charley, back, Chicago Cardinals (9)	1947–55
Tunnell, Emlen, def. back, Giants, Packers (14)	1948–61
Turner, Clyde (Bulldog), center, Bears (13)	1940–52
Unitas, John, quarterback, Colts (18)	1956–73
Van Brocklin, Norm, Qback, Rams, Eagles (12)	1949–60
Van Buren, Steve, back, Eagles (8)	1944–51
Waterfield, Bob, quarterback, Rams (8)	1945–52
Willis, Bill, Guard, Browns (8)	1946–53
Wilson, Larry, defensive back, Cardinals (13)	1960–72
Wojciechowicz, Alex, center, Lions, Eagles (13)	1938–50

N.F.L. INDIVIDUAL LIFETIME, SEASON AND GAME RECORDS
(Through 1978 American Football League marks were incorporated in N.F.L. records after merger in 1970)

All-Time Leading Scorers

	Yrs	TD	FG	PAT	Pts
George Blanda	26	9	335	943	2,002
Jim Turner	16	1	304	521	1,439
Jim Bakken	17	0	282	534	1,380
Fred Cox	15	0	282	519	1,365
Lou Groza	17	1	234	641	1,349
Jan Stenerud	13	0	279	394	1,231
Gino Cappelletti	11	42	176	350	1,130[1]
Bruce Gossett	11	0	219	374	1,031
Sam Baker	15	2	179	428	977
Lou Michaels	13	1	187	386	955[2]

1. Includes four 2-point conversions. 2. Includes one safety.

All-Time Leading Touchdown Scorers

	Yrs	Rush	Pass rec	Returns	TD
Jim Brown	9	106	20	0	126
Lenny Moore	12	63	48	2	113
Don Hutson	11	3	99	3	105
Jim Taylor	10	83	10	0	93
Bobby Mitchell	11	18	65	8	91
Leroy Kelly	10	74	13	3	90
Charley Taylor	13	11	79	0	90
Don Maynard	15	0	88	0	88
Lance Alworth	11	2	85	0	87
Paul Warfield	13	0	85	1	86

All-Time Leading Rushers

	Yrs	Att	Yds	Avg
Jim Brown	9	2,359	12,312	5.2
O.J. Simpson	10	2,258	10,643	4.7
Franco Harris	9	2,220	9,352	4.2
Jim Taylor	10	1,941	8,597	4.4
Walter Payton	6	1,865	8,386	4.5
Joe Perry	14	1,737	8,373	4.8
Larry Csonka	10	1,800	7,770	4.3
Leroy Kelly	10	1,727	7,274	4.2
Johnny Riggins	9	1,666	6,822	4.1
John Henry Johnson	13	1,571	6,803	4.3

All Time Leading Receivers

	Yrs	Pass rec	Yds	Avg
Charley Taylor	13	649	9,110	14.0
Don Maynard	15	633	11,834	18.7
Raymond Berry	13	631	9,275	14.7
Fred Biletnikoff	14	589	8,974	12.7
Lionel Taylor	10	567	7,195	12.7
Lance Alworth	11	542	10,266	18.9
Bobby Mitchell	11	521	7,954	15.3
Billy Howton	12	503	8,459	16.8
Tommy McDonald	12	495	8,410	17.0
Don Hutson	11	488	7,991	16.4

All-Time Leading Passers

	Comp	Pct comp	Yds	TD	Int	Rating
Roger Staubach	1,685	57.0	22,700	153	109	83.5
Sonny Jurgensen	2,433	57.1	32,224	255	189	82.8
Len Dawson	2,136	57.1	28,711	239	183	82.6
Fran Tarkenton	3,686	57.0	47,003	342	266	80.5
Bart Starr	1,808	57.4	24,718	152	138	80.3
Bert Jones	1,138	55,8	14,569	101	77	79.2

Ken Stabler	1,779	60.6	22,280	163	171	78.3
Johnny Unitas	2,830	54.6	40,239	290	253	78.2
Otto Graham	872	55.7	13,499	88	94	78.1
Ken Anderson	1,736	56.7	21,808	131	114	78.0

The passing ratings are based on performance standards established for completion percentage, interception percentage, touchdown percentage, and average pass gain. Passers are allocated points according to how their marks compare with those standards. This listing is based on 1,500 or more pass attempts.

Scoring

Most points scored, lifetime—2,002, George Blanda, Chicago Bears, 1949–58; Baltimore, 1950; Houston, 1960–66; Oakland, 1967–75 (9tds, 943 pat, 335 fgs).

Most points, season—176, Paul Hornung, Green Bay, 1960 (15 td, 41 pat, 15 fg).

Most points, game—40, Ernie Nevers, Chicago Cardinals, 1929 (6 td, 4 pat).

Most points, per quarter—29, Don Hutson, Green Bay, 1945 (4 td, 5 pat).

Most touchdowns, lifetime—126, Jim Brown, Cleveland, 1957–65.

Most touchdowns, season—23, O.J. Simpson, Buffalo, 1975.

Most touchdowns, game—6, Ernie Nevers, Chicago Cardinals, 1929; William Jones, Cleveland, 1951; Gale Sayers, Chicago Bears, 1965.

Most points after touchdown, lifetime—943, George Blanda, Chicago Bears, 1949–58; Baltimore, 1950; Houston, 1960–66; Oakland, 1967–75.

Most points after touchdown, game—9, Pat Harder, Chicago Cardinals, 1948; Bob Waterfield, Los Angeles, 1950; Charlie Gogolak, Washington, 1966.

Most consecutive points after touchdown—234, Tommy Davis, San Francisco, 1959–65.

Most points after touchdown, no misses, season—56, Danny Villanueva, Dallas, 1966.

Most field goals, lifetime—335, George Blanda, Chicago Bears 1949–58; Baltimore, 1950; Houston, 1960–66; Oakland 1967–75.

Most field goals, season—34, Jim Turner, New York Jets, 1968.

Most field goals, game—7, Jim Bakken, St. Louis, 1967.

Longest field goal—63 yards, Tom Dempsey, New Orleans, 1970.

Rushing

Most yards gained, lifetime—12,312, Jim Brown, Cleveland, 1957–65.

Most yards gained, season—2,003, O. J. Simpson, Buffalo, 1973.

Most yards gained, game—275, Walter Payton, Chicago, 1977.

Most touchdowns, lifetime—106, Jim Brown, Cleveland, 1957–65.

Most touchdowns, season—19, Earl Campbell, Houston, 1979; Jim Taylor, Green Bay, 1962.

Most touchdowns, game—6, Ernie Nevers, Chicago Cardinals, 1929.

Longest run from scrimmage—97 yards, Andy Uram, Green Bay, 1939; Bob Gage, Pittsburgh, 1949 (both for touchdowns).

Passing

Most passes completed, lifetime—3,686, Fran Tarkenton, Minnesota, 1961–66, 72–78; New York Giants, 1967–71.

Most passes completed, season—348, Dan Fouts, San Diego, 1980.

Most passes completed, game—37, George Blanda, Houston, 1964 (68 attempts).

Most consecutive passes completed—17, Bert Jones, Baltimore, 1974.

Most yards gained, lifetime—47,003, Fran Tarkenton, Minnesota, 1961–66, 72–78; New York Giants, 1967–71.

Most yards gained, season—4,715, Dan Fouts, San Diego, 1980.

Most yards gained, game—554, Norm Van Brocklin, Los Angeles, 1951

Most touchdown passes, lifetime—342, Fran Tarkenton, Minnesota, 1961–66, 72–78; New York Giants, 1967–71.

Most touchdown passes, season—36, George Blanda, Houston, 1961; Y. A. Tittle, New York Giants, 1963.

Most touchdown passes, game—7, Sid Luckman, Chicago Bears, 1943; Adrian Burk, Philadelphia, 1954; George Blanda, Houston 1961; Y.A. Tittle, New York Giants, 1963; Joe Kapp, Minnesota, 1969.

Most consecutive games, touchdown passes—47, John Unitas, Baltimore.

Most consecutive passes attempted, none intercepted—294, Bart Starr, Green Bay, 1964–65.

Longest pass completion—99 yards, Frank Filchock (to Andy Farkas), Washington, 1939; George Izo (to Bob Mitchell), Washington, 1963; Karl Sweetan (to Pat Studstill), Detroit, 1966; Sonny Jurgensen (to Gerry Allen), Washington, 1968, (all for touchdowns).

Most pass receptions, lifetime—649, Charley Taylor, Washington, 1964–75, 1977.

Most pass receptions, season—101, Charley Hennigan, Houston, 1964.

Most pass receptions, game—18, Tom Fears, Los Angeles, 1950.

Most consecutive games, pass receptions—105, Dan Abramowicz, New Orleans, 1967–73; San Francisco, 1973–74.

Most yards gained, pass receptions, lifetime—11,834, Don Maynard, New York Giants, 1958; New York Jets, 1960–72; St. Louis, 1973.

Most yards gained receptions, season—1,746, Charley Hennigan, Houston, 1961.

Most yards gained receptions, game—303, Jim Benton, Cleveland Rams, 1945.

Most touchdown pass receptions, lifetime—99, Don Hutson, Green Bay, 1935–45.

Most touchdown pass receptions, season—17, Don Hutson, Green Bay, 1942; Elroy Hirsch, Los Angeles, 1951; Bill Groman, Houston, 1961.

Most touchdown pass receptions, game—5, Bob Shaw, Chicago Cards, 1950.

Most consecutive games, touchdown pass receptions—11, Elroy Hirsch, Los Angeles, 1950–51; Buddy Dial, Pittsburgh, 1959–60.

Most pass interceptions, lifetime—79, Emlen Tunnell, New York Giants, 1948–58 (74); Green Bay, 1959–61 (5).

Most pass interceptions, season—14, Richard (Night Train) Lane, Los Angeles, 1952.

Most pass interceptions, game—4, by 15 players.

Longest pass interception return—102 yards, Bob Smith, Chicago Bears, 1949; Erich Barnes, New York Giants, 1961; Gary Barbaro, Kansas City, 1977.

Kicking

Longest punt—98 yards, Steve O'Neal, New York Jets, 1969.

Highest average punting, lifetime—45.10 yards, Sammy Baugh, Washington, 1937–52.

Longest punt return—98 yards, Gil LeFebvre, Cincinnati Reds, 1933; Charlie West, Minnesota, 1968; Dennis Morgan, Dallas, 1974.

Longest kick-off return—106 yards, Roy Green, St. Louis, 1979; Al Carmichael, Green Bay, 1956; Noland Smith, Kansas City, 1967.

TEAM NICKNAMES AND HOME FIELD STADIUM CAPACITIES

AMERICAN CONFERENCE

Eastern Division

Baltimore Colts	Memorial Stadium (G)	60,020
Buffalo Bills	Rich Stadium (AT)	80,020
Miami Dolphins	Orange Bowl (G)	75,449
New England Patriots	Schaefer Stadium (ST)[1]	61,297
New York Jets	Shea Stadium (G)	60,000

1. At Foxboro, Mass.

Central Division

Cincinnati Bengals	Riverfront Stadium (AT)	56,200
Cleveland Browns	Cleveland Stadium (G)	80,385
Houston Oilers	Astrodome (AT)	50,000
Pittsburgh Steelers	Three Rivers Stadium (TT)	50,350

Western Division

Denver Broncos	Mile High Stadium (G)	75,087
Kansas City Chiefs	Arrowhead Stadium (TT)	78,094
Oakland Raiders	County Coliseum (G)	54,615
San Diego Chargers	San Diego Stadium (G)	52,552
Seattle Seahawks	Kingdome (AT)	64,752

NATIONAL CONFERENCE

Eastern Division

Dallas Cowboys	Texas Stadium (TT)	65,101
New York Giants	Giants Stadium (AT)[2]	76,500
Philadelphia Eagles	Veterans Stadium (AT)	66,052
St. Louis Cardinals	Busch Mem. Stadium (AT)	51,392
Washington Redskins	R. F. Kennedy Stadium (G)	55,031

2. At East Rutherford, N.J.

Central Division

Chicago Bears	Soldier Field (AT)	58,064
Detroit Lions	Pontiac Silverdome (AT)	80,638
	Lambeau Field (G)	56,267
Green Bay Packers	Milwaukee Stadium (G)	55,958
Minnesota Vikings	Metropolitan Stadium (G)	48,446
Tampa Bay Buccaneers	Tampa Stadium (G)	72,112

Western Division

Atlanta Falcons	Atlanta-Fulton Stadium (G)	60,489
Los Angeles Rams[1]	Anaheim Stadium (G)	70,000
New Orleans Saints	Louisiana Superdome (AT)	71,330
San Francisco 49ers	Candlestick Park (G)	61,246

NOTE: Stadium playing surfaces in parentheses: AT = Astro-Turf; G = grass; ST = Super Turf; TT = TartanTurf.

1. Moved to Anaheim Stadium for 1980 season.V3,Sports—Basketball

FISHING

WORLD ALL-TACKLE FISHING RECORDS

Caught With Rod and Reel in Fresh Water

Source: International Game Fish Association

Species	lb–oz	Length	Girth	Where caught	Year	Angler
Bass, Largemouth	22–4	32½"	28½"	Montgomery Lake, Ga.	1932	George W. Perry
Bass, Peacock	14–4	—	—	Rio Ventuari, Venezuela	1980	Gustavo Lovera

Bass, Redeye	8–3	23"	16½"	Flint River, Ga.	1977	David A. Hubbard
Bass, Rock	3	13½"	10¾"	York River, Ontario	1974	Peter Gulgin
Bass, Smallmouth	11–15	27"	21⅔"	Dale Hollow Lake, Ky.	1955	David L. Hayes
Bass, Spotted	8–15	—	—	Smith Lake, Ala.	1978	Philip C. Terry Jr.
Bass, Striped (landlocked)	59–12	—	—	Colorado River, Ariz.	1977	Frank W. Smith
Bass, White	5–9	—	—	Colorado River, Texas	1977	David S. Cordill
Bass, Whiterock	20	—	—	Savannah River, Ga.	1977	Don Raley
Bass, Yellow	2–4	16¼"	12¾"	Lake Monroe, Ind.	1977	Donald L. Stalker
Bluegill	4–12	15"	18¼"	Ketona Lake, Ala.	1950	T. S. Hudson
Bowfin	21–8	—	—	Florence, N.C.	1980	Robert L. Harmon
Buffalo, Bigmouth	70–5	—	—	Bussey Brake, Bastrop, La.	1980	Delbert Sisk
Buffalo, Smallmouth	51	—	—	Lawrence, Kan.	1979	Scott Butler
Bullhead, Black	8	24"	17¾"	Lake Waccabuc, N.Y.	1951	Kani Evans
Bullhead, Brown	5–8	—	—	Veal Pond, Ga.	1975	Jimmy Andrews
Bullhead, Yellow	3	—	—	Nelson Lake, Wis.	1977	Mark Nessman
Burbot	18–4	—	—	Pickford, Mich.	1980	Thomas Courteman
Carp	55–5	42"	31"	Clearwater Lake, Minn.	1952	Frank J. Ledwein
Catfish, Blue	97	57"	37"	Missouri River, S.D.	1959	Edward B. Elliott
Catfish, Channel	58	47¼"	29⅛"	Santee-Cooper Res., S.C.	1964	W. B. Whaley
Catfish, Flathead	79–8	44"	27"	White River, Ind.	1966	Glenn T. Simpson
Catfish, White	10–5	25"	17½"	Raritan River, N.J.	1976	L. W. Lomerson
Char, Arctic	29–11	39¾"	26"	Arctic River, N.W.T.	1968	Jeanne P. Branson
Crappie, Black	6	—	—	Seaplane Canal, Westwego, La.	1969	Lettie Theresa Robertson
Crappie, White	5–3	21"	19"	Enid Dam, Miss.	1957	Fred L. Bright
Dolly Varden	32	40½"	29¾"	Lake Pend Oreille, Idaho	1949	N. L. Higgins
Drum, Freshwater	54–8	31½"	29"	Nickajack Lake, Tenn.	1972	Benny E. Hull
Gar, Alligator	279	93"	—	Rio Grande River, Tex.	1951	Bill Valverde
Gar, Florida	4	—	—	Hillsborough, Fla.	1980	W. R. (Ron) Haynes
Gar, Longnose	50–5	72¼"	22½"	Trinity River, Texas	1954	Townsend Miller
Gar, Shortnose	3–5	—	—	Lake Francis Case, S.D.	1977	J. Pawlowski
Grayling, Arctic	5–15	29⅞"	15⅛"	Katseyedie River, N.W.T.	1967	Jeanne P. Branson
Huchen	70–12	—	—	Carinthia, Austria	1980	Martin F. Esterl
Kokanee	6–9	24½"	14½"	Priest Lake, Idaho	1975	Jerry Verge
Muskellunge	69–15	64½"	31¾"	St. Lawrence River, N.Y.	1957	Arthur Lawton
Muskellunge, Tiger	51–3	—	—	Lac Vieux–Desert, Wis./Mich.	1919	John A. Knobla
Perch, White	4–12	19½"	13"	Messalonskee Lake, Me.	1949	Mrs. Earl Small
Perch, Yellow	4–3	—	—	Bordentown, N.J.	1865	Dr. C. C. Abbot
Pickerel, Eastern chain	9–6	31"	14"	Homerville, Ga.	1961	Baxley McQuaig, Jr.
Pike, Northern	62–8	—	—	Reuss-Weiher, Richenbach, Switz.	1979	Jurg Notzli
Redhorse, Northern	3–11	—	—	Missouri River, S.D.	1977	Philip Laumeyer
Redhorse, Silver	5–13	—	—	Betsie River, Frankfort, Mich.	1980	Darrell T. Hasler
Salmon, Atlantic	79–2	—	—	Tana River, Norway	1928	Henrik Henriksen
Salmon, Chinook	93	50"	39"	Kelp Bay, Alaska	1977	Howard C. Rider
Salmon, Chum	27–3	39⅜"	24½"	Raymond Cove, Alaska	1977	Robert A. Jahnke
Salmon Landlocked	22–8	36"	—	Sebago Lake, Me.	1907	Edward Blakely
Salmon CoHo	31	—	—	Cowichan Bay, B.C.	1947	Mrs. Lee Hallberg
Salmon, Pink	12–9	—	—	Moose and Kenai Rivers, Alaska	1974	Steven Alan Lee
Sauger	8–12	28"	15"	Lake Sakakawea, N.D.	1971	Mike Fischer
Shad, American	9–4	—	—	Delaware River, Pa.	1979	J. Edward Whitman
Splake	16–12	—	—	Island Lake, Colo.	1973	Del Canty
Sturgeon	407	—	—	Sacramento River, Colusa, Calif.	1979	Raymond Pihenger
Sturgeon, White	360	111"	86"	Snake River, Idaho	1956	Willard Cravens
Sunfish, Green	2–2	14¾"	14"	Stockton Lake, Mo.	1971	Paul M. Dilley
Sunfish, Redbreast	1–8	11"	12⅝"	Suwannee River, Fla.	1977	Tommy D. Cason, Jr.
Sunfish, Redear	4–8	16¼"	17¾"	Chase City, Va.	1970	Maurice E. Ball
Trout, Brook	14–8	31½"	11½"	Nipigon River, Ontario	1916	Dr. W. J. Cook
Trout, Brown	35–15	—	—	Nahuel Haupi, Argentina	1952	Eugenio Cavaglia
Trout, Cutthroat	41	39"	—	Pyramid Lake, Nev.	1925	John Skimmerhorn
Trout, Golden	11	28"	16"	Cook's Lake, Wyo.	1948	Charles S. Reed
Trout, Lake	65	52"	38"	Great Bear Lake, N.W.T.	1970	Larry Daunis
Trout, Rainbow or Steelhead	42–2	43"	23½"	Bell Island, Alaska	1970	David R. White
Trout, Sunapee	11–8	33"	21"	Lake Sunapee, N.H.	1954	Ernest Theoharis
Trout, Tiger	20–13	—	—	Lake Michigan, Wis.	1978	Pete M. Friedland
Walleye	25	41"	29"	Old Hickory Lake, Tenn.	1960	Mabry Harper
Warmouth	2–2	—	—	Douglas Swamp, S.C.	1973	Willie Singletary
Whitefish, Lake	13–1	—	—	Meaford Harbor, Meaford, Ont.	1978	Denis J. Bouchard
Whitefish, Mountain	5	19"	14"	Athabasca River, Alberta, Can.	1963	Orville Welch
Whitefish, Round	3–4	—	—	Leland Harbor, Mich.	1977	Vernon A. Bauer

Caught With Rod and Reel in Salt Water

Source: International Game Fish Association

Species	lb-oz	Length	Girth	Where caught	Year	Angler
Albacore	88–2	—	—	Canary Islands	1977	Siegfried Dickemann

Fish	Weight	Length	Girth	Location	Year	Angler
Amberjack	149	71"	41¾"	Bermuda	1964	Peter Simons
Barracuda	83	72¼"	29"	Lagos, Nigeria	1952	K. J. W. Hackett
Bass, Black Sea	8–12	—	—	Oregon Inlet, N.C.	1979	Joe W. Mizelle Sr.
Bass, Giant Sea	563–8	89"	72"	Anacapa Island, Calif.	1968	J. D. McAdam, Jr.
Bass, Striped	72	54½"	31"	Cuttyhunk, Mass.	1969	Edward J. Kirker
Blackfish (Tautog)	21–6	31½"	23½"	Cape May, N.J.	1954	R. N. Sheafer
Bluefish	31–12	47"	23"	North Carolina	1972	James M. Hussey
Bonefish	19	—	—	Zululand, S. Africa	1962	Brian W. Batchelor
Bonito, Atlantic	16–12	—	—	Canary Islands	1980	Rolf Fredderies
Bonito, Pacific	23–8	35¼"	23¼"	Victoria, Mahe	1975	Mrs. Anne Cochain
Cobia	110–5	—	—	Mombasa, Kenya	1964	Eric Tinworth
Cod	98–12	63"	41"	Isle of Shoals, N.H.	1969	Alphonse Bielevich
Conger	39–7	—	—	Pornichet—La Baule, France	1980	Jean–Claude Guilmineau
Dolphin	87	81⅔"	28"	Papapagalio Gulf, Costa Rica	1976	Manual Salazar
Drum, Black	113–1	53⅛"	43½"	Lewes, Del.	1975	G. M. Townsend
Drum, Red	90	55½"	38¼"	Rodanthe, N.C.	1973	Elvin Hooper
Flounder, Summer	22–7	—	—	Montauk, N.Y.	1975	Charles Nappi
Halibut, Atlantic	234	—	—	Scotland	1979	Colin Booth
Halibut, California	37–8	—	—	San Diego, Calif.	1979	William E. Williams
Halibut, Pacific	165–8	—	—	Sullivan Bay, B.C. Canada	1979	Stephanie Pollard
Jack, Horse–eye	22	—	—	Miami Beach, Fla.	1980	Donald C. Ball
Jack, Crevalle	51	—	—	Lake Worth, Fla.	1978	Stephen Schwenk
Jewfish	680	85½"	66"	Fernandina Beach, Fla.	1961	Lynn Joyner
Kawakawa	26	—	—	Merimbula, N.S.W., Australia	1980	Wally Elfring
Mackerel, King	90	—	—	Key West, Florida	1976	Norton I. Thomton
Marlin, Black	1560	174"	81"	Cabo Blanco, Peru	1953	A. C. Glassel, Jr.
Marlin, Atlantic Blue	1282	176"	76½"	St. Thomas, Virgin Islands	1977	Larry Martin
Marlin, Pacific Blue	1153	176"	73"	Ritidian Point, Guam	1969	Greg G. Perez
Marlin, Striped	417–8	139½"	52½"	Cavalli Island, New Zealand	1977	Phillip Bryers
Marlin, White	18–14	—	—	Victoria, Brazil	1979	Evandro Luiz Coser
Permit	51–8	—	—	Lake Worth, Fla.	1978	William M. Kenney
Pollack	16–1	—	—	Plymouth, England	1978	Peter J. Peck
Pollack (virens)	46–7	50½"	30"	Brielle, N.J.	1975	John T. Holton
Pompano, African	41–8	—	—	Fort Lauderdale, Fla.	1979	Wayne Sommers
Roosterfish	114	64"	33"	La Paz, Mexico	1960	Abe Sackheim
Runner, Rainbow	33–10	55¼"	22½"	Clarion Island, Mexico	1976	R. A. Mikkelsen
Sailfish, Atlantic	128–1	106¼"	34¼"	Luanda, Angola, Africa	1974	Harm Steyn
Sailfish, Pacific	221	129"	—	Santa Cruz Is., Galapagos Is.	1947	C. W. Stewart
Seabass, White	83–12	65½"	34"	San Felipe, Mexico	1953	L. C. Baumgardner
Seatrout, Spotted	16	32½"	21¾"	Mason's Beach, Va.	1977	William G. Katko
Shark, Blue	437	—	—	Catherine Bay, Australia	1976	Peter Hyde
Shark, Hammerhead	717	—	—	Jacksonville Beach, Fla.	1980	Richard Edward Morse
Shark, Mako	1080	—	—	Montauk, N.Y.	1979	James L. Melanson
Shark, Porbeagle	465	111"	56"	Padstow, Cornwall, England	1976	Jorge Potier
Shark, Thresher	739	106"	68"	Tutukaka, New Zealand	1975	Brian Galvin
Shark, Tiger	1780	166½"	103"	Cherry Grove, S.C.	1964	Walter Maxwell
Shark, White	2664	202"	114"	South Australia	1959	Alfred Dean
Skipjack, Black	14–8	—	—	Baja, Mexico	1977	Lorraine Carlton
Snapper, Cubera	60–12	—	—	Miami Beach, Fla.	1980	Dr. Richard A. Klein
Snook	53–10	—	—	Costa Rica	1978	Gilbert Ponzi
Spearfish	90–13	—	—	Madeira Island, Portugal	1980	Joseph Larkin
Swordfish	1182	179¼"	78"	Iquique, Chile	1953	L. E. Marron
Tanguigue	85–6	—	—	Western Australia	1978	Barry Wrightson
Tarpon	283	85⅜"	—	Lake Maracaibo, Venezuela	1956	M. Salazar
Tautog (See Blackfish)						
Trevally, Lowly	116	—	—	American Samoa	1978	William G. Foster
Tuna, Yellowfin	388–12	—	—	Mexico	1977	Curt Wiesenhutter
Tuna, Altantic Bigeye	375–8	—	—	Ocean City, Md.	1977	Cecil Browne
Tuna, Blackfin	42	—	—	Bermuda	1978	Alan J. Card
Tuna, Bluefin	1496	—	—	Nova Scotia, Canada	1979	Ken Fraser
Tuna, Dog–tooth	194	—	—	Kwan-Gall Island, Korea	1980	Kim Chul
Tuna, Longtail	65	—	—	Port Stephens, Australia	1978	Michael James
Tuna, Pacific Big-Eyed	435	93"	63½"	Cabo Blanco, Peru	1957	R.V. A. Lee
Tuna, Skipjack	39–15	39"	28"	Walker City, Bahamas	1952	R. Drowley
	40	38¾"	27½"	Baie du Tambeau, Mauritius	1971	Joseph R. Cabache
Tuna, Southern Bluefin	256–13	—	—	Mexico	1979	Rodney James Beard
Tunny, Little	27	39"	22"	Key Largo, Fla.	1976	William E. Allison
Wahoo	149	—	—	Cat Cay, Bahamas	1962	John Pirovano
Weakfish	17–14	—	—	Rye, N.Y.	1980	William N. Herold
Yellowtail, California	71–15	—	—	Alijos Rocks, Mexico	1979	Michael Carpenter
Yellowtail, Southern	111	—	—	Bay of Islands, New Zealand	1961	A. F. Plim

BASKETBALL

Basketball may be the one sport whose exact origin is definitely known. In the winter of 1891–92, Dr. James Naismith, an instructor in the Y.M.C.A. Training College (now Springfield College) at Springfield, Mass., deliberately invented the game of basketball in order to provide indoor exercise and competition for the students between the closing of the football season and the opening of the baseball season. He affixed peach baskets overhead on the walls at opposite ends of the gymnasium and organized teams to play his new game in which the purpose was to toss an association (soccer) ball into one basket and prevent the opponents from tossing the ball into the other basket. The game is fundamentally the same today, though there have been improvements in equipment and some changes in rules.

Because Dr. Naismith had eighteen available players when he invented the game, the first rule was: "There shall be nine players on each side." Later the number of players became optional, depending upon the size of the available court, but the five-player standard was adopted when the game spread over the country. United States soldiers brought basketball to Europe in World War I, and it soon became a world-wide sport.

College Basketball

NATIONAL COLLEGIATE A.A. CHAMPIONS

1939	Oregon	1949	Kentucky	1959	California	1975	U.C.L.A.
1940	Indiana	1950	C.C.N.Y.	1960	Ohio State	1976	Indiana
1941	Wisconsin	1951	Kentucky	1961	Cincinnati	1977	Marquette
1942	Stanford	1952	Kansas	1962	Cincinnati	1978	Kentucky
1943	Wyoming	1953	Indiana	1963	Loyola (Chicago)	1979	Michigan State
1944	Utah	1954	La Salle	1964	U.C.L.A.	1980	Louisville
1945	Oklahoma A & M	1955	San Francisco	1965	U.C.L.A.	1981	Indiana
1946	Oklahoma A & M	1956	San Francisco	1966	Texas Western		
1947	Holy Cross	1957	North Carolina	1967–73	U.C.L.A.		
1948	Kentucky	1958	Kentucky	1974	No. Carolina State		

NATIONAL INVITATION TOURNAMENT (NIT) CHAMPIONS

1939	Long Island U.	1951	Brigham Young	1962	Dayton	1973	Virginia Tech
1940	Colorado	1952	La Salle	1963	Providence	1974	Purdue
1941	Long Island U.	1953	Seton Hall	1964	Bradley	1975	Princeton
1942	West Virginia	1954	Holy Cross	1965	St. John's (Bklyn.)	1976	Kentucky
1943–44	St. John's (Bklyn.)	1955	Duquesne	1966	Brigham Young	1977	St. Bonaventure
1945	DePaul	1956	Louisville	1967	So. Illinois	1978	Texas
1946	Kentucky	1957	Bradley	1968	Dayton	1979	Indiana
1947	Utah	1958	Xavier (Cincinnati)	1969	Temple	1980	Virginia
1948	St. Louis	1959	St. John's (Bklyn.)	1970	Marquette	1981	Tulsa
1949	San Francisco	1960	Bradley	1971	North Carolina		
1950	C.C.N.Y.	1961	Providence	1972	Maryland		

N.C.A.A. MAJOR COLLEGE INDIVIDUAL SCORING RECORDS

Single Season Averages

Player, Team	Year	G	FG	FT	Pts	Avg
Pete Maravich, Louisiana State	1969–70	31	522[1]	337	1381[1]	44.5[1]
Pete Maravich	1968–69	26	433	282	1148	44.2
Pete Maravich	1967–68	26	432	274	1138	43.8
Frank Selvy, Furman	1953–54	29	427	355[1]	1209	41.7
Johnny Neumann, Mississippi	1970–71	23	366	191	923	40.1
Freeman Williams, Portland State	1976–77	26	417	176	1010	38.8
Billy McGill, Utah	1961–62	26	394	221	1009	38.8
Calvin Murphy, Niagara	1967–68	24	337	242	916	38.2
Austin Carr, Notre Dame	1969–70	29	444	218	1106	38.1

1. Record.

LONGEST FIELD GOAL IN COLLEGE BASKETBALL

What was the longest field goal ever scored in a college basketball game? Would you believe 89 ft 3 in.? That's only 4 ft 9 in. short of the regulation length of a court. It happened on January 21, 1980, at Tallahassee, Fla., and the shooter was Les Henson, a 6-ft-6-in. senior forward for Virginia Tech. He took the shot with only two seconds left in the game against Florida State and gave the Gobblers a 79–77 victory. Henson had just grabbed a rebound off the Florida State boards about a foot from the baseline. The normally left-handed-shooting Henson unleashed a right-handed shot in desperation and it went in. At first the shot was reported as 93 ft, but a later measurement established it at 89–3. "It was eerie while the ball was in the air," Henson later recalled. "Everything was quiet, you couldn't hear a thing in the arena. At first, I thought it was going to hit one of the light fixtures, but it didn't, and then it just swished through the hoop." It bettered the previous longest scoring shot of 88 ft by Rudy Williams of Providence College against Rhode Island on February 17, 1979.

N.C.A.A. CAREER SCORING TOTALS

Division I

Player, Team	Last year	G	FG	FT	Pts	Avg
Pete Maravich, Louisiana State	1970	83	1387[1]	893[1]	3667[1]	44.2[1]
Austin Carr, Notre Dame	1971	74	1017	526	2560	34.6
Oscar Robertson, Cincinnati	1960	88	1052	869	2973	33.8
Calvin Murphy, Niagara	1970	77	947	654	2548	33.1
Dwight Lanar[2]	1973	57	768	326	1862	32.7
Frank Selvy, Furman	1954	78	922	694	2538	32.5
Rick Mount, Purdue	1970	72	910	503	2323	32.3
Darrel Floyd, Furman	1956	71	868	545	2281	32.1
Nick Werkman, Seton Hall	1964	71	812	649	2273	32.0

1. Record. 2. Also played two seasons in college division.

Division II

Player, Team	Last year	G	FG	FT	Pts	Avg
Travis Grant, Kentucky State	1972	121	1760[1]	525	4045[1]	33.4[1]
John Rinka, Kenyon	1970	99	1261	729	3251	32.8
Florindo Vieira, Quinnipiac	1957	69	761	741	2263	32.8
Willie Shaw, Lane	1964	76	960	459	2379	31.3
Mike Davis, Virginia Union	1969	89	1014	730	2758	31.0
Henry Logan, Western Carolina	1968	107	1263	764	3290	30.7
Willie Scott, Alabama State	1969	103	1277	601	3155	30.6
Gregg Northington, Alabama State	1972	75	894	403	2191	29.2
Bob Hopkins, Grambling	1956	126	1403	953	3759	29.8

1. Record.

TOP SINGLE-GAME SCORING MARKS

Player, Team (Opponent)	Yr	Pts	Player, Team (Opponent)	Yr	Pts
Selvy, Furman (Newberry)	1954	100[1]	Floyd, Furman (Morehead)	1955	67
Williams, Portland State (Rocky Mtn.)	1978	81	Maravich, LSU (Tulane)	1969	66
Mikvy, Temple (Wilkes)	1951	73	Handlan, W & L (Furman)	1951	66
Williams, Portland State (So. Oregon)	1977	71	Roberts, Oral Roberts (N.C. A&T)	1977	66
Maravich, LSU (Alabama)	1970	69	Williams, Portland State (Geo. Fox Coll.)	1978	66
Murphy, Niagara (Syracuse)	1969	68	Roberts, Oral Roberts (Oregon)	1977	65

1. Record.

NATIONAL COLLEGIATE ATHLETIC ASSOCIATION (N.C.A.A.)—1981

DIVISION I

First Round—East

Brigham Young 60, Princeton 51
James Madison 61, Georgetown 55
Virginia Commonwealth 85, Louisiana State 69
Villanova 90, Houston 72

First Round—Mideast

Alabama–Birmingham 93, Western Kentucky 68
Boston College 93, Ball State 90
Maryland 81, Tennessee–Chattanooga 69
St. Joseph's (Pa.) 59, Creighton 57

First Round—Midwest

Arkansas 73, Mercer 67
Kansas 69, Mississippi 66
Lamar 71, Missouri 67
Wichita State 95, Southern Univ. 70

First Round—West

Kansas State 64, San Francisco 60
Northeastern 55, Fresno State 53
Pittsburgh 70, Idaho 69 (overtime)
Wyoming 78, Howard 43

Second Round—East

Brigham Young 78, U.C.L.A. 55
Notre Dame 54, James Madison 45

Virginia 54, Villanova 50
Tennessee 58, Virginia Commonwealth 56 (overtime)

Second Round—Mideast

Alabama–Birmingham 69, Kentucky 62
Boston College 67, Wake Forest 64
Indiana 99, Maryland 64
St. Joseph's 49, De Paul 48

Second Round—Midwest

Arkansas 74, Louisville 73
Louisiana State 100, Lamar 78
Kansas 88, Arizona State 71
Wichita State 60, Iowa 56

Second Round—West

Illinois 67, Wyoming 65
Kansas State 50, Oregon State 48
North Carolina 74, Pittsburgh 57
Utah 94, Northeastern 69

Third Round—East

Brigham Young 51, Notre Dame 50
Virginia 62, Tennessee 48

Third Round—Mideast

Indiana 87, Alabama–Birmingham 72
St. Joseph's 42, Boston College 41

Third Round—Midwest
Louisiana State 72, Arkansas 56
Wichita State 66, Kansas 65

Third Round—West
Kansas State 57, Illinois 52
North Carolina 61, Utah 56

Regional Finals
East—Virginia 74, Brigham Young 60
Mideast—Indiana 78, St. Joseph's 46
Midwest—Louisiana State 96, Wichita State 85
West—North Carolina 82, Kansas State 68

National Semifinals
(Philadelphia, March 28, 1981)
North Carolina 78, Virginia 65
Indiana 67, Louisiana State 49

Third Place
Virginia 78, Louisiana State 75

National Final
(Philadelphia, March 30, 1981)
Indiana 63, North Carolina 50

DIVISION II
Semifinals
Florida Southern 54, California Poly–St. Luis Obispo 51
Mount St. Mary's (Md.) 76, Wisconsin–Green Bay 60

Third Place
California Poly–St. Luis Obispo 62, Wisconsin–Green Bay 61 (2 overtimes)

Championship
(Springfield, Mass., March 21, 1981)
Florida Southern 73, Mount St. Mary's 68

DIVISION III
Semifinals
Augustana (Ill.) 93, Otterbein 81
Potsdam (N.Y.) State 63, Ursinus 61

Third Place
Ursinus 82, Otterbein 79

Championship
(Rock Island, Ill., March 21, 1981)
Potsdam State 67, Augustana 65 (overtime)

JUNIOR COLLEGES
Semifinals
Lincoln (Ill.) 70, Hiwassee (Tenn.) 63
Westark (Ark.) 78, Anderson (S.C.) 66

Third Place
Anderson 92, Hiwassee 87

Championship
(Hutchinson, Kan., March 21, 1981)
Westark 67, Lincoln 50

N.B.A. ALL-ROOKIE TEAM—1981

Forwards—Larry Smith, Golden State; Kevin McHale, Boston
Center—Joe Barry Carroll, Golden State
Guards—Darrell Griffith, Utah; Kelvin Ransey, Portland

ASSOCIATION FOR INTERCOLLEGIATE ATHLETICS FOR WOMEN
(A.I.A.W.—1981)

FIRST ROUND
Jackson State 68, Minnesota 65
U.C.L.A. 72, Oregon State 65
North Carolina State 85, Georgia State 66
Oregon 74, Colorado 67
Stephen F. Austin 88, Northwestern 67
Rutgers 99, Clemson 76
Kentucky 87, Syracuse 63
Illinois State 66, Texas 63

SECOND ROUND
Louisiana Tech 97, Jackson State 50
U.C.L.A. 73, Kansas 71
Cheyney State 88, North Carolina State 72
Southern California 67, Oregon 64
Old Dominion 60, Stephen F. Austin 54
Long Beach State 77, Rutgers 73
Maryland 83, Kentucky 82
Tennessee 78, Illinois State 53

THIRD ROUND
Old Dominion 76, Long Beach State 60
Louisiana Tech 87, U.C.L.A. 54
Southern California 67, Cheyney State 58
Tennessee 79, Maryland 67

NATIONAL SEMIFINALS
(Eugene, Ore., March 27, 1981)
Tennessee 68, Old Dominion 65
Louisiana Tech 66, Southern California 50

THIRD PLACE
Old Dominion 68, Southern California 65

CHAMPIONSHIP
(Eugene, Ore., March 29, 1981)
Louisiana Tech 79, Tennessee 59

DIVISION II
Final
(Dayton, Ohio)
William Penn College (Iowa) 64, College of Charleston (S.C.) 51

DIVISION III
Final
(La Crosse, Wis.)
Wisconsin–La Crosse 79, Mount Mercy College (Iowa) 71

N.B.A ALL-DEFENSIVE TEAM—1981

Forwards—Bobby Jones, Philadelphia; Caldwell Jones, Philadelphia
Center—Kareem Abdul-Jabbar, Los Angeles
Guards—Michael Ray Richardson, New York; Dennis Johnson, Phoenix

LEADING SCORERS—1980–81

N.C.A.A.—Division I

	FG	FT	Pts	Avg
Zam Fredrick, South Carolina	300	181	781	28.9
Mike Ferrara, Colgate	298	176	772	28.6
Kevin Magee, California-Irvine	280	183	743	27.5
Lewis Lloyd, Drake	298	166	762	26.3
Rob Williams, Houston	298	153	749	25.0
Rubin Jackson, Oklahoma City	293	133	719	24.8

N.C.A.A.—Division II

Gregory Jackson, St. Paul's	267	183	717	27.6
Steve Lingenfelter, So. Dakota St.	227	106	560	26.7
Izell Cleckley, Pratt Institute	237	160	634	25.4
Otto Porter, Southeast Missouri	287	103	677	25.1
Keith Bennett, Sacred Heart	295	117	707	24.4
Ernie Dewitt, Bryant	275	83	633	24.3
Tony Gonzalez, Southern Conn.	235	153	623	24.0

N.C.A.A.—Division III

Gerald Reece, William Penn	306	145	757	28.0
Ray Buckland, Boston State	288	122	698	25.9
Wil Peterson, St. Andrews	320	96	736	25.4
Tony Rychlec, Mass. Maritime	218	131	567	24.7
John Schelske, Kalamazoo	198	145	541	24.6
Kris Smith, Principia	253	101	607	24.3
Smooth Hammond, New Paltz	251	105	607	24.3

NATIONAL INVITATION TOURNAMENT

Semifinals

(March 23, 1981, Madison Square Garden, New York)
Syracuse 70, Purdue 63
Tulsa 89, West Virginia 87

Third Place

Purdue 75, West Virginia 72 (overtime)

Championship

(March 25, 1981, Madison Square Garden)
Tulsa 86, Syracuse 84 (overtime)

NATIONAL ASSOCIATION OF INTERCOLLEGIATE ATHLETICS—1981

Round of 16

Bethany Nazarene (Okla.) 88, Southern Tech (Ga.) 58
Alabama–Huntsville 67, Oregon College 62
Augsburg (Minn.) 81, Kearney State (Neb.) 77
Huron (S.D.) 52, Biola (Calif) 50
Wisconsin–Eau Claire 22, Waynesburg (Pa.) 21
Hillsdale (Mich.) 53, Briar Cliff (Iowa) 46

Midwestern (Tex.) 104, Lincoln Memorial (Tenn.) 87
Hanover (Ind.) 72, South Carolina–Spartanburg 60

Quarterfinals

Wisconsin–Eau Claire 35, Huron 29
Bethany Nazarene 84, Augsburg 69
Hillsdale 65, Midwestern 64
Alabama–Huntsville 94, Hanover 74

Semifinals

Bethany Nazarene 62, Wisconsin–Eau Claire 54
Alabama–Huntsville 65, Hillsdale 60

Third Place

Wisconsin–Eau Claire 90, Hillsdale 60

Championship

Bethany Nazarene 86, Alabama–Huntsville 85 (overtime)

A.A.U. CHAMPIONSHIP—MEN

(St. Augustine, Fla., April 1–5, 1981)

Quarterfinals

Hayden Sporting Goods (Chicago) 122, Hughes Bros. (Topeka, Kan.) 98
Jacksonville (Fla.) Spirit 122, Porter Skywalkers 115
Brewster's Packing (Washington) 104, Armed Forced 102
Hayden Sporting Goods 102, Whatcom (Bellingham, Wash.) 85
Burger King (Detroit) 92, Airliners 85
Custer Bros. (Columbus, Ohio) 104, Banker's Life 103

Semifinals

Custer Bros. 117, Hayden Sporting Goods 107
Brewster's Packing 117, Burger King 104

Third Place

Hayden Sporting Goods defeated Burger King

Championship

Brewster's Packing 108, Custer Bros. 106
Most valuable player—Wayne Smith, Brewster's Packing

Professional Basketball

NATIONAL BASKETBALL ASSOCIATION CHAMPIONS

Source: Matt Winick, Director of Media Information, National Basketball Association

The National Basketball Association was originally the Basketball Association of America. It took its current name in 1949 when it merged with the National Basketball League.

Season	Eastern Conference (W-L)	Western Conference (W-L)	Playoff Champions[1]
1946–47	Washington Capitols (49–11)	Chicago Stags (39–22)	Philadelphia Warriors
1947–48	Philadelphia Warriors (27–21)	St. Louis Bombers (29–19)	Baltimore Bullets
1948–49	Washington Capitols (38–22)	Rochester Royals (45–15)	Minneapolis Lakers
1949–50	Syracuse Nationals (51–13)	Indianapolis Olympians (39–25)	Minneapolis Lakers
1950–51	Philadelphia Warriors (40–26)	Minneapolis Lakers (44–24)	Rochester Royals
1951–52	Syracuse Nationals (40–26)	Rochester Royals (41–25)	Minneapolis Lakers
1952–53	New York Knickerbockers (47–23)	Minneapolis Lakers (48–22)	Minneapolis Lakers
1953–54	New York Knickerbockers (44–28)	Minneapolis Lakers (46–26)	Minneapolis Lakers
1954–55	Syracuse Nationals (43–29)	Ft. Wayne Pistons (43–29)	Syracuse Nationals
1955–56	Philadelphia Warriors (45–27)	Ft. Wayne Pistons (37–35)	Philadelphia Warriors
1956–57	Boston Celtics (44–28)	St. Louis Hawks (34–38)	Boston Celtics
1957–58	Boston Celtics (48–23)	St. Louis Hawks (41–31)	St. Louis Hawks
1958–59	Boston Celtics (52–20)	St. Louis Hawks (49–23)	Boston Celtics
1959–60	Boston Celtics (59–16)	St. Louis Hawks (46–29)	Boston Celtics
1960–61	Boston Celtics (57–22)	St. Louis Hawks (51–28)	Boston Celtics
1961–62	Boston Celtics (60–20)	Los Angeles Lakers (54–26)	Boston Celtics
1962–63	Boston Celtics (58–22)	Los Angeles Lakers (53–27)	Boston Celtics
1963–64	Boston Celtics (59–21)	San Francisco Warriors (48–32)	Boston Celtics

Season	Eastern Conference (W-L)	Western Conference (W-L)	Playoff Champions[1]
1964–65	Boston Celtics (62–18)	Los Angeles Lakers (49–31)	Boston Celtics
1965–66	Philadelphia 76ers (55–25)	Los Angeles Lakers (45–35)	Boston Celtics
1966–67	Philadelphia 76ers (68–13)	San Francisco Warriors (44–37)	Philadelphia 76ers
1967–68	Philadelphia 76ers (62–20)	St. Louis Hawks (56–26)	Boston Celtics
1968–69	Baltimore Bullets (57–25)	Los Angeles Lakers (55–27)	Boston Celtics
1969–70	New York Knickerbockers (60–22)	Atlanta Hawks (48–34)	New York Knicks
1970–71	Baltimore Bullets (42–40)	Milwaukee Bucks (66–16)	Milwaukee Bucks
1971–72	New York Knickerbockers (48–34)	Los Angeles Lakers (69–13)	Los Angeles Lakers
1972–73	New York Knickerbockers (57–25)	Los Angeles Lakers (69–22)	New York Knicks
1973–74	Boston Celtics (56–26)	Milwaukee Bucks (59–23)	Boston Celtics
1974–75	Washington Bullets (60–22)	Golden State Warriors (48–34)	Golden State Warriors
1975–76	Boston Celtics (54–28)	Phoenix Suns (42–40)	Boston Celtics
1976–77	Philadelphia 76ers (50–32)	Portland Trail Blazers (49–33)	Portland Trail Blazers
1977–78	Washington Bullets (44–38)	Seattle Super Sonics (47–35)	Washington Bullets
1978–79	Washington Bullets (54–28)	Seattle Super Sonics (52–30)	Seattle Super Sonics
1979–80	Philadelphia 76ers (59–23)	Los Angeles Lakers (60–22)	Los Angeles Lakers
1980–81	Boston Celtics (62–20)	Phoenix Suns (57–25)	Boston Celtics

1. Playoffs may involve teams other than conference winners.

INDIVIDUAL N.B.A. SCORING CHAMPIONS

Season	Player, Team	G	FG	FT	Pts	Avg
1953–54	Neil Johnston, Philadelphia Warriors	72	591	577	1759	24.4
1954–55	Neil Johnston, Philadelphia Warriors	72	521	589	1631	22.7
1955–56	Bob Pettit, St. Louis Hawks	72	646	557	1849	25.7
1956–57	Paul Arizin, Philadelphia Warriors	71	613	591	1817	25.6
1957–58	George Yardley, Detroit Pistons	72	673	655	2001	27.8
1958–59	Bob Pettit, St. Louis Hawks	72	719	667	2105	29.2
1959–60	Wilt Chamberlain, Philadelphia Warriors	72	1065	577	2707	37.6
1960–61	Wilt Chamberlain, Phildelphia Warriors	79	1251	531	3033	38.4
1961–62	Wilt Chamberlain, Philadelphia Warriors	80	1597	835	4029	50.4
1962–63	Wilt Chamberlain, San Francisco Warriors	80	1463	660	3586	44.8
1963–64	Wilt Chamberlain, San Francisco Warriors	80	1204	540	2948	36.9
1964–65	Wilt Chamberlain, San Francisco Warriors-Phila. 76ers	73	1063	408	2534	34.7
1965–66	Wilt Chamberlain, Philadelphia 76ers	79	1074	501	2649	33.5
1966–67	Rick Barry, San Francisco Warriors	78	1011	753	2775	35.6
1967–68	Dave Bing, Detroit Pistons	79	835	472	2142	27.1
1968–69	Elvin Hayes, San Diego Rockets	82	930	467	2327	28.4
1969–70	Jerry West, Los Angeles Lakers	74	831	647	2309	31.2
1970–71	Lew Alcindor,[1] Milwaukee Bucks	82	1063	470	2596	31.7
1971–72	Kareem Abdul-Jabbar, Milwaukee Bucks	81	1159	504	2822	34.8
1972–73	Nate Archibald, Kansas City-Omaha Kings	80	1028	663	2719	34.0
1973–74	Bob McAdoo, Buffalo Braves	74	901	459	2261	30.8
1974–75	Bob McAdoo, Buffalo Braves	82	1095	641	2831	34.5
1975–76	Bob McAdoo, Buffalo Braves	78	934	559	2427	31.1
1976–77	Pete Maravich, New Orleans Jazz	73	886	501	2273	31.1
1977–78	George Gervin, San Antonio Spurs	82	864	504	2232	27.2
1978–79	George Gervin, San Antonio	80	947	471	2365	29.6
1979–80	George Gervin, San Antonio	78	1024	505	2585	33.1
1980–81	Adrian Dantley, Utah Jazz	80	909	632	2452	30.7

1. (Kareem Abdul-Jabbar).

N.B.A. LIFETIME LEADERS
(Through June 1981)

Scoring

	Yrs	FG	FT	Pts
Wilt Chamberlain	14	12,681	6,057	31,419
Oscar Robertson	14	9,508	7,694	26,710
John Havlicek	16	10,513	5,394	26,395
Kareem Abdul-Jabbar	12	10,815	4,640	26,270
Jerry West	14	9,016	7,160	25,192
Elvin Hayes	13	9,875	4,794	24,547
Elgin Baylor	14	8,693	5,763	23,149
Hal Greer	15	8,504	4,578	21,586
Walt Bellamy	14	7,914	5,113	20,941
Bob Pettit	11	7,349	6,182	20,880

Scoring Average
(400 games or 10,000 points minimum)

	Games	Pts	Avg
Wilt Chamberlain	1,045	31,419	30.1
Kareem Abdul-Jabbar	935	26,270	28.1
Elgin Baylor	846	23,149	27.4
Jerry West	932	25,192	27.0
Bob McAdoo	599	15,792	26.5
Bob Pettit	792	20,880	26.4
Oscar Robertson	1,040	26,710	25.7
Pete Maravich	658	15,948	24.2
Rick Barry	794	18,395	23.2
Elvin Hayes	1,059	24,547	23.1

Field-Goal Percentage
(2,000 field goals minimum)

	Att	FG	Pct
Artis Gilmore	4,990	2,869	.575
Kareem Abdul–Jabbar	19,440	10,815	.556
Walter Davis	5,123	2,800	.546
Marques Johnson	5,115	2,773	.542
Adrian Dantley	5,801	3,135	.541
Wilt Chamberlain	23,497	12,681	.540
George Gervin	8,364	4,411	.524
Cliff Ray	4,450	2,333	.524
Walt Bellamy	15,340	7,914	.516
Paul Westphal	8,884	4,531	.510

Free-Throw Percentage
(1,400 free throws made minimum)

	Att	FT	Pct
Rick Barry	4,243	3,818	.900
Calvin Murphy	3,604	3,207	.890
Bill Sharman	3,557	3,413	.884
Mike Newlin	3,309	2,879	.870
Fred Brown	1,924	1,650	.863
Ricky Sobers	1,705	1,460	.856
Larry Siegfried	1,945	1,662	.854
Flynn Robinson	1,881	1,597	.849
Dolph Schayes	8,273	6,979	.844
Jack Marin	2,852	2,405	.843

Assists

Oscar Robertson	9,887
Lenny Wilkens	7,211
Bob Cousy	6,955
Guy Rodgers	6,917
Jerry West	6,238
John Havlicek	6,114
Dave Bing	5,397
Norm Van Lier	5,217
Walt Frazier	5,040
Gail Goodrich	4,805

Rebounds

Wilt Chamberlain	23,924
Bill Russell	21,620
Elvin Hayes	14,656
Nate Thurmond	14,464
Walt Bellamy	14,241
Wes Unseld	13,769
Kareem Abdul–Jabbar	13,167
Jerry Lucas	12,942
Bob Pettit	12,849
Paul Silas	12,357

N.B.A. MOST VALUABLE PLAYERS

1956	Bob Pettit	1966–68	Wilt Chamberlain	1975	Bob McAdoo, Buffalo
1957	Bob Cousy	1969	Wes Unseld	1976–77	Kareem Abdul–Jabbar, Los Angeles
1958	Bill Russell	1970	Willis Reed		
1959	Bob Pettit	1971–72	Lew Alcindor (Kareem Abdul–Jabbar)	1978	Bill Walton, Portland
1960	Wilt Chamberlain			1979	Moses Malone, Houston
1961–63	Bill Russell	1973	Dave Cowens	1980	Kareem Abdul–Jabbar, Los Angeles
1964	Oscar Robertson	1974	Kareem Abdul–Jabbar, Milwaukee		
1965	Bill Russell			1981	Julius Erving, Philadelphia

N.B.A. INDIVIDUAL RECORDS

Most points, game—100, Wilt Chamberlain, Philadelphia vs. New York at Hershey, Pa., 1962

Most points, quarter—33, George Gervin, San Antonio, 1978

Most points, half—59, Wilt Chamberlain, Philadelphia, 1962

Most free throws, game—28, Wilt Chamberlain, Philadelphia, vs. New York at Hershey, Pa. 1962

Most free throws, quarter—14, Rick Barry, San Francisco, 1966

Most free throws, half—19, Oscar Robertson, Cincinnati, 1964

Most field goals, game—28, Wilt Chamberlain, Philadelphia, 1962

Most consecutive field goals, game—18, Wilt Chamberlain, San Francisco, 1963; Wilt Chamberlain, Philadelphia, 1967

Most assists, game—29, Kevin Porter, New Jersey Nets, 1978

Most rebounds, game—55, Wilt Chamberlain, Philadelphia, 1963

N.B.A. TEAM RECORDS

Most points, game—173, Boston vs. Minneapolis, 1959

Most points, quarter—58, Buffalo vs. Boston, 1968

Most points, half—97, Atlanta vs. San Diego, 1970

Most points, overtime period—22, Detroit vs. Cleveland, 1973

Most field goals, game—72, Boston, 1959

Most field goals, quarter—23, Boston, 1959; Buffalo, 1972

Most field goals, half—40, Boston, 1959; Syracuse, 1963; Atlanta, 1979

Most assists, game—53, Milwaukee, 1978

Most rebounds, game—112, Philadelphia, 1959

Most points, both teams, game—316 (Philadelphia 169, New York 147), Hershey, Pa. 1962; (Cincinnati 165, San Diego 151), Cincinnati, 1970

Most points, both teams, quarter—96 (Boston 52, Minneapolis 44), 1959; (Detroit 53, Cincinnati 43), 1972

Most points, both teams, half—170 (Philadelphia 90, Cincinnati 80), Philadelphia, 1971

Longest winning streak—33, Los Angeles, 1971–72

Longest losing streak—20, Philadelphia, 1973

Longest winning streak at home—36, Philadelphia, 1966–67

Most games won, season—69, Los Angeles, 1971–72

Most games lost, season—73, Philadelphia, 1972–73

Highest average points per game—125.4, Philadelphia, 1961–62

BACKGAMMON

WORLD CHAMPIONSHIP—1981

Mrs. Lee Genud, New York City, defeated Joe Dwek, 25–19

NATIONAL BASKETBALL ASSOCIATION
FINAL STANDING OF THE CLUBS—1980–1981

EASTERN CONFERENCE
Atlantic Division

	W	L	Pct	Scoring For	Agst
Boston Celtics	62	20	.756	109.9	104.0
Philadelphia 76ers	62	20	.756	111.7	103.8
New York Knicks	50	32	.610	107.9	106.3
Washington Bullets	39	43	.476	105.6	105.6
New Jersey Nets	24	58	.293	106.9	113.0

Central Division

	W	L	Pct	For	Agst
Milwaukee Bucks	60	22	.732	113.1	105.9
Chicago Bulls	45	37	.549	109.0	107.0
Indiana Pacers	44	38	.537	107.6	106.2
Atlanta Hawks	31	51	.378	104.9	108.0
Cleveland Cavaliers	28	54	.341	105.7	110.6
Detroit Pistons	21	61	.256	99.7	106.0

WESTERN CONFERENCE
Midwest Division

	W	L	Pct	Scoring For	Agst
San Antonio Spurs	52	30	.634	112.3	109.4
Kansas City Kings	40	42	.488	106.9	106.9
Houston Rockets	40	42	.488	108.3	107.9
Denver Nuggets	37	45	.451	121.8	122.3
Utah Jazz	28	54	.341	101.2	107.1
Dallas Mavericks	15	67	.183	101.5	109.9

Pacific Division

	W	L	Pct	For	Agst
Phoenix Suns	57	25	.695	110.0	104.5
Los Angeles Lakers	54	28	.659	111.2	107.3
Portland Trail Blazers	45	37	.549	110.7	109.8
Golden State Warriors	39	43	.476	109.8	111.0
San Diego Clippers	36	46	.439	106.5	108.1
Seattle SuperSonics	34	48	.415	104.0	105.7

PLAYOFFS

EASTERN CONFERENCE
First Round

Chicago defeated New York, 2 games to 0
Philadelphia defeated Indiana, 2 games to 0

Semifinal Round

Boston defeated Chicago, 4 games to 0
Philadelphia defeated Milwaukee, 4 games to 3

Conference Final

Boston defeated Philadelphia, 4 games to 3
April 21—Philadelphia 105, Boston 104
April 22—Boston 118, Philadelphia 99
April 24—Philadelphia 110, Boston 100
April 26—Philadelphia 107, Boston 105
April 29—Boston 111, Philadelphia 109
May 1—Boston 100, Philadelphia 98
May 3—Boston 91, Philadelphia 90

WESTERN CONFERENCE
First Round

Houston defeated Los Angeles, 2 games to 1
Kansas City defeated Portland, 2 games to 1

Semifinal Round

Houston defeated San Antonio, 4 games to 3
Kansas City defeated Phoenix, 4 games to 3

Conference Final

Houston defeated Kansas City, 4 games to 1
April 21—Houston 97, Kansas City 78
April 22—Kansas City 88, Houston 79
April 24—Houston 92, Kansas City 88
April 26—Houston 100, Kansas City 89
April 29—Houston 97, Kansas City 88

Championship

Boston defeated Houston, 4 games to 2
May 5—Boston 98, Houston 95[1]
May 7—Houston 92, Boston 90[1]
May 9—Boston 94, Houston 71
May 10—Houston 91, Boston 86
May 12—Boston 109, Houston 80[1]
May 14—Boston 102, Houston 91
1. At Boston.

FIELD GOAL LEADERS
(Minimum 300 FG made)

	FG	Att	Pct
Artis Gilmore, Chicago	547	816	.670
Darryl Dawkins, Philadelphia	423	697	.607
Cedric Maxwell, Boston	441	750	.588
Bernard King, Golden State	731	1,244	.588
Kareem Abdul-Jabbar, L.A.	836	1,457	.574
Kermit Washington, Portland	325	571	.569
Adrian Dantley, Utah	909	1,627	.559
Bill Cartwright, New York	619	1,118	.554
Swen Nater, San Diego	517	935	.553
Marques Johnson, Milwaukee	636	1,153	.552

FREE THROW LEADERS
(Minimum 125 FT made)

	FT	Att	Pct
Calvin Murphy, Houston	206	215	.958
Ricky Sobers, Chicago	231	247	.935
Mike Newlin, New Jersey	414	466	.888
Jim Spanarkel, Dallas	375	423	.887
Junior Bridgeman, Milwaukee	213	241	.884
John Long, Detroit	160	184	.870
Charlie Criss, Atlanta	185	214	.864
Larry Bird, Boston	283	328	.863
Billy McKinney, Denver	162	188	.862

LEADING SCORERS

	G	FG	FT	Pts	Avg
Adrian Dantley, Utah	80	909	632	2,452	30.7
Moses Malone, Houston	80	806	609	2,222	27.8
George Gervin, San Antonio	82	830	512	2,221	27.1
Kareem Abdul-Jabbar, Los Ang.	80	836	423	2,095	26.2
David Thompson, Denver	77	734	489	1,967	25.5
Otis Birdsong	71	710	317	1,747	24.6
Julius Erving, Philadelphia	82	794	422	2,014	24.6
Mike Mitchell, Cleveland	82	853	302	2,012	24.5
Lloyd Free, Golden State	65	516	528	1,563	24.1
Alex English, Denver	81	768	390	1,929	23.8
Jamaal Wilkes, Los Angeles	81	786	254	1,827	22.6
Bernard King, Golden State	81	731	307	1,771	21.9
Dan Issel, Denver	80	614	519	1,749	21.9
John Drew, Atlanta	67	500	454	1,454	21.7
Mike Newlin, New Jersey	79	632	414	1,688	21.4
Larry Bird, Boston	82	719	283	1,741	21.2

	G				Avg
Darrel Griffith, Utah	81	716	229	1,671	20.6
Marques Johnson, Milwaukee	76	636	269	1,541	20.3
Bill Cartwright, New York	82	619	408	1,646	20.1
Ray Williams, New York	79	616	312	1,560	19.7

ASSISTS LEADERS
(Minimum 70 games or 400 assists)

	G	No.	Avg
Kevin Porter, Washington	81	734	9.1
Norm Nixon, Los Angeles	79	696	8.8
Phil Ford, Kansas City	66	580	8.8
Michael Ray Richardson, N.Y.	79	627	7.9
Nate Archibald, Boston	80	618	7.7
John Lucas, Golden State	66	464	7.0
Kelvin Ransey, Portland	80	555	6.9
Maurice Cheeks, Philadelphia	81	560	6.9

STEALS LEADERS
(Minimum 70 games or 125 steals)

	G	No.	Avg
Ervin Johnson, Los Angeles	37	127	3.43
Michael Ray Richardson, N.Y.	79	232	2.94
Quinn Buckner, Milwaukee	82	197	2.40
Maurice Cheeks, Philadelphia	81	193	2.38
Ray Williams, New York	79	185	2.34
Dudley Bradley, Indiana	82	186	2.27
Julius Erving, Philadelphia	82	173	2.11
Ron Lee, Detroit	82	166	2.02
Bob Reid, Houston	82	163	1.99
Larry Bird, Boston	82	161	1.96

THREE-POINT FIELD GOAL LEADERS
(Minimum 25 made)

	FG	FGA	Pct
Brian Taylor, San Diego	44	115	.383
Freeman Williams, San Diego	48	141	.340
Joe Hassett, Golden State	53	156	.340
Mike Bratz, Cleveland	57	169	.337
Henry Bibby, San Diego	32	95	.337
Kevin Grevey, Washington	45	136	.331
Chris Ford, Boston	36	109	.330
Scott Wedman, Kansas City	25	77	.325

REBOUND LEADERS
(Minimum 70 games or 800 rebounds)

	G	Off	Def	Total	Avg
Moses Malone, Houston	80	474	706	1,180	14.8
Swen Nater, San Diego	82	295	722	1,017	12.4
Phil Smith, Golden State	82	433	561	994	12.1
Larry Bird, Boston	82	191	704	895	10.9
Jack Sikma, Seattle	82	184	668	852	10.4
Austin Carr, Cleveland	81	260	575	835	10.3
Kareem Abdul–Jabbar, L.A.	80	197	624	821	10.3
Artis Gilmore, Chicago	82	220	608	828	10.1
Caldwell Jones, Philadelphia	81	200	613	813	10.0
Elvin Hayes, Washington	81	235	554	789	9.7

BLOCKED SHOTS LEADERS
(Minimum 70 games or 100 blocked shots)

	G	No.	Avg
George Johnson, San Antonio	82	278	3.39
Wayne Rollins, Atlanta	40	117	2.93
Kareem Abdul–Jabbar, L.A.	80	228	2.85
Robert Parish, Boston	82	214	2.61
Artis Gilmore, Chicago	82	198	2.41
Harvey Catchings, Milwaukee	77	184	2.39
Terry Tyler, Detroit	82	180	2.20
Mychal Thompson, Portland	79	170	2.15
Ben Poquette, Utah	82	174	2.12
Elvin Hayes, Washington	81	171	2.11

N.B.A. ALL-STAR TEAM—1981

First Team	Pos.	Second Team
Julius Erving, Philadelphia	F	Marques Johnson, Milwaukee
Larry Bird, Boston	F	Adrian Dantley, Utah
Kareem Abdul–Jabbar, Los Angeles	C	Moses Malone, Houston
George Gervin, San Antonio	G	Otis Birdsong, Kansas City
Dennis Johnson, Phoenix	G	Nate Archibald, Boston

WOMEN'S BASKETBALL LEAGUE
(Professional League)
FINAL STANDING OF THE TEAMS—1981

Coastal Division

	W	L	Pct
Dallas	27	9	.750
New Jersey	23	13	.639
New Orleans	18	19	.486
San Francisco	14	22	.389

Central Division

	W	L	Pct
Nebraska	27	9	.750
Chicago	18	18	.500
St. Louis	14	21	.400
Minnesota	7	28	.200

PLAYOFFS

Semifinal Round

Dallas defeated New Jersey, 2 games to 1
Nebraska defeated Chicago, 2 games to 0

Championship Series

Nebraska 89, Dallas 72
Dallas 106, Nebraska 93
Dallas 96, Nebraska 88
Nebraska 94, Dallas 93
Nebraska 99, Dallas 90
Nebraska won series, 3 games to 2

MOTORCYCLE RACING

WORLD CHAMPIONS—1981

350 c.c.—Anton Mang, West Germany
250 c.c.—Anton Mang, West Germany

SQUASH TENNIS

U.S. OPEN CHAMPION—1981

Men's open singles—Dave Stafford, Bronxville N.Y., defeated Bill Rubin, White Plains, N.Y., 9–15, 13–15, 16–14, 15–8, 15–10.

HOCKEY

Ice hockey, by birth and upbringing a Canadian game, is an offshoot of field hockey. Some historians say that the first ice hockey game was played in Montreal in December 1879 between two teams composed almost exclusively of McGill University students, but others assert that earlier hockey games took place in Kingston, Ontario, or Halifax, Nova Scotia. In the Montreal game of 1879, there were fifteen players on a side, who used an assortment of crude sticks to keep the puck in motion. Early rules allowed nine men on a side, but the number was reduced to seven in 1886 and later to six.

The first governing body of the sport was the Amateur Hockey Association of Canada, organized in 1887. In the winter of 1894–95, a group of college students from the United States visited Canada and saw the game played. They became enthused over the game and introduced it as a winter sport when they returned home. The first professional league was the International Hockey League, which operated in northern Michigan in 1904–06.

Until 1910, professionals and amateurs were allowed to play together on "mixed teams," but this arrangement ended with the formation of the first "big league," the National Hockey Association, in eastern Canada in 1910. The Pacific Coast League was organized in 1911 for western Canadian hockey. The league included Seattle and later other American cities. The National Hockey League replaced the National Hockey Association in 1917. Boston, in 1924, was the first American city to join that circuit. The league expanded to include western cities in 1967. The Stanley Cup was competed for by "mixed teams" from 1894 to 1910, thereafter by professionals. It was awarded to the winner of the N.H.L. playoffs from 1926–67 and now to the league champion. The World Hockey Association was organized in October 1972 and was dissolved after the 1978–79 season when the N.H.L. absorbed four of the teams.

STANLEY CUP WINNERS

Emblematic of World Professional Championship; N.H.L. Championship after 1967

1894	Montreal A.A.A.	1922	Toronto St. Patricks	1947–49	Toronto Maple Leafs
1895	Montreal Victorias	1923	Ottawa Senators	1950	Detroit Red Wings
1896	Winnipeg Victorias	1924	Montreal Canadiens	1951	Toronto Maple Leafs
1897–99	Montreal Victorias	1925	Victoria Cougars	1952	Detroit Red Wings
1900	Montreal Shamrocks	1926	Montreal Maroons	1953	Montreal Canadiens
1901	Winnipeg Victorias	1927	Ottawa Senators	1954–55	Detroit Red Wings
1902	Montreal A.A.A.	1928	N.Y. Rangers	1956–60	Montreal Canadiens
1903–05	Ottawa Silver Seven	1929	Boston Bruins	1961	Chicago Black Hawks
1906	Montreal Wanderers	1930–31	Montreal Canadiens	1962–64	Toronto Maple Leafs
1907	Kenora Thistles[1]	1932	Toronto Maple Leafs	1965–66	Montreal Canadiens
1907	Mont. Wanderers[2]	1933	N.Y. Rangers	1967	Toronto Maple Leafs
1908	Montreal Wanderers	1934	Chicago Black Hawks	1968–69	Montreal Canadiens
1909	Ottawa Senators	1935	Montreal Maroons	1970	Boston Bruins
1910	Montreal Wanderers	1936–37	Detroit Red Wings	1971	Montreal Canadiens
1911	Ottawa Senators	1938	Chicago Black Hawks	1972	Boston Bruins
1912–13	Quebec Bulldogs	1939	Boston Bruins	1973	Montreal Canadiens
1914	Toronto	1940	N.Y. Rangers	1974–75	Philadelphia Flyers
1915	Vancouver Millionaires	1941	Boston Bruins	1976–79	Montreal Canadiens
1916	Montreal Canadiens	1942	Toronto Maple Leafs	1980–81	New York Islanders
1917	Seattle Metropolitans	1943	Detroit Red Wings		
1918	Toronto Arenas	1944	Montreal Canadiens	1. January. 2. March.	
1919	No champion	1945	Toronto Maple Leafs		
1920–21	Ottawa Senators	1946	Montreal Canadiens		

NATIONAL HOCKEY LEAGUE YEARLY TROPHY WINNERS

The Hart Trophy—Most Valuable Player

1924	Frank Nighbor, Ottawa	1946	Max Bentley, Chicago
1925	Billy Burch, Hamilton	1947	Maurice Richard, Montreal Canadiens
1926	Nels Stewart, Montreal Maroons	1948	Buddy O'Connor, New York Rangers
1927	Herb Gardiner, Montreal Canadiens	1949	Sid Abel, Detroit
1928	Howie Morenz, Montreal Canadiens	1950	Chuck Rayner, New York Rangers
1929	Roy Worters, New York Americans	1951	Milt Schmidt, Boston
1930	Nels Stewart, Montreal Maroons	1952–53	Gordon Howe, Detroit
1931–32	Howie Morenz, Montreal Canadiens	1954	Al Rollins, Chicago
1933	Eddie Shore, Boston	1955	Ted Kennedy, Toronto
1934	Aurel Joliat, Montreal Canadiens	1956	Jean Beliveau, Montreal Canadiens
1935–36	Eddie Shore, Boston	1957–58	Gordon Howe, Detroit
1937	Babe Siebert, Montreal Canadiens	1959	Andy Bathgate, New York Rangers
1938	Eddie Shore, Boston	1960	Gordon Howe, Detroit
1939	Toe Blake, Montreal Canadiens	1961	Bernie Geoffrion, Montreal Canadiens
1940	Ebbie Goodfellow, Detroit	1962	Jacques Plante, Montreal Canadiens
1941	Bill Cowley, Boston	1963	Gordon Howe, Detroit
1942	Tom Anderson, New York Americans	1964	Jean Beliveau, Montreal Canadiens
1943	Bill Cowley, Boston	1965–66	Bobby Hull, Chicago
1944	Babe Pratt, Toronto	1967–68	Stan Mikita, Chicago
1945	Elmer Lach, Montreal Canadiens	1969	Phil Esposito, Boston

1970–72	Bobby Orr, Boston
1973	Bobby Clarke, Philadelphia
1974	Phil Esposito, Boston
1975–76	Bobby Clarke, Philadelphia
1977–78	Guy Lafleur, Montreal
1979	Bryan Trottier, N.Y. Islanders
1980	Wayne Gretzky, Edmonton
1981	Wayne Gretzky, Edmonton

Vezina Trophy—Leading Goalkeeper

1956–60	Jacques Plante, Montreal
1961	Johnny Bower, Toronto
1962	Jacques Plante, Montreal
1963	Glenn Hall, Chicago
1964	Charlie Hodge, Montreal
1965	Terry Sawchuk–Johnny Bower, Toronto
1966	Lorne Worsley–Charlie Hodge, Montreal
1967	Glenn Hall–Denis DeJordy, Chicago
1968	Lorne Worsley–Rogatien Vachon, Montreal
1969	Glenn Hall–Jacques Plante, St. Louis
1970	Tony Esposito, Chicago
1971	Ed Giacomin–Gilles Villemure, New York
1972	Tony Esposito–Gary Smith, Chicago
1973	Ken Dryden, Montreal
1974	Bernie Parent, Philadelphia, and Tony Esposito, Chicago
1975	Bernie Parent, Philadelphia
1976	Ken Dryden, Montreal
1977–79	Ken Dryden–Michel Larocque, Montreal
1980	Bob Sauve–Don Edwards, Buffalo
1981	Richard Sevigny, Denis Herron and Michel Larocque, Montreal

James Norris Trophy—Defenseman

1954	Red Kelly, Detroit
1955–58	Doug Harvey, Montreal
1959	Tom Johnson, Montreal
1960–62	Doug Harvey, Montreal, New York (62)
1963–65	Pierre Pilote, Chicago
1966	Jacques Laperriere, Montreal
1967	Harry Howell, New York
1968–75	Bobby Orr, Boston
1976	Denis Potvin, N.Y. Islanders
1977	Larry Robinson, Montreal
1978	Denis Potvin, N.Y. Islanders
1980	Larry Robinson, Montreal
1981	Randy Carlyle, Pittsburgh

Lady Byng Trophy—Sportsmanship

1960	Don McKenney, Boston
1961	Red Kelly, Detroit
1962–63	Dave Keon, Toronto
1964	Ken Wharram, Chicago
1965	Bobby Hull, Chicago
1966	Alex Delvecchio, Detroit
1967–68	Stan Mikita, Chicago
1969	Alex Delvecchio, Detroit
1970	Phil Goyette, St. Louis
1971	John Bucyk, Boston
1972	Jean Ratelle, New York
1973	Gil Perreault, Buffalo
1974	John Buyck, Boston
1975	Marcel Dionne, Detroit
1976	Jean Ratelle, N.Y. Rangers–Boston
1977	Marcel Dionne, Los Angeles
1978	Butch Goring, Los Angeles
1979	Bob MacMillan, Atlanta
1980	Wayne Gretzky, Edmonton
1981	Rick Kehoe, Pittsburgh

Calder Trophy—Rookie

1962	Bobby Rousseau, Montreal
1963	Kent Douglas, Toronto
1964	Jacques Laperriere, Montreal
1965	Roger Crozier, Detroit
1966	Brit Selby, Toronto
1967	Bobby Orr, Boston
1968	Derek Sanderson, Boston
1969	Danny Grant, Minnesota
1970	Tony Esposito, Chicago
1971	Gilbert Perreault, Buffalo
1972	Ken Dryden, Montreal
1973	Steve Vickers, New York Rangers
1974	Denis Potvin, N.Y. Islanders
1975	Eric Vail, Atlanta
1976	Bryan Trottier, N.Y. Islanders
1977	Willi Plett, Atlanta
1978	Mike Bossy, N.Y. Islanders
1979	Bobby Smith, Minnesota
1980	Ray Bourque, Boston
1981	Peter Stastny, Quebec

Art Ross Trophy—Leading scorer

1955	Bernie Geoffrion, Montreal
1956	Jean Beliveau, Montreal
1957	Gordie Howe, Detroit
1958–59	Dickie Moore, Montreal
1960	Bobby Hull, Chicago
1961	Bernie Geoffrion, Montreal
1962	Bobby Hull, Chicago
1963	Gordie Howe, Detroit
1964–65	Stan Mikita, Chicago
1966	Bobby Hull, Chicago
1967–68	Stan Mikita, Chicago
1969	Phil Esposito, Boston
1970	Bobby Orr, Boston
1971–74	Phil Esposito, Boston
1975	Bobby Orr, Boston
1976–78	Guy Lafleur, Montreal
1979	Bryan Trottier, N.Y. Islanders
1980	Marcel Dionne, Los Angeles
1981	Wayne Gretzky, Edmonton

N.H.L. CHAMPIONS
Prince of Wales Trophy

1939	Boston
1940	Boston
1941	Boston
1942	New York
1943	Detroit
1944–47	Montreal
1948	Toronto
1948–55	Detroit
1956	Montreal
1957	Detroit
1958–62	Montreal
1963	Toronto
1964	Montreal
1965	Detroit
1966	Montreal
1967	Chicago

Eastern Division

1968–69	Montreal
1970	Chicago
1971	Boston
1972	Boston
1973	Montreal
1974	Boston

Prince of Wales Conference

1975	Buffalo
1976–79	Montreal
1980	Buffalo
1981	Montreal

CAMPBELL BOWL
Western Division

1968	Philadelphia
1969	St. Louis
1970	St. Louis
1971–73	Chicago
1974	Philadelphia

Clarence Campbell Conference

1975	Philadelphia
1976–77	Philadelphia
1978–79	N.Y. Islanders
1980	Philadelphia
1981	New York Islanders

NATIONAL HOCKEY LEAGUE
Final Standing of the Clubs—1980–81

CLARENCE CAMPBELL CONFERENCE
Patrick Division

	W	L	T	GF	GA	Pts
New York Islanders	48	18	14	355	260	110
Philadelphia Flyers	41	24	15	313	249	97
Calgary Flames*	39	27	14	329	298	92
New York Rangers	30	36	14	312	317	74
Washington Capitals	26	36	18	286	317	70

Smythe Division

	W	L	T	GF	GA	Pts
St. Louis Blues	45	18	17	352	281	107
Chicago Black Hawks	31	33	16	304	315	78
Vancouver Canucks	28	32	20	289	301	76
Edmonton Oilers	29	35	16	328	327	74
Colorado Rockies	22	45	13	258	344	57
Winnipeg Jets	9	57	14	246	400	32

PRINCE OF WALES CONFERENCE
Norris Division

	W	L	T	GF	GA	Pts
Montreal Canadiens	45	22	13	332	232	103
Los Angeles Kings	43	24	13	337	290	99
Pittsburgh Penguins	30	37	13	302	345	73
Hartford Whalers	21	41	18	292	372	60
Detroit Red Wings	19	43	18	252	339	56

Adams Division

	W	L	T	GF	GA	Pts
Buffalo Sabres	39	20	21	327	250	99
Boston Bruins	37	30	13	316	272	87
Minnesota North Stars	35	28	17	292	263	87
Quebec Nordiques	30	32	18	314	318	78
Toronto Maple Leafs	28	37	15	322	367	71

*Atlanta franchise moved to Calgary, Alberta, after 1979–80 season.

Stanley Cup Playoffs

Preliminary Round
New York Islanders defeated Toronto, 3 games to 0
St. Louis defeated Pittsburgh, 3 games to 2
Edmonton defeated Montreal, 3 games to 0
New York Rangers defeated Los Angeles, 3 games to 1
Buffalo defeated Vancouver, 3 games to 0
Philadelphia defeated Quebec, 3 games to 2
Calgary defeated Chicago, 3 games to 0
Minnesota defeated Boston, 3 games to 0

Quarterfinal Round
New York Islanders defeated Edmonton, 4 games to 2
New York Rangers defeated St. Louis, 4 games to 2
Minnesota defeated Buffalo, 4 games to 1
Calgary defeated Philadelphia, 4 games to 3

Semifinal Round
New York Islanders defeated New York Rangers, 4 games to 0
   April 28—Islanders 5, Rangers 2[1]
   April 30—Islanders 7, Rangers 3[1]
   May 2—Islanders 5, Rangers 1
   May 4—Islanders 5, Rangers 2
1. At Nassau Coliseum, Uniondale, New York.
Minnesota defeated Calgary, 4 games to 2
   April 28—Minnesota 4, Calgary 1[1]
   April 30—Calgary 3, Minnesota 2[1]
   May 3—Minnesota 6, Calgary 4
   May 5—Minnesota 7, Calgary 4
   May 7—Calgary 3, Minnesota 1[1]
   May 9—Minnesota 5, Calgary 3
1. At Calgary.

Championship
New York Islanders defeated Minnesota, 4 games to 1
   May 12—New York Islanders 6, Minnesota 3[1]
   May 14—New York Islanders 6, Minnesota 3[1]
   May 17—New York Islanders 7, Minnesota 5
   May 19—Minnesota 4, New York Islanders 2

   May 21—New York Islanders 5, Minnesota 1[1]
1. At Nassau Coliseum, Uniondale, New York.

N.H.L. LEADING SCORERS—1980–1981

	GP	G	A	Pts
Wayne Gretzky, Edmonton	80	55	109	164
Marcel Dionne, Los Angeles	80	58	77	135
Kent Nilsson, Calgary	80	49	82	131
Mike Bossy, New York Islanders	79	68	51	119
Dave Taylor, Los Angeles	72	47	65	112
Peter Stastny, Quebec	77	39	70	109
Mike Rogers, Hartford	80	40	65	105
Charlie Simmer, Los Angeles	65	56	49	105
Bernie Federko, St. Louis	78	31	73	104
Jacques Richard, Quebec	78	52	51	103
Rick Middleton, Boston	80	44	59	103
Bryan Trottier, New York Islanders	73	31	72	103
Wilf Paiement, Toronto	77	40	57	97
Dennis Maruk, Washington	80	50	47	97
Wayne Babych, St. Louis	78	54	42	96
Darryl Sittler, Toronto	80	43	53	96
Mike Gartner, Washington	80	48	46	94
Bobby Smith, Minnesota	78	29	64	93

N.H.L. ALL-STAR TEAMS—1981

First Team	Pos.	Second Team
Mike Luit, St. Louis	G	Mario Lessard, Los Angeles
Denis Potvin, New York Islanders	D	Larry Robinson, Montreal
Randy Carlyle, Pittsburgh	D	Ray Bourque, Boston
Wayne Gretzky, Edmonton	C	Marcel Dionne, Los Angeles
Charlie Simmer, Los Angeles	LW	Billy Barber, Philadelphia
Mike Bossy, New York Islanders	RW	Dave Taylor, Los Angeles

OTHER N.H.L. AWARDS—1981

Selke (Best defensive forward)—Bob Gainey, Montreal
Smythe (Most valuable in playoffs)—Robert (Butch) Goring, New York Islanders

N.H.L. LEADING GOALTENDERS—1980–1981

	G	Min	GA	Avg
Richard Sevigny, Montreal	33	1,777	71	2.40
Rick St. Croix, Philadelphia	27	1,567	65	2.49
Don Edwards, Buffalo	45	2,700	133	2.96
Pete Peeters, Philadelphia	40	2,333	115	2.96
Michel Larocque, Montreal	28	1,623	82	3.03
*Glenn Resch, New York Islanders	32	1,817	93	3.07
Bob Sauve, Buffalo	35	2,100	111	3.17
Don Beaupre, Minnesota	44	2,585	139	3.20
Rejean Lemelin, Calgary	29	1,629	80	3.24
Mario Lessard, Los Angeles	64	3,746	203	3.25
Gilles Meloche, Minnesota	38	2,215	120	3.25
Billy Smith, New York Islanders	41	2,363	129	3.28

Top Team Scores

Montreal (Sevigny, Larocque, Herron, Wamsley)	80	4,800	232	2.90
Philadelphia (St. Croix, Peeters, Myre)	80	4,800	249	3.11

*Traded to Colorado Rockies during season.

N.H.L. CAREER SCORING LEADERS

(Listed in order of total points scored; figures in parentheses indicate the top 10 in goals scored)

	Yrs	Games	G	A	Pts
Gordie Howe (1)	26	1,767	801	1,049	1,850
Phil Esposito (2)	18	1,282	717	873	1,590
Stan Mikita (6)	22	1,407	541	926	1,467
John Bucyk (4)	24	1,540	556	813	1,369
Alex Delvecchio	23	1,549	456	825	1,281
Jean Ratelle (9)	20	1,281	491	776	1,267
Norm Ullman (10)	20	1,410	490	739	1,229
Jean Beliveau (8)	20	1,125	507	712	1,219
Bobby Hull (3)	16	1,063	610	560	1,170
Frank Mahovlich (7)	18	1,181	533	570	1,103
Marcel Dionne[1]	10	779	438	625	1,063
Henri Richard	20	1,256	358	688	1,046
Rod Gilbert	18	1,065	406	615	1,021
Guy Lafleur[1]	10	728	432	579	1,011
Bobby Clarke[1]	12	929	301	701	1,002
Andy Bathgate	17	1,069	349	624	973
Dave Keon[1]	17	1,218	388	579	967
Maurice Richard (5)	18	978	544	421	965
Gilbert Perreault[1]	11	809	360	568	928
Bobby Orr	12	657	270	645	915

1. Still active in N.H.L.

AMATEUR LEAGUES—1981

International League—Regular season: East Division: Saginaw; West Division: Kalamazoo. Playoffs: Saginaw defeated Kalamazoo, 4 games to 0.
Eastern League—Regular season: Erie. Playoffs: Erie defeated Richmond, 4 games to 0.
Western League—Regular season: West Division: Victoria; East Division: Regina. Playoffs: Victoria defeated Calgary, 4 games to 3.
Ontario Major League—Regular season: Leyden Division: S.S. Marie; Emms Division: Kitchener. Playoffs: Kitchener defeated S.S. Marie 9 to 3 in points. (Kitchener won 3 games and 3 games ended in a tie in best-of-seven series.)
Quebec Major League—Regular season: Lebel Division: Cornwall; Dilio Division: T. Rivieres. Playoffs: Cornwell defeated T. Rivieres, 4 games to 1.
Memorial Cup—Cornwall.

MINOR LEAGUE HOCKEY CHAMPIONS
American League—1981

	W	L	T	GF	GA	Pts
Northern Division						
Maine Mariners	45	28	7	319	290	97
New Brunswick Hawks	37	33	10	317	298	84
Nova Scotia Voyageurs	38	37	5	335	298	81
Springfield Indians	34	41	5	312	343	73
Southern Division						
Hershey Bears	47	24	9	357	299	103
Adirondack Red Wings	35	40	5	305	328	75
Binghamton Dusters	32	42	6	296	336	70
New Haven Nighthawks	29	40	11	293	321	69
Rochester Americans	30	42	8	295	316	68

CALDER CUP PLAYOFFS
Quarterfinals

Maine defeated Springfield, 4 games to 3
New Brunswick defeated Nova Scotia, 4 games to 2
Hershey defeated New Haven, 4 games to 0
Adirondack defeated Binghamton, 4 games to 2

Semifinals

Maine defeated New Brunswick, 4 games to 3
Adirondack defeated Hershey, 4 games to 2

Final

Adirondack defeated Maine, 4 games to 2

Central League—1981

	W	L	T	GF	GA	Pts
Dallas Black Hawks	56	16	7	356	333	119
Salt Lake City Golden Eagles	46	29	5	368	295	97
Indianapolis Checkers	44	30	6	306	238	94
Oklahoma City Stars	39	38	2	312	328	80
Tulsa Oilers	33	42	4	285	312	70
Wichita Wind	32	46	3	307	346	65
Fort Worth Texans	24	53	3	201	309	51
*Birmingham Bulls	17	37	4	204	277	38
**Houston Apollos	12	13	8	97	98	32

*Suspended operations Feb. 26, 1981.
**Suspended operations Jan. 4, 1981.

ADAMS CUP PLAYOFFS
Semifinals

Salt Lake defeated Tulsa, 4 games to 1
Wichita defeated Dallas, 4 games to 2

Final

Salt Lake defeated Wichita, 4 games to 3

COLLEGE CHAMPIONS—1981

N.C.A.A. Division I (Duluth, Minn.)—Final: Wisconsin defeated Minnesota, 6–3. Third place: Michigan Tech defeated Northern Michigan, 5–2. Semifinals: Minnesota defeated Michigan Tech, 7–2; Wisconsin defeated Northern Michigan, 5–1.
N.C.A.A. Division II (North Andover, Mass.)—Final: Lowell (Mass.) defeated Plattsburgh State, 5–4. Third place: Mankato State (Minn.) defeated Concordia (Minn.), 9–7.

E.C.A.C. Division I—Final: Providence defeated Cornell, 8–4. Semifinals: Providence defeated Clarkson, 4–3; Cornell defeated Colgate, 4–3. Quarterfinals: Providence defeated Boston College, 5–2; Clarkson defeated New Hampshire, 5–2; Colgate defeated Northeastern, 5–3; Cornell defeated Maine, 7–4.

C.C.H.A.—Final: Northern Michigan defeated Ohio State, 6–4, in two-game total-goals series. First game: Northern Michigan 2, Ohio State 2; Second game: Northern Michigan 4, Ohio State 2.

W.C.H.A.—Final: Minnesota defeated Michigan Tech.

FIGURE SKATING

WORLD CHAMPIONS

Men

1960	Alain Giletti, France
1961	No competition
1962	Donald Jackson, Canada
1963	Don McPherson, Canada
1964	Manfred Schnelldorfer, West Germany
1965	Alain Calmat, France
1966–68	Emmerich Danzer, Austria
1969–70	Tim Wood, United States
1971–73	Ondrej Nepela, Czechoslovakia
1974	Jan Hoffman, East Germany
1975	Sergei Yolkov, U.S.S.R.
1976	John Curry, Britain

1977	Vladimir Kovelov, U.S.S.R.
1978	Charles Tickner, United States
1979	Vladimir Kovalev, U.S.S.R.
1980	Jan Hoffman, East Germany
1981	Scott Hamilton, United States

Women

1956–60	Carol Heiss, United States
1961	No competition
1962–64	Sjoukje Dijkstra, Netherlands
1965	Petra Burka, Canada
1966–68	Peggy Fleming, United States
1969–70	Gabriele Seyfert, East Germany

1971–72	Beatrix Schuba, Austria
1973	Karen Magnusson, Canada
1974	Christine Errath, East Germany
1975	Dianne de Leeuw, Netherlands
1976	Dorothy Hamill, United States
1977	Linda Fratianne, United States
1978	Anett Poetzsch, East Germany
1979	Linda Fratianne, United States
1980	Anett Poetzsch, East Germany
1981	Denise Biellmann, Switzerland

U.S. CHAMPIONS

Men

1946–52	Richard Button
1953–56	Hayes Jenkins
1957–60	David Jenkins
1961	Bradley Lord
1962	Monty Hoyt
1963	Tommy Litz
1964	Scott Allen
1965	Gary Visconti
1966	Scott Allen
1967	Gary Visconti
1968–70	Tim Wood

1971	John M. Petkevich
1972	Ken Shelley
1973–75	Gordon McKellen
1976	Terry Kubicka
1977–80	Charles Tickner
1981	Scott Hamilton

Women

1943–48	Gretchen Merrill
1949–50	Yvonne Sherman
1951	Sonya Klopfer
1952–56	Tenley Albright

1957–60	Carol Heiss
1961	Laurence Owen
1962	Barbara Roles Pursley
1963	Lorraine Hanlon
1964–68	Peggy Fleming
1969–73	Janet Lynn
1974–76	Dorothy Hamill
1977–80	Linda Fratianne
1981	Elaine Zayak

WORLD CHAMPIONS—1981
(Hartford, Conn., March 4–8, 1981)

Men's singles—Scott Hamilton, Haverford, Pa.
Women's singles—Denise Biellmann, Switzerland
Pairs—Irina Vorobieva and Igor Lisovsky, Soviet Union
Dance—Jayne Torvill and Christopher Dean, Britain

UNITED STATES CHAMPIONS—1981
(San Diego, Calif., Feb. 3–8, 1981)

Men's singles—Scott Hamilton, Haverford, Pa.
Women's singles—Elaine Zayak, Paramus, N.J.
Pairs—Caitling and Peter Curruthers, Wilmington, Del.

BOWLING

AMERICAN BOWLING CONGRESS CHAMPIONS

Year	Singles	All-events	Year	Singles	All-events
1959	Ed Lubanski	Ed Lubanski	1971	Al Cohn	Al Cohn
1960	Paul Kulbaga	Vince Lucci	1972	Bill Pointer	Mac Lowry
1961	Lyle Spooner	Luke Karen	1973	Ed Thompson	Ron Woolet
1962	Andy Renaldo	Billy Young	1974	Gene Krause	Bob Hart
1963	Fred Delello	Bus Owalt	1975	Jim Setser	Bobby Meadows
1964	Jim Stefanich	Les Zikes, Jr.	1976	Mike Putzer	Jim Lindquist
1965	Ken Roeth	Tom Hathaway	1977	Frank Gadaleto	Bud Debenham
1966	Don Chapman	John Wilcox	1978	Rich Mersek	Chris Cobus
1967	Frank Perry	Gary Lewis	1979	Rick Peters	Bob Basacchi
1968	Wayne Kowalski	Vince Mazzanti	1980	Mike Eaton	Steve Fehr
1969	Greg Campbell	Eddie Jackson	1981	Rob Vital	Rod Toft
1970	Jake Yoder	Mike Berlin			

PROFESSIONAL BOWLERS ASSOCIATION

National Championship Tournament

1960	Don Carter	1966	Wayne Zahn	1972	Johnny Guenther	1978	Warren Nelson
1961	Dave Soutar	1967	Dave Davis	1973	Earl Anthony	1979	Mike Aulby
1962	Carmen Salvino	1968	Wayne Zahn	1974	Earl Anthony	1980	Johnny Petraglia
1963	Billy Hardwick	1969	Mike McGrath	1975	Earl Anthony	1981	Earl Anthony
1964	Bob Strampe	1970	Mike McGrath	1976	Paul Colwell		
1965	Dave Davis	1971	Mike Lemongello	1977	Tommy Hudson		

BOWLING PROPRIETORS' ASSOCIATION OF AMERICA—MEN

United States Open[1]

1971	Mike Lemongello	1974	Larry Laub	1977	Johnny Petraglia	1980	Steve Martin
1972	Don Johnson	1975	Steve Neff	1978	Nelson Burton, Jr.	1981	Marshall Holman
1973	Mike McGrath	1976	Paul Moser	1979	Joe Berardi		

1. Replaced All-Star tournament and is rolled as part of B.P.A. tour.

WOMEN'S INTERNATIONAL BOWLING CONGRESS CHAMPIONS

Year	Singles	All-events	Year	Singles	All-events
1959	Mae Ploegman	Pat McBride	1971	Ginny Younginer	Lorrie Koch
1960	Marge McDaniels	Judy Roberts	1972	D. D. Jacobson	Mildred Martorella
1961	Elaine Newton	Evelyn Teal	1973	Bobby Buffaloe	Toni Calvery
1962	Martha Hoffman	Flossie Argent	1974	Shirley Garms	Judy C. Soutar
1963	Dot Wilkinson	Helen Shablis	1975	Barbara Leicht	Virginia Park
1964	Jean Havlish	Jean Havlish	1976	Bev Shonk	Betty Morris
1965	Doris Rudell	Donna Zimmerman	1977	Akiko Yamaga	Akiko Yamaga
1966	Gloria Bouvia	Kate Helbig	1978	Mae Bolt	Annese Kelly
1967	Gloria Paeth	Carol Miller	1979	Betty Morris	Betty Morris
1968	Norma Parks	Susie Reichley	1980	Betty Morris	Cheryl Robinson
1969	Joan Bender	Helen Duval	1981	Virginia Norton	Virginia Norton
1970	Dorothy Fothergill	Dorothy Fothergill			

W.I.B.C. QUEENS TOURNAMENT CHAMPIONS

1961	Janet Harman	1967	Mildred Martorella	1973	Dorothy Fothergill	1979	Donna Adamek
1962	Dorothy Wilkinson	1968	Phyllis Massey	1974	Judy Soutar	1980	Donna Adamek
1963	Irene Monterosso	1969	Ann Feigel	1975	Cindy Powell	1981	Katsuko Sugimoto
1964	D.D. Jacobson	1970	Mildred Martorella	1976	Pamela Rutherford		
1965	Betty Kuczynski	1971	Mildred Martorella	1977	Dana Stewart		
1966	Judy Lee	1972	Dorothy Fothergill	1978	Loa Boxberger		

BOWLING PROPRIETORS' ASSOCIATION OF AMERICA—WOMEN

United States Open[1]

1971	Paula Carter	1974	Pat Costello	1977	Betty Morris	1980	Pat Costello
1972	Lorrie Nichols	1975	Paula Carter	1978	Donna Adamek	1981	Donna Adamek
1973	Mildred Martorella	1976	Pat Costello	1979	Diana Silva		

1. Replaced All-Star tournament.

AMERICAN BOWLING CONGRESS TOURNAMENT

(Memphis, Tenn., Feb. 28-May 25, 1981)

Regular Division

Singles—Rob Vital, Lancaster, Pa.	780
Doubles—Jim Kontos, Munster, Ind., and Al Bruder, Chicago	1,362
Bob Blaney and Ted Hannahs, Cambridge, Ohio	1,362
All events—Rod Toft, St. Paul, Minn.	2,107
Team—Strachota's Milshore Bowl, Milwaukee	3,188
Team All events—Cook County Tobacco No. 2, Chicago	9,695
Booster Team—Robey Tire, Ann Arbor, Mich.	2,833

MASTERS

(Memphis, Tenn., May 13-17, 1981)

Singles—Randy Lightfoot, St. Charles, Mo. (defeated Skip

Tucker, Merritt Island, Fla., 194–178, in final)
Third place—Tom Baker, Buffalo, N.Y.
Fourth place—Wayne Webb, Tucson, Ariz.
Fifth place—Dave Soutar, Kansas City, Mo.

WOMEN'S INTERNATIONAL BOWLING CONGRESS

(Baltimore, Md., April 2-May 26, 1981)

Open Division

Singles—Virginia Norton, South Gate, Calif.	672
Doubles—Donna Adamek, Duarte, Calif., and Nikki Gianulias, Vallejo, Calif.	1,305
All events—Virginia Norton, South Gate, Calif.	1,905
Team—Earl Anthony's Dublin Bowl, Dublin, Calif.	2,963

Division I

Singles—Dorothy Batey, East Orange, N.J.	651

Doubles—Jeri Gue, Townsend, Del., and Jo Ann Scott,
Wilmington, Del. — 1,181
All events—Ferol Streib, Leavenworth, Wash. — 1,738
Team—Gibson Specialty Co., Waterloo, Iowa — 2,796

Division II

Singles—Bonnie Bowley, Laurel, Md. — 594
Doubles—Constance Calveric, Sayre, Pa., and
Barbara White, Athens, Pa. — 1,050
All events—Doris Fletcher, Chestertown, Md. — 1,618
Team—Matinee Five, Severna Park, Md. — 2,631

QUEENS TOURNAMENT

Winner—Katsuko Sugimoto, Tokyo, Japan (defeated Virginia
Norton, South Gate, Calif., 166–158, in final).

COLLEGIATE
Association of College Unions—International
(Baltimore, Md., April 6, 1981)
Singles—Linda Painter, Michigan State — 596
Doubles—Michele Citro, Penn State, and Carol
Palangio, Robert Morris — 1,124
All events—Michele Citro, Penn State — 1,691

SKIING

ALPINE WORLD CUP OVERALL WINNERS

	Men	Women	Team
1967	Jean-Claude Killy, France	Nancy Greene, Canada	France
1968	Jean-Claude Killy, France	Nancy Greene, Canada	France
1969	Karl Schranz, Austria	Gertrude Gabl, Austria	Austria
1970	Karl Schranz, Austria	Michel Jacot, France	France
1971	Gustavo Thoeni, Italy	Annemarie Proell, Austria	France
1972	Gustavo Thoeni, Italy	Annemarie Proell, Austria	France
1973	Gustavo Thoeni, Italy	Annemarie Proell Moser, Austria	Austria
1974	Piero Gros, Italy	Annemarie Proell Moser, Austria	Austria
1975	Gustavo Thoeni, Italy	Annemarie Proell Moser, Austria	Austria
1976	Ingemar Stenmark, Sweden	Rosi Mittermaier, West Germany	Austria
1977	Ingemar Stenmark, Sweden	Lise-Marie Morerod, Switzerland	Austria
1978	Ingemar Stenmark, Sweden	Hanni Wenzel, Liechtenstein	Austria
1979	Peter Luescher, Switzerland	Annemarie Proell Moser, Austria	Austria
1980	Andreas Wenzel, Liechtenstein	Hanni Wenzel, Liechtenstein	Liechtenstein
1981	Phil Mahre, United States	Marie-Theres Nadig, Switzerland	Switzerland

UNITED STATES CHAMPIONSHIPS—1981

ALPINE
Men's Events

Downhill—Doug Powell, Chappaqua, N.Y. — 1:06.71
Slalom—Steve Mahre, Yakima, Wash. — 1:31.15
Giant Slalom—Phil Mahre, Yakima, Wash. — n.a.

Women's Events

Downhill—Holly Flanders, Deerfield, N.H. — 1:36.83
Slalom—Cindy Nelson, Lutsen, Minn. — 1:36.15
Giant Slalom—Tamara McKinney, Olympic Valley, Calif. — n.a.

NORDIC
Men's Cross-Country

15 kilometers—Bill Koch, Putney, Vt. — 40:37.13
30 kilometers—Bill Koch — 1:26:17
50 kilometers—Tim Caldwell, Putney, Vt. — 2:35:19
Relay—Douglas Peterson, H. Bean, Dan Simoneau,
Livermore Falls, Me. — n.a.
Veterans 15 km—Jim Fredericks, Craftsbury, Vt. — 46:11.39
Veterans 30 km—Jim Fredericks — 1:36:29
Veterans relay—Jim Fredericks, Hank Lange,
Brattleboro, Vt., Fred Fayette, Colchester, Vt. — 1:37:49.73

Women's Cross-Country

5 kilometers—Allison Owen-Spencer, East
Wenatchee, Wash. — 17:13.41
10 kilometers—Allison Owen-Spencer — 31:18
20 kilometers—Lynn Spencer Galanes, Vermont — 1:07:39
Relay—Allison Owen-Spencer, P. Engberg, J. Musolf — n.a.
Veterans 5 km—Gail Landgren — 21:07.03
Veterans 10 km—Jane Parrish, Fairbanks, Alaska — 40:17.67
n.a. = not available.

ALPINE WORLD CUP—1981

Overall—Men

	Pts
Phil Mahre, Yakima, Wash.	266
Ingemar Stenmark, Sweden	260
Aleksandr Zhirov, Soviet Union	185
Steve Mahre, Yakima, Wash.	155

Overall—Women

	Pts
Marie-Theres Nadig, Switzerland	289
Erika Hess, Switzerland	251
Hanni Wenzel, Liechtenstein	241
Christin Cooper, Ketchum, Idaho	198
6—Tamara McKinney, Olympic Valley, Calif.	176
8—Cindy Nelson, Lutsen, Minn.	168

Event Leaders—Men

	Pts
Downhill—Harti Weirataher, Austria	115
2—Steve Podborski, Canada	110
3—Peter Mueller, Switzerland	95
Slalom—Ingemar Stenmark, Sweden	120
2—Phil Mahre, Yakima, Wash.	97
3—Steve Mahre, Yakima, Wash.	80
Giant Slalom—Ingemar Stenmark, Sweden	125
2—Aleksandr Zhirov, Soviet Union	115
3—Phil Mahre, Yakima, Wash.	84

Event Leaders—Women

	Pts
Downhill—Marie-Theres Nadig, Switzerland	120
2—Doris DeAgostini, Switzerland	110

3—Cornelia Proell, Austria ... 78
Slalom—Erika Hess, Switzerland ... 125
2—Christin Cooper, Ketchum, Idaho ... 86
3—Perrine Pelen, France ... 81
Giant Slalom—Tamara McKinney, Olympic Valley, Calif. ... 102
2—Marie-Theres Nadig, Switzerland ... 97
3—Erika Hess, Switzerland ... 78

COLLEGIATE
Men—N.C.A.A.
(Park City, Utah)

Slalom—Scott Hoffman, Utah ... 1:26.80
Giant Slalom—Tor Melander, Vermont ... 2:08.41
Cross-country—Bernt Lund, Utah ... 49:48.6
Cross-country relay—Vermont (Jon Zdechlik, Todd Kempainen, Pal Sjulstad) ... 1:16:37.8
Team—Utah ... 183 pts

ALPINE NATIONS CUP—1981

	Pts
Overall—Switzerland	1,584
Austria	1,284
United States	1,276
Italy	738
West Germany	723
Liechtenstein	519
France	498
Soviet Union	421
Sweden	399
Canada	315
Men's Events—Austria	982
3. United States	517
8. Canada	208
Women's Events—Switzerland	922
2. United States	759
8. Canada	107

NORTH AMERICA TROPHY SERIES—1981

	Pts
Men's overall champion—Tiger Shaw, Stowe, Vt.	76
Women's overall champion—Tie between Noel Lyons, East Burke, Vt., and Brenda Buglione, Stowe, Vt.	71

HANNI AND ANDREAS WENZEL STARS OF WORLD CUP SKIING

Rarely in sport do a brother and sister excel the way Hanni and Andreas Wenzel of Liechtenstein did during the 1980 skiing season. They emerged as the world's top all-round skiers by winning the overall World Cup titles and excelling in the Winter Olympics.

It was the first time a brother and sister took the overall World Cup crowns. Hanni won her title with 311 points and Andreas won with 204. The 23-year-old Hanni also won two gold and one silver medal at the Winter Olympics. Andreas captured two gold medals at the Games at Lake Placid, N.Y.

Their triumphs put tiny Liechtenstein, a country with only seven ski lifts and 6,000 skiers, on the world sports map and placed it fourth in the overall standings of World Cup nations behind Austria, Switzerland, and the United States.

The Wenzels are an active family. There is another sister, Petra, 19, who is a World Cup skier of great promise. Hanni is also a brilliant tennis player, sports car buff, and motorcyclist. Andreas also enjoys tennis and motorcycling.

WEIGHT LIFTING

UNITED STATES WEIGHTLIFTING FEDERATION
MEN'S NATIONAL CHAMPIONSHIPS
(San Francisco, Calif., June 6–7, 1981)

	Snatch	C&J[1]	Total
114 lb—Wrenn Norvell, Chicago	148.5	198	346.5
123 lb—Albert Hood, Los Angeles	220	258.5	478.5
132 lb—Phil Sanderson, Billings, Mont.	236.5	291.5	528
148 lb—Cal Schake, Butler, Pa.	291.5	346.5	638
165 lb—Fred Lowe, East Lansing, Mich.	297	396	693
181 lb—Val Balison, Superior, Mont.	313.5	407	720.5
198 lb—Kevin Winter, San Jose, Calif.	352	401.5	753.5
220 lb—Ken Clark, Pacifica, Calif.	330	440	770
242 lb—Guy Carlton, Decatur, Ill.	352	440	792
Over 242 lb—Jerome Hannan, Colorado Springs, Colo.	385	478.5	863.5
Team—York Barbell Club, York, Pa.			

Outstanding lifter—Cal Schake, Butler, Pa.
1. Clean and jerk.

WOMEN'S NATIONAL CHAMPIONSHIPS
(Waterloo, Iowa, May 23, 1981)

	Snatch	C&J[1]	Total
97 lb—Joette Weber, Kokomo, Ind.	71.5	88	159.5
105.8 lb—Quin Burgess, Newnan, Ga.	82.5	110	192.5
114 lb—Mary Beth Cervenak, Malmstrom Air Force Base, Mont.	99	154	253
123 lb—Lisa Semm, Batavia, Ill.	66	104.5	170.5
132 lb—Kim Besuden, West Lafayette, Ind.	93.5	132	225.5
148¾ lb—Judy Glenney, Farmington, N.M.	165	214.5	379.5
165¼ lb—Karyn Bastiansen, New York City	143	176	319
181¾ lb—Karen Weaver, West Lafayette, Ind.	82.5	104.5	187
Over 181¾ lb—Lorna Griffin, Huntington Beach, Calif.	159.5	209	368.5
Team—Purdue University.			

Outstanding lifter—Judy Glenney, Farmington, N.M.
1. Clean and jerk.

SPEED SKATING

U.S. OUTDOOR CHAMPIONS

Men		1976	John Wurster	1967	Jean Ashworth
1959–60	Ken Bartholomew	1977	Jim Chapin	1968	Helen Lutsch
1961	Ed Rudolph	1978	Bill Heinkel	1969	Sally Blatchford
1962	Floyd Bedbury	1979	Erik Henriksen	1970–71	Sheila Young
1963	Tom Gray	1980	Greg Oly	1972	Ruth Moore, Nancy Thorne
1964	Neil Blatchford	1981	Tom Grannes	1973	Nancy Class
1965–66	Rich Wurster			1974	Kris Garbe
1967	Mike Passarella	**Women**		1975	Nancy Swider
1968–70	Peter Cefalu	1960	Mary Novak	1976	Connie Carpenter
1971	Jack Walters	1961	Jean Ashworth	1977	Liz Crowe
1972	Barth Levy	1962	Jean Omelenchuk	1978	Paula Class, Betsy Davis
1973	Mike Woods	1963	Jean Ashworth	1979	Gretchen Byrnes
1974	Leigh Barczewski, Mike Passarella	1964	Diane White	1980	Shari Miller
		1965	Jean Omelenchuk	1981	Lisa Merrifield
1975	Rich Wurster	1966	Diane White		

WORLD SPEED SKATING RECORDS

Men

Distance	Time	Skater	Place	Year
500 m	0:36.91	Yevgeny Kulikov, U.S.S.R.	Alma-Ata, U.S.S.R.	1981
1,000 m	1:13.39	Gaetan Boucher, Canada	Davos, Switzerland	1981
1,500 m	1:55.18	Jan Egil Storholt, Norway	Medeo, U.S.S.R.	1977
3,000 m	4:04.01	Eric Heiden, U.S.	Inzell, Austria	1978
5,000 m	6:56.90	Kay Arne Stenshjemmet, Norway	Medeo, U.S.S.R.	1977
10,000 m	14:25.71	Dmitri Ogloblin, U.S.S.R.	Alma Ata, U.S.S.R.	1980

Women

Distance	Time	Skater	Place	Year
500 m	0:40.18	Christa Rothenburger, E. Germany	Alma-Ata, U.S.S.R.	1981
1,000 m	1:20.81	Natalya Petruseva, U.S.S.R.	Alma-Ata, U.S.S.R.	1981
1,500 m	2:05.39	Natalya Petruseva, U.S.S.R.	Alma-Ata, U.S.S.R.	1981
3,000 m	4:21.70	Gabi Schoenbrunn, E. Germany	Alma-Ata, U.S.S.R.	1981

U.S. OUTDOOR CHAMPIONS
(Milwaukee, Wis., Jan. 31-Feb. 1, 1981)

Men—Tom Grannes, Minneapolis, Minn.
Women—Lisa Merrifield, Butte, Mont.
Intermediate men—Mike Jansen, West Allis, Wis.
Intermediate women—Bonnie Blair, Champaign, Ill.
Junior boys—Dan Jansen, West Allis, Wis.
Junior girls—Angela Zuckerman, Whitefish, Bay, Wis.

U.S. INDOOR CHAMPIONS
(Butte, Mont., March 21-22, 1981)

Men—Scott Drebes, Champaign, Ill.
Women—Mary Polaski, Colorado Springs, Colo.
Intermediate men—David Besteman, Madison, Wis.
Intermediate women—Bonnie Blair, Champaign, Ill.
Junior boys—Marty Pierce, St. Francis, Wis.
Junior girls—Becky Mane, Milwaukee, Wis.

NORTH AMERICAN OUTDOOR CHAMPIONS
(Winnipeg, Manitoba, Feb. 7-8, 1981)

Men—Kevin O'Brien, Prince Edward Isle
Women—Lisa Merrifield, Butte, Mont.
Intermediate men—Paul Grannes, Minneapolis, Minn.
Intermediate women—Katie Class, St. Paul, Minn.
Junior boys—Dan Jansen, West Allis, Wis.
Junior girls—Angela Zuckerman, Whitefish Bay, Wis.

NORTH AMERICAN INDOOR CHAMPIONS
(Midland, Mich., March 28-29, 1981)

Men—Gaetan Boucher, Quebec
Women—Margie Burns, Riverside, Ill.
Intermediate men—Guy Daignault, Quebec

Intermediate women—Louise Begin, Quebec
Junior boys—Marcel Tremblay, Quebec
Junior girls—Tie between Marie Martin, Quebec, and Nathalie Grondin, Quebec

WORLD CHAMPIONSHIPS—1981

Men

(Oslo, Norway, Feb. 14–15, 1981)

Champion—A. Sjobrend, Norway	167.781 pts
500 m—K.A. Stenshjemmet, Norway	0:38.72
1,500 m—A. Sjobrend, Norway	1:58.46
5,000 m—P. Kleine, Netherlands	7:16.17
10,000 m—S. Berezin, Soviet Union	14:51.38

Women

(Quebec City, Canada, Feb. 7–8, 1981)

Champion—Natalya Petruseva, Soviet Union	178.947 pts
500 m—Natalya Petruseva, Soviet Union	0:42.93
1,000 m—Natalya Petruseva, Soviet Union	1:25.90
1,500 m—Karin Enke, East Germany	2:13.58
3,000 m—A. Pleshkova, Soviet Union	4:44.51

WORLD SPRINT CHAMPIONSHIPS—1981
(Grenoble, France, Feb. 21–22, 1981)

Men's champion—Frode Roenning, Norway	153.700 pts
Women's champion—Karin Enke, East Germany	168.640 pts

WORLD JUNIOR CHAMPIONSHIPS—1981
(Elverum, Norway, Feb. 28-March 1, 1981)

Men's champion—Bjorn Nyland, Norway	170.398 pts
Women's champion—Sarah Docter, United States	179.525 pts

SPORTS ORGANIZATIONS AND INFORMATION BUREAUS

Amateur Athletic Union of the U.S. 3400 West 86th St., Indianapolis, Indiana 46862

Amateur Bicycle League of America. *See* United States Cycling Federation

Amateur Hockey Association of the U.S. 10 Lake Circle, Colorado Springs, Colo. 80906

Amateur Skating Union of the U.S. 4423 West Deming Place, Chicago, Ill. 60639

Amateur Softball Association. 2801 N.E. 50th St., P.O. Box 11437, Oklahoma City, Okla. 73111

Amateur Trapshooting Association of America. Vandalia, Ohio 45377

American Amateur Baseball Congress. Box 4, Battle Creek, Mich. 49016

American Association (baseball). P.O. Box 382, Wichita, Kan. 67201

American Bowling Congress. 5301 South 76th St., Greendale, Wis. 53129

American Canoe Association. 4260 East Evans Ave., Denver, Colo. 80222

American Fencers League of America. 249 Eton Place, Westfield, N.J. 07090

American Hockey League. P.O. Box 100, West Springfield, Mass. 01089

American Horse Shows Association. 527 Madison Ave., New York, N.Y. 10022

American Kennel Club. 51 Madison Ave., New York, N.Y. 10010

American League (baseball). 280 Park Ave., New York, N.Y. 10017

American Motorcycle Association. P.O. Box 141, Westerville, Ohio 43081

American Power Boat Association. 415 Burns Drive, Detroit, Mich. 48214

American Water Ski Association. State Route 550 at Carl Floyd Road, P.O. Box 191, Winter Haven, Fla. 33880

Association of Intercollegiate Athletics for Women. 1201 16th St. N.W., Washington, D.C.

Baseball Commissioner. 75 Rockefeller Plaza, New York, N.Y. 10019

Baseball Hall of Fame. Cooperstown, N.Y.

Bowling Proprietors' Association of America. P.O. Box 5802, Arlington, Texas 76011

Central Hockey League. 5740 Oakland Ave., St. Louis, Mo. 63110

Championship Auto Racing Teams (CART). 12626 US 12, Brooklyn, Mich., 49230

Eastern College Athletic Conference. P.O. Box 3, Centerville, Mass. 02632

Elias Sports Bureau. 500 Fifth Ave., New York, N.Y. 10036

Fish and Wildlife Service. Department of the Interior, Washington, D.C. 20240

Football Hall of Fame (college). Kings Mills, Ohio 45034

Football Hall of Fame (pro). Canton, Ohio 44708

International Amateur Athletic Federation. Halton House, 23 Holborn, London, E. C. 1, England

Intercollegiate (Big Ten) Conference (1896). 1111 Plaza Dr., Schaumburg, Ill. 60195

International Game Fish Association. 3000 East Las Olas Blvd., Fort Lauderdale, Fla. 33316

International League (baseball). Box 608, Grove City, Ohio 43123

International Motor Sports Association. P.O. Box 805, Fairfield, Conn. 06430

International Olympic Committee. Chateau de Vidy, Lausanne, Switzerland

The Jockey Club. 300 Park Ave., New York, N.Y. 10022

Ladies Professional Golf Association. 919 Third Ave., New York, N.Y. 10022

Little League Baseball. Williamsport, Pa. 17701

National Archery Association. 1951 Geraldson Drive, Lancaster, Pa. 17601

National Association for Girls and Women in Sports. 1201 16th St. N.W., Washington, D.C.

National Association of Amateur Oarsmen. 4 Boathouse Row, Philadelphia, Pa. 19130

National Association of Intercollegiate Athletics. 1221 Baltimore St., Kansas City, Mo. 64105

National Association of Professional Baseball Leagues (minors). P.O. Box A, St. Petersburg, Fla. 33731

National Association for Stock Car Auto Racing. P.O. Box K, Daytona Beach, Fla. 32015

National Baseball Congress. Wichita, Kan. 67201

National Basketball Association. Olympic Tower, 645 Fifth Ave., New York, N.Y. 10022

National Collegiate Athletic Association. P.O. Box 1906, Shawnee Mission, Kan. 66222

National Duck Pin Bowling Congress. 711–14th St. N.W., Washington, D.C. 20005

National Field Archery Association. Rt. 2, Box 514, Redlands, Calif. 92373

National Football Foundation. 201 East 42nd St., New York, N.Y. 10017. *See also:* Football Hall of Fame (college)

National Football League. 410 Park Ave., New York, N.Y. 10022

National Hockey League. 922 Sun Life Bldg., Montreal, Que., Canada

National Horseshoe Pitchers Association. Route 5, Lucasville, Ohio 45648

National Hot Rod Association. P.O. Box 150, North Hollywood, Calif. 91603

National Junior College Athletic Association. P.O. Box 1586, Hutchinson, Kan. 67501

National Lawn Tennis Hall of Fame. Newport Casino, Newport, R.I., 02840

National League (baseball). 1 Rockefeller Plaza, New York, N.Y. 10019

National Rifle Association of America. 1600 Rhode Island Ave., N.W., Washington, D.C. 20036

National Skeet Shooting Association. P.O. Box 28188, San Antonio, Tex. 78228

New York Racing Association. P.O. Box 90, Jamaica, N.Y. 11417

New York State Athletic Commission (boxing). 226 W. 47th St., New York, N.Y. 10036

National Shuffleboard Association. 5612 Plattsburg Road, Springfield, Ohio, 45505

North American Yacht Racing Union. *See* United States Yacht Racing Union

North American Soccer League. 1133 Avenue of the Americas, New York, N.Y. 10036

Pacific Coast League (baseball). 2509 South Shannon Drive, Tempe, Ariz., 85282

Professional Bowlers Association. 1720 Merriman Road, Akron, Ohio 44313

Professional Golfers' Association of America. Box 12458, Lake Park, Fla. 33403

Rodeo Cowboys Association. 2929 W. 19th Ave., Denver, Colo. 80204

Roller Skating Rink Operators Association. P.O. Box 81846, Lincoln, Neb. 68501

Sports Car Club of America. 6750 So. Emporia St., Englewood, Colo. 80112

Tennis Hall of Fame. *See* National Lawn Tennis Hall of Fame

Thoroughbred Racing Associations of the U.S. 3000 Marcus Ave., Lake Success, N.Y. 11040

Track and Field Association of the USA. 10920 Ambassador Drive, Kansas City, Mo., 64153

Track and Field Hall of Fame. Charleston, W.Va.

United States of America Roller Skating Confederation. 7700 "A" Street, Lincoln, Neb. 68501

United States Auto Club. 4910 West 16th Street, Speedway, Indiana, 46224

United States Badminton Association. 787 South Orange Grove Blvd., Unit 9, Pasadena, Calif. 91105

U.S. Chess Federation. 186 Route 9W, New Windsor, N.Y. 12550

U.S. Cycling Federation. Box 669, Wall Street Station, New York, N.Y. 10005

U.S. Figure Skating Association. 575 Boylston St., Boston, Mass. 02116

U.S. Golf Association. Far Hills, N.J. 07931

U.S. Handball Association. 4101 Dempster St., Skokie, Ill. 60077

U.S. Men's Curling Association. 12822 Water Street, Duluth, Minn., 55008

U.S. Olympic Committee. 1750 East Boulder Street, Colorado Springs, Colo. 80909

U.S. Olympic Training Center. P.O. Box 4000, Colorado Springs, Colo. 80930

U.S. Parachute Association. 806–15th St. N.W., Washington, D.C. 20005

U.S. Polo Association. 1301 W. 22nd St., Oak Brook, Ill. 60521

U.S. Ski Association. 1726 Champa St., Denver, Colorado 80202

U.S. Ski Team. P.O. Box 100, Park City, Utah 84060

U.S. Soccer Federation. 350 Fifth Ave., New York, N.Y. 10001

U.S. Squash Racquets Association. 211 Ford Road, Bala-Cynwyd, Pa., 19004

U.S. Table Tennis Association. 3466 Bridgeland Drive, Bridgeland Square Building, St. Louis, Mo. 63044

U.S. Tennis Association. 51 E. 42nd St., New York, N.Y. 10017

U.S. Touch and Flag Football Association. 2705 Normandy Drive, Youngstown, Ohio, 49511

U.S. Trotting Association. 750 Michigan Ave., Columbus, Ohio 43215

U.S. Volleyball Association. 557 Fourth Street, San Francisco, Calif. 94107

U.S. Women's Curling Association. 635 Chatham Road, Glenview, Ill. 60025

U.S. Yacht Racing Union. P.O. Box 209, Goat Island, Newport, R.I. 02840

Women's International Bowling Congress. 5301 S. 76th St., Greendale, Wis. 53129

STANDARD MEASUREMENTS IN SPORTS

BASEBALL

Home plate to pitcher's box: 60 feet 6 inches.
Plate to second base: 127 feet 3⅜ inches.
Distance from base to base (home plate included): 90 feet.
Size of bases: 15 inches by 15 inches.
Pitcher's plate: 24 inches by 6 inches.
Batter's box: 3 feet by 4 feet.
Home plate: 17 inches by 12 inches by 12 inches, cut to a point at rear.
Home plate to backstop: Not less than 60 feet (recommended).
Weight of ball: Not less than 5 ounces nor more than 5¼ ounces.
Circumference of ball: Not less than 9 inches nor more than 9¼ inches.
Bat: Must be round, not over 2¾ inches in diameter at thickest part, nor more than 42 inches in length, and of solid wood in one piece or laminated.

FOOTBALL

(N.C.A.A.)

Length of field: 120 yards. (including 10 yards of end zone at each end).
Width of field: 53⅓ yards (160 feet).
Height of goal posts: At least 20 feet.
Height of crossbar: 10 feet.
Width of goal posts (above crossbar): 23 feet 4 inches, inside to inside, and not more than 24 feet, outside to outside.
Length of ball: 11 to 11.25 inches (long axis).
Circumference of ball: 21.25 to 21.50 inches (middle); 28 to 28.5 inches (long axis).

LAWN TENNIS

Size of court: Rectangle 78 feet long and 27 feet wide (singles); 78 feet long and 36 feet wide (doubles).

Height of net: 3 feet in center, gradually rising to reach 3-foot 6-inch posts at a point 3 feet outside each side of court.
Ball: Shall be more than 2½ inches and less than 2⅝ inches in diameter and weight more than 2 ounces and less than 2¹/₁₆ ounces.
Service line: 21 feet from net.

HOCKEY

Size of rink: 200 feet long by 85 feet wide surrounded by a wooden wall not less than 40 inches and not more than 48 inches above level of ice.
Size of goal: 6 feet wide by 4 feet in height.
Puck: 1 inch thick and 3 inches in diameter; made of vulcanized rubber; weight 5½ to 6 ounces.
Length of stick: Not more than 58 inches from heel to end of shaft nor 12½ inches from heel to end of blade. Blade should not be more than 3 inches in width but not less than 2 inches, except goal keeper's stick, which shall not exceed 3½ inches in width except at the heel, where it must not exceed 4½ inches.

BOWLING

Lane dimensions: Overall length 62 feet 10³/₁₆ inches, measuring from foul line to pit (not including tail plank), with ½ inch tolerance permitted. Foul line to center of No. 1 pinspot 60 feet, with ½ inch tolerance permitted. Lane width, 41½ inches with a tolerance of ½ inch permitted. Approach, not less than 15 feet. Gutters, 9 ⁵/₁₆ inches wide with ³/₁₆ plus or ⁵/₁₆ minus tolerances permitted.
Ball: Circumference, not more than 27 inches. Weight, 16 pounds maximum.

GOLF

The ball, specifications: Broadened to require that the ball be designed to perform as if it were spherically symmetrical.

Velocity of ball: Not greater than 250 feet per second when tested on U.S.G.A. apparatus, with 2 percent tolerance.
Hole: 4¼ inches in diameter and at least 4 inches deep.
Clubs: 14 is the maximum number permitted.

BASKETBALL
(National Collegiate A.A. Rules)
Playing court: College: 94 feet long by 50 feet wide (ideal dimensions). High School: 84 feet long by 50 feet wide (ideal inside dimensions).
Baskets: Rings 18 inches in inside diameter, with white cord 12–mesh nets, 15 to 18 inches in length. Each ring is made of metal, is not more than ⅝ of an inch in diameter, and is bright orange in color.
Height of basket: 10 feet (upper edge).
Weight of ball: Not less than 20 ounces nor more than 22.
Circumference of ball: No greater than 30 inches and not less than 29½.

Free-throw line: 15 feet from the face of the backboard, 2 inches wide.

BOXING
Ring: Professional matches take place in an area not less than 18 nor more than 24 feet square including apron. It is enclosed by four covered ropes, each not less than one inch in diameter. The floor has a 2–inch padding of Ensolite (or equivalent) underneath ring cover that extends at least 6 inches beyond the roped area in the case of elevated rings. For A.A.U. boxing, not less than 16 nor more than 20 feet square within the ropes. The floor must extend beyond the ring ropes not less than 2 feet. The ring posts shall be connected to the ring ropes with the extension not shorter than 18 inches and must be properly padded.
Gloves: In professional fights, not less than 8–ounce gloves generally are used. A.A.U., not less than 10 ounces for all divisions; for international competition not less than 8 ounces.

BADMINTON

WORLD CHAMPIONS—1980
Men—Rudy Hartono, Indonesia
Women—Wiharjo Verawaty, Indonesia

U.S. BADMINTON ASSOCIATION CHAMPIONSHIPS—1980
(Offutt Air Force Base, Neb., April 16–19, 1980)
Men's singles—Gary Higgins, Alhambra, Calif.
Women's singles—Cheryl Carton, San Diego, Calif.
Men's doubles—Matt Fogarty, Duxbury, Mass., Mike Walker, Manhattan Beach, Calif.
Women's doubles—Pam Brady, Flint, Mich., Judianne Kelly, Costa Mesa, Calif.
Mixed doubles—Mike Walker, Manhattan Beach, Calif., Judianne Kelly, Costa Mesa, Calif.

Seniors
Men's singles—Jim Poole, Westminster, Calif.
Men's doubles—Don Paup, Washington D.C., Jim Poole, Westminster, Calif.
Women's doubles—Claire Bowyer, Canada, Ethel Marshall, Williamsville, N.Y.
Mixed doubles—Don Paup, Washington, D.C., Sondra Fogarty, Duxbury, Mass.

Masters
Men's singles—Ted Moehlmann, Warson Woods, Mo.
Men's doubles—James McQuie, Kirkwood, Mo., Ted Moehlmann, Warson Woods, Mo.
Mixed doubles—Jim Bell, Ypsilanti, Mich., Ethel Marshall, Williamsville, N.Y.

Grand Masters
Men's singles—Waldo Lyon, San Diego, Calif.
Men's doubles—Taylor Caffery, New Orleans, La., Roy Nusbaum, Granger, Ind.

ALL-ENGLAND CHAMPIONSHIPS—1980
(Wembley, England, March 19–22, 1980)
Men's singles—Prakash Padukone, India
Women's singles—Lene Koppen, Denmark
Men's doubles—Johan Wahjudi and Tjun Tjun, Indonesia
Women's doubles—Nora Perry and Gillian Gilks, England
Mixed doubles—Mike Tredgett and Nora Perry, England

WORLD CHAMPIONSHIPS—1980
(Jakarta, Indonesia, May 27-June 1, 1980)
Men's singles—Rudy Hartono, Indonesia
Women's singles—Wiharjo Verawaty, Indonesia
Men's doubles—Ade Chandra and Christian Hadinata, Indonesia
Women's doubles—Nora Perry and Jane Webster, England
Mixed doubles—Christian Hadinata and Imelda Wigoeno, Indonesia

ROLLER SKATING

NATIONAL CHAMPIONSHIPS—1980
Men's singles—Michael Glatz, San Diego, Calif.
Women's singles—Kathleen O'Brien DiFelice, Cherry Hill, N.J.
Men's figures—Tony St. Jacques, Virginia Beach, Va.
Women's figures—Anna Conklin, Bakersfield, Calif.
Junior men—Rick Monturo, Cleveland
Junior women—Gerry Goodman, Chula Vista, Calif.
Junior men's figures—Dallas Oskey, Flint, Mich.
Junior women's figures—Tammy DeWulf, Brighton, Mich.
Pairs—Paul Price and Tina Kneisley, Brighton, Mich.
Junior pairs—Rick Monturo and Valerie Acree, Cleveland
Dance—Harvey White and Beth Wahlig, Newark, Del.
Junior dance—Curt Cherry and Rae Marie Bonacci, Fountain Valley, Calif.
Free dance—Scott Oakley and Gladys Smith, East Meadow, N.Y.
International-style dance—Charles Kirchner and Linda Todd, Cherry Hill, N.J.
Esquire dance—Ralph Crews and Jean Meyers, Decatur, Ga.

Speed
Men—Robb Dunn, Farmington Hills, Mich.
Women—Linda Swaim, High Point, N.C.
2-man relay—Robb Dunn and Chuck Jackson, Farmington Hills, Mich.
2-woman relay—Sandra Dulaney and Karen Johnson, Santa Ana, Calif.
4-man relay—Chris Snyder, Mark Sutton, Marty Sutton, Mike Vouklizas, Irving, Tex.
4-woman relay—Kathy Katovich, Denise McLeod, Tammy Griffith, Sue Dooley, Farmington Hills, Mich.
Mixed couples relay—Robb Dunn, Denise McLeod, Farmington Hills, Mich.
Mixed-4 relay—Robb Dunn, Chuck Jackson, Kathy Katovich, Denise McLeod, Farmington Hills, Mich.

LACROSSE

NATIONAL INTERCOLLEGIATE CHAMPIONS

1946	Navy	1959	Army, Johns Hopkins, Maryland	1972	Virginia
1947–48	Johns Hopkins			1973	Maryland
1949	Johns Hopkins, Navy	1960	Navy	1974	Johns Hopkins
1950	Johns Hopkins	1961	Army, Navy	1975	Maryland
1951	Army, Princeton	1962–66	Navy	1976–77	Cornell
1952	Virginia, R.P.I.	1967	Johns Hopkins, Maryland, Navy	1978–80	Johns Hopkins
1953	Princeton			1981	North Carolina
1954	Navy	1968	Johns Hopkins		
1955–56	Maryland	1969	Army, Johns Hopkins	1. First year of N.C.A.A. Championship Tournaments.	
1957	Johns Hopkins	1970	Johns Hopkins, Navy, Virginia		
1958	Army	1971[1]	Cornell		

NATIONAL COLLEGIATE ATHLETIC ASSOCIATION CHAMPIONSHIPS

DIVISION I
Final

(Princeton, N.J., May 30, 1981)
North Carolina 14, Johns Hopkins 13

Semifinals

Johns Hopkins 10, Virginia 6
North Carolina 17, Navy 8

Quarterfinals

Navy 16, Army 10
North Carolina 13, Syracuse 6
Johns Hopkins 19, Maryland 14
Virginia 16, Massachusetts 12

ALL-AMERICAN TEAM

DIVISION I

Attack—Mike Burnett, North Carolina; Jeff Cook, Johns Hopkins; Syd Abernathy, Navy
Midfield—Brendan Schneck, Johns Hopkins; Peter Schmitz, Massachusetts; Tom Donahue, Syracuse; Doug Hall, North Carolina
Defense—Bob Henry, Army; Mike McLaughlin, Navy; Jeff McKee, Syracuse
Goal—Tom Sears, North Carolina

DIVISION II
Final

(Garden City, Long Island, N.Y., May 17, 1981)
Adelphi 17, Loyola of Baltimore 14

DIVISION II

Attack—Ken King, Adelphi; Ed Hughes, Adelphi; Gary Hanley, Loyola
Midfield—David Maynes, Loyola; Kevin Meinsen, Adelphi; Dave Leistman, Adelphi
Defense—Ed Henegaux, Adelphi; Tim Rotanz, Adelphi; Joe Carrier, Loyola
Goal—Steve McCloskey, Loyola

DIVISION III
Final

(Geneva, N.Y., May 24, 1981)
Hobart 10, Cortland (N.Y.) State 8

DIVISION III

Attack—Jeff Kraus, Hobart; Mark Koetzner, Cortland; Mike Bracken, Salisbury State
Midfield—Mark Darcangelo, Hobart; Bill Sipperly, Hobart; Glenn Norris, Salisbury State
Defense—Jerry Demeo, Cortland; Kevin Martin, Hobart; James Rhode, Roanoke
Goal—Guy Van Arsdale, Hobart

ASSOCIATION FOR INTERCOLLEGIATE ATHLETICS FOR WOMEN

DIVISION I
(State College, Pa., May 16, 1981)

Final
Maryland 5, Ursinus 3

DIVISION II
Final
Delaware 8, Lehigh 4

DIVISION III
Final
Trenton State 7, Franklin and Marshall 6

WATER POLO

FINA WORLD CUP—1981

Champion—Soviet Union (6–0–1, 13 pts); 2. Yugoslavia (5–1–1, 11); 3. Cuba (4–2–1, 9); 4. United States (3–2–2, 8); 5. Spain (2–2–3, 7); 6. Hungary (3–4–0, 6); 7. Australia (1–6–0, 2); 8. Bulgaria (0–7–0, 0)

RODEO

PROFESSIONAL RODEO COWBOY ASSOCIATION, ALL AROUND COWBOY

1953	Bill Linderman	1962	Tom Nesmith	1975	Leo Camarillo and Tom Ferguson
1954	Buck Rutherford	1963–65	Dean Oliver		
1955	Casey Tibbs	1966–70	Larry Mahan	1976–79	Tom Ferguson
1956–59	Jim Shoulders	1971–72	Phil Lyne	1980	Paul Tierney
1960	Harry Tompkins	1973	Larry Mahan		
1961	Benny Reynolds	1974	Tom Ferguson		

TENNIS

Lawn tennis is a comparatively modern modification of the ancient game of court tennis. Major Walter Clopton Wingfield thought that something like court tennis might be played outdoors on lawns, and in December, 1873, at Nantclwyd, Wales, he introduced his new game under the name of *Sphairistike* at a lawn party. The game was a success and spread rapidly, but the name was a total failure and almost immediately disappeared when all the players and spectators began to refer to the new game as "lawn tennis." In the early part of 1874, a young lady named Mary Ewing Outerbridge returned from Bermuda to New York, bringing with her the implements and necessary equipment of the new game, which she had obtained from a British Army supply store in Bermuda. Miss Outerbridge and friends played the first game of lawn tennis in the United States on the grounds of the Staten Island Cricket and Baseball Club in the spring of 1874.

For a few years, the new game went along in haphazard fashion until about 1880, when standard measurements for the court and standard equipment within definite limits became the rule. In 1881, the U.S. Lawn Tennis Association (whose name was changed in 1975 to U.S. Tennis Association) was formed and conducted the first national championship at Newport, R.I. The international matches for the Davis Cup began with a series between the British and United States players on the courts of the Longwood Cricket Club, Chestnut Hill, Mass., in 1900, with the home players winning.

Professional tennis, which got its start in 1926 when the French star Suzanne Lenglen was paid $50,000 for a tour, received full recognition in 1968. Staid old Wimbledon, the London home of what are considered the world championships, let the pros compete. This decision ended a long controversy over open tennis and changed the format of the competition. The United States championships were also opened to the pros and the site of the event, long held at Forest Hills, N.Y., was shifted to the National Tennis Center in Flushing Meadows, N.Y., in 1978. Pro tours for men and women became worldwide in play that continued throughout the year.

DAVIS CUP CHAMPIONSHIPS
No matches in 1901, 1910, 1915–18, and 1940–45.

1900	United States 3, British Isles 0	1929	France 3, United States 2	1958	United States 3, Australia 2
1902	United States 3, British Isles 2	1930	France 4, United States 1	1959	Australia 3, United States 2
1903	British Isles 4, United States 1	1931	France 3, Great Britain 2	1960	Australia 4, Italy 1
1904	British Isles 5, Belgium 0	1932	France 3, United States 2	1961	Australia 5, Italy 0
1905	British Isles 5, United States 0	1933	Great Britain 3, France 2	1962	Australia 5, Mexico 0
1906	British Isles 5, United States 0	1934	Great Britain 4, United States 1	1963	United States 3, Australia 2
1907	Australasia 3, British Isles 2	1935	Great Britain 5, United States 0	1964	Australia 3, United States 2
1908	Australasia 3, United States 2	1936	Great Britain 3, Australia 2	1965	Australia 4, Spain 1
1909	Australasia 5, United States 0	1937	United States 4, Great Britain 1	1966	Australia 4, India 1
1911	Australasia 5, United States 0	1938	United States 3, Australia 2	1967	Australia 4, Spain 1
1912	British Isles 3, Australasia 2	1939	Australia 3, United States 2	1968	United States 4, Australia 1
1913	United States 3, British Isles 2	1946	United States 5, Australia 0	1969	United States 5, Romania 0
1914	Australasia 3, United States 2	1947	United States 4, Australia 1	1970	United States 5, West Germany 0
1919	Australasia 4, British Isles 1	1948	United States 5, Australia 0	1971	United States 3, Romania 2
1920	United States 5, Australasia 0	1949	United States 4, Australia 1	1972	United States 3, Romania 2
1921	United States 5, Japan 0	1950	Australia 4, United States 1	1973	Australia 5, United States 0
1922	United States 4, Australasia 1	1951	Australia 3, United States 2	1974	South Africa (Default by India)
1923	United States 4, Australasia 1	1952	Australia 4, United States 1	1975	Sweden 3, Czechoslovakia 2
1924	United States 5, Australasia 0	1953	Australia 3, United States 2	1976	Italy 4, Chile 1
1925	United States 5, France 0	1954	United States 3, Australia 2	1977	Australia 3, Italy 1
1926	United States 4, France 1	1955	Australia 5, United States 0	1978	United States 4, Britain 1
1927	France 3, United States 2	1956	Australia 5, United States 0	1979	United States 5, Italy 0
1928	France 4, United States 1	1957	Australia 3, United States 2	1980	Czechoslovakia 3, Italy 2

FEDERATION CUP CHAMPIONSHIPS
World team competition for women conducted by International Lawn Tennis Federation

1963	United States 2, Australia 1	1969	United States 2, Australia 1	1975	Czechoslovakia 3, Australia 0
1964	Australia 2, United States 1	1970	Australia 3, West Germany 0	1976	United States 2, Australia 1
1965	Australia 2, United States 1	1971	Australia 3, Britain 0	1977	United States 2, Australia 1
1966	United States 3, West Germany 0	1972	South Africa 2, Britain 1	1978	United States 2, Australia 1
1967	United States 2, Britain 0	1973	Australia 3, South Africa 0	1979	United States 3, Australia 0
1968	Australia 3, Netherlands 0	1974	Australia 2, United States 1	1980	United States 3, Australia 0

FOUR PLAYERS WIN GRAND SLAM OF TENNIS

Only four players, two men and two women, have won the Grand Slam of Tennis by winning the Australian, French, Wimbledon, and United States singles championships. Rod Laver of Australia did it twice, in 1962 and again in 1969 when the tourneys were opens. Don Budge, an American, was the first to complete the slam in 1938. Maureen Connolly of California in 1953 was the first woman to take the four titles. Margaret Smith Court of Australia won them all in 1970.

U.S. CHAMPIONS

Singles—Men

NATIONAL

1881–87	Richard D. Sears	1915	William Johnston	1944–45	Frank Parker	1968	Arthur Ashe[3]
1888–89	Henry Slocum, Jr.	1916	R. N. William II	1946–47	Jack Kramer	1969	Stan Smith[3]
1890–92	Oliver S. Campbell	1917–18	R. Lindley Murray[2]	1948–49	Richard Gonzales		
		1919	William Johnston	1950	Arthur Larsen	**OPEN**	
1893–94	Robert D. Wrenn	1920–25	Bill Tilden	1951–52	Frank Sedgman	1968	Arthur Ashe
1895	Fred H. Hovey	1926–27	Jean Rene Lacoste	1953	Tony Trabert	1969	Rod Laver
1896–97	Robert D. Wrenn	1928	Henri Cochet	1954	Vic Seixas	1970	Ken Rosewall
1898–		1929	Bill Tilden	1955	Tony Trabert	1971	Stan Smith
1900	Malcolm Whitman	1930	John H. Doeg	1956	Ken Rosewall	1972	Ilie Nastase
1901–02	William A. Larned	1931–32	Ellsworth Vines	1957	Mal Anderson	1973	John Newcombe
1903	Hugh L. Doherty	1933–34	Fred J. Perry	1958	Ashley Cooper	1974	Jimmy Connors
1904	Holcombe Ward	1935	Wilmer L. Allison	1959–60	Neale Fraser	1975	Manuel Orantes
1905	Beals C. Wright	1936	Fred J. Perry	1961	Roy Emerson	1976	Jimmy Connors
1906	William J. Clothier	1937–38	Don Budge	1962	Rod Laver	1977	Guillermo Vilas
1907–11	William A. Larned	1939	Robert L. Riggs	1963	Rafael Osuna	1978	Jimmy Connors
1912–13	Maurice McLoughlin[1]	1940	Donald McNeill	1964	Roy Emerson	1979	John McEnroe
		1941	Robert L. Riggs	1965	Manuel Santana	1980–81	John McEnroe
1914	R. N. Williams II	1942	Fred Schroeder	1966	Fred Stolle		
		1943	Joseph Hunt	1967	John Newcombe		

Singles—Women

NATIONAL

1887	Ellen F. Hansel	1904	May Sutton	1931	Helen Wills Moody	1962	Margaret Smith
1888–89	Bertha Townsend	1905	Elisabeth H. Moore	1932–35	Helen Jacobs	1963–64	Maria Bueno
1890	Ellen C. Roosevelt			1936	Alice Marble	1965	Margaret Smith
1891–92	Mabel E. Cahill	1906	Helen Homans	1937	Anita Lizana	1966	Maria Bueno
1893	Aline M. Terry	1907	Evelyn Sears	1938–40	Alice Marble	1967	Billie Jean King
1894	Helen R. Helwig	1908	Maud Bargar-Wallach	1941	Sarah Palfrey Cooke	1968–69	Margaret Smith Court[3]
1895	Juliette P. Atkinson	1909–11	Hazel V. Hotchkiss	1942–44	Pauline Betz		
1896	Elisabeth H. Moore			1945	Sarah Cooke	**OPEN**	
		1912–14	Mary K. Browne	1946	Pauline Betz	1968	Virginia Wade
1897–98	Juliette P. Atkinson	1915–18	Molla Bjurstedt	1947	Louise Brough	1969–70	Margaret Court
		1919	Hazel Hotchkiss Wightman	1948–50	Margaret Osborne duPont	1971–72	Billie Jean King
1899	Marion Jones					1973	Margaret Court
1900	Myrtle McAteer	1920–22	Molla Bjurstedt Mallory	1951–53	Maureen Connolly	1974	Billie Jean King
1901	Elisabeth H. Moore			1954–55	Doris Hart	1975–78	Chris Evert
		1923–25	Helen N. Wills	1956	Shirley Fry	1979	Tracy Austin
1902	Marion Jones	1926	Molla B. Mallory	1957–58	Althea Gibson	1980	Chris Evert Lloyd
1903	Elisabeth H. Moore	1927–29	Helen N. Wills	1959	Maria Bueno	1981	Tracy Austin
		1930	Betty Nuthall	1960–61	Darlene Hard		

Doubles—Men

NATIONAL

1920	Bill Johnston–C. J. Griffin	1942	Gardnar Mulloy–Bill Talbert	1957	Ashley Cooper–Neale Fraser
1921–22	Bill Tilden–Vincent Richards	1943	Jack Kramer–Frank Parker	1958	Ham Richardson–Alex Olmedo
1923	Bill Tilden–B. I. C. Norton	1944	Don McNeill–Bob Falkenburg	1959–60	Neale Fraser–Roy Emerson
1924	H. O. Kinsey–R. G. Kinsey	1945	Gardnar Mulloy–Bill Talbert	1961	Chuck McKinley–Dennis Ralston
1925–26	Vincent Richards–R. N. Williams II	1946	Gardnar Mulloy–Bill Talbert		
		1947	Jack Kramer–Fred Schroeder	1962	Rafael Osuna–Antonio Palafox
1927	Bill Tilden–Frank Hunter	1948	Gardnar Mulloy–Bill Talbert	1963–64	Chuck McKinley–Dennis Ralston
1928	G. M. Lott, Jr.–V. Hennessy	1949	John Bromwich–William Sidwell		
1929–30	G. M. Lott, Jr.–J. H. Doeg			1965–66	Fred Stolle–Roy Emerson
1931	W. L. Allison–John Van Ryn	1950	John Bromwich–Frank Sedgman	1967	John Newcombe–Tony Roche
1932	E. H. Vines, Jr.–Keith Gledh			1968	Stan Smith–Bob Lutz[3]
1933–34	G. M. Lott, Jr.–L. R. Stoefen	1951	Frank Sedgman–Ken McGregor	1969	Richard Crealy–Allan Stone[3]
1935	W. L. Allison–John Van Ryn	1952	Vic Seixas–Mervyn Rose		
1936	Don Budge–Gene Mako	1953	Mervyn Rose–Rex Hartwig	**OPEN**	
1937	G. von Cramm–H. Henkel	1954	Vic Seixas–Tony Trabert	1968	Stan Smith–Bob Lutz
1938	Don Budge–Gene Mako	1955	Kosei Kamo–Atsushi Miyagi	1969	Fred Stolle–Ken Rosewall
1939	A. K. Quist–J. E. Bromwich	1956	Lewis Hoad–Ken Rosewall	1970	Nikki Pilic–Fred Barthes
1940–41	Jack Kramer–F. R. Schroeder				

1. Challenge round abandoned in 1912. 2. Patriotic Tournament in 1917. 3. With the inaugural of the Open Tournament in 1968, the United States Lawn Tennis Association held a national championship at Longwood, Chestnut Hill, Mass. which barred contract professionals in 1968 and 1969.

1971	John Newcombe–Roger Taylor	1975	Jimmy Connors–Ilie Nastase	1978	Bob Lutz–Stan Smith
1972	Cliff Drysdale–Roger Taylor	1976	Marty Riessen–Tom Okker	1979	John McEnroe–Peter Fleming
1973	John Newcombe–Owen Davidson	1977	Frew McMillan–Bob Hewitt	1980	Stan Smith–Bob Lutz
1974	Bob Lutz–Stan Smith			1981	John McEnroe–Peter Fleming

Doubles—Women

NATIONAL

1924	G. W. Wightman–Helen Wills	1942–47	A. Louise Brough–Margaret	**OPEN**	
1925	Mary K. Browne–Helen Wills		Osborne	1968	Maria Bueno–Margaret Court
1926	Elizabeth Ryan–Eleanor Goss	1948–50	A. Louise Brough–Margaret O.	1969	Darlene Hard–Francoise Durr
1927	L. A. Godfree–Ermyntrude		duPont	1970	Margaret Court–Judy Dalton
	Harvey	1951–54	Doris Hart–Shirley Fry	1971	Rosemary Casals–Judy Dalton
1928	Hazel Hotchkiss Wightman–Helen Wills	1955–57	A. Louise Brough–Margaret O. duPont	1972	Francoise Durr–Betty Stove
1929	Phoebe Watson–L. R. C. Michell	1958–59	Darlene Hard–Jeanne Arth	1973	Margaret Court–Virginia Wade
		1960	Darlene Hard–Maria Bueno	1974	Billie Jean King–Rosemary Casals
1930	Betty Nuthall–Sarah Palfrey	1961	Darlene Hard–Lesley Turner	1975	Margaret Court–Virginia Wade
1931	Betty Nuthall–E. B. Wittingstall	1962	Darlene Hard–Maria Bueno	1976	Linky Boshoff–Ilana Kloss
1932	Helen Jacobs–Sarah Palfrey	1963	Margaret Smith–Robyn Ebbern	1977	Martina Navratilova–Betty Stove
1933	Betty Nuthall–Freda James	1964	Karen Hantze Susman–Billie Jean Moffitt	1978	Billie Jean King–Martina Navratilova
1934	Helen Jacobs–Sarah Palfrey				
1935	Helen Jacobs–Sarah Palfrey Fabyan	1965	Nancy Richey–Carole Caldwell Graebner	1979	Betty Stove–Wendy Turnbull
1936	Marjorie G. Van Ryn–Carolin Babcock	1966	Nancy Richey–Maria Bueno	1980	Billie Jean King–Martina Navratilova
1937–40	Sarah Palfrey Fabyan–Alice Marble	1967	Billie Jean King–Rosemary Casals	1981	Kathy Jordan–Anne Smith
1941	Sarah Palfrey Cooke–Margaret Osborne	1968	Margaret Court–Maria Bueno[3]		
		1969	Margaret Court–Virginia Wade[3]		

1. Challenge round abandoned in 1912. 2. Patriotic Tournament in 1917. 3. With the inaugural of the Open Tournament in 1968, the United States Lawn Tennis Association held a national championship at Longwood, Chestnut Hill, Mass. which barred contract professionals in 1968 and 1969.

U.S. INDOOR CHAMPIONS

Singles—Men

1964	Charles McKinley	1972	Stan Smith
1965	Erik Lundquist	1973–75	Jimmy Connors
1966	Charles Pasarell	1976	Ilie Nastase
1967	Charles Pasarell	1977	Bjorn Borg
1968	Cliff Richey	1978–79	Jimmy Connors
1969	Stan Smith	1980	John McEnroe
1970	Ilie Nastase	1981	Gene Mayer
1971	Clark Graebner		

Singles—Women

1964	Mary Ann Eisel	1972	Not held
1965	Nancy Richey	1973	Evonne Goolagong
1966	Billie Jean King	1974	Billie Jean King
1967	Billie Jean King	1975	Martina Navratilova
1968	Billie Jean King	1976	Virginia Wade
1969	Mary Ann Eisel	1977–81	Not held
1970	Mary Ann Curtis		
1971	Billie Jean King		

Doubles—Men

1967	Arthur Ashe–Charles Pasarell
1968	Thomas Koch–Tom Okker
1969	Stan Smith–Bob Lutz
1970	Arthur Ashe–Stan Smith
1971	Manuel Orantes–Juan Gisbert
1972	Manuel Orantes–Andres Gimeno
1973	Juan Gisbert–Jurgen Fassbender
1974	Jimmy Connors–Frew McMillan
1975	Jimmy Connors–Ilie Nastase
1976–77	Sherwood Stewart–Fred McNair
1978	Brian Gottfried–Raul Ramirez
1979	Wojtek Fibak–Tom Okker
1980	John McEnroe–Brian Gottfried
1981	Gene Mayer–Sandy Mayer

Doubles—Women

1967	Carol Aucamp–Mary Ann Eisel
1968	Rosemary Casals–Billie Jean King
1969	Mary Ann Eisel–Valerie Ziegenfuss
1970	Peaches Bartkowicz–Nancy Richey
1971	Billie Jean King–Rosemary Casals
1972	Not held
1973	Olga Morozova–Marina Kroshina
1974	Not held
1975	Billie Jean King–Rosemary Casals
1976	Rosemary Casals–Francoise Durr
1977–81	Not held

BRITISH (WIMBLEDON) CHAMPIONS
(Amateur from inception in 1877 through 1967)

Singles—Men

1908–09	Arthur Gore	1929	Jean Cochet	1950	Budge Patty	1964–65	Roy Emerson
1910–13	A. F. Wilding	1930	Bill Tilden	1951	Richard Savitt	1966	Manuel Santana
1914	N. E. Brookes	1931	S. B. Wood	1952	Frank Sedgman	1967	John Newcombe
1919	G. L. Patterson	1932	Ellsworth Vines	1953	Vic Siexas	1968–69	Rod Laver
1920–21	Bill Tilden	1933	J. H. Crawford	1954	Jaroslav Drobny	1970–71	John Newcombe
1922	G. L. Patterson	1934–36	Fred Perry	1955	Tony Trabert	1972	Stan Smith
1923	William Johnston	1937–38	Don Budge	1956–57	Lewis Hoad	1973	Jan Kodes
1924	Jean Borotra	1939	Robert L. Riggs	1958	Ashley Cooper	1974	Jimmy Connors
1925	Rene Lacoste	1946	Yvon Petra	1959	Alex Olmedo	1975	Arthur Ashe
1926	Jean Borotra	1947	Jack Kramer	1960	Neale Fraser	1976–80	Bjorn Borg
1927	Henri Cochet	1948	R. Falkenburg	1961–62	Rod Laver	1981	John McEnroe
1928	Rene Lacoste	1949	Fred Schroeder	1963	Chuck McKinley		

Singles—Women

1919–23	Lenglen	1937	D. E. Round	1959–60	Maria Bueno	1972–73	Billie Jean King
1924	Kathleen McKane	1938	Helen Wills Moody	1961	Angela Mortimer	1974	Chris Evert
1925	Lenglen	1939	Alice Marble	1962	Karen Susman	1975	Billie Jean King
1926	Godfree	1946	Pauline M. Betz	1963	Margaret Smith	1976	Chris Evert
1927–29	Helen Wills	1947	Margaret Osborne	1964	Maria Bueno	1977	Virginia Wade
1930	Helen Wills Moody	1948–50	A. Louise Brough	1965	Margaret Smith	1978–79	Martina Navratilova
1931	Frl. C. Aussen	1951	Doris Hart	1966–67	Billie Jean King		
1932–33	Helen Wills Moody	1952–54	Maureen Connolly	1968	Billie Jean King	1980	Evonne Goolagong Cawley
1934	D. E. Round	1955	A. Louise Brough	1969	Ann Jones		
1935	Helen Wills Moody	1956	Shirley Fry	1970	Margaret Court	1981	Chris Evert Lloyd
1936	Helen Jacobs	1957–58	Althea Gibson	1971	Evonne Goolagong		

Doubles—Men

1953	K. Rosewall–L. Hoad	1963	Rafael Osuna–Antonio Palafox	1974	John Newcombe–Tony Roche
1954	R. Hartwig–M. Rose	1964	Fred Stolle–Bob Hewitt	1975	Vitas Gerulaitis–Sandy Mayer
1955	R. Hartwig–L. Hoad	1965	John Newcombe–Tony Roche	1976	Brian Gottfried–Raul Ramirez
1956	L. Hoad–K. Rosewall			1977	Ross Case–Geoff Masters
1957	Gardnar Mulloy–Budge Patty	1966	John Newcombe–Ken Fletcher	1978	Frew McMillan–Bob Hewitt
1958	Sven Davidson–Ulf Schmidt	1967	Bob Hewitt–Frew McMillan	1979	Peter Fleming–John McEnroe
1959	Roy Emerson–Neale Fraser	1968–70	John Newcombe–Tony Roche	1980	Peter McNamara–Paul McNamee
1960	Dennis Ralston–Rafael Osuna	1971	Rod Laver–Roy Emerson		
1961	Roy Emerson–Neale Fraser	1972	Bob Hewitt–Frew McMillan	1981	John McEnroe–Peter Fleming
1962	Fred Stolle–Bob Hewitt	1973	Jimmy Connors–Ilie Nastase		

Doubles—Women

1956	Althea Gibson–Angela Buxton	1965	Billie Jean Moffitt–Maria Bueno	1975	Ann Kiyomura–Kazuko Sawamatsu
1957	Althea Gibson–Darlene Hard				
1958	Althea Gibson–Maria Bueno	1966	Nancy Richey–Maria Bueno	1976	Chris Evert–Martina Navratilova
1959	Darlene Hard–Jeanne Arth	1967–68	Billie Jean King–Rosemary Casals		
1960	Darlene Hard–Maria Bueno			1977	Helen Cawley–JoAnne Russell
1961	Karen Hantze–Billie Jean Moffitt	1969	Margaret Court–Judy Tegart	1978	Wendy Turnbull–Kerry Reid
		1970–71	Billie Jean King–Rosemary Casals	1979	Billie Jean King–Martina Navratilova
1962	Karen Hantze Susman–Billie Jean Moffitt				
		1972	Billie Jean King–Betty Stove	1980	Kathy Jordan–Anne Smith
1963	Darlene Hard–Maria Bueno	1973	Billie Jean King–Rosemary Casals	1981	Martina Navratilova–Pam Shriver
1964	Margaret Smith–Les Turnerley	1974	Evonne Goolagong–Peggy Michel		

U.S. CHAMPIONSHIPS—1980

Open

(Flushing Meadows, N.Y., Aug. 26–Sept. 7, 1980)

Men's singles—Final: John McEnroe, Douglaston, N.Y., defeated Bjorn Borg, Sweden, 7–6, 6–1, 6–7, 5–7, 6–4. Semifinals: McEnroe defeated Jimmy Connors, Miami Beach, Fla., 6–4, 5–7, 0–6, 3–6, 7–6; Borg defeated Johan Kriek, South Africa, 4–6, 4–6, 6–1, 6–1, 6–1.

Women's singles—Final: Chris Evert Lloyd, Palm Springs, Calif. defeated Hana Mandlikova, Czechoslovakia, 5–7, 6–1, 6–1. Semifinals: Mrs. Lloyd defeated Tracy Auston, Rolling Hills, Calif., 4–6, 6–1, 6–1; Miss Mandlikova defeated Andrea Jaeger, Lincolnshire, Ill., 6–1, 3–6, 7–6.

Men's doubles—Final: Bob Lutz, San Clemente, Calif., and Stan Smith, Hilton Head Island, S.C., defeated McEnroe and Peter Fleming, Seabrook Island, S.C., 7–6, 3–6, 6–1, 3–6, 6–3.

Women's doubles—Final: Billie Jean King, New York City, and Martina Navratilova, Charlottesville, Va., defeated Pam Shriver, Lutherville, Md., and Betty Stove, Netherlands, 7–6, 7–5.

Mixed doubles—Final: Wendy Turnbull, Australia, and Marty Riessen, Boca West, Fla., defeated Miss Stove and Frew McMillan, South Africa, 7–6, 6–2.

Junior boys singles—Final: Mike Falberg, Santa Barbara, Calif., defeated Eric Wilborts, Netherlands, 6–7, 6–3, 6–3.

Junior girls singles—Final: Sue Mascarin, Grosse Point Shores, Mich., defeated Kathrine Keil, Albuquerque, N.M., 6–3, 6–4.

National Clay Court

(Indianapolis, Aug. 3–9, 1981)

Men's singles final—Jose–Luis Clerc, Argentina, defeated Ivan Lendl, Czechoslovakia, 4–6, 6–4, 6–2.
Women's singles final—Andrea Jaeger, Lincolnshire, Ill., defeated Virginia Ruzici, Romania, 6–1, 6–0.
Men's doubles final—Steve Denton, Driscoll, Tex., and Kevin Curren, South Africa, defeated Raul Ramirez, Mexico, and Van Winitsky, Lauderhill, Fla., 6–3, 5–7, 7–5.
Women's doubles final—Virginia Ruzici, Romania, and Joanne Russell, New York City, defeated Sue Barker, England, and Paula Smith, LaJolla, Calif., 6–2, 6–2.

World Championship Tennis

(Dallas, April 29–May 3, 1981)

Final—John McEnroe, Douglaston, N.Y., defeated John Kriek, Naples, Fla., 6–2, 6–4.

U.S. National Indoor

(Memphis, Tenn., Feb. 23–March 1, 1981)

Singles final—Gene Mayer, West Hampton, N.Y., defeated Roscoe Tanner, Lookout Mountain, Tenn., 6–2, 6–4. Doubles final—Gene Mayer and Sandy Mayer, Atherton, Calif., defeated Mike Cahill, Memphis, and Tom Gullikson, Palm Coast, Fla., 7–6, 6–7, 7–6.

U.S. Pro Indoor

(Philadelphia, Jan. 26–Feb. 1, 1981)

Singles final—Roscoe Tanner, Lookout Mountain, Tenn., defeated Wojtek Fibak, Poland, 6–2, 7–6, 7–5.

U.S. Pro

(Brookline, Mass., July 13–19, 1981)

Singles final—Jose–Luis Clerc, Argentina, defeated Hans Gildenmeister, Chile, 0–6, 6–2, 6–2. Doubles final—Raul Ramirez, Mexico, and Pavel Slozil, Czechoslovakia, defeated Gildemeister and Andres Domez, Ecuador, 6–4, 7–6.

OTHER 1981 CHAMPIONSHIPS

Wimbledon Open

Men's singles—John McEnroe, Douglaston, N.Y., defeated Bjorn Borg, Sweden, 4–6, 7–6, 7–6, 6–4.
Women's singles—Chris Evert Lloyd, Fort Lauderdale, Fla., defeated Hana Mandlikova, Czechoslovakia, 6–2, 6–2.
Men's doubles—John McEnroe and Peter Fleming, United States, defeated Bob Lutz and Stan Smith, United States, 6–4, 6–4, 6–4.
Women's doubles—Martina Navratilova and Pam Shriver, United States, defeated Kathy Jordan and Anne Smith, United States, 6–3, 7–6.
Mixed doubles—Frew McMillan, South Africa, and Betty Stove, Netherlands, defeated John and Tracy Austin, United States, 4–6, 7–6, 6–3.
Junior boys—Matt Anger, United States, defeated Pat Cash, Australia, 7–6, 7–5.
Junior girls—Zina Garrison, United States, defeated Rene Uys, South Africa, 6–4, 3–6, 6–0.

French Open

Men's singles—Bjorn Borg, Sweden, defeated Ivan Lendl, Czechoslovakia, 6–1, 4–6, 6–2, 3–6, 6–1.
Women's singles—Hana Mandlikova, Czechoslovakia, defeated Sylvia Hanika, West Germany, 6–2, 6–4.
Men's doubles—Balasz Taroczy, Hungary, and Heinz Gunthardt, Switzerland, defeated Eliot Teltscher and Terry Moor, United States, 6–2, 7–6, 6–3.
Women's doubles—Rosalyn Fairbank and Tanya Harford, South Africa, defeated Candy Reynolds and Paula Smith, United States, 6–1, 6–3.

Australian Open

(Men's events at Melbourne, Australia, Dec. 26, 1980-Jan. 4, 1981)
(Women's events at Melbourne, Australia, Nov. 24–30, 1980)

Men's singles—Brian Teacher, United States, defeated Kim Warwick, Australia, 7–5, 7–6, 6–2.
Women's singles—Hana Mandlikova, Czechoslovakia, defeated Wendy Turnbull, Australia, 6–0, 7–5.
Men's doubles—Kim Warwick and Mark Edmondson, Australia, defeated Peter McNamara and Paul McNamee, Australia, 7–5, 6–4.
Women's doubles—Martina Navratilova and Betsy Nagelsen, United States, defeated Candy Reynolds and Ann Kiyomura, United States, 6–4, 6–4.

1981 DAVIS CUP NON–ZONAL COMPETITION

First Round

Argentina 3, West Germany 2
Romania 3, Brazil 2
Britain 3, Italy 2
New Zealand 5, Korea 0
Sweden 5, Japan 0
Australia 3, France 2
Czechoslovakia 3, Switzerland 2
United States 3, Mexico 2

Quarterfinal Round

Argentina 3, Romania 2
Britain 4, New Zealand 1
Australia 3, Sweden 1
United States 4, Czechoslovakia 1
Semifinals were to be played Sept. 28 to Oct. 4, with the final to be arranged at a later date.

MEN'S FINAL TENNIS EARNINGS—1980

Player	Amount
John McEnroe	$602,383
Bjorn Borg	523,212
Jimmy Connors	409,641
Vitas Gerulaitis	317,441
Guillermo Vilas	302,126
Ivan Lendl	292,286
Wojtek Fibak	288,687
Gene Mayer	254,119
Vijay Amritraj	243,563
Brian Gottfried	232,760

WOMEN'S FINAL TENNIS EARNINGS—1980

Player	Amount
Martina Navratilova	$657,400
Tracy Austin	608,787
Chris Evert Lloyd	418,705
Hana Mandlikova	365,430
Billie Jean King	321,309
Wendy Turnbull	278,573
Andrea Jaeger	218,431
Evonne Goolagong Cawley	210,080
Virginia Ruzici	187,113
Kathy Jordan	178,593

BOXING

Whether it be called pugilism, prize fighting or boxing, there is no tracing "the Sweet Science" to any definite source. Tales of rivals exchanging blows for fun, fame or money go back to earliest recorded history and classical legend. There was a mixture of boxing and wrestling called the "pancratium" in the ancient Olympic Games and in such contests the rivals belabored one another with hands fortified with heavy leather wrappings that were sometimes studded with metal. More than one Olympic competitor lost his life at this brutal exercise.

There was little law or order in pugilism until Jack Broughton, one of the early champions of England, drew up a set of rules for the game in 1743. Broughton, called "the father of English boxing,"

also is credited with having invented boxing gloves. However, these gloves—or "mufflers" as they were called—were used only in teaching "the manly art of self-defense" or in training bouts. All professional championship fights were contested with "bare knuckles" until 1892, when John L. Sullivan lost the heavyweight championship of the world to James J. Corbett in New Orleans in a bout in which both contestants wore regulation gloves.

The Broughton rules were superseded by the London Prize Ring Rules of 1838. The 8th Marquis of Queensberry, with the help of John G. Chambers, put forward the "Queensberry Rules" in 1866, a code that called for gloved contests. Amateurs took quickly to the Queensberry Rules, the professionals slowly.

HISTORY OF WORLD HEAVYWEIGHT CHAMPIONSHIP FIGHTS

(Bouts in which a new champion was crowned)

Source: Nat Fleischer's Ring Boxing Encyclopedia and Record Book, published and copyrighted by The Ring Book Shop, Inc., 120 West 31st St., New York, N.Y. 10001.

Date	Where held	Winner, weight, age	Loser, weight, age	Rounds	Referee
Sept. 7, 1892	New Orleans, La.	James J. Corbett, 178 (26)	John L. Sullivan, 212 (33)	21	Prof. John Duffy
March 17, 1897	Carson City, Nev.	Bob Fitzsimmons, 167 (34)	James J. Corbett, 183 (30)	KO 14	George Siler
June 9, 1899	Coney Island, N.Y.	James J. Jeffries, 206 (24)[1]	Bob Fitzsimmons, 167 (37)	KO 11	George Siler
Feb. 23, 1906	Los Angeles	Tommy Burns, 180 (24)[2]	Marvin Hart, 188 (29)	20	James J. Jeffries
Dec. 26, 1908	Sydney, N.S.W.	Jack Johnson, 196 (30)	Tommy Burns, 176 (27)	KO 14	Hugh McIntosh
April 5, 1915	Havana, Cuba	Jess Willard, 230 (33)	Jack Johnson, 205½ (37)	KO 26	Jack Welch
July 4, 1919	Toledo, Ohio	Jack Dempsey, 187 (24)	Jess Willard, 245 (37)	KO 3	Ollie Pecord
Sept. 23, 1926	Philadelphia	Gene Tunney, 189 (28)[3]	Jack Dempsey, 190 (31)	10	Pop Reilly
June 12, 1930	New York	Max Schmeling, 188 (24)	Jack Sharkey, 197 (27)	WF 4	Jim Crowley
June 21, 1932	Long Island City	Jack Sharkey, 205 (29)	Max Schmeling, 188 (26)	15	Gunboat Smith
June 29, 1933	Long Island City	Primo Carnera, 260½ (26)	Jack Sharkey, 201 (30)	KO 6	Arthur Donovan
June 14, 1934	Long Island City	Max Baer, 209½ (25)	Primo Carnera, 263¼ (27)	KO 11	Arthur Donovan
June 13, 1935	Long Island City	Jim Braddock, 193¾ (29)	Max Baer, 209½ (26)	15	Jack McAvoy
June 22, 1937	Chicago	Joe Louis, 197¼ (23)	Jim Braddock, 197 (31)	KO 8	Tommy Thomas
June 22, 1949	Chicago	Ezzard Charles, 181¾ (27)[4]	Joe Walcott, 195½ (35)	15	Davey Miller
Sept. 27, 1950	New York	Ezzard Charles, 184½ (29)[5]	Joe Louis, 218 (36)	15	Mark Conn
July 18, 1951	Pittsburgh	Joe Walcott, 194 (37)	Ezzard Charles, 182 (30)	KO 7	Buck McTiernan
Sept. 23, 1952	Philadelphia	Rocky Marciano, 184 (29)[6]	Joe Walcott, 196 (38)	KO 13	Charley Daggert
Nov. 30, 1956	Chicago	Floyd Patterson, 182¼ (21)	Archie Moore, 187¾ (42)	KO 5	Frank Sikora
June 26, 1959	New York	Ingemar Johansson, 196 (26)	Floyd Patterson, 182 (24)	KO 3	Ruby Goldstein
June 20, 1960	New York	Floyd Patterson, 190 (25)	Ingemar Johansson, 194¾ (27)	KO 5	Arthur Mercante
Sept. 25, 1962	Chicago	Sonny Liston, 214 (28)	Floyd Patterson, 189 (27)	KO 1	Frank Sikora
Feb. 25, 1964	Miami Beach, Fla.	Cassius Clay, 210 (22)[7]	Sonny Liston, 218 (30)	KO 7	Barney Felix
March 4, 1968	New York	Joe Frazier, 204½ (24)[8]	Buster Mathis, 243½ (23)	KO 11	Arthur Mercante
April 27, 1968	Oakland, Calif.	Jimmy Ellis, 197 (28)[9]	Jerry Quarry, 195 (22)	15	Elmer Costa
Feb. 16, 1970	New York	Joe Frazier, 205 (26)[10]	Jimmy Ellis, 201 (29)	KO 5	Tony Perez
Jan. 22, 1973	Kingston, Jamaica	George Foreman, 217½ (24)	Joe Frazier, 214 (29)	KO 2	Arthur Mercante
Oct. 30, 1974	Kinshasa, Zaire	Muhammad Ali, 216½ (32)	George Foreman, 220 (26)	KO 8	Zack Clayton
Feb. 15, 1978	Las Vegas, Nev.	Leon Spinks, 197 (25)	Muhammad Ali, 224½ (36)	15	Howard Buck
June 9, 1978	Las Vegas, Nev.	Larry Holmes, 212 (28)[11]	Ken Norton, 220 (32)	15	Mills Lans
Sept. 15, 1978	New Orleans	Muhammad Ali, 221 (36)[12]	Leon Spinks, 201 (25)	15	Lucien Joubert
Oct. 20, 1979	Pretoria, S. Africa	John Tate, 240 (24)[13]	Gerrie Coetzee, 222 (24)	15	Carlos Berrocal
March 31, 1980	Knoxville, Tenn.	Mike Weaver, 207½ (27)	John Tate, 232 (25)	KO 15	Ernesto Magana Ansorena

1. Jeffries retired as champion in March 1905. He named Marvin Hart and Jack Root as leading contenders and agreed to referee their fight in Reno, Nev., on July 3, 1905, with the stipulation that he would term the winner the champion. Hart, 190 (28), knocked out Root, 171 (29), in the 12th round. 2. Burns claimed the title after defeating Hart. 3. Tunney retired as champion after defeating Tom Heeney on July 26, 1928. 4. After Louis announced his retirement as champion on March 1, 1949, Charles won recognition from the National Boxing Association as champion by defeating Walcott. 5. Charles gained undisputed recognition as champion by defeating Louis, who came out of retirement. 6. Retired as champion April 27, 1956. 7. The World Boxing Association later withdrew its recognition of Clay as champion and declared the winner of a bout between Ernie Terrell and Eddie Machen would gain its version of the title. Terrell, 199 (25), won a 15-round decision from Machen, 192 (32), in Chicago on March 5, 1965. Clay, 212¼ (25) and Terrell, 212½ (27) met in Houston on Feb. 6, 1967, Clay winning a 15-round decision. 8. Winner recognized by New York, Massachusetts, Maine, Illinois, Texas and Pennsylvania to fill vacated title when Clay was stripped of championship for failing to accept U. S. Induction. 9. Bout was final of eight-man tournament to fill Clay's place and is recognized by World Boxing Association. 10. Bout settled controversy over title. 11. Holmes won World Boxing Council title after W.B.C. had withdrawn recognition of Spinks, March 18, 1978, and awarded its title to Norton. W.B.C. said Spinks had reneged on agreement to fight Norton 12. Ali regained World Boxing Association championship. 13. Tate won W.B.A. title after Ali retired and left it vacant.

CHAMPIONSHIP BOUTS—1981

(Through July 31, 1981)

Junior Flyweight

(108 pound limit)

In the first title fight in San Francisco since 1962, Hilario Zapata of Panama, the World Boxing Council champion, scored a 15-round unanimous verdict over Rudolfo Crawford of Nicaragua to keep the title he won from Shigeo Nakajima of Japan on March 24, 1980. The 22-year-old Zapata was making his fifth defense and won easily, taking at least 11 rounds on the scorecards of each of the judges. The victory was his 17th against one loss. Almost a month earlier, Feb. 8 at Panama City, Zapata knocked out Joey Olivo of the United States in the 13th round. Zapata's continual punishment left lumps on both of Olivo's cheeks.

Pedro Flores of Mexico won the World Boxing Association title on March 8 at Tokyo with a stunning knockout of Yoko Gushiken of Japan in the 12th round. The American referee, Steve Crosson, was asked to stop the fight by Gushiken's manager after Gushiken had been knocked down in the 8th and 12th rounds and had taken severe punishment.

Flores's first defense proved unsuccessful. He was knocked out at 2 minutes 51 seconds of the 13th round by Kim Hwan Jin of South Korea at Seoul, July 19. Kim had Flores leaning helplessly against the ropes, and was scoring easily. The victory was Kim's 19th, with 2 draws. Flores's record was 15–5.

Flyweight

(112 pound limit)

Shoji Oguma of Japan survived cuts over both eyes in the 3rd round and went on to outpoint Park Chan Hee of South Korea to retain his W.B.C. crown. The 29-year-old champion, a southpaw, gained a majority decision in the 15-round bout on Feb. 3 in Tokyo. There were no knockdowns, but Oguma's superior power and speed dominated the late rounds, enabling him to pile up points en route to his 36th victory against eight losses and a draw. Park, a former champion, had a 15–3–2 record.

The W.B.A. championship changed hands on March 28 at Soweto, South Africa, when Santos Laciar of Argentina knocked out Peter Mathebula of Johannesburg in the 7th round. Mathebula had taken the title away from Kim Tae Shik of Korea on a split decision at Los Angeles on Dec. 13, 1980.

Laciar's reign was short. In his first defense on June 6 in Buenos Aires, he was outpointed by Luis Ibarra of Panama over 15 rounds. Ibarra thus regained the title he had lost on a 2nd-round knockout to Kim Tae Shik on Feb. 17, 1980, in Seoul, South Korea.

Junior Bantamweight

(115 pound limit)

Chul Ho Kim of South Korea became the W.B.C. champion by dethroning Rafael Orono of Venezuela with an 8th-round knockout on Jan. 24, at San Cristobal, Venezuela. Each fighter weighed the class limit for the bout.

Kim retained his title on July 29 at Pusan, South Korea, by stopping Willie Jensen of Las Vegas, Nev., at 1 minute 18 seconds of the 13th round. Jensen took charge in the middle rounds, but Kim regained the initiative in the 10th with counter body-punching. A barrage of rights and lefts to the body floored Jensen for the knockout.

Bantamweight

(118 pound limit)

Jeff Chandler made the first defense of the W.B.A. title he won by stopping Julian Solis in the 14th round at Miami on Nov. 14, 1980, and retained the crown with a unanimous 15-round decision over Jorge Lujan, a former champion from Panama, on Jan. 31 at Philadelphia. It was Chandler's 25th straight victory since fighting to a draw in his pro debut in 1976. Chandler weighed 113½ to Lujan's 118. The bout was the first for the bantamweight title in Philadelphia, Chandler's hometown, in almost 40 years. Chandler earned $70,000 and Lujan $25,000.

On Feb. 22, Mexico's Lupe Pintor, the W.B.C. champion, kept his title with a unanimous decision over Jose Uziga of Argentina at Houston. Uziga, never knocked down in a pro fight, maintained that record but had all he could do to stay on his feet as the bell saved him in the 15th after he had taken a pounding from the champion. Pintor, defending his title for the sixth time, earned $100,000. His record stood at 41–4–1. The challenger, with a 28–2–3 record, earned $20,000, his biggest payday.

Chandler made his second defense of the year on April 5 in Tokyo and held his title with a 15-round draw against Eijiro Murata of Japan. There were no knockdowns and Chandler held off the aggressive Murata with fast footwork and a sharp uppercut. Both fighters remained unbeaten. One judge scored the fight 145–142 for the champion, a second judge favored Murata 147–146. The referee, Ernesto Magana of Mexico, called it even at 146.

On July 26 at Atlantic City, Chandler knocked out Solis in the 7th round of a rematch. With 2 seconds left in the round, Chandler hit Solis with a right to the chin and Solis hit the canvas face down. In 25 fights Solis had lost only twice—both times to Chandler.

Junior Featherweight

(122 pound limit)

Sergio Palma of Argentina retained his W.B.A. crown with a unanimous 15-round victory over Leo Cruz in Buenos Aires. Palma took the title on Aug. 9, 1980, with a 5th-round knockout of Leo Randolph in Spokane, Wash. The defeat, in Randolph's first defense, prompted him to announce his retirement from boxing the next day. Randolph, then 22 and a 1976 Olympic gold medal winner, said he wanted to settle down to a "normal life" with his family.

Featherweight

(128 pound limit)

Eusebio Pedroza of Panama sent Patrick Ford of Guyana reeling to the canvas with a barrage of punches in the 13th round and scored a knockout that enabled him to keep the W.B.A. championship he had captured in 1978. Pedroza suffered a deep cut over an eyebrow, but he was dominant throughout and scored repeatedly to pile up points before the knockout on Feb. 14 in Panama City. His handlers said the cut came from a blow inflicted by Ford's elbow. Pedroza's record is 29–3. Ford has a 15–2 mark.

In his fifth successful defense in a year, Salvador Sanchez of Mexico, the W.B.C. champion, turned back the No. 1 contender, Roberto Castanon of Spain, with a knockout at 1 minute 9 seconds of the 10th round at Las Vegas, Nev., on March 22. Sanchez, 126 pounds, controlled the bout from the opening bell against Castanon's wild lunges. Sanchez won the title in Phoenix Ariz., on Feb. 3, 1980 with a 13th-round knockout of Danny (Little Red) Lopez.

Junior Lightweight

(130 pound limit)

On Aug. 2, 1980, Sammy Serrano of Puerto Rico was knocked out by Yasutsune Uehara of Japan in the 6th round and lost his W.B.A. title on a gala card at Joe Louis Arena in Detroit. The quick-punching Serrano and the clever Uehara staged a rematch in April at Wakayama, Japan, and this time Serrano regained the title with a 15-round decision.

Cornelius Boza-Edwards, a Ugandan who fights out of London, knocked down Rafael Limon of Mexico in the 5th round, then withstood a comeback effort by the Mexican and went on to take the W.B.C. title on March 8, at Stockton, Calif.

Then in his first defense, on May 30 at Las Vegas, Nev., Boza-Edwards battered Bobby Chacon of Oroville, Calif., until the challenger's manager asked the referee to stop the fight after the 13th round. Chacon, a former champion, scored well for the first six rounds, then tired and fell behind rapidly. The victory for Boza–Edwards, 129½ pounds, was his 31st against 2 losses, with 25 knockouts. Chacon, who weighed 130, had a record of 45–6–1, with 38 knockouts.

Serrano, in his first defense since regaining the title, scored a unanimous decision over Leonel Hernandez, a Venezuelan, in a 15-rounder in Caracas in June.

Lightweight

(135 pound limit)

At Atlantic City on April 12, Sean O'Grady, a 22-year-old Oklahoman, knocked down the previously unbeaten champion Hilmer Kenty of Detroit in the 2nd and 8th rounds and went on to win by a unanimous decision and become the new W.B.A. champion. It was O'Grady's second attempt to win the title. Kenty opened a cut on O'Grady's left eye with an accidental butt in the 5th round, and it made O'Grady fight harder. Kenty, who had won 20 pro bouts, won the title from Ernesto Espana of Venezuela on March 2, 1980. It was his fourth title defense. O'Grady's victory was his 75th against 2 losses.

The W.B.C. title also changed hands when Alexis Arguello of Nicaragua, now a resident of Miami, took the crown from James Watt at Wembley Arena in England on June 20. Arguello thus became only the sixth boxer to win a world title in three different divisions, having held the featherweight and junior lightweight crowns. The 29-year-old Arguello floored Watt for an 8-count in the 7th round. Watt, from Scotland, received $750,000 and Arguello $280,000. Watt weighed 134¾ pounds, Arguello 134½.

Junior Welterweight

(140 pound limit)

Saoul Mamby, 34-year-old W.B.C. champion from New York City, scored a unanimous 15-round victory over Jo Kimpuani of France on June 12 in Detroit to retain his title. The bout was part of the undercard for the Larry Holmes–Leon Spinks heavyweight championship fight. Mamby weighed 139¾ pounds and his 31-year-old opponent scaled 139¼.

Unbeaten Aaron Pryor floored Lennox Blackmoore three times in the first two rounds on June 27 at Las Vegas, Nev., and kept his W.B.A. title when the referee stopped the fight after 58 seconds of the 2nd round. Pryor, from Cincinnati, weighed 140. He stunned the challenger with a left hook that dropped him to the canvas only seconds after the fight began. Pryor, who earned $200,000, notched his 20th straight knockout and 26th in a career that boasts 28 triumphs.

Welterweight

(147 pound limit)

Sugar Ray Leonard retained his W.B.C. championship by stopping Larry Bonds of Denver in the 10th round of their scheduled 15-rounder at Syracuse, N.Y., on March 28. Leonard, the fighter of the year in 1979, was simply no match for the less experienced Bonds. Leonard, from Palmer Park, Md., weighed 145½, and Bonds 144¾.

Thomas Hearns, the 1980 boxer of the year, used his reach and superior punching power to knock out Randy Shields in the 13th round and keep his W.B.A. crown on April 25 at Phoenix, Ariz. Shields, who had never been knocked out before, was bleeding from both eyes from the 8th round on. He was standing in his corner, awaiting the 13th round when the referee, acting on advice from ring doctors, halted the bout. Hearns lifted his record to 31–0, with 29 knockouts.

Hearns returned to action on June 25 at Houston's Astrodome and scored an easy knockout of Pablo Baez, a Dominican living in Los Angeles, at 2 minutes 10 seconds of the 4th round.

Junior Middleweight

(154 pound limit)

Wilfred Benitez shot a crushing right to the head of Maurice Hope of England and scored a knockout at 1 minute 56 seconds of the 12th round on May 23 at Las Vegas, Nev., to win the W.B.C. title and become the fifth fighter in boxing history to hold three individual championships. He joined Henry Armstrong, Bob Fitzsimmons, Tony Canzoneri, and Barney Ross. But at 22, Benitez was the youngest to accomplish the feat.

Benitez, from Puerto Rico, defeated Tony Cervantes on March 6, 1976, for the junior welterweight title and became the youngest world champion in history. He won from Carlos Palomino Jan. 14, 1979 to take the welterweight title, which he later lost to Sugar Ray Leonard. Hope, a 29-year-old Antiguan who lives in London, won the title from Rocky Matioli in San Remo, Italy, March 4, 1979. He had lost on a knockout only once before.

Moving up in weight class Sugar Ray Leonard, the holder of the W.B.C. welterweight crown, became the holder of two titles when he stopped Ayub Kalule, a Ugandan who lives in Denmark, in the 9th round of a bout on the same card as the Hearns–Baez title fight at Houston June 25. The knockout gave Leonard the W.B.A. crown.

Middleweight

(160 pound limit)

Marvin Hagler of Brockton, Mass., the undisputed middleweight champion, retained his title in his first defense with a devastating knockout of Fulgencio Obelmejias of Venezuela at 20 seconds of the 8th round at the Boston Garden on Jan. 17. The referee stepped in to end the one-sided bout.

Hagler made his second title defense on June 13, again in Boston, and his opponent was Vito Antuofermo of Brooklyn, N.Y. A crowd of 9,000 turned out for the bizarre bout. Antuofermo, who has a history of bleeding easily, suffered a deep cut on the forehead over his left eye in the first minute of the fight and bled profusely. Antuofermo's corner claimed he had been intentionally butted by Hagler. However, in the 4th round Antuofermo suffered a cut under the right eye and he did not answer the bell for the 5th round, Hagler thus regaining the title on a knockout.

Light Heavyweight

(175 pound limit)

Matthew Saad Muhammad of Columbus, Ohio, scored his 21st knockout and retained his W.B.C. title for the sixth time on Feb. 28 at Atlantic City when the referee indicated that Vonzell Johnson could no longer continue at 2 minutes 23 seconds of the 11th round. Johnson, from Philadelphia, staggered the champion in the 1st round and seemed capable in the early rounds. But it was his first attempt to go more than 10 rounds and he tired badly. Johnson weighed 174 pounds, the champion 174¼. Saad Muhammad raised his record to 29–3–2.

Saad Muhammad scored another knockout in the same ring on April 25. He stopped Murray Sutherland, from Bay City, Mich., with a right-left combination to the jaw at 1 minute 16 seconds of the 9th round. The champion again started slowly and Sutherland split his lower lip in the 1st round. In the 7th, however, the champion dropped Sutherland for an 8-count and the tide turned. The victory was the 17th straight for Saad Muhammad, with 20 knockouts. Sutherland, who was born in Scotland, saw his record drop to 31–4, with 20 knockouts. He suffered only his second knockout.

On July 18 at Las Vegas, Nev., Michael Spinks, brother of Leon Spinks, the former heavyweight champion, dethroned Eddie Mustafa Muhammad with a unanimous 15-round decision and captured the W.B.A. championship. Unbeaten Spinks won his 17th bout. He controlled the final rounds, knocking Muhammad down in the 12th with an overhand right. Mustafa Muhammad had trouble making the weight limit. Two months earlier he had fought as a heavyweight and lost to Renaldo Snipes in a 10-rounder. He was forced to lose more than 20 pounds for the Spinks bout and 16½ hours before fight time he had to sweat off almost 2 pounds.

Heavyweight

Larry Holmes extended his unbeaten streak to 37 fights on April 11 at Las Vegas, Nev., with a 15-round unanimous verdict over Trevor Berbick of Halifax, Nova Scotia, and retained his W.B.C. crown. The bout, however, ended Holmes's record streak of eight straight knockout victories. Berbick's style appeared to bewilder Holmes. The challenger muscled and pushed and even taunted Holmes for most of the bout. Holmes

hit him freely in the later rounds and particularly in the 15th, but could not put him down. There were no knockdowns. It was Holmes's first fight since defeating Muhammad Ali Oct. 2, 1980, and he appeared rusty from the layoff.

Holmes proved he was a fighting champion on June 12 at Detroit when he tore into Leon Spinks, a former champion, and knocked him out at 2 minutes 34 seconds of the third round with an awesome display of punching power. It was Holmes's 38th pro fight, his 38th victory, 28th knockout, and 10th successful defense of the title. It was also the first heavyweight title bout in Detroit in 10 years.

OTHER WORLD BOXING TITLEHOLDERS

(Through July 31, 1981)

Light Heavyweight

1903	Jack Root, George Gardner	1941–48	Gus Lesnevich	1978	Victor Galindez (WBA), Mike
1903–05	Bob Fitzsimmons	1948–50	Freddie Mills		Rossman (WBA), Miguel
1905–12	Philadelphia Jack O'Brien[1]	1950–52	Joey Maxim		Cuello (WBC), Mate Parlov
1912–16	Jack Dillon	1952–61	Archie Moore[3]		(WBC), Marvin Johnson
1916–20	Battling Levinsky	1961–63	Harold Johnson		(WBC)
1920–22	Georges Carpentier	1963–65	Willie Pastrano	1979	Mike Rossman (WBA), Victor
1923	Battling Siki	1965–66	José Torres		Galindez (WBA), Marvin
1923–25	Mike McTigue	1966–67	Dick Tiger		Johnson (WBC), Matthew
1925–26	Paul Berlenbach	1968	Dick Tiger, Bob Foster		(Franklin) Saad
1926–27	Jack Delaney[2]	1969–70	Bob Foster		Muhammad (WBC)
1927	Mike McTigue	1971	Vicente Rondon (WBA), Bob	1980	Matthew Saad Muhammad
1927–29	Tommy Loughran		Foster (WBC)		(WBC), Marvin Johnson
1930	Jimmy Slattery	1972–73	Bob Foster (WBA, WBC)		(WBA), Eddie (Gregory)
1930–34	Maxie Rosenbloom	1974	John Conteh (WBA), Bob		Mustafa Muhammad
1934–35	Bob Olin		Foster (WBC)[1 4]		(WBA)
1935–39	John Henry Lewis	1975–76	Victor Galindez (WBA), John	1981	Matthew Saad Muhammad
1939	Melio Bettina		Conteh (WBC)		(WBC), Eddie Mustafa
1939–41	Billy Conn[2]	1977	Victor Galindez (WBA), John		Muhammad (WBA),
1941	Anton Christoforidis (NBA)		Conteh (WBC)[4], Miguel		Michael Spinks (WBA)
			Cuello (WBC)		

1. Retired. 2. Abandoned title. 3. NBA withdrew recognition in 1961, New York Commission in 1962; recognized thereafter only by California and Europe. 4. WBC withdrew recognition.

Middleweight

1867–72	Tom Chandler		Apostoli, Ceferino Garcia,	1965–66	Dick Tiger
1872–81	George Rooke		Ken Overlin, Billy Soose,	1966	Emile Griffith
1881–82	Mike Donovan[1]		Tony Zale[4]	1967	Nino Benvenuti, Emile Griffith
1884–91	Jack (Nonpareil) Dempsey	1941–47	Tony Zale	1968	Emile Griffith, Nino Benvenuti
1891–97	Bob Fitzsimmons[2]	1947–48	Rocky Graziano	1969	Nino Benvenuti
1908	Stanley Ketchel, Billy Papke	1948	Tony Zale	1970	Nino Benvenuti, Carlos Mon-
1908–10	Stanley Ketchel[3]	1948–49	Marcel Cerdan		zon
1913	Frank Klaus	1949–51	Jake LaMotta	1971–73	Carlos Monzon
1913–14	George Chip	1952	Ray Robinson, Randy Turpin	1974–75	Carlos Monzon (WBA),
1914–17	Al McCoy	1951–52	Ray Robinson[1]		Rodrigo Valdez (WBC)
1917–20	Mike O'Dowd	1953–55	Carl Olson	1976	Carlos Monzon (WBA, WBC),
1920–23	Johnny Wilson	1955–57	Ray Robinson[5]		Rodrigo Valdez (WBC)
1923–26	Harry Greb	1957	Gene Fullmer, Ray Robinson	1977	Carlos Monzon (WBA,
1926	Tiger Flowers	1957–58	Carmen Basilio		WBC)[1], Rodrigo Valdez
1926–31	Mickey Walker[2]	1958–60	Ray Robinson[6]		(WBA, WBC)
1931–41	Gorilla Jones, Ben Jeby,	1960–61	Paul Pender[7]	1978	Rodrigo Valdez, Hugo Corro
	Marcel Thil, Lou Brouillard,	1959–62	Gene Fullmer (NBA)	1979	Hugo Corro, Vito Antuofermo
	Vince Dundee, Teddy	1961–62	Terry Downes[1]	1980	Vito Antuofermo, Alan
	Yarosz, Babe Risko,	1962	Paul Pender[1]		Minter, Marvin Hagler
	Freddy Steele, Al Hostak,	1962–63	Dick Tiger	1981	Marvin Hagler
	Solly Kreiger, Fred	1963–65	Joey Giardello		

1. Retired. 2. Abandoned title. 3. Died. 4. National Boxing Association and New York Commission disagreed on champions. Those listed were accepted by one or the other until Zale gained world-wide recognition. 5. Ended retirement in 1954. 6. NBA withdrew recognition. 7. Recognized by New York, Massachusetts, and Europe.

Welterweight

1892–94	Mysterious Billy Smith	1900	Rube Ferns	1904–06	Joe Walcott
1894–96	Tommy Ryan	1900–01	Matty Matthews	1906–07	Honey Mellody
1896	Kid McCoy[2]	1901	Ruby Ferns	1907	Mike (Twin) Sullivan[2]
1896–		1901–04	Joe Walcott	1915–19	Ted Lewis
1900	Mysterious Billy Smith	1904	Dixie Kid[2]	1919–22	Jack Britton

1922–26	Mickey Walker	1951–54	Kid Gavilan	1975	José Napoles (WBA, WBC)[3], Angel Espada (WBA), John Stracey (WBC)
1926–27	Pete Latzo	1954–55	Johnny Saxton		
1927–29	Joe Dundee	1955	Tony DeMarco		
1929–30	Jackie Fields	1955–56	Carmen Basilio	1976	Angel Espada (WBA), José Cuevas (WBA), John Stracey (WBC), Carlos Palomino (WBC)
1930	Young Jack Thompson	1956	Johnny Saxton		
1930–31	Tommy Freeman	1956–57	Carmen Basilio[2]		
1931	Young Jack Thompson	1958	Virgil Akins		
1931–32	Lou Brouillard	1959–60	Don Jordan	1977–78	José Cuevas (WBA), Carlos Palomino (WBC)
1932–33	Jackie Fields	1960–61	Benny (Kid) Paret		
1933	Young Corbett 3rd	1961	Emile Griffith	1979	José Cuevas (WBA), Carlos Palomino (WBC), Wilfredo Benitez (WBC)
1933–34	Jimmy McLarnin, Barney Ross	1961–62	Benny (Kid) Paret		
1934–35	Jimmy McLarnin	1962–63	Emile Griffith, Luis Rodriguez		
1935–38	Barney Ross	1963–66	Emile Griffith[2]	1980	Jose Cuevas (WBA), Sugar Ray Leonard (WBC), Roberto Duran (WBC), Thomas Hearns (WBA)
1938–40	Henry Armstrong	1966–69	Curtis Cokes		
1940–41	Fritzie Zivic	1969	Curtis Cokes, José Napoles		
1941–46	Freddie Cochrane	1970	José Napoles, Billy Backus		
1946	Marty Servo[1]	1971	Billy Backus, José Napoles	1981	Ray Leonard (WBC), Thomas Hearns (WBA)
1946–51	Ray Robinson[2]	1972–74	José Napoles		
1951	Johnny Bratton (NBA)				

1. Retired. 2. Abandoned title. 3. WBA withdrew recognition.

Lightweight

1869–99	Kid Lavigne		Williams (NBA)	1973	Roberto Duran (WBA), Rodolfo Gonzalez (WBC)
1899–		1947–51	Ike Williams		
1902	Frank Erne	1951–52	James Carter	1974	Roberto Duran (WBA), Rodolfo Gonzalez (WBC), Guts Ishimatsu (WBC)
1902–08	Joe Gans	1952	Lauro Salas		
1908–10	Battling Nelson	1952–54	James Carter		
1910–12	Ad Wolgast	1954	Paddy DeMarco	1975	Roberto Duran (WBA), Guts Ishimatsu (WBC)
1912–14	Willie Ritchie	1954–55	James Carter		
1914–17	Freddy Welsh	1955–56	Wallace Smith	1976	Roberto Duran (WBA), Guts Ishimatsu (WBC), Esteban De Jesus (WBC)
1917–25	Benny Leonard[1]	1956–62	Joe Brown		
1925	Jimmy Goodrich	1962–65	Carlos Ortiz		
1925–26	Rocky Kansas	1965	Ismael Laguna	1977	Roberto Duran (WBA), Esteban De Jesus (WBC)
1926–30	Sammy Mandell	1965–68	Carlos Ortiz		
1930	Al Singer	1968	Teo Cruz	1978	Roberto Duran (WBA, WBC)
1930–33	Tony Canzoneri	1969	Teo Cruz, Mando Ramos	1979	Roberto Duran[2]; Jim Watt (WBC), Ernesto Espana (WBA)
1933–35	Barney Ross[2]	1970	Mando Ramos, Ismael Laguna, Ken Buchanan		
1935–36	Tony Canzoneri				
1936–38	Lou Ambers	1971	Ken Buchanan (WBA), Mando Ramos (WBC), Pedro Carrasco (WBC)	1980	Ernesto Espana (WBA), Hilmer Kenty (WBA), Jim Watt (WBC)
1938–39	Henry Armstrong				
1939–40	Lou Ambers				
1940–41	Lew Jenkins	1972	Ken Buchanan (WBA), Roberto Duran (WBA), Pedro Carrasco (WBC), Mando Ramos (WBC), Chango Carmona (WBC), Rodolfo Gonzalez (WBC)	1981	Hilmer Kenty (WBA), Sean O'Grady (WBA), James Watt (WBC), Alexis Arguello (WBC)
1941–42	Sammy Angott[1]				
1943–47	Beau Jack (N.Y.), Bob Montgomery (N.Y.), Sammy Angott (NBA), Juan Zurita (NBA), Ike				

1. Retired. 2. Abandoned title.

Featherweight

1889	Dal Hawkins[1]	1940–41	Harry Jefra, Joey Archibald	1972	Antonio Gomez (WBA), Ernesto Marcel (WBA), Kuniaki Shibata (WBC), Clemente Sanchez (WBC),[2] José Legra (WBC)
1890	Billy Murphy	1941–42	Chalky Wright		
1892–		1942–48	Willie Pep		
1900	George Dixon	1948–49	Sandy Saddler[2]		
1900–01	Terry McGovern	1949–50	Willie Pep	1973	Ernesto Marcel (WBA), José Legra (WBC), Eder Jofre (WBC)
1901	Young Corbett[1]	1950–57	Sandy Saddler		
1901–12	Abe Attell	1957–59	Kid Bassey		
1912–23	Johnny Kilbane	1959–63	Davey Moore	1974	Ernesto Marcel (WBA)[2], Ruben Olivares (WBA), Alexis Arguello (WBA), Eder Jofre (WBC), Bobby Chacon (WBC)
1923	Eugene Criqui	1963–64	Sugar Ramos		
1923–25	Johnny Dundee[1]	1964–67	Vicente Saldivar[2]		
1925–27	Louis (Kid) Kaplan[1]	1968	Howard Winstone, José Legra,[3] Paul Rojas (WBA), Sho Saijo (WBA)		
1927–28	Benny Bass			1975	Alexis Arguello (WBA), Bobby Chacon (WBC), Ruben Olivares (WBC), David Kotey (WBC)
1928	Tony Canzoneri	1969	Sho Saijo (WBA), Johnny Famechon[3]		
1928–29	Andre Routis	1970	Sho Saijo (WBA), Johnny Famechon,[3] Vicente Salvidar,[3] Kuniaki Shibata[3]		
1929–32	Battling Battalino[1]			1976	Alexis Arguello (WBA),[2] David Kotey (WBC), Danny Lopez (WBC)
1932	Tommy Paul (NBA), Kid Chocolate (N.Y.)				
1933–36	Freddie Miller	1971	Sho Saijo (WBA), Antonio Gomez (WBA), Kuniaki Shibata (WBC)		
1936–37	Petey Sarron			1977	Rafael Ortega (WBA), Danny
1937–38	Henry Armstrong[1]				
1938–40	Joey Archibald				

	Lopez (WBC)		Lopez (WBC)		Danny Lopez (WBC),
1978	Rafael Ortega (WBA), Cecilio	1979	Eusebio Pedrosa (WBA),		Salvador Sanchez (WBC)
	Lastra (WBA), Eusebio		Danny Lopez (WBC)	1981	Eusebio Pedroza (WBA),
	Pedrosa (WBA), Danny	1980	Eusebio Pedroza (WBA),		Salvador Sanchez (WBC)

1. Abandoned title. 2. Retired. 3. Recognized in Europe, Mexico, and Orient.

Bantamweight

1890–92	George Dixon[1]	1939–40	Sixto Escobar[2]		Romeo Anaya (WBA),
1894–99	Jimmy Barry[2]	1940–42	Lou Salica		Arnold Taylor (WBA)
1899–		1942–46	Manuel Ortiz		Rodolfo Martinez (WBC),
1900	Terry McGovern[1]	1947	Manuel Ortiz, Harold Dade		Rafael Herrera (WBC)
1901	Harry Harris[1]	1948–50	Manuel Ortiz	1974	Arnold Taylor (WBA), Soo
1902–03	Harry Forbes	1950–52	Vic Toweel		Hwan Hong (WBA), Rafael
1903–04	Frankie Neil	1952–54	Jimmy Carruthers[2]		Herrera (WBC), Rodolfo
1904	Joe Bowker[1]	1954–55	Robert Cohen		Martinez (WBC)
1905–07	Jimmy Walsh[1]	1956	Robert Cohen, Mario	1975	Soo Hwan Hong (WBA),
1910–14	Johnny Coulon		D'Agata, Raul Macias		Alfonso Zamora (WBA),
1914–17	Kid Williams		(NBA)		Rodolfo Martinez (WBC)
1917–20	Pete Herman	1957	Mario D'Agata, Alphonse	1976	Alfonso Zamora (WBA),
1920	Joe Lynch		Halimi		Rodolfo Martinez (WBC),
1920–21	Joe Lynch, Pete Herman,	1958–59	Alphonse Halimi		Carlos Zarate (WBC)
	Johnny Buff	1959–60	Jose Becerra[2]	1977	Alfonso Zamora (WBA),
1922	Johnny Buff, Joe Lynch	1960–61	Alphonse Halimi[4]		Jorge Lujan (WBA), Carlos
1923	Joe Lynch	1961–62	Johnny Caldwell[4]		Zarate (WBC)
1924	Joe Lynch, Abe Goldstein	1961–65	Eder Jofre	1978	Jorge Lujan (WBA), Carlos
1924	Abe Goldstein, Eddie	1965–68	Masahika (Fighting) Harada		Zarate (WBC)
	(Cannonball) Martin	1968	Masahika (Fighting) Harada,	1979	Jorge Lujan (WBA), Carlos
1925	Eddie (Cannonball) Martin,		Lionel Rose		Zarate (WBC), Lupe Pintor
	Charlie (Phil) Rosenberg[3]	1969	Lionel Rose, Ruben Olivares		(WBC)
1927–28	Bud Taylor (NBA)[1]	1970	Ruben Olivares, Chucho	1980	Jorge Lujan (WBA), Lupe
1929–34	Al Brown		Castillo		Pintor (WBC), Julian Solis
1935	Al Brown, Baltazar Sangchili	1971	Chucho Castillo, Ruben		(WBA) Jeff Chandler
1936	Baltazar Sangchili, Tony		Olivares		(WBA)
	Marino, Sixto Escobar	1972	Ruben Olivares, Rafael	1981	Lupe Pintor (WBC), Jeff
1937	Sixto Escobar, Harry Jeffra		Herrera, Enrique Pinder		Chandler (WBA)
1938	Harry Jeffra, Sixto Escobar	1973	Enrique Pinder (WBA),		

1. Abandoned title. 2. Retired. 3. Deprived of title for failing to make weight. 4. Recognized in Europe.

Flyweight

1916–23	Jimmy Wilde	1966–68	Charchai Chionoi		Shoji Oguma (WBC),
1923–25	Pancho Villa[1]	1969	Bernabe Villacampa, Efran		Miguel Canto (WBC)
1925	Frankie Genaro		Torres (WBA)	1976	Erbito Salavarria (WBA),
1925–27	Fidel La Barba[2]	1970	Bernabe Villacampa,		Alfonso Lopez (WBA),
1927–31	Corporal Izzy Schwartz,		Chartchai Chionoi, Erbito		Guty Espadas (WBA),
	Frankie Genaro, Emile		Salavarria, Berkrerk		Miguel Canto (WBC)
	(Spider) Pladner, Midget		Chartvanchai (WBA),	1977	Guty Espadas (WBA), Miguel
	Wolgast, Young Perez[3]		Masao Ohba (WBA)		Canto (WBC)
1932–35	Jackie Brown	1971	Masao Ohba (WBA), Erbito	1978	Guty Espadas (WBA), Betulio
1935–38	Bennie Lynch[4]		Salavarria (WBC)		Gonzalez (WBA), Miguel
1939	Peter Kane[4]	1972	Masao Ohba (WBA), Erbito		Canto (WBC)
1943–47	Jackie Paterson[1]		Salavarria (WBC), Betulio	1979	Betulio Gonzalez (WBA),
1947–50	Rinty Monaghan[2]		Gonzalez (WBA), Venice		Miguel Canto (WBC), Park
1950	Terry Allen		Borkorsor (WBC)		Chan-Hee (WBC)
1950–52	Dado Marino	1973	Masao Ohba (WBA),	1980	Luis Ibarra (WBA), Kim Tae
1952–54	Yoshio Shirai		Chartchai Chionoi (WBA),		Shik (WBA), Park
1954–60	Pascual Perez		Venice Borkorsor (WBC),		Chan-Hee (WBC), Shoji
1960–62	Pone Kingpetch		Betulio Gonzalez (WBC)		Oguma (WBC) Peter
1962–63	Masahika (Fighting) Harada	1974	Chartchai Chionoi (WBA),		Mathebula (WBA)
1963–64	Hiroyuki Ebihara		Susumu Hanagata (WBA),	1981	Shoji Oguma (WBC), Peter
1964–65	Pone Kingpetch		Betulio Gonzalez (WBC),		Mathebula (WBA), Santos
1965–66	Salvatore Burrini		Shoji Oguma (WBC)		Laciar (WBA), Luis Ibarra
1966	Walter McGown, Chartchai	1975	Susumu Hanagata (WBA),		(WBA)
	Chionoi		Erbito Salavarria (WBA),		

1. Died. 2. Retired. 3. Claimants to NBA and New York Commission titles. 4. Abandoned title.

JOE LOUIS, HEAVYWEIGHT CHAMPION FOR 12 YEARS, DIES AT 66

Joe Louis, who held the heavyweight title from 1937 to 1949, longer than any champion, died on April 12, 1981, of a heart attack in Las Vegas, Nev. He was 66 years old. Louis won the heavyweight championship by knocking out James J. Braddock in the eighth round on June 22, 1937, at Chicago. He retired undefeated as champion on March 1, 1949, after defending his title 25 times, a record. His last title defense was against Jersey Joe Walcott on June 25, 1948, at Yankee Stadium, New York. Louis knocked out Walcott in the 11th round.

After his retirement, Louis attempted a comeback. He fought Ezzard Charles on Sept. 27, 1950, for the title in Yankee Stadium and lost on a 15-round decision. In his last professional fight, Oct. 26, 1950, he lost to Rocky Marciano.

Louis was born Joseph Louis Barrow on May 13, 1914, in Lafayette, Ala., the eighth child of Munn and Lily Barrow. His father was a share-cropper. Later he moved with his family to Detroit where he became interested in boxing. Known as the Brown Bomber, he soon attracted national attention and rose quickly among contenders.

On June 19, 1936, Louis suffered his first professional defeat, a 12th-round knockout at the hands of Max Schmeling of Germany. Schmeling, who later in life praised and admired Louis, had been billed at the time as Hitler's emissary from Nazi Germany, then proclaiming its doctrine of the master race. On June 22, 1938, at Yankee Stadium, an enraged Louis bent on avenging his previous loss to Schmeling and dispelling the master race propaganda, knocked Schmeling out in 2 minutes 4 seconds of the first round, a record for turning back a challenger in a heavyweight title fight. Louis's terrific punches sent Schmeling to a hospital to recover from his injuries.

While he was champion, Louis's bouts grossed more than $4.6 million, of which he received about $800,000. Louis was a free-spender and did not invest his money wisely. His comeback in 1950 was prompted because he was short of funds and was heavily in debt to the Internal Revenue Service. Louis entered the Army as a private in World War II and rose to sergeant. Before entering service he fought several bouts, and parts of the purses went to Army and Navy Relief. As a soldier he traveled 21,000 miles and staged 96 exhibition bouts before 2 million soldiers. He won affection and praise for his patriotism.

Through a special dispensation issued by President Reagan, Louis was buried with military honors in Arlington National Cemetery.

JOE LOUIS' TITLE FIGHTS

June 22, 1937[1]	Jim Braddock, Chicago	KO	8	Feb. 17, 1941	Gus Dorazio, Philadelphia	KO	2
Aug. 30, 1937	Tommy Farr, Yankee Stadium	W	15	March, 21, 1941	Abe Simon, Detroit	KO	13
				April 8, 1941	Tony Musto, St. Louis	KO	9
Feb. 23, 1938	Nathan Mann, Mad. Sq. Garden	KO	3	May 23, 1941	Buddy Baer, Washington, D.C.	W disq.	7
April 1, 1938	Harry Thomas,Chicago	KO	5	June 18, 1941	Billy Conn, Polo Grounds	KO	13
June 22, 1938[2]	Max Schmeling, Yankee Stadium	KO	1	Sept. 29, 1941	Lou Nova, Polo Grounds	KO	6
Jan. 25, 1939	John Henry Lewis, Mad. Sq. Garden	KO	1	Jan. 9, 1942	Buddy Baer, Madison Sq. Garden	KO	1
April 17, 1939	Jack Roper, Los Angeles	KO	1	March 27, 1942	Abe Simon, Madison Sq. Garden	KO	6
June 28, 1939	Tony Galento, Yankee Stadium	KO	4	June 19, 1946	Billy Conn, Yankee Stadium	KO	8
Sept. 20, 1939	Bob Pastor, Detroit	KO	11	Sept. 18, 1946	Tami Mauriello, Yankee Stadium	KO	1
Feb. 9, 1940	Arturo Godoy, Mad. Sq. Garden	W	15	Dec. 5, 1947	Joe Walcott, Madison Sq. Garden	W	15
March 29, 1940	Johnny Paycheck, Mad. Sq. Garden	KO	2	June 25, 1948	Joe Walcott, Yankee Stadium	KO	11
June 20, 1940	Arturo Godoy, Yankee Stadium	KO	8	Sept. 27, 1950[3]	Ezzard Charles, Yankee Stadium	L	15
Dec. 16, 1940	Al McCoy, Boston	KO	6				
Jan. 31, 1941	Red Burman, Mad. Sq. Garden	KO	5				

1. Won title. 2. Schmeling had stopped Louis in 12th round of non-title fight, June 19, 1936. 3. After announcing retirement as champion on March 1, 1949, Louis returned to boxing and sought to regain title in bout with Charles.

BILLIARDS—1981

World 3–cushion champion (Cairo, Egypt, Feb. 3–8, 1981)—Ludo Dielis, Belgium

United States 3–cushion champion (Oak Park, Mich., Feb. 20–22, 1981)—George Ashby, Murrayville, Ill.

Men's world pocket billiards open—Mike Sigel, Towson, Md. (defeated Nick Varner, Owensboro, Ky., 150–55, in finals)

Women's world pocket billiards open—Loree–Jon Ogonowski, Garwood, N.J. (defeated Vicki Frechen, Grand Ledge, Mich., 75–55, in final)

Junior world pocket billiards—Christer Lofstrand, Fronlunda, Sweden (defeated Sal Butera, Canoga Park, Calif., 100–33, in final)

CURLING

WORLD CHAMPION—1981

(London, Ontario, March 29, 1981)

Men—Switzerland, Jury Tanner, skip (defeated United States, Superior, Wis., Bud Somerville, skip, 2–1, in final)

UNITED STATES CHAMPION

Women's Curling Association champion—Seattle, Wash., defeated Grafton, N.D., 9–5, in final

FIGHTER OF THE YEAR
Selected by *The Ring* Magazine.

1928	Gene Tunney	1941	Joe Louis	1955	Rocky Marciano	1969	Jose Napoles
1929	Tommy Loughran	1942	Ray Robinson	1956	Floyd Patterson	1970–71	Joe Frazier
1930	Max Schmeling	1943	Fred Apostoli	1957	Carmen Basilio	1972	Carlos Monzon and
1931	Tommy Loughran	1944	Beau Jack	1958	Ingemar Johansson		Muhammad Ali
1932	Jack Sharkey	1945	Willie Pep	1959	Ingemar Johansson	1973	George Foreman
1933	No award	1946	Tony Zale	1960	Floyd Patterson	1974–75	Muhammad Ali
1934	Barney Ross and	1947	Gus Lesnevich	1961	Joe Brown	1976	George Foreman
	Tony Canzoneri	1948	Ike Williams	1962	Dick Tiger	1977	Carlos Zarate
1935	Barney Ross	1949	Ezzard Charles	1963	Cassius Clay	1978	Muhammad Ali
1936	Joe Louis	1950	Ezzard Charles	1964	Emile Griffith	1979	Sugar Ray Leonard
1937	Henry Armstrong	1951	Ray Robinson	1965	Dick Tiger	1980	Thomas Hearns
1938	Joe Louis	1952	Rocky Marciano	1966	No award		
1939	Joe Louis	1953	Bobo Olson	1967	Joe Frazier		
1940	Billy Conn	1954	Rocky Marciano	1968	Nino Benvenuti		

BOXING'S BIGGEST GATES

Date	Winner, weight Loser, weight	Rounds	Site	Receipts	Attendance
Oct. 2, 1980	Holmes (211½)—Ali (217½)	KO 11	Las Vegas, Nev.	$6,000,000	24,790
Sept. 15, 1978	Ali (221)—Spinks (201)	15	Superdome, New Orleans	4,806,675	65,370
Sept. 22, 1927	Tunney (189½)—Dempsey (192½) (2d)	10	Soldier Field, Chicago	2,658,660	104,943
Sept. 28, 1976	Ali (221)—Norton (217½) (2d)	15	Yankee Stadium, New York	2,400,000	30,289
June 19, 1946	Louis (207)—Conn (187) (2d)	KO 8	Yankee Stadium, New York	1,925,564	45,266
Sept. 23, 1926	Tunney (189½)—Dempsey (190) (1st)	10	Sesquicentennial Stdm., Phila.	1,895,733	120,757
July 2, 1921	Dempsey (188)—Carpentier (172)	KO 4	Boyle's 30 Acres, Jersey City	1,789,238	80,183
Oct. 1, 1975	Ali (224½)—Frazier (214½) (3d)	KO 14	Manila, Philippines	1,600,000	25,000
March 8, 1971	Joe Frazier (205½)—Muhammad Ali (215)	15	New Madison Square Garden	1,352,951	20,455
Oct. 30, 1974	Ali (216½)—Foreman (220)	KO 8	Kinshasa, Zaire	1,200,000	65,000
Sept. 14, 1923	Dempsey (192½)—Firpo (216½)	KO 2	Polo Grounds, New York	1,188,603	82,000
July 21, 1927	Dempsey (194½)—Sharkey (196)	KO 7	Yankee Stadium, New York	1,083,530	75,000
Jan. 28, 1974	Ali (212) Frazier (209) (2d)	12	New Madison Square Garden	1,053,688	20,748
June 22, 1938	Louis (198¾)—Schmeling (193) (2d)	KO 1	Yankee Stadium, New York	1,015,012	70,043
Sept. 24, 1935	Louis (199¼)—Max Baer (210½)	KO 4	Yankee Stadium, New York	1,000,832	88,150
Sept. 21, 1955	Marciano (188¼)—Moore (188)	KO 9	Yankee Stadium, New York	948,117	61,574
June 25, 1948	Louis (213½)—Walcott (194¾) (2d)	KO 11	Yankee Stadium, New York	841,739	42,667
June 20, 1960	Patterson (190)—Johansson (194¾) (2d)	KO 5	Polo Grounds, New York	824,814	31,892
Sept. 12, 1951	Robinson (157½)—Turpin (159) (2d)	KO 10	Polo Grounds, New York	767,626	61,370
June 12, 1930	Schmeling (188)—Sharkey (197) (1st)	WF 4	Yankee Stadium, New York	749,935	79,222
June 22, 1937	Louis (197¼)—Braddock (197)	KO 8	Comiskey Park, Chicago	715,470	45,500
July 26, 1928	Tunney (192)—Heeney (203½)	KO 11	Yankee Stadium, New York	691,014	45,890
Sept. 25, 1962	Liston (214)—Patterson (189) (1st)	KO 1	Comiskey Park, Chicago	665,420	18,894
March 4, 1968	{ Frazier (206)—Mathis	KO 11	New Madison Square Garden	658,503	18,096
	Benvenuti (160)—Griffith (154½)	15			
Feb. 16, 1970	Joe Frazier (205)—Jimmy Ellis (201)	KO 5	New Madison Square Garden, N.Y.	647,997	18,079
Feb. 25, 1964	Clay (210½)—Liston (218) (1st)	KO 7	Miami Beach, Fla.	625,000	8,927
Dec. 7, 1970	Ali (212)—Bonavena (204)	KO 15	New Madison Square Garden, New York	615,401	19,417
Sept. 29, 1941	Louis (202¼)—Nova (202½)	KO 6	Polo Grounds, New York	583,711	56,549
Sept. 23, 1957	Basilio (153½)—Robinson (160) (1st)	15	Yankee Stadium, New York	556,467	38,072
June 19, 1936	Schmeling (192)—Louis (198) (1st)	KO 12	Yankee Stadium, New York	547,541	42,088
June 17, 1954	Marciano (187½)—Charles (185½) (1st)	15	Yankee Stadium, New York	543,092	47,585
June 17, 1974	Frazier (212)—Quarry (197½) (2d)	KO 5	New Madison Square Garden, N.Y.	517,006	14,611
Sept. 20, 1972	Ali (218)—Patterson (188½) (2d)	KO 7	New Madison Square Garden, N.Y.	512,361	17,378

NOTES: KO—won by knockout; WF—won on foul; ND—no decision; 1st—first bout; 2d—second bout; 3rd—third bout.

SOAP BOX DERBY

(Akron, Ohio, Aug. 15, 1981)

All–American senior division—Tonia Schlegel, Hamilton, Ohio, 28.23 seconds
All–American junior division—Howie Fraley, Portsmouth, Ohio, 28.90 seconds

Darts

U.S. OPEN—1980

Rick Ney, Pine Grove, Pa.
World champion—Stefan Lord, Sweden

HORSE RACING

Ancient drawings on stone and bone prove that horse racing is at least 3000 years old, but Thoroughbred Racing is a modern development. Practically every thoroughbred in training today traces its registered ancestry back to one or more of three sires that arrived in England about 1728 from the Near East and became known, from the names of their owners, as the Byerly Turk, the Darley Arabian, and the Godolphin Arabian. The Jockey Club (English) was founded at Newmarket in 1750 or 1751 and became the custodian of the Stud Book as well as the court of last resort in deciding turf affairs.

Horse racing took place in this country before the Revolution, but the great lift to the breeding industry came with the importation in 1798, by Col. John Hoomes of Virginia, of Diomed, winner of the Epsom Derby of 1780. Diomed's lineal descendants included such famous stars of the American turf as American Eclipse and Lexington. From 1800 to the time of the Civil War there were race courses and breeding establishments plentifully scattered through Virginia, North Carolina, South Carolina, Tennessee, Kentucky, and Louisiana.

The oldest stake event in North America is the Queen's Plate, a Canadian fixture that was first run in the Province of Quebec in 1836. The oldest stake event in the United States is The Travers, which was first run at Saratoga in 1864. The gambling that goes with horse racing and trickery by jockeys, trainers, owners, and track officials caused attacks on the sport by reformers and a demand among horse racing enthusiasts for an honest and effective control of some kind, but nothing of lasting value to racing came of this until the formation in 1894 of The Jockey Club.

"TRIPLE CROWN" WINNERS IN THE UNITED STATES[1]

(Kentucky Derby, Preakness and Belmont Stakes)

Year	Horse	Owner	Year	Horse	Owner
1919	Sir Barton	J. K. L. Ross	1946	Assault	Robert J. Kleberg
1930	Gallant Fox	William Woodward	1948	Citation	Warren Wright
1935	Omaha	William Woodward	1973	Secretariat	Meadow Stable
1937	War Admiral	Samuel D. Riddle	1977	Seattle Slew	Karen Taylor
1941	Whirlaway	Warren Wright	1978	Affirmed	Louis Wolfson
1943	Count Fleet	Mrs. John Hertz			

1. Statistics relative to thoroughbred racing in this publication are reproduced from the *American Racing Manual*, by special permission of the copyright owners. TRIANGLE PUBLICATIONS, INC. Reproduction prohibited.

KENTUCKY DERBY

Churchill Downs; 3-year-olds; 1 1/4 miles.

Year	Winner	Jockey	Wt.	Win val.	Year	Winner	Jockey	Wt.	Win val.
1875	Aristides	O. Lewis	100	$2,850	1909	Wintergreen	V. Powers	117	4,850
1876	Vagrant	R. Swim	97	2,950	1910	Donau	F. Herbert	117	4,850
1877	Baden Baden	W. Walker	100	3,300	1911	Meridian	G. Archibald	117	4,850
1878	Day Star	J. Carter	100	4,050	1912	Worth	C. H. Shilling	117	4,850
1879	Lord Murphy	C. Schauer	100	3,550	1913	Donerail	R. Goose	117	5,475
1880	Fonso	G. Lewis	105	3,800	1914	Old Rosebud	J. McCabe	114	9,125
1881	Hindoo	J. McLaughlin	105	4,410	1915	Regret	J. Notter	112	11,450
1882	Apollo	B. Hurd	102	4,560	1916	George Smith	J. Loftus	117	9,750
1883	Leonatus	W. Donohue	105	3,760	1917	Omar Khayyam	C. Borel	117	16,600
1884	Buchanan	I. Murphy	110	3,990	1918	Exterminator	W. Knapp	114	14,700
1885	Joe Cotton	E. Henderson	110	4,630	1919	Sir Barton	J. Loftus	112 1/2	20,825
1886	Ben Ali	P. Duffy	118	4,890	1920	Paul Jones	T. Rice	126	30,375
1887	Montrose	I. Lewis	118	4,200	1921	Behave Yourself	C. Thompson	126	38,450
1888	Macbeth II	G. Covington	115	4,740	1922	Morvich	A. Johnson	126	46,775
1889	Spokane	T. Kiley	118	4,970	1923	Zev	E. Sande	126	53,600
1890	Riley	I. Murphy	118	5,460	1924	Black Gold	J. D. Mooney	126	52,775
1891	Kingman	I. Murphy	122	4,680	1925	Flying Ebony	E. Sande	126	52,950
1892	Azra	A. Clayton	122	4,230	1926	Bubbling Over	A. Johnson	126	50,075
1893	Lookout	E. Kunze	122	4,090	1927	Whiskery	L. McAtee	126	51,000
1894	Chant	F. Goodale	122	4,020	1928	Reigh Count	C. Lang	126	55,375
1895	Halma	J. Perkins	122	2,970	1929	Clyde Van Dusen	L. McAtee	126	53,950
1896	Ben Brush	W. Simms	117	4,850	1930	Gallant Fox	E. Sande	126	50,725
1897	Typhoon II	F. Garner	117	4,850	1931	Twenty Grand	C. Kurtsinger	126	48,725
1898	Plaudit	W. Simms	117	4,850	1932	Burgoo King	E. James	126	52,350
1899	Manuel	F. Taral	117	4,850	1933	Brokers Tip	D. Meade	126	48,925
1900	Lieut. Gibson	J. Boland	117	4,850	1934	Cavalcade	M. Garner	126	28,175
1901	His Eminence	J. Winkfield	117	4,850	1935	Omaha	W. Saunders	126	39,525
1902	Alan-a-Dale	J. Winkfield	117	4,850	1936	Bold Venture	I. Hanford	126	37,725
1903	Judge Himes	H. Booker	117	4,850	1937	War Admiral	C. Kurtsinger	126	52,050
1904	Elwood	F. Prior	117	4,850	1938	Lawrin	E. Arcaro	126	47,050
1905	Agile	J. Martin	122	4,850	1939	Johnstown	J. Stout	126	46,350
1906	Sir Huon	R. Troxler	117	4,850	1940	Gallahadion	C. Bierman	126	60,150
1907	Pink Star	A. Minder	117	4,850	1941	Whirlaway	E. Arcaro	126	$61,275
1908	Stone Street	A. Pickens	117	$4,850	1942	Shut Out	W. D. Wright	126	64,225

Year	Winner	Jockey	Wt.	Win val.	Year	Winner	Jockey	Wt.	Win val.
1943	Count Fleet	J. Longden	126	60,725	1963	Chateaugay	B. Baeza	126	108,900
1944	Pensive	C. McCreary	126	64,675	1964	Northern Dancer	W. Hartack	126	114,300
1945	Hoop Jr.	E. Arcaro	126	64,850	1965	Lucky Debonair	W. Shoemaker	126	112,000
1946	Assault	W. Mehrtens	126	96,400	1966	Kauai King	D. Brumfield	126	120,500
1947	Jet Pilot	E. Guerin	126	92,160	1967	Proud Clarion	R. Ussery	126	119,700
1948	Citation	E. Arcaro	126	83,400	1968	Forward Pass[1]	I. Valenzuela	126	122,600
1949	Ponder	S. Brooks	126	91,600	1969	Majestic Prince	W. Hartack	126	113,200
1950	Middleground	W. Boland	126	92,650	1970	Dust Commander	M. Manganello	126	127,800
1951	Count Turf	C. McCreary	126	98,050	1971	Canonero II	G. Avila	126	145,500
1952	Hill Gail	E. Arcaro	126	96,300	1972	Riva Ridge	R. Turcotte	126	140,300
1953	Dark Star	H. Moreno	126	90,050	1973	Secretariat	R. Turcotte	126	155,050
1954	Determine	R. York	126	102,050	1974	Cannonade	A. Cordero, Jr.	126	274,000
1955	Swaps	W. Shoemaker	126	108,400	1975	Foolish Pleasure	J. Vasquez	126	209,600
1956	Needles	D. Erb	126	123,450	1976	Bold Forbes	A. Cordero, Jr.	126	165,200
1957	Iron Liege	W. Hartack	126	107,950	1977	Seattle Slew	J. Cruguet	126	214,700
1958	Tim Tam	I. Valenzuela	126	116,400	1978	Affirmed	S. Cauthen	126	186,900
1959	Tomy Lee	W. Shoemaker	126	119,650	1979	Spectacular Bid	R. Franklin	126	228,650
1960	Venetian Way	W. Hartack	126	$114,850	1980	Genuine Risk	J. Vasquez	126	250,550
1961	Carry Back	J. Sellers	126	120,500	1981	Pleasant Colony	J. Velasquez	126	317,200
1962	Decidedly	W. Hartack	126	119,650					

1. Dancer's Image finished first but was disqualified after traces of drug were found in system.

PREAKNESS STAKES

Pimlico; 3-year-olds; 1 3/16 miles; first race 1873.

Year	Winner	Jockey	Wt.	Win Val.	Year	Winner	Jockey	Wt.	Win val.
1919	Sir Barton	J. Loftus	126	$ 24,500	1956	Fabius	W. Hartack	126	84,250
1930	Gallant Fox	E. Sande	126	51,925	1957	Bold Ruler	E. Arcaro	126	65,250
1931	Mate	G. Ellis	126	48,225	1958	Tim Tam	I. Valenzuela	126	97,900
1932	Burgoo King	E. James	126	50,375	1959	Royal Orbit	W. Harmatz	126	136,200
1933	Head Play	C. Kurtsinger	126	26,850	1960	Bally Ache	R. Ussery	126	$121,000
1934	High Quest	R. Jones	126	25,175	1961	Carry Back	J. Sellers	126	126,200
1935	Omaha	W. Saunders	126	25,325	1962	Greek Money	J. Rotz	126	135,800
1936	Bold Venture	G. Woolf	126	27,325	1963	Candy Spots	W. Shoemaker	126	127,500
1937	War Admiral	C. Kurtsinger	126	45,600	1964	Northern Dancer	W. Hartack	126	124,200
1938	Dauber	M. Peters	126	51,875	1965	Tom Rolfe	R. Turcotte	126	128,100
1939	Challedon	G. Seabo	126	53,710	1966	Kauai King	D. Brumfield	126	129,000
1940	Bimelech	F.A. Smith	126	53,230	1967	Damascus	W. Shoemaker	126	141,500
1941	Whirlaway	E. Arcaro	126	49,365	1968	Forward Pass	I. Valenzuela	126	142,700
1942	Alsab	B. James	126	58,175	1969	Majestic Prince	W. Hartack	126	129,500
1943	Count Fleet	J. Longden	126	43,190	1970	Personality	E. Belmonte	126	151,300
1944	Pensive	C. McCreary	126	60,075	1971	Canonero II	G. Avila	126	137,400
1945	Polynesian	W.D. Wright	126	66,170	1972	Bee Bee Bee	E. Nelson	126	135,300
1946	Assault	W. Mehrtens	126	96,620	1973	Secretariat	R. Turcotte	126	129,900
1947	Faultless	D. Dodson	126	98,005	1974	Little Current	M. Rivera	126	156,000
1948	Citation	E. Arcaro	126	91,870	1975	Master Derby	D. McHargue	126	158,100
1949	Capot	T. Atkinson	126	79,985	1976	Elocutionist	J. Lively	126	129,700
1950	Hill Prince	E. Arcaro	126	56,115	1977	Seattle Slew	J. Cruguet	126	138,600
1951	Bold	E. Arcaro	126	83,110	1978	Affirmed	S. Cauthen	126	136,200
1952	Blue Man	C. McCreary	126	86,135	1979	Spectacular Bid	R. Franklin	126	165,300
1953	Native Dancer	E. Guerin	126	65,200	1980	Codex	A. Cordero	126	180,600
1954	Hasty Road	J. Adams	126	91,600	1981	Pleasant Colony	J. Velasquez	126	270,800
1955	Nashua	E. Arcaro	126	67,550					

BELMONT STAKES

Belmont Park; 3-year-olds; 1 1/2 miles.
Run at Jerome Park 1867 to 1890; at Morris Park 1890–94; at Belmont Park 1905–62; at Aqueduct 1963–67. Distance 1 5/8 miles prior to 1874; reduced to 1 1/2 miles, 1874; reduced to 1 1/4 miles, 1890; increased to 1 1/8 miles, 1893; increased to 1 1/4 miles, 1895; increased to 1 3/8 miles, 1896; reduced to 1 1/4 miles in 1904; increased to 1 1/2 miles, 1926.

Year	Winner	Jockey	Wt.	Win val.	Year	Winner	Jockey	Wt.	Win val.
1919	Sir Barton	J. Loftus	126	$ 11,950	1940	Bimelech	F.A. Smith	126	35,030
1930	Gallant Fox	E. Sande	126	66,040	1941	Whirlaway	E. Arcaro	126	39,770
1931	Twenty Grand	C. Kurtsinger	126	58,770	1942	Shut Out	E. Arcaro	126	44,520
1932	Faireno	T. Malley	126	55,120	1943	Count Fleet	J. Longden	126	35,340
1933	Hurryoff	M. Garner	126	49,490	1944	Bounding Home	G.L. Smith	126	55,000
1934	Peace Chance	W.D. Wright	126	43,410	1945	Pavot	E. Arcaro	126	56,675
1935	Omaha	W. Saunders	126	35,480	1946	Assault	W. Mehrtens	126	75,400
1936	Granville	J. Stout	126	29,800	1947	Phalanx	R. Donoso	126	78,900
1937	War Admiral	C. Kurtsinger	126	38,020	1948	Citation	E. Arcaro	126	77,700
1938	Pasteurized	J. Stout	126	34,530	1949	Capot	T. Atkinson	126	60,900
1939	Johnstown	J. Stout	126	37,020	1950	Middleground	W. Boland	126	61,350

Year	Winner	Jockey	Wt.	Win val.	Year	Winner	Jockey	Wt.	Win val.
1951	Counterpoint	D. Gorman	126	82,000	1967	Damascus	W. Shoemaker	126	104,950
1952	One Count	E. Arcaro	126	82,400	1968	Stage Door Johnny	H. Gustines	126	117,700
1953	Native Dancer	E. Guerin	126	82,500	1969	Arts and Letters	B. Baeza	126	104,050
1954	High Gun	E. Guerin	126	89,000	1970	High Echelon	J. Rotz	126	115,000
1955	Nashua	E. Arcaro	126	83,700	1971	Pass Catcher	R. Blum	126	97,750
1956	Needles	D. Erb	126	83,600	1972	Riva Ridge	R. Turcotte	126	93,540
1957	Gallant Man	W. Shoemaker	126	77,300	1973	Secretariat	R. Turcotte	126	90,120
1958	Cavan	P. Anderson	126	73,440	1974	Little Current	M. Rivera	126	101,970
1959	Sword Dancer	W. Shoemaker	126	93,525	1975	Avatar	W. Shoemaker	126	116,160
1960	Celtic Ash	W. Hartack	126	96,785	1976	Bold Forbes	A. Cordero, Jr.	126	117,000
1961	Sherluck	B. Baeza	126	$104,900	1977	Seattle Slew	J. Cruguet	126	109,080
1962	Jaipur	W. Shoemaker	126	109,550	1978	Affirmed	S. Cauthen	126	110,580
1963	Chateaugay	B. Baeza	126	101,700	1979	Coastal	R. Hernandez	126	161,400
1964	Quadrangle	M. Ycaza	126	110,850	1980	Temperence Hill	E. Maple	126	176,220
1965	Hail to All	J. Sellers	126	104,150	1981	Summing	G. Martens	126	170,580
1966	Amberoid	W. Boland	126	117,700					

1981 TRIPLE CROWN RACES

(For 3-year-olds, carrying 126 pounds; jockeys in parentheses)

Kentucky Derby (Churchill Downs, Louisville, Ky., May 2; gross purse $413,450; 1¼ miles)—1. Pleasant Colony (Jorge Velasquez), owned by Thomas Mellon Evans; mutuel returns: $9, 5.60, 4.40. 2. Woodchopper (Eddie Delahoussaye) $23.40, 13. 3. Partez (Sandy Hawley) $4. 4. Classic Go Go (Black). 5. Television Studio (Whited). 6. Pass the Tab (Pincay). 7. Splendid Spruce (McHargue). 8. Flying Nashua (Cordero). 9. Noble Nashua (Asmussen). 10. Bold Ego (Lively). 11. Double Sonic (Thornburg). 12. Hoedown Day (Chapman). 13. Beau Rit (Rubbicco). 14. Tap Shoes (Hernandez). 15. Cure the Blues (Shoemaker). 16. Well Decorated (MacBeth). 17. Mythical Ruler (Wirth). 18. Proud Appeal (Fell). 19. Top Avenger (Snyder). 20. Habano (Feliciano). 21. Golden Derby (Espinoza). Time: 2:02. Winner's purse: $317,200. Margin of victory: Three-quarters of a length. Attendance: 139,195.

Preakness Stakes (Pimlico, Baltimore, Md., May 16; gross purse $270,800; 1 3/16 miles)—1. Pleasant Colony (Jorge Velasquez), owned by Thomas Mellon Evans; mutuel returns: $5, 3.40, 3.20. 2. Bold Ego (Lively) $4.60, 4.20. 3. Paristo (Ashcroft) $17.80. 4. Thirty Eight Pieces (Passmore). 5. Partez (Hawley). 6. Highland Blade (Vasquez). 7. Escambia Bay (Pino). 8. Bare Knuckles (Evans). 9. Double Sonic (Thornburg). 10. A Run (Lovato). 11. Woodchopper (Delahoussaye). 12. Flying Nashua (Cordero). 13. Top Avenger (Romero). Time: 1:54 3/5. Winner's purse: $200,800. Margin of victory: 1 length. Attendance: 84,113.

Belmont Stakes (Elmont, N.Y., June 6; gross purse: $284,300; 1½ miles)—1. Summing (George Martens), owned by C.T. Wilson, Jr.; mutuel returns: $17.80, 7.80, 4.00. 2. Highland Blade (Vasquez) 11.40, 5.60. 3. Pleasant Colony (Velasquez) 2.80. 4. Woodchopper (Pincay). 5. Escambia Bay (Maple) 6. Tap Shoes (Hernandez). 7. Paristo (Cordero). 8. Bare Knuckles (Evans). 9. Stage Door Key (MacBeth). 10. Sezyou (Fell). 11. Bold Ego (Lively). Time: 2:09. Winner's purse: $170,580. Margin of victory: neck. Attendance: 61,000.

BIATHLON

WORLD CHAMPIONSHIPS—1981

(Lahti, Finland, Feb. 15–21, 1981)

Men's 20 kilometers—Heikki Ikola, Finland
Men's 10 kilometers—Frank Ullrich, East Germany
4 x 7.5 kilometer relay—Mathias Jung, Mathias Jacob, Frank Ullrich, Eberhard Roesch, East Germany
Junior 15 kilometers—Harri Eloranto, Finland
Junior 3 x 7.5 kilometer relay—Steffen Lundau, Frank–Peter Roetsch, Rolf Goethel, East Germany

Eclipse Awards—1980

The Eclipse Awards in thoroughbred racing are given on the basis of voting by three groups: the Daily Racing Form, the National Turf Writers Association, and the racing secretaries at tracks that are members of the Thoroughbred Racing Association.

Horse of the year and best older horse	Spectacular Bid
2-year-old colt	Lord Avie
2-year-old filly	Heavenly Cause
3-year-old colt	Temperence Hill
3-year-old filly	Genuine Risk
Older filly or mare	Glorious Song
Male turf horse	John Henry
Female turf horse	Just A Game II
Sprinter	Plugged Nickel
Steeplechase	Zaccio

QUARTER HORSE RACING—1981

Rainbow Futurity—Special Effort (W.R. Hunt, jockey)
Kansas Futurity—Special Effort (W.R. Hunt)
Kansas Derby—Easily Smashed (Jackie Martin)

JUDO

UNITED STATES CHAMPIONSHIPS—1981

(North Little Rock, Ark., April 27–29, 1981)

Men

132 lb—Rod Condurages, Wantagh, N.Y.
143 lb—James A. Martin, Alhambra, Calif.
156 lb—Mike Swain, Bridgewater, N.J.
172 lb—Nicky Yonezuka, Watchung, N.J.
189 lb—Robert Berland, Chicago, Ill.
Under 209 lb—Leo White, United States Army
Over 209 lb—Douglas Nelson, Englewood, N.J.
Open—Mitch Santa Maria, Roselle Park, N.J.

Women

106 lb—Darlene Anaya, Albuquerque, N.M.
114 lb—Robin Takemori, Alexandria, Va.
123 lb—Darlene Hill, Memphis, Tenn.
134 lb—Robin Chapman, Cranford, N.J.
145 lb—Chris Penick, San Jose, Calif.
158 lb—Heide Baversachs, New York, N.Y.
Over 158—Juanita Cardwell, Tallahassee, Fla.
Open—Karen Mackey, Sioux City, Iowa

TRACK AND FIELD

Running, jumping, hurdling and throwing weights—track and field sports, in other words—are as natural to young people as eating, drinking and breathing. Unorganized competition in this form of sport goes back beyond the Cave Man era. Organized competition begins with the first recorded Olympic Games in Greece, 776 B.C., when Coroebus of Elis won the only event on the program, a race of approximately 200 yards. The Olympic Games, with an ever-widening program of events, continued until "the glory that was Greece" had faded and "the grandeur that was Rome" was tarnished, and finally were abolished by decree of Emperor Theodosius I of Rome in A.D. 394. The Tailteann Games of Ireland are supposed to have antedated the first Olympic Games by some centuries, but we have no records of the specific events and winners thereof.

Professional contests of speed and strength were popular at all times and in many lands, but the widespread competition of amateur athletes in track and field sports is a comparatively modern development. The first organized amateur athletic meet of record was sponsored by the Royal Military Academy at Woolwich, England, in 1849. Oxford and Cambridge track and field rivalry began in 1864, and the English amateur championships were established in 1866. In the United States such organizations as the New York Athletic Club and the Olympic Club of San Francisco conducted track and field meets in the 1870s, and a few colleges joined to sponsor a meet in 1874. The success of the college meet led to the formation of the Intercollegiate Association of Amateur Athletes of America and the holding of an annual set of championship games beginning in 1876. The Amateur Athletic Union, organized in 1888, has been the ruling body in American amateur athletics since that time. In 1980, The Athletics Congress of the U.S.A. took over the governing of track and field from the A.A.U.

WORLD RECORDS—MEN

(Through Sept. 9, 1981)
Recognized by the International Athletic Federation
The I.A.A.F. decided late in 1976 not to recognize records in yards except for the one-mile run.
The I.A.A.F. also requires automatic timing for all records for races of 400 meters or less.

Event	Record	Holder	Home Country	Where Made	Date
Running					
100 m	0:09.95	Jim Hines	U.S.	Mexico City	Oct. 14, 1968
200 m	0:19.72	Pietro Mennea	Italy	Mexico City	Sept. 17, 1979
400 m	0:43.86	Lee Evans	U.S.	Mexico City	Oct. 18, 1968
800 m	1:41.72	Sebastian Coe	England	Oslo, Norway	July 5, 1979
1,000 m	2:12.40	Sebastian Coe	England	Oslo	July 11, 1981
1,500 m	3:31.36	Steve Ovett	England	Koblenz, W. Ger.	Aug. 27, 1980
1 mile	3:47.33	Sebastian Coe	England	Brussels	Aug. 28, 1981
2,000 m	4:51.4	John Walker	New Zealand	Oslo	June 30, 1976
3,000 m	7:32.1	Henry Rono	Kenya	Oslo	June 27, 1978
3,000 m steeplechase	8:05.4	Henry Rono	Kenya	Seattle, Wash.	May 13, 1978
5,000 m	13:08.4	Henry Rono	Kenya	Berkeley, Calif.	April 8, 1978
10,000 m	27:22.4	Henry Rono	Kenya	Vienna, Austria	June 11, 1978
25,000 m	1:13:55.8	Toshihiko Seko	Japan	Christchurch, N.Z.	March 22, 1981
30,000 m	1:29:18.8	Toshihiko Seko	Japan	Christchurch, N.Z.	March 22, 1981
20,000 m	57:24.2	Jos Hermans	Netherlands	Papandal, Neth.	May 1, 1976
1 hour	13 mi. 24 yd	Jos Hermans	Netherlands	Papandal, Neth.	May 1, 1976
Walking					
20,000 m	1:20.06.8	Daniel Bautista	Mexico	Montreal	Oct. 17, 1979
2 hours	17 mi. 881 yd	Jose Marin	Spain	Barcelona	Aug. 4, 1979
30,000 m	2:08:00	Jose Marin	Spain	Barcelona	Aug. 4, 1979
50,000 m	3:41:39	Raul Gonzales	Mexico	Bergen, Norway	May 25, 1979
Hurdles					
110 m	0:12.93	Renaldo Nehemiah	U.S.	Zurich, Switzerland	Aug. 19, 1981
400 m	0:47.13	Edwin Moses	U.S.	Milan, Italy	July 3, 1980
Relay Races					
400 m (4x100)	0:38.03	National Team	U.S.	Dusseldorf, W. Ger.	Sept. 3, 1977
800 m (4x200)	1:20.26	So. California	U.S.	Tempe, Ariz.	May 27, 1978
		(Joel Andrews, James Sanford, Billy Mullins, Clancy Edwards)			
1,600 m (4x400)	2:56.16	National Team	U.S.	Mexico City	Oct. 20, 1968
		(Vince Matthews, Ron Freeman, Larry James, Lee Evans)			
3,200 m (4x800)	7:08.1	National Team	U.S.S.R.	Podolsk, U.S.S.R.	Aug. 12, 1978
		(Vladimir Podolyakov, Nikolai Kirov, Vladimir Malozemlin, Anatoli Reshetnyak)			

Field Events

High jump	7 ft 8¾ in.	Gerd Wessig	East Germany	Moscow	Aug. 1, 1980
Long jump	29 ft 2½ in.	Bob Beamon	U.S.	Mexico City	Oct. 18, 1976
Triple jump	58 ft 8¼ in.	Joao Oliveira	Brazil	Mexico City	Oct. 15, 1975
Pole vault	19 ft 2 in. p	Konstantin Volkov	U.S.S.R.	Irkutsk, U.S.S.R.	Aug. 2, 1981
Shotput	72 ft 8 in.	Udo Beyer	East Germany	Goteborg, Sweden	July 6, 1978
Discus throw	233 ft 5 in.	Wolfgang Schmidt	East Germany	East Berlin	Aug. 9, 1978
Javelin throw	317 ft 4 in.	Ferenc Paragi	Hungary	Tata, Hungary	April 23, 1980
Hammer throw	268 ft 4 in.	Yuri Sedyky	U.S.S.R.	Moscow	July 31, 1980
Decathlon	8,649 pts	Guido Kratschmer	West Germany	Filderstadt, W. Ger.	July 13–14, 1980

p = mark is pending official acceptance.

WORLD RECORDS—WOMEN

Event	Record	Holder	Home Country	Where Made	Date
Running					
100 m	0:10.88	Marlies Goehr	East Germany	Dresden, E. Ger.	July 1, 1977
200 m	0:21.71	Marita Koch	East Germany	Karl Marx Stadt	June 10, 1979
400 m	0:48.60	Marita Koch	East Germany	Turin, Italy	Aug. 4, 1979
800 m	1:53.42	Nadezhda Olizaryenko	U.S.S.R.	Moscow	June 27, 1980
1,500 m	3:52.47	Tatyana Kazankina	U.S.S.R.	Zurich, Switz.	Aug. 13, 1980
1 mile	4:21.68	Mary Decker	U.S.	Auckland, N.Z.	Jan. 26, 1980
3,000 m	8:27.12	Lyudmila Bragina	U.S.S.R.	College Park, Md.	Aug. 7, 1976
5,000 m	15:28.43	Ingrid Christensen	Norway	Oslo	July 11, 1981
10,000 m	31:45.4	Loa Olafsson	Denmark	Copenhagen	April 6, 1978
Hurdles					
100 m	0:12.36	Grazyna Rabsztyn	Poland	Warsaw	June 13, 1980
400 m	0:54.28	Karin Rossley	East Germany	Jena, E. Ger.	May 17, 1980
Relay Races					
400 m (4x100)	0:41.60	National Team	East Germany	Moscow	Aug. 1, 1980
		(Romy Mueller, Barbel Woeckel, Ingrid Auerwald, Marlies Goehr)			
800 m (4x200)	1:28.15	National Team	East Germany	Jena, E. Ger.	July 9, 1980
		(Marlies Goehr, Romy Mueller, Barbel Woeckel, Marita Koch)			
1,600 m (4x400)	3:19.23	National Team	East Germany	Montreal	July 31, 1976
		(Doris Maletzki, Brigitte Rohde, Ellen Streidt, Christine Bremer)			
3,200 m (4x800)	7:52.3	National Team	U.S.S.R.	Podolsk, U.S.S.R.	Aug. 16, 1976
		(Tatyana Providokhina, Vera Gerasimova, Svetlana Styrkina, Tatyana Kazankina)			
Field Events					
High jump	6 ft 7 in.	Sara Simeoni	Italy	Brescia, Italy	Aug. 4, 1978
	6 ft 7 in.	Sara Simeoni	Italy	Prague, Czech.	Aug. 31, 1978
Long jump	23 ft 3¼ in.	Vilma Bardauskiene	U.S.S.R.	Prague, Czech.	Aug. 29, 1978
Shotput	73 ft 4¼ in.	Ilona Slupianek	East Germany	Celje, Yugoslavia	May 2, 1980
Discus throw	235 ft 7 in.	Maria Vergova	Bulgaria	Sofia, Bulgaria	July 13, 1980
Javelin throw	235 ft 10 in.	Antoanetta Todorova	Bulgaria	Zagreb, Yugoslavia	Aug. 15, 1981
Heptathlon	6,717 pts	Ramona Neubert	East Germany	Kiev, U.S.S.R.	June 27, 1981

AMERICAN RECORDS—MEN

Officially approved by The Athletics Congress; all listings are for automatic timing.

Event	Record	Holder	Where Made	Date
Running				
100 m	0:09.95	Jim Hines	Mexico City	Oct. 14, 1968
200 m	0:19.83	Tommie Smith	Mexico City	Oct. 16, 1968
400 m	0:43.86	Lee Evans	Mexico City	Oct. 16, 1968
800 m	1:43.9	Richard Wohlhuter	Stockholm	July 18, 1974
1,000 m	2:13.9	Richard Wohlhuter	Oslo	July 30, 1974
1,500 m	3:31.96	Steve Scott	Koblenz, W. Ger.	Aug. 26, 1981
1 mile	3:49.68	Steve Scott	Oslo, Norway	July 11, 1981
2,000 m	5:01.4	Steve Prefontaine	Coos Bay, Ore.	May 10, 1975
3,000 m	7:36.69	Steve Scott	Ingelheim, W. Ger.	Sept. 1, 1981
5,000 m	13:15.06	Martin Liquori	Dusseldorf, W. Ger.	Sept. 4, 1977
10,000 m	27:29.16	Craig Virgin	Paris	July 17, 1980
20,000 m	58:15.0	Bill Rodgers	Boston	Aug. 9, 1977
25,000 m	1:14:12	Bill Rodgers	Saratoga, Calif.	Feb. 21, 1979
30,000 m	1:31:50	Bill Rodgers	Saratoga, Calif.	Feb. 21, 1979
1 hour	12 mi. 997 yds	Bill Rodgers	Saratoga, Calif.	Feb. 21, 1979
3,000 m steeplechase	8:15.68	Henry Marsh	Eugene, Ore.	June 28, 1980

Hurdles

110 m	0:12.93	Renaldo Nehemiah	Zurich, Switzerland	Aug. 19, 1981
400 m	0:47.13	Edwin Moses	Milan, Italy	July 3, 1980

Relay Races

400 m (4x100)	0:38.03	U.S. Team	Dusseldorf, W. Ger.	Sept. 3, 1977
		(Bill Collins, Steve Riddick, Cliff Wiley, Steve Williams)		
800 m (4x200)	1:20.26	Southern California	Tempe, Ariz.	May 27, 1978
		(Joe Andrews, James Sanford, Billy Mullins, Clancy Edwards)		
1,600 m (4x400)	2:56.16	U.S. Team	Mexico City	Oct. 20, 1968
		(Vince Matthews, Ron Freeman, Larry James, Lee Evans)		
3,200 m (4x800)	7:10.4	U. of Chicago T.C.	Durham, N.C.	May 12, 1973
		(Tom Bach, Ken Sparks, Lowell Paul, Rick Wohlhuter)		

Field Events

High jump	7 ft 6½ in.	Dwight Stones	Munich	July 11, 1973
Long jump	29 ft 2½ in.	Bob Beamon	Mexico City	Oct. 18, 1968
Triple jump	57 ft 7½ in.	Willie Banks	Sacramento, Calif.	June 21, 1981
Pole vault	18 ft 8¼ in.	Dave Roberts	Eugene, Ore.	June 22, 1976
Shotput	72 ft 3 in.	Brian Oldfield	Modesto, Calif.	May 16, 1981
Discus throw*	232 ft 10 in.	Mac Wilkins	Helsinki, Finland	July 9, 1980
Javelin throw	300 ft	Mark Murro	Tempe, Ariz.	March 27, 1970
Hammer throw	237 ft 2 in.	Dave McKenzie	Leningrad	July 11, 1981

*Ben Plucknett threw the discus 237 ft 4 in. on May 16, 1981 at Modesto, Calif., for a world record, but the record was withdrawn by the I.A.A.F., charging Plucknett with using illegal steroids.

AMERICAN RECORDS—WOMEN

Event	Record	Holder	Where Made	Date
Running				
100 m	0:10.90	Evelyn Ashford	Colorado Springs	July 22, 1981
200 m	0:21.83	Evelyn Ashford	Montreal	Aug. 24, 1979
400 m	0:50.62	Rosalyn Bryant	Montreal	July 28, 1976
800 m	1:57.9	Madeline Jackson	College Park, Md.	Aug. 7, 1976
1,500 m	3:59.43	Mary Decker	Zurich, Switzerland	Aug. 13, 1980
1 mile	4:21.68	Mary Decker	Auckland, N.Z.	Jan. 26, 1980
3,000 m	8:38.73	Mary Decker	Philadelphia	July 17, 1980
5,000 m	15:33.8	Jan Merrill	Durham, N.C.	May 19, 1979
10,000 m	32:52.5	Mary Shea	Walnut, Calif.	June 15, 1979
Hurdles				
100 m	0:12.86	Deby LaPlante	Walnut, Calif.	July 16, 1979
400 m	0:56.16	Esther Mahr	Sittard, Netherlands	Aug. 15, 1980
Relay Races				
400 m (4x100)	0:42.87	U.S. Team	Mexico City	Oct. 20, 1968
		(Barbara Ferrell, Margaret Bailes, Mildrette Netter, Wyomia Tyus)		
800 m (4x200)	1:32.6	U.S. National Team	Bourges, France	June 23, 1979
		(Wanda Hooker, Karen Hawkins, Chandra Cheeseborough, Brenda Morehead)		
1,600 m (4x400)	3:22.81	U.S. Team	Montreal	July 31, 1976
		(Debra Sapenter, Sheila Ingram, Pam Jiles, Rosalyn Bryant)		
Field Events				
High jump	6 ft 5¼ in.	Pam Spencer	Wichita, Kans.	May 30, 1981
Long jump	22 ft 11½ in.	Jodi Anderson	Eugene, Ore.	June 28, 1980
Shotput	62 ft 7¾ in.	Maren Seidler	Walnut, Calif.	June 16, 1979
Discus throw	207 ft 5 in.	Lorna Griffin	Long Beach, Calif.	May 24, 1980
Javelin throw	227 ft 5 in.	Kathy Schmidt	Furth, W. Ger.	Sept. 11, 1977
Heptathlon	6,308 pts	Jane Frederick	Gotzis, Austria	May 23–24, 1981

HISTORY OF THE RECORD FOR THE MILE RUN

Time	Athlete	Country	Year	Location
4:36.5	Richard Webster	England	1865	England
4:29.0	William Chinnery	England	1868	England
4:28.8	Walter Gibbs	England	1868	England
4:26.0	Walter Slade	England	1874	England
4:24.5	Walter Slade	England	1875	London

4:23.2	Walter George	England	1880	London
4:21.4	Walter George	England	1882	London
4:18.4	Walter George	England	1884	Birmingham, England
4:18.2	Fred Bacon	Scotland	1894	Edinburgh, Scotland
4:17.0	Fred Bacon	Scotland	1895	London
4:15.6	Thomas Conneff	United States	1895	Travers Island, N.Y.
4:15.4	John Paul Jones	United States	1911	Cambridge, Mass.
4:14.4	John Paul Jones	United States	1913	Cambridge, Mass.
4:12.6	Norman Taber	United States	1915	Cambridge, Mass.
4:10.4	Paavo Nurmi	Finland	1923	Stockholm
4:09.2	Jules Ladoumegue	France	1931	Paris
4:07.6	Jack Lovelock	New Zealand	1933	Princeton, N.J.
4:06.8	Glenn Cunningham	United States	1934	Princeton, N.J.
4:06.4	Sydney Wooderson	England	1937	London
4:06.2	Gundar Hägg	Sweden	1942	Göteborg, Sweden
4:06.2	Arne Andersson	Sweden	1942	Stockholm
4:04.6	Gunder Hägg	Sweden	1942	Stockholm
4:02.6	Arne Andersson	Sweden	1943	Göteborg, Sweden
4:01.6	Arne Andersson	Sweden	1944	Malmö, Sweden
4:01.4	Gunder Hägg	Sweden	1945	Malmö, Sweden
3:59.4	Roger Bannister	England	1954	Oxford, England
3:58.0	John Landy	Australia	1954	Turku, Finland
3:57.2	Derek Ibbotson	England	1957	London
3:54.5	Herb Elliott	Australia	1958	Dublin
3:54.4	Peter Snell	New Zealand	1962	Wanganui, N.Z.
3:54.1	Peter Snell	New Zealand	1964	Auckland, N.Z.
3:53.6	Michel Jazy	France	1965	Rennes, France
3:51.3	Jim Ryun	United States	1966	Berkeley, Calif.
3:51.1	Jim Ryun	United States	1967	Bakersfield, Calif.
3:51.0	Filbert Bayi	Tanzania	1975	Kingston, Jamaica
3:49.4	John Walker	New Zealand	1975	Göteborg, Sweden
3:49.0	Sebastian Coe	England	1979	Oslo
3:48.8	Steve Ovett	England	1980	Oslo
3:48.53	Sebastian Coe	England	1981	Zurich, Switzerland
3:48.40	Steve Ovett	England	1981	Koblenz, W. Ger.
3:47.33	Sebastian Coe	England	1981	Brussels

WORLD'S FASTEST INDOOR MILES

Time	Athlete	Country	Date	Location
3:50.6	Eamonn Coghlan	Ireland	Feb. 20, 1981	San Diego
3:51.8	Steve Scott[1]	United States	Feb. 20, 1981	San Diego
3:52.6	Eamonn Coghlan	Ireland	Feb. 16, 1979	San Diego
3:52.8	John Walker[2]	New Zealand	Feb. 20, 1981	San Diego
3:52.9	Eamonn Coghlan	Ireland	Feb. 15, 1980	Los Angeles
3:53.0	Steve Scott[1]	United States	Feb. 15, 1980	Los Angeles
3:53.0	Eamonn Coghlan	Ireland	Feb. 6, 1981	New York
3:53.6	Ray Flynn[3]	Ireland	Feb. 20, 1981	San Diego
3:53.7	Steve Scott	United States	Feb. 6, 1981	New York
3:53.8	Ray Flynn	Ireland	Feb. 16, 1979	San Diego
3:54.1	Steve Scott[1]	United States	Jan. 30, 1981	Los Angeles
3:54.3	Eamonn Coghlan[1]	Ireland	Jan. 30, 1981	Los Angeles
3:54.4	Ray Flynn[2]	Ireland	Feb. 15, 1980	Los Angeles
3:54.5	Filbert Bayi[2]	Tanzania	Feb. 16, 1979	San Diego
3:54.7	Steve Lacy[2]	United States	Feb. 6, 1981	New York
3:54.7	Thomas Wessinghage[2]	West Germany	Feb. 13, 1981	Inglewood, Calif.
3:54.9	Ray Flynn	Ireland	Feb. 17, 1974	San Diego
3:55.0	Tony Waldrop	United States	Jan. 13, 1978	College Park, Md.
3:55.0	Dick Buerkle	United States	Feb. 9, 1979	New York
3:55.0	Eamonn Coghlan	Ireland	Feb. 6, 1981	New York
3:55.0	Steve Scott[3]	United States	Feb. 13, 1981	Inglewood, Calif.
3:55.2	John Walker[1]	New Zealand	Feb. 21, 1981	Daly City, Calif.
3:55.3	Steve Scott	United States	Jan. 28, 1977	Columbia, Mo.
3:55.4	Niall O'Shaughnessy	Ireland	Feb. 22, 1980	San Diego
3:55.5	Filbert Bayi	Tanzania	Feb. 21, 1981	Daly City, Calif.
3:55.5	Sydney Maree[1]	South Africa	Jan. 31, 1981	Dallas
3:55.55	Eamonn Coghlan	Ireland	Feb. 15, 1980	Los Angeles
3:55.6	Steve Lacy[3]	United States	Feb. 13, 1981	Toronto
3:55.63	Eamonn Coghlan	Ireland	Feb. 18, 1977	San Diego
3:55.7	Wilson Waigwa	Kenya	Feb. 22, 1980	San Diego
3:55.7	Eamonn Coghlan[1]	Ireland	Feb. 7, 1975	Philadelphia
3:55.8	Marty Liquori	United States		

3:55.8	John Walker[2]	New Zealand	Feb. 22, 1980	San Diego
3:55.87	Wilson Waigwa	Kenya	Jan. 31, 1981	Dallas
3:56.0	Eamonn Coghlan	Ireland	Feb. 17, 1978	San Diego
3:56.0	Tom Byers[2]	United States	Feb. 13, 1981	Inglewood, Calif.
3:56.1	Filbert Bayi	Tanzania	Feb. 27, 1976	New York
3:56.1	Eamonn Coghlan	Ireland	Jan. 20, 1979	Los Angeles

1. Finished second. 2. Finished third. 3. Finished fourth.

WORLD'S FASTEST OUTDOOR MILES

Time	Athlete	Country	Date	Location
3:47.33	Sebastian Coe	England	Aug. 28, 1981	Brussels
3:48.4	Steve Ovett	England	Aug. 26, 1981	Koblenz, W. Ger.
3:48.53	Sebastian Coe	England	Aug. 19, 1981	Zurich
3:48.8	Steve Ovett	England	July 1, 1980	Oslo
3:48.95	Sebastian Coe	England	July 17, 1979	Oslo
3:49.25	Steve Ovett	England	July 11, 1981	Oslo
3:49.4	John Walker	New Zealand	Aug. 12, 1975	Goteborg, Sweden
3:49.57	Steve Ovett	England	Aug. 31, 1979	London
3:49.66	Steve Ovett	England	July 14, 1981	Lausanne, Switz.
3:49.67	Jose-Luis Gonzalez[1]	Spain	July 11, 1981	Oslo
3:49.68	Steve Scott[2]	United States	July 11, 1981	Oslo
3:49.74	Mike Boit[1]	Kenya	Aug. 19, 1981	Zurich
3:49.94	Steve Cram[2]	England	Aug. 19, 1981	Zurich
3:50.12	John Walker[3]	New Zealand	Aug. 19, 1981	Zurich
3:50.26	John Walker[3]	New Zealand	July 11, 1981	Oslo
3:50.34	Todd Harbour[4]	United States	July 11, 1981	Oslo
3:50.38	Steve Cram[5]	England	Aug. 31, 1979	London
3:50.56	Thomas Wessinghage[1]	West Germany	Mar. 19, 1981	Auckland, N.Z.
3:50.58	John Walker	New Zealand	July 14, 1981	Lausanne, Switz.
3:50.87	Jose-Luis Gonzalez[1]	Spain	July 11, 1981	Oslo
3:50.91	Thomas Wessinghage[6]	West Germany	Aug. 19, 1981	Zurich
3:50.95	Thomas Wessinghage[4]	West Germany	May 17, 1975	Kingston, Jamaica
3:51.0	Filbert Bayi	Tanzania	June 23, 1967	Bakersfield, Calif.
3:51.1	Jim Ryun	United States	July 17, 1979	Oslo
3:51.11	Steve Scott[1]	United States	July 17, 1966	Berkeley, Calif.
3:51.3	Jim Ryun	United States	Aug. 22, 1980	Brussels
3:51.6	Steve Ovett	England	July 14, 1981	Lausanne, Switz.
3:51.77	Pierre Deleze[2]	Switzerland	July 14, 1981	Lausanne, Switz.
3:51.94	Suleiman Nyambui[3]	Tanzania	July 11, 1977	Dublin
3:51.98	John Walker[4]	New Zealand	July 17, 1979	Oslo
3:52.0	John Walker	New Zealand	June 23, 1981	Dublin
3:52.02	Craig Masback[2]	United States	July 2, 1973	Stockholm
3:52.11	Eamonn Coghlan	Ireland	May 17, 1975	Kingston, Jamaica
3:52.17	Ben Jipcho	Kenya	June 30, 1975	Stockholm
3:52.2	Marty Liquori[2]	United States	May 30, 1981	Villanova, Pa.
3:52.24	John Walker	New Zealand	Aug. 19, 1981	Zurich
3:52.26	Steve Scott	United States	May 30, 1981	Villanova, Pa.
3:52.31	Vittorio Fontanella[5]	Italy	July 11, 1981	Oslo
3:52.44	Sydney Maree[1]	South Africa	July 17, 1979	Oslo
3:52.44	John Robson[7]	Scotland	July 3, 1978	Stockholm
3:52.45	Eamonn Coghlan[3]	Ireland	May 10, 1981	Westwood, Calif.
3:52.50	Thomas Wessinghage	West Germany		
3:52.50	Steve Scott	United States		

1. Finished second. 2. Finished third. 3. Finished fourth. 4. Finished fifth. 5. Finished sixth. 6. Finished seventh. 7. Finished eighth.
NOTE: Professional marks not included.

LEWIS FIRST SINCE OWENS TO WIN FIELD AND TRACK EVENT IN SAME MEET

Carl Lewis of Houston became the first athlete since the late Jesse Owens to win meet titles in both a track and a field event during the National Collegiate Athletic Association outdoor championships at Baton Rouge, La., in 1981. Lewis ran the 100-meter dash in 9.99 seconds and captured the long jump with 27 feet 3/4 inch. Owens, competing for Ohio State, accomplished the feat in 1936. An oddity surrounded Lewis's feat. Although the N.C.A.A. championships were held outdoors and

Lewis won the 100-meter dash on an outdoor track, he was forced to do his high jumping indoors because of a thunderstorm. Suleiman Nyambui of Texas-El Paso surpassed a record also set by Owens in the same meet. By winning the 10,000 and 5,000 meter runs, Nyambui set a record of winning 10 individual N.C.A.A. career titles. Owens had shared the mark at eight with Gerry Lindgren of Washington State.

HISTORY OF THE POLE VAULT

(Some of early dates are the winning heights of A.A.U. champion for that year, used to show progression from one foot level to the next. Figures from A.A.U. records and *Track & Field News*.)

Bamboo Poles

1877	G. McNichol	9 ft 7 in.
1879	W. J. Van Houten	10 ft 4¾ in.
1883	Hugh Baxter	11 ft 0½ in.
1904	Norman Dole	12 ft 1³/₁₀ in.
1912	Robert Gardner	13 ft 1 in.
1927	Sabin Carr	14 ft 0 in.
1940	Cornelius Warmerdam	15 ft 1 in.
1942	Cornelius Warmerdam	15 ft 7¾ in.

Metal Poles

1957	Bob Gutowski	15 ft 8¼ in.
1960	Don Bragg	15 ft 9¼ in.

Fiberglas Poles

1961	George Davis	15 ft 10¼ in.
1962	John Uelses	16 ft 0¾ in.
1962	Dave Tork	16 ft 2 in.
1962	Pentti Nikula	16 ft 2½ in.
1963	John Pennel	16 ft 4 in.
1963	Brian Sternberg	16 ft 5 in.
1963	John Pennel	16 ft 6¾ in.
1963	Brian Sternberg	16 ft 8 in.

1963	John Pennel	16 ft 10 in.
1963	John Pennel	17 ft 0¾ in.
1964	Fred Hansen	17 ft 4 in.
1966	Bob Seagren	17 ft 5½ in.
1966	John Pennel	17 ft 6¼ in.
1967	Bob Seagren	17 ft 7 in.
1967	Paul Wilson	17 ft 7¾ in.
1968	Bob Seagren	17 ft 9 in.
1969	John Pennel	17 ft 10¼ in.
1970	Wolfgang Norwig	17 ft 10½ in.
1970	Chris Papanicolaou	18 ft 0¼ in.
1972	Kjell Isaksson	18 ft 1 in.
1972	Kjell Isaksson	18 ft 2 in.
1972	Kjell Isaksson, Bob Seagren	18 ft 4¼ in.
1972	Bob Seagren	18 ft 5¾ in.
1975	Dave Roberts	18 ft 6½ in.
1976	Earl Bell	18 ft 7¼ in.
1976	Dave Roberts	18 ft 8¼ in.
1980	Thierry Vigneron	18 ft 10¼ in.
1980	Philippe Houvion	18 ft 11 in.
1980	Wladyslaw Kozakiewicz	18 ft 11½ in.
1981	Thierry Vigneron	19 ft ¼ in.
1981	Vladimir Polyakov	19 ft ¾ in.
1981	Konstantin Volkov	19 ft 2 in.

UNITED STATES MARATHON CHAMPIONS

(26 miles, 385 Yards)

Boston Marathon

1970	Ron Hill, England	2:10:30
1971	Alvaro Meija, Colombia	2:18:45
1972	Olavi Suomalainen, Finland	2:15:39
1973	Jon Anderson, Eugene, Ore.	2:16:03
1974	Neil Cusack, Ireland	2:13:39
1975	William H. Rodgers, Boston	2:09:55
1976	Jack Fultz, Arlington, Va.	2:20:19
1977	Jerome Drayton, Toronto	2:14:46
1978	William H. Rodgers, Melrose, Mass.	2:10:13
1979	William H. Rodgers, Melrose, Mass.	2:09.27
1980	William H. Rodgers, Melrose, Mass.	2:12:11
1981	Toshihiko Seko, Japan	2:09:26

Amateur Athletic Union

1970	Bob Fitts, Wisconsin	2:24:11
1971	Ken Moore, Portland, Ore.	2:16:49
1972	Edmund Norris, Brockton, Mass.	2:24:42.8
1973	Doug Schmenk	2:15:48
1974	Ron Wayne, Eugene, Ore.	2:18:52
1975	Gary Tuttle, Beverly Hills Strider	2:17:27
1976	Gary Tuttle, Los Angeles	2:15:15
1977	Not Held	
1978	Carl Hatfield, West Va. T.C.	2:17.20
1979	Tom Antczak, Rockford, Ill.	2:15.28

The Athletics Congress

1980	Paul Richardson, Ames, Iowa	2:13:54*

*Time not recognized because course was too short.

CROSS COUNTRY RACE CHAMPIONS

Amateur Athletic Union

(10,000 Meters)

1971	Frank Shorter, Gainesville, Fla.; Florida T.C.
1972	Frank Shorter, Gainesville, Fla.; Florida T.C.
1973	Frank Shorter, Gainesville, Fla.; Florida T.C.
1974	John Ngeno, Kenya; Colorado T.C.
1975	Greg Fredericks, Philadelphia; Colorado T.C.
1976	Rick Rojas, San Diego; Jamul Toads
1977	Nick Rose, England; Colorado T.C.
1978	Greg Meyer, Boston; Mason Dixon A.C.
1979	Alberto Salazar, Boston; Greater Boston T.C.
1980	Jon Sinclair, Boulder, Colo. Victory A.C.

N.C.A.A. (University)

(10,000 meters)

1973	Steve Prefontaine, Oregon; Oregon
1974	Nick Rose, Western Kentucky; Oregon
1975	Craig Virgin, Illinois; Texas-El Paso

1976	Henry Rono, Wash. State; Texas-El Paso
1977	Henry Rono, Wash. State; Oregon
1978	Alberto Salazar, Oregon; Texas-El Paso
1979	Henry Rono, Washington State; Texas-El Paso
1980	Suleiman Nyambui, Texas-El Paso, Texas-El Paso

N.C.A.A. (College)

(10,000 meters)

1975	Div. II: Ralph Serna, Calif.-Irvine; Calif.-Irvine
	Div. III: Vin Fleming, Lowell; N. Central Illinois
1976	Div. II: Ralph Serna, Calif.-Irvine; Calif.-Irvine
	Div. III: Dale Cramer, Carleton; N. Central Illinois
1977	Div. II: Michael Bollman, N.D. State; E. Illinois
	Div. III: Dale Kramer, Carleton; Occidental
1978	Div. II: Jim Schankel, Cal Poly, San Luis Opisbo; Cal Poly, San Luis Opisbo
	Div. III: Dan Henderson, Wheaton; N. Cent. Illinois
1979	Div. II: Jim Schankel, Cal Poly, San Luis Opisbo
	Div. III: Steve Hunt, Boston State; North Central, Ill.

1980   Div. II: Gary Henry, Pembroke State; Humboldt State
       Div. III: Jeff Millman, North Central; Carleton

1979   Sam Montoya, Adams State; Adams State
1980   Pat Porter, Adams State; Adams State

N.A.I.A.

(5 Miles)

1973   Tony Brien, Marymount; Eastern New Mexico
1974   Mike Boit, Eastern New Mexico; Eastern New Mexico
1975   Mike Boit, Eastern New Mexico; Edinboro State
1976   John Kebiro, Eastern New Mexico; Edinboro State
1977   Garry Henry, Pembroke State; Adams State
1978   Kelly Jensen, So. Oregon; Pembroke State

CROSS-COUNTRY WORLD CHAMPIONSHIPS—1981

(Madrid, Spain, March 28, 1981)

Men—Craig Virgin, United States	35:05
Women—Grete Waitz, Norway	14:07
Junior men—Mohamed Chouri, Tunisia	22:04
Men's team—Ethiopia	81 pts
Women's team—Soviet Union	24 pts
Junior men's team—United States	23 pts

WORLD AND AMERICAN BEST PERFORMANCES IN INDOOR TRACK

The International Amateur Athletic Union does not recognize indoor records. The following best performances, often called world records, are from lists provided by The Athletics Congress of the United States and *Track and Field News*, published in Los Altos, Calif., Bert Nelson, editor and publisher.

MEN
Running

50 yards—Houston McTear, Toronto, 1978	0:05.25
60 yards—Stanley Floyd, Dallas, 1981	0:06.04
70 yards—Herb McFarland, Louisville, Ky.	0:06.7
100 yards—Don Quarrie, Pocatello, Idaho, 1971	0:09.3
Carl Lawson, Pocatello, Idaho, 1971	0:09.3
Cliff Branch, Pocatello, Idaho, 1972	0:09.3
300 yards—Terron Wright, Bloomington, Ind., 1981	0:29.26
440 yards—Tommie Smith, Louisville, Ky., 1967	0:46.2
Deon Hogan (Am.), Lincoln, Neb., 1981	0:47.20
500 yards—Lee Evans, College Park, Md., 1971	0:54.4
Pro—Larry James, Salt Lake City, Utah, 1973	0:53.9
600 yards—Martin McGrady, New York, 1970	1:07.6
880 yards—Ralph Doubell, Albuquerque N.M., 1969	1:47.9
Mark Belger (Am.), College Park, Md., 1978	1:48.1
Tom Von Ruden (Am.), College Park, Md., 1971	1:48.5
1,000 yards—Don Paige, New York, 1981	2:04.9
Mile—Eamonn Coghlan, San Diego, 1981	3:50.6
Steve Scott (Am.), San Diego, 1981	3:51.8
2 miles—Emiel Puttemans, Berlin, 1973	8:13.2
Terry O'Brien (Am.), San Diego, 1971	8:15.2
Steve Prefontaine (Am.), San Diego, 1974	8:20.4
3 miles—Emiel Puttemans, Pentin, Belgium, 1976	12:54.6
Alberto Salazar (Am.), New York, 1981	12:56.6

Running—Metric Distances

50 meters—Manfred Koket, East Germany, 1971	0:05.4
Bill Gaines (Am.), Highland Park, N.J., 1968	0:05.4
James Sanford (Am.), San Diego, 1981	0:05.61
60 meters—Houston McTear, New York, 1978	0:06.11
70 meters—Helmut Kornig, Germany, 1932	0:07.5
Ira Murchison (Am.), United States	0:07.5
Pro—John Carlos, Pocatello, Idaho, 1974	0:07.3
100 meters—Eugen Ray, East Berlin, 1976	0:10.16
Pro—Warren Edmonson, Pocatello, Idaho, 1973	0:10.2
200 meters—Karlh Wiesenseel, West Germany, 1978	0:21.11
Pietro Mennea, Italy, 1978	0:21.11
300 meters—Pietro Mennea, Italy, 1978	0:32.83
Cliff Wiley (Am.), Saskatchewan, 1981	0:33.33
400 meters—Hartmut Weber, West Germany, 1981	0:45.96
Bill Green (Am.), Sherbrooke, Quebec, 1981	0:46.08
500 meters—Herman Frazier, Long Beach, Calif., 1979	1:01.2
Pro—Lee Evans, Pocatello, Idaho, 1973	1:02
600 meters—Martin Bilham, England, 1969	1:17.7
Mark Winzenreid (Am.), England, 1975	1:18.3
Pro—Lee Evans, Pocatello, Idaho, 1977	1:16.7
800 meters—Sebastian Coe, England, 1981	1:46.0
Ted Nelson (Am.), Berlin, 1965	1:47.4
1,000 meters—Paul-Heinz Wellmann, West Germany, 1976	2:19.1

Adam Dixon (Am.), Allston, Mass., 1981	2:19.80
Pro—Chris Fisher, Daly City, Calif., 1973	2:19.7
1,500 meters—Eamonn Coghlan, San Diego, 1981	3:35.6
Steve Smith (Am.), San Diego, 1981	3:36.0
2,000 meters—Steve Scott, Louisville, Ky., 1981	4:58.6
3,000 meters—Emiel Puttemans, Berlin, 1973	7:39.2
Steve Scott (Am.), Long Beach, Calif., 1980	7:45.2
5,000 meters—Suleiman Nyambui, New York, 1981	13:20.4
Alberto Salazar (Am.), New York, 1981	13:22.6

Hurdles

50 yards—Renaldo Nehemiah, Toronto, 1981	0:05.98
60 yards—Renaldo Nehemiah, New York, 1979	0:06.89
50 meters—Renaldo Nehemiah, Edmonton, 1979	0:06.36
60 meters—Andre Prokofyev, Vilnius, 1979	0:07.54
Renaldo Nehemiah, (Am.), Montreal, 1979	0:07.62

Walking

1,500 meters—Todd Scully, New York, 1979	5:40.0
Mile—Neal Pyke, 1978	6:04.0
3,000 meters—Yevgeny Yavsyukov, Montreal, 1979	11:31.1
2 miles—Vittorio Visini, Italy, 1978	12:51.5
Todd Scully (Am.), New York, 1977	13:02.5
3 miles—Antoli Soloman, Toronto, 1978	19:40.0

Relays

1,600 meters—West Germany, Dortmund, West Germany, 1981	3:34.38
880 yards—Idaho State, Pocatello, Idaho, 1979	1:26.9
Mile—Pacific Coast Club, Pocatello, Idaho, 1971	3:09.4
2 miles—Univ. of Chicago, T.C., Louisville, Ky., 1974	7:20.8
4 miles—Villanova, Hanover, N.H., 1976	16:19
Sprint medley—Philadelphia T.C., New York, 1980	2:01.1
Distance medley—Villanova, Louisville, Ky., 1980	9:38.4

Field Events

High jump—Dietmar Mogenburg, West Germany, 1980	7 ft 8¾ in.
Jeff Woodard (Am.), New York, 1981	7 ft 7¾ in.
Long jump—Carl Lewis, Fort Worth, Tex., 1981	27 ft 10¼ in.
Triple jump—Keith Connor, Detroit, 1981	56 ft 9½ in.
Willie Banks (Am.), Tokyo, 1981	56 ft 5¾ in.
Pole vault—Thierry Vigneron, France, 1981	18 ft 8¼ in.
Konstantin Volkov, Moscow, 1980	18 ft 8¼ in.
Dan Ripley (Am.), Fort Worth, Tex., 1979	18 ft 5½ in.
Steve Smith (pro), New York, 1975	18 ft 5 in.
Shotput—George Woods, Inglewood, Calif., 1974	72 ft 2¾ in.
Brian Oldfield (pro), El Paso, Tex., 1975	72 ft 6½ in.

35-pound weight throw—Yuri Syedikh, Montreal, 1979	76 ft 11¾ in.
Ed Kania (Am.), Princeton, N.J., 1981	73 ft 4 in.

WOMEN
Running

50 yards—Andrea Lynch, Toronto, 1978	0:05.80
Deandra Carney (Am.), Toronto, 1978	0:05.68
Evelyn Ashford (Am.), Toronto, 1981	0:05.83
60 yards—Alice Brown, Dallas, Tex., 1981	0:06.62
100 yards—Marita Koch, East Berlin, 1979	0:10.40
Wilma Rudolph (Am.), Tennessee State, 1960	0:10.70
220 yards—Chandra Cheeseborough, New York, 1981	0:23.27
300 yards—Merlene Ottey, Lincoln, Neb., 1981	0:33.11
Lis Young (Am.), Columbia, Md., 1975	0:34.50
440 yards—Rosalyn Bryant, New York, 1977	0:53.20
500 yards—Rosalyn Bryant, San Diego, 1977	1:03.30
600 yards—Yvonne Saunders, Toronto, 1974	1:18.40
Robin Campbell (Am.), Toronto, 1974	1:19.30
880 yards—Mary Decker, San Diego, 1980	1:59.70
1,000 yards—Mary Decker, Inglewood, Calif., 1978	2:23.80
Mile—Francie Larrieu, Richmond, Va., 1975	4:28.50
2 miles—Francie Larrieu, New York, 1981	9:38.1

Running—Metric Distances

50 meters—Jeanette Bolden, Edmonton, Alberta, 1981	0:06.13
60 meters—Marlies Gohr, East Germany, 1980	0:07.10
Brenda Moorehead (Am.), Louisville, Ky., 1980	0:07.28
100 meters—Marlies Gohr, East Berlin, 1979	0:11.30
Mamie Rallins (Am.), San Diego, 1975	0:12.40
200 meters—Jarmila Kratochvilova, Vienna, Austria, 1981	0:22.76
300 meters—Merlene Ottey, Lincoln, Neb., 1981	0:33.12
Lori Green (Am.), Oklahoma City, 1979	0:35.32
400 meters—Jarmila Kratochvilova, Vienna, Austria, 1981	0:49.64
Sharon Dabney (Am.), Italy, 1978	0:53.27
500 meters—Lorna Forde, Hanover, N.H., 1978	1:10.50
600 meters—Anita Weiss, East Berlin, 1980	1:26.20
Chris Muller (Am.), Columbia, Mo., 1980	1:28.80
800 meters—Olga Vakrusheva, Moscow, 1980	1:58.40
Mary Decker (Am.), San Diego, 1980	1:58.90
1,000 meters—Bridgette Kraus, West Germany, 1978	2:34.80
Francie Larrieu (Am.), Los Angeles, 1975	2:40.20
1,500 meters—Mary Decker, New York, 1980	4:00.80
2,000 meters—Francie Larrieu, Edmonton, Alberta, 1981	5:55.2
3,000 meters—Jan Merrill, Montreal, 1978	8:57.60

Hurdles

50 yards—Johanna Klier, Toronto, 1978	0:06.20
Deby LaPlante (Am.), Toronto, 1978	0:06.37
60 yards—Stephanie Hightower, New York, 1980	0:07.47
70 yards—Mamie Rallins, Chicago, 1970	0:08.80
Deby LaPlante, Louisville, Ky., 1976	0:08.80
50 meters—Annelie Ehrhardt, Berlin, 1973	0:06.74
Sofia Bielczyzk, Grenoble, France, 1981	0:06.74
Candy Young (Am.), Edmonton, Alberta, 1979	0:06.95
60 meters—Sofia Bielczyzk, Poland, 1980	0:07.77
Stephanie Hightower, (Am.), San Diego, 1980	0:08.17
100 meters—Annelie Ehrhardt, East Germany, 1976	0:13.12
Patty van Wolvelaere (Am.), New York, 1974	0:13.20

Walking

Mile—Susan Brodock, New York, 1978	7:01.70
1,500 meters—Susan Brodock, Toronto, 1976	6:42.90

Relays

640 yards—Tennessee State, New York, 1981	1:08.99
880 yards—Tennessee State, Louisville, Ky., 1980	1:37.80
880 yard medley relay—Tennessee State, New York, 1981	1:42.17
Mile—Los Angeles Mercurettes, New York, 1981	3:40.46
2 miles—Soviet Union, 1972	8:41.60

Field Events

Long jump—Kasin Haenel, Grenoble, France, 1981	22 ft 2½ in.
Carol Lewis (Am.), Dallas, Tex., 1981	21 ft 7½ in.
High jump—Andrea Matay, Budapest, 1979	6 ft 6 in.
Joni Huntley (Am.), New York, 1981	6 ft 4¾ in.
Shotput—Helena Fibingerova, Czechoslovakia, 1977	73 ft 9¾ in.
Maren Seidler (Am.), West Germany, 1978	61 ft 2¼ in.

THE ATHLETICS CONGRESS NATIONAL CHAMPIONSHIPS

INDOOR
(Madison Square Garden, New York, Feb. 27, 1981)

Men's Events

60 yd—Stanley Floyd, Houston, unattached	0:06.15
600 yd—Mike Solomon, Philadelphia Pioneer Club	1:10.31
1,000 yd—William Martin, Athletics West	2:08.37
440 yd—Ed Yearwood, Long Island Alliance Track Club	0:48.12
Mile—Steve Scott, Tempe, Ariz.	3:57.3
3 Miles—Eamonn Coghlan, New York Athletic Club	12:54.80[1]
60-yd hurdles—Alejandro Casanas, Cuba	0:07.14
2-mile walk—Raymond Sharp, Kenosha, Wis., unattached	12:37.65
Sprint medley relay—Philadelphia Pioneer Club (Fred Taylor, Steve Riddick, Bill Collins, Tony Darden)	2:01.89
Mile relay—Philadelphia Pioneer Club (Cliff McKenzie, Robert Taylor, Charles Oliver, Herman Frazier)	3:12.36
2-mile relay—Athletics Attic (Lynn Brown, Palmer Simmons, Phil Rolle, Randy Wilson)	7:28.42
Long jump—Larry Myricks, Athletics Attic	26 ft 8¼ in.
Triple jump—Mike Marlow, Berkeley, Calif., unattached	54 ft 6½ in.
High jump—Jeff Woodard, Alabama, unattached	7 ft 7¾ in.[2]
Pole vault—Thierry Vigneron, France	18 ft 4½ in.[3]
Shot-put—Brian Oldfield, Univ. of Chicago Track Club	69 ft 4 in.
35 lb weight throw—Ed Kania, Pacific Coast Club	73 ft 4 in.[2]
Team—Philadelphia Pioneer Club	18 pts

1. Betters all-comers indoor record. 2. American indoor record. 3. Meet record.

Women's Events

60 yd—Evelyn Ashford, Los Angeles, unattached	0:06.63[1]
220 yd—Chandra Cheeseborough, Tennessee State	0:23.27[2]
440 yd—Diane Dixon, Atoms Track Club	0:55.38
Mile—Jan Merrill, Age Group Track Club	4:34.03[3]
2 miles—Francie Larrieu, Pacific Coast Club	9:38.1[2]
60 yd hurdles—Benita Fitzgerald, University of Tennessee	0:07.72
Mile walk—Susan Leirs-Westerfield, Island Track Club	7:05
640-yd relay—Tennessee State (Chandra Cheeseborough, Ernestine Davis, Judith Pollion, Sheryl Pernell)	1:08.99[2]
880-yd medley relay—Tennessee State (Ernestine Davis, Judith Pollion, Sheryl Pernell, Chandra Cheeseborough)	1:43.24
Mile relay—Los Angeles Mercurettes (Deann Gutowski, Paulette Clagon, Cindy Cumbess, Brenda Peterson)	3:40.46[4]

High jump—Joni Huntley, Pacific Coast Club — 6 ft 1½ in.
Long jump—Ana Alexander, Cuba — 20 ft 9¾ in.
Shot-put—Marita Walton, University of Maryland — 52 ft 11 in.
Team—Tennessee State — 19 pts
1. Championship record. 2. World best. 3. Meet record. 4. American indoor record.

ATHLETICS CONGRESS NATIONAL CHAMPIONSHIPS*

(June 18–21, 1981, Sacramento, Calif.)

OUTDOOR
Men's Events

100 m—Carl Lewis, Santa Monica Track Club	0:10.13
200 m—Jeff Phillips, Philadelphia Pioneers	0:20.36
400 m—Cliff Wiley, D.C. International	0:44.70[1]
800 m—James Robinson, Inner City Athletic Club	1:45.53
1,500 m—Sydney Maree, Athletic Attic	3:35.02[1]
3,000 m steeplechase—Henry Marsh, Athletics West	8:30.7
5,000 m—Matt Centrowitz, New York Athletic Club	13:28.86
10,000 m—Alberto Salazar, Athletics West	28:39.33
5,000–m walk—Ray Sharp, Athletic Attic	20:47.52
110–m hurdles—Greg Foster, Shaklee Track Club	0:13.39
400–m hurdles—Edwin Moses, unattached	0:47.59
High jump—Tyke Peacock, Modesto Junior College	7 ft 4½ in.
Pole vault—Billy Olson, Pacific Coast Club	17 ft 10½ in.
Long jump—Carl Lewis, Santa Monica Track Club	28 ft 3½ in.
Triple jump—Willie Banks, Athletics West	57 ft 7½ in.[2]
Shot-put—Dave Laut, Athletics West	70 ft 10½ in.
Discus—Ben Plucknett, Southern California Striders	226 ft 5 in.
Hammer—Richard Olsen, New York Athletic Club-Norway	235 ft 10 in.
Javelin—Bruce Kennedy, Pacific Coast Club	276 ft 8 in.

1. Meet record. 2. American record. *Previously under the sponsorship of the Amateur Athletic Union (A.A.U.).

Women's Events

100 m—Evelyn Ashford, Medalist Track Club	0:11.07
200 m—Evelyn Ashford	0:22.30[1]
400 m—Denean Howard, Shaklee Track Club	0:51.79
800 m—Madeline Manning, Oral Roberts Track Club	1:58.50
1,500 m—Jan Merrill, Age Group Athletic Association	4:14.62
3,000 m—Brenda Webb, Athletics West	9:04.54
10,000 m—Joan Benoit, Athletics West	33:37.5
100–m hurdles—Stephanie Hightower, Los Angeles Naturite	0:13.09
400–m hurdles—Sandy Myers, Los Angeles Naturite	0:56.43[1]
5,000–m walk—Susan Liers-Westerfield, Island Track Club	24:26.7
400–m relay—Shaklee Track Club (Brown, Griffith, Bisco, Bolden)	0:43.39[1]
800–m relay—Los Angeles Naturite	1:37.86
1,600–m relay—Los Angeles Naturite (Bryant, Pusey, Rich, Myers)	3:27.90
3,200–m relay—SportsWest (Sue Gregg, Smith, Joyce, Sandra Gregg)	8:36.94
High jump—Pam Spencer, Los Angeles Naturite	6 ft 4¾ in.[1]
Long jump—Jodi Anderson, Los Angeles Naturite	22 ft ¼ in.
Shot-put—Denise Wood, Knoxville Track Club	55 ft 5¾ in.
Discus—Leslie Deniz, Sun Devils Sports	182 ft 9 in.
Javelin—Karin Smith, Medalist Track Club	208 ft 1 in.

1. Meet record.

NATIONAL COLLEGIATE ATHLETIC ASSOCIATION

INDOOR

(Detroit, March 13–14, 1981)

60 yd—Carl Lewis, Houston	0:06.16
440 yd—Bert Cameron, Texas-El Paso	0:48.23
600 yd—Eugene Sanders, Mississippi Valley	1:09.84
880 yd—Sammy Koskei, Southern Methodist University	1:52.29
1,000 yd—Peter Lemashon, Texas-El Paso	2:12.29
Mile—Suleiman Nyambui, Texas-El Paso	4:01.85
2 miles—Doug Padilla, Brigham Young	8:26.52
3 miles—Michael Musyoki, Texas-El Paso	13:25.03
60–yd hurdles—Terron Wright, Memphis State	0:07.14
Mile relay—Seton Hall (Derrick Peynado, Linvall Francis, Mike Paul, Washington Njiri)	3:15.91
2–mile relay—Rutgers (Brian Grimes, Stan Belin, Walter Kirkland, James Westman)	7:30.95
Distance medley relay—Villanova (John Borgese, Willie Sydnor, Marcus O'Sullivan, Sydney Maree)	9:47.20
Long jump—Carl Lewis, Houston	27 ft 10 in.[1]
High jump—Leo Williams, Navy	7 ft 5¼ in.[2]
Pole vault—Ed Langford, Purdue	17 ft 9½ in.
Triple jump—Keith Connor, Southern Methodist University	56 ft 9½ in.[3]
35–lb weight throw—Robert Weis, Southern Methodist U.	73 ft 7 in.[2]
Shot-put—Michael Carter, Southern Methodist U.	69 ft 8½ in.[1]
Team—Texas-El Paso	76 pts

1. Meet record. 2. Collegiate record. 3. World indoor best.

Outdoor

(Baton Rouge, La., June 3–6, 1981)

100 m—Carl Lewis, Houston	0:09.99
200 m—Dwayne Evans, Arizona State	0:20.20
400 m—Bert Cameron, Texas-El Paso	0:44.58
800 m—Sammy Kofkel, Southern Methodist	1:46.41
1,500 m—Sydney Maree, Villanova	3:35.30
3,000 steeplechase—Solomon Chebor, Fairleigh Dickinson	8:23.34
5,000 m—Suleiman Nyambui, Texas-El Paso	13:38.8
10,000 m—Suleiman Nyambui, Texas-El Paso	28:34.23
110–m hurdles—Larry Cowling, California	0:13.60
400–m hurdles—Andre Phillips, U.C.L.A.	0:49.12
400–m relay—Northwestern Louisiana (Victor Oatis, Joe Delaney, Mario Johnson, Mark Duper)	0:39.32
1,600–m relay—Tennessee (Darryl Canady, Darryl Wilson, David Patrick, Anthony Blair)	3:03.08
Discus—Scott Crowell, Iowa State	206 ft 3 in.
Javelin—Mike Juskus, Glassboro (N.J.) State	273 ft 2 in.
Shot-Put—Michael Carter, Southern Methodist	68 ft 10 ¾ in.
Hammer—Richard Olsen, Southern Methodist	237 ft
Pole vault—David Volz, Indiana	17 ft 8¼ in.
High jump—Leo Williams, Navy	7 ft 4¼ in.

Triple jump—Steven Hanna, Texas–El Paso   55 ft 11 in.
Long jump—Carl Lewis, Houston   27 ft ¾ in.
Team—Texas–El Paso   70 pts

NATIONAL ATHLETIC CONGRESS RELAY CHAMPIONSHIPS

(Piscataway, N.J., July 5, 1981)

400 meters—Long Island Alliance (Mel Abernathy, Hubert Blue, Brady Crain, Ed Yearwood)   0:40.2[1]
800 meters—Long Island Alliance (Mel Abernathy, Hubert Blue, Brady Crain, Ed Yearwood)   1:23.6
1,600 meters—Brooklyn Over the Hill Athletic Association (Dennis Duckworth, Richard Lewis, Dave Cherry, Gordon Hinds)   3:07.6[1]
3,200 meters—Fort Lee (N.J.) Athletic Attic (Vince Forte, Kevin Burke, Bob Barratta, Tavo Rivera)   7:31.1[1]
Sprint medley—Concerned Athletes in Action (Demetrius Hallums, David Silas, Randy Williams, Fred Gore)   3:27.1
6,000 meters—New York Athletic Club (John Sullivan, Jim Shields, Luis Ostolozaga, Marcel Phillipe)   15:51.3[1]
Distance medley—New York Athletic Club (Jim DiRienzo, Bob Moffatt, Vince Draddy, Ross Donoghue)   9:50.9[1]
440–meter shuttle hurdles—Philadelphia Pioneers (Jack Pierce, Martin Booker, Kerry Bethel, Rod Wilson)   0:56.2[1]
1. Meet record.

NATIONAL ASSOCIATION OF INTERCOLLEGIATE ATHLETICS

Indoor

(Kansas City, Mo., Feb. 19–21, 1981)

60 yd—Larry White, Mississippi Valley State   0:06.22
440 yd—Kevin Jones, Northwood (Mich.) Institute   0:47.75[1]
600 yd—Eugene Sanders, Mississippi Valley State   1:09.63[1]
880 yd—Joel Ngetich, Wayland (Tex.) Baptist   1:53.04
1,000 yd—Clifton Perry, Texas Southern   2:13.53
Mile—John Esquibel, Adams State, Colo.   4:08.15[1]
2 miles—Kregg Einspahr, Concordia (Neb.)   8:50.88[1]
3 miles—Joel Marchand, Malone (Ohio)   13:59.86[1]
2–mile walk—Ray Sharp, Wisconsin–Parkside   12:56.86
60–yd hurdles—Dwayne Alenn, Harding (Ark.)   0:07.46
Mile relay—Texas Southern (Clifton Perry, Kenneth Williams, John Wallace, Tyrone Cross)   3:17.21
2–mile relay—Jackson (Miss.) State (Robert Wilson, Anthony Appoy, Napoleon Hooks, Michael Watson)   8:05.3
Distance medley relay—Oklahoma Christian (Greg Norman, Blake Smith, Tony Yates, Jerry Bellmyer)   10:11.23
Long jump—Britt Courville, Texas Southern   24 ft 4¾ in.
Triple jump—Cary Tyler, Viola (Calif.)   52 ft 2¾ in.
High jump—Albert Peacock, Ottawa (Kan.)   7 ft
Pole vault—Brad Pursley, Abilene Christian (Tex.)   17 ft ½ in.
Shot-put—Harold Ledet, Angelo State (Tex.)   60 ft 11¾ in.
Team—Texas Southern   80 pts
1. N.A.I.A. record.

ASSOCIATION FOR INTERCOLLEGIATE ATHLETICS FOR WOMEN

(Pocatello, Idaho, March 13–14, 1981)

Indoor

60 m—Merlene Ottey, Nebraska   0:07.24
300 m—Merlene Ottey, Nebraska   0:35.83
400 m—Pam Moore, Wisconsin   0:53.88
600 m—Dalisa Walton, Tennessee   1:26.56
800 m—Darlene Beckford, Harvard   2:05.75
1,000 m—Josephine White, Richmond   3:43.33
1,500 m—Jill Haworth, Virginia   4:25.20
3,000 m—Patricia Sharples, Idaho   9:33.96
5,000 m—Aileen O'Connor, Virginia   16:33.6
60–m hurdles—Candy Young, Fairleigh Dickinson   0:08.18
800–m relay—Florida State (Esmeralda Garcia, Marita Payne, Alice Bennett, Randy Givens)   1:36.88
1,600–m relay—Adelphi University (Marva Fearon, Cheryl Inniss, Marilyn Gilliard, June Griffith)   3:37.28
3,200–m relay—University of Wisconsin (Susan Beischel, Maryann Brenns, Ellen Brewster, Sue Spaltohlz)   8:44.26
Distance medley relay—Iowa State University (Wren Schafer, Sumetia Wells, Diane Vetter, Christine McMeekin)   11:24.04
Long jump—Pat Johnson, Wisconsin   21 ft
High jump—Colleen Reinstra, Arizona State   6 ft 3¼ in.
Shot-put—Meg Ritchie, Arizona   55 ft 2½ in.
Pentathlon—Patsy Walker, Houston   4,215 pts
Team—University of Virginia   48 pts

Outdoor

(Austin, Tex., May 27–30, 1981)

100 m—Merlene Ottey, Nebraska   0:11.20
200 m—Merlene Ottey   0:22.78[1]
400 m—Jackie Pusey, California State–Los Angeles   0:51.85
800 m—Leann Warren, Oregon   2:06.07
1,500 m—Leann Warren   4:15.0[1]
3,000 m—Regina Joyce, Washington   9:02.0[1]
5,000 m—Julie Shea, North Carolina State   16:11.04
10,000 m—Aileen O'Connor, Virginia   33:28.20
100–m hurdles—Benita Fitzgerald, Tennessee   0:13.12
400–m hurdles—Robin Marks, Arizona   0:58.41
400–m relay—Florida State (Esmeralda Garcia, Marita Payne, Auce Bennett, Randy Givens)   0:44.35[1]
800–m relay—Tennessee (Sharetta Barksdale, Cathy Rattray, Benita Fitzgerald, Delisa Walton)   1:36.70[1]
1,600–m relay—Tennessee (Cathy Rattray, Sharetta Barksdale, Joetta Clark, Delisa Walton)   3:31.70[1]
3,200–m relay—Wisconsin (Susan Beischal, Mariane Brenner, Ellen Brewster, Sue Spalthulc)   8:53.44
Javelin—Sally Harmon, Oregon   177 ft. 10 in.
Shot-put—Meg Ritchie, Arizona   57 ft. 1 in.[1]
Discus—Ria Stalman, Arizona State   198 ft. 3 in.
High jump—Coleen Reinstra, Arizona State   6 ft.
Long jump—Donna Thomas, North Texas State   20 ft. 9 3/4 in.
Team—Tennessee   61 pts
1. A.I.A.W. Record.

RACQUETBALL

AMERICAN AMATEUR RACQUETBALL ASSOCIATION—1981

Men's amateur champion—Ed Andrews, San Diego, Calif. (defeated Larry Fox, Cincinnati, 21–12, 21–13, in final)
Women's amateur champion—Cindy Baxter, Lewiston, Pa. (defeated Linda Emerick, Denver, 21–10, 21–3, in final)

WOMEN'S PRO RACQUETBALL ASSOCIATION—1981

Women's pro champion—Heather McKay, Toronto (defeated Lynn Adams, 3–0, 3–0, in final)
Women's amateur champion—Caryn McKinney, Atlanta (defeated Barbara Maltby, Philadelphia, 3–1, 3–1, in final)

MEN'S PRO CHAMPIONSHIP—1981

Leach Pro–Amateur champion—Marty Hogan, San Diego (defeated Craig McCoy, 21–19, 21–12, in final)

CHESS

WORLD CHAMPIONS

1894–1921	Emanuel Lasker, Germany
1921–27	Jose R. Capablanca, Cuba
1927–35	Alexander A. Alekhine, U.S.S.R.
1935–37	Dr. Max Euwe, Netherlands
1937–46	Alexander A. Alekhine, U.S.S.R.[1]
1948–57	Mikhail Botvinnik, U.S.S.R.
1957–58	Vassily Smyslov, U.S.S.R.
1958–60	Mikhail Botvinnik, U.S.S.R.
1960–61	Mikhail Tal, U.S.S.R.
1961–63	Mikhail Botvinnik, U.S.S.R.
1963–68	Tigran Petrosian, U.S.S.R.
1969–71	Boris Spassky, U.S.S.R.
1972–74	Bobby Fischer, Los Angeles
1975	Bobby Fischer[2]; Anatoly Karpov, U.S.S.R.
1976–81	Anatoly Karpov, U.S.S.R.[3]

1. Alekhine, a French citizen, died while champion. 2. Relinquished title. 3. In 1978, Karpov defeated Viktor Korchnoi 6 games to 5.

UNITED STATES CHAMPIONS

1909–36	Frank J. Marshall, New York
1936–44	Samuel Reshevsky, New York[1]
1944–46	Arnold S. Denker, New York
1946	Samuel Reshevsky, Boston
1948	Herman Steiner, Los Angeles
1951–52	Larry Evans, New York
1954–57	Arthur Bisguier, New York
1958–61	Bobby Fischer, Brooklyn, N.Y.
1962	Larry Evans, New York
1963–67	Bobby Fischer, New York
1968	Larry Evans, New York
1969–71	Samuel Reshevsky, Spring Valley, N.Y.
1972	Robert Byrne, Ossining, N.Y.
1973	Lubomir Kavelek, Washington; John Grefe, San Francisco
1974–77	Walter Browne, Berkeley, Calif.
1978–79	Lubomir Kavalek, New York
1980	Tie, Walter Browne, Berkeley, Calif. Larry Christiansen, Modesto, Calif. Larry Evans, Reno, Nev.
1981	Tie, Walter Browne Yasser Seirawan, Seattle, Wash.

1. In 1942, Isaac I. Kashdan of New York was co-champion for a while because of a tie with Reshevsky in that year's tournament. Reshevsky won the play-off.

SWIMMING

WORLD RECORDS—MEN

(Through Sept. 9, 1981)
Approved by International Swimming Federation (F.I.N.A.)
(F.I.N.A. discontinued acceptance of records in yards in 1968)

Distance	Record	Holder	Country	Where Made	Date
Freestyle					
100 Meters	0:49.36	Rowdy Gaines	U.S.	Austin, Tex.	April 3, 1981
200 Meters	1:49.16	Rowdy Gaines	U.S.	Austin, Tex.	April 11, 1980
400 Meters	3:50.49	Peter Szmidt	Canada	Etobicoke	July 16, 1980
800 Meters	7:56.49	Vladimir Salnikov	U.S.S.R.	Minsk	March 24, 1979
1,500 Meters	14:58.27	Vladimir Salnikov	U.S.S.R.	Moscow	July 22, 1980
Backstroke					
100 Meters	0:55.49	John Naber	U.S.	Montreal	July 19, 1976
200 Meters	1:59.19	John Naber	U.S.	Montreal	July 24, 1976
Breaststroke					
100 Meters	1:02.86	Gerald Moerken	West Germany	Jonkoepping, Sweden	Aug. 17, 1977
200 Meters	2:15.11	David Wilkie	Britain	Montreal	July 24, 1976
Butterfly					
100 Meters	0:53.81	William Paulus	U.S.	Austin, Tex.	April 3, 1981
200 Meters	1:58.01	Craig Beardsley	U.S.	Kiev, U.S.S.R.	Aug. 22, 1981
Individual Medley					
200 Meters	2:02.78	Alex Bauman	Canada	Heidelberg, W. Ger.	July 29, 1981
400 Meters	4:20.05	Jesse Vassallo	U.S.	West Berlin	Aug. 22, 1978
Freestyle Relays					
400 Meters	3:19.74	National Team	U.S.	West Berlin	Aug. 22, 1978
(Jack Babashoff, Rowdy Gaines, Jim Montgomery, David McCagg)					
800 Meters	7:20.82	National Team	U.S.	West Berlin	Aug. 24, 1978
(Bruce Furniss, Bill Forrester, Bobby Hackett, Rowdy Gaines)					
Medley Relay					
400 Meters	3:42.22	National Team	U.S.	Montreal	July 22, 1976

WORLD RECORDS—WOMEN

Freestyle

100 Meters	0:54.79	Barbara Krause	East Germany	Moscow	July 21, 1980
200 Meters	1:58.23	Cynthia Woodhead	U.S.	Tokyo	Sept. 3, 1979
400 Meters	4:06.28	Tracey Wickham	Australia	West Berlin	Aug. 24, 1978
800 Meters	8:24.62	Tracey Wickham	Australia	Edmonton, Canada	Aug. 5, 1978
1,500 Meters	16:04.49	Kim Linehan	U.S.	Ft. Lauderdale, Fla.	Aug. 19, 1979

Backstroke

100 Meters	1:00.86	Rica Reinisch	East Germany	Moscow	July 23, 1980
200 Meters	2:11.77	Rica Reinisch	East Germany	Moscow	July 27, 1980

Breaststroke

100 Meters	1:08.60	Ute Geweniger	East Germany	Split, Yugoslavia	Sept. 8, 1981
200 Meters	2:28.36	Lina Kachushite	U.S.S.R.	Potsdam	April 6, 1979

Butterfly

100 Meters	0:57.93	Mary T. Meagher	U.S.	Brown Deer, Wis.	Aug. 16, 1981
200 Meters	2:05.96	Mary T. Meagher	U.S.	Brown Deer, Wis.	Aug. 13, 1981

Individual Medley

200 Meters	2:11.73	Ute Geweniger	East Germany	East Berlin	July 4, 1981
400 Meters	4:36.29	Petra Schneider	East Germany	Moscow	July 26, 1980

Freestyle Relay

400 Meters	3:42.71	National Team	East Germany	Moscow	July 27, 1980
800 Meters	8:07.44	Mission Viejo A	U.S.	Milwaukee	Aug. 14, 1981

Medley Relay

400 Meters	4:06.67	National Team	East Germany	Moscow	July 20, 1980

U.S. SHORT–COURSE SWIMMING RECORDS
(Listed by Amateur Athletic Union)

MEN
Freestyle

50 yards—Robin Leamy, 1981	0:19.36
100 yards—Rowdy Gaines, 1981	0:42.38
100 yards—Rowdy Gaines, 1980	0:43.16
100 yards—Andy Coan, 1979	0:43.25
100 yards—Jonty Skinner, 1978	0:43.29[1]
100 yards—Joe Bottom, 1977	0:43.49
200 yards—Rowdy Gaines, 1981	1:33.80
200 yards—Rowdy Gaines, 1980	1:34.57
200 yards—Andy Coan, 1979	1:35.62
200 yards—Jim Montgomery, 1977	1:35.67
500 yards—Brian Goodell, 1978	4:16.40
500 yards—Brian Goodell, 1978	4:16.43
1,650 yards—Brian Goodell, 1979	14:47.27
1,650 yards—Rafael Escalas, 1981	14:53.90[1]
1,650 yards—Brian Goodell, 1979	14:54.13
1,650 yards—Brian Goodell, 1978	14:54.54

Backstroke

100 yards—Clay Britt, 1981	0:49.08
100 yards—John Naber, 1977	0:49.31
200 yards—Rick Carey, 1981	1:46.00
200 yards—John Naber, 1977	1:46.09

Breaststroke

100 yards—Steve Lundquist, 1981	0:52.93
100 yards—Steve Lundquist, 1980	0:53.59
100 yards—Steve Lundquist, 1979	0:54.08
100 yards—Graham Smith, 1977	0:54.91[1]
100 yards—Scott Spann, 1977	0:55.19
200 yards—Steve Lundquist, 1981	1:55.01
200 yards—Bill Barrett, 1980	1:58.43
200 yards—Steve Lundquist, 1979	1:59.18
200 yards—Graham Smith, 1977	2:00.05[1]
200 yards—Nick Nevid, 1978	2:00.53

Butterfly

100 yards—Scott Spann, 1981	0:47.22
100 yards—Par Arvidsson, 1980	0:47.34[1]
100 yards—Par Arvidsson, 1979	0:47.76[1]
100 yards—Joe Bottom, 1977	0:47.77
200 yards—Craig Beardsley, 1981	1:44.15
200 yards—Par Arvidsson, 1980	1:44.43[1]
200 yards—Mike Bruner, 1977	1:45.27

Individual Medley

200 yards—Bill Barrett, 1981	1:45.01
200 yards—Bill Barrett, 1980	1:46.25
200 yards—Scott Spann, 1977	1:48.26
400 yards—Jesse Vassallo, 1981	3:48.16
400 yards—Jesse Vassallo, 1979	3:48.24
400 yards—Brian Gpodell, 1979	3:50.80
400 yards—Jesse Vassallo, 1978	3:51.69

Relays

400-yard freestyle—Mission Viejo, 1981	2:53.86
400-yard freestyle—Tennessee, 1979	2:54.54
400-yard freestyle—Gatorade S.C., 1978	2:55.27
800-yard freestyle—Florida Aquatic Club, 1979	6:25.42
800-yard freestyle—Auburn, 1981	6:26.49
800-yard freestyle—Florida A.C., 1978	6:29.81
400-yard medley—Texas, 1981	3:12.93
400-yard medley—California-Berkeley, 1979	3:15.22[1]
400-yard medley—Indiana, 1977	3:17.14[1]
400-yard medley—Auburn, 1977	3:17.62

WOMEN
Freestyle

50 yards—Jill Sterkel, 1981	0:22.41
100 yards—Jill Sterkel, 1980	0:48.76

100 yards—Cynthia Woodhead, 1979	0:49.39
100 yards—Jill Sterkel, 1979	0:49.55
100 yards—Tracy Caulkins, 1978	0:49.58
200 yards—Cynthia Woodhead, 1979	1:44.10
200 yards—Stephanie Elkins, 1978	1:45.91
500 yards—Tracy Caulkins, 1979	4:36.25
500 yards—Cynthia Woodhead, 1978	4:39.94
1,650 yards—Kim Linehan, 1979	15:49.10
1,650 yards—Cynthia Woodhead, 1978	15:55.15

Backstroke

100 yards—Linda Jezek, 1978	0:54.94
200 yards—Linda Jezek, 1978	1:57.79

Breaststroke

100 yards—Tracy Caulkins, 1979	1:01.82
100 yards—Tracy Caulkins, 1979	1:02.06
100 yards—Tracy Caulkins, 1978	1:02.20
200 yards—Tracy Caulkins, 1980	2:11.46
200 yards—Tracy Caulkins, 1978	2:14.07

Butterfly

100 yards—Jill Sterkel, 1981	0:53.10
100 yards—Mary T. Meagher, 1980	0:53.18
100 yards—Jill Sterkel, 1979	0:53.76
100 yards—Diane Johannigman, 1978	0:54.11
200 yards—Mary T. Meagher, 1980	1:53.21
200 yards—Nancy Hogshead, 1978	1:55.74

Individual Medley

200 yards—Tracy Caulkins, 1979	1:57.86
200 yards—Tracy Caulkins, 1978	1:59.33
400 yards—Tracy Caulkins, 1979	4:08.09
400 yards—Tracy Caulkins, 1978	4:11.38

Relays

200—yard freestyle—Stanford, 1981	1:31.12
400—yard freestyle—Stanford, 1981	3:19.70
400—yard freestyle—Nashville A.C., 1979	3:20.51
400—yard freestyle—Nashville A.C., 1978	3:20.69
800—yard freestyle—Mission Viejo S.C., 1979	7:15.14
800—yard freestyle—U.S. Team, 1976	7:15.64
200—yard medley—North Carolina, 1981	1:42.63
400—yard medley—Nashville A.C., 1978	3:42.54

1. Open American record by non-U.S. competitors.

AMATEUR ATHLETIC UNION NATIONAL CHAMPIONSHIPS

(Boston, Mass., April 8–11, 1981)

INDOOR (SHORT COURSE)
Men

50—yd freestyle—Robin Leamy, Rancho Palos Verdes, Calif.	0:19.91
100—yd freestyle—Robin Leamy	0:43.58
200—yd freestyle—David Larson, Jesup, Ga.	1:36.04
500—yd freestyle—Peter Szmidt, Canada	4:21.10
1,000—yd freestyle—Brian Goodell, Mission Viejo, Calif.	8:58.54[1]
1,650—yd freestyle—Dave Sims, Joliet, Ill.	15:01.31
100—yd backstroke—Rick Carey, Mount Kisco, N.Y.	0:49.79
200—yd backstroke—Rick Carey	1:46.00[1]
100—yd butterfly—Matt Gribble, Miami	0:47.82
200—yd butterfly—Craig Beardsley, Harrington Park, N.J.	1:44.74
100—yd breaststroke—Steve Lundquist, Jonesboro, Ga.	0:53.83
200—yd breaststroke—Steve Lundquist	1:56.29

200—yd ind. med.—Bill Barrett, Alfaretta, Ga.	1:46.91
400—yd inv. med.—Jesse Vassallo, Mission Viejo, Calif.	3:50.31
400—yd freestyle relay—Mission Viejo A (Robin Leamy, David McCagg, Jerry Spencer, Bill Barrett)	2:53.86[1]
800—yd freestyle relay—Mission Viego A (David McCagg, Stuart MacDonald, Brian Goodell, Rich Saeger)	6:31.50
400—yd medley relay—Mission Viejo A (Jesse Vassallo, Bill Barrett, Brad Herring, Robin Leamy)	3:13.22

1. American record.

Women

50—yd freestyle—Jill Sterkel, Hacienda Heights, Calif.	0:22.51
100—yd freestyle—Jill Sterkel	0:49.24
200—yd freestyle—Jill Sterkel	1:46.13
500—yd freestyle—Kim Linehan, Austin, Tex.	4:38.80
1,000—yd freestyle—Kim Linehan	9:29.97
1,650—yd freestyle—Kim Linehan	15:50.23
100—yd backstroke—Susan Walsh, Hamburg, N.Y.	0:55.51
200—yd backstroke—Tracy Caulkins, Nashville, Tenn.	1:57.02[1]
100—yd breaststroke—Tracy Caulkins	1:01.13[1]
200—yd breaststroke—Kim Rhodenbaugh, Cincinnati	2:16.20
200—yd ind. med.—Tracy Caulkins	1:57.11[1]
400—yd ind. med.—Tracy Caulkins	4:04.63[1]
100—yd butterfly—Jill Sterkel	0:52.99[1]
200—yd butterfly—Mary T. Meagher, Louisville, Ky.	1:52.99[1]
400—yd medley relay—Nashville Aquatic Club (Macie Phillips, Tracy Caulkins, Patty King, Amy Caulkins)	3:43.69
400—yd freestyle relay—Mission Viejo A (Marybeth Linzmeier, Julie Williams, Susan Hebernigg, Cynthia Woodhead)	3:19.55[1]
800—yd freestyle relay—Mission Viejo A (Marybeth Linzmeier, Susan Habernigg, Julie Williams, Sherri Hanna)	7:12.62[1]

1. American record.

U.S. LONG-COURSE CHAMPIONSHIPS

(Schroeder Aquatic Center, Brown Deer, Wis., Aug. 13–16, 1981)

Men's Events

50—m freestyle—Robin Leamy, Mission Viejo, Calif.	0:22.57
100—m freestyle—Chris Cavanaugh, Saratoga, Calif.	0:50.71
200—m freestyle—David Larson, Gainesville, Fla.	1:50.86
400—m freestyle—Jeff Float, Sacramento, Calif.	3:54.99
800—m freestyle—Doug Towne, Tucson, Ariz.	8:05.07
1,500—m freestyle—Max Metzger, Mission Viejo, Calif.	15:23.85
100—m breaststroke—Nick Nevid, Elm Grove, Wis.	1:03.80
200—m breaststroke—Nick Nevid	2:19.27
100—m backstroke—Rick Carey, Mount Kisco, N.Y.	0:56.58
200—m backstroke—Jesse Vassallo, Mission Viejo, Calif.	2:01.50
100—m butterfly—Matt Gribble, Miami, Fla.	0:54.15
200—m butterfly—Craig Beardsley, Harrington Park, N.J.	1:59.01
200—m ind. medley—Bill Barrett, Mission Viejo, Calif.	2:03.26
400—m ind. medley—Jesse Vassallo	4:20.33
400—m medley relay—Longhorn Aquatic A (Nick Nevid, Clay Britt, William Paulus, Chris Kirschner)	3:45.70
800—m freestyle relay—Florida Aquatic A (David Larson, Kyle Millar, Don Hillencamp, Steve Wood)	7:30.23
400—m freestyle relay—Mission Viejo (Robin Leamy, Stuart MacDonald, Jerry Spencer, Bill Barrett)	3:22.99

Women's Events

50—m freestyle—Jill Sterkel, Hacienda Heights, Calif.	0:25.95
100—m freestyle—Jill Sterkel	0:56.25

200–m freestyle—Marybeth Linzmeier, Mission Viejo, Calif.	2:00.05
400–m freestyle—Tiffany Cohen, Mission Viejo, Calif.	4:09.88
800–m freestyle—Marybeth Linzmeier	8:27.80
1,500–m freestyle—Marybeth Linzmeier	16:16.86
100–m breaststroke—Tracy Caulkins, Nashville, Tenn.	1:10.77
200–m breaststroke—Tracy Caulkins	2:32.49
100–m backstroke—Theresa Andrews, Annapolis, Md.	1:03.04
200–m backstroke—Libby Kinkead, West Chester, Pa.	2:15.13
100–m butterfly—Mary T. Meagher, Louisville, Ky.	0:57.93[1]
200–m butterfly—Mary T. Meagher	2:05.96[1]
200–m ind. medley—Tracy Caulkins	2:14.18
400–m ind. medley—Tracy Caulkins	4:43.66
400–m medley relay—Mission Viejo A (Loran Rozowski, Shannon Orcutt, Sue Habernigg, Cynthia Woodhead)	4:13.83
800–m freestyle relay—Mission Viejo A (Marybeth Linzmeier, Sue Habernigg, Tiffany Cohen, Cynthia Woodhead)	8:07.44[2]
400–m freestyle relay—Mission Viejo (Sue Habernigg, Barb Major, Cynthia Woodhead, Julie Williams)	3:45.68

1. World record. 2. American record.

A.A.U. NATIONAL DIVING CHAMPIONSHIPS—1981

INDOOR

(Columbus, Ohio, April 14–18, 1981)

Men's Events

1 meter—Greg Louganis, Mission Viejo Nadadores
3 meter—Greg Louganis
Platform—Bruce Kimball, Ann Arbor, Mich.
High point winner—Greg Louganis
Team—Mission Viejo Nadadores

Women's Events

1 meter—Diane Dudeck
3 meter—Megan Neyer, Mission Viejo Nadadores
Platform—Wendy Wyland, Mission Viejo Nadadores
High point winner—Wendy Wyland
Team—Mission Viejo Nadadores

OUTDOOR

(Mission Viejo, Calif., Aug. 11–15, 1981)

Men's Events

1 meter—Greg Louganis, Mission Viejo, Calif.
3 meter—Greg Louganis
Platform—Bruce Kimball, Ann Arbor, Mich.
High point winner—Greg Louganis
Team—Mission Viejo, Calif.

Women's Events

1 meter—Kelly McCormick, Ohio State
3 meter—Megan Neyer, Mission Viejo, Calif.
Platform—Debbie Rush, Ohio State Diving Club
High point winner—Wendy Wyland, Mission Viejo, Calif.
Team—Mission Viejo, Calif.
Combined team—Mission Viejo, Calif.

NATIONAL COLLEGIATE ATHLETIC ASSOCIATION

(Austin, Tex., March 26–28, 1981)

50–yd freestyle—Kris Kirchner, Texas	0:19.66
100–yd freestyle—Ambrose (Rowdy) Gaines, Auburn	0:42.38[2]
200–yd freestyle—Ambrose Gaines	1:33.91
500–yd freestyle—Doug Towne, Arizona	4:16.54

1,650–yd freestyle—Rafael Escalas, U.C.L.A.	14:53.90[1]
100–yd backstroke—Clay Britt, Texas	0:49.08[2]
200–yd backstroke—Wade Flemons, Stanford	1:46.30
100–yd breaststroke—Steve Lundquist, Southern Methodist	0:52.93[2]
200–yd breaststroke—Steve Lundquist	1:55.01[2]
100–yd butterfly—Scott Spann, Texas	0:47.22[2]
200–yd butterfly—William Barrett, U.C.L.A.	1:45.01[2]
400–yd individual medley—Jesse Vassallo, Miami	3:48.16[2]
400–yd freestyle relay—Texas (Kris Kirchner, Eric Finical, Andy Schmidt, Scott Spann)	2:54.84
800–yd freestyle relay—Florida (Bill Sanchuk, John Hillencamp, Geoff Gaberino, David Larson)	6:27.02
400–yd medley relay—Texas (Clay Britt, Scott Spann, Bill Paulus, Kris Kirchner)	3:12.93[2]
1–m dive—Randy Ableman, Iowa	n.a.
3–m dive—Robert Bollinger, Indiana	540.70 pts
Team—Texas	259 pts

1. Meet record. 2. American record. n.a. = not available.

NATIONAL ASSOCIATION OF INTERCOLLEGIATE ATHLETICS

(Liberty, Mo., March 5–7, 1981)[1]

50–m freestyle—Steve Koga, Willamette (Ore.) University	0:23.361
100–m freestyle—Steve Koga	0:51.281
200–m freestyle—James Yount, Drury (Mo.) College	1:53.499
400–m freestyle—James Yount	4:02.051
1,500–m freestyle—Malcolm Crimp, Simon Fraser, Canada	15:59.454
100–m backstroke—Sean Allison, Drury	0:58.295
200–m backstroke—Nick Borelli, Simon Fraser	2:09.238
100–m breaststroke—Myron Luthringer, Westminster, Pa.	1:06.045
200–m breaststroke—Goran Jern, Denver University	2:25.422
100–m butterfly—Mark Hartung, Drury	0:57.402
200–m butterfly—Paul Eckenroad, Denver University	2:06.833
200–m ind. medley—Steve Boss, Bemidji (Minn.) State	2:10.741
400–m ind. medley—Malcolm Crimp, Simon Fraser	4:33.344
400–m freestyle relay—Drury College	3:28.211
400–m medley relay—Drury College	3:53.586
800–m freestyle relay—Drury College	7:39.442
1–meter dive—Mike Lewis, Drury College	437.80 pts
3–meter dive—Jeff Weber, Wisconsin–Eau Claire	410.40 pts
Team—Drury College	483 pts

1. Meet contested for first time at metric distances.

ASSOCIATION FOR INTERCOLLEGIATE ATHLETICS FOR WOMEN (A.I.A.W.)

(Columbia, S.C., March 18–21, 1981)

50–yd freestyle—Jill Sterkel, University of Texas	0:22.41[1]
100–yd freestyle—Jill Sterkel	0:48.91
200–yd freestyle—Jill Sterkel	1:48.18[1]
500–yd freestyle—Kim Linehan, University of Texas	4:42.33[1]
1,650–yd freestyle—Kim Linehan	15:58.52[1]
50–yd backstroke—Susan Walsh, University of North Carolina	0:25.97[1]
100–yd backstroke—Susan Walsh	0:55.60[1]
200–yd backstroke—Cheryl Gibson, Arizona State	2:00.23
50–yd breaststroke—Kathy Trieble, University of Florida	0:29.14[1]
100–yd breaststroke—Kathy Trieble	1:02.57[1]

200-yd breaststroke—Kathy Trieble	2:16.19	400-yd freestyle relay—Stanford	3:19.70[1]
50-yd butterfly—Jill Sterkel	0:24.22[1]	800-yd freestyle relay—Stanford	7:17.60[1]
100-yd butterfly—Jill Sterkel	0:53.10[1]	200-yd medley relay—North Carolina	1:42.63[1]
200-yd butterfly—Kim Linehan	1:58.68	400-yd medley relay—Arizona State	3:45.96
100-yd ind. medley—Carol Borgmann, University of Texas	0:56.97	1-meter dive—Karen Gorham, Univ. of Arkansas–Fayetteville	425.82 pts[1]
200-yd ind. medley—Diane Johnson, University of Arizona	2:02.55	3-meter dive—Crissy Gentz, Univ. of Minnesota–Minneapolis	447.03 pts
400-yd ind. medley—Cheryl Gibson	4:17.74	Team—University of Texas	587.5 pts
200-yd freestyle relay—Stanford	1:31.12[1]	1. Betters A.I.A.W. championship record.	

ROWING

Rowing goes back so far in history that there is no possibility of tracing it to any particular aboriginal source. The oldest rowing race still on the calendar is the "Doggett's Coat and Badge" contest among professional watermen of the Thames (England) that began in 1715. The first Oxford-Cambridge race was held at Henley in 1829. Competitive rowing in the United States began with matches between boats rowed by professional oarsmen of the New York water front. They were oarsmen who rowed the small boats that plied as ferries from Manhattan Island to Brooklyn and return, or who rowed salesmen down the harbor to meet ships arriving from Europe. Since the first salesman to meet an incoming ship had some advantage over his rivals, there was keen competition in the bidding for fast boats and the best oarsmen. This gave rise to match races.

Amateur boat clubs sprang up in the United States between 1820 and 1830 and seven students of Yale joined together to purchase a four-oared lap-streak gig in 1843. The first Harvard-Yale race was held Aug. 3, 1852, on Lake Winnepesaukee, N.H. The first time an American college crew went abroad was in 1869 when Harvard challenged Oxford and was defeated on the Thames. There were early college rowing races on Lake Quinsigamond, near Worcester, Mass., and on Saratoga Lake, N.Y., but the Intercollegiate Rowing Association in 1895 settled on the Hudson, at Poughkeepsie, as the setting for the annual "Poughkeepsie Regatta." In 1950 the I.R.A. shifted its classic to Marietta, Ohio, and in 1952 it was moved to Syracuse, N.Y. The National Association of Amateur Oarsmen, organized in 1872, has conducted annual championship regattas since that time.

INTERCOLLEGIATE ROWING ASSOCIATION REGATTA
(Varsity Eight-Oared Shells)

Rowed at 4 miles, Poughkeepsie, N.Y., 1895–97, 1899–1916, 1925–32, 1934–41. Rowed at 3 miles, Saratoga, N.Y., 1898; Poughkeepsie, 1921–24, 1947–49; Syracuse, N.Y., 1952–1963, 1965–67. Rowed at 2,000 meters, Syracuse, N.Y., 1964 and from 1968 on. Rowed at 2 miles, Ithaca, N.Y., 1920; Marietta, Ohio, 1950–51. Suspended 1917–19, 1933, 1942–46.

Year	Time	First	Second	Year	Time	First	Second
1895	21:25	Columbia	Cornell	1931	18:54 1/5	Navy	Cornell
1896	19:59	Cornell	Harvard	1932	19:55	California	Cornell
1897	20:47 4/5	Cornell	Columbia	1934	19:44	California	Washington
1898	15:51 1/2	Pennsylvania	Cornell	1935	18:52	California	Cornell
1899	20:04	Pennsylvania	Wisconsin	1936	19:09 3/5	Washington	California
1900	19:44 3/5	Pennsylvania	Wisconsin	1937	18:33 3/5	Washington	Navy
1901	18:53 1/5	Cornell	Columbia	1938	18:19	Navy	California
1902	19:03 3/5	Cornell	Wisconsin	1939	18:12 3/5	California	Washington
1903	18:57	Cornell	Georgetown	1940	22:42	Washington	Cornell
1904	20:22 3/5	Syracuse	Cornell	1941	18:53 3/10	Washington	California
1905	20:29	Cornell	Syracuse	1947	13:59 1/5	Navy	Cornell
1906	19:36 4/5	Cornell	Pennsylvania	1948	14:06 2/5	Washington	California
1907	20:02 2/5	Cornell	Columbia	1949	14:42 2/5	California	Washington
1908	19:24 1/5	Syracuse	Columbia	1950	8:07.5	Washington	California
1909	19:02	Cornell	Columbia	1951	7:50.5	Wisconsin	Washington
1910	20:42 1/5	Cornell	Pennsylvania	1952	15:08.1	Navy	Princeton
1911	20:10 4/5	Cornell	Columbia	1953	15:29.6	Navy	Cornell
1912	19:31 2/5	Cornell	Wisconsin	1954	16:04.4	Navy[1]	Cornell
1913	19:28 3/5	Syracuse	Cornell	1955	15:49.9	Cornell	Pennsylvania
1914	19:37 4/5	Columbia	Pennsylvania	1956	16:22.4	Cornell	Navy
1915	19:36 3/5	Cornell	Stanford	1957	15:26.6	Cornell	Pennsylvania
1916	20:15 2/5	Syracuse	Cornell	1958	17:12.1	Cornell	Navy
1920	11:02 3/5	Syracuse	Cornell	1959	18:01.7	Wisconsin	Syracuse
1921	14:07	Navy	California	1960	15:57	California	Navy
1922	13:33 3/5	Navy	Washington	1961	16:49.2	California	Cornell
1923	14:03 1/5	Washington	Navy	1962	17:02.9	Cornell	Washington
1924	15:02	Washington	Wisconsin	1963	17:24	Cornell	Navy
1925	19:24 4/5	Navy	Washington	1964	6:31.1	California	Washington
1926	19:28 3/5	Washington	Navy	1965	16:51.3	Navy	Cornell
1927	20:57	Columbia	Washington	1966	16:03.4	Wisconsin	Navy
1928	18:35 4/5	California	Columbia	1967	16:13.9	Pennsylvania	Wisconsin
1929	22:58	Columbia	Washington	1968	6:15.6	Pennsylvania	Washington
1930	21:42	Cornell	Syracuse	1969	6:30.4	Pennsylvania	Dartmouth

Year	Time	First	Second
1970	6:39.3	Washington	Wisconsin
1971	6:06	Cornell	Washington
1972	6:22.6	Pennsylvania	Brown
1973	6:21	Wisconsin	Brown
1974	6:33	Wisconsin	Mass. Inst. of Technology
1975	6:08.2	Wisconsin	M.I.T.
1976	6:31	California	Princeton
1977	6:32.4	Cornell	Pennsylvania
1978	6:39.5	Syracuse	Brown
1979	6:26.4	Brown	Wisconsin
1980	6:46	Navy	Northeastern
1981	5:57.3	Cornell	Navy

1. Disqualified.

COLLEGIATE—1981

Intercollegiate Rowing Association

(Lake Onondaga, Syracuse, N.Y., June 6–8, 1981)
(All races at 2,000 meters)

Eights—1. Cornell, 5 minutes 57.3 seconds. 2. Navy, 6:01.5. 3. Northeastern, 6:03. 4. Boston University, 6:05.6. 5. U.C.L.A., 6:06.2. 6. Dartmouth, 6:12.1.

Junior varsity eights—Navy	6:15.7
Freshman eights—Brown	6:22.1
Pairs with coxswain—Pennsylvania	7:48
Pairs without coxswain—Wisconsin	7:18.8
Fours with coxswain—Syracuse	6:51.7
Fours without coxswain—Cornell	6:45.4
Freshman fours—Pennsylvania A	7:07

U.S. MEN'S CHAMPIONSHIPS

National Association of Amateur Oarsmen

Lightweight ¼-mile dash—Larry Klecatsky, New York Athletic Club — 1:19.7
Intermediate doubles—Tom Rowlette and Ron Binder, Fairmount — 7:11.8
Intermediate lightweight doubles—Clay Ziegler and Jim Schultz, Undine Boat Club — 7:17.5
Intermediate fours with coxswain—Vesper Boat Club (Greg Lewis, Sam Bradford, Paul Hughes-Cromwick, George Meck) — 7:07.5
Elite lightweight fours without coxswain—Lightweight Camp A (Pete Kermond, Marshall McInnis, John Wohler, Tim Guiles) — 6:35.8
Elite fours without coxswain—New York Athletic Club (Robert Elsener, Michael Connors, Bill Donoho, Steven Hargis, Stephen Quagliano) — 6:46.5
Intermediate pairs without coxswain—Jay Collins and Mark Hanley, California–Irvine — 7:49.3
Elite lightweight singles—Paul Fuchs, Detroit A — 7:38.4
Intermediate lightweight singles—Jim Schultz, Undine — 8:15.4
Intermediate singles—Charles Bracken, Fairmount — 7:50.9
Elite pairs without coxswain—Dave Townsley and Dave Krmpotich, Univ. of Pennsylvania A — 7:16.4
Elite lightweight eights—Lightweight Camp (Mike Mellon, Marshall McInnis, John Dirvin, Bill Rubin, John Wohler, Chuck Gardiner, Pete Kermond, Tim Guiles, Chris Colville) — 6:16.8
Lightweight quads—New York Athletic Club (John Sonberg, Michael Verlin, Larry Klecatsky, Frank Pisani) — 6:32.5
Elite singles—Jim Dietz, New York Athletic Club — 7:28
Intermediate eights—Williamstown (Tom Knowlton, Peter Detwiler, Scott Schweighauser, Tomaz Remec, Sloane Graff, Cabby Tennis, George Baumgarten, Vinnie Sloman, Laura Yordy) — 6:26.6
Intermediate lightweight eights—Vesper B.C. (John Hooten, Sy Danberg, Andy Schultze Rhonhof, Rolf Glover, Al Guarino, Mark O'Connor, Greg Lewis, Dave Morton, Julian Halliday) — 6:28.4
Quarter–mile singles—Chris Richard, Detroit — 1:12.6
Senior doubles—Mike Corboy and Charles Bracken, Fairmount A — 7:07.9
Senior lightweight doubles—Brian Myers and Chuck Lange, Detroit — 7:02.8
Senior fours with coxswain—New York Athletic Club (Robert Elsener, Michael Connors, Bill Donoho, Steven Hargis, Stephen Quagliano) — 6:48.8
Elite fours without coxswain—Vesper B.C. (Mike Teti, Steve Barainyak, Russell Blount, Craig Leeds) — 6:31.1
Senior lightweight fours without coxswain—Lightweight Camp (Bill Rubin, John Dirvin, Mike Mellon, Chuck Gardiner) — 6:46.9
Senior quads—Fairmount (Mike Corboy, Jack Frackleton, Nat Trinsey, Charlie Bracken) — 6:25.5
Senior pairs without coxswain—Jay Collins and Mark Hanley, California–Irvine — 7:30.2
Elite doubles—William Belden and Jim Dietz, New York Athletic Club — 6:46.7
Elite pairs with coxswain—Mike Teti, Craig Leeds, George Meeck, Vesper B.C. — 7:30.4
Elite lightweight doubles—Larry Klecatsky and William Belden, New York Athletic Club — 6:57.9
Senior singles—Paul Enquist, Lake Washington — 7:39.8
Senior lightweight singles—Brennan Agajan, Vesper B.C. — 7:46.0
Elite lightweight fours with coxswain—Vesper B.C. (Hilary Langer, John Riechenback, Dan Hingley, Ed Gribbin, Sean Brennan) — 7:15.2
Elite lightweight pairs without coxswain—Charles Butt and Steve Schmitt, Vesper B.C. — 7:35.3
Senior lightweight eights—New York Athletic Club (Eric Jensen, Scott Scheinin, Vincent Ventura, Robert Florio, Brian Searchinger, David Filosa, Robert Tschinkel, Gregory Torelli, Lucy Sherry) — 6:23.7
Senior eights—New York Athletic Club (Vincent Houston, Robert Coords, David Barden, Michael Connors, Robert Elsener, Steven Hargis, Willard Donoho, Jim Dietz, Stephen Quagliano) — 6:11.9
Elite quads—New York Athletic Club (Larry Klecatsky, Jon Sonberg, William Belden, Michael Verlin) — 6:30.1
Elite eights—Lightweight Camp (Mike Mellon, Marshall McInnis, John Dirvin, Bill Rubin, John Wohler, Chuck Gardiner, Pete Kermond, Tim Guiles, Chris Colville) — 6:11.2

U.S. WOMEN'S CHAMPIONSHIPS

Varsity eights—Univ. of Washington (Debbie Moore, Madaline Hanson, Sue Broome, Karen Mohling, Pet Achterman, Kristi Norelius, Shyril O'Steen, Jane McDougall, Lisa Horn)	3:20.80
Junior varsity eights—Univ. of Washington	3:30.42
Varsity fours—California	3:44.09
Lightweight eights—Univ. of California–San Diego	3:38.72
Lightweight fours—Loyola Marymount Univ.	3:59.20

FISA INTERNATIONAL CHAMPIONSHIP

(Hazewinkle, Belgium, Aug. 12–18, 1980)

Lightweights

Single sculls—Christian Wahlrich, West Germany	7:00.94
Double sculls—Francesco Espositio and Ruggero Verroca, Italy	6:29.18
Fours without coxswain—Australia (Graham Gardiner, Charles Bartlett, Clyde Hefer, Simon Gillett)	6:12.35
Eights—Britain (Colin Barratt, David Hosking, Robert Downie, Nicholas Howe, Peter Zeun, Clive Roberts, Nigel Read, Stephen Simpole, Simon Jefferies (coxswain))	5:42.76

HANDBALL

U.S.H.A. NATIONAL FOUR-WALL CHAMPIONS

Singles

		1977	Naty Alvarado	1967–68	Jimmy Jacobs-Marty Decatur
		1978	Fred Lewis	1969	Lou Kramberg-Lou Russo
1960	Jimmy Jacobs	1979	Naty Alvarado	1970	Karl and Ruby Obert
1961	John Sloan	1980	Naty Alvarado	1971	Ray Neveau-Simie Fein
1962–63	Oscar Obert	1981	Fred Lewis	1972	Kent Fusselman-Al Drews
1964–65	Jimmy Jacobs			1973–74	Ray Neveau-Simie Fein
1966–67	Paul Haber	**Doubles**		1975	Marty Decatur-Steve Lott
1968	Simon (Stuffy) Singer			1976	Gary Rohrer-Dan O'Connor
1969–71	Paul Haber	1960	Jimmy Jacobs-Dick Weisman	1977	Skip McDowell-Matt Kelly
1972	Fred Lewis	1961	John Sloan-Vic Hershkowitz	1978	Stuffy Singer-Marty Decatur
1973	Terry Muck	1962–63	Jimmy Jacobs-Marty Decatur	1979	Stuffy Singer-Marty Decatur
1974	Fred Lewis	1964	John Sloan-Phil Elbert	1980	Skip McDowell-Harry Robert-
1975	Jay Bilyeu	1965	Jimmy Jacobs-Marty Decatur		son
1976	Vern Roberts, Jr.	1966	Pete Tyson-Bob Lindsay	1981	Tom Kopatich-Jack Roberts

U.S. HANDBALL ASSOCIATION FOUR-WALL CHAMPIONS

(Palatine, Ill., June 20–27, 1981)

Open singles—Fred Lewis, Tucson, Ariz. (defeated Naty Alvarado, Hesperia, Calif., 10–21, 21–12, 11–1, in final)

Open doubles—Tom Kopatich-Jack Roberts, Chicago (defeated Jim Vandenbos–Jim Barnett, Long Beach, Calif., 15–21, 21–15, 11–7, in final)

Women's singles—Rosemary Bellini, New York (defeated Rossanna Ettinger, Long Beach, Calif., 21–3, 21–4, in final)

Women's doubles—Rosemary Bellini, New York, and Sue Oak-

leaf, Texas, (defeated Allison Roberts and Glorian Motal, Houston, 21–19, 21–15, in final)

35 and over singles—Ernie Virgili, Wisconsin (defeated Ken Eby, Chicago, 21–20, 18–21, 11–10, in final)

23 and under singles—Alfonse Monreal, El Paso, Tex. (defeated Jon Kendler, Lake Forest, Ill., 21–12, 21–12, in final)

40 and over singles—Pat Kirby, Tucson, Ariz. (defeated Ted Gewertz, New York, 21–6, 21–15, in final)

40 and over doubles—Pat Kirby and Fred Munsch, Tucson, Ariz. (defeated Bruce McCormick and Roger Nickels, Ohio, 21–5, 21–11, in final).

CYCLING

NATIONAL AMATEUR CHAMPIONS

1951	Gus Gatto	1965	Jack Simes 3rd	1971–72	Gary Campbell
1952	Steve Hromjak	1966	Jack Disney	1973	Roger Young
1953	Ronald Rhoads	1967	Jack Simes, 3rd	1974–75	Steve Woznick
1954–58	Jack Disney	1968	Jack Disney	1976–79	Leigh Barczewski
1959–63	James Rossi	1969	Tim Mountford	1980	Mark Gorski
1964	Jack Simes, 3rd	1970	Harry Cutting	1981	Les Barczewski

U.S. NATIONAL CHAMPIONSHIPS

Road Racing

(Bear Mountain, N.Y., Aug. 7–9, 1981)

Senior men—Tom Broznowski, Seattle, Wash.
Senior women—Connie Carpenter, Boulder, Colo.
Veteran men—Kim Layton, Tahoe City, Calif.
Veteran women—Martha Stafford, Sausalito, Calif.
Junior men—Mike Jensen, La Crescente, Calif.
Junior women—Rebecca Twigg, Seattle, Wash.
Intermediate boys—Gordon Holtermann, Petersburg, Va.
Intermediate girls—Elizabeth Keyser, Aptos, Calif.

Time Trials

(Bear Mountain, N.Y., Aug. 3–4, 1981)

Senior men—Tom Doughty, Hobart, Ind.
Senior women—Connie Carpenter, Boulder, Colo.
Veteran men—Franz Hammer, Redmond, Wash.
Veteran women—Judie Layton, Tahoe City, Calif.
Junior men—Norman Alvis, Loomis, Calif.
Junior women—Rebecca Twigg, Seattle, Wash.
Team—American Machine Foundry (Thurlow Rogers, Granada Hills, Calif.; Kevin Lutz, San Gabriel, Calif.; Ron Kiefel, Denver, Colo., Tom Phren, Colorado Springs)

Track Racing

(Trexlertown, Pa., Aug. 11–16, 1981)

Kilometer—Brent Emery, Milwaukee
Pursuit—Leonard Nitz, Emmaus, Pa.
Women's pursuit—Rebecca Twigg, Seattle, Wash.
Sprint—Les Barczewski, Fort Collins, Colo.
Women's sprint—Sheila Young-Ochowicz, Pewaukee, Wis.
Points—John Beckman, Beaverton, Ore.
Women's points—Connie Carpenter, Boulder, Colo.
Junior men's omnium—Russ Dalbey, Seal Beach, Calif.
Junior women's omnium—Maria Wisser, Allentown, Pa.
Intermediate girls—Renee Duprel, North Bend, Wash.

Tour de France

Bernard Hinault, France

SOARING

U.S. CHAMPIONSHIPS—1980

Open division—Dick Butler, Tullahoma, Tenn.
15 meters—Karl Striedieck, Port Matilda, Pa.
Standard division—Karl Striedieck

HARNESS RACING

Oliver Wendell Holmes, the famous Autocrat of the Breakfast Table, wrote that the running horse was a gambling toy but the trotting horse was useful and, furthermore, "horse-racing is not a republican institution; horse-trotting is." Oliver Wendell Holmes was a born-and-bred New Englander, and New England was the nursery of the harness racing sport in America. Pacers and trotters were matters of local pride and prejudice in Colonial New England, and, shortly after the Revolution, the Messenger and Justin Morgan strains produced many winners in harness racing "matches" along the turnpikes of New York, Connecticut, Rhode Island, Massachusetts, Vermont, and New Hampshire.

There was English thoroughbred blood in Messenger and Justin Morgan, and, many years later, it was blended in Rysdyk's Hambletonian, foaled in 1849. Hambletonian was not particularly fast under harness but his descendants have had almost a monopoly of prizes, titles, and records in the harness racing game. Hambletonian was purchased as a foal with its dam for a total of $124 by William Rysdyk of Goshen, N.Y., and made a modest fortune for the purchaser.

Trotters and pacers often were raced under saddle in the old days, and, in fact, the custom still survives in some places in Europe. Dexter, the great trotter that lowered the mile record from 2:19¾ to 2:17¼ in 1867, was said to handle just as well under saddle as when pulling a sulky. But as sulkies were lightened in weight and improved in design, trotting under saddle became less common and finally faded out in this country.

WORLD RECORDS

Established in a Race or Against Time at One Mile
Source: Martin J. Evans, Research Specialist, United States Trotting Association

Trotting on Mile Track

	Record	Holder	Driver	Where Made	Year
All Age	1:54⅘¹	Lindy's Crown	Howard Beissinger	DuQuoin, Ill.	1980
	1:54⅘*	Nevele Pride	Stanley Dancer	Indianapolis	1969
2–year–old	1:56⅗*	Star Investment, f	William Herman	Lexington, Ky.	1979
3–year–old	1:55¹	Speedy Somolli	Howard Beissinger	DuQuoin, Ill.	1978
		Florida Pro	George Sholty	DuQuoin, Ill.	1978
4–year–old	1:54⅘¹	Lindy's Crown	Howard Beissinger	DuQuoin, Ill.	1980
	1:54⅘*	Nevele Pride	Stanley Dancer	Indianapolis	1969

Trotting on Five-Eighths Mile Track

	Record	Holder	Driver	Where Made	Year
All Age	1:57⅕¹	Lindy's Crown	Howard Beissinger	Wilmington, Del.	1980
2–year–old	2:00⅕¹	Smokin Yankee	Stanley Dancer	Laurel, Md.	1980
3–year–old	1:58⅕¹	Speedy Somolli	Howard Beissinger	Meadow Lands, Pa.	1978
		Florida Pro	George Sholty	Philadelphia	1978
4–year–old	1:57⅕¹	Lindy's Crown	Howard Beissinger	Wilmington, Del.	1980

Trotting on Half-Mile Track

	Record	Holder	Driver	Where Made	Year
All Age	1:56⅘¹	Nevele Pride	Stanley Dancer	Saratoga Springs, N.Y.	1969
2–year–old	2:00⅕¹	Ayres	John Simpson Sr.	Delaware, Ohio	1963
3–year–old	1:58⅜¹	Songcan	George Sholty	Delaware, Ohio	1972
4–year–old	1:56⅘¹	Nevele Pride	Stanley Dancer	Saratoga Springs, N.Y.	1969

Pacing on Mile Track

	Record	Holder	Driver	Where Made	Year
All Age	1:52⅘¹	Niatross	Clint Galbraith	Syracuse, N.Y.	1980
	1:49⅕*	Niatross	Clint Galbraith	Lexington, Ky.	1980
2–year–old	1:54¹	French Chef	Stanley Dancer	Indianapolis	1980
3–year–old	1:52⅕¹	Niatross	Clint Galbraith	Inglewood, Calif.	1980
	1:49⅕*	Niatross	Clint Galbraith	Lexington, Ky.	1980
4–year–old	1:52*	Steady Star	Joe O'Brien	Lexington, Ky.	1971

Pacing on Five-Eighths Mile Track

	Record	Holder	Driver	Where Made	Year
All Age	1:53⅖¹	Storm Damage	Joe O'Brien	Meadow Lands, Pa.	1980
2–year–old	1:56⅕¹	French Chef	Stanley Dancer	Columbus, Ohio	1980
3–year–old	1:53⅖¹	Storm Damage	Joe O'Brien	Meadow Lands, Pa.	1980
4–year–old	1:54⅖¹	Direct Scooter	Warren Cameron	Windsor, Ontario	1980

Pacing on Half-Mile Track

	Record	Holder	Driver	Where Made	Year
All Age	1:54⅘¹	Niatross	Clint Galbraith	Delaware, Ohio	1980
2–year–old	1:57⅖¹	Slapstick	Jack Parker Jr.	Louisville, Ky.	1980
		Icarus Lobell	Herve Filion	Louisville, Ky.	1981
3–year–old	1:54⅘¹	Niatross	Clint Galbraith	Delaware, Ohio	1980
4–year–old	1:55⅜¹	Albatross	Stanley Dancer	Delaware, Ohio	1972

1. Record set in race. *Record set in time trial. f=filly.

HARNESS RACING RECORDS FOR THE MILE

Trotters				Pacers		
Time	**Trotter, age, driver**		**Year**	**Time**	**Pacer, age, driver**	**Year**
2:00	Lou Dillon, 5, Millard Sanders		1903	2:00½	John R. Gentry, 7, W.J. Andrews	1896
1:58½	Lou Dillon, 5, Millard Sanders		1903	1:59¼	Star Pointer, 8, D. McClary	1897
1:58	Uhlan, 8, Charles Tanner		1912	1:59	Dan Patch, 6, M. E. McHenry	1903
1:58	Peter Manning, 5, T. W. Murphy		1921	1:56¼	Dan Patch, 7, M. E. McHenry	1903
1:57¾	Peter Manning, 5, T. W. Murphy		1921	1:56	Dan Patch, 8, H. C. Hersey	1904
1:57	Peter Manning, 6, T. W. Murphy		1922	1:55	Billy Direct, 4, Vic Fleming	1938
1:56¾	Peter Manning, 6, T. W. Murphy		1922	1:55	Adios Harry, 4, Luther Lyons	1955
1:56¾	Greyhound, 5, Sep Palin		1937	1:54⅗	Adios Butler, 4, Paige West	1960
1:56	Greyhound, 5, Sep Palin		1937	1:54	Bret Hanover, 4, Frank Ervin	1966
1:55¼	Greyhound, 6, Sep Palin		1938	1:53⅗	Bret Hanover, 4, Frank Ervin	1966
1:54⅘	Nevele Pride, 4, Stanley Dancer		1969	1:52	Steady Star, 4, Joe O'Brien	1971
				1:49⅕	Niatross, 3, Clint Galbraith	1980

HARNESS HORSE OF THE YEAR

Chosen in poll conducted by United States Trotting Association in conjunction with the U.S. Harness Writers Assn.

1959	Bye Bye Byrd, Pacer	1967	Nevele Pride, Trotter	1975	Savoir, Trotter
1960	Adios Butler, Pacer	1968	Nevele Pride, Trotter	1976	Keystone Ore, Pacer
1961	Adios Butler, Pacer	1969	Nevele Pride, Trotter	1977	Green Speed, Trotter
1962	Su Mac Lad, Trotter	1970	Fresh Yankee, Trotter	1978	Abercrombie, Pacer
1963	Speedy Scot, Trotter	1971	Albatross, Pacer	1979	Niatross, Pacer
1964	Bret Hanover, Pacer	1972	Albatross, Pacer	1980	Niatross, Pacer
1965	Bret Hanover, Pacer	1973	Sir Dalrae, Pacer		
1966	Bret Hanover, Pacer	1974	Delmonica Hanover, Trotter		

HISTORY OF TRADITIONAL HARNESS RACING STAKES

The Hambletonian

Three-year-old trotters. One mile. Guy McKinney won first race at Syracuse in 1926; held at Goshen, N.Y., 1930–1942, 1944–1956; at Yonkers, N.Y., 1943; at Du Quoin, Ill., 1957–1980. In 1981 the race was held at the Meadowlands in East Rutherford, N.J.

Year	Winner	Driver	Best time	Total purse
1967	Speedy Streak	Del Cameron	2:00	122,650
1968	Nevele Pride	Stanley Dancer	1:59⅖	116,190
1969	Lindy's Pride	Howard Beissinger	1:57⅗	124,910
1970	Timothy T.	John Simpson, Jr.	1:58⅖[1]	143,630
1971	Speedy Crown	Howard Beissinger	1:57⅖	129,770
1972	Super Bowl	Stanley Dancer	1:56⅖	119,090
1973	Flirth	Ralph Baldwin	1:57⅕	144,710
1974	Christopher T	Billy Haughton	1:58⅗	160,150
1975	Bonefish	Stanley Dancer	1:59²	232,192
1976	Steve Lobell	Billy Haughton	1:56⅖	263,524
1977	Green Speed	Billy Haughton	1:55⅗	284,131
1978	Speedy Somolli	Howard Beissinger	1:55	241,280
1979	Legend Hanover	George Sholty	1:56	300,000
1980	Burgomeister	Billy Haughton	1:56⅗	293,570
1981	Shiaway St. Pat	Ray Remmen	2:02⅕	838,000

1. By Formal Notice. 2. By Yankee Bambino.

Little Brown Jug

Three-year-old pacers. One Mile. Raced at Delaware County Fair Grounds, Delaware, Ohio.

Year	Winner	Driver	Best time	Total purse
1967	Best of All	Jim Hackett	1:59¹	84,778
1968	Rum Customer	William Haughton	1:59⅗	104,226
1969	Laverne Hanover	William Haughton	2:00⅖	109,731
1970	Most Happy Fella	Stanley Dancer	1:57⅕	100,110
1971	Nansemond	Herve Filion	1:57⅖	102,994
1972	Strike Out	Keith Waples	1:56⅗	104,916
1973	Melvin's Wo	Joe O'Brien	1:57⅗	120,000
1974	Ambro Omaha	Billy Haughton	1:57	132,630
1975	Seatrain	Ben Webster	1:57	147,813
1976	Keystone Ore	Stanley Dancer	1:56½²	153,799
1977	Governor Skipper	John Chapman	1:56½	150,000
1978	Happy Escort	William Popfinger	1:55⅖³	186,760
1979	Hot Hitter	Herve Filion	1:55⅗	226,455
1980	Niatross	Clint Galbraith	1:54⅘	104,717

1. By Nardin's Byrd. 2. By Armbro Ranger. 3. By Falcon Almahurst.

GYMNASTICS

NATIONAL COLLEGIATE ATHLETIC ASSOCIATION
(Lincoln, Neb., April 2–4, 1981)

DIVISION I

	Pts.
All around—Jim Hartung, Nebraska	115.90
Floor exercise—James Yuhashi, Oregon	9.90
Pommel horse—Steve Jennings, New Mexico	9.85
Still rings—Jim Hartung, Nebraska	9.90
Vault—Ron Galimore, Iowa State	10.00
Parallel bars—Phil Cahoy, Nebraska	9.70
Horizontal bar—Phil Cahoy	9.90
Team—Nebraska	284.60

DIVISION II

All around—Dan Nekich, Wisconsin-Oshkosh	52.35
Floor exercise—Tie between Evan Eklin, Wisconsin-Oshkosh, and Franklin Winstead, East Stroudsburg State	9.30
Pommel horse—Bob Jaquaint, Cortland (N.Y.) State	9.10
Still rings—Mike Viola, Springfield	9.30
Vault—Peter Shields, Cortland State	9.75
Parallel bars—Dave Pieper, Wisconsin-Oshkosh	8.90
Horizontal bar—Jeff Stark, Cortland State	9.25
Team—Wisconsin-Oshkosh	209.50

WORLD CUP
(Toronto, Oct. 24–26, 1980)

Men's Events

All around—Bogdan Makuz, Soviet Union
Floor exercise—Roland Brueckner, East Germany
Horizontal bar—Tie among Makuz, Koji Gushiken, Japan, and Toshiomi Nishikii, Japan
Still rings—Tie between Makuz and Yubin Huang, China
Pommel horse—Roland Brueckner, East Germany
Parallel bars—Yuejiu Li, China
Vault—Roland Brueckner, East Germany

Women's Events

All around—Stella Zakharova, U.S.S.R.
Floor exercise—Maxi Gnauck, East Germany
Balance beam—Elena Naymoushina, U.S.S.R.
Vault—Stella Zakharova, U.S.S.R.
Uneven parallel bars—Maxi Gnauck, East Germany

WORLD CHAMPIONSHIPS—1979*
(Fort Worth, Tex., Dec. 7–9, 1979)

Men's Events

	Pts
All around—Aleksandr Dityatin, Soviet Union	118.25
Floor exercises—Kurt Thomas, Indiana State	19.80
Pommel horse—Zoltan Magyar, Hungary	19.82
Still rings—Aleksandr Dityatin	19.80
Vault—Aleksandr Dityatin	19.72
Parallel bars—Bart Conner, United States	19.72
Horizontal bar—Kurt Thomas	19.77
Team—Soviet Union	587.50

Women's Events

All around—Nelli Kim, Soviet Union	78.65
Floor exercises—Emilia Eberle, Romania	19.80
Balance beam—Vera Cerna, Czechoslovakia	19.80
Uneven parallel bars—Yanhons Ma, China	19.82
Vault—Dumitrita Turner, Romania	19.77
Team—Romania	389.55

*Because of Olympics the world championships were not held in 1980. The 1981 world championships were scheduled for November in Moscow.

ASSOCIATION FOR INTERCOLLEGIATE ATHLETICS FOR WOMEN
(Salt Lake City, Utah, April 9–11, 1981)

DIVISION I

	Pts.
All around—Sharon Shapiro, U.C.L.A.	37.2
Balance beam—Laurie Carter, Oregon State	18.8
Floor exercise—Heidi Anderson, Penn State	19.05
Vault—Sharon Shapiro	18.875
Uneven parallel bars—Diane Dovas, U.C.L.A.	19.1
Team—Utah	145.65

DIVISION II
(Williamsburg, Va., April 2–4, 1981)

All around—Christie Clark, Southern Connecticut State	35.90
Balance beam—Karen Beer, Denver	18.45
Floor exercise—Margot Todd, Centenary	18.3
Vault—Margot Todd	18.5
Uneven parallel bars—Christie Clark	18.15
Team—Centenary	141.05

KURT THOMAS FIRST GYMNAST TO WIN SULLIVAN AWARD

Kurt Thomas, a graduate assistant gymnastics coach at Arizona State University, became the first gymnast to be named the outstanding amateur athlete in America in 1979. The 24-year-old Thomas won the James A. Sullivan Award by excelling in a sport generally dominated by Europeans and Japanese. The showing by the 5-ft-5-in., 127-lb Thomas in the world championships in December 1979 at Fort Worth, Tex., put him in the forefront. He won the gold medal in the horizontal bar, shared a gold in the floor exercises, took a silver medal in the pommel horse, shared a silver medal on the parallel bars, and won the second-place silver in the all-around championship. Thomas has a gymnastic trick named after him—"The Thomas Flair." He does it on the pommel horse. His legs whirl and then he goes into a scissors, a move that has been described as seeming to resemble a helicopter in action.

EQUESTRIAN EVENTS—1981

World Cup jumping—Mike Matz, Lafayette Hill, Pa. (riding Jet Run)
Almaden Garden State Grand Prix—Mike Matz (riding Honest Tom)

GOLF

It may be that golf originated in Holland—historians believe it did—but certainly Scotland fostered the game and is famous for it. In fact, in 1457 the Scottish Parliament, disturbed because football and golf had lured young Scots from the more soldierly exercise of archery, passed an ordinance that "futeball and golf be utterly cryit doun and nocht usit." James I and Charles I of the royal line of Stuarts were golf enthusiasts, whereby the game came to be known as "the royal and ancient game of golf."

The golf balls used in the early games were leather-covered and stuffed with feathers. Clubs of all kinds were fashioned by hand to suit individual players. The great step in spreading the game came with the change from the feather ball to the gutta-percha ball about 1850. In 1860, formal competition began with the establishment of an annual tournament for the British Open championship. There are records of "golf clubs" in the United States as far back as colonial days but no proof of actual play before John Reid and some friends laid out six holes on the Reid lawn in Yonkers, N.Y., in 1888 and played there with golf balls and clubs brought over from Scotland by Robert Lockhart. This group then formed the St. Andrews Golf Club of Yonkers, and golf was established in this country.

However, it remained a rather sedate and almost aristocratic pastime until a 20-year-old ex-caddy, Francis Ouimet of Boston, defeated two great British professionals, Harry Vardon and Ted Ray, in the United States Open championship at Brookline, Mass., in 1913. This feat put the game and Francis Ouimet on the front pages of the newspapers and stirred a wave of enthusiasm for the sport. The greatest feat so far in golf history is that of Robert Tyre Jones, Jr., of Atlanta, who won the British Open, the British Amateur, the U.S. Open, and the U.S. Amateur titles in one year, 1930.

U.S. OPEN CHAMPIONS

Year	Winner	Score	Where played	Year	Winner	Score	Where played
1895	Horace Rawlins	173	Newport	1938	Ralph Guldahl	284	Cherry Hills
1896	James Foulis	152	Shinnecock Hills	1939	Byron Nelson[1]	284	Philadelphia
1897	Joe Lloyd	162	Chicago	1940	Lawson Little[1]	287	Canterbury
1898[3]	Fred Herd	328	Myopia	1941	Craig Wood	284	Colonial
1899	Willie Smith	315	Baltimore	1942–45	No tournaments[5]		
1900	Harry Vardon	313	Chicago	1946	Lloyd Mangrum[1]	284	Canterbury
1901	Willie Anderson[1]	331	Myopia	1947	Lew Worsham[1]	282	St. Louis
1902	Laurie Auchterlonie	307	Garden City	1948	Ben Hogan	276	Riviera
1903	Willie Anderson[1]	307	Baltusrol	1949	Cary Middlecoff	286	Medinah
1904	Willie Anderson	303	Glen View	1950	Ben Hogan[1]	287	Merion
1905	Willie Anderson	314	Myopia	1951	Ben Hogan	287	Oakland Hills
1906	Alex Smith	295	Onwentsia	1952	Julius Boros	281	Northwood
1907	Alex Ross	302	Philadelphia	1953	Ben Hogan	283	Oakmont
1908	Fred McLeod[1]	322	Myopia	1954	Ed Furgol	284	Baltusrol
1909	George Sargent	290	Englewood	1955	Jack Fleck[1]	287	Olympic
1910	Alex Smith[1]	298	Philadelphia	1956	Cary Middlecoff	281	Oak Hill
1911	John McDermott[1]	307	Chicago	1957	Dick Mayer[1]	298	Inverness
1912	John McDermott	294	Buffalo	1958	Tommy Bolt	283	Southern Hills
1913	Francis Ouimet[1][2]	304	Brookline	1959	Bill Casper, Jr.	282	Winged Foot
1914	Walter Hagen	290	Midlothian	1960	Arnold Palmer	280	Cherry Hills
1915	Jerome D. Travers[2]	297	Baltusrol	1961	Gene Littler	281	Oakland Hills
1916	Charles Evans, Jr.[2]	286	Minikahda	1962	Jack Nicklaus[1]	283	Oakmont
1917–18	No tournaments[4]			1963	Julius Boros[1]	293	Country Club
1919	Walter Hagen[2]	301	Brae Burn	1964	Ken Venturi	278	Congressional
1920	Edward Ray	295	Inverness	1965	Gary Player[1]	282	Bellerive
1921	Jim Barnes	289	Columbia	1966	Bill Casper[1]	278	Olympic
1922	Gene Sarazen	288	Skokie	1967	Jack Nicklaus	275	Baltusrol
1923	R. T. Jones, Jr.[1][2]	296	Inwood	1968	Lee Trevino	275	Oak Hill
1924	Cyril Walker	297	Oakland Hills	1969	Orville Moody	281	Champions G. C.
1925	Willie Macfarlane[1]	291	Worcester	1970	Tony Jacklin	281	Hazeltine
1926	R. T. Jones, Jr.[2]	293	Scioto	1971	Lee Trevino[1]	280	Merion
1927	Tommy Armour[1]	301	Oakmont	1972	Jack Nicklaus	290	Pebble Beach
1928	Johnny Farrell[1]	294	Olympia Fields	1973	Johnny Miller	279	Oakmont
1929	R. T. Jones, Jr.[1][2]	294	Winged Foot	1974	Hale Irwin	287	Winged Foot
1930	R. T. Jones, Jr.[2]	287	Interlachen	1975	Lou Graham[1]	287	Medinah
1931	Billy Burke[1]	292	Inverness	1976	Jerry Pate	277	Atlanta A.C.
1932	Gene Sarazen	286	Fresh Meadow	1977	Hubert Green	278	Southern Hills
1933	John Goodman[2]	287	North Shore	1978	Andy North	285	Cherry Hills
1934	Olin Dutra	293	Merion	1979	Hale Irwin	284	Inverness
1935	Sam Parks, Jr.	299	Oakmont	1980	Jack Nicklaus	272	Baltusrol
1936	Tony Manero	282	Baltusrol	1981	David Graham	273	Merion
1937	Ralph Guldahl	281	Oakland Hills				

1. Winner in playoff. 2. Amateur. 3. In 1898, competition was extended to 72 holes. 4. In 1917, Jock Hutchison, with a 292, won an Open Patriotic Tournament for the benefit of the American Red Cross at Whitemarsh Valley Country Club. 5. In 1942, Ben Hogan, with a 271 won a Hale American National Open Tournament for the benefit of the Navy Relief Society and USO at Ridgemoor Country Club.

U.S. AMATEUR CHAMPIONS

Year	Winner	Year	Winner	Year	Winner	Year	Winner
1895	Charles B. Mac-donald	1920	Charles Evans, Jr.	1946	Ted Bishop	1965[2]	Robert Murphy, Jr.
1896–97	H. J. Whigham	1921	Jesse P. Guilford	1947	Robert Riegel	1966	Gary Cowan[1]
1898	Findlay S. Douglas	1922	Jess W. Sweetser	1948	Willie Turnesa	1967	Bob Dickson
1899	H. M. Harriman	1923	Max R. Marston	1949	Charles Coe	1968	Bruce Fleisher
1900–01	Walter J. Travis	1924–25	R. T. Jones Jr.	1950	Sam Urzetta	1969	Steven Melnyk
1902	Louis N. James	1926	George Von Elm	1951	Billy Maxwell	1970	Lanny Wadkins
1903	Walter J. Travis	1927–28	R. T. Jones Jr.	1952	Jack Westland	1971	Gary Cowan
1904–05	H. Chandler Egan	1929	H. R. Johnston	1953	Gene Littler	1972	Vinny Giles 3d
1906	Eben M. Byers	1930	R. T. Jones, Jr.	1954	Arnold Palmer	1973[3]	Craig Stadler
1907–08	Jerome D. Travers	1931	Francis Ouimet	1955–56	Harvie Ward	1974	Jerry Pate
1909	Robert A. Gardner	1932	Ross Somerville	1957	Hillman Robbins	1975	Fred Ridley
1910	W. C. Fownes, Jr.	1933	G. T. Dunlap, Jr.	1958	Charles Coe	1976	Bill Sander
1911	Harold H. Hilton	1934–35	Lawson Little	1959	Jack Nicklaus	1977	John Fought
1912–13	Jerome D. Travers	1936	John W. Fischer	1960	Deane Beman	1978	John Cook
1914	Francis Ouimet	1937	John Goodman	1961	Jack Nicklaus	1979	Mark O'Meara
1915	Robert A. Gardner	1938	Willie Turnesa	1962	Labron Harris, Jr.	1980	Hal Sutton
1916	Charles Evans, Jr.	1939	Marvin H. Ward	1963	Deane Beman	1981	Nathaniel Crosby
1919	S. D. Herron	1940	R. D. Chapman	1964	Bill Campbell		
		1941	Marvin H. Ward				

1. Winner in playoff. 2. Tourney switched to medal play through 1972. 3. Return to match play.

U.S. P.G.A. CHAMPIONS

Year	Winner	Year	Winner	Year	Winner	Year	Winner
1916	Jim Barnes	1939	Henry Picard	1955	Doug Ford	1970	Dave Stockton
1919	Jim Barnes	1940	Byron Nelson	1956	Jack Burke, Jr.	1971	Jack Nicklaus
1920	Jock Hutchison	1941	Victor Ghezzi	1957	Lionel Hebert	1972	Gary Player
1921	Walter Hagen	1942	Sam Snead	1958[2]	Dow Finsterwald	1973	Jack Nicklaus
1922–23	Gene Sarazen	1944	Bob Hamilton	1959	Bob Rosburg	1974	Lee Trevino
1924–27	Walter Hagen	1945	Byron Nelson	1960	Jay Hebert	1975	Jack Nicklaus
1928–29	Leo Diegel	1946	Ben Hogan	1961	Jerry Barber[1]	1976	Dave Stockton
1930	Tommy Armour	1947	Jim Ferrier	1962	Gary Player	1977	Lanny Wadkins[1]
1931	Tom Creavy	1948	Ben Hogan	1963	Jack Nicklaus	1978	John Mahaffey
1932	Olin Dutra	1949	Sam Snead	1964	Bobby Nichols	1979	David Graham[1]
1933	Gene Sarazen	1950	Chandler Harper	1965	Dave Marr	1980	Jack Nicklaus
1934	Paul Runyan	1951	Sam Snead	1966	Al Geiberger	1981	Larry Nelson
1935	Johnny Revolta	1952	Jim Turnesa	1967	Don January[1]		
1936–37	Denny Shute	1953	Walter Burkemo	1968	Julius Boros		
1938	Paul Runyan	1954	Chick Harbert	1969	Ray Floyd		

1. Winner in playoff. 2. Switched to medal play.

THE MASTERS TOURNAMENT WINNERS
Augusta National Golf Club, Augusta, Ga.

Year	Winner	Score	Year	Winner	Score	Year	Winner	Score
1934	Horton Smith	284	1952	Sam Snead	286	1968	Bob Goalby	277
1935	Gene Sarazen[1]	282	1953	Ben Hogan	274	1969	George Archer	281
1936	Horton Smith	285	1954	Sam Snead[1]	289	1970	Billy Casper[1]	279
1937	Byron Nelson	283	1955	Cary Middlecoff	279	1971	Charles Coody	279
1938	Henry Picard	285	1956	Jack Burke	289	1972	Jack Nicklaus	286
1939	Ralph Guldahl	279	1957	Doug Ford	283	1973	Tommy Aaron	283
1940	Jimmy Demaret	280	1958	Arnold Palmer	284	1974	Gary Player	278
1941	Craig Wood	280	1959	Art Wall, Jr.	284	1975	Jack Nicklaus	276
1942	Byron Nelson[1]	280	1960	Arnold Palmer	282	1976	Ray Floyd	271
1943–45	No Tournaments		1961	Gary Player	280	1977	Tom Watson	276
1946	Herman Keiser	282	1962	Arnold Palmer[1]	280	1978	Gary Player	277
1947	Jimmy Demaret	281	1963	Jack Nicklaus	286	1979	Fuzzy Zoeller[1]	280
1948	Claude Harmon	279	1964	Arnold Palmer	276	1980	Severiano Ballesteros	275
1949	Sam Snead	282	1965	Jack Nicklaus	271	1981	Tom Watson	280
1950	Jimmy Demaret	283	1966	Jack Nicklaus[1]	288			
1951	Ben Hogan	280	1967	Gay Brewer, Jr.	280			

1. Winner in playoff.

U.S. WOMEN'S AMATEUR CHAMPIONS

Year	Winner	Year	Winner	Year	Winner	Year	Winner
1916	Alexa Stirling	1926	Helen Stetson	1937	Mrs. J. A. Page, Jr.	1949	Mrs. D. G. Porter
1919–20	Alexa Stirling	1927	Mrs. M. B. Horn	1938	Patty Berg	1950	Beverly Hanson
1921	Marion Hollins	1928–30	Glenna Collett	1939–40	Betty Jameson	1951	Dorothy Kirby
1922	Glenna Collett	1931	Helen Hicks	1941	Mrs. Frank Newell	1952	Jacqueline Pung
1923	Edith Cummings	1932–34	Virginia Van Wie	1946	Mildred Zaharias	1953	Mary Lena Faulk
1924	Dorothy Campbell Hurd	1935	Glenna Collett Vare	1947	Louise Suggs	1954	Barbara Romack
1925	Glenna Collett	1936	Pamela Barton	1948	Grace Lenczyk	1955	Patricia Lesser
						1956	Marlene Stewart

Year	Winner	Year	Winner	Year	Winner	Year	Winner
1957	JoAnne Gunderson	1963	Anne Quast Welts	1970	Martha Wilkinson	1977	Beth Daniel
1958	Anne Quast	1964	Barbara McIntire	1971	Laura Baugh	1978	Cathy Sherk
1959	Barbara McIntire	1965	Jean Ashley	1972	Mary Ann Budke	1979	Carolyn Hill
1960	JoAnne Gunderson	1966	JoAnne Gunderson	1973	Carol Semple	1980	Juli Inkster
1961	Anne Quast Decker	1967	Lou Dill	1974	Cynthia Hill	1981	Juli Inkster
1962	JoAnne Gunderson	1968	JoAnne G. Carner	1975	Beth Daniel		
		1969	Catherine Lacoste	1976	Donna Horton		

U.S. WOMEN'S OPEN CHAMPIONS

Year	Winner	Score	Year	Winner	Score	Year	Winner	Score
1946	Patty Berg (match play)	—	1958	Mickey Wright	290	1970	Donna Caponi	287
1947	Betty Jameson	295	1959	Mickey Wright	287	1971	JoAnne Carner	288
1948	Mildred D. Zaharias	300	1960	Betsy Rawls	291	1972	Susie Berning	299
1949	Louise Suggs	291	1961	Mickey Wright	293	1973	Susie Berning	290
1950	Mildred D. Zaharias	291	1962	Murle Lindstrom	301	1974	Sandra Haynie	295
1951	Betsy Rawls	293	1963	Mary Mills	289	1975	Sandra Palmer	295
1952	Louise Suggs	284	1964	Mickey Wright[1]	290	1976	JoAnne Carner	292
1953	Betsy Rawls[1]	302	1965	Carol Mann	290	1977	Hollis Stacy	292
1954	Mildred D. Zaharias	291	1966	Sandra Spuzich	297	1978	Hollis Stacy	289
1955	Fay Crocker	299	1967	Catherine LaCoste	294	1979	Jerilyn Britz	284
1956	Katherine Cornelius[1]	302	1968	Susie Berning	289	1980	Amy Alcott	280
1957	Betsy Rawls	299	1969	Donna Caponi	294	1981	Pat Bradley	279

1. Winner in playoff. 2. Amateur.

BRITISH OPEN CHAMPIONS

(First tournament, held in 1860, was won by Willie Park, Sr.)

Year	Winner	Score	Year	Winner	Score	Year	Winner	Score
1920	George Duncan	303	1939	R. Burton	290	1964	Tony Lema	279
1921	Jock Hutchison[1]	296	1946	Sam Snead	290	1965	Peter Thomson	285
1922	Walter Hagen	300	1947	Fred Daly	294	1966	Jack Nicklaus	282
1923	A. G. Havers	295	1948	Henry Cotton	283	1967	Roberto de Vicenzo	278
1924	Walter Hagen	301	1949	Bobby Locke[1]	283	1968	Gary Player	289
1925	Jim Barnes	300	1950	Bobby Locke	279	1969	Tony Jacklin	280
1926	R. T. Jones, Jr.	291	1951	Max Faulkner	285	1970	Jack Nicklaus[1]	283
1927	R. T. Jones, Jr.	285	1952	Bobby Locke	287	1971	Lee Trevino	278
1928	Walter Hagen	292	1953	Ben Hogan	282	1972	Lee Trevino	278
1929	Walter Hagen	292	1954	Peter Thomson	283	1973	Tom Weiskopf	276
1930	R. T. Jones, Jr.	291	1955	Peter Thomson	281	1974	Gary Player	282
1931	Tommy Armour	296	1956	Peter Thomson	286	1975	Tom Watson[1]	279
1932	Gene Sarazen	283	1957	Bobby Locke	279	1976	Johnny Miller	279
1933	Denny Shute[1]	292	1958	Peter Thomson[1]	278	1977	Tom Watson	268
1934	Henry Cotton	283	1959	Gary Player	284	1978	Jack Nicklaus	281
1935	A. Perry	283	1960	Kel Nagle	278	1979	Severiano Ballesteros	283
1936	A. H. Padgham	287	1961	Arnold Palmer	284	1980	Tom Watson	271
1937	Henry Cotton	290	1962	Arnold Palmer	276	1981	Bill Rogers	276
1938	R. A. Whitcombe	295	1963	Bob Charles[1]	277			

1. Winner in playoff.

U.S. OPEN—MEN

(Merion Country Club, Ardmore, Pa., June 17–21, 1981)

David Graham	68	68	70	67—273	$55,000
George Burns	69	66	68	73—276	24,650
Bill Rogers	70	68	69	69—276	24,650
John Cook	68	70	71	70—279	16,200
John Schroeder	71	68	69	71—279	16,200
Frank Connor	71	72	69	68—280	9,920
Lon Hinkle	69	71	70	70—280	9,920
Jack Nicklaus	69	68	71	72—280	9,920
Sammy Rachels	70	71	69	70—280	9,920
Chi Chi Rodriguez	68	73	67	72—280	9,920

Leaders—18 holes: Jim Torpe, 66; 36 holes: George Burns, 135; 54 holes: George Burns, 203.

P.G.A. CHAMPIONSHIP

(Atlanta Athletic Club, Duluth, Ga., Aug. 6–9, 1981)

Larry Nelson	70	66	66	71—273	$60,000
Fuzzy Zoeller	70	68	68	71—277	40,000

Dan Pohl	69	67	73	69—278	25,000
Bob Gilder	74	69	70	66—279	13,146
Greg Norman	73	67	68	71—279	13,146
Tom Kite	71	67	69	72—279	13,146
Isao Aoki	75	68	66	70—279	13,146
Keith Fergus	71	71	69	68—279	13,146
Bruce Lietzke	70	70	71	68—279	13,146
Jack Nicklaus	71	68	71	69—279	13,146

MASTERS TOURNAMENT—MEN

(Augusta, Ga., April 9–12, 1981)

Tom Watson	71	68	70	71—280	$60,000
Jack Nicklaus	70	65	75	72—282	30,500
Johnny Miller	69	72	73	68—282	30,500
Greg Norman	69	70	72	72—283	16,000
Jerry Pate	71	72	71	70—284	12,667
Tom Kite	74	72	70	68—284	12,667
Dave Graham	70	70	74	71—285	11,167
Ray Floyd	75	71	71	69—286	9,667
Ben Crenshaw	71	72	70	73—286	9,667
John Mahaffey	72	71	69	74—286	9,667
Peter Jacobsen	71	70	72	74—287	7,333

Bruce Lietzke	72	67	73	75—287	7,333
George Archer	74	70	72	71—287	7,333
Hubert Green	70	70	74	73—287	7,333

BRITISH OPEN

(Sandwich, England, July 16–19, 1981)

Bill Rogers	72	66	67	71—276	$50,000
Bernhard Langer	73	67	70	70—280	35,000
Ray Floyd	74	70	69	70—283	23,500
Mark James	72	70	68	73—283	23,500
S. Torrance	72	69	73	70—284	17,000
M. Pinero	73	74	68	70—285	15,500
Bruce Leitzke	76	69	71	69—285	15,500
Ben Crenshaw	72	67	76	71—286	13,000
Brian Jones	73	76	66	71—286	13,000
Howard Clark	72	76	70	68—286	13,000
Lee Trevino	77	67	70	73—287	10,000
Isao Aoki	71	73	69	74—287	10,000
Nick Faldo	77	68	69	73—287	10,000

WOMEN'S OPEN

(La Grange, Ill., July 23–26, 1981)

Pat Bradley	71	74	68	66—279	$22,000
Beth Daniel	69	74	69	68—280	12,500
Kathy Whitworth	69	70	71	74—284	9,500
Cynthia Hill	76	70	69	72—287	7,000
Bonnie Lauer	72	67	72	76—287	7,000
Donna Caponi	71	74	72	73—290	4,562
Muriel Floyd	71	72	73	74—290	4,562
JoAnn Carner	73	71	72	74—290	4,562
P. Sheehan	74	74	72	70—290	4,562
Amelia Rorer	73	77	69	73—292	2,967
Sally Little	74	72	76	70—292	2,967
Hollis Stacy	73	75	69	75—292	2,967
Debbie Massey	71	72	72	77—292	2,967
Sandra Haynie	75	73	73	71—292	2,967
Sue Hamlin	70	75	75	72—292	2,967

L.P.G.A. CHAMPIONSHIP

(Jack Nicklaus Sports Center, Kings Island, Ohio, June 11–14, 1981)

Donna Caponi	69	68	70	73—280	$22,500
Jerilyn Britz	67	71	71	72—281	12,600
Pat Meyers	68	70	72	71—281	12,600
Debbie Massey	72	72	69	70—283	7,500
Beth Daniel	72	70	71	71—284	5,350
JoAnne Carner	72	69	73	70—284	5,350
Nancy Lopez–Melton	70	72	72	70—284	5,350
Sally Little	71	77	69	68—285	4,350
Amy Alcott	69	70	73	74—286	4,050
Sandra Palmer	73	70	72	72—287	3,600
Martha Hansen	69	74	72	72—287	3,600

MEN'S AMATEUR

(The Country Club of North Carolina, Pinehurst, N.C., Aug. 26–31, 1980)

Final (36 holes)—Hal Sutton, Shreveport, La., defeated Bob Lewis, Warren, Ohio, 9 and 8

Semifinals—Sutton defeated Jim Holtgrieve, Kirkwood, Mo., 3 and 2; Lewis defeated Dick Von Tacky, Titusville, Ga., 4 and 2

Quarterfinals—Holtgrieve defeated Fred Couples, Seattle, Wash., 5 and 3; Sutton defeated Jodie Mudd, Louisville, Ky., 2 up; Von Tacky defeated Clarence Rose, Goldsboro, N.C., 3 and 1; Lewis defeated Jay Sigel, Berwyn, Pa., 4 and 3

L.P.G.A. EARNINGS—1981

(Through July 31, 1981)

Player	Amount	Player	Amount
Pat Bradley	$154,182	Beth Daniel	110,252
Nancy Lopez–Melton	149,468	Sally Little	107,285
		Kathy Whitworth	101,617
Donna Caponi	136,595	Jane Blalock	83,480
JoAnne Carner	129,858	Jan Stephenson	75,488
Amy Alcott	117,327		

FINAL 1980 LEADING L.P.G.A. EARNINGS

Player	Amount	Player	Amount
Beth Daniel	$231,000	Pat Bradley	183,377
Donna Caponi	220,619	Sally Little	139,127
Amy Alcott	219,887	Jane Blalock	127,873
Nancy Lopez–Melton	209,078	Jo Ann Washam	107,063
JoAnne Carner	185,915	Sandra Post	102,822

P.G.A. EARNINGS—1981

(Through July 31, 1981)

Player	Amount	Player	Amount
Tom Watson	$335,982	Johnny Miller	183,778
Ray Floyd	324,754	Hale Irwin	180,774
Bruce Lietzke	275,612	Craig Stadler	179,145
Tom Kite	214,081	Curtis Strange	169,899
Jerry Pate	196,962	Bill Rogers	161,261

FINAL 1980 LEADING P.G.A. EARNINGS

Player	Amount	Player	Amount
Tom Watson	$530,808	Jerry Pate	222,976
Lee Trevino	385,814	George Burns	219,928
Curtis Strange	271,400	Craig Stadler	206,291
Andy Bean	269,033	Mike Reid	206,097
Ben Crenshaw	237,727	Ray Floyd	192,993

U.S.G.A. SENIORS CHAMPIONSHIP—1981

(Birmingham, Mich., July 9–13, 1981)
(For professionals and amateurs 50 and older)

*Arnold Palmer[1]	72	76	68	73—289	$26,000
Bob Stone[1]	72	71	74	72—289	9,586
Billy Casper[1]	73	72	71	73—289	9,586
Art Wall	71	72	73	74—290	6,736
Gene Littler	75	71	75	71—292	6,136
Miller Barber	74	71	74	74—293	5,636
Bob Goalby	71	71	76	76—294	5,136
Lionel Hebert	70	77	74	75—296	4,036
Mike Souchak	75	74	78	69—296	4,036
Stan Thirsk	73	77	75	71—296	4,036
Mike Fetchick	76	73	75	72—296	4,036

1. In 3-way 18-hole playoff. *Won playoff with round of 70; Stone shot 74, Casper 77.

1981 COLLEGIATE GOLF CHAMPIONS
N.C.A.A.

Division I—Brigham Young, 1,161
Division II—Florida Southern, 1,184
Division III—Stanislaus State, 1,262

A.I.A.W.

Division I—Florida State University
Division II—College of William and Mary
Division III—California State–Sacramento

OTHER 1981 P.G.A. TOUR WINNERS
(Through July 31, 1981)

Tucson Open—Johnny Miller (265)	$54,000
Bob Hope Classic—Bruce Lietzke (335)	50,000
Phoenix Open—David Graham (268)	54,000
Crosby Pro-Am—John Cook* (209)[1]	40,500
San Diego Open—Bruce Lietzke* (278)	45,000
Hawaiian Open—Hale Irwin (265)	58,500
Los Angeles Open—Johnny Miller (270)	54,000
Bay Hill Classic—Andy Bean (266)	54,000
Inverrary Classic—Tom Kite (274)	54,000
Doral Open—Ray Floyd (273)	45,000
Tournament Players Championship—Ray Floyd* (285)	72,000
Heritage Classic—Bill Rogers (278)	54,000
Greensboro Open—Larry Nelson* (281)	54,000
Tournament of Champions—Lee Trevino (273)	54,000
Tallahassee Open—Dave Eichelberger* (271)	18,000
New Orleans Open—Tom Watson (270)	63,000
Houston Open—Ron Streck (198)[1]	47,250
Nelson Classic—Bruce Lietzke* (281)	54,000
Colonial Invitational—Fuzzy Zoeller (274)	54,000
Memorial Tournament—Keith Fergus (284)	63,000
Kemper Open—Craig Stadler (270)	72,000
Atlanta Classic—Tom Watson* (277)	54,000
Westchester Classic—Ray Floyd (275)	72,000
Memphis Open—Jerry Pate (274)	54,000
Western Open—Ed Fiori (277)	54,000
Greater Milwaukee Open—Jay Haas (274)	45,000

Quad Cities Open—Dave Barr* (270)	36,000
Anheuser Busch Classic—John Mahaffey (276)	54,000
Canadian Open—Peter Oosterhuis (280)	60,000

*Won playoff. 1. Shortened by rain.

OTHER 1981 L.P.G.A. TOUR WINNERS
(Through July 31, 1981)

Whirlpool—Sandra Palmer (284)	$15,000
Arden Classic—Sally Little* (283)	18,750
S&H Classic—JoAnne Carner* (215)	15,000
Bent Tree Classic—Amy Alcott (276)	22,500
Olympia Gold—Sally Little (142)[1]	22,500
Arizona Copper—Nancy Lopez–Melton (278)	18,750
Sun City Classic—Patty Hayes (277)	15,000
Desert Inn Pro-Am—Donna Caponi (286)	30,000
Women's Kemper—Pat Bradley (284)	26,250
Colgate–Dinah Shore—Nancy Lopez–Melton (277)	37,500
American Defender—Donna Caponi (208)	18,750
Lady Citrus—Beth Daniel* (281)	15,000
Birmingham Classic—Beth Solomon* (206)	15,000
CPC International—Sally Little* (287)	18,750
Lady Michelob—Amy Alcott (209)	18,750
Coca-Cola Classic—Kathy Whitworth* (211)	18,750
Corning Classic—Kathy Hite (282)	18,750
Golden Lights—Cathy Reynolds (285)	18,750
McDonald's Classic—Sandra Post (282)	22,500
Lady Keystone—JoAnne Carner (203)	18,750
Sarah Coventry—Nancy Lopez–Melton (285)	18,750
Peter Jackson—Jan Stephenson (278)	30,000
Mayflower Classic—Debbie Austin (279)	22,500
W.U.I. Classic—Donna Caponi (282)	18,750
Danvers Classic—Donna Caponi (276)	22,500

*Won playoff. 1. Shortened by rain.

SOCCER

WORLD CUP

1930	Uruguay	1946	No competition		
1934	Italy	1950	Uruguay	1962	Brazil
1938	Italy	1954	West Germany	1966	England
1942	No competition	1958	Brazil	1970	Brazil
				1974	West Germany

1978 Argentina

MAJOR INDOOR SOCCER LEAGUE
FINAL STANDINGS—1981
Atlantic Division

	W	L	Pct.	GB
New York	35	5	.875	—
Baltimore	21	19	.525	14
Philadelphia	18	22	.450	17
Hartford	13	27	.325	22

Central Division

	W	L	Pct.	GB
St. Louis	25	15	.625	—
Cleveland	21	19	.525	4
Chicago	20	20	.500	5
Buffalo	20	20	.500	5

Western Division

	W	L	Pct.	GB
Wichita	23	17	.575	—
Phoenix	17	23	.425	6
Denver	16	24	.400	7
San Francisco	11	29	.275	12

CHAMPIONSHIP PLAYOFFS
Quarterfinals
New York defeated Phoenix, 2 games to 1
St. Louis defeated Buffalo, 2 games to 0

Wichita defeated Chicago, 2 games to 1
Baltimore defeated Cleveland, 2 games to 1

Semifinals
New York 10, Baltimore 1
St. Louis 8, Wichita 7 (shootout)

Final
New York 6, St. Louis 5

NORTH AMERICAN SOCCER LEAGUE
Outdoor Season
Final Standing—1981

EASTERN DIVISION

	W	L	GF	GA	BP[1]	Pts
Cosmos[2]	23	9	80	49	64	200
Montreal Manic[3]	15	17	63	57	55	141
Washington Diplomats	15	17	59	58	51	135
Toronto Blizzard	7	25	39	82	37	77

SOUTHERN DIVISION

	W	L	GF	GA	BP[1]	Pts
Atlanta Chiefs[4]	17	15	62	60	53	151
Fort Lauderdale Strikers[3]	18	14	54	46	44	144

Jacksonville Tea Men[3]	18	14	51	46	41	141
Tampa Bay Rowdies[3]	15	17	63	64	53	139

CENTRAL DIVISION

Chicago Sting[4]	23	9	84	50	63	195
Minnesota Kicks[3]	19	13	63	57	55	163
Tulsa Roughnecks[3]	17	15	60	49	54	154
Dallas Tornado	5	27	27	71	26	54

WESTERN DIVISION

San Diego Sockers[4]	21	11	68	49	55	173
Los Angeles Aztecs[3]	19	13	53	55	48	160
California Surf	11	21	60	77	51	117
San Jose Earthquake	11	21	44	78	42	108

NORTHWEST DIVISION

Vancouver Whitecaps[4]	21	11	74	43	62	186
Calgary[3]	17	15	59	54	51	151
Portland Timbers[3]	17	15	52	49	45	141
Seattle Sounders[3]	15	17	60	62	51	137
Edmonton Drillers	12	20	60	79	51	123

1. Bonus points—awarded for each goal to a maximum of three per team per game; teams receive 6 points for each victory. 2. Won league point title. 3. Qualified for playoffs. 4. Won division title.

CHAMPIONSHIP BOWL—1980

(R.F.K. Stadium, Washington, D.C., Sept. 21, 1980)
Cosmos 3, Fort Lauderdale 0
(Scoring: Chinaglia 2, Romero)

LEADING N.A.S.L. SCORERS—1981

	GP	G	A	Pts
Giorgio Chinaglia, Cosmos	32	29	16	74
Karl–Heinz Granitza, Chicago	31	19	17	55
Mike Stojanovic, San Diego	32	23	6	52
Brian Kidd, Atlanta	27	22	8	52
Franz Gerber, Calgary	25	20	10	50
Teofilo Cubillas, Fort Lauderdale	28	17	10	44
Arno Steffenhagen, Chicago	28	17	10	44
Gordon Hill, Montreal	30	16	12	44
Edi Kirschner, Edmonton	31	17	9	43
Duncan McKenzie, Tulsa	31	14	15	43

N.A.S.L. INDOOR SOCCER
Final Standing—1981

Central Division

	W	L	Pct	GB
Chicago	13	5	.722	—
Minnesota	12	6	.667	1
Detroit	7	11	.389	6

Eastern Division

	W	L	Pct	GB
Atlanta	13	5	.722	—
Tampa Bay	9	9	.500	4
Jacksonville	8	10	.444	5
Fort Lauderdale	1	17	.056	12

Northern Division

	W	L	Pct	GB
Vancouver	11	7	.611	—
Edmonton	10	8	.556	1
Calgary	10	8	.556	1
Toronto	5	13	.278	6

Southern Division

	W	L	Pct	GB
California	10	8	.556	—
Tulsa	9	9	.500	1
Dallas	7	11	.389	3
San Diego	6	12	.333	4

Western Division

	W	L	Pct	GB
Los Angeles	11	7	.611	—
Portland	10	8	.556	1
San Jose	10	8	.556	1
Seattle	9	9	.500	2

CHAMPIONSHIP PLAYOFFS
Quarterfinals
Edmonton defeated Los Angeles, 2 games to 0
Atlanta defeated Minnesota, 2 games to 0
Vancouver defeated California, 2 games to 1
Chicago defeated Portland, 2 games to 0

Semifinals
Edmonton defeated Vancouver, 2 games to 0
Chicago defeated Atlanta, 2 games to 1

Finals
Edmonton 9, Chicago 6
Edmonton 5, Chicago 4 (Edmonton won series 2 games to 0)

WRESTLING

A.A.U. NATIONAL CHAMPIONSHIPS

Freestyle
(Tempe, Ariz., April 16–18, 1981)
105.5 lb—Bill Rosado, Sunkist Kids
114.5 lb—Joe Gonzales, Sunkist Kids
125.5 lb—John Azevedo, Sunkist Kids
136.5 lb—Lee Roy Smith, Cowboys Wrestling Club
149.5 lb—Andrew Rein, Wisconsin Underdogs
163 lb—David Schultz, Oklahoma Underdogs
180.5 lb—Dan Zilverberg, Sunkist Kids
198 lb—Eric Wais, Oklahoma Underdogs
220 lb—Greg Gibson, United States Marines
Heavyweight—Jimmy Jackson, Sunkist Kids
Team—Sunkist Kids (132 points)
Outstanding wrestler—Dave Schultz

Greco-Roman
(Albany, N.Y., April 30–May 2, 1981)
105.5 lb—T.J. Jones, United States Navy
114.5 lb—Wilfredo Leivia, United States Marines
125.5 lb—Dan Mello, United States Marines
136.5 lb—Abdurrahim Kuzu, Nebraska Olympic Club
149.5 lb—Doug Yeats, Montreal
163 lb—David Schultz, Oklahoma Underdogs
180.5 lb—Dan Chandler, Twin Cities Wrestling Club
198 lb—Mike Houck, Minnesota Wrestling Club
220 lb—Jeff Blatnick, Adirondack Free-Style Wrestling Club
Unlimited—Ron Carlisle, United States Marines
Team—United States Marines
Outstanding wrestler—Jeff Blatnick

NATIONAL COLLEGIATE ATHLETIC ASSOCIATION
(Princeton, N.J., March 12–14, 1981)
118 lb—Gene Mills, Syracuse
126 lb—Dan Cuestas, California State–Bakersfield
134 lb—Jim Gibbons, Iowa State
142 lb—Andre Metzger, Oklahoma
150 lb—Nate Carr, Iowa State
158 lb—Rick Stewart, Oklahoma State
167 lb—Mark Schultz, Oklahoma
177 lb—Ed Banach, Iowa
190 lb—Tom Martucci, Trenton (N.J.) State
Heavyweight—Lou Banach, Iowa
Team—Iowa

National Sports Festival

(Syracuse, N.Y., July 24–29, 1981)

ARCHERY

Men—Darrell Pace, Cincinnati, Ohio
Women—Ruth Rowe, Gaithersburg, Md.
Men's Team—West
Women's Team—West

SWIMMING
Men's Events

100-m freestyle—Robin Leamy, Palos Verdes, Calif.	0:51.5
200-m freestyle—Mike Heath, Dallas, Tex.	1:54.51
400-m freestyle—Doug Towne, Tucson, Ariz.	4:00.04
1,500-m freestyle—Paul Budd, Memphis, Tenn.	15:55.20
100-m backstroke—Rick Carey, Mount Kisco, N.Y.	0:57.51
200-m backstroke—Rick Carey	2:04.54
100-m breaststroke—Bill Barrett, Alpharetta, Ga.	1:05.54
200-m breaststroke—John Moffet, Balboa, Calif.	2:24.96
100-m butterfly—Dave Cowell, Belpre, Ohio	0:55.96
200-m butterfly—John Denny, Fort Wayne, Ind.	2:04.37
200-m ind. med.—Bill Barrett, Alpharetta, Ga.	2:06.74
400-m ind. med. relay—Roger Von Jouanne, Renton, Wash.	4:37.81
400-m med. relay—West (John Engs, Lafayette, Calif.; Bill Barrett; Robin Leamy, Chris Cavanaugh, Mount View, Calif.)	3:53.33
400-m freestyle relay—West (Stuart MacDonald, Woodland Hills, Calif.; Rich Thornton, Meraga, Calif.; Robin Leamy, Chris Cavanaugh)	3:28.62
800-m freestyle relay—West A (Stuart MacDonald, Todd Trowbridge, Rich Thornton, Chris Cavanaugh)	7:41.80
Team—West	422 pts

Women's Events

100-m freestyle—Susie Thayer, Barstow, Fla.	0:58.48
200-m freestyle—Mary Wayte, Mercer Island, Wash.	2:04.12
400-m freestyle—Sabrina Sagehorn, Martinez, Calif.	4:20.57
800-m freestyle—Susan Andra, Wichita, Kan.	8:48.92
100-m backstroke—Theresa Andrews, Annapolis, Md.	1:04.76
200-m backstroke—Mary Wayte	2:19.62
100-m breaststroke—Terri Baxter, Palo Alto, Calif.	1:14.21
200-m breaststroke—Polly Winde, Elliot City, Pa.	2:40.57
100-m butterfly—Melanie Buddmeyer, Pittsburgh, Pa.	1:03.10
200-m butterfly—Sara Linke, Walnut Creek, Calif.	2:15.77
200-m ind. med.—Patty Gavin, Ardmore, Pa.	2:19.91
400-m ind. med.—Patty Gavin	4:53.45
400-m med. relay—Midwest (Kim Nicholson, Evansville, Ill.; Margaret Brown, Indianapolis, Ind.; Barbara Larsen, Mount Prospect, Ill.; Beth Washut, Jeffersonville, Ohio)	4:21.05
400-m freestyle relay—Midwest (Beth Washut; Diane Wallner, Roseville, Minn.; Tammy Thomas, Lawrence, Kan.; Suze Fila, Indianapolis, Ind.)	3:54.28
800-m freestyle relay—West (April Cox, Lynda White, Mary Wayte, Sara Linke)	8:24.36

SYNCHRONIZED SWIMMING

Solo—Tracie Ruiz, Bothell, Wash.
Figures—Tracie Ruiz
Duet—Candy Costie and Tracie Ruiz, Bothell, Wash.
Team—West

TRACK
Men's Events

100 m—James Sanford, Los Angeles	0:10.03
200 m—Dwayne Evans, Tempe, Ariz.	0:20.53
400 m—Tony Darden, Reno, Nev.	0:46.51
800 m—James Robinson, Berkeley, Calif.	1:47.53
1,500 m—Tom Byers, Eugene, Ore.	3:44.84[1]
3,000-m steeplechase—Henry Marsh, Eugene, Ore.	8:32.62[1]
5,000 m—Craig Virgin, Lebanon, Ill.	13:35.4
10,000 m—Greg Meyer, Holliston, Mass.	28:58.88[1]
20-kilometer walk—Todd Scully, Blacksburg, Va.	1:29:13[1]
50-kilometer walk—Vince O'Sullivan, New York City	4:28:58[1]
110-m hurdles—Renaldo Nehemiah, Scotch Plains, N.J.	0:13.00
400-m hurdles—Andre Phillips, Los Angeles	0:49.63
400-m relay—West (Ron Brown, Baldwin Park, Calif.; Eric Brown, Los Angeles; James Sanford; Dwayne Evans)	0:39.28
1,600-m relay—East (Neville Hodge, St. Thomas, U.S. Virgin Islands; Jeff White, Reading, Pa.; Jeff Hills, Philadelphia; Ed Yearwood, Stratford, Conn.)	3:03.60
Hammer throw—Dave McKenzie, Sacramento, Calif.	228 ft 5 in.[1]
Javelin—Bob Roggy, Eugene, Ore.	280 ft 7 in.
Long Jump—Larry Myricks, Clinton, Miss.	26 ft 11¼ in.
Pole vault—Dave Volz, Bloomington, Ind.	18 ft 2½ in.
Discus—John Powell, Los Angeles	214 ft 1 in.
High jump—Greg Seay, Oklahoma City, Okla.	7 ft 5 in.
Shotput—Brian Oldfield, Los Angeles	68 ft 5 in.
Triple jump—David McFadgen, Petersburg, Va.	54 ft 6 in.
Decathlon—Brian Mondschein, Huntington Beach, Calif.	7,532 pts
Modern pentathlon—Blair Driggs, San Antonio, Tex.	4,534 pts
Team—West	262 pts

Women's Events

100 m—Evelyn Ashford, Los Angeles	0:11.01
200 m—Florence Griffith, Los Angeles	0:23.02
400 m—Denean Howard, Granada Hills, Calif.	0:53.04
800 m—Madeline Manning Mimms, Clarksville, Tenn.	2:01.99
1,500 m—Cindy Bremser, Madison, Wis.	4:15.62
3,000 m—Kim Gallagher, Upper Darby, Pa.	9:19.67
100-m hurdles—Stephanie Hightower, Columbus, Ohio	0:13.05
400-m hurdles—Edna Brown, Philadelphia	0:58.50[1]
High jump—Pam Spencer, Northridge, Calif.	6 ft 3¼ in.
Javelin—Patty Kearney, Eugene, Ore.	175 ft 9 in.
Shotput—Denise Wood, Knoxville, Tenn.	53 ft 9 in.[1]
Discus—Denise Wood, Knoxville, Tenn.	n.a.
Long jump—Kathy McMillan-Ray, Clarksville, Tenn.	21 ft 2¾ in.
Heptathlon—Cindy Greiner, Lebanon, Ore.	5,574 pts
400-m relay—West (Alice Brown, Northridge, Calif.; Jeannette Bolden, Los Angeles; Florence Griffith, Los Angeles; Jackie Washington, Northridge, Calif.)	0:44.14
1,600-m relay—West (Paulette Clagon, Sacramento, Calif.; Arlise Emerson, Los Angeles; Rosalyn Bryant, Los Angeles; Denean Howard)	3:31.72
Marathon—Laura Dewald, Arlington, Va.	2:47:06[2]
Team—West	187 pts
Combined team—West	449 pts

1. National Sports Festival record. 2. Course record.
NOTE: n.a. = not available.

BASEBALL

BASEBALL PLAYERS' STRIKE HALTS SEASON FOR 7 WEEKS

A seven-week strike by major league players began on June 12 and disrupted the 1981 baseball season, canceled 713 games, caused heavy financial losses in all 26 big league cities, and created confusion and ill-feelings among fans, players, and officials.

The loss to players in salaries was estimated at $28 million. For example, the highest-paid player, Dave Winfield of the New York Yankees, lost $388,500 in salary. Although the club owners had strike insurance that reimbursed them $44 million for the canceled games, their net loss in revenues based on average ticket prices and concession sales amounted to $72 million.

The major issue concerned compensation for teams losing a player's services when he became a free agent. The owners insisted that a team be adequately compensated when it lost a quality player through free agency; the players insisted that their bargaining position would be weakened under such an arrangement. The players struck after having completed only about one third of the games scheduled for the regular season. The strike affected approximately 650 players, a small number in a labor stoppage, but the longer the strike lasted the greater was its impact on the economy. The strike forced postponement of the All-Star Game, originally scheduled in Cleveland July 14.

The two sides finally worked out an agreement and the strike ended on Aug. 1. A pool arrangement under which teams losing ranking free agents would receive professional players as compensation as well as a selection in the amateur free-agent draft was the key to the accord. It also resolved a service credit issue for the players for the time lost during the strike. Service credit is used to determine eligibility for free agency and salary arbitration. The players were allowed a week to get into condition and the season resumed on Aug. 10. The All-Star Game was played on Aug. 9 to a capacity crowd of 72,086 at Cleveland and enriched the players' pension fund by $2,139,000, a contributing factor in the settlement of the strike.

Rescheduling the championship season became a problem. Normally the regular-season winners in the two divisions—Eastern and Western—in the National and American leagues meet in a best-of-five-game playoff series for their respective league pennants.

Because the 162-game regular schedule was shortened, officials decided to split the season into two halves. The four leaders in the two leagues when the strike began were declared champions of the first half. The four leaders in the second half also would be declared champions. Those teams would play for their respective division titles in a preliminary playoff round. If a team won both halves of the split season, it would have to face the second-place team from the second half of the season for the division title in the preliminary playoff round. The survivors then would play for the league pennants. The World Series was scheduled to start Oct. 20.

RECORD OF WORLD SERIES GAMES

Source: The Book of Baseball Records, published by Seymour Siwoff, New York City.

Figures in parentheses for winning pitchers (WP) and losing pitchers (LP) indicate the game number in the series

1903—Boston A.L. 5 (Jimmy Collins); Pittsburgh N.L. 3 (Fred Clarke). WP—Bos.: Dinneen (2, 6, 8), Young (5, 7); Pitts.: Phillippe (1, 3, 4). LP—Bos.: Young (1), Hughes (3), Dinneen (4); Pitts.: Leever (2, 6), Kennedy (5), Phillippe (7, 8).

1904—No series.

1905—New York N.L. 4 (John J. McGraw); Philadelphia A.L. 1 (Connie Mack). WP—N.Y.: Mathewson (1, 3, 5); McGinnity (4); Phila.: Bender (2). LP—N.Y.: McGinnity (2); Phila.: Plank (1, 4), Coakley (3), Bender (5).

1906—Chicago A.L. 4 (Fielder Jones); Chicago N.L. 2 (Frank Chance). WP—Chi.: A.L.: Altrock (1), Walsh (3), White (6); Chi.: N.L.: Reulbach (2), Brown (4). LP—Chi. A.L.: White (2), Altrock (4); Chi.: N.L.: Brown (1, 6), Pfeister (3, 5).

1907—Chicago N.L. 4 (Frank Chance); Detroit A.L. 0 (Hugh Jennings). First game tied 3–3, 12 innings. WP—Pfeister (2), Reulbach (3), Overall (4), Brown (5). LP—Mullin (2, 5), Siever (3), Donovan (4).

1908—Chicago N.L. 4 (Frank Chance); Detroit A.L. 1 (Hugh Jennings). WP—Chi.: Brown (1, 4), Overall (2, 5); Det.: Mullin (3). LP—Chi.: Pfeister (3); Det.: Summers (1, 4), Donovan (2, 5).

1909—Pittsburgh N.L. 4 (Fred Clarke); Detroit A.L. 3 (Hugh Jennings). WP—Pitts.: Adams (1, 5, 7), Maddox (3); Det.: Donovan (2), Mullin (4, 6). LP—Pitts.: Camnitz (2), Leifield (4), Willis (6); Det.: Mullin (1), Summers (3, 5), Donovan (7).

1910—Philadelphia A.L. 4 (Connie Mack); Chicago N.L. 1 (Frank Chance). WP—Phila.: Bender (1), Coombs (2, 3, 5); Chi.: Brown (4). LP—Phila.: Bender (4); Chi.: Overall (1), Brown (2, 5), McIntyre (3).

1911—Philadelphia A.L. 4 (Connie Mack); New York N.L. 2 (John J. McGraw). WP—Phila.: Plank (2), Coombs (3), Bender (4, 6); N.Y.: Mathewson (1), Crandall (5). LP—Phila.: Bender (1), Plank (5); N.Y.: Marquard (2), Mathewson (3, 4), Ames (6).

1912—Boston A.L. 4 (J. Garland Stahl); New York N.L. 3 (John J. McGraw). Second game tied, 6–6, 11 innings. WP—Bos.: Wood (1, 4, 8), Bedient (5); N.Y.: Marquard (3, 6), Tesreau (7). LP—Bos.: O'Brien (3, 6), Wood (7); N.Y.: Tesreau (1, 4), Mathewson (5, 8).

1913—Philadelphia A.L. 4 (Connie Mack); New York N.L. 1 (John J. McGraw). WP—Phila.: Bender (1, 4), Bush (3), Plank (5); N.Y.: Mathewson (2); LP—Phila.: Plank (2); N.Y.: Marquard (1), Tesreau (3), Demaree (4), Mathewson (5).

1914—Boston N.L. 4 (George Stallings); Philadelphia A.L. 0 (Connie Mack). WP—Rudolph (1, 4), James (2, 3). LP—Bender (1), Plank (2), Bush (3), Shawkey (4).

1915—Boston A.L. 4 (Bill Carrigan); Philadelphia N.L. 1 (Pat Moran). WP—Bos.: Foster (2, 5), Leonard (3), Shore (4); Phila.: Alexander (1). LP—Bos.: Shore (1); Phila.: Mayer (2), Alexander (3), Chalmers (4), Rixey (5).

1916—Boston A.L. 4 (Bill Carrigan); Brooklyn N.L. 1 (Wilbert Robinson). WP—Bos.: Shore (1, 5), Ruth (2), Leonard (4); Bklyn.: Coombs (3). LP—Bos.: Mays (3); Bklyn.: Marquard (1, 4), Smith (2), Pfeffer (5).

1917—Chicago A.L. 4 (Clarence Rowland); New York N.L. 2 (John J. McGraw). WP—Chi.: Cicotte (1), Faber (2, 5, 6); N.Y.: Benton (3), Schupp (4). LP—Chi.: Cicotte (4), Faber (4); N.Y.: Sallee (1, 5), Anderson (2), Benton (6).

1918—Boston A.L. 4 (Ed Barrow); Chicago N.L. 2 (Fred Mitchell). WP—Bos.: Ruth (1, 4), Mays (3, 6); Chi.: Tyler (2), Vaughn (5). LP—Bos.: Bush (2), Jones (5); Chi.: Vaughn (1, 3), Douglas (4), Tyler (6).

1919—Cincinnati N.L. 5 (Pat Moran); Chicago A.L. 3 (William Gleason). WP—Cin.: Ruether (1), Sallee (2), Ring (4), Eller (5, 8); Chi.: Kerr (3, 6), Cicotte (7). LP—Cin.: Fisher (3), Ring (6), Sallee (7); Chi.: Cicotte (1, 4), Williams (2, 5, 8).

1920—Cleveland A.L. 5 (Tris Speaker); Brooklyn N.L. 2 (Wilbert Robinson). WP—Cleve.: Coveleski (1, 4, 7), Bagby (5), Mails (6); Bklyn.: Grimes (2), Smith (3). LP—Cleve.: Bagby (2), Caldwell (3). Bklyn.: Marquard (1), Cadore (4), Grimes (5, 7), Smith (3).

1921—New York N.L. 5 (John J. McGraw); New York A.L. 3 (Miller Huggins). WP—N.Y. N.L.: Barnes (3, 6), Douglas (4, 7), Nehf (8); N.Y. A.L.: Mays (1), Hoyt (2, 5). LP—N.Y. N.L.: Nehf (2, 5), Douglas (1). N.Y. A.L.: Quinn (3), Mays (4, 7), Shawkey (6), Hoyt (8).

1922—New York N.L. 4 (John J. McGraw); New York A.L. 0 (Miller Huggins). Second game tied 3–3, 10 innings. WP—Ryan (1), Scott (3), McQuillan (4), Nehf (5); LP—Bush (1, 5), Hoyt (3), Mays (4).

1923—New York A.L. 4 (Miller Huggins); New York N.L. 2 (John J. McGraw). WP—N.Y. A.L.: Pennock (2, 6), Shawkey (4), Bush (5); N.Y. N.L.:Ryan (1), Nehf (3). LP—N.Y. A.L.: Bush (1), Jones (3); N.Y. N.L.: McQuillan (2), Scott (4), Bentley (5), Nehf (6).

1924—Washington A.L. 4 (Bucky Harris); New York N.L. 3 (John J. McGraw). WP—Wash.: Zachary (2, 6), Mogridge (4), Johnson (3); N.Y.: Nehf (1), McQuillan (3), Bentley (5). LP—Wash.: Johnson (1, 5), Marberry (3); N.Y.: Bentley (2, 7), Barnes (4), Nehf (6).

1925—Pittsburgh N.L. 4 (Bill McKechnie); Washington A.L. 3 (Bucky Harris). WP—Pitts.: Aldridge (2, 5), Kremer (6, 7); Wash.: Johnson (1, 4), Ferguson (3). LP—Pitts.: Meadows (1), Kremer (3), Yde (4); Wash.: Coveleski (2), Ferguson (6), Johnson (7).

1926—St. Louis N.L. 4 (Rogers Hornsby); New York A.L. 3 (Miller Huggins). WP—St. L.: Alexander (2, 6), Haines (3, 7); N.Y.: Pennock (1, 5), Hoyt (4). LP—St. L.: Sherdel (1, 5), Reinhart (4); N.Y.: Shocker (2), Ruether (3), Shawkey (6), Hoyt (7).

1927—New York A.L. 4 (Miller Huggins); Pittsburgh N.L. 0 (Donie Bush). WP—Hoyt (1), Pipgras (2), Pennock (3), Moore (4). LP—Kremer (1), Aldridge (2), Meadows (3), Miljus (4).

1928—New York A.L. 4 (Miller Huggins); St. Louis N.L. 0 (Bill McKechnie). WP—Hoyt (1, 4), Pipgras (2), Zachary (3). LP—Sherdel (1, 4), Alexander (2), Haines (3).

1929—Philadelphia A.L. 4 (Connie Mack); Chicago N.L. 1 (Joe McCarthy). WP—Phila.: Ehmke (1), Earnshaw (2), Rommel (4), Walberg (5); Chi.: Bush (3). LP—Phila.: Earnshaw (3); Chi.: Root (1), Malone (2, 5), Blake (4).

1930—Philadelphia A.L. 4 (Connie Mack); St. Louis N.L. 2 (Gabby Street). WP—Phila.: Grove (1, 5), Earnshaw (2, 6); St. L.: Hallahan (3), Haines (4). LP—Phila.: Walberg (3), Grove (4); St. L.: Grimes (1, 5), Rhem (2), Hallahan (6).

1931—St. Louis N.L. 4 (Gabby Street); Philadelphia A.L. 3 (Connie Mack). WP—St. L.: Hallahan (2, 5), Grimes (3, 7); Phila.: Grove (1, 6), Earnshaw (4). LP—St. L.: Derringer (1, 6), Johnson (3); Phila.: Earnshaw (2, 7), Grove (5), Hoyt (5).

1932—New York A.L. 4 (Joe McCarthy); Chicago N.L. 0 (Charles Grimm). WP—Ruffing (1), Gomez (2), Pipgras (3), Moore (4). LP—Bush (1), Warneke (2), Root (3), May (4).

1933—New York N.L. 4 (Bill Terry); Washington A.L. 1 (Joe Cronin). WP—N.Y.: Hubbell (1, 4), Schumacher (2), Luque (5); Wash.: Whitehill (3). LP—N.Y.: Fitzsimmons (3); Wash.: Stewart (1), Crowder (2), Weaver (4), Russell (5).

1934—St. Louis N.L. 4 (Frank Frisch); Detroit A.L. 3 (Mickey Cochrane). WP—St. L.: J. Dean (1, 7), P. Dean (3, 6); Det.: Rowe (2), Auker (4), Bridges (5). LP—St. L.: W. Walker (2, 4), J. Dean (5); Det.: Crowder (1), Bridges (3), Rowe (6), Auker (7).

1935—Detroit A.L. 4 (Mickey Cochrane); Chicago N.L. 2 (Charles Grimm). WP—Det.: Bridges (2, 6), Rowe (3), Crowder (4); Chi.: Warneke (1, 5); LP—Det.: Rowe (1, 5); Chi.: Root (2), French (3, 6), Carleton (4).

1936—New York A.L. 4 (Joe McCarthy); New York N.L. 2 (Bill Terry). WP—N.Y. A.L.: Gomez (2, 6), Hadley (3), Pearson (4); N.Y. N.L.: Hubbell (1), Schumacher (5); LP—N.Y. A.L.: Ruffing (1), Malone (6); N.Y. N.L.: Schumacher (2), Fitzsimmons (3, 6), Hubbell (4).

1937—New York A.L. 4 (Joe McCarthy); New York N.L. 1 (Bill Terry). WP—N.Y. A.L.: Gomez (1, 5), Ruffing (2), Pearson (3); N.Y. N.L.: Hubbell (4). LP—N.Y. A.L.: Hadley (4); N.Y. N.L.: Hubbell (1), Melton (2, 5), Schumacher (3).

1938—New York A.L. 4 (Joe McCarthy); Chicago N.L. 0 (Gabby Hartnett). WP—Ruffing (1, 4), Gomez (2), Pearson (3). LP—Lee (1, 4), Dean (2), Bryant (3).

1939—New York A.L. 4 (Joe McCarthy); Cincinnati N.L. 0 (Bill McKechnie). WP—Ruffing (1), Pearson (2), Hadley (3), Murphy (4). LP—Derringer (1), Walters (2, 4), Thompson (3).

1940—Cincinnati N.L. 4 (Bill McKechnie); Detroit A.L. 3 (Del Baker). WP—Cin.: Walters (2, 6), Derringer (4, 7); Det.: Newsom (1, 5), Bridges (3). LP—Cin.: Derringer (1), Turner (3), Thompson (5); Det.: Rowe (2, 6), Trout (4), Newsom (7).

1941—New York A.L. 4 (Joe McCarthy); Brooklyn N.L. 1 (Leo Durocher). WP—N.Y.: Ruffing (1), Russo (3), Murphy (4), Bonham (5); Bklyn: Wyatt (2). LP—N.Y.: Chandler (2); Bklyn: Davis (1), Casey (3, 4), Wyatt (5).

1942—St. Louis N.L. 4 (Billy Southworth); New York A.L. 1 (Joe McCarthy). WP—St. L.: Beazley (2, 5), White (3), Lanier (4); N.Y.: Ruffing (1). LP—St. L.: Cooper (1); N.Y.: Bonham (2), Chandler (3), Donald (4), Ruffing (5).

1943—New York A.L. 4 (Joe McCarthy); St. Louis N.L. 1 (Billy Southworth). WP—N.Y.: Chandler (1, 5), Borowy (3), Russo (4); St. L.: Cooper (2). LP—N.Y.: Bonham (2); St. L.: Lanier (1), Brazle (3), Brecheen (4), Cooper (5).

1944—St. Louis N.L. 4 (Billy Southworth); St. Louis A.L. 2 (Luke Sewell). WP—St. L. N.L.: Donnelly (2), Brecheen (4), Cooper (5), Lanier (6); St. L. A.L.: Galehouse (1), Kramer (3). LP—St. L. N.L.: Cooper (1), Wilks (3); St. L. A.L.: Muncrief (2), Jakucki (4), Galehouse (5), Potter (6).

1945—Detroit A.L. 4 (Steve O'Neill); Chicago N.L. 3 (Charles Grimm). WP—Det.: Trucks (2), Trout (4), Newhouser (5, 7); Chi.: Borowy (1, 6), Passeau (3). LP—Det.: Newhouser (1), Overmire (3), Trout (6); Chi.: Wyse (2), Prim (4), Borowy (5, 7).

1946—St. Louis N.L. 4 (Eddie Dyer); Boston A.L. 3 (Joe Cronin). WP—St. L.: Brecheen (2, 6, 7), Munger (4); Bos.: Johnson (1), Ferriss (3), Dobson (5). LP—St. L.: Pollet (1), Dickson (3), Brazle (5); Bos.: Harris (2, 6), Hughson (4), Klinger (7).

1947—New York A.L. 4 (Bucky Harris); Brooklyn N.L. 3 (Burt Shotton). WP—N.Y.: Shea (1, 5), Reynolds (2), Page (7); Bklyn.: Casey (3, 4), Branca (6). LP—N.Y.: Newsom (3), Bevens (4), Page (6); Bklyn.: Branca (1), Lombardi (2), Barney (5), Gregg (7).

1948—Cleveland A.L. 4 (Lou Boudreau); Boston N.L. 2 (Billy Southworth). WP—Cleve.: Lemon (2, 6), Bearden (3), Gromek (4); Bos.: Sain (1), Spahn (5). LP—Cleve.: Feller (1, 5); Bos.: Spahn (2), Bickford (3), Sain (4), Voiselle (6).

1949—New York A.L. 4 (Casey Stengel); Brooklyn N.L. 1 (Burt Shotton). WP—N.Y.: Reynolds (1), Page (3), Lopat (4), Raschi (5); Bklyn.: Roe (2). LP—N.Y.: Raschi (2); Bklyn.: Newcombe (1, 4), Branca (3), Barney (5).

1950—New York A.L. 4 (Casey Stengel); Philadelphia N.L. 0 (Eddie Sawyer). WP—Raschi (1), Reynolds (2), Ferrick (3), Ford (4). LP—Konstanty (1), Roberts (2), Meyer (3), Miller (4).

1951—New York A.L. 4 (Casey Stengel); New York N.L. 2 (Leo Durocher). WP—N.Y. A.L.: Lopat (2, 5), Reynolds (4), Raschi (6); N.Y. N.L.: Koslo (1), Hearn (3). LP—N.Y. A.L.: Reynolds (1), Raschi (3); N.Y. N.L.: Jansen (2, 5), Maglie (4), Koslo (6).

1952—New York A.L. 4 (Casey Stengel); Brooklyn N.L. 3 (Chuck Dressen). WP—N.Y.: Raschi (2, 6), Reynolds (4, 7); Bklyn.: Black (1), Roe (3), Erskine (5). LP—N.Y.: Reynolds (1), Lopat (3), Sain (5); Bklyn.: Erskine (2), Black (4, 7), Loes (6).

1953—New York A.L. 4 (Casey Stengel); Brooklyn N.L. 2 (Chuck Dressen). WP—N.Y.: Sain (1), Lopat (2), McDonald (5), Reynolds (6); Bklyn.: Erskine (3), Loes (4). LP—N.Y.: Raschi (3), Ford (4); Bklyn.: Labine (1, 6), Roe (2), Podres (5).

1954—New York N.L. 4 (Leo Durocher); Cleveland A.L. 0 (Al Lopez). WP—Grissom (1), Antonelli (2), Gomez (3), Liddle (4). LP—Lemon (1, 4), Wynn (2), Garcia (3).

1955—Brooklyn N.L. 4 (Walter Alston); New York A.L. 3 (Casey Stengel). WP—Bklyn.: Podres (3, 7), Labine (4), Craig (5); N.Y.: Ford (1, 6), Byrne (2). LP—Bklyn.: Newcombe (1), Loes (2), Spooner (6); N.Y.: Turley (3), Larsen (4), Grim (5), Byrne (7).

1956—New York A.L. 4 (Casey Stengel); Brooklyn N.L. 3 (Walter Alston). WP—N.Y.: Ford (3), Sturdivant (4), Larsen (5), Kucks (7); Bklyn.: Maglie (1), Bessent (6), Labine (6). LP—N.Y.: Ford (1), Morgan (2), Turley (6); Bklyn.: Craig (3), Erskine (4), Maglie (5), Newcombe (7).

1957—Milwaukee N.L. 4 (Fred Haney); New York A.L. 3 (Casey Stengel). WP—Mil.: Burdette (2, 5, 7), Spahn (4); N.Y.: Ford (1), Larsen (3), Turley (6). LP—Mil.: Spahn (1), Buhl (3), Johnson (6); N.Y.: Shantz (2), Grim (4), Ford (5), Larsen (7).

1958—New York A.L. 4 (Casey Stengel); Milwaukee N.L. 3 (Fred Haney). WP—N.Y.: Larsen (3), Turley (5, 7), Duren (6); Mil.: Spahn (1, 4), Burdette (2). LP—N.Y.: Duren (1), Turley (2), Ford (4); Mil.: Rush (3), Burdette (5, 7), Spahn (6).

1959—Los Angeles N.L. 4 (Walter Alston); Chicago A.L. 2 (Al Lopez). WP—L.A.: Podres (3), Drysdale (4), Sherry (4, 6); Chi.: Wynn (1), Shaw (5). LP—L.A.: Craig (1), Koufax (5); Chi.: Shaw (2), Donovan (3), Staley (4), Wynn (6).

1960—Pittsburgh N.L. 4 (Danny Murtaugh); New York A.L. 3 (Casey Stengel). WP—Pitts.: Law (1, 4), Haddix (5, 7); N.Y.: Turley (2), Ford (3, 6). LP—Pitts.: Friend (2, 6), Mizell (3); N.Y.: Ditmar (1, 5), Terry (4, 7).

1961—New York A.L. 4 (Ralph Houk); Cincinnati N.L. 1 (Fred Hutchinson). WP—N.Y.: Ford (1, 4), Arroyo (3), Daley (5); Cin.: Jay (2). LP—N.Y.: Terry (2); Cin.: O'Toole (1, 4), Purkey (3), Jay (5).

1962—New York A.L. 4 (Ralph Houk); San Francisco N.L. 3 (Al Dark). WP—N.Y.: Ford (1), Stafford (3), Terry (5, 7); S.F.: Sanford (2), Larsen (4), Pierce (6). LP—N.Y.: Terry (2), Coates (4), Ford (6); S.F.: O'Dell (1), Pierce (3), Sanford (5, 7).

1963—Los Angeles N.L. 4 (Walter Alston); New York A.L. 0 (Ralph Houk). WP—Koufax (1, 4), Podres (2), Drysdale (3). LP—Ford (1, 4), Downing (2), Bouton (3).

1964—St. Louis N.L. 4 (Johnny Keane); New York A.L. 3 (Yogi Berra). WP—St. L.: Sadecki (1), Craig (4), Gibson (5, 7); N.Y.: Stottlemyre (2), Bouton (3, 6). LP—St. L.: Gibson (2), Schultz (3), Simmons (6); N.Y.: Ford (1), Downing (4), Mikkelsen (5), Stottlemyre (7).

1965—Los Angeles N.L. 4 (Walter Alston); Minnesota A.L. 3 (Sam Mele). WP—L.A.: Osteen (3), Drysdale (4), Koufax (5, 7); Minn.: Grant (1, 6), Kaat (2). LP—L.A.: Drysdale (1), Koufax (2), Osteen (6); Minn.: Pascual (3), Grant (4), Kaat (5, 7).

1966—Baltimore A.L. 4 (Hank Bauer); Los Angeles N.L. 0

(Walter Alston). WP—Drabowsky (1), Palmer (2), Bunker (3), McNally (4). LP—Drysdale (1, 4), Koufax (2), Osteen (3).

1967—St. Louis N.L. 4 (Red Schoendienst); Boston A.L. 3 (Dick Williams). WP—St. L.: Gibson (1, 4, 7), Briles (3); Bos.: Lonborg (2, 5); Wyatt (6). LP—St. L.: Hughes (2), Carlton (5), Lamabe (6); Bos.: Santiago (1, 4), Bell (3), Lonborg (7).

1968—Detroit A.L. 4 (Mayo Smith); St. Louis N.L. 3 (Red Schoendienst). WP—Det.: Lolich (2, 5, 7), McLain (6); St. L.: Gibson (1, 4), Washburn (3). LP—Det.: McLain (1, 4), Wilson (3); St. L.: Briles (2), Hoerner (5), Washburn (6), Gibson (7).

1969—New York N.L. 4 (Gil Hodges); Baltimore A.L. 1 (Earl Weaver). WP—N.Y.: Koosman (2, 5), Gentry (3), Seaver (4); Balt.: Cuellar (1). LP—N.Y.: Seaver (1); Balt.: McNally (2), Palmer (3), Hall (4), Watt (5).

1970—Baltimore A.L. 4 (Earl Weaver); Cincinnati N.L. 1 (Sparky Anderson) 1. WP—Balt.: Palmer (1), Phoebus (2), McNally (4), Cuellar (5); Cin.: Carroll (4). LP—Cin.: Nolan (1), Wilcox (2), Cloninger (3), Merritt (5); Balt.: Watt (4).

1971—Pittsburgh N.L. 4 (Danny Murtaugh); Baltimore A.L. 3 (Earl Weaver). WP—Pitts.: Blass (3, 7), Kison (4), Briles (5); Balt.: McNally (1, 6), Palmer (2). LP—Pitts.: Ellis (1), R. Johnson (2), Miller (6); Balt.: Cuellar (3, 7), Watt (4) McNally (5).

1972—Oakland A.L. 4 (Dick Williams); Cincinnati N.L. (Sparky Anderson) 3. WP—Oakland: Holtzman (1), Hunter (2, 7), Fingers (4); Cincinnati: Billingham (3), Grimsley (5, 6). LP—Oakland: Odom (3), Fingers (5), Blue (6); Cincinnati: Nolan (1), Grimsley (2), Carroll (4), Bordon (7).

1973—Oakland A.L. 4 (Dick Williams); New York N.L. 3 (Yogi Berra). WP—Oakland: Holtzman (1, 7), Lindblad (3), Hunter (6). New York: McGraw (2), Matlack (4), Koosman (5). LP—Oakland: Fingers (2), Holtzman (4), Blue (5). New York: Matlack (1, 7) Parker (3), Seaver (6).

1974—Oakland A.L. 4 (Al Dark); Los Angeles N.L. 1 (Walter Alston). WP—Oakland: Fingers (1), Hunter (3), Holtzman (4), Odom (5). Los Angeles: Sutton (2). LP—Oakland: Blue (2), Los Angeles: Messersmith (1, 4), Downing (3), Marshall (5).

1975—Cincinnati N.L. 4 (Sparky Anderson); Boston A.L. 3 (Darrell Johnson). WP—Cincinnati: Eastwick (2-3), Gullett (5), Carroll (7); Boston: Tiant (1–4), Wise (6). LP—Cincinnati: Gullett (1), Norman (4), Darcy (6); Boston: Drago (2), Willoughby (3), Cleveland (5), Burton (7).

1976—Cincinnati N.L. 4 (Sparky Anderson); New York A.L. 0 (Billy Martin). WP—Gullett (1), Billingham (2), Zachry (3), Nolan (4). LP—Alexander (1), Hunter (2), Ellis (3), Figueroa (4).

1977—New York A.L. 4 (Billy Martin); Los Angeles N.L. 2 (Tom Lasorda). WP—New York: Lyle (1), Torrez (3,6), Guidry (4); Los Angeles: Hooton (2), Sutton (5). LP—New York: Hunter (2), Gullett (5); Los Angeles: Rhoden (1), John (3), Rau (4), Hooton (6).

1978—New York A.L. 4 (Bob Lemon); Los Angeles N.L. 2 (Tom Lasorda). WP—New York: Guidry (3), Gossage (4); Beattie (5), Hunter (6); Los Angeles: John (1), Hooton (2). LP—New York: Figuero (1), Hunter (2); Los Angeles: Sutton (3-6), Welch (4), Hooton (5).

1979—Pittsburgh N.L. 4 (Chuck Tanner), Baltimore A.L. 3 (Earl Weaver); WP—Pittsburgh: D. Robinson (2), Blyleven (5), Candelaria (6), Jackson (7); Baltimore: Flanagan (1), McGregor (3), Stoddard (4). LP—Pittsburgh: Kison (1), Candelaria (3), Tekulve (4); Baltimore: Stanhouse (2), Flanagan (5), Palmer (6), McGregor (7).

1980—Philadelphia N.L. 4 (Dallas Green), Kansas City A.L. 2 (Jim Frey); WP—Philadelphia: Walk (1), Carlton (2), McGraw (5); Kansas City: Quisenberry (3). LP—Philadelphia: McGraw (3), Christenson (4); Kansas City: Leonard (1), Quisenberry (2), Quisenberry (5), Gale (6).

PARACHUTING

U.S. CHAMPIONS—1980

Men's overall—Matt O'Gwynn, Langley Air Force Base, Va. Women's overall—Cheryl Stearns, Fort Bragg, N.C.

WORLD SERIES CLUB STANDING (THROUGH 1980)

	Series	Won	Lost	Pct.		Series	Won	Lost	Pct.
Oakland (A)	3	3	0	1.000	New York (N-Giants)	14	5	9	.357
Pittsburgh (N)	7	5	2	.714	Washington (A)	3	1	2	.333
New York (A)	32	22	10	.687	Philadelphia (N)	3	1	2	.333
St. Louis (N)	12	8	4	.667	Chicago (N)	10	2	8	.200
Cleveland (A)	3	2	1	.667	Brooklyn (N)	9	1	8	.111
Boston (A)	8	5	3	.625	St. Louis (A)	1	0	1	.000
Philadelphia (A)	8	5	3	.625	San Francisco (N)	1	0	1	.000
Los Angeles (N)	7	3	4	.429	Minnesota (A)	1	0	1	.000
New York (N-Mets)	2	1	1	.500	Kansas City (A)	1	0	1	.000
Milwaukee (N)	2	1	1	.500					
Boston (N)	2	1	1	.500	**Recapitulation**				
Chicago (A)	4	2	2	.500					
Cincinnati (N)	8	4	4	.500					**Won**
Baltimore (A)	5	2	3	.400	American League				45
Detroit (A)	8	3	5	.375	National League				32

SINGLE GAME AND SINGLE SERIES RECORDS*

Most hits game—4, held by many players.

Most hits inning—2, held by many players.

Most hits series—13 (7 games) Bobby Richardson, New York A.L., 1964; Lou Brock, St. Louis N.L., 1968; 12 (6 games) Billy Martin, New York A.L., 1953; 12 (8 games) Buck Herzog, New York N.L., 1912; Joe Jackson, Chicago A.L., 1919; 10 (4 games) Babe Ruth, New York A.L., 1928; 9 (5 games) held by 7 players.

Most home runs, series—5 (6 games) Reggie Jackson, New York A.L., 1977; 4 (7 games) Babe Ruth, New York A.L., 1926; Duke Snider, Brooklyn N.L., 1952, 1955; Hank Bauer, New York A.L., 1958; Gene Tenace, Oakland A.L., 1972; 4 (4 games) Lou Gehrig, New York A.L., 1928; 3 (6 games) Babe Ruth, New York A.L., 1923; Ted Kluszewski, Chicago A.L., 1959; 3 (5 games) Donn Clendenon, New York Mets N.L., 1969; 2 (8 games) Patrick Dougherty, Boston A.L., 1903.

Most home runs, game—3, Babe Ruth, New York A.L., 1926 and 1928; Reggie Jackson, New York A.L., 1977.

Most strikeouts, series—12 (6 games) Willie Wilson, Kansas City A.L., 1980; 11 (7 games) Ed Mathews, Milwaukee N.L., 1958; Wayne Garrett, New York N.L., 1973; 10 (8 games) George Kelly, New York N.L., 1921; 9 (6 games) Jim Bottomley, St. Louis N.L., 1930; 8 (5 games) Rogers Hornsby, Chicago N.L., 1924; Duke Snider, Brooklyn N.L., 1949; 7 (4 games) Bob Muesel, New York A.L., 1927.

Most stolen bases, game—3, Honus Wagner, Pittsburgh N.L., 1909; Willie Davis, Los Angeles N.L., 1965; Lou Brock, St. Louis N.L., 1967 and 1968.

Most strikeouts by pitcher, game—17, Bob Gibson, St. Louis N.L. 1968.

Most strikeouts by pitcher in succession—6, Horace Eller, Cincinnati N.L., 1919; Moe Drabowsky, Baltimore A.L., 1966.

Most strikeouts by pitcher, series—35 (7 games) Bob Gibson, St. Louis N.L., 1968; 28 (8 games) Bill Dinneen, Boston A.L., 1903; 23 (4 games) Sandy Koufax, Los Angeles, 1963; 20 (6 games) Chief Bender, Philadelphia A.L., 1911; 18 (5 games) Christy Mathewson, New York N.L., 1905.

Most bases on balls, series—11 (7 games) Babe Ruth, New York A.L., 1926; Gene Tenace, Oakland A.L., 1973; 8 (6 games) Babe Ruth, New York A.L., 1923; 7 (5 games) James Sheckard, Chicago N.L., 1910; Mickey Cochrane, Philadelphia A.L., 1929; Joe Gordon, New York A.L. 1941.

Most consecutive scoreless innings, one series—27, Christy Mathewson, New York N.L., 1905.

* Through 1980.

LIFETIME WORLD SERIES RECORDS

Most hits—71, Yogi Berra, New York A.L., 1947, 1949–53, 1955–58, 1960–63.

Most runs—42, Mickey Mantle, New York A.L., 1951–53, 1955–58, 1960–64.

Most runs batted in—40, Mickey Mantle, New York A.L., 1951–53, 1955–58, 1960–64.

Most home runs—18, Mickey Mantle, New York A.L., 1951–53, 1955–58, 1960–64.

Most bases on balls—43, Mickey Mantle, New York A.L., 1951–53, 1955–58, 1960–64.

Most strikeouts—54, Mickey Mantle, New York A.L., 1951–53, 1955–58, 1960–64.

Most stolen bases—14, Eddie Collins, Philadelphia A.L. 1910–11, 13–14; Chicago A.L., 1917, 1919. Lou Brock, St. Louis N.L., 1964, 67–68.

Most victories, pitcher—10, Whitey Ford, New York A.L., 1950, 1953, 1955–58, 1960–64.

Most times member of winning team—10, Yogi Berra, New York A.L., 1947, 1949–53, 1956, 1958, 1961–62.

Most victories, no defeats—6, Vernon Gomez, New York A.L., 1932, 1936(2), 1937(2), 1938.

Most shutouts—4, Christy Mathewson, New York N.L., 1905 (3), 1913.

Most innings pitched—146, Whitey Ford, New York A.L., 1950, 1953, 1955–58, 1960–1964.

Most consecutive scoreless innings—33²/₃, Whitey Ford, New York A.L., 1960 (18), 1961 (14), 1962 (1²/₃).

Most strikeouts by pitcher—94, Whitey Ford, New York A.L., 1950, 1953, 1955–58, 1960–64.

1916 NEW YORK GIANTS HOLD WINNING STREAK RECORD AT 26

The longest winning streak in major-league history was registered by the New York Giants of the National League in 1916 when they reeled off 26 in a row, all at home. The American League record is held by the Chicago White Sox who posted 19 straight victories in 1906, 11 at home and 8 on the road. In the losing streak category, the American League mark is held by the 1906 Boston Red Sox who dropped 20 in order, 19 of them before the home fans. Cleveland lost 24, only 3 at home, in 1899 when it was a member of the National League.

AMERICAN LEAGUE HOME RUN CHAMPIONS

Year,	Player, team	No.	Year,	Player, team	No.	Year,	Player, team	No.
1901	Nap Lajoie, Phila.	13	1929	Babe Ruth, N.Y.	46	1957	Roy Sievers, Wash.	42
1902	Ralph Seybold, Phila.	16	1930	Babe Ruth, N.Y.	49	1958	Mickey Mantle, N.Y.	42
1903	Buck Freeman, Bost.	13	1931	Lou Gehrig, N.Y., and		1959	Rocky Colavito, Cleve., and	
1904	Harry Davis, Phila.	10		Babe Ruth, N.Y.	46		Harmon Killebrew, Wash.	42
1905	Harry Davis, Phila.	8	1932	Jimmy Foxx, Phila.	58	1960	Mickey Mantle, N.Y.	40
1906	Harry Davis, Phila.	12	1933	Jimmy Foxx, Phila.	48	1961	Roger Maris, N.Y.	61
1907	Harry Davis, Phila.	8	1934	Lou Gehrig, N.Y.	49	1962	Harmon Killebrew, Minn.	48
1908	Sam Crawford, Det.	7	1935	Jimmy Foxx, Phila., and		1963	Harmon Killebrew, Minn.	45
1909	Ty Cobb, Det.	9		Hank Greenberg, Det.	36	1964	Harmon Killebrew, Minn.	49
1910	J. Garland Stahl, Bost.	10	1936	Lou Gehrig, N.Y.	49	1965	Tony Conigliaro, Bost.	32
1911	Franklin Baker, Phila.	9	1937	Joe DiMaggio, N.Y.	46	1966	Frank Robinson, Balt.	49
1912	Franklin Baker, Phila.	10	1938	Hank Greenberg, Det.	58	1967	Carl Yastrzemski, Bost., and	
1913	Franklin Baker, Phila.	12	1939	Jimmy Foxx, Bost.	35		Harmon Killebrew, Minn.	44
1914	Franklin Baker, Phila., and		1940	Hank Greenberg, Det.	41	1968	Frank Howard, Wash.	44
	Sam Crawford, Det.	8	1941	Ted Williams, Bost.	37	1969	Harmon Killebrew, Minn.	49
1915	Robert Roth, Chi.-Cleve.	7	1942	Ted Williams, Bost.	36	1970	Frank Howard, Wash.	44
1916	Wally Pipp, N.Y.	12	1943	Rudy York, Det.	34	1971	Bill Melton, Chicago	33
1917	Wally Pipp, N.Y.	9	1944	Nick Etten, N.Y.	22	1972	Dick Allen, Chicago	37
1918	Babe Ruth, Bost., and		1945	Vern Stephens, St. L.	24	1973	Reggie Jackson, Oak.	32
	Clarence Walker, Phila.	11	1946	Hank Greenberg, Det.	44	1974	Dick Allen, Chicago	32
1919	Babe Ruth, Bost.	29	1947	Ted Williams, Bost.	32	1975	Reggie Jackson, Oak., and	
1920	Babe Ruth, N.Y.	54	1948	Joe DiMaggio, N.Y.	39		George Scott, Mil.	36
1921	Babe Ruth, N.Y.	59	1949	Ted Williams, Bost.	43	1976	Graig Nettles, N.Y.	32
1922	Ken Williams, St. L.	39	1950	Al Rosen, Cleve.	37	1977	Jim Rice, Boston	39
1923	Babe Ruth, N.Y.	41	1951	Gus Zernial, Chi.-Phila.	33	1978	Jim Rice, Boston	46
1924	Babe Ruth, N.Y.	46	1952	Larry Doby, Cleve.	32	1979	Gorman Thomas, Milwaukee	45
1925	Bob Meusel, N.Y.	33	1953	Al Rosen, Cleve.	43	1980	Reggie Jackson, N.Y., and	
1926	Babe Ruth, N.Y.	47	1954	Larry Doby, Cleve.	32		Ben Oglivie, Mil.	41
1927	Babe Ruth, N.Y.	60	1955	Mickey Mantle, N.Y.	37			
1928	Babe Ruth, N.Y.	54	1956	Mickey Mantle, N.Y.	52			

AMERICAN LEAGUE BATTING CHAMPIONS

Year,	Player, team	Avg.	Year,	Player, team	Avg.	Year,	Player, team	Avg.
1901	Nap Lajoie, Phila.	.422	1928	Goose Goslin, Wash.	.379	1955	Al Kaline, Det.	.340
1902	Ed Delahanty, Wash.	.376	1929	Lew Fonseca, Cleve.	.369	1956	Mickey Mantle, N.Y.	.353
1903	Nap Lajoie, Cleve.	.355	1930	Al Simmons, Phila.	.381	1957	Ted Williams, Bost.	.388
1904	Nap Lajoie, Cleve.	.381	1931	Al Simmons, Phila.	.390	1958	Ted Williams, Bost.	.328
1905	Elmer Flick, Cleve.	.306	1932	Dale Alexander, Det.-Bost.	.367	1959	Harvey Kuenn, Det.	.353
1906	George Stone, St. L.	.358	1933	Jimmy Foxx, Phila.	.356	1960	Pete Runnels, Bost.	.320
1907	Ty Cobb, Det.	.350	1934	Lou Gehrig, N.Y.	.363	1961	Norman Cash, Det.	.361
1908	Ty Cobb, Det.	.324	1935	Buddy Myer, Wash.	.349	1962	Pete Runnels, Bost.	.326
1909	Ty Cobb, Det.	.377	1936	Luke Appling, Chi.	.388	1963	Carl Yastrzemski, Bost.	.321
1910	Ty Cobb, Det.	.385	1937	Charley Gehringer, Det.	.371	1964	Tony Oliva, Minn.	.323
1911	Ty Cobb, Det.	.420	1938	Jimmy Foxx, Bost.	.349	1965	Tony Oliva, Minn.	.321
1912	Ty Cobb, Det.	.410	1939	Joe DiMaggio, N.Y.	.381	1966	Frank Robinson, Balt.	.316
1913	Ty Cobb, Det.	.390	1940	Joe DiMaggio, N.Y.	.352	1967	Carl Yastrzemski, Bost.	.326
1914	Ty Cobb, Det.	.368	1941	Ted Williams, Bost.	.406	1968	Carl Yastrzemski, Bost.	.301
1915	Ty Cobb, Det.	.369	1942	Ted Williams, Bost.	.356	1969	Rod Carew, Minn.	.332
1916	Tris Speaker, Cleve.	.386	1943	Luke Appling, Chi.	.328	1970	Alex Johnson, Calif.	.329
1917	Ty Cobb, Det.	.383	1944	Lou Boudreau, Cleve.	.327	1971	Tony Oliva, Minn.	.337
1918	Ty Cobb, Det.	.382	1945	George Sternweiss, N.Y.	.309	1972	Rod Carew, Minn.	.318
1919	Ty Cobb, Det.	.384	1946	Mickey Vernon, Wash.	.353	1973	Rod Carew, Minn.	.350
1920	George Sisler, St. L.	.407	1947	Ted Williams, Bost.	.343	1974	Rod Carew, Minn.	.364
1921	Harry Heilmann, Det.	.394	1948	Ted Williams, Bost.	.369	1975	Rod Carew, Minn.	.359
1922	George Sisler, St. L.	.420	1949	George Kell, Det.	.343	1976	George Brett, Kansas City	.333
1923	Harry Heilmann, Det.	.403	1950	Billy Goodman, Bost.	.354	1977	Rod Carew, Minn.	.388
1924	Babe Ruth, N.Y.	.378	1951	Ferris Fain, Phila.	.344	1978	Rod Carew, Minn.	.333
1925	Harry Heilmann, Det.	.393	1952	Ferris Fain, Phila.	.327	1979	Fred Lynn, Boston	.333
1926	Heinie Manush, Det.	.378	1953	Mickey Vernon, Wash.	.337	1980	George Brett, Kansas City	.390
1927	Harry Heilmann, Det.	.398	1954	Bobby Avila, Cleve.	.341			

CONSECUTIVE NO-HITTERS BY VANDER MEER

Johnny Vander Meer, a 23-year-old lefthander with the Cincinnati Reds, pitched consecutive no-hitters in June 1938, setting a mark of 18 innings of no-hit hurling. On June 11, in Cincinnati, he set down Boston without a hit as the Reds won, 3–0. Four days later, June 15, in the first night game in Brooklyn, he again held the opposition hitless as the Reds triumphed, 6–0. He was nicknamed Johnny (Double No-Hitter) Vander Meer.

NATIONAL LEAGUE HOME RUN CHAMPIONS

Year	Player, team	No.	Year	Player, team	No.	Year	Player, team	No.
1876	George Hall, Phila. Athletics	5	1911	Frank Schulte, Chi.	21	1946	Ralph Kiner, Pitts.	23
1877	George Shaffer, Louisville	3	1912	Henry Zimmerman, Chi.	14	1947	Ralph Kiner, Pitts., and	
1878	Paul Hines, Providence	4	1913	Cliff Cravath, Phila.	19		John Mize, N.Y.	51
1879	Charles Jones, Bost.	9	1914	Cliff Cravath, Phila.	19	1948	Ralph Kiner, Pitts., and	
1880	James O'Rourke, Bost., and		1915	Cliff Cravath, Phila.	24		John Mize, N.Y.	40
	Harry Stovey, Worcester	6	1916	Davis Robertson, N.Y., and		1949	Ralph Kiner, Pitts.	54
1881	Dan Brouthers, Buffalo	8		Fred Williams, Chi.	12	1950	Ralph Kiner, Pitts.	47
1882	George Wood, Det.	7	1917	Davis Robertson, N.Y., and		1951	Ralph Kiner, Pitts.	42
1883	William Ewing, N.Y.	10		Cliff Cravath, Phila.	12	1952	Ralph Kiner, Pitts., and	
1884	Ed Williamson, Chi.	27	1918	Cliff Cravath, Phila.	8		Hank Sauer, Chi.	37
1885	Abner Dalrymple, Chi.	11	1919	Cliff Cravath, Phila.	12	1953	Ed Mathews, Mil.	47
1886	Arthur Richardson, Det.	11	1920	Cy Williams, Phila.	15	1954	Ted Kluszewski, Cin.	49
1887	Roger Connor, N.Y., and		1921	George Kelly, N.Y.	23	1955	Willie Mays, N.Y.	51
	Wm. O'Brien, Wash.	17	1922	Rogers Hornsby, St. L.	42	1956	Duke Snider, Bklyn.	43
1888	Roger Connor, N.Y.	14	1923	Cy Williams, Phila.	41	1957	Henry Aaron, Mil.	44
1889	Sam Thompson, Phila.	20	1924	Jacques Fournier, Bklyn.	27	1958	Ernie Banks, Chi.	47
1890	Tom Burns, Bklyn., and		1925	Rogers Hornsby, St. L.	39	1959	Ed Mathews, Mil.	46
	Mike Tiernan, N.Y.	13	1926	Hack Wilson, Chi.	21	1960	Ernie Banks, Chi.	41
1891	Harry Stovey, Bost., and		1927	Hack Wilson, Chi., and		1961	Orlando Cepeda, San Fran.	46
	Mike Tiernan, N.Y.	16		Cy Williams, Phila.	30	1962	Willie Mays, San Fran.	49
1892	Jim Holliday, Cin.	13	1928	Hack Wilson, Chi., and		1963	Henry Aaron, Mil., and	
1893	Ed Delahanty, Phila.	19		Jim Bottomley, St. L.	31		Willie McCovey, San Fran.	44
1894	Hugh Duffy, Bost., and		1929	Chuck Klein, Phila.	43	1964	Willie Mays, San Fran.	47
	Robert Lowe, Bost.	18	1930	Hack Wilson, Phila.	56	1965	Willie Mays, San Fran.	52
1895	Bill Joyce, Wash.	17	1931	Chuck Klein, Phila.	31	1966	Henry Aaron, Atlanta	44
1896	Ed Delahanty, Phila., and		1932	Chuck Klein, Phila., and		1967	Henry Aaron, Atlanta	39
	Sam Thompson, Phila.	13		Mel Ott, N.Y.	38	1968	Willie McCovey, San Fran.	36
1897	Nap Lajoie, Phila.	10	1933	Chuck Klein, Phila.	28	1969	Willie McCovey, San Fran.	45
1898	James Collins, Bost.	14	1934	Mel Ott, N.Y., and		1970	Johnny Bench, Cin.	45
1899	John Freeman, Wash.	25		Rip Collins, St. L.	35	1971	Willie Stargell, Pitts.	48
1900	Herman Long, Bost.	12	1935	Wally Berger, Bost.	34	1972	Johnny Bench, Cin.	40
1901	Sam Crawford, Cin.	16	1936	Mel Ott, N.Y.	33	1973	Willie Stargell, Pitts.	44
1902	Tom Leach, Pitts.	6	1937	Mel Ott, N.Y., and Joe		1974	Mike Schmidt, Phila.	36
1903	James Sheckard, Bklyn.	9		Medwick, St. L.	31	1975	Mike Schmidt, Phila.	38
1904	Harry Lumley, Bklyn.	9	1938	Mel Ott, N.Y.	36	1976	Mike Schmidt, Phila.	38
1905	Fred Odwell, Cin.	9	1939	John Mize, St. L.	28	1977	George Foster, Cin.	52
1906	Tim Jordan, Bklyn.	12	1940	John Mize, St. L.	43	1978	George Foster, Cin.	40
1907	David Brain, Bost.	10	1941	Dolph Camilli, Bklyn.	34	1979	Dave Kingman, Chicago	48
1908	Tim Jordan, Bklyn.	12	1942	Mel Ott, N.Y.	30	1980	Mike Schmidt, Phila.	48
1909	John Murray, N.Y.	7	1943	Bill Nicholson, Chi.	29			
1910	Fred Beck, Bost., and		1944	Bill Nicholson, Chi.	33			
	Frank Schulte, Chi.	10	1945	Tommy Holmes, Bost.	28			

NATIONAL LEAGUE BATTING CHAMPIONS

Year	Player/Team	Avg	Year	Player/Team	Avg	Year	Player/Team	Avg
1876	Roscoe Barnes, Chicago	.404	1899	Ed Delahanty, Phila.	.408	1922	Rogers Hornsby, St. Louis	.401
1877	Jim White, Boston	.385	1900	Honus Wagner, Pittsburgh	.381	1923	Rogers Hornsby, St. Louis	.384
1878	Abner Dalrymple, Mil.	.356	1901	Jesse Burkett, St. Louis	.382	1924	Rogers Hornsby, St. Louis	.424
1879	Cap Anson, Chicago	.407	1902	Clarence Beaumont, Pitts.	.357	1925	Rogers Hornsby, St. Louis	.403
1880	George Gore, Chicago	.365	1903	Honus Wagner, Pittsburgh	.355	1926	Gene Hargrave, Cincinnati	.353
1881	Cap Anson, Chicago	.399	1904	Honus Wagner, Pittsburgh	.349	1927	Paul Waner, Pittsburgh	.380
1882	Dan Brouthers, Buffalo	.367	1905	Cy Seymour, Cincinnati	.377	1928	Rogers Hornsby, Boston	.387
1883	Dan Brouthers, Buffalo	.371	1906	Honus Wagner, Pittsburgh	.339	1929	Lefty O'Doul, Phila.	.398
1884	James O'Rourke, Buffalo	.350	1907	Honus Wagner, Pittsburgh	.350	1930	Bill Terry, N. Y.	.401
1885	Roger Connor, N. Y.	.371	1908	Honus Wagner, Pittsburgh	.354	1931	Chick Hafey, St. Louis	.349
1886	King Kelly, Chicago	.388	1909	Honus Wagner, Pittsburgh	.339	1932	Lefty O'Doul, Brooklyn	.368
1887	Cap Anson, Chicago	.421	1910	Sherwood Magee,		1933	Chuck Klein, Phila.	.368
1888	Cap Anson, Chicago	.343		Philadelphia	.331	1934	Paul Waner, Pittsburgh	.362
1889	Dan Brouthers, Boston	.373	1911	Honus Wagner, Pittsburgh	.334	1935	Arky Vaughan, Pittsburgh	.385
1890	John Glasscock, N. Y.	.336	1912	Henry Zimmerman, Chicago	.372	1936	Paul Waner, Pittsburgh	.373
1891	William Hamilton, Phila.	.338	1913	Jake Daubert, Brooklyn	.350	1937	Joe Medwick, St. Louis	.374
1892	Dan Brouthers, Bklyn., and		1914	Jake Daubert, Brooklyn	.329	1938	Ernie Lombardi, Cin.	.342
	Clarence Childs, Cleve.	.335	1915	Larry Doyle, New York	.320	1939	John Mize, St. Louis	.349
1893	Hugh Duffy, Boston	.378	1916	Hal Chase, Cincinnati	.339	1940	Debs Garms, Pittsburgh	.355
1894	Hugh Duffy, Boston	.438	1917	Edd Roush, Cincinnati	.341	1941	Pete Reiser, Brooklyn	.343
1895	Jesse Burkett, Cleveland	.423	1918	Zack Wheat, Brooklyn	.335	1942	Ernie Lombardi, Boston	.330
1896	Jesse Burkett, Cleveland	.410	1919	Edd Roush, Cincinnati	.321	1943	Stan Musial, St. Louis	.357
1897	Willie Keeler, Baltimore	.432	1920	Rogers Hornsby, St. Louis	.370	1944	Dixie Walker, Brooklyn	.357
1898	Willie Keeler, Baltimore	.379	1921	Rogers Hornsby, St. Louis	.397	1945	Phil Cavarretta, Chicago	.355

Year	Player/Team	Avg	Year	Player/Team	Avg	Year	Player/Team	Avg
1946	Stan Musial, St. Louis	.365	1958	Richie Ashburn, Phila.	.350	1970	Rico Carty, Atlanta	.366
1947	Harry Walker, St. L.-Phila.	.363	1959	Henry Aaron, Mil.	.355	1971	Joe Torre, St. Louis	.363
1948	Stan Musial, St. Louis	.376	1960	Dick Groat, Pittsburgh	.325	1972	Billy Williams, Chicago	.333
1949	Jackie Robinson, Brooklyn	.342	1961	Roberto Clemente, Pitts.	.351	1973	Pete Rose, Cincinnati	.338
1950	Stan Musial, St. Louis	.346	1962	Tommy Davis, L. A.	.346	1974	Ralph Garr, Atlanta	.353
1951	Stan Musial, St. Louis	.355	1963	Tommy Davis, L. A.	.326	1975	Bill Madlock, Chicago	.354
1952	Stan Musial, St. Louis	.336	1964	Roberto Clemente, Pitts.	.339	1976	Bill Madlock, Chicago	.339
1953	Carl Furillo, Brooklyn	.344	1965	Roberto Clemente, Pitts.	.329	1977	Dave Parker, Pittsburgh	.338
1954	Willie Mays, N. Y.	.345	1966	Matty Alou, Pittsburgh	.342	1978	Dave Parker, Pittsburgh	.334
1955	Richie Ashburn, Phila.	.338	1967	Roberto Clemente, Pitts.	.357	1979	Keith Hernandez, St. Louis	.344
1956	Henry Aaron, Mil.	.328	1968	Pete Rose, Cincinnati	.335	1980	Bill Buckner, Chicago	.324
1957	Stan Musial, St. Louis	.351	1969	Pete Rose, Cincinnati	.348			

AMERICAN LEAGUE PENNANT WINNERS

Year	Club	Manager	Won	Lost	Pct.	Year	Club	Manager	Won	Lost	Pct.
1901	Chicago	Clark C. Griffith	83	53	.610	1942	New York	Joseph V. McCarthy	103	51	.669
1902	Philadelphia	Connie Mack	83	53	.610	1943[1]	New York	Joseph V. McCarthy	98	56	.636
1903[1]	Boston	Jimmy Collins	91	47	.659	1944	St. Louis	Luke Sewell	89	65	.578
1904[2]	Boston	Jimmy Collins	95	59	.617	1945[1]	Detroit	Steve O'Neill	88	65	.575
1905	Philadelphia	Connie Mack	92	56	.622	1946	Boston	Joseph E. Cronin	104	50	.675
1906[1]	Chicago	Fielder A. Jones	93	58	.616	1947[1]	New York	Stanley R. Harris	97	57	.630
1907	Detroit	Hugh A. Jennings	92	58	.613	1948[1]	Cleveland	Lou Boudreau	97	58	.626
1908	Detroit	Hugh A. Jennings	90	63	.588	1949[1]	New York	Casey Stengel	97	57	.630
1909	Detroit	Hugh A. Jennings	98	54	.645	1950[1]	New York	Casey Stengel	98	56	.636
1910[1]	Philadelphia	Connie Mack	102	48	.680	1951[1]	New York	Casey Stengel	98	56	.636
1911[1]	Philadelphia	Connie Mack	101	50	.669	1952[1]	New York	Casey Stengel	95	59	.617
1912[1]	Boston	J. Garland Stahl	105	47	.691	1953[1]	New York	Casey Stengel	99	52	.656
1913[1]	Philadelphia	Connie Mack	96	57	.627	1954	Cleveland	Al Lopez	111	43	.721
1914	Philadelphia	Connie Mack	99	53	.651	1955	New York	Casey Stengel	96	58	.623
1915[1]	Boston	William F. Carrigan	101	50	.669	1956[1]	New York	Casey Stengel	97	57	.630
1916[1]	Boston	William F. Carrigan	91	63	.591	1957	New York	Casey Stengel	98	56	.636
1917[1]	Chicago	Clarence H. Rowland	100	54	.649	1958[1]	New York	Casey Stengel	92	62	.597
1918[1]	Boston	Ed Barrow	75	51	.595	1959	Chicago	Al Lopez	94	60	.610
1919	Chicago	William Gleason	88	52	.629	1960	New York	Casey Stengel	97	57	.630
1920[1]	Cleveland	Tris Speaker	98	56	.636	1961[1]	New York	Ralph Houk	109	53	.673
1921	New York	Miller J. Huggins	98	55	.641	1962[1]	New York	Ralph Houk	96	66	.593
1922	New York	Miller J. Huggins	94	60	.610	1963	New York	Ralph Houk	104	57	.646
1923[1]	New York	Miller J. Huggins	98	54	.645	1964	New York	Yogi Berra	99	63	.611
1924[1]	Washington	Stanley R. Harris	92	62	.597	1965	Minnesota	Sam Mele	102	60	.630
1925	Washington	Stanley R. Harris	96	55	.636	1966[1]	Baltimore	Hank Bauer	97	63	.606
1926	New York	Miller J. Huggins	91	63	.591	1967	Boston	Dick Williams	92	70	.568
1927[1]	New York	Miller J. Huggins	110	44	.714	1968[1]	Detroit	Mayo Smith	103	59	.636
1928[1]	New York	Miller J. Huggins	101	53	.656	1969	Baltimore[3]	Earl Weaver	109	53	.673
1929[1]	Philadelphia	Connie Mack	104	46	.693	1970[1]	Baltimore[3]	Earl Weaver	108	54	.667
1930[1]	Philadelphia	Connie Mack	102	52	.662	1971	Baltimore[4]	Earl Weaver	101	57	.639
1931	Philadelphia	Connie Mack	107	45	.704	1972[1]	Oakland[5]	Dick Williams	93	62	.600
1932[1]	New York	Joseph V. McCarthy	107	47	.695	1973[1]	Oakland[6]	Dick Williams	94	68	.580
1933	Washington	Joseph E. Cronin	99	53	.651	1974[1]	Oakland[6]	Alvin Dark	90	72	.556
1934	Detroit	Gordon Cochrane	101	53	.656	1975	Boston[4]	Darrell Johnson	95	65	.594
1935[1]	Detroit	Gordon Cochrane	93	58	.616	1976	New York	Billy Martin	97	62	.610
1936[1]	New York	Joseph V. McCarthy	102	51	.667	1977[1]	New York[7]	Billy Martin	100	62	.617
1937[1]	New York	Joseph V. McCarthy	102	52	.662	1978[1]	New York[7]	Billy Martin and Bob Lemon	100	63	.613
1938[1]	New York	Joseph V. McCarthy	99	53	.651						
1939[1]	New York	Joseph V. McCarthy	106	45	.702	1979	Baltimore[8]	Earl Weaver	102	57	.642
1940	Detroit	Delmar D. Baker	90	64	.584	1980	Kansas City[9]	Jim Frey	97	65	.599
1941[1]	New York	Joseph V. McCarthy	101	53	.656						

1. World Series winner. 2. No World Series. 3. Defeated Minnesota, Western Division winner, in playoff. 4. Defeated Oakland, Western Division Leader, in playoff. 5. Defeated Detroit, Eastern Division winner, in playoff. 6. Defeated Baltimore, Eastern Division winner, in playoff. 7. Defeated Kansas City, Western Division winner, in playoff. 8. Defeated California, Western Division winner, in playoff. 9. Defeated New York, Eastern Division winner, in playoff.

ASTROS WIN 1980 PLAYOFF FOR N.L. WESTERN TITLE

The Houston Astros defeated the Los Angeles Dodgers, 7–1, in a playoff for the 1980 National League Western Division crown after the Dodgers had swept three straight games from Houston and deadlocked the standing at the end of the regular season. It was Houston's first title since the franchise was started in 1962. It was only the fifth pennant or division playoff in more than 100 years in the National League.

NATIONAL LEAGUE PENNANT WINNERS

Year	Club	Manager	Won	Lost	Pct	Year	Club	Manager	Won	Lost	Pct
1876	Chicago	Albert G. Spalding	52	14	.788	1929	Chicago	Joseph V. McCarthy	98	54	.645
1877	Boston	Harry Wright	31	17	.646	1930	St. Louis	Gabby Street	92	62	.597
1878	Boston	Harry Wright	41	19	.683	1931	St. Louis[1]	Gabby Street	101	53	.656
1879	Providence	George Wright	55	23	.705	1932	Chicago	Charles J. Grimm	90	64	.584
1880	Chicago	Adrian C. Anson	67	17	.798	1933	New York[1]	William H. Terry	91	61	.599
1881	Chicago	Adrian C. Anson	56	28	.667	1934	St. Louis[1]	Frank F. Frisch	95	58	.621
1882	Chicago	Adrian C. Anson	55	29	.655	1935	Chicago	Charles J. Grimm	100	54	.649
1883	Boston	John F. Morrill	63	35	.643	1936	New York	William H. Terry	92	62	.597
1884	Providence	Frank C. Bancroft	84	28	.750	1937	New York	William H. Terry	95	57	.625
1885	Chicago	Adrian C. Anson	87	25	.777	1938	Chicago	Gabby Hartnett	89	63	.586
1886	Chicago	Adrian C. Anson	90	34	.726	1939	Cincinnati	William B. McKechnie	97	57	.630
1887	Detroit	W. H. Watkins	79	45	.637	1940	Cincinnati[1]	William B. McKechnie	100	53	.654
1888	New York	James J. Mutrie	84	47	.641	1941	Brooklyn	Leo E. Durocher	100	54	.649
1889	New York	James J. Mutrie	83	43	.659	1942	St. Louis[1]	William H. Southworth	106	48	.688
1890	Brooklyn	William H. McGunnigle	86	43	.667	1943	St. Louis	William H. Southworth	105	49	.682
1891	Boston	Frank G. Selee	87	51	.630	1944	St. Louis[1]	William H. Southworth	105	49	.682
1892	Boston	Frank G. Selee	102	48	.680	1945	Chicago	Charles J. Grimm	98	56	.636
1893	Boston	Frank G. Selee	86	44	.662	1946	St. Louis[1]	Edwin H. Dyer	98	58	.628
1894	Baltimore	Edward H. Hanlon	89	39	.695	1947	Brooklyn	Burton E. Shotton	94	60	.610
1895	Baltimore	Edward H. Hanlon	87	43	.669	1948	Boston	William H. Southworth	91	62	.595
1896	Baltimore	Edward H. Hanlon	90	39	.698	1949	Brooklyn	Burton E. Shotton	97	57	.630
1897	Boston	Frank G. Selee	93	39	.705	1950	Philadelphia	Edwin M. Sawyer	91	63	.591
1898	Boston	Frank G. Selee	102	47	.685	1951	New York	Leo E. Durocher	98	59	.624
1899	Brooklyn	Edward H. Hanlon	88	42	.677	1952	Brooklyn	Charles W. Dressen	96	57	.630
1900	Brooklyn	Edward H. Hanlon	82	54	.603	1953	Brooklyn	Charles W. Dressen	105	49	.682
1901	Pittsburgh	Fred C. Clarke	90	49	.647	1954	New York[1]	Leo E. Durocher	97	57	.630
1902	Pittsburgh	Fred C. Clarke	103	36	.741	1955	Brooklyn[1]	Walter Alston	98	55	.641
1903	Pittsburgh	Fred C. Clarke	91	49	.650	1956	Brooklyn	Walter Alston	93	61	.604
1904	New York[2]	John J. McGraw	106	47	.693	1957	Milwaukee[1]	Fred Haney	95	59	.617
1905	New York[1]	John J. McGraw	105	48	.686	1958	Milwaukee	Fred Haney	92	62	.597
1906	Chicago	Frank L. Chance	116	36	.763	1959	Los Angeles[1]	Walter Alston	88	68	.564
1907	Chicago[1]	Frank L. Chance	107	45	.704	1960	Pittsburgh[1]	Danny Murtaugh	95	59	.617
1908	Chicago[1]	Frank L. Chance	99	55	.643	1961	Cincinnati	Fred Hutchinson	93	61	.604
1909	Pittsburgh[1]	Fred C. Clarke	110	42	.724	1962	San Francisco	Alvin Dark	103	62	.624
1910	Chicago	Frank L. Chance	104	50	.675	1963	Los Angeles[1]	Walter Alston	99	63	.611
1911	New York	John J. McGraw	99	54	.647	1964	St. Louis[1]	Johnny Keane	93	69	.574
1912	New York	John J. McGraw	103	48	.682	1965	Los Angeles[1]	Walter Alston	97	65	.599
1913	New York	John J. McGraw	101	51	.664	1966	Los Angeles	Walter Alston	95	67	.586
1914	Boston[1]	George T. Stallings	94	59	.614	1967	St. Louis[1]	Red Schoendienst	101	60	.627
1915	Philadelphia	Patrick J. Moran	90	62	.592	1968	St. Louis	Red Schoendienst	97	65	.599
1916	Brooklyn	Wilbert Robinson	94	60	.610	1969	New York[1 3]	Gil Hodges	100	62	.617
1917	New York	John J. McGraw	98	56	.636	1970	Cincinnati[4]	Sparky Anderson	102	60	.630
1918	Chicago	Fred L. Mitchell	84	45	.651	1971	Pittsburgh[1 5]	Danny Murtaugh	97	65	.599
1919	Cincinnati[1]	Patrick J. Moran	96	44	.686	1972	Cincinnati[4]	Sparky Anderson	95	59	.617
1920	Brooklyn	Wilbert Robinson	93	61	.604	1973	New York[6]	Yogi Berra	82	79	.509
1921	New York[1]	John J. McGraw	94	59	.614	1974	Los Angeles[6]	Walter Alston	102	60	.630
1922	New York[1]	John J. McGraw	93	61	.604	1975	Cincinnati[1 4]	Sparky Anderson	108	54	.667
1923	New York	John J. McGraw	95	58	.621	1976	Cincinnati[7 1]	Sparky Anderson	102	60	.630
1924	New York	John J. McGraw	93	60	.608	1977	Los Angeles[7]	Tom Lasorda	98	64	.605
1925	Pittsburgh[1]	William B. McKechnie	95	58	.621	1978	Los Angeles[7]	Tom Lasorda	95	67	.586
1926	St. Louis[1]	Rogers Hornsby	89	65	.578	1979[1]	Pittsburgh[6]	Chuck Tanner	98	64	.605
1927	Pittsburgh	Donie Bush	94	60	.610	1980[1]	Philadelphia[8]	Dallas Green	91	71	.562
1928	St. Louis	William B. McKechnie	95	59	.617						

1. World Series winner. 2. No World Series. 3. Defeated Atlanta, Western Division winner, in playoff. 4. Defeated Pittsburgh, Eastern Division winner, in playoff. 5. Defeated San Francisco, Western Division winner, in playoff. 6. Defeated Cincinnati, Western Division winner, in playoff. 7. Defeated Philadelphia, Eastern Division winner, in playoff. 8. Defeated Houston, Western Division winner, in playoff.

Ted Williams' Major League Batting Record

(All games with Boston Red Sox)

	G	R	H	HR	RBI	Avg		G	R	H	HR	RBI	Avg		G	R	H	HR	RBI	Avg
1939	149	131	185	31	145[1]	.327	1950	89	82	106	28	97	.317	1958	129	81	135	26	85	.328[1]
1940	144	134[1]	193	23	113	.344	1951	148	109	169	30	126	.318	1959	103	32	69	10	43	.254
1941	143	135[1]	185	37[1]	120	.406[1]	1952	6	2	4	1	3	.400	1960	113	56	98	29	72	.316
1942	150	141[1]	186	36[1]	137[1]	.356[1]	1953	37	17	37	13	34	.407	Total	2292	1798	2654	521	1839	.344
1946	150	142[1]	176	38	123	.342	1954	117	93	133	29	89	.345							
1947	156	125[1]	181	32[1]	114[1]	.343[1]	1955	98	77	114	28	83	.356							
1948	137	124	188	25	127	.369[1]	1956	136	71	138	24	82	.345							
1949	155	150[1]	194	43[1]	159[2]	.343	1957	132	96	163	38	87	.388[1]							

1. Led league. 2. Tied for league lead.
NOTE: The years 1943–45 were spent in military service.

MAJOR LEAGUE ALL-STAR GAME

Year	Date	Winning league and manager	Runs	Losing league and manager	Runs	Winning pitcher	Losing pitcher	Site	Paid attendance
1933	July 6	A.L. (Mack)	4	N.L. (McGraw)	2	Gomez	Hallahan	Chicago A.L.	47,595
1934	July 10	A.L. (Cronin)	9	N.L. (Terry)	7	Harder	Mungo	New York N.L.	48,363
1935	July 8	A.L. (Cochrane)	4	N.L. (Frisch)	1	Gomez	Walker	Cleveland A.L.	69,831
1936	July 7	N.L. (Grimm)	4	A.L. (McCarthy)	3	J. Dean	Grove	Boston N.L.	25,556
1937	July 7	A.L. (McCarthy)	8	N.L. (Terry)	3	Gomez	J. Dean	Washington A.L.	31,391
1938	July 6	N.L. (Terry)	4	A.L. (McCarthy)	1	Vander Meer	Gomez	Cincinnati N.L.	27,067
1939	July 11	A.L. (McCarthy)	3	N.L. (Hartnett)	1	Bridges	Lee	New York A.L.	62,892
1940	July 9	N.L. (McKechnie)	4	A.L. (Cronin)	0	Derringer	Ruffing	St. Louis N.L.	32,373
1941	July 8	A.L. (Baker)	7	N.L. (McKechnie)	5	E. Smith	Passeau	Detroit A.L.	54,674
1942	July 6	A.L. (McCarthy)	3	N.L. (Durocher)	1	Chandler	Cooper	New York N.L.	34,178
1943	July 13[1]	A.L. (McCarthy)	5	N.L. (Southworth)	3	Leonard	Cooper	Philadelphia A.L.	31,938
1944	July 11[1]	N.L. (Southworth)	7	A.L. (McCarthy)	1	Raffensberger	Hughson	Pittsburgh N.L.	29,589
1946	July 9	A.L. (O'Neill)	12	N.L. (Grimm)	0	Feller	Passeau	Boston A.L.	34,906
1947	July 8	A.L. (Cronin)	2	N.L. (Dyer)	1	Shea	Sain	Chicago N.L.	41,123
1948	July 13	A.L. (Harris)	5	N.L. (Durocher)	2	Raschi	Schmitz	St. Louis A.L.	34,009
1949	July 12	A.L. (Boudreau)	11	N.L. (Southworth)	7	Trucks	Newcombe	Brooklyn N.L.	32,577
1950	July 11	N.L. (Shotton)	4	A.L. (Stengel)	3[3]	Blackwell	Gray	Chicago A.L.	46,127
1951	July 10	N.L. (Sawyer)	8	A.L. (Stengel)	3	Maglie	Lopat	Detroit A.L.	52,075
1952	July 8	N.L. (Durocher)	3	A.L. (Stengel)	2[4]	Rush	Lemon	Philadelphia N.L.	32,785
1953	July 14	N.L. (Dressen)	5	A.L. (Stengel)	1	Spahn	Reynolds	Cincinnati N.L.	30,846
1954	July 13	A.L. (Stengel)	11	N.L. (Alston)	9	Stone	Conley	Cleveland A.L.	68,751
1955	July 12	N.L. (Durocher)	6	A.L. (Lopez)	5[5]	Conley	Sullivan	Milwaukee N.L.	45,643
1956	July 10	N.L. (Alston)	7	A.L. (Stengel)	3	Friend	Pierce	Washington A.L.	28,843
1957	July 9	A.L. (Stengel)	6	N.L. (Alston)	5	Bunning	Simmons	St. Louis A.L.	30,693
1958	July 8	A.L. (Stengel)	4	N.L. (Haney)	3	Wynn	Friend	Baltimore A.L.	48,829
1959[2]	July 7	N.L. (Haney)	5	A.L. (Stengel)	4	Antonelli	Ford	Pittsburgh N.L.	35,277
	Aug. 3	A.L. (Stengel)	5	N.L. (Haney)	3	Walker	Drysdale	Los Angeles N.L.	55,105
1960[2]	July 11	N.L. (Alston)	5	A.L. (Lopez)	3	Friend	Monbouquette	Kansas City A.L.	30,619
	July 13	N.L. (Alston)	6	A.L. (Lopez)	0	Law	Ford	New York A.L.	38,362
1961[2]	July 11	N.L. (Murtaugh)	5	A.L. (Richards)	4[6]	Miller	Wilhelm	San Francisco N.L.	44,115
	July 31	N.L. (Murtaugh)	1	A.L. (Richards)	1[7]	—	—	Boston A.L.	31,851
1962[2]	July 10	N.L. (Hutchinson)	3	A.L. (Houk)	1	Marichal	Pascual	Washington A.L.	45,480
	July 30	A.L. (Houk)	9	N.L. (Hutchinson)	4	Herbert	Mahaffey	Chicago N.L.	38,359
1963	July 9	N.L. (Dark)	5	A.L. (Houk)	3	Jackson	Bunning	Cleveland A.L.	44,160
1964	July 7	N.L. (Alston)	7	A.L. (Lopez)	4	Marichal	Radatz	New York A.L.	50,850
1965	July 13	N.L. (March)	6	A.L. (Lopez)	5	Koufax	McDowell	Minnesota A.L.	46,706
1966	July 12	N.L. (Alston)	2	A.L. (Mele)	1[6]	Perry	Richert	St. Louis N.L.	49,926
1967	July 11	N.L. (Alston)	2	A.L. (Bauer)	1[8]	Drysdale	Hunter	Anaheim A.L.	46,309
1968	July 9	N.L. (Schoendienst)	1	A.L. (Williams)	0	Drysdale	Tiant	Houston N.L.	48,321
1969	July 23	N.L. (Schoendienst)	9	A.L. (M. Smith)	3	Carlton	Stottlemyre	Washington A.L.	45,259
1970	July 14	N.L. (Hodges)	5	A.L. (Weaver)	4[5]	Osteen	Wright	Cincinnati N.L.	51,838
1971	July 13	A.L. (Weaver)	6	N.L. (Anderson)	4	Blue	Ellis	Detroit A.L.	53,559
1972	July 25	N.L. (Murtaugh)	4	A.L. (Weaver)	3[6]	McGraw	McNally	Atlanta N.L.	53,107
1973	July 24[1]	N.L. (Anderson)	7	A.L. (Williams)	1	Wise	Blyleven	Kansas City A.L.	40,849
1974	July 23[1]	N.L. (Berra)	7	A.L. (Williams)	2	Brett	Tiant	Pittsburgh N.L.	50,706
1975	July 15[1]	N.L. (Alston)	6	A.L. (Dark)	3	Matlack	Hunter	Milwaukee A.L.	51,540
1976	July 13	N.L. (Anderson)	7	A.L. (D. Johnson)	1	R. Jones	Fidrych	Philadelphia N.L.	63,974
1977	July 19[1]	N.L. (Anderson)	7	A.L. (Martin)	5	Sutton	Palmer	New York A.L.	56,683
1978	July 11[1]	N.L. (Lasorda)	7	A.L. (Martin)	3	Sutter	Gossage	San Diego N.L.	51,549
1979	July 17[1]	N.L. (Lasorda)	7	A.L. (Lemon)	6	Sutter	Kern	Seattle A.L.	58,905
1980	July 8[1]	N.L. (Tanner)	4	A.L. (Weaver)	2	Reuss	John	Los Angeles N.L.	56,088
1981	Aug. 9[1]	N.L. (Green)	5	A.L. (Frey)	4	Blue	Fingers	Cleveland* A.L.	72,086

1. Night game. 2. Two games. 3. Fourteen innings. 4. Five innings, rain. 5. Twelve innings. 6. Ten innings. 7. Called because of rain after nine innings. 8. Fifteen innings. NOTE: No game in 1945. *Game was originally scheduled for July 14, but was put off because of players' strike.

PAWTUCKET WINS LONGEST GAME IN 33RD INNING

The Pawtucket Red Sox and the Rochester Red Wings of the International League played one of the most bizarre games and the longest in baseball history during 1981. Pawtucket won it, 3–2, after 33 innings, 67 days after it had begun. The teams made 39 hits in the marathon that lasted 8 hours 25 minutes of actual playing time. The Class AAA game started on April 18 at McCoy Stadium in Pawtucket, R.I., and was tied at 2–2 when it was called at 4:07 in the morning by order of the league

president. On Rochester's next visit to Pawtucket, June 23, the teams resumed the game and took only 18 minutes to decide the outcome. Miami and St. Petersburg of the Florida State League had played 29 innings on June 14, 1966, the previous longest game. Miami won, 4–3. In the major leagues the longest game was played on May 2, 1920, between the Brooklyn Dodgers and Boston Braves. It went 26 innings and was called with the teams tied at 1–1.

NATIONAL BASEBALL HALL OF FAME
Cooperstown, N.Y.

Fielders

Member	Active years	Member	Active years	Member	Active years
Anson, Adrian (Cap)	1876–1897	Duffy, Hugh	1888–1906	Maranville, Walter	
Appling, Lucius (Luke)	1930–1950	Evers, John	1902–1919	(Rabbit)	1912–1935
Averill, H. Earl	1929–1941	Ewing, William	1880–1897	Mathews, Edwin	1952–1968
Baker, J. Frank		Flick, Elmer	1898–1910	Mays, Willie	1951–1973
(Home Run)	1908–1922	Foxx, James	1925–1945	McCarthy, Thomas	1884–1896
Bancroft, David	1915–1930	Frisch, Frank	1919–1937	McGraw, John J.	1891–1906
Banks, Ernest	1953–1971	Gehrig, H. Louis (Lou)	1923–1939	Medwick, Joseph	
Beckley, Jacob	1888–1907	Gehringer, Charles	1924–1942	(Ducky)	1932–1948
Bell, James		Gibson, Josh[1]	1929–1946	Mize, John (The Big Cat)	1936–1953
(Cool Papa)[1]	1920–1947	Goslin, Leon (Goose)	1921–1938	Musial, Stanley	1941–1963
Berra, Lawrence (Yogi)	1946–1965	Greenberg, Henry		O'Rourke, James	1876–1894
Bottomley, James	1922–1937	(Hank)	1933–1947	Ott, Melvin	1926–1947
Boudreau, Louis	1938–1952	Hafey, Charles (Chick)	1924–1937	Rice, Edgar (Sam)	1915–1934
Bresnahan, Roger	1897–1915	Hamilton, William	1888–1901	Robinson, Jack	1947–1956
Brouthers, Dennis	1879–1896	Hartnett, Charles		Robinson, Wilbert	1886–1902
Burkett, Jesse	1890–1905	(Gabby)	1922–1941	Roush, Edd	1913–1931
Campanella, Roy	1948–1957	Heilmann, Harry	1914–1932	Ruth, George (Babe)	1914–1935
Carey, Max	1910–1929	Herman, William	1931–1947	Schalk, Raymond	1912–1929
Chance, Frank	1898–1914	Hooper, Harry	1909–1925	Sewell, Joseph	1920–1933
Charleston, Oscar[1]	1915–1954	Hornsby, Rogers	1915–1937	Simmons, Al	1924–1944
Clarke, Fred	1894–1915	Irvin, Monford (Monte)[1]	1939–1956	Sisler, George	1915–1930
Clemente, Roberto	1955–1972	Hugh Jennings	1891–1918	Snider, Edwin D. (Duke)	1947–1964
Cobb, Tyrus	1905–1928	Johnson, William (Judy)[1]	1921–1937	Speaker, Tristram	1907–1928
Cochrane, Gordon		Kaline, Albert W.	1953–1974	Terry, William	1923–1936
(Mickey)	1925–1937	Keeler, William		Thompson, Samuel	1885–1906
Collins, Edward	1906–1930	(Wee Willie)	1892–1910	Tinker, Joseph	1902–1916
Collins, James	1895–1908	Kelley, Joseph	1891–1908	Traynor, Harold (Pie)	1920–1937
Comiskey, Charles	1882–1894	Kelly, George	1915–1932	Wagner, John (Honus)	1897–1917
Combs, Earle	1924–1935	Kelly, Michael (King)	1878–1893	Wallace, Roderick	
Connor, Roger	1880–1897	Kiner, Ralph	1946–1955	(Bobby)	1894–1918
Crawford, Samuel	1899–1917	Klein, Charles H. (Chuck)	1928–1944	Waner, Lloyd	1927–1945
Cronin, Joseph	1926–1945	Lajoie, Napoleon	1896–1916	Waner, Paul	1926–1945
Cuyler, Hazen (Kiki)	1921–1938	Leonard, Walter (Buck)[1]	1933–1955	Ward, John (Monte)	1878–1894
Delahanty, Edward	1888–1903	Lindstrom, Frederick	1924–1936	Wheat, Zachariah	1909–1927
Dickey, William	1928–1946	Lloyd, John Henry[1]	1905–1931	Williams, Theodore	1939–1960
Dihigo, Martin[1]	1923–1945	Mantle, Mickey	1951–1968	Wilson, Lewis R. (Hack)	1923–1934
DiMaggio, Joseph	1936–1951	Manush, Henry (Heinie)	1923–1939	Youngs, Ross (Pep)	1917–1926

Pitchers

Member	Active years	Member	Active years	Member	Active years
Alexander, Grover	1911–1930	Grove, Robert (Lefty)	1925–1941	Pennock, Herbert	1912–1934
Bender, Charles (Chief)	1903–1925	Haines, Jesse	1918–1937	Plank, Edward	1901–1917
Brown, Mordecai		Hoyt, Waite	1918–1938	Radbourn, Charles	
(3-Finger)	1903–1916	Hubbell, Carl	1928–1943	(Hoss)	1880–1891
Chesbro, John	1899–1909	Johnson, Walter	1907–1927	Rixey, Eppa	1912–1933
Clarkson, John	1882–1894	Joss, Adrian	1902–1910	Roberts, Robert (Robin)	1948–1966
Coveleski, Stanley	1912–1928	Keefe, Timothy	1880–1893	Ruffing, Charles (Red)	1924–1947
Dean, Jerome (Dizzy)	1930–1947	Koufax, Sanford		Rusie, Amos	1889–1901
Faber, Urban (Red)	1914–1933	(Sandy)	1955–1966	Spahn, Warren	1942–1965
Feller, Robert	1936–1956	Lemon, Robert	1946–1958	Vance, Arthur (Dazzy)	1915–1935
Ford, Edward (Whitey)	1950–1967	Lyons, Theodore	1923–1946	Waddell, George	1897–1910
Foster, Andrew (Rube)	1897–1926	Marquard, Richard		Walsh, Edward	1904–1917
Galvin, James (Pud)	1876–1892	(Rube)	1908–1925	Welch, Michael (Mickey)	1880–1892
Gibson, Bob	1959–1975	Mathewson, Christopher	1900–1916	Wynn, Early	1939–1963
Gomez, Vernon (Lefty)	1930–1943	McGinnity, Joseph	1899–1908	Young, Denton (Cy)	1890–1911
Griffith, Clark	1891–1914	Nichols, Charles (Kid)	1890–1906		
Grimes, Burleigh	1916–1934	Paige, LeRoy (Satchel)[1]	1926–1965		

Officials and Others

Barrow, Edward[2,3]	Frick, Ford C.[7,3]	Landis, Kenesaw M.[7]	Stengel, Charles D.[8]
Bulkeley, Morgan G.[3]	Giles, Warren C.[3]	Lopez, Alfonso R.[8]	Weiss, George M.[3]
Cartwright, Alexander[3]	Harridge, William[3]	Mack, Connie[2,3]	Wright, George[6]
Chadwick, Henry[4]	Harris, Stanley R.[8]	MacPhail, Leland S.[3]	Wright, Harry[6,2]
Conlan, John[5]	Hubbard, R. Calvin[5]	McCarthy, Joseph V.[2]	Yawkey, Thomas[3]
Connolly, Thomas[5]	Higgins, Miller J.[2]	McKechnie, William B.[2]	
Cummings, William A.[6]	Johnson, B. Bancroft[3]	Rickey, W. Branch[2,3]	
Evans, William G.[5,3]	Klem, William[5]	Spalding, Albert G.[6]	

1. Negro league player selected by special committee. 2. Manager. 3. Executive. 4. Writer-statistician. 5. Umpire. 6. Early player. 7. Commissioner. 8. Player-manager.

MOST VALUABLE PLAYERS
(Baseball Writers Association selections)

American League

1931	Lefty Grove, Philadelphia
1932–33	Jimmy Foxx, Philadelphia
1934	Mickey Cochrane, Detroit
1935	Hank Greenberg, Detroit
1936	Lou Gehrig, New York
1937	Charlie Gehringer, Detroit
1938	Jimmy Foxx, Boston
1939	Joe DiMaggio, New York
1940	Hank Greenberg, Detroit
1941	Joe DiMaggio, New York
1942	Joe Gordon, New York
1943	Spurgeon Chandler, New York
1944–45	Hal Newhouser, Detroit
1946	Ted Williams, Boston
1947	Joe DiMaggio, New York
1948	Lou Boudreau, Cleveland
1949	Ted Williams, Boston
1950	Phil Rizzuto, New York
1951	Yogi Berra, New York
1952	Bobby Shantz, Philadelphia
1953	Al Rosen, Cleveland
1954–55	Yogi Berra, New York
1956–57	Mickey Mantle, New York
1958	Jackie Jensen, Boston
1959	Nellie Fox, Chicago
1960–61	Roger Maris, New York
1962	Mickey Mantle, New York
1963	Elston Howard, New York
1964	Brooks Robinson, Baltimore
1965	Zoilo Versalles, Minnesota
1966	Frank Robinson, Baltimore
1967	Carl Yastrzemski, Boston
1968	Dennis McLain, Detroit
1969	Harmon Killebrew, Minnesota
1970	John (Boog) Powell, Baltimore
1971	Vida Blue, Oakland
1972	Dick Allen, Chicago
1973	Reggie Jackson, Oakland
1974	Jeff Burroughs, Texas
1975	Fred Lynn, Boston
1976	Thurman Munson, New York
1977	Rod Carew, Minnesota
1978	Jim Rice, Boston
1979	Don Baylor, California
1980	George Brett, Kansas City

National League

1931	Frank Frisch, St. Louis
1932	Chuck Klein, Philadelphia
1933	Carl Hubbell, New York
1934	Dizzy Dean, St. Louis
1935	Gabby Hartnett, Chicago
1936	Carl Hubbell, New York
1937	Joe Medwick, St. Louis
1938	Ernie Lombardi, Cincinnati
1939	Bucky Walters, Cincinnati
1940	Frank McCormick, Cincinnati
1941	Dolph Camilli, Brooklyn
1942	Mort Cooper, St. Louis
1943	Stan Musial, St. Louis
1944	Marty Marion, St. Louis
1945	Phil Cavarretta, Chicago
1946	Stan Musial, St. Louis
1947	Bob Elliott, Boston
1948	Stan Musial, St. Louis
1949	Jackie Robinson, Brooklyn
1950	Jim Konstanty, Philadelphia
1951	Roy Campanella, Brooklyn
1952	Hank Sauer, Chicago
1953	Roy Campanella, Brooklyn
1954	Willie Mays, New York
1955	Roy Campanella, Brooklyn
1956	Don Newcombe, Brooklyn
1957	Henry Aaron, Milwaukee
1958–59	Ernie Banks, Chicago
1960	Dick Groat, Pittsburgh
1961	Frank Robinson, Cincinnati
1962	Maury Wills, Los Angeles
1963	Sandy Koufax, Los Angeles
1964	Ken Boyer, St. Louis
1965	Willie Mays, San Francisco
1966	Roberto Clemente, Pittsburgh
1967	Orlando Cepeda, St. Louis
1968	Bob Gibson, St. Louis
1969	Willie McCovey, San Francisco
1970	Johnny Bench, Cincinnati
1971	Joe Torre, St. Louis
1972	Johnny Bench, Cincinnati
1973	Pete Rose, Cincinnati
1974	Steve Garvey, Los Angeles
1975–76	Joe Morgan, Cincinnati
1977	George Foster, Cincinnati
1978	Dave Parker, Pittsburgh
1979	Willie Stargell, Pittsburgh
1979	Keith Hernandez, St. Louis
1980	Mike Schmidt, Philadelphia

CY YOUNG AWARD

1956	Don Newcombe, Brooklyn N.L.
1957	Warren Spahn, Milwaukee N.L.
1958	Bob Turley, New York A.L.
1959	Early Wynn, Chicago A.L.
1960	Vernon Law, Pittsburgh, N.L.
1961	Whitey Ford, New York A.L.
1962	Don Drysdale, Los Angeles N.L.
1963	Sandy Koufax, Los Angeles N.L.
1964	Dean Chance, Los Angeles A.L.
1965	Sandy Koufax, Los Angeles N.L.
1966	Sandy Koufax, Los Angeles N.L.
1967	Jim Lonborg, Boston A.L.; Mike McCormick, San Francisco N.L.
1968	Dennis McLain, Detroit A.L.; Bob Gibson, St. Louis N.L.
1969	Mike Cuellar, Baltimore, and Dennis McLain, Detroit, tied in A.L.; Tom Seaver, N.Y. N.L.
1970	Jim Perry, Minnesota A.L.; Bob Gibson, St. Louis N.L.
1971	Vida Blue, Oakland A.L.; Ferguson Jenkins, Chicago N.L.
1972	Gaylord Perry, Cleveland A.L.; Steve Carlton, Phila. N.L.
1973	Jim Palmer, Baltimore A.L.; Tom Seaver, New York N.L.
1974	Catfish Hunter, Oakland A.L.; Mike Marshall, Los Angeles N.L.
1975	Jim Palmer, Baltimore A.L.; Tom Seaver, New York N.L.
1976	Jim Palmer, Baltimore A.L.; Randy Jones, San Diego N.L.
1977	Sparky Lyle, N.Y., A.L.; Steve Carlton, Philadelphia N.L.
1978	Ron Guidry, N.Y., A.L.; Gaylord Perry, San Diego N.L.
1979	Mike Flanagan, Baltimore, A.L.; Bruce Sutter, Chicago, N.L.
1980	Steve Stone, Baltimore, A.L.; Steve Carlton, Philadelphia, N.L.

ROOKIE OF THE YEAR
(Baseball Writers Association selections)

American League

1949	Roy Sievers, St. Louis
1950	Walt Dropo, Boston
1951	Gil McDougald, New York
1952	Harry Byrd, Philadelphia
1953	Harvey Kuenn, Detroit
1954	Bob Grim, New York
1955	Herb Score, Cleveland
1956	Luis Aparicio, Chicago
1957	Tony Kubek, New York
1958	Albie Pearson, Washington
1959	Bob Allison, Washington
1960	Ron Hansen, Baltimore
1961	Don Schwall, Boston
1962	Tom Tresh, New York
1963	Gary Peters, Chicago
1964	Tony Oliva, Minnesota
1965	Curt Blefary, Baltimore
1966	Tommy Agee, Chicago
1967	Rod Carew, Minnesota
1968	Stan Bahnsen, New York
1969	Lou Piniella, Kansas City
1970	Thurman Munson, New York
1971	Chris Chambliss, Cleveland
1972	Carlton Fisk, Boston
1973	Alonzo Bumbry, Baltimore
1974	Mike Hargrove, Texas
1975	Fred Lynn, Boston
1976	Mark Fidrych, Detroit
1977	Eddie Murray, Baltimore
1978	Lou Whitaker, Detroit
1979	Alfredo Griffin, Toronto
1979	John Castino, Minnesota
1980	Joe Charboneau, Cleveland

National League

1949	Don Newcombe, Brooklyn
1950	Sam Jethroe, Boston
1951	Willie Mays, New York
1952	Joe Black, Brooklyn
1953	Jim Gilliam, Brooklyn
1954	Wally Moon, St. Louis
1955	Bill Virdon, St. Louis
1956	Frank Robinson, Cincinnati

1957	Jack Sanford, Philadelphia	1965	Jim Lefebvre, Los Angeles	1973	Gary Matthews, San Francisco
1958	Orlando Cepeda, San Francisco	1966	Tommy Helms, Cincinnati	1974	Bake McBride, St. Louis
1959	Willie McCovey, San Francisco	1967	Tom Seaver, New York	1975	John Montefusco, San Francisco
1960	Frank Howard, Los Angeles	1968	Johnny Bench, Cincinnati	1976	Pat Zachry, Cincinnati
1961	Billy Williams, Chicago	1969	Ted Sizemore, Los Angeles	1977	Andre Dawson, Montreal
1962	Ken Hubbs, Chicago	1970	Carl Morton, Montreal	1978	Bob Horner, Atlanta
1963	Pete Rose, Cincinnati	1971	Earl Williams, Atlanta	1979	Rick Sutcliffe, Los Angeles
1964	Richie Allen, Philadelphia	1972	Jon Matlack, New York	1980	Steve Howe, Los Angeles

MAJOR LEAGUE LIFETIME RECORDS

Source: The Book of Baseball Records, published and copyrighted by Seymour Siwoff, New York, N.Y. 10036.

Leading Batters, by Average
(Over 2,000 Hits)

	Years	At Bats	Hits	Avg
Ty Cobb	24	11,429	4,191	.367
Rogers Hornsby	23	8,173	2,930	.358
Dan Brouthers	19	6,725	2,349	.349
Ed Delahanty	16	7,493	2,593	.346
Tris Speaker	22	10,196	3,515	.345
Willie Keeler	19	8,564	2,955	.345
Ted Williams	19	7,706	2,654	.345
Billy Hamilton	14	6,262	2,157	.344
Harry Heilmann	17	7,787	2,660	.342
Babe Ruth	22	8,399	2,873	.342
Jesse Burkett	16	8,389	2,872	.342
Bill Terry	14	6,428	2,193	.341
Lou Gehrig	17	8,001	2,721	.340
George Sisler	15	8,267	2,812	.340
Nap Lajoie	21	9,589	3,251	.339
Cap Anson	22	9,084	3,081	.339
Sam Thompson	15	6,004	2,016	.336
Al Simmons	20	8,761	2,927	.334
Rod Carew[1][2]	15	7,315	2,440	.334
Eddie Collins	25	9,949	3,311	.333
Paul Waner	20	9,459	3,152	.333
Stan Musial	22	10,972	3,630	.331
Heinie Manush	17	7,653	2,524	.330
Hugh Duffy	17	6,999	2,307	.330
Honus Wagner	21	10,427	3,430	.329
Joe DiMaggio	13	6,821	2,214	.325
Jimmy Foxx	20	8,134	2,646	.325

Leading Pitchers
(Over 250 Victories)

	Years	W	L	Pct
Cy Young	22	511	315	.619
Walter Johnson	21	416	279	.599
Grover Alexander	20	373	208	.642
Christy Mathewson	17	373	188	.665
James Galvin	15	365	309	.542
Warren Spahn	21	363	245	.597
Charles Nichols	15	360	202	.641
Tim Keefe	14	346	225	.606
John Clarkson	12	328	175	.652
Eddie Plank	17	325	190	.631
Mickey Welch	13	316	214	.596
Hoss Radbourne	11	308	191	.617
Lefty Grove	20	300	141	.680
Early Wynn	23	300	244	.551
Gaylord Perry[*1]	20	295	234	.558
Robin Roberts	19	286	245	.539
Tony Mullane	14	282	221	.561
Jim Kaat[*1]	23	275	229	.546
Red Ruffing	22	273	225	.548
Burleigh Grimes	19	270	212	.560
Bob Feller	18	266	162	.621
Eppa Rixey	21	266	251	.515
Gus Weyhing	14	265	236	.529
Jim McCormick	10	264	217	.549
Ferguson Jenkins[*1]	17	263	200	.568
Ted Lyons	21	260	230	.531
Steve Carleton[*1]	17	258	171	.601
Red Faber	20	254	212	.545
Carl Hubbell	16	253	154	.622
Tom Seaver[*1]	15	252	143	.638
Bob Gibson	17	251	174	.591

*Through Aug. 13, 1981. 1. Active player. 2. Through 1980 season.

LEN BARKER OF CLEVELAND PITCHES PERFECT GAME

Len Barker, a 25-year-old right-hander whose fastball has been measured at 96 miles an hour, pitched the first perfect game in the major leagues since 1968 when he defeated the Toronto Blue Jays, 3–0, at Cleveland on May 15, 1981. The Indians' pitcher became only the 11th man in baseball history to accomplish the feat—retiring all 27 men to face him. In 1980, Barker led the American League in strikeouts with 187. He struck out 11 batters in his perfect game.

The previous perfect game in the majors was pitched by Jim (Catfish) Hunter of the Oakland A's, who beat the Minnesota Twins, 4–0, on May 8, 1968. Barker's no-hitter was the first by a Cleveland pitcher since Dennis Eckersley blanked California, 1–0, on May 30, 1977, and it was the first pitched against Toronto in its six-year history.

Only five days before Barker's perfect game, Charlie Lea of the Montreal Expos pitched a no-hitter against the San Francisco Giants.

DOG SHOWS

WESTMINSTER KENNEL CLUB
(Madison Square Garden, New York, Feb. 11, 1981)
Best in show—Ch. Dhandy's Favorite Woodchuck, pug, owned by Robert A. Hauslohner, Philadelphia, Pa.

INTERNATIONAL KENNEL CLUB
(Chicago, Ill., March 30, 1981)
Best in show—Ch. Dhandy's Favorite Woodchuck, pug, owned by Robert A. Hauslohner, Philadelphia, Pa.

MAJOR LEAGUE INDIVIDUAL ALL-TIME RECORDS

Highest Batting Average—.438, Hugh Duffy, Boston N.L., 1894 (Since 1900—.424, Rogers Hornsby, St. Louis N.L., 1924.)

Most Times at Bat—12,364, Henry Aaron, Milwaukee N.L., 1954–65; Atlanta N.L., 1966–74; Milwaukee A.L., 1975–76.

Most Years Batted .300 or Better—23, Ty Cobb, Detroit A.L., 1906–26, Philadelphia A.L., 1927–28.

Most hits—4,191, Ty Cobb, Detroit A.L., 1905–26, Philadelphia A.L., 1927–28.

Most Hits, Season—257, George Sisler, St. Louis A.L., 1920.

Most Hits, Game (9 innings)—7, Wilbert Robinson, Baltimore N.L., 6 singles, 1 double, 1892. Rennie Stennett, Pittsburgh N.L., 4 singles, 2 doubles, 1 triple, 1975.

Most Hits, Game (extra innings)—9, John Burnett, Cleveland A.L., 18 innings, 7 singles, 2 doubles, 1932.

Most Hits in Succession—12, Mike Higgins, Boston A.L., in four games, 1938; Walt Dropo, Detroit A.L., in three games, 1952.

Most Consecutive Games Batted Safely—56, Joe DiMaggio, New York A.L., 1941.

Most Runs—2,244, Ty Cobb, Detroit A.L., 1905–26, Philadelphia A.L., 1927–28.

Most Runs, Season—196, William Hamilton, Philadelphia N.L., 1894. (Since 1900—177, Babe Ruth, New York A.L., 1921.)

Most Runs, Game—7, Guy Hecker, Louisville A.A., 1886. (Since 1900—6, by Mel Ott, New York N.L., 1934, 1944; Johnny Pesky, Boston A.L., 1946; Frank Torre, Milwaukee N.L., 1957.)

Most Runs Batted In—2,297, Henry Aaron, Milwaukee N.L., 1954–1965; Atlanta N.L., 1966–74; Milwaukee A.L., 1975–76.

Most Runs Batted in, Season—190, Hack Wilson, Chicago N.L., 1930.

Most Runs Batted In, Game—12, Jim Bottomley, St. Louis N.L., 1924.

Most Home Runs—755, Henry Aaron, Milwaukee N.L., 1954–1965; Atlanta N.L., 1966–74; Milwaukee A.L., 1975–76.

Most Home Runs, Season—61, Roger Maris, New York A.L., 1961 (162-game season); 60, Babe Ruth, New York A.L., 1927 (154-game season)

Most Home Runs with Bases Filled—23, Lou Gehrig, New York A.L., 1927–39.

Most 2-Base Hits—793, Tris Speaker, Boston A.L., 1907–15, Cleveland A.L., 1916–26, Washington A.L., 1927, Philadelphia A.L., 1928.

Most 2-Base Hits, Season—67, Earl Webb, Boston A.L., 1931.

Most 2-base Hits, Game—4, by many.

Most 3-Base Hits—312, Sam Crawford, Cincinnati N.L., 1899–1902, Detroit A.L., 1903–17.

Most 3-Base Hits, Season—36, Owen Wilson, Pittsburgh N.L., 1912.

Most 3-Base Hits, Game—4, George Strief, Philadelphia A.A., 1885; William Joyce, New York N.L., 1897. (Since 1900—3, by many.)

Most Games Played—3,218. Henry Aaron, Milwaukee N.L., 1954–1965; Atlanta, N.L., 1966–74; Milwaukee A.L., 1975–76.

Most Consecutive Games Played—2,130, Lou Gehrig, New York A.L., 1925–39.

Most Bases on Balls—2,056, Babe Ruth, Boston A.L., 1914–19; New York A.L., 1920–34, Boston N.L., 1935.

Most Bases on Balls, Season—170, Babe Ruth, New York A.L., 1923.

Most Bases on Balls, Game—6, Walter Wilmot, Chicago N.L., 1891; Jimmy Foxx, Boston A.L., 1938.

Most Strikeouts—1,710, Mickey Mantle, New York A.L., 1951–68.

Most Strikeouts, Season—189, Bobby Bonds, San Francisco N.L., 1970.

Most Strikeouts, Game (9 innings)—5, by many.

Most Strikeouts, Game (extra innings)—6, Carl Weilman, St. Louis A.L., 15 innings, 1913; Don Hoak, Chicago N.L., 17 innings, 1956; Fred Reichardt, California A.L., 17, innings, 1966; Billy Cowan, California A.L., 20, 1971; Cecil Cooper, Boston A.L., 15, 1974.

Most pinch-hits, lifetime—144, Forrest Burgess, Chi.-Mil.-Cin.-Pitts., N.L., 1949, 1951–64; Chi., A.L., 1964–67.

Most Pinch-hits, season—25, Jose Morales, Montreal N.L., 1976.

Most consecutive pinch-hits—9, Dave Philley, Phil., N.L., 1958 (8), 1959 (1).

Most pinch-hit home runs, lifetime—18, Gerald Lynch, Pitt.-Cin. N.L., 1957–66.

Most pinch-hit home runs, season—6, Johnny Frederick, Brooklyn, N.L., 1932.

Most stolen bases, lifetime (since 1900)—938, Lou Brock, Chicago N.L. 1961–64; St. Louis, N.L. 1964–79.

Most stolen bases, season—156, Harry Stovey, Philadelphia, American Assn., 1888. Since 1900: 96, Ty Cobb, Detroit A.L. (156 games 1915); 118, Lou Brock, St. Louis, N.L. (162 games, 1974).

Most stolen bases, game—7, George Gore, Chicago N.L. 1881; William Hamilton, Philadelphia N.L. 1894. (Since 1900—6, Eddie Collins, Philadelphia A.L., 1912.)

Most times stealing home, lifetime—35, Ty Cobb, Detroit-Phil. A.L., 1905–28.

MAJOR LEAGUE ALL-TIME PITCHING RECORDS

Most Games Won—511, Cy Young, Cleveland N.L., 1890–98, St. Louis N.L., 1899–1900, Boston A.L., 1901–08, Cleveland A.L., 1909–11, Boston N.L., 1911.

Most Games Won, Season—60, Hoss Radbourne, Providence N.L., 1884. (Since 1900—41, Jack Chesbro, New York A.L., 1904.)

Most Consecutive Games Won—24, Carl Hubbell, New York N.L., 1936 (16) and 1937 (8).

Most Consecutive Games Won, Season—19, Tim Keefe, New York N.L., 1888; Rube Marquard, New York N.L., 1912.

Most Years Won 20 or More Games—16, Cy Young, Cleveland N.L., 1891–98, St. Louis N.L., 1899–1900, Boston A.L., 1901–04, 1907–08.

Most Shutouts—113, Walter Johnson, Wash. A.L., 1907–27.

Most Shutouts, Season—16, Grover Alexander, Philadelphia N.L., 1916.

Most Consecutive Shutouts—6, Don Drysdale, Los Angeles, N.L., 1968.

Most Consecutive Scoreless Innings—58, Don Drysdale, Los Angeles, N.L., 1968.

Most Strikeouts—3,508, Walter Johnson, Washington A.L. 1907–27.

Most Strikeouts, Season—505, Matthew Kilroy, Baltimore A.A., 1886. (Since 1900—383, Nolan Ryan, California, A.L., 1973.)

Most Strikeouts, Game—21, Tom Cheney, Washington A.L. 1962, 16 innings. Nine innings: 19, Charles McSweeney, Providence N.L., 1884; Hugh Dailey, Chicago U.A., 1884. (Since 1900—19, Steve Carlton, St. Louis N.L. vs. New York, Sept. 15, 1969; Tom Seaver, New York N.L. vs. San Diego, April 22, 1970; Nolan Ryan, California A.L. vs. Boston, Aug. 12, 1974.)

Most Consecutive Strikeouts—10, Tom Seaver, New York N.L. vs. San Diego, April 22, 1970.

Most Games, Season—106, Mike Marshall, Los Angeles, N.L., 1974.

Most Complete Games, Season—74, William White, Cincinnati N.L., 1879. (Since 1900—48, Jack Chesbro, New York A.L., 1904.)

MAJOR LEAGUE ATTENDANCE RECORDS

Single game—78,672, San Francisco at Los Angeles (N.L.), April 18, 1958. (At Memorial Coliseum.)
Doubleheader—84,587, New York at Cleveland (A.L.), Sept. 12, 1954.
Night—78,382, Chicago at Cleveland (A.L.), Aug. 20, 1948.
Season, home—3,347,845, Los Angeles (N.L.), 1978.
Season, road—2,461,240, New York (A.L.), 1980.

Season, league—22,371,979, American League, 1979.
Season, both leagues—43,550,398, 1979.
World Series, single game—92,706, Chicago (A.L.) at Los Angeles (N.L.), Oct. 6, 1959.
World Series, all games (6)—420,784, Chicago (A.L.) and Los Angeles (N.L.), 1959.

MOST HOME RUNS IN ONE SEASON
(45 or More)

HR	Player/Team	Year	HR	Player/Team	Year
61	Roger Maris, New York (AL)	1961	48	Jimmy Foxx, Philadelphia (AL)	1933
60	Babe Ruth, New York (AL)	1927	48	Harmon Killebrew, Minnesota (AL)	1962
59	Babe Ruth, New York (AL)	1921	48	Willie Stargell, Pittsburgh (NL)	1971
58	Jimmy Foxx, Philadelphia (AL)	1932	48	Dave Kingman, Chicago (NL)	1979
58	Hank Greenberg, Detroit (AL)	1938	48	Mike Schmidt, Philadelphia (NL)	1980
56	Hack Wilson, Chicago (NL)	1930	47	Babe Ruth, New York (AL)	1926
54	Babe Ruth, New York (AL)	1920	47	Ralph Kiner, Pittsburgh (NL)	1950
54	Babe Ruth, New York (AL)	1928	47	Ed Mathews, Milwaukee (NL)	1953
54	Ralph Kiner, Pittsburgh (NL)	1949	47	Ernie Banks, Chicago (NL)	1958
54	Mickey Mantle, New York (AL)	1961	47	Willie Mays, San Francisco (NL)	1964
52	Mickey Mantle, New York (AL)	1956	47	Henry Aaron, Atlanta (NL)	1971
52	Willie Mays, San Francisco (NL)	1965	47	Reggie Jackson, Oakland (AL)	1969
52	George Foster, Cincinnati (NL)	1977	46	Babe Ruth, New York (AL)	1924
51	Ralph Kiner, Pittsburgh (NL)	1947	46	Babe Ruth, New York, (AL)	1929
51	John Mize, New York (NL)	1947	46	Babe Ruth, New York (AL)	1931
51	Willie Mays, New York (NL)	1955	46	Lou Gehrig, New York (AL)	1931
50	Jimmy Foxx, Boston (AL)	1938	46	Joe DiMaggio, New York (AL)	1937
49	Babe Ruth, New York (AL)	1930	46	Ed Mathews, Milwaukee (NL)	1959
49	Lou Gehrig, New York (AL)	1934	46	Orlando Cepeda, San Francisco (NL)	1961
49	Lou Gehrig, New York (AL)	1936	46	Jim Rice, Boston (AL)	1978
49	Ted Kluszewski, Cincinnati (NL)	1954	45	Harmon Killebrew, Minnesota (AL)	1963
49	Willie Mays, San Francisco (NL)	1962	45	Willie McCovey, San Francisco (NL)	1969
49	Harmon Killebrew, Minnesota (AL)	1964	45	Johnny Bench, Cincinnati (NL)	1970
49	Frank Robinson, Baltimore (AL)	1966	45	Gorman Thomas, Milwaukee (AL)	1979
49	Harmon Killebrew, Minnesota (AL)	1969	45	Henry Aaron, Milwaukee (NL)	1962

PETE ROSE SURPASSES MUSIAL AS N.L. LEADER IN HITS

Pete Rose became the National League's leader in lifetime hits during the embattled 1981 season. Just before the 50-day player strike began on June 12, Rose had tied Musial's record of 3,630, which Musial compiled in 22 seasons with the St. Louis Cardinals. Rose, who was rookie of the year in 1963, the year Musial retired from baseball, broke the record on Aug. 10, the first day of the resumption of the season. He hit a single his fourth time up against the Cardinals' Bob Forsch at Philadelphia. A crowd of 60,561 turned out for the game, including Musial, who had made a promise to be present when Rose broke his record. The 40-year-old Rose has started at five different positions—left field, right field, third base, second base, and first base—in his 19 seasons. Only two other players have made more hits than Rose in baseball history—Ty Cobb, who leads all with 4,191, and Henry Aaron, with 3,771. Rose started his career with the Cincinnati Reds and became a Philadelphia Phillie in 1979. He is the holder of numerous records and was named the National League's most valuable player in 1973.

Some of Pete Rose's accomplishments:
Won batting titles in 1968 (.335), 1969 (.348), 1973 (.338).

Set modern National League record, hitting safely in 44 consecutive games (1978).
Only player in major league history to make 200 hits in 10 seasons.
All-time singles hitter in National League.
Holds major league record, highest fielding percentage, lifetime for an outfielder, 1,000 or more games (.992).
Holds all-time record of playing most seasons of 150 games (15).
Holds all-time record for most seasons with 600 at-bats (16) and most consecutive seasons with 600 at-bats.
Batted .300 or better in 14 of 18 seasons (prior to 1981).
Named to All-Star team 14 times.
Holds record for most hits and total bases lifetime for a switch-hitter and most home runs in National League for a switch-hitter.
Had consecutive-game playing streak of 678 (ninth longest in baseball history).
Led National League in hits six seasons (1965, 1968, 1970, 1972, 1973, 1976).
Led National League in runs scored four times (1969, 1974, 1975, 1976).

MAJOR LEAGUE BALL PARK STATISTICS

lf—Left–field foul line; cf—center field; rf—right–field foul line

Club, nickname, and grounds	Distance, feet			Seating capacity	Record Attendance[3]		
	lf	cf	rf		Day game	Double-header[2]	Night game
American League							
Baltimore Orioles—Memorial Stadium	309	405	309	52,137	51,798	46,796	51,649
Boston Red Sox—Fenway Park	315	420	302	33,524	36,350	41,766	36,228
California Angels—Anaheim Stadium	333	404	333	43,204	42,655	37,768	53,591
Chicago White Sox—Comiskey Park	352	400	352	46,550	50,754	55,555	53,940
Cleveland Indians—Municipal Stadium	320	400	320	76,997	74,420	84,587	78,382
Detroit Tigers—Tiger Stadium	340	440	325	54,220	57,888	58,369	56,586
Kansas City Royals—Royals Stadium	330	410	330	40,762	41,329	40,525	41,860
Milwaukee Brewers—County Stadium	320	402	315	46,000	55,120	49,054	52,968
Minnesota Twins—Metropolitan Stadium	330	410	330	45,921	46,963	43,419	45,890
New York Yankees—Yankee Stadium*	312	430	310	54,208	73,205	81,841	74,747
Oakland A's—Oakland Coliseum	330	400	330	50,000	48,758	33,477	47,741
Seattle Mariners—Kingdome	316	405	316	59,059	47,353	25,344	57,762
Texas Rangers—Arlington Stadium	330	400	330	35,698	40,078	24,241	41,097
Toronto Blue Jays—Exhibition Stadium	330	400	330	40,000	44,649	41,308	39,347
National League							
Atlanta Braves—Atlanta Stadium	330	400	330	52,744	51,275	46,489	53,775
Chicago Cubs—Wrigley Field	355	400	353	37,741	46,572	46,965	No lights
Cincinnati Reds—Riverfront Stadium	330	404	330	51,786	53,390	52,147	52,315
Houston Astros—Astrodome	340	406	340	45,000	49,442	42,648	50,908
Los Angeles Dodgers—Dodger Stadium[1]	330	395	330	56,000	78,672	53,856	67,550
Montreal Expos—Olympic Stadium	325	404	325	60,000	57,592	59,282	57,121
New York Mets—Shea Stadium	341	410	341	55,300	56,738	57,175	56,658
Philadelphia Phillies—Veterans Stadium	330	408	330	56,581	60,120	40,720	63,283
Pittsburgh Pirates—Three Rivers Stadium	335	400	335	50,230	51,726	49,412	48,846
St. Louis Cardinals—Busch Memorial Stadium	330	404	330	50,101	50,548	49,743	50,340
San Diego Padres—San Diego Stadium	330	410	330	48,460	42,142	43,373	50,569
San Francisco Giants—Candlestick Park	335	410	335	58,000	56,196	50,924	55,920

*Seating before rebuilding exceeded current capacity. 1. Played also in Los Angeles Coliseum. 2. Two day games. 3. Through 1980 season.

MAJOR LEAGUE FRANCHISE SHIFTS AND ADDITIONS

1953—Boston Braves (N.L.) became Milwaukee Braves. Home attendance, last season in Boston (1952), 281,278; first season in Milwaukee (1953), 1,826,397.

1954—St. Louis Browns (A.L.) became Baltimore Orioles. Home attendance, last season in St. Louis (1953), 297,238; first season in Baltimore (1954), 1,060,910.

1955—Philadelphia Athletics (A.L.) became Kansas City Athletics. Home attendance, last season in Phila. (1954), 627,-100; first season in K.C. (1955), 1,393,054.

1958—New York Giants (N.L.) became San Francisco Giants. Home attendance, last season in New York (1957), 653,923; first season in San Francisco (1958), 1,272,625.

1958—Brooklyn Dodgers (N.L.) became Los Angeles Dodgers. Home attendance, last season in Brooklyn (1957), 1,028,258; first season in Los Angeles (1958), 1,845,556.

1961—Washington Senators (A.L.) became Minnesota Twins. Home attendance, last season in Washington (1960), 743,-404; first season in Minneapolis-St. Paul (1961), 1,256,722.

1961—Los Angeles Angels (later renamed the California Angels) enfranchised by the American League.

1961—Washington Senators enfranchised by the American League (a new team, replacing the former Washington club, whose franchise was moved to Minneapolis-St. Paul).

1962—Houston Colt .45's (later renamed the Houston Astros) enfranchised by the National League.

1962—New York Mets enfranchised by the National League. Home attendance, first season (1962), 922,530.

1966—Milwaukee Braves (N.L.) became Atlanta Braves. Home attendance, last season in Milwaukee (1965), 555,584; first season in Atlanta (1966), 1,539,801.

1968—Kansas City Athletics (A.L.) became Oakland Athletics.

1969—Two major leagues each added two teams for totals of 12 and split into two divisions. American League additions: Kansas City Royals and Seattle Pilots; National League additions: Montreal Expos and San Diego Padres. The division leaders met for the league championship and the two league winners met in the World Series.

1970—Seattle franchise was shifted to Milwaukee, with final court approval coming on March 31. Club was renamed Milwaukee Brewers.

1971—Washington franchise shifted at end of season to Dallas-Fort Worth Texas Rangers with field at Arlington, Tex.

1977—Seattle and Toronto began play in American League.

LARSEN'S PERFECT GAME IN 1956 WORLD SERIES

Don Larsen of the New York Yankees pitched the only no-run no-hit game in World Series history in 1956 and hurled a perfect game in so doing. Facing the Brooklyn Dodgers at the Yankee Stadium in the fifth game before 64,519 on Oct. 8, Larsen retired 27 batters in a row. The Yankees won, 2 to 0.

AMERICAN LEAGUE
(FINAL FIRST–HALF STANDING—1981)
EASTERN DIVISION

Team	W	L	Pct.	GB
New York Yankees*	34	22	.607	—
Baltimore Orioles	31	23	.574	2
Milwaukee Brewers	31	25	.554	3
Detroit Tigers	31	26	.544	3½
Boston Red Sox	30	26	.536	4
Cleveland Indians	26	24	.520	5
Toronto Blue Jays	16	42	.276	19

WESTERN DIVISION

Team	W	L	Pct.	GB
Oakland A's*	37	23	.617	—
Texas Rangers	33	22	.600	1½
Chicago White Sox	31	22	.585	2½
California Angels	31	29	.517	6
Kansas City Royals	20	30	.400	12
Seattle Mariners	21	36	.368	14½
Minnesota Twins	17	39	.304	28

NATIONAL LEAGUE
(FINAL FIRST–HALF STANDINGS—1981)
EASTERN DIVISION

Team	W	L	Pct.	GB
Philadelphia Phillies*	34	21	.618	—
St. Louis Cardinals	30	20	.600	1½
Montreal Expos	30	25	.545	4
Pittsburgh Pirates	25	23	.521	5½
New York Mets	17	34	.333	15
Chicago Cubs	15	37	.288	17½

WESTERN DIVISION

Team	W	L	Pct.	GB
Los Angeles Dodgers*	36	21	.632	—
Cincinnati Reds	35	21	.625	½
Houston Astros	28	29	.491	8
Atlanta Braves	25	29	.463	9½
San Francisco Giants	27	32	.458	10
San Diego Padres	23	33	.411	12½

*Qualified for postseason playoffs.

OTHER LIFETIME BATTING, PITCHING, AND BASE–RUNNING RECORDS

Source: Baseball Record Book, published and copyrighted by The Sporting News, St. Louis, Mo. 63166.

Hits (3,000 or More)

Ty Cobb	4,191
Henry Aaron	3,771
Pete Rose*[1]	3,635
Stan Musial	3,630
Tris Speaker	3,515
Honus Wagner	3,430
Eddie Collins	3,311
Willie Mays	3,283
Nap Lajoie	3,251
Paul Waner	3,251
Carl Yastrzemski*[1]	3,152
Cap Anson	3,081
Lou Brock	3,023
Al Kaline	3,007
Roberto Clemente	3,000

Earned–Run Average

Walter Johnson	2.37
Grover Alexander	2.56
Tom Seaver[1] [2]	2.60
Jim Palmer[1] [2]	2.74
Whitey Ford	2.74
Stanley Coveleski	2.88
Juan Marichal	2.89
Wilbur Cooper	2.89
Bob Gibson	2.91
Carl Mays	2.92
Don Drysdale	2.95
Gaylord Perry[1] [2]	2.96

Runs Scored

Ty Cobb	2,244
Henry Aaron	2,174
Babe Ruth	2,174
Willie Mays	2,062
Stan Musial	1,949
Lou Gehrig	1,888
Tris Speaker	1,881
Pete Rose*[1]	1,880
Mel Ott	1,859
Eddie Collins	1,818

Ted Williams	1,798
Charley Gehringer	1,773
Jimmy Foxx	1,751
Honus Wagner	1,740
Willie Keeler	1,720
Cap Anson	1,712
Jesse Burkett	1,708
Billy Hamilton	1,690
Mickey Mantle	1,677
John McPhee	1,674
George Van Haltren	1,650

Strikeouts, Pitching

Walter Johnson	3,508
Gaylord Perry*[1]	3,308
Nolan Ryan*[1]	3,185
Bob Gibson	3,117
Steve Carleton*[1]	3,068
Tom Seaver*[1]	3,041
Ferguson Jenkins*[1]	2,946
Jim Bunning	2,855
Mickey Lolich	2,832
Cy Young	2,819
Don Sutton*[1]	2,709
Warren Spahn	2,583
Bob Feller	2,581
Phil Niekro*[1]	2,620
Tim Keefe	2,538

Home Runs (350 or More)

Henry Aaron	755
Babe Ruth	714
Willie Mays	660
Frank Robinson	586
Harmon Killebrew	573
Mickey Mantle	536
Jimmy Foxx	534
Ted Williams	521
Willie McCovey	521
Ernie Banks	512
Ed Mathews	512

Mel Ott	511
Lou Gehrig	493
Stan Musial	475
Willie Stargell*[1]	472
Billy Williams	426
Carl Yastrzemski*[1]	423
Reggie Jackson*[1]	416
Duke Snider	407
Al Kaline	399
Frank Howard	382
Orlando Cepeda	379
Norm Cash	377
Rocky Colavito	374
Gil Hodges	370
Ralph Kiner	369
Joe DiMaggio	361
Johnny Mize	359
Yogi Berra	358
Johnny Bench*[1]	356
Tony Perez*[1]	353
Richard Allen	351
Lee May*[1]	351

Shutouts

Walter Johnson	110
Grover Alexander	90
Christy Mathewson	83
Cy Young	77
Eddie Plank	64
Warren Spahn	63
Ed Walsh	58
James Galvin	57
Bob Gibson	56
Tom Seaver*[1]	54
Don Sutton*[1]	53
Gaylord Perry*[1]	52
Juan Marichal	52
Jim Palmer*[1]	51

Strikeouts, Batting

Willie Stargell[1] [2]	1,903
Lou Brock	1,730

Reggie Jackson[1] [2]	1,728
Bobby Bonds[1] [2]	1,713
Mickey Mantle	1,710
Harmon Killebrew	1,699
Tony Perez[1] [2]	1,628
Richard Allen	1,556
Willie McCovey	1,550
Lee May[1] [2]	1,538
Frank Robinson	1,532
Willie Mays	1,526
Ed Mathews	1,487

Bases on Balls

Babe Ruth	2,056
Ted Williams	2,019
Mickey Mantle	1,734
Mel Ott	1,708
Carl Yastrzemski[1] [2]	1,683
Eddie Yost	1,614
Stan Musial	1,599
Harmon Killebrew	1,559
Joe Morgan[1] [2]	1,559
Lou Gehrig	1,508
Willie Mays	1,464
Jimmy Foxx	1,452
Ed Mathews	1,444
Frank Robinson	1,420

Stolen Bases

Lou Brock	938
Billy Hamilton	937
Ty Cobb	892
Walter Latham	791
Harry Stovey	744
Eddie Collins	743
Max Carey	738
Honus Wagner	720
Tom Brown	697
Bert Campaneris[1] [2]	638

1. Active player. 2. Through 1980 season. * Through Aug. 13, 1981.

AMERICAN LEAGUE
(Final Standing—1980)

EAST DIVISION

Team	W	L	Pct	GB
New York Yankees	103	59	.636	—
Baltimore Orioles	100	62	.617	3
Milwaukee Brewers	86	76	.531	17
Boston Red Sox	83	77	.519	19
Detroit Tigers	84	78	.519	19
Cleveland Indians	79	81	.494	23
Toronto Blue Jays	67	95	.414	36

WEST DIVISION

Team	W	L	Pct	GB
Kansas City Royals	97	65	.599	—
Oakland A's	83	79	.512	14
Minnesota Twins	77	84	.478	19½
Texas Rangers	76	85	.472	20½
Chicago White Sox	70	90	.438	26
California Angels	65	95	.406	31
Seattle Mariners	59	103	.364	38

AMERICAN LEAGUE PLAYOFFS
1st game, Kansas City, Oct. 8

New York	020	000	000—2	10	1
Kansas City	000	000	12X—7	10	0

Guidry, Davis (4), Underwood (8); Gura. Winner: Gura; Loser: Guidry. Home runs: New York: Cerone, Piniella. Kansas City: G. Brett. Attendance: 42,598.

2nd game, Kansas City, Oct. 9

New York	000	200	000—2	8	0
Kansas City	003	000	00X—3	6	0

May; Leonard, Quisenberry (9). Winner: Leonard; Loser: May. Home runs: New York: Nettles. Kansas City: None. Attendance: 42,633.

3rd game, New York, Oct. 10

Kansas City	000	010	300—4	12	1
New York	000	002	000—2	8	0

Splittorff, Quisenberry (6); John, Gossage (7), Underwood (8). Winner: Quisenberry; Loser: Gossage. Home runs: Kansas City: White, G. Brett. New York: None. Attendance: 56,588.

AMERICAN LEAGUE LEADERS

Batting—George Brett, Kansas City	.390
Runs—Willie Wilson, Kansas City	134
Hits—Willie Wilson, Kansas City	230
Runs batted in—Cecil Cooper, Milwaukee	122
Doubles—Robin Yount, Milwaukee	49
Triples—Alfredo Griffin, Toronto	15
Home Runs—Ben Oglivie, Milwaukee	41
Reggie Jackson, New York	41
Stolen Bases—Rick Henderson, Oakland	100

Pitching

Victories—Steve Stone, Baltimore	25
Earned-run average—Rudy May, New York	2.46
Strikeouts—Len Barker, Cleveland	188
Shutouts—Tommy John, New York	6

NATIONAL LEAGUE
(Final standing—1980)

EAST DIVISION

Team	W	L	Pct	GB
Philadelphia Phillies	91	71	.562	—
Montreal Expos	90	72	.556	1
Pittsburgh Pirates	83	79	.512	8
St. Louis Cardinals	74	88	.457	17
New York Mets	67	95	.414	24
Chicago Cubs	64	98	.395	27

WEST DIVISION

Team	W	L	Pct	GB
*Houston Astros	93	70	.571	—
Los Angeles Dodgers	92	72	.564	1
Cincinnati Reds	89	73	.549	3½
Atlanta Braves	81	80	.503	11
San Francisco Giants	75	86	.466	17
San Diego Padres	73	89	.451	19½

*Won one-game playoff for division title.

NATIONAL LEAGUE PLAYOFFS
1st game, Philadelphia, Oct. 7

Houston	001	000	000—1	7	0
Philadelphia	000	000	21X—3	8	1

Forsch; Carlton, McGraw (8). Winner: Carlton; Loser: Forsch. Home runs: Philadelphia: Luzinski. Attendance: 65,277.

2nd game, Philadelphia, Oct. 8

Houston	001	000	110	4—7	8	1
Philadelphia	000	200	010	1—4	14	2

Ryan, Sambito (7), D. Smith (8), LaCorte (9), Andular (10); Ruthven, McGraw (8), Reed (9), Saucier (10). Winner: LaCorte; Loser: Reed. Home runs: None. Attendance: 65,476.

3rd game, Houston, Oct. 10

Philadelphia	000	000	000	00—0	7	1
Houston	000	000	000	01—1	6	1

Christenson, Noles (7), McGraw (8); Niekro, D. Smith (11). Winner: D. Smith; Loser: McGraw. Home runs: None. Attendance: 44,443.

4th game, Houston, Oct. 11

Philadelphia	000	000	030	2—5	13	0
Houston	000	110	001	0—3	5	1

Carlton, Noles (6), Saucier (7), Reed (7), Brusstar (8), McGraw (10); Ruhle, D. Smith (8), Sambito (8). Winner: Brusstar; Loser: Sambito. Home runs: None. Attendance: 44,952.

5th game, Houston, Oct. 12

Philadelphia	020	000	050	1—8	13	2
Houston	100	001	320	0—7	14	0

Bystrom, Brussat (6), Christenson (7), Reed (7), McGraw (8), Ruthven (9); Ryan, Sambito (8), K. Forsch (8), LaCorte (9). Winner: Ruthven; Loser: LaCorte. Home runs: None. Attendance: 44,802.

NATIONAL LEAGUE LEADERS

Batting—Bill Buckner, Chicago	.324
Runs—Keith Hernandez, St. Louis	111
Hits—Steve Garvey, Los Angeles	200
Runs batted in—Mike Schmidt, Philadelphia	121
Doubles—Pete Rose, Philadelphia	42
Triples—Rod Scott, Montreal	13
Oscar Moreno, Pittsburgh	13
Home runs—Mike Schmidt, Philadelphia	48
Stolen bases—Ron LeFlore, Montreal	97

Pitching

Victories—Steve Carlton, Philadelphia	24
Earned-run average—Don Sutton, Los Angeles	2.20
Strikeouts—Steve Carlton, Philadelphia	286
Shutouts—Jerry Reuss, Los Angeles	6

AMERICAN LEAGUE AVERAGES—1980
(Unofficial)

Batting—Club

	AB	R	H	HR	RBI	PCT
Kansas City	5,715	811	1,634	115	767	.286
Texas	5,690	756	1,616	124	720	.284
Boston	5,606	757	1,589	160	717	.283
Cleveland	5,471	737	1,516	89	692	.277
Milwaukee	5,656	811	1,555	204	772	.275
Detroit	5,618	824	1,534	142	764	.273
Baltimore	5,558	797	1,513	155	742	.272
New York	5,555	821	1,485	189	773	.267
Minnesota	5,531	670	1,467	98	637	.265
California	5,443	698	1,442	106	655	.265
Oakland	5,495	687	1,424	133	635	.259
Chicago	5,440	587	1,408	91	547	.259
Toronto	5,571	625	1,398	125	579	.251
Seattle	5,492	610	1,359	104	565	.247

Batting Leaders

Player/team	AB	R	H	HR	RBI	PCT
G. Brett, Kansas City	449	87	175	24	118	.390
Cooper, Milwaukee	622	96	219	25	122	.352
Dilone, Cleveland	528	87	180	0	40	.341
Rivers, Texas	630	96	210	7	60	.333
Carew, California	540	74	179	3	59	.331
B. Bell, Texas	489	76	161	17	83	.329
Wilson, Kansas City	705	134	230	3	50	.326
Stapleton, Boston	449	61	144	7	45	.321
Bumbry, Baltimore	641	117	205	9	53	.320
Oliver, Texas	656	96	209	19	117	.319
Hassey, Cleveland	390	42	124	8	65	.318
Watson, New York	469	62	144	13	68	.307
Wathan, Kansas City	453	57	138	6	58	.305
Molitor, Milwaukee	450	81	137	9	37	.304
Oglivie, Milwaukee	592	94	180	41	117	.304
Hargrove, Cleveland	589	86	179	11	85	.304
Henderson, Oakland	591	111	179	9	53	.303
Singleton, Baltimore	579	84	175	24	103	.302
Castino, Minnesota	546	67	165	13	64	.302
Murray, Baltimore	620	100	187	32	115	.302
Lynn, Boston	415	67	125	12	61	.301
Woods, Toronto	373	54	112	15	47	.300
Bochte, Seattle	520	62	156	13	78	.300
Staub, Texas	340	42	102	9	55	.300
R. Jackson, New York	514	94	154	41	111	.300
Hurdle, Kansas City	395	49	118	10	60	.299

Leading Pitchers
(15 or more decisions)

Player/team	IP	H	BB	SO	W	L	ERA
R. May, New York	175	144	39	133	15	5	2.46
M. Norris, Oakland	284	215	83	181	22	9	2.53
Darwin, Texas	109	98	50	103	13	4	2.63
Burns, Chicago	238	213	63	133	15	13	2.84
Keough, Oakland	250	218	93	122	16	13	2.92
Gura, Kansas City	283	271	76	112	18	10	2.95
Proly, Chicago	146	136	58	54	5	10	3.07
Quisenberry, Kansas City	128	129	27	37	12	7	3.09
Haas, Milwaukee	252	246	56	146	16	15	3.14
Clear, California	106	82	65	104	11	11	3.21
Stone, Baltimore	250	224	101	149	25	7	3.23
Erickson, Minnesota	191	198	56	97	7	13	3.25
Farmer, Chicago	99	92	56	54	7	9	3.25
Langford, Oakland	290	276	64	100	19	12	3.26
Clancy, Toronto	250	217	128	152	13	16	3.30
B. Stanley, Boston	179	186	52	71	10	8	3.32
McGregor, Baltimore	252	254	58	119	20	8	3.32
John, New York	265	270	56	78	22	9	3.43
F. Bannister, Seattle	217	200	66	154	9	13	3.47
Jenkins, Texas	198	190	52	129	12	12	3.55
Trout, Chicago	199	229	49	89	9	16	3.56
Guidry, New York	219	215	80	166	17	10	3.56
T. Underwood, New York	187	163	66	116	13	9	3.66
Sorensen, Milwaukee	195	242	45	54	12	10	3.68
Stied, Toronto	242	232	83	108	12	15	3.71

NATIONAL LEAGUE AVERAGES—1980
(Unofficial)

Batting—Club

	AB	R	H	HR	RBI	PCT
St. Louis	5,607	738	1,538	101	689	.274
Philadelphia	5,625	728	1,517	117	674	.270
Pittsburgh	5,518	666	1,466	117	625	.266
Los Angeles	5,570	663	1,461	148	635	.262
Cincinnati	5,518	704	1,446	112	667	.262
Houston	5,566	637	1,456	76	599	.262
Montreal	5,466	696	1,413	114	648	.259
New York	5,478	611	1,407	61	554	.257
San Diego	5,540	591	1,411	67	546	.255
Chicago	5,627	617	1,415	107	579	.252
Atlanta	5,396	629	1,354	144	597	.251
San Francisco	5,368	573	1,308	79	539	.244

Batting Leaders

Player/team	AB	R	H	HR	RBI	PCT
L. Smith, Philadelphia	298	69	101	3	20	.339
Easler, Pittsburgh	393	66	133	21	74	.338
Lacy, Pittsburgh	278	45	93	7	33	.335
Buckner, Chicago	578	69	187	10	68	.324
R. Smith, Los Angeles	311	47	100	15	55	.322
K. Hernandez, St. Louis	595	111	191	16	99	.321
Templeton, St. Louis	504	83	161	4	43	.319
Valentine, Montreal	311	40	99	13	67	.318
McBride, Philadelphia	554	68	171	9	87	.309
Cedeno, Houston	499	70	154	10	73	.309
Dawson, Montreal	577	96	178	17	87	.308
Johnstone, Los Angeles	251	31	77	2	20	.307
Garvey, Los Angeles	658	78	200	26	106	.304
Oberkfell, St. Louis	422	58	128	3	47	.303
Simmons, St. Louis	495	84	150	21	98	.303
Collins, Cincinnati	551	94	167	3	34	.303
Hendrick, St. Louis	572	73	173	25	109	.302
J. Cruz, Houston	612	79	185	11	91	.302
Richards, San Diego	642	91	193	4	41	.301
Walling, Houston	284	30	85	3	28	.299
Iorg, St. Louis	251	33	75	3	36	.299
Vail, Chicago	312	29	93	6	47	.298
Mumphry, San Diego	564	31	168	4	59	.298
Whitfield, San Francisco	321	38	95	4	26	.296
Parker, Pittsburgh	581	71	153	18	79	.295
Griffey, Cincinnati	544	90	160	13	85	.294
Baker, Los Angeles	579	80	170	29	97	.294

Leading Pitchers
(15 or more decisions)

Player/team	IP	H	BB	SO	W	L	ERA
Sutton, Los Angeles	212	163	47	128	13	5	2.20
Carlton, Philadelphia	304	243	90	286	24	9	2.34
Ruhle, Houston	158	148	30	54	12	4	2.39
Shone, Los Angeles	84	83	22	40	7	9	2.44
Reuss, Los Angeles	229	193	40	111	18	6	2.51
Hume, Cincinnati	137	121	38	64	9	10	2.56
Reardon, New York	110	96	47	104	8	7	2.61
Fingers, San Diego	103	101	32	68	11	9	2.80
Blue, San Francisco	224	202	61	129	14	10	2.97
Rogers, Montreal	281	247	85	147	16	11	2.98
Zachry, New York	165	145	58	88	6	10	2.99
Gullickson, Montreal	141	127	50	119	10	5	3.00
Soto, Cincinnati	190	126	84	181	10	8	3.07
Whitson, San Francisco	211	222	56	91	11	13	3.10
Sanderson, Montreal	211	206	56	124	16	11	3.11
Sosa, Montreal	94	106	21	58	9	6	3.16

Player/team	IP	H	BB	SO	W	L	ERA
K. Forsch, Houston	223	230	42	84	12	13	3.18
Pastore, Cincinnati	184	161	42	110	13	7	3.27
Welch, Los Angeles	213	190	79	141	14	9	3.28
Bibby, Pittsburgh	238	209	88	141	19	6	3.29
Tekulve, Pittsburgh	93	96	40	47	8	12	3.29
Ryan, Houston	233	205	98	200	11	10	3.35
Reuschel, Chicago	257	281	76	140	11	13	3.40
Vuckovich, St. Louis	222	203	68	131	12	9	3.40
Boggs, Atlanta	192	180	46	84	12	9	3.42

WORLD SERIES—1980

Philadelphia Phillies (NL) defeated Kansas City Royals (AL), 4 games to 2

1st Game—Philadelphia, Oct. 14

PHILADELPHIA (N)	AB	R	H	BI	KANSAS CITY (A)	AB	R	H	BI
Smith, lf	4	0	2	0	Wilson, lf	5	0	0	0
Gross, lf	1	0	0	0	McRae, dh	3	1	1	0
Rose, 1b	3	1	0	0	G. Brett, 3b	4	1	1	0
Schmidt, 3b	2	2	1	0	Aikens, 1b	4	2	2	4
McBride, rf	4	1	3	3	Porter, c	2	1	0	0
Luzinski, dh	3	0	0	0	Otis, cf	4	1	3	2
Maddox, cf	3	0	0	1	Hurdle, rf	3	0	1	0
Trillo, 2b	4	1	1	0	Wathan, rf	1	0	0	0
Bowa, ss	4	1	1	0	White, 2b	4	0	1	0
Boone, c	4	1	3	2	Washington, ss	4	0	0	0
Total	32	7	11	6	Total	34	6	9	6

Kansas City   0 2 2 0 0 0 0 2 0—6
Philadelphia   0 0 5 1 1 0 0 0 X—7
E—Leonard. DP—Philadelphia. LOB—Kansas City 4, Philadelphia 6. 2B—Boone 2, G. Brett. HR—Otis, Aikens 2, McBride. SB—Bowa, White. SF—Maddox.

	IP	H	R	ER	BB	SO
Kansas City						
Leonard (L)	3⅔	6	6	6	1	3
Martin	4	5	1	1	1	1
Quisenberry	⅓	0	0	0	0	0
Philadelphia						
Walk (W)	7	8	6	6	3	3
McGraw	2	1	0	0	0	1

WP—Walk. HBP—by Leonard (Rose), by Martin (Luzinski). Walk pitched to 2 batters in 8th. Times of game—3:01. Attendance—65,791.

2nd Game—Philadelphia, Oct. 15

KANSAS CITY (A)	AB	R	H	BI	PHILADELPHIA (N)	AB	R	H	BI
Wilson, lf	4	1	1	0	Smith, lf	3	0	0	0
Washington, ss	4	0	1	0	Unser, cf	1	1	1	1
G. Brett, 3b	2	0	2	0	Rose, 1b	4	0	0	0
Chalk, 3b	0	1	0	0	McBride, rf	3	1	1	1
Porter, ph	1	0	0	0	Schmidt, 3b	4	1	2	1
McRae, dh	4	1	3	0	Moreland, dh	4	1	2	1
Otis, cf	5	1	2	2	Maddox, cf	3	1	1	0
Wathan, c	3	0	0	1	Gross, lf	1	0	0	0
Aikens, 1b	3	0	1	0	Trillo, 2b	2	0	0	1
LaCock, 1b	0	0	0	0	Bowa, ss	3	0	1	1
Cardenal, rf	4	0	0	0	Boone, c	3	1	1	0
White, 2b	4	0	1	0	Total	29	6	8	6
Total	34	4	11	3					

Kansas City   0 0 0 0 0 1 3 0 0—4
Philadelphia   0 0 0 0 2 0 0 4 X—6
E—Trillo. DP—Kansas City 2, Philadelphia 4. LOB—Kansas City 11, Philadelphia 3. 2B—Maddox, Otis, Unser, Schmidt. SB—Wilson, Chalk. S—Washington. SF—Trillo, Wathan.

	IP	H	R	ER	BB	SO
Kansas City						
Gura	6	4	2	2	2	2
Quisenberry (L)	2	4	4	4	1	0
Philadelphia						
Carlton (W)	8	10	4	3	6	10
Reed	1	1	0	0	0	2

WP—Carlton. Time of game—3:01. Attendance—65,775.

3rd Game—Kansas City, Oct. 17

PHILADELPHIA (N)	AB	R	H	BI	KANSAS CITY (A)	AB	R	H	BI
L. Smith, lf	4	0	2	1	Wilson, lf	4	1	0	0
Gross, lf	0	0	0	0	White, 2b	5	0	0	0
Rose, 1b	4	0	1	1	G. Brett, 3b	4	1	2	1
Schmidt, 3b	5	1	1	1	Aikens, 1b	5	1	2	1
McBride, rf	5	0	2	0	McRae, dh	4	0	2	1
Moreland, dh	5	0	1	0	Otis, cf	4	1	2	1
Maddox, cf	4	0	1	0	Hurdle, rf	4	0	2	0
Trillo, 2b	5	1	2	0	Concepcion, pr	0	0	0	0
Bowa, ss	5	1	3	0	Cardenal, rf	0	0	0	0
Boone, c	4	0	1	0	Porter, c	4	0	0	0
Total	41	3	14	3	Washington, ss	4	0	1	0
					Total	38	4	11	4

Philadelphia   0 1 0 0 1 0 0 1 0 0—3
Kansas City   1 0 0 1 0 0 0 0 1 1—4
DP—Philadelphia 1, Kansas City 2. LOB—Philadelphia 15, Kansas City 7. 2B—Trillo, G. Brett. 3B—Aikens. HRs—G. Brett, Schmidt, Otis. SB—Hurdle, Bowa, Wilson. S—Gross.

	IP	H	R	ER	BB	SO
Philadelphia						
Ruthven	9	9	3	3	0	7
McGraw (L)	*⅔	2	1	1	2	1
Kansas City						
Gale	4⅓	7	2	2	3	3
Martin	3⅓	5	1	1	1	1
Quisenberry (W)	2⅓	2	0	0	2	0

*Two outs when winning run was scored. Time of game—3:19. Attendance—42,380.

1980 WORLD SERIES MATCHED CLUBS WHO HAD NEVER WON

The Kansas City Royals in 1980 competed in their first World Series since the franchise was started in 1968. Their opponents, the Philadelphia Phillies, had not appeared in the Series in 30 years, losing in four straight games to the New York Yankees in 1950. The confrontation between the Royals and Phillies marked the first time since 1920, when Cleveland met Brooklyn, that two teams that had not won a World Series faced each other. In Philadelphia's only other appearance in a Series, in 1915 against the Boston Red Sox, the Phillies won the first game with Grover Alexander pitching, then lost four in a row.

4th Game—Kansas City, Oct. 18

PHILADELPHIA (N)

	AB	R	H	BI
L. Smith, dh	4	0	0	0
Rose, 1b	4	1	2	0
McBride, rf	3	0	1	0
Schmidt, 3b	3	0	1	1
Unser, lf	4	0	1	0
Maddox, cf	4	0	1	0
Trillo, 2b	4	2	1	0
Bowa, ss	4	0	2	1
Boone, c	3	0	1	1
Total	33	3	10	3

KANSAS CITY (A)

	AB	R	H	BI
Wilson, lf	4	1	1	0
White, 2b	5	0	0	0
G. Brett, 3b	5	1	1	1
Aikens, 1b	3	2	2	3
McRae, dh	4	1	2	0
Otis, cf	4	0	2	1
Hurdle, rf	2	0	1	0
Porter, c	3	0	0	0
Washington, ss	4	0	1	0
Total	34	5	10	5

Philadelphia	010	000	110—3
Kansas City	410	000	00X—5

E—White, Christenson, Washington. DP—Kansas City 1. LOB—Philadelphia 5, Kansas City 10. 2B—McRae 2, Otis, Hurdle, McBride, Trillo, Rose. 3B—G. Brett. HR—Aikens 2. SB—Bowa. SF—Schmidt.

Philadelphia	IP	H	R	ER	BB	SO
Christenson (L)	1/3	5	4	4	0	0
Noles	4 2/3	5	1	1	2	6
Saucier	2/3	0	0	0	2	0
Brusstar	2 1/3	0	0	0	1	0
Kansas City						
Leonard (W)	7	9	3	2	1	2
Quisenberry	2	1	0	0	0	0

Time of game—2:37. Attendance—42,363.

5th Game—Kansas City, Oct. 19

PHILADELPHIA (N)

	AB	R	H	BI
Rose, 1b	4	0	0	0
McBride, rf	4	1	0	0
Schmidt, 3b	4	2	2	2
Luzinski, lf	2	0	0	0
L. Smith, lf	0	0	0	0
Unser, lf	1	1	1	1
Moreland, dh	3	0	1	0
Maddox, cf	4	0	0	0
Trillo, 2b	4	0	1	1
Bowa, ss	4	0	1	0
Boone, c	3	0	1	0
Total	33	4	7	4

KANSAS CITY (A)

	AB	R	H	BI
Wilson, lf	5	0	2	0
White, 2b	3	0	0	0
G. Brett, 3b	5	0	1	1
Aikens, 1b	3	0	0	0
Concepcion, pr	0	0	0	0
McRae, dh	5	0	1	0
Otis, cf	3	1	2	1
Hurdle, rf	3	1	1	0
Cardenal, rf	2	0	0	0
Porter, c	4	0	2	0
Washington, ss	3	1	2	1
Total	36	3	12	3

6th Game—Philadelphia, Oct. 21

KANSAS CITY (A)

	AB	R	H	BI
Wilson, lf	4	0	0	0
Washington, ss	3	0	1	1
G. Brett, 3b	4	0	2	0
McRae, dh	4	0	0	0
Otis, cf	3	0	0	0
Aikens, 1b	2	0	0	0
Concepcion, pr	0	0	0	0
Wathan, c	3	1	2	0
Cardenal, rf	4	0	2	0
White, 2b	4	0	0	0
Total	31	1	7	1

PHILADELPHIA (N)

	AB	R	H	BI
L. Smith, lf	4	2	1	0
Gross, lf	0	0	0	0
Rose, 1b	4	0	3	0
Schmidt, 3b	3	0	1	2
McBride, rf	4	0	1	0
Luzinski, dh	4	0	0	0
Maddox, cf	4	0	2	0
Trillo, 2b	4	0	0	0
Bowa, ss	4	1	1	0
Boone, c	2	1	1	1
Total	33	4	9	4

Kansas City	000	000	010—1
Philadelphia	002	011	00X—4

E—White, Aikens. DP—Kansas City 1, Philadelphia 2. LOB—Kansas City 9, Philadelphia 7. 2B—Maddox, L. Smith, Bowa. SF—Washington.

Kansas City	IP	H	R	ER	BB	SO
Gale (L)	2	4	2	1	1	1
Martin	2 1/3	1	1	1	1	0
Splittorff	1 2/3	4	1	1	0	0
Pattin	1	0	0	0	0	2
Quisenberry	1	0	0	0	0	0
Philadelphia						
Carlton (W)	7	4	1	1	3	7
McGraw	2	3	0	0	2	2

Time of game—3:00. Attendance—65,838.

Philadelphia	000	200	002—4
Kansas City	000	012	000—3

E—Aikens, G. Brett. DP—Kansas City 2. LOB—Philadelphia 4, Kansas City 13. 2B—Wilson, McRae, Unser. HRs—Schmidt, Otis. SB—G. Brett. S—White, Moreland. SF—Washington.

Philadelphia	IP	H	R	ER	BB	SO
Bystrom	5	10	3	3	1	4
Reed	1	1	0	0	0	0
McGraw (W)	3	1	0	0	4	5
Kansas City						
Gura	6 1/3	4	2	1	1	2
Quisenberry (L)	2 2/3	3	2	2	0	0

Time of game—2:51. Attendance—42,369.

BASEBALL'S PERFECTLY PITCHED GAMES[1]

(no opposing runner reached base)

John Richmond—Worcester vs. Cleveland (NL) June 12, 1880	
John M. Ward—Providence vs. Buffalo (NL) June 17, 1880	1–0
Cy Young—Boston vs. Philadelphia (AL) May 5, 1904	5–0
Addie Joss—Cleveland vs. Chicago (AL) Oct. 2, 1908	3–0
Ernest Shore[2]—Boston vs. Washington (AL) June 23, 1917	1–0
Charles Robertson—Chicago vs. Detroit (AL) April 30, 1922	4–0
Don Larsen[3]—New York (AL) vs. Brooklyn (NL) Oct. 8, 1956	2–0
Jim Bunning—Philadelphia vs. New York (NL) June 21, 1964	2–0
Sandy Koufax—Los Angeles vs. Chicago (NL) Sept. 9, 1965	6–0
Jim Hunter—Oakland vs. Minnesota (AL) May 8, 1968	1–0
Len Barker—Cleveland vs. Toronto (AL) May 15, 1981	4–0
	3–0

1. Harvey Haddix, of Pittsburgh, pitched 12 perfect innings against Milwaukee (NL), May 26, 1959 but lost game in 13th on error and hit. 2. Shore, relief pitcher for Babe Ruth who walked first batter before being ejected by umpire, retired 26 batters who faced him and baserunner was out stealing. 3. World Series.

BASEBALL—AMATEUR
1981 CHAMPIONS

N.C.A.A. Division I—Arizona State (defeated Oklahoma State, 7–4, in final)
N.C.A.A. Division II—Florida Southern (defeated Eastern Illinois, 9–0, in final)
N.C.A.A. Division III—Marietta (defeated Ithaca, 14–12, in final)

BASEBALL—MINOR LEAGUES—1980

CLASS AAA
AMERICAN ASSOCIATION
Eastern Division

	W	L	Pct.
Springfield (Cardinals)	75	61	.551
Evansville (Tigers)	61	74	.452
Iowa (White Sox)	59	77	.434
Indianapolis (Reds)	58	77	.430

Western Division

	W	L	Pct.
Denver (Expos)	92	44	.676
Oklahoma City (Phillies)	70	65	.519
Omaha (Royals)	66	70	.485
Wichita (Cubs)	61	74	.452

Playoff—Springfield defeated Denver, 4 games to 1

INTERNATIONAL LEAGUE

	W	L	Pct.
Columbus (Yankees)	83	57	.593
Toledo (Twins)	77	63	.550
Rochester (Orioles)	74	65	.532
Richmond (Braves)	69	71	.493
Charleston (Rangers)	67	71	.486
Tidewater (Mets)	67	72	.482
Pawtucket (Red Sox)	62	77	.446
Syracuse (Blue Jays)	58	81	.417

Playoffs

Semifinals—Columbus defeated Richmond, 3 games to 2
Toledo defeated Rochester, 3 games to 1
Final—Columbus defeated Toledo, 4 games to 1

PACIFIC COAST LEAGUE
North Division

First half winner—Hawaii (Padres)
Second half winner—Vancouver (Brewers)
Playoff—Hawaii defeated Vancouver

South Division

First half winner—Tucson (Rangers)
Second half winner—Albuquerque (Dodgers)

Playoff—Albuquerque defeated Tucson
Championship playoff—Albuquerque defeated Hawaii, 3 games to 2

MEXICAN LEAGUE[1]

Southeastern Division—Puebla
Southwestern Division—Mexico City
Northeastern Division—Aquascalientes
Northwestern Division—Juarez

1. Players' strike canceled regular season after July 3.

CLASS AA

Eastern League—Northern Division, first half: Buffalo (Pirates); second half: Holyoke (Brewers); playoff: Holyoke. Southern Division, first half: Waterbury (Reds); second half: Reading (Phillies); playoff: Waterbury. League championship: Holyoke defeated Waterbury, 2 games to 1

Southern League—Eastern Division, first half: Charlotte (Orioles); second half: Savannah (Braves); playoff: Charlotte. Western Division, first half: Memphis (Expos); second half: Nashville (Yankees); playoff: Memphis. League champion: Charlotte defeated Memphis, 3 games to 1

Texas League—Eastern Division, first half: Arkansas (Cardinals); second half: Jackson (Mets); playoff: Arkansas. Western Division, first half: San Antonio (Dodgers); second half: Amarillo (Padres); playoff: San Antonio. League championship: Arkansas defeated San Antonio, 3 games to 0

CLASS A

California League—Southern Division, first half: Fresno (Giants); second half: Visalia (Twins); playoff: Visalia. Northern Division, first half: Stockton (Brewers); second half: Stockton. League championship: Stockton defeated Visalia, 3 games to 0

Midwest League—Northern Division, first half, Waterloo (Indians); second half: Wisconsin Rapids (Twins); playoff: Waterloo. Southern Division, first half: Quad–Cities (Cubs); second half: Burlington (Brewers); playoff: Quad–Cities. League championship: Waterloo defeated Quad–Cities, 2 games to 1

New York–Penn League—Eastern Division, Oneonta (Yankees); Western Division, Geneva (Cubs). League championship: Oneonta defeated Geneva, 2 games to 1

Northwest League—Northern Division: Bellingham (Mariners). Southern Division: Eugene (Reds). Playoff: Teams declared co-champions after third game of two–of–three series was rained out. Seattle parent club refused extension of series. Each team had won a game.

South Atlantic League—Northern Division: Greensboro (Yankees) won first and second half. Southern Division: Charleston (Royals) won first and second half. League championship: Greensboro defeated Charleston, 3 games to 0

ROOKIE LEAGUES

Appalachian—Paintsville (Yankees)
Pioneer—Northern Division: Lethbridge (Dodgers). Southern Division: Billings (Reds)

LUGE

WORLD CHAMPIONSHIPS
(Hammarstrand, Sweden, Feb. 1–3, 1981)

Men—Sergei Damilin, Soviet Union
Women—Melitta Sollman, East Germany

UNITED STATES CHAMPIONSHIPS
(Lake Placid, N.Y., Feb. 14–16, 1981)

Men—Frank Masley, Newark, Del.	3:03.733
Women—Donna Burke, Lake Placid, N.Y.	2:46.322
Men's doubles—Terry Morgan, Saranac Lake, N.Y., and Beau Jamieson, Hudon, Ohio	1:24.941

LITTLE LEAGUE WORLD SERIES

1947	Williamsport, Pa.	1958	Monterrey, Mexico	1969	Taiwan (Nationalist China)
1948	Lock Haven, Pa.	1959	Hamtramck, Mich.	1970	Wayne, N.J.
1949	Hammonton, N.J.	1960	Levittown, Pa.	1971	Taiwan (Nationalist China)
1950	Houston, Tex.	1961	El Cajon, Calif.	1972	Taiwan (Nationalist China)
1951	Stamford, Conn.	1962	San Jose, Calif.	1973	Taiwan (Nationalist China)
1952	Norwalk, Conn.	1963	Granada Hills, Calif.	1974	Taiwan (Nationalist China)
1953	Birmingham, Ala.	1964	Staten Island, N.Y.	1975	Lakewood Township, N.J.
1954	Schenectady, N.Y.	1965	Windsor Locks, Conn.	1976	Tokyo, Japan
1955	Morrisville, Pa.	1966	Houston, Tex.	1977	Tapei, Taiwan
1956	Roswell, N.M.	1967	West Tokyo, Japan	1978–79	Pintung, Taiwan
1957	Monterrey, Mexico	1968	Wakayama, Japan	1980	Hua Lian, Taiwan

SOFTBALL

Source: Amateur Softball Association.

Amateur Champions

1959	Aurora (Ill.) Sealmasters	1968	Clearwater (Fla.) Bombers	1975	Rising Sun Hotel, Reading, Pa.
1960	Clearwater (Fla.) Bombers	1969	Raybestos Cardinals, Strat- ford, Conn.	1976	Raybestos Cardinals, Strat- ford, Conn.
1961	Aurora (Ill.) Sealmasters				
1962–63	Clearwater (Fla.) Bombers	1971	Welty Way, Cedar Rapids, Iowa	1977	Billard Barbell, Reading, Pa.
1964	Burch Gage & Tool, Detroit	1972	Raybestos Cardinals, Strat- ford, Conn.	1978	Reading, Pa.
1965	Aurora (Ill.) Sealmasters			1979	Midland, Mich.
1966	Clearwater (Fla.) Bombers	1973	Clearwater (Fla.) Bombers	1980	Peterbuilt Western, Seattle
1967	Aurora (Ill.) Sealmasters	1974	Santa Rosa (Calif.)		

AMATEUR SOFTBALL ASSOCIATION CHAMPIONS—1980

Men's major fast pitch—Peterbuilt Western, Seattle, Wash.
Women's major fast pitch—Raybestos Brakettes, Stratford, Conn.
Women's Class A fast pitch—Astros, San Diego, Calif.
Men's major slow pitch—Campbell's Carpets, Concord, Calif.
Women's major slow pitch—Rubi–Otts, Graham, N.C.
Men's major industrial slow pitch—Sikorsky, Stratford, Conn.
Men's Class A slow pitch—Wreckers, Houston, Tex.
Women's Class A slow pitch—Encore, Brandywine, Md.
Men's Class A industrial slow pitch—Local 761, Louisville, Ky.
Women's Class A industrial slow pitch—Provident Vets, Chattanooga, Tenn.
Modified—Cadillac, Atlanta, Ga.
Men's church slow pitch—West End Baptist, Houston, Tex.

Women's church slow pitch—Rock Creek Methodist, Snow Camp, N.C.

YOUTH TOURNAMENTS—1980

Boys 16–18 fast pitch—Schlitz Bulls, Springfield, Mo.
Boys 16–18 slow pitch—Gills's Insurance, Tifton, Ga.
Boys 13–15 fast pitch—Universal Corp., Baton Rouge, La.
Boys 13–15 slow pitch—The Mavericks, Tifton, Ga.
Girls 16–18 fast pitch—Nor-cal Tremors, Fairfield, Calif.
Girls 16–18 slow pitch—Chem-Nut Tom Boys, Tifton, Ga.
Girls 13–15 fast pitch—Aces, Eugene, Ore.
Girls 13–15 slow pitch—The Mets, Satellite Beach, Fla.

WORLD CHAMPION—1980

Men's fast pitch—Home Savings, Aurora, Ill.

SQUASH RACQUETS

1981 U.S. SQUASH RACQUETS CHAMPIONSHIPS

Men's Events (Amateur)

Singles—Mark Alger, Tacoma, Wash.
Singles, 35 and over—Leonard Bernheimer, Boston
Singles, 40 and over—Raul Sanchez, Mexico City
Singles, 45 and over—Les Harding, Mercer Island, Wash.
Singles, 50 and over—Henri Salaun, Boston
Singles, 55 and over—Charles Butt, Brunswick, Me.
Singles, 60 and over—Calvin MacCracken, Englewood, N.J.
Class B singles—Bruce Horowitz, New York City
Class C singles—William Alemoni, Forestville, Conn.
Doubles—Victor Harding–Peter Hall, Hamilton, Ontario
Veterans doubles—Edward Simmons, St. Louis, and Mel Sokolow, New York City
Seniors doubles—Donald Leggat–Charles Wright, Hamilton, Ontario
College A singles—John Nimick, Princeton
College B singles—George Lemmon, Harvard
College C singles—Clark Bain, Harvard
United States 5–man team—Mexico No. 1
College 6–man team—Harvard

Lapham Cup (singles)—United States 11, Canada 4
Grant Trophy (doubles)—Canada 4, United States 3

Professional and Open Events

U.S. Dunlop Professional singles—Michael Desaulniers, Montreal
World Professional Squash Association singles—Michael Desaulniers, Montreal
World Open doubles—Mohibullah Khan, Boston, and Clive Caldwell, Toronto
North American Open singles—Sharif Khan, Toronto

Women's Events

Singles—Barbara Maltby, Philadelphia
Class B singles—Mary McGuirk, Baltimore, Md.
Class C singles—Elizabeth O'Brien, Madison, Wis.
Intercollegiate singles—Jane Giammattei, Pine Manor
Doubles—Carol Thesieres, Broomall, Pa., and Joyce Davenport, King of Prussia, Pa.
Doubles, 40 and over—Carol Thesieres, Broomall, Pa., and Irma Brogan, Wynnewood, Pa.
Mixed Doubles—Ralph E. Howe, Cold Spring Harbor, N.Y., and Joyce Davenport, King of Prussia, Pa.

YACHTING

AMERICA'S CUP RECORD

First race in 1851 around Isle of Wight, Cowes, England. First defense and all others through 1920 held 30 miles off New York Bay. Races since 1930 held 30 miles off Newport, R.I. Conducted as one race only in 1851 and 1870; best four-of-seven basis, 1871; best two-of-three, 1876–1887; best three-of-five, 1893–1901; best four-of-seven, since 1930. Figures in parentheses indicate number of races won.

Year	Winner and owner	Loser and owner
1851	AMERICA (1), John C. Stevens, U.S.	AURORA, T. Le Marchant, England[1]
1870	MAGIC (1), Franklin Osgood, U.S.	CAMBRIA, James Ashbury, England[2]
1871	COLUMBIA (2), Franklin Osgood, U.S.[3]	LIVONIA (1), James Ashbury, England
	SAPPHO (2), William P. Douglas, U.S.	
1876	MADELEINE (2), John S. Dickerson, U.S.	COUNTESS OF DUFFERIN, Chas. Gifford, Canada
1881	MISCHIEF (2), J. R. Busk, U.S.	ATALANTA, Alexander Cuthbert, Canada
1885	PURITAN (2), J. M. Forbes-Gen. Charles Paine, U.S.	GENESTA, Sir Richard Sutton, England
1886	MAYFLOWER (2), Gen. Charles Paine, U.S.	GALATEA, Lt. William Henn, England
1887	VOLUNTEER (2), Gen. Charles Paine, U.S.	THISTLE, James Bell et al, Scotland
1893	VIGILANT (3), C. Oliver Iselin et al., U.S.	VALKYRIE II, Lord Dunraven, England
1895	DEFENDER (3), C. O. Iselin-W. K. Vanderbilt-E. D. Morgan, U.S.	VALKYRIE III, Lord Dunraven-Lord Lonsdale-Lord Wolverton, England
1899	COLUMBIA (3), J. P. Morgan-C. O. Iselin, U.S.	SHAMROCK I, Sir Thomas Lipton, Ireland
1901	COLUMBIA (3), Edwin D. Morgan, U.S.	SHAMROCK II, Sir Thomas Lipton, Ireland
1903	RELIANCE (3), Cornelius Vanderbilt et al., U.S.	SHAMROCK III, Sir Thomas Lipton, Ireland
1920	RESOLUTE (3), Henry Walters et al., U.S.	SHAMROCK IV (2), Sir Thomas Lipton, Ireland
1930	ENTERPRISE (4), Harold S. Vanderbilt et al., U.S.	SHAMROCK V, Sir Thomas Lipton, Ireland
1934	RAINBOW (4), Harold S. Vanderbilt, U.S.	ENDEAVOUR (2), T. O. M. Sopwith, England
1937	RANGER (4), Harold S. Vanderbilt, U.S.	ENDEAVOUR II, T. O. M. Sopwith, England
1958	COLUMBIA (4), Henry Sears et al., U.S.	SCEPTRE, Hugh Goodson et al., England
1962	WEATHERLY (4), Henry D. Mercer et al., U.S.	GRETEL (1), Sir Frank Packer et al., Australia
1964	CONSTELLATION (4), New York Y.C. Syndicate, U.S.	SOVEREIGN (0), J. Anthony Bowden, England
1967	INTREPID (4), New York Y.C. Syndicate, U.S.	DAME PATTIE (0), Sydney (Aust.) Syndicate
1970	INTREPID (4), New York Y.C. Syndicate, U.S.	GRETEL II (1), Sydney (Aust.) Syndicate
1974	COURAGEOUS (4), New York, N.Y. Syndicate, U.S.	SOUTHERN CROSS (0), Sydney (Aust.) Syndicate
1977	COURAGEOUS (4), New York, N.Y. Syndicate, U.S.	AUSTRALIA (0), Sun City (Aust.) Syndicate
1980	FREEDOM (4), New York, N.Y. Syndicate, U.S.	AUSTRALIA (1), Alan Bond et al, Australia

1. Fourteen British yachts started against America; Aurora finished second. 2. Cambria sailed against 23 U.S. yachts and finished tenth. 3. Columbia was disabled in the third race, after winning the first two; Sappho substituted and won the fourth and fifth.

SOUTHERN OCEAN RACING CONFERENCE—1981 OVERALL STANDING

Boat Skipper	Class Position	Pts
1—Intuition (Pat Malloy)	1-C	1,804.0
2—Locura (deGuardiola and Soverel)	2-C	1,802.0
3—Acadia (Burt Keenan)	1-D	1,795.0
4—Aries (Michael Swerdlow)	3-C	1,791.5
5—Stars & Stripes (Bill Martin)	2-D	1,784.0
6—Williwaw (Sinett and Conner)	1-B	1,783.5
7—Magic Flamenco (Guillermo Cryns)	4-C	1,761.0
8—Merrythought (Jack King)	3-B	1,754.5
9—High Roler (William Power)	7-C	1,738.5
10—Immigrant (Bill McAteer)	6-C	1,733.5
20—Celebration (Bruce and Pat Clark)	1-E	1,659.5
34—Running Tide (Al Van Metre)	1-A	1,586.0

BOBSLEDDING

WORLD CHAMPIONS—1981

Two-man—Bernhard Germeshausen and Hans Jurgen Gerhardt, East Germany		4:54.27
Four-man—Bernhard Germeshausen, Henry Gerlach, Martin Truebner, Hans Jurgen Gerhardt, East Germany		4:50.90

VOLLEYBALL

U.S. VOLLEYBALL ASSOCIATION CHAMPIONSHIPS

(Arlington, Tex., May 12–16, 1981)

National Champions

Men—Nautilus/Nike, Long Beach, Calif.; runnerup: Chuck's Steak House National, Los Angeles.

Women—Utah State, Logan Utah; runnerup: Palo Alto YMCA, Palo Alto, Calif.

Senior men—Legends Restaurant, Long Beach, Calif.; runnerup: Outrigger Canoe Club, Honolulu.

Senior women—South Bay Spoilers, Hermosa Beach, Calif.; runnerup: Mavericks, Los Angeles.

Golden Masters—Kansas City Masters, Kansas City, Mo.; runnerup: Ringwood VBC, Ringwood, N.J.

NATIONAL COLLEGIATE ATHLETIC ASSOCIATION CHAMPIONSHIPS

(Santa Barbara, Calif., May 8–9, 1981)

Final—U.C.L.A. defeated Southern California
Third place—Penn State defeated Ohio State

A.I.A.W. CHAMPIONSHIPS—1981

Division I—Southern California
Division II—California State–Northridge
Division III—California State–Sacramento

AUTO RACING

INDIANAPOLIS 500

Year	Winner	Car	Time	mph	Second place
1911	Ray Harroun	Marmon	6:42:08	74.59	Ralph Mulford
1912	Joe Dawson	National	6:21:06	78.72	Teddy Tetzloff
1913	Jules Goux	Peugeot	6:35:05	75.93	Spencer Wishart
1914	René Thomas	Delage	6:03:45	82.47	Arthur Duray
1915	Ralph DePalma	Mercedes	5:33:55.51	89.84	Dario Resta
1916[1]	Dario Resta	Peugeot	3:34:17	84.00	Wilbur D'Alene
1919	Howard Wilcox	Peugeot	5:40:42.87	88.05	Eddie Hearne
1920	Gaston Chevrolet	Monroe	5:38:32	88.62	René Thomas
1921	Tommy Milton	Frontenac	5:34:44.65	89.62	Roscoe Sarles
1922	Jimmy Murphy	Murphy Special	5:17:30.79	94.48	Harry Hartz
1923	Tommy Milton	H. C. S. Special	5:29:50.17	90.95	Harry Hartz
1924	L. L. Corum—Joe Boyer	Dusenberg Special	5:05:23.51	98.23	Earl Cooper
1925	Peter DePaolo	Dusenberg Special	4:56:39.45	101.13	Dave Lewis
1926[2]	Frank Lockhart	Miller Special	4:10:14.95	95.904	Harry Hartz
1927	George Souders	Dusenberg Special	5:07:33.08	97.54	Earl DeVore
1928	Louis Meyer	Miller Special	5:01:33.75	99.48	Lou Moore
1929	Ray Keech	Simplex Special	5:07:25.42	97.58	Louis Meyer
1930	Billy Arnold	Miller–Hartz Special	4:58:39.72	100.448	Shorty Cantlon
1931	Louis Schneider	Bowes Special	5:10:27.93	96.629	Fred Frame
1932	Fred Frame	Miller–Hartz Special	4:48:03.79	104.144	Howard Wilcox
1933	Louis Meyer	Tydol Special	4:48:00.75	104.162	Wilbur Shaw
1934	Bill Cummings	Boyle Products Special	4:46:05.20	104.863	Mauri Rose
1935	Kelly Petillo	Gilmore Special	4:42:22.71	106.240	Wilbur Shaw
1936	Louis Meyer	Ring Free Special	4:35:03.39	109.069	Ted Horn
1937	Wilbur Shaw	Shaw–Gilmore Special	4:24:07.80	113.580	Ralph Hepburn
1938	Floyd Roberts	Burd Piston Ring Special	4:15:58.40	117.200	Wilbur Shaw
1939	Wilbur Shaw	Boyle Special	4:20:47.39	115.035	Jimmy Snyder
1940	Wilbur Shaw	Boyle Special	4:22:31.17	114.277	Rex Mays
1941	Floyd Davis—Mauri Rose	Noc-Out Hose Clamp Special	4:20:36.24	115.117	Rex Mays
1946	George Robson	Thorne Engineering Special	4:21:26.71	114.820	Jimmy Jackson
1947	Mauri Rose	Blue Crown Special	4:17:52.17	116.338	Bill Holland
1948	Mauri Rose	Blue Crown Special	4:10:23.33	119.814	Bill Holland
1949	Bill Holland	Blue Crown Special	4:07:15.97	121.327	Johnnie Parsons
1950[3]	Johnnie Parsons	Wynn's Friction Proof Special	2:46:55.97	124.002	Bill Holland
1951	Lee Wallard	Belanger Special	3:57:38.05	126.244	Mike Nazaruk
1952	Troy Ruttman	Agajanian Special	3:52:41.88	128.922	Jim Rathmann
1953	Bill Vukovich	Fuel Injection Special	3:53:01.69	128.740	Art Cross
1954	Bill Vukovich	Fuel Injection Special	3:49:17.27	130.840	Jim Bryan
1955	Bob Sweikert	John Zink Special	3:53:59.13	128.209	Tony Bettenhausen
1956	Pat Flaherty	John Zink Special	3:53:28.84	128.490	Sam Hanks
1957	Sam Hanks	Belond Exhaust Special	3:41:14.25	135.601	Jim Rathmann
1958	Jimmy Bryan	Belond A–P Special	3:44:13.80	133.791	George Amick
1959	Rodger Ward	Leader Card 500 Roadster	3:40:49.20	135.857	Jim Rathmann
1960	Jim Rathmann	Ken–Paul Special	3:36:11.36	138.767	Rodger Ward
1961	A. J. Foyt	Bowes Special	3:35:37.49	139.130	Eddie Sachs
1962	Rodger Ward	Leader Card Special	3:33:50.33	140.293	Len Sutton
1963	Parnelli Jones	Agajanian Special	3:29:35.40	143.137	Jim Clark
1964	A. J. Foyt	Offenhauser Special	3:23:35.83	147.350	Rodger Ward
1965	Jim Clark	Lotus–Ford	3:19:05.34	150.686	Parnelli Jones
1966	Graham Hill	Lola–Ford	3:27:52.53	144.317	Jim Clark
1967[4]	A. J. Foyt	Coyote–Ford	3:18:24.22	151.207	Al Unser
1968	Bobby Unser	Eagle–Offenhauser	3:16:13.76	152.882	Dan Gurney
1969	Mario Andretti	STP Hawk–Ford	3:11:14.71	156.867	Dan Gurney
1970	Al Unser	P. J. Colt–Ford	3:12:37.04	155.749	Mark Donohue
1971	Al Unser	P. J. Colt–Ford	3:10:11.56	157.735	Peter Revson
1972	Mark Donohue	McLaren–Offenhauser	3:04:05.54	162.962	Al Unser
1973[5]	Gordon Johncock	Eagle–Offenhauser	2:05:26.59	159.036	Bill Vukovich
1974	Johnny Rutherford	McLaren–Offenhauser	3:09:10.06	158.589	Bobby Unser
1975[6]	Bobby Unser	Eagle–Offenhauser	2:54:55.08	149.213	Johnny Rutherford
1976[7]	Johnny Rutherford	McLaren–Offenhauser	1:42:52.48	148.725	A. J. Foyt
1977	A. J. Foyt	Coyote–Foyt	3:05:57.16	161.331	Tom Sneva
1978	Al Unser	Lola–Cosworth	3:05:54.99	161.363	Tom Sneva
1979	Rick Mears	Penske–Cosworth	3:08:27.97	158.899	A. J. Foyt
1980	Johnny Rutherford	Chaparral–Cosworth	3:29:59.56	142.862	Tom Sneva
1981[8]	Mario Andretti	Wildcat–Cosworth	3:35:41.78	139.029	Bobby Unser

1. 300 miles. 2. Race ended at 400 miles because of rain. 3. Race ended at 345 miles because of rain. 4. Race, postponed after 18 laps because of rain on May 30, was finished on May 31. 5. Race postponed May 28 and 29 was cut to 332.5 miles

because of rain, May 30. 6. Race ended at 435 miles because of rain. 7. Race ended at 255 miles because of rain. 8. Andretti was awarded the victory after Bobby Unser, whose car finished first, was penalized one lap and dropped from first place to second for passing other cars illegally under a yellow caution flag. Unser has appealed the decision which was still pending as this edition went to press.

U.S. AUTO CLUB
NATIONAL CHAMPIONS

1910	Ray Harroun	1925	Peter DePaolo	1946–48	Ted Horn	1963–64	A. J. Foyt
1911	Ralph Mulford	1926	Harry Hartz	1949	Johnnie Parsons	1965–66	Mario Andretti
1912	Ralph DePalma	1927	Peter DePaolo	1950	Henry Banks	1967	A. J. Foyt
1913	Earl Cooper	1928–29	Louis Meyer	1951	Tony Bettenhaus-	1968	Bobby Unser
1914	Ralph DePalma	1930	Billy Arnold		en	1969	Mario Andretti
1915	Earl Cooper	1931	Louis Schneider	1952	Chuck Stevenson	1970	Al Unser
1916	Dario Resta	1932	Bob Carey	1953	Sam Hanks	1971–72	Joe Leonard
1917	Earl Cooper	1933	Louis Meyer	1954	Jimmy Bryan	1973	Roger McCluskey
1918	Ralph Mulford	1934	Bill Cummings	1955	Bob Sweikert	1974	Bobby Unser
1919	Howard Wilcox	1935	Kelly Petillo	1956–57	Jimmy Bryan	1975	A. J. Foyt
1920	Gaston Chevrolet	1936	Mauri Rose	1958	Tony Bettenhaus-	1976	Gordon Johncock
1921	Tommy Milton	1937	Wilbur Shaw		en	1977–78	Tom Sneva
1922	James Murphy	1938	Floyd Roberts	1959	Rodger Ward	1979	A. J. Foyt
1923	Eddie Hearne	1939	Wilbur Shaw	1960–61	A. J. Foyt	1980	Johnny Rutherford
1924	James Murphy	1940–41	Rex Mays	1962	Rodger Ward		

NATIONAL ASSOCIATION FOR STOCK CAR AUTO RACING
(NASCAR) GRAND NATIONAL CHAMPIONS

1949	Red Byron	1955	Tim Flock	1964	Richard Petty	1971–72	Richard Petty
1950	Bill Rexford	1956–57	Buck Baker	1965	Ned Jarrett	1973	Benny Parsons
1951	Herb Thomas	1958–59	Lee Petty	1966	David Pearson	1974–75	Richard Petty
1952	Tim Flock	1960	Rex White	1967	Richard Petty	1976–78	Cale Yarborough
1953	Herb Thomas	1961	Ned Jarrett	1968–69	David Pearson	1979	Richard Petty
1954	Lee Petty	1962–63	Joe Weatherly	1970	Bobby Isaac	1980	Dale Earnhardt

WORLD GRAND PRIX DRIVER CHAMPIONS

1950	Giuseppe Farina, Italy, Alfa Romeo	1966	Jack Brabham, Australia, Brabham-Repco
1951	Juan Fangio, Argentina, Alfa Romeo	1967	Denis Hulme, New Zealand, Brabham-Repco
1952	Alberto Ascari, Italy, Ferrari	1968	Graham Hill, England, Lotus-Ford
1953	Alberto Ascari, Italy, Ferrari	1969	Jackie Stewart, Scotland, Matra-Ford
1955	Juan Fangio, Argentina, Maserati, Mercedes-Benz	1970	Jochen Rindt, Austria, Lotus-Ford
1955	Juan Fangio, Argentina, Mercedes-Benz	1971	Jackie Stewart, Scotland, Tyrrell-Ford
1956	Juan Fangio, Argentina, Lancia-Ferrari	1972	Emerson Fittipaldi, Brazil, Lotus-Ford
1957	Juan Fangio, Argentina, Maserati	1973	Jackie Stewart, Scotland, Tyrrell-Ford
1958	Mike Hawthorn, England, Ferrari	1974	Emerson Fittipaldi, Brazil, McLaren-Ford
1959	Jack Brabham, Australia, Cooper	1975	Niki Lauda, Austria, Ferrari
1960	Jack Brabham, Australia, Cooper	1976	James Hunt, Britain, McLaren-Ford
1961	Phil Hill, United States, Ferrari	1977	Niki Lauda, Austria, Ferrari
1962	Graham Hill, England, BRM	1978	Mario Andretti, Nazareth, Pa., Lotus
1963	Jim Clark, Scotland, Lotus-Ford	1979	Jody Scheckter, South Africa
1964	John Surtees, England, Ferrari	1980	Alan Jones, Australia
1965	Jim Clark, Scotland, Lotus-Ford		

GRAND PRIX—1981

(Through Aug. 2, 1981)

Formula One Competition

United States West (Long Beach, Calif., March 15)—Alan Jones, Australia; driving a Saudi–Williams; 1 hour, 50 minutes, 41.33 seconds; 87.6 miles per hour

Brazil (Rio de Janiero, March 29)—Carlos Reutemann, Argentina; Saudi–Williams; 2:23.66; 96.592 mph

Argentina (Buenos Aires, April 12)—Nelson Piquet, Brazil; Brabham; 1:34:32.74; 124.665 mph

San Marino (Imola, Italy, May 3)—Nelson Piquet, Brazil; Brabham; 1:51.23.97; 101.202 mph

Belgium (Zolder, Belgium, May 17)—Carlos Reutemann, Saudi–Williams; 1:16:31.61; 112.123 mph

Monaco (Monte Carlo, Monaco, May 31)—Gilles Villeneuve, France; Ferrari; 1:54.23.36; 82.021 mph

Spain (Jarama, June 21)—Gilles Villeneuve, France; Ferrari; 1:46:35.01; 92.682 mph

France (Dijon, France, July 5)—Alain Prost, France; Renault–Turbo; 1:35:48.13; 118.304 mph

Britain (Silverstone, England, July 18)—John Watson, Northern Ireland; McLaren; 1:26:54.80; 137.640 mph

Germany (Hockenheim, West Germany, Aug. 2)—Nelson Piquet, Brazil; Brabham; 1:25:55.60; 132.450 mph

U.S. AUTO CLUB

1981 Triple Crown Races

Indianapolis 500 (Indianapolis Motor Speedway, May 25, 500 miles)—1. Mario Andretti, Nazareth, Pa.; Wildcat-Cosworth; 200 laps; 3 hours 35 minutes 41.78 seconds; average speed: 139.029 mph; first-place prize: $262,424. 2.* Bobby Unser, Albuquerque, N.M.; Penske–Cosworth; 199 laps; $168,674. 3. Vern Schuppan, Australia; McLaren–Cosworth; 199 laps; $87,974. 4. Kevin Cogan, Redondo Beach, Calif.; Phoenix–Cosworth; 197 laps; $59,024. 5. Geoff Brabham, San Clemente, Calif.; Penske–Cosworth; 197 laps; $55,384.

Pocono 500 (Pocono International Raceway, Long Pond, Pa., June 21, 500 miles)—1. A.J. Foyt, Houston, Tex.; March–Cosworth; 2:13:23.16; 137.196 mph; 122 laps; $73,675. 2. Jack Brabham, Australia, Penske–Cosworth; 122 laps. 3. Tom Bigelow, Whitewater, Wis.; Penske–Chevrolet; 122 laps. 4. George Snider, Coyote–Cosworth; 121 laps; 5. Harry MacDonald, Lola–Cosworth; 120 laps.

* Unser was penalized one lap and dropped from first to second place for passing other cars illegally under yellow caution flag. He has appealed the decision.

WINSTON CUP GRAND NATIONAL LEADERS

(Through July 31, 1981)

	Pts
Bobby Allison	2,864
Darrell Waltrip	2,760
Harry Gant	2,612
Ricky Rudd	2,570
Dale Earnhardt	2,526
Richard Petty	2,519
Jody Ridley	2,424
Terry Labonte	2,403
Benny Parsons	2,293
Buddy Arrington	2,133

FINAL 1980 WINSTON CUP POINT STANDING

Dale Earnhardt	4,661
Cale Yarborough	4,642
Benny Parsons	4,278
Richard Petty	4,255
Darrell Waltrip	4,239
Bobby Allison	4,019
Jody Ridley	3,972
Terry Labonte	3,766
Dave Marcis	3,745
Richard Childress	3,742

NATIONAL ASSOCIATION FOR STOCK CAR AUTO RACING (NASCAR)—1981

Winston Western 500 (Riverside, Calif., Jan. 11, 311.78 miles)—Bobby Allison, Hueytown, Ala.; Chevrolet, 3 hours, 16 minutes, 18 seconds; average speed: 95.263 mph; total purse: $202,155; winner's purse: $24,600.

Daytona 500 (Daytona Beach, Fla., Feb. 15, 500 miles)—Richard Petty, Randleman, N.C., Buick; 2:56:50; 169.651 mph; $783,710; $90,575.

Richmond 400 (Richmond, Va., Feb. 22, 216.8 miles)—Darrell Waltrip, Franklin, Tenn., Buick; 2:49:53; 76.570 mph; $140,085; $18,800.

Carolina 500 (Rockingham, N.C., March 1, 500 miles)—Darrell Waltrip, Buick; 4:21:59; 114.594 mph; $192,935; $21,655.

Coca-Cola 500 (Atlanta, Ga., March 15, 500 miles)—Cale Yarborough, Timmonsville, S.C., Buick; 3:44:10; 133.619 mph; $271,110; $28,950.

Valleydale 500 (Bristol, Tenn., March 29, 266.5 miles)—Darrell Waltrip, Buick; 2:58:36; 89.530 mph; $149,835; $22,450.

Northwestern Bank 400 (North Wilkesboro, N.C., April 5, 250 miles)—Richard Petty, Buick; 2:55:41; 85.381 mph; $142,200; $18,850.

CRC Chemicals Rebel 500 (Darlington, S.C., April 12, 500 miles)—Morgan Shepherd, Conover, N.C., Pontiac; 3:30:10; 75.019 mph; $169,385; $24,525.

Winston 500 (Talladega, Ala., May 3, 500 miles)—Bobby Allison, Buick; 3:20:52; 149.376 mph; $346,600; $41,500.

Melling Tool 420 (Nashville, Tenn., May 9, 250 miles)—Benny Parsons, Ellerbe, N.C., Ford; 2:47:02; 89.756 mph; $124,485; $15,950.

Mason–Dixon 500 (Dover, Del., May 17, 500 miles)—Jody Ridley, Chatsworth, Ga., Ford; 4:17:18; 116.595 mph; $187,410; $22,560.

World 600 (Charlotte, N.C., May 24, 600 miles)—Bobby Allison, Buick; 4:38:22; 129.326 mph; $412,035; $60,200.

Budweiser NASCAR 400 (College Station, Tex., June 7, 400 miles)—Benny Parsons, Ford; 3:01:10; 132.475 mph; $212,310; $22,750.

Hodgdon 400 (Riverside, Calif., June 14, 248.9 miles)—Darrell Waltrip, Buick; 2:39:30; 93.597 mph; $180,685; $23,650.

Gabriel 400 (Brooklyn, Mich., June 21, 400 miles)—Bobby Allison, Buick; 3:03:47; 130.589 mph; $214,140; $24,075.

Firecracker 400 (Daytona Beach, Fla., July 4, 400 miles)—Cale Yarborough, Buick; 2:48:32; 142.588 mph; $24,625.

Mountain Dew 500 (Pocona, Pa., July 26, 500 miles)—Darrell Waltrip, Buick; 4:11:52; 119.111 mph; $207,385; $23,640.

LEADING NASCAR MONEY-WINNERS

(Through July 31, 1981)

Bobby Allison	$381,300
Darrell Waltrip	281,175
Richard Petty	269,680
Dale Earnhardt	247,110
Ricky Rudd	236,925
Benny Parsons	$183,370
Terry Labonte	161,865
Jody Ridley	149,440
Harry Gant	146,940
Cale Yarborough	124,660

FINAL 1980 NASCAR LEADING MONEY-WINNERS

Dale Earnhardt	$588,926
Cale Yarborough	537,358
Benny Parsons	385,140
Darrell Waltrip	382,138
Richard Petty	374,092
Bobby Allison	$356,050
Buddy Baker	264,200
Terry Labonte	215,889
Neil Bonnett	210,547
Jody Ridley	196,617

OTHER 1981 CHAMPIONSHIP CAR RACES

Norton 500 (Norton, Mich., July 25, 500 miles, CART)—Pancho Carter, Brownsburg, Ind.; Penske–Cosworth; 3 hours, 45 minutes, 45 seconds; 132,890 mph; $94,355

Kraco Twin 125's (Atlanta, Ga., June 28, 126.326 miles, CART)—First race: Rick Mears, Bakersfield, Calif.; Penske–Cosworth; 51:29; 150.139 mph; $15,052. Second race: Rick Mears, 45:20; 167.073; $15,052

Rex Mays 150 (Milwaukee, June 7, 150 miles, CART)—Mike Mosley, Fallbrook, Calif.; Chevrolet; 1:19:3.55; 113.838 mph; $16,050

Kraco Phoenix 150 (Phoeniz, Ariz., March 22, 150 miles, CART)—Johnny Rutherford, Fort Worth, Tex.; Chaparral–Cosworth; 1:17:08; 116.681 mph; $18,336

COURT TENNIS

UNITED STATES CHAMPIONS—1980

Men's open—Chris Ronaldson, England
Men's amateur—Gene Scott, New York
Men's seniors—William Vogt, Philadelphia
College—George de Bell, Harvard

FENCING

AMATEUR FENCERS LEAGUE OF AMERICA
1981 UNITED STATES CHAMPIONS
(Fort Worth, Tex., 1981)

Men's foil—Mark Smith, Atlanta Fencers Club
Men's epee—Lee Shelley, Salle Orsi, Rutherford, N.J.
Men's saber—Peter Westwood, New York Fencers Club, New York City
Women's foil—Jana Angelakis, Tanner City Fencing Club, Peabody, Mass.
Women's epee—Susan Badders, Salle Auriol, Portland, Ore.
Men's foil team—New York Fencers Club
Men's saber team—New York Fencers Club
Men's epee team—United States Modern Pentathlon, Fort Sam Houston, Tex.
Women's foil team—Itinerant Fencing and Chowder Society, Fort Worth, Tex.
Men's under-19 foil—Nestor Rosario, Challenge II, New York City
Men's under-19 epee—Bentley Storm, District of Columbia Fencers Club, Washington, D.C.
Men's under-10 saber—Michael Loftin, Salle Tanya, Freeport, N.Y.
Women's under-19 foil—Jana Angelakis

WORLD CHAMPIONSHIPS
(Claremont-Ferrand, France, 1981)

Men's foil—Vladimir Smironov, Soviet Union
Men's epee—Z. Szekely, Hungary
Men's saber—W. Wodke, Poland
Women's foil—Cornelia Haenisch, West Germany
Men's foil team—Soviet Union
Men's epee team—Soviet Union
Men's saber team—Hungary
Women's foil team—Soviet Union

INTERCOLLEGIATE CHAMPIONSHIPS
National Collegiate Athletic Association
(Kenosha, Wis., Feb. 19–21, 1981)

Foil—Ernest Simon, Wayne State
Epee—Gil Pezza, Wayne State
Saber—Paul Friedberg, Pennsylvania
Team—Pennsylvania

TABLE TENNIS

U.S. OPEN CHAMPIONSHIPS—1981
(Princeton, N.J., June 17–21, 1981)

Men's singles—Xie Saike, China
Women's singles—Tong Ling, China
Men's doubles—Si Hung Yoo and Kim Wan, South Korea
Women's doubles—Nam Sook Hwang and Hae Sook An, South Korea
Men's team—China
Women's team—China

WORLD CHAMPIONSHIPS
(Novi Sad, Yugoslavia, April 14–26, 1981)

Men's singles—Guo Yuehua, China
Women's singles—Tong Ling, China
Men's doubles—Li Zhenshi and Cai Zhenhua, China
Women's doubles—Zhang Deying and Cao Yanhua, China
Mixed doubles—Xie Saike and Huang Junqun, China
Men's team—China
Women's team—China

PLATFORM TENNIS

UNITED STATES CHAMPIONS—1981
AMERICAN PLATFORM TENNIS ASSOCIATION
(Montclair [N.J.] Golf Club, March 29, 1981)

Men's doubles—Steve Baird, Ryetown, N.Y., and Rich Maier, Allendale, N.J., defeated Greg Brents, White Plains, N.Y., and Greg Moore, Westfield, N.J., 7–6, 6–2, 0–6, 7–6
Women's doubles—Hilary Hilton, Glen Ellyn, N.Y., and Yvonne Hockenburg, Kalamazoo, Mich., defeated Robin Fulton, Norwalk, Conn., and Linda Wolf, New Canaan, Conn., 6–4, 7–5
Men's singles—Doug Russell, New York City, defeated Bob Kleinert, New Jersey, 1–6, 6–3, 6–3, in final

PADDLE TENNIS

Source: Murray Geller, Executive-Secretary, U.S. Paddle Tennis Association

NATIONAL OPEN CHAMPIONSHIPS—1981
(Santa Monica, Calif., Aug. 1–2, 1981)

Men's singles—Mark Rifenback, Los Angeles
Men's doubles—Jeff Fleitman, Brooklyn, N.Y., and Sol Hauptman, Los Angeles

WOMEN'S EASTERN CHAMPIONSHIPS—1981

Doubles—Sari Bleich and Dorothy Wasser, Brooklyn, N.Y.

ARCHERY

NATIONAL ARCHERY ASSOCIATION CHAMPIONSHIPS
(Oxford, Ohio, Aug. 4–7, 1981)

Men's Division

Pts	
Richard McKinney, Glendale, Ariz.	2,565
Darrell Pace, Cincinnati	2,538
Larry Smith, Shrewsbury, Pa.	2,495
Raymond Burk, Santa Ana, Calif.	2,475
Pete Grondin, Hamilton, Mich.	2,473

Women's Division

Debra Metzger, Lancaster, Pa.	2,576
Luann Ryon, Riverside, Calif.	2,510
Ruth Rowe, Gaithersburg, Md.	2,488
Cindy Vezzetti, Phoenix, Ariz.	2,477
Laura Cale, Orlando, Fla.	2,414

Other Champions

Intermediate boys—Johnny Kazak, Aurora, Ill.	2,481
Intermediate girls—Becky Liggett, Muncie, Ind.	2,344
Junior boys—Danny Stinnett, Mogadore, Ohio	2,458
Junior girls—Rhonda Liggett, Muncie, Ind.	2,306
Cadet boys—John Gardiner, Farmland, Ind.	2,366
Cadet girls—Katie Blum, Cincinnati	2,621

Crossbow

Men's Division—Ervin Myers, Dallastown, Pa.	3,415
Women's Division—Carol Pelosi, Greenbelt, Md.	3,152
King's Round—Alan Kaufhold, Smoketown, Pa.	
Queen's Round—LaRue Bruce, Natrona Heights, Pa.	

BOXING—AMATEUR

U.S. AMATEUR CHAMPIONSHIPS

U.S. Amateur Boxing Federation
(Concord, Calif., May 18–23, 1981)
106 lb—Jesse Benavides, Corpus Christi, Tex.
112 lb—Fred Perkins, U.S. Army
119 lb—Richard Savage, West Monroe, La.
125 lb—Guadalupe Suarez, Corpus Christi, Tex.
132 lb—Joe Manley, U.S. Army
139 lb—James Mitchell, U.S. Army
147 lb—Darryl Robinson, Houston, Tex.
156 lb—James Rayford, U.S. Navy
165 lb—Michael Grogan, Atlanta, Ga.
178 lb—Alex DeLucia, Portland, Ore.
Heavyweight—Mark Mahone, U.S. Navy
Superheavyweight (over 201 lb)—Tyrone Biggs, Philadelphia

NATIONAL FESTIVAL BOXING CHAMPIONS
(Syracuse, N.Y., July 23–29, 1981)
106 lb—Jesse Benavides, Corpus Christi, Tex.
112 lb—Fred Perkins, U.S. Army, Fort Bragg, N.C.
119 lb—Richard Savage, West Monroe, La.
125 lb—Benjamin Marquez, Denver, Colo.
132 lb—Vincent Pazienza, Cranston, R.I.
139 lb—Vincent Webb, University City, Mo.
147 lb—Mark Breland, Brooklyn, N.Y.
156 lb—Alfred Mayes, St. Louis, Mo.
165 lb—Randy Smith, Chicago
178 lb—Johnny Williams, Chicago
Heavyweight—Mark Mahone, U.S. Navy, Norfolk, Va.

SKEET SHOOTING

NATIONAL SKEET SHOOTING ASSOCIATION WORLD CHAMPIONSHIPS—1980
(Savannah, Ga., July 24–Aug. 1, 1980)

High Overall
Men—Al Magyar Jr., Taylor, Mich.	549
Women—Carla Brundage, San Antonio, Tex.	544
Senior—Jesse L. Vint, Tulsa, Okla.	541
Veteran—Barbee Ponder, Amite, La.	541
Junior—Bobby Wren, Punta Gorda, Fla.	544
Junior women—Vicky Cool, Louisville, Ky.	351
Collegiate—John Shima, San Antonio, Tex.	547

Individual Gun
12–gauge, men—Tito Killian, San Antonio, Tex.	250
12–gauge, women—Barbara Thomas, Brooklyn, N.Y.	250
20–gauge, men—Bruce Evans, Burnet, Tex.	100
20–gauge, women—Sandra McCurley, Mobile, Ala.	100
28–gauge, men—George Desatoff, Hacienda, Calif.	100
28–gauge, women—Ila Hill, Birmingham, Mich.	98
.410–gauge, men—Wayne Mayes, Cleveland, Tenn.	100
.410–gauge, women—Carla Brundage, San Antonio, Tex.	99

Champion of Champions
Men—Todd Bender, San Antonio, Tex.	100
Women—Sheri Confer, Warren, Mich.	98

DUCKPIN BOWLING

NATIONAL CHAMPIONSHIPS—1980
Men's singles—Jim Dion, Westport, Mass.	597
Women's singles—Brenda Wachtell, Hagerstown, Md.	500
Men's doubles—Doug Gosewisch—Kent Schwartz, Glen Burnie, Md.	989
Women's doubles—Dawn Healey—Bonnie Myers, Baltimore, Md.	875
Championship Team—Adams Five, Alexandria, Va.	2,089
Class A Teams—Norwich Duckpin, Norwich, Conn.	2,139
Class B Teams—Kelleher Realty, Waldorf, Md.	2,010
Class C Teams—4 Spares and A Strike, Bethesda, Md.	1,994
Class D Teams—Dean Construction, California, Md.	1,737

TRAPSHOOTING

1980 GRAND AMERICAN TOURNAMENT

Grand American Handicap
Men—William Hazlett, Sarven, Pa.
Women—Indika Morris, Wahpeton, S.D.
Junior—Todd Overstreet, St. Charles, Mo.
Veteran—Williard Koch, Upland, Neb.
Sub-Junior—Randy Wilhelm, Mt. Vernon, Ohio

All-Around
Men—Steve Carmichael, Raytown, Mo.
Women—Nyla Johnson, Chattaroy, Wash.
Junior—Stuart Welton, Meridian, Idaho

Overall
Men—Leo Harrison II, Hannibal, Mo.
Women—Nyla Johnson, Chattaroy, Wash.
Junior—Stuart Welton, Meridian, Idaho

Doubles
Men—Brian Robinson, Tahoka, Tex.
Women—Nyla Johnson, Chattaroy, Wash.
Junior—Stuart Welton, Meridian, Idaho

POLO

1980 CHAMPIONSHIPS
Gold Cup (18–22 goals)—Retama, San Antonio, Tex.
World Cup—Hallal of Nigeria
Cup of the Americas—Argentina
America Cup—Macondo, Colombia
Silver Cup—Retama
Delegate's Cup (8 goals)—Tennessee
North American Cup—Kingsville, Tex.
Men's college—York University, Toronto
Women's college—University of California—Davis

RUGBY—1980

United States—Old Blues, Berkeley, Calif.
Monterey Peninsula—James Bay, Vancouver, British Columbia
Boston 350—Dublin Wanderers
Test Match—Canada 16, United States 0

The Year's Top Trivia

Sanford Teller

Many Americans who are convinced that the nation is on the brink of economic collapse and social chaos have taken steps to prepare themselves for what they believe are the dark days ahead. They've stockpiled food, drinking water, gold, and ammunition.

Now there's welcome news for the dog lovers among them.

A Van Nuys, California, company introduced a line of dehydrated, high-protein dog foods, with a five-year shelf life. Each can of the canine gustatory delight has a picture of a dog wearing both a hungry look and a medieval helmet.

The name of the product is, not surprisingly, *Sir Vival.*

●

Leave it to American advertising genius to come up with a brilliant way to capitalize on the energy shortage.

The *Los Angeles Times* ran an ad for La Paz margarita mix, with an illustration of the product accompanied by the following copy: "SAVE GAS! Stay Home and Drink."

●

Whatever happened to Monopoly, electric trains, and doll houses?

As personal computers showed an enormous increase in popularity, manufacturers of software kept pace by turning out a huge assortment of home computer games. One of the most ingenious was *Castle Wolfenstein.* This novel adventure/fantasy game enables the player to act the role of an Allied soldier in Europe during World War II. As part of the game, the player is captured by Nazi soldiers and must come up with a way of both finding the enemy's secret plans and escaping from the castle's prison. To heighten the sense of reality, the game features such sound effects as guns firing and Nazis shouting—in German.

●

The owner of a Tokyo pet-grooming parlor, Shigenori Nasuda, launched a new service to help dogs, cats, raccoons, rabbits, and birds cope with the pressures of being a pet in the big city. He said that the stresses they were subjected to by living in small apartments often resulted in such problems as nervous depression, constant yapping, and obesity.

So, in order to help them unwind, relax, and feel more content, he's offering yoga classes for pets.

●

If the former President of France, Valéry Giscard d'Estaing, seemed a bit puzzled during the ceremonies marking the opening of the Gerald R. Ford Museum, in Grand Rapids, Michigan, he had reason to be.

Former President Ford had just told him how much he regretted never having visited France during his White House years. Evidently, Mr. Ford had forgotten that he had attended the 1975 summit conference of Western leaders in Rambouillet . . . France.

●

The Egg Board conducted a survey among the nation's restaurants to determine just how popular various egg dishes have become: 50% of the establishments featured scrambled eggs on their menus, while 43% had fried eggs, 39% had poached or boiled eggs, and 38% had omelets. But only 9% offered Eggs Benedict. The organization also revealed that the average American eats 283 eggs per year.

An Egg Board executive reported that she had visited a Seattle restaurant which served a $9 omelet. It would be difficult to take issue with her observation that, "When eggs cost six to eight cents each, you know they're making a profit."

●

On the feline front, the following ad appeared in a New York City newspaper: "After fire on Sat. night, August 22, fireman handed my cat to a Spanish lady who was watching at 248 E. 23rd Street. $50 reward for the return of my cat."

●

It's quite clear that the Central Intelligence Agency won't tolerate agents who violate the code of conduct as set forth by Emily Post and Amy Vanderbilt.

Francis Edward Terpil, a former CIA operative, was accused of being an instructor at a school for terrorists in Libya. The CIA did acknowledge that he had been one of its agents. But the agency was quick to point out that he was dismissed in 1971 . . . for "boasting and boorishness."

●

Some airline flight attendants are using humor to get passengers to pay attention to those familar announcements that many jaded travelers often fail to heed.

As her aircraft taxis to the terminal, Sandy Yaley, a United Airlines attendant, frequently uses the plane's P.A. system to inform passengers: "Keep your seats until the seatbelt sign has been turned off by the captain when we are parked at the gate. Anyone who gets up before the seatbelt sign goes off will not only be laughed at, but we will ask you to remain on board and help us clean this airplane.

"Once the sign does go off and you are free to get up, please check around you and make sure that you have all of your carry-on baggage, your coats, your hats and, especially, all of your children. If you should happen to forget anything, remember United does hold an auction at the end of each month and you will be able to buy it back at a very low price. Thank you."

●

Before his business trip to Moscow, a man identified as the "chief of one of Britain's biggest industrial concerns," said that a top English intelligence expert had warned him that the Russians might attempt to blackmail him by photographing him in a compromising situation with a gorgeous Soviet agent.

When he finished his trip and returned to London, he reported: "It was exactly as you predicted. At 11 p.m., there was a knock at my hotel door and there standing in the doorway was a blonde so luscious that I couldn't resist her. I told her to undress in the sitting room, while I undressed in the bedroom.

"When she came to join me, I had a pillow slip over my head with a couple of eye holes cut in it. I never took it off. So it doesn't matter what the hell they photographed."

COMPREHENSIVE INDEX

A

Abacus, 342
Abatement, 640
Abbreviations:
  Academic degrees, 749
  Postal, 628
  Rules for, 492
  Weights and measures, 345–46
Abidjan, Ivory Coast, 200
Abortions, 774
Absolute zero, 345, 349, 351
Abu Dhabi, United Arab Emirates, 262
Academic degrees. See Degrees
Academy Awards, 504–07
Academy of Natural Sciences of Philadelphia, 798
Acadia, 287
Acadia National Park, 636
Accidents:
  Aircraft accidents, 438, 643–45
  Deaths from, 641–45, 776–77
  Fires and explosions, 642–43
  Motor vehicle, 776–77
  Railroad accidents, 645, 776, 777
  Rates, 776–77
  Shipwrecks, 643
  See also Disasters
Accra, Ghana, 181
Aconcagua Peak, 134, 460
Acre, 346, 347, 348
Acropolis, 83
ACTION, 615
Actium, Battle of, 85
Actors, actresses:
  Awards for, 504–07
  Famous, 521–43
Adams, John, 570
  See also Headline History; Presidents (U.S.)
Adams, John Quincy, 571
  See also Headline History; Presidents (U.S.)
Adams National Historic Site, 307, 638
Adaptation, 640
Adding machine, 342
Addis Ababa, Ethiopia, 168, 169
Address, forms of, 492–94
Aden, Yemen, 276
Adenauer, Konrad, 180, 521
Administration, Office of, 613
Admirals (U.S.), 394, 401
  First admiral, 544
Adrenaline, isolation of, 342
Adulterants, 640
Advent (season), 387, 389
Advertising, 56, 57
  Expenditures, 56
  Leading agencies, 57
Aegean Islands, 182
Aerial combat, first, 438
Aerial photographers, first, 438
Afars and Issas. See Djibouti
Afghanistan, 131, 249
  See also Countries
AFL-CIO, 47–48, 101
Africa, 130, 457
  Explorations and discoveries, 453
  Map, 482–83
  Population, 112
  Portuguese territory, 235
  Southernmost point, 243
  See also Countries
African M. E. Church, 414
Agate (measure), 348
Age:
  Arrests by, 782, 783

At first marriage, 768
  Death rates by, 778, 780–81
  Life expectancy by, 111, 779–81
  Marriage prospects, 768
  Mothers of illegitimate children, 774
  Population by, 689, 750–51, 754
  School enrollment by, 706
Age limits:
  Driving licenses, 786
  Marriage licenses, 767
  Purchase of distilled spirits, 788
  School attendance, 707
Agencies, U.N., 327–28
Agencies (U.S.), 613–18
Aggtelek Cavern, 467
Agincourt, Battle of, 87
Aging. See Growing Older
Agnew, Spiro T., 584, 592, 593
  Resignation, 104
Agreements, international, 126–30
Agriculture:
  Animals on farms, 58
  Economic statistics, 41, 58–59, 562–67
  Education, 709
  Employment, 48, 49, 52
  Farm construction, 42
  Farm laborers, 48, 49, 52, 562–65
  Farm production, 562–65
  Farm property, 562–65
  Income, 59
  Production by state, 58
  See also Food
Agriculture, U.S. Dept. of, 614
  Secretaries of, 599–601
Air (atmosphere), 358, 363
Air brake, 342
Air charter flights, 298–99
Air conditioning, 342
Aircraft industries, 445
Air distances, cities, 312–15
Air Force, U.S., 391, 394, 401
  Aircraft types, 444
  See also Armed Forces
Air Force, U.S. Department of:
  Secretary of, 614
Air Force Academy, U.S., 392, 649
Airlines:
  Accident death rate, 776
  Charter flights, 298–99
  First scheduled passenger service, 439
  Freight, 63
  Passenger traffic, 64, 442
  Pilots, 443
  Transport planes, 443
  See also Travel
Airmail, 625
  Firsts, 439
  International, 627
  Priority mail, 625
  Stamps for, 626
Airplanes:
  Accident death rate, 776
  Accidents, 643–45
  Exports and imports, 70
  Invention, 342
  Military, 444
  Passenger traffic, 64, 442
  Pilots, 443
  Records, 441–42
  Types, 443–44
Air pollution, 629, 632
  Automobile emissions, 632
Airports, world's busiest, 442
Air transport company, first, 438
Akkadian civilization, 83, 84
Alabama, 646
  See also States of U.S.
Alabama River, 469

Alamo, Battle of the, 93, 658
Aland Islands, 170
Alaska, 646–47
  Discovered, 454, 646
  Maps, 473, 474
  Mountain peaks, 469
  National parks, 636–37
  Oil, 105, 647
  Volcanoes, 455
  See also States of U.S.
Albania, 132
  See also Countries
Alberta, Canada, 282, 283, 284, 286
Albuquerque, New Mexico, 677
Alcohol. See Liquor
Aldrin, Edwin E., Jr., 103, 374–75
Aleutian Islands, 91, 455, 646
  Map, 474
Alexander the Great, 84, 194, 453
  Map of empire, 487
Alexandria, Egypt, 165
Alexandria, Pharos of, 316
Alfred the Great, 86, 264
Algeria, 132–33
  Rebellion, 132–33, 173
  See also Countries
Alhambra, 317
Ali, Muhammad (Cassius Clay), 864, 871
Aliens, in U.S., 765
Allende, Salvador, 104, 150
Alliance for Progress, 102, 127
All Saints' Day, 386
All-Star Game, Baseball, 910
Alpha Centauri, 355
Alps, 171, 199, 254
  Tunnels under, 320
Altamaha-Ocmulgee River, 469
Altamira Cave, 467
Altiplano, 142
Altitude records, aircraft, 441–42
Altitudes. See Elevations
Aluminum:
  As element, 339
  Manufacture, electrolytic, 183
Amazon River, 143, 155, 454, 463
Amendments to Constitution, 553–57
  Civil rights, 553–54
  Right to bear arms, 553
  Search and seizure, 553
American Academy and Institute of Arts and Letters, 619, 796
American Federation of Labor, 101
American folklore, 545
American History. See United States History
American Independent Party, 591, 592, 593
American Indian, Museum of, 796
American Indians. See Indians
American League. See Baseball; Football
American Museum of Atomic Energy, 798
American Museum of Natural History, 796
American Red Cross, 623
American Revolution. See Revolutionary War
American Samoa, 673
American's Creed, The, 611
America's Cup, 924
Amish. See Mennonites
Amman, Jordan, 203
Ampere, 345, 348
Amphibians, endangered, 631
Amsterdam, Netherlands, 221
Amsterdam-Rhine Canal, 322
Amu Darya River, 464
Amur River, 151, 463

Amusement. *See* Recreation
Ancient empires, 84
  Map, 487
Ancient history, events, 83–85
Andaman Islands, 189
Andaman Sea, 461
Anderson, John B., 107, 595
Andes, 134, 150, 155, 231, 460–61
Andorra, 133
Anesthetic, first use of, 342
Angel Falls, 464
Angkor Wat, 317
Angola, 133–34, 235
Angstrom, 346, 348
Anguilla, 270–71
Animals:
  Classification, 342
  Endangered species, 630–31
  Farm, 58, 59, 565–67
  Gestation, incubation, longevity, 634
  Group terminology, 634
  Names of, 633
  Speed of, 633
  State animals, 646–72
Ankara, Turkey, 260
Annapolis, Md., 655, 656
  Naval Academy, 391–92, 656
Anniversaries, wedding, 445
Antananarivo, Madagascar, 212
Antarctica, 454, 457
  Australian Antarctic Territory, 136
  British Antarctic Territory, 268
  Exploration, 98, 454
  Falkland Islands, 269
  First flight over, 439
  French Antarctica, 176
  Icecap, 633
  Ross Dependency, 223
Antarctic Circle, 385, 454
Anthem, National, 559
Antibiotics, 342
Anti-Comintern Treaty, 99, 179, 202
Antietam, Battle of, 94
Antigua, 270
Antimony (element), 339
Antiparos Cavern, 467
Antipodes Islands, 223
Antiseptic, 342
Antitoxin, diphtheria, 342
Antoinette Perry Awards, 516
Antwerp, Belgium, 139
Anzio beachhead, 99
Apalachicola-Chattahoochee River, 469
Apartheid, 243–45
Apennine Mountains, 199
Apennine Tunnel, 320
Aphelion, 354, 365, 384–85
Apia, Western Samoa, 276
Apollo flights, 370, 374–76
Apollo/Soyuz Test Project, 104, 376
Apothecaries fluid measure, 346
Apothecaries weight, 346
Appalachian Trail, 639
Appeals, U.S. Court of, 602
Appendicitis, 776
Appleseed, Johnny, 545
Appomattox surrender, 94
Aqaba, Gulf of, 166, 197
Arabia, explored, 453
  See specific Arab countries for other data
Arabian Desert, 466
Arab-Israeli wars, 103, 104, 166–67
  Map, 480–81
  See also Egypt; Israel; Jordan; Lebanon
Arab League, 126
Arabs, 85, 86
Aral Lake, 462
Arbor Day, 388
Archery, 821, 901, 928
Architect of the Capitol, 618
Architecture. *See* Structures
Arctic Area:
  Exploration, 454

Islands, 465–66
First polar flight, 439
Icecap, 633
Arctic Circle, 385
Arctic Ocean, 461
Ardennes, 140
Area:
  Cities of U.S., 677–86
  Continents, 457
  Countries, 108–09, 131–281
  Deserts, 466
  Formulas for, 352
  Islands, 465–66
  Lakes, 462–63, 633
  Measure of, 345–47
  Oceans, seas, 461
  States of U.S., 646–72
  U.S. and territories, 750, 763
  U.S. growth, 750, 763
  World, 457
Argentina, 107, 134–35
  Volcanoes, 456
  See also Countries
Aristotle, 84
Arithmetic. *See* Mathematics
Arizona, 647
  See also States of U.S.
Arkansas, 647–48
  See also States of U.S.
Arkansas River, 454, 464, 469
Arlington National Cemetery, 569, 584
Armada, Spanish, 89, 250, 264
Armaments, 405
Armed Forces (U.S.), 390–406
  Airplanes, 444
  Allowances, 395, 396
  Construction, 42
  Defense expenditures, 398, 403
  History of, 390–91
  Insignia, 405
  Joint Chiefs of Staff, 614
  Military interventions, 399
  Officers, 394
  Pay, 394
  Ranks, 394, 401
  Service academies, 391–93
  Ships, 401
  Spending for, 60, 398, 403
  Strength, 390, 403
  Veterans' benefits, 396–97
  War casualties, 399–401
  Women 100, 397
  See also Defense; Selective Service; Veterans
Armenia, U.S.S.R., 246
Armenian Massacre, 98
Armenian Orthodox Churches, 296, 413
Armistice Day, 386, 388
Arms Control and Disarmament Agency, U.S., 617
Armstrong, Neil A., 103, 374–75
Army, U.S. Department of the, 390, 394, 401
  Expenditures, 60, 398, 403
  Secretary of, 614
  See also Armed Forces
Army-Navy games, 823
Arrests, 782–83
  See also Law enforcement; Crime
"Arsenal of the Nation," 649
Arson, arrests for, 782, 783
Art:
  Glossary and Movements, 790–91
  See individual artists listed in People section
Artemis, Temple of, 316
Arthur, Chester A., 575
  See also Headline History; Presidents (U.S.)
Articles of Confederation, 561
Art Institute of Chicago, 797
Art museums, 796–807
Art Ross Trophy, 847
Arts and Letters, American Academy

and Institute of, 619, 796
Arts and the Humanities, National Foundation on the, 616
Aruba, 222
Asama, Mount, 455
Asbestos, 640
Ascension Day, 386, 389
Ascension Island, 270
Ash Lawn, 307
Ash Wednesday, 385, 388, 389
Asia, 130, 455, 457
  Explorations and discoveries, 453
  Maps, 480–81, 484, 485, 486
  Population, 112
  See also Continents
Assassinations, attempts, 545
  See also Chronology
Assault, 782, 783, 784
Assemblies of God, 415
Assistance, public, 61–62, 698
Associations, 619–24
  Sports organizations, 855–56
Assyrian Empire, 83, 84, 194
Asteroids, 360, 377
Astronauts, 374–77
  See also Space Exploration
Astronomical signs, 363
Astronomical unit, 348, 354
Astronomy, 354–65
  Asteroids, 360, 377
  Atmosphere, 358, 363
  Auroras, 363
  Comets, 360–61
  Conjunctions, 364–65
  Constants, 354
  Constellations, 362–63
  Eclipses, 364
  Measures, 348–49, 354
  Meteors and meteorites, 361–62
  Moon, 356, 357, 364–65
  Phenomena (1982), 364–65
  Planets, 356–59
  Radio telescopes, 363
  Seasons, 358, 378, 384–85
  Stars, 355–57, 362–63,
  Sun, 356–57, 363, 364
  Telescopes, 363
  Terms, 354–55
  Universal time, 355
  Zodiac, 363
  See also Space Exploration
Asunción, Paraguay, 230
Aswan Dam, 166, 319, 323, 462
Atacama Desert, 150, 466
Athens, Greece, 182
  See also Cities (world)
Athletes. *See* Sports Personalities
Atlanta, Ga., 651, 677
  See also Cities (U.S.)
Atlantic Charter, 99
Atlantic Ocean, 461
  Hurricanes, 421, 426–27
  Islands, 465–66
  U.S. coastline, 472
  Volcanoes, 456
Atlas Mountains, 219
Atmosphere, 358, 363
  Water in, 633
Atom bomb, 99, 341
  Dropped on Japan, 99, 202, 341
Atomic Age, 341
Atomic energy, 341
  Legislation, 341
  Peaceful uses, 341
Atomic Energy, American Museum of, 798
Atomic Energy Act, U.S., 341
Atomic Energy Agency, International, 327
Atomic numbers, 339–40
Atomic theory, 342
Atomic weights, 339–40
Atonement, Day of, 386, 389
Attila the Hun, 85, 552
Attlee, Clement, 265, 266, 522

Attorneys General:
  State, 646–72
  United States, 597–601
Auckland Islands, 223
Augustus, Emperor, 85, 522
Auroras, 363
Austerlitz, Battle of, 92
Austin, Tex., 677
  See also Cities (U.S.)
Australasia. *See* Oceania
Australia, 135–36, 455
  Explored, 136, 454
  Islands of, 466
  Map, 485
  See also Continents; Countries
Australian Antarctic Territory, 136
Australian Desert, 136, 466
Austria, 136–37
  See also Countries
Authors:
  See Awards; People
Automobiles:
  Accident deaths, 776–77
  Drunken driving arrests, 782, 783
  Economic statistics, 65–67
  Exports and imports, 67, 70
  Industry, hours and wages, 53
  Inventions, 342
  Mileage, 334
  Pollutants emitted, 632
  Registrations, 65, 334
  Sales, 66–67
  Services, 45
  State laws, 786
  Theft statistics, 782–84
  U.S. production, 65–67
  See also Motor Vehicles
Auto racing, 925–27
Autumn (1982), 378
Avalanches, 641
Average, mathematical, 353
Aviation, 438–45
  Accident death rate, 776
  Accidents, 643–45
  Aircraft types, 443–44
  Airports, world's busiest, 442
  CAB, 615
  Firsts, 438–40
  Helicopter records, 445
  International Civil Aviation
    Organization, 327
  Inventions, 342–44
  National Air and Space Museum,
    797–98
  Pilots, 443
  Records, 441–42
  Traffic (passengers, freight), 63–64,
    442
  Women, 438, 440
  World records, 441–42
  See also Airlines; Airplanes
Avoirdupois weight, 346
Awards, 497–520
  Academy Awards, 504–07
  American Library Association, 518
  Antoinette Perry, 516
  Baseball Hall of Fame, 798, 911
  Bollingen (poetry), 520
  Broadcasting, 518
  Canadian, 297
  Cy Young, 912
  Emmy, 31
  Fermi, 516
  Fighter of Year, 871
  Hart Trophy, 846–47
  Heisman Trophy, 825
  Medal of Freedom, 519–20
  Most Valuable Player, baseball, 912
  Most Valuable Player, basketball,
    843
  Most Valuable Player, hockey,
    846–47
  Music, 503, 515–16, 732
  New York Drama Critics', 517–18
  Nobel Prizes, 497–502
  Peabody, 518

  Presidential Medal of Freedom,
    519–20
  Pulitzer Prizes, 508–16
  Rookie of the Year, baseball,
    912–13
  Sigma Delta Chi, 516
  Sullivan, 822, 894
  "Tony," 516
Axel Heiberg, 466
Axis Powers, 99
Azerbaijan, U.S.S.R., 246
Azores, 234
Azov, Sea of, 461
Aztecs, 87
Azuma, 455

B

Babylon, Hanging Gardens, 83, 316
Babylonian Empire, 83, 84, 194
Backgammon, 843
Bacteria, 336, 342
Badminton, 857
Baffin Bay, discovered, 454
Baffin Island, 465
Baghdad, Iraq, 194, 195
Baghdad Pact. *See* Central Treaty
    Organization
Bagnell Dam, 658
Bahá'í Faith, 415
Bahamas, 137–38
  See also Countries
Bahrain, 138
  See also Countries
Baikal, Lake, 462
Bakelite, 342, 343
Baker Island, 673
Bakke case, 105
Balance of payments, 67
Balaton, Lake, 187
Balearic Islands, 250
Bale (weight), 348
Balfour Declaration, 97, 197
Balkans, 278
Balkan Wars, 96
Balloons:
  Flights, 438, 439, 440
  Invention, 342
Ball-point pen, 342, 343
Baltic Sea, 461
Baltimore, Md., 656, 677
  See also Cities (U.S.)
Bamako, Mali, 215
Bangkok, Thailand, 257
  See also Cities (world)
Bangladesh, 138–39, 190, 228, 457
  See also Countries
Bangui, Central African Empire, 148
Banjul, Gambia, 176
Bank of America, 45, 648
Bank of North America, 544
Banks and banking:
  Firsts, 544
  Largest, 45, 648
Banks (island), 466
Baptist Churches, 412–13, 417–18
Barbados, 139
  See also Countries
Barker, Len, 913
Barometer, 342
Baseball, 902–23
  All-Star Game, 910
  Amateur, 922–23
  American League averages (1980),
    919
  Attendance records, 915, 916
  Barker's perfect game, 913
  Batting statistics, 905–08, 909,
    913–15, 917, 918, 919, 920,
    921
  Club standings (1980, 1981), 917,
    918
  Cy Young Award, 912
  Franchise shifts, additions, 916
  Hall of Fame, 798, 911

  Home run statistics, 905, 906, 907,
    914, 915, 917
  Individual all-time records, 914
  Larsen's perfect game, 916
  Little League World Series, 923
  Minor Leagues, 922
  Most Valuable Players, 912
  National League averages (1980),
    919
  No-hit and perfect games, 906, 913,
    916, 921
  Pennant winners, 908–09
  Pitching statistics, 902–05, 910,
    913–14, 917, 918, 919–20,
    921
  Records, 905–08, 909, 913–17
  Records (1980), 918–19
  Rookie of the Year, 912–13
  Rose's feats, 915
  Stadiums, 916
  Standard measurements, 856
  Strike, 1981, 902
  Williams' batting record, 909
  World Series (1903–80), 902–04
  World Series (1980), 920–21
  World Series records and standing,
    905
Baseball Hall of Fame, 798, 911
Basketball, 838–45
  College, 838–41
  History, 838
  Professional, 840, 841–45
  Standard measurements, 857
Bastille Day, 91
Basutoland. *See* Lesotho
Bataan surrender (1942), 99
Battlefields, National, 636, 638
Battle of Hastings, 86, 263
Battles. *See* specific battles
Bay of Pigs, 102, 158, 184
Beaumont-Port Arthur Canal, 322
Bechuanaland. *See* Botswana
Bedloe's Island, 309
Beef, food value, 80
Beer, age for purchase of, 788
Beethoven, Ludwig van, 91, 93
Begin, Menachem, 105, 196, 198–99
Beirut, Lebanon, 209–10
Belfast, Northern Ireland, 266
Belgian Congo. *See* Zaire
Belgium, 139–40
  See also Countries
Belgrade, Yugoslavia, 277
Belize, 140–41
  See also Countries
**Bell, Alexander Graham, 95, 344,
    522**
Belmont Stakes, 873–74
Benelux, 212
Benin, 141
  See also Countries
Bering Sea, 461
Bering Strait, 454
Berkeley Plantation, 307
Berlin, Congress of, 95
Berlin, East, 177, 181
Berlin, Germany, 179, 181
  Airlift (1948), 100, 180
  East Berlin uprising (1953), 101,
    177, 181
  Wall (1961), 102, 181
  World War II, 99
  See also Cities (world)
Berlin, Treaty of (1899), 673
Bermuda, 267–68
Bern, Switzerland, 254
Bessarabia, 236
Bessemer converter, 342
Bhutan, 141
  See also Countries
Biafra, 103, 225
Biathlon, 822, 874
Bible, 87, 89
  Books of the, 420
  Old Testament, 83, 84
Bicentennial, 104

Bicycles:
Deaths from collisions with motor vehicles, 777
Invention of, 342
See also Cycling
Bifocal lens, 342
Big Bend National Park, 636
Bikini Atoll, 101, 675
Biko, Steven, 105
Billiards, 870
Bill of Rights, 92, 553–54
Bills (Congressional):
How a bill becomes a law, 601
Procedure, 549, 601
Bills (money), 353
Billy the Kid, 545
Biodegradable, 640
Biographies:
Of U.S. Presidents, 570–82
Pulitzer Prizes for, 514–15
See also People
Biomass fuel, 329–30, 336
Birds:
Endangered species, 630–31
State birds, 646–72
Birmingham, Alabama, 646, 677–78
See also Cities (U.S.)
Birmingham, England, 262
Birth dates, places of, People, 86–102, 521–43
Birth rates, 73, 112, 773–75
Birthstones, 496
Births (U.S.):
Age of mother, 774
Live, 773–75
To unmarried women, 774
Bismarck, Otto von, 179
Bissau, Guinea-Bissau, 184
Black Death, 87, 264
Black Friday, 95
Black Hills, 667
Black hole, 355
Black Hole of Calcutta, 91
"Black Moon," 357
Blackouts, Northeast, 103
Black Rock Desert, 466
Black Sea, 461
Blacks in U.S.:
Armed forces, 397
Births, birth rates, 774, 775
Crime statistics, 783, 785
Employment, 49, 51–52
Population statistics, 750–51, 754, 763
School enrollment, 706
See also Civil rights; Nonwhite persons; Racial statistics; Racial violence; Slavery
Blanc, Mont, 171, 320
Bleeding, treatment of, 72, 79
Blood, circulation of, 342
Blood tests, 767
Blue Grotto, 467
Blue Nile, 169
Board foot (measure), 348
Bobsledding, 822, 924
Boers, 93, 96, 243
Boer War, 96, 243, 265
Bogotá, Colombia, 155
Bohemia, 160
Boiling points:
Elements, 339–40
Water, 351
Bolivia, 142
See also Countries
Bolsheviks, 97, 247
Bolt (measure), 348
Bolts and screws, 350
Bombay, India, 188, 190
See also Cities (world)
Bonaire, 222
Bonanza Creek, 290
Bonaparte, Napoleon, 92, 93, 172, 173, 523
Bonded debts, city, 677–86
Bonn, West Germany, 178, 180

Books:
Awards, 507, 512–15, 518
Notable (1980), 789
Reference, 451–52
Boone, Daniel, 523, 545, 654
Booth, John Wilkes, 523, 545, 574
Bophuthatswana, 244
See also Countries
Boquerón (volcano), 456
Borneo (island), 192, 214, 465
Brunei, 268
Boroughs, New York City, 683, 760
Bosnia, 278
Boston, Mass., 656, 678
Fire (1872), 642
Museums, 799, 800
See also Cities (U.S.)
Boston Massacre, 89
Boston Museum of Fine Arts, 799
Boston Tea Party, 89
Botanic garden, first, 544
Botanic Garden, U.S., 618
Botswana, 142–43
See also Countries
Boulder Dam. *See* Hoover Dam
Bounty, H.M.S., 92
Bourbon Kings of France, 172, 173
Bowl games (football), 823–25
Bowling, 850–52
Standard measurements, 856
Boxer Rebellion, 96, 152, 399
Boxing, 817–18, 821, 864–71, 929
Amateur, 929
Bare-knuckle, 864
Biggest gates, 871
Fighter of the Year, 871
Heavyweight champion fights, 818, 821, 864, 866–67, 870
History, 864
Louis, Joe, 870
Olympic Games, 817–18, 821
Professional, 864–71
Standard measurements, 857
Titleholders, 864–70
World championship fights, 864–67, 870
Boyne, Battle of, 90
Boy Scouts of America, 96, 620
Brahmaputra River, 138, 189, 463
Braille, 342
Brandt, Willy, 180, 523
Brazil, 142–43, 454
See also Countries
Brazos River, 469
Brazzaville, Congo, 156
Bread, food value, 80
Breeder, 640
Brest-Litovsk, Treaty of, 247
Brethren Churches, 415, 416, 417–18
Bretton Woods Conference, 100
Brezhnev, Leonid, 106, 245, 248, 249, 523
Bridges, 321–22
Bridgetown, Barbados, 139
British Columbia, 282, 283, 286
British Commonwealth. *See* Commonwealth of Nations
British Guiana. *See* Guyana
British Honduras. *See* Belize
British Indian Ocean Territory, 268
British Museum, 317
British New Guinea. *See* Papua New Guinea
British Open Champions, 897
British Solomon Islands. *See* Solomon Islands
British Thermal Unit, 332, 348
British Virgin Islands, 268
Broadcasting awards, 518
Broad jump. *See* Track and Field
Broadway theater:
Longest runs, 795
Brodie, Steve, 545
Bronx, The, 683, 760
Bronx Zoo, 634, 635

Brooklyn, 683, 760
Brooklyn Bridge, 95, 321
Brooklyn Museum, 796
Brown, John, 94
Brown v. Board of Education, 101
Brunei, 268
Brussels, Belgium, 139
See also Cities (world)
Bryan, William Jennings, 96, 524
Presidential candidate, 590
Secretary of State, 599
Bryce Canyon National Park, 636
BTU, 332, 348
Buchanan, James, 573
See also Headline History; Presidents (U.S.)
Bucharest, Romania, 235
Budapest, Hungary, 187
Buddha, Gautama, 83, 410–11, 529
Buddhism, 83, 85, 410–11
Followers, 298, 407, 412, 415
Budget, Federal, 34, 59–63
Budget, Office of Management and, 613
Budget. *See* Expenditures; Revenue
Budgets, family, 49
Buenos Aires, Argentina, 134
Buffalo, N.Y., 678
See also Cities (U.S.)
Buffalo Bill, 524, 545
Buffalo Museum of Science, 799
Buildings:
Canada's tallest, 297
New construction (U.S.), 42, 43
Structures, famous, 316–18
U.S.'s tallest, 320
Bujumbura, Burundi, 145
Bulganin, Nikolai A., 101, 246, 248
Bulgaria, 144–45
See also Countries
Bulge, Battle of the, 99
Bullet, 342
Bull Run, Battle of, 94
Bunyan, Paul, 545
Burger, Warren E., 603
Burgesses, House of, 544
Burglary, 782, 783, 784
Burma, 145
See also Countries
Burns, treatment of, 71
Burr, Aaron, 92, 524, 583, 588
Burundi, 145–46
See also Countries
Buses, 64, 65, 66, 334
Accident death rates, 776
Economic statistics, 64, 65, 66
Bush, George, 584, 595
Business, economy, 34–70
See also Current Events
Businesses:
Failures, 44
Number, 44
Retail sales, 45
See also Retail trade; Wholesale trade; Industry
Busing to achieve school integration, 103
Butter:
Calories and vitamins, 80
Economic statistics, 59
Byelorussia, U.S.S.R., 246, 247
Byrd, Richard E., 98, 439, 524
Byzantine architecture, 316–17
Byzantium, 83, 85

C

Cabinets (U.S.), 597–601
First woman member, 544
Salaries, 612
Cable television, 793, 803, 805
Caesar, Julius, 84, 85, 171, 524
Cairo, Egypt, 165
See also Cities (world)
Cairo Conference, 99

Calcutta, India, 188
Calder Trophy, 847
Calendar 378–79
  Chinese, 364
  History, 382–83
  Names of days and months, 384
  Perpetual, 380–81
  Three-year (1981–83), 378–79
Calgary, Alberta, Canada, 282, 286, 297
Calhoun, John C., 524, 588
California, 648
  Gold Rush, 93
  Mountain peaks, 469
  Museums, 799, 800–01, 802
  Volcanoes, 455
  See also States of U.S.
Californium, 339
Calories:
  Content of foods, 80–82
Calvin, John, 88, 524
Cambodia, 101, 103, 105, 106, 146–47, 208–09
  See also Countries
Cambrian Mountains, 263
Cambrian Period, 338
Camera, 95, 342
Cameroon, 147–48
  See also Countries
Camp Fire, Inc., 620
Canada, 282–97
  Automobiles, 292
  Awards, 297
  Buildings, tallest, 297
  Church membership, 296
  Distance between cities, 295–96
  Economy, 284–85, 291–94
  Flag, 291
  Geography, 282, 295, 296
  Government, 282–84, 285
  Economic growth, 293
  History, 282–84
  Holidays, 291
  Labor force, 294
  Latitude and longitude, 471
  Map, 473
  Motto, 291
  Museums, 291
  Parliament, 290
  Population, 282, 284, 292
  Provinces, 284, 286–90, 292
  Territories, 284, 286–90, 292
  Time zones, 384, 459
  Trade, 291
  Weather, 294–95
  See also Countries
Canadian River, 469
Canals, 322
Canary Islands, 250, 456, 644
Cancer, 77, 776
Cancer, Tropic of, 385
Candela, 345
Canoe racing, 821
Canton Island, 673
Canyonlands, National Park, 636
Cape Canaveral, 650
Cape Horn, 150, 454
Cape of Good Hope, 243, 453
Capetian Dynasty, 86, 171, 172
Cape Town, South Africa, 242
Cape Verde, 148, 456
  See also Countries
Capitalization, rules for, 491
Capital punishment, first state to abolish, 544
  See also Executions
Capitals, foreign, 131–281
Capitals of states, 646–72
Capitals of U.S.:
  Early capitals, 662, 665, 686
  Washington, D.C., 686
Capitol, Architect of the, 618
Capitol, U.S., 568
Capone, Al, 98
Capri, 467
Capricorn, Tropic of, 385

Caracas, Venezuela, 273
Carat (measure), 348–49
Carboniferous Period, 338
Carburetor, 342
Cardiac Pulmonary Resuscitation, 71–72
Caribbean area:
  Countries, 130
  Islands, 455
  Map, 478
  Volcanoes, 456
  See also specific countries
Caribbean Sea, 461, 466, 478
Carloadings, railroad, 64
Carlsbad Caverns, 467, 636, 662
Carnegie Institute, 799
Carnival season, 385
Caroline Islands, 485, 675
Carolingian Dynasty, 171, 172
Carpathian Mountains, 233, 236
Carriers, traffic by, 63–64
Carter, Jimmy (James E., Jr.), 581–82
  See also Headline History; Presidents (U.S.)
Carthage, 83, 84, 85
Cartoons:
  Awards for, 509
  First colored, 544
Casablanca, Morocco, 219
Casablanca Conference, 99
Caspian Sea, 193, 462
Castro, Fidel, 102, 157–59, 524
Casualties, war, 399–401
Catalytic converter, 640
Caterpillar Club, 439
Cathedrals, 316–18
Catholic churches, 407, 409, 413, 417–18
  See also Roman Catholic Church
Cattle, 58, 59, 565–67
Caucasus, 455
Cavaliers, 89
Caves, caverns, 467
Cayman Islands, 268
CB 10-Codes, 520
CEA, 613
Celanese, 342
Celebes, 192, 465
Celluloid, 342
Celsius (Centigrade) scale, 345, 349, 351
Cement, 117–18
Cemeteries, National, 639
  Arlington, 569, 639
Cenozoic Era, 339
Census. See Population
Census, Bureau of, 614
Centigrade (Celsius) scale, 345, 349, 351
CENTO, 127, 130
Central African Republic, 148–49
  See also Countries
Central America, 455
  Countries, 130
  Map, 478
  Volcanoes, 456
  See also specific countries
Central Intelligence Agency, 613
Central Powers, 97
Cerebrovascular diseases, 776
Cermak, Anton J., 98, 545
Certified mail, 626
Ceylon. See Sri Lanka
Chaco, 134, 230
Chad, 149–50
  See also Countries
Chad, Lake, 462
Chain (measure), 346, 349
Chamberlain, Neville, 99, 265, 525
Channel Islands, 268
Charlemagne, 85, 86, 171, 172, 179, 525
Charles I of England, 89, 264, 265, 663
Charlotte, N.C., 678

  See also Cities (U.S.)
Charter flights, 298–99
Cheese:
  Calories and vitamins, 80
  Economic statistics, 59
Chemicals, 41, 42, 54, 70
Chemistry:
  Discoveries and theories, 342–44
  Elements, 339–40
  Nobel Prizes for, 31, 499–501
Chesapeake Bay, 656
Chess, 885
Chiang Kai-shek, 99, 152, 155
Chicago, Ill., 652, 678
  Climate, 422
  Fire (1871), 95, 642
  Museums, 797
  St. Valentine's Day Massacre, 98
  See also Cities (U.S.)
Chickenpox, 79
Chickens:
  Calories and vitamins, 80–81
  Economic statistics, 58, 59
  Incubation and longevity, 634
Children:
  Birth statistics, 112, 773–75
  Death statistics, 776, 778, 779, 780
  Education statistics, 706–08
  Illegitimate births, 774
  Life expectancy, 111, 779, 780–81
  Medicaid, 701–02
  Number of, 754
  Runaways, 782, 783
  Social Security, 694–98
Children's Crusade, 86
Chile, 106, 150–51
  Volcanoes, 456
  See also Countries
China, 100, 151–54
  Boxer Rebellion, 96, 152, 399
  Great Wall, 84, 151, 317
  History, 151–54, 154–55, 453
  Japan and, 152, 154, 155
  Maps, 484, 485, 510
  Ming Dynasty, 87, 89, 151
  Nuclear weapons testing, 103, 104, 153
  Provinces and regions, 152
  Structures, 317
  U.S. and, 152, 153, 154
  U.S. military action in, 399
  See also Countries; Headline History
China Sea, 461
"China seat" (U.N.), 153, 155
China (Taiwan), 154–55, 457
  See also Countries; Taiwan
Chinese, new spelling, 151
Chinese in U.S.:
  Births, birth rates 775
  See also Nonwhite persons
Chinese-Japanese War (1895), 95, 152, 155
Chou En-lai. See Zhou Enlai
Christ. See Jesus Christ
Christian and Missionary Alliance, 415
Christian Church (Disciples of Christ), 415
Christianity, 85, 86, 407, 408–09
  Roman Empire, 85, 408
  World membership, 407
  See also Religion; Roman Catholic Church
Christian Science. See Church of Christ, Scientist
Christmas, 387, 388
Christmas Island, 136, 241
Chromium, 339
Chromosphere, 356–57
Chronology:
  For 1980–81, 11–31
  4500 B.C.—A.D. 1980, 83–107
  Space Age, 371–72, 374–77
Churches (buildings):
  Famous, 316–18
  In largest cities, 677–86

Churches (organizations), 407–18
  See also Religion
Churchill, Sir Winston, 99, 100, 101, 265, 266, 525
Church of Christ, Scientist, 415
Church of England, 88, 264
CIA, 613
Cimarron River, 469
Cimmerian civilization, 84
Cinncinnati, Ohio, 664, 678
  See also Cities (U.S.)
Cincinnati Art Museum, 799
CIO, 101
Circular measure, 346, 351–52
Circumference, formula for, 352
Cities (Canadian):
  Latitude and longitude, 471
  Time of day, 471
Cities (U.S.), 677–86
  Assessed valuations, 677–86
  Bridges, 321–22
  Buildings, tallest, 320
  Chambers of Commerce, 677–86
  Climate, 422–24
  Commissions, councils, 687
  Consumer Price Index, 39
  Crime rates, 784
  Distances between, 310–13
  Government statistics, 687
  Latitudes and longitudes, 471
  Mayors, managers, 677–86, 687
  Museums, 796–802
  Newspapers, 446–48
  Officials, terms and salaries, 687
  Police departments, 781
  Population figures:
    Largest, 677–86
    Largest by state, 646–72
    1970–80 (table), 756–62
  Population growth, 756–62
  Ports, 64
  Taxes, 437, 677–86
  Time of day, 471
  Tunnels, 320
  Zoos, 635
  See also specific cities
Cities (world):
  Bridges, 321–22
  Distances between, 314–15
  Largest, by country, 131–281
  Largest (table), 109–10
  Latitudes and longitudes, 458
  Population, 109–10, 131–281
  Southernmost, 150
  Time of day, 458
  Tunnels, 320
  Zoos, 634–35
  See also specific cities
City managers, 677–86, 687
Civil Aeronautics Board, 615
Civilian labor force, 36, 48–52, 56–57
Civil liberties, 123–26
Civil rights:
  Bill of rights, 553–54
  Education, 703–05
  Emancipation Proclamation, 559–60
  Other Constitutional provisions, 552, 554, 555, 557
Civil Rights, Commission on, 617
Civil Service Commission, U.S., 95
  See also Office of Personnel Management
Civil time, 355, 383–84
Civil War, American, 94, 400
  Confederate States, 560
  Gettysburg Address, 560
Civil War, English, 89, 265
Civil War, Russian, 97, 247
Civil War, Spanish, 99, 250
Claims Court, U.S., 602
Clark, Charles Joseph, 282, 283, 284, 290
Clay, Cassius. *See* Ali, Muhammad
Clay, Henry, 94, 525, 588
Cleopatra, 84

Clerical workers, 49, 52
Cleveland, Grover, 575
  See also Headline History; Presidents (U.S.)
Cleveland, Ohio, 664, 679
  Museums, 799
  See also Cities (U.S.)
Climate. *See* Weather
Clocks:
  Imports, 70
  Pendulum clock, 342
Cloisters (museum), 796
Clothing:
  Economic statistics, 36, 39, 42, 53, 57, 70
  Industry, hours and wages, 53
  Price indexes, 36, 39
Cloture rule, 601
Coal, 329, 332
  Economic statistics, 53, 54, 70, 115–16
  Industry, hours, wages, 53, 54
  World production, 115–16
Coast Guard Academy, U.S., 392
Coast Guard, U.S., 391, 394, 401
Coastline of U.S., 472
Cobalt, 339
Cochise, 647
Cocoa, 59, 70
  Calories and vitamins, 81
Cocos (Keeling) Islands, 136, 241
Code of Hammurabi, 83
C.O.D. mail, 626
Cody, William F., 525, 545
Coffee, 59, 70
  Calories and vitamins, 81
Coins, A1, A9–A11
  See also Money
Cold, common, 79
Collectibles, A1, A9–A14, A15–A16
Collect-on-delivery mail, 626
College graduates, 707, 709
Colleges and Universities, 710–49
  Accredited, 721–49
  Degrees, academic, 709, 749
  Endowments, 709
  Enrollments, 706, 708, 721–49
  Firsts, 544
  Graduates, 707, 709
  Junior, 710–20
  Libraries of, 708
  United States, 710–49
Colombia, 155–56
  Volcanoes, 456
  See also Countries
Colombo, Sri Lanka, 251
Colonial Williamsburg, 799
Colorado, 648–49
  Mountain peaks, 469
  See also States of U.S.
Colorado Desert, 466
Colorado River (Colorado-Mexico), 453, 464, 469
  Hoover Dam, 318
Colorado River (Texas), 469
Colorado Springs, Colo., 648
  Air Force Academy, U.S., 392, 649
Colors, of each state, 646–72
Colosseum (Rome), 85, 316
Colossus at Rhodes, 316
Columbia River, 464, 469, 670
  Grand Coulee Dam, 318, 670
Columbia (space shuttle), 366, 370, 377
Columbus, Christopher, 87, 453, 454
Columbus, Ohio, 679
  See also Cities (U.S.)
Columbus Day, 386, 388
Colville River, 469
Combustion, nature of, 342
Comets, 360–61
Cominform, 100
Comintern, 97, 100
Commerce. *See* Foreign trade; Interstate Commerce
Commerce, U.S. Dept. of, 614

Secretaries of, 599–601
Commissions, city, 687
Committees:
  Congressional, 610–11
  National, 591
Commodities, Producer Price Index, 41
Common Market, 102, 103, 127
  See also European Economic Community
Commonwealth of Nations, 127, 130
Commonwealth, Puritan, 264, 265
Commune, Revolutionary, 91
Communicable diseases, 79, 776
Communications:
  FCC, 616
  Industry, hours and wages, 53
  ITU, 328
  World, 121–22
  See also specific types of communication
Communist Internationals, 95, 97
Communist Manifesto, 93
Communist Party (U.S.S.R.), 246–47, 248
Community, European Economic, 102, 127, 130
Community Services Administration, 615
Como, Lake, 99, 199
Comoros, 156
  Volcanoes, 456
  See also Countries
Composers:
  Awards, 515–16
  See also People; Entertainment and Culture
Computer(s), 342
Comstock Lode, 660
Conakry, Guinea, 184
Conditioned reflex, 342
Confederate Memorial Day, 388
Confederate States, 94
  Flag, 569
  Secession, readmission dates, 560
Confucianism, 411
  Number of followers, 407
Confucius, 83, 151, 411, 525
Congo, 156–57
  See also Countries
Congo, Democratic Republic of the, *See* Zaire
Congo River, 453, 463
Congregational Christian Churches, 416, 417
Congress, Library of, 618
Congresses, Continental, 89, 546–47, 561
Congress of Industrial Organizations, 101
Congress of Vienna, 93, 137, 173
Congress (U.S.), 606–10
  Adjournment, 549
  Assembling time, 549
  Committees, 610–11
  Compensation and privileges, 549
  Constitutional provisions, 548–57
  First sessions, 561
  First women members, 544
  Legislative powers, 548, 555–57, 601
  Party strength, 606–10
  Powers and duties, 549–50
  Salary of members, 549, 612
  See also House of Representatives; Senate
Conjunctions (planetary), 364–65
Connecticut, 649
  See also States of U.S.
Connecticut River, 469
Constantinople, 86, 87, 88, 260
  See also Istanbul
Constellations, 362–63
Constitutions (state):
  Dates adopted, 646–72
  Firsts, 544, 649

Constitution (U.S.), 91, 548–57
  Amendment procedure, 552
  Amendments, 553–57
  Drafting of, 548, 561
  Ratification, 548, 553, 561
  Supremacy of, 552
Construction industry, 35, 36, 42, 43, 44, 50, 52
Consumer Price Index, 36, 39
Consumer Product Safety Commission, 615
Consumers:
  Credit, 43
  Metric conversion tables, 350–51
  Price indexes, 36, 39
  Spending, 57
Continental Congresses, 89, 546–47, 561
Continental Divide, 472
Continental Drift, 358, 454
Continents, 454–55
  Area, 457
  Dimensions, 457
  Elevations, 457
  Explorations, discoveries, 453–54
  Maps, 472–87
  Populations, 112, 457
  Religions, 407
  See also specific continents
Controllers (of states), 646–72
Conventions, National, 586–87
Converter, Bessemer, 342
Cook Islands, 223
Coolidge, Calvin, 577
  See also Headline History; Presidents (U.S.)
Cooper-Hewitt Museum, 796
Cooperstown, N.Y. (museums), 798, 800, 801
Copenhagen, Denmark, 161
Copper, 339
Coptic Christians, 169, 409
Copyrights, 495–96
Coral Sea Islands, 136
Corcoran Gallery of Art, 797
Core (of the Earth), 357
Corn:
  Economic statistics, 58, 120–21
  World production, 120–21
Corning Glass Center, 799
Corona of sun, 357
Corporations:
  Largest, 44–45
  Stocks, stockholders, 38, 43, 46
  Taxes, 434
Corpus Christi (holiday), 389
Corregidor, 99
Corsica, 171, 199
Cosmetics, 342
Cosmonauts, 374–77
Cosmos (satellite), 373
Costa Rica, 157
  See also Countries
Cost of living, international, 113
Cotopaxi, 456
Cotton, 58, 117–18
Cotton Bowl, 824
Cotton gin, 342
Council of Economic Advisors, 613
Council of Nicaea, 85, 408
Council of Trent, 88, 382
Council on Environmental Quality, 613
Councils, city, 687
Counterfeiting, 782, 783
Counties (per state), 646–72
Countries of world, 123–281
  Agriculture, 118–21, 131–281
  Areas, 108–09, 131–281
  Birth rates, 112
  Capitals, 131–281
  Cities, largest, 109–10, 131–281
  Death rates, 112
  Economic conditions, 131–281
  Explorations and discoveries of selected areas, 453–54
  Foreign trade, 114, 131–281

Freedom in, 123–26
Governments, 131–281
Groupings, 130
History, 131–281
Holidays, 387
Immigration to U.S., 764
Industry, 117–18, 131–281
Languages, 131–281
Life expectancy, 111
Maps, 472–87
Military forces, 403–04
Monetary units, 131–281
Natural features, 131–281
Petroleum, production of, 115–16, 333
Political parties, 131–281
Population densities, 131–281, 457
Populations, 131–281, 457
Population (table), 108–09
Premiers, prime ministers, 131–281
Presidents, 131–281
Rulers, 131–281
Structures, 316–23
Suicide rates, 113
U.N. members, 324
U.S. interventions in, 399
World Wars I and II, 97–100, 400–01
Zoos, 634–35
  See also Geography (world); History (world)
Court, International, 327
Courts:
  News events, 1980–81, 12–13
Courts (federal), 551–52, 602
  See also Supreme Court
Courts (state), 676
Court tennis, 927
Cows:
  Economic statistics, 58, 59
  Gestation and longevity, 634
  See also Cattle
"Coxey's Army," 95
CPI, 36, 39
CPR, 71–72
Crater Lake National Park, 455, 636, 665
Craters, meteorite, 362
Cream:
  Calories and vitamins, 81
  Economic statistics, 59
Credit, consumers, 43
Cretaceous Period, 338
Crete, 83, 84, 86, 182, 455
Crime:
  Assassinations and attempts, 545
  News events, 1980–81, 13–15
  Rates, 783, 784
  Statistics, 782–85, 787
  Tax fraud cases, 433
  Trial rights, 552
Crimean War, 94, 260, 265
Croatia, 278
Crockett, Davy, 93, 526, 545
Cromwell, Oliver, 89, 264, 265
Crossbow, 342
Cross Country Race Champions, 880
Crucifixion of Christ, 85
Crusades, 86
  Map, 86
Crust (of the Earth), 357
Cuba, 157–59
  Bay of Pigs invasion, 102, 158, 184
  Island, 466
  Missile crisis, 102, 158
  Refugees, 107, 159
  See also Countries
Cubic measure, 345, 346
Cubit (measure), 349
Cultural Revolution, 104, 153
Cumberland River, 469
Cuneiform, 83
Curaçao, 222
Curfew law arrests, 782, 783
Curling (sport), 870
Currency. See Money

Currency exchange, 122
Current events:
  Chronology of 1980–81, 11–31
Currier Gallery of Art, 799
Custer, Gen. George, 95, 526, 659, 664
Custer's Last Stand, 95, 659
Customs, declarations, 300–01
Customs Court, U.S., 602
Cycling, 821, 891
Cyclotron, 98, 342
Cyprus, 159–60, 182, 455
  Greek-Turkish crisis, 159–60, 260–61
  See also Countries
Cy Young Award, 912
Czechoslovakia, 160–61
  Warsaw Pact invasion of, 103, 161
  See also Countries

D

Dacca, Bangladesh, 138
Dahomey. See Benin
Dairy products:
  Calories and vitamins, 80–82
  Economic statistics, 59, 70
Dakar, Senegal, 239
Dalai Lama, 102
Dallas, Tex., 102, 422, 679
  See also Cities (U.S.)
Damascus, Syria, 255
Damavend, Mount, 193
Dams, 318–19, 323
Danube River, 137, 160, 178, 187, 236, 278, 463
Dardanelles, 260
Dare, Virginia, 544, 663
Dar es Salaam, Tanzania, 256
Darling River, 464
Darrow, Clarence, 526
Darts, 871
Dasht-e-Kavir Desert, 466
Dasht-e-Lut Desert, 466
Date line, 384
Davis, Jefferson, 94, 388, 526
Davis Cup, 859, 863
Daylight Savings Time, 378
Days:
  Names of, 384
  Sidereal and solar, 354, 383
D-Day, 99
Dead Sea, 196
Death dates of People, 521–43
Death penalty, 103, 104, 785, 787
Deaths and death rates, 73–74, 112, 113, 776–81
  Accidental, 776–77
  Countries, 112, 113
  Diseases, 776
  In disasters, 641–45
  Motor vehicle, 776–77
  War casualties, 399–401
Deaths in 1980–81, 32–33
Death Valley, 467, 637, 648
Debs, Eugene V., 95, 526, 590
Debts:
  City bonded debts, 677–86
  National, 60, 63
Decathlon. See Track and field
Decibel, 349
Decimals, fractions, 352
Declaration of Independence, 546–47
Decoration Day. See Memorial Day
Deerfield Massacre, 90
Defense, U.S. Dept. of, 614
  Expenditures, 59, 60, 398, 403
  Hotline, 624
  Secretaries, 600–01
  See also Armed Forces (U.S.)
Defense Budget, Major Programs, U.S., 398
de Gaulle, Charles, 102, 172, 173
Degrees, academic:
  Abbreviations, 749

First for women, 544
 Number conferred, 709
Delaware, 649–50
 See also States of U.S.
Delaware River, 470
Democratic Party:
 Members of Congress, 606–10
 National Committee chairmen, 591
 National conventions, 586–87
 Senate floor leaders, 612
Denali National Park, 636
Denmark, 161–62
 See also Countries
Densities of Population:
 United States, 750, 755
 World, 131–281, 457
Dentists, 50, 51, 74
Denver, Colo., 422, 648, 679
 Museums, 799–800
 See also Cities (U.S.)
Depression (1930s), 98
Desegregation in schools, 101, 102
Deserts, 466
Détente, 248
Detroit, Mich., 679
 Museums, 800
 See also Cities (U.S.)
Deuterium, 342
Devil's Hole, 467
Devonian Period, 338
Devon Island, 466
Diabetes mellitus, 776
Diamond mine (Arkansas), 647
Diamonds, 70, 496, A1, A9
Diesel engine, 95, 342
Dietary allowances, recommended
 daily, 78
Dillinger, John, 526
Dinaric Alps, 278
Diphtheria, 79, 776
 Antitoxin, 342
Directory, French, 91, 92
Dirigibles, 439
 Firsts, 438
Disability benefits, 396, 696–97
Disasters, 641–45
 Aircraft accidents, 643–45
 Avalanches, 641
 Earthquakes, 641
 Explosions, 642–43
 Fires, 642–43
 Floods, 641
 Miscellaneous, 645
 News events, 1980–81, 16–17
 Railroad accidents, 645
 Shipwrecks, 643
 Storms, 426–27, 642
 Tidal waves, 641
 Volcanic eruptions, 641
Disciples of Christ, 416
Discoveries:
 Chemical elements, 339–40
 Geographical, 453–54
 Scientific, 342–44
Discus throw. *See* Track and Field
Diseases:
 Communicable, 79, 776
 Deaths from, 776
 Medical discoveries, 342–44
Distance:
 Airplane records, 441
 Between cities, 295–96, 310–15
Distilled spirits. *See* Liquor
District of Columbia, 686
 See also Washington, D.C.
Diving. *See* Swimming
Divorce:
 Grounds for, 770–71
 State laws, 769–71
 Statistics, 766, 769–71
"Divorce capitals," 660
Djibouti, Republic of, 163
 See also Countries
DNA, 7–8, 342
Dnieper River, 246, 464
Doctors (physicians), 51, 74, 75

First woman, 544
 Income, 75
Dodecanese Islands, 182
Dog shows, 913
Dominica, 163, 270
Dominican Republic, 163–64
 U.S. interventions, 164, 399
 See also Countries
Don River, 246, 464
Dow Jones Industrials, 35
Draft evaders, 104
Drama. *See* Theater
Dram (measure), 346–48
Dred Scott case, 94
Dreyfus, Alfred, 95, 527
Drivers:
 Accidents, 776–77
 Arrests for drunkenness, 782, 783
 State laws, 786
Dropouts, high school, 706
Drowning, treatment of, 72
Drugs:
 Economic statistics, 70
 See also Narcotics
Drunkenness, arrests for, 782, 783
Dry measure, 346
Dublin, Ireland, 104, 195, 196
Duckpin bowling, 929
Duomo (Florence), 317
Durable goods, 36, 53
 Industry employment, 53
 See also individual item
Dutch East Indies. *See* Indonesia
Dutch Guiana. *See* Suriname
Dynamite, 94, 342
Dynamo, 342

E

Earhart, Amelia, 98, 99, 440, 527
Earth (planet), 356, 357–58
 Astronomical constants, 354
 Geological periods, 338–39
 Life on, 338–39
 Origin, 338, 357
 Scientific satellites, 368–69, 373
 See also Planets; World
Earthquake predictions, 788
Earthquakes, 456, 641
East China Sea, 461
Easter Island, 150
Eastern Front (World War I), 97
Eastern Orthodox churches, 296, 407,
 408–09, 412, 413
Easter Rebellion, 97, 196
Easter Sunday, 386, 389
East Germany. *See* Germany, East
Ebert, Friedrich, 179, 180
Eclipses, 364
Ecology, 640
 See also Environment
Economic Advisers, Council of, 613
Economic and Social Council, U.N.,
 326–27
Economic Community of West African
 States, 130
Economics, Nobel Prize for, 31, 502
Economic statistics (U.S.), 34–70,
 114–22, 561–68
Economic statistics (world), 67–69,
 114–22
Economic systems, 123–24
Economy, U.S., 34–70
"Economy in 1981," 34–35
Ecuador, 164–65
 Volcanoes, 456
 See also Countries
Ecumenical Councils, 102, 273, 408,
 409
 Council of Nicaea, 85, 408
 Council of Trent, 88
 Vatican Council I, 409
 Vatican Council II, 102, 273, 409
Eddy, Mary Baker, 415, 527

Eden, Anthony, Sir, 101, 265, 266
Edict of Nantes, 88, 90
Edinburgh, Scotland, 262
Edison, Thomas A., 95, 342, 343,
 527
Education, 703–49
 Attendance laws, 707
 Construction for, 42
 Consumer spending for, 57
 Degrees, academic, 709, 749
 Department of, 615
 Employment, payrolls, 59
 Enrollments, 706, 708, 721–49
 Exceptional children, 703–05, 708
 Expenditures, college, 709
 Federal aid, 705
 Graduates, 707, 709
 News events, 1980–81, 17
 Prayer in schools, 102
 School statistics, 706–09
 Service academies, 391–93
 Special education, 703–05, 708
 Supreme Court school decisions,
  101, 103, 105
 Teachers, 721–49
 Veterans' benefits, 396–97
 See also Colleges & Universities
Edward VIII, 99, 264, 265
EEC, 127, 130
Eggs:
 Calories and vitamins, 81
 Economic statistics, 59, 70
Egypt, Arab Republic of, 165–67
 Israel and, 100, 101–02, 103, 104,
  105, 166–67, 197–98
 Maps, 480, 482
 Pyramids, 316
 Suez Canal, 101–02, 165–67, 322
 See also Arab-Israeli wars; Countries
Egyptian Empire, 83, 84
 Map, 487
Eiffel Tower, 317
Einstein, Albert, 96, 99, 341, 342,
 344, 498, 527
 Theorem, 341, 342, 352
Eire. *See* Ireland (Republic)
Eisenhower, Dwight D., 578
 See also Headline History; Presidents
  (U.S.)
Eisenhower Doctrine, 102
Elbe River, 160, 178
Elbert, Mount, 469
Election Day, 378, 386, 388, 389
Elections, presidential, 588–96
 Election results, 1968–80, 592–95
Electoral College, 554, 556
 Voting, 586–87, 588–91, 592–95,
  596
Electrical appliances and equipment,
 45
Electricity:
 Economic statistics, 39
 Electric current, 345
 Hydroelectric plants, 319
 Inventions and discoveries, 342–44
 Nuclear power plants, 334
 World production, 331
Electrocution, first, 544
Electromagnet, 342
Electromagnetic waves, 344
Electron microscope, 343
Electrons, 342
Elementary schools, 706, 708
Elements, chemical, 339–40
Elevations:
 Canadian, highest, 295
 Cities of U.S., 677–86
 Continents, 457
 Deserts, 466
 Extremes of U.S., 467, 468
 Mountain peaks, 460–61
 States of U.S., 468
 Volcanoes, 455–56
Elevator (inventions), 342
Elizabeth I, 88, 89, 264
Elizabeth II, Queen, 100, 264, 266

Elks (BPOE), 621
Ellesmere Island, 465
Ellice Islands. *See* Tuvalu
Ell (measure), 349
El Paso, Tex., 668, 679–80
  See also Cities (U.S.)
El Salvador, 167–68
  Volcanoes, 456
  See also Countries
Emancipation Proclamation, 559–60
Embezzlement arrests, 782, 783
Emmy Awards, 31
Empire, Second (French), 94, 172, 173
Empires, ancient, 83–85
  Map, 487
Empire State Building, 320
Employment, 36, 48–56, 57
  Average weekly earnings, 53–54
  By race, occupation, 49
  Future job openings, 50–51
  Government, 59
  Labor force, 36, 48–52, 56–57
  Major occupations, 51–52
  Taxes, 429
  Unemployed, 36, 56, 57
  Unions, 47–48
  Women, 48, 49, 54–56
  See also Labor
Endangered species, 630–31
Enderbury Island, 673
Energy, 329–35
  Atomic, 334, 341
  Consumption, 115–16, 329, 331
  In 1980–81, 329–30
  News events, 1980–81, 17
  Producers, 331
  Solar, 330
  Thermal, 331
  U.S. Supply and disposition, 332
  World production, 115, 331
Energy, U.S. Department of, 615
Enewetak (Eniwetok) Atoll, 101, 675
Engine:
  Internal combustion, 342
  Steam, 342
Engineers, 50, 51
England, 262–71
  Area, population, 262, 263
  Rulers, 264
  Structures, 317
  See also United Kingdom
Engels, Friedrich, 93, 527
Enlightenment, The, 90
Enrollment, school. *See* Education
Entebbe, 104, 198, 262
Entente Cordiale, 96
Entertainment and culture, 789–802
  Art movements, 791–92
  Motion pictures, 794, 795
  Museums, 796–802
  Music, 792
  News events, 1980–81, 17–18
  Orchestras, symphony, 789
  Plays, 795
Environment, 629–40
  Endangered species, 630–31
  Federal funds, 632
  Glossary of terms, 640
  National Park System, 635–39
  News events, 1980–81, 18
  Pollutants, 632
  Quality index, 629–30
  World's water supply, 633
Environmental Protection Agency, 615
Environmental Quality, Council on, 613, 632
EPA, 615
Epiphany, 385
Episcopal Church. *See* Protestant Episcopal Church
"E pluribus unum," 561
Equal Employment Opportunity Commission, 615
Equatorial Guinea, 168
  See also Countries

Equestrian Events, 821, 894
Equinox(es), 358, 382, 383, 385
Equipment expenditures, 43
Ericson, Leif, 86, 282, 453
Erie, Lake, 462
  Battle of, 93
Erie Canal, 652, 662
Eritrea, Ethiopia, 169–70
Eros (asteroid), 360
Estate gift taxes, 429, 435, 436
Estonia, 99, 246, 247
Ether (anesthetic), 342
Ethical Culture Movement, 417
Ethiopia, 99, 168–70
  See also Countries
Etna, Mount, 199, 456
Etruscans, 83, 84
Euclid, 84, 343, 527
Euphrates River, 83, 194, 464
Eurasia, 455
Europe, 130, 455, 457
  Explorations and discoveries, 453
  Map, 476–77
  Population, 112
  See also Countries
European Economic Community, 102, 127, 130, 266
European Free Trade Assn., 127, 130
European Recovery Program, 100, 128
Evangelical churches, 416, 417
Evangelical United Brethren. *See* United Methodist Church
Everest, Mount, 101, 221, 457, 460
Everglades National Park, 636, 650
Evolution, theory of, 94, 98, 342
  Scopes trial, 98
Exceptional children, 703–05, 708
Executions:
  First electrocution, 544
  Methods by state, 785
  See also Capital punishment
Executive Departments and Agencies 613–18
Exosphere, 358
Expectation of life, 111, 779–81
Expenditures:
  Advertising, 56
  City governments, 677–86
  Consumer spending, 57
  Education, college, 709
  Federal government, 59–63, 632
  Gross national product, 37
  Plant and equipment, 43
  State governments, 646–72
Explorations, 453–54
Explorer (satellite), 102, 321, 363, 368
Explosions, 642–43
Explosives (inventions), 342–43
Export-Import Bank, 618
Exports:
  United States, 67, 70, 114
  Value by country, 67–69, 114
Express Mail, 625
Extradition between states, 552

F

Faeroe Islands, 162
Fahrenheit scale, 345, 351
Failures, business, 44
Falkland Islands, 269
Fall (1982), 378
Falling bodies:
  Formulas for, 352
  Law of, 342
Families:
  Characteristics, 765, 766, 772–73
  Income, 39, 41, 765, 772–73
  Of U.S. Presidents, 585
  Statistics, 39, 40, 41, 765, 771–73
Famous People, 521–43
  Sports Personalities, 806–08
  See also Awards; Headline History

Far East:
  Countries, 130
  Maps, 484, 485
  See also individual countries
Farm Credit Administration, 616
Farmers' Museum, 800
Farm Index, 41
Farms. *See* Agriculture
Farragut, David G., Adm., 94, 544
Fascists, 97
Fats and oils, 81
Fat Tuesday. *See* Shrove Tuesday
FBI, 104, 614
FCA, 616
FDIC, 616
Feasts, Jewish, 385–86, 387, 389
FEC, 616
Federal budget, 34, 59–63
  Foreign assistance, 63
  Public debt, 60, 63
  Social welfare expenditure, 61–62
Federal Bureau of Investigation, 614
Federal Communications Commission, 616
Federal Courts, 551–52, 602
  See also Supreme Court
Federal Deposit Insurance Corporation, 616
Federal Election Campaign Act, 104
Federal Election Commission, 616
Federal Energy Administration. *See* Department of Energy
Federal Government. *See* United States Government
Federalist papers, 571
Federalist Party, 570–71, 583–84, 588
Federal Maritime Commission, 616
Federal Mediation and Conciliation Service, 616
Federal Power Commission. *See* Department of Energy
Federal Reserve Board, 34, 35, 42, 616
Federal Reserve System, 96, 616
Federal Trade Commission, 96, 616
Fencing, 821, 928
Fermentation, 342
Fermi, Enrico, 100, 341, 343, 499, 528
Fernando Po, Equatorial Guinea. *See* Macias Nguema Biyogo
Fertilizers, 70
Festival of Lights, 387, 389
Fibers, man-made, 342–43
Fiction, awards for, 507, 512–13
Fifth Republic (French), 102, 172, 173
Fighter of the Year, 871
Figure skating, 818, 822, 850
Fiji, 170
  See also Countries
Filament, tungsten, 342
Filibusters, 601
Fillmore, Millard, 573
  See also Headline History; Presidents (U.S.)
Films. *See* Motion pictures
Fingal's Cave, 467
Finland, 170–71
  See also Countries
Firearms:
  As murder weapons, 785
  Domestic production and imports, 784
  Inventions, 342–44
"Fireballs," 361
Firemen, 59
Fires:
  Arson arrests, 782, 783
  Famous, 642–43
First Aid, 71–72, 79
First Fruits, Feast of, 386, 389
Firsts:
  In America, 544
  In aviation, 438–40

Fish:
Calories and vitamins, 81–82
Economic statistics, 70
Endangered species, 631
World production, 117–18
Fishing (sport):
Record catches, 835–37
Fission bombs, 341
Five and ten cents store, first, 544
Flag (Confederate), 569
Flag Day, 386, 388
Flag (U.S.), 569
Pledge to, 569
Flights:
First, 438–40
Orbital, 374–77
Records, 441–42
Floods, 641
Floor Leaders of Senate, 612
Florence, Italy, 87, 106, 199
Florida, 453, 650
See also States of U.S.
Flour:
Economic statistics, 59, 70
Flowers:
Canadian province, 286–92
State, 646–72
Fluorocarbons, 640
FMCS, 616
FM radio stations, 677–86
Folklore, American, 545
Food:
Calories and vitamins, 80–82
Economic statistics, 45, 57, 58, 59, 70
Industry, hours and wages, 53
Price indexes, 36, 39
Recommended daily dietary allowances, 78
U.S. consumption, 59
See also Agriculture
Food and Agriculture Organization, U.N., 327
Food and Drug Administration, 615
Food-choking, treatment of, 72
Food poisoning, 79
Football, 823–35
American League Champions, 832
Army-Navy games, 823
Bowl games, 823–25
Coaches, college, 827
College, 823–30
Heisman Memorial Trophy, 825
History, 823
National Football League, 830–35
National League Champions, 831–32
Nicknames of clubs, 835
Professional, 830–35
Records, college, 827–30
Records, professional, 834–35
Stadiums, 835
Standard measurements, 856
Super Bowl, 831
Ford, Gerald R., 104, 580–81
Assassination attempts, 104, 545
See also Headline History; Presidents (U.S.)
Ford, Henry, 96
Foreign aid (U.S.), 62–63
Foreign mail. See International mail
Foreign trade (U.S.), 67, 70
Foreign trade (world):
Each country's, 131–281, 291
Exports-imports table, 114
Foreign words and phrases, 494
Forests:
Resources of countries, 131–281
State forests, 646–72
Forgery, 782, 783
Formosa. See Taiwan
Forms of address, 492–94
Formulas, math, physics, 352
Fort Dodge, 653
Fort Sumter, Battle of, 94, 667
Fort Ticonderoga, 662, 669

Fort Worth, Tex., 680
See also Cities (U.S.)
Fossil fuels, 640
Fountain pen, 343
Four Freedoms, 99
Four Noble Truths, 410
Fourth of July, 386, 387, 388
Fractions, decimals, 352
France, 171–76
NATO, 173, 174
Rulers (table), 172
Structures, 317
See also Countries
Franco, Francisco, 99, 250, 528
Franco-Prussian War, 95, 173
Frankfurt, West Germany, 178
Franklin Institute, 798
Fraternity, first, 544
Freedom, Comparative Survey, 125–26
Freedom in the World, 123–26
"Freedom March," 646
Freedom of the press, 90, 553
Freedoms, Constitutional, 553–54
Freetown, Sierra Leone, 240
Freezing point of water, 351
Freight ton (measure), 349
Freight traffic, 63, 64
FRELIMO, 220
French and Indian War, 90, 653, 657, 658, 664, 668, 669, 671
French Guiana, 174
French Polynesia, 174
French Revolution, 91, 173
French Somaliland. See Djibouti
French Southern and Antarctic Lands, 176
French Sudan. See Mali
French Territory of the Afars and Issas. See Djibouti
Freud, Sigmund, 96, 97, 344, 528
Frick Collection, 796
Friendly Islands, 258
Friends (Quakers), 416, 417
Fritchie, Barbara, 545
FRS, 616
Fruit:
Calories and vitamins, 80–82
Economic statistics, 59, 70
FTC, 616
Fuel, 44, 46, 329–30, 334, 335
See also specific fuels
Fuel consumption, motor vehicle, 334
Fujiyama, 202, 455
"Fundamental Orders," 649
Fur, 70
Furniture:
Economic statistics, 41, 42, 45, 53
Industry, hour and wages, 53
Fusion bombs, 341

G

Gabon, 176
See also Countries
Gadsden Purchase, 647, 662, 763
Gagarin, Yuri A., 102, 248, 374
Galápagos Islands, 164, 454
Galaxy, 354–55
Galilee, Sea of, 196
Galileo, 89, 342, 354, 528
Gambia, 176–77
See also Countries
Gambia River, 177, 453
Gambier Island, 174
Gambling, 782, 783
Gandhi, Indira, 190–91, 528
Gandhi, Mohandas K., 100, 190, 528
Ganges River, 138, 189, 464
"Gang of Four," 105, 153
GAO, 618
Garfield, James A., 545, 575
See also Headline History; Presidents (U.S.)
Gas, natural, manufactured, 70, 331, 332

Gasohol, 329–30, 336
Gasoline, 335
Gasoline, motor vehicle, 334
Gasoline service stations, 45
Gasoline taxes, 786
Gator Bowl, 824
GATT, 327
Gaza Strip, 103, 166, 167, 197, 198
Gemini flights, 370, 374
Gemstones, A9
General Accounting Office, 618
General Agreement on Tariffs and Trade (GATT), 327
General Assembly, U.N., 326
General Services Administration, 616
General Sherman Tree, 648
Generals (U.S.), 394, 401
Generator, electric, 342
Genetics, 7–8, 336
Geneva, 97, 254, 255
Geneva, Lake, 254
Geneva Conference (1954), 101
Genghis Khan, 86, 131, 529
Genocide, 98
Geographic centers:
Of states, 646–72
Of United States, 467
Geographic Society, National, 621
Geography:
Caves and caverns, 467
Coastline of U.S., 472
Continental Divide, 472
Continents, 453–57, 459, 473–87
Deserts, 466
Elevations, 457
Explorations, discoveries, 453–54
Islands, 465–66
Lakes, 462–63
Map section, 472–88
Mountain peaks, 460–61
National Parks, 635–39
Oceans, seas, 461
Of countries, 131–281
Rivers, 463–64, 469–70
United States, 467–72
Volcanoes, 455–56, 469
Waterfalls, 464–65
World, 453–54
Geological periods, 338–39
Geological Survey, 614
Geometric formulas, 352
Geometry, 343
Georgetown, Guyana, 185
Georgia, 650–51
See also States of U.S.
Georgia, U.S.S.R., 246
Geriatrics. See Growing Older
Germany:
History, 177–78, 179–81
Nazi regime, 98–100, 179
Rulers (table), 180
World War I, 97
World War II, 99
Zoos, 634
See also Germany, East; Germany, West
Germany, East, 177–78
See also Countries
Germany, West, 178–81
See also Countries
Geronimo, 647
Gestation periods, animals. 634
Gettysburg, Battle of, 94, 560
Gettysburg Address, 560
Ghana, 181–82
See also Countries
Ghent, Treaty of, 93
Gibraltar, 269
Gift taxes, federal, 429, 435, 436
Gilbert Islands, 205, 223
See also Kiribati
Girl Scouts of U.S.A., 621
Giscard d'Estaing, Valéry, 172, 173–74
Glacier National Park, 636, 659
Glasgow, Scotland, 262

Glass:
  Economic statistics, 42, 70
Glass Center, Corning, 799
Glenn, John H., Jr., 102, 374
Glossaries:
  Art movements, 790–91
  Environment, 640
  Television and video, 805
  Weather, 425
GNP, 34, 37
Gobi Desert, 151, 466
Godwin Austen, Mount (K-2), 460
Golan Heights, 103, 166, 197, 255
Gold:
  As element, 339
  Karat (measure of purity), 349, 353
  Standard, 95
Gold Coast. *See* Ghana
Golden Gate Bridge, 321, 648
Gold Rush:
  Alaska, 647
  California, 93, 648
Golf, 895–99
  Earnings, 897–99
  History, 895
  Standard measurements, 856–57
  U.S. Amateur Champions, 896
  U.S. Open Champions, 895
  U.S. P.G.A. Champions, 896
Good Friday, 386, 389
Gorki, U.S.S.R., 245
Gospels, 85, 408
Gothic architecture, 317
Goths, 85
Gotland, Sweden, 253
Government, U.S. *See* United States Government
Government employment, 59
Government Printing Office, 618
Governments (foreign), 131–281
  Rulers, 131–281
Governors of states, 646–72, 675
  Birth dates, 675
  First woman Governor, 98, 544, 672
  Puerto Rico, 672
  Terms and salaries, 676
  U.S. Territories, 673–74
Graduates, high school, college, 707, 709
Grain, 70
  Food values, 80–82
  See also specific grains
Gram (measure), 345, 348, 350, 351
Grammy Awards, 503
Grand Canyon National Park, 636
Grand Coulee Dam, 318
  Hydroelectric plant, 319
Grand Prix (of auto racing), 926
Grand Teton National Park, 636
Grant, Ulysses S., 574
  See also Headline History; Presidents (U.S.)
Grants for education, 705
Graves, Presidential, 584
Gravitation, law of, 343
Great Arabian Desert, 466
Great Australian Desert, 466
Great Bear Lake, 462
Great Britain (country). *See* United Kingdom
Great Britain (island), 465
Great gross (measure), 349
Great Lakes, 462
Great Salt Lake, 463, 669
Great Salt Lake Desert, 466
Great Seal of U.S., 561
Great Slave Lake, 462
Great Smoky Mountains National Park, 636, 663
Great Sphinx of Egypt, 83, 316
Great Wall of China, 84, 151, 317
Greece, 182–83
  See also Countries
Greece, ancient, 83–84, 182, 809

Map, 487
  Persian Wars, 83
  Structures, 316
Greek Orthodox Church, 413
Greenback Party, 589
Greenhouse effect, 640
Greenland, 86, 162, 453, 465
Green Mountain Boys, 669
Green River (Ky.), 470
Green River (Wyoming-Utah), 470
Greenwich time, 384
Gregorian calendar, 382–83
Grenada, 183, 270
  See also Countries
Grocery stores, 45
Gross (measure), 349
Gross National Product, 34, 37
Growing Older, 688–702
  Elderly parents, 688–91
  Employment, 691, 697–98
  Facts, 691–94
  Finding help, 692–94
  Myths, 693
  Pensions, 692
  Social Security, 694–98
GSA, 616
Guadalcanal, 241
Guadalupe Mountains National Park, 636
Guadeloupe, 175
Guam, 485, 672–73
  Volcanoes, 456
  See also Countries
Guernsey, 268–69
Guevara, Ché, 142, 158
Guggenheim Museum, 796
Guiana, British. *See* Guyana
Guiana, Dutch. *See* Suriname
Guiana, French, 174
Guinea, Portuguese. *See* Guinea-Bissau
Guinea, Spanish. *See* Equatorial Guinea
Guinea-Bissau, 184–85, 235
  See also Countries
Guinea (republic), 184
  See also Countries
Gulf of Mexico, 217, 218, 461
Gulf of Tonkin Resolution, 101, 103
Gunpowder, 343
Guns. *See* Firearms
Gunter's chain (measure), 346, 349
Gupta, 85
Guyana, 185
  Jonestown, 185
  See also Countries
Gymnastics, 821, 894
Gyrocompass, 343
Gyroscope, 343

H

Hague, The Netherlands, 221
Hague Conventions, 96
Haile Selassie, 169, 530
Hailstone, largest, 424
Hainan Island, 151
Haiti, 92, 185–86
  U.S. intervention in, 186, 399
  See also Countries
Haleakala National Park, 636
Halicarnassus, Mausoleum at, 316
Hall of Fame, Baseball, 798, 911
Halley's Comet, 360–61
Halloween, 386
Hambletonian, 893
Hamburg, West Germany, 178
Hamilton, Alexander, 91, 92
Hammarskjöld, Dag, 101, 279, 326, 530
Hammer throw. *See* Track and Field
Hammurabi, Code of, 83
Handball, 891
Hand (measure), 349
Hanging as death penalty, 785

Hanging Gardens, 316
Hannibal, 84
Hanoi, Vietnam, 101, 274–76
Hanover, House of, 264
Hanukkah, 387, 389
Hapsburg, House of, 137, 187
Harding, Warren G., 576–77
  See also Headline History; Presidents (U.S.)
Hardware, 45
Harness racing, 892–93
Harpers Ferry raid, 94
Harrison, Benjamin, 575
  See also Headline History; Presidents (U.S.)
Harrison, William Henry, 572
  See also Headline History; Presidents (U.S.)
Hart Trophy, 846–47
Harvard University, 544
Harvest, Feast of, 386, 389
Hashemite Kingdom. *See* Jordan
Hastings, Battle of, 86, 263
Havana, Cuba, 157, 158, 159
Hawaii, 91, 651
  Map, 474
  U.S. military action in, 399
  Volcanoes, 456
  See also States of U.S.
Hawaii Volcanoes National Park, 636
Hayes, Rutherford B., 574–75
  See also Headline History, Presidents (U.S.)
Haymarket Riots, 95
Headline history, 83–107
Health, Education, and Welfare, U.S. Dept. of, 600–01
  Secretaries of, 600–01
  See also Health and Human Services, Dept. of; Education, Dept. of
Health and Human Services, Dept. of, 601, 615
Health and medicine:
  News events, 1980–81, 18–19
Health care, 73–75
  Expenditures, 75
Health Insurance (Medicare), 698, 700–02
HEAO, 368
Heard Island, 136
Heart, human:
  Disease, 776
  First artificial (1966), 103
  Transplants, 103
Heath, Edward, 265, 266
Hebrew Pentecost, 386, 389
Hebrides, 263
Hectare, 347
Hegira (Hijra), 85, 409
Heiden, Eric, 818
Heimlich Maneuver, 72
Heisman Memorial Trophy, 825
Helicopters:
  First flights, 440
  Invention, 343
  Records, 445
Helium, 339
  Discovered on sun, 343
  First use in balloon, 439
Helsinki, Finland, 170, 171
Helsinki Agreement, 127–28, 248
Herbicide, 640
Hercules, labors of, 789
Heredity, 94, 343
Hermitage, The (Andrew Jackson's home), 307, 584
Hertz (measure), 349
Herzegovina, 278
Hides, 41, 70
High Aswan Dam, 166, 319, 323, 462
High Energy Astronomy Observatory, 368
Highest points, U.S., 468
High jump. *See* Track and field

High schools, 706–08
  Graduates, 707
Highways:
  Construction, 42
  Road mileages, 310–11
Hijackings, 104, 442
Hijra. See Hegira
Hillary, Sir Edmund, 101, 530
Himalayas, 189, 191, 460–61
Hindenburg, Paul von, 179, 180, 530
Hindenburg (zeppelin), 643
Hinduism, 410
  Number of followers, 407
Hindu Kush range, 131
Hirohito, Emperor, 201, 530
Hiroshima, Japan:
  Atomic bombing, 99, 202, 341
Hispanics. See Spanish Origin, persons of
Hispaniola, 164, 186, 466
Historical parks and sites, 637, 638
History, headline, 83–107
History books, awards for, 513–15
History (U.S.). See United States History
History (world), 83–107, 131–281
  Ancient empires, 83–85, 487
  Chronology for 1980–81, 11–31
  Discoveries, 453–54
  Explorations, 453–54
  Headline history, 83–107
  Seven Wonders, 316
  See also Chronology
Hitler, Adolf, 97, 98, 99, 179, 180, 530
Hittite civilization, 84
Ho Chi Minh, 101, 275
Ho Chi Minh City, Vietnam, 274
Hockey, ice, 819–20, 846–50
  Amateur champions, 819–20, 849–50
  American victory at 1980 Winter Olympics, 819
  History, 846
  N.H.L. Trophy winners, 846–48
  Professional, 846–49
  Standard measurements, 856
Hogshead (measure), 349
Hokkaido, 202, 466
Holidays, 378, 385–89
  Calendar, 378, 389
  National, by country, 291, 387
  Religious, 385–89
Holland. See Netherlands
Holocaust, 98
Holocene Period, 339
Holy Roman Empire, 86, 88, 179
Holy Saturday, 389
Homer, 83, 531
Home run records, 905, 906, 907, 914, 915, 917
Homestake Mine, 667
Homestead Strike, 95
Homicide. See Murder
Honduras, 186–87
  See also Countries
Honduras, British. See Belize
Hong Kong, 269
Honolulu, Hawaii, 680
  See also Cities (U.S.)
Honshu, Japan, 202, 465
Hood, Mount, 455, 468, 665
Hoover, Herbert, 577
  See also Headline History; Presidents (U.S.)
Hoover Dam, 318, 660
  Lake Mead, 462, 660
Horn, Cape, 150, 454
Horsepower, 349
Horse racing, 872–74
  Belmont Stakes, 873–74
  History, 872
  Kentucky Derby, 872–73, 874
  Preakness Stakes, 873, 874
  Triple Crown, 872–74
  See also Harness Racing

Hospital insurance, 698, 700–02
Hospitals:
  Construction, 42
Hostages, American, 106, 107, 193–94
Hotels:
  Hours and wages, 53
"Hot Line," 102
Hot Springs National Park, 636
Households, 39, 54, 765, 771
Household operation, 57
House of Burgesses, 544
House of Representatives (U.S.), 548–49, 607–10
  Apportionment, 548, 554–55
  Committees, 611
  Eligibility, 548
  First woman member, 544
  Shooting on floor of, 101
  Speakers, 612
  See also Congress (U.S.)
Housing:
  Construction, 35, 42, 43
  Economic statistics, 36, 42, 43, 57
  Mortgages, 35, 47
Housing and Urban Development, U.S. Dept. of, 615
  Secretaries of, 600–01
Houston, Tex., 680
  See also Cities (U.S.)
Houston Canal, 322
Howland Island, 673
Hsi River (Si Kiang). See Xi Jiang
Hudson Bay, 282, 286, 288, 454, 461
Hudson River, 454, 662
Hudson's Bay Company, 282, 283, 286, 288, 290
Huguenots, 88, 90
Human Rights, 123–26
Humidity, relative, 422–24
Humphrey, Hubert H., 584, 592
"Hundred Days," 93
Hundred Years' War, 87, 171, 264
Hungary, 105, 187–88
  1956 uprisings, 102, 187
  See also Countries
Huns. See Mongols
Huntington Library and Art Gallery, 800
Huron, Lake, 282, 462, 657
Hurricanes, 421, 425, 426–27
Hus, Jan, 87, 160
Hussein, King, 204, 277, 531
Hwang Ho, 151, 463
Hyde Park, N.Y. (F.D.R.), 308, 584
Hydroelectric plants, 106, 319
Hydrogen, 339
  First use in balloon, 438
Hydrogen, heavy, 98, 342
Hydrogen bomb, 100, 101, 102, 103, 248, 341

I

ICC, 616
Icecaps, Arctic, Antarctic, 633
Ice Cave, 467
Ice hockey. See Hockey
Iceland, 86, 188, 453
  Island, 466
  Volcanoes, 456
  See also Countries
Ice skating. See Figure skating; Speed skating
Idaho, 651–52
  See also States of U.S.
Ikhnaton, 83
"Iliad," 83
Illinois, 652
  See also States of U.S.
Illinois River, 470
Illinois State Museum, 800
IMF, 328
Immigration:

Statistics, 762, 764, 765
Impeachments, 548–49, 551, 605
  Andrew Johnson, 574, 605
Imperial gallon, 347
Imports:
  United States, 67, 70, 114
  Value by country, 67–69, 114
Inca Empire, 87, 88, 142, 165, 231
Income:
  By occupation, 53–54
  Doctors, 75
  Family, 39, 41
  Farm income, 59
  Household, 39, 41
  National income, 40
  Per capita, 37, 39
  See also Revenue; Salaries; Wages
Income tax (city), 437
Income tax (federal), 60, 429–34
  Collections, 60
  Established, 428, 555
  New legislation, 428, 431–32, 434
Incorporations, new, 44
Incubation periods, animals, 634
Incubation periods, disease, 79
Independence, Declaration of, 546–47
Independence Day, 386, 387, 388
Independence Hall, 666
India, 91, 94, 100, 138–39, 188–91
  Structures, 317
  See also Countries
Indiana, 652–53
  See also States of U.S.
Indianapolis, Ind., 680
  See also Cities (U.S.)
Indianapolis "500," 925
Indian Ocean, 461
  Islands, 465–66
  Volcanoes, 456
Indians (American):
  Births and birth rates, 775
  Museum exhibits, 796–802
  Population of reservations, 765
  Reservations, 647, 765
Indochina. See Cambodia; Laos; Vietnam
Indonesia, 191–92
  See also Countries
Indus River, 189, 463
Industrial Revolution, 91
Industry:
  Construction, 42
  Employment, 36, 49
  Failures, 44
  Foreign countries, 131–281, 293
  Hours and wages, 53–54
  Labor force (world), 117–18
  Largest corporations, 44–45
  Plant and equipment costs, 43
  Production indexes, 41, 42
  See also individual industries
Infantile paralysis. See Poliomyelitis
Infant mortality, 776, 778, 779, 780–81
Inflation:
  Cost of Living, 435
  See also "The Economy in 1981"
Influenza, 79, 97, 776
Information bureaus, sports, 855–56
Information Please quiz show, 544
Ingathering, Feast of, 386, 389
Inini, 174
Inquisition, 86, 89
Insulin, 7, 105, 336, 343
Insurance:
  Largest companies, 45
  Life insurance, 41, 45
  Medicaid, 698, 701–02
  Medicare, 698, 700–02
  Social Security, 694–98
  Unemployment, 698–700
Insured mail, 626
Intelligence testing, 343
Intelsat, 368
Intercity railways, 64
Interest:

First mortgages, 47
Public debt, 60
Rates, 34–35, 38, 47, A1, A7–A9
Inter-Governmental Maritime
Consultative Organization, 327
Interior, U.S. Dept. of, 614
Secretaries of, 598–601
Internal Revenue Service. *See* Taxes
International affairs:
News events, 1980–81, 19–25
International Atomic Energy Agency,
327
International Bank, 327
International Civil Aviation
Organization, 327
International Communication Agency,
616
International Court, 327
International Date Line, 384
International Development Association,
328
International Development
Cooperation Agency, U.S., 617
International Finance Corp., 328
International Labor Organization, 328
International mail, 627
International Monetary Fund, 100,
328
International organizations, U.S.
Contributions to, 62
Internationals, 95, 97
International System of Units,
345–48, 350–51
International Telecommunication
Union, 328
International Trade Commission, U.S.,
617
International Treaties, Agreements,
and Organizations, 126–30
Interplanetary probes, 371–72
Interstate commerce, 63, 64
Interstate Commerce Commission,
616
Inventions and discoveries, 342–44
Inversion, 640
Investments. *See* Centerfold
Investment Section
Iolani Palace, 651
Ionian Islands, 182
Ionosphere, 358
Iowa, 653
See also States of U.S.
IQ tests, 704–05
IRA, 106, 196, 267
Iran, 106, 107, 192–94
Hostage crisis, 106, 107, 193–94
Maps, 481, 484, 486
Shah of, 193, 194
See also Countries; News events
Iraq, 107, 194–95
Map, 481
See also Countries; News events
Ireland, Northern, 103, 266–67
See also United Kingdom
Ireland (island), 466
Ireland (republic), 97, 104, 195–96
See also Countries
Irish Republican Army, 106, 196, 267
Iron:
As element, 340
Economic statistics, 53, 70
World production, 117–18
"Iron Curtain," 100
Irrawaddy River, 464
Irtish River, 463
Islam, 409–10
Number of Moslems, 407
Islamabad, Pakistan, 227
Islands, 465–66
See also specific islands
Isle of Man, 269
Isle Royale National Park, 636
Isotopes of elements, 339–40, 343
Israel, 196–99
Balfour Declaration, 97, 197
Entebbe rescue, 104, 198, 262

Independence (1948), 100, 197
Map, 480
Wars with Arabs, 100, 103, 104,
166–67, 197–99, 204
See also Countries; Headline History
Israel, ancient, 83, 197, 407–08
Istanbul, Turkey, 260
Italy, 199–200
Structures, 316–17
Volcanoes, 456
World War I, 97
World War II, 99
See also Countries; Roman Empire
Ivory Coast, 200–01
See also Countries
Iwo Jima, 455

J

Jackson, Andrew, 571–72
See also Headline History; Presidents
(U.S.)
Jackson, Miss., 658
Jacksonville, Fla., 680–81
See also Cities (U.S.)
Jack the Ripper, 95
Jakarta, Indonesia, 191
Jamaica, 201
See also Countries
James, Jesse, 531, 545
James River, 470
Jamestown, Va., 89, 454, 670
Jammu, 189, 190, 191
Japan, 201–03, 453
China and, 95, 98, 152, 202
Islands, 465–66
Russia and, 96, 202
Volcanoes, 455
War trial, 100
World War II, 99, 202
World War II peace treaty, 202
See also Countries
Japanese in U.S.:
Births and birth rates, 775
See also Nonwhite persons
Japan Sea, 461
Japurá River, 464
Jarvis Island, 673
Java, 192, 465
See also Indonesia
Javelin throw. *See* Track and Field
Jefferson, Thomas, 91, 570–71
Birthday, 388
See also Headline History; Presidents
(U.S.)
Jehovah's Witnesses, 416
Jenolan Caves, 467
Jersey (island), 268–69
Jerusalem, 83, 85, 86, 196, 197,
198, 407
Jesus Christ, 85, 408
Jet propulsion:
First use in aviation, 440
Invention, 343
Jewelry:
Birthstones, 496
Consumer spending, 57
Jewish holidays, 385–86, 387, 389
Jewish Museum, 796
Jewish New Year, 386, 389
Jews. *See* Judaism
Jihad, 86
Joan of Arc, 87, 171, 531
Jobs. *See* Employment
Jockeys. *See* Horse racing
Johnson, Andrew, 574
Impeachment, 574, 605
See also Headline History; Presidents
(U.S.)
Johnson, Lyndon B., 579
See also Headline History; Presidents
(U.S.)
Johnston Atoll, 673
Johnstown flood (1889), 95, 641
Joint Chiefs of Staff, 614

Jones, Casey, 545
Jones, Jim, 185
Jordan (kingdom), 203–04
See also Countries
Journalism awards, 508–12
Juan Fernández Islands, 150
Judaism, 407–08
Congregations, 413–14
Followers, 296, 407, 412
Holidays, 385–86, 387, 389
Organizations, 413–14
Judiciary, U.S., 602
Act of 1789, 544
Constitutional provisions, 551–52
See also Supreme Court
Judo, 821, 874
Julian Calendar, 382–83
Junior Colleges, 710–20
Jupiter (planet), 356, 359, 367
See also Planets
Jura Mountains, 254
Jurassic Period, 338
Jury trial, 552, 553–54
Justice, U.S. Department of, 614
Attorneys General, 597–601
Justices. *See* Supreme Court
Justinian Code, 85
Jutland, Battle of, 97

K

Kabul, Afghanistan, 131
Kalahari Desert, 466
Kamchatka, 455
Kampala, Uganda, 261
Kampuchea. *See* Cambodia
Kanawha-New River, 470
Kansas, 653–54
See also States of U.S.
Kansas City, Mo., 423, 681
See also Cities (U.S.)
Kansas-Nebraska Act, 94
Karafuto. *See* Sakhalin
Kara Kum Desert, 466
Karat (measure), 349, 353
Kariba Lake, 462
Kashmir, 189, 190, 191, 228
Katanga (now Shaba), 279
Katmandu, Nepal, 221
Kazakhstan, U.S.S.R., 246
Kellogg-Briand Pact, 98
Kelvin (scale), 345, 349
Kennedy, Cape. *See* Cape Canaveral
Kennedy, Edward M., 103, 610
Kennedy, Jacqueline. *See* Onassis,
Jacqueline
Kennedy, John F., 102, 545, 578–79
Death, 102, 106, 545, 579
Warren Report, 102–03
See also Headline History; Presidents
(U.S.)
Kennedy, Robert F., 103, 545
Kennedy International Airport, 442,
662
Kent's Cavern, 467
Kent State University, 103, 104, 106
Kentucky, 654
See also States of U.S.
Kentucky Derby, 95, 654, 872–73,
874
Kenya, 204–05
See also Countries
Kepler, Johannes, 89, 354, 361, 532
Key, Francis Scott, 532, 559
Kharkov, U.S.S.R., 245
Khartoum, Sudan, 95, 251
Khmer Republic. *See* Cambodia
Khomeini, Ayatollah, 106, 193–94
Krushchev, Nikita, 101, 102, 246,
248, 579
Kiel Canal, 322
Kiev, U.S.S.R., 245, 246, 247
Kigali, Rwanda, 236
Kilauea, 456
Kilogram, 345, 348, 351

Kilometer, 345, 347, 350, 351
Kindergarten, 706, 708
King, Rev. Martin Luther, Jr., 101, 103, 545
Kingman Reef, 673–74
Kings:
  Of England, 264
  Of France, 171–73
  Of Prussia, 180
Kings Canyon National Park, 636
Kingston, Jamaica, 201
Kinshasa, Zaire, 278
Kirghizia, U.S.S.R., 246
Kiribati, 205
  See also Countries
Kissinger, Henry A., 197, 198, 275, 497, 520, 532, 600–01
Kitty Hawk, N.C., 438, 663
Kiwanis International, 622
Kjölen Mountains, 253
Knights of Columbus, 622
Knights of Pythias, 622
Knot (measure), 349
Know-Nothing Party, 591
Knox, John, 88
Kohoutek (comet), 360, 361
Koran (Qur'an), 409
Korea, North, 205–06
  See also Countries; Korean War
Korea, South, 206–07, 457
  See also Countries; Korean War
Korean War, 100, 206, 207, 399
  Casualties, U.S., 400
  Unknown Soldier of, 569
Kosciusko, Mount, 136
Kosygin, Alexei N., 246, 248
Krakatau, 456, 641
Kremlin (structure), 316–17
K-2 (Mount Godwin Austen), 460
Kuala Lumpur, Malaysia, 213
Kublai Khan, 87, 151, 219
Ku Klux Klan, 97
Kunlun Mountains, 151
Kuomintang, 152, 154
Kurile Islands, 202, 455
Kuskokwim River, 470
Kuwait, 207–08
  See also Countries
Ky, Nguyen Cao. *See* Nguyen Cao Ky
Kyushu (island), 202, 466
Kyzyl Kum Desert, 466

L

Labor:
  Civilian labor force, 36, 48–52, 56–57
  ILO, 328
  NLRB, 617
  Statistics, 36, 48–56, 57, 59
  Strikes and lockouts, 48
  Unions, leading, 47–48
  World, 117–18
  See also Employment
Labor, U.S. Department of, 615
  Secretaries of, 599–601
Labor Day, 386, 388, 389
Labors of Hercules, 789
Labrador, 282, 287, 453
Laccadive Islands, 189
Lacrosse, 858
Lady Byng Trophy, 847
Laetrile, 105
Lagos, Nigeria, 225, 226
Lakes, 462–63
  Total volume, 633
  See also specific lakes
Lakeshores, National, 636, 639
"Lame Duck" Amendment, 556
Lamp, electric incandescent, 342
Lancaster, House of, 264
Land:
  Area of cities, 677–86
  Area of countries, 108–09, 131–281

Area of states, 646–72
Farmland, 562–64
World area, 457
Land rushes, 664
Languages:
  Foreign phrases, 494
  Use by country, 131–281
Laos, 208–09
  See also Countries
Lao-Tse, 83, 151
La Paz, Bolivia, 142
Larceny, 782, 783, 784
Larsen, Don, 916
Laser, 343
Lassen Peak, 455, 648
Lassen Volcanic National Park, 636
Lateran Treaty, 98, 273
Latin America:
  Alliance for Progress, 127
  Maps, 478, 479
  OAS, 128
  Population, 112
Latitudes of cities, 458, 471
Latter-day Saints, 416
Latvia, 99, 246, 247
Laundries, hours, wages, 53
Lausanne, Switzerland, 254
Law, codes of, 83, 85, 92
Law, first unconstitutional, 544
Law enforcement, 781–85, 787
  Officers killed, 787
  Prisoners under death sentence, 785, 787
  See also Crime; Arrests
Laws. *See* Bills (Congressional)
Lawyers, 50, 51
  First woman, 544
Lead, 340
League (measure), 349
League of Nations, 97, 98, 99, 100, 255
Leaning Tower of Pisa, 317
Leather:
  Economic statistics, 41, 42, 53
  Industry, hours and wages, 53
Lebanon, 209–10
  Civil War, 104, 209
  U.S. military action in, 209, 399
  See also Countries
Lee, Robert E., 94, 388, 533
Leeward Islands. *See* British Virgin Islands; Montserrat; West Indies Associated States
Legal holidays, 388–89
Legends, American folklore, 545
Legionnaire's disease, 104
Legislatures (state), 676
  Only unicameral, 659, 676
Legislatures (world), 131–281
  Oldest, 188
Lena River, 463
Lend-Lease, 99
Length, units of, 345–47
  Metric Systems, 345–47
Lenin, N., 97, 246, 247
Leningrad, U.S.S.R., 245, 247
  See also Cities (world)
Lens, bifocal, 343
Lent, 385
Leonardo da Vinci, 88, 106, 107
Leopold-Loeb case, 98
Lesbos, 182
Lesotho, 210
  See also Countries
Lesser Antilles, volcanoes, 456
Letters:
  Forms of address, 492–94
  Postal regulations, 625–28
Lewis and Clark expedition, 92, 454, 665, 670
Lexington-Concord, Battle of, 89
Liberia, 210–11
  See also Countries
Liberty, Statue of, 95, 309
Liberty Bell, 584, 666
Libraries, 708, 790

First circulating, 544
Presidential, 307–09
Number of librarians, 51
U.S. public, 790
Library of Congress, 618
Libreville, Gabon, 176
Libya, 211
  See also Countries
Libyan Desert, 466
Licenses:
  Auto license plates, 786
  Drivers' licenses, 786
  Marriage licenses, 767
Lidice, Czechoslovakia, 99
Lie, Trygve, 326
Liechtenstein, 211–12
  See also Countries
Life expectancy, 779–81
Life in outer space, 104
Life insurance, 41, 45
Life on earth, 338–39
Light:
  Discoveries, 343
  Velocity of, 343, 354
"Lighthouse of the Mediterranean," 456
Lightning, 367
Lightning rod, 343
Light-year, 349, 354
Lilongwe, Malawi, 213
Lima, Peru, 230
Lincoln, Abraham, 385, 388, 545, 573–74, 652
  Assassination, 94, 545
  Emancipation Proclamation, 559–60
  Gettysburg Address, 560
  Home, 308
  Lincoln-Douglas debates, 94
  See also Headline History; Presidents (U.S.)
Lincoln's Birthday, 385, 388
Lindbergh, Charles A., 98, 439
Lindbergh kidnapping, 98
Lindenwald, 307
Linear measure, 345–47
Linotype machine, 343
Lions Clubs, 622
Lipari Islands, 456
Liquid measure, 346–48, 350, 351
Liquor:
  Age for purchase of, 788
  Economic statistics, 45, 57, 70
  Law violations, 782, 783
  Taxes, 429
  See also Prohibition
Lisbon, Portugal, 234
  Earthquake (1755), 90, 641
Liter, 345, 347–48, 351
Literature:
  Authors. *See* Awards; People
Lithium, 340
Lithography, 343
Lithuania, 99, 246, 247
Little Big Horn, Battle of, 95, 659
Little Brown Jug, 893
Little League World Series, 923
Little Missouri River, 470
"Little White House," 651
Livestock, 58, 59
Loans:
  Educational loans, 705
  GI loans, 396
  Interest rates, 34, 38, 47
  Mortgages, 35, 47
Locarno Conferences, 98
Lockheed, 104
Lockouts, 48
Locomotive, 343
Logan, Mount, 282
Logarithm, 343
Lomé, Togo, 258
London, England, 262
  Fire (1666), 89, 642
  Great Plague, 89
  Structures, 317
  See also Cities (world)

London, Tower of, 317
Long, Huey P., 99, 533, 545
Long Beach, Calif., 681
  See also Cities (U.S.)
Longevity, animal, 634
Long Island, Battle of, 89
Longitude of cities, 458, 471
Long runs on Broadway, 795
Loom, 343
Lord's prayer, 102
Los Angeles, Calif., 423, 681
  Museums, 800–01, 802
  See also Cities (U.S.)
Lots, Feast of, 385, 389
Louisiana, 654–55
  See also States of U.S.
Louisiana Purchase, 97, 655, 763
Louisiana Superdome, 318
Louis XVI, 91, 172, 173
Louis, Joe, 864, 870, 871
Louisville, Ky., 654, 681
  See also Cities (U.S.)
Louvre, 317
Lowest points, U.S., 468
LST, 368
Luanda, Angola, 133
Luge, 822, 922
Lumber and wood:
  Economic statistics, 41, 42, 45, 53, 70
  Industry, hours and wages, 53
  See also Forests
Lunar flights, 370, 374–76
Lunar probes, 369–70, 371–72, 373, 374–76
Lunation, 382
Luray Cavern, 467
Lusaka, Zambia, 279–80
Lusitania, 97
Luther, Martin, 88, 179, 409
Lutheran Churches, 414, 417–18
Luxembourg, 212
  See also Countries
Luzon, Philippines, 231, 466
Lydian civilization, 84

M

Macao, 235
MacArthur, Douglas, 98, 100, 202, 206, 207
Maccabean revolt, 84
MacDonald, Ramsay, 265
Macedonia, 182, 278
Machine gun, 343
Machinery:
  Economic statistics, 41, 42, 45, 70
  Industry, hours and wages, 53
  Inventions, 342–44
Machu Picchu, Peru, 86
Macias Nguema Biyogo, 168
Mackenzie River, 454, 463
Mackinac Straits Bridge, 321
Macmillan, Harold, 265
Madagascar, 212–13, 465
  See also Countries
Madeira, Portugal, 234
Madeira River, 463
Madison, James, 571
  See also Headline History; Presidents (U.S.)
Madrid, Spain, 249
Magazines, 449
  Advertising, 56
Magellan, Ferdinand, 88, 454, 534
Maggiore, Lake, 199, 254
Magna Carta, 86, 263
Magnesium, 340
Magnum, 349
Mahabharata, 410
Mail:
  Air-mail route, first, 544
  Postal regulations, 625–28
  World statistics, 121–22
Maine, 655

  See also States of U.S.
Maine (battleship), 95, 158
Majorca, 250
Majority, plurality, 587
Malabo, Equatorial Guinea, 168
Malagasy, 213
Malawi, 213
  See also Countries
Malaya. *See* Malaysia
Malay Archipelago, 192
Malaysia, 213–14
  See also Countries
Malcolm X, 103
Maldives, 214–15
  See also Countries
Malé, Maldives, 214
Malenkov, Georgi M., 101, 246, 248
Mali, 215
  See also Countries
Mali Empire, 87
Malta, 215–16
  See also Countries
Mammals:
  Age of, 339
  Endangered, 630
Mammoth Cave, 467, 636, 654
Man, Isle of, 269
Management and Budget, Office of, 613
Managerial workers, 49, 51–52
Managua, Nicaragua, 223, 224
Manama, Bahrain, 138
Manchu Dynasty, 89, 96, 152, 202
Manchukuo, 152, 202
Manchuria, 96, 98, 151, 152, 202
Manganese, 340
Manhattan, 662, 683, 760
Manhattan Project, 99
Manila, Philippines, 231
Manitoba, 282, 283, 284, 285, 286–87
Manned space flights, 370, 373, 374–77
Manslaughter, 782, 783
Mantle (of the Earth), 357
Manufacturing. *See* Industry
Mao Tse-tung. *See* Mao Zedong
Mao Zedong, 152–54, 534
Maps, 459, 472–88
Maputo, Mozambique, 220
Marathon, Battle of, 83
Marathon champions, U.S., 880
Marconi, Guglielmo, 96, 344, 534
Marco Polo, 87, 453, 537
Mardi Gras, 385, 389
Margarine, 59, 81
Mariana Islands, 675
Marie Antoinette, 91, 534
Marine Corps, U.S., 391, 394, 401
  Actions, 96, 98, 102, 103, 104, 257, 399
  Commandant of, 614
  See also Armed Forces
Mariner space probes, 369, 371–72
Marne, Battle of, 97
Marquesas Islands, 174
Marriage:
  Prospects of, by age, 768
  State laws, 767
  Statistics, 766–71
Mars (planet), 356, 358–59, 360
  Space probes, 369, 370, 371–72, 373
  See also Planets
Marshall, John, 603
Marshall Islands, 675
Marshall Plan, 100, 128, 578
Martinique, 175
  Mount Pelée, 456, 641
Marx, Karl, 93, 94, 534
Mary, Queen of Scots, 89
Maryland, 655–56
  See also States of U.S.
Maseru, Lesotho, 210
Mason and Dixon's Line, 468
Mass:

Chemical elements, 339–40
Metric System, 345
Massachusetts, 656
  See also States of U.S.
Mass-energy theorem, 341, 352
Massive, Mount, 469
Masters Tournament (golf), 896
Match, 343
Maternal mortality, 776
Mathematics:
  Averages, 353
  Decimals and fractions, 352
  Formulas, 352
  Mean and median, 353
  Metric and U.S. equivalents, 346–48, 350, 351
  Prefixes and multiples, 352
  Prime numbers, 353
Matter-energy theorem, 341, 352
Mauna Kea, 456, 468, 651
Mauna Loa, 456, 651
Maundy Thursday, 389
Mauritania, 216
  See also Countries
Mauritius, 216–17
  See also Countries
Maximilian, Emperor, 94, 217, 534
Mayaguez incident, 104, 257
Mayflower (ship), 89
Mayflower Compact, 558
Mayors, U.S., 677–86, 687
Mayotte, Comoros, 156, 175
Mbabane, Swaziland, 265
McCarthy (Joseph) hearings, 101
McDonald Islands, 136
McHenry, Fort, 93, 559
McKinley, Mount, 461, 468, 469, 636, 647
McKinley, William, 545, 575
  See also Headline History; Presidents (U.S.)
McNary Dam, 665
Mean and median, 353
Measles, 79, 776
Measurement ton, 349
Measures, weights, 345–53
  Capacities and volumes, 347–48
  Conversion factors, 351
  Cooking, 350
Meat:
  Calories and vitamins, 80–82
  Economic statistics, 59, 70, 120–21
  World production, 120–21
Mecca, Saudi Arabia, 238, 239, 409
Medal of Freedom, 519–20
Mede civilization, 84
Media, 446–50
  Magazines, 449
  Newspapers, 446–48, 449–50
Mediation and Conciliation Service, Federal, 616
Medicaid, 701–02
Medical care:
  Economic statistics, 36, 57, 75
Medicare, 103, 698, 700–02
Medicine:
  Discoveries, 342–44
  Hospital facilities, 74–75
  Nobel Prizes for, 31, 501–02
Medina, Saudi Arabia, 239, 409
Mediterranean Sea, 461
  Volcanoes, 456
"Mein Kampf" (Hitler), 97, 98
Meir, Golda, 197, 535
Mekong River, 463
Melting points, of elements, 339–40
Melville Island, 466
Memorial Day, 386, 388
Memorial Day, Confederate, 388
Memorials, National, 636, 638–39
Memphis, Tenn., 681–82
  See also Cities (U.S.)
Mendelevium, 340
Mendelian Law, 343
Mennonites, 416, 417
Merced River, waterfalls, 464–65

Merchant Marine Academy, U.S., 393
Mercury (element), 340
Mercury (planet), 356, 358
  Flights, 369, 372
  See also Planets
Mercury-vapor lamp, 342
Meredith, James H., 102
Merrimack (ship), 94
Mesabi Range, 657
Mesa Verde National Park, 637
Mesopause, 358
Mesopotamia, 84, 194
  Map, 481
Mesopotamian Empire, 83
Mesosphere, 358
Mesozoic Era, 338
Metals:
  As elements, 339–40
  Economic statistics, 41, 42, 70
  Industry, hours and wages, 53
  Mineral wealth in countries,
    131–281
Meteors and meteorites, 361–62
  Showers, 361, 362
Meter, 345, 347, 351
Methodist Church. *See* United
  Methodist Church
Methodist churches, 414, 417–18
Metric System, 345–48, 350–51
  Conversion tables, 350–51
Metropolitan areas, 751–54
Metropolitan Museum of Art, 796
Metropolitan Opera, 95
Mexican Cession, 217, 763
Mexican War, 93, 217, 400
Mexico, 83, 84, 217–18
  Conquest of, 88, 217, 453
  Map, 478
  Revolution, 96
  U.S. military actions in, 217, 399
  Volcanoes, 456
  See also Countries
Mexico, Gulf of, 461
Mexico City, Mexico, 217
  See also Cities (world)
Miami, Fla., 423, 682
  Race riots, 107
  See also Cities (U.S.)
Michigan, 656–57
  See also States of U.S.
Michigan, Lake, 454, 462
Micronesia, 674–75
Microscope, compound, 343
Middle East;
  Arab-Israeli conflicts, 100, 101–02,
    103, 104, 105, 166–67,
    197–99, 204
  Countries, 130
  Maps, 480–81
Midway Islands, 674
Mileage:
  Canadian cities, between, 295
  U.S. cities, between, 310–11
  World cities, between, 314–15
Mile records:
  Race horses (harness), 892–93
  Runners, 877–79
Military. *See* National defense
Military Academy, U.S., 391
Military construction, 42
Military forces. *See* Armed Forces
Military interventions, U.S., 399
Military Parks, National, 636, 638
Military sales, 406
Military strength, U.S., 390, 403
Milk:
  Calories and vitamins, 81
  Economic statistics, 59
Milk River, 470
Milky Way, 354–55
Milwaukee, Wis., 682
  See also Cities (U.S.)
Milwaukee Art Center, 801
Mindanao, Philippines, 231, 466
Mindszenty, Jozsef Cardinal, 187,
  188

Minerals. *See* Coal; Metals
Minerals:
  Dietary allowances, 78
  Food value, 80–82
Ming Dynasty, 87, 89, 151
Mining:
  Hours and wages, 53
  Plant, equipment costs, 43
  Production, 42
  Union, 47
Minneapolis, Minn., 657, 682
  See also Cities (U.S.)
Minnesota, 657–58
  See also States of U.S.
Minoan culture, 83, 84
Minority Presidents, 596
Minsk, Byelorussia, 245, 246
Minutemen, 656
Miquelon. *See* St. Pierre
Mississippi, 658
  See also States of U.S.
Mississippi-Missouri-Red Rock River,
  463, 470
Mississippi River, 453, 454, 463,
  470
Missouri, 658–59
  See also States of U.S.
Missouri (battleship), 99
Missouri Compromise, 93, 571, 658
Missouri-Red Rock River, 463, 470
Missouri River, 463, 470
Mistletoe, 387
Mitterrand, François, 171, 172, 173,
  174
Mmabatho, Bophuthatswana, 244
Mobile-Alabama-Coosa River, 470
Mobile homes, 43
Modern Art, Museum of, 796
Mogadishu, Somalia, 241
Mohammed, 85, 239, 409–10
Mojave Desert, 466
Moldavia, U.S.S.R., 246
Mole, 345
Molecular genetics, 7–8
Moluccas Islands, 192
Monaco, 218–19, 457
  See also Countries
Mondale, Walter F., 584, 594, 595
Monetary Fund, International, 328
Money:
  Designs of U.S. bills, 353
  Of countries, 131–281
  Portraits on U.S. Bills, 353
Money orders, postal, 626
Mongolia, 219, 453
  See also Countries
Mongols, 85, 86, 87
Monitor (ship), 94
"Monkey Trial," 98
Monroe, James, 571
  See also Headline History; Presidents
    (U.S.)
Monroe Doctrine, 93, 558, 571
Monrovia, Liberia, 210
Montana, 659
  See also States of U.S.
Mont Blanc, 171
Mont Blanc Tunnel, 320
Monte Carlo, Monaco, 219
Montenegro, 278
Montevideo, Uruguay, 271
Months:
  Birthstones for, 496
  Name derivations, 384
  Sidereal and synodic, 354
Monticello, Va., 307, 670
Montreal, Quebec, Canada, 282, 284,
  289, 297
Montserrat, 269–70
"Monumental Mountain," 467
Monuments, National, 636, 637
Moon, 357
  Apollo program, 374–76
  Eclipses, 364
  First manned landing, 103, 375
  Lunar probes, 371–72

Map, 488
  Perigee and apogee, 364–65
  Phases, 364–65
  Phenomena, 364–65
  Symbols, 363
Moons of planets, 354, 357–59, 367,
  419
Moors, 86, 87
Moral Majority, 9, 10
Moravia, 160
Moravian Church, 416
Morgan Library, 797
Mormons, 93, 105, 416
Moro, Aldo, 105, 200
Morocco, 219–20
  See also Countries
Moroni, Comoros, 156
Morse, Samuel F.B., 93, 344, 535
Mortality. *See* Deaths
Mortgage terms, 35, 47
Moscow, U.S.S.R., 245, 247
  See also Cities (world)
Moses, 83
Moslem architecture, 317
Most Valuable Player:
  Baseball, 912
  Basketball, 843
  Hockey, 846–47
"Mother of Presidents," 670
Motion pictures:
  Awards, 504–07
  Income from, 794, 795
  Inventions, 343
  Stars of, 504–07, 521–43
  Top-grossing, 795
  Top rentals of 1980, 794
Motor, 343
Motorcycle, 343
Motorcycle racing, 845
Motor vehicles:
  Accident deaths, 776–77
  Canadian, 292
  Economic statistics, 65–67
  Fuel consumption, 334
  Registration, 65, 334
  State laws, 786
  Thefts, 782, 783, 784
  See also Automobiles; Buses
Mottoes:
  Canadian, 291
  National, 611
  State, 646–72
Mound State Monument Museum, 801
Mountains:
  United States, 461, 468, 469
  World, 460–61
  See also names of mountains;
    Volcanoes
Mount Evans Highway, 649
Mount McKinley National Park. *See*
  Denali National Park
Mount Rainier National Park, 637,
  670
Mount Vernon, Va., 307, 584, 670
Movies. *See* Motion pictures
Mozambique, 220–21, 235
  See also Countries
Mozart, Wolfgang Amadeus, 91, 536
Munich, West Germany, 178
  Beer hall putsch (1923), 97
Munich Conference (1938), 99, 179
Murder, 782, 783, 784, 787
Murray River, 464
Muscat, Oman, 227
Muscle Shoals plant, 646
Museums:
  First science museum, 544
  Presidential, 307–09
  United States, 796–802
Music:
  Classical, 792
  Popular, 792
  Pulitzer Prize for, 515–16
  U.S. Symphony orchestras, 789
Muslims. *See* Islam
Mussolini, Benito, 97, 99, 199
Mystic Seaport, Conn., 801

N

NAACP, 622–23
Nagasaki, Japan, 99, 202, 341
Nairobi, Kenya, 204
Names:
  Animal, 633
  States, origins of, 646–72
Namibia, 244–45
  See also Countries
Nantes, Edict of, 88, 90
Napoleon Bonaparte. *See* Bonaparte, Napoleon
Napoleonic Code, 92
Napoleonic Wars, 92, 93, 173
Narcotics, number of arrests, 782, 783
NASA, 616
NASCAR, 926, 927
Nashville, Tenn., 682
  See also Cities (U.S.)
Nassau, Bahamas, 137
Nasser, Gamal Abdel, 166, 197, 277
National Academy of Design, 796–97
National Aeronautics and Space Administration, 616
National Anthem, 559
National Basketball Association, 840, 841–45
National Capital Parks, 636, 639
National Cemeteries, 569
  Arlington, 569, 584, 639
National Committees, 591
National Conventions, 586–87
National debt, 60, 63
  Interest, 60
  Validity, 555
National defense, 398
  Sales to foreign countries, 406
  Spending for, 37, 59, 60, 398, 403
National Foundation on the Arts and Humanities, 616
National Gallery of Art, 798
National Guard, The, 393–94
National Historic Sites and Historical Parks, 635–39
National Hockey League, 846–49
National income, 40
National Labor Relations Board, 617
National League. *See* Baseball; Football
National Park System, 635–39
National Parkways, 636, 639
National Republican Party, 588
National Scenic Riverways, 636, 639
National Science Foundation, 617
National Security Council, 613
National Sports Festival, 901
National Transportation Safety Board, 617
National Zoo, 634, 635
NATO. *See* North Atlantic Treaty Organization
Natural features (of countries), 131–281
Natural gas, 331, 332
Natural history museums, 796–802
Naturalization statistics, 762
Natural resources:
  South America map, 479
  States of U.S., 646–72
Nauru, 221
  See also Countries
Nautilus (submarine), 101
Navaho Ceremonial Art, Museum of, 802
Naval Academy, U.S., 391–92, 656
Navy (U.S.), 92, 390, 394, 401
  Combatant vessels, 401
  Expenditures, 60
  First admiral, 544
  Secretaries of, 597–600, 614
  See also Armed Forces
Nazarene, Church of the, 415

Nazis, 98, 99, 100, 102, 179
N'Djamena, Chad, 149
"Neap tides," 357
Near East, maps, 477, 480–81
Nebraska, 659–60
  Kansas-Nebraska Act, 94
  See also States of U.S.
Nebuchadnezzar, 83, 316
Negev Desert, 196
Negroes. *See* Blacks
Nehru, Jawaharlal, 190, 536
Nelson Gallery of Art, 801
Nelson River, 464
Neosho River, 470
Nepal, 221
  See also Countries
Neptune (planet), 356, 359, 367
  See also Planets
Neptunium, 343
Netherlands, 221–22, 457
  See also Countries
Netherlands Antilles, 222–23
Networks, TV, 793
Neutron, discovery of, 343
Nevada, 660
  See also States of U.S.
Nevis, 270–71
New Amsterdam, 89
Newark, N.J., 682–83
  See also Cities (U.S.)
New Brunswick, 283, 284, 287
New Caledonia, 175
"New Colossus, The," 309
New Cornelia Tailings, 323, 647
New Deal, 98, 99, 577–78
New Delhi, India, 188
Newfoundland, 282, 283, 284, 285, 287, 466
New Freedom, 576
"New Frontier," 578
New Guinea. *See* Papua New Guinea
New Hampshire, 660–61
  See also States of U.S.
New Hebrides. *See* Vanuatu
New Jersey, 661
  See also States of U.S.
New Mexico, 661–62
  See also States of U.S.
New Orleans, 423, 683
  See also Cities (U.S.)
New Orleans, Battle of, 93, 655
New Party, 592
News:
  Chronology (4500 B.C. to A.D. 1980), 83–107
  Current Events, 11–31
Newspapers, 446–48, 449–50
  Advertising, 56
  Awards, 508–12
  Firsts, 544
  Oldest still published, 649
  Postal rates, 625
  World circulation, 121–22
Newsreel, first, 544
Newton, Isaac, 89, 343, 536
Newton (measure), 345
New Year, Jewish, 386, 389
New Year's Day, 385, 388
New York City, 662–63, 683, 760
  Boroughs, 683, 760
  Bridges, 321
  Buildings and structures, 317–18, 320
  Climate, 423
  Kennedy Airport, 442, 662
  Museums, 796–97
  Statue of Liberty, 309
  Tunnels, 320
  Tweed Ring, 95
  U.N. Headquarters, 325
  World's Fairs, 99, 795
  See also Cities (U.S.)
New York Drama Critics' Circle Awards, 517–18
New-York Historical Society, 797
New York (State), 662–63

  See also States of U.S.
New York State Historical Association, 801
New Zealand, 223
  First visited, 454
  Volcanoes, 455
  See also Countries
Niagara Falls, 465
Niamey, Niger, 224
Nicaea, Council of, 85, 408
Nicaragua, 107, 223–24
  U.S. military actions in, 224, 399
  Volcanoes, 456
  See also Countries
Nicene Creed, 85, 408
Nickel (element), 340
Nicknames:
  Football teams, 835
  States (U.S.), 646–72
Nicobar Islands, 189
Nicosia, Cyprus, 159
Niger, 224–25
  See also Countries
Nigeria, 225–26
  See also Countries
Niger River, 225, 463
Nile River, 165, 251, 463
  High Aswan Dam, 166, 319, 323
Niobara River, 470
Nirvana, 410
Nitroglycerin, 343
Niue (island), 223
Nixon, Richard M., 579–80
  Resignation, 104, 580
  See also Headline History; Presidents (U.S.)
NLRB, 617
Noatak River, 470
Nobel, Alfred, 94, 342, 497, 536
Nobel Prizes, 31, 96, 497–502
  For 1981, 31
Nonfiction (general), awards for, 515
Nonwhite persons in U.S.:
  Deaths and death rates, 778, 779, 780–81
  Life expectancy, 779–81
  Population statistics, 750–51, 754, 763
  See also Chinese; Indians; Japanese; Blacks in U.S.
Norfolk Island, 136
Normandy, House of, 264
Normandy Invasion, 99
Norris Trophy, 847
North America, 130, 455, 457
  Explorations, discoveries, 453–54
  Maps, 473, 474–75, 478
  Population, 112
  See also Countries
North Atlantic Treaty Organization, 100, 128, 130
  France and, 173, 174
  Military strength, 403, 405
  Warsaw Pact, military balance with, 405
North Canadian River, 470
North Carolina, 663
  See also States of U.S.
North Cascades National Park, 637
North Dakota, 663–64
  See also States of U.S.
Northeast Passage, 454
Northern Ireland, 262, 263, 266–67
  See also United Kingdom
"Northern lights," 363
Northern Rhodesia. *See* Zambia
North Island (New Zealand), 223, 465
North Platte River, 470
North Pole, 96, 454
  Flights over, 439, 440
  Reached, 93, 454
North Sea, 140, 161, 178, 222, 226, 263, 461
North West Company, 286
North West Mounted Police, 290

See also Royal Canadian Mounted Police
Northwest Passage, 454
Northwest Territories, 282, 283, 285, 288
Norway, 226–27
See also Countries
Notre-Dame de Paris, 317
Nouakchott, Mauritania, 216
Nova Scotia, 282, 283, 285, 288, 453
Novelists. *See* Awards; People
NRC, 617
NSF, 617
Nubian Desert, 466
Nuclear fission, 341, 343
Nuclear physics, discoveries and theories, 341, 343
Nuclear power plants, U.S., 334
Nuclear proliferation, 105
Nuclear reactors, 341, 343, 640
Nuclear Regulatory Commission, 617
Nuclear Test Ban Treaty, 129
Nuclear weapons, 341, 405
Test ban treaty, 129
Testing by country, 99, 100, 101, 103, 104
Nuku'alofa, Tonga, 258
Numbers:
Decimals and fractions, 352
Prime, 353
Roman, 353
Nuremberg laws, 98
Nuremberg war trial, 98, 100
Nurses, 74
Nutrition, 73–82
Contents of foods, 80–82
Dietary allowances, 78
Dietary guidelines, 75–77
Nuts, food value, 81
Nyasa, Lake, 462
Nyasaland. *See* Malawi
Nylon, 343

O

Oakland, Calif., 683
See also Cities (U.S.)
OAO, 368
OAS. *See* Organization of American States
Oaths:
Constitutional, 552–53
Presidential, 551
OAU. *See* Organization of African Unity
Oberlin College, 544
Ob River, 463
Occupational Safety and Health Review Commission, 618
Oceania, 455, 457
Countries, 130, 457
Elevations, 457
Explorations and discoveries, 454
Population, 112, 457
Religions, 407
Entries under Continents *may also apply*
Ocean liners. *See* Steamships
Oceans, 461
Volume of, 633
Odd Fellows, Independent Order of, 623
Oder-Neisse Line, 179, 180
Odessa, U.S.S.R., 245
"Odyssey," 83
Office of Personnel Management, 617
Offices, Executive, 613–18
Ohio, 664
See also States of U.S.
Ohio-Allegheny River, 464, 470
Ohio River, 470
Ohm, 349
Ohm's Law, 343
Oil (petroleum):
Crude production, 333

Economic statistics, 42, 53, 70, 115–16
First well in U.S., 544
Industry, hours and wages, 54
Imported directly from OPEC countries, 333
World production, 115–16, 333
Oils, fats, 59, 70
Food value, 81
O.K. Corral, 647
Okhotsk Sea, 461
Okinawa, 103, 202–03
Oklahoma, 664–65
See also States of U.S.
Oklahoma City, Okla., 683
.. *See also* Cities (U.S.)
Öland, 253
Old Age. *See* Growing Older
Old North Church, 656
Olympic Games, 809–22
History, sites, 96, 809
Munich Massacre, 103
1980 Games, 809–22
Olympic National Park, 637
Omaha, Neb., 659–60, 683–84
See also Cities (U.S.)
Oman, 227
See also Countries
Onassis, Aristotle, 219, 536
Onassis, Jacqueline, 536, 578, 585
Ontario, Canada, 282, 284–85, 289
Ontario, Lake, 462
OPEC, 35, 128, 130, 193, 239, 274, 329, 333
Map, 486
See also Economy in 1981
Opium War, 93
OPM, 617
Orange Bowl, 824
Orange River, 464
Orbiting Astronomical Observatory, 368
Orbiting Solar Observatory, 369
Orbits:
Comets, 360–61
Minor planets (asteroids), 360
Moon, 357
Planets, 354, 357–59
Orchestras, symphony, 789
Ordovician Period, 338
Oregon, 665
Volcanoes, 455
See also States of U.S.
Organization for Economic Cooperation and Development, 128, 130
Organization of African Unity, 128, 130
Organization of American States, 100, 128, 130, 150, 158
Dominican Republic and, 164
Organization of Petroleum Exporting Countries, 35, 128, 130, 193, 239, 274, 329, 333
Organizations, 619–24
International, 126–30
Sports, 855–56
Oriental Institute Museum, 797
Orinoco River, 155, 464
Orkney Islands, 263
Orthodox churches, 86, 389, 407, 408–09, 413, 417–18
Osage River, 470
Oscars (awards), 504–07
Oslo, Norway, 226
OSO, 369
Oswald, Lee Harvey, 102–03, 545, 579
Ottawa, Ontario, Canada, 282, 289
Ottoman Turks, 260
Ouachita River, 470
Ouagadougou, Upper Volta, 271
Outer Mongolia. *See* Mongolia.
Owen Falls Lake, 462
Ozark Mountains, 658
Ozone, discovery of, 343

Ozonosphere, 358

Pacific Islands (U.S.), 672–75
Pacific Ocean, 461
Discovery, 453
Islands, 465–66
Map, 485
"Ring of Fire," 455–56
U.S. coastline, 472
Volcanoes, 455–56
See also Oceania
Pacts. *See* Treaties
Paddle tennis, 928
Pagodas, 317
Painted Desert, 466
Painters. *See* People
Pakistan, 138–39, 190, 191, 227–28
See also Countries
Palau Islands, 675
Paleozoic Era, 338
Palestine, 197
Palestinian Liberation Organization, 104, 106, 197–98, 204, 209–10
Palm Sunday, 385, 389
Pamir Mountain Range, 460–61
Panama, 105, 228–29
U.S. military action in, 399
See also Countries
Panama Canal, 96, 105, 157, 228–29, 322
Treaties, 105, 128–29, 229
Panama City, Panama, 228
Panay (gunboat), 99
Pancake Tuesday, 385
Panel quiz radio show, first, 544
Panmunjom, North Korea, 206, 399
Pantheon, Rome, 316
Papal States, 273
Papeete, French Polynesia, 174
Paper:
Economic statistics, 41, 42, 53, 70
Industry, hours and wages, 53
Invention of, 343
Paper currency, portraits on, 353
Papua New Guinea, 229–30, 465
First visited, 454
See also Countries
Parachute, 343
Parachuting:
Caterpillar Club, 439
First jump, 438
Sports parachuting, 904
Paraguay, 230
See also Countries
Paraguay River, 230, 464
Paramaribo, Suriname, 252
Paraná River, 143, 230, 463
Parcel post, 625
Parícutin, 456
Paris, France, 171, 173
Structures, 317
World War I, 97
World War II, 99, 173
Paris, Peace of (1783), 89
Paris, Treaty of (1898), 95
Paris, Treaty of (1947), 100, 187
Parks:
Affiliated areas, 639
City-owned, 677–86
National Park System, 635–39
Provincial (Canada), 286–92
State parks, 646–72
Parliament (Great Britain), 87, 89, 92, 98, 263, 265
Parsec (measure), 349, 354
Parties, political (world), 131–281
Passover, 385, 389
Passports and Customs, 300–01
Patagonia, 134
Patent Appeals, U.S. Court of, 602
Patents, 496
Patients, hospital, 74–75
Paulo Afonso Falls, 143

Peace Corps, 615
Peace Prizes, Nobel, 31, 497
Peace River, 464
Peak Cavern, 467
Pearl Harbor attack, 99, 651
Peary, Robert, E., 96, 454, 537
Pedestrian deaths, 777
Pee Dee-Yadkin River, 470
Peking, China, 151, 152, 317
    Structures, 317
    See also Cities (world)
Pelée, Mount, 456
Peloponnesian War, 83
Penicillin, 98, 342, 343
Pennsylvania, 665–66
    See also States of U.S.
Pennsylvania Academy of Fine Arts, 798
Pennyweight, 346
Pensions:
    Veterans, 397
    See also Social Security
Pentagon, 614
Pentagon Papers, 101
Pentathlon, 813, 821
Pentecost, 386, 389
Pentecost, Hebrew, 386, 389
Pentecostal churches, 416, 417, 418
People, 28, 521–43
People's Party (Populists), 589–90
Per capita income, 37, 39
Performers. *See* People
Pericles, 83, 84
Perihelion, 354, 364, 384–85
Periodic law, 343
Periodic table, 343
Permian Period, 338
Perón, Juan D., 135
Perpetual calendar, 380–81
Persia, ancient, 83, 84
Persia, modern. *See* Iran
Persian Gulf States. *See* United Arab Emirates
Peru, 230–31, 454
    See also Countries
Pesticide, 640
Petition, right of, 553
Petrified Forest National Park, 637
Petroleum. *See* Oil
Petsamo, 247
P.G.A., Champions, 896
Pharos of Alexandria, 316
Philadelphia, Pa., 92, 665–66, 684
    Continental Congresses, 546, 561
    Liberty Bell, 584, 666
    Museums, 798
    See also Cities (U.S.)
Philippines, 231–32
    Tydings-McDuffie Act, 232
    U.S. Territory, 763
    Volcanoes, 455
    See also Countries
Philosophers. *See* People
Phnom-Penh, Cambodia, 106, 146, 147
Phoenician Empire, 84
Phoenix, Ariz., 423, 684
    See also Cities (U.S.)
Phoenix Islands, 205, 673
Phonographs:
    Invention, 95, 343
    Records, 792
Photography:
    Awards, 509–10, 516
    Equipment, 70
    First aerial, 438
    Inventions, 343
Photosphere, 356
Photovoltaics, 330
Phrygian civilization, 84
Physical Fitness, President's Council on, 618
Physicians, number in U.S., 51, 74
    See also Doctors
Physics:
    Inventions, discoveries, and theories,

442–44
    Nobel Prizes for, 31, 498–99
Pi (measure), 349, 352
Pica (measure), 349
Pierce, Franklin, 573
    See also Headline History; Presidents (U.S.)
Pigs, Bay of, 102, 158, 184
Pikes Peak, 469
Pilcomayo River, 464
Pilgrims, 89, 656
Pilots, number of, 443
Pindus Mountains, 182
Pioneer probes, 106, 369, 371–72, 377
Pipe (measure), 349
Pisa, Leaning Tower of, 317
Pitcairn Island, 92, 270
Pittsburgh, Pa., 684
    See also Cities (U.S.).
"Pittsburgh of the South," 646
"Pittsburgh of the West," 648
Plague, 85, 87, 89, 264
Planets, 354, 356–59
    Conjunctions, 364–65
    Exploration of, 367, 370, 371–73
    Minor planets (asteroids), 360, 377
    Moons of, 357–59, 367
    Origin of, 338, 356
    Symbols, 363
    See also Space Exploration; Astronomy
Plantagenet, House of, 264
Plants, classification of, 342
Plastics, 41, 42, 70, 343
Plata River, 143, 271
Platform tennis, 928
Plato, 84
Playwrights. *See* People
Pledge to flag, 569
Pleistocene Period, 339
PLO, 104, 106, 197–98, 204, 209–10
Plow, 343
Plurality, majority, 587
Pluto (planet), 367, 356, 359
    See also Planets
Plutonium, 340, 343
    Used in atomic bomb, 341
Plymouth Colony, 89, 656
Plymouth Rock, 89
Pneumonia, 79, 776
Pocket veto, 601
Poetry, awards for, 515, 520
Poets. *See* People; Awards
Poets Laureate of England, 503
Point Four program, 100
Point (measure), 349
Poisons, treatment of, 71
Poland, 91, 97, 232–34
    Poznan uprising (1956), 101, 233
    Workers Strike (1980), 107, 233–34
    World War II (1939), 99, 233
    See also Countries
Polar flights, 439, 440
Pole vault. *See* Track and Field
Policemen, statistics, 781, 787
Policy Development, White House Office of, 613
Poliomyelitis, 79
    Vaccines, 101, 343
Political parties (U.S.). *See* specific parties
Political parties (world), 131–281
Political rights, 123–26
Political systems, 123–24
Polk, James K., 572–73
    See also Headline History; Presidents (U.S.)
Poll tax, 557
Pollution, 629, 632, 640
Polo, 929
Polo, Marco, 87, 453, 537
Polymerization, 343
Polynesia, French, 174

Pompeii, 456
Pompidou, Georges, 172, 173
Pontiffs, Roman Catholic, 418–20
Pony Express, 628, 658
Popes, 418–20
    John XXIII, 102, 420
    John Paul I, 105, 420
    John Paul II, 105, 106, 233, 420
    Paul VI, 102, 105, 420
Popocatépetl, 456
Population (U.S.), 750–65
    Age, by, 689, 750–51, 754
    Black, 750–51, 754, 763
    Census required by Constitution, 548
    Census years, 750
    Cities:
        Largest, 677–86
        Largest of each state, 646–72
        1970–1980, 756–67
    Civilian labor force, 36, 48–52, 56–57
    Colonial estimates, 750
    Densities (1790–1980), 750, 755
    Family groups, 771
    Female, 750–51, 754
    Foreign-born, 750–51, 762, 764, 765
    Growth, 750–65
    Households, 771
        Income by age of head, 765
    Indians on reservations, 765
    Male, 750–51, 754
    Marital status, 766, 768, 771
    Married couples, 771
    Metropolitan areas, 751–54
    Nativity, 750–51
    Race, 750–51, 754, 763
    Sex, 750–51, 754
    Shifts, 755
    65 and over, 690, 750–51, 754
    Spanish origin, 754, 763
    States, 1790–1980, 755, 763
    Territories, 763
    Total, 763
    Urban, 751–54, 756–62
    Working population, 36, 48–52, 56–57
Population (world), 108–09, 112, 116
    Cities, by country, 131–281
    Cities, largest (table), 109–10
    Continents, 112, 457
    Countries, 131–281
    Countries (table), 108–09
    Densities, 131–281, 457
Populists. *See* People's Party
Porcupine River, 470
Port Arthur, Kwantung, 96, 151, 152
Port-au-Français, French Southern and Antarctic Lands, 176
Port-au-Prince, Haiti, 185
Portland, Ore., 684
    See also Cities (U.S.)
Port Louis, Mauritius, 216
Port Moresby, Papua New Guinea, 229
Port-of-Spain, Trinidad and Tobago, 259
Porto-Novo, Benin, 141
Portraits on U.S. currency, 353
Ports, U.S., commerce at, 64
Portsmouth, Treaty of, 96, 660
Portugal, 234–35
    See also Countries
Portuguese Guinea. *See* Guinea-Bissau
Portuguese West Africa. *See* Angola
Positron, 343
Post, Wiley, 440, 537
Postal regulations, 625–28
Postal Service, U.S., 92, 618
    Employment, 59
    Rates, 625–26, 627
Postal Union, Universal, 328

Post cards, 625
Postmasters General, 597–600
Post Office Department. See Postal Service
Postojna Grotto, 467
Potatoes:
  Calories and vitamins, 82
  Economic statistics, 58, 59
Potomac River, 470, 686
Potsdam Conference, 99, 129, 179
Poultry:
  Calories and vitamins, 80–82
  Economic statistics, 58, 59
Powder River, 470
Power failure of 1965, 103
Power loom, 343
Poznan, Poland, uprising, 101
Prague, Czechoslovakia, 160
Praia, Cape Verde, 148
Preakness Stakes, 873, 874
Precipitation, 294–95, 422–24
Premiers and Prime Ministers:
  Canada, 283
  Countries, 131–281
  Great Britain, 265
  Soviet Union, 246
Presbyterian churches, 88, 414, 417–18
Presidential candidates, 588–91
  First woman, 544
Presidential elections, 588–96
Presidential libraries and museums, 307–09
Presidential Medal of Freedom, 519–20
Presidential oath, 551
"Presidents, Mother of," 670
President's Council on Physical Fitness and Sports, 618
Presidents (foreign), 131–281
  France, 172, 173–74
  Germany, 180
Presidents (U.S.), 570–85
  Assassinations and attempts, 545
  Biographies, 570–82
  Burial places, 584
  Cabinets, 597–601
  Constitutional provisions, 550–51
  Continental Congresses, 561
  Election procedure, 550–51, 554, 586–87
  Elections, 588–96
  Families of, 585
  Homes, 307–09
  Libraries, 307–09
  Minority Presidents, 596
  Mount Rushmore carvings, 667
  Museums, 307–09
  National Historic Sites, 307–09, 638–39
  Nomination, 586
  Oath of Office, 551
  Portraits on currency, 353
  Powers, duties, 550–51
  Qualifications, 550
  Religious affiliations, 583
  Salary, 551, 612
  Succession to, 551, 557, 558
  Tabulated data, 583
  Term of office, 550, 556
  Wives and children, 585
  See also entries under Presidential
Press, freedom of, 553
Price Indexes:
  Consumer, 36, 39
  GNP deflator, 37
  Producer, 41
Prime Ministers. See Premiers
Prime numbers, 353
Prince Edward Island, 283, 289
Prince of Wales, 263
Prince of Wales Trophy, 847
Principe, 238
Printing:
  Economic statistics, 42, 53
  Industry, hours and wages, 53

Inventions, 343
Measures, 349
  See also Publishing
Priority mail. See Airmail
Private schools, 706, 708
Prizes. See Awards
Probes, lunar, deep space, 371–72
Production indexes:
  U.S. industries, 41, 42
  See also kind of industry or product
Professional Golfers Association Champions, 896
Professional personnel, 49, 50–52
Programming, information, 344
Progressive Party (1912, 1924, 1948), 590
Prohibition, 97, 98, 555, 556
Promontory Point, 669
Propeller, screw, 344
Prostitution, arrests for, 782, 783
Protestant Episcopal Church, 104, 416
Protestantism, 409
  Leading groups, 412–18
  Protestants, number of, 296, 407, 412
  Reformation, 88, 179, 409
Proton, 344
Prudhoe Bay, Alaska, 647
Prussia, 179, 180
  Kings of, 180
Psychoanalysis, 344
Public assistance, 61–62, 698
Public Health Service, 615
Public schools, 706, 708
Public utilities, 42, 334
  Employment, 36
  Hours and wages, 53
  Largest companies, 45, 334
Publishing:
  Magazines, 449
  Newspapers, 446–48, 449–50
  Notable books, 1980, 789
  Printed matter, 70
Pueblo (ship), 103, 206
Puerto Rico, 672
  Execution methods, 785
  Holidays, 388–89
Pulitzer Prizes, 508–16
Pullman strike, 95
Pulsars, 355
Punctuation, rules for, 489–91
Punic Wars, 84
Punjab, 189, 453
Pupils. See Students
Purim, 385, 389
Puritan Commonwealth, 264, 265
Purús River, 463
Pyongyang, North Korea, 100, 205
Pyramids of Egypt, 316

Q

Qatar, 235
  See also Countries
Quakers. See Friends
Quantum theory, 344
Quarks, 337
Quart, 346–48, 350–51
Quarter horse racing, 874
Quasars, 354, 367, 377
Quebec, Canada, 282, 283, 284–85, 289–90
Quebec, Que., 282, 289
  See also Cities (world)
Queens (NYC), 683, 760
Queensberry Rules, 864
Quintal (measure), 349
Quintuplets, Dionne (1934), 99
Quire, 349
Quisling, Maj. Vidkun, 226
Quito, Ecuador, 164
Quiz show, first panel, 544
Qur'an. See Koran

R

Rabbinical organizations, 414
Rabies, 344
Racial statistics, 49, 56, 57, 397, 706, 750–51, 754, 763, 771–775, 778–81, 783, 785
Racial violence (U.S.), 103, 107
Racing. See kind of racing
Racquetball, 884
Radar, 344
Radiation, 640
Radiation, doses, 334
Radiation, neutron-induced, 343
Radio:
  Advertising, 56
  Awards, 518
  Inventions, 344
  Number in countries, 121–22
  Receivers in U.S. cities, 677–86
  Stations in U.S. cities, 677–86
Radioactivity, 96, 344
Radio telescopes, 363
Railroad Retirement Board, 700
Railroads:
  Accidents; deaths, 645, 776, 777
  Construction, 42
  Economic statistics, 63–64
  Firsts, 544
  Legislation, 700
  Passengers, freight, 63–64
  Railroad tunnels, 320
Rainfall, greatest, 421
Rainier, Mount, 455, 468, 469, 670
Ramakrishna, 410
Ramayana, 410
Ranger probes, 370, 371
Rangoon, Burma, 145
Rape, 782, 783, 784
Rayon, 344
Reactors, nuclear, 334, 341, 343, 640
Reagan, Ronald, 545, 582
  See also Headline History; Presidents (U.S.)
Ream (measure), 349
Reaper, 344
Recommended Daily Dietary Allowances, 78
Reconstruction, 95
Reconstruction Finance Corporation (1932), 98
Records:
  Aviation, 441–42, 445
  See also Sports
Records (phonograph), 792
Recreation:
  Economic statistics, 57
  Government employment, 59
Recreation Areas, National, 636, 639
Red Cross, American, 623
Red Desert (An Nafud), 466
Red Guards (1966), 153
Red River (Okla.-La.), 470
Red Rock River, 470
Red Sea, 461
Redwood National Park, 637
Reference books, 451–52
Reformation, 88, 179, 409
Reformed churches, 417–18
Registered mail, 626
Reichstag fire, 98
Reign of Terror (1793–94), 91
Rejoicing of the Law, 386, 389
Relative humidity in cities, 422–24
Relativity theories, 96, 344
Religion, 28–29, 407–20
  Canadian church membership, 296
  Christian New Right, 9–10
  Churches in U.S., 412–18
  Churches in U.S. cities, 677–86
  Colleges, affiliation with, 721–49
  Consumer spending for, 57
  Freedom of religion, 553

Holidays, 385–89
Jewish organizations, 414
Moral Majority, 9, 10
News events, 1980–81, 28–29
Popes, 418–20
Practice by country, 131–281
World faiths, 407–12
See also specific religions and
 churches
Religious affiliations:
 Presidents, 583
 Supreme Court Justices, 603–05
Renaissance, 87, 88
 Architecture, 317
Rent, 36, 39, 40
Reparations (World War I), 97
Reporting, awards, 510–12
Representatives. *See* House of
 Representatives
Reptiles, Age of, 338
Reptiles, endangered, 631
Republic, oldest, 238
Republican Party:
 Founding, 94
 Members of Congress, 606–10
 National Committee chairmen, 591
 National conventions, 586–87
 Senate floor leaders, 612
Republican River, 470
Reservations, Indian, 647, 765
Residence requirements:
 For divorce, 769
 For voting, 596
Resources, world, by country,
 131–281
Restaurants, 45, 52
Retail trade:
 Establishments, 44–45
 Hours and wages, 53
 Largest companies, 44–45
 Sales, 45
Retired couples, budgets, 40
Retirement:
 Benefits, 694–96, 697–98
 Railroad workers, 700
 See Growing Older; Social Security
Réunion, 175, 456
Revenue:
 Bills for raising, 549
 City, 677–86
 National, 37, 60
 State, 646–72
Revolutionary War, American, 89, 91
 Casualties, 399
 Continental Congress, 546–47, 561
 Declaration of Independence,
  546–47
Revolver, 344
Reykjavik, Iceland, 188
Rhine River, 171, 178, 222, 254
Rhode Island, 666
 See also States of U.S.
Rhodes, Cecil, 280, 281, 538
Rhodes, Colossus at, 316
Rhodesia. *See* Zambia; Zimbabwe
Rhodope Mountains, 144
Rhône River, 171
Ribbon Falls, 464
Rice:
 Calories and vitamins, 82
 Economic statistics, 70
 World production, 118–19
Richmond (NYC). *See* Staten Island
Rifle, 344
Ringling Museums, 801–02
"Ring of Fire," 455–56
Rio de Janeiro, Brazil, 143
 See also Cities (world)
Rio de la Plata, 271
Rio Grande, 463, 470
Río Muni, 168
Riots. *See* Racial violence
Rivers:
 Dams, 318–19
 Total volume, 633
 U.S., 469–70

World, 463–64
Riyadh, Saudi Arabia, 238
Roads:
 Highway construction, 42
 Mileages, 310–11
Roanoke Island, 663
Roanoke River, 470, 663
Robbery, 782, 783, 784
Rockefeller Center, 317
Rocket engine flight, first, 439
Rocky Mountain National Park, 636
Rodeo, 858
Roentgen, Wilhelm Conrad, 95, 334
Roentgen (measure), 334, 349
Roller bearing, 344
Roller skating, 857
Roman Catholic Church, 407, 409,
 413
 Council of Nicaea, 85, 408
 Council of Trent, 88
 Great Schism, 87
 Inquisition, 86, 89
 Membership, 296, 407, 412
 Popes, 408, 418–20
 Vatican, 272–73, 317
 Vatican Council I, 409
 Vatican Council II, 102, 273, 409
Roman Empire, 84, 85
 Map, 487
 Structures, 316
Romania, 235–36
 See also Countries
Roman numerals, 353
Rome, Italy, 199
 Founded, 83
 Structures, 316–17
 World War II, 99
Rookie of the year (baseball), 912–13
Roosevelt, Eleanor, 539, 577, 585
Roosevelt, Franklin D., 545, 577
 See also Headline History; Presidents
  (U.S.)
Roosevelt, Theodore, 497, 545,
 575–76
 See also Headline History; Presidents
  (U.S.)
Roosevelt's (FDR) Birthday, 388
"Roots," 104
Rose Bowl, 823–24
Rosenberg trial, 100, 101
Rose, Pete, 915
Roses, Wars of the, 87, 264
Rosh Hashana, 386, 389
Rosicrucian Museum, 802
Ross, Betsy, 545, 569
Ross Dependency, 223
Ross Trophy, 847
Rotary International, 623
Rough Riders, 576
Rowing, 821, 889–90
Royal Canadian Mounted Police, 288
Rubber:
 Economic statistics, 41, 42, 70
 Vulcanized, 344
Ruby, Jack (1963), 102, 545
Rugby, 929
Rulers of countries, 131–281
Rumania. *See* Romania
Running. *See* Track and Field
Rupert's Land, 283, 290
Rushmore, Mount, 667
Russia:
 History, 247–49
 Kremlin (structure), 316–17
 Revolution, 97, 247
 Rulers, 246
 Structures, 316–17
 World War I, 97, 247
 World War II, 99, 247
 See also Countries; Soviet Union
Russian Orthodox Church, 413
Russo-Finnish War, 99, 170–71, 247
Russo-Japanese War, 96, 202, 247,
 576
 Treaty signed in Portsmouth, N.H.,
  96, 660

Russo-Turkish War, 95, 260
Rwanda, 236–37
 See also Countries
Ryukyu Islands, 202

S

Sabah, Malaysia, 214
Sabine River, 470
Sabin vaccine, 343
Sacco-Vanzetti case, 97
Sacramento River, 470
Sadat, Anwar el-, 31, 165, 166–67,
 198
Sagamore Hill National Historic Site,
 308, 638
Sahara, 453, 466
Saigon, Vietnam. *See* Ho Chi Minh City
St. Bartholomew Massacre, 88
St. Francis River, 470
St. George's, Grenada, 183
St. Helena, 270
St. John the Divine, Cathedral of, 317
St. Kitts-Nevis, 270–71
St. Lawrence River, 463
St. Helens, Mount, 337, 445, 469
St. Lawrence Seaway, 102, 322, 662
 Map, 475
St. Louis, Mo., 684
 Art museum, 802
 See also Cities (U.S.)
St. Lucia, 237, 270
 See also Countries
St. Mark's Cathedral, 316
St. Mihiel, Battle of, 97
St. Patrick's Cathedral, 318
St. Patrick's Day, 385
St. Paul, Minn., 657–58
 See also Cities (U.S.)
St. Peter, Basilica of, 88,317
St. Petersburg, Russia. *See* Leningrad
St. Pierre and Miquelon, 176
St. Thomas, V.I., 674
St. Valentine's Day, 385
St. Valentine's Day Massacre, 98
St. Vincent, 237–38, 270
Saipan, 675
Sakhalin, 466
Salamis, Battle of, 83
Salaries:
 Armed forces, 394–96
 Federal government, 612
 Industrial wages, 53–54
 National income and, 40
 State governments, 676
Sales, retail and wholesale, 45
Sales taxes:
 City, 437
 On motor vehicles, 786
 State, 436
Sales workers, 49, 52
Salisbury, Zimbabwe, 280
Salk vaccine, 101, 343
Salmon River, 470
SALT. *See* Strategic Arms Limitation
 Talks
Salvador, El. *See* El Salvador
Salvation Army, 417, 623
Salween River, 464
Salyut space station, 373
Samoa, American, 673
Samoa, Western, 276
Samoan archipelago, 456
Samos, 182
San'a', Yemen Arab Republic, 277
San Antonio, Tex., 685
 See also Cities (U.S.)
San Diego, Calif., 648, 685
 Museums, 802
 See also Cities (U.S.)
Sandinista guerrillas, 224
Sandwich Islands, 269
San Francisco, Calif., 685
 Bridges, 321
 Climate, 424

Earthquake (1906), 96, 641
  Museums, 799, 802
  See also Cities (U.S.)
San Jacinto, Battle of, 93, 658
San Joaquin River, 470
San Jose, Calif., 685
  See also Cities (U.S.)
San José, Costa Rica, 157
San Juan River, 470
San Marino, 238
  See also Countries
San Salvador, El Salvador, 167, 168
San Stefano, Treaty of, 95
Santa Claus, 387
Santee-Wateree-Catawba River, 470
Santiago, Chile, 150
Santiago de Cuba, 157
Santo Domingo, Dominican Rep., 163,
  164
São Francisco River, 143, 463
São Tomé and Príncipe, 238
  See also Countries
Saratoga, Battle of, 89
Sarawak, Malaysia, 214
Sardinia, 86, 199
SAS, 369
Saskatchewan, Canada, 282, 283,
  284, 290
Saskatchewan River, 464
Satellites, scientific, 105, 361,
  368–69, 373
Satellites (moons), 354, 357–59,
  367, 419
  Orbits defined, 354
"Saturday Night Massacre," 104
Saturn (planet), 356, 359, 367
  See also Planets
Saudi Arabia, 238–39
  See also Countries
Sault Ste. Marie Canal, 322, 657
Savings bank, first in U.S., 544
Savings rate, 38
Saxe-Coburg, House of, 264
Saxon kings, 264
SBA, 617
Scarlet fever, 79, 776
Scenic Riverways, National, 636, 639
Scenic Trail, National, 636, 639
Schism, Great, 87
Schmidt, Helmut, 178, 180–81
Schools:
  And Supreme Court, 102, 103
  Statistics, 706–09
  See also Colleges and universities;
  Education
Schuman Plan (1951), 100
Science, 336–44
  Chemical elements, 339–40
  Genetics, 7–8, 336
  Inventions, discoveries, and theories,
    342–44
  Metric System, 345–48, 350–51
  Museums, 544, 796–802
  News events, 1980–81, 29–30
  Nobel Prizes, 31, 498–502
  UNESCO, 328
  Weights and measures, 345–53
  See also Astronomy; Atomic energy;
  Chemistry; Mathematics; Medicine;
  Physics
Science and Industry, Museum of,
  797
Science and Technology, Office of,
  613
Science Foundation, National, 617
Scopes evolution trial, 98
Score (measure), 349
Scotland, 263–66
  See also United Kingdom
Scott, Dred, 94
Screw propeller, 344
Scythian civilization, 84
Seafood, food value, 81–82
Seal of U.S., Great, 561
Sears Tower, 320

Seas, 461
  Total volume, 633
Seashores, National, 636, 639
Seasons, 358, 378, 384–85
SEATO. *See* Southeast Asia Treaty
  Organization
Seattle, Wash., 424, 685
  See also Cities (U.S.)
SEC, 617
Secondary schools, 706–08
Second International, 95
Secretaries-General (U.N.), 326
Secret Army Organization (OAS), 133
Securities and Exchange Commission,
  617
Security Council, National, 613
Security Council, U.N., 326
Seine River, 171
Selassie, Haile. *See* Haile Selassie
Selective Service System, 99, 617
Seljuk Turks, 86
Senate (U.S.), 548–49, 606–07
  Birthdates of members, 606–07
  Committees, 610–11
  Eligibility, 548
  First woman member, 544
  Floor leaders, 612
  Impeachment cases, 548–49
  See also Congress (U.S.)
Senegal, 239–40
  See also Countries
Seoul, South Korea, 206
Sepoy Mutiny, 94, 190
Sequoia National Park, 637, 648
Serbia, 278
Service academies, 391–93
Service industries, 44
  Employment, 36
"Seven Cities of Gold," 647
Seventh-Day Adventists, 417
Seven Weeks' War, 94
Seven Wonders of World, 316
Seven Years' War, 90, 282
Seward, William, 545, 598, 646–47
"Seward's Folly," 647
Sexes, distribution by:
  Arrests, 782
  Colleges, 707, 721–49
  Death rates, 778, 779, 780–81
  Degrees received, 707
  Employment, 51–52, 54, 55, 56
  Graduates, 707
  Life expectancy, 779–81
  Marriage statistics, 766, 768
  Population in U.S., 754
  Ratio of men to women, 750–51
Sex offenses, arrests for, 782, 783
Seychelles, 240
Shaba, Zaire, 279
Shah of Iran, 193, 194
Shang Dynasty, 83
Shanghai, China, 151, 153
  See also Cities (world)
Shannon River, 195
Shasta, Mount, 455, 469
Shatt-al-Arab, 195, 464
Shavuot, 386, 389
Shemini Atseret, 389
Shenandoah (dirigible), 643
Shenandoah National Park, 637, 670
Sherman Antitrust Act, 95
Shetland Islands, 263, 453
Shikoku, 202
Shintoism, 411
  Number of followers, 407
Ship canals, 322
Shipping:
  Commerce, 64
Ships. *See* Steamships
Shipwrecks, famous, 643
Shock, treatment of, 71
Shooting, death rates from, 787
Shooting (sport). *See* kind of shooting
"Shooting stars," 361–68
Shoreline of U.S., 472
Shotput. *See* Track and Field

Shrove Tuesday, 385, 388, 389
Siam. *See* Thailand
Siberia, 246
Sicily, 86, 199
  Volcanoes, 456
Sidereal time, 354, 383
Sierra Leone, 240–41, 453
  See also Countries
Sihanouk, Norodom, 146-47
Si Kiang (river). *See* Xi Jiang River
Sikkim, 189, 191
Silurian Period, 338
Simhat Torah, 386, 389
Simplon Tunnel, 320
Sinai Peninsula, 102, 103, 166, 167,
  197, 198
  Map, 480
Singapore, 99, 214, 241, 457
  See also Countries
Singers. *See* People
Singing Cave, 467
Single persons, 768
Sino-Japanese War, 95
Sirhan, Sirhan Bishara, 103, 545
Sistine Chapel, 88, 317
Six-day war, 103, 197
  See also Arab-Israeli wars
Skating, ice, 818, 822, 850, 854
Skating, roller, 857
Skeet shooting, 929
Skiing, 819, 822, 852–53
  Olympic Games, 819, 822
  U.S. Championships, 852
  World Cup, 852–53
Skylab, 370, 376
Skyscrapers:
  First, 544
  In Canada, 297
  In U.S., 320
Slavery:
  Abolished in British Empire, 93
  Dred Scott case, 94
  Emancipation Proclamation, 559–60
  First slaves to America, 88, 544,
    670
  First state to forbid, 669
  Importation barred, 93
  Kansas-Nebraska Act, 94
  Prohibited in U.S., 554
Small Astronomy Satellite, 369
Small Business Administration, 617
Smallpox, and vaccination against, 79,
  92, 344
Smithsonian Institution, 618, 797–98
Smoky Hill River, 470
Snake River, 470
Snowdon, Mount, 263
Snowfall, greatest, 421
Snyder-Gray case, 98
Soap Box Derby, 871
Soaring, 891
Soccer, 899–900
Socialist parties, 590
Social Security, 694–98
  Medicaid, 701–02
  Medicare, 698, 700–02
Social workers, 51
Societies and associations, 619–24
Society Islands, 174
Socrates, 84, 540
Sofia, Bulgaria, 144
Softball, 923
Solar energy, 330
Solar system, 344, 356–60
Solar time, 354, 383
Solomon Islands, 24
Solstice, 358
Somalia, 241–42
  See also Countries
Somaliland, French. *See* Djibouti
Somme, Battle of, 97
Somoza Debayle, Gen. Anastasio, 224
Songs, state, 646–72
"Sooners," 664
Sophocles, 84, 540
Sorority, first, 544

Sound:
First flight faster than, 440
Speed of, 349, 352
Sources, reference, 451–52
South Africa, Rep. of, 96, 104, 105, 107, 242–44
See also Countries
South America, 130, 455, 457
Explorations, discoveries, 454
Map, 479
Natural resources and climate maps, 479
Southernmost point of, 150
See also Continents
South Carolina, 666–67
See also States of U.S.
South China Sea, 461
South Dakota, 667
See also States of U.S.
Southeast Asia, maps, 484, 485
Southeast Asia Nations, Association of, 130
Southeast Asia Treaty Organization, treaty signed, 101
Southeast Asia War. *See* Vietnam War
Southern Alps, 223
Southern Cameroons. *See* Nigeria
"Southern lights," 363
Southern Rhodesia. *See* Zimbabwe
Southern Yemen. *See* Yemen (People's Democratic Republic of)
South Georgia Island, 269
South Island (N.Z.), 223, 465
South Manchurian Railway, 152
South Orkney Islands, 268
South Platte River, 470
South Pole:
First flight over, 439
Reached, 96, 454
South Shetland Islands, 268
South-West Africa, 244–45
Southwest Museum, 802
Soviet Union, 245–49
Afghanistan invasion, 106, 107, 131, 249
Area, elevations, and population density, 457
Armed forces, 403
Constitution, 248
Germany, nonaggression pact with (1939), 99, 247
Government, 246–47
Hydrogen bomb (1961), 102
Maps, 477, 481, 484, 485, 486
Moscow Summer Olympics, 107, 249
Nuclear weapons testing, 100
Population growth, 112
Rulers, 246
Space programs, 366–67, 371–72, 373, 374–77
World War II, 99, 247
See also Countries; Russia
Soweto, South Africa, 104, 243
Soyuz flights, 373, 374–77
Space exploration, 366–77
Astronauts, 374–77
Chronology of unmanned probes, 371–72
First manned space station, 370
Highlights of 1981, 366–67, 377
Manned flights, 370, 373, 374–77
Moon landings and explorations, 370, 371–72, 375–76
Moon map, 488
Scientific satellites (Soviet Union), 373
Scientific satellites (U.S.), 368–69
Space shuttle, 366–67, 370
See also Astronomy
Spain, 83, 86, 87, 88, 94, 98, 249–51
See also Countries
Span (measure), 349
Spanish-American War, 95, 158, 400

Spanish Armada, 89, 250, 264
Spanish Civil War, 99, 250
Spanish origin, persons of:
Population, 754, 763
Spanish Succession, War of, 90
Sparta, 83
Spartacus, 84
Speakers of House, 612
Special-delivery mail, 626
Special Education, 703–05, 708
Special features, 7–10
Special Representative, Office of the U.S. Trade Representative, 613
Specific gravity of elements, 339–40
Spectrum, 344
Speech, freedom of, 553
Speed:
Of falling body, 352
Of light, 343, 354
Of sound, 349, 352
Speed records:
Airplanes, 441
See also individual sports
Speed skating, 818, 822, 854
Spelling, new Chinese, 151
Spermatozoa, 344
Sphinx, Great, 83, 316
Spinning inventions, 344
"Spiral nebula," 354
Spirit of St. Louis (plane), 439
Spitsbergen, 226, 454
Sports, 806–929
Memorabilia, A14
News events, 1980–81, 30–31
Olympic Games, 809–22
Organizations and information bureaus, 855–56
Personalities, 806–08
Standard measurements, 856–57
See also individual sports
Spring (1982), 378
"Spring tides," 357
Square, 349
Squash racquets, 923
Squash tennis, 845
Sri Lanka, 251, 466
See also Countries
Stadiums:
Baseball, 916
Football, 835
Stalin, Joseph, 97, 99, 100, 246, 247–48, 540
Stalingrad, Battle of, 99, 247
Stamp Act, 89
Stamps, postage, 544, 626, A1, A9–A11
United Nations, 627
Standard time, 384
Stanley Cup, 846, 848
Stars, 354–57
Brightest, 355
Constellations, 362–63
Twinkling of, 363
"Stars," of entertainment, 521–43
"Star-Spangled Banner," 559
State, Secretaries of (states), 646–72
State, U.S. Department of, 613
Secretaries of, 597–601
State and local governments, News Events, 1980–81, 31
Staten Island, 683, 760
See also New York City
States, Confederate, 560
States of U.S., 646–72
Agricultural production, 58
Areas, 646–72
Births and birth rates, 775
Coastlines, 472
Congress members, 606–10
Constitutional provisions, 550, 552
Deaths and death rates, 777
Distilled spirits, purchase age, 788
Divorce information, 769–71
Education, 707, 710–49
Elections, presidential, 592–95
Execution, methods of, 785

Firsts, 544
Government employment, 59
Government statistics, 676
Governors, 646–72, 675, 676
Highest court members, term and salary, 676
Holidays, 388–89
Marriage information, 767
Medicaid; Medicare, 701–02
Motor vehicle deaths, 777
Motor vehicle laws, 786
Motor vehicle registrations, 65
Newspapers, 449–50
Per capita personal income, 37
Population, 755, 763
Procedure for admitting new states, 552
Representatives, 607–10
School attendance laws, 707
Senators, 606–07
Taxes. *See* Taxes
Thirteen original, 548
Tourism offices, 304–06
Unemployment benefits, 699
Voting qualifications, 596
States' rights, 550, 552, 554
States' Rights Democratic Party, 590
Statistical History of the U.S., 561–68
Statue of Liberty, 95, 309
Steam engine, 91, 344
Steamship, 344
Steamships, disasters, 643
Steel, 53, 70, 117–18
Stock-car racing, 926, 927
Stockholm, Sweden, 253
Stock market, 35, 43, 46, A1–A7, A13
Companies, widely held, 46
Dow Jones Industrials, 35
50 leading stocks, 46
Shareholders, 38
Stonehenge, 83
Stone (measure), 349
Stores, retail. *See* Retail trade
Storms, 426–27, 642
Strategic Arms Limitation Talks, 106, 129, 248, 249
Stratopause, 358
Stratosphere, 358
Stratosphere, first flight into, 439
Strikes (labor), 48
First strike in U.S., 544
Stromboli, 456
Structures:
Bridges, 321–22
Buildings, tallest, 297, 320
Canals, 322
Dams, 318–19, 323
Famous, 316–23
Seven Wonders, 316
Tunnels, 320
Stuart, House of, 264
Students:
College and professional, 707–08, 721–49
Elementary and secondary schools, 706–08
Submarines, 97, 401
Disasters, 643
First atomic-powered, 101
Subways:
First in U.S., 544
Sucre, Bolivia, 142
Sudan, 251–52, 453
See also Countries
Suez Canal, 94, 95, 102, 104, 165–67, 197, 322, 480
Egypt seizes (1956), 101, 166
Suffrage. *See* Voting
Suffragettes, 96
Sugar:
Calories, 82
Economic statistics, 59, 70, 120–21
World production, 120–21
Sugar Bowl (football), 824
Suicides, 113

Sukarno, 192
Sukkot, 386, 389
Suleiman I, 88
Sulfa drugs, 344
Sullivan Award, 822, 894
Sumatra, 192, 465
Volcanoes, 456
Sumerian civilization, 83, 84
Summer (1982), 378
Sun, 354, 356–57
Eclipses, 364
Phenomena, 364–65
Seasons, 384–85
Symbol, 363
Time based on, 383–84
Sungari River, 464
Sunshine in cities, 422–24
Sun spots, 356
Sun Yat-sen, 96, 152, 541
Super Bowl, 831
Superdome, 318
Superior, Lake, 282, 462
Supersonic aircraft, 440
Supreme Courts, state, 676
Supreme Court (U.S.):
Constitutional provisions, 551–52
First law declared unconstitutional, 544
Justices, 602, 603–05
Major deicisions (1954–80), 101, 102, 103, 104, 105, 106, 107
Salaries, 612
Surgery, first antiseptic, 342
Suribachi, Mount, 455
Suriname, 252
See also Countries
Surveying measures, 346
Surveyor probes, 370, 371
Survivor benefits, 695–96
Susquehanna River, 470
Sutter's Mill, 648
Suva, Fiji, 170
Svendrup Islands, 283
Swains Island, 673
Swan Islands, 674
Swaziland, 253
See also Countries
Sweden, 253–54
See also Countries
Sweets, food value, 80–82
Swimming, 814–17, 820, 885–89, 901
Olympic Games, 814–17, 820
Switzerland, 254–55
See also Countries
Sydney, Australia, 135, 136
Symbionese Liberation Army, 104, 105
Symbols:
Astronomical, 363
Chemical elements, 339–40
Symphony orchestras, 789
Synodic month, 354
Synthetic fuels, 329–30
Syphilis, 79, 344, 776
Wassermann test, 344
Syria, 255–56
Map, 480–81
See also Countries
Syrian Orthodox churches, 413, 418

T

Tabernacles, Feast of, 386, 389
Table tennis, 928
Tabloid newspaper, first, 544
Tadzhikistan, U.S.S.R., 246
Taft, William Howard, 576
See also Headline History; Presidents (U.S.)
Tahiti, 174
Taipei, China, 154
Taiwan (Formosa), 154–55
Map, 485
See also China (Taiwan)

Taj Mahal, 317
Takla Makan Desert, 466
Talmud, 407–08
Tamerlane, 131, 541
Tananarive, Madagascar. See Antananarivo
Tana River, 470
Tanganyika. See Tanzania
Tanganyika, Lake, 453, 462
T'ang Dynasty, 151
Tannenberg, Battle of, 97
Tannu Tuva, 247
Tanzania, 256–57
See also Countries
Taoism, 83, 411–12
Number of followers, 407
Tarawa, 205
Tarbela Dam, 323
Tasmania, 136, 454, 466
Tax Court, U.S., 602
Taxes, 34, 428–37, A15–A16
Auto sales taxes, 786
Constitutional provisions for, 549–50, 555, 557
Corporation taxes, federal, 429, 434
Corporation taxes, state, 434–35
Estate taxes, federal, 429, 435, 436, A15
Excise, 429
Franchise taxes, state, 434–35
Fraud cases, 433
Gasoline taxes, state, 786
Gift taxes, federal, 429, 435, 436, A16
Gross receipts, state, 646–72
Income tax, city, 437
Income tax, federal, 38, 429–34
Income tax, history, 428
Individual returns, 433
Internal Revenue Service, 428–29
New legislation, federal 428, 431–32, 434, 435, A15–A16
Returns filed, 433
Sales and use taxes, state, 436
Sales tax, city, 437
Taylor, Zachary, 573
See also Headline History; Presidents (U.S.)
Tea, 70
Teachers, 721–55
Teapot Dome, 97, 577
Technology Assessment, Office of, 618
Tegucigalpa, Honduras, 186
Teheran, Iran, 192, 193, 194
See also Cities (world)
Teheran Conference (1943), 99
Tektites, 362
Tel Aviv, Israel, 196
Telegraph:
Economic statistics, 42
Invention, 344
Trans-Atlantic cable, 94
Telephones:
Economic statistics, 42, 53
Invention, 95, 344
Number in countries, 121–22
Telescope:
Invention, 344
Large Space Telescope, 368
Optical, radio, 363
Television:
Advertising, 56
Awards, 31, 518
Cable, 793, 803, 805
Color, 100, 344
Glossary, 805
Home video, 803–05
Inventions, 98, 344, 803–05
Networks, 793
Number in countries, 121–22
Prime time, 793–94
Sets in cities, 677–86
Stations in cities, 677–86
Viewing, 793–94
Teller, Sanford, 930

Telstar (satellite), 369
Temperatures:
In Canada, 294–95
International, 301–02
In U.S. cities, 422–24
Scales, 345, 349, 351
U.S. extremes, 421
World extremes, 421
Tenerife, Canary Islands, 456, 644
Tennessee, 667–68
See also States of U.S.
Tennessee River, 470
Tennessee Valley Authority, 617, 668
Tennis, 859–63
Earnings, 863
History, 859
Standard measurements, 856
Tennis, court, 927
Tennis, squash, 845
Tennis, table, 928
Teotihuacan, Mexico, 84
Territorial expansion of U.S., 763
Territories of U.S., 673–74
Areas, 763
Execution methods, 785
Population, 763
Terrorism, 103, 105, 107, 204, 209, 252, 262, 267, 272, 281
Tertiary Period, 339
Tests, educational:
Interpretation of, 704–05
Test-tube baby, 105
Texas, 668
War of Independence, 93, 668
See also States of U.S.
Textiles, economic statistics, 41, 42, 53, 70
Thailand, 257–58
See also Countries
Thames River, 263
Thanksgiving Day, 386, 388, 389
Thant, U, 279, 326
Thar Desert, 466
Thatcher, Margaret, 265, 266
Theater:
Awards, 513, 516, 517–18
Celebrities of, 521–43
First vaudeville, 544
Longest Broadway runs, 795
Thefts, 782–84
Theories, scientific, 342–44
Therm (measure), 349
Thermometer:
Invention, 344
Scales, 349, 351
Thermopylae, Battles of, 83, 84
Thermopause, 358
Thermosphere, 358
Thieu, Nguyen Van, 275
Thimphu, Bhutan, 141
Third Estate, 91
Third International, 97
"Third World," 278
Thirty Years' War, 89, 179, 254
Thomas, Kurt, 894
Three Mile Island, 106, 329
Tibet, 151, 453
Tidal shoreline of U.S., 472
Tidal waves, 425, 641
Tides, 357
Tien-Pamir Mountains, 246
Tien Shan Mountains, 151
Tierra del Fuego, 134, 150, 466
Tigris River, 83, 194, 464
Tikhonov, Nikolai, A., 245, 246
Time:
Kinds of, 383–84, 452
Universal and civil, 355, 383–84
Time of day, cities, 458, 471
Time zones, 383–84, 459
On U.S. map, 474–75
Timor, 235
Tin, 340
Tinian (island), 675
Tippecanoe, 653

Tirana, Albania, 132
Tires, pneumatic, 95, 344
Tiros (satellite), 369
Titanic (ship), 96, 643
Titicaca, Lake, 142, 462
Tito, Marshal, 100, 278
Tobacco:
  Consumer spending, 57
  Economic statistics, 42, 53, 58, 70
  In Connecticut, 649
  Taxes, 429
Tobago. *See* Trinidad and Tobago
Tocantins River, 464
Togo, 258
  See also Countries
Toilet, flush, 344
Tojo, Hideki (1948), 100
Tokelau Island, 223
Tokyo, Japan, 89, 201
  See also Cities (world)
Toledo, Ohio, 684, 685–86
  See also Cities (U.S.)
Toledo Museum of Art, 802
Tombigbee River, 470
Tomb of the Unknown Soldier, 569
Ton, 346, 348, 351
  Gross or long, 348, 351
  Metric, 348, 351
  Net or short, 348, 351
Tonga, 258
  See also Countries
"Tony" Awards, 516
Torah, 386, 407–08
Tornadoes, 425, 427
Toronto, Canada, 282, 289, 297
Toulouse, France, 171
Tourist information. *See* Travel
Tours, Battle of, 85
Tower of London, 317
Township (measure), 349
Toys and games, 70
Track and Field, 809–14, 875–84,
  901
  History, 875
  History of mile run, 877–78
  Indoor records, 881–82
  National AAU Championships,
    882–84
  Olympic Games, 809–14
Tractor, invented, 344
Trade. *See* Foreign trade; Interstate
  Commerce
Trade Commission, Federal, 616
Trade Commission, U.S. International,
  617
Trademarks, 496
Trade Negotiations, Office of the
  Special Representative for, 613
Trade unions. *See* Unions, labor
Trafalgar, Battle of, 92
Trains. *See* Railroads
Trans-Alaska Pipeline, 647
Transarctic flight, first, 439
Transatlantic flights, 438, 439, 440
Transcontinental flights, 439, 440
Transistor, 344
Transkei, 245
  See also Countries
Transpacific flight, 439
Transportation:
  Accident death rates, 776–77
  Economic statistics, 57, 63–67
  Employment, 36
  Freight traffic, 63, 64
  Fuel consumption, 334
  Industry, hours and wages, 53
  Inventions, 342–44
  Largest companies, 45
  Passenger traffic, 64
  See also kinds of transportation
Transportation, U.S. Department of,
  615
  Secretaries of, 600–01
Transportation equipment, 41, 42, 43,
  70
Trapshooting, 929

Travel, 298–315
  Air distances between cities, 312–15
  Charter flights, 298–99
  Countries visited, 303
  Currency exchange, 122
  Expenditures, 302, 303, 304
  Industry statistics, 299
  Information sources, 304–07
  Mileage, motor vehicle, 334
  Mileages between cities, 310–11
  Object of, 304
  Passports and Customs, 300–01
  Tourist arrivals, 301
  Volume of, 301
Treason defined, 552
Treasurers (of states), 646–72
Treasury, U.S. Dept. of, 613
  Secretaries, 597–601
Treaties, 126–30
Trees, state, 646–72
Triangle Shirtwaist Factory fire, 96
Triassic Period, 338
Trieste, 200
Trinidad and Tobago, 258–59
  See also Countries
Trinity River, 470
Trinity Sunday, 389
Triple Alliance, 95
Triple Crown (horse racing), 872–74
Triple jump. *See* Track and Field
Tripoli, Libya, 211
Tristan da Cunha, 270
Trivia, Year's Top, 930
Trojan War, 83
Tropical storms, 421
Tropical year, 354
Tropic of Cancer, 385
Tropic of Capricorn, 385
Tropopause, 358
Troposphere, 358
Trotsky, Leon, 97, 98, 99, 247, 542
Trotting. *See* Harness racing
Troy, ancient, 83
Troy weight, 346
Trucial States. *See* United Arab
  Emirates
Trucks and trucking, 63, 65, 66, 67,
  334
Trudeau, Pierre, E., 282, 283–84,
  290, 542
Truman, Harry S., 545, 577–78
  See also Headline History; Presidents
  (U.S.)
Truman Doctrine, 100
Trusteeship Council, U.N., 327
Trusteeships, U.N., 327, 674
Trust Territory of Pacific Islands,
  674–75
Tuberculosis, 79, 95, 776
Tucson, Ariz., 686
  See also Cities (U.S.)
Tudor, House of, 264
Tugela Falls, 464
Tulsa, Okla., 664, 686
  See also Cities (U.S.)
Tungsten filament, 342
Tunis, Tunisia, 259
Tunisia, 259
  See also Countries
Tun (measure), 349
Tunnels, 320
Turbojet, first flight, 440
Turkey, 259–61
  See also Countries
Turkish-Russian War, 95, 260
Turkmenistan, U.S.S.R., 246
Turks and Caicos Islands, 270
Turner, Nat, 93
Tuskegee Institute, 646
Tutankhamen, 83
Tuvalu, 261
  See also Countries
TVA, 617
Tweed Ring, 95
Twelfth Night, 385
Tydings-McDuffie Act (1934), 232

Tyler, John, 572
  See also Headline History; Presidents
  (U.S.)
Typhoid fever, 79, 776

U

Uganda, 261–62
  See also Countries
Ukraine, U.S.S.R., 246, 247
  See also Soviet Union
Ukrainian Orthodox Church, 413, 418
Ulan Bator, Mongolia, 219
Ulbricht, Walter, 177, 180
Ulster, Northern Ireland, 266–67
Umtala, Transkei, 245
Uncertainty principle, 344
Uncle Sam, 545
Unemployment, 36, 56, 57
  Insurance, 698–700
UNESCO, 328
Union Islands. *See* Tokelau Island
Union Labor Party, 589
Union of Soviet Socialist Republics.
  See Soviet Union
Unions, labor, 47–48
Unitarian Universalist Association, 417
United Arab Emirates, 262
  See also Countries
United Automobile Workers, 47
United Kingdom, 262–71
  Map, 476
  Prime Ministers, 265
  Rulers, 264
  Zoos, 635
  See also Countries
United Methodist Church, 414
United Nations, 324–28
  Agencies, 327–28
  Assessments of members, 325
  Budget, 325
  Charter, 326
  "China seat," 103, 153, 155
  Economic and Social Council, 326
  Established, 100
  Events, 100, 101, 103, 104, 106
  General Assembly, 326
  Headquarters, 325
  International Court, 327
  Member nations, 324
  Principal organs, 326–28
  Secretariat, 326
  Security Council, 326
  Stamps, 627
  Trusteeship Council, 327
  Trust territories, 229, 327, 674
  U.S. contributions to, 62, 325
United Nations Educational, Scientific,
  and Cultural Organization, 328
United States:
  Aliens admitted, 764, 765
  Area, 763
  Armed forces, 390–406
  Balance of payments, 69
  Birth statistics, 773–75
  Bridges, 321–22
  Buildings, tallest, 320
  Canals, 322
  Church memberships, 412
  Climate extremes, 421
  Coastline, 572
  Colleges, 710–49
  Crime statistics, 782–85, 787
  Dams, 318–19, 323
  Death statistics, 776–81
  Development statistics, 561–68
  Disasters, 441–45
  Divorce statistics, 766, 769–71
  Economic statistics, 34–70
  Education statistics, 705–09
  Exports, 67, 70
  Extreme points, 467
  Fairs and Expositions, 794, 795
  Family statistics, 40, 41, 771–73
  Flag, 569

Geography, 467–72
Growth, 763
Highest points, 468
Holidays, 385–89
Hospital statistics, 74–75
Immigration, 764, 765
Imports, 67, 70
Junior colleges, 710–20
Labor force, 36, 48–52, 56–57
Largest cities, 677–86
Latitudes and Longitudes, 471
Libraries, 790
Life expectancy in, 779–81
Lowest points, 468
Magazines, 449
Map, 474–75
Marriage statistics, 766–71
Mileages between cities, 310–11
Motor vehicle laws, 786
Museums, 796–802
National Anthem, 559
National Park System, 635–39
Naturalization statistics, 762
Newspapers, 446–48, 449–50
Passports and customs, 300-01
Population, 750–65
  For detailed listing, *see* Population
    (U.S.)
Postal regulations, 625–28
Religious groups, 412–18
Societies and associations, 619–24
State tourism offices, 304–06
Symphony orchestras, 789
Territories, 673–74, 763
Time zones, 459, 474–75
Travel information, 304–09
Tunnels, 320
Universities, 721–49
Weather and climate, 421–27
Zoos, 634–35
  See also Cities (U.S.); Foreign trade;
    Interstate commerce; States (U.S.);
    U.S. Government; U.S. History
United States Government:
  Armed forces, 390–406
  Cabinet, 597–601
  Congress. *See* Congress (U.S.)
  Constitution, 548–57
  Employment, 59
  Executive Departments, 613–18
  Expenditures and receipts, 59–63
  Federal budget, 60
  Foreign aid, 62–63
  Great Seal, 561
  Independent agencies, 615–18
  Judicial powers, 551–52
  Library of Congress, 618
  Majority and minority whips,
    606–10
  National Park System, 635–39
  News events, 1980–81, 25–28
  Presidents, 570–85
  Salaries of officials, 612
  Social Security, 694–98
  Supreme Court, 552, 602, 603–05
  Unemployment insurance, 698–700
  Veterans' benefits, 396–97
  Voting qualifications, 596
  See also individual entries elsewhere
    in index for more extensive listing
United States History:
  Armed services, 390–91
  Articles of Confederation, 561
  Assassinations and attempts, 545
  Atlantic Charter (1941), 99
  Cabinets, 597–601
  Chronology, 89–127
  Civil War, 94
  Colonization, 89
  Constitution, 548–57
  Continental Congresses, 89, 561
  Declaration of Independence,
    546–47
  Development statistics, 561–68
  Disasters, 641–45
  Discoveries and explorations,

453–54
  Elections, presidential, 588–96
  Emancipation Proclamation, 559–60
  Firsts, 544
  Flag, 569
  Gettysburg Address, 560
  Historical events, 88–107
  Impeachments, 605
  Mason and Dixon's Line, 468
  Mayflower Compact, 558
  Military interventions, 399
  Minority Presidents, 596
  Monroe Doctrine, 558
  National Committee chairmen, 591
  Presidents, 570–85
  Pulitzer Prizes for, 513–14
  Revolutionary War period, 89
  Speakers of the House, 612
  "Star-Spangled Banner," 559
  Statistics, 561–68
  Statue of Liberty, 309
  Territorial expansion, 763
  Unknown soldiers, 569
  War casualties, 399–401
    See also names of wars
  White House, 557, 639, 686
Universal Postal Union, 328
Universal time, 355
Universe, origin of, 355
Universities, United States, 721–49
  See also Colleges
Unknown, Tomb of the, 569
**Unleavened Bread, Feast of, 385,
  389**
Upanishads, 410
Upper Volta, 271
  See also Countries
Ural Mountains, 246
Ural River, 464
Uranium:
  As element, 340
  Used in atomic bomb, 341
Uranus (planet), 367, 356, 359
  See also Planets
Urey, Harold, 118, 342, 542
Uruguay, 271–72
  See also Countries
Uruguay River, 271
Utah, 668–69
  See also States of U.S.
Utilities, largest, 45
U-2 incident (1960), 102
Uzbekistan, U.S.S.R., 246

V

VA, 618
Vaccination, smallpox, 344
Vacuum tube, 344
Vaduz, Liechtenstein, 212
Valentine's Day, 385
Valentine's Day Massacre, 98
Valetta, Malta, 215
Valley Forge, Pa., 665
Valois, House of, 172
Van Allen Belt, 344, 363, 368
Van Buren, Martin, 572
  See also Headline History; Presidents
    (U.S.)
**Vancouver, B.C., Canada, 282, 286,
  297**
Vandalism arrests, 782, 783
Vandals, 85
Vanguard (satellite), 369
Vanuatu, 272
  See also Countries
Vatican City State, 272–73
  See also Countries; Roman Catholic
    Church
Vatican Council I, 409
Vatican Council II, 102, 273, 409
Vatican (Structures), 317
Vaudeville theater, first, 544
Vedanta Society, 418
Vedas, 410

V-E Day (1945), 99
Vegetables:
  Calories and vitamins, 80–82
  Economic statistics, 59, 70
Venda, 245
Venera probes, 371–72, 373
Venezuela, 273–74
  See also Countries
Venus (planet), 356, 358
  Space probes, 369, 371–72, 373
  See also Planets
Verdun, Battle of, 97
Vermont, 669
  See also States of U.S.
Vernal Equinox, 382, 383
Verrazano-Narrows Bridge, 321
Versailles, Palace of, 89, 317
Versailles, Treaty of, 97, 99, 179
Vesuvius, Mount, 456, 641
Veterans:
  Benefits, 396–97
  Education, 397, 705
  March (1932), 98
Veterans Administration, 618
Veterans' Day, 378, 386, 388
Veto power, 549, 601
Vezina Trophy, 847
Vice Presidents (U.S.):
  As Acting President, 557
  Election procedure, 550–51, 554
  List of, 583–84
  Nomination, 586
  Powers and duties, 548
  Salary, 612
  Succession to Presidency, 551, 556,
    557, 558
  Term of office, 556
  Much of what applies to Presidents
    (U.S.) *also applies to Vice*
    Presidents
Vichy, France, 172, 174, 275
Vicksburg, Battle of, 94
Victoria, Lake, 462
**Victoria, Queen, 93, 95, 96, 264,
  265**
Victoria, Seychelles, 240
Victoria Falls, 453, 465
Victoria (island), 465
Video, 803–05
Vienna, Austria, 136, 137
Vienna, Congress of, 93, 137, 173
Vientiane, Laos, 208
Viet Cong, 101, 275
Vietnam, 208, 274–76
  See also Countries; Chronology
Vietnam War, 101, 275, 399
  Casualties, U.S., 400
  See also Cambodia; Chronology;
    Laos; Thailand
Viking probes, 370, 372, 377
Vikings, 85, 86, 162, 226
Vinson Massif, 457
Virginia, 669–70
  See also States of U.S.
Virgin Islands, British, 268
Virgin Islands, U.S., 97, 674
Virgin Islands National Park, 637
VISTA, 615
Vitamins:
  Content of foods, 80–82
  Dietary allowances, 78
  Discoveries, 344
V-J Day (1945), 99
Volcanoes, 337, 641, 455–56, 469
  Famous eruptions, 641
  "Ring of Fire," 455–56
Volcano Islands, 455
Volga River, 463
  Hydroelectric plants on, 319
  Lakes, 462
Volleyball, 924
Volume:
  Formulas for, 352
  Measure of, 345–52
Volunteers of America, 418
Voskhod flights, 373, 374

Vostok flights, 373, 374
Voting:
　18-year-olds; 103, 557
　Plurality and majority, 587
　Presidential elections, 588–96
　Qualification by state, 596
　Rights, 555, 557
　Unusual voting results, 596
　Woman suffrage, 97, 544, 555
Voyager probes, 107, 367, 370, 372
Voyageurs National Park, 637

W

Wabash River, 470
Wadsworth Atheneum, 802
Wages, hours:
　Industrial, 53–54
　National income and, 40
　See also Income
Wake Island, 674
Waldheim, Kurt, 326
Wales, 263
　See also United Kingdom
Wales, Prince of, 263
Walking. *See* Track and Field
Wallace, George, 103, 545
Wallis and Futuna Islands, 176
Wall of China, 151, 317
War, U.S. Department of, Secretaries of, 597–600
War casualties, 399–401
War crimes, 98, 100
War of 1812, 93, 399
Warren, Earl, 542, 603
Warren Report (1965), 102–03
Wars. *See* individual wars
Warsaw, Poland, 232
Warsaw Ghetto, 98
Warsaw Pact, 103, 129, 130, 403, 405
Warsaw Pact and NATO military balance, 405
Warsaw Treaty Organization, 233, 236, 248
Wars of the Roses, 87, 264
War trials (1946), 100
Washington, D.C., 92, 93, 686
　Bonus march (1932), 98
　Civil rights rally (1963), 102
　Climate, 424
　Museums, 797–98
　Twenty-third Amendment, 556
　White House, 557, 639, 686
　See also Cities (U.S.); *much information under States also applies to Washington, D.C.*
Washington, George, 89, 91, 92, 570
　See also Headline History; Presidents (U.S.)
Washington, Mount, 468
Washington Birthplace National Monument, 307, 637
Washington-Lincoln Day, 388
Washington Monument, 568
Washington's Birthday, 385, 388
Washington (state), 670–71
　Mountains and volcanoes, 455, 469
　See also States of U.S.
Washita River, 470
Wassermann Test, 344
Water:
　Boiling and freezing points, 351
　World supply, 633
Waterfalls, 464–65
Watergate, 103–04, 580
Waterloo, Battle of, 93, 179, 265
Water polo, 858
Waterways, traffic on, 63, 64
Watt, 349
Watts riots (1966), 103
Watusi, 146
Weapons, 782, 783, 784, 787
Weather and climate, 337, 421–27, 642

Disastrous storms, 426–27, 642
Glossary, 425
Hurricanes, 421, 425, 426–27
Of U.S. cities, 422–24
South America climate map, 479
Tornadoes, 425, 427
Tropical storms, 421
World extremes, 421
Weaving cloth, 344
Wedding anniversaries, 445
Weight, desirable, 73, 77
Weight lifting, 821, 853
Weights, atomic, 339–40
Weights, measures, 345–53
　Capacities, volumes, 345–48
　Conversion factors, 351
Weimar Republic, 179
Welfare. *See* Public assistance
Wellington, New Zealand, 223
Wesleyan Church, 417
Westar (satellite), 369
Western Samoa, 276
　See also Countries
West Germany. *See* German, West
West Indies:
　Discovery, 453
　Map, 478
　Volcanoes, 456
　See also specific islands
West Indies Associated States, 270–71
West Irian, 191–92
Westminster Abbey, 317
West Point (U.S. Military Academy), 391
West Virginia, 671
　See also States of U.S.
Wheat, 58, 59, 70
　World production, 118–19
Wheat flour. *See* Flour
Wheel, 344
Wheelwright Museum, 802
Where to find out more, 451–52
Widows, widowers, Social Security benefits, 695–96
Whig Party (U.S.), 572–73, 589
Whipple theory, 360
Whiskey Insurrection, 92
White House, 557, 636, 639, 686
White House Office of Policy Development, 613
White River, 470
Whitney, Mount; 468, 469, 648
Whitney Museum, 797
Whitsunday, 386
WHO, 328
Wholesale trade:
　Employment, 36
　Hours and wages, 53
　Price indexes, 41
　Sales, 45
Whooping cough, 79, 776
Williams, Ted, 909
Williamsburg, Va., 670, 799
William the Conqueror, 86, 263, 264
William II, Kaiser, 179, 180
Wilson, Harold, 265, 266
Wilson, Woodrow, 576
　See also Headline History; Presidents (U.S.)
Wimbledon champions, 862, 863
Wind Cave National Park, 467, 637
Wind chill factor, 424, 425
Windhoek, South-West Africa, 244
Windmill, 344
Windsor, House of, 264
Wind velocities of hurricanes, 426–27
Windward Islands. *See* West Indies Associated States
Wine, Age for purchase of, 788
Winnie Mae (plane), 440
Winnipeg, Lake, 462
Winter (1982), 378
WIPO, 328
Wisconsin, 671–72
　See also States of U.S.

Wisconsin River, 470
Wives of Presidents, 585
WMO, 328
Wollaston Islands, 150
Women:
　Abortions, 774
　Armed forces, 100, 397
　Arrests, 782
　Death rates, 778, 779, 780–81
　Earnings, 41, 55–56
　Education, 55, 707
　Employment, 48, 49, 54–56
　Families maintained by, 54, 766, 771
　Famous, 521–43
　Firsts, 438, 440, 544
　Heads of families, 54, 766, 771
　Labor force, in, 48, 49, 54–56
　Life expectancy, 111, 779–80, 781
　Marriage statistics, 766, 768
　Mothers, 774
　Mothers employed, 49
　News Events, 1980–81, 31
　Number, 754
　Occupations, 51–52
　Political firsts, 544
　Presidents' wives, 585
　Ratio of men to women, 750–51
　Suffrage, 97, 544, 555
Women Voters, League of, 624
Wonders of World, Seven, 316
Wood. *See* Lumber and wood
Wood burning, 329–30
Wood pulp, 41, 70
Woolworth Building, 320
Working population, 36, 48–52, 56–57
World:
　Air distances, 314–15
　Area, 457
　Bridges, 321–22
　Canals, 322
　Caves, caverns, 467
　Climate extremes, 421
　Consumer Price Indexes, 115
　Countries of, 123–281
　Dams, 318–19, 323
　Defense expenditures, 403–04, 406
　Deserts, 466
　Dimensions, 457
　Disasters, 641–45
　Elevations, 457
　Energy production, 331
　Explorations, discoveries, 453–54
　Freedom in, 123–26
　Geography. *See* Geography (world)
　Highest mountain peaks, 460–61
　History. *See* History (world)
　Hydroelectric plants, 319
　Islands, 465–66
　Lakes, 462–63
　Maps, 472–87
　Population. *See* Population (world)
　Religion, 407–20
　Rivers, 463–64
　Seven Wonders of the, 316
　Statistics, 108–22
　Structures, famous, 316–23
　Tunnels, 320
　Volcanoes, 455–56
　Waterfalls, 464–65
　Water supply, 633
　Zoos, 634–35
　See also Cities (world); Countries; Earth; Governments (foreign)
World Bank (IBRD), 100, 327
World Court, International Court of Justice, 327
World Cup, Soccer, 899
World Health Organization, 328
World History, 83–107, 131–281
World Intellectual Property Organization (WIPO), 328
World Meteorological Org., 328
World Series:
　1980, 920–21

1903–80, 902–04
Records and standing, 905
World's Fairs, 794, 795
Chicago:
Century of Progress International Exposition (1933–34), 795
World's Columbia Exposition (1893), 795
New York:
Crystal Palace Exposition (1853), 795
Peace Through Understanding (1964–65), 795
World of Tomorrow (1939–40), 99, 795
World Time Zones, 383–84
Map, 459
World Trade Center, 318, 320
World War I, 96, 97
Casualties, 400, 400-01
Unknown Soldier of, 569
World War II, 99
Casualties, 400, 401
Chronology, 99
Declarations of war (U.S.), 99
Treaties, 100
Unknown, Tomb of the, 569
See also involved countries
Wounded Knee, S.D., 103
Wrangell, Mount, 455, 469
Wrestling, 821, 900
Wright, Orville and Wilbur, 96, 342, 438
Writers. *See* People
Writer's Guide, 489–96
Abbreviations, 492
Capitalization, 491
Punctuation, 489–91
Wyandotte Cave, 467, 653
Wyoming, 672
See also States of U.S.

X

Xavier, St. Francis, 453
Xenon, 340
Xerography, 344
Xhosa, 245
Xi Jiang River, 151, 464
X-rays, 95, 344

Y

Yachting, 821–22, 924
Yalta Conference, 99, 100, 129
Yangtze Kiang, 151, 463
Yaoundé, Cameroon, 147
Yasukuni, 411
Year, defined, 382–83
Year's Top Trivia, 930
Yellow River, 151, 463
Yellowstone National Park, 637
Yellowstone River, 470
Yemen, People's Democratic Republic of, 276–77
See also Countries
Yemen Arab Republic, 277
See also Countries
Yenisei River, 463
Yom Kippur, 386, 389
York, House of, 264
Yorktown, Battle of, 89
Yosemite, waterfalls, 464
Yosemite National Park, 637
Young, Brigham, 93, 543
Young Men's Christian Association, 624
Young Women's Christian Association, 624
Yugoslavia, 277–78
See also Countries

Yukon River, 463, 470
Yukon Territory, 282, 283, 290

Z

Zaire, 102, 278–79
U.N. action, 279
See also Countries
Zama, Battle of, 84
Zambezi River, 453, 464
Kariba Dam, 462
Zambia, 279–80
See also Countries
Zanzibar. *See* Tanzania
Zenger, John Peter, 90
Zeppelin:
First Flight, 438
Invention of, 342
Zero, 344
Zeus, statue of, 316
Zhou Enlai, 152–54, 543
Zimbabwe, 280–81
See also Countries
Zinc, 340
Zionism, 197
Zion National Park, 637
ZIP codes, 756–62
Zodiac, 362, 363
Zond probes, 371–72, 373
Zoological gardens, 634–35
Zoos, American, 634–35
Zoroaster, 543
Zoroastrians, 407
Zugspitze (peak), 178
Zwingli, Ulrich, 88